June 26–July 1, 2016
San Francisco, California, USA

Association for
Computing Machinery

Advancing Computing as a Science & Profession

SIGMOD'16

Proceedings of the 2016 International Conference on Management of Data

Sponsored by:

ACM SIGMOD

Supported by:

Microsoft, Oracle, Tableau, Alibaba, AT&T, Facebook, Google, IBM, Infosys, Platfora, Recruit, Salesforce, SAP, Snowflake, Amazon Web Services, Cloudera, Esgyn, Hewlett Packard, Intel, Linked In, LogicBlox, MemSQL, Splice Machine, VISA Research, Hewlett-Packard Enterprise, Morgan & Claypool, Elsevier, Springer, and National Science Foundation

Association for Computing Machinery

Advancing Computing as a Science & Profession

The Association for Computing Machinery
2 Penn Plaza, Suite 701
New York, New York 10121-0701

Notice to Past Authors of ACM-Published Articles
ACM intends to create a complete electronic archive of all articles and/or other material previously published by ACM. If you have written a work that has been previously published by ACM in any journal or conference proceedings prior to 1978, or any SIG Newsletter at any time, and you do NOT want this work to appear in the ACM Digital Library, please inform permissions@acm.org, stating the title of the work, the author(s), and where and when published.

ISBN: 978-1-4503-3531-7 (Digital)

ISBN: 978-1-4503-4606-1 (Print)

Additional copies may be ordered prepaid from:

ACM Order Department
PO Box 30777
New York, NY 10087-0777, USA

Phone: 1-800-342-6626 (USA and Canada)
+1-212-626-0500 (Global)
Fax: +1-212-944-1318
E-mail: acmhelp@acm.org
Hours of Operation: 8:30 am – 4:30 pm ET

Printed in the USA

Welcome Message from the SIGMOD Chairs

It is our great pleasure to welcome you to SIGMOD 2016, the 2016 edition of the ACM SIGMOD International Conference on Management of Data, at San Francisco, the heart of Silicon Valley. A unique bridge, cable cars, a sparkling bay, a famous prison, and steep streets with beautiful Victorian houses are just a few of the things that make San Francisco one of the world's greatest cities to visit. Located in the Bay Area along the Northern California coast, many attractions beyond those in the city can be easily reached: the world-famous wine country, including Napa and Sonoma Valley, beautiful beaches, the world's largest trees and wonderful hikes in nearby National Parks.

The conference itself is held in the Hyatt Regency Hotel, located in the financial district in downtown San Francisco. The hotel is very conveniently located nearby to many activities and landmarks, making this the ideal spot not only for an exciting conference but also for exploring the area. The banquet will be held in the California Academy of Sciences. The California Academy of Sciences is a Planetarium, Aquarium and Natural History Museum under a Living Roof in San Francisco, and it is among the largest museums of natural history in the world, housing over 26 million specimens.

This year's technical program features 137 papers in 22 sessions; 116 research papers, 17 industrial papers, and 4 invited papers. Research and industrial papers will be mixed together instead of separated into separate tracks as in past years. All papers will be presented at conference sessions, as well as at one of two plenary poster events. There are also 31 demos and 10 tutorials. Instead of running these concurrently with technical presentations, demos are now a separate plenary event in the conference and tutorials have been moved before and after the conference. There is just one panel, the Careers in Industry panel. Finally, this year's conference will feature one keynote, from the inimitable Jeff Dean (Google, USA), who will talk about how deep learning and software systems can support each other, with particular thoughts on the implications for data management. The net effect of these changes is that there are more plenary events, and at most three concurrent events ongoing (from 6 or more concurrent tracks in previous conferences). We hope this will make the SIGMOD experience more communal.

Other technical events of interest include the SIGMOD programming contest, featuring a $7,000 prize for the winning team plus a $3,000 dollar prize for the runner-up donated by Microsoft, with contest participants presenting their work during the poster session; the undergraduate poster competition, featuring 12 undergraduate posters from an outstanding group of young database researchers; the new research symposium on Tuesday night; and the business meeting, also on Tuesday evening.

We made a number of changes in the way we assembled this year's technical program with an eye towards improving review and paper quality. As in past years we had two submission deadlines, but we spread them out more (one in July and one in November). Each submission included one round of revisions, during which reviewers could request specific changes to papers. The vast majority of accepted papers underwent revision, which we believe significantly improved the quality of papers. All submissions were also discussed in a series of conference calls organized by our group leaders; this forced reviewers to defend their positions and helped achieve consensus. A post-review survey revealed 70% of reviewers felt this improved the review process, and 80% reported they worked harder in preparing and defending their reviews. We also asked reviewers and group leaders to request additional reviews when an additional opinion was needed; many papers received four reviews, and some papers received as many as six. Finally, we introduced an online conference organization tool, Confer, which we used to get the community's input about how papers should be grouped together, and which attendees can use throughout the conference to navigate the program.

SIGMOD 2016 is preceded and followed by 10 workshops, including the PhD symposium on Sunday, June 26. These workshops provide an opportunity for small groups of like-minded researchers to discuss areas of interest and new ideas, and we are pleased to see a diverse ecosystem of workshops with competitive submissions evolving at SIGMOD.

We are grateful to the many members of our community who made this technical program possible, especially the 247 reviewers whose hard work resulted in writing more than 2700 reviews for our research, industrial, and demo tracks. This work was coordinated by our fabulous program committee team, including our program track chairs, Alexandra Meliou (UMass Amherst, USA), and Tim Kraska (Brown University, USA), and our 14 group leaders, who coordinated conference calls and guided papers through the review process. The industrial program was created by Tyson Condie (UCLA, USA), and Carlo Curino (Microsoft, USA), and the demo program was organized by Jennie Duggan (Northwestern University, USA), and Aaron Elmore (University of Chicago, USA). Alexandros Labrinidis (University of Pittsburgh, USA), efficiently organized the tutorials program. The undergraduate poster competition was organized by Aditya Parameswaran (University of Illinois, Champaign Urbana, USA), and Anisoara Nice (SAP SE, Canada). Ken Salem organized this year's programming contest (finding shortest paths in a changing graph), and Peter Bailis (Stanford University, USA), and Andy Pavlo (Carnegie Mellon University, USA) organized the poster session. Anant Bhardwaj (MIT, USA), built the Confer online conference software. Finally, last but certainly not least Alekh Jindal helped organize the proceedings, tirelessly hounding authors to get their camera ready submissions uploaded!

SIGMOD is a volunteer effort and involved thousands of hours of work, thousands of emails, and thousands of hours in meetings during the last two years to put together. Please thank all these individuals involved if you see them around the conference. Also congratulate Alex Labrinidis, Alex Meliou, Melanie, Martin, Yunyao, and Stratos who became parents in the meantime.

We also acknowledge all members of the SIGMOD 2016 organizing committee, as well as the SIGMOD Executive Committee, for their invaluable help and guidance throughout the many months leading to the conference. The strong organizing team for SIGMOD 2016 includes finance chair Martin Theobald (University of Ulm, Germany), publicity chair Melanie Herschel (University of Stuttgart, Germany), social media chair Hakan Ferhatosmanoglu (Bilkent University, Turkey), sponsorship chairs Mohamed Mokbel (University of Minnesota, USA) and Stratos Idreos (Harvard University, USA), exhibit chair Huiping Cao (New Mexico State University, USA), local arrangements chairs Enela Pema (Facebook, USA) and Yunyao Li (IBM Research-Almaden, USA), registration chair Mohamed Sarwat (Arizona State University, USA) , workshop local arrangement chair Fei Chen (LinkedIn, USA), web chair Kostas Stefanidis (ICS-FORTH, Hellas), volunteer chair Maria Daltayanni (University of San Francisco, USA), and travel award committee chairs Eugene Wu (Columbia University, USA) and Peter Alvaro (University of California, Santa Cruz, USA. The success of this conference would be impossible without their hard work, persistent dedication, and hours of effort they committed to the conference. We also would like to thank K. Selçuk Candan for providing us with his advice and SIGMOD institutional memory, as well as for his help with logistics throughout the conference planning. We are also grateful to the Microsoft Research Conference Management Toolkit (CMT) team for their extremely prompt and helpful support throughout the complex conference reviewing process. We would also like to extend our appreciation to the student volunteers.

Finally, we would like to thank ACM, and particularly Fran Spinola and April Mosqus for helping with the conference logistics, Diana Brantuas for guidance and help with the budget, Stephanie Sabal for hotel site selection, Ann Lane for conference promotion, and Carolina Erazo for preparing the visa letters. Adrienne Griscti (ACM) and Lisa Tolles (Sheridan) have made the proceedings and the program booklet possible.

This year we are extremely grateful for all our corporate sponsors, whose contributions helped to keep the conference registration fees low, most significantly for student attendees. These include at the Platinum Level: Microsoft, Oracle, and Tableau; at the Gold Level: Alibaba.com, AT&T, Facebook, Google, IBM Research, Infosys, Platfora, Recruit, Salesforce, SAP, and Snowflake; and at the Silver Level: Amazon Web Services, Cloudera, esgyn, HP, Intel, LinkedIn, LogicBlox, memsql, Splice Machine, and Visa Research. Microsoft also supported the programming contest by providing the generous award to the winners. In addition, Microsoft, Google, the National Science Foundation and the SIGMOD Executive Committee have generously funded the SIGMOD 2016 student travel award program, Microsoft's donation provided 16 travel awards, Facebook's donation supported 4 travel awards, Snowflake's donation supported 1 travel award, and the NSF grant covered another 15 travel awards. Finally, the SIGMOD EC provided 27 awards, and covered all 63 free registrations for the student travel program awardees. Last but not least, we would like to thank Salesforce for organizing the reception at Exploratorium on Tuesday night for all SIGMOD attendees.

Welcome to San Francisco, and we hope you enjoy the conference!

Fatma Özcan	**Georgia Koutrika**	**Samuel Madden**	**Alekh Jindal**
General Chair	*General Chair*	*Program Chair*	*Proceedings Chair*

Table of Contents

Session 3 - Logical and Physical Database Design

Session 4 - New Storage and Network Architectures

Session 5 - Graphs 1: Infrastructure and Processing on Modern Hardware

Session 6 - Streaming 1: Systems and Outlier Detection

Session 7 - Approximate Query Processing

Session 8 - Networks and the Web

Session 9 - Data Discovery and Extraction

Session 10 - Data Integration / Cleaning

Session 11 - Spatio / Temporal Databases

Session 12 - Distributed Data Processing

Session 13 - Graphs 2: Subgraph-based Optimization Techniques

Session 14 - Main Memory Analytics

Session 15 - Interactive Analytics ....

Session 16 - Streaming 2: Sketches

Session 17 - Transaction Processing

Session 18 - Transactions and Consistency

Session 19 - Query Optimization

Session 20 - Graphs 3: Potpourri

Session 21: Hardware Acceleration and Query Compilation

Session 22 - Nearest Neighbors and Similarity Search

Demonstrations

Tutorials

Undergraduate Student Abstracts

2016 SIGMOD Conference Organization

General Chairs:	Fatma Özcan (IBM Research, USA) Georgia Koutrika (HP Labs, USA)
Program Chair:	Sam Madden (Massachusetts Institute of Technology, USA)
PC Track Chairs:	Tim Kraska (Brown University, USA) Alexandra Meliou (University of Massachusetts, Amherst, USA)
Proceedings Chair:	Alekh Jindal (Microsoft, USA)
Tutorials Chair:	Alex Labrinidis (University of Pittsburgh, USA)
Industrial Program Chairs:	Carlo Curino (Microsoft, USA) Tyson Condie (University of California, Los Angeles, USA)
Demonstration Chairs:	Aaron Elmore (University of Chicago, USA) Jennie Duggan (Northwestern University, USA)
Workshops Chairs:	Anastasia Ailamaki (EPFL, Switzerland) Barzan Mozafari (University of Michigan, USA)
Poster Chairs:	Andy Pavlo (Carnegie Mellon University, USA) Peter Bailis (Stanford University, USA)
Undergraduate Poster Competition Chairs:	Anisoara Nica (SAP SE, Canada) Aditya Parameswaran (University of Illinois at Urbana Champaign, USA)
Local Organization Chairs:	Yunyao Li (IBM Research, USA) Enela Pema (Facebook, USA)
Finance Chair:	Martin Theobald (University of Ulm, Germany)
Sponsorship Chairs:	Mohamed Mokbel (University of Minnesota, USA) Stratos Idreos (Harvard University, USA)
Publicity Chair:	Melanie Herschel (University of Stuttgart, Germany)
Social Media Chair:	Hakan Ferhatosmanoglu (Bilkent University, Turkey)
Exhibits Chair:	Huiping Cao (New Mexico State University, USA)
Registration Chair:	Mohamed Sarwat (Arizona State University, USA)
Web/Information Chair:	Kostas Stefanidis (ICS-FORTH, Greece)

Travel Award Selection Committee Chairs:	Eugene Wu (Columbia University, USA) Peter Alvaro (University of California, Santa Cruz, USA)
Programming Contest Chair:	Ken Salem (University of Waterloo, Canada)
New Researcher Symposium Chairs:	Julia Stoyanovich (Drexel University, USA) Fabian M. Suchanek (Telecom ParisTech University, France)
Volunteer Chair:	Maria Daltayanni (University of San Francisco, USA)
Local Workshops Chair:	Fei Chen (LinkedIn, Mountain View, USA)
Group Leaders:	Sihem Amer-Yahia (CNRS, France) Magdalena Balazinska (University of Washington, USA) Carsten Binnig (DHBW Mannheim, Germany) Mike Cafarella (University of Michigan, USA) Philippe Cudre-Mauroux (University of Fribourg, Switzerland) Amol Deshpande (University of Maryland, USA) Ihab Ilyas (University of Waterloo, Canada) Justin Levandoski (Microsoft Research, USA) Amelie Marian (Rutgers University, USA) Kyriakos Mouratidis(Singapore Management University, Singapore) Paolo Papotti (QCRI, Qatar) Daisy Zhe Wang (University of Florida, USA)
Program Committee:	Daniel Abadi (Yale, USA) Ashraf Aboulnaga (Qatar Computing Research Institute, Qatar) Foto Afrati (NTU Athens, Greece) Sameer Agarwal (Databricks, Inc, USA) Yanif Ahmad (Johns Hopkins University, USA) Reza Akbarinia (INRIA Sophia Antipolis, France) Gustavo Alonso (ETH Zurich, Switzerland) Peter Alvaro (UC Berkeley, USA) Sihem Amer-Yahia (CNRS/LIG, France) Aijun An (York University, Canada) Arvind Arasu (Microsoft Research, USA) Peter Bailis (UC Berkeley, USA) Magda Balazinska (University of Washington, USA) Zhuowei Bao (Facebook Inc., USA) Denilson Barbosa (University of Alberta, Canada) Srikanta Bedathur (IBM Research, India) Philip Bernstein (Microsoft Research, USA) Carsten Binnig (Brown University, USA) Spyros Blanas (Ohio State, USA) Michael Bohlen (University of Zurich, Switzerland) Francesco Bonchi (Yahoo Labs, Barcelona, Spain) Peter Boncz (CWI, Netherlands)

Program Committee (continued):

Angela Bonifati (Lille 1 University and INRIA, France)
Philippe Bonnet (IT University of Copenhagen, Denmark)
Stephane Bressan (NUS, Singapore)
Nico Bruno (Google, USA)
Michael Cafarella (University of Michigan, USA)
Mark Callaghan (Facebook, USA)
K. Selcuk Candan (Arizona State University, USA)
Kaushik Chakrabarti (Microsoft Research, USA)
Badrish Chandramouli (Microsoft Research, USA)
Kevin Chang (University of Illinois at Urbana-Champaign, USA)
Shimin Chen (ICT, Chinese Academy of Science, China)
Lei Chen (Hong Kong University of Science and Technology, Hong Kong)
James Cheng (CUHK, Hong Kong)
Alvin Cheung (University of Washington, USA)
Fei Chiang (McMaster University, Canada)
Sarah Cohen-Boulakia (LRI Universite Paris Sud, France)
Dario Colazzo (Universite Paris-Dauphine, France)
Tyson Condie (UCLA, USA)
Neil Conway (Typical Set LLC, USA)
Brian Cooper (Google, USA)
Philippe Cudre-Mauroux (University of Fribourg, Switzerland)
Bin Cui (Peking U., China)
Mahashweta Das (HP Labs, USA)
Sudipto Das (Microsoft Research, USA)
Antonios Deligiannakis (Technical University of Crete, Greece)
Amol Deshpande (University of Maryland, USA)
Stefan Dessloch (TU Kaiserslautern, Germany)
Jens Dittrich (Saarland University, Germany)
Luna Dong (Google, USA)
Chris Douglas (Microsoft, USA)
Eduard Dragut (Temple Univ., USA)
Jennie Duggan (Northwestern University, USA)
Curtis Dyreson (Utah State, USA)
Aaron Elmore (University of Chicago, USA)
Alan Fekete (U. Sydney, Australia)
Shel Finkelstein (UCSC, USA)
Peter Fischer (Universitat Freiburg, Germany)
Avrilia Floratou (IBM Almaden, USA)
Tim Furche (Oxford, United Kingdom)
Avigdor Gal (Technion, Israel)
Wolfgang Gatterbauer (CMU Tepper School of Business, USA)
Tingjian Ge (UMass Lowell, USA)
Floris Geerts (University of Antwerp, Belgium)
Rainer Gemulla (Max-Planck-Institut fur Informatik, Germany)
Boris Glavic (IIT Chicago, USA)
Lukasz Golab (University of Waterloo, Canada)

Program Committee (continued):

Todd Green (LogicBlox, USA)
Torsten Grust (U Tubingen, Germany)
Dimitrios Gunopulos (University of Athens, Greece)
Jiawei Han (UIUC, USA)
Wook-Shin Han (POSTECH, South Korea)
Carmem Hara (Universidade Federal do Parana, Brazil)
Oktie Hassanzadeh (IBM Research, USA)
Michael Hay (Colgate, USA)
Bingsheng He (Nanyang Technological University, Singapore)
Katja Hose (Aalborg University, Denmark)
Vagelis Hristidis (UC Riverside, USA)
Stratos Idreos (Harvard University, USA)
Ihab Ilyas (University of Waterloo, Canada)
Zachary Ives (University of Pennsylvania, USA)
Ruoming Jin (Kent State University, USA)
Alekh Jindal (MIT, USA)
Eser Kandogan (IBM Research, USA)
Panagiotis Karras (Skoltech, Russia)
Asterios Katsifodimos (TU Berlin, Germany)
Yannis Katsis (UC San Diego, USA)
Georgios Kellaris (Harvard, USA)
Anastasios Kementsietsidis (Google Inc., USA)
Alfons Kemper (University of Munich, Germany)
Oliver Kennedy (University at Buffalo, USA)
Eamonn Keogh (UC Riverside, USA)
Martin Kersten (CWI, Netherlands)
Daniel Kifer (Penn State, USA)
Christoph Koch (EPFL, Switzerland)
George Kollios (Boston University, USA)
Nick Koudas (University of Toronto, Canada)
Tim Kraska (Brown University, USA)
Hongrae Lee (Google, USA)
Wolfgang Lehner (TU Dresden, Germany)
Alberto Lerner (New York University, USA)
Justin Levandoski (Microsoft, USA)
Chengkai Li (UT Arlington, USA)
Feifei Li (University of Utah, USA)
Guoliang Li (Tsinghua University, China)
Yunyao Li (IBM Research, USA)
Erietta Liarou (EPFL, Switzerland)
Xuemin Lin (University of New South Wales, Australia)
Chengfei Liu (Swinburne University of Technology, Australia)
Eric Lo (Polytecnic University of Hong Kong, Hong Kong)
Guy Lohman (IBM Research, USA)
Jiaheng Lu (University of Helsinki, Finland)
Qiong Luo (Hong Kong University of Science & Technology, Hong Kong)

Program Committee (continued):

Shuai Ma (Beihang University, Beijing, China)
Ashwin Machanavajjhala (Duke U., USA)
Samuel Madden (MIT, USA)
Jayant Madhavan (Google, USA)
David Maier (Portland State University, USA)
Nikos Mamoulis (U. Hong Kong, Hong Kong)
Silviu Maniu (Universite Paris-Sud, France)
Essam Mansour (Qatar Computing Research Institute, Qatar)
Amelie Marian (Rutgers University, USA)
Davide Martinenghi (Politecnico di Milano, Italy)
Gianni Mecca (Universita della Basilicata, Italy)
Alexandra Meliou (UMass Amherst, USA)
Sergey Melnik (Google, USA)
Xiaofeng Meng (Renmin University of China, China)
Sebastian Michel (TU Kaiserslautern, Germany)
Umar Minhas (IBM Research, USA)
Zhou Minqi (East China Normal University, China)
Mohamed Mokbel (Northeastern University, USA)
Kyriakos Mouratidis (Singapore Management University, Singapore)
Barzan Mozafari (University of Michigan, USA)
Hannes Muhleisen (CWI, Netherlands)
Arnab Nandi (Ohio State University, USA)
Vivek Narasayya (Microsoft Research, USA)
Neha Narula (MIT, USA)
Felix Naumann (Hasso Plattner Institute, Germany)
Muhammad Naveed (University of Illinois at Urbana-Champaign, USA)
Rimma Nehme (Microsoft, USA)
Thomas Neumann (TU Munich, Germany)
Christopher Olston (Google, USA)
Dan Olteanu (Oxford University & LogicBlox, United Kingdom)
Beng Chin Ooi (National University of Singapore, Singapore)
Carlos Ordonez (University of Houston, USA)
M. Tamer Ozsu (University of Waterloo, Canada)
Ippokratis Pandis (Cloudera, USA)
Dimitris Papadopoulos (Boston University, USA)
Stavros Papadopoulos (Intel Labs and MIT, USA)
Olga Papaemmanouil (Brandeis University, USA)
Charalampos Papamanthou (UMD, USA)
Stelios Paparizos (Microsoft Research, USA)
Paolo Papotti (QCRI, Qatar)
Srinivasan Parthasarathy (Ohio State, USA)
Alex Passos (Google, USA)
Andy Pavlo (Carnegie Mellon University, USA)
Torben Bach Pedersen (Aalborg University, Denmark)
Jian Pei (Simon Fraser University, Canada)
Peter Pietzuch (Imperial College London, United Kingdom)

Program Committee (continued):

Holger Pirk (MIT, USA)
Evaggelia Pitoura (University of Ioannina, Greece)
Li Qian (Facebook, USA)
Jorge Quiane-Ruiz (Qatar Computing Research Institute, Qatar)
Karthik Ramachandra (Microsoft, USA)
Ravi Ramamurthy (Microsoft Research, USA)
Vijayshankar Raman (IBM Research, USA)
Christopher Re (Stanford University, USA)
Tore Risch (Uppsala Universitet, Sweden)
Florin Rusu (UC Merced, USA)
Russell Sears (PureStorage, USA)
Elaine Shi (Cornell University, USA)
Suvrit Sra (MIT, USA)
Ion Stoica (UC Berkeley, USA)
Kian-Lee Tan (National University of Singapore, Singapore)
Nesime Tatbul (Intel Labs and MIT, USA)
Anthony Tung (National University of Singapore, Singapore)
Daisy Zhe Wang (University of Florida, USA)
Jiannan Wang (UC Berkeley, USA)
Gerhard Weikum (Max-Planck-Institut fur Informatik, Germany)
Till Westmann (Oracle, USA)
Janet Wiener (Facebook, USA)
Xiaokui Xiao (Nanyang Technological University, Singapore)
Xiaochun Yang (Northeastern University, China)
Ken Yocum (Human Longevity, USA)
Cong Yu (Google Research, USA)
Matei Zaharia (MIT, USA)
Kai Zeng (UC Berkeley, USA)
Kevin Zheng (University of Queensland, Australia)
Jingren Zhou (Alibaba, USA)

Demo Program Committee:

Adam Silberstein (Trifacta, USA)
Alekh Jindal (MIT, USA)
Alexandros Labrinidis (University of Pittsburgh, USA)
Alvin Cheung (U. Washington, USA)
Arijit Khan (ETH Zurich, Switzerland)
Beng Chin Ooi (National University of Singapore, Singapore)
Danica Porobic (EPFL, Switzerland)
Darius Sidlauskas (EPFL, Switzerland)
Emad Soroush (Dato, USA)
Eugene Wu (Columbia University, USA)
Guy Lohman (IBM Almaden, USA)
Hannes Muhleisen (CWI, Netherlands)
Herodotos Herodotou (Cyprus University of Technology, Cyprus)
Holger Pirk (MIT, USA)
Isabel Cruz (Univ. of Illinois at Chicago, USA)

Demo Program Committee (continued):

Jagan Sankaranarayanan (NEC Labs, USA)
James Cheng (CUHK, Hong Kong)
Jens Teuber (TU Dortmund, Germany)
Jens Dittrich (Saarland, Germany)
Jeong-Hyon Hwang (SUNY Albany, USA)
Jiannan Wang (University of California, Berkeley, USA)
Jianyong Wang (Tsinghua, P.R. China)
Julia Stoyanovich (Drexel University, USA)
Junho Shim (Sookmyung Women's University, Rep. of Korea)
K. Selcuk Candan (Arizona State University, USA)
Kostis Kyzirakos (CWI, Netherlands)
Lei Chen (HKUST, Hong Kong)
Marco Serafini (QCRI, Qatar)
Martin Kersten (CWI, Netherlands)
Mike Carey (University of California - Irvine, USA)
Mohamed Mokbel (Univ of Minnesota, USA)
Mohamed Sarwat (Arizona State University, USA)
Paolo Papotti (QCRI, Qatar)
Pat Helland (Salesforce, USA)
Paul Brown (Paradigm4, USA)
Peter Bailis (University of California, Berkeley, USA)
Philippe Cudre-Mauroux (Univ. of Freiburg, Germany)
Pinar Tozun (IBM, USA)
Rachel Pottinger (University of British Columbia, Canada)
Ravi Ramamurthy (Microsoft Research, USA)
Reynold Cheng (Univ of Hong Kong, Hong Kong)
Ryan Stutsman (Microsoft Research, USA)
Shel Finkelstein (University of California, Santa Cruz, USA)
Spyros Blanas (Ohio State University, USA)
Sudeepa Roy (University of Washington, USA)
Sudipto Das (Microsoft Research, USA)
Christian Thomsen (Aalborg University, Denmark)
Tingjian Ge (U. Mass Lowell, USA)
Victor Alvarez (Saarland University, Germany)
Willis Lang (Microsoft Jim Gray Systems Lab, USA)
Yinghui Wu (Washington State University, USA)
Ziawasch Abedjan (MIT, USA)

Industrial Program Committee:

Philip Bernstein (Microsoft Research, USA)
Nico Bruno (Google, USA)
Michael Cafarella (University of Michigan, USA)
Mark Callaghan (Facebook, USA)
Neil Conway (Mesosphere, USA)
Brian Cooper (Google, USA)
Chris Douglas (Microsoft, USA)
Shel Finkelstein (UCSC, USA)
Konstantinos Karanasos (Microsoft, USA)
Guy Lohman (IBM Research, USA)
Ippokratis Pandis (Amazon Web Services, USA)
Karthik Ramachandra (Microsoft, USA)
Karthik Ramasamy (Twitter, USA)
Russell Sears (PureStorage, USA)
Till Westmann (Couchbase, USA)
Ken Yocum (Human Longevity, USA)
Jingren Zhou (Alibaba, USA)

Tutorials Program Committee:

Selçuk Candan (Arizona State University, USA)
Junghoo Cho (University of California, Los Angeles, USA)
Alex Delis (University of Athens, Greece)
AnHai Doan (University of Wisconsin, USA)
Luis Gravano (Columbia University, USA)
Guy Lohman (IBM Almaden, USA)
Qiong Luo (Hong Kong University of Science & Technology, Hong Kong)
Meral Ozsoyoglu (Case Western Reserve University, USA)
Alkis Polyzotis (Google, USA)
Mohamed Sharaf (University of Queensland, Australia)
Peter Triantafillou (University of Glasgow, UK)
Stratis Viglas (University of Edinburgh, UK)
Jun Yang (Duke University, USA)

Sponsors, Supporters, and Exhibitors

Sponsor:

Platinum Supporters:

Gold Supporters:

Silver Supporters:

Other Supporters:

Platinum Publisher:

Silver Publishers:

Student Travel Awards:

A Hybrid B+-tree as Solution for In-Memory Indexing on CPU-GPU Heterogeneous Computing Platforms

Amirhesam Shahvarani
Fakultät für Informatik
Technische Universität München
shahvara@in.tum.de

Hans-Arno Jacobsen
Fakultät für Informatik
Technische Universität München

ABSTRACT

An in-memory indexing tree is a critical component of many databases. Modern many-core processors, such as GPUs, are offering tremendous amounts of computing power making them an attractive choice for accelerating indexing. However, the memory available to the accelerating co-processor is rather limited and expensive in comparison to the memory available to the CPU. This drawback is a barrier to exploit the computing power of co-processors for arbitrarily large index trees.

In this paper, we propose a novel design for a B^+-tree based on the heterogeneous computing platform and the hybrid memory architecture found in GPUs. We propose a hybrid CPU-GPU B^+-tree, – HB^+-tree, – which targets high search throughput use cases. Unique to our design is the joint and simultaneous use of computing and memory resources of CPU-GPU systems. Our experiments show that our HB^+-tree can perform up to 240 million index queries per second, which is 2.4X higher than our CPU-optimized solution.

CCS Concepts

•Information systems → Data management systems; Data structures; •Computer systems organization → *Multicore architectures;*

Keywords

Heterogeneous Computing; Indexing; In-memory Database; B^+-tree

1. INTRODUCTION

The B^+-tree is a well known dynamic data structure, widely used as index in database management systems, data warehouses, online analytical processing (OLAP), decision support systems and data mining [10, 26, 4, 15]. Since the memory capacity of modern servers is sufficiently large, in many databases today, indexing information is kept in main memory in order to eliminate performance limitations arising from expensive disk I/O [35, 2]. Due to different characteristics of main memory, implementing an efficient in-memory B^+-tree involves different constraints [42].

Approaches that leverage GPUs to accelerate processing have become popular in many domains due to the superior computing power to price ratio offered by many GPUs [39, 41]. Also, in databases, several approaches have emerged to demonstrate the benefits of using GPUs to accelerate processing, such as, GPUTeraSort for sorting billion-record wide-key databases [17] and GPU-accelerated relational join processing [23][6]. Also, tree-based indexing, as a critical operation in databases, has been in the focus of recent approaches [27, 28, 13].

A GPU offers a higher memory bandwidth as compared to a CPU, which makes the GPU an attractive choice for database indexing. However, the efficient utilization of both memory bandwidth and computation resources of a GPU is a challenging endeavor because of distinct architecture of the GPU, which forces programmers to use the same arrangement of parallel threads for both computation and data transfer [7]. In addition, leveraging the GPU as a processing accelerator necessarily involves data transfer between main memory and GPU memory, resulting in additional latency [20].

In this paper, we present HB^+-tree (Hybrid B^+-tree), a modified B^+-tree, jointly leveraging CPU and GPU resources of the same compute platform. Our design is geared towards lookup intensive applications where tree updates are performed through bulk update processing, applicable to index updates in online analytical processing (OLAP), decision support systems and data mining [47, 48, 18].

Realizing indexing operations based on either CPU or GPU is subject to different trade-offs. CPU performance is bounded by *memory bandwidth* as the index grows beyond the size of the last level cache (LLC), while GPU performance is bounded by *memory capacity.* Although GPU's memory architecture is efficient enough enabling the GPU to reach higher throughput, the memory available to the GPU is more limited than CPU's main memory. Intuitively speaking, our design objective is to combine these characteristics of CPU and GPU memory to achieve high throughput for index tree operations over high volumes of data. We explore a hybrid design that scatters index data among CPU and GPU memory according to the volume and the frequency of accesses. Complementing this design, we proposed a heterogeneous CPU-GPU algorithm for searching the HB^+-tree. We develop a task pipelining method between CPU and GPU to

SIGMOD'16, June 26-July 01, 2016, San Francisco, CA, USA
© 2016 ACM. ISBN 978-1-4503-3531-7/16/06...$15.00
DOI: http://dx.doi.org/10.1145/2882903.2882918

overcome the communication cost between them. For better computation resource utilization, the task pipeline is further extended by double buffering, which is a concurrency design pattern for avoiding delay in data transfer [19]. We also design a load balancing scheme to improve resource utilization for systems with different GPU to CPU computation power ratios.

Furthermore, we propose two versions of HB$^+$-tree in this paper. In addition to the *regular* HB$^+$-tree, capable of efficiently performing bulk updates, we propose an array representation, referred to as *implicit* HB$^+$-tree, which is more efficient for high-throughput search-only applications. Moreover, we develop a bulk update mechanism for the regular HB$^+$-tree, which deals with the challenges of utilizing a hybrid memory architecture. For both regular and implicit HB$^+$-tree, we develop and evaluate a 64-bit and a 32-bit key versions of the tree. The data structure and algorithm designs we describe are based on using 64-bit keys; the design differences for the 32-bit tree version are summarized at the end of each section.

To the best of our knowledge, HB$^+$-tree is among the first indexing approaches to *jointly* leverage the heterogeneous computing power of CPU and GPU as well as *jointly* utilize their separate memories to achieve a higher aggregate bandwidth than using either memory alone.

Our approach has two main advantages over previous heterogeneous implementations of B$^+$-tree employing, for example, an APU (Accelerated Processing Unit) [13]. First, our design benefits from the hybrid memory architecture to improve memory bandwidth instead of relying on the CPU's main memory alone. Heterogeneous platforms increase the potential computing power of a system, but applications which are bandwidth bounded cannot leverage the extra compute resources unless the memory bandwidth is also improved [29]. Second, we accelerate the index search using a discrete GPU which provides higher computing power than an integrated GPU, as found in APUs. An APU is a system processor equipped with additional processing resources such as a FPGA (Field-Programmable Gate Array) or an integrated GPU to accelerate a specific kind of computation. However, the computing power of these integrated components are not comparable to high-end discrete FPGAs or GPUs that are interconnected with the system via the PCIe bus.

We opted to develop our approach using CUDA, which is the widely-used parallel computing platform and programming model developed by Nvidia for general purpose computing on GPUs [44]. However, there is no technical limitation in our design that prevents porting our approach to other GPU platforms, such as OpenCL [46].

To highlight the advantages of our hybrid solution, we further develop a CPU-optimized, multi-threaded B$^+$-tree, as baseline for comparison with our HB$^+$-tree. For this design, we also develop regular and implicit as well as 64-bit and 32-bit tree versions.

To ensure our CPU-optimized B$^+$-trees exhibits adequate performance, we also implement FAST – the fastest reported indexing performance of a comparable solution running on a single CPU [29] – and compare our implementations against it. Our CPU-optimized B$^+$-tree attains 1.3X higher throughput than FAST on average. Furthermore, for our CPU-optimized tree, we propose a novel tree structure optimization based on cache blocking and SIMD-enabled parallel search algorithm, and show how the use of huge pages help to increase the throughput of index search operations using a single CPU. Several components of the CPU-optimized B$^+$-tree are used in the implementation of our HB$^+$-trees.

We evaluate our solutions for varying number of tuples from 8M to 1B and show how each design decision affects the indexing performance.

HB$^+$-tree achieves up to 240 and 210 million queries per second for implicit and regular tree versions, respectively, which is 2.4X times higher than the results for our CPU-optimized B$^+$-tree.

The remainder of the paper is organized as follows. Section 2 surveys related approaches. Section 3 provides background information on B$^+$-tree. Section 4 presents our CPU-optimized design and implementation of B$^+$-tree. Section 5 introduces our HB$^+$-tree, including implementation details. Section 6 presents our experimental evaluation. Section 7 gives our conclusions and identifies future works.

2. RELATED WORK

A large body of work has been developed to optimize B-tree-like indexing. In this section, we focus on analyzing related work on in-memory indexing employing the power of parallel computing platforms.

B$^+$-tree is an indexing structure originally designed for systems with small main memory and comparatively large hard disks [8][15]. To optimize for costly disk I/O, B$^+$-tree operations are performed for entire disk blocks yielding fewer I/O transactions.

Flash-aware indexing trees such as BF-tree, FD-Tree, and LA-Tree have been proposed to reap performance benefits from the superior bandwidth and latency of solid state drives [5, 34, 1]. Furthermore, there exist many approaches for in-memory indexing in order to exploit the superior bandwidth and latency of system main memory. For example, Zhang et al. [22] provide a comprehensive review of data structures for in-memory data management such as for time-/space efficient indexing and concurrency control.

T-tree was proposed for databases where both indexing information and data records reside in main memory [31]. Lu et al. [36] showed that B$^+$-tree outperforms T-tree when concurrency control mechanisms are enforced. Rao et al. [42] introduce a cache-conscious indexing data structure, called Cache Sensitive Search Tree (CSS-tree), which is designed for predominantly static data. Later, Rao et al. [43] extended CSS-tree to CSB$^+$-tree to support incremental updates.

The Bw-tree is designed to exploit the caches of modern multi-core chips and the superior bandwidth of flash storage [33]. Zhou et al. [50] present an access buffering technique for in-memory tree-structured indexes that avoids cache thrashing. Mao et al. [37] introduced Masstree, a shared concurrent data structure combining B$^+$-tree and tries tailored to multi-cores. Hankins et al. [21] studied the effect of node size on cache misses, instruction count, and TLB misses for the CSB$^+$-tree. Based on their experiments, using nodes with sizes of 512 bytes and above, resulted in fewer TLB misses and better performance, while setting nodes size equal to the cache line width produced fewer cache misses but higher TLB misses. Chen et al. [11] explored how prefetching could improve operations in B$^+$-tree, also concluding that nodes wider than a single cache-line resulted in better performance. ART (Adaptive Radix

Tree) and FAST (Fast Architecture Sensitive Tree) are the latest data structures targeting high throughput in-memory indexing [32] [29]. ART is an adaptive radix tree (trie) for high speed in-memory indexing which exhibits better memory usage than previous radix trees. Alvarez et al. [3] compared the lookup throughput and memory footprint of ART to different data structures including B$^+$-tree and hash indexes. FAST is a static binary-tree developed for multi-core systems, which is configurable according to system characteristics such as cache-line size, memory page size and SIMD width. Sewall et al. [45] introduced PALM, a parallel latch-free modification of a B$^+$-tree designed for multi-core processors which is capable of concurrent search and update processing.

All these approaches are developed to utilize either a single-core or a multi-core CPU expect FAST which is capable to be configured for many-core GPU accelerators. But it is only able to operate on GPU resident data and assumes that the data fits into the GPU memory; it is therefore bounded by the GPU memory capacity. There are other GPU-accelerated index structures, which suffer from the same limitations. Fix et al. [16] presented an approach for a GPU-accelerated B$^+$-tree by proposing to modify the memory layout of the B$^+$-tree optimized for GPU memory. No GPU search throughput is reported, but a 9.4X to 19.2X speedup over a single-threaded CPU implementation is shown. Kaczmarski [27] proposed a GPU-specific implementation of B$^+$-tree which is capable of performing efficient updates. Although this approach performs bulk insertions faster than a CPU implementation, search throughput does not surpass 25.6 Kilo Queries Per Second (including copying keys from CPU to GPU and returning values back). Also in [28], the authors proposed a p-ary search with the goal of improving response time of query search using GPUs.

The limited capacity of GPU memory is addressed by other approaches. Daga et al. [13] utilize an APU (Accelerated Processing Unit) to accelerate search in a B$^+$-tree. Since the integrated many-core processor is directly accessing system main memory, their approach does not suffer from the penalty of having to move data between CPU and GPU memory and the limited capacity of GPU memory does not constitute a problem. However, it is still bounded by system main memory bandwidth, which is a critical problem for tree traversal as the tree grows [29]. Their implementation achieved up to 18 MQPS for a 6-core CPU and 70 MQPS for an APU (operating on system memory). Although, an APU is a heterogeneous computing platform, our solution based on a similar platforms has two main advantages. First, we are jointly utilizing two memory components, which is critical to improve the overall system memory bandwidth, while the APU approach is still relaying only on system main memory. Second, the computing power of high-end discrete GPUs is significantly higher than the integrated accelerator available in APUs.

3. B$^+$-TREE BACKGROUND

B$^+$-tree is a variation of B-tree which stores values only in leaf nodes, while inner nodes only comprise keys [15]. Hence, inner nodes and leaf nodes are represented by different data structures. Beside the characteristics adapted from B-tree such as height-balance and optimized memory access, B$^+$-tree offers faster range query support because of its sorted linked leaf nodes. The branching factor of the inner nodes is called the *order* of the B$^+$-tree. Inner nodes of order m, store up to $m-1$ keys and m child references.

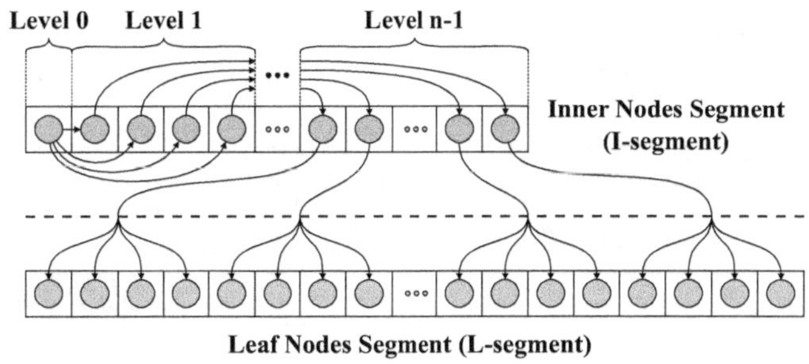

Figure 1: Arrangement of nodes in I-segment and L-segment.

Search in B$^+$-tree is a step-wise process, traversing the tree from the root node, each step consists of two parts: first, the search detects the child node associated with an interval which holds the targeted key, and, second, traversal proceeds to the next node. The process continues until the target key-value pair is found in a leaf node. To perform a range query on a B$^+$-tree, one can simply search for the first key in the range and then traverse leaf nodes until the last key is found.

Data structures in which the structural information is implicitly preserved in the way data is stored rather than explicitly through pointers, are called *implicit data structures* [38]. In implicit representation of B$^+$-tree, nodes are arranged in a breadth-first fashion in a one dimensional array. Since a node's child locations are known, and there is no need to store pointers, an implicit B$^+$-tree requires less memory and provides higher search throughput as compared to a regular B$^+$-tree. However, using an implicit representation leads to a linear time penalty for insert and delete operations. To distinguish the implicit representation from the one with pointers, we refer to the latter as the *regular* B$^+$-tree and the former the *implicit* B$^+$-tree in the rest of this paper.

The notations we use in this paper is summarized below.

H : Height of root node (leaves are at height zero).
S : Size of a variable (a key or a value) in bytes.
S_I : Size of an inner node in bytes.
S_L : Size of a leaf node in bytes.
F_I : Maximum fanout of an inner node.
P_L : Maximum capacity of key-value pairs in a leaf node.

4. CPU-OPTIMIZED B$^+$-TREE

In this section, we describe our parallel design of both, the implicit and the regular B$^+$-tree, optimized to exploit the features of a multi-core Intel CPU. Our CPU-optimized solutions serve as baseline in the evaluation of our hybrid solution, the HB$^+$-tree, described in the next section. The three main optimization we applied for the CPU-optimized solutions are : (1) an SIMD-enabled search algorithm based on the Intel AVX extension, (2) cache blocking to minimize cache misses, (3) huge page utilization to reduce TLB misses.

4.1 Tree Layout

The node structures of the CPU-optimized B$^+$-tree are designed with regards to minimizing both cache and TLB misses during search operations. We make use of huge pages by developing our own memory allocator which allows deter-

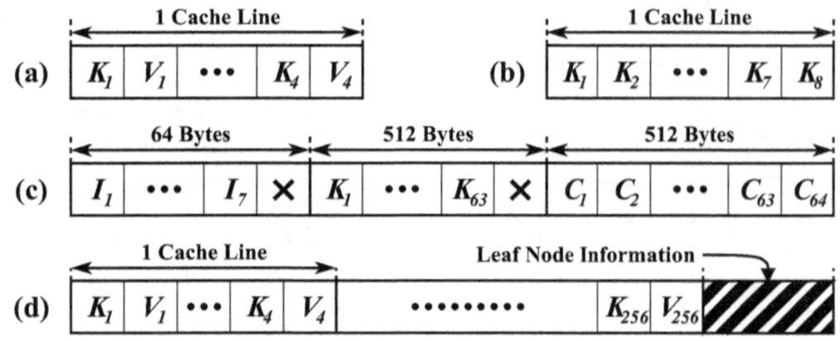

Figure 2: Node structure for CPU-optimized B$^+$-tree. (a) leaf node on implicit B$^+$-tree (b) inner node of implicit B$^+$-tree (c) inner node of regular B$^+$-tree (d) leaf node of regular B$^+$-tree (× indicates the element in fixed to maximum value).

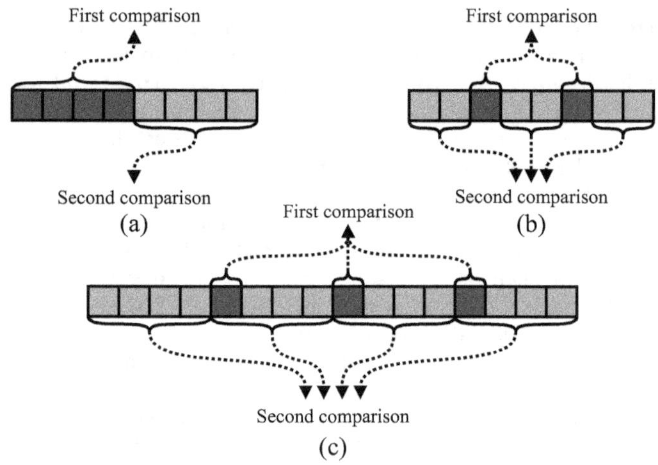

Figure 3: Node search using AVX unit. (a) linear 64-bit (b) hierarchical 64-bit (c) hierarchical 32-bit.

mining whether a node resides on a huge page or not. Coupled with our tree node segmentation, which separates inner and leaf nodes into different segments, our approach minimizes the cost of TLB misses. We also use cache-conscious node structures for better cache data utilization.

The nodes are split into two segments: Inner node segment (I-segment) and leaf node segment (L-segment). The I-segment is always allocated to huge pages, while the L-segment could be allocated to either a huge page or a 4KB page, depending on the total size of the B$^+$-tree. For a given set of N tuples, the space needed for the I-segment (I_{space}) and L-segment (L_{space}) is given in Equation 1 (assuming the tree is full). Since there are only four entries in the last level TLB for 1GB pages and to assure that accessing inner nodes cause no TLB misses, the I-segment must not be larger than 4GB.

$$I_{space} = \frac{N}{P_L(F_I - 1)} \times S_I, \; L_{space} = \frac{N}{P_L} \times S_L \qquad (1)$$

Query search starts from the I-segment, where the root resides, and after passing all inner nodes, continues in the L-segment to determine the target key-value pair in the leaf.

The total number of TLB misses depends on whether the L-segment is placed in a 1GB or a 4KB page. In case of using a 4KB page, since accessing the I-segment causes no TLB miss and each leaf node resides within its individual 4KB page, there is at most a single TLB miss per lookup. If the required memory to store both segments is not more than 4GB, the best option is to also allocate the L-segment on the huge page. Using such a configuration causes no TLB miss for the entire search operation. If the size of the tree exceeds 4GB and the L-segment is allocated to a huge page, the total number of misses depends on the sequence of input queries and the TLB replacement policy.

We design different inner node data structures for our implicit and regular B$^+$-tree, as detailed in Figure 2.

Implicit B$^+$-tree: Since in this tree organization, nodes are arranged in a breadth first fashion, the child node locations are implicitly known. If the node A is the i_{th} node of a tree at level m in breadth first order, then the j_{th} child of A is at position $Offset[m+1]+i\times F_I+j$, where $Offset[l]$ is pointing to the beginning of the l_{th}-level. As a result, it is possible to achieve a higher fanout using the same amount of memory in comparison to the regular B$^+$-tree. We dedicate one cache line per each inner or leaf node ($S_I = S_L = 64$). The only content of leaf nodes are key-value pairs as it shown in Figure 2(a). Since all nodes are fully occupied and they are placed in order, there is no need to explicitly maintain node size as well as next and previous node pointers for the linked list of leaves. Each inner node filled with eight keys as illustrated in Figure 2(b). The number of cache lines required per search query is $H + 1$, where $H = \lceil \log_9 (N/4 + 1) \rceil$.

Regular B$^+$-tree: The minimum amount of space required for an inner node with m children is equal to $(m - 1)S + mP$ bytes, where P is the reference size in bytes. Considering $S = P = 8$, the maximally achievable fanout using a single cache line is limited to 4. Such a small fanout leads to many random memory accesses during search operations. For better lookup performance, we propose a structure for inner nodes consisting of indexes, keys and child references. As illustrated in Figure 2(c), each inner node consist of 17 cache lines ($S_I = 1088$), where the first one is dedicated to indexes, while keys and references are arranged in the following sixteen cache lines ($F_I = 64$). Each index is assigned to the maximum value of the corresponding cache line ($I_s = K_{8s}$). Utilizing indexes, only three cache lines are retrieved to find the successor node. The search algorithm first searches indexes and, based on the comparison result, fetches the corresponding cache lines, which includes the targeted child reference.

We apply inner node fragmentation in order to achieve better memory and cache line data utilization. The data of each inner node is broken up into two fragments. One fragment contains key-value pairs and child references, and the other one contains the node size, parent and sibling references. Whenever an inner node is needed, our node memory allocator dedicates one of each fragment from two separated data structures in such a way that both fragments share the same index which can be used to retrieve both fragments later on. Also, we set all empty keys of each inner node to the maximum value in our implementation ($2^n - 1$ for an n-bit integer), so that the lookup algorithm is able to perform node search without knowing the inner node size.

The size of a leaf node in the regular B$^+$-tree impacts the range query performance. Moving to the successor leaf node in the implicit B$^+$-tree can be done very efficiently, as leaf nodes are arranged sequentially. But the small leaf node capacity of the regular B$^+$-tree causes a series of cache misses during range query execution and, thus, decreases performance, while leaf nodes bigger than a cache line lead to slower leaf node search. To address this problem, we designed bigger leaf nodes and make use of a dedicated memory pool manager for allocating leaf nodes and last level inner nodes so that both point and range queries can be realized efficiently. We pack 64 small leaf nodes into a bigger node, which we extend with another cache line to store leaf node information. Each last level inner node is only related to one big leaf node. Similar to the node fragmentation technique we used, here, our memory pool manager allocates leaf nodes and last level inner nodes from two different memory pools in such a way that both nodes share the same index. Consequently, the tree lookup algorithm can directly retrieve the cache line in the leaf node, where the targeted key is located, by using the index of the last inner node and the inner node search result. Moreover, we set all empty elements of a leaf node to the maximum value, which enables the lookup algorithm to search a leaf node without knowing the size of the leaf node. In case the search key is the maximum value, the lookup algorithm must read the node size to perform leaf node search. Although the capacity of the bigger leaf node is 256 key-value pairs, we consider $P_L = 4$ in our analysis since the addressable units from a last inner node are cache lines with a capacity of 4. The structures of implicit and regular B$^+$-tree are illustrated in Figure 2(a) and (d), respectively. The total number of cache lines needed for each query is $3H + 1$, where H (height of tree) is:

$$\left\lceil \log_{32}\left(\frac{N}{4}+1\right)\right\rceil \leq H \leq \left\lfloor \log_{16}\left(\frac{N/2+1}{2}\right)\right\rfloor + 1 \quad (2)$$

Using 32-bit variables, 16 keys or values can fit into a cache line. Consequently, an inner node's fanout increases to 17 and 256 for implicit and regular B$^+$-tree, respectively. The capacity of each cache line in leaf nodes increases to 8.

4.2 Utilizing SIMD Unit for Search

The Advanced Vector Extensions 2 (AVX2) is the latest enhancement to Intel x86 processors for SIMD operations. AVX2 is capable of operating on 256-bit registers, which is equivalent to eight 32-bit or four 64-bit integers.

Since the size of AVX registers is half the size of a cache line, it is not feasible to compare an entire cache line using a single AVX comparison operation. We propose two different approaches to employ the AVX unit: linear and hierarchical.

The linear approach divides the cache line into two equal parts and separately searches each one. In contrast, the hierarchical approach divides the array into three equal parts and uses the boundary keys to locate the part where the target is placed.

The hierarchical approach needs less data loaded into AVX2 registers, while the linear approach is control dependency free, which is safe for out-of-order execution. We also implemented sequential search as a baseline to measure the resulting speedup. Our AVX-enabled search algorithms are illustrated in Figure 3.

Software Pipelining is a method to improve loop performance by rearranging instructions such that the instructions of the modified loop are chosen from different iterations of the original loop [24]. Using this method, dependent instructions from a single iteration are scattered among multiple loop iterations, so that the CPU pipeline can be scheduled to reduce instruction stalls caused by memory latency. To this end, each CPU thread loads a batch of queries and resolves them concurrently. Using this configuration, the thread switches to resolving another query whenever the current search operation is blocked by a data access. The optimal size for batches depends on the system configuration. Small batch sizes cannot provide reasonable overlap, while large overlap leads to inefficient CPU register utilization. In our experiments, a size of 16 resulted in the best performance. The total number of concurrent queries is up to 16 × *CPU Threads*.

5. HYBRID CPU-GPU B$^+$-TREE

In this section, we introduce the design of our CPU-GPU hybrid B$^+$-tree. We describe the tree's memory layout and the heterogeneous CPU-GPU search algorithm. Finally, we present a load balancing method, as technique for fine-tuning our hybrid tree across systems with different GPU-to-CPU computation power ratios.

5.1 Overview

Current multi-purpose processors are heavily relying on cache units to mitigate the memory wall problem [49]. For trees which would fit entirely into the last level cache (LLC), caching is very effective and memory latency would almost vanish. However, search throughput drops noticeably as the tree size surpasses LLC capacity and becomes memory bound [29]. Although techniques such as prefetching and software pipelining are applicable for tree-based index search to alleviate the memory latency problem, the system performance is still bounded by the memory bandwidth [11, 29].

The results from previous efforts of implementing a B+-tree on GPUs demonstrate the realizable performance benefits [29]. Instead of relying on caching, GPUs use high degrees of multi-threading and fast context switching logic with near zero overhead, to hide memory latency [12]. Since this mechanism is not affected by the volume of data, the throughput of tree indexing using GPUs is more resilient against tree growth. As result, GPU-based approaches outperform CPU-based approaches for tree sizes larger than the LLC [29]. However, GPUs cannot maintain their performance advantage, because the amount of their memory is limited in comparison to CPUs. It is not feasible to make use of the computational capabilities of GPUs, when the tree grows beyond the GPU memory capacity using previous methods [13].

To address this dilemma, we propose a new B$^+$-tree, called HB$^+$-tree, leveraging the hybrid memory architecture and heterogeneous computing model of today's computing platforms. Here, we employ the computing power of discrete many-core accelerators for index searching on trees larger than the accelerator's dedicated memory. We design HB$^+$-tree based on a compute platform accelerated by GPUs. To achieve higher total memory bandwidth, we scatter the nodes across GPU *and* CPU memory in a way which enables the index search algorithm to utilize *both memories* concurrently. As a result, the effective system memory bandwidth is the aggregate of both memory units. Also, we design a heterogeneous search algorithm to minimize the communication overhead between processors and *utilize both* – GPU and CPU – simultaneously.

Since our target use cases are lookup-intensive and batch update processing dominated scenarios (e.g., data ware/-

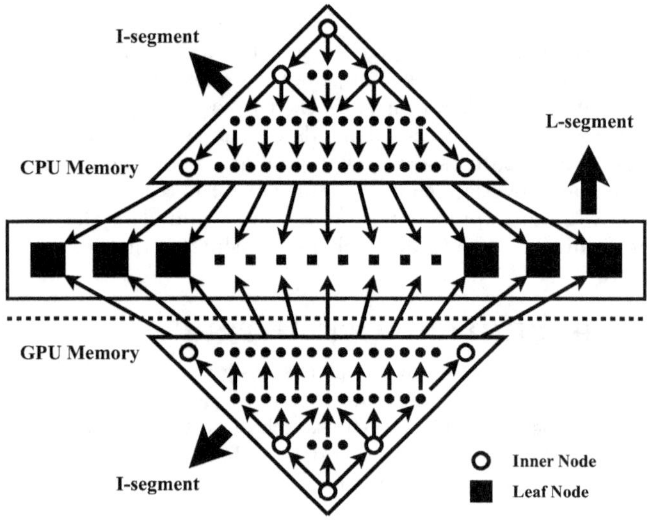

Figure 4: HB$^+$-tree node arrangement: The triangular area is the I-segment which is duplicated on both CPU and GPU memory and the rectangular area is the L-segment which resides only in the CPU memory.

houses), we envision that our indexes are integrated into existing systems based on passing query input and index output via CPU main memory. Also, all our HB$^+$-tree versions exhibits the same interface as our CPU-optimized B$^+$-tree; both follow the conventional B+-tree interface.

5.2 Tree Layout

Similar to the CPU-optimized tree, HB$^+$-tree also consist of I-segments and L-segments. The L-segment is configured based on the CPU search algorithm and only resides in CPU memory, while the I-segment resides in both GPU and CPU memory, i.e., it is mirrored across both memory units. The rationale for this design is that leaf nodes require more space than inner nodes for storage and are less frequently accessed; thus, we place them in CPU memory, which has a higher capacity but lower bandwidth.

Figure 4 illustrates the placement of inner and leaf nodes in the HB$^+$-tree. The leaf nodes of both, the regular and implicit HB$^+$-tree, are identical to the ones of the CPU-optimized version of the tree.

Unlike main memory, the GPU memory architecture does not have a fixed unit of transfer. As a warp executes an instruction accessing GPU memory, the GPU translates the access into one or more aligned data transfers of size 32, 64 or 128 bytes [40]. This limitation is a consequence of coalesced memory access, which results in higher bandwidth as well as higher latency.

We discovered that the best balance between thread scheduling efficiency and bandwidth utilization results from using transfers of size 64 bytes. Since our CPU-optimized B$^+$-tree nodes are also based on 64 byte transfers, the inner node structures of HB$^+$-tree are similar to our CPU-optimized B$^+$-tree. For the regular version, the inner nodes are identical, but we reduce fan-out of inner nodes in implicit HB$^+$-tree to 8, so that we can utilize the same thread hierarchy for both data access and node search and avoid warp divergence, and we set the last key (K_8) to the maximum representable value.

For the 32-bit version, F_I is increased to 16 and 256 for implicit and regular HB$^+$-tree, respectively.

5.3 Parallel Node Search on GPU

In this section, we first describe our search algorithm for an arbitrary sized array and then explain how it is used for search in HB$^+$-tree.

For a given *key* and a sorted *array* of s elements such that *key* is not bigger than the last element ($key \leq array[s]$), the parallel search algorithm finds the maximum index i such that $key \leq array[i]$. The possible values for i are $[1..s]$. To find the target index i, the search algorithm initializes s threads ($t_j : 1 \leq j \leq s$), where each thread is assigned to a single result value. First, each thread (t_j) compares *key* to the associated value ($array[j]$) to check whether *key* is less than or equal to $array[j]$ and stores the result ($r_t : 0, 1$) in a shared array. Based on the thread's local comparison result (r_t) and the result from the prior thread (r_{t-1}), each thread determines if it is assigned the final answer. If so (i.e., $r_t = 1$ and $r_{t-1} = 0$), the thread sets the final answer to its own index.

Because the last keys of all inner nodes of HB$^+$-tree are always set to the maximum ($2^n - 1$ for an n bit number), it is assured that all queries are less than or equal to the last key, and our search algorithm always returns a valid result.

Searching an inner node in the regular HB$^+$-tree is slightly different and requires three memory accesses instead of one and involves three steps. First, the parallel search algorithm is applied on indexes to determine the interval of keys containing the search query. Then, the corresponding interval is fetched from GPU memory and searched using the parallel algorithm to identify the next node position. Finally, the address of the next level node is retrieved using an extra memory transfer.

The total number of concurrent queries at the GPU is equal to $GPU\_Threads/T$, where the optimal number of $GPU\_Threads$ depends on the GPU specification and T is the number of threads dedicated per each query (8 for a 64-bit implementation and 16 for a 32-bit implementation).

5.4 Search Query Execution

Since we considered that the input queries are given in CPU memory, the first step is to transfer them into GPU memory, before the GPU starts executing a search operation. After GPU finished its task, the intermediate results, – references to nodes where the search operation must be resumed, – are transfered into main memory after the GPU completes the search operation. In the last step, the CPU continues the search operation to reach the target tuple. The execution of a search on the CPU is analogous to the implementation for the CPU-optimized B$^+$-tree.

The given queries are broken into buckets of size M which are processed independently according to the following steps, where $T_i, i = 1..4$ are times required for each step in our cost model.

1. Transfer bucket to GPU memory.
   $T_1 = T_{init} + (M \times S)/Bandwidt$
2. GPU traversal of all inner nodes of tree per each query.
   $T_2 = K_{init} + (M/SIMD_G) \times P_{GPU}$
3. Transfer of intermediate results to CPU memory.
   $T_3 = T_{init} + (M \times R)/Bandwidt$
4. CPU continues search in leaf nodes.
   $T_4 = (M/SIMD_C) \times P_{CPU}$

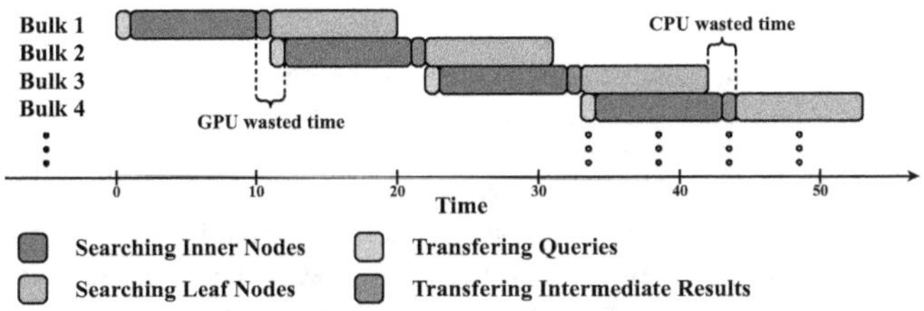

Figure 5: CPU-GPU pipelining.

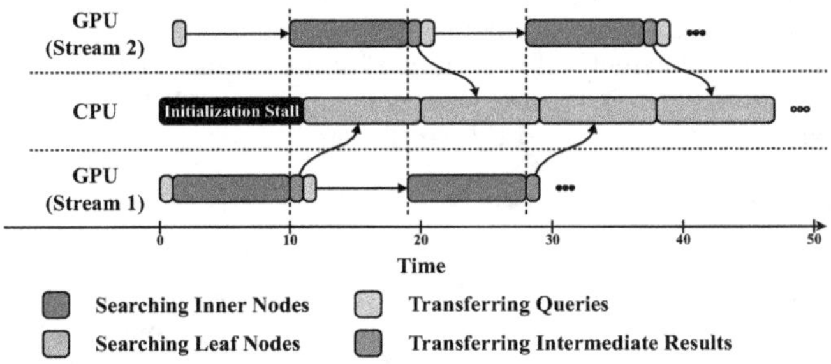

Figure 6: CPU-GPU pipelining with double buffering.

R	: Size of an intermediate result in bytes.
T_{init}	: Data transfer initialization time between main memory and GPU memory.
K_{init}	: GPU initialization time for search operation.
$SIMD_G$	: GPU SIMD width.
$SIMD_C$	: CPU SIMD width.
P_{GPU}	: Average processing time for a query on GPU.
P_{CPU}	: Average processing time for a query on CPU.
Bandwidth	: Data transfer bandwidth between main memory and GPU memory.

Assigning the proper value for M is important since both performance parameters, throughput and latency, are controlled by M. Small bucket sizes increase the influence of overhead constants (K_{init} and T_{init}) against effective computation time, leading to lower throughput; increasing M increases the cost of each step (T_i), resulting in higher latency.

Apart from how each bucket is processed, bucket scheduling is also important for optimal utilization of resources. The simplest approach is to load and resolve each query bucket sequentially. The drawbacks of using this approach are two-fold: (1) it is not feasible to utilize both processors concurrently, and (2) there is no opportunity of overlapping communication and computation to eliminate data transfer overhead. Thus, the cost for resolving each bucket is the aggregate of all steps ($T_S = \sum_{i=1}^{4} T_i$). We propose CPU-GPU pipelining and employ a double buffering technique to eliminate these drawbacks.

CPU-GPU pipelining improves system performance by overlapping the execution of buckets. As illustrated in Figure 5, the next bucket is loaded as soon as the intermediate result of the current bucket is transferred into CPU memory. In this way, CPU and GPU can be utilized concurrently. The average time needed to resolve queries within a bucket is reduced to $T_P = T_1 + \max(T_2 + T_3, T_4)$ (ignoring pipeline initialization stalls). Considering $T_2 = T_4$, T_P is equal to $T_1 + T_2 + T_3$, then CPU processing time has been eliminated.

Furthermore, we extend pipelining with double buffering to eliminate the data transfer time. The timeline for the enhanced pipelining approach is given in Figure 6. We initiate two GPU threads which are working on separated buffers but share the same processors, where each thread operates as a CPU-GPU pipelined approach. The average cost of processing each bucket is $T_P = \max(T_2, T_4)$, considering that data transfer time is smaller than computation time.

Although double buffering improves overall system throughput, it also increases processing latency because of prefetching of buckets. The average latency of the pipelined approach is $T_1 + T_2 + T_3 + \frac{T_4}{2}$, which increases to $2 \times T_2 + \frac{T_4}{2}$ by applying double buffering.

5.5 Load Balancing Scheme

Our HB$^+$-tree design is primarily targeting systems which are accelerated using sufficiently powerful GPUs and the system throughput is bounded by the CPU. Therefore, HB$^+$-tree devotes only a small share of the query load to the CPU, which is only searching leaf nodes while all inner nodes are processed by the GPU.

To offer a more generally applicable solution, we enhance HB$^+$-tree with a load balancing mechanism, which improves resource utilization on systems with an arbitrary GPU-to-CPU computation power ratio, refereed to as *load balanced* HB$^+$-tree.

With the load balancing scheme, the CPU starts traversing inner nodes up to a specific depth (D) and transfers the query and the intermediate inner node index to GPU memory. Then, the GPU resumes traversing up to the final inner node level and returns the leaf node index to the CPU. Finally, the CPU searches the leaf node to determine the target key-value pair. We prefer to dedicate the top inner nodes to the CPU since the space required for them is comparably lower than the inner nodes at the bottom of tree resulting in better cache utilization and lookup performance.

Let $I_{G,i}$ and $I_{C,i}$ be the average cost of searching at depth i for GPU and CPU, respectively, and let L_C be the average cost of searching a leaf node, then the average cost of a single search (C) is given according to Equation 3. Adjusting the parameter D is required to minimize C_{inner}.

$$C = \max(L_C + \sum_{0}^{D} C_{C,i}, \sum_{D+1}^{H} C_{G,i}) \tag{3}$$

Moreover, to provide a finer granularity for work load distribution, we divide each bucket into two parts. For the first part, $R \times M$ queries ($0 \leq R \leq 1$) of a bucket, the CPU searches only D levels of inner nodes, while for the rest of the queries ($M \times (1 - R)$), the CPU searches $D + 1$ levels. Using the new parameter R, the search cost C is updated to Equation 4.

$$C = \max(L_C + \sum_{0}^{D-1} C_{C,i} + R\, C_{C,D}, (1 - R)C_{G,D} + \sum_{D+1}^{H} C_{G,i}) \tag{4}$$

We develop a discovery algorithm to determine the values for D and R that minimize C. The algorithm starts from $D = 0$ and $R = 1$, where it dedicates the maximum possible load to the GPU. First, it linearly searches for the optimal value of D (coarser parameter). Then, it adjusts R (finer parameter) using binary search. The discovery algorithm is given in Algorithm 1.

Algorithm 1 Discovery algorithm

```
D ← 0, R = 1
(Time_GPU, Time_CPU) = getSample(D, R)†
while Time_GPU > Time_CPU do
    D ← D + 1
    (Time_GPU, Time_CPU) = getSample(D, R)
R ← 0.5
for step ← 2 to 5 do
    (Time_GPU, Time_CPU) = getSample(D, R)
    if Time_GPU > Time_CPU then
        R ← R + 1/(2^step)
    else
        R ← R − 1/(2^step)
```

† *getSample* runs the program for given D and R; it returns the time GPU and CPU require to perform their work share.

We also change the bucket handling strategy which is advantageous only for GPU bounded systems. The GPU must perform thread scheduling prior to starting effective kernel execution as a new kernel program is submitted to the GPU. Pre-submitting of a successor kernel before the current one is finished, enables the GPU to perform scheduling of the next kernel, concurrently to the previous kernel execution. For this to work, we require at least three concurrently operating buckets. Since this optimization technique is not effective for CPU bounded systems, we restrict the number of query buckets in the not-load-balanced version of HB$^+$-tree to two in order to reduce latency. However, we increase the number of query buckets to three in the load balanced implementation of the HB$^+$-tree for better GPU utilization.

5.6 Batch Update

The implicit B$^+$-tree is not capable of processing individual updates. Whenever an update is required, the entire tree must be re-built. The algorithm first builds both I-segment and L-segment in main memory based on the new dataset and, subsequently transfers the I-segment to GPU memory.

Efficiently processing concurrent batch updates with the regular HB$^+$-tree faces two challenges: (1) I-segment synchronization and (2) concurrency handling. The former is specific to HB$^+$-tree, while the latter is a general challenge for tree indexing. We propose two different tree update methods; their performances depends on the batch size.

We design an asynchronous parallel update method which first performs updates in main memory in parallel and then transfers the entire I-segment to GPU memory. The given update queries are processed in groups of size 16K. Each thread takes a query and searches the tree up to the last level inner node. At this point, the thread checks if the query execution causes any node merge or split. If not, it requests the lock assigned to the inner node and performs the update. Because of HB$^+$-tree's big leaf nodes (256 entries), more than 99% of the update queries can be resolved this way, on average. The remaining unresolved queries are processed subsequently using a single thread. When all queries are executed, the I-segment in GPU memory is updated. This method is more efficient for bigger batch sizes which often result in many inner node modifications. In these cases, it is more beneficial to transfer the entire I-segment once, instead of performing many small transfers for each inner node.

For smaller batch sizes, we propose a synchronized update method which is performed by two threads, a *modifying* and a *synchronizing* one. The modifying thread executes update queries and submits a request for each modified inner node to a shared queue. Upon receiving a request, the synchronizing thread updates the inner node in GPU memory according to the node's replica in main memory. Using this method, tree update and node synchronization proceed concurrently. Although, it is feasible to implement this method with multiple modifying and synchronizing threads, we found the performance of this method is bounded by the communication initialization latency between main memory and GPU memory which was not reduced by parallelism.

6. EVALUATION

We now present the performance evaluation of both CPU-optimized B$^+$-tree and HB$^+$-tree. First, we describe the experimental setup and workload. Then, we demonstrate the impact of various optimizations on the individual approaches, and finally, we compare the search operation performance of CPU-optimized B$^+$-tree and HB$^+$-tree considering latency and throughput.

6.1 Experimental Setup

We used two system setups for evaluating our approaches. The first machine (M_1) is equipped with Intel Xeon E5-2665 accelerated by the Nvidia Geforce 780 GTX. The second machine (M_2) is an Intel Core-i7 4800MQ accelerated by the Nvidia Geforce 770M GTX.

For all experiments except the experiment on skewed data, we generated multiple sets of key-value with 8M (2^{23}) to 1B (2^{30}) tuples, where keys and values are randomly generated according to a uniform distribution on $[0 - MAX]$ ($MAX = 2^n - 1$, n is number of bits: 32 or 64). After constructing the B$^+$-tree using this set, we randomly permuted the pairs using the Knuth shuffle [30]. Finally, we use the new sequence as the input for the search operation.

Our multi-threaded implementation is using OpenMP, an API for parallel computing based on the shared memory programming paradigm [14]. We also made use of PAPI to better understand the performance of our implementation. PAPI is an API for accessing available hardware counters inside the CPU [9].

6.2 CPU-optimized B$^+$-tree Evaluation

Memory Page Configuration. In this experiment, we aim to determine the memory page configuration that maximizes the search operation throughput. We evaluated our B$^+$-tree using three different configurations: (1) both I-segment and L-segment on small pages, (2) I-segment on huge pages and L-segment on small pages, (3) both I-segment and L-segment on huge pages.

To examine our expectation about the average TLB misses per query, we evaluated a single-threaded implementation of all three configurations and counted the TLB misses during search operations using PAPI. Since OpenMP library causes extra TLB misses, we excluded multi-threading to obtain more accurate measurement. We plot the average TLB miss per each query in Figure 7(a). Without utilizing huge pages, the misses increase as the tree grows. Also, it can be seen that searching in the implicit tree causes more TLB misses

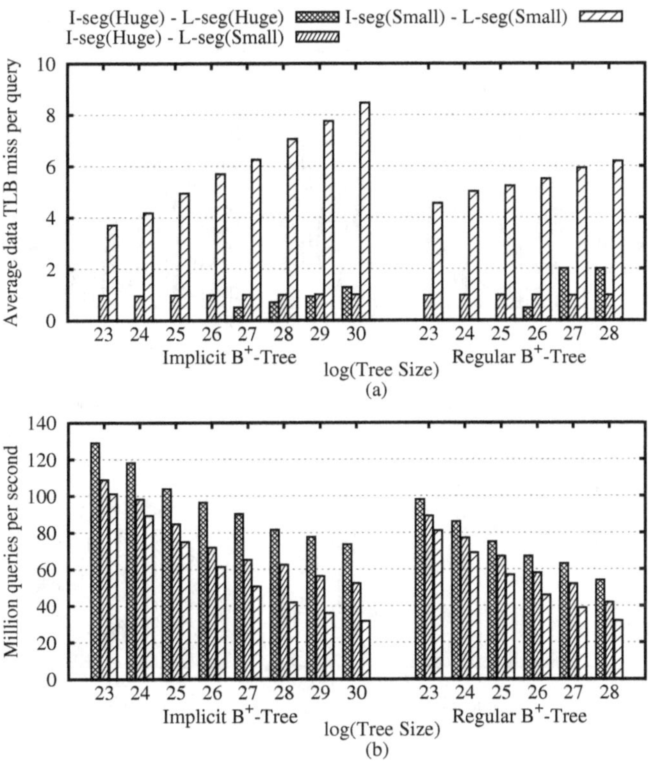

Figure 7: Memory page configuration evaluation. (a) TLB misses (b) Throughput.

than for the regular B^+-tree. The reason is the fanout of inner nodes in the implicit tree is inferior to the regular tree, consequently, the tree depth is higher. Allocating only inner nodes on huge pages, significantly reduces the number of misses. In this case, misses are independent of tree depth and they are bounded to one TLB miss per query. Allocating the entire tree on huge pages eliminates misses for smaller trees which do not need more than 4GB of space. As the required space exceeds this amount, the average miss rate increases and surpasses one miss per query. We conclude from Figure 7(a) that in terms of TLB misses, the second configuration is more robust against tree growth, while the third one is best for trees less than 4GB in size.

To determine the effect of TLB misses on tree search performance, we evaluated the multi-threaded tree search using the same configurations. The results are in Figure 7(b). As expected, the first configuration is the least performing. The fastest configuration is the third one, although, it generates more TLB misses than the second configuration for bigger trees. According to our analysis, this behavior is the consequence of the different costs of misses for 4K and 1G pages. As a TLB miss occurs, a page walk is required to retrieve the requested physical address. For 4K pages, five memory accesses are required to translate logical to physical address, while three accesses are sufficient for 1G pages [25]. Even if the TLB miss rate is higher in the third configuration, the penalty of a page walk is less significant, which results in better performance. This experiment indicates the superiority of using huge pages in this application.

SIMD Accelerated Node Search. We now examine the node search algorithms to determine the fastest one and measure the resulting improvements. A query search operation is evaluated using three different search algorithms: (1) sequential, (2) linear SIMD, and (3) hierarchical SIMD; software pipelining is applied in all of these configurations. To indicate the effectiveness of software pipelining in this application, we also evaluated sequential search without software pipelining. Since AVX2 support is required for the evaluation, we evaluated this experiment on M_2 (M_1 does not support AVX2). The result of the experiments are given in Figure 8.

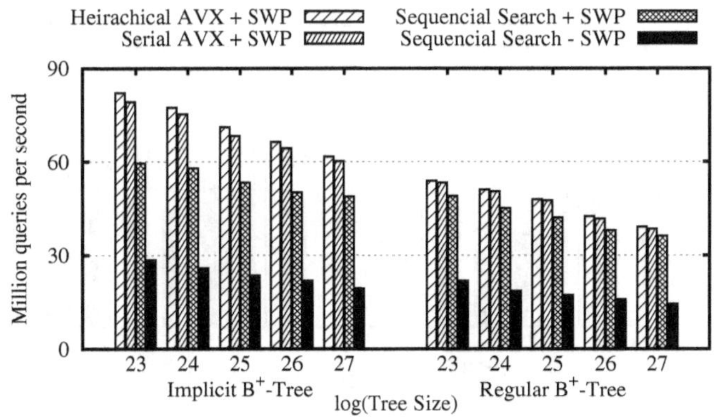

Figure 8: Software pipelining and node search comparison.

Enabling software pipelining is highly effective and improves the system throughout between 108%-152%, while it increased latency by 6X on average. Among the node search algorithms, the hierarchical SIMD approach, achieved the best result; it is slightly faster than linear search. Both SIMD implementations lose their advantage to sequential search as the tree size grows. This behavior confirms that tree processing becomes memory latency bounded for bigger trees, and memory optimization techniques are ever more important in this case.

Comparison with FAST. We compare our CPU-optimized implicit B^+-tree to FAST [29], the fastest reported indexing tree in the literature, – also an implicit structure, – to assure our CPU-optimized B^+-tree design is competitive enough to be used as a performance baseline. As shown in Figure 9, our B^+-tree achieved 1.3X higher throughput on average than FAST. Our different SIMD-enabled node search, which allows us to reach higher node fan-out and, consequently, better cache line utilization, is the source for this improvement. Even though our implementation achieves better performance than what FAST reported, we do not aim to challenge FAST in this work, since FAST is designed to be a configurable data structure, able to adapt to different hardware configurations, while our design is specifically tuned for the Intel architecture.

6.3 HB$^+$-tree Evaluation

Bucket Handling Strategies. In this experiment, we study three different bucket handling techniques: (1) sequential, (2) pipelining, and (3) pipelining with double buffering. With sequential bucket handling, it is neither feasible to employ CPU and GPU simultaneously, nor overlap communication and computation. This approach is the simplest; we use it as baseline in our evaluation. Resolving buckets using pipelining allows us to partially overlap CPU and GPU computations. Double buffering helps to overlap

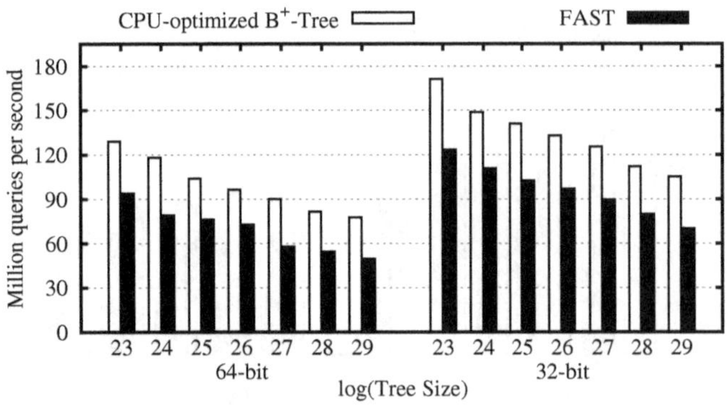

Figure 9: Comparison of FAST and implicit CPU-optimized B$^+$-tree.

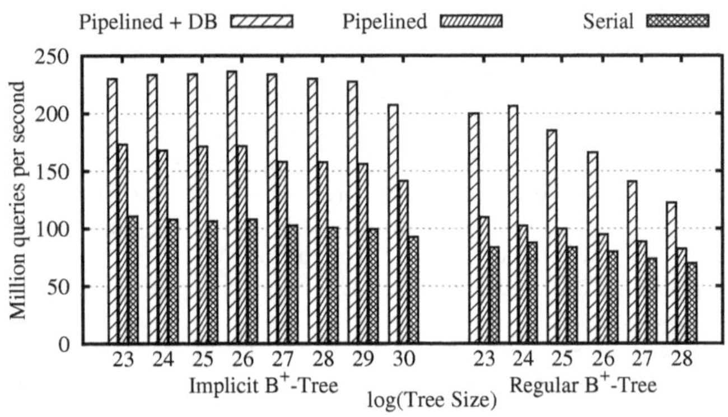

Figure 10: Bucket handling strategy evaluation.

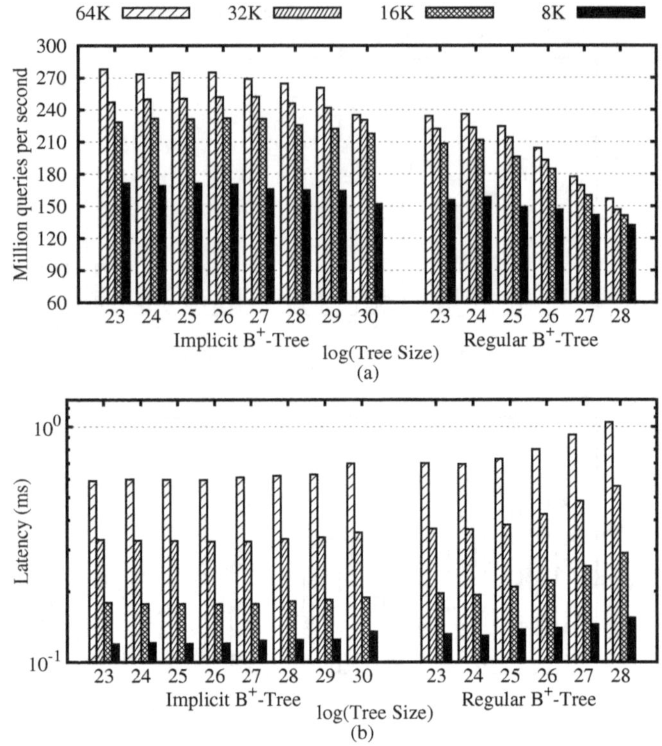

Figure 11: Experiment on varying size of buckets (a) throughput (b) latency.

data transfer and search, so that it improves resource utilization. We show the results for search using these techniques in Figure 10.

Sequential bucket handling is the least efficient. Pipelining is more effective for the implicit B$^+$-tree. It increases the throughput by 56% for implicit and by 20% for regular B$^+$-tree. The double buffering technique is effective for both tree versions. Using bucket pipelining extended by double buffering improves throughput by 110% over the baseline technique. Gaining twice the throughput in comparison to the sequential approach indicates that we successfully managed to simultaneously exploit the computation capabilities of both processors.

Bucket Size. The goal of this experiment is to determine the optimal bucket size considering both throughput and latency. Increasing the bucket size, diminishes the influence of communication and GPU initialization overheads, resulting in better system throughput, while at the same time, increases the system latency. We evaluated the search operation using M_1 for different bucket sizes: 8K, 16K, 32K, and 64K. As shown in Figure 11, search throughput grows, as bucket size increases for the implicit B$^+$-tree, while for the regular B$^+$-tree, the throughput is nearly the same for bucket sizes 16K, 32K, and 64K. Considering that the average latency also increases as the bucket size grows (2.7X for 64K and 1.7X for 32K), we use 16K as the optimal bucket size for the rest of our experiments.

Impact of Skewed Data. We studied HB$^+$-tree for several input data distributions, including Uniform, Normal($\mu = 0.5$, $\sigma^2 = 0.125$), Gamma($k = 3$, $\theta = 3$) and Zipf($\alpha = 2$). The generated random values are in the range $[0, 1]$. Before the values are given to search queries, they are linearly mapped to $[0, MAX]$. We used the Uniform distribution as the baseline and scaled the results of other distributions accordingly. The normalized results are illustrated in Figure 12.

The performance on all distributions, except Zipf, is within 1.1X of the Uniform distribution, while the performance for Zipf input data increases by up to 2.2X. When the data becomes more skewed, the same portion of the tree is accessed more frequently, which results in a higher cache hit rate. This behavior is even more pronounced for highly skewed data, such as the Zipf distribution.

Update Performance. In this experiment, we evaluate the performance of update query execution on HB$^+$-tree as compared to CPU-optimized B$^+$-tree for both regular and implicit tree versions.

We first present evaluations of the different update query execution methods for the regular HB$^+$-tree including both the single- and multi-threaded versions of the synchronous and asynchronous approach. Figure 13(a) illustrates the throughput of these methods for various tree sizes; the I-segment transfer time is excluded for the asynchronous approaches. Parallel execution is more effective in the asynchronous approach which results in 3X higher throughput in comparison with the single-threaded approach. The synchronous approach is only 30% faster than the multi-threaded one, which is bounded by the data transfer latency between CPU and GPU memory.

The I-segment synchronization times for different tree sizes are illustrated in Figure 13(b). To examine the effect of I-segment synchronization overhead, we measure the time required to perform batch updates with different batch sizes in a tree of size 64M. The results are shown in Figure 14.

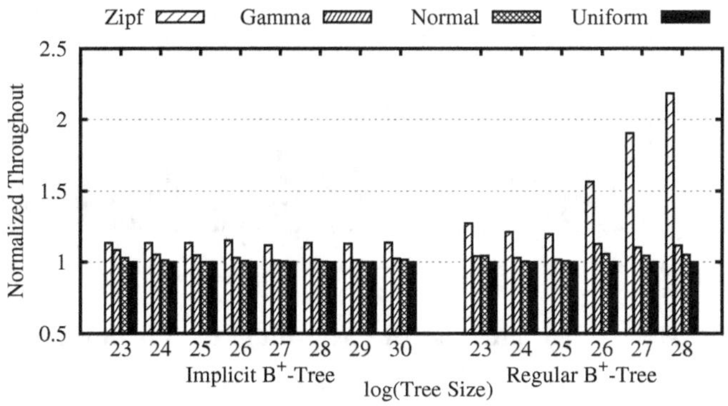

Figure 12: Experiment on different distributions.

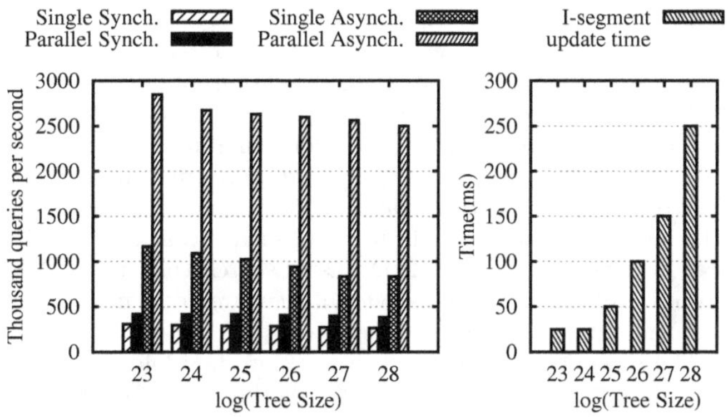

Figure 13: Evaluation of Regular B$^+$-tree update.

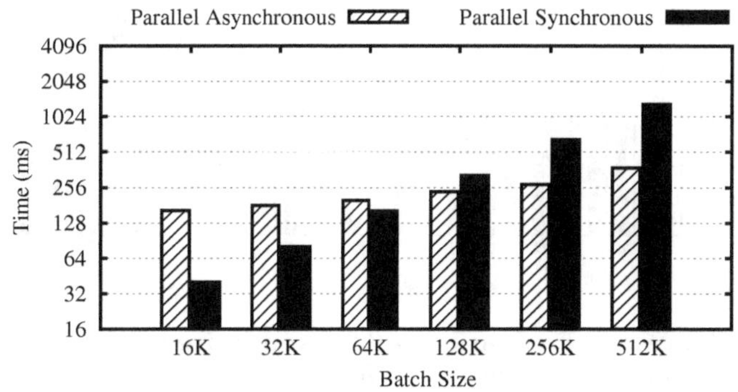

Figure 14: Regular B$^+$-tree update for different batch sizes.

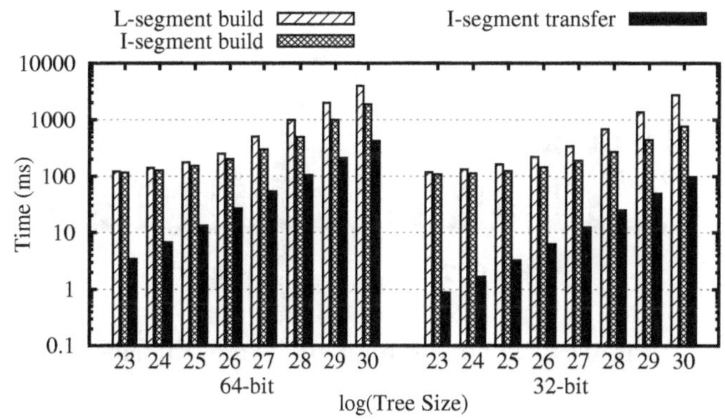

Figure 15: Implicit HB$^+$-tree update.

Up to a batch size of 64K, the synchronous approach performs better because of the slow I-segment transfer in the asynchronous approach. But for batches larger than 128K, the asynchronous is more effective, as the I-segment transfer cost is amortized by the larger number of queries processed. This experiment shows that the choice of update depends on the batch size. A synchronous update is more efficient for smaller batches while an asynchronous one performs better for larger batches.

To update implicit CPU-optimized B$^+$-tree, the entire tree has to be rebuilt, including the I-segment and L-segment. For implicit HB$^+$-tree, it is additionally required to transfer the I-segment to GPU memory. To compare the cost of updating these two trees, we measure the cost of each phase including L-segment rebuilding, I-segment rebuilding, and I-segment transfer separately as shown in Figure 15. The cost of transferring the I-segment is only 3 to 7 percent of tree reconstruction.

6.4 HB$^+$-tree vs. CPU-optimized B$^+$-tree

We now compare the search performance of HB$^+$-tree against the CPU-optimized B$^+$-tree in terms of throughput, latency and selectivity using M_1.

Throughput. Figures 16(a) and 16(b) show the search performance of both trees (for 64-bit and 32-bit variable sizes). The throughput of the implicit HB$^+$-tree is almost constant for different tree sizes, which indicates that the amount of time the GPU requires for traversing inner nodes is inferior to the time, the CPU requires for scheduling and searching leaf nodes. Consequently, the search performance is bounded by the computational power of the CPU. However, the regular HB$^+$-tree does not show similar behavior; similar to the CPU-optimized tree, its performance declines as the tree grows. The GPU accelerated approach outperforms the CPU-optimized approach by 2.4X and 2.1X higher throughput on average for 64-bit and 32-bit variables, respectively.

Latency. Figure 16(c) illustrates the query search latency for both HB$^+$-tree and CPU-optimized B$^+$-tree. The hybrid approach exhibits comparably higher latency, 67X on average, than the CPU-optimized one. The higher latency is the consequence of a different number of queries required for an effective utilization of each platform. The number of concurrent queries for CPU and GPU are 2^8 and 2^{14}, respectively, where the ratio (64) is almost the same as the latency ratio. The average latency of the hybrid approach is less than 0.18ms for the implicit B$^+$-tree and 0.25ms for regular the B$^+$-tree.

Range queries. In this experiment, we compare HB$^+$-tree against CPU-optimized B$^+$-tree in performing range queries for different numbers of matching keys per query for a total of 128M keys. Figure 17 shows the performance of range queries for the retrieval of 1 to 32 keys. Since range queries require more leaf node traversal, the ratio of the search time in inner nodes to the entire lookup time decreases for these queries. As a result, the lookup performance of implicit and regular tree versions becomes similar; also, HB$^+$-tree looses its advantage as more keys per query match. HB$^+$-tree is more than 80% faster than the CPU-optimized B$^+$-tree up to 8 matching keys per query and the performance advantage decreases to 22% for 32 matching keys per query.

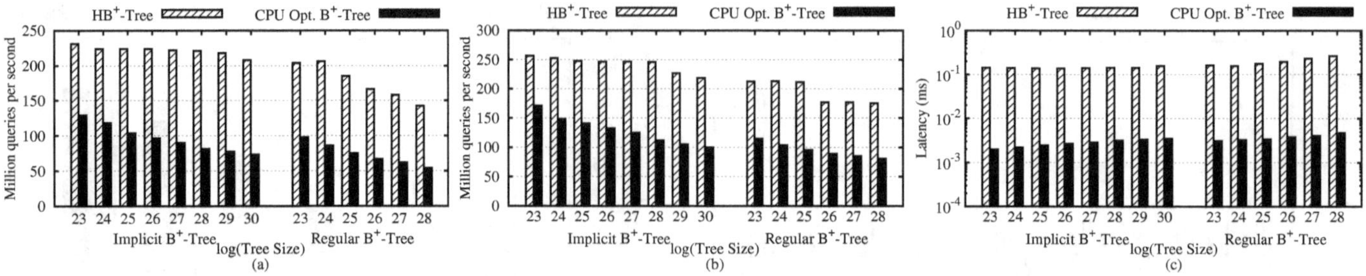

Figure 16: Evaluation of CPU-optimized B$^+$-tree and HB$^+$-tree. (a) Throughput (64-bit) (b) Throughput (32-bit) (c) Latency (64-bit).

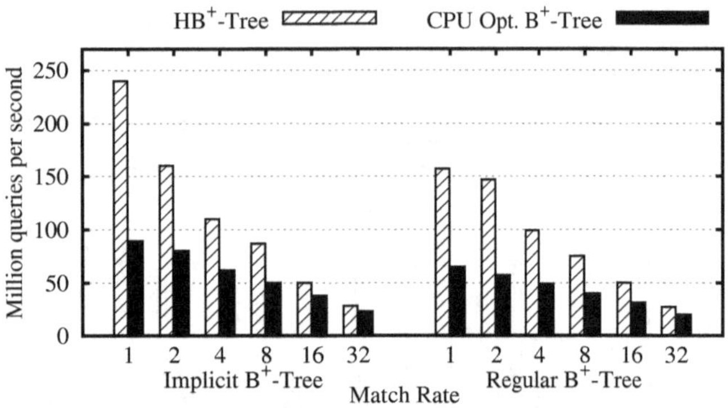

Figure 17: Throughput of Range queries.

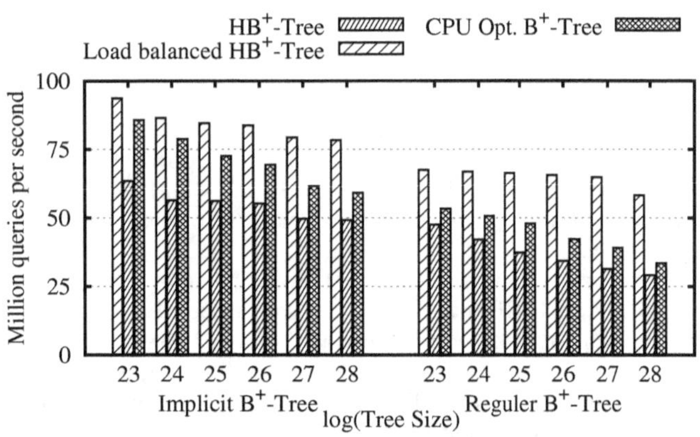

Figure 18: Evaluation of load balancing scheme.

6.5 Load Balancing Evaluation

We now examine the effectiveness of our load balancing scheme on heterogeneous platforms where the computation power is not bounded by the CPU. To this end, we used M_2 which is, relatively speaking, equipped with a less powerful GPU accelerator. Figure 18 shows the results. Without load balancing, HB$^+$-tree performs 25% slower than our CPU-optimized tree, on average. This indicates that the communication overhead between both processors is far higher than the acceleration provided by the GPU.

Applying load balancing scheme is highly effective and improves HB$^+$-tree throughput by 65% on average. In comparison to the CPU-optimized tree, the load balanced HB$^+$-tree performs up to 32% and 65% better for the implicit and regular approach, respectively.

7. CONCLUSIONS

In this paper, we presented an indexing structure, called HB$^+$-tree, specifically tailored to a heterogeneous computing platform with a hybrid memory architecture. Index search is accelerated by utilizing the resources of the hybrid GPU-CPU platform to aggregate the processing resources and memory bandwidth of both processing units. These improvements empower our approach to perform search faster for trees where the tree traversal performance approaches the memory bandwidth limit. In such situations, HB$^+$-tree performs on average 2.4X faster search than the CPU-optimized B$^+$-tree, with individual measurements improving performance by up to 2.9X.

The directions for our future work are two-fold: (1) Further support for parallel update queries and (2) development of a general leaf-stored tree processing framework using a CPU-GPU hybrid platform. In this paper, we primarily focused on realizing efficient search. So far, updates are performed sequentially by the CPU with asynchronous data transfer to the GPU; this could be further improved by employing GPU cycles in support of parallel update query execution. The other direction is to develop a general framework which enables the use of a CPU-GPU hybrid platform for any arbitrary leaf-stored tree structure, such that using the node structure and search/update function as input, the framework would determine the parameters for an approach that best utilizes the resources of both CPU and GPU.

8. REFERENCES

[1] D. Agrawal, D. Ganesan, R. Sitaraman, Y. Diao, and S. Singh. Lazy-adaptive tree: An optimized index structure for flash devices. *Proc. VLDB Endow.*, 2009.

[2] M.-C. Albutiu, A. Kemper, and T. Neumann. Massively parallel sort-merge joins in main memory multi-core database systems. *VLDB*, 2012.

[3] V. Alvarez, S. Richter, X. Chen, and J. Dittrich. A comparison of adaptive radix trees and hash tables. In *ICDE*, 2015.

[4] J. C. Anderson, J. Lehnardt, and N. Slater. *CouchDB: the definitive guide.* " O'Reilly Media, Inc.", 2010.

[5] M. Athanassoulis and A. Ailamaki. Bf-tree: Approximate tree indexing. *Proc. VLDB Endow.*, 2014.

[6] P. Bakkum and K. Skadron. Accelerating SQL database operations on a GPU with CUDA. In *GPGPU*, 2010.

[7] M. Bauer, H. Cook, and B. Khailany. CudaDMA: optimizing GPU memory bandwidth via warp specialization. In *SC*, 2011.

[8] R. Bayer and E. McCreight. Organization and maintenance of large ordered indices. In *SIGFIDET*, 1970.

[9] S. Browne, J. Dongarra, N. Garner, G. Ho, and P. Mucci. A portable programming interface for performance evaluation on modern processors. *IJHPCA*, 2000.

[10] S. Chaudhuri and U. Dayal. An overview of data warehousing and olap technology. *SIGMOD*, 1997.

[11] S. Chen, P. B. Gibbons, and T. C. Mowry. *Improving index performance through prefetching.* ACM, 2001.

[12] S. Cook. *CUDA programming: a developer's guide to parallel computing with GPUs.* Newnes, 2013.

[13] M. Daga and M. Nutter. Exploiting coarse-grained parallelism in b+ tree searches on an APU. In *SCC*, 2012.

[14] L. Dagum and R. Menon. OpenMP: an industry standard API for shared-memory programming. *Computational Science & Engineering, IEEE*, 1998.

[15] R. Elmasri. *Fundamentals of database systems.* Pearson Education India, 2008.

[16] J. Fix, A. Wilkes, and K. Skadron. Accelerating braided b+ tree searches on a GPU with CUDA. In *A4MMC*, 2011.

[17] N. Govindaraju, J. Gray, R. Kumar, and D. Manocha. GPUTeraSort: high performance graphics co-processor sorting for large database management. In *SIGMOD*, 2006.

[18] G. Graefe. Modern b-tree techniques. *Foundations and Trends in Databases*, 2011.

[19] M. Grand. *Patterns in Java: a catalog of reusable design patterns illustrated with UML*, volume 1. John Wiley & Sons, 2003.

[20] C. Gregg and K. Hazelwood. Where is the data? why you cannot debate CPU vs. GPU performance without the answer. In *ISPASS*, 2011.

[21] R. A. Hankins and J. M. Patel. Effect of node size on the performance of cache-conscious B+-trees. In *ACM SIGMETRICS Performance Evaluation Review*, 2003.

[22] B. C. O. K.-L. T. M. Z. Hao Zhang, Gang Chen. In-memory big data management and processing: A survey. *Knowledge and Data Engineering, IEEE Transactions on*, 2015.

[23] B. He, K. Yang, R. Fang, M. Lu, N. Govindaraju, Q. Luo, and P. Sander. Relational joins on graphics processors. In *SIGMOD*, 2008.

[24] J. L. Hennessy and D. A. Patterson. *Computer architecture: a quantitative approach.* Elsevier, 2012.

[25] Intel Corporation. *Intel® 64 and IA-32 Architectures Software Developer's Manual.* Number 253669-052US. September 2014.

[26] M. Jarke, M. Lenzerini, Y. Vassiliou, and P. Vassiliadis. *Fundamentals of data warehouses.* Springer Science & Business Media, 2013.

[27] K. Kaczmarski. B+-tree optimized for GPGPU. In *OTM*. 2012.

[28] T. Kaldewey, J. Hagen, A. Di Blas, and E. Sedlar. Parallel search on video cards. In *HotPar*, 2009.

[29] C. Kim, J. Chhugani, N. Satish, E. Sedlar, A. D. Nguyen, T. Kaldewey, V. W. Lee, S. A. Brandt, and P. Dubey. FAST: fast architecture sensitive tree search on modern CPUs and GPUs. In *SIGMOD*, 2010.

[30] D. E. Knuth. *Art of Computer Programming, Volume 2: Seminumerical Algorithms, The.* Addison-Wesley Professional, 2014.

[31] T. J. Lehman and M. J. Carey. A study of index structures for main memory database management systems. In *VLDB*, 1986.

[32] V. Leis, A. Kemper, and T. Neumann. The adaptive radix tree: Artful indexing for main-memory databases. In *ICDE*, 2013.

[33] J. J. Levandoski, D. B. Lomet, and S. Sengupta. The bw-tree: A b-tree for new hardware platforms. In *ICDE*, 2013.

[34] Y. Li, B. He, R. J. Yang, Q. Luo, and K. Yi. Tree indexing on solid state drives. *Proc. VLDB Endow.*, 2010.

[35] J. Lindström, T. Niklander, P. Porkka, and K. Raatikainen. A distributed real-time main-memory database for telecommunication. In *Databases in Telecommunications*. 2000.

[36] H. Lu, Y. Y. Ng, and Z. Tian. T-tree or b-tree: Main memory database index structure revisited. In *ADC*, 2000.

[37] Y. Mao, E. Kohler, and R. T. Morris. Cache craftiness for fast multicore key-value storage. In *EuroSys*, 2012.

[38] J. I. Munro and H. Suwanda. Implicit data structures for fast search and update. *Journal of Computer and System Sciences*, 1980.

[39] J. Nickolls and W. J. Dally. The GPU computing era. *IEEE micro*, 2010.

[40] C. Nvidia. NVIDIA CUDA programming guide (version 6.5). *NVIDIA Corporation*, 2014.

[41] J. D. Owens, M. Houston, D. Luebke, S. Green, J. E. Stone, and J. C. Phillips. GPU computing. 2008.

[42] J. Rao and K. A. Ross. Cache conscious indexing for decision-support in main memory. VLDB, 1999.

[43] J. Rao and K. A. Ross. Making B+-trees cache conscious in main memory. In *SIGMOD*, 2000.

[44] J. Sanders and E. Kandrot. *CUDA by example: an introduction to general-purpose GPU programming.* Addison-Wesley Professional, 2010.

[45] J. Sewall, J. Chhugani, C. Kim, N. Satish, and P. Dubey. PALM: Parallel architecture-friendly latch-free modifications to B+ trees on many-core processors. *Proc. VLDB Endowment*, 2011.

[46] J. E. Stone, D. Gohara, and G. Shi. OpenCL: A parallel programming standard for heterogeneous computing systems. *Computing in science & engineering*, 2010.

[47] A. Vaisman and E. Zimányi. Data warehouses: Next challenges. In *Business Intelligence*. Springer, 2012.

[48] P. Vassiliadis and A. Simitsis. Near real time ETL. In *New trends in data warehousing and data analysis.* Springer, 2009.

[49] W. A. Wulf and S. A. McKee. Hitting the memory wall: implications of the obvious. *ACM SIGARCH*, 1995.

[50] J. Zhou and K. A. Ross. Buffering accesses to memory-resident index structures. In *VLDB*, 2003.

APPENDIX

Here, we provide more details on our implementations of the SIMD-enabled node search using AVX unit, the GPU search kernel, and more evaluations.

A. SIMD ENABLED SEARCH

In this section, we present our SIMD enabled search algorithm in more detail. Considering `Node[0..7]` is an array of keys in an inner node and `query` is the given search query, Snippets 1 and 2 show the implementation of the linear and hierarchical approaches for 64-bit keys, respectively.

Snippet 1 Linear AVX search (64-bit)§.

```
1:  __m256i† Vquery =_mm_set1_epi64x(query);
2:  __m256i vec =_mm256_set_epi64x(node[0],
3:  node[1], node[2], node[3]);
4:  __m256i Vcmp =_mm256_cmpgt_epi64(Vquery,
        vec);
5:  int cmp = _mm256_movemask_epi8(Vcmp);
6:  cmp = cmp & x10101010;
7:  cmp = __builtin_popcount‡(cmp);
8:  int k = cmp;
9:  Vec = _mm256_set_epi64x(node[4], node[5],
10: node[6], node[7]);
11: Vcmp = _mm256_cmpgt_epi64(Vquery, vec);
12: cmp = _mm256_movemask_epi8(Vcmp);
13: cmp = cmp & x10101010;
14: cmp = __builtin_popcount (cmp);
15: k += cmp;
16: // k is the minimum i s.t. query <= node[i]
```

§Functions starting with _mm are SIMD instructions

†256-bit data type as four 64-bit integer values

‡method by GNU's Compiler Collection (GCC) determines the number of ones in the binary representation of a number

Snippet 2 Hierarchical AVX search (64-bit).

```
1:  __m128i† Vquery = _mm_set1_epi64x(query);
2:  __m128i Vec =_mm_set_epi64x(node[2], node
        [5]);
3:  __m128i Vcmp =_mm_cmpgt_epi64(Vquery, Vec);
4:  int cmp = _mm_movemask_epi8(cmpRes);
5:  cmp = cmp & 0x00001010;
6:  cmp = __builtin_popcount (cmp);
7:  int k = cmp * 3;
8:  Vec = _mm_set_epi64x(node[k], node[k + 1]);
9:  Vcmp = _mm_cmpgt_epi64(Vquery, Vec);
10: cmp = _mm_movemask_epi8(Vcmp);
11: cmp = cmp & 0x00001010;
12: cmp = __builtin_popcount (cmp);
13: k += cmp;
14: // k is the minimum i s.t. query <= node[i]
```

†128-bit data type as two 64-bit integer values

The linear approach first loads the `query` into an AVX vector in Line 1. In Lines 2-4, the first half of the key array (`Node[0..3]`) is loaded into a vector and compared to `key`. Then, the number of keys smaller or equal to the input are stored in variable `k` (cf. Lines 5-8). This process repeats for the second half of the key array adding the comparison result to `k` in Lines 9-15. At the end, `k` is the index of the child to resolve the query.

The hierarchical approach first compares the boundary keys which are `node[2]` and `node[5]` to `query` in Lines 2-4 and based on the comparison results, the search algorithm calculates the index of keys for the second comparison and stores it in `k`. Finally, it compares the `query` to the `node[k]` and `node[k+1]` to find the right child index.

B. ADDITIONAL EVALUATIONS

In this section, we provide further experimental results for our HB$^+$-tree and our CPU-optimized B$^+$-tree.

B.1 HB$^+$-tree lookup using CPU

Figure 19 shows a comparison of the lookup performance of CPU-optimized B$^+$-tree and HB$^+$-tree only using the CPU. The performance of the regular tree versions are identical since they are based on the same node structures. The CPU-optimized implicit B$^+$-tree results in better performance, due to better cache line data utilization. The fanout of inner nodes in HB$^+$-tree is decremented by one for the benefit of faster search with GPU.

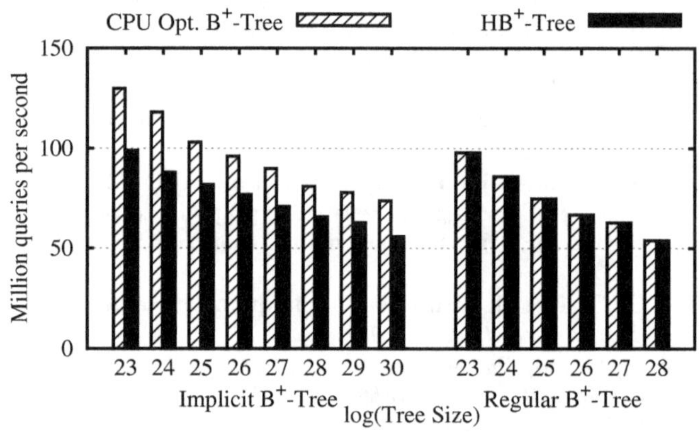

Figure 19: Evaluation of lookup in HB$^+$-tree using CPU.

B.2 Software Pipelining

In this experiment, we study the effect of software pipelining on lookup performance, that is, on throughput and latency. Software pipelining helps the processor to overlap execution with data fetching by executing multiple queries simultaneously, but at the same time, increases processing latency. Algorithm 2 shows how we apply software pipelining with prefetching for CPU-optimized B$^+$-tree lookup. Here, as a thread finishes searching a node, instead of waiting for the child node to be loaded into the cache, it switches to processing another query. Then, when the thread switches back to the same query, the child node is already loaded into cache.

Figure 20(a) illustrates the lookup throughput for various numbers of simultaneously processed queries ranging from 1 to 32. Increasing the number of queries from 1 to 16 continuously improves the throughput, which results in 2.5X better performance than without software pipelining. But due to the limited cache size, increasing the number of simultaneously processed queries from 16 to 32 is not effective and performance remains almost the same. The lookup latency for different software pipeline lengths is illustrated in Figure 20(b) which indicates the latency is quickly increasing with number of queries per thread. On average, the lookup

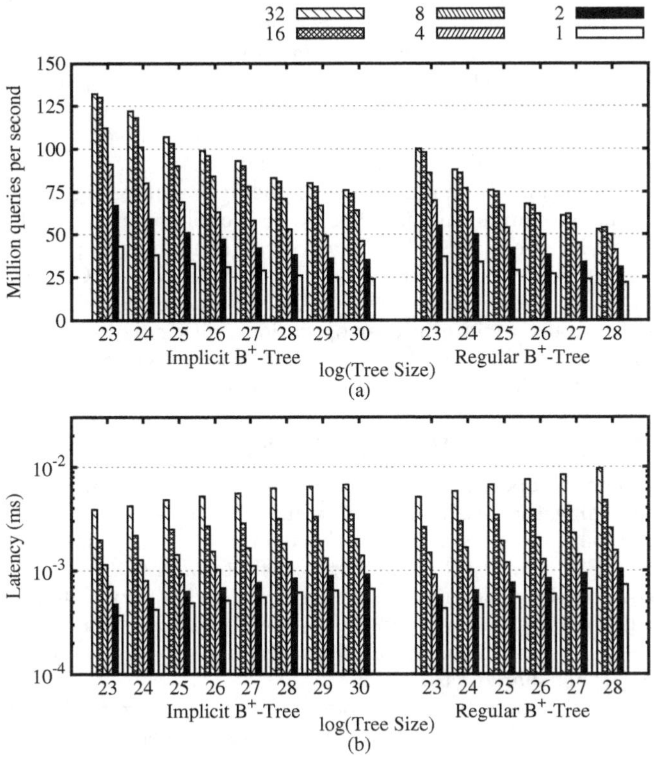

Figure 20: Evaluation of various software pipelining lengths: (a) throughput (b) latency.

latency using a software pipeline of length 16 is 6X higher than without software pipelining.

Algorithm 2 Software pipelining-enabled tree search

Input: P : length of software pipeline
Input: $keys[P]$: search queries
Input: H : height of B^{+}-tree

```
for i ← 1 to P do
    node[i] ← root
for step ← 1 to H − 1 do
    for i ← 1 to P do
        node[i] ← getNextNode(I-seg, node[i], keys[i])
        prefetch(node[i])
for i ← 1 to P do
    value[i] ← getValue(L-seg, node[i], key[i])
```

B.3 Concurrent Search and Update Queries

We now examine the performance of parallel search/update query execution in HB^{+}-tree utilizing only the CPU. We evaluate both synchronous and asynchronous approaches, where the I-segment transfer time is excluded for the asynchronous approach.

The synchronous approach consists of one synchronizing thread, which continuously updates the inner nodes in GPU memory and multiple query processing threads, while the asynchronous approach only consists of query processing threads. The query processing threads are based on the update algorithms given in Section 5.6, which are also capable of resolving search queries. The results are shown in Figure 21. As the ratio of update queries increases, the throughput of the synchronous approach decreases faster than the asynchronous one which is due to the high communication initialization overhead between GPU and main memory. The execution of buckets with 100% search queries in this evaluation is not as fast as our previously evaluated lookup methods which is due to the mutex locking and synchronization overhead in the query processing threads.

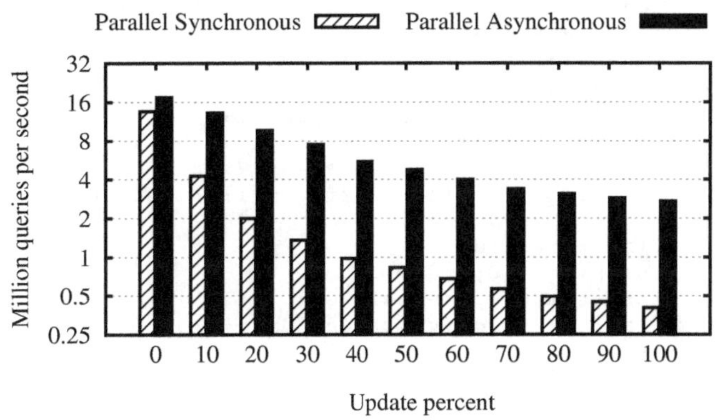

Figure 21: Evaluation of concurrent search/update queries.

C. CUDA PROGRAMMING MODEL

The CUDA programming model is based on hierarchical threading including the notions of *grid*, *block* and *thread*. At the top of the hierarchy is the grid which consists of *blocks* and each block is a group of threads. Threads are distinguished by two index values, `BlockIdx` and `ThreadIdx`, which define the runtime behavior of each thread.

Implementing efficient programs for CUDA requires good understanding of both the GPU memory architecture and the thread scheduling model. The unit of scheduling in CUDA is the *warp*, which is a set of 32 threads. Threads within the same warp are able to execute only a single instruction at a time. The situation called *warp divergence* results when threads of the same warp divert into different code paths, typically occurring for if-then-else statements. As a result, the warp has to be scheduled for both paths separately, which increases the total execution time. Proper index assignment, which directs threads of each warp into a single code path avoids this situation.

Since there is no message passing mechanism supported by CUDA, communication is only feasible via read/write operations on memory. Therefore, efficient bandwidth utilization is of great significance. The CUDA memory architecture is composed of different memory types, where the important ones for our work are *shared memory* and *device memory*.

Device memory, or GPU memory, is the biggest and slowest memory; it can be accessed by an entire grid. All accesses to device memory have to be done through either 32-, 64-, or 128-byte memory transactions. As a warp issues a device memory access, the GPU coalesces this access into transactions of these sizes. In the worst case, each access is translated into 32 separate memory transactions, which divide the device memory performance by 32. Relocating data, such that threads within a warp access adjacent memory locations, leads to more efficient device memory utilization. Shared memory is comparably faster than device memory but it is limited to a block. To provide higher

Snippet 3 GPU kernel code for searching inner nodes in implicit tree ($F_I = 8$)[§].

```
1: // teamQuery is the requested key
2: long teamQuery;
3: __shared__† char flag[9], result;
4: char selfFlag, i;
5: long selfKey, nodeIndex;
6: flag[threadIdx.x] = 0;
7: nodeIndex = 0; // root index
8: __syncthreads()‡;
9: for (i = 0; i < tree_depth; i++) {
10: // levelOffsets is an array stores the
11: // offsets of each level in tree
12: selfKey = tree[levelOffsets[i] + nodeIndex
      + threadIdx.x];
13: flag[threadIdx.x+1] = 0;
14: selfFlag = 0;
15: if (teamQuery <= selfKey) {
16: flag[threadIdx.y][threadIdx.x+1] = 1;
17: selfFlag = 1;
18: }
19: __syncthreads();
20: if (selfFlag == 1 &&
21: flag[threadIdx.x] == 0) {
22: result = threadIdx.x;
23: }
24: __syncthreads();
25: // threads traverse to the next node
26: nodeIndex = (nodeIndex + result)<<3;
27: }
28: // nodeIndex is the index of target leaf
      node
```

[§] This program is executed by eight threads concurrently with `threadIdx.x` = 0 to 7

[†] Shared variables are declared by `__shared__`

[‡] `__syncthreads` is a barrier synchronization primitive

bandwidth, shared memory is composed of multiple memory banks which can be accessed simultaneously. The highest bandwidth is achieved when accesses are equally separated among the memory banks. For inter-block communication, shared memory is the better option in comparison to the device memory due to lower access latency.

The Nvidia Tesla platform is explicitly targeting high performance computing and offers faster double precision floating point operations which is a critical requirement for many applications. However, we opted for the Nvidia Geforce processor family in this work, since index tree search algorithms only require integer operations, either 64-bit or 32-bit, and the Geforece platform offers a better computation-power-to-price ratio for these operations.

D. GPU SEARCH KERNEL

The Snippet 3 represents the GPU kernel function for searching the I-segment of the implicit HB$^+$-tree. The input parameters are `I-seg`: the reference to the I-segment in GPU memory, `levelOffsets`: offsets of each level in I-segment, and `teamQuery`: the given search query. Shared variables are declared by the keyword `__shared__` and barriers `__syncthreads` are used to avoid race conditions when accessing shared variables.

Search starts from the root node (`nodeIndex = 0`) and performs the parallel node search per each inner node. Each thread loads a key from the current node and stores it into local register (`selfKey`) in Line 12. After initializing flags, threads compare their local register to `teamQuery` and store the result in both local and shared flags. In Line 19, it is required to synchronize threads before they check the shared flag to avoid race conditions. In Lines 20-23, each thread deduces if it is assigned to the next level node. If so, the thread update the shared result variable. The operation is repeated for each level of inner nodes. At the end, `nodeIndex` is referring to the desired leaf node.

Low-Overhead Asynchronous Checkpointing in Main-Memory Database Systems

Kun Ren, Thaddeus Diamond, Daniel J. Abadi, Alexander Thomson
Yale University
kun.ren@yale.edu; thaddeus.diamond@aya.yale.edu; {dna,thomson}@cs.yale.edu

ABSTRACT

As it becomes increasingly common for transaction processing systems to operate on datasets that fit within the main memory of a single machine or a cluster of commodity machines, traditional mechanisms for guaranteeing transaction durability—which typically involve synchronous log flushes—incur increasingly unappealing costs to otherwise lightweight transactions. Many applications have turned to periodically checkpointing full database state. However, existing checkpointing methods—even those which avoid freezing the storage layer—often come with significant costs to operation throughput, end-to-end latency, and total memory usage.

This paper presents Checkpointing Asynchronously using Logical Consistency (CALC), a lightweight, asynchronous technique for capturing database snapshots that does not require a physical point of consistency to create a checkpoint, and avoids conspicuous latency spikes incurred by other database snapshotting schemes. Our experiments show that CALC can capture frequent checkpoints across a variety of transactional workloads with extremely small cost to transactional throughput and low additional memory usage compared to other state-of-the-art checkpointing systems.

1. INTRODUCTION

As the size of main memory on modern servers continues to expand, an increasingly large number of transactional, Web, and ERP applications can fit their datasets entirely in the physical memory of an individual server or across the main memories of a cluster of servers using a shared-nothing architecture. This has led to the release of a flurry of new main memory database products, including Microsoft Hekaton [4], SAP HANA [10], VoltDB [23], Hyper [7], several main memory NoSQL products, and even a refresh of Oracle TimesTen [8].

A fundamental issue that all main memory database systems face is how to guarantee the 'D'—durability—of ACID when all data sits in volatile main memory. Historically, main memory databases have done this by retaining the logging component of traditional database systems, and forcing log records to stable storage before committing each transaction. Unfortunately, this solution removes several of the advantages of having the data in memory—transactional latency is still bounded by the time it takes to force all log records generated by a transaction to stable storage, and the CPU and memory bandwidth required to generate the log records take a significant toll on the otherwise extremely low overhead main memory transactions. One study indicated that 30% of the CPU cycles of a transaction are devoted to generating log records [6].

Furthermore, as high availability becomes increasingly crucial, the newer generation of database systems tend to build replication into the system from the beginning in order to ensure continued operation of the system in the face of failures. This requirement is reinforced by the fact that another trend is to deploy databases on failure-prone commodity hardware or on virtual machines in the cloud. Once data is replicated, recovering from a log upon a failure is typically far slower than copying database state from a replica [9].

Some main-memory systems, such as H-Store [20] and the early versions of VoltDB [23], and even some disk-based systems like C-Store [19] and HARBOR [9] abandoned logging protocols such as ARIES[14] altogether and rely on "K-safety" mechanisms for guaranteeing durability. As long as the effect of a transaction has made it to K+1 replicas (even if it is only in main memory in all these replicas), the system can survive K failures and still ensure full durability of transactions.

Unfortunately, in many cases, failures are not independent events. Rather, they can highly correlated. Catastrophic failures such as cluster-wide power outages or deterministic bugs in the database code can cause more the K simultaneous failures, which can lead to disastrous losses if none of the data is on stable storage. Indeed, VoltDB moved away from K-safety-based durability and instead released a "command logging" feature [13]. This feature, which is based on deterministic database system research [21], causes the system to log all transactional input. After a failure, the recovery process replays all input transactions that occurred after the latest full checkpoint, which recreates the in-memory database state that existed before the failure. The advantage of such a protocol is that logging of transactional input is generally far lighter weight than full ARIES logging.

It is clear that to avoid traditional logging, modern main memory database systems must implement some sort of checkpointing or backup algorithm in order to avoid catastrophic data loss. For some applications, especially those running

SIGMOD'16, June 26-July 01, 2016, San Francisco, CA, USA

ISBN 978-1-4503-3531-7/16/06...$15.00

DOI: http://dx.doi.org/10.1145/2882903.2915966

on NoSQL database systems, checkpointing alone is sufficient: even though transactions that were committed after the checkpoint may be discarded, the application does not require full durability. For other applications, checkpointing combined with k-safety is sufficient—data will only be lost in the case of K+1 correlated failures, and even in this case, the checkpoint limits the amount of data that is lost. For yet other applications, checkpointing combined with a deterministic replay of post-checkpoint transactional input is required to ensure no loss of data at all.

For all three types of applications mentioned above, the database system must be able to checkpoint its state with extremely low overhead in order to receive the benefits of main memory execution without having to log transactional actions to stable storage.

The lack of a log makes database checkpointing much more challenging, as the majority of the high performance checkpointing literature in database systems take the approach of creating "fuzzy" or non-transactionally-consistent checkpoints, and rely on the log along with key data structures found in these checkpoints to recreate a consistent state of the database. Without the log, these fuzzy schemes cannot be used. Instead, traditional techniques such as quiescing the database system (as done in Oracle TimesTen), obtaining read locks on the entire database, or requiring a hot spare server to take the checkpoint can be used. However, the performance of these techniques is far from ideal.

Recent work by Cao et al. [2] presented some promising results for taking low overhead complete checkpoints of database state without requiring a database log. This work focused on applications that have frequent points of consistency, such as massive multiplayer online games that have distinct steps in game states. In particular, Cao et al. presented the Zigzag and Ping-Pong algorithms, which allow an asynchronous thread to capture a snapshot of the complete database state after a point of consistency while simultaneously allowing a separate mutator thread to make concurrent modifications to a different copy of the database state.

Unfortunately, most transactional applications do not guarantee frequent physical points of consistency. Furthermore, the implementation presented by Cao. et al. assumes that the database state is stored in fixed-width vectors, which is not flexible enough for relational tables that have variable length attributes. In addition, it requires multiple copies of the application state at all times.

In this paper, we present CALC, a checkpointing algorithm with significantly lower overhead than the state of the art, and which does not require physical points of consistency. In particular, our algorithms use "virtual" points of consistency. The basic idea is to declare a virtual point of consistency to exist at a particular place in the sequence of transaction commits. All state changes to the database by transactions that commit before this point are considered to be part of a checkpoint, while subsequent transactions' mutations are not reflected in the checkpoint. In order to achieve this, the first state change to each data item by a transaction after this point is redirected to a separate copy of the data item (so that the last value of the item before the checkpoint will not be overwritten, and can be captured by an asynchronous thread which reads this final value).

In addition to our algorithm for taking a low-overhead checkpoint at a virtual point of consistency, we are also able to further reduce the overhead of the checkpointing process by only taking partial checkpoints containing database state which may have changed since the last checkpoint. These partial checkpoints are merged together by a background thread, in order to reduce the checkpoint reconstruction cost at recovery time.

2. ASYNCHRONOUS CHECKPOINTING

When we refer to *checkpoints*, we denote a set of records, each uniquely identified by a primary key, that are written out to stable storage. The set of all of these records represents the full state of the database, also referred to as *application state*, at a given point in time, t.

It is desirable for checkpoint capture algorithms to have the following properties:

1. The process should not significantly impede the system's transactional throughput (even if the system is running at maximum capacity).
2. The process should not introduce unacceptable latencies in transaction or query execution.
3. Although the price of memory is rapidly dropping, it is still relatively expensive to store many OLTP applications entirely in main memory, and main memory becomes a limited resource. Therefore, complete multi-versioning (where database updates do not overwrite previous values, but rather add another version to a new place in memory) is likely to be too expensive in terms of memory resources for many applications. Ideally, the checkpointing process should require minimum additional memory usage.

In order to achieve the first two of these properties, it is desirable for checkpointing to occur asynchronously with respect to other transaction processing tasks. Since records continue to be updated during the process of logging the set of all records to disk, it is therefore important to consider methods of ensuring that a snapshot of the database remains available to the background thread performing the checkpoint. However, in order to achieve the third of these properties, this snapshot should be as small as possible, since complete database multi-versioning or application state replication in memory is not possible for many applications.

2.1 Physical versus virtual points of consistency

A database is defined as being at a *point of consistency* if its state reflects all changes made by all committed transactions, and no change made by any uncommitted, in-progress transaction. A checkpoint taken at a particular *point of consistency* is generally called "transaction-consistent (TC)".

Most database systems achieve asynchronous checkpointing by not taking transaction-consistent checkpoints. They rely on mechanisms such as fuzzy checkpointing that include snapshots of key data structures of database system operation so that it is possible to recreate a transaction-consistent state of the database with the help of the database log during recovery. However, without the help of the log, checkpointing algorithms that do not produce transaction-consistent checkpoints are unable to recreate a consistent state of the database.

Certain applications, such as many massive multiplayer online games, naturally reach points in the process of normal execution in which no transactions are actively executing. This is termed a *physical* point of consistency. Most applications, however, are not guaranteed to reach physical points of consistency at regular intervals. Although it is always possible to force the database system to reach such a point by quiescing it entirely (disallowing new transactions from beginning to execute until all currently active transactions complete), quiescing a database system can have significant detrimental effects on both throughput and latency. Therefore, one of the primary goals of the work discussed in this paper is to achieve fast checkpointing even in the absence of physical points of consistency.

We introduce the notion of a *virtual point of consistency*. A virtual point of consistency is a view of the database that reflects all modifications committed before a specified time and none after—but obtained without quiescing the system. Virtual points of consistency are instead created using full or partial multi-versioning.

Systems implementing snapshot isolation via MVCC implement *full multi-versioning*. In such schemes, a full view of database state can be obtained for any recent timestamp simply by selecting the latest versions of each record whose timestamp precedes the chosen timestamp. Since MVCC is specifically designed such that writes never block on reads, a virtual point of consistency can be obtained inexpensively for any timestamp.

However, as described above, many main memory database systems do not implement full multi-versioning since memory is an important and limited resource in these systems. Therefore, precise partial multi-versioning is preferable.

The general idea of precise partial multi-versioning is the following: while a checkpoint is being captured, track two versions of each record: (a) the *live* version, which represents the most current state of the record, and (b) a *stable* version, which represents the state of the record as of the virtual point of consistency. Any transaction that commits before the point of consistency must update both versions of each record it writes, while transactions that commit after the point of consistency only overwrites the live version. However, a mechanism is needed for ensuring that each transaction updates the correct version(s) of the record.

In the Zigzag and Ping-Pong algorithms presented by Cao et al., a global flag specifies whether the point of consistency has been reached yet. The flag (and certain other corresponding metadata) are only updated at a physical point of consistency—therefore any update operation is guaranteed to precede the point of consistency if and only if the transaction's commit will also occur before the point of consistency. Zigzag and Ping-Pong pre-allocate memory for two or three (respectively) copies of each record to use as live and stable versions of that record.

2.2 The CALC Algorithm

We present here the CALC (Checkpointing Asynchronously using Logical Consistency) algorithm, which is designed to have the advantages of asynchronous checkpointing but with four additional benefits:

- **No requirement for a database log.** CALC is able to create a transaction-consistent checkpoint without relying on any kind of database log except for a simple log containing the order in which transactions commit.
- **Uses virtual points of consistency.** CALC does not require quiescing of the database in order to achieve a physical point of consistency. It therefore is able to avoid throughput drops and latency spikes for transactions that are submitted during and after checkpoints, which is critical for maintaining database service level agreements.
- **Reduced memory usage.** At most two copies of each record are stored at any time. Memory usage is minimized by only storing one physical copy of a record when its live and stable versions are equal or when no checkpoint is actively being recorded.
- **Low overhead.** CALC's overhead is smaller than other asynchronous checkpointing algorithms.

CALC implements a storage structure where each record key is associated with two record versions—one live and one stable. Initially, the stable version is `empty`, indicating that the stable version is not actually different from the live version, and that a checkpointing thread may safely record the live version. CALC also needs to maintain a bit vector called *stable_status*. Each record corresponds to a bit in *stable_status* to indicate whether its stable version is empty[1]. For the purposes of this discussion, we assume that transactions are executed using a pessimistic (lock-based) concurrency control algorithm in a multi-threaded execution environment, since this is the most common concurrency control implementation. We also assume that there exists a `commit-log`, and each transaction commits by atomically appending a commit token to this log before releasing any of its locks.

A system running the CALC algorithm cycles through five states, or phases:

1. the *rest* phase, in which no checkpoint is being taken,
2. the *prepare* phase, immediately preceding a virtual point of consistency,
3. the *resolve* phase, immediately following a virtual point of consistency but before the asynchronous checkpoint capture has started,
4. the *capture* phase, during which a background thread records the checkpoint to disk, and meanwhile deletes stable versions,
5. the *complete* phase, which immediately follows the completion of *capture* phase.

Each transition between phases of the algorithm is marked by a token atomically appended to the transaction `commit-log`. Therefore it can always be unambiguously determined which phase the system was in when a particular transaction committed. Additionally, each transaction makes note of the phase during which it *begins* executing. The algorithm proceeds as follows.

2.2.1 Rest phase

While in the *rest* phase, every record stores *only* a live version. All stable versions are *empty*, and the bits in *stable_status* vector are always equal to *not_available*. Any transaction that begins during the *rest* phase uses only the live version for its read and write operations, regardless of when it commits.

[1]Inserts and deletes are handled via two additional bit vectors, called *add_status* and *delete_status*. However, we only focus on updates in our discussion to keep the explanation simple.

```
Initialized Database status:
    bit not_available = 0;
    bit available = 1;
    bit stable_status[DB_SIZE];
    foreach key in Database
        db[key].live contains actual record value;
        db[key].stable is empty;
        stable_status[key] = not_available;

function ApplyWrite(txn, key, value)
    if (txn.start−phase is PREPARE)
        if (stable_status[key] == not_available)
            db[key].stable = db[key].live;
    else if (txn.start−phase is RESOLVE OR CAPTURE)
        if (stable_status[key] == not_available)
            db[key].stable = db[key].live;
            stable_status[key] = available;
    else if (txn.start−phase is COMPLETE OR REST)
        if (db[key].stable is not empty)
            Erase db[key].stable;
    db[key].live = value

function Execute(txn)
    txn.start−phase = current−phase;
    request txn's locks;
    run txn logic, using ApplyWrite for updates;
    append txn commit token to commit−log;
    if (txn.start−phase is PREPARE)
        if (txn committed during PREPARE phase)
            foreach key in txn
                Erase db[key].stable;
        else if (txn committed during RESOLVE phase)
            foreach key in txn
                stable_status[key] = available;
    release txn's locks;

function RunCheckpointer()
    while (true)
        SetPhase(REST);
        wait for signal to start checkpointing;
        SetPhase(PREPARE);
        wait for all active txns to have
            start−phase == PREPARE;
        SetPhase(RESOLVE);
        wait for all active txns to have
            start−phase == RESOLVE ;
        SetPhase(CAPTURE);
        foreach key in db
            if (stable_status[key] == available)
                write db[key].stable to Checkpoint;
                Erase db[key].stable;
            else if (stable_status[key] == not_available)
                stable_status[key] = available;
                val = db[key].live;
                if (db[key].stable is not empty)
                    write db[key].stable to Checkpointing;
                    Erase db[key].stable;
                else if (db[key].stable is empty)
                    write val to Checkpointing;
        SetPhase(COMPLETE);
        wait for all active txns to have
            start−phase == COMPLETE;
        SwapAvailableAndNotAvailable ();
```

Figure 1: CALC algorithm pseudocode.

2.2.2 Prepare phase

When the checkpointing process is triggered to begin, the system enters the *prepare* phase. Transactions that start during the *prepare* phase read and write *live* record versions, just like transactions that started during the *rest* phase. However, before updating a record, if the stable version is currently empty and unavailable, a copy of the live version is stored in the stable version prior to the update. This is done because the system is not sure in which phase the transaction will be committed. For example, a transaction T_P that begins during the *prepare* phase and writes a record R_1—overwriting a previous value R_0—makes a copy of R_0 in its stable version before replacing R_0 in the live version. Immediately after committing, but before releasing any locks, a check is made: if the system is still in the *prepare* phase at the time the transaction is committed, the stable version is removed.

2.2.3 Resolve phase

The *prepare* phase lasts until all active transactions are running in *prepare* phase—that is, until all transactions that started during the *rest* phase have completed. At this point, the system transitions to the *resolve* phase (appending a phase-transition token to the `commit-log`). This transition marks the *virtual point of consistency.* All transactions that have committed before this point will have their writes reflected in the checkpoint, whereas transactions that commit subsequently will not.

If a transaction that started during the *prepare* phase commits in *resolve* phase, the stable version is not deleted, and the corresponding bit in *stable_status* is set to *available.* For example, suppose the transaction T_P (discussed above) committed during the *resolve* phase. When it performed its check to see what phase it committed in, it discovers this, and then sets the corresponding bit in *stable_status.* Now subsequent transactions will see R_1 as the live version, but the background checkpoint recorder will see R_0 as the stable value when it runs.

Transactions that start during the *resolve* phase are already beginning after the point of consistency, so they will certainly complete after the checkpoint's point of consistency. Therefore, they always copy any live version to the corresponding stable record version before updating it, unless the record already has an explicit stable version.

2.2.4 Capture phase

The *resolve* phase lasts until all transactions that began during the *prepare* phase have completed and released all their locks.

The system then transitions into the *capture* phase. Transaction write behavior is the same during the *capture* phase as during the *resolve* phase, both for new transactions, and for transactions that were already active when the *capture phase began.*

Once this phase has begun, a background thread is spawned that scans all records, recording stable versions (or live versions for record versions that have no explicit stable version) to disk. As it proceeds, it erases any explicit stable versions that it encounters. This can be accomplished with no additional blocking synchronization. The *capture* phase section of the `RunCheckpointer` function outlined in Figure 1 shows the pseudocode for this process. Note that the bit in *stable_status* is set to *available* after the background thread accesses the record. This prevents other transactions running during the *capture* phase from creating the stable version again.

2.2.5 Complete phase

Once the checkpoint capture has completed, the system transitions into the *complete* phase. Transaction write behavior reverts to being the same as in the *rest* phase. Once all transactions that began during the *capture* phase have completed, the system transitions back into the *rest* phase, and awaits the next signal to take a checkpoint.

However, before transitioning back to the *rest* phase, the function *SwapAvailableAndNotAvailable()* is called to swap the variables *not_available* and *available*, in order to reverse their mapping to '1' and '0' values in the bit vector. In one iteration of the checkpointing algorithm, *not_available* maps to "1" and *available* maps to "0"; in the next *not_available* maps to "0" and *available* maps to "1". This allows the system to avoid a full scan to reset the *stable_status* bits, since after the *capture* phase all the *stable_status* bits are set to *available*, but at the beginning of the *rest* phase we want all the *stable_status* bits to be set to *not_available*.

Figure 1 shows pseudocode for the CALC algorithm. In particular, it outlines the initialized database status and the status of variables that are used in CALC algorithm. It also shows the `ApplyWrite` function called directly by transaction logic, the `Execute` function, which outlines all steps taken by a worker thread executing a transaction, and the basic steps taken by the CALC background thread over the course of a checkpointing cycle (in the `RunCheckpointer` function).

2.3 Partial checkpoints

In the CALC algorithm described above, each capture phase takes a complete checkpoint of the entire database. Even though this can be done in an asynchronous background thread which runs with low overhead, if very few records were updated since the last checkpoint (either because there is transaction skew where the same records get updated repeatedly or because the workload is mostly 'read-only'), it is wasteful to take a complete checkpoint if there are very few differences from the last checkpoint.

Therefore, as an alternative to the CALC algorithm, we also propose a pCALC option, that takes partial checkpoints that contain only records that may have been changed since the most recent checkpoint. These partial checkpoints can be merged together to create a complete checkpoint either at recovery time or as a background process during normal operation.

In order to take partial checkpoints, pCALC keeps track of keys that were updated after the most recent virtual point of consistency. We explored three alternative data structures for keeping track of keys that are updated. In the first approach, we stored each updated key in a hash table. In the second approach, we used a bit vector where the ith bit is set if the ith value had been updated since the most recent checkpoint. In the third approach, we used a bloom filter to decrease the size of the aforementioned bit vector. The main disadvantage of the bit vector approach is that it always consumes one bit per record in the database — even if that record has not been updated. The first approach never wastes space on irrelevant records and the third approach falls somewhere in between these two extremes. Nonetheless, in practice we found that the bit vector approach usually outperformed the other two approaches. This is because the entire database already fits in main memory (since this is the application space for which we are designing CALC). If each record consumes 50 bytes (400 bits), then the bit vector only extends memory requirements by $1/400 = 0.25\%$. Although smaller data structures have better cache properties, we found that the additional work required by the other approaches were slightly more costly than the performance savings from improved cache locality. Therefore, we settled on the bit vector approach in our final implementation.

Bit vectors are atomically cleared during the checkpointing period. This can be accomplished with no blocking synchronization by keeping two copies of the structure, and flipping a bit specifying which is active at the beginning of the *resolve* phase, and clearing the inactive one during each checkpointing period. For transactions that start in the *prepare* phase and commit in the *prepare* phase, we update the bit vector associated with current upcoming partial checkpoint; for those that commit in the *resolve* phase, we update the bit vector associated with the later partial checkpoint. For those transactions that start in (or after) the *resolve* phase, the bit vector associated with the later partial checkpoint is updated.

Although the bit vector must be cleared during each checkpoint period, note that pCALC does not require a full scan of the database. This can lead to a significant reduction in overhead of checkpointing relative to CALC.

2.3.1 Background merging of partial checkpoints

The cost at recovery time of taking partial checkpoints can be ameliorated by periodically collapsing pCALC's partial snapshots in a background thread. This is done in a low-priority thread to take advantage of moments of sub-peak load, while refraining from limiting peak throughput. Furthermore, this task can optionally be offloaded to different machines that do *not* stand in the critical path of a high-volume OLTP application pipeline.

The collapsing process itself is a simple merge of two or more recent partial checkpoints, where the latest version is always used if a record appears in multiple partial checkpoints. Old checkpoints are discarded only once they have been collapsed. Thus a system failure during the collapsing process or before some recent set of partial snapshots has been collapsed has no effect on durability.

3. RECOVERY

Thus far we have discussed two types of checkpoints: CALC and pCALC. We now discuss how to recover from each type of checkpoint.

3.1 Recovery Using CALC

A CALC checkpoint is a complete snapshot of database state as of a particular point it time. It is guaranteed to be physically consistent — it reflects the state of the database after all transactions that committed prior to the checkpoint have been processed and no intermediate or temporary state from ongoing transactions that had not committed prior to the checkpoint. This makes recovery very easy for the use cases discussed in Section 1: for the use cases that find it acceptable to lose transactions that committed after the most recent checkpoint (e.g. the NoSQL and K-Safety use cases mentioned above), the database state is created via loading in the most recent **completed** checkpoint. For use cases that rely on determinism to avoid losing committed transactions [22, 13, 20, 23, 21], the database state is created via a two-step process. First, the most recent completed checkpoint is loaded to create a temporary database state. Then the commit log is read to see which transactions committed after this checkpoint that was loaded. These transactions are then replayed, leveraging determinism to ensure that the serialization order and states are equivalent to the original order before the crash.

Note that all of CALC's data structures — the "stable" record versions, the stable_status bit vector, etc., get wiped out along with the rest of volatile memory upon a crash. So there is no clean-up that has to occur upon recovery. The most recent completed checkpoint is loaded and all of CALC's data structures are initialized as shown in Figure 1.

3.2 Recovery Using pCALC

Recovery from partial checkpoints is slightly more complicated since there is not necessarily a single checkpoint which can be loaded in order to get a consistent database state.

A naive algorithm would be to collapse all partial checkpoints that exist on stable storage into a single checkpoint using the merge process described in Section 2.3.1. Obviously, although correct, this is unacceptably slow, since partial checkpoints are continuously generated since the beginning of the installation of the database system.

A less naive algorithm is to occasionally take a full checkpoint so that only the partial checkpoints that were taken since this full checkpoint need to be merged. This leads to a recovery time vs. runtime tradeoff. Full checkpoints are more expensive to generate than partial checkpoints, so optimizing for runtime implies that full checkpoints should be taken rarely. However, this increases recovery time since on average there will be more partial checkpoints to merge since the last full checkpoint.

Note that if a full checkpoint is merged with all partial checkpoints that were taken subsequent to it, the result is a new full checkpoint that is accurate as of the most recent partial checkpoint. Therefore, as an alternative to occasionally taking full checkpoints, the system can instead collapse a series of partial checkpoints and a older full checkpoint. This has the advantage of being a process that can be run entirely asynchronously, in the background. This is the approach that we take in our implementation. However, the recovery time vs. runtime tradeoff remains — it is now expressed as the size of the batch of partial checkpoints that are allowed to exist before performing this merge process. We revisit this tradeoff experimentally in Section 5.1.3.

Once a full checkpoint has been created via merging partial checkpoints, recovery proceeds as discussed in Section 3.1 above.

4. EXPERIMENTAL SETUP

To evaluate the CALC algorithm side-by-side with other state-of-the-art checkpointing approaches, we implemented a memory-resident key-value store with full transactional support. Transactions in our system are implemented as C++ stored procedures, and are executed by a pool of worker threads, using a pessimistic concurrency control protocol to ensure serializability. In order to eliminate deadlock as an unpredictable source of variation in our performance measurements, we implemented a deadlock-free variant of strict two-phase locking.

All experimental results shown here were obtained on Amazon EC2 using a c3.4xlarge instance, which has 16 virtual cores (Intel Xeon E5-2680 v2 (Ivy Bridge) Processors) running 64-bit Ubuntu 12.04.2 LTS with 30GB RAM and a 160GB magnetic disk that delivers approximately 100-150 MB/sec for sequential reads and writes. Of the 16 cores, we allocated 15 cores to transaction processing and checkpointing threads, and devote the remaining core to shared database components and infrastructure necessary to take statistics for these experiments.

4.1 Benchmarking CALC

In order to compare the performance of CALC under different transactional throughputs and contention rates, we implemented two different versions of our checkpointing scheme. The first, labeled CALC, is the rudimentary version of our algorithm. The second, labeled pCALC, is a version of our algorithm that captures partial checkpoints.

We compare the performance of CALC and pCALC to four other comparison points, described in the following sections.

4.1.1 Naive Snapshot

We implemented a simple version of "naive snapshot" in our database. A naively taken snapshot involves acquiring an exclusive lock on the entire database, iterating through every existing key, and writing its corresponding value to disk. Recent work by Lau et al. favors "round-robin" naive snapshot as a low-cost way of achieving durability in highly-replicated systems [9].

4.1.2 Fuzzy Checkpointing

The naive snapshot algorithm incurs a long interruption of normal processing during checkpointing. The fuzzy checkpointing algorithm was invented to avoid this, as it only interrupts normal processing to write two relatively small data structures to the log, instead of a full snapshot of database state. As a result, it has become an extremely popular (perhaps even the most popular) checkpointing algorithm used in database systems — especially those systems that use the ARIES recovery algorithm.

Although there exist several proposals and optimizations of fuzzy checkpointing, the simple version of the algorithm is done as follows [1, 18]: (1) The DBMS stops accepting new update, commit, and abort operations. (2) It creates a "checkpoint" log record which contains a list of all the dirty pages in the cache, and also a list of all active transactions along with pointers to the last log record that these active transactions have made. (3) It writes this checkpoint record to the log. (4) The DBMS allows normal operation to resume. At this point, the pages marked as dirty in the checkpoint record can be flushed to disk in parallel with the DBMS running new update, commit and abort operations.

It has repeatedly been pointed out in the literature that the traditional version of the fuzzy checkpointing algorithm is designed for disk resident DBMSs, and does not adapt well to main memory DBMSs [12, 5]. The main issue is that while the granularity of a write to disk is a page, the granularity of a write to main memory is typically a single record. Therefore, the dirty page table in the fuzzy checkpoint (along with the pageLSN header of disk pages) need to be modified to work with record-level granularity. This increases the size of these structures. Furthermore, the higher throughput of main memory database systems tend to result in more dirty records per checkpoint than seen in disk-based systems. Combined these two issues cause much more to be written to a checkpoint record, and therefore a longer interruption of normal database processing. There have therefore been several proposals for reducing the size of this interruption (e.g. splitting the checkpoint record to begin_checkpoint and end_checkpoint records) and to generally improve the performance of checkpointing in main memory database systems. We have implemented that which we believe to be the most performant of these proposals (IPP), which we describe in the next section. However, we nonetheless also run a version of basic fuzzy checkpointing since it can serve as familiar comparison point that is well-known to most database researchers.

Our implementation of fuzzy checkpointing uses bit vectors to keep track of dirty keys (like we do in pCALC — see Section 2.3). Furthermore, in order to directly compare this approach to our implementations of CALC and pCALC, we created full and partial versions of the fuzzy checkpointing. The default implementation is the partial version — pFuzzy — since that corresponds to the traditional approach to fuzzy checkpointing. To create the full version, we maintain an extra copy of the database in main memory which is the latest consistent snapshot, so the full checkpoint can be generated by merging dirty records with the latest snapshot.

4.1.3 Ping-Pong

As a third comparison point, we implemented the "Interleaved Ping-Pong" (IPP) checkpointing algorithm [2]. IPP is an asynchronous method that accomplishes the capture of entire snapshots of a database without key locking by triplicating application data and relying on *physical* points of consistency. In this scheme, the storage layer maintains an application state composed of a simple byte array, and two additional byte arrays of size equal to the application state labeled odd and even. In addition to representing application data, odd and even maintain a single dirty bit for each element in the array.

Data is initially stored in the application state and even arrays. In the latter, every key's bit is marked dirty. In addition, odd is marked as the current array. The application then proceeds to execute, during which time writes are performed not only on the application state array, but also on the array pointed to by current. Any key that is updated has the corresponding dirty bit turned to "on" in the current array. At a physically consistent point, even becomes the current array, marking the switch into the first checkpoint period. During this period, a background process asynchronously finds all the values that have been labeled as dirty during the first period, and merges them with the last consistent checkpoint in order to construct a new consistent checkpoint that can be written to disk. After each element is written to disk, the corresponding dirty bit is set to "off". Once completed, the process alerts the scheduler that at the next physical point of consistency the process can begin again.

4.1.4 Zig-Zag

As a fourth comparison point, we implemented the Zig-Zag checkpointing algorithm [2]. Zig-Zag starts with two identical versions of each record in the datastore: $AS[Key]_0$ and $AS[Key]_1$, plus two additional bit vectors, $MR[Key]$ and $MW[Key]$. $MR[Key]$ indicates which version should be used when reading a particular record, Key, and $MW[Key]$ indicates which version to overwrite when updating Key. New updates of Key are always written to $AS[Key]_{MW[Key]}$, and $MR[Key]$ is set equal to $MW[key]$ each time Key is updated. The bit vector MR is initialized with zeros and MW with ones, and each checkpoint period begins with setting $MW[Key]$ equal to $\neg MR[Key]$ for all keys in the database. Thus $AS[Key]_{MW[Key]}$ always stores the latest version of the record, and the asynchronous checkpointing thread can therefore safely write $AS[Key]_{\neg MW[Key]}$ to disk.

IPP and Zigzag make several assumptions about the application and data layers that do not necessarily apply to all use cases. First, they assume that the application layer has some *physical* point of consistency at which the database does not contain any state that has been written by a transaction that is not yet committed. For applications that do not naturally have such points of consistency, the database can enforce one by blocking any incoming transactions from starting until after all existing operations finish.

Second, IPP and Zigzag assume that the storage layer uses simple array storage using fixed-length values. Although some applications are possible to be implemented over fixed-length array-based storage (including the massive multiplayer online game applications for which IPP and Zigzag were designed), many applications have data that cannot easily be managed via array-based storage (which is why most modern database systems do not use array-storage backends). In order to be general and make an apples-to-apples comparison, we implemented a modified version of IPP and Zigzag that use the same hash-table-based storage engine that is used for CALC. Nonetheless, we maintain the cache optimizations of these algorithms For example, IPP stores all three copies of each record continuously in memory in order to keep as much data as possible for a record in the same cache line. We maintain the same optimization — maintaining all three copies of each record contiguously in the same hash entry of the database.

IPP and Zigzag both take full checkpoints and are thus best compared to CALC. However, in order to additionally compare them with pCALC, we implemented a second version of the IPP and Zigzag implementations that take only partial snapshots using the same bit vectors as used for pCALC. In this way, the advantage of pCALC of not having to write entire database snapshots to disk at each checkpoint can also be attained by IPP and Zigzag. These secondary implementations are labeled "pIPP" and "pZigzag" in the experiments.

5. EXPERIMENT RESULTS

In this section we run experiments to benchmark CALC against the naive snapshot, fuzzy, IPP and Zigzag algorithms described in the previous section. We run our experiments using two benchmarking applications: The first is a microbenchmark similar to the one used in recently published transactional database system papers [22, 16]. The second is TPC-C, which we implemented by writing stored procedures in C++.

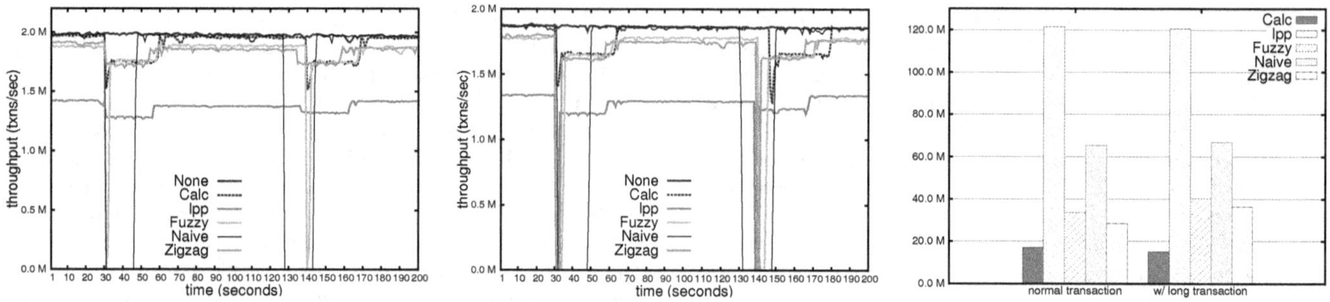

(a) Throughput over time, no long xacts (b) Throughput over time, long xacts (c) Transactions lost.

Figure 2: Full checkpointing, Microbenchmark experiments.

5.1 Microbenchmark experiments

The microbenchmark operates on a collection of 20 million records, where each record is 100 bytes and has an 8 byte key. We experiment with two versions of the microbenchmark. The first version consists entirely of transactions that read and update 10 records from the database, and do some simple computing operations. The second version contains 99.999% of transactions that are the same type as the first version, but 0.001% of transactions are long-running batch-writes which take approximately two seconds to complete. We keep contention low for both versions of the microbenchmark. This enables worker threads to fully utilize all cores on the experimental system, instead of becoming blocked on acquiring locks. This ensures that the overhead of checkpointing is clearly visible.

5.1.1 Full Checkpointing

We first compare CALC with the other checkpointing algorithms for the "full" checkpoint case, where each scheme must create a complete snapshot of the database before the end of the checkpoint interval. Figure 2(a) shows the system throughput over time for the first version of the microbenchmark (the version without long-running transactions). Figure 2(b) shows the results for the second version of the microbenchmark (the version with .001% long-running transactions). This experiment runs over the course of a 200 second period, where the first checkpoint is taken, starting at time 30 seconds, and the second checkpoint is taken 80 seconds after the first one. We run database system under peak workload (the database system is 100% busy).

For the naive snapshot algorithm, the throughput drops to 0 transactions per second while the checkpoint is being taken. However, the time to take this checkpoint is very small, since all database resources are devoted to creating the checkpoint during this period. After the checkpoint completes, database throughput returns to normal.

For the fuzzy checkpointing algorithm, the database system is quiesced to write the dirty record table to disk (which results in a sharp drop in database throughput), but then continues to process transactions after the data structure is written. Since the size of the dirty record table is much smaller than the size of a full database checkpoint, the time that the database is quiesced is smaller for the fuzzy case than the naive snapshot case. However, after the database returns to processing transactions, database throughput does not fully return to normal, since some processing resources need to be allocated to asynchronously creating the full checkpoint from the data structures written out in the previous step.

The IPP algorithm's performance (even before the checkpoint period begins) is around 25% worse than the no-checkpoint baseline, since it needs to maintain two copies of the database state at all times, which involves memory copy operations during normal operation. Even though we utilize the IPP optimization of ensuring that both copies of each record are stored contiguously in memory, and thus this copy operation is as cache-local as possible, nonetheless the overhead is noticeable given the write-intensive nature of the workload.

We found that the Zigzag algorithm performed better than IPP. At rest, before the checkpoint period begins, Zigzag results in only a 4% decrease in throughput relative to the baseline. This is because, unlike IPP, Zigzag only has to perform writes once, without any additional copying. The only extra ongoing cost at rest is that it needs to read and update two bit vectors that control access to the two copies of the data. Once the checkpoint period begins, its drop in throughput relative to its baseline is larger than the corresponding drop for IPP. Nonetheless, since its baseline is so much higher than IPP for this workload, its throughput remains higher than IPP throughout the experiment.

The naive algorithm has to quiesce the database system to perform the entire checkpoint, and the fuzzy checkpointing algorithm has to quiesce the system while certain data-structures are written (see above). These needs to quiesce the system are mostly independent from the workload. Therefore, the precipitous drop in throughput during this quiescence period is approximately the same in Figure 2(a) and Figure 2(b) for both the naive and fuzzy algorithms. In contrast, IPP and Zigzag only have to quiesce the system until all active transactions at the start of a checkpoint complete (this enables the system to get into a physical point of consistency which are required by these algorithms). This type of quiescence is very workload dependent. When every active transaction is short (as for the workload in Figure 2(a)), the period of time for which the database must quiesce is essentially invisible. However, where there are long-running transactions in the workload (as for Figure 2(b)), the period of time for which the database has to reject new transactions until these long transactions complete is noticeable. Therefore, there is a visible drop to zero transactions a second at the beginning of the checkpoint period for both IPP and Zigzag in Figure 2(b) but not in Figure 2(a).

In contrast, CALC does not require physical points of consistency, instead relying on a virtual point of consistency. Therefore, the performance of CALC is similar for both ver-

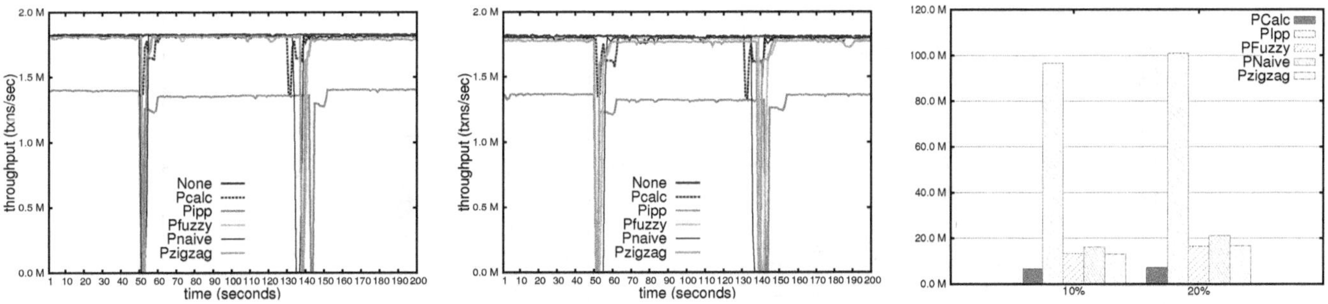

(a) 10% of records modified since last checkpoint. (b) 20% of records modified since last checkpoint. (c) Transactions lost.

Figure 3: Partial checkpointing with Long-running transactions.

sions of the microbenchmark in Figures 2(a) and Figure 2(b). Furthermore, it does not suffer from performance degradation in baseline performance, since unlike IPP and Zigzag, it does not have to maintain multiple copies of the data outside of checkpoint periods — either via making multiple copies of each write, or by controlling access to different copies though bit vectors. It does, however, have a 10% performance degradation relative to its baseline during the asynchronous parts of the checkpoint process. This drop relative to its baseline is slightly larger than the corresponding drops for the other algorithms because in addition to writing the checkpoint, CALC requires some additional memory copy operations during the checkpoint period (in particular, it has to copy the live version to the stable version in the database the first time a record is written after the beginning of the checkpoint period).

In general, the different checkpointing algorithms have different shapes in Figures 2(a) and Figure 2(b). Some have short periods of zero transactions per second being run, while some have longer periods of reduced performance during asynchronous checkpointing processes, and some have both. In general, the total transactions that were completed is the area underneath each line in the graph, and the total cost of checkpointing is thus the difference between these areas. Therefore, in order to present the total cost of checkpointing, we measured, for each algorithm, the total number of transactions that were completed during the 200 second window of our experiment. We then subtracted this number from the total number of transactions that would have completed if no checkpointing code had been performed. The result is the total cost of checkpointing — the number of transactions that were not processed during this period in order to devote database resources to checkpointing.

Figure 2(c) shows the result of this cost summary calculation. It is perhaps more clear from this graph than the previous graphs how much lower overhead CALC has relative to the other algorithms. Even relative to Zigzag for the workload without long transactions (when Zigzag does not have to noticeably quiesce the database), CALC still significantly outperforms Zigzag by almost 40%.

5.1.2 Partial Checkpointing

We now compare the partial versions of the checkpointing algorithms. In this case, instead of being required to create a full snapshot of the database at each checkpoint, the algorithms only have to checkpoint the records that had been modified since the most recent checkpoint.

The write locality conditions can make a big difference for the partial checkpointing schemes. High write locality means that most transactions update the same "hot" subset of the records in the database, so that the total number of records modified between two consecutive checkpoints is small. Hence, the size of the partial checkpoints will also be small. It is very common to see this kind of skew in data access patterns in real-world applications.

Therefore we vary the write locality conditions for our partial checkpoint experiments. Figure 3(a), 3(b) shows the performance of the partial checkpointing algorithms where there is 10% and 20% data access skew respectively. The workload we run is the microbenchmark with long-running transactions. Similarly to the previous experiment, the experiment lasts 200 seconds and contains 2 checkpoints.

Overall, the relative performance of CALC vs. Zigzag, IPP, fuzzy, and naive are the same for this set of experiments as they were for the previous set of experiments. The only difference is that the amount of time spent writing the checkpoint data is smaller for all 5 algorithms, since only modified records need to be written. For Zigzag, IPP, fuzzy, and CALC, this results in a much shorter window of time that the system is running at 7% to 10% lower than maximum capacity. For naive, this results in a much shorter window of time that the system must be quiesced.

In all five cases, the total cost of checkpointing is proportionally reduced, as shown in Figure 3(c). Interestingly, as data access skew increases, the relative cost of CALC vs. the other algorithms improves, since the time to take a checkpoint gets increasingly small for all four algorithms, and therefore baseline performance and the time required to manufacture a physical point of consistency start to dominate the overall checkpointing cost. Since CALC has almost no overhead at rest and does not require a physical point of consistency, its relative performance to the other algorithms improves.

5.1.3 Recovery Time

Section 3 discussed the recovery time vs runtime tradeoff for CALC vs. pCALC. In both cases, recovery involves loading a complete checkpoint, and (potentially) replaying committed transactions since this checkpoint. Since both the loading cost and the replaying of committed transactions is a constant for both CALC and pCALC, and their costs are entirely independent of the checkpointing scheme, we ignore them from our recovery time analysis.

Thus, the recovery time for CALC is effectively zero in

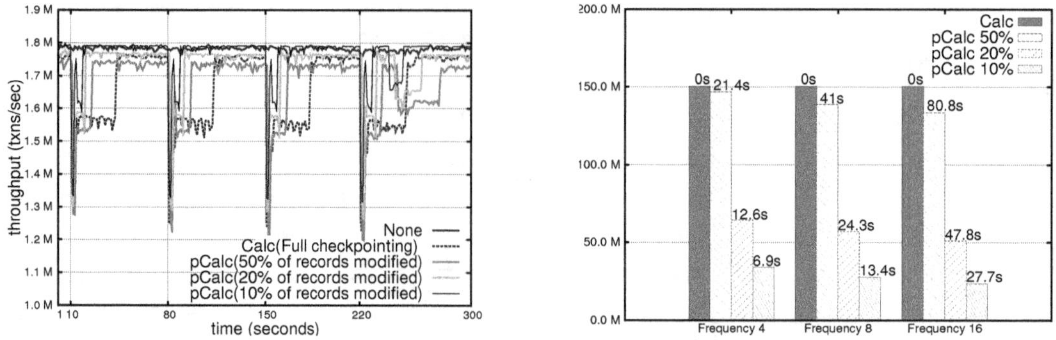

(a) Throughput over time.

(b) Transactions lost.

Figure 4: Full checkpointing vs. Partial checkpointing.

our analysis — no additional work has to occur aside from loading the most recent checkpoint and replaying committed transactions. However, if the most recent checkpoint is a partial checkpoint instead of a full checkpoint, additional work must be performed in order to merge all partial checkpoints that have occurred since the most recent full checkpoint. As mentioned in Section 3.2, we can use a background process during runtime to continuously merge together partial checkpoints so that the distance to the most recent full checkpoint is limited. However, there remains a recovery time vs runtime tradeoff — the less frequently this background merge process happens, the less cost there is at runtime, but the longer the recovery time.

To investigate this process further, we experimented with three different configurations for this background process — it runs after 4, 8, and 16 partial checkpoints have been taken.

Figure 4(a) shows the results of this experiment when partial checkpoints are merged with the most recent full checkpoint after every 4 partial checkpoints. The experiment lasts 300 seconds and checkpoints are taken at 10 seconds, 80 seconds, 150 seconds and 220 seconds. For the pCALC algorithm, the four partial checkpoints are merged together with the most recent full checkpoint 5 seconds after the fourth checkpoint completes. We benchmark with three write locality skew cases(10%, 20% and 50% of records modified).

The left 4 bars in Figure 4(b) summarizes the number of transactions lost for this graph, analogously to how Figure 2(c) showed the transactions lost for Figures 2(a) and 2(b). The number of transactions lost is an indication of the runtime cost for each experiment. Above each bar in the graph shows the recovery time needed in the worst case scenario were all four partial checkpoints have to be merged at recovery time in order generate a full checkpoint. The remaining 8 bars in Figure 4(b) summarize the runtime and recovery time costs for the case of partial checkpoints being merged after 8 and 16 partial checkpoints have been taken.

When focusing on runtime, it is clear that despite the additional time to merge the partial checkpoints, the overall cost of checkpointing is much smaller for the partial checkpointing algorithms than the full checkpointing algorithm with higher locality skew(10% and 20%). However, there is less advantage for pCALC with lower locality skew(50%).

The runtime vs recovery time tradeoff is clear as one compares the three different sets of bars corresponding to the partial checkpoint batch sizes of 4, 8, and 16. pCALC's runtime improvement relative to CALC increases as the batch size of partial checkpoints to merge increases. However, recovery time increases linearly. Nonetheless, we expect that pCALC with batch sizes within our experimental range will be the preferred option for most workloads, since the background merge process keeps the recovery time tractable.

5.1.4 Transaction Latency

Next, we measure transaction latency for each checkpointing algorithm. We collect transaction latency from the experiments run in Section 5.1.1, in which we run the database system for 100 seconds and take a checkpoint at the 30 second mark. Figures 5(a) and 5(b) show cumulative distribution functions for latencies observed when the database receives transactions at a rate that keeps it running at 90% of its maximum capacity. We also measure transaction latency for a less intense input transactional workload that keeps the database at 70% maximum capacity in Figures 5(c) and 5(d).

When the input transactional workload is intense (keeping the database system at 90% of its maximum capacity) the latencies of the naive and fuzzy schemes are very poor. This is because the naive and fuzzy schemes quiesce the database temporarily during the checkpoint period. All transactions that enter the system during this period thus get queued and wait for the database to resume processing. This queue gets continuously bigger during the checkpoint period. After the database resumes processing, the transactions in this queue get processed. However, new transactions continue to the enter the system and get placed at the end of the queue. Since the input transactional workload is so close to the database system's maximum capacity, the database never gets a chance to "catch up" and shrink the size of the queue. Therefore, all transactions that enter the system after the first time the database is quiesced experience the latency of the quiesce period — even those transactions that enter the system substantially after this period has ended. Thus, the latencies for the naive algorithm are the worst, since its quiesce period is the longest. However, even Zigzag and IPP, which temporarily quiesce the database to create a physical point of consistency when there exist long-running transactions in the database system, experience poor latency in Figure 5(b).

Figures 5(c) and 5(d) show the latencies in perhaps the more realistic scenario, where the database is not running at full capacity, and can use its additional headroom to catch up after transactions get queued during periods of unavailability. In these figures, the latencies of Zigzag, IPP, fuzzy, and naive are much better than than the previous case, but

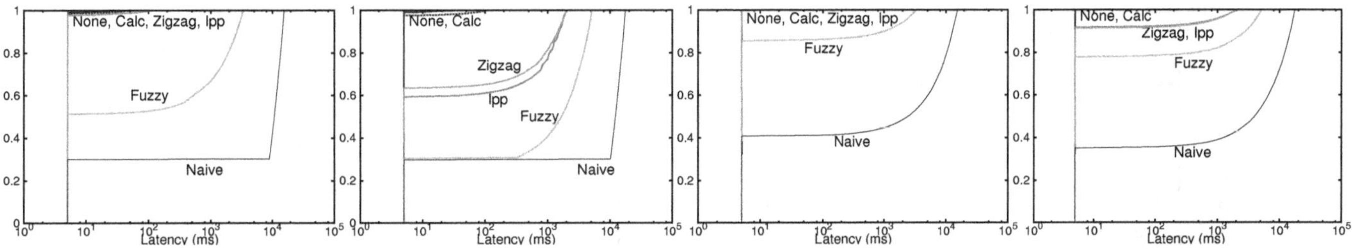

(a) No long xacts, 90% load (b) Long xacts, 90% load (c) No long xacts, 70% load (d) Long xacts, 70% load

Figure 5: Latency distribution.

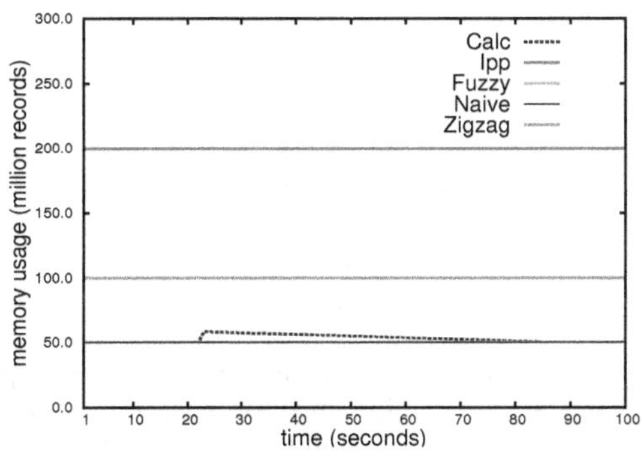

Figure 6: Memory used for record storage over time.

the short period of unavailability while the database was quiesced, in addition to the short catch-up period thereafter, do take their toll on the latency distribution.

For all of these latency experiments, CALC performs very similarly with the "no checkpointing" scheme because CALC does not require physical points of consistency, and never has to quiesce the database system. This experiment shows a major advantage of CALC relative to the other checkpointing schemes. While it is common for main memory database systems to experience hiccups in latency during checkpointing periods, *CALC manages to avoid these hiccups entirely.*

5.1.5 Scalability

We also ran some experiments to see if the database size effects the overhead of CALC. In particular, experimented with database sizes of 10 million records, 50 million, 100 million, and 150 million. We found that the checkpoint duration was linearly correlated with database size. This is not surprising — if the database is larger, so too is the checkpoint. Thus if the database is twice as large, twice as much work has to happen during checkpointing as far as scanning through the stable records and writing them to disk. Accordingly, the total overhead of checkpointing, expressed in terms of total transactions lost, is also linear in database size. Due to lack of space and lack of surprise in the results, we do not present these results in more detail here. However, more detailed results are provided in Appendix A.

5.1.6 Physical Memory usage

One advantage of the naive and fuzzy checkpointing schemes is that they do not need to keep around extra copies of the data in memory.

In contrast, IPP requires keeping 3 copies of all records. Furthermore, during the checkpointing period, IPP must merge the updated records with the last consistent checkpoint in order to construct a new consistent checkpoint that can be written to disk. Therefore, in practice, IPP requires up to 4 copies of the database in memory. Zigzag requires keeping 2 copies of all records.

In the worst case, CALC requires two copies of each record to be stored. However, in practice, the actual memory needed is much less than this. CALC does not require any extra memory until the checkpoint process begins. When CALC enters the *prepare* phase, transactions begin inserting stable record versions on all writes. Once the *capture* phase begins, the checkpointing thread begins erasing these stable versions. Thus CALC only requires extra space for records written during the short period of time in between these two phases, which is generally much smaller than the total number of records updated since the last checkpoint.

Figure 6 summarizes the space required for each algorithm over the course of a 100 second experiment where a checkpoint is taken at 20 seconds for a 50 million record database. Naive, fuzzy, IPP, and Zig-zag all require constant space. Naive and fuzzy require almost no extra space beyond the original database size. Zigzag and IPP require 2X and 4X database size, respectively. CALC requires no extra space most of the time, but requires around 1.2X database size during its peak requirements during the checkpointing period.

In practice, in order to avoid frequently allocating and erasing stable records, our implementation pre-allocates a pool of space for stable records, so that when a transaction needs to insert stable record, it simply allocates memory for the stable record from the pool. When transactions need to erase the stable record, they simply release the space back into the pool. Therefore, in practice, CALC's memory usage is also flat — it needs as much space as peak requirements — 1.2X database size. Nonetheless, it is clear that its overall memory requirements are much smaller than IPP and Zigzag and similar to Naive and Fuzzy.

5.2 TPC-C experiments

Finally, we examined the overhead of the checkpointing schemes on the TPC-C benchmark at a scale of 50 TPC-C warehouses. For this experiment, we run a mix of 50% NewOrder and 50% Payment transactions. These two transactions make up 88% of the default TPC-C mix and are the most relevant transactions when experimenting with checkpointing algorithms since they are write-intensive. Figure 7(a) shows TPC-C throughput under maximum load for each checkpointing scheme when a checkpoint is taken at the 50 second mark, and Figure 7(b) plots the total transactions lost during the checkpoint period of Figure 7(a).

The result is very similar to our earlier results for the microbenchmark without long-running transactions, since

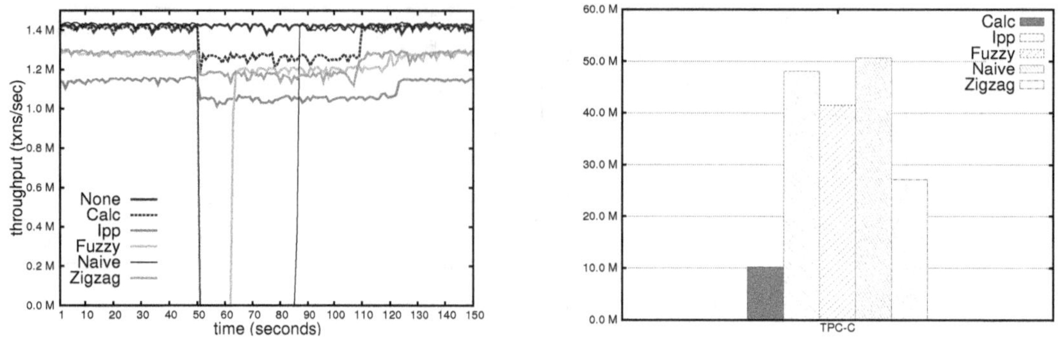

(a) Throughput over time.

(b) Transactions lost.

Figure 7: TPC-C workload.

TPC-C does not have a non-read-only transaction of substantial length. However, one interesting difference between these results and the microbenchmark is that Zigzag performs relatively worse relative to CALC on TPC-C. This is because the TPC-C New Order transaction (the most common transaction in the workload) contains many more writes to records than the microbenchmark, which introduces more overhead for Zigzag since it needs to maintain two copies of the record upon each write, even when checkpointing is not actively ongoing.

6. RELATED WORK

There have been several previous attempts to capture checkpoints asynchronously. Dewitt et al. [3] discuss the implementation of a main memory system that uses checkpoints to prevent massive data loss due to system interruptions and crashes. Their scheme begins writing values to stable storage, marking pages in the buffer pool that have been updated after being checkpointed as belonging to a set ΔMem. Once the checkpoint completes, the pages in ΔMem are written to their old location on disk. However, this algorithm not only requires a physical point of consistency to record the time at which a checkpoint begins, it also requires at worst a doubling of disk IO in order to reconcile the inconsistent state created by pages in ΔMem.

Granular tuple locking allowing for incremental checkpoint captures has also been previously investigated by Pu [15]. However, this "on-the-fly" checkpointing does not allow transactions that touch checkpointed and non-checkpointed keys to execute. This causes numerous non-deterministic aborts, possibly causing the throughput to drop dramatically during the checkpoint period.

Some other asynchronous methods have traditionally relied on the availability of a spare hot server to duplicate transactions and intermittently quiesce the database to capture a full snapshot [24]. However, despite the assumption that there exists an available spare server to perform no tasks other than checkpointing, this technique is extremely vulnerable to network delays or failures, which could result in costly latency spikes.

Zheng et al. presented SiloR [25], a logging, checkpointing, and recovery subsystem for a very fast in-memory database. However, they do not create transaction-consistent checkpoints.

VoltDB [13] proposed an asynchronous checkpointing technique which takes checkpoints by making every database record 'copy-on-write'. However, like many of the other schemes presented in the paper, it requires a physical point of consistency — a key requirement that CALC drops. Furthermore, their scheme relies on VoltDB's deterministic design, and is thus not generally applicable to all database systems.

Fuzzy checkpointing has become an extremely popular checkpointing algorithm in database systems. There have been several proposals for applying it to main memory [12, 5, 11]. Salem et al. argues that fuzzy checkpointing is the most efficient [17]. Oracle's main memory database TimesTen[8] also supports fuzzy checkpointing. However, fuzzy checkpointing requires a database log, a requirement that we avoided in our work.

Microsoft's main memory database system, Hekaton [4], proposed a fast partial checkpoint algorithm. The basic idea is to continually scan the tail of the log and create data and delta checkpoint files. In contrast, CALC is designed for an entirely different type of main memory system — a system that does not have any redo log at all. Furthermore, the Hekaton technique is specifically designed for multi-versioning systems, while CALC is more general.

Hyper proposed a consistent snapshot mechanism through a UNIX system call to fork(), and OS-based copy-on-update [7]. However, it requires the physical point of consistency and does not support partial checkpoints.

7. CONCLUSION

We have presented CALC and pCALC, novel methods for asynchronous checkpointing that require minimum additional memory usage, no physical point of consistency in the application state, and extremely low runtime overhead. Our experiments show that CALC and pCALC have an overhead that is 2-10X less than alternative approaches — even promising approaches that were introduced recently. Furthermore, it avoids the temporary latency spikes that are common in other checkpointing approaches.

Acknowledgements. This work was sponsored by the NSF under grant IIS-1527118.

8. REFERENCES

[1] P. Bernstein and E. Newcomer. *Principles of Transaction Processing*. seconod edition edition, 2009.

[2] T. Cao, M. Vaz Salles, B. Sowell, Y. Yue, A. Demers, J. Gehrke, and W. White. Fast checkpoint recovery algorithms for frequently consistent applications. In

Proceedings of the 2011 international conference on Management of data, SIGMOD '11, pages 265–276, 2011.

[3] D. J. DeWitt, R. H. Katz, F. Olken, L. D. Shapiro, M. R. Stonebraker, and D. A. Wood. Implementation techniques for main memory database systems. In *Proceedings of the 1984 ACM SIGMOD international conference on Management of data*, SIGMOD '84, pages 1–8, New York, NY, USA, 1984. ACM.

[4] C. Diaconu, C. Freedman, E. Ismert, P. ÃĚke Larson, P. Mittal, R. Stonecipher, N. Verma, and M. Zwilling. Hekaton: Sql server's memory-optimized oltp engine. In *SIGMOD*, 2013.

[5] R. B. Hagmann. A crash recovery scheme for a memory-resident database system. *IEEE Trans. Comput.*, 35:839–843, September 1986.

[6] S. Harizopoulos, D. J. Abadi, S. R. Madden, and M. Stonebraker. OLTP through the looking glass, and what we found there. In *SIGMOD*, 2008.

[7] A. Kemper and T. Neumann. Hyper: A hybrid OLTP&OLAP main memory database system based on virtual memory snapshots. *Proc. of ICDE*, pages 195–206, June 2011.

[8] T. Lahiri, M.-A. Neimat, and S. Folkman. Oracle timesten: An in-memory database for enterprise applications. *In IEEE Data Engineering Bulletin.*, June 2013.

[9] E. Lau and S. Madden. An integrated approach to recovery and high availability in an updatable, distributed data warehouse. In *Proc. of VLDB*, pages 703–714, 2006.

[10] J. Lee, M. Muehle, N. May, F. Faerber, V. Sikkal, H. Plattner, J. Krueger, and M. Grund. High-performance transaction processing in sap hana. *In IEEE Data Engineering Bulletin.*, June 2013.

[11] X. Li and M. H. Eich. Post-crash log processing for fuzzy checkpointing main memory databases. In *Procceedings of the Ninth International Conference on Data Engineering*, Apr. 1993.

[12] J.-L. Lin and M. H. Dunham. Segmented fuzzy checkpointing for main memory databases. In *Procceedings of the ACM Symposium on Applied Computing*, February 1996.

[13] N. Malviya, A. Weisberg, S. Madden, and M. Stonebraker. Rethinking main memory oltp recovery. In *Proc. of ICDE*, 2014.

[14] C. Mohan, D. Haderle, B. Lindsay, H. Pirahesh, and P. Schwarz. Aries: a transaction recovery method supporting fine-granularity locking and partial rollbacks using write-ahead logging. *ACM Trans. Database Syst.*, 17:94–162, March 1992.

[15] C. Pu. On-the-fly, incremental, consistent reading of entire databases. In *Proceedings of the 11th international conference on Very Large Data Bases - Volume 11*, VLDB '85, pages 369–375. VLDB Endowment, 1985.

[16] K. Ren, A. Thomson, and D. J. Abadi. An evaluation of the advantages and disadvantages of deterministic database systems. PVLDB 7(10): 821-832, 2014.

[17] K. Salem and H. Garcia-Molina. Checkpointing memory-resident databases. In *In Proc. ICDE*, 1989.

[18] A. Silberschatz, H. Korth, and S. Sudarshan. *Database Systems Concepts*. 5 edition, 2006.

[19] M. Stonebraker, D. J. Abadi, A. Batkin, X. Chen, M. Cherniack, M. Ferreira, E. Lau, A. Lin, S. R. Madden, E. J. O'Neil, P. E. O'Neil, A. Rasin, N. Tran, and S. B. Zdonik. C-store: A column-oriented dbms. In *VLDB*, pages 553–564, Trondheim, Norway, 2005.

[20] M. Stonebraker, S. R. Madden, D. J. Abadi, S. Harizopoulos, N. Hachem, and P. Helland. The end of an architectural era (it's time for a complete rewrite). In *VLDB*, Vienna, Austria, 2007.

[21] A. Thomson and D. J. Abadi. The case for determinism in database systems. *VLDB*, 2010.

[22] A. Thomson, T. Diamond, P. Shao, K. Ren, S.-C. Weng, and D. J. Abadi. Calvin: Fast distributed transactions for partitioned database systems. In *SIGMOD*, 2012.

[23] VoltDB. http://voltdb.com.

[24] A. Whitney, D. Shasha, and S. Apter. High Volume Transaction Processing Without Concurrency Control, Two Phase Commit, SQL or C++. In *Int. Workshop on High Performance Transaction Systems*, 1997.

[25] W. Zheng and S. Tu. Fast databases with fast durability and recovery through multicore parallelism. In *OSDI*, 2014.

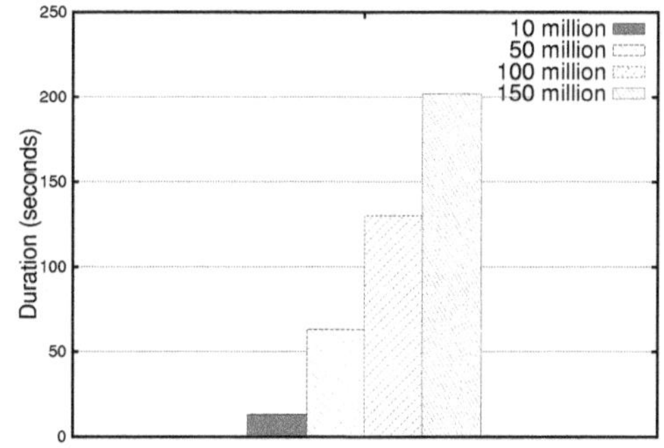

(a) Checkpoint duration.

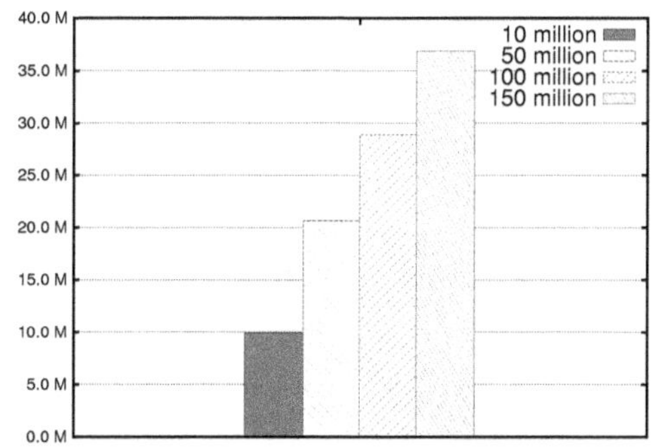

(b) Transactions lost.

Figure 8: Scalability.

APPENDIX

A. SCALABILITY RESULTS

Figure 8 shows the result of an experiment in which we examine the scalability for the CALC algorithm. We scale from 10 million records to 150 million records. We measure the checkpoint duration and total transactions lost for each database size setting when running 300 seconds that contains one full checkpoint. As can be seen, the CALC algorithm is linearly scalable. If the database is twice as large, twice as much work has to happen during checkpointing as far as scanning through the stable records and writing them to disk. Accordingly, the total overhead of checkpointing, expressed in terms of total transactions lost, is also linear in database size.

Note that since the recording of a checkpoint is limited by disk bandwidth in our system, the time to complete a checkpoint is a direct measure of total disk IO. Therefore, using higher bandwidth disks will reduce both the checkpoint duration and transactions lost.

T-Part: Partitioning of Transactions for Forward-Pushing in Deterministic Database Systems

Shan-Hung Wu, Tsai-Yu Feng, Meng-Kai Liao, Shao-Kan Pi, Yu-Shan Lin
National Tsing Hua University
shwu@cs.nthu.edu.tw, kayfeng@appier.com,
{mkliao,skpi,yslin}@netdb.cs.nthu.edu.tw

ABSTRACT

Deterministic database systems have been shown to yield high throughput on a cluster of commodity machines while ensuring the strong consistency between replicas, provided that the data can be well-partitioned on these machines. However, data partitioning can be suboptimal for many reasons in real-world applications. In this paper, we present T-Part, a transaction execution engine that *partitions transactions* in a deterministic database system to deal with the unforeseeable workloads or workloads whose data are hard to partition. By modeling the dependency between transactions as a *T-graph* and continuously partitioning that graph, T-Part allows each transaction to know which later transactions on other machines will read its writes so that it can *push forward* the writes to those later transactions *immediately after committing*. This forward-pushing reduces the chance that the later transactions stall due to the unavailability of remote data. We implement a prototype for T-Part. Extensive experiments are conducted and the results demonstrate the effectiveness of T-Part.

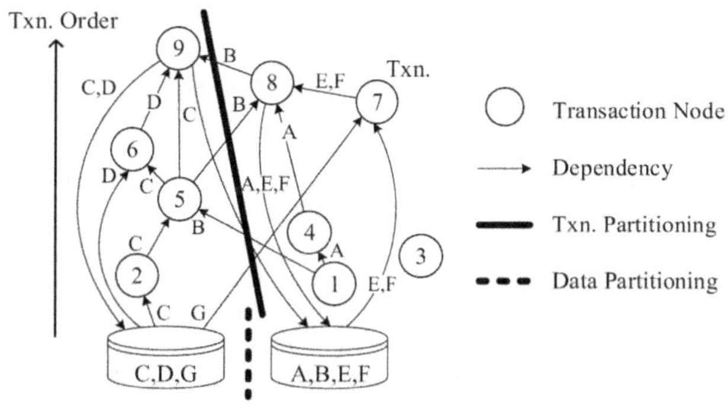

Figure 1: Partitioning of transactions and the forward-pushing.

1. INTRODUCTION

Modern OLTP workloads have two salient features. First, most transactions are short and drawn from predefined stored procedures consisting of no user interaction/stall [27]. Applications use stored procedures to cut down on the number of round trips between themselves and the database systems. Second, the data being accessed change over time and may not be easily partitionable [9,31]. For example, it is difficult to partition the data for social networking applications, as their schemas often consist of many n-to-n relationships.

The first feature motivates re-examination of the *deterministic database systems* [15,29,30], a type of distributed OLTP database systems that requires different machines (holding data partitions or replicas) to process all relevant transactions in the same total order (or an equivalent one). This allows transactions to produce the same results on different machines, avoids costly 2PC for data synchronization, and significantly increases system throughput on a large cluster of commodity machines while guaranteeing strong consistency between replicas. On the other hand, the totally ordered execution of transactions makes the throughput vulnerable to long transactions [29], as short transactions ordered after a long one cannot be reordered on-the-fly to complete first and to prevent the long transaction from hurting throughput.

While OLTP transactions are generally short, there are two common cases that a transaction will be prolonged in a distributed database system: when it is executed on an overloaded machine/storage and when the data being accessed span multiple machines. To work around these cases, most existing deterministic database systems require that the data in storage are well-partitioned *at all times* so the loads of machines are balanced and the number of distributed transactions is minimized.

Unfortunately, in practice it is hard to keep the data well-partitioned at all times. The second feature of modern OLTP workloads makes static, coarse-grained data partitioning insuffcient, and motivates studies on dynamic, fined-grained data partitioning driven by workloads [9,20,21,34]. The basic idea is to employ the data access patterns in the workload traces to determine better partitions. However, due to its "looking back" nature, the workload-driven data partitioning only finds good partitions *in the past*, and gives no guarantee on the quality of partitions when facing the changing workloads. Furthermore, due to the large volume of data, frequent data partitioning (so to keep up with changing workloads) may incur unacceptable computing/data migration cost.

In this paper, we present *T-Part*, a transaction execution engine for deterministic database systems that achieves high throughput in the presence of dynamic workloads and imperfect data partitions. Observe that before executing a transaction, each machine in a deterministic database system needs to assign that transaction a place in the total order (follow in which all machines execute transactions) and to analyze the read and write sets of that transaction. Therefore, the dependency between *pending transactions*

SIGMOD '16, June 26–July 1, 2016, San Francisco, CA, USA.

DOI: http://dx.doi.org/10.1145/2882903.2915227

(i.e., transactions that have entered the system but not yet executed) can be known early. Using this dependency, T-Part *partitions pending transactions*, by first establishing a *T-graph* whose nodes and edges denote transactions and their dependency respectively, and then finds the partitions of that graph. Figure 1 gives an example of transaction partitioning. T-Part ensures that 1) nodes/transactions spread evenly among partitions, so that machines, each assigned a partition of transactions, are evenly loaded; and 2) there exists as few cross-partition edges as possible, so that execution of transactions requires less remote data access.

Based on the partitioning results, each transaction can know exactly which later transactions will read its writes, and can "push forward" those writes *immediately after its execution*. For example, the transaction 1 in Figure 1 can push forward the object B to transaction 5 right after committing. So transaction 5, upon execution, need not pull data from other machines. This early forward-pushing reduces the *synchronization between machines* (i.e., one machine stops to wait for the others to catch-up and send data it needs), a major cause of slowdown in a deterministic database system when executing distributed transactions.

T-Part also opens up numerous opportunities for sophisticated optimization of data movement and transaction execution. In terms of optimizing data movement, T-Part moves data by *looking forward*. The read/write sets of pending transactions are modeled into the T-graph. So, finding partitions of pending transactions effectively finds the partitions of the in-memory data *to be accessed in the near future*. In addition, the number of nodes/transactions in the T-graph is much smaller than the number of records in the storage. Thus, transaction partitioning can be performed much more frequently than data partitioning.[1] The above augments the workload-driven data partitioning techniques [9, 20, 21, 34] and make the system robust to changing workloads. Following summarizes our contributions:

- We propose T-Part, which allows transactions to push forward their writes to later transactions early to avoid machine synchronization. T-Part is compatible with existing deterministic database systems [15, 29, 30] and works alongside any storage with the CRUD interface and any data partitioning scheme.
- We discuss numerous performance optimization techniques enabled by T-Part, such as the principles to obtain a better T-graph.
- We implement a prototype for T-Part based on our implementation of Calvin [30]. We devise efficient partitioning algorithms that can be run by individual machines continuously without accounting for more than 0.25% of the transaction latency in general. Furthermore, these algorithms are deterministic to the total order of transactions. So different machines need not communicate with each other to reach consensus on the partitioning. T-Part supports systems with fully distributed architecture.
- Extensive experiments are conducted and the results show that T-Part is able to make the baseline systems (with and without fine-grained, dynamic data partitioning) much more scalable when given the hard-to-partition workloads like TPC-E. In particular, it is able to eliminate more than 50% distributed transactions having network stall (due to unavailable remote data on local machines).

The rest of paper is organized as follows. Section 2 discusses the advantages and limitations of existing deterministic database systems. Section 3 introduces T-Part while Section 4 describes optimization techniques for improving the system performance. We discuss implementation challenges/pitfalls in Section 5. Section 6 evaluates the performance of T-Part and Section 7 discusses related work. Finally, Section 8 concludes the paper.

[1] In fact, the transaction partitioning is continuous in T-Part.

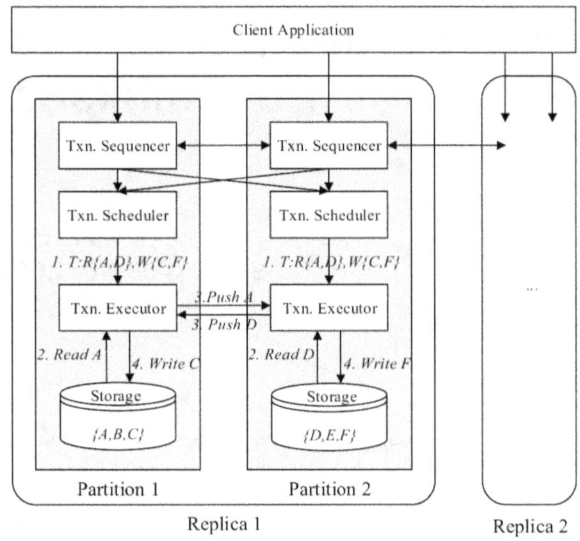

Figure 2: System architecture of Calvin [29, 30]. Each scheduler receives *all* transactions from the sequencers but only forwards a *part* of them (that touch data in the local storage) to the local executor.

2. BACKGROUND AND CHALLENGES

In this section, we review the deterministic database systems and discuss their practical limitations when facing imperfect data partitions.

2.1 Deterministic Database Systems

Assuming that all transactions are short and defined as stored procedures without user stall, recent studies [15, 29, 30] show that the deterministic database systems can be advantageous to high scalability and availability. Here, we briefly review the architecture of Calvin [30], shown in Figure 2, based on which we build T-Part. In this architecture, data are fully replicated across multiple data centers separated geographically for availability. A data center has a cluster of machines. To avoid hot spots, each machine holds a partition of data. Upon arrival of a transaction request, it is assigned a place in the total order and replicated to all data centers, both done by the sequencers in the system. The sequencers forward the replicated requests to all schedulers by following the total order. Each scheduler, when receiving a request, determines its read set and write set by analyzing the stored procedure,[2] and forwards the request to the local executor if the read and write sets cover any data stored locally. By *determinism* we mean that 1) all executors in the system process transactions following the total order (or an equivalent one) decided by the sequencers; and 2) there is no reason other than the stored procedure logic that can cause the transaction to abort. So, the commit/abort decision and the written values of each transaction are deterministic. Note that each scheduler receives *all* transactions from the sequencers but

[2] In order to determine the read and write sets of a transaction before its execution, the scheduler may break the transaction into multiple ones. For more details, please refer to [29, 30].

each executor processes only *partial* transactions which touch data in the local storage. The above system offers some nice features:

Lightweight distributed transactions. Execution of distributed transactions (i.e., transactions accessing data on multiple partitions) can be simplified with the aid of *peer-pushing* and *local writes*. For example, suppose a transaction T reading data $\{A, D\}$ and writing $\{C, F\}$ is being executed by two machines holding partitions 1 and 2 respectively (Figure 2(1)). Both machines recognize that this transaction is a distributed transaction and, additionally, which objects are missing on the other side in order to execute that transaction. They both perform local reads first (Figure 2(2)), and then *push* to the peer those missing objects (Figure 2(3)). Once obtaining $\{A, D\}$, these machines can execute the transaction *locally*—there is no need for some expensive data synchronization protocols (e.g., 2PL and 2PC), as the determinism ensures that these two machines will always reach the same conclusion on whether to commit the transaction or not and, if so, write the same values for C and F. Furthermore, each machine needs only write objects local to its storage (Figure 2(4)).

Cross-WAN data replication with strong consistency. By replicating the transaction *requests* rather than the post-execution *writes*, the system needs *no* agreement protocol (e.g., 2PC or the group-commit protocol [17]) between replicas to commit a transaction. Note that the delay incurred by the total-ordering protocol (e.g., Paxos [8] or its variants [14, 22]) for ordering a transaction does *not* count into the contention footprint of that transaction during the concurrency control. Therefore, such delay has no impact on the system throughput. Data centers can be placed across WAN to survive from geographical disasters. Furthermore, by determinism, different replicas will always see/produce the same snapshot of data at a given total order, preserving strong consistency.

The system has a fully distributed architecture, thereby preventing a single point failure. In addition, it supports any storage engine (either memory- or disk-based) with the CRUD interface. Study [30] demonstrates its improved performance over traditional (R*-like) systems on a large cluster of commodity machines.

2.2 The Synchronization Problem

The totally ordered execution of transactions makes the system throughput vulnerable to long transactions [29], as short transactions ordered after a long one cannot be reordered on-the-fly in the concurrency control module to prevent the long transaction from blocking others. Although OLTP workloads do not tend to have long transactions, in practice a transaction can be prolonged due to either a hot machine, slow I/Os (over hot data), or remote data access. This leads to the *synchronization problem*. Recall that when processing the transaction T (Figure 2(3)), the participating machines need to collect the read set from remote ones. If *any* machine falls behind, then *all* others need to wait for that machine to catch up and to push the missing data. Later transactions conflicting with T will be blocked until the progress of participating machines becomes synchronous, which could damage the throughput badly. Figures 8(a) and (c) show the impacts of distributed transactions and skewness of machine loads on the throughput of our Calvin implementation, respectively. We can see that the occurrence of distributed transactions and workload skewness significantly degrade the throughput. The settings and further discussions will be detailed in Section 6.

One way to avoid the synchronization problem is to find good data partitions such that 1) data access spreads evenly among partitions, so that the machines have balanced loads without hot spot; and 2) the need for cross-partition data access is minimized, so that the system encounters as few distributed transactions as possible. However, as discussed in Section 1, it is hard to find good data partitions at all times in many OLTP workloads. It is crucial to have a new transaction processing technique for deterministic database systems that can cope with the synchronization problem itself.

3. OVERVIEW OF T-PART

In this section, we introduce *T-Part*, a new transaction execution engine for deterministic database systems.

T-Part consists of two components, the *scheduler* and *executor*, for the architecture shown in Figure 2. This is how T-Part works in general:

As in Calvin, a T-Part scheduler receives all transactions [3] from the sequencers and decides which of them will be routed to the executor on the local machine. It analyzes and models transaction dependency as a *T-graph*, finds the balanced partitioning of that graph, and forwards to the local executor a *push plan* along with the transactions assigned to the current machine. Then, the T-Part executor processes the received transactions and *push forward* their writes to other machine by following the push plan.

T-Part is designed to work alongside any deterministic database system with architecture similar to the one shown in Figure 2 (Calvin), any storage with the CRUD interface, and any data partitioning scheme. The outputs of T-Part schedulers and executors are deterministic to the total order of transactions so to support fully distributed architecture. Since the T-Part schedulers face all transactions (requests), they are designed to be very efficient in computing. Note that unlike Calvin, each transaction will be executed only once in some executor.

Next, we provide more details about some important steps.

3.1 Constructing T-Graph

To maximize the throughput of a total-ordering protocol, each sequencer in existing deterministic database systems [29, 30] periodically compiles its requests arriving within a time interval into a *batch* (in which the order of requests are decided), and uses the total-ordering protocol to determine the total order of that batch only. Therefore, the totally ordered transactions actually come to the schedulers *in batches*. This allows the schedulers to analyze the dependency between transactions before forwarding them to the executors.[4]

By analyzing the read set and write set of each transaction,[5] the T-Part scheduler models the transactions and their dependency as the nodes and edges respectively in a graph, called *T-graph*. Since we are looking for the chances of pushing writes from one machine to another, we model the write-read conflicts (wr-conflicts for short) as edges. Figure 3(a) gives an example T-graph based on the following transactions:

$$\begin{array}{ll} T1: W\{A, B\}, & T2: R\{B, C\}, W\{C\}, \\ T3: R\{C\}, W\{C\}, & T4: R\{A\}, W\{A, E\}, \\ T5: R\{B, C\}, W\{B, C\}, & T6: R\{C\}, W\{D\}, \\ T7: W\{G\}, & T8: R\{A, B\}, W\{F\}. \end{array}$$

An *forward-push edge* from $T1$ to $T2$ means "a wr-conflict such that if $T1$ and $T2$ are assigned to difference machines (after the T-graph is partitioned), the machine executing $T1$ could push the

[3] Specifically, transaction requests. For simplicity, we do not distinguish transaction requests from transactions if doing so does not lead to confusion.

[4] If the transactions come individually, the schedulers can still buffer each transaction for a short time to analyze its dependency with the others. The buffering delay does *not* add to the contention footprint of transactions, and has no impact to the system throughput.

[5] As in traditional deterministic database systems [29,30], to obtain the read and write sets T-Part may break a dependent transaction into multiple ones, interleaved by the "reconnaissance" queries.

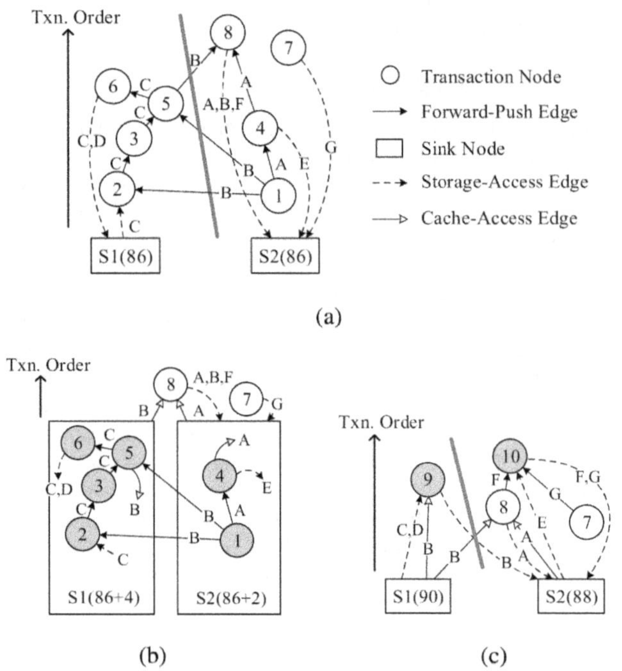

Figure 3: T-graph. (a) An example. (b) Sinking of transactions 1 to 6. (c) Arrival of transactions 9 and 10.

commonly accessed data (object B) to the machine where $T2$ resides. "

Nodes and edges are associated with weights. The weight of a node represents the processing cost of a transaction while the weight of an edge denotes the synchronization cost. For simplicity, here we assume that all node/edge weights equal to 1. We will discuss other weighting rules in Section 4.1.

T-Part works with any data partitioning strategy in the storage, and models each data partition held by a machine using a *sink node*. For example, $S1$ and $S2$ in Figure 3(a) represent two data partitions held by machines 1 and 2, with data:

$$S1 : \{C, D\}, \quad S2 : \{A, B, E, F, G\},$$

respectively. The weight of a sink node denotes the load of the corresponding machine. It is defined as the sum of weights of nodes that have already been sent to the executor on that machine, but not committed yet. In our example, we assume that both machines 1 and 2 have 86 running transactions, so the weights of $S1$ and $S2$ are 86. If a transaction reads an object not written by previous transactions, it needs to read the object from the storage on some machine (e.g., $T2$ reads C from $S1$). This is modeled in T-graph by a *storage-access edge* from the corresponding sink node (where the object belongs to) to the transaction. Conversely, when a transaction writes an object that will not be read nor overwritten by later transactions, it needs to write back the object to the storage (e.g., $T4$ writes E back to $S2$). This is modeled by another storage-access edge in the opposite direction. The storage-access edges can be weighted differently than the forward-push edges to reflect the storage access cost. Note that, even if $T6$ does not write C, it needs to write back C to storage as C was written by previous transactions but had not been written back yet. Similarly, $T8$ needs to write back A and B. We will discuss this behavior in Section 4.2.

3.2 Partitioning T-Graph

After obtaining a T-graph, the T-Part scheduler finds the balanced partitioning of that graph, as shown by the thick line in Figure 3(a), such that: 1) the sums of the weights of nodes in different partition are similar, so that each executor, once assigned a partition of nodes/transactions, is not overloaded; and 2) the sum of the weights of cross-partition edges is minimized, so that execution of transactions requires the least remote data access. Note that, by taking the weights of storage-access edges into account, T-Part tends to *move transactions to machines holding the data to be accessed.*

The balanced graph partitioning is an NP-hard problem. In practice, there exist software such as METIS [16] that can solve the problem efficiently using heuristics. However, our problem here differs from the conventional one in that it has *disconnectivity* constraints; that is, two sink nodes (denoting two data partitions on different machines) *cannot* be put into the same partition. So we cannot directly apply the software to our problem. We devise a new partitioning algorithm based on the *streaming graph partitioning* [26], which is very efficient and gives quality partitions comparable to those of METIS. Our results show that the algorithm accounts for no more than 0.25% of the transaction latency in general. We will discuss more about the challenges/pitfalls and the algorithm in Section 5.1.

3.3 Sinking & Push-Plan Generation

As transactions keep arriving from the sequencers, the partition assignment of each transaction changes over time. The T-Part scheduler periodically *sink* a batch[6] of the earliest transactions in T-graph by fixing their assignment and merging them into the sink nodes, as shown in Figure 3(b) (suppose the batch size is 6). The weight of each sink node is increased by the sum of weights of the transactions sunk to that node. Notice that some edges are transformed into the *cache-access edges* during the sinking process. We will discuss such transformation in Section 3.4.

After sinking transactions, the T-Part scheduler generates a *push plan* for the local executor. For example, the plan for the executor on machine 1 is as follows:

$T2$: Read B from cache; C from storage. Write C to cache.
$T3$: Read C from cache. Write C to cache.
$T5$: Read B, C from cache. Write B, C to cache.
$T6$: Read C from cache. Write C, D to storage.

And the plan for machine 2 is:

$T1$: Write A to cache. Push B to $T2$ and $T5$ on $S1$.
$T4$: Read A from cache. Write A to cache; E to storage.

The scheduler then forwards the plan and the sunk transactions to the local executor. Each executor receives only the plan and transactions local to a T-graph partition.

It is important to note that each sinking process needs be *deterministic* so that different schedulers under a distributed architecture (like the one shown in Figure 2) do not generate inconsistent push plans. To ensure the determinism, we require a scheduler to trigger the sinking process *whenever it sees a fixed number of totally ordered transactions in T-graph.* We call this number the *sink size.* By taking advantage of total ordering, the schedulers will generate consistent plans during each sinking process, as they are based on the same transactions in the system. However, this creates a subtle issue: the schedulers will stop sinking transactions if there are not enough transactions available in the T-graph due to the silence of clients (and sequencers too). To solve this issue, we require each

[6]The batch size need not be the same as the size of request batches from sequencers.

sequencer to add *dummy requests* into every batch to be sent to the total-ordering protocol if there are not enough requests from the clients. The schedulers discard these dummy requests when generating a push plan.

3.4 Push-Plan Execution

Upon receiving a batch of sunk transactions along with their push plan, the T-Part executor processes the transactions by following the plan.

The T-Part executor implements a key-value *cache area* (above the buffer manager of the storage engine) in memory to store the objects that are either 1) written by the earlier transactions on the same machine (e.g., $T3$ reads C in Figure 3(b)); or 2) pushed from the remote machines (e.g., $T5$ reads B). Upon execution, a transaction either reads an object from the storage (if that object has not been written by earlier transactions) or the cache area (otherwise). The transaction stalls if the object is not available in memory yet. Note that once accessed by a transaction, an object will stay in the cache until it is not used by any transaction in the T-graph. This prevents repeated storage access to the hot records, and avoids unnecessary buffer/index/file manipulation. We will discuss the cache management in more detail in Section 5.2 and its implication to failure handling in Section 5.4.

T-Part does *not* use the conservative locking for concurrency control as in Calvin. Rather, it makes use of the cache manager to implement a version-based deterministic concurrency control. The idea is to let each transaction access a unique version of a targeted record that is created by some of it's preceding transactions which writes the record last. If that version is not available yet, the current transaction stalls. More details are given in Section 5.2.

Unlike Calvin, each transaction in T-Part is processed by only one executor, and it does *not* wait for the *peer-pushing* from other machines, which requires precise machine synchronization, to obtain the remote data it needs. In T-part, transactions access remote data from *previous* transactions. This allows the data to be prepared *early* so that they are likely to be available in the local cache of machines executing later transactions. Consider those transactions that are sunk in a batch. When processing a transaction in that batch, the executor knows which later transactions in the same batch will read the objects written by current transaction. The executor can push those objects to later transactions *immediately after the current transaction commits*. For example, in 3(b), right after committing $T1$ the executor local to $S2$ pushes forward the object B to $T2$ on another machine. This early *forward-pushing* reduces the need for machine synchronization.

Note that, since the partitions of unsunk nodes (e.g., $T7$ and $T8$ in Figure 3(b)) are subject to change, transactions (e.g., $T5$) writing objects that will read by the unsunk nodes do not know where to push the objects. During the sinking process, the T-Part scheduler transforms all forward-push edges (e.g., the edge from $T5$ to $T8$ in Figure 3(a)) from the sunk to unsunk nodes into the *cache-access edges* (e.g., the cache-write edge from $T5$ to $S1$ in Figure 3(b)). So transactions sunk in the next batch will read the objects from the cache (e.g., the cache-read edge from $S1$ to $T8$) rather than the storage.

The above transformation should not affect the partitioning decided earlier (otherwise transactions will not be executed optimally from the graph partitioning point of view). To ensure this, we leverage the fact that the cache-write edges have no impact on the quality of partitioning since they are local. So, the partitioning will be unchanged if the cache-read edges have the same weights as those of the corresponding forward-push edges before the transformation. Setting the weight of each cache-read edge to the weight of the original forward-push edge is realistic since these two edges share the same endpoints at which only the memory access is involved.

The T-graph construction, partitioning, and sinking processes discussed above repeat for the continuously arriving transactions. When building the T-graph, we have to write back the data read from the sink nodes that have been cached due to the above transformation. For example, suppose two new transactions arrive:

$$T9 : R\{B, C, D\}, W\{B\}, \quad T10 : R\{E, F, G\}.$$

The updated T-graph is shown in Figure 3(c). Notice that $T9$ needs to write back B to the storage holding $S2$, as B is read from the cache.

3.5 Merits

T-Part allows each transaction to *push forward* the data needed by the later transactions early. This early forward-pushing reduces the chance of transaction stalls due to the asynchronous machines and makes the system robust to the progress skew among machines.

T-Part also augments existing data partitioning by instructing the movement of data that will be accessed in the near future. Note the the number of nodes in a T-graph is much smaller than the number of records in storage. So the T-graph can be partitioned much more efficiently and frequently than the data in storage. This alleviates the need for frequent data partitioning in order to keep up with the changing workloads, which may incur high computing/data migration cost.

Furthermore, T-Part opens up numerous opportunities for the sophisticated optimization of transaction execution, to be discussed next.

4. OPTIMIZATION

In this section, we discuss techniques enabled by T-Part that can improve transaction execution.

4.1 Refining Weights

Let w_i be the weight of a node v_i, where i is an index in the total order of transactions to be executed, and $w_{i,j}$ be the weight of an edge $e_{i,j}$ from v_i to v_j. We did not observe significant performance gain in tuning the node weights. This is because OLTP transactions are usually short and lack of user interaction.

On the other hand, edge weights have impact on the system performance. The weight $w_{i,j}$ of an edge $e_{i,j}$ should reflect the machine synchronization cost, which can be roughly defined as the amount of time v_j stalls to wait for the push from v_i. Intuitively, the larger the *transaction distance* $(j - i)$, the lower the weight should be. However, in a real system, there are many reasons that can affect the progress of a machine, and it is very hard to know the exact cost between two specific nodes. Our approach is to regard $w_{i,j}$ as a function of $(j - i)$, and fit the function to the inverse of our measurements. Figures 4(a) and (b) show the average and maximum stalls we observed over different $(j - i)$'s, which can be fitted by the linear and Sigmoid functions (notice the jump around $(j - i) = 200$) respectively.[7] We choose the linear fitting in our prototype due to its simplicity, and leave the latter our future work.

4.2 Modeling Principles

[7]Note there are some peaks at large distance. In each of these cases, v_i is a (relatively) long transaction and should excluded from the fitting. Also, there are two levels in Figure 4(b) when the distance is above 200. These are contributed by the remote and local pushes respectively. Since we care only about the remote pushes, the Sigmoid function should be fitted to the higher level.

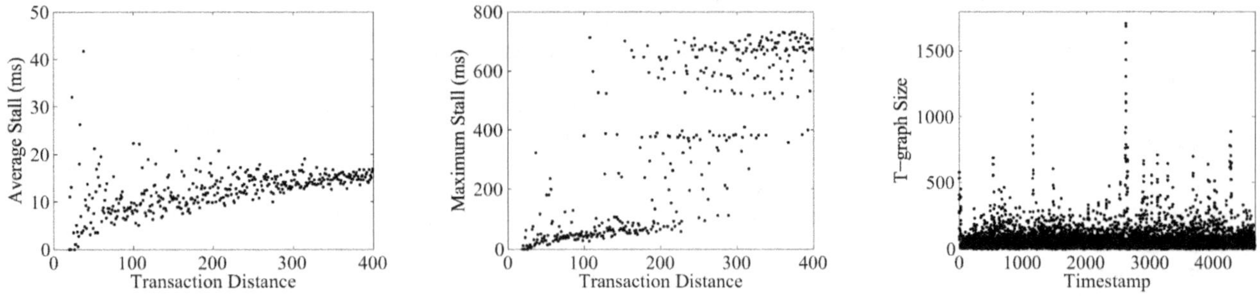

(a) (b) (c)

Figure 4: Measurements of a system over 9 Amazon EC2 machines, giving throughput 350,000 txn/min under a microbenchmark. (a) Average stall. (b) Maximum stall. (c) T-graph size.

We can model a given set of transactions into different T-graphs. For example, in Figure 3(a), $T5$ can either read B from $T1$ or $T2$. T-Part chooses to create an edge from $T1$ to $T5$ based on the *reading-from-the-earliest* principle, which prefers the source node to be the earliest transaction that sees the version of data required by the destination node. The intuition behind this is that, if the edge becomes a cross-partition edge after partitioning, then the source node can push the object as early as possible to prevent the stall at destination.

T-Part also employs the *writing-back-the-latest* principle when creating the storage-write edges, which requires only the latest node writing an object to have an storage-write edge. For example, in Figure 3(a), despite that all transactions $T2$, $T3$, $T5$ and $T6$ update the object C, only $T6$ needs to write it back to the storage. This avoids unnecessary storage-access edges that could mislead T-Part to bad partitions, and does not damage the recoverability of transactions as long as their operations and commit decisions are logged.

4.3 Plan Optimization

After generating a push plan and before sending it to the executor, the scheduler can optimize the plan by eliminating the cross-partition edges if local reads are possible. For example, in Figure 3(b), we can eliminate a cross-partition edge from $T1$ to $T5$ by creating another local edge from from $T2$ to $T5$. Plan optimization further reduces the synchronization between machines. Note that each machine only needs to optimize the plans for its owning partition.

5. IMPLEMENTATION

In this section, we briefly discuss some of the key engineering challenges and design decisions we made when building T-Part.

5.1 Real-Time Partitioning

As discussed in Section 3.2, the problem of partitioning T-graph differs from conventional balanced graph partitioning in that the former has the disconnectivity constraints prohibiting the sink nodes from going to the same partition.

To partition the T-graph, our initial direction is to reduce the problem to the conventional one, then apply the off-the-shelf graph partitioning software like METIS [16]. We first introduce a virtual node, called the *pin node*, for each sink node and connect them using a virtual edge, called the *tie edge*. Then, by giving sufficiently large weights to all the tie edges, we can ensure that each pair of the sink and pin nodes will go to the same partition. Furthermore, by giving sufficiently large weights to the pin nodes we can ensure that two pins never go to the same partition, neither do the sinks.

However, this approach has some shortcomings. First, the large pin weights dilute the weights of normal nodes, so we may not find very balanced partitions. Second, whenever new nodes arrive, we need to repartition the T-graph from scratch, which is not preferred in a large-scale system.

We therefore take another direction in extending the *streaming graph partitioning* algorithms [26]. These algorithms assume that the nodes enter a graph as a stream, and build partitions incrementally. We extend a greedy algorithm (called "weighted deterministic greedy" in [26]) that is shown to work well for various types of graphs. Our partitioning algorithm works as follows.

ALGORITHM 1 (T-PART PARTITIONING). *First, assign a sink node to each partition. Upon arrival of a node v, calculate the total weight of edges between v and each partition. Assign v to the partition having the smallest total weight.*[8] *If there is a tie, then assign v to the partition having the smallest total weight of nodes in that partition. Break tie again by assigning v deterministically to a partition with smaller ID (which could be the ID of the machine).*

The performance comparison of our METIS- and Streaming-based algorithms under our simplified TPC-E workload is given as follows:

	Streaming-based			METIS-based		
#Txn	Time	Cut	Skew	Time	Cut	Skew
100	0.14	474	114	5.1	464	25
1000	1.1	4914	94	18.1	4704	201
10000	12.7	59125	46	185.8	72909	242

The time, cut, and skew denote the time (in milliseconds) required to update partitions after arrival of a batch of nodes, the number of cross-partition edges, and the maximum difference between the loads of machines (in total weight of nodes on a machine) respectively. These metrics are measured against different numbers of unsunk transactions in the system. Normally, the number of unsunk transactions (i.e., the size of T-graph) is under 200, as shown in Figure 4(c). Based on the above facts, the streaming-based algorithm offers both speed and quality advantages in spite of its simplicity.

5.2 Cache Management

As discussed in Section 3.4, each executor in T-Part implements a key-value cache area to store the hot data and to prevent repeated

[8]The total weight of a partition can be normalized by the capacity of the corresponding machine. Our deployment consists of homogeneous machines. So we do not perform the normalization.

storage access. We now discuss how T-Part manages the cache area to keep its minimum size small and, when necessary, to trade more cache space for improved performance.

The value of an cache entry is an object value. Each cache access in a push plan needs to specify a key. For example, the push plan for machine holding $S2$ in Section 3.4 can be formally written as:

$T1$: Write cache: <$A, T1, T4$>;
Push to $S1$: <$B, T1, T2$>, <$B, T1, T5$>.
$T4$: Read cache: <$A, T1, T4$>;
Write cache: <$A, Sink1$>; storage: E.

Each forward-push edge involves entries with keys of the form: <*obj key, source txn, destination txn*>, a triple consisting of the primary key of the object, the order of source transaction who writes the object, and the order of destination transaction who will read the object. By the definition of its key, each entry of this kind will be read by only the destination transaction. So, after reading an object from the cache area, the destination transaction can invalidate the enclosing entry immediately.

The cache-access edges (e.g., the edge from $T4$ to $S2$ carrying A in Figure 3(b)) involve entries with keys of the form: <*obj key, sink number*>, where a sink number p denotes the p-th sinking process. Assuming that the above plan is generated by the first sinking process, $T4$ writes A using the key <A, $Sink1$>. The purpose of the sink number is to ensure that the later transactions to be sunk in the next batch will read the correct version of data. For example, in Figure 3(c), there will be a line:

$T8$: Read cache: <A, $Sink1$>, <B, $Sink1$>

in the plan generated by the next sinking process to instruct $T8$ to read A and B from the batch in the right front. Upon reading the these objects, $T8$ can invalidate the corresponding entries immediately.

Version-based Deterministic CC. Since each transaction stalls whenever the desired entry is not available in the cache area, T-Part does *not* require the conservative 2PL for concurrency control as in Calvin. Instead, the serializability is guaranteed by allowing each transaction to know which specific version (recorded in the *source txn* field of a cache entry for an forward-push edge, for example) of the object it needs to access. To ensure the serializability and recoverability, a transaction can only write to cache if it knows that it will commit eventually.

Sticky Caching. From the above, all essential cache entries are invalidated once they are accessed. This helps keeping a limited cache size. Actually, we observe that, the total size of the essential cache entries on each machine is proportional to the working set of the transactions assigned to that machine.

We can introduce more cache entries to improve the performance of storage access. Consider the plan for $T6$:

$T6$: Read cache: <$C, T5, T6$>;
Write storage: C, D.

If a new transaction $T20$ reading C enters the system after $T6$ is sunk, then it needs to read C from the storage, causing unnecessary storage access. We observe that such "immediate storage reads after write" are frequent under some workloads, where there exists locality in data access but the access interval of an object is longer than that of the sinking process. T-Part deals with this problem by creating a *sticky entry* that caches the data being written back for a fixed small amount of time. For example, it first changes the plan for $T6$ to the following:

$T6$: Read cache: <$C, T5, T6$>;
Write sticky cache: <C>, <D>;
Write storage: C, D.

Instead of waiting $T6$ to commit or waiting the C from being read form the storage, $T20$ now can obtain C immediately by searching for the stick entry containing C.

5.3 Handling Transaction Aborts

Next, we discuss how T-Part handles transaction aborts while ensuring the correctness of transaction execution. Recall that a deterministic database system eliminates all the cases of system-initiated transaction aborts apart from that the transaction aborts initiated by its own logic [29, 30]. So, each transaction, upon execution, can know whether its net effect will persist in the system or not by simply looking at its own commit/abort decision hard-coded in the transaction logic. Leveraging this, we require each transaction in T-Part to *read the objects it writes*, and, if it decides to abort, push the read data forward. So, whether a transaction commits or not will *not* change the structure of a T-graph (but only the values of the pushed data), and the T-Part schedulers can partition the T-graph without worrying the commit/abort decisions of transaction execution in the future.

5.4 Handling Failure

The properties of deterministic database systems that simplify the task of fault tolerance have been discussed in [30]. First, if machine failure happens, the failover process can be done immediately because a failed machine can be taken over by an active replica. Second, by logging each transaction request, the failed machine can recover by acquiring a snapshot of data from replicas (if they exist) and/or *replaying* the logged requests to get the latest data back. There is no need for REDO-logging the transaction operations. Moreover, various checkpointing methods are supported, such as the Zig-Zag algorithm [7].

T-Part inherits all the above properties from existing deterministic database systems. We only summarize the difference here. Recall from Section 5.2 that all storage access is actually done by the write-back procedures rather than normal transactions. In T-Part, only the operations of write-back procedures need to be UNDO-logged. Normal transactions do not need any log .

When a failed machine decides to replay transactions (during, say, the REDO phase in the recovery procedure), it cannot replay the transactions that were assigned to itself alone, as 1) the partitioning information is lost; and 2) some transactions need to read the pushes from other machines, which already happened. In T-Part, the transaction requests are logged only after they are partitioned, and each machine *logs only those requests that are assigned to itself.* Furthermore, T-Part requires each executor to create a *PUSH-log* upon receiving a push in order to remember the object value. Therefore, each machine in T-Part can replay its transactions locally during the recovery.

6. PERFORMANCE EVALUATION

In this section, we evaluate the performance of T-Part.

Implementation and Systems. We implement T-Part on a distributed database system called ElaSQL [2], a Java implementation of Calvin [30]. Note that the Calvin source code available from GitHub [1] focuses on the distributed transaction handling and simplifies many low-level database operations (e.g., storage access, buffering, latching, logging, indexing, etc.) by using simulations. ElaSQL, on the other hand, employs VanillaDB [5] as its core on each machine. VanillaDB is a single-node, IBM-System-R-like database system for research purpose. Both ElaSQL and VanillaDB have *no* simulated component. So we believe that building T-Part on ElaSQL can give more realistic performance results.

We implemented Zab [14, 22], a well-known simplification of Paxos, as our total ordering protocol in our communication module. In order to avoid the possible overuse of CPU caused by the leader in Zab, we pull the leader out of the database nodes as a standalone node. We compare the default implementation of ElaSQL (which we denote "Calvin") and Calvin with T-Part (denoted as "Calvin+TP") in the following experiments.

6.1 Scalability

We first evaluate the scalability of T-Part by using the well-known TPC-C and TPC-E benchmarks. To make the results comparable to those published in the Calvin paper [30], we run experiments on machines/environment similar to that adopted in the Calvin paper. We rent 46 Amazon EC2 C3.xlarge dedicated instances, each promises 7.5 GB of memory and 14 EC2 Compute Units[9] (4 virtual cores with 3.5 EC2 Compute Units each), and reserve 15 instances to run the clients (named Remote Terminal Emulator (RTE) in the TPC terminology), 30 instances as DB nodes, and one as the Zab leader. Note that, although we strive to create a comparable environment, the actual capability/provision of an EC2 instance changes overtime thus our environment may still be different from that used in the Calvin paper.

6.1.1 TPC-C

The TPC-C benchmark simulates a warehouse management system, and its data are known to be partitionable based on warehouses because each transaction has only 10% probability to access the data in more than one warehouses. While T-Part focuses on the hard-to-partition data, we show that it can also achieve the same level of transaction throughput as Calvin does.

Figure 5(a) shows the system throughput of the New-Order transactions given by T-Part and Calvin over different numbers of machines.[10] As we can see, both Calvin and T-Part can scale out up to 30 machines. This implies that T-Part incurs little overhead on a deterministic database system where data are well-partitioned. It is safe to turn it on even with easy workloads.

Note that our Calvin implementation, without simulated components, verifies the trends reported in the original Calvin paper [30]. However, the absolute values of our throughput readings are generally only one-third of those reported in [30]—the per-core throughput of our implementation and the study is 208 and 625 transactions per second in the above figure, respectively.[11] This give a sense how much the other components, such as index maintenance and file system operations, may impact the performance of a deterministic database system.

6.1.2 TPC-E

TPC-E emulates the behavior of customers, brokers, and markets in a financial brokerage system, and, as compared to TPC-C, has more complicated and long-running transactions, non-uniform data access, and *hard-to-partition data*.

Because there is no well-known best partitioning method for TPC-E, we partition each table horizontally based on the hash value of the primary key of each record. Among all types of TPC-E transactions, we focus on the Trade-Order and Trade-Result transactions, as they are two most representative transaction types. Normally, almost all transactions of TPC-E are distributed transactions. And a record read by a transaction could be on any machine; that is, almost all operations of a TPC-E transaction are remote operations. Moreover, the EGen program provided by TPC generates non-uniform customer ID, thus the data access pattern is skewed. The above characteristics fit well to other types of applications such as the social networking services.

The throughput of T-Part and Calvin given up to 30 nodes are shown in Figure 5(b). We can see that Calvin can only scale out up to 4 machines. When the number of machines go beyond five, Calvin starts to saturate. On the other hand, T-Part is still scalable, and the linear scalability preserves up to 22 machines.[12] The reason for this drastic change in trend is twofold. First, the forward-pushing technique in T-Part significantly reduces the chance of transaction stalls due to unavailable remote data, and mitigates the machine synchronization problem in the presence of workload skewness. We will further verify the effectiveness of forward-pushing in later sections. Another reason, less obvious but still important, is that T-Part does *not* let multiple machines execute the same distributed transaction collaboratively (via peer-pushing, as described in paragraph 2 in Section 2.1). Instead, it assigns each transaction to only one machine, and that machine collects necessary data from either previous transactions or storage on different machines. So, the benefit is that it saves the computing resources from processing the same transaction logic multiple times. In TPC-C, this benefit doesn't make much difference because each transaction is short and the portion of distributed transactions is low. However, in TPC-E where the portion of distributed transactions is high and each distributed transaction accesses data spanning almost *all* machines, Calvin requires almost all machines to participate in every distributed transaction, resulting in huge overhead.

Parameter	Default Value
#Records per Machine	1,000,000
#RTEs (i.e., #client processes)	4000
#Server / #Client Machines	20 / 10
Buffer Size per Server Machine	390 MB
#Records Accessed per Txn.	10
#Remote Records per Distributed Txn.	9
#Write Records per Read-write Txn.	5
Distributed Txn. Rate	1.0
Read-write Txn. Rate	0.5
Skewed Txn. Rate	0.3
Txn. Conflict Rate	1% (10k hot rec.)
Sink Size (T-Part parameter)	100

Table 1: Default parameters of the Microbenchmark.

6.2 Comparison with Data Partitioning / Moving Methods

Here we demonstrate the advantages of T-Part over conventional data partitioning methods in the presence of hard-to-partition workloads. Figure 6 compares the 10-minute-average throughput of T-Part against those of various data partitioning/moving techniques

[9]One EC2 Compute Unit provides the equivalent CPU capacity of a 1.0-1.2 GHz 2007 Opteron or 2007 Xeon processor.

[10]We focus on the New-Order transactions because it is a major limiting factor of the system scalability in TPC-C. For more discussions, please refer to [29].

[11]Note that the capability of machines we used on AWS differs from that of machines used in [30]. The machines they used are of the C1.xlarge type while we were using the C3.xlarge machines. According to the documentation, each C1.xlarge machine consists of 8 virtual cores and a C3.xlarge has 4. So, if we consider the per-core throughput of TPC-C on 10 nodes, the original Calvin and our implementation give 625 txs/sec and 208 txs/sec respectively.

[12]Notice that the performance of T-Part fluctuates when the number of machines is large. This is because that not all EC2 instances yield equivalent performance, and this issue has been reported in the Calvin paper [30] as well as other industrial articles [4]. Given hard-to-partition workloads like TPC-E, any slowdown of a single machine could have an impact on the overall system performance. And, as the number of machines increases, this impact can be more significant, as we can see in the figure.

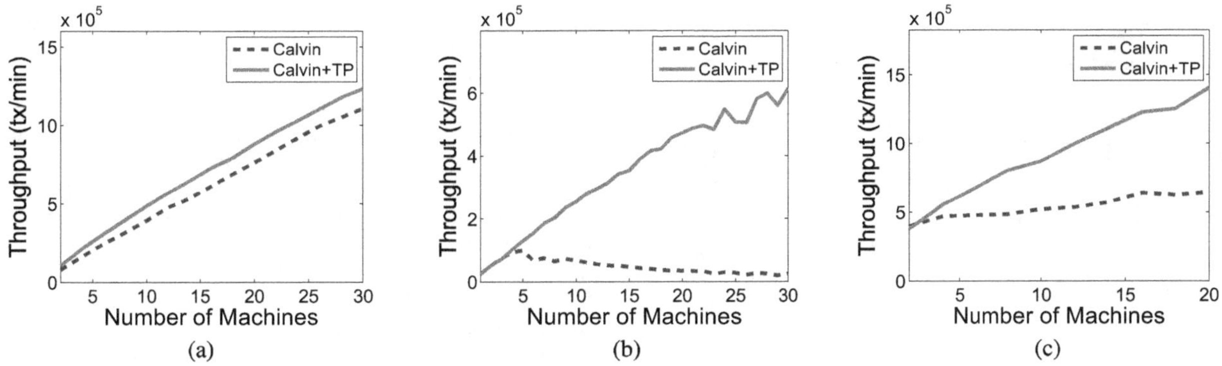

Figure 5: System throughput with the (a) TPC-C benchmark (New-Order transactions); (b) TPC-E benchmark; and (c) Microbenchmark (default parameters).

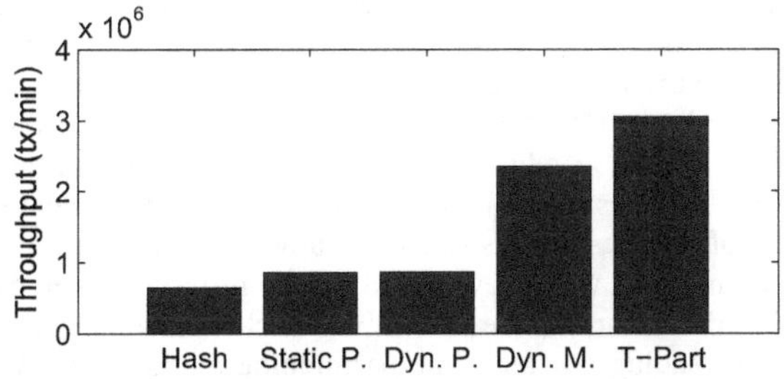

Figure 6: System throughput with (a) static hash-based data partitioning, (b) static graph-based data partitioning (Schism [9]), (c) dynamic graph-based data partitioning, (d) dynamic data movement (G-Store [10]), and (e) T-Part.

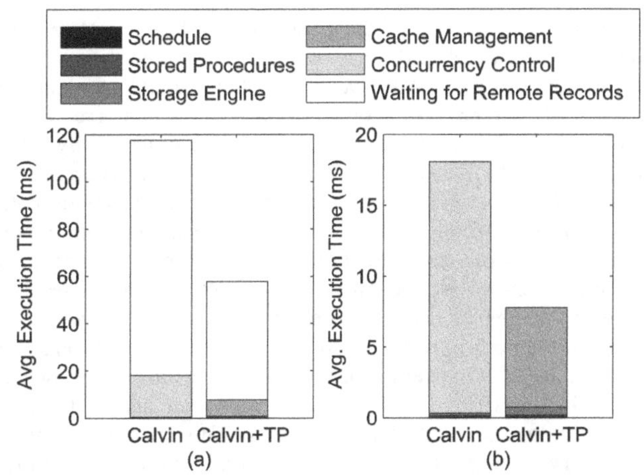

Figure 7: Breakdowns of the average execution time (a) with and (b) without transaction stalls due to the unavailable remote records.

(other than the basic hash-based data partitioning) under the TPC-E workloads. The experiments are ran on 20 machines of our own. Each machine is equipped with an Intel Core i5-4460 3.2 GHz CPU and 8 GB RAM and running CentOS 7.

Static Graph-based Data Partitioning (Schism). In this experiment, we follow Schism [9] to model the trace of 300K transactions into a graph, then employ METIS [16] (a multi-way graph partitioning algorithm) to partition the graph and obtain data partitions. As shown in Figure 6(b), Schism gives about 60% performance boost as compared to the basic hash-based data partitioning.

Dynamic Graph-based Data Partitioning. One obvious way to further improve the quality of data partitions is to run Schism periodically. In this experiment, we re-generate the data partitions every 3 minutes. Note that we pre-generate all the data partitions offline, so the reported throughout will *not* take into account the data migration cost and be optimistic. Even so, the resultant throughput does not change much, as shown in Figure 6(c), because TPC-E does not render much temporal locality.

Dynamic Data Movement (G-Store). Another approach to deal with hard-to-partition data is to use the dynamic data movement approach proposed by G-Store [10], which transfers all relevant records to a single machine and execute the corresponding transactional operations on demand. However, this approach requires the clients to specify explicitly a certain group of data that is going to be accessed together in the near future *before* issuing the corresponding transactions, which is not possible in TPC-E. In fact, G-Store is proposed only for the NoSQL database systems. Therefore, we can only simulate this dynamic data movement approach by moving the read-sets and write-sets of a group of transactions to a single machine, executing the transactions, and then moving the records back to their original machines. To determine the transaction group without users' specifications, we make it as a transaction partition in a T-graph. In effect, this simplification reduces to T-Part with the sink size 1, and, as shown in Figure 6(d), gives 270% performance boost as compared to the dynamic graph-based data partitioning. This demonstrates the importance of joint optimization of transaction execution and data movement.

T-Part. T-Part, with sink size larger than 1, additionally takes into account the locality of data access between subsequent transactions and move transactions around to avoid unnecessary storage reads/writes. This gives yet another 30% boost in system throughput, as shown in Figure 6(e), and demonstrates the effectiveness of T-Part in replacing the storage reads/writes with the forward-pushes.

6.3 Microbenchmark

To further investigate the factors that affect the T-Part performance, we implemented a Microbenchmark that has several adjustable parameters whose default values are summarized in Table 1. This Microbenchmark consists of one table that are horizontally and evenly partitioned across different machines. The size of each record is 164 bytes. We split each data partition into the *hot* set and *cold* set. We distinguish transactions from different aspects: 1) read-only vs. read-write; 2) local vs. distributed; and 3) non-skewed vs. skewed. A read-only transactions reads a constant 10 records; while a read-write transaction, after reading 10 records,

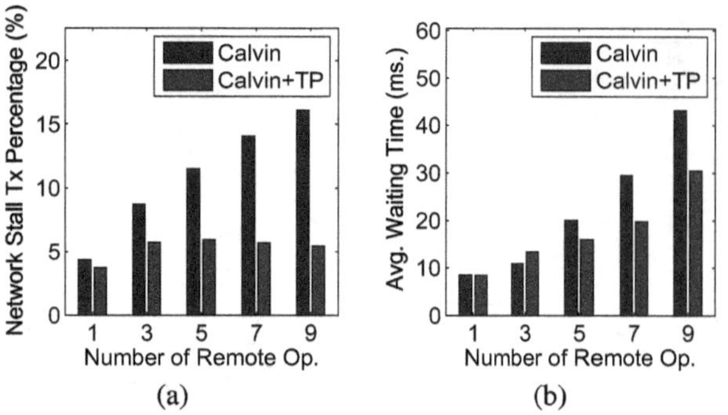

Figure 9: The impact of the number of remote operations under a TPC-C-like workload. (a) Network-stalled transaction percentage. (b) Average waiting time.

randomly writes back 5 of them back to the storage. A transaction is deemed distributed if any of the accessed records is located on a remote machine. A skewed transaction has 50% probability of accessing remote records on machines that are numbered in the first one-fifth. We control the conflict rate of transactions by varying the size of the hot sets—the 10 records read by each transaction consists of one record in a hot set (called hot record) and 9 in a cold set. So, the smaller the hot sets, the higher transaction conflict rate.

Like the previous experiments, these experiments are also ran on the same machine described in Section 6.2. We carefully select the default parameter values so that we can re-produce the same trends shown in Figure 5(b) using the Microbenchmark. The throughput of T-Part and Calvin over the default Microbenchmark is shown in Figure 5(c). Looking into the parameters, we see high distributed transaction and skewed transaction rates. This is consistent with our observations in TPC-E, where almost all transactions are distributed and the skewness are high due to the non-uniform customer ID generator.

6.3.1 Execution Time Breakdown

Running Microbenchmark on our own machines allows us to break down the behavior of T-Part and Calvin in detail. We inject the probing code to the codebases of T-Part and Calvin to record the execution time of every major component. The results are shown in Figure 7. Note that we do not include the time spent in the total-ordering protocol Zab because it remains around 150 milliseconds in both Calvin and Calvin+TP.

We can see that, the main cause of the transaction delay is the time spent in waiting for remote records. And T-Part can reduce about 50% of this cost thanks to the partitioning of T-graph and the forward-pushing technique. Note that the delay of T-graph analysis and partitioning (covered in "Schedule" component) is almost neglectable (less than 0.05% of the overall delay). These together justify the effectiveness and efficiency of our run-time partitioning algorithm, as described in Section 5.1.

Note that the role of concurrency control is replaced by the (multi-version) cache management layer in T-Part, as described in Section 5.2. Comparing the cost of the cache management in T-Part against the concurrency control in Calvin, we can see that our multi-version design yields better implementation efficiency than conservative locking. Also note that, since T-Part spends less time in communication, the storage engine is better utilized thus contributing more to the delay.

6.3.2 Distributed Transactions

Next, we investigate the impact of distributed transactions on system throughout. We conduct two experiments: one with varying distributed transaction rate, and another with distributed transactions accessing a varying number of remote records. The results are shown in Figures 8(a) and (b) respectively. As we can see, T-Part leads to 60%~120% speedup when either the distributed transaction rate or the remote operation number is high. The improvement becomes significant when the distributed transaction rate is above 0.2 and when there are more than 5 remote records in a transaction. This justifies the effectiveness of our 1) T-graph partitioning, so the machine workloads be can indeed be balanced and the (cross machine) storage reads/writes can be optimized; and 2) forward-pushing of records, so the chance of transaction stall due to unavailable remote records can be reduced. Recall that "bad" data partitioning is a major reason of a high distributed transaction rate and a high number of remote operations. T-Part mitigates the synchronization problem of existing deterministic database systems and make them applicable to workloads where data are hard to partition.

Note that, when all transactions are local, the throughput of Calvin is little higher than T-Part. This is because 1) in the absence of distributed transactions, the cache management in T-Part becomes relatively costly; and 2) with default workload skewness (see Table 1), the schedulers in T-Part attempts to balance the load between machines (see Algorithm 1) and thus may create a small number of unnecessary distributed transactions. However, the gap is very small and we believe that it can be further reduced by optimizing the T-Part source code about cache management, or by further extending our real-time partitioning algorithm (to be described in Section 6.3.6).

6.3.3 Network Stall

To further investigate whether T-Part decreases the chance of network stall that happening when a distributed transaction needs a record from a remote machine. We vary the number of remote operations under a TPC-C-like workload and a TPC-E-like workload separately and record how many transactions need to wait for remote records and the average waiting time of them. We call these transactions the *network-stalled transactions* here. Followings are our results.

TPC-C-like Workloads. We create such workloads by setting the skewed transaction rate to 0.0 and the remote transaction rate to 0.1. The results are reported in Figure 9. As the number of remote operations increases, one would expect more network-stalled transactions since there are more remote records to wait. This is the case for Calvin, but *not* for Calvin+TP, as shown in Figure 9(a). As the number of remote operations increases, the T-Part gradually shifts its focus from balancing the machine workloads to minimizing the cross-partition edges when partitioning the T-graphs. So the number of network-stalled transactions decreases slightly. This validates the benefits of T-graph partitioning. In addition, Figure 9(b) shows that Calvin+TP is able to reduce more than 30% of the average waiting time when the number of remote records is high. This validates the effectiveness of the forward-pushing technique.

TPC-E-like Workloads. Now we step back to the default parameters of the Microbenchmark, which simulates the TPC-E. The results are shown in Figure 10. The percentage of the network-stalled transactions doesn't change significantly in Calvin. We believe this is because that the transaction throughput of Calvin has already been saturated (as shown in 5(b)). On the other hand, Calvin+TP gives a decreasing number of network-stalled transactions again, validating the benefits of T-graph partitioning in this case. And, as shown in Figure 10(b),[13] the forward-pushing tech-

[13]Note that the delay reported here is higher than that reported in Figure 7, because Figure 7 takes into account all transactions while we consider only the network-stalled transactions here.

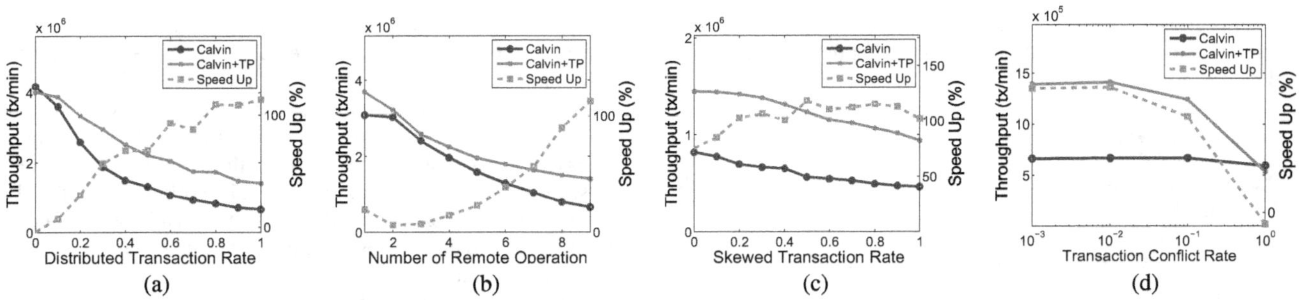

Figure 8: (a) Impact of distributed transaction ratio. (b) Impact of the number of remote operations in a distributed transaction. (c) Impact of skewness. (d) Impact of transaction conflict rate.

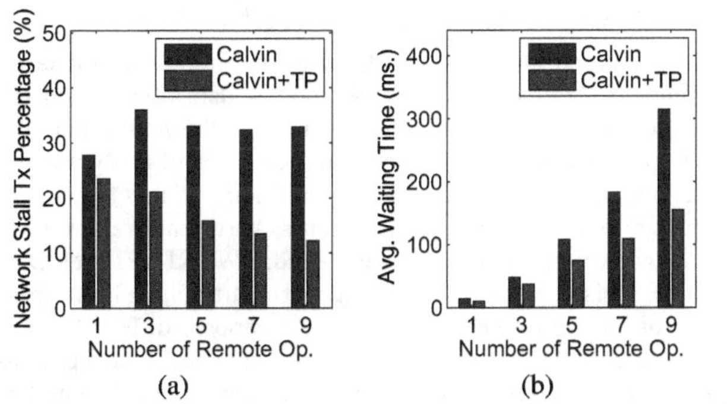

Figure 10: The impact of the number of remote operations under a TPC-E-like workload. (a) Network-stalled transaction percentage. (b) Average waiting time.

nique adopted by Calvin+TP is able to reduce more than 50% of the average waiting time when the number of remote records is high.

6.3.4 Workload Skewness

Another negative impact of "bad" partitioning is the imbalanced workloads across machines, as most records accessed by a transaction may reside on few particular machines. Theses machines would fall behind easily and make the synchronization problem worse. We study the impact of workload skewness on system throughput and conduct experiments with varying skew transaction rate. The results are shown in Figure 8(c). Again, T-Part significantly outperforms Calvin when the skewness is high. This justifies the effectiveness of Algorithm 1 on balancing machine loads.

6.3.5 Transaction Conflict Rate

Next, we study how transaction conflict rate affects the system throughput. We conduct experiments with varying hot set size (recall that each transaction access one hot record so we can change the size of hot set to control the transaction conflict rate).[14]

The results are given in Figure 8(d). While the main paper [30] of Cavlin reports that the transaction conflict rate has significant impact on performance under TPC-C-like workloads, we do *not* observe similar results here under TPC-E-like workloads. We believe this is because that Calvin has already been saturated by the communication overhead due to distributed transactions and numerous remote operations. On the other hand, the Calvin+TP performance can be affected by a high transaction conflict rate. This is because that, at a high conflict rate, the T-graph becomes very dense and hard to partition. However, with mild conflict rates T-Part is still able to keep the T-graph partitioning beneficial, by reducing the cross-machine links.

[14]The actual transaction conflict rate may be slightly higher, because two transactions may conflict with each other when accessing the same cold record. However, due to the large amount of cold records, the chance may be too low to be noticeable.

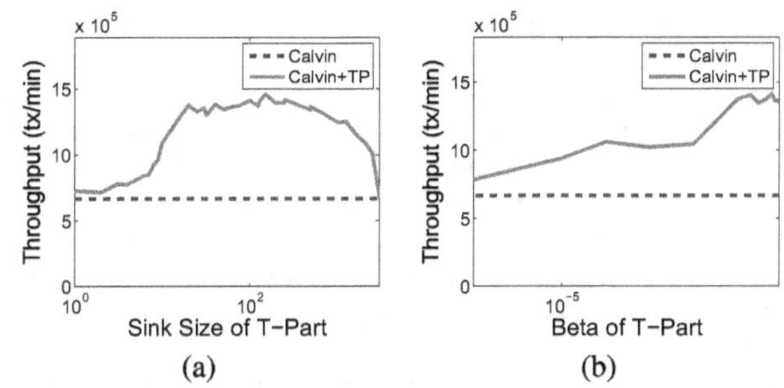

Figure 11: The effects of T-Part parameters: (a) Sink Size; (b) β.

6.3.6 Parameter Tuning

The sink size in T-Part is an adjustable parameter. We study the impact of this parameter by conducting experiments with varying sink size. The results are shown in Figure 11(a). We can see that either a too large or too small sink size has negative impact on the system throughput. When the sink size is too large, the T-graph becomes very large thus its partitioning overhead increases; on the other hand, when the sink size is too small, the T-graph may be too small to have enough forward-push edges to improve the efficiency of transaction executors. Note that except with extreme values, the sink size does not impact the system throughput too much. One can easily pick a value around 100 to have good performance.

Recall that Algorithm 1's goal is to minimize the cross-machine edges *and* to balance the workloads between machines. Given that most of the transaction execution time is spent in communication (see Figure 7), it may seem that minimizing the cross-machine edges is more important than balancing machine workloads. However, we observe that the latter is vital to good performance in the presence of hard-to-partition data. We extend Algorithm 1 by dispatching each transaction to the partition having the maximum weight:

$$(\text{total edge weight}) + \beta(\text{total node weight}),$$

where the total-edge-weight denotes the sum of weights of edges between the transaction and the partition, and the total-node-weight denotes the sum of weights of nodes/transactions that has been assigned to the partition previously. The smaller the β, the more T-Part prefer minimizing the cross-machine edges than balancing machine workloads. We conduct experiments with varying β and the results are shown in Figure 11(b). As we can see, the throughput is high only β is sufficiently large, justifying the importance of load balancing.

7. RELATED WORK

Our partitioning algorithms are based on the streaming graph partitioning algorithms [26].

7.1 Transaction Execution Altering

A main contribution of T-Part is the design of transaction execution framework that allows the forward-pushing and reduces machine synchronization in a deterministic database system. There are other studies that alter the execution of transactions to improve the system performance. NuoDB [3] can dispatch/route transactions to different machines on-the-fly. However, T-Part leverages the determinism so to allow more sophisticated optimization—the forward-pushing. G-Store [10] executes a group of transactions that access the same data (called a *key group*) on the same machine and move data around beforehand. It assumes that the data can be perfectly partitioned into key groups and each client can tell exactly which key group to access before issuing a transaction. T-Part, on the other hand, does not have such assumptions and finds the optimal "transaction groups" by partitioning the T-graph. Studies [12, 13] explicitly create transaction dependency graphs for multi-versioned deterministic database systems in order to increase data access locality in multi-core settings; while T-Part uses dependency graphs for increasing data access locality for multi-machine settings.

7.2 Pre-Fetching

The T-graph, having data-access links, is related to the pre-fetching techniques. In the pre-fetching techniques, the storage system pre-fetches a batch of blocks upon detecting some data access pattern. Smith [24] develop an algorithm using the sequentiality of data access. Nightingale et al. [18] implement a speculative execution for file systems so to increase the I/O throughput by masking the I/O latency. Soundararajan et al. [25] propose QuickMine, which improves pre-fetching by capturing application contexts, such as a transaction or query. There are many other work on improving the effectiveness of pre-fetching under particular settings. For example, PROMISE [23] improves pre-fetching by predicting the query behavior in OLAP systems, and Scout [28] improves pre-fetching by capturing the latent structure behind spatial data.

T-Part differs from most of the above work in that it decides not only the policy for pre-fetching (realized by the storage-read edges in a T-graph), but also 1) the relay of modified data (realized by the forward-push edges) and 2) the writeback (realized by the storage-write edges). This jointly optimizes the management of data in memory, in storage, and across machines (e.g., not to write back certain data in one machine to avoid repeated fetching *and* to reduce remote wait).

7.3 Content-Aware Request Dispatching

To partition the T-graph, T-Part employs the streaming-based partitioning algorithms that dispatches the nodes to partitions upon their arrival, therefore is related to the work on content-aware request dispatching. Studies, LARD [19] and HACC [35], propose content-aware request dispatching protocols in the middleware and dispatcher layers for clustered servers. In replicated database systems with lazy replication, Amza et al. [6] propose to route the read request to the replica with the up-to-date data and with the least load. Similar to T-Part, it totally orders the requests and processes the conflict transactions following this order. Zuikeviciute et al. [36] consider dispatching the update transaction to the machine which has processed some conflicting transaction in order to reduce the abort rate. Yamamuro et al. [32] explore the working set information of transaction to dispatch the requests. Tashkent+ [11] uses the query engine to estimate the working sets of each transaction type, and then assigns a set of transaction types (forming a transaction group) to replicas such that the memory is large enough to serve the composite working set. This work shares with T-Part a similar idea of partitioning the transaction workload (rather than partitioning the data). However, the partition unit in Tashkent+ is the coarse-grained transaction group.

T-Part differs from all of the above work in that it does *not* finalize the dispatch decisions on previous requests until it sink a batch of requests. This allows T-Part to change the dispatch decisions on previous requests to get better overall dispatch results.

7.4 Graph-based Data Partitioning

The T-graph modeling is related to the graph-based data partitioning techniques. Schism [9] models data objects and their common access in the past transactions as the nodes and edges of a graph respectively, and finds the partitions of this graph such that 1) nodes spread evenly among partitions, so that the machine loads are balanced; and 2) edges across partitions are the fewest, so the communication cost is minimized. SWORD [21] , an extension of Schism, supports dynamic data re-partitioning by swapping pairs of data in different partitions and chooses different replication strategies based on the data update frequency. It also proposes grouping the nodes to increase the efficiency of partitioning large graphs. Yang et al. [33] propose a two-level partitioning technique for large graphs, which uses the static primary and dynamic secondary partitions together to fit the changing workload. It replicates the hotspot in different graph partitions to decrease the cross-partition queries.

The design goals of T-Part are very different from the graph-based data partitioning. First, it deals with a much smaller graph but requires the graph to be partitioned in real-time (and continuously). Second, T-Part does not change the data placement, but how data are accessed and where transactions are executed.

8. CONCLUSIONS

This paper presents T-Part, a transaction execution engine for the deterministic database systems. T-Part partitions pending transactions to keep the balanced loads on machines while minimizing the communication cost between them. By following the push plan, each transaction can push forward the data to later transactions immediately after its execution. Our experiments demonstrate that T-Part reduces machine synchronization and makes the system robust to the unforeseeable workloads or workloads whose data are hard to partition.

There are some points in T-Part that deserves further investigation. First, as discussed in Section 4.1, the maximum stall due to transaction i that a transaction j will encounter depends on $(j - i)$ and can be approximated by a Sigmoid function. It remains unclear how the performance of T-Part will be affected if we set the edge weights using this model. Second, although not shown in Figure 2, data partitions may be replicated within a data center to survive from machine failure and/or to avoid hot spots due to reads. The replication of transactions in a T-graph may be further extended to work with the data replicas inside a data center. The above matters are our future inquiry.

9. ACKNOWLEDGMENT

We thank Mr. Ching Tsai (ctsai@netdb.cs.nthu.edu.tw) for helping setup environments and run experiments.

10. REFERENCES

[1] Calvin source code. https://github.com/yaledb/calvin.

[2] Elasql. http://www.elasql.org.

[3] Nuodb. http://www.nuodb.com.

[4] The top 5 aws ec2 performance problems. http://www.datadoghq.com/wp-content/uploads/2015/06/Top-5-AWS-Ec2-Performance-Problems-Guide-Ebook.pdf.

[5] Vanilladb. http://www.vanilladb.org.

[6] C. Amza, A. L. Cox, and W. Zwaenepoel. Conflict-aware scheduling for dynamic content applications. In *USENIX Symposium on Internet Technologies and Systems*, volume 21, page 22, 2003.

[7] T. Cao, M. Vaz Salles, B. Sowell, Y. Yue, A. Demers, J. Gehrke, and W. White. Fast checkpoint recovery algorithms for frequently consistent applications. In *Proc. of SIGMOD*, pages 265–276. ACM, 2011.

[8] T. Chandra, R. Griesemer, and J. Redstone. Paxos made live-an engineering perspective (2006 invited talk). In *Proc. of PODC*, volume 7, 2007.

[9] C. Curino, E. Jones, Y. Zhang, and S. Madden. Schism: a workload-driven approach to database replication and partitioning. *Proc. of the VLDB Endowment*, 3(1-2):48–57, 2010.

[10] S. Das, D. Agrawal, and A. El Abbadi. G-store: A scalable data store for transactional multi key access in the cloud. In *Proceedings of the 1st ACM Symposium on Cloud Computing*, SoCC '10, pages 163–174, New York, NY, USA, 2010. ACM.

[11] S. Elnikety, S. Dropsho, and W. Zwaenepoel. Tashkent+: Memory-aware load balancing and update filtering in replicated databases. *ACM SIGOPS Operating Systems Review*, 41(3):399–412, 2007.

[12] J. M. Faleiro and D. J. Abadi. Rethinking serializable multiversion concurrency control. *Proc. of the VLDB Endowment*, 8(11):1190–1201, 2015.

[13] J. M. Faleiro, A. Thomson, and D. J. Abadi. Lazy evaluation of transactions in database systems. In *Proc. of SIGMOD*, pages 15–26. ACM, 2014.

[14] P. Hunt, M. Konar, F. P. Junqueira, and B. Reed. Zookeeper: wait-free coordination for internet-scale systems. In *Proc. of the 2010 USENIX conference on USENIX annual technical conference*, volume 8, pages 11–11, 2010.

[15] R. Kallman, H. Kimura, J. Natkins, A. Pavlo, A. Rasin, S. Zdonik, E. P. Jones, S. Madden, M. Stonebraker, Y. Zhang, et al. H-store: a high-performance, distributed main memory transaction processing system. *Proc. of the VLDB Endowment*, 1(2):1496–1499, 2008.

[16] G. Karypis and V. Kumar. A fast and high quality multilevel scheme for partitioning irregular graphs. *SIAM journal on Scientific Computing*, 20(1):359–392, 1999.

[17] B. Kemme and G. Alonso. Don't be lazy, be consistent: Postgres-r, a new way to implement database replication. In *Proc. of VLDB*, pages 134–143, 2000.

[18] E. B. Nightingale, P. M. Chen, and J. Flinn. Speculative execution in a distributed file system. *ACM Transactions on Computer Systems (TOCS)*, 24(4):361–392, 2006.

[19] V. S. Pai, M. Aron, G. Banga, M. Svendsen, P. Druschel, W. Zwaenepoel, and E. Nahum. Locality-aware request distribution in cluster-based network servers. In *ACM Sigplan Notices*, volume 33, pages 205–216. ACM, 1998.

[20] A. Pavlo, C. Curino, and S. Zdonik. Skew-aware automatic database partitioning in shared-nothing, parallel oltp systems. In *Proc. of SIGMOD*, pages 61–72. ACM, 2012.

[21] A. Quamar, K. A. Kumar, and A. Deshpande. Sword: scalable workload-aware data placement for transactional workloads. In *Proc. of EDBT*, pages 430–441. ACM, 2013.

[22] B. Reed and F. P. Junqueira. A simple totally ordered broadcast protocol. In *Proc. of the 2nd Workshop on Large-Scale Distributed Systems and Middleware*, page 2. ACM, 2008.

[23] C. Sapia. Promise: Predicting query behavior to enable predictive caching strategies for olap systems. In *Proc. of Data Warehousing and Knowledge Discovery*, pages 224–233. Springer, 2000.

[24] A. J. Smith. Sequentiality and prefetching in database systems. *ACM Transactions on Database Systems (TODS)*, 3(3):223–247, 1978.

[25] G. Soundararajan, M. Mihailescu, and C. Amza. Context-aware prefetching at the storage server. In *Proc. of the USENIX Annual Technical Conference*, pages 377–390, 2008.

[26] I. Stanton and G. Kliot. Streaming graph partitioning for large distributed graphs. In *Proc. of SIGKDD*, pages 1222–1230. ACM, 2012.

[27] M. Stonebraker, S. Madden, D. J. Abadi, S. Harizopoulos, N. Hachem, and P. Helland. The end of an architectural era:(it's time for a complete rewrite). In *Proc. of the VLDB Endowment*, pages 1150–1160. VLDB Endowment, 2007.

[28] F. Tauheed, T. Heinis, F. Schürmann, H. Markram, and A. Ailamaki. Scout: Prefetching for latent structure following queries. *Proc. of the VLDB Endowment*, 5(11):1531–1542, 2012.

[29] A. Thomson and D. J. Abadi. The case for determinism in database systems. *Proc. of the VLDB Endowment*, 3(1-2):70–80, 2010.

[30] A. Thomson, T. Diamond, S.-C. Weng, K. Ren, P. Shao, and D. J. Abadi. Calvin: Fast distributed transactions for partitioned database systems. In *Proc. of SIGMOD*, pages 1–12. ACM, 2012.

[31] E.-J. van Baaren. Wikibench: A distributed, wikipedia based web application benchmark. *Master's thesis, VU University Amsterdam*, 2009.

[32] T. Yamamuro, Y. Suga, N. Kotani, T. Hitaka, and M. Yamamuro. Buffer cache de-duplication for query dispatch in replicated databases. In *Database Systems for Advanced Applications*, pages 352–366. Springer, 2011.

[33] S. Yang, X. Yan, B. Zong, and A. Khan. Towards effective partition management for large graphs. In *Proc. of SIGMOD*, pages 517–528. ACM, 2012.

[34] G.-W. You, S.-W. Hwang, and N. Jain. Ursa: Scalable load and power management in cloud storage systems. *ACM Transactions on Storage*, 9(1):1, 2013.

[35] X. Zhang, M. Barrientos, J. B. Chen, and M. Seltzer. Hacc: An architecture for cluster-based web servers. In *Proc. of the USENIX Windows NT Symposium*, volume 3, pages 16–16. USENIX Association, 1999.

[36] V. Zuikeviciute and F. Pedone. Conflict-aware load-balancing techniques for database replication. In *Proc. of ACM SAC*, pages 2169–2173. ACM, 2008.

Reducing the Storage Overhead of Main-Memory OLTP Databases with Hybrid Indexes

Huanchen Zhang
Carnegie Mellon University
huanche1@cs.cmu.edu

David G. Andersen
Carnegie Mellon University
dga@cs.cmu.edu

Andrew Pavlo
Carnegie Mellon University
pavlo@cs.cmu.edu

Michael Kaminsky
Intel Labs
michael.e.kaminsky@intel.com

Lin Ma
Carnegie Mellon University
lin.ma@cs.cmu.edu

Rui Shen
VoltDB
rshen@voltdb.com

ABSTRACT

Using indexes for query execution is crucial for achieving high performance in modern on-line transaction processing databases. For a main-memory database, however, these indexes consume a large fraction of the total memory available and are thus a major source of storage overhead of in-memory databases. To reduce this overhead, we propose using a two-stage index: The first stage ingests all incoming entries and is kept small for fast read and write operations. The index periodically migrates entries from the first stage to the second, which uses a more compact, read-optimized data structure. Our first contribution is hybrid index, a dual-stage index architecture that achieves both space efficiency and high performance. Our second contribution is Dual-Stage Transformation (DST), a set of guidelines for converting any order-preserving index structure into a hybrid index. Our third contribution is applying DST to four popular order-preserving index structures and evaluating them in both standalone microbenchmarks and a full in-memory DBMS using several transaction processing workloads. Our results show that hybrid indexes provide comparable throughput to the original ones while reducing the memory overhead by up to 70%.

1. INTRODUCTION

Main-memory database management systems (DBMSs) target on-line transaction processing (OLTP) workloads that require high throughput and low latency—performance that is only available if the working set fits in memory. Although the price of DRAM has dropped significantly in recent years, it is neither free nor infinite. Memory is a non-trivial capital cost when purchasing new equipment, and it incurs real operational costs in terms of power consumption. Studies have shown that DRAM can account for up to 40% of the overall power consumed by a server [36].

Improving memory efficiency in a DBMS, therefore, has two benefits. First, for a fixed working set size, reducing the required memory can save money, both in capital and operating expenditures. Second, improving memory efficiency allows the DBMS to keep more data resident in memory. Higher memory efficiency allows for a larger working set, which enables the system to achieve higher performance with the same hardware.

Index data structures consume a large portion of the database's total memory—particularly in OLTP databases, where tuples are relatively small and tables can have many indexes. For example, when running TPC-C on H-Store [33], a state-of-the-art in-memory DBMS, indexes consume around 55% of the total memory. Freeing up that memory can lead to the above-mentioned benefits: lower costs and/or the ability to store additional data. However, simply getting rid of all or part of the indexes is suboptimal because indexes are crucial to query performance.

This paper presents **hybrid index**, a dual-stage index architecture that substantially reduces the per-tuple index space with only modest costs in throughput and latency (and, indeed, is actually faster for some workloads) even when the reclaimed memory is not exploited to improve system performance. Although the idea of using multiple physical data structures to construct a logical entity has been explored before [4, 28, 29, 43, 44, 47], to the best of our knowledge, we are the first to show the benefits of applying it to indexes in main-memory OLTP DBMSs.

The dual-stage architecture maintains a small dynamic "hot" store to absorb writes and a more compact, but read-only store to hold the bulk of index entries. Merge between the stages is triggered periodically and can be performed efficiently. Unlike prior work [20, 35, 39, 47, 53], our design offers low latency and high throughput for the point queries and short-range scans that typify the OLTP workloads used with main-memory databases [34, 50].

Hybrid index leverages the skew typically found in OLTP workloads. This skew manifests itself with respect to item popularity [23, 49]: certain data items are accessed more often than others and thus are more likely to be accessed again in the near future. This observation has been used extensively to move cold data from memory to block-based storage [23, 27, 48], and to store data efficiently by compressing the cold data in a main-memory database [29]. To our knowledge, however, previous work has not exploited skew to shrink the indexes themselves, particularly for purely in-memory structures. Because the indexes can take more than half the memory for an OLTP workload, doing so has the potential to save a considerable amount of still-expensive DRAM without significant performance penalty.

To facilitate building hybrid indexes, we provide **Dual-Stage Transformation (DST)**, a set of guidelines that can convert any order-preserving index structure to a hybrid index. We applied DST to four order-preserving index structures: B+tree, Masstree [41], Skip List [46], and ART [37]. Using both YCSB-based microbench-

SIGMOD'16, June 26-July 01, 2016, San Francisco, CA, USA

http://dx.doi.org/10.1145/2882903.2915222

	Tuples	Primary Indexes	Secondary Indexes
TPC-C	42.5%	33.5%	24.0%
Articles	64.8%	22.6%	12.6%
Voter	45.1%	54.9%	0%

Table 1: Percentage of the memory usage for tuples, primary indexes, and secondary indexes in H-Store using the default indexes (DB size ≈ 10 GB).

marks and by integrating them into the H-Store OLTP DBMS [33], we find that hybrid indexes meet the goals, achieving performance comparable to the original indexes while reducing index memory consumption by up to 70% (Section 6). Also, by using hybrid indexes, H-Store is able to sustain higher throughput for OLTP workloads for more transactions and with fewer performance interruptions due to memory limitations (Section 7).

The contributions of this paper are as follows. First, we propose hybrid index, a dual-stage index architecture that can improve the memory efficiency of indexes in main-memory OLTP databases. Second, we introduce DST, a set of guidelines that includes a simple dynamic-to-static transformation to help design hybrid indexes from existing index data structures. Third, we applied DST to four index structures and show the effectiveness and generality of our method. Finally, the dual-stage architecture provides the opportunity to use compact/compressed static data structures (e.g., succinct data structures [32]) for database indexing.

2. THE CASE FOR HYBRID INDEXES

The overhead of managing disk-resident data has given rise to a new class of OLTP DBMSs that store the entire database in main memory [24, 25, 28, 50]. These systems outperform traditional disk-oriented DBMSs because they eschew the legacy components that manage data stored on slow, block-based storage [30]. Unfortunately, this improved performance is achievable only when the database is smaller than the amount of physical memory available in the system. If the database does not fit in memory, then the operating system will move virtual memory pages out to disk, and memory accesses will cause page faults [48]. Because these page faults are transparent to the DBMS, the threads executing transactions will stall while the page is fetched from disk, degrading the system's throughput and responsiveness. Thus, the DBMS must use memory efficiently to avoid this performance bottleneck.

Indexes are a major factor in the memory footprint of a database. OLTP applications often maintain several indexes per table to ensure that queries execute quickly. This is important in applications that interact with users and other external systems where transactions must complete in milliseconds [50]. These indexes consume a significant fraction of the total memory used by a database. To illustrate this point, Table 1 shows the relative amount of storage used for indexes in several OLTP benchmarks deployed in a main-memory DBMS [3]. We used the DBMS's internal statistics API to collect these measurements after running the workloads on a single node until the database size ≈ 10 GB. Indexes consume up to 58% of the total database size for these benchmarks, which is commensurate with our experiences with real-world OLTP systems.

Designing memory-efficient indexes is thus important for improving database performance and reducing costs. Achieving space-efficient indexes is, however, non-trivial because there are trade-offs between function, performance, and space. For example, hash tables are fast and potentially more space-efficient than tree-based data structures, but they do not support range queries, which prevents them from being ubiquitous.

A common way to reduce the size of B+trees is to compress their nodes before they are written to disk using a general-purpose compression algorithm (e.g., LZMA) [8]. This approach reduces the I/O cost of fetching pages from disk, but the nodes must be decompressed once they reach memory so that the system can interpret their contents. To the best of our knowledge, the only compressed main-memory indexes are for OLAP systems, such as bitmap [20] and columnar [35] indexes. These techniques, however, are inappropriate for the write-heavy workload mixtures and small-footprint queries of OLTP applications [50]. As we show in Section 6, compressed indexes perform poorly due to the overhead of decompressing an entire block to access a small number of tuples.

An important aspect of these previous approaches is that the indexes treat all of the data in the underlying table equally. That is, they assume that the application will execute queries that access all of the table's tuples in the same manner, either in terms of frequency (i.e., how many times it will be accessed or modified in the future) or use (i.e., whether it will be used most in point versus range queries). This assumption is incorrect for many OLTP applications. For example, a new tuple is likely to be accessed more often by an application soon after it was added to the database, often through a point query on the index. But as the tuple ages, its access frequency decreases. Later, the only time it is accessed is through summarization or aggregation queries.

One could handle this scenario through multiple partial indexes on the same keys in a table that use different data structures. There are several problems with this approach beyond just the additional cost of maintaining more indexes—foremost is that developers might need to modify their application so that each tuple specifies what index it should be stored in at runtime. This information is necessary because some attributes, such as a tuple's creation timestamp, may not accurately represent how likely it will be accessed in the future. Second, the DBMS's query optimizer might not be able to infer what index to use for a query since a particular tuple's index depends on this identifying value. If a complex query accesses tuples from multiple partial indexes that each has a portion of the table's data, then the system will need to retrieve data from multiple sources for that query operator. This type of query execution is not possible in today's DBMSs, so the system would likely fall back to scanning the table sequentially.

We argue that a better approach is to use a single logical hybrid index that is composed of multiple data structures. This approach gives the system more fine-grained control over data storage without requiring changes to the application. To the rest of the DBMS, a hybrid index looks like any other, supporting a conventional interface and API. Previous work showed the effectiveness of using multiple physical data structures or building blocks to construct a higher-level logical entity. Most notable are log-structured merge-trees [44]. More recent examples include SILT [39], a flash-based key-value store that achieves both memory-efficiency and high-performance by combining three basic stores with different optimization focuses to effectively overcome each others' deficiencies. Anvil [40] offers a toolkit for building database backends out of specialized storage modules, each of which is optimized for different workload objectives. OctopusDB [26] and WiredTiger [17] take a similar approach, but at a table-level granularity.

Applying these ideas to database indexes is a natural fit, especially for in-memory OLTP systems. In these applications, transactions' access patterns vary over time with respect to age and use. Index entries for new tuples go into a fast, write-friendly data structure since they are more likely to be queried again in the near future. Over time, the tuples become colder and their access patterns change, usually from frequent modification to occasional read [23]. Aged tuples thus eventually migrate to a more read-friendly and more compact data structure to save space [47].

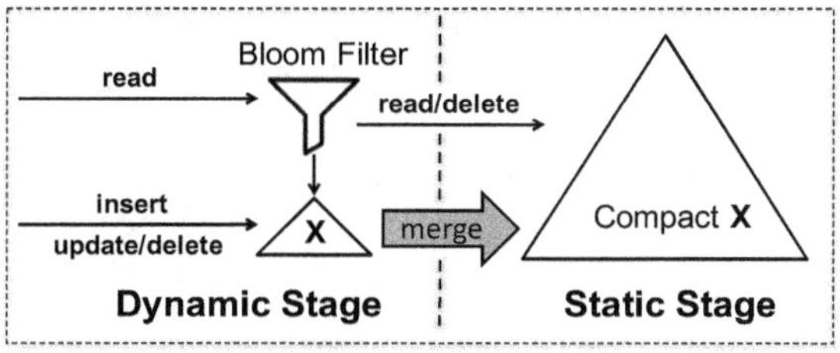

Figure 1: Dual-Stage Hybrid Index Architecture – All writes to the index first go into the dynamic stage. As the size of the dynamic stage grows, it periodically merges older entries to the static stage. For a read request, it searches the dynamic stage and the static stage in sequence.

Given this, we present our dual-stage architecture for hybrid indexes in the next section. Section 4 introduces a set of transformation guidelines for designing compact, read-optimized data structures. Section 5 discusses the techniques for migrating data between stages.

3. THE DUAL-STAGE ARCHITECTURE

As shown in Figure 1, the dual-stage hybrid index architecture is comprised of two stages: the *dynamic* stage and the *static* stage. New entries are added to the dynamic stage. This stage is kept small so that queries to the most recent entries, which are likely to be accessed and modified in the near future, are fast. As the size of the dynamic stage grows, the index periodically triggers the merge process and migrates aged entries from its dynamic stage to the static stage which uses a more space-efficient data structure to hold the bulk of the index entries. The static stage does not support direct key additions or modifications. It can only incorporate key updates in batches through the merge process.

A hybrid index serves read requests (point queries, range queries) by searching the stages in order. To speed up this process, it maintains a Bloom filter for the keys in the dynamic stage so that most point queries search only one of the stages. Specifically, for a read request, the index first checks the Bloom filter. If the result is positive, it searches the dynamic stage and the static stage (if necessary) in sequence. If the result is negative, the index bypasses the dynamic stage and searches the static stage directly. The space overhead of the Bloom filter is negligible because the dynamic stage only contains a small subset of the index's keys.

A hybrid index handles value updates differently for primary and secondary indexes. To update an entry in a primary index, a hybrid index searches the dynamic stage for the entry. If the target entry is found, the index updates its value in place. Otherwise, the index inserts a new entry into the dynamic stage. This insert effectively overwrites the old value in the static stage because subsequent queries for the key will always find the updated entry in the dynamic stage first. Garbage collection for the old entry is postponed until the next merge. We chose this approach so that recently modified entries are present in the dynamic stage, which speeds up subsequent accesses. For secondary indexes, a hybrid index performs value updates in place even when the entry is in the static stage, which avoids the performance and space overhead of having the same key valid in both stages.

For deletes, a hybrid index first locates the target entry. If the entry is in the dynamic stage, it is removed immediately. If the entry is in the static stage, the index marks it "deleted" and removes it at the next merge. Again, depending on whether it is a unique index or not, the DBMS may have to check both stages for entries.

This dual-stage architecture has two benefits over the traditional single-stage indexes. First, it is space-efficient. The periodically-triggered merge process guarantees that the dynamic stage is much smaller than the static stage, which means that most of the entries are stored in a compact data structure that uses less memory per entry. Second, a hybrid index exploits the typical access patterns in OLTP workloads where tuples are more likely to be accessed and modified soon after they were added to the database (Section 2). New entries are stored in the smaller dynamic stage for fast reads and writes, while older (and therefore unchanging) entries are migrated to the static stage only for occasional look-ups.

More importantly, the dual-stage architecture opens up the possibility of using compact/compressed static data structures that have not yet been accepted for database indexing, especially in OLTP databases. These data structures, including succinct data structures for example, provide excellent compression rates but suffer the drawback of not being able to support dynamic operations such as inserts and updates efficiently. A hybrid index can use these specialized data structures in its static stage—leveraging their compression to gain additional memory efficiency while amortize their performance impact by applying updates in batches. This paper examines several general purpose data structures, but we leave exploration of more esoteric data structures as future work.

To facilitate using the dual-stage architecture to build hybrid indexes, we provide the following Dual-Stage Transformation (DST) guidelines for converting any order-preserving index structure to a corresponding hybrid index:

- **Step 1:** Select an order-preserving index structure (**X**) that supports dynamic operations efficiently for the dynamic stage.
- **Step 2:** Design a compact, read-optimized version of **X** for the static stage.
- **Step 3:** Provide a merge routine that can efficiently migrate entries from **X** to compact **X**.
- **Step 4:** Place **X** and compact **X** in the dual-stage architecture as shown in Figure 1.

We describe the process to accomplish Step 2 of DST in the next section. We note that these steps are a manual process. That is, a DBMS developer would need to convert the index to its static version. Automatically transforming any arbitrary data structure is outside the scope of this paper.

4. DYNAMIC-TO-STATIC RULES

As described in Section 3, the static stage is where the index stores older entries in a more memory-efficient format. The cost of this efficiency is that the set of keys in the data structure cannot change. The only way to add new entries is to rebuild the data structure.

The ideal data structure for the static stage must have three properties: First, it must be memory-efficient (i.e., have low space overhead per entry). Second, it must have good read performance for both point queries and range queries. This is particularly important for primary indexes where guaranteeing key uniqueness requires checking the static stage for every insert. Third, the data structure must support merging from the dynamic stage efficiently. This not only means that the merge process is fast, but also that the temporary memory use is low. These three properties have trade-offs, and it is difficult to achieve all three in a single data structure (e.g., more compact data structures are usually slower). Our design, therefore, aims to strike a balance; alternate application-specific two-stage designs that make a different trade-off are possible.

Although any data structure with the above properties can be used in the static stage, using one that inter-operates well with dynamic stage's index simplifies the design and improves merge performance. Therefore, we present the Dynamic-to-Static (D-to-S)

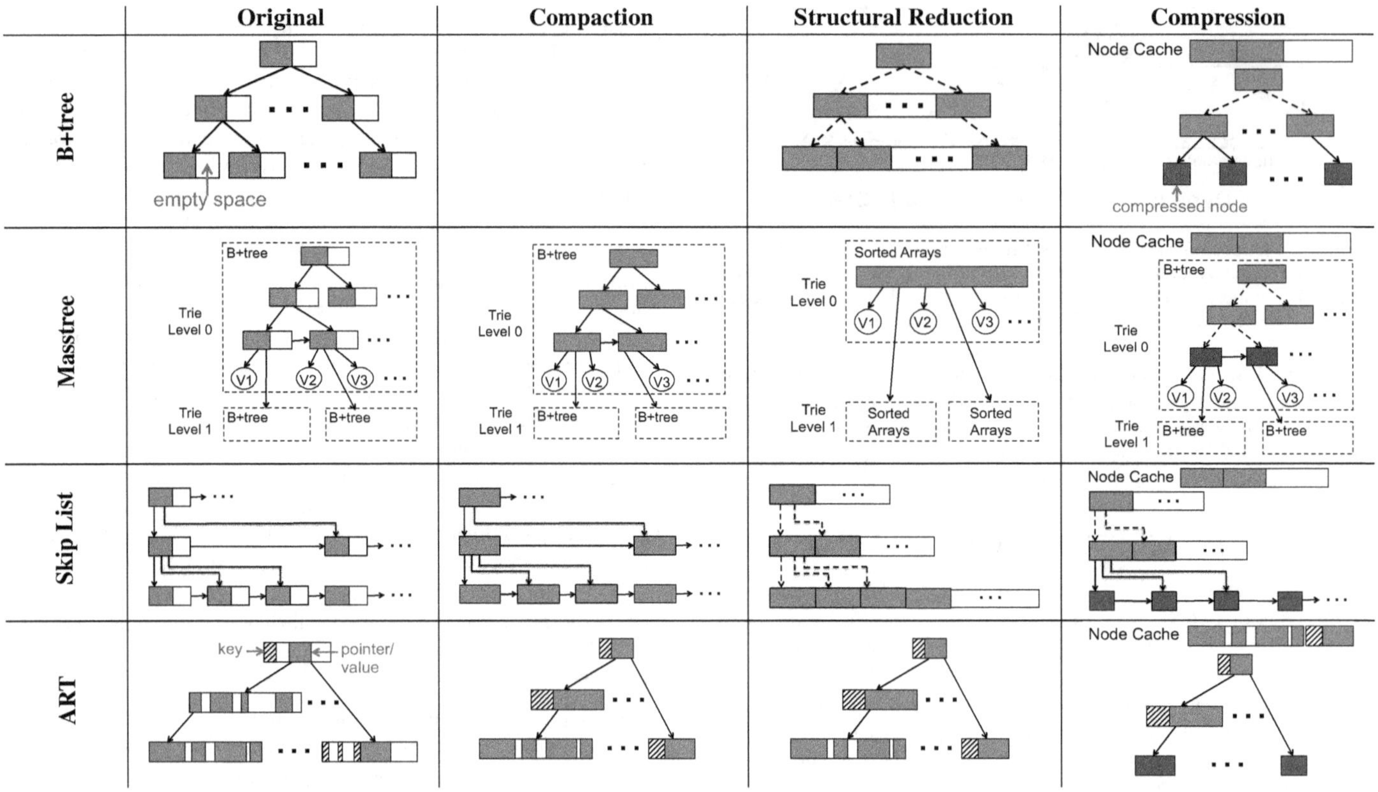

Figure 2: Examples of Applying the Dynamic-to-Static Rules – Solid arrows are pointers; dashed arrows indicate that the child node location is calculated rather than stored in the structure itself. The second column shows the starting points: the original dynamic data structures. After applying the Compaction Rule, we get intermediate structures in column three. We then applied the Structural Reduction Rule on those intermediate structures and obtain more compact final structures in column four. Column five shows the results of applying the Compression Rule, which is optional depending on workloads.

rules to help convert a dynamic stage data structure to a smaller, immutable version for use in the static stage.

The crux of the D-to-S process is to exploit the fact that the static stage is read-only and thus extra space allocated for efficient dynamic operations can be removed from the original structure. We observe two major sources of wasted space in dynamic data structures. First, dynamic data structures allocate memory at a coarse granularity to minimize the allocation/reallocation overhead. They usually allocate an entire node or memory block and leave a significant portion of that space empty for future entries. Second, dynamic data structures contain a large number of pointers to support fast modification of the structures. These pointers not only take up space but also slow down certain operations due to pointer-chasing.

Given a dynamic data structure, the D-to-S rules are:

- **Rule #1: Compaction** – Remove duplicated entries and make every allocated memory block 100% full.
- **Rule #2: Structural Reduction** – Remove pointers and structures that are unnecessary for efficient read-only operations.
- **Rule #3: Compression** – Compress parts of the data structure using a general purpose compression algorithm.

A data structure created by applying one or more of these rules is a good data structure for the static stage. First, it is more memory-efficient than the dynamic stage's index. Second, the data structure preserves the "essence" of the original index (i.e., it does not fundamentally change its core design). This is important because applications sometimes choose certain index structures for certain workload patterns. For example, one may want to use a trie-based data structure to efficiently handle variable-length keys that have common prefixes. After applying the D-to-S rules, a static trie is still a trie. Moreover, the similarity between the original and the compact structure enables an efficient merge routine to be implemented and performed without significant space overhead.

In the rest of this section, we describe how to apply the D-to-S rules to create static versions of four different indexes.

4.1 Example Data Structures

We briefly introduce the data structures that we applied the D-to-S rules on. Their structures are shown in Figure 2.

B+tree: The B+tree is the most common index structure that is used in almost every OLTP DBMS [21]. It is a self-balancing search tree, usually with a large fanout. Although originally designed for disk-oriented databases to minimize disk seeks, B+trees have maintained their prevalence in the main-memory DBMSs (Appendix A). For our analysis, we use the STX B+tree [19] as our baseline implementation. We found in our experiments that a node size of 512 bytes performs best for in-memory operations.

Masstree: Masstree [41] is a high-performance key-value store that also supports range queries. Masstree combines B+trees and tries to speed up key searches. The trie design makes the index particularly efficient in terms of both performance and space when handling keys with shared prefixes. In the diagram shown in Figure 2, the dashed rectangles in Masstree represent the individual B+trees that conceptually form a trie. The keys are divided into fixed-length 8-byte keyslices and are stored at each trie level. Unique key suffixes are stored separately in a structure called a *keybag*. Each B+tree leaf node has an associated keybag with a maximum capacity equal to the fanout of the B+tree. A value pointer in a

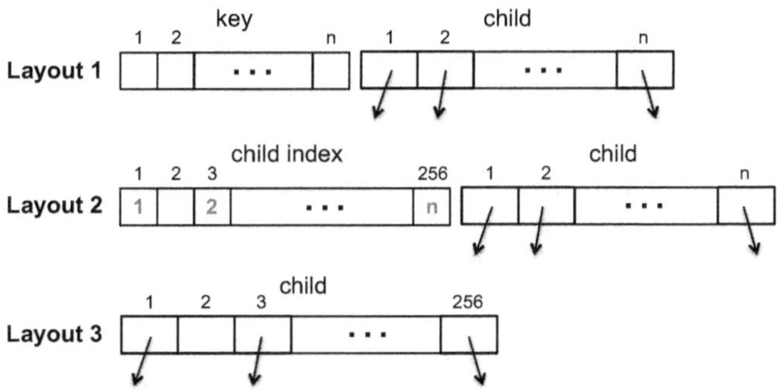

Figure 3: ART Node Layouts – Organization of the ART index nodes. In Layout 1, the key and child arrays have the same length and the child pointers are stored at the corresponding key positions. In Layout 2, the current key byte is used to index into the child array, which contains offsets/indexes to the child array. The child array stores the pointers. Layout 3 has a single 256-element array of child pointers as in traditional radix trees [37].

leaf node can point to either a data record (when the corresponding keyslice is uniquely owned by a key), or a lower-level B+tree.

Skip List: The Skip List was introduced in 1990 as an alternative to balanced trees [46]. It has recently gained attention as a lock-free index for in-memory DBMSs [45]. The internal structure of the index is a linked hierarchy of subsequences that is designed to "skip" over fewer elements. The algorithms for insertion and deletion are designed to be more simple and potentially faster than equivalent operations in balanced trees. For our analysis, we use an implementation [2] of a variation of Skip List (called a *paged-deterministic Skip List* [42]) that resembles a B+tree.

Adaptive Radix Tree: The Adaptive Radix Tree (ART) [37] is a fast and space-efficient data structure designed for in-memory databases. ART is a 256-way radix tree (i.e., each level represents one byte of the key). Unlike traditional radix trees (or tries) where each node is implemented as a fixed-size (256 in this case) array of child pointers, ART uses four node types (`Node4`, `Node16`, `Node48`, and `Node256`) with different layouts and capacities adaptively to achieve better memory efficiency and better cache utilization. Figure 3 illustrates the three node layouts used in ART. `Node4` and `Node16` use the representation in Layout 1 with n=4, 16, respectively. `Node48` uses Layout 2 (n=48), and `Node256` uses Layout 3.

4.2 Rule #1: Compaction

This first rule seeks to generate a more efficient layout of an index's entries by minimizing the number of memory blocks allocated. This rule includes two steps. The first is to remove duplicate content. For example, to map multiple values to a single key (for secondary indexes), dynamic data structures often store the same key multiple times with different values. Such key duplication is unnecessary in a static data structure because the number of values associated with each key is fixed. The second step is to fill all allocated memory blocks to 100% capacity. This step may include modifications to the layouts of memory blocks/nodes. Memory allocation is done at a fine granularity to eliminate gaps between entries; furthermore, leaving spacing for future entries is unnecessary since the data structure is static. The resulting data structure thus uses fewer memory blocks/nodes for the same entries.

As shown in Figure 2, a major source of memory waste in a B+tree, Masstree, Skip List, or ART is the empty space in each node. For example, the expected node occupancy of a B+tree is only 69% [54]. We observed similar occupancies in the Masstree and Skip List. For ART, our results show that its node occupancy

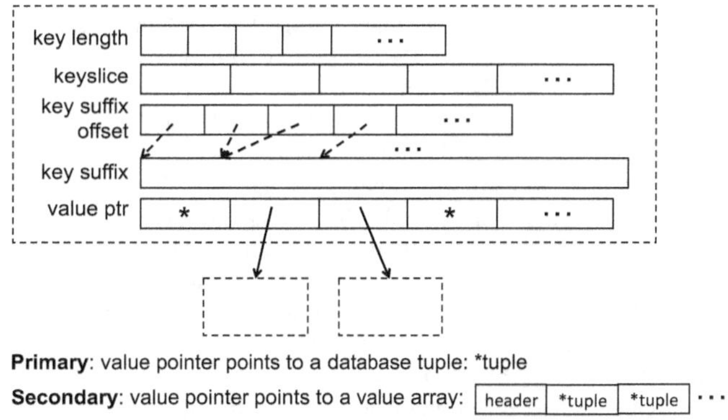

Figure 4: Compact Masstree – The internal architecture of the Masstree index after applying the Compaction and Structural Reduction Rules.

is only 51% for 50 million 64-bit random integer keys. This empty space is pre-allocated to ingest incoming entries efficiently without frequent structural modifications (i.e., node splits). For B+tree, Masstree and Skip List, filling every node to 100% occupancy, as shown in Figure 2 (column 3), reduces space consumption by 31% on average without any structural changes to the index itself.

ART's prefix tree structure prevents us from filling the fixed-sized nodes to their full capacity. We instead customize the size of each node to ensure minimum slack space. This is possible because the content of each node is fixed and known when building the static structure. Specifically, let n denote the number of key-value pairs in an ART node ($2 \leq n \leq 256$). We choose the most space-efficient node layout in Figure 3 based on n. If $n \leq 227$, Layout 1 with array length n is used; otherwise, Layout 3 is used.

Because of the multi-structure design, compacting Masstree's memory blocks is a more complicated process: both its internal nodes and its dynamically-allocated keybags for suffixes require modification. We found that the original implementation of Masstree allocates memory for the keybags aggressively, which means that it wastes memory. Thus, for this rule, we instead only allocate the minimum memory space to store these suffixes.

For secondary indexes where a key can map to multiple values, the only additional change to the indexes is to remove duplicated entries by storing each key once followed by an array of its associated values.

4.3 Rule #2: Structural Reduction

The goal of this next rule is to minimize the overhead inherent in the data structure. This rule includes removing pointers and other elements that are unnecessary for read-only operations. For example, the pointers in a linked list are designed to allow for fast insertion or removal of entries. Thus, removing these pointers and instead using a single array of entries that are stored contiguously in memory saves space and speeds up linear traversal of the index. Similarly, for a tree-based index with fixed node sizes, we can store the nodes contiguously at each level and remove pointers from the parent nodes to their children. Instead, the location of a particular node is calculated based on in-memory offsets. Thus, in exchange for a small CPU overhead to compute the location of nodes at runtime we achieve memory savings. Besides pointers, other redundancies include auxiliary elements that enable functionalities that are unnecessary for static indexes (e.g., transaction metadata).

We applied this rule to our four indexes. The resulting data structures are shown in Figure 2 (column four). We note that after the reduction, the nodes in B+tree, Masstree, and Skip List are stored contiguously in memory. This means that unnecessary pointers are gone (dashed arrows indicate that the child nodes' locations in memory are calculated rather than stored). For ART, however, because its nodes have different sizes, finding a child node requires a "base + offset" or similar calculation, so the benefit of storing nodes contiguously is not clear. We, therefore, keep ART unchanged here and leave exploring other layouts as future work.

There are additional opportunities for reducing the space overhead with this rule. For example, the internal nodes in the B+tree, Masstree, and Skip List can be removed entirely. This would provide another reduction in space but it would also make point queries slower. Thus, we keep these internal nodes in B+tree and Skip List. For the Masstree, however, it is possible to do this without a significant performance penalty. This is because most of the trie nodes in Masstree are small and do not benefit from a B+tree structure. As a result, our compacted version of Masstree only stores the leaf nodes contiguously as an array in each trie node. To perform a look-up, it uses binary search over this array instead of a B+tree walk to find the appropriate entries. Our results show that performing a binary search is as fast as searching a B+tree in Masstree. We also note that this rule does not affect Masstree's overall trie, a distinguishing feature of Masstree compared to B+trees and Skip Lists.

We also need to deal with Masstree's keybags. In Figure 4, we provide a detailed structure of the compacted Masstree. It concatenates all the key suffixes within a trie node and stores them in a single byte array, along with an auxiliary offset array to mark their start locations. This reduces the structural overhead of maintaining multiple keybags for each trie node.

4.4 Rule #3: Compression

The final rule is to compress internal nodes or memory pages used in the index. For this step, we can use any general-purpose compression algorithm. We choose the ones that are designed to have fast decompression methods in exchange for a lower compression rate, such as Snappy [14] or LZ4 [5]. Column five of Figure 2 shows how we apply the Compression Rule to the B+tree, Masstree, Skip List and ART. Only the leaf nodes are compressed so that every point query needs to decompress at most one node. To minimize the cost of an expensive decompress-node operation, we maintain a cache of recently decompressed nodes. The node cache approximates LRU using the CLOCK replacement algorithm.

This rule is not always necessary for hybrid indexes because of its performance overhead. Our results in Sections 6 and 7 show that using compression for in-memory data structures is expensive even with performance optimizations, such as node caching. Furthermore, the compression ratio is not guaranteed because it depends heavily on the workload, especially the key distribution. For many applications, the significant degradation in throughput may not justify the space savings; nevertheless, compression remains an option for environments with significant space constraints.

5. MERGE

This section focuses on Step 3 of the Dual-Stage Transformation guidelines: merging tuples from the dynamic stage to the static stage. Although the merge process happens infrequently, it should be fast and efficient on temporary memory usage. Instead of using standard copy-on-write techniques, which would double the space during merging, we choose a more space-efficient merge algorithm that blocks all queries temporarily. There are trade-offs between blocking and non-blocking merge algorithms. Blocking algorithms are faster but hurt tail latency while non-blocking algorithms execute more smoothly but affect more queries because of locking and latching. Implementing non-blocking merge algorithms is out of the scope of this paper, and we defer it to future work.

The results in Section 6.3 show that our merge algorithm takes 60 ms to merge a 10 MB B+tree into a 100 MB Compact B+tree. The merge time increases linearly as the size of the index grows. The space overhead of the merge algorithm, however, is only the size of the largest array in the dynamic stage structure, which is almost negligible compared to the size of the entire dual-stage index. Section 5.1 describes the merge algorithm. Section 5.2 discusses two important runtime questions: (1) what data to merge from one stage to the next; and (2) when to perform this merge.

5.1 Merge Algorithm

Even though individual merge algorithms can vary significantly depending on the complexity of the data structure, they all have the same core component. The basic building blocks of a compacted data structure are sorted arrays containing all or part of the index entries. The core component of the merge algorithm is to extend those sorted arrays to include new elements from the dynamic stage. When merging elements from the dynamic stage, we control the temporary space penalty as follows. We allocate a new array adjacent to the original sorted array with just enough space for the new elements from the dynamic stage. The algorithm then performs in-place merge sort on the two consecutive sorted arrays to obtain a single extended array. The temporary space overhead for merging in this way is only the size of the smaller array, and the in-place merge sort completes in linear time.

The steps for merging B+tree and Skip List to their compacted variations are straightforward. They first merge the leaf-node arrays using the algorithm described above, and then rebuild the internal nodes. The internal nodes are constructed based on the merged leaf nodes so that the balancing properties of the structures are maintained. Merging Masstree and ART to their compacted versions, however, are more complicated. When merging two trie nodes, the algorithms (depth-first) recursively create new merging tasks when two child nodes (or leaves/suffixes) require further merging. We present the detailed algorithms in Appendix B.

5.2 Merge Strategy

In this section, we discuss two important design decisions: (1) what to merge, and (2) when to merge.

What to Merge: On every merge operation, the system must decide which entries to move from the dynamic stage to the static stage. Strategy one, called merge-all, merges the entire set of dynamic stage entries. This choice is based on the observation that many OLTP workloads are insert-intensive with high merge demands. Moving everything to the static stage during a merge makes room for the incoming entries and alleviates the merge pressure as much as possible. An alternative strategy, merge-cold, tracks key popularity and selectively merges the cold entries to the static stage.

The two strategies interpret the role of the dynamic stage differently. Merge-all treats the dynamic stage as a write buffer that absorbs new records, amortizing the cost of bulk insert into the static stage. Merge-cold, however, treats the dynamic stage as a write-back cache that holds the most recently accessed entries. Merge-cold represents a tunable spectrum of design choices depending on how hot and cold are defined, of which merge-all is one extreme.

The advantage of merge-cold is that it creates "shortcuts" for accessing hot entries. However, it makes two trade-offs. First, it typically leads to higher merge frequency because keeping hot entries renders the dynamic stage unable to absorb as many new records before hitting the merge threshold again. The merge itself will also be slower because it must consider the keys' hot/cold status. Second, merge-cold imposes additional overhead for tracking an entry's access history during normal operations.

Although merge-cold may work better in some cases, given the insert-intensive workload patterns of OLTP applications, we consider merge-all to be the more general and more suitable approach. We compensate for the disadvantage of merge-all (i.e., some older yet hot tuples reside in the static stage and accessing them requires searching both stages in order) by adding a Bloom filter atop the dynamic stage as described in Section 3.

When to Merge: The second design decision is what event triggers the merge process to run. One strategy to use is a ratio-based trigger: merge occurs whenever the size ratio between the dynamic and the static stages reaches a threshold. An alternative strategy is to have a constant trigger that fires whenever the size of the dynamic stage reaches a constant threshold.

The advantage of a ratio-based trigger is that it automatically adjusts the merge frequency according to the index size. This strategy prevents write-intensive workloads from merging too frequently. Although each merge becomes more costly as the index grows, merges happen less often. One can show that the merge overhead over time is constant. The side effect is that the average size of the dynamic stage gets larger over time, resulting in an increasingly longer average search time in the dynamic stage.

A constant trigger works well for read-intensive workloads because it bounds the size of the dynamic stage ensuring fast look-ups. For write-intensive workloads, however, this strategy leads to higher overhead because it keeps a constant merge frequency even though merging becomes more expensive over time. We found that a constant trigger is not suitable for OLTP workloads due to too frequent merges. We perform a sensitivity analysis of the ratio-based merge strategy in Appendix C. Although auto-tuning is another option, it is beyond the scope of this paper.

6. MICROBENCHMARK EVALUATION

For our evaluation, we created five hybrid indexes using our DST guidelines proposed in Section 3. We use X to represent either B+tree, Masstree, Skip List, or ART. *Hybrid-Compact* (or simply *Hybrid*) X means that the static stage uses the Compaction and Structural Reduction D-to-S Rules from Section 4. *Hybrid-Compressed* means that the static stage structure is also compressed using Snappy [14] according to the Compression Rule. We implemented Hybrid-Compact for all four data structures. We only implemented Hybrid-Compressed B+tree for this evaluation to verify our conclusion that using general-purpose compression is not a viable solution for improving space-efficiency of indexes in main-memory OLTP databases.

We evaluate hybrid indexes in two steps. In this section, we evaluate the hybrid index as stand-alone key-value data structure using YCSB-based microbenchmarks. We first show the separate impact on performance and space of a hybrid index's building blocks. We then compare each hybrid index to its original structure to show the performance trade-offs made by adopting a hybrid approach for better space efficiency. We did not use an existing DBMS for this section because we did not want to taint our measurement with features that are not relevant to the evaluation.

In Section 7, we evaluate hybrid indexes inside H-Store, a state-of-the-art main-memory OLTP database system. We replace the default STX B+tree with the corresponding transformed hybrid indexes and evaluate the entire DBMS end-to-end.

6.1 Experiment Setup & Benchmarks

We used a server with the following configuration in our evaluation:

CPU: 2×Intel® Xeon® E5-2680 v2 CPUs @ 2.80 GHz
DRAM: 4×32 GB DDR3 RAM
Cache: 256 KB L2-cache, 26 MB L3-cache
Disk: 500 GB, 7200 RPM, SATA (used only in Section 7)

We used a set of YCSB-based microbenchmarks to mimic OLTP index workloads. The Yahoo! Cloud Serving benchmark (YCSB) approximates typical large-scale cloud services [22]. We used its default workloads **A** (*read/write*, 50/50), **C** (*read only*), and **E** (*scan/insert*, 95/5) with Zipfian distributions, which have skewed access patterns common to OLTP workloads. The initialization phase in each workload was also measured and reported as the *insert-only* workload. For each workload, we tested three key types: 64-bit random integers, 64-bit monotonically increasing integers, and email addresses with an average length of 30 bytes. The random integer keys came directly from YCSB while the email keys were drawn from a large email collection. All values are 64-bit integers to represent tuple pointers. To summarize:

Workloads: insert-only, read-only, read/write, scan/insert
Key Types: 64-bit random int, 64-bit mono-inc int, email
Value: 64-bit integer (tuple pointers)

All experiments in this section are single-threaded without any network activity. An initialization phase inserts 50 million entries into the index. Then the measurement phase executes 10 million key-value queries according to the workload. Throughput results in the bar charts are the number of operations divided by the execution time; memory consumption is measured at the end of each trial. All numbers reported are the average of three trials.

6.2 Compaction & Compression Evaluation

We analyze hybrid indexes by first evaluating their building blocks. As mentioned in Section 4, the data structure for the static stage must be both space-efficient and fast for read operations. To test this, we compare the data structures created by applying the D-to-S (Compact/Compressed X) rules to the original data structures (X) using the *read-only* workloads described in Section 6.1. Here, X represents either B+tree, Masstree, Skip List, or ART . Note that this is an evaluation of the data structures alone without the runtime merging process that is needed to move data from the dynamic stage to the static stage. We consider the complete hybrid index architecture (with merging) in Section 6.4.

As Figure 5 shows, the read throughput for the compact indexes is up to 20% higher in most cases compared to their original data structures. This is not surprising because these compact versions inherit the core design of their original data structures but achieve a more space-efficient layout with less structural overhead. This results in fewer nodes/levels to visit per look-up and better cache performance. The only compact data structure that performs slightly worse is the Compact ART for random integer (4%) and email keys (1%). This is because unlike the other three compact indexes, Compact ART uses a slightly different organization for its internal nodes that causes a degradation in performance in exchange for a greater space saving (i.e., Layout 1 is slower than Layout 3 for look-ups – see Section 4.2).

Figure 5 also shows that the compact indexes reduce the memory footprint by up to 71% (greater than 30% in all but one case). The savings come from higher data occupancy and less structural waste (e.g., fewer pointers). In particular, the Compact ART is only half the size for random integer and email keys because ART has relatively low node occupancy (54%) compared to B+tree and Skip List (69%) in those cases. For monotonically increasing (mono-inc) integer keys, the original ART is already optimized for space.

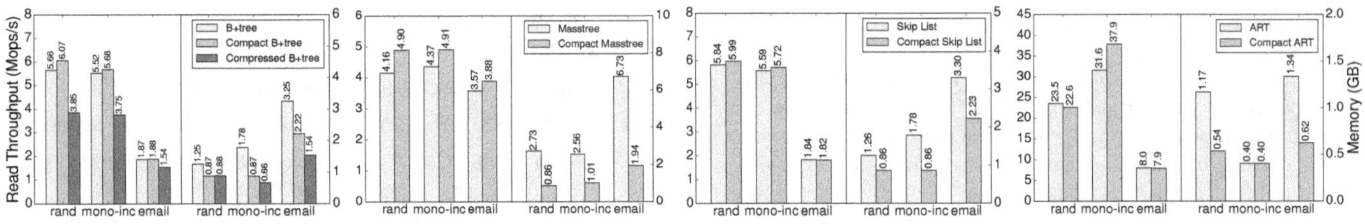

(a) B+tree (b) Masstree (c) Skip List (d) ART

Figure 5: Compaction & Compression Evaluation – Read performance and storage overhead for the compacted and compressed data structures generated by applying the D-to-S rules. Note that the figures have different Y-axis scales (rand=random integer, mono-inc=monotonically increasing integer).

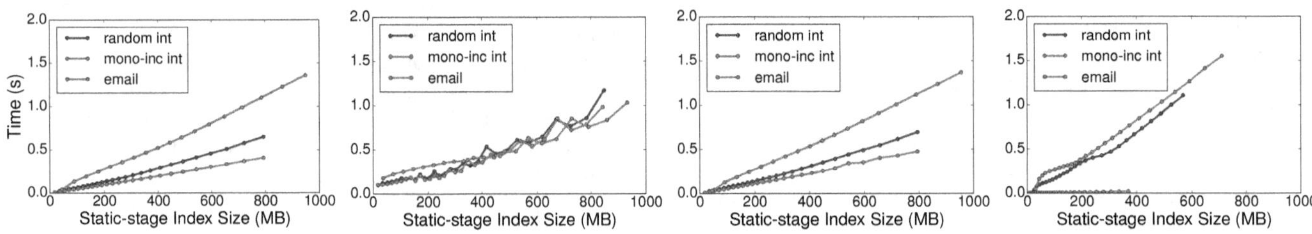

(a) B+tree (b) Masstree (c) Skip List (d) ART

Figure 6: Merge Overhead – Absolute merge time given the static-stage index size. Dynamic-stage index size = $\frac{1}{10}$ static-stage index size.

	Instructions	IPC	L1 Misses	L2 Misses
B+tree	4.9B	0.8	262M	160M
Masstree	5.4B	0.64	200M	174M
Skip List	4.5B	0.78	277M	164M
ART	2.1B	1.5	58M	26M

Table 2: Point Query Profiling – CPU-level profiling measurements for 10M point queries of random 64-bit integer keys for B+tree, Masstree, Skip List, and ART (B=billion, M=million).

The Compact Masstree has the most space savings compared to the others because its internal structures (i.e., B+trees) are completely flattened into sorted arrays.

We also tested the Compression Rule (Section 4.4) on the B+tree. As shown in Figure 5a, although the Compressed B+tree saves additional space for the mono-inc (24%) and email (31%) keys, the throughput decreases from 18–34%. Since the other data structures have the same problems, we choose not to evaluate compressed versions of them and conclude that naïve compression is a poor choice for in-memory OLTP indexes. Thus, for the rest of this paper, when we refer to a "Hybrid" index, we mean one whose static stage-structure is compacted (not compressed, unless explicitly stated).

Overall we see that ART has higher point query performance than the other three index structures. To better understand this, we profiled the 10 million point queries of random 64-bit integer keys for the four original data structures using `PAPI` [10]. Table 2 shows the profiling results for total CPU instructions, instructions per cycle (IPC), L1 cache misses and L2 cache misses. We observe that ART not only requires fewer CPU instructions to perform the same load of point queries, but also uses cache much more efficiently than the other three index structures.

6.3 Merge Strategies & Overhead

We next evaluate the merge process that moves data from the dynamic stage to the static stage at runtime. We concluded in Section 5.2 that ratio-based triggers are more suitable for OLTP applications because it automatically adjusts merge frequency according to the index size. We show a sensitivity analysis of the ratio-based merge strategy in Appendix C. Based on the analysis, we choose 10 as the default merge ratio for all hybrid indexes in the subsequent experiments in this paper.

Using the default merge strategy, we next measure the cost of the merge process. We used the *insert-only* workload in this experiment because it generates the highest merge demand. For all four hybrid indexes and all three key types, we recorded the absolute time for every triggered merge operation along with the static-stage index size at the time of the execution to measure the merge speed. Note that the size of the dynamic stage is always $\frac{1}{10}$ of that of the static stage at merge.

Figure 6 illustrates how the merge time changes with the size of the static stage of the indexes. In general, the time to perform a merge increases linearly with the size of the index. Such linear growth is inevitable because of the fundamental limitations of merging sorted arrays. But merging occurs less frequently as the index size increases because it takes longer to accumulate enough new entries to reach the merge ratio threshold again. As such, the amortized cost of merging remains constant over time. We also observe an interesting exception when running hybrid ART using mono-inc integer keys. As Figure 6d shows, the merge time (red line) is much lower than the other key types. This is because the hybrid ART does not store nodes at the same level contiguously in an array in the same manner as the other data structures (see Figure 2). Hence, the merge process for ART with mono-inc integers only needs to create and rebuild a few number of nodes to complete the merge, which is faster than readjusting the entire array.

6.4 Hybrid Indexes vs. Originals

Lastly, we compare the hybrid indexes to their corresponding original structures to show the trade-offs of adopting a hybrid approach. We evaluated each of these indexes using the same set of YCSB-based workloads described in Section 6.1 with all three key types. We conducted separate experiments using the data structures as both primary key (i.e., unique) and secondary key (i.e., non-unique) indexes. We present the primary key index evaluation here. Results for secondary key indexes can be found in Appendix E.

Figure 7 shows the throughput and memory consumption for hybrid indexes used as primary key indexes. The main takeaway is that all of the hybrid indexes provide comparable throughputs (faster in some workloads, slower in others) to their original structures while consuming 30–70% less memory. Hybrid-Compressed B+tree achieves up to 30% additional space saving but loses a sig-

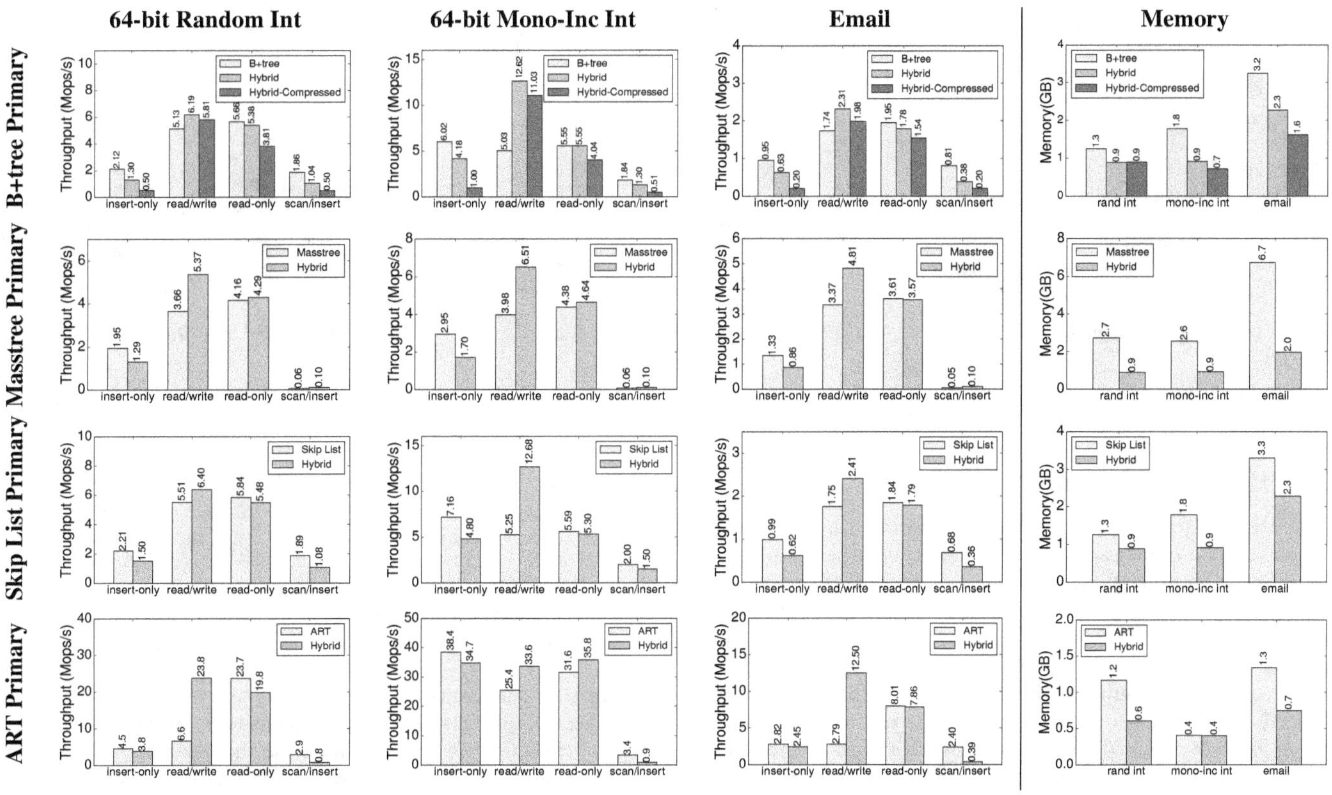

Figure 7: Hybrid Index vs. Original (Primary Indexes) – Throughput and memory measurements for the different YCSB workloads and key types when the data structures are used as primary key (i.e., unique) indexes. Note that the figures have different Y-axis scales.

nificant fraction of the throughput. This trade-off might only be acceptable for applications with tight space constraints.

Insert-only: One disadvantage of a hybrid index is that it requires periodic merges. As shown in Figure 7, all hybrid indexes are slower than their original structures under the insert-only workloads since they have the highest merge demand. The merging, however, is not the main reason for the performance degradation. Instead, it is because a hybrid index must check both the dynamic and static stages on every insert to verify that a key does not already exist in either location. Such key uniqueness check causes about a 30% insert throughput drop. For the Hybrid-Compressed B+tree, however, merge remains the primary overhead because of the decompression costs.

Read/Write: Despite having to check for uniqueness in two locations on inserts, the hybrid indexes' dual-stage architecture is better at handling skewed updates. The results for this workload show that all of the hybrid indexes outperform their original structures for all key types because they store newly updated entries in the smaller (and therefore more cache-friendly) dynamic stage.

Read-only: We already compared the point-query performance for the dynamic and static stage data structures in Section 6.2. When we put these structures together in a single hybrid index, the overall point-query performance is only slightly slower than the static stage alone because a query may have to check both data structures. We, therefore, use a Bloom filter in front of the dynamic stage to ensure that most reads only search one of the stages. We evaluate the impact of this filter in Appendix D.

Scan/Insert: This last workload shows that the hybrid indexes have lower throughput for range queries. This is expected because their dual-stage design requires comparing keys from both the dynamic and static stages to determine the "next" entry when advancing the iterator. This comparison operation is particularly inefficient for hybrid ART because the data structure does not store the full keys in the leaf nodes. Therefore, performing full-key comparison requires fetching the keys from the records first. We also note that range query results are less optimized in Masstree because it does not provide the same iterator API that the other index implementations support. We do not believe, however, that there is anything inherent to Masstree's design that would make it significantly better or worse than the other data structures for this workload.

Memory: All of the hybrid indexes use significantly less memory than their original data structures. An interesting finding is that although the random and mono-inc integer key data sets are the same size, the B+tree and Skip List use more space to store the mono-inc integer keys. This is because the key insertion pattern of mono-inc integers produces B+tree nodes that are only 50% full (instead of 69% on average). The paged-deterministic Skip List that we used has a similar hierarchical structure as the B+tree and thus has a similar node occupancy. ART, however, uses less space to store mono-inc keys than the random keys because of prefix compression. This also reduces memory for the email keys as well.

7. FULL DBMS EVALUATION

This section shows the effects of integrating hybrid indexes into the in-memory H-Store OLTP DBMS [3, 33]. The latest version of H-Store uses B+tree as its default index data structure. We show that switching to hybrid B+tree reduces the DBMS's footprint in memory and enables it to process transactions for longer without having to use secondary storage. We omit the evaluation of the other hybrid data structures because they provide similar benefits.

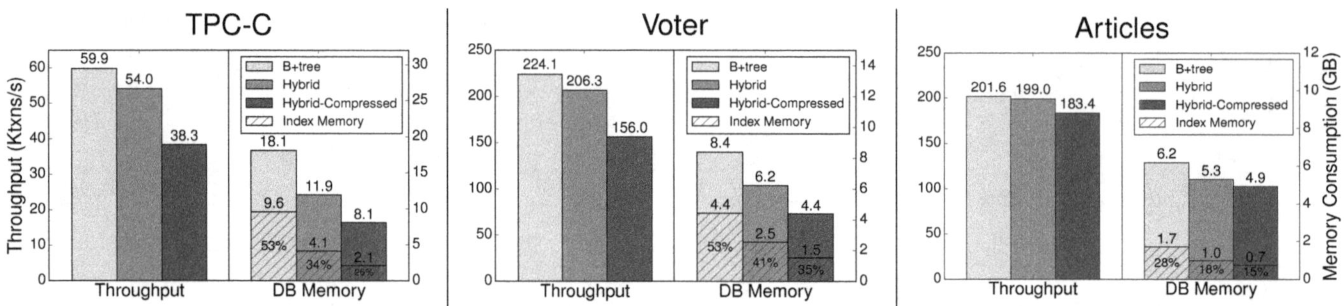

(a) TPC-C Throughput + Memory

(b) Voter Throughput + Memory

(c) Articles Throughput + Memory

Figure 8: In-Memory Workloads – Throughput and memory measurements of the H-Store DBMS using the default B+tree, Hybrid, and Hybrid-Compressed B+tree when running workloads that fit entirely in memory. The system runs for 6 min in each benchmark trial.

7.1 H-Store Overview

H-Store is a distributed, row-oriented DBMS that supports serializable execution of transactions over main memory partitions [33]. It is optimized for the efficient execution of workloads that contain transactions invoked as pre-defined stored procedures. Client applications initiate transactions by sending the procedure name and input parameters to any node in the cluster. Each partition is assigned a single-threaded execution engine that is responsible for executing transactions and queries for that partition. A partition is protected by a single lock managed by its coordinator that is granted to transactions one-at-a-time based on the order of their arrival timestamp.

Anti-caching is a memory-oriented DBMS design that allows the system to manage databases that are larger than the amount of memory available without incurring the performance penalty of a disk-oriented system [23]. When the amount of in-memory data exceeds a user-defined threshold, the DBMS moves data to disk to free up space for new data. To do this, the system dynamically constructs blocks of the coldest tuples and writes them asynchronously to the anti-cache on disk. The DBMS maintains in-memory "tombstones" for each evicted tuple. When a running transaction attempts to access an evicted tuple through its tombstone, the DBMS aborts that transaction and fetches the tuple from the anti-cache without blocking other transactions. Once the data that the transaction needs is in memory, the system restarts the transaction.

7.2 Benchmarks

The experiments in this section use H-Store's built-in benchmarking framework to explore three workloads:

TPC-C: The TPC-C benchmark is the current industry standard for evaluating the performance of OLTP systems [51]. Its five stored procedures simulate a warehouse-centric order processing application. Approximately 88% of the transactions executed in TPC-C modify the database. We configure the database to contain eight warehouses and 100,000 items.

Voter: This benchmark simulates a phone-based election application. It is designed to saturate the DBMS with many short-lived transactions that all update a small number of records. There are a fixed number of contestants in the database. The workload is mostly transactions that update the total number of votes for a particular contestant. The DBMS records the number of votes made by each user based on their phone number; each user is only allowed to vote a fixed number of times.

Articles: This workload models an on-line news website where users submit content, such as text posts or links, and then other users post comments to them. All transactions involve a small number of tuples that are retrieved using either primary key or secondary indexes. We design and scale the benchmark so that the transactions coincide roughly with a week of Reddit's [11] traffic.

	B+tree	**Hybrid**	**Hybrid-Compressed**
50%-tile	10 ms	10 ms	11 ms
99%-tile	50 ms	52 ms	83 ms
MAX	115 ms	611 ms	1981 ms

Table 3: Latency Measurements – Transaction latencies of H-Store using the default B+tree, Hybrid B+tree, and Hybrid-Compressed B+tree as indexes for the TPC-C workload (same experiment as in Figure 8a).

7.3 In-Memory Workloads

We first show that using hybrid indexes helps H-Store save a significant amount of memory. We ran the aforementioned three DBMS benchmarks on H-Store (anti-caching disabled) with three different index types: (1) B+tree, (2) Hybrid B+tree, and (3) Hybrid-Compressed B+tree. Each benchmark warms up for one minute after the initial load and then runs for five minutes on an 8-partition H-Store instance (one CPU core per partition). We deployed eight clients on the same machine using another eight cores on the other socket to exclude network factors. We compared throughput, index memory consumption, and total database memory consumption among the three index types. Figure 8 shows the results. The throughput results are the average throughputs during the execution time (warm-up period excluded); memory consumption is measured at the end of each benchmark. We repeated each benchmark three times and compute the average for the final results.

As shown in Figure 8, both Hybrid and Hybrid-Compressed B+tree have a smaller memory footprint than the original B+tree: 40–55% and 50–65%, respectively. The memory savings for the entire database depend on the relative size of indexes to database. Hybrid indexes favor workloads with small tuples, as in TPC-C and Voter, so the index memory savings translate into significant savings at the database level.

Hybrid B+tree incurs a 1–10% average throughput drop compared to the original, which is fairly small considering the memory savings. Hybrid-Compressed B+tree, however, sacrifices throughput more significantly to reap its additional memory savings. These two hybrid indexes offer a throughput-memory tradeoff that may depend on the application's requirements.

The results in Figure 8 are consistent with our findings in the microbenchmark evaluation (Section 6). The throughput drops associated with hybrid indexes are more noticeable in the TPC-C (10%) and Voter (8%) benchmarks because they are insert-intensive and contain a large fraction of primary indexes. Referring to the *insert-*

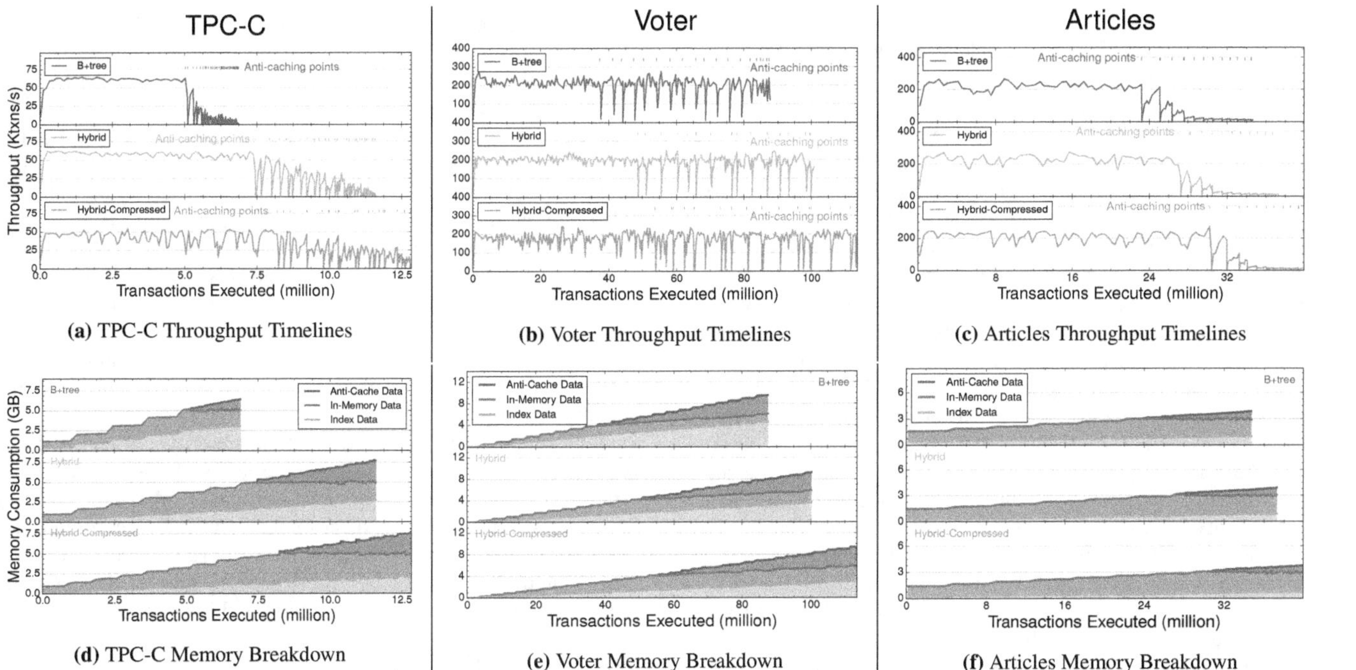

(a) TPC-C Throughput Timelines

(b) Voter Throughput Timelines

(c) Articles Throughput Timelines

(d) TPC-C Memory Breakdown

(e) Voter Memory Breakdown

(f) Articles Memory Breakdown

Figure 9: Larger-than-Memory Workloads – Throughput and memory measurements of the H-Store DBMS using B+tree, Hybrid, and Hybrid-Compressed B+tree as index structures when running workloads that are larger than the amount of memory available to the system. H-Store uses its anti-caching component to evict cold data from memory out to disk. The system runs 12 minutes in each benchmark trial.

only workloads in Figure 7, we see that hybrid indexes are slower when used as primary indexes because of the key-uniqueness check. The Articles benchmark, however, is more read-intensive. Since hybrid indexes provide comparable or better read throughput (see Figure 7), the throughput drop in Figure 8c is small (1%).

Table 3 lists the 50%-tile, 99%-tile, and MAX latency numbers for the TPC-C benchmark. Hybrid indexes have little effect on 50%-tile and 99%-tile latencies. For example, the difference in 99% latency between Hybrid B+tree and the original is almost negligible. The MAX latencies, however, increase when switching to hybrid indexes because our current merge algorithm is blocking. But the infrequency of merge means that the latency penalty only shows up when looking at MAX.

7.4 Larger-than-Memory Workloads

The previous section shows the savings from using hybrid indexes when the entire database fits in memory. Here, we show that hybrid indexes can further help H-Store with anti-caching enabled expand its capacity when the size of the database goes beyond physical memory. When both memory and disk are used, the memory saved by hybrid indexes allows the database to keep more hot tuples in memory. The database thus can sustain a higher throughput because fewer queries must retrieve tuples from disk.

We ran TPC-C, Voter, and Articles on H-Store with anti-caching enabled for all three index configurations: B+tree, Hybrid B+tree, and Hybrid-Compressed B+tree. Each benchmark executes for 12 minutes after the initial load. We used the same client-server configurations as in Section 7.3. We set the anti-caching eviction threshold to be 5 GB for TPC-C and Voter, 3 GB for Articles so that the DBMS starts anti-caching in the middle of the execution. The system's eviction manager periodically checks whether the total amount of memory used by the DBMS is above this threshold. If it is, H-Store selects the coldest data to evict to disk. Figure 9 shows the experiment results; note that we use the **total number of transactions executed** on the x-axis rather than time.

Using hybrid indexes, H-Store with anti-caching executes more transactions than the original B+tree index during the same 12-minute run. We note that the B+tree and Hybrid B+tree configurations cannot execute the Voter benchmark for the entire 12 minutes because the DBMS runs out of memory to hold the indexes as only the database tuples can be paged to disk.

Two features contribute to H-Store's improved capacity when using hybrid indexes. First, with the same anti-caching threshold, hybrid indexes consume less memory, allowing the database to run longer before the first anti-caching eviction occurs. Second, even during periods of anti-caching activity, H-Store with hybrid indexes sustains higher throughput because the saved index space allows more tuples to remain in memory.

H-Store's throughput when using anti-caching depends largely on whether the workload reads evicted tuples [23]. TPC-C is an insert-heavy workload that mostly reads new data. Thus, TPC-C's throughput decreases relatively slowly as the tuples are evicted to disk. Voter never reads evicted data, so the throughput remains constant. Articles, however, is relatively read-intensive and occasionally queries cold data. These reads impact throughput during anti-caching, especially at the end of the run when a significant number of tuples have been evicted. The throughput fluctuations for hybrid indexes (especially Hybrid-Compressed indexes) before anti-caching are due to index merging. After anti-caching starts, the large throughput fluctuations are because of the anti-caching evictions since the current version of anti-caching is a blocking process; all transactions are blocked until eviction completes.

8. RELATED WORK

Previous research explored unifying multiple underlying physical data structures, each with different optimization focuses, to construct a single logical entity. Some of the first examples include log-structured engines such as log-structured merge (LSM) trees [44], LevelDB [4] and LHAM [43]. Our hybrid index approach differs from these techniques in several ways. First, log-structured engines are storage management systems that leverage the storage hierarchy while a hybrid index is an index data structure that resides only in memory. Such difference greatly influences a number of design decisions. For example, unlike LSM-trees, hybrid indexes avoid having too many stages/levels (unless the workload is extremely skewed) because the additional stages cause the worst case read latency to increase proportionally to the number of stages. In addition, log-structured engines focus on speeding up writes while hybrid indexes target at saving memory space.

SILT is a flash-based key-value store that achieves high performance with a small memory footprint by using a multi-level storage hierarchy with different data structures [39]. The first level is a log-structured store that supports fast writes. The second level is a transitional hash table to perform buffering. The final level is a compressed trie structure. Hybrid indexes borrow from this design, but unlike SILT, a hybrid index does not use a log-structured storage tier because maximizing the number of sequential writes is not a high priority for in-memory databases. Hybrid indexes also avoid SILT's heavyweight compression because of the large performance overhead. Similar systems include Anvil, a modular framework for database backends to allow flexible combinations of the underlying key-value stores to maximize their benefits [40].

The Dynamic-to-Static Rules are inspired by work from Bentley and Saxe [18]. In their paper, they propose general methods for converting static structures to dynamic structures; their goal is to provide a systematic method for designing new, performance-optimized dynamic data structures. In this paper, we use a different starting point, a dynamic data structure, and propose rules for creating a static version; furthermore, our focus is on creating space-optimized instead of performance-optimized variants.

Several DBMSs use compressed indexes to reduce the amount of data that is read from disk during query execution. There has been considerable work on space-efficient indexes for OLAP workloads to improve the performance of long running queries that access large segments of the database [20, 53]. SQL Server's columnar indexes use a combination of dictionary-based, value-based, and run-length encoding to compress the column store indexes [35]. MySQL's InnoDB storage engine has the ability to compress B-tree pages when they are written to disk [8]. To amortize compression and decompression overhead, InnoDB keeps a modification log within each B-tree page to buffer incoming changes to the page. This approach differs from hybrid indexes, which focus on structural reduction rather than data compression. Because hybrid indexes target in-memory databases and their concomitant performance objectives, data compression is prohibitive in most cases.

Other in-memory databases save space by focusing on the tuple stores rather than the index structures. One example is SAP's HANA hybrid DBMS [28, 47]. In HANA, all new data is first inserted into a row-major store engine that is optimized for OLTP workloads. Over time, the system migrates tuples to dictionary-compressed, in-memory columnar store that is optimized for OLAP queries. This approach is also used in HyPer [29]. Hybrid indexes take a similar approach to migrate cold data from the write-optimized index to the compact, read-only index. Both these techniques are orthogonal to hybrid indexes. A DBMS can use hybrid indexes while still moving data out to these compressed data stores.

Other work seeks to reduce the database's storage footprint by exploiting the access patterns of OLTP workloads to evict cold tuples from memory. These approaches differ in how they determine what to evict and the mechanism they use to move data. The anti-caching architecture in H-Store uses an LRU to track how often tuples are accessed and then migrates cold data to an auxiliary, on-disk data store [23]. Although the tuple data is removed from memory, the DBMS still has to keep all of the index keys in-memory. A similar approach was proposed for VoltDB (the commercial implementation of H-Store) where the database relies on the OS's virtual memory mechanism to move cold pages out to disk [48]. The Siberia Project for Microsoft's Hekaton categorizes hot/cold tuples based on sampling their access history [49] and can also migrate data out to an on-disk data store [27]. Hekaton still uses a disk-backed index, so cold pages are swapped out to disk as needed using SQL Server's buffer pool manager and the remaining in-memory index data is not compressed. Hybrid indexes do not rely on any tracking information to guide the merging process since it may not be available in every DBMS. It is future work to determine whether such access history may further improve hybrid indexes' performance.

Dynamic materialized views materialize only a selective subset of tuples in the view based on tuple access frequencies to save space and maintenance costs [55]. Similarly, database cracking constructs self-organizing, discriminative indexes according to the data access patterns [31]. Hybrid indexes leverage the same workload adaptivity by maintaining fast access paths for the newly inserted/updated entries to save memory and improve performance.

9. FUTURE WORK

Our work can be extended in several directions. First, developing space-efficient non-blocking merge algorithms for hybrid indexes can further satisfy the needs for tail-latency-sensitive applications. Second, with the non-blocking merge algorithms, it would be worthwhile attempting to make the entire hybrid index concurrent so that it can be applied to a concurrent main-memory DBMS. Third, the hybrid index architecture opens up the research opportunity to apply highly-compressed static data structures, including succinct data structures, to database indexes.

10. CONCLUSION

A hybrid index uses the dual-stage architecture to combine two data structures with different optimization emphasis to create a memory-efficient and high-performance order-preserving index structure. It uses a fast dynamic data structure as a write buffer in its dynamic stage to provide fast inserts and accesses to the recently added entries. For the second stage, it uses a compact, read-optimized data structure to serve reads for colder data. This design captures the characteristics of OLTP workloads, where newly inserted entries are likely to be accessed/modified frequently in the near future while older entries are mostly accessed through occasional lookups. We provide a set of guidelines, called the Dual-Stage Transformation (DST), to help index designers convert any order-preserving index structure to a hybrid index. Experimental results show that hybrid indexes created by applying the DST guidelines provide throughput comparable to the original index structures while using significantly less memory. We hope that the various techniques discussed in the paper can form an important step towards a hybrid approach for index design in main-memory databases.

ACKNOWLEDGMENTS

This work was supported by funding from U.S. National Science Foundation under awards IIS-1409802, CNS-1345305, and CCF-1535821, as well as Intel via the Intel Science and Technology Center for Cloud Computing (ISTC-CC).

For questions or comments about this paper, please call the CMU Database Hotline at `+1-844-88-CMUDB`**.**

11. REFERENCES

[1] ALTIBASE Index Documentation. http://aid.altibase.com/display/migfromora/Index.

[2] Cache-Optimized Concurrent Skip list. http://sourceforge.net/projects/skiplist/files/Templatized%20C%2B%2B%20Version/.

[3] H-Store. http://hstore.cs.brown.edu.

[4] Leveldb. http://www.leveldb.org.

[5] LZ4. https://code.google.com/p/lz4/.

[6] MemSQL Documentation. http://docs.memsql.com/latest/concepts/indexes/.

[7] MySQL Memory Storage Engine. http://dev.mysql.com/doc/refman/5.7/en/memory-storage-engine.html.

[8] Mysql v5.5 – how compression works for innodb tables. http://dev.mysql.com/doc/refman/5.5/en/innodb-compression-internals.html.

[9] Overview of TimesTen Index Types. https://docs.oracle.com/cd/E21901_01/timesten.1122/e21633/comp.htm#TTOPR380.

[10] Performance Application Programming Interface. http://icl.cs.utk.edu/papi/index.html.

[11] Reddit. http://www.reddit.com.

[12] Redis Index. http://redis.io/topics/indexes.

[13] SAP Hana Indexes. http://saphanawiki.com/2015/09/2160391-faq-sap-hana-indexes/.

[14] Snappy. https://github.com/google/snappy.

[15] SQLite Documentation. https://www.sqlite.org/docs.html.

[16] VoltDB Blog. https://voltdb.com/blog/best-practices-index-optimization-voltdb.

[17] WiredTiger. http://wiredtiger.com.

[18] J. L. Bentley and J. B. Saxe. Decomposable searching problems I: static-to-dynamic transformation. *J. Algorithms*, 1(4):301–358, 1980.

[19] T. Bingmann. STX B+ tree C++ template classes. http://panthema.net/2007/stx-btree/.

[20] C.-Y. Chan and Y. E. Ioannidis. Bitmap index design and evaluation. SIGMOD, pages 355–366, 1998.

[21] D. Comer. Ubiquitous b-tree. *ACM Comput. Surv.*, 11(2):121–137, June 1979.

[22] B. F. Cooper, A. Silberstein, E. Tam, R. Ramakrishnan, and R. Sears. Benchmarking cloud serving systems with YCSB. In *SoCC*, pages 143–154, 2010.

[23] J. DeBrabant, A. Pavlo, S. Tu, M. Stonebraker, and S. Zdonik. Anti-caching: A new approach to database management system architecture. *VLDB*, 6(14):1942–1953, Sept. 2013.

[24] D. J. DeWitt, R. H. Katz, F. Olken, L. D. Shapiro, M. R. Stonebraker, and D. Wood. Implementation techniques for main memory database systems. *SIGMOD Rec.*, 14(2):1–8, 1984.

[25] C. Diaconu, C. Freedman, E. Ismert, P.-A. Larson, P. Mittal, R. Stonecipher, N. Verma, and M. Zwilling. Hekaton: SQL Server's Memory-Optimized OLTP Engine. In *SIGMOD*, pages 1–12, 2013.

[26] J. Dittrich and A. Jindal. Towards a one size fits all database architecture. In *CIDR*, pages 195–198, 2011.

[27] A. Eldawy, J. J. Levandoski, and P. Larson. Trekking through siberia: Managing cold data in a memory-optimized database. *PVLDB*, 7(11):931–942, 2014.

[28] F. Färber, S. K. Cha, J. Primsch, C. Bornhövd, S. Sigg, and W. Lehner. Sap hana database: data management for modern business applications. *SIGMOD Rec.*, 40(4):45–51, Jan. 2012.

[29] F. Funke, A. Kemper, and T. Neumann. Compacting transactional data in hybrid oltp&olap databases. *VLDB*, 5(11):1424–1435, July 2012.

[30] S. Harizopoulos, D. J. Abadi, S. Madden, and M. Stonebraker. OLTP through the looking glass, and what we found there. In *SIGMOD*, pages 981–992, 2008.

[31] S. Idreos, M. L. Kersten, and S. Manegold. Database cracking. In *CIDR*, pages 68–78, 2007.

[32] G. J. Jacobson. Succinct static data structures. 1980.

[33] R. Kallman, H. Kimura, J. Natkins, A. Pavlo, A. Rasin, S. Zdonik, E. P. C. Jones, S. Madden, M. Stonebraker, Y. Zhang, J. Hugg, and D. J. Abadi. H-Store: A High-Performance, Distributed Main Memory Transaction Processing System. *VLDB*, 1(2):1496–1499, 2008.

[34] J. Krueger, C. Kim, M. Grund, N. Satish, D. Schwalb, J. Chhugani, H. Plattner, P. Dubey, and A. Zeier. Fast updates on read-optimized databases using multi-core cpus. *VLDB*, 5(1):61–72, Sept. 2011.

[35] P.-A. Larson, C. Clinciu, E. N. Hanson, A. Oks, S. L. Price, S. Rangarajan, A. Surna, and Q. Zhou. Sql server column store indexes. SIGMOD, pages 1177–1184, 2011.

[36] C. Lefurgy, K. Rajamani, F. Rawson, W. Felter, M. Kistler, and T. W. Keller. Energy management for commercial servers. *Computer*, 36(12).

[37] V. Leis, A. Kemper, and T. Neumann. The adaptive radix tree: Artful indexing for main-memory databases. ICDE, pages 38–49, 2013.

[38] J. Levandoski, D. Lomet, S. Sengupta, A. Birka, and C. Diaconu. Indexing on modern hardware: Hekaton and beyond. SIGMOD, pages 717–720, 2014.

[39] H. Lim, B. Fan, D. G. Andersen, and M. Kaminsky. SILT: A memory-efficient, high-performance key-value store. SOSP '11, pages 1–13, 2011.

[40] M. Mammarella, S. Hovsepian, and E. Kohler. Modular data storage with anvil. SOSP, pages 147–160, 2009.

[41] Y. Mao, E. Kohler, and R. T. Morris. Cache craftiness for fast multicore key-value storage. EuroSys, pages 183–196, 2012.

[42] J. I. Munro, T. Papadakis, and R. Sedgewick. Deterministic skip lists. the third annual ACM-SIAM symposium on Discrete algorithms, 1992.

[43] P. Muth, P. O'Neil, A. Pick, and G. Weikum. The lham log-structured history data access method. *The VLDB Journal*, 8(3-4):199–221, Feb. 2000.

[44] P. O'Neil, E. Cheng, D. Gawlick, and E. O'Neil. The log-structured merge-tree (lsm-tree). *Acta Inf.*, 33(4):351–385, June 1996.

[45] A. Prout. The story behind memsql's skiplist indexes. http://blog.memsql.com/the-story-behind-memsqls-skiplist-indexes/.

[46] W. Pugh. Skip lists: A probabilistic alternative to balanced trees. *Communications of the ACM*, 33(6):668–676, 1990.

[47] V. Sikka, F. Färber, W. Lehner, S. K. Cha, T. Peh, and C. Bornhövd. Efficient transaction processing in sap hana database: The end of a column store myth. SIGMOD, pages 731–742, 2012.

[48] R. Stoica and A. Ailamaki. Enabling efficient os paging for main-memory oltp databases. DaMoN, 2013.

[49] R. Stoica, J. J. Levandoski, and P.-A. Larson. Identifying hot and cold data in main-memory databases. ICDE, pages 26–37, 2013.

[50] M. Stonebraker, S. Madden, D. J. Abadi, S. Harizopoulos, N. Hachem, and P. Helland. The end of an architectural era: (it's time for a complete rewrite). In *VLDB*, pages 1150–1160, 2007.

[51] The Transaction Processing Council. TPC-C Benchmark (Revision 5.9.0). http://www.tpc.org/tpcc/, June 2007.

[52] S. Tu, W. Zheng, E. Kohler, B. Liskov, and S. Madden. Speedy transactions in multicore in-memory databases. In *Proceedings of the Twenty-Fourth ACM Symposium on Operating Systems Principles*, SOSP '13, pages 18–32, 2013.

[53] T. Westmann, D. Kossmann, S. Helmer, and G. Moerkotte. The implementation and performance of compressed databases. *SIGMOD Rec.*, 29(3):55–67, Sept. 2000.

[54] A. C.-C. Yao. On random 2-3 trees. *Acta Informatica*, 9:159–170, 1978.

[55] J. Zhou, P.-A. Larson, J. Goldstein, and L. Ding. Dynamic materialized views. ICDE, pages 526–535, 2007.

	Year	Supported Index Types
ALTIBASE [1]	1999	**B-tree/B+tree**, R-tree
H-Store [3]	2007	**B+tree**, hash index
HyPer [29]	2010	**Adaptive Radix Tree**, hash index
MSFT Hekaton [38]	2011	**Bw-tree**, hash index
MySQL (MEMORY) [7]	2005	**B-tree**, hash index
MemSQL [6]	2012	**skip list**, hash index
Redis [12]	2009	linked list, hash, skip list
SAP HANA [13]	2010	**B+tree/CPB+tree**
Silo [52]	2013	**Masstree**
SQLite [15]	2000	**B-tree**, R*-tree
TimesTen [9]	1995	**B-tree**, T-tree, hash index, bitmap
VoltDB [16]	2008	**Red-Black Tree**, hash index

Table 4: Index Types – The different type of index data structures supported by major commercial and academic in-memory OLTP DBMSs. The year corresponds to when the system was released or initially developed. The default index type for each DBMS is listed in **bold**.

APPENDIX

A. INDEX TYPES

In order to better understand how modern DBMSs use indexes, we examined several of the major commercial and academic in-memory OLTP DBMSs that were developed in the last two decades. Our listing in Table 4 shows the index types (i.e., data structures) supported by 12 DBMSs and the year that they were released. We also include which index type is used as the default when the user does not specify any hints to the DBMS; that is, the data structure that the DBMS uses when application invokes the CREATE INDEX command. Our survey shows that the order-preserving data structures are the most common, with the B+tree as the most popular default index type supported in these systems. This is notable since B+trees were originally designed for disk-oriented DBMSs in the 1970s [21]. We also note that In addition, most of the listed DBMSs support hash indexes, but none of them use this as their default option. Four of the systems do not even expose a hash index to the application developer, although they do use on internally for operator execution (e.g., joins). We attribute this to the fact that hash indexes cannot support range queries and thus may provide unexpected performance for users.

B. DETAILED MERGE ALGORITHMS

This section extends Section 5.1 by providing more details about the merge algorithms for the different data structures.

As we mentioned in Section 5.1, the algorithm for merging B+tree to Compact B+tree is straightforward. The first step is to merge the new items from the dynamic stage to the leaf-node array of the Compact B+tree in the static stage, using the in-place merge sort algorithm. Then, based on the merged leaf-node array, the algorithm rebuilds the internal nodes level by level bottom up. Skip List merging uses a similar algorithm.

For Masstree and ART, merging uses recursive algorithms. Figure 10 shows the pseudo code for merging Masstree to Compact Masstree. The algorithm is a combination of merging sorted arrays and merging tries. We define three merge tasks that serve as building blocks for the merge process: merge two trie nodes, insert an item into a trie node, and create a trie node to hold two items. Note that the "==" sign between items in the pseudo code means that they have equivalent keyslices.

The initial task is to merge the root nodes of the two tries, as shown in the *merge_nodes(root_m, root_n)* function in Figure 10. Merging any two trie nodes, including the root nodes, involves merging the sorted arrays of keys within the nodes. Conceptually, the algorithm proceeds as in a typical merge sort, except that it recursively (depth-first) creates new tasks when the child nodes (or suffixes) require further merging. The merge process ends once the root node merge completes.

```
merge_nodes(node m, n, parent):
  //merge the sorted arrays together
  merge_arrays(m, n)
  link n to parent

merge_arrays(node m, n):
  //2 running cursors: x for m, y for n
  for item x in m and item y in n:
    if x == y:                  //equal keyslice
      recursively invoke:
        case 1: both x and y have child:
          merge_nodes(x.child, y.child, n)
        case 2: x has child, y has suffix:
          add_item(y.suffix, x.child, n)
        case 3: y has child, x has suffix:
          add_item(x.suffix, y.child, n)
        case 4: x.suffix != y.suffix:
          create_node(x.suffix, y.suffix, n)
    else
      move min(x, y) to new position in n
```

```
add_item(item x, node n, parent):
  //insert item x to the sorted arrays in n
  insert_one(x, n)
  link n to parent

insert_one(item x, node n):
  if x == (any item y in n):
    recursively invoke:
    case 1: y has child:
      add_item(x.suffix, y.child, n)
    case 2: y has suffix:
      create_node(x.suffix, y.suffix, n)
  else
    insert x to appropriate position in n
```

```
create_node(item x, y, node parent):
  //create a new node to hold x and y
  n = new_node(x, y)
  if x == y:
    create_node(x.suffix, y.suffix, n)
  link n to parent
```

Figure 10: Algorithm of merging Masstree to Compact Masstree – A recursive algorithm that combines trie traversal and merge sort.

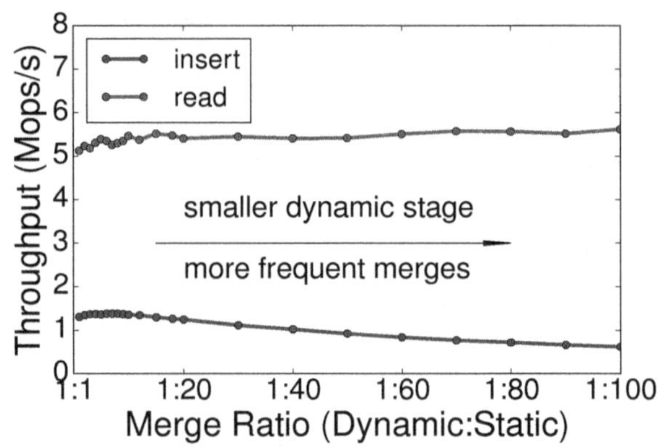

Figure 11: Merge Ratio – A sensitivity analysis of hybrid index's ratio-based merge strategy. The index used in this analysis is Hybrid B+tree.

Merging ART to Compact ART adopts a slightly more complicated recursive algorithm. Instead of checking the key suffixes directly within the node (as in Masstree), ART has to load the full keys from the records and extract the suffixes based on the current trie depth. The two optimizations (lazy expansion and pass compression) in ART [37] further complicates the algorithm because child nodes of the same parent can be at different levels.

C. SENSITIVITY ANALYSIS OF RATIO-BASED MERGE STRATEGY

This section extends Section 6.3 by providing a sensitivity analysis of the ratio-based merge strategy. To determine a good default merge ratio that balances read and write throughput, we use the *insert-only* workload followed by the *read-only* workload with 64-bit integer keys to test ratios ranging from 1 to 100. For each ratio setting, we adjust the number of entries inserted so that the dynamic stage is about 50% "full" right before the read-only workload starts. We measure the average throughput of the hybrid index for the insert-only and read-only phases separately for each ratio. We only show the results for hybrid B+tree because they are sufficient

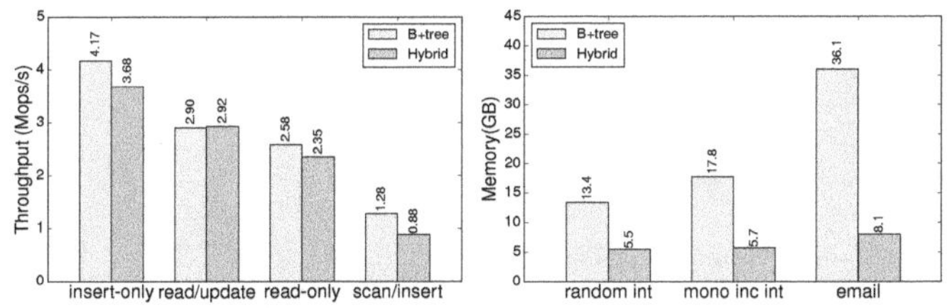

(a) Throughput (b) Memory

Figure 13: Hybrid Index vs. Original (Secondary Indexes) – Throughput and memory measurements for different YCSB workloads using 64-bit random integer keys when the data structures are used as secondary (i.e., non-unique) indexes. The data set contains 10 values for each unique key.

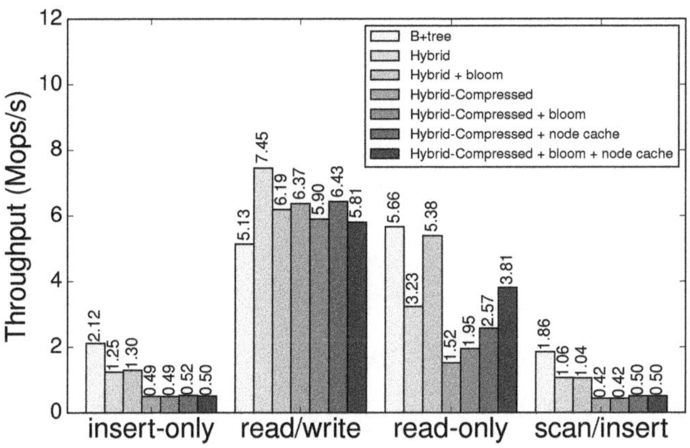

Figure 12: Auxiliary Structures – This figure is an extended version of the figure in the (B+tree Primary, 64-bit random int) cell of Figure 7 that shows the effects of the Bloom filter and the node cache in the hybrid index architecture.

to demonstrate the relationship between read/write throughput and merge ratio.

The results in Figure 11 show that a larger merge ratio leads to slightly higher read throughput and lower write throughput. A larger ratio keeps the dynamic stage smaller, thereby speeding up traversals in the dynamic stage. But it also triggers merges more frequently, which reduces the write throughput. As the merge ratio increases, the write throughput decreases more quickly than the read throughput increases. Since OLTP workloads are generally write-intensive, they benefit more from a relatively small ratio. Based on this finding, we use 10 as the merge ratio for all indexes in the subsequent experiments in this paper.

D. AUXILIARY STRUCTURES

This section is an extension of Section 6.4, where we show the effects of two auxiliary structures presented in the hybrid index architecture: Bloom filter (see Figure 1) and node cache (see Figure 2). We extend the experiment shown in the (B+tree Primary, 64-bit random int) cell of Figure 7 by making the inclusion of Bloom filter or node cache controlled variables to show separately their effects on performance.

Figure 12 presents the results. We first focus on the read-only workload. For all variants of the hybrid index, the throughput improves significantly when adding the Bloom filter; similarly, adding a node cache also improves throughput over the same index variant without a node cache. In addition, Bloom filter and node cache improve read performance without noticeable overhead for other non-read-only workloads.

E. SECONDARY INDEXES EVALUATION

This section is an extension of Section 6.4, where we provide the experiment results for hybrid indexes used as secondary indexes. The experiment setup is described in Section 6.4. We insert ten values (instead of one, as in primary indexes) for each unique key. Because we implement multi-value support for all indexes in the same way (described in Section 4.2), we only show the result for hybrid B+tree in the 64-bit random integer key case as a representative to demonstrate the differences between using hybrid indexes as primary and secondary indexes.

As shown in Figure 13, the secondary index results are consistent with the primary index findings with several exceptions. First, the insert throughput gap between the original and hybrid B+tree shrinks because secondary indexes do not require a key-uniqueness check for an insert, which is the main reason for the slowdown in the primary index case. Second, hybrid B+tree loses its large throughput advantage in the read/write (i.e., update-heavy) workload case because it handles these value updates in-place rather than inserting new entries into the dynamic stage (as for primary indexes). In-place updates prevent the same key from appearing in both stages with different sets of values, which would require a hybrid index to search both stages to construct a complete value list for a key. Third, the memory savings of hybrid B+tree are more significant in the secondary index case because the original B+tree stores duplicate keys while Compact B+tree does not.

Design Principles for Scaling Multi-core OLTP Under High Contention

Kun Ren
Yale University
kun.ren@yale.edu

Jose M. Faleiro
Yale University
jose.faleiro@yale.edu

Daniel J. Abadi
Yale University
dna@cs.yale.edu

ABSTRACT

Although significant recent progress has been made in improving the multi-core scalability of high throughput transactional database systems, modern systems still fail to achieve scalable throughput for workloads involving frequent access to highly contended data. Most of this inability to achieve high throughput is explained by the fundamental constraints involved in guaranteeing ACID — the addition of cores results in more concurrent transactions accessing the same contended data for which access must be serialized in order to guarantee isolation. Thus, linear scalability for contended workloads is impossible. However, there exist flaws in many modern architectures that exacerbate their poor scalability, and result in throughput that is much worse than fundamentally required by the workload.

In this paper we identify two prevalent design principles that limit the multi-core scalability of many (but not all) transactional database systems on contended workloads: the multi-purpose nature of execution threads in these systems, and the lack of advanced planning of data access. We demonstrate the deleterious results of these design principles by implementing a prototype system, ORTHRUS, that is motivated by the principles of separation of database component functionality and advanced planning of transactions. We find that these two principles alone result in significantly improved scalability on high-contention workloads, and an order of magnitude increase in throughput for a non-trivial subset of these contended workloads.

1. INTRODUCTION

The maximum throughput that a database system is able to achieve is dependent on many factors, from the hardware on which it runs to the particular implementation details of the database software. While most of these factors can be overcome by spending more money, on better hardware or better software developers, throughput will always be fundamentally limited by the presence of *contended operations* in a workload.

The definition of a "contended operation" may vary depending on the user's requested isolation level of transactions, the ability of the database to prevent reads from conflicting with writes via multi-versioning and the semantic commutativity of operations. Nonetheless, unless no isolation whatsoever is required, there will always be certain operations that cannot be executed concurrently and the presence of many of these contended operations in a workload will necessarily limit throughput. Thus, adding more processors to a system, which enables more transactions to be processed in parallel, only increases throughput if the additional transactions that can be run do not conflict with the existing transactions that are currently running.

For decades, database systems had been designed for single processor machines. These conventional database architectures were ill suited for the abundant parallelism in multi-core hardware. As a consequence, they could not achieve scalable throughput across the entire spectrum of transactional workloads. Particularly problematic was the fact that conventional database architectures were not able to scale throughput on *low contention* workloads, despite the fact that low contention workloads have no fundamental limit to scalability. To address this gap between hardware and database software, most work on multi-core database systems has focused on eliminating fundamental scalability bottlenecks in these systems's design [21,23,48]. As a result of this research, today's state-of-the-art systems can achieve close to linear scalability in transactional throughput on low contention workloads.

Unfortunately, as recently demonstrated by Yu et al., multi-core database systems continue to be plagued by performance problems on *high contention* workloads [53]. For the fundamental reason described above, it is impossible to achieve linear scalability in high contention workloads; the throughput of a database system should taper as cores are added under high contention. However, the *actual* shortfall relative to linear scalability on high contention workloads is much worse than what is theoretically required by the nature of the contention in the workload. In some cases, in fact, throughput actually *decreases* as more cores are added. The problem is that the overhead of managing transactions, particularly that of concurrency control, is proportional to the amount of workload contention. At high levels of contention, concurrency control overhead takes up a non-trivial fraction of each transaction's total execution time. As a consequence, modern multi-core database systems achieve nowhere near the theoretical performance determined by the achievable concurrency in high contention workloads.

We attribute this poor performance under high contention to two design decisions that, to the best of our knowledge, are present in every widely-used transactional database system available today. First, despite compelling proposals to the contrary [17,37,38], database systems tend to assign responsibility for a particular transaction to a single thread [18]. Assigning a transaction to a single thread *conflates database functionality*, which leads to poor instruction and data cache locality [17]. Worse, this conflated functionality causes workload contention to directly impact physical contention in the database system (§2.1).

Second, database systems allow dynamic access of data without advanced planning of transactions' data access patterns. The negative side-effects of this design decision are most clearly present in database systems that use pessimistic concurrency control pro-

SIGMOD'16, June 26-July 01, 2016, San Francisco, CA, USA

ISBN 978-1-4503-3531-7/16/06...$15.00

DOI: http://dx.doi.org/10.1145/2882903.2882958

tocols based on logical locking. Such systems dynamically acquire each transaction's logical locks in an arbitrary order, which makes transactions susceptible to deadlocks. Any system which employs dynamic lock acquisition must therefore include a mechanism for handling deadlocks. Under high contention workloads, deadlock handling mechanisms are a significant source of overhead and can lead to wasted work due to transaction aborts (§2.2).

This paper proposes two design principles to address these overheads. First, we propose that database systems *partition functionality* across the cores of a single machine. Instead of using a single thread to perform both a transaction's logic *and* concurrency control on behalf of the transaction, we dedicate a set of threads to perform *only* concurrency control, and another set of threads to execute transaction logic. Concurrency control and execution threads cooperatively process transactions using explicit message-passing.

Second, we propose that database systems analyze transactions prior to their execution in order to predict their access patterns. These access patterns are used to coordinate access to data. Since almost all widely-used database systems use pessimistic locking to protect at least some types of data access, our focus in this paper is particularly within the context of pessimistic locking protocols. In this context, planning data access enables the implementation of a deadlock avoidance protocol, which circumvents the overhead of deadlock detection and resolution.

We built a prototype database system, ORTHRUS, based on the design principles of partitioned functionality and deadlock freedom. A notable aspect of ORTHRUS's design is the use of message passing between cores devoted to different functionalities. Although the use of explicit message-passing among a system's cores has been used in the context of multi-core operating systems [2,51] and programming models [5,33], to the best of our knowledge, ORTHRUS is the first multi-core database system to successfully use explicit message-passing to avoid physical contention on shared concurrency control data structures in the database system.

To summarize, the contributions of this paper are as follows:

- We identify two sources of overhead in state-of-the-art multi-core database systems that severely limit throughput under high contention workloads: conflated functionality (§2.1) and dynamic data access (§2.2).
- We propose two design principles to address this overhead; partitioning database functionality (§3.1) and planned data access (§3.2).
- Based on these design principles, we implement a prototype database system, ORTHRUS. We discuss techniques to make our design principles practical to implement (§3.3 and §3.4).
- We perform an extensive set of experiments in order to evaluate the multi-core scalability of ORTHRUS relative to an archetypal modern multi-core database system (§4).

2. PROBLEMS WITH EXISTING DESIGNS

2.1 Conflated functionality

As mentioned above, in most database systems, a single thread processes an individual transaction [18]. This single thread manages both the execution of the transaction's logic and the necessary interactions with the concurrency control module of the database system (e.g. a lock manager or the shared data structures needed for OCC validation). Several such threads concurrently execute on a single multi-core system. These concurrently executing threads make requests of the same concurrency control module[1]. This design pattern of multiple threads globally sharing a single concurrency control module can lead to severe scalability bottlenecks. We discuss these bottlenecks in this section.

Synchronization overhead. We first discuss the overhead associated with synchronization on concurrency control meta-data. In order to control the interleaving of concurrent transactions, any concurrency control protocol must associate some meta-data with the database's logical entities. The meta-data used is protocol dependent. For example, pessimistic locking protocols use a hash-table of lock requests on records [15], while optimistic and multi-version protocols associate timestamps with records [29, 48]. As part of the concurrency control protocol, several concurrent threads may need to read or write the meta-data associated with a particular database object. Concurrent threads must therefore synchronize their access to concurrency control meta-data. Note that synchronization is *not* implementation dependent; instead, it is intrinsic to any concurrency control protocol whose meta-data can be read or written by any database thread. Since meta-data is associated with database objects (such as records), contention for concurrency control meta-data is directly affected by workload contention; if a particular database record is popular, then threads will need to frequently synchronize on that record's meta-data. Unfortunately, on modern multi-core hardware, contention significantly degrades the performance of *atomic instructions* [4, 12, 13, 48]. These atomic instructions – such as *fetch-and-increment* and *compare-and-swap* – are the basic building blocks of both latch based and latch-free algorithms. Thus, under contention, both classes of algorithms are susceptible to severe performance degradation.

Data movement overhead. In addition to synchronization on concurrency control meta-data, another source of overhead in conventional database architectures is the *movement* of this meta-data across multiple cores. In order to access an object's meta-data, a thread must move the memory words corresponding to the meta-data into its CPU core's local cache. As multiple threads request access to a particular object's meta-data, the memory words corresponding to the meta-data are moved between cores. The movement of data between a machine's cores occurs because multiple threads are allowed to read or write the data. If a thread requires access to a latch-protected data-structure, the thread must first acquire the latch and then move the data-structure to its core. Only when these two steps complete can the thread actually access the data-structure. Since the latch is acquired first, it is held for the time it takes to move the data-structure. As a consequence, data-movement extends the duration for which latches are held. In the presence of contention, the increase in latch hold times can contribute to a decrease in concurrency.

In order to validate the deleterious effects of synchronization and data movement overhead, we ran a simple experiment to measure the scalability of short read-only transactions under two-phase locking on a high contention workload (see Appendix A.1 for a detailed description of the experimental setup). Since transactions are read-only, the workload is conflict free (despite the presence of contention). Figure 1 shows the results of the experiment. Two-phase

[1]The discussion that follows assumes a shared-memory architecture where all threads have access to the same shared memory where the concurrency control data structures sit. It should be noted that some database systems, such as H-Store [44] and Hyper [24], use a shared-nothing architecture across threads. Such systems do not suffer from the overheads associated with conflated functionality discussed in this section. However, they introduce other performance problems — namely agreement protocols across threads necessary to handle transactions that access data in multiple separate partitions. We explore this further in §4.

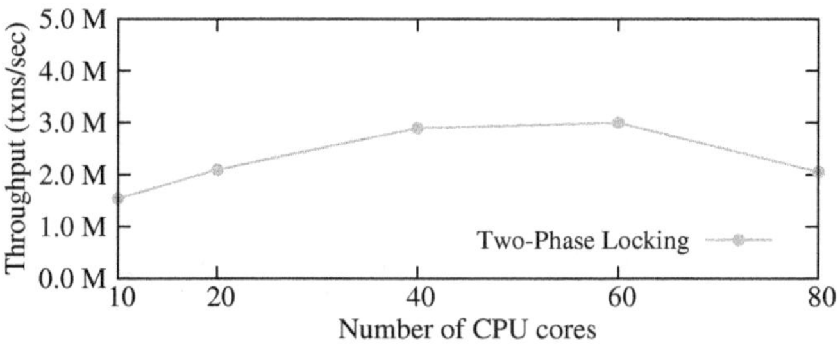

Figure 1: Scalability of read-only transactions under two-phase locking on a high contention workload.

locking is unable to scale beyond 40 cores despite the absence of conflicts and surprisingly *decreases* in performance. The inability to scale is due to synchronization and data movement overhead. The source of synchronization overhead is two-phase locking's use of atomic instructions on contended memory words to manipulate the table of lock requests. Data movement overhead is a consequence of multiple cores manipulating the same list of lock requests (due to multiple cores requesting read locks on the same records).

Instruction and data cache pollution. If a single thread executes both concurrency control and transaction logic, then the thread's CPU core must cache data and instructions corresponding to each of these two functions. The data and instructions corresponding to concurrency control, and transaction logic thus compete for a single core's cache. Concurrency control cache-lines therefore evicts transaction logic cache-lines, and vice-versa. This has the overall effect of increasing the duration of each transaction, which in turn decreases overall throughput.

All three reasons for performance degradation — synchronization overhead, data movement overhead, and cache pollution — have the effect of increasing a transaction's execution time. Not only does this increase in execution time per transaction necessarily reduce throughput by occupying system resources for longer periods of time, but the throughput reduction is compounded by the fact that increasing transaction time is particularly harmful in high contention settings. This is because conflicting transactions either have to block (in pessimistic schemes) or abort (in optimistic schemes). The longer it takes to execute a transaction, the higher the probability that a later conflicting transaction will abort or block behind the original transaction.

2.2 Dynamic concurrency control

Most database systems allow transactions to dynamically request records to read and write as they execute. This lack of advanced planning precludes opportunities to coordinate access to contended items in order to maximize concurrency. The clearest example of this are in systems that use two-phase locking (2PL) for concurrency control, where locks are acquired for a transaction as each data access request is processed. Allowing transactions to dynamically request access to records necessitates dynamic lock acquisition, which can lead to deadlocks. These systems must therefore implement mechanisms to deal with deadlocks.

Under high contention workloads, deadlock handling logic is a significant source of overhead. There are two reasons for this overhead: first, deadlock handling logic extends the duration for which locks are held; second, deadlocks waste useful work performed by transactions that must be aborted.

- Since a transaction cannot deadlock unless it has already acquired locks, any deadlock handling logic must be executed while locks are held. Therefore, deadlock handling logic extends the duration for which locks are held. The increased lock hold time means that conflicting transactions must wait longer to execute. Therefore, deadlock handling logic imposes a performance penalty regardless of whether a deadlock has actually occurred.
- If deadlock handling logic aborts a transaction, then any work performed by the transaction is wasted. Furthermore, if a transaction is allowed to directly write records (i.e., if transactions do not buffer their writes), then the database must also undo the aborted transaction's writes. In addition to wasted work, aborted transactions induce unnecessary waiting on conflicting transactions; if a conflicting transaction is made to wait on a transaction that is eventually aborted, then in retrospect the conflicting transaction could have been allowed to make progress without delay. Finally, under high contention workloads, deadlocks are simply more prevalent. Therefore, the wasted work and unnecessary waiting due to transaction aborts occur more often under such workloads.

3. ARCHITECTURE

In this section, we describe the architecture of a proof-of-concept system that we built, ORTHRUS. ORTHRUS is designed to ameliorate the scalability bottlenecks described in §2. ORTHRUS is not a complete database system — we did not build a relational query processor, a client communications manager, or many of the shared utilities that are present in most database systems. Instead, we just built the transaction management component of the system, with a particular focus on concurrency control, since the main impediment to scalability under high contention is concurrency control.

ORTHRUS implements locking-based pessimistic concurrency control. We choose a pessimistic scheme because ORTHRUS is targeted at workloads with high contention, and optimistic schemes are well-known to perform poorly under high contention due to excessive aborts — even recent proposals for multi-core optimized optimistic schemes (such as Silo [48] and Hekaton [29]) perform poorly under high contention [13].

Like most recently proposed architectures for transactional database systems, ORTHRUS assumes that the working set of data accessed by transactions can be held in main memory, since memory sizes are growing faster than transactional working sets [44]. As a consequence, ORTHRUS does not incur stalls to access data from disk. ORTHRUS therefore creates exactly the same number of threads as physical CPU cores and pins each thread to a single core, as is done in several other main-memory database systems [13, 14, 24, 34, 37, 38, 41, 44, 48, 53].

ORTHRUS's first key design feature is that it *partitions functionality* across the cores of a single machine. The thread pinned to each core on the server is devoted to a single narrow component of transaction processing. Since our focus in this paper is on concurrency control, ORTHRUS assigns cores one of two possible roles; concurrency control or transaction execution. Note, however, that this philosophy can extend to other roles within a database system. For instance, StagedDB successfully separated functionality across cores in the query processor component of the database system [17]. In ORTHRUS, concurrency control and transaction execution cores do not share any data-structures; concurrency control cores cannot read or write any data-structures on execution cores, and vice-versa. Instead of implicitly communicating through shared-memory, ORTHRUS uses explicit message-passing between concurrency control and execution threads.

The second key design feature of ORTHRUS is data access planning for the purpose of deadlock avoidance. In the rest of this section, we discuss these two key features of ORTHRUS's architecture in more detail.

3.1 Partitioned functionality

Logically, concurrency control threads perform the same function as that of a centralized lock manager. ORTHRUS partitions responsibility for database objects across concurrency control threads such that each database object is controlled by single thread. Thus, each concurrency control thread maintains meta-data for a disjoint subset of the database's objects. The meta-data on each concurrency control thread is exactly the same as in a centralized lock manager; each thread maintains a hash-table which maps keys to a list of transaction lock requests.

Execution threads do not contain instructions nor data pertaining to concurrency control; they are only responsible for performing each transaction's logic. Each transaction is assigned to a single execution thread, which is responsible for processing the transaction's logic in its entirety. Execution threads request locks by sending messages to the concurrency control threads responsible for those locks[2]. Message passing between execution threads and concurrency control threads is mediated via queues. Space is allocated in shared memory for an input queue to each concurrency control thread and an output queue from each concurrency control thread. Messages are passed via reads and writes to these queues.

Note that a naïve implementation of these queues leads to the same type of synchronization bottlenecks observed in traditional systems. If every transaction execution thread is allowed to write to a single input queue (for a particular concurrency control thread), then synchronization overhead will prevent a scalable implementation of message passing. To overcome this pitfall, our implementation assigns each concurrency control thread a *separate* queue for each execution thread. Thus, while we mention a single *logical* input queue to each concurrency control thread, its implementation consists of N physical queues, where N is the number of execution threads.

With the above implementation, each queue has only one writer (the associated execution thread) and one reader (the associated concurrency control thread). The queue can be therefore implemented using a standard latch-free circular buffer [33] to avoid synchronization between the reader and writer except in the rare case where the queue fills up. Consequently, our message passing implementation does not suffer from the synchronization costs that contended writes to shared-memory usually encounter.

Concurrency control threads serially process requests from their logical input queues. On dequeuing a request for locks from its input queue, a concurrency control thread checks the requested set of locks, and determines which of these locks are requested on objects in its local partition. For each lock on an object in its logical partition, the concurrency control inserts a lock request into its local hash-table. The concurrency control thread responds to an acquisition request only after it has granted all locks from the request of an individual transaction. Note that the response may take a while; the lock acquisition request may have to wait for prior conflicting requests to release locks (just as in conventional locking protocols). Instead of waiting for responses from concurrency control threads, execution threads begin working on other transactions. The interaction between execution and concurrency control threads during lock release is similar; the only difference is that concurrency control threads respond immediately because lock release requests are satisfied immediately.

Figure 2 shows an example of the interaction between a concurrency control thread and an execution thread. Transaction T_1's execution thread, E_1, requests locks on records A, B, and C (see §3.2 for why multiple requests are made together; for simplicity, we omit the details of the *lock mode* required on each of these records). E_1 writes these lock requests in a message that we label with name of the transaction (T_1). In order to acquire a lock on A, E_1 enqueues message T_1 in CC_1's input queue (**Step 1**). CC_1 dequeues T_1 from its input queue (**Step 2**) and checks the locks requested by T_1. In this particular example, of the locks requested by T_1 (A, B, and C), only A resides on CC_1's partition. CC_1 thus inserts a lock request on record A into its local lock table (**Step 3**). The details of how locks B and C are acquired, and how these requests end up in the input queues of the other concurrency control threads will be explained in §3.3.

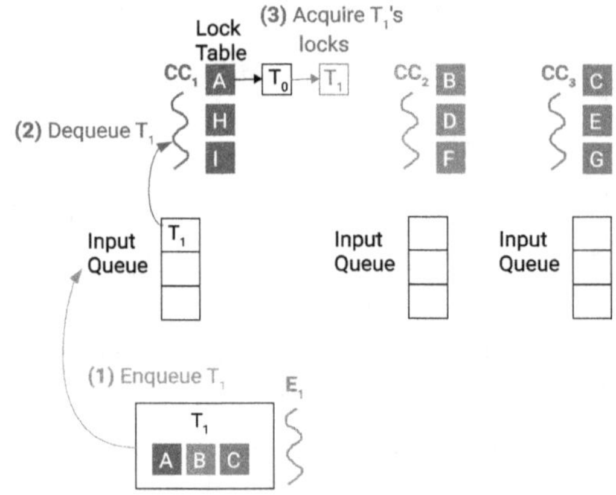

Figure 2: Concurrency control thread acquiring locks on behalf of an execution thread.

The communication pattern between execution and concurrency control threads is much like client-server communication in distributed systems; execution threads behave as clients, and concurrency control threads behave as servers. An execution thread's "request" is an explicit message asking the concurrency control thread to acquire or release a lock on behalf of a particular transaction. While centralized lock managers and ORTHRUS's concurrency control threads perform the same logical function (acquire and release logical locks), they each use two fundamentally different communication mechanisms. In conventional database systems, threads use the abstraction of a shared-address space to implicitly share data. Intuitively, data is shared *by default*. Since data is globally shared, each database thread can directly manipulate the data. In contrast, in ORTHRUS, the default mode of operation is to *eliminate* shared data among threads of different types; execution and concurrency control threads do not share any data. In order to acquire and release locks on database objects, an execution thread must request concurrency control threads to acquire locks on its behalf.

As a result of its physical separation of concurrency control and transaction execution concerns across threads, ORTHRUS guarantees that data is *never* implicitly shared across concurrency control and execution threads; the only way to share data is via message-passing. The consequence of this design principle is that ORTHRUS completely eliminates all overheads associated with conflated functionality (§2.1):

- **Synchronization overhead.** ORTHRUS partitions database objects across concurrency control threads. As a consequence, every lock acquisition and release request for a particular object is serviced by a single concurrency control thread; reads and writes of an object's meta-data are restricted to one thread. Therefore, this thread does not need to synchronize its access to any of the

[2]Since responsibility for objects is disjointedly partitioned across concurrency control threads, the set of locks required by a single transaction may reside on multiple concurrency control threads.

objects' meta-data it is responsible for. If multiple execution threads concurrently request locks on the same record, then the requests are handled by the same concurrency control thread.

- **Data movement overhead.** Since the locking operations on a particular database object are performed by a single thread, concurrency control meta-data (linked-lists of lock requests in the lock table) never need to move between threads. As a result, ORTHRUS does not suffer from any data movement overhead (for concurrency control).
- **Instruction and data cache pollution.** In ORTHRUS, execution and concurrency control threads perform two different functions. Execution threads are completely isolated from concurrency control threads; these two types of threads do not share any instructions nor data. As a consequence, ORTHRUS avoids the cache pollution that is inherent in conventional database implementations.

3.2 Deadlock avoidance

§2.2 discussed the various overheads associated with handling deadlocks in pessimistic locking-based concurrency control protocols. The fundamental problem behind the cost of deadlocks is the dynamic nature of data access, which in turn stems from a lack of advanced planning. Motivated by this observation, ORTHRUS plans data access prior to transaction execution, and leverages this advanced planning to perform a deadlock avoidance protocol instead of deadlock detection and resolution.

In more detail, ORTHRUS guarantees that deadlocks never occur by enforcing a locking discipline on execution threads. Execution threads must acquire locks on behalf of transactions in some well-defined order. To enforce this locking discipline, an execution thread cannot start to make lock requests (by sending messages to concurrency control threads) until it knows the complete set of locks requests that it will make for a particular transaction. Once an execution thread knows the complete set of locks requests, it can request locks from the appropriate concurrency control threads in order of the threads' unique identifiers. In order to avoid deadlock, these requests to concurrency control threads cannot occur concurrently — locks are requested from the next concurrency control thread after the locks from the previous thread have been granted.

In some cases, the set of locks that a transaction will request cannot be determined via a simple inspection of the transaction logic. Rather, there is a data-dependent access such that a part of the transaction needs to be executed before it can be determined what locks will be requested. In such a situation ORTHRUS uses the OLLP technique proposed by Thomson et al. in the context of Calvin [46]. In OLLP, a transaction is partially executed in "reconnaissance" mode in order to generate an estimate of the access footprint of the transaction. No locks are acquired during this reconnaissance, so no writes to the database state occur, and all reads are not assumed to be consistent (this is why the resulting access footprint is just an estimate and not a guarantee). This access estimate is then annotated as part of the transaction, which is submitted to the system to be actually run. Before starting to process a transaction, ORTHRUS acquires the locks that are indicated by the access estimate annotation. If, over the course of processing the transaction, an execution thread notices that it needs to access a record that it did not acquire a lock for at the beginning of the transaction (that is, the access estimate it received was incorrect), ORTHRUS updates the annotation, and then aborts and restarts the transaction with a new estimate. Ren et al. have shown that the extra overhead of OLLP (the reconnaissance phase) is generally a small percentage of actual transaction processing and that aborts due to incorrect access estimates are rare in practice [42].

A disadvantage of ORTHRUS's approach relative to dynamic lock acquisition is that there is a risk of locks being held for a longer period of time. This is because ORTHRUS immediately acquires all locks at the beginning of a transaction, while dynamic locking can acquire one lock at a time, interleaving lock acquisition with transaction execution. For example, if a lock on a highly contended record is only needed for the last operation of a transaction, dynamic lock acquisition only needs to hold the lock for a very short period of time (just the end of the transaction). Meanwhile ORTHRUS must hold the lock for the entire transaction.

Note that increased lock hold time is not a disadvantage under low contention. Increased lock hold time only hurts performance under high contention workloads. However, it is precisely under high contention that deadlocks are more frequent, and the cost of deadlock detection increases (§2.2). We hypothesize that ORTHRUS's increased lock hold time is more than offset by avoiding the decrease in concurrency and wasted work due to deadlock detection and aborts, respectively, in dynamic locking. We experiment with this hypothesis in §4.

3.3 Optimizations

ORTHRUS's design philosophy of partitioning concurrency control and execution functionality across the threads of a database server addresses several sources of overhead in conventional database systems. However, since concurrency control and execution threads communicate with each other via explicit message-passing, ORTHRUS introduces new sources of overhead. The single biggest source of overhead we had to overcome was that of *asynchrony* in the interactions between execution and concurrency control threads.

In ORTHRUS, concurrency control threads run a tight loop which sequentially processes requests for lock acquisition or release. At any given point in time, a concurrency control thread may have multiple outstanding lock acquisition or release requests. Thus, execution threads' requests may experience queuing delay before being processed. To prevent these queuing delays from wasting CPU cycles, execution threads do not synchronously wait on responses from concurrency control threads. After sending a request to a concurrency control thread, an execution thread checks whether any older requests have received responses. If yes, the execution thread resumes the execution of the corresponding transaction. If not, the execution thread begins executing a new transaction. Consequently, when a concurrency control thread does eventually respond to a lock request, the execution thread will likely be in the middle of working on a different transaction, and does not resume the original transaction immediately. Execution threads' lock acquisition and release requests are therefore *asynchronous*.

On its own, asynchrony is not a source of overhead. However, the interaction of asynchrony with the higher level concept of logical locking can hamper concurrency. The queuing delays experienced by requests and responses extend the duration for which logical locks are held. For instance, if an execution thread requests a lock on record A for transaction T, the time between when the lock is acquired by the appropriate concurrency control thread, and the time the execution thread resumes the execution of T represents time for which the lock on A is needlessly held. Furthermore, the overhead due to queuing delay is compounded when an execution thread requests locks from multiple concurrency control threads. This is because our deadlock avoidance mechanism requires that lock requests to these concurrency control threads occur sequentially (as explained in §3.2). For instance, if the execution thread from the example above subsequently requests locks on B and C, the lock on A is held while requests and responses on B and C experience queuing delays.

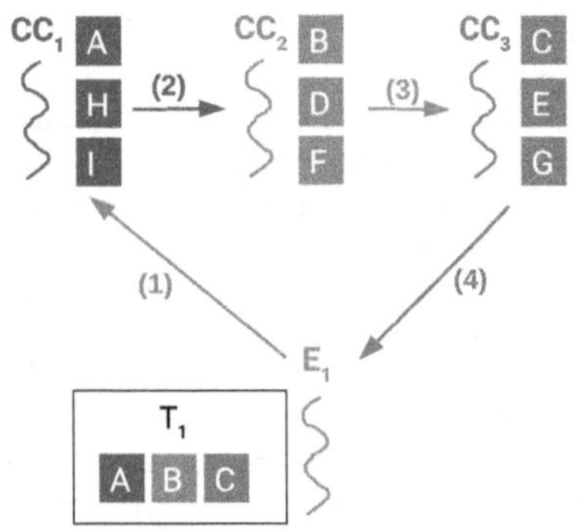

Figure 3: Concurrency control thread acquiring locks on behalf of an execution thread.

In order to reduce the impact of queuing delay, ORTHRUS minimizes the number of messages sent between threads. The basic idea is to allow concurrency control threads to forward lock request messages to other concurrency control threads on behalf of an execution thread. In other words, instead of paying two message delays for all concurrency control threads involved in a transaction, each concurrency control thread forwards the request directly to the next thread involved in that transaction (which reduces the number of message delays per concurrency control thread to one).

Figure 3 shows an example of how multiple locks are acquired. Transaction T_1 requires locks on records A, B, and C. As mentioned in §3.2, to avoid deadlocks, ORTHRUS requires all transactions to request locks from concurrency control threads in a well-defined order. In Figure 3, this order is CC_1, followed by CC_2, followed by CC_3[3].

Execution threads request the first of these concurrency control threads to acquire locks on its partition. E_1 therefore requests CC_1 to acquire T_1's locks (**Step 1**). For every lock required on later concurrency control threads, the concurrency control thread itself forwards the request. For instance, in order to acquire a lock on record B, CC_1 forwards T_1 to CC_2 (**Step 2**). Similarly, after acquiring a lock on record B, CC_2 forwards T_1 to CC_3 (**Step 3**). The last concurrency control thread that needs to acquire a lock on a transaction returns the transaction back to the execution thread. In this case, CC_3 returns T_1 to E_1 (**Step 4**).

If this optimization were not in place, E_1 would have to request locks to each concurrency control thread directly. First it would send a message to CC_1 to acquire a lock on A. CC_1 then responds to E_1 once the lock on A has been acquired by T_1. E_1 then repeats this process for each concurrency control thread. The number of messages per execution-concurrency control thread interaction would thus be two. Therefore, the total number of messages sent in the case of execution thread mediated lock acquisition is $2(N_{cc})$ (where N_{cc} is the number of concurrency control threads from which the execution thread requires locks). On the other hand, ORTHRUS's optimized lock acquisition procedure requires $N_{cc} + 1$ messages (one message to each concurrency control thread, and one last message to the execution thread). The reduced number of messages is directly correlated with decreased waiting due to asynchrony.

Note that concurrency control threads may be subject to over- and under-utilization due to workload skew [39]. ORTHRUS can reuse prior techniques for addressing utilization imbalance in shared-nothing systems [6,39,45] in order to partition data among concurrency control threads.

[3]In Figure 3, each thread is assumed to have its own input queue (as in Figure 2). However, we do not show them in the figure.

3.4 Alternative architectures

In ORTHRUS, the set of database objects is partitioned across concurrency control threads. This design ensures that concurrency control threads do not share any data, thereby avoiding data movement and synchronization overhead (§2.1). Note, however, that partitioning objects across concurrency control threads is orthogonal to the design principle of separating functionality. ORTHRUS's use of partitioning is just one possible implementation of locking-based concurrency control.

A plausible alternative implementation would be to share a single lock table across all concurrency control threads. A single concurrency control thread could then obtain all the logical locks needed by a particular transaction. Execution threads could request any one of several concurrency control threads to acquire locks on its behalf. Although such an implementation would be subject to synchronization and data movement overhead, this synchronization is only across the concurrency control threads — a much smaller number of threads than the total number of threads in the system. Furthermore, the database system has the flexibility to limit the impact of these synchronization overheads. For example, the system could choose to assign concurrency control threads to execute on cores within a single NUMA socket.

Note that this flexibility to choose the number of threads to dedicate to each function is a direct consequence of the design principle of separating functionality. Conventional database systems do not have this flexibility because a single thread performs all the work entailed in executing a transaction. Furthermore, the separation of functionality enables a single system to support more than one implementation of a particular sub-system (such as the partitioned and non-partitioned lock table). Since components interact through narrow message-passing interfaces, the actual deployed implementation of a sub-system, such as concurrency control, can vary depending on system parameters, such as number of cores, number of NUMA sockets, and so forth.

4. EVALUATION

We run our experiments on a single 80-core machine, consisting of eight 10-core Intel E7-8850 processors and 128GB of memory. The operating system used is Ubuntu 14.04. All our experiments are performed in memory (none of our implementations utilize secondary storage). In all experiments, the number of threads used is equal to the number of cores; we pin a single long running thread to each CPU core (see §3.1).

We compare ORTHRUS against an implementation of two-phase locking (2PL) within the same ORTHRUS transaction management codebase. Our 2PL implementation uses a lock-table to store information about the locks acquired and requested by transactions. The lock-table is implemented as a hash-table. We implemented two important multi-core specific optimizations to improve the scalability of our 2PL implementation. First, the lock manager hash-table uses per-bucket latches instead of a single latch to protect the entire table. Per-bucket latches allow our 2PL implementation to avoid contention and overly conservative serialization on a single global latch. In addition to per-bucket latches, our 2PL implementation does not acquire high-level intention locks; transactions only acquire fine-grained logical locks on individual records. As a consequence, latch contention occurs only when multiple threads try to acquire or release logical locks on the same record. Second, our 2PL implementation *never* interacts with a memory allocator. Each database thread manually manages a pre-allocated thread-local pool of memory. Avoiding interaction with a memory allocator (such as malloc) removes superfluous synchronization in the operating system's memory management logic and the memory allocator's logic. This allows us to isolate the sources of synchronization overhead to those in our own implementation.

To evaluate the overhead of deadlock handling in 2PL, we implement three different deadlock detection/avoidance mechanisms:

Wait-for graph. We use a graph to track the dependencies between transactions waiting to acquire logical locks, and the current holders of the lock. We only add edges to the wait-for graph if a transaction requests a lock, but finds that the lock is currently held in a conflicting mode by another transaction. The presence of a cycle in the wait-for graph implies that the transactions that constitute the cycle have deadlocked. In order to scale across multiple cores, our implementation avoids the use of a global latch to protect the entire graph. Instead, each database thread maintains a local partition of the wait-for graph, as is done by Yu et al. [53].

Wait die. Unlike the wait-for graph deadlock detection technique, which allows transactions to deadlock, and then detects and resolves deadlocks after the fact, wait die proactively avoids deadlocks by aborting transactions if they are suspected to be involved in a deadlock. In wait die, each transaction is assigned a timestamp prior to its execution, and the timestamp is used to determine whether or not the transaction is allowed to wait for a logical lock. If a transaction fails to immediately acquire a lock, then wait die only allows the transaction to wait on prior transactions if its timestamp is smaller than that of the current lock holder. If not, the transaction is aborted and restarted. Thus, wait die prioritizes older transactions (transactions with smaller timestamps), over younger transactions (transactions with larger timestamps). Each database thread uses the local timestamp counter on its CPU core to assign transactions their timestamps. Reading from the the core-local timestamp counter is low-overhead and contention-free. Core-local timestamp counters are therefore a cheap scalable source of monotonically increasing timestamps.

Dreadlocks. This state-of-the-art deadlock detection technique was proposed by Koskinen et al. in the context of mutual exclusion spin locks [26] and is used in the multi-core optimized version of the Shore database system (Shore-MT) [22]. Each transaction, T, maintains a digest, a data-structure which indicates the set of *other* transactions that T waits on for locks. Intuitively, a transaction's digest is a compact representation of its localized wait-for graph; T's digest contains the *transitive closure* of the transactions it waits for. If T fails to acquire a lock, T performs a set-union of its digest with the digest of the current lock holder. If T ever finds itself in its own digest, then it means that T's transitive closure contains a cycle, and a deadlock has occurred. Note that digests are amenable to a simple bitmap representation, and that a particular transaction's digest is always updated by the thread responsible for running the transaction. However, other threads can *read* the transaction's digest. As a consequence, updates to a transaction's digest can be performed without the use of latches [26].

We also include a version of 2PL that uses the deadlock avoidance protocol described in §3.2. We call this baseline *Deadlock-free locking*. This deadlock-free implementation analyzes each transaction prior to its execution in order to obtain its read- and write-sets and acquires locks in the lexicographical order in advance of transaction execution (as described in §3.2). Thus, we can compare our version of deadlock avoidance with three other widely-used techniques for handling deadlocks in 2PL systems.

4.1 Quantifying deadlock handling overhead

We begin our evaluation with experiments to show the overhead of the three deadlock handling mechanisms we implemented — wait-for graph, wait die, and dreadlocks — and compare them with

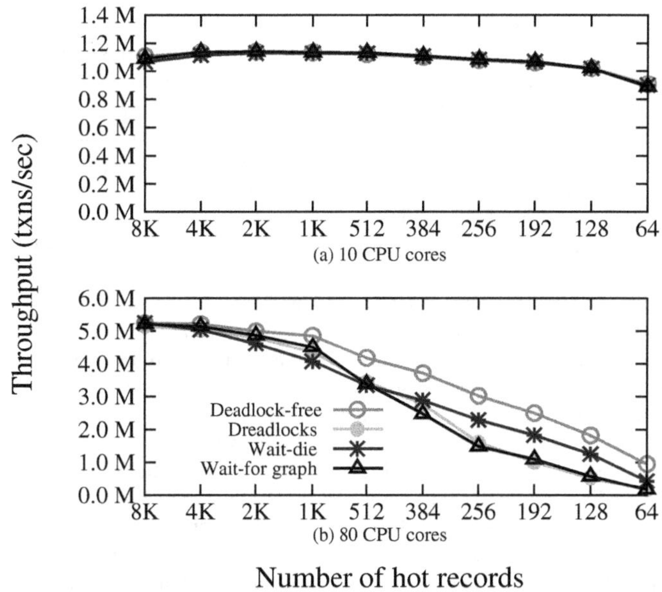

Figure 4: Throughput while varying the number of hot records in the database. (a) Number of database cores = 10. (b) Number of database cores = 80.

the simple, deadlock-free implementation of 2PL discussed above. We measure the throughput of these mechanisms under varying levels of contention.

Our benchmark uses a single table of 10,000,000 records. Each record's size is 1,000 bytes. The workload consists of transactions that each perform read-modify-write operations on ten records. Of the ten records updated by each transaction, we pick two records uniformly at random from a set of "hot" records, while the remaining eight are selected uniformly at random from a set of "cold" records. We vary the level of contention in the workload by varying the number of hot records. Intuitively, if transactions pick two records from a small set of hot records, then the probability that they will conflict is higher than if the set is large. We run two experiments, the first dedicates 10 CPU cores to the database system, while the second uses all 80 CPU cores of our test machine.

Figure 4(a) shows the throughput of each deadlock handling protocol when the database runs on 10 CPU cores. The number of hot records decreases as we move from left to right along the x-axis. As a consequence, contention *increases* from left to right. As expected, each system's throughput decreases with increasing contention, because as contention increases, the likelihood of conflicts between transactions increases. This, in turn, limits the amount of concurrency the database system is able to exploit. However, the relative difference in throughput between each deadlock handling mechanism is small.

Next, we perform the same experiment with 80 CPU cores. Figure 4(b) shows the results. Increasing the core count has two effects. First, it increases overall contention in the system since there are more active threads competing for the same logical data and internal data structures. Note that this is a different type of contention increase than the x-axis in the graphs which are generated via increasing logical contention by reducing the hot-set size. By increasing the number of active transactions, the overhead of the deadlock management schemes all increase as the data structures that they have to access (e.g., linked lists of waiting transactions) all become larger. (2) It causes the system to encounter NUMA effects as different cores are located in different NUMA sockets, increasing the cost of passing active data between cores (the 10 cores in the previous experiment are located on a single socket). So, for example, the cost to acquire a latch on the data structures maintained by the deadlock handling schemes increases. Combined, these two effects (1) increase the overhead of the deadlock handling schemes, and (2) increase logical contention to the point where deadlock is more frequent, such that avoiding deadlocks a priori is superior to *dynamically* avoiding or detecting them.

The performance of the wait-for graph mirrors that of dreadlocks across the spectrum of contention. Both wait-for graph and dreadlocks effectively use the same algorithm to detect deadlocks — they only use different data-structures to represent the same information (a bitmap vs. an explicit dependency graph). Logically, however, the two algorithms are equivalent: both abort transactions upon detecting a cycle in their respective graph representations. Hence, both have poor performance at the right-hand side of the graph when logical contention is high, and deadlocks are frequent.

Wait-for graph and dreadlocks outperform wait die in the low to medium range of contention (the left-hand side of Figure 4(b)). This is because wait die suffers from false positives — it aborts transactions despite the absence of deadlocks. However, on the right-hand side of the graph, deadlocks are frequent, and the delay inherent in the dreadlocks and wait-for graph schemes, because they first detect deadlocks before resolving them, causes locks to be held by deadlocked transactions for longer periods of time before they abort, further exacerbating the effect of high contention. Thus, the wait-die approach of "giving up" early has the benefit of not allowing deadlocks to increase lock hold times.

Most importantly, Figure 4(b) indicates that *Deadlock-free locking always* outperforms all three deadlock handling mechanisms. There are two reasons for this. First, when deadlocks do not occur too often (in the middle of the graph), *Deadlock-free locking* outperforms the other schemes due to its low-overhead. *Deadlock-free locking* only has to analyze transactions's read- and write-sets in advance, and request locks in the correct order, while the other schemes are burdened by running deadlock handling logic (wait-for graph and dreadlocks) and aborting transactions due to false positives (wait die). Second, by eliminating the possibility of deadlocks, *Deadlock-free locking* does not suffer from aborts, and the subsequent wasted work due to retries. *Deadlock-free locking*'s advantage over deadlock handling techniques grows with increasing contention. At the right-most point in the graph, *Deadlock-free locking*'s throughput is 2.2x, 5.5x and 5.5x times that of wait die, dreadlocks and the wait-for graph, respectively.

Figure 4(b) validates the fact that under high contention workloads, deadlock handling logic is a significant impediment to multicore throughput; dynamic deadlock handling techniques are *always* outperformed by *Deadlock-free locking*. Furthermore, the fact that throughput drops so drastically from 10 to 80 CPU cores indicates the problem will only get worse with increasing core counts.

Appendix B presents additional experiments on deadlock overhead on alternative workloads.

4.2 Tradeoffs in thread allocation

Until this point, we have experimented with just the benefit of deadlock avoidance in high contention scenarios. We now experiment with the full system design of ORTHRUS including its partitioned functionality.

ORTHRUS's partitioned functionality means that each database thread can be assigned one of two roles; concurrency control or transaction execution. Given a fixed number of threads, ORTHRUS must apportion threads to either concurrency control or execution. This section shows the performance implications of various concurrency control and execution thread allocations. We run one experiment in which 80 threads (corresponding to our test machine's 80 physical CPU cores) are made available to ORTHRUS. We experiment with multiple ORTHRUS configurations. In each configuration, we fix the number of concurrency control threads, and measure throughput while varying the number execution threads.

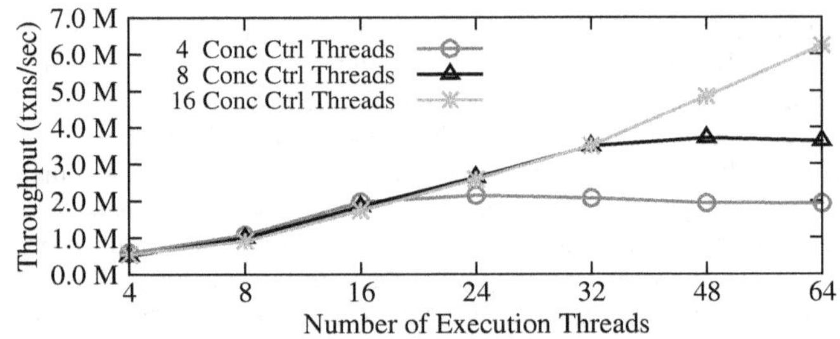

Figure 5: Execution thread scalability in ORTHRUS under various fixed concurrency control thread configurations.

We configure the database with a single table of 10,000,000 rows, each of size 1,000 bytes. The workload consists of transactions performing 10 read-modify-write operations on unique records. The records in transactions' read- and write-sets are selected uniformly at random from the set of 10,000,000 database rows. Each transaction acquires all its locks from a single concurrency control thread (we experiment with transactions that acquire locks on multiple concurrency control threads in §4.3, and §4.4).

Figure 5 shows the results of the experiment. We experiment with three concurrency control configurations, each corresponding to a curve in Figure 5. In each concurrency control configuration, throughput initially increases with increasing execution thread count. This is because on the left-hand-side of Figure 5, there are not enough execution threads to fully utilize the available concurrency control threads. Throughput continues increasing until a sufficient number execution threads saturate the available concurrency control threads. At this point, throughput plateaus. The point at which each curve plateaus is directly proportional to the number of concurrency control threads; more concurrency control threads can sustain a higher aggregate throughput than fewer concurrency control threads.

While ORTHRUS provides the flexibility to configure the number of concurrency control and execution threads, the choice of the optimal division of threads between concurrency control and execution is not obvious. Too few execution threads causes underutilization of concurrency control threads, and vice-versa. Fortunately, ORTHRUS uses a staged event driven architecture (SEDA) [50]; ORTHRUS's concurrency control and execution modules correspond to SEDA stages communicating via explicit-message passing. Systems based on SEDA are amenable to dynamic allocation of resources (such as threads) based on load. In order to decide on the optimal allocation of threads between concurrency control and execution, therefore, ORTHRUS can use techniques for dynamic resource allocation on SEDA systems.

4.3 Multi-partition transactions

This section explores the cost of multi-partition transactions (transactions that need locks located on multiple concurrency control threads) in ORTHRUS. We compare performance against *Deadlock-free locking* (which has no partitioning whatsoever), and a fully-partitioned, "shared-nothing" system, where no memory is shared between partitions. Our implementation is based on the single-node (not distributed) version of the architecture of H-Store/VoltDB and HyPer [24,44]. This *Partitioned-store* baseline is similar to the corresponding implementation by Tu et al. in Silo [48]. *Partitioned-store* physically partitions data across database worker threads, such

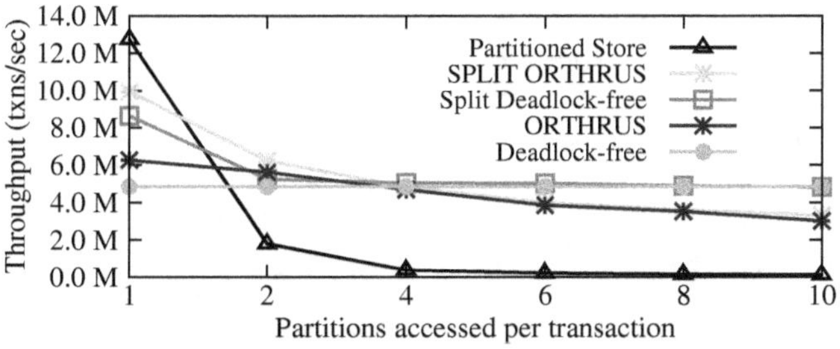

Figure 6: Performance of ORTHRUS and *Partitioned-store* as the number of partitions accessed per transaction is varied.

that each worker has its own local hash-table index. For concurrency control, *Partitioned-store* associates a coarse-grain partition-level spinlock with each worker. In order to execute a transaction, a worker thread obtains partition-level spinlocks on every partition that the transaction needs to access. If every transaction is single-partition, the corresponding workers will only acquire their own partition-level spinlocks. In the single-partition case, therefore, workers' lock acquisitions never conflict with each other. Furthermore, in the single-partition case, spinlock acquisition has minimal overhead because the lock is cached by the corresponding worker.

We run two experiments, both highlighting the effect of multi-partition transactions on performance. The first experiment compares the throughput of each system while varying the number of partitions accessed by each transaction. The second varies the fraction of multi-partition transactions in the workload.

The experiments in this section use a database which consists of a single table with 10,000,000 records of size 1,000 bytes each. These 10,000,000 records are uniformly spread across *Partitioned-store*'s physical partitions. Similarly, 10,000,000 logical locks are uniformly spread across ORTHRUS's concurrency control threads. Both experiments use transactions which perform 10 read-modify-write operations. In *Partitioned-store*, multi-partition transactions span physical partitions. Similarly, multi-partition transactions in ORTHRUS request locks from multiple concurrency control threads.

Vary partitions per transaction. Figure 6 shows the performance of ORTHRUS, *Partitioned-store* and *Deadlock-free locking* while varying the number of partitions accessed by each transaction. When transactions are restricted to a single partition, *Partitioned-store* outperforms ORTHRUS and *Deadlock-free locking*. There are two primary reasons for this. First, *Partitioned-store* requires no concurrency control when transactions are restricted to a single partition. Second, *Partitioned-store* index structures have better cache locality because indexes are physically partitioned across worker threads. As transactions access two or more partitions, however *Partitioned-store* experiences a sharp drop in throughput. *Partitioned-store*'s drop in throughput is due to its use of coarse-grain concurrency control. *Partitioned-store* isolates transactions at the level of partitions; a pair of transactions conflict if they both access the same partition. In contrast, ORTHRUS and *Deadlock-free locking* isolate transactions at the granularity of read- and write-conflicts on individual records.

We also find that ORTHRUS's throughput decreases as transactions access more partitions. However, unlike *Partitioned-store*, ORTHRUS's drop in throughput is more modest. ORTHRUS's throughput drops because of the increase in the number of messages required to acquire a transaction's locks. In the single-partition case, each transaction acquires its locks from a single concurrency control thread. However, as transactions' locks are distributed over a greater number of concurrency control threads, the number of message hops during lock acquisition increases. In particular, the number of messages required to acquire a transaction's locks is equal to $N_{cc} + 1$, where N_{cc} is the number of concurrency control threads on which a transaction's locks reside (§3.3). Clearly, as N_{cc} increases, the number of messages involved in acquiring a single transaction's locks increases. Figure 6 also shows that *Deadlock-free locking*'s throughput remains unchanged as the number of partitions accessed by a transaction increases. *Deadlock-free locking* is a shared-everything system, and hence is not subject to additional overhead in the presence of multi-partition transactions.

To better understand the performance characteristics of the curves in Figure 6, we physically partitioned indexes across ORTHRUS and *Deadlock-free locking*'s worker threads[4]. These curves are marked SPLIT ORTHRUS and *Split Deadlock-free*, respectively. This optimization puts all three systems on the same level as *Partitioned-store* with respect to cache locality, and any remaining difference between *Partitioned-store* and these two new curves can be attributed to concurrency control.

When analyzing the difference between *Partitioned-store* and SPLIT ORTHRUS/*Split Deadlock-free* and comparing this difference to the difference between *Partitioned-store* and ORTHRUS/*Deadlock-free locking*, we can conclude that when transactions are restricted to a single partition, *Partitioned-store*'s main advantage over ORTHRUS and *Deadlock-free locking* is due to the smaller cache footprint of partitioned indexes. *Partitioned-store*'s throughput is about 2x and 2.6x that of ORTHRUS and *Deadlock-free locking*, respectively, while its advantage over SPLIT ORTHRUS and *Split Deadlock-free* is a more modest 1.3x and 1.5x, respectively. Furthermore, as transactions access more partitions, the performance of the partitioned variants of ORTHRUS and *Deadlock-free locking* converge to their non-partitioned counterparts. This confirms that *Partitioned-store*'s poor performance under multi-partition transactions is due to its use of coarse-grain concurrency control.

It should be noted that a big advantage of ORTHRUS and *Deadlock-free locking* over *Partitioned-store* is that these systems by default do not require a user to be concerned about finding a near-perfect data partitioning such that the vast majority of a transactions in a workload will only access a single-partition. However, if a good or near-perfect partitioning is available for a particular workload, there is no reason why ORTHRUS and *Deadlock-free locking* cannot benefit from it by partitioning their indexes across worker threads accordingly. In other words, although our primary motivation for introducing SPLIT ORTHRUS and *Split Deadlock-free* was in order to break down the performance differences between *Partitioned-store* and ORTHRUS/*Deadlock-free locking*, if a good data partitioning is available for a workload, SPLIT ORTHRUS could be used instead of ORTHRUS, and achieve much closer performance to partitioned stores on single-partitioned transactions, while maintaining its significant advantages over partitioned-stores for multi-partition transactions.

Vary fraction of multi-partition transactions. Although Figure 6 shows the effect of multi-partition transactions on each system's throughput, realistic workloads involve a mix of single-partition and multi-partition transactions. In this experiment, we evaluate a workload consisting of both single- and multi-partition transactions. We vary the percentage of multi-partition transactions in the workload. Multi-partition transactions run on exactly two partitions.

Figure 7 shows the result of the experiment. As in the previous experiment, we find that *Partitioned-store* outperforms ORTHRUS and *Deadlock-free locking* when all transactions are single-partition (0% multi-partition transactions). *Partitioned-store*'s throughput decreases as the fraction of multi-partition transactions increases.

[4]Tu et al. perform a similar analysis in Silo [48]

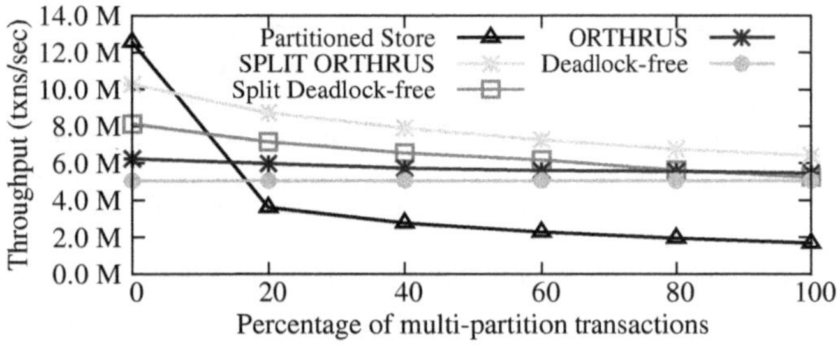

Figure 7: Performance of ORTHRUS and *Partitioned-store* as the percentage of multi-partition transactions is varied.

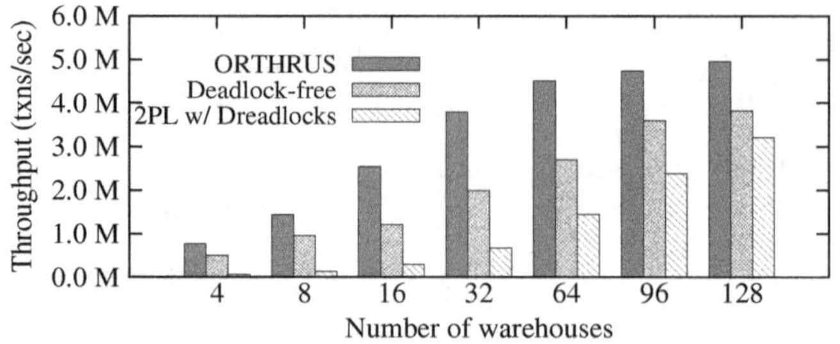

Figure 8: TPC-C NewOrder and Payment throughput, varying number of warehouses. Each system uses 80 CPU cores.

This is expected because we already saw in Figure 6 that *Partitioned-store*'s performance decreases dramatically as soon an transactions access more than one partition.

ORTHRUS's throughput also decreases as the fraction of multi-partition transactions increases. As elaborated in the previous experiment, this is due to the increase in the number of messages required to acquire transactions' locks. However, despite the decrease in throughput, ORTHRUS *always* outperforms *Deadlock-free locking* (even when the percentage of multi-partition transaction is 100%). Although both ORTHRUS and *Deadlock-free locking* use the same underlying locking-based protocol, ORTHRUS's partitioned functionality allows concurrency control and execution threads to better utilize data- and instruction-caches (§3.1).

Finally, Figure 7 also evaluates SPLIT ORTHRUS and *Split Deadlock-free*. These curves reinforce the fact that *Partitioned-store*'s main advantage relative to ORTHRUS and *Deadlock-free locking* is cache locality, and this advantage can be duplicated by ORTHRUS and *Deadlock-free locking* if a good data partitioning is available. Nonetheless, *Partitioned-store*'s total elimination of concurrency control for single-partition transactions prevents SPLIT ORTHRUS and *Split Deadlock-free* from matching its performance at the extreme left-hand side of the graph.

4.4 Performance under contention

This section evaluates the performance of ORTHRUS under contention. We compare ORTHRUS against *Deadlock-free locking*, and 2PL with dreadlocks. The experiments in this section run a subset of the TPC-C benchmark, while we experiment with the YCSB benchmark in Appendix A. As is common practice, our TPC-C implementation does not model client "think" time, and transactions are executed as one-shot stored procedures [1,41,44,48]. We restrict our evaluation to TPC-C's NewOrder and Payment transactions. These two transactions make up the vast majority of the benchmark; approximately 45% and 43% of transactions in the full TPC-C mix are NewOrder and Payment transactions, respectively. Furthermore, NewOrder and Payment are short update transactions[5], and thereby put greater stress on concurrency control. Our evaluation therefore uses an equal mix of NewOrder and Payment transactions; both types of transaction are equally likely to occur.

TPC-C's database conforms to a tree-based schema [44]. Most tables in TPC-C have a foreign key dependency on the "root" Warehouse table. Excluding the Warehouse table itself, out of eight tables in the TPC-C database, only one, Item, does not contain a foreign key dependency on the Warehouse table. TPC-C's Item table is read-only. Hence, none of our baselines perform any concurrency control on reads to Item table's rows. In TPC-C, the $warehouse\_id$ attribute is the primary key of the Warehouse table, and foreign key in all other tables (apart from Item). ORTHRUS partitions database tables across concurrency control threads based on each row's $warehouse\_id$ attribute. Our evaluation adheres to the TPC-C specification of requiring 10% of NewOrder and 15% of Payment transactions to span two warehouses. Therefore, approximately 12.5% of transactions in our evaluation require locks from two concurrency control threads. Some Payment transactions' read- and write-sets are deducible only upon reading the value of a secondary index. In particular, 60% of Payment transactions must find a Customer by a secondary index on customers' last name. For this subset of transactions, ORTHRUS must speculatively read this secondary index in order to obtain the transaction's read- and write-sets using the OLLP protocol described in §3.2.

4.4.1 *Throughput under varying contention*

Since the TPC-C database schema is tree-based, and rooted at the Warehouse table, contention on all tables (except the read-only Items table) can be controlled by varying the number of records in the Warehouse table; decreasing the number of warehouses increases the level of contention in the workload. Figure 8 shows the throughput of each system while varying the number of warehouses. The number of warehouses increases from left to right along the x-axis, therefore, contention *decreases* from left to right.

When the number of warehouses is small, we find that ORTHRUS significantly outperforms 2PL. When the number of warehouses is small, both transactions update highly contended records. Payment updates two records, one each from the Warehouse and District tables. NewOrder updates a single District record. *Deadlock-free locking* suffers from latching overhead associated with acquiring logical locks on each of these records (synchronization overhead). Furthermore, the linked-list corresponding to a bucket in the lock table must also be moved across cores (data movement overhead).

In addition to suffering from the same sources of overhead as *Deadlock-free locking*, 2PL with dreadlocks must also execute deadlock handling logic, which further reduces throughput (see §4.1). Dreadlocks requires all transactions waiting on a particular logical lock to spin on the lock holder's digest. When the lock holder eventually releases the lock, it updates its digest, which propagates to the threads spinning on the digest. In order to read the new value of the digest, the readers' cached values of the digest must be invalidated and then reloaded with the new value. Note that this cache coherence overhead is *in addition* to the cache coherence overhead associated with latch acquisition and linked-list traversal experienced by *Deadlock-free locking*. Furthermore, we found that the actual occurrence of deadlocks on the TPC-C workload was rare. 2PL with Dreadlocks is thus subject to severe cache coherence overhead despite the fact that the workload itself is mostly deadlock free.

Unlike 2PL, ORTHRUS does not experience cache-coherence induced overhead. In ORTHRUS, a single concurrency control thread is responsible for processing every lock operation on a particular record. Concurrency control threads therefore require no synchronization to process lock acquisition or release requests. Further-

[5]Compared to long running transactions such as StockLevel

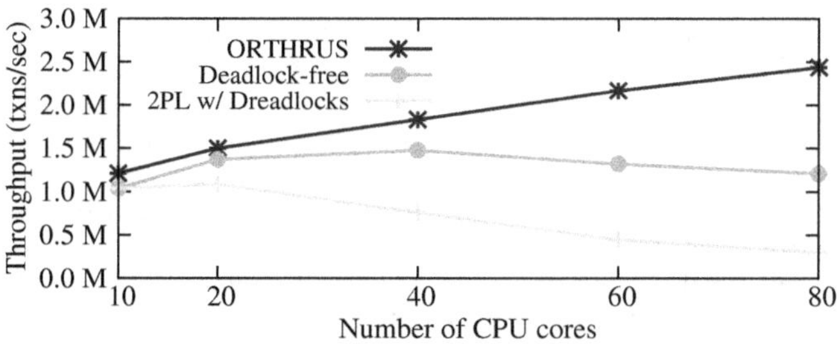

Figure 9: TPC-C throughput while increasing core count. Number of warehouses = 16.

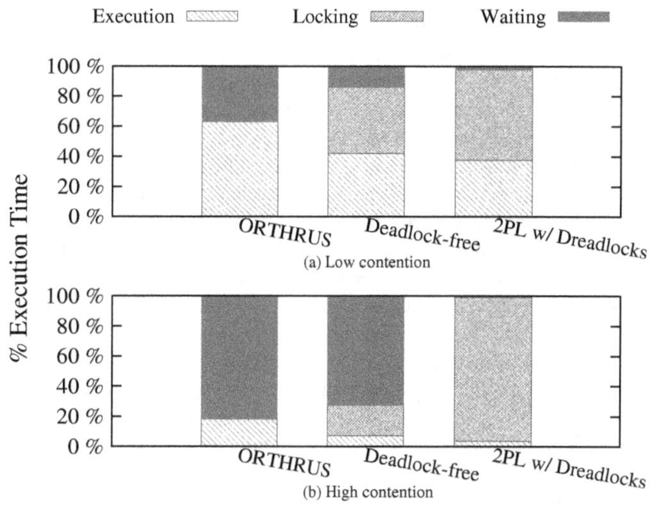

Figure 10: Execution thread CPU time breakdown on TPC-C with 80 threads. (a): 128 Warehouses (low contention). (b): 16 Warehouses (high contention)

more, the meta-data associated with the locks (the linked list of lock requests) does not need to move across cores. On the contrary, since Warehouse and District records are popular, the linked lists of lock requests on these records experience good cache locality on concurrency control threads. As mentioned previously, 10% of NewOrder and 15% of Payment transactions span two warehouses. Since we assign a single concurrency control thread to a particular warehouse, this subset of NewOrder and Payment transactions must interact with two concurrency control threads. These transactions are therefore subject to greater lock hold times on popular records due to asynchrony (§3.3). Despite the longer duration for which contended locks are held, ORTHRUS is able to significantly outperform both locking implementations.

As the number of warehouses increases, the level of contention in the workload decreases. As a consequence, both locking systems experiences lower synchronization overhead. However, despite the decrease in contention, we find that ORTHRUS maintains a significant advantage over both locking systems. At 128 warehouses, ORTHRUS's throughput is 1.3x and 1.5x that of *Deadlock-free locking* and 2PL, respectively. We attribute this remaining advantage to the lower instruction- and data-cache footprint entailed by partitioned functionality (§2.1 and §3.1).

4.4.2 Scalability under high contention

Next, we compare the scalability of ORTHRUS, *Deadlock-free locking* and 2PL under high contention. We set the total number of warehouses to 16 and vary the number of cores used by the system. Figure 9 shows the results of the experiment. When each system uses 10 CPU cores, we find that *Deadlock-free locking* and 2PL's throughput is identical (as explained in §4.1). On increasing the number of CPU cores, we find that 2PL's throughput begins to drop because of the overhead of deadlock handling logic. As mentioned above, deadlocks occur with negligible frequency on the TPC-C benchmark. However, despite the negligible frequency of deadlocks, we find a significant difference between 2PL and *Deadlock-free locking*; this difference validates our claim that deadlock handling logic is a significant source of overhead, even on workloads which are devoid of deadlocks. Despite the significant level of contention in the workload ORTHRUS's throughput scales with additional CPU cores. At 80 cores, ORTHRUS outperforms *Deadlock-free locking* and 2PL by 2x and nearly an *order of magnitude*, respectively.

4.4.3 Execution time breakdown

We conclude our experimental evaluation by showing the breakdown of CPU time on database execution threads in ORTHRUS, *Deadlock-free locking*, and 2PL. Figure 10 shows that 2PL spends significantly more time locking records than *Deadlock-free locking*. This is due to the fact the the dreadlocks algorithm spends time spinning on threads' digests in the lock manager. The difference between these two baselines is only that 2PL spends time waiting within the lock manager, while *Deadlock-free locking* spends time waiting outside the lock manager.

ORTHRUS's execution threads spend more cycles doing useful work than both *Deadlock-free locking* and 2PL under both high contention and low contention. Under high contention all three systems spend a large fraction of their time waiting on locks. However, ORTHRUS's execution threads spend significantly more time executing transactions (in comparison to *Deadlock-free locking* and 2PL). In particular, ORTHRUS's execution threads spend 18% of their time executing transactions. In comparison, *Deadlock-free locking* and 2PL threads spend just 7.2% and 3.7% of their time doing useful work. Thus, ORTHRUS's execution thread utilization is about 2.5x and 5x greater than that *Deadlock-free locking* and 2PL, respectively. It should be noted that as a consequence of its partitioned functionality, ORTHRUS uses fewer execution threads than *Deadlock-free locking* and 2PL. In both experiments, ORTHRUS uses 16 concurrency control threads and 64 execution threads. In contrast, the other systems utilize all 80 threads for execution. However, despite having 20% fewer execution threads at its disposal, ORTHRUS outperforms *Deadlock-free locking* and 2PL by much better utilizing its available execution threads.

5. RELATED WORK

Synchronization. Remote Core Locking (RCL) is a technique for reducing synchronization overhead and increasing data locality in contended critical sections [33]. RCL classifies a subset of a machine's CPU cores as "server" cores, and assigns contended critical sections to server cores. Threads request server cores to execute critical sections on their behalf. Flat combining is a synchronization technique that addresses the same problem as RCL; the impact of contended critical sections on synchronization overhead and data locality [19]. Unlike RCL, flat combining does not dedicate CPU cores for the sole purpose of critical section execution. Instead, a single "combiner" thread is dynamically chosen to execute critical sections on behalf of others. Both RCL and flat combining use the design principle of dedicating a single thread to repeatedly execute critical sections for the purposes of exploiting instruction- and data-cache locality, and reducing synchronization overhead. ORTHRUS uses the same design principle; RCL's server cores, and flat combining's combiner are analogous to ORTHRUS's concurrency control threads. However, both RCL and flat combining address high contention in critical sections without regard to any higher level functionality. In contrast, ORTHRUS's concurrency control threads implement logical locking, and must therefore carefully address harmful interactions between logical locking and asynchronous message-passing (§3.3).

Operating systems. Barrelfish is a multi-core operating system kernel that forbids shared-memory-based inter-core communication altogether [2]. Barrelfish forces cores to communicate using explicit message passing. One of the motivations for Barrelfish's deisgn was shared-memory operating system kernels's inability to reason about contention at scale. Wentzlaff et al. propose a factored operating system (fos), which assigns operating system functions to specific cores of a single machine [51]. fos's design is intended to reduce contention, and improve instruction- and data-cache locality. ORTHRUS shares some of the motivation behind Barrelfish and fos: synchronization overhead, and poor locality due to conflated functionality (§2.1). However, Barrelfish and fos address overheads in operating system kernels, while ORTHRUS addresses overheads in database concurrency control.

Partitioned functionality. Bernstein and Das, and Ding et al. proposed optimistic distributed DBMSs in which validation is performed by a dedicated set of processes, independent from those that execute transactions's logic [3, 11]. Faleiro et al. proposed techniques for lazy transaction evaluation [14], and multi-version concurrency control [13], that separate concurrency control and transaction execution. None of these systems advocated for explicit message-passing as an inter-thread communication mechanism on a single multi-core machine. Moreover, this paper analyzes the broader implications of separating concurrency control from transaction execution, while these prior systems used separate concurrency control and execution threads in the narrower context of distributed optimistic concurrency control, lazy transaction evaluation, and multi-version concurrency control.

Staged DBMSs. Harizopoulos et al. identified several sources of overhead with thread-based query execution architectures [17]. Chief among these was poor instruction- and data-cache locality due to thread context switching. To address this overhead, they proposed StagedDB, a staged event-driven query execution architecture. StagedDB uses long-lived threads to exploit inter-query instruction- and data-cache locality. ORTHRUS uses a similar design; it dedicates long-lived threads to perform concurrency control and transaction execution logic respectively. These threads are pinned to physical CPU cores in order to exploit instruction- and data-cache locality. ORTHRUS differs from StagedDB in that it addresses bottlenecks in transaction processing, not query execution. Furthermore, ORTHRUS addresses transaction processing overheads on modern multi-core machines, such as synchronization, data movement, and deadlock handling.

Several distributed DBMSs have adopted a staged event driven architecture (SEDA) [10, 20, 28, 54]. SEDA is a natural fit for distributed database systems, which must *necessarily* use message-passing as a communication mechanism. In contrast, ORTHRUS uses a staged message-passing among threads on a *single node*.

Multi-core optimized DBMSs. Several researchers have recently proposed techniques to address synchronization overhead and improve cache-locality in multi-core databases [25, 30–32, 35, 40, 47, 49]. Johnson et al. devised a technique to reduce the frequency of contended latch acquisitions in conventional lock managers [21]. Their technique, speculative lock inheritance, passes contended logical locks between transactions without requiring calls to the lock manager (consequently decreasing the frequency of contended latch acquisition within the lock manager). Jung et al. devised scalable latch-free algorithms for conventional lock managers [23]. Larson et al. address several scalability bottlenecks in both pessimistic and optimistic concurrency control protocols [29]. For instance, their optimistic validation protocol does not require the use of a global critical section (as required by conventional protocols [27]). Tu et al. propose Silo, an optimistic main-memory multi-core database system designed to eliminate contended centralized data-structures [48]. All of these systems use a conventional shared-memory design. In contrast, ORTHRUS mediates communication among concurrency control and execution threads using explicit message-passing.

Semantics-aware concurrency control. Several researchers have argued for reasoning about conflicts using the semantics of operations [1,7,8,36,43]. Doppel is a main-memory database system that exploits commutative operations on contended records [34]. Contended records are replicated across a machine's cores, and commutative operations on these records are satisfied by any core. In order to process non-commutative operations, the state on each replica is periodically aggregated. In contrast, ORTHRUS is designed to address high contention in workloads where semantic knowledge about conflicts is not available (beyond reads, and writes to records).

Shared-nothing systems. Prior research found that the cost of two-phase locking was prohibitively expensive on main-memory database systems [16]. Several researchers subsequently recommended doing away with two-phase locking altogether, and advocated for serial transaction execution. H-Store is an example of a database system which employs serial transaction execution, and works best when workloads are perfectly partitionable [44]. HyPer is another example of a single-thread transaction processing system, but its design is meant to simultaneously support OLTP and OLAP workloads [24] (note that the latest version of HyPer abandons a shared-nothing design in favor of shared-everyting optimistic multi-versioning [35]). Since these systems do away with concurrency control altogether, they do not suffer from any of the overheads described in this paper. However, for the same reason, they cannot adequately utilize multi-core systems when a workload contains a non-trivial fraction of distributed transactions.

Pandis et al. propose a shared-nothing transaction processing architecture to avoid contention on locking meta-data (DORA) [37] and indexes (PLP) [38]. Unlike conventional designs where a single thread performs a transaction's logic, their work proposes that a transaction is collectively processed by the partitions on which it must execute. A transaction's logic is broken into smaller sub-transactions such that an entire sub-transaction is restricted to a single partition. Unlike ORTHRUS, DORA assigns a single thread to perform both concurrency control and execution within a partition. Furthermore, this paper advocates for *partitioned functionality*, which does not necessarily preclude shared-data among concurrency control or execution threads (§3.4). PLP is complimentary to our work; we do not address index contention.

6. CONCLUSIONS

The vast majority of database systems adhere to the design principle of assigning a single thread the responsibility of performing all logic on behalf of a transaction. This design principle leads to severe scalability problems on main-memory multi-core databases due to synchronization overhead, data movement overhead, and cache pollution. Furthermore, these systems allow dynamic access of data which necessitates expensive deadlock handling mechanisms. ORTHRUS addresses these limitations by partitioning functionality across a machine's cores and eliminating the need for handling deadlocks. Our experimental evaluation shows that ORTHRUS's design enables it to outperform conventional database systems by upto an order of magnitude on high contention workloads.

Acknowledgements. This work was sponsored by the NSF under grant IIS-1527118. We thank the anonymous SIGMOD 2016 reviewers for their insightful feedback.

7. REFERENCES

[1] P. Bailis, A. Fekete, M. J. Franklin, A. Ghodsi, J. M. Hellerstein, and I. Stoica. Coordination avoidance in database systems. *PVLDB*, 8(3), 2014.

[2] A. Baumann, P. Barham, P.-E. Dagand, T. Harris, R. Isaacs, S. Peter, T. Roscoe, A. Schüpbach, and A. Singhania. The multikernel: A new OS architecture for scalable multicore systems. In *SOSP*, 2009.

[3] P. A. Bernstein and S. Das. Scaling optimistic concurrency control by approximately partitioning the certifier and log. *DE Bull*, 38(1), 2015.

[4] S. Boyd-Wickizer, M. F. Kaashoek, R. Morris, and N. Zeldovich. Non-scalable locks are dangerous. In *Linux OLS*, 2012.

[5] I. Calciu, D. Dice, T. Harris, M. Herlihy, A. Kogan, V. Marathe, and M. Moir. Message passing or shared memory: Evaluating the delegation abstraction for multicores. In *OPODIS*. 2013.

[6] A. Cheung, S. Madden, O. Arden, and A. C. Myers. Automatic partitioning of database applications. *PVLDB*, 5(11), 2012.

[7] A. T. Clements, M. F. Kaashoek, N. Zeldovich, R. T. Morris, and E. Kohler. The scalable commutativity rule: Designing scalable software for multicore processors. In *SOSP*, 2013.

[8] N. Conway, W. R. Marczak, P. Alvaro, J. M. Hellerstein, and D. Maier. Logic and lattices for distributed programming. In *SoCC*, 2012.

[9] B. F. Cooper, A. Silberstein, E. Tam, R. Ramakrishnan, and R. Sears. Benchmarking cloud serving systems with YCSB. In *SoCC*, 2010.

[10] G. DeCandia, D. Hastorun, M. Jampani, G. Kakulapati, A. Lakshman, A. Pilchin, S. Sivasubramanian, P. Vosshall, and W. Vogels. Dynamo: Amazon's highly available key-value store. In *SOSP*, 2007.

[11] B. Ding, L. Kot, A. Demers, and J. Gehrke. Centiman: Elastic, high performance optimistic concurrency control by watermarking. In *SoCC*, 2015.

[12] J. M. Faleiro and D. J. Abadi. FIT: A distributed database performance tradeoff. *DE Bull*, 38(1), 2015.

[13] J. M. Faleiro and D. J. Abadi. Rethinking serializable multiversion concurrency control. *PVLDB*, 8(11), 2015.

[14] J. M. Faleiro, A. Thomson, and D. J. Abadi. Lazy evaluation of transactions in database systems. In *SIGMOD*, 2014.

[15] J. Gray and A. Reuter. *Transaction processing*. Morgan Kaufmann Publishers, 1992.

[16] S. Harizopoulos, D. Abadi, S. Madden, and M. Stonebraker. OLTP through the looking glass, and what we found there. In *SIGMOD*, 2008.

[17] S. Harizopoulos and A. Ailamaki. A case for staged database systems. In *CIDR*, 2003.

[18] J. M. Hellerstein, M. Stonebraker, and J. Hamilton. *Architecture of a database system*. Now Publishers, 2007.

[19] D. Hendler, I. Incze, N. Shavit, and M. Tzafrir. Flat combining and the synchronization-parallelism tradeoff. In *SPAA*, 2010.

[20] R. Huebsch, B. N. Chun, J. M. Hellerstein, B. T. Loo, P. Maniatis, T. Roscoe, S. Shenker, I. Stoica, and A. R. Yumerefendi. The architecture of PIER: An internet-scale query processor. In *CIDR*, 2005.

[21] R. Johnson, I. Pandis, and A. Ailamaki. Improving OLTP scalability using speculative lock inheritance. *PVLDB*, 2(1), 2009.

[22] R. Johnson, I. Pandis, N. Hardavellas, A. Ailamaki, and B. Falsafi. Shore-MT: A scalable storage manager for the multicore era. In *EDBT*, 2009.

[23] H. Jung, H. Han, A. D. Fekete, G. Heiser, and H. Y. Yeom. A scalable lock manager for multicores. In *SIGMOD*, 2013.

[24] A. Kemper and T. Neumann. Hyper: A hybrid OLTP & OLAP main memory database system based on virtual memory snapshots. In *ICDE*, 2011.

[25] H. Kimura. FOEDUS: OLTP engine for a thousand cores and NVRAM. In *SIGMOD*, 2015.

[26] E. Koskinen and M. Herlihy. Dreadlocks: Efficient Deadlock Detection. In *SPAA*, 2008.

[27] H.-T. Kung and J. T. Robinson. On optimistic methods for concurrency control. *ACM TODS*, 6(2), 1981.

[28] A. Lakshman and P. Malik. Cassandra: A decentralized structured storage system. *ACM SIGOPS OSR*, 44(2), 2010.

[29] P.-A. Larson, S. Blanas, C. Diaconu, C. Freedman, J. M. Patel, and M. Zwilling. High-performance concurrency control mechanisms for main-memory databases. *PVLDB*, 5(4), 2011.

[30] V. Leis, A. Kemper, and T. Neumann. Exploiting hardware transactional memory in main-memory databases. In *ICDE*, 2014.

[31] J. Levandoski, D. Lomet, S. Sengupta, R. Stutsman, and R. Wang. Multi-version range concurrency control in deuteronomy. *PVLDB*, 8(13), 2015.

[32] D. B. Lomet, S. Sengupta, and J. J. Levandoski. The bw-tree: A b-tree for new hardware platforms. In *ICDE*, 2013.

[33] J.-P. Lozi, F. David, G. Thomas, J. L. Lawall, G. Muller, et al. Remote core locking: Migrating critical-section execution to improve the performance of multithreaded applications. In *USENIX ATC*, 2012.

[34] N. Narula, C. Cutler, E. Kohler, and R. Morris. Phase reconciliation for contended in-memory transactions. In *OSDI*, 2014.

[35] T. Neumann, T. Mühlbauer, and A. Kemper. Fast serializable multi-version concurrency control for main-memory database systems. In *SIGMOD*, 2015.

[36] P. E. O'Neil. The escrow transactional method. *TODS*, 11(4), 1986.

[37] I. Pandis, R. Johnson, N. Hardavellas, and A. Ailamaki. Data-oriented transaction execution. *PVLDB*, 3(1-2), 2010.

[38] I. Pandis, P. Tözün, R. Johnson, and A. Ailamaki. Plp: page latch-free shared-everything oltp. *PVLDB*, 4(10), 2011.

[39] A. Pavlo, C. Curino, and S. Zdonik. Skew-aware automatic database partitioning in shared-nothing, parallel oltp systems. In *SIGMOD*, 2012.

[40] D. Porobic, I. Pandis, M. Branco, P. Tözün, and A. Ailamaki. Oltp on hardware islands. *PVLDB*, 5(11), 2012.

[41] K. Ren, A. Thomson, and D. J. Abadi. Lightweight locking for main memory database systems. *PVLDB*, 6(2), 2012.

[42] K. Ren, A. Thomson, and D. J. Abadi. An evaluation of the advantages and disadvantages of deterministic database systems. *PVLDB*, 7(10), 2014.

[43] S. Roy, L. Kot, G. Bender, B. Ding, H. Hojjat, C. Koch, N. Foster, and J. Gehrke. The homeostasis protocol: Avoiding transaction coordination through program analysis. In *SIGMOD*, 2015.

[44] M. Stonebraker, S. R. Madden, D. J. Abadi, S. Harizopoulos, N. Hachem, and P. Helland. The end of an architectural era (it's time for a complete rewrite). In *VLDB*, 2007.

[45] R. Taft, E. Mansour, M. Serafini, J. Duggan, A. J. Elmore, A. Aboulnaga, A. Pavlo, and M. Stonebraker. E-store: Fine-grained elastic partitioning for distributed transaction processing systems. *PVLDB*, 8(3), 2014.

[46] A. Thomson, T. Diamond, S. chun Weng, K. Ren, P. Shao, and D. J. Abadi. Calvin: Fast distributed transactions for partitioned database systems. In *SIGMOD*, 2012.

[47] P. Tözün, I. Atta, A. Ailamaki, and A. Moshovos. Addict: Advanced instruction chasing for transactions. *PVLDB*, 7(14), 2014.

[48] S. Tu, W. Zheng, E. Kohler, B. Liskov, and S. Madden. Speedy Transactions in Multicore In-memory Databases. In *SOSP*, 2013.

[49] Z. Wang, H. Qian, J. Li, and H. Chen. Using restricted transactional memory to build a scalable in-memory database. In *Eurosys*, 2014.

[50] M. Welsh, D. Culler, and E. Brewer. Seda: An architecture for well-conditioned, scalable internet services. In *SOSP*, 2001.

[51] D. Wentzlaff and A. Agarwal. Factored operating systems (fos): the case for a scalable operating system for multicores. *ACM SIGOPS OSR*, 43(2), 2009.

[52] C. Yan and A. Cheung. Leveraging lock contention to improve OLTP application performance. *PVLDB*, 9(5), 2016.

[53] X. Yu, G. Bezerra, A. Pavlo, S. Devadas, and M. Stonebraker. Staring into the abyss: An evaluation of concurrency control with one thousand cores. *PVLDB*, 8(3), 2014.

[54] L.-Y. Yuan, L. Wu, J.-H. You, and Y. Chi. Rubato DB: A highly scalable staged grid database system for OLTP and big data applications. In *CIKM*, 2014.

APPENDIX

A. YCSB EVALUATION

In this section, we compare ORTHRUS's performance against that of *Deadlock-free locking* and 2PL on the Yahoo! Cloud Serving Benchmark (YCSB) [9].

This set of experiments uses a single table of 10,000,000 records, each 1,000 bytes in size. Since YCSB transactions execute over a single table, the benchmark implicitly assumes a "flat" schema. This is in contrast to the *tree schema* from TPC-C that we experimented with in §4.4. The key difference between flat and tree schemas is that it is easier to partition data in a tree schema such that multi-partition transactions are rare.

To avoid assumptions about the partitionability of the data, we run ORTHRUS under three different configurations; single partition, dual partition, and random. In the single partition configuration all the locks required by a particular transaction are guaranteed to reside on a single concurrency control thread. The single partition configuration represents a perfectly partitionable tree schema. In the dual partition configuration, all the locks required by a transaction are guaranteed to reside on exactly two concurrency control threads. The dual partition configuration forces *every* transaction

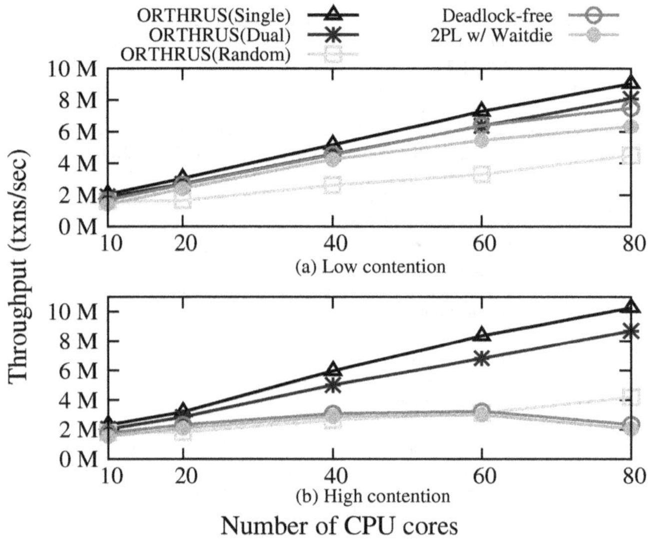

Figure 11: YCSB read-only transaction scalability.

to acquire locks from exactly two concurrency control threads. The dual partition configuration thus represents a workload in which *every* transaction is distributed due to the involvement of an ad-hoc pairing of real-world entities involved in the transaction. Under the random configuration, a transaction's locks are randomly distributed across concurrency control threads and could potentially access many more than two threads. This corresponds to complex transactions involving many real-world entities whose joint-involvement in transactions are not predictable in advance.

A.1 Read-only transactions

This experiment compares ORTHRUS's throughput against that of 2PL with wait-die[6] and *Deadlock-free locking* on a workload consisting of read-only transactions. Each transaction reads 10 records. We run both low and high contention experiments. In the low contention experiment, the 10 records in a transaction's read-set are selected uniformly at random from the set of 10,000,000 records. In the high contention experiment, each transaction picks two records from a set of hot records, and the remaining eight records from a set of cold records (locks on two hot records are acquired before locks on cold records). We set the number of hot records to 64. In both low, and high contention experiments, 2PL's deadlock handling logic is *never* invoked. This is because read-only transactions do not conflict with each other. Hence, this experiment is designed to explore the overhead of conflated functionality in conventional concurrency control protocols in the absence of deadlock handling logic.

Figure 11(a) shows the results of the low contention experiment. All the schemes that we compare use lock-based concurrency control. However, since all transactions are read-only, all locks that are acquired are shared-locks, and no lock request is ever denied. Thus, one may expect that all schemes should perform similarly. Surprisingly, this is not the case. Read-only transactions are extremely short in YCSB. As a consequence, concurrency control overhead — the process of requesting and immediately receiving a shared lock — takes up a non-trivial fraction of each transaction's total execution time. Single partition ORTHRUS outperforms all other baselines, which indicates that its concurrency control overhead is the least among all the other baselines when only one concurrency control thread is involved in a transaction. This is because it doesn't require synchronized access to shared memory concurrency control meta-data.

§3.3 explained that the number of message delays required in order for a transaction to acquire its locks in ORTHRUS is $N_{cc} + 1$, where N_{cc} is the number of concurrency control threads on which a transaction's locks reside. The number of message delays required for lock acquisition directly affects the time spent acquiring locks; more message delays correspond to more time spent acquiring locks. Since each transaction in single partition ORTHRUS acquires *all* its locks from a single concurrency control thread, the number of message delays per transaction in single partition ORTHRUS is 2. The number of message delays per transaction in dual partition ORTHRUS is 3 (because every transaction must acquire its locks from two concurrency control threads, but the threads forward messages to eliminate one extra message). Finally, in random ORTHRUS, the number of concurrency control threads that a single transaction acquires its locks from is, on average, a factor of 3 higher than in dual ORTHRUS. The difference in throughput of each of these systems is therefore directly attributable to the difference in the number of message delays required for lock acquisition.

Figure 11(a) also shows that both *Deadlock-free locking* and 2PL outperform random ORTHRUS. The reason is that messaging overhead in ORTHRUS when there are 8-10 messages per transaction exceeds the overhead of latch acquisition and data movement in the 2PL and *Deadlock-free locking* baselines. However, single and dual partition ORTHRUS (when there are only 2-3 messages per transaction) outperform both 2PL and *Deadlock-free locking*, indicating that the reduction in synchronization and data movement overhead does indeed pay off for many workloads, even under low contention.

Figure 11(b) compares each of these systems under high contention. Since read-only transactions never conflict with one another, the increase in contention does not affect the number of actual conflicts in the workload (which remains zero). In this case, the throughput of each ORTHRUS configuration increases slightly. The increase in throughput is due to better cache locality in concurrency control and execution threads. Concurrency control threads experience better locality because they often update the same meta-data across different transactions (corresponding to contended records). Execution threads experience better locality because they read the same contended records across transactions.

However, unlike ORTHRUS, *Deadlock-free locking* and 2PL do not scale beyond 60 cores. Instead, their throughput *decreases* after 60 cores. This decrease in throughput occurs despite the absence of conflicts among read-only transactions. *Deadlock-free locking* and 2PL do not scale because of contention for concurrency control meta-data. In order to acquire or release a logical lock, both locking implementations must acquire a latch. This latch protects the hash-bucket in which requests for a particular lock reside. Under high contention, database threads will contend for the latches protecting the meta-data corresponding to popular records. Furthermore, as the number of cores allocated to the database increases, latch contention increases because more threads attempt to acquire the same set of latches. As §2.1 explained, contention on memory words – such as those corresponding to latches – leads to significant cache coherence overhead, which in turn inhibits *Deadlock-free locking* and 2PL's scalability[7]. Note that *Deadlock-free locking*'s throughput is nearly identical to that of 2PL because 2PL's deadlock handling logic is never invoked due to the absence of logical conflicts among read-only transactions.

[6] We also evaluated the throughput of 2PL with the wait-for graph, and dreadlocks algorithms, but found that wait-die outperformed both these schemes on this benchmark.

[7] Note that while our implementation uses latches, latch-free algorithms are subject to the same cache-coherence overhead [13,48].

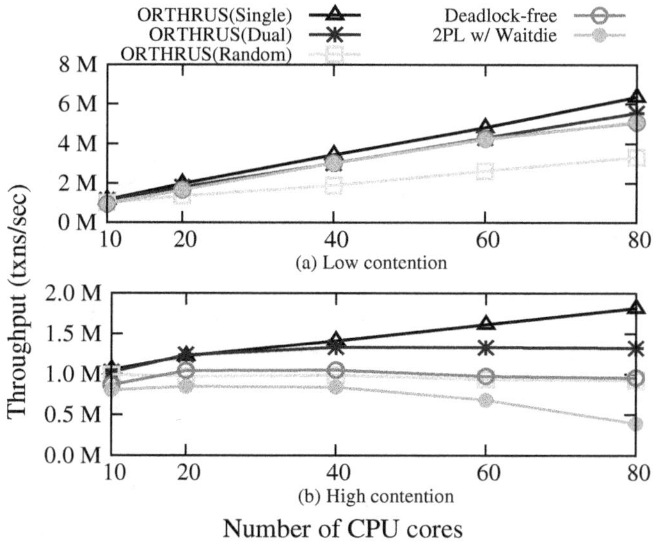

Figure 12: YCSB 10RMW scalability.

A.2 10RMW transactions

We now compare ORTHRUS's throughput with that of *Deadlock-free locking* and 2PL when transactions perform 10 read-modify-write (RMW) operations. As in §A.1, we perform both low contention and high contention experiments. Records in transactions' read- and write-sets are picked in the same manner as the read-only experiment, where the hot set for the high contention experiment is 64 records. Note that unlike read-only transactions which never logically conflict, a pair of 10RMW transactions conflict with each other if their read-/write-sets intersect.

Figure 12(a) shows the results of the low contention experiment. Each system's performance trend is similar to that in the low contention read-only experiment (§A.1). However, the absolute throughput of each system is less than its throughput in the low contention read-only experiment. This is because 10RMW transactions take longer than read-only transactions since they both read and write 10 records while read-only transactions only read 10 records.

Figure 12(b) shows the throughput of each system under high contention. Under high contention, 2PL does not scale beyond 20 cores. On the contrary, its throughput begins to *drop* as more cores are added. *Deadlock-free locking*'s throughput also does not scale beyond 20 cores. However, unlike 2PL, its throughput plateaus at 1,000,000 transactions per second. We attribute the difference between *Deadlock-free locking* and 2PL to deadlock handling overhead. 2PL uses the wait-die deadlock avoidance algorithm, which aborts a transaction if it requests a lock held by an older transaction (§4). Therefore, in addition to suffering from synchronization and data-movement overheads associated with lock acquisition, 2PL suffers additional overhead due to deadlock handling (in particular, wasted work due to transaction aborts).

As expected, single and dual partition ORTHRUS outperform random ORTHRUS. This is because transactions in single and dual partition ORTHRUS request locks from fewer concurrency control threads (relative to random ORTHRUS), and therefore hold contended locks for shorter durations (§3.3). Single partition ORTHRUS outperforms dual partition ORTHRUS configuration for the same reason.

At 80 cores, the difference between 2PL and random, dual, and single partition ORTHRUS is 2.3x, 3.35x, and 4.65x, respectively.

B. DEADLOCK EXPERIMENTS

This section analyzes the pros and cons various deadlock handling mechanisms in greater detail. §4 explained that *Deadlock-free locking* eliminates the possibility of deadlock by acquiring locks in lexicographic order. This lexicographic order does not necessarily match the order in which locks are actually required by a transaction's logic. For instance, if the last operation performed by a transaction is an update to a contended record, then a conventional locking protocol would acquire a lock on this record at the end of the transaction. In contrast, *Deadlock-free locking* may need to acquire this contended lock before other locks because the contended lock may occur earlier in the lexicographic order. In the worst case, the lexicographic order may force the contended lock to be acquired at the *beginning* of the transaction. Thus, although lexicographically ordered lock acquisition avoids deadlocks, it may force transactions to hold contended locks for longer. This section analyzes this tradeoff in detail.

The workload used in this section consists of transactions which perform 10 read-modify-write operations (RMW) on 1000-byte sized records (as in §A.2). One or two of the records in each transaction's write-set are chosen from a set of hot records. The remainder – nine or eight, respectively – are chosen from a set of cold records. We vary contention in the workload by decreasing the number of hot records in the database. For each experiment, we plot the throughput of each system against the number of hot records. In each graph, the number of hot records decreases along the x-axis, which corresponds to increasing contention.

Figure 13 shows the results of the experiments. We run experiments corresponding to different points at which transactions update the hot record(s). In Figure 13(a) and Figure 13(d), hot records are updated at the beginning of transactions. In Figure 13(b) and Figure 13(e), hot records are updated at the end of transactions. In Figure 13(c) and Figure 13(f), hot record updates are randomly distributed across transactions' writesets.

When hot records are updated at the beginning of transactions (Figure 13(a) and Figure 13(d)), we find that *Deadlock-free locking* outperforms two-phase locking (2PL) with every variant of deadlock handling algorithm. This is because *Deadlock-free locking* and 2PL are forced to acquire locks on hot records at the beginning of transactions, which mostly eliminates their advantage over *Deadlock-free locking* which is also forced to acquire its locks at the beginning of the transaction. Meanwhile the 2PL variants must additionally execute deadlock handling logic, which was shown to be expensive in §4.1. Furthermore, when transactions access two hot records (Figure 13(a)), deadlocks occur more frequently than in the case when transactions access one hot record. Thus, in Figure 13(a), 2PL-based systems waste additional cycles on transactions that are eventually aborted. As a consequence, the relative difference between *Deadlock-free locking* and the best performing 2PL system is higher when transactions update two hot records (2.2x) than when transactions update one hot record (1.4x).

The higher probability of deadlocks when transactions update two hot records (Figure 13(a)) also explains the relative performance between the wait-die and the dreadlocks/wait-for graph deadlock handling mechanisms. Wait-die conservatively aborts transactions that wait on locks held by older transactions. These conservative aborts minimize the wasted work involved in forcing a transaction to wait for a lock, only to have the same transaction later abort due to a deadlock. As a consequence, wait-die outperforms both the dreadlocks and wait-for graph deadlock detection algorithms in Figure 13(a). However, when transactions update a single hot record (Figure 13(d)), conservatively aborting transactions in anticipation of deadlocks does not pay off because deadlocks are rare.

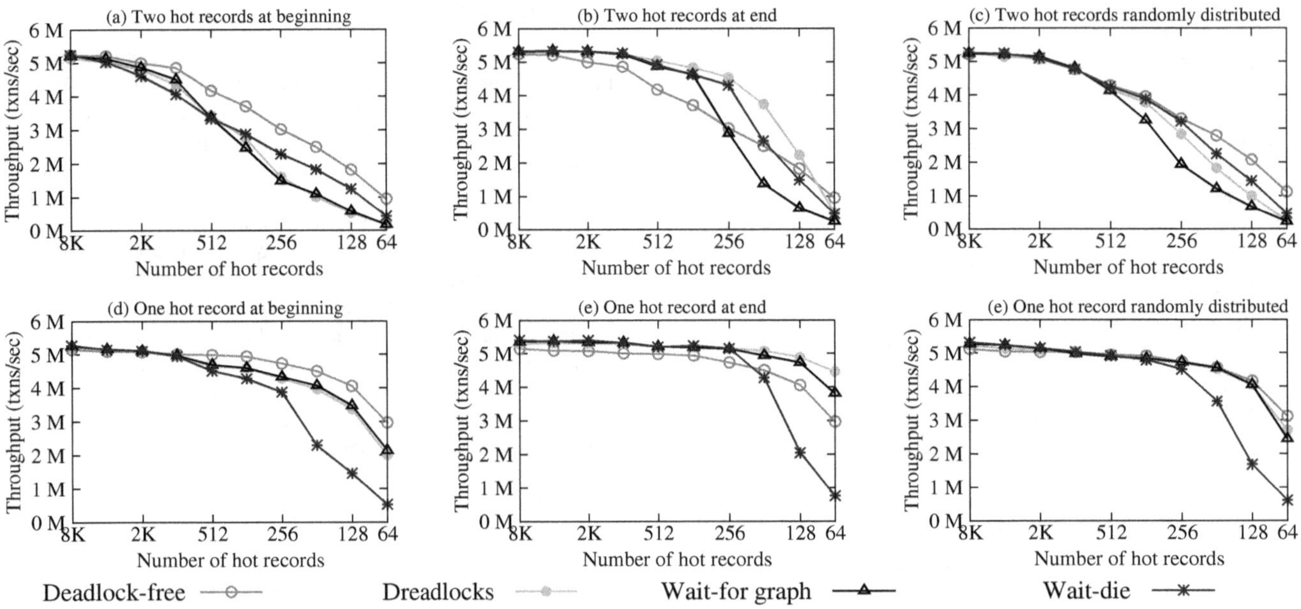

Figure 13: Throughput while varying number of hot records at 80 CPU cores.

Thus, both dreadlocks and wait-for graph outperform wait-die in Figure 13(d).

Figure 13(b) and Figure 13(e) show the results of experiments where updates to two hot records, and one hot record, respectively, occur at the end of each transaction. These experiments represent the best-case behavior for the 2PL systems because they hold locks on contended data for the least possible duration (the time taken to update the data) [52]. Meanwhile, because it acquires locks in lexicographic order, *Deadlock-free locking* cannot wait until the end of the transaction to acquire locks on hot records. Indeed, in Figure 13(b), when transactions update two hot records, we find that 2PL initially outperforms *Deadlock-free locking*. However, at the highest level of contention (at 64 hot records), the 2PL baselines are more susceptible to deadlocks, which in turn causes them to waste cycles on transactions that will abort. At this point, despite the fact it holds contended locks for longer durations, *Deadlock-free locking* outperforms all 2PL implementations.

In Figure 13(e), however, only a single hot record is updated at the end of each transaction. This experiment represents the *best-case* scenario for the 2PL schemes for two reasons. First, 2PL holds contended locks for the shortest possible duration. Second, deadlocks are rare. Accordingly, 2PL with dreadlocks and wait-for graph outperform *Deadlock-free locking* by 1.5x and 1.3x respectively. Despite the fact it holds locks for longer duration, *Deadlock-free locking* outperforms 2PL with wait-die at high levels of contention because wait-die spuriously aborts transactions that are not involved in deadlocks.

Note that when locks for hot records are acquired at the end of transactions, the performance of the wait-for graph and dreadlock approaches to deadlock control are no longer identical. §4.1 explained that both algorithms effectively search for cycles in the transitive closure of transactions waiting for locks. Even though the dreadlocks and wait-for graph algorithms are equivalent, they use very different graph representations — a bitmap to represent a transaction's transitive closure of wait-for dependencies, and an explicit distributed dependency graph of transactions, respectively. Computing the transitive closure of the explicit graph involves traversing the graph of transactions, which is distributed across the cores of a machine. In contrast, dreadlocks only spins on the bitmap of the most recent preceding transaction (the transitive closure computation is effectively memoized in each bitmap) — a much lighter-weight process. The extra overhead of the graph traversal in the wait-for graph approach is hidden when the hot records are accessed at the beginning of the transaction, because the traversal can take place in parallel with the transaction that is holding the lock performing the rest of the transaction. However, when the hot record locks are acquired at the end of the transaction, the original transaction may complete while the graph traversal is ongoing, making this graph traversal overhead more visible.

Finally, Figure 13(c) and Figure 13(f) show the results of experiments where the positions of updates to hot records are randomly distributed across transactions. In both these experiments, *Deadlock-free locking* outperforms all variants of 2PL. As in prior experiments, *Deadlock-free locking* has a greater advantage over 2PL when transactions update two hot records because deadlocks are more likely.

In conclusion, these experiments indicate that *Deadlock-free locking*'s lexicographic lock acquisition can cause locks on hot records to be held for longer, which can translate into poorer performance (relative to 2PL) in cases where hot records are accessed at the end of transactions. However, when deadlocks are actually prevalent (experiments with two hot records), *Deadlock-free locking* outperforms 2PL, even when hot records are updated at the end of transactions. Furthermore, when operations on hot records are not restricted to the end of transactions, *Deadlock-free locking always* outperforms 2PL (Figure 13(a), Figure 13(c), Figure 13(d), and Figure 13(f)). These results make a strong case for eliminating deadlock handling logic from pessimistic locking protocols; for the most part, the benefits of eliminating deadlocks significantly outweigh any concurrency disadvantage due to increased lock hold times.

Furthermore, it should be noted that the lack of flexibility of *Deadlock-free locking* in these experiments, in particular the requirement to acquire locks on hot records before they are actually needed, could be overcome with further improvements to the algorithm. In particular, it is possible to envision an algorithm that *renames* hot records such that they appear at the end of the lexicographic order relative to the other records in the database. This would further increase the advantage of *Deadlock-free locking* relative to the 2PL-based deadlock handling schemes.

DBSherlock: A Performance Diagnostic Tool for Transactional Databases*

Dong Young Yoon Ning Niu Barzan Mozafari

University of Michigan, Ann Arbor

{dyoon, nniu, mozafari}@umich.edu

ABSTRACT

Running an online transaction processing (OLTP) system is one of the most daunting tasks required of database administrators (DBAs). As businesses rely on OLTP databases to support their mission-critical and real-time applications, poor database performance directly impacts their revenue and user experience. As a result, DBAs constantly monitor, diagnose, and rectify any performance decays.

Unfortunately, the manual process of debugging and diagnosing OLTP performance problems is extremely tedious and non-trivial. Rather than being caused by a single slow query, performance problems in OLTP databases are often due to a large number of concurrent and competing transactions adding up to compounded, non-linear effects that are difficult to isolate. Sudden changes in request volume, transactional patterns, network traffic, or data distribution can cause previously abundant resources to become scarce, and the performance to plummet.

This paper presents a practical tool for assisting DBAs in quickly and reliably diagnosing performance problems in an OLTP database. By analyzing hundreds of statistics and configurations collected over the lifetime of the system, our algorithm quickly identifies a small set of potential causes and presents them to the DBA. The root-cause established by the DBA is reincorporated into our algorithm as a new causal model to improve future diagnoses. Our experiments show that this algorithm is substantially more accurate than the state-of-the-art algorithm in finding correct explanations.

Keywords

Transactions; OLTP; performance diagnosis; anomaly detection

1. INTRODUCTION

Many enterprise applications rely on executing transactions against their database backend to store, query, and update data. As a result, databases running online transaction processing (OLTP) workloads are some of the most mission-critical software components for enterprises. Any service interruptions or performance hiccups in these databases often lead directly to revenue loss.

Thus, a major responsibility of database administrators (DBAs) in large organizations is to constantly monitor their OLTP workload for any performance failures or slowdowns, and to take appropriate actions promptly to restore performance. However, diagnosing the root cause of a performance problem is generally tedious, as it requires the DBA to consider many possibilities by manually inspecting queries and various log files over time. These challenges are exacerbated in OLTP workloads because performance problems cannot be traced back to a few demanding queries or their poor execution plans, as is often the case in analytical workloads. In fact, most transactions take only a fraction of a millisecond to complete. However, tens of thousands of concurrent transactions competing for the same resources (e.g., CPU, disk I/O, memory) can create highly non-linear and counter-intuitive effects on database performance. Minor changes in an OLTP workload can push the system into a new performance regime, quickly making previously abundant resources scarce.

However, it can be quite challenging for most DBAs to explain (or even investigate) such phenomena. Modern databases and operating systems collect massive volumes of detailed statistics and log files over time, creating an exponential number of subsets of DBMS variables and statistics that may explain a performance decay. For instance, MySQL maintains over 260 different statistics and variables (see Section 2.1) and commercial DBMSs collect thousands of granular statistics (e.g., Teradata [12]). Unfortunately, existing databases fail to provide DBAs with effective tools for analyzing performance problems using these rich datasets, aside from basic visualization and monitoring mechanisms. As a consequence, highly-skilled and highly-paid DBAs (a scarce resource themselves) spend many hours diagnosing performance problems through different conjectures and manually inspecting various queries and log files, until the root cause is found [13].

To avoid this tedious, error-prone, and adhoc procedure, we propose a performance explanation framework called `DBSherlock` that combines techniques from outlier detection and causality analysis to assist DBAs in diagnosing performance problems more easily, more accurately, and in a more principled manner. Through `DBSherlock`'s visual interface, the user (e.g., a DBA) specifies certain instances of past performance that s/he deems abnormal (and optionally, normal). `DBSherlock` then automatically analyzes large volumes of past statistics to find the most likely causes of the user-perceived anomaly, presenting them to the user along with a confidence value, either in the form of (i) concise predicates describing the combination of system configurations or workload characteristics causing the performance anomaly, or (ii) high-level diagnoses based on the existing causal models in the system. The DBA can then identify the actual cause within these few possibilities. Once the actual cause is confirmed by the DBA, his/her feedback is inte-

*`DBSherlock` is now open-sourced at http://dbseer.org.

SIGMOD'16, June 26-July 01, 2016, San Francisco, CA, USA

ISBN 978-1-4503-3531-7/16/06... $15.00

DOI: http://dx.doi.org/10.1145/2882903.2915218

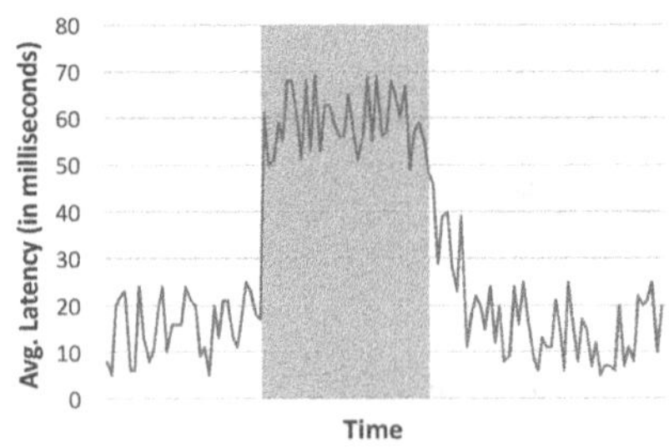

Figure 1: Identifying the root cause of a performance anomaly is non-trivial, as different causes may lead to the same performance pattern.

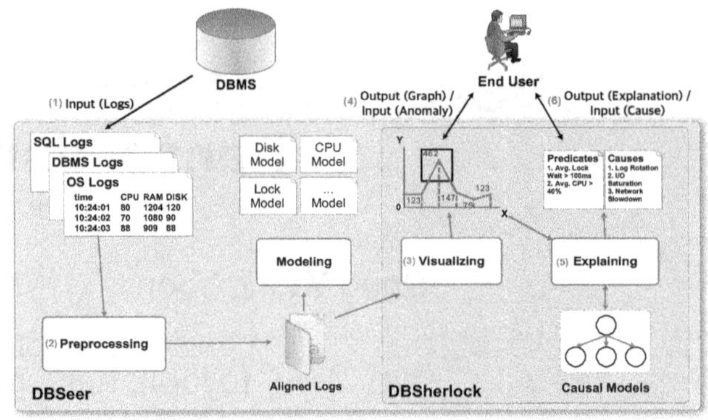

Figure 2: The workflow in DBSherlock.

grated back into DBSherlock to improve its causal models and future diagnoses.

As an example, consider Figure 1, which is a graph of average transaction latencies over time. In practice, finding the root cause of this latency spike can be quite challenging. In fact, we observe nearly the same performance plot in the following situations: (i) if the overall workload suddenly spikes, (ii) if the number of poorly written queries spikes, or (iii) if a network hiccup occurs. To establish the correct cause, the DBA has to plot several other performance metrics during the same timespan as the latency spike. This means choosing among hundreds of DBMS, OS, and network telemetry, and even inspecting several queries manually. However, DBSherlock can significantly narrow this search space by generating appropriate explanatory predicates that help the DBA distinguish between the different possible causes. In the particular example of Figure 1, DBSherlock's statistical analysis will lead to different predicates depending on the cause. When (i) has occurred, DBSherlock generates a predicate showing an increase in the number of lock waits and running DBMS threads compared to normal. In the case of (ii), DBSherlock's predicates indicate a sudden rise of next-row-read-requests as well as the CPU usage of the DBMS. Finally, (iii) leads to a predicate showing a lower than usual number of network packets sent or received during a specific time. In other words, DBSherlock's predicates help explain the root cause by bringing appropriate signals and metrics to the DBA's attention. (In Section 6, we show how DBSherlock can also provide human-readable causes in addition to raw predicates.)

Note that designing a tool for performance diagnosis is a challenging task due to the exponential number of combinations of variables and statistics that may explain the cause of a performance decay, making a naïve enumeration algorithm infeasible. Though off-the-shelf algorithms for feature selection exist, they are primarily designed to maximize a machine learning algorithm's predictive power rather than its explanatory and diagnostic power. Similarly, decision trees (e.g., PerfXplain [34]) and robust statistics (e.g., PerfAugur [41]) have been used for automatic performance explanation of map-reduce jobs and cloud services, respectively. However, such models are more likely to find secondary symptoms when the root cause of the anomaly is outside the database and not directly captured by the collected statistics. (In Section 6, we show that constructing and using causal models leads to significantly more relevant explanations.) Finally, while sensitivity-analysis-based techniques (e.g., Scorpion [46]) are highly effective in finding the individual tuples most responsible for extreme aggregate values in scientific computations, they are not applicable to performance diagnosis of OLTP workloads. This is because databases often avoid prohibitive logging overheads by maintaining aggregate statistics rather than detailed statistics for individual transactions. For instance, instead of recording each transaction's wait time for locks, MySQL and Postgres only record the total wait time for locks across all transactions. Thus, listing individual transactions is impractical (and often unhelpful for diagnosis, due to the complex interactions among concurrent transactions).

In this paper, we make the following contributions:

1. To the best of our knowledge, we propose the first algorithm specifically designed to explain and diagnose performance anomalies in highly-concurrent and complex OLTP workloads.

2. We adopt the notion of causality from the artificial intelligence (AI) literature, and treat user feedback as causal models in our diagnostic tool. We formally define a notion of *confidence* to combine predicate-based explanations and causal model predictions in a principled manner.

3. We propose a new automatic anomaly detection algorithm with a competitive accuracy to that of an expert. We also introduce a framework to prune secondary symptoms using basic forms of domain knowledge.

4. We evaluate DBSherlock against the state-of-the-art performance explanation technique, across a wide range of performance problems. DBSherlock's predicates on average achieve 28% (and up to 55%) higher F1-measures[1] than those generated by previous techniques.

Section 2 describes the high-level overview of DBSherlock. Sections 3 and 4 present our criterion and algorithm for generating predicate-based explanations, respectively. Section 5 describes our technique for incorporating domain knowledge and pruning secondary symptoms from our explanations. Section 6 explains how our system incorporates user feedback (when available) in the form of casual models in order to provide higher-level, descriptive explanations. Section 7 explains how automatic anomaly detection techniques can be combined with DBSherlock. Section 8 describes our experimental results.

2. SYSTEM OVERVIEW

DBSherlock's workflow for performance explanation and diagnosis consists of six steps, as shown in Figure 2.

1. **Data Collection.** DBSherlock collects various log files, configurations, and statistics from the DBMS and OS.

2. **Preprocessing.** The collected logs are summarized and aligned by their timestamps at fixed time intervals (e.g., every second).

[1]F1-measure (a.k.a. balanced F-score) is a commonly used measure of a test's accuracy. It considers both the precision p and the recall r of the test, and is defined as: $F_1 = 2 \cdot \frac{p \cdot r}{p+r}$.

3. **Visualization.** Through DBSherlock's graphical user interface, our end user (e.g., a DBA) can generate scatter plots of various performance statistics of the DBMS over time.

4. **Anomaly Detection.** If the end user deems any of the performance metrics of the DBMS unexpected, abnormal, or suspicious in any period of time, s/he can simply select that region of the plot and ask DBSherlock for an explanation of the observed anomaly. Alternatively, users can also rely on DBSherlock's automatic anomaly detection feature.

5. **Anomaly Explanation.** Given the user-perceived region of anomaly, DBSherlock analyzes the collected statistics and configurations over time and explains the anomaly using either descriptive predicates or actual causes.

6. **Anomaly Diagnosis and User Feedback.** Using DBSherlock's explanations as diagnostic clues, the DBA attempts to identify the root cause of the observed performance problem. Once s/he has diagnosed the actual cause, s/he provides evaluative feedback to DBSherlock. This feedback is then incorporated in DBSherlock as a causal model and used for improving future explanations.

Next, we discuss these steps in more detail: steps 1–2 in Section 2.1, steps 3–4 in Section 2.2, and steps 5–6 in Section 2.3. Then, we list the current limitations of DBSherlock in Section 2.4.

2.1 Data Collection and Preprocessing

We have implemented DBSherlock as a module for DBSeer [1]. DBSeer is an open-source suite of database administration tools for monitoring and predicting database performance [37, 38, 47]. We have integrated our DBSherlock into DBSeer for two reasons. First, adding performance diagnosis and explanation features will greatly benefit DBSeer's current users in gaining deeper insight into their workloads. Second, DBSherlock can simply rely on DBSeer's API for collecting and visualizing various performance statistics from MySQL and Linux (the systems used in our experiments). Here, we briefly describe the data collection and preprocessing steps performed by DBSeer and used by DBSherlock, i.e., components (1) and (2) in Figure 2.

DBSeer collects various types of performance data by passively observing the DBMS and OS *in situ* (i.e., as they are running in operation), via their standard logging features. Specifically, DBSeer collects the following data at one-second intervals [37]:

(i) Resource consumption statistics from the OS (in our case, *Linux*'s /proc data), e.g., per-core CPU usage, number of disk I/Os, number of network packets, number of page faults, number of allocated/free pages, and number of context switches.

(ii) Workload statistics from the DBMS (in our case, *MySQL*'s global status variables), e.g., number of logical reads, number of **SELECT**, **UPDATE**, **DELETE**, and **INSERT** commands executed, number of flushed and dirty pages, and the total lock wait-time.[2]

(iii) Timestamped query logs, containing start-time, duration, and the SQL statements executed by the system, as well as the query plans used for each query.

(iv) Configuration parameters from the OS and the DBMS, e.g., environment variables, kernel parameters, database server configurations, network settings, and (relevant) driver versions.

DBSeer further processes this data. First, it computes aggregate statistics about transactions executed during each time interval (e.g., their average and quantile latencies, total transaction counts, etc.).[3] These transaction aggregates are then aligned with the OS and DBMS statistics and configurations according to their timestamps, using the following format:

(Timestamp, $\texttt{Attr}_1$, . . . , $\texttt{Attr}_k$)

where Timestamp marks the starting time of the 1-second interval during which these data were collected, and {$\texttt{Attr}_1$, ..., $\texttt{Attr}_k$} are the attributes, comprised of the transaction aggregates and other categorical and numerical metrics collected from the database and operating system. DBSherlock uses these timestamped data for its performance explanation and diagnosis purposes.

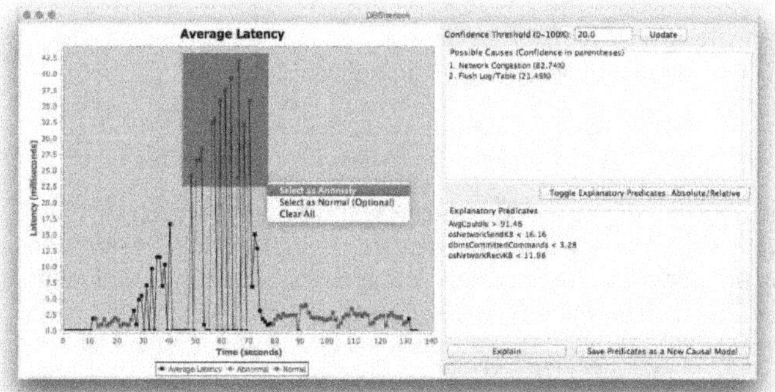

Figure 3: DBSherlock's user interface.

2.2 User Interface

DBSherlock comes with a graphical user interface, where users can plot a graph of various performance metrics over their time window of interest. This is shown as component (3) in Figure 2. For example, users might plot the average or 99% latency of transactions, number of disk I/Os, or CPU usage over the past hour, day or week. Figure 3 is an example of a scatter plot of the average latency of transactions over time. After inspecting this plot, the user can select some region(s) of the the graph where s/he finds some database metrics abnormal, suspicious, counter-intuitive, or simply worthy of an explanation. Regardless of the user's particular reason, we simply call the selected region(s) an *anomaly* (or call them *abnormal* regions). Optionally, the user can also select other areas of the graph that s/he thinks are normal (otherwise, the rest of the graph is implicitly treated as normal). After specifying the regions, the user asks DBSherlock to find likely causes or descriptive characteristics that best explain the observed *anomaly*.

When users cannot manually specify or detect the anomaly, DBSherlock relies on automatic anomaly detection (see Section 7).

2.3 System Output

Given a user-perceived anomaly, DBSherlock provides explanations in one of the following forms:

(i) predicates over different attributes of the input data; or

(ii) likely causes (and their corresponding confidence) based on existing causal models.

First, DBSherlock generates a number of predicates that identify anomalous values of some of the attributes that best explain the anomaly (Sections 3 and 4). For human readability, DBSherlock returns a conjunct of simple predicates to the user.[4] For example,

[2]To avoid performance overheads, DBSeer does not collect expensive statistics that are not maintained by default, e.g., fine-grained locking information.

[3]Since the number of transactions per second varies, we do not use individual query plans as attributes. Rather, we use their aggregate statistics, e.g., average cost estimates, number of index lookups.

[4]More complex predicates (e.g., with disjunction or negation) can easily overwhelm an average user, defeating DBSherlock's goal of being an effective tool for practitioners.

DBSherlock may explain an anomaly caused by a network slowdown by generating the following predicates:

$$\texttt{network\_send} < \texttt{10KB} \;\wedge\; \texttt{network\_recv} < \texttt{10KB} \;\wedge\; \texttt{client\_wait\_times} > \texttt{100ms} \;\wedge\; \texttt{cpu\_usage} < \texttt{5}$$

showing that there are active clients waiting without much CPU activity. (In Section 6, we show that with causal models, DBSherlock can provide even more descriptive diagnoses.) Once the user identifies the actual problem (network congestion, in this example) using these predicates as diagnostic hints, s/he can provide feedback to DBSherlock by accepting these predicates and labeling them with the actual *cause* found. This 'cause' and its corresponding predicates comprise a causal model, which will be utilized by DBSherlock for future diagnoses.

When there are any causal models in the system (i.e., from accepted and labeled predicates during previous sessions), DBSherlock calculates the *confidence* of every existing causal model for the given anomaly. This *confidence* measures a causal model's fitness for the given situation. DBSherlock then presents all existing causes in their decreasing order of confidence (as long as greater than a minimum threshold). When none of the causal models yield a sufficiently large confidence, DBSherlock does not show any causes and only shows the generated predicates to the user.

Note that DBSherlock's output in either case is only a *possible* explanation/cause of the anomaly, and it is ultimately the end user's responsibility to diagnose the *actual* root cause. The objective of DBSherlock is to provide the user with informative clues to *facilitate* fast and accurate diagnosis. In the rest of this paper, we use the terms *possible explanation* and *explanation* interchangeably, but always make a clear distinction between *possible* and *actual causes* as they are quite different from a causality perspective.

2.4 Current Limitations

The current implementation of DBSherlock has two limitations:
(i) DBSherlock finds an explanation for an anomaly if the anomaly affects at least one of the statistics available to the system.

(ii) Invariant characteristics of the system (e.g., fixed parameters or hardware specifications of the database server) are *not* considered a valid explanation of an anomaly.

It is straightforward to see the reason behind (i): if the anomaly does not manifest itself in any of the gathered statistics, DBSherlock has no means of distinguishing between abnormal and normal regions. Similarly for (ii), since the invariants of the system remain unchanged across the abnormal and normal regions, they cannot be used to distinguish the two. However, such invariants may have ultimately contributed to the anomaly in question. For instance, with a small buffer pool, dirty pages are flushed to disk frequently. Thus, when the number of concurrent transactions spikes, the pages may be flushed even more frequently. The increase in disk IOs may then affect transaction latencies. In such a case, DBSherlock reports the workload spike as the explanation for the increased latencies. While one might argue that small memory was the root cause of the problem, DBSherlock does not treat the memory size as a cause, as it is unchanged before and after the anomaly. Here, the workload spike can distinguish the two regions (see Section 3) and is hence returned as a cause to the user (i.e., with the justification that the memory was sufficient for the normal workload).

However, DBSherlock's reported cause can still be quite helpful even in the cases above. For example, even when presented with workload spike as an explanation of the performance slowdown, an experienced DBA may still rectify the problem by modifying system invariants (e.g., provisioning a larger memory or faster disk) or throttling the additional load.

3. PREDICATE GENERATION CRITERION

Given an abnormal region A, a normal region N, and input data T, we aim to generate a conjunct of predicates, where each predicate Pred is in one of the following forms: $\texttt{Attr}_i < \texttt{x}$, $\texttt{Attr}_i > \texttt{x}$, or $\texttt{x} < \texttt{Attr}_i < \texttt{y}$ when $\texttt{Attr}_i$ is numeric, and $\texttt{Attr}_i \in \{\texttt{x}_1, \ldots, \texttt{x}_c\}$ when $\texttt{Attr}_i$ is categorical. Intuitively, we desire a predicate that segregates the input tuples in A well from those in N. We formally define this quality as the separation power of a predicate.

Separation power of a predicate. Let T_N and T_A be the input tuples in the normal and abnormal regions, respectively. Also, let Pred(T) be the input tuples satisfying predicate Pred. Then the separation power (SP) of a predicate Pred is defined as:

$$\texttt{SP(Pred)} = \frac{|\texttt{Pred}(T_A)|}{|T_A|} - \frac{|\texttt{Pred}(T_N)|}{|T_N|} \quad (1)$$

In other words, a predicate's separation power is the ratio of the tuples in the abnormal region satisfying the predicate, subtracted by the ratio of the tuples in the normal region satisfying the predicate. A predicate with higher separation power is more capable of distinguishing (i.e., separating) the input tuples in the abnormal region from those in the normal one. Thus, DBSherlock's goal is to filter out individual attributes with low separation power.[5]

Identifying predicates with high separation power is challenging. First, one cannot find a predicate of high separation power by simply comparing the values of an attribute in the raw dataset.This is because real-world datasets and OS logs are noisy and attribute values often fluctuate regardless of the anomaly. Second, due to human error, users may not specify the boundaries of the abnormal regions with perfect precision. The user may also overlook smaller areas of anomaly, misleading DBSherlock to treat them as normal regions. These sources of error compound the problem of noisy datasets. Third, one cannot easily conclude that predicates with high separation power are the actual cause of an anomaly. They may simply be correlated with, or be symptoms themselves of the anomaly, and hence, lead to incorrect diagnoses. The following section describes our algorithm for efficiently finding predicates of highest separation power, while accounting for the first two sources of error. We deal with the third type of error in Section 5.

4. ALGORITHM

Our algorithm takes the aligned tuples as input (described in Section 2.1), which are separated between the abnormal and the normal regions (other tuples are ignored by DBSherlock).

Figure 4 illustrates a high-level overview of our predicate generation algorithm. The majority of our attributes are numeric (i.e., statistics), which are significantly noisier than our categorical attributes. As a result, our algorithm uses two additional steps for numeric attributes (Steps 3 and 4). (In our discussion, we highlight the differences for categorical attributes when applicable.) The first step is to discretize the domain of each attribute into a number of partitions (Step 1). Based on the user-specified abnormal and normal regions, DBSherlock labels each partition of an attribute as **Abnormal**, **Normal**, or **Empty** (Step 2 in Figure 4). Next, for numeric attributes, DBSherlock filters out some of the **Abnormal** and **Normal** partitions, which are mingled at this point, to find a predicate with high separation power (Step 3 in Figure 4). If the previous step is successful, the algorithm then fills the gap between the two separated sets of partitions and generates the candidate predicate accordingly (Steps 4 and 5 in Figure 4). The formal pseudo code of

[5]This strategy is similar to *single-variable classifiers* in machine learning literature, whereby variables' individual predictive power is used for feature selection [27].

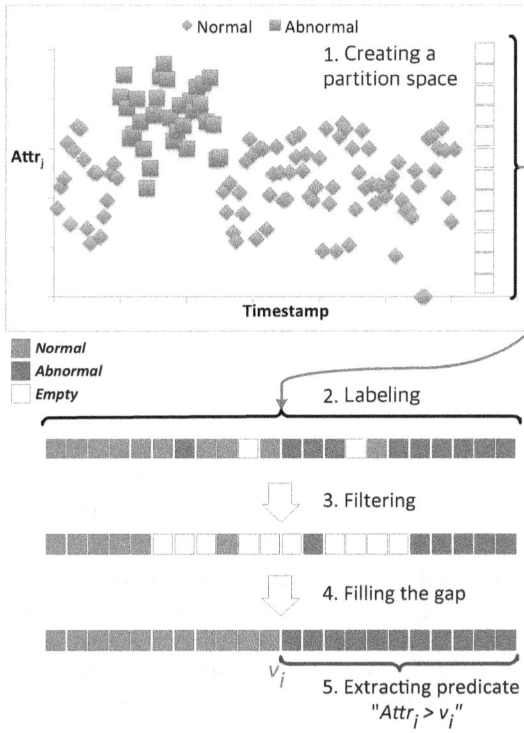

Figure 4: Example of finding a predicate over an attribute in the partition space. (Steps 3 & 4 are only applied to numeric attributes.)

these steps is presented in Algorithm 1. In the rest of this section, we explain each of these steps in detail.

Algorithm 1: Predicate Generation.

Inputs: T: input tuples (with k attributes)
A: abnormal region
N: normal region
R: number of partitions
θ: normalized difference threshold
δ: anomaly distance multiplier
Output: π: list of predicates with high separation power

$\pi \leftarrow \emptyset$ **// start with no predicate**
foreach $\texttt{Attr}_i \in \{\texttt{Attr}_1, \ldots, \texttt{Attr}_k\}$ **do**
  if $\texttt{Attr}_i$ is numeric **then**
    $P \leftarrow$ create a partition space for $Attr_i$ with R partitions
    $P_L \leftarrow$ label P based on tuples T and regions A, N
    $P_{L,Filtered} \leftarrow$ filter P_L
    $P^* \leftarrow$ fill the gap in $P_{L,Filtered}$ based on δ
    Norm($\texttt{Attr}_i$) $\leftarrow$ Normalization of $\texttt{Attr}_i$ into $[0, 1]$ values
    $\mu_A \leftarrow$ Average of Norm($\texttt{Attr}_i$) for tuples in A
    $\mu_N \leftarrow$ Average of Norm($\texttt{Attr}_i$) for tuples in N
    $d \leftarrow |\mu_A - \mu_N|$
    if P^* contains a single block of consecutive abnormal partitions ***and*** $d > \theta$
    then
      Pred $\leftarrow$ extract a candidate predicate from P^*
      $\pi \leftarrow \pi \cup$ Pred **// add Pred into the list**
    end
  else if $\texttt{Attr}_i$ is categorical **then**
    $P \leftarrow$ create a partition space for $Attr_i$ with $|Unique(\texttt{Attr}_i)|$ partitions
    $P_L \leftarrow$ label P based on tuples T and regions A, N
    if P_L has at least one abnormal partition
    then
      Pred $\leftarrow$ extract a candidate predicate from P_L
      $\pi \leftarrow \pi \cup$ Pred **// add Pred into the list**
    end
  end
end
return π

4.1 Creating a Partition Space

DBSherlock starts by creating a discretized domain for each attribute, called a *partition space*.

For each numeric attribute $\texttt{Attr}_i$, we create R equi-width partitions $\texttt{P} = \{\texttt{P}_1, \ldots, \texttt{P}_R\}$ that range from $\texttt{Min}(\texttt{Attr}_i)$ to $\texttt{Max}(\texttt{Attr}_i)$. The width of each partition is

$$\frac{\texttt{Max}(\texttt{Attr}_i) - \texttt{Min}(\texttt{Attr}_i)}{R}$$

We denote the lower and upper bounds of partition $\texttt{P}_j$ as $\texttt{lb}(\texttt{P}_j)$ and $\texttt{ub}(\texttt{P}_j)$, respectively. $\texttt{P}_j$ contains any value val of $\texttt{Attr}_i$ where $\texttt{lb}(\texttt{P}_j) \leq \texttt{val} < \texttt{ub}(\texttt{P}_j)$.

For example, if the values of an attribute range from 0 to 100 and we discretize them into buckets of size 20, their partition space will be {[0,20), [20,40), [40,60), [60,80), [80,100)}. We use equi-width partitions to preserve and map the distribution of input tuples in the abnormal and normal regions into the partition space, as shown in Figure 4. A secondary goal of our discretization step is to reduce the influence of having more tuples with normal values than with abnormal values. Thus, our discretization enables us to focus on the distribution of an attribute's value across the two regions.

Here, the number of partitions, R, is an important parameter, which decides the trade-off between our algorithm's computation time (see Section 4.6) and the ability of the individual partitions to distinguish normal from abnormal tuples. By default, DBSherlock uses 1,000 partitions (R=1,000) for numeric attributes, which is large enough to separate abnormal and normal tuples, yet small enough to optimize computation time. (We study the effect of different values of R on our predicate accuracy and run time in Appendix D.)

For each categorical attribute $\texttt{Attr}_i$, we create $|Unique(\texttt{Attr}_i)|$ number of partitions. Here, $|Unique(\texttt{Attr}_i)|$ is the number of unique values found in our dataset for $\texttt{Attr}_i$, i.e., one partition per each value of the attribute. We use $\texttt{C}_j$ to denote the (categorical) value represented by partition $\texttt{P}_j$. Unlike numeric attributes, the order of partitions for categorical attributes is unimportant.

4.2 Partition Labeling

Once the partition space is created, the next step is to mark each partition with one of three labels: {**Empty**, **Normal**, **Abnormal**}. For a numeric attribute $\texttt{Attr}_i$, an input tuple belongs to partition $\texttt{P}_j$, if the tuple's value for $\texttt{Attr}_i$ lies within $\texttt{P}_j$'s boundaries. If every tuple belonging to $\texttt{P}_j$ lies in the abnormal region specified by the user, $\texttt{P}_j$ is labeled as **Abnormal**. Conversely, if every tuple belonging to $\texttt{P}_j$ lies in the normal region, $\texttt{P}_j$ is labeled as **Normal**. Otherwise, the partition label is left **Empty**. (See Figure 4.)

For a categorical attribute, an input tuple belongs to a partition $\texttt{P}_j$, if the tuple's value for $\texttt{Attr}_i$ equals the category value of the partition, i.e., $\texttt{Attr}_i = \texttt{C}_j$. Since our categorical attributes are less noisy, we use a simpler labeling strategy. Let $\texttt{P}_j(\texttt{A})$ and $\texttt{P}_j(\texttt{N})$ be the number of tuples belonging to $\texttt{P}_j$ in the abnormal and normal

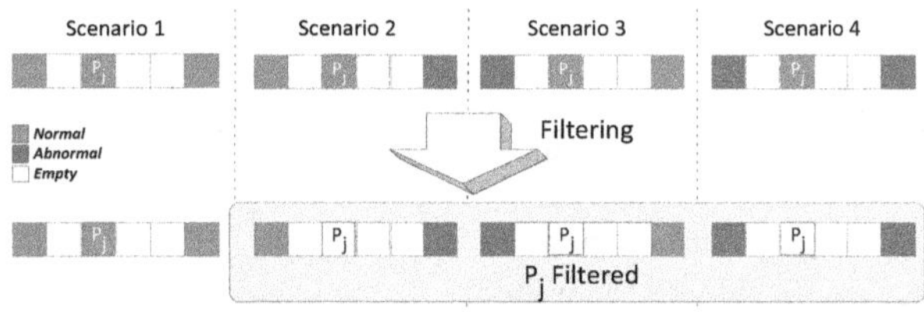

Figure 5: Different scenarios of filtering P_j in the partition space.

regions, respectively. P_j is labeled as `Abnormal` if $\mathsf{P}_j(\mathsf{A}) > \mathsf{P}_j(\mathsf{N})$. Similarly, P_j is labeled as `Normal` if $\mathsf{P}_j(\mathsf{A}) < \mathsf{P}_j(\mathsf{N})$. Otherwise, the partition label is left with an `Empty` label. For categorical attributes, our algorithm extracts a candidate predicate from the partition space right after the labeling step (see Section 4.5), skipping the next two steps.

4.3 Partition Filtering

After labeling, we filter some of the `Normal` and `Abnormal` partitions by replacing their labels with an `Empty` one. The filtering step is only applied to our numeric attributes, which are quite noisy. During this step, a partition P_j's label is replaced with `Empty`, if its original label is different from either of its two non-`Empty` adjacent partitions (i.e., the closest non-`Empty` partitions on the left and right side of P_j in the partition space). Figure 5 demonstrates various cases where a partition P_j is filtered out. Note that the only case where P_j remains unchanged is when both of its non-`Empty` adjacent partitions have the same label as P_j itself (shown as Scenario 1 in Figure 5). If we only have a single `Normal` or `Abnormal` partition to begin with, we deem it significant and do not filter it. Once all non-`Empty` partitions are processed, their labels are changed to `Empty` *simultaneously*. We do not perform this procedure incrementally to prevent a situation where partitions continuously filter each other out. If filtering is performed incrementally, the two partitions at each end of the partition space will also get filtered in Scenarios 2 and 3 in Figure 5.

Our filtering strategy aims to separate the `Normal` and `Abnormal` partitions that are originally mixed across the partition space (e.g., due to the noise in the data or user errors). If there is a predicate on attribute Attr_i that has high separation power, the `Normal` and `Abnormal` partitions are very likely to form well-separated clusters after the filtering step. This step mitigates some of the negative effects of noisy data or user's error, which could otherwise exclude a predicate with high separation power from the output. This idea is visually shown in Figure 4.

4.4 Filling the Gaps

This step is only applied to numeric attributes. After the filtering step, there will be larger blocks of consecutive `Abnormal` and `Normal` partitions, separated by `Empty` partitions. These `Empty` partitions were either initially `Empty` or were filtered out during the filtering step. Our algorithm fills these gaps before the predicate generation by labeling these `Empty` partitions as either `Normal` or `Abnormal` as follows.

We compare the distance of each `Empty` partition P_j to its two adjacent non-`Empty` partitions. If both adjacent partitions have the same label or if P_j has only one adjacent non-`Empty` partition (i.e., j=1 or j=R), P_j will receive the same label as its adjacent non-`Empty` partition(s) at the end of this step. If P_j's two adjacent non-`Empty` partitions have different labels, we calculate P_j's distance to each partition and assign it the label of the closer partition.

There is a special case where only `Abnormal` partitions remain after the filtering step. In this case, if we naïvely fill the gaps, every partition will become `Abnormal` and the algorithm will not find any predicates for the attribute. To handle this special case, we calculate the average value of the attribute over the input tuples in the normal region and label the partition that contains this average value as `Normal` regardless of its previous label. Then we fill the gaps according to the previously described procedure. (Without any `Normal` partitions, we will not be able to determine the direction of the predicate in the next step of the algorithm, i.e., whether Attr_i < v or Attr_i > v.)

To control the behavior of our algorithm, we also introduce a parameter δ, called the *anomaly distance multiplier*. When the `Empty` partition P_j is processed by the above procedure, we multiply its distance to its adjacent `Abnormal` partition by δ. Thus, δ>1 will cause more `Empty` partitions to be labeled as `Normal` while δ<1 results in more `Empty` partitions being labeled as `Abnormal`. In other words, with parameter δ, we can tune our predicates: δ<1 for more general predicates (i.e., more likely to flag tuples as abnormal) and δ>1 for more specific ones (i.e., less likely to flag tuples as abnormal). By default, DBSherlock uses δ = 10. (We study the effect of different values of δ on our predicates in Appendix D.)

4.5 Extracting Predicates from Partitions

This step is applied to both numeric and categorical attributes using slightly different procedures. For numeric attributes, the previous filtering step allows us to find attributes that have a predicate with high separation power, but there is still a possibility that some of these attributes are not related to the actual cause of the anomaly. To mitigate this problem, we perform the following procedure. First, we normalize each numeric attribute Attr_i by subtracting its minimum value from its original values val_i and dividing them by the attribute's range:

$$\mathsf{Norm}(\mathsf{val}_i) = \frac{\mathsf{val}_i - \mathsf{Min}(\mathsf{Attr}_i)}{\mathsf{Max}(\mathsf{Attr}_i) - \mathsf{Min}(\mathsf{Attr}_i)} \quad (2)$$

This results in the values of an attribute to range in $[0, 1]$. Let μ_A and μ_N be the average values of Norm(Attr_i) for tuples in the abnormal and normal regions, respectively. DBSherlock extracts a candidate predicate from Attr_i's partition space only if $|\mu_A - \mu_N| > \theta$, where θ is a parameter called the *normalized difference threshold*. The user can tune this threshold to adjust the selectivity of DBSherlock in finding predicates (we study the effect of this parameter in Appendix D).

After performing these normalization and thresholding procedures, we can extract candidate predicates from the partition space, as follows. As noted in section 3, we only seek predicates of the form Attr_i < x, Attr_i > x, and x < Attr_i < y. In the partition space, these types of predicates correspond to a single block of consecutive `Abnormal` partitions. Therefore, we extract a candidate predicate Pred for an attribute Attr_i if and only if there is a single block of consecutive `Abnormal` partitions.

For categorical attributes, our procedure for extracting a candidate predicate is much simpler. DBSherlock traverses the partition space of such attributes and extracts each category value C_j if its partition P_j is labeled as `Abnormal`. A predicate for a categorical attribute is of the form $\mathsf{Attr}_i \in \{c_1, \ldots, c_l\}$, where l is the number of partitions labeled as `Abnormal` and c_i's are their corresponding category values.

4.6 Time Complexity

For each attribute, our predicate generation algorithm scans the input tuples to label each partition. Then, it iterates over these partitions twice in the subsequent steps (i.e., 'Filtering' and 'Filling the gap' in Figure 4). Thus, the time complexity of DBSherlock's predicate generation algorithm is $O(k(X+R))$, where R is the number of partitions,[6] X is the number of input tuples, and k is the number of attributes. In Appendix D, we study the effectiveness and run-time of our algorithm for different values of these parameters.

5. INCORPORATING DOMAIN KNOWLEDGE

Our algorithm extracts predicates that have a high diagnostic power (see Section 8). However, some of these predicates may be secondary symptoms of the root cause, which if removed, can make the diagnosis even easier. This is because the fact that $\texttt{Pred}_i$ **implies** an anomaly, we cannot conclude that it also **causes** it. In fact, there could be another predicate, say $\texttt{Pred}_j$, causing both $\texttt{Pred}_i$ and the anomaly.

Thus, to further improve the accuracy of our predicates and prune secondary symptoms, DBSherlock allows for incorporating domain knowledge of attributes' semantics into the system. However, note that this mechanism is an optional feature, and as we show in our experiments, DBSherlock produces highly accurate explanations even without any domain knowledge (see Section 8.3). Also, DBSherlock is bootstrapped with domain knowledge only once for each specific version of OS or DBMS. In other words, DBAs do not need to modify this, as the semantics of DBMS and OS variables do not depend on the workload, e.g., OS CPU Usage always has the same meaning regardless of the specific workload.

Every piece of domain knowledge is encoded as a rule: $\texttt{Attr}_i \rightarrow \texttt{Attr}_j$. Each rule must satisfy the following conditions:

i. If predicates $\texttt{Pred}_i$ and $\texttt{Pred}_j$ (corresponding to attributes $\texttt{Attr}_i$ and $\texttt{Attr}_j$, respectively) are both extracted, $\texttt{Pred}_j$ is likely to be a secondary symptom of $\texttt{Pred}_i$.

ii. $\texttt{Attr}_i \rightarrow \texttt{Attr}_j$ and $\texttt{Attr}_j \rightarrow \texttt{Attr}_i$ cannot coexist.

For instance, if $\texttt{Attr}_i$ is the 'DBMS CPU Usage' and $\texttt{Attr}_j$ is the 'OS CPU Usage', then $\texttt{Attr}_i \rightarrow \texttt{Attr}_j$ is a valid rule since DBMS CPU usage effects OS CPU usage, but not vice versa.

However, given a rule $\texttt{Attr}_i \rightarrow \texttt{Attr}_j$, and the corresponding predicates $\texttt{Pred}_i$ and $\texttt{Pred}_j$, whether $\texttt{Pred}_j$ will be filtered out will require further analysis, since the domain knowledge may not be a perfect reflection of the reality either. For instance, the rule 'DBMS CPU Usage' → 'OS CPU Usage' may occasionally break. For example, there might be other attributes, such as 'Number of Processes' or 'Number of Threads' that are not utilized by the DBMS, but may affect 'OS CPU Usage'.

As a solution, DBSherlock tests the independence between $\texttt{Attr}_i$ and $\texttt{Attr}_j$ based on their continuous (or categorical) values. For continuous attributes, we discretize the two attributes $\texttt{Attr}_i$ and $\texttt{Attr}_j$ with γ equi-width bins for each attribute. We then construct a two-dimensional joint histogram from the input data, estimating the joint probability distribution of the two attributes. For categorical attributes, a joint histogram is constructed from the input data. For testing independence, we use the joint probability distribution of the two attributes to calculate their *mutual information*.

We denote the mutual information of two attributes $\texttt{Attr}_i$ and $\texttt{Attr}_j$ by $\texttt{MI}(\texttt{Attr}_i, \texttt{Attr}_j)$, defined as:

$$\texttt{MI}(\texttt{Attr}_i, \texttt{Attr}_j) = H(\texttt{Attr}_i) + H(\texttt{Attr}_j) - H(\texttt{Attr}_i, \texttt{Attr}_j)$$

where $H(\texttt{Attr}_i)$ is the entropy of the attribute $\texttt{Attr}_i$ and $H(\texttt{Attr}_i, \texttt{Attr}_j)$ is the joint entropy of the two attributes [18]. An independence factor $\kappa(\texttt{Attr}_i, \texttt{Attr}_j)$ of the two attributes is then calculated as follows:

$$\kappa(\texttt{Attr}_i, \texttt{Attr}_j) = \frac{\texttt{MI}(\texttt{Attr}_i, \texttt{Attr}_j)^2}{H(\texttt{Attr}_i)H(\texttt{Attr}_j)}$$

[6] A similar analysis applies if the number of partitions differ.

The value of κ will be 0, if the two attributes are independent and approaches 1 with higher dependence. We perform the independence test by comparing the value of κ with a threshold κ_t (by default, we use $\kappa_t = 0.15$), and the two attributes pass the test if $\kappa < \kappa_t$. If the two attributes do not pass the independence test, we conclude that the rule $\texttt{Attr}_i \rightarrow \texttt{Attr}_j$ is indeed valid, and $\texttt{Pred}_j$ is merely a secondary symptom of $\texttt{Pred}_i$ and filter out $\texttt{Pred}_j$. If the two attributes pass the independence test, we conclude that the rule $\texttt{Attr}_i \rightarrow \texttt{Attr}_j$ does not apply, and leave both predicates in the output.

For MySQL on Linux, the following four rules are sufficient to encode such relationships:

1. DBMS CPU Usage → OS CPU Usage
2. OS Allocated Pages → OS Free Pages
3. OS Used Swap Space → OS Free Swap Space
4. OS CPU Usage → OS CPU Idle

The first rule encodes the subset relationship. The last three rules encode the fact that one attribute is always a constant value minus the other attribute, and is thus uninteresting. In Section 8.6, we show that even without these rules, DBSherlock's accuracy drops by only 2–3%. We evaluate the effectiveness of this approach in pruning secondary symptoms in Appendix F.

6. INCORPORATING CAUSAL MODELS

Previous work on performance explanation [34] has only focused on generating explanations in the form of predicates. DBSherlock improves on this functionality by generating substantially more accurate predicates (20-55% higher F1-measure; see Section 8.4). However, a primary objective of DBSherlock is to go beyond raw predicates, and offer explanations that are more human-readable and descriptive. For example, the cause of a performance hiccup could be a network congestion due to a malfunctioning network router. Initially, the user will rely on DBSherlock's generated predicates as diagnostic clues to identify the actual cause of the performance problem more easily. However, once the root cause is diagnosed, s/he can notify DBSherlock as to what the actual cause was. DBSherlock then relates the generated predicates to the actual cause and saves them in the form of a causal model. This model will be consulted in future diagnoses to provide a human-readable explanation (i.e., 'malfunctioning router') for similar situations.

To utilize the user feedback, DBSherlock uses a simplified version of the *causal model* proposed in the seminal work of Halpern and Pearl [28]. Our causal model consists of two parts: *cause variable* and *effect predicates*. The *cause variable* is a binary, exogenous variable[7] labeled by the end user. When the *cause variable* is set to *true*, it activates all of its *effect predicates*. For example, Figure 6 is a causal model with 'Log Rotation' as the *cause variable* and three *effect predicates*. According to this model, if there is an event of 'Log Rotation' (i.e. *cause variable* is *true*) then these three *effect predicates* will also be true.

The following example describes how such causal models are constructed and used in DBSherlock. Consider a scenario where the user selects an abnormal region for which DBSherlock returns the following predicates:

$\texttt{CpuWait} > 50\% \wedge \texttt{Latency} > 100\text{ms} \wedge \texttt{DiskWrite} > 5\text{MB/s}$

[7] An exogenous variable is a variable whose values are determined by factors outside the model [28].

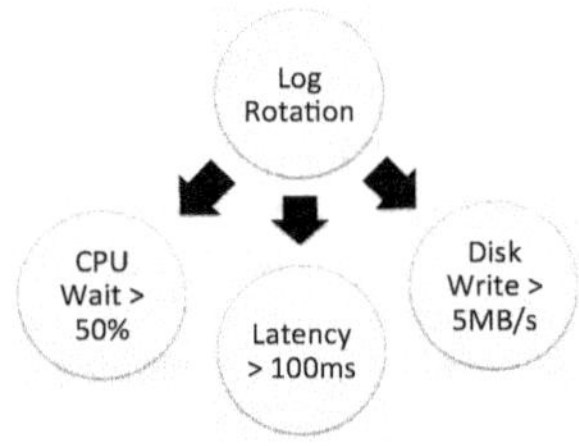

Figure 6: An example of a causal model in `DBSherlock`.

Also, suppose that the user is able to diagnose the actual cause of the problem with the help of these predicates; assume that by inspecting the recent system logs she establishes that the cause was the rotation of the redo log file.[8] Once this feedback is received from the user, `DBSherlock` can link this cause with these predicates as shown in Figure 6. After that, for every diagnosis inquiry in the future, `DBSherlock` calculates the *confidence* of this causal model and 'Log Rotation' is reported as a possible cause if its confidence is higher than a threshold λ. By default, `DBSherlock` displays only those causes whose confidence is higher than λ=20%. However, the user can modify λ as a knob (i.e., using a sliding bar) to interactively view fewer or more causes.

Over time, additional causal models might be added in the system as a result of inspecting new performance problems. When multiple causal models are available in the system, `DBSherlock` consults all of them (i.e., computes their confidence) and returns those models whose confidence is higher than λ to the user, presented in their decreasing order of confidence. When none of the causes offered by the existing models are deemed helpful by the user, she always has the option of asking `DBSherlock` to simply show the original predicates instead. Also, when none of the causal models achieve a confidence higher than λ (e.g., when the given anomaly has not been previously observed in the system), `DBSherlock` only displays the generated predicates. Again, once the cause is diagnosed and shared with the system, `DBSherlock` creates a new causal model to be used in the future. (See Figure 2 in Section 2.)

We evaluate the accuracy of the generated explanations in Section 8. Next, we explain how `DBSherlock` computes the confidence of each causal model (Section 6.1), and how it merges multiple models to improve their explanatory power (Section 6.2).

6.1 Confidence of a Causal Model

In `DBSherlock` we define the confidence of a causal model as the average `separation` power of its *effect predicates* in the partition space. Note that, unlike equation (1), here we use the partition space instead of the input tuples to reduce the effect of the noise in real-world data (see Section 4.1). Formally:

Confidence of a causal model. Let $\{\texttt{Pred}_1, \ldots, \texttt{Pred}_n\}$ be the *effect predicates* of a given causal model $\mathcal{M}$, where $\texttt{Pred}_i$ is defined over $\texttt{Attr}_i$. Also, let $P_{i,N}$ and $P_{i,A}$ be the partitions labeled as **`Normal`** and **`Abnormal`** in the partition space of $\texttt{Attr}_i$, respectively. We define the *confidence* $\mathcal{C}_\mathcal{M}$ of the causal model $\mathcal{M}$ as:

$$\mathcal{C}_\mathcal{M} = \frac{\sum_{i=1}^{n} \frac{|\texttt{Pred}_i(P_{i,A})|}{|P_{i,A}|} - \frac{|\texttt{Pred}_i(P_{i,N})|}{|P_{i,N}|}}{n} \tag{3}$$

where $\texttt{Pred}(P)$ is the set of partitions in P that satisfy predicate `Pred`.

The idea behind this definition is to estimate the likelihood of a *cause variable* being true given the normal and abnormal partitions, based on the assumption that if the model's *cause variable* is true, then its *effect predicates* are also likely to exhibit high separation power in their partition spaces.

[8]In MySQL, log rotations can cause performance hiccups when the adaptive flushing option is disabled.

6.2 Merging Causal Models

Among the *effect predicates* of a causal model, some predicates may have less or no relevance to the actual cause, e.g., some predicates could simply be a side-effect of the actual cause. Also, since the *effect predicates* of a single causal model reflect the specific values observed in a particular instance of an anomaly, they may not be applicable to other instances of the same cause. In `DBSherlock`, multiple causal models might be created for the same cause while analyzing different anomalies over time. `DBSherlock` can improve such causal models by merging them into a single one.

Merging causal models eliminates some of the unnecessary and less relevant *effect predicates*, while enabling relevant *effect predicates* to apply to different anomaly instances caused by the same cause. We merge two causal models by:

1. keeping only those *effect predicates* that are on attributes common to both models; and
2. merging two predicates on the same attribute into a single predicate that includes the boundaries (or categories) of both.

Suppose that we have two causal models with the same cause: $\mathcal{M}_1$ with the *effect predicates* {`A` > `10`, `B` > `100`, `C` > `20`, `E` ∈ {'`xx`', '`yy`', '`zz`'}}, and $\mathcal{M}_2$ with the *effect predicates* {`A` > `15`, `C` > `15`, `D` < `250`, `E` ∈ {'`xx`', '`zz`'}}. To merge $\mathcal{M}_1$ and $\mathcal{M}_2$, we only keep {`A` > `10`, `C` > `20`, `E` ∈ {'`xx`', '`yy`', '`zz`'}} from $\mathcal{M}_1$ and {`A` > `15`, `C` > `15`, `E` ∈ {'`xx`', '`zz`'}} from $\mathcal{M}_2$ since attributes `A`, `C` and `E` are common to both models.

Next, we compare the two predicates on the same attribute and merge them such that the merged predicate includes both. Here, merging {`A` > `10`} and {`A` > `15`} leads to {`A` > `10`} and merging {`C` > `20`} and {`C` > `15`} leads to {`C` > `15`}. Likewise, merging {`E` ∈ {'`xx`', '`yy`', '`zz`'}} and {`E` ∈ {'`xx`', '`zz`'}} leads to {`E` ∈ {'`xx`', '`zz`'}}. Thus, in this example, the *effect predicates* of the merged causal model will be {`A` > `10`, `C` > `15`, `E` ∈ {'`xx`', '`yy`', '`zz`'}}. Note that numeric predicates with different directions (e.g., {`A` > `10`} and {`A` < `30`}) are considered inconsistent. Such predicates are not merged and will be discarded.

We study the effect of merging causal models in Section 8.5, where we show that the merged causal models are on average 30% more accurate than the original models.

7. AUTOMATIC ANOMALY DETECTION

Sometimes, an anomaly may not be visually obvious to a human user inspecting a performance plot. In such situations, users may mistakenly specify a normal region as abnormal and vice versa. To aid with these cases, `DBSherlock` also provides an option for automatic anomaly detection. Thus, users can either (i) rely on `DBSherlock` to find and suggest anomalies to them, or (ii) continue to manually find anomalies but compare them with those found by `DBSherlock` for reassurance.

There is much work on outlier detection in different contexts [15, 19, 33, 40, 41, 42, 43, 44, 45, 46, 48]. In `DBSherlock`, we introduce an algorithm for the automatic detection of the anomaly regions. Our algorithm utilizes the DBSCAN clustering algorithm [25] and works as follows.

First, we normalize each attribute $\texttt{Attr}_i$, which is equivalent to the normalization step in our predicate generation algorithm (Equation (2) in Section 4.5). We then choose relevant attributes to detect possible anomalies, which are characterized by a subsequence in the time series with an abrupt change in the values. For attributes that we cannot identify such a behavior, we exclude them from our analysis as they are likely to have an insignificant separation power. We quantify this behavior and call it a *potential power* of an attribute, denoted as $PP(\texttt{Attr}_i)$.

To calculate $PP(\texttt{Attr}_i)$, we first define a sliding window $w(\tau)$ as a subsequence of size τ in the time series. We also denote the median of $\texttt{Attr}_i$ as $\texttt{Median}(\texttt{Attr}_i)$ and denote the median of the values within a sliding window $w(\tau)$ as $\texttt{Median}(\texttt{Attr}_i,\ w)$. Then $PP(\texttt{Attr}_i)$ is calculated as follows:

$$PP(\texttt{Attr}_i) = \max_{w \in W} |\texttt{Median}(\texttt{Attr}_i) - \texttt{Median}(\texttt{Attr}_i,\ w)| \tag{4}$$

where W represents the set of all possible sliding windows of size τ. Equation (4) uses a median filter to calculate the maximum absolute difference between the overall median and the median of values in each window. We only include attributes with a potential power greater than a threshold $PP_t \in [0, 1]$. (DBSherlock uses $\tau = 20$ and $PP_t = 0.3$ as default values.)

We use DBSCAN to build clusters with the selected attributes from the previous step. DBSCAN takes two parameters, ϵ and $minPts$. For our algorithm, we fix $minPts$ to 3 and use the *k-dist* function to build a list L_k of the distances of the *k-th nearest neighbors*, as suggested in [25], to determine ϵ. We have empirically found $\epsilon = \max(L_k)/4$ to perform well in DBSherlock.

Given the clusters formed by DBSCAN, our algorithm returns the points in all clusters whose sizes are less than 20% of the total number of data items. This is under the assumption that the abnormal region is relatively smaller than the normal region. In Appendix E, we evaluate DBSherlock's accuracy when using automatic anomaly detection against a manually selected anomaly and another anomaly detection algorithm, PerfAugur [41].

8. EVALUATION

In this section, we empirically evaluate the effectiveness of DBSherlock. The goals of our experiments are to show that:

(i) Our causal models produce accurate explanations (Section 8.3).

(ii) Even without causal models, the raw predicates generated by DBSherlock are more accurate than those generated by the state-of-the-art explanation framework (Section 8.4).

(iii) Our idea of merging causal models improves the quality of our explanations significantly (Sections 8.5).

(iv) Incorporating domain knowledge allows DBSherlock to achieve higher accuracy (Section 8.6).

(v) DBSherlock is able to explain compound situations where multiple anomalies arise simultaneously (Section 8.7).

(vi) Using our predicates, users can diagnose the actual cause of performance anomalies much more accurately (Section 8.8).

We have included additional experiments in the Appendix for interested readers.

8.1 Experiment Setup

To collect log data with different types of anomalies, we ran different mixtures of the TPC-C benchmark [5] on Microsoft Azure [2] virtual machine instances. In all our experiments, we have used two Microsoft Azure A3-tier instances, each with 4 CPU cores of 2.1Ghz (AMD Opteron 4171H) and 7GB of RAM running Ubuntu 14.04. We employed one of the two A3 instances to run MySQL 5.6.20 and the other to simulate clients (using OLTPBenchmark framework [3, 21]). For stress-based experiments, we also used a tool called stress-ng [4] which can artificially stress the system by taking up excessive CPU, I/O and network resources when needed. Each individual experiment (called a *dataset* in this paper) consisted of two minutes of normal activity plus one or more abnormal situations (of varying length). We ran our experiments using both TPC-C and TPC-E. Due to space constraints and the similarity of the results, here we only report our TPC-C results and defer TPC-E results to Appendix A. The default setting used in our TPC-C workload was a scale factor of 500 (i.e., 50GB) with 128 terminals. We also experimented with different scale factors (from 16 to 500) and number of terminals (from 16 to 128). The results were consistent across these different settings, and thus we only report our results using the default setting described above. In each dataset, we intentionally created various abnormal situations on the server, as described next.

8.2 Test Cases

To test our algorithm, we created 10 different classes of anomalies to represent some of the important types of real-world problems that can deteriorate the performance of a database. During the two-minute run of the normal workload in each dataset, we invoked the actual cause of an anomaly with different start times and durations. For each type of anomaly, we collected 11 different datasets by varying the duration when possible (e.g., stressing system resources) or its start time (i.e., the time when the cause of an anomaly is triggered) when the actual duration was impossible to control (e.g., running *mysqldump*). The duration or start time of the anomalies ranged from 30 to 80 seconds with the increment of 5 seconds, yielding 11 datasets (i.e., 30, 35, $\cdots$, 80) for each type of anomaly (a total of 110 datasets). For each dataset, we manually selected a region of anomaly via visual inspection; the region left unselected automatically became the normal region.

Table 1 lists the types and descriptions of the different classes of anomalies that we tested within our experiments. These anomalies are designed to reflect a wide range of realistic scenarios that can negatively impact the performance of a transactional database.

8.3 Accuracy of Single Causal Models

Our goal in this section is to evaluate the effectiveness of our causal models in producing correct explanations. It is quite common that an anomaly from a certain cause is only observable a few times over the lifetime of a database operation. This makes log samples of such anomalies quite scarce in many cases (e.g., disk failure) and thus necessitates that our framework identifies the correct cause even when our causal model is created from a single dataset. Thus, in each test case we only used a single dataset to construct a causal model with θ=0.2 (which is the normalized difference threshold, see Section 4.5). This is the default value of θ in DBSherlock chosen to aggressively filter out attributes with insignificant behavior in the anomaly region. We applied the constructed causal model on all the remaining 109 datasets to obtain its confidence in each test case. We repeated this process until every dataset was chosen to construct a causal model.

With our algorithm, the correct causal models achieve the highest confidence in all 10 test cases (i.e., the correct cause was shown as the most likely cause to the user). The margin (i.e., positive difference) of confidence between the correct model and the highest among incorrect models is on average 13.5%. In other words, not only does the correct model achieve the highest confidence (and is shown to the user as the most likely cause), but its confidence is also well separated from the highest-ranked incorrect model. (In Section 8.5, we show that our model merging technique improves this margin even further.) Figure 7 shows the margin of confidence of

Type of anomaly	Description
Poorly Written Query	Execute a poorly written JOIN query, which would run efficiently if written properly.
Poor Physical Design	Create an unnecessary index on tables where mostly INSERT statements are executed.
Workload Spike	Greatly increase the rate of transactions and the number of clients simulated by OLTPBenchmark (128 additional terminals with transaction rate of 50,000).
I/O Saturation	Invoke stress-ng, which spawns multiple processes that spin on write()/unlink()/sync() system calls.
Database Backup	Run *mysqldump* on the TPC-C database instance to dump the table to the client machine over the network.
Table Restore	Dump the pre-dumped *history* table back into the database instance.
CPU Saturation	Invoke stress-ng, which spawns multiple processes calling poll() system calls to stress CPU resources.
Flush Log/Table	Flush all tables and logs by invoking *mysqladmin* commands ('flush-logs' and 'refresh').
Network Congestion	Simulate network congestion by adding an artificial 300-milliseconds delay to every traffic over the network via Linux's *tc* (Traffic Control) command.
Lock Contention	Change the transaction mix to execute *NewOrder* transactions only on a single warehouse and district.

Table 1: Ten types of performance anomalies used in our experiments.

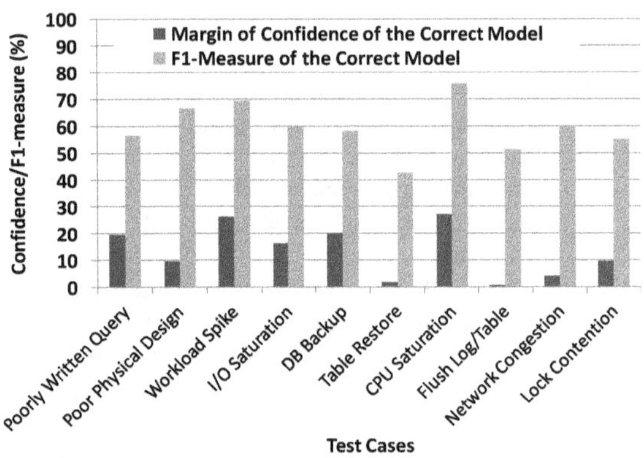

Figure 7: The margin of confidence and the average F1-measure of the correct causal model for different anomalies.

the correct causal model, which compares the average confidence of the correct causal model to the highest confidence among all other (incorrect) models for different types of anomalies.

Here, anomalies caused by 'Table Restore' and 'Flush Log/Table' proved most illusive, as they yielded the lowest confidence among the causal models. This was because the two anomalies shared the common characteristic that the DBMS performed too many disk I/Os. However, even in this case, `DBSherlock` could correctly distinguish the correct cause from the incorrect ones.

Overall, this challenging experiment is an extremely encouraging result showing that `DBSherlock` is capable of generating the correct explanation even with a single dataset as a training sample and in the presence of 9 other competing models.

8.4 DBSherlock Predicates versus PerfXplain

We compared the accuracy of our predicates with predicates generated by the state-of-the-art performance explanation framework, PerfXplain [34]. Since PerfXplain is designed to work with MapReduce logs, we had to re-implement PerfXplain's algorithm to fit into our context. Originally, PerfXplain operates on pairs of MapReduce jobs. Instead, we modified it to use pairs of our input tuples. We used the following query for PerfXplain:

```
EXPECTED avg_latency_difference = insignificant
OBSERVED avg_latency_difference = significant
```

where two average latencies are deemed significant if their difference is at least 50% of the smaller value. We chose the same parameters for PerfXplain as suggested in [34] (i.e., we used 2,000 samples and a weight value of 0.8 for its scoring rules). We also varied the number of predicates from 1 to 10 and chose 2, which yielded the best results for PerfXplain. With 11 datasets for each case, we used 10 datasets to generate predicates and the accuracy of generated predicates was tested on the remaining dataset. Figure 9 demonstrates the average precision, recall and F1-measure in comparison. Our predicates achieved better accuracy than PerfXplain in nearly all cases (except for recall on one test case). Most notably, `DBSherlock` improves on PerfXplain's F1-measure by upto 55% (28% on average). This shows that performance explanation and diagnosis for OLTP workloads requires drastically different techniques than those developed for OLAP and map-reduce workloads.

8.5 Effectiveness of Merged Causal Models

When multiple causal models are available (from diagnosing different datasets), `DBSherlock` tries to merge them as much as possible in order to further improve the relevance and accuracy of the generated explanations. To evaluate the effectiveness of our merging strategy, we conducted a series of experiments, each using multiple datasets as training samples. We randomly assigned about 50% of the datasets from each type of anomaly (i.e., 5 out of 11 datasets) to construct and merge causal models for each type. Merged causal models were then used to calculate the confidence on the remaining 6 datasets. The process was repeated 50 times, resulting in 300 instances of explanations for each test case. We used a lower value of θ, namely $\theta = 0.05$, for our merged causal models (in contrast to 0.20 used for our single causal models). With a lower value of θ, we can maximize the effect of merging causal models by having more predicates for each causal model at the start.

The results of these experiments are summarized in Figure 8a, showing that merging significantly increases the average margin of confidence against the second-highest confidence in all test cases.

To compare the accuracy of each explanation, we counted the number of cases where the correct cause was included in the top-k possible causes shown to a user. As shown in Figure 8b, `DBSherlock` presented the correct cause as the top explanation in almost every instance. In other words, k=1 would always be sufficient for achieving an accuracy greater than 98%. If we allow `DBSherlock` to list the top-2 possible explanations, then it identifies the correct cause in 99% of the cases.

We also studied the effectiveness of merging causal models with respect to the number of datasets used in constructing each causal model. As shown in Figure 8c, the accuracy of the merged causal models increases with more datasets. The accuracy quickly reaches 95% with only two datasets if only the top cause is returned, and it reaches 99% if the top two causes are returned. This experiment highlights that `DBSherlock` only requires a few manual diagnoses of an anomaly to construct highly accurate causal models.

In summary, the merging of causal models greatly improves the accuracy and quality of our explanations, generating predicates that

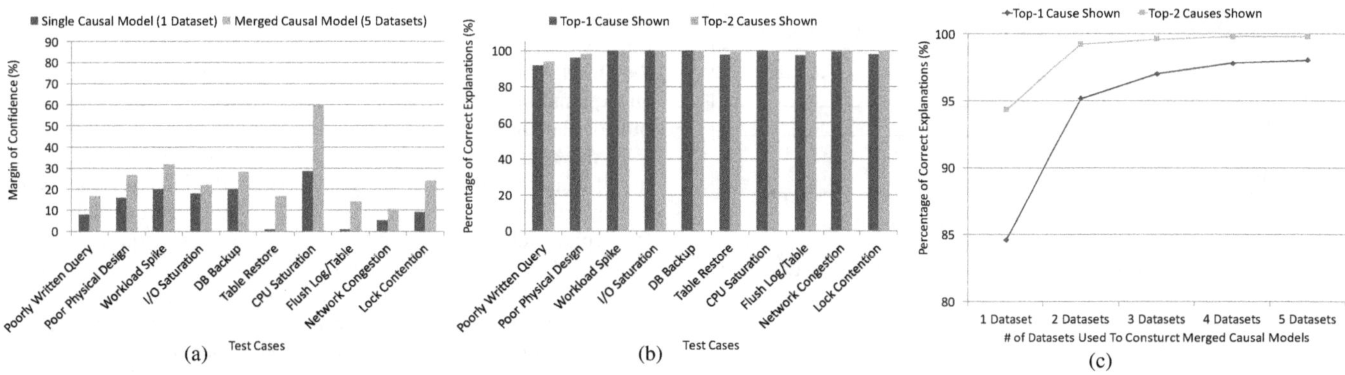

Figure 8: (a) The margin of confidence for single versus merged causal models, (b) the ratio of correct explanations for merged causal models (if the top-k possible causes are shown to the user), and (c) the effect of the number of datasets (i.e., number of manual diagnoses required) on the accuracy of the casual model.

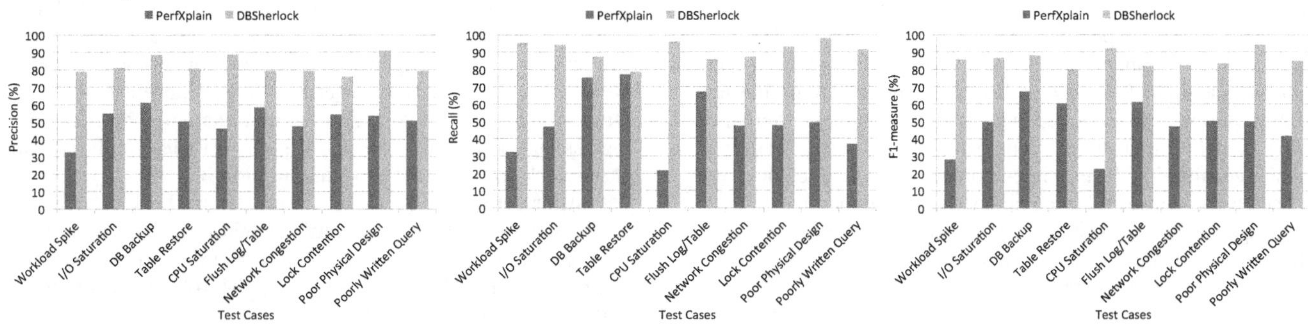

Figure 9: Average precision, recall and F1-measure of predicates generated by `DBSherlock` and PerfXplain.

are more relevant to the cause. Only a few datasets of the same anomaly are needed to construct a merged causal model that achieves an accuracy greater than 95%.

8.6 Effect of Incorporating Domain Knowledge

To study the effect of incorporating domain knowledge, we incorporated the four rules introduced in Section 5 into `DBSherlock`, and constructed single causal models with and without these rules, similar to the setup of Section 8.3.

	Accuracy if shown top-1 cause	Accuracy if shown top-2 causes
With Domain Knowledge	85.3%	94.8%
Without Domain Knowledge	82.7%	93.2%

Table 2: Ratio of correct causes with & without domain knowledge.

Table 2 reports the accuracy of single causal models with and without domain knowledge. Domain knowledge removed predicates that were a secondary symptom, and thus less relevant for the correct diagnosis of a given anomaly, improving the accuracy of causal models by 2.6% if shown the top-1 cause and 1.6% if shown the top-2 causes. On the other hand, this experiment shows that, in practice, `DBSherlock` works surprisingly well even without any domain knowledge. (To fully evaluate the effect of domain knowledge in removing secondary symptoms, we report additional experiments in Appendix F using synthetic data.)

8.7 Explaining Compound Situations

It is not uncommon in a transactional database that multiple problems occur simultaneously. These compound situations add a new level of difficulty to diagnostic systems. We ran an experiment to address the framework's capability in such compound situations. We created six cases, where two or three anomalies happen at the same time during the two-minute run of our normal workload. For this experiment, causal models were constructed for each individual test case by merging causal models from every dataset. Explanations were then generated for the compound test cases.

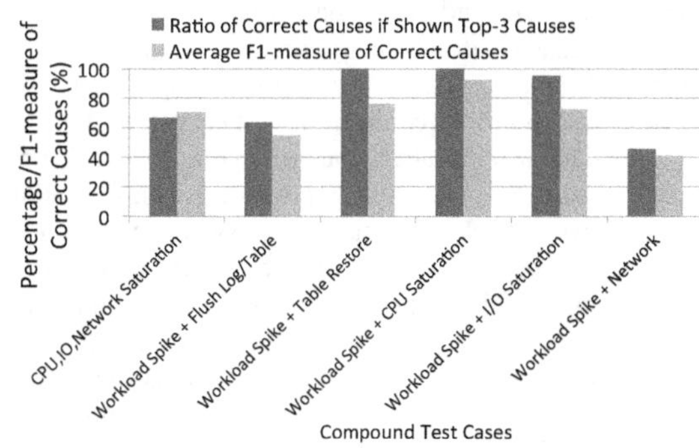

Figure 10: Ratio of the correct causes and their average F1-measure for compound situations (when top-3 causes are shown to the user).

Figure 10 demonstrates the ratio and the average F1-measure of correct causes (when three possible causes were offered to the user). On average, our explanation contained more than two-thirds of the correct causes, except for 'Workload Spike + Network Congestion'. For this dataset, `DBSherlock` missed the 'Workload Spike' and only returned 'Network Congestion' as the correct cause. This was because 'Network Congestion' had reduced the impact of 'Workload Spike' on the system (by slowing down the rate of incoming

Background	# of participants	Avg. # of correct answers (out of 10)
Baseline (No Predicates)	N/A	2.5
Preliminary DB Knowledge	20	7.5
DB Usage Experience	15	7.8
DB Research or DBA Experience	13	7.8

Table 3: The summary of the user study.

queries), and hence made it difficult for DBSherlock to identify their simultaneous occurrence.

8.8 User Study

We also performed a user study to evaluate the ability of our generated predicates in helping users diagnose the actual cause of performance problems. We asked various people who had some experience with databases to participate in a web-based questionnaire. We categorized the participants into three levels of competency based on their experience: *Preliminary DB Knowledge* (e.g., SQL knowledge or undergraduate course on databases), *DB Usage Experience*, and *DB Research or DBA Experience*. We used a few trivial questions to filter out spammers from genuine participants, leaving us with a total of 20 participants in our study. The questionnaire consisted of 10 multiple-choice questions. Each question had one correct cause and three randomly chosen incorrect causes. In each question, we presented a graph of average latency to our participants, with a pre-specified anomaly region and DBSherlock's generated predicates explaining the anomaly.

Table 3 shows the summary of the user study. Here, the first row represents the random baseline, i.e., where no predicates are presented to the user. Participants with preliminary database knowledge were able to identify the correct cause in 75% of the cases. Participants with practical database usage or above identified the correct cause in 78% of the cases. This promising result shows that the predicates generated by DBSherlock can help the end user correctly diagnose anomalies in practice.

9. RELATED WORK

Our work incorporates recent research in the fields of causality, performance diagnosis, and outlier detection.

Causality. Our work draws on the notion of causality proposed by Halpern and Pearl [28, 29]. We apply a simplified version of their causal model to introduce the notion of causality in our explanations. In the database literature, the notion of causality is brought together with data provenance [14, 17]. Meliou et al. [36] adapt the notion of causality to explain the cause of answers and non-answers in the output of database queries. In the context of probabilistic databases, Kanagal et al. [32] define the notion of an input tuple's *influence* on a query result. Scorpion [46] explains outliers in aggregate results of a query by unifying the concepts of *causality* and *influence*. Our notions of *normal* and *anomaly* are similar to Scorpion's *hold-out* and *outlier* sets, respectively.

Performance diagnosis. There have been many applications of performance diagnosis in databases [22], such as tuning query performance [8, 30], diagnosing databases that run on storage area networks [11], or parameter tuning [23]. Benoit [9] and Dias et al. [20] propose tools for automatic diagnosis of performance problems in commercial databases. However, [9] requires DBAs to provide a set of manual rules and [20] relies on detailed internal performance measurements from the DBMS (e.g., time spent in various modules of Oracle to process a query). More importantly, these tools lack explanatory features to answer 'why' a performance problem has occurred. In contrast, DBSherlock produces accurate explanations even without manual rules and using only aggregate statistics. Also, previous work has not accounted for the interaction of the DBMS with the machine that it is running on. DBSherlock gives an explanation based on every statistic it can gather both inside and outside the DBMS.

In the context of MapReduce, there is work on automatic tuning of MapReduce programs [7, 31]. Here, the most relevant work is PerfXplain [34], which generates predicate-based explanations. PerfXplain helps debug MapReduce jobs, answering questions such as 'Why Job A is faster than Job B?'. DBSherlock is designed for OLTP workloads, its predicates are more accurate than those of PerfXplain (see Section 8.4), and can incorporate causal models.

There has been much work on automated performance diagnosis in other areas. Gmach et al. [26] use a *fuzzy controller* to remedy exceptional situations in an enterprise application. Their controller, however, requires the rules to be hard-coded and pre-defined by experts. In contrast, DBSherlock allows for causal models to be added, merged, and refined as new anomalies occur in the future. Further, while DBSherlock allows for incorporating domain knowledge, it can provide accurate explanations even without domain knowledge (see Section 8.6). Mahimkar et al. [35] propose a tool for troubleshooting IPTV networks, but assume that large correlation and regression coefficients among pairs of attributes imply causality. DBSherlock does not make this assumption.

Outlier detection. DBSherlock uses a simple but effective outlier detection strategy to autonomously monitor database performance (Section 7). Allowing users to choose from additional outlier detection algorithms (e.g., [15, 19, 33, 40, 41, 42, 43, 44, 45, 46, 48]) will make an interesting future work.

10. CONCLUSION

Performance diagnosis of database workloads is one of the most challenging tasks DBAs face on a daily basis. Besides basic visualization and logging mechanisms, current databases provide little help in automating this adhoc, tedious, and error-prone task. In this paper, we presented DBSherlock, a framework that explains performance anomalies in the context of a complex OLTP environment. A user can select a region in a performance graph, which s/he thinks is abnormal, and ask DBSherlock to provide a diagnostic explanation for the observed anomaly. DBSherlock explains the anomaly in the form of predicates and possible causes produced by causal models. These explanations aid our users in diagnosing the correct cause of the performance problems more easily and more accurately. We also demonstrated that the confidence of our causal models can be increased via merging multiple causal models sharing the same cause. Our extensive experiments show that our algorithm is highly effective in identifying the correct explanations and is more accurate than the state-of-the art algorithm. As a much needed tool for coping with the increasing complexity of today's DBMS, DBSherlock is released as an open-source module in our workload management toolkit [1].

An important future work is to enable automatic actions for rectifying simple forms of performance anomaly (e.g., throttling certain tenants or triggering a migration), once they are detected and diagnosed with high confidence. We also plan to extend DBSherlock to go beyond creating causal models upon successful diagnoses, by documenting and storing the actions taken by the DBA to use as a suggestion for future occurrences of the same anomaly. Finally, DBSherlock's ideas might also be applicable to analytical workloads, e.g., in explaining performance problems caused by workload drifts [39].

Acknowledgements. This work is in part funded by National Science Foundation (IIS-1553169).

11. REFERENCES

[1] DBSeer. http://www.dbseer.org.

[2] Microsoft Azure. https://azure.microsoft.com/.

[3] OLTPBenchmark. http://oltpbenchmark.com/.

[4] stress-ng. http://tinyurl.com/pw59xs3.

[5] TPC-C benchmark. http://www.tpc.org/tpcc/.

[6] TPC-E benchmark. http://www.tpc.org/tpce/.

[7] S. Babu. Towards automatic optimization of mapreduce programs. In *SoCC*, 2010.

[8] P. Belknap, B. Dageville, K. Dias, and K. Yagoub. Self-tuning for sql performance in oracle database 11g. In *ICDE*, 2009.

[9] D. G. Benoit. Automatic diagnosis of performance problems in database management systems. In *ICAC*, 2005.

[10] K. A. Bollen. Structural equations with latent variables. 1989.

[11] N. Borisov, S. Uttamchandani, R. Routray, and A. Singh. Why did my query slow down. In *CIDR*, 2009.

[12] D. P. Brown, A. Richards, and D. Galeazzi. Teradata active system management, 2008.

[13] D. P. Brown and P. Sinclair. White paper: Real-time diagnostic tools for teradata's parallel query optimizer. Technical report, Teradata Solutions Group, 2000.

[14] P. Buneman, S. Khanna, and T. Wang-Chiew. Why and where: A characterization of data provenance. In *ICDT*. 2001.

[15] L. Cao, Q. Wang, and E. A. Rundensteiner. Interactive outlier exploration in big data streams. *PVLDB*, 7, 2014.

[16] S. Chen, A. Ailamaki, M. Athanassoulis, P. B. Gibbons, R. Johnson, I. Pandis, and R. Stoica. Tpc-e vs. tpc-c: Characterizing the new tpc-e benchmark via an i/o comparison study. *ACM SIGMOD Record*, 39(3):5–10, 2011.

[17] J. Cheney, L. Chiticariu, and W.-C. Tan. Provenance in databases: Why, how, and where. *Foundations and Trends in Databases*, 2007.

[18] T. M. Cover and J. A. Thomas. Entropy, relative entropy and mutual information. *Elements of Information Theory*, pages 12–49, 1991.

[19] A. Deligiannakis, V. Stoumpos, Y. Kotidis, V. Vassalos, and A. Delis. Outlier-aware data aggregation in sensor networks. In *ICDE*, 2008.

[20] K. Dias, M. Ramacher, U. Shaft, V. Venkataramani, and G. Wood. Automatic performance diagnosis & tuning in oracle. In *CIDR*, 2005.

[21] D. E. Difallah, A. Pavlo, C. Curino, and P. Cudre-Mauroux. Oltp-bench: An extensible testbed for benchmarking relational databases. *Proceedings of the VLDB Endowment*, 7(4):277–288, 2013.

[22] S. Duan, S. Babu, and K. Munagala. Fa: A system for automating failure diagnosis. In *ICDE*, 2009.

[23] S. Duan, V. Thummala, and S. Babu. Tuning database configuration parameters with ituned. *PVLDB*, 2, 2009.

[24] O. D. Duncan. Introduction to structural equation models. 1975.

[25] M. Ester, H.-P. Kriegel, J. Sander, and X. Xu. A density-based algorithm for discovering clusters in large spatial databases with noise. In *Kdd*, volume 96, pages 226–231, 1996.

[26] D. Gmach, S. Krompass, A. Scholz, M. Wimmer, and A. Kemper. Adaptive quality of service management for enterprise services. *ACM Transactions on the Web (TWEB)*, 2(1):8, 2008.

[27] I. Guyon and A. Elisseeff. An introduction to variable and feature selection. *JMLR*, 3, 2003.

[28] J. Y. Halpern and J. Pearl. Causes and explanations: a structural-model approach. part i: causes. In *UAI*, 2001.

[29] J. Y. Halpern and J. Pearl. Causes and explanations: a structural-model approach. part ii: explanations. In *IJCAI*, 2001.

[30] H. Herodotou and S. Babu. Xplus: a sql-tuning-aware query optimizer. *PVLDB*, 3, 2010.

[31] E. Jahani, M. J. Cafarella, and C. Ré. Automatic optimization for mapreduce programs. *PVLDB*, 4, 2011.

[32] B. Kanagal, J. Li, and A. Deshpande. Sensitivity analysis and explanations for robust query evaluation in probabilistic databases. In *SIGMOD*, 2011.

[33] E. Keogh, J. Lin, A. W. Fu, and H. Van Herle. Finding unusual medical time-series subsequences: Algorithms and applications. *Information Technology in Biomedicine, IEEE Transactions on*, 10(3):429–439, 2006.

[34] N. Khoussainova, M. Balazinska, and D. Suciu. PerfXplain: Debugging mapreduce job performance. *PVLDB*, 2012.

[35] A. A. Mahimkar, Z. Ge, A. Shaikh, J. Wang, J. Yates, Y. Zhang, and Q. Zhao. Towards automated performance diagnosis in a large IPTV network. In *ACM SIGCOMM Computer Communication Review*, volume 39, pages 231–242. ACM, 2009.

[36] A. Meliou, W. Gatterbauer, and D. Suciu. Bringing provenance to its full potential using causal reasoning. In *TaPP*, 2011.

[37] B. Mozafari, C. Curino, A. Jindal, and S. Madden. Performance and resource modeling in highly-concurrent OLTP workloads. In *SIGMOD*, 2013.

[38] B. Mozafari, C. Curino, and S. Madden. DBSeer: Resource and performance prediction for building a next generation database cloud. In *CIDR*, 2013.

[39] B. Mozafari, E. Z. Y. Goh, and D. Y. Yoon. CliffGuard: A principled framework for finding robust database designs. In *SIGMOD*, 2015.

[40] A. Rogge-Solti and G. Kasneci. Temporal anomaly detection in business processes. In *Business Process Management*. 2014.

[41] S. Roy, A. C. König, I. Dvorkin, and M. Kumar. PerfAugur: Robust diagnostics for performance anomalies in cloud services. In *ICDE*, 2015.

[42] S. Sarawagi. Explaining differences in multidimensional aggregates. In *VLDB*, 1999.

[43] Y. Tan, X. Gu, and H. Wang. Adaptive system anomaly prediction for large-scale hosting infrastructures. In *PODC*, 2010.

[44] L. Wei, N. Kumar, V. N. Lolla, E. J. Keogh, S. Lonardi, and C. A. Ratanamahatana. Assumption-free anomaly detection in time series. In *SSDBM*, volume 5, pages 237–242, 2005.

[45] L. Wei, W. Qian, A. Zhou, W. Jin, and X. Jeffrey. Hot: Hypergraph-based outlier test for categorical data. In *AKDDM*. 2003.

[46] E. Wu and S. Madden. Scorpion: Explaining away outliers in aggregate queries. *PVLDB*, 6, 2013.

[47] D. Y. Yoon, B. Mozafari, and D. P. Brown. DBSeer: Pain-free database administration through workload intelligence. *PVLDB*, 2015.

[48] J. X. Yu, W. Qian, H. Lu, and A. Zhou. Finding centric local outliers in categorical/numerical spaces. *KAIS*, 9, 2006.

APPENDIX

Our appendix provides supplementary experiments for interested readers. Appendix A demonstrates the performance of `DBSherlock` on a different workload (i.e., TPC-E). Appendix B shows the effectiveness of merged causal models and discusses the possible issue of over-fitting. Appendix C demonstrates the robustness of `DBSherlock` against input errors. Appendix D describes the effect of tuning parameters on our predicate generation algorithm. Appendix E evaluates `DBSherlock`'s performance, when using automatic anomaly detection. Appendix F demonstrates the effectiveness of domain knowledge in pruning secondary symptoms.

A. ACCURACY FOR OTHER WORKLOADS

To confirm whether `DBSherlock`'s capability of producing accurate explanations extends to other workloads besides TPC-C, we conducted additional experiments using the TPC-E benchmark [6]. Here, we used TPC-E with 3,000 customers, resulting in a 50GB data size. We generated the datasets and constructed merged causal models using a similar setup as in Section 8.5 (i.e., 5 datasets to construct merged causal models and 300 instances of explanations).

Type of Workload	Accuracy if shown top-1 cause	Accuracy if shown top-2 causes
TPC-C	98.0%	99.7%
TPC-E	92.5%	99.6%

Table 4: `DBSherlock`'s accuracy for TPC-C and TPC-E workloads.

Table 4 compares the percentage of correct answers when the top-1 or top-2 causes are returned to the user for both TPC-C and TPC-E. When only the top-1 cause was shown to the user, the accuracy for the TPC-E workload slightly dropped to 92.5% on average. This was mainly due to DBSherlock's lower accuracy for 'Poor Physical Design' with TPC-E, as the effects of 'Poor Physical Design' and 'Lock Contention' on the system were not as significant as they were with TPC-C. The was due to the fact that TPC-E is much more read-intensive than TPC-C [16]. Nonetheless, DBSherlock still achieved an impressive accuracy of 99% on average with the TPC-E workload when the top-2 causes were shown to the user.

B. OVER-FITTING AND MERGED CAUSAL MODELS

To verify if adding more datasets could further improve our merged models, we also ran a leave-one-out cross validation experiment. With 11 datasets for each case, we constructed causal models from 10 datasets and merged them. The final causal model then calculated confidence on the remaining dataset of each test case. Overall, the average confidence of the correct model increased slightly as shown in Figure 11a, but at the same time, the average margin of confidence decreased in some test cases as shown in Figure 11b.

The decrease in the average margin of confidence in some test cases suggests that merging more models than necessary can be ineffective. In other words, our proposed technique for merging causal models continues to widen the scope of relevant predicates while filtering irrelevant ones out. Once every irrelevant predicate has been filtered out, merging more models is not as effective. This is similar to the over-fitting phenomenon in machine learning. Nonetheless, DBSherlock still succeeded in returning the correct cause among its top two explanations in every instance (except for 'Network Congestion'), as demonstrated in Figure 11c.

C. RARE ANOMALIES AND ROBUSTNESS AGAINST INPUT ERRORS

As explained in Section 2.2, the user selects the abnormal regions manually after visual inspection of the performance plots. (We have used the same method in our experiments—Section 8.2.) However, users may not specify the regions with perfect precision. To understand how robust DBSherlock is to input errors caused by human mistakes, we conducted the following experiment. Using the same setup as Appendix B, we extended the boundaries of the original anomaly region by 10% in one experiment and shortened them by 10% in another. We also ran a third experiment where we randomly chose only two seconds of the original abnormal region as our input anomaly. The goal of this test case was to evaluate DBSherlock's effectiveness in diagnosing anomalies that are rare or only last a few seconds. For each dataset, we repeated each experiment 10 times and averaged the result.

Width of Abnormal Region	Accuracy if shown top-1 cause	Accuracy if shown top-2 causes
Original	94.6%	99.1%
10% Longer	95.5%	100%
10% Shorter	95.5%	97.3%
Two Seconds	74.6%	86.4%

Table 5: DBSherlock's robustness against rare and imperfect inputs.

Table 5 reports the percentage of correct answers when the top-1 or 2 causes are returned to the user. The accuracy did not change significantly when the span of the abnormal region was shorter or longer than the original one by 10%. More surprisingly, DBSherlock achieved reasonable accuracy even when the abnormal region was only two seconds long (e.g., the top-2 causes contained the correct explanation in 85% of the cases). These experiments show that DBSherlock remains effective even when the abnormal regions are not perfectly aligned with the actual anomaly or only last a very short period.

D. DIFFERENT PARAMETERS/STEPS IN DBSHERLOCK

We conducted various experiments to study the effect of the individual steps and configurable parameters of our predicate generation algorithm on its accuracy.

To evaluate the different steps of our algorithm (from Section 4), we compared it against its simpler variants by omitting some of the steps each time. Since steps 1, 2 and 5 (i.e., *Creating a Partition Space*, *Partition Labeling* and *Extracting Predicates*) form the skeleton of our algorithm and cannot be excluded easily, we omitted the other two steps (i.e., *Partition Filtering* and *Filling the Gaps*). Table 6 reports the average margin of confidence and accuracy of each variant. Skipping either of the *Partition Filtering* or *Filling the Gaps* steps lowers the accuracy of our algorithm significantly (down to 0–10%). Without both, our algorithm fails to find any relevant predicates for explaining the given anomaly. This experiment underlines the significant contribution of these two steps towards our algorithm's overall accuracy.

Algorithms	Overall avg. margin of confidence	Accuracy if shown top-1 cause
Original (all 5 steps)	37.4	94.6%
Without *Filling the Gaps*	9.3	10.1%
Without *Partition Filtering*	0.7	0%
Without *Filling the Gaps* & *Partition Filtering*	0	0%

Table 6: Contributions of the different steps of our predicate generation algorithm to the overall accuracy.

Our predicate generation algorithm has three configurable parameters: the number of partitions (R), the anomaly distance multiplier (δ) and the normalized difference threshold (θ). We conducted experiments to study the effect of these parameters on the generated explanations. We ran our algorithm on every dataset with different values of each parameter and averaged its confidence, computation time, and number of generated predicates. For each experiment, we used 10 datasets to construct merged causal models and calculated their confidence on the remaining dataset. We used the default values of $\{R, \delta, \theta\} = \{250, 10, 0.2\}$.

We varied R using the following values {125, 250, 500, 1000, 2000}. As shown in Figure 12a, $R > 1000$ increased the computation time significantly, without much improvement in confidence. We also varied δ using the following values {0.1, 0.5, 1, 5, 10}. As shown in Figure 12b, and as expected, $\delta > 1$ favored more specific predicates and led to higher confidence.

Lastly, we varied the value of θ using the following values {0.01, 0.05, 0.1, 0.2, 0.4}. As shown in Figure 12c, increasing the value of θ reduced the number of generated predicates but increased their confidence slightly. However, the confidence dropped significantly

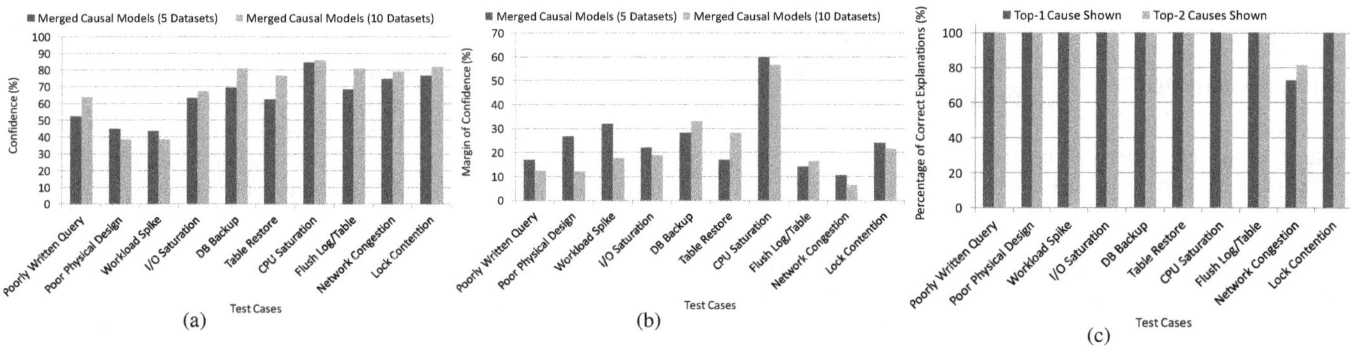

Figure 11: Evaluation of a merged causal model with 10 datasets in terms of (a) confidence, compared to a merged causal model with 5 datasets, (b) margin of confidence, compared to a merged causal model with 5 datasets, and (c) accuracy if top-k causes are returned.

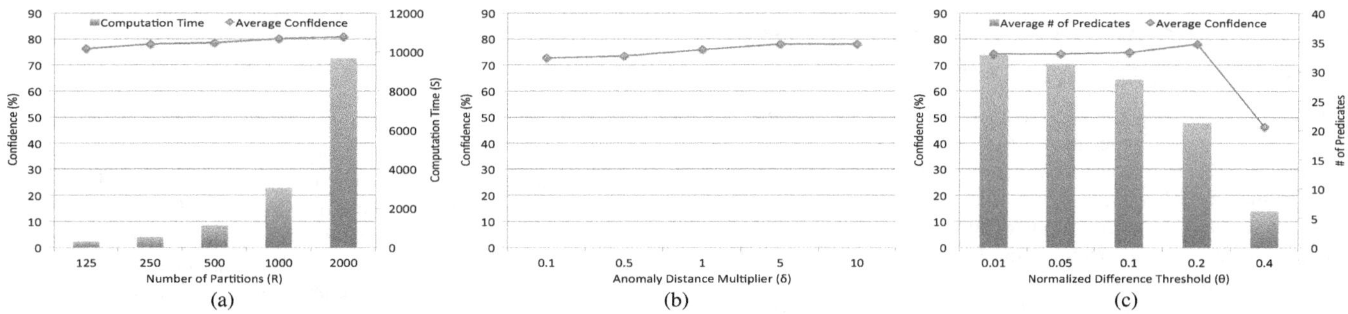

Figure 12: The effect of (a) the number of partitions on our algorithm's average confidence and computation time, (b) the anomaly distance multiplier on its confidence, and (c) the normalized difference threshold on its average confidence and number of generated predicates.

with $\theta = 0.4$. This is because a large value of θ filters out most predicates, leaving only a few predicates that are too specific to their training dataset and do not generalize to others.

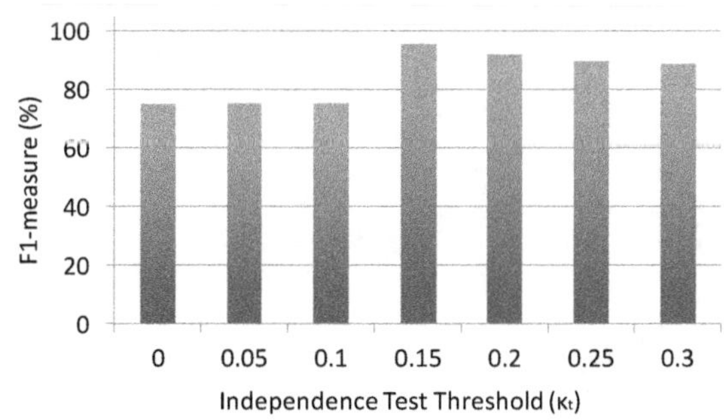

Figure 13: The effect of the parameter κ_t to average F1-measure.

We also performed a sensitivity analysis with the parameter κ_t that we use to filter secondary symptoms with the domain knowledge. We compared the average F1-measures with different values of κ_t using the same experiment setup as described in Appendix F. As demonstrated in Figure 13, the value of 0.15 for κ_t gave the highest average F1-measure.

E. DBSHERLOCK'S ACCURACY WITH AUTOMATIC ANOMALY DETECTION

We conducted an experiment to test DBSherlock's accuracy when automatic anomaly detection is used and also compared against another anomaly detection algorithm, PerfAugur. For PerfAugur, we supplied the overall average latency as its performance indicator variable and used their naïve algorithm with the original scoring function to compute the abnormal region.

For this experiment, we have generated datasets with the longer duration (i.e., 10 minutes) of the normal workload to ensure that the normal region is larger than the abnormal region, necessary for automatic detection algorithm to distinguish between both. Then, causal models were constructed for each individual test case by merging the causal models from 10 datasets. Abnormal regions were manually specified with our 'ground-truth' knowledge of each test case, to simulate a perfect user diagnosing the problem. The anomaly detection algorithm described in Section 7 and PerfAugur then identified abnormal regions for the remaining dataset of each test case. This leave-one-out cross validation set-up is designed to test the effectiveness of DBSherlock using merged causal models, but in the absence of any user input. DBSherlock used the automatically detected region of anomaly as its input and generated explanations for each test case.

Detection Algorithms	Accuracy if shown top-1 cause	Accuracy if shown top-2 causes
Manual Anomaly Detection	94.6%	99.1%
Automatic Anomaly Detection	90%	95.5%
PerfAugur	77.3%	88.2%

Table 7: Ratio of the correct causes for different strategies.

As shown in Table 7, DBSherlock identified about 95% of the correct causes on average with our algorithm, when top-2 possi-

		Actual	
		Positive	**Negative**
Domain Knowledge Test	**Pruned**	91.6%	0.9%
	Not Pruned	8.4%	99.1%

Table 8: Confusion matrix for finding secondary symptoms using incorporated domain knowledge.

ble causes were shown to a user. Our anomaly detection algorithm also performed substantially better than PerfAugur's detection algorithm. This promising result demonstrates that DBSherlock can be used in an automated setting once it has enough user feedback for well-constructed causal models. An interesting future work is to integrate a domain-specific and a more sophisticated anomaly detection algorithm in DBSherlock.

F. TESTING DOMAIN KNOWLEDGE WITH SYNTHETIC DATASET

To test DBSherlock's ability to remove secondary symptoms, we conducted a separate experiment using a synthetic dataset. Using a real dataset for this experiment is non-trivial since the 'ground-truth' casual model is unknown to us. With a synthetic dataset, however, we can define the 'ground-truth' causality between variables and hence, correctly evaluate our framework's ability to prune secondary symptoms. We created the synthetic dataset using a randomly generated *linear causal graph*. A linear causal graph is a directed acyclic graph, where the causal relationship of variables in the graph is defined by a linear structural equation model (SEM) [10, 24]. Using this graph, we randomly generated the domain knowledge to classify which predicates to prune (called **'Actual Positive'**) or keep (called **'Actual Negative'**) before running the experiment.

Now, we give a detailed description of our experimental setup. Our experiment consisted of multiple runs, where we randomly generated synthetic datasets. This bootstrap testing model enables us to empirically evaluate DBSherlock's ability to incorporate domain knowledge in various scenarios. For each run, we generate a linear causal graph $G = \{V_1, V_2, \cdots, V_k\}$, where k is the number of variables in the system. We used $k = 7$. Each node V_i in G represents a variable and corresponds to an attribute $\texttt{Attr}_i$ in our input data. Note that we treat the node V_k specially as an *effect variable*, which is the node with no outgoing edges and at least one incoming edge. From the effect variable V_k, we also define *root cause variables*, denoted as C. Root cause variables are the root nodes of the effect variable V_k (i.e., the ancestors of V_k with no incoming edges). They are the variables causing anomalies. For these variables, we randomly draw their values from $\mathcal{N}(10, 10)$ except 10% of their values are drawn from $\mathcal{N}(100, 10)$, which are contiguous and aligned among the root cause variables, representing an abnormal region of the data.

A variable V_i that is not a root cause variable is defined by a linear structural equation of the form:

$$V_i = \sum_j c_{ji} V_j + \epsilon_i \tag{5}$$

where c_{ji} is a *cause coefficient*, which represents the effect of V_j on V_i and ϵ_i is an error term for the variable V_i. c_{ji} takes a non-zero integer value randomly drawn in [-10, 10]. ϵ_i is drawn from the standard normal distribution (i.e., $\mathcal{N}(0, 1)$). Starting from the root cause variables and applying linear structural equations in order, we generate a synthetic dataset for DBSherlock in the format described in Section 2.1 (i.e., (Timestamp, $\texttt{Attr}_1$, . . . , $\texttt{Attr}_k$)). The synthetic dataset we used for the experiment had 600 tuples, representing data collected for 10 minutes with 1-second intervals. 60 consecutive tuples are selected as an abnormal region (i.e., their root cause variables have the distribution of $\mathcal{N}(100, 10)$), representing the anomaly that lasts for a minute.

Now given the root cause variables C, we construct the domain knowledge D by randomly generating rules for the attributes corresponding to the root cause variables, each attribute becoming the cause variable of a rule. Random attributes then become effect attributes to create multiple rules obeying the two conditions of the rule in Section 5. We consult C, D and G to classify which predicates should be pruned (**'Actual Positive'**) or not (**'Actual Negative'**) before running the experiment. A predicate should be pruned only if its attribute is an effect attribute in D and there exists a path to it from its cause variable in G. They are secondary symptoms that we should remove using our domain knowledge. Conversely, a predicate should not be pruned only if its attribute is an effect attribute in D and there exists no path to it from its cause variable in G.

We studied the impact of incorporating domain knowledge on 10,000 randomly generated linear causal graphs (i.e., 10,000 runs). We evaluated the performance of our technique from Section 5 using the confusion matrix shown in Table 8. Our technique for pruning secondary symptoms achieves a 91.6% precision and a 99.1% recall. This experiment demonstrates the effectiveness of our technique in correctly pruning secondary symptoms, as well as its robustness against incorrect domain knowledge (thanks to checking the independence between attributes in the data itself).

TARDiS: A Branch-and-Merge Approach To Weak Consistency

Natacha Crooks[‡] Youer Pu[‡] Nancy Estrada[†]
Trinabh Gupta[‡] Lorenzo Alvisi[‡] Allen Clement[§]
[‡]The University of Texas at Austin [†]MPI-SWS [§]Google,inc.

ABSTRACT

This paper presents the design, implementation, and evaluation of TARDiS (**T**ransactional **A**synchronously **R**eplicated **Di**vergent **S**tore), a transactional key-value store explicitly designed for weakly-consistent systems. Reasoning about these systems is hard, as neither causal consistency nor per-object eventual convergence allow applications to deal satisfactorily with write-write conflicts. TARDiS instead exposes as its fundamental abstraction the set of conflicting branches that arise in weakly-consistent systems. To this end, TARDiS introduces a new concurrency control mechanism: branch-on-conflict. On the one hand, TARDiS guarantees that storage will appear sequential to any thread of execution that extends a branch, keeping application logic simple. On the other, TARDiS provides applications, when needed, with the tools and context necessary to merge branches atomically, when and how applications want. Since branch-on-conflict in TARDiS is fast, weakly-consistent applications can benefit from adopting this paradigm not only for operations issued by different sites, but also, when appropriate, for conflicting local operations. We find that TARDiS reduces coding complexity for these applications and that judicious branch-on-conflict can improve their local throughput at each site by two to eight times.

1. INTRODUCTION

This paper describes the design, implementation, and evaluation of TARDiS, an asynchronously replicated, multi-master, transactional key-value store designed for applications built above weakly-consistent and often non-transactional systems, such as Riak [10], MongoDB [37], or Cassandra [6]. TARDiS renounces the one-size-fits-all abstraction of sequential storage and instead exposes applications, when appropriate, to concurrency and distribution. This unconventional design is predicated on a simple notion: to help developers resolve the anomalies that arise in such applications, *each replica should faithfully store the full context necessary to understand how the anomalies arose in the first place, but only expose that context to applications when needed.*

In light of the CAP theorem [14, 23], many wide-area services and applications [16] choose to renounce strong consistency and focus instead on providing the ALPS properties [31] of **A**vailability, low **L**atency, **P**artition tolerance, and high **S**calability. Distributed

SIGMOD'16, June 26-July 01, 2016, San Francisco, CA, USA

DOI: http://dx.doi.org/10.1145/2882903.2882951

ALPS applications, however, are hard to reason about. Geographically distinct replicas can issue conflicting operations, and the read-write and write-write conflicts that can ultimately result from these operations may cause replicas' states to diverge.

Many prior systems have attempted to insulate applications from this complexity by relying on a combination of two techniques: *causal consistency* [4, 9, 21, 32, 44, 47] to mitigate the effects of read-write conflicts, and per-object *eventual convergence* [20, 31, 33, 34, 44, 48] to address write-write conflicts. These systems strive to keep complexity in check by aggressively preserving the familiar abstraction that an application's state evolves through a linear sequence of updates. Any perturbation to this abstraction is nipped in the bud, either within the storage layer—by enforcing per-object convergence through simple deterministic resolution policies—or by asking the application to resolve the state of objects with conflicting updates as soon as conflicts arise [20, 25, 48, 31].

These techniques, however, are not sufficient to uphold the abstraction of sequential storage in the presence of concurrent updates. Worse, causal order and per-object convergence provide no support for meaningfully resolving conflicts between concurrent sequences of updates that involve multiple objects: indeed, they often destroy information that could have helped the application address these anomalies. For example, deterministic writer-wins, a common technique to achieve convergence [31], hides write-skew from applications (§2). Similarly, exposing multivalued objects without context obscures cross-object semantic dependencies (§2).

Anomalies like write-skew are intrinsic to ALPS applications. The issue is then neither how to prevent them (one can't), nor how to resolve them transparently (application-specific knowledge is often indispensable): rather, it is how to provide ALPS applications with the best possible system support when merging conflicting states.

To this end, TARDiS deliberately abandons a strictly sequential view of storage, and instead gives applications flexibility. If all is well, storage at each replica appears sequential; when conflicts must be resolved, however, the intricate details of distribution become available. As in Git [24], users operate on their own branch and explicitly request (when convenient) to see concurrent modifications, using the history recorded by the underlying branching storage to help them resolve conflicts. Unlike Git, however, branching in TARDiS does not rely on specific user commands, but occurs implicitly, to preserve availability in the presence of conflicts, using three core mechanisms: (*i*) branch-on-conflict, (*ii*) inter-branch isolation, and (*iii*) application-driven cross-object merge.

Branch-on-conflict lets TARDiS logically fork its state whenever it detects conflicting operations, and store the conflicting branches explicitly. Inter-branch isolation guarantees that storage will appear as sequential to any thread of execution that extends a

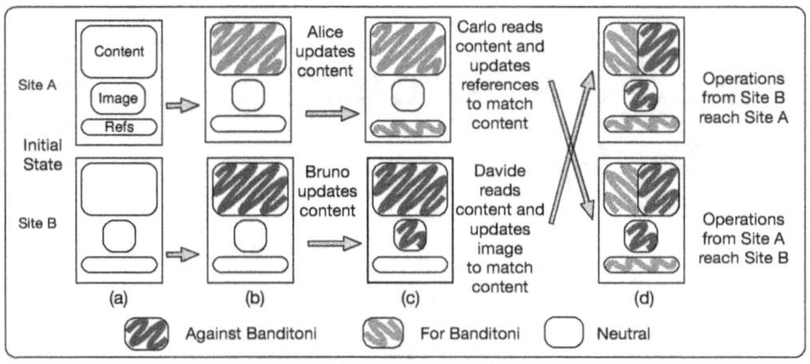

Figure 1: Weakly-consistent Wikipedia

branch, keeping application logic simple. Finally, TARDiS leaves the task of deciding if, when, and how divergent branches should be merged to the application, rather than to the storage layer, which is generally unsuited to leverage relevant semantic information.

At first glance, TARDiS' design may appear counter-intuitive: isn't a simpler abstraction, such as sequential storage, easier to reason about? Our view is that abstractions should indeed be made as simple as possible—but no simpler: a simplistic abstraction that overlooks critical context can actually make reasoning harder. Through its richer interface, TARDiS gives applications access to context that is essential to reasoning about concurrent updates, reducing the complexity of programming ALPS applications and improving their performance. It does so via the following four key properties.

TARDiS knows history. Each TARDiS site stores a DAG that records all branches generated during an execution, and uses a new algorithm, *DAG compression*, to track the minimal information needed to support branch merges. This context, which traditional storage systems hastily discard, can prove invaluable when programming ALPS applications (§7). We find, for example, that using TARDiS rather than BerkeleyDB [38] to implement CRDTs [42]—a library of scalable, weakly-consistent datatypes—cuts code size by half, improves performance by four to eight times, and reduces development time by a factor of three.

TARDiS merges branches, not objects. Prior systems that, like TARDiS, admit parallel versions of the same object [3, 20, 34, 48] have systematically taken a strictly per-object view of multiversions. With no support for enforcing the cross-object consistency demands expressed in many application invariants, such systems make conflict resolution more difficult and error prone. To efficiently construct and maintain branches, TARDiS introduces the notion of *conflict tracking*. By summarizing branches as a set of fork points and merge points, conflict tracking significantly reduces the metadata overhead experienced by many systems that enforce causal consistency [8, 21].

TARDiS is expressive. Despite exposing a different abstraction, TARDiS supports many isolation levels (serializability, snapshot isolation, read-committed [11]) and consistency guarantees (read-my-writes [46], causal consistency [4]). It does so with minimal changes to applications' code and with performance comparable to that of BerkeleyDB, a commercially available Java database. TARDiS achieves this flexibility by reformulating isolation and consistency requirements as a set of pre- and post- conditions.

TARDiS improves performance of the local site. A unique feature of TARDiS is that it allows ALPS applications to apply weak-consistency principles end-to-end, by triggering branch-on-conflict not only for operations issued by different sites, but also for locally conflicting operations. When so configured, TARDiS handles local conflicts not through abort/rollback and locking, but by logically forking the local datastore, which in our implementation is a very fast operation. Of course, this feature is not beneficial to all applications, as producing a large number of additional branches may increase merging complexity dramatically. However, we find that the ALPS applications that TARDiS targets, where weak consistency and merging are first-order concerns, can leverage this feature to increase their throughput significantly: applying this technique to Retwis [41], a commonly used Twitter-like ALPS application [39, 41, 44, 51], yields a three-fold improvement in throughput with negligible increase in complexity. TARDiS enables this speedup by extending the copy-on-write techniques present in multiversioned systems to support not just stale snapshots, but also branches.

2. THE GAP BETWEEN CAUSALITY AND REALITY

In the classic example used to illustrate the virtues of causal consistency, Alice gains assurance that Bob, whom she had defriended before posting her Spring-break photos, will not be able to access her pictures, even though Alice and Bob access the photo-sharing application using different sites [8, 17, 31]. ALPS applications, however, face another class of anomalies—write-write-conflicts—that causal consistency cannot prevent, detect, or repair.

To illustrate, consider the process of updating a Wikipedia page consisting of multiple HTML objects (Figure 1(a)). The page in our example, about a controversial politician, Mr. Banditoni, is frequently modified, and is thus replicated on two sites, A and B. Assume, for simplicity, that the page consists of just three objects—the content, references, and an image. Alice and Bruno, who respectively strongly support and strongly oppose Mr. Banditoni, concurrently modify the content section of the webpage on sites A and B to match their political views (Figure 1(b)). Carlo reads the content section on site A, which now favors Mr. Banditoni, and updates the reference section accordingly by adding links to articles that praise the politician. Similarly, Davide reads the update made by Bruno on site B and chooses to strengthen the case made by the content section by updating the image to a derogatory picture of Mr. Banditoni (Figure 1(c)). Eventually, the operations reach the other site and, although nothing in the preceding sequence of events violates causal consistency, produce the inconsistent state shown in Figure 1(d): a content section that exhibits a write-write conflict; a reference section in favor of Mr. Banditoni; and an image that is against him. Worse, there is no straightforward way for the application to detect the full extent of the inconsistency: unlike the explicit conflict in the content sections, the discrepancy between image and references is purely semantic, and would not trigger an automatic resolution procedure.

To the best of our knowledge, this scenario presents an open challenge to existing weakly-consistent systems, which exhibit at least one of the following two properties:

(*i*) *Syntactic conflict resolution.* To maintain the abstraction of sequential storage, many systems use fixed, syntactic resolution policies to reconcile write-write conflicts [31]. Deterministic writer-wins (DWW), for example, resolves write-write conflicts identically at all sites, ensuring that applications never see conflicting writes and guaranteeing eventual convergence. In our example, this policy would choose Bruno's update. However, this is not sufficient to restore consistency, as it ignores the relationship between the content, references, and images of the webpage. The datastore's greedy attempt at syntactic conflict resolution is not only inadequate to bridge this semantic gap, but leads to losing valuable information (here, Alice's update).

(*ii*) *Lack of cross-object semantics.* Some systems choose to push conflict resolution to the application [20, 48], but on a per-object

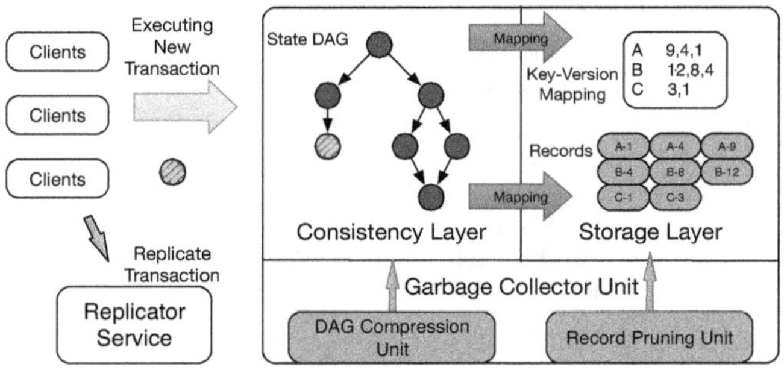

Figure 2: TARDiS architecture

basis only. Though more flexible than a purely syntactic solution, this approach, which reduces conflict resolution to the merging of explicitly conflicting writes, is still overly narrow. For example, it would not address the inconsistencies, such as the one between the references and the image, that do not produce a write-write conflict. Yet, the effects of a write-write conflict on an object do not end with that object: Carlo and Davide update references and images as they do because they have *read* the conflicting updates to the original content section. Indeed, any operation that depends on one of two conflicting updates is potentially incompatible with all the operations that depend on the other: the shockwaves from even a single write-write conflict may spread to affect the state of the entire database.

There is currently no straightforward way for applications to resolve consistently the kind of multi-object, indirect conflicts that our example illustrates. Transactions [31, 32], an obvious candidate, are powerless when the objects that directly or indirectly reflect a write-write conflict are updated, as in our example, by different users. After Bruno's update, the application has no way to know that Davide's update is forthcoming: it must therefore commit Bruno's transaction, forcing Bruno's and Davide's updates into separate transactions. Nor would it help to change the granularity of the object that defines the write-write conflict—in our example, by making that object be the entire page. It would be easy to correspondingly scale up the example, using distinct pages that link each other. Short of treating the entire database as the "object", it is futile to try to define away these inconsistencies by redrawing the objects' semantic boundaries.

3. BRIDGING THE GAP: BRANCHES

TARDiS' design is motivated by the belief that isolating ALPS applications from the harsh but inescapable reality of independent conflicting writes, and from the resolution process that they require, is a well-intentioned fallacy. TARDiS instead embraces transparency. By default, applications execute on a branch, and hence perceive storage as sequential. But when anomalies arise, TARDiS provides two novel features that simplify reconciliation.

First, it exposes applications to the resulting independent branches, and to the states at which the branches are created (*fork points*) and merged (*merge points*). Second, it supports atomic merging of conflicting branches and lets applications choose when and how to reconcile them (§3.1). These features allow TARDiS to offer ALPS applications the opportunity to pursue, down to each site's local datastore, an intriguing notion: that of turning weak consistency, through a bit of system-design judo, from a weakness to an unlikely strength (§3.2).

3.1 State branching and merging

As the discussion in Section 2 has illustrated, even a single write-write conflict has the potential to affect the entire state of a database. In essence, conflicting operations fork the entire state of the system, creating distinct *branches*, each tracking the linear evolution of the datastore according to a separate thread of execution. The Wikipedia example hence consists of two branches: one in support of Banditoni, and one against him. Elevating branches to the datastore's fundamental abstraction has two complementary advantages. First, users that operate within a given thread of execution continue to perceive the application's state as evolving linearly. Second, when it becomes necessary to alert users to the existence of concurrent updates that conflict with that linear view, branches are the natural unit of merging.

Resolving conflicts in ALPS applications often requires semantic context. Replicas, however, only see a sequence of read/write operations and are unaware of the application-level logic and invariants that relate these operations [5]. Therefore, they should avoid deterministic quick fixes, and instead give applications the information they need to decide what is best. Branches, together with their fork and merge points, naturally encapsulate such information: they make it easy to identify all the objects to be considered during merging and pinpoint when and how the conflict developed. This context can reduce the complexity and improve the efficiency of automated merging procedures, as well as help system administrators when user involvement is required. In our example, a Wikipedia moderator presented with the two conflicting branches would be able to reconstruct the events that led to them and handle the conflicting sources according to Wikipedia's guidelines [50]. Note that merging need not simply involve deleting one branch. Indeed, branching and merging states enables merging strategies with richer semantics than aborts or rollbacks [44].

3.2 Weak consistency end-to-end

Write-write conflicts in distributed systems are not restricted to remote sites: conflicting operations can also happen locally. Unlike remote conflicts, however, they are immediately detectable, and hence they are typically handled by the datastore through locking or rollback. When considering the specific nature of ALPS applications, however, two observations bring this common-sense approach into question. First, desirable as it may be, the abstraction of a sequential store cannot be preserved end-to-end: at the distributed system level, it falls apart. Second, the design complexity of having to program against the possibility of remote conflicts is already factored into ALPS applications, whose semantics often support simple merging procedures.

These observations lead us to explore an unconventional proposition: design and implement a datastore for ALPS applications with branching as its fundamental abstraction, used to model conflicts end-to-end, from the level of the distributed system down to that of local storage. This stance does not simply have an aesthetic appeal: eliminating locks and rollbacks from the performance critical path offers the potential, through a lightweight implementation of branching, to improve throughput at local sites.

Accordingly, TARDiS gives ALPS applications the option of handling local conflicts through branch-on conflict, rather than syncronization. Naturally, one must tread carefully: out-of-control branching can turn reasoning about the state of the system into a nightmare. TARDiS thus lets applications tune the degree of local branching allowed, so they can strike the balance between performance and complexity that best meets their requirements.

3.3 System Goals

The challenge is then to develop a datastore that can keep track of independent execution branches, record fork and merge points, facilitate reasoning about branches and, as appropriate, atomically

Constraint	B	E	Description
Any	√	√	Always Satisfies
Serializability		√	Guarantees Serializability
Snapshot Iso		√	Guarantees Snapshot Isolation
Read Committed		√	Guarantees Read Committed
No Branching		√	State has no children
K-Branching		√	State has fewer than k-1 children
Parent	√		State where client last committed
Ancestor	√		Child of client's last committed state
State Identifier	√		State ID matches the specified ID

Table 1: Begin (B) and end (E) constraints supported by TARDiS

merge them—while keeping performance and resource overheads comparable to those of weakly-consistent systems. Such a system should satisfy the following three requirements:

- **Simple interface** The datastore should expose an interface that allows developers to navigate and manipulate branches; that interface should minimize any increase in complexity and need to modify legacy code.
- **Good Performance** The datastore should efficiently create, track, and merge branches; its performance should match or surpass that of a storage system that is strictly sequential and does not keep track of history.
- **Minimal Space Overhead** The datastore should have a reasonable memory footprint and manage efficiently the space overhead associated with keeping multiple executions and their fork points.

The rest of this paper presents the design of TARDiS, focusing on how it satisfies these three requirements.

4. TARDiS ARCHITECTURE

The TARDiS transactional key-value store tracks conflicting execution branches using three mechanisms: *branch-on-conflict*, *inter-branch isolation*, and *application-specific merge*. TARDiS uses multi-master asynchronous replication: transactions first execute locally at a specific site, and are then asynchronously propagated to all other replicas. Each replica consists of four components: a storage layer, a consistency layer, a garbage collector unit, and a replicator service (Figure 2).

The *storage layer* stores records in a disk-backed B-Tree. Currently, every site stores a full copy of the database, though TARDiS can be extended to support data partitioning (§6.4). TARDiS is a multiversioned system: every update operation creates a new record version. The mapping between versions and keys is stored in an in-memory cache for fast traversal.

The *consistency layer* tracks branches with the help of a directed acyclic graph, whose vertices correspond to logical *states* of the datastore: each transaction that updates a record generates a new state. TARDiS' logic is geared towards efficiently mapping the consistency layer to the storage layer: when a transaction creates a new state, it extends the State DAG by appending the state to its chosen branch of execution. Any newly created record version is marked by this state's identifier. When a transaction executes a get operation, it uses information contained in the State DAG to determine which object versions are visible to its branch.

TARDiS' *garbage collector unit* comprises a DAG compression submodule and a record pruning submodule. DAG compression periodically discards intermediate states that are no longer needed, and record pruning then removes the associated object versions. Garbage collection allows TARDiS' to maintain memory and storage overheads that are comparable to traditional weakly-consistent systems that do not track history.

S	M	return type	method
√		transaction	begin(*beginConstraint*)
	√	transaction	beginMerge(*beginConstraint*)
√	√	void	put(*key, value*)
√		value	get(*key*)
	√	value	getForID(*key, StateID[]*)
	√	key[]	findConflictWrites(*StateID[]*)
	√	forkPoints[]	findForkPoints(*StateID[]*)
√	√	abort|commit	commit(*endConstraint*)

Table 2: TARDiS API - S:single mode, M:merge mode

Finally, the *replicator service* propagates committed transactions and applies remote transactions as appropriate.

5. USING TARDiS

To help weakly-consistent applications deal with the complexity of resolving the conflicts they encounter, TARDiS' API (Table 2) addresses three competing concerns: (*i*) minimizing programming complexity, (*ii*) simplifying reasoning about concurrent branches, and (*iii*) controlling the degree of local branching.

5.1 Interface

To ease programming, TARDiS can operate in either *single mode* or *merge mode*. In the default *single mode*, the programmer is allowed to (transactionally) read from and write to a single branch. Programming proceeds exactly as in traditional transactional systems, except that programmers must now select a branch to operate on. Thus, porting an application to TARDiS requires only adding a branch-selection call. Figure 3 illustrates this point by sketching the implementation of a simple counter. The two single mode operators, `increment` and `decrement`, now take as parameters predicates that specify the properties of the desired branch (more on these predicates below), but these operators are otherwise implemented exactly as one would on sequential storage.

In *merge mode*, programmers can instead explicitly reconcile conflicting branches via *merge transactions*, that read from multiple states and write back to a single, merged state. TARDiS' merge mode allows users to perform cross-object resolution atomically: this simplifies conflict resolution significantly, much like transactions simplify application logic by allowing users to modify multiple objects atomically.

When reconciling branches, applications will typically (*i*) detect conflicting objects; (*ii*) identify where branches forked; and (*iii*) determine the values of conflicting keys at this fork point (§3). To help applications obtain the information that they need for merging, TARDiS adds three new API calls: `findConflictWrites`, `findForkPoints`, and `getForID`. `findConflictWrites` returns the list of objects with conflicting values across all selected branches, freeing programmers from the need to implement application-level mechanisms for tracking what has to be resolved. `findForkPoints` returns, for a given set of states, the structured set of fork points that reveals the branching structure of the corresponding State DAG. For simplicity, in this paper we restrict ourselves to the case where `findForkPoints` returns a single fork point. Finally, `getForID` allows the application to request any object version, freeing application programmers from the need to track how the datastore evolves. We expect applications to call this function primarily to obtain object values at the fork point(s), and to use this information to resolve conflicts in an application-specific way before writing the merged value back. Though TARDiS supports concurrent merges for full flexibility, we expect that, for simplicity, most applications will restrict merging to a single site.

```
func increment(counter)
  Tx t = begin(AncestorConstraint)
  int value = t.get(counter)
  t.put(counter, value + 1)
  t.commit(SerializabilityConstraint)

func decrement(counter)
  Tx t = begin(AncestorConstraint)
  int value = t.get(counter)
  t.put(counter, value - 1)
  t.commit(SerializabilityConstraint)

func merge()
  Tx t = beginMerge(AnyConstraint)
  forkPoint forkPt =
           t.findForkPoints(t.parents).first
  int forkVal = t.getForID(counter,forkPt)
  list<int> currentVals =
           t.getForID(counter, t.parents)
  int result = forkVal
  foreach c in currentVals
    result += (c - forkVal)
  t.put(counter,result)
  t.commit(SerializabilityConstraint)
```

Figure 3: TARDiS' counter implementation

TARDiS helps applications reason about concurrent execution branches and control the degree of local branching through *begin* and *end constraints*—predicates associated with begin and commit commands that specify which branch a transaction can execute from. Intuitively, begin constraints select what states the transaction can read, while end constraints specify what conditions must hold upon commit. TARDiS supports the constraints listed in Table 1: along with their union and intersection, they are sufficiently flexible to express traditional database isolation levels, such as serializability and snapshot isolation [11], as well as distributed-system guarantees such as read-my-writes [46]. For example, an application could use the *Ancestor* begin constraint and the union of the *Serializability* and *No Branching* end constraint to mimic the local behavior of a traditional sequential storage and achieve causal consistency globally. Similarly, applications using the *Ancestor* begin constraint and the *Snapshot Isolation* end constraint would always see their own writes and maintain snapshot isolation within a branch. Alternatively, the *K-Branching* constraint explicitly bounds the degree of branching in the system, giving developers the ability to balance the performance benefit of allowing local branching with the degree of divergence that this entails.

By default, TARDiS uses the *Ancestor* begin constraint and *Serializability* end constraint. Though some applications may benefit from multiple consistency levels [47], in most cases this default will let programmers write almost unmodified code, without explicitly specifying constraints.

5.2 Coding with TARDiS

TARDiS' greater fidelity in capturing the context that leads to conflicting operations is key to reducing the complexity of developing ALPS applications and improving their performance. This feature is evident even in simple programs, such as the counter presented in Figure 3. In a traditional, non-branching causally consistent system, counters are often implemented as two separate vector clocks (one for increment operations, the other for decrement operations) with an entry for each replica [42]. Reading the value of a counter requires adding the values in the increment vector and substracting those in the decrement vector. Similarly, applying a remote operation requires merging the local increment and decrement vectors with those of the incoming remote operation by taking the maximum of each corresponding vector element. Thus, all operations, including non-conflicting reads, in effect involve a merge: the

```
func buy(customer, item, cart)
  Tx t = client.begin(AncestorConstraint)
  list<itemId> items = t.get(cart.items)
  items += item.itemId
  t.put(cart.items, items)
  int stock = t.get(item.stock)
  t.put(item.stock, stock-1)
  list<cartId> carts = t.get(item.carts)
  carts += cartId
  t.put(item.carts, carts)
  t.commit(SerializabilityConstraint)

func merge()
  Tx t = client.beginMerge(AnyConstraint)
  list<item> conflictItems =
            t.findConflictWrites(t.parents)
  forkPoint forkP =
            t.findForkPoints(t.parents).first
  foreach item in conflictItems
    list<int> stockVals = new list
    int forkPtStock = t.getForID(item.stock,forkP)
    foreach branch in t.parents:
      stockVals.add(t.getForID(item.stock,branch))
      int newStock = mergeCounter(stockVals,
            forkPtStock)
    if(newStock > 0)
      t.put(item.stock,newStock)
      confirmItem(item.itemId, item.carts)
    else
      // get orders since fork point
      set<cartId> carts = new set
      foreach branch in t.parents:
        carts+= t.get(item.carts)
      carts = carts - t.getForID(item.carts,forkP)
      carts.sortBy(valueOfCart)
      foreach cart in carts
        if (forkPtStock > 0)
          // confirm item until run out
          --forkPtStock
          confirmItem(item.itemId, cart.cartId)
        else
          // apologize to other users
          removeRelatedItems(item,cart)
          sendApology(cart.clientId)
      t.put(item.stock,0)
  t.commit(SerializabilityConstraint)
```

Figure 4: TARDiS' shopping cart implementation

system must reconstruct the global view from each replica's local view, at a cost linear in the number of replicas.

In TARDiS, instead, single mode and merge mode are cleanly separated. In single mode (see Figure 3), increment and decrement operations access a single field, just as they would in a non-distributed scenario. Access to fork points makes merge operations both simpler and more flexible. In TARDiS, merging distinct counter branches is easy: one can simply compute the merged value by summing, for all branches, the difference between the value of the counter at the fork point and the current value for the branch. The application can then choose to merge branches periodically, during periods of low load, or to do so more frequently, if the counter nears boundary values.

The benefits of the TARDiS API become especially notable in examples that involve multiple objects with richer semantics. Consider the case of an online game store that sells both board games and extension packs that are only playable after buying the corresponding board game. The store tracks inventory by keeping a counter object per each item it sells, and associates each customer with a shopping cart. Suppose Alice and Bruno have, on different sites, both bought the last copy of a boardgame. Bruno has additionally bought an extension pack. Figure 4 gives the simplified pseudocode of the merging process.[1] On a merge, the application iterates over the keys in conflict and detects which items have been

[1]For clarity of explanation, we assume two branches only.

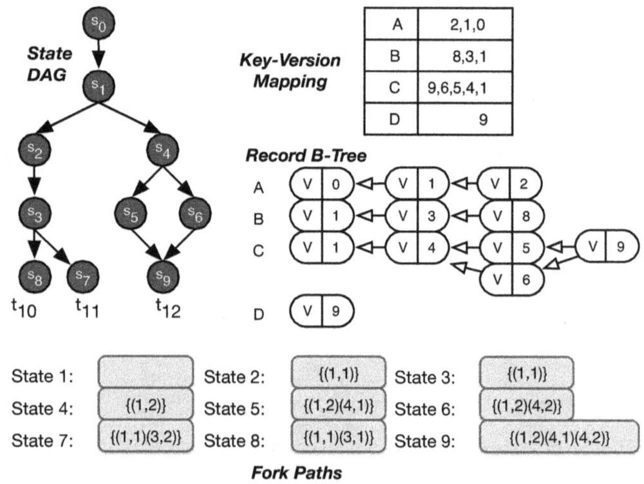

Figure 5: Main system datastructures

bought on different sites (lines 19-44), reconciling counter values through the merging process discussed above (lines 22-24). When the counter for a particular item falls below zero, as in our scenario, the merging logic must select the shopping cart from which the oversold items should be removed, while maintaining the invariant that no user should buy the extension pack without the game. The application has several options: it can choose, as does the pseudocode in Figure 4 (lines 30-44), to leave Bruno with both the game and the expansion pack, and send an apology to Alice, maximizing its overall profit. Alternatively, it can observe that Alice is a better customer than Bruno, and choose to privilege customer loyalty.

In current systems, merging that spans conflicts across multiple objects and requires application involvement is not achievable without significant engineering effort. Through the combination of branch-on-conflict, inter-branch isolation, and application-specific merge, TARDiS makes it easy for applications to acquire the context that led to such conflicts and empowers them with the flexibility and expressiveness necessary to meaningfully reconcile them.

6. DESIGN AND IMPLEMENTATION

To ensure that branches are cheaply created, maintained, and merged, TARDiS proceeds as follows. A transaction starts by identifying a most recent state that satisfies its begin constraint: this is the state from which the transaction can read (its *read state*). Likewise, upon commit, the transaction identifies a most recent state since its read state that satisfies the end constraint (the *commit state*). Since this process is identical for all transactions and independent of concurrently executing transactions, it naturally leads to state forking and to transactions aborting. If two concurrent transactions select the same state from which to commit, a new branch is created; alternatively, if no state satisfies a transaction's end constraint, the transaction aborts. There is thus no conceptual difference between sequential execution and forking, and TARDiS' design ensures that the implementation is similarly uniform. We describe this process in further detail below, focusing on the life of a particular transaction and relying on Figure 5 to illustrate the TARDiS' main datastructures.

6.1 Basic Operation

6.1.1 Begin Transaction: Read State Selection

A TARDiS transaction begins by selecting a branch. To choose one among the most recent suitable states, the transaction conducts a breadth-first search through the State DAG from its leaves up, looking for a state that satisfies the transaction's begin constraint. For example, given the State DAG in Figure 6(a), a newly executing transaction (t_{13}) would visit, in order, s_8, s_7, and s_4 and select the latter—the first state to satisfy the transaction's begin constraint—as its read state. Some constraints may require states to store additional information beyond pointers to their parents or children: the *Parent* and *StateID* constraints, for example, require all states in the DAG to be uniquely identifiable. Similarly, the *Serializability* and *Snapshot Isolation* (end) constraints demand to store, with each state, the read and write sets of the transaction responsible for creating it. In practice, there is often a unique state that satisfies the begin constraint; if instead multiple states are suitable, TARDiS simply selects one of them at random.

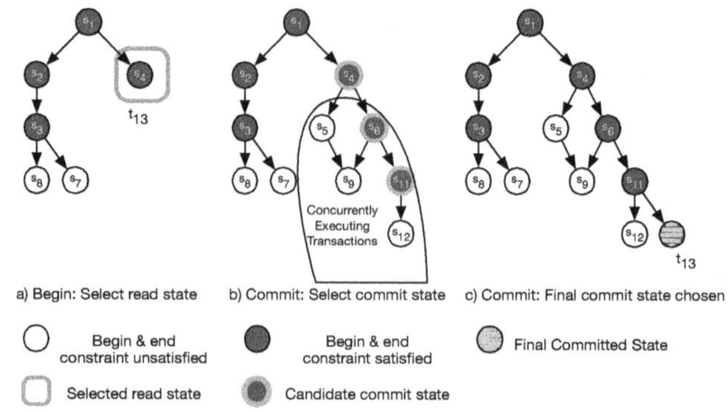

Figure 6: Transaction commit logic

6.1.2 Commit Transaction: Commit State Selection

The process for committing a transaction is similar: it requires identifying the most recent state, since the read state, that satisfies the end constraint. At commit, the transaction first checks whether its read state satisfies the end constraint. If it does not, the transaction aborts, as it read from an invalid state. Otherwise, the transaction checks whether more recent states also satisfy the end constraint. In effect, starting from its read state, the transaction "ripples" down the DAG, stopping before the first state that no longer satisfies the end constraint. Figure 6(b) illustrates the process. Transaction t_{13} first checks that the read state s_4 satisfies the end constraint, and then ripples down through states s_6 and s_{11} until it encounters s_{12}. As s_{12} does not satisfy t_{13}'s end constraint, t_{13} commits after s_{11}, creating a new branch (Figure 6(c)).

6.1.3 Reading records

Logically, non-read-only transactions create a new database state every time they execute. Storing each of these states as physically distinct instances is unsustainable. Write operations therefore simply create new record versions, and TARDiS relies on system logic to reconstruct the appropriate state for reads. This copy-on-write approach is similar to that of most multiversioned concurrency control (MVCC) systems [12], but with one key difference: TARDiS must not only provide support for stale snapshots, but also for divergent snapshots. As in traditional MVCC systems, to read a record a transaction must determine the most recent record version in the key-version map. Unlike MVCC systems, however, TARDiS must also ensure that the record version belongs to the branch it has selected. The selected version is then read from the record B-tree and returned.

To quickly determine whether a record version belongs to the selected branch, TARDiS abandons traditional dependency checking [21, 31, 34], which quickly becomes a bottleneck in causally

```
descendantCheck(x, y):
    if x.id = y.id then return true
    else if x.id > y.id then return false
    else if x.path ⊈ y.path then return false
    else return true
```

Figure 7: Check if state y can see records associated with state x

consistent systems [8, 21], and instead relies on *fork point checking*. In TARDiS, a branch is summarized only by its fork points (§3). A fork point is a tuple (i, b), indicating that the current state is a descendant of the bth child of state i. Together, the set of fork points for a branch denotes its *fork path*. A record version belongs to the selected branch if the fork path of the state associated with this record version is a subset of the fork path of the transaction's read state (see pseudocode in Figure 7). Figure 5 shows the fork path associated with each state: one can quickly determine that s_7 is on the same branch as s_3, as the fork path of s_3 is a subset of that of s_7. Similarly, s_9 is on the same branch as both s_5 and s_6.

By capturing *conflicts* (fork points) instead of dependencies, fork paths allow TARDiS to track concurrent branches efficiently. The small size of fork paths (conflicts are a small percentage of the total number of operations) not only limits memory overhead, but makes it possible to check quickly whether two states are on the same branch.

To guarantee that transactions select the most recent version, TARDiS keeps a topological sort of versions in each key-version mapping entry. Consider, for example, key C in Figure 5. The list stored in the key-version mapping is a topological order of the true structure of C's record versions, as saved in the record B-tree. As transactions iterate through the list, the first record version identified as belonging to the selected branch will necessarily be that branch's most recent version.

Putting this together, consider Figure 5. It shows three transactions t_{10}, t_{11}, and t_{12}, with respective read states s_8, s_7, and s_9. t_{10} would read *v2* for key A, *v8* for B, *v1* for C, and *empty* for D. Similarly, t_{11} would read *v2*, *v3*, *v1*, and *empty* respectively for keys A to D. Finally, t_{12} would read *v1*, *v1*, *v9*, and *v9*.

6.1.4 Writing values

To handle uniformly branching and non-branching scenarios, TARDiS's write logic ensures (*i*) that writes, whether conflicting or not, never block, and (*ii*) that updating the appropriate record on the correct branch is cheap.

Both aims can be very simply achieved by pushing most of the work to reads. As long as writes preserve the topological order of versions in the key-version mapping, the read logic ensures that the appropriate version is returned. Hence, a write operation in TARDiS simply creates a new record version storing the transaction's state identifier and the pertinent data, inserts it into the record B-tree, and appropriately updates the corresponding key-version mapping. Since state identifiers (and thus record identifiers) are monotonically increasing along a branch, TARDiS can cheaply maintain a topological order as a sorted list (more precisely, as a lock-free skip list). Thus, independently of whether conflicting writes occurred, all a transaction needs to do to complete a write is to insert the new version into the skip list.

Read-only Transactions Since read-only transactions cannot induce conflicts, TARDiS does not add them to the State DAG. This optimization limits unnecessary DAG growth, easing pressure on the garbage collector.

6.2 Merge Transactions

Merge transactions in TARDiS function similarly to single mode, but with a key difference: they select multiple read states, and hence operate on multiple branches. In merge mode, the application is thus directly exposed to any conflicting writes that forked the state of the datastore.

Merge transactions must atomically reconcile all conflicting objects, writing back a single merged state. As stated previously (§3), merging often requires providing the application with detailed information about the structure of the State DAG, including how branches diverged and the values of conflicting objects at the branches' fork points. This information must be made available efficiently, as a slow merge will stop applications from seeing up-to-date values. TARDiS thus provides an API to aid applications understand branch divergence. It consists of three operations: `findForkPoints`, to identify the fork point(s) of a set of branches; `findConflictWrites`, to list conflicting keys across branches; and `getForID`, to obtain, at the specified state, the record corresponding to a given key. TARDiS leverages the properties of the existing storage and consistency layers to make these operations fast. It implements `findForkPoints` by identifying the fork point(s) of the merge transaction's read states. For `findConflictWrites`, TARDiS similarly identifies the fork points of the branches and computes the conflicting key list from the write set of each intermediate state. Finally, for `getForID`, it uses the key-version mapping to select the appropriate record for a given state.

6.3 Garbage Collection

Most traditional databases store only the active frontier of records, keeping space overhead manageable as old transactions commit. TARDiS, on the contrary, stores by default all stale and parallel versions or states. For performance and efficiency under finite storage, TARDiS implements an aggressive, three-pronged garbage collection policy that runs concurrently with regular operations: (*i*) users place *ceilings* on specific states, promising never to use any state that precedes them as a read state; (*ii*) a path-compression algorithm compresses the State DAG to remove all states that are neither fork points nor leaf states; and (*iii*) a record-promotion algorithm removes record versions that are no longer visible because of ceilings or path compression.

Path Compression Path compression relies on one core heuristic: since most merging policies only require the fork points and the leaf states of a given execution, all intermediate states can be safely removed from the State DAG. In effect, this reduces the DAG to explicitly tracking the *nearest conflict dependency* using a three-staged process (Figure 8).

First, a *ceiling marking* bottom-up pass marks all the states above a recently placed ceiling. Marked states can no longer be selected as read states, ensuring that no new transaction starts above a ceiling (Figure 8(b)). Second, a *safe to garbage-collect* top-down pass labels as *safe-to-gc* all marked states (*i*) that are not currently selected as read states by some executing transaction and (*ii*) whose ancestors are also safe to garbage collect. This pass prevents committing transactions from rippling down deleted states and ensures that a state will only be deleted after all its ancestors have been deleted (Figure 8(c)). Finally, a *garbage collecting pass* marks safe-to-gc states that are not fork points as *garbage collectable* (*gc-able*). Garbage-collectable states are then "promoted" by mapping their state identifier to that of their most recent non-deleted child. All accesses looking up a deleted state are henceforth forwarded to the promoted state. In effect, the child node takes over the identity of its parent as well as its own, allowing for the parent to be garbage collected (Figure 8(d.e.f)). Consider in Figure 8 an object D that is last modified in s_1. Its state identifier is therefore 1. All transactions whose read states are a descendant of s_1 see D. But, when s_1

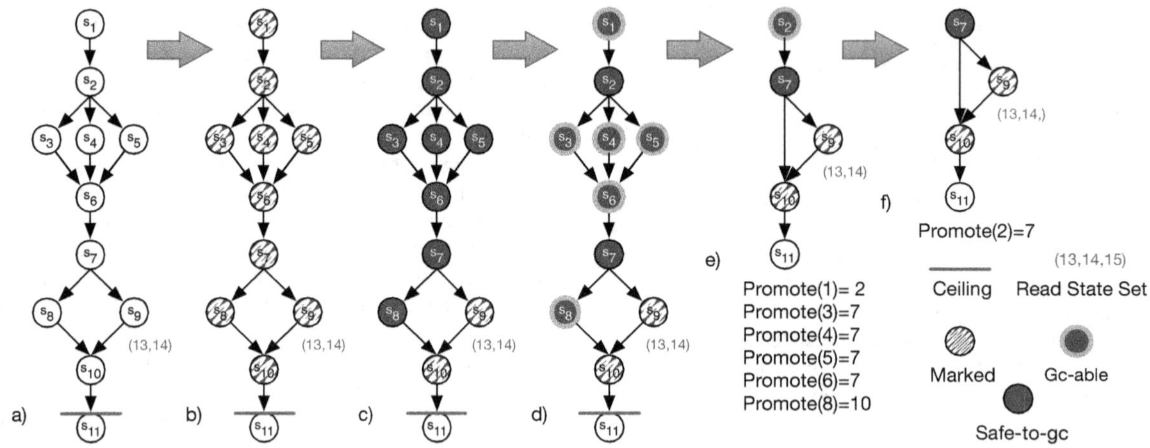

Figure 8: Path Compression Algorithm - Ceiling placed above s_{11}. s_8 and ancestors are marked as safe-to-gc; since s_{10} is the read state for several pending transactions, it cannot be marked as safe-to-gc. Non fork points safe-to-gc states are marked as gc-able and deleted.

is garbage collected, any transaction that tries to read D and thus looks up the fork path of s_1 would fail. Promoting s_1 to s_7 ensures that any such transaction is redirected to s_7. Once promoted, garbage collectable states can safely be removed.

Record Promotion Next, TARDiS deletes record versions that are no longer needed. Record versions associated with previously deleted states are promoted to their first non-garbage-collected descendants and updated to reflect their new identifier. This promotion creates long chains of records with the same state identifier. Since TARDiS' get/put algorithm returns only the most recent visible record, none but the first of the promoted records that share an identifier will ever be accessed: the rest can therefore be safely discarded. A full record-promotion pass, as in path compression, hence ensures that the only record versions maintained are those that are either current or at a fork point.

6.4 Replication

The Replicator (§4) uses a gossip protocol [1] to asynchronously propagate locally executing transactions. These transactions carry a *StateID* constraint that specifies the state to which they should be applied. The Replicator applies a newly received transaction if the required parent state is present. If not, the transaction is cached to be appended later. The *StateID* constraint removes the need to track expensive dependency meta-data: it reduces dependency checking to looking up whether the state with the corresponding id is present in the remote DAG, which can be done in constant time.

Garbage collection is triggered by each local Replicator and can operate either optimistically or pessimistically. When pessimistic, TARDiS garbage collects states only after receiving unanimous consent from all Replicators [34]. As this can cause garbage collection to trail significantly during partitions, optimistic mode lets sites garbage collect states independently. If a replica later needs a state it garbage-collected, the replica simply retrieves the missing information from the appropriate replica. This may cause some transactions to block. If an application erroneously places a ceiling that causes states to be prematurely garbage collected, TARDiS simply aborts the transactions that try accessing the missing states.

The current prototype of TARDiS does not support data partitioning, but it can be extended to support this feature by using an approach similar to the one taken by COPS [31]—in essence, by executing distributed transactions within a datacenter (with the State DAG collocated with the transaction manager) and replicating transactions asynchronously across datacenters.

6.5 Fault Tolerance and Recovery

TARDiS guarantees consistency, atomicity, and (optionally) durability if, at all times, the write operations of all transactions present in the State DAG are observable by future transactions. TARDiS maintains this invariant across failures by logging, at transaction commit time, the id of the corresponding commit state, its parent state(s) ids, and the transaction's write set keys.

Recovery During recovery, TARDiS reconstructs the State DAG and key-version mapping by iterating chronologically over the log. For each log entry, the recovery process (*i*) inserts a new state in the DAG with matching id and adds it as a child of the states with matching parent ids; and (*ii*) adds a new entry in the key-version mapping for each key in the recorded write set. Iterating over the log chronologically guarantees that no child is recovered before its parents; the skip-list implementation of the key-version mapping guarantees that the order of entries in the key-version mapping is preserved across failures.

Asynchrous Flush To mitigate the overheads of writing to disk, TARDiS offers the option of asynchronously flushing both record updates and the commit log (at the cost of durability). To preserve atomicity, TARDiS ensures that the commit log is flushed sequentially and further checks, on recovery, whether each entry in the write set has been made persistent to stable storage. If only part of a transaction's effect has been made persistent, the corresponding state and all subsequent states are discarded. Orphaned records (resulting from operations that belong to, or depend on, partially applied transactions) have no effect on correctness, as it is the DAG and key-version mapping that determine what can be read. These records are simply eventually garbage collected.

Checkpointing To reduce log size, TARDiS periodically takes non-blocking checkpoints by (*i*) selecting a state id s_c, (*ii*) flushing all outstanding writes, and (*iii*) saving every DAG state with id smaller than s_c.

Replication To recover transactions that have committed elsewhere but are lost locally, the recovery process broadcasts a vector with the id of the latest surving state received from each Replicator. Replicas respond by sending states and records more recent than their corresponding entry in the vector. If these states have already been garbage collected, it may be necessary to send the full DAG.

6.6 Implementation notes

Our prototype consists of 15K lines of Java in two configurations. In TARDiS-BDB, record persistence to disk is via BerkeleyDB with concurrency control turned off, while TARDiS-MDB depends on MapDB [35]. We rely on Google Protobuffers v2.4.5 for message serialization and on the Netty networking library for inter-site communication.

7. EVALUATION

TARDiS proposes branching as the fundamental abstraction to model conflicts end-to-end. To quantify the cost and benefits of this new abstraction with respect to both performance and complexity, we first benchmark the performance of the system itself. We then use the abstraction to program two representative ALPS applications: CRDTs [42], a library of scalable, weakly consistent datatypes (counters, sets, maps, and more); and Retwis [41], a Twitter clone. We find that using state branching/merging cuts the number of lines of code in half, while judicious branch-on-conflict yields a speedup of between two and eight times.

7.1 Microbenchmarks

Our microbenchmarks answer the following questions:

(i) What are the overheads of tracking state? (§7.1.2,§7.1.5)
(ii) When does local branching improve performance? (§7.1.3)
(iii) What impact has expressiveness on performance? (§7.1.4)
(iv) How does the system scale for multiple sites? (§7.1.6)

7.1.1 *Evaluation Setup*

Unless otherwise stated, we run our experiments on a shared local cluster of machines equipped with a 2.67GHz Intel Xeon CPU X5650 with 48GB of memory and connected by a 2Gbps network. Inter-machine ping latencies average 0.15 ms. Each experiment is run with three dedicated server machines, three dedicated Replicators and with clients spread equally among separate machines. To the best of our ability, all runs were performed in the absence of interfering workloads.

We compare TARDiS with both BerkeleyDB v6.2.31 Java Edition (**BDB**) and a custom OCC implementation (**OCC**) that uses BDB as its backend. BerkeleyDB, as a widely-used, pure-Java ACID datastore, provides a sound basis for comparison against our TARDiS prototype. We configure BerkeleyDB so that *(i)* read-write transactions are flushed to disk asynchronously; and *(ii)* all requests hit the cache. Our OCC implementation is based on a modified version of Kung et al.'s algorithm [28] that does not require read-write transactions to be verified against read-only transactions.

Each client issues transactions consisting of six operations in a closed loop, running for two minutes. We use a set of clients large enough to saturate the system. Read-only transactions contain only reads; read-write transactions contain three reads and three writes. We consider four transaction mixes differentiated by the ratio of read-only transactions to read-write transactions: Read-only (R-O, 100/0), Read-heavy (R-H, 75/25), Mixed (M, 25/75), and Write-Heavy (W-H, 0/100). We report only on the read-heavy and write-heavy workloads. We further consider two access patterns from the YCSB benchmark [18]: uniform and Zipfian (p=0.99). We report on TARDiS-BDB only: the performance of TARDiS-MDB is similar (approximately 10% better).

7.1.2 *Baseline TARDiS performance*

We begin by establishing a baseline for the performance of TARDiS: we want to determine how it compares, when local branch-on-conflict is not enabled, against both our simple implementation of OCC and a commercial system like BDB. Transactions use *Ancestor* as begin constraint and the union of *Serializability* and *No Branching* as end constraint. We expect this setup to

Workload		Begin	Get	Put	Commit
RH-Uniform	TARDiS	0.6	0.6	1	0.2
	BDB	0.3	0.4	1.2	0.1
	OCC	0.5	0.6	1.1	3.5
WH-Uniform	TARDiS	1	1.2	1.1	1.8
	BDB	0.6	0.8	2.7	0.1
	OCC	0.9	1.2	1.1	6.7
WH-Zipfian	TARDiS	1	1.4	1.2	0.8
	BDB	0.6	8	23	0.1
	OCC	0.4	0.9	1.2	9

Table 3: Per-operation latency breakdown ($\times 10^{-2}ms$)

be common: it guarantees that each application sees its own writes and that the execution is serializable.

The throughput-latency graph in Figure 9 shows that, despite tracking the full system's history and paying the overhead of selecting a read and commit state, TARDiS-BDB performs similarly to BDB for both read-heavy and write-heavy workloads. TARDiS incurs a 10% slowdown as its begin and commit phase are more costly than in BDB. As contention increases, however, TARDiS-BDB's lock-free writes reduce the performance gap. In both cases, our OCC implementation lags behind. For the read-heavy workload, OCC must verify read-only transactions, which increases latency and reduces throughput. For the write-heavy workload, OCC suffers from a long validation phase. Though also optimistic, TARDiS's validation phase (commit state identification) is less costly: it requires checking only the write set of those transactions that already committed as children of the selected read state. In contrast, OCC requires checking against all concurrently committing transactions.

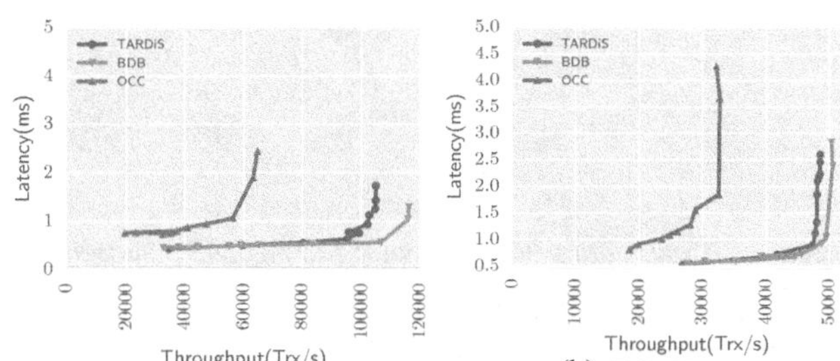

(a) Read-Heavy (b) Write-Heavy

Figure 9: TARDiS-BDB vs BerkeleyDB vs OCC

7.1.3 *Impact of branching*

TARDiS lets ALPS applications choose to branch on conflict rather than abort. Unsurprisingly, we find that the relative benefits of branching increase with contention. Results are shown in Figure 10 (all transactions run with branch-on-conflict enabled and with *Ancestor* and *Serializability* as, respectively, their begin and end constraint). Table 3 provides a per-operation breakdown of the same experiments, excluding network latency and retries. Figure 10(a) shows that, when contention is low, branching indeed does not help: TARDiS's performance is slightly lower than BDB's. By contrast, with higher contention (Figure 10(b)), TARDiS outperforms BDB by 35%. The performance of BDB drops by half, as transactions wait longer for locks to become available, increasing the cost of gets and puts by a factor of almost two (Table 3 shows that reads take 0.004ms in the R-H workload, and 0.008ms in the W-H workload). The 37% throughput drop in TARDiS is due to several factors. First, the lack of read-only transactions: since all transactions now have to identify a commit state, the commit cost of the transaction increases (from Table 3: from 0.002ms to 0.018ms). Second, reads become more expensive, as more record versions

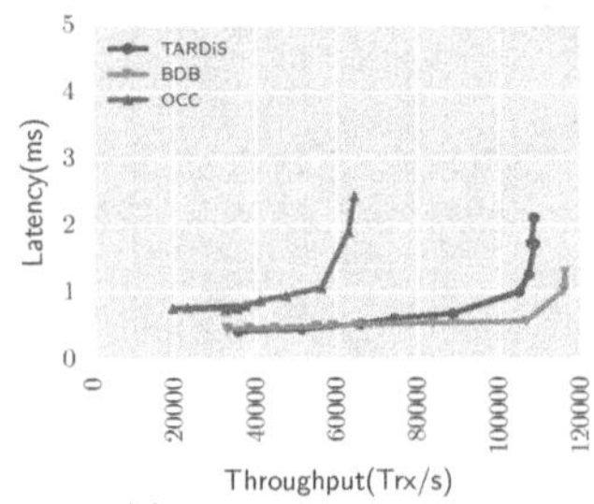

(a) Uniform Read-Heavy

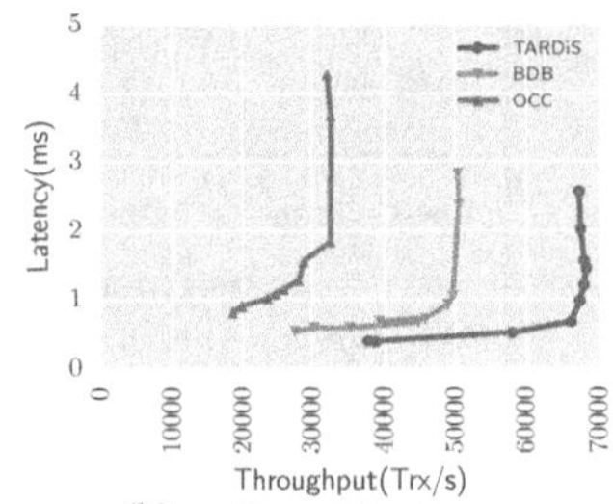

(b) Uniform Write-Heavy

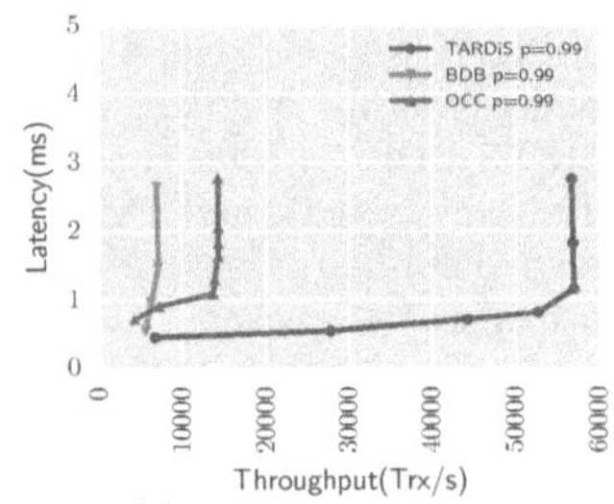

(c) Zipfian Write-Heavy

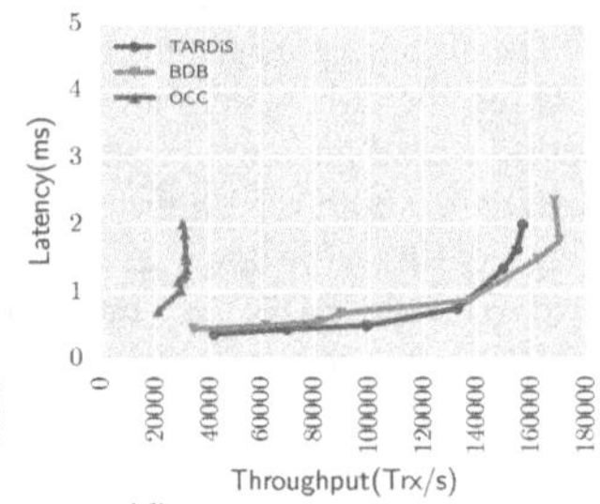

(d) Uniform Blind Writes

Figure 10: Benefit of branching as a function of workload

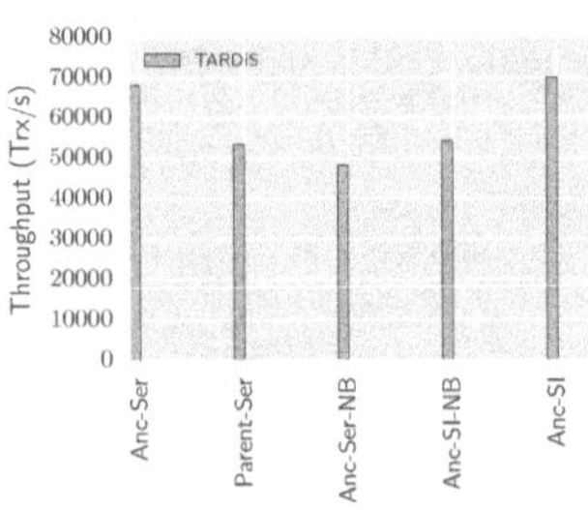

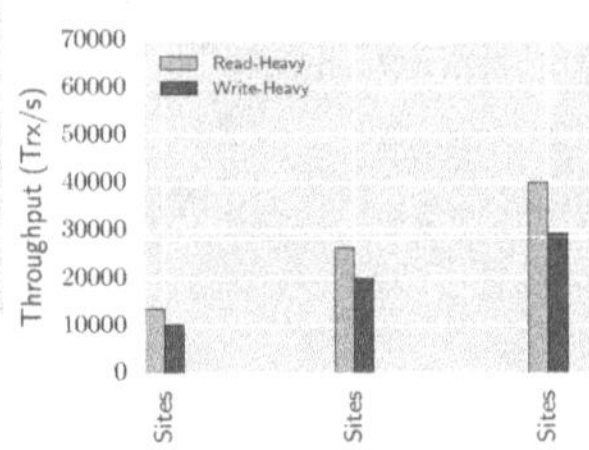

Figure 11: Constraint Choice *Figure 12: TARDiS Scalability*

need to be checked (from 0.006ms to 0.012ms). With both low and high contention, the throughput of OCC is bottlenecked by the verification phase. The relative performance increase of branching over sequential storage is most marked when requests follow a Zipfian workload in which a small number of objects, accessed very frequently, experience a high degree of contention (Figure 10(c)). In this scenario, TARDiS outperforms BDB by a factor of eight. Whereas moving from a uniform to a Zipfian distribution causes BDB's performance to collapse (7x throughput decrease), TARDiS' throughput is much less affected: the lock-free implementation of the write skip-list ensures that writes never block, even when conflicting. Table 3 confirms this: the cost of writes increases only moderately in TARDiS (from 0.011ms to 0.012ms). Similarly, the use of fork points to efficiently summarize the DAG means that, despite an eight-fold increase in the branching factor in the Zipfian workload, the cost of reads only increases by 16%. In contrast, locking causes the read and write time for BDB to increase by a factor of ten. OCC performs comparatively better, as it ensures that (*i*) at least one transaction will always commit, and (*ii*) readers will not block writers. Nonetheless, its high abort rate and expensive validation phase limit its throughput to a fifth of TARDiS'.

Branching, however, is not always beneficial. In the workload of Figure 10(d) transactions consist of a single write accessing the database uniformly, conflicts are rare, and locks are held for a very short period of time: here, branching does not help, but still incurs the cost of tracking past states. Since the current implementation of TARDiS' garbage collector is unable to keep up with the speed

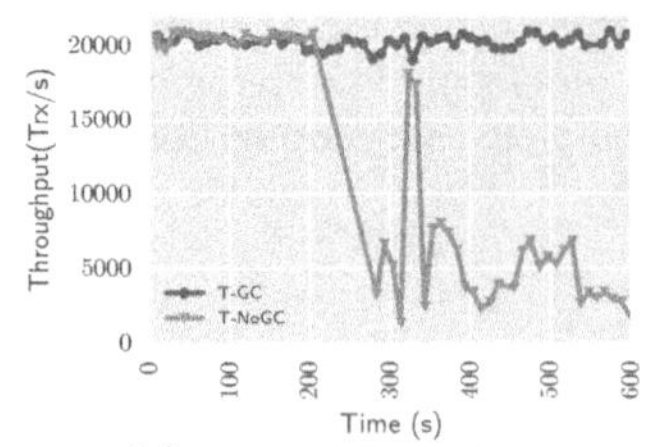

(a) Throughput over time

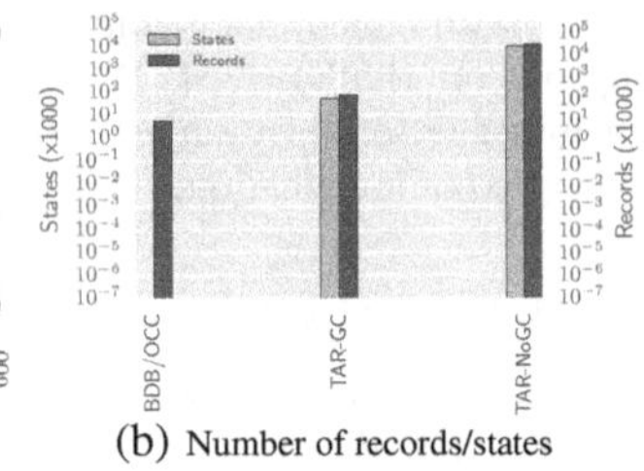

(b) Number of records/states

Figure 13: Impact of garbage collection

at which new states are generated, the increased memory pressure grows the number of stalls induced by garbage collection, causing TARDiS to perform 10% worse than BDB.

7.1.4 Impact of Constraint Choice

The choice of begin and end constraints involves a complex trade-off between consistency and performance. To shed some light on this trade-off for our current implementation, we plot in Figure 11 the throughput of TARDiS for several different constraint choices for the same configuration (15 machines, each with seven clients) that led TARDiS to reach the elbow in the write-heavy throughput/latency graphs of Figures 9 and 10. We focus on the *Ancestor* and *Parent* begin constraints because we expect them to be the most popular. *Ancestor* ensures that clients will see their own writes, along with those of any non-conflicting clients. In the Wikipedia example, this would allow Alice to read back Carlo's operations, but not Davide's or Bruno's. *Parent* results in a behavior very much akin to that of a local Git branch, as clients will see their own operations only. A detailed per-operation performance breakdown (omitted for lack of space) gives us clues for why, despite commit selection being 30% cheaper in *Parent* (as only the read state can satisfy it), *Ancestor* still outperforms *Parent* by 21%. First, read state selection is 40% more expensive in *Parent*, as it requires a look-up over the full DAG rather than one that only involves its leaves. Second, since *Parent* results in more branches, fork path checking becomes more expensive, increasing the cost of reads by 15%. Finally, *Parent* prevents states from being quickly garbage collected.

Unlike begin constraints, we find that end constraints, as long as they do not cause transactions to abort, do not significantly affect throughput or latency: throughput results for the (branching) *Serializability* and *Snapshot Isolation* constraints are within 5% of each other, mostly because the former, by creating twice as many branches, increases the cost of reads by 10%. Non-branching serializability and snapshot isolation both perform poorly in comparison. Though each individual operation is cheap, they see repeated aborts due to write-write or read-write conflicts.

7.1.5 Garbage Collection

Figures 13(a) and 13(b) report, respectively, the throughput and number of DAG states and records generated by a single server running TARDiS, with and without garbage collection, over a ten minute run with *Ancestor* begin constraint, *Serializability* end constraint, and clients placing ceilings (§6.3) every 1000 transactions. Without DAG compression, throughput drops dramatically after three minutes, since old and new generation Java garbage collection pause TARDiS constantly. With DAG compression, throughput instead remains constant, as (*i*) states are removed from the DAG and their underlying datastructures recycled for incoming transactions, and (*ii*) record promotion/deletion keeps the key-version mapping structure small. Compression should ideally bound the DAG size to the product of the number of clients times the ceiling placing interval (i.e., $30 \times 1000 = 30,000$ states) but, as Figure 13(b) shows, the DAG is $55,000$—98% fewer states than without garbage collection, but still two times higher than the ideal. This mismatch is due to record compression. Though, in principle, states can be removed from the DAG as soon as they become garbage-collectible, in practice the promotion table must first be flushed, which can only happen after a full record promotion pass. Unfortunately, these records are often not present in the cache and must be read from disk, causing the record promotion threads to trail behind. Likewise, the storage size in TARDiS is 15x larger than in OCC or BDB. We are currently investigating alternative schemes that do not have this drawback.

7.1.6 *Replication*

We measure the scalability of TARDiS when running in geographically distinct replicas. We use a Google Cloud Services cluster of three machines (2.5GHz Intel Xeon E5 v2 machines with 60GB of memory), running in three geographical zones (us-central1-f, europe-west1-b, asia-east-1). Figure 12 shows how the aggregated throughput scales with the number of sites. As transactions are asynchronously replicated, latency is unchanged from the single site experiments. TARDiS scales linearly with the number of sites, as its design ensures that transactions, when applied to remote sites, do not contend with local transactions.

7.2 Applications

In porting ALPS applications to TARDiS, we answer two questions: *(i)* Do explicit state branching and merging simplify conflict resolution? *(ii)* Can ALPS applications use local branch-on-conflict to improve their performance?

7.2.1 *Simplifying Merging: CRDTs*

Convergent Replicated Data Types (CRDTs) [42] are a family of data types that support lazy replication by including a set of semantically meaningful conflict resolution functions. A variety of CRDTs have been developed [40, 42], including counters, sets, registers, and trees. To date, they have been incorporated into cooperative text editing tools [40] and in the Riak key-value store [26].

We followed the algorithms developed Shapiro et al. [42] to implement, on top of both TARDiS and BDB, a subset of CRDTs sufficient to design realistic applications. The TARDiS implementation proved easier to write and required less code, often by a factor of two or more (Figure 14(a)): the entire effort took less than a day with TARDiS, compared to over three days with BDB. Two features of TARDiS account for this: *StateID* replication and conflict tracking. *StateID* replication guarantees that operations that execute locally on a given state will execute on the same state at all remote sites, and therefore eliminates the need to capture and replicate side-effects. In turn, conflict tracking makes it easy, for each CRDT replica implemented in TARDiS, to access, through the State DAG, a consistent view of the updates that need to be merged. Implementations on flat storage systems like BDB, in contrast, need to explicitly track the updates applied at each replica and make sure that the state of the CRDTs is replicated consistently everywhere. Consider, for example, the counter CRDT, which is modeled as two separate increment and decrement vectors, containing an entry per replica. On BDB, it is up to the CRDT developer to ensure that, as new operations are applied, the global state is tracked correctly at each replica. TARDiS instead tracks the necessary information by design. With access to the fork point, merging becomes as easy as adding, for each branch, the difference between the counter's value at the fork point and at the current state.

To guarantee eventual convergence, CRDTs implemented on sequential storage must mutate local state atomically and sequentially (e.g., new vector clocks must be created atomically to guarantee causal delivery, and updating counters requires read-modify-write operations). Each replica must consequently be serializable, thus limiting the throughput at each site. Branch-on-conflict removes this limitation without sacrificing consistency. For a workload consisting of 90% reads and 10% writes, with transactions configured to use the *Ancestor* and *Serializability* constraint set and periodic merging, TARDiS' CRDT implementations achieve a four to eight times speedup over their sequential counterparts (Figure 14(b)). Three factors contribute to this speedup. First, each individual operation is simpler: for instance, reading or updating a counter no longer involves manipulating a vector, but simply requires reading or writing an integer. Second, operations are no longer serialized, but fork on conflict, and are later merged back. Finally, merges can be batched. Traditional CRDTs require a merge for every remote operation received; in TARDiS, merges need only take place periodically, as operations are consistently recorded in separate branches. These effects are displayed in Figure 14(d). It shows, for a CRDT counter implemented in TARDiS, BDB, and OCC, the percentage of *useful work*, measured as the time spent executing committed transactions (i.e., excluding time spent waiting on locks, aborted transactions, and merge transactions): useful work in TARDiS is at 0.96, while for BDB and OCC almost half the time is wasted.

7.2.2 *Pushing weak consistency down: Retwis*

To understand the performance implications of building ALPS applications in TARDiS, we implemented Retwis [41], a popular Twitter clone [39, 44, 51]. Retwis users can create accounts (*createAccount*), follow users (*followUser*), post new content (*post*), and read their own timeline (*readOwnTimeline*), which includes their own tweets and those of the users they follow. In our implementation, *readOwnTimeline* returns the 50 most recent posts. Contention primarily arises when a user posts new content, as the Retwis implementation must ensure that the tweet becomes visible to all the user's followers. Retwis, like many ALPS applications, has relatively weak consistency requirements: as long as posts are not incorrectly attributed and are presented in causal order, users can tolerate small delays in seeing posts. Porting Retwis on TARDiS was straightforward. We simply extended each transactional call to take the *Ancestor* begin constraint and *Serializability* end constraint, and implemented a separate conflict resolver that periodically merges conflicting branches by resolving duplicate user ids and merging timelines (preserving the order of posts).

Figure 14(c) shows the throughput of Retwis on TARDiS, BDB, and OCC, for three workloads: read-only (100% reads), read-heavy (85% reads, 5% follows, and 10% posts), and post-heavy (65% reads, 5% follows, and 30% posts). Branching does not benefit the read-only workload, but it significantly softens the performance blow caused by contention in the remaining two workloads. An analysis of the per-transaction behavior (omitted for lack of space) reveals that the throughput of *readOwnTimeline* operations drops by 70% for OCC in the read-heavy workload, as *posts* cause these transactions to abort, and by 80% in BDB, as write operations block both reads and other writes (causing in turn read operations to block for longer). These effects are amplified in the post-heavy workload. Moving to Figure 14(d), we see that TARDiS, by branching and merging asychronously, is able to maintain a much higher fraction of useful work than OCC and BDB for both of these worklods because, unlike waiting on locks, merging does not prevent the system from making progress. The small drop in TARDiS' throughput is due to the need to identify commit states for *posts*. Thus, for ALPS

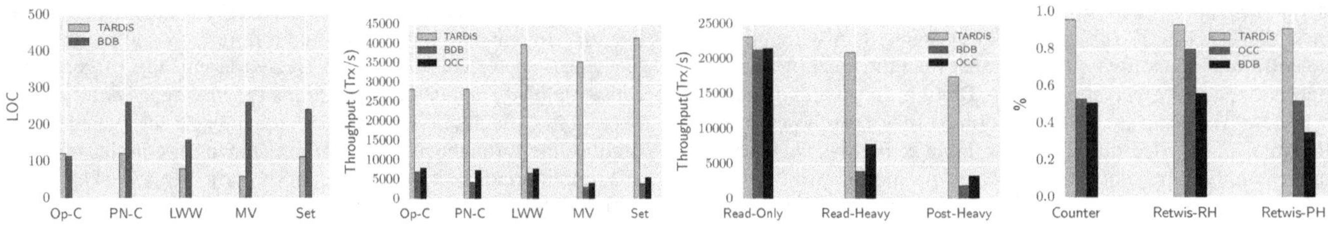

(a) CRDT Lines of Code (b) CRDT Throughput (c) Retwis Throughput (d) Application Goodput

Figure 14: Applications on BerkeleyDB and TARDiS. Op-C:Operation Based Counter, PN-C: State Based Counter, LWW: Last-Writer-Wins Register, MV: Multivalued Register, Set: Or-Set

applications, executing conflicting transactions optimistically and reconciling them later can improve scalability within a site, much like weak consistency improves scalability across sites.

8. RELATED WORK

Avoiding Conflicts The core challenge in geo-replication is handling conflicts at different sites. One option is to preemptively ensure that conflicts do not happen, either through strong synchronization [2, 13, 19] or through scheduling transactions to avoid conflicts (using static analysis [53] or upon admission [49]). TARDiS explicitly targets applications whose availability or latency constraints preclude this option.

Weakening Consistency Systems designed for ALPS applications trade-off strong consistency for performance and provide weaker guarantees such as causal consistency [4, 20], timeline consistency [17], parallel snapshot isolation [44], and non-monotonic snapshot isolation [7]. Others have sought to give applications the flexibility of adapting the consistency level required as a function of the operation (Pileus [47], Red-Blue Consistency [29], MDCC [27]) or the object (Continuous Consistency Model [52], CRDTs [42], Escrow Transactions [43]). TARDiS instead allows for general conflict resolution strategies defined by the application.

Resolving Conflicts When conflicts are allowed, most systems resolve conflicting executions by projecting them onto sequential storage. COPS [31] adopts a first-writer-wins policy; Ficus [25], Dynamo [20], and Bayou all leave resolution up to the users; and operational transforms [45] leverage specific textual properties. Unlike in TARDiS, these resolution functions are per-object and do not allow programmers to see and resolve the entire state atomically.

Branching Conflicts in a distributed system introduce implicit branching that must be reconciled when conflicts are detected. A number of systems expose this branching: version control systems (Git) allow users to operate on different branches; the Olive [3] file-system allows users to create/and fork snapshots efficiently; and ORI [36] tracks possibly divergent histories across multiple devices. They contrast with TARDiS as their branching is explicit (git branch) rather than implicit: explicit branching requires synchronization, which is precisely what ALPS applications want to avoid. Some causally consistent systems also allow for concurrent writes to be exposed to the users (Ficus [25], Dynamo [20]). This is a limited notion of branching, which forks individual objects rather than a state. These systems, as a result, provide neither conflict tracking nor branches, and increase complexity for the application by systematically exposing it to multiple values. By contrast, in TARDiS programmers only deal with multivalued objects if they explicitly request it in merge mode. In the Byzantine context, SUNDR [30] and FAUST [15] develop fork consistency/linearizability to isolate clients that see different values in a faulty server, and Depot [34] extends SUNDR's model to support fork-joining. Depot does not, however, expose the abstraction of branches, and provides no support for cross-object atomic merges, unlike TARDiS. Finally, Sporc [22] does provide atomic joining of forks, but only for the restricted case of collaborative text applications, and uses operational transformation to resolve conflicts.

9. CONCLUSIONS AND FUTURE WORK

This paper introduced TARDiS, a novel transactional key-value store designed to support weakly-consistent systems. By explicitly tracking concurrent branches and exposing them, when needed, to applications, TARDiS simplifies conflict resolution. By giving applications the option of applying weak consistency principles end-to-end, TARDiS can significantly improve the performance of the local site.

TARDiS nonetheless lacks several features. First and foremost, its replicas do not support distributed transactions: we are currently investigating how to add this feature to the system. More generally, we believe that TARDiS' ability to efficiently distinguish between concurrent threads of execution makes it a strong candidate for concurrency control systems based on speculation. We hope to investigate whether speculation can alleviate many of the throughput issues in wide-area strongly consistent systems.

10. ACKNOWLEDGEMENTS

We would like to thank the anonymous reviewers and Phil Bernstein, Ionel Gog, Steven Hand, Kim Keeton, Akbar Syed Mehdi, Reinhard Munz, Clement Pit-Claudel, Daniel Porto, Rodrigo Rodrigues, Marco Serafini, Chunzhi Su, Malte Schwarzkopf, Chao Xie, Michael Walfish, John Wilkes, and Emmett Witchell for their insightful comments and feedback on earlier drafts of this work. This work was supported by the National Science Foundation under grant number CNS-1409555 and by a Google Cloud Platform credit award. Natacha Crooks was partially supported by a Google European Fellowship in Distributed Computing. A significant portion of this work was done while Allen Clement and Natacha Crooks were at MPI-SWS.

11. REFERENCES

[1] Gossip-based computer networking. *ACM SIGOPS Operating Systems Review*, 41(5), 2007.

[2] M. K. Aguilera, A. Merchant, M. Shah, A. Veitch, and C. Karamanolis. Sinfonia: A new paradigm for building scalable distributed systems. In *Proceedings of the 21st ACM Symposium on Operating Systems Principles*, SOSP '07, pages 159–174.

[3] M. K. Aguilera, S. Spence, and A. Veitch. Olive: Distributed point-in-time branching storage for real systems. In *Proceedings of the 3rd USENIX Symposium on Networked Systems Design and Implementation - Volume 3*, NSDI '06.

[4] M. Ahamad, G. Neiger, J. E. Burns, P. Kohli, and P. Hutto. Causal memory: Definitions, implementation and programming. Technical report, Georgia Institute of Technology, 1994.

[5] P. Alvaro, P. Bailis, N. Conway, and J. M. Hellerstein. Consistency without borders. In *Proceedings of the 4th ACM Symposium on Cloud Computing*, SOCC '13, pages 23:1–23:10.

[6] Apache. Cassandra. http://cassandra.apache.org/.

[7] M. S. Ardekani, P. Sutra, and M. Shapiro. Non-monotonic snapshot isolation: Scalable and strong consistency for geo-replicated transactional systems. In *Proceedings of the 32nd International Symposium on Reliable Distributed Systems*, SRDS '13, pages 163–172.

[8] P. Bailis, A. Fekete, A. Ghodsi, J. M. Hellerstein, and I. Stoica. The potential dangers of causal consistency and an explicit solution. In *Proceedings of the 3rd ACM Symposium on Cloud Computing*, SOCC '12, pages 22:1–22:7.

[9] P. Bailis, A. Ghodsi, J. M. Hellerstein, and I. Stoica. Bolt-on causal consistency. In *Proceedings of the 2013 ACM SIGMOD International Conference on Management of Data*, SIGMOD '13.

[10] Basho. Riak. http://basho.com/products/.

[11] H. Berenson, P. Bernstein, J. Gray, J. Melton, E. O'Neil, and P. O'Neil. A critique of ANSI SQL isolation levels. In *ACM SIGMOD Record*, volume 24, pages 1–10, 1995.

[12] P. A. Bernstein and N. Goodman. Multiversion concurrency control;theory and algorithms. *ACM Transactions on Database Systems*, 8(4):465–483, 1983.

[13] P. A. Bernstein, V. Hadzilacos, and N. Goodman. *Concurrency control and recovery in database systems*. 1987.

[14] E. A. Brewer. Towards robust distributed systems (abstract). In *Proceedings of the 19th ACM Symposium on Principles of Distributed Computing*, PODC '00.

[15] C. Cachin, I. Keidar, and A. Shraer. Trusting the cloud. *SIGACT News*, 40(2):81–86, June 2009.

[16] Cassandra. Cassandra Use Cases. http://www.planetcassandra.org/apache-cassandra-use-cases/.

[17] B. F. Cooper, R. Ramakrishnan, U. Srivastava, A. Silberstein, P. Bohannon, H.-A. Jacobsen, N. Puz, D. Weaver, and R. Yerneni. PNUTS: Yahoo!'s hosted data serving platform. *Proceedings of the VLDB Endowment*, 1(2):1277–1288, 2008.

[18] B. F. Cooper, A. Silberstein, E. Tam, R. Ramakrishnan, and R. Sears. Benchmarking cloud serving systems with YCSB. In *Proceedings of the 1st ACM Symposium on Cloud Computing*, SoCC '10, pages 143–154.

[19] J. C. Corbett, J. Dean, M. Epstein, A. Fikes, C. Frost, J. J. Furman, S. Ghemawat, A. Gubarev, C. Heiser, P. Hochschild, W. Hsieh, S. Kanthak, E. Kogan, H. Li, A. Lloyd, S. Melnik, D. Mwaura, D. Nagle, S. Quinlan, R. Rao, L. Rolig, Y. Saito, M. Szymaniak, C. Taylor, R. Wang, and D. Woodford. Spanner: Google's globally-distributed database. In *Proceedings of the 10th USENIX Symposium on Operating Systems Design and Implementation*, OSDI '12, pages 251–264.

[20] G. DeCandia, D. Hastorun, M. Jampani, G. Kakulapati, A. Lakshman, A. Pilchin, S. Sivasubramanian, P. Vosshall, and W. Vogels. Dynamo: Amazon's highly available key-value store. In *Proceedings of 21st ACM Symposium on Operating Systems Principles*, SOSP '07, pages 205–220.

[21] J. Du, C. Iorgulescu, A. Roy, and W. Zwaenepoel. Gentlerain: Cheap and scalable causal consistency with physical clocks. In *Proceedings of the ACM Symposium on Cloud Computing*, SOCC '14, pages 4:1–4:13.

[22] A. J. Feldman, W. P. Zeller, M. J. Freedman, and E. W. Felten. SPORC: Group collaboration using untrusted cloud resources. In *Proceedings of the 9th USENIX Symposium on Operating Systems Design and Implementation*, OSDI '10.

[23] S. Gilbert and N. Lynch. Brewer's conjecture and the feasibility of consistent, available, partition-tolerant web services. *SIGACT News*, 33(2):51–59, June 2002.

[24] Git. Git: the fast version control system. http://git-scm.com.

[25] R. G. Guy, J. S. Heidemann, W. Mak, T. W. Page, Jr., G. J. Popek, and D. Rothmeir. Implementation of the Ficus Replicated File System. In *Proceedings of the Summer 1990 USENIX Conference*, pages 63–72, 1990.

[26] R. Klophaus. Riak core: Building distributed applications without shared state. In *ACM SIGPLAN Commercial Users of Functional Programming*, CUFP '10.

[27] T. Kraska, G. Pang, M. J. Franklin, S. Madden, and A. Fekete. Mdcc: multi-data center consistency. In *Proceedings of the 8th ACM European Conference on Computer Systems*, EuroSys '13, pages 113–126.

[28] H. Kung and J. T. Robinson. On optimistic methods for concurrency control. *ACM Transactions on Database Systems*, 6(2):213–226, June 1981.

[29] C. Li, D. Porto, A. Clement, J. Gehrke, N. Preguiça, and R. Rodrigues. Making geo-replicated systems fast as possible, consistent when necessary. In *Proceedings of the 10th USENIX Symposium on Operating Systems Design and Implementation*, OSDI '12, pages 265–278.

[30] J. Li, M. Krohn, D. Mazières, and D. Shasha. Secure untrusted data repository (SUNDR). In *Proceedings of the 6th USENIX Symposium on Operating Systems Design and Implementation - Volume 6*, OSDI '04.

[31] W. Lloyd, M. J. Freedman, M. Kaminsky, and D. G. Andersen. Don't settle for eventual: scalable causal consistency for wide-area storage with COPS. In *Proceedings of the 23rd ACM Symposium on Operating Systems Principles*, SOSP '11, pages 401–416.

[32] W. Lloyd, M. J. Freedman, M. Kaminsky, and D. G. Andersen. Stronger semantics for low-latency geo-replicated storage. In *Proceedings of the 10th USENIX Symposium on Networked Systems Design and Implementation*, NSDI '13, pages 313–328.

[33] P. Mahajan, L. Alvisi, and M. Dahlin. Consistency, availability, convergence. Technical Report TR-11-22, Computer Science Department, University of Texas at Austin, May 2011.

[34] P. Mahajan, S. Setty, S. Lee, A. Clement, L. Alvisi, M. Dahlin, and M. Walfish. Depot: Cloud storage with minimal trust. *ACM Transactions on Computer Systems*, 29(4):12, 2011.

[35] MapDB. MapDB: Embedded Database Engine. http://www.mapdb.org/.

[36] A. J. Mashtizadeh, A. Bittau, Y. F. Huang, and D. Mazières. Replication, History, and Grafting in the Ori File System. In *Proceedings of the 24th ACM Symposium on Operating Systems Principles*, SOSP '13, pages 151–166.

[37] MongoDB. Agility, Performance, Scalibility. Pick three. https://www.mongodb.org/.

[38] M. A. Olson, K. Bostic, and M. Seltzer. Berkeley DB. In *Proceedings of the Annual Conference on USENIX Annual Technical Conference*, ATEC '99.

[39] R. Padilha and F. Pedone. Augustus: Scalable and robust storage for cloud applications. In *Proceedings of the 8th ACM European Conference on Computer Systems*, EuroSys '13, pages 99–112.

[40] N. Preguica, J. M. Marques, M. Shapiro, and M. Letia. A commutative replicated data type for cooperative editing. In *Proceedings of the 29th IEEE International Conference on Distributed Computing Systems*, ICDCS '09, pages 395–403.

[41] Retwis. Twitter-like Clone. http://retwis.redis.io/.

[42] M. Shapiro, N. Preguiça, C. Baquero, and M. Zawirski. A comprehensive study of Convergent and Commutative Replicated Data Types. Rapport de recherche RR-7506, INRIA, Jan. 2011.

[43] L. Shrira, H. Tian, and D. Terry. Exo-leasing: escrow synchronization for mobile clients of commodity storage servers. In *Proceedings of the 9th ACM/IFIP/USENIX International Conference on Middleware*, Middleware '08, pages 42–61.

[44] Y. Sovran, R. Power, M. K. Aguilera, and J. Li. Transactional storage for geo-replicated systems. In *Proceedings of the 23rd ACM Symposium on Operating Systems Principles*, SOSP '11, pages 385–400.

[45] C. Sun and C. Ellis. Operational transformation in real-time group editors: issues, algorithms, and achievements. In *Proceedings of the 1998 ACM Conference on Computer Supported Cooperative Work*, CSCW '98, pages 59–68.

[46] D. B. Terry, A. J. Demers, K. Petersen, M. J. Spreitzer, M. M. Theimer, and B. B. Welch. Session guarantees for weakly consistent replicated data. In *Proceedings of the 3rd International Conference on on Parallel and Distributed Information Systems*, PDIS '94, pages 140–150.

[47] D. B. Terry, V. Prabhakaran, R. Kotla, M. Balakrishnan, M. K. Aguilera, and H. Abu-Libdeh. Consistency-based service level agreements for cloud storage. In *Proceedings of the 24th ACM Symposium on Operating Systems Principles*, SOSP '13, pages 309–324.

[48] D. B. Terry, M. M. Theimer, K. Petersen, A. J. Demers, M. J. Spreitzer, and C. H. Hauser. Managing update conflicts in Bayou, a weakly connected replicated storage system. In *Proceedings of the 15th ACM Symposium on Operating Systems Principles*, SOSP '95, pages 172–182.

[49] A. Thomson, T. Diamond, S.-C. Weng, K. Ren, P. Shao, and D. J. Abadi. Calvin: Fast distributed transactions for partitioned database systems. In *Proceedings of the 2012 ACM SIGMOD International Conference on Management of Data*, SIGMOD '12, pages 1–12.

[50] Wikipedia. Wikipedia: Conflicting Sources. http://en.wikipedia.org/wiki/Wikipedia:Conflicting_sources.

[51] Z. Wu, M. Butkiewicz, D. Perkins, E. Katz-Bassett, and H. V. Madhyastha. Spanstore: Cost-effective geo-replicated storage spanning multiple cloud services. In *Proceedings of the 24th ACM Symposium on Operating Systems Principles*, SOSP '13, pages 292–308.

[52] H. Yu and A. Vahdat. Design and evaluation of a continuous consistency model for replicated services. In *Proceedings of the 4th USENIX Symposium on Operating Systems Design and Implementation - Volume 4*, OSDI '00.

[53] Y. Zhang, R. Power, S. Zhou, Y. Sovran, M. K. Aguilera, and J. Li. Transaction chains: Achieving serializability with low latency in geo-distributed storage systems. In *Proceedings of the 24th ACM Symposium on Operating Systems Principles*, SOSP '13, pages 276–291.

TicToc: Time Traveling Optimistic Concurrency Control

Xiangyao Yu
CSAIL MIT
yxy@csail.mit.edu

Andrew Pavlo
Carnegie Mellon University
pavlo@cs.cmu.edu

Daniel Sanchez
CSAIL MIT
sanchez@csail.mit.edu

Srinivas Devadas
CSAIL MIT
devadas@csail.mit.edu

ABSTRACT

Concurrency control for on-line transaction processing (OLTP) database management systems (DBMSs) is a nasty game. Achieving higher performance on emerging many-core systems is difficult. Previous research has shown that timestamp management is the key scalability bottleneck in concurrency control algorithms. This prevents the system from scaling to large numbers of cores.

In this paper we present TicToc, a new optimistic concurrency control algorithm that avoids the scalability and concurrency bottlenecks of prior T/O schemes. TicToc relies on a novel and provably correct data-driven timestamp management protocol. Instead of assigning timestamps to transactions, this protocol assigns read and write timestamps to data items and uses them to lazily compute a valid commit timestamp for each transaction. TicToc removes the need for centralized timestamp allocation, and commits transactions that would be aborted by conventional T/O schemes. We implemented TicToc along with four other concurrency control algorithms in an in-memory, shared-everything OLTP DBMS and compared their performance on different workloads. Our results show that TicToc achieves up to 92% better throughput while reducing the abort rate by 3.3× over these previous algorithms.

1. INTRODUCTION

Multi-core systems are now pervasive, as parallelism has become the main approach to increase system performance. Systems with tens to hundreds of CPU cores are already on the market [2, 12], and thousand-core chips will be available in the near future [10]. Conventional DBMSs, however, still scale poorly beyond a few cores. The key bottleneck of on-line transaction processing (OLTP) DBMSs is their concurrency control algorithm. Prior work has shown that common concurrency control algorithms suffer from both fundamental and artificial scalability bottlenecks [34, 37, 29]. Although recent work ameliorates some artificial bottlenecks [20, 21, 24, 28, 32, 35], fundamental bottlenecks remain.

Ideally, concurrency control schemes should restrict the inherent parallelism in transactional workloads as little as possible, while incurring small management overhead that scales well with the number of cores. Most of the recently-proposed concurrency control schemes are based on *timestamp ordering* (T/O) [5]. T/O schemes assign a unique, monotonically-increasing timestamp to each transaction. The DBMS then uses these timestamps to process conflicting operations in the proper order. The two most common variants of T/O are multi-version concurrency control (MVCC) [30] and optimistic concurrency control (OCC) [22].

T/O algorithms are popular because they allow significant concurrency, but suffer from a fundamental scalability bottleneck: timestamp allocation. Using a shared-memory counter to produce timestamps limits T/O schemes to a few million transactions per second, orders of magnitude lower than modern OLTP workload requirements [35, 37]. Prior work has proposed hardware and software techniques to increase timestamp allocation throughput, but both approaches have serious limitations. On the hardware side, centralized asynchronous counters [37], remote atomic memory operations [2, 18], and fully-synchronized clocks [19] alleviate the timestamp allocation bottleneck, but they are challenging to implement and are not available in current systems. On the software side, coarse-grained timestamp epochs with group commit [35] reduces the frequency of timestamp allocations, but still limits concurrency in common scenarios as we show later.

In this paper we present **TicToc**, a new concurrency control algorithm that achieves higher concurrency than state-of-the-art T/O schemes and completely eliminates the timestamp allocation bottleneck. The key contribution of TicToc is a technique that we call *data-driven timestamp management*: instead of assigning timestamps to each transaction independently of the data it accesses, TicToc embeds the necessary timestamp information in each tuple to enable each transaction to compute a valid commit timestamp after it has run, right before it commits. This approach has two benefits. First, each transaction infers its timestamp from metadata associated to each tuple it reads or writes. No centralized timestamp allocator exists, and concurrent transactions accessing disjoint data do not communicate, eliminating the timestamp allocation bottleneck. Second, by determining timestamps *lazily* at commit time, TicToc finds a logical-time order that enforces serializability even among transactions that overlap in physical time and would cause aborts in other T/O-based protocols. In essence, TicToc allows commit timestamps to move forward in time to uncover more concurrency than existing schemes without violating serializability.

We present a high-performance, OCC-based implementation of TicToc, and prove that it enforces serializability. We also design several optimizations that further improve TicToc's scalability. Finally, we compare TicToc with four other modern concurrency control schemes in the **DBx1000** main-memory DBMS [1], using two different OLTP workloads on a multi-socket, 40-core system. Our results show that TicToc achieves up to 92% higher throughput than prior algorithms under a variety of workload conditions.

SIGMOD'16, June 26-July 01, 2016, San Francisco, CA, USA

DOI: http://dx.doi.org/10.1145/2882903.2882935

2. BACKGROUND

OLTP DBMSs support the part of an application that interacts with end users. End users send requests to the application to perform some function (e.g., post a comment, purchase an item). The application processes these requests and then executes transactions in the DBMS to read or write to the database. A *transaction* in the context of one of these systems is the execution of a sequence of one or more operations (e.g., SQL queries) on a shared database to perform some higher-level function [15].

A *concurrency control scheme* is the protocol that a DBMS uses to interleave the operations of simultaneous transactions in such a way to provide the illusion that each transaction is running exclusively on the database. There are two classes of concurrency control algorithms [5]: two-phase locking and timestamp ordering.

Two-phase locking (2PL) was the first method proven to ensure correct execution of concurrent DBMS transactions [6, 13]. Under this scheme, transactions have to acquire locks for a particular element in the database before they are allowed to execute a read or write operation on that element. 2PL is considered a pessimistic approach because it assumes that transactions will conflict and thus they need to acquire locks to avoid this problem. If a transaction is unable to acquire a lock for an element, then it is forced to wait until the lock becomes available. If this waiting is uncontrolled, then the DBMS can incur deadlocks. Thus, a major difference among 2PL variants is their deadlock-avoidance strategy.

Timestamp ordering (T/O) concurrency control schemes generate a serialization order of transactions a priori based on monotonically increasing timestamps. The DBMS uses these timestamps to process conflicting operations in the proper order (e.g., read and write operations on the same element, or two separate write operations on the same element) [5].

Although 2PL has been widely adopted in traditional DBMSs (e.g., IBM DB2, Microsoft SQL Server, MySQL), the contention introduced by locks severely hurts performance in today's many-core systems [37]. Almost every OLTP DBMS released in the last decade that we are aware of, including all but a few of the NewSQL DBMSs [3], uses a T/O-based concurrency control scheme.

We next discuss T/O algorithms in further detail to understand their key bottlenecks. We then discuss state-of-the-art algorithms in Section 2.2. This will provide the necessary background for our presentation of the TicToc algorithm in Section 3.

2.1 Timestamp Allocation

The execution of transactions must obey certain ordering constraints. In the strictest isolation level (i.e., serializable), the execution schedule must be equivalent to a schedule where all the transactions are executed sequentially. In a T/O-based concurrency control algorithm, this serial order is expressed using timestamps. Each transaction is assigned a unique and monotonically increasing timestamp as the serial order that is used for conflict detection. Multi-versioning (MVCC) and optimistic (OCC) concurrency control algorithms are both timestamp based.

In traditional T/O-based algorithms, a centralized timestamp allocator assigns a unique timestamp to each transaction. A common way to implement the allocator is through an *atomic add* instruction that increments a global counter for each new transaction. This approach, however, is only able to generate less than 5 million instructions per second on a modern multi-core system due to the long latency incurred by the CPU's cache coherence protocol [11, 35]. As such, most state-of-the-art T/O-based algorithms suffer from the timestamp allocation bottleneck [37].

Hardware support can alleviate the timestamp allocation bottleneck. For example, Tilera processors support remote atomic operations [14] that can increment the timestamp counter without incurring extra cache coherence traffic [2, 18]. In practice, this achieves 100 million timestamps per second [11]. A second option is to add a special hardware timestamp counter on the multi-core chip (which does not exist in any CPUs today). This approach is able to allocate one billion timestamps per second according to simulations [37]. The third option is to produce timestamps using a clock that is synchronized across all cores. In fact, small-scale Intel systems have a synchronized clock [19]. However, fully-synchronized clocks are challenging to maintain in large-scale, multi-socket systems, which use different clock sources that drift over time. Keeping these clocks completely synchronized would require either an unreasonable amount of communication for adjustments, or a global clock source with an impractically low frequency.

All the hardware solutions described here require some hardware support that either does not exist in any CPUs or only exists in a subset of the CPUs today. Even for those CPU architectures that do have this support, it is not guaranteed that the support will still exist in the future considering that its cost increases with the number of cores. Moreover, even if this hardware support exists in all processors, a T/O-based concurrency control algorithm may still achieve suboptimal performance. In these algorithms, timestamps are statically assigned to transactions and the assignment does not depend on the data access pattern. At runtime, the actual dependency between two transactions may not agree with the assigned timestamp order and thus transactions may be unnecessarily aborted, which hurts performance (see example in Section 3.1).

2.2 Optimistic Concurrency Control

The original OCC algorithm was proposed in 1981 [22], but it has only recently been adopted in high-performance OLTP DBMSs. By contrast, MVCC, the other T/O-based algorithm, has been used in DBMSs for several decades (e.g., Oracle, Postgres).

Under OCC, the DBMS executes a transaction in three phases: *read*, *validation*, and *write*. In the *read phase*, the transaction performs read and write operations to tuples without blocking. The DBMS maintains a separate private workspace for each transaction that contains its read set and write set. All of a transaction's modifications are written to this workspace and are only visible to itself. When the transaction finishes execution, it enters the *validation phase*, where the OCC scheme checks whether the transaction conflicts with any other active transaction. If there are no conflicts, the transaction enters the *write phase* where the DBMS propagates the changes in the transaction's write set to the database and makes them visible to other transactions.

Many algorithms have been proposed to refine and improve the original OCC algorithm [8, 17, 26, 31]. The first OCC derivatives from the 1980s dealt with improving transaction validation for single-threaded systems with limited memory [17, 31].

One OCC-based protocol that bears some similarity to our proposed TicToc algorithm is the *dynamic timestamp allocation* (DTA) approach [4, 7]. Instead of assigning a specific timestamp to a transaction, DTA allows the transaction to take a range of timestamps and adjusts the commit timestamp during the validation phase. This approach was revisited in the 1990s for "real-time" DBMSs to give higher priority in the validation phase to certain transactions [23, 25]. Similar to TicToc, DTA-based OCC can reduce the number of aborts compared to a traditional OCC. The key difference is that DTA only assigns timestamps to transactions and not to tuples. As a result, DTA-based OCC requires the DBMS to use a global critical section for coordination among concurrently-validating transactions. This is a major scalability bottleneck on multi-core and multi-socket systems [37].

Silo is a state-of-the-art OCC algorithm that achieves high throughput by avoiding bottlenecks caused by global locks or timestamp allocation [35]. In Silo, a global timestamp (called an *epoch*) is allocated at coarse time granularity (every 40 ms) and is used to indicate the serial order among transactions. Within an epoch, transaction IDs are used to identify data versions as well as to detect conflicts. These IDs, however, do not reflect the relative order among transactions. This is because they only capture read-after-write dependencies, but not write-after-read dependencies (anti-dependencies). Silo is still able to enforce serializable execution, but only able to exploit a limited amount of parallelism.

To tackle the above issues, we now present a new OCC variant that uses decentralized data-driven timestamp management.

3. THE TICTOC ALGORITHM

Like other T/O-based algorithms, TicToc uses timestamps to indicate the serial order of the transactions. But unlike these previous approaches, it does not assign timestamps to transactions using a centralized allocator. Instead, a transaction's timestamp is calculated *lazily* at its commit time in a *distributed* manner based on the tuples it accesses. There are two key advantages of this timestamp management policy. First, its distributed nature avoids all of the bottlenecks inherent in timestamp allocation [37], making the algorithm highly scalable. Second, laziness makes it possible for the DBMS to exploit more parallelism in the workload, thereby reducing aborts and improving performance.

3.1 Lazy Timestamp Management

To see why lazy timestamp management can reduce conflicts and improve performance, we consider the following example involving two concurrent transactions, A and B, and two tuples, x and y. The transactions invoke the following sequence of operations:

1. A read(x)
2. B write(x)
3. B commits
4. A write(y)

This interleaving of operations does not violate serializability because transaction A can be ordered before B in the serial order. But A cannot commit after B in the serial order because the version of x read by A has already been modified by B.

Traditional OCC algorithms assign timestamps to transactions statically, essentially agreeing on a fixed sequential schedule for concurrent transactions. This eases conflict detection, but limits concurrency. In this example, if transaction A is assigned a lower timestamp than transaction B, then A can commit since the interleaving of operations is consistent with timestamp order. However, if transaction A is assigned a higher timestamp than transaction B, A must eventually abort since committing it would violate the schedule imposed by timestamp order.

By contrast, TicToc does not allocate timestamps statically, so it does not restrict the set of potential orderings. It instead calculates the timestamp of each transaction lazily at the transaction's commit time by inspecting the tuples it accessed. In our example, when transaction A reaches its commit point, TicToc calculates the commit timestamp using the versions of the tuple x and y it actually read/wrote rather than the latest version in the database right now. And since the version of tuple x read by A is older than the one written by B, A will be ordered before B and can commit.

To encode the serialization information in the tuples, each data version in TicToc has a valid range [4] of timestamps bounded by the write timestamp (*wts*) and the read timestamp (*rts*). Specifically, a particular version is created at timestamp *wts* and is valid

Algorithm 1: Read Phase

Data: read set RS, tuple t

$r = RS.get\_new\_entry()$

$r.tuple = t$

 # Atomically load wts, rts, and value

< *r.value = t.value, r.wts = t.wts, r.rts = t.rts* >

until timestamp *rts*. A version read by a transaction is valid if and only if that transaction's commit timestamp is in between the version's *wts* and *rts*. And a write by a transaction is valid if and only if the transaction's commit timestamp is greater than the *rts* of the previous version. Formally, the following invariant must hold for transaction T to commit:

$$\begin{aligned} &\exists\ commit\_ts, \\ &\quad (\forall v \in \{versions\ read\ by\ T\}, v.wts \leq commit\_ts \leq v.rts) \\ &\quad\quad \wedge (\forall v \in \{versions\ written\ by\ T\}, v.rts < commit\_ts) \end{aligned} \quad (1)$$

This policy leads to serializable execution because all the reads and writes within a transaction occur at the same timestamp. A read always returns the version valid at that timestamp and a write is ordered after all the reads to older versions of the same tuple.

3.2 Protocol Specification

Like standard OCC algorithms, each transaction in TicToc accesses the database without acquiring locks during normal operation. This is known as the *read phase*. When the transaction invokes the commit operation, the protocol then takes the transaction through the *validation phase* to check whether it should be allowed to commit. If it does, then it enters the *write phase* where the transaction's changes are applied to the shared database.

We now discuss these phases in further detail.

3.2.1 Read Phase

The DBMS maintains a separate read set and write set of tuples for each transaction. During this phase, accessed tuples are copied to the read set and modified tuples are written to the write set, which is only visible to the current transaction. Each entry in the read or write set is encoded as $\{tuple, data, wts, rts\}$, where $tuple$ is a pointer to the tuple in the database, $data$ is the data value of the tuple, and *wts* and *rts* are the timestamps copied from the tuple when it was accessed by the transaction. For a read set entry, TicToc maintains the invariant that the version is valid from *wts* to *rts* in timestamp order.

Algorithm 1 shows the procedure for a tuple access request in the read phase. The pointer to the tuple is stored in the read or write set depending on the request type. The data value and read and write timestamps are also recorded. Note that the value and timestamps must be loaded atomically to guarantee that the value matches the timestamps. We explain in Section 3.6 how to efficiently perform this operation in a lock-free manner.

3.2.2 Validation Phase

In the validation phase, TicToc uses the timestamps stored in the transaction's read and write sets to compute its commit timestamp. Then, the algorithm checks whether the tuples in the transaction's read set are valid based on this commit timestamp.

The first step for this validation, shown in Algorithm 2, is to lock all the tuples in the transaction's write set in their primary key order to prevent other transactions from updating the rows concurrently. Using this fixed locking order guarantees that there are no deadlocks with other transactions committing at the same time. This technique is also used in other OCC algorithms (e.g., Silo [35]).

Algorithm 2: Validation Phase

```
Data: read set RS, write set WS
# Step 1 – Lock Write Set
for w in sorted(WS) do
  | lock(w.tuple)
end
# Step 2 – Compute the Commit Timestamp
commit_ts = 0
for e in WS ∪ RS do
  | if e in WS then
  |   | commit_ts = max(commit_ts, e.tuple.rts +1)
  | else
  |   | commit_ts = max(commit_ts, e.wts)
  | end
end
# Step 3 – Validate the Read Set
for r in RS do
  | if r.rts < commit_ts then
  |   | # Begin atomic section
  |   | if r.wts ≠ r.tuple.wts or (r.tuple.rts ≤ commit_ts and
  |   | isLocked(r.tuple) and r.tuple not in W) then
  |   |   | abort()
  |   | else
  |   |   | r.tuple.rts = max(commit_ts, r.tuple.rts)
  |   | end
  |   | # End atomic section
  | end
end
```

The second step in the validation phase is to compute the transaction's commit timestamp from the timestamps stored within each tuple entry in its read/write sets. As discussed in Section 3.1, for a tuple in the read set but not in the write set, the commit timestamp should be no less than its *wts* since the tuple would have a different version before this timestamp. For a tuple in the transaction's write set, however, the commit timestamp needs to be no less than its current *rts* $+ 1$ since the previous version was valid till *rts*.

In the last step, the algorithm validates the tuples in the transaction's read set. If the transaction's *commit_ts* is less than or equal to the *rts* of the read set entry, then the invariant *wts* $\leq$ *commit_ts* $\leq$ *rts* holds. This means that the tuple version read by the transaction is valid at *commit_ts*, and thus no further action is required. If the entry's *rts* is less than *commit_ts*, however, it is not clear whether the local value is still valid or not at *commit_ts*. It is possible that another transaction has modified the tuple at a logical time between the local *rts* and *commit_ts*, which means the transaction has to abort. Otherwise, if no other transaction has modified the tuple, *rts* can be extended to be greater than or equal to *commit_ts*, making the version valid at *commit_ts*.

Specifically, the local *wts* is first compared to the latest *wts*. If they are different, the tuple has already been modified by another transaction and thus it is not possible to extend the *rts* of the local version. If *wts* matches, but the tuple is already locked by a different transaction (i.e., the tuple is locked but it is not in the transaction's write set), it is not possible to extend the *rts* either. If the *rts* is extensible or if the version is already valid at *commit_ts*, the *rts* of the tuple can be extended to at least *commit_ts*. Note that the whole process must be done atomically to prevent interference from other transactions. The DBMS also does not need to validate tuples that are only in the write set since they are already protected by the locks acquired at the beginning of the validation phase.

In TicToc, there is no centralized contention point during transaction execution. The locks and atomic sections protect only the tuples that a transaction touches. In Section 5, we present optimizations to further reduce the contention caused by these operations.

Algorithm 3: Write Phase

```
Data: write set WS, commit timestamp commit_ts
for w in WS do
  | write(w.tuple.value, w.value)
  | w.tuple.wts = w.tuple.rts = commit_ts
  | unlock(w.tuple)
end
```

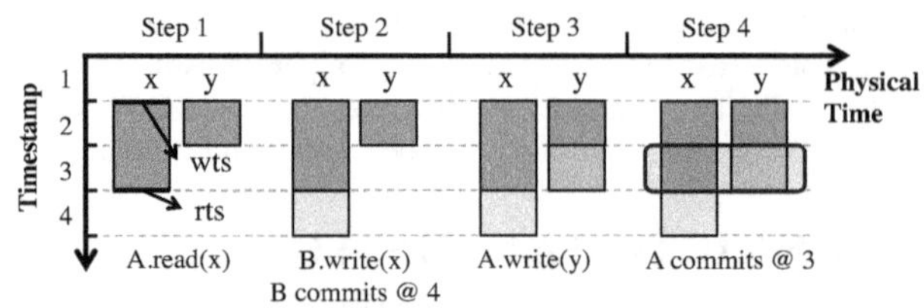

Figure 1: An example of two transactions executing using TicToc.

3.2.3 *Write Phase*

Finally, if all of the tuples that the transaction accessed pass validation, then the transaction enters the write phase. As shown in Algorithm 3, in this phase the transaction's write set is written to the database. For each tuple in the transaction's write set, the DBMS sets their *wts* and *rts* to *commit_ts*, indicating that it is a new version. All locks that were acquired during the validation phase are then released, making the changes visible to all other transactions.

3.3 Example

We now revisit the example in Section 3.1 and explain how TicToc is able to commit both transactions A and B even though previous OCC algorithms could not. Fig. 1 shows a step-by-step diagram. In this example, one operation occurs in each physical step. The *wts* and *rts* for tuples x and y are encoded as the start and end point of the vertical bands.

Step 1: Transaction A reads tuple x. The current version of x and its timestamps (*wts* $= 2$ and *rts* $= 3$) are stored in A's read set.

Step 2: Transaction B writes to tuple x and commits at timestamp 4. The version of x will be overwritten and both the *wts* and *rts* of the new version will become 4.

Step 3: Transaction A writes to tuple y. Since the previous version of y has *rts* $= 2$, the new version can be written at timestamp 3. At this point, the new version of y is only stored in the write set of transaction A and is not visible to other transactions yet.

Step 4: Transaction A enters the validation phase. According to Algorithm 2, the commit timestamp should be the maximum of the read tuple's *wts* and write tuple's *rts* $+1$, which is timestamp 3 in this example. Then, transaction A validates the read set by checking whether the version of tuple x it read is valid at timestamp 3. Since transaction A's version of tuple x is valid at timestamp 2 and 3, it passes the validation phase and commits.

Note that when the DBMS validates transaction A, it is not even aware that tuple x has been modified by another transaction. This is different from existing OCC algorithms (including Hekaton [24] and Silo [35]) which always recheck the tuples in the read set. These algorithms would abort transaction A in this example because tuple x has already been modified since transaction A last read it.

3.4 Spurious Aborts

A transaction may not always be able to validate its read set during the validation phase, which leads to aborts that may seem spurious. For example, if tuple y in Fig. 1 was originally valid from timestamps 1 to 4, then transaction A's *commit_ts* has to be 5. And since x's *rts* cannot be extended to 5, A has to abort. In this case, A aborts not because of the timestamps and not data values.

In general, the reason that these aborts occur is because other transactions violate serializability. For the example above, imagine that there exists a transaction C reading tuple x and y after B commits but before A commits. C is able to commit at timestamp 4 as it observes B's write to x and the original value of y. C will extend the *rts* of y to 4. This means that A cannot commit now without violating serializability because there is a dependency cycle between A, B and C[1]. Note that when A enters the validation phase, it does not know that C exists or that A would form a dependency cycle with other committed transactions.

Note that in TicToc a transaction aborts only if a tuple it reads or writes is overwritten by another transaction that enters the validation phase first. So only concurrent transactions (i.e., one starts before the other commits) can cause aborts. If a transaction commits, then all transactions that start after it will observe its changes.

3.5 Discussion

Beyond scalability and increased concurrency, TicToc's protocol has two other distinguishing features. Foremost is that the transaction's logical commit timestamp order may not agree with the physical commit time order. In the example from shown in Fig. 1, transaction A commits physically after transaction B, but its commit timestamp is less than transaction B's commit timestamp. This means that A precedes B in the serial schedule. This also indicates that TicToc is not *order-preserving* serializable, since the serial order may not be the commit order.

Another feature of TicToc is that logical timestamps grow more slowly than the number of committed transactions. Moreover, the rate at which the logical timestamp advances is an indicator of the contention level in the workload. This is because different transactions may commit with the same logical timestamp. Such a scenario is possible if two transactions have no conflicts with each other, or if one transaction reads a version modified by the other transaction. At one extreme, if all transactions are read-only and thus there is no contention, all transactions will have the same commit timestamp. At the other extreme, if all the transactions write to the same tuple, each commit would increase the tuple's *wts* by one, and the logical timestamp would increase at the same rate as the number of committed transactions. Since most OLTP workloads have some contention, the DBMS's logical timestamps will increase more slowly than the number of committed transactions; the higher the contention, the faster logical timestamps advance. We will show this in Section 6.5.

3.6 Implementation

As shown in Algorithms 1 and 2, both the read and validation phases require the DBMS to atomically read or write tuples' timestamps. But implementing these atomic sections using locks would degrade performance. To avoid this problem, TicToc adopts an optimization from Silo [35] to encode a lock bit and a tuple's *wts* and *rts* into a single 64-bit word (`TS_word`) of the following form:

[1] $A<B$ due to write-after-read on x, $B<C$ due to read-after-write on x, and $C<A$ due to write-after-read on y.

Algorithm 4: Atomically Load Tuple Data and Timestamps

Data: read set entry r, tuple t

do
  v1 = *t.read_ts_word()*
  read(r.data, t.data)
  v2 = *t.read_ts_word()*
while $v1 \neq v2$ *or v1.lock_bit* == 1;
r.wts = *v1.wts*
r.rts = *v1.wts* + *v1.delta*

`TS_word[63]`: Lock bit (1 bit).
`TS_word[62:48]`: *delta* = *rts* − *wts* (15 bits).
`TS_word[47:0]`: *wts* (48 bits).

The highest-order bit is used as the lock bit. *wts* is stored as a 48-bit counter. To handle *wts* overflows, which happens at most once every several weeks for the most active workloads, the tuples in the database are periodically loaded in the background to reset their *wts*. This process is infrequent and can be performed concurrently with normal transactions, so its overhead is negligible.

Algorithm 4 shows the lock-free implementation of atomically loading the data and timestamps for the tuple read operation from Algorithm 1. `TS_word` is loaded twice, before and after loading the data. If these two `TS_word` instances are the same and both have the lock bit unset, then the data value must not have changed and is still consistent with the timestamps. Otherwise, the process is repeated until both timestamps are consistent. There are no writes to shared memory during this process. To avoid starvation, one could revert to more heavy-weight latching if this check repeatedly fails.

Similarly, Algorithm 5 shows the steps to atomically extend a tuple's *rts* in TicToc's validation phase (Algorithm 2). Recall that this operation is called if *commit_ts* is greater than the local *rts*; the DBMS makes the local version valid at *commit_ts* by extending the *rts* of the tuple. The first part of the algorithm is the same as explained in Section 3.2.2; validation fails if the tuple's *rts* cannot possibly be extended to *commit_ts*.

Since we only encode *delta* in 15 bits in `TS_word`, it may overflow if *rts* and *wts* grow far apart. If an overflow occurs, we also increase *wts* to keep *delta* within 15 bits without affecting the correctness of TicToc. Intuitively, this can be considered a dummy write to the tuple at the new *wts* with the same data. Inserting such a dummy write does not affect serializability. Increasing *wts*, however, may increase the number of aborts since another transaction may consider the version as being changed while it has not actually changed. This effect is more problematic the fewer bits *delta* uses. Although not shown in the paper, our experiments indicate that 15 bits is enough for the overflow effect to be negligible.

Finally, the new *wts* and *delta* are written to a new `TS_word` and atomically applied to the tuple. The DBMS uses an atomic *compare-and-swap* instruction to make sure that the `TS_word` has not been modified by other transactions simultaneously.

Scanning tuples in a database may miss tuples being inserted because they are not observed by the scanning transaction. Standard techniques for solving this problem include using locks in indexes [31] or rescanning the tuples during the validation phase [24]. Both techniques incur significant performance overhead. This can be avoided by running the transactions at lower isolation levels (e.g., snapshot isolation) if the application allows it. We believe that it is possible to apply the data-driven timestamp management concept used in TicToc to order-preserving indexes to avoid this phantom anomaly for serializable transactions. This exploration is outside of the scope of this paper and is left for future work.

Algorithm 5: Read-Set Validation

```
Data: read set entry r, write set W, commit timestamp
      commit_ts
do
    success = true
    v2 = v1 = r.tuple.read_ts_word()
    if r.wts ≠ v1.wts or (v1.rts ≤ commit_ts and
    isLocked(r.tuple)) and r.tuple not in W then
        Abort()
    end
    # Extend the rts of the tuple
    if v1.rts ≤ commit_ts then
        # Handle delta overflow
        delta = commit_ts − v1.wts
        shift = delta − delta ∧ 0x7fff
        v2.wts = v2.wts + shift
        v2.delta = delta − shift
        # Set the new TS word
        success = compare_and_swap(r.tuple.ts_word, v1, v2)
    end
while not success;
```

3.7 Logging and Durability

The TicToc algorithm can support logging and crash recovery in a similar way as traditional concurrency control algorithms. The DBMS can use the canonical ARIES approach if there is only a single log file [27]. But ARIES cannot provide the bandwidth required in today's multi-core systems [39]. Implementing arbitrarily scalable logging is out of the scope of this paper and is left for future work. In this section, we briefly discuss one idea of implementing parallel logging with multiple log files on TicToc.

Parallel logging has been studied in other DBMSs [36, 39]. The basic idea is to perform logging in batches. All transactions in a previous batch must be ordered before any transaction in a later batch, but the relative ordering among transactions within the same batch can be arbitrary. For each batch, logs are written to multiple files in parallel. A batch is considered durable only after all the logs within that batch have been written to files.

In TicToc, the batching scheme requires that transactions in a later batch must have commit timestamps greater than transactions in a previous batch. This can be achieved by setting a minimum commit timestamp for transactions belonging to the new batch. To start a new batch, each worker thread should coordinate to compute the minimum commit timestamp that is greater than the commit timestamps of all transactions in previous batches. Each transaction in the new batch has a commit timestamp greater than this minimum timestamp. Setting a minimum timestamp does not affect the correctness of TicToc since timestamps only increase in this process, and transactions are properly ordered based on their timestamps. The performance of this parallel logging scheme should be the same as with other concurrency control algorithms [36, 39].

4. PROOF OF CORRECTNESS

In this section, we prove that the TicToc algorithm is able to correctly enforce serializability.

4.1 Proof Idea

To prove that a schedule is serializable in TicToc, we need to show that the schedule is equivalent to another schedule where all the transactions are executed serially. Previous T/O concurrency control algorithms use the transaction's unique timestamps to determine the serial order. In TicToc, however, the commit timestamp is derived from the accessed tuples and no global coordination takes place, and thus two transactions may commit with the same timestamp. Therefore, transactions cannot be fully ordered based on their commit timestamps alone.

Our proof instead uses a combination of the timestamp and physical time orders [38]. A transaction's logical commit time is its *commit timestamp*; its *physical commit time* is the physical time between a transaction's validation phase and write phase. We define the following specific serial order.

DEFINITION 1 (SERIAL ORDER). *Using $<_s$, $<_{ts}$ and $<_{ps}$ to indicate serial order, commit timestamp order, and physical commit time order, respectively, the serial order between transaction A and B is defined as follows:*

$$A <_s B \triangleq A <_{ts} B \vee (A =_{ts} B \wedge A \leq_{pt} B)$$

The serial order defined in Definition 1 is a total order among all the transactions. Transaction A is ordered before transaction B if A has a smaller commit timestamp or if they have the same commit timestamp but A commits before B in physical time. If A and B both have the same logical and physical commit time, then they can have arbitrary serial order.

The goal of the correctness proof is summarized as follows:

THEOREM 1. *Any schedule in TicToc is equivalent to the serial schedule defined in Definition 1.*

To prove this, we show that the dependencies in the actual schedule are maintained as the dependencies in the equivalent serial schedule. Specifically, a read in the actual schedule always returns the value of the last store in the serial schedule. We also prove that transactions having the same commit timestamp and physical commit time do not have conflicts.

4.2 Formal Proofs

We first prove a useful lemma that will be used to prove subsequent Lemmas 2 and 3.

LEMMA 1. *Transactions writing to the same tuple must have different commit timestamps.*

PROOF. According to Algorithms 2 and 3, a tuple is locked while being written, therefore only one transaction can write to that tuple at any time. According to line 3 in Algorithm 3, both *wts* and *rts* of the modified tuple become its commit timestamp.

According to line 7 in Algorithm 2, if another transaction writes to the same tuple at a later time, its commit timestamp must be strictly greater than the tuple's current *rts*. Since *rts* never decreases in the TicToc algorithm, the commit timestamp of the later transaction must be greater than the commit timestamp of the earlier transaction. Therefore, transactions writing to the same tuple must have different commit timestamps. □

As discussed in the previous section, two requirements are needed to prove Theorem 1. First, transactions that have the same commit timestamp and physical time must not conflict. Second, a read always returns the latest write in the serial order. We now prove these two requirements for TicToc:

LEMMA 2. *Transactions that commit at the same timestamp and physical time do not conflict with each other.*

PROOF. According to Lemma 1, write-write conflicting transactions must have different commit timestamps. Therefore, we only need to show that all read-write or write-read conflicting transactions commit at different logical or physical time.

Consider a pair of transactions committing at the same physical time. One reads a tuple and the other writes to the same tuple. Then, the commit timestamp of the reading transaction must be less than or equal to the tuple's current *rts*. And the commit timestamp of the writing transaction must be greater than the tuple's current *rts*. Therefore, they have different commit timestamps. □

LEMMA 3. *A read operation from a committed transaction returns the value of the latest write to the tuple in the serial schedule.*

PROOF. We first prove that if a committed transaction's read observes another transaction's write, then the reading transaction must be ordered after the writing transaction in the serial schedule.

A tuple's *wts* is always updated together with its value, and the *wts* is always the commit timestamp of the transaction that writes the value. Line 9 in Algorithm 2 states that if another transaction reads the value, then its commit timestamp must be greater than or equal to *wts*. If the commit timestamp equals *wts*, then the reading transaction still commits after the writing transaction in physical time because the writing transaction only makes its writes globally visible after its physical commit time. By Definition 1, the reading transaction is always ordered after the writing transaction in the serial schedule.

We next show that the write observed by the following read is the latest write in the serial schedule. In other words, if the writing transaction has timestamp t_1 and the reading transaction has timestamp t_2, no other write to the same tuple happens at timestamp t, such that $t_1 \leq t \leq t_2$.

According to Algorithm 2, when the reading transaction commits, it can observe a consistent view of the tuple's `TS_word` with *wts* and *rts*, where $t_1 = wts$ and $t_2 \leq rts$. This implies that so far in physical time, no write to the same tuple has happened between t_1 and t_2 in logical time because otherwise the *wts* of the tuple would be greater than t_1. No such write can happen in the future either because all future writes will have timestamps greater the tuple's *rts* and thus greater than t_2. □

PROOF OF THEOREM 1. According to Lemma 2, transactions with the same commit timestamp and physical commit time do not conflict. Thus, all serial orders among them are equivalent.

According to Lemma 3, for transactions with different commit timestamps or physical commit times, a read in a transaction always returns the latest write in the serial schedule. According to Lemma 1, only one such latest write can exist so there is no ambiguity. Then, for each transaction executed in the actual schedule, all the values it observes are identical to the values it would observe in the serial schedule. Hence, the two schedules are equivalent. □

5. OPTIMIZATIONS

The TicToc algorithm as presented so far achieves good performance when tested on a multi-socket system (Section 6). There are, however, still places in the validation phase that may create unnecessary contention and thus hurt performance. For example, locking the transaction's write set during the validation phase may cause thrashing for write-intensive benchmarks.

In this section, we discuss several optimizations that we developed for TicToc to minimize contention. We also discuss how TicToc works for weaker isolation levels for those applications that do not need strong serializability.

5.1 No-Wait Locking in Validation Phase

In TicToc's validation phase (Algorithm 2), tuples in a transaction's write set are locked following the primary key order. This is essentially the same process as a 2PL protocol where a transaction may wait if the next lock that it needs to acquire is not immediately available. Waiting for locks, however, may create thrashing problems at high core counts, even if locks are acquired in primary key order [37]. Thrashing happens when a transaction already holds locks and waits for the next lock. The locks it already holds, however, may block other transactions.

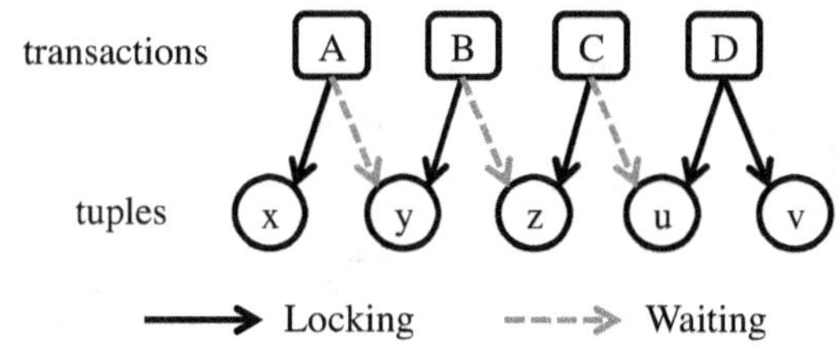

Figure 2: An example of lock thrashing in a 2PL protocol.

Consider a pathological case shown in Fig. 2 where each transaction tries to lock two tuples. Transaction D has already acquired both of the locks that it needs, while transactions A, B, and C are waiting for locks held by other transactions. When transaction D commits, C is able to acquire the lock and make forward progress. Transactions A and B, however, still need to wait. The end result is that the four transactions are validated sequentially.

Note that, in this particular example, it is actually possible to abort transactions A and C so that B and D can acquire the locks and run in parallel. After they finish, A and C can also run in parallel. This schedule only takes half the execution time compared to the pathological schedule, but it requires an additional deadlock detection thread to quickly identify these scenarios.

A better approach to avoid the thrashing problem is to use a 2PL variant based on non-waiting deadlock prevention in TicToc's validation phase [5]. This protocol optimization, which we refer to as **no-wait**, is like running a mini concurrency control algorithm inside of the TicToc algorithm. With no-wait, if a transaction fails to acquire a lock for a tuple in its write set during the validation phase, the validation is immediately aborted (releasing any locks) and then TicToc restarts the validation phase. The transaction sleeps for a short period (1 μs) before retrying to reduce restarts. Our experiments show that the algorithm's performance is not overly sensitive to the length of this sleep time as long as it is not too large.

The no-wait optimization minimizes the blocking and allows more transactions to validate simultaneously. In the example in Fig. 2, if no-wait is used, then A or B may run in parallel with D.

5.2 Preemptive Aborts

The first step of the validation phase (Algorithm 2) locks the tuples in the transaction's write set before it examines the read set. If a transaction ends up aborting because read set validation fails, then this locking potentially blocked other transactions unnecessarily. We observe that for some transactions the decision to abort can actually be made before locking the write set tuples. We call this optimization **preemptive abort**. Since all the serialization information is already stored in the tuples' timestamps, it can be used to make early abort decisions, thereby reducing contention.

To better understand this, consider a transaction with one tuple in its read set. This transaction will fail the validation phase if this tuple's local *rts* is less than the transaction's commit timestamp and its local *wts* does not match the tuple's latest *wts*. A tuple's latest *wts* can be atomically read from the `TS_word` of the tuple. The transaction's commit timestamp, however, cannot be accurately determined before the write set is locked because a tuple's *rts* in the write set might be changed by a different transaction. The key observation here is that we just need to find an approximate commit

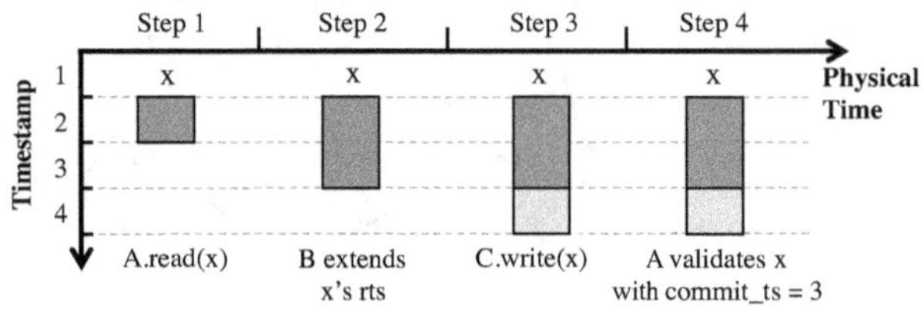

Figure 3: Using a tuple's timestamp history to avoid aborting.

timestamp. Thus, this optimization achieves some early aborts, but does not catch all the transactions that will fail read set validation.

We compute the approximate commit timestamp using the local *wts* and *rts* in the read and write sets. For each tuple in the read set, the approximate commit timestamp is no less than the tuple's local *wts*; for each tuple in the write set, the approximate commit timestamp is no less than the tuple's local *rts* $+1$. Note that the actual commit timestamp is no less than our approximation, because the latest timestamps in the tuples cannot be less than the local timestamps. Once an approximate commit timestamp is determined, it is used to determine if the transaction should be preemptively aborted.

5.3 Timestamp History

TicToc always aborts a transaction if its local *rts* of a tuple is less than *commit_ts* and the local *wts* does not match the latest *wts*. There are some cases, however, where the latest *wts* is greater than *commit_ts* and the local version is still valid at *commit_ts*. Such transactions can actually commit without violating serializability.

Fig. 3 shows such an example. Transaction A first reads tuple x with *wts* $=$ 2 and *rts* $=$ 2. Later, tuple x's *rts* is extended to timestamp 3 due to the validation of transaction B. Then, tuple x is modified by transaction C and thus the latest *wts* and *rts* both become 4. Finally, transaction A enters the validation phase and validates tuple x at *commit_ts* $=$ 3 (not 2 because transaction A accessed other tuples not shown in the figure). At this point, transaction A only has the local timestamps of x (*wts* $=$ 2 and *rts* $=$ 2) and knows that the local version is valid at timestamp 2, but does not know if it is still valid at timestamp 3. From transaction A's perspective, it is possible that the local version has been extended to timestamp 3 by some other transaction; it is also possible, however, that some other transaction did a write that is only valid at timestamp 3. Based on all the information transaction A has, these two situations are indistinguishable.

To prevent these unnecessary aborts, we can extend TicToc to maintain a history of each tuple's *wts* rather than just one scalar value. When a new version is created for a tuple, the *wts* of the old version is stored in a history buffer. The value of the old version does not need to be stored since transactions in TicToc always read the latest data version. Therefore, the storage overhead of this optimization in TicToc is smaller than that of MVCC. In our implementation, the history buffer is a per-tuple array that keeps a fixed number of the most recent *wts*'s, and thus the DBMS does not have to perform garbage collection.

During a transaction's validation phase, if a read tuple's local *rts* is less than *commit_ts* and the *wts* does not match the latest *wts*, then the DBMS checks if the *wts* matches any version in the tuple's history buffer. If so, the valid range of that version is from the local *wts* to the next *wts* in the history buffer. If *commit_ts* falls within that range, the tuple can still be validated.

5.4 Lower Isolation Levels

The TicToc algorithm described in Section 3 provides serializable isolation, which is the strictest isolation level in ANSI SQL. With minimal changes, TicToc can also support lower isolation levels for those applications that are willing to sacrifice isolation guarantees in favor of better performance and lower abort rate.

Snapshot Isolation: This level mandates that all of a transaction's reads see a consistent snapshot of the database, and that the transaction will commit only if it does not conflict with any concurrent updates made since that snapshot. In other words, all the read operations should happen at the same timestamp (*commit_rts*) and all the write operations should happen at a potentially later timestamp (*commit_wts*), and the written tuples are not modified between *commit_rts* and *commit_wts*.

To support snapshots, instead of using a single *commit_ts* and verifying that all reads and writes are valid at this timestamp, two commit timestamps are used, one for reads (*commit_rts*) and one for writes (*commit_wts*). The algorithm verifies that all reads are valid at *commit_rts* and all writes are valid at *commit_wts*. It also guarantees that, before the transaction writes to a tuple, its previous *wts* is less than or equal to *commit_rts*. All of these can be implemented with minor changes to Algorithm 2.

Repeatable Reads: With this weaker isolation level, a transaction's reads do not need to happen at the same timestamp even though writes should still have the same commit timestamp. This means there is no need to verify the read set in the validation phase. For a tuple read and updated by the same transaction, however, the DBMS still needs to guarantee that no other updates happened to that tuple since the transaction last read the value.

6. EXPERIMENTAL EVALUATION

We now present our evaluation of the TicToc algorithm. For these experiments, we use the DBx1000 OLTP DBMS [1]. This is a multi-threaded, shared-everything system that stores all data in DRAM in a row-oriented manner with hash table indexes.

DBx1000 uses worker threads (one per core) that invoke transactions from a fixed-length queue. Each transaction contains program logic intermixed with query invocations. Queries are executed serially by the transaction's worker thread as they are encountered in the program logic. Transaction statistics, such as throughput and abort rates, are collected after the system achieves a steady state during the warm-up period. The abort rate is calculated as the total number of aborts divided by the total number of transaction attempts (both committed and aborted transactions).

DBx1000 includes a pluggable lock manager that supports different concurrency control schemes. This allows us to compare five approaches all within the same system:

TICTOC: Time traveling OCC with all optimizations
SILO: Silo OCC [35]
HEKATON: Hekaton MVCC [24]
DL_DETECT: 2PL with deadlock detection
NO_WAIT: 2PL with non-waiting deadlock prevention

We deployed DBx1000 on a 40-core machine with four Intel Xeon E7-4850 CPUs and 128 GB of DRAM. Each core supports two hardware threads, for a total of 80 threads. The experiments with more than 40 threads (shaded areas in the throughput graphs) use multiple threads per core, and thus may scale sub-linearly due to contention. To minimize memory latency, we use `numactl` to ensure each thread allocates memory from its own socket.

6.1 Workloads

We next describe the two benchmarks that we implemented in the DBx1000 DBMS for this analysis.

TPC-C: This workload is the current industry standard to eval-

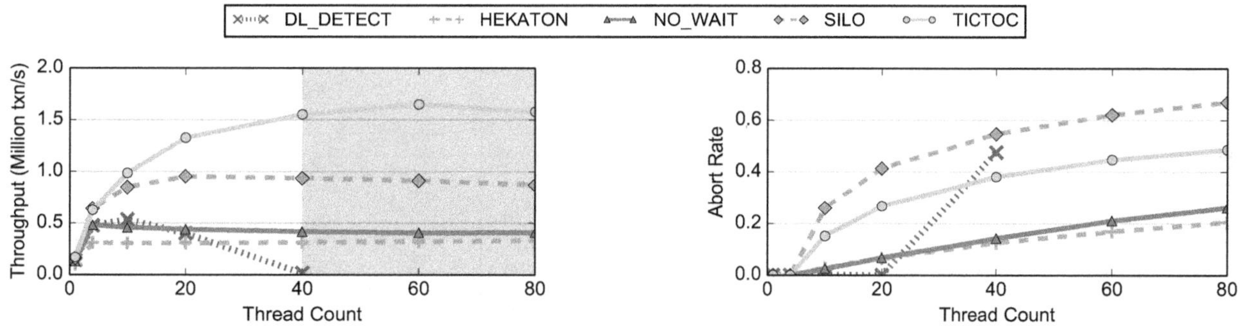

(a) Throughput

(b) Abort Rate

Figure 4: TPC-C (4 Warehouses) – Scalability of different concurrency control algorithms on TPC-C workload with 4 warehouses.

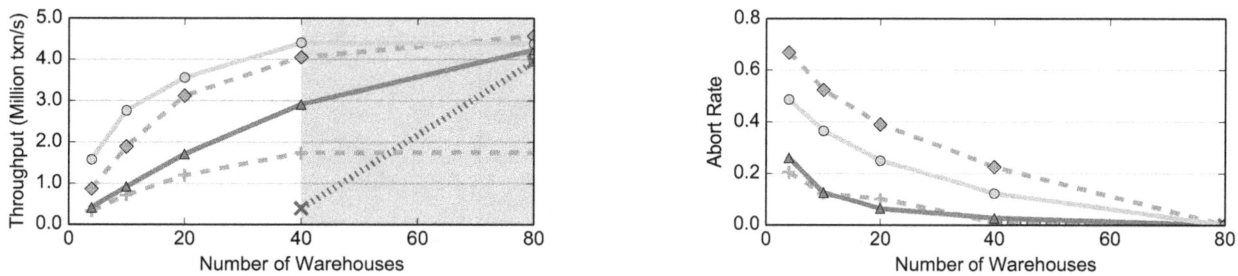

(a) Throughput

(b) Abort Rate

Figure 5: TPC-C (Variable Warehouses) – Scalability of different concurrency control algorithms on TPC-C when sweeping the number of warehouses. The number of worker threads in DBx1000 is fixed at 80.

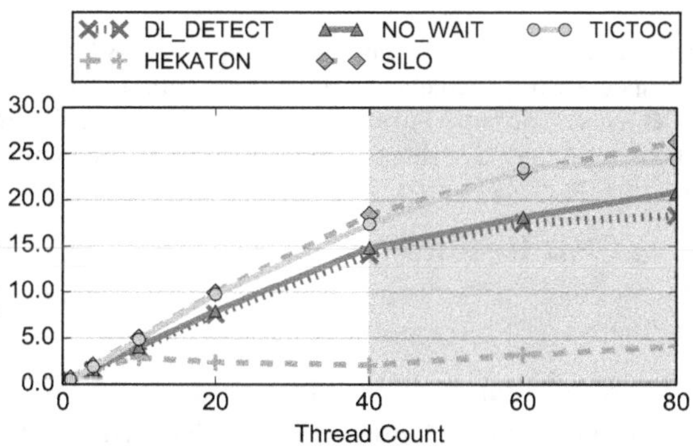

Figure 6: YCSB (Read-Only) – Results for a read-only YCSB workload for the different concurrency control schemes and the *atomic add* timestamp allocator.

uate OLTP systems [33]. It consists of nine tables that simulate a warehouse-centric order processing application. Only two (`Payment` and `NewOrder`) out of the five transactions in TPC-C are modeled in our simulation, with the workload comprised of 50% of each type. These two make up 88% of the default TPC-C mix and are the most interesting in terms of complexity for our evaluation.

YCSB: The Yahoo! Cloud Serving Benchmark is representative of large-scale on-line services [9]. Each query accesses a single random tuple based on a Zipfian distribution with a parameter ($theta$) that controls the contention level in the benchmark [16]. We evaluate three different variations of this workload:

1. **Read-Only:** Two read queries per transaction and a uniform access distribution ($theta$=0).
2. **Medium Contention:** 16 queries per transaction (90% reads and 10% writes) with a hotspot of 10% tuples that are accessed by ~60% of all queries ($theta$=0.8).
3. **High Contention:** 16 queries per transaction (50% reads and 50% writes) with a hotspot of 10% tuples that are accessed by ~75% of all queries ($theta$=0.9).

For all of the YCSB experiments in this paper, we used a ~10 GB database containing a single table with 10 million records. Each tuple has a single primary key column and then 10 additional columns each with 100 bytes of randomly generated string data.

6.2 TPC-C Results

We first analyze the performance of all the concurrency control algorithms on the TPC-C benchmark.

The number of warehouses in TPC-C determines both the size of the database and the amount of concurrency. Each warehouse adds ~100 MB to the database. The warehouse is the root entity for almost all of the tables in the database. We follow the TPC-C specification where ~10% of the `NewOrder` transactions and ~15% of the `Payment` transactions access a "remote" warehouse.

We first run TPC-C with four warehouses, as this is an example of a database that has a lot of contention. We then run an experiment where we fix the number of threads and scale the number of warehouses in the database. This measures how well the algorithms scale when the workload has more parallelism opportunities.

6.2.1 4 Warehouses

The results in Fig. 4 show that the performance improvements of additional threads are limited by contention on the `WAREHOUSE` table. Each `Payment` transaction updates a per-warehouse tuple in this table and each `NewOrder` transaction reads that tuple. Since there are only four such tuples in the entire database, they become the bottleneck of the whole system.

The `Payment` transaction is simpler faster than `NewOrder` transactions. In SILO, when the `NewOrder` transaction enters the validation phase, it is likely that a `Payment` transaction has already modified the tuple in the `WAREHOUSE` table. Therefore, SILO (like other

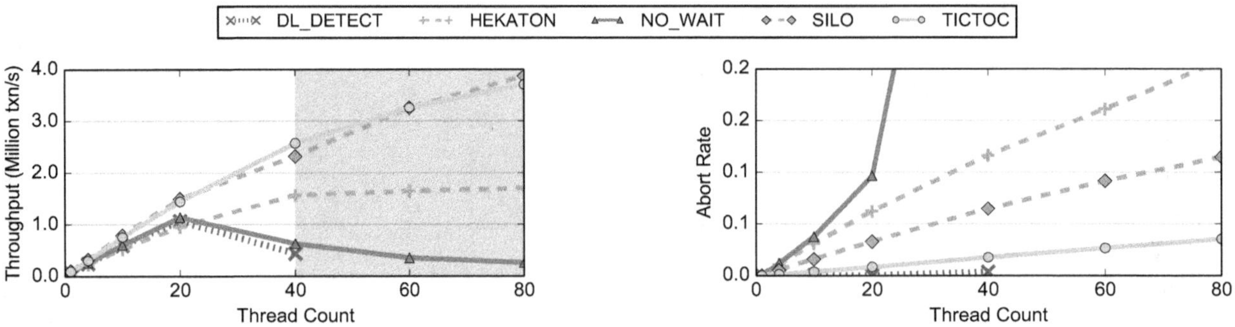

(a) Throughput (b) Abort Rate

Figure 7: YCSB (Medium Contention) – Results for a read-write YCSB workload with medium contention. Note that DL_DETECT is only measured up to 40 threads.

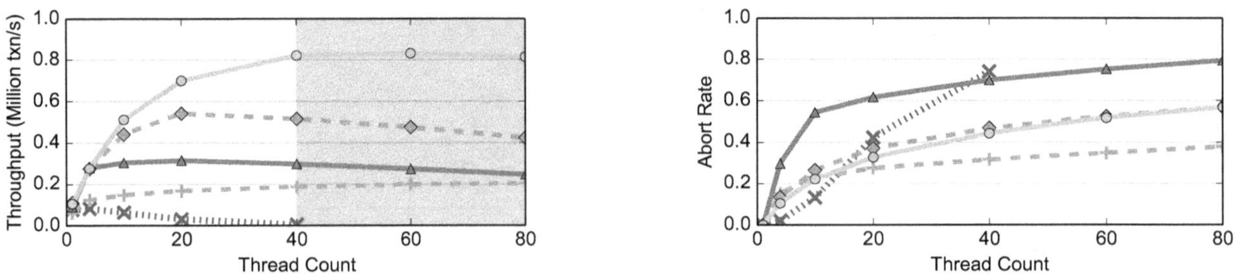

(a) Throughput (b) Abort Rate

Figure 8: YCSB (High Contention) – Results for a read-write YCSB workload with high contention. Note that DL_DETECT is only measured up to 40 threads.

traditional OCCs) frequently aborts these NewOrder transactions.

In TICTOC, the NewOrder transaction would also see that the WAREHOUSE tuple has been modified. But most of the time the transaction can find a common timestamp that satisfies all the tuples it accesses and thus is able to commit. As shown in Fig. 4, TICTOC achieves 1.8× better throughput than SILO while reducing its abort rate by 27%. We attribute this to TICTOC's ability to achieve better parallelism by dynamically selecting the commit timestamp.

The figure also shows that DL_DETECT has the worst scalability of all the algorithms. This is because DL_DETECT suffers from the thrashing problem discussed in Section 5.1. Thrashing occurs because a transaction waits to acquire new locks while holding other locks, which cause other transactions to block and form a convoy. NO_WAIT performs better than DL_DETECT as it avoids this thrashing problem by not waiting for locks. HEKATON also supports non-blocking reads since a transaction can always access a previous version and transactions that perform conflicting writes are immediately aborted. Since rolling back an aborted transaction in an in-memory DBMS is a relatively fast operation, these increased aborts do not significantly hurt performance. But NO_WAIT still performs worse than TICTOC and SILO due to the usage of locks. Similarly, HEKATON is slower because of the overhead of maintaining multiple versions.

6.2.2 *Variable Warehouses*

As we increase the number of warehouses while fixing the number of worker threads, the contention in the system will decrease. In Fig. 5 the number of warehouses is swept from 4 to 80 but the number of worker threads is fixed to 80.

When the number of warehouses is small and contention is high, TICTOC performs consistently better than SILO for the same reason as in Section 6.2.1. As the number of warehouses grows, parallelism in TPC-C becomes plentiful, so the advantage of TICTOC over SILO decreases and eventually disappears at 80 warehouses. With respect to the scheme's measured abort rate, shown in Fig. 5b, TICTOC has consistently fewer aborts than SILO for fewer than 80 warehouses because it is able to adjust timestamps to commit transactions that SILO aborts.

6.3 YCSB Results

We now compare TicToc to other concurrency control schemes under different YCSB scenarios.

6.3.1 *Read-Only*

We executed a YCSB workload comprising read-only transactions with a uniform access distribution. This provides a baseline for each concurrency control scheme before we explore more complex workload arrangements.

The results in Fig. 6 show that all of the algorithms except for HEKATON scale almost linearly up to 40 threads. Beyond that point, scaling is sub-linear as the threads executing on the same physical core contend for pipeline resources. TICTOC and SILO achieve better absolute performance than the other algorithms because they do not have locking overheads. HEKATON is limited by its centralized timestamp allocation component. It uses a single *atomic add* instruction on a global counter, which causes threads accessing the counter from different cores to incur cache coherence traffic on the chip. In our 4-socket system, this limits HEKATON to ~5 million timestamps per second.

6.3.2 *Medium Contention*

In a read-only workload, transactions do not conflict with each other and thus any algorithm without artificial bottlenecks should scale. For workloads with some contention, however, the ways that the algorithms handle conflicts affect the DBMS's performance.

Fig. 7 shows the throughput and abort rate of the medium contention YCSB workload. The results in Fig. 7a show that SILO and

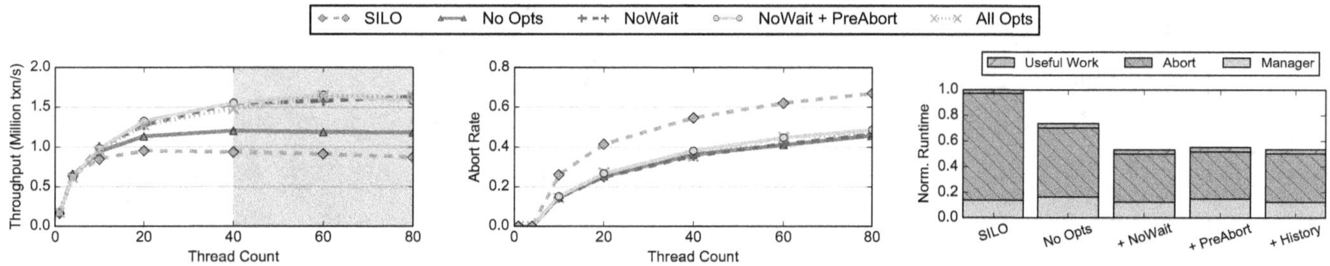

(a) Throughput (b) Abort Rate (c) Execution Time Breakdown (80 threads)

Figure 9: TicToc Optimizations (TPC-C) – Throughput measurements of TicToc using the different optimizations from Section 5 for TPCC with 4 warehouses.

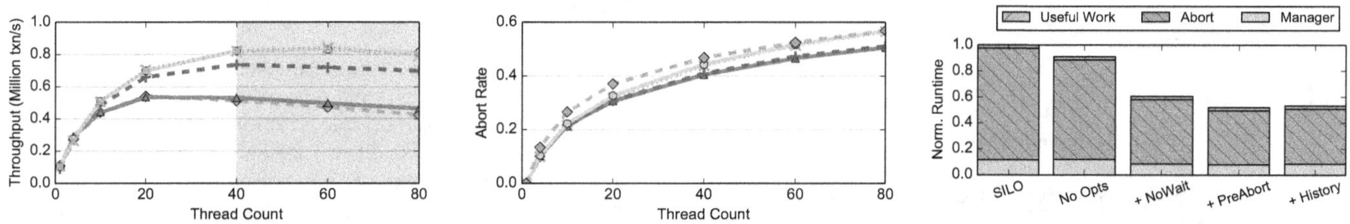

(a) Throughput (b) Abort Rate (c) Execution Time Breakdown (80 threads)

Figure 10: TicToc Optimizations (YCSB) – Throughput measurements of TicToc using the different optimizations from Section 5 for a high contention read-write YCSB workload.

TICTOC both scale well and achieve similar throughput. But the graph in Fig. 7b shows that TICTOC has a $\sim$3.3$\times$ lower abort rate than SILO. This is due to TICTOC's data-driven timestamp management, as transactions can commit at the proper timestamp that is not necessarily the largest timestamp so far.

The throughput measurements show that DL_DETECT again has the worst scalability of all the algorithms due to lock trashing. Since NO_WAIT does better since transactions can get immediately restarted when there is a deadlock. HEKATON performs better than the 2PL schemes since multiple versions allows more read operations to succeed (since they can access older versions) which leads to fewer transaction aborts. But this adds overhead that causes HEKATON to perform worse than TICTOC and SILO.

6.3.3 High Contention

We now compare the algorithms on a YCSB workload with high contention. Here, conflicts are more frequent and the workload has lower inherent parallelism, which stresses the DBMS and allows us to more easily identify the main bottlenecks in each algorithm.

As expected, the results in Fig. 8 show that all algorithms are less scalable than in the medium contention workload. We note, however, that the performance difference between TICTOC and SILO is more prominent. As we discuss next, this performance gain comes from the optimizations we presented in Section 5.

Both TICTOC and SILO have similar abort rates in Fig. 8b under high contention. The timestamp management policy in TICTOC does not reduce the abort rate because the workload is too write-intensive and the contention level is so high that both algorithms have similar behaviors in terms of aborting transactions.

6.4 TicToc Optimizations

We now evaluate the optimizations we presented in Section 5 to determine their individual effect on TicToc's overall performance. To do this, we run DBx1000 multiple times using TicToc but enable the optimizations one-at-a-time. We use four different configurations in this experiment:

1. **No Opts:** TicToc without any optimizations.
2. **NoWait:** TicToc with no-wait locking described in Section 5.1.
3. **NoWait + PreAbort:** TicToc with no-wait locking and preemptive aborts from Section 5.2.
4. **All Opts:** TicToc with no-wait locking, preemptive aborts, and timestamp history from Section 5.3.

Recall that this last configuration is the default setting for TicToc in all of the other experiments in this paper. We also include the performance measurements for SILO from Fig. 8a for comparison.

The results in Fig. 9 show the performance, abort rate, and time breakdown (at 80 cores) for the TPC-C workload with four warehouses. At 80 threads, TICTOC without optimizations achieves 35.6% higher throughput than SILO, and has a 32% lower abort rate. This gain comes from the greater parallelism exploited by the TICTOC's timestamp management policy. Using the no-wait optimization for locking transactions' write sets provides another 38% performance gain at 80 threads while not affecting the abort rate. In Fig. 9c, we see that the gains of basic TICTOC over SILO mainly come from reducing the abort rate. Optimizations do not reduce TICTOC's abort rate further, but they do reduce the amount of time wasted in aborting transactions. These optimizations effectively make each abort take a shorter amount of time.

Fig. 10 shows the same experiments on high contention YCSB workload. Here we see similar performance improvement as in TPC-C but it comes from different aspects of TICTOC. TICTOC without any optimizations only performs 10% better than SILO, and most of the performance improvement comes from the no-wait and preemptive abort optimizations. In contrast to Fig. 9, using preemptive aborts provides a larger performance gain in YCSB. This is partly because in YCSB each transaction locks more tuples during the validation phase. Preemptive aborts alleviate the contention caused by these locks.

A key finding is that the timestamp history optimization does not provide any measurable performance gain in either workload. This was initially surprising to us, but upon further investigation we are convinced that this is indeed correct. In a way, TICTOC without this optimization already stores multiple versions of a tuple in each transaction's private workspace. This means that each transaction

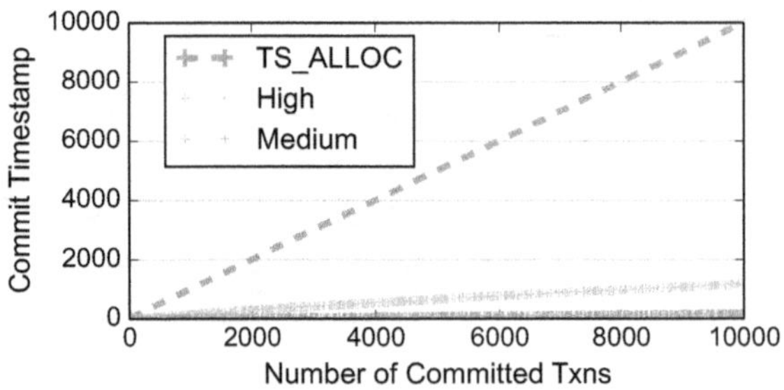

Figure 11: Logical Time Analysis – Comparison of the growth rate of the timestamps in TICTOC versus TS_ALLOC.

	DL_DETECT	HEKATON	NO_WAIT	SILO	TICTOC
SR	0.43	1.55	0.63	2.32	2.57
SI	–	1.78	–	–	2.69
RR	0.72	1.88	1.89	2.45	2.69

(a) Throughput (Million txn/s)

	DL_DETECT	HEKATON	NO_WAIT	SILO	TICTOC
SR	0.35%	11.6%	63.2%	6.47%	1.76%
SI	–	1.96%	–	–	1.54%
RR	0.10%	1.94%	9.9%	0.71%	0.72%

(b) Abort Rate

Table 1: Isolation Levels (Medium Contention) – Performance measurements for the concurrency control schemes running YCSB under different isolation levels with 40 threads.

can commit in parallel using its own version. Although in theory timestamp history can enable more concurrency, in practice there is no clear performance benefit for the workloads we evaluated.

6.5 Logical Time Analysis

We analyze how TicToc's commit timestamps grow over time under different levels of contention. Ideally, we would like timestamps to grow slowly over time relative to the total number of committed transactions, indicating that synchronization among transactions is relatively infrequent. For this experiment, we execute the medium and high contention YCSB workloads from Section 6.3 and track the values of the transactions' commit timestamps over time. We also include TS_ALLOC as a baseline where each transaction is assigned a unique timestamp using an atomic add instruction. This is representative of the timestamp growth rate in other T/O-based algorithms, such as HEKATON.

Fig. 11 shows the relationship between logical timestamps and the number of committed transactions for the three configurations. With the TS_ALLOC protocol, the number of committed transactions and logical timestamps increase at the same rate. In TicToc, however, logical timestamps increase at a slower rate: 64× and 10× slower for low and high contention levels in YCSB, respectively. What is interesting about these measurements is that the rate of growth of logical timestamps indicates the inherent level of parallelism in a workload that can be exploited by TicToc. In the high contention workload, for example, this ratio is 10×. This corroborates our results in Fig. 8a that show the DBMS was only able to achieve 7.7× better throughput from running multiple threads in the high contention YCSB workload.

6.6 Isolation Levels

All of the experiments so far have used serializable isolation. Serializable is the strictest isolation level and thus usually has less concurrency opportunities than lower isolation levels. We now

	DL_DETECT	HEKATON	NO_WAIT	SILO	TICTOC
SR	0.005	0.18	0.30	0.52	0.82
SI	–	0.23	–	–	0.90
RR	0.010	0.23	0.35	0.80	1.04

(a) Throughput (Million txn/s)

	DL_DETECT	HEKATON	NO_WAIT	SILO	TICTOC
SR	74.0%	34.4%	69.9%	46.8%	44.3%
SI	–	30.9%	–	–	40.1%
RR	74.3%	30.4%	71.3%	42.3%	39.7%

(b) Abort Rate

Table 2: Isolation Levels (High Contention) – Performance measurements for the concurrency control schemes running YCSB under different isolation levels with 40 threads.

compare the DBMS's performance when transactions execute under snapshot isolation (SI) and repeatable read isolation (RR) levels versus the default serializable isolation (SR). All five algorithms support the RR level. For SI, we are only able to test the TICTOC and HEKATON algorithms. This is because supporting SI requires the DBMS to maintain multiple versions for each tuple, and thus this requires significant changes to the other algorithms. We use the medium- and high-contention YCSB workloads from Section 6.3.

The medium-contention YCSB results are shown in Table 1. For this setting, the workload has enough parallelism and thus all the optimistic T/O-based algorithms only see small improvements when running at a lower isolation level (4.7% for TICTOC and 5.6% for SILO), whereas for the pessimistic 2PL algorithms the improvement is more pronounced (67.4% for DL_DETECT and 200.0% for NO_WAIT). HEKATON only has a 21.3% improvement from SR to RR. The abort rate measurements in Table 1b show that the lower isolation levels achieve lower abort rates because there are fewer conflicts between transactions. As expected, all the algorithms have the fewest number of aborted transactions under RR since it is the most relaxed isolation level.

The high-contention YCSB results are shown in Table 2. Lower isolation levels have better performance than serializable isolation. Again, the throughput of the RR isolation level is slightly better than SI's. In general, for this workload setting we found that different isolation levels do not cause large reductions in abort rates due to the significant amount of contention on hotspot tuples.

7. CONCLUSION

In this paper we have presented TicToc, a new OCC-based concurrency control algorithm that eliminates the need for centralized timestamp allocation. TicToc instead uses a novel *data-driven timestamp management* approach that decouples logical timestamps and physical time by deriving transaction commit timestamps from data items. This enables an OLTP DBMS to exploit more parallelism than other OCC-based algorithms. We have also presented several optimizations that leverage this timestamp management policy to further improve TicToc's performance. Our evaluation results show that, compared to another state-of-the-art OCC algorithm, TicToc achieves up to 92% higher throughput while reducing transaction abort rates by up to 3.3× under different workload conditions.

ACKNOWLEDGMENTS

This research was funded (in part) by the Intel Science and Technology Center for Big Data and the U.S. National Science Foundation (CCF-1438955, CCF-1438967).

For questions or comments about this paper, please call the CMU Database Hotline at `+1-844-88-CMUDB`.

8. REFERENCES

[1] DBx1000. https://github.com/yxymit/DBx1000.

[2] Tile-gx family of multicore processors. http://www.tilera.com.

[3] M. Aslett. How will the database incumbents respond to NoSQL and NewSQL? The 451 Group, April 2011.

[4] R. Bayer, K. Elhardt, J. Heigert, and A. Reiser. Dynamic timestamp allocation for transactions in database systems. In *2nd Int. Symp. on Distributed Databases*, pages 9–20, 1982.

[5] P. A. Bernstein and N. Goodman. Concurrency control in distributed database systems. *ACM Comput. Surv.*, 13(2):185–221, 1981.

[6] P. A. Bernstein, D. Shipman, and W. Wong. Formal aspects of serializability in database concurrency control. *IEEE Transactions on Software Engineering*, 5(3):203–216, 1979.

[7] C. Boksenbaum, M. Cart, J. Ferrié, and J.-F. Pons. Concurrent certifications by intervals of timestamps in distributed database systems. *Software Engineering, IEEE Transactions on*, (4):409–419, 1987.

[8] M. J. Carey. Improving the performance of an optimistic concurrency control algorithm through timestamps and versions. *Software Engineering, IEEE Transactions on*, SE-13(6):746–751, June 1987.

[9] B. F. Cooper, A. Silberstein, E. Tam, R. Ramakrishnan, and R. Sears. Benchmarking cloud serving systems with YCSB. In *SoCC'10*, pages 143–154.

[10] W. J. Dally. GPU Computing: To Exascale and Beyond. In *Supercomputing '10, Plenary Talk*, 2010.

[11] T. David, R. Guerraoui, and V. Trigonakis. Everything you always wanted to know about synchronization but were afraid to ask. In *Symposium on Operating Systems Principles*, pages 33–48, 2013.

[12] B. D. de Dinechin, R. Ayrignac, P.-E. Beaucamps, P. Couvert, B. Ganne, P. G. de Massas, F. Jacquet, S. Jones, N. M. Chaisemartin, F. Riss, and T. Strudel. A clustered manycore processor architecture for embedded and accelerated applications. In *Proc. of the High Performance Extreme Computing Conference*, 2013.

[13] K. P. Eswaran, J. N. Gray, R. A. Lorie, and I. L. Traiger. The notions of consistency and predicate locks in a database system. *CACM*, 19(11):624–633, 1976.

[14] A. Gottlieb, R. Grishman, C. P. Kruskal, K. P. McAuliffe, L. Rudolph, and M. Snir. The NYU Ultracomputer: Designing an MIMD Shared Memory Parallel Computer. *IEEE Trans. Comput.*, 100(2), 1983.

[15] J. Gray. The transaction concept: Virtues and limitations. In *VLDB*, pages 144–154, 1981.

[16] J. Gray, P. Sundaresan, S. Englert, K. Baclawski, and P. J. Weinberger. Quickly generating billion-record synthetic databases. SIGMOD, pages 243–252, 1994.

[17] T. Härder. Observations on optimistic concurrency control schemes. *Inf. Syst.*, 9(2):111–120, Nov. 1984.

[18] H. Hoffmann, D. Wentzlaff, and A. Agarwal. Remote store programming. In *High Performance Embedded Architectures and Compilers*, pages 3–17. Springer, 2010.

[19] Intel. Intel 64 and IA-32 Architectures Software Developer's Manual, Volume 3B, 17.14.1 Invariant TSC, 2015.

[20] R. Johnson, I. Pandis, N. Hardavellas, A. Ailamaki, and B. Falsafi. Shore-MT: a scalable storage manager for the multicore era. EDBT, pages 24–35, 2009.

[21] H. Kimura. Foedus: Oltp engine for a thousand cores and nvram. SIGMOD '15, pages 691–706, 2015.

[22] H. T. Kung and J. T. Robinson. On optimistic methods for concurrency control. *ACM Trans. Database Syst.*, 6(2):213–226, June 1981.

[23] K.-W. Lam, K.-Y. Lam, and S.-L. Hung. Real-time optimistic concurrency control protocol with dynamic adjustment of serialization order. In *Real-Time Technology and Applications Symposium*, pages 174–179. IEEE, 1995.

[24] P.-A. Larson, S. Blanas, C. Diaconu, C. Freedman, J. M. Patel, and M. Zwilling. High-performance concurrency control mechanisms for main-memory databases. *VLDB*, 5(4):298–309, Dec. 2011.

[25] J. Lee and S. H. Son. Using dynamic adjustment of serialization order for real-time database systems. In *Real-Time Systems Symposium*, pages 66–75. IEEE, 1993.

[26] D. A. Menascé and T. Nakanishi. Optimistic versus pessimistic concurrency control mechanisms in database management systems. *Information Systems*, 7(1):13–27, 1982.

[27] C. Mohan, D. Haderle, B. Lindsay, H. Pirahesh, and P. Schwarz. Aries: a transaction recovery method supporting fine-granularity locking and partial rollbacks using write-ahead logging. *TODS*, 17(1):94–162, 1992.

[28] I. Pandis, R. Johnson, N. Hardavellas, and A. Ailamaki. Data-oriented transaction execution. *Proc. VLDB Endow.*, 3:928–939, September 2010.

[29] D. Porobic, I. Pandis, M. Branco, P. Tözün, and A. Ailamaki. OLTP on Hardware Islands. *Proc. VLDB Endow.*, 5:1447–1458, July 2012.

[30] D. P. Reed. *Naming and synchronization in a decentralized computer system*. PhD thesis, Massachusetts Institute of Technology, 1978.

[31] M. Reimer. Solving the phantom problem by predicative optimistic concurrency control. VLDB '83, pages 81–88, 1983.

[32] M. Stonebraker, S. Madden, D. J. Abadi, S. Harizopoulos, N. Hachem, and P. Helland. The end of an architectural era: (it's time for a complete rewrite). In *VLDB*, pages 1150–1160, 2007.

[33] The Transaction Processing Council. TPC-C Benchmark (Revision 5.9.0), June 2007.

[34] A. Thomasian. Concurrency control: Methods, performance, and analysis. *ACM Comput. Surv.*, 30(1):70–119, Mar. 1998.

[35] S. Tu, W. Zheng, E. Kohler, B. Liskov, and S. Madden. Speedy transactions in multicore in-memory databases. In *SOSP*, 2013.

[36] T. Wang and R. Johnson. Scalable logging through emerging non-volatile memory. *Proceedings of the VLDB Endowment*, 7(10):865–876, 2014.

[37] X. Yu, G. Bezerra, A. Pavlo, S. Devadas, and M. Stonebraker. Staring into the abyss: An evaluation of concurrency control with one thousand cores. volume 8, pages 209–220. VLDB Endowment, 2014.

[38] X. Yu and S. Devadas. TARDIS: timestamp based coherence algorithm for distributed shared memory. In *International Conference on Parallel Architectures and Compilation Techniques*, 2015.

[39] W. Zheng, S. Tu, E. Kohler, and B. Liskov. Fast databases with fast durability and recovery through multicore parallelism. In *Proceedings of the 11th USENIX Conference on Operating Systems Design and Implementation*, OSDI'14, pages 465–477. USENIX Association, 2014.

APPENDIX: DYNAMIC TIMESTAMP ALLOCATION

As discussed in Section 2.2, the original DTA technique [4] was designed to resolve and detect deadlocks using dependency graph analysis. It was first used in deadlock detection and prevention for 2PL algorithms. In DTA, timestamps are associated with each transaction and are compared when two transactions conflict with each other. Timestamps are not associated with tuples in DTA like they are in TicToc.

DTA was then adapted to OCC algorithms [7] and was later studied in the context of real-time DBMSs [23, 25]. In these designs, DTA was used to detect conflicts and determine the relative ordering among transactions. Similar to TicToc, DTA OCC also reorders transactions in logical time, which may not agree with physical time. However, since timestamps are only associated with transactions but not tuples, the DBMS has to maintain a dependency graph of all active transactions. This dependency graph is updated whenever there is a conflicting access. All the DTA OCC algorithms proposed in the literature have this critical section that becomes a serious performance bottleneck as thread count increases.

We modeled DTA OCC in our DBx1000 system and compared it against TicToc. Our implementation of DTA OCC is idealized since we modeled an empty critical section where a full-blown DTA OCC requires considerable logic in the critical section. As a result, our implementation provides an upper bound on the performance of DTA OCC. For this experiment, we used the same medium-contention YCSB workload that we use in Section 6.3.2. The results in Fig. 12 show that, as expected, DTA OCC fails to scale beyond 20 cores due to this critical section bottleneck. This matches previous studies that have shown that algorithms with shared global resources are unable to scale beyond 16–32 active threads [37].

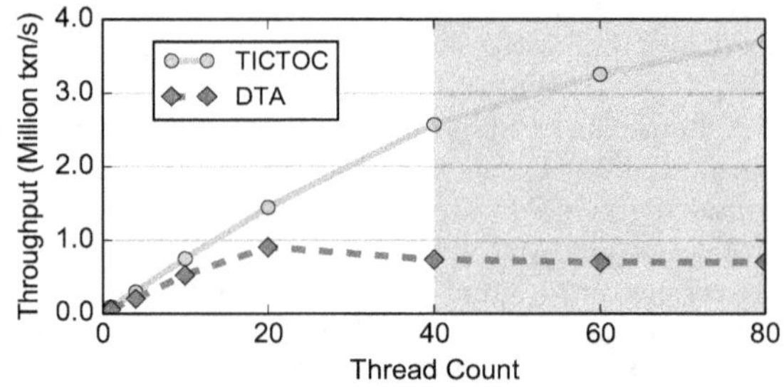

Figure 12: Dynamic Timestamp Allocation – Performance comparison of the DTA OCC and TicToc algorithms for the YCSB workload with medium contention.

Scaling Multicore Databases via Constrained Parallel Execution

Zhaoguo Wang, Shuai Mu, Yang Cui, Han Yi †, Haibo Chen†, Jinyang Li
New York University, † Shanghai Jiao Tong University

ABSTRACT

Multicore in-memory databases often rely on traditional concurrency control schemes such as two-phase-locking (2PL) or optimistic concurrency control (OCC). Unfortunately, when the workload exhibits a non-trivial amount of contention, both 2PL and OCC sacrifice much parallel execution opportunity. In this paper, we describe a new concurrency control scheme, interleaving constrained concurrency control (IC3), which provides serializability while allowing for parallel execution of certain conflicting transactions. IC3 combines the static analysis of the transaction workload with runtime techniques that track and enforce dependencies among concurrent transactions. The use of static analysis simplifies IC3's runtime design, allowing it to scale to many cores. Evaluations on a 64-core machine using the TPC-C benchmark show that IC3 outperforms traditional concurrency control schemes under contention. It achieves the throughput of 434K transactions/sec on the TPC-C benchmark configured with only one warehouse. It also scales better than several recent concurrent control schemes that also target contended workloads.

1. INTRODUCTION

Rapid increase of memory volume and CPU core counts have stimulated much recent development of multi-core in-memory databases [42, 15, 20, 27, 48, 51, 34, 55]. As the performance bottleneck has shifted from I/O to CPU, how to maximally take advantage of the CPU resources of multiple cores has become an important research problem.

A key challenge facing multi-core databases is how to support serializable transactions while maximizing parallelism so as to scale to many CPU cores. Popular concurrency control schemes are based on two-phase locking (2PL) [5, 19] or optimistic concurrency control (OCC) [26, 5]. Both achieve good parallel execution when concurrent transactions rarely conflict with each other. Unfortunately, when the workload exhibits contention, the performance of both schemes crumbles. 2PL makes transactions grab read/write locks, thus it serializes the execution of transactions as soon as they make a conflicting access to some data item. OCC performs worse under contention because it aborts and retries conflicted transactions.

There is much parallelism left unexploited by 2PL and OCC in contended workloads. As an example, suppose transactions 1 and 2 both modify data items A and B. One can safely interleave their execution as long as both transactions modify items A and B in the same order. Under 2PL or OCC, their execution is serialized. This paper presents IC3, a concurrency control scheme for multi-core in-memory databases, which unlocks such parallelism among conflicting transactions.

A basic strategy for safe interleaving is to track dependencies that arise as transactions make conflicting data access and to enforce tracked dependencies by constraining a transaction's subsequent data access. This basic approach faces several challenges in order to extract parallelism while guaranteeing serializability: How to know which data access should be constrained and which ones should not? How to ensure transitive dependencies are not violated without having to explicitly track them (which is expensive)? How to guarantee that tracked dependencies are always enforceable at runtime?

IC3's key to solving these challenges is to combine runtime techniques with a static analysis of the transaction workload to be executed. IC3's static analysis is based on the foundation laid out by prior work on transaction chopping [4, 7, 6, 41]. In particular, it constructs a static conflict graph (SC-graph) in which a transaction is represented as a series of atomic pieces each making one or more database accesses. Two pieces of different transactions are connected if both access the same table and one of the accesses is a write. A cycle involving multiple pieces of some transaction (i.e. an SC-cycle) indicates a potential violation of serializability when interleaving the execution of those pieces involved in the SC-cycle. Transaction chopping precludes any SC-cycle in a workload by merging pieces into a larger atomic unit. By contrast, IC3 permits most types of SC-cycles and relies on its runtime to render them harmless by constraining the execution of the corresponding pieces.

The runtime of IC3 only tracks and enforces direct dependencies; this is more efficient and scalable than explicitly tracking and enforcing transitive dependencies, as is done in [33]. Without the aid of static analysis, this simplified runtime does not expose much parallelism: once a transaction T becomes dependent on another T', T has no choice but to wait for T' to finish in order to prevent potential

SIGMOD'16, June 26-July 01, 2016, San Francisco, CA, USA

DOI: http://dx.doi.org/10.1145/2882903.2882934

violations of transitive dependencies. Static analysis helps unlock the parallelism inherent in a workload. If there exists an SC-cycle connecting the next piece p of T to some piece p' of the dependent transaction T', then IC3 can shortcut the wait and execute p as soon as p' has finished without waiting for the rest of T'. As most SC-cycles are among instances of the same type of transaction, this shortcut is very common and is crucial for IC3's performance. Static analysis also helps IC3 ensure all tracked dependencies are enforceable at runtime. In particular, we identify a class of SC-cycles as deadlock-prone in that they may cause deadlocks when IC3 tries to constrain piece execution. We remove the subset of SC-cycles that are deadlock-prone by combining pieces.

We contrast IC3's approach to existing work [36, 2, 47, 45, 16] that also expose parallelism among contended transactions (see § 7 for a more complete discussion). Dependency-aware transaction memory (DATM) [36] and Ordered shared lock [2] permit safe interleaving should it arise at runtime and otherwise abort. As such aborts may cascade, IC3's approach to pro-actively constraining execution for safe interleaving is more robust. Deterministic database [47, 45, 16] generates a dependency graph that deterministically orders transactions' conflicting record access in accordance with transactions' global arrival order. This fine-grained runtime technique avoids certain unnecessary constraining incurred by IC3 because static analysis cannot accurately predict actual runtime conflict. However, as the dependency graph is generated by one thread, deterministic database does not scale as well as IC3 when running on a large number of cores.

We have implemented IC3 in C++ using the codebase of Silo [48]. Evaluations on a 64-core machine using microbenchmarks and TPC-C [44] show that IC3 outperforms traditional 2PL and OCC under moderate to high amounts of contention. For the TPC-C benchmark configured with 1 warehouse, IC3 achieves 434K transactions/sec on 64 threads while the throughput of 2PL and OCC is under 50K transactions/sec. IC3 also scales better than deterministic lazy evaluation [16] and DATM [36] under high contention.

2. MOTIVATION AND APPROACH

In this section, we consider those parallel execution opportunities that are not exploited by 2PL and OCC. We discuss the challenges in enabling safe interleaving (§ 2.1) and explain IC3's key ideas at a high level(§ 2.2).

2.1 Parallelism Opportunity and Challenges

When concurrent transactions make conflicting database access, much opportunity for parallelism is lost when using traditional concurrency control protocols like 2PL and OCC. Consider two transactions, T_1 and T_2, each of which reads and modifies records A and B, i.e. T_1=$R_1(A)$, $W_1(A)$, $R_1(B)$, $W_1(B)$ and T_2=$R_2(A)$, $W_2(A)$, $R_2(B)$, $W_2(B)$. Both 2PL and OCC effectively serialize the execution of T_1 and T_2. However, safe parallel execution of T_1 and T_2 exists, as shown by the example in Figure 1a. In this example, once T_2 reads record A after T_1's write, T_2's subsequent read from record B will be constrained to occur after that of T_1's write to B, thereby ensuring serializability. Some existing protocols, such as Commit conflicting transactions [36] and Ordered sharing lock [2], augment OCC or 2PL to permit the safe interleaving in Figure 1a should it happen at runtime. However, if the actual interleaving happens to be unsafe (e.g. $W_1(A) \rightarrow R_2(A)$ but $R_2(B) \rightarrow W_1(B)$), these protocols [36, 2] abort offending transactions, resulting in a cascading effect because interleaved data access have read uncommitted writes. To avoid costly cascading aborts, it is better to actively constrain the interleaving to guarantee safety instead of passively permitting interleaving that happens to be safe.

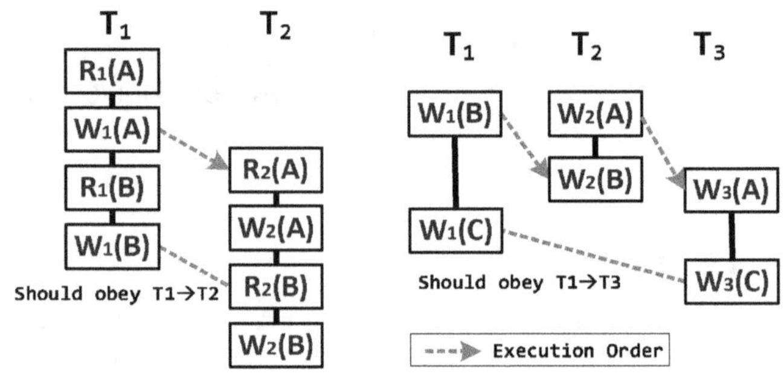

(a) An example of safe parallel execution of two conflicting transactions

(b) Transitive dependency makes it difficult to track and enforce dependency.

Figure 1: Opportunity & Challenge.

The example of Figure 1a suggests an intuitive, albeit naive, solution to exploit parallelism. Specifically, the database could track the dependencies among transactions as they make conflicting data accesses (including read-write or write-write conflicts). It would then ensure that tracked dependencies are not violated later (i.e. no dependency cycles arise) by delaying a transaction's subsequent data access when necessary. For the example in Figure 1a, we would track $T_1 \rightarrow T_2$ when T_2 performs $R_2(A)$ after $W_1(A)$. Subsequently, the database would block $R_2(B)$ until $W_1(B)$ has finished in order to enforce the dependency $T_1 \rightarrow T_2$. While this naive approach works for the example in Figure 1a, it does not work for general transactions, due to the following challenges.

Knowing which data access to enforce dependency on. In order to minimize unnecessary blocking, we need to know the series of records to be accessed by a transaction beforehand. In the example of Figure 1a, if T_2 knows that its dependent transaction T_1 will update record B (and T_1 makes no other access to B), T_2 only needs to wait for $W_1(B)$ to finish before performing its own access $R_2(B)$. If a transaction's record access information is not known, T_2 must wait for T_1 to finish its execution in entirety, leaving no opportunities for interleaving.

Handling transitive dependencies. The naive approach is not correct for general transactions, because it does not handle transitive dependencies. To see why, let us consider the example in Figure 1b, in which T_3 becomes dependent on T_2 (i.e. $T_2 \rightarrow T_3$) after T_3 has written to record A after T_2. During subsequent execution, T_2 becomes dependent on another transaction T_1, resulting in the transitive dependency $T_1(\rightarrow T_2) \rightarrow T_3$. This transitive dependency needs to be enforced by delaying T_3's write to record C after that of T_1. Techniques for tracking transitive dependencies at runtime have been proposed in the distributed setting [33], but the required computation would impose much overhead when used in the multi-core setting.

Tracked dependencies are not always enforceable. The naive approach assumes that it is always possible to enforce tracked dependencies. While this assumption holds for some workloads, it is not the case for arbitrary real-world transaction workloads. For example, if $T_1 = W_1(A), W_1(B)$ and $T_2 = W_2(B), W_2(A)$, no safe interleaving of T_1 and T_2 exists. If the database permits both to execute concurrently, it is impossible to enforce the tracked dependencies later.

2.2 IC3's Approach

To solve the challenges of safe parallel execution, one could rely solely on the runtime to analyze transactions' record access information and to enforce the dependency among them. Deterministic databases [47, 45, 16] take such an approach. They generate a dependency graph that deterministically orders transactions' conflicting record access in accordance with transactions' global arrival order and enforces the dependency during execution, sometimes lazily [16]. While this approach can enforce dependency precisely, it does not scale well to a large number of cores, as the dependency analysis is performed by one thread and can become a performance bottleneck (§ 6). IC3 uses a different approach that augments runtime techniques with an offline static analysis of the workload. Below, we discuss the main ideas of IC3.

Static analysis. Most OLTP workloads consist of a mix of known transaction types. For each type of transaction, we typically know which table(s) the transaction reads or writes [4, 41, 33, 54]. Utilizing such information, static analysis chops each transaction into pieces, each of which makes an atomic data access. IC3's runtime decides which pair of pieces needs to be constrained (e.g. if both make conflicting access to the same table) to enforce tracked dependencies. Moreover, static analysis can also determine when there may exist no safe interleaving at runtime and take preemptive steps to ensure all tracked dependencies are enforceable. The upside of static analysis is that it simplifies IC3's runtime dependency tracking and enforcement. The downside is that it can cause the runtime to unnecessarily constrain certain safe interleaving. We discuss techniques to mitigate the performance cost of over constraining (§ 4.1).

Efficient runtime dependency tracking and enforcement. IC3 tracks and enforces only direct dependencies which occur between two transactions when they make consecutive, conflicting access to the same record. By augmenting these direct dependencies with information from offline static analysis, IC3 can ensure all transitive dependencies are obeyed without explicitly tracking them.

To see how static analysis helps, let us consider a naive scheme that can obey all transitive dependencies while only tracking direct ones. In this scheme, every transaction T must wait for its directly dependent transactions to commit before T is allowed to commit or perform subsequent data access. Such conservative waiting ensures that all transitive dependencies are obeyed. For example, in Figure 1b, T_3 waits for its directly dependent transaction T_2 to commit before it proceeds to write to record C. Because T_2 also waits for its directly dependent transaction T_1 to commit before T_2 commits, we are able to ensure $T_1 \rightarrow T_3$ for their corresponding access to record C without ever explicitly tracking and discovering the transitive dependency $T_1 \rightarrow T_2 \rightarrow T_3$.

The naive scheme kills the parallel execution opportunity shown in Figure 1a. For example, it will prevent the interleaved execution in Figure 1a, as T_2 waits for T_1 to commit before it is allowed to perform $R_2(B)$. The key to make direct dependency enforcement work well is to leverage the static analysis of the workload. With the help of static analysis, we add two rules that bypass the default behavior of making T_2 wait for its direct dependency T_1 to commit. 1) if static analysis shows that no *potential* transitive dependencies may arise between T_1 and T_2 due to T_2's next data access, the runtime can safely let T_2 perform that access without blocking for T_1. 2) if static analysis shows that T_2's next data access might potentially conflict with some of T_1's later access, then T_2 only needs to wait for the corresponding access of T_1 to finish instead of waiting for the entirety of T_1 to finish and commit. The second rule applies to Figure 1a to allow its interleaving. Both rules are crucial for achieving good performance for practical workloads. We will elaborate the combined static analysis and runtime techniques in the next section (§ 3) and provide intuitions for their correctness.

3. BASIC DESIGN

This section describes the design of IC3. We discuss how IC3 analyzes static conflict information (§ 3.1), how its runtime utilizes this information to track and enforce dependency (§ 3.2), and lastly, how IC3 ensures that all tracked dependencies are enforceable (§ 3.3). We provide a proof sketch for correctness in § 3.5.

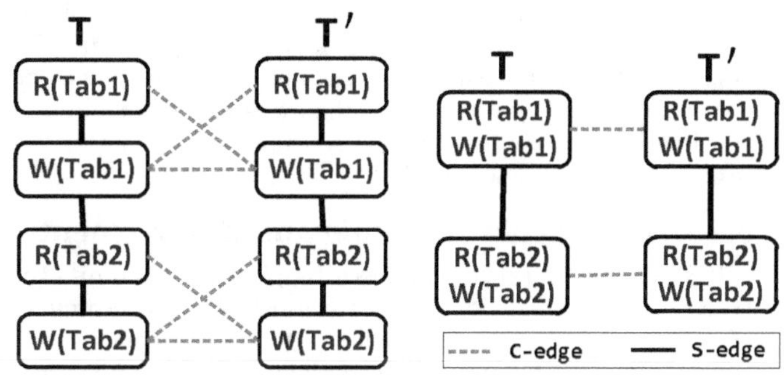

(a) SC-graph when considering each operation as a single piece

(b) SC-graph after merging

Figure 2: SC-graph [41] with two instances of the same transaction type.

3.1 Static Analysis

IC3 is an in-memory database with a one-shot transaction processing model, i.e., a transaction starts execution only when all its inputs are ready Many existing databases have the same transaction model (e.g., H-store [42], Calvin [45, 47], Silo [48]). IC3's current API provides transactions over sorted key/value tables whose primitives for data access are: *Get*("tableName", key), *Put*("tableName", key, value), *Scan*("tableName", keyRange)[1].

In this paper, we assume the transaction workload is static and known before the execution of any transaction. We relax this assumption and propose techniques to handle dynamic workloads and ad-hoc transactions in the technical report [50]. IC3 performs the static analysis by first constructing a static conflict graph (SC-graph), which is introduced by prior work on transaction chopping [4, 7, 6, 41]. In an SC-graph, each transaction is represented as a series of atomic *pieces* each making one or more data access. Pieces

[1]Get/Put/Scan also optionally take column names as parameters to restrict access the specified subset of columns.

within a transaction are connected by a S(ibling)-edge. To construct an SC-graph for a given workload, we include *two* instances of each transaction type and connect two pieces belonging to different transactions with a C(onflict)-edge if they *potentially* conflict, i.e., two pieces access the same column of the same database table and one of which is a write access. IC3 analyzes user transaction code to decompose each transaction into pieces and to construct the resulting SC-graph (see details in § 5). Suppose the example of Figure 1a corresponds to a workload consisting of the following one type of transaction:

MyTransaction(k_1,v_1,k_2,v_2):
  v_1 =**Get**("Tab1", k_1)
  Put("Tab1", k_1, v_1')
  v_2 =**Get**("Tab2", k_2)
  Put("Tab2", k_2, v_2')

The corresponding SC-graph for this workload is shown in Figure 2a. SC-graphs reveal potential violations of serializability at runtime. Specifically, if there exists an SC-cycle [41] which contains both S- and C-edges, then a corresponding cyclic dependency (i.e., a violation of serializability) may arise at runtime. Figure 2a has an SC-cycle containing two instances of the same transaction, therefore, there is a danger for T_1 and T_2 (two instances of T) to enter a cyclic dependency at runtime, e.g., with execution order $R_1(A)$, $W_1(A)$, $R_2(A)$, $W_2(A)$, $R_2(B)$, $W_2(B)$, $R_1(B)$, $W_1(B)$. While transaction chopping combines pieces to eliminate all SC-cycles, IC3 renders SC-cycles harmless at runtime by constraining piece execution to prevent the corresponding dependency cycles.

3.2 Dependency Tracking and Enforcement

IC3 executes a transaction piece-by-piece and commits the transaction after all its pieces are finished. The atomicity of each piece is guaranteed using traditional concurrency control (OCC). IC3 ensures the serializability of multi-piece transactions by tracking and enforcing dependencies among concurrent transactions. To control performance overhead and improve multi-core scaling, IC3 only tracks and enforces direct dependencies at runtime. Without static analysis, a transaction T must wait for *all* its dependent transaction to commit before T can perform *any* subsequent data access, which precludes most scenarios for safe parallel execution. Static analysis helps IC3 avoid or shorten such costly wait in many circumstances.

Algorithm 1 shows how IC3 executes each piece and Algorithm 2 shows how IC3 executes and commits a multi-piece transaction. Together, they form the pseudo-code of IC3. IC3 uses several data structures to perform direct dependency tracking. First, each transaction T maintains a dependency queue, which contains the list of transactions that T is directly dependent on. Second, the database maintains an accessor list [36], one per record, which contains the set of not-yet-committed transactions that have either read or written this record.

Piece execution and commit. The execution of each piece consists of three phases, as shown in Algorithm 1:

Algorithm 1: RunPiece(p, T):

```
   Input: p is a piece of transaction T
1
2  // Wait Phase:
3   if p does not have any C-edge                   // case-1
4     skip to execute phase
5   foreach T' in T.depqueue:
6     if ∃ p' of T' and p has a C-edge with p'  // case-2
7       wait for p' to commit
8     else                                          // case-3
9       wait for T' to commit
10
11 // Execute Phase
12  run user code to execute p
13
14 // Commit Phase
15  lock records in p's read+writeset (using a sorted order)
16  validate p's readset
17  foreach d in p.readset:
18    T_w ← last write tx in DB[d.key].acclist
19    T.depqueue += T_w
20    DB[d.key].acclist += (T,"reader")
21  foreach d in p.writeset:
22    T_rw ← last read/write tx in DB[d.key].acclist
23    T.depqueue += T_rw
24    DB[d.key].acclist += (T,"writer")
25    DB[d.key].stash = d.val
26  release grabbed locks
27
28 return status //whether p has committed or aborted
```

- *Wait Phase (lines 3-9).* Once a transaction T has become dependent on another transaction T', how long should T wait before executing its next piece p? There are three cases, as determined by information from the static analysis. In the first case (lines 3-4), piece p does not have any C-edges and thus is not part of any SC-cycle involving T and T'. This means one cannot violate $T' \to T$ by executing p immediately, without constraints. In the second case, piece p is part of an SC-cycle that involves only T and its dependent transaction T'. In other words, p has a C-edge connecting to some piece p' in T'. For case-2, p only needs to wait for p' to finish (line 6-7). The third case is when neither case-1 or case-2 applies (line 8-9), then T has to wait for T' to finish all pieces and commit. The intuition for why p only needs to wait for p' in the second case is subtle; basically, if IC3 ensures that no (direct) dependencies are violated due to the SC-cycle involving only T and T', then no transitive dependencies are violated due to SC-cycles involving T, T' and some other transaction(s). To see why, we refer readers to the proofs (§ 3.5 and Appendix A). Note that case 2 is actually quite common; SC-cycles are most likely to occur among instances of the same transaction type (Figure 2a shows such an example). These SC-cycles make case-2 applicable.

- *Execution Phase (line 12).* In this phase, IC3 executes user code, and accesses database records. In the database, the value of a record reflects the write of the last committed transaction. In addition, each record also keeps a stashed value, which reflects the write of the last committed piece. A read of the record returns its stashed value, instead of the actual value. This ensures that a transaction T can read the writes of

Algorithm 2: RunTransaction(T):

```
1  // Execute Phase
2  foreach p in T:
3      RunPiece(p, T)
4      retry p if p is aborted (due to contention)
5
6  // Commit Phase
7  foreach T' in T.depqueue:
8      wait for T' to commit
9  foreach d in T.writeset:
10     DB[d.key].value = d.val
11     delete T from DB[d.key].acclist
12
13 return status //whether T has committed or aborted
```

completed pieces in another transaction T' before T' commits. This allows for more interleavings that are not available to 2PL or OCC. All the writes of a piece are simply buffered locally.

- *Commit Phase (lines 15-25).* First, IC3 must check that p has executed atomically w.r.t. other concurrent pieces. We perform the validation according to OCC: IC3 grabs all locks on the piece's readset and writeset (line 15) and checks if any of its reads has been changed by other pieces (line 16, with details ignored).

  Second, we augment T's dependency queue (*T.depqueue*) due to any write-read relations that arise from p's reads. Specifically, for each record in p's readset, we append to *T.depqueue* the last writer according to the record's accessor list (line 18-19). We then add T to the record's accessor list.

  Third, we update *T.depqueue* and the corresponding accessor lists based on p's writeset. This update is similar to that done for p's readset, except we must account for both read-write and write-write relations (lines 22-24). We then update the record's stashed value with the write value (line 25).

Transaction commit. After all its pieces have finished, transaction T proceeds to commit. First, T must wait for all its dependent transactions to finish their commits (lines 7-8). This is crucial because we must ensure that T's writes are not overwritten by transactions that are ordered before T in the serialization order. Then, it updates the value of the corresponding record in the database according to its writeset and removes itself from the record's accessor list (lines 10-11). We note that, unlike 2PL or OCC, the commit phase does not require holding locks across its writeset. This is safe because 1) T explicitly waits for all transactions serialized before itself to finish, and 2) conflicting transactions that are to be serialized after T wait for T's writes explicitly during piece execution (lines 5-9).

Examples. Now we use the examples in Figure 1a and Figure 1b again to see how IC3 works. After merging the deadlock-prone SC-cycles shown in Figure 2a into Figure 2b (details in § 3.3), we can enforce the interleaving as follows: after T_1 has executed the piece $RW_1(A)$, IC3 appends T_1 to record A's accessor list. When T_2's first piece, $RW_2(A)$, finishes, IC3 checks A's accessor list and puts T_1 in T_2's dependency queue. When T_2 tries to execute its next piece, $RW_2(B)$, it will have to wait for $RW_1(B)$ to finish because the two pieces are connected by a C-edge and $RW_1(B)$'s transaction (T_1) appears in T_2's dependency queue. In Figure 1b, T_2 is in T_3's dependency queue when T_3 is about to execute $W_3(C)$. Since, $W_3(C)$ has a C-edge with some transaction but not with T_2, it has to wait for T_2 to finish all pieces and commit. As T_2 can only commit after its dependent transaction T_1 commits, $W_3(C)$ only executes after T_1 has finished, thereby ensuring $W_1(C) \rightarrow W_3(C)$ and guaranteeing serializability.

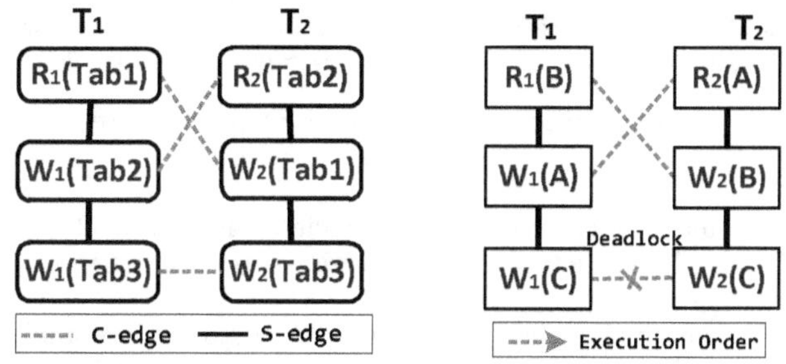

(a) $R1, W1, R2, W2$ is a deadlock-prone SC-cycle.

(b) An example runtime interleaving with deadlocks.

Figure 3: A deadlock-prone SC-cycle suggests potential runtime deadlock.

3.3 Ensuring Tracked Dependencies are Enforceable

As we discussed earlier, tracked dependencies are not always enforceable at runtime for arbitrary workloads. When this happens, the basic IC3 algorithm encounters deadlocks as pieces enter some cyclic wait pattern. The traditional approach is to run a deadlock detection algorithm and abort all deadlocked transactions. Unlike 2PL, however, in the context of IC3, aborts have a cascading effect: not only must we abort all deadlocked transactions, we must also abort all transactions that have seen the writes of aborted transactions and so forth. A number of concurrency control protocols adopt such an approach [2, 36]. However, as we see in § 6, cascading aborts can be devastating for performance when the workload has a moderate amount of contention.

IC3 adopts a different approach to prevent deadlocks. Again, we leverage the static analysis to identify those pieces that can cause potential deadlocks. We combine those pieces (belonging to the same transaction) together into one larger atomic piece. This ensures all tracked dependencies enforceable at runtime with no risks of deadlocks.

Given an SC-graph, what patterns suggest potential deadlocks? Consider the example in Figure 3a in which T_1 accesses table $Tab1$ before $Tab2$ and T_2 does the opposite. In the underlying SC-graph, this corresponds to an SC-cycle whose conflicting pieces access different tables in an inconsistent order. We refer to this SC-cycle as a deadlock-prone SC-cycle. Deadlock-prone SC-cycles indicate potential runtime deadlocks. Figure 3b gives an example execution that is deadlocked: T_1 reads record B before T_2's write to B ($T_1 \rightarrow T_2$) while at the same time T_2 reads record A before T_2's write to A ($T_2 \rightarrow T_1$). This cyclic dependency will eventually manifest itself as a deadlock when T_1 and T_2 try to commit. In the example of Figure 3b, the deadlock appears earlier as T_1 and T_2 wait for each other before they attempt to modify record C. In addition to accessing different tables

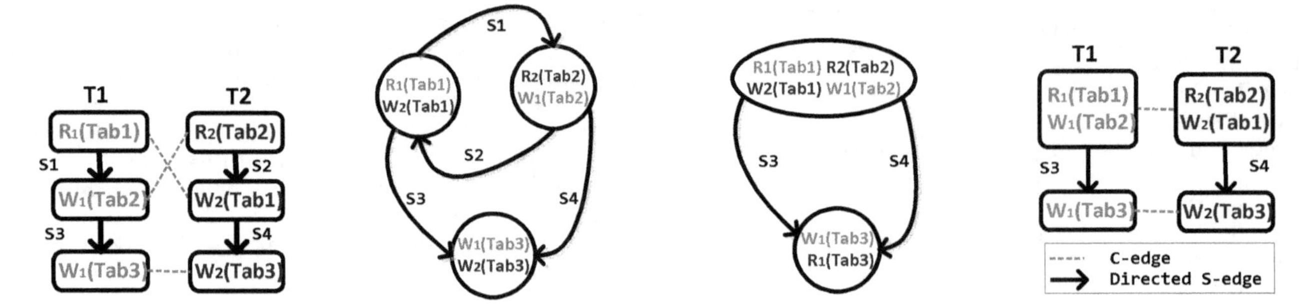

(a) Make S-edge directed to reflect the execution order within a transaction. (b) Put pieces connected with C-edges into the same vertex (c) Make the graph acyclic by merging the vertexes involved in a cycle (d) For each merged vertex, combine pieces of the same transaction into one piece.

Figure 4: How to combine pieces to remove deadlock-prone SC-cycles and avoid runtime deadlock.

in an inconsistent order, an SC-cycle is also deadlock-prone if multiple conflicting pieces of a transaction access the same table.

To eliminate deadlock-prone SC-cycles, IC3 combines pieces into a larger atomic piece using the following algorithm. First, we add direction to each S-edge to reflect the chronological execution order of a transaction(Figure 4a). Second, we put all pieces connected by C-edges into a single vertex. The first two steps result in a directed graph whose edges are the original S-edges (Figure 4b). Third, we iteratively merge all the vertexes involved in the same directed cycle into one vertex until the graph is acyclic (Figure 4c). Last, we combine those pieces of a merged vertex that belong to the same transaction into a single piece. Figure 4d shows the resulting SC-graph of Figure 3a after combining those pieces. Note that there are no longer deadlock-prone SC-cycles in Figure 4d, so IC3 is guaranteed to encounter no deadlocks when enforcing tracked dependencies.

3.4 Applicability of IC3

IC3 is not beneficial for all application workloads; it is only effective for contentious workloads that access multiple tables within a single transaction. For these workloads, the static analysis is likely to produce transactions containing multiple pieces, thereby allowing IC3 to exploit the parallelism opportunity overlooked by 2PL/OCC by interleaving the execution of conflicting pieces. For workloads that only access a single table within a transaction, IC3 does not provide any performance gains over traditional concurrency control such as 2PL or OCC. For example, if all transactions only do read and then modify a single database record, then static analysis merges the two accesses so that all transactions consist of a single (merged) piece. As a result, IC3 behaves identically to the traditional concurrency control protocol which it uses to ensure the atomicity of a piece.

Workloads that access multiple tables within a transaction are quite common in practice. For example, all transactions in the popular TPC-C benchmarks access multiple tables and thus contain multiple pieces (§ 6 gives more details). We have also manually analyzed the 14 most popular Ruby-on-Rails applications on GitHub and found most of them contain transactions accessing multiple tables (Appendix C).

3.5 Proof Sketch

Due to space limitations, we only give a proof sketch here. A more rigorous proof is included in the appendix. We are going to prove that IC3 always ensures serializability by only generating acyclic serialization graph.

In a proof by contradiction we assume there is a cycle in the serialization graph, denoted by $T_1 \to T_2 \to ... \to T_n \to T_1$. Treating each piece as a sub-transaction, the cycle can be expanded as $q_1..p_1 \to q_2..p_2 \to ... \to q_n..p_n \to q_1$. Because we use OCC to protect the atomicity of each piece, the directed edge in the cycle reflects the chronological commit order of pieces, therefore there must be at least a pair of q_i and p_i such that they are not the same piece. Then this cycle corresponds to an SC-cycle in the SC-graph, which means no piece in the cycle can skip checking direct dependent transactions in Algorithm 1. Moreover, the cycle necessarily implies a deadlock at transaction commit time, so none of the transaction in the cycle can commit.

Consider a fragment $p_i \to q_j \to p_j$ in that cycle. For p_j, because it can neither skip the checking phase nor successfully wait for T_i to commit (T_i can never commit due to deadlock), p_j can only execute after it waits for the commit of a piece r_i in T_i that has a C-edge connection to itself. Our static analysis ensures that this r_i must be chronologically later than p_i, otherwise there will be a non-existent cycle $q_j \to p_j \to q_j$ in the SC-graph.

Using the above property, we can inductively "shrink" the cycle until there is no $q_i \to p_i$ in the cycle. Eventually after m ($m < n$) times iteration, we will get a new cycle, represented as $q_1^m \leftarrow p_1^m \to q_2^m \leftarrow p_2^m \to ... \to q_{n-m}^m \leftarrow p_{n-m}^m \to q_1^m$, which necessarily implies a directed cycle in the SC-graph we have already eliminated, which is a contradiction to the result of static analysis. As a result, a cycle in the serialization graph cannot exist; it means IC3's scheduling is always serializable.

4. OPTIMIZATION AND EXTENSIONS

This section introduces several important performance optimizations and extends IC3 to support user-initiated aborts.

4.1 Constraining Pieces Optimistically

Static analysis can cause the runtime to unnecessarily constrain certain safe interleaving. Figure 5a shows an example runtime execution for the SC-graph in Figure 2. T_1 and T_2 write to the same record A in Tab1 but write to different records (B and B') in Tab2. However, under Algorithm 1, as T_2 is dependent on T_1 after both write to A, T_1 can not execute $W_2(B')$ until $W_1(B)$ is finished. Such unnecessary constraining sacrifices parallelism.

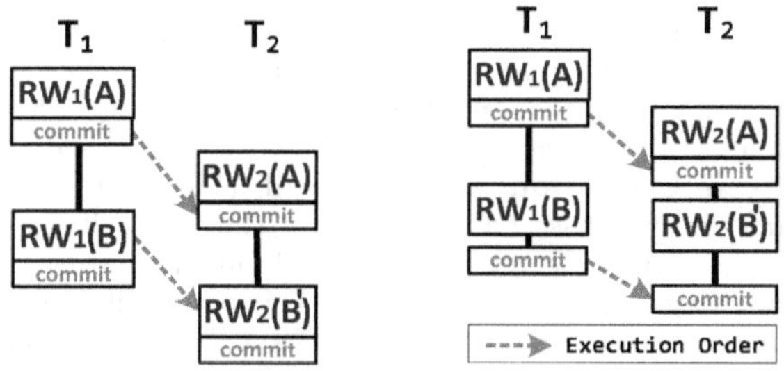

(a) Static analysis may constrain piece execution unnecessarily.

(b) Constrain piece optimistically by moving the waiting phase to be after piece execution and before its commit.

Figure 5: Constrain the interleaving optimistically to reduce false constraint

As each piece is protected by OCC, we can constrain its execution optimistically to unlock more parallelism. The basic idea to constrain each piece's commit phase instead of its execution phase. This can be done by reordering the wait phase and execution phase in Algorithm 1. For each piece, it first optimistically executes the piece without blocking (execute phase). Then, it waits according to the rules of the wait phase. Last, it will validate and commit the piece.

Figure 5b shows the allowed interleaving of the previous example with optimistic constraining. Unlike before, $W_2(B')$ can execute concurrently with $W_1(B)$. However, before T_2 commits its second piece, it needs to wait for T_1's second piece to finish committing. As the commit time of each piece is typically shorter than its execution time, this optimization reduces the size of critical section in which execution needs to be serialized.

4.2 Rendezvous Piece

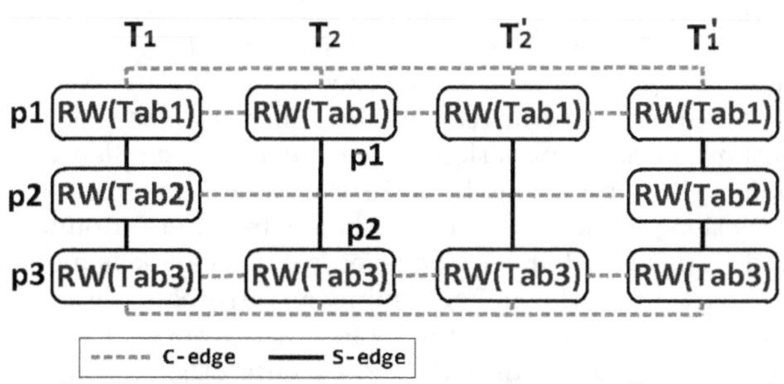

Figure 6: The SC-graph involving two types of transactions. T_2's P2 is the rendezvous piece of T_1's P2 and T_1''s P2.

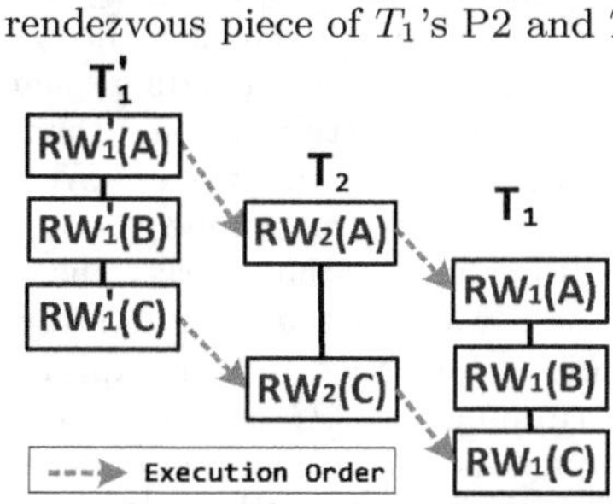

Figure 7: Constrain the interleaving with the rendezvous piece. Before T execute $W_1(B)$, it only needs wait T_2 finishes $W_2(C)$

When executing a piece p in T that is potentially involved in any conflicts (Algorithm 1, line 5-9), IC3 needs to find T's dependent transaction T', and then either 1) wait for a piece in T' that may potentially cause conflicts with p to finsih, or 2) wait for the entire T' to commit if no such pieces in T' exist. In the latter case, the wait could be expensive depending on how soon T' will commit. As an optimization to reduce this cost, we introduce a concept named *rendezvous piece*. For piece p in transaction T, its rendezvous piece in another transaction T' works as a promise that after this rendezvous piece finishes, T' can form no more conflicts with T involving p. More specifically, if we can find a later piece q in T (after p) and another piece r in T', such that q and r are connected by an C-edge in static analysis, r will be a rendezvous piece of p in T'. We then can use r to synchronize T with T'. In this case, IC3 can simply wait for r to finish before committing p, and doing so is sufficient to ensure no undesirable interference could ever happen.

During static analysis, after merging operations, IC3 looks for rendezvous pieces of every piece in other transaction types, and tags the information in the generated SC-graph. Afterwards, IC3 can leverage this information at runtime to cut down waiting time. As an example, Figure 6 shows an SC-graph with two types of transactions T_1 and T_2. The piece p_2 of T_1 has no C-edge directly connecting to T_2, but a later piece p_3 of T_1 directly connects the p_2 of T_2. During static analysis, p_2 is identified as the rendezvous piece of p_2 of T_1. Afterwards, during the execution, before T_1 executes p_2, it only needs to wait until T_2 finishes p_2, as shown in Figure 7.

4.3 Commutative Operation

Two write pieces commute if different execution orders produce the same database state. Therefore, it may seem unnecessary to constrain the interleaving of commutative pieces. However, this is not correct as write pieces do not commute with read operations that IC3 uses to generate a periodic consistent snapshot in the background [2]. IC3 solves this issue by deferring the execution of commutative operation to the transaction commit phase[3]. In our current implementation, users make commutativity explicitly by using a new data access interface, *Update*("tableName", key, value, *op*) where *op* is user-specified commutative accumulation function such as addition.

4.4 Handling User-initiated Aborts

So far, we have presented IC3 on the assumption that transactions are never aborted by users and thus can always be retried until they eventually succeed. We now explain how IC3 handles user-initiated aborts.

In IC3, when a transaction is aborted (by the user), all the transactions that depend on it must also be aborted. IC3 supports this cascading aborts by using an abort bit for each entry in the accessor list. When a transaction aborts, it unlinks its own entry from each accessor list that it has updated and sets the abort bit for all the entries appearing after itself. Before a transaction commits, it checks the abort bits of all its accessorlist entries. If any of its entry has the abort bit, then the transaction aborts itself.

[2]IC3 runs read-only transactions separately from read-write transactions by using thse snapshots, same as is done in Silo [48].

[3]Such deferring is always possible because commutative write pieces do not return any values used by later pieces. Otherwise they do not commute.

5. IMPLEMENTATION

We have built the IC3 runtime in C++ and implemented the static analyzer in Python. This section describes the basic implementation that performs static analysis in a separate pre-processing stage. We have also extended IC3 to perform online analysis in order to handle dynamic workloads, the details of which are given in [50].

5.1 Pre-processing and Static Analysis

The static analysis is done by a Python script in the pre-processing stage, before the system is to execute any transaction. Therefore, the overhead of static analysis does not affect IC3's runtime performance. The analyzer parses the stored procedures (in C++) to determine the scope of transaction piece and construct the corresponding SC-graph. The granularity of the analysis is at the level of columns, i.e. two pieces are connected by a C-edge if they both access the same column and at least one of them is write. To simplify the analysis, users are currently required to explicitly define the names of tables and columns accessed via the Get/Put/Scan API. This restriction enables the analyzer to easily identify each database access, label each access as an individual piece, and determine which pieces are connected via C-edges. When processing an `if-else` statement, the analyzer includes the table access of both branches in the corresponding transaction in the SC-graph. For table accesses within a `for` loop, they are grouped into one piece (it is possible to split loops using known compiler techniques, but we did not implement it.)

After the analyzer obtains the raw SC-graph by parsing the stored procedures, it applies the algorithm in § 3.3 to merge some pieces if necessary. For each table access, the final output of the analyzer contains its corresponding piece identifier and its C-edge information (i.e., the identifiers for those pieces with a C-edge to it). The IC3 runtime loads the C-edge information based on the analyzer's output prior to execution. We currently rely on manual annotation to associate the piece identifier with each table access. If a piece contains more than one table access, users must enclose those accesses within a pair of `begin_piece` and `end_piece` statements. As a result of the pre-processing, the IC3 runtime has sufficient information to implement line 3 and 6 in Algorithm 1.

5.2 Runtime Implementation

IC3's runtime implementation is based on the codebase of Silo [48], a high-performance in-memory database. Silo implements OCC on top of Masstree [31], a concurrent B-tree like data structure. We change the concurrency control protocol to IC3 and reuse Silo's implementation to support read-only transactions using snapshots, durability, and garbage collection.

IC3 uses a *tuple* to represent each table record and its meta-data. Among others, the meta-data includes the record's accessor list (implemented as a linked list), the stashed value and a version number for ensuring piece atomicity using OCC.

IC3 uses n worker threads to execute transactions, where n is the number of cores in the machine. We implement MCS lock [32], a type of spinlock that scales well to many cores [9]. Each tuple is associated with a separate MCS lock which protects the atomicity of operations on the tuple.

Each running transaction is associated with a data structure, referred to as its context, that holds information such as the transaction ID, its dependency queue, the current piece being executed, and its status. The context data structure has a fixed size and is reused for a new transaction.

Piece Execution and Commit (Lines 11-26, Algorithm 1). IC3 uses OCC to ensure the atomicity of each piece. During piece execution, IC3 buffers writes in the piece's write-set and copies the version number of each record being read in the piece's read-set. To commit piece p, IC3 first acquires the MCS locks for all tuples corresponding to p's read- and write-set. Then, IC3 checks whether the version numbers in the read-set differ from those currently stored in the tuples. Suppose validation succeeds for piece p of transaction T. Then, for each record accessed by p, IC3 adds the piece's transaction ID (T) to the tuple's accessor list, updates the tuple' stash value if the corresponding access is a write, and copies the transaction ID of the last conflicting entry in the tuple's accessor list to T's dependency queue (lines 17-25, Algorithm 1). Last, IC3 releases the MCS locks.

Piece wait (lines 2-9, Algorithm 1). There are three cases for how long a piece should wait before execution. The IC3 runtime can determine which case applies to piece p by examining p's C-edge information. This information is calculated by the static analyzer during pre-processing and loaded in the runtime's memory prior to execution.

By default, the worker thread waits by spinning. If piece p needs to wait for its dependent transaction T' to commit (line 8, Algorithm 1), the worker thread continuously reads several pieces of information in T''s context and checks 1) whether the status of T' becomes "committed". 2). whether the transaction ID stored in the context of T' has been changed; this occurs when T' finishes and its context data structure is re-used by other transactions. If piece p needs to wait for a specific piece p' in T' to commit (line 6-7, Algorithm 1), the worker thread also additionally spins to check whether the current piece being executed by T' is after p'. If so, piece p can proceed to execution without waiting for T' to commit. Each read of the spin variables (i.e., transaction status, transaction ID, or current piece identifier) is done without locking because the underlying memory instructions involving no more than 8-bytes are atomic. IC3 adds a memory barrier whenever a spin variable is modified.

Apart from the default spin-wait strategy, we also explored a suspend-wait strategy in which a worker thread suspends a blocked transaction to execute others. The implementation of suspend-wait is done using C++ co-routines. If a piece needs to wait, the worker thread puts the current transaction in the thread's pending queue and switches to execute other runnable transactions (that the worker has previously suspended) or a new one. We implement the pending queue as a lock-free queue so that suspending a transaction will not block other worker threads.

We choose spin-wait as the default strategy because it leads to better performance in our experiments. For example, when running TPC-C new-order transactions with 64 worker threads accessing one warehouse, the spin-wait strategy has 2.14X throughput than the suspend-wait strategy (340K TPS vs. 158K TPS). This is because the overhead of the context switching and lock-free queue manipulation out-weights the overhead of spin-wait for short waits which are the case in TPC-C. Suspend-wait may be beneficial for workloads involving long waits.

5.3 Secondary Index Implementation

The current implementation of IC3 relies on users to update and lookup in secondary indexes, similar to what is done in Silo [48] and Calvin [16]. Specifically, users need to represent each secondary index as a separate table that maps secondary keys to the records' primary keys. To ensure consistency, one must access the secondary index table in the same user transaction that reads or writes the base table. For example, in our implementation of the TPC-C benchmark, the new-order transaction inserts into the base *order table* and then inserts to the *order table*'s secondary index, all in the same transaction. Because secondary indexes are read or updated as part of regular user transactions, we can use the same static analysis and runtime implementation.

6. EVALUATION

This section measures the performance and scalability of IC3. We first compare IC3 to OCC and 2PL using microbenchmarks and TPC-C. We use the OCC implementation of Silo [48]. We implement 2PL ourselves by associating each record with a scalable read-write lock [4]. Then, we present the comparison with other alternatives with contended workloads. Last, we analyze the effect of different optimization methods. Due to space limitation, we leave evaluations on the TPC-E benchmark, the effect of user-initiated aborts (which may cascade) and transitive dependencies in the technical report [50].

6.1 Experiment Setup

Hardware. Our experiments are conducted on a 64-core AMD machine with 8 NUMA nodes. Each node has 8 cores (Opteron-6474). Each core has a private 16KB L1 cache and every two cores share a 2MB L2 cache. Each NUMA node has a 8MB L3 cache and 16GB local memory (128GB in total). The machine runs a 64-bit 4.0.5 Linux kernel.

Workloads and metrics. This evaluation includes two benchmarks, a microbenchmark which does simple updates and the TPC-C [44] benchmark. We use TPC-C to compare the performance of IC3 with alternatives.

For each benchmark, we first evaluate the performance of IC3 with increasing contention rate. Then, we study system scalability under high contention.

Throughput is the primary metric in this evaluation. Every trial is run for a fixed duration (i.e., 30 seconds) to record a *sustainable throughput.* We manually pin each thread to a single core, and ensure that the number of worker threads equals to the number of cores. When disk logging is enabled, IC3 can only scale up to 16 cores due to the limitation of I/O bandwidth (two disks) in our test machine; thus, we disable logging by default.

6.2 Microbenchmark

We begin our evaluation with a simple microbenchmark involving one type of transaction. Each transaction executes a controllable number of pieces and each different piece accesses a different table. Each piece randomly updates 4 distinct records from the same table. Each piece is protected using 2PL. To avoid deadlock, the records are sorted when each piece starts. Each table has 1M records. Each record has a 100-byte value and a 64-bit primary key.

[4]Our implementation of 2PL eliminates the chance of deadlock by sorting the locks in a consistent order

For each piece, the contention rate is controlled by varying the selection scope of its first operation between 10 and 1M. When a piece selects a record out of 10, it has 10% contention rate. Figure 8(a) shows the performance of workloads with each transaction with moderate size (10 pieces). When the selecting scope is 1,000,000 (contention rate is nearly 0), IC3's throughput is about 15% lower than that of 2PL and OCC (167K vs. 196K vs. 189K TPS). This extra cost is mainly from manipulating the linked list for dependency tracking. When the contention rate increases to 1% with 100 records to select from, the performance of IC3 remains unchanged (167K TPS) , while 2PL and OCC have 23% and 52% performance slowdown accordingly (149K vs. 196K and 93K vs.189K TPS). OCC's performance drops greater than 2PL because the 1% contention rate among pieces can cause 65% transaction aborts in OCC. When the contention rate is greater than 1%, IC3's performance degrades more gracefully. With 10% contention rate, IC3 has 45% performance loss, (90K vs. 167K TPS), while the throughput of 2PL and OCC drops 86% and 90% respectively (27K vs. 196K and 18K vs. 189K TPS).

We also evaluate IC3's performance speedup with concurrent execution under highly contended workload. Figure 8(b) shows the throughput improvement under highly contented workload (10% abort rate) with an increasing number of worker threads. The throughput of IC3 keeps growing to 64 worker threads, while 2PL and OCC can only scale to 16 cores. With 64 worker threads, IC3 outperforms its single thread version by 9X (90K vs. 9.9K TPS), while 2PL gets 3X speedup (29K vs. 10K TPS) and OCC only gets 1.5X speedup (16K vs. 10K TPS).

We also analyze the effect of transaction length on performance. For the workload with short transactions having only 2 pieces, it has 70% performance degradation when the contention rate is increased from 0 to 10% (1350K vs. 410K TPS). Under high contention level with 10% abort rate, IC3 achieves 10X speedup with 64 worker threads compared with the performance with only 1 thread (43K TPS vs. 410K TPS). For the workload with the longer transaction containing 64 pieces, it has 37% performance degradation when the contention rate is increased from 0 to 10% (23K vs. 15K TPS). For highly contended workloads with 10% abort rate, IC3 achieves 15X speedup (1K vs. 15K TPS) over a single thread. IC3 can improve the workloads' performance for workload under high contention regardless of the number of pieces in the transaction. However, IC3 achieves more speedup for longer transactions.

6.3 TPC-C

In the TPC-C benchmark, three out of five transactions are read-write transactions that are included in the static analysis and processed by IC3's main protocol. The SC-graph is shown in Appendix B. The other two are read-only transactions and are supported by the same snapshot mechanism in Silo [48]. In TPC-C, we decrease the number of warehouses from 64 to 1 to increase the contention rate. When there are 64 warehouses, each worker thread is assigned with a local warehouse, so each thread will make most of the orders using its local warehouse. Only a small fraction of transactions will access remote warehouses. When there is only one warehouse, all worker threads make orders from this global shared warehouse, suggesting a high contention rate.

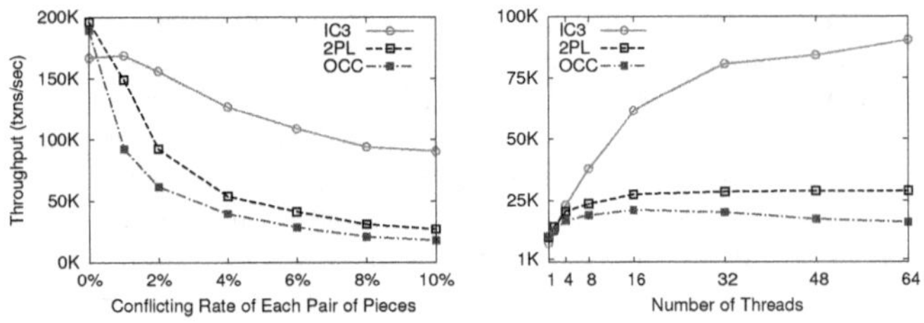

(a) Throughput with increasing contention rate.

(b) Throughput with increasing number of worker threads.

Figure 8: *Microbenchmark*

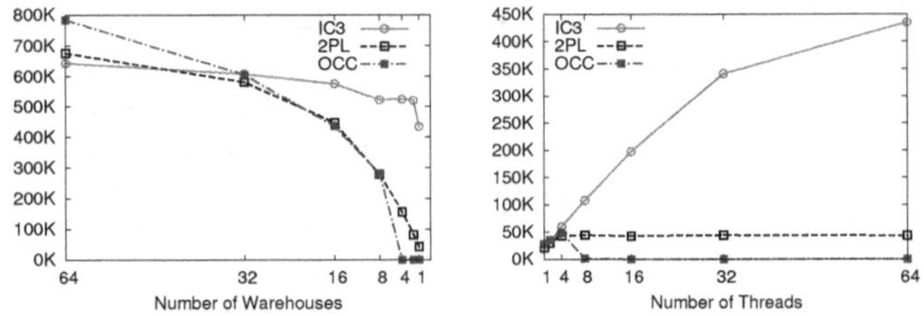

(a) Throughput with increasing contention rate.

(b) Throughput with increasing number of threads.

Figure 9: *TPC-C Benchmark*

Figure 9(a) shows throughput of 64 worker threads with the increasing contention rate. Under low contention, IC3's throughput is 6% lower than 2PL due to the overhead of dependency tracking. However, both IC3 and 2PL have around 15% performance degradation than OCC due to mandating locks on read-only accesses. For IC3, except manipulating the accessor list, it also needs to acquire the lock on read-only operations if the access is included in the conflict piece. For 2PL, it needs to acquire the read lock before each read-only access.

Under high contention rate, IC3 performs much better than 2PL and OCC. As the number of warehouses decreases to 1, the throughput of IC3 only drops by 32% (643K vs. 435KTPS). In contrast, the performance of 2PL and OCC degrades dramatically when the total number of warehouses is less than 16. OCC suffers 64% throughput degradation at 8 warehouses with 63% abort rate. When there are only 4 or less warehouses, OCC has only a few hundreds of TPS (e.g. 341 TPS for 4 warehouses) as the abort rate is more than 99%. For 2PL, its performance degrades 59% with 8 warehouses and 93% with 1 warehouse.

Figure 9(b) shows the scalability of IC3 when sharing a global warehouse. IC3 can scale to 64 threads with 22X speedup over one thread (435K vs. 19K TPS)). However, the performance is only improved by 27% from 32 cores to 64 cores. The major reason is that all payment transactions update the same warehouse record and contend on the same cache line. This can be further optimized by distributing the record, such as phase reconciliation [34]. One may find that IC3's scalability with TPC-C is better than in our microbenchmarks. This is because not all pieces' execution in TPC-C will be constraint (i.e., commutative pieces, read-only pieces and read-only transactions). Such pieces can be concurrently executed with the conflicting pieces, which increases the concurrency. Both OCC and 2PL can only scale to 4 cores, with 49K TPS and 43K TPS accordingly. After 4 threads, the performance of 2PL does not change notably, but the performance of OCC degrades drastically because conflicting transactions are frequently aborted.

6.4 Comparison with Alternative Approaches

This subsection continues to use TPC-C to compare IC3 with four important alternative approaches under highly contended workloads.

Transaction chopping: We first apply transaction chopping [41] to TPC-C and merge pieces to eliminate SC-cycles. Each merged piece is protected using 2PL or OCC. We also exclude C-edges between any commutative operations. Figure 10a shows the performance when all worker threads share a global warehouse. Transaction chopping with 2PL only gets marginal benefit compared to 2PL: it cannot scale beyond 8 threads, as most operations of new-order and delivery transaction need to be merged. After 8 threads, IC3 scales better than transaction chopping and its performance is 4X under 64 threads(435K vs. 100K TPS). When using OCC to protect the merged piece (Chopping-OCC in Figure 10a), it has similar performance as chopping-2PL when the number of threads is less than 8. With 8 worker threads, its performance is worse than chopping-2PL (75K vs. 99K TPS) due to piece aborts and retries. As contention further increases with more than 8 worker threads, the throughput of chopping-OCC degrades significantly.

Deterministic database with lazy evaluation: We also compare against the deterministic database with lazy evaluation [16]. Deterministic database divides each transaction into two phases: now phase and later phase. The system needs to execute all transactions' now phases sequentially to generate a global serialized order and analyze the dependency of their later phases. Then the later phases can be executed deterministically according to the dependency graph generated in the now phase. Execute high conflicting operations in the now phase can improve the temporal locality and increase the concurrency of later phases.

We use the implementation released with the paper. Figure 10b shows the scaling performance of deterministic database under one global TPC-C warehouse. We use one extra worker thread to run all the transaction's now phases and use the same number of worker threads with IC3 to run the later phase concurrently. We tune the setting such that the number of transaction can be buffered in the now phase and choose the threshold (i.e., 100) with the highest throughput. We issue 1M transactions to the system for processing to get the throughput result.

With a single thread, lazy evaluation is better than IC3 (38K vs. 19K TPS). This is because: 1) One extra thread is used to execute all highly contended operations which parallelise the execution and achieve good cache locality; 2) Some operations are deferred and even never executed; 3) Different code base for both benchmark and system implementation also contribute the performance difference. When the size of transaction batch is 100, their system achieves highest throughput under 16 worker threads (318K) [5]. However, its performance degrades after 16 threads and IC3 can even achieve better performance after 32 threads.

Using OCC to ensure serializability across pieces. We evaluate another strategy, called Nested OCC, that

[5]This number is lower than what is reported in [16] because their evaluation used a more powerful CPU (Intel Xeon E7-8850)

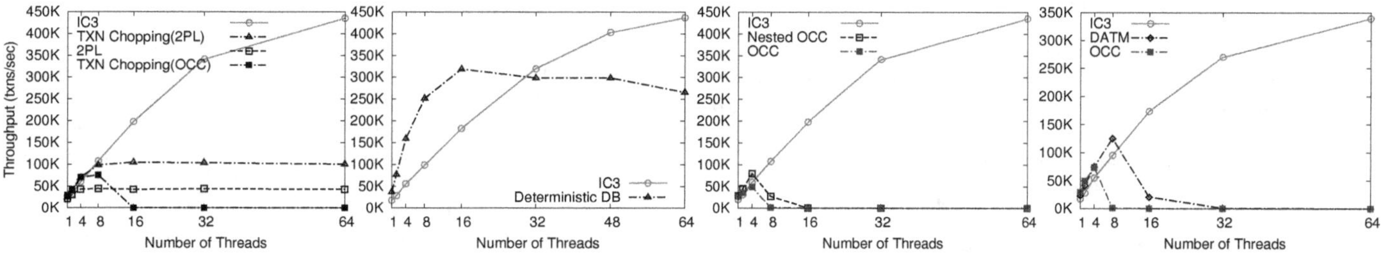

(a) Transaction chopping (b) *Lazy evaluation* (c) OCC across pieces (d) Dependency-aware OCC

Figure 10: *Comparison with prior approaches under high contention. New-order only for dependency-aware OCC*

chops each transaction into pieces and uses OCC to ensure atomicity within and across pieces. At the end of each piece, it validates the records read by the piece and retries the piece if validation fails. At the end of the transaction, it validates the records read in all pieces. Similar to IC3, commutative operations are not included in the conflicting pieces.

Figure 10c shows performance of Nested OCC for TPC-C under high contention. Since the contention within a piece only causes the re-execution of the piece instead of the whole transaction, Nested OCC has slower abort rate than OCC with 4 worker threads (15% vs. 42%). As a result, its performance is 62% better than OCC and 30% better than IC3 with 4 worker threads. With an increasing number of threads, the throughput of Nested OCC drops significantly like OCC due to dramatically increased abort rate. With 64 worker threads, its abort rate is 98% which is the same as OCC. This is because, with more worker threads, pieces are more likely to interleave in a non-serializable manner, thereby causing aborts. By contrast, as IC3 enforces the execution order among the concurrent conflicting pieces, thereby avoiding aborts and achieving good scalability with many threads.

Dependency-aware transactional memory (DATM) [36] is the last compared algorithm. Under DATM, a transaction can observe the update of conflicting uncommitted transactions. All conflicting transactions will commit successfully, if the interleaving of the conflicting operations are safe. However, this method also allows unsafe interleaving which will incur cascading abort.

We port DATM by modifying OCC to be dependency aware. Each record keeps an accessor list to track the accessed transactions. However, since original algorithm targets software transaction memory, we make slightly optimized choices for our implementation of DATM. Our implementation only keeps the memory pointers of the received or written value. We can check if a read is stale by checking the memory pointer, which saves the cost from memory compare. Like [36], we use timeout for deadlock prevention.

As DATM is designed for software transactional memory, it does not support range query and deletion. Thus we only evaluate it with new-order transactions in TPC-C under high contention: all workers share the same warehouse. After profiling with different timeout thresholds, we found the best performance can be achieved when the timeout threshold is set to 0.45 ms on our 2.2GHz CPU. Figure 10d shows the performance. We also include OCC and 2PL as reference. Since DATM can manage dependency among uncommitted conflicting transactions, DATM scales to 8 threads with 125K TPS, which is better than all others. With 8 threads, IC3 gets 95K TPS, while 2PL and OCC

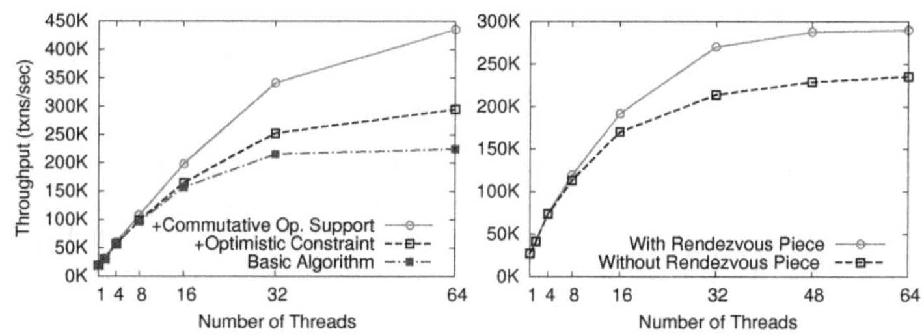

(a) Optimistic interleaving constraint & Defer the commutative operation. (b) Rendezvous piece

Figure 11: *Analysis the effect of each optimization method. Optimization is applied from bottom to top for each group.*

achieve 105K TPS and 1K TPS accordingly. However, the performance of DATM degrades with the increasing number of cores, mainly due to more cascading aborts and an increased cost per abort. With 16 threads, the abort rate is 81% and the abort rate increases to 99% (with 92% for observing an aborted transaction's update).

6.5 Factor Analysis

To understand the overhead and the benefit of each optimization, we show an analysis with TPC-C (Figure 11) when all threads share one warehouse (high contention). Figure 11a shows the analysis result. "Basic" is the performance of the basic algorithm(§ 3.2). Enforcing the interleaving optimistically ("+Optimistic Constraint") improves the performance by 32% with 64 threads (224K vs. 296K TPS). The performance is improved by 40% (296K vs. 435K) if we run the commutative operations without constraints.

Optimization with rendezvous piece. Because TPC-C contains no rendezvous pieces, we modified the benchmark to include a new transaction called *last-order-status*; it checks the status of the latest order made by some new-order transaction. This transaction contains three pieces: it first reads *next_o_id* from a random district, then uses this id to read records from the *ORDER* table, and lastly, it reads from the *ORDERLINE* table. The SC-graph involving new-order and last-order-status is shown in Figure 12 (Appendix B). The second and third pieces of last-order-status are rendezvous pieces for the new-order transaction. We configure a benchmark with 50% new-order and 50% last-order-status. Figure 11b shows the evaluation result. Compared with the basic protocol, the performance is improved by 23% with rendezvous piece with 64 cores (289K vs. 235K TPS).

7. RELATED WORK

One purpose of concurrency control is constraining interleavings among transactions to preserve some serial order, using various approaches like 2PL [1, 26, 8, 14], timestamp ordering [10, 5, 29] and commit ordering [37, 38]. One main difference with prior approaches is that IC3 constrains interleavings at a much finer granularity, i.e., a transaction piece. This exposes more concurrency for database transactions, while still preserving serializability.

IC3 is built upon prior work on statically analyzing transactions to assist runtime concurrency control. Bernstein et al. [7, 6] use a conflict graph to analyze conflicting relationships among transaction operations and preserve serializability by predefining orders of transactions. However, they handle cyclic dependency by quiescing all other transactions other than a transaction in the cycle, while IC3 dynamically constrains interleaving of transaction pieces to preserve serializability, which may lead to more concurrency. Others have proposed decomposing transactions into pieces [18, 4, 13, 41]. To preserve serializability after chopping, Garcia-Molina [17] shows that if all pieces of a decomposed transaction commute, then a safe interleaving exists. This, however, is a strong condition and many OLTP workloads do not suffice. Shasha et al. [41] show that serializability can be preserved if there is no SC-cycle in an SC-graph. Zhang et al. [54] further extends this theory to achieve lower latency in distributed systems. In contrast, IC3 tracks dependency at runtime and constrain the interleaving with SC-graph. Cheung et al. [11] also use static analysis to optimize database applications. However they target the code quality of the database applications which are running on application servers.

There exist some approaches [36, 2] that try to improve performance by being aware of dependencies. Ordered sharing lock [2] allows transactions to hold locks concurrently. It ensures serializability by enforcing order protected operation and lock releasing must obey the lock acquired order . Ramadan et al. [36] developed a dependency aware software transactional memory. They avoid false aborts by tracking dependency. However, both permit unsafe interleaving which cause cascading aborts. IC3 only permits safe interleaving during the execution. Callas [52] is a piece of work done concurrently with ours that also constrains the interleaving of transaction pieces to ensure serializability. Although the basic algorithms of Callas, called runtime pipelining, is very similar to IC3, they are applied in different settings (distributed vs. multicore). Furthermore, the details of the algorithms are different, e.g. Callas does not support dynamic workloads via online analysis [50] and does not include the technique of § 4.1.

Deterministic database [47, 46, 45] leverages a sequencing layer to pre-assign a deterministic lock ordering to eliminate a commit protocol for distributed transactions. Faleiro et al. [16] proposes a deterministic database with lazy evaluation on multicore settings. However, they only allow concurrency after the system knows exactly the data accessed information [40]. Thus, the sequencing layer can become a performance bottleneck with large number of cores.

Recently, there has been work to re-schedule or reconcile conflicting transactions to preserve serializability. For example, Mu et al. [33] reduces conflicts by reordering conflicting pieces of contended transactions to achieve serializability. However, they require the entire dependency graph is generated to before reordering. This approach is not practicable on multicore settings. Narula et al. [34] utilize commutativity of special transaction pieces to mitigate centralized contention during data updating. Compared to this work, IC3 is more general and can be applied to general transactions.

Researchers have applied techniques to reduce or even eliminate concurrency control [24, 12, 3]. H-store and its relatives [42, 24, 20, 49] treat each partition as a standalone database; local transactions can run to completion without any concurrency control. Cross-partition transactions can then be executed using a global lock. Hence, performance highly depends on whether the partition of database fit the workload and the performance would degrade noticeably when cross-partition transactions increase [48]. Granola [12] requires no locking overhead for a special type of distributed transactions called independent transactions.

IC3 continues this line of research by optimizing transaction processing in multicore and in-memory databases [35, 25, 27, 28, 15, 48, 30, 55, 53]. Recently, some databases start to improve multicore scalability by eliminating centralized locks and latches [22, 23, 39, 21] for databases implemented using 2PL. However, the inherent limitation of 2PL such as read locking constrains its performance under in-memory settings. Several recent systems instead use OCC [1, 26] to provide speedy OLTP transactions, using fine-grained locking [48] or hardware transaction memory to protect the commit phase [29, 51]. As shown in this paper, IC3 notably outperforms both OCC and 2PL under contention.

Subasu et al. [43] describe a hybrid design by using several replicated database engines, each running on a subset of cores, where a primary handles normal requests and other synchronized replicas handle read-only requests. In this case, IC3 could be used to accelerate the primary copy. Dora [35] uses a thread-to-data assignment policy to run each piece accessing a partition to reduce contention on the centralized lock manager. Though it also decomposes the execution of a transaction into pieces, each piece still uses locks to ensure an execution as a whole, while each piece in IC3 executes concurrently with others rather than respecting the synchronization constraints.

8. CONCLUSION

Multi-core in-memory databases demand its concurrency control mechanism to extract maximum parallelism to utilize abundant CPU cores. This paper described IC3, a new concurrency control scheme that constrains interleavings of transaction pieces to preserve serializability while allowing parallel execution under contention. The key idea of IC3 is to combine static analysis with runtime techniques to track and enforce dependencies among concurrent transactions. To demonstrate its effectiveness, we have implemented IC3 and evaluations on a 64-core machine using TPC-C showed that IC3 has better and more scalable performance than OCC, 2PL, and other recently proposed concurrent control mechanisms under moderate or high levels of contention.

Acknowledgements. The authors would like to thank Dennis Shasha, Lidong Zhou and all the reviewers for their insightful comments and feedback on this work. This work is supported in part by National Science Foundation under award CNS–1218117.

References

[1] D. Agrawal, A. J. Bernstein, P. Gupta, and S. Sengupta. Distributed optimistic concurrency control with reduced rollback. *Distributed Computing*, 2(1):45–59, 1987.

[2] D. Agrawal, A. El Abbadi, R. Jeffers, and L. Lin. Ordered shared locks for real-time databases. *The VLDB Journal*, 4(1):87–126, 1995.

[3] P. Bailis, A. Fekete, M. J. Franklin, A. Ghodsi, J. M. Hellerstein, and I. Stoica. Coordination avoidance in database systems. *Proceedings of the VLDB Endowment*, 8(3), 2014.

[4] A. J. Bernstein, D. S. Gerstl, and P. M. Lewis. Concurrency control for step-decomposed transactions. *Information Systems*, 24(8):673–698, 1999.

[5] P. A. Bernstein, V. Hadzilacos, and N. Goodman. *Concurrency control and recovery in database systems.* Addison-wesley New York, 1987.

[6] P. A. Bernstein and D. W. Shipman. The correctness of concurrency control mechanisms in a system for distributed databases (sdd-1). *ACM Transactions on Database Systems (TODS)*, 5(1):52–68, 1980.

[7] P. A. Bernstein, D. W. Shipman, and J. B. Rothnie Jr. Concurrency control in a system for distributed databases (SDD-1). *ACM Transactions on Database Systems (TODS)*, 5(1):18–51, 1980.

[8] H. Boral, W. Alexander, L. Clay, G. Copeland, S. Danforth, M. Franklin, B. Hart, M. Smith, and P. Valduriez. Prototyping bubba, a highly parallel database system. *Knowledge and Data Engineering, IEEE Transactions on*, 2(1):4–24, 1990.

[9] S. Boyd-Wickizer, M. F. Kaashoek, R. Morris, and N. Zeldovich. Non-scalable locks are dangerous. In *Linux Symposium*, 2012.

[10] M. J. Carey. Modeling and evaluation of database concurrency control algorithms. 1983.

[11] A. Cheung, S. Madden, A. Solar-Lezama, O. Arden, and A. C. Myers. Using program analysis to improve database applications. *IEEE Data Eng. Bull.*, 37(1):48–59, 2014.

[12] J. Cowling and B. Liskov. Granola: low-overhead distributed transaction coordination. In *Proceedings of the 2012 USENIX conference on Annual Technical Conference*, pages 21–21. USENIX Association, 2012.

[13] C. T. Davies. Data processing spheres of control. *IBM Systems Journal*, 17(2):179–198, 1978.

[14] D. J. DeWitt, S. Ghandeharizadeh, D. A. Schneider, A. Bricker, H.-I. Hsiao, and R. Rasmussen. The gamma database machine project. *Knowledge and Data Engineering, IEEE Transactions on*, 2(1):44–62, 1990.

[15] C. Diaconu, C. Freedman, E. Ismert, P.-A. Larson, P. Mittal, R. Stonecipher, N. Verma, and M. Zwilling. Hekaton: SQL ServerâĂŹs memory-optimized OLTP engine. In *Proc. SIGMOD*, 2013.

[16] J. M. Faleiro, A. Thomson, and D. J. Abadi. Lazy evaluation of transactions in database systems. In *Proceedings of the 2014 ACM SIGMOD international conference on Management of data*, pages 15–26. ACM, 2014.

[17] H. Garcia-Molina. Using semantic knowledge for transaction processing in a distributed database. *ACM Transactions on Database Systems (TODS)*, 8(2):186–213, 1983.

[18] H. Garcia-Molina and K. Salem. *Sagas*, volume 16. ACM, 1987.

[19] J. Gray and A. Reuter. Transaction processing: concepts and techniques, 1993.

[20] S. Harizopoulos, D. J. Abadi, S. Madden, and M. Stonebraker. OLTP through the looking glass, and what we found there. In *Proc. SIGMOD*, pages 981–992. ACM, 2008.

[21] T. Horikawa. Latch-free data structures for DBMS: design, implementation, and evaluation. In *Proc. SIGMOD*, pages 409–420. ACM, 2013.

[22] R. Johnson, I. Pandis, N. Hardavellas, A. Ailamaki, and B. Falsafi. Shore-MT: a scalable storage manager for the multicore era. In *Proc. EDBT*, pages 24–35. ACM, 2009.

[23] H. Jung, H. Han, A. D. Fekete, G. Heiser, and H. Y. Yeom. A scalable lock manager for multicores. In *Proc. SIGMOD*, pages 73–84. ACM, 2013.

[24] R. Kallman, H. Kimura, J. Natkins, A. Pavlo, A. Rasin, S. Zdonik, E. P. Jones, S. Madden, M. Stonebraker, Y. Zhang, et al. H-store: a high-performance, distributed main memory transaction processing system. *VLDB Endowment*, 1(2):1496–1499, 2008.

[25] A. Kemper and T. Neumann. Hyper: A hybrid oltp&olap main memory database system based on virtual memory snapshots. In *Data Engineering (ICDE), 2011 IEEE 27th International Conference on*, pages 195–206. IEEE, 2011.

[26] H.-T. Kung and J. T. Robinson. On optimistic methods for concurrency control. *ACM Transactions on Database Systems (TODS)*, 6(2):213–226, 1981.

[27] P.-Å. Larson, S. Blanas, C. Diaconu, C. Freedman, J. M. Patel, and M. Zwilling. High-performance concurrency control mechanisms for main-memory databases. In *Proc. VLDB*, 2011.

[28] J. Lee, M. Muehle, N. May, F. Faerber, V. Sikka, H. Plattner, J. Krueger, and M. Grund. High-performance transaction processing in sap hana. *IEEE Data Eng. Bull.*, 36(2):28–33, 2013.

[29] V. Leis, A. Kemper, and T. Neumann. Exploiting Hardware Transactional Memory in Main-Memory Databases. In *Proc. ICDE*, 2014.

[30] J. Lindström, V. Raatikka, J. Ruuth, P. Soini, and K. Vakkila. Ibm soliddb: In-memory database optimized for extreme speed and availability. *IEEE Data Eng. Bull.*, 36(2):14–20, 2013.

[31] Y. Mao, E. Kohler, and R. T. Morris. Cache craftiness for fast multicore key-value storage. In *Proc. EuroSys*, pages 183–196, 2012.

[32] J. M. Mellor-Crummey and M. L. Scott. Algorithms for scalable synchronization on shared-memory multiprocessors. *ACM Transactions on Computer Systems (TOCS)*, 9(1):21–65, 1991.

[33] S. Mu, Y. Cui, Y. Zhang, W. Lloyd, and J. Li. Extracting more concurrency from distribted transactions. In *Proceedings of the 11th USENIX conference on Operating Systems Design and Implementation*, pages 479–494. USENIX Association, 2014.

[34] N. Narula, C. Cutler, E. Kohler, and R. Morris. Phase reconciliation for contended in-memory transactions. In *Proceedings of the 11th USENIX conference on Operating Systems Design and Implementation*, pages 511–524. USENIX Association, 2014.

[35] I. Pandis, R. Johnson, N. Hardavellas, and A. Ailamaki. Data-oriented transaction execution. *VLDB Endowment*, 3(1-2):928–939, 2010.

[36] H. E. Ramadan, I. Roy, M. Herlihy, and E. Witchel. Committing conflicting transactions in an stm. In *ACM Sigplan Notices*, volume 44, pages 163–172. ACM, 2009.

[37] Y. Raz. The principle of commitment ordering, or guaranteeing serializability in a heterogeneous environment of multiple autonomous resource managers using atomic commitment. In *VLDB*, volume 92, pages 292–312, 1992.

[38] Y. Raz. Serializability by commitment ordering. *Information processing letters*, 51(5):257–264, 1994.

[39] K. Ren, A. Thomson, and D. J. Abadi. Lightweight locking for main memory database systems. *Proceedings of the VLDB Endowment*, 6(2):145–156, 2012.

[40] K. Ren, A. Thomson, and D. J. Abadi. An evaluation of the advantages and disadvantages of deterministic database systems. *Proceedings of the VLDB Endowment*, 7(10):821–832, 2014.

[41] D. Shasha, F. Llirbat, E. Simon, and P. Valduriez. Transaction chopping: Algorithms and performance studies. *ACM Transactions on Database Systems (TODS)*, 20(3):325–363, 1995.

[42] M. Stonebraker, S. Madden, D. J. Abadi, S. Harizopoulos, N. Hachem, and P. Helland. The end of an architectural

era:(it's time for a complete rewrite). In *Proc. VLDB*, pages 1150–1160, 2007.
[43] T. Subasu and J. Alonso. Database engines on multicores, why parallelize when you can distribute. In *Proc. Eurosys*, 2011.
[44] The Transaction Processing Council. TPC-C Benchmark (Revision 5.9.0). http://www.tpc.org/tpcc/, 2007.
[45] A. Thomson and D. J. Abadi. The case for determinism in database systems. *Proceedings of the VLDB Endowment*, 3(1-2):70–80, 2010.
[46] A. Thomson and D. J. Abadi. Modularity and Scalability in Calvin. *IEEE Data Engineering Bulletin*, page 48, 2013.
[47] A. Thomson, T. Diamond, S.-C. Weng, K. Ren, P. Shao, and D. J. Abadi. Calvin: fast distributed transactions for partitioned database systems. In *Proceedings of the 2012 ACM SIGMOD International Conference on Management of Data*, pages 1–12. ACM, 2012.
[48] S. Tu, W. Zheng, E. Kohler, B. Liskov, and S. Madden. Speedy Transactions in Multicore In-Memory Databases. In *Proc. SOSP*, 2013.
[49] L. VoltDB. Voltdb technical overview, 2010.
[50] Z. Wang, S. Mu, Y. Cui, H. Yi, H. Chen, and J. Li. Scaling multicore databases via constrained parallel execution. Technical Report TR2016-981, New York University, 2016. http://ic3.news.cs.nyu.edu/techreport16.pdf.
[51] Z. Wang, H. Qian, J. Li, and H. Chen. Using restricted transactional memory to build a scalable in-memory database. In *Proc. EuroSys*, 2014.
[52] C. Xie, C. Su, C. Littley, L. Alvisi, M. Kapritsos, and Y. Wang. High-performance acid via modular concurrency control. In *Proceedings of the 25th Symposium on Operating Systems Principles*, pages 279–294. ACM, 2015.
[53] X. Yu, G. Bezerra, A. Pavlo, S. Devadas, and M. Stonebraker. Staring into the abyss: An evaluation of concurrency control with one thousand cores. *Proceedings of the VLDB Endowment*, 8(3):209–220, 2014.
[54] Y. Zhang, R. Power, S. Zhou, Y. Sovran, M. K. Aguilera, and J. Li. Transaction chains: achieving serializability with low latency in geo-distributed storage systems. In *Proc. SOSP*, pages 276–291. ACM, 2013.
[55] W. Zheng, S. Tu, E. Kohler, and B. Liskov. Fast databases with fast durability and recovery through multicore parallelism. In *Proceedings of the 11th USENIX conference on Operating Systems Design and Implementation*, pages 465–477. USENIX Association, 2014.

Appendix A: Proof

Definition: Let each S-edge in an SC-graph become directed following the chronological order of pieces. Also, repeatedly merge vertexes (pieces) connected by C-edges to a single vertex. Afterwards, a cycle in the graph is defined as an *x-cycle*. Similarly, a path is defined as an *x-path*.

FACT 1. *The offline static analysis ensures there is no x-cycle.*

We use the concept of serialization graph as a tool to prove serializability. A schedule is serializable iff the serialization graph is acyclic. Because we use OCC to protect the execution of each piece, if we consider each piece as a (sub-)transaction, we have the following property.

FACT 2. *The serialization graph of pieces is acyclic.*

If two pieces p_i and p_j from two different transactions are connected as $p_i \rightarrow p_j$ in the serialization graph, they have a chronological commit order as $t_c(p_i) < t_c(p_j)$, and p_i, p_j should be also connected by a C-edge in the SC-graph. We can denote the chronological commit order as $p_i \overset{c}{\rightarrow} p_j$.
If two pieces q_i and p_j are connected by an S-edge in the SC-graph, and q_i is ahead of p_i in chronological order, we denote this as $q_i \overset{s}{\rightarrow} p_j$.

FACT 3. *IC3 tracks per-record longest path in the serialization graph.*

If $T_i \rightarrow T_j$ (expanded as $p_i \rightarrow p_j$) is a longest path in the serialization graph, after p_j is committed, T_i will appear in T_j's depqueue. This also suggests that T_j will only enter its commit phase after T_i commits.

THEOREM 1. *The schedule of IC3 is serializable as it always generates acyclic serialization graph.*

Now we are going to prove IC3 is serializable by proving the serialization graph is acyclic. Assume there is a cycle in the serialization graph, let it be $T_1 \rightarrow T_2 \rightarrow ... \rightarrow T_n \rightarrow T_1$; We are going to prove that the cycle necessarily implies there is an x-cycle in the SC-graph, which leads to a contradiction to Fact 1.
Expand each transaction in the cycle $T_1 \rightarrow T_2 \rightarrow ... \rightarrow T_n \rightarrow T_1$ to pieces, as

$$q_1 \overset{s}{+} p_1 \overset{c}{\rightarrow} q_2 \overset{s}{+} p_2 \overset{c}{\rightarrow} ... \overset{c}{\rightarrow} q_n \overset{s}{+} p_n \overset{c}{\rightarrow} q_1$$

The symbol "$\overset{s}{+}$" above (between a pair of $q_i \overset{s}{+} p_i$) represents following three possible cases:

1. q_i and p_i are the same piece, i.e. $q_i = p_i$.
2. q_i and p_i are different pieces, they are connected by an S-edge, and q_i is chronologically ahead of p_i, denoted by $q_i \overset{s}{\rightarrow} p_i$.
3. q_i and p_i are different pieces, they are connected by an S-edge, and q_i is chronologically behind p_i, denoted by $q_i \overset{s}{\leftarrow} p_i$.

To simplify without loss of accuracy, we use the symbol $\overset{s}{\nrightarrow}$ to represent the combination of the first and second cases; $\overset{s}{\nleftarrow}$ to represent the first and third cases.

LEMMA 1. *No transaction in cycle can commit.*

According to Fact 3, the cycle $T_1 \rightarrow T_2 \rightarrow ... \rightarrow T_n \rightarrow T_1$ necessarily implies an chronological cycle in the commit order, i.e. $t_c(T_1) < t_c(T_2) < ... t_c(T_n) < t_c(T_1)$, which is not possible. According to IC3's protocol, a cycle in the serialization graph will necessarily cause a deadlock in transaction commit phase, which means no transaction is able to commit. Actually, such deadlock can never form in the first place. The following part explains that.

LEMMA 2. $\exists\ i : q_i \neq p_i$

Assume for every pair of q_i and p_i, they are the same piece. Then the cycle leads a contradiction: the cycle should not exist according to Fact 2.

LEMMA 3. $\exists\ i, j : q_i \overset{s}{\rightarrow} p_i$ *and* $p_j \overset{s}{\rightarrow} q_j$

Proof by contradiction. Without loss of generality, assume $\forall i : q_i \overset{s}{\rightarrow} p_i$. Then the cycle will necessary imply an x-cycle in static analysis, which contradicts with Fact 1.

LEMMA 4. *For a fragment* $p_i \overset{c}{\rightarrow} q_j \overset{s}{\rightarrow} p_j \overset{c}{\rightarrow} q_k$*, there will be a piece* r_i *in* T_i*, such that* $p_i \overset{c}{\rightarrow} r_i \overset{c}{\rightarrow} q_k$.

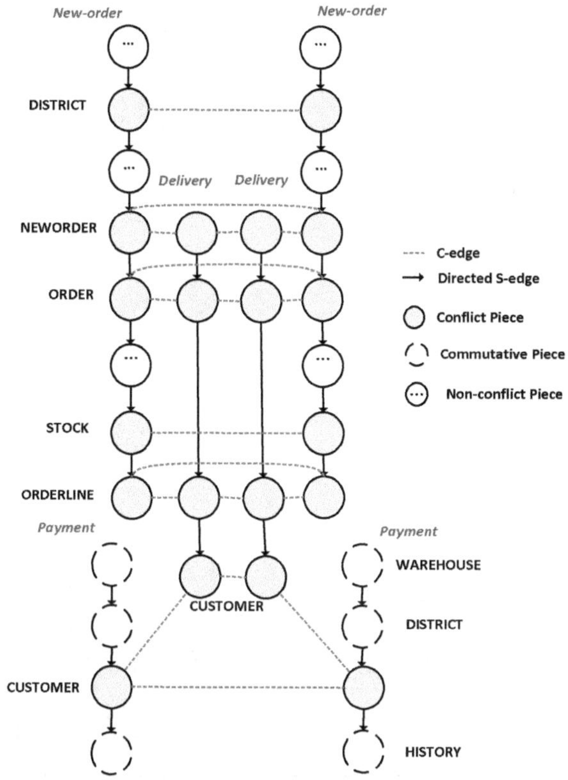

Figure 13: *The SC-graph of 3 Read Write Transactions in TPC-C*

$q_j \overset{s}{\rightarrow} p_j$ refers to that before p_j executes, q_j already commits, leaving T_i in T_j's depqueue. Therefore, when p_j commits, it shall either wait T_i commits, or it waits until all pieces in T_j that has C-connection to itself commits. According to Lemma 1 it has to be the latter case. Assume the last piece in T_i that has C-connection to p_j is r_i. r_i cannot be neither be p_i or any piece before p_i. Otherwise $r_i \overset{s}{\nrightarrow} p_i \overset{c}{\rightarrow} q_j \overset{s}{\rightarrow} p_j \overset{c}{\leftarrow} r_i$ will form a x-cycle, which contradicts with Fact 1.

With Lemma 4, we can inductively prove the cycle in serialization graph will necessarily implies an x-cycle in static analysis.

In the cycle:

$$q_1 \overset{s}{\not-} p_1 \overset{c}{\rightarrow} q_2 \overset{s}{\not-} p_2 \overset{c}{\rightarrow} \ldots \overset{c}{\rightarrow} q_n \overset{s}{\not-} p_n \overset{c}{\rightarrow} q_1$$

If there exists j that $q_j \overset{s}{\rightarrow} p_j$, without loss of generosity, we can safely assume $j = n$. We can shrink the cycle following Lemma 4, then the cycle becomes as follows.

$$q_1 \overset{s}{\not-} p_1 \overset{c}{\rightarrow} q_2 \overset{s}{\not-} p_2 \overset{c}{\rightarrow} \ldots \overset{c}{\rightarrow} q_{n-1} \overset{s}{\not-} p_{n-1} \overset{s}{\rightarrow} r_{n-1} \overset{c}{\rightarrow} q_1$$

Transform the above cycle into:

$$q_1^1 \overset{s}{\not-} p_1^1 \overset{c}{\rightarrow} q_2^1 \overset{s}{\not-} p_2^1 \overset{c}{\rightarrow} \ldots \overset{c}{\rightarrow} q_{n-1}^1 \overset{s}{\not-} p_{n-1}^1 \overset{c}{\rightarrow} q_1^1$$

Repeatedly reduce the cycle following Lemma 4, for m times ($m < n$), until we have:

$$q_1^m \overset{s}{\nleftarrow} p_1^m \overset{c}{\rightarrow} q_2^m \overset{s}{\nleftarrow} p_2^m \overset{c}{\rightarrow} \ldots \overset{c}{\rightarrow} q_{n-m}^m \overset{s}{\nleftarrow} p_{n-1}^m \overset{c}{\rightarrow} q_1^m$$

Consider each pair of $q_i^m \overset{s}{\nleftarrow} p_i^m$ in the above cycle, there exists at least one pair of q_i^m and p_i^m such that $q_i^m \neq p_i^m$. Otherwise we will have $q_1^m \overset{c}{\rightarrow} q_2^m \overset{c}{\rightarrow} \ldots \overset{c}{\rightarrow} q_{n-m}^m \overset{c}{\rightarrow} q_1^m$, which is not possible. Then means the above cycle necessarily implies an x-cycle in the SC-graph, which is a contradiction to the result of static analysis.
Q.E.D.

Appendix B: SC-graph of TPC-C benchmark

Figure 13 shows the SC-graph for the 3 read-write transactions in the TPC-C benchmark. Each piece includes at least one operation. For the delivery transaction, the for loop is split into four small loops and each one only accesses one table.
Figure 12 shows the SC-graph of a modified TPC-C benchmark including the new-order transaction with a new transaction called last-order-status.

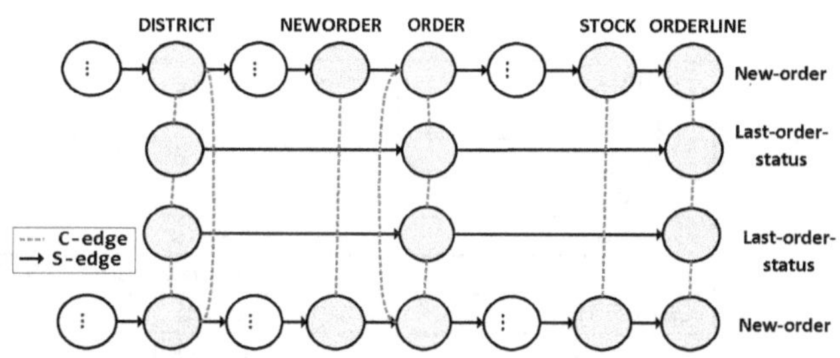

Figure 12: SC-graph with new-order and last-order-status

Appendix C: Web Applications Analysis

To determine if real-world applications can potentially benefit from IC3, we analyze the user-defined transactions in 14 most popular ruby-on-rails web applications on GitHub according to their GitHub stars. As most applications use the active record interface instead of SQL, we analyze the user defined transactions manually. Table 1 shows the results. 10 out of 14 applications have transactions that access more than one table. We construct the SC-graphs of these 11 applications and classify the SC-cycles found. As shown in Table 1, the SC-cycles found in most of these applications are *not* deadlock-prone. Thus, these workloads are likely to benefit from IC3. Even for workloads that contain deadlock-prone SC-cycles, there is much opportunity for parallel execution. For example, the most complex workload Canvas LMS has 46 user defined transactions, 30 of which access more than one table. Among these 46 transactions, 12 transactions are involved in a deadlock-prone SC-cycle. After merging the deadlock-prone SC-cycles into atomic pieces, there are still 20 transactions which have more than one conflicting piece. All of them can benefit from IC3.

Name	Description	Total	Mul-Tables	D-SC	Safe-SC	GitHub Stars
Canvas LMS	Education	46	30	12	20	1,542
Discourse	Community discussion	36	28	3	26	16,019
Spree	eCommerce	7	3	-	3	6,802
Diaspora	Social network	2	1	-	1	10,331
Redmine	Pro ject management	17	8	-	8	1,560
OneBody	Church portal	2	1	-	1	1,229
Community Engine	Social networking	2	-	-	-	1,117
Publify	Blogging	5	1	-	1	1,497
Browser CMS	Content management	4	3	-	3	1,200
GitLab	Code management	8	5	-	5	16,523
Insoshi	Social network	3	-	-	-	1,585
Teambox	Project management	4	1	-	1	1,873
Radiant	Content management	2	-	-	-	1,609
GitLab CI	Continuous integration	2	-	-	-	1,420

Table 1: Ruby-on-rails applications used in analysis (**Total**: the total number of user defined transactions in the workload. **Mul-Tables**: the number of transactions which access more than one table. **D-SC**: The number of transactions which are involved in a deadlock-prone SC-Cycle. **Safe-SC**: The number of transactions which are involved in a non-deadlock-prone SC-Cycle and can benefit from IC3. **GitHub stars** records the number of stars on GitHub as of October 2015.).

Towards a Non-2PC Transaction Management in Distributed Database Systems

Qian Lin[†] Pengfei Chang[§] Gang Chen[§] Beng Chin Ooi[†] Kian-Lee Tan[†] Zhengkui Wang[†¶*]

[†]National University of Singapore [§]Zhejiang University [¶]Singapore Institute of Technology

[†]{linqian, ooibc, tankl, wangzhengkui}@comp.nus.edu.sg [§]{changpeng3336, cg}@cs.zju.edu.cn

ABSTRACT

Shared-nothing architecture has been widely used in distributed databases to achieve good scalability. While it offers superior performance for local transactions, the overhead of processing distributed transactions can degrade the system performance significantly. The key contributor to the degradation is the expensive two-phase commit (2PC) protocol used to ensure atomic commitment of distributed transactions. In this paper, we propose a transaction management scheme called LEAP to avoid the 2PC protocol within distributed transaction processing. Instead of processing a distributed transaction across multiple nodes, LEAP converts the distributed transaction into a local transaction. This benefits the processing locality and facilitates adaptive data repartitioning when there is a change in data access pattern. Based on LEAP, we develop an online transaction processing (OLTP) system, L-Store, and compare it with the state-of-the-art distributed in-memory OLTP system, H-Store, which relies on the 2PC protocol for distributed transaction processing, and H^L-Store, a H-Store that has been modified to make use of LEAP. Results of an extensive experimental evaluation show that our LEAP-based engines are superior over H-Store by a wide margin, especially for workloads that exhibit locality-based data accesses.

1. INTRODUCTION

The past decade has witnessed an increasing interest in adopting shared-nothing database technology to handle fast growing business data. By horizontally partitioning data across different physical machines, shared-nothing systems are highly scalable for non-transactional and analytical workloads which are "embarrassingly partitionable". For OLTP workloads, shared-nothing systems conventionally depend on the 2PC protocol for preserving the atomicity and serializability of distributed transactions [31]. Although these systems offer superior performance for local transactions (i.e., transactions whose data are hosted on a single node), overhead of processing distributed transactions (i.e., transactions whose data are spread over multiple nodes) can degrade the system performance significantly [10, 26, 30]. The key contributor to the degradation is the 2PC protocol [20, 26, 3, 29]. To commit a distributed transaction, the 2PC protocol requires multiple network round-trips between all participant machines which typically take a much longer time than the local transaction processing. As such, much work has been done to address this bottleneck [10, 30]. On the one hand, systems such as Calvin [30] seek to improve the scalability of distributed transaction processing by trading latency for a higher throughput [30]. On the other hand, fine-grained partitioning of the data can be performed offline to reduce the number of distributed transactions [10]. These techniques can reduce but cannot eliminate distributed transactions completely and hence the expensive distributed commit procedure must still be performed.

In this paper, we propose *LEAP* (Localizing Executions via Aggressive Placement of data) as a solution towards non-2PC distributed transaction processing in a shared-nothing architecture, particularly in our epiC system [19]. LEAP converts a distributed transaction into a local transaction to eliminate the expensive distributed commit procedure. To localize the execution of a distributed transaction, LEAP aggressively places all cross-node data needed for the transaction on a single node (i.e., the node issuing the transaction). By doing so, the transaction executor would physically hold all the data it uses during the transaction execution and can easily commit or abort the transaction without worrying about the distributed consensus as in the 2PC protocol. We design LEAP in anticipation of the wide availability of modern fast networks (e.g., 10 Gigabit Ethernet, InfiniBand) to provide latency and bandwidth guarantees.

LEAP is motivated by the following key observations. First, OLTP queries typically involve only a small number of data records [5, 14, 25]. Therefore, the number of records to migrate is small. Second, depending on applications, the data record size may be comparable with the size of a "sub-transaction". This means it is no more expensive to migrate records to the processing node than sending sub-transactions to multiple nodes for processing. Third, data access in real-world distributed transactions typically exhibits some form of locality. For example, if a person accesses his/her domestic account when traveling overseas, it is likely that he/she will repeatedly access the data in this account via a series of transactions issued from his/her place of travel.

LEAP always maintains a single copy of each data record. Each distributed server manages two meta-data structures:

*This work was done while Zhengkui was at NUS.

SIGMOD '16, June 26–July 1, 2016, San Francisco, CA, USA.

ACM ISBN 978-1-4503-3531-7/16/06.

DOI: http://dx.doi.org/10.1145/2882903.2882923

data table and owner table. The *data table* stores the application's records in memory, and the *owner table* is a key-value store where each pair associates a record in the data table (identified by its primary key) with its access owner (i.e., a transaction server serving read/write requests for that record). At any time, each data record only has a single access owner. The owner table is partitioned among all transaction servers using standard distributed key-value store techniques. To process a transaction, a processing node S first searches its local storage and checks whether the data is in the local storage. If yes, the transaction is a local transaction and thus can be performed immediately. Otherwise, the transaction is a distributed transaction, and S will then send requests to the owners of those records and ask them to yield data ownership. When S collects all the required data ownership, it processes the transaction locally.

The contributions of this paper are threefold:

- We propose LEAP, a transaction management scheme that localizes any distributed transaction processing to a single node. LEAP facilities efficient distributed transaction processing by eliminating the need of costly distributed commit protocol and inter-node intermediate results exchange during transaction processing.
- Based on LEAP, we propose a practical OLTP engine designed for a shared-nothing database architecture. Specifically, we provide the detailed techniques of enabling LEAP by using a ownership transfer scheme and ensuring concurrency control by employing a lock-based mechanism.
- We conduct extensive experiments to evaluate our LEAP-based systems against a 2PC-based system, H-Store, on a cluster of 64 machines. Results show that LEAP-based transaction processing outperforms that of 2PC-based approach in terms of throughput, latency and scalability.

The rest of the paper is organized as follows: Section 2 introduces distributed transaction processing using the 2PC protocol. In Section 3, we present our proposed LEAP protocol. In Section 4, we provide the system design of the LEAP-based OLTP engine. Section 5 presents results of an experimental study. We discuss related works in Section 6 and conclude in Section 7.

2. PRELIMINARIES

Transactions in a shared-nothing database are classified into two types: *local transactions*, which only access data within a single node, and *distributed transactions*, which access data spanning multiple nodes. Local transactions are efficient to process while distributed transactions are expensive due to the cost of the 2PC protocol typically used to enforce atomicity.

Figure 1 shows an example of 2PC-based transaction processing. This example will also be used to illustrate our proposed strategy in the next section. In Figure 1, the database has two partitions served by two nodes S_1 and S_2. A transaction T submitted at S_1 will access data records r_1 and r_2 stored in two partitions. Here, S_1 (the node where T is submitted) serves as the *coordinator* and S_2 as a *participant*. Then, a two-step strategy is employed to execute T.

(Step 1) Task Distribution: The coordinator first divides the transaction into multiple sub-transactions, each of which is sent to one participant for execution. In our example, T is divided into T_1 and T_2 where T_1 is executed at the coordinator and T_2 is executed at the participant. Therefore, in this step, the coordinator sends a message containing the sub-transaction T_2 to the participant for execution (message 1 in Figure 1).

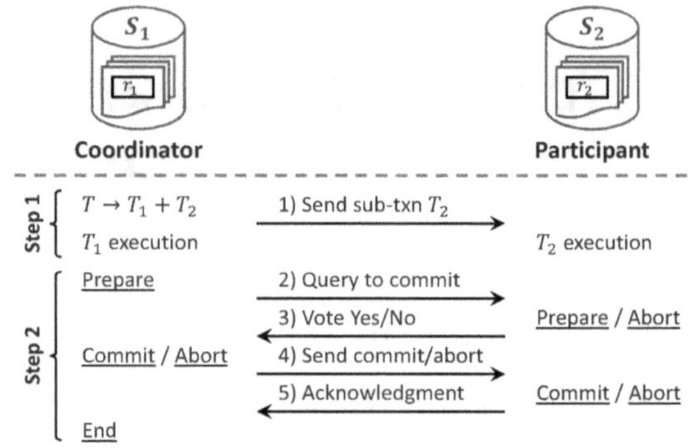

Figure 1: Distributed transaction processing with 2PC. The underlined operations need to force-write related log entries to stable storage.

(Step 2) Atomic Commit: When the transaction is ready to commit, it enters into the commit step consisting of the voting phase and the completion phase. In the voting phase, the coordinator polls all participants for their readiness to commit (message 2 in Figure 1), and waits for their responses. Meanwhile, after receiving the request, each participant replies with its vote (Yes or No) to the coordinator (message 3 in Figure 1). Before voting positively, the participant prepares to commit by persisting changes to stable storage. Otherwise, the participant aborts immediately. In the completion phase, the coordinator collects all the votes. If all the votes are Yes, the coordinator decides to commit and sends a global commit message to all the participants. Otherwise, it sends an abort message to all the participants (message 4 in Figure 1). Each participant acts accordingly based on the decision it receives and the acknowledgement message is sent to the coordinator.

The 2PC protocol is simple but introduces significant delay due to the communication costs and uncertainty. During the execution, all communications between the coordinator and the participants are achieved by inter-node messages. In our running example, each participant incurs at least four messages. Note that the protocol can still function correctly without the acknowledgement message (message 5 in Figure 1) which is used to enable servers to delete stale coordinator information. Furthermore, participants may be blocked for a long time when failures occur. This happens when the coordinator and at least one participant fail after all non-failed nodes voted Yes; these nodes have no clue about the global decision – it could be a commit decision (if the failed nodes have voted Yes) or an abort decision (if the failed nodes have not voted or voted No). Moreover, for complex multistep transactions, the 2PC-based processing may have to exchange intermediate results among the coordinator and the participants, which would incur additional inter-node message passing.

3. DISTRIBUTED TRANSACTION PROCESSING: THE LEAP WAY

In this section, we present LEAP for distributed transaction processing. We first give an overview of LEAP, and then describe the data structure and protocol to realize it.

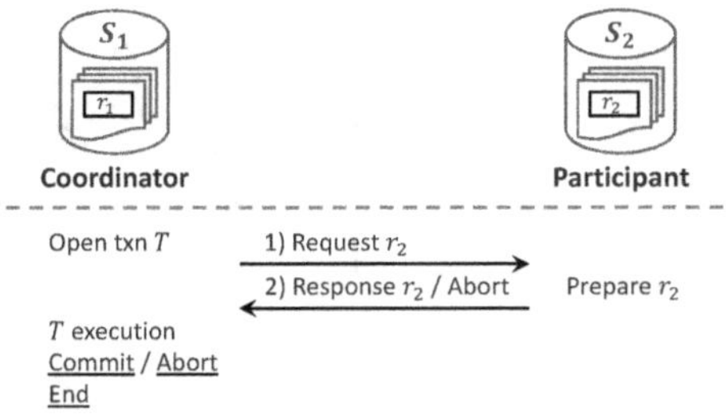

Figure 2: An overview of LEAP for distributed transaction processing.

3.1 The Big Picture

The main goal of LEAP is to eliminate the expensive 2PC protocol. What LEAP does is to do away with 2PC completely by turning all distributed transactions into local transactions. To achieve this, LEAP aggressively migrates data requested by a distributed transaction to a single node at runtime. In other words, the system dynamically places data at the nodes where the transactions need them.

LEAP employs the concept of an *owner* of a record.

Definition 1 (Owner). Given a data record r, the owner of r is the single server node S where r is placed. Moreover, S is granted exclusive access to r.

By definition, except for the owner, no other servers can access the data record and, at any given time, each record is assigned to a unique owner. Therefore, if a node S_1 wants to access a record r owned by another node S_2, it has to issue a request to S_2 for ownership transfer. When S_2 gives up its ownership of r, it sends r to S_1; only then can S_1 access r, which turns out to be a local access.

Under LEAP, a distributed transaction is processed as follows: the coordinator (where the transaction is submitted) aggressively requests from the participants for the data to be migrated to its site; once these data are placed at the coordinator site, it executes the transaction locally. To illustrate this idea, we refer the reader to the previous running example again. In Figure 1, data are partitioned into two partitions that are placed at two nodes, S_1 and S_2, which own records r_1 and r_2 respectively. To execute the transaction T which accesses r_1 and r_2, as shown in Figure 2, the coordinator S_1 triggers a migration process to S_2 by requesting to be the owner of r_2 (i.e, message 1 in Figure 2). Once S_2 receives the request, it decides whether the transfer can be carried out. If the migration can be performed, S_2 transfers the ownership of r_2 to S_1, by transmitting to S_1 a ownership transfer granted message (i.e., message 2 in Figure 2) along with the requested data (i.e., r_2). At this point, S_1 owns all data requested by T and processes T locally. When T commits, it commits locally without interfering other distributed nodes. Comparing with 2PC, LEAP uses fewer messages (two in this example) to execute the transaction and thus reduces the processing latency.

At first sight, it seems that LEAP's aggressive dynamic data placement approach is costly. However, this strategy is practical and feasible due to three reasons. First, OLTP queries only touch a small number of data records. Therefore, the cost of transferring data is comparable to the communication overhead under 2PC (In 2PC, we need to transfer sub-transactions as well as the intermediate results). Second, advances in networking technologies such as 10 Gigabit Ethernet and InfiniBand continually reduces the time required for data transmission. Third, subsequent transactions in the same node that access the same records can avoid remote accesses. Therefore, it is worthwhile to trade a little bit more data transmission for fewer inter-node messages.

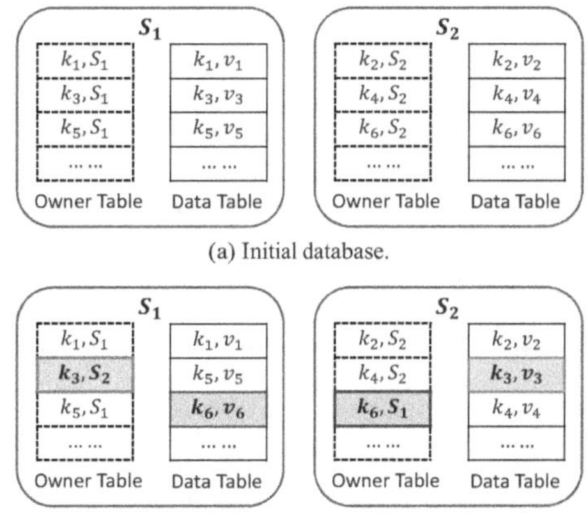

(b) After ownership transfer.

Figure 3: Example of ownership transfer.

The LEAP design and the analytical model assume modern network infrastructure which offers sufficient bandwidth and low-latency communication. Such fast networks are widely available in most local area networks (LANs).

3.2 Managing Ownership and Data Placement

The first challenge to realize LEAP is to ensure that the ownership and data placement can be effectively managed. For example, how can we find the location of a record if it is being moved frequently? Towards this end, we decouple the meta-data (on ownership) from the data, and employ two types of tables: an *owner table* which maintains owner information and a *data table* which stores the actual data records. For each record, represented as a key-value pair $r = (k, v)$, we store two pieces of information in the aforementioned two tables: 1) a data owner record $r_o = (k, o)$ where o is the identifier (e.g., IP address) of the owner of r in the owner table, and 2) a data record $r_d = (k, v)$ in the data table. The owner table is partitioned across all nodes using any standard data partitioning techniques (e.g., hash or range) on k. The data table is also partitioned across the nodes; however, a data record r_d is stored at its owner's local data table.

Initially, a record r's owner is assigned to the node that hosts the owner record r_o, namely r_d is stored along with r_o. Subsequently, whenever ownership transfer occurs, the data record r_d will be moved to its new owner's local data table. The owner record r_o, on the other hand, is never moved; instead, it remains at the node where the record was initially placed. The owner record r_o is essentially used for tracking the current owner of r.

Figure 3.a shows the initial storage layout of a cluster, where the data and its corresponding owner information are stored in the same node in S_1 or S_2. Figure 3.b shows the updated storage layout after some ownership transfers. For instance, after record $\langle k_3, v_3 \rangle$ is migrated from S_1 to S_2, the owner information still remains in S_1 with an updated owner information. Similarly, transferring record $\langle k_6, v_6 \rangle$ to S_1 results in the new owner information in S_2.

To minimize storage utilization, there is actually no need to physically store the owner information when the records and the owner information collocate. Only when a record is transferred to other nodes do we need to maintain its owner information in the owner table. In other words, by default the owner of one record is the node that holds its owner information. For example, under this optimized scheme, all entries in the owner tables of both S_1 and S_2 are eliminated in Figure 3.a, and only entries of $\langle k_3, S_2\rangle$ and $\langle k_6, S_1\rangle$ remain in the owner tables of S_1 and S_2 respectively in Figure 3.b. Furthermore, a good partitioning strategy of the keys may reduce the size of the owner table, as most records may remain in the node where they were initially placed.

3.3 Ownership Transfer

Our proposed LEAP scheme exploits an ownership transfer protocol. To introduce the ownership transfer protocol, we first provide the following definitions.

Definition 2 (Requester). A node is referred to as the *requester*, if the node requests data that are owned by other nodes.

Definition 3 (Partitioner). A node is referred to as the *partitioner* of a record r, if the node holds the ownership information of r.

Recall that given a transaction T, if the node is the owner of all the data that T requires, the transaction can be directly executed by the node without incurring any ownership transfer. Ownership transfer only happens when the node needs to request the data owned by other nodes. To transfer ownership from other nodes, the requester runs a ownership transfer protocol which conceptually consists of the following 4 steps.

- *Owner Request:* The partitioner figures out who the current owner of the requesting record is by performing a standard key-value lookup over the owner table.
- *Transfer Request:* After finding the current owner of the record, the ownership transfer request is sent to the owner to request for ownership transfer to the requester.
- *Response:* Once the owner receives the ownership transfer request, it checks the status of the requesting data. When the ownership cannot be granted to the requester (e.g., due to contention[1]), the owner sends a reject message to the requester. Otherwise, the owner sends a response message to the requester along with the requested data. Once the data is sent to the requester, it automatically becomes invalidated at the old owner's node that will be garbage collected in the future.
- *Inform:* After receiving the data, the requester informs the partitioner to update the ownership with respect to the ownership transfer. Note that during the above three steps, the ownership is not updated in the partitioner. Only when the ownership is transferred successfully and the inform message is received, then will the partitioner update the ownership accordingly. This guarantees the ownership consistency in terms of node failure during the ownership transfer. Moreover, the requester will also inform the partitioner about the failure of ownership transfer if either the owner request or the transfer request is rejected (e.g., due to concurrency control); and the partitioner will retain the ownership. Therefore, the ownership of data is maintained in a consistent state.

[1]Contention happens when multiple transactions request the same record and cannot be granted together. To prevent deadlock, one of the transactions has to abort. More details will be discussed in Section 4.1.2.

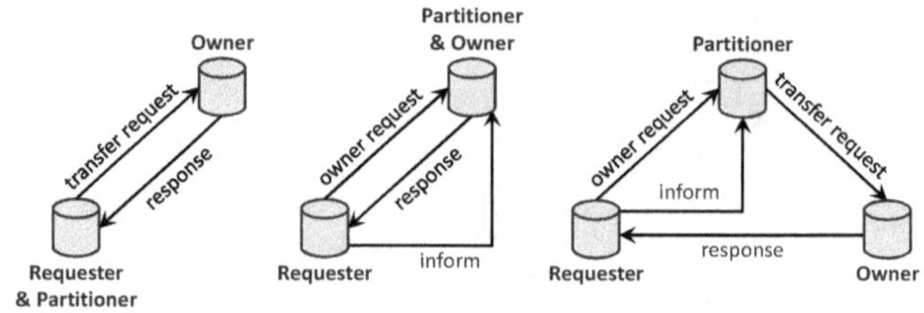

(a) RP-O. (b) R-PO. (c) R-P-O.

Figure 4: Ownership transfer cases.

Before a message is transmitted, it is logged locally at the sender site. When failure happens, any message loss is handled by resending the message after a predetermined timeout period. Note that the response step is the only step that may lead to data loss. To address this issue, we allow the original owner to maintain a backup of the invalidated data for a longer timeout until deletion. Therefore, when the response message is lost, the original owner can recover the data. Appendix D provides more details on how message loss is handled in LEAP.

The above four steps compose the general processing procedure for handling one ownership transfer. For ownership transfer, there are three different situations depending on who the requester, partitioner and owner are. Figure 4 illustrates these three situations, namely RP-O, R-PO and R-P-O. They may incur different overheads with respect to the number of remote messages generated. RP-O is when the requester is the same as the partitioner. In this case, the owner request step and the inform step are efficiently conducted within the requester itself, and the other two steps can be achieved by using two inter-node messages. R-PO arises when the partitioner remains the same as the owner but is different from the requester. In this case, each of the owner request, response and inform steps needs one inter-node message. In R-P-O, when the requester, partitioner and owner are three different nodes, each step utilizes one inter-node message.

Recall that once the requester obtains the ownership of the data, it automatically becomes the owner of the data. The owner will own and keep the data locally as long as the ownership is not transferred to others. This ensures the data can serve multiple instances of the same transactions at the owner node and avoids frequent data transfer.

For ease of discussion, we first consider data access via primary key. How to support data access via non-primary keys in the ownership transfer of LEAP is discussed in Appendix B.

3.4 Comparison with 2PC

Benefiting from the modern high speed network technology, the latency of network transmission becomes nearly indistinguishable for transferring small data (e.g., a tuple or an SQL statement). Given the fact that network I/O still remains orders of magnitude slower than main memory operation, the number of sequential messages passed mainly determines the cost of distributed in-memory transaction processing. As can be seen from Figure 1 and Figure 4, LEAP shows its superiority over 2PC in terms of the number of sequential messages passed.

3.4.1 Theoretical Analysis

To better appreciate LEAP-based transaction processing, we further provide a theoretical analysis with regards to the *latency expectation* of each individual transaction to evaluate the transaction processing efficiency of the two different techniques. Here, the latency consists of two components: transaction processing and transaction commit. We ignore the cost of sending query statement in the initial stage since its cost is the same for both LEAP and 2PC. Appendix C summarizes the notations used throughout the analysis.

To simplify the analysis and focus on the comparison between LEAP and 2PC, we make the following assumptions:

- **(A1)** Time for local processing is negligible compared with the distributed data communication. In other words, the cost of distributed data communication dominates the overall performance.
- **(A2)** The cost of sending an SQL query is the same as the cost of sending one tuple. This assumption generally holds due to the fast networking enabled by modern network infrastructure.
- **(A3)** Each OLTP transaction only accesses a small subset of the entire database, and does not perform full table scans or large distributed joins [25]. Specifically, we assume each transaction performs n data accesses whose footprints (e.g., keys of the tuples) are given in the transaction statement. In particular, for a LEAP transaction, all its data accesses can be processed in parallel since all its required tuples are known upfront, and thus the expected latency of one data access reflects the expected latency of all the n data accesses within the transaction.

Consider a partition-based database. We define data access to be *local* if the data being accessed was initially assigned to the node that the transaction is currently running on. Otherwise, data access is defined to be *remote*. Note that though LEAP would migrate data during transaction processing, the above definitions always refer to the initial state of database partitioning. Moreover, we further define whether a remote data access is with locality. Suppose node S_1 requests data r from node S_2. This remote data access is referred to be *with locality* if r will be only accessed by transactions in S_1 in the near future. In contrast, it is referred to be *without locality* if r will be frequently requested by nodes other than S_1.

First, we consider the LEAP-based transaction processing. Let $P(R)$ be the probability of data access being remote and $P(L|R)$ be the probability of remote data access with locality. Then the probabilities of different types of data access are calculated as follows:

- $P_l = 1 - P(R)$: probability of local data access.
- $P_{rl} = P(R) \cdot P(L|R)$: probability of remote data access with locality.
- $P_{rnl} = P(R) \cdot \big(1 - P(L|R)\big)$: probability of remote data access without locality.

Accordingly, we analyze the cost estimation of each type of data access. For local data access, based on assumption A1, the cost only includes accessing the data that are previously transferred to other nodes via remote data access without locality. Thus, the cost of the local data access can be calculated as

$$t_l = \alpha \cdot X \cdot P(R) \cdot \big(1 - P(L|R)\big)$$

where α is the average number of sequential messages passed within a protocol round-trip and X of one-time network communication is used for all kinds of message passing based on assumption A2. For LEAP, α can be 2, 3 or 4 according to the ownership transfer cases as shown in Figure 4.

Similarly, the same estimation for remote data access with locality is as follows:

$$t_{rl} = \alpha \cdot X \cdot P(R) \cdot \big(1 - P(L|R)\big)$$

This is because the accessed data is expected to become locally available as long as they have been migrated to the requesting node.

Finally, for remote data access without locality, the data are expected to be at the remote node. Although there is a chance that the accessed data may have been transferred to the requesting node through some prior data accesses, we ignore such a chance as it is expected to be rare. Thus, the cost for this type of data access is as follows:

$$t_{rnl} = \alpha \cdot X$$

Since LEAP converts every distributed transaction into a local transaction, transaction commit can be performed locally and with negligible cost. Therefore, under assumption A3, we can derive the latency expectation of LEAP-based transaction processing as the sum of different types of data access with their corresponding probabilities, i.e.,

$$\begin{aligned} T_{LEAP} &= t_l \cdot P_l + t_{rl} \cdot P_{rl} + t_{rnl} \cdot P_{rnl} \\ &= \alpha \cdot X \cdot P(R) \cdot \overline{P(L|R)} \cdot \big(2 - P(R) \cdot \overline{P(L|R)}\big) \end{aligned} \tag{1}$$

where $\overline{P(L|R)} = 1 - P(L|R)$ represents the probability of remote data access not preserving locality.

Next, we consider the 2PC-based transaction processing. Recall that 2PC is only needed when one transaction involves data access from more than one node. With assumption A1, we only need to deal with the case where the transaction processing involves multiple nodes. With n data accesses, the probability of a transaction being distributed is

$$P_{dt} = 1 - \big(1 - P(R)\big)^n$$

Furthermore, since 2PC-based distributed transaction processing may involve multiple threads residing in different nodes, a multistep transaction may need to exchange intermediate result among the distributed threads. Suppose i steps in a multistep transaction requiring intermediate result transfer, each of which involves at least one message passing. Therefore, we can derive the latency expectation of 2PC-based transaction processing as

$$\begin{aligned} T_{2PC} &= \beta \cdot X \cdot P_{dt} + i \cdot X \cdot P_{dt} \\ &= (\beta + i) \cdot X \cdot \Big[1 - \big(1 - P(R)\big)^n\Big] \end{aligned} \tag{2}$$

where β is the number of sequential messages passed within the 2PC procedure. As shown in Figure 1, β equals to 5 in a normal 2PC protocol[2].

The above analysis on latency expectation provides three insights for LEAP/2PC-based transaction processing. First, without considering the locality of remote data access (e.g., $P(L|R) = 0$), T_{LEAP} grows with $P(R) \cdot \big(2 - P(R)\big)$, whereas T_{2PC} grows with $1 - \big(1 - P(R)\big)^n$. This implies the superiority of LEAP over 2PC becomes significant when remote

[2]For simplicity, the log-writing cost is omitted in the cost.

data access increases (as illustrated in Appendix F). Second, remote data access with locality would benefit T_{LEAP}, whereas it does not affect T_{2PC}. Third, 2PC-based processing becomes more expensive when transactions involve intermediate result transfer, whereas the LEAP-based one does not suffer from such an issue.

4. LEAP-BASED OLTP ENGINE

In this section, we introduce the design of L-Store, a LEAP-based OLTP engine. Figure 5 shows the architecture of L-Store which consists of N nodes and one distributed in-memory storage. There are four main functional components in each node as follows.

- **Application Layer:** This layer provides the interface to interact with the client applications.
- **Storage Engine:** L-Store employs an in-memory storage. To facilitate efficient data access, lightweight indexes (e.g., hash index) are utilized to facilitate speedy retrieval of the data tables, the owner tables and the locks.
- **Transaction Engine:** This engine handles transaction execution. It adopts multi-threading to process transactions in order to increase the degree of parallelism. It interacts with the storage engine to fetch/write the data and the node management component to detect the data locks and send the ownership transfer request.
- **Node Management:** This layer manages the entire node including controlling the locks and running the LEAP protocol. It also serves as the agent for inter-node communication. Its implementation applies the Actor model [17] to interact with the messages for ownership transfer.

Based on the above architecture, we further present the key designs on concurrency control, transaction isolation, and fault tolerance.

4.1 Concurrency Control

Concurrency control ensures that database transactions can be performed concurrently without violating data integrity. In this section, we introduce a lock-based distributed concurrency control scheme in the system. Evaluating L-Store with other concurrency control techniques such as multiversion-based protocols is left as a future work.

In each node of L-Store, the concurrency control is achieved by maintaining two data structures: data lock and owner dispatcher. The *data lock* is designed to control the ongoing data access. Considering each OLTP transaction typically accesses only a few tuples and is unlikely to clash with other concurrent transactions, the lock granularity is applied to tuples. The data lock scheme uses read-write lock mechanism [33]. The *owner dispatcher* is designed to handle concurrent ownership transfer requests of the same tuple from different nodes. When these concurrent requests are sent to the partitioner, the owner dispatcher in the partitioner would decide which one to process first according to the deadlock prevention strategy. The main property of the owner dispatcher is to guarantee that only one request is forwarded to the data owner to complete the data transfer.

4.1.1 Life Cycle of a Transaction

Now, we introduce the life cycle of one transaction execution in L-Store. To guarantee serial equivalence and high-level transaction ***isolation***, we employ the strict two-phase locking scheme (S2PL) [31] which guarantees serializability and recoverability of transaction processing. In S2PL, a transaction holds on to all granted locks until it commits or aborts. Transaction execution proceeds in the following phases.

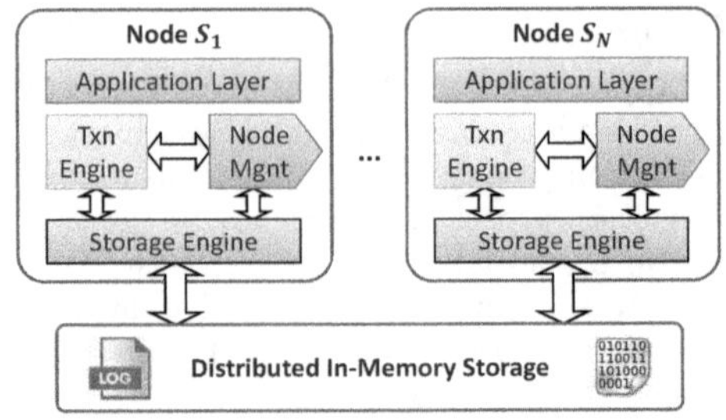

Figure 5: Architecture of L-Store.

- **Begin:** In the initial phase, the transaction executor thread will initialize the transaction and analyze the execution plan (e.g., local/distributed transaction, number of intermediate steps, data required in the first step, etc).
- **Data Preparation:** Next, the transaction executor will check whether the required data is locally available. This is performed by checking the local in-memory storage. If the data is stored in the local memory, it indicates the current node is the owner and the transaction can be executed with the local data. The executor will then send the data request to the lock manager to lock the data for use. However, if any of the requesting data is not available locally, the executor thread will send an ownership transfer request to the corresponding partitioner to remotely grab the data.

  During this phase, if the executor receives one abort signal due to conflict through either ownership transfer protocol or deadlock prevention mechanism, the transaction will directly enter the abort phase.
- **Execution:** In this phase, a transaction can access or update any data item from the local store. It is sometimes impossible to predict at the start of a transaction which objects will be used. This is generally the case in interactive applications. Therefore, under such a scenario, the transaction may re-enter the previous phase to get the data in the middle of the transaction execution. When this phase finishes, it will enter the commit phase.
- **End: a.) Commit:** The transaction enters the commit phase when the whole transaction has completed successfully. All the data updates are applied in the local memory. In addition, the write-ahead logging technique is applied to write the transaction log into the distributed persistent storage. Once the log is written successfully, the transaction is considered to be completed and a commit flag is set to the transaction log in the end. Meanwhile, all the locked data are released.

  b.) Abort: On conflict, the transaction is rolled back to cancel all the updates during the transaction execution. Meanwhile, all the locked data is released.

  The commit and abort strategies provide the ***atomic*** transaction execution where either all operations in one transaction are committed or aborted.

4.1.2 Deadlock Prevention

Deadlock happens when two or more competing processes

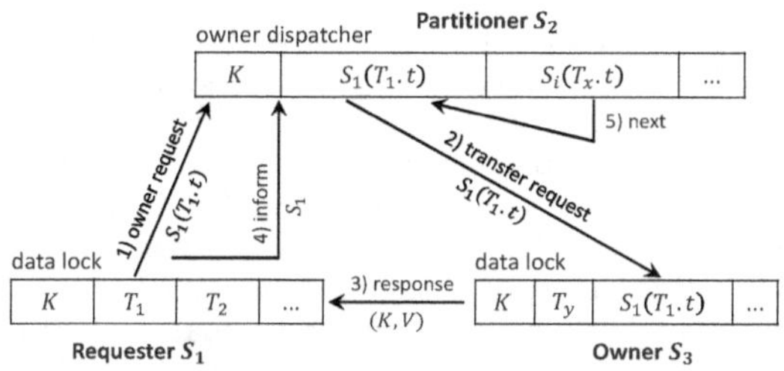

Figure 6: Ownership transfer with contention.

(i.e., transactions or ownership transfer requests in L-Store) are waiting for each other to finish, and thus neither ever does. To tackle this problem, we adopt a timestamp-based deadlock prevention technique [31] to manage requests for resources so that at least one process is always able to get all the resources it needs. In L-Store, each transaction is assigned a globally unique timestamp according to the time it arrives at the execution node (see Appendix J for implementation details). Based on the transaction timestamps, the deadlock prevention is implemented using the *Wait-Die* policy to handle conflicts. The intuitive idea is to set the priority of the transactions. An older transaction with a smaller timestamp is endowed with higher priority than a younger one. In the Wait-Die policy, higher-priority transaction waits for the data held by a lower-priority transaction, whereas lower-priority transaction aborts immediately if the data is held by a higher-priority transaction. To simplify the presentation, we define a Wait-Die based conflict handling operation that will be used in the rest of this section.

Suppose transaction T_1 is holding the lock of record K and transaction T_2 requests to access K. Under the Wait-Die policy, the conflict handling function CH between T_1 and T_2 is defined as follows.

$$CH(T_1, T_2) = \begin{cases} T_1 \text{ waits} & \text{if } T_1.t < T_2.t \\ T_1 \text{ aborts} & \text{if } T_1.t > T_2.t \end{cases} \quad (3)$$

where t is the timestamp of transaction.

Moreover, every aborted transaction is restarted with its initial timestamp so that starvation is avoided.

4.1.3 Handling Concurrent Requests

In L-Store, concurrent requests may arise in two situations. First, transactions within a node concurrently access the local data. Second, transactions concurrently access data that require ownership transfer. The second case also includes the situation where multiple nodes concurrently request the ownership of the same data.

The first category of the concurrent request can be easily handled by traditional centralized lock-based concurrency control mechanisms like the Wait-Die policy. L-Store differs from other lock-based distributed systems in handling the second category of concurrent requests.

For ease of presentation, we first assume that there is one transaction in the requester that needs a remote record. We will generalize to the case where multiple transactions at a node may request for remote records later. We will use the following running example in our discussion.

Requester Side: Suppose transaction T_1 in node S_1 requires one record K that is currently held in node S_3 as shown in Figure 6. Before S_1 sends the ownership transfer request, it first builds a new "request" lock item in the data lock to indicate that one ownership transfer request of K from S_1 has been sent. The difference between this request lock and other data lock is that this locked key does not have data in the local storage yet. For deadlock prevention, the timestamp of the request transaction is also attached to the message (i.e., $S_1(T_1.t)$).

Partitioner Side: In the partitioner side, there could be multiple ownership transfer requests sent from different nodes at the same time (i.e., $S_1(T_1.t)$ from S_1 and $S_i(T_x.t)$ from S_i). One of the main design principles is to process the request sequentially. In other words, at any time, only one request is sent to the owner and the others have to wait until the previous one finishes and sends out the inform message to the partitioner. This is to avoid the overheads of re-sending requests: if multiple requests are all sent to the owner, only one of them will be granted ownership while the rest have to resend again (since there is a new owner).

To prevent deadlock, the Wait-Die policy is also applied here to handle the conflict among different requests using Equation 3. To reduce the abort rate, another design principle is to choose the request attached with the biggest timestamp to process first. Assume $T_1.t > T_x.t$ and then $S_1(T_1.t)$ will be processed first. Here, the one that is being processed is analogous to holding one process "lock". And all the rest (e.g., $S_i(T_x.t)$) have to wait in the waiting queue.

In addition, before the partitioner S_2 receives the inform message acknowledging the completion of $S_1(T_1.t)$, all the new emerging requests for the same K apply the Wait-Die handling check by comparing with $T_1.t$ to determine whether it can wait in the queue or has to abort. After receiving the inform message, the owner dispatcher would pick another requests with the biggest timestamp from the waiting queue to process until all the requests have been processed.

Owner Side: After receiving the ownership transfer request of K, S_3 handles the request in a manner similar to a local transaction applying for an exclusive lock. First, it checks whether K is currently locked by another local transaction. If not, the data is directly granted to the request by sending one response message with the data to S_1. Otherwise, it enters the next step to determine whether the request can wait or abort. Assume T_y is locking K when $S_1(T_1.t)$ arrives. This step compares the timestamp of the transaction holding the lock and the timestamp attached in the request using the conflict handling function $CH(T_y, S_1(T_1.t))$ as defined in Equation 3. If the decision is abort, then the owner does not allow $S_1(T_1.t)$ to wait but reject the request via sending one abort response message to S_1.

Generalization: Now, we are ready to see how to handle the situation where multiple transactions at the requester accessing the same remote data. For instance, when transactions T_1 and T_2 both request K in S_1, a straightforward approach is to send multiple ownership transfer requests to the partitioner. However, this would incur high ownership transfer overhead, as the system has to handle two requests from the same node. To tackle this issue, our approach is to only send one request for the multiple transactions. The approach is similar to what is employed in the owner dispatcher, where the transaction with the biggest timestamp is chosen to process the request and the rest have to wait in a waiting queue. For instance, if $T_1.t > T_2.t$, T_1 is chosen to send the request and T_2 has to wait. Similarly, if a new transaction (e.g., T_z) emerging in S_1 requires K as well, it has to do the deadlock prevention using the $CH(T_1, T_z)$ to determine whether T_z should wait or abort.

Based on the message received from S_3, S_1 would take an appropriate action accordingly. When the message is an abort message, S_1 would abort the transaction T_1 and pick another transaction (i.e., T_2) with the biggest timestamp from the waiting queue to resend the ownership transfer request. Otherwise, the "request" lock is converted into a normal data lock to serve the local transaction. In this case, the data has been granted and can serve all the waiting transactions in the queue.

4.2 Fault Tolerance

L-Store is designed to run over large-scale clusters, and provides fault tolerance guarantee. As L-Store employs an in-memory storage, data stored in memory may be lost when data node crashes. To tackle this challenge, we adopt data logging and checkpointing techniques for data ***durability*** as what has been widely used in database literature [32].

Conceptually, L-Store only has "local" transactions execution in the sense that all transactions hold all the data in the same place. This enables the transaction processing to be logged efficiently. Unlike other shared-nothing databases that require multiple log writes during the 2PC as shown in Figure 1, L-Store only writes the update data log once at the commit phase for each transaction. Two important factors ensure the correctness of this logging mechanism. First, there is no need for distributed synchronization during the commit phase, as all the data and updates are in local storage. Second, partial update of the transaction during any node crash is not visible to transactions at other nodes, which ensures that no rollback operation is needed during failure recovery.

For checkpointing, adopting the distributed storage in L-Store simplifies the mechanism. The system makes periodic checkpoint to the distributed storage. When node crash happens, the latest version of the checkpoint and the data logs are utilized to perform the recovery together.

We employ Zookeeper [18] to detect node crashes and coordinate the recovery. When one node S_i crashes, how to handle the failed message delivery has been discussed in Section 3.3. Now, we present the recover mechanism of handling another two types of data. The first type is the data that is currently owned by S_i. The other type is the owner table that traces which nodes own the data initially from S_i.

Recovering owned data. When S_i crashes, the data in S_i are lost from the volatile storage. These data can be recovered by using the latest checkpoint and the transaction logs. The logs are replayed from the latest checkpoint to recreate the state of the node prior to the crash.

Recovering owner table. When S_i crashes, the owner table is lost as well. In order to recover the owner table, Zookeeper sends a request to every node to write the data that belong to S_i into the distributed storage. When a new node is ready to replace the failed S_i, it would retrieve all these data from the distributed storage on demand, in which case the new node becomes the owner for those data and starts to build its own owner table again.

For more details on how the LEAP design handles data loss, interested readers may refer to Appendix D.

5. PERFORMANCE EVALUATION

In this section, we present results of an experimental study to investigate the effectiveness of LEAP. We implement the LEAP-based OLTP engine in Java as a stand-alone system, namely *L-Store*, and compare it with the state-of-the-art distributed in-memory OLTP system, H-Store [21], whose distributed transaction processing relies on 2PC. L-Store supports multi-threaded processing for database partitions where the number of threads being used is independent of the number of partitions deployed. In contrast, H-Store applies single-threaded processing for each partition [21, 20, 26]. Towards fair comparison, we additionally integrate the core of L-Store into H-Store to replace its 2PC-based transaction processing while retaining the single-threaded processing for each partition. We term this modified H-Store as H^L*-Store*. The comparison between H^L-Store and H-Store aims to verify the benefits of the proposed LEAP strategy under the same degree of parallelism in transaction processing. The comparison between L-Store and H-Store further shows the superiority of LEAP-based transaction processing when a larger number of threads is exploited to optimize the system resource utilization.

5.1 Experimental Setup

Environment. Our experiments are conducted on an in-house cluster with 64 nodes. Each node consists of an Intel Xeon X3430 @ 2.4 GHz CPU running Centos 5.11 with 8 GB memory. The cluster is connected using 10 Gigabit Ethernet. By default, we use 16 nodes to run the experiments.

Workloads. Two benchmarks are used throughout the experiments: TPC-C and YCSB.

The TPC-C benchmark [1] is an industry-standard benchmark for evaluating the performance of OLTP systems. It consists of nine tables and five stored procedures that simulate a warehouse-centric parts-supply application. The specification of TPC-C benchmark [1] defines the workload as five stored procedures. In particular, the `NewOrder` and `Payment` transactions (comprising 88% of the total workload as defined in the specification) contain remote data access to the `CUSTOMER` and `STOCK` tables, and the remaining types of transactions interact with local data only. Thus, to focus on the study of distributed transactions, we only generate the `NewOrder` and `Payment` transactions with uniform distribution in the experiments. Meanwhile, we control the percentage and access pattern of remote data access in these two types of transactions for evaluation purposes.

The Yahoo! Cloud Serving Benchmark (YCSB) [8] was initially designed for testing key-value data stores. It consists of a single table and two key-value operations (read/update). The table is partitioned based on the primary key. We extend the benchmark to add support for multistep transaction that is configurable for the number of intermediate results exchange among nodes. This is implemented by batching several key-value operations into steps and enforcing that the search keys of each step (except the first step) are derived from the result of the prior step. Each step involves data access to one arbitrarily chosen remote partition.

Metrics. The throughput is measured by counting the number of committed transactions within a time unit. The latency is measured by capturing the time span between transaction initialization and commit, which includes all the retrials of a transaction.

Settings. For the TPC-C benchmark, we deploy one warehouse per partition, and the total number of warehouses is proportional to the number of nodes used in the experiments. Figure 7 shows the impact of performance of H-Store

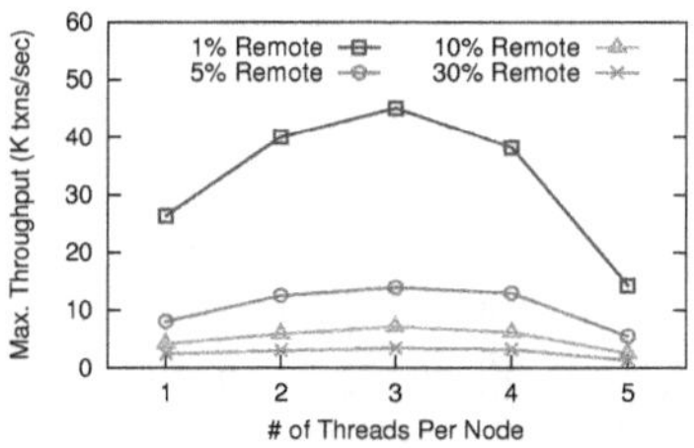

Figure 7: Impact of the number of threads used in H-Store.

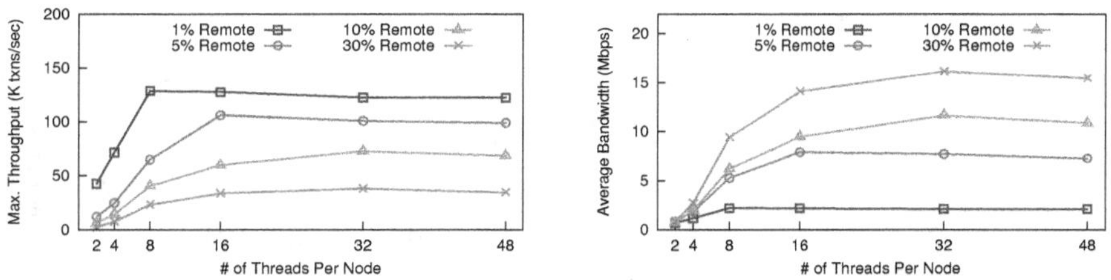

(a) Throughput.

(b) Bandwidth.

Figure 8: Impact of the number of threads used in L-Store.

by varying the number of partitions deployed on a 4-node cluster. We show results for 1%, 5%, 10% and 30% remote data access. Recall that the single-threaded execution model in H-Store implies the number of threads per node for transaction processing equal to the number of partitions deployed in that node. From the results, we can see that with 4 cores in each node, H-Store achieves best performance by using one partition per core and allowing one core to do the system coordination, which is consistent with the setting from [21, 26]. Therefore, in our experiments, we deploy three partitions in each node for H-Store to perform optimally. Accordingly, we also deploy three partitions per node for both L-Store and H^L-Store[3].

For pure performance evaluation on transaction processing and transaction commit, we remove the settings of admission control, user initiated abort, transaction sleeping and timeout in the experimental workloads. Moreover, for all three systems (L-Store, H^L-Store and H-Store), whether a partition is local or remote is based on the node it resides in rather than its assigned core. We strictly enforce the remote data access to be inter-node with respect to the initial state of database partitioning (since LEAP would migrate data during transaction processing).

5.2 Impact of Multi-Threaded Processing

As L-Store supports multi-threaded transaction processing, this set of experiments aim to study how the usage of threads affects the system throughput and bandwidth.

Throughput. Figure 8.a provides the maximum throughput of L-Store for the TPC-C workload with 1%, 5%, 10% and 30% of remote data access when we vary the number of threads per node from 2 to 48 with the number of partitions per node unchanged. From the result, we can see that the throughput initially increases with increasing number of threads (from 4 to 32) but decreases or remains stable beyond 32 threads. For any thread running a distributed transaction, it is suspended during ownership transfer. Thus using more threads for more concurrent execution would reduce CPU idle time so that computation resources can be better utilized towards higher throughput. However, deploying too many threads would incur significant overhead of thread scheduling. Moreover, higher concurrency would bring in higher contention of data, which could lead to more transaction abort due to deadlock prevention. Transaction abort not only wastes the CPU cycles spent on partial processing but also consumes extra CPU cycles to perform transaction rollback. Hence, setting the number of threads to an appropriate range could balance the trade-off between efficiency and effectiveness of computation resource usage. Based on the result shown in Figure 8.a, we set 32 threads per node as the default setting of L-Store for the rest of the experiments.

Bandwidth Usage. To study the communication cost incurred by inter-node message passing in L-Store, we further examine the bandwidth usage under different number of threads. Note that the cost of ownership transfer dominates the overall bandwidth. We gather three insights from the result given by Figure 8.b. First, higher percentage of remote data access results in higher bandwidth usage. This is expected as more remote data accesses incur more ownership transfers. Second, the bandwidth usage shows a similar curve as the throughput with respect to varying number of threads. This is because the bandwidth usage is basically proportional to the number of remote data accesses within a time unit, which is implicitly constrained by the system throughput. Third, the network traffic generated by the ownership transfer is small and acceptable. The result in Figure 8.b indicates that even with 32 threads, the bandwidth usage for running the workload with 30% remote data access is around 17 Mbps. With modern network infrastructure such as 10 Gigabit Ethernet, the bandwidth usage in L-Store is not likely to become a bottleneck even in a large-scale system setting.

5.3 Impact of Distributed Transactions

Next, we study the impact of distributed transactions by observing the maximum throughput and mean latency when the percentage of remote data access varies from 0% to 100% (without preserving locality of data access) for the TPC-C workload. Figure 9.b and Figure 9.c show that L-Store and H^L-Store have comparative throughput and latency with H-Store when all transactions are local, i.e., 0% remote data access[4]. On the other hand, with increasing percentage of remote data access, the throughput for all three systems decreases while the latency increases. This is expected as executing local transactions is much faster than processing distributed transactions. However, we observe that L-Store and H^L-Store outperform H-Store by a wide margin once distributed transactions are involved. For instance, L-Store (resp. H^L-Store) exhibits 2.5x to 20x (resp. 1.2x to 6x) speedup over H-Store when the percentage of remote data access varies from 1% to 50% as shown in Figure 9.b. As analyzed in Section 3.4.1, the performance of 2PC-based transaction processing is sensitive to the proportion of distributed transactions in the workload. Figure 9.a indicates that the percentage of distributed transactions grows rapidly with the increment of remote data access. For example, 1% remote data access results in about 10% distributed trans-

[3]H^L-Store is therefore set with three threads per node for transaction processing.

[4]Appendix G provides additional evaluation on the performance of local transaction processing.

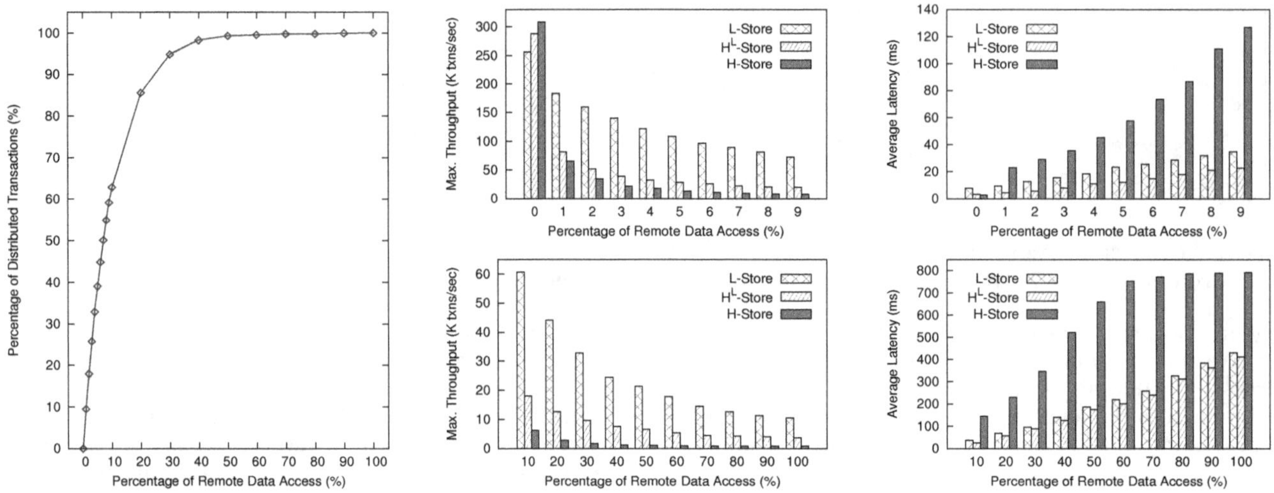

(a) Distributed transactions. (b) Throughput. (c) Latency.

Figure 9: Impact of the percentage of remote data access.

Table 1: Transaction abort and trials in L-Store.

Remote	Abort Rate	1 Trial	2 Trials	$\geq$ 3 Trials
1%	3.43%	96.89%	2.95%	0.16%
5%	3.71%	96.52%	3.34%	0.14%
10%	3.49%	96.74%	3.15%	0.11%
30%	2.68%	97.62%	2.33%	0.05%

actions, 10% remote data access results in about 63% distributed transactions, and 50% of remote data access results in nearly 100% distributed transactions. The rapid increase in the number of distributed transactions greatly raises the latency of H-Store (as shown in Figure 9.c) and consequently leads to the dramatic decrease of its throughput (as shown in Figure 9.b). This is caused by the frequent invocation of the expensive 2PC protocol in H-Store for committing distributed transactions. On the contrary, we observe that the throughput of L-Store and H^L-Store decreases at a much slower rate as the percentage of remote data access increases. This confirms that LEAP enables L-Store and H^L-Store to handle distributed transaction processing much more efficiently than H-Store.

The throughput gap between L-Store and H^L-Store is due to the CPU utilization. When the maximum throughput is reached, both L-Store and H-Store utilize CPU at nearly 100%, whereas H^L-Store utilizes CPU at around 30%. This result is consistent with Figure 8.a where the LEAP-based processing suffers from blocking due to the usage of locks. On the other hand, H^L-Store provides lower latency than L-Store. This is because the processing in H^L-Store does not require thread scheduling.

We further evaluate the concurrency control of the LEAP-based engine. Taking L-Store as the example, Table 1 shows the transaction abort rate and the distribution of different number of transaction trials for transactions to successfully commit. The results are collected after the system is saturated, i.e., running with the maximum throughput. As can be seen, the abort rate is lower than 4% in all the test instances. The aborts are caused by the Wait-Die policy in resolving data contention (i.e., deadlock prevention and ownership transfer failure). Moreover, every issued transaction gets committed eventually. For all the committed transactions, over 96% successfully commit without any prior abort, and around 3% get to commit in their second trial of execution. The maximum number of transaction trials observed in the experiments is 6. These results clearly show that LEAP is effective in not only having low abort rates, but the number of retrials for aborted transactions is also acceptable.

5.4 Impact of Locality of Remote Data Access

Using the TPC-C workload containing remote data accesses, we further study how the locality of these remote data accesses affect the performance. Recall that a remote data access is considered to be with locality if the data being requested at the remote partition are exclusively accessible to the requesting node, and a remote data access is considered to be without locality if the data is accessed randomly over the global database. This set of experiments are conducted using the TPC-C workload with 10% remote data access. Figure 10 provides the throughput and latency of L-Store, H^L-Store and H-Store as we vary the locality level from 0% to 90%. The locality level is simulated as the probability of remote data access being with locality during transaction generation.

As can be seen from the results, LEAP-based systems (i.e., L-Store and H^L-Store) outperform 2PC-based system (i.e., H-Store) by a big margin when the locality level is high. This is expected as LEAP enables the migrated data to be reaccessed by subsequent transactions in the same node without additional remote requests. Consequently, the percentage of remote data access is significantly reduced. High locality of remote data access benefits high possibility of trivially turning a remote data access into a local data access without issuing any remote request once the data is available in the requesting node due to prior migration. On the other hand, while the performance of LEAP-based processing (i.e., in L-Store and H^L-Store) increases with the increment of locality of remote data access, the change of locality is agnostic to the 2PC-based processing (i.e., in H-Store). This is because, in the 2PC-based processing, remote data access would always remain remote as the data would not be automatically repartitioned.

For micro evaluation on ownership transfer of LEAP, interested readers may refer to Appendix E.

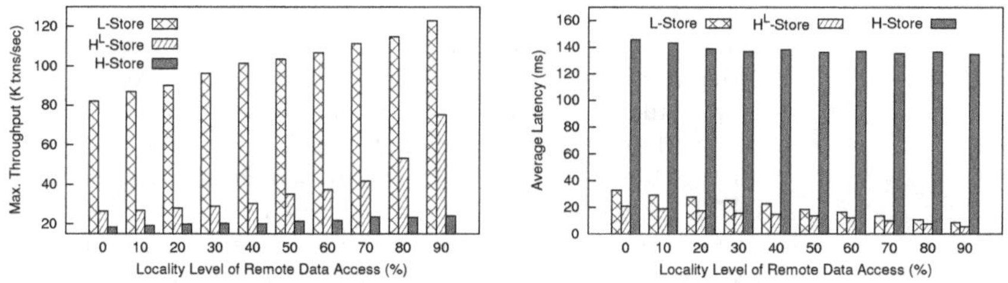

(a) Throughput. (b) Latency.

Figure 10: Impact of the locality level of remote data access.

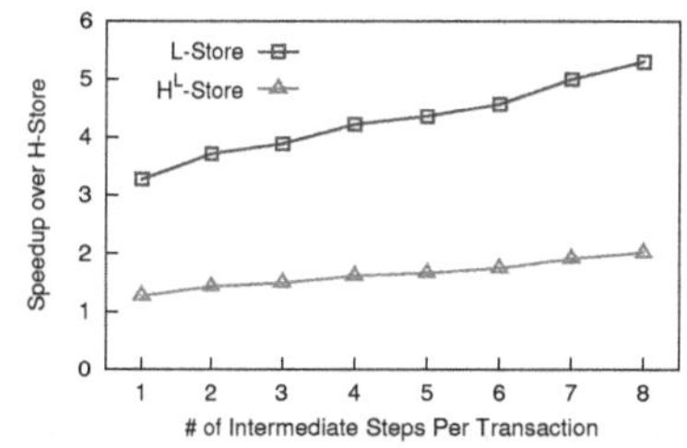

Figure 11: Impact of the number of intermediate results.

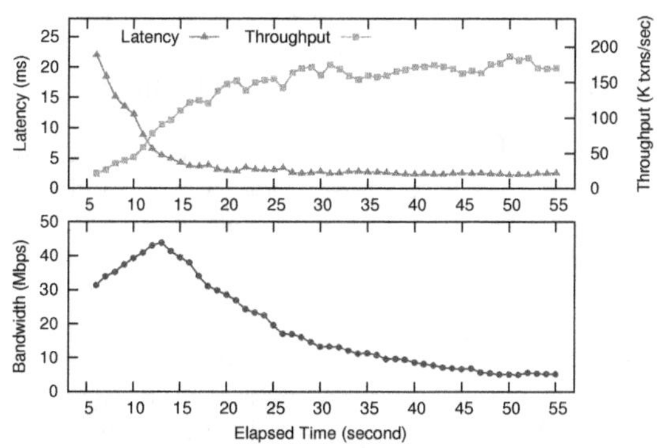

Figure 12: Automatic data repartitioning.

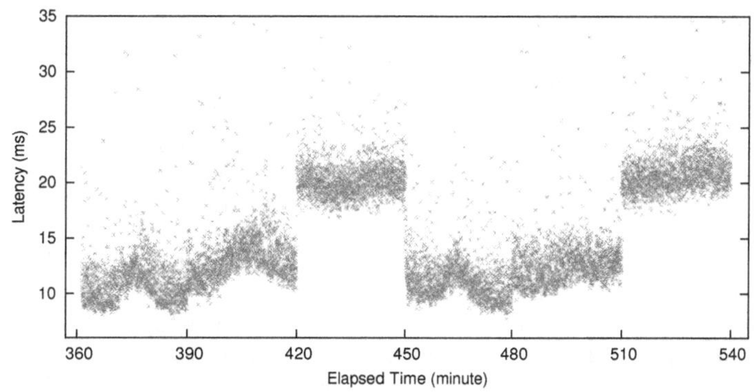

Figure 13: Impact of access pattern.

5.5 Impact of Intermediate Result Transfer

Next, we study the performance impact of intermediate result transfer within the distributed transaction processing. This set of experiments are conducted by running our extended YCSB workload with 10% remote data accesses. Figure 11 shows the speedup of L-Store and H^L-Store over H-Store, when we vary the number of steps involving intermediate result transfer within each transaction. Each step involves one remote data access and one tuple of intermediate result. From the result, we can see that as the amount of intermediate result transfer increases, the LEAP-based processing exhibits increment of speedup over the 2PC-based processing. For instance, the speedup of L-Store (resp. H^L-Store) over H-Store increases from 3.2x (resp. 1.2x) to 5.1x (resp. 1.9x) when the number of intermediate result steps varies from 1 to 8. The performance degradation of the 2PC-based processing is caused by the increased inter-node communication for intermediate result transfer. On the other hand, since LEAP always gathers the required data of a transaction for processing within a single thread, it naturally avoids the transfer of intermediate results within the transaction. This further confirms the superiority of LEAP-based distributed transaction processing.

5.6 Impact of Access Pattern

As LEAP exploits data migration to convert distributed transactions into local transactions, a side-effect of data migration in LEAP is to automatically repartition the database with respect to the workload. We conduct an experimental study to verify the effectiveness of database auto-repartitioning within the LEAP-based transaction processing. Figure 12 illustrates the real-time latency, throughput and bandwidth usage changes when H^L-Store runs the TPC-C workload with initially 10% remote data access and 100% locality of remote data access. Transaction generator feeds in 16,000 transactions per second. At the beginning, the latency is relatively high due to the frequent ownership transfer. This makes sense because the distributed transactions are aggressively migrating data from remote partitions to local partitions. As expected, as time goes by, the bandwidth usage drops dramatically and reduces to almost zero in the end. This confirms that all the remote data have been migrated to the same node with respect to the locality of remote data access. As a consequence, subsequent transactions contain no remote data access and thus the system retains high throughput and low latency.

Besides the locality of remote data access, the pattern of data access will also impact the system performance. Figure 13 shows the real-time latency along L-Store's long-time execution with periodic alternation of three data access patterns: each remote data access is limited to (1) one, (2) two and (3) all stated partitions respectively. Each access pattern lasts for 30 minutes. The result is a segment sample of a 3-hour run. As can be seen, LEAP can adapt to the changes of data access pattern towards good performance. This results from the fact that data contention increases from (1) to (3). In case (1), each data ownership is mainly accessible from two nodes, while it may be accessed by three nodes (resp. all nodes in the cluster) in case (2) (resp. case (3)). When the number of nodes requesting the same data increases, the contention increases accordingly and thus incurs more overhead of ownership transfer.

5.7 Scalability

Finally, we evaluate the scalability of L-Store, H^L-Store and H-Store when the size of the cluster changes. Figure 14.a shows the throughput changes for running the TPC-C workload with 10% remote data access as the number of nodes varies from 4 to 64. The results illustrate that L-Store scales much better than H-Store. For instance, the throughput of H-Store with 64 nodes is only 8 times faster than the

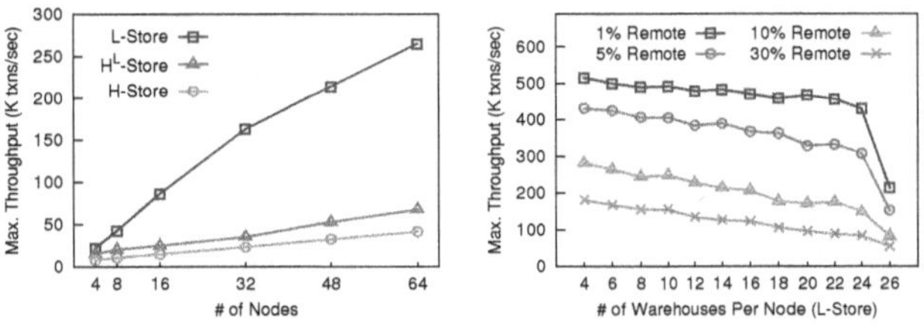

(a) Over nodes. (b) Over database sizes.

Figure 14: Scalability.

one with 4 nodes. On the other hand, we observe that the throughput of L-Store grows almost linearly when the number of nodes increases from 4 to 32. Although H^L-Store manifests similar scalability as H-Store, H^L-Store greatly underutilizes the CPU resources due to its restricted usage of threads (recalling that both H^L-Store and H-Store allocate a single thread for each partition). On the other hand, both L-Store and H-Store fully utilize the CPU resources when reaching the maximum throughput.

Furthermore, we evaluate the system scalability with increasing size of database. To this end, we still use the TPC-C workload as above but raise the database size beyond 3 warehouses per node. The experiments are run on a 64-node cluster by varying the amount of warehouses deployed. We first test H-Store and find that it cannot scale beyond 320 warehouses (i.e., 5 warehouses per node). This is consistent with the result as shown in Figure 7. Next, we test L-Store by augmenting the database size until the system reaches its limit of in-memory processing. The results are shown in Figure 14.b, with the percentage of remote data access set to 1%, 5%, 10% and 30%. As can be seen, with 512 GB memory capacity of the cluster, L-Store can scale out up to 1536 warehouses (i.e., 24 warehouses per node) whose data volume is around 450 GB in total. This confirms that L-Store is highly scalable when the cluster memory is sufficient.

6. RELATED WORK

There has been much interest in developing scalable distributed databases. One class of systems achieves good scalability by removing the transactional support, such as Dynamo [13] and Cassandra [23]. Another batch of systems only provides limited transactional support. For example, Bigtable [7] supports single-row transactional updates, and Megastore [4] offers transaction access over a small subset of a database. These systems provide linear outward scalability by sacrificing the complete transactional support.

H-Store [21] and its commercial successor VoltDB [27] are distributed main-memory systems that support ACID properties through data partitioning and replication. While these systems process local transactions efficiently, their performance degenerates with increasing number of distributed transactions due to usage of the expensive 2PC protocol.

Calvin [30] is a transaction scheduling and data replication layer that uses a deterministic ordering guarantee to reduce the contention costs associated with distributed transactions. Calvin does not use any distributed commit protocols; instead, it employs a deterministic locking mechanism that executes (sub)transactions in the same order across all nodes. However, this results in high transaction delay as the transactions can only be executed after agreeing on a transaction execution order.

L-Store is similar in spirit to G-Store [11]. Both systems transfer all the keys forming a group to a single node in order to allow efficient multi-key access. However, G-Store is specially designed for web application (e.g., online gaming) rather than OLTP workload. It requires the group to collect all the keys before the execution, which does not work in OLTP workload as the keys may not be known in advance. In G-Store, transactions are limited to one group and the techniques are tailored for long-lived transactions, while L-Store is designed to OLTP workload where transactions are short-lived.

Our work is also related to the research on data migration and database partitioning. Zephyr [15] performs live migration in a shared-nothing transactional database. It aims to reduce the system downtime while migrating tenants between hosts. Pavlo et al. [26] proposed an automatic database partitioning algorithm based on an adaptation of the neighborhood search technique, and a cost model that estimates the coordination cost and load distribution for a sample workload. E-Store [28] provides a two-tier data placement strategy to prioritize hot data and adopts a live reconfiguration technique [16] to repartition the database. ElasTraS [12] recursively partitions the database with tree-structured scheme towards minimizing remote data accesses, and adopts the 2PC protocol to handle distributed transactions. L-Store differentiates itself from these works by automatically transferring the data to the computation according to the transaction execution request.

Non-2PC distributed transaction processing has been studied in the context of shared-data databases [6, 24]. For example, Loesing et al. [24] proposed a design of distributed transaction processing by leveraging the in-memory shared-data storage. It shares similarity with L-Store in the mechanism of transaction processing such that it gathers all required data of a transaction from the storage to a node and processes the transaction locally. With shared-data storage, this design can achieve load balancing since the execution of each transaction is independent of the location of data. However, this design requires the shared-data storage to provide atomic data access primitives to resolve contention among parallel updates. This renders the solution less applicable to vanilla in-memory storage systems that are not necessary to guarantee atomicity of data access. In contrast, in L-Store, the logic of transaction processing and concurrency control are decoupled from the underlying storage layer, making L-Store friendly to all kinds of distributed in-memory storage. In Appendix I, we provide an experimental comparison between LEAP and the scheme in [24].

7. CONCLUSION

We proposed a distributed transaction management scheme called LEAP which facilitates low latency and good scalability. LEAP always converts a distributed transaction into a local transaction to eliminate the expensive commit protocol. Based on LEAP, we developed a distributed in-memory OLTP engine L-Store with full ACID support. L-Store enables a good scalability with a shared-nothing database engine and no single-node failure problem by employing a distributed in-memory storage. Furthermore, we presented a lock-based distributed concurrency control scheme to handle concurrent requests in L-Store. The experimental evaluation highlighted the superiority of the LEAP-based distributed transaction processing over 2PC-based systems like H-Store.

Acknowledgments

We would like to thank Dawei Jiang for initiating the idea of this research in February 2014, and Chang Yao and Meihui Zhang for their early tests. We would also like to thank our reviewers and shepherd of the paper, and H. V. Jagadish, for their insightful feedback that helped improve the paper. This research is funded by the National Research Foundation Singapore under its Campus for Research Excellence and Technological Enterprise (CREATE) programme with the SP2 project of the E2S2 programme, and the National Research Foundation, Prime Minister's Office, Singapore under its Competitive Research Programme (CRP Award No. NRF-CRP8-2011-08).

APPENDIX

A. REFERENCES

[1] Tpc-c benchmark. http://www.tpc.org/tpcc/.

[2] A. Adya et al. Efficient optimistic concurrency control using loosely synchronized clocks. In *Proc. of SIGMOD*, 1995.

[3] P. Bailis et al. Coordination avoidance in database systems. In *Proc. of VLDB*, 2015.

[4] J. Baker et al. Megastore: Providing scalable, highly available storage for interactive services. In *Proc. of CIDR*, 2011.

[5] Y. Cao et al. Es2: A cloud data storage system for supporting both oltp and olap. In *Proc. of ICDE*, 2011.

[6] S. Chandrasekaran et al. Shared cache - the future of parallel databases. In *Proc. of ICDE*, 2003.

[7] F. Chang et al. Bigtable: A distributed storage system for structured data. *ACM Trans. on Computer Systems*, 26(2):4:1–4:26, 2008.

[8] B. F. Cooper et al. Benchmarking cloud serving systems with ycsb. In *Proc. of SoCC*, 2010.

[9] J. C. Corbett et al. Spanner: Google's globally-distributed database. In *Proc. of OSDI*, 2012.

[10] C. Curino et al. Schism: A workload-driven approach to database replication and partitioning. In *Proc. of VLDB*, 2010.

[11] S. Das et al. G-store: A scalable data store for transactional multi key access in the cloud. In *Proc. of SoCC*, 2010.

[12] S. Das et al. Elastras: An elastic, scalable, and self-managing transactional database for the cloud. *ACM Trans. on Database Systems*, 38(1):5:1–5:45, 2013.

[13] G. DeCandia et al. Dynamo: Amazon's highly available key-value store. In *Proc. of SOSP*, 2007.

[14] D. E. Difallah et al. Oltp-bench: An extensible testbed for benchmarking relational databases. In *Proc. of VLDB*, 2014.

[15] A. J. Elmore et al. Zephyr: Live migration in shared nothing databases for elastic cloud platforms. In *Proc. of SIGMOD*, 2011.

[16] A. J. Elmore et al. Squall: Fine-grained live reconfiguration for partitioned main memory databases. In *Proc. of SIGMOD*, 2015.

[17] C. Hewitt et al. A universal modular actor formalism for artificial intelligence. In *Proc. of IJCAI*, 1973.

[18] P. Hunt et al. Zookeeper: Wait-free coordination for internet-scale systems. In *Proc. of USENIX ATC*, 2010.

[19] D. Jiang et al. epic: An extensible and scalable system for processing big data. In *Proc. of VLDB*, 2014.

[20] E. P. Jones et al. Low overhead concurrency control for partitioned main memory databases. In *Proc. of SIGMOD*, 2010.

[21] R. Kallman et al. H-store: A high-performance, distributed main memory transaction processing system. In *Proc. of VLDB*, 2008.

[22] J. F. Kurose et al. *Computer networking: a top-down approach.* Pearson Education, 2012.

[23] A. Lakshman et al. Cassandra: Structured storage system on a p2p network. In *Proc. of PODC*, 2009.

[24] S. Loesing et al. On the design and scalability of distributed shared-data databases. In *Proc. of SIGMOD*, 2015.

[25] A. Pavlo. *On Scalable Transaction Execution in Partitioned Main Memory Database Management Systems.* PhD thesis, Brown University, 2014.

[26] A. Pavlo et al. Skew-aware automatic database partitioning in shared-nothing, parallel oltp systems. In *Proc. of SIGMOD*, 2012.

[27] M. Stonebraker et al. The voltdb main memory dbms. *IEEE Data Engineering Bulletin*, 36(2):21–27, 2013.

[28] R. Taft et al. E-store: Fine-grained elastic partitioning for distributed transaction processing systems. In *Proc. of VLDB*, 2015.

[29] K.-L. Tan et al. In-memory databases: Challenges and opportunities from software and hardware perspectives. *ACM SIGMOD Record*, 44(2):35–40, 2015.

[30] A. Thomson et al. Calvin: Fast distributed transactions for partitioned database systems. In *Proc. of SIGMOD*, 2012.

[31] G. Weikum et al. *Transactional Information Systems: Theory, Algorithms, and the Practice of Concurrency Control and Recovery.* Elsevier, 2001.

[32] C. Yao et al. Adaptive logging: Optimizing logging and recovery costs in distributed in-memory databases. In *Proc. of SIGMOD*, 2016.

[33] H. Zhang et al. In-memory big data management and processing: A survey. *IEEE Trans. on Knowledge and Data Engineering*, 27(7):1920–1948, 2015.

B. DATA ACCESS VIA NON-PRIMARY KEYS

Our proposal in LEAP with data access via primary key can be easily extended for transactional workloads with data access via non-primary keys using secondary indexes. To this end, existing techniques of building and manipulating distributed index can be exploited to construct the secondary indexes. Each secondary index entry records the primary key of the data record so that the secondary indexes facilitate identifying the primary key via non-primary keys. As a consequence, data access via the non-primary key is done in two steps: retrieving the primary key through the secondary index and then accessing the data through the LEAP protocol using the obtained primary key. Therefore, the corresponding process of ownership transfer can reduce to the one described in the paper.

C. SYMBOLIC NOTATIONS

Table 2 lists the notations used in Section 3.4.1.

Table 2: List of notations.

Sym.	Description
T	Latency expectation of a transaction.
n	Number of data accesses within a transaction.
i	Number of steps dependent on intermediate results.
R	Event of remote data access.
L	Event of remote data access appearing locality.
X	Cost of one-time network communication.

D. FAULT TOLERANCE SCHEME

As an addendum to Section 4.2, we shall further elaborate on the fault tolerance of LEAP, particularly on its handling of data and message loss.

Handling Message Loss. The LEAP design handles message loss with two levels of guarantees. First, in the transmission level, LEAP relies on TCP for inter-node message passing, which has been shown to be reliable [22].

Second, in the protocol level, LEAP adopts a timeout-and-resend strategy. Every owner/transfer request is accompanied with a timeout setting. When there is a timeout waiting for a corresponding response, the owner/transfer request will be resent. Note that the response to an owner request is either the requested data or a transaction abort signal, and the response to a transfer request is an inform message indicating whether the ownership transfer succeeds or not. With the resent requests, the process of ownership transfer can be replayed once message loss occurs. However, resending requests may introduce the issue of duplicate requests. To address this issue in LEAP, duplicate messages are filtered out at the receiver site based on the processing logic. Referring to Figure 6, we enumerate the cases of duplicate elimination with respect to the four types of messages in the general case of ownership transfer (i.e., R-P-O).

- Suppose S_2 receives an owner request from S_1, e.g., $S_1(T_1.t)$ for K. If S_2 detects that $S_1(T_1.t)$ is already in the waiting queue for K or S_1 is already the owner of K, the ownership request will be ignored. Otherwise, S_2 will add $S_1(T_1.t)$ into the waiting queue for K, or send a corresponding transfer request to S_3, or send an abort signal of T_1 to S_1.
- Suppose S_3 receives a transfer request $S_1(T_1.t)$ for K from S_2. If S_3 detects that $S_1(T_1.t)$ is already in the waiting queue for K, the transfer request will be ignored. Otherwise, S_3 will either transfer (a copy of) K to S_1 or send an abort signal of T_1 to S_1. Note that after K is transferred out of S_3, S_3 still maintains a backup of K for a longer timeout until deletion.
- Suppose S_1 receives the requested K or an abort signal of T_1. After T_1 completes (i.e., commits or aborts), S_1 will inform S_2 whether the ownership transfer of K succeeds or not. Note that no duplicate elimination is performed in this case.
- Suppose S_2 receives an inform message from S_1 for K. If S_2 detects that the ongoing ownership transfer is not for S_1, the inform message will be ignored. Otherwise, based on the inform message, S_2 will update the owner table entry for K and invoke a pending owner request, if any, from the waiting queue for K.

In brief, the message-passing-based ownership transfer can be guaranteed by the reliable transmission of TCP and the timeout-and-resend strategy of LEAP.

Handling Data Loss. Considering the general case of ownership transfer (i.e., R-P-O), we discuss all possible failures in requester, partitioner and owner during the protocol. Note that the protocol starts with the owner request being sent by the requester and ends with the inform message being confirmed by the partitioner. Our current implementation of L-Store only considers the mechanism of handling single-node failure.

- *Requester failure* may occur in the cases based on the status of receiving the response message (associating either the requested data or a transaction abort signal).
- *Partitioner failure* may occur in the cases based on the status of receiving the owner request, sending the transfer request and receiving the inform message.
- *Owner failure* may occur in the cases based on the status of receiving the transfer request and sending the response message.

Due to space constraint, we only elaborate on two cases, and the remaining ones follow the similar processing pattern. For example, suppose the partitioner fails before the owner request arrives. In this case, once the requester waiting for the response message is timed out, it will resend the owner request. This procedure repeats until the partitioner resumes. Once the partitioner resumes and receives the owner request, the protocol proceeds as normal. For another example, suppose the requester fails before the response message arrives. In this case, once the partitioner waiting for the inform message is timed out, it will resend the transfer request and then the owner will resend the response message with (a backup copy of) the data. This procedure repeats until the requester resumes. Once the requester resumes and receives the response message, the protocol proceeds as normal.

Moreover, we specially elaborate on node recovery with respect to its data. While the data owned by the failed node can be recovered through the log, it is possible that some data have been transferred out prior to the node failure:

- If the data transferred out belongs to the failed node (i.e., the failed node is the partitioner of the data), then the new owner of the data will flush the data (after its running transaction completes) to the distributed storage after it is informed about the failure. When the failed node resumes, it will retrieve the data from the distributed storage on demand (i.e., when the data is requested but the owner table entry is missing, which by default means the data locates at the partitioner). In other words, the data is "indirectly" transferred back to the partitioner.
- If the data transferred out does not belong to the failed node (i.e., the failed node is not the partitioner of the data), then the data is owned by a new owner and the recovery of the failed node (i.e., the old owner) does not affect the protocol.

E. EVALUATING OWNERSHIP TRANSFER

Figure 15 illustrates the breakdown of ownership transfer cases referring to Figure 4. The experiment is conducted on a 16-node cluster by running L-Store with the TPC-C workload. Each result is measured after the system has been saturated for 15 minutes. Figure 15.a and Figure 15.b show

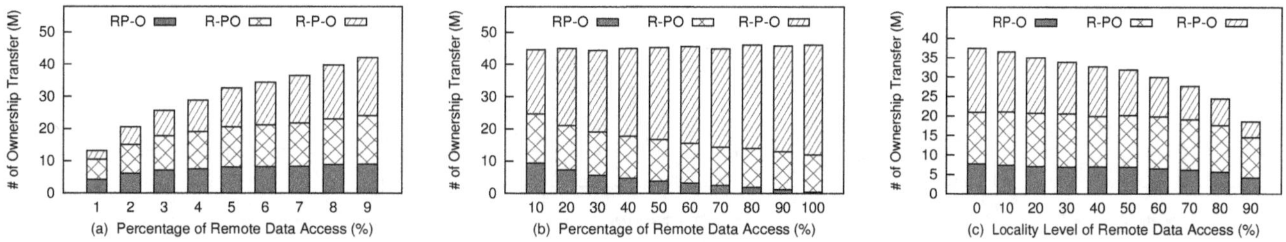

Figure 15: Breakdown of ownership transfer cases. (Case types referring to Figure 4)

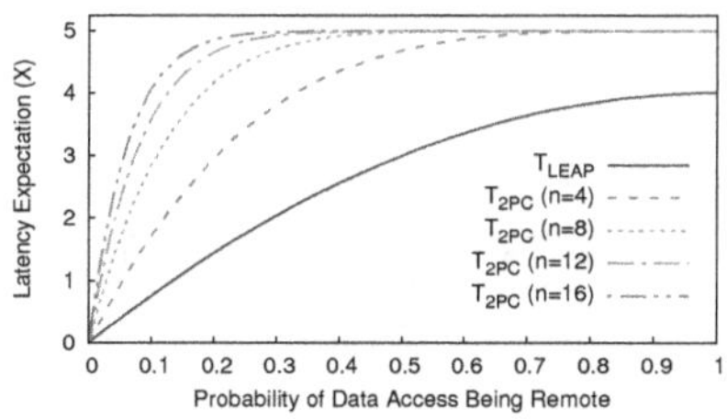

Figure 16: Comparison of latency expectation.

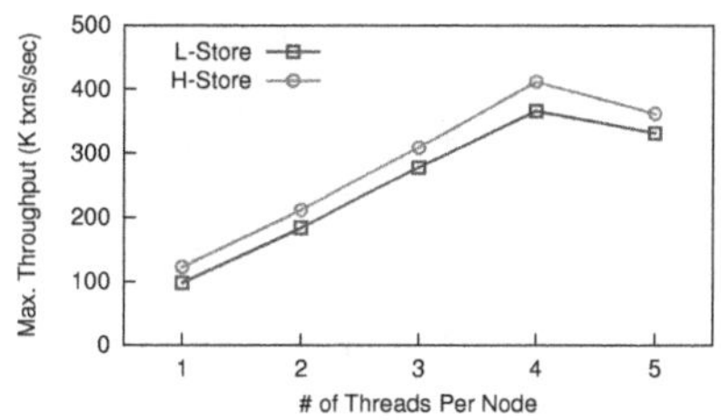

Figure 17: Performance of local transaction processing.

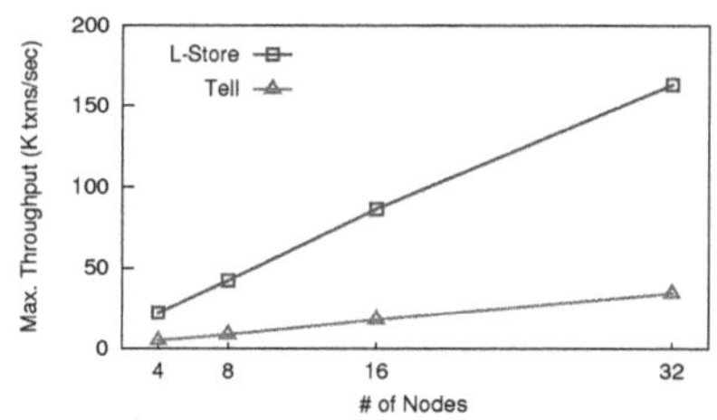

Figure 18: Comparison of scalability with Tell [24].

the results when varying the percentage of remote data access from 1% to 100% with the locality level set to be 0%. When remote data accesses are rare (e.g., less than 10% as in Figure 15.a), the number of ownership transfers increases obviously along the increment of remote data access. When remote data accesses become frequent (e.g., more than 10% as in Figure 15.b), the total amount of ownership transfers remains nearly the same in spite of the increment of remote data access. This is due to the exploitation of locality of remote data access in LEAP. (Although the locality of all data accesses in Figure 15.a and Figure 15.b are not advisedly preserved, the randomization of data access naturally contributes some degree of locality.) Moreover, the portion of R-P-O of ownership transfer increases steadily along the increment of remote data access. This explains the performance loss of LEAP-based transaction processing when remote data access rises but the total amount of ownership transfer remains stable, because R-P-O of ownership transfer is most expensive comparing with RP-O and R-PO.

Furthermore, Figure 15.c shows the results when varying the locality level from 0% to 90% with 10% remote data access. The rise of locality decreases the amount of ownership transfer, especially those of R-P-O. This confirms the gain of the LEAP protocol due to the locality of data accesses.

F. LATENCY EXPECTATION

Figure 16 illustrates the comparison of latency expectation between LEAP-based and 2PC-based transaction processing. The plots are based on Equation 1 and Equation 2 with $\alpha = 4$ and $\beta = 5$ respectively. The locality of remote data access is ignored, i.e., $P(L|R) = 0$. Each transaction only contains single step (i.e., $i = 1$). Recall that n is the number of data access within a transaction and X is the estimated average cost of one-time network communication.

G. LOCAL TRANSACTION PROCESSING

To evaluate how local transactions affect the overall performance, Figure 17 provides the result of maximum throughput when L-Store and H-Store process the TPC-C workload with local transactions only. The experiment is conducted on a 16-node cluster. The percentage of remote data access is set to 0% (i.e., all generated transactions are local), and the number of threads per node varies from 0 to 5. From the result we obtain two insights. First, H-Store outperforms L-Store with local transaction only workloads. The performance difference is mainly contributed by the overhead of locking. To handle data contention, H-Store applies the warehouse-granule locks along with its single-threaded processing for each warehouse, whereas L-Store applies the tuple-granule locks in the design to support multi-threaded processing. Moreover, once H-Store figures out that a transaction is local, it does not actually perform locking [20, 26] since only one thread is manipulating the data in the same warehouse and thus no contention exists. This makes H-Store more efficient than L-Store when processing local transactions. Second, the scalability curves of both H-Store and L-Store share a similar pattern. Especially, the performance peak appears with 4 threads per node. This is rational because each node is equipped with 4 physical cores. Specially, for H-Store, the thread for coordinating the processing of distributed transactions is always idle since no distributed transaction is generated. As a consequence, all the cores can fully participate in processing local transactions.

Additionally, we measure the latency under the same settings as above. With the number of threads per node varying from 1 to 4, the latency remains around 3.2 ms and 2.6 ms for L-Store and H-Store respectively. This is because each thread processes local transactions independently and no thread scheduling is performed over the cores. However, with 5 threads per node, the latency increases to 3.5 ms for L-Store and 3.1 ms for H-Store due to the overhead of thread scheduling.

H. MEMORY USAGE OF OWNER TABLE

Figure 20 shows the memory consumption of owner table when L-Store runs the TPC-C workload in a 16-node cluster. The percentage of remote data access varies from 0% to 100%, and the locality level of remote data access is set to 0% (i.e., no locality is preserving). Each result is measured

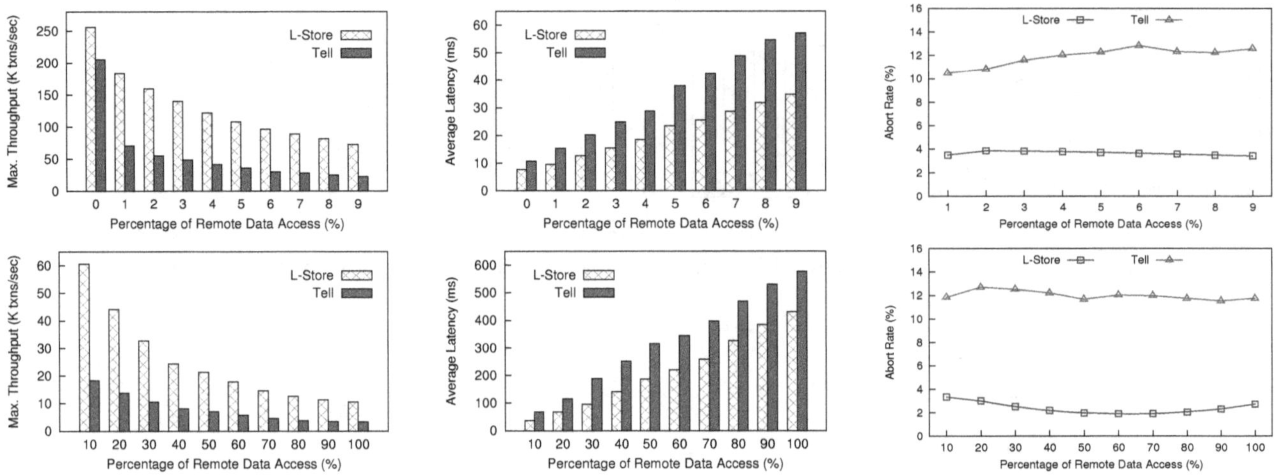

(a) Throughput. (b) Latency. (c) Abort Rate.

Figure 19: Comparison of performance with Tell [24].

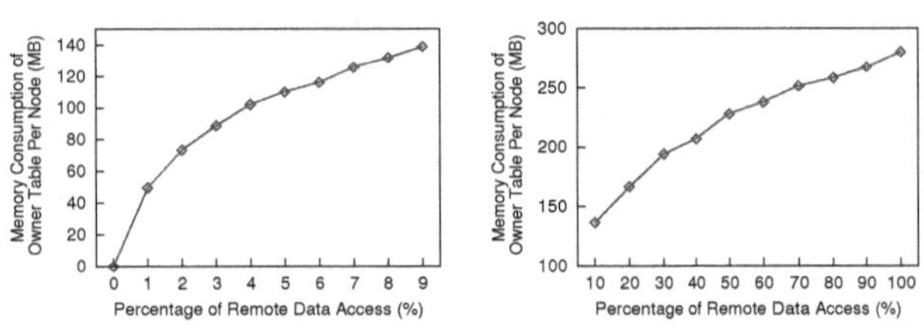

Figure 20: Memory consumption of owner table.

after the system has been saturated for 15 minutes. As can be seen from the result, the owner tables do not consume any memory when the system processes local transactions only (i.e., with 0% remote data access). This confirms the memory optimization as discussed in Section 3.2. Furthermore, the memory consumption increases along the increment of remote data access. This is expected with respect to the ownership transfer protocol.

I. COMPARISON WITH SHARED-DATA OLTP SYSTEM

Here, we shall evaluate L-Store against a state-of-the-art shared-data OLTP system, Tell [24]. For Tell, each physical node consists of two logical nodes: one processing node and one storage node[5]. Additionally, two nodes are exclusively used as the commit manager and the management node, and they are not counted in the experiments. We conduct experiments by running the TPC-C workload.

We first compare the performance with various settings of remote data access. Figure 19 shows the results of throughput, latency and abort rate by varying the percentage of remote data access from 0% to 100%. L-Store outperforms Tell in throughput and latency due to the following two reasons. First, although L-Store and Tell share similarity in turning every distributed transaction into a local one for processing, Tell does not exploit any locality of data access since it always retrieves data acquired by the transactions from the storage. Second, Tell resolves write-contention in the storage layer when transactions commit. This leads to high abort rate of Tell in comparison with L-Store, as shown in Figure 19.c. The high abort rate of Tell inversely affects its throughput and latency, since the throughput refers to only the committed transactions and the latency includes all the retrials of the aborted transactions.

Next, we compare the scalability. The result in Figure 18 shows that Tell also exhibits nearly linear scalability as L-Store does. This is expected as the design of Tell is specially proposed for good scalability [24].

[5]In the experiments, we only count the physical nodes.

J. ASSIGNING GLOBAL TIMESTAMPS

Current implementation of L-Store assigns a timestamp to each issued transaction of the format of $\langle node\_time, node\_id \rangle$. Specifically, *node_time* is the local wall-time in nanoseconds when the transaction arrives at the execution node, and *node_id* is the unique node identifier. We assume each node can accept at most one transaction per nanosecond, which is practical in general. Thus, the timestamp of each transaction is globally unique.

The timestamp ordering is determined by the comparison between timestamps. For transactions in the same node, their timestamps are naturally ordered by the *node_time*'s. For transactions in different nodes, the timestamp ordering is primarily based on *node_time* and secondarily based on *node_id*. Although this is an easy-to-implement approach, it suffers from two disadvantages. First, all clocks of the nodes have to be synchronized to make the timestamp ordering among different nodes meaningful. This is known to be hard in practice, especially for maintaining the synchronization strictly all the time. In the experiments of this paper, we only synchronize the clocks at the beginning of each running instances. Second, the comparison based on *node_id* is biased towards nodes with identifiers of high preference. But its impact is limited since it is only used for breaking ties when the *node_time*'s appear to be equal.

An alternative solution is to assign a global order for each transaction through a central coordinator [20]. But the central coordinator could be a bottleneck of the system. Using multiple coordinators with synchronization protocols (e.g., loosely synchronized clocks [2] or TrueTime [9]) could mitigate the issue. We leave the optimized implementation to future work, and only adopt the simple method as described above in this paper.

ERMIA: Fast Memory-Optimized Database System for Heterogeneous Workloads

Kangnyeon Kim† Tianzheng Wang† Ryan Johnson‡ Ippokratis Pandis*

†University of Toronto knkim,tzwang@cs.utoronto.ca
‡LogicBlox ryan.johnson@logicblox.com
*Amazon Web Services ippo@amazon.com

ABSTRACT

Large main memories and massively parallel processors have triggered not only a resurgence of high-performance transaction processing systems optimized for large main-memory and massively parallel processors, but also an increasing demand for processing heterogeneous workloads that include *read-mostly* transactions. Many modern transaction processing systems adopt a lightweight optimistic concurrency control (OCC) scheme to leverage its low overhead in low contention workloads. However, we observe that the lightweight OCC is not suitable for heterogeneous workloads, causing significant starvation of read-mostly transactions and overall performance degradation.

In this paper, we present ERMIA, a memory-optimized database system built from scratch to cater the need of handling heterogeneous workloads. ERMIA adopts snapshot isolation concurrency control to coordinate heterogeneous transactions and provides serializability when desired. Its physical layer supports the concurrency control schemes in a scalable way. Experimental results show that ERMIA delivers comparable or superior performance and near-linear scalability in a variety of workloads, compared to a recent lightweight OCC-based system. At the same time, ERMIA maintains high throughput on read-mostly transactions when the performance of the OCC-based system drops by orders of magnitude.

1. INTRODUCTION

Modern systems with massively parallel processors and large main memories have inspired a new breed of high-performance in-memory transaction processing systems [23, 24, 28, 31, 36, 46]. These systems leverage spacious main memory to fit the whole working set or even the whole database in DRAM with streamlined memory-friendly data structures. Multicore and multi-socket hardware optimizations further allow a much higher level of parallelism compared to conventional systems. With disk overheads and delays removed, transaction latencies drop precipitously and threads can usually execute transactions to completion without interruption. The result is a welcome reduction in contention at the logical level and less pressure on whatever the concurrency control (CC) scheme might be in place. A less welcome result is an increasing pressure for scalable data structures and algorithms to cope with the growing number of threads that concurrently execute transactions and need to communicate with each other [19].

SIGMOD'16, June 26-July 01, 2016, San Francisco, CA, USA

DOI: http://dx.doi.org/10.1145/2882903.2882905

Interactions at the logical level. Many designs exploit the reduction in the pressure on CC, by employing lightweight optimistic concurrency control (OCC) schemes, boosting even further the performance of these systems on suitable workloads [11, 25, 46]. But, as is usually the case, it appears that database workloads stand ready to absorb any and all concurrency gains the memory-optimized systems have to offer. In particular, there is high demand for database systems that can readily serve heterogeneous workloads, blending the gap between transaction and analytical processing [14, 27, 41]. These workloads often combine long *read-mostly* transactions for operational analytic with short and write-intensive transactions.

Lightweight OCC can be problematic in such workloads. First, its unfair (albeit lightweight) contention resolution, where a writer wins over a reader, leads to starvation of read-intensive transactions, as transactions have to abort if any portion of their read footprint is overwritten before they commit [49]. We believe that fairness among different types of transactions should be treated as a first-class citizen when serving heterogeneous workloads. Moreover, the lightweight OCC usually aborts loser transactions at commit time, wasting precious CPU cycles on long transactions that are destined to abort [1]. Consequently, heavyweight read-mostly transactions often lead to significant overall performance degradation as well. Therefore, going forward and as the industry shifts to heterogeneous workloads served by memory-optimized engines, it is vital for them to employ more effective CC schemes.

Interactions at the physical level. But it is not only the interaction at the logical level that should be central to the design of a memory-optimized database system. As commodity servers become increasingly parallel, many low-level issues (such as latching and thread scheduling) and design decisions—at the system architecture level—need to be revisited. The form of logging/recovery used, the storage management architecture, and scheduling policies for worker threads can impose drastic constraints on which forms of CC can be implemented at all, let alone efficiently. It can be difficult or impossible to adopt a different CC scheme without significant changes to the rest of the system. Thus, a physical layer should be designed with full awareness of consequences for CC and recovery, in addition to scalability efforts.

Desired properties. Considering the challenges, we argue that transaction processing systems should be designed with the following basic requirements:

- To provide robust and balanced concurrency control for the logical interactions over heterogeneous transactions.
- To address the physical interactions between threads in a scalable way and have a lightweight recovery methodology.

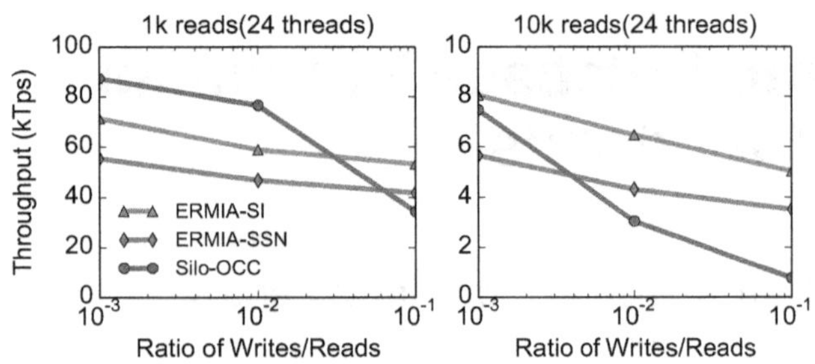

Figure 1: Performance of lightweight optimistic concurrency control and multi-version concurrency control at different transaction read-set sizes, as the ratio of writes increases. 1K reads (left); 10K reads (right).

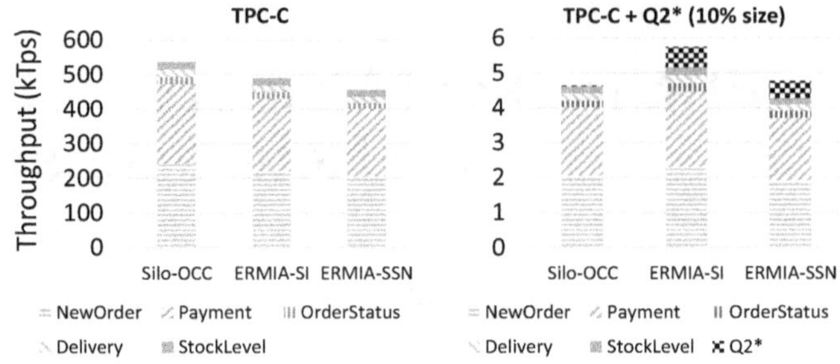

Figure 2: Breakdown of the commit rate of the TPC-C transactions (left) as well as when we add a read-intensive transaction (Q2*) to the mix (right). Silo achieves a very low commit rate, almost no progress, of the Q2* transaction.

1.1 ERMIA

In this paper, we present a novel memory- and multicore-optimized OLTP database, called ERMIA [1], to support the aforementioned desired properties. It employs a snapshot-isolation (SI) CC scheme that provides the following valuable features for heterogeneous workloads: (1) robustness against contention; (2) harmonious co-existence between readers and writers; and (3) early detection of doomed transactions to minimize the amount of wasted work. On top of the vanilla SI, ERMIA also provides serializability by adopting a recent proposal, called Serial Safety Net (SSN) [48].

We also present the design of a physical layer that interacts with the CC schemes efficiently and achieves multicore scalability in a memory-optimized design. The key components are (1) a scalable centralized log manager that provides global ordering; (2) latch-free indirection arrays which provide low overhead multi-versioning and efficient infrastructure for recovery; and (3) epoch managers that handle resource allocation and recycling.

As the detailed evaluation in Section 4 shows, ERMIA addresses inefficiencies of systems with lightweight OCC. In particular, Figure 1 demonstrates how the performance of Silo [46], a representative of the camp of memory-optimized systems with lightweight OCC, degrades as transactions have larger read footprint or when contention increases (experimental setup details in Section 4). As a comparison, Figure 1 shows the performance of ERMIA with snapshot isolation (ERMIA-SI) and serializable SI(ERMIA-SSN). Figure 1 shows that it just takes 0.1% or 1% of the touched records to be updates for the transaction throughput to drastically drop in Silo. The sharply decreasing curves of Silo in the figure indicate OCC's sensitivity to contention.

Further, Figure 2 demonstrates the unfairness of lightweight OCC schemes. The left graph shows the commit rate of each individual transaction of TPC-C under Silo as well as the ERMIA flavors. We can see that the commit rates are comparable under TPC-C. On the other hand, on the right side we add a read-mostly transaction in the mix, labeled at Q2*. We see that the commit rate of that read-intensive transaction starves in Silo, while for ERMIA it is quite high (the Q2* transaction is presented in Section 4.2). Also, given the drastic drop in overall TPS after we added Q2* transaction which takes more than 90% out of total cycles, Figure 2 also implies that Silo just wasted a huge number of cycles on aborted Q2* transactions while ERMIA spent most of its time on useful work.

[1] Stemmed from the two major components our system is built upon: ***E***poch-based ***R***esource ***M***anagement and ***I***ndirection ***A***rray.

1.2 Contributions and paper organization

In summary, this paper makes the following contributions:

- Highlights the mismatch between existing OCC mechanisms and heterogeneous workloads, and revisits snapshot isolation with cheap serializability guarantee as a solution.
- Presents a system architecture to efficiently support CC schemes in a scalable way with latch-free indirection arrays, scalable centralized logging, and epoch-based resource managers.
- Presents a comprehensive performance evaluation that studies the impact of CC and physical layer in various workloads, from the traditional OLTP benchmarks to heterogeneous workloads.

The rest of this paper is organized as follows. In Section 2 we lay out the design principles for memory-optimized engines to handle heterogeneous workloads on modern hardware. Section 3 discusses the detailed design of ERMIA. Section 4 compares the performance of ERMIA against an OCC-based memory-optimized system in a variety of transactional workloads. We discuss related work in Section 5 and conclude in Section 6.

2. DESIGN DIRECTIONS

In this section we discuss the design directions of database engines optimized for main-memory and multicores. We focus on three areas: the CC scheme that determines the interaction between concurrent transactions at the logical level; the mechanism that controls the interaction and communication among threads at the physical level; and recovery.

Shared-everything database. Some systems sidestep the issues of logical and physical contention entirely—along with the accompanying implementation complexity—by adopting physical partitioning and a single-threaded transaction execution model [23, 24]. This execution model introduces a different set of problems for mixed workloads and for workloads that are inherently difficult to partition. Given the developments in scaling-out the performance of distributed OLTP systems, especially for easy-to-partition workloads, e.g. [2, 8, 42], as well as for high availability and cost-effectiveness reasons, we predict that the successful architectures will combine scale-out solutions built on top of non-partitioning-based scale-up engines within each node. Therefore, we focus on the performance of non-partitioning-based memory-optimized engines within a single node.

Snapshot isolation and serializability. Broadly speaking, there are two camps of CC methods: the pessimistic, e.g. two-phase locking (2PL), and the optimistic (OCC). Past theory work [1] has shown that pessimistic methods are superior to optimistic ones under high contention. In practice, this result requires that pessimistic methods can be implemented with sufficiently low overhead relative to their optimistic counterparts, which is not easy to achieve in practice. For example, a study of the SHORE storage manager reports roughly 25% overhead for locking-based pessimistic methods [16]. Having said that, typical memory-optimized engines that employ lightweight OCC and running on modern commodity servers, leave some room for exploration. There are different flavors of optimistic, or opportunistic, CC. Many recent systems adopt a lightweight read validation step at the end of the transaction, during pre-commit.

However, read validation is very opportunistic, and somewhat brittle, leaving the system vulnerable to workloads where writers are likely to overwrite readers (causing them to abort). The vulnerability against contention does not appear in the TPC-C benchmark where tiny transaction footprints and precipitous reduction in transaction latency offered by main-memory systems collectively minimize CC pressure (transaction contentions). Also, the unfair contention resolution of the lightweight OCC, a writer always wins over a reader, can be problematic in heterogeneous workloads. It is quite common that read-intensive analytic transactions are mixed with short, update-intensive transactions. The extreme favor for writers can cause massive aborts or even starvation of read-intensive transactions, consequently. Another problem is lazy transaction coordination policy that affects overall performance drastically. During forward processing, transactions keep all footprints locally and validate them only at the pre-commit time. Committed changes to a transaction's read set are not visible until the reader starts to validate its reads, wasting CPU cycles on long readers that are destined to abort. Regardless optimistic or pessimistic, the CC mechanism should not only have a low false positive rate detecting conflicts, but it should allow the system to detect doomed transactions as early as possible to minimize the amount of wasted work.

To recap, the following features are desirable for CC to orchestrate heterogeneous transactions: 1) robustness against contention, 2) balanced contention resolution over reader and writer and 3) early detection of abort conditions to minimize the amount of wasted work. Based on that, we believe that snapshot isolation based CC schemes satisfy all those requirements. Under snapshot isolation, reader-writer contention never happen by distributing transactions to multiple versions, bringing significantly higher throughput of read-intensive transactions. Also, it can recognize write-write conflicts as early as possible, possibly reducing the amount of wasted work on aborts.

Nevertheless, snapshot isolation still has remaining concerns. First of all, in presence of cyclic transaction dependency, SI can generate "write-skew" phenomenon which can violate serializable schedule. Generally SSI proposals in literature ensure serializability by tracking the "dangerous structure" that must exist in every serial dependency cycle under snapshot isolation. But their expensive tracking methods are usually prohibitively expensive for memory-optimized systems and tendency of aborting the "pivot" update transaction can starve writers [48], violating the fairness requirement. We argue that a cheap, fair certifier that can be overlaid on top of SI is the desired approach to serializability. We adopt such a certified, the Serial Safety Net [48] and describe it in Section 3. Also, efficient infrastructures in underlying physical layer are essential to make the SI-based CC schemes efficiently. We introduce physical layer supports in the following paragraphs.

Scalable centralized logging. Log managers are a well-known source of complexity and bottlenecks in a database system. The in-memory log buffer is a central point of communication that simplifies a variety of other tasks in the system, but which tends to kill scalability. Past work has attempted to optimize [21] or distribute [47] the log, with partial success and significant additional complexity. Systems such as H-Store [23] (and its commercial version, VoltDB) largely dispense with logging and rely instead on replication. These systems replace the logging bottleneck with a transaction dispatch bottleneck. Silo avoids the logging bottleneck by giving up the traditional total order in transactions. Avoiding total ordering is efficient but prevents the system from using any but the simplest of CC schemes—there is no practical way to implement repeatable read or snapshot isolation, for example.

We advocate a sweet spot between the extremes of fully coordinated logging (multiple synchronization points per transaction) and fully uncoordinated logging (no synchronization at all): latch-free logging with single synchronization point per transaction. A transaction with a reasonably small write footprint can acquire a totally ordered commit timestamp, and reserve all needed space in the log, using a single global atomic memory operation. While technically a potential bottleneck, our experimental results will prove that such a system can scale to *hundreds of thousands* of commits per second, while still preserving global ordering information that enables SI-based concurrency control schemes. We present this log manager in Section 3.

Latch-free indirection arrays. Transaction processing systems typically depend on their low-level storage manager component to mediate thread interactions at the physical level. The implementation of the storage manager is extremely tightly coupled to the CC scheme, making it difficult to modify or extend the CC schemes of legacy systems. Internal infrastructure matters terribly. It decides whether it is even possible to implement a particular CC scheme, and also which implementable schemes can be made practical. For example, the effort to enhance Postgres with serializable snapshot isolation (SSI) required a very large implementation effort, since the team had to integrate what it is essentially a lock manager with a purely multi-versioned system. Even then, the achieved performance borders on unusable, due to severe bottlenecks in multiple parts of the system (including a globally serialized pre-commit phase, latch contention in the new lock manager, and existing scalability problems in the log manager).

One promising technique that provides desirable properties for both SI-based CC schemes and physical contention is the notion of an *indirection array* [11, 40] for mapping logical object IDs to physical locations of records. Most of all, it is suitable for the physical implementation of CC for multi-versioned systems, as a single compare-and-swap (CAS) operation suffices to install a new version of an object without the use of heavyweight locking methods. Similarly, presence of an uncommitted version makes write-write conflicts easy to detect and manage.

Also, indirection can reduce the amount of logging required for an update in append-only systems. Update only requires installing a new physical pointer at the appropriate indirection array entry. Without the indirection, creating a new version requires updating every reference to that record, amplifying the amount of log records.

Moreover, it can reduce update pressure in (especially secondary) indexes; by storing a logical address (OID) of a tuple, indexes are isolated from update, as an OID of an updated tuple remains the same. Even though modern indexes leverage latch-free thread coordination for higher parallelism [30] [33], concurrent update still comes at an additional cost. Therefore, it is beneficial to offload the concurrent update pressure from the indexes to indirection arrays which have cheaper thread coordination. When it comes to secondary index maintenance, some systems maintain secondary indexes by mapping primary keys and secondary keys to avoid the update-propagation, however, it shifts burden to readers; secondary index access has to entail additional primary index probe.

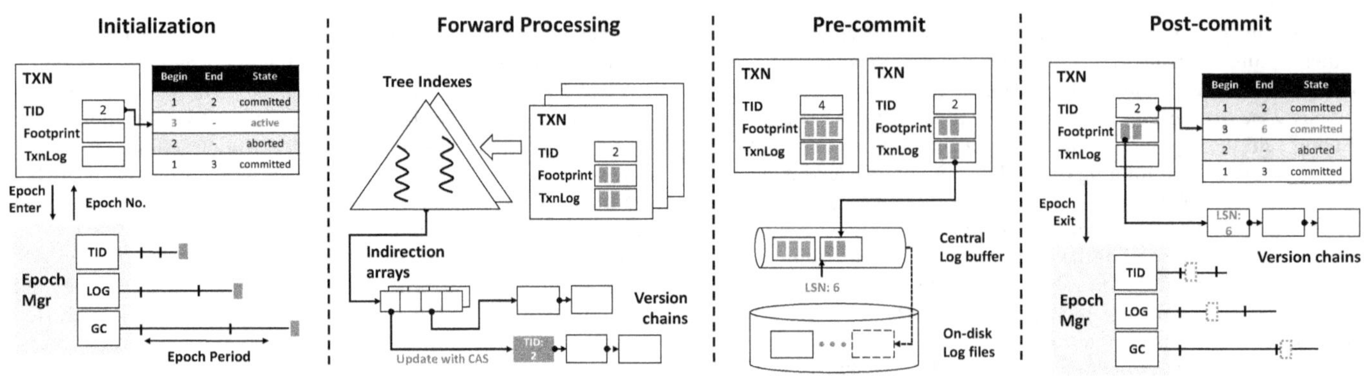

Figure 3: Architecture of ERMIA and transaction lifecycle.

Append-only storage. Append-only storage allows drastic simplifications of both I/O patterns and corner cases in the code. Combining a carefully designed log manager and indirection arrays produces a single-copy system where the log is a significant fraction of the database. Records graduate from the log to secondary storage only if they go a long time with no updates. The resulting system is also easier to recover, as both undo and redo are largely unnecessary—the log can be truncated at the first hole without losing any committed work.

Epoch-based resource management. Resource management is a key concern in any storage manager, and one of the most challenging aspects of it is ensuring that all threads in the system have a consistent view of the available resources, without imposing heavy per-access burdens. The infamous "ABA problem" [17] from the lock-free literature is one example of what can go wrong if the system does not maintain invariants about the presence and status of in-flight accesses. Epoch-based resource management schemes such as RCU [34] achieve this tracking at low cost by requiring only that readers inform the system whether they are *active* (possibly holding references to resources) or *quiescent* (definitely not holding any references to resources). These announcements can be made fairly infrequently, for example when a transaction commits or a thread goes idle. Resource reclamation then follows two phases: the system first makes the resource unreachable to new arrivals, but delays reclaiming it until all threads have quiesced at least once (thus guaranteeing that all thread-private references have died). Epoch-based resource management is especially powerful when combined with multi-versioning, as writers can coexist relatively peacefully with readers. Although epochs are traditionally fairly coarse-grained (e.g. hundreds of ms in Silo), we have implemented an epoch manager that is lightweight enough to use even at very fine time scales. As discussed in Section 3.4, ERMIA instantiates several epoch managers, all running at different time scales, to simplify all types of resource management in the system.

3. ERMIA

In this section, we start with an overview of ERMIA, and then describe its key pieces, with a focus on why we choose the design trade-offs we do.

3.1 Overview

ERMIA is designed around latch-free indirection arrays, epoch-based resource management and extremely efficient centralized logging. For indexing, it uses Masstree which is a concurrent and cache-efficient index structure, as Silo does [33]. We next briefly describe how ERMIA processes transactions using the components shown in Figure 3.

Initialization. When a transaction enters the system, it first joins three epoch-based resource managers: (1) the log manager, (2) transaction ID (TID) manager, and (3) the garbage collector. These resource managers then start to track the transaction to make sure that their resources (log buffers, TIDs and versions, respectively) are allocated/reclaimed correctly. Upon start, each transaction acquires a private log buffer, a TID and a begin timestamp—the current log sequence number (LSN). The transaction then calls in to the TID manager for initializing its transaction context and stores the begin timestamp in the context for CC interactions. The transaction is then ready to begin forward processing.

Forward processing. In ERMIA, transactions access the database through tree indexes. We associate each index/table with an indirection array. Different from traditional designs which give access to data in the leaf nodes, we store object IDs (OIDs) in the leaf level. Indexed by object IDs (OIDs), each array entry points to a chain of historic versions of the object (i.e., database record). Dictated by the underlying CC scheme, the transaction performs read/insert/update/delete operations on these structures (detailed in Section 3.2 and Section 3.6). To install a new version, the transaction stores its TID into the version's creation timestamp field. Other transactions who encounter the TID-stamped version have to follow the owner transaction's context with the TID to check if the version is visible. Each transaction accumulates the *descriptors* of its inserts and updates in the private log buffer to avoid log buffer contention. The garbage collector periodically goes over all indirection arrays to remove versions that are not needed by any transaction.

Pre-commit. We divide the commit process into two parts: pre-commit and post-commit. During pre-commit, the transaction first obtains a commit LSN from the log manager to fix its global order among all transactions and to reserve the space for storing its logs in the centralized log buffer. This is achieved by using a single atomic `fetch-and-add` instruction, which advances the current LSN by the size of the transaction's write footprint. Note that in most cases, this is the only global synchronization point in the log during a transaction life cycle. The transaction then goes through the underlying CC's commit protocol (detailed in Section 3.6), and follows the descriptors in its private log buffer to populate log records in its space reserved in the centralized log buffer. After this, the transaction switches its state to "committed"; all updates are visible to other transactions atomically after this point.

Post-commit. If a transaction survives pre-commit, it iterates versions in write-set, replacing its TID in the versions' creation timestamp field with its commit LSN, so that other transactions can directly check visibility on the LSN-stamped versions without accessing the owner transaction's context. Finally, the transaction concludes by returning all resources and de-registering from epoch managers. If the transaction needs to abort, it changes its state to "aborted" and removes write-set versions from the version chains.

3.2 Indirection arrays

The indirection arrays used in ERMIA are linear arrays and similar to the ones proposed in the literature [11, 40]. All logical objects (database records) are identified by an OID that maps to a slot in an indirection array. The slot contains a physical pointer to data. The pointer may reference a chain of versions stored in memory, or stable storage (e.g., the durable log on disk). ERMIA leverages a latch-free singly linked list structure to provide cheap multi-versioning support. We next illustrate how insert, update, and read operations are handled with the structures.

Insert. The transaction first obtains a new OID from the OID manager and generates a new version. It then will store the new version's address to the corresponding slot in the table's indirection array. Note that this process is completely contention-free: it simply means writing to an element in an array of OIDs because no two threads will be allocated with the same new OID. After setting up the OID entry, the insert finishes by inserting to indexes using a key provided by the application.

Update/delete. To update a record, the transaction needs to create a new version out-of-place, and then follow the index and indirection array to reach the version chain. The new version is installed by an atomic `compare-and-swap` instruction against the corresponding OID slot in the indirection array, because the entry stores the address of the head version. An uncommitted head version acts as a write lock, so that write-write conflicts can be detected. Delete is treated as an update with tombstone marking. The garbage collector periodically scans the indirection arrays and removes any versions that are not needed (including deleted ones). Note that whether a transaction can update a record is dictated by the underlying CC scheme.

Read/scan. Once a transaction found an OID with a given key through index probe, it accesses the corresponding OID slot to fetch the first version in the version chain. While traversing the chain, the underlying CC scheme dictates read operations. It returns the appropriate version that should be read by a transaction based on the begin timestamp of the transaction and the version's creation timestamp. Scans are handled similarly, except that the transaction will first conduct a range query (instead of a point query) in the index to figure out which records (i.e., indirection array entries) to access.

Admittedly the use of another level of indirection will impose extra cache misses. But it is still promising in that database changes are largely absorbed by the indirection array; the updates are not propagated to other parts of database including indexes, as OIDs in the indexes remain same as before. Consequently, it can reduce the amount of log data and thread contentions in the indexes (usually concurrent trees).

3.3 Logging

The log manager is a pivotal component in most databases. It provides a centralized point of coordination that other pieces of the system build off of and depend on. Although its central nature can simplify recovery and provide transaction ordering for SI-based CC schemes, the log is also a notorious source of contention in many systems. ERMIA's log manager retains the benefits of a serial "history of the world" while largely avoiding the contention issues

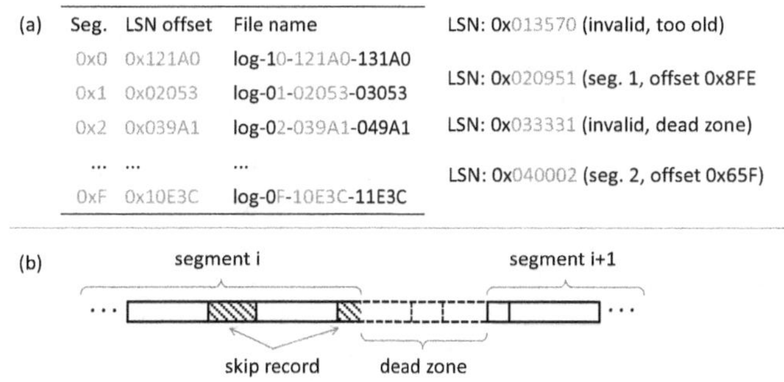

Figure 4: LSN space management.

that normally accompany it. In particular, ERMIA's log manager features the following four useful features:

1. Communication in the log manager is extremely sparse. Most update transactions will issue just one global atomic fetch-and-add before committing, even in the presence of high contention and corner cases such as full log buffer or log file rotations.
2. Transactions maintain log records privately while in flight, and aggregate them into large blocks before inserting them into the centralized log.
3. Transactions can acquire their commit LSN before entering pre-commit, thus simplifying the latter significantly (as all committing transactions agree on their relative commit order).
4. Large object writes can be diverted to secondary storage, requiring only an indirect pointer in the actual log.

The central feature of the log—*a single global atomic operation per insert*—rests on a key observation: while the LSN space must be monotonic, it need not be contiguous as long as sequence numbers can be translated efficiently to physical locations on disk. Therefore, each LSN consists of two parts: the higher-order bits identify an offset in a logical LSN space, while the lowest-order bits identify the physical log segment file the offset maps to. There are a fixed number of log segments in existence at any time (16 in our prototype), but segments may be arbitrarily large and are sized independently of each other.[2] Placing the segment number in low-order bits preserves the total of log offsets.

Figure 4 (a) illustrates how the system converts between LSN and physical file offsets. Each modulo segment number is assigned a physical log segment, which consists of a start and end offset, and the name of the file that holds the segment's log records. The file name is chosen so the segment table can be reconstructed easily at start up/recovery time, even if the current system's log segment size is different than that of the existing segments. Given the mapping table, LSN can be validated and converted to file offsets using a constant-time look up into the table.

Because we allow holes in the LSN space, acquiring space in the log is a two-step process. First, the thread claims a section of the LSN space by incrementing a globally shared log offset by the size of the requested allocation. Then, having acquired this block of logical LSN space, the transaction must validate it against various corner cases:

- Log segment full. If the block straddles the end of the current segment file, it cannot be used and a skip record is written in its place to "close" the segment. The thread competes to open the next segment file (see below) before requesting a new LSN.

[2] A system can thus scale log segment sizes upward to handle higher loads, and downward to conserve disk space.

- Between segments. Threads that acquire a log block that starts after the current segment file must compete to open the next segment. Blocks preceding the winner's block must be discarded as they do not correspond to a valid location on disk; losers retry.
- Log buffer full. The transaction retains its LSN but must wait for the corresponding buffer space to drain before using it.

Once a thread validates its LSN offset, it combines the segment and offset to form a valid LSN. A transaction can request log space at any time, for example to enter pre-commit with a valid commit LSN or to spill an oversized write footprint to disk; should it later abort, it simply writes a skip record.

Figure 4 (b) illustrates the various types of log blocks that might exist near a log segment boundary. Skip records in the middle of the segment come from aborted transactions (or are overflow blocks disguised as skip records). The skip record at the end of the segment "closes" the segment and points to the first valid block of the next segment. The "dead zone" between segments i and $i+1$ contains blocks that lost the race to open segment $i+1$; these do not map to any location on disk and should never be referenced.

Decoupling LSN offsets from log buffer and log file management simplifies the log protocol to the point that a single atomic operation suffices in the common case. There are only two times a transaction might require additional atomic operations: (a) Occasionally, a segment file will close and several unlucky transactions will race to open the next one. This case is very rare, as segment files can be hundreds of GB in size if desired. (b) A large write transaction may not be able to fit all of its log records in a single block, and so would be forced to write some number of overflow log blocks in a backward-linked list before committing. We expect this case to *reduce* contention, because a thread servicing large transactions—even with overflow blocks—will not visit the log nearly as often as a thread servicing short requests.

Because the log allocation scheme is fully non-blocking, there is no reliable way to know whether a thread has left. A thread with a reference to a segment that is about to be recycled could end up accessing invalid data (e.g. from segment $i+16$ rather than segment i). Therefore, we use an epoch manager to ensure that stragglers do not suffer the ABA problem when the system recycles modulo segment numbers, and that background cleaning has migrated live records to secondary storage before a segment is reclaimed (reassigning its modulo segment number effectively removes it from the log's "address space").

3.4 Epoch-based resource management

Epoch-based memory management–exemplified by RCU [34]—allows a system to track readers efficiently, without requiring readers to enter a critical section at every access. Updates and resource reclamation occur in the background once the system can prove no reader can hold a reference to the resource in question. Readers inform the system when they become *active* (intend to access managed resources soon) and *quiescent* (no longer hold any references to managed resources). These announcements are decoupled from actual resource accesses in order to amortize their cost, as long as they are made reasonably often. Ideal points in a database engine would include transaction commit or a worker thread going idle. Resource reclamation then follows two phases: the system first makes the resource unreachable to new arrivals, but delays reclaiming it until all threads have quiesced at least once (thus guaranteeing that all thread-private references have died). Once a resource is proven safe to reclaim, reclamation proceeds very flexibly: worker threads are assigned to reclaim the resources they freed and a daemon thread performs cleanup in the background.

We have developed a lightweight epoch management system that can track multiple time lines of differing granularities in parallel. A multi-transaction-scale epoch manager implements garbage collection of dead versions and deleted records, a medium-scale epoch manager implements read-copy-update (RCU) that manages physical memory and data structure usages [34], and a very short timescale epoch manager tracks transaction IDs , which we recycle aggressively (see details in Section 3.5).

The widespread and fine-grained use of epoch managers is enabled by a very lightweight design we developed for ERMIA. It has three especially useful characteristic. First, the protocol for a thread to report activation and quiescent points is lock-free and threads interact with the epoch manager through thread-private state they grant it access to. Thus, activating and quiescing a thread is inexpensive. Second, threads can announce conditional quiescent points: if the current epoch is not trying to close, a read to a single shared variable suffices. This allows highly active threads to announce quiescent points frequently (allowing for tighter resource management) with minimal overhead in the common case where the announcement is uninteresting. Third, and most importantly, ERMIA tracks three epochs at once, rather than the usual two.

In a traditional epoch management scheme, the "open" epoch accepts new arrivals, while a "closed" epoch will end as soon as the last straggler leaves. Unfortunately, this arrangement cannot differentiate between a straggler (a thread that has not yet quiesced in a long time) and a busy thread (one which quiesces often but is likely to be active at any given moment). Thus, when an epoch closes, most busy threads in the system will be flagged as stragglers—in addition to any true stragglers—and will be forced to participate in an expensive straggler protocol designed to deal with non-responsive threads. The ERMIA epoch manager, in contrast tracks a third epoch, situated between the other two, which we call "closing." When a new epoch begins, all currently active threads become part of the "closing" epoch but are otherwise ignored. Only when a third epoch begins does the "closing" epoch transition to "closed" and check for stragglers. Active threads will have quiesced and migrated to the current (open) epoch, leaving only true stragglers—if any—to participate in the straggler protocol.

Although the three-phase approach tracks more epochs, the worst-case duration of any epoch remains the same: it cannot be reclaimed until the last straggler leaves. In the common case where stragglers are rare, epochs simply run twice as often (to reflect the fact that threads have two epoch-durations to quiesce).

3.5 Transaction management

At its lowest level, the transaction manager is responsible to provide information about transactions that are currently running, or which recently ended, and this is partly achieved by allocating TIDs to all transactions and mapping those TIDs to the corresponding transaction's state. In our system, this is especially important because the CC scheme (see below) makes heavy use of TIDs to avoid corner cases.

Similar to the LSN allocation scheme the log manager uses, ERMIA's transaction manager assigns a TID to each transaction that combines an offset into a fixed-size table (where transaction state is held) with an epoch that identifies the transaction's "generation" (distinguishing it from other transactions that happened to use the same slot of the TID table).

Each entry in the TID table records the transaction's full TID (to identify the current owner), begin timestamp (an LSN), end timestamp (if one exists), and current status. The latter two fields are the most heavily used by the CC scheme, as transactions stamp records they create with their TID and only change that stamp to a commit timestamp during post-commit. During the cleanup period, other transactions will encounter TID-stamped versions and must call into the transaction manager to learn the true commit status/stamp. Such inquiries about a transaction's state can have three possible outcomes: (a) the transaction could still be in flight, (b) the transaction has ended and the end stamp is returned, or (c) the supplied TID is invalid (from a previous generation). In the latter case, the caller should re-read the location that produced the TID—the transaction in question has finished post-commit and so the location is guaranteed to contain a proper commit stamp.

The TID table has limited capacity (currently 64k entries), and so the generation number will change frequently in a high-throughput environment. The TID manager thus tracks which TIDs are currently in use—allowing them to span any number of generations—and recycles a given slot only once it has been released. Because the system only handles a limited number of in-flight transactions at a time (far fewer than 64k), at most a small fraction of the TID table is occupied by slow transactions.

To serve TID inquiries and handle allocation/deallocation of TIDs across multiple generations (all of which are quite frequent), we use only lock-free protocols. An epoch manager running at the time scale of a typical TID allocation detects and deals with stragglers who are delayed while trying to allocate a TID. This is only possible because the epoch manager is so lightweight. Without an epoch manager, a mutex would be required to prevent bad cases such as double allocations and thread inquiries returning inaccurate results.

3.6 Concurrency control

ERMIA's physical layer allows efficient implementations of a variety of CC schemes, including read-set validation and multi-version CC. In this paper, we focus on handling *read-mostly* workloads gracefully with SI-based CC schemes. Different components in the physical layer work together to support them efficiently; indirection arrays allow cheap (almost free) multi-versioning at an extremely low overhead; the log gives total ordering which is the key to implement snapshot-based CC mechanisms. To guarantee serializability, we adopt the Serial Safety Net (SSN) [48], a recent serializability certifier that can be overlaid on top of SI. We first give a brief overview of SI, and then explain in detail how SSN works and how we prevent phantoms.

3.6.1 Snapshot Isolation

Although not serializable [4], snapshot isolation (SI) is an ideal choice to start from: long, read-mostly transactions will have much higher chance to survive compared to lightweight OCC schemes.

Under SI, reads and writes never block each other. Reads are done by traversing the version chains: the reader transaction needs to perform visibility check directly on LSN-stamped versions by comparing its begin timestamp and the version's creation timestamp. If the version's creation timestamp predates the visitor's begin timestamp, the transaction will read it. Otherwise it moves on to the next version. In case the version's creation timestamp is a TID, the visitor has to access the owner transaction's context for visibility check. If the owner transaction is committed (but have not finished post-commit, i.e., it is still filling in the creation timestamp for new versions), and its commit timestamp predates the visitor's begin timestamp, the version is also visible. Otherwise the visitor has to move on to check the next version (which must be a committed version). Each update is done by installing a new version at the head of the chain. We forbid a transaction to update a record that has a committed head version later than its begin timestamp. We follow the "first-updater-wins" rule, so write-write conflicts are detected if the head version is uncommitted. The doomed updater will abort

Algorithm 1 SSN commit protocol [48]

```
def ssn_commit(T):
  t.cstamp = next_timestamp() # begin pre-commit

  for v in t.writes: # finalize η(T)
    t.pstamp = max(t.pstamp, v.pstamp)

  # finalize π(T)
  t.sstamp = min(t.sstamp, t.cstamp)
  for v in t.reads:
    t.sstamp = min(t.sstamp, v.sstamp)

  if t.sstamp <= t.pstamp:
    t.abort()

  t.status = COMMITTED

  # update η(V)
  for v in t.reads:
    v.pstamp = max(v.pstamp, t.cstamp)

  for v in t.writes:
    v.prev.sstamp = t.sstamp # update π(V)
    # initialize new version
    v.cstamp = v.pstamp = t.cstamp
```

immediately to avoid dirty write, minimizing the amount of wasted work on aborts.

Since our SI scheme makes sure that dirty reads never happen and write-write conflicts have already been avoided on every update, if a transaction can successfully finish all of its updates, it enters pre-commit, following the process we have mentioned in earlier paragraphs to obtain a commit LSN, changes its status to "committed", and finishes its post-commit phase.

3.6.2 Serializability

Compared to OCC, SI can achieve better performance when handling heterogeneous workloads. However, it is not serializable. The existing state-of-the-art to make SI serializable is Serializable SI (SSI) [6], which tracks the "dangerous structure" that will cause possible non-serializable executions under SI. Despite its effectiveness, SSI could starve writers because it tends to abort the "pivot" (writer) transaction when there are concurrent readers in the dangerous structure. Instead, ERMIA adopts a recent proposal, the Serial Safety Net (SSN) [48], which provides both serializability and balanced reader/writer performance to guarantee serializability.

The Serial Safety Net. SSN is a cheap certifier that can be overlaid on top of any CC mechanism that prevents lost updates and dirty reads. The underlying CC scheme (e.g., SI) still dictates transaction access patterns; SSN only adds additional checks during transaction execution and at commit time to avoid non-serializable executions, which indicate a cycle in the corresponding dependency graph, where conflicting transactions represented by vertices are connected by dependency edges. Transactions are added to the graph once committed. To detect cycles, for each transaction T SSN maintains an easily-computed *priority stamp* $\pi(T)$ that summarizes all dependent transactions that committed *before*, but must be serialized *after* T. During transaction execution (i.e., when handling reads and writes) and at commit time, T will apply an *exclusion window* test against T's most-recent committed transaction U that conflicts with and committed before T. If U's commit timestamp (`cstamp`) is later than $\pi(T)$, then committing T might form a cycle in the dependency graph. Intuitively, SSN ensures that a "predecessor" (U) will not at the same time be a "successor" of T, which if committed might close a cycle in the dependency graph.

As noted in [48], the exclusion window test can be simplified as comparing a pair of timestamps: $\pi(T)$ and $\eta(T)$ which records T's most-recent predecessor: $\pi(T) \leq \eta(T)$ is forbidden. This observation leads to the commit protocol depicted in Algorithm 1. After getting a commit timestamp, the transaction will go over its write set to finalize its $\eta(T)$. Note that record versions also maintain their π (`sstamp`) and η (`pstamp`) values, which are recorded by the corresponding transaction which overwrote or read the versions. Similarly, the transaction then examines its read set to finalize its `sstamp`. If the transaction survives the exclusion window test, it will proceed to update all read versions' `pstamp` with its `cstamp`. The commit protocol then finishes by updating overwritten versions' `sstamp` and initializing new versions with the `cstamp`.

Compared to SSI, SSN provides balanced performance for both readers and writers, and does not exaggerate the starvation of writers. Specifics about SSN vs. SSI are out of the scope of this paper; interested readers may refer to [48] for details.

Phantom protection. Although SSN prevents serialization dependency cycles, non-serializable executions can still arise due to *phantoms*, or insertion of new records into a range previously read by an in-flight transaction. ERMIA is amenable to various phantom protection strategies, such as hierarchical and key-range locking [26, 32]. We inherit Silo's tree-version validation strategy [46]. The basic idea is to track and verify tree node versions, taking advantage of the fact that any insertion into an index will change the version number of affected leaf nodes. As Silo does, ERMIA also maintains a *node set*, which maps from leaf nodes that fall into the range query to node versions. The node set is examined after pre-commit. If any node's version has changed, the transaction must abort to avoid a potential phantom. Interested readers may refer to [46] for details.

3.7 Recovery

Recovery in ERMIA is straightforward because the log contains only committed work; OID arrays are the only real source of complexity. The OID array objects are updated in place to avoid overloading the log, and are thus effectively volatile in-memory data structures. However, they are needed to find all other objects in the system (including themselves), so ERMIA employs a combination of fuzzy checkpointing and logical logging to maintain OID arrays properly across crashes and restarts. All OID arrays are periodically copied (non-atomically) and the disk address of each valid OID entry is dumped to secondary storage after recording a checkpoint-begin record in the log. A checkpoint-end record records the location of the fuzzy snapshot once the latter is durable. The location of the most recent checkpoint record is also recorded in the name of an empty checkpoint marker file in the file system. During recovery, the system decodes the checkpoint marker, restores the OID snapshots from the checkpoint, then rolls them forward by scanning the log after the checkpoint and replaying the allocator operations implied by insert and delete records. The replay process examines only log block headers which take less than 10% out of total space and does *not* replay the insertions or deletions themselves (which are safely stored in the log already). A similar process could potentially be applied to other internal data structures in the system, such as indexes, but we leave that exploration to future work. It is important to note that the process of restoring OID arrays is exactly the same when coming up from either a clean shutdown or a crash—the only difference is that a clean shutdown might have a more recent checkpoint available.

In summary, because the log is the database [3, 5], recovery only needs to rebuild the OID arrays in memory using sequential I/O; anti-caching [10] can take care of loading the actual data, though background pre-loading is highly recommended to minimize cold start effects.

4. EVALUATION

In this section, we evaluate the performance of ERMIA using various benchmarks including both traditional, update-heavy and emerging heterogeneous workloads. We compare the performance of ERMIA and Silo [46], a representative lightweight OCC implementation optimized for main-memory and multicore hardware. Through the experiments, we are interested in revealing and confirming the mismatch between lightweight OCC and heterogeneous workloads, and showing that ERMIA achieves its design goals of providing robustness and fairness, while maintaining high performance. Therefore, our experiments focus on two perspectives: (1) the capability to serve heterogeneous workloads (in particular, avoiding starvation of read-mostly transactions) and (2) scalability of the physical layer on massively parallel hardware.

4.1 Experimental setup

We run our experiments on a quad-socket server with four Intel Xeon E7-4807 processors (24 physical threads in total) and 64GB of RAM. All worker threads are pinned to a dedicated core to minimize context switch penalties and inter-socket communication costs. Log records are written to *tmpfs* asynchronously. We measure the performance of three systems with different CC schemes: Silo (Silo-OCC), ERMIA with SI (ERMIA-SI), and ERMIA with SSN (ERMIA-SSN). For Silo, read-only snapshots are enabled to handle read-only transactions. We also improved Silo's transaction abort handling and string manipulation mechanisms, which improves the throughput in TPC-C by $\sim$15% (in workloads where abort count is high, the impact of the optimization is higher than 15%). To achieve fair comparison, ERMIA uses the same benchmark code and phantom prevention mechanism as Silo's.

4.2 Benchmarks

We run a microbenchmark, TPC-C and TPC-E benchmarks on all system variants. For TPC benchmarks, we run both the original version described by the specifications [43, 44] and modified versions that contain synthesized read-mostly transactions. For each run, we load data from scratch on a pre-faulted memory pool and run the benchmark for 30 seconds. All runs are repeated for three times and we report the average numbers.

Microbenchmark. We use the the Stock table in TPC-C benchmark to build a synthesized workload. The microbenchmark consists of a single transaction that randomly picks a subset of the Stock table to read and a smaller fraction of it to update. The purpose is to create read-write conflicts. We have discussed the results from this benchmark in Section 1.

TPC-C. It is well-known that TPC-C is update-heavy with small transaction footprints. TPC-C is also a partitionable workload: conflicts can be reduced by partitioning and single-threading on local partitions. In such a environment, the only source of contention is cross-partition transactions. However, its impact is dampened by the small footprints, avoiding the majority of read-write conflicts. In this benchmark, we partition the database by warehouse ID and assign each worker thread a local warehouse, but 1% of the NewOrder transactions and 15% of Payment transactions are cross-partition.

TPC-C-hybrid. To simulate heterogeneous workloads, we adopt a modified version of the Query2 transaction (TPC-CH-Q2*) in TPC-CH [13] benchmark. The original version of Q2 lists suppliers in a certain region and their items having the lowest stock-level. We modify the query by enforcing it to pick a random region and update items in the stock table having lower quantity than a certain

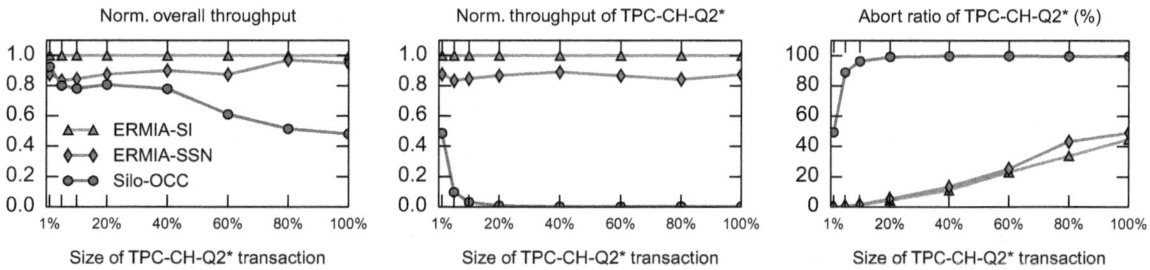

Figure 5: TPC-C-hybrid performance. Overall performance (left); TPC-CH-Q2* xct performance (middle), Abort ratio of TPC-CH-Q2* xct (right), varying size of TPC-CH-Q2* transaction. Performances are normalized to ERMIA-SI (see Table 1 for absolute numbers of overall TPS for ERMIA-SI).

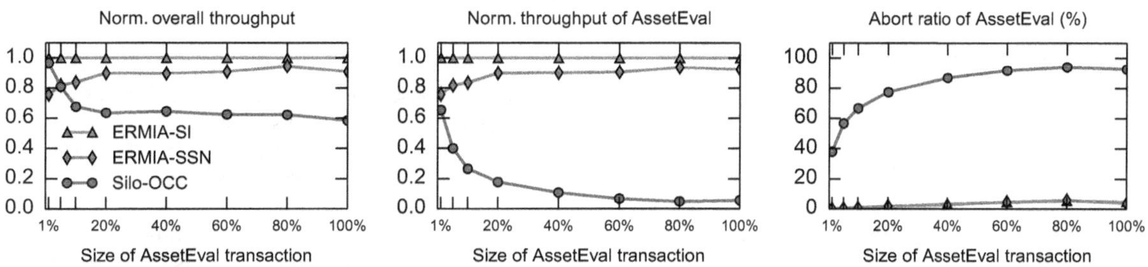

Figure 6: TPC-E-hybrid performance. Overall performance (left); AssetEval xct performance (middle), Abort ratio of AssetEval xct (right), varying size of AssetEval transaction. Performances are normalized to ERMIA-SI. (see Table 1 for absolute numbers of overall TPS for ERMIA-SI).

threshold. We vary the fraction of the Supplier table to be scanned by TPC-CH-Q2* to adjust transaction footprint size. The new transaction mix consists of 40% of NewOrder, 38% of Payment, 10% of TPC-CH-Q2*, and 4% of OrderStatus, StockLevel and Delivery each. The access pattern of TPC-CH-Q2* is determined by supplier ID, not by partitioning field (warehouse ID), thus, it is often cross-partition, interfering with local worker threads. Because of the majority of TPC-CH-Q2*'s access is in the Item and Stock tables, a TPC-CH-Q2* transaction will conflict frequently with NewOrder and other TPC-CH-Q2* transactions.

TPC-E. Although TPC-C has been dominantly used to evaluate OLTP systems, TPC-E is designed to be a more realistic OLTP benchmark with modern features. It models brokerage firm activities and has more sophisticated schema and transaction execution control [44]. It is also known for higher read-to-write ratio than TPC-C (~10:1 vs. ~2:1 [7]). The parameters we set for TPC-E experiments are 5000 customers, 500 scale factor and 10 initial trading days (the initial trading day parameter was limited by our machine's memory capacity).

TPC-E-hybrid. Similar to the changes we made to TPC-C, we also augment TPC-E with a new read-mostly transaction (AssetEval). AssetEval evaluates the aggregate assets for random customer accounts and inserts the results into a newly added AssetHistory table. The total asset of an account is computed by joining the HoldingSummary and LastTrade tables. The vast majority of contentions will occur between AssetEval and TradeResult transactions. To vary the degree of contention and the footprint size of AssetEval, we adjust the size of a customer account group in the CustomerAccount table to be scanned by AssetEval. The revised workload mix is as follows: BrokerVolume (4.9%), CustomerPosition (8%), MarketFeed (1%), MarketWatch (13%), SecurityDetail (14%), TradeLookup (8%), TradeOrder (10.1%), TradeResult (10%), TradeStatus (9%), TradeUpdate (2%) and AssetEval (20%).

	1%	5%	10%	20%	40%	60%	80%	100%
TPC-C-hybrid	70,319	12,938	5,698	2,435	1,173	868	750	647
TPC-E-hybrid	37,151	7,675	4,298	2,142	1,090	705	524	429

Table 1: Overall TPS of ERMIA-SI in TPC-C-hybrid and TPC-E-hybrid over varying sizes of read-mostly transactions.

4.3 Impact of CC schemes

We explore how ERMIA and Silo react to heterogeneous workloads with the different CC schemes they employ. We first examine the throughput of read-mostly transactions in all the three CC schemes. We extract performance numbers of TPC-CH-Q2* and AssetEval transactions from TPC-C-hybrid and TPC-E-hybrid benchmarks, respectively, and normalize them to the numbers of ERMIA-SI. As shown in Figure 5 (middle), Silo-OCC only produces half TPC-CH-Q2* commits in ERMIA, even at the smallest footprint size. As we increase the size of TPC-CH-Q2* transaction, Silo-OCC quickly collapses, converging to nearly zero throughput for this transaction. Starting from 40%, Silo-OCC produces two orders of magnitudes lower commits than ERMIA. Figure 6 (middle) shows a relatively modest curve for Silo-OCC because TPC-E-hybrid has less contention than TPC-C-hybrid. Nevertheless, Silo-OCC becomes quickly vulnerable in high contention scenarios and the throughput of AssetEval quickly drops to unacceptable level, the same as in TPC-C-hybrid.

Figure 5 (right) and Figure 6 (right) show the percentage of aborted TPC-CH-Q2* and AssetEval transactions out of their number of total executions. We find strong correlation between abort ratio and the throughput of read-mostly transactions. In TPC-E-hybrid, 40% of AssetEval transactions are aborted by Silo-OCC

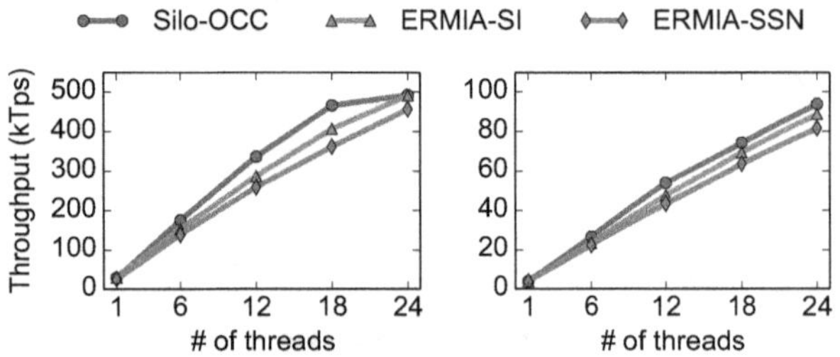

Figure 7: Throughput when running TPC-C (left); TPC-E (right). ERMIA achieves near-linear scalability over 24 cores and comparable peak performance to Silo.

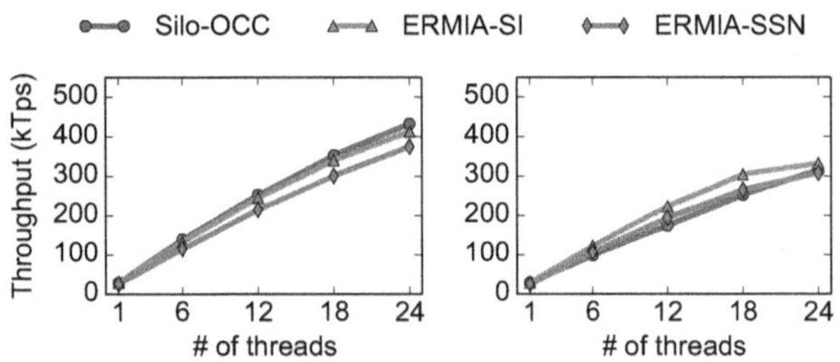

Figure 8: Throughput when running TPC-C with uniformly random access (left); TPC-C with 80-20 access skew (right). Due to robust CC schemes, ERMIA is less sensitive to contention.

at the smallest footprint size and it keeps increasing as the size of AssetEval grows. TPC-C-hybrid shows a much sharper increase of abort ratio under Silo-OCC due to frequent conflicts with NewOrder. ERMIA generally commits most read-intensive transactions. Note that ERMIA's abort ratio also increases when TPC-CH-Q2*'s footprint size passes the 40% mark. Since read-write conflicts never happen under SI, the majority of the aborts in ERMIA-SI came from write-write conflicts between TPC-CH-Q2* transactions, which are inevitable under any CC scheme that prevents dirty reads and lost updates. SSN adds slightly more aborts on top of it, but the number of the additional aborts due to serializability violation is marginal. This verifies that contention imposed heavy pressure on the CC and lightweight OCC is not a good match for heterogeneous workloads because of unacceptable performance penalty for read-mostly transactions due to unfair contention resolution. Read-mostly transactions are unlikely to commit as a result of extreme favor for short, update-intensive transactions. Meanwhile, ERMIA effectively protects read-intensive transactions from updaters with SI.

Figure 5 (left) and Figure 6 (left) show the normalized overall throughput when varying the size of TPC-CH-Q2* and AssetEval transactions. ERMIA-SI performs the best at all transaction sizes and ERMIA-SSN pays an additional cost for serializability guarantee; this comes from the trade-off between strong consistency and performance. ERMIA maintains superior overall performance while committing most heavyweight, read-mostly transactions, while Silo-OCC rarely commits them. Note that higher commits for read-mostly transactions do not significantly contribute to overall throughput due to their limited fractions out of workload mix. The figure also highlights OCC's reader starvation and lazy communication problems. As shown in Figure 6 (left), the performance gap between ERMIA and Silo-OCC closes when we hit the

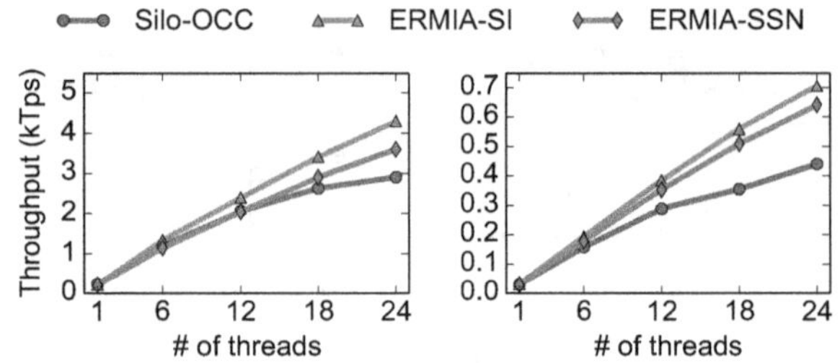

Figure 9: Throughput when running TPC-E-hybrid with 10% AssetEval transaction (left); with 60% AssetEval transaction (right). CC pressure deteriorates scalability of Silo in heterogeneous workloads.

5% mark for AssetEval footprint size. After this point, Silo-OCC becomes worse than ERMIA's. A similar trend is found in Figure 5 (left), with an earlier break-even point at 1% to 5%. These trends show that Silo-OCC's growing loss on read-mostly transactions affects overall performance.

Another interesting finding is that Silo-OCC is still slower than ERMIA despite its negligible commits from read-mostly transactions. If the underlying CC had detected read-mostly transactions that are destined to abort in a timely manner, it should have skipped the uncomfortable transactions and switched to other (much shorter) transactions as early as possible, reaping more commits from other transactions. Unlike SI and SSN, the lightweight OCC schemes cannot detect conflicts until commit time. Hence, heavyweight read-mostly transactions often lead to unnecessary domination of CPUs, instead of giving more CPU cycles to other transactions that are more likely to commit. On the other hand, ERMIA can detect write-write conflicts on every update, giving some transactions early-out and avoids most read-write conflicts. This is evidenced by Figure 5 (left and right): starting from the 20% mark on the x-axis, the increasing performance gap between ERMIA and Silo does not indicate Silo-OCC's sudden slowdown, but rather shows that ERMIA minimized the amount of wasted work on aborted TPC-CH-Q2* transactions, by capturing write-write conflicts early and switching to other transactions. This result proves that OCC's validate-at-commit scheme can have a huge impact on overall performance, wasting a tremendous amount of CPU cycles.

4.4 Scalability

In this section, we measure scalability of all systems in diverse workloads, from original TPC benchmarks to mixed workloads we introduced. We start from original TPC benchmarks where lightweight OCC shines, as those workloads impose little pressure on the OCC scheme.

We measure overall throughput in TPC-C and TPC-E, varying the number of worker threads. Figure 7 shows that ERMIA achieves comparable peak performance and scalability trends to Silo-OCC in both TPC-C and TPC-E. Silo-OCC shows the best performance by taking advantages of its low-overhead CC and physical layer when little CC pressure exists. On ERMIA, indirection arrays brought more cache-misses and SSN paid additional serializability guarantee cost. In TPC-E, Silo-OCC avoided most of read-write conflicts by forwarding read-only transactions to read-only snapshots although TPC-E is more contentious than TPC-C (when read-only snapshots are turned off, Silo-OCC delivers similar performance to ERMIA-SSN).

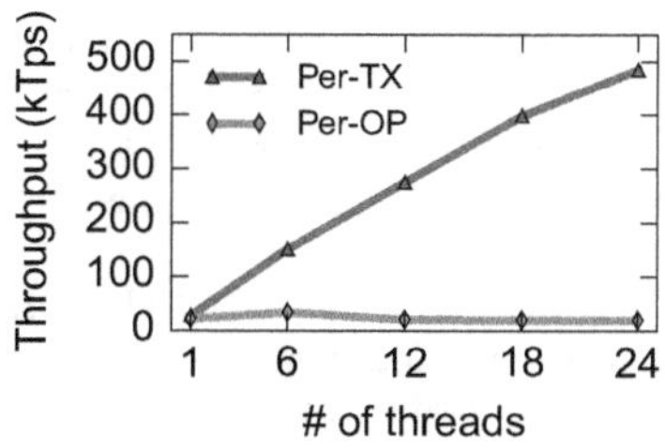

Figure 10: Throughput of ERMIA-SI with per-transaction logging and per-operation logging when running TPC-C.

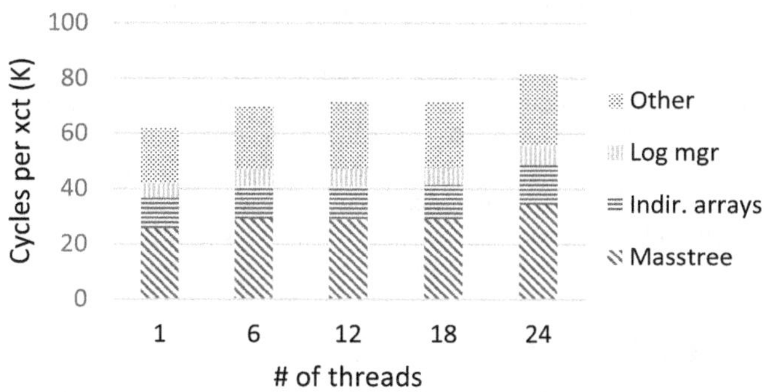

Figure 11: Cycle breakdown of the various components of ERMIA-SI when running an increasing number of threads run TPC-C.

To investigate the impact of skew-induced contentions on scalability, we enforce workers to pick up target partition randomly in TPC-C, following uniform and 80-20 random distribution, each time transactions start. In Figure 8, we can find that growing access skew suppresses Silo-OCC's scalability more than ERMIA; Silo-OCC is dragged down to performance of ERMIA-SI with uniform random access and to performance of ERMIA-SSN performance with highly skewed access.

We also study the impact of heavy read-mostly transaction on scalability in heterogeneous workloads. Figure 9 shows scalability at different sizes, 10% and 60%, of AssetEval transaction in TPC-E-hybrid, increasing the number of concurrent workers. Overwhelmed by CC-pressure, Silo-OCC does not achieve linear scalability and it becomes worse as we run larger read-mostly transactions. ERMIA benefits from its robust CC scheme and scalable storage manager. This figure shows that not only the scalability of underlying physical layer, but also CC scheme performance dictates overall performance.

Figure 10 shows efficiency of ERMIA's log manager. Unlike the WAL protocol, ERMIA log manager has only single round-trip to centralized log buffer at pre-commit to reduce contention. As comparison, we emulate the traditional way of logging by enforcing log buffer round-trip for every single update operation. As shown in the figure, the impact of per-transaction logging is drastic in memory-optimized systems. The per-operation logging did not scale at all, even without log buffer latching (single atomic instruction was used to reserve log buffer space).

Figure 11 illustrates CPU cycle breakdown per transaction of ERMIA-SI in TPC-C. With growing parallelism, the critical components maintain quite steady overhead. It indicates that the building blocks of ERMIA are generally scalable over 24 cores. As shown in the figure, Masstree takes the biggest bottleneck (41%) out of total

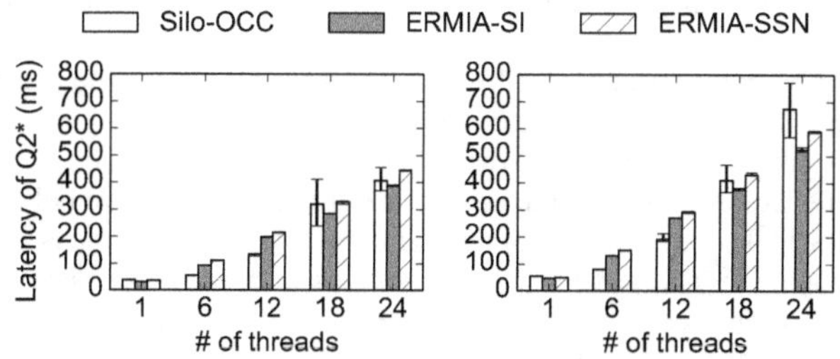

Figure 12: Latency of TPC-CH-Q2* at 60% size (left); 80% size (right), varying the number of threads. Under Silo-OCC, latency fluctuates with larger transaction size and higher concurrency.

cycles. At the expense of robust CC schemes, ERMIA pays 16% overhead as indirection costs which mainly came from additional last-level cache misses (32% of cache misses occurred in the indirection arrays). The overhead of log manager consistently takes 8 9% at all points; it proves that fully-decentralized logging and giving up total ordering are not necessarily required to achieve scalability over 24 cores. Although we ran the experiments on a 24-core machine, we do not expect that log manager's overhead will skyrocket over 32 cores. The cost of epoch-based resource managers are negligible (less than 1%). Resource management does not suffer from thread contentions at all.

4.5 Latency analysis

In this section, we perform latency analysis. Figure 12 shows latency of TPC-CH-Q2* over varying number of threads with 60% and 80% transaction size. We calculated average latency of the transaction within a run and presented the median value out of three runs in the figure. The maximum and minimum values are represented with error bars. Note that latency of TPC-CH-Q2* transaction is proportional to the number of threads in TPC-C-hybrid workload because the Stock table which is heavily accessed by the transaction grows proportionally to scale factor, and we give the same number of scale factor with the number of threads.

Let us take a look on latency variance first. Both ERMIA-SI and ERMIA-SSN have negligible variance in all cases. Under Silo-OCC, the transaction latency is consistent in general, however, in the cases where the transaction is large and the number of concurrent threads are high, we can observe latency fluctuation (noticeable variance tends to appear when the transaction takes more than 200ms). Also, latency increases more quickly than ERMIA with increasing parallelism, as shown in Figure 12. Considering growing size of the transaction, ERMIA delivers consistent latency regardless of concurrent threads indeed.

One of the main reasons for the results is read-write contention. During commit protocol, lightweight OCC grabs write locks on their write set first, validates read set and releases the write locks after installation of the write set. Meanwhile, readers facing the locked tuples have to wait for them to be released. Since both larger transaction size and higher concurrency possibly trigger more read-write contention, they often lead to larger latency variance and performance burden. In the worst case, heavy read-mostly transactions can hold write locks for a long time until read validation on their huge footprint is completed, blocking other transactions to proceed upon read-write conflict. Fundamentally, it is a problem of single-versioned database and might not be a serious problem when serving short transactions only. However, in the presence of heavy read-mostly transactions, it could bring huge latency variance and slowdown, as confirmed by Figure 12.

Another factor that possibly affects latency in Silo is the use of spinlock in coordinating read-write contention. Spinlock generally does not consider fairness over waiters; some unlucky readers could wait excessively due to the random nature of spinlock. We believe MCS lock could be a promising alternative for its fairness and multicore friendliness [35]. In addition, we also found that Masstree relies on spinlock for concurrent access coordination, which partly causes latency increases.

5. RELATED WORK

In terms of concurrency control, one of the most important studies has been [1]. This modeling study shows that if the overhead of pessimistic two-phase locking can be comparable to the overhead of optimistic methods then the pessimistic one is superior. The same study shows that it is beneficial to abort transactions that are going to abort as soon as possible. For higher concurrency, snapshot isolation has been widely used in practice, despite of its non-serializable scheduling in presence of cyclic transaction dependency. There have been some proposals that guarantee serializability with snapshot isolation [6, 12, 15, 39].

Many of the memory-optimized systems adopt lightweight optimistic concurrency control schemes that are suitable only for a small fraction of transactional workloads. Silo[46], Hekaton[11] and Foedus[25] employ lightweight optimistic concurrency control schemes that perform validations at pre-commit. As a comparison with ERMIA, Silo performs in place updates: under normal circumstances the system maintains only a single committed version of an object, in addition to some number of uncommitted private copies (only one of which can be installed). In order to support large read-only transactions, a heavyweight copy-on-write snapshot mechanism must be invoked. These snapshots are too expensive to use with small transactions, and unusable by transactions that perform any writes. Similarly, Microsoft Hekaton[11] employs similar multi-versioning CC [28]. It is technically multi-versioned, but the snapshot-plus-read-validation CC scheme it uses means that older versions become unusable to update transactions as soon as any overwrite commits. Foedus keeps logically-equivalent snapshots in NVRAM for OLAP queries. For all practical purposes, these systems are multi-versioned only for read-only transactions.

H-Store (and its commercial version, VoltDB) is a characteristic partitioning-based system [23]. H-Store physically partitions each database to as many instances as the number of available processors, and each processor executes each transaction in serial order without interruption. Performance issues raise when the system has to execute multi-site transactions that touch data from two or more separate database instances. Lots of work has been put in the area, including low overhead concurrency control mechanisms [22], deterministic transaction execution to avoid two-phase commit overhead [42], and partitioning advisors that help to co-locate data that are frequently accessed in the same transactions, thereby reducing the frequency of multi-site transactions, e.g. [9, 38, 45].

For scaling up, many proposals have focused on exploiting multicore parallelism. DORA [36] employs logical partitioning and PLP [37] extends the data-oriented execution principle, by employing physiological partitioning. Under PLP, the logical partitioning is reflected at the root level of the B+tree indexes that now are essentially multi-rooted. Both DORA and PLP use Shore-MT's codebase [20], which is a scalable but disk-optimized storage manager. Hence, their performance lacks in comparison with the memory-optimized proposals. Additionally, even though only logical, there is a certain overhead in the performance due to the partitioning mechanism employed. Aether is an holistic approach for scalable logging, minimizing centralized log buffer contention [18]. It combined several techniques such as early lock release, log buffer pipelining and consolidation buffer. Wang et al. [47] proposed distributed logging with non-volatile memory to improve logging performance even further.

HANA[41] and Hyrise[14] are OLAP-OLTP hybrid engines with more focus on analytic side. Commonly, they append delta records to row-store partitions and gradually transform the delta to columnar compressed main tables. Krueger et al. suggested an efficient merge operation between the delta partitions and main tables, exploiting multicore parallelism as well [27]. Hyper [24] follows H-Store's single-threaded execution principle. It exploits "copy-on-write" functionality to generate snapshots for read-only queries. To scale up to multi-cores, they employ the hardware transactional memory capabilities of the latest generation of processors [29].

The indirection array, which is central to ERMIA's design, is a well-known technique, for example presented in [40]. It is worth mentioning that Hekaton also uses a technique similar to the indirection map. ERMIA relies on Masstree for indexing. Masstree[33] is a trie-based index structure, designed with lock-free technique for concurrent thread coordination. In Hekaton, Bw-tree[30] exploits indirection map and delta records to achieve lock-free design.

6. CONCLUSION

In this paper, we underlined the mismatch between the lightweight OCC currently in vogue with memory-optimized systems and emerging heterogeneous workloads that include read-mostly transactions. To address the challenge, we proposed ERMIA, a memory-optimized transaction processing system built from scratch, to accommodate heterogeneous workloads. It provides robust and balanced CC schemes to orchestrate heterogeneous transactions. Also its physical layer supports the CC schemes efficiently and achieves near-linear scalability over parallel processors with scalable centralized log manager, latch-free indirection arrays and epoch-based resource managers. Experimental results confirm that ERMIA can maintain high performance for long read-mostly transactions, while achieving comparable or superior overall performance and (near-linear) scalability in various transactional workloads.

7. REFERENCES

[1] R. Agrawal, M. J. Carey, and M. Livny. Concurrency control performance modeling: alternatives and implications. *ACM TODS*, 12(4), 1987.

[2] P. Bailis, A. Fekete, J. M. Hellerstein, A. Ghodsi, and I. Stoica. Scalable atomic visibility with ramp transactions. In *SIGMOD*, 2014.

[3] M. Balakrishnan, D. Malkhi, V. Prabhakaran, T. Wobbler, M. Wei, and J. D. Davis. CORFU: A shared log design for flash clusters. In *NSDI*, 2012.

[4] H. Berenson, P. Bernstein, J. Gray, J. Melton, E. O'Neil, and P. O'Neil. A critique of ANSI SQL isolation levels. In *SIGMOD*, 1995.

[5] P. A. Bernstein, C. W. Reid, and S. Das. Hyder - a transactional record manager for shared flash. In *CIDR*, January 2011.

[6] M. J. Cahill, U. Röhm, and A. D. Fekete. Serializable isolation for snapshot databases. In *SIGMOD*, 2008.

[7] S. Chen, A. Ailamaki, M. Athanassoulis, P. B. Gibbons, R. Johnson, I. Pandis, and R. Stoica. TPC-E vs. TPC-C: Characterizing the new TPC-E benchmark via an I/O comparison study. *SIGMOD Record*, 39, 2010.

[8] J. C. Corbett et al. Spanner: Google's globally-distributed database. In *OSDI*, 2012.

[9] C. Curino, E. Jones, Y. Zhang, and S. Madden. Schism: a workload-driven approach to database replication and partitioning. *PVLDB*, 3, 2010.

[10] J. DeBrabant, A. Pavlo, S. Tu, M. Stonebraker, and S. Zdonik. Anti-caching: A new approach to database management system architecture. *PLVDB*, 2013.

[11] C. Diaconu, C. Freedman, E. Ismert, P.-A. Larson, P. Mittal, R. Stonecipher, N. Verma, and M. Zwilling. Hekaton: SQL Server's memory-optimized OLTP engine. In *SIGMOD*, 2013.

[12] J. M. Faleiro and D. J. Abadi. Rethinking serializable multiversion concurrency control. *PVLDB*, 8(11), 2015.

[13] F. Funke, A. Kemper, and T. Neumann. Benchmarking hybrid OLTP&OLAP database systems. In *BTW*, 2011.

[14] M. Grund, J. Krüger, H. Plattner, A. Zeier, P. Cudre-Mauroux, and S. Madden. HYRISE—A main memory hybrid storage engine. *PVLDB*, 4, 2010.

[15] H. Han, S. Park, H. Jung, A. Fekete, U. Rohm, and H. Yeom. Scalable serializable snapshot isolation for multicore systems. pages 700–711, March 2014.

[16] S. Harizopoulos, D. J. Abadi, S. Madden, and M. Stonebraker. OLTP through the looking glass, and what we found there. In *SIGMOD*, 2008.

[17] M. Herlihy and N. Shavit. *The Art of Multiprocessor Programming*. Morgan Kaufmann Publishers Inc., San Francisco, CA, USA, 2008.

[18] R. Johnson et al. Aether: a scalable approach to logging. *PVLDB*, 3, 2010.

[19] R. Johnson, I. Pandis, and A. Ailamaki. Eliminating unscalable communication in transaction processing. *The VLDB Journal*, 2013.

[20] R. Johnson, I. Pandis, N. Hardavellas, A. Ailamaki, and B. Falsafi. Shore-MT: a scalable storage manager for the multicore era. In *EDBT*, 2009.

[21] R. Johnson, I. Pandis, R. Stoica, M. Athanassoulis, and A. Ailamaki. Aether: a scalable approach to logging. *PVLDB*, 3, 2010.

[22] E. Jones, D. J. Abadi, and S. Madden. Low overhead concurrency control for partitioned main memory databases. In *SIGMOD*, 2010.

[23] R. Kallman, H. Kimura, J. Natkins, A. Pavlo, A. Rasin, S. Zdonik, E. P. C. Jones, S. Madden, M. Stonebraker, Y. Zhang, J. Hugg, and D. J. Abadi. H-Store: a high-performance, distributed main memory transaction processing system. *PVLDB*, 2008.

[24] A. Kemper and T. Neumann. HyPer – a hybrid OLTP&OLAP main memory database system based on virtual memory snapshots. In *ICDE*, 2011.

[25] H. Kimura. FOEDUS: OLTP engine for a thousand cores and NVRAM. In *SIGMOD*, 2015.

[26] H. Kimura, G. Graefe, and H. Kuno. Efficient locking techniques for databases on modern hardware. In *ADMS*, 2012.

[27] J. Krueger, C. Kim, M. Grund, N. Satish, D. Schwalb, J. Chhugani, H. Plattner, P. Dubey, and A. Zeier. Fast updates on read-optimized databases using multi-core CPUs. *PVLDB*, 5(1), 2011.

[28] P.-A. Larson, S. Blanas, C. Diaconu, C. Freedman, J. M. Patel, and M. Zwilling. High-performance concurrency control mechanisms for main-memory databases. *PVLDB*, 5(4), 2011.

[29] V. Leis, A. Kemper, and T. Neumann. Exploiting hardware transactional memory in main-memory databases. In *ICDE*, 2014.

[30] J. Levandoski, D. Lomet, and S. Sengupta. The Bw-tree: A B-tree for new hardware. In *ICDE*, 2013.

[31] J. Levandoski, D. Lomet, S. Sengupta, R. Stutsman, and R. Wang. High performance transactions in deuteronomy. In *CIDR*, 2015.

[32] D. B. Lomet. Key range locking strategies for improved concurrency. In *VLDB*, 1993.

[33] Y. Mao, E. Kohler, and R. T. Morris. Cache craftiness for fast multicore key-value storage. In *EuroSys*, 2012.

[34] P. E. McKenney and J. D. Slingwine. Read-copy update: Using execution history to solve concurrency problems. *Parallel and Distributed Computing and Systems*, 1998.

[35] J. M. Mellor-Crummey and M. L. Scott. Algorithms for scalable synchronization on shared-memory multiprocessors. *ACM Trans. Comput. Syst.*, 9(1), 1991.

[36] I. Pandis, R. Johnson, N. Hardavellas, and A. Ailamaki. Data-oriented transaction execution. *PVLDB*, 3(1), 2010.

[37] I. Pandis, P. Tözün, R. Johnson, and A. Ailamaki. PLP: page latch-free shared-everything OLTP. *PVLDB*, 4(10), 2011.

[38] A. Pavlo, E. P. C. Jones, and S. Zdonik. On predictive modeling for optimizing transaction execution in parallel OLTP systems. *PVLDB*, 5(2), 2011.

[39] D. R. K. Ports and K. Grittner. Serializable snapshot isolation in postgresql. *PLVDB*, 5(12), 2012.

[40] M. Sadoghi, K. A. Ross, M. Canim, and B. Bhattacharjee. Making updates disk-I/O friendly using SSDs. *PVLDB*, 6, 2013.

[41] V. Sikka, F. Färber, W. Lehner, S. K. Cha, T. Peh, and C. Bornhövd. Efficient transaction processing in SAP HANA database: the end of a column store myth. In *SIGMOD*, 2012.

[42] A. Thomson and D. J. Abadi. The case for determinism in database systems. *PVLDB*, 3, 2010.

[43] TPC. TPC benchmark C (OLTP) standard specification, revision 5.11, 2010. Available at http://www.tpc.org/tpcc.

[44] TPC. TPC benchmark E standard specification, revision 1.12.0, 2010. Available at http://www.tpc.org/tpce.

[45] K. Q. Tran, J. F. Naughton, B. Sundarmurthy, and D. Tsirogiannis. JECB: A join-extension, code-based approach to OLTP data partitioning. In *SIGMOD*, 2014.

[46] S. Tu, W. Zheng, E. Kohler, B. Liskov, and S. Madden. Speedy transactions in multicore in-memory databases. In *SOSP*, 2013.

[47] T. Wang and R. Johnson. Scalable logging through emerging non-volatile memory. *PVLDB*, 2014.

[48] T. Wang, R. Johnson, A. Fekete, and I. Pandis. The Serial Safety Net: Efficient concurrency control on modern hardware. In *DaMoN*, 2015.

[49] X. Yu, G. Bezerra, A. Pavlo, S. Devadas, and M. Stonebraker. Staring into the abyss: An evaluation of concurrency control with one thousand cores. *PVLDB.*, 8(3), 2014.

Transaction Healing: Scaling Optimistic Concurrency Control on Multicores

Yingjun Wu, Chee-Yong Chan, Kian-Lee Tan
School of Computing, National University of Singapore
{yingjun, chancy, tankl}@comp.nus.edu.sg

ABSTRACT

Today's main-memory databases can support very high transaction rate for OLTP applications. However, when a large number of concurrent transactions contend on the same data records, the system performance can deteriorate significantly. This is especially the case when scaling transaction processing with optimistic concurrency control (OCC) on multicore machines. In this paper, we propose a new concurrency-control mechanism, called *transaction healing*, that exploits program semantics to scale the conventional OCC towards dozens of cores even under highly contended workloads. Transaction healing captures the dependencies across operations within a transaction prior to its execution. Instead of blindly rejecting a transaction once its validation fails, the proposed mechanism judiciously restores any non-serializable operation and heals inconsistent transaction states as well as query results according to the extracted dependencies. Transaction healing can partially update the membership of read/write sets when processing dependent transactions. Such overhead, however, is largely reduced by carefully avoiding false aborts and rearranging validation orders. We implemented the idea of transaction healing in THEDB, a main-memory database prototype that provides full ACID guarantee with a scalable commit protocol. By evaluating THEDB on a 48-core machine with two widely-used benchmarks, we confirm that transaction healing can scale near-linearly, yielding significantly higher transaction rate than the state-of-the-art OCC implementations.

1. INTRODUCTION

Optimistic concurrency control (OCC) is gaining popularity in the development of modern main-memory databases that target at supporting OLTP transactions on multicore machines [21, 35, 42, 55]. By clearly detaching the computation of a transaction from its commitment, OCC greatly shortens its lock-holding duration and therefore yields very high transaction rate when processing low-contention workloads.

Unfortunately, such performance benefits diminish for workloads with significant data contention, where multiple concurrent transactions access the same data record with at least one transaction modifying the record. A transaction using OCC protocol has to validate the consistency of its read set before commitment in order to ensure that no other committed concurrent transaction has modified any record that is read by the current transaction. If a transaction fails the validation, the transaction has to be aborted and restarted from scratch. Moreover, any partial work done prior to the abort will be discarded, wasting the resources that have been put into running the transaction. Such performance penalty can be exacerbated if the accessed records are highly contended, forcing a transaction to repeatedly abort and restart.

In this paper, we present *transaction healing*, a new concurrency-control mechanism that scales the conventional OCC towards dozens of cores even under highly contended workloads. The key observation that inspires our proposal is the fact that most OLTP applications contend on a few hot records [37], and the majority of transactions failing OCC's validation phase is due to the inconsistency of a very small portion of its read set. By exploiting program semantics of the transactions, expensive transaction aborts-and-restarts can be prevented by restoring only those *non-serializable operations*, whose *side effects*, i.e., the value returned by a read operation or the update performed by a write operation, are (indirectly) affected by a certain inconsistent read. Subsequently, inconsistent transaction states as well as query results can be healed without resorting to the expensive abort-and-restart mechanism. This approach significantly improves the resource-utilization rate in transaction processing, yielding superior performance for any type of workloads.

A key design decision in transaction healing is to maintain a thread-local structure, called *access cache*, to track the runtime behavior of each operation within a transaction. This structure facilitates the operation restoration in transaction healing from two aspects. First, the recorded side effects of each operation can be re-utilized to shorten the critical path for healing transaction inconsistencies; second, the cached memory addresses of the accessed records can be leveraged to eliminate any unnecessary index lookups for accessing targeted records. In particular, the maintenance of this data structure is very lightweight, which is confirmed by our experimental studies.

Transaction healing can partially update the membership of read-/write sets when processing dependent transactions[1]. Observing the high expense brought by such update, transaction healing avoids unnecessary overhead by carefully analyzing the false invalidation. While membership update can result in transaction abort due to deadlock prevention, our proposed schema-based optimization mechanism leverages the access patterns within the database applications to greatly reduce the likelihood of deadlock occurrences.

Different from the state-of-the-art OCC optimization techniques

[1]A dependent transaction is a transaction where its read/write set cannot be determined from a static analysis of the transaction [53].

SIGMOD'16, June 26-July 01, 2016, San Francisco, CA, USA

DOI: http://dx.doi.org/10.1145/2882903.2915202

that address scalability bottlenecks caused by redundant serial-execution points [21, 35, 55], the emphasis of transaction healing is to reduce the high cost of aborts-and-restarts from data contentions. This essentially renders OCC effective for a wider spectrum of OLTP workloads. The design of transaction healing is also a departure from existing hybrid OCC schemes [28, 52, 60]. Instead of executing restarted transactions with lock-based protocols, transaction healing attempts to re-utilize the execution results without restarting the invalidated transactions from scratch.

We implemented transaction healing in THEDB, a main-memory database prototype built from the ground up. Results of an extensive experimental study on two popular benchmarks, TPC-C and Smallbank, confirmed THEDB's remarkable performance especially under highly contended workloads.

This paper is organized as follows: Section 2 demonstrates transaction healing through a running example. Section 3 introduces the static analysis mechanism and Section 4 describes the runtime execution of transaction healing. We report extensive experiment results in Section 5. Section 6 reviews related works and Section 7 concludes this work.

2. TRANSACTION HEALING OVERVIEW

Transaction healing aims at scaling the conventional optimistic concurrency control (OCC) towards dozens of cores even under highly contended workloads. Inheriting the success of the state-of-the-art OCC protocols [21, 35, 55] in eliminating redundant serial-execution points, transaction healing further strengthens OCC's capability in tackling data conflicts by exploiting program semantics.

Optimistic concurrency control. The conventional OCC proposed by Kung and Robinson [34] splits the execution of a transaction into three phases: (1) a read phase, which tracks the transaction's read/write set using a thread-local data structure; (2) a validation phase, which certifies the consistency of its read set; and (3) a write phase, which installs all its updates atomically. While the detachment between computation and commitment shortens the lock-holding time during execution, the absence of lock protection in the read phase can compromise the consistency of an uncommitted transaction if certain record in its read set is modified by any committed concurrent transaction. Conventional OCC tackles such problem with a straightforward abort-and-restart strategy once inconsistency is detected. We illustrate the mechanism with a running example depicted in Figure 1a[2].

```
1.  PROCEDURE Transfer(srcId){
2.      dstId<-read(Client, srcId)
3.      srcVal<-read(Balance, srcId)
4.      dstVal<-read(Balance, dstId)
5.      tmp<-0.01*srcVal
6.      write(Balance, srcId, srcVal-tmp)
7.      write(Balance, dstId, dstVal+tmp)
8.      bonus<-read(Bonus, srcId)
9.      write(Bonus, srcId, bonus+1)
10. }
```

(a) Stored procedure.

Table: Client	
Amy	Dan

Table: Balance	
Amy	2,000
Dan	1,200

Table: Bonus	
Amy	18

(b) Initial database state.

Figure 1: Bank-transfer example.

Given the initial database state shown in Figure 1b, a transaction T_1 issued with argument Amy first assigns `dstId` with the value Dan (Line 2) and then transfers \$20 to Dan's Balance account (Lines 3-7). Finally, \$1 is returned back to Amy's Bonus account (Lines 8-9). During the validation phase, T_1 will be determined as inconsistent if a concurrent transaction T_2 gets committed with Amy's balance modified from \$2,000 to, say, \$2,500. In this scenario, abort-and-restart mechanism is applied to ensure a serializable execution of T_1. Unfortunately, such a scheme can severely degrade the system performance if a certain data record is intensively updated, causing invalidated transactions to be repeatedly restarted from scratch.

Transaction Healing. Confronting the pros and cons of conventional OCC, transaction healing leverages program semantics to remedy OCC's weakness in addressing data conflicts. This is achieved with the help of static analysis at compile time that extracts operation dependencies hidden within the stored procedures.

Figure 2 compares the runtime execution of transaction healing with that of conventional OCC. Instead of directly rejecting an invalidated transaction, transaction healing resorts to an additional healing phase to handle any detected inconsistency by restoring the transaction's non-serializable operations. Given an invalidated transaction T, a read/write operation o in T is defined to be a *non-serializable operation* if the outcome of o would be different when T is re-executed. The healing phase aims to re-utilize as many of an invalidated transaction's execution results as possible to heal its inconsistent transaction state as well as its query results according to the extracted dependencies. The forward progress of any in-flight transaction is guaranteed by the design principle of transaction healing, as will be elaborated further in the following sections.

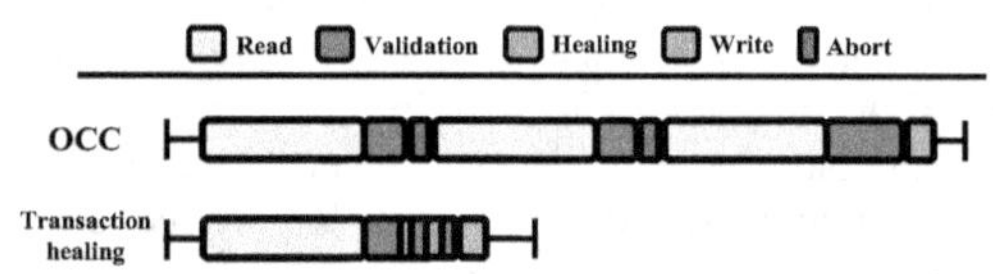

Figure 2: A comparison between OCC and transaction healing.

As an illustration, we discuss how transaction healing addresses the data conflicts exhibited in the running example with minimal execution overhead. Transaction healing maintains a thread-local access cache to track the behavior of every operation that is executed by T_1. On detecting the modification of Amy's balance during the validation phase of T_1, the operations in Line 3 and Lines 6-7 (see Figure 1a) are determined to be non-serializable. This is because the operation in Line 3 assigns Amy's balance to `srcVal`, which is subsequently used in Lines 6-7. Transaction healing therefore directly corrects the side effects made by these three operations without restarting the whole transaction. This strategy works as the maintained access cache records the runtime behavior of every operation in the transaction, and the results generated by those serializable operations can still be reused. Meanwhile, the invoked operation restoration does not trigger any expensive index lookups, since all the records that are read or written by the corresponding operation are logged in the access cache. Hence, the system overhead is greatly reduced.

THEDB overview. We implemented transaction healing in a main-memory database prototype called THEDB, which is specifically designed for modern multicore architecture. THEDB is designed to optimize the execution of transactions that are issued from *stored procedures* and it provides full support for ad-hoc queries. THEDB maintains locks with a per-record strategy. For each database record, THEDB maintains the following three metadata fields: (1) a *timestamp* field indicating the commit timestamp of the last transaction that writes the record; (2) a *visibility* bit in-

[2]For simplicity, we respectively abstract the *read* and *write* operations in a stored procedure as `var←read(Tab, key)` and `write(Tab, key, val)`. Both operations search records in table `Tab` using the accessing key called `key`. The read operation assigns the retrieved value to a local variable `var`, while the write operation updates the corresponding value to `val`.

dicating whether the record is visible to other transactions[3]; and (3) a *lock* bit indicating the lock status of the record. As we shall see, these additional fields enable an efficient implementation of the healing phase in THEDB.

In the following sections, we formalize the mechanism of transaction healing and show how this proposed technique improves the performance of THEDB without bringing costly runtime overhead.

3. STATIC ANALYSIS

THEDB performs static analysis [7] to extract operation dependencies from each predefined stored procedure prior to transaction processing. The goal is to help identify the inconsistent transaction states as well as the query results for any uncommitted transaction that fails its validation, which is elaborated in Section 4. For ease of presentation and to focus on the key ideas, this paper considers only stored procedures without conditional branches; details for handling more general procedures are given in the extended version of this paper [57].

THEDB classifies the dependencies among program operations into two categories: *key dependencies* and *value dependencies*. A key dependency captures the relation between two operations where the preceding operation directly determines the accessing key of the subsequent operation. A value dependency captures the relation between two operations where the generated output of the preceding operation determines the non-key value to be used in the subsequent operation. The dependencies in a program are extracted using a static analysis process and they are represented by a graph referred to as a *program dependency graph*. Figure 3 shows such a graph for the bank-transfer example listed in Figure 1a. We say that the operations in Lines 4 and 7 are key-dependent on the preceding operation in Line 2, because Line 2 generates `dstId` that is further used as accessing key in Lines 4 and 7. Operations in Lines 8 and 9, in contrast, depict a value-dependency relation, since the preceding read operation defines the variable `bonus` that is later used as update value in the subsequent write operation.

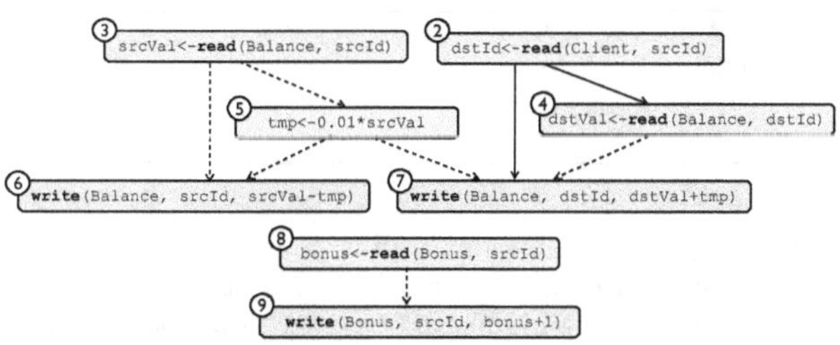

Figure 3: Program dependency graph. Solid lines represent key dependencies, while dashed lines represent value dependencies.

Given a stored procedure's program dependency graph, THEDB can leverage the extracted dependency information for healing the procedure's transactions that fail to pass the validation phase. The detailed mechanism is discussed in Section 4.

THEDB aborts any transaction that violates the integrities enforced by either application logic (e.g., user-defined constraints) or database constraints (e.g., functional dependencies). This is achieved by encoding additional dependencies for any enforced integrities in the program dependency graph. The whole transaction will be aborted once the restoration of any non-serializable operation results in the violation of integrities.

[3]The visibility bit for a record R is set to 0 iff R has been deleted by a committed transaction or R is newly inserted by a yet-to-be-committed transaction.

4. RUNTIME EXECUTION

This section describes the runtime execution of THEDB, our multicore database prototype that supports scalable transaction processing on multicores. THEDB serializes concurrent transactions using the transaction-healing protocol, which generally splits the execution of a transaction into three phases, including a read phase, a validation phase, and a write phase. During the validation phase, an additional healing phase is invoked to restore non-serializable operations once any inconsistent read is detected. This is achieved by leveraging a combination of the statically extracted dependency graph and the dynamically obtained execution information that is explicitly monitored during the transaction's execution.

In this section, we first explain transaction healing by modeling transactions using simple read and write operations where records are accessed given their key values (Sections 4.1-4.6). Specifically, Section 4.1 explains how transaction healing tracks runtime information during the read phase of the transaction execution, and Sections 4.2-4.6 show how the validation, healing, and write phases are designed and optimized to facilitate transaction processing under highly contended workloads. To show the generality of transaction healing, we discuss the support for generic database operations (e.g., inserts, deletes, and range queries) as well as ad-hoc transactions in Sections 4.7-4.8.

4.1 Tracking Operation Behaviors

Similar with conventional OCC, transaction healing tracks the read/write set of a transaction and buffers all the write effects during the read phase of its execution [11]. In particular, a read/write set is a thread-local data structure (i.e., a structure that is privately updated by a single thread) where each element in the set is represented by the main-memory address of some data record accessed by the transaction. In addition, the following metadata is maintained for each accessed record in the transaction's read/write set: (1) a *mode* field indicating the access type (i.e., read (R), write (W), or read-write (RW)) to the data record; (2) an *R-timestamp* field recording the value of the timestamp metadata of the data record at the time it was read; and (3) a *bookmark* field uniquely identifying the transaction's operation that first reads the record; if the record is created by a blind-write operation, its bookmark value is $null$. For simplicity, throughout the paper, we represent a bookmark value by the line number in the corresponding stored procedure.

In addition to the read/write set, transaction healing further maintains a lightweight thread-local *access cache* to keep track of the runtime behavior of each operation. Each operation invokes an index lookup to retrieve a certain number of database records. By using the outputs of preceding operations or the input arguments to its stored procedure, a read operation *op* returns certain values that will be either consumed by the operations that are dependent on *op* or used as query results, while a write operation yields update effects that will be buffered to the local copy of its accessed record. In transaction healing, the access cache monitors inputs, outputs, as well as update effects to capture each operation's behavior. Each operation further maintains an access set in the access cache to log the memory addresses of all the records it reads or writes. The access cache facilitates the restoration of an operation as follows: on the one hand, recording the runtime behavior for each operation helps re-utilize the execution results yielded by those serializable operations; on the other hand, caching the memory addresses of the accessed records eliminates the need for invoking an index lookup to access a record as long as the accessing key of the operation remains the same.

Figure 4 shows the thread-local data structures maintained for transaction T_1 that is created in the bank-transfer example (see Sec-

ACCESS CACHE

Bookmark	Inputs	Effects	Outputs	Access set
Line 2	*Amy*	-	*Dan*	{0xAAAA}
Line 3	*Amy*	-	*2000*	{0xBBBB}
Line 4	*Dan*	-	*1200*	{0xCCCC}
Line 6	*Amy, 1980*	*1980*	-	{0xBBBB}
Line 7	*Dan, 1220*	*1220*	-	{0xCCCC}
Line 8	*Amy*	-	*18*	{0xDDDD}
Line 9	*Amy, 19*	*19*	-	{0xDDDD}

READ/WRITE SET

Address	Mode	R-Timestamp	Bookmark
0xAAAA	R	25	Line 2
0xBBBB	RW	27	Line 3
0xCCCC	RW	10	Line 4
0xDDDD	RW	14	Line 8

Figure 4: Thread-local data structures.

tion 2). The execution of the read operation in Line 2 accesses a single data record stored at address `0xAAAA` and produces the value Dan that will be used by subsequent operations dependent on this read operation. Similarly, the write operation in Line 6 consumes two input arguments and updates the local copy of its corresponding record to \$1,980. In this example, although each entry in the access cache is associated with exactly one element in the read-/write set, in general, range queries in a transaction could retrieve multiple records and therefore each entry in the access cache can map to multiple elements.

As we shall see shortly, with the runtime information maintained in these thread-local data structures, transaction healing is able to restore any non-serializable operation efficiently during the validation phase without resorting to abort-and-restart mechanism that can lead to extremely low resource-utilization rate.

4.2 Restoring Non-Serializable Operations

4.2.1 *Validation Phase*

The read phase in the transaction execution is performed in a consistency-oblivious manner. That is, any committed concurrent transaction can modify the global copy of a data record in the database without notifying any concurrent transaction that has a local copy of the same record in its read/write set. Thus, transaction healing, similar to conventional OCC, resorts to a validation phase to check the consistency of every record that is read by a transaction before committing that transaction. We briefly depict transaction healing's validation phase in Algorithm 1.

Algorithm 1: Validation phase in transaction healing.

Data: Read/write set $\mathcal{S}$ of the current transaction.

Validation Phase:
foreach r **in** sorted($\mathcal{S}$) **do**
    Lock data record located at $r.address$;
    if r is accessed by any read operation **then**
        if Validation of r fails **then**
            Invoke healing phase for r;

In the validation phase for a transaction T, the data record corresponding to each element in T's read/write set will be locked and the locks are only released after the commit or abort of T. Locking of data records during the validation, healing, and write phases is necessary as multiple transactions could be concurrently validated and committed. Since the data records accessed by a transaction are known from its read/write set, deadlocks due to locking is avoided in THEDB by ordering the lock acquisitions following a global order that is applied to all transactions. In our implementation, the global order is based on an ascending order of the memory addresses of the data records [55].

For each element r in the read/write set $\mathcal{S}$, the validation phase first locks the data record R corresponding to r by turning on its lock bit. If R was retrieved by a read operation, the consistency of r is then validated by comparing the timestamps of R and r. A read inconsistency is detected if these timestamps are not equal, implying that a committed concurrent transaction has updated the same record. In this case, conventional OCC would abort and restart the entire transaction from scratch, wasting resources that have been put into running the transaction. Our proposed protocol, in contrast, detects and restores non-serializable operations by leveraging the data structures maintained in the thread-local workspace. This is achieved with the assistance of the healing phase.

4.2.2 *Healing Phase*

Algorithm 2: Healing inconsistent access during validation.

Data: Inconsistent element r, read/write set $\mathcal{S}$, access cache $\mathcal{C}$, and program dependency graph $\mathcal{G}$ of the current transaction.

Healing Phase:
Retrieve operation *op* $= r.bookmark$;
Restore *op*;
Retrieve child operation list $\mathcal{O}$ for *op* w.r.t. $\mathcal{G}$;
Initialize FIFO healing queue $\mathcal{H} = \mathcal{O}$;
while $\mathcal{H} \neq \emptyset$ **do**
    heal_op = PopFront($\mathcal{H}$);
    if *heal_op* is key-dependent on its parent operation **then**
        Update *heal_op*'s access set $\mathcal{M}$ through re-execution;
        foreach m **in** $\mathcal{M}$ **do**
            if $m.address < r.address$ **then**
                if Attempting to lock m fails **then**
                    Abort();
            Insert m into $\mathcal{S}$ and update $\mathcal{C}$;
    else
        Restore *heal_op*;
    Retrieve child operation list $\mathcal{P}$ for *heal_op*;
    foreach p **in** $\mathcal{P}$ **do**
        Insert p into $\mathcal{H}$;

Algorithm 2 shows how the healing phase works. On detecting an inconsistent element r that is read by an operation *op* in the transaction, the healing phase first corrects the outputs for *op*, which is the initial non-serializable operation whose side effect is influenced by the inconsistency of r. The modification on the record pointed by r can affect *op*'s outputs, subsequently influencing the behavior of the operations that are dependent on *op*. Instead of restoring *op* with a straightforward operation re-execution, transaction healing corrects *op*'s outputs by directly visiting the memory addresses maintained in the access cache. This approach fully eliminates the potential overhead brought by index lookup. Meanwhile, transaction serializability is still preserved. The key reason is that *op*'s accessing key remains the same despite of the raised inconsistency, and therefore the corresponding access set is still unchanged[4]. The effect of *op*'s restoration must be propagated to all operations dependent on *op*, which can be identified using the statically-extracted program dependency graph. On retrieving an operation list $\mathcal{O}$ comprising the operation that are directly dependent on *op*, transaction healing selects the correct healing strategy

[4]This statement is still valid even if inserts, deletes, or range queries exist. See Section 4.7 for a detailed explanation.

for each operation according to the dependency type with *op*, as described below.

Restoring value-dependent operations. The restoration of an operation *heal_op* that is value-dependent on *op* simply requires a direct access to the corresponding memory addresses maintained in the access cache. This is because while the restoration can modify *op*'s outputs that will be consumed as inputs by *heal_op*, the access set cached for *heal_op* remains the same, due to the invariance of *heal_op*'s accessing key.

For a transaction issued from the stored procedure in Figure 1a, transaction healing merely restores operations in Lines 8 and 9 once detecting the inconsistency of Amy's bonus account. Such restoration is lightweight, as the access cache maintains the corresponding record pointers that will be used by these operations, and the index lookup overhead is consequently eliminated.

Restoring key-dependent operations. The restoration of an operation *heal_op* that is key-dependent on *op* calls for a more sophisticated mechanism. This is because *op*'s output directly serves as the accessing key for *heal_op*, and therefore the correction of *op*'s output can affect the composition or even the size of *heal_op*'s access set. Consequently, the maintained access cache should not be used for accelerating the restoration of *heal_op*. Transaction healing solves this problem by invoking a complete re-execution of *heal_op*, where the latest access set is retrieved through index lookup. Such re-execution also updates the membership of the transaction's read/write set.

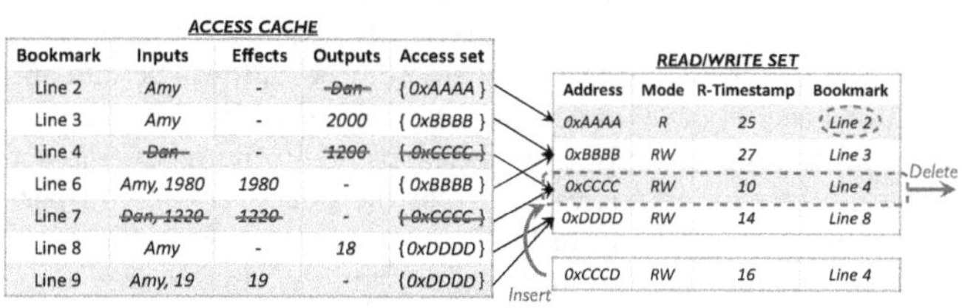

Figure 5: Healing inconsistency for the bank-transfer example.

We still use the bank-transfer procedure in Figure 1a to give a detailed explanation. Figure 5 shows the scenario where the validation of an instantiated transaction fails due to the detection that a committed concurrent transaction has updated Amy's client to $Dave$. The healing phase first corrects the output value from Dan to $Dave$ for the operation in Line 2. As this output is used as the accessing key in Lines 4 and 7, transaction healing further re-executes these two operations to retrieve the correct access set. In particular, the re-execution triggers an index lookup with the accessing key $Dave$. This also leads to a partial update to the membership of the read/write set, where the original element pointing to the memory address `0xCCCC` is replaced by a new one referring to the address `0xCCCD`. The healing phase terminates by correcting the update effects and outputs for these two operations.

Note that membership updates can cause deadlocks. Let us consider that a healing phase is invoked after detecting an inconsistent element r in the read/write set during validation. At this point, every element with a smaller memory address compared to r would have been locked, as is guaranteed by the global order of the validation phase. However, if a new element r_n containing a smaller memory address than r is inserted into the read/write set during the healing phase, the global order will be violated when attempting to lock r_n. Consequently, potential deadlocks can occur. Transaction healing resolves this problem using a no-waiting deadlock prevention technique [11, 61]. On confronting a failure when attempting to acquire the lock for r_n, transaction healing directly aborts the whole transaction instead of blindly spinning. This mechanism can be further optimized by setting an upper bound controlling the maximum number of times the lock request is attempted.

The read inconsistency within a transaction can be propagated through (indirect) operation dependencies. Transaction healing therefore recursively checks and restores all the possibly non-serializable operations by traversing the statically extracted program dependency graph in a breath-first approach. This essentially guarantees that any non-serializable operation is restored exactly once, and the healing overhead is minimized. The execution of a transaction resumes its validation once the healing phase completes. The forward progress of the validation is guaranteed because of the finite capacity of a transaction's read/write set. A transaction is allowed to commit if all the elements in its read/write set have been successfully validated. Transaction healing aborts a transaction only if the deadlock-prevention mechanism is triggered during the healing phase, where the membership of the read/write set is partially updated.

4.3 Committing Transactions at Scale

The commitment of a transaction installs all the locally buffered write effects to the database state. In addition, all the updates will also be flushed to the persistent storage for ensuring database durability. Transaction healing leverages a variation of epoch-based protocol [55] for committing transactions in a concurrent manner. The detailed mechanism is presented in Algorithm 3.

Algorithm 3: Commit protocol in transaction healing.

Data: Read/write set S of the current transaction.

Write Phase:
Generate global timestamp $glocal\_ts$;
Compute commit timestamp $commit\_ts$;
foreach r **in** sorted(S) **do**
    if r is accessed by any write operation **then**
        Install writes for data record R located at $r.address$;
        Dump writes to persistent storage;
        Overwrite timestamp of R with $commit\_ts$;

foreach r **in** sorted(S) **do**
    Unlock data record located at $r.address$;

In transaction healing, a commit timestamp is a 64-bit unsigned integer, where the higher order 32 bits contain a global timestamp and the lower order 32 bits contain a local timestamp. The global timestamp is assigned with the value of a global epoch number E that is periodically (e.g., every 10 ms) advanced by a designated thread in the system, and the local timestamp is generated according to the specific thread ID. As an example, given three threads for executing transactions, the first thread generates a local timestamp from the list $0, 3, 6, ..., 3m, ...$, while the third thread generates a local timestamp from the list $2, 5, 8, ..., 3n + 2, ...$. When committing a transaction, the corresponding thread will assign the transaction with the smallest commit timestamp that is larger than (a) the commit timestamp attached in any record read or written by the transaction and (b) the thread's most recently generated commit timestamp. On obtaining the commit timestamp $commit\_ts$, a transaction installs all the buffered writes to the database and assigns the corresponding records with $commit\_ts$. In particular, each thread persists its committed transactions independently, and updates from transactions assigned with a same global epoch number E can be dumped to the persistent storage as a group. When a transaction finishes its commitment, it releases all its locks.

4.4 Guaranteeing Serializability

This section sketches an argument that transaction healing provides full serializability for transaction processing.

Compared with OCC, transaction healing restores non-serializable operations to heal inconsistent transaction states and query results. When processing a transaction whose read/write set does not overlap with that of any concurrent one, the effect of transaction healing is essentially equivalent to that of OCC. Now let us assume that an inconsistent element r that is read by the transaction is detected during the validation. At this point, we denote the set of elements with smaller memory address than r as E_s, and the set of elements with larger memory address as E_l. To restore the initial non-serializable operation *op* that first reads the inconsistent r, transaction healing directly reloads the latest value of the record's global copy, which is referred to by r. This action does not compromise database serializability, because the lock bit associated with this record has already been acquired by the current thread. After restoring *op*, transaction healing begins to restore all the operations that are (possibly indirectly) dependent on *op*. Restoring operation op_v that is value-dependent on its parent operation only requires retrieving the latest values of the records pointed by the access cache. This action does not affect the serializability. On the one hand, if a record accessed by op_v is pointed by an element in E_s, then the record access is consistent, because the current thread has exclusive privilege for accessing the record; on the other hand, if a record accessed by op_v is pointed by an element in E_l, then the record access can be inconsistent. However, the remaining part of the validation phase will lock and validate any element in E_l. Therefore, the raised inconsistency will be healed. The restoration of an operation that is key-dependent on its parent operation, however, can partially update the membership of read/write set. The potential deadlock brought by such membership update is prevented by transaction healing, as transaction healing attempts to lock any newly inserted element r_i with a smaller memory address than that of r. An uncommitted transaction will be aborted once any lock-acquisition attempt fails during the membership update. Transaction healing guarantees forward progress and final termination of transaction processing. This is because the read/write set of any transaction maintains a finite number of elements, and the validation phase certifies the consistency of any element for exactly once. To conclude, transaction healing guarantees serializability when restoring non-serializable operations, and the effect of transaction healing is equivalent to that of OCC.

4.5 Optimizing Dependent Transactions

Transaction healing optimizes the execution of dependent transactions, which must perform reads for determining their full read-/write sets [53, 54]. Compared with their independent counterparts, dependent transactions usually require more efforts for resolving conflicting accesses, since the restoration of non-serializable key-dependent operations can partially update the membership of the read/write set, and transaction aborts can be invoked by the deadlock-prevention mechanism. Transaction healing reduces these overheads by (1) avoiding unnecessary membership update by eliminating false invalidations and (2) reducing the likelihood of deadlock occurrences by rearranging global validation orders.

Eliminating false invalidations. During the validation phase, a false invalidation can occur if any concurrent transactions accessing the same record modify a column that is not read by the current transaction. Figure 6 shows a simplified example of such a case.

While transactions T_1 and T_2 both access record R, T_1's read is not compromised by T_2's write. However, conventional OCC can still invalidate T_1's access when checking R's timestamp field.

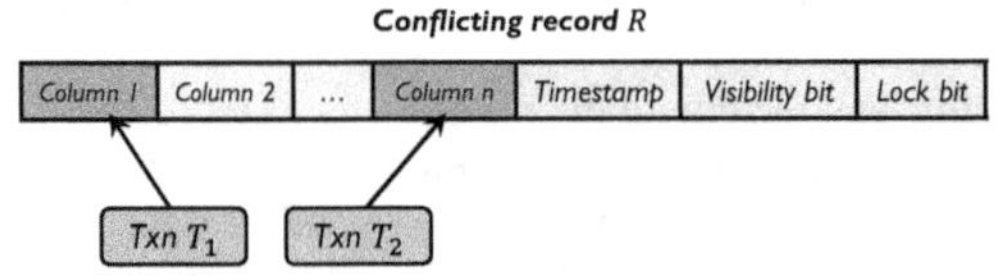

Figure 6: False invalidation. Transaction T_1 reads the first column while transaction T_2 writes the nth one. T_1 is invalidated although the write installed by T_2 does not affect T_1's correctness.

Such false invalidation is tolerable when processing independent transactions, but the invoked healing phase can bring high overhead for dependent transactions because of the partial membership update of the read/write set. Transaction healing eliminates such overhead by maintaining a local copy for each read operation. Once the validation of a certain element fails, transaction healing directly checks the value of the read column to determine whether a false invalidation occurs. This proposed mechanism may incur additional overhead inherited from memory allocation. However, our experiments confirm that such overhead is negligible.

Rearranging validation orders. Transaction healing can abort an uncommitted transaction when partially updating the membership of the read/write set, which is invoked by the restoration of an inconsistent key-dependent operation. The key reason is that the record accessing order in the healing phase may not be aligned with the global validation order, and therefore attempts will be made to lock any record with comparatively smaller memory address (see Section 4.2). Observing that most stored procedures in certain applications access tables based on a *tree schema* [20, 50], transaction healing consequently sorts the elements in the read/write set according to any topological order of the tree structure. In particular, elements pointing to the records extracted from the same table are ordered based on the memory address. In this way, only records with larger order are inserted into the read/write set during the membership update. As a result, the likelihood of deadlock occurrences is greatly reduced.

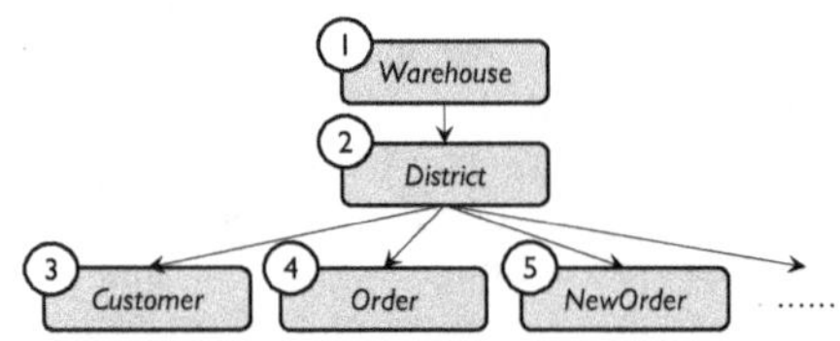

Figure 7: Validation order in the TPC-C benchmark. The stored procedures modeled in this benchmark touch `Warehouse` table and `District` table before accessing any other tables.

Figure 7 shows the tree schema for the TPC-C benchmark. As the restoration of an operation accessing `District` table never affects those accessing `Warehouse` table, no deadlock can occur when healing the inconsistency of an element pointing to the record from `District` table. Based on this principle, the possibility of transaction abort caused by deadlock prevention can be significantly reduced.

4.6 Optimizing Independent Transactions

Transaction healing achieves optimal performance when processing independent transactions, whose read/write sets can be determined according to the input arguments prior to execution [18, 53, 54]. As transaction abort happens only when confronting membership update during the healing phase, independent transactions processed using the transaction healing protocol are guaranteed to be committed due to the absence of key-dependency relations. Based on this observation, transaction healing further optimizes the execution of such transactions by combining the validation phase with its subsequent write phase. Accordingly, any write effect of a transaction can be directly applied to the database state once the corresponding element in the read/write set has passed validation. As a result, transaction healing reduces lock-holding duration for independent transactions, increasing the overall level of concurrency when supporting OLTP workloads.

4.7 Supporting Database Operations

As a general database system, THEDB supports the full spectrum of database operations that are expressible by the SQL language. In this subsection, we discuss how different operations are implemented in THEDB.

4.7.1 Inserts and Deletes

When committing a transaction T, the timestamp of each record modified or created by T is updated to the transaction's commit timestamp. In addition, the visibility bit of each record that is deleted by T is turned off. THEDB further relies on a garbage collector to periodically clean up all the deleted records. To guarantee the correctness of garbage collection, a reference counter is maintained for each record to count the number of transactions that are currently accessing the record. A deleted record can be safely removed from the database once its reference counter drops to 0.

We further explain how THEDB handles insert operations in the presence of conflicting operations using three scenarios.

In the first scenario, consider an insertion of a new record R by transaction T_1 followed by a read operation by another concurrent transaction T_2 to read R. To insert R, T_1 performs the insertion during its read phase, with the visibility bit of R set to false. When T_2 reads R, although R is added to T_2's read set, R is not visible to T_2 due to its visibility value (i.e., R does not exist from T_2's perspective). When T_1 commits, the visibility bit of R will be turned on, indicating that R is now visible to other transactions. During the validation phase of T_2, T_2's read operation that accesses R would be detected to be non-serializable, and the healing phase will be triggered to restore all the affected non-serializable operations.

In the second scenario, consider the reverse of the first scenario where a transaction T_1 first attempts to read a non-existent record R followed by a concurrent transaction T_2 that inserts R. When T_1 attempts to read the non-existent R, THEDB will create a dummy empty record R_e to represent R with the visibility bit of R_e set to off, and an element corresponding to R_e is inserted to T_1's read set. If T_2 attempts to insert R into the database, it must acquire the lock on R_e before performing the real insertion. Once T_2 has passed the validation, record insertion is executed by directly copying R's content to R_e. Suppose that T_1 commits before T_2. Both transactions can commit successfully without confronting validation failure. However, if T_2 commits before T_1, T_1 will detect the modification of R's timestamp during its validation phase, and a healing phase will be triggered to heal the detected inconsistency.

In the third scenario, we consider the case where two concurrent transactions attempt to insert the same record R. Suppose that T_1's insertion is performed before T_2's insertion during their read phases. Similar to the discussion for the second scenario, a dummy empty record R_e would be created by T_1's insertion with its visibility bit turned off. Subsequently, when T_2 attempts to insert R, it would detect the presence of R_e and an element that points to R_e will be added to T_2's read/write set. Should T_2 validate and commit before T_1, T_2's insertion will be committed and the visibility bit for R_e will be turned on. Subsequently, T_1's validation will fail on detecting the modification of R_e's timestamp; in this case, T_1 will be aborted due to the integrity constraint violation.

We have demonstrated that THEDB guarantees serializability in all the cases where inserts are performed concurrently with conflicting operations. We conclude that database serializability can be preserved with the existence of inserts and deletes.

4.7.2 Range Queries and Phantoms

The design of transaction healing naturally supports range queries that access a collection of records in a table. However, range queries can result in the phantom problem [23]. Instead of utilizing the *next-key locking* mechanism [40] that is specifically designed for two-phase locking protocol, THEDB solves this problem by leveraging a mechanism that is first proposed by Silo [55]. THEDB records a version number on each leaf node of a B+-tree to detect structural modifications to the B+-tree. Any structural modification caused by inserts, deletes, or node splits will increase the version number. When performing a range query in a transaction, transaction healing records both the version number and the leaf node pointers to the read/write set. During the validation phase, on detecting a structural change that is indicated by the version mismatch, transaction healing attempts to heal the inconsistency by restoring the corresponding non-serializable operations.

4.8 Supporting Ad-Hoc Transactions

In real-world applications, a database user can submit ad-hoc transactions without invoking stored procedures that are defined prior to execution. THEDB processes such type of transactions using the conventional OCC scheme, which is fully compatible with the transaction-healing mechanism. In the case that all the incoming transactions are ad-hoc, THEDB is equivalent to a database system that implements conventional OCC for serializing transactions. While it is technically possible to enable transaction healing for ad-hoc transactions by building an efficient program analyzer that extracts dependency graphs at runtime, there still exists two factors that may restrict the system's effectiveness. First, a database user may issue SQL statements within a transaction interactively, making the extraction of dependency graphs difficult due to the absence of complete knowledge of the transaction program. Second, most ad-hoc transactions may be executed only once, and the overhead introduced by runtime program analysis can potentially outweigh the benefits brought by transaction healing, making it unnecessary to perform transaction healing to execute ad-hoc transactions. At current stage, we restrict the scope of transaction healing to transactions that are issued from stored procedures, and leave the investigation of supporting ad-hoc transactions as a future work.

5. EVALUATION

We implemented THEDB from the ground up in C++. As a highlight, we automated the static analysis in THEDB with the LLVM Pass framework [1]. In this section, we evaluate the effectiveness of THEDB, by seeking to answer the following key questions:

1. Why do the state-of-the-art OCC protocols not scale well under highly contended workloads?
2. Can THEDB scale linearly under different workloads?

All the experiments were performed on a multicore machine running Ubuntu 14.04 with four 12-core AMD Opteron Processor 6172 clocked at 2.1 GHz, yielding a total of 48 physical cores. Each core owns a private 64 KB L1 cache and a private 256 KB L2 cache. Every 6 cores share a 5 MB L3 cache and a 8 GB local

DRAM. The machine has a 2 TB SATA hard disk. We compare THEDB with the following five systems:

THEDB-OCC. THEDB-OCC implements the conventional OCC with several optimization techniques applied [61]. We have implemented the scalable timestamp-allocation mechanism proposed by Silo [55] to improve system concurrency.

THEDB-SILO. THEDB-SILO faithfully implements Silo's design [55] on THEDB. It adopts a variation of OCC and improves concurrency level by eliminating the necessity for tracking anti-dependency relations.

THEDB-2PL. THEDB-2PL implements the widely accepted two-phase locking (2PL) mechanism [11]. We adopt no-waiting strategy for avoiding transaction deadlocks. We note that this strategy is reported as the most scalable deadlock-prevention approach for 2PL-based protocols [61].

THEDB-HYBRID. THEDB-HYBRID is a system that adopts a hybrid concurrency-control mechanism [28, 52, 60] for optimized performance. THEDB-HYBRID first executes an incoming transaction using OCC, and switches over to executing it using 2PL protocol should the transaction aborts due to OCC validation failure.

THEDB-DT. THEDB-DT is a partitioned deterministic database that follows the design of existing works [32, 33, 54]. It leverages coarse-grained partition-level locks to serialize transaction executions. In particular, several optimization mechanisms, including replication of read-only tables, were adopted [19, 45].

We adopted two well-known benchmarks, namely TPC-C [4] and Smallbank [6], to evaluate the system performance. For the TPC-C benchmark, we control the workload contention by varying the number of warehouses. Specifically, the contention degree increases with the decrease in the number of warehouses. For the Smallbank benchmark, the degree of workload contention is controlled by a parameter θ, which indicates the skewness of the Zipfian distribution. Increasing θ yields more contended workload. Our query-generation approach faithfully follows that employed by several previous works [55, 61].

5.1 Existing Performance Bottlenecks

We begin our evaluation with a detailed performance analysis on the state-of-the-art OCC protocols. We measure the transaction throughput of THEDB-OCC and THEDB-SILO with different degrees of workload contentions using the TPC-C benchmark. Figure 8 shows the results produced with 46 cores[5]. By decreasing the warehouse count from 48 to 2, the performance of both systems drops drastically. Specifically, when setting the number of warehouses to 2, these two systems respectively yield only 150 K and 60 K transactions per second (tps), reflecting high system sensitivity to workload contentions. To investigate how transaction aborts influence system performance, we disable the validation phase of the OCC protocols in both systems. Such modification can result in non-serializable results due to the absence of consistency checking, but the achieved transaction rates essentially indicate the peak performance that could be attained without any aborts. As shown in Figure 8, disabling the validation phase essentially yields 3 (THEDB-OCC) to 12 (THEDB-SILO) times higher transaction rate for highly contended workloads (see THEDB-OCC$^-$ and THEDB-SILO$^-$). In particular, the peak performance achieved by THEDB-SILO can be 10-15% higher than that of THEDB-OCC after disabling the validation phase. The key reason is that the commit protocol of THEDB-SILO by design eliminates the necessity for tracking anti-dependency relations [55], consequently leading to reduced locking overhead. Note that the transaction rate of both systems can still deteriorate even after disabling the validation phase. This is mainly because of lock thrashing effects [11, 61], where concurrent transactions are waiting for the access privilege of contended locks. Such a phenomenon exists universally in modern concurrency-control mechanisms that require fine-grained locking scheme [61]. While the recently proposed deterministic partitioned databases can prevent such overhead [32, 33, 53, 54], the management of coarse-grained locks in these databases incurs costly overhead when processing cross-partition transactions. This is confirmed by our experiments presented later in Section 6.2.

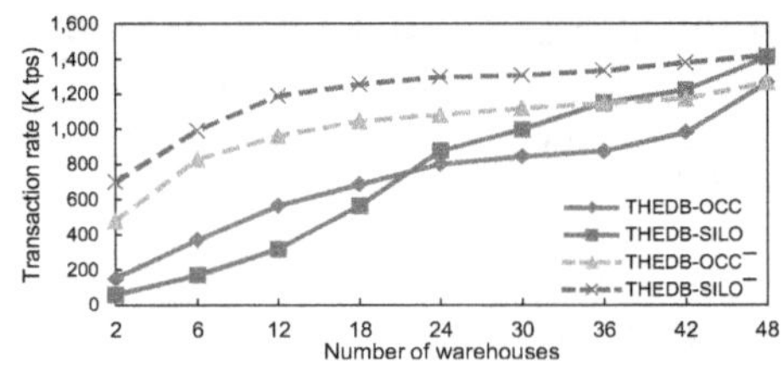

Figure 8: Transaction rate with different degree of contentions. The number of cores is set to 46.

We next analyze the overheads incurred by OCC protocols due to their abort-and-restart mechanism. Figure 9a depicts the percentage of the total execution time spent on transaction abort-and-restart. With the number of warehouses set to 2, THEDB-OCC and THEDB-SILO respectively spent 69% and 91% of their execution time on aborting-and-restarting transactions due to validation failure. This result confirms that the abort-and-restart mechanism is the key contributor to the inefficiency of the state-of-the-art OCC protocols. Figure 9b illustrates that both THEDB-OCC and THEDB-SILO achieve similarly high abort rate[6] which increases as expected with increasing data contention (i.e., lower number of warehouses). Given the relatively weaker performance of THEDB-SILO under highly contended workloads compared to THEDB-OCC, this indicates that THEDB-SILO is more sensitive to high abort rate. The main reason is that THEDB-SILO starts its validation phase for a transaction only after locking its entire write set, which therefore incurs more wasted effort for an aborted transaction. Indeed, the concurrency-control protocol adopted in Silo can be considered as a *more optimistic* OCC scheme. While this design achieves comparatively higher transaction throughput for low-contention workloads, its design suffers significant performance penalty when the workload is highly contended.

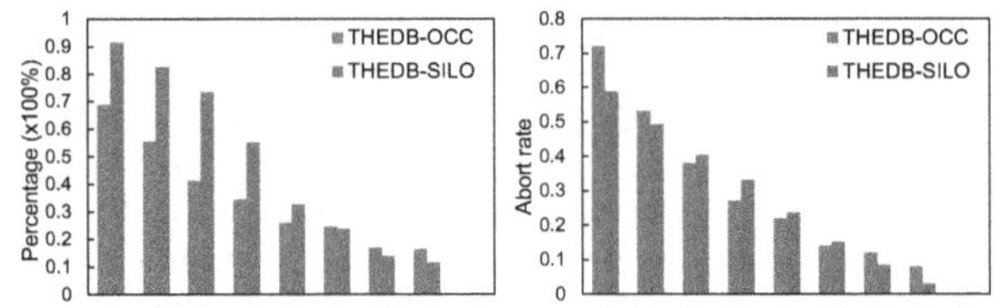

(a) Percentage of allocated time. (b) Abort rate.

Figure 9: Overhead of the abort-and-restart mechanism with different degree of contentions. The number of cores is set to 46.

In the experiments above, we confirm that the existing OCC protocols are not scalable on multicore architectures due to the expensive abort-and-restart mechanism. Given this, THEDB is designed

[5]We leave two cores for handling OS-related tasks.

[6]The abort rate is calculated as the number of transaction restarts divided by the number of committed transactions.

and implemented to achieve high scalability even under highly contended workloads by reducing the abort-and-restart overhead.

5.2 Scalability

This subsection evaluates the scalability of THEDB. Specifically, we attempt to address the following questions: (1) whether THEDB yields high transaction rate under workloads with different contentions; (2) whether THEDB achieves low latency when processing transactions; (3) whether THEDB sustains high performance in the presence of ad-hoc transactions; (4) whether THEDB achieves satisfactory performance in benchmarks comprising short-duration transactions; and (5) how each proposed mechanism affects the system performance.

5.2.1 Transaction Rate

We first investigate the robustness of THEDB using the TPC-C benchmark with 46 cores. We set the percentage of cross-partition transactions to 0 and change the number of warehouses from 2 to 48 to decrease the workload contention. Figure 10 shows the results. All the systems in comparison achieve near-linear scalability with the number of warehouses set to 48. In particular, THEDB-DT yields the highest transaction rate, due to the absence of cross-partition transactions. However, with the increase of workload contention, the performance of THEDB-OCC, THEDB-SILO, THEDB-2PL, THEDB-HYBRID, and THEDB-DT drop sharply, especially when the number of warehouses is set to 2. THEDB, in contrast, sustains a relatively high transaction rate that is very close to THEDB-OCC's peak performance (denoted as THEDB-OCC$^-$) where the validation phase of the OCC protocol is disabled. This observation essentially confirms that the transaction healing protocol adopted in THEDB brings little overhead to the system runtime, and it can scale well even when the workload is highly contended.

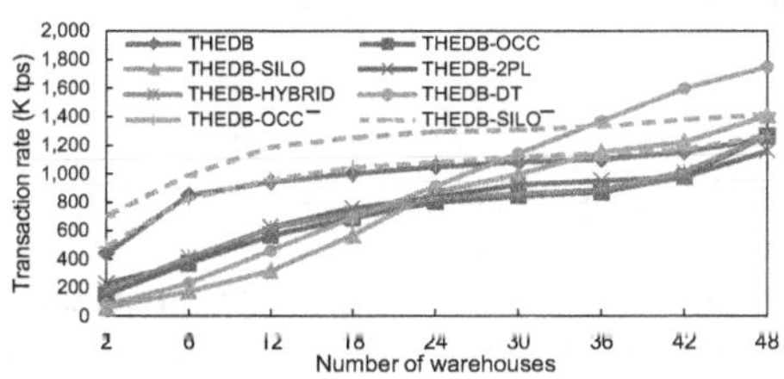

Figure 10: Transaction rate with different degree of contentions. The number of cores is set to 46.

Figure 11 further presents the system scalability using the same benchmark. Under the highly contended workload shown in Figure 11a, THEDB achieves much higher transaction rate than that of the other five systems. In contrast, THEDB-SILO achieves the worst performance. This is because THEDB-SILO's commit protocol is vulnerable to frequent transaction aborts, as explained in Section 6.1. Although THEDB-2PL achieves 25% higher transaction rate compared to THEDB-OCC, its long-duration locks decrease the concurrency degree, making it less effective on multicore architecture. THEDB-HYBRID also achieves unsatisfactory results, since its performance is severely restricted by the combination of OCC and 2PL protocols. While the percentage of cross-partition transactions is set to 0 in this experiment, THEDB-DT still yields a low performance. The major reason is that the execution model of THEDB-DT forbids concurrent execution on a single partition, and therefore the number of cores that can be utilized for processing transactions is strictly limited by the number of warehouses in the TPC-C benchmark, consequently resulting in low resource utilization rate. Compared to these systems, THEDB scales near linearly towards 46 cores, achieving respectively 2.3 and 6.2 times higher throughput than that of THEDB-2PL and THEDB-SILO. This is because the transaction-healing protocol adopted by THEDB heals any inconsistency that is detected during the validation phase, and the expensive overhead caused by abort-and-restart is completely eliminated with the help of the proposed optimization mechanisms. Figures 11b and 11c further illustrate that, while the performance of the other five systems improves under low-contention workload, THEDB maintains a high transaction throughput when scaling to 46 cores, demonstrating THEDB's high scalability and robustness.

While THEDB achieves a comparatively high transaction rate when supporting high-contention workloads, the experimental results reported above indicate that THEDB still suffers from performance degradation due to lock thrashing [11, 61]. While recent research has proposed deterministic database systems to overcome this problem, the management of coarse-grained locks in such database systems incurs additional overhead when processing cross-partition transactions. Figure 12 shows the transaction rate of each system with different percentage of cross-partition transactions. In this set of experiments, the number of cores is set to 46. While all the other systems achieve a stable performance that is not affected by the percentage of cross-partition transactions, THEDB-DT suffers from a significant drop in performance when cross-partition transactions are introduced. Specifically, regardless of the workload contentions, THEDB-DT achieves a low transaction rate when the percentage of cross-partition transactions increases to 10%. This is because the coarse-grained locking mechanism adopted by THEDB-DT requires a transaction to lock all the partitions that it accesses until it completes. Consequently, any concurrent transaction that needs to access one of the locked partitions would be blocked. This experiment demonstrates that existing deterministic databases cannot perform well when supporting cross-partition transactions.

5.2.2 Transaction Latency

Next, we analyze the transaction latency of THEDB when processing highly contended workloads. We execute the TPC-C benchmark with the number of warehouses set to 4, and measure the processing durations for `NewOrder` transactions and `Delivery` transactions. Both types of transactions are dependent transactions, which must perform read operations to obtain its full read/write set. In particular, the program logic of `Delivery` transactions is more complicated, and the processing latency can be much longer compared to `NewOrder` transactions.

Table 1 shows the transaction latencies of different systems for processing `NewOrder` transactions. Compared with THEDB-OCC THEDB-SILO, and THEDB-2PL, THEDB incurs a much shorter latency with over 95% of the `NewOrder` transactions committed within 80 μs. In contrast, the latencies for THEDB-OCC, THEDB-SILO, and THEDB-2PL are more varied, ranging from below 20 μs to over 640 μs. This is because the conventional abort-and-restart mechanism adopted by these two systems could incur a high overhead when the same transaction has to be re-executed multiple times. Table 1 also presents the latencies achieved by THEDB-OCC and THEDB-SILO with the validation phase disabled (denoted as THEDB-OCC$^-$ and THEDB-SILO$^-$). The reported numbers are very close to that obtained by THEDB, showing that the adopted transaction-healing protocol incurs little overhead to the system runtime. To conclude, THEDB enables efficient transaction processing as any transaction that fails the validation will be healed without getting restarted from scratch.

We further analyze the latencies achieved by different systems when processing `Delivery` transactions, which comprise

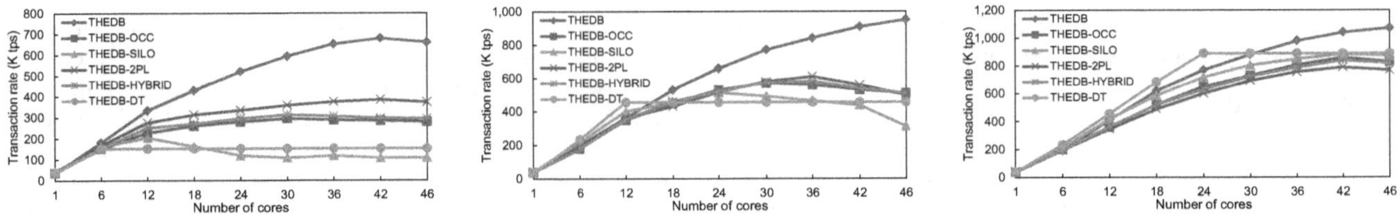

(a) 4 warehouses. (b) 12 warehouses. (c) 24 warehouses.

Figure 11: Transaction rate for TPC-C benchmark with different degree of workload contentions.

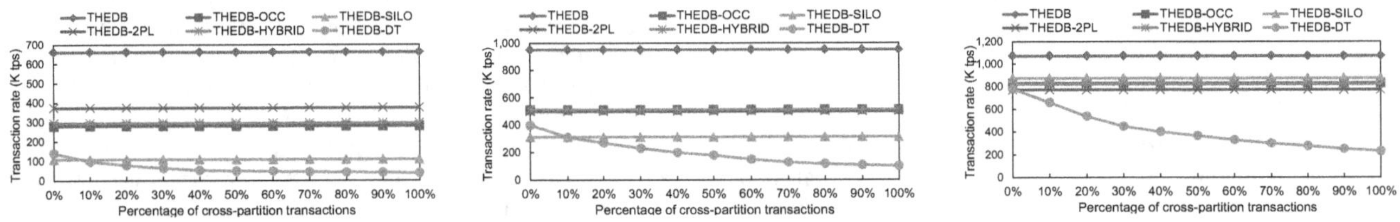

(a) 4 warehouses. (b) 12 warehouses. (c) 24 warehouses.

Figure 12: Transaction rate for TPC-C benchmark with different percentage of cross-partition transactions.

complex dependencies among operations. As shown in Table 1, by disabling the validation phase, THEDB-OCC commits 84.1% of the `Delivery` transactions within 320 μs (denoted as THEDB-OCC$^-$). In this scenario, no consistency check is performed during the execution, and therefore transactions will always be committed without being any restarts. However, enabling the validation phase significantly increases the transaction latency, and only 14.1% and 16.0% of the transactions are committed within 320 μs respectively by THEDB-OCC and THEDB-SILO. This result demonstrates the inefficiency of the abort-and-restart mechanism. Compared with these two systems, THEDB could achieve a much lower transaction latency. While the healing of inconsistencies for dependent transactions could cause membership updates of the read/write sets, THEDB is still able to commit nearly 90% of the transactions within 640 μs. In addition, the transaction latency is strictly bounded within 1280 μs, and hence the overall system performance is much better than that achieved by THEDB-OCC, THEDB-SILO, and THEDB-2PL.

The experiments reported above demonstrate that the transaction-healing protocol adopted by THEDB does not incur high latency when processing different types of transactions.

5.2.3 Ad-Hoc Queries

THEDB processes ad-hoc transactions using conventional OCC protocol, which is fully compatible with transaction healing. On detecting inconsistency during validation phase, ad-hoc transactions will be directly aborted and restarted from scratch. In this experiment, we randomly taint some transactions as ad-hoc transactions, and examine how the transaction rate of THEDB is influenced by the percentage of ad-hoc transactions. Figure 13 shows the result with the number of warehouses set to 4. By changing the percentage of ad-hoc transactions from 0% to 100%, the performance of THEDB deteriorates smoothly, and finally degrades to the performance of conventional OCC protocol. This is because THEDB's transaction-processing scheme is essentially equivalent to that of THEDB-OCC when all the incoming transactions are ad-hoc. Given the fact that most transactions in modern applications are generated from stored procedures [50], we conclude that transaction healing can provide a great performance boost when supporting real-world OLTP workloads.

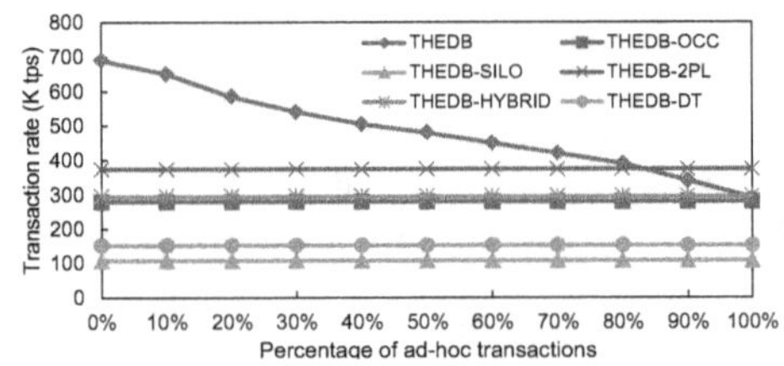

Figure 13: Transaction rate with different percentages of ad-hoc transactions. The number of cores is set to 46.

5.2.4 Short-Duration Transactions

In the following experiments, we use the Smallbank benchmark to evaluate the performance of THEDB for workloads with short-duration transactions. Recall that the workload contention of the Smallbank benchmark is controlled by a parameter θ, which indicates the skewness of the Zipfian distribution. Table 2 shows the percentage of accesses to different keys based on the various Zipfian distributions by varying θ. Here, the number of records in each table is set to 1,000. Note that the workload contention grows exponentially with θ. The results in Table 2 show that the abort rates of THEDB-OCC and THEDB-SILO climb rapidly from 0.007 to 0.324 and 0.403, respectively. Different from these two systems, THEDB did not abort any transaction as all the detected validation failures were resolved with the healing phase.

Figure 14 shows the transaction rate of different systems with θ varying from 0.1 to 0.9. In this experiment, the number of cores is set to 24. With θ set to 0.1, THEDB-SILO achieves around 5% higher throughput compared to THEDB and THEDB-OCC. This is because the design of THEDB-SILO's concurrency-control protocol eliminates the necessity for checking anti-dependency relations. However, the tradeoff for such an extreme optimistic protocol is that it underperforms for high-contention workloads. In particular, when $\theta = 0.9$, THEDB-SILO yields the lowest transaction throughput among all the systems being compared. However, the performance of THEDB remains stable for different workload contentions. Under highly contended workload, the transaction throughput achieved by THEDB is 4.5 times higher than other systems, and this performance is very close to the peak throughput

Transaction type	Latency (µs)	THEDB	THEDB-OCC	THEDB-SILO	THEDB-2PL	THEDB-OCC$^-$	THEDB-SILO$^-$
`NewOrder`	10 - 20	0.2%	0%	3.5%	1.1%	0%	4.8%
	20 - 40	36.7%	13.7%	25.9%	29.2%	34.0%	45.3%
	40 - 80	59.1%	32.1%	28.8%	41.4%	62.8%	42.0%
	80 - 160	2.7%	28.4%	28.1%	19.9%	3.2%	7.7%
	160 - 320	1.3%	17.9%	7.8%	6.7%	0%	0.2%
	320 - 640	0%	5.6%	4.7%	1.5%	0%	0%
	640 - INF	0%	2.3%	1.2%	0.3%	0%	0%
`Delivery`	10 - 80	0%	0.3%	0.8%	1.4%	0%	0%
	80 - 160	0.3%	0%	0%	1.6%	0.6%	1.4%
	160 - 320	41.1%	14.1%	16.0%	29.6%	84.1%	69.3%
	320 - 640	48.4%	31.4%	24.2%	38.1%	14.0%	22.7%
	640 - 1280	10.2%	34.6%	37.9%	21.3%	1.2%	6.6%
	1280 - 2560	0%	13.8%	16.8%	7.5%	0%	0%
	2560 - 5120	0%	4.0%	3.9%	0.6%	0%	0%
	5120 - INF	0%	1.7%	0.5%	0%	0%	0%

Table 1: Transaction latency for TPC-C benchmark. The number of warehouses is set to 4, and the number of cores is set to 46.

θ	1st	2nd	10th	100th	Abort rate
0.1	0.25%	0.24%	0.20%	0.16%	0 / 0.007 / 0.007
0.2	0.45%	0.39%	0.29%	0.18%	0 / 0.008 / 0.008
0.3	0.78%	0.63%	0.40%	0.19%	0 / 0.009 / 0.009
0.4	1.34%	1.02%	0.55%	0.22%	0 / 0.013 / 0.010
0.5	2.26%	1.60%	0.74%	0.22%	0 / 0.016 / 0.012
0.6	3.70%	2.45%	0.95%	0.24%	0 / 0.024 / 0.023
0.7	5.86%	3.60%	1.20%	0.23%	0 / 0.047 / 0.084
0.8	8.91%	5.17%	1.48%	0.23%	0 / 0.251 / 0.347
0.9	13.01%	7.06%	1.72%	0.21%	0 / 0.324 / 0.403

Table 2: The percentage of accesses to the first, second, 10th, and 100th most popular keys in Zipfian distributions for different values of θ. The last column shows the abort rates of THEDB, THEDB-OCC, and THEDB-SILO respectively.

θ	Percentile	THEDB	THEDB-OCC	THEDB-SILO
0.5	25%	4.86 µs	4.79 µs	5.45 µs
	80%	8.52 µs	8.57 µs	9.02 µs
	95%	10.63 µs	11.12 µs	11.58 µs
0.7	25%	4.55 µs	4.25 µs	3.20 µs
	80%	9.12 µs	8.43 µs	7.75 µs
	95%	11.84 µs	12.74 µs	12.34 µs
0.9	25%	4.57 µs	2.60 µs	2.21 µs
	80%	9.14 µs	5.22 µs	4.50 µs
	95%	11.45 µs	36.14 µs	42.54 µs

Table 3: Transaction latency for Smallbank benchmark. The number of cores is set to 24.

that is achieved by disabling OCC's validation phase. This result essentially demonstrates the low overhead of transaction healing.

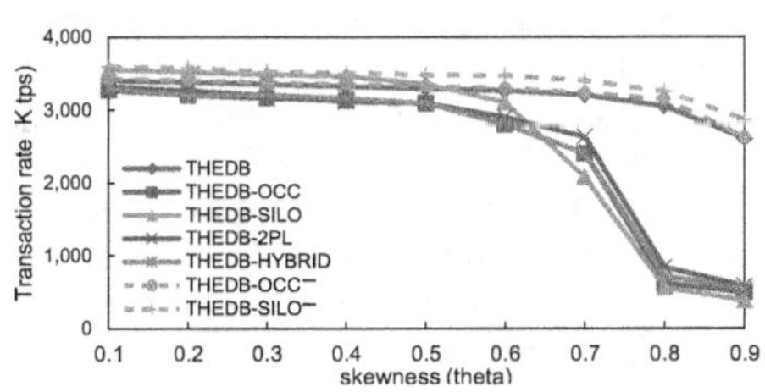

Figure 14: Transaction rate with different degree of contentions. The number of cores is set to 24.

We further compare the transaction latency of THEDB with that of THEDB-OCC and THEDB-SILO in Table 3. When θ = 0.5, the three systems in comparison yield similar transaction latency. In THEDB, 25% of the transactions are committed within 4.86 µs. This number is very close to that achieved by THEDB-OCC and THEDB-SILO, which are 4.79 µs and 5.45 µs, respectively. This result essentially indicates that transaction healing brings little overhead to the system runtime when processing workloads with low contentions. When supporting highly contended workloads, THEDB generates remarkably lower latency compared to the other systems. Specifically, 95% of the transactions executed by THEDB complete within 11.45 µs when θ = 0.9; in contrast, the latency for THEDB-OCC and THEDB-SILO increases to 36.14 µs and 42.54 µs, respectively. This result indicates that the state-of-the-art OCC protocols cannot process each transaction uniformly, and the abort-and-restart mechanism severely hurts the latency of some transactions in the workload, hence causing degradation to the overall system performance.

5.2.5 *Runtime Overhead*

In this section, we analyze the runtime overhead incurred by transaction healing in THEDB. Compared with OCC, transaction healing maintains an additional access cache during the read phase of the transaction execution. In addition, a local copy of any record that is read by the transaction is held to eliminate potential overhead caused by false invalidation when processing dependent transactions. Such overheads can potentially cause observable performance degradation when processing low-contention workloads. To precisely measure the performance overhead associated with transaction healing, we executed the TPC-C benchmark with the number of warehouses set to be equal to the core count. To minimize conflicting actions, we allocate each thread to be responsible for processing transactions associated with a single warehouse. Table 1 shows the experimental results. Without maintaining the access cache and local copies for read operations, THEDB yields 1139 K tps when processing transactions with 46 cores (denoted by Normal). Maintaining the access cache incurs little overhead to the system runtime, and THEDB still achieves 1087 K tps with 46 cores enabled (denoted by +Access Cache). Similarly, the overhead caused by the maintenance of local copies for read operations is also negligible, and less than 2% performance degradation is observed (denoted by +Read Copy). Hence, we conclude that transaction healing brings little overhead to the system runtime when processing low-contention workloads.

The experiments presented above demonstrate that the

#cores	8	16	24	32	40	46
Normal (K tps)	328	606	840	971	1088	1139
+Access Cache (K tps)	325	602	811	937	1036	1087
+Read Copy (K tps)	314	588	790	924	1015	1067

Table 4: Transaction rate when processing the TPC-C benchmark. The number of warehouses is set to be equal to the core count.

transaction-healing protocol can achieve both high scalability and robustness for transaction processing on multicores, with little performance overhead brought to the system runtime.

6. RELATED WORK

Multicore databases. Concurrency-control protocols have been investigated in the last thirty years [11]. To facilitate the performance in disk-based OLTP databases, several works [29, 30, 31, 43, 44] have been proposed to remove centralized locking bottlenecks. With the evolution of hardware architecture, researchers have shifted their attentions to improve performance in multicore main-memory databases. Ren et al. [48] removed contention bottlenecks in centralized lock manager by proposing a lightweight per-tuple 2PL scheme. Yao et al. [59] extracted concurrency control from execution to accelerate the multicore processing of OLTP workloads. Larson et al. [35] recently revisited two multi-version concurrency-control (MVCC) algorithms, and their study further settled the foundation for Microsoft's Hekaton database [21]. Faleiro et al. [25] proposed a technique for lazily evaluating transactions, and this technique improves database performance for certain kinds of workloads. Based on a similar design principle, the same authors improved the MVCC performance by decoupling concurrency control and version management from transaction execution [24]. Levandoski et al. [36] presented an efficient range concurrency-control scheme that extends multi-version timestamp ordering to support range resources and fully supports phantom prevention. As a departure from the traditional database architectures, several deterministic databases, including H-Store [32], Hyper [33], and Calvin [53, 54], have been proposed. These databases divide the underlying storage into multiple partitions, each of which is protected by a lock and is assigned a single-threaded execution engine with exclusive access. To optimize system performance, different partitioning schemes [19, 45] were proposed to reduce the number of cross-partition transactions. Unlike these databases, THEDB leverages static analysis to optimize database performance.

Optimistic concurrency control. Optimistic concurrency control (OCC) was first proposed by Kung and Robinson [34]. Witnessing its vulnerability to contended workloads, several works have been introduced to reduce OCC's abort rate. Agrawal et al. [5] adopted a multi-versioned protocol to allow inconsistent access to the database records. Herlihy [28] eliminated successive abort-and-restart in OCC by resorting to pure lock-based protocol once transaction abort occurs. Different from these proposals, THEDB exploits program semantics to partially re-execute transactions instead of blindly restarting the entire transaction from the scratch. In recent years, OCC have been widely adopted in main-memory databases. As a representative system, Silo [55] achieves high transaction rate by avoiding anti-dependency tracking and taking advantage of a main-memory index [39]. Hekaton [21] facilitates the OCC's performance by exploiting multi-versioning to avoid installing writes until commit time. Hyder [12] adopts a variant of OCC protocol called meld [13] that is specifically designed for log-structured databases. Absorbing the design benefits from these systems, THEDB lays its major contribution to improve OCC's scalability and robustness to the contended workloads by leveraging static analysis to the transaction programs. Some other recent works focus on optimizing OCC in distributed environments and new system architecture. For example, Bernstein et al. [9, 10] improved OCC's performance in distributed log-structured databases without storage partitioning. Ding et al. [22] introduced a new elastic distributed transaction processing mechanism that separates the validation layer from storage layer. Wang et al. [56] leveraged restricted transactional memory to optimize the OCC performance.

Program analysis. Many works have been proposed to adopt program partitioning and transformation to optimize system performance [8, 15, 16, 17, 26, 27, 46]. Among them, one widely adopted technique is transaction chopping [49], which analyzes possible transaction conflicts using SC-cycles. In fact, the database community has investigated various types of transaction partitioning mechanisms for improved system performance [8, 26, 27]. Transaction chopping is also applied to several modern database applications. Zhang et al. [62] proposed transaction chain to achieve serializability in geo-distributed databases, and Mu et al. [41] tracked dependencies between concurrent transactions to optimize distributed transactions in high contention scenario. Several other works also resorted to program analysis for improved performance. Doppel [42] splits transaction execution into two phases, and processes commutative operations in parallel for higher transaction rate. Wu et al. [58] leveraged program analysis to parallelize command-log recovery on multicores. Unlike these previous works, THEDB only requires simple static analysis that extracts the dependencies within a program, and ad-hoc queries are naturally supported.

Transactional memory. In the area of transactional memory systems, researchers also adopt OCC to facilitate the performance of transactional execution. Blundell et al. [14] adopted symbolic tracking to commit transactions in the case of data conflicts by re-executing read instructions in the programs. However, their approach is restricted to only "non-critical conflicts" occurring on auxiliary or bookkeeping data. Litz et al. [38] resorted to snapshot isolation for reduced abort rate, but their approach inevitably sacrifices program consistency. Ramadan et al. [47] proposed conflict serializability to reduce aborts by relaxing concurrency control. While their approach reduce abort rates in certain cases, it is not general enough to provide full capability of tolerating all the read-write conflicts. Different from these works, THEDB is specifically designed for supporting OLTP applications and can be generalized to support all kinds of database operations. Meanwhile, system durability is guaranteed by its effective commit protocol.

7. CONCLUSION

We have introduced a new concurrency-control mechanism, called *transaction healing*, that scales the conventional OCC towards dozens of cores even under highly contended workloads. Transaction healing leverages the statically extracted program dependency graph to restore any non-serializable operations once inconsistency is detected during validation. By maintaining a thread-local access cache, the overhead for committing conflicting transactions is significantly reduced. Our experimental study confirms that transaction healing can scale near-linearly, yielding much higher transaction rate than the state-of-the-art OCC implementations.

Acknowledgment

We appreciate the reviewers' insightful comments. This research is supported in part by MOE Grant R-252-000-583-112. The source code is available at https://github.com/Cavalia/Cavalia.

8. REFERENCES

[1] http://llvm.org/docs/passes.html.

[2] https://github.com/apavlo/h-store.

[3] https://github.com/stephentu/silo.

[4] http://www.tpc.org/tpcc/.

[5] D. Agrawal, A. J. Bernstein, P. Gupta, and S. Sengupta. Distributed optimistic concurrency control with reduced rollback. *Distributed Computing*, 2(1), 1987.

[6] M. Alomari, M. Cahill, A. Fekete, and U. Röhm. The cost of serializability on platforms that use snapshot isolation. In *ICDE*, 2008.

[7] T. M. Austin and G. S. Sohi. Dynamic dependency analysis of ordinary programs. In *ISCA*, 1992.

[8] A. J. Bernstein, D. S. Gerstl, and P. M. Lewis. Concurrency control for step-decomposed transactions. *Information Systems*, 24(8), 1999.

[9] P. A. Bernstein and S. Das. Scaling optimistic concurrency control by approximately partitioning the certifier and log. *IEEE Data Eng. Bull*, 38(1), 2015.

[10] P. A. Bernstein, S. Das, B. Ding, and M. Pilman. Optimizing optimistic concurrency control for tree-structured, log-structured databases. In *SIGMOD*, 2015.

[11] P. A. Bernstein, V. Hadzilacos, and N. Goodman. *Concurrency control and recovery in database systems*. 1987.

[12] P. A. Bernstein, C. W. Reid, and S. Das. Hyder-a transactional record manager for shared flash. In *CIDR*, 2011.

[13] P. A. Bernstein, C. W. Reid, M. Wu, and X. Yuan. Optimistic concurrency control by melding trees. In *VLDB*, 2011.

[14] C. Blundell, A. Raghavan, and M. M. Martin. Retcon: transactional repair without replay. In *ISCA*, 2010.

[15] A. Cheung, S. Madden, O. Arden, and A. C. Myers. Automatic partitioning of database applications. In *VLDB*, 2012.

[16] A. Cheung, S. Madden, and A. Solar-Lezama. Sloth: Being lazy is a virtue (when issuing database queries). In *SIGMOD*, 2014.

[17] A. Cheung, S. Madden, A. Solar-Lezama, O. Arden, and A. C. Myers. Using program analysis to improve database applications. *IEEE Data Eng. Bull.*, 37(1), 2014.

[18] J. Cowling and B. Liskov. Granola: low-overhead distributed transaction coordination. In *USENIX ATC*, 2012.

[19] C. Curino, E. Jones, Y. Zhang, and S. Madden. Schism: a workload-driven approach to database replication and partitioning. In *VLDB*, 2010.

[20] S. Das, D. Agrawal, and A. El Abbadi. Elastras: An elastic, scalable, and self-managing transactional database for the cloud. *TODS*, 38(1), 2013.

[21] C. Diaconu, C. Freedman, E. Ismert, P.-A. Larson, P. Mittal, R. Stonecipher, N. Verma, and M. Zwilling. Hekaton: Sql server's memory-optimized oltp engine. In *SIGMOD*, 2013.

[22] B. Ding, L. Kot, A. Demers, and J. Gehrke. Centiman: Elastic, high performance optimistic concurrency control by watermarking. In *SoCC*, 2015.

[23] K. P. Eswaran, J. N. Gray, R. A. Lorie, and I. L. Traiger. The notions of consistency and predicate locks in a database system. *Communications of the ACM*, 19(11), 1976.

[24] J. M. Faleiro and D. J. Abadi. Rethinking serializable multiversion concurrency control. In *VLDB*, 2015.

[25] J. M. Faleiro, A. Thomson, and D. J. Abadi. Lazy evaluation of transactions in database systems. In *SIGMOD*, 2014.

[26] H. Garcia-Molina. Using semantic knowledge for transaction processing in a distributed database. *TODS*, 8(2), 1983.

[27] H. Garcia-Molina and K. Salem. Sagas. In *SIGMOD*, 1987.

[28] M. Herlihy. Apologizing versus asking permission: Optimistic concurrency control for abstract data types. *TODS*, 15(1), 1990.

[29] T. Horikawa. Latch-free data structures for dbms: design, implementation, and evaluation. In *SIGMOD*, 2013.

[30] R. Johnson, I. Pandis, N. Hardavellas, A. Ailamaki, and B. Falsafi. Shore-mt: A scalable storage manager for the multicore era. In *EDBT*, 2009.

[31] H. Jung, H. Han, A. D. Fekete, G. Heiser, and H. Y. Yeom. A scalable lock manager for multicores. In *SIGMOD*, 2013.

[32] R. Kallman, H. Kimura, J. Natkins, A. Pavlo, A. Rasin, S. Zdonik, E. P. C. Jones, S. Madden, M. Stonebraker, Y. Zhang, J. Hugg, and D. J. Abadi. H-store: A high-performance, distributed main memory transaction processing system. In *VLDB*, 2008.

[33] A. Kemper and T. Neumann. Hyper: A hybrid oltp&olap main memory database system based on virtual memory snapshots. In *ICDE*, 2011.

[34] H.-T. Kung and J. T. Robinson. On optimistic methods for concurrency control. *TODS*, 6(2), 1981.

[35] P.-Å. Larson, S. Blanas, C. Diaconu, C. Freedman, J. M. Patel, and M. Zwilling. High-performance concurrency control mechanisms for main-memory databases. In *VLDB*, 2011.

[36] J. Levandoski, D. Lomet, S. Sengupta, R. Stutsman, and R. Wang. Multi-version range concurrency control in deuteronomy. In *VLDB*, 2015.

[37] J. J. Levandoski, P.-A. Larson, and R. Stoica. Identifying hot and cold data in main-memory databases. In *ICDE*, 2013.

[38] H. Litz, D. Cheriton, A. Firoozshahian, O. Azizi, and J. P. Stevenson. Si-tm: reducing transactional memory abort rates through snapshot isolation. In *ASPLOS*, 2014.

[39] Y. Mao, E. Kohler, and R. T. Morris. Cache craftiness for fast multicore key-value storage. In *EuroSys*, 2012.

[40] C. Mohan. Aries/kvl: A key-value locking method for concurrency control of multiaction transactions operating on b-tree indexes. In *VLDB*, 1990.

[41] S. Mu, Y. Cui, Y. Zhang, W. Lloyd, and J. Li. Extracting more concurrency from distributed transactions. In *OSDI*, 2014.

[42] N. Narula, C. Cutler, E. Kohler, and R. Morris. Phase reconciliation for contended in-memory transactions. In *OSDI*, 2014.

[43] I. Pandis, R. Johnson, N. Hardavellas, and A. Ailamaki. Data-oriented transaction execution. In *VLDB*, 2010.

[44] I. Pandis, P. Tözün, R. Johnson, and A. Ailamaki. Plp: page latch-free shared-everything oltp. In *VLDB*, 2011.

[45] A. Pavlo, C. Curino, and S. Zdonik. Skew-aware automatic database partitioning in shared-nothing, parallel oltp systems. In *SIGMOD*, 2012.

[46] K. Ramachandra, R. Guravannavar, and S. Sudarshan. Program analysis and transformation for holistic optimization of database applications. In *SOAP*, 2012.

[47] H. E. Ramadan, C. J. Rossbach, and E. Witchel. Dependence-aware transactional memory for increased concurrency. In *MICRO*, 2008.

[48] K. Ren, A. Thomson, and D. J. Abadi. Lightweight locking

for main memory database systems. In *VLDB*, 2012.

[49] D. Shasha, F. Llirbat, E. Simon, and P. Valduriez. Transaction chopping: Algorithms and performance studies. *TODS*, 20(3), 1995.

[50] M. Stonebraker, S. Madden, D. J. Abadi, S. Harizopoulos, N. Hachem, and P. Helland. The end of an architectural era: (it's time for a complete rewrite). In *VLDB*, 2007.

[51] R. H. Thomas. A majority consensus approach to concurrency control for multiple copy databases. *TODS*, 4(2), 1979.

[52] A. Thomasian. Distributed optimistic concurrency control methods for high-performance transaction processing. *TKDE*, 10(1), 1998.

[53] A. Thomson and D. J. Abadi. The case for determinism in database systems. In *VLDB*, 2010.

[54] A. Thomson, T. Diamond, S.-C. Weng, K. Ren, P. Shao, and D. J. Abadi. Calvin: Fast distributed transactions for partitioned database systems. In *SIGMOD*, 2012.

[55] S. Tu, W. Zheng, E. Kohler, B. Liskov, and S. Madden. Speedy transactions in multicore in-memory databases. In *SOSP*, 2013.

[56] Z. Wang, H. Qian, J. Li, and H. Chen. Using restricted transactional memory to build a scalable in-memory database. In *EuroSys*, 2014.

[57] Y. Wu, C.-Y. Chan, and K.-L. Tan. Transaction healing: Scaling optimistic concurrency control on multicores (extended version). In *CoRR*, 2016.

[58] Y. Wu, W. Guo, C.-Y. Chan, and K.-L. Tan. Parallel database recovery for multicore main-memory databases. In *CoRR*, 2016.

[59] C. Yao, D. Agrawal, P. Chang, G. Chen, B. C. Ooi, W.-F. Wong, and M. Zhang. Dgcc: A new dependency graph based concurrency control protocol for multicore database systems. In *CoRR*, 2015.

[60] P. S. Yu and D. M. Dias. Analysis of hybrid concurrency control schemes for a high data contention environment. *TSE*, 18(2), 1992.

[61] X. Yu, G. Bezerra, A. Pavlo, S. Devadas, and M. Stonebraker. Staring into the abyss: An evaluation of concurrency control with one thousand cores. In *VLDB*, 2014.

[62] Y. Zhang, R. Power, S. Zhou, Y. Sovran, M. K. Aguilera, and J. Li. Transaction chains: Achieving serializability with low latency in geo-distributed storage systems. In *SOSP*, 2013.

APPENDIX

A. BENCHMARKS

In our experimental study, we use two benchmarks, namely, TPC-C and Smallbank, to evaluate the system performance. We briefly describe these benchmarks here.

TPC-C. This benchmark is a widely-recognized industry standard for evaluating the performance of OLTP workloads. It contains nine tables and simulates a warehouse-centric order processing application. Three out of the five stored procedures, namely, `NewOrder`, `Delivery`, and `Payment`, contain write operations. The workload contention is controlled by the number of warehouses, and smaller number of warehouses indicates higher level of contention. The ratio of cross-partition transactions is controlled by changing the probability of accessing remote warehouses in the `NewOrder` transactions.

Smallbank. The Smallbank benchmark models a simple banking application containing three tables and six stored procedures. Transactions in this benchmark perform simple read and update operations on customers' accounts. Only a small number of items are involved in each transaction. The workload contention is controlled by a parameter θ, which indicates the skewness of the Zipfian distribution.

B. PROGRAM DEPENDENCY GRAPH

Figure 15a and Figure 15b respectively show the program dependency graphs for `NewOrder` transactions and `Delivery` transactions. In these two figures, solid lines represent key dependencies, while dashed lines represent value dependencies. Compared with `NewOrder` transactions, `Delivery` transactions access more data records, and the dependency relations among operations are more complicated. Therefore, healing the inconsistencies that are detected in `Delivery` transactions can require more efforts compared to `NewOrder` transactions.

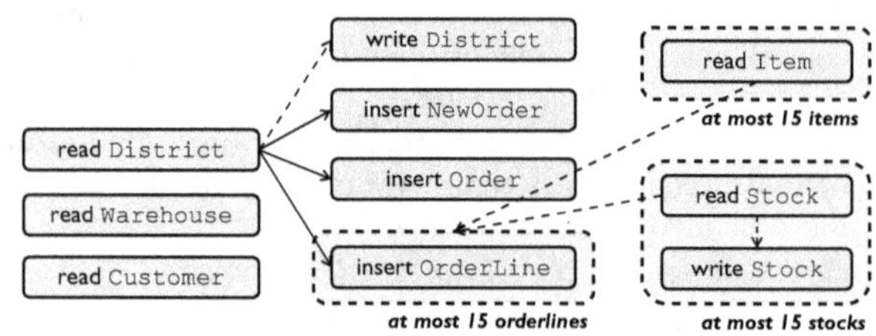

(a) `NewOrder` transactions.

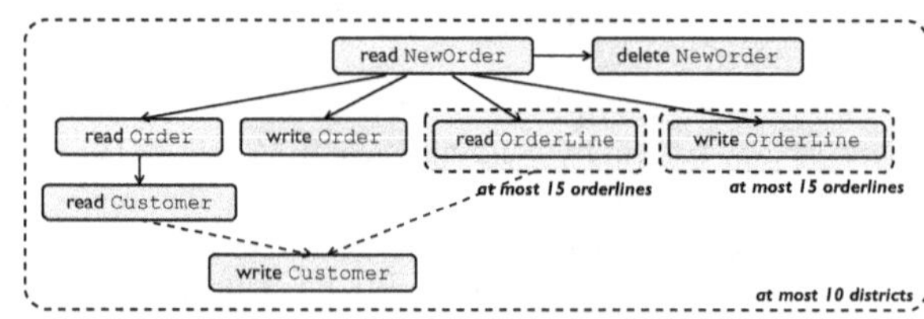

(b) `Delivery` transactions.

Figure 15: Program dependency graphs.

C. DURABILITY

This section first discusses how THEDB achieves system durability with minimum runtime overhead, and then demonstrates the efficiency of the adopted mechanisms through careful experiments.

C.1 Design

THEDB employs both checkpointing and value-logging during transaction execution to avoid loss of committed transaction updates in the event of machine failure or power outage. THEDB periodically checkpoints its in-memory database states to bound the maximum failure-recovery time. Meanwhile, all the update effects along with their timestamps are logged to the persistent storage, as is described in Section 4.3. In particular, transactions assigned with the same epoch number are persisted together, reducing the overhead that is caused by frequent storage access. Query result generated by a transaction is returned to the client only until the transaction's write effects have already been dumped to the underlying storage. Once machine failure occurs, THEDB reloads the most recent transaction-consistent checkpoint from the persistent storage. The reloading time is correlated to the checkpoint size and storage access speed, and parallelism can be achieved by using multiple storage devices or other new hardware. THEDB's logging mechanism ensures that log-recovery can be performed in parallel.

After reloading the corresponding log file to its local workspace, each thread re-instates the values of committed records concurrently. Specifically, each record in the database is attached with a timestamp indicating its last updater. When attempting to update a record with timestamp t_1, the write effect will be ignored if the updater's timestamp t_2 is smaller than t_1. The correctness of this approach is guaranteed by the Thomas write rule [51].

C.2 Experiments

This subsection evaluates the effectiveness of THEDB's durability. While the logging mechanism in a database system is largely influenced by the throughput of the underlying persistent storage, we focus on investigating whether the proposed commit protocol in transaction healing can bring any bottleneck that can bound the system performance. Figure 16 shows the logging overhead in THEDB when processing the TPC-C benchmark. Each thread directly dumps its logging data to an in-memory data structure, therefore, the generated result will not be influenced by the hardware (of the persistent devices like disk, SSD) throughput. As shown in the figure, the adopted value-logging mechanism yields similar transaction rate compared with command logging, indicating that the commit protocol in transaction healing is scalable. In fact, without considering the hardware throughput, the major overhead in THEDB's logging mechanism is memory allocation and string serialization, which can be addressed with sophisticated implementation. This result confirms that the logging mechanism in THEDB will not become a system bottleneck if provided with high-throughput persistent devices.

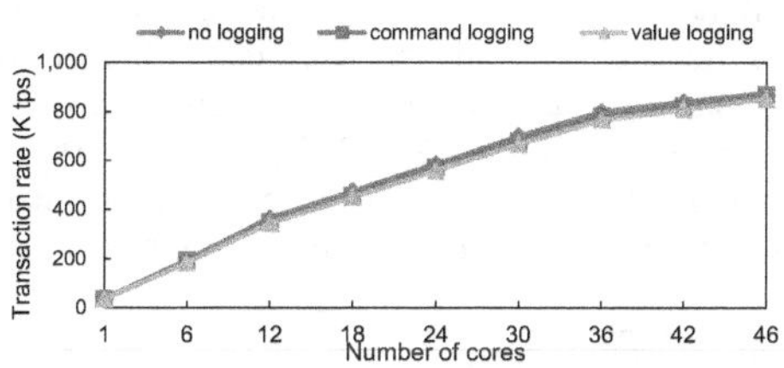

Figure 16: Transaction rate with different logging mechanisms. The number of warehouses is set to 12.

D. SYSTEM COMPARISON

In our experimental study, all the systems in comparison share exactly the same underlying framework. Therefore, the fairness of our experiments are guaranteed.

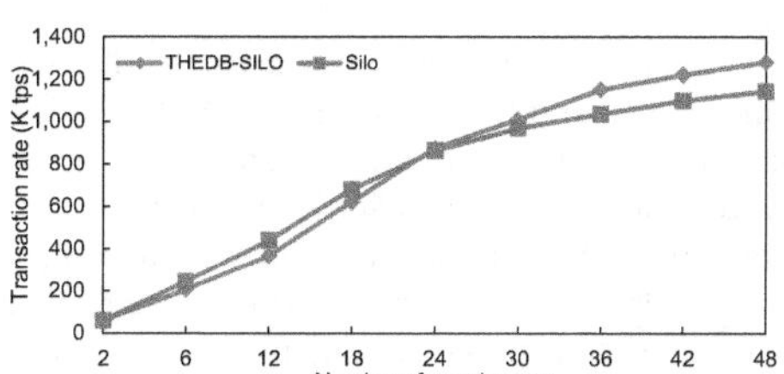

Figure 17: Performance comparison between THEDB-SILO and Silo. The number of cores is set to 46.

We adopted a self-implemented THEDB to compare transaction healing with the concurrency-control protocol that is proposed by Silo [55]. To confirm that our own implementation can precisely capture the behavior of Silo, we show the transaction rate of THEDB and the open-sourced version of Silo [3] in Figure 17.

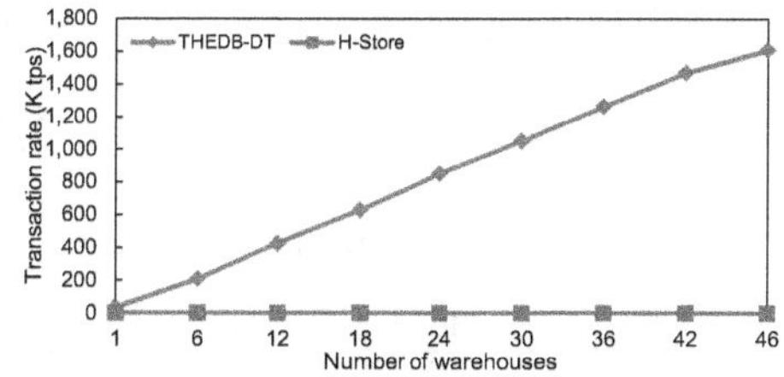

Figure 18: Performance comparison between THEDB-DT and H-Store. The number of cores is set to 46.

In this experiment, we set the number of cores to 46, and vary the number of warehouses to change the workload contention. As the result indicates, neither of these two systems can achieve a satisfactory performance when processing highly contended workloads. Meanwhile, the transaction rates of both systems scale smoothly with the decrease of workload contention. When the number of warehouses is set to 48, THEDB-SILO achieves around 10% higher transaction rate compared to Silo. This result confirms that our implementation of THEDB-SILO is efficient, and the runtime behavior of Silo's concurrency-control protocol can be precisely captured.

Next, we show a performance comparison between THEDB-DT and H-Store [32], which is a deterministic database that resorts to coarse-grained partition-level locking for achieving high performance. THEDB-DT faithfully follows the design of H-Store, and is specifically optimized for multicore architecture. In our experimental study, we did not directly use H-Store to measure the performance of deterministic databases. This is because H-Store cannot achieve satisfactory performance on multicore machines, and it suffers from additional performance penalty from network communication. Figure 18 shows a comparison between THEDB-DT and the open-sourced version of H-Store [2]. In this experiment, the ratio of cross-partition transactions is set to 0. That is, the workload can be perfectly partitioned. By varying the number of warehouses from 1 to 46, the transaction rate of THEDB-DT increases linearly. However, H-Store only achieves around 4.8 K tps regardless of the number of warehouses. This is because the performance of H-Store is strictly bounded by the network client. Therefore, we adopt the self-implemented THEDB-DT in our study.

E. TRANSACTION LATENCY

In this section, we analyze the transaction latency of THEDB when processing low-contention workloads. Table 5 shows the transaction latencies of different systems when processing `NewOrder` and `Delivery` transactions.

Similar with the results achieved when processing high-contention workloads, THEDB still yields a shorter latency compared with THEDB-OCC, THEDB-SILO, and THEDB-2PL. Specifically, around 95% of `NewOrder` and `Delivery` transactions processed by THEDB are committed within 80 ns and 640 ns, respectively. While the generated latency is much shorter than that achieved under high-contention workloads (see Section 5.2.2), THEDB-OCC, THEDB-SILO, and THEDB-2PL yet cannot maintain a stable transaction latency, and the produced latency can range from less than 20 ns to over 640 ns. In fact, the reported result generated by THEDB is very close to that achieved by THEDB-OCC and THEDB-SILO with the validation phase disabled (denoted as THEDB-OCC^{-} and THEDB-SILO^{-}). This result confirms that THEDB can achieve high performance when processing low-contention workloads.

Transaction type	Latency (μs)	THEDB	THEDB-OCC	THEDB-SILO	THEDB-2PL	THEDB-OCC⁻	THEDB-SILO⁻
NewOrder	10 - 20	0.9%	2.0%	9.0%	4.4%	2.1%	9.8%
	20 - 40	42.4%	37.4%	47.9%	38.6%	50.2%	53.7%
	40 - 80	54.2%	47.3%	36.9%	44.2%	45.3%	35.2%
	80 - 160	2.4%	12.2%	4.9%	11.9%	1.9%	1.2%
	160 - 320	0%	1.0%	1.3%	0.7%	0.2%	0%
	320 - 640	0%	0%	0%	0%	0.1%	0%
	640 - INF	0%	0%	0%	0.1%	0%	0%
Delivery	10 - 80	0%	1.5%	1.3%	4.2%	0%	0%
	80 - 160	0%	0%	0%	0%	0.7%	0.5%
	160 - 320	65.7%	28.2%	54.9%	40.3%	83.3%	74.3%
	320 - 640	29.0%	50.7%	29.8%	49.6%	14.9%	24.9%
	640 - 1280	5.2%	18.3%	13.4%	3.7%	0.8%	0.3%
	1280 - 2560	0%	0.5%	0.5%	2.2%	0.3%	0%
	2560 - 5120	0%	0.8%	0%	0%	0%	0%
	5120 - INF	0%	0%	0%	0%	0%	0%

Table 5: Transaction latency for TPC-C benchmark. The number of warehouses is set to 24, and the number of cores is set to 46.

F. RUNTIME BREAKDOWN

Figure 19 depicts the time breakdown of THEDB and THEDB-OCC using the TPC-C benchmark. In this set of experiments, we set the number of warehouses to 4 in order to generate contended workloads.

As shown in Figure 19a, THEDB-OCC spends respectively over 60% and 20% of its runtime in executing the read and write phases when the number of cores is set to 1. However, with 46 cores utilized in processing the workload, over 40% of the time is taken by the execution of the validation phase. This is because, under highly contended workloads, more transactions fail the validation phase due to inconsistent reads, and consequently much time is wasted in performing resource cleanups, such as lock releasing and memory deallocation. As a result, the transaction rate (i.e., the proportion of transactions that successfully completed the write phase) is reduced as contention increases.

Figure 19b shows the runtime breakdown of THEDB using the same workload configurations. As the number of cores increases, the proportion of time spent on the healing phase also increases. However, the percentage of time spent on the write phase is still maintained at around 20%, as most of the transactions that pass the validation phase can be committed. This result confirms the effectiveness of transaction healing when processing highly contended workloads.

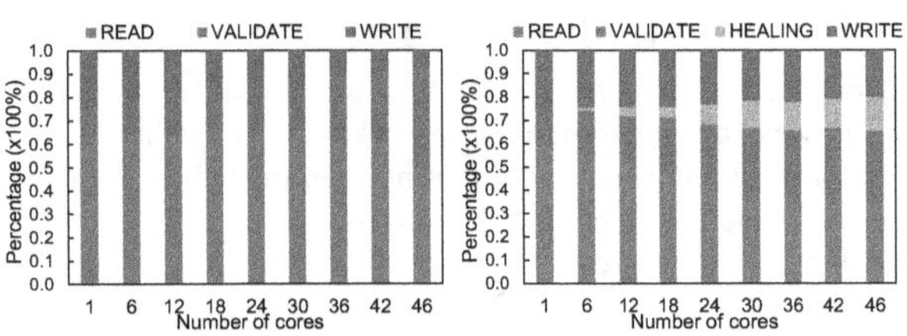

(a) THEDB-OCC. (b) THEDB.

Figure 19: Breakdown of transaction processing time using the TPC-C benchmark.

G. ABORT RATE

he following experiment exploits the performance improvement brought by validation-order rearrangement using the TPC-C benchmark. While we can hardly control the likelihood of deadlock occurrence, we can measure the *worst case* scenario where validation-order rearrangement is disabled. To construct such a scenario, we directly reverse the validation order. That is, instead of validating the consistency of the records following the table order: `Warehouse` → `District` → `Customer` → ... (shown in Figure 7, as is done when validation-order rearrangement is enabled), THEDB validates the consistency of the accessed records in a reversed order: ... → `Customer` → `District` → `Warehouse`. This is essentially the worst case, as once any update to the read-/write set's membership occurs, the healing phase is more likely to trigger transaction abort for the prevention of deadlocks. Figure 20 shows the result. Even under the worst case (see THEDB-W), THEDB still achieves 2X higher transaction rate compared to THEDB-OCC, especially when the workload is highly contended. With validation-order rearrangement enabled, THEDB's performance is improved by around 25%. This result confirms the effectiveness of order rearrangement. Moreover, the performance benefits brought by transaction healing is further confirmed.

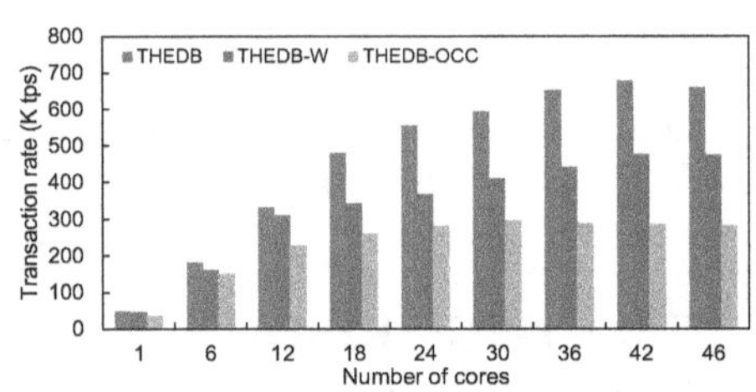

Figure 20: Performance improvement brought by rearranging validation orders.

Table 6 exhibits the abort rate caused by deadlock-prevention strategy in the transaction healing protocol. With order rearrangement disabled, in the worst case, the abort rate in THEDB can raise to 0.16 with the number of cores set to 46. However, with order rearrangement enabled, the abort rate is drastically dropped to less than 0.01 even under highly contended workloads. This result further confirms the effectiveness of validation-order rearrangement.

#cores	8	16	24	32	40	46
THEDB	0.0009	0.0017	0.0019	0.0021	0.0023	0.0024
THEDB-W	0.01	0.03	0.09	0.11	0.14	0.16

Table 6: Transaction abort rate caused by deadlock prevention.

Enabling Incremental Query Re-Optimization

Mengmeng Liu*
@WalmartLabs
liumengmeng@gmail.com

Zachary G. Ives
University of Pennsylvania
zives@cis.upenn.edu

Boon Thau Loo
University of Pennsylvania
boonloo@cis.upenn.edu

ABSTRACT

As declarative query processing techniques expand to the Web, data streams, network routers, and cloud platforms, there is an increasing need to re-plan execution in the presence of unanticipated performance changes. New runtime information may affect which query plan we prefer to run. Adaptive techniques require innovation both in terms of the *algorithms used to estimate costs*, and in terms of the *search algorithm* that finds the best plan. We investigate how to build a cost-based optimizer that recomputes the optimal plan *incrementally* given new cost information, much as a stream engine constantly updates its outputs given new data. Our implementation especially shows benefits for stream processing workloads. It lays the foundations upon which a variety of novel adaptive optimization algorithms can be built. We start by leveraging the recently proposed approach of formulating query plan enumeration as a set of *recursive datalog queries*; we develop a variety of novel optimization approaches to ensure effective pruning in both static and incremental cases. We further show that the lessons learned in the declarative implementation can be equally applied to more traditional optimizer implementations.

1. INTRODUCTION

Today, query optimization is being applied to many settings beyond traditional databases. Consider declarative cloud data processing systems [5, 22] and data stream processing [7, 23] platforms, where data properties and the status of cluster compute nodes may be constantly changing. Here it is very difficult to effectively choose a good plan for query execution: data statistics may be unavailable or highly variable; cost parameters may change due to resource contention or machine failures; and in fact a *combination* of query plans might perform better than any single plan. Given the complexities of cost estimation, work in the early 2000s was done on *self-tuning* so the performance of a query or set of queries can be improved [1, 6, 21]. More recently, the focus has been on generating "robust" rather than optimal plans [12] or selecting database designs that yield robust plans [24].

Nonetheless, there is need for *adaptive* techniques that can adjust to runtime conditions during query processing — *adaptive query processing* [11]. Adaptivity requires three orthogonal building blocks: (1) techniques for acquiring information about performance (ideally, performing accurate cost estimation) and trading off *exploration vs. exploitation* as we seek to determine the most efficient plan, (2) a planner capable of taking new information and rapidly re-estimating the most efficient plan, (3) an execution system whose computation can be adapted in mid-execution. Most recent work focused on the first and last problems: namely, new methods for better statistics collection and costs estimation during query execution [4, 6, 17, 18, 21, 30]; and techniques for adapting execution [10]. Our goal is to explore the second capability: how to support *incremental* techniques for re-optimization, whereby an optimizer, given new cost information, would only re-explore the minimal set of query plans whose costs may be affected. Given any existing set of cost estimation techniques, pruning heuristics, and transformation rules, matched with an execution engine, our approach will always incrementally recompute the *same optimal plan* (based on the cost model) as a full-blown optimization.

In this paper, we consider incremental re-optimization for two main settings: (1) *data stream management systems* where data may be bursty, and its distributions may vary over time — meaning that different query plans may be preferred over different segments. Here it is vital to optimize frequently based on recent data distribution and cost information; (2) traditional OLAP database settings when the same query (or highly similar queries) gets executed frequently, as in a prepared statement. Here we may wish to re-optimize the plan after each iteration, given increasingly accurate information about costs, and we would like this optimization to have minimal overhead. Our focus in the paper is not on novel optimizer strategies or cost estimation techniques per se, but on redesigning the planning components of the optimizer to incrementally recompute the best plan given *any preferred strategy that would be used in a standard optimizer*.

The main contribution of this paper is to show how an *incremental* re-optimizer can be developed, and how it can be useful in adaptive query processing scenarios matching the application domains cited above. Our incremental re-optimizer implements the basic capabilities of a modern database query optimizer, and could easily be extended to support other more advanced features and estimators; our main goal is to show that an incremental optimizer following our model can be competitive with a standard optimizer implementation for *initial* optimization, and significantly faster for *repeated* optimization — for any choice of cost model and estimation techniques. Moreover, in contrast to randomized or heuristics-based optimization methods, we **still guarantee the discovery of the best plan** according to the cost model. Since our work is oriented towards adaptive query processing, we evaluate the system in a variety of settings in conjunction with a basic pipelined query engine for stream and stored data.

We implement incremental re-optimization using a novel approa-

*This work was done while the author was at UPenn.

SIGMOD '16, June 26–July 1, 2016, San Francisco, CA, USA.

DOI: http://dx.doi.org/10.1145/2882903.2915212

ch, which is based on the observation that query optimization is essentially a recursive process involving the derivation and subsequent pruning of state (namely, alternative plans and their costs). If one is to build an *incremental* re-optimizer, this requires preservation of state (i.e., the optimizer memoization table) across optimization runs — but moreover, it must be possible to determine what plans have been *pruned* from this state, and to re-derive such alternatives and test whether they are now viable.

One way to achieve such "re-pruning" capabilities is to carefully define a semantics for how state needs to be tracked and recomputed in an optimizer. However, we observe that this task of "re-pruning" in response to updated information looks remarkably similar to the database problem of *view maintenance* through aggregation [15] and recursion as studied in the database literature [16]. In fact, recent work [9] has shown that query optimization can itself be captured in recursive datalog. Thus, we initially formulate our approach to developing an incremental re-optimizer using a *declarative specification*. **A key benefit of the declarative approach is that it enables us to identify state-pruning strategies agnostic to the order of control and data flow during plan enumeration.**

More precisely, we express the optimizer as a recursive datalog program consisting of a set of rules, and leverage the existing database query processor to actually execute the declarative program. In essence, this is optimizing a query optimizer using a query processor. Our implementation approaches the performance of conventional procedural optimizers for reasonably-sized queries. Our implementation recovers the initial overhead during subsequent re-optimizations by leveraging *incremental view maintenance* [16, 20] techniques. It only recomputes portions of the search space and cost estimates that might be affected by the cost updates. Frequently, this is only a small portion of the overall search space, and hence we often see order-of-magnitude performance benefits.

Given this setting, we tackle the problem of pruning while recursively computing the optimal plan. We develop a variety of novel *incremental* and *recursive* optimization techniques to capture the kinds of pruning used in a conventional optimizer, and more importantly, to generalize them to the incremental case. Our approach achieves pruning levels that rival or best bottom-up (as in System-R [27]) and top-down (as in Volcano [13, 14]) plan enumerations with branch-and-bound pruning. Our techniques are of broader interest to incremental evaluation of recursive queries as well.

Finally, we use insights gained from our declarative implementation to form a *specification for pruning and state management* that we use to retrofit standard optimizer architectures with incremental re-optimization capabilities. Here we still *guarantee optimality* of the pruning techniques based on their equivalence to the declarative implementation. We make the following contributions:

- A rule-based, declarative approach to query (re)optimization as an *incremental view maintenance problem*, which relaxes traditional restrictions on search order and pruning.
- Novel strategies to prune the state of an executing recursive query, such as a declarative optimizer: *aggregate selection* with *tuple source suppression*; *reference counting*; and *recursive bounding*.
- An implementation over a query engine developed for recursive stream processing [20], with a comprehensive evaluation of performance against alternative approaches, over a diverse workload.
- "Porting" techniques from incremental re-optimization to conventional cost-based adaptive query processing techniques [17, 30].

2. INCREMENTAL RE-OPTIMIZATION

We show our query processing architecture in Figure 1. We assume a set of **transformation rules** and **initial statistics**, using any existing strategy for statistics collection and cost estimation. Our specific implementation uses histograms on join attributes and

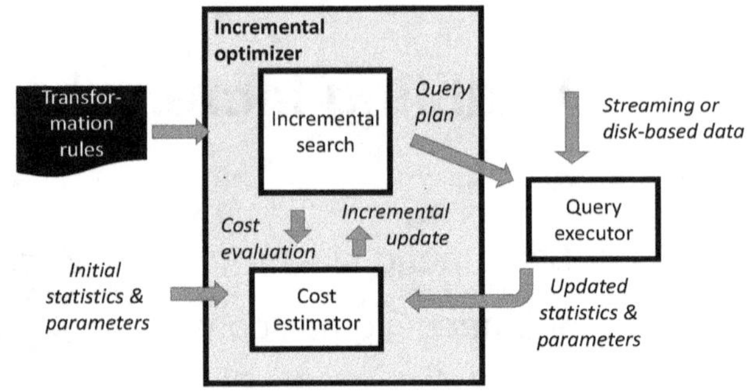

Figure 1: Query processing architecture

standard heuristics [8]. The implemented transformation space includes hash and nested loops join and group-by, as well as a sort *enforcer* and merge joins. Our focus is on the **incremental search** module: we develop strategies that — given updated runtime conditions from the **query executor** — can trigger an *incremental update* to the search, which still *guarantees the choice of the lowest-estimated-cost plan in the search space*, i.e., that exactly mirror what a non-incremental optimizer would have done. The **query executor** in our system [20] supports streaming, favors pipelined execution, and supports runtime monitoring of statistics.

In subsequent sections, we first consider a *declarative* implementation of the incremental re-optimizer, which enables us to decouple search and pruning from any particular order of search. Next we show how to take the same strategies and incorporate them into a traditional, procedural query optimizer implementation.

3. DECLARATIVE QUERY OPTIMIZATION

Our goal is an optimizer that incrementally maintains information about best (sub)plans and takes advantage of pruning opportunities. Restated, it performs *incremental state management* of (recursively computed) plan costs, in response to updates to query plan cost information. Incremental update propagation is a very well-studied problem for recursive queries, with a clean semantics and many efficient implementations. Thus we consider a model in which our optimizer is itself formulated as a recursive, incrementally maintainable query. (In Section 5.4 we show how to adapt ideas to a more traditional optimizer setting.)

Prior work has also demonstrated the feasibility of a datalog-based query optimizer [9]. Hence, rather than re-inventing incremental recomputation techniques we have built our optimizer as a series of recursive rules in datalog, executed in the query engine that already exists in the DBMS. In contrast to the prior work, our focus is not on formulating every aspect of query optimization in datalog, but rather on capturing the state management and pruning as datalog rules — so we can adapt incremental view maintenance (delta rules) and develop novel sideways information passing techniques, respectively. Other optimizer features that are not reliant on state that changes at runtime, such as cardinality estimation, breaking expressions into subexpressions, etc., are specified as built-in auxiliary functions. As a result, we specify an entire optimizer in only three stages and 10 rules (dataflow is illustrated in Figure 2).

Plan enumeration (SearchSpace). Searching the space of possible plans has two aspects. In the *logical phase*, the original query is recursively broken down into a full set of alternative relational algebra subexpressions[1]. The decomposition is naturally a "top-down" type of recursion: it starts from the original query expression, which then breaks down into subexpressions, and so on. The *physical phase* takes as input a query expression from the logical phase, and creates physical plans by enumerating the set of possible physical operators that satisfy any constraints on the output

[1]Alternatively, only *left-linear* expressions may be considered [27].

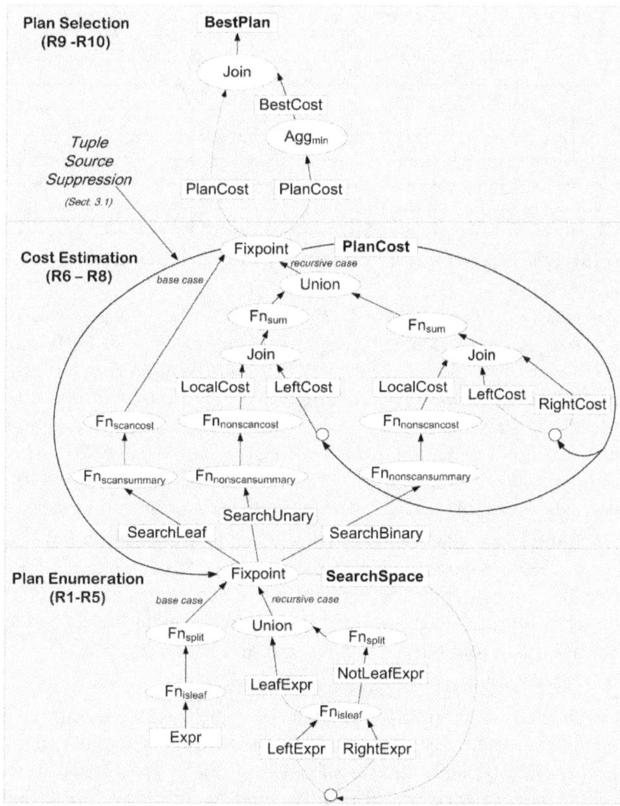

Figure 2: Query plan of our declarative query optimizer. Operators are in ellipses; views are in rectangles. Plan enumeration (SearchSpace) **consists of 5 rules, cost estimation** (PlanCost) **3 rules, and plan selection** (BestPlan) **2 rules. See Appendix.**

properties [14] or "interesting orders" [27] (e.g., the data must be sorted by a particular attribute). Without physical properties, the extension from logical plans to physical plans can be computed either top-down or bottom-up; however, the properties are more efficiently computed in goal-directed (top-down) manner.

Cost estimation (PlanCost). This phase determines the cost for each physical plan in the search space, by recursively merging the statistics and cost estimates of a plan's subplans. It is naturally a bottom-up type of recursion, as the plan subexpressions must already have been cost-estimated before the plan itself. Here we can encode in a table the mapping from a plan to its cost.

Plan selection (BestPlan). As costs are estimated, the program produces the plan that incurs the lowest estimated cost.

In our declarative approach to query optimization, we treat optimizer state as data, use rules to specify what a query optimizer is, and leverage a database query processor to actually perform the computation. Figure 2 shows a (simplified) query plan for the datalog rules. As we can see, the declarative program is by nature recursive, and is broken into the three stages mentioned before (with Fixpoint operators between stages). Starting from the bottom of the figure, **plan enumeration** recursively generates a SearchSpace table containing plan specifications, by decomposing the query and enumerating possible output properties; enumerated plans are then fed into the **plan estimation** component, PlanCost, which computes a cost for each plan, by building from leaf to complex expressions; **plan selection** computes a BestCost and BestPlan entry for each query expression and output property, by aggregating across the PlanCost entries.

This basic datalog program can be evaluated in a conventional datalog engine, augmented with a few user-defined functions. However, it will likely perform poorly due to limited pruning of plan alternatives. A major contribution of this paper is to develop new strategies for pruning of recursive computations like planning. We use an example to help explain the overall evaluation process.

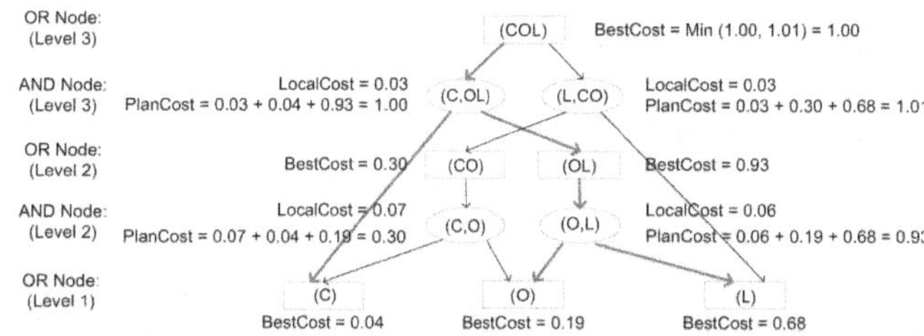

Figure 3: The and-or-graph for Q3S. Red edges denote the best plan. Rectangles and ovals denote "OR" and "AND" nodes respectively. Each "OR" node is labeled with its BestCost **and each "AND" node is labeled with its** LocalCost **and** PlanCost**.**

EXAMPLE 1. *As our driving example, consider a simplified TPC-H Query 3 with its aggregates and functions removed, called Q3S.*

```
SELECT L_orderkey, O_orderdate, O_shippriority
FROM Customer C, Orders O, Lineitem L
WHERE C_mktsegment = 'MACHINERY' and C_custkey =
    O_custkey and O_orderkey = L_orderkey and
    O_orderdate < '1995-03-15' and L_shipdate > '
    1995-03-15'
```

3.1 Plan Enumeration

Plan enumeration takes as input the original query expression as Expr, and then generates as output the set of alternative plans. As with many optimizers, it is divided into two levels:

Logical search space. The logical plan search space contains all the logical plans that correspond to subexpressions of the original query expression up to any logically equivalent transformations (e.g., commutativity and associativity of join operators). In traditional query optimizers such as Volcano [14], a data structure called an *and-or-graph* is maintained to represent the logical plan search space. The and-or-graph can capture both tree- and DAG-structured query plans [26]. Bottom-up dynamic programming optimizers do not physically store this graph, but it is still conceptually relevant.

EXAMPLE 2. *Figure 3 shows an example and-or-graph for Q3S, which describes a set of alternative subplans and subplan choices using interleaved levels. "AND" nodes represent alternative subplans (typically with join operator roots) and the "OR" nodes represent decision points where the cheapest AND-node was chosen.*

Our implementation captures each node in a table SearchSpace. As we discuss next, we supplement this information with further information about the output properties and *physical plan*. (We explain why we combine the results from both stages in Section 3.3.)

Physical search space. The physical search space extends the logical one in that it enumerates all the physical operators for each algebraic logical operator. For example, in our figure above, each "AND" node denotes a logical join operator, but it may have multiple physical implementations such as pipelined-hash, indexed nested-loops, or sort-merge join. If the physical implementation is not symmetric, exchanging the left and right child would become a different physical plan. A physical plan has not only a root physical operator, but also a set of physical properties over the data that it maintains or produces; if we desire a set of output properties, this may constrain the physical properties of the plan's inputs.

EXAMPLE 3. *Table 1 shows the* SearchSpace *content for a subset of Figure 3. The AND logical operators are either joins (with*

*Expr	*Prop	*Index	LogOp	*PhyOp	lExpr	lProp	rExpr	rProp
(COL)	–	1	join	sort-merge	(C)	C_custkey order	(OL)	O_custkey order
(COL)	–	2	join	indexed nested-loop	(L)	index on L_orderkey	(CO)	–
(OL)	O_custkey order	1	join	pipelined-hash	(O)	–	(L)	–
(CO)	–	1	join	pipelined-hash	(C)	–	(O)	–
(CO)	–	1	join	sort-merge	(C)	–	(O)	–
(O)	O_custkey order	–	scan	local scan	–	–	–	–
(L)	index on L_orderkey	–	scan	index scan	–	–	–	–
(C)	C_custkey order	–	scan	local scan	–	–	–	–

Table 1: A simplified SearchSpace relation encoding the and-or-graph for Q3S's search space. Primary keys are denoted by *.

2 child expressions), or tablescans (with selection predicates applied). Each expression Expr *may have multiple Indexed alternatives. Prop and PhyOp represent the physical properties of a plan and its root physical operator, respectively.*

For instance, expression SearchSpace(COL) *has encodes an "OR" node with two alternatives the first "AND" (join) child is* SearchSpace(C, OL) *and the second is* SearchSpace(L, CO). *For the first* SearchSpace *tuple, the left expression is C and the right expression is OL. The tuple indicates a Sort-Merge join, whose left and right inputs' physical properties require a sort order based on $C\_custkey$ and $O\_custkey$, respectively. The second alternative uses an Indexed Nested-Loop Join as its physical operator. The left expression refers to the inner join relation indexed on $L\_orderkey$, while there are no ordering restrictions on the right expression.*

We enumerate plans using a single recursive query (bottom of Figure 2). Given an expression, the $\mathsf{Fn_{split}}$ function enumerates all the algebraically equivalent rewritings for the given expression, as well as the possible physical operators and their interesting orders. Fixpoint is reached when Expr has been decomposed down to leaf-level scan operations over a base relation (checked using $\mathsf{Fn_{isleaf}}$).

3.2 Cost Estimation and Plan Selection

The cost estimation component computes an estimated cost for every physical plan. Given the SearchSpace tuples generated in the plan enumeration phase, three datalog rules (R6 - R8) are used to compute PlanCost (corresponding to a more detailed version of the "AND" nodes in Figure 3, with physical operators considered and all costs enumerated), and two additional rules (R9 - R10) select the BestPlan (corresponding to an "OR" node). Cost estimates are recursively computed by summing up the children costs and operation costs. The computed sum for each physical plan is stored in PlanCost.

In addition to the search space, cost estimation requires a set of *summaries* (statistics) on the input relations and indexes, e.g., cardinality of a (indexed) relation, selectivity of operators, data distribution, etc. These summaries are computed using functions $\mathsf{Fn_{scansummary}}$ and $\mathsf{Fn_{nonscansummary}}$. The former computes the leaf level summaries over base tables, and the latter computes the output summaries of an operator based on input summaries. Given the statistics, the cost of a plan can be computed by combining factors such as CPU, I/O, bandwidth and energy into a single cost metric. We compute the cost of each physical operator using functions $\mathsf{Fn_{scancost}}$ and $\mathsf{Fn_{nonscancost}}$ respectively.

Given the above functions, cost estimation becomes a recursive computation that sums up the cost of children expressions and the root cost, to finally compute a cost for the entire query plan. At each step, $\mathsf{Fn_{sum}}$ is used to sum up the PlanCost of its child plans with LocalCost. The particular form of the operation depends on whether the plan root is a leaf node, a unary or a binary operator.

EXAMPLE 4. *To illustrate the process of cost estimation, we revisit Figure 3, which shows a simplified logical search space (omitting physical operators and properties) for our simplified TPC-H Q3S. For every "AND" node, we compute the plan cost by summing up the cost of the join operator, with the best costs of computing its two inputs (e.g., the level 2 "AND" node (C, O) sums up its local cost 0.07, its left best cost 0.04, and its right best cost 0.19, and gets its plan cost 0.30). For every "OR" node, we determine the alternative with minimum cost among its "AND" node children (e.g., the level 3 "OR" node (COL) computes a minimum over its two input plan costs 1.00 and 1.01, and gets its best cost 1.00). After the best cost is computed for the root "OR" node in the graph, the optimization process is done, and an optimal plan tree is chosen.*

Once the PlanCost for every "AND" node are generated, the final two rules compute the BestCost for every "OR" node by computing a min aggregate over PlanCost of its alternative "AND" node derivations, and output the BestPlan for each "AND" node by computing a join between BestCost and PlanCost.

3.3 Execution Strategy

Given a query optimizer specified in datalog, the natural question is how to actually execute it. We seek to be general enough to incorporate typical features of existing query optimizers, to rival their performance and flexibility, and to only develop implementation techniques that generalize. We adopt two strategies and develop novel execution techniques to support them:

Merging logical and physical plan enumeration. The physical plan elaborates on the logical plan. Since both logical and physical enumeration are top-down types of recursion, and there is no pruning information from the physical stage that should be propagated back to the logical one, we can merge the logical and physical enumeration stages into a single recursive query.

As we enumerate each logical subexpression, we simultaneously join with the table representing the possible physical operators that can implement it. This generates the entire set of possible physical query plans. To make it more efficient to generate multiple physical plans from a single logical expression, we use *caching* to memoize the results of $\mathsf{Fn_{nonscansummary}}$ and $\mathsf{Fn_{split}}$.

Decoupling of cost estimation and plan enumeration. Cost estimation requires bottom-up evaluation: a cost estimate can *only* be obtained once cost estimates and statistics are obtained from child expressions. The enumeration stage naturally produces expressions in the order from parent to child, yet estimation must be done from child to parent. We *decouple* the execution order among plan enumeration and cost estimation, making the connections between these two components flexible. For example, some cost estimates may happen before all related plans have been enumerated. Cost estimates may even be used to *prune* portions of the plan enumeration space (and hence also further prune cost estimation itself) in an opportunistic way.

4. ACHIEVING PRUNING

We now consider how to incorporate *pruning* of the search space into pipelined execution of our query optimizer. Our approach is based on the idea of *sideways information passing*, in which the computation of one portion of the query plan may be made more efficient by filtering against information computed elsewhere, but not connected directly by pipelined dataflow. Specifically, we incorporate the technique of aggregate selection [28] from the deductive database literature, which we briefly review; we extend it to perform further pruning; and we develop two new techniques for recursive queries that enable tracking of dependencies and computation of bounds. Beyond query optimization, our techniques are broadly useful in the evaluation of recursive datalog queries. In the next section we make these strategies *incrementally maintainable*.

Section 4.1 reviews aggregate selection, which removes non-viable plans from the optimizer state if they are not cost-effective, and shows how we can use it to achieve the similar effects to dynamic programming in bottom-up style optimizers. There we also introduce a novel technique called *tuple source suppression*. In the remainder of the section we show how to introduce two familiar notions into datalog execution: namely, *reference counting* that enables us to remove plan subexpressions once all of their parent expressions have been pruned (Section 4.2), and *recursive bounding*, which lets the datalog engine incorporate branch-and-bound pruning as in a typical top-down query optimizer (Section 4.3). Our approaches relax the traditional restrictions on the search order and pruning techniques in either Volcano's [14] top-down traversal or System R's [27] bottom-up dynamic programming approaches. For example, a top-down search algorithm can have a depth-first order, breadth-first order or another order.

4.1 Pruning Suboptimal Plan Expressions

Dating back to System-R [27], every modern query optimizer uses dynamic programming techniques (although some via memoization [14]). Dynamic programming is based on the *principle of optimality*, i.e. an optimal plan can be decomposed into sub-plans that must themselves be optimal solutions. This property is vital to optimizer performance, because the same subexpression may appear repeatedly in many parent expressions. Formally:

PROPOSITION 5. *Given a query expression E and property p, consider a plan tree $T\langle E, p\rangle$ that evaluates E with output property p. For this and other propositions, we assume that plans have distinct costs. Here one such T will have the minimum cost: call that T_{OPT}. Suppose E^s is a subexpression of E, and consider a plan tree $T^s\langle E^s, p^s\rangle$ that evaluates E^s with output property p^s. Again one such T^s will have the minimum cost: call that T^s_{OPT}. If T^s is* not *T^s_{OPT}, then T^s must* not *be the subtree of T_{OPT}.*

This proposition ensures that we can safely discard suboptimal subplans without affecting the final optimal plan. Consider the and-or-graph of example query Q3S (Figure 3). The red (bolded) subtree is the optimal plan for the root expression (COL). The subplan of the level 3 "AND" node (L, CO) has suboptimal cost 1.00. If there exists a super-expression containing (COL), then the only viable subplan is the one marked in the figure. State for any alternative subplan for (COL) may be pruned from SearchSpace and PlanCost. We prune both relations via two novel techniques.

Pruning PlanCost **via aggregate selection.** Refer back to Figure 2: each BestCost tuple encodes the minimum cost for a given query expression-property pair, over all the plans associated with this pair in PlanCost. To avoid enumerating unnecessary PlanCost tuples, one can wait until the BestCost of subplans are obtained before computing a PlanCost for a root plan. This is how System R-style dynamic programming works. However, this approach constrains the order of evaluation.

We instead extend a logic programming optimization technique called *aggregate selection* [28], to achieve dynamic programming-like benefits for any arbitrary order of implementation. In aggregate selection, we "push down" a selection predicate into the input of an aggregate, such that we can prune results that exceed the current minimum value or are below the current maximum value. In our case (as shown in the middle box of Figure 2), the current best-known cost for any equivalent query expression-property pair is maintained within our Fixpoint operator (which also performs the non-blocked **min** aggregation). We only propagate a newly generated PlanCost tuple if its cost is smaller than the current minimum. This does not affect the computation of BestCost, which still outputs the minimum cost for each expression-property pair. Since pruning bounds are updated upon every newly generated tuple, there is no restriction on evaluation order. As with pruning strategies used in Volcano-style optimizers, the amount of state pruned varies depending on the order of exploration: the sooner a min-cost plan is encountered, the more effective the pruning is.

Pruning SearchSpace **via tuple source suppression.** Enumeration of the search space will generally happen in parallel with enumeration of plans. Thus, as we prune tuples from PlanCost, we may be able to remove related tuples (e.g., representing subexpressions) from SearchSpace, possibly preventing enumeration of their subexpressions and/or costs. We achieve such pruning through *tuple source suppression*, along the arcs indicated in Figure 2. Any PlanCost tuples pruned by aggregate selection should also trigger cascading deletions to the *source tuples* by which they were derived from the SearchSpace relation. To achieve this, since PlanCost contains a superset of the attributes in SearchSpace, we simply project out the cost field and propagate a deletion to the corresponding SearchSpace tuple.

4.2 Pruning Unused Plan Subexpressions

The techniques described in the previous section remove *suboptimal plans* for specific expression-property pairs. However, some *optimal plans* for certain expressions may be unused in the final query execution plan. Consider in Figure 3 the level 2 "AND" node (C, O): this node is not in the final plan because its "OR" node parent expression (CO) does not appear in the final result. In turn, this is because (CO)'s parent "AND" nodes (in this example, just a single plan (L, CO)) do not contribute to the final plan. Intuitively, we may prune an "AND" node if all of its parent "AND" nodes (through only one connecting "OR" node) have been pruned.

We would like to remove such plans once they are discovered, which requires a form of *reference counting* within the datalog engine executing the optimizer. Every tuple in SearchSpace is annotated with a *count*: this count represents the number of **parent plans** still present in the SearchSpace. For example, in Table 1, the plan entry of $O \bowtie L$ has reference count of 1, because it only has one parent plan, which is $C \bowtie OL$; on the other hand, the plan entry of (O) has reference count of 2, because it has two parent plans, which are $O \bowtie L$ and $C \bowtie O$.

PROPOSITION 6. *Given a query expression E with output property p: let T^s be a plan tree for E's subexpression E^s with property p^s. If T^s has reference count of zero, then T^s must not be a subtree of the optimal plan tree for the query E with property p.*

The proposition ensures that a plan with a reference count of zero can be safely deleted. Note that a deleted plan may make more reference counts to drop to zero, hence the deletion process may be recursive. Our reference counting scheme is more efficient than the *counting* algorithm of [16], which uses a count representing the *total number of derivations* of each tuple in bag semantics. Our count represents the number of *unique parent plans from which a subplan may be derived*, and can typically be incrementally updated in a single recursive step (whereas **counting** often requires multiple recursive steps to compute the whole derivation count).

Our reference counting mechanism complements the pruning techniques discussed in Section 4.1. Following an insertion (exploration) or deletion (pruning) of a SearchSpace tuple, we update the reference counts of relevant tuples accordingly; cascading insertions or deletions of SearchSpace (and further PlanCost) tuples may be triggered because their reference counts may be raised

r1: ParentBound($lExpr, lProp, bound - rCost - localCost$) :-
Bound($expr, prop, bound$), BestCost($rExpr, rProp, rCost$),
LocalCost($expr, prop, index, lExpr, lProp, rExpr,$
$rProp, -, localCost$);
r2: ParentBound($rExpr, rProp, bound - lCost - localCost$) :-
Bound($expr, prop, bound$), BestCost($Expr, lProp, lCost$),
LocalCost($expr, prop, index, lExpr, lProp, rExpr,$
$rProp, -, localCost$);
r3: MaxBound($expr, prop, max < bound >$) :-
ParentBound($expr, prop, bound$);
r4: Bound($expr, prop, min < minCost, maxBound >$) :-
BestCost($expr, prop, minCost$),
MaxBound($expr, prop, maxBound$);

Figure 4: Datalog rules to express bounds computation

above zero (or dropped to zero). Finally, the optimal plan computed by the query optimizer is unchanged, but more tuples in SearchSpace and PlanCost are pruned. Indeed, by the end of the process, the combination of aggregate selection and reference counts ensure SearchSpace and PlanCost *only* contain those plans that are on the final optimal plan tree. Such "garbage collection" greatly reduces the optimizer's state and the number of data items that must be updated incrementally, as described in Section 5.

4.3 Full Branch-and-Bound Pruning

Our third innovation generalizes *branch-and-bound pruning*, as in top-down optimizers like Volcano, during cost estimation of physical plans. Branch-and-bound pruning uses *prior exploration* of related plans to prune the exploration of new plans: a physical plan for a subexpression is pruned if its cost already exceeds the cost of a plan for the equivalent subexpression (or its parent, grandparent, or other ancestor expression). Typically, branch-and-bound pruning assumes a single-recursive descent execution thread during its enumeration. We develop a branch-and-bounding solution independent of the search order, which supports parallel enumeration.

Previous work [9] has shown that it is possible to do a limited form of branch-and-bound pruning in a declarative optimizer, by initializing a bound based on the cost of the parent expression, and then pruning subplan exploration whenever the cost has exceeded an *equivalent* expression. This can actually be achieved by our aggregate selection approach described in Section 4.1.

We seek to generalize this to prune against the *best* known bound for an expression-property pair — which may be from a plan for an equivalent expression, or from any ancestor plan that *contains* the subplan corresponding to this expression-property pair. (Recall that there may be several parent plans for a subplan: this introduces some complexity as each parent plan may have different cost bounds, and at certain point in time we may not know the costs for some of the parent plans.) The bound should be continuously *updated* as different parts of the search space are explored via pipelined execution. In this section, we assume that bounds are initialized to infinity and *monotonically decreasing*. In Section 5.3 we will relax this requirement.

Our solution, *recursive bounding*, creates and updates a single recursive relation Bound, whose values form the *best-known* bound on each expression-property pair (each "OR" node). This bound is the minimum of (1) known costs of any equivalent plans; (2) the highest bound of any parent plan's expression-property pair, which in turn is defined recursively in terms of parents of this parent plan. Figure 4 shows how we can express the bounds table using recursive datalog rules. ParentBound propagates cost bounds from a parent expression-property pair to child expression-property pairs, through LocalCost, while the child bound also takes into account the cost of the local operator, and the best cost from the sibling side. MaxBound finds the highest of bounds from parent plans, and Bound maintains the minimum bounding information derived from BestCost or MaxBound, allowing for more strict pruning.

Given the definition of Bound, we can reason about the viability of certain physical plans below:

PROPOSITION 7. *Given a query expression E with desired output property p: let T^s be a plan tree that produces E's subexpression E^s and yields property p^s. If T^s has a cumulative cost that is larger than Bound $\langle E^s, p^s \rangle$, then T^s cannot be a sub-tree of the optimal plan tree for the query E, for property p.*

Based on Proposition 7, recursive bounding may safely remove any plan that exceeds the bound for its expression-property pair. Indeed, with our definition of the bounds, this strategy is a generalization of the aggregate selection strategy discussed in Section 4.1. However, bounds are recursively defined here and a single plan cost update may result in a number of changes to bounds for others.

Overall the execution flow of pruning PlanCost and SearchSpace via recursive bounding is similar to that described in Section 4.1. Specifically, PlanCost is pruned inside the Fixpoint operator, where an additional comparison check PlanCost $<$ Bound is performed before propagating a newly generated PlanCost. Updates over other Bound tuples derived from a given PlanCost tuple are computed separately. SearchSpace is again pruned via sideways information passing where the pruned PlanCost tuples are directly mapped to deletions over SearchSpace.

5. INCREMENTAL RE-OPTIMIZATION

The previous section described how we achieve pruning at a level comparable to a conventional query optimizer, without being constrained to the standard data and control flow of a top-down or bottom-up procedural implementation. In this section, we discuss *incremental* maintenance during both query optimization and re-optimization. In particular, we seek to incrementally update not only the state of the optimizer, but also the state that affects pruning decisions, e.g., reference counts and bounds.

Initial query optimization takes a query expression and metadata like summaries, and produces a set of tables encoding the plan search space and cost estimates. During execution, pruning bounds will always be monotonically decreasing. Now consider *incremental* re-optimization, where the optimizer is given updated cost (or cardinality) estimates based on information collected at runtime after partial execution. This scenario commonly occurs in adaptive query processing, where we monitor execution and periodically re-optimize based on the updated status. For simplicity, our discussion of the approaches assumes that a single *cost parameter* (operator estimated cost, output cardinality) changes, though our architecture is able to handle multiple such changes simultaneously.

Given a change to a cost parameter, our goal is in principle to re-evaluate the costs for all affected query plans. Some of these plans might have previously been pruned from the search space, meaning they will need to be re-enumerated. Some of the pruning bounds might need to be adjusted, as some plans become more expensive and others become cheaper. As the bounds are changed, we may in turn need to re-introduce further plans that had been previously pruned, or to remove plans that had previously been viable. This is where our declarative query optimizer formulation is extremely helpful: we use *incremental view maintenance* techniques to only recompute the necessary results, while guaranteeing correctness.

Incremental maintenance enabled via datalog. From the declarative point of view, initial query optimization and query re-optimization can be considered the same task, if the datalog program is **extended** to handle updates (insertions, deletions and replacements). Indeed, incremental query re-optimization can be specified using a delta rules formulation like [16]. This requires extensions to the database query processor to support **direct processing of deltas**: instead of processing standard tuples, each operator in the query processor must be extended to process delta tuples encoding changes.

A delta tuple of a relation R may be an insertion (R[+x]), deletion (R[-x]), or update (R[x→x']). For example, a new plan generated in SearchSpace is an insertion; a pruned plan in PlanCost is a deletion; an updated cost of BestCost is an update.

We extend the query processor following standard conventions from continuous query systems [19] and stream management systems [23]. The extended query operators consume and emit deltas largely as if they were standard tuples. For stateful operators, we maintain for each encountered tuple value a *count*, representing the cumulative total of how many times the tuple has been inserted and deleted. Insertions increment the count and deletions decrement it; counts may temporarily become negative if a deletion is processed out of order with its corresponding insertion, though ultimately the counts converge to nonnegative values, since every deletion is linked to an insertion. A tuple only affects the output of a stateful operator if its count is positive.

Upon receiving a series of delta tuples, every query operator (1) updates its corresponding state, if necessary; (2) performs any internal computations such as predicate evaluation over the tuple or against state; (3) constructs a set of output delta tuples. Joins follow the rules established in [16]. For aggregation operators that compute minimum (or maximum) values, we must further extend the internal state management to keep track of *all* values encountered — such that, e.g., we can recover the "second-from-minimum" value. If the minimum is deleted, the operator should propagate an update delta, replacing its previous output with the next-best-minimum for the associated group (and conversely for maximum).

Challenge: recomputation of pruned state. While datalog allows us to propagate updates through rules, a major challenge is that the pruning strategies of Section 4 are achieved *indirectly*. In this section we detail how we incrementally re-create pruned state as necessary. Section 5.1 shows how we incrementally maintain the output of aggregate selection and "undo" tuple source suppression. Section 5.2 describes how to incrementally adjust the reference counts and maintain the pruned plans. Section 5.3 shows how we can incrementally modify the pruning bounds and the affected plans. Finally, Section 5.4 discusses how we leverage the ideas gained from the declarative perspective solving the problem into more traditional procedural-based query optimization frameworks and several optimization techniques.

5.1 Incremental Aggregate Selection

Aggregate selection [28] prunes state against bounds and does not consider how incremental maintenance might change the bound itself. Our incremental aggregate selection algorithm is a generalization of the non-incremental case we describe in Section 4.1. Recall that we push down a selection predicate, PlanCost < BestCost, within the Fixpoint operator that generates PlanCost. To illustrate how this works, consider how we may revise BestCost and BestPlan after encountering an insertion, deletion or update to PlanCost. There are four possible cases:

1. Upon an *insertion* PlanCost[+c], set BestCost to **min** (c, current BestCost).
2. Upon a *deletion* PlanCost[-c], set BestCost to the next-best PlanCost iff the current BestCost is equal to c.
3. Upon a *cost update* PlanCost[c→c'], if $c < c'$, set BestCost to **min** (c', next-best PlanCost) iff the current BestCost is equal to c.
4. Upon a *cost update* PlanCost[c→c'], if $c > c'$, if the current BestCost is equal to c, then set BestCost to c'; else set BestCost to **min** (c', current BestCost).

Each PlanCost tuple denotes a newly computed cost associated with a physical plan, and a BestCost tuple denotes the best cost that has been computed so far for this physical plan's expression-property pair. We update BestCost based on the current state of PlanCost. In Cases 1 and 4, we can directly compute updates to BestCost. To support Cases 2 and 3, we modify the aggregate operator to buffer *multiple* alternative PlanCost tuples, including those that are non-minimal; we use view-maintenance techniques to determine when we should replace the current minimum-value with the next-best value or a new value [20]. In our implementation we use a priority queue to order the candidate "minimum" tuples.

We may also need to re-introduce tuples in SearchSpace that were suppressed when they led to PlanCost tuples that were pruned, we achieve this by propagating an insertion (rather than deletion as in Section 4.1) to the previous stage.

5.2 Incremental Reference Checking

Once we have updated the set of viable plans for given expressions in the search space, we must consider how this impacts the viability of their subplans: we must incrementally update the reference counts on the child expressions to determine if they should be left the same, re-introduced, or pruned. As before, we simplify this process and make it order-independent through the use of incremental maintenance techniques.

We incrementally and recursively maintain the reference counts for each expression-property pair whenever an associated plan in the PlanCost relation is inserted, deleted or updated. When a new entry is inserted into PlanCost, we increment the count of each of its child expression-property pairs; similarly, whenever an existing entry is deleted from PlanCost, we decrement each child reference count. Replacement values for PlanCost entries do not change the reference counts, but may recursively affect the PlanCost entries for super-expressions. Whenever a count goes from 0 to 1 (or drops from 1 to 0) we recompute (prune, respectively) all of the physical plans associated with this expression-property pair.

If we combine this strategy with aggregate selection, only the best-cost plan needs to be pruned or re-introduced (all others are pruned via aggregate selection). Similar to Section 5.1, the aggregate operators internally maintain a record of all PlanCost tuples they have received as input, so "next-best" plans can be retrieved if the best-cost entry gets deleted or updated to a higher cost value. During incremental updates, we only propagate changes affecting the old and new best-cost plan and all recursively dependent plans.

5.3 Incremental Branch-and-bounding

We next consider how to incrementally maintain the branch-and-bound pruning structure of Section 4.3: as new costs for any operation are discovered, we must recursively recompute the bounds for all super-expressions. As necessary we then update PlanCost and SearchSpace tuples based on the updated bounds. Recall from Figure 4 that the Bound relation's contents are computed recursively based on the **max** bounds derived from parent plans; and also based on the **min** values for equivalent plan costs. Hence, an update to LocalCost or BestCost may affect the entries in Bound. Here we again rely in part on the fact that Bound is a recursive query and we can incrementally maintain it, then use its new content to adjust the pruning. We illustrate the handling of cost updates by looking at what happens when a cost *increases*.

Suppose a plan's LocalCost increases. As a consequence of the rules in Figure 4, the ParentBound of this plan's children may increase due to rules r1 and r2. MaxBound is then updated by r3 to be the maximum of the ParentBound entries: hence it may also increase. As in the previous cases, the internal aggregate operator for ParentBound maintains all input values; thus, it can recompute the new minimum bound and output a corresponding update from old to new value. Finally, as a result of the updated ParentBound, Bound in r4 may also increase. The process may continue recursively to this plan's descendant expression-property pairs, until Bound has converged to the correct bounds for all expression-property pairs.

Alternatively, suppose an expression-property pair's BestCost estimate increases (e.g., due to discovering the machine is heavily loaded). This may trigger an update to the corresponding entry in Bound (via rule r4). Moreover, via rules r1 and r2, an update to this bound may affect the bounds on the parent expression, i.e., ParentBound, and thus affecting any expression whose costs were pruned via ParentBound.

The cases for handling cost *decreases* are similar. Sometimes we may get simultaneous changes in both directions. Consider, for instance, that an expression's cost bound may increase, as in the previous paragraph. At the same time, perhaps the expression-property pair's ParentBound may decrease. Any equivalent plan (sibling expression) for our original expression-property pair is bounded *both* by the bounds of sibling expressions and parents. As ParentBound decreases, MaxBound and Bound may also potentially decrease through r3 and r4. The results are guaranteed to converge to the best of the sibling and parent bounds.

So far we focused only on how to update bounds given updated cost information; of course, there is the added issue of updating the pruning results. Recall in Section 4.3 that we evaluate the following predicate ϕ before propagating a newly generated PlanCost value: if PlanCost < Bound then set Bound to PlanCost. When PlanCost or Bound is updated, we can end up in any of 3 cases:

1. Upon a plan cost update PlanCost[+c],PlanCost[-c] or PlanCost[c→c']: if predicate ϕ's result changes from false to true, then emit an insertion of the PlanCost tuple; otherwise if ϕ's result changes from true to false, then emit a deletion. Incrementally update the corresponding Bound entry, including its aggregated cost value, as a result.
2. Upon an update on Bound[b→b'] where $b < b'$: for those tuples t in PlanCost where $b < t.cost < b'$, re-insert t into PlanCost and re-insert t's counterpart in SearchSpace to *undo* tuple source suppression.
3. Upon an update on Bound[b→b'] where $b > b'$: for those tuples t in PlanCost where $b > t.cost > b'$, prune tuple t from PlanCost and delete t's counterpart from SearchSpace via tuple source suppression.

The first step resembles incremental aggregate selection (Section 5.1), except that here the condition check is not on BestCost but rather on Bound. Essentially we want to incrementally update Bound based on the current bounding status, hence a sorted list of PlanCost tuples needs to be maintained.

An interesting observation of Cases 2 and 3 is that an update on Bound may affect the pruned or propagated plans as well. If a bound is raised, it may re-introduce previously pruned plans; if a bound is lowered, it may incrementally prune previously viable plans. If incremental aggregate selection is used, then only the optimal plan among the pruned plans needs to be revisited. SearchSpace is again updated via sideways information passing.

5.4 Adapting Traditional Optimizers

Our declarative query re-optimizer enabled us to define pruning strategies independently from execution flow, and guaranteed correctness. This has given us a specification for pruning that we can "retrofit" into traditional bottom-up or top-down query optimizers. We can modify the procedural query optimizer to incrementally recompute portions of a query plan (and the contents of the memoization table), and propagate control flow upwards or downwards as appropriate to propagate the effects of a change. Then a variety of our techniques from the prior sections can similarly be adapted:

- *Incremental aggregate selection* can be used to memoize suboptimal plans as well as optimal ones, and only propagate changes that affect the choice of a "best" alternative plan for a given expression.
- *Incremental branch-and-bound* can maintain a table of bounds for subplans, which can be used for pruning.
- Separating the bounds computation enables it to be updated during enumeration both of alternative plans and superplans, as well as smaller subplans.

For both declarative and procedural-based query optimizers, we can also apply two main optimizations to minimize recomputation and bookkeeping. We term the first idea *lazy propagation*: only propagate cost changes if they might affect the choice of a super-plan; keep any remaining changes local to a node. For example, if we know in advance that an optimal subplan has not changed or it has even decreased in cost, we only need to consider alternative (previously suboptimal) plans whose costs may also have decreased.

The second optimization is to trade-off memoization versus recomputation, to reduce the cost of bookkeeping for suboptimal plans. On one extreme, if we memoize nothing during pre-optimization, then re-optimization will always need to do a full recomputation. On the other extreme, if we memoize everything, we might use up too much memory for bookkeeping. Hence in some cases, we can choose to only memoize the suboptimal plans most likely to become viable if small changes are made; and choose to discard the other alternatives, later recomputing them as necessary. This is a time and space complexity trade-off, but often a small amount of memoization can limit the recomputation to a few nodes in the and-or graph. We can also cache the output when a recomputation occurs, to avoid multiple revisits of the same node during re-optimization.

6. EVALUATION

In this section, we discuss the implementation and evaluate the performance of our incremental re-optimizer both versus other strategies, and as a primitive for adaptive query processing. (Note that we reuse existing adaptive query processing technologies from [17, 30]; our focus is to show that incremental re-optimization *improves* these systems.) We also demonstrate that our ideas work in both declarative and procedural query optimizer implementations.

We implemented the declarative optimizer in 10 datalog rules (see Appendix) with 8 auxiliary functions (including histogram generation, cost estimation, expression decomposition and so forth). Our goal was to implement as a proof of concept the **common core** of optimizer techniques — not an exhaustive set. We executed the optimizer in a modified version of the ASPEN system's query engine [20]. To support the pruning and incremental update propagation features in this paper, we added approximately 10K lines of code to the query engine. In addition, we developed a plan generator to translate the declarative optimizer into a dataflow graph as in Figure 2. Our experiments were performed on a single local node.

For comparison, we implemented in Java both a Volcano-style top-down query optimizer with branch-and-bound pruning, and a System-R-style bottom-up dynamic programming optimizer, which both reuse the histogram generation, cost estimation, and other core components as auxiliary functions in our declarative optimizer. We also built a variant of our declarative optimizer that only uses the pruning strategies of the Evita Raced declarative optimizer [9]. Wherever possible we used common code across the implementations to make fair comparisons. Finally, we extended this optimizer to support incremental computation using the declarative implementation as a reference.

Experimental Workload. For **repeated optimization** scenarios we use TPC-H queries, with data from the TPC-H and skewed TPC-D data generators [25] (Scale Factor 1, with Zipfian skew factor 0 for the latter). We focused on the single-block SQL queries: Q1, 3, 5, 6 and 10. (Q1 and 6 are aggregation-only queries; Q3

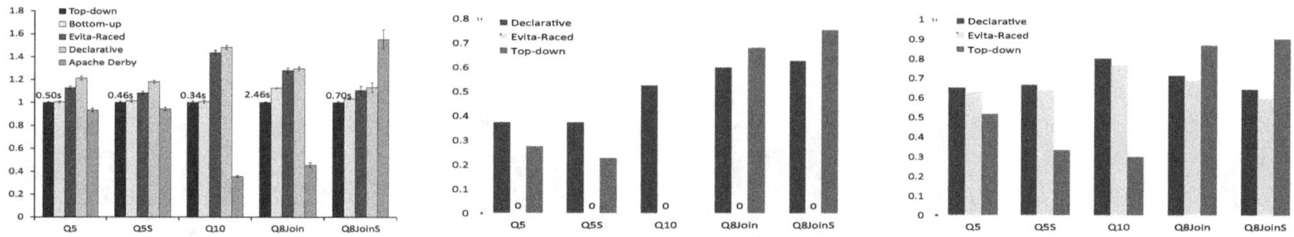

(a) Execution time (normalized to top-down style) (b) Pruning ratio: plan table entries (c) Pruning ratio: plan alternatives

Figure 5: Performance comparison for initial query optimization, across different optimizer architectures

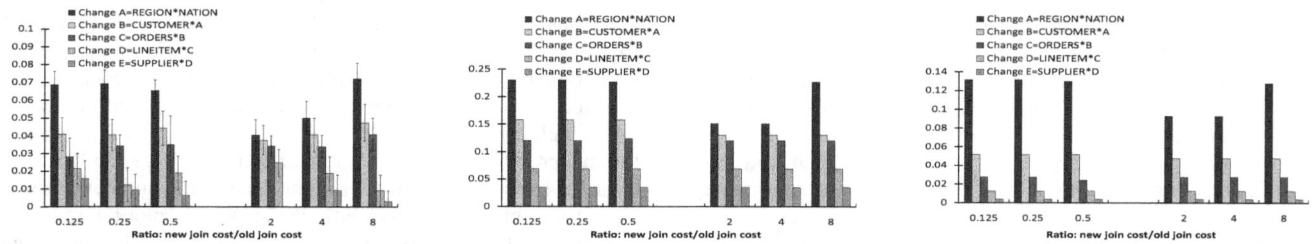

(a) Execution time (normalized to top-down style) (b) Update ratio: plan table entries (c) Update ratio: plan alternatives

Figure 6: Performance during incremental re-optimization of TPC-H Q5 — change to join selectivity estimate

joins 3 relations; Q10 joins 4; and Q5 joins 6 relations). Our experiments showed that Q1, 3, and 6 are all simple enough to optimize that (1) there is not a compelling need to adapt, since there are few plan alternatives; (2) they completed in under 80msec on all implementations. (The declarative approach tended to add 10-50msec to these settings, as it has higher initialization costs.) Thus we focus our presentation on join queries with more than 3-way joins. To create greater query diversity, we modified the 4-way and larger join queries by removing aggregation — we constructed a simplified query Q5S. Finally, to test scale-up to larger queries, we manually constructed an eight-way join query, Q8Join, and its simplified version (removing aggregates), Q8JoinS. For **adaptive stream processing** we used the Linear Road benchmark [2]: We modified the largest query, called SegToll, into SegTollS. We show the TPC-H and LinearRoad benchmark queries used in our experiments in Table 5 in Appendix B.

Experimental Methodology. We aim to answer five questions:

- Can a declarative query optimizer perform at a rate competitive with procedural optimizers, for 4-way-join queries and larger?
- Does incremental query re-optimization show running time and search space benefits versus non-incremental re-optimization, for repeated query execution-over-static-data scenarios?
- How does each of our three pruning strategies (aggregate selection, reference counting, and recursive bounding) contribute to the performance?
- Can the ideas of incremental re-optimization studied from the declarative perspective be applied to traditional procedural-based query optimization frameworks, and what is their performance versus their non-incremental counterparts?
- Does incremental re-optimization improve the performance of cost-based adaptive query processing techniques for streaming?

The TPC-H benchmark experiments are conducted on a single local desktop machine: a dual-core Intel Core 2 2.40GHz with 2GB memory running 32-bit Windows XP Professional, and Java JDK 1.6. The Linear Road benchmark experiments are conducted on a single server machine: a dual-core Intel Xeon 2.83GHz with 8 GB memory running 64-bit Windows Server Standard. Performance results are averaged across 10 runs, and 95% confidence intervals are shown. We mark as 0 any results that are exactly zero.

6.1 Declarative Optimization Performance

Our initial experiments focus on the question of **whether our declarative query optimizer can be competitive with procedural optimizers** based on bottom-up style enumeration through dynamic programming and top-down style enumeration with memoization and branch-and-bound pruning models. To show the value of the pruning techniques developed in this paper, we also measure the performance when our engine is limited to the pruning techniques developed in Evita Raced [9] (where pruning is only done against logically equivalent plans for the same output properties). Recall that all of our implementations share the same procedural logic (e.g., histogram derivation); their differences are in search strategy, dataflow, and pruning techniques.

We begin with a running time comparison among top-down style, bottom-up style, and declarative implementations (one using our sideways information passing strategies, and one based on the Evita Raced pruning heuristics) — shown in Figure 5 (a). This graph is normalized against the running times for our top-down style implementation (which is also included as a bar for visual comparison of the running times). Actual top-down running times are shown directly above the bar. Observe from the graph that the top-down strategy is always the fastest, though bottom-up style enumeration often approaches its performance due to simpler (thus, slightly faster) exploration logic. Our declarative implementation is not quite as fast as the dedicated procedural optimizers, with an overhead of 10-50%, but this is natural given the extra overhead of using a general-purpose engine and supporting incremental update processing. The Evita Raced-style declarative implementation is marginally faster in this setting, as it does less pruning. We also measure the query optimization performance of Apache Derby (chosen because it is a state of the art open-source DBMS implemented in Java, like our engine) to show how a well-known DBMS performs the same query, as a reference.[2] We shall see in later experiments that there are significant benefits to our more aggressive strategies during re-optimization — which is our focus in this work.

To understand the contributions of the different options, we next study their effectiveness in *pruning* the search space. We divide this into two parts: (1) pruning of expression-property entries in

[2]While some commercial DBMSs offer richer statistical or machine learning techniques, such capabilities are reliant on static data or predictable workloads.

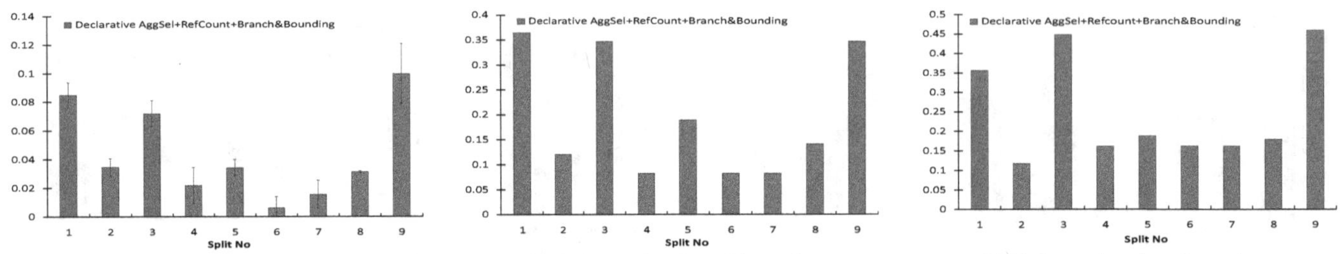

(a) Execution time (normalized to top-down style) (b) Update ratio: plan table entries (c) Update ratio: plan alternatives

Figure 7: Performance during incremental re-optimization of TPC-H Q5 — updates to costs based on real execution over skewed data

the plan table, such that we do not need to compute and maintain *any* plans for a particular expression yielding a particular property; (2) pruning of *plan alternatives* for a particular expression-property pair. In terms of the and-or graph formulation of Figure 3, the first case prunes or-nodes and the second prunes and-nodes. We show these two cases in Figure 5 parts (b) and (c). We omit bottom-up style optimizers from this discussion, as they use a dynamic programming-based pruning model is not directly comparable.

Part (b) shows that our declarative implementation achieves pruning of approximately 35-80% of the plan table entries, resulting in large reductions in state (and, in many cases, reduced computation). We compare with the strategies used by Evita Raced, which never prunes plan table entries, and with our top-down style implementation. Our pruning strategies, which are flexible with respect to order of evaluation, are often more effective than the top-down strategy, which is limited to top-down enumeration with branch-and-bound pruning. (All pruning strategies' effectiveness depends on the specific order in which nodes are explored, and may be non-deterministic: better pruning is achieved when inexpensive options happen to be considered early. However, in the common case, high levels of pruning are observed, as we see next.)

Part (c) shows that our implementation prunes approximately 55-75% of the plans (95% confidence intervals are plotted but are extremely tight). It exceeds the pruning ratios obtained by the Evita Raced strategies by 4-8%, and often results in significantly greater pruning than the top-down style.

We conclude from these results that a declarative optimizer can be competitive in terms of running time and pruning.

6.2 Incremental Re-optimization

We next study the trade-offs in processing incremental changes to costs. A typical setting in a non-streaming context would be the repeated execution of a prepared statement query, where a bound variable affects costs. We measure, for a given update, how expensive it is to re-optimize the query and produce the new, predicted-optimal plan. Note that there exist no comparable techniques for incremental cost-based re-optimization, so we compare the gains versus those of re-running a complete optimization (as is done in [17, 30]). In these experiments, we consider running time — versus the running times for the best-performing initial optimization strategy, namely that of our top-down style implementation — as well as how much of the total search space gets re-enumerated. We consider re-optimization under "microbenchmark"-style simulated changes to costs, for synthetic updates as well as observed execution conditions over skewed data. We measured performance across the **full suite of queries** in our workload. However, since the results are representative, we focus our presentation on query Q5. We show more experimental results in the appendix.

6.2.1 Synthetic Changes to Subplan Costs

We first simulate what happens if we discover that an operator's output is not in accordance with our original selectivity estimates. Figures 6 (a)-(c) show the impact of synthetically injecting changes for each join expression's selectivity, and therefore the PlanCost of the related plans and their super-plans. For conciseness in the graph captions, we assign a symbol with each expression, e.g., the first join $Region \bowtie Nation$ is expression A, and the second join expression combines the output of A with data from the $Customer$ table, yielding $B = Customer \bowtie A$. We expect that changes to smaller subplans will take longer to re-optimize, and changes to larger subplans will take less time (due to the number of recursive propagation steps involved). We separately plot the results of changing each expression's selectivity value, as we change it along a range from 1/8 the predicted size through 8 times larger than the predicted size. Running times in part (a) are plotted relative to the top-down implementation's performance: we see that the speedups are at least a factor of 12, when the lowest-level join cost is updated; going up to over 300, when the topmost join operator's selectivity is changed. In general the speedups confirm that larger expressions are cheaper to update. We can observe from these last two figures that we recompute only a small portion of the search space.

6.2.2 Changes based on Real Execution

We now look at what happens when costs are updated according to an actual query execution. We took TPC-H Q5 and to gain better generality, we divided its input into 10 partitions (each having uniform distribution and independent variables) that would result in equal-sized output. We optimized the query over one such partition, using histograms from the TPC-H dataset. Then we ran the resulting query over different partitions of **skewed data** (Zipf skew factor 0.5, from the Microsoft Research skewed TPC-D generator [25]); each of which exhibits different properties. At the end we re-optimized the given the cumulatively observed statistics from the partition. We performed re-optimization on each of such interval, given the current plan and the revised statistics.

Figure 7 (a) shows the execution times for each round of incremental re-optimization, normalized against the running time of top-down style. We see that, as with the join re-estimation experiments of Figure 6, there are speedups of a factor of 10 or greater. In terms of throughput, the top-down model takes 500msec to perform one optimization, meaning it can perform 2 re-optimizations per second; whereas our declarative incremental re-optimizer can achieve 20-60 optimizations per second, and it can respond to changing conditions in 10-100msec. Again, Figure 7 (b) and (c) show that the speedup is due to significant reductions in the amount of state that must be recomputed.

Table 2 shows overall performance for this setting, over TPC-D scale factor 10 data. We omit the cost of initial optimization, and show (top row) the *overall cost* of incremental re-optimization plus execution for each split, vs. (bottom row) the cost of simply executing the originally optimized plan over the same data split. This corresponds to running a prepared statement, with selection predicates over different parts of the data, using incremental re-optimization given costs for the selected data – vs. a single query plan over all of the data.

6.3 Contributions of Pruning Strategies

Here we investigate how each of our pruning and incremental

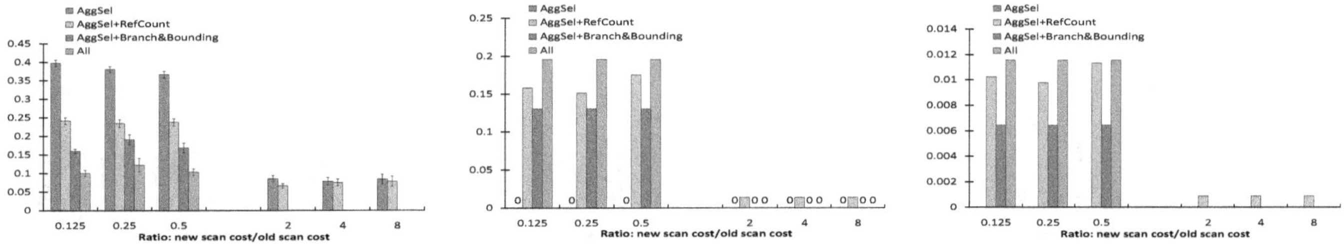

(a) Execution time (vs top-down style) (b) Pruning ratio: plan table entries (c) Pruning ratio: plan alternatives

Figure 8: Contributions of pruning techniques for re-optimization of Q5 when $Orders$ has updated scan cost

Split number								
1	*2*	*3*	*4*	*5*	*6*	*7*	*8*	*9*
2.07	**2.91**	**2.05**	2.02	2.91	2.02	**2.04**	**2.04**	**2.06**
2.77	3.49	2.66	2.04	2.95	2.01	2.23	2.86	3.01

Table 2: Query processing time (s) of incrementally re-optimized vs. single-stage TPCH-Q5, for splits of Fig. 7

strategies from Sections 4 and 5 contribute to the overall performance of our declarative optimizer. We systematically considered all techniques individually and in combination, unless they did not make sense (e.g., reference counting must be combined with one of the other techniques, and branch-and-bound requires aggregate selection to perform pruning of the search space). See Figure 8, where *AggSel* refers to aggregate selection with source tuple suppression; *RefCount* refers to reference counting; and *Branch&-Bounding* refers to recursive bounding. We consider aggregate selection in isolation and with the other techniques.

The incremental setting — shown for Q5 and changes to the orders table, in Figures 8 (a)-(c) — shows benefits in running time and pruned search space. In contrast to our other graphs for incremental re-optimization, plots (b) and (c) isolate the amount of pruning performed, rather than showing the total state updated. Our different techniques work best in combination, and each increases the amount of pruning.

Query	Num of Joins	Pruning Strategy	Space (KB)
Q10	4	No pruning	2211
		AggSel	253
		All pruning	412
Q5	6	No pruning	3046
		AggSel	266
		All pruning	445
Q8Join	8	No pruning	DNC
		AggSel	1046
		All pruning	1669

Table 3: Overhead of memoized state in declarative optimizer

Table 3 shows the total state size in our declarative optimizer. We measure the size of the objects instead of the JVM memory to alleviate the effects of garbage collection. We measure the space overhead of TPC-H Q10, Q5 and Q8Join, with 4, 6, 8 joins respectively. Since we employ the same memoization scheme for initial query pre-optimization and query re-optimization in the declarative approach, these numbers both relate to pre-optimization and re-optimization. The table shows the size of the unpruned state. (Here since the optimization time for Q8Join without pruning did not complete within over 2 minutes, due to a complete lack of pruning.) If we only prune by using AggSel, we have less state to maintain than the full pruning scenario, but the optimization time is worse, as shown in Figure 8.

6.4 Incrementalizing a Conventional Optimizer

To this point, we have focused on the performance of our datalog-based query optimizer implementation. As described in Section 5.4, some of the ideas from this implementation can also be retrofitted into more conventional optimizers (both top-down and bottom-up). Thus we measure, in Figure 9, how a traditional optimizer, retrofitted with incremental re-optimization, performs versus an equivalent non-incremental implementation.

In this experiment, we see the cost of re-optimization if a join's actual cost is discovered to vary (by a factor ranging from 1/8th to 8x of its estimated cost) for TPC-H query Q5. In our procedural implementation we memoize not only the best plans, but alternative subplans. Figure 9 (a) shows the running time for incremental query re-optimization (normalized to the time for non-incremental counterparts), for several different queries. The "(BU)" entries are bottom-up implementations, whereas "(TD)" references a comparable top-down implementation. Observe that incremental re-optimization is 4-20 times faster than a complete optimization. As expected, the results validate that top-down strategies are generally superior to bottom-up ones, because they enable greater amounts of pruning. The only exception to this is the last data point, where we change the join cost of $E = Supplier * D$: here, increasing this join cost causes the top-down re-optimizer to recompute a larger number of nodes than the bottom-up implementation.

We can see this in more detail in Figure 9 (b), which shows the proportion of *updated* plan table entries (OR nodes), and in (c), which shows the proportion of *recomputed* plan alternatives (AND nodes). In general, the larger the subexpression for which a join cost changes, the less work is required to re-compute and update, and the more benefit provided by incremental re-optimization. Bottom-up re-optimizers generally incur the same amount of updated plan table entries as the non-incremental approach due to lack of pruning, and constantly recompute less than 60% of the plan alternatives; top-down re-optimizers usually incur far less updates and recomputations when a join cost decreases and more updates when a join cost increases.

6.5 Incremental Reoptimization for AQP

A major motivation for our work was to facilitate better *cost-based adaptive query processing*, especially for continuous optimization of stream queries. Our goal is to show the benefits of incremental reoptimization; we leave as future work a broader comparison of adaptive query processing techniques. Our final set of experiments shows how our techniques can be used within a standard cost-based adaptive framework, one based on the *data-partitioned* model of [17] where the optimizer periodically pauses plan execution, forming a "split" point from which it may choose a new plan and continue execution. In general, if we change plans at a split point, there is a challenge of determining how to combine state across the split. In contrast to [17] we chose *not* to defer the cross-split join execution until the end: rather, we used CAPE's *state migration* strategy [30] to transfer all existing state from the prior plan into the current one. As necessary, new intermediate state is computed. Note that our data-partitioned model could be combined with other cost-based adaptive schemes such as [18, 21].

To evaluate this setting, we combine unfold the various views comprising the SegToll query from the Linear Road benchmark [2]

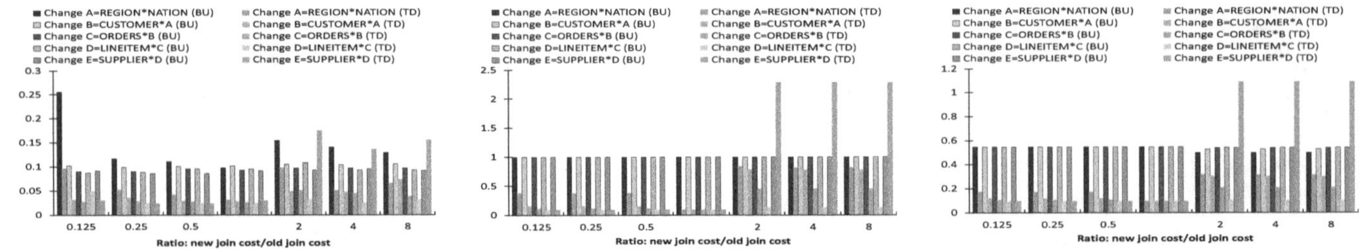

(a) Optimization time ratio to non-incremental counterparts (b) Update ratio: plan table entries (c) Recompute ratio: plan alternatives

Figure 9: Performance of top-down vs bottom-up style procedural incremental re-optimization of TPC-H Q5 — upon change to join cost value

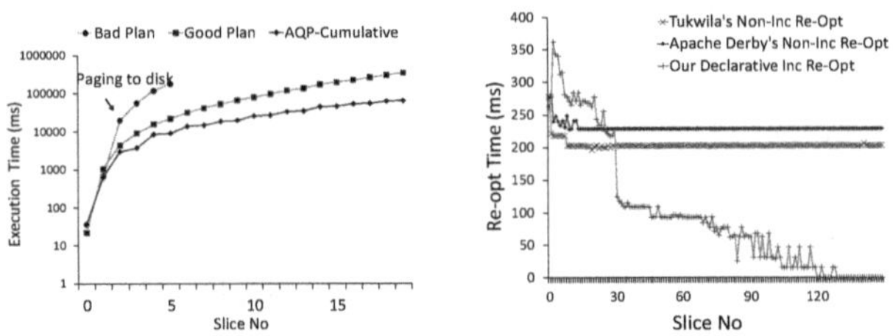

Figure 10: AQP execution (left) and re-optimization times

— resulting in a 5-way join plan SegTollS with multiple windowed aggregates. We use the standard Linear Road data generator to synthesize data whose characteristics frequently change.

In the adaptive setting, our goal is to have the optimizer start with zero statistical information on the data, and find a sequence of plans whose running time equals or betters the *single best static plan* that it would pick given complete information (e.g., histograms).

On the left of Figure 10, we see that our incremental AQP scheme provides **superior performance to the single best plan** ("good single plan"), if we re-optimize every 1 second. This is because the adaptive scheme has a chance to "fit" its plan to the local characteristics of whatever data is currently in the window, rather than having to choose one plan for all data.

Per Slice	Re-Opt Time	N.C. Exec Time	Total Time
1s	5.75s	2.20s	7.95s
5s	1.23s	6.82s	8.05s
10s	0.63s	13.35s	13.98s

Table 4: Frequency of Adaptation (20 sec stream)

A natural question is where the "sweet spot" is between query execution versus optimizer overhead. We measured, for several slice sizes, the total query processing time *over each new slice of data* (not considering the additional overhead of state migration, which depends on how similar the plans are). Table 4 shows significant gains in shrinking the interval from 10sec to 5sec, but little more gain to be had in going down to 1sec. Figure 10 shows that as we re-optimize and execute, the overhead of a non-incremental re-optimizer remains constant (about 200 msec each time), whereas the incremental re-optimization time drops off rapidly, going to nearly zero as the plan stabilizes. This means that the system has essentially *converged on a plan* and that new executions do not affect the final plan. We measure the performance against Tukwila-style query optimizer implementation [17], as well as the Apache Derby query optimizer. We see that the majority of incremental re-optimizations are much faster than the non-incremental baselines.

6.6 Experimental Conclusions

We summarize the answers to questions posed at the start of this section. First, our declarative query optimizer performs respectably when compared to a procedural query optimizer, for initial optimization: despite the overhead of a full query processor, it gets within 10-50% of the running times of a dedicated optimizer. It more than recovers this overhead during incremental re-optimization, where it typically shows an order-of-magnitude speedup or better. Such gains are largely due to having to re-enumerate a much smaller space of plans. In addition, our pruning techniques of Section 4 and Section 5 each contribute in a meaningful way to the overall performance of incremental re-optimization. We also successfully adapted our novel pruning techniques to a procedural implementation, providing speedup factors of more than 4. Finally, our incremental re-optimization techniques enable *finer-grained* adaptivity and hence better overall performance. Overhead decreases as the system *converges on a single plan.*

7. RELATED WORK

Our work takes a first step towards supporting continuous adaptivity in a distributed (e.g., cloud) setting where correlations and runtime costs may be unpredictable at each node. Fine-grained adaptivity has previously only been addressed in the query processing literature via heuristics, such as flow rates [3, 29], that continuously "explore" alternative plans rather than using long-term cost estimates. Exploration adds overhead even when a good plan has been found; moreover, for joins and other stateful operators, the flow heuristics has been shown to result in state that later incurs significant costs [10]. Other strategies based on filter reordering [4] are provably optimal, but only work for selection-like predicates. Full-blown cost-based re-optimization can avoid these future costs but was previously only possible on a coarse-grained (high multiple seconds) interval [17, 30].

Our use of declarative techniques to specify the optimizer was inspired in part by the Evita Raced [9] system. However, their work aims to construct an entire optimizer using reprogrammable datalog rules, whereas our goal is to effectively perform incremental maintenance of the output query plan. We seek to fully match the pruning techniques of conventional optimizers following the System R [27] and Volcano [14] models. Our results show for the first time that a declarative optimizer *can* be competitive with a procedural one, even for one-time "static" optimizations, and produce large benefits for future optimizations.

8. CONCLUSIONS AND FUTURE WORK

To build large-scale, pipelined query processors that are reactive to conditions across a cluster, we must develop new adaptive query processing techniques. This paper represents the first step towards that goal: namely, a fully cost-based architecture for incrementally re-optimizing queries. As future work, we plan to study how our declarative execution model parallelizes across multi-core hardware and clusters, and how it can be extended to consider the cost of *changing* a plan given existing query execution state.

9. ACKNOWLEDGMENTS

This work was funded in part by grants NSF IIS-0713267, IIS-1050448, CNS-0845552, CNS-1218066, CNS-1513679, and NIH 1U01EB020954-01.

References

[1] S. Agrawal, S. Chaudhuri, and V. R. Narasayya. Automated selection of materialized views and indexes in SQL databases. In *VLDB*, 2000.

[2] A. Arasu, M. Cherniack, E. Galvez, D. Maier, A. S. Maskey, E. Ryvkina, M. Stonebraker, and R. Tibbetts. Linear road: a stream data management benchmark. In *VLDB*, pages 480–491, 2004.

[3] R. Avnur and J. M. Hellerstein. Eddies: Continuously adaptive query processing. In *SIGMOD*, 2000.

[4] S. Babu, R. Motwani, K. Munagala, I. Nishizawa, and J. Widom. Adaptive ordering of pipelined stream filters. In *SIGMOD*, 2004.

[5] A. Behm, V. R. Borkar, M. J. Carey, R. Grover, C. Li, N. Onose, R. Vernica, A. Deutsch, Y. Papakonstantinou, and V. J. Tsotras. Asterix: towards a scalable, semistructured data platform for evolving-world models. *Distributed and Parallel Databases*, 29(3):185–216, 2011.

[6] N. Bruno and S. Chaudhuri. Exploiting statistics on query expressions for optimization. In *SIGMOD*, 2002.

[7] S. Chandrasekaran, O. Cooper, A. Deshpande, M. J. Franklin, J. M. Hellerstein, W. Hong, S. Krishnamurthy, S. Madden, V. Raman, F. Reiss, and M. A. Shah. TelegraphCQ: Continuous dataflow processing for an uncertain world. In *CIDR*, 2003.

[8] S. Chaudhuri. An overview of query optimization in relational systems. In *PODS*, pages 34–43, 1998.

[9] T. Condie, D. Chu, J. M. Hellerstein, and P. Maniatis. Evita raced: metacompilation for declarative networks. *PVLDB*, 1(1):1153–1165, 2008.

[10] A. Deshpande and J. M. Hellerstein. Lifting the burden of history from adaptive query processing. In *VLDB*, pages 948–959, 2004.

[11] A. Deshpande, Z. Ives, and V. Raman. Adaptive query processing. *Foundations and Trends in Databases*, 2007.

[12] A. Dutt and J. R. Haritsa. Plan bouquets: query processing without selectivity estimation. In *SIGMOD*, pages 1039–1050, 2014.

[13] G. Graefe. The Cascades framework for query optimization. *IEEE Data Eng. Bull.*, 18(3):19–29, 1995.

[14] G. Graefe and W. J. McKenna. The Volcano optimizer generator: Extensibility and efficient search. In *ICDE*, pages 209–218, 1993.

[15] A. Gupta, H. Jagadish, and I. S. Mumick. In P. Apers, M. Bouzeghoub, and G. Gardarin, editors, *EDBT*. Berlin / Heidelberg, 1996.

[16] A. Gupta, I. S. Mumick, and V. S. Subrahmanian. Maintaining views incrementally. In *SIGMOD*, pages 157–166, 1993.

[17] Z. G. Ives, A. Y. Halevy, and D. S. Weld. Adapting to source properties in processing data integration queries. In *SIGMOD*, pages 395–406, 2004.

[18] N. Kabra and D. J. DeWitt. Efficient mid-query re-optimization of sub-optimal query execution plans. In *SIGMOD*, pages 106–117, 1998.

[19] L. Liu, C. Pu, R. Barga, and T. Zhou. Differential evaluation of continual queries. Technical Report TR95-17, University of Alberta, June 1995.

[20] M. Liu, N. E. Taylor, W. Zhou, Z. G. Ives, and B. T. Loo. Recursive computation of regions and connectivity in networks. In *ICDE*, 2009.

[21] V. Markl, V. Raman, G. Lohman, H. Pirahesh, D. Simmen, and M. Cilimdzic. Robust query processing through progressive optimization. In *SIGMOD*, 2004.

[22] S. Melnik, A. Gubarev, J. J. Long, G. Romer, S. Shivakumar, M. Tolton, and T. Vassilakis. Dremel: Interactive analysis of web-scale datasets. *PVLDB*, 3(1):330–339, 2010.

[23] R. Motwani, J. Widom, A. Arasu, B. Babcock, S. Babu, M. Datar, G. Manku, C. Olston, J. Rosenstein, and R. Varma. Query processing, resource management, and approximation in a data stream management system. In *CIDR*, 2003.

[24] B. Mozafari, E. Z. Y. Goh, and D. Y. Yoon. Cliffguard: A principled framework for finding robust database designs. In *SIGMOD*, pages 1167–1182, New York, NY, USA, 2015.

[25] V. Narasayya. TPC-D skewed data generator. 1999.

[26] P. Roy, S. Seshadri, S. Sudarshan, and S. Bhobe. Efficient and extensible algorithms for multi query optimization. In *SIGMOD*, volume 29(2), pages 249–260, 2000.

[27] P. G. Selinger, M. M. Astrahan, D. D. Chamberlin, R. A. Lorie, and T. G. Price. Access path selection in a relational database management system. In *SIGMOD*, pages 23–34, 1979.

[28] S. Sudarshan and R. Ramakrishnan. Aggregation and relevance in deductive databases. In *VLDB*, 1991.

[29] S. D. Viglas and J. F. Naughton. Rate-based query optimization for streaming information sources. In *SIGMOD*, pages 37–48, 2002.

[30] Y. Zhu, E. A. Rundensteiner, and G. T. Heineman. Dynamic plan migration for continuous queries over data streams. In *SIGMOD*, 2004.

APPENDIX

A. DATALOG RULES FOR OPTIMIZER

R1: $\mathsf{SearchSpace}(expr, prop, index, logOp, phyOp, lExpr, lProp, rExpr, rProp)$:-
$\mathsf{Expr}(expr, prop)$, $\mathsf{Fn\_isleaf}(expr, false)$,
$\mathsf{Fn\_split}(expr, prop, \underline{index}, \underline{logOp}, \underline{phyOp}, \underline{lExpr}, \underline{lProp}, \underline{rExpr}, \underline{rProp})$;

R2: $\mathsf{SearchSpace}(expr, prop, index, logOp, phyOp, lExpr, lProp, rExpr, rProp)$:-
$\mathsf{SearchSpace}(-, -, -, -, -, expr, prop, -, -)$,
$\mathsf{Fn\_isleaf}(expr, false)$,
$\mathsf{Fn\_split}(expr, prop, \underline{index}, \underline{logOp}, \underline{phyOp}, \underline{lExpr}, \underline{lProp}, \underline{rExpr}, \underline{rProp})$;

R3: $\mathsf{SearchSpace}(expr, prop, index, logOp, phyOp, lExpr, lProp, rExpr, rProp)$:-
$\mathsf{SearchSpace}(-, -, -, -, -, -, -, expr, prop)$,
$\mathsf{Fn\_isleaf}(expr, false))$,
$\mathsf{Fn\_split}(expr, prop, \underline{index}, \underline{logOp}, \underline{phyOp}, \underline{lExpr}, \underline{lProp}, \underline{rExpr}, \underline{rProp})$;

R4: $\mathsf{SearchSpace}(expr, prop, -, 'scan', phyOp, -, -, -, -))$:-
$\mathsf{SearchSpace}(-, -, -, -, -, expr, prop, -, -)$,
$\mathsf{Fn\_isleaf}(expr, true)$, $\mathsf{Fn\_phyOp}(prop, \underline{phyOp})$;

R5: $\mathsf{SearchSpace}(expr, prop, -, 'scan', phyOp, -, -, -, -)$:-
$\mathsf{SearchSpace}(-, -, -, -, -, -, -, expr, prop)$,
$\mathsf{Fn\_isleaf}(expr, true)$, $\mathsf{Fn\_phyOp}(prop, \underline{phyOp})$;

R6: $\mathsf{PlanCost}(expr, prop, index, logOp, phyOp, -, -, -, -, md, cost)$:-
$\mathsf{SearchSpace}(expr, prop, index, logOp, phyOp, -, -, -, -)$,
$\mathsf{Fn\_scansummary}(expr, prop, \underline{md})$,
$\mathsf{Fn\_scancost}(expr, prop, md, \underline{cost})$;

R7: $\mathsf{PlanCost}(expr, prop, index, logOp, phyOp, lExpr, lProp, -, -, md, cost)$:-
$\mathsf{SearchSpace}(expr, prop, index, logOp, phyOp, lExpr, lProp, -, -$, $\mathsf{Fn\_isleaf}(lExpr, false)$,
$\mathsf{PlanCost}(lExpr, lProp, -, -, -, -, -, -, -, lMd, lCost)$,
$\mathsf{Fn\_nonscansummary}(expr, prop, index, logOp, lMd, -, \underline{md})$,
$\mathsf{Fn\_nonscancost}(expr, prop, index, logOp, phyOp, lExpr, lProp, -, -, md, \underline{localCost})$,
$\mathsf{Fn\_sum}(lCost, null, localCost, \underline{cost})$;

Q1: SELECT l_returnflag, l_linestatus, sum(l_quantity) as sum_qty, sum(l_extendedprice) as sum_base_price, sum(l_extendedprice*(1-l_discount)) as sum_disc_price, sum(l_extendedprice*(1-l_discount)*(1+l_tax)) as sum_charge, avg(l_quantity) as avg_qty, avg(l_extendedprice) as avg_price, avg(l_discount) as avg_disc, count(*) as count_order FROM lineitem WHERE l_shipdate ≤ '1998-09-01' GROUPBY l_returnflag, l_linestatus;
Q3: SELECT l_orderkey, sum(l_extendedprice*(1-l_discount)) as revenue, o_orderdate, o_shippriority FROM customer, orders, lineitem WHERE c_mktsegment = 'MACHINERY' and c_custkey = o_custkey and l_orderkey = o_orderkey and o_orderdate < '1995-03-15' and l_shipdate > '1995-03-15' GROUPBY l_orderkey, o_orderdate, o_shippriority;
Q5: SELECT n_name, sum(l_extendedprice * (1 - l_discount)) as revenue FROM customer, orders, lineitem, supplier, nation, region WHERE c_custkey = o_custkey and l_orderkey = o_orderkey and l_suppkey = s_suppkey and c_nationkey = s_nationkey and s_nationkey = n_nationkey and n_regionkey = r_regionkey and r_name = 'AMERICA' and o_orderdate ≥ CAST('1993-01-01' and o_orderdate < '1994-01-01' GROUPBY n_name;
Q5S: SELECT n_name, l_extendedprice * (1 - l_discount) FROM customer, orders, lineitem, supplier, nation, region WHERE c_custkey = o_custkey and l_orderkey = o_orderkey and l_suppkey = s_suppkey and c_nationkey = s_nationkey and s_nationkey = n_nationkey and n_regionkey = r_regionkey and r_name = 'AMERICA' and o_orderdate ≥ '1993-01-01' and o_orderdate < '1994-01-01';
Q6: SELECT sum(l_extendedprice*l_discount) as revenue FROM lineitem WHERE l_shipdate ≥ '1994-01-01' and l_shipdate < '1995-01-01' and l_discount ≥ 0.06 - 0.01 and l_discount ≤ 0.06 + 0.01 and l_quantity < 24.2;
Q10: SELECT c_custkey, c_name, sum(l_extendedprice * (1 - l_discount)) as revenue, c_acctbal, n_name, c_address, c_phone, c_comment FROM customer, orders, lineitem, nation WHERE c_custkey = o_custkey and l_orderkey = o_orderkey and o_orderdate ≥ '1993-06-01' and o_orderdate < '1993-09-01' and l_returnflag = 'R' and c_nationkey = n_nationkey GROUPBY c_custkey, c_name, c_acctbal, c_phone, n_name, c_address, c_comment;
Q8Join: SELECT c_name, p_name, ps_availqty, s_name, o_custkey, r_name, n_name, sum(l_extendedprice * (1 -l_discount)) FROM orders, lineitem, customer, part, partsupp, supplier, nation, region WHERE o_orderkey = l_orderkey and c_custkey = o_custkey and p_partkey = l_partkey and ps_partkey = p_partkey and s_suppkey = ps_suppkey and r_regionkey = n_regionkey and s_nationkey = n_nationkey GROUPBY c_name, p_name, ps_availqty, s_name, o_custkey, r_name, n_name;
Q8JoinS: SELECT c_name, p_name, ps_availqty, s_name, o_custkey, r_name, n_name, l_extendedprice * (1 -l_discount) FROM orders, lineitem, customer, part, partsupp, supplier, nation, region WHERE o_orderkey = l_orderkey and c_custkey = o_custkey and p_partkey = l_partkey and ps_partkey = p_partkey and s_suppkey = ps_suppkey and r_regionkey = n_regionkey and s_nationkey = n_nationkey;
SegTollS: SELECT r1_expway, r1_dir, r1_seg, COUNT(distinct r5_xpos) FROM CarLocStr [size 300 time] as r1, CarLocStr [size 1 tuple partition by expway, dir, seg] as r2, CarLocStr [size 1 tuple partition by caid] as r3, CarLocStr [size 30 time] as r4, CarLocStr [size 4 tuple partition by carid] as r5 WHERE r2_expway = r3_expway and r2_dir = 0 and r3_dir = 0 and r2_seg < r3_seg and r2_seg > r3_seg - 10 and r3_carid = r4_carid and r3_carid = r5_carid and r1_expway = r2_expway and r1_dir = r2_dir and r1_seg = r2_seg GROUP BY r5_carid, r2_expway, r2_dir, r2_seg;

Table 5: Queries modified based on TPC-H and LinearRoad benchmark queries used in our experiments

R8: $\mathsf{PlanCost}(expr, prop, index, logOp, phyOp,$
$lExpr, lProp, rExpr, rProp, md, cost)$:-
$\mathsf{SearchSpace}(expr, prop, index, logOp, phyOp,$
$lExpr, lProp, rExpr, rProp),$
$\mathsf{Fn\_isleaf}(lExpr, false), Fn\_isleaf(rExpr, false),$
$\mathsf{PlanCost}(lExpr, lProp, -, -, -, -, -, -, lMd, lCost),$
$\mathsf{PlanCost}(rExpr, rProp, -, -, -, -, -, -, -, rMd, rCost),$
$\mathsf{Fn\_nonscansummary}(expr, prop, index, logOp, lMd, rMd, \underline{md}),$
$\mathsf{Fn\_nonscancost}(expr, prop, index, logOp, phyOp,$
$lExpr, lProp, rExpr, rProp, md, \underline{localCost}),$
$\mathsf{Fn\_sum}(lCost, rCost, localCost, \underline{cost});$
R9: $\mathsf{BestCost}(expr, prop, min < cost >)$:-
$\mathsf{PlanCost}(expr, prop, index, logOp, phyOp,$
$lExpr, lProp, rExpr, rProp, md, cost);$
R10: $\mathsf{BestPlan}(expr, prop, index, logOp, phyOp,$
$lExpr, lProp, rExpr, rProp, md, cost)$:-
$\mathsf{BestCost}(expr, prop, cost),$
$\mathsf{PlanCost}(expr, prop, index, logOp, phyOp,$
$lExpr, lProp, rExpr, rProp, md, cost);$

B. EXPERIMENTAL QUERIES

Table 5 shows our experimental query workload, which consists of the main select-project-join-aggregate queries from TPC-H (queries 1, 3, 5, 6, 8, and 10) with some modifications; as well as a streaming query from Linear Road [2].

C. PROOFS OF PROPOSITIONS IN SECTION 3

PROOF OF PROPOSITION 5. $\Rightarrow$: Prove by contradiction. If T^s is T^s_{OPT}, then suppose T^s is *not* the subtree of T_{OPT}. Let T'^s be the subtree of T_{OPT}. Since $T^s = T^s_{OPT}$, then we must have $\mathsf{PlanCost}(T^s\langle E^s, p^s\rangle) < \mathsf{PlanCost}\ (T'^s\langle E^s, p^s\rangle)$. If we substitute T'^s with T^s in the tree T_{OPT}, we get a new tree T'', with $\mathsf{PlanCost}(T''\langle E, p\rangle) < \mathsf{PlanCost}\ (\ T_{OPT}\ \langle E, p\rangle)$. Contradiction to the definition of T_{OPT}.

$\Leftarrow$: Prove by contradiction. If T^s is the subtree of T_{OPT}, then suppose T^s is *not* T^s_{OPT}, since plans have distinct costs, we have $\mathsf{PlanCost}(T^s\langle E^s, p^s\rangle) > \mathsf{PlanCost}(T^s_{OPT}\langle E^s, p^s\rangle)$. If we substitute subtree T^s with subtree T^s_{OPT} in the tree T_{OPT}, we get a new plan tree T', which has $\mathsf{PlanCost}\ (T'\langle E, p\rangle) < \mathsf{PlanCost}\ (T_{OPT}\langle E, p\rangle)$. Contradiction to the definition of T_{OPT}. ☐

PROOF OF PROPOSITION 6. $\Rightarrow$: Prove by contradiction. If $\mathsf{RefCount}\ \langle E^s, p^s\rangle = 0$, then any plan tree whose root is the AND node representing the parent of $\langle E^s, p^s\rangle$ is pruned. Suppose T^s is a subtree of $T_{OPT}\langle E, p\rangle$, then consider the immediate parent node of T^s in T_{OPT}, let it be $T^{s'}$. According to Proposition 5, $T^{s'} = T^{s'}_{OPT}$. This means it has the minimal cost to subexpression $\langle E^{s'}, p^{s'}\rangle$, is on the optimal tree of the final optimal plan, but has been pruned. Contradiction.

$\Leftarrow$: Prove by contradiction. If T^s is *not* a subtree of T_{OPT}, according to Proposition 5, T^s is not T^s_{OPT}. Hence, $\mathsf{PlanCost}(T^s_{OPT}) < \mathsf{PlanCost}(T^s)$. Suppose T^s has the reference count other than zero, then it must have at least a parent plan that has not been pruned. Suppose that parent plan is $T'^{s'}$. If we substitute T^s with T^s_{OPT} in $T'^{s'}$, we get a plan tree $T''^{s'}$ that has a smaller cost than $T'^{s'}$. Hence $T'^{s'}$ can be pruned in the final result because it is suboptimal to $T''^{s'}$. Contradiction. ☐

PROOF OF PROPOSITION 7. $\Rightarrow$: Prove by contradiction. Suppose $\mathsf{PlanCost}(T^s) > \mathsf{Bound}\langle E, p\rangle$. And suppose T^s is a subtree of the optimal plan tree T_{OPT}, according to Proposition 5, T^s is T^s_{OPT}. Hence, $\mathsf{PlanCost}(T^s_{OPT}) > \mathsf{Bound}\langle E, p\rangle$. Now we prove by induction that if T^s is a subtree of T' of subexpression $E^{s'}$ and property $p^{s'}$, then $\mathsf{PlanCost}(T'_{OPT}) > \mathsf{Bound}\langle E^{s'}, p^{s'}\rangle$.

First, the base case $\mathsf{PlanCost}(T^s_{OPT}) > \mathsf{Bound}\langle E^s, p^s\rangle$ holds. Now, if $\mathsf{PlanCost}(T^s_{OPT}) > \mathsf{Bound}\langle E^s, p^s\rangle$, according to the definition of Bound where $\mathsf{Bound}\langle E^s, p^s\rangle = \min(\mathsf{BestCost}(T^s),$

$\mathsf{maxBound}\langle E^s, p^s\rangle$), we have $\mathsf{Bound}\langle E^s, p^s\rangle = \mathsf{MaxBound}\langle E^s, p^s\rangle < \mathsf{PlanCost}(T^s_{OPT})$. According to the definition of MaxBound, $\mathsf{MaxBound}\langle E^s, p^s\rangle = \max(\mathsf{ParentBound}\langle E^s, p^s\rangle)$, therefore, for any arbitrary sibling OR node of T^s, $Sib(T^s)$, and corresponding parent AND node of T^s, $Par(T^s)$ of expression $E^{s'}$ and property $P^{s'}$, we have $\mathsf{Bound}\langle E^{s'}, p^{s'}\rangle$ - $\mathsf{BestCost}(Sib(T^s))$ - $\mathsf{LocalCost}(Par(T^s)) \leq \mathsf{MaxBound}\langle E^s, p^s\rangle < \mathsf{PlanCost}(T^s_{OPT})$. Hence, $\mathsf{Bound}\langle E^{s'}, p^{s'}\rangle < \mathsf{BestCost}(Sib(T^s))$ + $\mathsf{BestCost}(T^s)$ + $\mathsf{LocalCost}$ $(Par(T^s))$. Because this holds for any sibling and parent, we have $\mathsf{Bound}\langle E^{s'}, p^{s'}\rangle < \min(\mathsf{BestCost}(Sib(T^s))$ + $\mathsf{BestCost}(T^s)$ + $\mathsf{LocalCost}(Par(T^s)))$ = $\mathsf{BestCost}(Par(T^s))$ = $\mathsf{PlanCost}(Par(T^s)_{OPT})$.

By applying this induction we prove that if T^s is a subtree of T' of subexpression $E^{s'}$ and property $p^{s'}$, then $\mathsf{PlanCost}(T'_{OPT}) > \mathsf{Bound}\langle E^{s'}, p^{s'}\rangle$. Since T^s is a subtree of the optimal plan tree T_{OPT}, hence $\mathsf{PlanCost}(T_{OPT}) > \mathsf{Bound}\langle E, p\rangle$. However, as T_{OPT} is the root, it has no parent, according to the definition of Bound, it should have $\mathsf{Bound}(T_{OPT}) = \mathsf{PlanCost}(T_{OPT})$. Contradiction.

$\Leftarrow$: Prove by contradiction. Suppose T^s is *not* a subtree of T_{OPT}, according to Proposition 5, T^s is not T^s_{OPT}, hence, $\mathsf{PlanCost}(T^s) > \mathsf{PlanCost}(T^s_{OPT})$. Suppose $\mathsf{PlanCost}(T^s) \leq \mathsf{Bound}\langle E^s, p^s\rangle$, then we have $\mathsf{PlanCost}(T^s_{OPT}) < \mathsf{PlanCost}(T^s) \leq \mathsf{Bound}\langle E^s, p^s\rangle$. According to the definition of Bound, $\mathsf{Bound}\langle E^s, p^s\rangle = \min(\mathsf{BestCost}(T^s), \mathsf{maxBound}\langle E^s, p^s\rangle)$, we have $\mathsf{PlanCost}(T^s_{OPT}) < \mathsf{BestCost}(T^s)$, contradiction to the definition of T^s_{OPT}. □

D. ADDITIONAL EXPERIMENTAL RESULTS

As a supplement to the figures in Section 6.3, Figures 11 (a)-(c) compare the three pruning strategies when performing initial query *pre-optimization* on various TPC-H queries. It can be observed that each of the pruning techniques adds a small bit of runtime overhead (never more than 10%) in this setting, as each requires greater computation and data propagation. Parts (b) and (c) show that each technique adds greater pruning capability, however.

For greater completeness, we show additional experimental results to gain more insights over a full range of TPC-H queries under different scenarios.

Figure 12 is a supplement to Figure 8 where it measures the performance breakdown of different pruning strategies during incremental re-optimization of TPC-H query Q5 when a different table, $Suppliers$, other than $Orders$, has updated its scan cost from 1/8 to 8x of the original. We can observe in the figure that each pruning strategy contributes in a meaningful way to the effectiveness of incremental re-optimization, as well.

Figure 13 and Figure 14 show a full range of incremental re-optimization performance upon a scan cost change of each base relation, for TPC-H query Q10 (a 4-way join query) and Q8Join (a 8-way join query as shown in Table 5) respectively. We can see from Figure 13 (a) and Figure 14 (a) that incremental re-optimization has at least 3x of speedup compared to a top-down style non-incremental optimizer. (b) and (c) show the numbers of plan table entries and plan alternatives updated during incremental re-optimization, to gain more insights on where the speedup comes from.

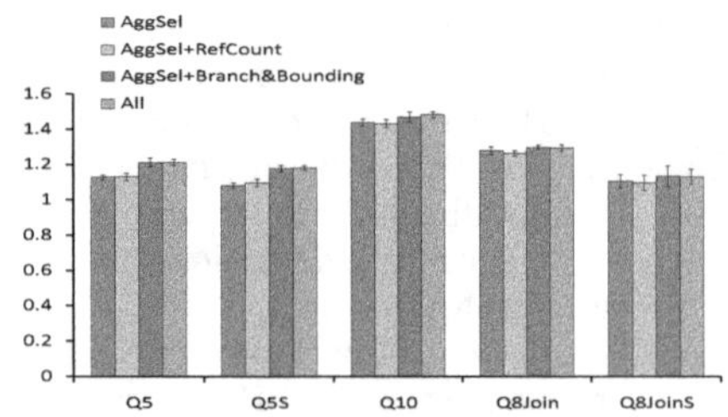

(a) Execution time (normalized to top-down style)

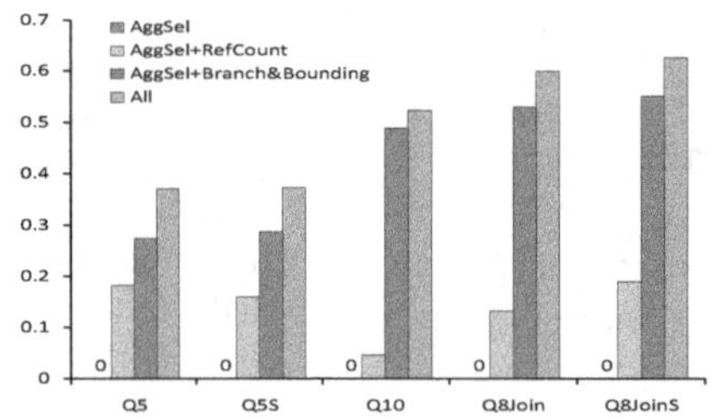

(b) Pruning ratio: plan table entries

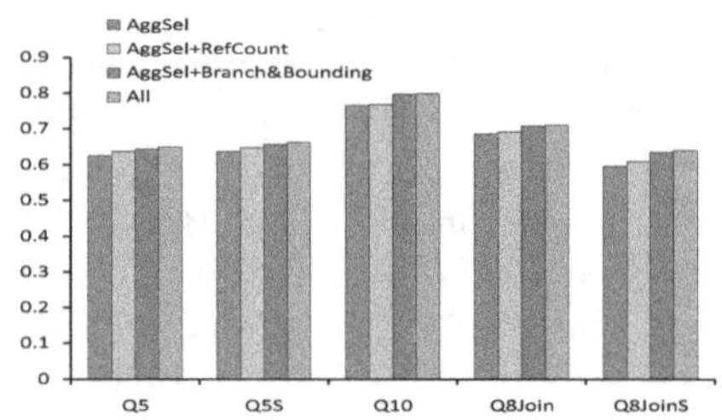

(c) Pruning ratio: plan alternatives

Figure 11: Performance breakdown of pruning techniques for initial optimization, across full query workload

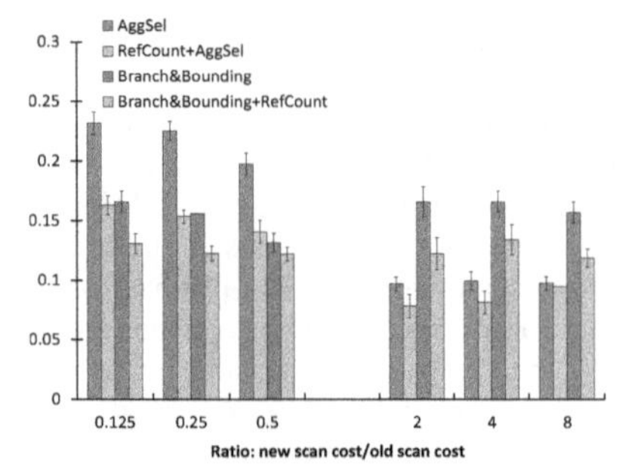

(a) Execution time (normalized to top-down style)

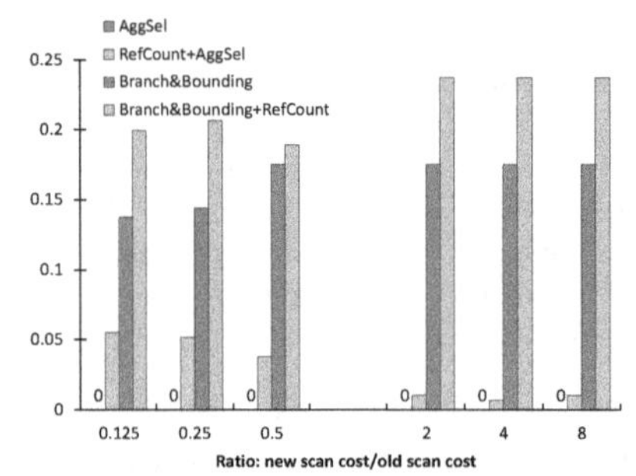

(b) Pruning ratio: plan table entries

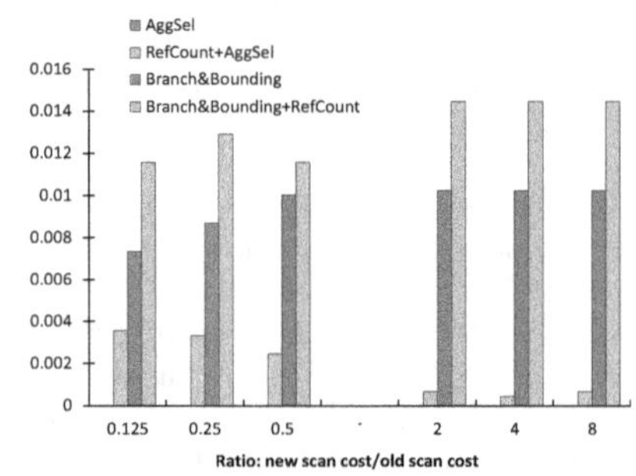

(c) Pruning ratio: plan alternatives

Figure 12: Performance breakdown of pruning techniques during incremental re-optimization of Q5 when $Suppliers$ **has updated scan cost**

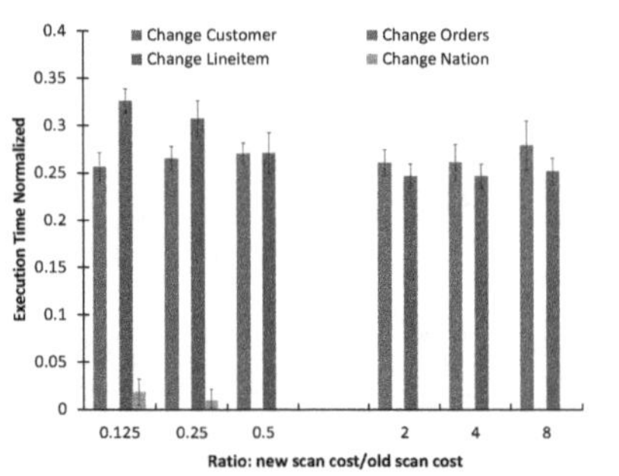

(a) Execution time (normalized to top-down style)

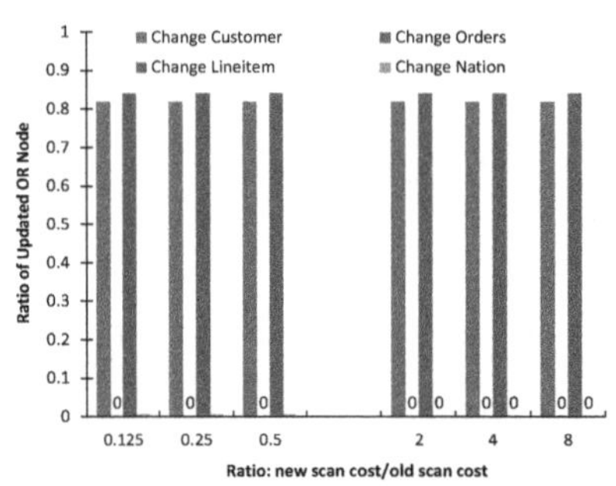

(b) Update ratio: plan table entries

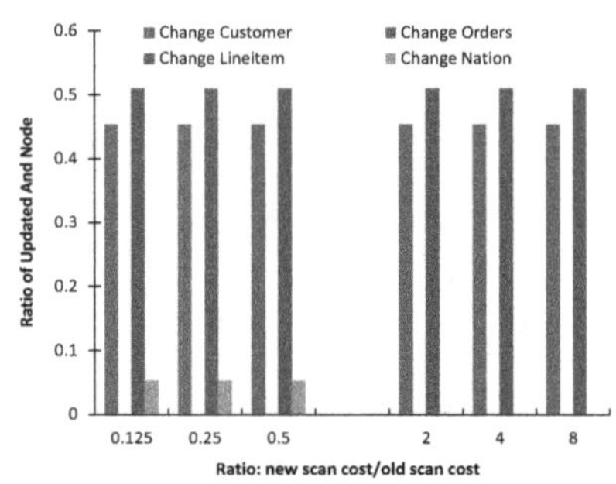

(c) Update ratio: plan alternatives

Figure 13: Performance during incremental re-optimization of TPC-H Q10 — changes to a base scan relation cardinality estimate

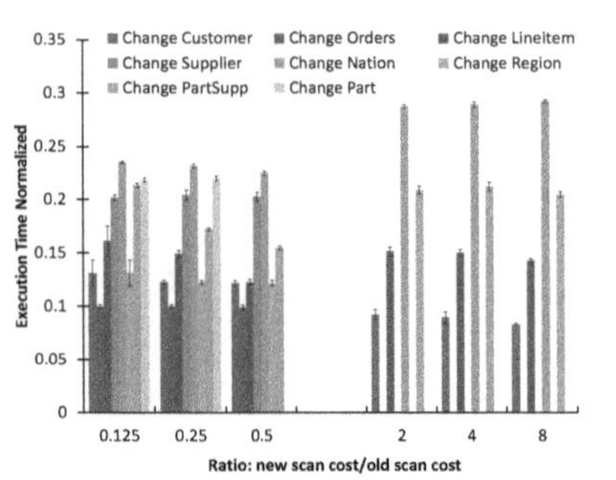

(a) Execution time (normalized to top-down style)

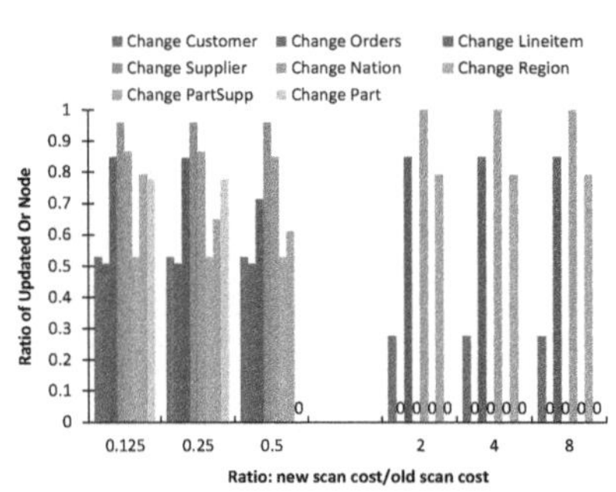

(b) Update ratio: plan table entries

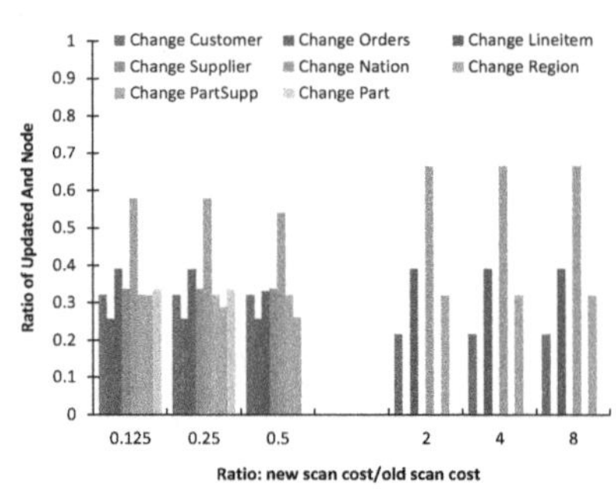

(c) Update ratio: plan alternatives

Figure 14: Performance during incremental re-optimization of TPC-H Q8Join — changes to a base scan relation cardinality estimate

Sampling-Based Query Re-Optimization

Wentao Wu Jeffrey F. Naughton Harneet Singh
Department of Computer Sciences, University of Wisconsin-Madison
{wentaowu, naughton, harneet}@cs.wisc.edu

ABSTRACT

Despite of decades of work, query optimizers still make mistakes on "difficult" queries because of bad cardinality estimates, often due to the interaction of multiple predicates and correlations in the data. In this paper, we propose a low-cost post-processing step that can take a plan produced by the optimizer, detect when it is likely to have made such a mistake, and take steps to fix it. Specifically, our solution is a sampling-based iterative procedure that requires almost no changes to the original query optimizer or query evaluation mechanism of the system. We show that this indeed imposes low overhead and catches cases where three widely used optimizers (PostgreSQL and two commercial systems) make large errors.

1. INTRODUCTION

Query optimizers rely on decent cost estimates of query plans. Cardinality/selectivity estimation is crucial for the accuracy of cost estimates. Unfortunately, although decades of research has been devoted to this area and significant progress has been made, cardinality estimation remains challenging. In current database systems, the dominant approach is to keep various statistics, primarily histograms, about the data. While histogram-based approaches have worked well for estimating selectivities of local predicates (i.e., predicates over a column of a base table), query optimizers still make mistakes on "difficult" queries, often due to the interaction of multiple predicates and correlations in the data [28].

Indeed, there is a great deal of work in the literature exploring selectivity estimation techniques beyond histogram-based ones (see Section 6). Nonetheless, histogram-based approaches remain dominant in practice because of its low overhead. Note that, query optimizers may explore hundreds or even thousands of candidates when searching for an optimal query plan, and selectivity estimation needs to be done for each candidate. As a result, a feasible solution has to improve cardinality estimation quality without significantly increasing query optimization time.

In this paper, we propose a low-cost post-processing step that can take a plan produced by the optimizer, detect when it is likely to have made such a mistake, and take steps to fix it. Specifically, our solution is a sampling-based iterative procedure that requires almost no changes to the original query optimizer or query evaluation mechanism of the system. We show that this indeed imposes low overhead and catches cases where three widely used optimizers (PostgreSQL and two commercial systems) make large errors.

In more detail, sampling-based approaches (e.g., [11, 20, 27]) automatically reflect correlation in the data and between multiple predicates over the data, so they can provide better cardinality estimates on correlated data than histogram-based approaches. However, sampling also incurs higher overhead. In previous work [39, 40, 41], the authors investigated the effectiveness of using sampling-based cardinality estimates to get better query running time predictions. The key observation is the following: while it is infeasible to use sampling for all plans explored by the optimizer, it is feasible to use sampling as a "post-processing" step after the search is finished to detect potential errors in optimizer's original cardinality estimates for the final chosen plan.

Inspired by this observation, our basic idea is simple: if significant cardinality estimation errors are detected, the optimality of the returned plan is then itself questionable, so we go one step further to let the optimizer re-optimize the query by also feeding it the cardinality estimates refined via sampling. This gives the optimizer second chance to generate a different, perhaps better, plan. Note that we can again apply the sampling-based validation step to this new plan returned by the optimizer. It therefore leads to an iterative procedure based on feedback from sampling: we can repeat this optimization-then-validation loop until the plan chosen by the optimizer does not change. The hope is that this re-optimization procedure can catch large optimizer errors *before* the system even begins executing the chosen query plan.

A couple of natural concerns arise regarding this simple query re-optimization approach. First, how efficient is it? As we have just said, sampling should not be abused given its overhead. Since we propose to run plans over samples iteratively, how fast does this procedure converge? To answer this question, we conduct a theoretical analysis as well as an experimental evaluation. Our theoretical study suggests that, the expected number of iterations can be bounded by $O(\sqrt{N})$, where N is the number of plans considered by the optimizer in its search space. In practice, this upper bound can rarely happen. Re-optimization for most queries tested in our experiments converges after only a few rounds of iteration, and the time spent on re-optimization is ignorable compared with the corresponding query running time.

Second, is it useful? Namely, does re-optimization really generate a better query plan? This raises the question of how to evaluate the effectiveness of re-optimization. Query optimizers appear to do well almost all of the time. But the experience of optimizer developers we have talked to is that there are a small number of "difficult" queries that cause them most of the pain. That is, most

SIGMOD'16, June 26-July 01, 2016, San Francisco, CA, USA
 ISBN 978-1-4503-3531-7/16/06... $15.00
DOI: http://dx.doi.org/10.1145/2882903.2882914

of the time the optimizer is very good, but when it is bad, it is very bad. Indeed, Lohman [28] recently gave a number of compelling real-world instances of optimizers that, while presumably performing well overall, make serious mistakes on specific queries and data sets. It is our belief that an important area for optimizer research is to focus precisely on these few "difficult" queries.

We therefore choose to evaluate re-optimization over those difficult, corner-case queries. Now the hard part is characterizing exactly what these "difficult" queries look like. This will inevitably be a moving target. If benchmarks were to contain "difficult" queries, optimizers would be forced to handle them, and they would no longer be "difficult," so we cannot look to the major benchmarks for examples. In fact, we implemented our approach in PostgreSQL and tested it on the TPC-H benchmark database, and we did observe significant performance improvement for certain TPC-H queries (Section 5.2). However, for most of the TPC-H queries, the re-optimized plans are exactly the same as the original ones. We also tried the TPC-DS benchmark and observed similar phenomena (Appendix A.2). Using examples of real-world difficult queries would be ideal, but we have found it impossible to find well-known public examples of these queries and the data sets they run on.

It is, however, well-known that many difficult queries are made difficult by correlations in the data — for example, correlations between multiple selections, and more likely correlations between selections and joins [28]. This is our target in this paper. It is in fact very easy to generate examples of these queries and data sets that confuse all the optimizers (PostgreSQL and two commercial RDBMS) that we tested — such examples are the basis for our "optimizer torture test" presented in Section 4. We observed that re-optimization becomes superior on these cases (Section 5.3). While original query plans often take hundreds or even thousands of seconds to finish, after re-optimization all queries can finish in less than 1 second. We therefore hope that our re-optimization technique can help cover some of those corner cases that are challenging to current query optimizers.

The idea of query re-optimization goes back to two decades ago (e.g. [25, 30]). The main difference between this line of work and our approach is that re-optimization was previously done *after* a query begins to execute whereas our re-optimization is done *before* that. While performing re-optimization during query execution has the advantage of being able to observe accurate cardinalities, it suffers from (sometimes significant) runtime overhead such as materializing intermediate results that have been generated. Meanwhile, runtime re-optimization frameworks usually require significant changes to query optimizer's architecture. Our compile-time re-optimization approach is more lightweight. The only additional cost is due to running tentative query plans over samples. The modification to the query optimizer and executor is also limited: our implementation in PostgreSQL needs only several hundred lines of C code. Furthermore, we should also note that our compile-time re-optimization approach actually does not conflict with these previous runtime re-optimization techniques: the plan returned by our re-optimization procedure could be further refined by using runtime re-optimization. It remains interesting to investigate the effectiveness of this combination framework.

The rest of the paper is organized as follows. We present the details of our iterative sampling-based re-optimization algorithm in Section 2. We then present a theoretical analysis of its efficiency in terms of the number of iterations it requires and the quality of the final plan it returns in Section 3. To evaluate the effectiveness of this approach, we further design a database (and a set of queries) with highly correlated data in Section 4, and we report experimental evaluation results on this database as well as the TPC-H benchmark databases in Section 5. We discuss related work in Section 6 and conclude the paper in Section 7.

2. THE RE-OPTIMIZATION ALGORITHM

In this section, we first introduce necessary background information and terminology, and then present the details of the re-optimization algorithm. We focus on using sampling to refine selectivity estimates for join predicates, which are the major source of errors in practice [28]. The sampling-based selectivity estimator we used is tailored for join queries [20], and it is our goal in this paper to study its effectiveness in query optimization when combined with our proposed re-optimization procedure. Nonetheless, sampling can also be used to estimate selectivities for other types of operators, such as aggregates (i.e., "Group By" clauses) that require estimation of the number of distinct values (e.g. [11]). We leave the exploration of integrating other sampling-based selectivity estimation techniques into query optimization as interesting future work.

2.1 Preliminaries

In previous work [39, 40, 41], the authors used a sampling-based selectivity estimator proposed by Haas et al. [20] for the purpose of predicting query running times. In the following, we provide an informal description of this estimator.

Let R_1, ..., R_K be K relations, and let R_k^s be the sample table of R_k for $1 \leq k \leq K$. Consider a join query $q = R_1 \bowtie \cdots \bowtie R_K$. The selectivity ρ_q of q can be estimated as

$$\hat{\rho}_q = \frac{|R_1^s \bowtie \cdots \bowtie R_K^s|}{|R_1^s| \times \cdots \times |R_K^s|}.$$

It has been shown that this estimator is both unbiased and strongly consistent [20]: the larger the samples are, the more accurate this estimator is. Note that this estimator can be applied to joins that are sub-queries of q as well.

2.2 Algorithm Overview

As mentioned in the introduction, cardinality estimation is challenging and cardinality estimates by optimizers can be erroneous. This potential error can be noticed once we apply the aforementioned sampling-based estimator to the query plan generated by the optimizer. However, if there are really significant errors in cardinality estimates, the optimality of the plan returned by the optimizer can be in doubt.

If we replace the optimizer's cardinality estimates with sampling-based estimates and ask it to re-optimize the query, what would happen? Clearly, the optimizer will either return the same query plan, or a different one. In the former case, we can just go ahead to execute the query plan: the optimizer does not change plans even with the new cardinalities. In the latter case, the new cardinalities cause the optimizer to change plans. However, this new plan may still not be trustworthy because the optimizer may still decide its optimality based on erroneous cardinality estimates. To see this, let us consider the following example.

EXAMPLE 1. *Consider the two join trees T_1 and T_2 in Figure 1. Suppose that the optimizer first returns T_1 as the optimal plan. Sampling-based validation can then refine cardinality estimates for the three joins: $A \bowtie B$, $A \bowtie B \bowtie C$, and $A \bowtie B \bowtie C \bowtie D$. Upon knowing these refined estimates, the optimizer then returns T_2 as the optimal plan. However, the join $C \bowtie D$ in T_2 is not observed in T_1 and its cardinality has not been validated.*

Hence, we can again apply the sampling-based estimator to this new plan and repeat the re-optimization process. This then leads to an iterative procedure.

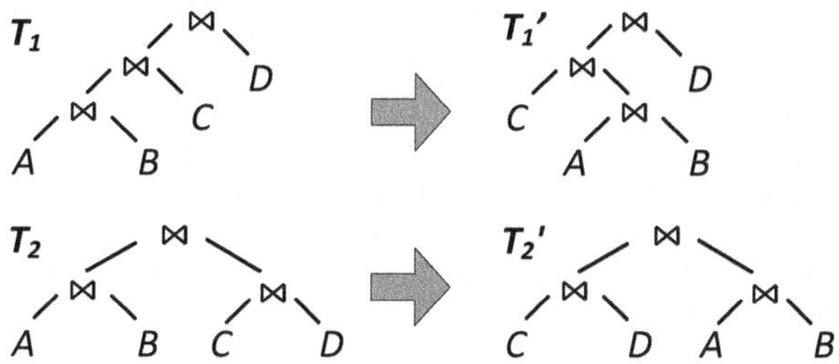

Figure 1: Join trees and their local transformations.

Algorithm 1 outlines the above idea. Here, we use Γ to represent the sampling-based cardinality estimates for joins that have been validated by using sampling. Initially, Γ is empty. In the round i ($i \geq 1$), the optimizer generates a query plan P_i based on the current information preserved in Γ (line 5). If P_i is the same as P_{i-1}, then we can terminate the iteration (lines 6 to 8). Otherwise, P_i is new and we invoke the sampling-based estimator over it (line 9). We use Δ_i to represent the sampling-based cardinality estimates for P_i, and we update Γ by merging Δ_i into it (line 10). We then move to the round $i+1$ and repeat the above procedure (line 11).

Algorithm 1: Sampling-based query re-optimization

Input: q, a given SQL query
Output: P_q, query plan of q after re-optimization
1 $\Gamma \leftarrow \emptyset$;
2 $P_0 \leftarrow$ null;
3 $i \leftarrow 1$;
4 **while** *true* **do**
5   $P_i \leftarrow GetPlanFromOptimizer(\Gamma)$;
6   **if** *P_i is the same as P_{i-1}* **then**
7   **break**;
8   **end**
9   $\Delta_i \leftarrow GetCardinalityEstimatesBySampling(P_i)$;
10   $\Gamma \leftarrow \Gamma \cup \Delta_i$;
11   $i \leftarrow i + 1$;
12 **end**
13 Let the final plan be P_q;
14 **return** P_q;

Note that this iterative process has as its goal improving the selected plan, not finding a new globally optimal plan. It is certainly possible that the iterative process misses a good plan because the iterative process does not explore the complete plan space — it only explores neighboring transformations of the chosen plan. Nonetheless, as we will see in Section 5, this local search is sufficient to catch and repair some very bad plans.

3. THEORETICAL ANALYSIS

In this section, we present an analysis of Algorithm 1 from a theoretical point of view. We are interested in two aspects of the re-optimization procedure:

- *Efficiency*, i.e., how many rounds of iteration does it require before it terminates?
- *Effectiveness*, i.e., how good is the final plan it returns compared to the original plan, in terms of the cost metric used by the query optimizer?

Our following study suggests that (i) the expected number of rounds of iteration in the worst case is upper-bounded by $O(\sqrt{N})$ where N is the number of query plans explored in the optimizer's search space (Section 3.3); and (ii) the final plan is guaranteed to be no worse than the original plan if sampling-based cost estimates are consistent with the actual costs (Section 3.4).

3.1 Local and Global Transformations

We start by introducing the notion of local/global transformations of query plans. In the following, we use $\text{tree}(P)$ to denote the *join tree* of a query plan P. A join tree is the logical skeleton of a physical plan, which is represented as the set of *ordered* logical joins contained in P. For example, the representation of T_2 in Figure 1 is $T_2 = \{A \bowtie B, C \bowtie D, A \bowtie B \bowtie C \bowtie D\}$.

DEFINITION 1 (LOCAL/GLOBAL TRANSFORMATION). *Two join trees T and T' (of the same query) are* local *transformations of each other if T and T' contain the same set of* unordered *logical joins. Otherwise, they are global transformations.*

In other words, local transformations are join trees that subject to only exchanges of left/right subtrees. For example, $A \bowtie B$ and $B \bowtie A$ are different join trees, but they are local transformations. In Figure 1 we further present two join trees T_1' and T_2' that are local transformations of T_1 and T_2. By definition, a join tree is always a local transformation of itself.

Given two plans P and P', we also say that P' is a local/global transformation of P if $\text{tree}(P')$ is a local/global transformation of $\text{tree}(P)$. In addition to potential exchange of left/right subtrees, P and P' may also differ in specific choices of physical join operators (e.g., hash join vs. sort-merge join). Again, by definition, a plan is always a local transformation of itself.

3.2 Convergence Conditions

At a first glance, even the convergence of Algorithm 1 is questionable. Is it possible that Algorithm 1 keeps looping without termination? For instance, it seems to be possible that the re-optimization procedure might alternate between two plans $P1$ and $P2$, i.e., the plans generated by the optimizer are $P1$, $P2$, $P1$, $P2$, ... As we will see, this is impossible and Algorithm 1 is guaranteed to terminate. We next present a sufficient condition for the convergence of the re-optimization procedure. We first need one more definition regarding plan coverage.

DEFINITION 2 (PLAN COVERAGE). *Let P be a given query plan and $\mathcal{P}$ be a set of query plans. P is* covered *by $\mathcal{P}$ if*

$$\text{tree}(P) \subseteq \bigcup\nolimits_{P' \in \mathcal{P}} \text{tree}(P').$$

That is, all the joins in $\text{tree}(P)$ are included in the join trees of $\mathcal{P}$. As a special case, any plan that belongs to $\mathcal{P}$ is covered by $\mathcal{P}$.

Let P_i ($i \geq 1$) be the plan returned by the optimizer in the i-th re-optimization step. We have the following convergence condition for the re-optimization procedure:

THEOREM 1 (CONDITION OF CONVERGENCE). *Algorithm 1 terminates after $n+1$ ($n \geq 1$) steps if P_n is covered by $\mathcal{P} = \{P_1, ..., P_{n-1}\}$.*

PROOF. If P_n is covered by $\mathcal{P}$, then using sampling-based validation will not contribute anything new to the statistics Γ. That is, $\Delta_n \cup \Gamma = \Gamma$. Therefore, P_{n+1} will be the same as P_n, because the optimizer will see the same Γ in the round $n+1$ as that in the round n. Algorithm 1 then terminates accordingly (by lines 6 to 8). □

Note that the convergence condition stated in Theorem 1 is sufficient by not necessary. It could happen that P_n is not covered by

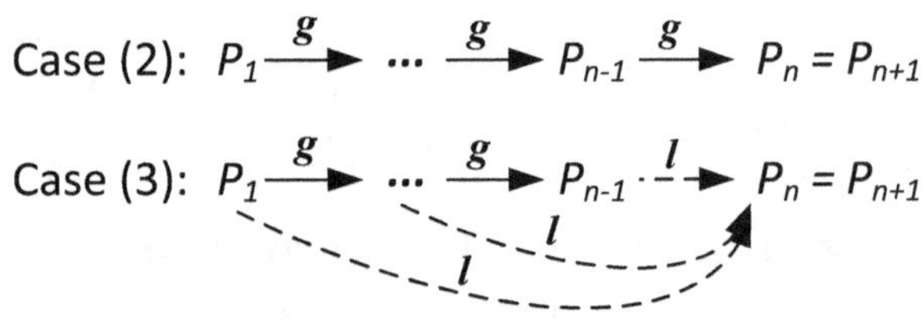

Figure 2: Characterization of the re-optimization procedure (g and l stand for global and local transformations, respectively). For ease of illustration, P_i is only noted as a global transformation of P_{i-1}, but we should keep in mind that P_i is also a global transformation of all the P_j's with $j < i$.

the previous plans $\{P_1, ..., P_{n-1}\}$ but $P_{n+1} = P_n$ after using the validated statistics (e.g., if there are no significant errors detected in cardinality estimates of P_n).

COROLLARY 1 (CONVERGENCE GUARANTEE). *Algorithm 1 is guaranteed to terminate.*

PROOF. Based on Theorem 1, Algorithm 1 would only continue if P_n is not covered by $\mathcal{P} = \{P_1, ..., P_{n-1}\}$. In that case, P_n should contain at least one join that has not been included by the plans in $\mathcal{P}$. Since the total number of possible joins considered by the optimizer is finite, $\mathcal{P}$ will eventually reach some fixed point if it keeps growing. The re-optimization procedure is guaranteed to terminate upon that fixed point, again by Theorem 1. □

Theorem 1 also implies the following special case:

COROLLARY 2. *The re-optimization procedure terminates after $n+1$ ($n \geq 1$) steps if $P_n \notin \mathcal{P}$ but P_n is a local transformation of some $P \in \mathcal{P} = \{P_1, ..., P_{n-1}\}$.*

PROOF. By definition, if P_n is a local transformation of some $P \in \mathcal{P}$, then tree(P_n) and tree(P) contain the same set of unordered logical joins. By Definition 2, P_n is covered by $\mathcal{P}$. Therefore, the re-optimization procedure terminates after $n+1$ steps, by Theorem 1. □

Also note that Corollary 2 has covered a common case in practice that P_n is a local transformation of P_{n-1}.

Based on Corollary 2, we next present an important property of the re-optimization procedure.

THEOREM 2. *When the re-optimization procedure terminates, exactly one of the following three cases holds:*

(1) It terminates after 2 steps with $P_2 = P_1$.

(2) It terminates after $n+1$ steps ($n > 1$). For $1 \leq i \leq n$, P_i is a global transformation of P_j with $j < i$.

(3) It terminates after $n+1$ steps ($n > 1$). For $1 \leq i \leq n-1$, P_i is a global transformation of P_j with $j < i$, and P_n is a local transformation of some $P \in \mathcal{P} = \{P_1, ..., P_{n-1}\}$.

That is, when the procedure does not terminate trivially (Case (1)), it can be characterized as a sequence of global transformations with *at most* one more local transformation before its termination (Case (2) or (3)). Figure 2 illustrates the latter two nontrivial cases. A formal proof of Theorem 2 is included in [1].

One might raise the question here that why we separate Case (3) from Case (2) in Theorem 2. Why would the fact that there might be one local transformation be interesting? The interesting point here is not that we may have one local transformation. Rather, it is that local transformation can occur at most once, and, if it occurs, it must be the last one in the transformation chain. Actually, we have observed in our experiments that re-optimization of some queries only involves (one) local transformation. This, however, by no means suggests that local transformations do not lead to any significant optimizations. For instance, sometimes even just replacing an index-based nested loop join by a hash join (or vice versa) can result in nontrivial performance improvement.

3.3 Efficiency

We are interested in how fast the re-optimization procedure terminates. As pointed out by Theorem 2, the convergence speed depends on the number of *global* transformations the procedure undergoes. In the following, we first develop a probabilistic model that will be used in our analysis, and then present analytic results for the general case and several important special cases.

3.3.1 A Probabilistic Model

Consider a queue of N balls. Originally all balls are not marked. We then conduct the following procedure:

PROCEDURE 1. *In each step, we pick the ball at the head of the queue. If it is marked, then the procedure terminates. Otherwise, we mark it and randomly insert it back into the queue: the probability that the ball will be inserted at the position i ($1 \leq i \leq N$) is uniformly $1/N$.*

We next study the expected number of steps that Procedure 1 would take before its termination.

LEMMA 1. *The expected number of steps that Procedure 1 takes before its termination is:*

$$S_N = \sum_{k=1}^{N} k \cdot (1 - \frac{1}{N}) \cdots (1 - \frac{k-1}{N}) \cdot \frac{k}{N}. \quad (1)$$

We include a proof of Lemma 1 in [1]. We can further show that S_N is upper-bounded by $O(\sqrt{N})$.

THEOREM 3. *The expected number of steps S_N as presented in Lemma 1 satisfies $S_N = O(\sqrt{N})$.*

The proof of Theorem 3 is in [1]. In Figure 3, we plot S_N by increasing N from 1 to 1000. As we can see, the growth speed of S_N is very close to that of $f(N) = \sqrt{N}$.

3.3.2 The General Case

In a nutshell, query optimization can be thought of as picking a plan with the lowest estimated cost among a number of candidates. Different query optimizers have different search spaces, so in general we can only assume a search space with N different join trees that will be considered by an optimizer.[1] Let these trees be T_1, ..., T_N, ordered by their estimated costs. The re-optimization procedure can then be thought of as shuffling these trees based on their refined cost estimates. This procedure terminates whenever (or even before) the tree with lowest estimated cost reoccurs, that is, when some tree appears at the head position for the second time. Therefore, the probabilistic model in the previous section applies here. As a result, by Lemma 1, the expected number of steps for this procedure to terminate is S_N. We formalize this result as the following theorem:

[1]By "different" join trees, we mean join trees that are global transformations of each other. We use this convention in the rest of the paper unless specific clarifications are noted.

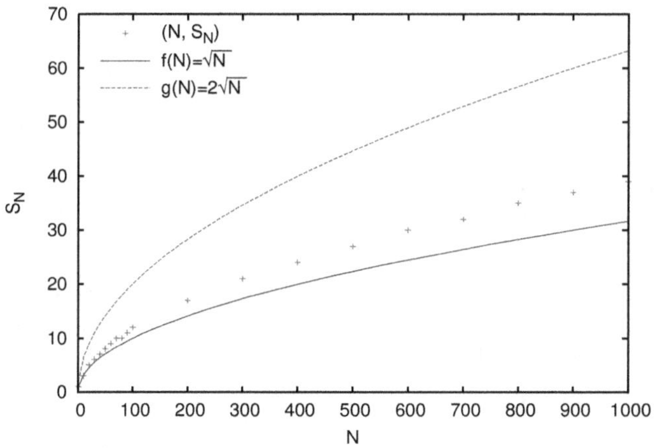

Figure 3: S_N with respect to the growth of N.

THEOREM 4. *Assume that the position of a plan (after sampling-based validation) in the ordered plans with respect to their costs is uniformly distributed. Let N be the number of different join trees in the search space.* [2] *The expected number of steps before the re-optimization procedure terminates is then S_N, where S_N is computed by Equation 1. Moreover, $S_N = O(\sqrt{N})$ by Theorem 3.*

We emphasize that the analysis here only targets worst-case performance, which might be too pessimistic. This is because Procedure 1 only simulates the Case (3) stated in Theorem 2, which is the worst one among the three possible cases. In our experiments, we have found that all queries we tested require less than 10 rounds of iteration, most of which require only 1 or 2 rounds.

Remark: The uniformity assumption in Theorem 4 may not be valid in practice. It is possible that a plan after sampling-based validation (or, a marked ball in terms of Procedure 1) is more likely to be inserted into the front/back half of the queue. Such cases imply that, rather than with an equal chance of overestimation or underestimation, the optimizer tends to overestimate/underestimate the costs of all query plans (for a particular query). This is, however, not impossible. In practice, significant cardinality estimation errors usually appear locally and propagate upwards. Once the error at some join is corrected, the errors in all plans that contain that join will also be corrected. In other words, the correction of the error at a single join can lead to the correction of errors in many candidate plans. In Appendix B, we further present analysis for two extreme cases: all local errors are overestimates/underestimates. To summarize, for left-deep join trees, we have the following two results:

- If all local errors are overestimates, then in the worst case the re-optimization procedure will terminate in at most $m + 1$ steps, where m is the number of joins contained in the query.
- If all local errors are underestimates, then in the worst case re-optimization is expected to terminate in $S_{N/M}$ steps. Here N is the number of different join trees in the optimizer's search space and M is the number of edges in the join graph.

Note that both results are better than the bound stated in Theorem 4. For instance, in the underestimation-only case, if $N = 1000$ and $M = 10$, we have $S_N = 39$ but $S_{N/M} = 12$.

However, in reality, overestimates and underestimates may co-exist. For left-deep join trees, by following the analysis in Appendix B, we can see that such cases sit in between the two extreme cases. Nonetheless, an analysis for plans beyond left-deep trees (e.g., bushy trees) seems to be challenging. We leave this as one possible direction for future work.

3.4 Optimality of the Final Plan

We can think of the re-optimization procedure as progressive adjustments of the optimizer's direction when it explores its search space. The search space depends on the algorithm or strategy used by the optimizer. So does the impact of re-optimization. But we can still have some general conclusions about the optimality of the final plan regardless of the search space.

ASSUMPTION 1. *The cost estimates of plans using sampling-based cardinality refinement are consistent. That is, for any two plans P_1 and P_2, if $\text{cost}^s(P_1) < \text{cost}^s(P_2)$, then $\text{cost}^a(P_1) < \text{cost}^a(P_2)$. Here, $\text{cost}^s(P)$ and $\text{cost}^a(P)$ are the estimated cost based on sampling and the actual cost of plan P, respectively.*

We have the following theorem based on Assumption 1. The proof is included in [1].

THEOREM 5. *Let P_1, ..., P_n be a series of plans generated during the re-optimization procedure. Then $\text{cost}^s(P_n) \leq \text{cost}^s(P_i)$, and thus, by Assumption 1, it follows that $\text{cost}^a(P_n) \leq \text{cost}^a(P_i)$, for $1 \leq i \leq n - 1$.*

That is, the plan after re-optimization is guaranteed to be better than the original plan. Nonetheless, it is difficult to conclude that the plans are improved monotonically, namely, in general it is not true that $\text{cost}^s(P_{i+1}) \leq \text{cost}^s(P_i)$, for $1 \leq i \leq n - 1$. However, we can prove that this is true if we only have overestimates during re-optimization (proof in [1]):

COROLLARY 3. *Let P_1, ..., P_n be a series of plans generated during the re-optimization procedure. If in the re-optimization procedure only overestimates occur, then $\text{cost}^s(P_{i+1}) \leq \text{cost}^s(P_i)$ for $1 \leq i \leq n - 1$.*

Our last result on the optimality of the final plan is in the sense that it is the best among all the plans that are local transformations of the final plan (proof in [1]).

THEOREM 6. *Let P be the final plan the re-optimization procedure returns. For any P' such that P' is a local transformation of P, it holds that $\text{cost}^s(P) \leq \text{cost}^s(P')$.*

3.5 Discussion

We call the final plan returned by the re-optimization procedure the *fixed point* with respect to the initial plan generated by the optimizer. According to Theorem 5, this plan is a *local optimum* with respect to the initial plan. Note that, if $\mathcal{P} = \{P_1, ..., P_n\}$ covers the whole search space, that is, any plan P in the search space is covered by $\mathcal{P}$, then the locally optimal plan is also globally optimal. However, in general, it is difficult to give a definitive answer

[2]Theoretically N could be as large as $O(2^m)$ where m is the number of join operands, assuming that the optimizer uses the bottom-up dynamic programming search strategy. Nonetheless, this may not always be the case. For example, some optimizers use the Cascades framework that leverages a top-down search strategy [18]. An optimizer may even use different search strategies for different types of queries. For example, PostgreSQL will switch from the dynamic programming search strategy to a randomized search strategy based on genetic algorithm, when the number of joins exceeds a certain threshold (12 by default) [2]. For this reason, we choose to characterize the complexity of our algorithm in terms of N rather than m.

to the question that how far away the plan after re-optimization is from the *true* optimal plan. It depends on several factors, including the quality of the initial query plan, the search space covered by re-optimization, and the accuracy of the cost model and sampling-based cardinality estimates.

A natural question is then the impact of the initial plan. Intuitively, it seems that the initial plan can affect both the fixed point and the time it takes to converge to the fixed point. (Note that it is straightforward to prove that the fixed point must exist and be unique, with respect to the given initial plan.) There are also other related interesting questions. For example, if we start with two initial plans with similar cost estimates, would they converge to fixed points with similar costs as well? We leave all these problems as interesting directions for further investigation.

Moreover, the convergence of the re-optimization procedure towards a fixed point can also be viewed as a validation procedure of the costs of the plans $\mathcal{V}$ that can be covered by $\mathcal{P} = \{P_1, ..., P_n\}$. Note that $\mathcal{V}$ is a subset of the whole search space explored by the optimizer, and $\mathcal{V}$ is induced by P_1 — the initial plan that is deemed as optimal by the optimizer. It is also interesting future work to study the relationship between P_1 and $\mathcal{V}$, especially how much of the complete search space can be covered by $\mathcal{V}$.

4. OPTIMIZER "TORTURE TEST"

Evaluating the effectiveness of a query optimizer is challenging. As we mentioned in the introduction, query optimizers have to handle not only common cases but also difficult, corner cases. However, we found it impossible to find well-known public examples of these corner-case queries and the data sets they run on. Regarding this, in this section we create our own data sets and queries based on the well-known fact that many difficult queries are made difficult by correlation in the data [28]. We call it "optimizer torture test" (OTT), given that our goal is to sufficiently challenge the cardinality estimation approaches used by current query optimizers. We next describe the details of OTT.

4.1 Design of the Database and Queries

Since we target cardinality/selectivity estimation, we can focus on queries that only contain selections and joins. In general, a selection-join query q over K relations R_1, ..., R_K can be represented as

$$q = \sigma_F(R_1 \bowtie \cdots \bowtie R_K),$$

where F is a selection predicate as in relational algebra (i.e., a boolean formula). Moreover, we can just focus on equality predicates, i.e., predicates of the form $A = c$ where A is an attribute and c is a constant. Any other predicate can be represented by unions of equality predicates. As a result, we can focus on F of the form

$$F = (A_1 = c_1) \wedge \cdots \wedge (A_K = c_K),$$

where A_k is an attribute of R_k, and $c_k \in \text{Dom}(A_k)$ $(1 \leq k \leq K)$. Here, $\text{Dom}(A_k)$ is the domain of the attribute A_k.

Based on the above observations, our design of the database and queries is as follows:

(1) We have K relations $R_1(A_1, B_1)$, ..., $R_K(A_K, B_K)$.

(2) We use A_k's for selections and B_k's for joins.

(3) Let $R'_k = \sigma_{A_k=c_k}(R_k)$ for $1 \leq k \leq K$. The queries of our benchmark are then of the form:

$$R'_1 \bowtie_{B_1=B_2} R'_2 \bowtie_{B_2=B_3} \cdots \bowtie_{B_{K-1}=B_K} R'_K. \quad (2)$$

The remaining question is how to generate data for R_1, ..., R_K so that we can easily control the selectivities for the selection and join predicates. This requires us to consider the joint data distribution for $(A_1, ..., A_K, B_1, ..., B_K)$. A straightforward way could be to specify the contingency table of the distribution. However, there is a subtle issue of this approach: we cannot just generate a large table with attributes A_1, ..., A_K, B_1, ..., B_K and then split it into different relations $R_1(A_1, B_1)$, ..., $R_K(A_K, B_K)$. The reason is that we cannot infer the joint distribution $(A_1, ..., A_K, B_1, ..., B_K)$ based on the (marginal) distributions we *observed* on (A_1, B_1), ..., (A_K, B_K). In Appendix C we further provide a concrete example to illustrate this. This discrepancy between the observed and true distributions calls for a new approach.

4.2 The Data Generation Algorithm

The previous analysis suggests that we can only generate data for each $R_k(A_k, B_k)$ separately and independently, without resorting to their joint distribution. To generate correlated data, we therefore have to make A_k and B_k correlated, for $1 \leq k \leq K$. Because our goal is to challenge the optimizer's cardinality estimation algorithm, we choose to go to the extreme of this direction: let B_k be the same as A_k. Algorithm 2 presents the details of this idea.

Algorithm 2: Data generation for the OTT database

Input: $\Pr(A_k)$, the distribution of A_k, for $1 \leq k \leq K$
Output: $R_k(A_k, B_k)$: tables generated, for $1 \leq k \leq K$
for $1 \leq k \leq K$ **do**
  Pick a seed independently for the random number generator;
  Generate A_k with respect to $\Pr(A_k)$;
  Generate $B_k = A_k$;
end
return $R_k(A_k, B_k)$, $1 \leq k \leq K$;

We are now left with the problem of specifying $\Pr(A_k)$. While $\Pr(A_k)$ could be arbitrary, we should reconsider our goal of sufficiently challenging the optimizer. We therefore need to know some details about how the optimizer estimates selectivities/cardinalities. Of course, different query optimizers have different implementations, but the general principles are similar. In the following, we present the specific technique used by PostgreSQL, which is used in our experimental evaluation in Section 5.

4.2.1 PostgreSQL's Approaches

PostgreSQL stores the following three types of statistics for each attribute A in its `pg_stats` view [3], if the `ANALYZE` command is invoked for the database:

- the number of distinct values $n(A)$ of A;
- most common values (MCV's) of A and their frequency;
- an equal-depth histogram for the other values of A except for the MCV's.

The above statistics can be used to estimate the selectivity of a predicate over a single attribute in a straightforward manner. For instance, for the predicate $A = c$ in our OTT queries, PostgreSQL first checks if c is in the MCV's. If c is present, then the optimizer simply uses the (exact) frequency recorded. Otherwise, the optimizer assumes a uniform distribution over the non-MCV's and estimates the frequency of c based on $n(A)$.

The approach used by PostgreSQL to estimate selectivities for join predicates is more sophisticated. Consider an equal-join predicate $B_1 = B_2$. If MCV's for either B_1 or B_2 are not available, then the optimizer uses an approach first introduced in System R [35] by estimating the reduction factor as $1/\max\{n(B_1), n(B_2)\}$. If, on the other hand, MCV's are available for both B_1 and B_2, then PostgreSQL tries to refine its estimate by first "joining" the two lists of MCV's. For skewed data distributions, this can lead to much better estimates because the join size of the MCV's, which is accurate, will be very close to the actual join size. Other database systems, such as Oracle [7], use similar approaches.

To combine selectivities from multiple predicates, PostgreSQL relies on the well-known attribute-value-independence (AVI) assumption, which assumes that the distributions of values of different attributes are independent.

4.2.2 The Distribution $\Pr(A_k)$ And Its Impact

From the previous discussion we can see that whether $\Pr(A_k)$ is uniform or skewed will have little difference in affecting the optimizer's estimates if MCV's are leveraged, simply because MCV's have recorded the *exact* frequency for those skewed values. We therefore can just let $\Pr(A_k)$ be uniform. We next analyze the impact of this decision by computing the differences between the estimated and actual cardinalities for the OTT queries.

Let us first revisit the OTT queries presented in Equation 2. Note that for an OTT query to be non-empty, the following condition must hold: $B_1 = B_2 = \cdots = B_{K-1} = B_K$. Because we have intentionally set $A_k = B_k$ for $1 \le k \le K$, this then implies

$$A_1 = A_2 = \cdots = A_{K-1} = A_K. \quad (3)$$

The query size can thus be controlled by the values of the A's. The query is simply empty if Equation 3 does not hold. In Appendix D, we further present a detailed analysis of the query size when Equation 3 holds. To summarize, we are able to control the difference between the query sizes when Equation 3 holds or not. Therefore, we can make this gap as large as we wish. However, the optimizer will give the same estimate of the query size regardless of if Equation 3 holds or not. In our experiments (Section 5) we further used this property to generate instance OTT queries.

5. EXPERIMENTAL EVALUATION

We present experimental evaluation results of our proposed re-optimization procedure in this section.

5.1 Experimental Settings

We implemented the re-optimization framework in PostgreSQL 9.0.4. The modification to the optimizer is small, limited to several hundred lines of C code, which demonstrates the feasibility of including our framework into current query optimizers. We conducted our experiments on a PC with 2.4GHz Intel dual-core CPU and 4GB memory, and we ran PostgreSQL under Linux 2.6.18.

5.1.1 Databases and Performance Metrics

We used both the standard version and a skewed version [4] of the TPC-H benchmark database, as well as our own OTT database described in Section 4.

TPC-H Benchmark Databases. We used TPC-H databases at the scale of 10GB in our experiments. The generator for skewed TPC-H database uses a parameter z to control the skewness of each column by generating Zipfian distributions. The larger z is, the more skewed the generated data are. $z = 0$ corresponds to a uniform distribution. In our experiments, we generated a skewed database by setting $z = 1$.

OTT Database. We created an instance of the OTT database in the following manner. We first generated a standard 1GB TPC-H database. We then extended the 6 largest tables (*lineitem, orders, partsupp, part, customer, supplier*) by adding two additional columns A and B to each of them. As discussed in Section 4.2, we populated the extra columns with uniform data. The domain of a column is determined by the number of rows in the corresponding table: if the table contains r rows, then the domain is $\{0, 1, ..., r/100 - 1\}$. In other words, each distinct value in the domain appears roughly 100 times in the generated column. We further created an index on each added column.

Performance Metrics. In our experiments, we measured the following performance metrics for each query on each database:

(1) the original running time of the query;

(2) the number of iterations the re-optimization procedure requires before its termination;

(3) the time spent on the re-optimization procedure;

(4) the total query running time including the re-optimization time.

Based on studies in the previous work [40], in all of our experiments we set the sampling ratio to be 0.05, namely, 5% of the data were taken as samples.

5.1.2 Calibrating Cost Models

The previous work [40] has also shown that, after proper calibration of the cost models used by the optimizer, we could have better estimates of query running times. An interesting question is then: would calibration also improve query optimization?

In our experiments, we also investigated this problem. Specifically, we ran the offline calibration procedure (details in [40]) and replaced the default values of the five cost units (*seq_page_cost, random_page_cost, cpu_tuple_cost, cpu_index_tuple_cost*, and *cpu_operator_cost*) in `postgresql.conf` (i.e., the configuration file of PostgreSQL server) with the calibrated values. In the following, we also report results based on calibrated cost models.

5.2 Results on the TPC-H Benchmark

We tested 21 TPC-H queries. (We excluded Q15, which is not supported by our current implementation because it requires to create a view first.) For each TPC-H query, we randomly generated 10 instances. We cleared both the database buffer pool and the file system cache between each run of each query.

5.2.1 Results on Uniform Database

Figure 4 presents the average running times and their standard deviations (as error bars) of these queries over the uniform database.

We have two observations. First, while the running times for most of the queries almost do not change, we can see significant improvement for some queries. For example, as shown in Figure 4(a), even without calibration of the cost units, the average running time of Q9 drops from 4,446 seconds to only 932 seconds, a 79% reduction; more significantly, the average running time of Q21 drops from 20,746 seconds (i.e., almost 6 hours) to 3,508 seconds (i.e., less than 1 hour), a 83% reduction.

Second, calibration of the cost units can sometimes significantly reduce the running times for some queries. For example, comparing Figure 4(a) with Figure 4(b) we can observe that the average

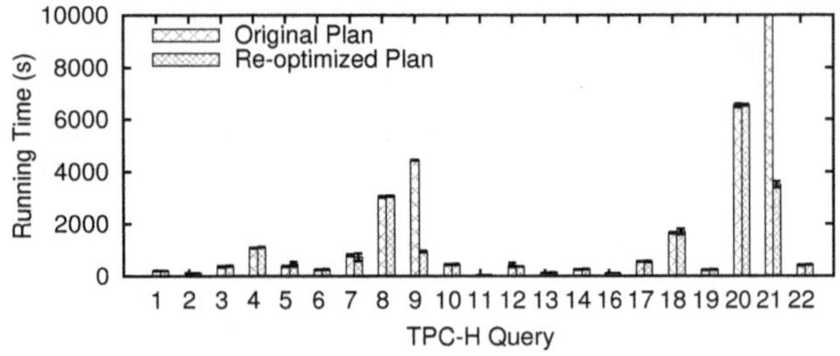

(a) Without calibration of the cost units

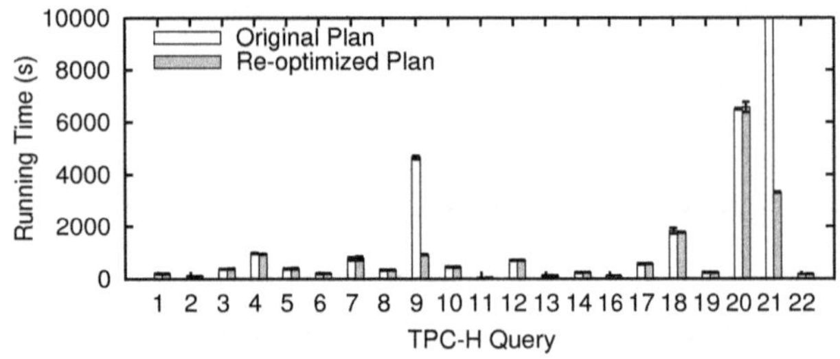

(b) With calibration of the cost units

Figure 4: Query running time over uniform 10GB TPC-H database ($z = 0$).

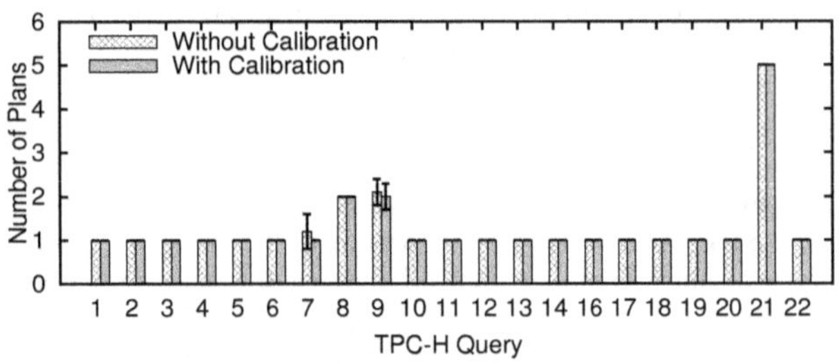

Figure 5: The number of plans generated during re-optimization over uniform 10GB TPC-H database.

running time of Q8 drops from 3,048 seconds to only 339 seconds, a 89% reduction, by just using calibrated cost units without even invoking the re-optimization procedure.

We further studied the re-optimization procedure itself. Figure 5 presents the number of plans generated during re-optimization. It substantiates our observation in Figure 4: for the queries whose running times were not improved, the re-optimization procedure indeed picked the same plans as those originally chosen by the optimizer. Figure 6 further compares the query running time excluding/including the time spent on re-optimization. For all the queries we tested, re-optimization time is ignorable compared to query execution time, which demonstrates the low overhead of our re-optimization procedure.

5.2.2 Results on Skewed Database

On the skewed database, we have observed results similar to that on the uniform database. Figure 7 presents the running times of the queries, with or without calibration of the cost units.[3] While it looks quite similar to Figure 4, there is one interesting phenomenon

[3]We notice that Q17 in Figure 7 has a large error bar. The error bars represent variance due to different instances of the query template (different constants in the query). Q17 therefore has a large variance, because we used a skewed TPC-H database. The variance is much smaller when a uniform database is used (see Figure 4).

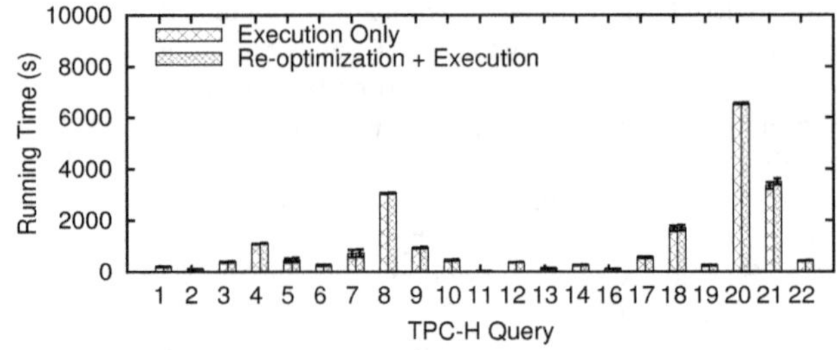

(a) Without calibration of the cost units

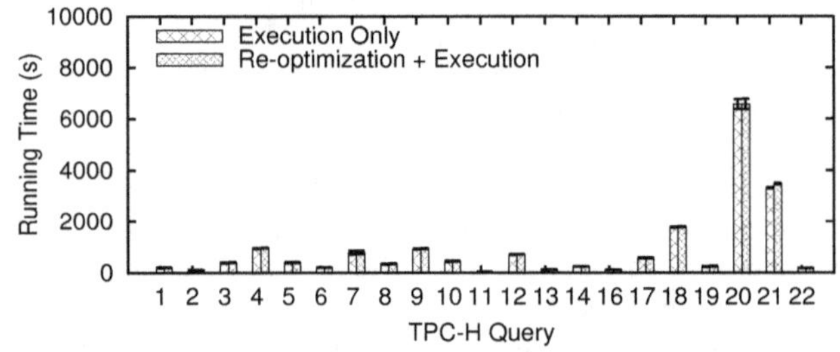

(b) With calibration of the cost units

Figure 6: Query running time excluding/including re-optimization time over uniform 10GB TPC-H database ($z = 0$).

not shown before. In Figure 7(a) we see that, without using calibrated cost units, the average running times for Q8 and Q9 actually increase after re-optimization. Recall that in Section 3.4 we have shown the local optimality of the plan returned by the re-optimization procedure (Theorem 5). However, that result is based on the assumption that sampling-based cost estimates are consistent with actual costs (Assumption 1). Here this seems not the case. Nonetheless, after using calibrated cost units, both the running times of Q8 and Q9 were significantly improved (Figure 7(b)).

We further present the number of plans considered during re-optimization in Figure 8. Note that re-optimization seems to be more active on skewed data. Figure 9 shows the running times excluding/including the re-optimization times of the queries. Again, the additional overhead of re-optimization is trivial.

5.2.3 Discussion

While one might expect the chance for re-optimization to generate a better plan is higher on skewed databases, our experiments show that this may not be the case, at least for TPC-H queries. There are several different situations, though. First, if a query is too simple, then there is almost no chance for re-optimization. For example, Q1 contains no join, whereas Q16 and Q19 involve only one join so only local transformations are possible. Second, the final plan returned by the re-optimization procedure heavily relies on the initial plan picked by the optimizer, which is the seed or starting point where re-optimization originates. Note that, even if the optimizer has picked an inefficient plan, re-optimization cannot help if the estimated cost of that plan is not significantly erroneous. One question is if this is possible: the optimizer picks an inferior plan whose cost estimate is correct? This actually could happen because the optimizer may (incorrectly) overestimate the costs of the other plans in its search space. Another subtle point is that the inferior plan might be robust to certain degree of errors in cardinality estimates. Previous work has reported this phenomenon by noticing that the plan diagram (i.e., all possible plans and their governed optimality areas in the selectivity space) is dominated by just a couple of query plans [33].

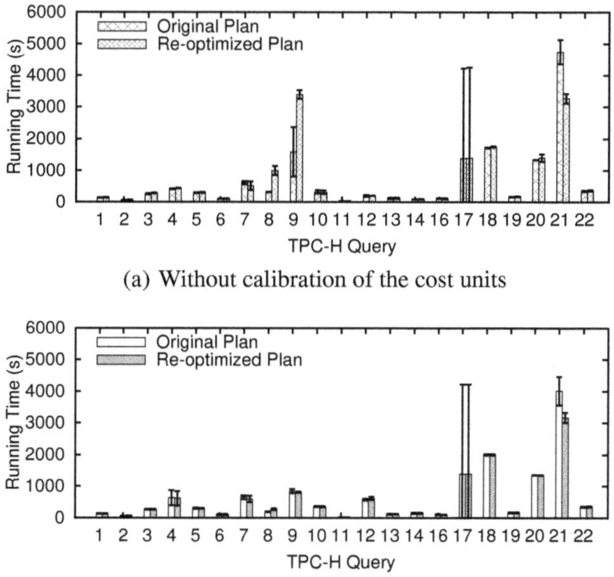

(a) Without calibration of the cost units

(b) With calibration of the cost units

Figure 7: Query running time over skewed 10GB TPC-H database ($z = 1$).

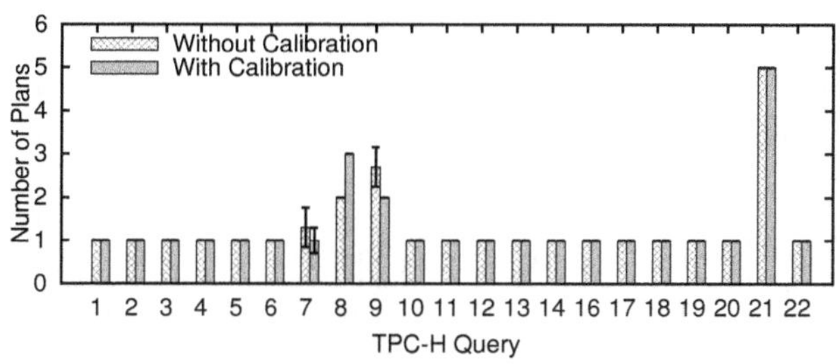

Figure 8: The number of plans generated during re-optimization over skewed 10GB TPC-H database.

In summary, the effectiveness of re-optimization depends on factors that are out of the control of the re-optimization procedure itself. Nevertheless, we have observed intriguing improvement for some long-running queries by applying re-optimization, especially after calibration of the cost units.

5.3 Results of the Optimizer Torture Test

We created queries following our design of the OTT in Section 4.1. Specifically, if a query contains n tables (i.e., $n-1$ joins), we let m of the selections be $A = 0$ ($A = 1$), and let the remaining $n - m$ selections be $A = 1$ ($A = 0$). We generated two sets of queries: (1) $n = 5$ (4 joins), $m = 4$; and (2) $n = 6$ (5 joins), $m = 4$. Note that the maximal non-empty sub-queries then contain 3 joins over 4 tables with result size of roughly $100^4 = 10^8$ rows.[4] However, the size of each (whole) query is 0. So we would like to see the ability of the optimizer as well as the re-optimization procedure to identify the empty/non-empty sub-queries.

Figure 10 and 11 present the running times of the 4-join and 5-join queries, respectively. We generated in total 10 4-join queries and 30 5-join queries. Note that the y-axes are in log scale and we do not show queries that finish in less than 0.1 second. As we can see, sometimes the optimizer failed to detect the existence of empty sub-queries: it generated plans where empty join predicates were evaluated after the non-empty ones. The running times of these queries were then hundreds or even thousands of seconds. On the other hand, the re-optimization procedure did an almost perfect job in detecting empty joins, which led to very efficient query plans where the empty joins were evaluated first: all the queries after re-optimization finished in less than 1 second.

[4]Recall that a non-empty query must have equal A's (Equation 3) and we generated data with roughly 100 rows per distinct value (Section 5.1).

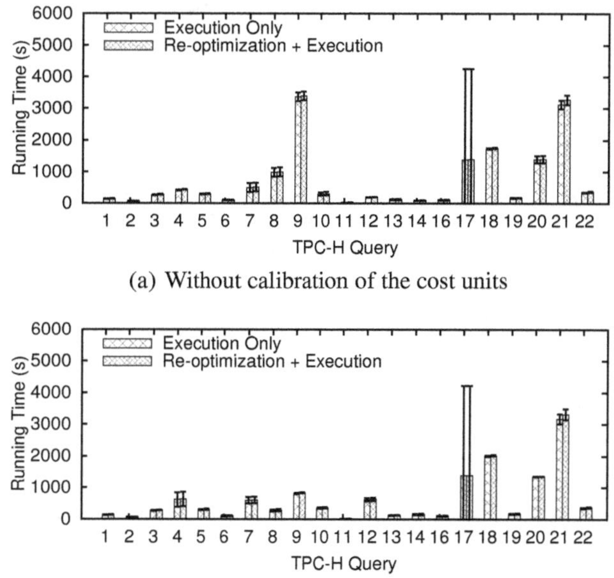

(a) Without calibration of the cost units

(b) With calibration of the cost units

Figure 9: Query running time excluding/including re-optimization time over skewed 10GB TPC-H database ($z = 1$).

We also did similar studies regarding the number of plans generated during re-optimization and the time it consumed. Due to space constraints, we refer the readers to Appendix A.1 for the details.

One might argue that the OTT queries are really contrived: these queries are hardly to see in real-world workloads. While this might be true, we think these queries serve our purpose as exemplifying extremely hard cases for query optimization. Note that hard cases are not merely long-running queries: queries as simple as sequentially scanning huge tables are long-running too, but there is nothing query optimization can help with. Hard cases are queries where efficient execution plans do exist but it might be difficult for the optimizer to find them. The OTT queries are just these instances. Based on the experimental results of the OTT queries, re-optimization is helpful to give the optimizer second chances if it initially made a bad decision.

Another concern is if commercial database systems could do a better job on the OTT queries. In regard of this, we also ran the OTT over two major commercial database systems. The performance is very similar to that of PostgreSQL (Figure 12 and 13). We therefore speculate that commercial systems could also benefit from our re-optimization technique proposed in this paper.

5.3.1 A Note on Multidimensional Histograms

Note that even using multidimensional histograms (e.g., [10, 31, 32]) may not be able to detect the data correlation presented in the OTT queries, unless the buckets are so fine-grained that the exact joint distributions are retained. To understand this, let us consider the following example.

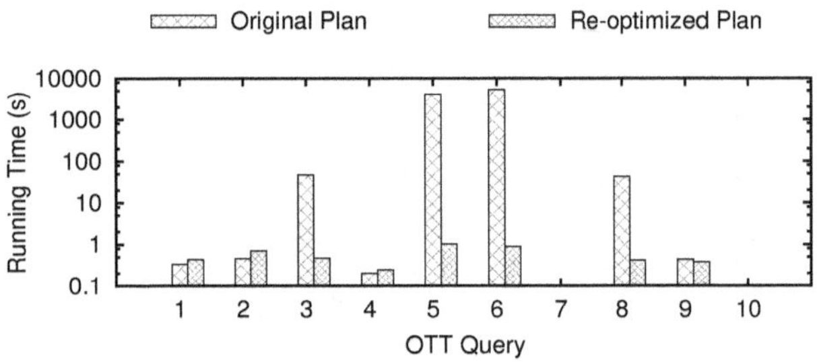

(a) Without calibration of the cost units

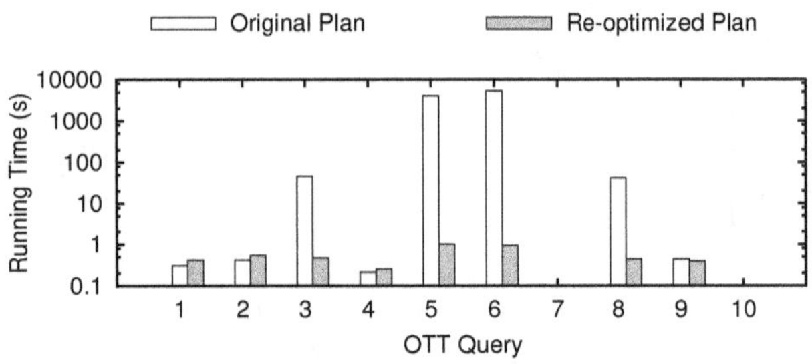

(b) With calibration of the cost units

Figure 10: Query running times of 4-join queries.

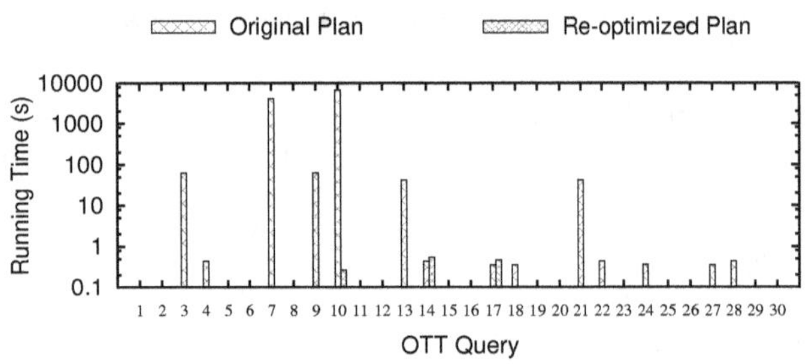

(a) Without calibration of the cost units

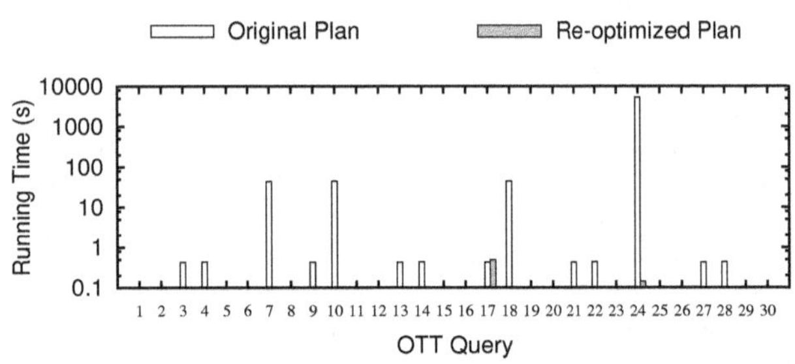

(b) With calibration of the cost units

Figure 11: Query running times of 5-join queries.

EXAMPLE 2. *Following our design of OTT, suppose that now we only have two tables $R_1(A_1, B_1)$ and $R_2(A_2, B_2)$. Moreover, suppose that each A_k (and thus B_k) contains $m = 2l$ distinct values, and we construct (perfect) 2-dimensional histograms on (A_k, B_k) ($k = 1, 2$). Each dimension is evenly divided into $\frac{m}{2} = l$ intervals, so each histogram contains l^2 buckets. The joint distribution over (A_k, B_k) estimated by using the histogram is then:*

$$\begin{cases} \Pr(2r-2 \le A_k < 2r, 2r-2 \le B_k < 2r) = \frac{1}{l}, & 1 \le r \le l; \\ \Pr(a_l \le A_k < a_2, b_1 \le B_k < b_2) = 0, & \textit{otherwise.} \end{cases}$$

For instance, if $m = 100$, then $l = 50$. So we have $\Pr(0 \le A_k < 2, 0 \le B_k < 2) = \cdots = \Pr(98 \le A_k < 100, 98 \le B_k < 100) = \frac{1}{50}$, while all the other buckets are empty. On the other hand, the actual joint distribution is

$$\Pr(A_k = a, B_k = b) = \begin{cases} \frac{1}{m}, & \textit{if } a = b; \\ 0, & \textit{otherwise.} \end{cases}$$

Now, let us consider the selectivities for two OTT queries:

(q_1) $\sigma_{A_1=0 \wedge A_2=1 \wedge B_1=B_2}(R_1 \times R_2)$;

(q_2) $\sigma_{A_1=0 \wedge A_2=0 \wedge B_1=B_2}(R_2 \times R_2)$.

We know that q_1 is empty but q_2 is not. However, the estimated selectivity (and thus cardinality) of q_1 and q_2 is the same by using the

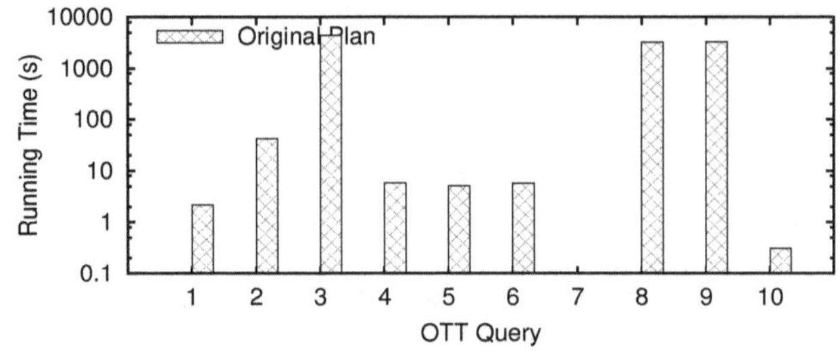

(a) 4-join OTT queries

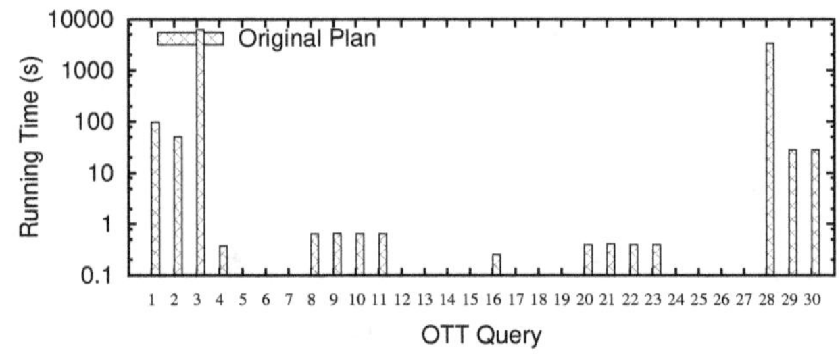

(b) 5-join OTT queries

Figure 12: Query running times of the OTT queries on the commercial database system A.

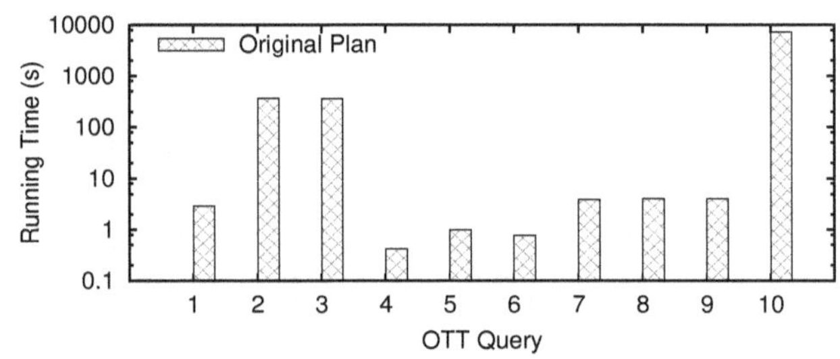

(a) 4-join OTT queries

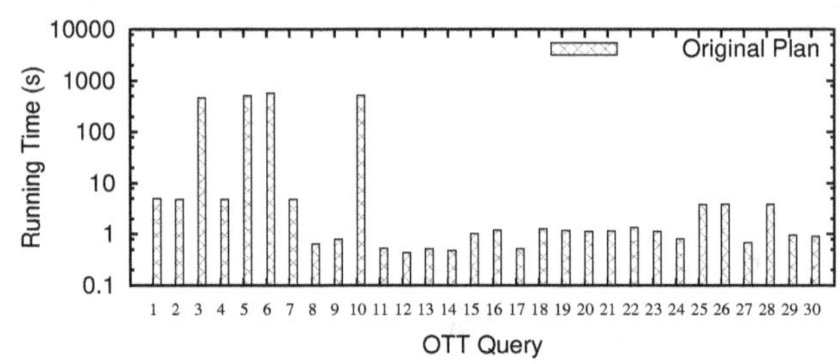

(b) 5-join OTT queries

Figure 13: Query running times of the OTT queries on the commercial database system B.

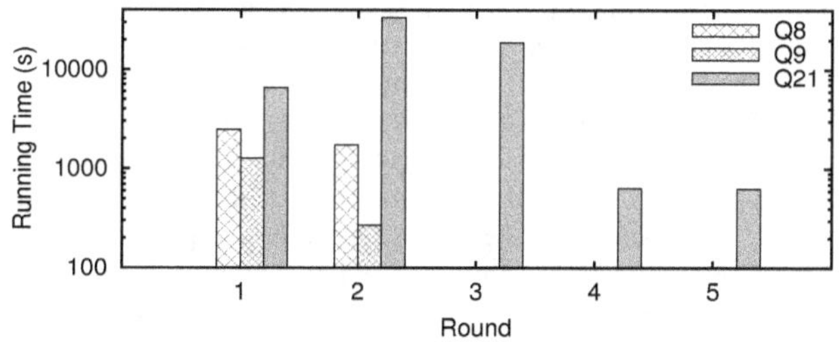

Figure 14: Running time of plans generated in re-optimization for TPC-H queries ($z = 0$) without calibration of cost units.

2-dimensional histogram, because of the assumption used by histograms that data inside each bucket is uniformly distributed.[5] *With the setting used in our experiments, $m = 100$ and thus $l = 50$. So each 2-dimensional histogram contains $l^2 = 2,500$ buckets. However, even such detailed histograms cannot help the optimizer distinguish empty joins from nonempty ones. Furthermore, note that our conclusion is independent of m, while the number of buckets increases quadratically in m. For instance, when $m = 10^4$ which means we have histograms containing 2.5×10^7 buckets, the optimizer still cannot rely on the histograms to generate efficient query plans for OTT queries.*

5.4 Effectiveness of Iteration

One interesting further question is how much benefit iteration brings in. Since running plans over samples incurs additional cost, we may wish to stop the iteration as early as possible rather than wait until its convergence. To investigate this, we also tested execution times for plans generated during re-optimization on the original databases. We focus on queries for which at least two plans were generated. Figure 14 presents typical results for TPC-H queries Q8, Q9, and Q21, and Figure 15 presents typical results for the OTT queries. For each query, the plan in the first round is the original one returned by the optimizer.

We have the following observations. While the plan returned in the second round of iteration (i.e., the first different plan returned by re-optimization) often dramatically reduces the query execution time, it is not always the case. Sometimes it takes additional rounds before an improved plan is found while the plans generated in between have similar execution times (e.g., 4-join OTT query Q8 and 5-join OTT query Q13). In the case of TPC-H Q21, the execution times of intermediate plans generated during re-optimization are even not non-increasing. The plans returned by the optimizer in the second and third round are even much worse than the original plan. (Note that the y-axis of Figure 14 is in log scale.) Fortunately, by continuing with the iteration, we can eventually reach a plan that is much better than the original one.

The above observations give rise to the question why worse plans might be generated during re-optimization. To understand this, note that in the middle of re-optimization, the plans returned by the optimizer are based on statistics that are *partially* validated by sampling. The optimizer is likely to generate an "optimal" plan due to underestimating the costs of joins that have not been covered by plans generated in previous rounds. This phenomenon has also been observed in previous work [13]. It is the essential reason that we cannot make Theorem 5 stronger. As long as there exist uncovered joins, there is no guarantee on the plan returned by the optimizer. Only upon the convergence of re-optimization we can say that the final plan is locally optimal.

[5] It is easy to verify that the selectivity estimates are $\hat{s}_1 = \hat{s}_2 = \frac{1}{8l^2}$.

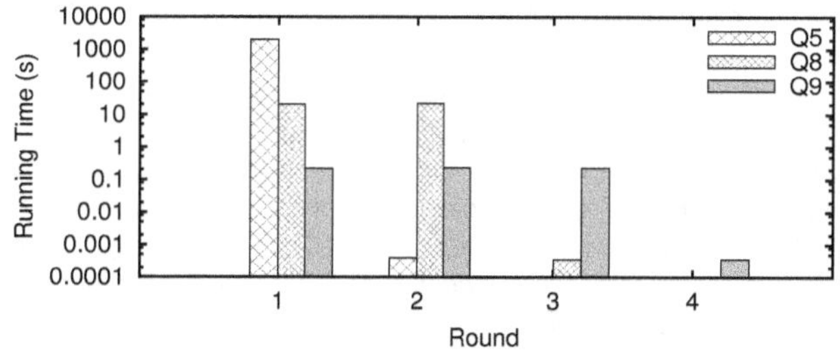

(a) 4-join queries

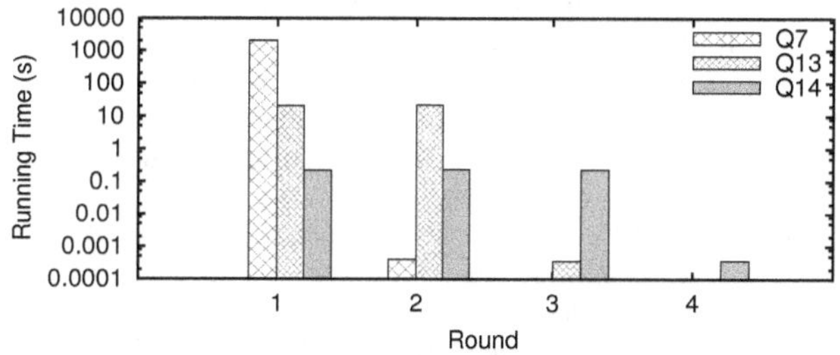

(b) 5-join queries

Figure 15: Running time of plans generated in re-optimization for the OTT queries without calibration of cost units.

Nevertheless, in practice we can still have various strategies to control the overhead of re-optimization. For example, we can stop re-optimization if it does not converge after a certain number of rounds, or if the time spent on re-optimization has reached some timeout threshold. We then simply return the best plan among the plans generated so far, based on their cost estimates by using refined cardinality estimates from sampling [40]. As another option, it might even be worth considering not doing re-optimization at all if the estimated query execution time is shorter than some threshold, or only doing it if we run that plan and get past that threshold without being close to done.

6. RELATED WORK

Query optimization has been studied for decades, and we refer the readers to [12] and [22] for surveys in this area.

Cardinality estimation is a critical problem in cost-based query optimization, and has triggered extensive research in the database community. Approaches for cardinality estimation in the literature are either static or dynamic. Static approaches usually rely on various statistics that are collected and maintained periodically in an off-line manner, such as histograms (e.g., [23, 32]), samples (e.g., [11, 20, 27]), sketches (e.g., [5, 34]), or even graphical models (e.g. [17, 37]). In practice, approaches based on histograms are dominant in the implementations of current query optimizers. However, histogram-based approaches have to rely on the notorious attribute-value-independence (AVI) assumption, and they often fail to capture data correlations, which could result in significant errors in cardinality estimates. While variants of histograms (in particular, multidimensional histograms, e.g., [10, 31, 32]) have been proposed to overcome the AVI assumption, they suffer from significantly increased overhead on large databases. Meanwhile, even if we can afford the overhead of using multidimensional histograms, they are still insufficient in many cases, as we discussed in Section 5.3.1. Compared with histogram-based approaches, sampling is better at capturing data correlation. One reason for this is that sampling evaluates queries on real rather than summarized data. There are many sampling algorithms, and in this paper we just picked a simple one (see [38] for a recent survey). We do not try to explore more advanced sampling techniques (e.g. [16]), which we believe could further improve the quality of cardinality estimates.

On the other hand, dynamic approaches further utilize information gathered during query runtime. Approaches in this direction include dynamic query plans (e.g., [14, 19]), parametric query optimization (e.g. [24]), query feedback (e.g., [8, 36]), mid-query re-optimization (e.g. [25, 30]), and quite recently, plan bouquets [15]. The ideas behind dynamic query plans and parametric query optimization are similar: rather than picking one single optimal query plan, all possible optimal plans are retained and the decision is deferred until runtime. Both approaches suffer from the problem of combinatorial explosion and are usually used in contexts where expensive pre-compilation stages are affordable. The recent development of plan bouquets [15] is built on top of parametric query optimization so it may also incur a heavy query compilation stage.

Meanwhile, approaches based on query feedback record statistics of past queries and use this information to improve cardinality estimates for future queries. Some of these approaches have been adopted in commercial systems such as IBM DB2 [36] and Microsoft SQL Server [8]. Nonetheless, collecting query feedback incurs additional runtime overhead as well as storage overhead of ever-growing volume of statistics.

The most relevant work in the literature is the line along mid-query re-optimization [25, 30]. The major difference is that re-optimization was previously carried out at runtime over the actual database rather than at query compilation time over the samples. The main issue is the trade-off between the overhead spent on re-optimization and the improvement on the query plan. In the introduction, we have articulated the pros and cons of both techniques. In some sense, our approach can be thought of as a "dry run" of runtime re-optimization. But it is much cheaper because it is performed over the sampled data. As we have seen, cardinality estimation errors due to data correlation can be caught by the sample runs. So it is perhaps an overkill to detect these errors at runtime by running the query over the actual database. Sometimes optimizers make mistakes that involve a bad ordering that results in a larger than expected result from a join or a selection. It is true that runtime re-optimization can detect this, but this may require the query evaluator to do a substantial amount of work before it is detected. For example, if the data is fed into an operator in a non-random order, because of an unlucky ordering the fact that the operator has a much larger than expected result may not be obvious until a substantial portion of the input has been consumed and substantial system resources have been expended. Furthermore, it is non-trivial to stop an operator in mid-flight and switch to a different plan — for this reason most runtime query re-optimization deals with changing plans at pipeline boundaries. Running a bad plan until a pipeline completes might be very expensive.

Nonetheless, we are not claiming that we should just use our approach. Rather, our approach is complementary to runtime re-optimization techniques: it is certainly possible to apply those techniques on the plan returned by our approach. The hope is that, after applying our approach, the chance that we need to invoke more costly runtime re-optimizaton techniques can be significantly reduced. This is similar to the "alerter" idea that has been used in physical database tuning [9], where a lightweight "alerter" is invoked to determine the potential performance gain before the more costly database tuning advisor is called. There is also some recent work on applying runtime re-optimization to Map-Reduce based systems [26]. The "pilot run" idea explored in this work is close to our motivation, where the goal is also to avoid starting with a bad plan by collecting more accurate statistics via scanning a small amount of samples. However, currently "pilot run" only collects statistics for leaf tables. It is then interesting to see if "pilot run" could be further enhanced by considering our technique.

In some sense, our approach sits between existing static and dynamic approaches. We combine the advantage of lower overheads from static approaches and the advantage of more optimization opportunities from dynamic approaches. This compromise leads to a lightweight query re-optimization procedure that could bring up better query plans. However, this also unavoidably leads to the co-existence of both histogram-based and sampling-based cardinality estimates during re-optimization, which may cause inconsistency issues [29]. Somehow, this is a general problem when different types of cardinality estimation techniques are used together. For example, an optimizer that also uses multi-dimensional histograms (in addition to one-dimensional histograms) may also have to handle inconsistencies. Previous runtime re-optimization techniques are also likely to suffer similar issues. In this sense, this is an orthogonal problem and we do not try to address it in this paper. In spite of that, it is interesting future work to see how much more improvement we can get if we further incorporate the approach based on the maximum entropy principle [29] into our re-optimization framework to resolve inconsistency in cardinality estimates.

Finally, we note that we are not the first that investigates the idea of incorporating sampling into query optimization. Ilyas et al. proposed using sampling to detect data correlations and then collecting joint statistics for those correlated data columns [21]. However, this seems to be insufficient if data correlation is caused by specific selection predicates, such as those OTT queries used in our experiments. Babcock and Chaudhuri also investigated the usage of sampling in developing a robust query optimizer [6]. While robustness is another interesting goal for query optimizer, it is beyond the scope of this paper.

7. CONCLUSION

In this paper, we studied the problem of incorporating sampling-based cardinality estimates into query optimization. We proposed an iterative query re-optimization procedure that supplements the optimizer with refreshed cardinality estimates via sampling and gives it second chances to generate better query plans. We show the efficiency and effectiveness of this re-optimization procedure both theoretically and experimentally.

There are several directions worth further exploring. First, as we have mentioned, the initial plan picked by the optimizer may have great impact on the final plan returned by re-optimization. While it remains interesting to study this impact theoretically, it might also be an intriguing idea to think about varying the way that the query optimizer works. For example, rather than just returning one plan, the optimizer could return several candidates and let the re-optimization procedure work on each of them. This might make up for the potentially bad situation currently faced by the re-optimization procedure that it may start with a bad seed plan. Second, the re-optimization procedure itself could be further improved. As an example, note that in this paper we let the optimizer unconditionally accept cardinality estimates by sampling. However, sampling is by no means perfect. A more conservative approach is to consider the uncertainty of the cardinality estimates returned by sampling as well. The previous work [41] has investigated the problem of quantifying uncertainty in sampling-based query running time estimation. It is very interesting to study a combination of that framework with the re-optimization procedure proposed in this paper. We leave all these as promising areas for future work.

Acknowledgements. We thank the anonymous reviewers for their valuable comments, and we thank Heng Guo for his help with the proof of Theorem 3. This work was supported in part by a Google Focus Award.

8. REFERENCES

[1] http://arxiv.org/abs/1601.05748.

[2] http://www.postgresql.org/docs/9.0/static/runtime-config-query.html.

[3] http://www.postgresql.org/docs/9.0/static/view-pg-stats.html.

[4] Skewed tpc-h data generator. ftp://ftp.research.microsoft.com/users/viveknar/TPCDSkew/.

[5] N. Alon, P. B. Gibbons, Y. Matias, and M. Szegedy. Tracking join and self-join sizes in limited storage. In *PODS*, 1999.

[6] B. Babcock and S. Chaudhuri. Towards a robust query optimizer: A principled and practical approach. In *SIGMOD*, pages 119–130, 2005.

[7] W. Breitling. Joins, skew and histograms. http://www.centrexcc.com/Joins,SkewandHistograms.pdf.

[8] N. Bruno and S. Chaudhuri. Exploiting statistics on query expressions for optimization. In *SIGMOD*, pages 263–274, 2002.

[9] N. Bruno and S. Chaudhuri. To tune or not to tune? A lightweight physical design alerter. In *VLDB*, pages 499–510, 2006.

[10] N. Bruno, S. Chaudhuri, and L. Gravano. Stholes: A multidimensional workload-aware histogram. In *SIGMOD*, pages 211–222, 2001.

[11] M. Charikar, S. Chaudhuri, R. Motwani, and V. R. Narasayya. Towards estimation error guarantees for distinct values. In *PODS*, pages 268–279, 2000.

[12] S. Chaudhuri. An overview of query optimization in relational systems. In *PODS*, pages 34–43, 1998.

[13] S. Chaudhuri, V. R. Narasayya, and R. Ramamurthy. A pay-as-you-go framework for query execution feedback. *PVLDB*, 1(1):1141–1152, 2008.

[14] R. L. Cole and G. Graefe. Optimization of dynamic query evaluation plans. In *SIGMOD*, pages 150–160, 1994.

[15] A. Dutt and J. R. Haritsa. Plan bouquets: query processing without selectivity estimation. In *SIGMOD*, 2014.

[16] C. Estan and J. F. Naughton. End-biased samples for join cardinality estimation. In *ICDE*, 2006.

[17] L. Getoor, B. Taskar, and D. Koller. Selectivity estimation using probabilistic models. In *SIGMOD*, 2001.

[18] G. Graefe. The cascades framework for query optimization. *IEEE Data Eng. Bull.*, 18(3):19–29, 1995.

[19] G. Graefe and K. Ward. Dynamic query evaluation plans. In *SIGMOD Conference*, pages 358–366, 1989.

[20] P. J. Haas, J. F. Naughton, S. Seshadri, and A. N. Swami. Selectivity and cost estimation for joins based on random sampling. *J. Comput. Syst. Sci.*, 52(3):550–569, 1996.

[21] I. F. Ilyas, V. Markl, P. J. Haas, P. Brown, and A. Aboulnaga. CORDS: automatic discovery of correlations and soft functional dependencies. In *SIGMOD*, pages 647–658, 2004.

[22] Y. E. Ioannidis. Query optimization. *ACM Comput. Surv.*, 28(1):121–123, 1996.

[23] Y. E. Ioannidis. The history of histograms (abridged). In *VLDB*, pages 19–30, 2003.

[24] Y. E. Ioannidis, R. T. Ng, K. Shim, and T. K. Sellis. Parametric query optimization. In *VLDB*, pages 103–114, 1992.

[25] N. Kabra and D. J. DeWitt. Efficient mid-query re-optimization of sub-optimal query execution plans. In *SIGMOD*, pages 106–117, 1998.

[26] K. Karanasos, A. Balmin, M. Kutsch, F. Ozcan, V. Ercegovac, C. Xia, and J. Jackson. Dynamically optimizing queries over large scale data platforms. In *SIGMOD*, pages 943–954, 2014.

[27] R. J. Lipton, J. F. Naughton, and D. A. Schneider. Practical selectivity estimation through adaptive sampling. In *SIGMOD*, pages 1–11, 1990.

[28] G. Lohman. Is query optimization a "solved" problem? http://wp.sigmod.org/?p=1075.

[29] V. Markl, P. J. Haas, M. Kutsch, N. Megiddo, U. Srivastava, and T. M. Tran. Consistent selectivity estimation via maximum entropy. *VLDB J.*, 16(1):55–76, 2007.

[30] V. Markl, V. Raman, D. E. Simmen, G. M. Lohman, and H. Pirahesh. Robust query processing through progressive optimization. In *SIGMOD*, pages 659–670, 2004.

[31] M. Muralikrishna and D. J. DeWitt. Equi-depth histograms for estimating selectivity factors for multi-dimensional queries. In *SIGMOD*, pages 28–36, 1988.

[32] V. Poosala and Y. E. Ioannidis. Selectivity estimation without the attribute value independence assumption. In *VLDB*, 1997.

[33] N. Reddy and J. R. Haritsa. Analyzing plan diagrams of database query optimizers. In *VLDB*, 2005.

[34] F. Rusu and A. Dobra. Sketches for size of join estimation. *ACM Trans. Database Syst.*, 33(3), 2008.

[35] P. G. Selinger, M. M. Astrahan, D. D. Chamberlin, R. A. Lorie, and T. G. Price. Access path selection in a relational database management system. In *SIGMOD*, 1979.

[36] M. Stillger, G. M. Lohman, V. Markl, and M. Kandil. LEO - DB2's learning optimizer. In *VLDB*, 2001.

[37] K. Tzoumas, A. Deshpande, and C. S. Jensen. Lightweight graphical models for selectivity estimation without independence assumptions. *PVLDB*, 4(11):852–863, 2011.

[38] D. Vengerov, A. C. Menck, M. Zaït, and S. Chakkappen. Join size estimation subject to filter conditions. *PVLDB*, 8(12):1530–1541, 2015.

[39] W. Wu, Y. Chi, H. Hacigümüs, and J. F. Naughton. Towards predicting query execution time for concurrent and dynamic database workloads. *PVLDB*, 6(10):925–936, 2013.

[40] W. Wu, Y. Chi, S. Zhu, J. Tatemura, H. Hacigümüs, and J. F. Naughton. Predicting query execution time: Are optimizer cost models really unusable? In *ICDE*, pages 1081–1092, 2013.

[41] W. Wu, X. Wu, H. Hacigümüs, and J. F. Naughton. Uncertainty aware query execution time prediction. *PVLDB*, 7(14):1857–1868, 2014.

APPENDIX

A. ADDITIONAL RESULTS

In this section, we present additional experimental results for the OTT queries. We also performed the same experiments for TPC-DS queries, and we report the results here.

A.1 Additional Results on OTT Queries

For OTT queries, we also did similar studies regarding the number of plans generated during re-optimization and the time it consumed. Figure 16 presents the number of plans generated during the re-optimization procedure for the 4-join and 5-join OTT queries. Figure 17 and 18 further present the comparisons of the running times by excluding or including re-optimization times for these queries (the y-axes are in log scale).

A.2 Results on the TPC-DS Benchmark

We conducted the same experiments on the TPC-DS benchmark. Specifically, we use a subset containing 29 TPC-DS queries that are supported by PostgreSQL and our current implementation, and we use a 10GB TPC-DS database. The experiments were performed on a PC with 3.4GHz Intel 4-core CPU and 8GB memory, and we ran PostgreSQL under Linux 2.6.32.

We again use a sampling ratio of 5%. Figure 19 presents the execution time of each TPC-DS query. The time spent on running query plans over the samples is again trivial and therefore is not plotted. Figure 20 further presents the number of plans generated during re-optimization.[6]

[6]The results we show here are based on the TPC-DS database with only indexes on primary keys of the tables. The TPC-DS benchmark specification does not recommend any indexes, which potentially could have impact on the optimizer's choices. Regarding this,

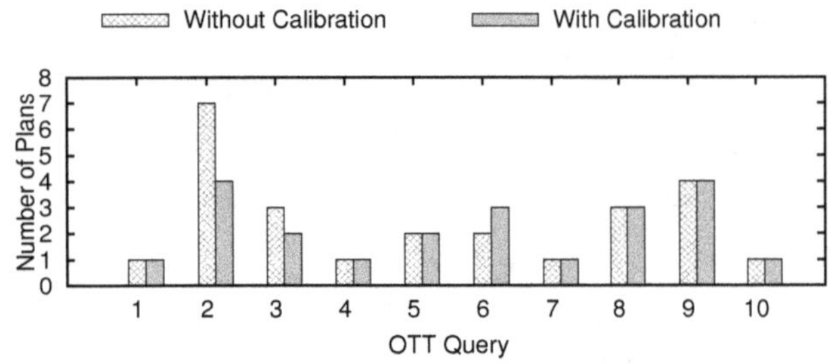

(a) 4-join queries

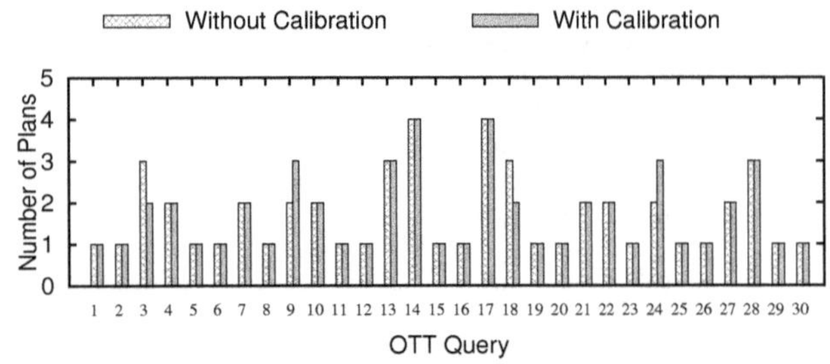

(b) 5-join queries

Figure 16: The number of plans generated during re-optimization for the OTT queries.

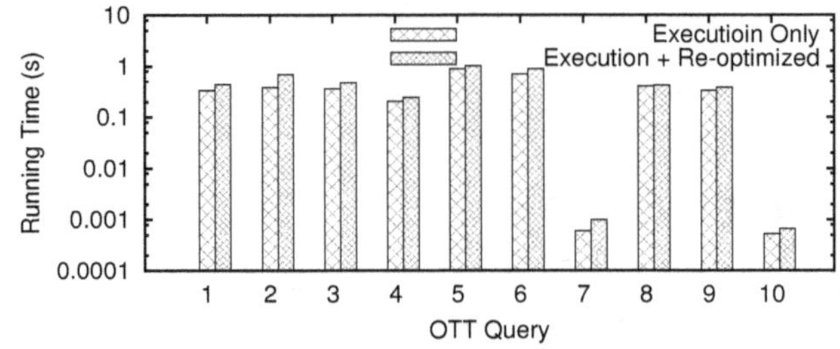

(a) Without calibration of the cost units

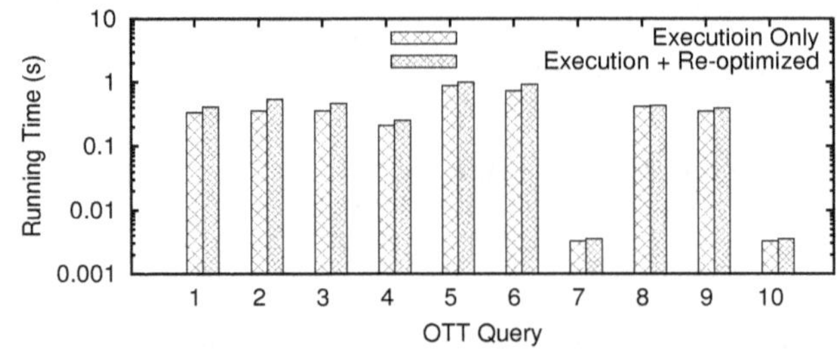

(b) With calibration of the cost units

Figure 17: Query running time excluding/including re-optimization time for the 4-join OTT queries.

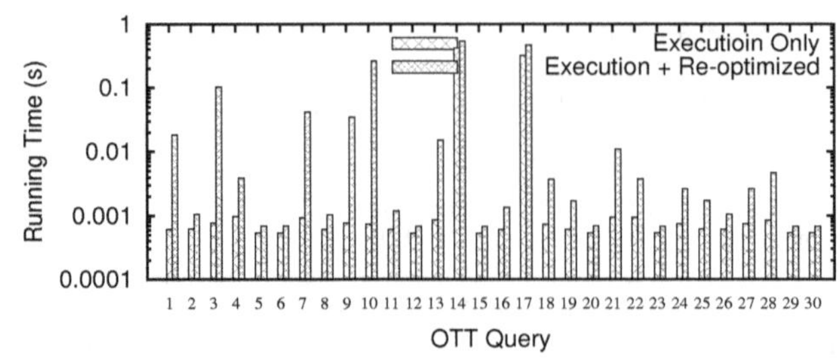

(a) Without calibration of the cost units

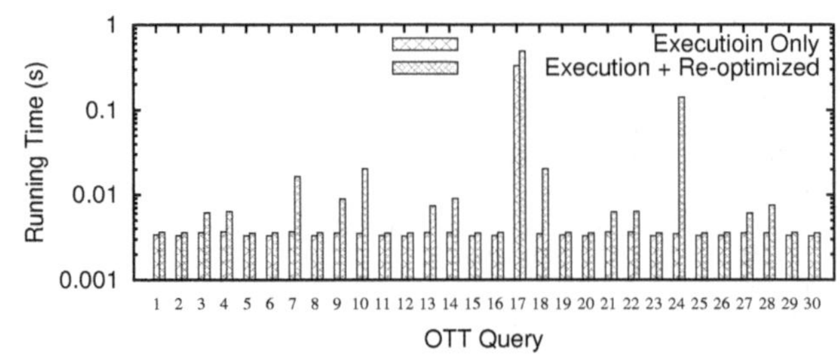

(b) With calibration of the cost units

Figure 18: Query running time excluding/including re-optimization time for the 5-join OTT queries.

Unfortunately, we do not observe remarkable improvement over the TPC-DS queries we tested by using re-optimization. There are several reasons. First, the majority of the queries are short-running ones, though some of them are quite complicated in terms of their query plans. There is little room for improvement on these queries. Second, for the four relatively long-running queries Q28, Q50, Q55, and Q65 (with running time above 100 seconds), three of them (Q28, Q55, and Q65) are a bit trivial for re-optimization to have impact. Q28 only accesses one table, while Q55 joins a fact table with two small dimension tables. Q65 involves joins between a fact table and three small dimension tables, but its execution time is dominated by a self-join over the fact table. Meanwhile, after checking the plans, we found that all cardinality estimates are on track. We therefore cannot observe a plan change for any of these three queries (see Figure 20). Third, even if there are significant errors in cardinality estimates, they may not lead to significant improvement on the query plan. This is the case for Q50, which involves joins over two fact tables and three dimension tables. The execution time is then dominated by the join between the two fact tables. The optimizer's cardinality estimate for that join is indeed inaccurate, and the error was successfully detected by using sampling. As a result, re-optimization did generate different access paths for the rest of the plan. However, the execution time of the plan remains to be dominated by that huge join, and the remaining execution time after that dominant join was done is trivial.

We actually further tweaked Q50 by modifying the predicates over the dimension tables so that the selectivity estimates were changed. By doing this, we did identify cases where re-optimization significantly reduced query execution times. We show one such variant of Q50 (i.e., Q50') in Figure 19. The execution time of Q50' dropped from around 300 seconds to around 130 seconds after re-optimization, a 57% reduction. Tweaking the other queries may also give more opportunities for re-optimization. Another way is to further change the distribution that governs the underlying data generation. We do not pursue these options any further, for it remains debatable that these variants might just be contrived. A more systematic way could be to identify a particular class of queries that the current optimizers do not handle well, figure out how to handle these queries, then move on to find other kinds of queries that are still not handled well. We suspect (and hope) that this is one way optimizers will improve over time — our work on creating the "optimizer torture test" in Section 4 is one step in this direction. We leave the study of other types of "difficult" queries as important direction for future work.

we actually further tried to build indexes on columns that are referenced by the queries. However, the results we obtained are very similar to the ones we present here.

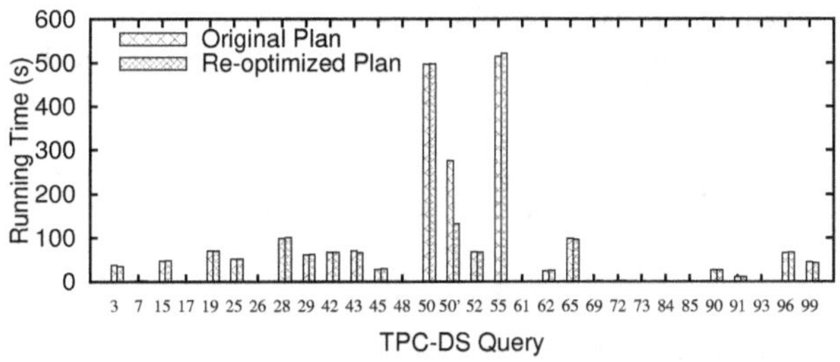

(a) Without calibration of the cost units

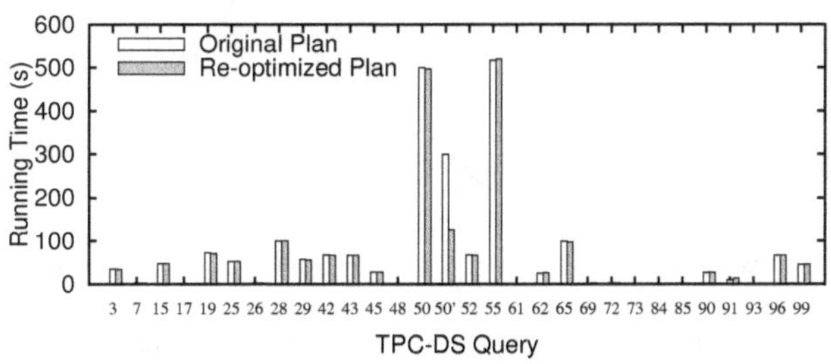

(b) With calibration of the cost units

Figure 19: Query running time over 10GB TPC-DS database.

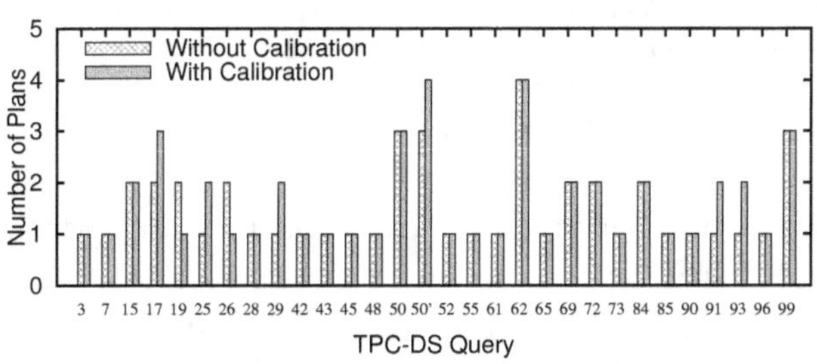

Figure 20: The number of plans generated during re-optimization over 10GB TPC-DS database.

B. ADDITIONAL ANALYSIS

Continuing with our study of the efficiency of the re-optimization procedure in Section 3.3, we now consider two special cases where the optimizer significantly overestimates or underestimates the selectivity of a particular join in the returned optimal plan. We focus our discussion on left-deep join trees. Before we proceed, we need the following assumption of cost functions.

ASSUMPTION 2. *Cost functions used by the optimizer are monotonically non-decreasing functions of input cardinalities.*

We are not aware of a cost function that does not conform to this assumption, though.

B.1 Overestimation Only

Suppose that the error is an overestimate, that is, the actual cardinality is smaller than the one estimated by the optimizer. Let that join operator be O, and let the corresponding subtree rooted at O be $\text{tree}(O)$. Now consider a candidate plan P in the search space, and let $\text{cost}(P)$ be the estimated cost of P. Note that the following property holds:

LEMMA 2. $\text{cost}(P)$ *is affected (i.e., subject to change) only if* $\text{tree}(O)$ *is a subtree of* $\text{tree}(P)$.

Moreover, under Assumption 2, the refined cost estimate $\text{cost}'(P)$ satisfies $\text{cost}'(P) < \text{cost}(P)$ because of the overestimate. Therefore, if we let the set of all such plans P be $\mathcal{P}$, then the next optimal plan picked by the optimizer must be from $\mathcal{P}$. We thus can prove the following result:

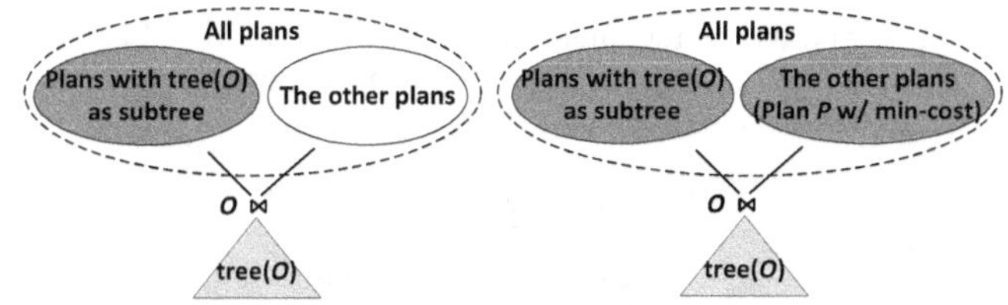

(a) Overestimation Only (b) Underestimation Only

Figure 21: Comparison of the space of candidate optimal plans when local estimation errors are overestimation-only or underestimation-only. Candidate optimal plans are shaded.

THEOREM 7. *Suppose that we only consider left-deep join trees. Let m be the number of joins in the query. If all estimation errors are overestimates, then in the worst case the re-optimization procedure will terminate in at most $m + 1$ steps.*

The proof of Theorem 7 is included in [1]. We emphasize that $m+1$ is a worst-case upper bound. The intuition behind Theorem 7 is that, for left-deep join trees, the validated subtree belonging to the final re-optimized plan can grow by at least one more level (i.e., with one more validated join) in each re-optimization step.

B.2 Underestimation Only

Suppose that, on the other hand, the error is an underestimate, that is, the actual cardinality is larger than the one estimated by the optimizer. Then things become more complicated: not only those plans that contain the subtree rooted at the erroneous node but the plan with the lowest estimated cost in the rest of the search space (which is not affected by the estimation error) also has the potential of being the optimal plan, after the error is corrected (see Figure 21). We next again focus on left-deep trees and present some analysis in such context.

Suppose that the join graph G contains M edges. We partition the join trees based on their first joins, which must be the edges of G. So we have M partitions in total.

Let s_i be the state when a plan returned by the optimizer uses the i-th edge in G ($1 \leq i \leq M$) as its first join. The re-optimization procedure can then be thought of as transitions between these M states, i.e., a Markov chain. Assume that the equilibrium state distribution $\pi(s_i)$ of this Markov chain exists, subject to

$$\sum\nolimits_{i=1}^{M} \pi(s_i) = 1.$$

$\pi(s_i)$ therefore represents the probability that a plan generated in the re-optimization procedure would have its first join in the partition i ($1 \leq i \leq M$). We can then estimate the expected number of steps before the procedure terminates as

$$S = \sum\nolimits_{i=1}^{M} \pi(s_i) \cdot N_i,$$

where N_i is the number of steps/transitions confined in the partition i before termination. Since we only consider left-deep trees, $N_i = N_j$ for $1 \leq i, j \leq M$. As a result, S can be simplified as $S = N_i$. So we are left with estimating N_i.

N_i is the expected number of steps before termination if the transitions (i.e., re-optimization steps) are confined in the partition i. We can divide this process into stages, and each stage contains one more join than the previous stage. If there are m joins, then we will have m stages. In each stage, we go through every plan until we finish, and the average number of plans we considered is S_{K_j} as computed by Equation 1, where K_j is the number of join-trees (actually subtrees) in the stage j ($1 \leq j \leq m$). So

$$S = N_i = \sum_{j=1}^{m} S_{K_j}.$$

As an upper bound, we have $S \leq S_{N/M}$, where N is the total number of different join trees considered by the optimizer, and $S_{N/M}$ is computed by Equation 1. This is obtained by applying Theorem 4 to each partition. $S_{N/M}$ is usually much smaller than S_N, according to Figure 3. Again, we emphasize that the analysis here only targets worst-case expectations, which might be too pessimistic.

C. JOINT/MARGINAL DISTRIBUTIONS

To see why the straightforward approach that first generates a relation $(A_1, ..., A_K, B_1, ..., B_K)$ based on the joint distribution and then splits it into different relation $R_1(A_1, B_1)$, ..., $R_K(A_K, B_K)$ is incorrect, let us consider the following example.

EXAMPLE 3. *Suppose that we need to generate binary values for two attributes A_1 and A_2, with the following joint distribution:*

(1) $p_{00} = \Pr(A_1 = 0, A_2 = 0) = 0.1$;

(2) $p_{01} = \Pr(A_1 = 0, A_2 = 1) = 0$;

(3) $p_{10} = \Pr(A_1 = 1, A_2 = 0) = 0$;

(4) $p_{11} = \Pr(A_1 = 1, A_2 = 1) = 0.9$.

Assume that we generate 10 tuples (A_1, A_2) according to the above distribution. Then we will expect to obtain a multiset of tuples: $\{1 \cdot (0,0), 9 \cdot (1,1)\}$. Here the notation $1 \cdot (0,0)$ means there is one $(0,0)$ in the multiset. If we project the tuples onto A_1 and A_2 (without removing duplicates), we have $A_1 = A_2 = \{1 \cdot 0, 9 \cdot 1\}$. Now what is the joint distribution of (A_1, A_2) once we see such a database? Note that we have no idea about the true *joint distribution that governs the generation of the data, because we are only allowed to see the* marginal *distributions of A_1 and A_2. A natural inference of the joint distribution may be to consider the cross product $A_1 \times A_2$. In this case we have*

$$\begin{aligned} A_1 \times A_2 &= \{1 \cdot 0, 9 \cdot 1\} \times \{1 \cdot 0, 9 \cdot 1\} \\ &= \{1 \cdot (0,0), 9 \cdot (0,1), 9 \cdot (1,0), 81 \cdot (1,1)\}. \end{aligned}$$

Hence, the "observed" joint distribution of A_1 and A_2 is:

(1) $p'_{00} = \Pr'(A_1 = 0, A_2 = 0) = 1/100 = 0.01$;

(2) $p'_{01} = \Pr'(A_1 = 0, A_2 = 1) = 9/100 = 0.09$;

(3) $p'_{10} = \Pr'(A_1 = 1, A_2 = 0) = 9/100 = 0.09$;

(4) $p'_{11} = \Pr'(A_1 = 1, A_2 = 1) = 81/100 = 0.81$.

The "observed" joint distribution is indeed "the" joint distribution when tables are joined. It might be easier to see this if we rewrite the query in Equation 2 as

$$\sigma_{A_1=c_1 \wedge \cdots \wedge A_K=c_K \wedge B_1=B_2 \wedge \cdots \wedge B_{K-1}=B_K}(R_1 \times \cdots \times R_K). \quad (4)$$

The previous example shows that there is information loss when marginalizing out attributes, which is somewhat similar to the notion of lossless/lossy joins in database normalization theory.

D. ANALYSIS OF THE OTT QUERIES

We now compute the query size when Equation 3 holds. Consider a specific query q where the constants in the selection predicates are fixed. Let us compute the cardinality of q, which is equivalent to computing the selectivity of the predicate in Equation 4.

In probabilistic sense, the selectivity s can be interpreted as the chance that a (randomly picked) tuple from $R_1 \times \cdots \times R_K$ making the selection predicate true. That is,

$$s = \Pr(A_1 = c_1, \cdots, A_K = c_K, B_1 = \cdots = B_K).$$

LEMMA 3. *When Equation 3 holds, we have*

$$s = \prod_{k=1}^{K} \frac{1}{n(A_k)}.$$

The proof of Lemma 3 is included in [1]. As a result, the size of the query q is

$$|q| = s \cdot \prod_{k=1}^{K} |R_k| = \prod_{k=1}^{K} \frac{|R_k|}{n(A_k)}.$$

To summarize, we have

$$|q| = \begin{cases} \prod_{k=1}^{K} \frac{|R_k|}{n(A_k)}, & \text{if } c_1 = \cdots = c_K; \\ 0, & \text{otherwise.} \end{cases}$$

Now what will be the query size estimated by the optimizer? Again, let us compute the estimated selectivity $\hat{s}$, assuming that the optimizer knows the exact histograms of the A_k and B_k ($1 \leq k \leq K$). Note that this assumption is stronger than the case in Section 4.2.1, where the optimizer possesses exact histograms only for MCV's. We have the following result:

LEMMA 4. *Suppose that the AVI assumption is used. Assuming that* $\mathrm{Dom}(B_k)$ *is the same for* $1 \leq k \leq K$ *and* $|\mathrm{Dom}(B_k)| = L$, *the estimated selectivity* $\hat{s}$ *is then*

$$\hat{s} = \frac{1}{L^{K-1}} \prod_{k=1}^{K} \frac{1}{n(A_k)}.$$

The proof of Lemma 4 is included in [1]. Hence, the estimated size of the query q is

$$\widehat{|q|} = \hat{s} \cdot \prod_{k=1}^{K} |R_k| = \frac{1}{L^{K-1}} \prod_{k=1}^{K} \frac{|R_k|}{n(A_k)}.$$

Note that this is regardless of if Equation 3 holds or not. In our experiments (Section 5) we further used this property to generate instance OTT queries.

Comparing the expressions of $|q|$ and $\widehat{|q|}$, if we define

$$d = \left| \, |q| - \widehat{|q|} \, \right|,$$

it then follows that

$$d = \begin{cases} \left(1 - \frac{1}{L^{K-1}}\right) \cdot \prod_{k=1}^{K} \frac{|R_k|}{n(A_k)}, & \text{if } c_1 = \cdots = c_K; \\ \frac{1}{L^{K-1}} \cdot \prod_{k=1}^{K} \frac{|R_k|}{n(A_k)}, & \text{otherwise.} \end{cases}$$

Let us further get some intuition about how large d could be by considering the following specific example.

EXAMPLE 4. *For simplicity, assume that $M = |R_k|/n(A_k)$ is the same for $1 \leq k \leq K$. M is then the number of tuples per distinct value of A_k ($1 \leq k \leq K$). In this case,*

$$d = \begin{cases} \left(1 - 1/L^{K-1}\right) \cdot M^K, & \text{if } c_1 = \cdots = c_K; \\ M^K / L^{K-1}, & \text{otherwise.} \end{cases}$$

If $L = 100$ and $M = 100$, it then follows that

$$d = \begin{cases} 100^K - 100, & \text{if } c_1 = \cdots = c_K; \\ 100, & \text{otherwise.} \end{cases}$$

For $K = 4$ (i.e., just 3 joins), $d \approx 10^8$ if it happens to be that $c_1 = \cdots = c_K$. Moreover, if $c_1 = \cdots = c_K$, then $|q| > \widehat{|q|}$. Therefore, the optimizer will significantly underestimate the size of the join (by 10^8). So it is likely that the optimizer would pick an inefficient plan that it thought were efficient.

A Fast Randomized Algorithm for Multi-Objective Query Optimization

Immanuel Trummer and Christoph Koch
{firstname}.{lastname}@epfl.ch
École Polytechnique Fédérale de Lausanne

ABSTRACT

Query plans are compared according to multiple cost metrics in multi-objective query optimization. The goal is to find the set of Pareto plans realizing optimal cost tradeoffs for a given query. So far, only algorithms with exponential complexity in the number of query tables have been proposed for multi-objective query optimization. In this work, we present the first algorithm with polynomial complexity in the query size.

Our algorithm is randomized and iterative. It improves query plans via a multi-objective version of hill climbing that applies multiple transformations in each climbing step for maximal efficiency. Based on a locally optimal plan, we approximate the Pareto plan set within the restricted space of plans with similar join orders. We maintain a cache of Pareto-optimal plans for each potentially useful intermediate result to share partial plans that were discovered in different iterations. We show that each iteration of our algorithm performs in expected polynomial time based on an analysis of the expected path length between a random plan and local optima reached by hill climbing. We experimentally show that our algorithm can optimize queries with hundreds of tables and outperforms other randomized algorithms such as the NSGA-II genetic algorithm over a wide range of scenarios.

Keywords

Query optimization; multi-objective; randomized algorithms

1. INTRODUCTION

Multi-objective query optimization compares query plans according to multiple cost metrics. This is required to model scenarios such as cloud computing where users care about execution time and monetary fees for cloud resources [18]. Another example is approximate query processing where users care about execution time and result precision [1]. The goal of multi-objective query optimization is then to find the set of Pareto-optimal plans, i.e. the query plans realizing optimal cost tradeoffs for a given query. The optimal cost tradeoffs can either be visualized to the user for a manual selection [19] or the best plan can be selected automatically out of that set based on a specification of user preferences (i.e., in the form of cost weights and cost bounds [18]).

So far, exhaustive algorithms [7, 20] and several approximation schemes [18, 19] have been proposed to solve the generic multi-objective query optimization problem. The exhaustive algorithms formally guarantee to find the full Pareto frontier while the approximation schemes formally guarantee to approximate the Pareto frontier with a certain minimum precision. Those quality guarantees come at a cost in terms of optimizer performance: all existing algorithms for multi-objective query optimization have at least exponential time complexity in the number of tables (potentially higher depending on the number of Pareto plans). This means that they cannot be applied for queries with elevated number of tables.

For the traditional query optimization problem with one cost metric, there is a rich body of work proposing heuristics and randomized algorithms [17, 16, 9, 2]. Those algorithms offer no formal quality guarantees on how far the generated plans are from the theoretical optimum but often generate good plans in practice. They have polynomial complexity in the number of tables and can be applied to much larger queries than exhaustive approaches. Up to date, corresponding approaches for multi-objective query optimization are missing entirely (and we will show later that algorithms for traditional query optimization perform poorly for the multi-objective case). In this paper, we close that gap and present the first randomized algorithm for multi-objective query optimization with polynomial time complexity.

Existing algorithms for single- or multi-objective query optimization typically exploit only one out of two fundamental insights about the query optimization problem: dynamic programming based algorithms [14, 11, 18, 19, 20] exploit its decomposability, i.e. the fact that a query optimization problem can be split into smaller sub-problems such that optimal solutions (query plans) for the sub-problems can be combined into optimal solutions for the original problem. Randomized algorithms such as iterative improvement, simulated annealing, or two-phase optimization exploit a certain near-convexity (also called well shape [8]) of the standard cost functions when using suitable neighboring relationships in the query plan space. There is no reason why both insights shouldn't be exploited within the same algorithm and we do so: our algorithm improves plans using a multi-objective generalization of hill climbing, thereby exploiting near-convexity. It also maintains a plan cache storing partial

SIGMOD'16, June 26-July 01, 2016, San Francisco, CA, USA

DOI: http://dx.doi.org/10.1145/2882903.2882927

Pareto-optimal plans generating potentially useful intermediate results. Newly generated plans are decomposed and dominated sub-plans are replaced by partial plans from the cache. Therefore we exploit decomposability as well.

Our algorithm is iterative and performs the following steps in each iteration. First, a query plan is randomly generated. Second, the plan is improved using local search until a local optimum is reached. Third, based on the locally optimal plan we restrict the plan space to plans that are similar in certain aspects (we provide details in the following paragraphs). We approximate the Pareto plan set within that restricted plan space. For that approximation, we might reuse partial plans that were generated in prior iterations if they realize a better cost tradeoff than the corresponding sub-plans of the locally optimal plan.

For the second step, we use a multi-objective version of hill climbing that exploits several properties of the query optimization problem to reduce time complexity significantly compared to a naive version. First, we exploit the multi-objective principle of optimality for query optimization [7] stating that replacing a sub-plan by another sub-plan whose cost is not Pareto-optimal cannot improve the cost of the entire plan. This allows to quickly discard local mutations that will not improve the overall plan. Second, we exploit that query plans can be recursively decomposed into sub-plans for which local search can be applied independently. This allows to apply many beneficial mutations simultaneously in different parts of the query tree and therefore reduces the number of complete query plans that need to be generated on the path from the random plan to a local optimum. Those optimizations reduce the time complexity comparing with a naive version and we found them to be critical to achieve good optimizer performance.

For the third step, we restrict the plan space to plans that generate a similar set of intermediate results as the locally optimal plan that results from the second step. We consider plans that use the same join order as the locally optimal plan but different operator combinations. Also, we consider the possibility to replace sub-plans by plans from a cache (those plans can use a different join order than the locally optimal plan). The cache stores non-dominated partial plans for each potentially useful intermediate result we encountered during optimization so far. Finding the full Pareto plan set even within the restricted plan space may lead to prohibitive computational cost (the number of Pareto plans within the restricted space may grow exponentially in the number of query tables). We therefore approximate the Pareto plan set by a subset of plans (whose size grows polynomially in the number of query tables) realizing representative cost tradeoffs. The precision of that approximation is slowly refined over the iterations. This enables our algorithm to quickly find a coarse-grained approximation of the full Pareto plan set for the given query; at the same time, as we refine precision, the approximation converges to the real Pareto set.

The insights underlying the design of our algorithm are the following: on the one hand, we observe that the same join order can often realize many Pareto-optimal cost tradeoffs when using different operator configurations. This is why we approximate in the third step a Pareto frontier based on a restricted set of join orders. On the other hand, the full Pareto frontier cannot be covered using only one join order. This is why we generate new plans and join orders in each iteration.

We analyze our randomized algorithm experimentally, using different cost metrics, query graph structures, and query sizes. We compare against dynamic programming based approximation schemes that were previously proposed for multi-objective query optimization. While approximation schemes are preferable for small queries, we show that only randomized algorithms can handle larger query sizes. We evaluate our algorithm with queries joining up to 100 tables considering an unconstrained bushy plan space. Even in case of one cost metric, dynamic programming based approaches do not scale to such search space sizes. We also compare our algorithm against other randomized algorithms: the non-dominated sort genetic algorithm 2 (NSGA-II) [6] is a very popular multi-objective optimization algorithm for the number of plan cost metrics that we consider in our experiments. Genetic algorithms have been very successful for traditional query optimization [2] so a comparison against NSGA-II (using the combination and mutation operators proposed for traditional query optimization) seems interesting. We also compare our algorithm against other multi-objective generalizations of well known randomized algorithms for traditional query optimization such as iterative improvement, simulated annealing, and two-phase optimization [16]. Our randomized algorithm outperforms all competitors significantly, showing that the combination of local search with plan decomposition is powerful.

We analyze the time complexity of our algorithm and show that each iteration has expected polynomial complexity. Our analysis includes in particular a study of the expected path length from a random plan to the nearest local optimum. Based on a simple statistical model of plan cost distributions, we can show that the expected path length grows at most linearly in the number of query tables.

In summary, the original scientific contributions of this paper are the following:

- We present the first polynomial time algorithm for multi-objective query optimization: a randomized algorithm that exploits several properties of the query optimization problem.
- We analyze that algorithm formally, showing that each iteration (resulting in at least one query plan) has polynomial complexity in the number of query tables.
- We evaluate our algorithm experimentally against previously published approximation schemes for multi-objective query optimization and several randomized algorithms. We show that our algorithm outperforms the other algorithms over a wide range of scenarios.

The remainder of this paper is organized as follows. We give an overview of related work in Section 2. In Section 3, we introduce the formal model used in pseudo-code and formal analysis. We introduce the first randomized algorithm for multi-objective query optimization in Section 4 and analyze its complexity in Section 5. In Section 6, we experimentally evaluate our algorithm in comparison with several baselines.

2. RELATED WORK

Most work in query optimization treats the single-objective case, meaning that query plans are compared according to only one cost metric (usually execution time) [2, 3, 14, 16,

17, 21]. This problem model is however often insufficient: in a cloud scenario, users might be able to reduce query execution time when willing to pay more money for renting additional resources from the cloud provider [10]. On systems that process multiple queries concurrently, the tradeoff between the amount of dedicated system resources and query execution time needs to be considered [18]. In those and other scenarios, query optimization becomes a multi-objective optimization problem.

Query optimization algorithms that have been designed for the case of one cost metric cannot be applied to the multi-objective case. They return only one optimal plan while the goal in multi-objective query optimization is usually to find a set of Pareto-optimal plans [12, 20, 19]. This allows in particular to let users choose their preferred cost tradeoff out of a visualization of the available tradeoffs [19]. We will use several variations of single-objective randomized query optimization algorithms as baselines for our experiments. Note that mapping multi-objective optimization into a single-objective optimization problem using a weighted sum over different cost metrics with varying weights will not yield the Pareto frontier but at most a subset of it (the convex hull).

One exhaustive optimization algorithm and multiple approximation schemes have been proposed for multi-objective query optimization [7, 18, 19, 20]. They are based on dynamic programming and have all exponential complexity in the number of query tables. This means that they do not scale to large query sizes. In traditional single-objective optimization, randomized algorithms and heuristics are used for query sizes that cannot be handled by exhaustive approaches. No equivalent is currently available for multi-objective query optimization. In this work, we close that gap and propose the first polynomial time heuristic for multi-objective query optimization.

One of the most popular randomized algorithms for single-objective query optimization is the genetic algorithm [2]. Also, multi-objective genetic algorithm variants are very popular for multi-objective optimization in general [4]. It seems therefore natural to use the crossover and mutation operators that have been proposed for traditional query optimization within a multi-objective genetic algorithm variant. We implemented a version of the widely used non-dominated sort genetic algorithm II (NSGA-II) [6] for our experiments.

We focus in this paper on query optimization in the traditional sense, i.e. the search space is the set of available join orders and the selection of scan and join operators. This distinguishes our work for instance from work on multi-objective optimization of workflows [10, 15] which does not consider alternative join orders. Prior work by Papadimitriou and Yannakakis [12] also aims at optimizing operator selections for a fixed join order and addresses therefore a different problem than we do. We focus on generic multi-objective query optimization as defined in our prior work [18] and our algorithm is not bound to specific combinations of cost metrics or scenarios such as precision-time [1] or energy-time tradeoffs [22].

3. FORMAL MODEL

A query q is modeled as a set of tables that need to be joined. This query model is simplistic but often used in query optimization [17, 7, 18]; extending a query optimization algorithm that optimizes queries represented as table sets to more complex query models is standard [14]. A query plan p for a query q specifies how the data described by the query can be generated by a series of scan and join operations. The plan describes the join order and the operator implementation used for each scan and join. We write ScanPlan(q, op) to denote a plan scanning the single table q ($|q| = 1$) using scan operator op. We write JoinPlan$(outer, inner, op)$ to denote a join plan that joins the results produced by an outer plan *outer* with the results produced by an inner plan *inner* using join operator *op*.

We denote by $p.rel$ the set of tables joined by a plan p. It is ScanPlan$(q, op).rel = q$ and JoinPlan$(po, pi, op).rel = po.rel \cup pi.rel$. For join plans we denote by $p.outer$ the outer plan and by $p.inner$ the inner plan. The property $p.isJoin$ yields **true** for join plans (where $|p.rel| > 1$) and **false** for scan plans (where $|p.rel| = 1$).

We compare query plans according to their execution cost. We consider multiple cost metrics that might for instance include monetary fees (in a cloud scenario [10]), energy consumption [22], or various metrics of system resource consumption such as the number of used cores or the amount of consumed buffer space [18] in addition to execution time. We consider cost metrics in the following, meaning that a lower value is preferable. It is straight forward to transform a quality metric on query plans such as result precision [1] into a cost metric (e.g., result precision can be transformed into the precision loss cost metric as shown in our prior work [18]). Hence we study only cost metrics in the following without restriction of generality.

We denote by $p.cost \in \mathbb{R}^l$ the cost vector associated with a query plan. Each vector component represents cost according to a different cost metric out of l cost metrics. We focus on optimization in this paper and assume that cost models for all considered cost metrics are available. The algorithms that we discuss in this paper are generic and can be applied to a broad set of plan cost metrics.

In the special case of one cost metric, we say that plan p_1 is better than plan p_2 if the cost of p_1 is lower. Pareto-dominance is the generalization to multiple cost metrics. In case of multiple cost metrics, we say that plan p_1 dominates p_2, written $p_1 \preceq p_2$ if p_1 has lower or equivalent cost to p_2 according to each considered cost metric. We say that p_1 strictly dominates p_2, written $p_1 \prec p_2$, if $p_1 \preceq p_2$ and $p_1.cost \neq p_2.cost$, meaning that p_1 has lower or equivalent cost than p_2 according to each metric and lower cost in at least one metric. We apply the same terms and notations to cost vectors in general, e.g. we write $c_1 \preceq c_2$ for two cost vectors c_1 and c_2 to express that there is no cost metric for which c_1 contains a higher cost value than c_2.

Considering a set P of alternative plans generating the same results, we call each plan $p \in P$ Pareto-optimal if there is no other plan $\widetilde{p} \in P$ that strictly dominates p. For a given query, the Pareto plan set is the set of plans for q that are Pareto-optimal within the set of all possible query plans for q. The full Pareto plan set is often too large to be calculated in practice. This is why we rather aim at approximating the Pareto plan set. The following definitions are necessary to establish a measure of how well a given plan set approximates the real Pareto set.

A plan p_1 approximately dominates a plan p_2 with approximation factor $\alpha \geq 1$, written $p_1 \preceq_\alpha p_2$, if $p_1.cost \preceq \alpha \cdot p_2.cost$. This means that the cost of p_1 is not higher than the cost of p_2 by more than factor α according to each

```
// Returns approximate Pareto plan set for query q
function RandomMOQO(q)
    // Initialize partial plan cache and iteration counter
    P ← ∅
    i ← 1
    // Refine frontier approximation until timeout
    while No Timeout do
        // Generate random bushy query plan
        plan ←RandomPlan(q)
        // Improve plan via fast local search
        optPlan ←ParetoClimb(plan)
        // Approximate Pareto frontier
        P ←ApproximateFrontiers(optPlan, P, i)
        i ← i + 1
    end while
    return P[q]
end function
```

Algorithm 1: Main function.

cost metric. Considering a set P of plans, an α-approximate Pareto plan set $P_\alpha \subseteq P$ is a subset of P such that $\forall p \in P \exists \widetilde{p} \in P_\alpha : \widetilde{p} \preceq_\alpha p$, i.e. for each plan p in the full set there is a plan in the subset that approximately dominates p. The (approximate) Pareto frontier are the cost vectors of the plans in the (approximate) Pareto set.

The goal of multi-objective query optimization is to find α-approximate Pareto plan sets for a given input query q. We compare different incremental optimization algorithms in terms of the α values (i.e., how well the plan set generated by those algorithms approximates the real Pareto set) that they produce after certain amounts of optimization time.

4. ALGORITHM DESCRIPTION

We describe a randomized algorithm for multi-objective query optimization. Section 4.1 describes the main function, the following two subsections describe sub-functions. Section 4.2 describes a multi-objective hill climbing variant that executes multiple plan transformations in one step for maximal efficiency. Section 4.3 describes how we generate a local Pareto frontier approximation for a given join order, using non-dominated partial plans from a plan cache and trying out different operator configurations.

4.1 Overview

Algorithm 1 is the main function of our optimization algorithm. The input is a query q and the output a set of query plans that approximate the Pareto plan set for q.

Our algorithm is iterative and refines the approximation of the Pareto frontier in each iteration. Each iteration consists of three principal steps: a random query plan is generated (local variable *plan* in the pseudo-code), it is improved via a multi-objective version of hill climbing, and afterwards the improved plan (local variable *optPlan*) is used as base to generate a local Pareto frontier approximation. For the latter step, a plan cache (local variable P in the pseudo-code) is used that stores for each intermediate result (i.e., a subset $s \subseteq q$ of joined tables) that we encountered so far a set of non-dominated partial plans. For the locally optimal plan resulting from hill climbing, we consider plans that can be obtained by varying the operator configurations but not the join order. In addition, we consider replacing sub-plans by non-dominated partial plans from the plan cache.

Within that restricted plan space, we do not search for the entire Pareto frontier as its size can be exponential in the number of query tables. Instead, we search for an approximation that has guaranteed polynomial size in the number of query tables. The precision of those approximations is refined with increasing number of iterations: our goal is to obtain a coarse-grained approximation of the entire Pareto frontier quickly so we start with a coarse approximation precision to quickly explore a large number of join orders. In later iterations, the precision is refined to allow to better exploit the set of join orders that was discovered so far. As the frontier approximation precision depends on the iteration number, function ApproximateFrontiers obtains the iteration counter i as input parameter in addition to the locally optimal plan and the plan cache. All non-dominated partial plans generated during the frontier approximation are inserted into the plan cache P and might be reused in following iterations.

After the timeout, the result plan set is contained in the plan cache and associated with table set q, the entire query table set (we use the array notation $P[q]$ to denote the set of cached Pareto plans that join table set q). Note that we can easily use different termination conditions than a timeout. In particular, in case of interactive query optimization where users choose an execution plan based on a visualization of available cost tradeoffs [19], optimization ends once the user selects a query plan for execution from the set of plans generated so far.

Our algorithm exploits two ideas that have been very successful in traditional query optimization but are typically used in separate algorithms: our algorithm exploits a certain near-convexity of typical plan cost functions [8] by using local search (function ParetoClimb) to improve query plans. It exploits however at the same time that the query optimization problem can be decomposed into sub-problems, meaning that Pareto-optimal plans joining table subsets can be combined into Pareto-optimal plans joining larger table sets. It is based on the insight that the same join order often allows to construct multiple Pareto-optimal cost tradeoffs by varying operator implementations but takes into account at the same time that not all optimal cost tradeoffs can be found considering only one join order. We describe the two principal sub-functions of Algorithm 1, function ParetoClimb and function ApproximateFrontiers, in more detail in the following subsections.

Note finally that the algorithm can easily be adapted to consider different join order spaces (e.g., left-deep plans) by exchanging the random plan generation method and the set of considered local transformations.

4.2 Pareto Climbing

Algorithm 2 shows the pseudo-code of function ParetoClimb (and of several auxiliary functions) that is used by Algorithm 1 to improve query plans via local search. The input is a query plan p to improve and the output is a locally optimal query plan that was reached from the input plan using a series of local transformations.

Hill climbing was already used in traditional query optimization [17] but our hill climbing variant differs from the traditional version in several aspects that are discussed in the following. A first obvious difference is that we consider multiple cost metrics on query plans while traditional query optimization considers only execution time. In case of one

```
// Plan p1 is better than p2 if it produces the same
// data format as p2 and has dominant cost.
function BETTER(p1, p2)
    return SAMEOUTPUT(p1, p2) ∧ (p1 ≺ p2)
end function
// Keeps one Pareto plan per output format.
function PRUNE(plans, newPlan)
    if ∄p ∈ plans : BETTER(p, newPlan) then
        plans ← {p ∈ plans | ¬BETTER(newPlan, p)}
        plans ← plans ∪ {newPlan}
    end if
    return plans
end function
// Improve plan p by parallel local transformations
function PARETOSTEP(p)
    // Initialize optimal mutations of this plan
    pPareto ← ∅
    if p.isJoin then
        // Improve sub-plans by recursive calls
        outerPareto ← PARETOSTEP(p.outer)
        innerPareto ← PARETOSTEP(p.inner)
        // Iterate over all improved sub-plan pairs
        for outer ∈ outerPareto do
            for inner ∈ innerPareto do
                p.outer ← outer
                p.inner ← inner
                // Mutations for specific sub-plan pair
                for mutated ∈ MUTATIONS(p) do
                    pPareto ← PRUNE(pPareto, mutated)
                end for
            end for
        end for
    else
        // p is single-table scan
        for mutated ∈ MUTATIONS(p) do
            pPareto ← PRUNE(pPareto, mutated)
        end for
    end if
    return pPareto
end function
// Climbs until plan p cannot be improved further.
function PARETOCLIMB(p)
    improving ← true
    while improving do
        improving ← false
        mutations ← PARETOSTEP(p)
        if pm ∈ mutations : pm ≺ p then
            p ← pm
            improving ← true
        end if
    end while
    return p
end function
```

Algorithm 2: Fast multi-objective hill climbing performing mutations in independent plan sub-trees simultaneously.

cost metric, hill climbing moves from one plan to a neighbor plan (i.e., a plan that can be reached via a local transformation [16]) if the neighbor plan has lower cost than the first one. Our multi-objective version moves from a first plan to a neighbor if the neighbor strictly dominates the first one in the Pareto sense, i.e. the second plan has lower or equivalent cost according to all metrics and lower cost according to at least one.

In principle, there can be multiple neighbors that strictly dominate the start plan while different neighbors do not necessarily dominate each other. In such cases, it cannot be determined which neighbor is the best one to move to and all neighbors might be required for the full Pareto frontier. In order to avoid a combinatorial explosion, we still chose to arbitrarily select one neighbor that strictly dominates the start plan instead of opening different path branches during the climb. The goal of function PARETOCLIMB within Algorithm 1 is to find one good plan while function APPROXIMATEFRONTIERS (which is discussed in the next subsection) will take care of exploring alternative cost tradeoffs.

Unlike most prior hill climbing variants used for traditional query optimization [17, 16], we chose to exhaustively explore all neighbor plans in each step of the climb instead of randomly sampling a subset of neighbors. We initially experimented with random sampling of neighbor plans which led however to poor performance. We believe that this is due to the fact that dominating neighbors become more and more sparse as the number of considered cost metrics grows. Using the simple statistical model that we introduce in Section 5, the probability of finding a dominating neighbor decreases exponentially in the number of cost metrics. Furthermore, sampling introduces overhead and makes it harder if not impossible to use the techniques for complexity reduction that we describe next.

Reducing the time complexity of local search as much as possible is crucial as function PARETOCLIMB is called in each iteration of Algorithm 1. We exploit properties of the multi-objective query optimization problem in order to make our implementation of local search much more efficient than a naive implementation. A naive hill climbing algorithm iterates the following steps until a local optimum is reached: in each step, it traverses all nodes of the current query plan tree and applies to each node a fixed set of local mutations. For each mutation and plan node, a new complete neighbor plan is created and its cost is calculated. Based on that cost, the next plan is selected among the neighbors. This naive approach has per step quadratic complexity in the number of plan nodes (which is linear in the number of query tables).

For a first improvement, we can exploit the principle of optimality for multi-objective query optimization [7]. After applying a local transformation to one specific node in the query tree, it is not always necessary to calculate the cost of the completed plan (at the tree root) in order to determine whether that mutation reduces the plan cost. Due to the principle of optimality, improving a sub-plan cannot worsen the entire plan (we assume for the current discussion that all alternative plans produce the same data representation, neglecting for instance the impact of interesting orders [14]). In many cases, reducing the cost of a sub-plan even guarantees that the cost of the overall plan decreases as well[1]. This means that we can at least exclude that a certain mutation reduces the cost of the entire plan if it

[1]This is guaranteed for cost metrics such as energy consumption, monetary cost, precision loss, and execution time when considering plans without parallel branches [18] where the cost of a plan is calculated as weighted sum or product over the cost of its sub-plans. It might not hold in special cases (e.g., when replacing a sub-plan that is not on the critical path in a parallel execution scenario by a faster one).

worsens the cost of the sub-plan to which it was applied. As the cost of the sub-plan can be recalculated in constant time (when treating the number of cost metrics as a constant as it is common in multi-objective query optimization [18]), this simple optimization already reduces the complexity per step from quadratic in the number of tables to linear whenever the chances that a local cost improvement does not yield a global improvement are negligible.

While the last optimization reduces the complexity per climbing step, the optimization discussed next tends to reduce the number of steps required to reach the nearest local optimum. Query plans are represented as trees and we can simultaneously apply mutations in independent sub-trees; it is not necessary to generate complete query trees after each single mutation which is what the naive hill climbing variant does. If we reduce the cost of several sub-trees simultaneously then the cost of the entire plan cannot worsen either due to the principle of optimality. Applying multiple beneficial transformations in different parts of the query tree simultaneously reduces the number of completed query trees that are created on the way to the local optimum.

Note that all discussed optimizations are also useful to improve the efficiency of local search for traditional query optimization with one cost metric. Local search has already been used for traditional query optimization but we were not able to find any discussion of the aforementioned issues in the literature while they have significant impact on the performance (the second optimization alone reduced the average time for reaching local optima from randomly selected plans by over one order of magnitude for queries with 50 tables in a preliminary benchmark).

Algorithm 2 integrates all of the aforementioned optimizations. Function PARETOCLIMB performs plan transformations until the plan cannot be improved anymore, i.e. there is no neighbor plan with dominant cost. Function PARETOSTEP realizes one transformation step. It may return multiple Pareto-optimal plan mutations that produce data in different representations (e.g., materialized versus non-materialized). We must do so since sub-plans producing different data representations cannot be compared as the data representation can influence the cost (or applicability) of other operations higher-up in the plan tree. We assume that the standard mutations for bushy query plans [16] are considered for each node in the plan tree. Function PARETOSTEP might however mutate multiple nodes in the tree during one call: when treating join plans then the outer and the inner sub-plan are both replaced by dominant mutations via a recursive call. We try out each combination of potentially improved sub-plans and try all local transformations for each combination. The resulting plans are pruned such that only one non-dominated plan is kept for each possible output data representation. Function BETTER is used during pruning to compare query plans and returns **true** if and only if a first plan produces the same output data representation as a second (tested using function SAMEOUTPUT) and the cost vector of the first plan strictly dominates the one of the second.

The following example illustrates how Algorithm 2 works.

EXAMPLE 1. *We assume for simplicity that only one plan cost metric is considered, that we have only one scan and join operator implementation such that only join order matters, and that the only mutation is the exchange of outer and inner join operands. We invoke function* PARETOCLIMB *on an initial query plan* $(S \bowtie T) \bowtie (R \bowtie U)$. *Function* PARETOCLIMB *invokes function* PARETOSTEP *to improve the initial plan. The root of the initial query plan is a join between* $(S \bowtie T)$ *and* $(R \bowtie U)$. *Function* PARETOSTEP *tries to improve the two operands of that join via recursive calls before considering mutations at the plan root. Hence one instance of* PARETOSTEP *is invoked to improve the outer operand* $(S \bowtie T)$ *and another instance is invoked to improve the inner operand* $(R \bowtie U)$. *The instance of function* PARETOSTEP *treating* $(S \bowtie T)$ *spawns new instances for improving the two join operands* S *and* T. *As we consider no scan operator mutations here, those invocations do not have any effect. After trying to improve* S *and* T, *the instance treating* $(S \bowtie T)$ *tries the mutation* $(T \bowtie S)$. *Assume that this mutation reduces cost. Then the improved sub-plan* $(T \bowtie S)$ *will be returned to the instance of function* PARETOSTEP *treating the initial plan. Assume that the sub-plan* $(R \bowtie U)$ *cannot be improved by exchanging outer and inner join operand. Then the top-level instance of function* PARETOSTEP *will try the mutation* $(R \bowtie U) \bowtie (T \bowtie S)$ *and compare its execution cost to the cost of* $(T \bowtie S) \bowtie (R \bowtie U)$. *The cheaper plan is returned to function* PARETOCLIMB *which detects that the initial plan has been improved. This function performs another iteration of the main loop as changing the initial plan can in principle enable new transformations that yield further improvements. This is not possible in the restricted setting of our example and hence function* PARETOCLIMB *terminates after two iterations.*

4.3 Frontier Approximation

The goal of Pareto climbing is to find one plan that is at least locally Pareto-optimal. Having such a plan, it is often possible to obtain alternative optimal cost tradeoffs by varying the operator implementations while reusing the same join order[2]. We exploit that fact in function APPROXIMATEFRONTIERS whose pseudo-code is shown in Algorithm 3.

Function APPROXIMATEFRONTIERS obtains a query plan p whose join order it exploits, the plan cache P mapping intermediate results to non-dominated plans generating them, and the iteration counter i (counting iterations of the main loop in Algorithm 1) as input. The output is an updated plan cache in which the non-dominated plans generated in the current invocation have been inserted for the corresponding intermediate results.

Function APPROXIMATEFRONTIERS starts by choosing the approximation factor α which depends on the iteration number i. A higher approximation factor reduces the time required for approximation but a lower approximation factor yields a more fine-grained approximation. We will see in Section 5 that APPROXIMATEFRONTIERS has dominant time complexity within each iteration so a careful choice of the approximation factor is crucial. Multi-objective query op-

[2]More precisely, this is possible when choosing an appropriate formalization of the plan space: when considering tradeoffs between buffer space consumption and execution time, we can for instance introduce different versions of the standard join operators that work with different amounts of buffer space. When considering tradeoffs between result precision and execution time in approximate query processing, we might introduce different scan operator versions associated with different sample densities. In a cloud scenario, we can introduce operator versions that are associated with different degrees of parallelism, allowing to trade monetary cost for execution time.

```
// Checks if plan p1 is significantly better than p2
// using coarsening factor α for cost comparison.
function SigBetter(p1, p2, α)
    return SameOutput(p1, p2) ∧ p1 ⪯α p2
end function
// Returns an α-approximate Pareto frontier.
function Prune(plans, newP, α)
    // Can we approximate the cost of the new plan?
    if ∄p ∈ plans :SigBetter(p, newP, α) then
        plans ← {p ∈ plans | ¬SigBetter(newP, p, 1)}
        plans ← plans ∪ {newP}
    end if
    return plans
end function
// Approximates the Pareto frontier for each
// intermediate result that appears in plan p,
// using partial plans from the plan cache P.
// The precision depends on the iteration count i.
function ApproximateFrontiers(p, P, i)
    // Calculate target approximation precision
    α ← 25 · 0.99^⌊i/25⌋
    if p.isJoin then
        // Approximate outer and inner plan frontiers
        P ←ApproximateFrontiers(p.outer, P, i)
        P ←ApproximateFrontiers(p.inner, P, i)
        // Iterate over outer Pareto plans
        for outer ← P[p.outer.rel] do
            // Iterate over inner Pareto plans
            for inner ← P[p.inner.rel] do
                // Iterate over applicable join operators
                for op ∈JoinOps(outer, inner) do
                    // Generate new plan and prune
                    np ←JoinPlan(outer, inner, op)
                    P[p.rel] ←Prune(P[p.rel], np, α)
                end for
            end for
        end for
    else
        // Iterate over applicable scan operators
        for op ∈ScanOps(p.rel) do
            np ←ScanPlan(p.rel, op)
            P[p.rel] ←Prune(P[p.rel], np, α)
        end for
    end if
    // Return updated plan cache
    return P
end function
```

Algorithm 3: Approximating the Pareto frontiers of all intermediate results occuring within given plan.

timization can be an interactive process in which alternative cost tradeoffs are visualized to the user such that he can make his choice [19]. Especially in such scenarios, it is beneficial to rather obtain a coarse-grained approximation of the entire Pareto frontier quickly than to obtain a very fine-grained approximation of only a small part of it. As approximating the entire Pareto frontier requires in general considering many join orders (see our remark at the end of this subsection), we do not want to spend too much time at the beginning exploiting one single join order. For that reason we start with a coarse-grained approximation factor that is reduced as iterations progress. We have tried different formulas for choosing α and the formula given in the pseudo-code worked best for a broad range of scenarios.

Having chosen the approximation precision, the function approximates the Pareto frontier for scan plans by trying out all available scan operators on the given table. For join plans, a frontier is first generated for the outer and inner operand using recursive calls (so we traverse the query plan tree in post-order). After that, we consider each possible pair of a plan from the outer frontier with a plan from the inner frontier and each applicable join operator and generate one new plan for each such combination. Newly generated plans are pruned again but the definition of the pruning function differs from the one we used in Algorithm 2. For the same output data properties, the pruning function in Algorithm 3 might now keep multiple plans that realize different optimal cost tradeoffs. However, in contrast to the previous pruning variant, new plans are only inserted if their cost cannot be approximated by any of the plans already in the pruned plan set. We will see in Section 5 that this pruning function guarantees that the number of plans stored for a single table set is bounded by a polynomial in the number of query tables.

Note that function ApproximateFrontiers does not only try different operator combinations for a given join order. Instead, we consider all non-dominated plans that are cached for the intermediate results generated by the input plan p. The plans we consider might have been inserted into the plan cache in prior iterations of the main loop and might therefore use different join orders. The plan cache is our mean of sharing information across different iterations of the main loop. As iterations continue, the content of the plan cache will more and more resemble the set of partial plans that is generated by dynamic programming based approximation schemes proposed for multi-objective query optimization [18, 19]. However, instead of approximating the frontier for each possible intermediate result (implying exponential complexity), we only treat table sets that are used by locally Pareto-optimal plans.

Note finally that it is in general not possible to obtain all Pareto optimal query plans by varying operators for a fixed join order. Considering again the tradeoff between buffer space and execution time, a left-deep plan using pipelining might for instance minimize execution time while a non-pipelined bushy plan achieves the lowest buffer footprint. Or in case of approximate query processing, different tradeoffs between result precision and execution time can be achieved by varying the sample size generated by scan operators so the output size for each table and hence the optimal join order depends on the operator configurations. This means that we need to consider different join orders in order to obtain the full Pareto set; we cannot decompose query optimization into join order selection followed by operator selection. Our algorithm respects that fact.

5. COMPLEXITY ANALYSIS

We analyze the time and space complexity of the algorithm presented in Section 4. We call that algorithm short RMQ for randomized multi-objective query optimizer.

We denote by n the number of query tables to be joined. The number of cost metrics according to which query plans are compared is specified by l. Similar to prior work [18, 19], we treat n as a variable and l as a constant: users choose the query size but the set of relevant cost metrics is usually determined by the query processing context. As in prior work [7], we simplify the following formulas by assuming only one join operator while the generalization is straightforward. We also neglect interesting orders such that query plans joining the same tables are only compared according to their cost vectors.

We analyze the time complexity of one iteration. Each iteration consists of three steps (random plan generation, local search, and frontier approximation); we analyze the complexity of each of those steps in the following. Random plan sampling (function RANDOMPLAN in Algorithm 1) can be implemented with linear complexity as shown by the following lemma.

LEMMA 1. *Function* RANDOMPLAN *executes in* $O(n)$ *time.*

PROOF. Query plans are labeled binary trees whose leaf nodes represent input tables. Quiroz shows how to generate binary trees in $O(n)$ [13]. Labels representing input tables and operators can be selected in $O(n)$ as well. Estimating the cost of a query plan according to all cost metrics is in $O(ln) = O(n)$ time (as l is a constant). □

Next we analyze the complexity of local search, realized by function PARETOCLIMB in Algorithm 1. We first analyze the complexity of function PARETOSTEP realizing a single step on the path to the next local optimum.

LEMMA 2. *Function* PARETOSTEP *executes in* $O(n)$ *time.*

PROOF. We apply a constant number of mutations at each of the $O(n)$ plan nodes. We assume that plans are only pruned based on their cost values such that each instance of function PARETOSTEP returns only one non-dominated plan. Plan comparisons take $O(l) = O(1)$ time which leads to the postulated complexity. □

The expected time complexity of local search depends of course on the number of steps required to reach the next local Pareto optimum (a plan that is not dominated by any neighbor). We analyze the expected path length based on a simple statistical model in the following: we model the cost of a random plan according to one cost metric as random variable and assume that the random cost variables associated with different metrics are independent from each other. This assumption is simplifying but standard in the analysis of multi-objective query optimization algorithms [7, 20].

LEMMA 3. *The probability that a randomly selected plan dominates another is* $(1/2)^l$.

PROOF. The probability that a randomly selected plan dominates another plan according to one single cost metric is 1/2. Assuming independence between different cost metrics, the probability that a random plan dominates another one according to all l cost metrics is $(1/2)^l$. □

LEMMA 4. *The probability that none of n plans dominates all plans in a plan set of cardinality i is* $(1-(1/2)^{li})^n$.

PROOF. The probability that one plan dominates another is $(1/2)^l$ according to Lemma 3. The probability that one plan dominates all of i other plans is $(1/2)^{li}$, assuming independence between the dominance probabilities between different plan pairs. The probability that a plan does not dominate all of i other plans is $1-(1/2)^{li}$. The probability that none of n plans dominates all of i plans is $(1-(1/2)^{li})^n$. □

We denote by $u(n,i) = (1-(1/2)^{li})^n$ the probability that none of n plans dominates all i plans. We simplify in the following assuming that each plan has exactly n neighbors.

THEOREM 1. *The expected number of plans visited by the hill climbing algorithm until finding a local Pareto optimum is* $\sum_{i=1..\infty} i \cdot u(n,i) \cdot \prod_{j=1..i-1}(1-u(n,j))$.

PROOF. Our hill climbing algorithm visits a sequence of plans such that each plan is a neighbor of its predecessor and dominates its predecessor. Pareto dominance is a transitive relation and hence, as each plan dominates its immediate predecessor, each plan dominates all its predecessors. Then the probability of one additional step corresponds to the probability that at least one of the neighbors of the current plan dominates all plans encountered on the path so far. The probability that a local optimum is reached after i plan nodes is the probability that none of the n neighbors of the i-th plan dominates all i plans on the path which is $u(n,i)$. The a-priori probability for visiting i plans in total is then $u(n,i) \cdot \prod_{j=1..i-1}(1-u(n,j))$. The expected number of visited plans is $\sum_{i=1..\infty} i \cdot u(n,i) \cdot \prod_{j=1..i-1}(1-u(n,j))$. □

We bound the formula given by Theorem 1.

THEOREM 2. *The expected path length from a random plan to the next local Pareto optimum is in* $O(n)$.

PROOF. Assume that the hill climbing algorithm encounters at least n plans on its path to the local Pareto optimum. We can write the expected number of additional steps as $\sum_{i=0..\infty} i \cdot u(n,n+i) \cdot \prod_{j=0..i-1}(1-u(n,j+n))$. Note that each additional step requires that one of the neighbors dominates at least n plans on the path. Since $u(n,j) \leq 1$, we can upper-bound the additional steps by $\sum_{i=0..\infty} i \cdot \prod_{j=0..i-1}(1-u(n,j+n))$. Since $(1-u(n,j))$ is anti-monotone in j, we can upper-bound that expression by $\sum_{i=0..\infty} i \cdot (1-u(n,n))^i$. This expression contains the first derivative of the infinite geometric series and we obtain $(1-u(n,n))/(1-(1-u(n,n)))^2 \leq 1/(1-(1-u(n,n)))^2 = 1/u(n,n)^2$ for the additional steps. We study how quickly that expression grows in n. It is $1/u(n,n)^2 = 1/(1-(1/2)^{ln})^{2n} \leq 1/(1-(1/2)^n)^{2n} \in O((1/(1-1/n)^n)^2) = O((1/e)^2) = O(1)$. The expected number of additional steps after n steps is a constant. □

We finally calculated the expected time complexity of local search. Note that we make the pessimistic assumption that only one mutation is applied per path step while our algorithm allows in fact to apply many transformations together in one step.

THEOREM 3. *Function* PARETOCLIMB *has expected time complexity in* $O(n^2)$.

PROOF. We combine the expected path length (see Theorem 2) with the complexity per step (see Lemma 2). □

At this point it might be interesting to compare the overhead of hill climbing, calculated before, with the benefit it provides by reducing the search space. The factor by which the search space size is reduced when focusing on local optima is given by the following lemma.

LEMMA 5. *The probability that a randomly selected plan is a local Pareto optimum is in* $O((1-(1/2)^l)^n)$.

PROOF. A plan is a local Pareto optimum if none of its neighbors dominates the plan. The neighbor plans are created by applying a constant number of mutations at each plan node. For a plan joining n tables, the number of neighbors is therefore in $O(n)$. We simplify by assuming that the probability that a plan is dominated by one of its neighbors corresponds to the probability that it is dominated by a random plan which is $(1/2)^l$ according to Lemma 3. The probability that a plan is not dominated by one of its neighbors is $1-(1/2)^l$ and the probability that it is not dominated by any of its neighbors is in $O((1-(1/2)^l)^n)$. □

Multi-objective hill climbing leads to an exponential reduction of search space size while the expected path length to the next local Pareto optimum grows only linearly in the number of query tables. Next we analyze the complexity of generating a frontier approximation. We denote by α the precision factor that is used in the analyzed iteration. The next lemma is based on a proof from prior work [18] (Lemma 2 in the previous paper) that bounds the number of query plans such that no plan approximately dominates another. Using the same notation, we denote by m the cardinality of the largest base table in the current database.

LEMMA 6. *The plan cache associates $O((n \log_\alpha m)^{l-1})$ plans with a table set of cardinality n.*

PROOF. New plans are only inserted into the plan cache if they are not approximately dominated by other plans joining the same tables, using approximation factor α. The bound of $O((n \log_\alpha m)^{l-1})$ on the number of plans joining n tables such that no plan approximately dominates another [18] applies therefore to the plan cache. □

We denote by $b(n)$ the asymptotic bound on the number of plans stored per table set. Note that $b(n)$ grows monotonically in n.

THEOREM 4. *Function* APPROXIMATEFRONTIER *has time complexity $O(n \cdot b(n)^3)$.*

PROOF. The function treats each plan node in bottom up order. For each node a set of new plans is generated and pruned by comparing it with alternative plans from the cache joining the same tables. We retrieve plans joining at most n tables such that the number of plans retrieved for each table set is bounded by $b(n)$. Comparing one new plan against $b(n)$ stored plans is in $O(b(n))$. The complexity for treating inner nodes of the query plan tree (representing joins) is higher than the complexity of treating leaf nodes (representing scans). We generate $O(b(n)^2)$ new plans for an inner node which yields a per-node complexity of $O(b(n)^3)$ when taking pruning into account. Summing over all query plan nodes leads to the postulated complexity. □

The operation with dominant time complexity is the generation of the approximate frontier. This justifies that we start with a coarse-grained precision factor in order to explore a sufficient number of join orders quickly. The per-iteration complexity of RMQ follows immediately.

COROLLARY 1. *RMQ has time complexity $O(n \cdot b(n)^3)$ per iteration.*

We finally analyze the space complexity of RMQ. We analyze the accumulated space consumed after i iterations. We assume that $b(n)$ designates the bound on the number of plans cached per table set for the precision factor α that is reached after i iterations.

THEOREM 5. *RMQ has space complexity $O(i \cdot n \cdot b(n))$.*

PROOF. Each plan generates $O(n)$ intermediate results. We approximate the Pareto frontiers of all intermediate results that are used by one locally optimal plan in each iteration. Each iteration therefore adds at most $O(n)$ plan sets to the plan cache. The number of plans cached for each intermediate result is bounded by $b(n)$ and each plan requires $O(1)$ space (as its sub-plans are already stored). □

Considering multiple operator implementations changes time but not space complexity. We denote the number of implementations per operator by r. The asymptotic number of neighbor plans multiplies by r and so does the expected path length to the nearest local optimum (this can be seen by substituting n by $r \cdot n$ in Theorems 1 and 2). Hence the time complexity of local search multiplies by r^2. The time complexity of the frontier approximation multiplies by r as we iterate over the operators in the innermost loop. Note that the number of plan cost metrics is traditionally treated as constant in multi-objective query optimization [18, 19].

6. EXPERIMENTAL EVALUATION

We describe our experimental setup in Section 6.1 and discuss the results in Section 6.2.

6.1 Experimental Setup

We compare our RMQ algorithm against other algorithms for multi-objective query optimization. We compare algorithms in terms of how well they approximate the Pareto frontier for a given query after a certain amount of optimization time. We measure the approximation quality in regular intervals during optimization to compare algorithms in different time intervals. This allows to identify algorithms that quickly find reasonable solutions as well as algorithms that take longer to produce reasonable solutions but yield a better approximation in the end.

We judge the set of query plans produced by a certain algorithm by the lowest approximation factor α such that the produced plan set is an α-approximate Pareto plan set. A lower α means a better approximation of the real Pareto frontier. This quality metric is equivalent to the ε metric that was recommended in a seminal paper by Zitzler and Thiele [23] (setting $\alpha = 1 + \varepsilon$). Choosing that metric also makes our comparison fair since the dynamic programming based approximation schemes [18] against which we compare have been developed for that metric. As it is common in the area of multi-objective optimization, we often deal with test cases where finding the full set of Pareto solutions is computationally infeasible. We therefore compare the output of each algorithm against an approximation of the real Pareto frontier that is obtained by running all algorithms that we describe in the following for three seconds and taking the union of the obtained result plans.

We compare RMQ against two classes of algorithms: dynamic programming based approximation schemes [18] and generalizations of randomized algorithms that have been proposed for single-objective query optimization [16]. The approximation schemes guarantee to produce a Pareto frontier approximation whose α value does not exceed a user-

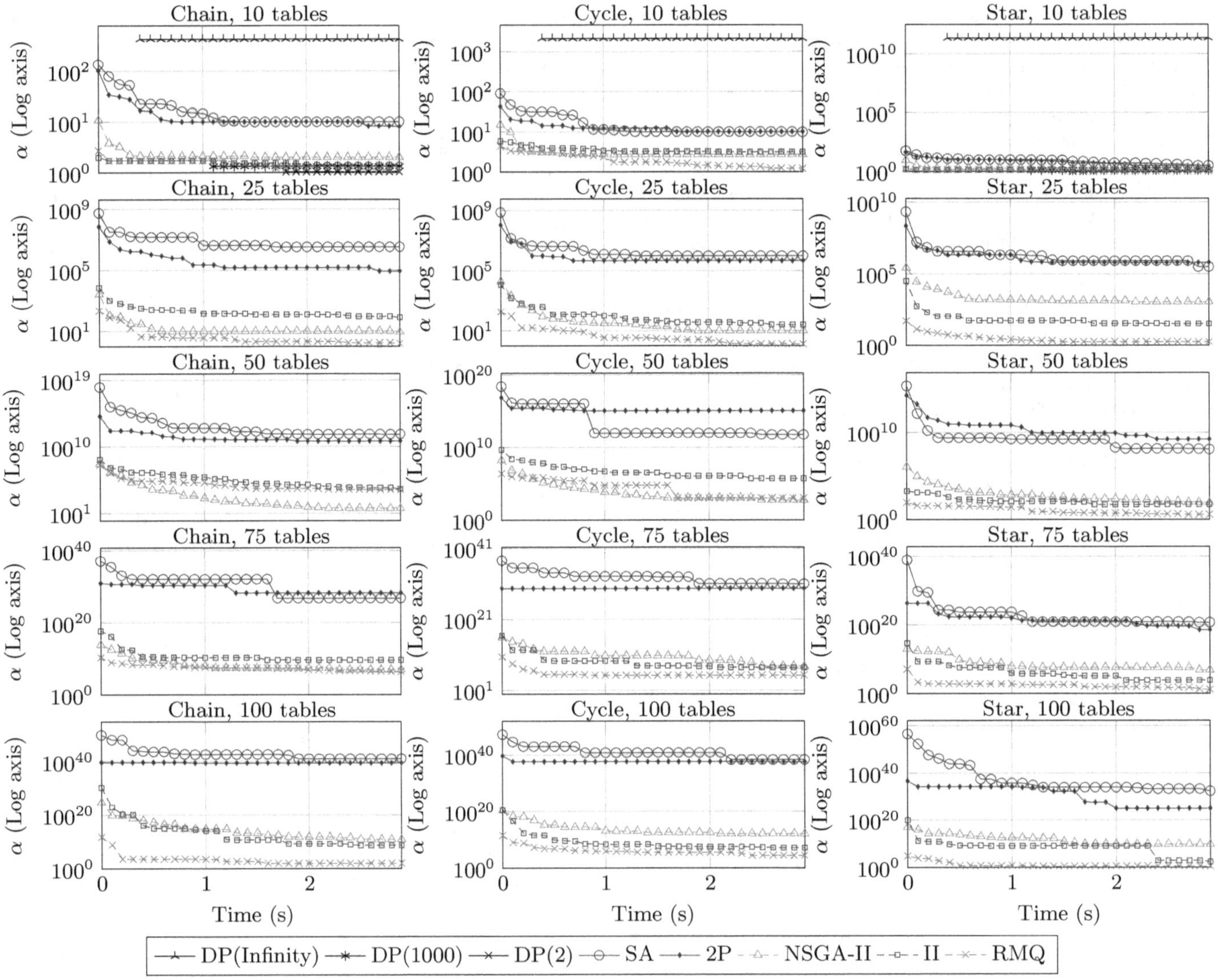

Figure 1: Median of approximation error for two cost metrics as a function of optimization time.

specified threshold. We denote by DP(α) the approximation scheme with threshold α. Choosing a higher value for α decreases optimization time but choosing a lower value leads to better result quality. We report results for different values of α in the following.

We experiment with four randomized algorithms (in addition to RMQ itself). By II we denote a generalization of iterative improvement [16] in which we iteratively walk towards local Pareto optima in the search space starting from random query plans. By SA we denote a generalization of the SAIO variant of simulated annealing, described by Steinbrunn et al. [16]. The original algorithm uses the difference between the scalar cost value of the current plan and the cost of a randomly selected neighbor to decide whether to move towards the neighbor plan, based additionally on the current temperature. Our generalization uses the average cost difference between the current plan and its neighbor, averaging over all cost metrics. By 2P we abbreviate the two phase optimization algorithm for query optimization [16]. It executes the II algorithm in a first phase and continues with SA in a second phase. We switch to the second phase after ten iterations of II [16] and choose the initial temperature for SA as described by Steinbrunn et al. [16]. By NSGA-II we abbreviate the Non-Dominated Sort Genetic Algorithm II [6], a genetic algorithm for multi-objective query optimization that has been very successful for scenarios with the same number of cost metrics that we consider.

All our algorithms that are based on local search use the plan transformations for bushy query plans that were described by Steinbrunn et al. [16]. All algorithms using hill climbing (II and 2P) use the same efficient climbing function (see Algorithm 2) as our own algorithm. NSGA-II uses an ordinal plan encoding and a corresponding single-point crossover [16]. Our implementation of NSGA-II follows closely the pseudo-code given in the original paper [5] and we use the same settings for mutation and crossover probabilities. We use populations of size 200. We experimented with several configurations for each of the randomized algorithms (e.g., experimenting with different population sizes for NSGA-II and different number of examined

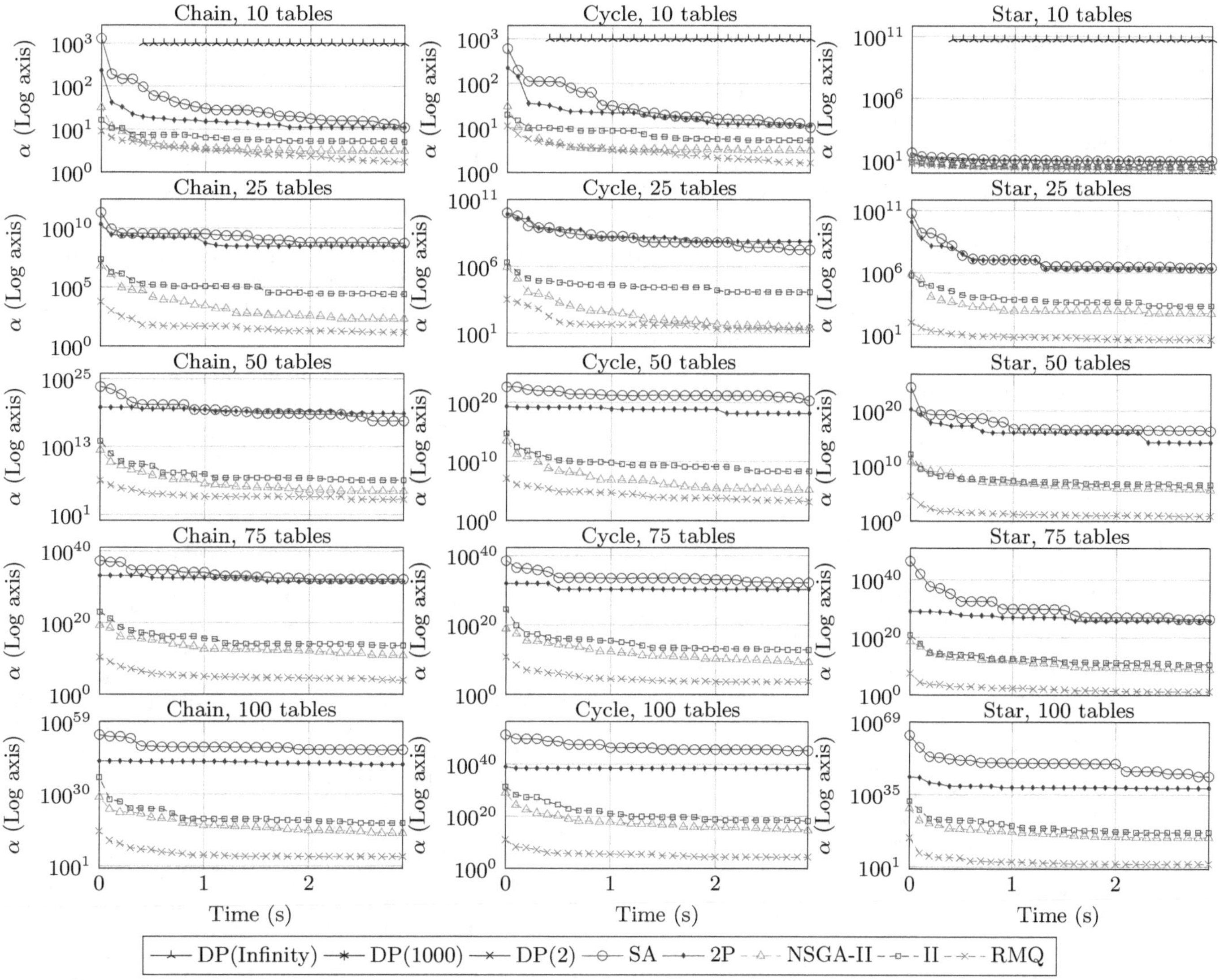

Figure 2: Median of approximation error for three cost metrics as a function of optimization time.

neighbors for II, SA, and 2P) and report for each algorithm only the configuration that led to optimal performance.

We generate random queries with a given number of tables in the same way as in prior evaluations of query optimization algorithms [16, 3]: we experiment with different join graph structures and use stratified sampling to pick table cardinalities, using the same distribution as Steinbrunn et al. [16]. We consider up to three cost metrics on query plans that were already used for other experimental evaluations in the area of multi-objective query optimization [18]: query execution time, buffer space consumption, and disc space consumption. We report in the following plots median values from 20 test cases per data point. For less than three cost metrics, we select the specified number of cost metrics with uniform distribution from the total set of metrics for each test case.

All algorithms were implemented in Java 1.7 and executed using the Java HotSpot(TM) 64-Bit Server Virtual Machine version on an iMac with i5-3470S 2.90GHz CPU and 16 GB of DDR3 RAM. We run each algorithm consecutively on all test cases after forcing garbage collection and after a ten seconds code warmup on randomly selected test cases in order to benchmark steady state performance[3].

6.2 Experimental Results

Figure 1 reports results for two cost metrics and Figure 2 reports our results for three cost metrics. We report separate results for different query sizes (measured by the number of tables being joined) and join graph structures (chain, cycle, and star shape). We allow up to three seconds of optimization time which might seem excessive for single-objective query optimization but is well within the range that multi-objective query optimizers are typically evaluated on [18, 19]. The experiments for producing the data shown in Figures 1 and 2 took around eight hours of optimization time.

Dynamic programming based approximation schemes for multi-objective query optimization have so far been evaluated only on queries joining up to around 10 tables [18,

[3]http://www.ibm.com/developerworks/library/j-benchmark1/

20, 19]. For 10 table queries, DP(2) finds the best frontier approximation among all evaluated algorithms if two cost metrics are considered. For three cost metrics, DP(2) cannot finish optimization within the given time frame. For queries joining 25 tables and more, none of the approximation schemes finishes optimization within the given time frame. Note that the optimization time required by the approximation schemes we compare against constitutes a lower bound for the optimization time required by the incremental approximation algorithm proposed in our prior work [19] for reaching the same approximation quality. As the non-incremental approximation schemes cannot finish optimization within the given time frame, even when setting $\alpha = \infty$, the incremental versions will not be able to do so either. This is not surprising as we reach a query size where randomized algorithms would already be used for single-objective query optimization which is computationally far less expensive than multi-objective query optimization. This shows the need for randomized algorithms for multi-objective query optimization such as RMQ.

Among the randomized algorithms that generalize popular randomized algorithms for single-objective query optimization (II, SA, 2P, and NSGA-II), II and NSGA-II generate the best approximations with a large gap to SA and 2P (note the logarithmic y axis for approximation error). It is interesting that II outperforms 2P unlike in traditional query optimization where the roles are reversed. However, SA and 2P both spend most of their time improving one single query plan (2P after limited initial sampling) and are therefore intrinsically based on the assumption that only one very good plan needs to be found as result. Approximating the Pareto frontier requires however to generate a diverse set of query plans which is better accomplished by the seemingly naive II which starts each iteration with a new random plan. NSGA-II usually performs better than II, SA, and 2P. This is not surprising since NSGA-II is a popular algorithm for multi-objective optimization with a moderate number of cost metrics and genetic algorithms have been shown to perform well for classical query optimization [2].

Our own algorithm, RMQ, outperforms all other algorithms in the majority of cases. The gap to the other algorithms increases in the number of query tables and in the number of cost metrics. For two cost metrics (see Figure 1), RMQ is competitive and often significantly better than all other algorithms over the entire optimization time period starting from more than 50 join tables. For star-shaped query graphs, RMQ is better than competing algorithms starting from 25 join tables already. Considering three cost metrics (see Figure 2) increases the gap between RMQ and all other algorithms. Starting from 25 join tables, RMQ dominates over the entire optimization time period. The gap in terms of approximation error reaches many orders of magnitude for large queries.

Figures 3 shows additional statistics: on the left side we see that the average path length from a random plan to the nearest Pareto optimum (using function ParetoClimb) grows slowly in the number of query tables as postulated in our formal analysis. On the right side, we see that the number of Pareto plans grows in the number of query tables which corroborates prior results [18]. This tendency explains why the approximation error of randomized algorithms increases in the query size: having more Pareto plans makes it harder to obtain a good approximation.

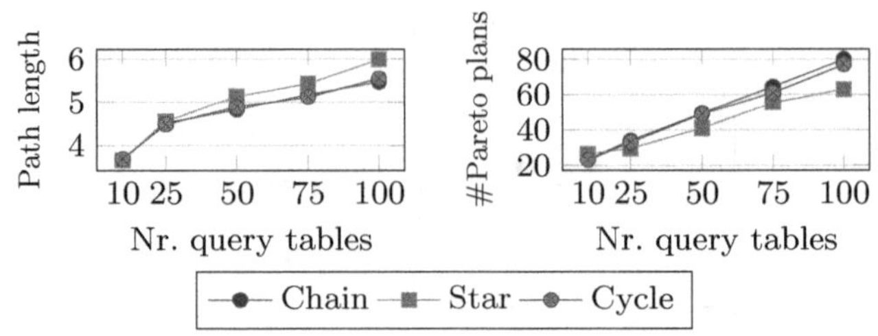

Figure 3: Median path length from random plan to next local Pareto optimum and median number of Pareto plans found by RMQ for three cost metrics.

We summarize the main results of our experimental evaluation. Dynamic programming based algorithms for multi-objective query optimization are only applicable for small queries. Using randomized algorithms, we were able to approximate the Pareto frontier for large queries joining up to 100 tables. The algorithm proposed in this paper performs best among the randomized algorithms over a broad range of scenarios. Among the remaining randomized algorithms, a general-purpose genetic algorithm for multi-objective optimization performs best, followed closely by an iterative improvement algorithm that uses the efficient hill climbing function that was introduced in this paper as well.

So far we have compared algorithms for a few seconds of optimization time. It is generally advantageous to minimize optimization time as it adds to execution time. In the context of multi-objective query optimization, it is even more important as query optimization can be an interactive process in which users have to wait until optimization finishes [19]. We have however also compared algorithms for up to 30 seconds of optimization time and present the corresponding results in the appendix. Until now we compared algorithms in terms of how well they approximate an approximated Pareto frontier since calculating the real Pareto frontier would lead to prohibitive computational costs for many of the query sizes we consider. We show results for small queries where we calculated the real Pareto frontier in the appendix. Furthermore, the appendix contains results for different query generation methods. The main results of our experiments are stable across all scenarios.

7. CONCLUSION

The applicability of multi-objective query optimization has so far been severely restricted by the fact that all available algorithms have exponential complexity in the number of query tables. We presented, analyzed, and evaluated the first polynomial time heuristic for multi-objective query optimization. We have shown that our algorithm scales to queries that are by one order of magnitude larger than the ones prior multi-objective query optimizers were so far evaluated on. We envision our algorithm being used in future multi-objective query optimizers that apply dynamic programming based algorithms for small queries and switch to randomized algorithms starting from a certain number of query tables, similar to single-objective optimizers today.

8. ACKNOWLEDGMENTS

This work was supported by ERC grant 279804. I. Trummer is supported by a Google European PhD Fellowship.

9. REFERENCES

[1] S. Agarwal, A. Iyer, and A. Panda. Blink and it's done: interactive queries on very large data. In *VLDB*, volume 5, pages 1902–1905, 2012.

[2] K. Bennett, M. Ferris, and Y. Ioannidis. *A genetic algorithm for database query optimization.* 1991.

[3] N. Bruno. Polynomial heuristics for query optimization. In *ICDE*, pages 589–600, 2010.

[4] C. a. Coello Coello. Evolutionary multi-objective optimization: a historical view of the field. *Computational Intelligence Magazine*, 1(1):28–36, 2006.

[5] K. Deb, S. Agrawal, A. Pratap, and T. Meyarivan. A fast elitist non-dominated sorting genetic algorithm for multi-objective optimization: NSGA-II. *Parallel Problem Solving from Nature PPSN VI*, pages 849–858, 2000.

[6] K. Deb, A. Pratap, S. Agarwal, and T. Meyarivan. A fast and elitist multiobjective genetic algorithm: NSGA-II. *IEEE Transactions on Evolutionary Computation*, 6(2):182–197, 2002.

[7] S. Ganguly, W. Hasan, and R. Krishnamurthy. Query optimization for parallel execution. In *SIGMOD*, pages 9–18, 1992.

[8] Y. Ioannidis and Y. Kang. Left-deep vs. bushy trees: An analysis of strategy spaces and its implications for query optimization. *SIGMOD*, pages 168–177, 1991.

[9] Y. E. Ioannidis and Y. Kang. Randomized algorithms for optimizing large join queries. In *SIGMOD Record*, volume 19, pages 312–321, 1990.

[10] H. Kllapi, E. Sitaridi, M. M. Tsangaris, and Y. E. Ioannidis. Schedule Optimization for Data Processing Flows on the Cloud. In *SIGMOD*, 2011.

[11] D. Kossmann and K. Stocker. Iterative Dynamic Programming: a New Class of Query Optimization Algorithms. *Trans. on Database Systems*, 1(212), 2000.

[12] C. Papadimitriou and M. Yannakakis. Multiobjective query optimization. In *PODS*, pages 52–59, 2001.

[13] A. J. Quiroz. Fast random generation of binary, t-ary and other types of trees. *Journal of Classification*, 6(1):223–231, 1989.

[14] P. G. Selinger, M. M. Astrahan, D. D. Chamberlin, R. A. Lorie, and T. G. Price. Access path selection in a relational database management system. In *SIGMOD*, pages 23–34, 1979.

[15] A. Simitsis, K. Wilkinson, U. Dayal, and M. Castellanos. Optimizing ETL workflows for fault-tolerance. In *ICDE*, pages 385–396. Ieee, 2010.

[16] M. Steinbrunn, G. Moerkotte, and A. Kemper. Heuristic and randomized optimization for the join ordering problem. *VLDBJ*, 6(3):191–208, 1997.

[17] A. Swami and A. Gupta. Optimization of large join queries. In *SIGMOD*, pages 8–17, 1988.

[18] I. Trummer and C. Koch. Approximation schemes for many-objective query optimization. In *SIGMOD*, pages 1299–1310, 2014.

[19] I. Trummer and C. Koch. An incremental anytime algorithm for multi-objective query optimization. In *SIGMOD*, pages 1941–1953, 2015.

[20] I. Trummer and C. Koch. Multi-objective parametric query optimization. *VLDB*, 8(3):221–232, 2015.

[21] B. Vance and D. Maier. Rapid bushy join-order optimization with Cartesian products. *SIGMOD*, 25(2):35–46, 1996.

[22] Z. Xu, Y. C. Tu, and X. Wang. PET: Reducing Database Energy Cost via Query Optimization. *VLDB*, 5(12):1954–1957, 2012.

[23] E. Zitzler and L. Thiele. Performance assessment of multiobjective optimizers: An analysis and review. *Evolutionary Computation*, 7(2):117–132, 2003.

APPENDIX

The performance of query optimization algorithms may depend on the probability distribution over predicate selectivity values used during random query generation. For our experiments in Section 6, we used the original method proposed by Steinbrunn et al. [16] to select the selectivity of join predicates. We performed an additional series of experiments in which we select predicate selectivity according to the MinMax method proposed by Bruno instead [3]. Using that method, each join has an output cardinality between the cardinalities of the two input relations. The purpose of those additional experiments is to verify whether our experimental results from Section 6 generalize. We report the results of the second series of experiments in Figures 4 and 5. The experimental setup is the same as described in Section 6.1 except for the choice of selectivity values. We focus on queries joining between 25 to 100 tables where randomized algorithms become better than dynamic programming variants.

The results are largely consistent with the results we obtained in our first series of experiments. Our own algorithm outperforms all other approaches significantly for large queries and many cost metrics, in particular during the first second of optimization time. NSGA-II performs well for smaller queries while its approximation error is by many orders of magnitude sub-optimal for large queries. II comes close to NSGA-II in certain scenarios while the two randomized algorithms based on simulated annealing, SA and 2P, perform badly. The approximation schemes do not scale to queries of 25 tables and more.

Multi-objective query optimization needs to integrate user preferences in order to determine the optimal query plan. One possibility to integrate user preferences is to present an approximation of the plan Pareto frontier for a given query to the user such that the user can select the preferred cost tradeoff [19]. This means that users have to wait after submitting a query until optimization finishes in order to make their selection. In that scenario, an optimization time of only a few seconds is desirable. If users formalize their preferences before optimization starts (e.g., in the form of cost weights and cost bounds [18]) then longer optimization times can be acceptable. The second scenario motivates us to compare the query optimization algorithms for longer periods of optimization time.

We executed another series of experiments giving each algorithm 30 seconds of optimization time. We reduced the number of test cases per scenario from 20 to 10 and only experimented with two query sizes in order to decrease the time overhead for the experiments. Figures 6 and 7 report the development of the median approximation error over 30 seconds of optimization time. We restrict the y domain of the figures and only show errors up to $\alpha = 10^{10}$. Using that

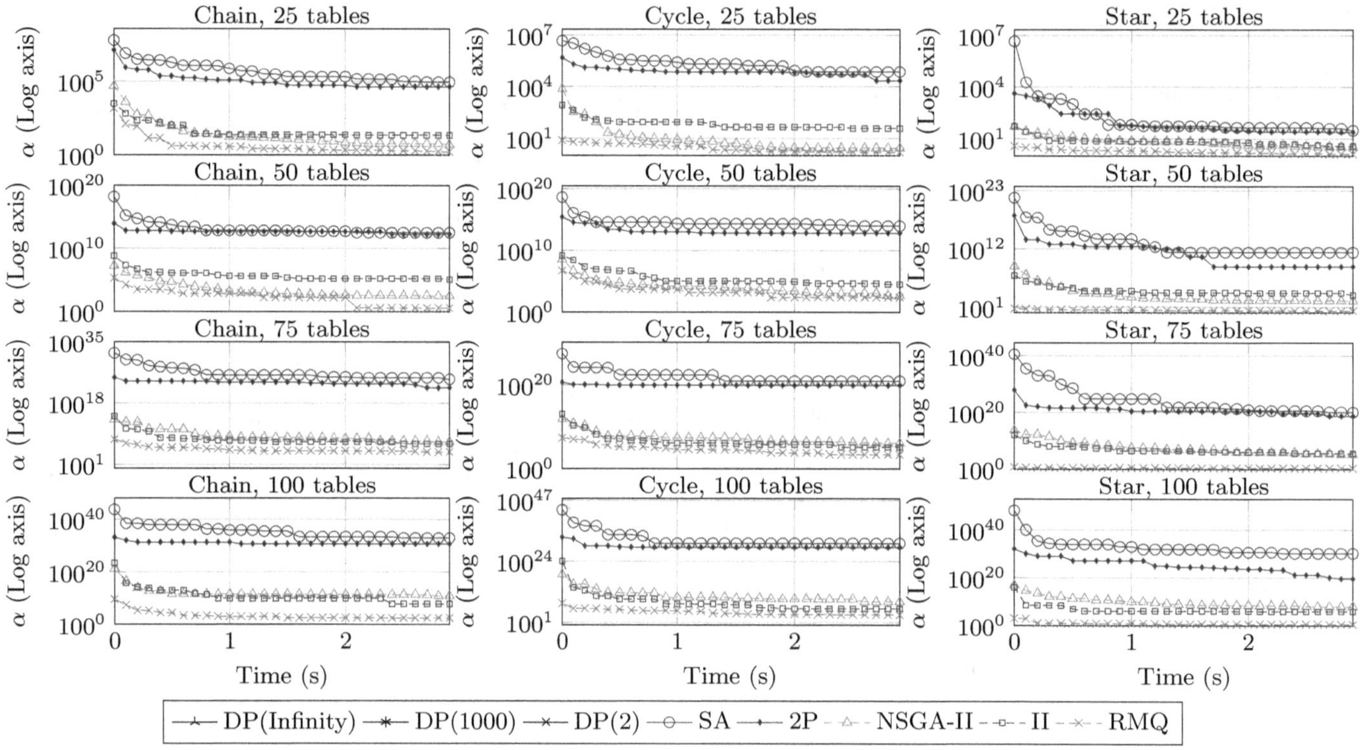

Figure 4: Median of approximation error for two cost metrics as a function of optimization time (MinMax joins).

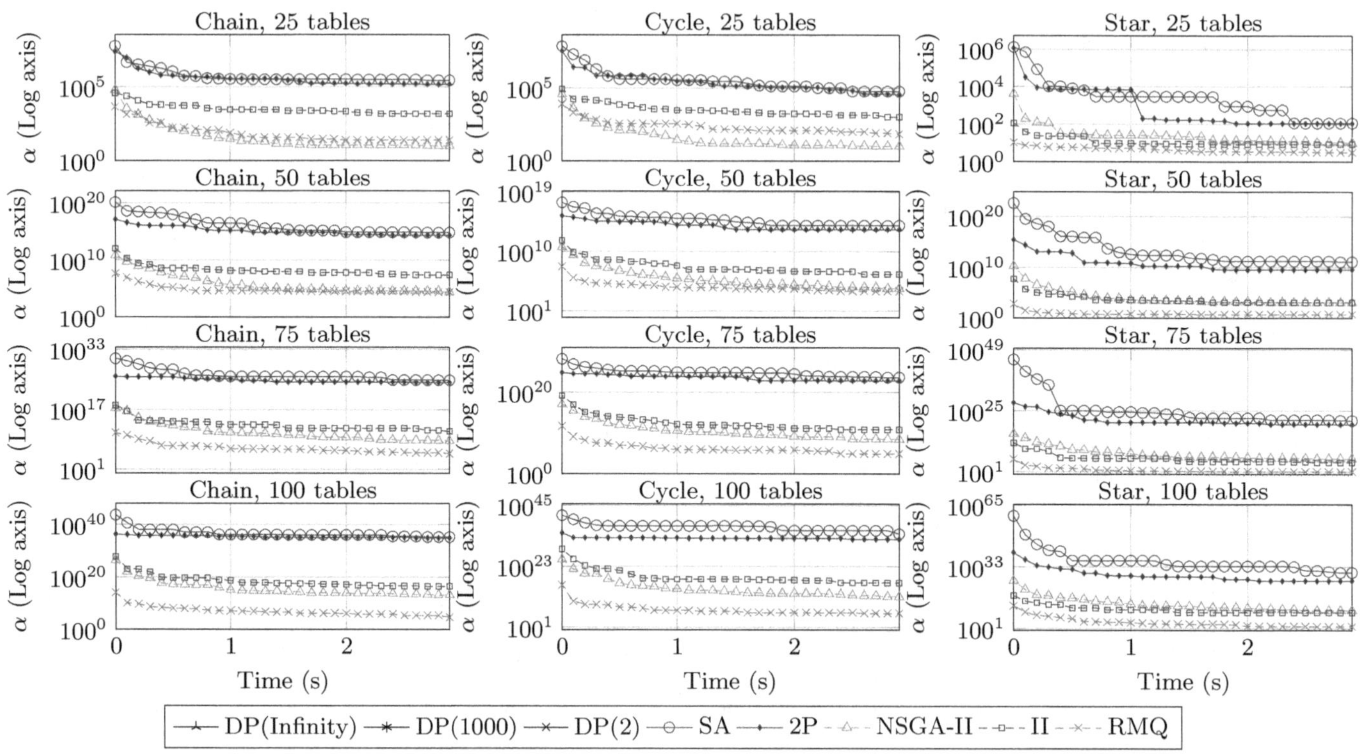

Figure 5: Median of approximation error for three cost metrics as a function of optimization time (MinMax joins).

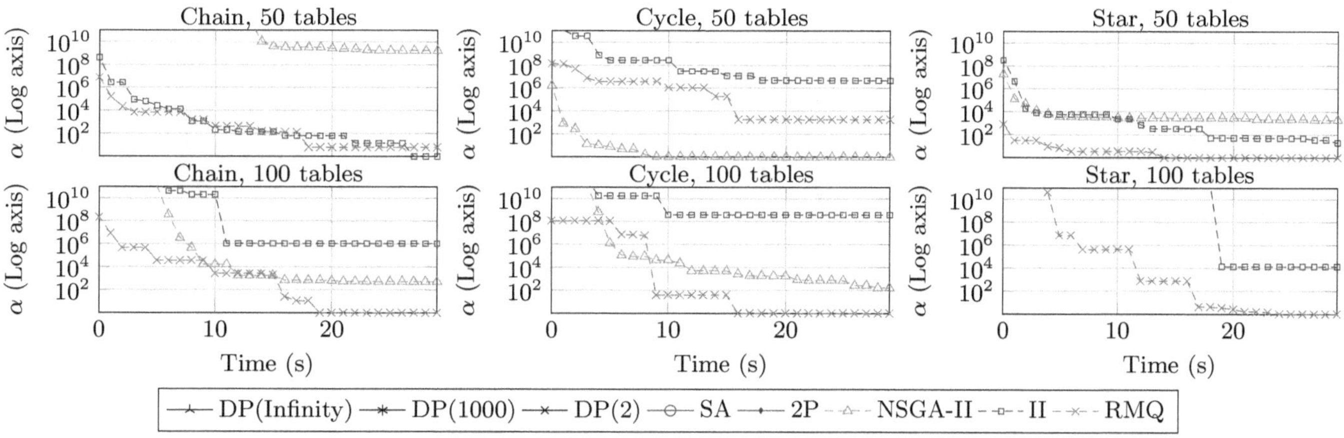

Figure 6: Median of approximation error in the interval $[1, 10^{10}]$ for two cost metrics and up to 30 seconds of optimization time.

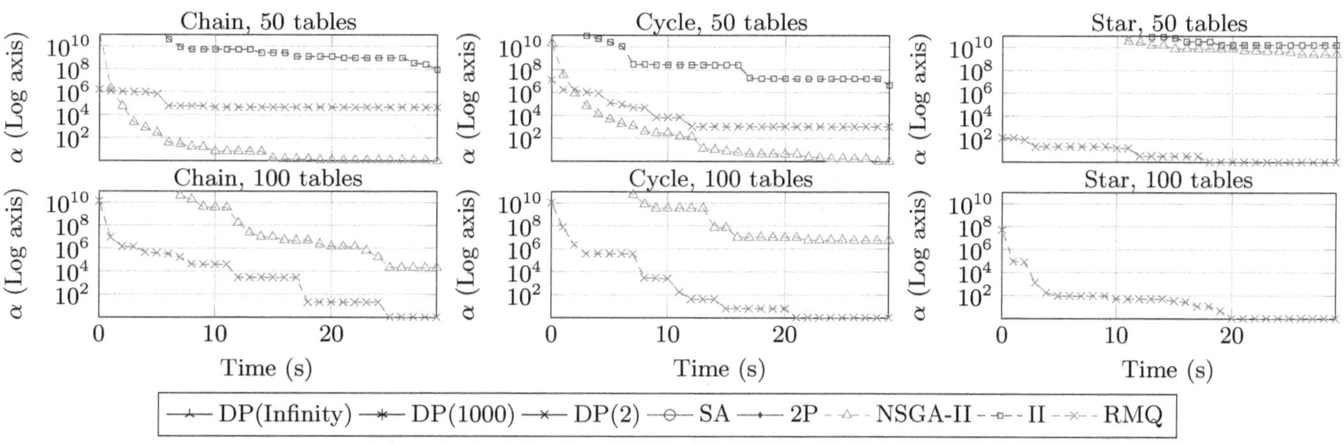

Figure 7: Median of approximation error in the interval $[1, 10^{10}]$ for three cost metrics and up to 30 seconds of optimization time.

thresholds allows us to visualize performance difference between the well performing algorithms that would otherwise become indistinguishable even though they are significant. Albeit we ran the same algorithms as in the previous plots on all test cases, the plots only show data points for a subset of those algorithms. For the dynamic programming variants, the reason for not being represented in the plots is that they did not return any results even within 30 seconds of optimization time. For simulated annealing and two-phase optimization, the reason for not being represented in the plots is that their approximation error is significantly above the threshold of 10^{10} (often more than 10^{110}).

The tendencies remain the same: our randomized algorithm, the genetic algorithm, and iterative improvement with our fast climbing function are the best randomized algorithms. RMQ is usually better than iterative improvement. For queries with up to 50 tables, it depends on the number of cost metrics and the join graph structure whether RMQ or the genetic algorithm perform better. For more than 50 tables, RMQ outperforms all other algorithms over most of the optimization time period, the margin increases in the number of plan cost metrics.

We have finally run an additional test series in which we calculate the approximation error more precisely than in the previous experiments. For large queries, we have no choice but to evaluate approximation precision with regards to an approximated Pareto frontier that is generated by the same randomized algorithms that we evaluate. For small queries, we can use the dynamic programming based approximation schemes to calculate an approximated Pareto frontier with formal guarantees on how closely it is approximated. For the last series of experiments, we calculate the approximated Pareto frontier by the approximation scheme, setting $\alpha = 1.01$. This means that the calculated approximation error is guaranteed to be precise within a very small tolerance. We restrict ourselves to small queries joining between four and eight tables. Note that the size of the Pareto frontier produced by the approximation scheme reaches several hundreds of Pareto plans already for such small queries.

Figures 8 and 9 show the results. We allow again 30 seconds of optimization time and restrict the plots to the domain $[1, 2]$ for the approximation error. This has the same implications as discussed in the previous paragraphs: algorithms with exceedingly high errors are not shown in order not to obfuscate the performance differences between

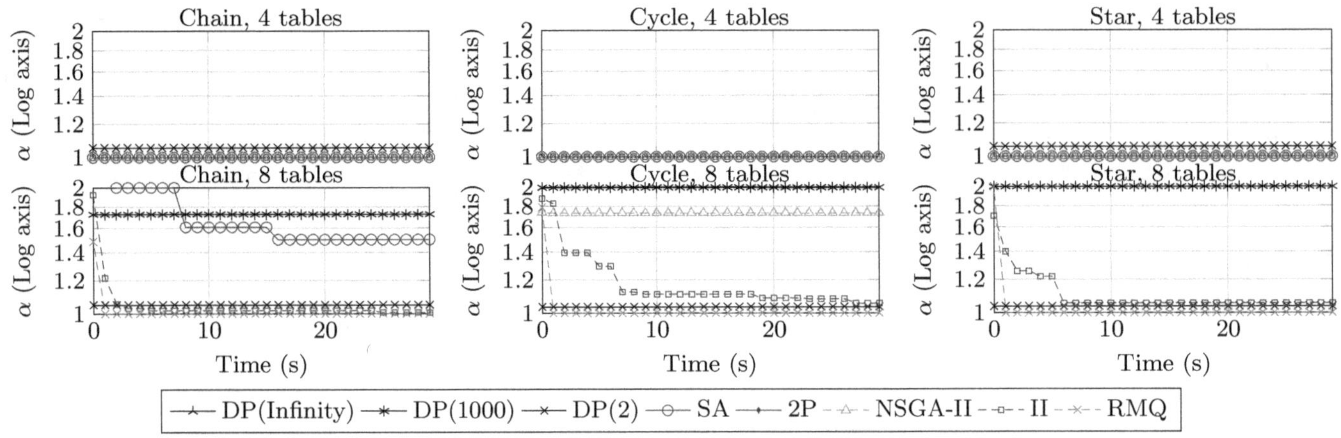

Figure 8: Median of precise approximation error in the interval $[1,2]$ for small queries and two cost metrics.

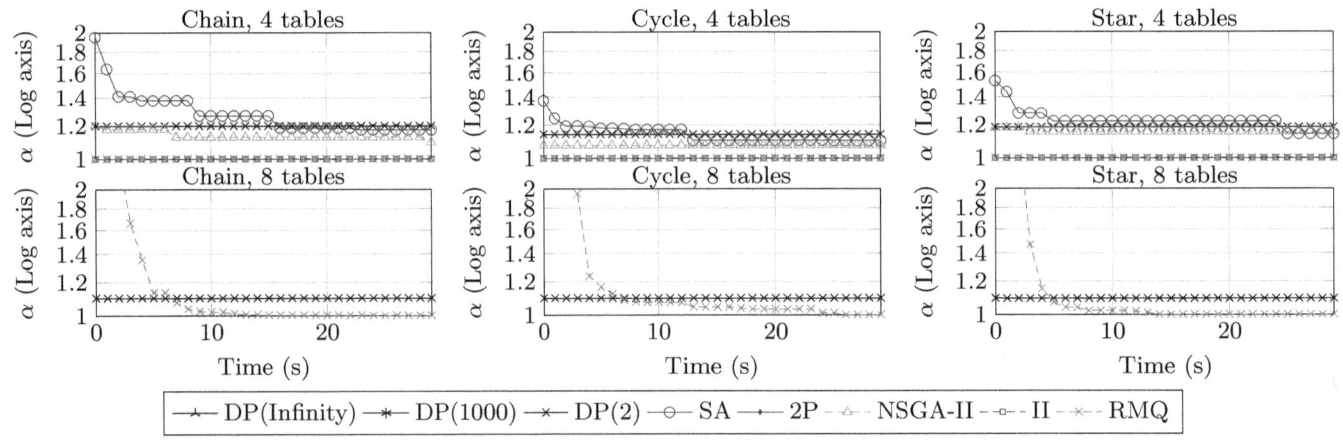

Figure 9: Median of precise approximation error in the interval $[1,2]$ for small queries and three cost metrics.

the competitive algorithms. We are primarily interested in whether or not the randomized algorithms converge to the reference Pareto frontier for small queries; therefore we choose to show a small error range above $\alpha = 1$.

We find that our algorithms converges in average to a perfect approximation with $\alpha = 1$ while this is not always the case for the other algorithms. In particular for queries joining eight tables and three plan cost metrics, our algorithm is the only one among all randomized algorithms that achieves a perfect approximation. The dynamic programming based approximation scheme with $\alpha = 2$ performs well for small queries. It generates output nearly immediately and the approximation error is much lower than the theoretical worst case bound. The approximation scheme configuration using $\alpha = 1.01$, the one generating the reference frontier, produces its solutions after less than two seconds of optimization time in average, even for three cost metrics and eight tables. We do not show results for that algorithm in the plots as its approximation error is minimal by definition. We conclude that approximation schemes often outperform randomized algorithms for small queries.

Operator and Query Progress Estimation in Microsoft SQL Server Live Query Statistics

Kukjin Lee[§] Arnd Christian König[§] Vivek Narasayya[§] Bolin Ding[§] Surajit Chaudhuri[§]
Brent Ellwein[§] Alexey Eksarevskiy[§] Manbeen Kohli[§] Jacob Wyant[§] Praneeta Prakash[§]
Rimma Nehme[§] Jiexing Li[∓] Jeff Naughton[∓]

[§]Microsoft Corp., Redmond
{kulee,chrisko,viveknar,bolind,surajitc,brellwei,alexek,makohli,jacobwy,pprakash,rimman}@microsoft.com

[∓]Univ. of Wisconsin, Madison
{jxli,naughton}@cs.wisc.edu

ABSTRACT

We describe the design and implementation of the new *Live Query Statistics* (LQS) feature in Microsoft SQL Server 2016. The functionality includes the display of *overall* query progress as well as progress of *individual operators* in the query execution plan. We describe the overall functionality of LQS, give usage examples and detail all areas where we had to extend the current state-of-the-art to build the complete LQS feature. Finally, we evaluate the effect these extensions have on progress estimation accuracy with a series of experiments using a large set of synthetic and real workloads.

1. INTRODUCTION

Accurate online estimates of the overall progress of execution of a SQL query is valuable to database administrators (DBAs), application developers and end users of applications. For example, a DBA (or an automated agent) can use query progress information to help decide whether a long-running, resource intensive query should be terminated or allowed to run to completion. There has been extensive work in SQL query progress estimation, e.g., [6, 18, 23, 24].

In addition to overall query progress information, it can also be valuable to provide progress estimates for *individual operators* in a query execution plan [12]. Such an operator-level progress indicator can aid in live troubleshooting of performance issues due to a poorly chosen execution plan: similarly to how accurate progress estimation allows database administrators to identify long-running queries early in their execution, having accurate progress estimates for individual operators allows DBAs to rapidly identify issues with operators that require significantly more time or resources than expected. For example, a database administrator might observe a nested loop operator that is not only executing for a significant amount of time, but, according to the progress estimate, has only completed a small fraction of its work. Based on this, she may then compare the number of rows seen so far on the outer side of the join and discover that these are already much larger than the optimizer estimate for the total number of outer rows, indicating an cardinality estimation problem. This may then trigger various remedial actions on the side of the DBA, such as creating additional statistics, the use of plan hints or a reformulation of the query. The same determination could obviously also be made using the operator duration information only, obtained *after* execution; however, having online operator-level progress information enables a DBA to identify potential issues much more quickly and easily.

In this paper we describe the design and implementation of operator and query level progress estimation included as part of Microsoft SQL Server 2016, available via the new Live Query Statistics (LQS) feature that is part of SQL Server Management Studio (SSMS). This feature enables the scenarios discussed above by providing estimates of both query and operator level progress. These progress estimates as well as the row counts are exposed to users through a query plan visualization. LQS can work with both Microsoft SQL Server 2014 as well as Microsoft SQL Server 2016.

1.1 Overview and Organisation

In the following, we will describe the new Live Query Statistics feature in detail; first, in Section 2, we will give an overview of the LQS functionality, including a description of the different components working together, and show examples of the output surfaced to the user. Subsequently, in Section 3, we will formally introduce the relevant technical background and then describe the particular challenges we faced when building the LQS feature. In particular, we will identify all aspects in which we needed to extend the current state-of-the-art to arrive at the desired functionality and level of accuracy. We will then go through the details of how we addressed each of these challenges in Section 4 and experimentally evaluate the effect of the resulting techniques in Section 5. Finally, we briefly discuss future work in Section 7.

2. OVERVIEW OF LQS

In this section, we will give an overview of the *Live Query Statistics* functionality as well as the different instrumented components. The progress estimator itself is a client-side component, which consumes all required counters for currently executing queries exposed via *dynamic management views* (DMV) on the server side (see Figure 1). The progress estimate for both the entire query as well as each individual operator is then computed in the client and displayed visually together with the query plan.

SIGMOD '16, June 26–July 1, 2016, San Francisco, CA, USA.

ACM 978-1-4503-3531-7/16/06...$15.00

DOI: http://dx.doi.org/10.1145/2882903.2903728

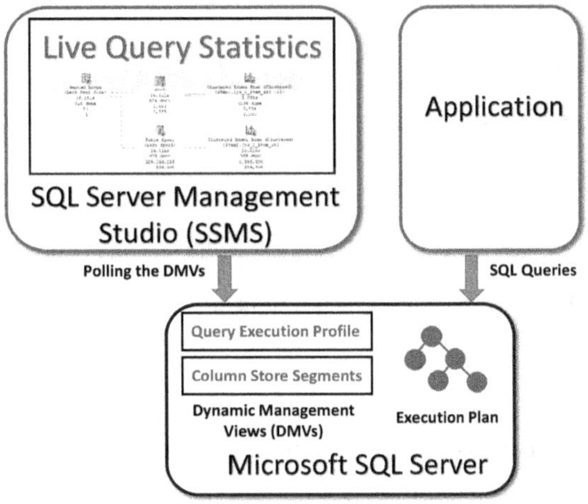

Figure 1: Architecture Overview.

2.1 Server Side DMVs

The counters required for progress estimation are collected within the Microsoft SQL Server engine process; most of them are exposed by the dynamic management view *sys.dm_exec_query_profiles* introduced first in Microsoft SQL Server 2014[1]. This view returns counters for each operator in a *currently executing query* (at the granularity of individual threads), such as the estimated and actual number of rows, the total elapsed time and CPU time for an operator, the number of physical reads, etc. Each counter is dynamically updated while the query executes. LQS supports the display of progress estimates for multiple, concurrently executing queries, each of them being given their own dedicated window.

2.2 Progress Estimation in SSMS

The progress estimation itself is implemented as a client-side module which is part of the SQL Server Management Studio. This model queries the DMV *sys.dm_exec_query_profiles* every 500ms to obtain up-to-date information on each executing operator/thread and, in addition, uses information extracted from a query's *showplan* (such as estimated cardinalities as well as CPU and I/O cost estimates) as well as additional system meta-data (such as e.g., the DMV *sys.column_store_segments*). The fact that progress estimation is client code (with the required information exposed by the server) has the advantage that the progress estimation module can evolve independently of the server code. Further, it allows for the development of other first-party or third-party client side tools that use the same data sources.

The main disadvantage lies in the fact that some information that is potentially useful for progress estimation (such as more detailed information on the internal state of *Sort* and *Hash* operators) is not exposed via *sys.dm_exec_query_profiles* at this time. Because the progress estimation is client code, it has no visibility into some aspects of operator state. We will touch on some of these limitations in Section 7.

2.3 Visualization

In SQL Server Management Studio, progress estimates are shown combined with *query showplan* output, showing an estimate of progress of the overall query (i.e., percentage completion) as well as an progress estimate for each operator as well. An example can be seen in Figure 2. In this example, the query is TPC-H Query 1, and the *showplan* for this query is shown in the bottom window. Below each operator, its progress is displayed – in this example, the Columnstore *Index Scan* and *Compute Scalar* operators have executed for 42.58 seconds and are at 5% progress, whereas all operators further up the plan have not started execution yet. The overall query progress is displayed on the top left-hand corner of the *showplan* window (3% in this example).

2.3.1 Visualization and Usage Examples

The LQS interface animates the links between all currently executing operators, thereby making it easy to identify which pipelines in the query plan are active at any moment. For example, in Figure 3 we can see that the upper two pipelines have already completed execution; here, the arrows between two operators are solid and their thickness corresponds to the number of tuples having flown between them. In contrast, the lower pipeline has dotted, animated arrows between the operators, meaning that it is still executing and – since all operators in the pipeline are still at 0% progress after 40 seconds of execution – likely long-running. Especially for complex query plans, this functionality allows DBAs to identify potential bottlenecks and opportunities for tuning very quickly.

In Figure 4 we demonstrate a different example scenario for LQS: here, in addition to the output we described earlier in the context of Figure 2, we also show the estimated cardinality and the total number of rows output so far for each operator in the plan[2] for illustration. As we can see, while the upper *Clustered Index Scan* operator has already finished execution (we can see the progress of the operator being reported as 100%), the *Table Spool* and lower *Clustered Index Scan* operator are still executing and show very significant errors in estimated cardinality; this cardinality information allows the DBA to identify nodes and the corresponding predicates with significant estimation errors which potentially may contribute to sub-optimal plans.

As we can see in Figure 4, the progress estimates at the *Table Spool* and lower *Clustered Index Scan* operators themselves are not accurate, which in turn leads to over-estimation of the fraction of work done at these nodes. We chose this example to illustrate that even when we do not have accurate estimates of node cardinality and e.g., overestimate the work done by an operator, LQS can still guide a database administrator to problematic nodes in the execution plan: in this example, the progress estimates at these nodes initially go up to 99% and then stay at that estimate for a significant time time. This in itself is enough to alert a DBA to the inaccuracy and potentially trigger an investigation of the nodes in question.

3. CHALLENGES

In this section we will describe the challenges encountered during the implementation of the LQS functionality. In particular, we will describe where the current state-of-the-art in research either needed to be extended or did not yield sufficient accuracy for some of the real workloads we used to evaluate the LQS system. To give this overview, we will first introduce some necessary background on progress estimation.

3.1 Background

3.1.1 Operators and Pipelines

Current progress estimation techniques [6,7,12,15,21–24] model a running query Q using a tree of physical operators and base their estimates of a query's progress on the number of tuples or bytes

[1]See `https://msdn.microsoft.com/en-us/library/-dn223301.aspx` for details.

[2]In the current interface, this information is is available by hovering the mouse over the operators in the *showplan*.

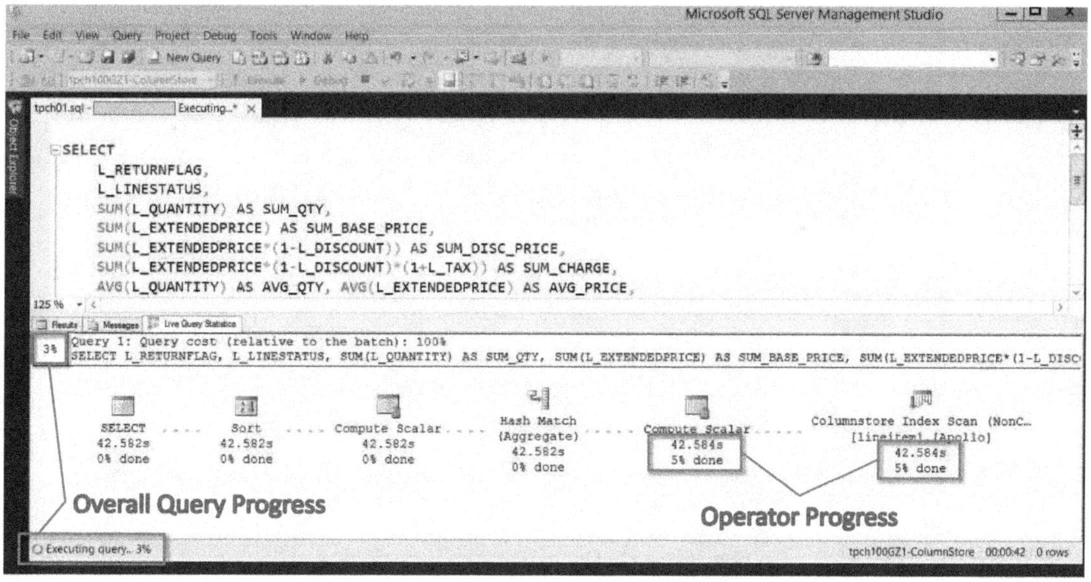

Figure 2: Query and Operator Progress in Live Query Statistics

processed by (a subset of) these operators at various points in time. We use $Nodes(\mathcal{Q})$ to enumerate the operators in the execution plan. To capture the notion of the sets of operators in a query plan which execute concurrently, prior work defined *Pipelines* or *Segments* (defined in [7], and [22], respectively), which correspond to maximal subtrees of concurrently executing operators in a (physical) operator tree.

For each pipeline (or segment), the nodes that are the sources of tuples operated upon by the remaining nodes (i.e., typically all leaf nodes of the pipeline, with the exception of the inner subtree of nested loop operators) are referred to as the *driver nodes* (or *dominant input*) of the pipeline; we use the notation $DriverNodes(\mathcal{Q}) \subseteq Nodes(\mathcal{Q})$ to denote these. An example operator tree with 3 pipelines is shown in Figure 5; the shaded nodes correspond to driver nodes. The notion of segments was further refined in [23].

3.1.2 Model of Work Done

Operators in a query execution plan of a modern RDBMS are typically implemented using a demand driven iterator model [11], where each physical operator in the execution plan exports a standard interface for query processing (including Open(), Close() and GetNext()). For the purposes of progress estimation, we follow the $GetNext$ model of work done by an operator, introduced in [7]. In the $GetNext$ model, at any point during the execution of the query the true progress of an *operator o* is defined as:

$$Prog(o) = \frac{k}{N} \qquad (1)$$

where k is the number of rows output by the operator thus far, and N is the total number of rows that will be output by the operator when query execution is complete. Similarly, the true progress of a *query* Q in the $GetNext$ model is:

$$Prog(Q) = \frac{\sum_{i \in Nodes(\mathcal{Q})} w_i k_i}{\sum_{i \in Nodes(\mathcal{Q})} w_i N_i} \qquad (2)$$

The summation is taken over all operators in the query execution plan. w_i is a *weight* associated with operator i that can be used to capture the fact that different operators perform different amount of work *per tuple* output relative to other operators.

While the k_i values can be measured precisely and with negligible overhead at query time, the N_i values are typically derived using the estimates of query optimizer, meaning that the accuracy of progress estimation is closely tied to the accuracy of cardinality estimation itself [15], which is know to erroneous in many cases. One of the ways this challenge has been alleviated has been by only considering driver nodes in the summation in equation 2 [7]. Because the cardinalities of driver nodes are typically known exactly when their pipeline starts execution (although there are notable exceptions which we will discuss in subsequent sections), this reduces the error in progress estimation for executing pipelines significantly. The main requirement for this approach to work is that the progress at the driver nodes closely matches the progress over all nodes of the pipeline.

3.2 Progress Estimation for Individual Operators

While previous work in progress estimation only concentrated on estimating the overall progress of queries (with the exception of [12]), Live Query Statistics also surfaces progress estimates for each individual operator. Providing operator-level progress estimates is conceptually similar to the *GetNext* based scheme described above (see Equation 1), when limited to single nodes, but creates a number of additional challenges, which we will describe below.

3.3 Challenges and Contributions

In order to enable the LQS functionality, there were a number of challenges we had to address. First, a key challenge for any progress estimation technique that ties their measure of progress to the number of rows output or processed by each operator is to accurately estimate the total number of rows to be output/processed, which is closely tied to the known hard problem of cardinality estimation. This challenge is made more difficult in our case by the fact that LQS provides operator-level progress estimates and hence requires accurate cardinality estimates for *all* operators in a plan; the

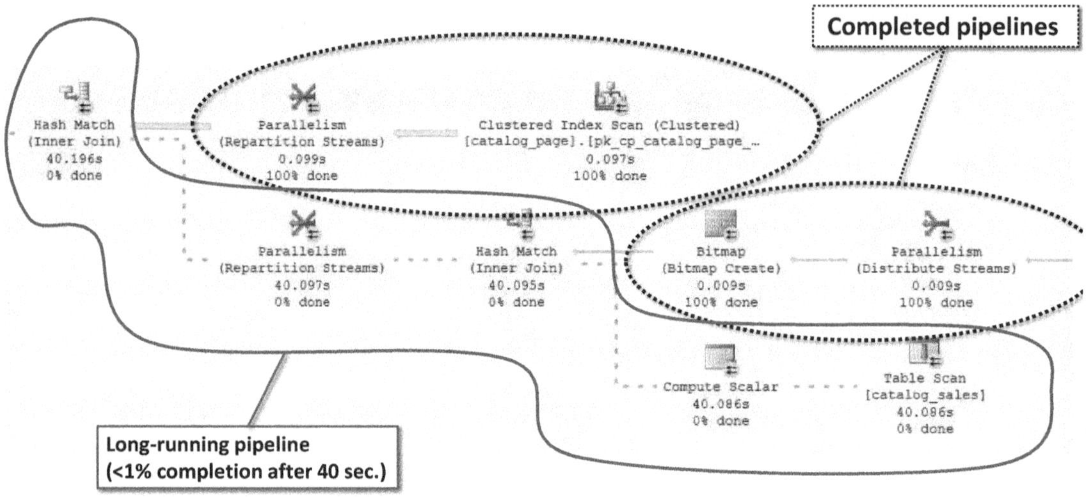

Figure 3: Live Query Statistics in Action

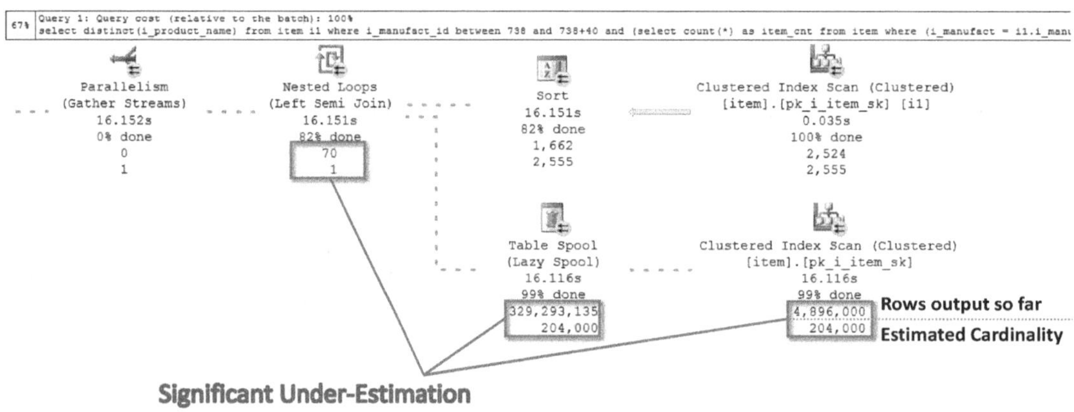

Figure 4: Live Query Statistics in Action

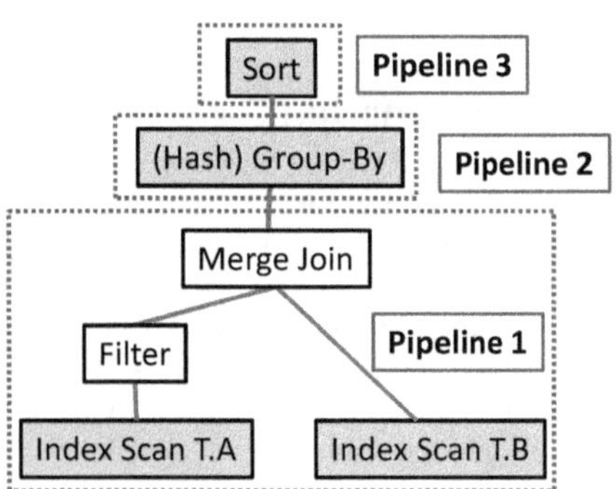

Figure 5: Example execution plan with multiple pipelines.

"trick" described above of only considering driver nodes can not be applied here, unlike for progress estimation of the entire query (or pipeline).

While the challenge of inaccurate cardinality estimates cannot be overcome generally, there is one unique aspect of progress estimation that can be leveraged here: unlike the cardinality estimation inside the query optimizer [5], progress estimation has the opportunity to observe execution characteristics of operators *in flight*, and use this feedback to dynamically *refine* cardinality estimates for both the executing operators and operators further up in the query plan. Earlier approaches to progress estimation [6, 15, 23] have used this to propose techniques that dynamically refine cardinality estimates as the query executes. For LQS, we propose a cardinality refinement approach of the same type, which uses a different model (described in Section 4.1) and in practice demonstrates fast convergence to the true cardinality. We combine this technique with the (worst-base) bounding techniques proposed in [7] based on algebraic properties of the operators (which we describe in Section 4.2). The combination of both techniques can help us mitigate many cases where there are egregious errors in the initial optimizer cardinality estimates.

Second, for accurate estimates of *operator* level progress, we needed to develop new techniques for modeling blocking operators (e.g. *Hash*, *Sort*), whose progress is in general insufficiently characterized by the number of tuples output by the operator itself. Here, the unmodified *GetNext* model as described in Section 3.1.2 is not sufficient to give accurate progress estimates, even when cardinalities are known. In addition, similar but not identical challenges are posed by *semi-blocking* operators (e.g., *Exchange*, *Nested Loops*) that can buffer inputs and break key assumptions made by earlier progress estimation techniques. We describe the techniques used to address these challenges in Sections 4.4 and 4.5.

Third, due to the often vastly different (per-row) resource requirements of different operators, we need to determine an appropriate weight for each operator in a query to obtain accurate overall query progress. For this challenge, we adopt a variant of the technique of [18], which leverages per-tuple CPU and I/O cost estimates by the optimizer and models the overlap between CPU and I/O as the basis for automatically determining an appropriate weight for an operator (or pipeline of operators).

Finally, we need to handle a number of additional cases not addressed in prior work but common in practice, including: (a) Scan operators containing filters evaluated at the storage engine level (e.g., *Bitmap* filters) whose selectivity may initially be estimated incorrectly, (b) operators such as *Scans* of *Columnstore indexes* [16, 17] that execute in *batch mode* rather than one row at a time. We will describe how we address each of these challenges in the next section.

4. ADDRESSING THE TECHNICAL CHALLENGES

In Section 3.3, we have identified a number of different challenges to accurate progress estimation as well as some scenarios not addressed by prior work; in this section, we will describe different techniques used to address these and improve the accuracy of progress estimation.

4.1 Cardinality Refinement

As described in Section 3.1.2, the N_i terms in the progress estimator (see Equation 2) are based on optimizer estimates, which may be very inaccurate for the long-running and often complex queries that progress estimation is targeted at. The use of *driver nodes* discussed in Section 3.1.1 alleviates this concern only partially; this approach assumes that the overall progress in a pipeline is proportional to the progress of the driver nodes, which can be violated in practice (see [15], Section 4.4.1, for a more detailed discussion). Moreover, providing operator-level progress estimates requires accurate estimates of the N_i terms on all nodes, not just the driver nodes.

While there exist large numbers of techniques to improve cardinality estimates by leveraging feedback from other executing queries in the research literature (such as [4, 8, 14, 20, 27, 28]), many of which are applicable in the context of progress estimation, our current technique only leverages the data structures and statistics already available in the target database engines; we leave the integration of novel statistical summaries as future work.

Instead, we leverage the observation that, unlike query optimization, progress estimation can leverage improved N_i estimates obtained *after* a query has started execution. The basic technique we use is to refine the estimate of N_i at runtime by treating the input tuples seen at a node i as a random sample of all tuples processed by this operator (similarly, to e.g., [13] for $COUNT$ aggregate queries) and scale the corresponding k_i up by the (inverse of the) fraction α of the tuples consumed at the driver node(s) of the corresponding pipeline:

$$\alpha = \frac{\sum_{i \in \text{DriverNodes}} k_i}{\sum_{i \in \text{DriverNodes}} N_i} \tag{3}$$

Here, we use only the driver nodes to estimate the scale-up factor, as for them the N_i are typically known with high accuracy, making the estimate of the total cardinality $N_i = k_i/\alpha$. The refinement of the total cardinality N_i at node i, i.e., $N_i = k_i/\alpha$, can be interpreted as *population estimation* using sampling without replacement. The intuition is that, each row output by a driver node (by a *GetNext* call) may trigger the output of zero, one, or more rows at node i. So assuming future drive-node rows trigger the output of rows at node i at *the same rate*, the total number of rows output by node i becomes k_i/α.

Of course, rows are output at node i at varying rates during the whole process and thus we need to estimate the *average rate*. Formally, let

$$TotalRows_{\text{DN}} = \sum_{i \in \text{DriverNodes}} N_i$$

be the total number of rows output by driver nodes, and

$$SeenRows_{\text{DN}} = \sum_{i \in \text{DriverNodes}} k_i$$

be the number of rows output by them so far. Let N_i^{true} be the true cardinality at node i. Our estimation N_i thus can be rewritten as

$$N_i = \frac{k_i}{\frac{SeenRows_{\text{DN}}}{TotalRows_{\text{DN}}}} = \frac{k_i}{SeenRows_{\text{DN}}} \cdot TotalRows_{\text{DN}}.$$

The true cardinality N_i^{true} can be rewritten similarly to be

$$N_i^{true} = \frac{N_i^{true}}{TotalRows_{\text{DN}}} \cdot TotalRows_{\text{DN}},$$

where $N_i^{true}/TotalRows_{\text{DN}}$ is the average rate of rows being output at node i. We essentially estimate this true average rate as $k_i/SeenRows_{\text{DN}}$, which decides how much error there is in our estimation of N_i relative to N_i^{true}.

If rows from driver nodes are randomly permuted, $k_i/SeenRows_{\text{DN}}$ is a reasonably accurate estimation of $N_i^{true}/TotalRows_{\text{DN}}$ with the estimation error bounded by the *Central Limit Theorem* or *Hoeffding inequality*. The order of these rows, unfortunately, depends on the physical layout of database tables which is fixed in advance and cannot be assumed to be totally random. Still, refining cardinalities in this manner is still a valid strategy for the vast majority of possible orderings: we have been able to show that among all possible orders of these rows, in the majority of them, $k_i/SeenRows_{\text{DN}}$ is very close to $N_i^{true}/TotalRows_{\text{DN}}$.

Formally, an order of rows from driver nodes is said to be a *bad order* iff $\frac{|N_i - N_i^{true}|}{N_i^{true}} > \epsilon$. Among all possible orders of rows being output from driver nodes, the portion of bad orders is proportional to $\frac{1}{\epsilon^2 \cdot SeenRows_{\text{DN}}}$ (where the exact equation depends on a number of additional, data-dependent parameters), which decreases quickly as we get more and more rows from driver nodes (i.e., as $SeenRows_{\text{DN}}$ increases).

Obviously, as also pointed out in [12], extrapolating the N_i from observations in this manner requires initially observing sufficiently many tuples at node i as well to allow us to estimate the operator selectivity accurately. As a result, we only invoke the cardinality refinement if the following guard conditions are met: First, similar to [12], we require a minimum number of tuples observed for all inputs to any operator. Second, for any filter or join operator, we only trigger refinement if we have observed *both* tuples satisfying the join/filter condition as well as tuples not satisfying it.

One thing to note is that a different techniques for online refinement of cardinality estimates in progress estimates have been proposed previously [22]. Unlike this approach, we do not use linear interpolation between the initial optimizer estimate and the scaled-up estimate, as we found these estimates to converge very slowly for highly erroneous initial estimates.

Finally, for any nested loop iterations, we make an additional modification to the technique, refining the cardinality estimates on the inner side of the nested loop by scaling the average number of $GetNext$ calls per input tuple by the corresponding $1/\alpha$ for the outer side; this is merely reflecting the fact that for nested loops, the outer side of the loop governs how often the inner side is invoked (as opposed to the child node). In case of multiple nested loops within a pipeline we have to apply this logic multiple times, from the outer to the inner nodes.

4.2 Cardinality Bounding

In addition to online cardinality refinement, we use the techniques described in [7] to maintain *worst-case* lower and upper bounds on the number of $GetNext$ calls possible for each operator, based on the number of tuples seen so far at each operator and the size of the input(s). If the value of any N_i ever falls outside of these bounds, it is set to the nearest boundary value. We describe the computation of the cardinality bounds on a per-operator basis in Appendix A.

Since these bounds are derived based on the algebraic properties of the operators alone, they are conservative, and therefore tend to only kick in for operators in the later pipelines in a query plan; for these operators, the initial cardinality estimation often requires computing selectivities for multiple joins and filter predicates, meaning that the cardinality estimates often have significant errors. In these cases, cardinality bounding can reduce these errors significantly: for example, after a first pipeline is complete, we know the exact cardinality of the input to the leaf node(s) of the second pipeline. In such cases, the resulting upper bound on the corresponding N_i for any node in the second pipeline can be significantly lower than the initial optimizer estimate of these N_i, in turn improving the cardinalities used during progress estimation. Similarly, these bounding techniques can improve estimates in case of cardinality underestimation as well. As we will show in the experimental evaluation (see Section 5.1), cardinality bounding results in noticeable increase in overall progress estimation accuracy.

4.3 Predicates evaluated in the Storage Engine

A special case for progress estimation are predicates that are pushed down to the storage engine. One important example of this are *bitmap filters*, which are common in data warehousing workloads. Bitmap filters are a type of semi-join reduction in which rows on the inner side of the join that cannot join with rows on the outer side, are eliminated prior to the join operator. In a typical case, the bitmap filter is created when the build input of a *Hash Join* is executed, and the bitmap filter is evaluated when scanning the probe side input. An example of a bitmap filter that has been pushed into the scan is shown in Figure 6.

There are many other examples of such filters, such as complex combinations of conjunctions and disjunctions, predicates on out-of-model scalar functions, etc., all of which may be pushed to the storage engine.

Because these predicates filter out rows as part of the initial data access, the assumption that we base driver nodes on, namely, that we have accurate estimates of the number of rows output by a driver node, is not valid any more. In fact, the bitmap filters and other complex predicates of this type often have very large estimation errors. As a result, using these driver nodes to compute query progress or as part of cardinality refinement for other nodes becomes problematic.

Therefore, we use a different technique when estimating the progress at nodes of this type: as long as only predicates are pushed to the storage engine that cannot be supported by an index, we know that

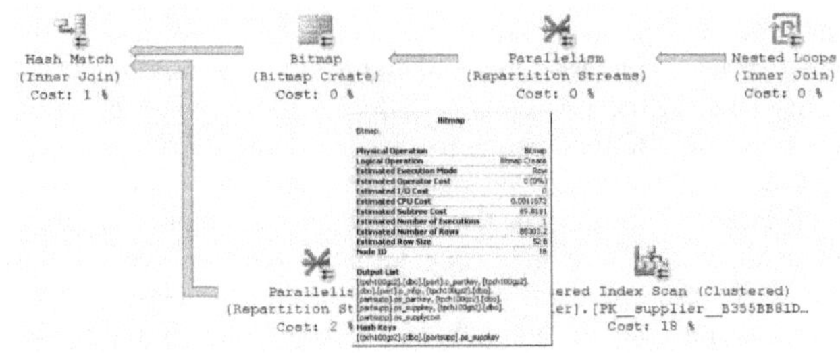

Figure 6: Plan with Bitmap Filter Evaluation in Index Scan.

the entirety of the table has to be accessed by the *Scan* operator (even if many rows may be filtered as part of the scan); hence, we instead compute the number of logical I/O operations required to scan the underlying table and based the current measure of progress at the *Scan* node in question on the fraction of these I/O requests issued at this point. This approach has turned out to be highly accurate and a significant improvement over the initial approach.

4.4 Semi-blocking Operators

Some operators such as *Sort* and *Hash* are stop-and-go, i.e., they are blocking. Other operators are pipelined in their execution, however, they buffer their output, which causes them to behave similar to blocking operators for subsets of their output. We refer to such operators as *semi-blocking*. Examples of such semi-blocking operators include *Nested Loops* (when the inner operator is an Index Seek) and *Parallelism* (aka. *Exchange*).

To illustrate this issue, consider the query pipelines shown in Figure 7: without any buffering, we would expect the number of *GetNext* calls in the *Parallelism* operator and its *Nested Loop* child to be identical. However, this is not the case in practice: in Figure 8 we plot the number of *GetNext* calls for both operators over time – as we can see, the *Parallelism* operator 'lags' behind its child noticeably. Note that while the curves follow each other closely on the time-scale, because of the steep trajectory of the curve, the difference in the number of *GetNext* calls between the operators can be very significant; for example, for the two measurements highlighted in Figure 8, the ratios between the *GetNext* calls of the *Nested Loop* and the *Parallelism* operator are about 88x and 12x, respectively. This, in turn, can significantly hurt the accuracy of progress estimation for two main reasons.

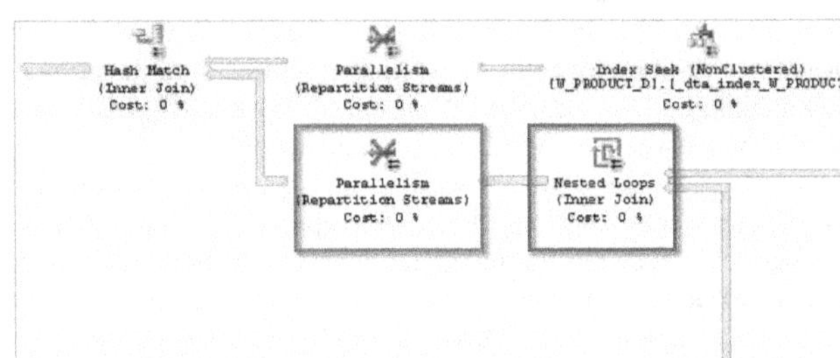

Figure 7: The *Parallelism* operator in this plan progresses significantly slower than its child node (*Nested Loop*)

First, they break the central assumption underlying the use of *driver nodes*, namely that the progress measured using driver nodes only corresponds to the progress over all nodes in a pipeline. To illustrate this, consider the case of a pipeline consisting of a single index nested loop join, with the scan of the outer side being the sole driver node. In this scenario, the buffering can lead to the

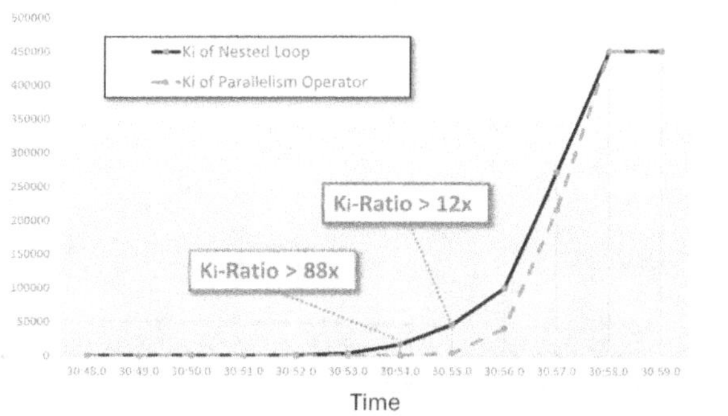

Figure 8: The difference in the *GetNext* calls between the two nodes from Figure 7 over time

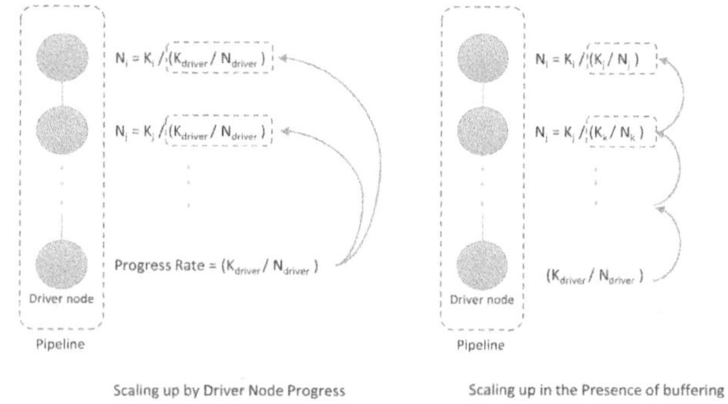

Figure 9: Scaling up N_i estimates using driver nodes vs. immediate child nodes.

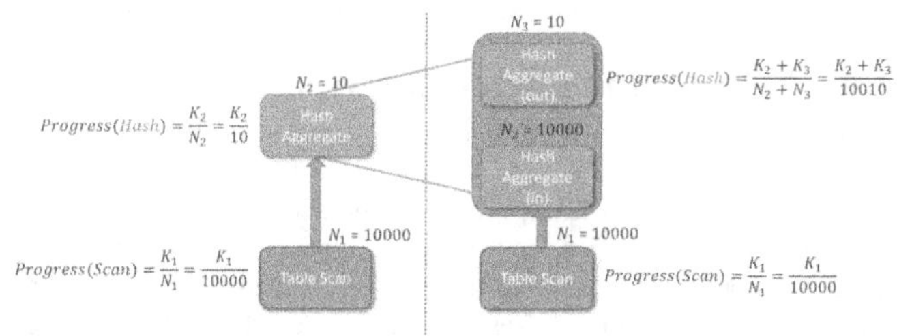

Figure 10: Modeling Hash Aggregation Progress in Two Phases.

scenario where all tuples from the outer side have been consumed and buffered before any tuples on the inner side were accessed, meaning that the progress at the driver node is 100%, yet the query may still be far from completion. This is a scenario we observe often in practice.

Second, when significant buffering occurs, the method described in Section 4.1 of refining the N_i estimates by scaling the corresponding k_i by the (inverse) driver-node progress is not accurate any more; especially when multiple semi-blocking operators occur in sequence in a query pipeline, this will lead to significant over-estimation of the N_i terms, as the 'correct' scale-factor becomes smaller and smaller with every semi-blocking operator between the node whose cardinality we are trying to refine and the driver nodes of the corresponding pipeline.

To address these issues, we modify the techniques described so far for pipelines containing semi-blocking operators as follows:
(1) For progress estimation of *Nested Loop* joins (which buffer tuples coming from the outer side), we treat the inner side of the join as a driver node as well. Similar modifications were proposed in [15] and were shown to yield significant improvements across a wide range of workloads there.
(2) For the purpose of improving initial estimates of the N_i counts using the cardinality refinement techniques of Section 4.1, we scale-up the k_i counts of a node that is separated from the leaves of its pipeline by at least one semi-blocking operator, using the progress at its *immediate child*. This is in contrast to using the progress of the driver node to scale-up the k_i counts. This difference in scale-up logic is illustrated in Figure 9. In case of nodes with multiple children (e.g., *Merge Joins*) we use both children's progress to compute the corresponding α.
(3) Finally, we adjust the scale-up factor for tuples on the inner side of a nested loop join to adjust for the fraction of tuples buffered on the outer side of the operator.

4.5 Improvements for Blocking Operators

One challenge introduced by operator-level progress is the accurate modelling of progress for blocking operators. For many blocking operators, the fraction of work done by the operator itself is very poorly characterized by the fraction of tuples output by the operator. For example, in case of *Hash Aggregates*, once tuples have started to be output, typically most of the processing and I/O associated with the operator have been completed already. When considering query-level progress, this issue is often, but not always, masked by the fact that the I/O and processing associated with tuples being input to a blocking operator is modelled as part of its child's operator(s). However, for operator-level progress, this does not apply any more.

Earlier work [12] has dealt with this scenario by introducing two new terms: "blocking time", which specifies the amount of time required before an operator outputs tuples, and "blocking progress", which specifies the fraction of total work done before tuples are output. The approach we chose in this work is different: because the relative per-tuple processing overhead for input and output tuples can be significantly different and change as a function of the width of output rows, complexity and number of aggregate expressions and grouping columns, etc., we model operators of this type (such as *Sort* and *Hash*) as two distinct phases. The first phase progresses in proportion to the fraction of input tuples consumed, whereas the second phase progresses in proportion to the fraction of tuples output by the operator.

We show the change compared to earlier approaches in Figure 10. On the left side we show the earlier progress model for a *Hash Aggregate* operator which inputs 10K tuples and outputs 10. In this model, the progress for this operator is 0 until tuples are output. In the new model, shown on the right side, the input and output phases of the *Hash Aggregate* are modelled separately, with the input executing synchronously with the child *Scan* operator and the output executing subsequently. To illustrate the effect of this change in practice, we plot the example progress for a *Hash Aggregate* operator (used in the execution of TPC-DS Query 13) in Figure 11 over the time the operator is active; in the figure, the dotted line represents a perfect estimate. Whereas the original model (using the output N_i only) reports no progress throughout nearly the entire time (and only changes when output is produced at the very end of execution), the new progress model (based on both input and output tuples) shows the operator making progress before any output is produced and correlates much better with time.

Note that the new model still can be an over-simplification, for example, for large sorts with multiple merge steps even more intri-

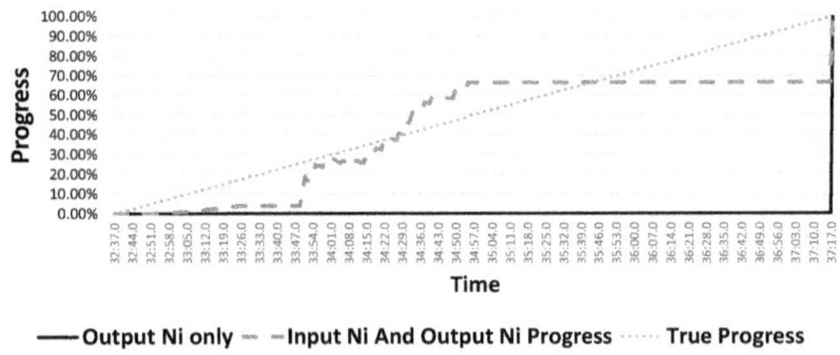

Figure 11: The effect of the refined model for Hash Aggregation

cate models may be needed; however, it performs well in practice across a variety of workloads and significantly improves upon our earlier models, as we demonstrate in the experimental evaluation.

4.6 Selecting the Operator Weights

While the accuracy of single-operator progress mainly depends on accurate estimation of the N_i (and – for blocking operators – how we "break" them into pipelines), the accuracy of the overall query progress requires us to assess the relative "speeds" at which different pipelines iterate over tuples; these speeds in turn depend on the corresponding row sizes and the amount of processing done at each individual operator in a pipeline.

We model these differences in speeds by changing the corresponding w_i terms in equation 2 accordingly. For this, we adopt the framework first introduced in [18]; here, the query workload is divided up into *speed-independent* pipelines, which are defined as groups of connected operators that execute concurrently and process tuples at a speed independent of the speeds of other operators (in other pipelines). The relative weights for each such pipeline are then set using estimates of I/O and CPU cost of the corresponding operators by the optimizer and the notion of 'overlapping' work: we make the (simplifying) assumption that I/O and CPU cost within a single operator are overlapping, meaning that only their maximum is used to weigh a pipeline.

In addition, the overall duration of a query depends only on the duration of its "longest" path (i.e., the path of speed-independent pipelines from the top operator in a query to the leaf level which requires the longest time among all such paths). As a result, we maintain this path (based on optimizer cost estimates of I/O and CPU cost per tuple and refined N_i counts) among all pipelines and use only the set of nodes along it to compute the overall query progress.

Because the weights we use are derived from optimizer cost estimates, they do not model transient effects not considered by it (e.g., effects of caching due to the buffer pool).

To illustrate the difference that this weighting scheme can make on progress estimation, we plotted the progress estimates over time for query 21 from the TPC-DS benchmark in Figure 12. As we can see in Figure 12, the un-weighted estimator severely underestimates query progress until the very end of query execution. In contrast, the weighted operator progress correlates much better with time. Examining the query plan in question in more detail, we see that it consists of 6 pipelines; one of them is not part of the longest path, so it is ignored. Two of the pipelines have very small CPU and I/O costs (and also only small numbers of tuples), so they don't affect progress estimation significantly. However, for the remaining 3 pipelines, which make up the majority of the execution, the corresponding weights differ by more than an order of magnitude, with the first two pipelines in the query plan having

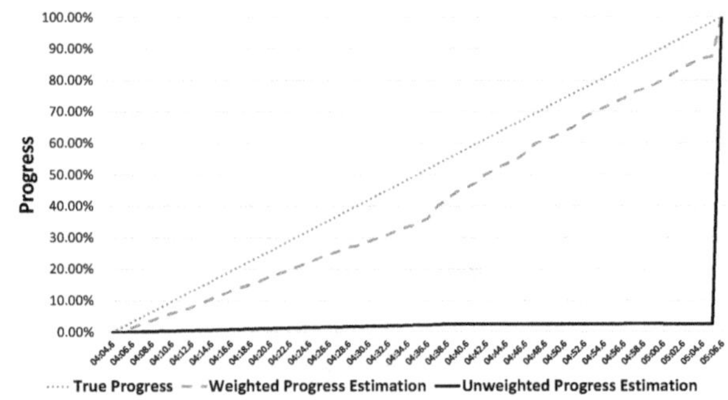

Figure 12: Progress for TPCDS Q21 with and w/o operator weights

high weights and each corresponding to nearly half of the execution time in the query (which can be seen by the two distinct 'angles' in the progress estimate in Figure 12); the effect of modelling these weights better (in combination with an initial over-estimate of the cardinality of the third pipeline, whose importance is decreased due to the adjusted weights) results in the improved accuracy of the progress estimates. We will evaluate the overall effects of using operator weights in Section 5.

4.7 Progress Estimation for Data with Column-store Indexes

In addition to the traditional row-at-a-time execution model, Microsoft SQL Server supports processing data in batches of rows when operating on data stored in columnar format, thereby greatly reducing CPU time and cache misses when processing large data sets [16, 17]. These changes affect progress estimation as well, as progress for these operators cannot be based on $GetNext$ calls any more; instead, we use a more coarse-grained approach in which we base the progress estimates for these operators/pipelines on the fraction of column segments processed at any point in time. The dynamic management view *sys.dm_exec_query_profiles* exposes the counters required for computing the numbers of segments processed by an operator as well, while the total number of segments in the underlying index can be computed from the dynamic management view *sys.column_store_segments*.

5. EXPERIMENTS

In this section, we will evaluate the various techniques described in Section 4 using both real-world and synthetic workloads.

Workloads: In order for this evaluation to cover a wide range of query plans and data distributions, we use 5 different workloads; the set of workloads we selected is skewed towards decision-support scenarios, since progress estimation is generally most important for longer-running queries. The workloads we use are

- A 100 GB instance of the TPC-H benchmark, with the data generated with a skew-parameter of $Z = 1$ [1].
- A 100 GB instance of the TPC-DS decision support benchmark.
- "*REAL-1*": a real-world decision-support and reporting workload over a 9GB Sales database. Most of the queries in this workload involve joins of 5-8 tables as well as nested sub-queries. The workload contains 477 distinct queries.
- "*REAL-2*" is a different real-life decision-support workload on 12GB dataset with even more complex queries (with a

typical query involving 12 joins). This workload contains a total of 632 queries.

- *"REAL-3"*: a 3rd real-life decision-support workload using a 97 GB dataset; this workload contains a total of 40 join and group by queries.

Error Metrics: In the following experiments, we will consider two different error metrics, depending on which aspect of our algorithm we seek to evaluate.

First, in scenarios where we evaluate the accuracy of techniques designed to improve the estimation of the N_i denominators in equation 2, we compare the accuracy of an *unweighted* (i.e., $\forall i : w_i = 1$) progress estimator $Prog$ to the progress estimate we obtain when we replace all estimated N_i with the exact values $\bar{N}_i$ (which we can determine after a query's completion). We measure this error at a number of evenly spaced time-intervals, recording the progress estimates as well as the k_i and N_i for every second of a query's runtime. We use the notation set $Observations(\mathcal{Q})$ to denote the set of all such measurements for a query $\mathcal{Q}$; for simplicity of notation, we denote each measurement using an index $t, t \in Observations(\mathcal{Q})$. For each measurement t, we denote the corresponding number of *GetNext* calls at a node i by k_i^t. We average the resulting error per query over all measurements and over all queries. This measure of accuracy thus becomes:

$$Error_{count} :=$$

$$\frac{1}{|\mathcal{Q}|} \sum_{\mathcal{Q} \in \text{Workload}} \left(\sum_{t \in Observations(\mathcal{Q})} \left| \left(Prog(Q,t) - \frac{\sum_{i \in Nodes(\mathcal{Q})} k_i^t}{\sum_{i \in Nodes(\mathcal{Q})} \bar{N}_i} \right) \right| \right)$$

Second, in practice many users of progress estimates mainly care about how well the estimates correlate with the time required to execute this query. In addition, a number of the techniques discussed in Section 4, such as the selection of different weights w_i for each operator i are aimed at improving the correlation between execution time and progress (and would remain important even if all N_i were estimated without error). Here, for each measurement t we use $Time(t)$ to denote the time the measurement was taken and $Time(t_{start}(\mathcal{Q}))$ to denote the start and $Time(t_{end}(\mathcal{Q}))$ to denote the end of execution for a query $\mathcal{Q}$. We introduce a second error measure that evaluates how well a progress estimator $Prog$ correlates with time, defined as

$$Error_{time} := \frac{1}{|\mathcal{Q}|} \sum_{\mathcal{Q} \in \text{Workload}}$$

$$\left(\sum_{t \in Observations(\mathcal{Q})} \left| \left(Prog(Q,t) - \frac{Time(t) - Time(t_{start}(\mathcal{Q}))}{Time(t_{end}(\mathcal{Q})) - Time(t_{start}(\mathcal{Q}))} \right) \right| \right)$$

We also consider use operator-specific variants of each error measure, where we only consider the error over all operators of a specific type.

For both metrics, all queries are executed in isolation. Note that for both metrics, the maximum error is small; for $Error_{count}$, it cannot exceed 1.0 and for $Error_{time}$ it cannot exceed 0.5. Hence, even an improvement of 0.1 or even 0.05 is significant in terms of real-life progress estimation accuracy. To illustrate this, we have plotted the progress estimators for two estimators on TPC-DS query 36 in Figure 13, with the difference in error between them being 0.1.

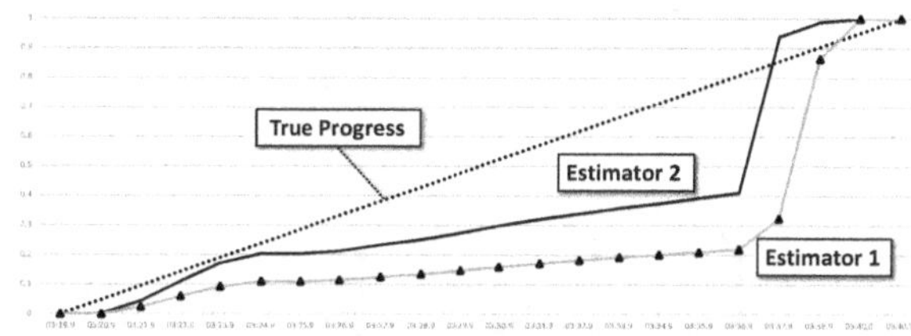

Figure 13: Two example progress estimates with 0.1 difference in Error

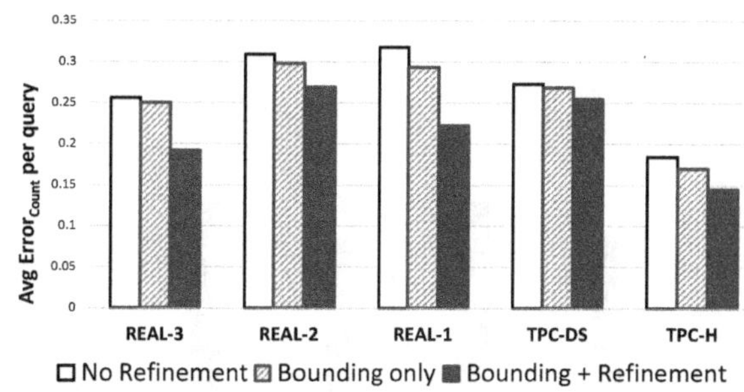

Figure 14: Evaluating the effect of cardinality refinement

5.1 Evaluation of Cardinality Refinement

First, we evaluate the effect of the various techniques used to obtain more accurate estimates of the N_i terms in Equation 2, namely the online cardinality refinement discussed in Section 4.1 and the cardinality bounding described in Section 4.2.

In Figure 14 we show the overall $Error_{count}$ when comparing the overall query progress computed with *exact* knowledge of the correct N_i terms to progress estimates based on three different models: (a) the "Total GetNext" (TGN) Model (which corresponds to Equation 2 with all w_i terms set to 1), (b) the TGN model with cardinality bounding and (c) the query progress model based on *driver nodes* only (DNE), using both online cardinality refinement as well as cardinality bounding. The results are shown in Figure 14. As we can see, both online cardinality refinement as well as bounding both substantially improve the quality of progress estimation across all workloads.

In Figure 15 we show the effect of cardinality refinement broken down by each operator type; we plot the average $Error_{count}$ for each operator when using (a) no refinement, (b) only the refinement based on the techniques described in Section 4.1 and (c) when using the basic cardinality refinement techniques combined with the modifications geared towards addressing the challenges posed by semi-blocking operators (see Section 4.4).

As we can see, while cardinality refinements improve estimates for some operators (most notably *Nested Loop Joins* and the *Bitmap* filter operators associated with *Hash Joins*), they also cause the average accuracy for some operators to degrade, e.g., when the fraction of tuples output by an operator is significantly correlated with time. Still, as shown by Figure 14, even the simple refinement techniques noticeably improve progress estimates when compared to no refinement when averaged over all operators.

Now, adding the techniques that address semi-blocking operators improves the effect of refinement across the board (with only one exception: *Merge Join* operators), in many cases significantly; this illustrates the importance of dealing with this type of buffering, which – in the context of cardinality refinement – has not been addressed in prior work.

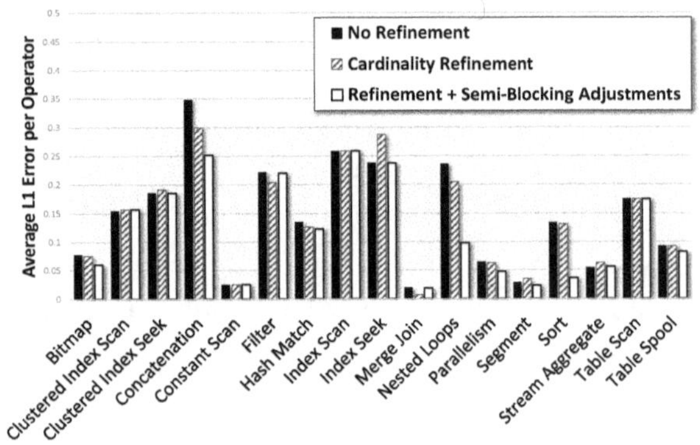

Figure 15: Effect of Cardinality Refinement by Operator

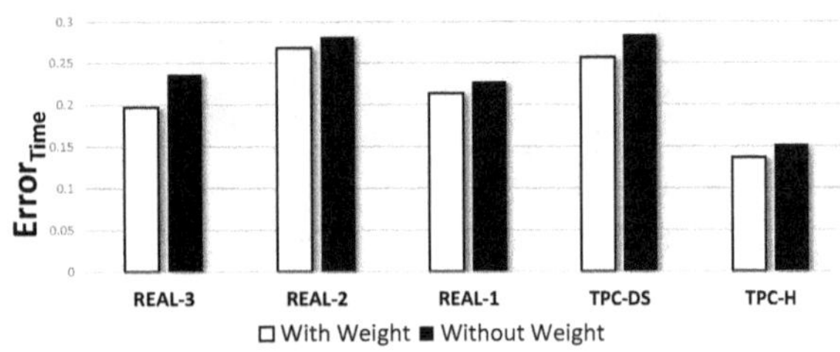

Figure 16: Evaluating the effect of operator weights

5.2 Evaluation of Operator weights

In this experiment, we evaluate the effect of the techniques using the relative operator cost when combining the progress estimates across pipelines on overall per-query accuracy. For this purpose, we evaluated all 5 workloads both with no weights (i.e., $\forall i : w_i = 1$) and compared the resulting accuracy to the weighting scheme described in Section 4.6. Because weights are intended to model the variations in speed across pipelines, we use the $Error_{time}$ metric here. The results are shown in Figure 16. As we can see, applying the weighting scheme improves the correlation between progress estimates and time noticeably across all workloads.

5.3 Evaluation: Improvements for Blocking Operators

In this experiment, we evaluate the effectiveness of the techniques described in Section 4.5 to improve the modelling of blocking operators. For this purpose, we measured $Error_{time}$ for both the original model as well as the improved one over all instances of *Sort* and *Hash Aggregation* operators over all 5 workloads; the results are shown in Figure 17. As we can see, the new model does noticeably improve the modelling of both *Hash* and *Sort* operators; at the same time, the absolute errors are still significant, suggesting that a more refined model of these operators utilizing more information on the internal operator state as future work.

5.4 Evaluation: Progress Estimation for Batch-Mode Operations

In this experiment, we evaluate the effect that the presence of Columnar Indexes has on progress estimation: for this purpose, we executed the TPC-H workload over two different physical designs: (a) the design obtained when building all indexes recommended for this workload by the Microsoft SQL Server Database Tuning Advisor [3] (DTA) and (b) the design obtained where we only construct a non-clustered Columnstore Index on each table in

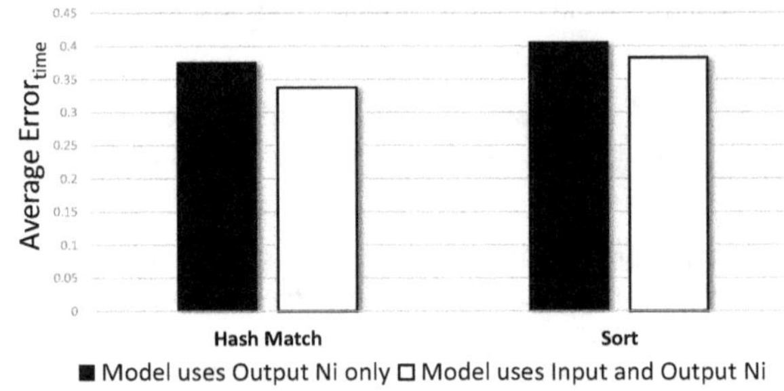

Figure 17: Evaluating the new model for blocking operators

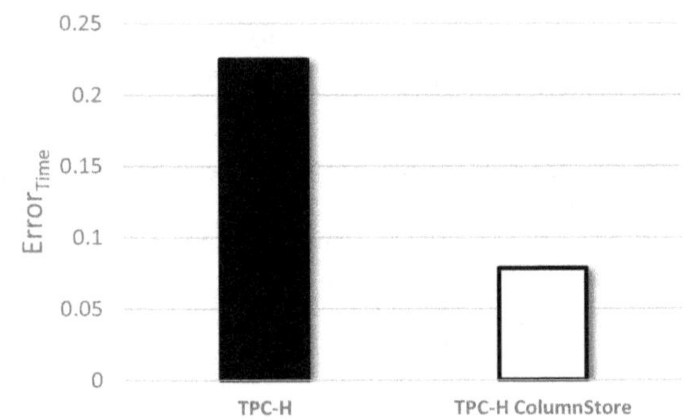

Figure 18: Average Error with and without Columnstore Indexes

the TPC-H benchmark. The average $Error_{Time}$ over the entire TPC-H workload is shown in Figure 18.

As we can see, the average error is reduced significantly; this turns out to be due to two main factors: for one, the distribution of operators for this workload has changed significantly: in Figure 19 we plotted the counts of each operator across the TPC-H workload for the two different physical designs; as we can see, the non-Columnstore design induces query plans with much more significant variation in the types of operators, whereas the Columnstore design results in query plans which mostly consist of *Index Scans* and *Hash Join* operators and much fewer *Nested Loops* or *Index Seek* operators.

Furthermore, the distribution of progress estimation errors changed significantly as well: in Figure 20, we plot the $Error_{Time}$ broken

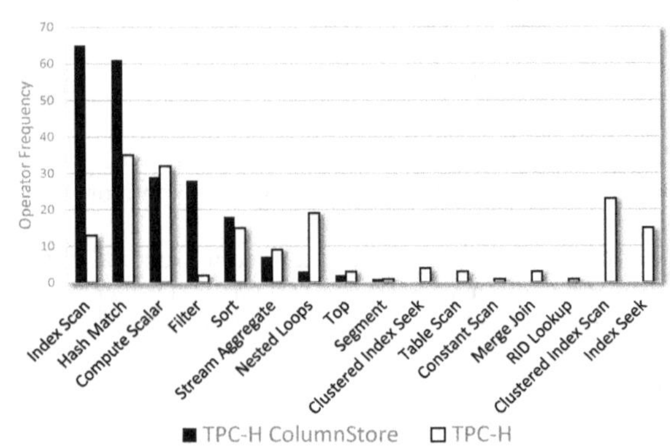

Figure 19: Operator Distribution with and without Columnar Indexes

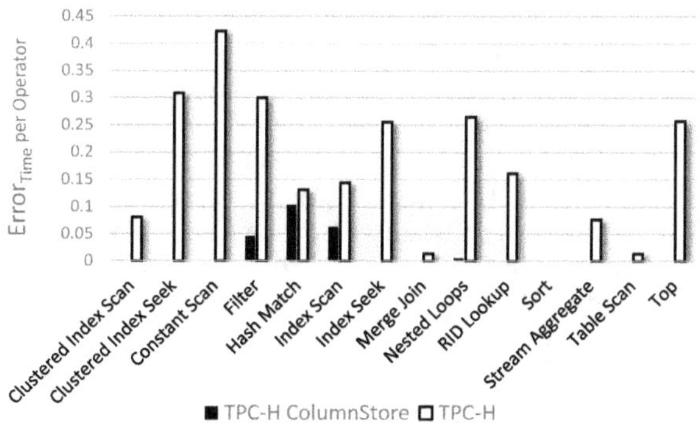

Figure 20: Average Error per Operator with and without Columnar Indexes

down by each operator. We can see that the per-operator error is significantly reduced for all operators occurring in the design based on Columnstore Indexes.

6. RELATED WORK

The problem of progress estimation for database queries was first proposed and studied in [7] and [22], with further refinements in [6,23,24]. In addition to the work on query progress estimation itself, there has been considerable research interest in techniques estimating the execution time of queries outright; however, these techniques either require the pre-computation of uniform random samples for all tables touched by a query [29,30], which can be prohibitively expensive in practice, or rely on statistical models trained on prior instances of the same query template and therefore do not generalize to new ad-hoc queries [9,10].

A statistical approach to progress estimation, that attempts to pick among a set of existing estimators dynamically using machine learning, has been described in [15]. [21] extended query progress estimation to multi-query scenarios, and [19,25,26] study progress estimation in *MapReduce* systems, both of which are scenarios that are beyond the scope of this paper.

Other database engines, e.g., *Oracle* expose server side views that provide real time monitoring of actual and estimated cardinality for currently executing query plans similar to the DMVs discussed in this paper. *Oracle* also exposes a dynamic view (*v$session_longops*) that – similar to *dm_exec_query_profiles* – provides statistical information and progress estimation for database operations such as backup/recovery functions, statistics gathering, and certain types of SQL operators [2]. However, not all operators in SQL queries are covered and therefore (often) no estimate of *overall* query progress is possible.

7. DISCUSSION AND FUTURE WORK

While the experimental evaluation demonstrated the improvements over the earlier state-of-the-art realized as a result of the techniques described in Section 4, they also point to opportunities for further improvements in progress estimates. Because the current design computes a query's progress as part of a client process, most of these improvements require the Microsoft SQL Server engine to expose additional counters beyond the set contained as part of *sys.dm_exec_query_profiles* already. These include:

- More fine-grained information on the internal state of blocking operators such as *Hash* and *Sort*. As illustrated in Figure 11, these operators can perform significant processing that is not concurrent with them outputting rows, meaning that it is not captured well by the *GetNext* model.
- Counters exposing how many tuples are being buffered and how many tuples have been passed on for all semi-blocking operators such as *Nested Loop* joins or *Parallelism*.
- In cases where we have combinations of filters evaluated at a leaf node, we need additional information on the selectivities of these filters: in order to apply the technique described in Section 4.3 in these scenarios, we ideally require the cardinality resulting from the filters that leverage indexes in their execution *only* to adjust the number of logical reads used in the technique described in Section 4.3 accordingly.

Other potential future improvements include (a) the improved propagation of cardinality estimate refinements *across* pipeline boundaries, as we currently only propagate worst-case bounds beyond blocking operators, but not refined cardinalities themselves, and (b) the ability to use feedback from prior executions of queries to adjust the weights that model the relative costs of CPU and I/O overhead when estimating query-level progress, (c) extending the refined model of Section 4.5 to additional operators and (d) improved cardinality-refinement logic for special cases where it is known that the number of *GetNext* calls (per driver node tuple) is highly correlated with time, such as cases of *Merge Joins* where one of the inputs contains large regions of non-joining tuples before the first joining tuple is seen, or filters with predicates on the column the input data is sorted on.

Acknowledgements: We are grateful for the feedback from the anonymous reviewers, which improved this paper significantly.

8. REFERENCES

[1] Program for TPC-H data generation with Skew. ftp://ftp.research.microsoft.com/users/viveknar/TPCDSkew/.

[2] V$SESSION_LONGOPS. http://docs.oracle.com/cd/B19306_01/server.102/b14237/-dynviews_2092.htm#REFRN30227.

[3] S. Agrawal, S. Chaudhuri, L. Kollar, A. Marathe, V. Narasayya, and M. Syamala. Database Tuning Advisor for Microsoft SQL Server 2005. In *VLDB*, pages 1110 1121, 2004.

[4] N. Bruno, S. Chaudhuri, and L. Gravano. STHoles: A Multidiemsnional Workload-Aware Histogram. In *ACM SIGMOD*, 2001.

[5] S. Chaudhuri. An overview of Query Optimization in Relational Systems. In *ACM PODS*, 1998.

[6] S. Chaudhuri, R. Kaushik, and R. Ramamurthy. When can we trust Progress Estimators for SQL queries? In *Proceedings of the 2005 ACM SIGMOD international conference on Management of data*, pages 575–586. ACM, 2005.

[7] S. Chaudhuri, V. Narasayya, and R. Ramamurthy. Estimating Progress of Execution for SQL queries. In *Proceedings of the 2004 ACM SIGMOD international conference on Management of data*, pages 803–814. ACM, 2004.

[8] C. M. Chen and N. Roussoploulos. Adaptive Selectivity Estimation Using Query Feedback. In *Proceedings of the ACM SIGMOD Conference*, pages 161–172, May 1994.

[9] J. Duggan, U. Cetintemel, O. Papaemmanouil, and E. Upfal. Performance Prediction for Concurrent Database Workloads. In *Proceedings of the 2011 ACM SIGMOD International Conference on Management of data*, pages 337–348. ACM, 2011.

[10] A. Ganapathi, H. Kuno, U. Dayal, J. L. Wiener, A. Fox, M. I. Jordan, and D. Patterson. Predicting Multiple Metrics for Queries: Better Decisions enabled by Machine Learning. In *Data Engineering, 2009. ICDE'09. IEEE 25th International Conference on*, pages 592–603. IEEE, 2009.

[11] G. Graefe. Query Evaluation Techniques for Large Databases. *ACM Computing Surveys (CSUR)*, 25(2):73–169, 1993.

[12] R. H. Güting. Operator-Based Query Progress Estimation. Technical Report 343-2/2008, FernUniversität Hagen, February 2008.

[13] J. M. Hellerstein, P. J. Haas, and H. J. Wang. Online Aggregation. *ACM SIGMOD Record*, 26(2):171–182, 1997.

[14] A. König and G. Weikum. Combining Histograms and Parametric Curve Fitting for Feedback-Driven Query Result-size Estimation. In *25th International Conference on Very Large Databases*, 1999.

[15] A. C. König, B. Ding, S. Chaudhuri, and V. Narasayya. A Statistical Approach towards Robust Progress Estimation. *Proceedings of the VLDB Endowment*, 5(4):382–393, 2011.

[16] P.-A. Larson, C. Clinciu, C. Fraser, E. N. Hanson, M. Mokhtar, M. Nowakiewicz, V. Papadimos, S. L. Price, S. Rangarajan, R. Rusanu, and M. Saubhasik. Enhancements to SQL Server Column Stores. In *ACM SIGMOD*, 2013.

[17] P.-A. Larson, C. Clinciu, E. N. Hanson, A. Oks, S. L. Price, S. Rangarajan, A. Surna, and Q. Zhou. Sql Server Column Store Indexes. In *ACM SIGMOD*, 2011.

[18] J. Li, R. Nehme, and J. Naughton. GSLPI: A Cost-based Query Progress Indicator. In *Data Engineering (ICDE), 2012 IEEE 28th International Conference on*, pages 678–689. IEEE, 2012.

[19] J. Li, R. V. Nehme, and J. F. Naughton. Toward Progress Indicators on Steroids for Big Data Systems. In *CIDR*, 2013.

[20] L. Lim, M. Wang, and J. S. Vitter. SASH: a Self-adaptive Histogram Set for Dynamically Changing Workloads. In *VLDB*, 2003.

[21] G. Luo, J. Naughton, and P. Yu. Multi-query SQL Progress Indicators. In *EDBT*, pages 921–941, 2006.

[22] G. Luo, J. F. Naughton, C. J. Ellmann, and M. W. Watzke. Toward a progress indicator for database queries. In *Proceedings of the 2004 ACM SIGMOD international conference on Management of data*, pages 791–802. ACM, 2004.

[23] G. Luo, J. F. Naughton, C. J. Ellmann, and M. W. Watzke. Increasing the Accuracy and Coverage of SQL Progress Indicators. In *Data Engineering, 2005. ICDE 2005. Proceedings. 21st International Conference on*, pages 853–864. IEEE, 2005.

[24] C. Mishra and N. Koudas. A Lightweight Online Framework for Query Progress Indicators. In *Data Engineering, 2007. ICDE 2007. IEEE 23rd International Conference on*, pages 1292–1296. IEEE, 2007.

[25] K. Morton, M. Balazinska, and D. Grossman. ParaTimer: a Progress Indicator for Mapreduce DAGs. In *Proceedings of the 2010 ACM SIGMOD International Conference on Management of data*, pages 507–518. ACM, 2010.

[26] K. Morton, A. Friesen, M. Balazinska, and D. Grossman. Estimating the Progress of MapReduce Pipelines. In *26th International Conference on Data Engineering (ICDE)*. IEEE, 2010.

[27] M. Stillger, G. Lohman, V. Markl, and M. Kandil. LEO - DB2's Learning Optimizer. In *Proceedings of the 27th Conference on Very Large Databases, Rome, Italy*, 2001.

[28] N. Thaper, S. Guha, P. Indyk, and N. Koudas. Dynamic Multidimensional Histograms. In *Proceedings of ACM SIGMOD Conference, Madison, USA*, pages 428–439, 2002.

[29] W. Wu, Y. Chi, H. Hacígümüş, and J. F. Naughton. Towards Predicting Query Execution Time for Concurrent and Dynamic Database Workloads. *Proceedings of the VLDB Endowment*, 6(10):925–936, 2013.

[30] W. Wu, Y. Chi, S. Zhu, J. Tatemura, H. Hacigumus, and J. F. Naughton. Predicting Query Execution Time: Are Optimizer Cost Models really Unusable? In *Data Engineering (ICDE), 2013 IEEE 29th International Conference on*, pages 1081–1092. IEEE, 2013.

APPENDIX

A. CARDINALITY BOUNDING LOGIC

In this section, we will describe the logic used to the compute worst-case bounds on cardinalities during query execution described in Section 4.2. The following table describes how we compute the lower bound LB_i and upper bound UB_i for a node i, broken down by the type of logical operator node i corresponds to. We use the offset $i-1$ to denote the direct child of node i. For *Nested Loops* and *Hash joins*, we use $i-1$ to denote the outer and $i-2$ the inner child. Finally, for nodes with variable number of children, we use the offset j to iterate over all of them (i.e., $\sum_j$).

Logical Operator	$\mathbf{LB_i}$	$\mathbf{UB_i}$
Inner Join	K_i	$(UB_{i-1}K_{i-1}) \cdot UB_{i-2} + K_i$
Left Anti Semi Join	K_i	$(UB_{i-1}K_{i-1}) \cdot UB_{i-2} + K_i$
Left Semi Join	K_i	$(UB_{i-1}K_{i-1}) \cdot UB_{i-2} + K_i$
Right Outer Join	K_i	$(UB_{i-1}K_{i-1}) \cdot UB_{i-2} + K_i$
Right Semi Join	K_i	$(UB_{i-1}K_{i-1}) \cdot UB_{i-2} + K_i$
Full Outer Join	K_i	$(UB_{i-1}K_{i-1}) \cdot UB_{i-2} + K_i$
Concatenation	$\sum_j K_j$	$\sum_j UB_j$
Clustered Index Seek Index Seek Index Scan	K_i	$TableSize$, or, when on inner side of join: $TableSize \cdot UB_{i-1}$
Table Scan	Table Size	$TableSize$
Constant Scan	N_i	N_i
Eager Spool Lazy Spool	K_i	∞
Filter	K_i	$(UB_{i-1}K_{i-1}) + K_i$
Distribute Streams	K_i	$(UB_{i-1}K_{i-1}) + K_i$
Gather Streams	K_i	$(UB_{i-1}K_{i-1}) + K_i$
Repartition Streams	K_i	$(UB_{i-1}K_{i-1}) + K_i$
Segment	K_i	$(UB_{i-1}K_{i-1}) + K_i$
Distinct Sort	K_i	$(UB_{i-1}K_{i-1}) + K_i$
Sort	K_{i-1}	UB_{i-1}
Top N Sort	K_{i-1}	$\min\{N, UB_{i-1}\}$
Bitmap Create	K_{i-1}	UB_{i-1}
Aggregate Partial Aggregate	$\max(1, K_i)$	$UB_{i-1} - \max(1, K_i)$
Compute Scalar	K_{i-1}	UB_{i-1}
Top N Sort	K_{i-1}	$\min\{N, UB_{i-1}\}$
RID Lookup	K_i	UB_{i-1}
Eager Spool Lazy Spool	LB_{i-1}	UB_{i-1}, or, when on inner side of join: $UB_{i-1} \cdot UB_{i-2}$

Table 1: Bounding logic for each operator

Optimization of Nested Queries using the NF² Algebra

Jürgen Hölsch Michael Grossniklaus Marc H. Scholl

Department of Computer and Information Science, University of Konstanz
P.O. Box 188, 78457 Konstanz, Germany

{juergen.hoelsch,michael.grossniklaus,marc.scholl}@uni-konstanz.de

ABSTRACT

A key promise of SQL is that the optimizer will find the most efficient execution plan, regardless of how the query is formulated. In general, query optimizers of modern database systems are able to keep this promise, with the notable exception of nested queries. While several optimization techniques for nested queries have been proposed, their adoption in practice has been limited. In this paper, we argue that the NF^2 (non-first normal form) algebra, which was originally designed to process nested tables, is a better approach to nested query optimization as it fulfills two key requirements. First, the NF^2 algebra can represent all types of nested queries as well as both existing and novel optimization techniques based on its equivalences. Second, performance benefits can be achieved with little changes to existing transformation-based query optimizers as the NF^2 algebra is an extension of the relational algebra.

1. INTRODUCTION

One of the reasons why declarative languages are popular and successful in query processing is the fact that developers do not need to worry about performance. As long as they can formulate a query that returns the desired result, the query optimizer of the database system promises to find the best possible execution plan. In the case of SQL, modern query optimizers are, for the most part, able to deliver on that promise. Still the exception to this general rule are nested queries, for which the actual formulation can have a large impact on execution time.

In order to close this gap, several optimization techniques for nested queries have been proposed. These techniques either work at the level of SQL [14, 20], define new operators [3, 9] and algebras [4] that are specifically targeted at nested queries, or build on entirely different formalisms, *e.g.*, comprehension calculus [8, 12, 13]. We argue that these approaches all have drawbacks that have limited their adoption in database systems. Using tailor-made algebras and operators requires considerable changes to the query optimizer for a single class of optimizations, whereas introducing an entirely different formalism can even lead to a complete rewrite. Finally, approaches that work at the level of SQL restrict the space of possible optimizations by addressing nested queries in isolation from other optimizations. As an example, consider the following query, which returns all parts that are cheaper and bigger than the average of parts of the same type, according to the schema of the TPC-H benchmark[1], which we use for examples throughout this paper.

```
SELECT P1.p_name
FROM Part P1
WHERE P1.p_retailprice <
        (SELECT AVG(P2.p_retailprice)
         FROM Part P2 WHERE P2.p_type = P1.p_type)
AND P1.p_size >
        (SELECT AVG(P3.p_size)
         FROM Part P3 WHERE P3.p_type = P1.p_type)
```

Both subqueries can be unnested according to Kim [14], which will result in the following SQL query.

```
SELECT P1.p_name
FROM Part P1,
  (SELECT p_type, AVG(p_retailprice) AS avg_price
   FROM Part GROUP BY p_type) AS P2,
  (SELECT p_type, AVG(p_size) AS avg_size
   FROM Part GROUP BY p_type) AS P3
WHERE P1.p_retailprice < avg_price AND P1.p_size > avg_size
  AND P1.p_type = P2.p_type AND P1.p_type = P3.p_type
```

Since both subqueries access the same relation, they can be merged (coalesced) into a single subquery. The result of this transformation is as follows.

```
SELECT P1.p_name
FROM Part P1,
  (SELECT p_type, AVG(p_retailprice) AS avg_price,
                  AVG(p_size) AS avg_size
   FROM Part GROUP BY p_type) AS P2
WHERE P1.p_retailprice < avg_price AND P1.p_size > avg_size
  AND P1.p_type = P2.p_type
```

Even if query optimizers can perform both of these steps in isolation, our experiments (*cf.* Section 7) have shown that they are not able to combine them. Since the inner workings of commercial query optimizers are well-kept company secrets, we can only speculate about the precise reasons for these limitations. We note, however, that both nesting and grouping are concepts of SQL that cannot be represented

[1] http://www.tpc.org/tpch/ (November 18, 2015)

SIGMOD'16, June 26-July 01, 2016, San Francisco, CA, USA

ISBN 978-1-4503-3531-7/16/06...$15.00

DOI: http://dx.doi.org/10.1145/2882903.2915241

by the relational algebra in its original form [6]. As query plan enumeration typically relies on transformations that are based on equivalences of the relational algebra, it is at least conceivable that optimizations, which cannot be expressed algebraically, are performed in separate phases.

Nesting (in the `WHERE` clause) and grouping are concepts that have been part of SQL since the beginning. Over time, many other extensions were made to the language, which are also not covered by the relational algebra. In this paper, we therefore argue that it is time to re-think the choice of the original relational algebra as a basis for query execution plan enumeration. Rather than defining yet another specialized algebra, we show how an existing algebra, which was developed for the NF^2 (non-first normal form) data model [18], can be used for the uniform optimization of nested SQL queries. Even though it was not their originally intended use, the operators defined by the NF^2 algebra to access nested relations can also be used to represent nested queries.

While the focus of this paper is mainly on nested queries, we note that the NF^2 algebra can also be used to represent SQL concepts such as grouping, `CASE` statements, and window functions with the `PARTITION BY` clause. Furthermore, the NF^2 algebra naturally represents operations provided by object-relational database systems, such as Oracle and PostgreSQL. As a consequence, we argue that the NF^2 algebra is a much better match to the current state of SQL than the original relational algebra. Also, since the NF^2 algebra is an extension of the relational algebra, all existing equivalences remain valid. Finally, all logical operators described in this paper can be implemented by the physical operators that are present in any relational database system, which is a key distinction of our approach with respect to some of the previous proposals. Specifically, the contributions of this paper are as follows.

- We show how all types of nested queries supported by SQL, *i.e.*, nesting in the `SELECT`, `FROM`, and `WHERE` clause, are represented by NF^2 expressions (Section 3).
- We define NF^2 equivalences that formalize existing optimization techniques, which were previously described as edit operations at the SQL code level (Section 4).
- Beyond the current state of the art, we introduce new optimization techniques, which are made possible by the NF^2 approach (Section 5).
- We demonstrate the feasibility of the proposed approach by discussing the necessary changes to a query optimizer that is based on Cascades framework (Section 6).
- We quantify the performance benefits of our approach by measuring the execution times of nested queries in four major database systems and comparing them to execution times of the corresponding queries that were optimized as proposed in this paper (Section 7).

We begin in the next section with a short overview of the NF^2 algebra and the notation used throughout this paper. Related work is presented in Section 8 and concluding remarks as well an an outlook on future work are given in Section 9.

2. NF² ALGEBRA OVERVIEW

For the sake of a self-contained presentation, this section introduces the concepts and notation of the NF^2 algebra that are used in this paper. A detailed introduction to the NF^2 algebra can be found, for example, in Schek and Scholl [18]. The NF^2 algebra is an extension of the traditional relational algebra. In the scope of this paper, the extended selection and projection operator, which both support nested subexpressions, are most relevant.

The following NF^2 expression introduces the notation for a selection operator that contains a subexpression in its selection condition.

$$\sigma[\text{c\_custkey} \in \pi[\text{o\_custkey}](\text{Orders})](\text{Customer})$$

For every tuple of the Customer relation, the subexpression in the selection condition is evaluated. If the key of the customer is contained in the result set of the subexpression, the customer tuple is added to the result set of the outer selection operator. The NF^2 expression above is equivalent to the following SQL statement.

```
SELECT *
FROM Customer
WHERE c_custkey IN (SELECT o_custkeyr FROM Orders)
```

The following NF^2 expression introduces the notation for a projection operator that contains a subexpression in its projection list.

$$\pi[\text{c\_custkey}, G := \sigma[\text{o\_custkey} = \text{c\_custkey}](\text{Orders})](\text{Customer})$$

The expression creates a new attribute G that contains all orders of a customer by evaluating the subexpression for each tuple of relation Customer and selecting all order tuples containing the corresponding customer key.

3. NF² REPRESENTATION OF NESTED QUERIES

Both generation-based and transformation-based optimizers use algebraic equivalences to enumerate query plans in the search space [16]. As a first step, a SQL statement therefore needs to be transformed into an algebraic expression. In this section, we first show how `GROUP BY`s can be represented in the NF^2 algebra. Then, we discuss how the different types of nested queries in the `WHERE` clause are represented by NF^2 expressions. Finally, we introduce the NF^2 representation for subqueries in the `SELECT` and `FROM` clause.

3.1 Preliminary Definitions

Aggregation functions are an important feature of SQL. However, since they are not part of the original NF^2 algebra, we define them for the purpose of this work.

Definition 3.1.1 (Aggregation Function) *Let f be an aggregation function and $\mathcal{D}$ a domain of numeric values. The input of f is a list of atomic values and the output of f is a single atomic value.*

$$f : \mathcal{P}(\mathcal{D}) \rightarrow \mathcal{D}$$

In SQL, aggregation functions are typically used together with the `GROUP BY` clause. Grouping can be represented in the NF^2 algebra using a nested projection.

Definition 3.1.2 (Grouping) *Let R be a relation and $A = \{A_1, \ldots, A_n\} \subseteq attr(R)$ a set of atomic attributes. Further, $R' := \pi[A'_1 := A_1, \ldots, A'_n := A_n, attr(R) \setminus A](R)$ is a relation obtained by renaming the attributes of R. The grouping of R by the attributes A is then defined as follows:*

$$\pi[A, G := \pi[attr(R') \setminus \{A'_1, \ldots, A'_n\}](\sigma[A'_1 = A_1 \wedge \ldots \wedge A'_n = A_n](R'))](R).$$

For each outer tuple t of R, the subset of tuples of R' that have the same values in the attributes $A'_1, \ldots, A'_n$ as t in its attributes $A_1, \ldots, A_n$ is selected. In order to prevent naming conflicts, the attributes of R' are renamed from $A_1, \ldots, A_n$ to $A'_1, \ldots, A'_n$. By applying an aggregation function f on an attribute of G, the groups of G can be aggregated.

Example 3.1.1 *Consider the relation Orders given below.*

o_orderkey	*o_custkey*	*o_totalprice*
1	*5*	*100*
2	*5*	*500*
3	*2*	*30*
4	*2*	*60*

The NF[2] expression to group the relation on the attribute o_custkey is as follows.

$$\pi[o\_custkey, G := \pi[attr(Orders') \setminus \{o\_custkey'\}](\sigma[o\_custkey' = o\_custkey](Orders'))](Orders)$$

The result is shown in the following relation.

o_custkey	*G*	
	o_orderkey'	*o_totalprice'*
2	*3*	*30*
	4	*60*
5	*1*	*100*
	2	*500*

The logical group-by/aggregate operator is defined by combining a nested projection with an aggregation function. This representation enables further transformations on the logical level, *e.g.*, the removal of redundant groupings (*cf.* Section 5). The following definition introduces a dedicated operator to abbreviate the corresponding logical group-by/aggregate NF[2] expression. Note that this operator directly corresponds to the physical group-by/aggregate operator of a relational database system.

Definition 3.1.3 (Group-By/Aggregate Operator) *Let R be a relation, $A = \{A_1, \ldots, A_n\} \subseteq attr(R)$, $\{B_1, \ldots, B_k\} \in attr(R) \setminus A$ a set of attributes, and $F = \{f_1, \ldots, f_k\}$ a set of aggregation functions. The group-by/aggregate operator $\gamma[A; F](R)$ groups R on the attributes of A and computes the functions $f_1, \ldots, f_k$ on the attributes $B_1, \ldots, B_k$:*

$$\gamma[A; F](R) := \pi[A, agg_{f_1} := f_1(\pi[B_1](G)), \ldots, agg_{f_k} := f_k(\pi[B_k](G))](\pi[A, G := \pi[attr(R') \setminus \{A'_1, \ldots, A'_n\}](\sigma[A'_1 = A_1 \wedge \ldots \wedge A'_n = A_n](R'))](R)).$$

As an abbreviation, the set braces in the expression

$$\gamma[\{A_1, \ldots, A_n\}; \{f_1, \ldots, f_k\}](R)$$

are ignored. Instead we write

$$\gamma[A_1, \ldots, A_n; f_1, \ldots, f_k](R).$$

Example 3.1.2 *The expression*

$$\gamma[o\_custkey; MAX(o\_totalprice)](Orders)$$

groups the orders table (cf. Example 3.1.1) on the attribute o_custkey and computes the most expensive order for each customer. The result is shown in the following relation.

o_custkey	agg_{max}
2	*60*
5	*500*

3.2 WHERE Clause Subqueries

Subqueries in the `WHERE` clause can occur in combination with quantifiers such as `ANY`, `ALL`, and `EXISTS`. In this subsection, we present how these different types of nested queries can be represented by NF[2] expressions.

3.2.1 Representation of the IN Operator

The `IN` comparison operator returns true, if the value of the selected column is contained in the result set of the subquery.

Example 3.2.1 *The query below returns all parts delivered by a supplier. This is the case, if the key of a part tuple is contained in the PartSupp relation.*

```
SELECT p_name
FROM Part
WHERE p_partkey IN (SELECT ps_partkey FROM PartSupp)
```

This query is represented by the following NF[2] expression:

$$\pi[p\_name](\sigma[p\_partkey \in \pi[ps\_partkey](PartSupp)](Part)).$$

Definition 3.2.1 *Consider the following SQL statement containing a subquery S in the* `WHERE` *clause that projects on an attribute, which has the same data type as attribute A.*

```
SELECT L FROM R WHERE A IN (S)
```

This query is represented by the following NF[2] expression, in which S' is an NF[2] expression that is equivalent to the SQL statement S:

$$\pi[L](\sigma[A \in S'](R)).$$

3.2.2 Representation of the EXISTS Quantifier

The `EXISTS` quantifier holds, if the result set of the corresponding subquery is not empty.

Example 3.2.2 *The query given below is an alternative formulation of the query from Example 3.2.1.*

```
SELECT p_name
FROM Part
WHERE EXISTS (SELECT *
              FROM PartSupp
              WHERE ps_partkey = p_partkey)
```

In the NF[2] algebra, this query is represented by the following expression:

$$\pi[p\_name](\sigma[COUNT(\sigma[ps\_partkey = p\_partkey](PartSupp)) \neq 0](Part)).$$

Definition 3.2.2 *Consider the following SQL statement containing a subquery S in the* `WHERE` *clause.*

```
SELECT L FROM R WHERE EXISTS (S)
```

This query is represented by the following NF² expression, in which S' is an NF² expression that is equivalent to the SQL statement S:

$$\pi[L](\sigma[COUNT(S') \neq 0](R)).$$

Note that for NOT EXISTS the predicate COUNT(S') $\neq 0$ has to be changed to COUNT(S') $= 0$. Alternatively, EXISTS (or NOT EXISTS) could be represented by S' $\neq \emptyset$ (or S' $= \emptyset$).

3.2.3 Representation of the ANY Quantifier

The ANY quantifier can be used in selection conditions, which compare the value of a given column to the result set of a subquery. The quantifier holds if *at least one* tuple of the subquery result set satisfies the comparison condition.

Example 3.2.3 *The following query returns all parts that are cheaper than the most expensive part.*

```
SELECT p_name
FROM Part
WHERE p_retailprice < ANY (SELECT p_retailprice FROM Part)
```

This query is expressed in the NF² algebra as follows:

$$\pi[p\_name](\sigma[p\_retailprice < MAX(\pi[p\_retailprice'](Part'))](Part)).$$

Definition 3.2.3 *Consider the following SQL statement containing a subquery S in the* WHERE *clause that projects on an attribute which has the same data type as attribute A. Let $\theta \in \{<, \leq, >, \geq, =\}$ be a comparison operator.*

SELECT L FROM R WHERE A θ ANY (S)

Depending on θ, there are three cases that define how the ANY *quantifier is represented as an NF² expression. Again, S' is an NF² expression that is equivalent to the SQL statement S.*

1. $\theta \in \{<, \leq\} : \pi[L](\sigma[A\ \theta\ MAX(S')](R))$
2. $\theta \in \{>, \geq\} : \pi[L](\sigma[A\ \theta\ MIN(S')](R))$
3. $\theta \in \{=\} : \pi[L](\sigma[A \in S'](R))$

3.2.4 Representation of the ALL Quantifier

The ALL quantifier can be used in selection conditions, which compare the value of a given column with the result set of a subquery. The quantifier holds if *all* tuples of the subquery result set satisfy the corresponding condition.

Example 3.2.4 *The following query returns the most expensive part.*

```
SELECT p_name
FROM Part
WHERE p_retailprice >= ALL (SELECT p_retailprice FROM Part)
```

This query is expressed in the NF² algebra as follows:

$$\pi[p\_name](\sigma[p\_retailprice \geq MAX(\pi[p\_retailprice'](Part'))](Part)).$$

Definition 3.2.4 *Consider the following SQL statement containing a subquery S in the* WHERE *clause that projects on an attribute which has the same data type as attribute A. Let $\theta \in \{<, \leq, >, \geq\}$ be a comparison operator.*

SELECT L FROM R WHERE A θ ALL (S)

Depending on θ, there are two cases that define how the ALL *quantifier is represented as an NF² expression. Again, S' is an NF² expression that is equivalent to the SQL statement S.*

1. $\theta \in \{<, \leq\} : \pi[L](\sigma[A\ \theta\ MIN(S')](R))$
2. $\theta \in \{>, \geq\} : \pi[L](\sigma[A\ \theta\ MAX(S')](R))$

3.3 SELECT and FROM Clause Subqueries

Originally, SQL only supported nesting in the WHERE clause. In an effort to make the language more orthogonal, subqueries were allowed in the SELECT and FROM clause as well.

Example 3.3.1 *The given query returns the total number of orders for each customer.*

```
SELECT o_custkey, (SELECT COUNT(*) FROM Orders O2
    WHERE O2.o_custkey = O1.o_custkey) AS nrOrders
FROM Orders O1
```

Note that this SQL statement can be directly represented by the nested projection operator.

$$\pi[o\_custkey, nrOrders := COUNT(\sigma[o\_custkey' = o\_custkey](Orders'))](Orders)$$

Definition 3.3.1 *Consider a SQL statement with a subquery in the SELECT clause.*

SELECT L, (S) AS Y FROM R

The query is represented by the following NF² expression, in which S' is an NF² expression that is equivalent to the SQL statement S:

$$\pi[L, Y := S'](R).$$

A subquery in the *FROM* clause can be directly represented as an input of the corresponding NF² operator.

Definition 3.3.2 *Consider a SQL statement with a subquery S in the* FROM *clause.*

SELECT L FROM S WHERE F

The query is represented by the following NF² expression, in which S' is an NF² expression that is equivalent to the SQL statement S:

$$\pi[L](\sigma[F](S')).$$

4. EQUIVALENCES FOR NESTED QUERY OPTIMIZATION TECHNIQUES

In the previous section, we defined the algebraic representation of SQL subqueries in terms of NF² expressions. Based on this representation, we now derive equivalence rules for well-know nested query optimization techniques.

4.1 Unnesting Subqueries

The work of Kim [14] describes how nested queries in the WHERE clause can be replaced by joins. The transformations are directly applied on the SQL code of the given query. Kim classifies the WHERE clause subqueries into five categories (Type N, J, A, JA, and D). In this paper, we define equivalence rules for the transformations of the Types N, J, A, and JA. Since Type D queries contain the relational division operator, which is no longer supported by the current SQL standard, we do not provide equivalence rules for queries of this type.

4.1.1 Unnesting Type N and Type J Subqueries

A subquery is of Type N, if it occurs in the WHERE clause in combination with the IN comparison operator and has no aggregation. If the subquery is additionally correlated with the outer query, the subquery is of Type J. The following example illustrates a Type J subquery and its equivalent NF^2 expression.

Example 4.1.1 *The query given below returns all parts delivered by a supplier.*

```
SELECT p_name, s_name
FROM Part, Supplier
WHERE p_partkey IN (SELECT ps_partkey
                    FROM PartSupp
                    WHERE ps_suppkey = s_suppkey)
```

The equivalent NF^2 expression is as follows:

$$\pi[p\_name,\ s\_name](\sigma[p\_partkey \in \pi[ps\_partkey](\sigma[ps\_suppkey = s\_suppkey](PartSupp))](Part \times Supplier)).$$

As described by Kim, this subquery can be replaced by a join. Example 4.1.2 shows the result of the transformation and the equivalent NF^2 expression.

Example 4.1.2

```
SELECT p_name, s_name
FROM Part, Supplier, PartSupp
WHERE p_partkey = ps_partkey AND ps_suppkey = s_suppkey
```

Below, the corresponding expression of the NF^2 algebra is given. Note that this is not the most efficient expression, since there is still a cross product. The cross product can be removed, however, based on equivalences defined by the traditional relational algebra.

$$\pi[p\_name,\ s\_name](PartSupp \bowtie_{p\_partkey=ps\_partkey \wedge ps\_suppkey=s\_suppkey} (Part \times Supplier))$$

In Definition 4.1.1, the equivalence rule for unnesting Type J and N subqueries is introduced.

Definition 4.1.1 (Unnesting Type N/J Subqueries) *Let Inner and Outer be NF^2 expressions, $A \in attr(Outer)$ and $B \in attr(Inner)$ attributes, and F a condition. The equivalence rule for unnesting a Type N or J subquery is defined as follows (for Type N, F is true; for Type J, F is a correlation condition):*

$$\sigma[A \in \pi[B](\sigma[F](Inner))](Outer) \equiv \pi[attr(Outer)](Outer \bowtie_{A=B \wedge F} Inner).$$

4.1.2 Unnesting Type A Subqueries

A subquery with aggregation, but without correlation is of Type A. Example 4.1.3 shows a Type A subquery.

Example 4.1.3 *The following query returns all parts with a price greater than the average price of parts.*

```
SELECT p_name
FROM Part P1
WHERE P1.p_retailprice > (SELECT AVG(P2.p_retailprice)
                          FROM Part P2)
```

The equivalence rule given in Definition 4.1.2 can be used to transform a Type A subquery into an expression, in which the aggregation value of the subquery is computed once. This precomputing is possible because the subquery is independent from the outer query and returns a single value as a result.

Definition 4.1.2 (Unnesting Type A Subqueries) *Let Inner and Outer be NF^2 expressions, $A \in attr(Outer)$ and $B \in attr(Inner)$ attributes, f an aggregation function, and $\theta \in \{<, \leq, >, \geq, =, \neq\}$ a comparison operator. The equivalence rule for unnesting Type A subqueries is defined as follows:*

$$\sigma[A\ \theta\ f(\pi[B](Inner))](Outer) \equiv \pi[attr(Outer)](\sigma[A\ \theta\ agg](Outer \times (agg := f(\pi[B](Inner)))).$$

4.1.3 Unnesting Type JA Queries

A Type JA subquery is correlated with the outer query and uses aggregation. Example 4.1.4 shows a Type JA subquery and its equivalent NF^2 expression.

Example 4.1.4 *The following query returns all parts with a price greater than the average price of parts of the same type.*

```
SELECT P1.p_name
FROM Part P1
WHERE P1.p_retailprice > (SELECT AVG(P2.p_retailprice)
                          FROM Part P2
                          WHERE P2.p_type = P1.p_type)
```

The equivalent NF^2 expression contains a relation Part', which is a renamed relation of Part. The renaming is necessary to unambiguously define to which relation (inner or outer relation) an attribute belongs to.

$$\pi[p\_name](\sigma[p\_retailprice > AVG(\pi[p\_retailprice'](\sigma[p\_type' = p\_type](Part')))](Part))$$

According to Kim, the nested query of Example 4.1.4 can be transformed as follows. The relation of the subquery is grouped by the attribute that is contained in the correlation condition. For each group, the value of the aggregation function is computed. Afterwards, the original subquery in the WHERE clause is removed and the grouping is added as a new subquery to the FROM clause of the outer query. Example 4.1.5 shows the result of this transformation.

Example 4.1.5

```
SELECT P1.p_name
FROM Part P1, (SELECT p_type, AVG(p_retailprice) AS avg_price
               FROM Part
               GROUP BY p_type) P2
WHERE P2.p_type = P1.p_type
      AND P1.p_retailprice > P2.avg_price
```

This query is represented using the NF^2 algebra as follows:

$$\pi[p\_name](\sigma[p\_retailprice > avg\_price](Part \bowtie_{p\_type'=p\_type} \gamma[p\_type';\ avg\_price := AVG(p\_retailprice')](Part'))).$$

In Definition 4.1.3, the equivalence rules that can be used to unnest Type JA subqueries are introduced. As pointed out by Ganski and Wong [10], subqueries that use the COUNT aggregation function and/or have inequality join predicates need to be treated separately. These different cases lead to three equivalence rules for Type JA subqueries.

Definition 4.1.3 (Unnesting Type JA Subqueries) *Let Inner and Outer be NF^2 expressions, $A \in attr(Outer)$ and $B \in attr(Inner)$ attributes, f an aggregation function, and $\theta \in \{<, \leq, >, \geq, =, \neq\}$ be a comparison operator. Assume that F is the condition that creates the correlation between the outer and inner query. Depending on the aggregation function f and the condition F, the equivalence rules for unnesting Type JA subqueries are defined as follows.*

1. *$f \neq COUNT$ and F consists of conjunctive subconditions $A_i = B_j$ with $A_i \in attr(Outer)$, $B_j \in attr(Inner)$. The set G contains the attributes $B_j \in attr(Inner)$.*

$$\begin{aligned} &\sigma[A\ \theta\ f(\pi[B](\sigma[F](Inner)))](Outer) \\ &\equiv \pi[attr(Outer)](\\ &\quad \sigma[A\ \theta\ agg](Outer \bowtie_F \gamma[G; agg := f(B)](Inner))) \end{aligned}$$

2. *$f \neq COUNT$ and F consists of conjunctive subconditions $A_i\ \theta'\ B_j$ with $\theta' \in \{<, >, \neq\}$, $A_i \in attr(Outer)$, and $B_j \in attr(Inner)$. The set G contains the attributes $A_i \in attr(Outer)$.*

$$\begin{aligned} &\sigma[A\ \theta\ f(\pi[B](\sigma[F](Inner)))](Outer) \\ &\equiv \pi[attr(Outer)](\sigma[A\ \theta\ agg](\\ &\quad Outer \bowtie \gamma[G; agg := f(B)](Outer \bowtie_F Inner))) \end{aligned}$$

3. *$f = COUNT$ and F consists of conjunctive subconditions $A_i\ \theta'\ B_j$ with $\theta' \in \{<, >, =, \neq\}$, $A_i \in attr(Outer)$, and $B_j \in attr(Inner)$. The set G contains the attributes $A_i \in attr(Outer)$.*

$$\begin{aligned} &\sigma[A\ \theta\ f(\pi[B](\sigma[F](Inner)))](Outer) \\ &\equiv \pi[attr(Outer)](\sigma[A\ \theta\ agg](\\ &\quad Outer \bowtie \gamma[G; agg := f(B)](Outer ⟗ Inner))) \end{aligned}$$

4.2 Subquery Coalescing

Bellamkonda *et al.* [2] describe which types of redundant subqueries can be merged. In this context the term "redundant" means that both subqueries access the same relations. Based on the work of Bellamkonda *et al.*, we define equivalence rules that can be used to merge redundant subqueries. Example 4.2.1 shows a query with two subqueries that can be merged into a single subquery.

Example 4.2.1 *The following query returns all orders that are at least as expensive as orders with high and medium priority.*

```
SELECT *
FROM Orders
WHERE o_totalprice >= ALL (
        SELECT o_totalprice
        FROM Orders
        WHERE o_orderpriority = '2-HIGH'
) AND o_totalprice >= ALL (
        SELECT o_totalprice
        FROM Orders
        WHERE o_orderpriority = '3-MEDIUM'
)
```

This query can be represented by the following NF^2 expression.

$$\begin{aligned} &\sigma[o\_totalprice \geq MAX(\pi[o\_totalprice'](\\ &\quad \sigma[o\_orderpriority = \text{'2-HIGH'}](Orders'))) \wedge \\ &\quad o\_totalprice \geq MAX(\pi[o\_totalprice'](\\ &\quad \sigma[o\_orderpriority = \text{'3-MEDIUM'}](Orders')))](Orders) \end{aligned}$$

In order to eliminate the redundant table access, the predicate of the second subquery is combined with the predicate of the first subquery. Afterwards, the second subquery can be removed. In the following, the transformed query is shown.

```
SELECT *
FROM Orders
WHERE o_totalprice >= ALL (
        SELECT o_totalprice
        FROM Orders
        WHERE o_orderpriority = '2-HIGH'
            OR o_orderpriority = '3-MEDIUM'
)
```

The NF^2 expression that is equivalent to this query is:

$$\begin{aligned} &\sigma[o\_totalprice \geq MAX(\pi[o\_totalprice'](\\ &\quad \sigma[o\_orderpriority' = \text{'2-HIGH'} \vee \\ &\quad o\_orderpriority' = \text{'3-MEDIUM'}](Orders')))](Orders). \end{aligned}$$

There are three equivalence rules that cover the different cases in which subqueries in the WHERE clause can be merged into a single subquery. In the following definitions, the different cases that are covered by a rule are represented by a triple of the form $(\theta_1, \theta_2, \theta_3)$. θ_1 is the comparison operator that is used in the outer query to compare the result of the subquery with an outer column. θ_2 corresponds to the Boolean operator connecting both subqueries. Finally, θ_3 denotes the aggregation function which is used in the subqueries.

The rule given in Definition 4.2.1 covers the cases, in which two subqueries can be merged into a single subquery by combining their predicates with OR. We already applied this rule to transform the query shown in Example 4.2.1. In the following definitions the function $val(E)$ returns the result set of tuples of an expression E.

Definition 4.2.1 (Subquery Merge I) *Let F_1 and F_2 be conditions with $val(\sigma[F_1](Inner)) \not\subseteq val(\sigma[F_2](Inner))$ and $val(\sigma[F_2](Inner)) \not\subseteq val(\sigma[F_1](Inner))$. In addition, $\theta_1 \in \{<, \leq, >, \geq, =, \neq\}$, $\theta_2 \in \{\wedge, \vee\}$, and $\theta_3 \in \{MIN, MAX, COUNT\}$ are given. For the assignments $(\neq, \vee, COUNT)$, $(=, \wedge, COUNT)$, $(<, \wedge, MIN)$, $(>, \wedge, MAX)$, $(<, \vee, MAX)$, and $(>, \vee, MIN)$ for $(\theta_1, \theta_2, \theta_3)$, the following equivalence holds:*[2]

$$\begin{aligned} &\sigma[(A\ \theta_1\ \theta_3(\pi[B](\sigma[F_1](Inner)))\ \theta_2 \\ &\quad (A\ \theta_1\ \theta_3(\pi[B](\sigma[F_2](Inner)))](Outer) \\ &\equiv \sigma[A\ \theta_1\ \theta_3(\pi[B](\sigma[F_1 \vee F_2](Inner))](Outer). \end{aligned}$$

The rule given in Definition 4.2.2 covers the cases, in which the second of two subqueries can be removed.

Definition 4.2.2 (Subquery Merge II) *Let F_1 and F_2 be conditions with $val(\sigma[F_2](Inner)) \subseteq val(\sigma[F_1](Inner))$. In addition, $\theta_1 \in \{<, \leq, >, \geq, =, \neq\}$, $\theta_2 \in \{\wedge, \vee\}$, and*

[2]If θ_3 equals $COUNT$, then A is zero.

$\theta_3 \in \{MIN, MAX, COUNT\}$ *is given. For the assignments* $(\neq, \vee, COUNT)$, $(=, \wedge, COUNT)$, $(<, \wedge, MIN)$, $(>, \wedge, MAX)$, $(<, \vee, MAX)$, *and* $(>, \vee, MIN)$ *for* $(\theta_1, \theta_2, \theta_3)$, *the following equivalence holds:*[2]

$$\begin{aligned}&\sigma[(A\ \theta_1\ \theta_3(\pi[A](\sigma[F_1](Inner)))\ \theta_2\\ &\quad (A\ \theta_1\ \theta_3(\pi[A](\sigma[F_2](Inner)))](Outer)\\ &\equiv \sigma[A\ \theta_1\ \theta_3(\pi[A](\sigma[F_1](Inner))](Outer).\end{aligned}$$

The rule given in Definition 4.2.3 covers the cases, in which the first of two subqueries can be removed.

Definition 4.2.3 (Subquery Merge III) *Let* F_1 *and* F_2 *be conditions with* $val(\sigma[F_2](Inner)) \subseteq val(\sigma[F_1](Inner))$. *In addition,* $\theta_1 \in \{<, \leq, >, \geq, =, \neq\}$, $\theta_2 \in \{\wedge, \vee\}$, *and* $\theta_3 \in \{MIN, MAX, COUNT\}$ *is given. For the assignments* $(\neq, \wedge, COUNT)$, $(=, \vee, COUNT)$, $(<, \vee, MIN)$, $(>, \vee, MAX)$, $(<, \wedge, MAX)$, *and* $(>, \wedge, MIN)$ *for* $(\theta_1, \theta_2, \theta_3)$, *the following equivalence holds:*[2]

$$\begin{aligned}&\sigma[(A\ \theta_1\ \theta_3(\pi[A](\sigma[F_1](Inner)))\ \theta_2\\ &\quad (A\ \theta_1\ \theta_3(\pi[A](\sigma[F_2](Inner)))](Outer)\\ &\equiv \sigma[A\ \theta_1\ \theta_3(\pi[A](\sigma[F_2](Inner))](Outer).\end{aligned}$$

In the previous definitions, whenever $>$ or $<$ is valid, the corresponding cases for $\geq$ and $\leq$ are also valid. In order to demonstrate how the correctness of these rules can be proven, a sample proof for a specific case of Definition 4.2.1 is included in Appendix C.

5. NEW OPTIMIZATION POSSIBILITIES

Up to now, we have demonstrated how the NF^2 algebra and its equivalences can be used to represent existing nested query optimizations. In this section, we present additional optimization techniques that are made possible at the algebraic level by our approach. We begin by introducing four auxiliary equivalence rules that we need for the definition of these new algebraic optimization possibilities.

5.1 Auxiliary Equivalence Rules

The first equivalence rule can be used to move a projection out of a join.

$$\pi[L_1](R) \bowtie_F \pi[L_2](S) \equiv \pi[L_1, L_2](R \bowtie_F S) \qquad (5.1.1)$$

The second equivalence rule can be used to eliminate a redundant equi-join. A join between a relation R and its renamed relation R' can be removed, if the subsequent operators (*e.g.*, a projection) are only accessing attributes of R.

Equi-join Elimination. *Let* R *be a relation,* $A_1, \ldots, A_n \in attr(R)$ *atomic attributes, and* $L \subseteq attr(R)$ *a projection list. In addition,* $R' := \pi[L'](R)$ *with* $L' = \{A' | A \in attr(R)\}$ *is given. Then the following holds:*

$$\pi[L](R \bowtie_{A_1 = A'_1 \wedge \ldots \wedge A_n = A'_n} R') \equiv \pi[L](R). \qquad (5.1.2)$$

The next equivalence rule combines two projections in cases where the inner projection generates a nested attribute which the outer projection is accessing.

$$\begin{aligned}&\pi[L, \langle op\rangle(E)](\pi[L, E := \langle expr\rangle](R))\\ &\equiv \pi[L, E := \langle op\rangle(\langle expr\rangle)](R)\end{aligned} \qquad (5.1.3)$$

The last equivalence rule moves a redundant subexpression of a projection into a separate projection. As a result, the subexpression is computed only once and the result is stored in a nested attribute.

$$\begin{aligned}&\pi[L, \langle op_1\rangle(\langle expr\rangle), \langle op_2\rangle(\langle expr\rangle)](R)\\ &\equiv \pi[L, \langle op_1\rangle(E), \langle op_2\rangle(E)](\pi[L, E := \langle expr\rangle](R))\end{aligned} \qquad (5.1.4)$$

5.2 Redundant GROUP BY Elimination

The following query returns the price of the cheapest and most expensive order for each customer.

```
SELECT O1.o_custkey, max_price, min_price
FROM (SELECT o_custkey, MAX(o_totalprice) AS max_price
      FROM Orders
      GROUP BY o_custkey) O1,
     (SELECT o_custkey, MIN(o_totalprice) AS min_price
      FROM Orders
      GROUP BY o_custkey) O2
WHERE O1.o_custkey = O2.o_custkey
```

Obviously, this SQL statement is not an efficient formulation of the query as there is a redundant GROUP BY in the FROM clause. Nevertheless, as this query computes the correct result, a modern query optimizer should be able to remove this redundancy in order to obtain the best possible execution plan. As our experiments show, however, most current database systems do not perform this optimization (*cf.* Section 7).

The following NF^2 expression represents the above query. In the expression, "O" is an abbreviation for the Orders table (O' is the renamed Orders table).

$$\begin{aligned}&\pi[\text{o\_custkey, max\_price, min\_price}](\\ &\quad \pi[\text{o\_custkey, max\_price} := \text{MAX}(\pi[\text{o\_totalprice'}](\text{G}))](\\ &\qquad \pi[\text{o\_custkey, G} := \sigma[\text{o\_custkey'} = \text{o\_custkey}](\text{O'})](\text{O}))\\ &\quad \bowtie_{\text{o\_custkey=o\_custkey''}}\\ &\quad \pi[\text{o\_custkey''} := \text{o\_custkey, min\_price} :=\\ &\qquad \text{MIN}(\pi[\text{o\_totalprice'}](\text{G}))](\pi[\text{o\_custkey, G} :=\\ &\qquad\quad \sigma[\text{o\_custkey'} = \text{o\_custkey}](\text{O'})](\text{O})))\end{aligned}$$

The above expression is the result of strictly applying the definitions from Section 3 to the SQL statement. As a consequence, the grouping and the computation of the aggregation values are represented by two separate nested projections. In order to further transform and optimize the expressions, these projections have to be merged into a single projection, which can be achieved by applying Rule 5.1.3 from Section 5.1. While this intermediate step is included here for reasons of understandability, it is not necessary to implement this transformation (*cf.* Section 6) as it can be performed at the time when the SQL statement is translated into an NF^2 expression.

$$\begin{aligned}&\overset{(5.1.3)}{\equiv} \pi[\text{o\_custkey, max\_price, min\_price}](\\ &\quad \pi[\text{o\_custkey, max\_price} :=\\ &\qquad \text{MAX}(\pi[\text{o\_totalprice'}](\\ &\qquad\quad \sigma[\text{o\_custkey'} = \text{o\_custkey}](\text{O'})))](\text{O})\\ &\quad \bowtie_{\text{o\_custkey=o\_custkey''}}\\ &\quad \pi[\text{o\_custkey''} := \text{o\_custkey, min\_price} :=\\ &\qquad \text{MIN}(\pi[\text{o\_totalprice'}](\\ &\qquad\quad \sigma[\text{o\_custkey'} = \text{o\_custkey}](\text{O'})))](\text{O}))\end{aligned}$$

In the next step, the projections of the two group-by operators are moved outside the join using Rule 5.1.1.

$$\overset{(5.1.1)}{\equiv} \pi[\text{o\_custkey, max\_price, min\_price}](\\ \pi[\text{o\_custkey}, \\ \text{max\_price} := \text{MAX}(\pi[\text{o\_totalprice'}](\\ \sigma[\text{o\_custkey'} = \text{o\_custkey}](\text{O'}))), \\ \text{min\_price} := \text{MIN}(\pi[\text{o\_totalprice'}](\\ \sigma[\text{o\_custkey'} = \text{o\_custkey}](\text{O'})))](\\ \text{O} \bowtie_{\text{o\_custkey=o\_custkey"}} \text{O"}))$$

Now, the redundant join can be removed by applying Rule 5.1.2.

$$\overset{(5.1.2)}{\equiv} \pi[\text{o\_custkey, max\_price, min\_price}](\\ \pi[\text{o\_custkey}, \\ \text{max\_price} := \text{MAX}(\pi[\text{o\_totalprice'}](\\ \sigma[\text{o\_custkey'} = \text{o\_custkey}](\text{O'}))), \\ \text{min\_price} := \text{MIN}(\pi[\text{o\_totalprice'}](\\ \sigma[\text{o\_custkey'} = \text{o\_custkey}](\text{O'})))](\text{O}))$$

Finally, the group-by/aggregate operator is split into two projections using the rule from Definition 3.1.3 in Section 3. While this step illustrates how these projections can be mapped to the physical group-by/aggregate operator, it is again not necessary to implement a transformation rule for this step (*cf.* Section 6).

$$\overset{(5.1.4)}{\equiv} \pi[\text{o\_custkey, max\_price} := \text{MAX}(\pi[\text{o\_totalprice'}](\text{G})), \\ \text{min\_price} := \text{MIN}(\pi[\text{o\_totalprice'}](\text{G})](\\ \pi[\text{o\_custkey, G} := \\ \sigma[\text{o\_custkey'} = \text{o\_custkey}](\text{O'}))](\text{O})$$

$$\overset{(3.1.3)}{\equiv} \gamma[\text{o\_custkey; max\_price} := \text{MAX(o\_totalprice)}, \\ \text{min\_price} := \text{MIN(o\_totalprice)}](\text{O})$$

To conclude, below the SQL statement that is equivalent to the NF^2 expression above is shown.

```
SELECT o_custkey, max_price, min_price
FROM (SELECT o_custkey, MAX(o_totalprice) AS max_price,
                        MIN(o_totalprice) AS min_price
      FROM Orders
      GROUP BY o_custkey) O1
```

5.3 SELECT Clause Subquery Elimination

The example given in this section shows how a correlated subquery in the SELECT clause can be eliminated. For each part type the following query returns the number and the average price of the corresponding parts.

```
SELECT p_type, AVG(p_retailprice), (SELECT COUNT(*)
                FROM Part P2 WHERE P2.p_type = P1.p_type)
FROM Part P1
GROUP BY p_type
```

The equivalent NF^2 expression is as follows:

$$\pi[\text{p\_type}, \text{AVG}(\pi[\text{p\_retailprice'}](G)), \text{COUNT}(\\ \sigma[\text{p\_type'} = \text{p\_type}](\text{P'}))](\\ \pi[\text{p\_type}, G := \sigma[\text{p\_type'} = \text{p\_type}](\text{P'})](\text{P})).$$

First, the projections can be merged by applying Rule 5.1.3.

$$\overset{(5.1.3)}{\equiv} \pi[\text{p\_type}, \\ \text{AVG}(\pi[\text{p\_retailprice'}](\sigma[\text{p\_type'} = \text{p\_type}](\text{P'}))), \\ \text{COUNT}(\sigma[\text{p\_type'} = \text{p\_type}](\text{P'}))](\text{P})$$

Now, the aggregation functions have the same groupings as input. Therefore, the redundant groupings can be removed and added as a separate projection.

$$\overset{(5.1.4)}{\equiv} \pi[\text{p\_type}, \text{AVG}(\pi[\text{p\_retailprice'}](G)), \text{COUNT}(G)](\\ \pi[\text{p\_type}, G := \sigma[\text{p\_type'} = \text{p\_type}](\text{P'})](\text{P}))$$

$$\overset{(3.1.3)}{\equiv} \gamma[\text{p\_type}; \text{AVG(p\_retailprice)}, \text{COUNT}(*)](\text{P})$$

Finally, the SQL statement that is equivalent to the above NF^2 expression is shown below.

```
SELECT p_type, AVG(p_retailprice), COUNT(*)
FROM Part
GROUP BY p_type
```

6. IMPLEMENTATION

In order to demonstrate the feasibility of our approach, we extended an existing optimizer, which is based on the Cascades framework designed by Graefe [11]. We chose this optimizer framework for two reasons. First, its general and modular architecture was specifically designed to support the definition of new operators and transformation rules. Second, the Cascades framework has been used to build commercial query optimizers such as the one of Microsoft SQL Server.

As a starting point for our NF^2 optimizer, we use an existing implementation of the Cascades framework that is based on the operators and transformation rules of the traditional relational algebra. As the NF^2 algebra is an extension of the relational algebra, it is only necessary to extend this implementation at three points.

First, we have to define how NF^2 algebra expressions are represented. In Cascades, expressions are modeled by class `EXPR` that consists of an operator and its input expressions. The number of input expressions that an operator can have is defined by its arity. In order to work with NF^2 expressions, nested selections and nested projections need to be introduced. Representing nested selections does not require any changes to the data structures, as the Cascades implementation described by Graefe already represents selection conditions as an expression tree consisting of so-called item operators. Accommodating nested projections with minimal changes is more challenging. In contrast to selection conditions, Graefe models the projection list as a parameter to the projection operator, rather than a (list of) input expressions. Unlike input expressions, operator parameters are not explored and therefore not optimized. A reason for this design is the fact that it would lead to a projection operator with variable arity, which is at odds with the static patterns used to match transformation rules to expressions. In order to keep the arity of the projection constant, while enabling nested expression, we introduce a new `GET_NESTED_EXPR` logical operator, which models the subexpressions in the projection list without affecting the rule engine. Figure 1 illustrates this design for a simple nested projection on relation R.

Second, we have to slightly adapt the control flow of the optimizer. The optimization algorithm of the Cascades frame-

Figure 1: Representation of a nested projection.

work is structured as a set of tasks. For our NF^2 optimizer, we have to modify the existing "optimize expression" task (class `O_EXPR`), which applies all relevant transformation rules to an expression in order to enumerate equivalent expressions. As described by Graefe, this task does not traverse expressions built from item operators. However, since the comparison operator that has the nested query as an input is an item operator, this behavior has to be changed.

Finally, transformation rules for the NF^2 equivalences have to be added to the optimizer. In principle, each equivalence gives rise to two transformations, depending on the direction it is applied. For the subquery unnesting and coalescing rules, we only implement the direction that removes a nesting or redundancy, since it is obvious which variant is more efficient. Note that the three subquery coalescing rules (*cf.* Definitions 4.2.1, 4.2.2, 4.2.3) can be implemented as one transformation rule. As they share the same input pattern, the output pattern can be created depending on the case. In order to apply some of our optimizations, projections need to be *pushed up* to move them out of a join. This transformation is in contradiction to the optimizer's general strategy of *pushing down* projections. This conflict is resolved by adding a compound rule that both moves the projection out of the join and performs the subsequent optimization. Some equivalences (*cf.* Definition 4.1.1) rely on set semantics, *i.e.*, it is important to consider the handling of duplicates in their implementation as a transformation rule. To obtain equivalent results, these rules insert explicit duplicate-elimination operators that enforce set semantics, if necessary.

To conclude this implementation section, we study the impact of our extensions on the code complexity of the optimizer. Originally, the optimizer consisted of 5972 LOC, whereas the extended optimizer has 7630 LOC. This constitutes an increase of 27.8%. However, most of this additional code implements the new transformation rules and only 48 LOC were added to the control flow of the optimization algorithm. Additionally, we study the cyclomatic complexity [15] of our extensions. The original optimizer had an average cyclomatic complexity of 2.241, whereas the value for the extended optimizer is 2.398, *i.e.*, an increase of 7%.

7. EVALUATION

In order to quantitatively evaluate the performance benefits that can be obtained with our approach in commercial database systems, we first define a set of eleven nested queries on the schema of the TPC-H benchmark. For each query, we use our optimizer to generate an optimized NF^2 expression, which is translated back to its equivalent SQL statement. We execute both the original and the optimized SQL query in four state-of-the-art database systems. In this way, we can show that our NF^2 optimizer is able to find more efficient execution strategies than the optimizers of these systems. Finally, we study how NF^2 transformation rules impact the optimization time and the memory usage of our optimizer.

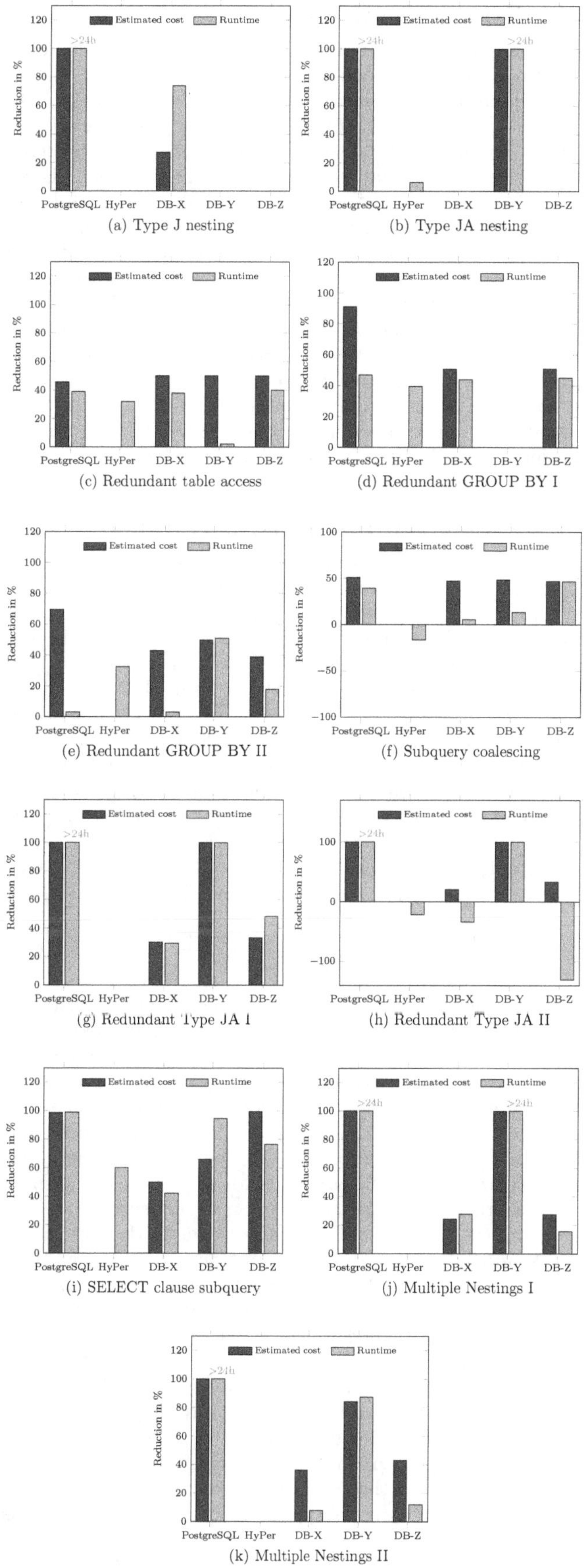

Figure 2: Reduction of estimated cost and runtime.

7.1 Experimental Setup

All experiments presented in this work were performed on a Mac Pro with a 3.5 GHz 6-Core Intel Xeon E5 processor with 64 GB main memory. In our evaluation, we use PostgreSQL Version 9.4.2, the in-memory database HyPer[3] and three market-leading commercial database systems. Due to license terms, the commercial systems are referred to as "DB-X", "DB-Y", and "DB-Z". PostgreSQL, DB-X, DB-Y and DB-Z were installed in a 64-bit Windows 8.1 virtual machine. HyPer was installed in a 64-bit Ubuntu 14.04 LTS virtual machine. 32 GB main memory were allocated to both virtual machines. For all systems, except HyPer, the buffer pool size was set to 2 GB[4]. For all systems, a 10 GB TPC-H database was stored on external storage. Runtime measurements for each of the eleven queries were repeated five times. In order to reduce the bias induced by caching, the queries were executed in random order. Out of the five measurements, the smallest and largest value was discarded and the average of the remaining values was computed.

7.2 Cost and Runtime of the Queries

For each database system, we determine the execution time of the original and the transformed query. With the exception of HyPer, we also determine the cost (estimated by the optimizer of the corresponding system) of the original and the transformed query. To the best of our knowledge, it is not possible to access the estimated cost in HyPer. In order to obtain a measure that is relevant in practical applications, the optimization time needed by our NF^2 optimizer is added to the execution time. In the following, we simply refer to this sum of optimization and execution time as "runtime". The optimization times for the original and transformed query are measured by deactivating and activating the NF^2 rules in our optimizer. Figure 2 plots the reduction of estimated costs and runtime for each query, which is computed as

$$\frac{(\text{value original query} - \text{value transformed query})}{\text{value original query}} * 100,$$

where "value original query" denotes the estimated cost/runtime of the original query and "value transformed query" denotes the estimated cost/runtime of the corresponding transformed query. Table 1 gives the absolute runtimes of the original and transformed queries. In the table, "–" is used to indicate that the execution plan of the original and transformed query is the same. In this case, the query was not executed at all. The SQL statements for both the original and the transformed query are given in Appendix A.

Query (a) contains a Type J subquery. HyPer, DB-X, DB-Y and DB-Z are all able to optimize this query. However, HyPer and DB-X use different join orderings and join implementations for the original and transformed query. In DB-X, the transformed query leads to a performance increase, whereas the runtime in HyPer is not reduced by the alternative plan. DB-Y and DB-Z execute the original and transformed query in the same way. For that reason, there is no reduction in the runtime and the estimated costs. However, PostgreSQL cannot transform the original query. Instead, it executes the subquery for each outer tuple. Even after 24 hours the original query did not terminate and was stopped manually. For each query that was manually aborted after 24 hours, the label ">24h" is added in the corresponding chart. The query transformed by our NF^2 optimizer was executed in 17 seconds by PostgreSQL.

Query (b) contains a Type JA subquery. As before, PostgreSQL cannot transform this query. Again, the original query was aborted after 24 hours, whereas the transformed query executed in 22 seconds. The other systems are able to perform a subquery unnesting. Interestingly, DB-Y finds a better plan for the query when given our transformed query than when it performs the same transformation itself. In the former case, a hash join is used to implement the join that results from the transformation, whereas in the latter case a nested-loops join is used. As a consequence, the original query was aborted after 24 hours. Likewise, HyPer produces a different plan for the original and transformed query.

Query (c) contains two subqueries in the `FROM` clause that access the same relation, but compute different aggregation functions. None of the systems can merge these subqueries into a single subquery. The transformed query, which has only one subquery, reduced the runtime in PostgreSQL, HyPer, DB-X and DB-Z by about 40%. While DB-Y estimates a reduction of about 50%, the transformed query does not lead to a substantial reduction of the runtime.

Query (d) from Section 5 uses a redundant `GROUP BY` in the `FROM` clause. Only DB-Y is able to remove the redundancy. Hence, for all other systems, the transformed query containing only one `GROUP BY` leads to a runtime reduction of around 50%.

Query (e) is an extension of Query (d), in which the `WHERE` clause of the subqueries have different predicates. The two subqueries can be merged into a single subquery by moving the predicates into the aggregation function as `CASE` statements and by adding an additional predicate to the outer query. None of the systems can eliminate this type of redundancy. For PostgreSQL and DB-X, we can again observe that the cost estimation does not accurately reflect the actual runtimes.

Query (f) has redundant subqueries in the `WHERE` clause that can be merged using the technique described by Bellamkonda *et al.* [2]. Surprisingly, no system eliminates this redundancy, even though they estimate a performance increase of about 50%. Although the transformed query leads to a reduction of the actual execution time in HyPer, the increase of the optimization time reduces the overall performance. This is due to the fact that the runtime of a query in HyPer falls within the scope of milliseconds. Therefore, the increase of the optimization time reduces the performance.

Query (g), which we introduced as a motivating example in Section 1, contains two redundant Type JA queries. As the query uses different predicates to compare an outer column value to the result of a subquery, the subquery coalescing proposed by Bellamkonda *et al.* cannot be applied. Instead, our NF^2 optimizer eliminates the redundant subquery by first unnesting both subqueries. As a result, two subqueries with the same `GROUP BY` clause are contained in the `FROM` clause, which can be merged into one subquery. As stated, no current database system features an optimizer that can perform all of these steps. Although DB-Y is able to do a subquery unnesting and a removal of redundant `GROUP BY`s, it cannot combine these steps to optimize the given query. PostgreSQL was aborted after 24 hours, whereas the transformed query executed in 3 seconds. Another significant

[3]http://www.hyper-db.de (February 16, 2016)

[4]One system was unable to execute the queries in reasonable time using a smaller buffer pool size.

Database	Query (a)	Query (b)	Query (c)	Query (d)	Query (e)	Query (f)	Query (g)	Query (h)	Query (i)	Query (j)	Query (k)
PostgreSQL	> 24 h	> 24 h	9896	58611	34108	17710	> 24 h	> 24 h	96228	> 24 h	> 24 h
	17377	22057	6070	31155	33050	10770	3216	3355	1292	7079	18315
HyPer	131	233	78	96	92	160	137	145	55	156	×
	134	218	53	58	62	186	133	176	22	158	×
DB-X	4817	–	1402	5152	2581	1471	588	418	506	1038	8525
	1261	–	869	2887	2503	1390	415	559	292	751	7853
DB-Y	–	> 24 h	29700	–	45224	23470	1177484	1171713	40908	> 24 h	395831
	–	8907	29076	–	21979	20353	3509	2965	2240	2522	50065
DB-Z	–	–	1273	14590	7948	72747	1006	301	1597	9987	4740
	–	–	760	8079	6551	38901	519	694	377	8426	4178

Table 1: Runtimes (in ms) of the original queries (top) and the transformed queries (bottom).

performance gain is achieved in DB-Y, where the original query is a factor 350 slower than the query transformed by our NF^2 optimizer. Due to the increase of the optimization time, there is no performance gain in HyPer.

Query (h) is an extension of Query (g), where the Type JA subqueries have different predicates in their `WHERE` clause. Again, the NF^2 optimizer unnests both subqueries. Then, the redundant `GROUP BY` with different predicates can be removed (*cf.* Query (e)). No system is able to remove this type of redundancy. For PostgreSQL and DB-Y, a significant performance increase can be achieved by executing the transformed query. Even though they estimate a performance benefit, the execution time of the transformed query is larger in DB-X and DB-Z. The reason for the performance decrease could be that the predicates in the original query are very selective. Therefore, only a small amount of tuples have to be grouped by each of the two `GROUP BY` statements. However, in the transformed query the grouping is performed on all tuples of the input relation. Tuples that should not be in the input of the aggregation function are then removed using a `CASE` statement. Again, in HyPer there is no performance gain, since the increase of the optimization time dominates the overall performance.

Query (i) from Example 3.3.1 uses a subquery in the `SELECT` clause. In section 5 we showed, how this type of subquery can be removed. However, no system performed this optimization. Therefore, the transformed query of our NF^2 optimizer led to a performance increase in all systems. For PostgreSQL, the original query is a factor 75 slower than the transformed query. For DB-Y the original query is a factor 18 slower and for DB-Z the original query is a factor 4 slower than the transformed query.

Query (j) has multiple subqueries within other subqueries. PostgreSQL and DB-Y were aborted after 24 hours, whereas the transformed query executed in less than 10 seconds in both systems. Again, due to the increase of the optimization time, there is no performance increase in HyPer.

Query (k) combines different types of nested queries. PostgreSQL was aborted after 24 hours. HyPer could not execute Query (k) and returned an abstract syntax tree error (denoted by "×" in Table 1).

7.3 NF^2 Optimization Time and Memory

In order to quantify the implications of our approach to the query optimizer itself, we measured the optimization time and the memory consumption with and without NF^2 rules.

Figure 3 (top) plots the optimization time required by our NF^2 optimizer for each query with NF^2 rules activated and deactivated. For Query (a) to (e) and Query (i), there is only a small increase when the NF^2 rules are activated. For the

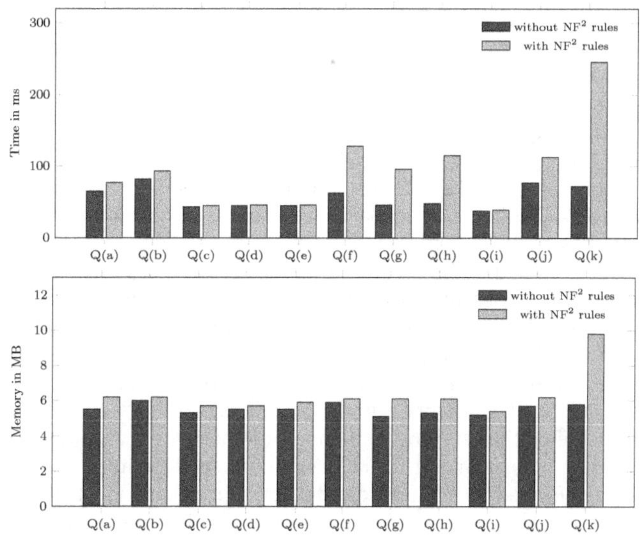

Figure 3: Optimization time (top) and memory usage (bottom) of the NF^2 optimizer.

other queries, the increase in optimization time is larger. The cause is that the implementation of the Cascades framework that we extended never merges expression groups, even if they contain equivalent expressions. For example, the search space for Query (k) currently consists of 2,058 groups. However, if redundant groups were merged during optimization, only 146 groups would be required. We are therefore integrating this functionality into our NF^2 optimizer.

Figure 3 (bottom) shows the memory usage of our NF^2 optimizer for each query with NF^2 rules activated and deactivated. Only Query (k) uses notably more memory when NF^2 rules are activated. Again, this is due to the fact that equivalent expression groups are not merged. The memory usage of the other queries is stable at around 5 to 6 MB.

7.4 Discussion and Limitations

To conclude this section, we discuss limitations of the presented evaluation that we are aware of. One possible weakness is the set of queries that we used to quantify the performance benefits of our approach. Since the queries of the TPC-H benchmark do not cover all optimization techniques that have been proposed in the literature, we defined our own set of eleven queries. Our first goal was to cover all types of nested queries for which optimizations have been proposed in the literature. Next, we aimed at covering all types of nesting that are possible in SQL. Finally, we introduced queries that combine different types of nesting, requiring different combinations of optimizations. We argue that this methodology is sound and that our set of queries can be used to identify the optimization opportunities that are still present in current database systems w.r.t. nested query optimization. At the same time, we cannot make any claims as to the relevance or frequency of these queries in practice.

Furthermore, our query set does not include queries that use disjunction, non-inner-joins, or non-equi-joins. Such queries can be executed using either nested-loops evaluation or special physical operators. In this paper, we do not claim to improve the state of the art at the physical level, but we clearly demonstrate that there is still much to be gained at the logical level by using the NF^2 algebra to represent and transform nested queries. This claim even holds for database systems that have special physical operators for nested queries (*e.g.*, SQL Server [9] and HyPer [17]). If such special physical operators exist, they can be incorporated into our approach by appropriate implementation rules.

Another limitation of our evaluation is its focus on nested queries. While this approach is appropriate to quantify the benefits of the optimization technique that we propose, it does not shed light on potential drawbacks it might have, if our NF^2 optimizer was applied in a setting with mostly non-nested queries. Although we acknowledge that such a study could be conducted, we also point out that it is possible to determine at parse-time whether or not a SQL query has subqueries. Since our Cascades-based NF^2 optimizer implementation supports the dynamic activation and deactivation of transformation rules, this parse-time information could be used to configure different "optimization profiles", which could mitigate some of the overhead introduced by our approach, when it is not needed.

8. RELATED WORK

The optimization techniques for nested queries that have been proposed over the last 30 years can be categorized into three classes. Approaches of the first category perform transformations at the level of SQL (or a query representation close to SQL). Approaches of the second category extend the relational algebra with new logical and physical operators that are specifically designed to represent nested queries. Finally, approaches of the third category address nested query optimization using an entirely different formalism.

Kim [14] is the first to address the optimization of nested SQL queries. His approach falls into the first catergory as it uses stepwise edits of the SQL code with the goal of replacing subqueries with joins. Our approach can express all transformations described by Kim, given that they are still possible in the current version of SQL. Zuzarte *et al.* [20] describe how certain subqueries can be replaced by window functions. Even though not included in this paper, our approach can also support these transformations (*cf.* Appendix B). Finally, Bellamkonda *et al.* [2] describe under which conditions subqueries in the `WHERE` clause can be merged. Their approach is implemented in Oracle based on their cost-based query transformation framework that uses "*query trees, which are different from algebraic operator trees in that query trees retain all the declarativeness of SQL*" [1]. In Section 4, we showed how subquery coalescing is realized in our approach. In contrast to these approaches, however, our transformation are integrated into the logical optimization phase, rather than performed at the level of SQL.

The work of Dayal [7], which falls into the second category, extends the relational algebra with special join and aggregation operators. It also sketches how these operators could be implemented in a database system. Cluet and Moerkotte [5] define an algebra and equivalences to optimize nested queries in object databases. Whereas most of the operators that they propose are nowadays supported by database systems, they also introduce a special join (*d-join*) to perform unnesting. Galindo-Legaria and Joshi [9] describe how Microsoft SQL Server transforms nested queries. They extend the relational algebra with the so-called apply operator that is used to algebraically represent nested queries in the `WHERE` clause. Both Brantner *et al.* [3] and Neumann and Kemper [17] extend the relational algebra with new operators to algebraically represent subquery unnestings. In the latter case, these operators use sideways information passing to execute nested queries more efficiently. Similar to our work, the approaches of Wang *et al.* [19] and Cao and Badia [4] also propose the use of nested relational algebras, but assume the presence of physical nest and unnest operators. Compared to these approaches of the second category, our approach performs only logical optimizations and every logical operator that we use can be mapped to a physical operator found in any current database system. For that reason, the plans generated by our NF^2 optimizer can be executed in every existing relational database system.

Instead of extending the relational algebra, approaches of the third category introduce an entirely different formalism by extending the relational calculus. For example, Fegaras and Maier [8] propose the monoid comprehension calculus and demonstrate how it can be used to remove any form of nesting in OQL. Similarly, the work of Grust and Scholl [13] extends monad comprehension calculus for which it can also be shown that normalization is complete [12]. Since the relational algebra rather than the relational calculus is the formal foundation of existing query optimizers, the goal of our work is to express unnesting rules in a formalism that fosters their practical adoption.

9. CONCLUSION AND FUTURE WORK

In this paper, we presented how nested queries can be optimized algebraically by representing them in the NF^2 algebra and applying transformation rules that are based on the equivalences of this algebra. A key advantage of this approach is that the optimization of nested queries can be performed as part of the logical plan enumeration phase. Furthermore, since the NF^2 algebra is an extension of the traditional relational algebra, all existing equivalences (and the corresponding transformation rules) are still valid and can work hand-in-hand with new rules. We demonstrated how this approach can be integrated into a Cascades-based query optimizer with little effort. Finally, we used this implementation to quantify the potential performance benefits that current database systems can achieve based on our approach.

Although we have focused on the optimization of nested queries in this paper, the applications of the NF^2 algebra in the context of SQL are not limited to this use case. As another line of future work, we therefore plan to extend our definitions to other SQL concepts, which then could be similarly optimized by algebraic transformation rules. For example, the `CUBE` or `ROLLUP` operator could be represented by NF^2 expressions and new transformation rules could be derived to optimize OLAP queries.

10. REFERENCES

[1] R. Ahmed, A. Lee, A. Witkowski, D. Das, H. Su, M. Zait, and T. Cruanes. Cost-based Query Transformation in Oracle. In *Proc. Intl. Conf. on Very Large Data Bases (VLDB)*, pages 1026–1036, 2006.

[2] S. Bellamkonda, R. Ahmed, A. Witkowski, A. Amor, M. Zait, and C.-C. Lin. Enhanced Subquery Optimizations in Oracle. In *Proc. Intl. Conf. on Very Large Data Bases (VLDB)*, volume 2, pages 1366–1377, 2009.

[3] M. Brantner, N. May, and G. Moerkotte. Unnesting Scalar SQL Queries in the Presence of Disjunction. In *Proc. Intl. Conf. on Data Engineering (ICDE)*, pages 46–55, 2007.

[4] B. Cao and A. Badia. SQL Query Optimization Through Nested Relational Algebra. *ACM Transactions on Database Systems (TODS)*, 32, 2007.

[5] S. Cluet and G. Moerkotte. Nested Queries in Object Bases. In *Proc. Intl. Workshop on Database Programming Languages (DBPL)*, pages 226–242, 1993.

[6] E. F. Codd. A Relational Model of Data for Large Shared Data Banks. *Communications of the ACM*, 13:377–387, 1970.

[7] U. Dayal. Of Nests and Trees: A Unified Approach to Processing Queries That Contain Nested Subqueries, Aggregates, and Quantifiers. In *Proc. Intl. Conf. on Management of Data (SIGMOD)*, pages 197–208, 1987.

[8] L. Fegaras and D. Maier. Optimizing Object Queries Using an Effective Calculus. *ACM Trans. Database Syst.*, 25(4):457–516, 2000.

[9] C. Galindo-Legaria and M. Joshi. Orthogonal Optimization of Subqueries and Aggregation. In *Proc. Intl. Conf. on Management of Data (SIGMOD)*, pages 571–581, 2001.

[10] R. A. Ganski and H. K. T. Wong. Optimization of Nested SQL Queries Revisited. In *Proc. Intl. Conf. on Management of Data (SIGMOD)*, pages 23–33, 1987.

[11] G. Graefe. The Cascades Framework for Query Optimization. *Data Engineering Bulletin*, 18:19–29, 1995.

[12] T. Grust. *Comprehending Queries*. PhD thesis, University of Konstanz, 1999.

[13] T. Grust and M. H. Scholl. How to Comprehend Queries Functionally. *J. Intell. Inf. Syst.*, 12(2-3):191–218, 1999.

[14] W. Kim. On Optimizing an SQL-like Nested Query. *ACM Transactions on Database Systems (TODS)*, 7:443–469, 1982.

[15] T. J. McCabe. A Complexity Measure. In *Proc. Intl. Conf. on Software Engineering (ICSE)*, pages 308–320, 1976.

[16] G. Moerkotte. Building Query Compilers. Available at: http://pi3.informatik.uni-mannheim.de/~moer/querycompiler.pdf, Dec. 2014. Under Construction.

[17] T. Neumann and A. Kemper. Unnesting Arbitrary Queries. In *Proc. Datenbanksysteme für Business, Technologie und Web (BTW)*, 2015.

[18] H.-J. Schek and M. H. Scholl. The Relational Model with Relation-Valued Attributes. *Information Systems*, 11:137–147, 1986.

[19] Q. Wang, D. Maier, and L. Shapiro. Algebraic Unnesting for Nested Queries. *CSETech. Paper 252*, 1999.

[20] C. Zuzarte, H. Pirahesh, W. Ma, Q. Cheng, L. Liu, and K. Wong. Winmagic: Subquery Elimination Using Window Aggregation. In *Proc. Intl. Conf. on Management of Data (SIGMOD)*, pages 652–656, 2003.

APPENDIX

In this appendix, the eleven queries used in the evaluation, NF^2 representations of additional SQL concepts, and a sample proof for an equivalence rule are given.

A. QUERIES

In this section, we present the queries that were used in the evaluation of this work. For each query, we also show the transformed version generated by our NF^2 optimizer.

Query (a): Type J Nesting

This query returns all parts delivered by suppliers from the region 'America'.

Original query

```
SELECT s_name, p_name
FROM Part, Supplier, Nation, Region
WHERE s_nationkey = n_nationkey AND n_regionkey = r_regionkey
    AND r_name = 'AMERICA'
    AND p_partkey IN (SELECT ps_partkey
                      FROM PartSupp
                      WHERE ps_suppkey = s_suppkey)
```

Transformed query

```
SELECT DISTINCT p_name, s_name
FROM Part, Supplier, PartSupp, Nation, Region
WHERE p_partkey = ps_partkey AND ps_suppkey = s_suppkey
    AND s_nationkey = n_nationkey
    AND n_regionkey = r_regionkey
    AND r_name = 'AMERICA'
```

Query (b): Type JA Nesting

This query returns all parts delivered by suppliers from Asia that are more expensive than the average price of parts of the same type delivered by suppliers from the region 'America'.

Original query

```
SELECT P1.p_name
FROM Part P1, PartSupp, Supplier, Nation, Region
WHERE p_partkey = ps_partkey AND ps_suppkey = s_suppkey
  AND s_nationkey = n_nationkey AND n_regionkey = r_regionkey
AND r_name = 'ASIA' AND P1.p_retailprice > (
  SELECT AVG(P2.p_retailprice)
  FROM Part P2, PartSupp PS2,
    Supplier S2, Nation N2, Region R2
  WHERE P2.p_type = P1.p_type
    AND P2.p_partkey = PS2.ps_partkey
    AND PS2.ps_suppkey = S2.s_suppkey
    AND S2.s_nationkey = N2.n_nationkey
    AND N2.n_regionkey = R2.r_regionkey
    AND R2.r_name = 'AMERICA')
```

Transformed query

```
SELECT P1.p_name
FROM Part P1, PartSupp PS1, Supplier S1, Nation N1,
```

```
  Region R1, (SELECT p_type, AVG(p_retailprice) AS avg_price
   FROM Part, PartSupp, Supplier, Nation, Region
   WHERE p_partkey = ps_partkey AND ps_suppkey = s_suppkey
    AND s_nationkey = n_nationkey
    AND n_regionkey = r_regionkey
    AND r_name = 'AMERICA'
   GROUP BY p_type) P2
WHERE P2.p_type = P1.p_type
   AND P1.p_retailprice > P2.avg_price
   AND P1.p_partkey = PS1.ps_partkey
   AND PS1.ps_suppkey = S1.s_suppkey
   AND S1.s_nationkey = N1.n_nationkey
   AND N1.n_regionkey = R1.r_regionkey
   AND R1.r_name = 'ASIA'
```

Query (c): Redundant Table Access

This query returns the price of the cheapest and most expensive order.

Original query

```
SELECT min_price, max_price
FROM (SELECT MIN(o_totalprice) AS min_price
      FROM Orders) O1,
     (SELECT MAX(o_totalprice) AS max_price
      FROM Orders) O2
```

Transformed query

```
SELECT min_price, max_price
FROM (SELECT MIN(o_totalprice) AS min_price,
      MAX(o_totalprice) AS max_price
     FROM Orders) O1
```

Query (d): Redundant GROUP BY I

This query returns the cheapest and most expensive order for each customer.

Original query

```
SELECT O1.o_custkey, max_price, min_price
FROM (SELECT o_custkey, MAX(o_totalprice) AS max_price
      FROM Orders
      GROUP BY o_custkey) O1,
     (SELECT o_custkey, MIN(o_totalprice) AS min_price
      FROM Orders
      GROUP BY o_custkey) O2
WHERE O1.o_custkey = O2.o_custkey
```

Transformed query

```
SELECT o_custkey, max_price, min_price
FROM (SELECT o_custkey, MAX(o_totalprice) AS max_price,
       MIN(o_totalprice) AS min_price
      FROM Orders
      GROUP BY o_custkey) O1
```

Query (e): Redundant GROUP BY II

This query returns for each customer the fraction between the urgent orders and the total number of orders. Compared to the previous query, the two subqueries of this query contain different predicates in the WHERE clause.

Original query

```
SELECT O1.o_custkey, nrUrgentOrders/nrOrders
FROM (SELECT o_custkey, COUNT(*) AS nrOrders
      FROM Orders
      GROUP BY o_custkey) O1,
     (SELECT o_custkey, COUNT(*) AS nrUrgentOrders
      FROM Orders
      WHERE o_orderpriority = '1-URGENT'
      GROUP BY o_custkey) O2
WHERE O1.o_custkey = O2.o_custkey
```

Transformed query

```
SELECT o_custkey, nrUrgentOrders/nrOrders AS ratio
FROM
  (SELECT o_custkey, COUNT(*) AS nrOrders, COUNT(
   CASE WHEN o_orderpriority = '1-URGENT' THEN 1 END)
    AS nrUrgentOrders
   FROM Orders
   GROUP BY o_custkey) O1
WHERE nrUrgentOrders <> 0
```

Query (f): Subquery Coalescing

This query returns all orders from customers located in Asia that are at least as expensive as the most expensive orders with urgent, high and medium priority. In contrast to the previous queries, the redundancy is now contained in the WHERE clause.

Original query

```
SELECT o_orderkey
FROM Orders, Customer, Nation, Region
WHERE o_custkey = c_custkey AND c_nationkey = n_nationkey
    AND n_regionkey = r_regionkey AND r_name='ASIA'
    AND o_totalprice >= (
        SELECT MAX(o_totalprice)
        FROM Orders
        WHERE o_orderpriority = '1-URGENT'
) AND o_totalprice >= (
        SELECT MAX(o_totalprice)
        FROM Orders
        WHERE o_orderpriority = '2-HIGH'
) AND o_totalprice >= (
        SELECT MAX(o_totalprice)
        FROM Orders
        WHERE o_orderpriority = '3-MEDIUM'
)
```

Transformed query

```
SELECT o_orderkey
FROM Orders, Customer, Nation, Region
WHERE o_custkey = c_custkey AND c_nationkey = n_nationkey
    AND n_regionkey = r_regionkey AND r_name='ASIA'
AND o_totalprice >= (
        SELECT MAX(o_totalprice)
        FROM Orders
        WHERE o_orderpriority = '1-URGENT'
              OR o_orderpriority = '2-HIGH'
              OR o_orderpriority = '3-MEDIUM'
)
```

Query (g): Redundant Type JA I

This query returns all parts that are cheaper and bigger than the average of parts of the same type. In contrast to the previous query, the aggregation functions of the subqueries are computed on different attributes.

Original query

```
SELECT P1.p_name
FROM Part P1
WHERE P1.p_retailprice < (
        SELECT AVG(P2.p_retailprice)
        FROM Part P2
        WHERE P2.p_type = P1.p_type
) AND P1.p_size > (
        SELECT AVG(P2.p_size)
        FROM Part P2
        WHERE P2.p_type = P1.p_type
)
```

Transformed query

```
SELECT p_name
FROM Part P1,
  (SELECT p_type, AVG(p_size) AS avg_size,
   AVG(p_retailprice) AS avg_price
  FROM Part
  GROUP BY p_type) P2
WHERE P1.p_type = P2.p_type
   AND p_retailprice < avg_price AND p_size > avg_size
```

Query (h): Redundant Type JA II

This query returns all parts that are cheaper than the average price of parts of the same type of brand "Brand#13" and that are bigger than the average size of parts of the same type of brand "Brand#14". Compared to the previous query, the two subqueries of this query contain different predicates in the WHERE clause.

Original query

```
SELECT P1.p_name
FROM Part P1
WHERE P1.p_retailprice < (
    SELECT AVG(P2.p_retailprice)
    FROM Part P2
    WHERE P2.p_type = P1.p_type
      AND P2.p_brand = 'Brand#13'
) AND P1.p_size > (
    SELECT AVG(P2.p_size)
    FROM Part P2
    WHERE P2.p_type = P1.p_type
      AND P2.p_brand = 'Brand#14'
)
```

Transformed query

```
SELECT p_name
FROM Part P1,
  (SELECT p_type,
   AVG(CASE WHEN p_brand = 'Brand#14' THEN p_size END)
    AS avg_size
   AVG(CASE WHEN p_brand = 'Brand#13' THEN p_retailprice
    END) AS avg_price
   FROM Part
   GROUP BY p_type) P2
WHERE P1.p_type = P2.p_type AND p_retailprice < avg_price
      AND p_size > avg_size
      AND avg_size IS NOT NULL AND avg_price IS NOT NULL
```

Query (i): SELECT Clause Subquery

This query returns for each part type the number of parts and the average price.

Original query

```
SELECT p_type, AVG(p_retailprice),
(SELECT COUNT(*) FROM Part P2 WHERE P2.p_type = P1.p_type)
FROM Part P1
GROUP BY p_type
```

Transformed query

```
SELECT p_type, AVG(p_retailprice), COUNT(*)
FROM Part
GROUP BY p_type
```

Query (j): Multiple Nestings I

This query returns all suppliers from the United States delivering parts that are cheaper and bigger than the average of parts of the same type.

Original query

```
SELECT s_suppkey, s_name
FROM Supplier, Nation
WHERE s_nationkey = n_nationkey
        AND n_name = 'UNITED STATES'
        AND s_suppkey IN (
                SELECT ps_suppkey
                FROM PartSupp
                WHERE ps_partkey IN (
                        SELECT p_partkey
                        FROM Part P1
                        WHERE P1.p_retailprice < (
                                SELECT AVG(P2.p_retailprice)
                                FROM Part P2
                                WHERE P2.p_type = P1.p_type
                        ) AND P1.p_size > (
                                SELECT AVG(P3.p_size)
                                FROM Part P3
                                WHERE P3.p_type = P1.p_type
                        )
                )
        )
```

Transformed query

```
SELECT DISTINCT s_suppkey, s_name
FROM Supplier, Nation, PartSupp, Part P1,
    (SELECT p_type, AVG(p_retailprice) AS avg_price
                    AVG(p_size) AS avg_size
    FROM Part
    GROUP BY p_type) P2
WHERE s_nationkey = n_nationkey
    AND n_name='UNITED STATES'
    AND s_suppkey = ps_suppkey
    AND ps_partkey=P1.p_partkey AND P1.p_type = P2.p_type
    AND P1.p_retailprice < avg_price
    AND P1.p_size > avg_size
```

Query (k): Multiple Nestings II

This query returns all parts delivered by a supplier from the United States that are cheaper and bigger than the average of parts of the same type. In addition, the price of a part has to be less than the price of the most expensive orders with urgent, high and medium priority.

```
SELECT s_name, p_name
FROM Part P1, Supplier, Nation
WHERE s_nationkey = n_nationkey
```

```
    AND n_name = 'UNITED STATES' AND p_partkey IN (
        SELECT ps_partkey
        FROM PartSupp
        WHERE ps_suppkey = s_suppkey
    ) AND P1.p_retailprice > (
        SELECT AVG(P2.p_retailprice)
        FROM Part P2
        WHERE P2.p_type = P1.p_type
    ) AND P1.p_retailprice < ALL (
        SELECT o_totalprice
        FROM Orders
        WHERE o_totalprice >= (
            SELECT MAX(o_totalprice)
            FROM Orders
            WHERE o_orderpriority = '1-URGENT'
        ) AND o_totalprice >= (
            SELECT MAX(o_totalprice)
            FROM Orders
            WHERE o_orderpriority = '2-HIGH'
        ) AND o_totalprice >= (
            SELECT MAX(o_totalprice)
            FROM Orders
            WHERE o_orderpriority = '3-MEDIUM'))
```

Transformed query

```
SELECT DISTINCT s_name, p_name
FROM Part P1, Supplier, Nation, PartSupp, (
    SELECT p_type, AVG(p_retailprice) AS avg_price
    FROM Part
    GROUP BY p_type
) P2
WHERE s_nationkey = n_nationkey
    AND n_name='UNITED STATES'
    AND P1.p_partkey = ps_partkey AND ps_suppkey = s_suppkey
    AND P1.p_type = P2.p_type AND P1.p_retailprice > avg_price
    AND P1.p_retailprice < ALL
        (SELECT o_totalprice
         FROM Orders
         WHERE o_totalprice >=
            (SELECT MAX(o_totalprice)
             FROM Orders
             WHERE o_orderpriority='1-URGENT'
                OR o_orderpriority='2-HIGH'
                OR o_orderpriority='3-MEDIUM'))
```

B. OTHER SQL CONCEPTS

B.1 CASE Statements

CASE statements can be represented with a projection containing a selection as subexpression in its projection list. The following example shows a SQL query with a CASE statement and the equivalent NF^2 expression.

Example B.1.1 *The following query returns for each part type the number of parts that are larger than a given size.*

```
SELECT p_type, COUNT(CASE WHEN p_size > 100 THEN 1 END)
FROM Part
GROUP BY p_type
```

The equivalent NF^2 expression is as follows.

$$\pi[p\_type, \text{COUNT}(\sigma[p\_size > 100 \wedge p\_type' = p\_type](Part'))](Part)$$

B.2 Window Functions

Window functions can be represented by combining nested selections with projections.

Definition B.2.1 (Window Function) *Let R be a relation, $L \subseteq attr(R)$ and $A = \{A_1, ..., A_k\} \subseteq attr(R)$ sets of attributes, f an aggregation function and R' the renamed relation of R. In addition, the following query is given.*

```
SELECT L, f(B) OVER(PARTITION BY A)
FROM R
```

This query can be represented by the NF^2 expression

$$\pi[L, \omega[A; f(B)](R')](R).$$

The window function ω inside the projection is defined by:

$$\omega[A; f(B)](R') := f(\pi[B](\sigma[A_1' = A_1 \wedge ... \wedge A_k' = A_k](R'))).$$

C. EXAMPLE PROOF

In this subsection, we demonstrate how the correctness of the subquery coalescing rules defined in Section 4 can be proven. As an example, we proove the correctness of the following case from Definition 4.2.1.

$$\begin{aligned}&\sigma[(A > \text{MAX}(\pi[B](\sigma[F_1](Inner))) \wedge \\ &\quad (A > \text{MAX}(\pi[B](\sigma[F_2](Inner)))](Outer) \\ &\equiv \sigma[A > \text{MAX}(\pi[B](\sigma[F_1 \vee F_2](Inner))](Outer)\end{aligned}$$

PROOF. Consider the expressions

$$\begin{aligned}E_1 := \sigma[(A > \text{MAX}(\pi[B](\sigma[F_1](Inner))) \\ \wedge (A > \text{MAX}(\pi[B](\sigma[F_2](Inner)))](Outer)\end{aligned}$$

and $E_2 := \sigma[A > \text{MAX}(\pi[B](\sigma[F_1 \vee F_2](Inner)))](Outer)$.

In order that $E_1 \equiv E_2$ is vaild, $sch(E_1) = sch(E_2)$ and $val(E_1) = val(E_2)$ have to hold (*i.e.*, both expressions have the same schema and return the same tuples). For both expressions the outer operator is a selection on the relation "Outer". For that reason, $sch(E_1) = sch(E_2)$ holds. As a next step, we have to show that $val(E_1) = val(E_2)$ holds. W.l.o.g. m_1 is the maximum of the first subexpression of E_1 and m_1' the maximum of the second subexpression of E_1. Additionally, m_2 is the maximum of the subexpression of E_2.

- $val(E_1) \subseteq val(E_2)$: Let $t \in val(E_1)$ be a tuple. Then $t(A) > m_1$ and $t(A) > m_1'$ have to hold (t(A) is the value of tuple t in attribute A). Since $m_1 \in val(\pi[B](\sigma[F_1](Inner)))$ and $m_1' \in val(\pi[B](\sigma[F_2](Inner)))$ hold, m_1, $m_1' \in val(\pi[B](\sigma[F_1 \vee F_2](Inner)))$ also have to hold. As a consequence, $m_2 = max\{m_1, m_1'\}$ and $t(A) > m_2$ follow. Hence, $t \in val(E_2)$ holds. Consequently, $val(E_1) \subseteq val(E_2)$ holds.
- $val(E_2) \subseteq val(E_1)$: Let $t \in val(E_2)$ be a tuple. Then $t(A) > m_2$ has to hold. Since $m_2 = max\{val(\pi[B](\sigma[F_1 \vee F_2](Inner)))\}$ holds, it follows that $m_2 = max\{m_1, m_1'\}$ holds. Consequently, $t(A) > m_1$ and $t(A) > m_1'$ hold. Therefore, $t \in val(E_1)$ is fulfilled and $val(E_2) \subseteq val(E_1)$ holds.

□

The other cases of Definition 4.2.1 can be proven analogously.

Extracting Equivalent SQL from Imperative Code in Database Applications

K. Venkatesh Emani
Subhro Bhattacharya†

Karthik Ramachandra*
S. Sudarshan

Indian Institute of Technology, Bombay
{venkateshek, sudarsha}@cse.iitb.ac.in, {karthik.s.ramachandra, subhro.bhattacharya}@gmail.com

ABSTRACT

Optimizing the performance of database applications is an area of practical importance, and has received significant attention in recent years. In this paper we present an approach to this problem which is based on extracting a concise algebraic representation of (parts of) an application, which may include imperative code as well as SQL queries. The algebraic representation can then be translated into SQL to improve application performance, by reducing the volume of data transferred, as well as reducing latency by minimizing the number of network round trips. Our techniques can be used for performing optimizations of database applications that techniques proposed earlier cannot perform. The algebraic representations can also be used for other purposes such as extracting equivalent queries for keyword search on form results. Our experiments indicate that the techniques we present are widely applicable to real world database applications, in terms of successfully extracting algebraic representations of application behavior, as well as in terms of providing performance benefits when used for optimization.

1. INTRODUCTION

Database applications are written using a mix of declarative SQL queries and imperative code written in languages such as Java. Techniques that optimize across the declarative and imperative parts of a database application are referred to as holistic optimization techniques. Such holistic techniques, which exploit program analysis and rewriting in conjunction with query rewriting, can perform optimizations that are beyond the scope of a database query optimizer or an optimizing compiler for the imperative language.

*Current affiliation: Microsoft Gray Systems Lab
†Current affiliation: Citrix Systems

SIGMOD'16, June 26-July 01, 2016, San Francisco, CA, USA

ISBN 978-1-4503-3531-7/16/06... $15.00

DOI: http://dx.doi.org/10.1145/2882903.2882926

In this paper, we present a novel holistic optimization technique which derives algebraic representations, or expressions, for program variables in database applications. The algebraic representation (D-IR) captures the effect of multiple program statements on a variable as a single expression. D-IR is then translated into a functional representation (F-IR) based on relational algebra and `fold`. Various transformation rules are presented to optimize F-IR, which is then translated into SQL. Our techniques have multiple applications, listed below.

Optimization of database applications: Our techniques allow many operations performed in imperative code in database backed applications to be translated to SQL queries making use of selections, joins, projections, and aggregate operations. Our techniques can detect when conditional execution, nested loops, and collection of results into an aggregate variable can be translated into SQL, reducing data transfer and even the number of queries executed.

There has been recent work by Cheung et al. [4] to transform parts of application logic into SQL queries, with a focus on database applications using Hibernate [13]. They rely on program synthesis technology, which is very resource intensive. Our techniques, on the other hand, rely on static program analysis, which is cheaper. For all programs that our techniques could successfully optimize, our techniques extracted equivalent SQL in much less time than [4], as shown by our experiments. Radoi et al. [17] proposed techniques for translating imperative code into MapReduce programs. While we use a functional representation which is similar to theirs, our goal is to infer SQL queries, so the techniques we propose are different. A detailed comparison with [4, 17], and other techniques for finding equivalent SQL queries, is given in Section 6.

Enhancing applicability of existing techniques: When the results of one query do not directly feed as parameters to another query, batching [11] is unable to combine these two queries into a single query. Techniques in this paper resolve assignments to intermediate variables and allow query parameters to be expressed in terms of program inputs or results of other queries. This enhances the applicability of batching as well as hybrid approaches proposed in [18], by combining related queries.

Keyword Search: Keyword search systems such as [6] accept a manually extracted set of queries for each form, along with mappings of form parameters to query parameters as input. Our algebraic representations can be used to automate extraction of equivalent SQL queries for keyword search.

Contributions: The key novel contributions of this paper are as follows:

1. We present (in Section 3) a DAG based intermediate representation (D-IR) for application code, that expresses the value of a variable at a point in the program as an expression in terms of values available at an earlier point in the program. D-IR represents straight line and conditionally evaluated code algebraically, while loops have a non algebraic representation (only cursor loops are considered). We present techniques for deriving D-IR representations for program variables. Our techniques are based on program regions (refer Section 3.1), and can be applied to complex programs that include function calls.

2. We show (in Section 4) how to translate D-IR for cursor loops into a functional representation which uses `fold` along with relational algebra (we call it fold intermediate representation, or F-IR). F-IR is a convenient declarative representation for imperative code.

3. We present (in Section 5) transformation rules for F-IR, which help us in moving computation out of cursor loops and generating equivalent SQL queries. We then describe (in Section 5.2) how to rewrite the source program to use equivalent SQL. Our techniques are able to extract equivalent SQL partially for some variables that are amenable to algebraic analysis, while leaving other parts of code intact. Our techniques can translate many instances of nested loops where the inner loop computes aggregation for each value of the outer loop, into a `GROUP BY` query; earlier techniques are unable to perform such translations.

4. Our techniques have been implemented in the DBridge [2] system, to analyze and optimize Java programs that use JDBC or Hibernate. (The techniques themselves are not specific to any language or API.)

5. We present (in Section 7) an experimental evaluation of the proposed techniques on real world applications, which show the applicability of our techniques and their impact on application performance.

Section 2 presents an overview of our approach. We discuss related work in Section 6, and conclude the paper in Section 8.

2. OVERVIEW

An overview of our system is given in Figure 1. Given the source program (fragment), we first construct our

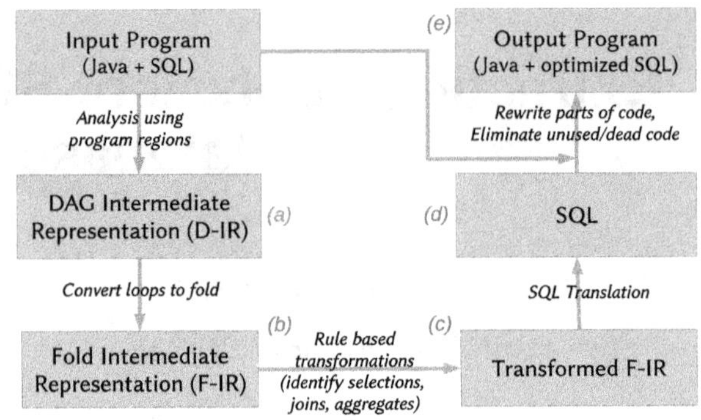

Figure 1: System Overview

DAG-based intermediate representation (which we call D-IR) for program variables. D-IR serves two purposes: (i) it resolves intermediate variable assignments, so the value of each variable at any program point is expressed in terms of values of variables at the beginning of the program, and (ii) it provides a semantic representation of the program.

For a variable whose computation we wish to optimize, its D-IR is translated into a functional representation using `fold` and relational algebra (F-IR), provided the required preconditions are met. The motivations behind translation of D-IR into F-IR are twofold: (i) F-IR provides a convenient declarative representation of the imperative program which is easy to translate into SQL. (ii) Transformations on F-IR are easy to describe and reason about, as F-IR uses higher order functions, which have well established properties. This makes it easy to prove correctness of transformation rules.

Rule based transformations are applied on the F-IR to push computation into the relational algebra query where possible; when no more transformations can be done, the rewritten F-IR representation is translated into SQL. The original program is then rewritten to derive the value of that particular variable, using the extracted equivalent SQL. Parts of the original program which are now rendered redundant/unused are removed. Translation of imperative code into SQL can greatly reduce the number of queries executed, and the amount of data transferred from the database, as compared to the original program.

Consider the code fragment shown in Figure 2, which is extracted from an open source gaming tournament software [15][1]. Variable types have not been displayed in this code, for ease of presentation (we will stick to this practice throughout the paper). It is part of a ranking page generator which tries to find the highest score across all tables in a round of the game Mahjong, where there are four players per table. The original code also finds the player who has the highest score along with

[1]Some changes have been made from the actual code for ease of presentation: (i) queries are made explicit and (ii) schema of the class `Board` has been simplified. Also, we use an abstract syntax for queries, which uses the pseudo function `executeQuery` that takes an SQL/HQL query, executes it and returns the result set/list of objects. Our implementation uses the actual source code.

```
findMaxScore(){
  boards = executeQuery("from Board as b
      where b.rnd_id = 1");
  scoreMax = 0;
  for(t : boards) {
    p1 = t.getP1();
    p2 = t.getP2();
    p3 = t.getP3();
    p4 = t.getP4();

    score = Math.max(p1, p2);
    score = Math.max(score, p3);
    score = Math.max(score, p4);
    if(score > scoreMax)
      scoreMax = score;
  }
  return scoreMax;
}
```

Figure 2: Code for highest score calculation

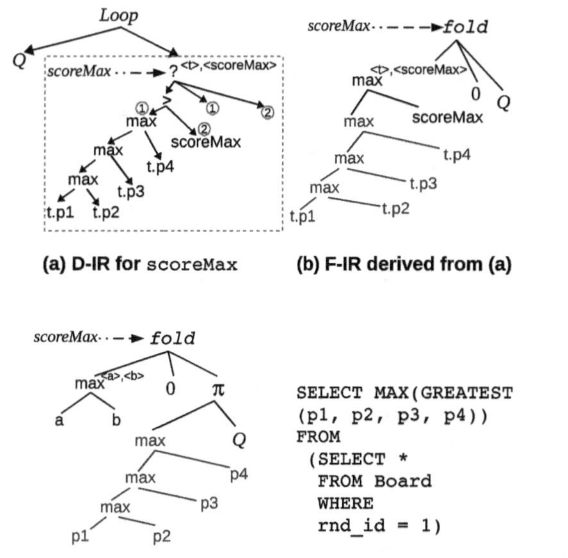

(a) D-IR for scoreMax (b) F-IR derived from (a)

(c) Transformed F-IR (d) Equivalent SQL

Figure 3: Walk-through of equivalent SQL derivation. Q denotes the query $\sigma_{rnd\_id=1}(Board)$

the score itself, for each round. Appendix B discusses how to generate equivalent SQL for such cases.

The optimized SQL for the `scoreMax` is shown in Figure 3(d)[2]. Parts (a), (b) and (c) show the various intermediate stages from the source code to optimized SQL, each of which will be described in detail in future sections. In parts (b) and (c), `max` is a function which returns the greatest of two elements.

The discussion in this paper targets loops that iterate over a collection, which we call *cursor loops*. If the iterated collection can be inferred (directly or indirectly) as equivalent to the result of a database query, we use the query to represent the collection. Otherwise, it is possible to create a temporary table at the database with the contents of the collection, and use a query (Q) on the temporary table to represent the collection. For simplicity, in this paper, we focus on the former case. For the latter case, we assume that Q is available. We omit details.

Furthermore, our discussion focuses on aggregates/collections built inside cursor loops. In addition to building aggregates/collections, another common use of cursor loops is to print values as they are computed in the loop. In such cases, we preprocess the program to replace output statements with appends to a (global) string (which can be treated as an ordered collection), and print its contents at the end of the program. The preprocessed program is then optimized using our techniques. We defer details to Appendix B.

Query execution calls are usually enclosed within exception handling code. Our implementation conservatively considers code that lies within a `try-catch` block, so that exception handling behavior is not altered due to optimizations. We also assume that loops do not contain unconditional exit statements like `break`, although certain cases of loop exit can be handling by some more engineering effort. Our experiments show that despite these restrictions, techniques presented in this paper have wide applicability. Inferring equivalent SQL across multiple `try-catch` blocks is work in progress.

[2]We illustrate using the `GREATEST` function of PostgreSQL. Translation into other dialects is possible using similar functions, or using `CASE..WHEN` construct.

3. DAG BASED IR

The goal of the first intermediate representation we use is to represent the values of program variables as algebraic expressions. We use a DAG representation that allows sharing of common sub-expressions between multiple expressions. We refer to our DAG-based intermediate representation as D-IR. DAG representation for basic blocks has been used in various code optimization techniques in traditional compilers [1]. We extend it to construct DAG representations for other program regions (Section 3.3).

In this section, we first present a background on program regions. We then discuss our D-IR representation and describe an algorithm for D-IR construction.

3.1 Background

A *Control Flow Graph* (CFG) is a directed graph in which nodes correspond to basic blocks in the program and edges correspond to control flow [1]. There are two specially designated nodes: the *Start* node, through which control enters into the graph, and the *End* node, through which all control flow leaves. CFGs are usually built on intermediate representations such as Java bytecode. Our techniques apply to any CFG; our implementation uses CFGs built on a representation called Jimple, provided by the Soot optimization framework [25].

Regions represent structured fragments of programs such as basic blocks, if-else blocks, loops, functions etc. A region in a flow graph is a set of nodes that includes a *header* that dominates all other nodes in the region,

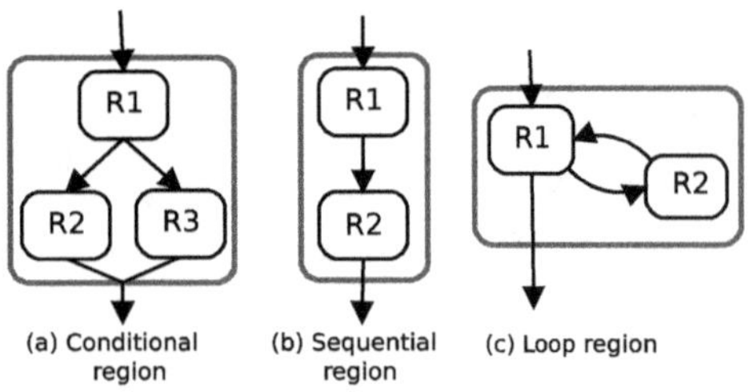

Figure 4: Types of regions

and has a single entry and exit. Regions are constructed from the CFG using rules described in [12]. Alternatively, it is possible to use an abstract syntax tree to identify program regions.

In our work, we handle four types of regions: basic block, sequential region, conditional region, and loop region (see Figure 4). In Figure 4, *R1*, *R2* and *R3* represent constituent regions of a parent region.

- **Basic Block Region**: A basic block represents a maximal group of consecutive statements that are executed together with sequential control flow between them. By definition, basic blocks cannot contain conditional constructs (if-else), loops or jumps of any sort. Regions R1, R2, R3 and R4 in Figure 5(a) represent basic blocks.

- **Sequential Region**: Sequential regions are regions composed of two sub-regions with sequential control flow between them (Figure 4(b)). In Figure 5(a), R6 is a sequential region.

- **Conditional Region**: A conditional region is comprised of three sub-regions (Figure 4(a)). The first sub-region (*R1*) contains the condition. The second sub-region (*R2*) is executed if the condition evaluates to true, otherwise the third sub-region (*R3*) is executed. We refer to *R1* as the "condition region", *R2* as the "true region" and *R3* as the "false region". In Figure 5(a), *R*5 is a conditional region composed of the condition region *R*2, true region *R*3 and false region *R*4.

- **Loop Region**: Loop regions are composed of two regions (loop header and loop body) with a cycle, as shown in Figure 4(c). Control flow starts at the loop header which contains the looping condition. If the condition evaluates to true, the loop body is executed, and control returns to the loop header to re-evaluate the condition. This is repeated until the condition becomes false, and then the loop exits.

By definition, regions compose other regions. We note that the program as a whole is also a region.

3.2 D-IR

D-IR is an intermediate representation for imperative code which may also contain database queries. It has two components: equivalent expression DAG (*ee-DAG*) and variable-expression map (*ve-Map*). Each region in

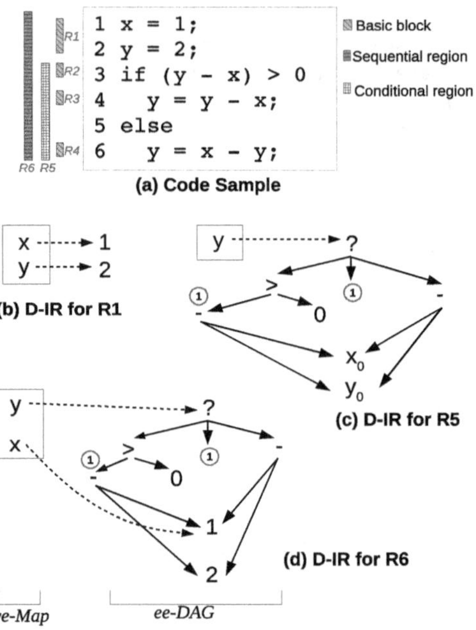

Figure 5: D-IR construction for a simple code fragment

the program has an ee-DAG and its associated ve-Map. We describe these data structures below.

3.2.1 ee-DAG

We define an equivalent expression DAG (ee-DAG) as a directed acyclic graph in which each node represents an *expression*. An expression (i) is a constant, a variable or a query attribute (base case) (ii) consists of an operator and its operands; each operand can in turn be an expression. The operator is connected to its operands through directed edges.

Consider the code sample shown in Figure 5(a). The ee-DAG for the program is shown in Figure 5(d). Circled numerals denote pointers to another part of the ee-DAG (to avoid clutter).

Parameterized queries in the source program can be treated as parameterized expressions in the multiset relational algebra. All relational algebraic operators (project (π), project (σ), join ($\bowtie$) etc.) are available in ee-DAG. Note that in this paper, π denotes projection without duplicate elimination. We also include extended relational algebraic operators for aggregation (γ), sorting (τ) and eliminating duplicates (δ) [27][3].

Relational operators do not guarantee that the order of input tuples is preserved in the output, unless explicitly sorted using τ. However, in this paper, we assume that for the operator π (projection without duplicate elimination), the input ordering is preserved in the output.

All arithmetic operators (+, −, ∗, / etc.), and logical operators (<, >, ==, AND, OR etc.), are available

[3]Usage: ${}_G\gamma_{Agg(E)}(R)$ groups R on G and performs aggregations in Agg (G could be empty), $\tau_L(R)$ sorts R on L, and $\delta(R)$ eliminates all duplicate rows from R.

in the ee-DAG. In addition, we introduce the following operators to enable representation of imperative code constructs:

- Conditional evaluation ("?"): Its semantics are similar to ternary operator or if-else in imperative languages like Java/C.
- Cursor loop (*Loop*): The *Loop* operator represents computations inside cursor loops. It accepts two operands.. The first operand is the relation or query result over which the loop iterates. The second operand represents the loop body. Unlike other operators, the *Loop* operator does not represent a single value. In this sense, the *Loop* operator is not algebraic. The loop body is represented by enclosing it inside a dotted rectangle (refer Figure 3(a)). Expressions inside this rectangle correspond to a single iteration of the loop.

Since our implementation can take imperative programs with rich language features as input, equivalent ee-DAG operators are necessary to model semantics of source program statements. We chose Java programs to demonstrate the working of our tool, so equivalent ee-DAG operators were created for the following Java constructs:

- String operations, addition/deletion of elements into/from collections (Array, List and Set), getter and setter functions for object attributes
- Important library functions – for example, in Figure 2, our system understands that `Math.max` is a function which returns the maximum of two numbers. This is modeled in D-IR using the `max` operator. Adding support for more library functions is not hard, and our ee-DAG can easily evolve as needed.

In our ee-DAG, an operator is represented as a node, and its operands are represented as children of the operator node. For example, in Figure 5(c), the condition `y - x > 0` is represented by the node rooted at >, and the operation `y - x` is represented by the node rooted at −. Similarly, in Figure 3(c), the ee-DAG rooted at π represents the query $\pi_{\,\mathtt{max(max(max(}p1,p2\mathtt{)},p3\mathtt{)},p4\mathtt{)}}(Q)$.

3.2.2 ve-Map

The ve-Map is a key-value data structure where a key is the label of a program variable (v) and its value is a pointer to a node e in the ee-DAG. The expression e when evaluated gives the value of variable v, in terms of values available at the beginning of the region. We refer to this ee-DAG expression as the equivalent ee-DAG expression (or simply the *equivalent expression*) of the program variable. In the illustrations in this paper, we denote ve-Map values (pointers) with dotted arrows. Note that these dotted arrows are not part of the ee-DAG edges. The ve-Map for the program in Figure 5(a) is shown in Figure 5(d). In this paper, we skip showing entries in the ve-Map for variables in which we are not interested (to make diagrams more readable).

3.3 Algorithm for D-IR Construction

D-IR construction works on top of the region hierarchy. Construction of regions was discussed in Section 3.1. We now outline a bottom up recursive algorithm for D-IR construction for a region. Appendix D describes the algorithm in full detail.

1. Construct D-IR (ee-DAG and ve-Map) for each constituent region (sub-region). All leaves in the ee-DAG which are variables are marked as region inputs.
2. Merge D-IRs of sub-regions appropriately (depending on type of parent region) to obtain D-IR for the parent region. The aim of merging is to replace region inputs with their ee-DAG expressions, which are expressed terms of inputs to a preceding region.

In the illustrations in this paper, region inputs are denoted by tagging them with a subscript 0, for example, $\mathtt{x}_0$ and $\mathtt{y}_0$ in Figure 5(c).

The smallest sub-region in a program is a single statement. Thus, D-IR construction for a program starts by constructing D-IR for simple statements, which are merged to get D-IR for basic blocks, which are merged to get D-IR for other composite regions. This process halts when the variable values are expressed in terms of inputs to the outermost region of interest.

We consider each simple source program statement as consisting of an expression (comprising of an operator and its operands) whose value is assigned to an optional target variable. For example, the statement `sum = 5 + 10` consists of an addition operation involving the operator + and its operands `5` and `10`, with `sum` as the target variable. A source language expression is represented in D-IR using an equivalent ee-DAG operator and equivalent expressions for operands as its children. Assignment is captured by adding an entry in ve-Map for the target variable (or updating, if an entry already exists), with its value as the ee-DAG expression.

We now outline the steps for D-IR construction for each type of region.

For a sequential region R comprising of regions R_1 and R_2 such that R_2 follows R_1, the ee-DAG for R is obtained by replacing each leaf variable (region input) in the ee-DAG of R_2, with the ee-DAG of the variable from R_1. For a conditional region R comprising of a condition c, true region R_1 and false region R_2, the ee-DAG for each variable in R is obtained by creating a conditional evaluation node ("?") with its three children as c, ee-DAG of variable from R_1 and ee-DAG of variable from R_2. For a loop region, the ee-DAG is obtained by creating a "*Loop*" parent node with its two children as the looping query and the loop body. Two ve-Maps are merged by creating a union of entries from both ve-Maps. In case of duplicate keys, entries from the following region are retained.

Consider the code sample shown in Figure 5(a). Figures 5(b), (c) and (d) show the step by step construction of D-IR for the program. In Figure 5(c), the variables `x` and `y` are leaves, so they are marked as region inputs (by tagging them with a subscript 0). These are resolved to constants in Figure 5(d), while merging with the preceding basic block *R1*. Note that in the final D-IR (Figure 5(d)), all intermediate variable references have been resolved to inputs at the beginning of the program. In order to efficiently check the existence of a node in the ee-DAG, a composite id – comprising of id's of its operator and operands – is assigned to each node, and a hash table is used for searching.

User defined functions/procedures are also handled by our techniques. D-IR is separately constructed for a user defined function/procedure. It is then merged with the preceding region at the caller location, by considering them to form a sequential region, taking into account actual to formal parameter mapping. We defer details to Appendix D.

4. F-IR REPRESENTATION

As we have described in Section 3.3, D-IR gives an algebraic representation for computations in sequential and conditional regions. However, the *Loop* operator used to represent cursor loops in D-IR is not algebraic. We now describe our second intermediate representation, which we call the *fold intermediate representation* (F-IR). F-IR combines D-IR and `fold` function to enable algebraic/functional representation of cursor loops. F-IR abstracts away details about imperative logic while still retaining the result ordering, unlike relational algebra. This allows easy translation from cursor loops to F-IR. Our transformation rules then operate on F-IR (Section 5). There has been earlier work on using `fold` to represent loops [17].

We use the following textual notation to represent a dag/tree. In general, $\triangle$ represents an ee-DAG, and e represents an expression tree. We write $op[c_1, c_2, \ldots]$ to describe an expression with root node as op, and $c_1, c_2, \ldots$ as its children. Angular brackets $\langle\rangle$ denote a parameter. Thus, $op[c, \langle p\rangle]$ denotes that the second child of op is a parameter p. Similarly, we use $e^{\langle p_1\rangle,\langle p_2\rangle,\ldots}$ to denote an expression, where values of some operands in the expression are given by parameters p_1, p_2 etc. A parameterized expression (say, $\mathtt{f}^{\langle p_1\rangle,\langle p_2\rangle}$) can be treated as a function taking parameters (p_1 and p_2). These parameters are substituted when the expression is evaluated with actual values. Parentheses are used to denote invocation of a function or a parameterized expression with actual values, for example, $\mathtt{f}(v_1, v_2)$ denotes a call to function `f` with parameter values v_1 and v_2, and $e(v)$ denotes evaluating the parameterized expression $e^{\langle p\rangle}$ by substituting p with v.

4.1 Fold

The `fold` function is a higher order function i.e., a function which can take other functions as parameters and can return functions as return values. `fold` takes 3 arguments: a folding function `f`, an identity element (id) and a recursive data structure on which `fold` is to be applied. In the context of lists, the `fold` function processes each element in an input list and combines the results into a single return value. The list elements can be processed from first to last, or last to first, depending on whether it is a left fold (`foldl`), or right fold (`foldr`). In this paper, by `fold`, we mean `foldl`. `foldl` is more suitable for representing computations on lists in imperative programs, as the elements are usually processed from first to last. `fold` on lists is defined recursively, as follows:

$\mathtt{fold}\ [\ \mathtt{f},\ id,\ [\,]\ ] = id$
$\mathtt{fold}\ [\ \mathtt{f},\ id,\ [a_1]\ ] = \mathtt{f}(id,\ a_1)$
$\mathtt{fold}\ [\ \mathtt{f},\ id,\ [a_1, .., a_{n+1}]\ ] =$
$\quad \mathtt{f}(\ \mathtt{fold}\ [\ \mathtt{f},\ id,\ [a_1, .., a_n]\ ],\ a_{n+1})$

Note that [and] are used both to denote lists, and to enclose arguments to the higher order function `fold`. (In the latter case, we could have used parentheses in place of [ ], or omitted them altogether, as is customary in the functional programming community, but we use [ ] to improve readability of our transformation rules.) For example, $\mathtt{fold}\ [\ +,\ 0,\ [1,2,3,4,5]\ ]$ evaluates to

$$((((0 + 1) + 2) + 3) + 4) + 5 = 15.$$

The definition of `fold` can be easily extended to operate on results of queries, which are ordered/unordered collections, instead of lists.

We extend ee-DAG to allow the use of a `fold` operator. We refer to D-IR extended with `fold` operator as F-IR. The `fold` operator takes three arguments, corresponding to each argument of a `fold` function. Note that the first argument can be a parameterized expression, which is treated as a function. Input queries are expressed using extended relational algebra. For example, the ee-DAG rooted at `fold` in Figure 3(c) is written as

$$\mathtt{fold}\ [\ \mathtt{max},\ 0,\ Q'\ ]$$

where `max` is the binary maximum function, and Q' denotes $\pi_{\mathtt{max}(\mathtt{max}(\mathtt{max}(p1,p2),p3),p4)}(\sigma_{rnd\_id=1}(Board))$.

4.2 Converting Loops to Fold

In this section, we describe how to use `fold` to precisely represent cursor loops, in F-IR. Equivalent SQL cannot be extracted for collections other than those constructed from query results (directly or indirectly), so we focus on cursor loops. Our system currently supports the following aggregations inside cursor loops: set/multiset insertion (`insert`), appending to list (`append`) or scalar aggregation (`min`, `max`, `sum`).

Before we present the algorithm for D-IR to F-IR translation (Figure 6), we describe a few terms commonly used in program analysis. A *loop carried flow dependency* is said to exist between two statements S_1 and S_2 in a loop, if S_2 follows S_1 in the control flow, and S_2 writes to a location which is read by S_1 in a future iteration. An *external dependency* is said to exist between S_1 and S_2 if both the statements access the same external location (file, database etc.), and at least one of S_1 or S_2 writes to the external location. For the purpose of dependence analysis, we conservatively treat the entire database/file as a single location. This is required since writes to a relation may trigger updates on another relation. Also, reading/writing an element in a collection is treated as accessing the entire collection. A *data dependence graph*(DDG) [16] of a program is a directed multi-graph in which program statements are nodes, and the edges represent data dependencies between the statements. Directions and labels on edges

procedure toFIR(R):

R: A program region.
Let $R.\triangle$ be the ee-DAG for R, and $R.M$ be its ve-Map.
begin
 foreach sub-region C of R
  toFIR(C)
 if R is not a (cursor) loop region, return
 else loopToFold(R)
end

procedure loopToFold(R):

R: A cursor loop region
begin
 foreach variable v that is updated in R {
  Let S = slice(R, l, v) represent a slice for v over R, where l is the program point at the end of R
  Let S_{acc} be the subset of statements from S updating v.
  Let D_S be the part of the data dependence graph for R that corresponds to statements from S.
  if all the preconditions below are satisfied in D_S:
   (P1) there should be a cycle of dependencies containing S_{acc} and a loop carried flow dependence (*lcfd*) edge (E).
   (P2) there should be no other *lcfd* edge apart from E and the *lcfd* edge due to update of the loop cursor variable.
   (P3) there should be no external dependencies.
  {
  Extract the expression tree $e = Loop[Q, e_{acc}]$ from the ee-DAG given by $R.M$.lookup(v).
  Let v_0 be the initial value of v at beginning of the loop.
  $foldExpr$ = fold$[e'^{\langle v\rangle,\langle t\rangle}_{acc}, v_0, Q]$
   where, e'_{acc} is obtained from e_{acc} by replacing each reference to attributes of Q, with reference to corresponding attributes of t (t is a new tuple variable).
  Add *foldEpr* to $R.\triangle$
  Update the entry for v in $R.M$ to point to *foldEpr*
  Replace pointers to v in $R.\triangle$ with pointers to *foldEpr*
  Insert statement(s_{fold}) "v = *foldExpr*" at the end of R
  updateDDG(R) /**reconstruct the DDG for R by ignoring unused/dead code (see description)**/
  }
 }
end

Figure 6: Algorithm for Conversion to F-IR

identify the direction and type of dependence, respectively. A program slice S = slice(P, n, v) is defined [26] as the subset (S) of all statements and control predicates of the program P that directly or indirectly affect the value of a variable v at the program point n. For example, in Figure 7(a), let the program point at the end of line 7 be l_7. Let P_{37} represent the loop, which contains lines 3 to 7. Then, slice(P_{37}, l_7, agg) = {*S3,S4*}. Similarly, slice(P_{37}, l_7, dummyVal) = {*S3,S4,S6*}. The algorithm is given in Figure 6.

Given a program region R, the algorithm attempts to translate all variables updated in R into F-IR. Updates to variables in a loop are translated into fold using the loopToFold procedure. The statement "v = *foldExpr*" (labeled s_{fold}) is a stub. The goal is to translate *foldExpr*

```
1 rs = executeQuery(Q);
2 agg = 0;
3 while(rs.next()){ //S3
4   agg += rs.getInt("x"); //S4
5   prettyPrint(rs.getString("y"),
                rs.getString("z")); //S5
6   dummyVal += agg; //S6
7 }
```

Q: SELECT x, y, z from R

(a) Code Sample

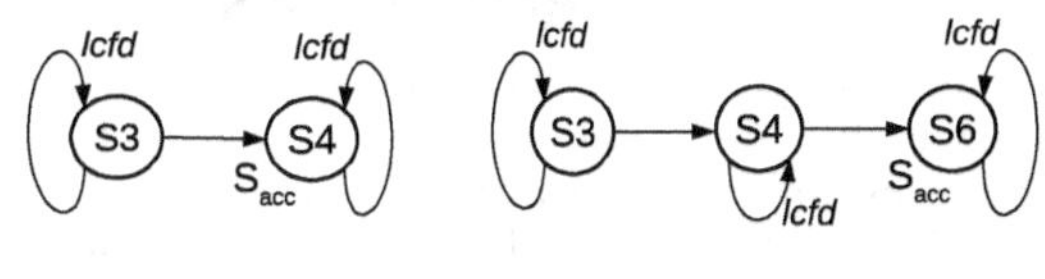

(b) Slice for agg **(c) Slice for dummyVal**

Figure 7: Demonstration of preconditions for translation into F-IR

into SQL. However, for the purpose of dependence analysis, we treat *foldExpr* as an algebraic expression.

Dead code [5] refers to code whose results are not used in any other computation. It may be transitive, i.e., identifying a part of the code as dead may reveal more dead code. Let S_{dead} denote the set of all statements which are rendered dead, due to insertion of s_{fold}. The actual decision of whether to use equivalent SQL (and remove S_{dead}) or not, happens after F-IR transformations on *foldExpr* (Section 5.1). However, dependences due to S_{dead} may cause preconditions to fail in an enclosing region. The procedure updateDDG reconstructs the DDG by ignoring statements in S_{dead} and including s_{fold}. Note that if the preconditions fail for a variable, the algorithm proceeds to attempt F-IR translation for other variables in the loop.

Theorem 1: Given a cursor loop region R, the value of a variable v after termination of the loop is equivalent to the result of *foldExpr* for v obtained by loopToFold(R), when executed on the same input.
A proof sketch for this theorem is given in Appendix A.

Consider the code sample shown in Figure 7(a). Figure 7(b) shows that the loop body slice for agg at the end of the loop satisfies the preconditions for translation into F-IR. The F-IR representation for agg is given as: fold [f, 0, Q] where f$^{\langle v\rangle,\langle t\rangle}$ = + [v, $t.x$].

The slice for dummyVal, as shown in Figure 7(c) violates P2, due to the presence of an additional *lcfd* edge from *S4* to itself. Thus, the ee-DAG for dummyVal cannot be translated into F-IR. We note that although our preconditions disallow an F-IR representation for dummyVal, in general, it is possible to represent dummyVal as a fold, where the folding function aggregates a pair of values (agg and dummyVal). However, SQL translation of dummyVal is not possible (without using a custom aggregation function), as it is dependent on agg. In Appendix B, we describe how some cases of dependent aggregations can be handled.

Note that the structure "if (*expr OP v*) then v = *expr*" is often used to implement min and max aggregations in a loop, where OP is one of <, >, <=, >=. This structure is translated into $v = OP_1(v, expr)$ where OP_1 is `max` for >, >=, and `min` for <, <=. If the program uses $v\ OP\ expr$, then it can easily be translated to the form $expr\ OP\ v$ before applying the above translation. Translation into F-IR is done after applying the above translation.

5. F-IR TRANSFORMATIONS

In this section, we present a number of transformations on F-IR representation. Our transformations are expressed as equivalence rules. Each rule has an input F-IR which can be replaced by an equivalent output F-IR by applying the rule. The aim of our transformations is to obtain an optimized F-IR from the given F-IR. By optimized F-IR, we mean an F-IR which when translated into SQL, reduces the number of queries and/or data transferred as compared to the original F-IR.

5.1 Transformation Rules

We now present transformation rules. Many of these rules specify a pattern for the relational algebra input to `fold`. The actual input may not directly match this pattern. However, standard relational algebra transformations can be used to bring the input query to the required structure to apply transformations.

Rule T1 (Simplification): If **append** denotes the list append operator, **insert** denotes the set insertion operator, and δ denotes the duplicate elimination operator,

$\texttt{fold}[\ \texttt{append},\ [\,],\ Q\ ] = Q$ (Rule T1.1)

$\texttt{fold}[\ \texttt{insert},\ \{\},\ Q\ ] = \delta(Q)$ (Rule T1.2)

Rule T2 (Predicate push):

If $\texttt{f}^{\langle v\rangle,\langle t\rangle} = ?[\ pred(t),\ \texttt{g}\ ]$, then

$\texttt{fold}\ [\ \texttt{f},\ id,\ \pi_L(\tau_Z(Q))\ ]$

$\equiv \texttt{fold}\ [\ \texttt{g},\ id,\ \pi_L(\tau_Z(\sigma_{pred}(Q)))\ ]$

where $pred(t)$ is a predicate expression parameterized only on attributes of tuple t, and τ is the relational sort operator (Section 3.2.1). Z can be empty, which signifies absence of ordering on Q.

The selection predicate $pred$ is obtained from $pred(t)$ by replacing references to attributes of t with corresponding attributes of Q. We will use the terms $pred(t)$ and $pred$ in similar contexts in other transformation rules, without describing them again.

Rule T3 (Push scalar functions into the query):

If $\texttt{f}^{\langle v\rangle,\langle t\rangle} = \texttt{g}(v,\ \texttt{h}(t.A))$, then

$\texttt{fold}\ [\ \texttt{f},\ id,\ \pi_A(Q)\ ]$

$\equiv \texttt{fold}\ [\ \texttt{g},\ id, \pi_{\texttt{h}(A)}(Q)]$

This rule can easily be extended to the case when **h** operates on more than one attribute of tuple t.

Rule T4 (Join identification)

(Rule T4.1 – list append):

If $\texttt{f}^{\langle v\rangle,\langle t\rangle} = \texttt{fold}\ [\ \texttt{append},\ v, \pi_L(\tau_{Z_2}(\sigma_{pred(t)}(Q_2)))\ ]$, then $\texttt{fold}\ [\ \texttt{f},\ [\,],\ \tau_{Z_1}(Q_1)\ ]$

$\equiv \pi_L(\tau_{Z_1,Q_1.K,Z_2}(Q_1 \bowtie_{pred} Q_2))$

provided Q_1 has a unique key K, where **append** is the list append operator. Z_2 can be empty.

This rule is the same as the join identification rule used by Cheung et al. [4], but the output should be sorted on $(Z_1, Q_1.K, Z_2)$, and not just (Z_1, Z_2).

For insertion into a set, the result ordering does not matter, but duplicates should be eliminated. Thus, the rule can be given as follows.

(Rule T4.2 – set insertion):

If $\texttt{f}^{\langle v\rangle,\langle t\rangle} = \texttt{fold}\ [\ \texttt{insert},\ v,\ \pi_L(\tau_{Z_2}(\sigma_{pred(t)}(Q_2)))\ ]$, then

$\texttt{fold}\ [\ \texttt{f},\ \{\},\ \tau_{Z_1}(Q_1)\ ] \equiv \delta(\pi_L(Q_1 \bowtie_{pred} Q_2))$

Z_1 and Z_2 can be empty. In the case of multiset **insert**, duplicate elimination is not required, so the RHS would simply be $\pi_L(Q_1 \bowtie_{pred} Q_2)$ (Rule T4.3).

Rule T5 (Aggregations)

(Rule T5.1 – entire relation):

$\texttt{fold}[\ op,\ id,\ \pi_A(Q)\ ] \equiv \gamma_{op\_agg(A)}(Q)$

where op_agg is the relational aggregation operator corresponding to the binary operator op, id is the identity element for op. For op=+, op_agg = `sum`; for op = `max`, op_agg = `max`; for op = `min`, op_agg = `min`. Note that we overloaded `max` to represent both binary and aggregation operators.

(Rule T5.2 – group by):

If $\texttt{f}^{\langle v\rangle,\langle t\rangle} = \texttt{append}[v,\ (t.B, \gamma_{op\_agg(A)}(\sigma_{pred(t)}(Q_2)))\ ]$, then $\texttt{fold}\ [\texttt{f},\ [\,],\ Q_1\ ] \equiv$

$\pi_{Q_1.B,\ op\_agg(Q_2.A)}(Q_1.{*}\gamma_{op\_agg(Q_2.A)}\ (Q_1 ⟕_{pred} Q_2))$

provided the order of Q_1 is not deterministic, and Q_1 has a key. This rule can be extended easily to handle **insert** in the place of **append**.

Note that the above transformation works with standard SQL semantics for aggregates involving NULL values. The general case that Q_1 may not have a key, and may be ordered can be handled using extensions to techniques for decorrelation of aggregate queries [7]. We omit details for lack of space. In rules T5.1 and T5.2, the initial variable value (second argument) passed to `fold` was the identity element for the folding function. In Appendix B, we discuss transformation rule T6 that enables us to handle the case when the above assumption does not hold.

Rule 5.2 is used to translate a common implementation of group by in imperative code, where there are two nested cursor loops, the outer loop defines the groups, and the inner loop performs aggregation of rows in the group, and appends the aggregated result to a result list. Appendix B describes how to handle another common case where, in addition to the aggregated value, a tuple of values from the row containing the aggregated value is returned (for example, one may want the name of a student who scored the highest marks in a test, along with his/her marks).

We present some more transformation rules which are used in our implementation, in Appendix B. Similar to database query optimizer rules, more transformations can be added to exploit other opportunities for inferring relational operations performed in imperative code.

5.2 Generating and Using Equivalent SQL

After a program has been translated into F-IR, we use a top down traversal of its regions to rewrite the program to use equivalent SQL, by processing the parent region first, and then its sub-regions, as follows.

For a region R, we consider each statement (s_{fold}) "$v = foldExpr$" that is directly inside R (inserted during F-IR translation), and apply transformations (Section 5.1) on *foldExpr*. Let *transExpr* denote the resultant F-IR obtained after all transformations have been applied. If *transExpr* does not contain any `folds` (i.e., it is a relational algebra expression), and all functions in *transExpr* have equivalent SQL functions, then translation of *transExpr* into SQL is straight forward. In some cases, if the folding function does not have an equivalent SQL aggregate function, it is possible to use a custom aggregation function (either as a user defined function inside the database, or as a stored procedure defined in the application source language, if the database allows it). In other cases, SQL translation fails.

If an SQL query (Q) could be obtained from *transExpr*, we replace the stub s_{fold} with the statement (s_{sql}) "$v =$ `executeQuery`(Q)"[4]. Parts of region R which are now rendered dead due to s_{sql} are removed by dead code elimination. If SQL translation for *transExpr* fails, then the assignment "$v = foldExpr$" is removed. The original code for v remains intact.

Replacing the original source with SQL generated from transformed F-IR is most often a good idea. However, from an optimization view point, the decision to replace should be taken in a cost based manner, in general, as discussed in the next section.

5.3 Application of Transformation Rules

In our implementation, we apply transformation rules in the left to right direction. Our transformation rules match the LHS for a syntactic pattern, and replace it with the RHS. We assume that translation into SQL is always beneficial.

In case multiple transformation rules are applicable for a given program fragment, we choose any one of the applicable rules and proceed. In the current set of rules (T1 through T7), a transformation from LHS to RHS does not destroy any syntactic patterns in the LHS, which are amenable for transformation by other rules. So, the order of application of the competing rules does not matter. Thus, the rule set is confluent. It can be verified that our current set of rules always push computation from the folding function into the query, and not in the other direction. Thus, infinite derivations are not possible, and neither are cyclic derivations. Thus, our current rule set always terminates. However, addition of new transformation rules may result in cycles.

Translation into SQL may not be beneficial for all programs. For example, consider the code sample from Figure 7(a). Our techniques will extract a separate query for the aggregated variable `agg`, but the entire data still has to be fetched to print other information with rich formatting. In this case, the cost of an additional query will outweigh the benefit of pushing aggregation into the database.

For this particular case, a simple heuristic can be used to decide whether or not to do the transformation: transform only if equivalent SQL could be extracted for all variables inside the loop that use query results. However, in general, a cost based exploration of the space of possible rewrites of the program is necessary, to choose the best possible rewrite. This is an important area of future work. We sketch an approach to a cost based choice of rewriting which we plan to implement, in Appendix C. This approach uses a top down search algorithm using an AND-OR DAG, based on the Volcano/Cascades query optimizer [9, 10].

5.4 Limitations

Our techniques focus on optimization of programs that iterate over a query result, performing actions that can be translated into SQL. Our system cannot handle cases where there are language constructs that cannot be represented in F-IR, like custom comparators, type based selection, retrieving the i'th element in a list etc. Expanding F-IR to address some of these cases is an area of future work. We note, however, that other parts of the program may still be amenable to optimization.

There are complex F-IR expressions that cannot be translated into SQL. One such example where the order of print statements needs to be preserved is discussed in Appendix B. Often, data structures in imperative programs are over-specified (for example, using a list in place of a set). Respecting such over-specification sometimes makes our transformation rules inapplicable. Techniques for "weakening" the data structures (for example, using a set instead of a list), which could make our rules applicable, are part of future work.

6. RELATED WORK

Wiederman et al. [28] propose a source-to-source program transformation technique that analyzes programs using Hibernate to identify conditions under which retrieved data is used, and rewrites the program to use explicit queries where the conditions are included in the query. However, they do not extract queries for other relational operations such as joins and aggregations expressed in imperative code.

There has also been recent work on inferring SQL queries from procedural code using program synthesis by Cheung et al. [4]. Their approach generates possible equivalent SQL queries and uses the Sketch framework [24] to check for equivalence. This approach is quite powerful, but, as evidenced by their results, can be quite expensive. While Cheung et al. identify continuous code fragments which can be replaced by an SQL query, our techniques can also transform intermittent fragments of code into SQL, thus enhancing their applicability. Cheung et al. developed a Theory of Ordered Relations (TOR) as an intermediate representation to express loop invariants and post conditions before con-

[4] `executeQuery` is a short form notation described earlier in footnote 1

verting to SQL. Our intermediate representation (F-IR), on the other hand, does not need a new algebra, and makes use of `fold` and existing operators from extended relational algebra.

Zhang et al. [30] propose techniques to infer queries, using the output table and database schema information by treating the source code (query) that generated the result as a black box. However, with this approach, guarantees for correctness of the query cannot be given for all inputs, since test inputs may not be exhaustive.

Recently, Radoi et al. [17] have proposed an approach for automatic translation of sequential array-based code into a parallel MapReduce framework. They use a functional intermediate representation (IR) and present rewrite rules that enable parallelism and translate the IR into Scala MapReduce code. Although their IR is similar to our F-IR based representation, their goals are quite different from ours. Our transformation rules are designed with the aim of inferring relational operations from the IR, while they focus on enabling parallelism and extracting map and reduce operations. Also, the work of Radoi et al. is suited purely for batch processing programs, while our work, in addition, considers application code where data access is interspersed with presentation (UI) logic, such as Web and mobile applications.

Iu et al. [14] propose a syntax (JQS) through which certain complex SQL queries can be expressed using normal (imperative) Java constructs. Similarly, Giorgidze et al. [8] present a Haskell library which allows developers to express database queries using Haskell constructs. However, an important difference of our techniques from [14] and [8] is that our techniques automatically infer which parts of imperative code can be pushed into the database. In contrast, [14] and [8] require developers to provide this information, in a syntax that uses source language constructs. Some of the techniques of Cheney et al. [3], for translating XQuery to SQL, could be useful for handling print statements as discussed in Appendix B. However, their goals and techniques are otherwise very different from ours.

Shi et al. [22] propose the UniAD system to unify execution of imperative code and queries at a single execution engine. They target only ad-hoc data processing tasks with small data sets, and use a custom database engine, hence they cannot leverage the query optimization capabilities of popular database systems.

Simhadri et al. [23] proposed techniques to algebraize imperative constructs in user defined functions (UDFs). Their aim was to extract a single relational algebra expression for the entire UDF body. Our techniques are applicable over a much richer set of imperative constructs including objects and collections.

Guravannavar et al. [11] proposed program analysis and transformation methods to exploit set oriented query execution to improve performance of iterative execution of parameterized queries. Ramachandra et al. [19] proposed a technique to prefetch query results across function calls. As discussed in Section 1, our techniques can be used in conjunction with the techniques of [11, 18, 19], to further enhance application performance.

7. EXPERIMENTAL EVALUATION

Our implementation is in Java. We used the Soot framework [25] for program analysis, and we incorporated a region based analysis framework in Soot. Our framework builds a hierarchical region tree over the CFG, and provides the infrastructure for traversing through regions, as well as merging the results of our analysis across regions.

For evaluation, we used our tool on code samples adapted from four real world applications namely, Wilos [29] – an orchestration software, Matoso [15] – a ranking software for Mahjong tournaments, *AcadPortal* and *JobPortal* – two real world applications in production use at IIT Bombay; and two benchmark applications namely, RuBiS [21] – a bidding system modeled after *ebay.com*, and RuBBoS [20] – a bulletin board like *slashdot.org*. Our experiments were run on a machine with 8GB RAM with Intel Core i7-3770, 3.40GHz CPU running Ubuntu Linux, with MySQL 5.5 database server. The client was on the same machine.

We use *EqSQL* to refer to techniques in this paper, and QBS to denote techniques by Cheung et al. [4].

7.1 Applicability

The techniques presented in this paper can be used with any language and data access API. We have implemented our techniques for database backed applications written in Java. Our implementation supports applications using Hibernate for database access.

Experiment 1 (Comparison with Cheung et al. [4]): Cheung et al. [4] reported the applicability of their techniques for code samples extracted from Wilos, an open source application that uses Hibernate. We tested our implementation on the same code samples. The results are shown in Table 1. The values in these columns denote time taken for equivalent SQL extraction in cases where the system succeeded. The numbers for QBS have been taken from [4]. "–" denotes that a particular code sample could not be optimized due to limitations in the techniques. ✓denotes that the code fragment can be handled by the techniques we propose, although they are not handled by our current implementation.

While QBS could automatically extract equivalent SQL in 21/33 cases, our system succeeded in 17/33 cases, although there are 7 further cases which can be handled by our techniques, but are not handled by our current implementation; we are working on extending our implementation to handle such cases. In 6 of the cases where our current implementation is able to extract equivalent SQL, QBS fails.

Techniques in [4] and those presented in this paper do not handle database updates. However, while [4] entirely rejects code fragments involving database updates, our tool partially optimizes such code fragments by keeping update statements intact, and extracting equivalent SQL for other variables in the code fragment, provided the update statements do not introduce a dependency between other statements. Similar to [4], our techniques fail for code samples 5 and 7 that contain polymorphic type comparison and selection using custom comparator, which are not handled in EqSQL.

Sl.	File (Line No.)	QBS	EqSQL
1	ActivityService (401)	–	< 1
2	ActivityService (328)	–	< 1
3	Guidance Service (140)	–	< 1
4	Guidance Service (154)	–	< 1
5	ProjectService (266)	–	–
6	ProjectService (297)	19	< 1
7	ProjectService (338)	–	–
8	ProjectService (394)	21	< 2
9	ProjectService (410)	39	< 1
10	ProjectService (248)	150	< 1
11	AffectedtoDao (13)	72	< 2
12	ConcreteActivityDao (139)	–	–
13	ConcreteActivityService (133)	–	✓
14	ConcreteRoleAffectationService (55)	310	✓
15	ConcreteRoleDescriptorService (181)	290	–
16	ConcreteWorkBreakdownElementService(55)	–	–
17	ConcreteWorkProductDescriptorService(236)	284	–
18	IterationService (103)	–	< 1
19	LoginService (103)	125	< 2
20	LoginService (83)	164	< 2
21	ParticipantBean (1079)	31	< 2
22	ParticipantBean (681)	121	–
23	ParticipantService (146)	281	✓
24	ParticipantService (119	301	< 2
25	ParticipantService (266)	260	–
26	PhaseService (98)	–	< 2
27	ProcessBean (248)	82	< 2
28	ProcessManagerBean (243)	50	< 2
29	RoleDao (15)	–	–
30	RoleService (15)	150	✓
31	WilosUserBean (717)	23	✓
32	WorkProductsExpTableBean (990)	52	✓
33	WorkProductsExpTableBean (974)	50	✓

Table 1: Comparison of time taken (s) by QBS (128GB RAM, 32 cores) and EqSQL (8GB RAM, 8 cores) for SQL extraction

Experiment 2 (Comparison with [11, 18, 19]): Our techniques can perform optimizations, which existing holistic optimization techniques like batching [11], prefetching of queries [19], and hybrid techniques [18] cannot perform.

Batching is applicable only when there is parameterized iterative query invocation from a loop. If the loop iterates over a query result, batching is able to extract a join query. In addition to the above case, EqSQL can identify more optimization opportunities for pushing selections, projections and aggregations into the database. We examined all code samples from Wilos listed in Table 1, and identified that batching is applicable in 7/33 cases, whereas EqSQL is applicable in 24/33 cases. In 4 cases where both batching and EqSQL are applicable, EqSQL will perform better or same as batching. This is because, in addition to extracting a join query, EqSQL also pushes selections and projections into the database, unlike batching. However, while techniques in this paper are applicable only on cursor loops, batching can handle while loops also, using loop split transformations. It is possible to extend our techniques, to be used in conjunction with loop split transformations.

Prefetching is possible in all cases we examined. However, prefetching by itself does not push any computation from imperative code into SQL, so data transfer is not reduced, although a hybrid technique described in [18] can combine batching and prefetching.

Experiment 3 (Extraction of equivalent SQL for keyword search systems): As mentioned in Section 1, keyword search systems for form interfaces require an SQL query, which would retrieve exactly the data printed by the form interface. The form can contain imperative code along with SQL queries. This was done manually in [6]. In this set of experiments, our goal was to evaluate whether our techniques can automatically extract equivalent SQL queries from servlets. One difference from the earlier cases is that in keyword search systems, ordering of data is not relevant.

We have analyzed the source code of three applications. The fraction of servlets where all queries were extracted by our tool was 17/17 for RuBiS, 16/16 for RuBBoS and 58/79 for *AcadPortal*. The cases where we were not able to derive queries were mainly due to limitations in our implementation such as the presence of operations which are not yet supported.

We have compared the output of our tool with manually extracted queries on the *AcadPortal* application and found that in about 20% of the cases, the manually extracted query was less precise than that extracted automatically by our tool, as the manual queries fetched more data than what is printed by the form interface.

Approaches for batching and prefetching are not suitable for this purpose. QBS can be used, but we are unable to give a comparison as we do not have access to their source code.

7.2 Performance Impact

In this section, we first compare our tool with QBS [4] based on time taken for optimization. We do not have the queries generated by QBS, so we could not directly compare the queries generated by our tool and QBS. However, we manually verified that for each of these cases, (i) queries generated by our system are correct, (ii) whenever a code fragment could entirely be translated into SQL, our system succeeded in doing so.

Experiment 4 (Comparison of optimization time with QBS): As shown in Table 1, for the code samples that we could successfully optimize, our techniques extract equivalent SQL in much less time than those of [4], even when run on a less powerful machine. The significant difference in time is because QBS relies on synthesis technology, which is resource intensive, while our system uses static program analysis, which is much cheaper.

The next three experiments present the impact of our transformations on applications using Hibernate, in terms of execution time and network data transfer.

Experiment 5 (Selection): We use code based on sample #6 from Table 1 which computes the list of unfinished projects, where all tuples are fetched, and filtered inside Java code. Our tool optimizes it to fetch only the required tuples by pushing the predicate into the query. The results, shown in Figure 8, indicate that the transformed code not only runs faster, but also transfers less data compared to the original code. We used 20% selectivity for the query in this experiment. The performance gain achieved is larger/smaller as the selectivity of the query is less/more.

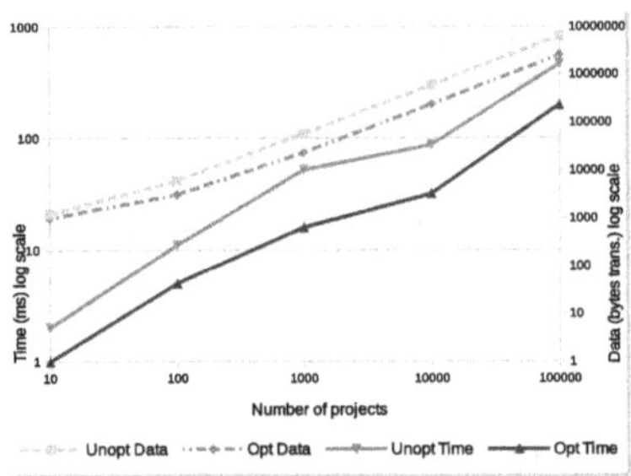

Figure 8: Selection

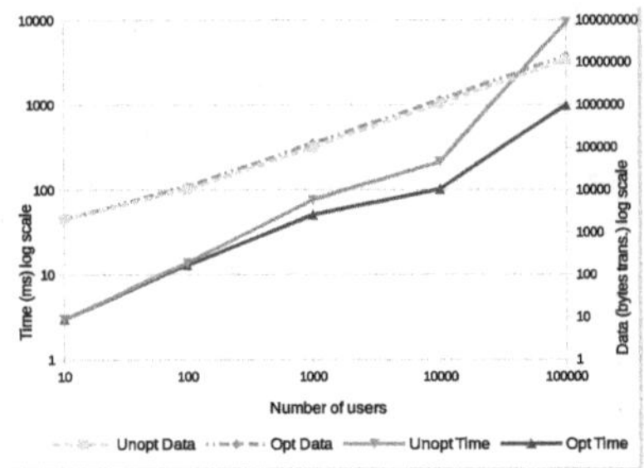

Figure 9: Join

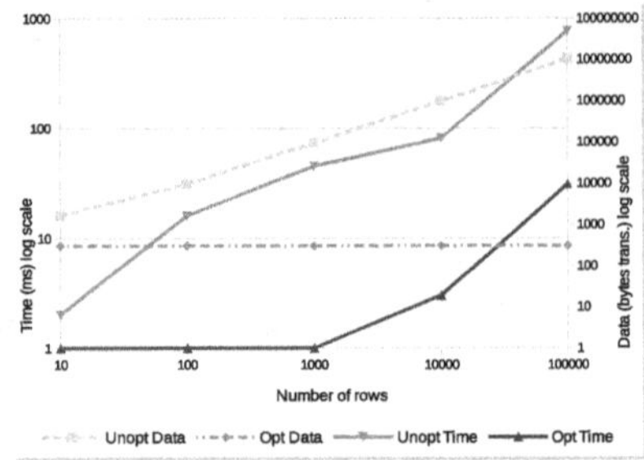

Figure 10: Aggregation

Performance impact of our transformations

Experiment 6 (Join): We consider code based on sample #30 from Table 1 (slightly simplified to be handled by our current implementation). This code computes a join of two tables `WilosUser` and `Role` (ratio of sizes 40:1), and projects the `WilosUser` entity, along with the role name from `Role`. The original code fetches all rows of both tables, and combines them using nested loops in the application, based on a condition. It is rewritten using our transformations, into a join query. The results are shown in Figure 9. The transformed code performs faster than the original code, as the database engine is allowed to choose the best join plan. However, the amount of data transferred is marginally more in the transformed code, because attributes of `Role` get replicated for each row of `WilosUser`.

Experiment 7 (Aggregation): We consider the code sample from Figure 2 which is based on a ranking page generator from Matoso. The results are shown in Figure 10. The data transferred for the optimized query is constant, as only the single result value is transferred in all cases. In contrast, data transfer for the original query increases linearly with increase in table size.

Experiment 8 (Comparison with batching [11] and prefetching [19]): In this experiment, we discuss the improvements due to equivalent SQL extraction over batching and prefetching. We extracted a code sample from the *JobPortal* application where there is opportunity for optimization by all three techniques, namely prefetching, batching and equivalent SQL extraction. This code fetches all relevant applicants for a job based on a search criteria. It then iterates over the results of the above query, and (conditionally) executes multiple scalar queries to fetch relevant information about that particular applicant. The pseudocode for this sample is shown in Figure 12 of Appendix B. The results are shown in Figure 11. In the figure, *Batch* refers to optimizations using techniques described in [11], *Prefetch* refers to techniques in [19]. Though existing techniques do lead to improved performance, they are limited in their applicability, as discussed in Appendix B. EqSQL enhances performance by upto two orders of magnitude compared to the original program, and upto one order of magnitude compared to other optimizations.

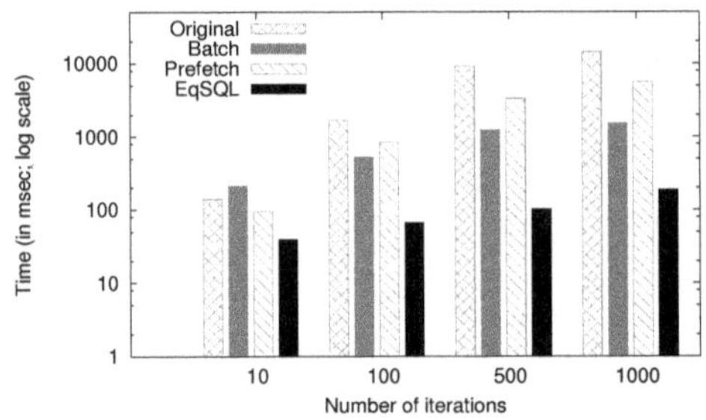

Figure 11: Comparison With Existing Techniques

8. CONCLUSION AND FUTURE WORK

In this paper, we have described novel techniques based on program regions, to translate imperative code to SQL. We presented algorithms to translate the source program into an algebraic/functional intermediate representation (F-IR) that uses `fold` and extended relational algebra to represent cursor loops. Transformation rules on F-IR identify relational operations performed in imperative code, and translate them into equivalent SQL. Our experiments show that techniques in this paper are widely applicable and useful in real world applications, and provide performance improvements that existing approaches cannot provide, on many programs.

Apart from addressing the limitations mentioned in Section 5.4, future work includes extracting equivalent SQL for database update operations performed in imperative code, and deciding in a cost-based manner, whether to rewrite parts of the code into SQL, as sketched in Appendix C.

Acknowledgments

The work of K. Venkatesh Emani is supported by a fellowship from Tata Consultancy Services. The work of Karthik Ramachandra was supported by a fellowship from Microsoft Research, India. We thank Uday Khedker for his valuable guidance, Tarun Jain and Tejas Deshpande for help with implementation, Prasanna Kumar for his inputs, and Kunal Shah for his work which motivated the techniques proposed in this paper.

9. REFERENCES

[1] A. V. Aho, M. S. Lam, R. Sethi, and J. D. Ullman. *Compilers: Principles, Techniques, and Tools.* Addison-Wesley, 2006.

[2] M. Chavan, R. Guravannavar, K. Ramachandra, and S. Sudarshan. Dbridge: A program rewrite tool for set-oriented query execution. In *ICDE*, pages 1284–1287, 2011.

[3] J. Cheney, S. Lindley, and P. Wadler. Query shredding: Efficient relational evaluation of queries over nested multisets. In *SIGMOD*, pages 1027–1038, 2014.

[4] A. Cheung, A. Solar-Lezama, and S. Madden. Optimizing database-backed applications with query synthesis. PLDI, pages 3–14, 2013.

[5] S. K. Debray, W. Evans, R. Muth, and B. De Sutter. Compiler techniques for code compaction. *ACM Trans. Program. Lang. Syst.*, 22(2):378–415, Mar. 2000.

[6] C. Duda, G. Frey, D. Kossmann, and C. Zhou. Ajaxsearch: crawling, indexing and searching web 2.0 applications. *PVLDB*, 1(2):1440–1443, 2008.

[7] C. A. Galindo-Legaria and M. Joshi. Orthogonal optimization of subqueries and aggregation. In *SIGMOD*, pages 571–581, 2001.

[8] G. Giorgidze, T. Grust, T. Schreiber, and J. Weijers. Haskell boards the ferry. In *Implementation and Application of Functional Languages*, pages 1–18. Springer, 2011.

[9] G. Graefe. The cascades framework for query optimization. *IEEE Data Eng. Bull.*, 18(3):19–29, 1995.

[10] G. Graefe and W. J. McKenna. The volcano optimizer generator: Extensibility and efficient search. In *Data Engineering*, pages 209–218. IEEE, 1993.

[11] R. Guravannavar and S. Sudarshan. Rewriting Procedures for Batched Bindings. In *Procs. VLDB*, pages 1107–1123, 2008.

[12] M. S. Hecht and J. D. Ullman. Flow graph reducibility. STOC, pages 238–250, 1972.

[13] Hibernate http://www.hibernate.org.

[14] M.-Y. Iu, E. Cecchet, and W. Zwaenepoel. Jreq: Database queries in imperative languages. In R. Gupta, editor, *Compiler Construction*, volume 6011 of *LNCS*, pages 84–103. Springer, 2010.

[15] MAhjong TOurnament SOftware https://code.google.com/p/matoso/.

[16] S. S. Muchnick. *Advanced Compiler Design and Implementation.* Morgan Kaufmann, 1997.

[17] C. Radoi, S. J. Fink, R. Rabbah, and M. Sridharan. Translating imperative code to mapreduce. In *OOPSLA*, pages 909–927. ACM, 2014.

[18] K. Ramachandra, M. Chavan, R. Guravannavar, and S. Sudarshan. Program transformations for asynchronous and batched query submission. *TKDE*, 27(2):531–544, 2015.

[19] K. Ramachandra and S. Sudarshan. Holistic optimization by prefetching query results. In *SIGMOD*, pages 133–144, 2012.

[20] ObjectWeb Consortium. Rice University bulletin board system http://jmob.objectweb.org/rubbos.html.

[21] ObjectWeb Consortium. Rice University bidding system http://rubis.objectweb.org/.

[22] X. Shi, B. Cui, G. Dobbie, and B. C. Ooi. Towards unified ad-hoc data processing. In *SIGMOD*, pages 1263–1274, 2014.

[23] V. Simhadri, K. Ramachandra, A. Chaitanya, R. Guravannavar, and S. Sudarshan. Decorrelation of user defined function invocations in queries. In *ICDE*, pages 532–543, March 2014.

[24] A. Solar-Lezama, L. Tancau, R. Bodik, S. Seshia, and V. Saraswat. Combinatorial sketching for finite programs, 2006.

[25] Soot: A Java Optimization Framework http://www.sable.mcgill.ca/soot (Oct 2014).

[26] F. Tip. A survey of program slicing techniques. Technical report, 1994.

[27] J. D. Ullman and J. Widom. *A First Course in Database Systems.* Pearson, 2007.

[28] B. Wiedermann, A. Ibrahim, and W. R. Cook. Interprocedural query extraction for transparent persistence. In *OOPSLA*, pages 19–36, 2008.

[29] Wilos Orchestration Software http://www.ohloh.net/p/6390.

[30] M. Zhang, H. Elmeleegy, C. M. Procopiuc, and D. Srivastava. Reverse engineering complex join queries. In *SIGMOD*, pages 809–820, 2013.

APPENDIX

A. PROOF SKETCH FOR LOOP TO FOLD TRANSLATION

We now present a sketch of the proof of correctness for theorem 1. We reuse the terms from Figure 6, without describing them here again.

Theorem 1: Given a cursor loop region R, the value of a variable v after termination of the loop is equivalent to the result of *foldExpr* for v obtained by `loopToFold`(R), when executed on the same input.

Proof Sketch: The proof is given in two parts. Part (a) proves correctness in the case of a single loop, and part (b) proves correctness in the presence of nested loops.

Part (a): Here, we prove that F-IR translation for a single variable in a cursor loop using `fold` is correct. Since `loopToFold` operates on one variable at a time, correctness for multiple variables follows. We use induction on the number of iterations of the loop (i.e., the number of rows in the result set, in order).

The base case is 0 rows (empty result set). For the inductive step, let Q_k denote the top k rows of query Q, v_k denote the value of u after k iterations of the loop, and t_k denote the k'th record of Q. Assume correctness for k iterations. We refer to preconditions P1 and P2 to claim that v_{k+1} depends only on v_k and the current tuple (t_{k+1}). Thus,

$v_{k+1} = e'_{acc}(v_k, t_{k+1})$
$= e'_{acc}(\texttt{fold}[\ e'_{acc}\ v_0\ Q_k\ ], t_{k+1})$
$= \texttt{fold}[\ e'_{acc},\ v_0,\ Q_{k+1}\ ]$ /* *defn of* fold */
Hence, proved.

Part (b): The procedure toFIR first translates all subregions for a given region into F-IR, before translating the region itself. In the case of a loop, all inner loops, if any, are translated into F-IR before translation is attempted for the loop. Thus, at any point of time, F-IR translation happens only for a single loop, whose correctness was proved in Part (a). Hence, correctness for nested loops follows.

B. MORE TRANSFORMATION RULES

In this section, we present some more transformation rules that we used in our implementation apart from those in Section 5.1, and then discuss some extensions to handle common cases in database applications.

Rule T6 (fold with non-id): Consider an F-IR expression fold[f, x, Q]. In some cases, the initial value passed to fold (x) may not be the identity element of the folding function (f). This limits the applicability of some of our transformation rules which assume that x must be the identity element for f. The following transformation rule allows fold to be expressed in terms of the identity element (id) for f.

If f is associative and $x \neq id$,
then
$\texttt{fold}\ [\ \texttt{f}, x,\ Q\ ] \equiv \texttt{f}\ [\ x,\ \texttt{fold}\ [\texttt{f},\ id,\ Q]\ ]$

Examples of associative functions include +, max, min, append etc.

Before we present Rule T7, we describe the outer apply construct. The outer apply construct [7], which we denote by Q_1 *OApply* $Q_2(t)$, accepts two arguments: an outer query (Q_1), and an inner query (or expression) which is parameterized on the outer query ($Q_2(t)$). For each row t_1 in Q_1, *OApply* evaluates $Q_2(t_1)$, and for each tuple t_2 in $Q_2(t_1)$, it adds t_1 concatenated with t_2 to the result. However, if $Q_2(t_1)$ is empty, t_1 concatenated with NULLs for attributes from Q_2 is added to the result. We use the outer apply syntax of SQL Server in our SQL queries; this is equivalent to the left outer join version of the lateral construct in SQL.

We now present Rule T7, which is used to extract a query for a common pattern in database applications, when the data is organized as a star schema. An example is given in Figure 12 in Appendix B.

Rule T7 (Outer Apply):
If $\texttt{f}^{\langle v \rangle, \langle t \rangle} = \textbf{append}[\ v,\ \textbf{g}(\ \pi^s_{L_1}(Q_2(t)), \pi^s_{L_2}(Q_3(t))\ )\ ]$
then $\texttt{fold}[\ \texttt{f}, [\ ],\ \tau_{Z_1}(Q_1)\ ] \equiv$
$\pi_{\textbf{g}(L_1,L_2)}(\tau_{Z_1}((Q_1\ \mathit{OApply}\ Q'_2)\ \mathit{OApply}\ Q'_3))$

where append is the list append operator, π^s represents scalar projection (single row), and $Q_2(t)$, $Q_3(t)$ are parameterized queries. Q'_2 and Q'_3 are obtained from $Q_2(t)$ and $Q_3(t)$ respectively by replacing references to attributes of t with reference to corresponding attributes of Q_1. This rule can also be used for insert (set insertion operator), in place of append.

Extensions: As we mentioned in Section 5.1, similar to database query optimizers, more transformation rules can easily be added to our system to exploit other opportunities for inferring relational operations performed in imperative code. We now discuss some extensions to our rules presented so far, which can be used to handle some common cases in database applications.

Checking for existence using cursor loops: So far, the focus of our discussion was to extract equivalent SQL from cursor loops that build the value of an aggregate/collection. However, in some cases, a single boolean value is conditionally assigned to a variable (v) inside the cursor loop. For example, a variable v may be initialized to false, and the loop may have a statement of the form "if ($pred(t)$) then v=true". Such an assignment can be treated as $v = v \vee pred(t)$, which can be handled using our techniques. Similarly, a variable initialized to true and set conditionally to false can be handled using $v = v \wedge pred(t)$.

A common use of the above constructs is for checking for existence/non-existence of a tuple in a table. Our implementation contains transformation rules to infer EXISTS and NOT EXISTS queries from the F-IR.

Sometimes, the loop can have an early exit, i.e., it may return/break immediately after a value is assigned once. Currently, we do not handle early exits. However, if the only computation inside the loop is the boolean value assignment, the return/break can potentially be removed, and equivalent SQL can be extracted using our techniques. We omit details.

Dependent Aggregations: In database applications, especially in reporting contexts, it is a common requirement to return a tuple of values from the row containing the aggregated value, along with the value itself. Specifically, if the aggregating function is max or min, this is an argmax/ argmin on a column for all rows in the relation. For example, one may want the name of a student who scored the highest marks in a test, along with his/her marks.

However, our techniques, described thus far, disallow conversion of D-IR to F-IR in the above case, because the tuple of row attributes to be returned depends on the aggregated value (causing a loop carried flow dependence, refer Section 4.2). We relax this precondition as follows.

If a variable v is being aggregated in a cursor loop, and another variable w has a loop carried dependence due to v, then the values of v and w after the loop can be represented in F-IR, using a folding function which returns a pair (v', w'). This allows us to obtain an F-IR from D-IR, which can then be transformed to optimized F-IR, to extract optimized SQL.

In general, this fold can then be translated into SQL using user defined aggregates. (Most databases today allow users to define user defined aggregates that can return a tuple.) However, for the special case of argmax, we can obtain an equivalent SQL query using any of several techniques such as sub-query, a combination of

```
ResultSet rs = fetchJobApplicants() //Q1
while(rs.next()) {
  String id = rs.getString("applicantId");
  String applnMode = rs.getString("applnMode");

  fetchAndPrintPersonalDetails(id); //Q2
  fetchAndPrintCommittee1Feedback(id); //Q3
  fetchAndPrintCommittee2Feedback(id); //Q4

  if(applnMode = "online")
    fetchAndPrintEducationalQualifs(id); //Q5
}
```

Figure 12: Cursor loop with nested scalar queries

ORDER BY and LIMIT, or using a construct like SQL's RANK if the SQL dialect supports it. We omit details.

Handling Output Ordering: It is not uncommon to find cases in database applications, that avoid intermediate collections by printing values as they are computed, in loops. In such cases, we preprocess the program to replace output statements with appends to a (global) string (which can be treated as an ordered collection), and print its contents at the end of the program. The preprocessed program is then optimized using our techniques.

When all output statements are present in the same level of loop nesting, this is straight forward. We now discuss optimization of database applications in the case where output statements may be distributed across different nesting levels of multiply nested loops. This approach can also be used for collection variables, when there is an ordering requirement on the contents of a collection.

Consider the sample program shown in Figure 12. This code is extracted from an administrative portal in production use at our organization. It fetches a list of job applicants (Q1), and for each applicant, it (conditionally) fetches and prints further information about the applicant using parameterized scalar queries (Q2, Q3, Q4, and Q5). We note that this is a frequent occurrence when data is organized as a star schema.

Although batching and prefetching techniques are applicable to this program, benefit due to batching is limited because of the overhead of creating four parameter tables, while prefetching is unable to chain queries Q1 and Q5, since parameters from Q1 feed into Q5 through the condition `applnMode == "online"`. However, using techniques described in this paper (Rule T7), a single SQL query can be extracted to fetch the required data for this code sample. The query is shown in Figure 13. As all the queries inside the cursor loop of Q1 in Figure 12 are scalar queries, Rule T7 is applicable. The source program is rewritten to refer to corresponding attributes from the extracted query, instead of attributes from the original queries (Q1 to Q5).

If some queries inside the cursor loop can return multiple rows, then combining them using the apply construct can result in cross products of the results of the

```
((((Q1 outer apply Q2 on Q1.applicantId
= Q2.applicantId)
outer apply Q3 on Q1.applicantId=Q3.applicantId)
outer apply Q4 on Q1.applicantId=Q4.applicantId)
outer apply Q5 on Q1.applicantId=Q5.applicantId
            and Q1.applnMode = 'online')
```

Figure 13: Optimized query for data access in Figure 12

sub-queries. This would be very inefficient, and not preserve ordering. In such cases, it is still possible to retrieve the data with proper ordering using techniques borrowed from [3]. Implementation of these techniques is part of future work. We note that batching and prefetching techniques may be applicable to such programs, even if our techniques are not applicable.

C. COST BASED APPLICATION OF TRANSFORMATIONS

We briefly sketch an approach that we are currently exploring for cost-based application of transformations.

Our approach is based on the Volcano/Cascades framework [10] for optimization of algebraic expressions, which is based on equivalence rules. This framework allows the optimizer implementor to specify rules that state the equivalence of two algebraic expressions; examples of such rules include join commutativity and join associativity.

One of the key ideas underlying the framework is an AND-OR DAG representation of the space of alternative expressions. Each OR-node can have multiple children representing alternative ways of computing the same result, while each AND-node represents the root operator of a tree that computes the result. The children of an OR-node can only be AND-nodes, and vice versa.

The framework allows transformations to be applied on an expression, and retains the old and all new expressions in the AND-OR DAG framework; as a result, the order in which transformations are applied is immaterial. Efficient techniques for detecting duplicate derivations of an expression are also a key part of the framework.

Although designed to deal with algebraic representations, the Volcano/Cascades framework can be used with the region-based representation that we use. Each region can be thought of as logically taking in input variables, and returning values for output variables; there are many ways of computing the same result. Thus, a region is mapped to an OR-node (also called equivalence node) in the AND-OR representation. Each way to compute the results in a region can be modeled as an operation node (AND node) in the Volcano/Cascades framework, with the children of the operation node being the child regions.

Similarly, an expression in the F-IR representation represents a specific way of computing a logical result. The logical result is represented by an OR-node; for each logically equivalent way of computing the result, which may be initially present or generated by transformation rules, the top-level operation is represented as a child operation node of the OR-node. Implementation of this approach is an area of future work.

D. D-IR CONSTRUCTION

In Section 3.3, we gave an outline of D-IR construction for various types of regions. We now describe the algorithms for D-IR construction in detail.

D.1 Simple Statement

Let s be a simple source language statement, with op being the operator of the contained source language expression, and n_1, n_2 etc. being its operands. The ee-DAG for s is a node with the equivalent ee-DAG operator for op as the root, and equivalent ee-DAGs for n_1, n_2 etc., as children. A ve-Map is created with a single entry, with key as the target variable, and value as a pointer to the ee-DAG root.

D.2 Basic Block

A basic block is treated as a special case of a sequential region (which we describe next) with each statement being a sub-region. Initially, the first two statements are merged to form a sequential region, and the result is merged with the next statement repeatedly, until the entire block results in a single region.

D.3 Sequential Region

Given two regions *r1* and *r2*, with *eeDag1* and *eeDag2* being their corresponding ee-DAGs, *veMap1* and *veMap2* being their corresponding ve-Maps, such that *r1* and *r2* (in order) form a sequential region r, the ee-DAG and ve-Map for r are obtained using the following algorithm.

- For each leaf in *eeDag2* that is a 0 subscripted variable (i.e., initial value), check and if present, replace it with ee-DAG obtained from a lookup in *veMap1* with the variable as key.
- The ee-DAG for r is the single ee-DAG obtained after step 1. In case *eeDag1* and *eeDag2* are disjoint after step 1, we combine them into a single ee-DAG using the NOP operator.
- Create a new map that is a union of entries from *veMap1* and *veMap2*. In case of duplicate keys, the entry from *veMap2* is retained. This map constitutes the ve-Map for r.

D.4 Conditional Region

Consider three regions *rc*, *rt* and *rf* that form a conditional region r, with *rc* containing the condition c, *rt* being the true region, and *rf* being the false region, *eeDag-t* and *eeDag-f* being the ee-DAGs, and *veMap-t* and *veMap-f* being the ve-Maps for *rt* and *rf* respectively, the ee-DAG and ve-Map for r are obtained using the following algorithm.

- Create a new ee-DAG and ve-Map for r.
- For each non local variable v modified inside r, create a conditional evaluation expression with c as the condition, expression for v in *eeDag-t* as its true operand, and expression for v in *eeDag-f* as its false operand (obtained by looking up in respective ve-Maps). Add this node to the ee-DAG of r.
- If there is no entry for v in one of *veMap1* or *veMap2*, then use its value at the beginning of the region (v_0).
- After creating the conditional evaluation expression, make an entry in the ve-Map of r with v as the key and a pointer to the conditional evaluation expression as its value.

D.5 Loop Region

The ee-DAG for a loop region can be created as follows:

- Create a *Loop* node with the looping query and the loop body as its two children.
- For each variable v that is a key in the ve-Map of the loop body and is also live at the program point immediately after the loop, add an entry *(v, ND)* to the ve-Map of the loop region.

Here, *ND* stands for not yet determined. Uses of v after the loop region will point to *ND* temporarily, until an expression for v over all iterations of the loop is obtained.

D.6 Functions

We classify functions into the following categories.

Library functions: Library functions that have an equivalent ee-DAG operator are represented using that operator. If there is so such operator, then D-IR construction fails for the target variable (v) of that statement, and target variables of statements which read the value of v after this assignment.

User defined functions: For a user defined function, we use the following approach:

1. Create the IR separately for the function. Let e denote the ee-DAG expression for the return value of the function. If an unknown statement is encountered inside the function, fail. Formal parameters are region inputs, so their initial values are denoted by appending a 0 subscript to the variable name.
2. If the above step succeeds, merge the function with its preceding region at the caller location, by considering them to form a sequential region. We update the value of the target variable (which is assigned the return value of the function, if any) in the ve-Map of the caller region to point to e. Formal parameters are mapped to actual parameters and resolved during the merge.

User defined procedures: User defined procedures, in addition to returning a value, can also modify the input parameters such that the change in their values is reflected at the caller location. They can be handled similar to functions, with the following additional step.

3. Remove all entries for local variables in the ve-Map for the procedure. Now, merge the procedure with its preceding region at the caller location, by considering them to form a sequential region (as described in Section D.3).

Generating Preview Tables for Entity Graphs

[1]Ning Yan* [2]Sona Hasani [2]Abolfazl Asudeh [2]Chengkai Li

[1]Huawei U.S. R&D Center [2]The University of Texas at Arlington

ning.yan.uta@gmail.com {sona.hasani,ab.asudeh}@mavs.uta.edu cli@uta.edu

ABSTRACT

Users are tapping into massive, heterogeneous entity graphs for many applications. It is challenging to select entity graphs for a particular need, given abundant datasets from many sources and the oftentimes scarce information for them. We propose methods to produce preview tables for compact presentation of important entity types and relationships in entity graphs. The preview tables assist users in attaining a quick and rough preview of the data. They can be shown in a limited display space for a user to browse and explore, before she decides to spend time and resources to fetch and investigate the complete dataset. We formulate several optimization problems that look for previews with the highest scores according to intuitive goodness measures, under various constraints on preview size and distance between preview tables. The optimization problem under distance constraint is **NP**-hard. We design a dynamic-programming algorithm and an Apriori-style algorithm for finding optimal previews. Results from experiments, comparison with related work and user studies demonstrated the scoring measures' accuracy and the discovery algorithms' efficiency.

1. INTRODUCTION

We witness an unprecedented proliferation of massive, heterogeneous *entity graphs* that represent entities and their relationships in many domains. For instance, in Fig. 1—a tiny excerpt of an entity graph, the edge labeled *Actor* between nodes Will Smith and Men in Black captures the fact that the person is an actor in the film. Real-world entity graphs include knowledge bases (e.g., DBpedia [2], YAGO [16], Probase [18], Freebase [4] and Google's Knowledge Vault [8]), social graphs, biomedical databases, and program analysis graphs, to name just a few. Numerous applications are tapping into entity graphs in domains such as search, recommendation systems, business intelligence and health informatics.

Entity graphs are often represented as RDF triples, due to heterogeneity of entities and the often lacking schema. The Linking Open Data community has interlinked billions of RDF triples spanning over several hundred datasets (http://linkeddata.org). Many other entity graph datasets are also available from data repositories such as the NCBI databases (http://www.ncbi.nlm.nih.gov), Amazon's

*Work done while at the University of Texas at Arlington.

SIGMOD'16, June 26-July 01, 2016, San Francisco, CA, USA

© 2016 ACM. ISBN 978-1-4503-3531-7/16/06...$15.00

DOI: http://dx.doi.org/10.1145/2882903.2915221

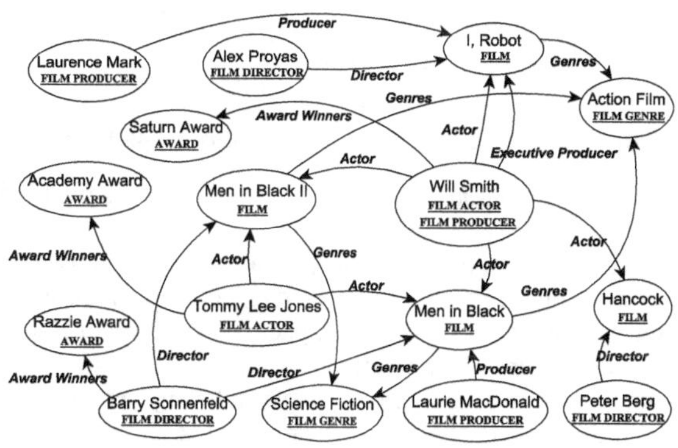

Figure 1: An excerpt of an entity graph.

Public Data Sets (http://aws.amazon.com/publicdatasets) and Data.gov (http://www.data.gov).

It is challenging to select entity graphs for a particular need, given abundant datasets from many sources and oftentimes scarce information available about them. While sources such as the aforementioned data repositories often provide dataset descriptions, one cannot get a direct look at an entity graph before fetching it. Downloading a dataset and loading it into a database can be a daunting task. A data worker may need to tackle many challenges before they can start any real work on an entity graph.

In this paper, we propose methods to automatically produce ***preview tables*** for entity graphs. Given an entity graph with a large number of entities and relationships, our methods select from the many entity types a few important ones and produce a table for each chosen entity type. Such a table comprises a set of attributes, selected among many candidates, each of which corresponds to a relationship associated with the corresponding entity type. A tuple in the table consists of an entity belonging to the entity type and its related entities for the table attributes.

Fig. 2 is a possible preview of the entity graph in Fig. 1. It consists of two preview tables—the upper table has attributes FILM, *Director* and *Genres*, and the lower table has attributes FILM ACTOR and *Award Winners*. In this preview, entities of types FILM and FILM ACTOR are deemed of central importance in the entity graph. Hence, FILM and FILM ACTOR are the *key attributes* of the two tables, respectively, marked by the underlines beneath them. Attributes *Director* and *Genres* in the upper table are considered highly related to FILM entities. Similarly, *Award Winners* in the lower table is highly related to FILM ACTOR entities. The two tables contain 4 and 2 tuples, respectively. For instance, the first tuple of the upper table is $t_1 = \langle$Men in Black, Barry Sonnenfeld, {Action Film, Science Fiction}$\rangle$. The tuple indicates that entity Men in Black belongs to type FILM and

	FILM	*Director*	*Genres*
t_1	Men in Black	Barry Sonnenfeld	{Action Film, Science Fiction}
t_2	Men in Black II	Barry Sonnenfeld	{Action Film, Science Fiction}
t_3	Hancock	Peter Berg	-
t_4	I, Robot	Alex Proyas	{Action Film}

	FILM ACTOR	*Award Winners*
t_5	Will Smith	Saturn Award
t_6	Tommy Lee Jones	Academy Award

Figure 2: A 2-table preview of the entity graph in Fig. 1. (Upper and lower tables for subgraphs #1 and #2 in Fig. 3, respectively.)

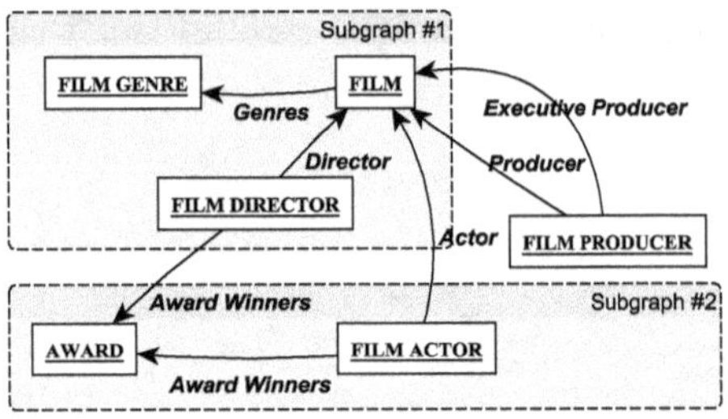

Figure 3: The schema graph for the entity graph in Fig. 1.

has a relationship *Director* from Barry Sonnenfeld and has relationship *Genres* to both Action Film and Science Fiction.

Data workers browse and explore data under inevitable display space constraints on mobile devices and desktop monitors. The proposed preview tables are for compact presentation of important types of entities and their relationships in an entity graph. They assist data workers in attaining a quick and rough preview of the schema of the data, before they decide to spend more time, money and resources to fetch and investigate the complete entity graph. The tuples in the tables further facilitate an intuitive understanding of the data. (Our approach shows a few randomly sampled tuples in each preview table. How to selectively display important tuples is left to future study.)

To this end, two other approaches are arguably less adequate for gaining a quick overview of an entity graph.

(1) One solution is to show a schema graph corresponding to the data graph. Fig. 3 is the schema graph for the entity graph in Fig. 1. While its definition is given in Sec. 2, we note that it is generated by merging same-type entity graph vertices (i.e., entities) and edges (i.e., relationships). Although a schema graph is much smaller than the corresponding entity graph, it is not small enough for easy presentation and quick preview. For instance, in a snapshot of the "film" domain of Freebase, there are 190K vertices and 1.6M edges. The corresponding schema graph consists of 50 entity types and 136 relationship types.

(2) Another approach is to present a summary of the schema graph, by schema summarization techniques [19, 20, 21, 17, 22]. Some of these methods [19, 20, 21] work on relational and semi-structured data, instead of graph data. Some [21, 17, 22] produce trees or graphs as output instead of flat tables. It is unclear how to apply these methods on an entity graph or its schema graph, due to differences in data models. Although it is plausible that some of these approaches can be adapted for entity graphs, several reasons can render them ineffective. *First*, schema summary can still be quite large. The most closely related work, [19, 20], clusters the tables in a database but does not reduce the number of tables or the complexity of database schema. If we treat each entity type as a table and its neighboring entity types in the schema graph as the table attributes, the number of tables would equal the number of entity types. For the aforementioned "film" domain in Freebase, it means one would have to understand the result of clustering 50 tables. *Second*, schema summarization is for helping database administrators and programmers in gaining a detailed understanding of a database in order to form queries. Our goal is to assist data workers in attaining a quick and rough understanding of an entity graph, before they decide to grasp such a detailed understanding. Therefore, our work can be viewed as an approach of finding a succinct representation of the schema graph (instead of clustering it). We are not aware of such an approach in previous studies.

In our definition (details in Sec. 2), a *preview* is a set of preview tables, each of which has a *key attribute* (corresponding to an entity type) and a set of *non-key attributes* (each corresponding to a relationship type). Given an entity graph and its schema graph, there is thus a large space of possible previews. Our goal is to find an "optimal" preview in the space. To this end, we tackle several challenges: (1) We discern what factors contribute to the goodness of a preview and propose several scoring functions for key and non-key attributes as well as preview tables. The scoring functions are based on several intuitions related to how much information a preview conveys and how helpful it is to users. (2) Based on the scoring measures, a preview's score is maximized when it includes as many tables and attributes as possible. However, the purpose of having a preview is to help users attain a quick understanding of data and thus a preview must fit into a limited display space. Considering the tradeoff, we enforce a constraint on preview size. Furthermore, we consider enforcing an additional constraint on the pairwise distance between preview tables. Given the spaces of all possible previews, we formulate the optimization problem of finding an preview with the highest score among those satisfying the constraints. The optimization is non-trivial, as we prove that it is **NP**-hard under distance constraint. (3) The search space of previews grows exponentially by data size and the constraints. A brute-force approach is thus too costly. For efficiently finding optimal previews, we designed a dynamic programming algorithm and an Apriori [1]-style algorithm.

In summary, this paper makes the following contributions:

- We motivated a novel concept of preview for entity graphs.
- We proposed ideas for measuring the goodness of previews based on several intuitions. (Sec. 3)
- We formulated optimal preview discovery problem, and proved its **NP**-hardness under distance constraint. (Sec. 4)
- We developed a dynamic-programming algorithm and an Apriori-style algorithm for finding optimal previews. (Sec. 5)
- Extensive experiments, comparison with related work, and user study verified the scoring measures' accuracy, the algorithms' efficiency, and the effectiveness of discovered previews. (Sec. 6)

2. PREVIEW DISCOVERY PROBLEM

An *entity graph* is a directed multigraph $G_d(V_d, E_d)$ with vertex set V_d and edge set E_d. Each vertex $v \in V_d$ represents an entity and each edge $e(v, v') \in E_d$ represents a directed relationship from entity v to v'. G_d is a multigraph since there can be multiple edges between two vertices. (E.g., in Fig. 1, there are two edges *Actor* and *Executive Producer* from entity Will Smith to entity I, Robot.)

Each entity is labeled by a name. For simplicity and intuitiveness of presentation, we shall mention entities by their names, assuming all entities have distinct names, although in reality they are distinguished by unique identifiers such as URIs. Each entity belongs to one or more *entity types*, underlined in Fig. 1. (E.g., Will Smith belongs to types FILM ACTOR and FILE PRODUCER and I, Robot belongs to type FILM.) Each relationship belongs to a *relationship type*. (E.g., the edge from Will Smith to Men in Black has type *Actor*.) The type of a relationship determines the types of its two end entities. For instance, an edge of type *Actor* is always from an entity belonging to FILE ACTOR to an entity belonging to FILM. We will mention edges by the surface names of their relationship types.

$G_d(V_d, E_d)$	an entity graph
$v \in V_d$	an entity
$e(v, v') \in E_d$	a directed relationship from entity v to entity v'
$G_s(V_s, E_s)$	a schema graph
$\tau \in V_s$	an entity type
$\gamma(\tau, \tau') \in E_s$	a relationship type from entity type τ to entity type τ'
T	a preview table
$T.key$	the key attribute of T
$T.nonkey$	the non-key attributes of T
$T.\tau$	the set of entities of type τ—the key attribute of T
$t \in T$	a tuple t in preview table T
$t.\tau$	t's value on τ which is the key attribute of T
$t.\gamma$	t's value on non-key attribute γ
$\mathcal{P} = \{\mathcal{P}[1], ..., \mathcal{P}[k]\}$	a preview, which consists of k preview tables
$\mathcal{P}_{opt}$	an optimal preview
$S(\mathcal{P})$	the score of preview $\mathcal{P}$
$S(T)$	the score of preview table T
$S_{cov}(\tau), S_{walk}(\tau)$	score of key attribute τ based on coverage/random-walk
$S^{\tau}_{cov}(\gamma), S^{\tau}_{ent}(\gamma)$	score of non-key attribute γ based on coverage/entropy
$\mathbb{T}$	the space of all possible preview tables
$\mathbb{P}$	the space of all possible previews
$dist(\tau, \tau')$	distance between τ and τ' in schema graph G_s

Table 1: Notations.

Two different relationship types may have the same surface name for intuitively expressing their meanings, although underlyingly they have different identifiers. For instance, the *Award Winners* edge from Will Smith to Saturn Award and the *Award Winners* edge from Barry Sonnenfeld to Razzie Award belong to two different relationship types. The former is for relationships from FILM ACTOR to AWARD, while the latter is for relationships from FILM DIRECTOR to AWARD.

Given an entity graph $G_d(V_d, E_d)$, its *schema graph* is a directed graph $G_s(V_s, E_s)$, where each vertex $\tau \in V_s$ represents an entity type and each directed edge $\gamma(\tau, \tau') \in E_s$ represents a relationship type from entity type τ to τ'. An edge $\gamma(\tau, \tau') \in E_s$ if and only if there exists an edge $e(v, v') \in E_d$ where e has type γ, v has type τ and v' has type τ'. Fig. 3 shows the schema graph corresponding to the entity graph in Fig. 1. A schema graph is a multigraph as there can be multiple relationship types between two entity types. (E.g., two relationship types—*Producer* and *Executive Producer*—are from entity type FILM PRODUCER to FILM.) It is clear from the above definitions that, given a data graph, the corresponding schema graph is uniquely determined.

Definition 1 (Preview Table and Preview). Given an entity graph $G_d(V_d, E_d)$ and its schema graph $G_s(V_s, E_s)$, a *preview table* T has a mandatory *key attribute* (denoted $T.key$) and at least one *non-key attributes* (denoted $T.nonkey$). T corresponds to a star-shape subgraph of the schema graph $G_s(V_s, E_s)$. The key attribute corresponds to an entity type $\tau \in V_s$, and each non-key attribute corresponds to a relationship type $\gamma(\tau, \tau') \in E_s$ or $\gamma(\tau', \tau) \in E_s$. Note that the edges from and to an entity are both important. Hence, a non-key attribute corresponds to either $\gamma(\tau, \tau')$ or $\gamma(\tau', \tau)$.

The preview table T consists of a set of tuples. The number of tuples equals the number of entities of type τ (the key attribute of T), i.e., $|T| = |T.\tau|$ and $T.\tau = \{v | v \in V_d \wedge v \text{ has type } \tau\}$. Given an arbitrary tuple $t \in T$, we denote t's key attribute value by $t.\tau$. Each tuple t attains a distinct value of $t.\tau$. Its value on a non-key attribute $\gamma(\tau, \tau')$, denoted $t.\gamma(\tau, \tau')$ or simply $t.\gamma$, is a set—the set of entities in entity graph G_d incident from $t.\tau$ through an edge of type $\gamma(\tau, \tau')$. More formally, $t.\gamma(\tau, \tau') = \{u | u \in V_d \wedge e(t.\tau, u) \in E_d \wedge u \text{ belongs to type } \tau'\}$. Symmetrically, its value on a non-key attribute $\gamma(\tau', \tau)$ is the set of entities in G_d incident to $t.\tau$ through an edge of type $\gamma(\tau', \tau)$, i.e., $t.\gamma(\tau', \tau) = \{u | u \in V_d \wedge e(u, t.\tau) \in E_d \wedge u \text{ belongs to type } \tau'\}$.

A *preview* $\mathcal{P}$ is a set of preview tables, i.e., $\mathcal{P} = \{\mathcal{P}[1], ..., \mathcal{P}[k]\}$, where $\forall i \neq j, \mathcal{P}[i].key \neq \mathcal{P}[j].key$, $k \leqslant |V_s|$ is the total number of preview tables. Note that $|V_s|$ is the number of vertices in G_s, i.e., the number of entity types in G_d. □

According to Definition 1, the upper and lower tables in Fig. 2 correspond to the star-shape subgraphs #1 and #2 in Fig. 3, respectively. The key attribute in the upper table is FILM and the non-key attributes are *Director* and *Genres*. The key attribute in the lower table is FILM ACTOR and its non-key attribute is *Award Winners*. It is worth noting that, although each tuple's value on the key attribute is non-empty, unique and single-valued, its value on a non-key attribute can be empty (e.g., t_3.*Genres* in Fig. 2), duplicate (e.g., t_1.*Director* and t_2.*Director* in Fig. 2) and multi-valued (e.g., t_1.*Genres* and t_2.*Genres* in Fig. 2). It also follows that a preview table is not a relational table.

By Definition 1, every vertex τ in a schema graph can serve as the key attribute of a candidate preview table, which also includes at least one non-key attribute—an edge incident on τ. We use $\mathbb{T}$ to denote the space of all possible preview tables. A preview is a set of preview tables. We use $\mathbb{P}$ to denote the space of all possible previews. Note that $\mathbb{P} \subset 2^{\mathbb{T}}$, i.e., not every member of the power set $2^{\mathbb{T}}$ is a valid preview, because by Definition 1 preview tables in a preview cannot have the same key attribute.

Problem Statement: Given an entity graph $G_d(V_d, E_d)$ and its corresponding schema graph $G_s(V_s, E_s)$, the *preview discovery problem* is to find $\mathcal{P}_{opt}$—the optimal preview among all possible previews. We shall develop the notions of goodness and optimality for a preview and define goodness measures in Sec. 3.

Note that the preview discovery problem focuses on selecting key and non-key attributes for preview tables. It does not select tuples. As our goal is to help users attain a good initial understanding of the schema of an entity graph, we argue that it is only necessary to show a small number of tuples instead of all. Our current approach is to randomly select a few. How to choose the most representative tuples is left for future work.

3. SCORING MEASURES FOR PREVIEWS

In this section, we discuss the scoring functions for measuring the goodness of previews for entity graphs. The measures are based on the intuition that a good preview should 1) relate to as many entities and relationships as possible and 2) help users understand an entity graph and its schema graph. The first intuition is obvious, as a preview relating to only a small number of entities or relationships will inevitably lose lots of information and thus lead to poor comprehensibility of the original graph. The second intuition models the goodness of previews according to users' behavior in browsing entity and schema graphs.

3.1 Preview Scoring

The score of a preview $\mathcal{P} = \{\mathcal{P}[1], ..., \mathcal{P}[k]\}$ is simply aggregated from individual preview tables' scores, by summation:

$$S(\mathcal{P}) = \sum_{i=1}^{k} S(\mathcal{P}[i]), \quad (1)$$

where $S(\mathcal{P}[i])$ is the score of a preview table $\mathcal{P}[i]$, defined as:

$$S(\mathcal{P}[i]) = S(\tau) \times \sum_{\gamma \in \mathcal{P}[i].nonkey} S^{\tau}(\gamma), \quad (2)$$

where $S(\tau)$ is the score of the key attribute of $\mathcal{P}[i]$ (i.e., $\mathcal{P}[i].key$=τ) and $S^{\tau}(\gamma)$ is the score of a non-key attribute γ in $\mathcal{P}[i]$. $S(\tau)$ and $S^{\tau}(\gamma)$ are defined and elaborated in Sec. 3.2 and Sec. 3.3.

In the above definition, the score of a preview table equals the product of its key attribute's score and the summation of its non-key attributes' scores. The definition gives the key attribute τ much higher importance than any individual non-key attribute, because the preview table centers around the entities of type τ and describes their non-key attributes, i.e., their relationships with other entities.

It is possible to propose many viable scoring functions for previews, key attributes and non-key attributes. Furthermore, techniques such as learning-to-rank [12] may be applied in ranking previews by features related to key and non-key attributes, although the feasibility of collecting many labelled data is less clear in this case. We leave it to future work to explore this direction. Nevertheless, we note that the results on the optimization problems in Section 4 and the algorithms in Section 5 will stand, as long as the scoring function replacing Eq. 1 and Eq. 2 is monotonic with regard to $S(\tau)$ and $S^{\tau}(\gamma)$, and the measures defining $S(\tau)$ and $S^{\tau}(\gamma)$ do not affect the results.

3.2 Key Attribute Scoring

Coverage-based scoring measure: Given an entity graph $G_d(V_d, E_d)$ and its corresponding schema graph $G_s(V_s, E_s)$, the key attribute τ of a candidate preview table T corresponds to an entity type, i.e., $\tau \in V_s$. If the entity graph consists of many entities of type τ, including T in the preview makes the preview relevant to all those entities. The coverage-based scoring measure thus defines the score of τ as the number of entities bearing that type:

$$S_{cov}(\tau) = |\{v|v \in V_d \wedge v \text{ has type } \tau\}|$$

For example, given the entity graph in Fig. 1 and the corresponding schema graph in Fig. 3, the coverage-based score of the key attribute FILM is $S_{cov}(\text{FILM}) = 4$.

Random-walk based scoring measure: We consider a *random-walk process* over a graph G converted from the schema graph $G_s(V_s, E_s)$, inspired by the PageRank algorithm [5] for Web page ranking and many related ideas. Similar to G_s, vertices in G are entity types and edges are relationship types. Different from G_s, the edges are undirected. As explained in Def. 1, the edges from and to an entity are both important to the entity. The edge between τ_i and τ_j in G is weighted by the number of relationships (i.e., the number of edges) in the entity graph between entities of types τ_i and τ_j. We denote the weight by w_{ij}, defined as follows.

$$w_{ij} = w_{ji} = \sum_{\gamma(\tau_i,\tau_j)\in E_s} |\{e|e \in E_d \wedge e \text{ has type } \gamma(\tau_i, \tau_j)\}| + \sum_{\gamma(\tau_j,\tau_i)\in E_s} |\{e|e \in E_d \wedge e \text{ has type } \gamma(\tau_j, \tau_i)\}|$$

In the $|V_s| \times |V_s|$ *transition matrix* M, an element M_{ij} corresponds to the *transition probability* from τ_i to τ_j in G. M_{ij} equals the ratio of w_{ij} to the total weight of all edges incident on τ_i in G:

$$M_{ij} = w_{ij} / \sum_k w_{ik}$$

For example, based on Fig. 3, the transition probability from FILM to FILM GENRE is $M_{\text{FILM,FILM GENRE}} = w_{\text{FILM,FILM GENRE}}/(w_{\text{FILM,FILM GENRE}} + w_{\text{FILM,FILM ACTOR}} + w_{\text{FILM,FILM DIRECTOR}} + w_{\text{FILM,FILM PRODUCER}}) = 5/(5+6+4+3) = 0.28$. The transition probability from FILM to FILM PRODUCER is $M_{\text{FILM,FILM PRODUCER}} = w_{\text{FILM,FILM PRODUCER}}/(w_{\text{FILM,FILM GENRE}} + w_{\text{FILM,FILM ACTOR}} + w_{\text{FILM,FILM DIRECTOR}} + w_{\text{FILM,FILM PRODUCER}}) = 3/(5+6+4+3) = 0.17$.

Suppose a random walker traverses in G, either by going from an entity type τ_i to another entity type τ_j through the edge between them with probability M_{ij} or by jumping to a random entity type. Entity types that are more likely to be visited by the user are of higher importance. The random walk process will converge to a stationary distribution which represents the chances of entity types being visited. The stationary distribution π of the random walk process is given as follows. Note that a similar idea was applied in [19] for ranking relational tables by importance.

$$\pi = \pi M$$

The random-walk based score of a candidate key attribute τ_i is: $S_{walk}(\tau_i) = \pi_i$, where π_i is the stationary probability of τ_i.

3.3 Non-Key Attribute Scoring

Coverage-based scoring measure: The coverage-based scoring measure for non-key attribute is similar to that for key attribute. Given an entity graph $G_d(V_d, E_d)$ and its schema graph $G_s(V_s, E_s)$, consider a candidate preview table T with key attribute τ. A non-key attribute γ of T corresponds to a relationship type, i.e., $\gamma \in E_s$. If the entity graph contains many edges (i.e., relationships) belonging to type γ, incorporating such a relationship type into table T makes it relevant to all those relationships and their corresponding entities. The coverage-based scoring measure thus defines the score of γ as the number of relationships bearing that type:

$$S^{\tau}_{cov}(\gamma) = |\{e|e \in E_d \wedge e \text{ has type } \gamma\}|$$

For example, given the entity graph in Fig. 1 and the schema graph in Fig. 3, the coverage-based scores of non-key attributes *Director* and *Genres* are $S^{\text{FILM}}_{cov}(\textit{Director}) = 4$ and $S^{\text{FILM}}_{cov}(\textit{Genres}) = 5$.

The coverage-based scoring measure for non-key attribute is symmetric, i.e., given $\gamma(\tau, \tau')$ (or $\gamma(\tau', \tau)$) $\in T.nonkey$, $S^{\tau}_{cov}(\gamma) \equiv S^{\tau'}_{cov}(\gamma)$. Both τ and τ' can be the key attribute of a different preview table, in which γ is a non-key attribute. The scores of γ in the two tables are equal.

Entropy-based scoring measure: For a preview table T with key attribute τ, we measure the goodness of a non-key attribute $\gamma(\tau, \tau')$ (or $\gamma(\tau', \tau)$) by how much information it provides to T, for which the *entropy* of γ ($H(\gamma)$) is a natural choice of measure:

$$S^{\tau}_{ent}(\gamma) = H(\gamma) = \sum_{j=1} \frac{n_j}{|t.\gamma|} \log(\frac{|t.\gamma|}{n_j}),$$

where n_j is the number of tuples in T that attain the same jth attribute value u on non-key attribute $\gamma(\tau, \tau')$ (or $\gamma(\tau', \tau)$), i.e., $u \in V_d \wedge u$ has type τ' and $n_j = |\{v|v \in T.\tau \wedge e(v, u) \in E_d$ (or $e(u, v) \in E_d) \wedge e$ has type $\gamma\}|$. $|t.\gamma|$ is the number of tuples in T with non-empty values on $\gamma(\tau, \tau')$ (or $\gamma(\tau', \tau)$). Continue the running example. The entropy-based scores of non-key attributes *Director* and *Genres* are $S^{\text{FILM}}_{ent}(\textit{Director}) = (2/4)\log(4/2) + (1/4)\log(4/1) + (1/4)\log(4/1) = 0.45$, and $S^{\text{FILM}}_{ent}(\textit{Genres}) = (2/3)\log(3/2) + (1/3)\log(3/1) = 0.28$. Note that for two values on a multi-valued attribute (e.g., {Action Film, Science Fiction} and {Action Film} for FILM.*Genres* in Fig. 2), we consider them equivalent if and only if they have the same set of component values. By definition, the entropy-based scoring measure for non-key attribute is asymmetric, i.e., given $\gamma(\tau, \tau')$ (or $\gamma(\tau', \tau)$) $\in T.nonkey$, $S^{\tau}_{ent}(\gamma) \not\equiv S^{\tau'}_{ent}(\gamma)$.

4. OPTIMAL PREVIEWS UNDER SIZE AND DISTANCE CONSTRAINTS

In this section, based on the scoring measures defined in Sec. 3, we formulate several optimization problems that look for the optimal previews with best scores under various constraints on preview size and distance between preview tables. We prove that some of these optimization problems are **NP**-hard.

By Eq. 1 (or any other monotonic aggregate function), the score of a preview monotonically increases by its member preview tables—the more preview tables in a preview, the higher its score. Similarly by Eq. 2, the score of a preview table monotonically increases by its non-key attributes. The properties are formally stated in the following two propositions. Recall that $\mathbb{P}$ and $\mathbb{T}$ denote the space of all possible previews and all possible preview tables.

Proposition 1. Given previews $\mathcal{P}_1, \mathcal{P}_2 \in \mathbb{P}$, if $\mathcal{P}_1 \supseteq \mathcal{P}_2$, then $S(\mathcal{P}_1) \geq S(\mathcal{P}_2)$.

Proposition 2. Given preview tables $T_1, T_2 \in \mathbb{T}$, if $T_1.key = T_2.key$ and $T_1.nonkey \supseteq T_2.nonkey$, then $S(T_1) \geq S(T_2)$.

By the above propositions, a preview's score is maximized when it includes as many tables and attributes as possible. However, a preview must fit into a limited display space, due to constraints posed by mobile devices and desktop monitors. Therefore the size and the goodness score of a preview present a tradeoff. Considering the tradeoff, we enforce a constraint on preview size, given by a pair of integers (k, n), where k is the number of allowed preview tables and n is the number of allowed non-key attributes in the tables. Their values may be either manually chosen by interactive users or automatically suggested based on the size of a display space. The previews satisfying the size constraint are called *concise previews.*

An alternative size constraint is a maximally allowed number of attributes per preview table. However, we do not consider such a constraint in this paper. We argue that forcing each preview table to have the same width can cause two problems—on the one hand, the allocated space for some preview tables may be wasted because they do not have as many important non-key attributes; on the other hand, the fixed space is insufficient for other preview tables with more important non-key attributes.

Further, for obtaining either a coherent or a diverse preview, we enforce an additional constraint on the pairwise distance between preview tables. The distance between two preview tables T_1 and T_2 (denoted $dist(T_1, T_2)$) is the length of the shortest undirected path[1] between their key attributes $T_1.key$ and $T_2.key$ in schema graph G_s. (Recall that the key attributes are vertices (i.e., entity types) in G_s.) For example, the distance between the two tables in Fig. 2 is 1, which is the shortest path length between FILM and FILM ACTOR in the schema graph in Fig. 3. Similarly, for the two tables whose key attributes are FILM and AWARD, their distance would be 2.

Based on the above notion of distance, the constraint on table distance is given by an integer d, which is the maximum (resp. minimum) distance between preview tables. The previews satisfying the distance constraint are called *tight (resp. diverse) previews.* Intuitively speaking, the preview tables in a tight preview are highly related to each other due to their short pairwise distance, while the preview tables in a diverse preview are not tightly related to each other and cover different types of concepts. Arguably, both types of previews are useful for understanding an entity graph. We shall compare them empirically in Sec. 6.

Below we formally define the three types of previews and the corresponding optimization problems. Note that we assume the constraints k, n, d are given. While it is intuitive for a user to specify desired values for these constraints, it is helpful if a system can automatically suggest values. We leave it to future work.

Definition 2 (Concise, Tight and Diverse Previews). Given the size constraint (k, n), a *concise preview* has k preview tables (i.e., key attributes) and no more than n non-key attributes in the tables.[2] The space of all concise previews is

$$\mathbb{P}_{k,n} = \{\mathcal{P} \mid \mathcal{P} \in \mathbb{P}, |\mathcal{P}| = k, \sum_{i=1}^{k} |\mathcal{P}[i].nonkey| \leq n\}.$$

Given the size constraint (k, n) and the distance constraint d, a *tight preview* (*diverse preview*) is a concise preview in which the distance between any pair of preview tables is smaller (greater) than or equal to d. The space of all tight previews is

$$\mathbb{P}_{k,n,\leq d} = \{\mathcal{P} \mid \mathcal{P} \in \mathbb{P}_{k,n}, \forall T_1, T_2 \in \mathcal{P}, dist(T_1, T_2) \leq d\}.$$

The space of all diverse previews is

$$\mathbb{P}_{k,n,\geq d} = \{\mathcal{P} \mid \mathcal{P} \in \mathbb{P}_{k,n}, \forall T_1, T_2 \in \mathcal{P}, dist(T_1, T_2) \geq d\}. \quad \square$$

[1] An undirected path in a directed graph is a path in which the edges are not all oriented in the same direction. [2] A preview with less than n non-key attributes may outscore another preview with exactly n non-key attributes. Further, a set of k entity types may have only less than n edges in the schema graph. Hence, the condition $|\mathcal{P}[i].nonkey| \leq n$ instead of $|\mathcal{P}[i].nonkey| = n$. On the other hand, it is safe to assume that an entity graph with practical significance always has more than k entity types under any reasonably small k. Therefore an optimal preview always should have exactly k preview tables, given the monotonic scoring function (cf. Eq. 1).

Given the spaces of concise, tight and diverse previews, we formulate three optimization problems—finding an *optimal preview* with the highest score in the corresponding space of previews.

Definition 3 (Optimal Preview Discovery Problem). The optimization problem of finding an *optimal preview* is defined as follows, where $\mathbb{P}$ can be any of the aforementioned three spaces—$\mathbb{P}_{k,n}$, $\mathbb{P}_{k,n,\leq d}$ and $\mathbb{P}_{k,n,\geq d}$.

$$\mathcal{P}_{opt} \in \arg\max_{\mathcal{P} \in \mathbb{P}} S(\mathcal{P}) \quad (3)$$

Note that the arg max function may return a set of optimal previews due to ties in scores. □

For example, given the entity graph in Fig. 1, using coverage-based scoring measures for both key and non-key attributes, an optimal concise preview consisting of 2 tables and 6 non-key attributes (i.e., k=2, n=6) is $\mathcal{P} = \{T_1$: FILM, *Actor*, *Genres*, *Director*, *Producer*; T_2 : FILM ACTOR, *Actor*, *Award Winners*$\}$. The edge *Actor* is a non-key attribute in both T_1 and T_2, in different directions. An optimal diverse preview under the same size constraint (k=2, n=6) and distance constraint d=2 is $\mathcal{P} = \{T_1$: FILM, *Actor*, *Genres*, *Director*, *Producer*, *Executive Producer*; T_2 : AWARD, *Award Winners*$\}$.

4.1 NP-hardness of the Optimal Tight and Diverse Preview Discovery Problems

The optimal preview discovery problem is non-trivial. Particularly, the problem in the spaces of both tight previews ($\mathbb{P}_{k,n,\leq d}$) and diverse previews ($\mathbb{P}_{k,n,\geq d}$) is **NP**-hard.

Theorem 1. Optimal tight preview discovery is **NP**-hard.

Proof. The decision version of the optimal tight preview discovery problem is $TightPreview(G_s, k, n, d, s)$—Given a schema graph G_s, decide whether there exists such a preview $\mathcal{P}$ that (1) $\mathcal{P}$ has k tables and no more than n non-key attributes; (2) the distance between every pair of preview tables is not greater than d; and (3) the preview's score is at least s, i.e., $S(\mathcal{P}) \geq s$.

We construct a reduction, in polynomial-time, from the **NP**-hard Clique problem to $TightPreview(G_s, k, n, d, s)$. Recall that the decision version of $Clique(G, k)$ is to, given a graph $G(V, E)$, decide whether there exists a clique in G with k vertices. The reduction is by constructing a schema graph G_s from G. For simplicity of exposition, in both this proof and the proof of Theorem 2, we assume the schema graph G_s is undirected and every edge γ in G_s corresponds to the same relationship type. This assumption is made without loss of generality. Note that our following proof casts no requirement on the score of a preview (i.e., $s = 0$) and thus no requirement on the scores of key and non-key attributes in G_s. Hence, edge orientation and its corresponding relationship type bears no significance in the proof.

Formally, we construct a schema graph $G_s(V_s, E_s)$ from G through a vertex bijection $f : V \to V_s$:

- $\forall e(v, v') \in E$, there exists an edge (i.e., relationship type) $\gamma(\tau, \tau') \in E_s$, where $\tau = f(v)$ and $\tau' = f(v')$.
- $\forall \gamma(\tau, \tau') \in E_s$, there exists an edge $e(v, v') \in E$, where $v = f^{-1}(\tau)$ and $v' = f^{-1}(\tau')$.

$Clique(G, k)$ is thus reduced to $TightPreview(G_s, k, k, 1, 0)$ by the above bijections. □

The **NP**-hardness of the optimal diverse preview discovery problem is also based on a reduction from the Clique problem, although the proof is more complex.

Theorem 2. Optimal diverse preview discovery is **NP**-hard.

Proof. The decision version of the optimal diverse preview discovery problem is $DiversePreview(G_s, k, n, d, s)$—Given a schema graph G_s, decide whether there exists such a preview $\mathcal{P}$ that (1) $\mathcal{P}$

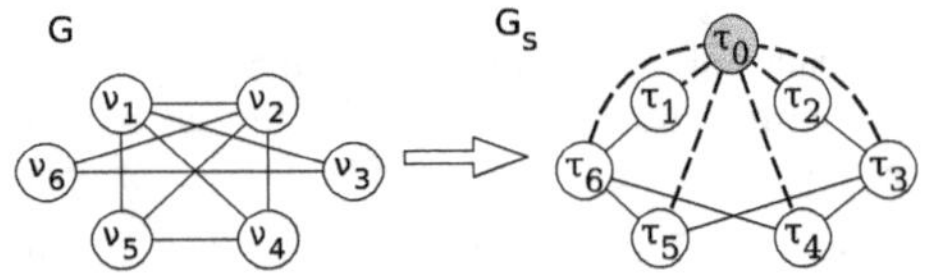

Figure 4: Construction of G_s from G, for reduction from the clique problem to the optimal diverse preview discovery problem.

has k tables and no more than n non-key attributes; (2) the distance between every pair of preview tables is not smaller than d; and (3) the preview's score is at least s, i.e., $S(\mathcal{P}) \geq s$.

We construct a reduction, in polynomial-time, from the **NP**-hard $Clique(G, k)$ to $DiversePreview(G_s, k, n, d, s)$. The reduction is also by constructing a schema graph $G_s(V_s, E_s)$ from G. It is similar to the reduction for $TightPreview(G_s, k, n, d, s)$ in Theorem 1, but also bears two important differences. (1) G_s contains a special vertex, denoted τ_0, that is directly connected to every other vertex in G_s. (2) Barring τ_0 and all its incident edges, G_s is the complement graph of G—There is still a vertex bijection $f : V \rightarrow V_s$, but an edge exists between two vertices in G_s if and only if there is no edge between the corresponding vertices in G. Formally, the construction of G_s from G is as follows:

- $\forall \tau, \tau' \in V_s \backslash \{\tau_0\}$, $\gamma(\tau, \tau') \in E_s$ if and only if $\nexists e(v, v') \in E$, where $v = f^{-1}(\tau)$ and $v' = f^{-1}(\tau')$.
- $\forall \tau \in V_s \backslash \{\tau_0\}$, $\gamma(\tau_0, \tau) \in E_s$.

$Clique(G, k)$ is thus reduced to $DiversePreview(G_s, k, k, 2, 0)$ by the above construction of G_s. □

Fig. 4 can help understand the reduction from $Clique(G, k)$ to $DiversePreview$ $(G_s, k, k, 2, 0)$ in the above proof. The figure shows an example with G (left) and the constructed schema graph G_s (right), where the gray vertex in G_s is τ_0. Consider an arbitrary pair of vertices (v, v') in G and their corresponding vertices (τ, τ') in G_s. On the one hand, if v and v' are not directly connected in G (e.g., v_1 and v_6), an edge between τ and τ' (i.e., τ_1 and τ_6) is included into G_s. When finding a diverse preview where pairwise table distance must be at least 2, τ and τ' will never be chosen together as the key attributes of two tables in the preview. Correspondingly, this means a clique must not include both v and v'. On the other hand, if v and v' are directly connected in G (e.g., v_1 and v_2), there must not be a direct edge between τ and τ' (i.e., τ_1 and τ_2) in G_s. The distance between τ and τ' is exactly 2, since they are only indirectly connected through τ_0. They will thus be considered in choosing the key attributes of two tables in a diverse preview where pairwise table distance must be at least 2. Correspondingly, the directly connected v and v' are considered together in forming a clique.

5. ALGORITHMS

In this section we discuss algorithms for solving the optimal preview discovery problem. As given in Eq. 3, the problem is to find a preview with the highest score among candidate previews, where the space of candidates can be concise previews ($\mathbb{P}_{k,n}$), tight previews ($\mathbb{P}_{k,n,\leq d}$) or diverse previews ($\mathbb{P}_{k,n,\geq d}$). Recall that we use $S(\tau)$ to denote the score of a candidate key attribute τ for a preview table T and $S^{\tau}(\gamma)$ to denote the score of a candidate non-key attribute $\gamma(\tau, \tau')$ (or $\gamma(\tau', \tau)$) for T whose key attribute is τ.

Our effort focuses on reducing the cost in finding optimal previews. Both the schema graph and the scoring measures defined in Sec. 3 are computed before optimal preview discovery. This is a realistic assumption, since the schema graph and scoring measures do not change by the size and distance constraints k, n, d. Furthermore, they can be incrementally updated when the underlying entity graph is updated (detailed discussion omitted). On the other hand, the optimal previews cannot be incrementally updated.

Algorithm 1: Brute-force algorithm for optimal preview discovery

Input : schema graph G_s, size constraint (k, n)
Output: an optimal preview $\mathcal{P}_{opt}$

1 **foreach** $\tau \in V_s$ **do**
2     $\langle \gamma_1^{\tau}, \gamma_2^{\tau}, \ldots \rangle \leftarrow$ sort the candidate non-key attributes $\gamma_j^{\tau} \in \Gamma^{\tau}$ by their scores $S^{\tau}(\gamma_j^{\tau})$;
3 $max\_score \leftarrow 0$; $\mathcal{P}_{opt} \leftarrow \varnothing$;
4 **foreach** *k-subset of V_s (denoted V)* **do**
5     $score \leftarrow 0$; $\mathcal{P} \leftarrow \varnothing$; $i \leftarrow 1$;
6   **foreach** $\tau \in V$ **do**
7         $\mathcal{P}[i].key = \tau$;
8         $\mathcal{P}[i].nonkey = \{\gamma_1^{\tau}\}$;
9         $score = score + S(\tau) \times S^{\tau}(\gamma_1^{\tau})$;
10         $i \leftarrow i + 1$;
11     $\Gamma \leftarrow$ top-$(n-k)$ candidate non-key attributes from all $\tau \in V$ in descending order of $S(\tau) \times S^{\tau}(\gamma_j^{\tau})$;
12   **foreach** $\gamma_j^{\tau} \in \Gamma$, *where* $\tau = \mathcal{P}[x].key$ **do**
13         $score \leftarrow score + S(\tau) \times S^{\tau}(\gamma_j^{\tau})$;
14         $\mathcal{P}[x].nonkey \leftarrow \mathcal{P}[x].nonkey \bigcup \{\gamma_j^{\tau}\}$;
15   **if** $score > max\_score$ **then**
16         $max\_score \leftarrow score$;
17         $\mathcal{P}_{opt} \leftarrow \mathcal{P}$;
18 **return** $\mathcal{P}_{opt}$;

Before we present the algorithms, consider the space of all possible previews. Every entity type τ can be the key attribute of a preview table T. Let Γ^{τ} denote the set of all edges (i.e., relationship types) incident on τ in schema graph G_s. Any $\gamma \in \Gamma^{\tau}$ can be a candidate for the non-key attributes of T. By the scoring function in Eq. 2 and the problem formulation in Eq. 3, the non-key attributes of T must have the highest scores among the candidates in Γ^{τ}. This property, stated in Theorem 3, is important to our algorithms.

Theorem 3. Suppose an optimal (concise, tight or diverse) preview $\mathcal{P}_{opt}$ contains a preview table $T \in \mathbb{T}$ with key attribute τ. If T has m non-key attributes, they must be the top-m non-key attributes by scores, i.e., $\forall \gamma, \gamma' \in \Gamma^{\tau}$, if $\gamma \in T.nonkey$ and $\gamma' \notin T.nonkey$, then $S^{\tau}(\gamma) \geq S^{\tau}(\gamma')$.

5.1 A Brute-Force Algorithm

Alg. 1 is a brute-force algorithm for the optimal preview discovery problem. It enumerates all possible k-subsets of entity types, as the k entity types in each subset form the key attributes of k preview tables in a preview $\mathcal{P}$ (Line 4). For a candidate key attribute τ, the elements in the set of its candidate non-key attributes Γ^{τ} are ordered by their scores. We denote these candidates in descending order of scores by γ_1^{τ}, γ_2^{τ}, and so on (Line 2). Suppose preview table T uses τ as its key attribute. Each table must contain at least one non-key attribute, according to Definition 1. Hence, γ_1^{τ} (i.e., the candidate non-key attribute with the highest score) must be included into $T.nonkey$ (Line 8), by Theorem 3. Further, among the remaining candidate non-key attributes for the k entity types, the top-$(n-k)$ candidates by scores must be included into $\mathcal{P}$ (Lines 11–14), by Theorem 3. Note that, since the sorted list of candidate non-key attributes for each τ is already created (Line 2), it is unnecessary to do a full sorting in order to determine the top-$(n-k)$ candidates Γ. Instead, a simple merge operation on the k sorted lists will get Γ.

The algorithm has an exponential complexity $O(KN \log N + \binom{K}{k}(k + n))$, where $K = |V_s|$ is the number of candidate key attributes, $N = 2|E_s|$ is the number of candidate non-key attributes for all candidate key attributes, $\binom{K}{k}$ is the number of k-subsets, and $KN \log N$ is for sorting individual lists of candidates (Line 2), in which each list contains at most N elements.

Algorithm 2: Dynamic-programming algorithm for optimal concise preview discovery

```
Input  : schema graph G_s, size constraint (k, n)
Output: an optimal concise preview P_opt
foreach x ← 1 to K do
    ⟨γ_1^{τx}, γ_2^{τx}, ...⟩ ← sort the candidate non-key attributes γ_j^{τx} ∈ Γ^{τx} by
    their scores S^{τx}(γ_j^{τx});
for x ← 1 to K do
    for i ← 1 to min(k, x) do
        for j ← i to n do
            P_opt(i, j, x) ← P_opt(i, j, x − 1);
            for m ← 1 to min(j − i + 1, |Γ^{τx}|) do
                T_x^m.key ← τ_x;
                T_x^m.nonkey ← top-m candidate non-key attributes in Γ^{τx};
                P ← P_opt(i − 1, j − m, x − 1) ∪ {T_x^m};
                if S(P) > S(P_opt(i, j, x)) then
                    P_opt(i, j, x) ← P;
P_opt ← P_opt(k, n, K);
return P_opt;
```

Alg. 1 is for finding one of the optimal previews. To find all optimal previews, it needs simple extension to deal with ties in scores, which we will not further discuss.

The same brute-force algorithm is applicable for optimal preview discovery in all three types of spaces—concise, tight and diverse previews. The pseudo code in Alg. 1 is for concise previews and does not enforce distance constraint, for simplicity of presentation. Enforcing distance constraint for tight/diverse previews is straightforward, by performing distance check on every pair of preview tables in each k-subset of entity types.

5.2 A Dynamic-Programming Algorithm for Concise Preview Discovery Problem

As the combinatorial number of k-subsets grows exponentially, the performance of the above brute-force algorithm becomes unacceptable for finding an optimal preview under modest size constraints. We thus developed a dynamic-programming algorithm to discover optimal concise previews more efficiently.

Consider an arbitrary order on all K entity types—$\tau_1, \ldots, \tau_K$. We use $\mathcal{P}_{opt}(k, n, x)$ to denote an optimal concise preview among the first x entity types $\tau_1, \ldots, \tau_x$. The optimal concise preview discovery problem is to find $\mathcal{P}_{opt}(k, n, K)$. $\mathcal{P}_{opt}(k, n, x)$ can be constructed from the solutions to smaller problems, in two ways: (1) It can be equal to $\mathcal{P}_{opt}(k, n, x-1)$, i.e., its k tables and n non-key attributes are from the first $x-1$ entity types and the x-th entity type τ_x does not contribute anything; (2) It can also be the union of $\mathcal{P}_{opt}(k-1, n-m, x-1)$ and a table T_x^m, where $\mathcal{P}_{opt}(k-1, n-m, x-1)$ is an optimal preview with $k-1$ tables and $n-m$ non-key attributes among the first $x-1$ entity types, and T_x^m is the table whose key attribute is τ_x and whose non-key attributes are the top-m elements in Γ^{τ_x}—the sorted list of candidate non-key attributes for τ_x. The number m is between 1 and $n-(k-1)$ (or less if there are less than $n-(k-1)$ elements in Γ^{τ_x}), since each of the $k-1$ tables in $\mathcal{P}_{opt}(k-1, n-m, x-1)$ must contribute at least one non-key attribute. The optimal substructure of the problem is as follows. (We omit boundary cases ($k = 1$ or $x = 1$ or $n = k$) for brevity.)

$$\mathcal{P}_{opt}(k,n,x) = \underset{\mathcal{P} \in \mathbb{P}(k,n,x)}{\arg\max}\ S(\mathcal{P})$$

$$\mathbb{P}(k,n,x) = \left\{ \begin{array}{l} \mathcal{P}_{opt}(k, n, x-1), \\ \mathcal{P}_{opt}(k-1, n-1, x-1) \bigcup \{T_x^1\}, \\ \mathcal{P}_{opt}(k-1, n-2, x-1) \bigcup \{T_x^2\}, \\ \ldots \\ \mathcal{P}_{opt}(k-1, k-1, x-1) \bigcup \{T_x^{n-(k-1)}\} \end{array} \right\},$$

Algorithm 3: Apriori-style Algorithm for optimal tight/diverse preview discovery

```
Input  : schema graph G_s, size constraint(k, n), distance constraint d
Output: an optimal tight/diverse preview P_opt
1  L_2 ← ∅;
2  foreach i ← 1 to K do
3      foreach j ← i + 1 to K do
4          if dist(τ_i, τ_j) ≤ d then        /* ≥ d for diverse preview */
5              L_2 ← L_2 ∪ {⟨i j⟩};
6  i ← 3;
7  while i ≤ k and L_{i−1} ≠ ∅ do
8      L_i ← ∅;
9      foreach A, B ∈ L_{i−1} s.t. (∀j < i − 1 : A[j] = B[j]) and
       (A[i − 1] < B[i − 1]) do
           /* ≥ d for diverse preview */
10         if dist(τ_{A[i−1]}, τ_{B[i−1]}) ≤ d then
11             L_i ← L_i ∪ {⟨A[1] ... A[i − 1] B[i − 1]⟩};
12     i ← i + 1;
13 if L_k = ∅ then
14     return ∅;
15 max_score ← 0;
16 foreach A ∈ L_k do
17     P ← ComputePreview(A);
18     if score(P) > max_score then
19         max_score ← score(P);
20         P_opt ← P;
21 return P_opt;
```

where $T_x^m.key = \tau_x$ and $T_x^m.nonkey$ = top-m candidate non-key attributes in Γ^{τ_x}. Note that the optimal substructure is inapplicable when previews must satisfy distance constraint in addition to size constraint (details omitted). Therefore the dynamic-programming algorithm is for concise previews but not tight/diverse previews.

The pseudo code of the dynamic-programming algorithm is shown in Alg. 2. Its complexity is $O(KN \log N + Kkn^2)$. Similar to Alg. 1, Alg. 2 is for finding one optimal preview. Finding all optimal previews requires simple extension to deal with ties in scores, which we will not further discuss.

Both Alg. 1 and 2 assume that, given any k entity types (key attributes), they always together have at least n non-key attributes. That may not be true in reality. In fact, for two previews with the same number of tables, the preview with less non-key attributes may have the higher score than the other preview. Note that, in Eq. 3, the optimal preview is not required to have exactly n non-key attributes. It is simple to extend Alg. 1 and 2 to fully comply with the definition. Given any entity type τ, if it has less than n candidate non-key attributes, we can simply pad the sorted list Γ^{τ} by pseudo non-key attributes with zero scores.

5.3 An Apriori-style Algorithm for Tight / Diverse Preview Discovery Problem

Since the dynamic-programming algorithm is inapplicable when previews must satisfy distance constraint, we propose an efficient algorithm for optimal tight/diverse preview discovery, shown in Alg. 3. It consists of two steps: (1) finding k-subsets of entity types (i.e., vertices in G_s) satisfying the distance constraint (Lines 1–14); (2) for each qualifying k-subset of entity types, forming a preview under the size constraint, computing its score and choosing a preview with the highest score (Lines 15– 20).

The first step is essentially finding k-cliques in a graph converted from the schema graph G_s, in which vertices are considered adjacent if they are within distance d (for tight previews) or apart by at least distance d (for diverse previews). The k-clique problem is well-studied and many efficient algorithms have been designed in the past. Our method is inspired by the well-known Apriori

Domain	# of vertices	# of edges
books	6M / 91	15M / 201
film	2M / 63	18M / 136
music	27M / 69	187M / 176
TV	2M / 59	17M / 177
people	3M / 45	17M / 78
basketball	19K / 6	557K / 21
architecture	133K / 23	432K / 48

Table 2: Sizes of entity/schema graphs.

Domain	Coverage	Entropy
books	0.8	0.786
film	0.2	0.25
music	0.528	0.589
TV	0.622	0.379
people	0.708	0.606

Table 3: MRR of non-key attribute scoring.

	key attribute			non-key attribute	
Domain	YPS09	Coverage	Random Walk	Coverage	Entropy
books	0.4	0.55	0.43	0.43	0.43
film	-0.01	0.48	0.25	0.35	0.35
music	0.37	0.33	0.46	0.42	0.41
TV	0.37	0.69	0.65	0.47	0.47
people	0.36	0.31	0.29	0.43	0.43

Table 4: PCC of key and non-key attribute scoring.

algorithm [1] for frequent itemset mining. In [11], an algorithm was proposed for finding k-cliques (where edges correspond to metabolite correlations) by similar ideas, although the connection to Apriori was not made. Their experimental results demonstrated superior efficiency in comparison with the more well-known Bron-Kerbosch algorithm [6]. Nevertheless, the two broad steps of our optimal tight/diverse preview discovery algorithm are independent from each other, and thus any more efficient or even approximate algorithm for finding k-cliques can be plugged into it to further improve its execution efficiency.

In more details, the first step of Alg. 3 iteratively generates a k-subset of entity types by merging two $(k-1)$-subsets. Entity types are arbitrarily ordered as $\tau_1, \ldots, \tau_K$. In the i-th iteration of the algorithm, if two $(i-1)$-subsets A and B only differ by their last entity types $\tau_{A[i-1]}$ and $\tau_{B[i-1]}$, and the distance between their last entity types satisfies the distance constraint, a candidate i-subset is generated by appending $\tau_{B[i-1]}$ to the end of A.

In the second step, for each candidate k-subset of entity types, a preview is computed ($ComputePreview(A)$ in Line 17 of Alg. 3). The details of function $ComputePreview$ are omitted. It follows Theorem 3 and is essentially the same as Lines 5– 14 in Alg. 1. The score of each preview is computed (the same as in Lines 5– 14 of Alg. 1) and a preview with the highest score is returned.

The worst-case complexity of Alg. 3 is the same as that of Alg. 1. However, as Sec. 6 shows, in practice it significantly outperforms the brute-force algorithm, since Line 10 could filter out many combinations that do not satisfy the distance constraint.

6. EVALUATION

We conducted experiments to evaluate the preview scoring measures' accuracy (Sec. 6.1), the preview discovery algorithms' efficiency (Sec. 6.2), and the overall quality of discovered previews (Sec. B). All experiments were run on a Dell T100 server running Ubuntu 8.10. The server has a Dual Core Xeon E3120 processor, 6MB cache, 4GB RAM, and two 250GB RAID1 SATA hard drivers. All algorithms are implemented in C++ and compiled with '-O2' optimization in GCC-4.3.2.

The entity graph used in our experiment is a dump of Freebase at September 28, 2012.[3] The dataset is imported into an MySQL database. In Freebase, the entire entity graph is partitioned into many domains. Our experiments were conducted on seven domains. The sizes of the entity and schema graphs in these domains are shown in Table 2. Our work currently is limited to named entities, thus all numeric attribute values from the data dump have been removed. Note that a schema graph may be disconnected. To ensure the convergence of random walk in such a graph, we added a small transition probability 10^{-5} to every pair of entity types.

6.1 Accuracy of Preview Scoring Measures

We conducted two experiments to evaluate the accuracy of the scoring measures for both key and non-key attributes presented in Sec. 3. One experiment compares the ranking orders of candidate key (non-key) attributes by the scoring measures with gold standard ranking orders. The other calculates the correlation between two pairwise ordering results on candidate key (non-key) attributes—one by the scoring measures and the other collected through crowdsourcing. In both experiments, we used both measures proposed in this paper and an adaptation of the approach in [19].

6.1.1 Adaptation of [19]

Yang et al. [19] proposed an algorithm to summarize relational databases, specifically the tables in TPC-E benchmark. [4] Their approach works in three steps. First they define an importance value for each table considering both information content of the tables and join relationships between the tables. Second, they measure the similarity/distance between tables. Finally, they use a weighted k-center clustering algorithm to place the tables into k clusters. The k cluster centers are the summary of the database. We implemented their algorithm. We compared the results on TPC-E tables with those reported in [19] and validated our own implementation.

We adapted [19] for the entity graphs in the aforementioned Freebase domains. Since [19] was designed to summarize relational databases only, we converted each entity graph into a relational database, as follows. For each entity type τ, we created a relational table, of which the first column takes entities belonging to τ as its values. Furthermore, a column is created for each relationship type incident on τ in the scheme graph. The values in such a column are the entities adjacent to the entities in the first column through the corresponding relationship type. For each entity belonging to τ, a number of tuples are inserted into the table, which are essentially a Cartesian product of distinct values on all these columns.

6.1.2 Comparison with Gold Standard

Key attributes:

We collected gold standard data for 5 largest entity domains in Freebase—"books", "film", "music", "TV" and "people". For each domain, Freebase offers an entrance page showing 6 major entity types in that domain. A user can choose to browse entities in any of the 6 types. [5] As such entrance pages were manually created by Freebase, our conjecture is that they are of high quality and reflect the most popular entity types. We thus treated the 6 entity types listed in the entrance page of a domain as the gold standard for top-6 key attributes in that domain. The schema of the tables in the gold standard can be found in Table 10 in the Appendix.

For both the coverage-based and the random-walk based scoring measures in Sec. 3.2, we ranked all candidate key attributes by their scores. We calculated the accuracy of a scoring measure by several widely-used measures, including Precision-at-K (P@K), Average Precision (AvgP) and Normalized Discounted Cumulative Gain (nDCG) [13]. An approach that ranks accurate results higher is expected to receive better values under these measures. For a scoring measure for key attributes, P@K is the percentage of its top-K results that belong to the aforementioned gold standard top-6 key attributes. For the adaptation of [19], we use the ranked

[3] https://developers.google.com/freebase/data

[4] http://www.tpc.org/tpce/ [5] The entrance pages were all under "Featured Data" on Freebase.com. For instance, http://www.freebase.com/view/film was the entrance page for domain "film". We collected these pages shortly after September 28, 2012, which is the timestamp of the Freebase entity graph dump used in our experiments. These pages have become unavailable lately.

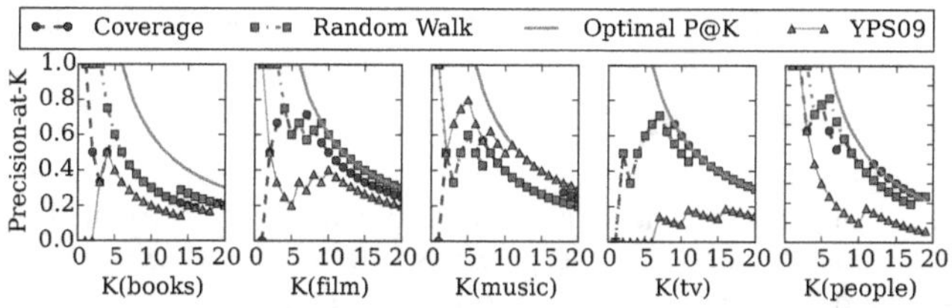

Figure 5: Precision-at-K of key attribute scoring.

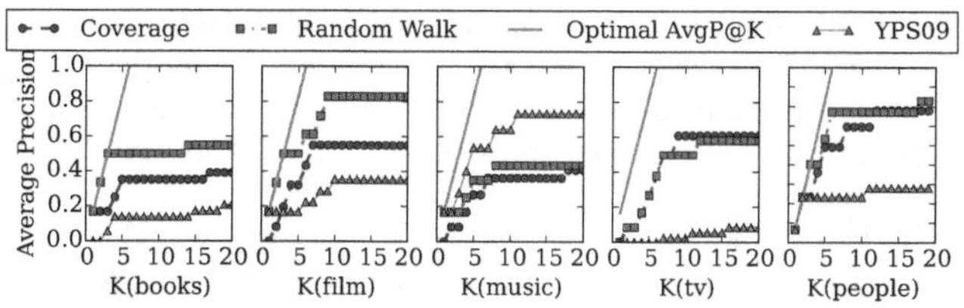

Figure 6: Average precision of key attribute scoring.

list by their table importance scoring. The results are in Fig. 5. The topmost curves ("Optimal P@K") represent the best possible P@K that can be archived by any method. For instance, P@10 can be at most 0.6, since there are only 6 gold standard key attributes in each domain, as mentioned above. Fig. 5 shows that both the coverage-based and the random-walk based scoring measures had P@10 close to 0.6 in 4 out of the 5 domains. They both had significantly higher P@K values than [19] (denoted "YSP09") in 4 out of the 5 domains and similar values in the remaining domain.

We also used AvgP and nDCG to gauge the accuracy of the scoring measures for key attributes. The results are as follows:

- Average Precision (AvgP): The average precision of the top-k results is given by AvgP= $\frac{\sum_{i=1}^{k} \text{P@}i \times rel_i}{\text{size of ground truth}}$, where rel_i equals 1 if the result at rank i is in the ground truth and 0 otherwise. Fig. 6 shows significantly higher AvgP for both the coverage-based and the random-walk based scoring measures, compared to [19], in 4 out of 5 domains.
- Normalized Discounted Cumulative Gain (nDCG): The cumulative gain of the top-k results is $\text{DCG}_k = rel_1 + \sum_{i=2}^{k} \frac{rel_i}{\log_2(i)}$. It penalizes the results if a ground truth result is ranked low. DCG_k is normalized by IDCG_k, the cumulative gain for an ideal ranking of the top-k results. Thus $\text{nDCG}_k = \frac{\text{DCG}_k}{\text{IDCG}_k}$. It is shown in Fig. 7 that both the coverage-based and the random-walk based scoring measures had clearly higher nDCG, in comparison with [19], in 4 out of the 5 domains.

Non-key attributes:

For each entity type, Freebase offers a table for users to browse and query the entities belonging to that type. [6] The table always has 3 common columns for recording names, types and article contents of entities. It also has 3 or less type-dependent non-key attributes manually selected by Freebase editors. Although Freebase allows users to add more attributes into this table, we believe the original 3 type-dependent attributes in general bear higher quality. We thus treated these attributes as the gold standard for top non-key attributes for that entity type.

For both the coverage-based and the entropy-based scoring measures in Sec. 3.3, we ranked all candidate non-key attributes by their scores. There is no comparison with [19] regarding non-key attributes, since it does not have an component that can be adapted for discovering non-key attributes. We calculated the accuracy of a scoring measure by Mean Reciprocal Rank (MRR) [13] instead of P@K as there are only 3 or less gold standard answers for top non-

[6] http://www.freebase.com/music/artist?instances=, for instance, would display a table for type ARTIST in "music" domain.

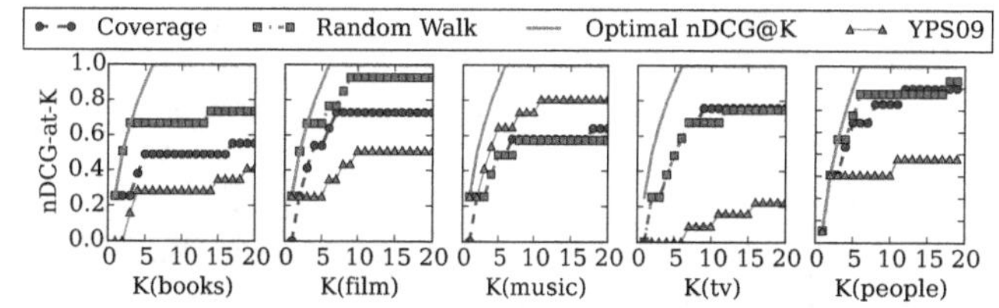

Figure 7: nDCG of key attribute scoring.

key attributes in each entity type. For a scoring measure for non-key attributes, the reciprocal rank is the multiplicative inverse of the rank of the first gold standard non-key attribute among its ranking results. MRR is the average reciprocal rank across all entity types with at least 5 candidate non-key attributes. (If an entity type has only less than 5 candidates, the gold standard answers are ranked deceptively high. Thus we exclude such entity types, to obtain more accurate evaluation.) The results are shown in Table 3. In every domain except "film" and for both the coverage-based and the entropy-based measures, MRR is above 0.5. This means in average a gold standard non-key attribute appeared in the top-2 ranked results. The lower MRR for "film" domain is from only one entity type and thus is not truly indicative, since only that entity type has at least 5 candidate non-key attributes.

6.1.3 *Correlation with Crowd Ranking*

We conducted an extensive study in Amazon Mechanical Turk (AMT)—a popular crowdsourcing service—and measured the correlation between our scoring measures and users' opinions with regard to key and non-key attributes ranking. We explain the procedure for evaluating key attribute ranking in one domain, since the procedure is repeated for all 5 gold standard domains and is the same for both key and non-key attribute ranking.

Given a domain, we randomly generated 50 pairs of entity types, i.e., candidate key attributes. Each pair was presented to 20 AMT workers. The workers were asked which of the 2 entity types in the pair is more important. To help them understand the tasks, we provided a few examples to explain what are considered more important in common sense. The workers were also asked to answer a few screening questions that test their common knowledge. They must answer the screening questions correctly, otherwise their responses are not considered.

We collected $1,000$ opinions (50 pairs $\times$ 20 workers per pair) in total. We then constructed two lists—X and Y, each of which contains 50 values corresponding to the 50 pairs. A value in X represents the difference in the ranking positions (by our scoring measures, or by the table importance measure in [19]) of the two entity types in the corresponding pair. A value in Y represents the difference in the numbers of AMT workers favoring the two entity types. The correlation between X and Y is measured by Pearson Correlation Coefficient (PCC) [7] as follows.

$$PCC = \frac{\text{E}(XY) - \text{E}(X)\text{E}(Y)}{\sqrt{\text{E}(X^2) - (\text{E}(X))^2}\sqrt{\text{E}(Y^2) - (\text{E}(Y))^2}} \quad (4)$$

The PCC value ranging from -1 to 1 indicates the degree of correlation between the pairwise ranking orders produced by our scoring methods and the pairwise preferences given by AMT workers. A PCC value in the ranges of [0.5,1.0], [0.3,0.5) and [0.1,0.3) indicates a strong, medium and small positive correlation, respectively. PCC values for the 5 gold standard domains are in Table 4. For all 5 domains, the results show at least a medium positive correlation between our scoring measures and AMT workers. For 4 out of the 5 domains, the coverage-based and/or the random walk-based measures had significantly higher PCC values than the adaptation of [19]("YPS09"), which even demonstrated slightly negative correlation in the "film" domain.

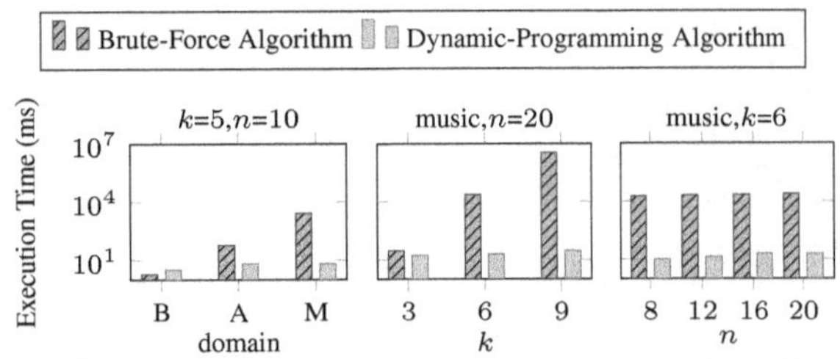

Figure 8: Execution time of optimal concise preview discovery algorithms.

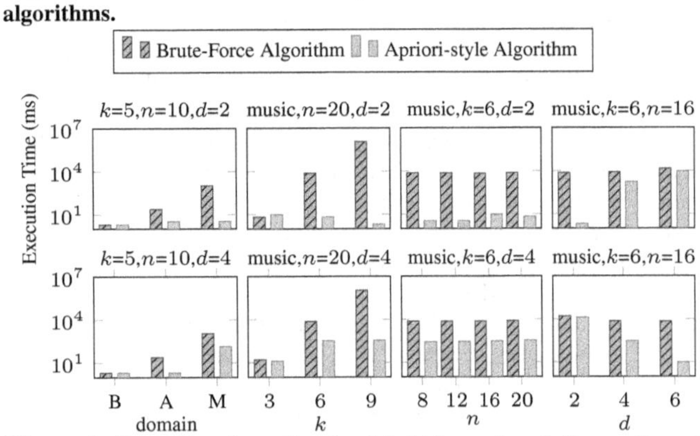

Figure 9: Execution time of optimal tight (upper) and diverse (lower) preview discovery algorithms.

6.2 Efficiency of Algorithms

This section presents results on the efficiency of the optimal preview discovery algorithms in Sec. 5. On optimal concise preview discovery, we compared the Brute-Force Alg. 1 and the Dynamic-Programming Alg. 2. Specifically, we compared their execution times by varying: (1) size of schema graph (i.e., number of candidate key attributes (K) and number of candidate non-key attributes (N)); (2) number of preview tables (i.e., key attributes) in a preview (k); and (3) maximum number of non-key attributes in a preview (n). For (1), we fixed k=5, n=10 and experimented with 3 domains—"basketball" (B), "architecture" (A), and "music" (M). They differ greatly in the sizes of their schema graphs (B: K=6, N=21; A: K=23, N=48; M: K=69, N=176). For (2), we varied k from 3 to 9, fixed n=20 and used "music" domain. For (3), we varied n from 8 to 20, fixed k=6 and used "music" domain.

On optimal tight/diverse preview discovery, we compared the Brute-Force Alg. 1 and the Apriori-style Alg. 3, by varying not only the aforementioned 3 parameters but also the distance constraint on d. When we varied other parameters, d is fixed at 2 and 4 for tight and diverse previews, respectively. When we fixed other parameters, d was varied from 2 to 6.

The results are in Figs. 8 and 9. In all results, the execution time is averaged across 3 runs, and execution time less than 1 millisecond is rounded to 1 millisecond. The results show that both the Dynamic-Programming and the Apriori-style algorithms outperformed the Brute-Force algorithm by orders of magnitude in most cases. The exceptions are the smallest domain "basketball" and when the number of requested preview tables is small (k=3). In these cases, the overheads of complex data structures and calculations in the advanced algorithms outweighed their benefits.

Fig. 9 shows that the Apriori-style algorithm did not perform well for d=6 in tight preview discovery and d=2 in diverse preview discovery. It is due to the excessive number of candidate k-subsets that satisfy the distance constraint in such cases. For instance, the diameter of a schema graph typically is not large. In the schema graph of "film" domain, the longest path length is 7 and the average path length is around 3–4. Setting distance constraint d=6 in finding tight previews will make most previews "tight". It is unnecessary to enforce such a distance constraint.

6.3 User Study

We conducted an extensive user study to compare seven different approaches, including concise previews ("Concise"), tight previews ("Tight"), diverse previews ("Diverse"), Freebase gold standard ("Freebase", cf. Sec. 6.1.2 and Table 10 in Appendix), hand-crafted previews by experts ("Experts"), schema summarization based on [19] ("YPS09"), and directly using schema graphs ("Graph"). For each approach, we created a website for presenting schema information using the approach and collecting participants' responses, on the five domains—"books", "film", "music", "TV", and "people".

To produce hand-crafted previews, we used a group of 10 experts (Ph.D. students in the database area at the authors' institution). Each expert participant was rewarded a $20 gift card. For each domain, we set the expected numbers of key attributes (K) and non-key attributes (N) to be the same as the values in the Freebase gold standard. Each expert was requested to produce preview tables under the size constraints given by K and N. During the process, the experts had access to the Freebase website, to help them understand the data. After the experts worked on all the five domains, they were asked to discuss and submit one consolidated preview for each domain. We use the consolidated previews as the hand-crafted previews in the ensuing user study. On average an expert spent about 10 minutes on the simplest domain "people" and more than 30 minutes on the most complex domain "film". After that, the experts spent about 2 hours to discuss. The preview tables from the experts have a reasonable overlap with the "Freebase" gold standard, but they also differ substantially, as shown in Tables 22 and 23 in Appendix. The substantial amount of time spent by the experts individually and as a group suggests that it is a challenging and time-consuming process to generate preview tables. This motivates the need for an automatic approach.

The participants of the user study include 84 computer science graduate students in the authors' institution. They all have taken database courses. None of them was affiliated with the authors' research group or exposed to the research project. Each participant was rewarded a $15 gift card.

Each participant was randomly assigned to use one of the aforementioned seven approaches (websites). Each approach received 10 to 13 participants. Before a participant started their session, they were given a 20-minute introduction on the approach of presenting schema information that they are using. The participant used the assigned approach to work on all five domains, in the order of "books", "film", "music", "TV", and "people". For each domain they were requested to answer 4 existence test questions about the existence/nonexistence of some specific information in the schema and 4 user experience questions. Hence each domain collected 40 to 52 responses to existence test questions (shown in Table 5), and 40 to 52 responses to user experience questions.

6.3.1 Existence Test Questions

The existence test questions were designed to measure how helpful the various approaches are in assisting the participants to acquire a good understanding of the data. An example existence test question is "Based on this schema summary, I know the dataset provides the awards of a musician." The participants were requested to provide a Boolean yes/no answer.

Time spent by participants: We first verify if the approaches are convenient to use, in terms of how much time the participants must spend to answer the existence test questions. For every existence test question that a participant worked on, we recorded the time

	books	film	music	TV	people
Concise	n=52 c=0.730	n=52 c=0.865	n=52 c=0.903	n=52 c=0.884	n=52 c=0.788
Tight	n=48 c=0.687	n=48 c=0.854	n=48 c=0.979	n=48 c=0.875	n=48 c=0.666
Diverse	n=52 c=0.846	n=51 c=0.921	n=52 c=0.730	n=48 c=0.75	n=48 c=0.875
Freebase	n=44 c=0.818	n=44 c=0.954	n=44 c=0.931	n=44 c=0.909	n=44 c=0.681
Experts	n=48 c=0.604	n=48 c=0.833	n=48 c=0.895	n=48 c=0.812	n=48 c=0.687
YPS09	n=52 c=0.692	n=52 c=0.884	n=52 c=0.923	n=52 c=0.692	n=52 c=0.634
Graph	n=40 c=0.975	n=40 c=0.875	n=40 c=0.875	n=40 c=0.9	n=40 c=0.85

Table 5: Sample sizes and conversion rates for all approaches and domains. (For "Diverse" and "film", 51 instead of 52 responses were recorded. One response was lost, likely due to imperfect implementation of session management in the data collection website.)

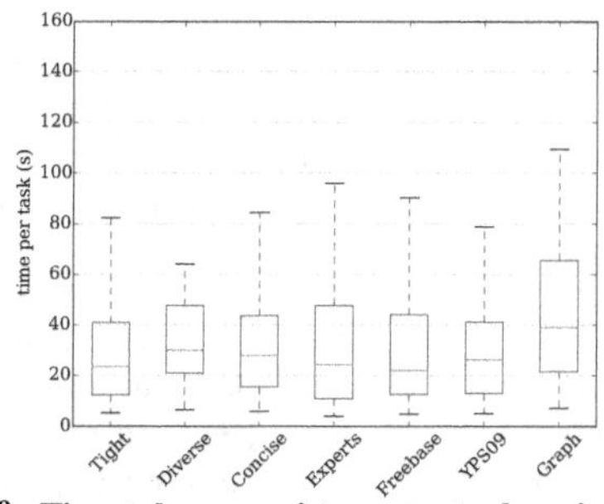

Figure 10: Time taken on existence tests, domain="music".

spent by the participant on the question. All participants worked on all the five domains in the same order. As a participant gets gradually more familiar with the tasks, they tend to spend more time on the initial domains and less on the later domains. This bias, due to budget and human resource constraints, makes it less meaningful to compare the time on existence tests across different domains. A future study that allows every participant to work on only one domain can shed further light on how the complexity of a domain determines the time needed for its existence tests.

The time per question for domain "music" is displayed in the boxplots in Fig. 10, and the results for other domains are included in the Appendix (Figs. 11 to 14). Table 6 provides a summary of the results. For each domain, it sorts all seven approaches in ascending order by the median time spent by participants on the existence test questions. Tight preview appears to be the most convenient approach, as its participants needed the least amount of time in three out of five domains and the second least in a fourth domain. The Freebase gold standard also did well, as expected. Surprisingly the previews produced by experts did not fare well. This may indicate the challenges in generating truly useful previews by hands, even though the experts spent a lot of time. "Diverse" and "Concise" are ranked in the middle. In general "YPS09" and "Graph" are the least convenient approaches. For "YPS09", the table for each entity type includes all relationships incident on the entity type, as explained in Sec. 6.1.1. Since [19] only clusters the tables and does not discern the importance of different attributes for each table, the tables are wide. Therefore they are less convenient in existence tests. For "Graph", its inconvenience may not be difficult to understand, given the complexity of a schema graph.

Accuracy of participants: We measured the effectiveness of the seven approaches by *conversion rate*, which is the percentage of existence test questions correctly answered by the participants. The conversion rates are shown in Table 5. Based on their values, we compare the seven approaches in a pairwise fashion. Table 7 reports the results for the "music" domain. The results for other

Domain	1	2	3	4	5	6	7
books	Graph	Freebase	Diverse	Tight	Concise	YPS09	Experts
film	Tight	Freebase	Diverse	Concise	Experts	Graph	YPS09
music	Freebase	Tight	Experts	YPS09	Concise	Diverse	Graph
TV	Tight	YPS09	Experts	Graph	Diverse	Concise	Freebase
people	Tight	Freebase	Concise	Diverse	Experts	YPS09	Graph

Table 6: Systems sorted in ascending order by the median time spent on existence test questions.

	Tight	Diverse	Freebase	Experts	YPS09	Graph
Concise	z=1.59 p=0.0559	z=−2.28 p=0.0113	z=0.49 p=0.3121	z=−0.13 p=0.4483	z=0.36 p=0.3594	z=−0.43 p=0.3336
Tight		z=−3.48 p=0.0003	z=−1.12 p=0.1314	z=−1.69 p=0.0455	z=−1.282 p=0.0999	z=−1.93 p=0.0268
Diverse			z=2.57 p=0.0051	z=2.10 p=0.0179	z=2.60 p=0.0047	z=1.70 p=0.0446
Freebase				z=−0.61 p=0.2709	z=−0.15 p=0.4404	z=−0.87 p=0.1922
Experts					z=0.49 p=0.3121	z=−0.29 p=0.3859
YPS09						z=−0.77 p=0.2206

Table 7: Pairwise comparisons of seven approaches' conversion rates, domain="music".

domains can be found in Tables 13 to 16 in Appendix. In the tables, each cell shows the hypothesis testing outcome when we compare the two approaches indicated by the corresponding column label and row label. If a cell is in light blue, users of the approach corresponding to the cell's row label are more accurate in existence tests than users of the approach corresponding to the column label, and the outcome is statistically significant. If a cell is in dark blue, it is the opposite. If a cell is not colored, we cannot make a statistically significant conclusion regarding which of the two approaches leads to more accurate users. Below we explain the hypothesis testing in more detail.

Each cell shows a z-score and a p-value, which are the outcomes of a two-proportion one-tailed z-test with significance level α=0.1. Such a hypothesis testing is proper, since our samples (responses from participants using different approaches) are independent and the sample sizes are large enough. Consider a cell at the intersection of column A and row B. The hypothesis testing for the difference between the two proportions for A and B is as follows. We assume that answering the existence test questions follows a Bernoulli trial with the probabilities of success p_A and p_B for approaches A and B, respectively. The observed conversion rates of A and B, c_A and c_B, are in Table 5. For $c_A > c_B$ (resp., $c_A < c_B$), the null hypothesis is H_0: $p_A \leq p_B$ (resp., $p_A \geq p_B$) and the alternative hypothesis is H_a: $p_A > p_B$ (resp., $p_A < p_B$). According to the sample sizes (n_A and n_B) and observed conversion rates (c_A and c_B) in Table 5, we calculate the z-score. For calculating the p-value, if the z-score is positive (i.e., $c_A > c_B$), we use a right-tailed z-test; otherwise we use a left-tailed z-test. Suppose the p-value is less than α. Then H_0 will be rejected and the data significantly supports the claim that users of A (resp., B) have a higher chance of answering existence tests correctly, if $c_A > c_B$ (resp., $c_B > c_A$).

The hypothesis testing outcomes for different domains exhibit certain degree of diversity. In domain "music" (Table 7), "Tight" outperformed all but "Freebase". In comparison with "Freebase", the conversion rate of "Tight" is actually higher, although we cannot reject the null hypothesis. On the other hand, "Diverse" performed poorly in this domain, as it is statistically significantly worse than all other approaches. In domain "books" (Table 13), "Graph" had the best performance, and "Diverse" did well too. In this domain "Tight" and "Experts" did poorly. In domain "film", "Freebase" did well (Table 14). In domain "TV", "YPS09" had the worst performance and no approach positively stood out (Table 15). In domain "people" (Table 16), both "Graph" and "Diverse" per-

Likert Scale Score	Q1: How easy was it to read the schema summary of this domain?	Q2: How much understanding of the data in this domain can you gain from the schema summary?	Q3: How helpful was the schema summary in assisting you to understand the data of this domain?	Q4: Is the schema summary missing important information about data in this domain?
1	Very hard	Very little	Not helpful at all	It provides very little important information.
2	Hard	A Little	Did not help much	It provides some important information.
3	Neutral	Neutral	Neutral	Neutral
4	Easy	Some	Somewhat helpful	It provides most of the important information.
5	Very easy	Very much	Very helpful	It provides all important information.

Table 8: User experience questionnaire.

Question	1	2	3	4	5	6	7
Q1	Freebase	Diverse	Graph	Experts	YPS09	Concise	Tight
Q2	Graph	Freebase	YPS09	Diverse	Concise	Tight	Experts
Q3	Graph	Freebase	YPS09	Diverse	Experts	Concise	Tight
Q4	YPS09	Concise	Experts	Graph	Tight	Freebase	Diverse

Table 9: Systems sorted in descending order by average user experience scores across five domains.

formed very well. Across all domains, it is quite surprising that "Experts" was never statistically significantly better than any other approach, except for "Diverse" in domain "music".

6.3.2 *User Experience Questions*

In each domain, we asked every participant four user experience questions, after the four existence test questions. The four questions Q1–Q4 are listed in Table 8. Each question comes with five options, specifying the level of satisfaction a participant may have regarding the particular aspect of the approach measured by the question. We assign a score to every option, based on the Likert scale shown in Table 8. The least favourable experience with respect to each question is assigned a score of 1, and the most favourable experience is assigned a score of 5. For a certain approach, the overall user experience score for each question is measured by averaging the scores obtained for that question from all the participants using that approach.

Results for individual domains can be found in the Appendix (Tables 17 to 21). The results for different domains are diverse, likely due to their different sizes and complexities. Hence, we summarize the results in Table 9. For each user experience question, Table 9 sorts all seven approaches in descending order by their average user experience scores across all five domains. Overall, the results suggest a mismatch between the participants' perception and their efficacy in answering existence test questions. The only exception appears to be "Freebase", of which the participants' perception largely agrees with their performance in using the approach. This may not be surprising, given that "Freebase" is the gold standard. Regarding Q1, while Table 6 indicates that "Tight" is the most convenient approach, the participants' perception suggests the opposite. Regarding Q2 and Q3, although the hypothesis testing results discussed earlier favor "Tight" in many situations, it once again did not fare well in leaving a satisfactory impression on the participants. The participants believed they acquired more understanding of the data when they used "Graph" and "YPS09", although the hypothesis testing results suggest that they typically answered the existence test questions more accurately when they use approaches such as "Tight". Regarding Q4, it is interesting that the participants favored "YPS09" the most, although they answered the questions less accurately using "YPS09" than using approaches such as "Tight". A logical explanation to these mismatches might be that the more complex presentation used in "Graph" and "YPS09" triggered the participants to believe that they had better understanding of the data and they had seen more complete information. A similar observation was made regarding "Tight" and "Diverse"—"Tight" clearly helped participants to do existence tests more accurately and quickly, but the participants had better impression of "Diverse". More thorough and robust explanation of these observations is the goal of future investigation, which likely will need to involve larger-scale user study and in-person interviews.

7. RELATED WORK

There have been several studies on schema summarization for relational databases [19, 20, 21], XML [21] and general graph data [17, 22]. [21] produces schema summarization for relational databases and XML data. The notion of summary in [19, 20] refers to clustering the tables in a database by their semantic roles and similarities as well as identifying direct join relationships and indirect join paths between the tables. The graph summarization in [17, 22] groups graph nodes based on their attribute similarity and allows users to browse the summary from different grouping granularities. As explained in Sec. 1, these methods are inapplicable or ineffective for producing preview tables from entity graphs, due to differences in input/output data models and goals.

There are many works on graph clustering [15]. They are not effective for generating preview tables, since clustering focuses on partitioning but does not present a concise structure. On the contrary, a preview only selects a small number of key attributes (vertices) and non-key attributes (edges) from a schema graph.

[14] proposed the concept of queried units ("qunits") for representing desired query results on a database. For automatic derivation of qunits, [14] discussed several ideas. One idea is to utilize the concept of queriability [10] which measures the importance of a schema entity by its schema connectedness and its data cardinality. The measure is thus similar to our key attribute scoring measures (Sec. 3.2). ObjectRank [3] applies authority-based ranking to keyword search in databases. Part of its ranking formula is extended from PageRank. The table importance measure in [19] and our random-walk based scoring measure (Sec. 3.2) bear similar ideas.

[9] studied how to generate query result snippets in XML search. Similar to [21], they focus on semi-structured data. Differently, they produce snippets of query results while [21] summarizes schema. In [9], the problem of generating snippets is formulated as maximizing information under an upper bound on snippet size. At high level, this is similar to our problem of finding optimal previews under size constraint, although its detailed problem formulation, solution, and data model are different.

8. CONCLUSION

This paper studies how to generate preview tables for entity graphs. The problem is challenging due to the scale and complexity of such graphs. We proposed effective scoring measures for preview tables. We proved that the optimal preview discovery problem under distance constraint is **NP**-hard. We designed efficient algorithms for discovering optimal previews. The experiments and user study verified the effectiveness of our methods.

There can be several future directions worth pursuing. (1) Guidelines and automatic techniques for choosing between tight and diverse previews. (2) Selecting representative entity tuples for preview tables. (3) Incorporating numeric attributes into preview tables. (4) Suggesting values of various parameters, including N, K and distance constraints for tight and diverse previews.

Acknowledgments The authors have been partially supported by NSF grants 1018865, 1408928 and NSF-China grant 61370019. Any opinions, findings, and conclusions in this publication are those of the authors and do not necessarily reflect the views of the funding agencies. We also thank Rudresh Ajgaonkar and Aaditya Kulkarni for contributions in user study.

9. REFERENCES

[1] R. Agarwal and R. Srikant. Fast algorithms for mining association rules. In *VLDB*, pages 487–499, 1994.

[2] S. Auer, C. Bizer, G. Kobilarov, J. Lehmann, R. Cyganiak, , and Z. Ives. DBpedia: A nucleus for a Web of open data. In *ISWC*, pages 722–735, 2007.

[3] A. Balmin, V. Hristidis, and Y. Papakonstantinou. Objectrank: Authority-based keyword search in databases. In *VLDB*, pages 564–575, 2004.

[4] K. Bollacker, C. Evans, P. Paritosh, T. Sturge, and J. Taylor. Freebase: a collaboratively created graph database for structuring human knowledge. In *SIGMOD*, pages 1247–1250, 2008.

[5] S. Brin and L. Page. The anatomy of a large-scale hypertextual web search engine. In *WWW*, pages 107–117, 1998.

[6] C. Bron and J. Kerbosch. Algorithm 457: finding all cliques of an undirected graph. *CACM*, 16(9):575–577, Sept. 1973.

[7] J. Cohen. *Statistical Power Analysis for the Behavioral Sciences*. Academic Press, 1988.

[8] X. Dong, E. Gabrilovich, G. Heitz, W. Horn, N. Lao, K. Murphy, T. Strohmann, S. Sun, and W. Zhang. Knowledge vault: A web-scale approach to probabilistic knowledge fusion. In *KDD*, pages 601–610, 2014.

[9] Y. Huang, Z. Liu, and Y. Chen. Query biased snippet generation in xml search. In *SIGMOD*, pages 315–326, 2008.

[10] M. Jayapandian and H. V. Jagadish. Automated creation of a forms-based database query interface. *PVLDB*, 1(1):695–709, Aug. 2008.

[11] F. Kose, W. Weckwerth, T. Linke, and O. Fiehn. Visualizing plant metabolomic correlation networks using clique-metabolite matrices. *Bioinformatics*, 17(12):1198–1208, Dec. 2001.

[12] T.-Y. Liu. Learning to rank for information retrieval. *Found. Trends Inf. Retr.*, 3(3):225–331, Mar. 2009.

[13] C. D. Manning, P. Raghavan, and H. Schtze. *Introduction to Information Retrieval*. Cambridge University Press, 2008.

[14] A. Nandi and H. V. Jagadish. Qunits: queried units in database search. In *CIDR*, 2009.

[15] S. E. Schaeffer. Survey: Graph clustering. *Comput. Sci. Rev.*, 1(1):27–64, Aug. 2007.

[16] F. M. Suchanek, G. Kasneci, and G. Weikum. YAGO: a core of semantic knowledge unifying WordNet and Wikipedia. In *WWW*, pages 697–706, 2007.

[17] Y. Tian, R. A. Hankins, and J. M. Patel. Efficient aggregation for graph summarization. In *SIGMOD*, pages 567–580, 2008.

[18] W. Wu, H. Li, H. Wang, and K. Q. Zhu. Probase: a probabilistic taxonomy for text understanding. In *SIGMOD*, pages 481–492, 2012.

[19] X. Yang, C. M. Procopiuc, and D. Srivastava. Summarizing relational databases. *PVLDB*, 2(1):634–645, 2009.

[20] X. Yang, C. M. Procopiuc, and D. Srivastava. Summary graphs for relational database schemas. *PVLDB*, 4(11):899–910, 2011.

[21] C. Yu and H. V. Jagadish. Schema summarization. In *VLDB*, pages 319–330, 2006.

[22] N. Zhang, Y. Tian, and J. M. Patel. Discovery-driven graph summarization. In *ICDE*, pages 880–891, 2010.

APPENDIX

A. SCHEMATA OF THE TABLES IN THE FREEBASE GOLD STANDARD

The schema of the tables in the "Freebase" gold standard can be found in Table 10.

Key attributes	Non-key attributes
Domain="books", k=6, n=15	
BOOK	*Characters, Genre, Editions*
BOOK EDITION	*Publication Date, Publisher, Credited To*
SHORT STORY	*Genre, Characters*
POEM	*Characters, Meter, Verse Form*
SHORT NON-FICTION	*Mode Of Writing, Verse Form*
AUTHOR	*Series Written (Or Contributed To), Works Edited, Works Written*
Domain="film", k=6, n=9	
FILM	*Directed By, Tagline, Initial Release Date*
FILM ACTOR	*Film performances*
FILM GENRE	*Films of this genre*
FILM DIRECTOR	*Films directed*
FILM PRODUCER	*Films Executive Produced, Films Produced*
FILM WRITER	*Film Writing Credits*
Domain="music", k=6, n=18	
COMPOSITION	*Includes, Lyricist, Composer*
CONCERT	*Venue, Start Date, Concert Tour*
MUSIC VIDEO	*Song, Initial release date, Artist*
MUSICAL ALBUM	*Release Type, Initial Release Date, Artist*
MUSICAL ARTIST	*Albums, Place Musical Career Began, Musical Genres*
MUSICAL RECORDING	*Length, Featured artists, Recorded by*
Domain="TV", k=6, n=9	
TV PROGRAM	*Program Creator, Air Date Of First Episode, Air Date Of Final Episode*
TV ACTOR	*Starring TV Roles*
TV CHARACTER	*Programs In Which This Was A Regular Character*
TV WRITER	*TV Programs (Recurring Writer)*
TV PRODUCER	*TV Programs Produced*
TV DIRECTOR	*TV Episodes Directed, TV Segments Directed*
Domain="people", k=6, n=16	
PERSON	*Profession, Country Of Nationality, Date Of Birth*
DECEASED PERSON	*Cause Of Death, Place Of Death, Date Of Death*
CAUSE OF DEATH	*People Who Died This Way, Includes Causes Of Death, Parent Cause Of Death*
ETHNICITY	*Geographic Distribution, Includes Group(S), Included In Group(S)*
PROFESSION	*Specializations, Specialization Of, People With This Profession*
PROFESSIONAL FIELD	*Professions In This Field*

Table 10: Gold standard ("Freebase"). For each domain, there are 6 key attributes and at most 3 non-key attributes for each key-attribute.

B. SAMPLE OPTIMAL PREVIEWS

To demonstrate the combined effectiveness of both scoring measures and preview discovery algorithms, Table 11 presents the optimal concise previews in 3 selected domains by 3 different combinations of key attribute scoring (KS) and non-key attribute scoring (NKS) measures. The size constraint is set as k=5 and n=10. All result previews show that the selected key and non-key attributes have covered important entity types and their important relationship types. Further, Table 12 shows the optimal tight (d=2) and diverse (d=4) previews in "film" domain by one particular choice of key and non-key attribute scoring measures. We see that, in the tight preview result, the chosen key attributes are all highly related to one entity type FILM. In the diverse preview result, the chosen key attributes are far less related to each other. Both verify the effectiveness of the concepts of tight/diverse previews.

Note that in the generated previews, certain non-key attributes represent relationship types involving more than two entity types. An example in Table 11 is *Portrayed in films*, which is a non-key

Key attributes	Non-key attributes (Target entity types)
Domain="film", KS=Coverage, NKS=Coverage, k=5, n=10	
Film Character	*Portrayed in films* (Film, Film Actor)
Film Actor	*Film performances* (Film, Film Character)
Film	*Performances* (Film actor, Film Character), *Genres* (Film Genre), *Runtime* (Film Cut), *Country of origin* (Country), *Directed by* (Film Director), *Languages* (Human Language)
Film Director	*Films directed* (Film)
Film Crewmember	*Films crewed* (Film, Film crew role)
Domain="music", KS=Random Walk, NKS=Coverage, k=5, n=10	
Musical Recording	*Releases* (Musical Release), *Tracks* (Release Track), *Recorded by* (Musical Artist)
Musical Release	*Tracks* (Musical Recording), *Track list* (Release Track)
Release Track	*Release* (Musical Release), *Recording* (Musical Recording)
Musical Artist	*Tracks recorded* (Musical Recording)
Musical Album	*Releases* (Musical Release), *Release type* (Musical Album Type)
Domain="TV", KS=Random Walk, NKS=Entropy, k=5, n=10	
TV Episode	*Previous episode* (TV Episode), *Next episode* (TV Episode), *Performances* (TV Actor, TV Character), *Season* (TV Season), *Series* (TV Program) , *Personal appearances* (Person, Personal Appearance Role)
TV Program	*Regular acting performances* (TV Actor, TV Character, TV Season)
TV Season	*Episodes* (TV Episode)
TV Actor	*TV episode performances* (TV Episode, TV Character)
TV Director	*TV episodes directed* (TV Episode)

Table 11: Sample optimal concise previews.

attribute of entity type Film Character. Different from other non-key attribute such as *Films directed*, it represents a 3-way relationship among Film Character, Film and Film Actor. For instance, Agent J is a Film Character played by Film Actor Will Smith in Film Men in Black. To present the values of such a *multi-way* non-key attribute in a preview table, we employ a simple approach of presenting values for all participating entity types in this relationship. It is arguable that this approach widens the preview table, which to some extent violates a given size constraint. An alternative solution is to use separate preview tables for all multi-way relationships. These pose interesting directions for our future work.

C. ADDITIONAL USER STUDY RESULTS

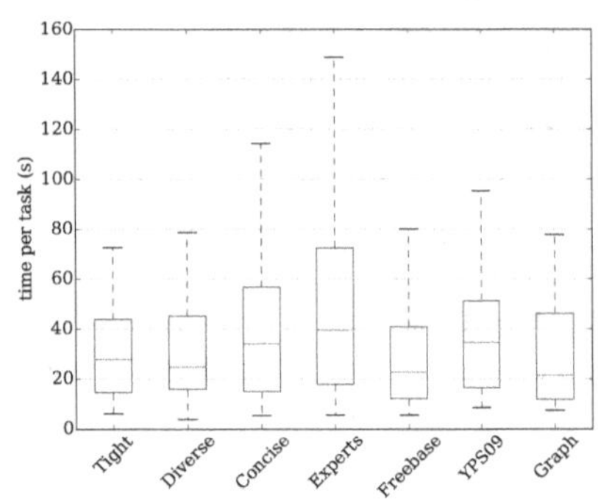

Figure 11: Time taken on existence tests, domain="books".

Key attributes	Non-key attributes (Target entity types)
Domain="film", KS=Coverage, NKS=Coverage, k=5, n=10, d=2	
Film	*Performances* (Film Character, Film Actor), *Genres* (Film Genre), *Runtime* (Film Cut), *Country of origin* (Country), *Directed by* (Film Director), *Languages* (Human Language)
Film Director	*Films directed* (Film)
Film Producer	*Films produced* (Film)
Film Writer	*Film writing credits* (Film)
Film Editor	*Films edited* (Film)
Domain="film", KS=Coverage, NKS=Coverage, k=5, n=10, d=4	
Film Character	*Portrayed in films* (Film, Film Actor), *Portrayed in films (dubbed)* (Film, Film Actor)
Film Crewmember	*Films crewed* (Film, Film Crew Role)
Person or Entity appearing in Film	*Films appeared in* (Film, Type of Appearance)
Film Festival	*Individual festivals* (Film Festival Event), *Location* (Location), *Focus* (Film Festival Focus), *Sponsoring organization* (Sponser)
Film Company	*Films* (Film)

Table 12: Sample optimal tight (upper) and diverse previews (lower).

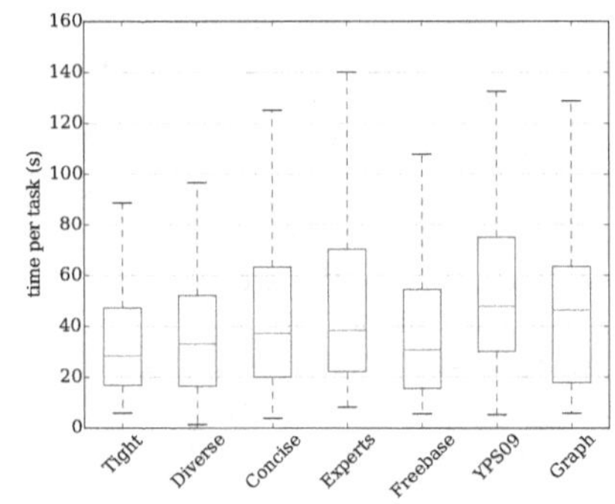

Figure 12: Time taken on existence tests, domain="film".

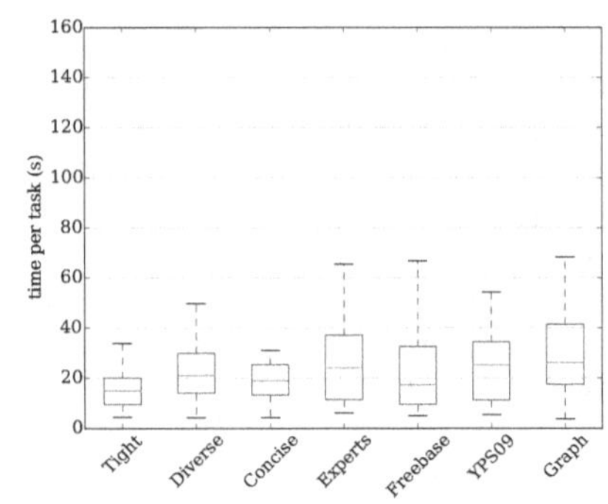

Figure 13: Time taken on existence tests, domain="TV".

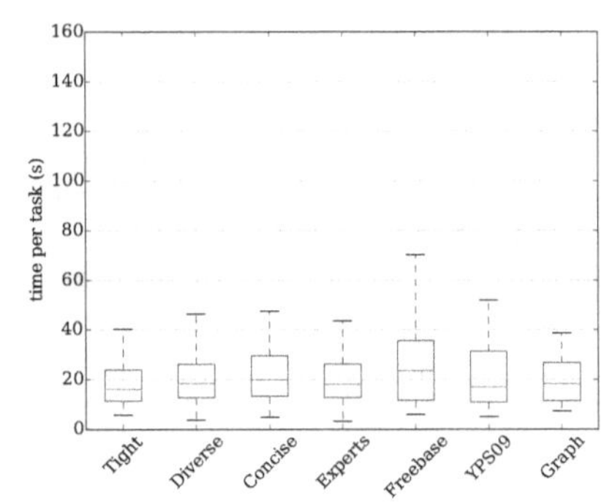

Figure 14: Time taken on existence tests, domain="people".

	Tight	Diverse	Freebase	Experts	YPS09	Graph
Concise	z=−0.47 p=0.3192	z=1.45 p=0.0735	z=1.02 p=0.1539	z=−1.34 p=0.0901	z=−0.43 p=0.3336	z=3.15 p=0.0008
Tight		z=1.89 p=0.0294	z=1.45 p=0.0735	z=−0.85 p=0.1977	z=0.05 p=0.4801	z=3.49 p=0.0002
Diverse			z=−0.37 p=0.3557	z=−2.72 p=0.0033	z=−1.86 p=0.0314	z=2.06 p=0.0197
Freebase				z=−2.25 p=0.0122	z=−1.42 p=0.0778	z=2.32 p=0.0102
Experts					z=0.92 p=0.1788	z=4.13 p=0.0000
YPS09						z=3.47 p=0.0003

Table 13: Pairwise comparisons of seven approaches' conversion rates, domain="books".

	Tight	Diverse	Freebase	Experts	YPS09	Graph
Concise	z=−0.16 p=0.4364	z=0.92 p=0.1788	z=1.49 p=0.0681	z=−0.45 p=0.3264	z=0.29 p=0.3859	z=0.14 p=0.4443
Tight		z=1.06 p=0.1446	z=1.61 p=0.0537	z=−0.28 p=0.3897	z=0.45 p=0.3264	z=0.29 p=0.3859
Diverse			z=0.66 p=0.2546	z=−1.34 p=0.0901	z=−0.63 p=0.2643	z=−0.73 p=0.2327
Freebase				z=−1.86 p=0.0314	z=−1.23 p=0.1093	z=−1.31 p=0.0951
Experts					z=0.73 p=0.2327	z=0.55 p=0.2912
YPS09						z=−0.13 p=0.4483

Table 14: Pairwise comparisons of seven approaches' conversion rates, domain="film".

	Tight	Diverse	Freebase	Experts	YPS09	Graph
Concise	z=−0.14 p=0.4443	z=−1.74 p=0.0409	z=0.40 p=0.3446	z=−1.01 p=0.1562	z=−2.40 p=0.0082	z=0.24 p=0.4052
Tight		z=−1.57 p=0.0582	z=0.52 p=0.3015	z=−0.85 p=0.1977	z=−2.21 p=0.0136	z=0.37 p=0.3557
Diverse			z=2.01 p=0.0222	z=0.73 p=0.2327	z=−0.65 p=0.2578	z=1.82 p=0.0344
Freebase				z=−1.33 p=0.0918	z=−2.61 p=0.0045	z=−0.14 p=0.4443
Experts					z=−1.38 p=0.0838	z=1.16 p=0.1230
YPS09						z=2.40 p=0.0082

Table 15: Pairwise comparisons of seven approaches' conversion rates, domain="TV".

	Tight	Diverse	Freebase	Experts	YPS09	Graph
Concise	z=−1.37 p=0.0853	z=1.16 p=0.1230	z=−1.19 p=0.1170	z=−1.15 p=0.1251	z=−1.73 p=0.0418	z=0.76 p=0.2236
Tight		z=2.43 p=0.0075	z=0.15 p=0.4404	z=0.22 p=0.4129	z=−0.34 p=0.3669	z=1.98 p=0.0239
Diverse			z=−2.25 p=0.0122	z=−2.23 p=0.0129	z=−2.78 p=0.0027	z=−0.34 p=0.3669
Freebase				z=0.06 p=0.4761	z=−0.48 p=0.3156	z=1.82 p=0.0344
Experts					z=−0.56 p=0.2877	z=1.79 p=0.0367
YPS09						z=2.31 p=0.0104

Table 16: Pairwise comparisons of seven approaches' conversion rates, domain="people".

System	Q1	Q2	Q3	Q4
Concise	3.5	4.0769	3.9231	3.6154
Tight	3.5833	3.9167	4	3.3333
Diverse	3.9231	3.8462	4.0769	3.6364
Freebase	3.8182	4.0909	4	3.6
Experts	3.3333	3.75	4.2727	3.5
YPS09	3.75	3.8333	3.8462	3.5385
Graph	4.4	4.1	4.1	3.3333

Table 17: Responses to user experience questions, domain="books".

System	Q1	Q2	Q3	Q4
Concise	4	4.0909	4.4167	3.7692
Tight	4.0833	4.6667	4.5	3.75
Diverse	4.1538	4.4615	4.4615	3.3846
Freebase	4.1818	4.3636	4.2727	3.4545
Experts	4	4.0833	4.25	3.2727
YPS09	3.5385	4.3077	4.2308	4
Graph	3.8	4.7	4.6	4

Table 18: Responses to user experience questions, domain="film".

System	Q1	Q2	Q3	Q4
Concise	3.8462	3.8462	4.1538	3.5833
Tight	3.6667	3.8333	4.0833	3.75
Diverse	3.75	3.75	3.9167	3
Freebase	3.8182	4.2727	4.4545	3.5455
Experts	4.1667	4.1667	4.5	4.3333
YPS09	4.3077	4.5385	4.4615	3.8333
Graph	3.6	4.6	4.5	3.9

Table 19: Responses to user experience questions, domain="music".

System	Q1	Q2	Q3	Q4
Concise	3.7692	4	3.7692	3.7692
Tight	4.1667	4.1667	4.1667	3.6667
Diverse	4.0833	4.25	4.4167	3.6667
Freebase	4.5455	4.3636	4.2727	3.2727
Experts	4.1667	3.8333	3.8333	3.6667
YPS09	3.5385	3.6154	3.7692	3
Graph	3.5	4.6	4.4	3.9

Table 20: Responses to user experience questions, domain="TV".

System	Q1	Q2	Q3	Q4
Concise	4.2308	4.3846	4.3077	4
Tight	2.9167	3.6364	3.4545	2.9167
Diverse	4.0833	4.1667	4.0833	3.5833
Freebase	3.9091	4.0909	4.0909	3.4545
Experts	3.9167	4.0833	4.0833	3.75
YPS09	4.3333	4.4615	4.6923	4.3846
Graph	4.5	4.1	4	3.1

Table 21: Responses to user experience questions, domain="people".

K	books	film	music	TV	people
1	1	1	1	1	1
2	0.5	0.5	1	1	1
3	0.334	0.334	1	1	0.664
4	0.25	0.5	1	0.75	0.5
5	0.2	0.6	1	0.6	0.6
6	0.333	0.5	0.833	0.5	0.5

Table 22: Precision-at-K of key attribute scoring in "Freebase", using "Experts" as ground truth.

K	books	film	music	TV	people
1	1	1	1	1	1
2	1	0.5	1	1	0.5
3	0.667	0.667	1	0.667	0.667
4	0.5	0.75	1	0.75	0.75
5	0.4	0.6	0.8	0.6	0.6
6	0.333	0.5	0.833	0.5	0.5

Table 23: Precision-at-K of key attribute scoring in "Experts", using "Freebase" as ground truth.

Speedup Graph Processing by Graph Ordering

Hao Wei, Jeffrey Xu Yu, Can Lu
Chinese University of Hong Kong
Hong Kong, China
{hwei,yu,lucan}@se.cuhk.edu.hk

Xuemin Lin
The University of New South Wales
Sydney, Australia
lxue@cse.unsw.edu.au

ABSTRACT

The CPU cache performance is one of the key issues to efficiency in database systems. It is reported that cache miss latency takes a half of the execution time in database systems. To improve the CPU cache performance, there are studies to support searching including cache-oblivious, and cache-conscious trees. In this paper, we focus on CPU speedup for graph computing in general by reducing the CPU cache miss ratio for different graph algorithms. The approaches dealing with trees are not applicable to graphs which are complex in nature. In this paper, we explore a general approach to speed up CPU computing, in order to further enhance the efficiency of the graph algorithms without changing the graph algorithms (implementations) and the data structures used. That is, we aim at designing a general solution that is not for a specific graph algorithm, neither for a specific data structure. The approach studied in this work is graph ordering, which is to find the optimal permutation among all nodes in a given graph by keeping nodes that will be frequently accessed together locally, to minimize the CPU cache miss ratio. We prove the graph ordering problem is NP-hard, and give a basic algorithm with a bounded approximation. To improve the time complexity of the basic algorithm, we further propose a new algorithm to reduce the time complexity and improve the efficiency with new optimization techniques based on a new data structure. We conducted extensive experiments to evaluate our approach in comparison with other 9 possible graph orderings (such as the one obtained by METIS) using 8 large real graphs and 9 representative graph algorithms. We confirm that our approach can achieve high performance by reducing the CPU cache miss ratios.

1. INTRODUCTION

Graph processing has been extensively studied in the recent years given a large number of real applications developed over online social networks, location-based social networks, semantic web, biological networks, and road networks. In the literature, the reported studies have focused on new graph algorithms to process large graphs and has shown that they can achieve high efficiency. We list the graph algorithms that we investigate in this paper including Breadth-First Search (*BFS*) [20], Depth-First Search (*DFS*) [20], Strongly Connected Component (*SCC*) detection [48], Shortest Path (*SP*) by Bellman-Ford algorithm [20], PageRank (*PR*) [39], Dominating Set (*DS*) [19], graph decomposition (*Kcore*) [6] and graph diameter (*Diam*). Here, *BFS*, *DFS*, *SCC* and *SP* are primitive graph algorithms. On top of them, many graph algorithms are designed. *PR* is widely used in many applications. *DS* is a representative of the set cover problem in graph which is NP-hard, and there are greedy algorithms to solve it [17]. *Kcore* is a graph decomposition algorithm, which is to find every subgraph H of a graph G such that the degree of nodes in H is $\geq k$. *Diam* is one of the most important pieces of information about the graph structure. The graph algorithms listed have been extensively studied, and are efficient to process large graphs.

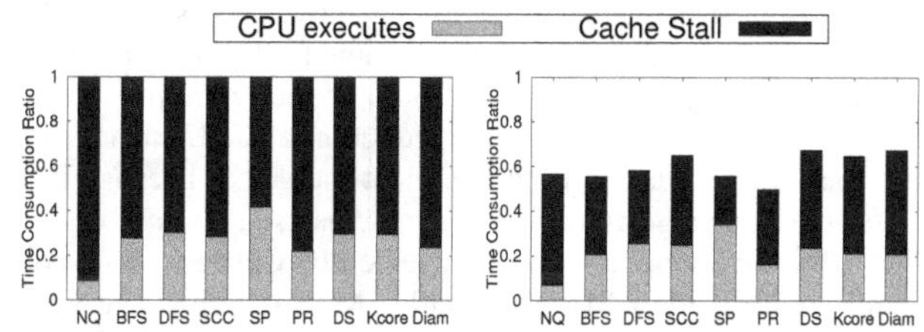

(a) The original order (b) Gorder

Figure 1: CPU execution and CPU Cache Stall over sd1-arc

In this paper, we focus on the following questions. Given the efficiency of the algorithms developed, can we make graph processing even faster? In addition, is there any general approach to enhance graph processing for all graph algorithms, rather than for some specific graph processing tasks only? To address these questions, we first show the potential to improve the efficiency significantly.

As observed in [2], a lot of time is wasted on CPU cache latency in database query processing. We also observe that graph algorithms waste a lot of time on CPU cache latency, and such time wasting cannot be handled by graph algorithms themselves. We show our finding in Fig. 1(a) by testing *NQ* (a primitive operation to access the neighbors of a node in a graph) as well as *BFS*, *DFS*, *SCC*, *SP*, *PR*, *DS*, *Kcore* and *Diam* using a hyperlink graph dataset `sd1-arc` with 94.94 millions of nodes and 1.9 billions of edges. The graph processing for the 9 tasks are different. To show the percentages of CPU cache stall (the CPU time waiting for the requested data due to the cache miss) and the CPU execution time while the CPU keeps computing, we normalize the entire graph processing time of each task to be 1. As shown in Fig. 1(a), CPU only works in the range of 10% and 45% (on average 30%) of the overall processing time, and wastes time in the range of 90% and 55% (on average 70% time) waiting for the desired data to be accessed in CPU cache in all algorithms tested.

The percentage of wasting CPU time is much higher than ex-

SIGMOD'16, June 26-July 01, 2016, San Francisco, CA, USA

DOI: http://dx.doi.org/10.1145/2882903.2915220

pected, which motivates us to study how to speedup CPU processing for graph computing. In this work, we explore how to reduce the time consumption on CPU cache stall by improving the CPU cache hit rate in graph computing, without changing the graph algorithms (implementations) and the data structures used. In other words, we do not aim at designing something that is for a specific graph algorithm, or for a specific data structure, or for a specific CPU cache mechanism. We seek a general solution for different graph algorithms. The main idea of our approach is to arrange nodes in graph in an order that nodes to be accessed is very likely to be in the CPU cache which is of considerably small size in comparison with the large graph size. We call our graph ordering Gorder. Fig. 1(b) shows the testing results by Gorder which rearranges all nodes in sd1-arc. Here, for comparison, the entire processing time by Gorder is normalized according to the entire processing time by the original order used. Take *NQ* as an example, The total processing time for *NQ* by Gorder is about 60% of the entire processing time in Fig. 1(a). The saving is the reduction of CPU cache stall, where the CPU execution time is almost the same, because it is done for the same algorithm over the same dataset. As can be seen in Fig. 1(b), the efficiency can be enhanced by Gorder, which significantly reduces the CPU cache stalls. More details about CPU cache are discussed in the appendix.

Related Works: The CPU cache performance has been studied in database systems. Ailamaki et al. show that cache miss latency takes half of the execution time in database systems [2], and Cieslewicz and Ross survey the CPU cache performance in [18]. There are many reported studies in literature that deal with trees [13, 15, 23, 35, 42, 43]. Rao et al. design cache sensitive search trees for searching in [42], and they also study cache sensitive B^+-trees for index structure in [43]. The cache performance is improved by fitting tree nodes into cache lines and removing most child pointers of tree nodes to reduce space. Lindstrom et al. generate cache-oblivious layout for binary search tree by optimizing a measure function with a locality measure to mimic the cache miss probability [35]. Ghoting et al. propose cache-conscious prefix tree to allocate the prefix tree in the memory [23]. Chen et al. propose Prefetching B^+-tree which uses the cache prefetch when loading the nodes of the B^+-tree, to reduce latency time [13], which can also be used to improve the hash join [12]. However, these works are designed to support searching for data that is with a total order, and they cannot be effectively used to support all different graph algorithms over complex graphs.

To deal with graphs, there are works on specific graph algorithms to improve CPU cache performance. Park et al. propose several strategies to optimize the cache performance of Floyd-Warshall, Bellman-Ford, Prim, and Bipartite matching algorithms in [40]. Then et al. optimize the multi-source breadth-first search (*BFS*) algorithm by sharing the common computation across concurrent *BFS*s to improve the cache hit rate [50]. However, these approaches are designed for some specific graph algorithms, and can not be used to support any graph algorithms in general. Some existing works improve the graph computing by graph ordering and node clustering. Banerjee et al. propose a node ordering scheme by the children-depth-first traversal method to improve the efficiency of the DAG traversal [4]. Auroux et al. propose to reorder the node set by BFS [3]. Mendelzon et al. propose a heuristic method for clustering nodes in the local area in the same disk page to minimize the number of I/Os needed to access the graph [38]. In addition, graph compression has been studied to reduce the number of bits per edge by placing nodes in a specific way. Kang et al. takes a graph decomposition approach to remove the hub nodes iteratively from the graph [29]. Boldi et al. study several ordering strategies for graph compression in [8], and use label propagation techniques to compute the clusters of the graph [7], where every node is assigned to the cluster having most neighbor nodes with it. Chierichetti et al. in [14] formulate graph compression as the variation of the graph bandwidth problem [16, 22], which finds the optimal permutation π of the node set minimizing $\max\{|\pi(u) - \pi(v)| : (u, v) \in E(G)\}$. The graph compression problem is closely related to the Minimum Linear Arrangement problem and its variants [27], which is NP-hard. Many heuristics have been proposed in literature [11, 32, 41, 44] but most existing approaches cannot process large graph successfully. The ideas presented here share the similarity with graph partitioning to minimize the number of edge-cuts, [30, 49, 51, 52, 53], which we discuss in detail later.

Major contribution: First, we explore a general approach to reduce the CPU cache miss ratio for graph algorithms with their implementation and data structures unchanged. This problem is challenging, because graphs are rather complex where there is no total order among data to follow and the graph algorithms designed are based on different techniques. It is worth noting that our general approach can be used together with other specialized optimizations for the specific algorithms. Second, we propose a solution by graph ordering, which is to find the optimal permutation ϕ among all nodes in a given graph G by keeping nodes that will be frequently accessed together in a window of size w, in order to minimize the CPU cache miss ratio. We use the ordering to renumber the node IDs as well as sort the nodes inside every adjacent lists. We will discuss in details that the same cannot be achieved by graph partitioning. Third, we prove the graph ordering problem to be studied is NP-hard, and give a basic algorithm with a bounded $\frac{1}{2w}$-approximation in time complexity of $O(w \cdot d_{max} \cdot n^2)$, where d_{max} is the maximum in-degree and n is the number of nodes in graph G. To further improve the performance, we propose a new priority queue (PQ) based algorithm, which is with the same $\frac{1}{2w}$-approximation but with $O(\sum_{u \in V}(d_O(u))^2)$ time complexity, where $d_O(u)$ is the out-degree of node u in G. We propose several optimization techniques including lazy-update to significantly reduce the cost of maintaining the priority queue. Fourth, we conducted extensive experimental studies to evaluate our approach in comparison with other 9 possible graph orderings (such as the one obtained by METIS) using 8 large real graphs and 9 representative graph algorithms. We confirm that our approach can achieve high performance by reducing the CPU cache miss ratio. In nearly all testings, our graph ordering outperforms other graph orderings for different graph algorithms over different datasets. The best speedup is > 2 comparing our graph ordering over others when testing graph algorithms over large real graphs.

The paper organization: The remainder of the paper is organized as follows. We discuss graph ordering in Section 2 in which we discuss the issues related to graph partitioning and graph ordering, give problem statement on graph ordering, and show the hardness of the problem. We give our algorithms in Section 3 in which we first give the approximation of our algorithm, and show we can significantly reduce the computational cost. We have conducted extensive testings, and report the experimental studies in Section 4. The paper is concluded in Section 5.

2. GRAPH ORDERING

In this paper, we model a graph as a directed graph $G = (V, E)$, where $V(G)$ represents the set of nodes and $E(G)$ represents the set of edges. The number of nodes and edges are denoted as $n = |V(G)|$ and $m = |E(G)|$, respectively. In addition, we use $N_O(u)$ and $N_I(u)$ to denote the out-neighbor set and in-neighbor set of u, such as $N_O(u) = \{v \mid (u,v) \in E(G)\}$ and $N_I(u) = \{v \mid (v,u) \in E(G)\}$, respectively. The in-degree, out-degree, and the degree of a node u is denoted as, $d_I(u) = |N_I(u)|$, $d_O(u) = |N_O(u)|$, and $d(u) = d_I(u) + d_O(u)$. Two nodes, u and v, are sibling nodes if they share a common in-neighbor. It is worth mentioning that our approach to be discussed can deal with undirected graphs, since an undirected graph can be represented by a directed graph.

Our key idea for CPU speedup for graph computing is to find a way to represent a graph that can reduce the CPU cache miss ratio and is independent of any graph algorithms and the data structure they use. Here, reducing the CPU cache miss ratio is to reduce the number of times of copying data from main memory to cache, or from slower cache to faster cache. To achieve this goal is to keep nodes frequently accessed together stored closely in main memory so that they are more likely to be loaded into cache together by one single cache line transfer. A possible solution is to group nodes of the graph into blocks using graph partition algorithm which divides graph into partitions to minimize edge-cut which is the number of edges that cross different partitions. *METIS* [30] is a widely-used graph partition algorithm and is used to place nodes in blocks in the existing works [51, 52]. However, such graph partition algorithms can not serve the purpose of reducing CPU cache miss ratio effectively for the following reasons. First, a recent study [34] shows the real graphs do not have good edge-cut due to the power-law degree distribution and the existence of nodes with high degree. The neighbors of a node with high degree must be dispersed in different partitions because one single partition is not enough to accommodate all neighbors of such high degree nodes. Second, in dealing with large graphs in distributed or I/O contexts where graph partitioning works well [51, 52], the size of a partition is rather large, e.g., 64 kilobytes (64KB). In such cases, the algorithms can be designed to deal with the nodes/edges in a partition in a way to achieve efficiency. However, for CPU cache, a cache line is fixed to be 64 bytes (64B), which is very small, and it is very difficult for user programs to control the CPU cache. Third, there is an issue of deciding the number of partitions or the number of nodes to be kept in one graph partition, given the small CPU cache line of 64B. A simple way is to keep 16 nodes in one partition, assuming a node is represented by an integer of 4 bytes. However, it does not work for all graph algorithms. Consider *PR*, a node needs to be associated with its degree and a PageRank value, which may end up additional 4+8 bytes. In other words, a partition can only keep 5 nodes in a partition to feed the 64B size CPU cache line. Fourth, assuming we can keep all nodes in all 64B partitions one followed by another, it does not necessarily mean it can reduce the CPU cache miss ratio much, since CPU has its own mechanism to align the data into the 64B CPU cache lines in main memory, which may be different from the way of the partitions allocated. In other words, a partition may be allocated into more than one CPU cache line, though the partition size is equal to cache line size. Note that CPU alignment is difficult to be controlled by user programs.

In this work, we propose graph ordering to arrange all nodes in an order, aiming at reducing CPU cache miss ratio, for any graph algorithms with any data structure they use in general. The main idea behind graph ordering is to reflect the CPU access of graph in a sequential manner, since CPU accesses data in sequence no matter how complex the graph is, and at the same time to maintain locality of nodes that will be frequently accessed together closely in graph ordering, which is the focus of this work we will discuss in detail. It is important to note that the graph ordering only affects the way of arranging nodes in main memory, and is independent from graph algorithm, algorithm implementation, and the data structure used.

Example 2.1: A graph $G = (V, E)$ is shown in Fig. 2 as a running example. There are 12 nodes numbered from 1 to 12, which is considered as one possible graph ordering. Given such numbering, the graph can be represented by either adjacency-matrix or adjacency-list in Fig. 10, where $n = 12$ and the node numbered i will be placed at the i-th position in the corresponding array. □

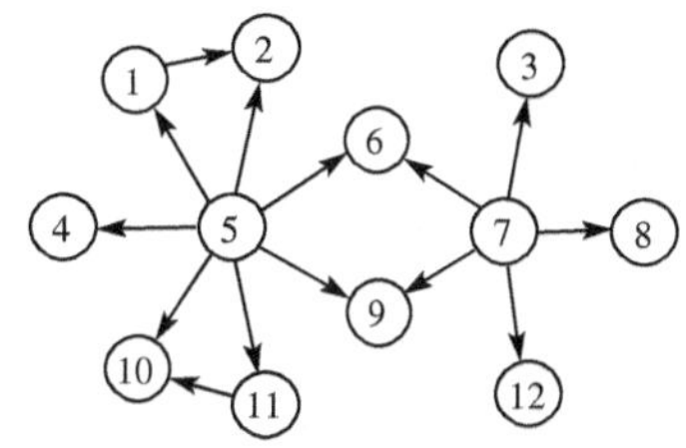

Figure 2: An Example

As illustrated in the example, in graph computing, a node will be assigned with an ID. Two vertices will be stored closely if they have similar IDs in main memory. In the following, the node v_i is assumed to have an ID i, for simplicity.

Next, we discuss locality of a graph that needs to be maintained in graph ordering. To capture the locality, we look at the common statement that is used in graph algorithms below.

```
1: for each node v ∈ N_O(u) do
2:     the program segment to compute/access v
```

This pattern appears in *BFS*, *DFS*, *PR*, and *SP*, to name a few, when it needs to access nodes v in an out-neighbor set $N_O(u)$, and indicates that these nodes are the nodes that need to be maintained locally to reduce the CPU cache miss ratio. When looking at the statement carefully, there are two relationships, namely, neighbor relationship and sibling relationship. Supposed $v_1, \cdots, v_{d_O(u)}$ are in the out-neighbor set of u, u and v_i are in neighbor relationship for $1 \leq i \leq d_O(u)$, and any two v_i and v_j in $N_O(u)$ are in sibling relationship. Both neighbor relationship and sibling relationship play an important role in locality, since they will be accessed together. One fact is that the sibling relationship is a dominating factor since there are $d_O(u)$ neighbor relationships and $\binom{d_O(u)}{2}$ combinations of sibling relationships, and $\binom{d_O(u)}{2} \gg d_O(u)$ in general. In order to measure the closeness of two nodes, u and v, in terms of locality, we define a score function.

$$S(u,v) = S_s(u,v) + S_n(u,v) \tag{1}$$

Here, $S_s(u,v)$ is the number of the times that u and v co-exist in sibling relationships, which is the number of their common in-neighbors, $|N_I(u) \cap N_I(v)|$. And $S_n(u,v)$ is the number of times that u and v in the neighbor relationship, which is either 0, 1, or 2, since both edge (u,v) and (v,u) may co-exist in a directed graph. One thing about the score function is that two nodes should be considered to be placed together, if they are in many sibling relationship, even though there is no edge between them.

Based on the score function, our problem is to maximize the locality of two nodes to be placed closely. And this is to find a permutation function $\phi(\cdot)$, to maximize the sum of the score, $S(\cdot)$, for close node pairs in G, where $\phi(u)$ assigns every node u with an unique number in $[1, n]$, assume there are n nodes in G.

Problem Statement: Find the optimal graph ordering (permutation), $\phi(\cdot)$, that maximizes Gscore (the sum of locality score), $F(\cdot)$,

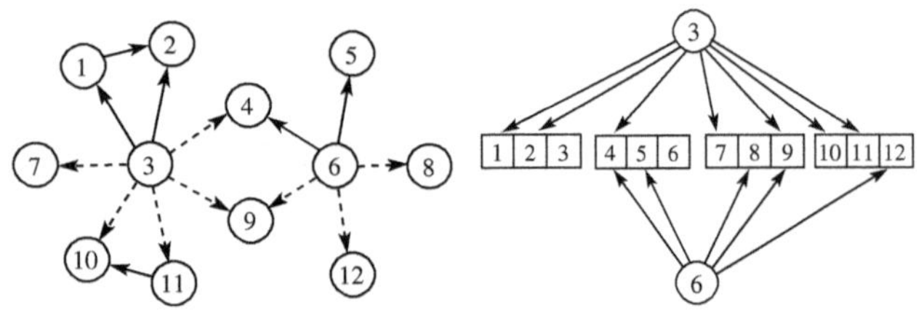

(a) Minimize Edge-Cuts (b) Graph Partition

Figure 3: By Graph Partitioning

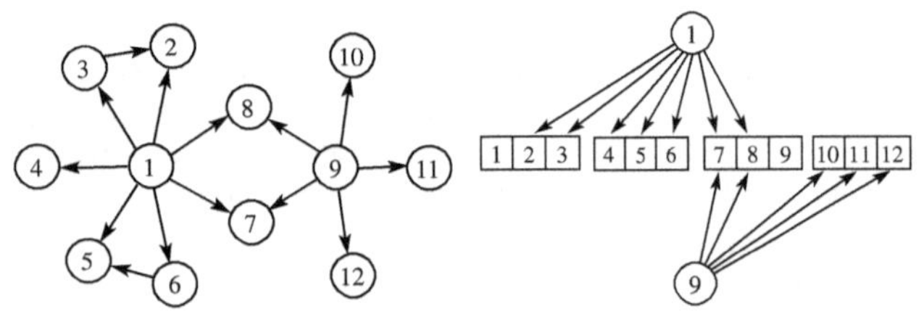

(a) Maximize $F(\phi)$ (b) Partition Representation

Figure 4: By Graph Ordering

based on a sliding window model with a window size w.

$$F(\phi) = \sum_{0<\phi(v)-\phi(u)\leq w} S(u,v) \tag{2}$$

$$= \sum_{i=1}^{n} \sum_{j=\max\{1,i-w\}}^{i-1} S(v_i, v_j) \tag{3}$$

We discuss more on the problem formulation. We adopt a sliding window model with a window size w ($w > 0$). Assume two nodes, u and v, are assigned with IDs in the graph ordering, denoted as $\phi(u)$ and $\phi(v)$, and u appears before v ($\phi(v) > \phi(u)$). With the sliding window, for any node v in G, as a pivot, we maximize the score function $S(u, v)$ for the pair of node v and any other node u in G that appears before v in the sliding window of size w (Eq.(2)). In fact, implicitly by the sliding window, at the same time, we also maximize $S(u, v)$ for the pair of node v and any other node u in G that appears after v, where the role of u and v are reversed when u becomes a pivot. Suppose $\phi(v_i) = i$. Eq. (2) can be rewritten as Eq. (3). Let ϕ_w denotes a permutation ϕ maximizing $F(\phi)$ with a window size w. It is worth noting that $F(\phi_w)$ will be different for a different window size w and $F(\phi_w) > F(\phi_{w'})$ if $w > w'$. As confirmed in our testings, we use $w = 5$, which ensures high reduction of CPU cache miss ratio because two nodes within distance 5 is likely to be located in the same cache line.

The window used in graph ordering is different from the partition used in graph partitioning. The window we use is based on a sliding window, whereas the partition is a non-overlapping window. Consider graph partitioning. With the non-overlapping partitions, nodes within a partition can be placed randomly since they are considered locally and there is no difference where they are placed in the same partition. Furthermore, the last node in a partition can possibly be far away from the first node in its next partition, in terms of distance in graph. On the other hand, consider graph ordering, with the sliding window, the locality is considered for any node in a window before and after its appearance in a continuous way. Such continuity can significantly reduce the CPU catch miss ratio. Consider any two v_i and v_j, for $0 < j - i \leq 2w$, where $\phi(v_i) = i$ and $\phi(v_j) = j$. The overlap range of windows between them is $2w + 1 - (j - i)$. Such high overlapping increases the chances to reduce the CPU cache miss ratio.

Below, we show the difference between graph partitioning and graph ordering using the graph G in Fig. 2. As shown in Fig. 2, there are 12 nodes and 14 edges in G, and G is a power-law graph, which has two nodes, v_5 and v_7, with high out-degree, 7 and 5, respectively. Note that there is no edge between v_6 and v_9. But v_6 and v_9 are siblings and share two in-neighbors, v_5 and v_7. Here, every node v_i in G is with an ID of i, which is a graph permutation number. However, such a permutation given in Fig. 2 does not preserve much locality. For example, v_2 is placed before v_3, which is supposed to be accessed/computed together, but v_2 is far away from v_3 in graph. Assumed one CPU cache line holds 3 nodes. Let partition size and window size be 3.

Consider graph partitioning. We need to partition the graph G in Fig. 2 into 4 partitions by minimizing the number of edges across partitions. Based on the graph partitioning, we can obtain a graph permutation by assigning two nodes in the same partition with close permutation numbers. The optimal graph partitioning for G in Fig. 2 is illustrated in Fig. 3(a), where the two graphs in Fig. 2 and Fig. 3(a) have the identical topological structure but are with different permutations. As shown in Fig. 3(a), the edges shown as dash-lines are the edges that cross two partitions to be cut. There are 4 partitions, $\{v_1, v_2, v_3\}$, $\{v_4, v_5, v_6\}$, $\{v_7, v_8, v_9\}$, $\{v_{10}, v_{11}, v_{12}\}$ in Fig. 3(a). Fig. 3(b) shows the 4 partitions of Fig. 3(a). From Fig. 3(b), we can see that if a graph algorithm accesses the out-neighbors of node v_3, $N_O(v_3) = \{v_1, v_2, v_4, v_7, v_9, v_{10}, v_{11}\}$, it needs to access all the 4 partitions in 4 CPU cache lines. If it needs to access the out-neighbors of node v_6, $N_O(v_6) = \{v_4, v_5, v_8, v_9, v_{12}\}$, it needs to access 3 partitions in 3 CPU cache lines.

Consider graph ordering. Fig. 4(a) shows the optimal permutation by graph ordering that maximizes $F(\phi)$, with the window size $w = 3$, for G shown in Fig. 2, where the two graphs in Fig. 2 and Fig. 4(a) have the identical topological structure but are with different permutations. Fig. 4(b) shows the 4 partitions of Fig. 4(a), as the result of graph ordering. From Fig. 4(b), we can see that if the graph algorithm accesses the out-neighbors of node v_1, $N_O(v_1) = \{v_2, v_3, v_4, v_5, v_6, v_7, v_8\}$, it needs to access 3 CPU cache lines. If the graph algorithm needs to access the out-neighbors of node v_9, $N_O(v_9) = \{v_7, v_8, v_{10}, v_{11}, v_{12}\}$, it needs to access 2 CPU cache lines. The graph ordering outperforms graph partitioning as shown in this example.

An acute reader may find that the graph ordering problem we study in this work can be solved by graph partitioning. First, we show that it is possible provided the partition size is given. In graph ordering, the score function $S(\cdot)$ (Eq. (1)) takes both neighbor relations and sibling relations, whereas graph partitioning is to minimize the edge cut, which implies that the neighbor relationship, $S_n(u, v)$, is the only concern. For graph partitioning to deal with the sibling relationships, $S_s(u, v)$, it can convert G into a graph G' by adding all edges between every pair of v_i and v_j if they are siblings. In this way, graph partitioning by minimizing the number of edges across different partitions in G' can be considered as a way to determine a graph permutation. Second, we show that it is infeasible in practice, since the number of edges in G' can be huge. Supposed a node u has 100,000 out-neighbors in a graph. The number of additional edges in G' to represent the sibling relationships of u will be up to 10 billion, which is unacceptable for both the computation cost and the space cost.

The graph ordering problem of maximizing $F(\phi)$ is NP-hard.

Theorem 2.1: *Maximizing $F(\phi)$ to obtain an optimal permutation $\phi(\cdot)$ for a directed graph G is NP-hard.*

The proof sketch is given in Appendix.

3. THE ALGORITHMS

In this section, we focus on efficient algorithms and data structures for solving the graph ordering problem for large graphs with millions/billions of nodes and edges. We give approximate algorithms due to the NP-hard time complexity of the problem.

The optimal graph ordering, for the window size $w = 1$, by maximizing $F(\phi)$ is equivalent to the maximum traveling salesman problem, denoted as *maxTSP* for short. Serdyukov proposes a $\frac{3}{4}$-approximation algorithm for *maxTSP* in [46]. It needs $O(n^3)$ time complexity to compute the maximum cycle cover and maximum matching which is too costly for large graphs. Alternatively, Fisher et al. propose the best-neighbor heuristic, to achieve $\frac{1}{2}$-approximation for the *maxTSP* in [21]. It starts with a randomly chosen node, and inserts it into a queue. Then, it greedily selects a node that has the maximum edge weight with the node just inserted into the queue repeatedly.

In general, the problem of finding the optimal graph ordering by maximizing $F(\phi)$ is the problem of solving *maxTSP-w* with a window size w as a variant of the *maxTSP* problem. To solve the graph ordering problem as *maxTSP-w*, we can construct an edge-weighted complete undirected graph G_w from G. Here, $V(G_w) = V(G)$, and there is an edge $(v_i, v_j) \in E(G_w)$ for any pair of nodes in $V(G_w)$. The edge-weight for an edge (v_i, v_j) in G_w, denoted as s_{ij}, is $S(v_i, v_j)$ computed for the two nodes in the original graph G. Then the optimal *maxTSP-w* over G is the solution of *maxTSP* over G. Note that *maxTSP* only cares the weight between two adjacent nodes, whereas *maxTSP-w* cares the sum of weights within a window of size w.

In this work, instead of constructing the large complete graph G_w, we adapt the main idea of the best-neighbor heuristic that used to solve *maxTSP* to deal with graph ordering as *maxTSP-w* for a window size $w > 1$. We adapt the best-neighbor heuristic, because it can be used to deal with large graphs with millions/billions of nodes and edges, even though the best-neighbor heuristic is $\frac{1}{2}$-approximation, which is worse than $\frac{3}{4}$-approximation by Serdyukov's algorithm [46]. In fact, it is difficult to extend the Serdyukov's algorithm to deal with the case that $w > 1$ in general.

3.1 The *GO* Algorithm

We give an approximate algorithm to compute a graph ordering ϕ by maximizing $F(\phi)$. Maximizing $F(\phi)$ is done by greedily inserting the node v that has the largest score $\sum S(u, v)$ with nodes u that have recently inserted in the window with size w repeatedly, based on the idea of the best-neighbor heuristic. The algorithm is called *GO* (Graph Ordering) and is given in Algorithm 1. The algorithm takes three inputs, the graph G, the window size w, and the score function $S(\cdot,\cdot)$ (Eq.(1)). Given an array P of size n, the node v placed at $P[i]$ is assigned to a permutation number i. The algorithm first randomly selects a node v, and inserts it into $P[1]$ as the first node in the permutation (line 1). Let V_R represents the set of nodes for the remaining nodes that have not yet been inserted into the array of P. In the while statement line 3-10 when finding the node v_i that should be placed at $P[i]$, it computes the sum of score k_v for every $v \in V_R$

$$k_v = \sum_{j=\max\{1,i-w\}}^{i-1} S(v_j, v) \tag{4}$$

where v_j is a node in the window of size w that has been inserted before v_i, represented as $P[j]$ in the *GO* algorithm. The node v_{max} is the node with the largest k_v selected from V_R. The algorithm inserts the node v_{max} into $P[i]$ repeatedly, and terminates until all nodes in G are placed in P. The permutation ϕ is obtained such that $\phi(v) = i$, if v is placed at $P[i]$.

Algorithm 1 *GO* $(G, w, S(\cdot,\cdot))$

1: select a node v as the start node, $P[1] \leftarrow v$;
2: $V_R \leftarrow V(G) \setminus \{v\}$, $i \leftarrow 2$;
3: **while** $i \leq n$ **do**
4:     $v_{max} \leftarrow \emptyset$, $k_{max} \leftarrow -\infty$;
5:     **for each node** $v \in V_R$ **do**
6:         $k_v \leftarrow \sum_{j=\max\{1,i-w\}}^{i-1} S(P[j], v)$;
7:         **if** $k_v > k_{max}$ **then**
8:             $v_{max} \leftarrow v$, $k_{max} \leftarrow k_v$;
9:     $P[i] \leftarrow v_{max}$, $i \leftarrow i + 1$;
10:    $V_R \leftarrow V_R \setminus \{v_{max}\}$;

We discuss the approximation of the algorithm *GO*, and give the approximation of *GO* in Theorem 3.1.

Theorem 3.1: *The algorithm GO gives $\frac{1}{2w}$-approximation for maximizing $F(\phi)$ to determine the optimal graph ordering.*

Proof Sketch: The optimal graph ordering with a window size w is the same with the optimal *maxTSP-w* problem, except that the former takes the permutation and the latter tries to find a circuit. Let F_w denotes the score of the optimal solution on G for *maxTSP-w* problem. And let F_{go} denotes the Gscore $F(\cdot)$ of the graph ordering by the *GO* algorithm. We give an upper bound $\overline{F}_w$ of F_w by formulating the below optimization problem.

$$\begin{aligned} \overline{F}_w = \quad & \text{maximize} \quad \sum_{i=1}^{n-1} \sum_{j>i} s_{ij} x_{ij} \\ & \text{subject to} \quad \sum_{j>i} x_{ij} + \sum_{j<i} x_{ji} = 2w, i \in [1, n] \\ & \qquad\qquad 0 \leq x_{ij} \leq 1, \qquad i, j \in [1, n] \end{aligned} \tag{5}$$

Here, s_{ij} represents $S(v_i, v_j)$ between nodes v_i and v_j in G. On one hand, the optimal solution of *maxTSP-w* is a feasible solution of Eq. (5), which satisfies the two constraints by setting $x_{ij} = 1$ if v_i and v_j are located within the window of size w, and $x_{ij} = 0$ otherwise. On the other hand, Eq. (5) is a generalized form of *maxTSP-w* problem. This is because it only requires $\sum_{j>i} x_{ij} + \sum_{j<i} x_{ji} = 2w$, for any $i \in [1, n]$. In other words, consider v_i and let W_i denotes the set of w nodes before v_i, plus the set of w nodes after v_i, and plus v_i itself, such that $|W_i| = 2w + 1$. Eq. (5) finds the max $\overline{F}_w$ where it is possible that $W_i \cap W_{i+1} = \emptyset$ for two adjacent nodes v_i and v_{i+1}. However, the *maxTSP-w* problem requires that $|W_i \cap W_{i+1}| = |W_i| - 1$. Besides, x_{ij} is not required to be either 0 or 1. Hence, we have $F_w \leq \overline{F}_w$. We further give an upper bound of $\overline{F}_w$ by the Lagrangian duality.

$$\begin{aligned} \overline{F}_w &\leq \max_{0 \leq x_{ij} \leq 1} \sum_{i=1}^{n-1} \sum_{j>i} s_{ij} x_{ij} + \sum_{i=1}^{n} \alpha_i (2w - \sum_{j>i} x_{ij} - \sum_{j<i} x_{ji}) \\ &= \max_{0 \leq x_{ij} \leq 1} \sum_{i=1}^{n-1} \sum_{j>i} (s_{ij} - \alpha_i - \alpha_j) x_{ij} + 2w \sum_{i=1}^{n} \alpha_i \end{aligned} \tag{6}$$

Here, α_i is the Lagrange multiplier and Eq. (6) is true for all $\alpha_i \in R$. Assume the graph ordering by *GO* is $v_1, v_2, \cdots, v_n$, where $\phi(v_i) = i$. In Eq. (6), α_i is given as the sum of the weights between v_{i+1} and the last up to w just before v_{i+1} by *GO* algorithm, such that $\alpha_i = \sum_{j=\max\{1,i-w+1\}}^{i} s_{j,i+1}$ for $i \in [1, n-1]$ and $\alpha_n = 0$.

We have $\alpha_i \geq 0$ and $\sum_{i=1}^{n} \alpha_i = F_{go}$. Since v_i is placed before v_j in the graph ordering by the algorithm *GO* for $1 \leq i < j \leq n$, we have $s_{ij} - \alpha_i \leq 0$ according to the best-neighbor heuristic, and hence $s_{ij} - \alpha_i - \alpha_j \leq 0$. Therefore, we have $F_w \leq \overline{F}_w \leq 2w \sum_{i=1}^{n} \alpha_i = 2w \cdot F_{go}$, which leads to the $\frac{1}{2w}$-approximation. □

In practice, we find that the lower bound of the approximation ratio of *GO* does not reflect the real performance of *GO*, and the Gscore F_{go} of the graph ordering by *GO* is very close to the optimal result. For the graph in Fig. 2, F_{go}, the optimal score F_w, and the upper bound of the optimal score $\overline{F}_w$ by Eq. (5) are 27, 32, and 35, respectively, with $w = 3$. We also compare F_{go} with the upper bound of the optimal score $\overline{F}_w$ using real datasets, since the optimal score F_w cannot be computed due to the NP-hard complexity. We analyze two small datasets: Facebook with 4,039 nodes and 88,234 edges from SNAP[1] and AirTrafficControl with 1,226 nodes and 2,615 edges from KONECT[2], given Eq. (5) needs $O(n^2)$ variables and $O(n)$ constraints. Table 1 shows F_{go} and $\overline{F}_w$ with different w. We can see that $F_{go}/\overline{F}_w$ is larger than 0.6, which indicates that the real performance of F_{go} is very close to the optimal score F_w in large graphs, given $F_{go} \leq F_w \leq \overline{F}_w$.

	$w=3$		$w=5$		$w=7$	
	F_{go}	$\overline{F}_w$	F_{go}	$\overline{F}_w$	F_{go}	$\overline{F}_w$
Facebook	149,073	172,526	231,710	275,974	308,091	373,685
AirTraffic	2,420	3,468	2,993	4,697	3,465	5,545

Table 1: F_{go} **and** $\overline{F}_w$

Theorem 3.2: *The GO Algorithm 1 is in* $O(w \cdot d_{max} \cdot n^2)$*, where* d_{max} *denotes the maximum in-degree of the graph G.*

The proof sketch is given in Appendix.

3.2 The Priority Queue based Algorithm

The computational cost of the *GO* algorithm is high as given in Theorem 3.2 in $O(w \cdot d_{max} \cdot n^2)$ where d_{max} is the maximum in-degree of G. The *GO* algorithm is impractical to be used to compute graph ordering for large graphs. The high computational cost is contributed by line 5-6 in Algorithm 1. We discuss it from two aspects. First, it repeatedly computes Eq. (4) w times for the same pair (v_j, v) while v_j is in the window of size w. Second, it scans every node v in the set of remaining nodes V_R in every iteration when computing Eq. (4). In other words, it scans every node $v \in V_R$ that has neighbor/sibling relationship with the nodes v_j in the window of size w, as well as the nodes v that has no neighbor/sibling relationship with the nodes v_j in the window of size w. Obviously, the latter is unnecessary. We give Example-A in the Appendix to discuss the two drawbacks in details.

Based on the observations, we propose a priority queue (PQ) based algorithm called *GO-PQ* (Algorithm 2). Like *GO*, we use an array of P to keep the graph ordering (permutation). The permutation ϕ is obtained such that $\phi(v) = i$, if v is placed at $P[i]$. Unlike *GO*, we efficiently compute line 5-6 in Algorithm 1, using a priority queue denoted as $\mathcal{Q}$. In the priority queue, $\mathcal{Q}[v]$ keeps a key which is k_v (Eq.(4)) for node v during computing, and the node v_{max} with the largest k_{max} will be popped up first from $\mathcal{Q}$ to be appended at the end of P. Consider two nodes, u and v in $\mathcal{Q}$, u will appear before v (or in other words pop before v), if $k_u > k_v$ regarding the current window of size w. We denote the key of v by $\mathsf{key}(v)$. In computing the graph ordering, to address the two drawbacks of *GO*, we incrementally update $\mathsf{key}(v)$ regarding the sliding windows shown below.

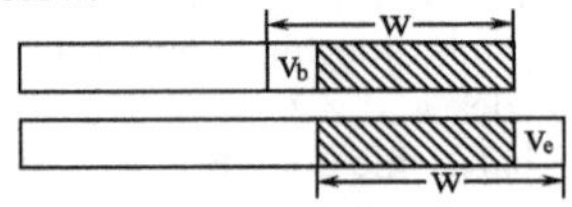

While the window is sliding, suppose v_b is the node to leave the window, and v_e is the node to join the window. We incrementally update $\mathsf{key}(v)$ for v in three ways.

Increase key: When v_e is newly placed in the permutation P, v in $\mathcal{Q}$ will increase its key value by 1 if v and v_e are considered local, based on the neighbor/sibling relationship. For the neighbor relationship, it means either there is an edge from v to v_e or there is an edge from v_e to v. For the sibling relationships, it means v and v_e share a common in-neighbor node. We denote the key increment by 1 for v in $\mathcal{Q}$ as $\mathcal{Q}.\mathsf{incKey}(v)$.

Decrease key: When v_b is about to leave the window while the window is sliding to the next position, v in $\mathcal{Q}$ will decrease its key value by 1 if v and v_b are considered local, based on the neighbor/sibling relationship as discussed in the case for increasing key. We denote the key decrement by 1 for v in $\mathcal{Q}$ as $\mathcal{Q}.\mathsf{decKey}(v)$. The updating ensures that the node to be selected next from $\mathcal{Q}$ is the one v_{max} with the largest k_{max} among the nodes that have not been selected.

Find the max key: Finding the node v_{max} with largest k_v (Eq. (4)) from the set of remaining nodes is to pop up the top node from $\mathcal{Q}$. We denote it by $\mathcal{Q}.\mathsf{pop}()$.

The *GO-PQ* algorithm is given in Algorithm 2, which uses these three operations as shown in line 6-20 to replace line 5-6 of Algorithm 1 by *GO*. The *GO-PQ* algorithm gives the same result of *GO* with the same $\frac{1}{2w}$-approximation for a window of size w.

The *GO-PQ* algorithm takes the same three inputs, the graph G, the window size w, and the score function $S(\cdot,\cdot)$ (Eq.(1)). Given an array P of size n, the node v placed at $P[i]$ is assigned to a permutation number i. In *GO-PQ*, initially, it inserts all nodes of G into the priority queue $\mathcal{Q}$ where the key of each node is initialized to be zero. Then, it randomly selects a node v, and inserts it into $P[1]$ as the first node in the permutation before deleting the node v from $\mathcal{Q}$ (line 3). In the while loop (line 5-22), it updates the keys of the nodes only if they are related to two nodes, v_b and v_e, where v_b is the node to leave the sliding window, and v_e is the node to join the sliding window. In brief, first, in line 7-12, regarding v_e, if a node u is a neighbor of v_e, it increases its key by $\mathsf{incKey}(u)$; and if a node v is a sibling of v_e, it increases its key by $\mathsf{incKey}(v)$. Second, in line 13-20, regarding v_b, if a node u is a neighbor of v_b, it decreases its key by $\mathsf{decKey}(u)$; and if a node v is a sibling of v_b, it decreases its key by $\mathsf{decKey}(v)$. Finally, following the updates, in the while loop, it places the node v_{max} into the array P where v_{max} is selected by popping the top node from $\mathcal{Q}$ line 21. A example is given in Example-B in the Appendix.

Compared with *GO*, *GO-PQ* significantly reduces the computational cost. We give the time complexity of *GO-PQ* algorithm in Theorem 3.3.

Theorem 3.3: *The time complexity of the GO-PQ algorithm is* $O(\mu \cdot \sum_{u \in V}(d_O(u))^2 + n \cdot \varrho)$*, where* μ *denotes the time complexity for the updates* ($\mathsf{incKey}(\cdot)$ *and* $\mathsf{decKey}(\cdot)$) *and* ϱ *denotes the time complexity for finding the max node* ($\mathsf{pop}()$).

The proof sketch is given in Appendix.

We will discuss the priority queue $\mathcal{Q}$ itself and its operations in Section 3.3. Below, we discuss the effectiveness of the window size w, selecting the first node, reducing the computational cost for updates, and dealing with huge nodes that have large outdegree.

[1]snap.stanford.edu/

[2]konect.uni-koblenz.de/networks/

Algorithm 2 *GO-PQ* $(G, w, S(\cdot,\cdot))$

```
1: for each node v ∈ V(G) do
2:     insert v into Q such that key(v) ← 0;
3: select a node v as the start node, P[1] ← v, delete v from Q;
4: i ← 2;
5: while i ≤ n do
6:     v_e ← P[i − 1];
7:     for each node u ∈ N_O(v_e) do
8:         if u ∈ Q then Q.incKey(u);
9:     for each node u ∈ N_I(v_e) do
10:        if u ∈ Q then Q.incKey(u);
11:        for each node v ∈ N_O(u) do
12:            if v ∈ Q then Q.incKey(v);
13:    if i > w + 1 then
14:        v_b ← P[i − w − 1];
15:        for each node u ∈ N_O(v_b) do
16:            if u ∈ Q then Q.decKey(u);
17:        for each node u ∈ N_I(v_b) do
18:            if u ∈ Q then Q.decKey(u);
19:            for each node v ∈ N_O(u) do
20:                if v ∈ Q then Q.decKey(v);
21:    v_max ← Q.pop();
22:    P[i] ← v_max, i ← i + 1;
```

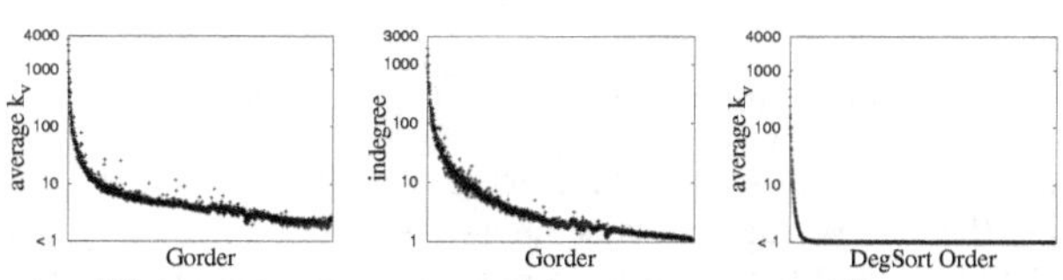

(a) $S()$ by *GO-PQ* (b) $d_I(u)$ Distri. (c) $S()$ by degsort

Figure 5: The Permutation and its In-degree Distri. on Flickr

Effectiveness of the window size w: It is important to note that the approximation of *GO* and *GO-PQ* is the same $\frac{1}{2w}$-approximation as proved. In *GO-PQ*, the window size w determines how the node v_b is defined which is related to k_v (Eq. (4)). However, in *GO-PQ*, the time complexity is not related to w. In other words, the window size w has no impacts on the time complexity.

Selecting the first node: The selection of the first node has impacts on the overall graph ordering. We select the node v_1 with the largest in-degree as the first node to start the ordering for the following two reasons. First, the node v_1 with the largest in-degree $d_I(v_1)$ (or largest $N_I(v_1)$) indicates that v_1 is highly likely to be a sibling node of another node v_i that shares common in-neighbor nodes in $N_I(v_1)$. Second, because $N_I(v_1)$ is large, v_1 will be frequently accessed together with its sibling nodes in the graph computing because there are a large number of in-coming edges pointing to v_1. The first node selected will lead the nodes selected in the following, and the nodes selected in the following iterations are more likely to be large in-degree nodes. Given the Flickr dataset with over 2.3M nodes, we compute the permutation by *GO-PQ*, denoted as Gorder, and show the in-degree distribution and the average scores of nodes comparing with the average scores of nodes by sorting nodes with decreasing in-degree in Fig. 5. In Fig. 5, a value in x-axis represents 1,000 nodes, and a value in y-axis represents the average k_v for the 1,000 nodes. Fig. 5(a) and Fig. 5(b) show the average score (Eq. (4)) and the average in-degree (d_I) of every 1,000 nodes. The nodes appear on the top of the permutation are with high score and high in-degree, and they are supposed to be locally stored in main memory following the permutation. Such high $F(\cdot)$ by summing all the score (Eq. (4)) cannot be achieved by simply sorting all nodes by in-degree, as shown in Fig. 5(c).

Reducing the computational cost: In *GO-PQ*, we have shown the main idea of the PQ-based algorithm. We can further reduce computational cost to make it efficient. Consider a node u that is a common in-neighbors of the two nodes, v_e and v_b, in the window before v_b leaves. In Algorithm 2, it first does incKey(v) w.r.t v_e followed by decKey(v) w.r.t v_b for every node in $N_O(u)$. Obviously, such pair of incKey(v) and decKey(v), will not change the key of such node v in $N_I(u)$, and such computing is unnecessary. To avoid such unnecessary computing, we can simply add the condition of "**if** $v_b \notin N_O(u)$ **then**" for line 11-12 to ensure that line 11-12 will only be executed when the condition is true. In a similar way, we add the condition of "**if** $v_e \notin N_O(u)$ **then**" for line 19-20 to ensure that line 19-20 will only be executed when the condition is true. In practice, since the window size w is rather small and v_e and v_b share many in-neighbors due to their close positions in the permutation, this can reduce cost significantly.

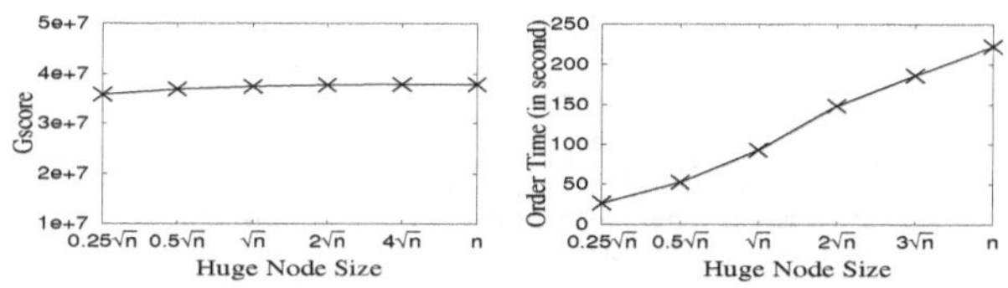

(a) Gscore (b) Graph Ordering Time

Figure 6: Huge Nodes on Flickr

Dealing with huge nodes: Real large graphs follow power-law degree distribution, with a small number of nodes having a large out-degree and a large number of nodes having a small out-degree. Supposed a node u has a large set of out-neighbors, $N_O(u)$. When one of its out-neighbors, $v \in N_O(u)$, is to join in/leave from the window, the key of every out-neighbor in $N_O(u)$ needs to update (line 11-12 and line 19-20 in Algorithm 2). This incurs high overhead for nodes that are with high out-degree $d_O(u)$, which is also indicated by the time complexity $O(\sum_u (d_O(u))^2)$. In this work, we take a high out-degree node as a **huge node** if its out-degree is greater than $\sqrt{n}$. For a large graph with millions of nodes, $\sqrt{n}$ is at least 1,000. To save such high computational cost, we do not compute the huge nodes when updating the key for the out-neighbors of these huge nodes. This is to add the condition of "**if** $d_O(u) \leq \sqrt{n}$ **then**" after line 9 and line 17 to ensure that line 10-12 and line 18-20 will only be executed when the condition is true. Such reduction of computing does not affect the quality of the chosen v_{max} to be placed into the array of P next, because the candidate nodes to be selected as v_{max} are likely to be the out-neighbors of huge nodes. Such reduction of computing those out-neighbors of huge nodes will reduce the similar amount of updates to all candidates that can possibly be the next v_{max}. Given two graph orderings, one is ϕ_1 by *GO-PQ* without special consideration to huge nodes, and the other is ϕ_2 by *GO-PQ* with special consideration to huge nodes discussed above. We measure the difference between the two using the Kendall tau coefficient [31]. Consider the two orderings ϕ_1 and ϕ_2, (v_i, v_j) is called the concordant pair if it is true that $\phi_1(v_i) > \phi_1(v_j)$ and $\phi_2(v_i) > \phi_2(v_j)$, or $\phi_1(v_i) < \phi_1(v_j)$ and $\phi_2(v_i) < \phi_2(v_j)$. Otherwise, (v_i, v_j) is called the discordant pair. Let C denotes the set of concordant pairs and D denotes the set of discordant pairs. The Kendall tau coefficient is

$$\tau(\phi_1, \phi_2) = \frac{2(|C| - |D|)}{n(n-1)} \quad (7)$$

where n is the size of permutation. The Kendall tau coefficient between ϕ_1 and ϕ_2 over Flickr is 0.7. This suggests that reduction of computing large out-degree nodes does not affect the quality of graph ordering obtained. In addition, on Flickr, we show the total score $F(\cdot)$ and the time to compute such $F(\cdot)$ for different huge

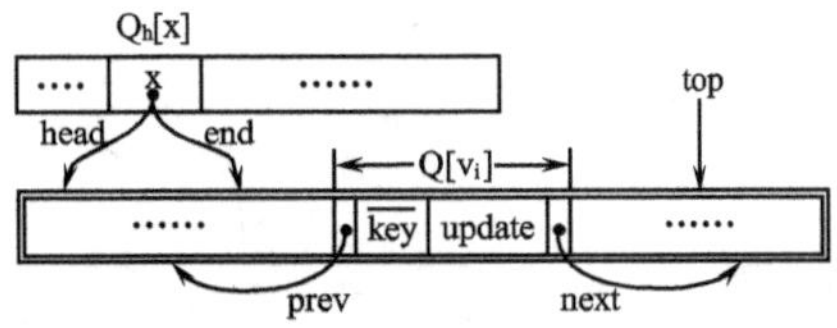

Figure 7: The Priority Queue: $\mathcal{Q}$, $\mathcal{Q}_h$, and top

node sizes in Fig. 6, where a huge node v is a node such that $d_O(v)$ is greater than either $\frac{1}{4}\sqrt{n}$, $\frac{1}{2}\sqrt{n}$, $\sqrt{n}$, $2\sqrt{n}$, $4\sqrt{n}$, or n. Note that the last one, $d_O(v) > n$, means not to reduce computing cost for huge nodes, since no nodes can be pruned. In Fig. 6, the x-axis is $\frac{1}{4}\sqrt{n}$, $\frac{1}{2}\sqrt{n}$, $\sqrt{n}$, $2\sqrt{n}$, $4\sqrt{n}$, and n. We take $F(\cdot)$ and the computing time regarding the one without pruning as the basis. Fig. 6(a) shows that $F(\cdot)$ computed for different huge node sizes change marginally. However, Fig. 6(b) shows that the reduction of computing time is significant. One question is whether dealing with huge nodes affects the approximation ratio given in Theorem 3.1. On one hand, Fig. 6(a) shows that dealing with the huge nodes has little influence to the quality of the output graph ordering in practice, even though Algorithm 2 with the special consideration of huge nodes may possibly fail to choose the real v_{max} during the iterations. On the other hand, the theoretical guarantee by Theorem 3.1 is just a lower bound. As shown in datasets Facebook and AirTrafficControl in Section 3.1, $F(\cdot)$ of the output graph ordering is much better than the given theoretical guarantee in practice. Given the limit influence of huge nodes, the graph ordering generated by pruning the huge nodes can still be better than the bound given by Theorem 3.1.

3.3 The Priority Queue and its Operations

We discuss the priority queue $\mathcal{Q}$ and its operations. There are three operations, namely, incKey(v), decKey(v), and pop(). Behind the operations, there is an implicit operation that is to access the key of a node requested irrespective of its position in $\mathcal{Q}$. One way to design $\mathcal{Q}$ is to adapt the same data structure used in [10] as follows. First, to ensure accessing the key of a node v in constant time, the priority queue $\mathcal{Q}$ is designed as an array of the size n. Given a node v_i in the graph G, the key value is stored in $\mathcal{Q}[v_i]$. Second, in order to maintain the max value at the top, every node v_i may be re-positioned. To do so, $\mathcal{Q}$ is designed as a double-linked data structure. That is, in $\mathcal{Q}[v_i]$, where v_i is the original node ID, it has two pointers, namely, prev(v_i) and next(v_i), in addition to the key value of key(v_i). Third, to access nodes by a specific key value, on top of $\mathcal{Q}$, there is a head table, denoted as $\mathcal{Q}_h$, where $\mathcal{Q}_h[x]$ points to the first node in $\mathcal{Q}$ whose key is x. This data structure can be used to support incKey(), decKey(), and pop() in $O(1)$, $O(1)$, and $O(n)$, respectively. However, we observe that the number of pop() is much smaller than the number of incKey() and decKey(). Take the data structure used in [10] as an example. Although it can achieve $O(1)$ for updates by incKey() and decKey(), it needs to adjust the linked list for every incKey() and every decKey(), and the number of possible updates is $O(\sum_u (d_O(u))^2)$, which is very high.

The issue is whether we can reduce the number of times of adjusting the linked list while keeping the time complexity for all the three operations the same. In this paper, we propose a lazy-updating strategy by which we reduce the number of adjusting linked list significantly.

Fig. 7 shows the $\mathcal{Q}$ data structure we use in this work. First, in every $\mathcal{Q}[v_i]$, in addition to the two components, prev(v_i) and next(v_i), we use $\overline{\text{key}}(v_i)$ and update(v_i) together instead of maintaining key(v_i), such that key(v_i) $=$ $\overline{\text{key}}(v_i)$ $+$ update(v_i). The priority queue $\mathcal{Q}$ is represented as a doubly linked list by prev($\cdot$) and next($\cdot$) with decreasing $\overline{\text{key}}(\cdot)$ values. The main idea here is that when we update key values, we keep the difference in the update where possible. By this, we only adjust the doubly linked list when $\overline{\text{key}}(v_i)$ has to be changed, and do not adjust the doubly linked list for every updates. Second, in the head table $\mathcal{Q}_h$, we maintain two pointers in $\mathcal{Q}_h[x]$, namely, head(x) and end(x). Here, head(x) and end(x) point to the first and the last element in $\mathcal{Q}$ such that every node v that has the same key value (key(v) $= x$) is positioned between head(x) and end(x) in the doubly linked list. Note that the length of $\mathcal{Q}_h$ can be as large as the maximum key value, which is far smaller than n in practice. Third, we add a new pointer top that always points to the node having the largest $\overline{\text{key}}(\cdot)$.

With the above data structure, when popping v_{max}, we maintain the true key(v_i) for a node v_i by $\overline{\text{key}}(v_i)$ $+$ update(v_i) such that (a) for the top node, key(top) $=$ $\overline{\text{key}}$(top), and (b) for any other node v_i, key(v_i) $\leq$ $\overline{\text{key}}(v_i)$. Following the conditions below,

$$\begin{aligned} \text{update}(\text{top}) &= 0 \\ \text{update}(v_i) &\leq 0 \quad \text{for } v_i \neq \text{top} \\ \overline{\text{key}}(\text{top}) &\geq \overline{\text{key}}(v_i) \\ \overline{\text{key}}(\text{top}) + \text{update}(\text{top}) &\geq \overline{\text{key}}(v_i) + \text{update}(v_i) \end{aligned} \tag{8}$$

for any $v_i \neq$ top in $\mathcal{Q}$, we guarantee that the top in $\mathcal{Q}$ is the one having the largest true key value key($\cdot$). We do not need to adjust the doubly linked list when updating every time. There are only two cases we need to adjust the doubly linked list. First, when update(v_i) > 0 after updating v_i, we have to make update(v_i) ≤ 0. In this process, we do $\overline{\text{key}}(v_i) \leftarrow \overline{\text{key}}(v_i)$ $+$ update(v_i) and update(v_i) $\leftarrow 0$. Since $\overline{\text{key}}(v_i)$ is changed, we need to adjust the doubly linked list. Second, when selecting v_{max} to be popped, we make update(top) $= 0$ as given in Eq. (8), and therefore the adjustment of doubly linked list is needed.

Note that we increase the computational cost for pop marginally within the same time complexity of $O(n)$, and at the same time we significantly reduce the number of adjusting doubly linked list, since the number of updates is huge. We discuss the priority queue operations below.

First, for decKey(v_i), we only reduce the value in update(v_i) by 1 to maintain key(v_i) $=$ $\overline{\text{key}}(v_i)$ $+$ update(v_i). Here, since update(v_i) ≤ 0, there is no need to update $\overline{\text{key}}(v_i)$.

Algorithm 3 decKey (v_i)

1: update(v_i) $\leftarrow$ update(v_i) $- 1$;

Second, for incKey(v_i), we show it in Algorithm 4. We increase the update value by 1. We only adjust doubly linked list when update(v_i) > 0. Since at this point update(v_i) $= 1$, we increase $\overline{\text{key}}(v_i)$ by 1 and make update(v_i) $= 0$. This ensures $\overline{\text{key}}(v_i) = \overline{\text{key}}(v_i) +$ update(v_i) and update(v_i) ≤ 0. Also, since $\overline{\text{key}}(v_i)$ is changed, its position in $\mathcal{H}$ needs to be adjusted. We adjust the position by deleting/inserting it from/into $\mathcal{Q}$. Accordingly, we adjust the head table $\mathcal{Q}_h$ and adjust top if the new $\overline{\text{key}}(v_i)$ is greater than $\overline{\text{key}}$(top), if needed.

Third, for pop() (Algorithm 5), recall that the true key(top) is $\overline{\text{key}}$(top) if update(top) $= 0$, because key(top) $=$ $\overline{\text{key}}$(top) $+$ update(top). When popping the node with the max true key value, we simply return the node pointed by top if update(top) $= 0$. However, when update(top) < 0, we need to check whether the node pointed by top is the node with the max true key value. (i) we make $\overline{\text{key}}(v_i)$ as the true key value by $\overline{\text{key}}(v_i) \leftarrow \overline{\text{key}}(v_i) +$

Algorithm 4 incKey (v_i)

1: update(v_i) $\leftarrow$ update(v_i) + 1;
2: **if** update(v_i) > 0 **then**
3: update(v_i) $\leftarrow 0$, $x \leftarrow \overline{\text{key}}(v_i)$, $\overline{\text{key}}(v_i) \leftarrow \overline{\text{key}}(v_i) + 1$;
4: delete v_i from $\mathcal{Q}$;
5: insert v_i into $\mathcal{Q}$ in the position just before head$[x]$;
6: update the head $\mathcal{Q}_h$ array accordingly;
7: **if** $\overline{\text{key}}(v_i) > \overline{\text{key}}(\text{top})$ **then**
8: top $\leftarrow v_i$;

Algorithm 5 pop ()

1: **while** update(top) < 0 **do**
2: $v_t \leftarrow$ top;
3: $\overline{\text{key}}(v_t) \leftarrow \overline{\text{key}}(v_t)$ + update(v_t);
4: update(v_t) $\leftarrow 0$;
5: **if** $\overline{\text{key}}(\text{top}) \leq \overline{\text{key}}(\text{next(top)})$ **then**
6: adjust the position of v_t and insert v_t just after u in $\mathcal{Q}$, such that $\overline{\text{key}}(u) \geq \overline{\text{key}}(\text{top})$ and $\overline{\text{key}}(\text{next}(u)) < \overline{\text{key}}(\text{top})$;
7: top $\leftarrow$ next(top);
8: update the head array;
9: $v_t \leftarrow$ top;
10: remove the node pointed by top from $\mathcal{Q}$ and update top $\leftarrow$ next(top);
11: **return** v_t;

update(v_i) followed by changing update(v_i) to be zero (line 3-4). (ii) we reposition the node v_t pointed by the current top to a new position in $\mathcal{Q}$ following the sorting order of the $\overline{\text{key}}$ values, and update top pointer to point to the node having the largest $\overline{\text{key}}$ value currently. We repeat it until update(top) = 0. The node returned by pop() is the node with the max true key value.

An example is given in Example-C in the Appendix.

Given the specific priority queue operations, we show the time complexity of *GO-PQ* below.

Theorem 3.4: *The time complexity of GO-PQ is* $O(\sum_{u \in V}(d_O(u))^2)$.

The proof sketch is given in Appendix.

The Constant factor: Comparing the data structure used in [10], the key difference is we shift the cost from updates (incKey and decKey) to pop while keeping all the operations in the same time complexity. The reason is that the number of updates (decKey(v_i) and incKey(v_i)) is much larger than the number of pop(). The former is $O(\sum_{u \in V}(d_O(u))^2)$ whereas the latter is $O(n)$. Note that pop() (Algorithm 5) only takes a few iterations for the while loop to stop in practice, because the linked list is sorted in the decreasing order of $\overline{key}$, even though it is $O(n)$. We discuss how much we can save in updates. Since decKey(v_i) only needs to update update(v_i) in constant time $O(1)$, we focus on Algorithm 4 for incKey(v_i). There is a condition of update > 0 in line 2. The adjustment of doubly linked list is done only when the condition is true. The question is how much we can save by this condition. To analyze the saving, we consider a key update sequence by incKey(v_i) and decKey(v_i) for a given v_i before v_i is adjusted by pop. During the period in $\mathcal{Q}$, the number of incKey(v_i) depends on the insertion of node v_e into the window, and the number of decKey(v_i) depends on the deletion of node v_b from the window, and v_e will become v_b after w iterations. Therefore, in the sequence, the number of incKey(v_i) is similar to the number of decKey(v_i). Based on this observation, we assume that the key updates on a given v_i has 0.5 probability to be incKey and 0.5 probability to be decKey. Suppose the total number of updates for a given node v_i is L, and the total number of updates that need to adjust the doubly linked list following the condition of update(v_i) > 0 is $\lambda_{v_i}^L$. There are two extreme cases of the key update sequence with the equal numbers of incKey and decKey w.r.t. a node v_i. Let +1 and -1 represent incKey and decKey. The best case: incKey and decKey occur one by one alternatively in the sequence, (+1, -1, +1, -1, ...). Here, the first incKey triggers the adjustment of doubly linked list and sets update(v_i) to be 0. In the following sequence, for any update, update(v_i) ≤ 0 because the sum of its previous operations is ≤ 0, and therefore no adjustment is needed. The total number of doubly linked list needed is 1 not matter how large L is. The worst case: all incKey followed by all decKey. Here, we need to adjust the doubly linked list for every incKey in total of $\frac{L}{2}$ times. We can save a half of link adjustments in the worst case. Below we show the worst case hardly occurs, and give the expected number of adjustments $\lambda_{v_i}^L$ in Theorem 3.5.

Dataset	$\lvert V(G) \rvert$	$\lvert E(G) \rvert$	d_{avg}
Pokec	1.63M	30.62M	18.8
Flickr	2.30M	33.14M	14.4
LiveJournal	4.84M	68.47M	14.1
wikilink	11.19M	340.24M	30.4
Google+	28.94M	462.99M	16.0
pld-arc	42.88M	623.05M	14.5
twitter	61.57M	1,468.00M	23.8
sd1-arc	94.94M	1,937.00M	20.4

Table 2: Real Graphs

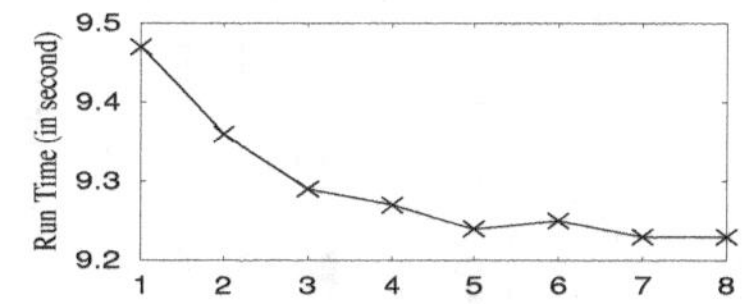

Figure 8: Window Size w

Theorem 3.5: *For a given node v_i over the random key update sequence of length L on v_i, and a sufficiently large L, the expected number of adjusting doubly linked list is as follows.*

$$E(\lambda_{v_i}^L) \sim \sqrt{\frac{2L}{\pi}} \quad (9)$$

The proof sketch is given in Appendix.

We tested the performance of lazy-update strategy in Flickr. There are over 8 billion key update operations in total. By our lazy-update strategy, only 0.66 billion key updates really trigger the adjustments of doubly linked list, and about 40% computing time is saved as shown in Section 4. This indicates that the constant factor of key update operations by *GO-PQ* is very small, which allows us to handle large graphs with billions of nodes and edges.

Finally, the space complexity of *GO-PQ* is $O(n)$, because the size of the priority queue is linear with the number of nodes, and array P keeping the output permutation result is at most as large as the node set.

4. EVALUATION

We evaluate our Gorder by the *GO-PQ* algorithm, in comparison with other 9 ordering approaches, using 8 real large graphs and 9 graph algorithms. The graph data is stored in *compressed sparse row* (CSR) format [1], which is equivalent to adjacency list. All implementations for graph algorithms and graph orderings are done using C++ and compiled by G++ 4.9.2. The extensive experiments have been conducted on two machines, (a) a Linux server with Intel Core i7-4770@3.40GHz CPU and 32 GB memory, (b) a Linux server with Intel Xeon X5550@2.67GHz CPU and 24 GB memory. We report our findings on the configuration of (a), since all the results obtained in these two machines are similar. The L1, L2, L3 cache size of the machine (a) is 64KB, 256KB, 8MB, re-

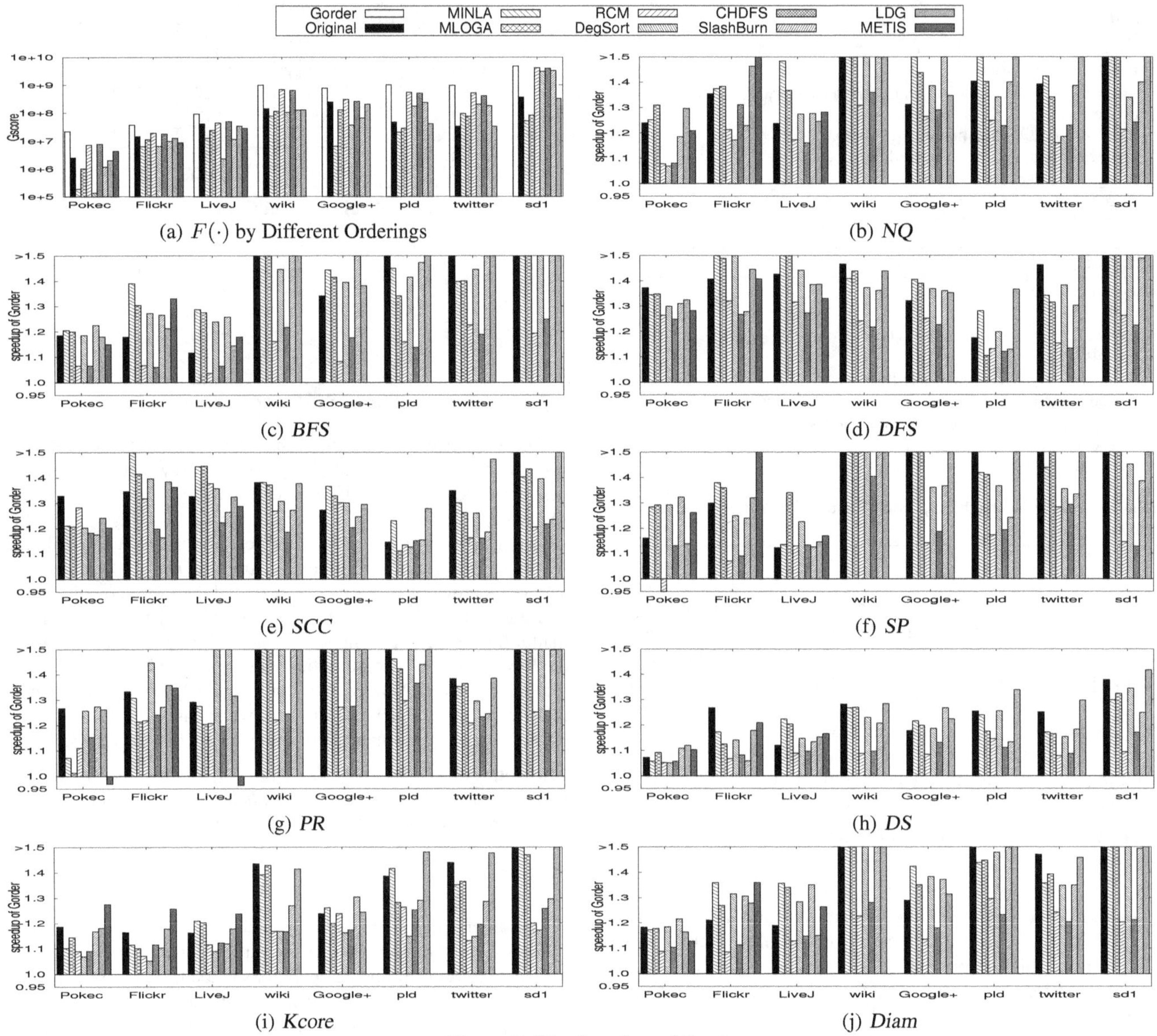

Figure 9: The Speedup of Gorder

Order	L1-ref	L1-mr	L3-ref	L3-r	Cache-mr
Original	11,109M	52.1%	2,195M	19.7%	5.1%
MINLA	11,110M	58.1%	2,121M	19.0%	4.5%
MLOGA	11,119M	53.1%	1,685M	15.1%	4.1%
RCM	11,102M	49.8%	1,834M	16.5%	4.1%
DegSort	11,121M	58.3%	2,597M	23.3%	5.3%
CHDFS	11,107M	49.9%	1,850M	16.7%	4.4%
SlashBurn	11,096M	55.0%	2,466M	22.2%	4.3%
LDG	11,112M	52.9%	2,256M	20.3%	5.4%
METIS	11,105M	50.3%	2,235M	20.1%	5.2%
Gorder	11,101M	**37.9%**	**1,280M**	**11.5%**	**3.4%**

Table 3: Cache Statistics by *PR* over Flickr **(M = Millions)**

Order	L1-ref	L1-mr	L3-ref	L3-r	Cache-mr
Original	623.9B	58.4%	180.0B	28.8%	18.6%
MINLA	628.8B	62.5%	196.6B	31.2%	14.8%
MLOGA	620.0B	62.1%	189.6B	30.5%	14.3%
RCM	628.9B	44.9%	103.8B	16.5%	10.2%
DegSort	632.2B	55.1%	149.5B	23.6%	15.9%
CHDFS	630.3B	38.0%	101.2B	16.1%	10.9%
SlashBurn	628.8B	44.5%	121.0B	19.3%	13.7%
LDG	637.9B	58.4%	186.2B	29.2%	18.6%
Gorder	620.3B	**31.5%**	**79.5B**	**12.8%**	**8.2%**

Table 4: Cache Statistics by *PR* over sd1-arc **(B = Billions)**

spectively. The efficiency is measured by the CPU time and the CPU cache miss ratio.

The eight real datasets we tested are with at least 1 million nodes and 30 million edges as shown in Table 2. They are mainly from SNAP (Pokec, LiveJournal) and KONECT (Flickr, wikilink). Here, Pokec, Flickr, LiveJournal, Google+[3][24] and twitter[4] are online social networks. wikilink is the hyperlink graph inside the English Wikipedia, and pld-arc and sd1-arc are two large hypelink graphs crawled in 2012[5]. The average degree is in the range from 14 to 30. twitter and sd1-arc are two billion-edge graphs.

[3] www.cs.berkeley.edu/~stevgong/dataset.html

[4] an.kaist.ac.kr/traces/WWW2010.html

[5] webdatacommons.org/hyperlinkgraph/

Order	NQ	BFS	DFS	SCC	SP	PR	DS	Kcore	Diam
Pokec	8.7	2.0	2.5	5.2	1.3	12.3	10.4	6.6	1,003
Flickr	5.1	1.5	1.8	3.7	1.0	9.1	8.6	5.3	620
LiveJ	19.4	4.9	5.9	12.1	4.6	26.4	24.0	16.8	2,556
wikilink	56.1	10.0	14.3	28.5	35.3	81.9	85.7	50.0	5,932
Google+	134	35.0	43.3	87.6	28.6	210	183	131	17,936
pld-arc	199	45.2	55.7	115	40.4	305	251	177	14,389
twitter	467	79.2	80.9	158	74.4	819	535	378	32,808
sd1-arc	492	83.7	104	218	120	665	587	430	30,202

Table 5: Running time by Gorder (in second)

The night graph algorithms: The graph algorithms being tested are Neighbors Query (*NQ*), Breadth-First Search (*BFS*) [20], Depth-First Search (*DFS*) [20], Strongly Connected Component (*SCC*) detection [48], Shortest Paths (*SP*) by the Bellman-Ford algorithm [20], PageRank (*PR*) [39], Dominating Set (*DS*) [19], graph decomposition (*Kcore*) [6] and graph diameter (*Diam*). All of them are fundamental for graph computing and provide the basis for the design of other advanced graph algorithms. For the accuracy of the collected information, except *NQ*, PageRank and *Diam*, we repeat these algorithms 10 times when running the experiments and report the total running time and the cache statistics. *NQ* randomly chooses $10n$ nodes for each dataset and accesses their out-neighbors. PageRank algorithm is stopped after 100 iterations in every dataset. The approximate graph diameter is obtained by finding the longest shortest distance of 5,000 randomly chosen nodes.

The night orderings: We compare our Gorder with the following 9 graph orderings: Original, MINLA, MLOGA, RCM, DegSort, CHDFS, SlashBurn, LDG, and METIS. Original uses the node IDs that come with the real graphs. MINLA is the node ordering π for the Minimum Linear Arrangement problem, which is to minimize $\sum_{(u,v)\in E(G)} \|\pi(u) - \pi(v)\|$. We have tried several existing solutions for this problem [41, 44], but none of them can be scalable to deal with large graphs effectively. Instead, we use simulated annealing technique to compute the result, which has good scalability and shows comparable performance with the state-of-the-art solutions. MLOGA is the node ordering for the Minimum Logarithmic Arrangement problem [45], that is to minimize $\sum_{(u,v)\in E(G)} \log_2(\|\pi(u) - \pi(v)\|)$. Similarly, we use simulated annealing to generate the node ordering. RCM is ordered by the reverse Cuthill-McKee algorithm [22], which is the well known solution for reducing graph bandwidth. DegSort is the node orders by sorting nodes in descending order of in-degree. CHDFS is obtained by children-depth-first traversal which is proposed in [4]. SlashBurn is the graph ordering used in graph compression algorithm [29]. LDG is the state-of-the-art streaming graph partitioner [49]. METIS is the de-facto standard offline graph partitioner [30] which is widely used in many applications. We set the partition size to be 64 for the two graph partitioners LDG and METIS to fit the size of cache line. Our Gorder is computed by *GO-PQ* with the window size $w = 5$. To determine the window size, we show the performance by different window sizes when testing *PR* in 100 iterations over Flickr in Fig. 8. The performance of *PR* improves when the window size becomes larger. But when $w > 5$, the improvement of running time is marginal. It is similar when we test other algorithms over different datasets. These orderings are used to renumber the node IDs in the datasets.

Exp-1 The Gscore and the CPU Cache Miss Ratio: We show the Gscore (Eq. (3)) by different orderings in Fig. 9(a), where the y-axis is in logarithmic. The Gscore of Gorder by *GO-PQ* is the highest in all the 8 real datasets, and it can achieve one order of magnitude higher than the Original ordering. RCM and CHDFS are second to Gorder but their Gscore are only a half of the Gscore by Gorder in most datasets. The higher Gscore means the better

Order	NQ	BFS	DFS	SCC	SP	PR	DS	Kcore	Diam
Original	50.8	15.3	5.4	7.8	21.5	52.1	21.9	20.8	14.9
MINLA	51.8	18.0	5.5	8.1	24.6	58.1	22.1	21.5	17.9
MLOGA	41.7	16.3	5.1	7.2	21.9	53.1	21.1	20.6	16.4
RCM	49.1	12.1	4.6	6.6	15.9	49.7	20.3	20.2	12.4
DegSort	45.7	16.7	4.8	7.0	24.9	58.3	21.4	18.6	17.0
CHDFS	42.1	12.3	4.1	5.8	18.5	49.9	21.1	20.6	12.9
SlashBurn	46.2	16.0	4.5	6.2	22.1	55.0	20.7	21.3	15.8
LDG	50.7	15.9	5.8	8.2	21.8	52.9	22.4	21.2	14.9
METIS	63.0	18.2	7.7	10.1	20.8	50.3	23.0	21.7	16.7
Gorder	**35.4**	**11.1**	**3.6**	**5.2**	**12.8**	**37.9**	**18.7**	**18.1**	**10.9**

Table 6: L1 Cache Miss Ratio on Flickr (in percentage %)

Order	NQ	BFS	DFS	SCC	SP	PR	DS	Kcore	Diam
Original	76.5	20.0	9.4	13.0	17.5	58.4	21.7	20.0	17.5
MINLA	76.0	22.7	10.2	12.8	20.7	62.5	21.8	20.5	18.3
MLOGA	76.0	21.7	9.4	12.3	19.8	62.1	21.8	20.6	18.5
RCM	61.6	14.4	7.5	8.7	**8.9**	44.9	18.2	17.5	11.7
DegSort	59.3	18.7	8.0	12.1	16.6	55.1	21.9	16.9	15.5
CHDFS	50.0	14.2	5.1	8.3	13.2	38.0	18.4	16.1	10.4
SlashBurn	56.6	16.8	6.7	9.3	10.2	44.5	18.9	16.8	13.5
LDG	74.7	22.7	10.0	13.6	18.7	58.4	22.0	20.3	17.9
Gorder	**40.0**	**12.1**	**4.6**	**7.2**	10.8	**31.5**	**16.9**	**14.5**	**9.5**

Table 7: L1 Cache Miss Ratio on sd1-arc (in percentage %)

graph locality which makes the graph accesses are more likely to be hit by the fast L1, L2 cache. Table 3 and Table 4 show the CPU cache statistics of running *PR* on two datasets, Flickr and sd1-arc, respectively, where M and B denote million and billion. Note that we do not show METIS in Table 4, because METIS fails to compute the graph partitions for the other 5 larger graph except Pokec, Flickr and LiveJournal, due to its excessive memory consumption. The cache statistics are collected by the perf tool.[6] Here, L1-ref denotes the number of L1 cache references, which is the total cache access number, because all cache accesses must be checked by the L1 cache firstly. L1-mr denotes the L1 cache miss ratio (the % of L1 cache miss numbers over L1-ref). L3-ref is the number of L3 cache reference. L3-r is the ratio of the cache reference checked in L3 cache, such that L3-r = L3-ref/L1-ref. A small L3-r means that most cache references are hit by the first two level fast cache, and can be effectively used to measure the performance of the first 2 level fast cache. Cache-mr denotes the percentage of cache references missed in all level of cache over the L1-ref.

In Table 3 and Table 4, L1-refs are similar by different orderings. This is because cache access numbers for the same algorithm to be tested are similar. The best results for the other measures are highlighted in **bold**. Gorder achieves the smallest cache miss numbers in all levels of cache, and reduces the cache miss ratio significantly, especially in the first two cache levels. Compared with Original, Gorder reduces over 30% cache miss numbers in every cache level for Flickr and nearly 50% cache miss numbers for sd1-arc. As indicated by Fig. 9(a) from the viewpoint of Gscore, RCM and CHDFS are second to Gorder. From the number of cache misses, RCM occurs 30% more cache miss numbers than Gorder in Flickr and CHDFS occurs 20% more cache miss numbers than Gorder in sd1-arc. The cache misses of MINLA, MLOGA and DegSort are nearly 2 times of Gorder, and METIS orderings occur 30% more cache misses than Gorder on average.

Exp-2 The running time speedup by *GO-PQ*: We show the speedup by Gorder comparing with the other orderings. As the basis of comparison, we first show the running time in second by Gorder for all graph algorithms over the large real graphs in Table 5. Fig. 9 shows the speedup of Gorder over the other 9 orderings, for every one of the 9 algorithms on the 8 large graphs. Here, the speedup

[6] perf.wiki.kernel.org/index.php

	Pokec	Flickr	LiveJ	wiki	G+	pld	twitter	sd1
T_w	13.4s	32.3s	39.5s	181s	719s	0.70h	1.48h	1.57h
T_{wo}	40.6s	140.8s	97.4s	536s	0.74h	1.84h	6.02h	4.24h
R_w	93%	92%	91%	82%	93%	97%	96%	97%

Table 8: Computing Time of *GO-PQ* (s: second, h: hour)

	Pokec	Flickr	LiveJ	wiki	G+	pld	twitter	sd1
MINLA	445	510	828	1,796	2,099	2,437	4,134	6,876
MLOGA	5,377	4,324	5,001	14,869	6,431	9,424	12,077	33,169
RCM	1.45	1.75	3.48	14.95	29.39	45.46	144	120
DegSort	0.14	0.17	0.44	1.01	2.86	4.35	5.92	9.72
CHDFS	0.53	0.45	1.34	3.52	10.60	13.47	27.68	36.82
SlashBurn	1,309	231	2,110	5,471	18,363	10,690	12,986	22,649
LDG	12.00	21.82	103	586	4,351	9,987	21,078	25,024
METIS	209	571	492	–	–	–	–	–
Gorder	13.43	32.30	39.54	181	719	2,502	5,339	5,665

Table 9: Graph Ordering Time (in second)

of Gorder over another ordering X is shown as the relative difference of $\frac{T(X)}{T(\text{Gorder})}$, where $T(X)$ indicates the running time of algorithm on the ordering X. Note that the running time of $T(\text{Gorder})$ is shown in Table 5 as the basis. In Fig. 9, for an ordering X, if its y-axis value $\beta > 1$, it means that Gorder outperforms the ordering X in β times. Otherwise, the ordering X outperforms Gorder. There are in total 72 (8×9) pairs of graph algorithms and graph datasets. From Fig. 9, we see that the graph algorithms run fastest using Gorder. Gorder can achieve the best with the positive speedup (> 1) compared to the other orderings over 69 out of 72 cases, in nearly every testing. The best speedup of Gorder over the Original ordering is larger than 2. There are only 3 out of 72 cases that Gorder fails to win the best (speedup < 1) but Gorder is very close to the best results (speedup ≥ 0.92). Besides, we have the following observations. (a) The speedup of the running time by Gorder becomes more significant while the graph size increases. Compared with Pokec, Flickr and LiveJournal, the other 5 datasets are much larger with at least 10 million nodes and 300 million edges. Given the small CPU cache, only limited graph information can be located within the CPU cache and hence the effect of the cache usage becomes more significant for large graphs. (b) Gorder shows different speedup performance for different graph algorithms. *DS* and *Kcore* algorithms use a heap-like data structure which is not cache friendly in nature and thus influences the speedup of Gorder. RCM is ordered by a BFS-like graph ordering method and so it has comparable performance with Gorder in *BFS* and *SP* algorithms. (c) The speedup results are consistent with the cache performance of different orderings shown in the Table 3 and Table 4. Furthermore, to give the details, we show the L1 CPU cache miss ratio of all the 10 orderings when testing the 9 graph algorithms over Flickr and sd1-arc in Table 6 and Table 7. These results confirm that the running time of graph algorithms is greatly influenced by the cache performance.

Exp-3: Computing Gorder **by** ***GO-PQ*****:** We show the computing time to compute Gorder based on $F(\cdot)$. The basic algorithm Algorithm 1 cannot process the large datasets within the limited time and the results are omitted. We use *GO-PQ* algorithm to compute the graph orderings and show the effectiveness of our new priority queue operations by lazy-update strategy. Let T_w and T_{wo} be the computing time for *GO-PQ* with and without the lazy-update strategy, and let R_w denote the ratio of key update operations pruned by the lazy-update strategy. Table 8 shows that over 90% operations are pruned in most cases. With the lazy-update, *GO-PQ* runs very fast for Pokec, Flickr and LiveJournal that have millions of nodes and edges. For the largest billion-edge graphs like twitter (61.57 millions of nodes and 1,468 millions of edges) and sd1-arc (94.94 millions of nodes and 1,937 millions of edges), the computing time T_w are about 1.5 hours. The computing time of the other orderings are listed in Table 9. DegSort is the fastest because it simply sorts the node set based on the degree information. RCM and CHDFS are also faster than Gorder because both of them are obtained by the variants of BFS traversal. However, it is important to note all graph orderings, including Gorder by *GO-PQ*, are computed offline. The cost saving by using Gorder for graph algorithm is huge, as it is the total number of times of running a graph algorithm multiplied by the cost saving for a single execution of the graph algorithm. For some graph algorithms which require long computation time, the time saving in a single execution is huge enough to cover the offline ordering time, for example, *Diam*. We test *Diam* and show the results in Table 10. For large datasets twitter and sd1-arc, Gorder can save more than 6,000 seconds computing time even comparing with RCM and CHDFS.

Order	Pokec	Flickr	LiveJ	wiki	G+	pld	twitter	sd
Original	1,187	750	3,040	10,503	23,128	21,961	48,238	50,784
MINLA	1,176	843	3,471	10,322	25,543	20,698	44,536	48,218
MLOGA	1,181	787	3,427	10,121	24,229	20,829	45,698	48,899
RCM	1,091	673	2,883	7,272	20,371	18,657	40,730	36,334
DegSort	1,188	815	3,281	9,500	24,799	21,278	44,228	47,723
CHDFS	1,107	690	2,934	7,600	21,150	17,732	39,517	36,585
SlashBurn	1,219	810	3,452	10,031	24,616	21,564	44,261	45,134
LDG	1,168	793	2,940	10,137	23,569	22,740	47,841	55,234
METIS	1,131	843	3,232	–	–	–	–	–
Gorder	**1,003**	**620**	**2,556**	**5,932**	**17,936**	**14,389**	**32,808**	**30,202**

Table 10: Running Time of *Diam* (in second)

Four additional experiments are given in Appendix. We demonstrate that Gorder can further accelerate a specialized BFS algorithm, which aims to optimize the cache performance during the graph traversal. Besides, we test the performance of Gorder under multicore environment and graph systems. We also run graph algorithms with profiling tools in datasets with Gorder. At the end, we study Gorder in dynamic scenario with graph updates.

5. CONCLUSION

In this paper, we explore a general approach to reduce the CPU cache miss ratio for graph algorithms with their implementations and data structures unchanged. This problem is challenging, given graphs are rather complex and the graph algorithms designed are based on different techniques. We study graph ordering, which is to find the optimal permutation ϕ among all nodes in a given graph G by keeping nodes that will be frequently accessed together locally in a window of size w, in order to minimize the CPU cache miss ratio. We prove the graph ordering problem is NP-hard, and give a new *GO-PQ* algorithm with a bounded $\frac{1}{2w}$-approximation in time complexity $O(\sum_{u \in V}(d_O(u))^2)$, where $d_O(u)$ is the out-degree of node u in G. Since the number of updates is huge, we further propose the lazy-update strategy to reduce the cost of maintaining the priority queue significantly. We conducted extensive experimental studies to evaluate our approach in comparison with other 9 possible graph orderings using 8 large real graphs and 9 representative graph algorithms. We confirm the efficiency of our graph ordering. In nearly all testings, our graph ordering outperforms others. The best speedup is > 2 in testing different graph algorithms over large real graphs.

ACKNOWLEDGEMENTS: We thank Zhigang Wang to help conducting the experiments in graph systems. This work was partially supported by the grant of the Research Grants Council of the Hong Kong SAR, China No. 14209314 and Xuemin Lin was partially supported by ARC DP150102728, DP140103578 and NSFC 61232006.

6. REFERENCES

[1] *The Boost Graph Library: User Guide and Reference Manual.* Addison-Wesley Longman Publishing Co., Inc., 2002.

[2] A. Ailamaki, D. J. DeWitt, M. D. Hill, and D. A. Wood. Dbmss on a modern processor: Where does time go? In *Proc. of VLDB'99*, 1999.

[3] L. Auroux, M. Burelle, and R. Erra. Reordering very large graphs for fun & profit. In *International Symposium on Web AlGorithms*, 2015.

[4] J. Banerjee, W. Kim, S. Kim, and J. F. Garza. Clustering a DAG for CAD databases. *IEEE Trans. Software Eng.*, 1988.

[5] A. I. Barvinok, D. S. Johnson, G. J. Woeginger, and R. Woodroofe. The maximum traveling salesman problem under polyhedral norms. In *Proc. of IPCO'98*, 1998.

[6] V. Batagelj and M. Zaversnik. An o(m) algorithm for cores decomposition of networks. *CoRR*, cs.DS/0310049, 2003.

[7] P. Boldi, M. Rosa, M. Santini, and S. Vigna. Layered label propagation: a multiresolution coordinate-free ordering for compressing social networks. In *Proc. of WWW'11*, 2011.

[8] P. Boldi, M. Santini, and S. Vigna. Permuting web graphs. In *Proc. of WAW'09*, 2009.

[9] S. Borkar, P. Dubey, K. Kahn, D. Kuck, H. Mulder, S. Pawlowski, and J. Rattner. Platform 2015: Intel processor and platform evolution for the next decade. *Technology*, 2005.

[10] L. Chang, J. X. Yu, L. Qin, X. Lin, C. Liu, and W. Liang. Efficiently computing k-edge connected components via graph decomposition. In *Proc. of SIGMOD'13*, 2013.

[11] M. Charikar, M. T. Hajiaghayi, H. Karloff, and S. Rao. l2 spreading metrics for vertex ordering problems. In *Proc. of SODA'06*, 2006.

[12] S. Chen, A. Ailamaki, P. B. Gibbons, and T. C. Mowry. Improving hash join performance through prefetching. In *Proc. of ICDE'04*, 2004.

[13] S. Chen, P. B. Gibbons, and T. C. Mowry. Improving index performance through prefetching. In *Proc. of SIGMOD'01*, 2001.

[14] F. Chierichetti, R. Kumar, S. Lattanzi, M. Mitzenmacher, A. Panconesi, and P. Raghavan. On compressing social networks. In *Proc. of KDD'09*, 2009.

[15] T. M. Chilimbi, M. D. Hill, and J. R. Larus. Cache-conscious structure layout. In *Proceedings of PLDI, Atlanta, Georgia, USA*, 1999.

[16] P. Z. Chinn, J. Chvatalova, A. K. Dewdney, and N. E. Gibbs. The bandwidth problem for graphs and matrices - a survey. *Journal of Graph Theory*, 6(3), 1982.

[17] V. Chvatal. A greedy heuristic for the set-covering problem. *Mathematics of operations research*, 4(3), 1979.

[18] J. Cieslewicz and K. Ross. Database optimizations for modern hardware. *Proc of the IEEE*, 96(5), 2008.

[19] E. Cockayne. Domination of undirected graphs - a survey. In *Theory and Applications of Graphs*, pages 141–147. Springer, 1978.

[20] T. H. Cormen, C. E. Leiserson, R. L. Rivest, and C. Stein. *Introduction to algorithms*. MIT press Cambridge, 2 edition, 2001.

[21] M. Fisher, G. Nemhauser, and L. Wolsey. An analysis of approximations for finding a maximum weight hamiltonian circuit. *Operations Research*, 27(4), 1979.

[22] A. George and J. W. Liu. Computer solution of large sparse positive definite. 1981.

[23] A. Ghoting, G. Buehrer, S. Parthasarathy, D. Kim, A. Nguyen, Y.-K. Chen, and P. Dubey. Cache-conscious frequent pattern mining on a modern processor. In *Proc. of VLDB'05*, 2005.

[24] N. Z. Gong, W. Xu, L. Huang, P. Mittal, E. Stefanov, V. Sekar, and D. Song. Evolution of social-attribute networks: measurements, modeling, and implications using google+. In *Proc. of IMC'12*, 2012.

[25] J. E. Gonzalez, Y. Low, H. Gu, D. Bickson, and C. Guestrin. Powergraph: Distributed graph-parallel computation on natural graphs. In *OSDI Hollywood, CA, USA*, 2012.

[26] C. M. Grinstead and J. L. Snell. *Introduction to probability*. American Mathematical Soc., 2012.

[27] L. H. Harper. Optimal assignments of numbers to vertices. *Journal of the Society for Industrial and Applied Mathematics*, 1964.

[28] R. Hassin and S. Rubinstein. An approximation algorithm for the maximum traveling salesman problem. *Inf. Process. Lett.*, 67(3), 1998.

[29] U. Kang and C. Faloutsos. Beyond 'caveman communities': Hubs and spokes for graph compression and mining. In *Proc. of ICDM'11*, 2011.

[30] G. Karypis and V. Kumar. Multilevel k-way partitioning scheme for irregular graphs. *J. Parallel Distrib. Comput.*, 48(1), 1998.

[31] M. G. Kendall. A new measure of rank correlation. *Biometrika*, 1938.

[32] Y. Koren and D. Harel. A multi-scale algorithm for the linear arrangement problem. In *Graph-Theoretic Concepts in Computer Science*. Springer, 2002.

[33] A. Kyrola, G. E. Blelloch, and C. Guestrin. Graphchi: Large-scale graph computation on just a PC. In *OSDI Hollywood, CA, USA*, 2012.

[34] J. Leskovec, K. J. Lang, A. Dasgupta, and M. W. Mahoney. Statistical properties of community structure in large social and information networks. In *Proc. of WWW'08*, 2008.

[35] P. Lindstrom and D. Rajan. Optimal hierarchical layouts for cache-oblivious search trees. In *Proc. of ICDE'14*, 2014.

[36] C.-K. Luk and T. C. Mowry. Compiler-based prefetching for recursive data structures. In *Proc. of ASPLOS'96*, 1996.

[37] The Apache Software Foundation. Giraph website. http://giraph.apache.org.

[38] A. O. Mendelzon and C. G. Mendioroz. Graph clustering and caching. In *Computer Science 2*. Springer, 1994.

[39] L. Page, S. Brin, R. Motwani, and T. Winograd. The pagerank citation ranking: Bringing order to the web. 1999.

[40] J. Park, M. Penner, and V. K. Prasanna. Optimizing graph algorithms for improved cache performance. *IEEE Trans. Parallel Distrib. Syst.*, 15(9), 2004.

[41] J. Petit. Experiments on the minimum linear arrangement problem. *Journal of Experimental Algorithmics (JEA)*, 2003.

[42] J. Rao and K. A. Ross. Cache conscious indexing for decision-support in main memory. In *Proc. of VLDB'99*, 1999.

[43] J. Rao and K. A. Ross. Making b+- trees cache conscious in main memory. In *Proc. of SIGMOD'00*, 2000.

[44] I. Safro, D. Ron, and A. Brandt. Multilevel algorithms for linear ordering problems. *Journal of Experimental Algorithmics (JEA)*, 2009.

[45] I. Safro and B. Temkin. Multiscale approach for the network compression-friendly ordering. *Journal of Discrete Algorithms*, 2011.

[46] A. I. Serdyukov. An algorithm with an estimate for the traveling salesman problem of the maximum. *Upravlyaemye Sistemy*, 25:80–86, 1984.

[47] Y. Shao, B. Cui, and L. Ma. PAGE: A partition aware engine for parallel graph computation. *IEEE Trans. Knowl. Data Eng.*, 27(2), 2015.

[48] M. Sharir. A strong-connectivity algorithm and its applications in data flow analysis. *Computers & Mathematics with Applications*, 7(1), 1981.

[49] I. Stanton and G. Kliot. Streaming graph partitioning for large distributed graphs. In *Proc. of KDD'12*, 2012.

[50] M. Then, M. Kaufmann, F. Chirigati, T.-A. Hoang-Vu, K. Pham, A. Kemper, T. Neumann, and H. T. Vo. The more the merrier: Efficient multi-source graph traversal. *PVLDB*, 8(4), 2014.

[51] Y. Tian, A. Balmin, S. A. Corsten, S. Tatikonda, and J. McPherson. From "think like a vertex" to "think like a graph". *PVLDB*, 7(3), 2013.

[52] W. Xie, G. Wang, D. Bindel, A. Demers, and J. Gehrke. Fast iterative graph computation with block updates. *PVLDB*, 6(14), 2013.

[53] D. Yan, J. Cheng, Y. Lu, and W. Ng. Blogel: A block-centric framework for distributed computation on real-world graphs. *PVLDB*, 7(14), 2014.

APPENDIX

CPU caches: In computer systems, the CPU cache plays a very important role to speedup computing by loading data from comparative low speed main memory to high speed CPU cache and keeping frequently accessed data in the CPU cache. In brief, most modern CPUs are equipped with three-level caches, namely, L1/L2/L3, where an individual core is associated with its L1 and L2 caches, and many cores share the same L3 cache. With the three-level CPU

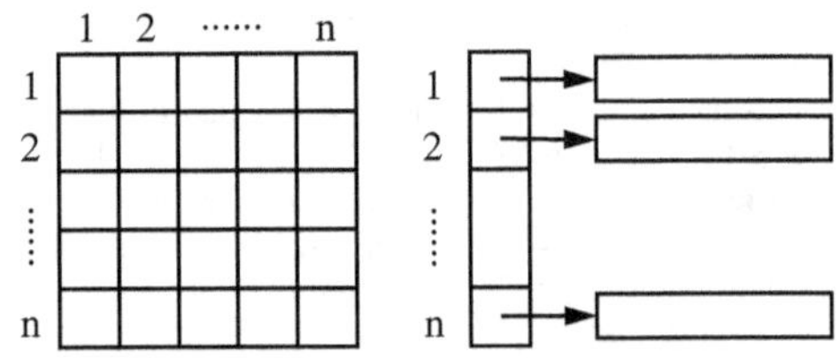

(a) Adjacent Matrix (b) Adjacent List

Figure 10: Graph Representations

cache, in computing, the CPU checks whether the requested data is in the fastest L1 cache, then L2 cache and the slowest L3 cache. If all CPU caches do not have the data, then the CPU copies a unit of data pieces containing the requested data from the main memory to the CPU cache. The unit of data to be transferred between the CPU cache and the main memory is a CPU cache line, which is small in size, e.g., 64 bytes (64B). In general, the L1 cache is smallest and fastest, the L2 cache is relative larger and comparative slower, and the L3 cache is the largest and is the slowest. Take Intel CPU since Core i3 as an example. The sizes of L1 and L2 are 64KB and 256KB, and the size of L3 is in the range of 3MB to 20MB. The latency of L1, L2, L3 cache and memory is about 1, 3, 10, and 60 nanoseconds, respectively, if the corresponding cache miss occurs.[7] The latency of memory is high due to the fact that the CPU needs to copy the cache line containing data from main memory to the CPU cache. Given the fact that there exists a wide speed gap between the CPU cache and the memory, reducing the cache miss ratio on all three level CPU caches can significantly improve the performance. On the other hand, the long latency of the memory access will exist in a long period of time due to the "memory wall" effect, which is caused by the fact that the slow improvement of memory access time in chip industry cannot follow the pace of the processor's increasing clock frequency [9].

Graph algorithm implementation: To implement graph algorithms, the well-known data structures to represent a graph $G = (V, E)$ are adjacency-matrix and adjacency-list [20]. The adjacency-matrix is not the first choice in practice since it represents a graph using a matrix which consumes large memory space, $n \times n$, where n is the number of nodes (Fig. 10(a)). The adjacency-list maintains a graph G using an array of n lists. First, there is an array *Adj* of size n to maintain all nodes. Second, for any node v in the array *Adj*, denoted as $Adj[v]$, there is a list of neighbor nodes u, if there is an edge (v, u) in E. Such a list of neighbor nodes can be represented by either an array or a linked list, and the array representation (Fig. 10(b)) is desirable to avoid the pointer-chasing problem which causes the CPU cache miss [36]. It is worth noting that, in addition to the list of neighbor nodes, graph algorithms may maintain some additional information in $Adj[v]$ to achieve efficiency. For example, for *PR*, in $Adj[v]$, it may maintain the node degree as well as the PageRank value for every node v to compute PraageRank iteratively, where the degree is represented by an integer type of 4 bytes and the PageRank value is represented by a double type of 8 bytes. In short, graph algorithms are implemented by the best data structure to achieve high efficiency in dealing with complex large graphs.

The proof sketch of Theorem 2.1: We prove it by showing that the special case when window size $w = 1$ is NP-hard. Consider the window size $w = 1$. To maximize $F(\phi)$ (Eq.(3)), for any v in G, we only consider the node u immediately appears before v in the permutation regarding $S(u, v)$. In order to do so, we construct an edge-weighted complete undirected graph G_w from G. Here, $V(G_w) = V(G)$, and there is an edge $(u, v) \in E(G_w)$ for any pair of nodes in $V(G_w)$. The edge-weight for an edge (u, v) in G_w is $S(u, v)$ computed for the two nodes in the original graph G. With G_w constructed, finding a graph ordering ϕ over G by maximizing $F(\phi)$ becomes a maximum traveling salesman problem without returning to the start node over G_w, which is to find the longest traveling salesman path over all nodes in G_w. The maximum traveling salesman problem is NP-hard [5, 28] and it does not change the computational complexity when it does not need to return to the start node. □

The proof sketch of Theorem 3.2: It requires $O(n)$ iterations to compute the permutation iteratively (line 3-10). In each iteration, it scans the set of the remaining nodes V_R (line 5-8) in $O(n)$, and computes the scores between the scanned node and the nodes in the window (line 6) in $O(w \cdot d_{max})$. The total time complexity of *GO* (Algorithm 1) is $O(w \cdot d_{max} \cdot n^2)$. □

The proof sketch of Theorem 3.3: Regarding time complexity, there are two terms. The first term is related to the updates (incKey and decKey). For every node $v \in G$, the updates occur only twice for v's neighbors and siblings, one for incKey and one for decKey, when v is to join/leave the window. Overall, computing neighboring relationships in G is $O(m)$, and computing sibling relationships in G is $O(\sum_v \sum_{u \in N_I(v)} d_O(u))$. Here, $O(\sum_v \sum_{u \in N_I(v)} d_O(u)) = O(\sum_{(u,v) \in E} d_O(u)) = O(\sum_u (d_O(u))^2)$. Thus, we have $O(m + \sum_v \sum_{u \in N_I(v)} d_O(u)) = O(m + \sum_u (d_O(u))^2) = O(\sum_u (d_O(u))^2)$, since $m < \sum_u (d_O(u))^2$. The second term is related to inserting v_{max} into P by popping it from Q in all n iterations. The time complexity for *GO-PQ* is $O(\mu \cdot \sum_{u \in V} (d_O(u))^2 + n \cdot \varrho)$. □

The proof sketch of Theorem 3.4: Let's see the time complexity got by Theorem 3.3. First, the time complexity of μ related to updates is $O(1)$, because both decKey(v_i) and incKey(v_i) are in $O(1)$, as Algorithm 3 and Algorithm 4. The pop() needs to adjust the linked list when update(top) < 0. When update(top) < 0, by key(top) $\leftarrow$ key(top) + update(top), update(top) will be set to zero. Here the time complexity of pop() is $O(n)$ in the worst case. However, pop() is in the reverse of incKey which increases the key values. The total key value decreased by pop() cannot be larger than the total key values increased by incKey. In other words, the total time consumption on pop() for all nodes, related to $O(\varrho \cdot n)$, cannot be larger than the overall time consumption on incKey. Since the overall time consumption on incKey is at most as large as the number of neighboring and sibling relationship pairs, $O(m + \sum_{u \in V} (d_O(u))^2) = O(\sum_{u \in V} (d_O(u))^2)$, the time complexity of *GO-PQ* algorithm is in $O(\sum_{u \in V} (d_O(u))^2)$. □

The proof sketch of Theorem 3.5: We consider the sequence of key updates over v_i as a one-dimensional random walk, which starts at 0 and moves +1 (incKey(v_i)) or -1 (decKey(v_i)) with equal probability at each step. Let M_L be the max number that the random walk reaches after L steps. It is worth noting that M_L indicates the number of data structure adjustments in incKey(v_i) that satisfies the condition of update(v_i) > 0. We have $M_L \geq 0$ and $\lambda_{v_i}^L \geq 0$. The step of moving +1 corresponds to incKey whereas the step of moving -1 corresponds to decKey. For every step of moving -1, it does not affect the max number of M_L. For every step of moving +1, M_L increases further only when the sum of the previous moving steps is larger than the current M_L, and adjusting the doubly linked list for v_i only occurs when M_L further

[7] software.intel.com/sites/products/collateral/hpc/vtune/performance_analysis_guide.pdf

(a) The priority queue $\mathcal{Q}$

Node ID	prev	next	key	update
v_1	$\emptyset$	$\emptyset$	3	0
v_2	$\emptyset$	$\emptyset$	4	0
v_3	v_7	v_8	2	-2
v_4	$\emptyset$	v_{10}	3	0
v_5	$\emptyset$	$\emptyset$	2	0
v_6	$\emptyset$	$\emptyset$	0	0
v_7	v_{11}	v_3	2	-2
v_8	v_3	v_{12}	2	-2
v_9	$\emptyset$	$\emptyset$	2	0
v_{10}	v_4	v_{11}	3	0
v_{11}	v_{10}	v_7	3	0
v_{12}	v_8	$\emptyset$	2	-2

(b) The head $\mathcal{Q}_h$

key	head	end
0	$\emptyset$	$\emptyset$
1	$\emptyset$	$\emptyset$
2	v_7	v_{12}
3	v_4	v_{11}
4	$\emptyset$	$\emptyset$

Table 11: A snapshot of $\mathcal{Q}$

increases. Hence, we have $E(\lambda_{v_i}^L) = E(M_L)$. Based on the result in [26] (Page 481), we have $E(M_L) \sim \sqrt{\frac{2L}{\pi}}$ for a sufficiently large L, which completes the proof. □

Example-A: Consider the example G in Fig. 2. Supposed the *GO* algorithm has already inserted (v_6, v_9, v_5, v_1, v_2) into the array of P after 5 iterations and the window size $w = 3$. The current window consists of the last three nodes, (v_5, v_1, v_2). Here, v_2 is the newest node inserted into the window and will be removed from the window after 3 new nodes to be inserted in the following 3 iterations. In these 3 iterations in the *GO* algorithm, the locality score between v_2 and the remaining nodes that have not been inserted into P need to be repeatedly computed in line 5-6. On the other hand, the *GO* algorithm wastes time to compute it for v_3, v_7, v_8 and v_{11} in line 5-6, although they have no neighbor/sibling relationships with the nodes in the window.

Example-B: To reduce the cost for the repeated computation, the *GO-PQ* algorithm uses a data structure to record the locality scores between every remaining node and the nodes of the window, and only updates the locality scores of the necessary nodes. Since the data structure needs to efficiently find the node with the highest locality score in every iteration, it is implemented as a priority queue denoted as Q. Assume that *GO-PQ* has inserted (v_6, v_9, v_5, v_1, v_2) into the array P. In the next iteration in the *GO-PQ* algorithm, we insert v_4, which is the node having the largest score, into P, and perform incKey($\cdot$) operations for all neighbors and siblings of v_4 that have not been inserted yet, namely, v_{10} and v_{11}. Node v_5 is the oldest node in the current window. So the *GO-PQ* algorithm removes v_5 from the window and perform decKey($\cdot$) operations for all neighbors and siblings of v_5 that have not been inserted, namely, v_{10} and v_{11}. No computation is needed for the nodes v_3, v_7, v_8 and v_{11}. Finally, the resulting graph ordering is $\phi = (v_6, v_9, v_5, v_1, v_2, v_4, v_{10}, v_{11}, v_7, v_3, v_8, v_{12})$. □

Example-C: Supposed the *GO-PQ* algorithm has already inserted (v_6, v_9, v_5, v_1, v_2) into the array of P and the window of size $w = 3$ contains v_5, v_1, and v_2. Table 11 shows the snapshot of $\mathcal{Q}$, where the top points to v_4 which will be returned as the node v_{max} with the max true key value in this iteration. Since the update($\cdot$) for v_3, v_7, v_8, v_{12} is -2, at least, the next two incKey($\cdot$) for them do not need to adjust the doubly linked list. □

Additional Exp-A: Optimized *BFS* and multicore performance: The recent work [50] designs a specialized *BFS* algorithm aiming to improve the cache performance during graph traversal. Gorder can further improve the cache usage of the optimized graph traversal algorithms. Fig. 11(a) shows the speedup of Gorder when applied for the best optimized BFS algorithm of [50], BFS256. It utilizes SIMD instructions and 256-bit wide registers. Here, the

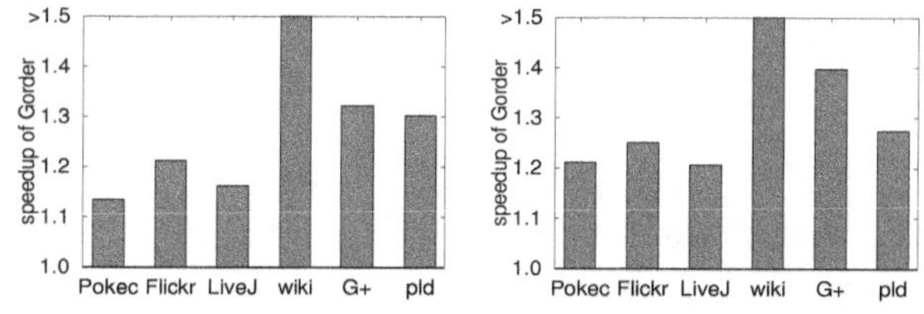

(a) BFS256 (b) BFS256 (4 threads)

Figure 11: Optimized BFS

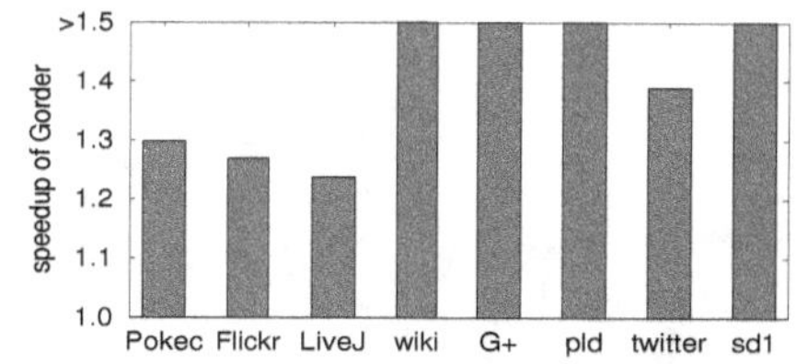

Figure 12: PageRank (4 threads)

speedup of Gorder is the ratio of the running time by BFS256 using the original datasets over the running time by BFS256 in the datasets with Gorder. BFS256 cannot deal with the largest 2 dataset twitter and sd1-arc. The speedup of Gorder in BFS256 algorithm in Fig. 11(a) is close to that in basic *BFS* algorithm in Fig. 9(c). It shows that Gorder can be used to further support the algorithms like BFS256 to enhance the performance. Furthermore, we test the performance of Gorder under multicore environment and run the BFS256 and *PR* with 4 threads (the machine used has 4 physical core). Fig. 11(b) and Fig. 12 show the speedup results which are similar with those by the single thread versions. In Fig. 12, the speedup of Gorder in wikilink and sd1-arc is larger than 2.

The cache performance in a multicore environment is also the bottleneck of the graph computing, as shown in the single core graph computing in Fig. 1. This is because in a multicore environment, even though every core has its own L1/L2 cache, all cores share the same L3 cache which makes the cache resource even more limited to every core.

Additional Exp-B: Graph Systems: In real applications, graph data can be too large to be fit into one machine's memory. Many graph systems have been developed in recent years to support scalable graph computing. We conduct testing using two graph systems, GraphChi [33] and PowerGraph [25]. Here, GraphChi is a graph system developed on just a PC by storing the graph data in the external disk and loading the requested graph data into the memory when necessary. On the other hand, PowerGraph is the representatives of distributed graph system, which partitions the large graph into several partitions and store them separately in a cluster of machines. For testing GraphChi, we install GraphChi on the same Linux server to be used for all testing. For testing PowerGraph, we install them in a cluster of 32 machines which are equipped with Intel Core i3-2100 CPU and 8GB memory.

Fig. 13(a) shows the speedup of Gorder when running the PageRank algorithm in GraphChi. The speedup of Gorder in wikilink and sd1-arc is more than 1.8 times. Compared with Fig. 9(g), we can see that the improvement of cache performance by Gorder on GraphChi is significant. This is because GraphChi attempts to optimize the random access program and Gorder is able to reduce the random access problem greatly by storing the nodes with high locality.

Fig. 13(b) shows the speedup of Gorder when running the PageRank algorithm in PowerGraph. The speedup results for the two

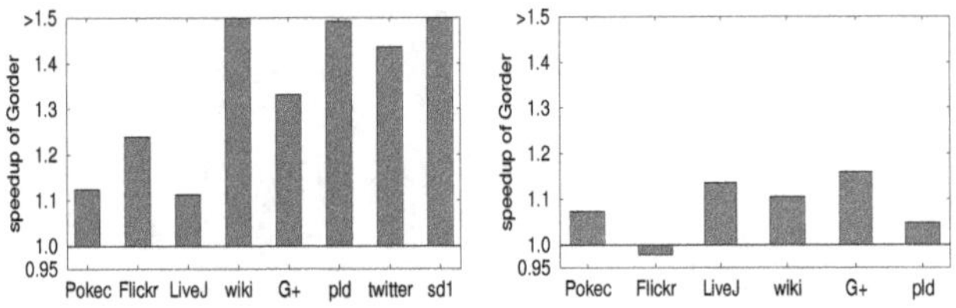

(a) GraphChi (b) PowerGraph

Figure 13: PageRank on Graph Systems

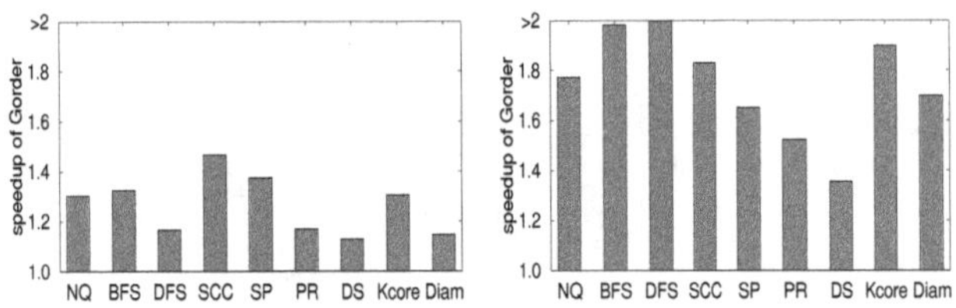

(a) Profiling in Flickr (b) Profiling in sd1-arc

Figure 14: Profiling

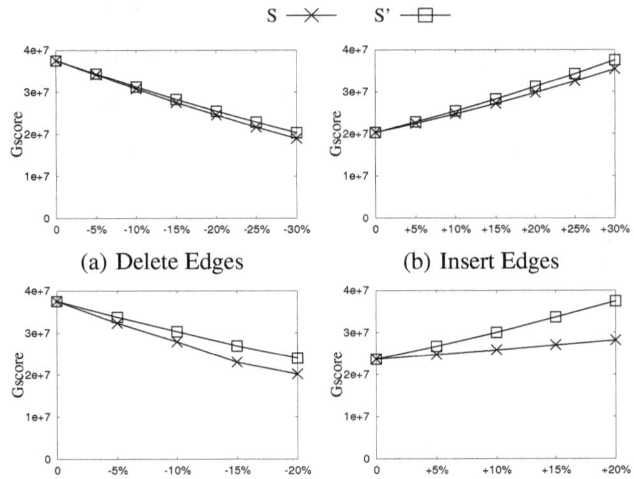

(a) Delete Edges (b) Insert Edges

(c) Delete Nodes (d) Insert Nodes

Figure 15: Graph Updates in Flickr

largest graphs twitter and sd1-arc are missing, because the 32 machine cluster used cannot run the two datasets successfully due to the excessive memory usage on node replication. It is worth mentioning that PowerGraph has its own mechanism to partition the graph into the clusters of machines. This implies that nodes with close IDs, as done by Gorder, are not necessary to be allocated into the same machine. Nevertheless, Gorder provides a good initial ordering, which boosts the PowerGraph system to generate a good graph partitions and the graph algorithms running on the system can benefit from Gorder through the good partition. On the other hand, we find that the improvement by Gorder on Giraph [37] is less obvious. Here, Giraph is optimized for simple partition strategies and a high quality graph partition may not lead to the good performance. It is the implementation issues according to the empirical study of [47].

In general, the issue of applying Gorder to a distributed graph system is rather complicated. A key issue is whether the graph partitioning used in a distributed graph system can take the advantage of Gorder, among many factors that influence the performance of distributed graph system, such as load balancing. We plan to study it as our future work.

Additional Exp-C: Gorder **with Profiling:** Profiling tool can record the statistics information, including the frequency of function calls, the function workload and branch probability, during the previous runs of the graph algorithms. The compiler GCC can use these historical statistics information to optimize the code if the program is compiled with the GCC parameter -fprofile-generate and -fprofile-use.[8] We compile the program with the GCC profiling tools and run the graph algorithms in datasets with original order and Gorder to make the comparisons. The results are shown in Fig. 14. Profiling information does improve the graph computing time when running the optimized code in original datasets. Also profiling information can help graph algorithms running with our Gorder even faster. In Fig. 14, the speedup of Gorder for every graph algorithm is nearly the same comparing with the speedup result running without profiling information shown in Fig. 9. As the analysis of Exp-2 in Section 4, in Fig. 14, the speedup of Gorder in large dataset sd1-arc is much more significant than the results in small dataset Flickr because the cache can hold very limited information of large graph when running the graph algorithms.

Additional Exp-D: Graph Update: In practice, graphs need to be updated by insertion/deletion of nodes/edges. It is costly to recompute the Gorder for every update of the graph. Here, we show the performance of Gorder, without any recomputing, when nodes/edges are inserted/deleted. In other words, we do not update the Gorder for any edge insertion/deletion and node removal. The node IDs remain unchanged in these cases. For node insertion, we simply put the node to be inserted at the end of Gorder and assign it with a new node ID in order. For node deletion, we simply remove the nodes from the datasets. To test node-deletion and node-insertion, we do the following. We randomly delete nodes up to 20% of the total number of nodes in a graph dataset for node deletion, and then we insert the deleted nodes back to the graph incrementally for node insertion. To test edge-deletion and edge-insertion, we also randomly delete edges up to 30% of the total number of edges in a graph dataset for edge deletion, and then we insert the deleted edges back to the graph incrementally for edge insertion. In the figures, we show the difference with and without recomputing. Here, S denote the Gscore of the node ordering without recomputing, and S' denote the Gscore of the node ordering by recomputing after updates. Fig. 15 shows the results in Flickr. Fig. 15(a) shows the influence of Gscore after deleting 5%-30% edges randomly from the original graph. Fig. 15(b) shows the influence of Gscore after adding back 5%-30% edges randomly selected. Gorder is not sensitive to the edge insertion/deletion. Fig. 15(c) and Fig. 15(d) show the results of node insertion/deletion. Note that deleting $x\%$ nodes causes deleting about $2x\%$ adjacent edges. Inserting a large number the new nodes at the end has impacts on the performance. Based on the results, the recomputing timing can be determined.

[8] gcc.gnu.org/onlinedocs/gcc/Optimize-Options.html

ROLL: Fast In-Memory Generation of Gigantic Scale-free Networks*

Ali Hadian‡ Sadegh Nobari§ Behrooz Minaei-Bidgoli‡ Qiang Qu§

‡Iran University of Science and Technology, Iran §Innopolis University, Russia

hadian@comp.iust.ac.ir sadegh@sqnco.com b_minaei@iust.ac.ir qu@innopolis.ru

ABSTRACT

Real-world graphs are not always publicly available or sometimes do not meet specific research requirements. These challenges call for generating synthetic networks that follow properties of the real-world networks. Barabási-Albert (BA) is a well-known model for generating scale-free graphs, i.e graphs with power-law degree distribution. In BA model, the network is generated through an iterative stochastic process called preferential attachment. Although BA is highly demanded, due to the inherent complexity of the preferential attachment, this model cannot be scaled to generate billion-node graphs.

In this paper, we propose ROLL-tree, a fast in-memory roulette wheel data structure that accelerates the BA network generation process by exploiting the statistical behaviors of the underlying growth model. Our proposed method has the following properties: (a) Fast: It performs +1000 times faster than the state-of-the-art on a single node PC; (b) Exact: It strictly follows the BA model, using an efficient data structure instead of approximation techniques; (c) Generalizable: It can be adapted for other "rich-get-richer" stochastic growth models. Our extensive experiments prove that ROLL-tree can effectively accelerate graph-generation through the preferential attachment process. On a commodity single processor machine, for example, ROLL-tree generates a scale-free graph of 1.1 billion nodes and 6.6 billion edges (the size of Yahoo's Webgraph) in 62 minutes while the state of the art (SA) takes about four years on the same machine.

1. INTRODUCTION

The study of complex networks is an impressive but young field of research. While the first contributions to the field date back to the early 1900 since the development of graph theory, new applications of network modeling have given rise to considerable efforts in understanding the structure and properties of complex networks.

The main feature that distinguishes complex networks from other types of networks, such as random graphs and lattices, is their non-trivial properties, i.e. complex networks have irregular characteristics which dynamically evolve in time [7]. For example, a common property of many large networks is that the vertex connectivities follow a scale-free (or power-law) distribution, i.e., the proportion of nodes $P(k)$ connected to k other nodes follows a power-law distribution $P(k) \sim k^{-\gamma}$ where $2 < \gamma < 3$ [6]. A number of theoretical models are proposed to explain how scale-free networks grow over time, including the Barabási-Albert model [6], fitness model [8, 12], tinkering [44], optimization [24, 47], Chung-Lu [1], BTER [30], R-MAT [16], hyperbolic unit disk [49], and the highly optimized tolerance model [15].

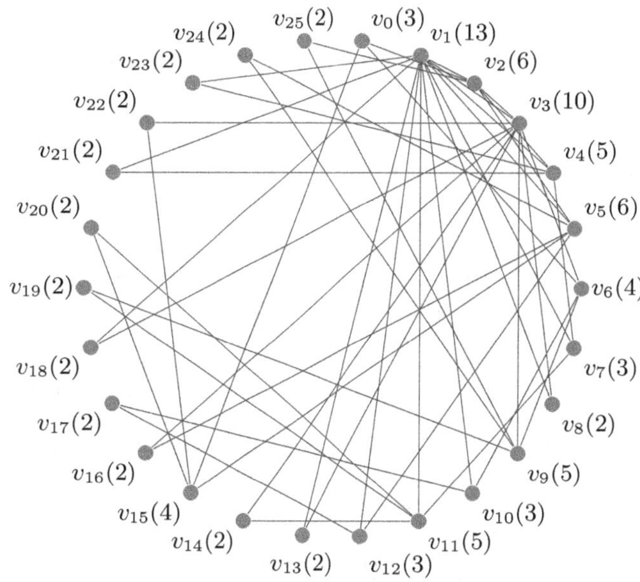

Figure 1: A Barabási-Albert graph with 25 nodes in which $v_i(d)$ has d connections ($m = m_0 = 2$)

Graph growth models not only provide theoretical abstractions for studying natural complex graphs, but also can be used to *generate* synthetic graphs for further analysis and simulation. In the last two decades, various randomized algorithms have been developed to generate synthetic graphs for different growth models. The primary motivation for recent interest in generating synthetic graphs is that, real-world networks are hardly accessible to researchers due to privacy concerns. In addition, synthetic graph generators can be used to create multiple independent graphs with similar statistical properties. These multiple independent graphs are useful for statistical tests, e.g. significance tests and cross-validation [49]. Recently, research is being shifted towards modeling gigantic networks, because small input graphs may not exhibit the same properties that can be found in large-scale graphs [4, 32].

*Supported by RFBR grant 16-37-60089.

SIGMOD'16, June 26-July 01, 2016, San Francisco, CA, USA

© 2016 ACM. ISBN 978-1-4503-3531-7/16/06...$15.00

DOI: http://dx.doi.org/10.1145/2882903.2882964

In this paper, we specifically focus on one of the most referred models, the Barabási-Albert (BA) model, which is a well-known model for scale-free network generation [5, 13, 17, 46, 55]. Figure 1 is a BA network that we use as our running example in this paper. The BA model generates a random scale-free graph using a preferential attachment mechanism: graph nodes are generated one by one, and each time attached to one or more existing nodes in the graph. The attachment is done in a "rich-get-richer" manner, such that the more connected a node is, the more likely it is to receive new connections. Roughly speaking, the probability for a new node to be connected to an existing node is proportional to the degree of the node. Although the fact that the BA model has been widely used in various research areas [5, 17, 46, 55], few studies have paid attention to its efficiency. While many graph generation models have subquadratic computational complexities, the complexity of Barabási-Albert is $O(|V|^2)$, which makes it infeasible for very large graphs. The algorithm is currently implemented in a number of graph-analysis software packages, such as iGraph [1] and graph-tool [2], and is being used for many research works in which the graph size is sufficiently small, e.g. $|V| < 10^7$. However, when the size of the graph goes beyond this range, e.g. for generating big synthetic web-graphs, current implementations cannot be used due to BA's $O(|V|^2)$ complexity.

The computationally intensive part of the algorithm is the degree-proportionate selection, a.k.a. *roulette wheel selection*, i.e. finding the node that is correspondent to the given random number. In this paper, we propose ROLL-tree, a novel data structure for fast random selection from dynamic roulette wheels where the probabilities follow a long-tailed distribution. We suggest two modifications to the basic roulette wheel. First, we propose a bucketing technique that drastically reduces the time required to compute the partial sums by reducing the size of the roulette wheel. Second, we suggest an efficient tree-based data structure along with a novel method for weighted random sampling on the dynamic roulette wheel. ROLL-tree can be applied to various problems with large dynamic roulette wheels, such as random graph generation [10,13,31,34,43,45] and simulation of random events [52, 54]. The advantages of our proposed method are **i) Fast**: It performs +1000 times faster than the state-of-the-art on a single node PC; **ii) Exact**: It strictly follows the BA model, using an efficient data structure instead of approximation techniques; **iii) Generalizable**: It can be adapted for other "rich-get-richer" growing models.

The remainder of this paper is organized as follows. The literature is briefly reviewed in Section 2. Section 3 describes the baseline and state-of-the-art roulette wheel selection methods for scale-free graph generation using the BA model. The proposed method is provided in detail in Section 4. Section 5 discusses the theoretical analysis and experimental evaluation results. Finally, Section 6 concludes the paper with directions for future work.

2. RELATED WORK

Data processing in memory is becoming increasingly important in many applications such as spatial data processing [41] and trajectory data management [50] for two reasons. First, main memory has grown gigantically that many datasets fit into it directly. Second, in-memory data generation is a necessary part of any data generation algorithm. Data generators can produce the data in parts that can fit in memory and then merge the partitions. Therefore, speeding up the in-memory data generation helps to substantially speed up any data generator as a whole as well. This paper focuses on increasing the speed of generating a well-know scale-free graph model by proposing a data structure that exploits memory. Subsequently we first cover the popular graph generators then we point to state-of-the-art advancement for the existing models.

2.1 Existing Graph Generation Models

Synthetically generated graphs are used in many applications, such as null-model, simulation, extrapolation, sampling, anonymization, visualization, and summarization [13,33]. Recently, there has been a great deal of work focused on the development of generative models for scale-free networks [1,16,21,24,30,40]. We briefly review the literature.

2.1.1 Random graph models

Research in graph generators started with Erdős-Rényi models, the two simple yet elegant models for generating random graphs. Paul Erdős and Alfréd Rényi proposed the $\Gamma_{v,e}$ model [21], while E. N. Gilbert proposed, at the same time, the $\Gamma_{v,p}$ model [26]. The former, noted as $\Gamma_{v,e}$, chooses a graph uniformly at random from the set of graphs with v vertices and e edges. The latter, noted as $\Gamma_{v,p}$, chooses a graph uniformly at random from the set of graphs with v vertices where each edge has the same independent probability p to exist. The Erdős-Rényi models generate a pure random graph that has a Binomial degree distribution, not power-law, and generally lacks clustering when generating sparse networks. As a result, multiple attempts as follows have been made to develop algorithms that generate graphs with realistic network properties.

2.1.2 Complex network models

Complex networks have statistical and structural properties in common, such as power law degree distribution and shrinking diameter. Moreover, specific groups of complex networks, e.g. social networks or scientific collaboration networks, share additional properties like modular community structures [39], bursty and self-similar edge/weight additions [16, 38], snapshot power-law [38], and many others [2,3]. Note that various complex networks are not structurally the same, and not every complex network exhibit all the above properties.

Random graph models, i.e. Erdős-Rényi, cannot exhibit all the properties of a real-world complex network. Several models are proposed to generate networks holding such properties. In the following, we briefly describe various complex graph models.

Generative models.

The Barabási-Albert (BA) model [24] is one of the most referred models that generates scale-free networks [5, 13, 17, 46, 55]. This model generates scale-free networks in a preferential attachment setting. A Barabási-Albert graph is generated as follows: (i) it starts with a small number of nodes (m_0); and (ii) each new node is connected to m existing nodes with probabilities proportional to their current degrees. Besides power-law degree distribution, networks generated by the BA model follow some other real-world network properties including average path length and clustering coefficients [28]. For instance, the average path length increases approximately logarithmically with the size of a network, which yields that the BA model has a systematically shorter average path length than a random graph [24]. Moreover, the BA model comes with the flexibility to generate networks with degree distributions with any exponent in $(2, \infty)$ [23].

Another well-known generative model is the Chung-Lu model, which generates a network that has a provable expected degree distribution equal to a given degree distribution [1, 18]. In the Chung-Lu model, the probability of an edge is proportional to the product

[1] http://igraph.sourceforge.net/

[2] https://graph-tool.skewed.de/

of the degrees of its two vertices. Edges can be generated independently by picking vertices proportional to their desired degrees. If all degrees are the same, Chung-Lu reduces to the Erdős-Rényi model. The Chung-Lu model has the problem of preserving clustering coefficients, and compared with the BA model, the Chung-Lu model requires a set of parameters. In recent years, various extensions to the BA model have been proposed, such as spatial and geometric attachment models, in order to support more networks properties [49].

Various other methods can be used for generating synthetic graphs as well. For example, The Block Two-Level Erdős-Rényi (BTER) model [11] is able to capture two network properties, degree distribution and clustering coefficients. BTER is designed based on an assumption derived from the two properties. The Chung-Lu model can be regarded as a special case of the BTER model [30].

A recent model, the hyperbolic unit-disk model, generates random hyperbolic graphs in a fast way [49]. This model uses a spatial data structure, i.e. a polar quadtree adapted to hyperbolic space, to improve the process of all pairwise distance calculation.

Recursive models.

Another popular approach for graph generation is the family of recursive graph models, which is applied to the adjacency matrix of a graph. Recursive MATrix method (R-MAT) model is an example [16]. Further developments on recursive methods include kronecker product and tensor products [3, 33]. Recursive models are efficiently computable. However, as mentioned by a recent study [30], the model has important drawbacks concerning realism and preservation of properties over different graph sizes [30], such as 1) it is expensive to fit to real data, and 2) it rarely closes wedges (a wedge is a path of length 2 and a close wedge forms a triangle in a graph) such that the clustering coefficients are much smaller than that in realistic networks.

Complexity comparison.

For a detailed discussion of graph generation models, readers are referred to [27]. To sum up, we briefly review some of the most popular graph generation models, shown in Table 1 along with corresponding time complexities.

Algorithm	Best Complexity
Erdős-Rényi [21]	$O(\|V\|^2)$
Watts-Strogatz [51]	$O(\|E\|)$
Barabási-Albert [24]	$O(\|V\|^2)$
Chung-Lu [1]	$O(\|V\| + \|E\|)$
R-MAT [16]	$O(\|E\| \log \|V\|)$
BTER [30]	$O(\|V\| + \|E\| \times d_{max})$
Hyperbolic unit disk [49]	$O((\|V\|^{3/2} + \|E\|) \log n)$

Table 1: The complexity of graph generation models. Note that d_{max} is the maximum vertex degree.

2.1.3 Special-purpose models

Following a different line of work, synthetic graphs can be generated using empirical data instead of pure statistical models. For instance, nodes and edges can be sampled using an empirical probability distribution (histogram). Empirical data can be used for more realistic and straightforward generation of multi-relational and RDF datasets, such as social networks. Nevertheless, data-driven methods are for special purpose and not easy to generalize for generating a diverge family of graphs. Moreover, in many domains, empirical data are not available, or are too specific that graph models overfit.

Data-driven approaches, however, are a good fit for generating specific graphs. For example, members of the LDBC council propose various data-enhanced graph generators, such as S3G2 [42] and DataGen [14] that leverage empirical distribution and correlation statistics of Facebook data. For generating heterogeneous information networks, a data-driven graph generator is a popular choice, since theoretical approaches are not matured for multi-relational and multi-type graphs [20].

2.1.4 Other observations

The above discussion provides a broad set of graph generators that rely on sampling from a probability distribution, such as Barabási-Albert, Chung-Lu, S3G2, and DataGen. We can further categorize the graph generators based on the probability distribution to static and dynamic. In the former, the set of items and their probabilities are fixed, e.g. Zipf or Geometric distribution, and data-driven distributions obtained from empirical data. On the other hand, sampling from a dynamic (evolving) probability distribution is challenging. For example, the BA model heavily relies on sampling an existing node with probabilities proportionate to the node's degree. Since the probabilities are changing over time, sampling from a dynamic and long-tailed distribution is computationally expensive. Also, such mechanism comes with strong dependencies that contradict with parallelism, as discussed in the following section.

For many natural graphs that are based on strong rich-get-richer effect, the BA model would be a good fit. Moreover, the BA model is a handy option for growing an existing network while maintaining the network properties, since BA leverages the existing network's degree distribution. Growing an existing method is not straightforward for other approaches, such as R-MAT and Kronecker product.

2.2 Scaling Graph Generation

Generating very large graphs is significant for many research communities. Therefore, efforts are being made to propose efficient parallel and distributed implementations for graph generation models, which focus on both theoretical and practical aspects of the graph models for efficient parallelization [4,36,37,40].

Simple graph generators that are based on sampling having a fixed probability distribution, such as Geometric or empirical Facebook distributions, can be easily converted into parallel versions, because picking multiple samples are independent and can be done in parallel. For instance, the data generators used by the LDBC council such as S3G2 and DataGen are inherently parallel because, for example, generating social degree for each user is independent from others.

Also, methods that are based on matrix operations, such as Kronecker product and recursive graph models are easy to be parallelized. Nevertheless, many other important graph models could not fit a parallelization framework. A large group of generative graph models that are based on dynamic sample selection, such as the preferential attachment models (like BA) are inherently sequential.

Few studies have been done on parallel preferential attachment. Yoo and Henderson [53] propose parallel version of the BA and Kronecker graph generators. The parallel BA algorithm, called PBA, is an approximate method that ignores the sequential nature of the algorithm. PBA is designed to reduce the communication cost in a large cluster: graph vertices are distributed between the processing units, and random selection is done in two steps: 1)inter-processor selection: choose one of the processor in random according to the weight of their items; 2)intra-processor selection: pick one of the items from among the items that are assigned to the chosen processor. Alam et al. [4] claim the first distributed-memory parallel algorithms for generating random graphs with exact preferential attachment growth. However, the algorithm obtained reasonable speedup in comparison to the baseline algorithm only when they employ more than 100 processors. Also, Lo et al. propose a distributed version for preferential attachment, which is based on approximation [36].

Studies by Lo et al. shows that the effects of approximation techniques and computationally unsafe (no-lock) parallelization should be carefully considered in parallel versions of BA models, as many parallel configurations result in networks that do not exhibit some properties of the original models, such as degree distribution. Thus, instead of approximation, we focus on proposing exact data structures that can accelerate dynamic roulette wheel selection.

Our goal is to propose a novel sequential algorithm that can significantly outperform the state-of-the-art sequential algorithm in a commodity machine. Our proposed method can be used either as a fast serial algorithm, or as a building block inside two-step parallel generative models, such as PBA. In other words, both the inter-process and intra-process operations in any parallel BA require a fast dynamic roulette wheel, therefore ROLL can substantially improve PBA and other distributed preferential attachment methods [36, 53].

3. THE BASELINE ALGORITHM

In this section, we explain two sequential algorithms, baseline and state-of-the-art, for generating scale-free graphs under Barabási-Albert (BA) model. The former employs a simple roulette wheel (SimpleRW) and the latter is based on stochastic acceptance (SA).

Preliminaries and notations.

Let $G = (V, E)$ be an undirected unweighted graph such that $V = \{v_1, ..., v_n\}$ is the set of nodes and E is the set of edges. The cardinality of vertices and edges is denoted by $|V| = n$ and $|E|$, respectively. For each node v_i, $deg(v_i)$ denotes the degree of v_i, that is the number of edges that are connected to v_i. Also, let $\mathbf{B}$ be the *set of unique degrees* for all nodes in the graph, that is $\{deg(v_i) : 1 \leq i \leq n\}$. $|\mathbf{B}|$ is hence the number of unique degree values in the graph.

As discussed further, the *nodes* of a graph are represented as *items* in its corresponding roulette wheel, so we use these two terms interchangeably. We further suggest a tree data structure that contains groups of nodes, called **buckets**. In order not to confuse the nodes of such trees with the nodes of the graph, we use Rnode for pointing to nodes of a tree (i.e. branches and leafs). Table 2 briefly summarizes the notations used in this paper.

Notation	Description
$\lvert V\rvert = n$	# of nodes (items)
$\lvert E\rvert$	# of edges
$\lvert B\rvert$	# of unique degrees
m_0	# of initial nodes
m	# of links per node
L_{CW}	Average code word length [3].
$deg(v_i)$	Degree of node v_i
S_n	Total degrees $= \sum_{i=1}^{n} deg(v_i)$

Table 2: Brief description of notations

[3] Average code word length of a tree with weighted leaf nodes is the weighted average distance of leaf nodes to the root node. See Section 4.2.2

The BA model has three parameters: the number of nodes in the final graph $n = |V|$, the number of initial nodes m_0 and the number of connections per new node m. The networks generated by BA model are called BA networks. BA networks have power law degree distribution. A degree distribution is defined power law iff the probability of a node with degree d is given by $P(k) \sim k^{-\gamma}$ where γ is a positive constant.

3.1 SimpleRW Algorithm (Baseline)

To generate a synthetic scale-free graph using the Barabási-Albert model, we begin with an empty network having m_0 nodes and no edges. For the next $n - m_0$ nodes, each node is connected to m distinct nodes among all the existing nodes in the graph. The probability of node v_i for being linked to the new node is proportional to the degree of the node $deg(v_i)$. Algorithm 1 describes this procedure in detail.

Algorithm 1 BA model

```
1:  Input: n = |V|, m, m_0
2:  Output: G(V, E): A scale-free graph containing n nodes
3:  Add m_0 nodes to G
4:  for i from (m_0 + 1) to n do
5:      Create new node v_i
6:      for j from 1 to m do          ▷ Connect v_i to m existing nodes
7:          Select a node v_k ∈ {v_1..v_{i-1}}/{v_j|(v_k, v_j) ∈ E}
        based on probability in Equation 1.
8:          E ← (v_i, v_k)                          ▷ Add the new edge
9:              deg(v_i) ← deg(v_i) + 1
10:             deg(v_k) ← deg(v_k) + 1
```

Consider a set of k nodes $v_1, v_2, ..., v_k$. When the next node v_{k+1} is created, it is connected with m new edges to m distinct nodes among $v_1, v_2, ..., v_k$. For each new edge from the new node, the probability for each of the existing graph nodes for being selected as the target of the edge and being attached to v_{k+1} is proportional to the degree of the node.

$$p(v_i) = \frac{deg(v_i)}{\sum_{l=1}^{k} deg(v_l)} \tag{1}$$

The m nodes that are to be connected to each node should be sampled without replacement, i.e. if a node is selected to be connected to the newborn node, its selection probability in the consecutive selections become zero. This mechanism is simply handled via rejection sampling: If the selected node has already been connected to the newborn node, the sampling is rejected and repeated again. Nonetheless, in most problems such as the Barabási-Albert algorithm we have $m \ll n$, hence the rejection probability (i.e. the probability that one of the already selected nodes are selected again) is very low and thus the rejection rarely happens.

The preferential attachment algorithm described above adopts a roulette wheel mechanism to select the target nodes. We briefly explain the simple roulette wheel method for selecting a random node (Algorithm 1, line 7). A roulette wheel is a list of items with their corresponding selection probabilities. In order to select a random item, we should generate a random number $0 < x \leq 1$ and select v_k for which $P(v_{k-1}) < x \leq P(v_k)$. Note that $P(v_i)$ denotes the cumulative probability, i.e. $P(v_k) = \sum_{i=1}^{k} p(v_i)$.

As an example, consider the sample graph in Figure 1 which has 26 nodes generated by the BA algorithm ($m_0 = m = 2$). The total degree of the nodes in the graph is $S_n = \sum_{i=1}^{n} deg(v_i) = 2|E| = 2m(n - m_0) = 2 \times 2(26 - 2) = 96$. To continue the

v_i	$w_i = \deg(v_i)$	$p(v_i)$	$P(v_i)$	$\sigma_i(v_i)$
v_0	3	0.03	0.03	3
v_1	13	0.14	0.17	16
v_2	6	0.06	0.23	22
v_3	10	0.10	0.33	32
⋮	⋮	⋮	⋮	⋮
v_{12}	3	0.03	0.71	68
v_{13}	2	0.02	0.73	70
⋮	⋮	⋮	⋮	⋮
v_{24}	2	0.02	0.98	94
v_{25}	2	0.02	1.00	96

Table 3: Roulette wheel of the graph in Figure 1

growth of the graph, the next new node v_{26} should be connected to $m = 2$ nodes among $\{v_1, ..., v_{25}\}$. Table 3 shows the degree-proportionate roulette wheel corresponding to this graph. We want to sample two nodes from the roulette wheel and connect them to v_{26}. For each random selection, a random number should be generated. Suppose that the generated random numbers for the first and second connections are 0.30 and 0.72, respectively. According to the roulette wheel in Table 3, the first target node is v_3 $(0.23 < 0.30 \leq 0.33 = P(v_3))$ and the second node is v_{13} $(0.71 < 0.72 \leq 0.73 = P(v_{13}))$.

In the above example, we had to compute $P(v_1)$ through $P(v_{13})$ in order to find the item that is corresponding to the generated random number (0.72). When a node is added to the network, it is also added to the roulette wheel. Also, whenever a new edge connects two nodes in the graph, the probability of nodes at its both ends are increased according to their new degrees and the probability of all other items in the roulette wheel should be updated as well to ensure that the total probabilities sum to one. As a result, the roulette wheel will change after each selection and the cumulative probabilities need to be recomputed in the next iteration. To alleviate this problem, the denominator in Equation 1 can be eliminated because it is constant. Hence, the probabilities $p(v_1), \ldots, p(v_n)$ can be converted into weights $w_1, \ldots, w_n$ such that $w_i = deg(v_i) = S_n \times p(v_i)$. Similarly, instead of cumulative probabilities, we can compute partial sums $\sigma_1, \ldots, \sigma_n$ where $\sigma_i = S_n \times P(v_i) = \sum_{j=1}^{i} w_j$ (see Table 3). To sample from the roulette wheel, we generate a random integer $r \in [1..S_n]$ and select v_k for which $\sigma_{k-1} < r \leq \sigma_k$.

The advantage of using weights in place of probabilities is that some partial sums do not change and do not need to be re-calculated. For instance, in the previous example it is not required to re-compute σ_0 through σ_2 since they are not changed after increasing the degrees of v_3 and v_{13}. Besides, using weights (i.e. degree of nodes) instead of the probabilities is more efficient because weights are stored as integer values. The simple roulette wheel algorithm for preferential attachment is illustrated in Algorithm 2. Whenever a node v_k is connected to the new node v_n, the partial sums for $\sigma_k, ..., \sigma_{n-1}$ are incremented by one and σ_n is incremented by two. As a result, the computational complexity of updating partial sums for each link is $O(n = |V|)$. Also, the random number generation requires a constant time, which is $O(1)$. Therefore, the total time taken to generate the whole graph containing $|E|$ links is $O(|E| \cdot (|V| + 1)) = O(mn^2)$.

3.2 SA Algorithm (State-of-the-art)

Lipowski and Lipowska recently proposed an alternative roulette-wheel selection algorithm based on stochastic acceptance instead of

Algorithm 2 SimpleRW Algorithm

Input: A set of items $\{v_1, ..., v_n\}$ with their weights $\{w_1, ..., w_n\}$
Output: A randomly chosen item v_k.
$S_n = \sum_{i=1}^{n} w_i$ ▷ In Barabási-Albert alg., $S_n = 2 \times |E|$
Initialize $\sigma_0 \leftarrow 0$
Uniformly generate a random number $r \in [1..S_n]$
for i from 1 to n **do**
  $\sigma_i \leftarrow \sigma_{i-1} + w_i$
  if $\sigma_i \geq r$ **then**
    Return v_i

searching [35]. In this algorithm, the target node is selected in an iterative two-step procedure, as follows:

1. Uniformly select a random node v_i.
2. Accept the selection with probability $p_{acc}(v_i) = w_i/w_{max}$, where w_{max} is the maximum weight in the roulette wheel. If the node is not accepted, then go to step 1.

This method is effective and is applied in various applications.

Complexity of SA. In general, the complexity of SA for selecting a single item from a roulette wheel is $O(w_{max}/\overline{w})$ where $\overline{w}$ is the average weight of items in the roulette wheel. In the Barabási-Albert model, the expected weight (i.e. average degree of nodes) is $\overline{w} = 2|E|/|V| = 2(mn - m_0)/n \approx 2m$. Also, the expected value of w_{max} (maximum degree) for a graph with power law degree distribution $(p(k) \sim k^{-\gamma})$ is $\mathbb{E}(w_{max}) \approx n^{1/(\gamma-1)}$ [9]. In Barabási-Albert graphs, $\gamma \approx 3$, thus $\mathbb{E}(w_{max}) \approx \sqrt{n}$. Putting these together, the complexity of SA for selecting one node from the roulette wheel, when the items are generated using the Barabási-Albert model, is $O(\sqrt{n}/m)$. In order to construct the entire graph, BA uses the roulette wheel $n \times m$ times, thus the total complexity is $O(n^{3/2})$.

Even though the complexity of the SA is better than the simple roulette wheel, it is still not efficient for generating Barabási-Albert graphs. Roughly speaking, the distribution of weights follows a power law, which implies that $w_i \lll w_{max}$ for most nodes. Therefore, the acceptance probability $p_{acc}(v_i)$ is usually very low, so while it is not required to traverse or modify a large part of the roulette wheel items, we have to re-sample until after the final node is reached. Such re-sampling for large graphs $(|V| > 10^6)$ is a time-consuming operation.

4. THE PROPOSED METHOD

In this section we describe our proposed roulette-wheel data structures for accelerating the preferential attachment algorithm. This data structure is designed to speed-up the Barabási-Albert algorithm, but in general it can be used for dynamic roulette wheels where the selection probability of items follows an arbitrary long-tailed distribution.

Sampling from a roulette wheel is easy when the selection probabilities of items are fixed. However, when the roulette wheel is dynamic, i.e. the selection probabilities of items change during the random process, it takes a long time to re-compute the cumulative probabilities (or partial sums of weights). In other words, we need a roulette wheel data structure that efficiently provides two operations: 1) *Sample* a random node and 2) *Update* the weight of an item, e.g. when a connection is made between two nodes in a Barabási-Albert graph, the degree of both nodes is increased, so their weights in the roulette wheel should be incremented as well.

In this section, we provide two modifications on the SimpleRW algorithm, which make random selections faster. The first modification is to reduce the problem size by grouping together items with the same probabilities. In our second modification, we suggest a different algorithm for sampling from a dynamic list of items in which the target item is selected using multiple random binary decisions instead of computing cumulative probabilities. This is done by a specific data structure named ROLL-tree, which allows for efficient selection of the target node in a divide-and-conquer manner.

4.1 Roulette Wheel Buckets (ROLL-bucket)

The intuition behind ROLL-bucket is that if the number of items inside a roulette wheel are very large and their selection probabilities are rational numbers with common denominator, large groups of nodes have the same selection probabilities. For example, recall that the degree distribution of scale-free graphs follows a power law and the degrees are integers. Theoretically speaking, the expected fraction of nodes that are connected to exactly k edges is $p(k) \sim k^{-\gamma}$. As a consequence, large groups of nodes, especially those with low degrees, have the same degree and thus have equal selection probabilities.

Following this intuition, our idea is to group the nodes into buckets (i.e. subsets of nodes) such that the nodes with the same weight, are stored in the same bucket, say $B_d = \{v_i | w_i = d\}$. Therefore, we keep a list of buckets $\mathbf{B}$ that contains all non-empty buckets. For example, in the graph of Figure 1, the 26 nodes are grouped into 7 buckets, as shown in Table 4. In this table, $p(B_d)$ and $P(B_d)$ are the probability density function (PDF) and cumulative density function (CDF) of B_d, respectively.

The sampling procedure can be broken into two phases. At first, a bucket is selected among all the available buckets. Then, one of the items inside the selected bucket is randomly selected. The chance of each bucket for being selected is the total chances of the items it contains. More precisely, the probability of selecting a bucket B_d is $p(B_d) = (d \times |B_d|)/S_n$, where $|B_d|$ is the number of items in B_d. Recall that $S_n = \sum_{i=1}^{n} w_i$ is constant and can be eliminated by converting probabilities to weights. If the selected bucket contains multiple items, one of its items is randomly chosen with equal probability. The proof of correctness of this two phases approach is explained in Theorem 1.

Whenever the weight of an item in ROLL-bucket changes, it should be moved from its current bucket to the bucket corresponding to its new weight. Particularly for the Barabási-Albert algorithm, when a node is connected to a new edge and its degree increases from d to $d+1$, it should be moved from B_d to B_{d+1}. The procedure is illustrated in Algorithm 3.

Theorem 1. *The two-stage sampling in ROLL-bucket is equivalent to the original roulette wheel selection, i.e the selection probability of items is equal.*

Proof. Given an item v_i with weight w_i, the probability of selecting v_i in the roulette wheel is $\frac{w_i}{S_n}$. For the two-stage sampling, the chance of selection equals the probability of selecting bucket B_{w_i} (which is $\frac{w_i \times |B_{w_i}|}{S_n}$) times the probability that v_i is selected from all items in B_{w_i}, that is $\frac{1}{|B_{w_i}|}$. Hence:

$$p(v_i) = \underbrace{\frac{w_i \times |B_{w_i}|}{S_n}}_{p(B_{w_i})} \times \underbrace{\frac{1}{|B_{w_i}|}}_{p(v_i|B_{w_i})} = \frac{w_i}{S_n}$$

□

Algorithm 3 ROLL-bucket

Input: Set of buckets: $\mathbf{B} = \{B_i | \exists v, deg(v) = i\}$
Output: A randomly chosen node v_k.
$\mathbf{S_n} = 2 \times |E|$
Initialize $\sigma = 0$ ▷ The partial sum
Uniformly generate a random number $r \in [1..S_n]$
for each $|B_i| \in \mathbf{B}$ **do**
    $deg(B_i) \leftarrow i \times |B_i|$
    if $\sigma + deg(B_i) \geq r$ **then** ▷ Target node is inside B_i
        Generate $r' \in [1..|B_i|]$ with uniform distribution
        $v_k \leftarrow r'$th node in B_i
        Move v_k from B_i to B_{i+1}
        Return v_k
    else
        $\sigma \leftarrow \sigma + deg(B_i)$ ▷ Updating the partial sum

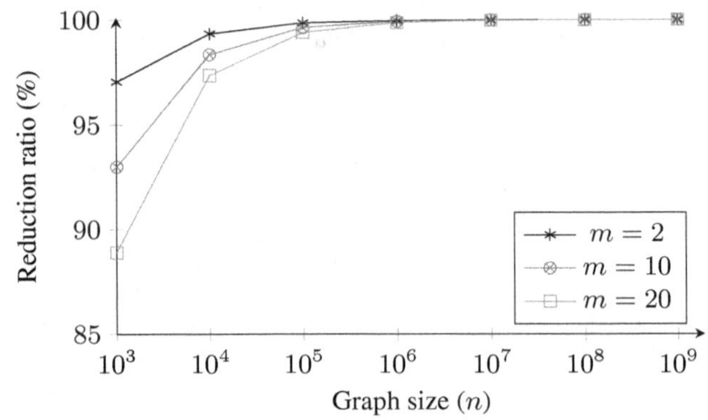

Figure 2: Ratio of items reduced to buckets in ROLL-bucket while varying n and $m = m_0$.

ROLL-bucket effectively reduces the problem space. Because the selection probabilities of all items inside each bucket are equal, it is not necessary to count the partial sums (i.e. cumulative probabilities) inside buckets. The partial sums are only computed over buckets, and since the number of buckets is very small compared to the number of items, a shorter list is traversed for finding the target item. For the case of Barabási-Albert preferential attachment, ROLL-bucket reduces the complexity of single node selection from $O(|V|)$ to $O(|\mathbf{B}|)$ where $|\mathbf{B}|$ is the number of unique weights, e.g. number of unique degrees in the graph. Figure 2 illustrates ratio of items reduced to buckets in ROLL-bucket for various m and n values. Reduction ratio is $(1 - \frac{|B|}{n}) \times 100$. This figure shows the advantage of bucketing approach in ROLL-bucket for reducing the problem size by more than 98% when $n = 10^4$. This figure also shows that the larger the graph, the more reduction we obtain, thanks to the power-law degree distribution.

In order to speedup ROLL-bucket, we have to traverse the buckets in a way that minimizes the number of buckets that are traversed before reaching the target one. A greedy approach would be to select buckets according to their weights in descending order, so that a large portion of partial sums are scanned by visiting few buckets. However, keeping buckets sorted by their weights is costly. An alternative to this method, as already suggested in Algorithm 3, is to traverse buckets by their degree, starting from the lightest bucket, i.e. B_m. Figure 3 compares the number of buckets traversed by each of the two options, as well as the generation time. Results show that while scanning buckets in decreasing order of their weights examines fewer number of buckets, it is slower in practice due to the cost of keeping buckets sorted by their weights.

Bucket	Degree d	#Nodes	$p(B_d)$ (PDF)	$P(B_d)$ (CDF)	Nodes
B_2	2	13	$26/96$	$26/96$	$\{v_8, v_{13}, v_{14}, v_{16}, v_{17}, v_{18}, v_{19}, v_{20}, v_{21}, v_{22}, v_{23}, v_{24}, v_{25}\}$
B_3	3	4	$12/96$	$38/96$	$\{v_0, v_7, v_{10}, v_{12}\}$
B_4	4	2	$8/96$	$46/96$	$\{v_6, v_{15}\}$
B_5	5	3	$15/96$	$61/96$	$\{v_4, v_9, v_{11}\}$
B_6	6	2	$12/96$	$73/96$	$\{v_2, v_5\}$
B_{10}	10	1	$10/96$	$83/96$	$\{v_3\}$
B_{13}	13	1	$13/96$	$96/96$	$\{v_1\}$

Table 4: ROLL-buckets for selecting the next node for the graph in Figure 1

As a results, our suggested algorithm for ROLL-bucket scans buckets in ascending order of their degrees, which is described before.

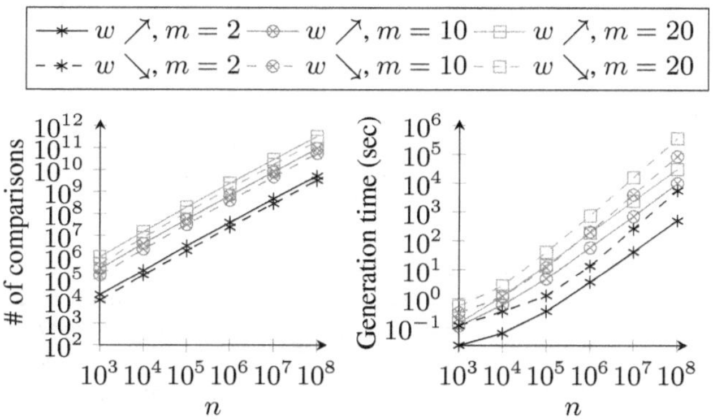

Figure 3: ROLL-bucket with sorting by degrees in ascending order ($d \nearrow$) or by weights in descending order ($w \searrow$).

4.2 ROLL-tree

Although ROLL-bucket can significantly reduce the problem size, still the buckets should be sequentially traversed to calculate the partial sums over the buckets. In other words, if the target node corresponding to a random number is in B_i, then it is inevitable to compute the partial sums of all non-empty buckets between B_1 and B_i. Hence, the complexity of this linear search is $O(|\mathbf{B}|)$.

Algorithm 4 Random selection with ROLL-tree

```
Input: Tree: The ROLL-tree containing all items
Output: A randomly chosen node v_k.
Rnode ← Tree.root
while Rnode is not a bucket do
    Uniformly generate r ∈ [1 ... (Rnode.w_R + Rnode.w_L)]
    if r ≤ Rnode.w_L then
        Rnode ← Rnode.Lchild
    else
        Rnode ← Rnode.Rchild
            ▷ Perform binary selections until a leaf is reached.
B_i ← bucket(Rnode)
v_k ← Uniformly select an item in B_i
Return v_k
```

We suggest a novel roulette wheel data structure, named ROLL-tree. Instead of ROLL, which keeps a sequential list of buckets in memory, ROLL-tree stores the buckets in a weighted binary tree. At first, we describe the random selection algorithm on the ROLL-tree. Figure 4, shows a ROLL-tree corresponding to the toy graph of Figure 1, which has 7 leafs (buckets) containing 26 items (The buckets are the same as in ROLL, shown in Table 4). Every leaf in the tree is a bucket and its weight is the same as in ROLL, i.e. $w_i = i \times |B_i|$. the weight of an internal node is the sum of the weights of its left and right children, which is the total weight of buckets in its subtree. To avoid confusing the nodes of ROLL-tree with nodes of the generated graph, we denote ROLL-tree nodes as Rnode, which consists of both buckets (leafs) and internal nodes.

4.2.1 *Sampling from ROLL-tree*

In ROLL-tree, random selection is done using a divide and conquer approach. Starting from the root Rnode, we know that the target item is in either the right or left subtrees, so we select one of the subtrees according to their weights. The weight of each subtree is the total probability that one of its leafs are selected. This procedure is repeated until a leaf is reached. The ROLL-tree's random selection algorithm is described in Algorithm 4.

We explain this algorithm on our toy example. Suppose that we want to randomly select a random node among $v_0, \dots, v_{25}$ to be connected to the newborn node v_{26}. Assume that the random generator draws the following numbers uniformly between $[0, 1]$: $\{0.83, 0.12, 0.54, 0.39, ...\}$. We first start from the root Rnode and select either its right or left children with probabilities proportional to their weights. In root Rnode, the probabilities for selecting the right and left children are $\frac{49}{96}$ and $\frac{47}{96}$, respectively. According to the first random number, the right child of the root Rnode is selected ($\frac{49}{96} < 0.83$). Now we consider the right subtree of the root Rnode. Similarly, we select its left subtree if the random number is below $\frac{27}{27+20}$, or its right subtree otherwise. According to the sequence of the generated random numbers, in both the second and third binary decision, the left branches are selected. ($\frac{27}{47} > 0.12$, $\frac{15}{27} > 0.54$). As a result, B_5 is returned by ROLL-tree as the selected bucket. Now we should select one of the three nodes in B_5, namely v_4, v_9, and v_{11}. According to the next random number (0.39), the second node (v_9) is chosen. Recall that since the selection probability of nodes inside a bucket are equal, there is no need to compute the partial sums inside a bucket.

The advantage of ROLL-tree is that it avoids traversing a large list of buckets. Instead, it stores a summary of buckets in the internal nodes, such that each internal node in ROLL-tree contains the total weight of all buckets in its subtree.

4.2.2 *Updating ROLL-tree*

When the weight of a bucket changes, the value of the internal Rnodes that are its ancestors should be updated accordingly. In Barabási-Albert algorithm, for example, whenever a node v_k with degree d is selected and connected to the newborn node, its degree increases, so it should be moved from B_d to B_{d+1} and the internal Rnodes that are an ancestor of either B_d or B_{d+1} should be updated accordingly. Consider the previous example and suppose that v_9 is selected and its degree is incremented by one. We should move v_9 from B_5 to B_6. Now the weight of B_5 and B_6 should be updated, i.e. $w_{B_5} = 5 \times (3 - 1) = 10$, $w_{B_6} = 6 \times (2 + 1) = 18$. Similarly, the weight of their parent, grandparent, and the root Rnode is updated as $27 \to 28$, $47 \to 48$, and $96 \to 97$, respectively in a bottom-up order. This procedure is described in Algorithm 5.

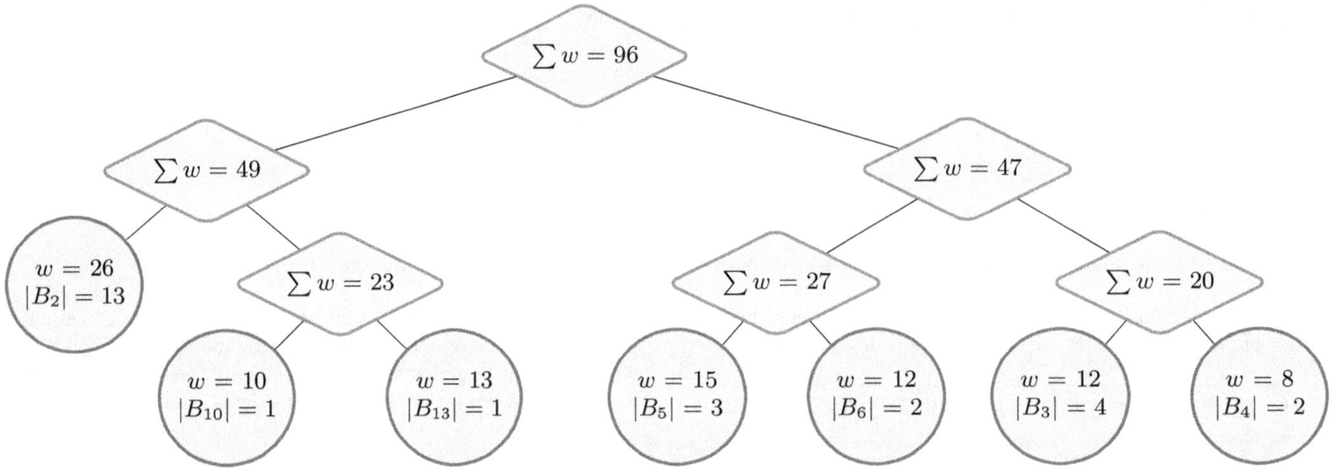

Figure 4: ROLL-tree of 26 nodes in 7 buckets when $m_0 = m = 2$. The internal nodes (diamonds) are decision nodes holding sum of weight of left and right child. The leaf nodes (circles) store w and $|B_d|$, weight and the number of nodes with degree d respectively.

Algorithm 5 Updating the weight of an item in ROLL-tree

```
Input: Tree, v, w_old, w_new
B_{w_old} ← B_{w_old} − v                      ▷ Remove v from the old bucket.
if B_{w_old} is empty now then
    Delete(Tree,Rnode(B_{w_old}))              ▷ Algorithm 7
else
    Rnode = Rnode(B_{w_old})
    Rnode.w = w_old × |B_{w_old}|
    while Rnode ≠ Tree.root do                 ▷ Update weights of parents
        Rnode ← Rnode.parent
        Rnode.w = Rnode.Rchild + Rnode.Lchild
B_{w_new} ← B_{w_new} ∪ v                      ▷ Add v to the new bucket
if Rnode(B_{w_new}) is not in the Tree then
    Insert(Tree,Rnode(B_{w_new}))              ▷ Algorithm 6
else
    Rnode = Rnode(B_{w_new})
    Rnode.w = w_new × |B_{w_new}|
    while Rnode ≠ Tree.root do                 ▷ Update weights of parents
        Rnode ← Rnode.parent
        Rnode.w = Rnode.Rchild + Rnode.Lchild
```

Whenever an item gets a new weight w_{new} and $B_{w_{\text{new}}}$ does not exist in the tree, it is *inserted* into the ROLL-tree as a new leaf. Similarly, in case that the previous bucket $B_{w_{\text{old}}}$ becomes empty after removing its last item, it should be *removed* from the ROLL-tree. These two tree operations, i.e. insertion and removal, are explained in the followings, respectively.

Inserting to ROLL-tree.

The insertion can be done in several ways. Obviously, any binary tree that contains all the elements can be used to select random items. Generally, the complexity of reaching a bucket in an arbitrary binary tree is $O(L_{CW})$, where L_{CW} is the average code word length of the tree, i.e. $\frac{1}{|\mathbf{B}|}\sum_{i=1}^{N} w_i \times L_{B_i}$. A simple solution would be to keep the buckets in a *complete* binary tree, such that new buckets are added at the end of the tree in the first available free space. This will ensure that the depth of the tree is $\log n$, so the complexity of insertion, deletion, and random selection would be $O(\log n)$. In case that the selection probability of all leaf Rnodes are equal, it is the optimal solution. However, since the weights of buckets are not equal, e.g. $w_{B_k} = k \times k^{-\gamma} = k^{1-\gamma}$ in scale-free graphs, putting all leafs in the same depth is not optimal. Instead, we should put leafs with higher selection probability in a shorter depth so that they are fetched easier. Since our objective is to increase the efficiency, we might think of a tree which minimizes the time taken to reach the target nodes. Apparently, the amount of time taken to sample a node is proportional to the distance of its corresponding bucket from the root node, which is how many times we perform a binary decision between the right and left subtrees. To reduce the sampling time, buckets that are more likely to be selected, i.e. have higher weights, should be closer to the root node. This idea recalls the concept of Huffman coding tree, in which the distance of more-frequent symbols is closer to root, and thus their assigned code word has a shorter length. More specifically, each bucket can be assigned a unique binary code, in which a 0/1 in i'th index represents moving to the left/right subtree in the i'th depth of the ROLL-tree. In Figure 4, for example, B_3 is assigned the code 110 which means "right → right → left", that represents the path from the root node to B_3. The random selection in ROLL-tree can be thought of as stochastically finding a path from the root to a bucket. In other words, our objective is to minimize the average code word length.

In the following, we first discuss about Huffman coding trees, which gives the theoretically optimal tree having minimum expected number of samplings. Then, we criticize the high computational cost of using Huffman trees. Finally, we propose a light greedy approach that is close to the optimal bound of Huffman.

Optimal ROLL-tree (Huffman). Our objective is to insert an Rnode into the tree such a way that the average code word length is kept minimized. If the roulette wheel were static, the Huffman coding tree would be proved to be the optimal solution [19]. However, Huffman tree is not efficient for our problem due to its large computation cost. The main reason is that the original Huffman tree is not adaptive, hence we need to re-build the tree once the selection probability is changed, e.g. when the degree of a node is increased or a new node is created.

In order to design an online solution for weigh-balancing the tree, one may think of *adaptive* Huffman coding algorithms, such as FGK [4] algorithm [22, 25, 29] and the Vitter [48], which allow updating the probabilities. These methods guarantee that the in-

[4]Faller-Gallagher-Knuth

sertion time has $O(L_{CW})$ complexity. However, adaptive coding algorithms have an important shortcoming: they do not support removing an item (code) or down-weighting an item. Recall that many buckets become empty and hence they have to be removed from ROLL-tree. Also, when an item is sampled from a bucket, its degree is increased and it is moved to the bucket with higher degree. Therefore, the old bucket loses an item and its weight should be decreased accordingly. To our knowledge, there is no adaptive Huffman coding algorithm that efficiently supports deleting codes (i.e. Rnodes). As a result, we are unable to use adaptive Huffman tree algorithms for weight-balancing the tree.

Optimality $\neq$ Performance. In order to minimize the execution time of the algorithm, we should minimize the time taken by the roulette wheel to sample buckets, plus the tree maintenance time, i.e. the time taken to update the weights in the tree, add new buckets and remove the empty ones. While shorter average code word length results in faster sampling, other operations for tree maintenance should be lightweight as well. Roughly speaking, the rationale behind using a weigh-balanced tree is to reduce the execution time, hence the weight-balancing procedure should not take too much time itself. Therefore, a computationally expensive weigh-balancing algorithms that over-optimize the average code word length by sacrificing time, such as adaptive Huffman encoders, are not suitable for this problem.

We use neither adaptive Huffman coding nor any rotation-based algorithm for weigh-balancing the tree. Instead, we turn our attention on how the stochastic behavior of the preferential attachment algorithm can help us in keeping ROLL-tree weight-balanced. We focus on some interesting properties that are observed in the preferential attachment process. For example, buckets with small index values, corresponding to low degrees such as B_2 and B_3 have higher selection probabilities. Note that $P(B_k) = k^{1-\gamma}$ where $2 < \gamma < 3$, hence the less the index value, the more the expected selection probability. As a consequence, buckets with lower degree should have smaller code-word lengths and should be kept closer to the root. Moreover, Low-degree buckets are more stable and almost never become empty. On the contrary, a bucket with a large index value, e.g. B_{100m} and above, usually contains a single element, and this single element is likely to be selected soon and then the bucket should be removed from the tree.

As an example, in our toy graph, it is very unlikely for B_2 to be removed, as it already have 13 elements. Also, B_2 has the highest selection chance in the round which means it should be close to the root. On the contrary, B_{13} is very unstable. While it also has a considerable selection chance, it becomes empty right after its single node (v_1) is selected, and then we should remove B_{13} and insert the new bucket B_{14}.

Performance-aware ROLL-tree maintenance. Inspired by the above, we adopt a greedy approach that heuristically keeps the ROLL-tree almost weight-balanced, thanks to the gradual insertions. The heuristic is to always insert the new bucket to the lighter subtree. ROLL-tree gradually grows by inserting new buckets of single item by a top-down traversal from root. At each level of this top-down traversal, the heuristic inserts the new bucket to the subtree that is lighter. This procedure is repeated until a leaf is reached. Then, the leaf is replaced by a new Rnode that has this leaf Rnode and the new bucket as its children. The heuristic is shown in Algorithm 6.

The above heuristic not only incurs substantially smaller processing cost in comparison to the Huffman tree, but also results to a near optimal tree, i.e. minimized code-word length, as observed in our empirical experiments. Figure 5 compares the code word length of ROLL-tree and its ideal value (Huffman code word length) for Barabási-Albert graph generation. Based on the result, the average code-word length in ROLL-tree is very close to its optimal value (Huffman) for various n and m.

Algorithm 6 Inserting Rnode in ROLL-tree

```
Input: Tree, newTNode
Rnode ← Tree.root
while Rnode is not leaf do
    if Rnode.Rchild.w > Rnode.Lchild.w then
        Rnode ← Rnode.Lchild
    else
        Rnode ← Rnode.Rchild
branchRnode ← Initialize a new internal Rnode
branchRnode.Parent ← node.Parent
branchRnode.Rchild ← node
branchRnode.Lchild ← newNode
for pRnode ∈ newRnode.ancestors() do    ▷ In bottom-up order
    pRnode.w ← pRnode.Lchild.w + pRnode.Rchild.w
```

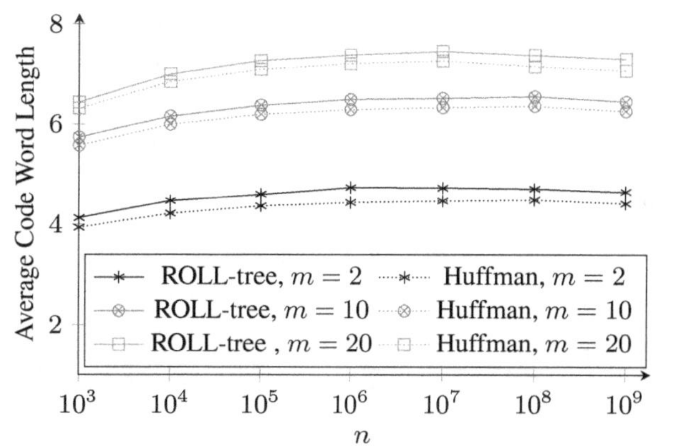

Figure 5: Comparison of the code-word length in ROLL-tree and Huffman tree, regarding to the final weight of items at the end of the process

Deleting from ROLL-tree.

In order to delete a bucket from the tree, we simply disconnect its corresponding Rnode from the tree. Then, the sibling of the deleted Rnode is replaced by its parent. This will ensure that none of the internal Rnodes have a null child and the tree is kept full. This procedure is shown in Algorithm 7. Note that while removing random Rnodes from the tree might decrease the balance, i.e. increase the average code word length, but this balance will be recovered as new Rnodes are inserted.

Algorithm 7 Deleting Rnode from ROLL-tree

```
Input: Tree, emptyTNode
Rnode ← emptyTNode.Parent
Rnode.removeChild(emptyTNode)
if Rnode ≠ Tree.root then
    Remove Rnode.parent and replace it with Rnode
for pRnode ∈ Rnode.ancestors() do    ▷ In bottom-up order
    pRnode.w ← pRnode.leftChild.w + pRnode.rightChild.w
```

Decreasing tree operations.

Finally, we improve ROLL-tree by compensating deletion and insertion of Rnodes by replacement of buckets. Given a ROLL-

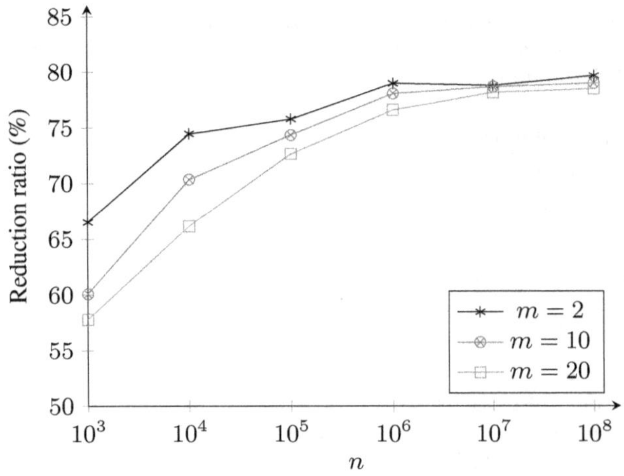

Figure 6: Ratio of the skipped tree operations on ROLL-tree

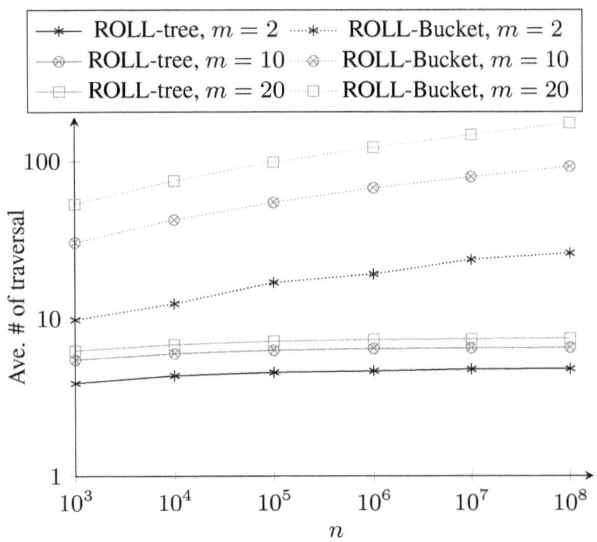

Figure 7: Average # of items traversed to the target sample

tree T, this replacement is possible if we sample an item i from a bucket B_d that only contains i and $B_{d+1} \notin T$, like $v_1 \in B_{13}$ in our toy example. When item i in bucket B_d is sampled, its degree is increased by one and thus it should be moved to B_{d+1}. If B_{d+1} does not exist in ROLL-tree, instead of deleting B_d then inserting B_{d+1} we replace B_d with B_{d+1}. Figure 6 shows how significantly this replacement reduces the number of deletion and insertion of Rnodes. In this figure reduction ratio is $(1 - \frac{rep}{del+ins}) \times 100$ such that rep, del and ins are replacement, deletion and insertion of Rnodes, respectively. Figure 7 compares the number of items traversed in ROLL-bucket and ROLL-tree. Experiments show that the idea of using ROLL-tree, along with the techniques for minimizing the code word length, effectively minimize the number of operations for each sampling.

5. ANALYSIS

In this section, we evaluate the two proposed algorithms along with the baseline method (SimpleRW) and the state of the art (SA) described in Section 3. We perform theoretical study, followed by experimental evaluations, in order to get a more complete view on the performance of our algorithms.

Algorithm	Sample	Maintenance
SimpleRW	$O(n^2m)$	$O(nm)$
SA	$O(n^{3/2})$	$O(nm)$
ROLL-bucket	$O(nm \times \lvert B \rvert)$	$O(nm \times \lvert B \rvert)$
ROLL-tree	$O(nm \times \lvert L_{CW} \rvert)$	$O(nm \times \lvert L_{CW} \rvert)$

Table 5: Complexity of the roulette wheel algorithms for sampling and maintenance

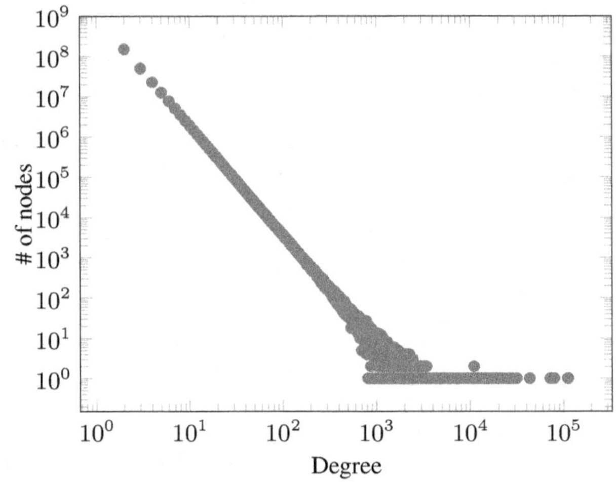

Figure 8: Degree distribution of the generated BA network with $n = 10^9$, $m = 2$ via ROLL-tree.

5.1 Theoretical Analysis

We summarize time and memory complexities of the four algorithms and then provide experimental results to verify the results.

Time Complexity. The generation time is the time taken to sample from the data structure, plus the time for maintaining the roulette wheels, such as updating the weights, buckets, and trees. The complexities are summarized in Table 5.

Memory Complexity. As discussed before, the complexity of all four algorithms are the same, because they all need to keep the weight of buckets in memory. The memory complexity of SimpleRW and SA is $O(n)$. ROLL-bucket and ROLL-tree take some additional memory for the buckets, hence their complexity is $O(n + |B|)$ which is effectively equal to to that of SimpleRW and SA because $|B| << n$.

Degree distribution. We measured the degree distribution of a one billion node graph resulted by ROLL-tree in Figure 8 with parameters $n = 10^9, m = m_0 = 2$. This figure shows a heavy tailed distribution of the generated graph that is a feature of the real-world power-law networks. In order to verify the scale-free distribution of the generated graph, we compute the γ exponent of this distribution which certifies the accuracy of the BA model generated via ROLL-tree. The value of γ, as measured by curve fitting, is $\gamma = 2.72$ which satisfies the condition $2 < \gamma < \infty$.

5.2 Experimental Analysis

In this section, we conduct experiments to study the performance of the algorithms. First, we perform a micro-level analysis in order to study the effect of the parameters. Then, we experimentally compare the performance of the proposed methods against other methods [5].

[5] Source code is available at https://github.com/alihadian/ROLL

$\lvert V \rvert$	Items Traversed in SimpleRW	Uniform Samples in SA	Buckets Traversed in ROLL-bucket	Depth of Bucket in ROLL-tree
10^3	171	14	9.3	3.87
10^4	1,665	42	12.6	4.34
10^5	16,631	135	16.4	4.51
10^6	166,740	442	19.5	4.69
10^7	1,666,500	1,320	22.5	4.71
10^8	-	3,769	26.2	4.71
10^9	-	-	-	4.86

Table 6: Comparison of the *average* number of items, i.e. node (in SimpleRW & SA) or bucket (in ROLL-*), traversed for each random node selection ($m = 2$)

5.2.1 Experimental Setup

In this work, our main focus is on efficiency, since the stochastic properties of all compared methods are the same, i.e. they randomly select a random node according to its weight. Therefore, we only compare the execution times of the algorithms. The experiments were performed on a commodity machine with Intel Xeon 2.66 GHz processor with 32GB of available main memory, running Linux 3.5.0. Note that only one thread is used in our experiments because the algorithms are inherently sequential. All algorithms were developed with Java 1.8 SDK. The quantities were measured five times and the average is reported.

An important limitation of preferential attachment is that we need to store either the index or weight of all elements in the main memory, thus the space complexity of the algorithms are approximately $O(|V|)$. For example, if the node indexes are stored as 32-bit integers, in order to generate a one-billion-node graph, at least 4GB will be required to keep the roulette wheel in memory. Therefore, we only managed to generate graphs with up to 1 billion nodes in our commodity machine.

For all algorithms, the generated graphs are persisted as a stream of edge lists, i.e. each line contains two nodes "v_i, v_j" that represent an edge $E_{i,j}$ between v_i and v_j. The resulting output stream is then pipelined to an external consumer process. We did not include the time taken to persist the graph, because the graph might be presented in different formats (e.g. edge list, adjacency list, etc.), that is application-dependent, or it is even not persisted in many applications. For the m_0 parameter, we set $m_0 = m$ as its default value. To be noted, the value of m_0 does not affect the degree distribution, hence the performance.

5.2.2 Micro-level Analysis

The majority of the preferential attachment models follow the so-called "rich-get-richer" phenomenon, i.e. nodes that have been selected more in the past are more likely to be selected in the future. Such a model results in a long-tailed probability distribution over the roulette wheel items. The performance of each of the roulette wheel algorithms discussed before highly depends on the statistical properties of the probability distribution corresponding to the generation model. For example, the performance of SA depends on the average acceptance rate, i.e. how many times, on average, we need to select a random item until the selection is accepted, which in turn depends on the estimate of both the maximum and the average probability among roulette wheel items. Similarly, the performance of the ROLL-bucket depends on our estimate of $|B|$. Performance analysis of ROLL-tree is even harder because we have to know the

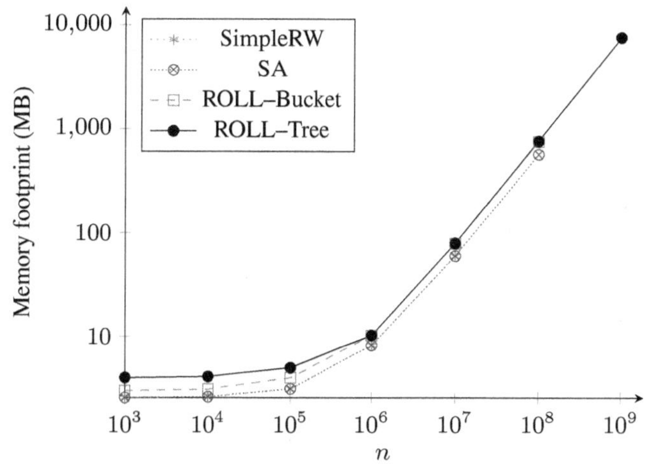

Figure 9: Memory footprints ($m = 2$)

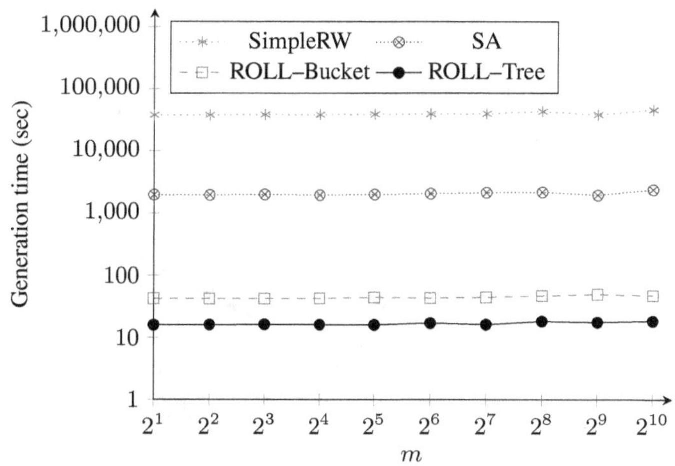

Figure 10: Generation time for various m_0, while $m = 2, n = 10^7$

probability distribution of the buckets and its growth model over time.

In this section, we experimentally analyze how different roulette wheel algorithms perform for Barabási-Albert graph generation. More specifically, we focus on the parameters that affect the performance of the algorithms, such as the number of operations performed in each of the algorithms for selecting an item from the roulette wheel. Table 6 illustrates how many comparisons are performed by each of the algorithms to select an item from the roulette wheel. For example, to generate a Barabási-Albert graph with 10 million nodes using the simple roulette wheel algorithm, about 1.6 million items in the roulette wheel are traversed in average to sample each single item (target node) from the roulette wheel, where SA tries 1320 uniformly sampled items in average until a selection is accepted. Similarly, the average number of buckets that are traversed in ROLL-bucket and the average depth of the target bucket in ROLL-tree are 22.5 and 4.71, respectively.

In the following, we consider the memory footprints and execution times of the four algorithms discussed in the paper for generating Barabási-Albert graphs.

5.2.3 Memory Footprint Comparison

Figure 9 illustrates the memory footprints of the four algorithms. The memory consumption of SimpleRW and SA are almost equal, while ROLL-bucket and ROLL-tree consume about 30% more mem-

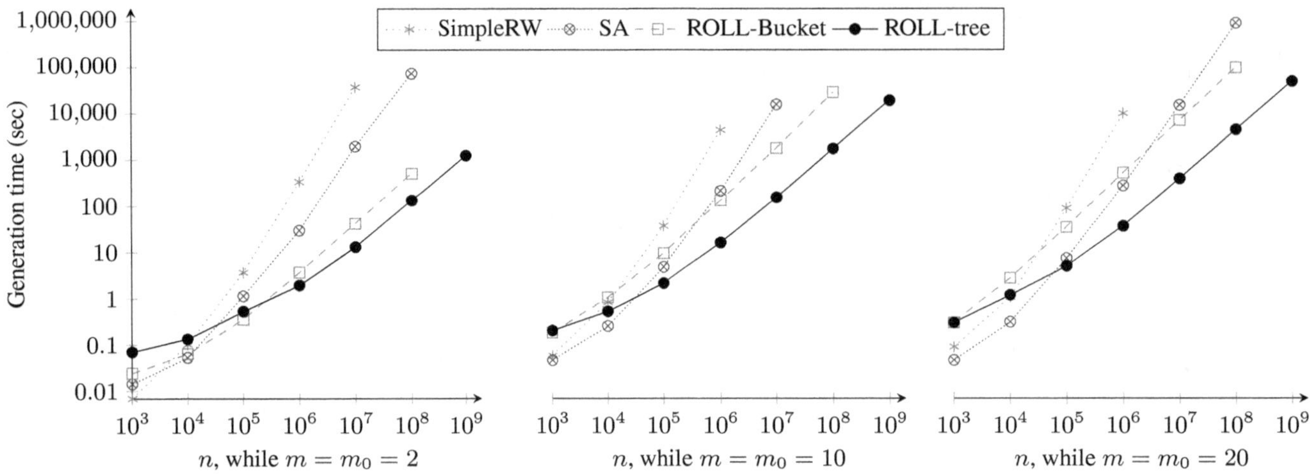

Figure 11: Generation time for various n values

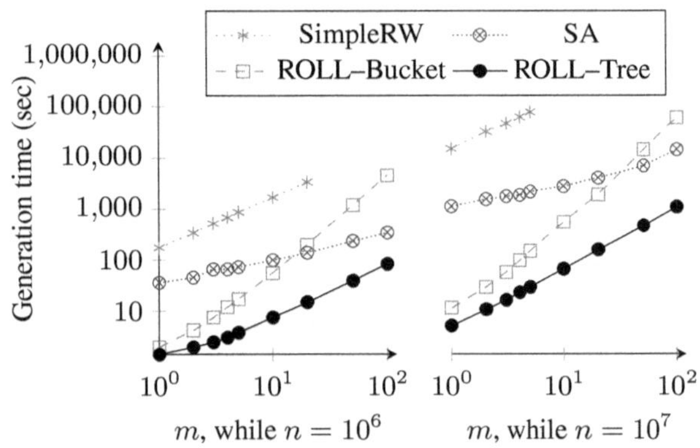

Figure 12: Generation time for various m values

ory space, which is mainly because the items inside each bucket are stored in dynamic arrays. These arrays reserve space for more entries than the actual number of items.

SimpleRW and SA only need a list of size n that contains the degree of items. Therefore, we use simple arrays for the sake of performance and cache efficiency. In ROLL-bucket, the list of buckets is stored in a red-black tree, which allows ordered traversal and is fast for lookup, delete, and insert. Items inside each bucket are stored in dynamic arrays that grow on demand.

5.2.4 *Performance Comparison*

The execution time for $m = 2$ and $m = 20$ is given in Figure 11. Results show that ROLL-tree outperforms all other algorithms with large margin for large graphs. For small-sized graphs, however, stochastic acceptance is faster than ROLL-tree, especially when m is relatively large. In general, ROLL-tree is the only algorithm that grows approximately linearly with n.

Figure 10 shows generation time of various m_0 values and further verifies that this time is almost independent of m_0. Figure 12 illustrates how graph generation time grows with m. Generally, the execution time of any roulette wheel algorithm is expected to grow linearly with m, since the roulette wheel is called $m(n - m_0)$ times and thus the number of roulette wheel invocations grows with m as well. The only exception is SA. As discussed in Section 3.2, the average number of uniform samples in SA until getting an acceptance is inversely proportional to m, i.e. $O(\sqrt{n}/m)$, which means that for larger m values, selecting from the roulette wheel is faster. However, since the stochastic rejection rate is generally too high, the stochastic acceptance algorithm is much slower than ROLL-bucket and ROLL-tree in real-world problems. Moreover, by increasing m after some threshold, that depends on n, the graph becomes so dense that it is no more scale-free. Thus, practically we are interested in generating BA graphs with m substantially smaller than n. For instance, there are hundreds of billions of nodes in the world wide web, while the average out-links (m) of each page is not more than 150. Figure 11 illustrates that when the graph is large ($n > 10^6$), ROLL-tree is the outperforming algorithm for any m.

6. CONCLUSION AND FUTURE WORK

The lack of gigantic scale-free graph input calls for scalable graph generation methods. This paper proposes an in-memory solution, ROLL-tree, a fast roulette wheel data structure to accelerate the Barabási-Albert Model. ROLL-tree is a fast, exact and generalizable method for preferential attachment processes. The experimental findings proved that ROLL-tree performs considerably faster than its rival. Instead of the baseline method that has a complexity of $O(|V|^2)$, the execution time of ROLL-tree is almost linear, which enables very large scale-free graph construction. For instance, on a single commodity machine we successfully generated a graph with 1 billion nodes in 62 minutes.

ROLL-tree is a general dynamic roulette wheel data structure, hence its not only applicable to random graph generation process but also to other random processes. For instance, many physical events can be modeled using random events that are similar to preferential attachment, e.g. simulating the motions of an object in water considering the diffusion effect in fluid. This study provides fundamentals and sheds a light in this direction. However, various applications may have specific constraints that requires further study in a generalized framework for future work.

ROLL-tree provides an exact serial roulette wheel data structure with no approximation. However, it can shed the light on the scalability requirements of generating gigantic graphs without losing precision. In other words, ROLL can be used as a building-block for parallel and distributed preferential attachment which effectively speeds up both the inter-machine and intra-machine operations by reducing the problem space from $O(n)$ to $O(|B|)$ and even very close to the lower bound of Huffman code word length over the bucket weights.

7. REFERENCES

[1] W. Aiello, F. Chung, and L. Lu. A random graph model for massive graphs. In *STOC*, pages 171–180, 2000.

[2] L. Akoglu and C. Faloutsos. RTG: A recursive realistic graph generator using random typing. *Data Mining and Knowledge Discovery*, 19(2):194–209, 2009.

[3] L. Akoglu, M. McGlohon, and C. Faloutsos. RTM: Laws and a recursive generator for weighted time-evolving graphs. In *ICDM*, pages 701–706, 2008.

[4] M. Alam, M. Khan, and M. V. Marathe. Distributed-memory parallel algorithms for generating massive scale-free networks using preferential attachment model. In *HPC*, pages 1–12, 2013.

[5] A. Arora, M. Sachan, and A. Bhattacharya. Mining statistically significant connected subgraphs in vertex labeled graphs. In *SIGMOD*, pages 1003–1014, 2014.

[6] A.-L. Barabási and R. Albert. Emergence of scaling in random networks. *Science*, 286(5439):509–512, 1999.

[7] S. Boccaletti, V. Latora, Y. Moreno, M. Chavez, and D.-U. Hwang. Complex networks: Structure and dynamics. *Physics reports*, 424(4):175–308, 2006.

[8] M. Boguná and R. Pastor-Satorras. Class of correlated random networks with hidden variables. *Physical Review E*, 68(3):036112, 2003.

[9] M. Boguná, R. Pastor-Satorras, and A. Vespignani. Cut-offs and finite size effects in scale-free networks. *The European Physical Journal B*, 38(2):205–209, 2004.

[10] P. Buesser and M. Tomassini. Supercooperation in evolutionary games on correlated weighted networks. *Physical Review E*, 85(1):16107–16107, 2012.

[11] T. G. K. C. Seshadhri and A. Pinar. Community structure and scale-free collections of Erdős-Rényi graphs. *Physical Review E*, 85(5):056109, 2012.

[12] G. Caldarelli, A. Capocci, P. De Los Rios, and M. A. Muñoz. Scale-free networks from varying vertex intrinsic fitness. *Physical review letters*, 89(25):258702, 2002.

[13] C. Campbell, K. Shea, and R. Albert. Comment on "control profiles of complex networks". *Science*, 346(6209):561, 2014.

[14] M. Capotă, T. Hegeman, A. Iosup, A. Prat-Pérez, O. Erling, and P. Boncz. Graphalytics: A big data benchmark for graph-processing platforms. In *GRADES*, 2015.

[15] J. M. Carlson and J. Doyle. Highly optimized tolerance: A mechanism for power laws in designed systems. *Physical Review E*, 60(2):1412, 1999.

[16] D. Chakrabarti, Y. Zhan, and C. Faloutsos. R-MAT: A recursive model for graph mining. In *SDM*, pages 442–446, 2004.

[17] H.-H. Chen, Y.-B. Ciou, and S.-D. Lin. Information propagation game: A tool to acquire humanplaying data for multiplayer influence maximization on social networks. In *SIGKDD*, pages 1524–1527, 2012.

[18] F. Chung and L. Lu. The average distances in random graphs with given expected degrees. *PNAS*, 99(25):79–82, 2002.

[19] I. Csiszar and J. Körner. *Information theory: coding theorems for discrete memoryless systems*. Cambridge University Press, 2011.

[20] N. Du, H. Wang, and C. Faloutsos. Analysis of large multi-modal social networks: patterns and a generator. In *ECML-PKDD*, pages 393–408. 2010.

[21] P. Erdős and A. Rényi. On random graphs I. *Publicationes Mathematicae*, 6:290–297, 1959.

[22] N. Faller. An adaptive system for data compression. In *Asilomar Conference*, pages 593–597, 1973.

[23] I. Fazekas and B. Porvázsnyik. Scale-free property for degrees and weights in a preferential attachment random graph model. *Journal of Probability and Statistics*, 2013.

[24] R. Ferrer-Cancho and R. V. Solé. Optimization in complex networks. *Statistical Mechanics of Complex Networks*, 625:114–126, 2003.

[25] R. G. Gallager. *Information theory and reliable communication*. Wiley, 1968.

[26] E. N. Gilbert. Random graphs. *The Annals of Mathematical Statistics*, 30(4):1141–1144, 1959.

[27] A. Goldenberg, A. X. Zheng, S. E. Fienberg, and E. M. Airoldi. A survey of statistical network models. *Foundations and Trends in Machine Learning*, 2(2):129–233, 2010.

[28] K. Klemm and V. M. Eguiluz. Growing scale-free networks with small-world behavior. *Physical Review E*, 65(5):057102, 2002.

[29] D. E. Knuth. Dynamic huffman coding. *Journal of algorithms*, 6(2):163–180, 1985.

[30] T. G. Kolda, A. Pinar, T. Plantenga, and C. Seshadhri. A scalable generative graph model with community structure. *SIAM*, 36(5):424–452, 2014.

[31] C. León, C. Machado, and A. Murcia. Assessing systemic importance with a fuzzy logic inference system. *ISAFM*, 2015.

[32] J. Leskovec. *Dynamics of large networks*. PhD thesis, Carnegie Mellon University, 2008.

[33] J. Leskovec, D. Chakrabarti, J. Kleinberg, C. Faloutsos, and Z. Ghahramani. Kronecker graphs: An approach to modeling networks. *JMLR*, 11:985–1042, 2010.

[34] J. Li, H. Wang, S. U. Khan, Q. Li, and A. Y. Zomaya. A fully distributed scheme for discovery of semantic relationships. *IEEE Trans. on Services Computing*, 6(4):457–469, 2013.

[35] A. Lipowski and D. Lipowska. Roulette-wheel selection via stochastic acceptance. *Physica A*, 391(6):2193–2196, 2012.

[36] Y.-C. Lo, H.-C. Lai, C.-T. Li, and S.-D. Lin. Mining and generating large-scaled social networks via MapReduce. *Social Network Analysis and Mining*, 3(4):1449–1469, 2013.

[37] A. Lumsdaine, D. Gregor, B. Hendrickson, and J. Berry. Challenges in parallel graph processing. *Parallel Processing Letters*, 17(01):5–20, 2007.

[38] M. McGlohon, L. Akoglu, and C. Faloutsos. Weighted graphs and disconnected components: patterns and a generator. In *SIGKDD*, pages 524–532, 2008.

[39] M. E. Newman. Modularity and community structure in networks. *Proceedings of the National Academy of Sciences*, 103(23):8577–8582, 2006.

[40] S. Nobari, X. Lu, P. Karras, and S. Bressan. Fast random graph generation. In *EDBT*, pages 331–342, 2011.

[41] S. Nobari, F. Tauheed, T. Heinis, P. Karras, S. Bressan, and A. Ailamaki. TOUCH: in-memory spatial join by hierarchical data-oriented partitioning. In *SIGMOD*, pages 701–712, 2013.

[42] M.-D. Pham, P. Boncz, and O. Erling. S3G2: A scalable structure-correlated social graph generator. In *TPCTC*, pages 156–172. 2013.

[43] J. Poncela, J. Gómez-Gardenes, Y. Moreno, and L. M. Floria. Cooperation in the prisoner's dilemma game in random scale-free graphs. *IJBC*, 20(03):849–857, 2010.

[44] R. V. Solé, R. Ferrer-Cancho, J. M. Montoya, and S. Valverde. Selection, tinkering, and emergence in complex networks. *Complexity*, 8(1):20–33, 2002.

[45] K. Soramäki and S. Cook. Sinkrank: An algorithm for identifying systemically important banks in payment systems. *Economics*, 7(28), 2013.

[46] S. Trißl and U. Leser. Fast and practical indexing and querying of very large graphs. In *SIGMOD*, pages 845–856, 2007.

[47] S. Valverde, R. F. Cancho, and R. V. Sole. Scale-free networks from optimal design. *EuroPhysics Letters*, 60(4):512–517, 2002.

[48] J. S. Vitter. Design and analysis of dynamic huffman codes. *JACM*, 34(4):825–845, 1987.

[49] M. von Looz, C. L. Staudt, H. Meyerhenke, and R. Prutkin. Fast generation of dynamic complex networks with underlying hyperbolic geometry. *CoRR*, 2015.

[50] H. Wang, K. Zheng, X. Zhou, and S. W. Sadiq. SharkDB: An in-memory storage system for massive trajectory data. In *SIGMOD*, pages 1099–1104, 2015.

[51] D. J. Watts and S. H. Strogatz. Collective dynamics of small-world networks. *Nature*, 393(6684):440–442, 1998.

[52] X. Yang, J. Cao, and Z. Yang. Synchronization of coupled reaction-diffusion neural networks with time-varying delays via pinning-impulsive controller. *SIAM Journal on Control and Optimization*, 51(5):3486–3510, 2013.

[53] A. Yoo and K. W. Henderson. Parallel generation of massive scale-free graphs. *CoRR*, 2010.

[54] F. Yuan-Yuan, W. Liang, and Z. Shi-Qun. Synchronization of phase oscillators in networks with certain frequency sequence. *CTP*, 61(3):329–333, 2014.

[55] F. Zhu, Z. Zhang, and Q. Qu. A direct mining approach to efficient constrained graph pattern discovery. pages 821–832, 2013.

Functional Dependencies for Graphs

Wenfei Fan[1,2] Yinghui Wu[3] Jingbo Xu[1,2]
[1]University of Edinburgh [2]RCBD and NLSDE Lab, Beihang University [3]Washington State University
{wenfei@inf, jingbo.xu@}.ed.ac.uk, yinghui@eecs.wsu.edu

ABSTRACT

We propose a class of functional dependencies for graphs, referred to as GFDs. GFDs capture both attribute-value dependencies and topological structures of entities, and subsume conditional functional dependencies (CFDs) as a special case. We show that the satisfiability and implication problems for GFDs are coNP-complete and NP-complete, respectively, no worse than their CFD counterparts. We also show that the validation problem for GFDs is coNP-complete. Despite the intractability, we develop parallel scalable algorithms for catching violations of GFDs in large-scale graphs. Using real-life and synthetic data, we experimentally verify that GFDs provide an effective approach to detecting inconsistencies in knowledge and social graphs.

Keywords

Functional dependencies; graphs; implication; satisfiability; validation

1. INTRODUCTION

Data dependencies have been well studied for relational data. In particular, our familiar functional dependencies (FDs) are found in every database textbook, and have been extended to XML [9]. Their revisions, such as conditional functional dependencies (CFDs) [16], have proven effective in capturing semantic inconsistencies in relations [15].

The need for FDs is also evident in graphs, a common source of data. Unlike relational databases, real-life graphs typically do not come with a schema. FDs specify a fundamental part of the semantics of the data, and are hence particularly important to graphs. Moreover, (1) FDs help us detect inconsistencies in knowledge bases [45], which need to be identified as violations of dependencies [15]. (2) For social networks, FDs help us catch spams and manage blogs [11].

Example 1: Consider the following examples taken from real-life knowledge bases and social graphs.

SIGMOD'16, June 26-July 01, 2016, San Francisco, CA, USA
© 2016 ACM. ISBN 978-1-4503-3531-7/16/06...$15.00
DOI: http://dx.doi.org/10.1145/2882903.2915232

(1) *Knowledge bases*, where inconsistencies are common [45]:

- Flight A123 has two entries with the same departure time 14:50 and arrival time 22:35, but one is from Paris to NYC, while the other from Paris to Singapore [40].
- Both Canberra and Melbourne are labeled as the capital of Australia [13].
- It is marked that all birds can fly, and that penguins are birds [26], despite their evolved wing structures.

We will see that all these inconsistencies can be easily captured by FDs defined on entities with a graph structure.

(2) *Social graphs.* When a blog Z with photo Y is posed, a social network company defines a status X with attachment Y. It is required that the annotation X.text of X must match the description Y.desc of Y. That is,

- Blog: if Z has_status X, Z has_photo Y, and if X has_attachment Y, then X.text = Y.desc.

This is essentially an FD on graph-structured data.

Functional dependencies are also useful in catching spams.

- Fake account [11]: If account x' is confirmed fake, both accounts x and x' like blogs $P_1, \ldots, P_k$, x posts blog y, x' posts y', and if y and y' have a particular keyword c, then x is also identified as a fake account.

This rule to identify fake accounts is an FD on graphs. □

No matter how important, however, the study of FDs for graphs is still in its infancy, from formulation to classical problems to applications. It is more challenging to define FDs for graphs than for relations, since real-life graphs are semi-structured and typically do not have a schema. Moreover, for entities represented by vertices in a graph, FDs have to specify not only regularity between attribute values of the entities, but also the topological structures of the entities.

Contributions. We study functional dependencies for graphs, from their fundamental problems to applications.

(1) We propose a class of functional dependencies for graphs, referred to as GFDs (Section 3). As opposed to relational FDs, a GFD specifies two constraints: (a) a topological constraint in terms of a graph pattern (Section 2), to identify entities on which the dependency is defined, and (b) an extension of CFDs to specify the dependencies of the attribute values of the entities. We show that GFDs subsume FDs and CFDs as special cases, and capture inconsistencies between attributes of the same entity and across different entities.

(2) We settle two classical problems for GFDs (Section 4). For a set Σ of GFDs, we study (a) its satisfiability, to decide

whether there exists a non-empty graph that satisfies all the GFDs in Σ, and (b) its implication, to decide whether a GFD is entailed by Σ. We show that the satisfiability and implication problems for GFDs are coNP-complete and NP-complete, respectively. The results tell us that reasoning about GFDs is no harder than their relational counterparts such as CFDs, which are also intractable [16].

(3) As one of applications of GFDs, we study the validation problem, to detect errors in graphs by using GFDs as data quality rules (Section 5). We show that it is coNP-complete to decide whether a graph contains no violation of a set of GFDs. Despite the intractability, we develop algorithms that are *parallel scalable*, *i.e.,* they guarantee to take less time when more processors are used. They are 2-approximation algorithms for a bi-criteria optimization problem, to balance workload and minimize communication costs (Section 6). These make it feasible to detect errors in large-scale graphs.

(4) Using real-life and synthetic graphs, we experimentally verify the effectiveness and efficiency of our GFD techniques (Section 7). We find the following. (a) Inconsistency detection with GFDs is feasible in real-life graphs. It takes 156 (resp. 326) seconds over replicated (resp. partitioned) YAGO [44] with 20 processors, for a set of 50 GFDs. (b) Our algorithms are parallel scalable: they are on average 2.4 and 3.7 times faster on fragmented and replicated real-life graphs, respectively, when processors increase from 4 to 20. (c) Our optimization techniques are effective: they improve performance by up to 1.9 times. (d) GFDs catch a variety of inconsistencies in real-life graphs, validating the need for combining topological constraints and value dependencies.

We contend that GFDs are a natural extension of traditional FDs, by incorporating graph topological structures. GFDs provide us with primitive dependencies for graphs, to specify fundamental semantics and to detect inconsistencies. This work also provides the first complexity bounds for reasoning about GFDs. Moreover, we develop the first parallel scalable algorithms to make practical use of GFDs.

Related work. We categorize related work as follows.

FDs *on graphs*. Extensions of FDs and CFDs have been studied for RDF [8, 10, 12, 23, 24, 49]. The definitions of FDs in [8, 12, 24] are based on RDF triple embedding and the coincidence of variable valuations. FDs are extended [49] to specify value dependencies on clustered values via, *e.g.,* path patterns; similarly for extensions of CFDs [23]. A schema matching framework is proposed in [10], for transformations between RDF and relations. It defines FDs as trees in which each node denotes an attribute in a corresponding relation.

Our work differs from the prior work in the following. (1) We define GFDs with graph patterns to express topological constraints of (property) graphs, beyond RDF. (2) GFDs capture inconsistencies in graph-structured entities identified by patterns. In contrast, the FDs of [8, 12, 24] are value-based regardless of what entities carry the values, and the reasoning techniques of [24] are based on relational encoding of RDF data. Moreover, these FDs cannot express equality with constants (semantic value binding) as in CFDs, *e.g.,* x.city = "Edi", while GFDs subsume CFDs. The FDs of [10] are defined as trees and assume a relational schema. They do not support general topological constraints; similarly for [23,49]. (3) We provide complexity bounds for GFD analyses and parallel scalable algorithms for error detection in graphs, which were not studied by the prior work.

Closer to this work is [14] on keys for graphs [14], which differ from GFDs in the following. (1) Keys are defined simply as a graph pattern $Q[x]$, with a designated variable x denoting an entity. In contrast, GFDs have the form $(Q[\bar{x}], X \rightarrow Y)$, where $\bar{x}$ is a list of variables, and X and Y are conjunctions of equality atoms with constants and variables in $\bar{x}$. GFDs cannot be expressed as keys, just like that relational FDs are not expressible as keys. Moreover, keys of [14] are recursively defined to identify entities, while GFDs are an extension of conventional FDs and are not recursively defined. (2) Keys are defined on RDF triples (s, p, o), while GFDs are defined on property graphs, *e.g.,* social networks. (3) Keys are interpreted in terms of three isomorphic mappings: two from subgraphs to Q, and one between the two subgraphs. In contrast, GFDs needs a single isomorphic mapping from a subgraph to Q. In light of the different semantics, algorithms for GFDs and keys are radically different. (4) We study the satisfiability and implication for GFDs; these classical problems were not studied for keys [14].

Inconsistency detection has been studied for relations (see [15] for a survey), and recently for knowledge bases (linked data) [23,32,35,37,42,45]. The methods for knowledge bases employ either rules [23, 32, 35, 42, 45], or probabilistic inferences [37]. (1) Datalog rules are used [42] to extract entities and detect inconsistent "facts". SOFIE [45] maintains the consistency of extracted facts by using rules expressed as first-order logic (FO) formulas along with textual patterns, existing ontology and semantic constraints. Pellet [35] checks inconsistencies by using inference rules in description logic (*e.g.,* OWL-DL). Dependency rules are used to detect inconsistencies in attribute values in semantic Web [32] and RDF [23]. BigDansing [28] supports user-defined rules for repairing relational data. To clean graph-structured entities, it needs to represent graphs as tables and encode isomorphic functions beyond relational query languages. (2) The inference method of [37] uses Markov logic to combine FO and probabilistic graphical models, and detects errors by learning and computing joint probability over structures.

Our work differs from the prior work as follows. (1) GFDs are among the first data-quality rules on (property) graphs, not limited to RDF, by supporting topological constraints with graph patterns. (2) GFDs aim to strike a balance between complexity and expressivity. Reasoning about GFDs is much cheaper than analyzing FO formulas. (3) We provide the complexity and characterizations for satisfiability and implication of GFDs; these are among the first results for reasoning about graph dependencies in general, and about data quality rules for graphs in particular. (4) We develop parallel scalable algorithms for error detection and new strategies for workload assignment, instead of expensive large-scale inference and logic programming. These make error detection feasible in large graphs with provable performance guarantees, which are not offered by the prior work.

Parallel algorithms related to GFD validation algorithms are (1) algorithms for detecting errors in distributed data [17, 18], and (2) algorithms for subgraph enumeration, subgraph isomorphism and SPARQL [5, 20, 22, 25, 30, 31, 39, 41, 46].

(1) Algorithms of [17, 18] (incrementally) detect errors in (horizontally or vertically) partitioned relations based on CFDs. The methods work on relations, but do not help GFDs

that require subgraph isomorphism computation. Indeed, our algorithms are radically different from those of [17, 18].

(2) Closer to this work are parallel algorithms for subgraph enumeration [5, 30, 36, 41]. (a) MapReduce algorithms are proposed via conjunctive multi-way join operations [5] and decomposed edge joins [36]. The strategy is effective for triangle counting [47]. (b) To reduce excessive partial answers for general patterns, a MapReduce solution in [30] decomposes a pattern into twin twigs (single edge or two incident edges), and adopts a left-deep-join strategy to join multiple edges as stars. To cope with skewed nodes, the neighborhoods of high-degree nodes are partitioned, replicated and distributed. Decomposition strategies are used to reduce MapReduce rounds and I/O cost. (c) A BSP framework is developed in [41] via vertex-centric programming. It adopts an online greedy strategy to assign partial subgraphs to workers that incur minimum overall workload, and optimization strategies to reduce subgraph instances.

(3) A number of parallel algorithms are developed for subgraph isomorphism [39, 46] and SPARQL queries [20, 22, 25, 31]. Twig decomposition is used to prune the intermediate results and reduce the latency in Trinity memory cloud [46]. The in-memory algorithm of [39] parallelizes a backtracking procedure by (a) evenly distributing partial answers among threads for local expansion, and (b) copying the partial answers to a global storage for balanced distribution in the next round. Hash-based partitioning, query decomposition and load balancing strategies are introduced for parallel SPARQL on RDF [20, 25]. Query decomposition and plan generation techniques are studied in [22], which avoid communication cost by replicating graphs. Optimization techniques for multi-pattern matching are provided in [31], by extracting common sub-patterns. Many of these techniques leverage RDF schema and SPARQL query semantics, which are not available for GFDs and general property graphs.

This work differs from the prior work in the following. (a) GFD validation in distributed graphs is a bi-criteria optimization problem, to balance workload and minimize communication cost, with combined complexity from subgraph enumeration of *disconnected* patterns and dependency checking in fragmented graphs. It is more challenging than graph queries studied in the prior work. (b) We introduce a workload assignment strategy for the intractable optimization problem, with approximation bounds, instead of treating workload balancing and communication cost minimization separately [30, 41]. (c) We warrant parallel scalability, which is not guaranteed by the prior algorithms.

On the other hand, this work can benefit from prior techniques for fast parallel subgraph matching and listing, *e.g.,* query decomposition strategies [22, 30, 46] and multi-thread in-memory algorithm [39], for local error detection at each worker. We have adopted the optimization techniques of [31], and will incorporate others into GFD tools.

(4) There has also been work on characterizing the effectiveness of parallel algorithms, in terms of communication costs of MapReduce algorithms [6], constraints on MapReduce computation/communication cost (MRC [27], MMC [48] and SGC [38]), and the polynomial fringe property of recursive programs [4]. We adopt the notion of parallel scalability [29], which measures speedup by parallelization over multiple processors, in terms of both computation and communication costs. It is for generic parallel algorithms not

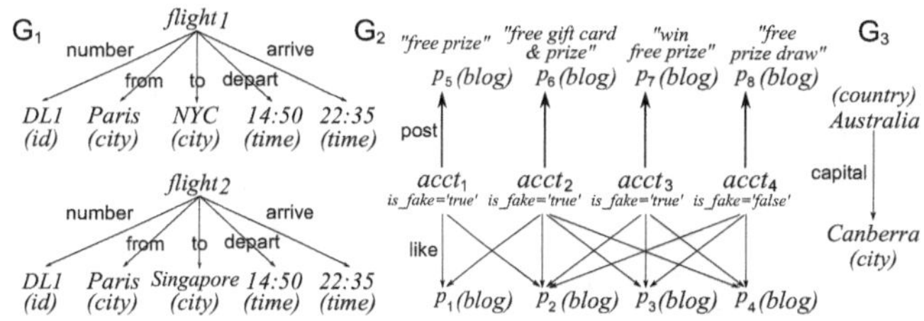

Figure 1: Graphs

limited to MapReduce. A parallel scalable algorithm guarantees to scale with large graphs by adding processors. However, parallel scalability is beyond reach for certain graph computations [19]. We show that GFD validation is parallel scalable, by providing such algorithms.

Static analyses. Over relations, the satisfiability and implication problems are known to be in $O(1)$ and linear time for FDs, NP-complete and coNP-complete for CFDs, $O(1)$ time and PSPACE-complete for inclusion dependencies (INDs), respectively. The validation problem is in PTIME for FDs, CFDs and INDs (cf. [3, 15]). We show that for GFDs on graphs, validation, satisfiability and implication for GFDs are coNP-complete, coNP-complete and NP-complete, respectively. As will be seen in Section 4, the complexity of GFDs comes from the interactions between graph patterns (subgraph isomorphism); it is not inherited from CFDs.

2. PRELIMINARIES

We start with a review of basic notations.

Graphs. We consider directed *graphs* $G = (V, E, L, F_A)$ with labeled nodes and edges, and attributes on its nodes. Here (1) V is a finite set of nodes; (2) $E \subseteq V \times V$ is a set of edges; (3) each node v in V (resp. edge e in E) carries label $L(v)$ (resp. $L(e)$), and (4) for each node v, $F_A(v)$ is a tuple $(A_1 = a_1, \ldots, A_n = a_n)$, where a_i is a constant, A_i is an *attribute* of v written as $v.A_i = a_i$, carrying the content of v such as properties, keywords, blogs and rating, as found in social networks, knowledge bases and property graphs.

Example 2: Three graphs are depicted in Fig. 2: (a) G_1 is a fragment of a knowledge graph, where each flight entity (*e.g.,* flight_1) has id (with value val = DL1), departure city (Paris), destination (NYC), and departure and arrival time; each node has attribute val (not shown) for its value; (b) G_2 records fake accounts; each account has an attribute is_fake that is "true" if the account is fake, and "false" otherwise; an account may post blogs that contain keywords (*e.g.,* blog p_5 has attribute keyword = "free prize"), and may like other blogs; and (c) G_3 depicts a country entity and its capital, carrying attribute val (not shown) for their values. □

We review two notions of subgraphs.

- A graph $G' = (V', E', L', F'_A)$ is a *subgraph of* $G = (V, E, L, F_A)$, denoted by $G' \subseteq G$, if $V' \subseteq V$, $E' \subseteq E$, and for each node $v \in V'$, $L'(v) = L(v)$ and $F'_A(v) = F_A(v)$; similarly for each edge $e \in E'$, $L'(e) = L(e)$.
- We say that G' is *a subgraph induced by* a set V' of nodes if $G' \subseteq G$ and E' consists of all the edges in G whose endpoints are both in V'.

Graph patterns. A *graph pattern* is defined as a directed graph $Q[\bar{x}] = (V_Q, E_Q, L_Q, \mu)$, where (1) V_Q (resp. E_Q) is a

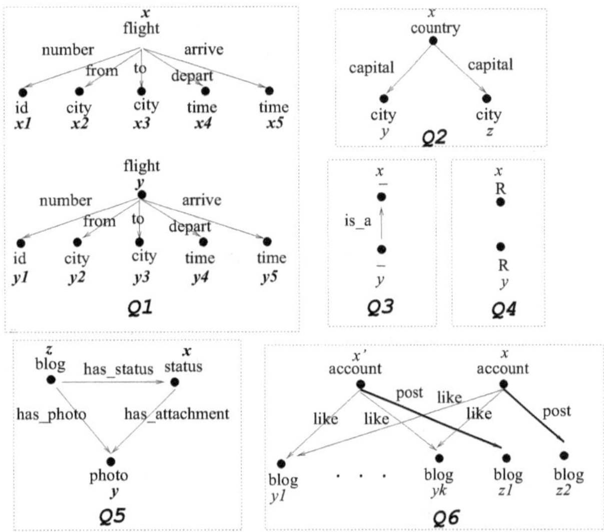

Figure 2: Graph patterns

set of pattern nodes (resp. edges), (2) L_Q is a function that assigns a label $L_Q(u)$ (resp. $L_Q(e)$) to each pattern node $u \in V_Q$ (resp. edge $e \in E_Q$), (3) $\bar{x}$ is a list of variables such that its arity $\|\bar{x}\|$ is equal to the number $|V_Q|$ of nodes, and (4) μ is a bijective mapping from $\bar{x}$ to V_Q, *i.e.*, it assigns a distinct variable to each node v in V_Q. For $x \in \bar{x}$, we use $\mu(x)$ and x interchangeably when it is clear in the context.

In particular, we allow wildcard '_' as a special label.

Example 3: Figure 2 depicts six graph patterns Q_1–Q_6: (1) Q_1 specifies two flight entities, where μ maps x to a flight, x_1–x_4 to its id, departure city, destination, departure time and arrival time, respectively; similarly for y and y_1–y_5; (2) Q_2 depicts a country entity with two distinct capitals; (3) Q_3 shows a generic is_a relationship, in which two nodes are labeled wildcard '_'; (4) Q_4 depicts two tuples of relation R represented as vertices in a graph, labeled with R; (5) Q_5 shows a blog entity z including photo y, and z is described by a status x; and (6) Q_6 specifies relationships between accounts x, x' and blogs $y_1, \ldots, y_k$ and z_1, z_2, where x and x' both like k blogs, x' posts a blog z_1 and x posts z_2. □

Graph pattern matching. We adopt the conventional semantics of matching via subgraph isomorphism. A *match* of pattern Q in graph G is a subgraph $G' = (V', E', L', F'_A)$ of G that is isomorphic to Q, *i.e.*, there exists a *bijective function* h from V_Q to V' such that (1) for each node $u \in V_Q$, $L_Q(u) = L'(h(u))$; and (2) $e = (u, u')$ is an edge in Q if and only if $e' = (h(u), h(u'))$ is an edge in G' and $L_Q(e) = L'(e')$. In particular, $L_Q(u) = L'(h(u))$ always holds if $L_Q(u)$ is '_', *i.e.*, wildcard matches any label to indicate generic entities, *e.g.*, is_a in Q_3 of Example 3; similarly for edge labels.

We also denote the match as a vector $h(\bar{x})$, consisting of $h(x)$ (*i.e.*, $h(\mu(x))$) for all $x \in \bar{x}$, in the same order as $\bar{x}$. Intuitively, $\bar{x}$ is a list of entities to be identified by Q, and $h(\bar{x})$ is such an instantiation in G, one node for each entity.

Example 4: A match of Q_1 of Example 3 in G_1 of Fig. 2 is h_1: $x \mapsto \text{flight}_1$, $y \mapsto \text{flight}_2$, $x_3 \mapsto$ NYC, $y_3 \mapsto$ Singapore, and similarly for the other variables in Q_1.

When $k = 2$, a match of Q_6 in G_2 is h_2: ($x' \mapsto \text{acct}_3, x \mapsto \text{acct}_4$, $y_1 \mapsto \text{p}_3$, $y_2 \mapsto \text{p}_4$, $z_1 \mapsto \text{p}_7, z_2 \mapsto \text{p}_8$). □

The notations of this paper are summarized in Table 1.

symbols	notations
G	graph (V, E, L, F_A)
$Q[\bar{x}]$	graph pattern (V_Q, E_Q, L_Q, μ)
φ, Σ	GFD $\varphi = (Q[\bar{x}], X \to Y)$, Σ is a set of GFDs
$h(\bar{x}) \models X \to Y$	a match $h(\bar{x})$ of Q satisfies $X \to Y$
Σ_Q	a set of GFDs of Σ embedded in pattern Q
Vio(Σ, G)	all the violations of GFDs Σ in graph G
$t(\|\Sigma\|, \|G\|)$	sequential time for computing Vio(Σ, G)
$T(\|\Sigma\|, \|G\|, n)$	parallel time for Vio(Σ, G), using n processors
$W(\Sigma, G)$	workload for computing Vio(Σ, G)
PV(φ)	a pivot vector $(\bar{z}, \bar{c}_Q)$ of GFD φ
$w = \langle \bar{v}_z, G_{\bar{z}} \rangle$	work unit ($\bar{v}_z$: candidate; $G_{\bar{z}}$: neighbors of $\bar{v}_z$)

Table 1: Notations

3. GFDS: SYNTAX AND SEMANTICS

We now define *functional dependencies for graphs* (GFDs).

GFDs. A GFD φ is a pair $(Q[\bar{x}], X \to Y)$, where

- $Q[\bar{x}]$ is a graph pattern, called the *pattern* of φ; and
- X and Y are two (possibly empty) sets of literals of $\bar{x}$.

Here a *literal* of $\bar{x}$ has the form of either $x.A = c$ or $x.A = y.B$, where $x, y \in \bar{x}$, A and B denote attributes (not specified in Q), and c is a constant. We refer to $x.A = c$ as a *constant literal*, and $x.A = y.B$ as a *variable literal.*

Intuitively, GFD φ specifies two constraints:

- a *topological constraint* imposed by pattern Q, and
- *attribute dependency* specified by $X \to Y$.

Recall that the "scope" of a relational FD $R(X \to Y)$ is specified by a relation schema R: the FD is applied only to instances of R. Unlike relational databases, graphs do not have a schema. Here Q specifies the scope of the GFD, such that the dependency $X \to Y$ is imposed only on the attributes of the vertices in each subgraph identified by Q. Constant literals $x.A = c$ enforce bindings of semantically related constants, along the same lines as CFDs [16].

Example 5: To catch the inconsistencies described in Example 1, we define GFDs with patterns Q_1–Q_6 of Fig. 2.

<u>*(1) Flight*:</u> GFD $\varphi_1 = (Q_1[x, x_1\text{-}x_5, y, y_1\text{-}y_5],\ X_1 \to Y_1)$, where X_1 is $x_1.\text{val} = y_1.\text{val}$, and Y_1 consists of $x_2.\text{val} = y_2.\text{val}$ and $x_3.\text{val} = y_3.\text{val}$. Here val is an attribute for the content of a node. By Q_1, x_1, x_2 and x_3 denote the flight id, departing city and destination of a flight x, respectively; similarly for y_1, y_2 and y_3 of entity y. Hence GFD φ_1 states that for all flight entities x and y, if they share the same flight id, then they must have the same departing city and destination.

<u>*(2) Capital*:</u> GFD $\varphi_2 = (Q_2[x, y, z],\ \emptyset \to y.\text{val} = z.\text{val})$. It is to ensure that for all country entities x, if x has two capital entities y and z, then y and z share the same name.

<u>*(3) Generic* is_a:</u> GFD $\varphi_3 = (Q_3[x, y],\ \emptyset \to x.A = y.A)$. It enforces a general property of is_a relationship: if entity y is_a x, then for any property A of x (denoted by attribute A), $x.A = y.A$. Observe that x and y in Q_3 are labeled with wildcard '_', to match arbitrary entities. Along the same lines, GFDs can enforce inheritance relationship subclass.

In particular, if x is labeled with bird, y with penguin, and A is can_fly, then φ_3 catches the inconsistency described in Example 1: penguins cannot fly but are classified as bird.

<u>*(4)* FDs *and* CFDs.</u> Consider an FD $R(X \to Y)$ over a relation schema R [3]. When an instance of R is represented as a graph in which each tuple is denoted by a node labeled R, we write $\varphi_4 = (Q_4[x, y],\ X' \to Y')$. Here Q_4 consists of two vertices x and y denoting two tuples of R, X' consists of

$x.A = y.A$ for all $A \in X$, and Y' includes $x.B = y.B$ for all $B \in Y$. Note that φ_4 is defined with variable literals only.

Using constant literals, GFDs can express CFDs [16]. For instance, $R(\text{country} = 44, \text{zip} \rightarrow \text{street})$ is a CFD defined on relation R, stating that in the UK, zip code uniquely determines street [16]. It can be written as GFD $\varphi'_4 = (Q_4[x, y], X' \rightarrow Y')$, where X' consists of $x.\text{country} = 44$, $y.\text{country} = 44$, and $x.\text{zip} = y.\text{zip}$, and Y' is $x.\text{street} = y.\text{street}$.

As another example, CFD $R(\text{country} = 44, \text{area\_code} = 131 \rightarrow \text{city} = \text{Edi})$ states that in the UK, if the area code of a city is 131, then the city is Edi [16]. It can be expressed as a GFD $\varphi''_4 = (Q''_4[x], X'' \rightarrow Y'')$, where Q''_4 consists of a single node x labeled R, and X'' includes $x.\text{country} = 44$ and $x.\text{area\_code} = 131$, while Y'' is $x.\text{city} = \text{Edi}$.

(5) Blogs: $\varphi_5 = (Q_5[x, y, z], \emptyset \rightarrow x.\text{text} = y.\text{desc})$. It states that if entities x, y and z satisfy the topological constraint of Q_5 depicted in Fig. 3, then the annotation of status x of blog z must match the description of photo y included in z.

(6) Fake account: $\varphi_6 = (Q_6[x, x', y_1, \ldots, y_k, z_1, z_2], X_6 \rightarrow Y_6)$, where X_6 includes $x'.\text{is\_fake} = \text{true}$, $z_1.\text{keyword} = c$, $z_2.\text{keyword} = c$, and Y_6 is $x.\text{is\_fake} = \text{true}$; here c is a constant indicating a peculiar keyword. It states that for accounts x and x', if the conditions in X_6 are satisfied, including that x' is confirmed fake, then x is also a fake account. □

Semantics. To interpret GFDs, we use the following notations. Consider a GFD $\varphi = (Q[\bar{x}], X \rightarrow Y)$. Consider a match $h(\bar{x})$ of Q in a graph G, and a literal $x.A = c$. We say that $h(\bar{x})$ *satisfies* the literal if *there exists* attribute A at the node $v = h(x)$ *and* $v.A = c$; similarly for literal $x.A = y.B$. We denote by $h(\bar{x}) \models X$ if $h(\bar{x})$ satisfies *all* the literals in X; similarly for $h(\bar{x}) \models Y$. Here we write $h(\mu(x))$ as $h(x)$, where μ is the mapping in Q from $\bar{x}$ to nodes in Q.

A graph G *satisfies* GFD φ, denoted by $G \models \varphi$, if *for all* matches $h(\bar{x})$ of Q in G, if $h(\bar{x}) \models X$ then $h(\bar{x}) \models Y$. We write $h(\bar{x}) \models X \rightarrow Y$ if $h(\bar{x}) \models Y$ whenever $h(\bar{x}) \models X$.

Observe the following. (1) For a literal $x.A = c$ in X, node $h(x)$ does not necessarily have attribute A. If $h(x)$ has *no* attribute A, $h(\bar{x})$ trivially satisfies $X \rightarrow Y$. This allows us to accommodate the semi-structured nature of graphs. (2) In contrast, when $x.A = c$ is in Y and $h(\bar{x}) \models Y$, then $h(x)$ must have attribute A by the definition of satisfaction above; similarly for $x.A = y.B$. (3) When X is $\emptyset$, $h(\bar{x}) \models X$ for any match $h(\bar{x})$ of Q in G; similarly for $Y = \emptyset$.

Example 6: Consider GFDs φ_1, φ_2 and φ_6 of Example 5 and G_1, G_2, G_3 of Fig. 2. One can verify the following.

(a) $G_1 \not\models \varphi_1$. Indeed, the match h_1 given in Example 4 satisfies X_1 since $h_1(x_1).\text{val} = h_1(y_1).\text{val}$, but it does not satisfy Y_1 since $h_1(x_3).\text{val} \neq h_1(y_3).\text{val}$. Similarly, $G_2 \not\models \varphi_6$, as witnessed by match h_2 of Example 4. Note that there are other matches of Q_6 in G_2 that satisfy $X_6 \rightarrow Y_6$, *e.g.*, when we map $x' \mapsto \text{acct}_1$ and $x \mapsto \text{acct}_2$, However, $G_2 \models \varphi_6$ only if *all* matches of Q_6 in G_2 satisfy $X_6 \rightarrow Y_6$.

(b) $G_3 \models \varphi_2$ since there exists *no* match of Q_2 in G_3: the country in G_3 has a unique capital, and trivially satisfies φ_2.

Observe the following: (a) entities in the same match of Q may be far apart; *e.g.*, flight_1 and flight_2 are *disconnected* from each other; and (b) $X \rightarrow Y$ is imposed only on matches of Q (satisfying its topological constraint), *e.g.*, φ_2. □

We say that a graph G *satisfies* a set Σ of GFDs if for all $\varphi \in \Sigma$, $G \models \varphi$, *i.e.*, G satisfies every GFD in Σ.

Special cases. GFDs subsume the following special cases.

(1) As shown by φ_4, φ'_4 and φ''_4 in Example 5, relational FDs and CFDs are special cases of GFDs, when tuples in a relation are represented as nodes in a graph. In fact, GFDs are able to express equality-generating dependencies (EGDs) [3].

(2) A GFD $(Q[\bar{x}], X \rightarrow Y)$ is called a *constant* GFD if X and Y consist of constant literals of $\bar{x}$ only. It is called a *variable* GFD if X and Y consist of variable literals only. Intuitively, constant GFDs subsume constant CFDs [16], and variable GFDs are analogous to traditional FDs [3].

In Example 5, φ_1-φ_5 are variable GFDs, φ''_4 and φ_6 are constant GFDs, while φ'_4 is neither constant nor variable.

(3) GFDs can specify certain type information. For an entity x of type τ, GFD $(Q[x], \emptyset \rightarrow x.A = x.A)$ enforces that x must have an A attribute, where Q consists of a single vertex labeled τ and denoted by variable x. However, GFDs *cannot* enforce that x has a finite domain, *e.g.*, Boolean.

4. REASONING ABOUT GFDS

We next study the satisfiability and implication problems for GFDs. These are classical problems associated with any class of data dependencies. Our main conclusion is that these problems for GFDs are no harder than for CFDs.

4.1 The Satisf ability Problem for GFDs

A set Σ of GFDs is *satisfiable* if Σ has a *model*; that is, a graph G such that (a) $G \models \Sigma$, and (b) for each GFD $(Q[\bar{x}], X \rightarrow Y)$ in Σ, there exists a match of Q in G.

The *satisfiability problem* for GFDs is to determine, given a set Σ of GFDs, whether Σ is satisfiable.

Intuitively, it is to check whether the GFDs are "dirty" themselves when used as data quality rules. A model G of Σ requires all patterns in the GFDs of Σ to find a match in G, to ensure that the GFDs do not conflict with each other.

Over relational data, a set Σ of CFDs may not be satisfiable [16]. The same happens to GFDs on graphs.

Example 7: Consider two GFDs defined with the same pattern Q_7 depicted in Fig. 3: $\varphi_7 = (Q_7[x], \emptyset \rightarrow x.A = c)$ and $\varphi'_7 = (Q_7[x], \emptyset \rightarrow x.A = d)$, where c and d are distinct constants. Then there exists no graph G that includes a τ entity v and satisfies both φ_7 and φ'_7. For if such a node v exists, then by φ_7, v has an attribute A with value c, while by φ'_7, $v.A$ must take a different value d, which is impossible.

As another example, consider GFDs $\varphi_8 = (Q_8[x, y, z], \emptyset \rightarrow x.A = c)$ and $\varphi_9 = (Q_9[x, y, z, w], \emptyset \rightarrow x.A = d)$ for distinct c and d, where Q_8 and Q_9 are shown in Fig. 3. One can verify that each of φ_8 and φ_9 has a model, when taken alone. However, they are not satisfiable when put together. Indeed, if they have a model G, then there must exist isomorphic mappings h and h' from Q_8 and Q_9 to G, respectively, such that $h(x) = h'(x) = v$ for some node v in G. Then again, v is required to have attribute A with distinct values. □

As shown in Example 7, GFDs defined with different graph patterns may interact with each other. Indeed, Q_8 and Q_9 are different, but φ_8 and φ_9 can be enforced on the same node, since Q_8 is isomorphic to a subgraph of Q_9. This tells us that the satisfiability analysis has to check subgraph

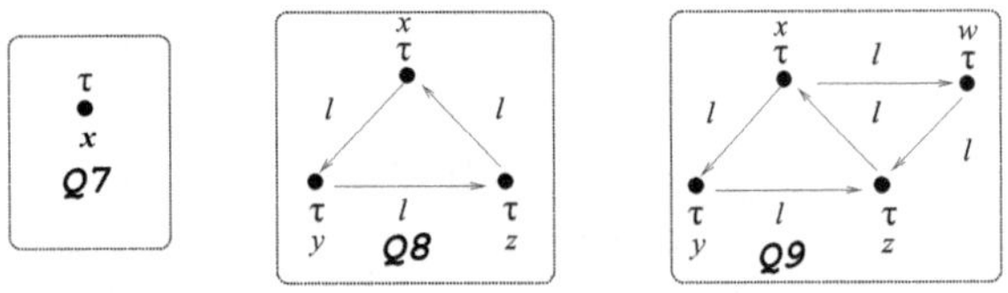

Figure 3: Graph patterns in GFDs

isomorphism among the patterns of the GFDs, which is NP-complete (cf. [34]). In light of this, we have the following.

Theorem 1: *The satisfiability problem is* coNP*-complete for* GFDs. □

One might think that the problem would become simpler if Σ consists of constant GFDs only (see Section 3), or when all patterns in Σ are acyclic directed graphs (DAGs). However, the complexity bound is rather robust.

Corollary 2: *The satisfiability problem is* coNP*-complete for constant* GFDs *that are defined with DAG patterns.* □

The complexity of GFDs is not inherited from CFDs. Indeed, the satisfiability analysis of CFDs is NP-hard only under a schema that enforces attributes to have a *finite domain* [16], *e.g.,* Boolean, *i.e.,* when CFDs and finite domains are put together. In contrast, graphs do not come with a schema; while GFDs subsume CFDs, they cannot specify finite domains. That is, the satisfiability problem for GFDs is already coNP-hard in the absence of a schema.

The upper bound proofs are nontrivial. It needs the following notations and a lemma.

(1) A pattern $Q' = (V'_Q, E'_Q, L'_Q, \mu')$ is *embeddable* in $Q = (V_Q, E_Q, L_Q, \mu)$ if there exists an isomorphic mapping f from (V'_Q, E'_Q) to a subgraph of (V_Q, E_Q), preserving node and edge labels. If Q' is embeddable in Q via f, then for any GFD $\varphi' = (Q'[\bar{x}'], X' \rightarrow Y')$ defined with Q', $(Q[\bar{x}], f(X') \rightarrow f(Y'))$ is an *embedded* GFD of φ' in Q, where $f(X')$ substitutes $f(x')$ for each x' in X'; similarly for $f(Y')$. Here again we use variable x and node $\mu(x)$ interchangeably.

(2) For a pattern Q and a set Σ of GFDs, a set Σ_Q of GFDs is said to be *embedded in* Q *and derived from* Σ if for each $\phi \in \Sigma_Q$, the pattern of ϕ is Q, and moreover, there exists $\varphi \in \Sigma$ such that ϕ is an embedded GFD of φ in Q.

(3) For a set Σ_Q of GFDs embedded in the same pattern Q, we define a set $\mathsf{enforced}(\Sigma_Q)$ of literals inductively as follows:

- if $(Q[\bar{x}], \emptyset \rightarrow Y)$ is in Σ_Q, then $Y \subseteq \mathsf{enforced}(\Sigma_Q)$, *i.e.,* all literals of Y are included in $\mathsf{enforced}(\Sigma_Q)$; and
- if $(Q[\bar{x}], X \rightarrow Y)$ is in Σ_Q and if all literals of X can be derived from $\mathsf{enforced}(\Sigma_Q)$ via the transitivity of equality atoms, then $Y \subseteq \mathsf{enforced}(\Sigma_Q)$.

As an example of transitivity, if $x.A = c$ and $y.B = c$ are in $\mathsf{enforced}(\Sigma_Q)$, then $X.A = y.B \in \mathsf{enforced}(\Sigma_Q)$. Intuitively, $\mathsf{enforced}(\Sigma_Q)$ is a set of equality atoms that have to be enforced on a graph G that satisfies Σ (and hence Σ_Q).

One can verify that given Σ_Q, $\mathsf{enforced}(\Sigma_Q)$ can be computed in polynomial time (PTIME) along the same lines as how closures for traditional FDs are computed (see, *e.g.,* [3]).

We say that Σ_Q is *conflicting* if there exist $(x.A, a)$ and $(x.A, b)$ in $\mathsf{enforced}(\Sigma_Q)$ such that $a \neq b$.

(4) A set Σ of GFDs is *conflicting* if *there exist* a pattern Q and a set Σ_Q of GFDs that are embedded in Q and derived from Σ, such that Σ_Q is *conflicting.*

Conflicting GFDs characterizes the satisfiability of GFDs.

Lemma 3: *A set* Σ *of* GFDs *is satisfiable if and only if* Σ *is not conflicting.* □

Proof of Theorem 1. Based on the lemma, we develop an algorithm that, given a set Σ of GFDs, returns "yes" if Σ is *not* satisfiable, *i.e.,* the complement of GFD satisfiability. (a) Guess (i) a set $\Sigma' \subseteq \Sigma$, (ii) a pattern Q such that Q carries labels that appear in Σ and $|Q|$ is at most the size of the largest pattern in Σ, and (iii) a mapping from the pattern of each GFD in Σ' to Q. (b) Check whether the mappings are isomorphic to subgraphs of Q. (c) If so, derive the set Σ_Q of GFDs embedded in Q from Σ' and the guessed mappings. (d) Check whether Σ_Q is conflicting; if so, return "yes". The algorithm is correct by Lemma 3. It is in NP as steps (b), (c) and (d) are in PTIME. Thus GFD satisfiability is in coNP.

The lower bound is verified by reduction from subgraph isomorphism to the complement of the satisfiability problem. The reduction uses constant GFDs defined with DAG patterns only, and hence proves Corollary 2 as well. □

Tractable cases. We next identify special cases when the satisfiability analysis can be carried out efficiently.

Corollary 4: *A set* Σ *of* GFDs *is always satisfiable if one of the following conditions is satisfied:*

- Σ *consists of variable* GFDs *only, or*
- Σ *includes no* GFDs *of the form* $(Q[\bar{x}], \emptyset \rightarrow Y)$.

It is in PTIME *to check whether* Σ *is satisfiable if* Σ *consists of* GFDs *defined with tree-structured patterns only,* i.e., *if for each* GFD $(Q[\bar{x}], X \rightarrow Y)$ *in* Σ, Q *is a tree.* □

4.2 The Implication Problem for GFDs

We say that a set Σ of GFDs *implies* another GFD φ, denoted by $\Sigma \models \varphi$, if for all graphs G such that $G \models \Sigma$, we have that $G \models \varphi$, *i.e.,* φ is a logical consequence of Σ.

We assume *w.l.o.g.* the following: (a) Σ is satisfiable, since otherwise it makes no sense to consider $\Sigma \models \varphi$; and (b) X is a satisfiable set of literals, where $\varphi = (Q[\bar{x}], X \rightarrow Y)$, since otherwise φ trivially holds. We will see that these do not increase the complexity of the implication problem.

The *implication problem* for GFDs is to determine, given a set Σ of GFDs and another GFD φ, whether $\Sigma \models \varphi$.

In practice, the implication analysis helps us eliminate redundant data quality rules defined as GFDs, and hence, optimize our error detection process by minimizing rules.

Example 8: Consider a set Σ of two GFDs $(Q_8[x, y, z], x.A = y.A \rightarrow x.B = y.B)$ and $(Q_9[x, y, z, w], x.B = y.B \rightarrow z.C = w.C)$. Consider GFD $\varphi_{11} = (Q_9[x, y, z, w], x.A = y.A \rightarrow z.C = w.C)$, where patterns Q_8 and Q_9 are given in Fig. 3. One can verify that $\Sigma \models \varphi_{11}$. □

The implication analysis of GFDs is NP-complete. In contrast, the problem is coNP-complete for CFDs [16].

Theorem 5: *The implication problem for* GFDs *is* NP*-complete.* □

As suggested by Example 8, to decide whether $\Sigma \models \varphi$, we have to consider the interaction between their graph patterns even when φ and all GFDs in Σ are variable GFDs, and when none of them has the form $(Q[\bar{x}], \emptyset \rightarrow Y)$. Thus the implication analysis of GFDs is more intriguing than their satisfiability analysis, in contrast to Corollary 2.

Corollary 6: *The implication problem is* NP*-complete for constant* GFDs *alone, and for variable* CFDs *alone, even* *when all the* GFDs *are defined with DAG patterns and when none of them has the form* $(Q[\bar{x}], \emptyset \to Y)$. □

To prove these, consider a set Σ of GFDs and a GFD $\varphi = (Q[\bar{x}], X \to Y)$. We define the following notations.

(1) We assume that φ is in *the normal form, i.e.,* when Y consists of a single literal $x.A = y.B$ or $y.B = c$ that is not a tautology $x.A = x.A$. This does not lose generality. Indeed, if Y consists of multiple literals, then φ is equivalent to a set of GFDs $(Q[\bar{x}], X \to l)$, one for each literal $l \in Y$. If Y is $\emptyset$ or a tautology, then $\Sigma \models \varphi$ trivially holds.

(2) For a set Σ_Q of GFDs embedded in Q, we define a set $\mathsf{closure}(\Sigma_Q, X)$ of literals inductively as follows:

- $X \subseteq \mathsf{closure}(\Sigma_Q, X)$, *i.e.,* all literals of X are in it; and
- if $(Q[\bar{x}'], X' \to Y')$ is in Σ_Q and if all literals of X' can be derived from $\mathsf{closure}(\Sigma_Q, X)$ via the transitivity of equality atoms, then $Y' \subseteq \mathsf{closure}(\Sigma_Q, X)$.

Note that $\mathsf{closure}(\Sigma_Q, X)$ differs from $\mathsf{enforced}(\Sigma_Q)$ only in the base case: the former starts with a given set X of literals, while the latter uses X from GFDs with $\emptyset \to X$.

Along the same lines as closures of relational FDs [3], one can verify that $\mathsf{closure}(\Sigma_Q, X)$ can be computed in PTIME.

(3) Recall that Y is a literal by the normal form defined above. We say that Y is *deducible* from Σ and X if *there exists* a set Σ_Q of GFDs that are embedded in Q and derived from Σ, such that $Y \in \mathsf{closure}(\Sigma_Q, X)$.

We characterize the implication analysis as follows.

Lemma 7: *For* $\varphi = (Q[\bar{x}], X \to Y)$ *and a set* Σ *of* GFDs, $\Sigma \models \varphi$ *if and only if* Y *is deducible from* Σ *and* X. □

The proof of the lemma is an extension of its relational FD counterpart (see [3] for relational FDs).

Proof of Theorem 5. For the upper bound, we give an algorithm for deciding $\Sigma \models \varphi$ as follows. (a) Guess a set $\Sigma' \subseteq \Sigma$, and a mapping from the pattern of each GFD in Σ' to the pattern Q of φ. (b) Check whether the mappings are isomorphic to subgraphs of Q. (c) If so, derive the set Σ_Q of GFDs embedded in Q from Σ' and the guessed mappings (d) Check whether $Y \in \mathsf{closure}(\Sigma_Q, X)$; if so, return "yes". The algorithm is in NP since steps (b), (c) and (d) are in PTIME. Its correctness follows from Lemma 7.

When the assumption about the satisfiability of Σ and X in φ is lifted, the algorithm can be extended with two initial steps: (i) check whether Σ is not satisfiable in NP; if so, return "invalid", and otherwise continue; (ii) check whether X is satisfiable, in PTIME; if so, continue; otherwise return "yes". The extended algorithm is still in NP. That is, the assumption does not increase the complexity bound.

The lower bound is verified by reduction from a variant of subgraph isomorphism, which is shown NP-complete. The reduction uses constant GFDs only or variable CFDs only, all defined with DAGs. Thus it also proves Corollary 2. □

<u>*Tractable cases*</u>. An efficient special case is as follows.

Corollary 8: *The implication problem is in* PTIME *for* GFDs *defined with tree-structured patterns.* □

5. INCONSISTENCY DETECTION

As an application of GFDs, we detect inconsistencies in graphs based on the validation analysis of GFDs. Our main conclusion is that while the validation problem for GFDs is intractable, it is feasible to efficiently detect errors in real-life graphs by means of parallel scalable algorithms.

5.1 GFD Validation and Error Detection

Given a GFD $\varphi = (Q[\bar{x}], X \to Y)$ and a graph G, we say that a match $h(\bar{x})$ of Q in G is a *violation* of φ if $G_h \not\models \varphi$, where G_h is the subgraph induced by $h(\bar{x})$. For a set Σ of GFDs, we denote by $\mathsf{Vio}(\Sigma, G)$ the set of all violations of GFDs in G, *i.e.,* $h(\bar{x}) \in \mathsf{Vio}(\Sigma, G)$ if and only if there exists a GFD φ in Σ such that $h(\bar{x})$ is a violation of φ in G. That is, $\mathsf{Vio}(\Sigma, G)$ collects all entities of G that are inconsistent when the set Σ of GFDs is used as data quality rules.

The *error detection problem* is stated as follows:

- *Input*: A set Σ of GFDs and a graph G.
- *Output*: The set $\mathsf{Vio}(\Sigma, G)$ of violations.

Its decision problem, referred to as *the validation problem* for GFDs, is to decide whether $G \models \Sigma$, *i.e.,* whether $\mathsf{Vio}(\Sigma, G)$ is empty. The problem is nontrivial.

Proposition 9: *Validation of* GFDs *is* coNP*-complete.* □

Proof: We show that it is NP-hard to check, given G and Σ, whether $G \not\models \Sigma$, by reduction from subgraph isomorphism. For the upper bound, we give an algorithm that returns "yes" if $G \not\models \Sigma$: (a) guess a GFD $(Q[\bar{x}], X \to Y)$ from Σ and a mapping h from Q to a subgraph of G; (b) check whether h is isomorphic; (c) if so, check whether $h(\bar{x}) \models X$ but $h(\bar{x}) \not\models Y$; if so, return "yes". This is in NP. □

In contrast, validation is in PTIME for FDs and CFDs, and errors can be detected in relations by two SQL queries that can be automatically generated from FDs and CFDs [16]. That is, error detection is more challenging in graphs.

A sequential algorithm. We give an algorithm that, given a set Σ of GFDs and a graph G, computes $\mathsf{Vio}(\Sigma, G)$ with a single processor. It is denoted as detVio and works as follows. (1) It starts with $\mathsf{Vio}(\Sigma, G) = \emptyset$. (2) For each $(Q[\bar{x}], X \to Y)$ in Σ, it enumerates all matches $h(\bar{x})$ of Q in G, and checks whether $h(\bar{x}) \not\models X \to Y$; if so, it adds $h(\bar{x})$ to $\mathsf{Vio}(\Sigma, G)$.

The cost of detVio is dominated by enumerating matches $h(\bar{x})$ of $Q[\bar{x}]$ in Σ. It is exponential and prohibitive for big G.

5.2 Parallel Scalability

Is error detection feasible in large-scale graphs? Our answer is affirmative, by using parallel algorithms to compute $\mathsf{Vio}(\Sigma, G)$. To characterize the effectiveness of parallelization, we adopt a notion of *parallel scalability* [29]. Denote by

- $W(\Sigma, G)$ the *workload, i.e.,* the necessary amount of work needed to compute $\mathsf{Vio}(\Sigma, G)$ for any algorithm;
- $t(|\Sigma|, |G|)$ the running time of a "best" *sequential algorithm* to compute $\mathsf{Vio}(\Sigma, G)$, *i.e.,* among all such algorithms, it has the least worst-case complexity; and
- $T(|\Sigma|, |G|, n)$ the time taken by a parallel algorithm to compute $\mathsf{Vio}(\Sigma, G)$ by using n processors.

An error detection algorithm is *parallel scalable* if

$$T(|\Sigma|, |G|, n) = \frac{c * t(|\Sigma|, |G|)}{n} + (n|\Sigma||W(\Sigma, G)|)^l,$$

such that $\frac{c*t(|\Sigma|,|G|)}{n} \geq (n(|\Sigma||W(\Sigma, G)|)^l$ when $n \leq |G|$ as found in practice, where c and l are constants. It reduces running time when n gets larger. Intuitively, such an algorithm guarantees that for a (possibly large) graph G, the more processors are used, the less time it takes to compute $\mathsf{Vio}(\Sigma, G)$. Hence it makes error detection feasible.

Workload model. To characterize the cost of error detection, we first introduce a model to quantify its workload.

We start with notions. Consider a GFD $\varphi = (Q[\bar{x}], X \rightarrow Y)$, where $(Q_1, \ldots, Q_k)$ are (maximum) connected components of Q. Consider $\bar{z} = (z_1, \ldots, z_k)$, where for $i \in [1, k]$, z_i is a variable in $\bar{x}$ such that $\mu(z_i)$ is a node in Q_i, where μ is the mapping from variables to nodes in Q (see Section 2). We fix a $\bar{z}$, referred to as the *pivot* of φ, by picking z_i with the minimum radius in Q_i, where the *radius* is the longest shortest distance between $\mu(z_i)$ and any node in Q_i. We use $\mathsf{PV}(\varphi)$ to denote $((z_1, c_Q^1), \ldots, (z_k, c_Q^k))$, referred to as the *pivot vector* of φ, where c_Q^i is the radius of Q_i at $\mu(z_i)$.

Observe the following. (a) By the locality of subgraph isomorphism, for any graph G, match $h(\bar{x})$ of Q in G, and any node $v = h(x)$ for $x \in \bar{x}$, v is within c_Q^i hops of some $h(z_i)$. (b) Vector $\mathsf{PV}(\varphi)$ can be computed in $O(|Q|^2)$ time, where Q is much smaller than G in real life. (c) Pattern Q typically has 1 or 2 connected components, and 99% of the components have radius at most 2 [21]. Hence in $\mathsf{PV}(\varphi)$, the arity $\|\bar{z}\|$ and each radius c_Q^i are typically 1 or 2.

Example 9: For GFDs of Example 5, $\mathsf{PV}(\varphi_1)$, $\mathsf{PV}(\varphi_2)$, $\mathsf{PV}(\varphi_4)$ and $\mathsf{PV}(\varphi_6)$ are $((x,1),(y,1))$, $((x,1))$, $((x,0),(y,0))$ and $((x,3))$, respectively (see Fig. 2); in particular, we take account x as a pivot of Q_6; similarly for φ_3 for φ_5. □

A *work unit* w for checking φ in a graph G is characterized by an one-to-one mapping σ from $\bar{z}$ to nodes in G, where $\bar{z}$ is the pivot in $\mathsf{PV}(\varphi)$, such that for each $z_i \in \bar{z}$, $\sigma(z_i)$ and $\mu(z_i)$ share the same label, *i.e.*, $\sigma(z_i)$ is a *candidate* of $\mu(z_i)$. More specifically, $w = \langle \bar{v}_z, G_{\bar{z}} \rangle$, where (a) $\bar{v}_z = \sigma(\bar{z})$; and (b) $G_{\bar{z}}$ is the fragment of G that includes, for each $z_i \in \bar{z}$, the c_Q^i*-neighbor* of $\sigma(z_i)$, *i.e.*, the subgraph of G induced by all the nodes within c_Q^i hops of $\sigma(z_i)$. Intuitively, $G_{\bar{z}}$ is a data block in G that has to be checked to validate φ.

We refer to $\bar{v}_z$ as a *pivot candidate* for φ in G.

The *workload* $W(\varphi, G)$ for checking φ in G, denoted by $W(\varphi, G)$, is the set of work units $\langle \bar{v}_z, G_{\bar{z}} \rangle$ when $\bar{v}_z$ ranges over all pivot candidates of φ in G. The *workload* $W(\Sigma, G)$ of a set Σ of GFDs in G is $\bigcup_{\varphi \in \Sigma} W(\varphi, G)$.

Observe the following. (a) To validate GFD φ in a graph G, it suffices to enumerate matches $h(\bar{x})$ of Q in data block $G_{\bar{z}}$ of each work unit of φ, by the locality of subgraph isomorphism. That is, *we enumerate in small* $G_{\bar{z}}$ *instead of in big* G. (b) The sequential cost $t(|\Sigma|, |G|)$ is the sum of $|G_{\bar{z}}|^{|\Sigma|}$ for all $G_{\bar{z}}$'s that appear in $W(\Sigma, G)$. (c) The size $|W(\Sigma, G)|$ is at most $|G|^k$, where k is the maximum arity of $\bar{z}$ in all $\mathsf{PV}(\varphi)$ of $\varphi \in \Sigma$. As argued earlier, typically $k \leq 2$. Hence $|W(\Sigma, G)|$ is *exponentially smaller* than $t(|\Sigma|, |G|)$. (d) For a match $h(\bar{x})$, checking whether $h(\bar{x}) \models X \rightarrow Y$ takes $O((|X| + |Y|)\log(|X| + |Y|))$ time, and $|X| + |Y| \leq |\varphi|$. Since the size $|\varphi|$ of φ is much smaller than $|G|$, $W(\varphi, G)$ suffices to assess the amount of work for checking φ in G.

Challenges. Computing $\mathsf{Vio}(\Sigma, G)$ is a bi-criteria optimization problem. (a) *Workload balancing*, to evenly partition $W(\Sigma, G)$ over n processors; it is to avoid "skewed" partitions, *i.e.*, when a processor gets far more work units than others, and hence, to maximize parallelism. (b) *Minimizing data shipment*, to reduce communication cost, which is often a bottleneck [4]. When a graph G is fragmented and distributed across processors, to process a work unit $w = \langle \bar{v}_z, G_{\bar{z}} \rangle$, we need to ship data from one processor to another to assemble $G_{\bar{z}}$. The cost, denoted by $\mathsf{CC}(w)$, is measured by $c_s * |M|$, where c_s is a constant and M is the data shipped.

Parallel scalable error detection. We tackle these challenges in the following two settings, which are practical parallel paradigms as demonstrated by [22]. We show that parallel scalability is within reach in these settings.

<u>Replicated G.</u> Graph G is replicated at each processor [22]. We study *error detection with replicated* G (Section 6.1), to balance workload $W(\Sigma, G)$ over n processors such that the overall parallel time for computing $\mathsf{Vio}(\Sigma, G)$ is minimized.

Theorem 10: *There exists a parallel scalable algorithm that given a set* Σ *of* GFDs *and a graph* G *replicated at* n *processors, computes* $\mathsf{Vio}(\Sigma, G)$ *in* $O(\frac{t(|\Sigma|, |G|)}{n} + |W(\Sigma, G)|(n + \log|W(\Sigma, G)|))$ *parallel time.* □

<u>Partitioned G.</u> When G is partitioned across processors, data shipment in inevitable. We study *error detection with partitioned* G (Section 6.2), with *bi-criteria* objective to (a) minimize data shipment and (2) balance the workload.

Theorem 11: *There exists a parallel scalable algorithm that given a set* Σ *of* GFDs, *a partitioned graph* G *and* n *processors, computes* $\mathsf{Vio}(\Sigma, G)$ *in* $O(\frac{t(|\Sigma|, |G|)}{n} + n|W(\Sigma, G)|^2 \log|W(\Sigma, G)| + |\Sigma||W(\Sigma, G)|)$ *parallel time.* □

6. PARALLEL ALGORITHMS

We next develop parallel scalable algorithms for error detection in the settings given above, as proofs of Theorems 10 and 11 in Sections 6.1 and 6.2, respectively. Such algorithms make it feasible to detect errors in large-scale graphs. We should remark that there exist other criteria for measuring the effectiveness of parallel algorithms (see Section 1).

6.1 Parallel Algorithm for Replicated Graphs

We start with an algorithm in the setting when G is replicated at each processor. In this setting, the major challenge is to balance the workload for each processor. The idea is to partition workload $W(\Sigma, G)$ in parallel, and assign (approximately) equal amount of work units to n processors.

Algorithm. The algorithm is denoted as repVal and shown in Fig. 4. Working with a coordinator S_c and n processors $S_1, \ldots, S_n$, it takes the following steps. (1) It first estimates workload $W(\Sigma, G)$, and creates a balanced partition $W_i(\Sigma, G)$ of $W(\Sigma, G)$ for $i \in [1, n]$, by invoking a parallel procedure bPar (line 1). It then sends $W_i(\Sigma, G)$ to processor S_i (line 2). (2) Each processor S_i detects its set of local violations, denoted by $\mathsf{Vio}_i(\Sigma, G)$, by a procedure localVio in parallel (line 3), which only visits the data blocks specified in $W_i(\Sigma, G)$. (3) When all processors S_i return $\mathsf{Vio}_i(\Sigma, G)$, S_c computes $\mathsf{Vio}(\Sigma, G)$ by taking a union of all $\mathsf{Vio}_i(\Sigma, G)$ (lines 4-5). It then returns $\mathsf{Vio}(\Sigma, G)$ (line 6).

We next present procedures bPar and localVio.

Workload balancing. Procedure bPar balances workload in two phases: estimation and partition, in parallel.

<u>Workload estimation.</u> Procedure bPar first estimates workload $W(\Sigma, G)$ in parallel, following the three steps below.

(1) At coordinator S_c, for each GFD $\varphi \in \Sigma$, bPar constructs a pivot vector $\mathsf{PV}(\varphi) = (\bar{z}, \bar{c}_Q)$. It then balances the computation for workload estimation at n processors as follows.

Algorithm repVal

Input: A set Σ of GFDs, coordinator S_c, n processors $S_1, \ldots, S_n$, a graph G replicated at each processor

Output: Violation set $\mathsf{Vio}(\Sigma, G)$.

```
bPar(Σ, G);   /*balance workload in parallel*/
/*executed at coordinator Sc*/
send Wi(Σ, G) to processor Si;
invoke localVio(Σ, Wi(Σ, G)) at each processor Si for i ∈ [1, n];
if every processor Si returns answer Vioi(Σ, G) then
    Vio(Σ, G): = ∪i∈[1,n] Vioi(Σ, G));
return Vio(Σ, G);

Procedure localVio(Σ, Wi(Σ, G))
/*executed at each processor Si in parallel*/
set Vioi(Σ, G) := ∅;
for each w = ⟨vz̄, |Gz̄|⟩ ∈ Wi(Σ, G) for GFD φ ∈ Σ do
    enumerate matches h(x̄) by accessing Gz̄;
    for each h(x̄) such that h(x̄) ⊭ X → Y do
        Vioi(Σ, G):= Vioi(Σ, G) ∪ {h(x̄)};
return Vioi(Σ, G);
```

Figure 4: Algorithm repVal

(a) For each variable z in the pivot $\bar{z}$, it extracts the frequency distribution of *candidates* $C(\mu(z))$, *i.e.*, those nodes in G that have the same label as $\mu(z)$. This can be supported by statistics of G locally stored at S_c.

(b) For each $\mathsf{PV}(\varphi) = ((z_1, c_Q^1), \ldots, (z_k, c_Q^k))$ and each z_i, it evenly partitions candidates $C(\mu(z_i))$ into m sets, for a predefined number m. More specifically, it derives an m-balanced partition $R_{\mu(z_i)} = \{r_1, \ldots, r_m\}$ of value ranges of a selected attribute of $C(\mu(z_i))$, such that the number of candidates in $C(\mu(z_i))$ whose attribute values fall in each range r_j is even. This is done by using *e.g.*, precomputed equi-depth histogram (*e.g.*, [33]). It then constructs a set M of messages of the form $\langle \mathsf{PV}(\varphi), \overline{r}_z \rangle$, where φ is a GFD, $\overline{r}_z = \langle r_{z_1}, \ldots r_{z_k} \rangle$, and each $r_{z_i} \in R_{\mu(z_i)}$ is a *range* of $C(\mu(z_i))$ for z_i. Removing duplicates, M contains at most m^k messages for φ, where $k \leq 2$ in practice (see Section 5).

(c) The set M is evenly distributed to n processors; each processor S_i receives a subset M_i of about $\frac{|M|}{n}$ messages.

Example 10: Consider GFD φ_1 of Example 5, where $\mathsf{PV}(\varphi_1) = ((x, 1), (y, 1))$ (*i.e.*, $k = 2$). Consider graph G including 9 flights flight_1–flight_9. For $n = 3 = m$, procedure bPar balances the estimation $W(\varphi_1, G)$ as follows.

(1) It determines a 3-range partition R_{flight} for flight entities as *e.g.*, $\{[\mathsf{flight}_1, \mathsf{flight}_3]$, $[\mathsf{flight}_4, \mathsf{flight}_6]$, $[\mathsf{flight}_7, \mathsf{flight}_9]\}$, for both $\mu(x)$ and $\mu(y)$, based on attribute $\mu(x).\mathsf{val}$ and $\mu(y).\mathsf{val}$.

(2) It yields a set M of 6 messages $\langle \mathsf{PV}(\varphi_1), (r_{\mathsf{flight}}, r'_{\mathsf{flight}}) \rangle$ after removing duplicates (since the two connected components in Q_1 (Fig. 2) of φ_1 are isomorphic, $(\mathsf{PV}(\varphi_1), r_i, r_j)$ and $(\mathsf{PV}(\varphi_1), r_j, r_i)$ are duplicates for ranges r_i and r_j).

It then evenly distributes M to 3 processors, *e.g.*, S_1 receives $M_1 = \{\langle \mathsf{PV}(\varphi_1), ([\mathsf{flight}_1, \mathsf{flight}_3], [\mathsf{flight}_1, \mathsf{flight}_3]) \rangle$, $\langle \mathsf{PV}(\varphi_1), ([\mathsf{flight}_1, \mathsf{flight}_3], [\mathsf{flight}_4, \mathsf{flight}_6]) \rangle\}$. □

(2) Procedure bPar then identifies work units at each processor S_i, in parallel. For each message $\langle \mathsf{PV}(\varphi), \overline{r}_z \rangle$ in M_i, S_i finds (a) all pivot candidates $v_{\bar{z}}$ of $\bar{z}$ such that for each $z_i \in \bar{z}$, *its candidate* $v_{\bar{z}}[z_i]$ in $v_{\bar{z}}$ has attribute value in the range $r_{z_i} \in \overline{r}_z$; and (b) the c_Q^i-neighbors $G_{\bar{z}}$ for each $v_{\bar{z}}$.

Each processor S_i then sends a message M'_i to the coordinator S_c. Here M'_i is a set of $\langle v_{\bar{z}}, |G_{\bar{z}}| \rangle$, each encoding a pivot candidate and *the size* of the data block for a unit. Note that $|G_{\bar{z}}|$ is sent, not $G_{\bar{z}}$. Moreover, S_i keeps track of $G_{\bar{z}}$ to facilitate local error detection (to be seen shortly).

Example 11: For $\langle \mathsf{PV}(\varphi_1), ([\mathsf{flight}_1, \mathsf{flight}_3], [\mathsf{flight}_1, \mathsf{flight}_3]) \rangle$, processor S_1 finds 3 candidates $\{\mathsf{flight}_1, \mathsf{flight}_2, \mathsf{flight}_3\}$ in the range $[\mathsf{flight}_1, \mathsf{flight}_3]$, and their 1-hop neighbors. These yield $v_{\bar{z}}[x]$ as $(\mathsf{flight}_i, \mathsf{flight}_j)$ ($i \in [1, 3]$, $j \in [1, 3]$, and $i < j$ to remove duplicates) and correspondingly, 3 work units encoded with $|G_{\bar{z}}|$, where $|G_{\bar{z}}|$ is the total size of the 1-hop neighbors of flight_i and flight_j in $v_{\bar{z}}[x]$. For example, a unit w_1 is $\langle (\mathsf{flight}_1, \mathsf{flight}_2), 22 \rangle$, where $G_{\bar{z}}$ for w_1 is graph G_1 in Fig. 2, which has 22 nodes and edges in total. □

(3) Procedure bPar, at the coordinator S_c, collects a set of messages $\langle v_{\bar{z}}, |G_{\bar{z}}| \rangle$ from all the processors, denoted by $W(\Sigma, G)$. It encodes the set of work units to be partitioned.

Workload partition. This gives rise to a load balancing problem. An n-partition $\mathcal{W}$ of $W(\Sigma, G)$ is a set of n pair-wisely disjoint work unit sets $\{W_1(\Sigma, G), \ldots, W_n(\Sigma, G)\}$, such that $W(\Sigma, G) = \bigcup_{i \in [1,n]} W_i(\Sigma, G)$. It is *balanced* if the cost $t(|\Sigma|, W_i(\Sigma, G))$, estimated as the sum of $|G_{\bar{z}}|^{|\Sigma|}$ for all $G_{\bar{z}}$ in $W_i(\Sigma, G))$, is approximately equal. The *load balancing problem* is to find a balanced n-partition $\mathcal{W}$ for a given $W(\Sigma, G)$.

Refer to the largest cost incurred at a processor as the *makespan* of the parallel processing. The load balancing problem is "equivalent to" makespan minimization [7], by setting the capacity of each processor as $\frac{t(|\Sigma|, |G|)}{n}$, via PTIME reductions. The problem is intractable, but approximable.

Proposition 12: *(1) The load balancing problem is* NP-*complete. (2) There is a 2-approximation algorithm to find a balanced workload partition in* $O(n|W(\Sigma, G)| + |W(\Sigma, G)| \log |W(\Sigma, G)|)$ *parallel time for given* Σ, n *and* $W(\Sigma, G)$. □

Given $W(\Sigma, G)$, procedure bPar computes a balanced n-partition with a greedy strategy, following an approximation algorithm of [7] for makespan minimization. (1) It first associates a weight $|G(\bar{z})|$ with each work unit $w = \langle v_{\bar{z}}, |G_{\bar{z}}| \rangle$. It then sorts all the work units, in descending order of the weights. With each processor it associates a load, initially 0. (2) It greedily picks a work unit w with the smallest weight and a processor S_i with the minimum load, assigns w to S_i and updates the load of S_i by adding the weight of w. (3) The process proceeds until all work units are distributed. This yields a 2-approximation algorithm, by approximation-factor preserving reduction to its counterpart of [7].

Example 12: Suppose that coordinator S_c receives 9 work units $\{w_1, \ldots, w_9\}$ in total, with estimated size $\{22, 22, 26, 26, 30, 30, 24, 28, 28\}$, respectively. The greedy assignment strategy of bPar generates a 3-partition of the work units as $\{\{w_1, w_3, w_9\}, \{w_2, w_4, w_5\}, \{w_6, w_7, w_8\}\}$, with balanced block sizes as 76, 78, 82, respectively. Then S_c assigns the 3 partitions to processors S_1, S_2, S_3, respectively. □

Local error detection. Upon receiving the assigned $W_i(\Sigma)$, procedure localVio computes the local violation set $\mathsf{Vio}_i(\Sigma, G)$ at each processor S_i in parallel. For each work unit $\langle v_{\bar{z}}, |G_{\bar{z}}| \rangle \in W_i(\Sigma, G)$ for GFD φ, it (a) enumerates matches $h(\bar{x})$ of the pattern in φ such that $h(\bar{x})$ includes $v_{\bar{z}}$, by only accessing $G_{\bar{z}}$, and (b) checks whether $h(\bar{x}) \models X \rightarrow Y$ of φ. It collects in $\mathsf{Vio}_i(\Sigma, G)$ all violations detected, and sends $\mathsf{Vio}_i(\Sigma, G)$ to coordinator S_c at the end of the process.

Example 13: Consider GFD $\varphi_1 = (Q_1[\bar{x}], X_1 \rightarrow Y_1)$ (Example 5) and work unit w_1 (Example 11) assigned to processor S_1. Procedure localVio inspects G_1 (Fig. 2) for w_1, and finds a match $h_1(\bar{x})$ of Q_1 in G_1, where h_1 is given in Example 4. As shown there, $h_1(\bar{x}) \not\models X_1 \rightarrow Y_1$. Thus localVio adds $h_1(\bar{x})$ to $\mathsf{Vio}_1(\Sigma, G)$. Similarly, S_1 processes w_3 and w_9 assigned to it, and finally returns $\mathsf{Vio}_1(\Sigma, G)$ to S_c. □

Proof of Theorem 10. By the locality of subgraph isomorphism, procedure bPar identifies all work units, and localVio computes all violations. From these the correctness of repVal follows. For the complexity, one can verify the following: (a) procedure bPar estimates $W(\Sigma, G)$ in $O(\frac{|W(\Sigma,G)|}{n})$ parallel time, by using a balanced partition; the partitioning takes $O(n|W(\Sigma, G)| + |W(\Sigma, G)| \log |W(\Sigma, G)|)$ time [7]; and (b) procedure localVio takes $O(\frac{t(|\Sigma|,|G|)}{n})$ parallel time, via a balanced workload partition. Thus repVal has the complexity stated in Theorem 10 and is parallel scalable. □

6.2 Algorithm for Fragmented Graphs

Graph G may have already been fragmented and distributed across n processor, especially when it is too costly to replicate G at each processor. In this setting, we have a *bi-criteria error* detection problem. Given a set Σ of GFDs and a fragmented graph G, it is to compute $\mathsf{Vio}(\Sigma, G)$ in parallel, such that (1) the communication cost is minimized, and (2) the workload for n processors is balanced.

Consider a fragmentation $(F_1, \ldots, F_n)$ of $G(V, E, L, F_A)$ such that (a) each $F_i(V_i, E_i, L, F_A)$ is a subgraph of G, (b) $\bigcup E_i = E$ and $\bigcup V_i = V$, and (c) F_i resides at processor S_i ($i \in [1, n]$). Assume *w.l.o.g.* that the sizes of F_i's are approximately equal. Moreover, F_i keeps track of (a) *in-nodes* $F_i.I$, *i.e.*, nodes in V_i to which there exists an edge from another fragment, and (b) *out-nodes* $F_i.O$, *i.e.*, nodes in another fragment to which there is an edge from a node in V_i. We refer to nodes in $F_i.I$ or $F_i.O$ as *border nodes*.

Algorithm. We provide an error detection algorithm for fragmented G, denoted as disVal. It differs from repVal in workload estimation and assignment, and in local error detection, to minimize communication and computation costs.

Algorithm disVal works with a coordinator S_c and n processors $S_1, \ldots, S_n$. (1) It first estimates and partitions workload $W(\Sigma, G)$ via a procedure disPar, such that the workload $W_i(\Sigma, G)$ at each S_i is balanced, with minimum communication cost. (2) Each processor S_i uses a procedure dlovalVio to detect local violation $\mathsf{Vio}_i(\Sigma, G)$, in parallel, with data exchange. (3) Finally, $\mathsf{Vio}(\Sigma, G) = \bigcup_{i \in [1,n]} \mathsf{Vio}(\Sigma_i, G)$.

We next present procedures disPar and dlovalVio.

Bi-criteria assignment. Procedure disPar extends its counterpart bPar by supporting (a) workload estimation with communication cost, and (b) bi-criteria assignment.

Workload estimation. Procedure disPar estimates $W(\Sigma, G)$ at each S_i in parallel. For each pivot vector $\mathsf{PV}(\varphi) = ((z_1, c_Q^1), \ldots, (z_k, c_Q^k))$ and each z_l in $\bar{z}$, it finds (a) local candidates $C(\mu(z_l))$ of $\mu(z_l)$ in F_i, (b) the c_Q^l-neighbors $G_{\bar{z}}[z_l]$ for each candidate of $C(\mu(z_l))$, and (c) border nodes $B_{\bar{z}}[z_l]$ from $G_{\bar{z}}[z_l]$ to some nodes in $G_{\bar{z}}[z_l]$. It encodes *partial work unit* w_φ as $\langle v_{\bar{z}}, \overline{|G_{\bar{z}}|}, \overline{B_{\bar{z}}} \rangle$, where (i) $v_{\bar{z}}$ is a pivot candidate of $\bar{z}$ in F_i; if $C(\mu(z_l))$=$\emptyset$, $v_{\bar{z}}[z_j]$ takes a placeholder $\perp$; (ii) $\overline{|G_{\bar{z}}|}$ is the list of $|G_{\bar{z}}[z_l]|$; and (iii) $\overline{B_{\bar{z}}}$ is the list of border nodes $B_{\bar{z}}[z_l]$, for all $z_l \in \bar{z}$, indicating "missing data". Each S_i then sends a message M_i to coordinator S_c, with all units, along with the sizes of c-neighbors of border nodes in $F_i.I$, where c ranges over the radius of patterns Q in Σ.

Upon receiving M_i's, disPar builds $W(\varphi, G)$, the set of complete work units at S_c. A work unit $\langle v_{\bar{z}}, |G_{\bar{z}}|, B_{\bar{z}} \rangle$ is added to $W(\varphi, G)$ if for each $z_l \in \bar{z}$, $v_{\bar{z}}[z_l]$ is a candidate $v_{\bar{z}}^i[z_l]$ from a unit w_φ^i of M_i such that $v_{\bar{z}}^i[z_l] \neq \perp$, $|G_{\bar{z}}|$ is the sum of $|G_{\bar{z}}^i[z_l]|$ (extracted from $\overline{|G_{\bar{z}}^i|}$), and $B_{\bar{z}}$ is the union of $B_{\bar{z}}^i[z_l]$ (extracted from $\overline{B_{\bar{z}}^i}$), for all $i \in [1, n]$ and $\varphi \in \Sigma$. That is, disPar assembles $v_{\bar{z}}^i[z_l]$ into work units. It also marks $|G_{\bar{z}}^i[z_l]|$ and $B_{\bar{z}}^i[z_l]$ with its source w_φ^i.

Workload assignment. The *bi-criteria assignment problem* is to find an n-partition of $W(\Sigma, G)$ into $W_i(\Sigma, G)$ for $i \in [1, n]$, such that (a) $W_i(\Sigma, G)$ is balanced, and (b) its communication cost CC_i is minimized, where CC_i denotes the amount of data that needs to be shipped to processor S_i if $W_i(\Sigma, G)$ is assigned to S_i. It should ensure that for each pivot candidate $v_{\bar{z}}$, there exists a unique unit $\langle v_{\bar{z}}, |G_{\bar{z}}|, B_{\bar{z}} \rangle$ in all of $W_i(\Sigma, G)$, *i.e.*, the candidate is checked only once.

Cost CC_i is estimated as follows. For each $\langle v_{\bar{z}}, |G_{\bar{z}}|, B_{\bar{z}} \rangle$ in $W_i(\Sigma, G)$ and each $z_l \in \bar{z}$, define $\mathsf{CC}_{v_{\bar{z}}}[z_l]$ to be the sum of (a) $|G_{\bar{z}}^j[z_l]|$ if $j \neq i$, *i.e.*, $G_{\bar{z}}^j[z_l]$ has to be fetched from fragment j; (b) $|G_{(c_Q^l, b)}|$ for each border node $v_b \in B_{\bar{z}}[z_l]$, which also demands data fetching. These are identified by using the sources w_φ^i recorded above. Let $\mathsf{CC}_{v_{\bar{z}}}$ be the sum of $\mathsf{CC}_{v_{\bar{z}}}[z_l]$ for all $z_l \in \bar{z}$. Then CC_i is the sum of all $\mathsf{CC}_{v_{\bar{z}}}$ for candidates $v_{\bar{z}}$ in $W_i(\Sigma, G)$. Care is taken so that each data block is counted only once for CC_i.

While bi-criteria assignment is more intriguing than load balancing, it is within reach in practice via approximation.

Proposition 13: *(1) The bi-criteria assignment problem is* NP*-complete. (2) There exists a 2-approximation algorithm to find a balanced workload assignment with minimized communication cost in $O(n|W(\Sigma, G)|^2 \log(|W(\Sigma, G)|))$ time.* □

Extending a strategy for makespan minimization [43], procedure disPar computes an n-partition of $W(\Sigma)$ (after unit grouping) into $W_i(\Sigma, G)$, sent to processor S_i for $i \in [1, n]$.

Local error detection. Upon receiving $W_i(\Sigma, G)$, procedure dlovalVio computes local violations $\mathsf{Vio}_i(\Sigma, F_i)$ at processor S_i, by selecting the following evaluation schemes.

Prefetching. For a work unit $w = \langle v_{\bar{z}}, |G_{\bar{z}}|, B_{\bar{z}} \rangle$, it first fetches $G_{\bar{z}}$ and $G_{(c,b)}$ for $F_i.O$ nodes in $B_{\bar{z}}$ from other fragments. It ensures that each node (edge) is retrieved only once. After the data is in place, it detects errors locally as in localVio to compute $\mathsf{Vio}_i(\Sigma, F_i)$.

Partial detection. We can also ship partial matches instead of data blocks. The idea is to estimate the size of partial matches via *graph simulation* [19] from pattern $Q[\bar{x}]$ in a GFD φ to F_i. If the number of partial matches is not large, S_i exchanges such matches with other processors in a pipelined fashion, and updates $\mathsf{Vio}_i(\Sigma, F_i)$ as soon as a complete match can be formed from partial ones.

For a unit $w \in W_i(\Sigma, G)$ for GFD φ at S_i, procedure dlovalVio selects a strategy that incurs smaller (estimated) communication cost $\mathsf{CC}(w)$ (see Appendix for the estimation of $\mathsf{CC}(w)$). Intuitively, dlovalVio decides to process each unit either locally or at a remote processor, whichever incurs smaller data shipment.

Our algorithms also support optimization strategies for skewed graphs and workload reduction (see Appendix).

We verify Theorem 11 by showing that disVal is correct and has the desired complexity, similar to Theorem 10.

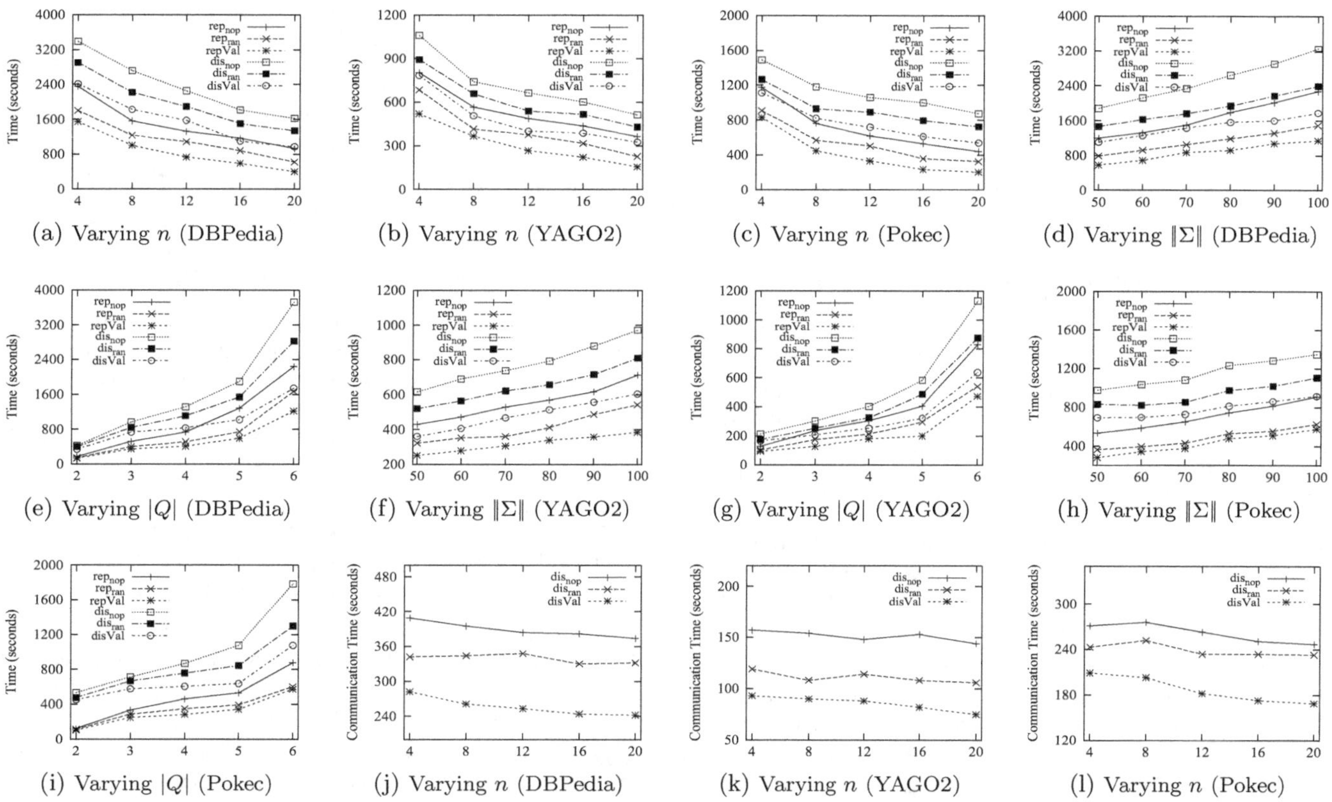

(a) Varying n (DBPedia) (b) Varying n (YAGO2) (c) Varying n (Pokec) (d) Varying $\|\Sigma\|$ (DBPedia)
(e) Varying $|Q|$ (DBPedia) (f) Varying $\|\Sigma\|$ (YAGO2) (g) Varying $|Q|$ (YAGO2) (h) Varying $\|\Sigma\|$ (Pokec)
(i) Varying $|Q|$ (Pokec) (j) Varying n (DBPedia) (k) Varying n (YAGO2) (l) Varying n (Pokec)

Figure 5: Performance evaluation

7. EXPERIMENTAL STUDY

Using real-life and synthetic graphs, we experimentally evaluated (1) the parallel scalability, (2) workload partition, (3) communication costs, (4) scalability of our algorithms, and (5) the effectiveness of GFDs for error detection.

Experimental setting. We used three real-life graphs: (a) *DBpedia*, a knowledge graph [1] with 28 million entities of 200 types and 33.4 million edges of 160 types, (b) *YAGO2*, an extended knowledge base of YAGO [44] with 3.5 million nodes of 13 types and 7.35 million edges of 36 types, (c) *Pokec* [2], a social network with 1.63 million nodes of 269 different types, and 30.6 million edges of 11 types. We removed meaningless nodes and labels for a compact representation. We then inserted new edges by repeatedly dereferencing HTTP URIs over a set of sampled entities to further enlarge *DBpedia* (resp. *YAGO2*), to 12.3 million (resp. 3.2 million) entities and 32.7 million (resp. 7.1 million) edges.

We also developed a generator to produce synthetic graphs $G = (V, E, L, F_A)$ following the power-law degree distribution. It is controlled by the numbers of nodes $|V|$ (up to 50 million) and edges $|E|$ (up to 100 million), with L drawn from an alphabet $\mathcal{L}$ of 30 labels, and F_A assigning 5 attributes with values from an active domain of 1000 values.

GFDs *generator*. We generated sets Σ of GFDs $(Q[\bar{x}], X \to Y)$, controlled by (a) $\|\Sigma\|$, the number of GFDs, and (b) $|Q|$, the average size of graph patterns Q in Σ, with 1 or 2 connected components. For each real-life graph, (1) we first mined frequent features, including edges and paths of length up to 3. We selected top-5 most frequent features as "seeds", and combined them to form patterns Q of size $|Q|$. (2) For each Q, we constructed dependency $X \to Y$ with literals composed of the node attributes. We generated 100 GFDs on each real-life graph in this way. For synthetic graphs, we generated 50 GFDs with labels drawn from $\mathcal{L}$.

Algorithms. We implemented the following, all in Java: (1) sequential algorithm detVio (Section 5), (2) parallel algorithm repVal (Fig. 4), versus its two variants (a) rep_{ran}, which randomly assigns work units to processors, and (b) rep_{nop}, which does not support optimization strategies (multi-query processing [31] and workload reduction; see Appendix), and (3) parallel algorithm disVal (Section 6.2), versus its two variants dis_{ran} and dis_{nop} similar to their counterparts in (2).

We deployed the algorithms on Amazon EC2 c4.2xlarge instances, each is powered by an Intel Xeon processor with 2.6GHz. We used up to 20 instances. Each experiment was run 5 times and the average is reported here.

Experimental results. We next report our findings.

Exp-1: Parallel scalability. We first evaluated parallel algorithms repVal and disVal, versus their variants. Fixing $|Q|$=5 and $\|\Sigma\|$=50, we varied the number n of processors from 4 to 20. We replicated and fragmented G for repVal and disVal, respectively. Figures 5(a), 5(b) and 5(c) report their performance on real-life *DBpedia*, *YAGO2* and *Pokec*, respectively. We find the following. (1) Both repVal and disVal substantially reduce parallel time when n increases: they are on average 3.7 and 2.4 times faster for n from 4 to 20, respectively. These validate Theorems 10 and 11. (2) Both repVal and disVal outperform their variants: repVal (resp. disVal) is on average 1.9 and 1.4 times (resp. 1.5 and 1.3 times) faster than rep_{nop} and rep_{ran} (resp. dis_{nop} and dis_{ran}), respectively. These verify the effectiveness of our optimization and load balancing techniques. (3) Algorithm repVal is

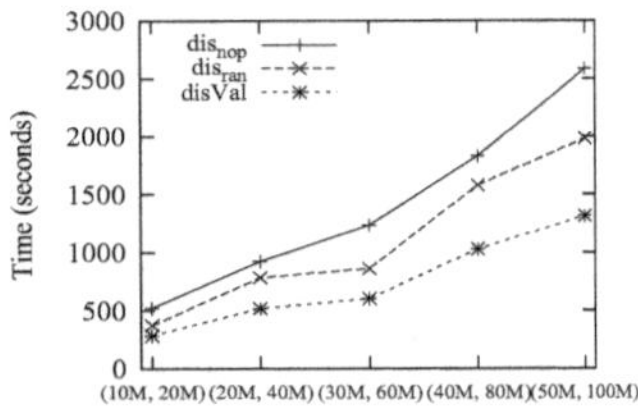

Figure 6: Scalability: Varying $|G|$ (synthetic)

faster than disVal, since it requires no data exchange by trading with replicated G. (4) Both repVal and disVal work well on large real-life graphs. For example, repVal (resp. disVal) takes 156 (resp. 326) seconds on *YAGO2* with 20 processors. In contrast, sequential algorithm detVio does not terminate on any of the three graphs within 6000 seconds. On average parallel graph replication (not shown) takes 21.3, 89 and 75 seconds for *YAGO2*, *DBpedia* and *Pokec*, respectively. The replication is performed once and is reused for all queries.

Exp-2: Workload complexity. We next evaluated the impact of the complexity of GFDs on workload estimation and partition, by varying $\|\Sigma\|$, the number of GFDs, and $|Q|$, the average pattern size. We fixed $n = 16$.

Varying $\|\Sigma\|$. Fixing $|Q| = 5$, we varied $\|\Sigma\|$ from 50 to 100. As shown in Figures 5(d), 5(f) and 5(h) on *DBpedia*, *YAGO2* and *Pokec*, respectively, (a) all the algorithms take longer time over larger Σ, as expected, and (b) repVal (resp. disVal) behaves better than $\mathsf{rep}_{\mathsf{ran}}$ and $\mathsf{rep}_{\mathsf{nop}}$ (resp. $\mathsf{dis}_{\mathsf{ran}}$ and $\mathsf{dis}_{\mathsf{nop}}$), by balancing workload and minimizing communication. However, detVio does not terminate within 120 minutes on any of the three graphs when $\|\Sigma\| \geq 80$.

Varying $|Q|$. Fixing $\|\Sigma\| = 50$, we varied $|Q|$ from 2 to 6. As shown in Figures 5(e), 5(g) and 5(i), all the algorithms take longer over larger $|Q|$, due to larger work units. However, repVal (resp. disVal) outperforms $\mathsf{rep}_{\mathsf{nop}}$ and $\mathsf{rep}_{\mathsf{ran}}$ (resp. $\mathsf{dis}_{\mathsf{nop}}$ and $\mathsf{dis}_{\mathsf{ran}}$) in all the cases, for the same reasons given above. Again, detVio does not terminate in 120 minutes when $|Q| \geq 6$ on all the three graphs.

Exp-3: Communication cost. In the same setting as Exp-1, we evaluated the total communication cost (measured as parallel data shipment time) of disVal, $\mathsf{dis}_{\mathsf{ran}}$ and $\mathsf{dis}_{\mathsf{nop}}$ over the three datasets, reported in Figures 5(j), 5(k) and 5(l), respectively. We omit repVal since it does not require data exchange. We find the following: (a) the total amount of data shipped (not shown) is far smaller than the size of the underlying graphs; this confirms our estimate of communication costs (Sections 5 and 6); (b) the communication cost takes from 12% to 24% of the overall error detection cost when n changes from 4 to 20; this is one of the reasons why adding processors does not always reduce parallel running time [19], since using more processors introduce more data exchange among different processors; and (c) although more data is shipped with larger n, the communication time is not very sensitive to n due to parallel shipment.

Exp-4: Synthetic G. We also evaluated the performance of algorithm disVal over large synthetic graphs of 50M nodes and 100M edges. We only tested the setting when G is partitioned, due to limited storage capacity for replicated G.

Fixing $n = 16$, we varied $|G|$ from (10M, 20M) to (50M, 100M). As shown in Fig. 6, (1) all the algorithms take longer time over larger $|G|$, as expected; (2) error detection is feasible in large graphs: disVal takes 21 minutes when $|G| =$ (50M, 100M); (3) disVal is on average 1.9 and 1.5 times faster than $\mathsf{dis}_{\mathsf{ran}}$ and $\mathsf{dis}_{\mathsf{nop}}$, respectively; this is consistent with the results on real-life graphs; and (4) sequential algorithm detVio does not run to completion when $|G| \geq$ (30M, 60M) within 120 minutes with one processor.

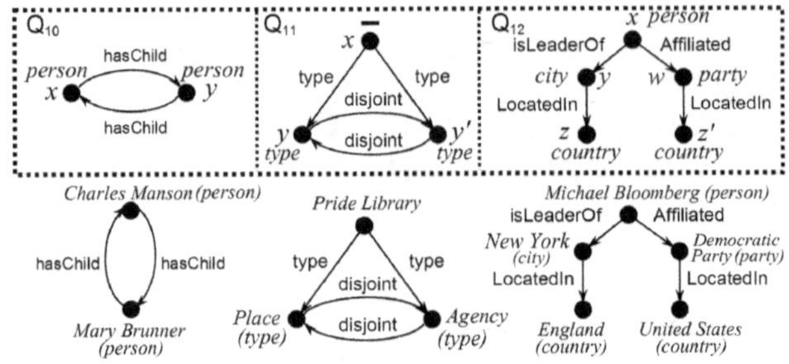

Figure 7: Real-life GFDs

Exp-5: Effectiveness. To demonstrate the effectiveness of GFDs in error detection, we show in Fig. 7 three real-life GFDs and error caught by them. Another set of experiments is reported in Appendix, comparing with other methods.

<u>GFD *1*</u> is $(Q_{10}[\bar{x}], \emptyset \rightarrow x.\mathsf{val} = c \ \wedge \ y.\mathsf{val} = d)$ for distinct c and d, (*i.e.*, $x.\mathsf{val} = c \ \wedge \ y.\mathsf{val} = d$ is false, stating that a person x cannot have y as both a child and a parent. It catches inconsistency in *YAGO2* shown in Fig. 7.

<u>GFD *2*</u> is $(Q_{11}[\bar{x}], \emptyset \rightarrow y.\mathsf{val} = y'.\mathsf{val})$, stating that an entity cannot have two disjoint types (with no common entities). It identifies an inconsistency at the "schema" level of *DBpedia* that contradicts a disjoint relationship.

<u>GFD *3*</u> is $(Q_{12}[\bar{x}], \emptyset \rightarrow z.\mathsf{val} = z'.\mathsf{val})$. It ensures that if a person is the mayor of a city in a country z, and is affiliated to a party of a country z', then z and z' must be the same country. It detects an error in *YAGO2* that associates different countries with New York city (NYC) and Democratic Party, witnessed by the mayor of NYC.

Summary. From the experimental results we find the following. (1) Error detection with GFDs is feasible in real-life graphs, *e.g.*, repVal (resp. disVal) takes 156 (resp. 326) seconds on *YAGO2* with 20 processors. (2) Better still, they are parallel scalable, with response time improved by 3.7 and 2.4 times, respectively, when the number of processors increase from 4 to 20. (3) Our optimization techniques improve the performance of $\mathsf{rep}_{\mathsf{nop}}$ and $\mathsf{dis}_{\mathsf{nop}}$ by 1.9 and 1.5 times, respectively; and workload balancing improves $\mathsf{rep}_{\mathsf{ran}}$ and $\mathsf{dis}_{\mathsf{ran}}$ by 1.4 and 1.3 times, respectively. (4) GFDs are capable of catching inconsistencies in real-world graphs.

8. CONCLUSION

The work is a first step towards a dependency theory for graphs. We have proposed GFDs, established complexity bounds for their classical problems, and provided parallel scalable algorithms for their application. Our experimental results have verified the effectiveness of GFD techniques.

One topic for future work is to develop effective algorithms for GFD discovery in real-life graphs. Another topic is to provide a sound and complete axiom system for GFDs, along the same lines as Armstrong's axioms for relational FDs [3]. A third topic is to re-investigate the satisfiability and implication problems for GFDs in the presence of types and other semantic constraints commonly found in knowledge bases.

Acknowledgments. Fan and Xu are supported in part by ERC 652976, 973 Program 2014CB340302 and 2012CB316200, NSFC 61133002 and 61421003, EPSRC EP/J015377/1 and EP/M025268/1, NSF III 1302212, Shenzhen Peacock Program 1105100030834361, Guangdong Innovative Research Team Program 2011D005, Shenzhen Science and Technology Fund JCYJ20150529164656096, Guangdong Applied R&D Program 2015B010131006, Beijing Advanced Innovation Centre for Big Data and Brain Computing, and a research grant from Huawei Technologies. Wu is supported by Google Faculty Research Award.

9. REFERENCES

[1] Dbpedia. *http://wiki.dbpedia.org/Datasets.*

[2] Pokec social network. *http://snap.stanford.edu/data/soc-pokec.html.*

[3] S. Abiteboul, R. Hull, and V. Vianu. *Foundations of Databases.* Addison-Wesley, 1995.

[4] F. N. Afrati, V. Borkar, M. Carey, N. Polyzotis, and J. D. Ullman. Map-reduce extensions and recursive queries. In *EDBT*, 2011.

[5] F. N. Afrati, D. Fotakis, and J. D. Ullman. Enumerating subgraph instances using map-reduce. In *ICDE*, 2013.

[6] F. N. Afrati and J. D. Ullman. Optimizing joins in a map-reduce environment. In *EDBT*, pages 99–110, 2010.

[7] G. Aggarwal, R. Motwani, and A. Zhu. The load rebalancing problem. In *SPAA*, 2003.

[8] W. Akhtar, A. Cortés-Calabuig, and J. Paredaens. Constraints in RDF. In *SDKB*, pages 23–39, 2010.

[9] M. Arenas and L. Libkin. A normal form for XML documents. In *PODS*, pages 85–96, 2002.

[10] D. Calvanese, W. Fischl, R. Pichler, E. Sallinger, and M. Šimkus. Capturing relational schemas and functional dependencies in RDFS. In *AAAI*, 2014.

[11] Q. Cao, M. Sirivianos, X. Yang, and T. Pregueiro. Aiding the detection of fake accounts in large scale social online services. In *NSDI*, pages 197–210, 2012.

[12] A. Cortés-Calabuig and J. Paredaens. Semantics of constraints in RDFS. In *AMW*, pages 75–90, 2012.

[13] O. Etzioni, M. Cafarella, D. Downey, S. Kok, A.-M. Popescu, T. Shaked, S. Soderland, D. S. Weld, and A. Yates. Web-scale information extraction in KnowItAll. In *WWW*, 2004.

[14] W. Fan, Z. Fan, C. Tian, and L. X. Dong. Keys for graphs. In *PVLDB*, 2015.

[15] W. Fan and F. Geerts. *Foundations of Data Quality Management.* Morgan & Claypool Publishers, 2012.

[16] W. Fan, F. Geerts, X. Jia, and A. Kementsietsidis. Conditional functional dependencies for capturing data inconsistencies. *TODS*, 33(1), 2008.

[17] W. Fan, F. Geerts, S. Ma, and H. Müller. Detecting inconsistencies in distributed data. In *ICDE*, pages 64–75, 2010.

[18] W. Fan, J. Li, N. Tang, and W. Yu. Incremental detection of inconsistencies in distributed data. *TKDE*, 26(6), 2014.

[19] W. Fan, X. Wang, and Y. Wu. Distributed graph simulation: Impossibility and possibility. *PVLDB*, 2014.

[20] L. Galárraga, K. Hose, and R. Schenkel. Partout: a distributed engine for efficient RDF processing. In *WWW*, 2014.

[21] M. A. Gallego, J. D. Fernández, M. A. Martínez-Prieto, and P. de la Fuente. An empirical study of real-world SPARQL queries. In *USEWOD workshop*, 2011.

[22] M. Hammoud, D. A. Rabbou, R. Nouri, S.-M.-R. Beheshti, and S. Sakr. DREAM: distributed RDF engine with adaptive query planner and minimal communication. *PVLDB*, 2015.

[23] B. He, L. Zou, and D. Zhao. Using conditional functional dependency to discover abnormal data in RDF graphs. In *SWIM*, pages 1–7, 2014.

[24] J. Hellings, M. Gyssens, J. Paredaens, and Y. Wu. Implication and axiomatization of functional and constant constraints. *Ann. Math. Artif. Intell.*, pages 1–29, 2015.

[25] J. Huang, D. J. Abadi, and K. Ren. Scalable SPARQL querying of large RDF graphs. *PVLDB*, 4(11):1123–1134, 2011.

[26] S. Huang, Q. Li, and P. Hitzler. Reasoning with inconsistencies in hybrid MKNF knowledge bases. *Logic Journal of IGPL*, 2012.

[27] H. Karloff, S. Suri, and S. Vassilvitskii. A model of computation for MapReduce. In *SODA*, pages 938–948, 2010.

[28] Z. Khayyat, I. F. Ilyas, A. Jindal, S. Madden, M. Ouzzani, P. Papotti, J.-A. Quiané-Ruiz, N. Tang, and S. Yin. Bigdansing: A system for big data cleansing. In *SIGMOD*, 2015.

[29] C. P. Kruskal, L. Rudolph, and M. Snir. A complexity theory of efficient parallel algorithms. *TCS*, 71(1):95–132, 1990.

[30] L. Lai, L. Qin, X. Lin, and L. Chang. Scalable subgraph enumeration in MapReduce. *PVLDB*, 8(10):974–985, 2015.

[31] W. Le, A. Kementsietsidis, S. Duan, and F. Li. Scalable multi-query optimization for SPARQL. In *ICDE*, 2012.

[32] L. Mendoza. A rule-based approach to address semantic accuracy problems on linked data. 2004.

[33] H. Mousavi and C. Zaniolo. Fast and accurate computation of equi-depth histograms over data streams. In *EDBT*, 2011.

[34] C. H. Papadimitriou. *Computational Complexity.* Addison-Wesley, 1994.

[35] B. Parsia and E. Sirin. Pellet: An OWL DL reasoner. In *ISWC-Poster*, volume 18, 2004.

[36] T. Plantenga. Inexact subgraph isomorphism in MapReduce. *J. Parallel Distrib. Comput.*, 73(2):164–175, 2013.

[37] H. Poon and P. Domingos. Joint inference in information extraction. In *AAAI*, volume 7, pages 913–918, 2007.

[38] L. Qin, J. X. Yu, L. Chang, H. Cheng, C. Zhang, and X. Lin. Scalable big graph processing in MapReduce. In *SIGMOD*, 2014.

[39] R. Raman, O. van Rest, S. Hong, Z. Wu, H. Chafi, and J. Banerjee. Pgx. iso: parallel and efficient

in-memory engine for subgraph isomorphism. In *GRADES*, pages 1–6, 2014.

[40] A. Rula and A. Zaveri. Methodology for assessment of linked data quality. In *LDQ@SEMANTiCS*, 2014.

[41] Y. Shao, B. Cui, L. Chen, L. Ma, J. Yao, and N. Xu. Parallel subgraph listing in a large-scale graph. In *SIGMOD*, 2014.

[42] W. Shen, A. Doan, J. F. Naughton, and R. Ramakrishnan. Declarative information extraction using datalog with embedded extraction predicates. In *VLDB*, 2007.

[43] D. B. Shmoys and É. Tardos. An approximation algorithm for the generalized assignment problem. *Mathematical Programming*, 62(1-3):461–474, 1993.

[44] F. M. Suchanek, G. Kasneci, and G. Weikum. Yago: a core of semantic knowledge. In *WWW*, pages 697–706, 2007.

[45] F. M. Suchanek, M. Sozio, and G. Weikum. SOFIE: a self-organizing framework for information extraction. In *WWW*, pages 631–640, 2009.

[46] Z. Sun, H. Wang, H. Wang, B. Shao, and J. Li. Efficient subgraph matching on billion node graphs. *PVLDB*, 2012.

[47] S. Suri and S. Vassilvitskii. Counting triangles and the curse of the last reducer. In *WWW*, pages 607–614, 2011.

[48] Y. Tao, W. Lin, and X. Xiao. Minimal MapReduce algorithms. *SIGMOD*, pages 529–540, 2013.

[49] Y. Yu and J. Heflin. Extending functional dependency to detect abnormal data in RDF graphs. In *ISWC*. 2011.

[50] A. Zaveri, D. Kontokostas, M. A. Sherif, L. Bühmann, M. Morsey, S. Auer, and J. Lehmann. User-driven quality evaluation of dbpedia. In *ICSS*, pages 97–104, 2013.

Appendix

Optimization Strategies

We next present optimization strategies employed by our algorithms.

Skewed graphs. Real-life graphs, *e.g.,* social networks, may exhibit skewed distribution, *i.e.,* most nodes have few neighbors while a small fraction of nodes are adjacent to a large fraction of the edges. Such skewed distribution may lead to a small number of large data blocks $G_{\bar{z}}$, and hence skewed workload.

Procedures bPar and disPar can readily adapt to skewed graphs, by applying a *replicate and split* strategy for large $G_{\bar{z}}$. (a) We set a threshold θ for $|G_{\bar{z}}|$. (b) For work units w with $G_{\bar{z}}$ exceeding θ, we replicate w with the same $\bar{z}$, but split $G_{\bar{z}}$ to subgraphs with size at most θ. (c) The original w is replaced by these new units. For these units, localVio and dlovalVio detect errors in G_z by shipping partial matches rather than data blocks.

We experimentally evaluated dlovalVio over skewed graphs. We generate synthetic graphs G controlled by skew measuring the "skewness" of G, quantified as a ratio $\frac{|G_{dm}|}{|G_{dm'}|}$, where $|G_{dm}|$ (resp. $|G_{dm'}|$) is the average size of top 10% smallest (resp. largest) d-hop neighbors of the nodes in G (we set d=3). It estimates the unbalance degree of data block sizes of work units. The smaller skew, the more unbalanced.

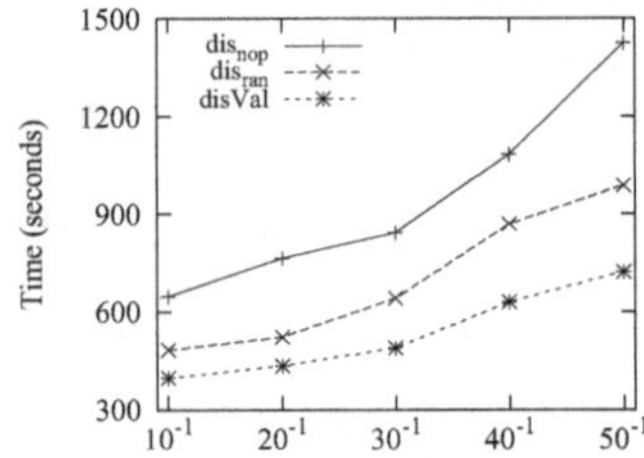

Figure 8: The impact of skewed graphs

Fixing $|G|$ = (10M, 20M) and n = 16, we varied skew from 0.1 to 0.02. Figure 8 shows that all the algorithms deteriorate when skew gets smaller ("more skewed"), due to unbalanced workload, as expected. However, disVal is more "robust" to skew: its running time only grows 1.7 times when G becomes 5 times more "skewed", as opposed to 2.0 times by $\mathsf{dis}_{\mathsf{ran}}$ and 2.2 by $\mathsf{dis}_{\mathsf{nop}}$. This verifies the effectiveness of our "replicate and split strategy".

Multi-query processing. There has been work on optimizing muilti-pattern matching by extracting common sub-patterns [31]. Algorithm repVal and disVal use some of the techniques, *e.g.,* pattern containment and sub-pattern scheduling, to process common sub-patterns in Σ, and to remove redundant work units (*e.g.,* Example 10).

Workload reduction. The implication analysis of GFDs can help us further reduce workload. Given a set Σ of GFDs, if $\Sigma \setminus \{\varphi\} \models \varphi$, we can safely remove φ from Σ without impacting Vio(Σ, G). As shown in Theorem 5, the implication problem is intractable. Nonetheless, it is in PTIME if the patterns in Σ are trees (Corollary 8), and moreover, there are heuristic algorithms to conduct the analysis efficiently.

Compared with Other Approaches

<u>GFDs *vs. other models*</u>. We evaluated the effectiveness of GFDs for error detection with *YAGO2*, by comparing with (a) the extension of CFDs to RDF [23], referred to as GCFDs, and (b) BigDansing [28]. Since the complete set of "true" errors in *YAGO2* is unknown, we sampled a set of entities. For each sampled entity x, we randomly injected noise (with probability 2%, 2690 errors in total) into *YAGO2* as suggested by [50]: (a) *attribute inconsistency*, by changing the value of an attribute $x.A$; (b) *type inconsistency*, by revising the type of x; and (c) *representational inconsistency*, by revising the value of either $x.A$ or $x'.A$ if $x.A$=$x'.A$ and x and x' are of the same type. Denote the set of entities with noise as Vio, we define the *precision* (resp. *recall*) of an error detection method $\mathcal{A}$ as $\frac{|\mathsf{Vio} \cap \mathsf{Vio}(\mathcal{A})|}{|\mathsf{Vio}(\mathcal{A})|}$) (resp. $\frac{|\mathsf{Vio} \cap \mathsf{Vio}(\mathcal{A})|}{|\mathsf{Vio}|}$, where Vio$(\mathcal{A})$ denotes the inconsistent entity set detected by $\mathcal{A}$.

We constructed (1) a set Σ of 10 GFDs on *YAGO2* with frequent patterns that match a fraction of sampled entities and with constants from the original values before noise injection; and (2) a set of 7 GCFDs over sampled entities following [23], including *all* GFDs in Σ with conjunctive paths (GCFDs do not allow general graph patterns). (3) We hardcoded the GFDs as user-defined functions for each GFD in Σ, as BigDansing does not support subgraph isomorphism.

We report the running time and accuracy of these methods in Fig. 9, with n = 16 on *YAGO2* extended with noise. We find that (a) GFDs has higher accuracy (91%) than GCFDs,

model	recall	prec.	time
GFD	**0.91**	**1.0**	**131s**
GCFD	0.57	1.0	106s
BigDansing	0.91	1.0	609s

Figure 9: Running time and accuracy

since it catches inconsistencies with general patterns not expressible by GCFDs; (b) it takes comparable time for GFDs and GCFDs; and (c) BigDansing is 4.6 times slower, because it had to cast subgraph isomorphic testing as relational joins. It reports the same accuracy as our algorithm since it hard-coded the same set Σ of GFDs.

Real-world GFDs. Observe the following about the GFDs depicted in Fig. 7.

GFD *1* is not expressible as (a) a GCFD since Q_{10} is a cyclic pattern, or (b) a CFD or denial constraint (DC) of BigDansing, since otherwise it gets false negative if subgraph isomorphism is not enforced.

GFD *2* is not expressible as GCFD, CFD or DC for the same reason as GFD 1.

GFD *3* is is not expressible as GCFD although Q_{12} is a tree, since GCFD cannot do the test z.id $= z'$.id; similarly for CFD and DC of BigDansing.

Summary. From the experimental results we can see the following. (1) GFDs are more accurate than GCFDs in error detection. (2) BigDansing requires users to code GFDs and subgraph isomorphism, and is 4.6 times slower than our algorithm.

SLING: A Near-Optimal Index Structure for SimRank

Boyu Tian
Shanghai Jiao Tong University
China
bytian@umich.edu

Xiaokui Xiao
Nanyang Technological University
Singapore
xkxiao@ntu.edu.sg

ABSTRACT

SimRank is a similarity measure for graph nodes that has numerous applications in practice. Scalable SimRank computation has been the subject of extensive research for more than a decade, and yet, none of the existing solutions can efficiently derive SimRank scores on large graphs with provable accuracy guarantees. In particular, the state-of-the-art solution requires up to a few seconds to compute a SimRank score in million-node graphs, and does not offer any worst-case assurance in terms of the query error.

This paper presents *SLING*, an efficient index structure for SimRank computation. *SLING* guarantees that each SimRank score returned has at most ε additive error, and it answers any single-pair and single-source SimRank queries in $O(1/\varepsilon)$ and $O(n/\varepsilon)$ time, respectively. These time complexities are *near-optimal*, and are significantly better than the asymptotic bounds of the most recent approach. Furthermore, *SLING* requires only $O(n/\varepsilon)$ space (which is also near-optimal in an asymptotic sense) and $O(m/\varepsilon + n\log\frac{n}{\delta}/\varepsilon^2)$ pre-computation time, where δ is the failure probability of the preprocessing algorithm. We experimentally evaluate *SLING* with a variety of real-world graphs with up to several millions of nodes. Our results demonstrate that *SLING* is up to 10000 times (resp. 110 times) faster than competing methods for single-pair (resp. single-source) SimRank queries, at the cost of higher space overheads.

1. INTRODUCTION

Assessing the similarity of nodes based on graph topology is an important problem with numerous applications, including social network analysis [21], web mining [16], collaborative filtering [5], natural language processing [26], and spam detection [27]. A number of similarity measures have been proposed, among which *SimRank* [14] is one of the most well-adopted. The formulation of SimRank is based on two intuitive arguments:

- A node should have the maximum similarity to itself;
- The similarity between two different nodes can be measured by the average similarity between the two nodes' neighbors.

Formally, the SimRank score of two nodes v_i and v_j is defined as:

SIGMOD'16, June 26-July 01, 2016, San Francisco, CA, USA

ISBN 978-1-4503-3531-7/16/06... $15.00

DOI: http://dx.doi.org/10.1145/2882903.2915243

$$s(v_i, v_j) = \begin{cases} 1, & \text{if } v_i = v_j \\ \dfrac{c}{|I(v_i)| \cdot |I(v_j)|} \displaystyle\sum_{a \in I(v_i), b \in I(v_j)} s(a, b), & \text{otherwise} \end{cases} \tag{1}$$

where $I(v)$ denotes the set of in-neighbors of a node v, and $c \in (0, 1)$ is a decay factor typically set to 0.6 or 0.8 [14, 23]. Previous work [5, 8, 16, 21, 22, 26, 27, 33, 35] has applied SimRank (and its variants) to various problem domains, and has demonstrated that it often provides high-quality measurements of node similarity.

1.1 Motivation

Despite of the effectiveness of SimRank, computing SimRank scores efficiently on large graphs is a challenging task, and has been the subject of extensive research for more than a decade. In particular, Jeh and Widom [14] propose the first SimRank algorithm, which returns the SimRank scores of all pairs of nodes in the input graph G. The algorithm incurs prohibitive costs: it requires $O(n^2)$ space and $O(m^2 \log\frac{1}{\varepsilon})$ time, where n and m denote the numbers of nodes and edges in G, respectively, and ε is the maximum additive error allowed in any SimRank score. Subsequently, Lizorkin et al. [23] improve the time complexity of the algorithm to $O(\log\frac{1}{\varepsilon} \cdot \min\{nm, n^3/\log n\})$, which is further improved to $O(\log\frac{1}{\varepsilon} \cdot \min\{nm, n^\omega\})$ by Yu et al. [34], where $\omega \approx 2.373$. However, the space complexity of the algorithm remains $O(n^2)$, as is inherent in any algorithm that computes *all-pair* SimRank scores.

Fogaras and Rácz [8] present the first study on *single-pair* SimRank computation, and propose a Monte-Carlo method that requires $O(n\log\frac{1}{\delta}/\varepsilon^2)$ pre-computation time and space. The method returns the SimRank score of any node pair in $O(\log\frac{1}{\delta}/\varepsilon^2)$ time, where δ is the failure probability of the Monte-Carlo method. Subsequently, Li et al. [20] propose a deterministic algorithm for single-pair SimRank queries; it has the same time complexity with Jeh and Widom's solution [14], but provides much better practical efficiency. However, existing work [24] show that neither Li et al.'s [20] nor Fogaras and Rácz's solution [8] is able to handle million-node graphs in reasonable time and space. There is a line of research [10, 13, 19, 30–32] that attempts to mitigate this efficiency issue based on an alternative formulation of SimRank, but the formulation is shown to be *incorrect* [17], in that it does not return the same SimRank scores as defined in Equation (1).

The most recent approach to SimRank computation is the *linearization* technique [24] by Maehara et al., which is shown to considerably outperform existing solutions in terms of efficiency and scalability. Nevertheless, it still requires up to a few seconds to answer a single-pair SimRank query on sizable graphs, which is inadequate for large-scale applications. More importantly, the

Table 1: Comparison of SimRank computation methods with at most ε additive error and at least $1-\delta$ success probability.

Algorithm	Query Time		Space Overhead	Preprocessing Time
	Single Pair	Single Source		
Fogaras and Rácz [8]	$O(\log\frac{1}{\varepsilon}\log\frac{n}{\delta}/\varepsilon^2)$	$O(n\log\frac{1}{\varepsilon}\log\frac{n}{\delta}/\varepsilon^2)$	$O(n\log\frac{1}{\varepsilon}\log\frac{n}{\delta}/\varepsilon^2)$	$O(n\log\frac{1}{\varepsilon}\log\frac{n}{\delta}/\varepsilon^2)$
Maehara et al. [24] (under heuristic assumptions)	$O(m\log\frac{1}{\varepsilon})$	$O(m\log^2\frac{1}{\varepsilon})$	$O(n+m)$	no formal result
this paper	$O(1/\varepsilon)$	$O(n/\varepsilon)$ (Algorithm 3) $O(m\log^2\frac{1}{\varepsilon})$ (Algorithm 6)	$O(n/\varepsilon)$	$O(m/\varepsilon+n\log\frac{n}{\delta}/\varepsilon^2)$
lower bound	$\Omega(1)$	$\Omega(n)$	$\Omega(n)$	-

technique is unable to provide any worst-case guarantee in terms of query accuracy. In particular, the technique has a preprocessing step that requires solving a system L of linear equations; assuming that the solution to L is *exact*, Maehara et al. [24] show that the technique can ensure ε worst-case query error, and can answer any single-pair and single-source SimRank queries in $O(m\log\frac{1}{\varepsilon})$ and $O(m\log^2\frac{1}{\varepsilon})$ time, respectively. (A single-source SimRank query from a node v_i asks for the SimRank score between v_i and every other node.) Unfortunately, as we discuss in Section 3.3, the linearization technique cannot precisely solve L, nor can it offer non-trivial guarantees in terms of the query errors incurred by the imprecision of L's solution. Consequently, the technique in [24] only provides heuristic solutions to SimRank computation. In summary, after more than tens years of research on SimRank, there is still no solution for efficient SimRank computation on large graphs with provable accuracy guarantees.

1.2 Contributions and Organization

This paper presents *SLING* (*SimRank via Local Updates and Sampling*), an efficient index structure for SimRank computation. *SLING* guarantees that each SimRank score returned has at most ε additive error, and answers any single-pair and single-source SimRank queries in $O(1/\varepsilon)$ and $O(n/\varepsilon)$ time, respectively. These time complexities are *near-optimal*, since any SimRank method requires $\Omega(1)$ (resp. $\Omega(n)$) time to output the result of any single-pair (resp. single-source) query. In addition, they are significantly better than the asymptotic bounds of the states of the art (including Maehara et al.'s technique [24] under their heuristic assumptions), as we show in Table 1. Furthermore, *SLING* requires only $O(n/\varepsilon)$ space (which is also near-optimal in an asymptotic sense) and $O(m/\varepsilon+n\log\frac{n}{\delta})$ pre-computation time, where δ is the failure probability of the preprocessing algorithm.

Apart from its superior asymptotic bounds, *SLING* also incorporates several optimization techniques to enhance its practical performance. In particular, we show that its preprocessing algorithm can be improved with a technique that estimates the expectation of a Bernoulli variable using an *asymptotically optimal* number of samples. Additionally, its space consumption can be heuristically reduced without affecting its theoretical guarantees, while its empirical efficiency for single-source SimRank queries can be considerably improved, at the cost of a slight increase in its query time complexity. Last but not least, its construction algorithms can be easily parallelized, and it can efficiently process queries even when its index structure does not fit in the main memory.

We experimentally evaluate *SLING* with a variety of real-world graphs with up to several millions of nodes, and show that it significantly outperforms the the states of the art in terms of query efficiency. Specifically, *SLING* requires at most 2.3 milliseconds to process a single-pair SimRank query on our datasets, and is up to 10000 times faster than the linearization method [24]. To our knowledge, this is the first result in the literature that demonstrates millisecond-scale query time for single-pair SimRank computation on million-node graphs. For single-source SimRank queries, *SLING* is up to 110 times more efficient than the linearization method. As a tradeoff, *SLING* incurs larger space overheads than the linearization method, but it is a still much more favorable choice in the common scenario where query time and accuracy (instead of space consumption) are the main concern.

The remainder of the paper is organized as follows. Section 2 defines the problem that we study. Section 3 discusses the major existing methods for SimRank computation. Section 4 presents the *SLING* index, with a focus on single-pair queries. Section 5 proposes techniques to optimize the practical performance of *SLING*. Section 6 details how *SLING* supports single-source queries. Section 7 experimentally evaluates *SLING* against the stats of the art

2. PRELIMINARIES

Let G be a directed and unweighted graph with n nodes and m edges. We aim to construct an index structure on G to support *single-pair* and *single-source* SimRank queries, which are defined as follows:

- A single-pair SimRank query takes as input two nodes u and v in G, and returns their SimRank score $s(u,v)$ (see Equation 1).
- A single-source SimRank query takes as input a node u, and returns $s(u,v)$ for each node v in G.

Following previous work [8, 23, 24, 33], we allow an additive error of at most $\varepsilon\in(0,1)$ in each SimRank score returned for any SimRank query.

For ease of exposition, we focus on single-pair SimRank queries in Sections 3-5, and then discuss single-source queries in Section 6. Table 2 shows the notations frequently used in the paper. Unless otherwise specified, all logarithms in this paper are to base e.

3. ANALYSIS OF EXISTING METHODS

This section revisits the three major approaches to SimRank computation: the *power method* [14], the *Monte Carlo method* [8], and the *linearization method* [17, 24, 25, 33]. The asymptotic performance of the Monte Carlo method and the linearization method has been studied in literature, but to our knowledge, there is no formal analysis regarding their space and time complexities when ensuring ε worst-case errors. We remedy this issue with detailed discussions on each method's asymptotic bounds and limitations.

3.1 The Power Method

The power method [14] is an iterative method for computing the SimRank scores of all pairs of nodes in an input graph. The method

Table 2: Table of notations.

Notation	Description
G	the input graph
n, m	the numbers of nodes and edges in G
v_i	the i-th node in G
$I(v)$	the set of in-neighbors of a node v in G
$s(v_i, v_j)$	the SimRank score of two nodes v_i and v_j in G
c	the decay factor in the definition of SimRank
ε	the maximum additive error allowed in a SimRank score
δ	the failure probability of a Monte-Carlo algorithm
$M(i,j)$	the entry on the i-th row and j-th column of a matrix M
d_k	the correction factor for node v_k
$h^{\ell}(v_i, v_j)$	the hitting probability (HP) from node v_i to node v_j at step ℓ (see Section 4.2)

uses a $n \times n$ matrix S, where the element $S(i,j)$ on the i-th row and j-th column ($i, j \in [1, n]$) denotes the SimRank score of the i-th node v_i and j-th node v_j. Initially, the method sets

$$S(i,j) = \begin{cases} 1, & \text{if } i = j \\ 0, & \text{otherwise} \end{cases}$$

After that, in the t-th ($t \geq 1$) iteration, the method updates S based on the following equation:

$$S(i,j) = \begin{cases} 1, & \text{if } i = j \\ \dfrac{c}{|I(v_i)||I(v_j)|} \displaystyle\sum_{v_k \in I(v_i), v_\ell \in I(v_j)} S(k, \ell), & \text{otherwise} \end{cases}$$

Let $S^{(t)}$ denote the version of S right after the t-th iteration. Lizorkin et al. [23] establish the following connection between t and the errors in the SimRank scores in $S^{(t)}$:

LEMMA 1 ([23]). *If* $t \geq \log_c(\varepsilon \cdot (1-c)) - 1$, *then for any* $i, j \in [1, n]$, *we have* $\left|S^{(t)}(i,j) - s(v_i, v_j)\right| \leq \varepsilon$. □

Based on Lemma 1 and the fact that each iteration of the power method takes $O(m^2)$ time, we conclude that the power method runs in $O(m^2 \log \frac{1}{\varepsilon})$ time when ensuring ε worst-case error. In addition, it requires $O(n^2)$ space (caused by S). These large complexities in time and space make the power method only applicable on small graphs.

3.2 The Monte Carlo Method

The Monte Carlo method [8] is motivated by an alternative definition of SimRank scores [14] that utilizes the concept of *reverse random walks*. Given a node w_0 in G, a reverse random walk from w_0 is a sequence of nodes $W = \langle w_0, w_1, w_2, \ldots \rangle$, such that w_{i+1} ($i \geq 0$) is selected uniformly at random from the in-neighbors of w_i. We refer to w_i as the i-th *step* of W.

Suppose that we have two reverse random walks W_i and W_j that start from two nodes v_i and v_j, respectively, and they *first meet* at the τ-th step. That is, the τ-th steps of W_i and W_j are identical, but for any $\ell \in [0, \tau)$, the ℓ-th step of W_i differs from the ℓ-th step of W_j. Jeh and Widom [14] establishes the following connection between τ and the SimRank score of v_i and v_j:

$$s(v_i, v_j) = \mathbb{E}[c^{\tau}], \tag{2}$$

where $\mathbb{E}[\cdot]$ denotes the expectation of a random variable.

Based on Equation (2), the Monte Carlo method [8] pre-computes a set $\mathcal{W}_i$ of reverse random walks from each node v_i in G, such that (i) each set $\mathcal{W}_i$ has the same number n_w of walks, and (ii) each walk in $\mathcal{W}_i$ is truncated at step t, i.e., the nodes after the t-th step are omitted. (This truncation is necessary to ensure that the walk is computed efficiently.) Then, given two nodes v_i and v_j, the method estimates their SimRank score as

$$\hat{s}(v_i, v_j) = \frac{1}{n_w} \sum_{\ell=0}^{n_w} c^{\tau_\ell},$$

where τ_ℓ denotes the step at which the ℓ-th walk in $\mathcal{W}_i$ first meets with the ℓ-th walk in $\mathcal{W}_j$. Fogaras and Rácz [8] show that, with at least $1 - 2\exp(-\frac{6}{7} n_w \varepsilon^2)$ probability,

$$\left|\hat{s}(v_i, v_j) - \mathbb{E}\left[\hat{s}(v_i, v_j)\right]\right| \leq \varepsilon. \tag{3}$$

However, we note that $\mathbb{E}\left[\hat{s}(v_i, v_j)\right] \neq s(v_i, v_j)$, due to the truncation imposed on the reverse random walks in W_i and W_j. To address this issue, we present the following inequality:

$$\begin{aligned} \left|\mathbb{E}\left[s(v_i, v_j)\right] - \hat{s}(v_i, v_j)\right| &= \left|\mathbb{E}[c^{\tau}] - \Pr[\tau \leq t] \cdot \mathbb{E}[c^{\tau} \mid \tau \leq t]\right| \\ &= \left|Pr[\tau > t] \cdot \mathbb{E}[c^{\tau} \mid \tau > t]\right| \\ &\leq c^{t+1} \end{aligned} \tag{4}$$

By Equations (3) and (4) and the union bound, it can be verified that when $t > \log_c \frac{\varepsilon}{2}$ and $n_w \geq \frac{14}{3\varepsilon^2}\left(\log \frac{2}{\delta} + 2 \log n\right)$,

$$\left|\hat{s}(v_i, v_j) - s(v_i, v_j)\right| \leq \varepsilon$$

holds for all pairs of v_i and v_j with at least $1 - \delta$ probability. In that case, the space and preprocessing time complexities of the Monte Carlo method are both $O(n_w \cdot t) = O(\frac{n}{\varepsilon^2} \log \frac{1}{\varepsilon} \log \frac{n}{\delta})$. In addition, the method takes $O(\frac{1}{\varepsilon^2} \log \frac{1}{\varepsilon} \log \frac{n}{\delta})$ time to answer a single-pair SimRank query, and $O(\frac{n}{\varepsilon^2} \log \frac{1}{\varepsilon} \log \frac{n}{\delta})$ time to process a single-source SimRank query. These space and time complexities are rather unfavorable under typical settings of ε in practice (e.g., $\varepsilon = 0.01$). Fogaras and Rácz [8] alleviate this issue with a *coupling technique*, which improves the practical performance of the Monte Carlo method in terms of pre-computation time and space consumption. Nevertheless, the method still incurs significant overheads, due to which it is unable to handle graphs with over one million nodes, as we show in Section 7.

3.3 The Linearization Method

Let S and P be two $n \times n$ matrices, with $S(i,j) = s(v_i, v_j)$ and

$$P(i,j) = \begin{cases} 1/|I(v_j)|, & \text{if } v_i \in I(v_j) \\ 0, & \text{otherwise} \end{cases} \tag{5}$$

Yu et al. [34] show that Equation (1) (i.e., the definition of SimRank) can be rewritten as

$$S = (cP^{\top} SP) \vee I, \tag{6}$$

where I is an $n \times n$ identity matrix, $P^{\top}$ is the transpose of P, and $\vee$ is the *element-wise maximum* operator, i.e., $(A \vee B)(i,j) = \max\{A(i,j), B(i,j)\}$ for any two matrices A and B and any i, j.

Maehara et al. [24] point out that solving Equation (6) is difficult since it is a *non-linear* problem due to the $\vee$ operator. To circumvent this difficulty, they prove that there exists a $n \times n$ diagonal matrix D (referred to as the *diagonal correction matrix*), such that

$$S = cP^{\top} SP + D. \tag{7}$$

Furthermore, once D is given, one can uniquely derive S based on the following lemma by Maehara et al. [24]:

LEMMA 2 ([24]). *Given the diagonal correction matrix D,*

$$S = \sum_{\ell=0}^{+\infty} c^{\ell} \left(P^{\ell}\right)^{\top} D P^{\ell}, \tag{8}$$

where P^{ℓ} denotes the ℓ-th power of P. □

Given Lemma 2, Maehara et al. [24] propose the linearization method, which pre-computes D and then uses it to answer SimRank queries based on Equation (8). In particular, for any two nodes v_i and v_j, Equation (8) leads to

$$s(v_i, v_j) = \sum_{\ell=0}^{+\infty} c^{\ell} \left(P^{\ell} \cdot \vec{e_i}\right)^{\top} D \left(P^{\ell} \cdot \vec{e_j}\right), \tag{9}$$

where $\vec{e_k}$ denotes a n-element column vector where the k-th element equals 1 and all other elements equal 0. To avoid the infinite series in Equation (9), the linearization method approximates $s(v_i, v_j)$ with

$$\tilde{s}(v_i, v_j) = \sum_{\ell=0}^{t} c^{\ell} \left(P^{\ell} \cdot \vec{e_i}\right)^{\top} D \left(P^{\ell} \cdot \vec{e_j}\right), \tag{10}$$

which can be computed in $O(m \cdot t)$ time. It can be shown that if D is precise and $t \geq \log_c(\varepsilon \cdot (1-c)) - 1$, then

$$\left|\tilde{s}(v_i, v_j) - s(v_i, v_j)\right| \leq \varepsilon. \tag{11}$$

Therefore, given an exact D, the linearization method answers any single-pair SimRank query in $O(m \log \frac{1}{\varepsilon})$ time. With a slight modification of Equation 10, the method can also process any single-source SimRank query in $O(m \log^2 \frac{1}{\varepsilon})$ time.

Unfortunately, the linearization method do not precisely derive D, due to which the above time complexities does not hold in general. Specifically, Maehara et al. [24] formulate D as the solution to a linear system, and propose to solve an *approximate* version of the system to derive an estimation $\widetilde{D}$ of D. However, there is no formal analysis on the errors in $\widetilde{D}$ and their effects on the accuracy of SimRank computation. In addition, the technique used to solve the approximate linear system does not guarantee to *converge*, i.e., it may not return $\widetilde{D}$ in bounded time. Furthermore, even if the technique does converge, its time complexity relies on a parameter that is unknown in advance, and may even dominate n, m, and $1/\varepsilon$. This makes it rather difficult to analyze the pre-computation time of the linearization method. We refer interested readers to Appendix A for detailed discussions on these issues.

In summary, the linearization method by Maehara et al. [24] does not guarantee ε worst-case error in each SimRank score returned, and there is no non-trivial bound on its preprocessing time. This problem is partially addressed in recent work [33] by Yu and McCann, who propose a variant of the linearization method that does not pre-compute the diagonal correction matrix D, but implicitly derives D during query processing. Yu and McCann's technique is able to ensure ε worst-case error in SimRank computation, but as a trade-off, it requires $O\left(mn \log \frac{1}{\varepsilon}\right)$ time to answer a single-pair SimRank query, which renders it inapplicable on any sizable graph.

4. OUR SOLUTION

This section presents our *SLING* index for SimRank queries. *SLING* is based on a new interpretation of SimRank scores, which we clarify in Section 4.1. After that, Sections 4.3-4.5 provide details of *SLING* and analyze its theoretical guarantees.

4.1 New Interpretation of SimRank

Let c be the decay factor in the definition of SimRank (see Equation (1)). Suppose that we perform a reverse random walk from any node u in G, such that

- At each step of the walk, we stop with $1 - \sqrt{c}$ probability;
- With the other $\sqrt{c}$ probability, we inspect the in-neighbors of the node at the current step, and select one of them uniformly at random as the next step.

We refer to such a reverse random walk as a *$\sqrt{c}$-walk* from u. In addition, we say that two $\sqrt{c}$-walks *meet*, if for a certain $\ell \geq 0$, the ℓ-th steps of the two walks are identical. (Note the 0-th step of a $\sqrt{c}$-walk is its starting node.) The following lemma shows an interesting connection between $\sqrt{c}$-walks and SimRank.

LEMMA 3. *Let W_i and W_j be two $\sqrt{c}$-walks from two nodes v_i and v_j, respectively. Then, $s(v_i, v_j)$ equals the probability that W_i and W_j meet.* □

The above formulation of SimRank is similar in spirit to the one used in the Monte Carlo method [8] (see Section 3.2), but differs in one crucial aspect: each $\sqrt{c}$-walk in our formulation has an expected length of $\frac{1}{1-\sqrt{c}}$, whereas each reverse random walk in the previous formulation is infinite. As a consequence, if we are to estimate $s(v_i, v_j)$ using a sample set of $\sqrt{c}$-walks from v_i and v_j, we do not need to truncate any $\sqrt{c}$-walk for efficiency; in contrast, the Monte Carlo method [8] must trim each reverse random walk to trade estimation accuracy for bounded computation time. In fact, if we incorporate $\sqrt{c}$-walks into the Monte Carlo method, then its query time complexities are immediately improved by a factor of $\log \frac{1}{\varepsilon}$. Nonetheless, the space and time overheads of this revised method still leave much room for improvement, since it requires $O(\log \frac{n}{\delta}/\varepsilon^2)$ $\sqrt{c}$-walks for each node, where δ is the upper bound on the method's failure probability. This motivates us to develop the *SLING* method for more efficient SimRank computation, which we elaborate in the following sections.

4.2 Key Idea of *SLING*

Let $h^{(\ell)}(v_a, v_b)$ denote the probability that a $\sqrt{c}$-walk from v_a arrives at v_b in its ℓ-th step. We refer to $h^{(\ell)}(v_a, v_b)$ as the *hitting probability (**HP**)* from v_a to v_b at step ℓ. Observe that, for any two $\sqrt{c}$-walks W_i and W_j from two nodes v_i and v_j, respectively, the probability that they meet at v_k at the ℓ-th step is

$$h^{(\ell)}(v_i, v_k) \cdot h^{(\ell)}(v_j, v_k).$$

Since $s(v_i, v_j)$ equals the probability that W_i and W_j meet, one may attempt to compute $s(v_i, v_j)$ by taking the the probability that W_i and W_j meet over all combinations of meeting nodes and meeting steps, i.e.,

$$s^*(v_i, v_j) = \sum_{\ell=0}^{+\infty} \sum_{k=1}^{n} \left(h^{(\ell)}(v_i, v_k) \cdot h^{(\ell)}(v_j, v_k)\right). \tag{12}$$

However, this formulation is incorrect, because the events that "W_i and W_j meet at node v_x at step ℓ" and "W_i and W_j meet at node v_y at step $\ell' > \ell$" are *not* mutually exclusive. For example, assume that $v_i = v_j$, and v_i has only in-neighbor v_k. In that case, W_i and W_j have 100% probability to meet at v_i at the 0-th step, and a non-zero probability to meet at v_k at the first step. This leads to $s^*(v_i, v_j) > 1$, whereas $s(v_i, v_j) = 1$ by definition.

Interestingly, Equation (12) can be fixed if we substitute $h^{(\ell)}(v_i, v_k) \cdot h^{(\ell)}(v_j, v_k)$ with the probability of the event that "W_i and W_j meet at v_k at step ℓ, *but never meet again afterwards*".

To explain this, observe that the above event indicates that W_i and W_j *last meet* at v_k at step ℓ. If we change v_k (resp. ℓ) in the event, then W_i and W_j should last meet at a different node (resp. step), in which case the changed event and the original one are mutually exclusive. Based on this observation, the following lemma presents a remedy to Equaiton (12).

LEMMA 4. *Let d_k be the probability that two $\sqrt{c}$-walks from node v_k do not meet each other after the 0-th step. Then, for any two nodes v_i and v_j,*

$$s(v_i, v_j) = \sum_{\ell=0}^{\infty}\sum_{k=1}^{n}\left(h^{(\ell)}(v_i, v_k)\cdot d_k \cdot h^{(\ell)}(v_j, v_k)\right). \quad (13)$$

In what follows, we refer to d_k as the *correction factor* for v_k.

Based on Lemma 4, we propose to pre-compute approximate versions of d_k and HPs $h^{(\ell)}(v_i, v_k)$, and then use them to estimate SimRank scores based on Equation (4). The immediate problem here is that there exists an infinite number of HPs $h^{(\ell)}(v_i, v_k)$ to approximate, since we need to consider all $\ell \geq 0$. However, we observe that if we allow an additive error in the approximate values, then most of the HPs can be estimated as zero and be omitted. In particular, we have the following observation:

OBSERVATION 1. *For any node v_i and $\ell \geq 0$, there exist at most $(\sqrt{c})^\ell/\varepsilon_h$ nodes v_k such that $h^{(\ell)}(v_j, v_k) \geq \varepsilon_h$.* □

To understand this, recall that each $\sqrt{c}$-walk has only $(\sqrt{c})^\ell$ probability to *not* stop before the ℓ-th step, i.e.,

$$\sum_{k=1}^{n} h^{(\ell)}(v_j, v_k) = (\sqrt{c})^\ell.$$

Therefore, at most $(\sqrt{c})^\ell/\varepsilon_h$ of the HPs at step ℓ can be larger than ε_h. Even if we take into account all $\ell \geq 0$, the total number of HPs above ε_h is only

$$\sum_{\ell=0}^{+\infty}(\sqrt{c})^\ell/\varepsilon_h = O(1/\varepsilon_h).$$

In other words, we only need to retain a constant number of HPs for each node, if we permit a constant additive error in each HP.

Based on the above analysis, we propose the *SLING* index, which pre-computes an approximate version $\tilde{d}_k$ of each correction factor d_k, as well as a constant-size set $H(v_i)$ of approximate HPs for each node v_i. To derive the SimRank score of two nodes v_i and v_j, *SLING* first retrieves $\tilde{d}_k$, $H(v_i)$, and $H(v_j)$, and then estimates $s(v_i, v_j)$ in constant time based on an approximate version of Equation (13). The challenge in the design of *SLING* is threefold. First, how can we derive an accurate estimation of $\tilde{d}_k$? Second, how can we efficiently construct $H(v_i)$ without iterating over all HPs? Third, how do we ensure that all $\tilde{d}_k$ and $H(v_i)$ can jointly guarantee ε worst-case error in each SimRank score computed? In Sections 4.3-4.5, we elaborate how we address these challenges.

Before we proceed, we note that there is an interesting connection between Lemmas 2 and 4:

LEMMA 5. *Let P and D be as in Lemma 2, and d_k and $h^{(\ell)}(v_i, v_k)$ be as in Lemma 4. For any $i, k \in [1, n]$, $h^{(\ell)}(v_i, v_k) = (\sqrt{c})^\ell \cdot P(k, i)$, and d_k equals the k-th diagonal element in D.* □

In other words, $h^{(\ell)}(v_i, v_k)$ (resp. d_k) can be regarded as a random-walk-based interpretation of the entries in P (resp. diagonal elements in D). Therefore, Lemmas 2 and 4 are different interpretations of the same result. The main advantage of our new interpretation is that it gives a physical meaning to d_k which, as we show in Section 4.3, enables us to devise a simple and rigorous algorithm to estimate d_k to any desired precision. In contrast, the only existing method for approximating D [24] fails to provide any non-trivial guarantees in terms of accuracy and efficiency, as we discuss in Section 3.3.

Algorithm 1: *A sampling method for estimating d_k*

Input: a node v_k, an error bound ε_d, and a failure probability δ_d
Output: an estimation version $\tilde{d}_k$ of d_k with at most ε_d error, with at least $1-\delta_d$ probability

Let $n_r = \dfrac{2c^2 + c\cdot\varepsilon_d}{\varepsilon_d^2}\log\dfrac{2}{\delta_d}$;
Let $cnt = 0$;
for $x = 1, 2, \cdots, n_r$ **do**
  Select two nodes v_i and v_j from $I(v_k)$ uniformly at random;
  if $v_i \neq v_j$ **then**
    Generate two $\sqrt{c}$-walks from v_i and v_j, respectively;
    if *the two $\sqrt{c}$-walks meet* **then**
      $cnt = cnt + 1$;
return $\tilde{d}_k = 1 - \dfrac{c}{|I(v_i)|} - c\cdot\dfrac{cnt}{n_r}$;

4.3 Estimation of d_k

Let W and W' be two $\sqrt{c}$-walks from v_k. By definition, $1 - d_k$ is the probability that any of the following events occurs:

1. W and W' meet at the first step.
2. In the first step, W and W' arrive at two different nodes v_i and v_j, respectively; but sometime after the first step, W and W' meet.

Note that the above two events are mutually exclusive, and the first event occurs with $\frac{c}{|I(v_k)|}$ probability. For the second event, if we fix a pair of v_i and v_j, then the probability that W and W' meet after the first step equals the probability that a $\sqrt{c}$-walk from v_i meets a $\sqrt{c}$-walk from v_j; by Lemma 3, this probability is exactly $s(v_i, v_j)$. Therefore, we have

$$d_k = 1 - \frac{c}{|I(v_k)|} - \frac{c}{|I(v_k)|^2}\sum_{\substack{v_i, v_j \in I(v_k)\\ v_i \neq v_j}} s(v_i, v_j). \quad (14)$$

Equation (14) indicates that, if we are to estimate d_k, it suffices to derive an estimation of

$$\mu = \frac{1}{|I(v_k)|^2}\sum_{v_i, v_j \in I(v_k) \wedge v_i \neq v_j} s(v_i, v_j) \quad (15)$$

by sampling $\sqrt{c}$-walks from v_i and v_j. In particular, as long as μ is estimated with an error no more than ε_d/c, the resulting estimation of d_k would have at most ε_d error. Motivated by this, we propose a sampling method for approximating d_k, as shown in Algorithm 1.

In a nutshell, Algorithm 1 generates n_r pairs of $\sqrt{c}$-walks, such that each walk starts from a randomly selected node in $I(v_k)$; after that, the algorithm counts the number cnt of pairs that meet at or after the first step; finally, it returns $\tilde{d}_k = 1 - \frac{c}{|I(v_i)|} - c\cdot\frac{cnt}{n_r}$ as an estimation of d_k. By the Chernoff bound (see Appendix D) and the properties of $\sqrt{c}$-walks, we have the following lemma on the theoretical guarantees of Algorithm 1.

LEMMA 6. *Algorithm 1 runs in $O\left(\frac{1}{\varepsilon_d^2}\log\frac{1}{\delta_d}\right)$ expected time, and returns $\tilde{d}_k$ such that $|\tilde{d}_k - d| \leq \varepsilon_d$ holds with at least $1-\delta_d$ probability.* □

Algorithm 2: *A local update method for constructing* $H(v_i)$

Input: G and a threshold θ
Output: A set $H(v_i)$ of approximate HPs for each node v_i in G

1 Initialize $H(v_i) = \emptyset$ for each node v_i;
2 **for** *each node* v_k *in* G **do**
3 Initialize a set $R_k = \emptyset$ for storing approximate HPs;
4 Insert $\tilde{h}^{(0)}(v_k, v_k) = 1$ into R_k;
5 **for** $\ell = 0, 1, 2, \ldots$ **do**
6 **for** *each* $\tilde{h}^{(\ell)}(v_x, v_k) \in R_k$ **do**
7 **if** $\tilde{h}^{(\ell)}(v_x, v_k) \leq \theta$ **then**
8 remove $\tilde{h}^{(\ell)}(v_x, v_k)$ from R_k;
9 **continue**;
10 **for** *each out-neighbor* v_i *of* v_x **do**
11 **if** $\tilde{h}^{(\ell)}(v_i, v_k) \notin R_k$ **then**
12 Insert $\tilde{h}^{(\ell+1)}(v_i, v_k) = \sqrt{c} \cdot \frac{\tilde{h}^{(\ell)}(v_x, v_k)}{|I(v_i)|}$ into R_k;
13 **else**
14 Increase $\tilde{h}^{(\ell+1)}(v_i, v_k)$ by $\sqrt{c} \cdot \frac{\tilde{h}^{(\ell)}(v_x, v_k)}{|I(v_i)|}$;
15 **if** R_k *does not contain any HP at step* $\ell + 1$ **then**
16 **break**;
17 **for** *each* $\tilde{h}^{(\ell)}(v_i, v_k) \in R_k$ **do**
18 Insert $\tilde{h}^{(\ell)}(v_i, v_k)$ into $H(v_i)$;

4.4 Construction of $H(v_i)$

As mentioned in Section 4.2, we aim to construct a constant-size set $H(v_i)$ for each node v_i, such that $H(v_i)$ contains an approximate version $\tilde{h}^{(\ell)}(v_i, v_x)$ of each HP $h^{(\ell)}(v_i, v_x)$ that is sufficiently large. Towards this end, a relatively straightforward solution is to sample a set $\mathcal{W}_i$ of $\sqrt{c}$-walks from each v_i, and then use $\mathcal{W}_i$ to derive approximate HPs. This solution, however, requires $O(1/{\varepsilon_h}^2)$ walks in $\mathcal{W}_i$ to ensure that the additive error in each $\tilde{h}^{(\ell)}(v_i, v_x)$ is at most ε_h, which leads to considerable computation costs when ε_h is small.

Instead of sampling $\sqrt{c}$-walks, we devise a deterministic method for constructing all $H(v_i)$ in $O(m/\varepsilon_h)$ time while allowing at most ε_h additive error in each approximate HP. The key idea of our method is to utilize the following equation on HPs:

$$h^{(\ell+1)}(v_i, v_k) = \frac{\sqrt{c}}{|I(v_i)|} \sum_{v_x \in I(v_i)} h^{(\ell)}(v_x, v_k), \tag{16}$$

for any $\ell \geq 0$. Intuitively, Equation (16) indicates that once we have derived the HPs to v_k at step ℓ, then we can compute the HPs to v_k at step $\ell + 1$. Based on this intuition, our method generates approximate HPs to v_k by processing the steps ℓ in ascending order of ℓ. We note that our method is similar in spirit to the *local update* algorithm [4,9,15] for estimating *personalized PageRanks* [15], and we refer interested readers to Appendix B for a discussion on the connections between our method and those in [4,9,15].

Algorithm 2 shows the pseudo-code of our method. Given G and a threshold θ, the algorithm first initializes $H(v_i) = \emptyset$ for each node v_i (Line 1). After that, for each node v_k, the algorithm performs a graph traversal from v_k to generates approximate HPs from other nodes to v_k. Specifically, for each v_k, it first initializes a set $R_k = \emptyset$, and then inserts an HP $\tilde{h}^{(0)}(v_k, v_k) = 1$ into R_k, which captures the fact that every $\sqrt{c}$-walk from v_k has 100% probability to hit v_k itself at the 0-th step (Lines 3-4). Then, the algorithm enters an iterative process, such that the ℓ-th iteration ($\ell \geq 0$) processes the HPs to v_k at step ℓ that have been inserted into R_k.

Algorithm 3: *An algorithm for single-pair SimRank queries*

Input: $\tilde{d}_k$, $H(v_k)$, and two nodes v_i and v_j
Output: An approximate SimRank score $\tilde{s}(v_i, v_j)$

Let $\tilde{s}(v_i, v_j) = 0$;
for *each* $\tilde{h}^{(\ell)}(v_i, v_k) \in H(v_i)$ **do**
if *there exists* $\tilde{h}^{(\ell)}(v_j, v_k) \in H(v_j)$ **then**
$\tilde{s}(v_i, v_j) = \tilde{s}(v_i, v_j) + \tilde{h}^{(\ell)}(v_i, v_k) \cdot \tilde{d}_k \cdot \tilde{h}^{(\ell)}(v_j, v_k)$;
return $\tilde{s}(v_i, v_j)$;

In particular, in the ℓ-the iteration, the algorithm first identifies the approximate HPs $\tilde{h}^{(\ell)}(v_x, v_k)$ in R_k that are at step ℓ, and processes each of them in turn (Lines 6-16). If $\tilde{h}^{(\ell)}(v_x, v_k) \leq \theta$, then it is removed from R_k, i.e., the algorithm omits an approximate HP if it is sufficiently small. Meanwhile, if $\tilde{h}^{(\ell)}(v_x, v_k) > \theta$, then the algorithm inspects each out-neighbor v_i of v_x, and updates the approximate HP from v_i to v_k at step $\ell + 1$, according to Equation (16). After all approximate HPs at step ℓ are processed, the algorithm terminates the iterative process on ℓ. Finally, the algorithm inserts each $\tilde{h}^{(\ell)}(v_i, v_k) \in R$ into $H(v_i)$, after which it proceeds to the next node v_{k+1}.

The following lemma states the guarantees of Algorithm 2.

LEMMA 7. *Algorithm 2 runs in $O(m/\theta)$ time, and constructs a set $H(v_i)$ of approximate HPs for each node v_i, such that $|H(v_i)| = O(1/\theta)$. In addition, for each $\tilde{h}^{(\ell)}(v_i, v_k) \in H(v_i)$, we have*

$$0 \geq \tilde{h}^{(\ell)}(v_i, v_k) - h^{(\ell)}(v_i, v_k) \geq -\frac{1 - (\sqrt{c})^\ell}{1 - \sqrt{c}} \cdot \theta.$$

4.5 Query Method and Complexity Analysis

Given an approximate correction factor $\tilde{d}_k$ and a set $H(v_k)$ of approximate HPs for each node v_k, we estimate the SimRank score between any two nodes v_i and v_j according to a revised version of Equation (13):

$$\tilde{s}(v_i, v_j) = \sum_{\ell=0}^{\infty} \sum_{k=1}^{n} \left(\tilde{h}^{(\ell)}(v_i, v_k) \cdot \tilde{d}_k \cdot \tilde{h}^{(\ell)}(v_j, v_k) \right). \tag{17}$$

Algorithm 3 shows the details of our query processing method.

To analyze the accuracy guarantee of Algorithm 3, we first present a lemma that quantifies the error in $\tilde{s}(v_i, v_j)$ based on the errors in $\tilde{d}_k$ and $H(v_k)$.

LEMMA 8. *Suppose that $\left|\tilde{d}_k - d_k\right| \leq \varepsilon_d$ for any k, and*

$$0 \geq \tilde{h}^{(\ell)}(v_k, v_x) - h^{(\ell)}(v_k, v_x) \geq -\varepsilon_h^{(\ell)},$$

for any k, x, ℓ. Then, we have $|\tilde{s}(v_i, v_j) - s(v_i, v_j)| \leq \varepsilon$ if

$$\frac{\varepsilon_d}{1 - c} + 2 \sum_{\ell=0}^{+\infty} \left((\sqrt{c})^\ell \cdot \varepsilon_h^{(\ell)} \right) \leq \varepsilon.$$

Combining Lemmas 6, 7, and 8, we have the following theorem.

THEOREM 1. *Suppose that we derive each $\tilde{d}_k$ using Algorithm 1 with input ε_d and δ_d, and we construct each $H(v_k)$ using Algorithm 2 with input θ. If $\delta_d \leq \delta/n$ and*

$$\frac{\varepsilon_d}{1 - c} + \frac{2\sqrt{c}}{(1 - \sqrt{c})(1 - c)} \theta \leq \varepsilon,$$

then Algorithm 3 incurs an additive error at most ε in each SimRank score returned, with at least $1 - \delta$ probability. □

By Theorem 1, we can ensure ε worst-case error in each SimRank score by setting $\varepsilon_d = O(\varepsilon)$, $\theta = O(\varepsilon)$, and $\delta_d = \delta/n$. In that case, our *SLING* index requires $O(m/\varepsilon + n\log\frac{n}{\delta})$ precomputation time and $O(n/\varepsilon)$ space, and it answers any single-pair SimRank query in $O(1/\varepsilon)$ time. The space (resp. query time) complexity of *SLING* is only $O(1/\varepsilon)$ times larger than the optimal value, since any SimRank method (that ensures ε worst-case error) requires $\Omega(n)$ space for storing the information about all nodes, and takes at least $\Omega(1)$ time to output the result of a single-pair SimRank query.

5. OPTIMIZATIONS

This section presents optimization techniques to (i) improve the efficiency of estimating each correction factors d_k (Section 5.1), (ii) reduce the space consumption of *SLING* (Section 5.2), (iii) enhance the accuracy of *SLING* (Section 5.3), and (iv) incorporate parallel and out-of-core computation into *SLING*'s index construction algorithm (Section 5.4).

5.1 Improved Estimation of d_k

As discussed in Section 4.3, Algorithm 1 generates an approximate correction factor $\tilde{d}_k$ in $O\left(\varepsilon_d^{-2}\log\delta_d^{-1}\right)$ expected time, where ε_d is the maximum error allowed in $\tilde{d}_k$, and δ_d is the failure probability. As the algorithm's time complexity is quadratic to $1/\varepsilon_d$, it is not particularly efficient when ε_d is small. This relative inefficiency is caused by the fact the algorithm requires $O\left(\varepsilon_d^{-2}\log\delta_d^{-1}\right)$ pairs of $\sqrt{c}$-walks to estimate the value μ (in Equation 15) with ε_d/c worst-case error.

However, we observe that we can often use a much smaller number of $\sqrt{c}$-walk pairs to derive an estimation of μ with at most ε_d/c error. Specifically, by the Chernoff bound (see Appendix D), we only need $O\left((\mu+\varepsilon_d)\cdot\varepsilon_d^{-2}\log\delta_d^{-1}\right)$ pairs of $\sqrt{c}$-walks to estimate μ. Apparently, this number is much smaller than $O\left(\varepsilon_d^{-2}\log\delta_d^{-1}\right)$ when $\mu \ll 1$ (which is often the case in practice). For example, if $\mu \le \varepsilon_d$, then the number of $\sqrt{c}$-walk pairs required is only $O(\varepsilon_d^{-1}\log\delta_d^{-1})$. The main issue here is that we do not know μ in advance. Nevertheless, if we can derive an upper bound of μ, and we use it to decide an appropriate number of $\sqrt{c}$-walks needed.

Based on the above observation, we propose an improved algorithm for computing $\tilde{d}_k$, as shown in Algorithm 4. The algorithm first generates $n_r = O(\varepsilon_d^{-1}\log\delta_d^{-1})$ pairs of $\sqrt{c}$-walks from randomly selected nodes in $I(v_k)$, and counts the number *cnt* of pairs that meet (Lines 1-8). Then, it computes $\hat{\mu} = cnt/n_r$ as an estimation of μ. If $\hat{\mu} \le \varepsilon_d$, then the algorithm determines that n_r pairs of $\sqrt{c}$-walks are sufficient for an accurate estimation of μ; in that case, it terminates and returns an estimation of d_k based on $\hat{\mu}$ (Lines 9-11).

On the other hand, if $\hat{\mu} > \varepsilon_d$, then the algorithm proceeds to generate a larger number of $\sqrt{c}$-walks to derive a more accurate estimation of μ. Towards this end, it first computes $\mu^* = \hat{\mu} + \sqrt{\hat{\mu}\cdot\varepsilon}$ as an upper bound of μ, and uses μ^* to decide the total number $n_r^* = O(\mu^*\varepsilon_d^{-2}\log\delta_d^{-1})$ of $\sqrt{c}$-walk pairs that are needed (Lines 12-13). After that, it increases the total number of $\sqrt{c}$-walk pairs to n_r^*, and recounts the number *cnt* of pairs that meet (Lines 14-19). Finally, it derives $\tilde{u} = cnt/n_r^*$ as an improved estimation of μ, and returns an approximate correction factor $\tilde{d}_k$ computed based on $\tilde{\mu}$ (Lines 20-21).

The following lemmas establish the asymptotic guarantees of Algorithm 4.

LEMMA 9. *With at least $1-\delta_d$ probability, Algorithm 4 returns $\tilde{d}_k$ such that $|\tilde{d}_k - d| \le \varepsilon_d$ holds.* □

Algorithm 4: *An improved method for estimating d_k*

Input: a node v_k, an error bound ε_d, and a failure probability δ_d
Output: an estimation version $\tilde{d}_k$ of d_k with at most ε_d error, with at least $1-\delta_d$ probability

1 Let $n_r = \frac{14c}{3\varepsilon_d}\log\frac{4}{\delta_d}$;
2 Let $cnt = 0$;
3 **for** $x = 1, 2, \cdots, n_r$ **do**
4   Select two nodes v_i and v_j from $I(v_k)$ uniformly at random;
5   **if** $v_i \ne v_j$ **then**
6   Generate two $\sqrt{c}$-walks from v_i and v_j, respectively;
7   **if** *the two $\sqrt{c}$-walks meet* **then**
8             $cnt = cnt + 1$;
9 Let $\hat{\mu} = cnt/n_r$;
10 **if** $\hat{\mu} \le \varepsilon_d$ **then**
11   **return** $\tilde{d}_k = 1 - \frac{c}{|I(v_i)|} - c\cdot\hat{\mu}$;
12 Let $\mu^* = \hat{\mu} + \sqrt{\hat{\mu}\cdot\varepsilon_d}$;
13 Let $n_r^* = \frac{2c^2\cdot\mu^* + \frac{2}{3}c\cdot\varepsilon_d}{\varepsilon_d^2}\log\frac{4}{\delta_d}$;
14 **for** $x = 1, 2, \cdots, n_r^* - n_r$ **do**
15   Select two nodes v_i and v_j from $I(v_k)$ uniformly at random;
16   **if** $v_i \ne v_j$ **then**
17   Generate two $\sqrt{c}$-walks from v_i and v_j, respectively;
18   **if** *the two $\sqrt{c}$-walks meet* **then**
19             $cnt = cnt + 1$;
20 $\tilde{\mu} = cnt/n_r^*$;
21 **return** $\tilde{d}_k = 1 - \frac{c}{|I(v_i)|} - c\cdot\tilde{\mu}$;

LEMMA 10. *Algorithm 4 generates $O(\frac{\mu+\varepsilon_d}{\varepsilon_d^2}\log\frac{1}{\delta_d})$ $\sqrt{c}$-walks in expectation, and runs in $O(\frac{\mu+\varepsilon_d}{\varepsilon_d^2}\log\frac{1}{\delta_d})$ expected time.* □

By Lemma 9, Algorithm 4 uses a number of $\sqrt{c}$-walks that is roughly $\max\{\mu, \varepsilon_d\}$ times the number in Algorithm 1, which leads to significantly improved efficiency. In addition, we note that Algorithm 4 can be easily revised into a general method that estimates the expectation μ_z of a Bernoulli distribution by taking $O(\frac{\mu_z+\varepsilon}{\varepsilon^2}\log\frac{1}{\delta})$ samples, while ensuring at most ε estimation error with at least $1-\delta$ success probability. In particular, the only major change needed is to replace each $\sqrt{c}$-walk pair in Algorithm 4 with a sample from the Bernoulli distribution. In this context, we can prove that the number of samples used by Algorithm 4 is *asymptotically optimal*.

Specifically, let $z_1, z_2, \ldots$ be a sequence of i.i.d. Bernoulli random variables, and $\mu_Z = \mathbb{E}[z_i]$. Let $\mathcal{A}$ be an algorithm that inspects z_i in ascending order of i, and stops at a certain z_j before returning an estimation $\tilde{\mu_Z}$ of μ_Z. In addition, for any possible sequence of z_i, $\mathcal{A}$ runs in finite expected time, and ensures that $|\tilde{\mu_Z} - \mu_Z| \le \varepsilon$ with at least $1-\delta$ probability. It can be verified that the revised Algorithm 4 is an instance of $\mathcal{A}$. The following lemma shows that no other instance of $\mathcal{A}$ can be asymptotically more efficient than Algorithm 4.

LEMMA 11. *Any instance of $\mathcal{A}$ has $\Omega(\frac{\max\{\mu_z,\varepsilon\}}{\varepsilon^2}\log\frac{1}{\delta})$ expected time complexity when $\mu_z < 0.5$.* □

Our proof of Lemma 11 utilizes an important result by Dagum et al. [7] that establishes a lower bound of the expected time complexity of $\mathcal{A}$, when it provides a worst-case guarantee in terms of the relative error (instead of absolute error) in $\tilde{\mu_z}$. Dagum et al. [7] also provide a sampling algorithm whose time complexity matches

Algorithm 5: *An algorithm for constructing* $H'(v_i)$

Input: a node v_i
Output: A set $H'(v_i)$ of precise HPs from v_i at steps 1 and 2

Initialize $H'(v_i) = \emptyset$;
Insert $h^{(0)}(v_i, v_i) = 1$ into $H'(v)$;
for *each node* $v_x \in I(v_i)$ **do**
  Insert $h^{(1)}(v_i, v_x) = \frac{c}{|I(v_i)|}$ into $H'(v)$;
  for *each node* $v_y \in I(v_x)$ **do**
    if $h^{(2)}(v_i, v_y) \notin H'(v_i)$ **then**
      Insert $h^{(2)}(v_i, v_y) = \sqrt{c} \cdot \frac{h^{(1)}(v_i, v_x)}{|I(v_x)|}$ into $H'(v_i)$;
    else
      Increase $h^{(2)}(v_i, v_y)$ by $\sqrt{c} \cdot \frac{h^{(1)}(v_i, v_x)}{|I(v_x)|}$ in $H'(v_i)$;
return $H'(v_i)$

their lower bound, but the algorithm is inapplicable in our context, since it requires as input a relative error bound, which cannot be translated into an absolute error bound unless μ_z is known.

5.2 Reduction of Space Consumption

Recall that our *SLING* index pre-computes a set $H(v_i)$ of approximate HPs for each node v_i, such that each $\tilde{h}^{(\ell)}(v_i, v_k) \in H(v_i)$ is no smaller than a threshold $\theta = O(\varepsilon)$. The total size of all $H(v_i)$ is $O(n/\varepsilon)$, which is asymptotically near-optimal, but may still be costly from a practical perspective (especially when ε is small). To address this issue, we aim to reduce the size of $H(v_i)$ without affecting the time complexity of *SLING*.

We observe that, in each $H(v_i)$, a significant portion of the approximate HPs are in the form of $\tilde{h}^{(1)}(v_i, v_k)$ or $\tilde{h}^{(2)}(v_i, v_k)$, i.e., they concern the HPs from v_i to the nodes within two hops away from v_i. On the other hand, such HPs can be easily computed using a two-hop traversal from v_i, as we will show shortly. This leads to the following idea for space reduction: we remove from $H(v_i)$ all approximate HPs that are at steps 1 and 2, and we recompute those HPs *on the fly* during query processing. The re-computation may lead to slightly increased query cost, but as long as it takes $O(1/\varepsilon)$ time, it would not affect the asymptotic performance of *SLING*. In the following, we clarify how we implement this idea.

First, we present a simple and *precise* algorithm for computing the set $H'(v_i)$ of HPs from node v_i to other nodes at steps 1 and 2, as shown in Algorithm 5. The algorithm first initializes a set $H'(v_i) = \emptyset$ for storing HPs, and then inserts $h^{(0)}(v_i, v_i) = 1$ into $H'(v)$. After that, for each in-neighbor v_x of v_i, it sets $h^{(1)}(v_i, v_x) = \frac{\sqrt{c}}{|I(v_i)|}$, which is the exact probability that a $\sqrt{c}$-walk from v_i would hit v_x at step 1. In turn, for each in-neighbor v_y of v_x, the algorithm initializes $h^{(2)}(v_i, v_y) = \sqrt{c} \cdot \frac{h^{(1)}(v_i, v_x)}{|I(v_x)|}$ in $H'(v_i)$, if it is not yet inserted into $H'(v_i)$; otherwise, the algorithm increases $h^{(2)}(v_i, v_y)$ by $\sqrt{c} \cdot \frac{h^{(1)}(v_i, v_x)}{|I(v_x)|}$ in $H'(v_i)$. This reason is that if a $\sqrt{c}$-walk from v_i hits v_x at step 1, then it has $\frac{\sqrt{c}}{|I(v_x)|}$ probability to hit v_y at step 2. After all of v_i's in-neighbors are processed, the algorithm terminates and returns $H'(v_i)$.

Algorithm 5 runs in time linear to the total number $\eta(v_i)$ of incoming edges of v_i and its in-neighbors, i.e.,

$$\eta(v_i) = |I(v_i)| + \sum_{v_x \in I(v_i)} |I(v_x)|.$$

If $\eta(v_i) = O(1/\varepsilon)$, then we can omit all step-1 and step-2 approximate HPs in $H(v_i)$, and compute them with Algorithm 5 during query processing without degrading the time complexity of *SLING*; otherwise, we need to retain all approximate HPs in $H(v_i)$. In our implementation of *SLING*, we set a constant $\gamma = 10$, and we exclude step-1 and step-2 HPs from $H(v_i)$ whenever $\eta(v_i) \le \gamma/\theta$, where $\theta = \Omega(\varepsilon)$ is the HP threshold used in the construction of $H(v_i)$ (see Algorithm 2). Notice that each $\eta(v_i)$ can be computed in $O(|I(v_i)|)$ time by inspecting v_i and all of its in-neighbors; therefore, the total computation cost of all $\eta(v_i)$ is $O(m)$, which does not affect *SLING*'s preprocessing time complexity. Furthermore, the on-the-fly computation of step-1 and step-2 HPs does not degrade *SLING*'s accuracy guarantee, since all HPs returned by Algorithm 5 are precise.

5.3 Enhancement of Accuracy

The approximation error of each $H(v_i)$ arises from the fact that it omits the HPs from v_i that are smaller than a threshold θ. A straightforward solution to reduce this error is to decrease θ, but it would degrade the space overhead of $H(v_i)$. Instead, we propose to generate *additional* HPs in $H(v_i)$ *on-the-fly* during query processing, to increase the accuracy of query results.

Specifically, for each node v_i, after $H(v_i)$ is constructed (with the space reduction procedure in Section 5.2 applied), we inspect the set of approximate HPs $\tilde{h}^{(\ell)}(v_i, v_j)$ in $H(v_i)$ such that v_j has no more than $1/\sqrt{\varepsilon}$ in-neighbors, and then *mark* the $1/\sqrt{\varepsilon}$ largest HPs in the set. After that, whenever a SimRank query requires utilizing $H(v_i)$, we substitute $H(v_i)$ with an enhanced version $H^*(v_i)$ constructed on-the-fly. In particular, we first set $H^*(v_i) = H(v_i)$. Then, for every marked HP $\tilde{h}^{(\ell)}(v_i, v_j)$ in $H(v_i)$, we process each in-neighbor v_k of v_j as follows:

- If there exists $\tilde{h}^{(\ell+1)}(v_i, v_k)$ in $H(v_i)$, then we omit v_k;
- If $\tilde{h}^{(\ell+1)}(v_i, v_k)$ is not in $H(v_i)$ and has not been inserted into $H^*(v_i)$, then we set $\tilde{h}^{(\ell+1)}(v_i, v_k) = \frac{\sqrt{c}}{|I(v_j)|} h^{(\ell)}(v_i, v_j)$, and insert it into $H^*(v_i)$;
- Otherwise, we update $\tilde{h}^{(\ell+1)}(v_i, v_k)$ in $H^*(v_i)$ as follows: $\tilde{h}^{(\ell+1)}(v_i, v_k) = \tilde{h}^{(\ell+1)}(v_i, v_k) + \frac{\sqrt{c}}{|I(v_j)|} h^{(\ell)}(v_i, v_j)$.

In other words, if $H(v_i)$ does not contain an approximate HP from v_i to v_k, then we generate $\tilde{h}^{(\ell+1)}(v_i, v_k)$ in $H^*(v_i)$.

It can be verified that $0 < \tilde{h}^{(\ell+1)}(v_i, v_k) \le h^{(\ell+1)}(v_i, v_k)$, and hence, $H^*(v_i)$ provides higher accuracy than $H(v_i)$. In addition, the construction of $H^*(v_i)$ requires only $O(1/\varepsilon)$ time, and hence, it does not affect the $O(1/\varepsilon)$ query time complexity of *SLING*. Furthermore, marking HPs in all $H(v_i)$ requires only $O(n/\sqrt{\varepsilon})$ space and $O(n \log(1/\varepsilon)/\varepsilon)$ preprocessing time, which does not degrade the $O(n/\varepsilon)$ space and $O(m/\varepsilon + n \log \frac{n}{\delta} / \varepsilon^2)$ preprocessing time complexity of *SLING*.

5.4 Parallel and Out-of-Core Constructions

The preprocessing algorithms of *SLING* (i.e., Algorithms 1, 2, and 4) are *embarrassingly parallelizable*. In particular, Algorithm 1 (and Algorithm 4) can be simultaneously applied to multiple nodes v_k to compute the corresponding approximate correction factors $\tilde{d}_k$. Meanwhile, the main loop of Algorithm 2 (i.e., Lines 2-16) can be parallelized to construct the "reverse" HP sets R_k for multiple nodes v_k at the same time.

Furthermore, *SLING* does not require the complete index structure to fit in the main memory. Instead, we only need to keep all approximate correction factors $\tilde{v_k}$ ($k \in [1, n]$) in the memory, but can store the approximate HP set $H(v_x)$ for each node v_x on the disk. To process a single-pair SimRank query on two nodes v_i and

v_j, we retrieve $H(v_i)$ and $H(v_j)$ from the disk and combine them with $\tilde{v_k}$ to derive the query result, which incurs a constant I/O cost, since $H(v_i)$ and $H(v_j)$ takes only $O(1/\varepsilon)$ space. In addition, the index construction process of *SLING* does not require maintaining all HP sets $H(v_x)$ simultaneously in the memory. Specifically, in Algorithm 2, we can construct each "reverse" HP set R_k in turn and write them to the disk; after that, we can construct all approximate HP sets $H(v_x)$ in a batch, by using an external sorting algorithm to sort all HPs $\tilde{h}^{(\ell)}(v_x, v_k)$ by v_x. This process requires only $O(\frac{n}{\varepsilon}\log\frac{n}{\varepsilon})$ I/O accesses, since the total size of all $H(v_x)$ is $O(n/\varepsilon)$.

6. EXTENSION TO SINGLE-SOURCE QUERIES

Given the *SLING* index introduced in Sections 4, we can easily answer any single-source SimRank query from a node v_i, by invoking Algorithm 3 n times to compute $s(v_i, v_j)$ for each node v_j. This leads to a total query cost of $O(n/\varepsilon)$, which is near-optimal since any single-source SimRank method requires $\Omega(n)$ time to output the results. This straightforward algorithm, however, can be improved in terms of practical efficiency. To explain this, let us consider two nodes v_i and v_j, such that $H(v_i)$ and $H(v_j)$ do not contain any HPs to the same node at the same step, i.e.,

$$\nexists v_k, \ell,\ \tilde{h}^{(\ell)}(v_i, v_k) \in H(v_i) \wedge \tilde{h}^{(\ell)}(v_j, v_k) \in H(v_j).$$

Then, *SLING* would return $\tilde{s}(v_i, v_j) = 0$. We say that $H(v_i)$ and $H(v_j)$ do not *intersect* in this case. Intuitively, if we can avoid accessing those HP sets $H(v_j)$ that do not intersect with $H(v_i)$, then we can improve the efficiency of the single-source SimRank query from v_i. For this purpose, a straightforward approach is to maintain, for each combination of v_k and ℓ, an *inverted list* $L(v_k, \ell)$ that records the approximate HPs $\tilde{h}^{(\ell)}(v_x, v_k)$ from any node v_x to v_k. Then, to process a single-source SimRank query from node v_i, we first examine each approximate HP $\tilde{h}^{(\ell)}(v_i, v_k) \in H(v_i)$ and retrieve $L(v_k, \ell)$, based on which we compute $\tilde{s}(v_i, v_j)$ for any node v_j with $\tilde{s}(v_i, v_j) > 0$.

Although the inverted list approach improves efficiency for single-source SimRank queries, it doubles the space consumption of *SLING*, since the inverted lists have the same total size as the approximate HP sets $H(v_i)$. Furthermore, the approach cannot be combined with the space reduction technique in Section 5.2, because the former requires storing all approximate HPs in the inverted lists, whereas the latter aims to omit certain HPs to save space. To address this issue, we propose a single-source SimRank algorithm for *SLING* that finds a middle ground between the inverted list approach and the straightforward approach. The basic idea is that, given node v_i, we first retrieve all approximate HPs $\tilde{h}^{(\ell)}(v_i, v_k) \in H(v_i)$, and then apply a variant of Algorithm 2 to compute the HPs from other nodes to each v_k; after that, we combine all HPs obtained to derive the query results. In other words, we construct the inverted lists relevant for the single-source query *on the fly*, instead of pre-computing them in advance.

Algorithm 6 shows the details of our method. It takes as input a query node v_i and the threshold θ used in constructing $H(v_i)$ (see Algorithm 2), and returns an approximate SimRank score $\tilde{s}(v_i, v_j)$ for each node v_j. The algorithm starts by initializing $\tilde{s}(v_i, v_j) = 0$ for all v_j (Line 1). Then, it identifies the steps ℓ such that there is at least one step-ℓ approximate HP in $H(v_i)$; after that, it processes each of those steps in turn (Lines 2-10). The general idea of processing is as follows. By Equation 13, if v_i has a positive HP to a node v_k at step ℓ, then for any other node v_j with a positive HP to v_k at step ℓ, we have $s(v_i, v_j) > 0$. To identify such nodes v_j

Algorithm 6: *An algorithm for single-source SimRank queries*

Input: query node v_i and threshold θ
Output: an approximate SimRank score $\tilde{s}(v_i, v_j)$ for each node v_j

1 Initialize $\tilde{s}(v_i, v_j) = 0$ for all v_j;
2 **for** *each ℓ such that $H(v_i)$ contains some approximate HP at step ℓ* **do**
3   **for** *each node v_k such that $\tilde{h}^{(\ell)}(v_i, v_k) \in H(v_i)$* **do**
4   Initialize $\rho^{(0)}(v_k) = \tilde{h}^{(\ell)}(v_i, v_k) \cdot d_k$;
5   **for** $t = 1$ *to* ℓ **do**
6   **for** *each node v_x such that $\rho^{(t-1)}(v_x) > (\sqrt{c})^\ell \cdot \theta$* **do**
7   **for** *each out-neighbor v_y of v_x* **do**
8   **if** *$\rho^{(t)}(v_y)$ does not exist* **then**
9                     $\rho^{(t)}(v_y) = \frac{\sqrt{c}}{|I(v_y)|} \cdot \rho^{(t-1)}(v_x)$;
10   **else**
11                     $\rho^{(t)}(v_y) = \rho^{(t)}(v_y) + \frac{\sqrt{c}}{|I(v_y)|} \cdot \rho^{(t-1)}(v_x)$;
12   **for** *each v_j such that $\rho^{(\ell)}(v_j) > 0$* **do**
13         $\tilde{s}(v_i, v_j) = \tilde{s}(v_i, v_j) + \rho^{(\ell)}(v_j)$;
14 **return** $\tilde{s}(v_i, v_j)$ for each node v_j;

and their SimRank scores with v_i, we can apply the local update approach in Algorithm 2 to traverse ℓ steps from v_k; however, the local update procedure needs to be slightly modified to deal with the fact that we may need to traverse from multiple v_k simultaneously, i.e., when v_i have positive HPs to multiple nodes at step ℓ.

Specifically, for each particular ℓ, Algorithm 6 first identifies each node v_k such that $\tilde{h}^{(\ell)}(v_i, v_k) \in H(v_i)$, and initializes a temporary score $\rho^{(0)}(v_k) = \tilde{h}^{(\ell)}(v_i, v_k)$ for v_k (Line 3). After that, it traverses ℓ steps from all v_k simultaneously (Lines 5-8). In the t-th step ($t \in [1, \ell]$), it inspects the temporary scores created in the $(t-1)$-th step, and omit those scores that are no larger than $(\sqrt{c})^\ell \cdot \theta$ (Line 6). This omission is similar to the pruning of HPs applied in Algorithm 2, except that the threshold used here is $(\sqrt{c})^\ell$ times smaller than the threshold θ used in Algorithm 2. The reason is that the local update procedure in Algorithm 2 starts from a node whose approximate HP equals 1, whereas the procedure in Algorithm 6 begins from a node whose temporary score $\rho^{(0)}(v_k) \le (\sqrt{c})^\ell$, due to which we need to scale down the threshold to ensure accuracy.

For each temporary score $\rho^{(t-1)}(v_x)$ that is above the threshold, Algorithm 2 examines each out-neighbor v_y of v_x, and checks whether the temporary score of v_y at step t (denoted as $\rho^{(t)}(v_y)$) exists. If it does not exist, then the algorithm initializes it as $\rho^{(t)}(v_y) = \frac{\sqrt{c}}{|I(v_y)|} \cdot \rho^{(t-1)}(v_x)$; otherwise, the algorithm increases it by $\frac{\sqrt{c}}{|I(v_y)|} \cdot \rho^{(t-1)}(v_x)$ (Lines 7-11). (Observe that this update rule is identical to that in Algorithm 2.) Finally, after the ℓ-step traversal is finished, the algorithm adds each temporary score $\rho^{(\ell)}(v_j)$ at step ℓ into $\tilde{s}(v_i, v_j)$, and then proceeds to consider the next ℓ (Lines 12-14). Once all steps ℓ are processed, the algorithm returns each $\tilde{s}(v_i, v_j)$ as the final result.

We have the following lemma regarding the theoretical guarantees of Algorithm 6.

LEMMA 12. *Algorithm 6 runs in $O\left(m \log^2 \frac{1}{\varepsilon}\right)$ time, and ensures that each SimRank score returned has ε worst-case error.* □

The time complexity of Algorithm 6 is not as attractive as those of the inverted list approach and the straightforward approach, but is roughly comparable to the latter when $m = O(n/\varepsilon)$ (as is often the case in practice). In addition, we note that the time complexity of Algorithm 6 matches that of the more recent method for single-source SimRank queries [24], even though the latter relies on heuristic assumptions that do not hold in general (see Section 3.3).

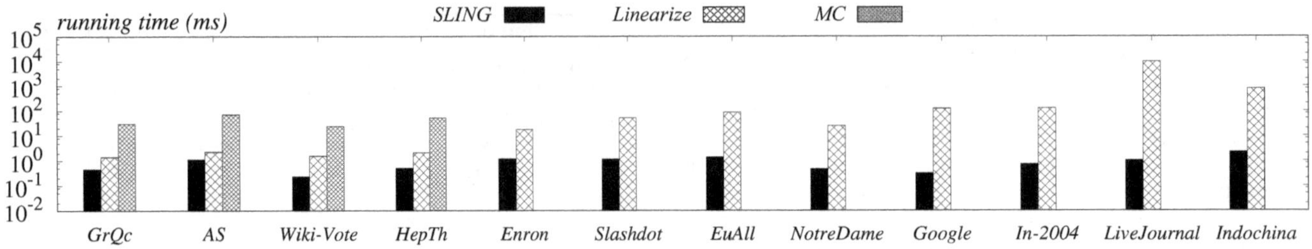

Figure 1: Average query costs for single-pair SimRank queries.

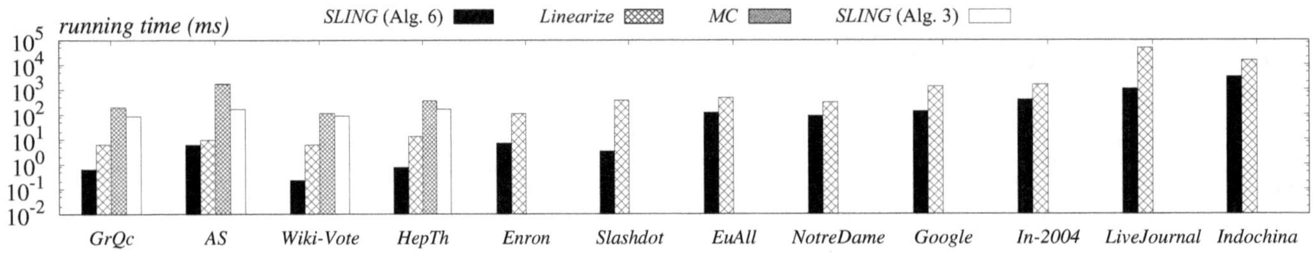

Figure 2: Average query costs for single-source SimRank queries.

Table 3: Datasets.

Dataset	Type	n	m
GrQc	undirected	5,242	14,496
AS	undirected	6,474	13,895
Wiki-Vote	directed	7,155	103,689
HepTh	undirected	9,877	25,998
Enron	undirected	36,692	183,831
Slashdot	directed	77,360	905,468
EuAll	directed	265,214	400,045
NotreDame	directed	325,728	1,497,134
Google	directed	875,713	5,105,049
In-2004	directed	1,382,908	17,917,053
LiveJournal	directed	4,847,571	68,993,773
Indochina	directed	7,414,866	194,109,311

7. EXPERIMENTS

This section experimentally evaluates *SLING*. Section 7.1 clarifies the experimental settings, and Section 7.2 presents the experimental results.

7.1 Experimental Settings

Datasets and Environment. We use twelve graph datasets that are publicly available from [1, 2] and are commonly used in the literature. Table 3 shows the statistics of each graph. We conduct all of experiments on a Linux machine with a 2.6GHz CPU and 64GB memory. All methods tested are implemented in C++. (Our code is available at [3].)

Methods and Parameters. We compare *SLING* against two state-of-the-art methods for SimRank computation: the linearization method [24, 25] (referred to as *Linearize*) and the Monte Carlo method [8] (referred to as *MC*). *Linearize* has three parameters T, R, and L. Following the recommendations in [24], we set $T = 11$, $R = 100$, and $L = 3$. In addition, we set the decay factor c in the SimRank model to 0.6, as suggested in previous work [23,24,31–33]. Under this setting, *Linearize* ensures a worst-case error $\varepsilon = c^T/(1-c) \approx 0.01$ in each SimRank score, *if it is able to derive an exact diagonal correction matrix D*. However, as we discuss in Section 3.3, *Linearize* utilizes an approximate version of D that provides no quality assurance, due to which the above error bound does not hold.

For *SLING*, we set its maximum error $\varepsilon = 0.025$, which is roughly comparable to the quality assurance of the linearization method given a precise D. Towards this end, we set $\varepsilon_d = 0.005$ and $\theta = 0.000725$, which ensures $\varepsilon < 0.025$ by Theorem 1. In addition, we set $\delta_d = 1/n^2$, which guarantees that the preprocessing algorithm of *SLING* succeeds with at least $1 - 1/n$ probability. For *MC*, we set $\varepsilon = 0.025$, as in *SLING*.

7.2 Experimental Results

In the first set of experiments, we randomly generate 1000 single-pair SimRank queries on each dataset, and evaluate the average computation time of each method in answering the queries. Figure 1 shows the results. We omit *MC* on all but the four smallest datasets, since its index size exceeds 64GB on the large graphs. Observe that the query time of *SLING* is at most 2.2ms in all cases, and is often several orders of magnitude smaller than that of *Linearize*. In particular, on *LiveJournal*, *SLING* is around 10000 times faster than *Linearize*. This is consistent with the fact that *SLING* and *Linearize* has $O(1/\varepsilon)$ and $O(m \log \frac{1}{\varepsilon})$ query time complexities, respectively. Meanwhile, *Linearize* incurs a smaller query cost than *MC* on the four smallest datasets, which is also observed in previous work [24].

Our second set of experiments evaluates the average computation cost of each method in answering 500 random single-source SimRank queries. For *SLING*, we consider two different methods: one that directly uses Algorithm 6, and another one that invokes Algorithm 3 once for each node. Figure 2 illustrates the results. Notice that the method that applies Algorithm 3 is significantly slower than Algorithm 6, even though the former (resp. latter) runs in $O(n/\varepsilon)$ time (resp. $O(m \log^2 \frac{1}{\varepsilon})$ time). This is in accordance with our analysis in Section 6, which shows that adopting Algorithm 3 for single-source queries would incur unnecessary overheads and lead to inferior query time. Since the method that employs Algorithm 3 is not competitive, we omit it on all but the four smallest datasets.

Among all methods for single-source SimRank queries, *SLING* (with Algorithm 6) achieves the best performance, but its improvement over *Linearize* is less pronounced when compared with the case of single-pair queries. This, as we mention in Section 6, is because the local update procedure in Algorithm 6 incurs superlinear overheads, due to which the algorihtm's time complexity is the same as *Linearize*'s. Nonetheless, *SLING* is still at least 9 times

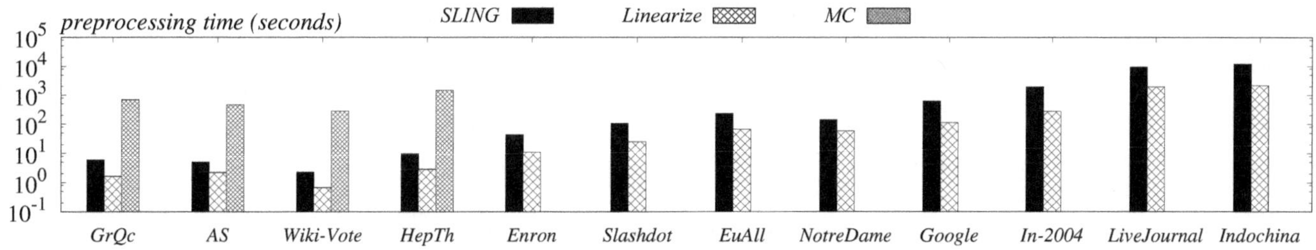

Figure 3: Preprocessing cost of each method.

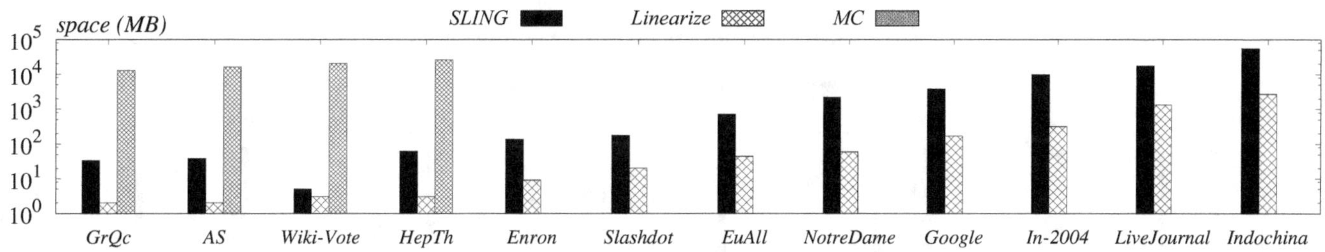

Figure 4: Space consumption of each method.

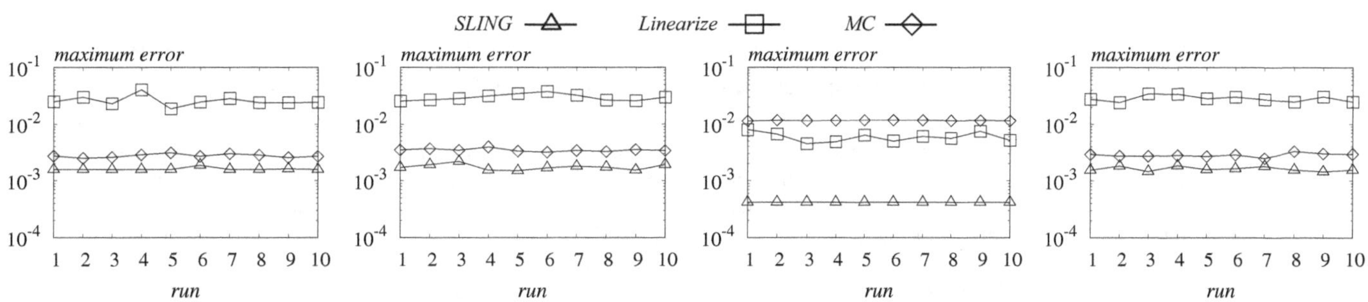

(a) GrQc (b) AS (c) Wiki-Vote (d) HepTh

Figure 5: Maximum SimRank error of each method measured in 10 different runs.

faster than *Linearize* on 7 out of the 12 datasets, and is 110 times more efficient on *Slashdot*. Meanwhile, *MC* is consistently outperformed by *Linearize*.

Next, we plot the the preprocessing cost (resp. space consumption) of each method in Figure 3 (resp. Figure 4). *Linearize* incurs a smaller pre-computation cost than *SLING* does; in turn, *SLING* is more efficient than *MC* in terms of pre-computation. The index size of *SLING* is considerably larger than *Linearize*, since *SLING* has an $O(n/\varepsilon)$ space complexity, while *Linearize* only incurs $O(n+m)$ space overhead. Nevertheless, *SLING* outperforms *MC* in terms of space efficiency. Overall, *SLING* is inferior to *Linearize* in terms of space overheads and preprocessing costs, but this is justified by the fact that *SLING* offers superior query efficiency and rigorous accuracy guarantee, whereas *Linearize* incurs significantly larger query costs and does not offer non-trivial bounds on its query errors. Furthermore, the pre-computation algorithm of *SLING* can be easily parallelized, as we discuss in Section 5.4 and demonstrate in Appendix C.

Our last three experiments focus on the query accuracy of each method. We first apply the power method (see Section 3.1) on each of the four smallest graphs to compute the SimRank score of each node pair, setting the number of iterations in the method to 50 (which results in a worst-case error below 10^{-11}). We take the SimRank scores thus obtained as the ground truth, and use them to gauge the error of each method computing all-pair SimRank scores. We do not repeat this experiment on larger graphs, due to the tremendous overheads in computing all-pair SimRank results.

Figure 5 illustrates the maximum query error incurred by each method in all-pair SimRank computation over 10 different runs, where each run rebuilds the index of each method from scratch. Observe that the maximum error of *SLING* is always below 0.0025, which is considerably smaller than the stipulated error bound $\varepsilon = 0.025$. *MC*'s maximum error is also below $\varepsilon = 0.025$, but is consistently larger than that of *SLING*, and is over 0.01 on *Wiki-Vote*. In contrast, the maximum error of *Linearize* is above 0.025 in most runs on *GrQc*, *AS*, and *Hepth*, which is consistent with our analysis that *Linearize* does not offer any worst-case guarantee in terms of query accuracy.

To further assess each method's query accuracy, we divide the ground-truth SimRank scores into three groups S_1, S_2, and S_3, such that S_1 (resp. S_2) contains SimRank scores in the range of $[0.1, 1]$ (resp. $[0.01, 0.1]$), while S_3 concerns SimRank scores smaller than 0.01. Intuitively, the scores in S_1 and S_2 are more important than those in S_3, since the former correspond to node pairs that are highly similar. Figure 6 shows the average query errors of each method for S_1, S_2, and S_3. Observe that, compared with *Linearize*, *SLING* incurs much smaller (resp. slightly smaller) errors on S_1 (resp. S_2). This indicates that *SLING* is more effective than *Linearize* in measuring the similarity of important node pairs. Meanwhile, *MC* is less accurate than *SLING* on S_1, and is considerably outperformed by both *SLING* and *Linearize* on *Wiki-Vote*.

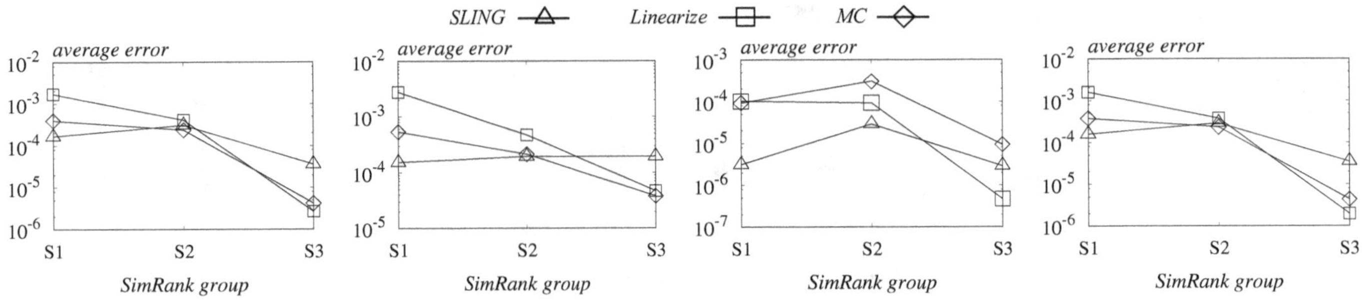

(a) GrQc (b) AS (c) Wiki-Vote (d) HepTh

Figure 6: Average SimRank error vs. SimRank group.

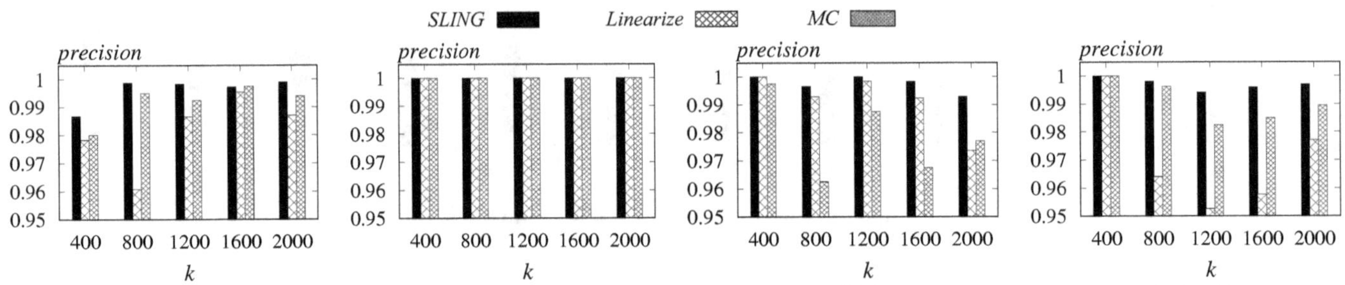

(a) GrQc (b) AS (c) Wiki-Vote (d) HepTh

Figure 7: Precision of the top-k SimRank pairs returned by each method.

Finally, we use the all-pair SimRank scores computed by each method to identify the k node pairs with the highest SimRank scores[1], and we measure the *precision* of those k pairs, i.e., the fraction of them among the ground-truth top-k pairs. Figure 7 illustrates the results when k varies from 400 to 2000. The precision of *SLING* is never worse than that of *Linearize*, and is up to 4% higher than the latter in many cases. This is consistent with our results in Figure 6 that, for node pairs with large SimRank scores, *SLING* provides much higher accuracy than *Linearize* does. Meanwhile, *MC* yields lower accuracy than *SLING* does, and is significantly outperformed by both *SLING* and *Linearize* on *Wiki-Vote*. These results are also in agreement with those in Figure 6.

8. OTHER RELATED WORK

The previous sections have discussed the existing techniques that are most relevant to ours. In what follows, we survey other related work on SimRank computation. First, there is a line of research [10,13,19,30–32] on SimRank queries based on the following formulation of SimRank:

$$S = cP^{\top}SP + (1-c)I,$$

where S, P, and T are $n \times n$ matrices such that $S(i,j) = s(v_i, v_j)$ for any i, j, P is as defined in Equation 5, and I is an identity matrix. However, as point out by Kusumoto et al. [17], the above formulation is *incorrect* since it assumes that $(1-c)I$ equals the diagonal correction matrix D (see Equation 7), which does not hold in general. As a consequence, the methods in [10,13,19,30–32] fail to offer any guarantees in terms of the accuracy of SimRank scores, due to which we do not consider them in this paper.

Second, several variants [5,8,22,33,35] of SimRank have been proposed to enhance the quality of similarity measure and mitigate certain limitations of SimRank. Antonellis et al. [5] present *SimRank++*, which extends SimRank by taking into account the weights of edges and prior knowledge of node similarities. Jin et al. [16] introduce *RoleSim*, which guarantees to recognize automorphically or structurally equivalent nodes. Fogaras and Rácz [8] propose *PSimRank*, which improves the quality of SimRank by allowing random walks that are close to each other to have a higher probability to meet. Yu and McCann [33] present *SimRank*$^{\#}$, which defines the similarity between two nodes based on the *consine similarity* of their neighbors. Zhao et al. [35] introduce *P-Rank*, which consider both in-neighbors and out-neighbors of two nodes when measuring their similarity.

Finally, there is existing work [10,17,18,25,28,36] that studies *top-k SimRank queries* and *SimRank similarity joins*. In particular, a top-k SimRank queries takes as input a node v_i, and asks for the k nodes v_j with the largest SimRank score $s(v_i, v_j)$. Meanwhile, a SimRank similarity join asks for all pairs of nodes whose SimRank scores are among the largest k, or are larger than a predefined threshold. Techniques designed for these two types of queries are generally inapplicable for single-pair and single-source SimRank queries.

9. CONCLUSIONS

This paper presents the *SLING* index for answering single-pair and single-source SimRank queries with ε worst-case error in each SimRank score. *SLING* requires $O(n/\varepsilon)$ space and $O(m/\varepsilon + n\log\frac{n}{\delta}/\varepsilon^2)$ pre-computation time, and it handles any single-pair (resp. single-source) query in $O(1/\varepsilon)$ (resp. $O(n/\varepsilon)$) time. The space and query time complexities of *SLING* are near-optimal, and are significantly better than those of the existing solutions. In addition, *SLING* incorporates several optimization techniques that considerably improves its practical performance. Our experiments show that *SLING* provides superior query efficiency against the states of the art. For future work, we plan to (i) investigate techniques to reduce the index size of *SLING*, and (ii) extend *SLING* to handle other similarity measures for graphs.

[1]Note that we ignore any node pair containing two nodes that are identical.

10. REFERENCES

[1] http://snap.stanford.edu/data/index.html.
[2] http://law.di.unimi.it/datasets.php.
[3] https://sourceforge.net/projects/slingsimrank/.
[4] R. Andersen, F. R. K. Chung, and K. J. Lang. Local graph partitioning using pagerank vectors. In *FOCS*, pages 475–486, 2006.
[5] I. Antonellis, H. G. Molina, and C. C. Chang. Simrank++: query rewriting through link analysis of the click graph. *PVLDB*, 1(1):408–421, 2008.
[6] F. R. K. Chung and L. Lu. Concentration inequalities and martingale inequalities: A survey. *Internet Mathematics*, 3(1):79–127, 2006.
[7] P. Dagum, R. M. Karp, M. Luby, and S. M. Ross. An optimal algorithm for monte carlo estimation. *SIAM J. Comput.*, 29(5):1484–1496, 2000.
[8] D. Fogaras and B. Rácz. Scaling link-based similarity search. In *WWW*, pages 641–650, 2005.
[9] D. Fogaras, B. Rácz, K. Csalogány, and T. Sarlós. Towards scaling fully personalized pagerank: Algorithms, lower bounds, and experiments. *Internet Mathematics*, 2(3):333–358, 2005.
[10] Y. Fujiwara, M. Nakatsuji, H. Shiokawa, and M. Onizuka. Efficient search algorithm for simrank. In *ICDE*, pages 589–600, 2013.
[11] G. H. Golub and C. F. Van Loan. *Matrix Computations*. Johns Hopkins University Press, 3 edition, 2012.
[12] P. Gupta, A. Goel, J. Lin, A. Sharma, D. Wang, and R. Zadeh. WTF: the who to follow service at twitter. In *WWW*, pages 505–514, 2013.
[13] G. He, H. Feng, C. Li, and H. Chen. Parallel simrank computation on large graphs with iterative aggregation. In *KDD*, pages 543–552, 2010.
[14] G. Jeh and J. Widom. Simrank: a measure of structural-context similarity. In *SIGKDD*, pages 538–543, 2002.
[15] G. Jeh and J. Widom. Scaling personalized web search. In *WWW*, pages 271–279, 2003.
[16] R. Jin, V. E. Lee, and H. Hong. Axiomatic ranking of network role similarity. In *KDD*, pages 922–930, 2011.
[17] M. Kusumoto, T. Maehara, and K. Kawarabayashi. Scalable similarity search for simrank. In *SIGMOD*, pages 325–336, 2014.
[18] P. Lee, L. V. S. Lakshmanan, and J. X. Yu. On top-k structural similarity search. In *ICDE*, pages 774–785, 2012.
[19] C. Li, J. Han, G. He, X. Jin, Y. Sun, Y. Yu, and T. Wu. Fast computation of simrank for static and dynamic information networks. In *EDBT*, pages 465–476, 2010.
[20] P. Li, H. Liu, J. X. Yu, J. He, and X. Du. Fast single-pair simrank computation. In *SDM*, pages 571–582, 2010.
[21] D. Liben-Nowell and J. M. Kleinberg. The link prediction problem for social networks. *JASIST*, 58(7):1019–1031, 2007.
[22] Z. Lin, M. R. Lyu, and I. King. Matchsim: a novel similarity measure based on maximum neighborhood matching. *KAIS*, 32(1):141–166, 2012.
[23] D. Lizorkin, P. Velikhov, M. N. Grinev, and D. Turdakov. Accuracy estimate and optimization techniques for simrank computation. *VLDB J.*, 19(1):45–66, 2010.
[24] T. Maehara, M. Kusumoto, and K. Kawarabayashi. Efficient simrank computation via linearization. *CoRR*, abs/1411.7228, 2014.
[25] T. Maehara, M. Kusumoto, and K. Kawarabayashi. Scalable simrank join algorithm. In *ICDE*, pages 603–614, 2015.
[26] S. Rothe and H. Schütze. Cosimrank: A flexible & efficient graph-theoretic similarity measure. In *ACL*, pages 1392–1402, 2014.
[27] N. Spirin and J. Han. Survey on web spam detection: principles and algorithms. *SIGKDD Explorations*, 13(2):50–64, 2011.
[28] W. Tao, M. Yu, and G. Li. Efficient top-k simrank-based similarity join. *PVLDB*, 8(3):317–328, 2014.
[29] B. Tian and X. Xiao. SLING: A near-optimal index structure for simrank. *CoRR*, abs/1604.04185, 2016.
[30] W. Yu, X. Lin, and W. Zhang. Fast incremental simrank on link-evolving graphs. In *ICDE*, pages 304–315, 2014.
[31] W. Yu, X. Lin, W. Zhang, L. Chang, and J. Pei. More is simpler: Effectively and efficiently assessing node-pair similarities based on hyperlinks. *PVLDB*, 7(1):13–24, 2013.
[32] W. Yu and J. A. McCann. Efficient partial-pairs simrank search for large networks. *PVLDB*, 8(5):569–580, 2015.

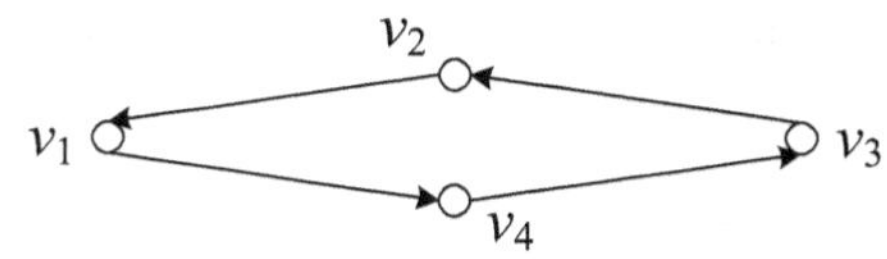

Figure 8: An adversarial case for the linearization method.

[33] W. Yu and J. A. McCann. High quality graph-based similarity search. In *SIGIR*, pages 83–92, 2015.
[34] W. Yu, W. Zhang, X. Lin, Q. Zhang, and J. Le. A space and time efficient algorithm for simrank computation. *World Wide Web*, 15(3):327–353, 2012.
[35] P. Zhao, J. Han, and Y. Sun. P-rank: a comprehensive structural similarity measure over information networks. In *CIKM*, pages 553–562, 2009.
[36] W. Zheng, L. Zou, Y. Feng, L. Chen, and D. Zhao. Efficient simrank-based similarity join over large graphs. *PVLDB*, 6(7):493–504, 2013.

APPENDIX

A. LIMITATIONS OF THE LINEARIZATION METHOD

Recall that the linearization method [24] requires pre-computing the diagonal correction matrix D. Maehara et al. [24] prove that the diagonal elements in D satisfy the following linear system:

$$\text{for all } k \in [1, n], \qquad \sum_{\ell=0}^{\infty}\sum_{i=1}^{n} c^{\ell}\left(p_{k,i}^{(\ell)}\right)^2 D(i,i) = 1, \tag{18}$$

where $p_{k,i}^{(\ell)}$ is the probability that v_i is the ℓ-th step of a reverse random walk from v_k. Based on this, the linearization method estimates $p_{k,i}^{(\ell)}$ with a set of reverse random walks, and then incorporates the estimated values into a truncated version of Equation (18):

$$\text{for all } k \in [1, n], \qquad \sum_{\ell=0}^{t}\sum_{i=1}^{n} c^{\ell}\left(\tilde{p}_{k,i}^{(\ell)}\right)^2 D(i,i) = 1, \tag{19}$$

where $\tilde{p}_{k,i}^{(\ell)}$ denotes the estimated version of $p_{k,i}^{(\ell)}$. After that, it applies the Gauss-Seidel technique [11] to solve Equation (19), and obtains an $n \times n$ diagonal matrix $\widetilde{D}$ that approximates D.

The above approach for deriving $\widetilde{D}$ is interesting, but it fails to provide any worst-case guarantee in terms of the pre-computation time and the accuracy of SimRank queries, due to the following reasons. First, because of the sampling error in $\widetilde{p}_{k,i}^{(\ell)}$ and the truncation applied in Equation (19), $\widetilde{D}$ could differ considerably from D, which may in turn lead to significant errors in SimRank computation. There is no formal result on how large the error in $\widetilde{D}$ could be. Instead, Maehara et al. [24] only show that the error in $\widetilde{p}_{k,i}^{(\ell)}$ can be bounded by using a sufficiently large sample set of reverse random walks; however, it does not translate into any accuracy guarantee on $\widetilde{D}$.

Second, even if $\widetilde{p}_{k,i}^{(\ell)} = p_{k,i}^{(\ell)}$ and Equation (19) is not truncated, the Gauss-Seidel technique [11] used by the linearization method to solve Equation (19) may not converge. In particular, if we define an $n \times n$ matrix M as

$$M(k,i) = \sum_{\ell=0}^{\infty}\sum_{i=1}^{n} c^{\ell}\left(p_{k,i}^{(\ell)}\right)^2,$$

then the linearization method requires that M should be diagonally dominant, i.e., for any i, $|M(i,i)| \geq \sum_{j \neq i} |M(i,j)|$. However, this requirement is not always satisfied. For example, consider the graph in Figure 8. The linear system corresponding to the graph is

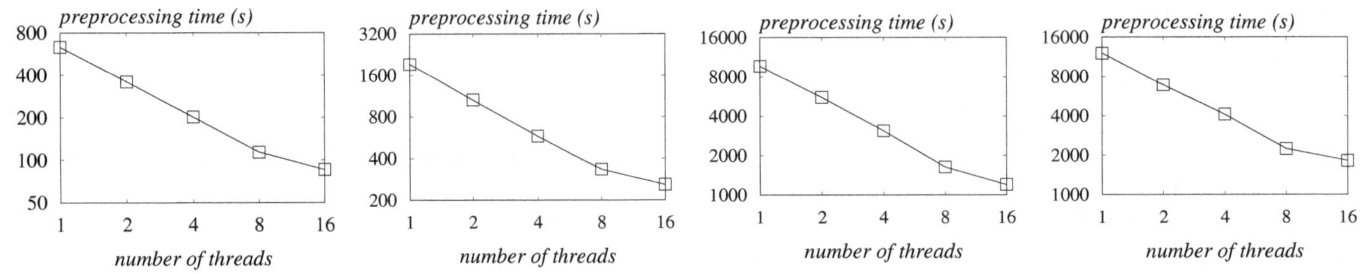

(a) Google (b) In-2004 (c) LiveJournal (d) Indochina

Figure 9: Preprocessing time vs. number of threads.

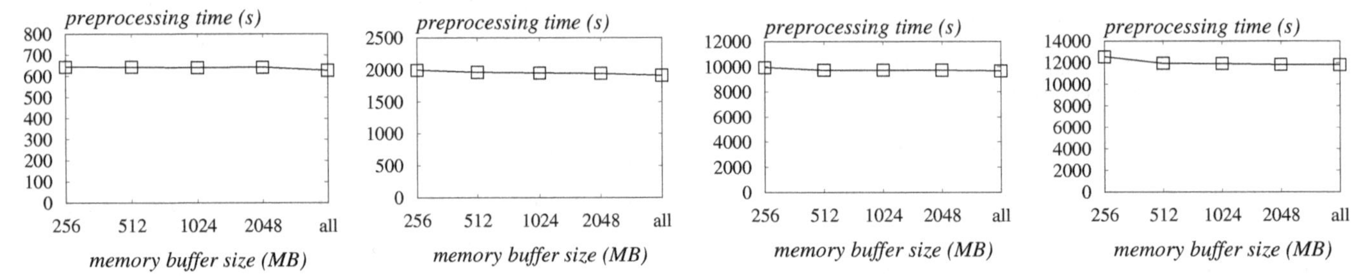

(a) Google (b) In-2004 (c) LiveJournal (d) Indochina

Figure 10: Preprocessing time vs. memory buffer size.

$$\frac{1}{1-c^4}\begin{pmatrix} 1 & c & c^2 & c^3 \\ c^3 & 1 & c & c^2 \\ c^2 & c^3 & 1 & c \\ c & c^2 & c^3 & 1 \end{pmatrix}\begin{pmatrix} D(1,1) \\ D(2,2) \\ D(3,3) \\ D(4,4) \end{pmatrix} = \begin{pmatrix} 1 \\ 1 \\ 1 \\ 1 \end{pmatrix}$$

It can be verified the matrix 4×4 matrix M on the left hand side is not diagonally dominant when $c = 0.6$.

Finally, the number of iterations required by the Gauss-Seidel method is $O(\log \varepsilon^* / \log \rho)$, where ε^* is the maximum error allowed in the solution to the linear system, and ρ is the spectral radius of the iteration matrix used by the method [11]. The value of ρ depends on the input graph, and might be very close to 1, in which case $\log \varepsilon^* / \log \rho$ can be an extremely large number.

B. HITTING PROBABILITIES VS. PERSONALIZED PAGERANKS

Suppose that we start a random walk from a node v_i following the outgoing edges of each node, with $1 - c_p$ probability to stop at each step. The probability that the walk stops at a node v_j is referred to as the *personalized PageRank (PPR)* [15] from v_i to v_j. PPR is well-adopted as a metric for measuring the *relevance* of nodes with respect to the input node v_i, and it has important applications in web search [15] and social network analysis [12].

Our notion of hitting probabilities (HP) bears similarity to PPR, but differs in the following aspect:

1. HP concerns the probability that the random walk reaches node v_j at a particular step ℓ, but disregards whether the random walk stops at v_j;

2. PPR only concerns the endpoint v_j of the random walk, and disregards all nodes before it.

Our Algorithm 2 for computing approximate HPs is inspired by the *local update* algorithm [4, 9, 15] proposed for computing approximate PPRs. Specifically, given a node v_j and an error bound ε, the local update algorithm returns an approximate version of the PPRs from other nodes to v_j, with ε worst-case errors. The algorithm starts by assigning a *residual* 1 to v_j, and 0 to any other node. Subsequently, the algorithm iteratively propagates the residual of each node to its in-neighbors, during which it computes the approximate PPR from each node to v_j. When the largest residual in all nodes is smaller than ε, the algorithm terminates. This algorithm is similar in spirit to our Algorithm 2, but it cannot be directly applied in our context, due to the inherent differences between PPRs and HPs.

C. ADDITIONAL EXPERIMENTS

In this section, we evaluate the parallel and out-of-core algorithms for constructing the index structures of *SLING* (presented in Section 5.4), using the four largest datasets in Table 3. First, we implement a multi-threaded version of *SLING*'s pre-computation algorithm, and measure its running time when the number of threads varies from 1 to 16 and all 64GB main memory on our machine is available. (The total number of CPU cores on our machine is 16.) Figure 9 illustrates the results. Observe that the algorithm achieves a near-linear speed-up as the number of threads increases, which is consistent with our analysis (in Section 5.4) that *SLING* preprocessing algorithm is embarrassingly parallelizable.

Next, we implement an I/O-efficient version of *SLING*'s preprocessing algorithm, based on our discussions in Section 5.4. Then, we measure the running time of the algorithm when it uses one CPU core along with a memory buffer of a pre-defined size. (We assume that the input graph is memory-resident, and we exclude it when calculating the memory buffer size.) Figure 10 shows the processing time of the algorithm as the buffer size varies. Observe that the algorithm can efficiently process all tested graphs even when the buffer size is as small as 256MB. In addition, the overhead of the algorithm does not increase significantly when the buffer size decreases, since the algorithm is CPU-bound. In particular, its only I/O cost is incurred by (i) writing each entry in the index once to the disk, and (ii) performing an external sort on the entries.

D. CONCENTRATION INEQUALITIES

This section introduces the concentration inequalities used in our proofs. We start from the classic Chernoff bound.

LEMMA 13 (CHERNOFF BOUND [6]). *For any set $\{x_i\}$ ($i \in [1, n_x]$) of i.i.d. random variables with mean μ and $x_i \in [0,1]$,*

$$\Pr\left\{\left|\sum_{i=1}^{n_x} x_i - n_x\mu\right| \geq n_x\varepsilon\right\} \leq \exp\left(-\frac{n_x \cdot \varepsilon^2}{\frac{2}{3}\varepsilon + 2\mu}\right).$$

Our proofs also use a concentration bound on *martingales*, as detailed in the following.

DEFINITION 1 (MARTINGALE). *A sequence of random variables $y_1, y_2, y_3, \cdots$ is a martingale if and only if $\mathbb{E}[y_i] < +\infty$ and $\mathbb{E}[y_{i+1}|y_1, y_2, \cdots, y_i] = y_i$ for any i.* □

LEMMA 14 ([6]). *Let $y_1, y_2, y_3, \cdots$ be a martingale, such that $|y_1| \leq a$, $|y_{j+1} - y_j| \leq a$ for any $j \in [1, i-1]$, and*

$$Var[y_1] + \sum_{j=2}^{i} Var[y_j \mid y_1, y_2, \cdots, y_j - 1] \leq b_i,$$

where $Var[\cdot]$ denotes the variance of a random variable. Then, for any $\lambda > 0$,

$$\Pr\{y_i - \mathbb{E}[y_i] \geq \lambda\} \leq \exp\left(-\frac{\lambda^2}{\frac{2}{3}a\lambda + 2b_i}\right)$$

E. PROOFS

This section presents the proofs of the theorems and lemmas in the paper. Due to space constraints, we omit the proofs of Lemmas 9-12 but include them in our technical report [29].

Proof of Lemma 3. Let $s'(v_i, v_j)$ be the probability that W_i and W_j meet. If $v_i = v_j$, then $s'(v_i, v_j) = 1$, since W_i and W_j always meet at the first step. Suppose that $v_i \neq v_j$. Then, $s'(v_i, v_j)$ is the probability that W_i and W_j meet at or after the second step. Assume without loss of generality that the second steps of W_i and W_j are v_k and v_ℓ, respectively. By definition, $s'(v_k, v_\ell)$ equals the probability that W_i and W_j meet at or after v_k and v_ℓ. Taking into account all possible second steps of W_i and W_j, we have

$$\begin{aligned}
s'(v_i, v_j) &= \sum_{v_k \in I(v_i), v_\ell \in I(v_j)} \frac{\sqrt{c}}{|I(v_i)|} \cdot \frac{\sqrt{c}}{|I(v_j)|} \cdot s'(v_k, v_\ell) \\
&= \frac{c}{|I(v_i)| \cdot |I(v_j)|} \sum_{v_k \in I(v_i), v_\ell \in I(v_j)} s'(v_k, v_\ell).
\end{aligned}$$

As such, $s'(v_i, v_j)$ have the same definition as $s(v_i, v_j)$ (see Equation (1)), which indicates that $s'(v_i, v_j) = s(v_i, v_j)$. □

Proof of Lemma 4. First, we define the following events:

- $E(v_i, v_j)$: Two $\sqrt{c}$-walks starting from v_i and v_j, respectively, meet each other.
- $L(v_i, v_j, v_k, \ell)$: Two $\sqrt{c}$-walks starting from v_i and v_j, respectively, *last meet* each other at the ℓ-th step at v_k.

As we discuss in Section 4.2, two different events $L(v_i, v_j, v_k, \ell)$ and $L(v_i, v_j, v_k', \ell')$ are mutually exclusive whenever $v_k \neq v_k'$ or $\ell \neq \ell'$. Therefore,

$$\Pr\{E(v_i, v_j)\} = \sum_{\ell=0}^{+\infty} \sum_{k=1}^{n} \Pr\{L(v_i, v_j, v_k, \ell)\}$$

Observe that the probability of $L(v_i, v_j, v_k, \ell)$ can be computed by multiplying the following two probabilities:

1. The probability that two $\sqrt{c}$-walks W_i and W_j from v_i and v_j, respectively, meet at v_k at step ℓ.
2. Given that W_i and W_j meet at v_k step ℓ, the probability that they do not meet at steps $\ell+1, \ell+2, \ldots$.

The first probability equals $h^{(\ell)}(v_i, v_k) \cdot h^{(\ell)}(v_i, v_k)$. Meanwhile, since the $(x+1)$-th step of any $\sqrt{c}$-walk depends only on its x-th step, the second probability should equal the probability that two $\sqrt{c}$-walks from v_k never meet after the 0-th step, which in turn equals d_k. Hence, we have

$$\begin{aligned}
s(v_i, v_j) = \Pr\{E(v_i, v_j)\} &= \sum_{\ell=0}^{+\infty} \sum_{k=1}^{n} \Pr\{L(v_i, v_j, v_k, \ell)\} \\
&= \sum_{\ell=0}^{+\infty} \sum_{k=1}^{n} \left(h^{(\ell)}(v_i, v_k) \cdot d_k \cdot h^{(\ell)}(v_j, v_k)\right),
\end{aligned}$$

which completes the proof. □

Proof of Lemma 5. Let $R = \sqrt{c} \cdot P$, and R^ℓ be the ℓ-th power of R. We have

$$R^0(k, i) = \begin{cases} 1 & \text{if } i = k \\ 0 & \text{otherwise} \end{cases}$$

Hence, $R^0(k,i) = h^{(0)}(v_i, v_k)$ for all v_i and v_k. Assume that for a certain ℓ, we have $R^\ell(k,i) = h^{(\ell)}(v_i, v_k)$ for all v_i and v_k. Then,

$$\begin{aligned}
R^{\ell+1}(k, i) &= \left(\sqrt{c} \cdot P \cdot R^\ell\right)(k, i) \\
&= \sum_{j=1}^{n} \left(\sqrt{c} \cdot P(k, j) \cdot R^\ell(j, i)\right) \\
&= \sum_{\text{each out-neighbor } v_j \text{ of } v_k} \left(\frac{\sqrt{c}}{|I(v_j)|} \cdot h^{(\ell)}(v_i, v_j)\right) \\
&= h^{(\ell+1)}(v_i, v_k).
\end{aligned}$$

Therefore, $R^\ell(k,i) = h^{(\ell)}(v_i, v_k)$ for all v_i, v_k, and ℓ.

Let $\tilde{D}$ be the $n \times n$ diagonal matrix whose k-th diagonal element is d_k. Then, Equation (13) can be written as:

$$S = \sum_{\ell=0}^{+\infty} \left(\left(R^\ell\right)^\top \tilde{D} R^\ell\right)$$

By multiplying $R^\top$ and R on the left and right, respectively, on both side of the equation, we have

$$S = R^\top S R + \tilde{D} = cP^\top S P + \tilde{D}.$$

This indicates that $\tilde{D}$ is a diagonal correction matrix. Since the diagonal correction matrix is unique [24], we have $\tilde{D} = D$. □

Proof of Lemma 6. By the Chernoff Bound in Lemma 13,

$$\begin{aligned}
\Pr\left\{\left|\frac{cnt}{n_r} - \mu\right| \geq \varepsilon/c\right\} &\leq 2\exp\left(-\frac{n_r(\varepsilon/c)^2}{\frac{2}{3}\varepsilon/c + 2\mu}\right) \\
&= 2\exp\left(-\frac{\frac{2}{3}\varepsilon/c + 2}{\frac{2}{3}\varepsilon/c + 2\mu} \log\frac{2}{\delta_d}\right) \\
&= \delta_d
\end{aligned}$$

Therefore, $|\tilde{d_k} - d_k| = c \cdot |\frac{cnt}{n_r} - \mu| \leq \varepsilon$ with at least $1 - \delta_d$ probability. □

Proof of Lemma 7. According to Algorithm 2, for all $\tilde{h}^{(\ell)}(v_i, v_j) \in H(v_i)$, we have

$$\theta \le \tilde{h}^{(\ell)}(v_i, v_j) \le h^{(\ell)}(v_i, v_j).$$

Then, for each node v_i and each step ℓ,

$$\sum_{v_j \in V} \tilde{h}^{(\ell)}(v_i, v_j) \le \sum_{v_j \in V} h^{(\ell)}(v_i, v_j) = \sqrt{c}^{\ell}$$

Therefore, there are at most $(\sqrt{c})^{\ell}/\theta$ nodes v_j such that $\tilde{h}^{(\ell)}(v_i, v_j) \in H(v_i)$. Therefore, the size of $H(v_i)$ is

$$|H(v_i)| \le \sum_{\ell=0}^{+\infty} \frac{(\sqrt{c})^{\ell}}{\theta} = O(1/\theta)$$

Let $\bar{d}$ be the average out-degree of the G. Since a local update is performed on each entry $\tilde{h}^{(\ell)}(v_i, v_j) \in H(v_i)$, the running time of the algorithm is $O(\bar{d}n/\theta) = O(m/\theta)$.

Let ε_ℓ be the upper bound of $|\tilde{h}^{(\ell)}(v_i, v_j) - h^{(\ell)}(v_i, v_j)|$ for all nodes v_i and v_j at step ℓ. When $\ell = 0$, we have $\varepsilon_0 \le \frac{1-(\sqrt{c})^0}{1-\sqrt{c}}\theta$. Assume that $\varepsilon_\ell \le \frac{1-(\sqrt{c})^{\ell}}{1-\sqrt{c}}\theta$ holds for a certain ℓ. Then,

$$\varepsilon_{\ell+1} \le \sqrt{c} \cdot \varepsilon_\ell + \theta = \frac{1-\sqrt{c}^{\ell+1}}{1-\sqrt{c}}\theta.$$

Thus, the lemma is proved. □

Proof of Lemma 8. Given that $\left|\tilde{d}_k - d_k\right| \le \varepsilon_d$ and $-\varepsilon_h^{(\ell)} \le \tilde{h}^{(\ell)}(v_k, v_x) - h^{(\ell)}(v_k, v_x) \le 0$ for any k, x, ℓ, we have

$$\begin{aligned}
&\tilde{h}^{(\ell)}(v_i, v_k) \cdot \tilde{d} \cdot \tilde{h}^{(\ell)}(v_j, v_k) - h^{(\ell)}(v_i, v_k) \cdot d_k \cdot h^{(\ell)}(v_j, v_k)\\
&\le h^{(\ell)}(v_i, v_k) \cdot \tilde{d}_k \cdot h^{(\ell)}(v_j, v_k) - h^{(\ell)}(v_i, v_k) \cdot d_k \cdot h^{(\ell)}(v_j, v_k)\\
&\le h^{(\ell)}(v_i, v_k) \cdot \varepsilon_d \cdot h^{(\ell)}(v_j, v_k).
\end{aligned}$$

Therefore,

$$\begin{aligned}
\tilde{s}(v_i, v_j) - s(v_i, v_j) &\le \sum_{\ell=0}^{+\infty}\sum_{k=1}^{n} h^{(\ell)}(v_i, v_k) \cdot \varepsilon_d \cdot h^{(\ell)}(v_j, v_k)\\
&\le \sum_{\ell=0}^{+\infty} \varepsilon_d \cdot (\sqrt{c})^{\ell} \cdot (\sqrt{c}^{\ell}) = \frac{\varepsilon_d}{1-c}.
\end{aligned}$$

Meanwhile,

$$\begin{aligned}
&h^{(\ell)}(v_i, v_k) \cdot d_k \cdot h^{(\ell)}(v_j, v_k) - \tilde{h}^{(\ell)}(v_i, v_k) \cdot \tilde{d} \cdot \tilde{h}^{(\ell)}(v_j, v_k)\\
&\le h^{(\ell)}(v_i, v_k) \cdot d_k \cdot h^{(\ell)}(v_j, v_k)\\
&\quad - \left(h^{(\ell)}(v_i, v_k) - \varepsilon_h^{(\ell)}\right) \cdot (d_k - \varepsilon_d) \cdot \left(h^{(\ell)}(v_j, v_k) - \varepsilon_h^{(\ell)}\right)\\
&= \left(h^{(\ell)}(v_i, v_k) - \varepsilon_h^{(\ell)}\right) \cdot \varepsilon_d \cdot \left(h^{(\ell)}(v_j, v_k) - \varepsilon_h^{(\ell)}\right)\\
&\quad + \varepsilon_h^{(\ell)} \cdot d_k \cdot \left(h^{(\ell)}(v_j, v_k) - \varepsilon_h^{(\ell)}\right) + \varepsilon_d \cdot \varepsilon_h^{(\ell)} \cdot h^{(\ell)}(v_i, v_k)
\end{aligned}$$

Hence,

$$\begin{aligned}
&s(v_i, v_j) - \tilde{s}(v_i, v_j)\\
&= \sum_{\ell=0}^{+\infty}\sum_{k=1}^{n}\Big(\left(h^{(\ell)}(v_i, v_k) - \varepsilon_h^{(\ell)}\right) \cdot \varepsilon_d \cdot \left(h^{(\ell)}(v_j, v_k) - \varepsilon_h^{(\ell)}\right)\\
&\quad + \varepsilon_h^{(\ell)} \cdot d_k \cdot \left(h^{(\ell)}(v_j, v_k) - \varepsilon_h^{(\ell)}\right) + \varepsilon_d \cdot \varepsilon_h^{(\ell)} \cdot h^{(\ell)}(v_i, v_k)\Big)\\
&\le \sum_{\ell=0}^{+\infty}\left((\sqrt{c})^{\ell} \cdot \varepsilon_d \cdot (\sqrt{c}^{\ell}) + 2 \cdot \varepsilon_h^{(\ell)} \cdot (\sqrt{c})^{\ell}\right)\\
&= \frac{\varepsilon_d}{1-c} + 2\sum_{\ell=0}^{+\infty}\left((\sqrt{c}^{\ell}) \cdot \varepsilon_h^{(\ell)}\right).
\end{aligned}$$

This completes the proof. □

Proof of Theorem 1. By Lemma 7, for all k, x, l,

$$-\frac{1-(\sqrt{c})^{\ell}}{1-\sqrt{c}}\theta \le \tilde{h}^{(\ell)}(v_k, v_x) - h^{(\ell)}(v_k, v_x) \le 0.$$

Then,

$$\begin{aligned}
&\frac{\varepsilon_d}{1-c} + 2\sum_{\ell=0}^{+\infty}\left((\sqrt{c})^{\ell} \cdot \varepsilon_h^{(\ell)}\right)\\
&= \frac{\varepsilon_d}{1-c} + 2\sum_{\ell=0}^{+\infty}\left((\sqrt{c})^{\ell} \cdot \frac{1-(\sqrt{c})^{\ell}}{1-\sqrt{c}}\theta\right)\\
&= \frac{\varepsilon_d}{1-c} + \frac{2\sqrt{c}}{(1-c)(1-\sqrt{c})}\theta.
\end{aligned}$$

By Lemma 6, $\left|\tilde{d}_k - d_k\right| \le \varepsilon_d$ holds with at least $1-\delta_d$ probability. Since $\delta_d \le \delta/n$, with at least $1-\delta$ probability,

$$\left|\tilde{d}_k - d_k\right| < \varepsilon_d \text{ , for all } k$$

Therefore, By Lemma 8, $|\tilde{s}(v_i, v_j) - s(v_i, v_j)| \le \varepsilon$ holds with at least $1-\delta$ probability. □

Query Planning for Evaluating SPARQL Property Paths

Nikolay Yakovets Parke Godfrey Jarek Gryz
York University
Toronto, Canada
{hush, godfrey, jarek}@cse.yorku.ca

ABSTRACT

The extension of SPARQL in version 1.1 with *property paths* offers a type of *regular path query* for RDF graph databases. Such queries are difficult to optimize and evaluate efficiently, however. We have embarked on a project, WAVEGUIDE, to build a cost-based optimizer for SPARQL queries with property paths. WAVEGUIDE builds a query plan—which we call a *waveplan* (WP)—which *guides* the query evaluation. There are numerous choices in the construction of a plan, and a number of optimization methods, so the space of plans for a query can be quite large. Execution costs of plans for the same query can vary by orders of magnitude. A WP's costs can be estimated, which opens the way to cost-based optimization. We demonstrate that the plan space of WAVEGUIDE properly subsumes existing techniques and that the new plans it adds are relevant.

1. INTRODUCTION

Graph data is becoming rapidly prevalent with the rise of the Semantic Web, social networks, and data-driven exploration in life sciences. There is need for natural, expressive ways to query over these graphs. Standards are coming into place for this. The Resource Description Framework (RDF) [21] provides a data model for graph data. An RDF *store* is a set of *triples* that describes a directed, edge-labeled multi-graph. A triple, $\langle \mathsf{s}, \mathsf{r}, \mathsf{o} \rangle$, denotes an *edge* from *node* "s" (the *subject*) to node "o" (the *object*), with the edge labeled by "r" (the *role*, also called *label* or *predicate*). The SPARQL query language [20] correspondingly provides a formal means to query over RDF stores. A query defines sub-graph match criteria; its evaluation over an RDF store returns all embedded sub-graphs meeting the criteria. For example, the query

$$\text{?friend :friendOf Charles .} \qquad (\mathcal{Q}_1)$$

evaluates to a list of people (nodes binding to variable "?friend") who are friends of (role ":friendOf") "Charles" (a named node, so a constant).

SIGMOD'16, June 26-July 01, 2016, San Francisco, CA, USA

DOI: http://dx.doi.org/10.1145/2882903.2882944

In its latest version, 1.1, SPARQL's expressiveness is extended with *property paths* [14]. This effectively introduces the concept of *regular path queries* (RPQs)—well studied before the advent of RDF and SPARQL—into the query language. Instead of specifying the path of interest *explicitly* between nodes, one may now specify it *implicitly* via a *regular expression*. For example, the query

$$\text{?friend :friendOf+ Charles .} \qquad (\mathcal{Q}_2)$$

evaluates to a list of people who are friends of "Charles", or friends of people who are friends of "Charles", and so forth (that is, a *transitive closure* over ":friendOf").

While SPARQL provides the expressiveness we desire, such queries are more challenging to optimize well. Query $\mathcal{Q}_1$ could be evaluated just by extracting the triples with "r = :friendOf" and "o = Charles". For even a slightly more complicated query, however, it may not be straightforward to find a *plan* to evaluate it efficiently. $\mathcal{Q}_2$ is more challenging in requiring transitive closure over ":friendOf" with respect to the graph.

Property path evaluation is a tale of two methods: two quite different approaches appear in the literature. For RPQs, the seminal work [18] which introduced the G+ query language shows how to use a *finite state machine* effectively as a plan to guide the *graph walk* for the query's evaluation. We call this approach FA. Subsequent work on RPQs have followed this idea.

SPARQL with property paths is much more recent. Systems for SPARQL query evaluation have followed a second approach, based essentially on the seminal work of [17]. These extend the *relational algebra* to accommodate the translation of a property path's regular expression, and then use dynamic programming over the (extended) relational-algebra parse to devise a plan. Added is an "α" operator, which provides transitive closure over a relation to accommodate regular expressions's Kleene star. Thus, we call this approach α-RA, the relational algebra extended by "α".

Which approach is better? We shall show that the effective "plan spaces" that result from FA and α-RA are incomparable. Sometimes, for a given query and graph, an FA plan will be the better choice. Other times, an α-RA plan will be. Our goal is to formalize the notion of plan space for both, to be able to choose the best plan. We shall show that a richer plan space can be had that properly subsumes FA and α-RA, and offers more plans existing in neither ("mixed" plans), which sometimes are the best plans.

We have designed a system called WAVEGUIDE with the goal to provide viable cost-based query optimization and

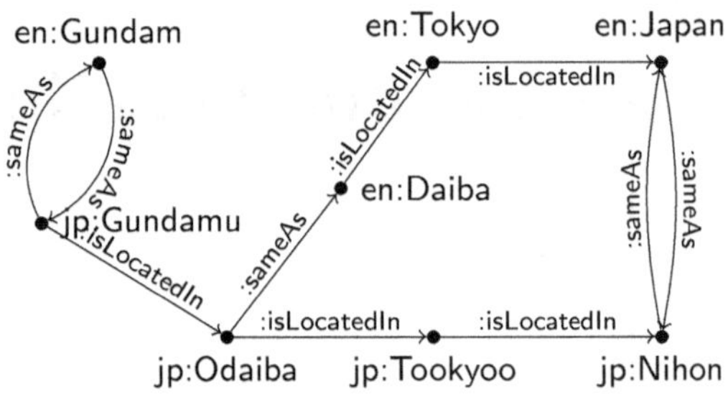

Figure 1: An example graph database.

evaluation for SPARQL over RDF stores that is on par with the state of the art for relational database systems. In this paper, we address the first but critical step of this endeavor, defining a *plan space*—the space of query plans, *waveplans* (WPs)—for SPARQL queries. We focus on single-path, property-path queries, essentially the RPQ fragment of SPARQL 1.1. We consider a set semantics—the distinct directive in each query—and thus do not consider aggregation.

Our contributions are as follows.

1. *plan space.* (§2—§4)
   (a) *Summarize* the state of the art for evaluation of RPQs and SPARQL property paths. (§2)
   (b) *Establish* why none suffices. (§3.1)
   (c) *Devise* WAVEGUIDE's place space, and *demonstrate* that it *subsumes* the state of the art, and extends beyond it. (§3)
   (d) *Model* the *cost factors* that determine the efficiency of plans, and *present* the powerful optimizations offered by WAVEGUIDE plans. (§4)
2. *performance study.* (§5)
   (a) Provide a *microbenchmark* over a pertinent RPQ template with realistic queries over real RDF stores / graphs.
   (b) *Substantiate* the optimizations of our approach.
   (c) *Justify* the *necessity* of the richer plan space.

2. BACKGROUND & RELATED WORK

2.1 Path Queries

Regular path queries[1] have been considered since *semi-structured* data models were first introduced [2, 6, 13, 18]. The complexity of RPQs for graph databases particularly has been well studied [4, 7]. In [16], the idea of employing NFAs to guide search for RPQ evaluation appears. In [25], a fixpoint evaluation for property paths is presented.

Regular path queries provide a useful mechanism for querying data in many application domains. For example, consider the knowledge base dataset of the Linked Open Data (LOD) cloud. LOD is a community effort which aims to interlink the structural information available in various datasets on the Web (such as Wikipedia and WordNet), and make it available as a single RDF graph. RPQs prove useful in querying such linked data by providing a convenient declarative mechanism which can be used to answer queries without prior knowledge of the underlying data paths.

[1]A *regular path query* Q is a tuple (x, r, y) for which x and y are free variables (that range over nodes) and r is a regular expression.

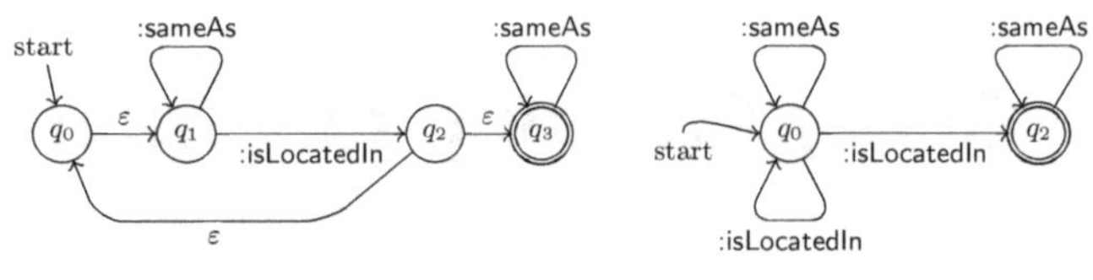

a) an ε-NFA b) a minimized NFA

Figure 2: An ε-NFA and corres. minimized NFA for $\mathcal{Q}_3$.

EXAMPLE 1. *Consider the part of a LOD graph database as presented in Fig. 1. This represents information about the Gundam robot statue in Odaiba in Tokyo. The data has been integrated from two datasets, identified by the prefixes* en *and* jp, *standing for the English and Japanese Wikipedia, respectively. The entities between these two datasets are interlinked by using OWL ontology terms. Equivalent entities are connected with* owl:sameAs *edges. In this case, the Japanese dataset contains richer spatial information related to the statue than does the English dataset.*

Say a user wants to know in which country this Gundam statue is located. Since there are no direct :isLocatedIn *edges outgoing from* en:Gundam*—as is often the case in linked data—the graph needs to be* searched. *During the search, equivalent data entities need to be resolved by following* :sameAs *edges. Likewise, a spatial hierarchy needs to be computed by following* :isLocatedIn *edges. This search can be defined by the following* SPARQL *query pattern:*

$$\text{en:Gundam (:sameAs*/:isLocatedIn)+ /:sameAs* ?place .} \qquad (\mathcal{Q}_3)$$

Query $\mathcal{Q}_3$ *computes the spatial hierarchy starting from node* en:Gundam, *using information from both interlinked datasets to resolve equivalent entity closures.*

2.2 Types of Query Plans

The literature on path queries over graphs, as is pertinent to property paths, comes from two distinct sources: evaluation strategies for *regular path queries* (RPQs); and SPARQL platforms extended for version 1.1 to handle *property paths.* We consider each in turn.

FA Plans. Research on RPQs, which well precedes RDF and SPARQL, mostly focused on theoretical aspects, but little on performance issues for evaluating such queries in practice. The seminal work which introduced the G+ query language [18] exploited the natural observation that, where there is a regular expression, there is a *finite automaton* (FA), that is, a *recognizer* for it. In essence, an FA corresponding to the query's regular expression provides a plan for its evaluation.

EXAMPLE 2. *Recall query* $\mathcal{Q}_3$ *from Ex. 1. As shown in Fig. 2, an automaton construction for this query is a two-step procedure. First, traversing the parse-tree of* r *bottom up, the* ε-NFA *is built up, from the base case and the inductive rules. Second, the resulting* ε-NFA *is then* minimized *to an* NFA, *which typically has smaller size, and hence, is more efficient to process.*

The idea of employing a product automaton for RPQ evaluation over graphs has been used in [9, 15, 16, 18, 19, 27] and over data trees (such as XML/XPath) in [5, 22, 23].

α-RA Plans. Work on evaluating property paths—much newer by virtue of the fact that the SPARQL 1.1 standard

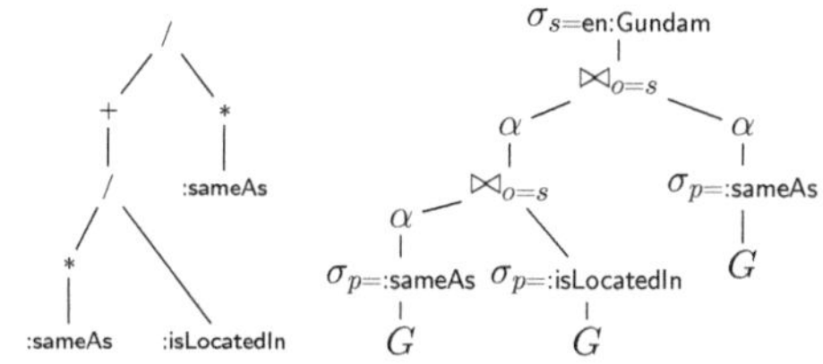

a) a parse tree b) an α-RA tree

Figure 3: A parse tree and α-RA tree for query $\mathcal{Q}_3$.

is quite recent—has mirrored the dynamic-programming approach behind the algorithm presented in [17]. This can be modeled by the *relational algebra* (RA) extended by an operator α for *transitive closure* (α-RA) [3]. The full power of relational algebra, extended with α, can then be employed to devise an evaluation plan—an α-RA-expression tree—based on the regular expression of the property path. This general approach is found behind many SPARQL platforms as it follows relational techniques well.

The α operator computes the transitive closure of a relation. Let the graph be represented as a relation of triples $G(s, p, o)$. Let $T = \pi_{1,3}G$; thus T consists of pairs of nodes $\langle s, o\rangle$ such that the pair is connected by a directed edge in the graph. Then α applied to T computes the *least fixpoint*:

$$T^+ = T \cup \pi_{1,3}(T^+ \bowtie_{T^+.o=T.s} T) \qquad (\mathcal{E}_1)$$

Thus, $\alpha(T)$ results in all pairs of nodes such that, for the nodes of each pair, there *exists* a path between them in graph G. If we were to evaluate the fixpoint by a semi-naïve evaluation, each iteration of evaluation is over paths of length one greater than of the previous iteration. The process stops when no new pairs are added; i.e., the fixpoint has been reached.

Given the relational algebra extended with the α operator, one can evaluate the RPQ $Q = (x, L(r), y)$ over graph $G = (N, E)$ by the algorithm proposed in [17]. This traverses the syntax tree of expression r bottom-up. Let s be the sub-expression of r represented by a given node in a parse tree. The binary relation $R_s \subseteq N \times N$ is computed so that node pair $(u, v) \in R_s$ *iff* there exists a path from u to v in G matching s.

EXAMPLE 3. *Given query $\mathcal{Q}_3$ and the database G from Ex. 1, the corresponding α-RA tree is shown in Fig. 3.*

The α-RA-based RPQ evaluation can be directly implemented in most relational databases and relational triple-stores. In [25], a method is proposed that translates RPQs as defined by SPARQL property paths into recursive SQL. A similar approach is used in [11] for the evaluation of provenance-aware RPQs by a relational engine.

3. QUERY PLANS & EVALUATION

Work on property-path evaluation has been remiss in not drawing the connection to RPQs. How do the FA and α-RA approaches compare? Does one subsume the other? Or are they *incomparable*? If so, a combined approach might be superior. A generalized approach might offer new plans that neither FA nor α-RA can produce with superior performance.

Both the FA and α-RA approaches effectively provide evaluation plans for property-path queries. However, the *plan*

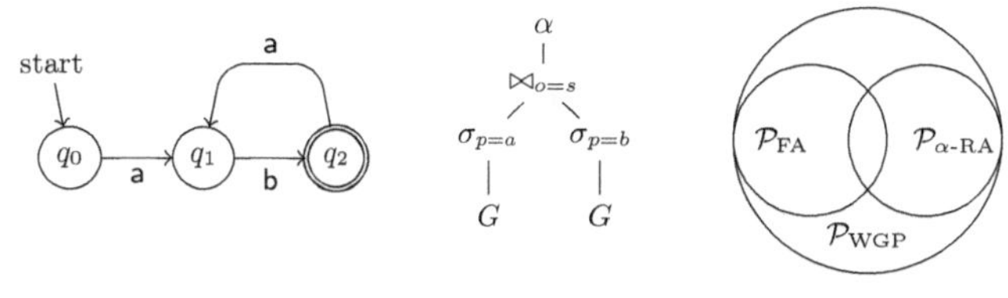

a) an FA plan b) an α-RA plan c) plan space classes

Figure 4: Example plans.

spaces that are implicit in these approaches have not been considered. In FA, choosing a different (but still correct) automaton for the plan might offer a significantly more efficient plan. In systems taking the α-RA approach, planning is done over the α-RA expression tree that results from the property path's translation, but no planning specific to the semantics of property paths takes place.

In §3.1, we show the approaches of FA and α-RA are, indeed, incomparable. We next describe WAVEGUIDE, which is a generalized approach to query planning and evaluation for SPARQL property-path queries, and which properly subsumes the FA and α-RA approaches. In §3.2, we discuss WAVEGUIDE's evaluation model. In §3.3, we present WAVEGUIDE's plans. In §3.4, we show that WAVEGUIDE's plan space properly subsumes FA $\cup$ α-RA.

3.1 Limitations

The FA and α-RA approaches each entail a *plan space*; that is, the plans the approach produces over all possible property-path queries. Let $\mathcal{P}_{\mathsf{FA}}$ and $\mathcal{P}_{\alpha\text{-}\mathsf{RA}}$ denote the plan spaces for FA and α-RA, respectively. To understand how the approaches are related—for instance, whether one approach subsumes the other, or whether they are incomparable—we consider these plan spaces. The Venn diagram of how they are related is shown in Fig. 4c.[2]

CLAIM 1. *$\mathcal{P}_{FA}$ and $\mathcal{P}_{\alpha\text{-}RA}$ are* incomparable *($\mathcal{P}_{FA} - \mathcal{P}_{\alpha\text{-}RA} \neq \emptyset$ and $\mathcal{P}_{\alpha\text{-}RA} - \mathcal{P}_{FA} \neq \emptyset$), but* overlap *($\mathcal{P}_{FA} \cap \mathcal{P}_{\alpha\text{-}RA} \neq \emptyset$).*

Of course, we are taking liberties; the place spaces should be over the same *domain* of plans. As we have presented things, however, they are not; we have presented FA plans as automata and α-RA plans as algebraic trees. To prove formally CLAIM 1, we would need to establish an isomorphism between FA and α-RA plans, or have a canonical form for plans to which each plan type could be mapped. This can be done. The formalism for waveguide plans we present in §3.3 would suffice for this mapping. DATALOG, or the *relational algebra* extended by *while loops* (established to be expressively equivalent to DATALOG) [1], would provide an even more universal domain that would suffice.

We can easily establish informally that these spaces are distinct. Consider this *generic* property-path pattern:

$$\text{?x (a/b)+ ?y .} \qquad (\mathcal{Q}_4)$$

Here, "a" and "b" are stand-ins for labels. It matches node-pairs that are connected by some path labeled ab, abab, or ababab, and so forth. While quite simple, this already demonstrates the complexities of planning.

[2] The diagram's claim that $\mathcal{P}_{\mathsf{WP}}$ properly subsumes both $\mathcal{P}_{\mathsf{FA}}$ and $\mathcal{P}_{\alpha\text{-}\mathsf{RA}}$ is taken up in §3.4.

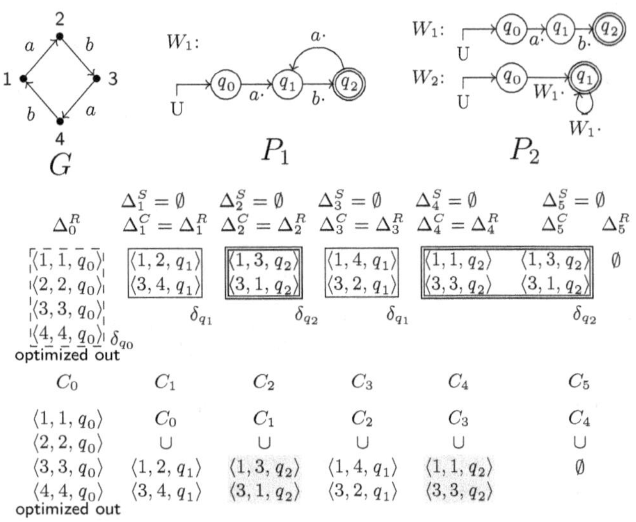

Figure 5: Two waveplans, P_1 & P_2, over graph G, with an evaluation trace of P_1.

```
WAVEGUIDESEARCH(G, P_Q)
Δ_0^R ← seed(G);
C_0 ← Δ_0^R;
i ← 0;
while |Δ_i^R| ≥ 0 do
    Δ_{i+1}^S ← seed(Δ_i^R);
    Δ_{i+1}^C ← crank(Δ_{i+1}^S, Δ_i^R, G, C_i, P_Q);
    Δ_{i+1}^R ← reduce(Δ_{i+1}^C, Δ_i^R, C_i);
    C_{i+1} ← cache(Δ_{i+1}^R, C_i);
    i ← i + 1;
done;
return extract(C_i);
```

Figure 6: WAVEGUIDE's evaluation procedure.

Consider the FA plan for query $\mathcal{Q}_4$ in Fig. 4a. There is no α-RA plan that could be equivalent to it, however; none would ever evaluate aba, ababa, and so forth as state q_1 does in the FA plan. α-RA plans cannot compute transitive closure in a *pipelined* fashion as the FA plan is doing; the α operator acts over an entire relation.

Now consider the α-RA plan for query $\mathcal{Q}_4$ in Fig. 4b. There is no FA plan that could be equivalent to it, however; no state transition in its automata can represent the "join" with ab. FA plans do not encompass *views* (that is, materialized parts of the query that can be reused), while the α-RA plan does by effectively materializing ab to join repeatedly on it.

Meanwhile, FA and α-RA have many plans in common: any query that is restricted to transitive closure over single labels, for example, results in common FA and α-RA plans.

3.2 WAVEGUIDE's Evaluation

WAVEGUIDE's evaluation strategy is based on an *iterative search algorithm*, and variations thereof.

Wavefronts. In WAVEGUIDE, we perform efficiently path search while *simultaneously* recognizing the path expressions. WAVEGUIDE's input is a graph database G and a *waveplan* P_Q which *guides* a number of search *wavefronts* that explore the given graph. We introduce the term *wavefront* to refer to a part of the plan that evaluates breadth-first during the evaluation. This graph exploration, driven by an iterative search procedure, is inspired by the semi-naïve bottom-up strategy used in evaluation of linear recursive expressions based on *fixpoint*, as is done for the α operator for α-RA, described in §2.2.

The key idea is, given a *seed*—a set of nodes in the graph from which this wavefront begins its search—as a start, to expand repeatedly the search wavefronts until no new answers are produced; i.e., we reach fixpoint. Each search wavefront is guided by an *automaton* in the plan, a finite state machine based on an NFA. In Fig. 4a, the plan consists of a single wavefront automaton. We shall see examples below of multi-wavefront plans; e.g., plan P_2 in Fig. 5. This is akin to the FA approach discussed in §2.2. Different, though, from NFAs which are used as recognizers of regular expressions on strings, wavefront automata have features directed to evaluation of regular expressions over graphs.

Expanding a Wavefront.

Each search wavefront has a seed as its initialization. A seed can be either *universal* or *restricted.* A wavefront with a universal seed conducts its search *virtually*[3] starting from *every* node in a graph. A wavefront with a restricted seed starts the search from a fixed set of nodes. (A restricted seed is defined by the results of other wavefronts or by constants used in a query.) Graphically, a seed is represented as an incoming edge to starting state q_0 of the wavefront. We use the label "U" to denote a universal seed; any other label on this incoming edge denotes a restriction placed on the seed, thus a restricted seed.

The graph exploration (*walk*) is performed by an iterative procedure *guided* by a waveplan, as illustrated in Fig. 6. Consider the example from Fig. 5 with an example graph G and two plans P_1 and P_2 for evaluating query $Q = (x, (ab)+, y)$ ($\mathcal{Q}_4$). Waveplan P_1 consists of a single wavefront automaton (W_1), which is analogous to the plan that results from the FA method. Fig. 5 also presents the evaluation trace by the procedure in Fig. 6 using plan P_1 over graph G.

During the search, intermediate results are kept in a *cache*, denoted as C_i for iteration i. This is the collection of tuples $\langle u, v, s\rangle$ for which u and v are nodes in G and s is a state in the plan. The newly discovered tuples found in the current iteration are denoted by *delta* Δ_i. We use C_i and Δ_i to eliminate answers already seen in the search. Delta tuples produced by crank are denoted Δ^C, and those surviving reduce are Δ^R.

To begin, all the universal seeds are initialized (but never materialized!); Δ_0^R is assigned the set of $\langle u, u, q_0\rangle$ for all $u \in N$. Note that q_0 is the starting state for all wavefronts with universal seeds. We then iterate, performing four operations per iteration:

1. seed. Determine the set of nodes from which to search.
2. crank. Perform a step of the fixpoint operation, the breadth-first search.
3. reduce. Eliminate node pairs seen before.
4. cache: Update the set of pairs of nodes seen already in the evaluation.

[3]Effectively all nodes in a graph are never materialized due to *first-hop* optimization which restricts the starting nodes according to the transition labels originating from q_0.

The iteration continues until fixpoint is reached. Thus, this is a guided semi-naïve evaluation [1].

The seed step populates the restricted seeds, according to their respective seed conditions. The crank step transitions from the previous delta to the current, $\Delta_i^R \rightarrow \Delta_{i+1}^C$. For each node v in $\langle u, v, s\rangle \in \Delta_i^R$, for edge $\langle v, a, w\rangle \in G$ and automaton transition $\langle s, a, t\rangle \in W_1$, $\langle u, w, t\rangle$ is added to Δ_{i+1}^C. Thus crank advances the search *simultaneously* in the graph *and* in the automaton.

To prevent unbounded computation over cyclic graphs, the delta is *reduced*: Δ_{i+1}^C is checked against both the previous delta Δ_i^R and the cache C_i; tuples that are seen in either Δ_i^R or C_i are removed to produce Δ_{i+1}^R. Lastly, the cache is updated C_{i+1} by adding the tuples in the reduced delta Δ_{i+1}^R to it (C_i). The iteration halts once Δ^R is empty.

It can be established by structural induction that, for any tuple $\langle u, v, s\rangle$ in the cache (C) such that s is an accepting state, the pair of nodes $\langle u, v\rangle$ must have a path between them in the graph that conforms to r. Thus, WAVEGUIDE produces the correct results. The answer set can be then *extracted* from the cache by selecting the tuples $\langle u, v, s\rangle$ for all accepting states s of automaton W_1.

EXAMPLE 4. *Consider the evaluation trace presented on Fig. 5. First, universal seeds in Δ_0^R are optimized out by the first-hop optimization which builds Δ_1^C directly by selecting the tuples from G which match the label (a) of the first transition $\langle q_0, a\cdot, q_1\rangle$ in P_1. The search proceeds by iterating crank, reduce and cache to produce Δ_i^C, Δ_i^R and C_i at each iteration i. The search stops at the 5th iteration when reduced delta Δ_5^R is empty. Those cache tuples in accepting state q_2 (shaded) at the end are then extracted as the answer set.*

3.3 Waveplans

Guiding a Wavefront. The construction of the NFA forces an order to the query evaluation. A "wrong" choice of NFA can lead to an inefficient evaluation plan. In WAVEGUIDE, we aim to minimize the search space explored by considering the possible orders of graph exploration by search wavefronts. To achieve this, we use wavefront automata which can use transitions that expand the wavefront in the direction opposite to the direction of the edges of the graph.

Consider a graph transition $\langle s, l, t\rangle$ in a wavefront as illustrated in Fig. 7a. Edge label l has a general form $\cdot a$ or $a\cdot$, where a is an edge label in G and the position of a dot '$\cdot$' specifies a direction of a search wavefront and denotes prepend ($\cdot a$) or append ($a\cdot$) transition. A prepend transition expands in the opposite direction to the edges in the graph. On the other hand, an append transition guides a wavefront that expands in the same direction as the edges in the graph.

Hence, wavefronts enable automaton transitions that explore the graph in a specified direction. This allows a wavefront to initiate evaluation from any label in the given regular expression and iteratively expand by appending or prepending path labels. This gives us the power to explore all different expansion orders of a single wavefront.

Wavefront Interaction. Often, the search space is constrained even further if several wavefronts are employed in the evaluation, each evaluating parts[4] of a given regular expression. A WAVEGUIDE plan enables this by defining a number of automata, one for each search wavefront.

[4]This decomposition of a regular expression can be determined by graph statistics such as cardinalities of its labels.

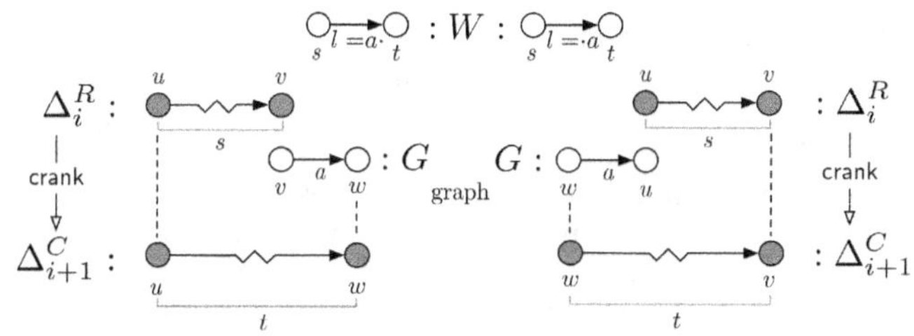

(a) Prepending vs. appending by expanding the wavefront using tuples from graph G.

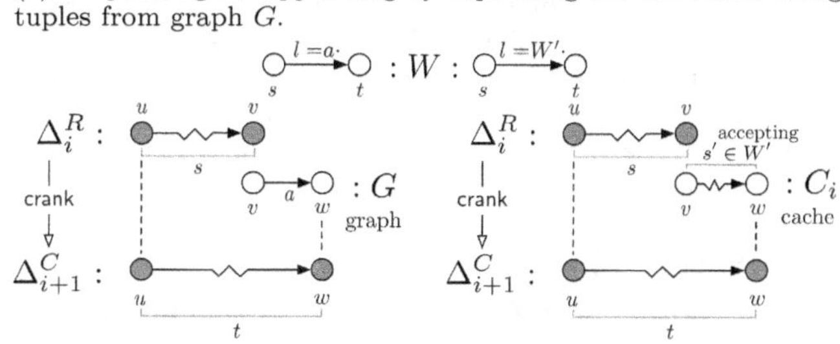

(b) Expanding the wavefront by appending and using the tuples from G (over the graph) vs. from search cache C (over the view).

Figure 7: Types of transitions used in a wavefront.

In addition to transitions over graph edge labels, waveplans allow transitions over *path views*, by using cached result sets produced by other wavefronts. Consider Fig. 7b and automaton transition $\langle s, l, t\rangle$. If l is an edge label a in G, then this *graph* transition expands the wavefront by using the tuples from *graph G*. Otherwise, if l is a wavefront W' then this *view* transition expands the wavefront by employing the tuples produced by the corresponding wavefront (W').

These new types of transitions offer powerful choices in WPs for guiding the search. The search can have *multiple* wavefronts originating from different starting points *and* expanding in different directions. Further, each wavefront can employ the cache through transitions over views to avoid recomputation. (This is also known as *memoization.*)

EXAMPLE 5. *Consider the wavefront search in Fig. 5 for a query Q with regular expression $r = (ab)+$ ($\mathcal{Q}_4$). P_1 is a basic WP embodying an NFA that recognizes r. From P_1, we can design a more efficient WP, P_2: first, compute (ab) with wavefront W_1; then use a loop-back path-view transition to compute the closure (ab)+ (with wavefront W_2). It can be shown that P_2 explores a smaller search space than P_1.*

3.4 WAVEGUIDE's Plan Space

We claim that the space of waveguide plans subsumes that of the FA and α-RA approaches, as the Venn diagram in Fig. 4 shows (and with the caveats as discussed in §3.1).

CLAIM 2. $\mathcal{P}_{WP}$ properly subsumes *the union of* $\mathcal{P}_{FA}$ *and* $\mathcal{P}_{\alpha\text{-}RA}$ ($\mathcal{P}_{WP} \supsetneq \mathcal{P}_{FA} \cup \mathcal{P}_{\alpha\text{-}RA}$).

That $\mathcal{P}_{WP}$ subsumes each of $\mathcal{P}_{FA}$ and $\mathcal{P}_{\alpha\text{-}RA}$ is straightforward; we devised WP so that we could express both FA- and α-RA- type plans. WP extends the FA model. WP encompasses α-RA by the addition of *path views*; what the α operator offers, transitive closure over an arbitrary relation, can be accomplished by view-labeled transitions.

$\mathcal{P}_{\mathsf{WP}}$ properly subsumes the union of $\mathcal{P}_{\mathsf{FA}}$ and $\mathcal{P}_{\alpha\text{-}\mathsf{RA}}$ because there is a waveguide plan that corresponds to neither an FA plan nor an α-RA plan. We have demonstrated that in the discussions above: any WP with multiple wavefronts and some wavefront with a long loop-back is such a plan; FA plans are essentially single wavefront by the FA model, and pipelined loop-backs are outside the scope of α-RA. Likewise, any WP, even single wavefront, that is "mixed", that combines views and long loop-backs, corresponds to no FA plan and to no α-RA plan. (In Fig. 11 below, P_2 with partial loop-caching is such a plan.) These very types of waveguide plans that FA and α-RA miss can be the most efficient plans.

In §4, we explain why this rich plan space is relevant. In §5, we we compare plans for real queries over real graph data to establish that this is true in practice, as well.

4. PLAN COSTS

We present a *cost framework* for WAVEGUIDE search, *search cost factors* that can magnify the cost (properties of the graph and of resulting pre-paths computed during evaluation), and *optimization methods* that are enabled by WPs which address the search factors, in turn.

4.1 Cost Framework

Recall the three steps in Fig. 6 of the search iteration: crank, reduce, and cache. Assume that the search completes in n iterations. The cost of crank, $\mathbf{C}_{\mathsf{crank}}$, corresponds to the total number of *edge walks* performed. This *search size* is the sum of sizes of the deltas (Δ^C's). The cost of reduce, has two components: duplicate removal within a delta ($\mathbf{C}^{\Delta}_{\mathsf{reduce}}$) and for the delta against the search cache ($\mathbf{C}^{C}_{\mathsf{reduce}}$). The cost of cache, $\mathbf{C}_{\mathsf{cache}}$, is associated with search cache maintenance procedures (e.g., indexing). The functions f_{1-4} are placeholders that weigh the costs:

Step	Generalized Cost
$\mathbf{C}_{\mathsf{crank}}$	$\sum_{i=0}^{n} f_1(\lvert\Delta_i^R\rvert, \lvert G\rvert, \lvert C_i\rvert)$
$\mathbf{C}^{\Delta}_{\mathsf{reduce}}$	$\sum_{i=1}^{n} f_2(\lvert\Delta_i^C\rvert)$
$\mathbf{C}^{C}_{\mathsf{reduce}}$	$\sum_{i=1}^{n} f_3(\lvert\Delta_i^C\rvert, \lvert C_i\rvert)$
$\mathbf{C}_{\mathsf{cache}}$	$\sum_{i=1}^{n} f_4(\lvert\Delta_i^R\rvert, \lvert C_i\rvert)$

The cost functions f_{1-4} above are monotone over their parameters; these simply abstract the actual costs as based upon the underlying implementation of WAVEGUIDE's data structures and algorithms. For example, in a relational-based system, assuming tree indexes on C_i and G, functions f_{1-4} can be approximated as:

	Example Implementation	Complexity
f_1	Index-nested loop joins: $\Delta_i^R \bowtie_{P_Q} G$ and $\Delta_i^R \bowtie_{P_Q} C_i$.	$O(\lvert\Delta_i^R\rvert \cdot (\log\lvert G\rvert + \log\lvert C_i\rvert))$
f_2	Sort Δ_i^C, remove duplicates.	$O(\lvert\Delta_i^C\rvert \cdot \log\lvert\Delta_i^C\rvert)$
f_3	Scan Δ_i^C, probe C_i's index.	$O(\lvert\Delta_i^C\rvert \cdot \log\lvert C_i\rvert)$
f_4	Scan Δ_i^R, insert into C_i's index.	$O(\lvert\Delta_i^R\rvert \cdot \log\lvert C_i\rvert)$

In this scenario, crank is implemented as joins of Δ_i^R with G (for graph transitions) and C_i (for view transitions). The predicates of these joins are dictated by the WP P_Q. Since usually $\Delta_i^C \ll C$, reduce$^{\Delta}$ typically occurs in-memory. On the other hand, reduce^C is more expensive since it requires probing C's index. Finally, cache involves updating C's index with new Δ_i^R's tuples.

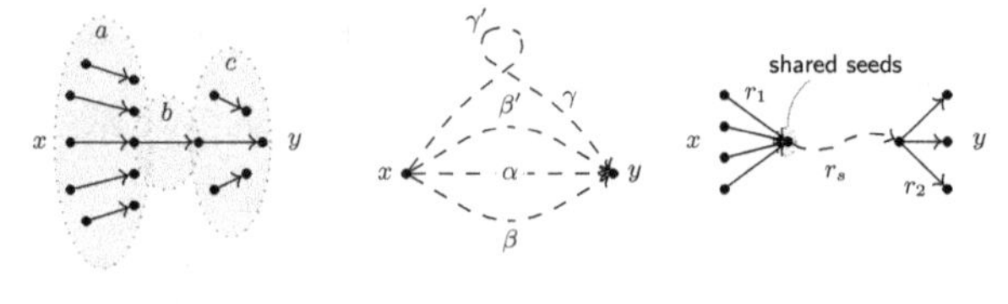

a) search cardinality b) solution redundancy c) sub-path sharing

Figure 8: Types of search cost factors.

4.2 Search Cost Factors

Properties of the graph and of the WP chosen will determine the evaluation cost.

Search Sizes. The wavefronts that we choose for the search determine the intermediate Δ_i (pairs of nodes connected by valid pre-paths) that we collect in each iteration i. Just as with different join orders in relational query evaluation, different wavefronts will result in different cardinalities of Δ_i. These intermediate cardinalities can vary widely from plan to plan and affect all four costs f_{1-4}.

Solution Redundancy. After much deliberation, the W3C has adopted a *non-counting* semantics for SPARQL property-path queries. Each node pair appears only once in the answer, even when there are several paths between the node pair satisfying the given regular expression.

Answer-path redundancy arises from two sources. First, in dense graphs, solutions are re-discovered by following conforming, yet different paths. Second, nodes are revisited by following cycles in the graph. Thus, the same answer pair may be discovered repeatedly during evaluation, which increases both $|\Delta_i|$ and $|C_i|$. It is critical to detect such duplicate solutions early in order to keep the costs f_{1-4} low.

Sub-path Redundancy. In *solution redundancy*, an answer pair could have multiple paths justifying it. Likewise, the paths justifying multiple answer pairs may *share* significant segments (*sub-paths*) in common. This arises, for instance, in dense graphs and with hierarchical structures (e.g., *isA* and *locatedIn* edge labels). Consider a query "?p :locatedIn+ Canada". Every person located in the neighborhood of the Annex in the city of Toronto qualifies, since the Annex is located in Toronto which is located in Ontario which is located in Canada. The sub-path "Annex :locatedIn+ Canada" is shared by the answer path for each Annex resident. Because we keep only node-pairs (plus state) in the search deltas, and not explicitly the paths themselves,[5] we may walk these sub-paths many times, recomputing "Annex :locatedIn+ Canada" for each Annex resident, thus unnecessary increasing both $|\Delta_i|$ and $|C|$.

4.3 Plan Optimizations

We consider WP-optimization methods in relation to the search cost factors above.

Choice of Wavefronts. The direction in which we follow edges, and where we start in the graph, with respect to the regular expression will result in different $|\Delta_i|$ we encounter during the search. Our choice of automata in the WP dictates the wavefront(s). For example, consider query $Q = (x, (abc), y)$ and a fragment of a graph shown in Fig. 8a.

[5]Note this design choice in our evaluation strategy is critical for good performance due to solution redundancy!

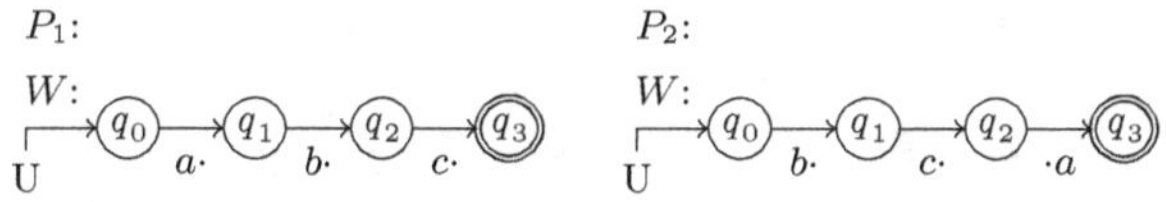

Figure 9: Choosing the wavefronts.

Since labels a, b and c have different frequencies, different wavefronts will have different search sizes. Consider two plans P_1 and P_2 that evaluate Q shown in Fig. 9. P_1 has a single wavefront that explores the graph starting from a, appending b and then c. On the other hand, P_2 has a wavefront that starts from the low frequency label b, appends c and then prepends a. Observe that, in this scenario, P_2 results in fewer edge walks than P_1.

To reduce overall search size, we need to choose wavefronts that result in fewer edge walks. Wavefronts can be costed to estimate their search sizes based on statistics about the graph, such as 1-gram and 2-gram label frequencies. (Such graph statistics can be computed offline for this purpose.)

Reduce. WAVEGUIDE's evaluation strategy is designed to counter solution redundancy. As shown in Fig. 8b, we consider several types of redundant solutions based on a path which was followed to obtain each solution. Path α is the shortest path. Paths β and β' are of the same length, but go through different nodes. Finally, path γ' shares some nodes with path γ, but it is longer due to a cycle.

In WAVEGUIDE, redundancy of *candidate* solutions is addressed by removal of duplicates against both C and Δ by the reduce operation. Assuming a BFS search strategy, duplicate solutions obtained by following paths of the same length (β, β') are removed within a Δ. On the other hand, duplicates obtained by following paths of different lengths (α, β) are removed when Δ is compared against C. This also includes paths with cycles such as γ and γ' as they also have different lengths.

As a further optimization, once a solution seed-target pair has been discovered, *first-path pruning* (fpp) removes the *seed* from further expansion by the search wavefronts. In our example, once path α has been discovered and solution (x, y) has been obtained, all longer paths $(\beta, \beta', \gamma, \gamma')$ are never even materialized.

Threading. To counter *sub-path redundancy* requires us to decompose a query into sub-queries. We call this decomposition *threading*, and our WPs accommodate this.

Consider query $Q = (x, (r_1 r_s r_2), y)$ where sub-path r_s is shared among many solutions as shown in Fig. 8c. This query can be threaded as follows. First, pre-path r_1 is computed by wavefront W_{r_1}. Then, the portion of the regular expression that will result in sub-paths that will be shared by many answer paths can be computed by a separate wavefront $W_{r_1:r_s}$. Here, W_{r_1} seeds wavefront $W_{r_1:r_s}$ which computes a shared path r_s for each of the partial solutions produced by W_{r_1}. Finally, the complete path is pieced together by wavefront W_{join}. Sub-path sharing can be predicted by graph statistics to indicate when threading is useful.

Partial Caching. Delta results are cached during evaluation as we need to check against C for redundantly computed pairs. For large intermediate $|\Delta_i|$, this can be a significant cost. However, some of this cost can be eliminated. In particular, not every state in the WP's automata needs to have its node-pairs cached. Caching is only needed when

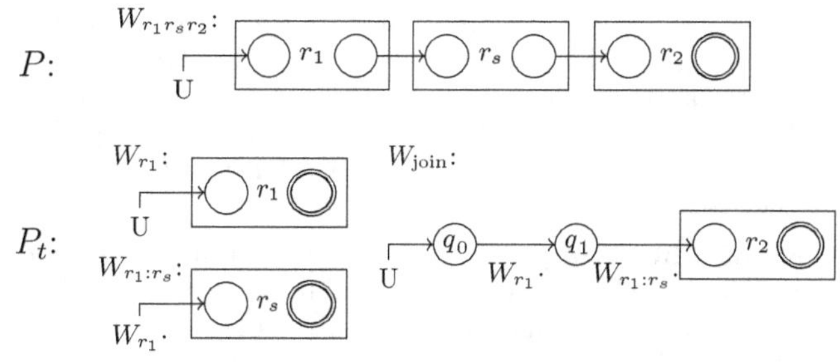

Figure 10: Threading a shared sub-path.

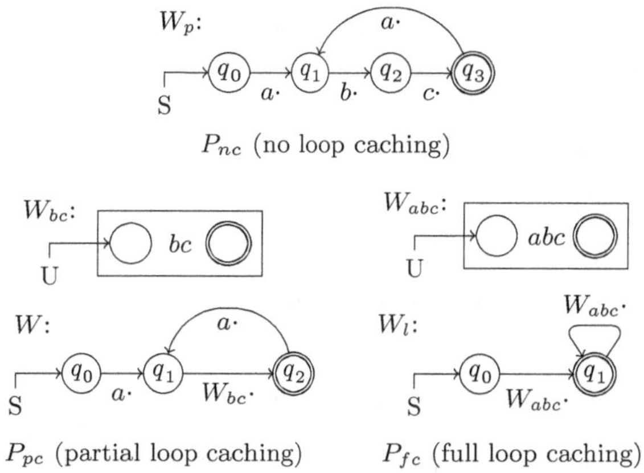

Figure 11: Types of loop caching.

unbounded redundancy is possible, due to cycles in the wavefront automata or in the graph. States without cycles need not be cached.

Loop Caching. Transitions over views in wavefront automata allows us to cache and re-use some of the intermediate node pairs we encounter during the search. Such named result sets are useful in reducing unnecessary re-computation by employing an optimization we call *loop caching.*

In transitive query $Q = (x, (r)+, y)$, the expression r is evaluated repeatedly until no new solutions are found. Loop caching rewrites an evaluation plan so that the base r is cached either fully or partially to speed up the transitive evaluation of $(r)+$.

Consider three plans P_{nc}, P_{pc} and P_{fc} for query $Q = (x, (abc)+, y)$ shown in Fig. 11. Plan P_{nc} has no loop caching as it evaluates full expression (abc) in a pipeline with W_p. Plan P_{pc} uses a separate wavefront to evaluate (bc) first, then these results are used in a loop to evaluate transitive $(abc)+$. Finally, plan P_{fc} caches the full base expression (abc) in W_{abc}, which is then used in evaluation of a transitive expression in a loop by W_l.

4.4 Cost Analysis

Consider deltas Δ_i^C, Δ_i^R and cache C_i for all iterations in the evaluation of WP P_Q over graph G. These determine the overall cost of P_Q according to the framework in §4.1.

We define a *logical* delta δ_s over state s to be a set of delta tuples $(u, v, s) \in \delta_s$ such that $\delta_s \subseteq \bigcup_{i=0}^{n} \Delta_i$ (assuming n total iterations of the search). In other words, from all *physical* deltas Δ_i we encountered during the search, we *select* delta tuples which occur in state s. Logical delta δ_S over set of states S is a union of logical deltas over all states in S, i.e. $\bigcup_{s \in S} \delta_s$. Similarly, δ_W over wavefront W is a union $\bigcup_{s \in W} \delta_s$. For example, consider a breakdown of Δ into δ for an execution of P_1 as shown on Fig. 5. Here, for each state $q \in P_1$, δ_q is shown by encasing the Δ tuples in a dashed, single and double rectangles for δ_{q0}, δ_{q1} and δ_{q2}, respectively.

Cost of Threading. Given a plan P with a single wavefront $W_{r_1 r_s r_2}$ which computes a regular expression of a form $r = r_1/r_s/r_2$, threading rewrites it into a plan P_t with three wavefronts W_{r_1}, $W_{r_1:r_s}$ and W_{join} as described in Section 4.3. We partition states in $W_{r_1 r_s r_2}$ into three subsets: S_{r_1}, S_{r_s} and S_{r_2} which are responsible for evaluation of expressions r_1, $r_1 r_s$ and $r_1 r_s r_2$, respectively.

To analyze the cost of threading, we partition edge walks into logical deltas for both P and P_t as follows:

$$P : \sum_{i=0}^{n} |\Delta_i'^C| = |\delta^C_{W_{r_1 r_s r_2}}| = |\delta^C_{S_{r_1}}| + |\delta^C_{S_{r_s}}| + |\delta^C_{S_{r_2}}| \quad (1)$$

$$P_t : \sum_{i=0}^{n_t} |\Delta_i''^C| = |\delta^C_{W_{r_1}}| + |\delta^C_{W_{r_1:r_s}}| + |\delta^C_{W_{\text{join}}}| \quad (2)$$

From construction (Fig.10), we have:

$$|\delta^C_{W_{r_1}}| = |\delta^C_{S_{r_1}}| \quad (3)$$

$$|\delta^C_{W_{\text{join}}}| = |\delta^C_{q0}| + |\delta^C_{q1}| + |\delta^C_{S_{r_2}}| \quad (4)$$

We define a *multiplicity* ratio of an expression r_1 in graph G, which is computed by analyzing the paths in G:

$$\mathcal{M}(G, r_1) = \frac{|S_s|}{|S_o|},$$

where S_s and S_o is a set of subjects and objects, respectively, connected in G with paths conforming to r_1. Then, $\mathcal{M}(G, r_1) > 1$, would indicate that, on average, there are many subjects connected to a single object in G, while $\mathcal{M}(G, r_1) < 1$ would indicate that the opposite is true. The greater $\mathcal{M}$ is, the more subjects are connected to the same object by path r_1, and, hence, more subjects share a path r_s which originates from this object. Hence, we can estimate:

$$|\delta^C_{S_{r_s}}| = \mathcal{M}(G, r_1) \cdot |\delta^C_{W_{r_1:r_s}}| \quad (5)$$

We define a *gain* $\mathcal{G}_t$ introduced by threading in P as difference in a number of edge walks performed in P and P_t. From (1-5), this gain is:

$$\mathcal{G}_t = \underbrace{(\mathcal{M}(G, r_1) - 1) \cdot |\delta^C_{W_{r_1:r_s}}|}_{\textbf{A}\text{: savings due to threading}} - \underbrace{(|\delta^C_{q0}| + |\delta^C_{q1}|)}_{\textbf{B}\text{: extra join}}$$

If a shared sub-path r_s is accurately identified, then the total reduction of number of edge walks in P_t (**A**) is sufficiently large to offset the cost of the extra join (**B**), i.e. $\mathcal{G}_t > 0$.

To maximize **A**, we need to maximize both $\mathcal{M}(G, r_1)$ and $|\delta_{W_{r_1:r_s}}|$. For the latter, one useful metric to consider is an average length $\mathcal{L}(G, r_s)$ of a path which conforms to r_s in G. A longer shared sub-path r_s can increase the cardinality $|\delta_{W_{r_1:r_s}}|$; hence, more potential savings in edge walks can be realized by a threading split on r_s.

Thus, given $\mathcal{M}$ and $\mathcal{L}$ for sub-expressions of r in G, the identification of an efficient threading split $r = r_1/r_s/r_2$ becomes an $(\mathcal{M}, \mathcal{L})$ maximization problem.

Cost of Loop Caching. Given a plan with a single wavefront which computes closure $(r)+$ of a regular expression r, loop caching rewrites it into a plan in which parts of r are pre-computed, cached, and then used in an iterative evaluation of the closure. For example, consider the differences in evaluation of query $Q = (x, (abc)+, y)$ with plans P_{nc}, P_{pc} and P_{fc} shown in Fig. 11. P_{nc} defines a single wavefront, which, due to absence of transitions over views, can be executed pipelined. On the other hand, P_{pc} and P_{fc} first compute (bc) and (abc), respectively, in separate wavefronts, the results of which are used in a wavefront which computes the final closure.

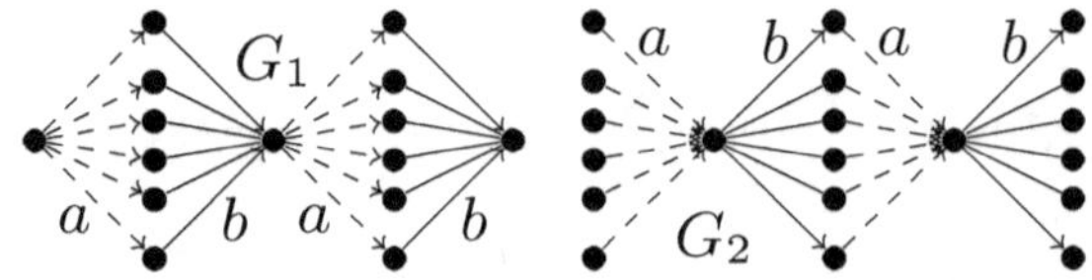

G_1	$\lvert\Delta_1^C\rvert$	$\lvert\Delta_1^R\rvert$	$\lvert\Delta_2^C\rvert$	$\lvert\Delta_2^R\rvert$	$\lvert\Delta_3^C\rvert$	$\lvert\Delta_3^R\rvert$	$\lvert\Delta_4^C\rvert$	$\lvert\Delta_4^R\rvert$	Σ^C
P_{nc}	12	12	12	2	6	6	6	1	**36**
P_{fc}	12	12	12	2	1	1			**25**

G_2	$\lvert\Delta_1^C\rvert$	$\lvert\Delta_1^R\rvert$	$\lvert\Delta_2^C\rvert$	$\lvert\Delta_2^R\rvert$	$\lvert\Delta_3^C\rvert$	$\lvert\Delta_3^R\rvert$	$\lvert\Delta_4^C\rvert$	$\lvert\Delta_4^R\rvert$	Σ^C
P_{nc}	12	12	72	72	36	6	36	36	**156**
P_{fc}	12	12	72	72	216	36			**300**

Figure 12: Lensing.

As previously, to analyze the cost of loop caching, we partition edge walks into logical deltas for both P_{nc} and P_{fc}[6]:

$$P_{nc} : \sum_{i=0}^{n_{nc}} |\Delta_i'^C| = |\delta^C_{q0 \in W_p}| + \underbrace{|\delta^C_{q1 \in W_p}| + |\delta^C_{q2 \in W_p}| + |\delta^C_{q3 \in W_p}|}_{\textbf{C}}$$

$$P_{fc} : \sum_{i=0}^{n_{fc}} |\Delta_i''^C| = \underbrace{|\delta^C_{W_{abc}}|}_{\textbf{D}} + |\delta^C_{q0 \in W_l}| + \underbrace{|\delta^C_{q1 \in W_l}|}_{\textbf{E}}$$

From construction (Fig.11), we have:

$$|\delta^C_{q0 \in W_p}| = |\delta^C_{q0 \in W_l}|$$

It follows that the gain $\mathcal{G}_{lc}$ of loop caching is the difference in a number of edge walks in P_{nc} and P_{fc}:

$$\mathcal{G}_{lc} = \textbf{C} - (\textbf{D} + \textbf{E})$$

In order for cached plan P_{fc} to be faster, the sum of edge walks associated with computation of base (abc) paths (**D**) and looped evaluation of $(abc)+$ paths (**E**) should be less than the sum of edge walks associated with evaluation of $(a), (ab), (abc), (abca), \ldots$ paths (**C**) in pipelined plan P_{nc}.

Interestingly, values of terms **C** and **E** can significantly differ depending on the general shape of the graph. For example, consider two basic graphs G_1 and G_2 as presented in Fig. 12. Both G_1 and G_2 have the same frequencies of labels a and b, but are different in terms of their *shape*. G_1 exhibits *lensing* with focal points on concatenations b/a, while G_2 has lensing in a/b. Intermediate cardinalities of Δ^C (number of edge walks) of the WAVEGUIDE search are presented for plans with (P_{fc}) and without (P_{nc}) loop caching. Observe that loop caching optimization is beneficial for search in G_1 with 30% fewer edge walks. On the other hand, loop caching performs worse in G_2 with 92% more edge walks. This can be explained by analyzing the edge walks and pruned tuples during the concatenation sequence $(\ldots/a/b)$ which is

[6]We omit the comparison with P_{pc} as it follows the same pattern.

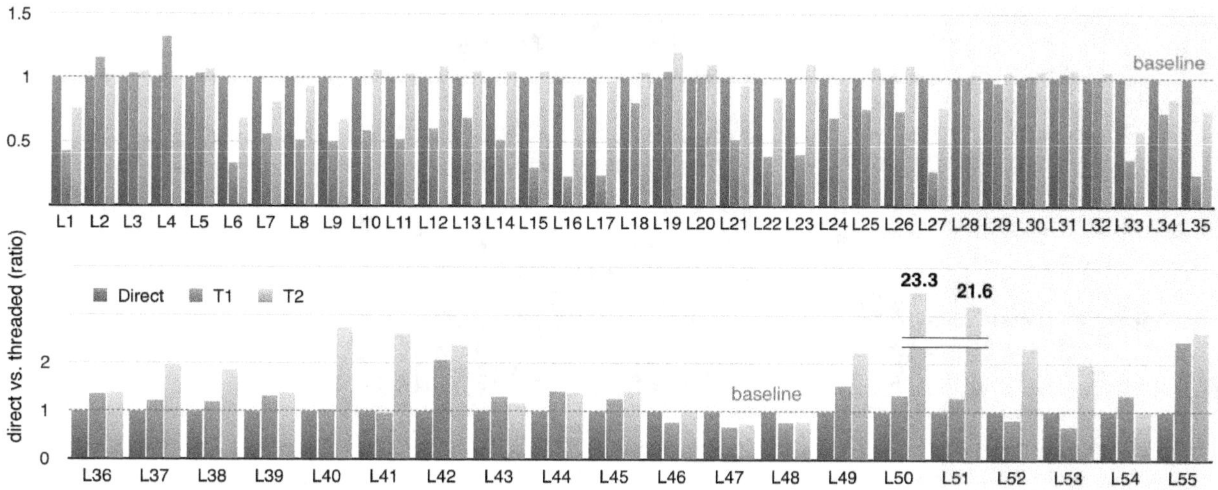

Figure 13: Benchmarking Threading.

performed in P_{nc}, but not in P_{fc}. In G_1, $(\ldots/a/b)$ computes a large number of intermediate tuples, most of which are later pruned due to the focal point in b/a. Meanwhile, in G_2, $(\ldots/a/b)$ first prunes many tuples due to the focal point in a/b, hence reducing the total number of edge walks performed later in the search.

Lastly, we consider queries with constants. In pipelined plan P_{nc}, this constant can be pushed to seed condition S of its wavefront, therefore reducing term **C**. On the other hand, plans P_{pc} and P_{fc} allow at most partial constant pushdown, since cached relations must be computed (term **D**) with universal seed to ensure completeness of the final closure.

5. PERFORMANCE STUDY

5.1 The Experimental Setup

The WAVEGUIDE Prototype. We have prototyped a system [26] that implements the methodology from §3 in order to benchmark waveguide plans to study their performance. In this WAVEGUIDE system, resource-intensive tasks are delegated to POSTGRESQL via SQL and *procedural* SQL routines.

Fig. 17 (in the Appendix) shows the architecture. It consists of two layers: *application* and *RDBMS*. The application layer provides a user front-end, preprocessing the graph data, parsing user queries, generating WPs, and visualizing key steps during the search. The RDBMS layer provides postprocessing of the graph data and performing the iterative WAVEGUIDE graph search for the given WP.

Our implementation of WAVEGUIDE 's operations matches the example implementations (f_1–f_4) given in §4.1.

Methodology. We test our implementation of WAVEGUIDE by running a collection of realistic path queries over real-world datasets YAGO2s [24] and DBPedia [10]. The datasets were preprocessed by removing invalid and duplicate triples. After preprocessing, YAGO2s had 242M triples and DBPedia had 463M triples, with 104 and 65K distinct predicates, respectively. Sufficiently large number of predicates (> 100) makes these datasets well suited for benchmarking of path queries.

At the time of this paper, we could not find any available benchmarks for SPARQL property-path queries. We therefore generate path queries based on data patterns we identified in real-world graphs. The goal of these experiments is to verify the gains offered by WAVEGUIDE optimizations, and show that they correspond to our cost framework (§4.1) and analysis (§4.4).

5.2 The Optimizations

Threading. We benchmark the threading optimization by executing a query of the following template:

$$?x \ p/p_1+/p_2+ \ ?y \qquad (\mathfrak{Q}_5)$$

over the YAGO2s dataset, with "p", "p_1" and "p_2" as variable predicates. We chose this template because it contains the concatenation of two transitive closures, which makes it difficult to predict the average length of the paths in the answer.

We group p candidates in two sets: the first (queries **L1**–**L35**) having an $\mathcal{M}$ value greater than 10; and the second (queries **L36**–**L55**) having an $\mathcal{M}$ value less than 1. Each of the queries is executed with three different plans: D, a direct evaluation with a single wavefront with no threading; T_1 threads on shared path (p_1+/p_2+); and T_2 threads on (p_2+) to illustrate the effect of potentially shorter $\mathcal{L}$ than in T_1. Given p, predicates p_1 and p_2 are chosen such that the running time of $\mathfrak{Q}_5$ is between 0.5 and 5 minutes.

The relative running times for queries **L1**–**L55** executed with plans D (the baseline), T_1, and T_2 are presented in Fig. 13. As anticipated, the evaluation of queries in the first group is significantly (up to 75%) faster threaded than direct, and with T_1 being faster than T_2. This can be attributed to the fact that the length of the shared path $\mathcal{L}$ is shorter in T_2 due to a "later" threading split in the query expression. Also as anticipated, queries in the second group show bad results for T_1. Indeed, picking a predicate with $\mathcal{M} < 1$ for a threading split will generally be bad due to few shared paths. Further, some queries (**L50**, **L51**) are evaluated significantly more slowly (up to 23 times!) when threaded in T_2. This illustrates the importance of choosing the correct threading split.

Loop Caching. We benchmark the loop-caching optimization by executing a collection of queries of the simple template $Q_{(ab)+} = (x, (ab)+, y)$ ($\mathfrak{Q}_4$) with two WPs P_{nc} and

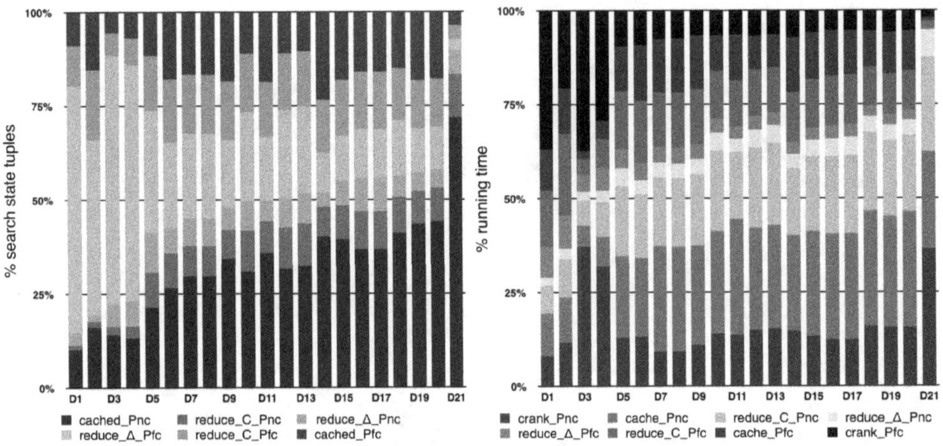

(a) Edge walks vs. runtime in plans w/ & w/o loop caching in DBPedia.

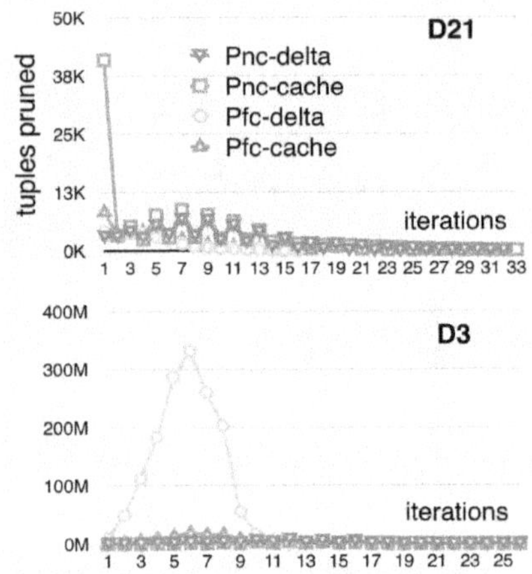

(b) Tuples pruned in P_{fc} vs. P_{nc}.

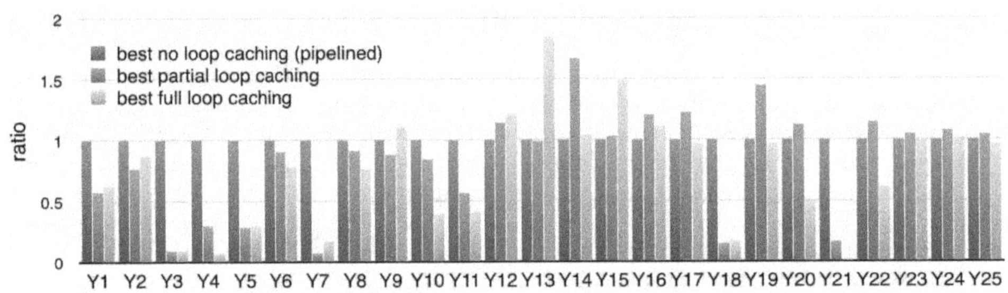

(c) Best pipelined, partially and fully cached plans for queries over YAGO2s.

Figure 14: Benchmarking Loop Caching.

P_{fc}, which specify executions of $Q_{(ab)+}$ with no loop caching and with full loop caching, respectively.

Values for a and b were chosen by iterative pruning of predicates appearing in the DBPedia dataset. First, we excluded predicates with very high (more than 25M) and low (less than 75K) cardinalities, to keep query running times reasonable. Then, we ran query $Q_{abab} = (x, (abab), y)$ and recorded those (a, b) predicate pairs for which the result of Q_{abab} was not empty. DBPedia had 1171 such pairs, which indicates a high number of $(ab)+$ paths in this dataset. For each of these pairs, we ran the full closure query $Q_{(ab)+}$ to obtain its *expansion ratio*,

$$r_{\text{exp}} = \frac{|Q_{(ab)+}|}{|Q_{ab}|} \qquad (\mathcal{E}_2)$$

where $|Q|$ denotes the cardinality of a query result.

Recall that both P_{nc} and P_{fc} initially evaluate (ab) paths in the same way, while the rest of the closure $(ab)+$ is computed differently. Hence, in order to show the differences between these plans, we chose predicate pairs with $r_{\text{exp}} > 2$, so that the computation of the rest of the closure constitutes at least 50% of the plan execution time. We identified 21 such queries by analyzing graph patterns in DBPedia.

We evaluated each one of these queries with P_{nc} and P_{fc} plans and recorded the *running time*, *edge walks* and *pruning statistics*. Due to widely varying absolute values for these statistics across queries, we present their relative percentage breakdowns in Fig. 14a, as follows. Each query is represented by a multi-colored bar, which shows the percentage breakdown of statistics values between P_{nc} and P_{fc} executions. In this way, we present edge walks (in the left chart) and running-time execution (in the right chart). We enumerate the queries from **D1** to **D21** by sorting ascending with respect to the percentage of edge walks performed in the P_{nc} execution relative to the P_{fc} execution. Hence, in query **D1**, the P_{nc} execution resulted in significantly fewer edge walks relative to P_{fc} execution, with the opposite true for query **D21**. For edge walks, we perform a further breakdown for each query of the total number of edge walks into the number of tuples which were cached, were reduced against the cache, or were reduced against the delta. This breakdown is represented by different shades of the color associated with P_{nc} or P_{fc} executions, respectively. Similarly, for each query, we break down its running time into total times of crank, cache, reduce^C and reduce$^\Delta$ steps to illustrate the costs of each in relation to the framework presented in §4.1.

Our first observation is that, in general, the loop caching optimization can both significantly increase *or* decrease the total number of edge walks performed by the search. In our benchmark, loop caching resulted in fewer edge walks in 10 queries, with almost an order of magnitude reduction, in the best case. On the other hand, in 11 queries, loop caching resulted in more edge walks, with a more than 5X increase, in the worst case.

Our second observation is that the real cost of WAVEGUIDE search corresponds to the approximations of costs f_1–f_4 given in §4.1. Consider queries **D1**–**D11** in which loop caching resulted in a higher total number of edge walks. However, the majority of these queries still ran faster than their pipelined counterparts due to the fact that the bulk of edge walks produced duplicate tuples, which were removed by reduce$^\Delta$. Indeed, such in-memory removals are

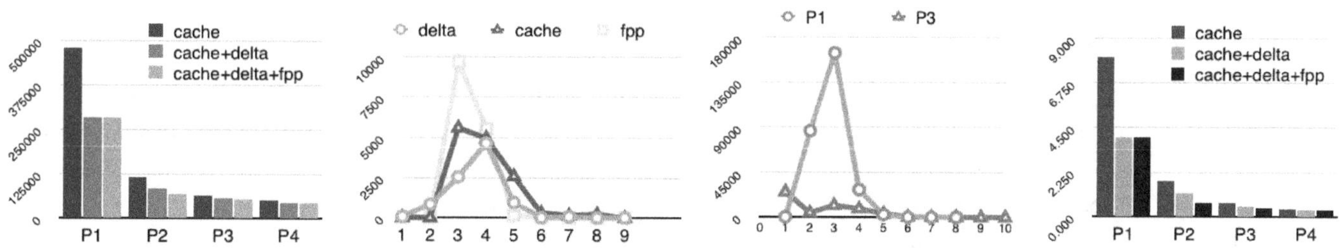

a) Search size for different plans and pruning types
b) Redundancy pruning (by type) over iterations of P2
c) Delta sizes over iterations
d) Total query time

Figure 15: Effect of plans on query evaluation.

inexpensive according to f_2. Further, we observe that expensive (f_1,f_3 and f_4) disk-based operations crank, reduce^C and cache which require probing or maintaining a tree index contribute significantly to the overall cost.

Finally, we study the effect of lensing by analyzing the degree of delta and cache pruning. Fig. 14b plots pruning over iterations for the queries which exhibit lensing: **D3** and **D21**. Query **D3** has $\mathcal{M}(G, a) = 10.58$ and $\mathcal{M}(G, b) = 0.33$, which suggests lensing with focal point on the concatenation a/b. As discussed in §4.4, this can significantly increase amount of pruning for loop caching, which is indeed what we observe. On the other hand, **D21** has $\mathcal{M}(G, a) = 0.07$ and $\mathcal{M}(G, b) = 5.34$, which suggests lensing with focal point on the concatenation b/a. This lensing benefits loop caching by decreasing the amount of pruning over iterations, which is what we observe.

Partial Loop Caching. In previous section we have shown experimentally that plans from both FA and α-RA spaces need to be considered in query evaluation. In this section, we aim to show that plans which are not in FA nor in α-RA often also require consideration.

We design a collection of queries over YAGO2s dataset which are based on the template:

$$?x\ (a/b/c)+\ ?y \qquad (\mathcal{Q}_6)$$

We pick values for a, b and c by iterative pruning of predicates appearing in the YAGO2s dataset similar to the process discussed in §5.2. As a result, we came up with 25 queries **Y1**–**Y25** which follow template $\mathcal{Q}_6$.

The results of the benchmark are presented on Fig.14c. We group plans into three categories: no loop caching (pipelined), partial loop caching and full loop caching. For each category we pick a best plan as judged by a total number of edge walks performed. Due to wide differences in absolute values, we present the best pipelined plan as a baseline and present the other two groups in relation to it.

As expected, pipelined plans are often not the best choice in evaluation of open-ended queries like $\mathcal{Q}_6$. Here, pipelined plans win for five out of 25 queries. This is explained by the strict evaluation order imposed by such plans. For a query like $\mathcal{Q}_6$, there are only two legal pipelined plans, direct and inverse pipelines. Hence, often these plans lose to other plans which allow more flexibility in evaluation order. Fully loop cached plans, which allow the most flexibility in evaluation order (we generate 20 such plans for $\mathcal{Q}_6$), are fastest in 11 queries out of 25, sometimes by an order of magnitude. Finally, in nine queries out of 25, partially loop cached plans are the fastest, sometimes by a large margin. Hence, these plans, which are exclusive to WAVEGUIDE, need to be considered as well.

Combined Optimizations. We illustrate the impact of combining WAVEGUIDE optimizations over the example query

$$?p\ :marriedTo/:diedIn/:locatedIn+/:dealsWith+\ USA \qquad (\mathcal{Q}_7)$$

over the YAGO2s dataset. We instantiate p as follows.
P_1: single inverse wavefront USA $\rightarrow$?p.
P_2: single direct wavefront ?p $\rightarrow$ USA.
P_3: two wavefronts
?p $\rightarrow$:locatedIn+/:dealsWith+ $\leftarrow$ USA.
P_4: P_2 but with a threaded sub-path
:locatedIn+/:dealsWith+ USA.

Fig. 15a shows the effect of wavefront choice on search cardinality. Note the order of magnitude difference between the best, P_4, versus the worst, P_1. The three types of redundancy pruning—cache, delta, and fpp—are illustrated for each plan. Fig. 15b plots search size across iterations for P_2 with pruning; over 40% of tuples are pruned! Fig. 15c plots delta sizes over iterations for P_1 and P_3. Note how the selective search of P_3 is better behaved than the rapid expansion of P_1. In Fig. 15d, the total execution time for each plan is presented. This demonstrates the significant improvement in performance achievable by careful design of the plan.

5.3 Comparison with Other Systems

We design a microbenchmark to analyze the performance of the WAVEGUIDE prototype in comparison with two RDF stores: VIRTUOSO [12] and JENA TDB [8]. Both VIRTUOSO and JENA TDB are well known and widely used today to store and query RDF data. VIRTUOSO is an example of an RDF store which is backed by a relational database, which makes it similar to WAVEGUIDE prototype. On the other hand, JENA TDB is a native solution developed specifically to handle graph data.

We design three experiments which aim to benchmark two main aspects of property path evaluation: 1) transitive closure computation and 2) query planning.

Transitive Closure. Computation of transitive closure is one of the main operations which are encountered during evaluation of property paths. Hence, it is important to handle this operation efficiently in order to be able to answer property path queries quickly. Our benchmark consists of a number of realistic simple transitive closure queries over YAGO2s dataset which follow the template:

$$?entity\ :locatedIn+\ \mathit{place} \qquad (\mathcal{Q}_8)$$

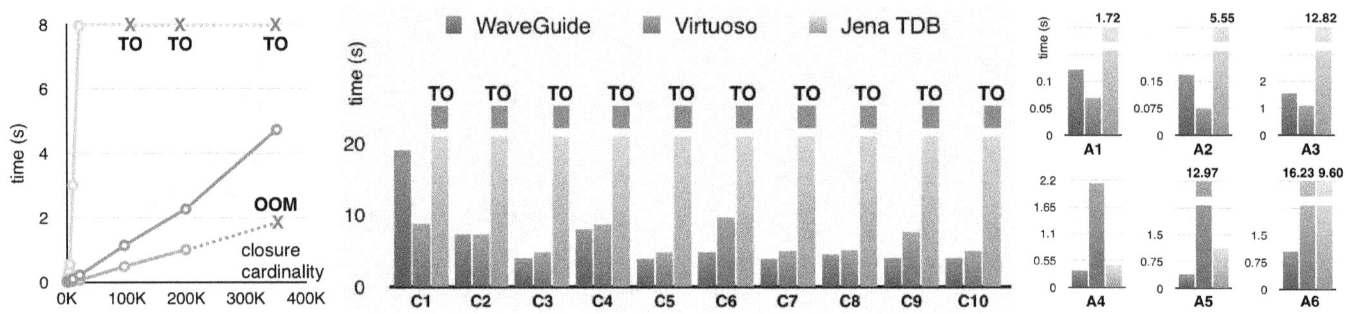

(a) Transitive closure. (b) Analytical query planning. (c) More complex queries.

Figure 16: Benchmarking vs. state of the art.

Here, $\mathfrak{Q}_8$ finds all entities transitively located in a certain place, which is given as a query constant. By varying this constant, we design transitive closure queries with increasing answer cardinalities, which allow us to benchmark the efficiency of transitive closure computation in a given system.

The benchmark results are presented on Fig.16a. VIRTUOSO has the fastest transitive closure computation engine. This is expected as VIRTUOSO is based on high-performance relational database written in C. Moreover, all its transitive closure computations are performed completely in main memory without spilling to disk. However, this can be a serious performance bottleneck for large cardinality property path queries, where VIRTUOSO runs out of memory (**OOM**). WAVEGUIDE prototype is roughly two times slower than VIRTUOSO. While our prototype is also based on a high-performance relational database, POSTGRESQL, we utilize stored procedures, which are less efficient than inline SQL or the in-memory computations used by VIRTUOSO. Lastly, JENA TDB did not scale well for transitive closures, timing out (**TO**) on all but the smallest cardinality queries.

Query Planning. This experiment aims to highlight the importance of planning in evaluation of property path queries. We design a number of queries over YAGO2s dataset which are based on the following template:

```
select distinct ?x ?y {                       (Q9)
        ?x :locatedIn+ place .          [Q8]
        ?x (a/b/c)+ ?y . }              [Q6]
```

Observe that $\mathfrak{Q}_9$ is a conjunction of templates $\mathfrak{Q}_8$ and $\mathfrak{Q}_6$. We could not use just $\mathfrak{Q}_6$ because of VIRTUOSO's limitation requiring property path queries to be bound on at least one variable. In $\mathfrak{Q}_9$, that binding is done by $\mathfrak{Q}_8$.

First, we set *place* in $\mathfrak{Q}_8$ to :Earth, to simulate an *analytical* workload by placing a *loose* binding on ?x in property path $\mathfrak{Q}_6$. Second, we set values of *a*, *b* and *c* to those used in queries **Y1–Y10** in §5.2 to produce queries **C1–C10**. The benchmark results are presented in Fig.16b. We observe that JENA TDB did not finish in the allotted time frame (timed out, TO) for any of the queries. We attribute this to JENA TDB's limited scalability of transitive closure computations. On the other hand, despite having a faster transitive closure computation engine, VIRTUOSO is slower than WAVEGUIDE in many of the queries, sometimes significantly. We attribute this to the limited plan space considered by VIRTUOSO, which requires transitive queries to be bound by one of the variables. VIRTUOSO was evaluating $\mathfrak{Q}_8$ first, and then *pipelining* the results to $\mathfrak{Q}_6$. As discussed in §5.2, such pipelined plans often do not perform well for loosely bound queries.

Query Planning vs. Transitive Closure. The goal of our third experiment is to understand the capacity in which the efficiency of transitive closure and query planning affect query evaluation. We design a set of six real-world queries over YAGO2s dataset which we split into two groups. Queries in the first group (**A1**–**A3**) are simple as they contain one or two non-transitive and one transitive predicate. Therefore, efficient transitive closure computation plays a bigger role than query planning for this group. Queries in the second group are more complex as they either contain two or more transitive (**A5**, **A6**) or a single transitive and three non-transitive predicates (**A4**). For these, a good evaluation plan is more important.

The benchmark results are presented in Fig. 16c. Due to the simplicity of the queries in the first group, all three engines used identical plans to evaluate them. VIRTUOSO, with the fastest transitive closure, had the lowest evaluation time. For queries in the second group, WAVEGUIDE was the fastest engine for all of the queries. The slight increase in query complexity from single (**A4**) to two or more transitive predicates (**A5**, **A6**) allowed WAVEGUIDE to gain a significant advantage over the two other systems. This shows the importance of the richer plan space considered by WAVEGUIDE.

6. CONCLUSIONS

We have devised a rich domain of evaluation plans for property-path queries (RPQs) in SPARQL, and have shown it extends significantly over the state of the art. WAVEGUIDE's plans, which encompasses powerful optimization techniques, offer a solid step towards building a full-fledged, cost-based query optimizer for SPARQL with property paths. Our next steps in this project are to construct an *enumerator* that can enumerate efficiently through the WP space for a given query and to devise a *cost estimator* for WPs so the better plans can be identified. For the cost estimator, we need to determine an array of graph *statistics* that can be evaluated offline that enable estimation that is good enough to distinguish between good and bad plans.

The rising prominence of graph data raises many challenges. As the community rose in the past to accomplish the "impossible" for relational data, for semi-structured, and for unstructured search, we too will meet these new challenges.

7. REFERENCES

[1] S. Abiteboul, R. Hull, and V. Vianu. *Foundations of databases*, volume 8. Addison-Wesley, 1995.

[2] S. Abiteboul, D. Quass, J. McHugh, J. Widom, and J. L. Wiener. The Lorel query language for semistructured data. *International Journal on Digital Libraries*, 1(1):68–88, 1997.

[3] R. Agrawal. Alpha: An extension of relational algebra to express a class of recursive queries. *Software Engineering, IEEE Transactions on*, 14(7):879–885, 1988.

[4] P. Barcelo, L. Libkin, A. W. Lin, and P. T. Wood. Expressive languages for path queries over graph-structured data. *Transactions on Database Systems*, 37(4):31, 2012.

[5] M. Bojanczyk. Automata for data words and data trees. In *RTA*, pages 1–4, 2010.

[6] P. Buneman, S. Davidson, G. Hillebrand, and D. Suciu. A query language and optimization techniques for unstructured data. *SIGMOD Record*, 25(2):505–516, 1996.

[7] D. Calvanese, G. De Giacomo, M. Lenzerini, and M. Y. Vardi. Rewriting of regular expressions and regular path queries. In *Proceedings of the Symposium on Principles of Database Systems*, pages 194–204. ACM, 1999.

[8] J. J. Carroll, I. Dickinson, C. Dollin, D. Reynolds, A. Seaborne, and K. Wilkinson. Jena: implementing the semantic web recommendations. In *Proceedings of the 13th international World Wide Web conference on Alternate track papers & posters*, pages 74–83. ACM, 2004.

[9] M. P. Consens, A. O. Mendelzon, D. Vista, and P. T. Wood. Constant propagation versus join reordering in datalog. In *Rules in Database Systems*, pages 245–259. Springer, 1995.

[10] The DBpedia knowledge base. http://dbpedia.org/.

[11] S. Dey, V. Cuevas-Vicenttín, S. Köhler, E. Gribkoff, M. Wang, and B. Ludäscher. On implementing provenance-aware regular path queries with relational query engines. In *Proceedings of the Joint EDBT/ICDT 2013 Workshops*, pages 214–223. ACM, 2013.

[12] O. Erling and I. Mikhailov. Virtuoso: RDF Support in Native RDBMS. *Semantic Web Information Management*, 1:501, 2010.

[13] D. Florescu, A. Y. Levy, and A. O. Mendelzon. Database techniques for the world-wide web: A survey. *SIGMOD Record*, 27(3):59–74, 1998.

[14] S. Harris and A. Seaborne. SPARQL 1.1 query language. W3C working draft. http://www.w3.org/TR/sparql11-query/, November 2012.

[15] K. J. Kochut and M. Janik. Sparqler: Extended sparql for semantic association discovery. In *The Semantic Web: Research and Applications*, pages 145–159. Springer, 2007.

[16] A. Koschmieder and U. Leser. Regular path queries on large graphs. In *Scientific and Statistical Database Management*, pages 177–194. Springer Berlin Heidelberg, 2012.

[17] K. Losemann and W. Martens. The complexity of evaluating path expressions in SPARQL. In *Proceedings of the 31st symposium on Principles of Database Systems*, pages 101–112. ACM, 2012.

[18] A. Mendelzon and P. Wood. Finding regular simple paths in graph databases. *SIAM Journal on Computing*, 24(6):1235–1258, 1995.

[19] J. Pérez, M. Arenas, and C. Gutierrez. nSPARQL: A navigational language for rdf. *Web Semantics: Science, Services and Agents on the World Wide Web*, 8(4):255–270, 2010.

[20] E. Prud'Hommeaux, A. Seaborne, et al. SPARQL query language for RDF. *W3C Recommendation*, 15, 2008.

[21] W3C: Resource Description Framework (RDF). http://www.w3.org/TR/rdf-concepts/, 2004.

[22] L. Segoufin. Automata and logics for words and trees over an infinite alphabet. In *Computer Science Logic*, pages 41–57. Springer, 2006.

[23] L. Segoufin. Static analysis of XML processing with data values. *ACM Sigmod Record*, 36(1):31–38, 2007.

[24] YAGO2s: A high-quality knowledge base. http://yago-knowledge.org/resource/. Max Planck Institut Informatik.

[25] N. Yakovets, P. Godfrey, and J. Gryz. Evaluation of SPARQL property paths via recursive SQL. In L. Bravo and M. Lenzerini, editors, *AMW*, volume 1087 of *CEUR Workshop Proceedings*. CEUR-WS.org, May 2013.

[26] N. Yakovets, P. Godfrey, and J. Gryz. WAVEGUIDE: evaluating SPARQL property path queries. In *Proceedings of the 18th International Conference on Extending Database Technology, EDBT 2015, Brussels, Belgium, March 23-27, 2015.*, pages 525–528, 2015.

[27] H. Zauner, B. Linse, T. Furche, and F. Bry. A RPL through RDF: expressive navigation in RDF graphs. In *Web Reasoning and Rule Systems*, pages 251–257. Springer, 2010.

APPENDIX

A. SYSTEM SETUP

A.1 Architecture

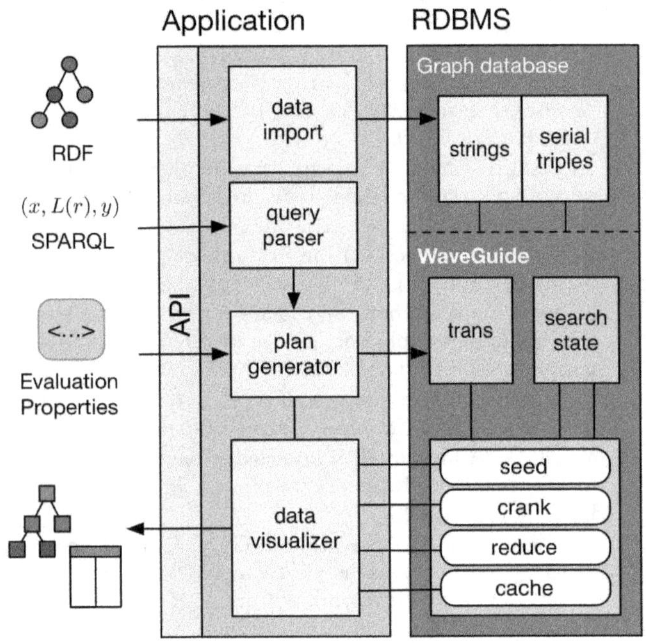

Figure 17: Overview of the prototype system.

A.2 Hardware

Our benchmark was executed on a host 2xXeon E5-2640v2 CPU server with 10x7200RPM HDDs running CentOS 6. PostgreSQL, OpenLink Virtuoso and Jena TDB were executed in their own virtual machines which were given 4 CPU cores, 4GB of RAM and 1TB of HDD space.

A.3 Software

WAVEGUIDE prototype planner was implemented in Java 1.8. WAVEGUIDE database execution engine was based on PostgreSQL 9.3. VIRTUOSO was built against open source distribution of version 07.20.3215-pthreads (latest at the time of submission of this paper) which is maintained by OpenLink on GitHub. Similarly, we obtained the latest version (3.0.1) of JENA TDB for our tests. Both DBPedia and YAGO2s were fully indexed on all systems to ensure indexed access paths for all queries used in benchmarks. In the transitive closure experiments, we limited the amount of RAM available to each system to 100MB. In VIRTUOSO, we have modified the source code to change the default transitive memory limit from 1GB to 100MB. This limit was raised to 4GB in the rest of the experiments, since all available memory in the VM (4GB) was allowed to be used for all systems. OOM abbreviation means the system ran out of allocated memory while executing a given query. For all queries in §5.3, a timeout (TO) was set to 10 minutes.

B. QUERIES

B.1 Threading

L	p	p_1	p_2
1	byTransport	rdf:type	owl:disjointWith
2	happenedIn	hasCapital	created
3	happenedIn	hasCapital	owns
4	happenedIn	hasCapital	rdf:type
5	happenedIn	hasCapital	participatedIn
6	happenedIn	dealsWith	rdf:type
7	happenedIn	dealsWith	hasCapital
8	happenedIn	rdf:type	owl:disjointWith
9	hasWonPrize	rdf:type	owl:disjointWith
10	hasWordnetDomain	rdf:type	owl:disjointWith
11	isCitizenOf	hasCapital	created
12	isCitizenOf	hasCapital	owns
13	isCitizenOf	hasCapital	rdf:type
14	isCitizenOf	hasCapital	participatedIn
15	isCitizenOf	dealsWith	rdf:type
16	isCitizenOf	dealsWith	hasCapital
17	isCitizenOf	rdf:type	owl:disjointWith
18	isLocatedIn	hasCapital	created
19	isLocatedIn	hasCapital	owns
20	isLocatedIn	hasCapital	rdf:type
21	isLocatedIn	dealsWith	hasCapital
22	isLocatedIn	rdf:type	owl:disjointWith
23	isPoliticianOf	hasCapital	created
24	isPoliticianOf	hasCapital	owns
25	isPoliticianOf	hasCapital	rdf:type
26	isPoliticianOf	hasCapital	participatedIn
27	isPoliticianOf	rdf:type	owl:disjointWith
28	rdfs:subClassOf	rdf:type	owl:disjointWith
29	wasBornIn	hasCapital	created
30	wasBornIn	hasCapital	owns
31	wasBornIn	hasCapital	rdf:type
32	wasBornIn	hasCapital	participatedIn
33	wasBornIn	dealsWith	rdf:type
34	wasBornIn	dealsWith	hasCapital
35	wasBornIn	rdf:type	owl:disjointWith
36	created	hasChild	isMarriedTo
37	created	influences	isMarriedTo
38	created	influences	hasChild
39	created	isMarriedTo	hasChild
40	hasChild	influences	isMarriedTo
41	hasChild	influences	hasChild
42	hasChild	isMarriedTo	hasChild
43	hasChild	hasChild	isMarriedTo
44	influences	hasChild	isMarriedTo
45	influences	isMarriedTo	hasChild
46	influences	influences	isMarriedTo
47	influences	influences	hasChild
48	isKnownFor	hasChild	isMarriedTo
49	isKnownFor	isMarriedTo	hasChild
50	isKnownFor	influences	isMarriedTo
51	isKnownFor	influences	hasChild
52	isMarriedTo	influences	isMarriedTo
53	isMarriedTo	influences	hasChild
54	isMarriedTo	hasChild	isMarriedTo
55	isMarriedTo	isMarriedTo	hasChild

B.2 Loop Caching

D	a	b
1	formerTeam	name
2	region	candidate
3	clubs	currentMember
4	starring	title
5	successor	predecessor
6	successor	before
7	associatedMusicalArtist	currentMembers

Loop Caching (continued)

D	a	b
8	associatedBand	currentMembers
9	associatedActs	currentMembers
10	after	predecessor
11	successor	successor
12	before	successor
13	before	successor
14	successor	after
15	currentMembers	associatedBand
16	before	predecessor
17	after	successor
18	imageCaption	ordo
19	imageCaption	order
20	label	subdivisionName
21	candidate	region

B.3 Partial Loop Caching

Y/C	a	b	c
1	isLocatedIn	hasCapital	owns
2	isConnectedTo	isLocatedIn	owns
3	dealsWith	participatedIn	isLocatedIn
4	isLocatedIn	owns	created
5	participatedIn	isLocatedIn	dealsWith
6	hasCapital	isLocatedIn	dealsWith
7	happenedIn	hasCapital	participatedIn
8	owns	isConnectedTo	isLocatedIn
9	dealsWith	hasCapital	isLocatedIn
10	participatedIn	happenedIn	hasCapital
Y	a	b	c
11	owns	isLocatedIn	dealsWith
12	hasCapital	participatedIn	happenedIn
13	isLeaderOf	dealsWith	participatedIn
14	dealsWith	owns	isLocatedIn
15	created	isLocatedIn	owns
16	hasCapital	owns	isLocatedIn
17	owns	isLocatedIn	hasCapital
18	hasAcademicAdvisor	isInterestedIn	influences
19	isInterestedIn	influences	hasAcademicAdvisor
20	isMarriedTo	hasChild	influences
21	influences	hasAcademicAdvisor	isInterestedIn
22	isMarriedTo	influences	hasChild
23	hasChild	influences	isMarriedTo
24	influences	isMarriedTo	hasChild
25	owns	created	isLocatedIn

B.4 State of the art Planning

A	query
1	select distinct ?p {?p :diedIn/:isLocatedIn+ :France .}
2	select distinct ?p {?p :wasBornIn/:isLocatedIn+ :France .}
3	select distinct ?p {?p :wasBornIn/:isLocatedIn+/:type :Europe .}
4	select distinct ?p {?p :isMarriedTo/:diedIn/:isLocatedIn+/dealsWith :United_States .}
5	select distinct ?p {?p :isMarriedTo/:diedIn/:isLocatedIn+/:dealsWith/:isLocatedIn+ :Earth .}
6	select distinct ?p {?p :livesIn/(owl:sameAs*/:locatedIn)+/owl:sameAs*/:dealsWith/ (owl:sameAs*/:locatedIn)+/owl:sameAs* :Earth .}

Robust Query Processing in Co-Processor-accelerated Databases

Sebastian Breß[*]
German Research Center for Artificial Intelligence
Germany
sebastian.bress@dfki.de

Henning Funke
TU Dortmund University
Germany
henning.funke@tu-dortmund.de

Jens Teubner
TU Dortmund University
Germany
jens.teubner@cs.tu-dortmund.de

ABSTRACT

Technology limitations are making the use of *heterogeneous computing devices* much more than an academic curiosity. In fact, the use of such devices is widely acknowledged to be the only promising way to achieve application-speedups that users urgently need and expect. However, building a robust and efficient query engine for heterogeneous co-processor environments is still a significant challenge.

In this paper, we identify two effects that limit performance in case co-processor resources become scarce. *Cache thrashing* occurs when the working set of queries does not fit into the co-processor's data cache, resulting in performance degradations up to a factor of 24. *Heap contention* occurs when multiple operators run in parallel on a co-processor and when their accumulated memory footprint exceeds the main memory capacity of the co-processor, slowing down query execution by up to a factor of six.

We propose solutions for both effects. *Data-driven operator placement* avoids data movements when they might be harmful; *query chopping* limits co-processor memory usage and thus avoids contention. The combined approach—*data-driven query chopping*—achieves robust and scalable performance on co-processors. We validate our proposal with our open-source GPU-accelerated database engine CoGaDB and the popular star schema and TPC-H benchmarks.

1. INTRODUCTION

Modern processors hit the *power wall*, which forces vendors to optimize a processor's performance within a certain energy budget [6]. As a consequence, processor manufactures started to specialize processors. Thus, experts predict that future machines will consist of a set of heterogeneous processors, where each processor is optimized for a certain application scenario [6]. This trend has already become commodity, e.g., in the form of graphics processors (GPUs), many integrated cores architectures (MICs), or field-programmable gate arrays (FPGAs). Not taking advantage of them for query processing means to leave available resources unused.

[*]Work done when author was working at TU Dortmund.

SIGMOD'16, June 26-July 01, 2016, San Francisco, CA, USA

DOI: http://dx.doi.org/10.1145/2882903.2882936

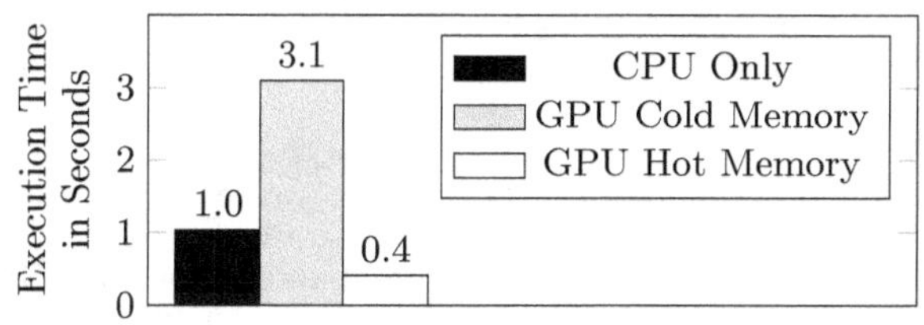

Figure 1: Impact of different query execution strategies on performance of a star schema benchmark query (Q3.3) on a database of scale factor 20. Using a GPU slows the system down in case input data is not cached on the GPU.

The potential of heterogeneous systems is often limited by the capacity of the communication channel between the co-processor and its host system [11]. We illustrate this problem in Figure 1 for a GPU-based co-processor, which we use as a poster child in the context of this work.

We obtained this figure by executing Query 3.3 from the Star Schema Benchmark *(a)* on a commodity CPU; *(b)* using a GPU accelerator, assuming a *cold-cache* scenario (i.e., all data has to be transferred to the GPU before an operator starts, which is very likely for ad-hoc queries); and *(c)* using the GPU accelerator in a *hot-cache* setting (more details on our experimentation platform follow later in the text). Clearly, while a GPU co-processor has the potential to speed up query execution by a factor of 2.5 (consistent with earlier results on GPU-accelerated query processing [13]), data transfer costs turn the situation into a performance degradation by more than a factor of three.

Techniques for co-processor acceleration typically make two assumptions:

1. The input data is cached on the co-processor and the working set fits into the co-processor memory.
2. Concurrent queries do not access the co-processor simultaneously.

Co-processors can slow down query processing significantly if these assumptions are violated, which is especially likely for ad-hoc queries. The goal of this paper is to understand *why* performance degrades under realistic conditions and *how* we can automatically detect when co-processors will slow down the DBMS (e.g., for many ad-hoc queries) and when co-processors will improve performance (e.g., for re-occuring or ad-hoc queries accessing the data cached on the co-processor).

In this work, we identify two problems: *cache thrashing* and *heap contention*. *Cache thrashing* occurs if the working set of the DBMS does not fit into the memory of a co-processor (assumption 1 violated), causing expensive evictions and re-caching. *Heap contention* is the situation where too many operators use the co-processor in parallel (assumption 2 violated), so their combined heap memory demand exceeds the device's memory capacity.

We show how existing techniques from other domains can mitigate the problem and thus achieve robust query processing in heterogeneous systems. First, we *place data before query execution*, according to the workload pattern; we assign operators only to (co-)processors where necessary data is already cached, thus avoiding the cache thrashing problem. Second, we defer *operator placement* to the query execution time, so we can dynamically react to faults. This way, we can react to out-of-memory situations and limit heap space usage to avoid heap contention. Third, we limit the number of parallel running operators on a co-processor to reduce the likelihood that *heap contention* occurs. The main benefit of our approaches lies in optimizing the worst-case execution time and thus, make it feasible to use co-processors in practice.

To validate the effect of the strategies, we provide a detailed experimental evaluation based on our open-source database engine *CoGaDB*[1]. CoGaDB is a from-scratch implementation of a column-oriented in-memory database engine, with GPU support from the ground.

The remainder of the paper is structured as follows. In Section 2, we present the state of the art on co-processing in databases. Then, we discuss our techniques: data-driven operator placement in Section 3, run-time placement in Section 4, and the query chopping technique in Section 5. Then, we present our extensive experimental evaluation in Section 6. Finally, we present related work in Section 7 and conclude in Section 8.

2. STATE OF THE ART

In this section, we provide a brief overview of the basics of co-processors, their resource limitations, the operator placement problem, and the evaluation system CoGaDB.

2.1 Co-Processors

Compared to CPUs, today's co-processors are specialized processors spending more chip space to light-weighted cores than on control logic such as branch prediction and pipelining [34]. In order to feed these cores, co-processors need high-bandwidth memory, which in turn means that the total memory capacity is relatively small (up to 16 GBs for high end GPUs or Xeon Phis) to achieve reasonable monetary costs. Since co-processors are separate processors, they are usually connected to the CPU by the PCIe bus, which often ends up being the bottleneck in CPU/co-processor systems [11].

A common optimization is to use part of the co-processor memory as cache, which can reduce the data volume that needs to be transferred to the co-processor. The remaining part of the co-processor's memory is used as heap for intermediate data structures and results. Naturally, the caching strategy cannot avoid the cost of moving results back from the co-processor to the host system.

2.2 Resource Limitations

The limited resource capacity of co-processors poses a major problem for database operators. For instance, the probability that an operator runs out of memory on a co-processor is significantly higher compared to a CPU operator. In case memory becomes scarce, operators will fail resource allocations and have to abort and clean up.

[1]cogadb.cs.tu-dortmund.de/wordpress/download

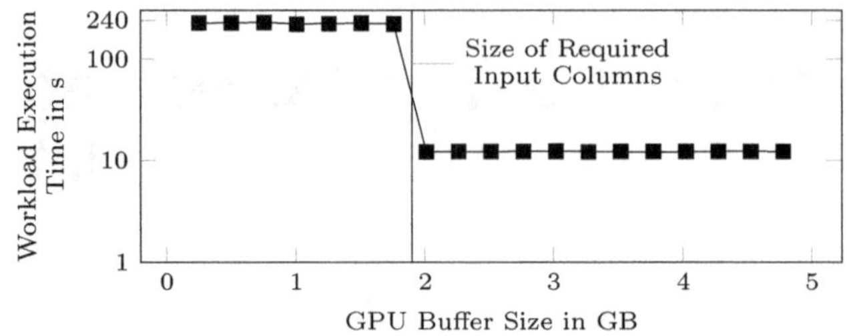

Figure 2: Execution time of selection workload. The performance degrades by a factor of 24 if not all input columns fit into the cache.

To be practically useful, database engines must have a mechanism to deal with such fault situations. Previous work [35] did so by aborting and re-starting the entire query. However, such simplistic solutions will hardly meet user expectations in realistic settings. As the use of GPU acceleration proliferates (and more users share the co-processor), the probability for resource contention sharply increases, resulting in starvation and other problems.

CoGaDB offers a more sophisticated mechanism for fault handling. In case of resource exhaustion, the system will have to re-start only the single failed operator. This way, we avoid losing already computed results and continue query processing immediately.

2.3 Query Processing

Most approaches for co-processor acceleration assume that first, the input data fits into the co-processor cache and second, no concurrent queries access the co-processor simultaneously. Next, we show the performance penalties that occur if these assumptions are not met, which is more the norm than the exception.

Cache Thrashing Figure 2 shows the query execution time of a workload of selection operators on the GPU with varying GPU buffer size. The workload consists of eight selections, which filter on eight different columns. Furthermore, the selections are executed interleaved, a common scenario in databases where different queries access different data. As input data, we chose the fact table of the star schema benchmark (scale factor 10). We provide the detailed workload in Section B.1. All required input columns have a total size of 1.9 GB. In the case that not all input columns fit into the co-processor's data cache, we observe a performance degradation of a factor of 24 due to *cache thrashing*. Caches commonly use a least-recently-used strategy, a least-frequently-used strategy or variants of the two strategies. For both strategies, at least one column needs to be evicted from the cache if the cache size is smaller than the accumulated memory footprint of required input columns (1.9 GB). Evicting the least recently used column practically makes the cache useless in case the memory footprint exceeds the cache size. This is because the evicted columns will be accessed by the next query of the workload (cf. Appendix B.1), which results in a copy operation.

Heap Contention Even if we solve the cache thrashing problem, we run into a similar effect in case we execute operators in parallel. We illustrate the problem with a selection workload on a GPU with increasing number of parallel users. The selection queries require four different operators to be executed consecutively to compute the result. All selections filter the same input columns to avoid the cache-trashing effect. The workload is fixed and consists of 100 queries,

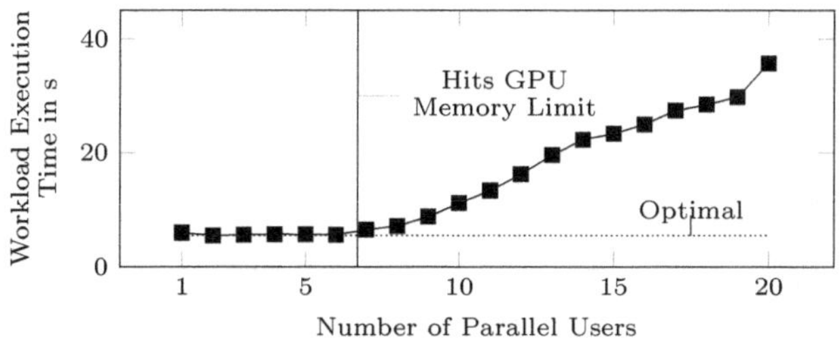

Figure 3: Execution time of a selection workload. With increasing parallelism, more operators allocate memory on the GPU, which leads to performance degradation when memory capacity is exceeded.

but we increase the number of parallel user sessions that execute the workload. We discuss the detailed workload in Appendix B.2.

Since all workloads contain the same amount of work, an ideal system could execute all workloads in the same time. Figure 3 shows the actual effect on our execution platform. Clearly visible is a performance degradation of up to factor six compared to a single user execution.

What we observe here is that the intermediate data structures of the parallel running operators exceed the co-processor's memory when seven or more users use the graphics processor concurrently (assumption 2 violated), which causes operators to run out of memory.

Once this happens, operator execution will be aborted on the GPU and moved to another processor instead, which increases the IO on the bus and degrades performance. We call this effect *heap contention.*

It is clearly visible that co-processors can slow down database query processing significantly, if we have no additional mechanism. To achieve robust query processing, we need to ensure that co-processors will never slow down the DBMS and that co-processors improve performance with increasing fraction of the working set that fits into their memory.

2.4 Operator Placement

All co-processor-accelerated database systems either process all queries on the co-processor (e.g., GPUDB [37], Multi-Qx-GPU [35], and Red Fox [36]), or try to balance the processing tasks between processors (e.g., CoGaDB, GPUQP [13], MapD [24]) by performing *operator placement* (i.e., a complete query plan is analyzed and each operator is assigned to a processor). Both strategies use the same principles: First, they create a query plan that is fixed during query execution. Second, the execution engine is responsible to transfer data to the processors where the operators are executed. Since data movement can be very expensive, this strategy is combined with data caching on co-processors.

2.5 Evaluation System: CoGaDB

CoGaDB is a main memory database system using a column-oriented data layout, has an SQL interface, and a Selinger-style optimizer. Similar to other OLAP DBMSs such as MonetDB [17], CoGaDB is an interpreter-based engine and processes queries by calling an operator-specific function for each operator in the query execution plan. The operator functions consume the complete input and materialize their output. Thus, CoGaDB does not employ pipelining. In case an operator contains two or more child operators, the child operators are evaluated in parallel (inter-operator parallelism). CoGaDB makes use of all CPU cores (or GPU cores, respectively) to speed up query processing (intra-operator parallelism). Furthermore, CoGaDB uses the hardware-oblivious query optimizer HyPE to solve the operator placement problem [7, 9]. We compare the performance of CoGaDB to the GPU-accelerated database engine MonetDB/Ocelot in Section A.

2.5.1 Fault Tolerance

In error situations (e.g., an operator runs out of memory), CoGaDB restarts the operator on a CPU. This is in contrast to the earlier system of Wang and others, which handled out-of-memory situations by aborting entire queries [35]. Thus, to cope with the resource restriction of GPUs, we provide a CPU-based fallback handler for every operator. This way, query processing can always continue though at a two-fold cost: First, the aborted operator will run slower than anticipated; second, the query processor performs more data transfer operations than expected.

Note that it is not practical to use a wait-and-admit approach for memory allocation. Since we cannot provide a concise upper bound for many database operators (e.g., joins), we are forced to allocate memory in several steps and hold onto already allocated memory. If this is done in parallel for multiple operators, the DBMS will run into deadlocks. Thus, CoGaDB aborts operators immediately if an allocation fails to avoid the overhead of deadlock detection.

2.5.2 Operator Placement

He and others early recognized the importance of operator placement and data movement [13]. To address the problem, they performed backtracking for sub-query plans and combined optimal sub plans to the final query plan [13]. From our experience in CoGaDB, this backtracking approach can be very time consuming. Thus, CoGaDB uses an iterative refinement optimizer that only considers query plans where multiple successive operators are executed on the same processor, a technique that already proved very useful in distributed databases because it limits communication between processors/nodes. We use this established approach for query optimization as a baseline for the experiments in the remainder of this paper.

2.5.3 Performance Optimizations for Data Transfer

CoGaDB implements the recommended optimizations to reduce data transfer bottlenecks [1]. It uses asynchronous data transfers via CUDA streams, which is required to get the full PCIe bus bandwidth and allows for parallel data transfer and computation on GPUs. For this, it is required to copy data into page-locked host memory as staging area, which cannot be swapped to disk by the OS. *Unified Virtual Addressing* (UVA) performs data transfers implicitly and transparently to the application but pays the same data transfer cost as manual data placement.

3. DATA-DRIVEN OPERATOR PLACEMENT

All of the heuristics in Section 2.5.2 assume that data placement is *operator-driven.* That is, for each operator the optimizer first decides on a processor, then—if necessary—moves required data to that processor. In case the hot data of the workload does not fit in the co-processor's data cache, the system runs into the cache thrashing effect.

In this section, we discuss how we can completely avoid the cache thrashing effect by first, deciding on a *data placement* and second, perform *operator placement* according to the data placement. For this, we analyze the workloads access pattern and place the most frequently accessed data in the co-

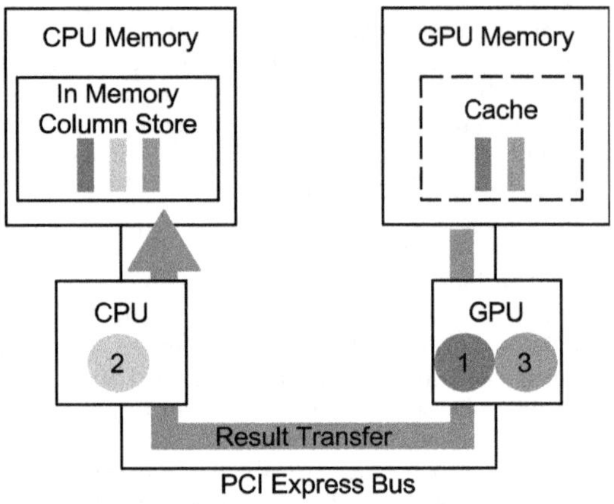

Figure 4: Principle of Data-Driven operator placement. Operators 1 and 3 are pushed to the cached data on the co-processor, whereas the data of operator 2 is not cached and must run on a CPU.

processor cache. Then, we place operators on the co-processor if and only if their input data is cached. Consequently, excessive evictions and re-caching cannot happen because the data placement is decided by one central component: the data placement manager.

3.1 Data-Driven: Push Operators to Data

As an alternative strategy to operator-driven data placement, we propose a *Data-Driven Operator Placement* (in short *Data-Driven*). The idea is that a storage adviser pins frequently used access structures to the co-processor's data cache and the query processor automatically places operators on the co-processor, if and only if the input data is available on the co-processor. Otherwise, the query processor executes the operator on a CPU. This strategy assumes that operators run faster on the co-processor if the data is cached on the co-processor. However, this is consistent with many studies (e.g., He and others [13]) and with our experiments in Section 6 and Section A in the appendix. In case the input data is *not* cached, join operators running on a co-processor can outperform their CPU counterparts, but most operators running on co-processors will not [13]. We illustrate *Data-Driven* in Figure 4. Here, we have three operators, where the input data of operators 1 and 3 are cached on the co-processor, whereas the input data of operator 2 is not. Therefore, operators 1 and 3 are pushed to the co-processor, whereas operator 2 must be executed on a CPU. This is similar to data-oriented transaction execution [29], where each processor core is responsible for processing transactions on a certain database partition. Similarly, we pin certain database access structures such as columns to the co-processor to profit from a perfect cache hit rate.

3.2 Automatic Data Placement

When we only execute operators on a co-processor in case their input is cached on that co-processor, then we need a background job that analyzes the access patterns of the query workload and automatically places frequently required access structures on a co-processor. We keep the data-placement strategy simple and use a least-frequently-used strategy. For this, the storage manager keeps statistics about how frequently and how recently access structures were used by the query processor. Each column in the database has an access counter, which is incremented each time an

Algorithm 1 Data placement updates the coprocessor's cache content using the access counts from query processing.

Input: Columns C, Cache State CS

$K = \text{sort}_{\text{access\_count,descending}}(C)$
used_buffer=0
$C_{cacheold} = CS$.cached_columns
$C_{cachenew} = \emptyset$
for $i = 1$; used_buffer + K_i.size $\leq CS$.buffer_size and $i < |K|$; $i++$ **do**
    $C_{cachenew} = C_{cachenew} \cup K_i$
    used_buffer+=K_i.size
end for
CS.evict($C_{cacheold} \setminus C_{cachenew}$)
CS.cache($C_{cachenew} \setminus C_{cacheold}$)

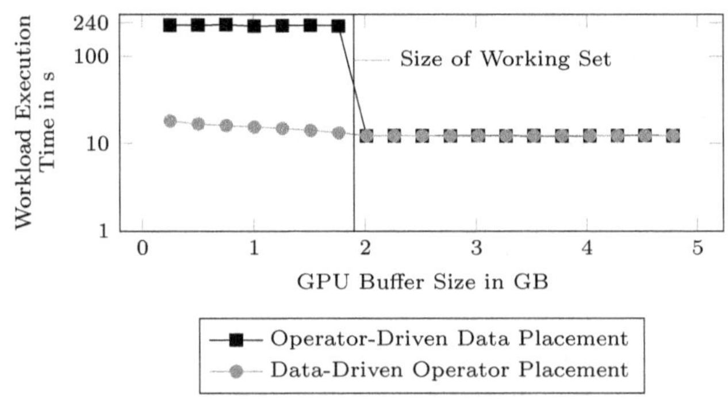

Figure 5: Execution time of selection workload. The performance degradation can be avoided by data-driven operator placement.

operator accesses a column. We show the cache management in Algorithm 1. Periodically, we fill the cache with the most frequently queried columns and access structures. This strategy commonly caches join columns and frequently used filter columns of dimension tables. Note that LRU and LFU strategies perform similarly well, as we show in Section E. Note that running queries can continue execution when the background job adjusts the data placement. We use reference counters for access structures to determine when they are no longer in use and can clean up evicted data when it is no longer used during query processing. Furthermore, we use fine-grained latching to avoid that running queries block when accessing the cache.

3.3 Query Processing

A consequence of *Data-Driven* is that operators are automatically chained (e.g., consecutive operators are executed on the same processor) from the leaf operators, until an n-ary operator ($n \geq 1$) is found where at least one input column is not available in the co-processor memory. Then, the operator chain is not continued and the remaining part of the query is processed on a CPU. This is because *Data-Driven* requires that *all* input columns are resident in the co-processor memory. *Data-Driven* can process the complete query on a co-processor in case the memory capacity is sufficient. If not all input data fits in the co-processor's memory, the co-processor is only used to the degree where the input data fits in the co-processor's memory, avoiding delays by transfer operations and ensuring graceful degradation.

We illustrate the behavior of *Data-Driven* on our two problem cases from the introduction in Figure 5 and 7, respectively. *Data-Driven* eliminates the performance degradation,

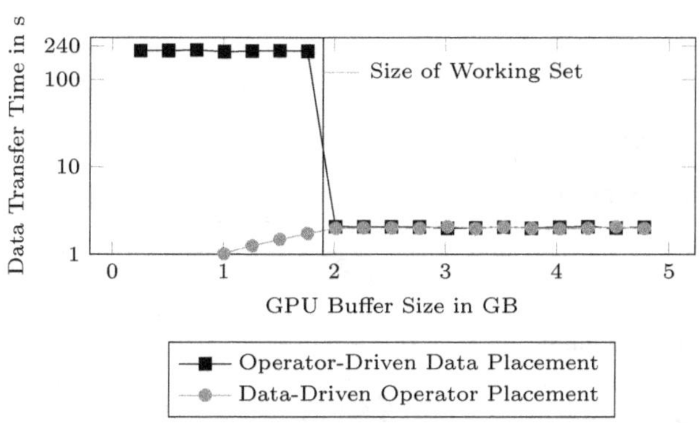

Figure 6: Time spent on data transfers in the selection workload.

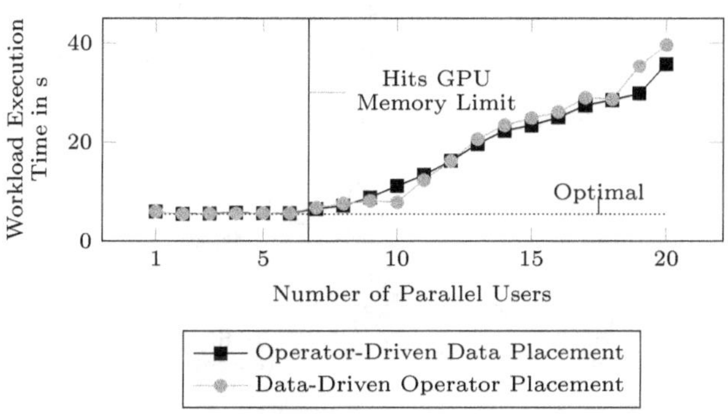

Figure 7: Execution time of a selection workload. *Data-Driven* has the same performance degradation as operator-driven data placement.

which we observed for the classic approach: operator-driven data placement. We show in Figure 6 that the performance degradation is caused by the enormous data transfer times caused by *cache thrashing.* However, with *Data-Driven* this cannot happen because the co-processor is not used for an operator, when its input data is not cached. We also observe that with increasing buffer size, *Data-Driven* gets faster with the number of input columns that fit into the cache, until it reaches the optimum.

3.4 Problems in Concurrent Workloads

The second problem case, where we observe performance degradation with an increasing number of concurrent operators on a co-processor, is not solved with *Data-Driven* as illustrated by Figure 7. This effect is caused by an increased data transfer overhead due to operator aborts on co-processors. In case too many operators run in parallel, their collective memory demand exceeds the co-processors memory capacity (*heap contention*).

In case of the parallel selection workload, we require a column C as input data. CoGaDB implements the GPU selection algorithm of He and others [13], which requires a memory footprint of 3.25 times the size of the input column. For n parallel queries, a column size C of 218 MB (fact table columns of star schema benchmark for scale factor 10), and a GPU memory capacity M of $5GB$, we can execute $n = \frac{|M|}{3.25 \cdot |C|} \approx 7$ parallel users without running in the memory limit. This is exactly the point where the performance starts to degrade in Figure 7.

In case of more than 7 parallel queries, some operators run out of memory and are restarted on a CPU. Since the operator placement decisions were all done during *query*

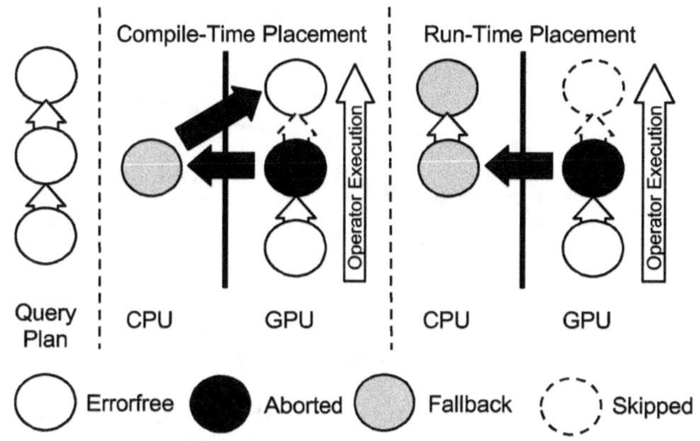

Figure 8: Flexibility of run-time placement. Compile-time heuristics force the query processor to switch back to the GPU after an operator aborts, whereas run-time heuristics avoid this overhead.

compile-time, the successor operator is still executed on the co-processor, which causes additional data transfers that were not anticipated by the optimizer. We discuss how we can solve this issue by performing operator placement at query run-time in the next section.

4. RUN-TIME OPERATOR PLACEMENT

Until now, we discussed heuristics for the operator placement problem applied at query *compile-time*, i.e., they decide on a fixed operator placement *before* a query runs. This strategy has three drawbacks:

1. It cannot predict error situations such as out of memory scenarios, where a co-processor operator needs to abort.
2. Compile-time heuristics need to rely on sufficiently accurate cardinality estimates to estimate the data transfer volume. However, it is still very difficult to provide cardinality estimations.
3. GPU code is particularly sensitive to environment parameters such as current load or usage of heap memory. Inherently, those parameters cannot be known before the actual execution time the classical dilemma of multi-query optimization.

A way to escape this dilemma has been proposed by Boncz and others [4]. By separating query optimization into strategical and tactical decisions, many important runtime parameters can be considered for the optimization process. Whereas the database optimizer performs the strategic optimization (e.g., the structure of the query plan), a run-time optimizer conducts the tactical optimization (e.g., operator placement and algorithm selection).[2] Therefore, run-time placement can dynamically react to unforeseen events (e.g., out of memory conditions) and does not need any cardinality estimates, because it performs operator placement after all input relations are available. In this section, we discuss how run-time operator placement helps a query processor to react to faults during operator execution on co-processors.

4.1 Run-Time Flexibility

If the optimizer performs operator placement decisions at run-time, it can dynamically react to unforeseen events, such as aborting co-processor operators. Since memory is scarce in co-processors, there is always the possibility that an operator cannot allocate enough memory. In this case, CoGaDB

[2]This separation requires the DBMS to use operator- or vector-at-a-time processing, which is the case for CoGaDB.

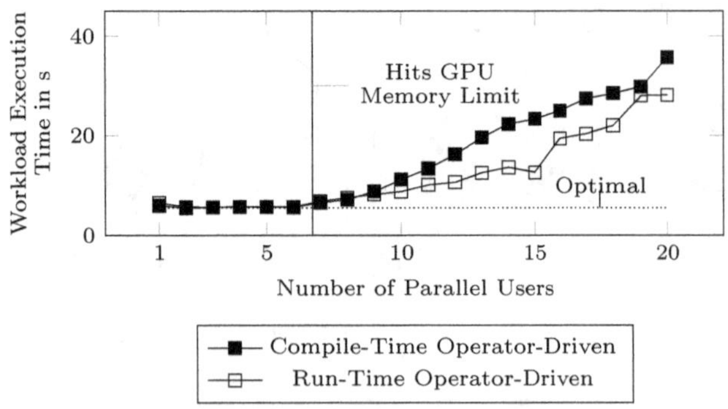

Figure 9: Run-time operator placement improves performance, but does not achieve the optimum.

discards the work of the operator and restarts the operator on the CPU. This mechanism is very efficient, because operators typically start with the allocation of memory for their input data and data structures. So most of the time, co-processor operators abort without wasting any resources.

Run-time resource contention interacts poorly with compile-time operator placement. We illustrate the problem in Figure 8. We assume a simple query execution plan that is placed completely on the GPU. The second operator runs out of memory and aborts, so CoGaDB creates a fall back operator and executes it on the CPU. The problem is that the third operator is still placed on the GPU, and requires to copy the result data to the GPU. In contrast, a run-time placement heuristic schedules the third operator, after the second operator aborted, and hence, places the third operator on the CPU to avoid the copy cost. Note that this procedure can repeat itself multiple times in the same query, and may cause large performance degradations.

4.2 Query Processing

We illustrate in Figure 9 that run-time operator placement reduces the performance penalty of concurrent running queries of up to a factor of two. However, run-time placement is still more than two times slower than the optimal case. The reason for this is that run-time placement avoids data transfer overhead in case of operator aborts. Instead, the aborted operators are restarted and lose their co-processor acceleration, so we still pay a performance penalty.

5. MINIMIZING OPERATOR ABORTS

In this section, we discuss how we can reduce the overhead of running multiple queries in parallel by reducing the probability that operators abort. Based on this, we present our technique *query chopping*, which reduces the maximum number of operators that can run in parallel by using the thread pool pattern.

5.1 Probability of Operator Aborts

To avoid operator aborts, we reduce the probability that an operator runs out of memory. One way to achieve this is to prohibit the DBMS to execute multiple GPU operators concurrently (e.g., He and others [13]). However, Wang and others showed that we can improve the performance of query processing by allowing moderate parallel execution [35]. Wang and others proposed to use an admission control mechanism for queries, limiting the total number of queries in the DBMS and hence, the number of parallel queries that concurrently access the co-processor. While we cannot use this approach on an operator granularity, we can put an upper

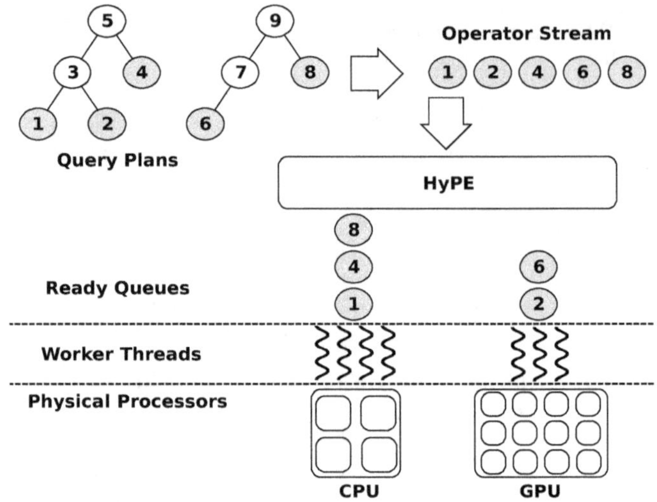

Figure 10: Query Chopping.

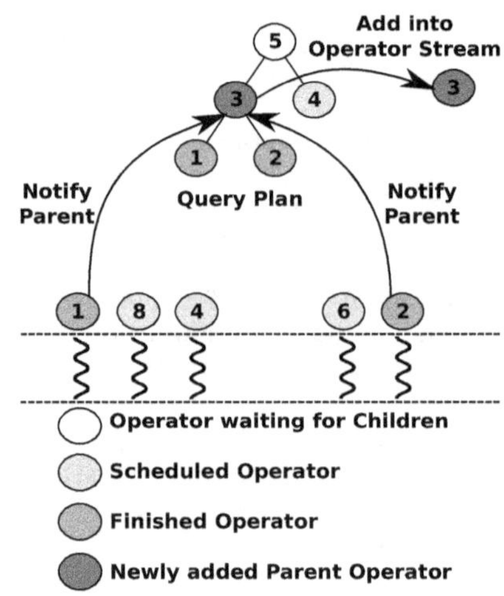

Figure 11: Query Chopping: Finished operators pull their parents into the global operator stream.

bound on the number of operators concurrently executing on a co-processor by using the thread pool pattern. Here, processing tasks are not *pushed* towards the processor, but *pulled* by the processor. If no worker thread is available for an operator, it is kept in a queue, until a prior operator finishes execution. This way, we do not artificially limit the number of concurrent queries in the DBMS, but still avoid that queries run into resource contention problems due to the use of co-processors.

5.2 Query Chopping

Based on our discussions, we now present our novel technique *query chopping* (*Chopping*), which is essentially a progressive query optimizer that performs operator placement at query run-time and limits the number of operators executing in parallel via a thread pool.

Our goal is to accelerate a workload of queries by using the available (co-)processors, but avoid that these accelerators can slow down query processing. We implemented *Chopping* as an additional layer between the strategic optimizer of CoGaDB and the hardware oblivious query optimizer HyPE. *Chopping* takes n queries, chops off their leaf operators, and inserts them into a global operator stream. Since the leaf operators have no dependencies, they can immediately start their execution independent of each other. HyPE then schedules the operators on the available processors, and selects for each operator a suitable algorithm. We summarize our discussion in Figure 10.

When an operator finishes execution, it notifies its parent. After all children of an operator completed, the operator inserts itself into the global operator stream. Once the root operator of a query plan has finished execution, the query result is returned. We illustrate this procedure in Figure 11.

This technique works for single-query and multi-query workloads. The virtue of the strategy is that we always know the exact input cardinalities during the tactical optimization, which increases the accuracy of HyPE's cost models and, hence, its operator placement and algorithm selection. Furthermore, we can fully benefit from HyPE's load balancing capabilities.

Additionally, *Chopping* manages the concurrency on a processor at the operator level. HyPE's execution engine virtualizes the physical processors, e.g., we can create multiple worker threads per processor to achieve inter-operator parallelism. For each physical processor, we maintain a *ready queue*, where all worker threads of that processor pull new operators from. This mechanism can also be used to decide on the number of threads for a single operator. In a workload with low concurrency, an algorithm could decide to use more threads to execute faster, whereas in highly parallel workloads, each operator would use only a single thread. To balance the load between CPU and GPU, we keep track of the load on each processor by estimating the completion time of each processor's ready queue.

A thread pool avoids that operators run out of memory by accumulated memory usage, but does not guarantee that single operators get enough heap memory. However, the heap memory usage of operators directly corresponds to the database size. When the input columns exceed a certain memory capacity, the operators cannot allocate enough memory for intermediate data structures and results, which forces the system to process the workload on CPU only. Therefore, a thread pool is sufficient to solve the heap contention problem.

Chopping puts only an upper bound to the concurrency of operators: It is up to the operating system or the co-processor's driver when and how many operators are executed in parallel. Thus, *Chopping* steers the parallelism on all processors and leaves it to the scheduling mechanisms of the OS to place threads on a certain CPU socket to a specific core. Thus, *Chopping* seamlessly integrates with existing approaches.

5.3 Query Processing

We illustrate in Figure 12 that *Chopping* achieves near optimal performance. This is because *Chopping* also limits the number of operators that can run concurrently on a co-processor. This significantly reduces the probability that operators run into the heap contention effect and need to abort. We illustrate this in Figure 13. It is clearly visible that operator-driven data placement at compile-time leads to the most operator aborts. Simple run-time placement reduces this overhead, as it continues query processing on the CPU if an operator aborts, thus relieving the GPU heap. If we additionally limit the inter-operator parallelism we achieve near optimal results.

5.4 Data-Driven Query Chopping

We now discuss how *Data-Driven* and *Chopping* work together. The combined strategy places frequently used access structures in the co-processor's data cache using a periodic background job to avoid cache thrashing. Then, starting from the leaf operators of the query, all operators are pushed on the co-processor if the input data of an operator is cached and on the CPU otherwise. The operator is then put into the ready queue of the selected processor. After a worker thread executed an operator, it notifies its completion to the parent operator and fetches the next operator from the ready queue. The parent operator is processed in the same way, when all child operators completed execution. This procedure is continued until all operators of the query finished. The trick is that when operator aborts are detected, query processing continues on the CPU, because the output data no longer resides on the co-processor. Thus, the combined strategy avoids memory thrashing and heap contention.

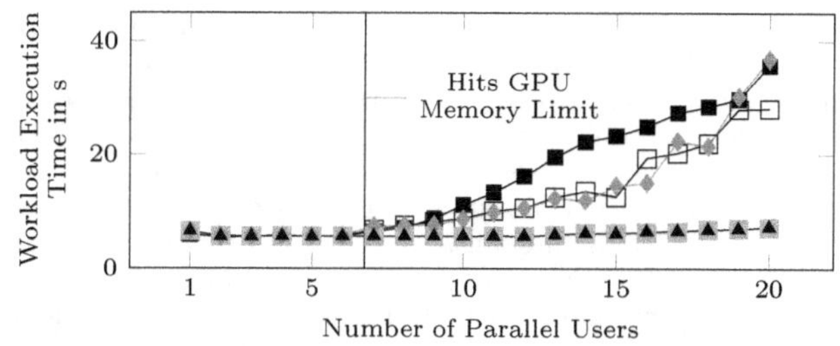

Figure 12: Dynamic reaction to faults and limiting the number of parallel running GPU operators achieves near optimal performance.

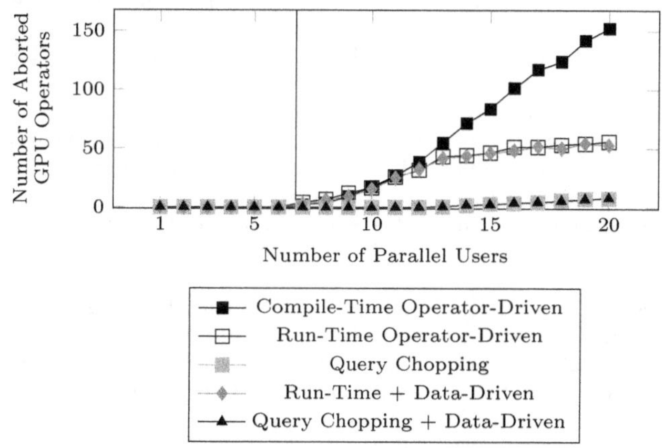

Figure 13: Run-time placement reduces heap contention by continuing execution in the CPU. *Chopping* limits the number of parallel running GPU operators and further decreases the abort probability.

5.5 Applicability To Other Processing Models

Aside from operator-at-a-time processing, two alternative processing models have been proposed in the past: vector-a-time processing and query compilation. An inherent property of many real world queries is that they contain multiple *pipeline breakers*, which force the DBMS to materialize intermediate results, regardless of the processing model. In this cases, cache thrashing and heap contention can lead to the same performance penalties observed in this paper.

Vectorized Execution. Vector-at-a-time processing works on cache-resident chunks of columns (vectors), avoids materialization cost of operator-at-a-time processing, and supports pipelining [5]. Support of *Data-Driven* is straightforward: Cached vectors would be processed on the co-processors and the remaining vectors on the CPU. In case the co-processor finished its cached vectors, we can exploit an additional optimization: The vector-at-a-time scheme can overlap data transfer and computation on the co-processor, which allows to process vectors on all processors (e.g., Chen and others [10]). We expect that such a cross-processor database engine would significantly boost performance, but the observations in this paper are still valid in such a system. Heap contention is reduced to pipeline-breaking operators, but for a reasonable complex query workloads the DBMS is still required to deal with this problem.

Compiled Execution. Query compilation generates C or assembly code for a specific query and executes the compiled program [21, 27]. Operators that can be pipelined are compiled to a single function (called pipeline), which typically processes data in a single pass. Thus, intermediate results are only materialized for pipeline breakers [27]. These pipelines then need to be placed on a (co-)processor. In this scenario, *Data-Driven Chopping* is still required to avoid cache trashing and heap contention. An extension of the morsel framework [22] would lead to the option of streaming data to co-processors as it is a vector-at-a-time processing using compiled pipelines. Therefore, the reasoning for vector-at-a-time execution applies for query compilation as well.

Summary. In summary, the cache thrashing and heap contention effects are inherent to all database engines regardless of their processing model. Therefore, our discussed approaches are useful in all co-processor-accelerated database engines.

6. EFFECTS ON FULL WORKLOAD

In this section, we quantitatively assess the performance of our proposed approaches on two more complex workloads: the star schema benchmark and the TPC-H benchmark.

6.1 Experimental Setup

As evaluation platform, we use a machine with an Intel Xeon CPU E5-1607 v2 with four cores @3.0 GHz (Ivy Bridge), 32 GB main memory, and an NVIDIA GTX 770 GPU with 4 GB of device memory. On the software side, we use Ubuntu 14.04.2 (64 Bit) as operating system and the NVIDIA CUDA driver 331.113 (CUDA 5.5). Before starting the benchmark, we pre-load the database into main memory and access structures in the GPU memory, until the GPU buffer size is reached.

For each SSBM workload, we run all SSBM queries (Q1.1-Q4.3). In case of the TPC-H workload, we run a subset of the queries (Q2-Q7). The remaining TPC-H queries are not fully supported in the current version of CoGaDB. We elaborate details about the benchmarks and the selection of queries in Appendix C. For each experiment, we run a workload two times to warm up the system. Then, we run the workload 100 times, and show the execution time of the workload and the time to transfer data over the PCIe bus. We focus our discussions on *Data-Driven*, *Chopping*, and *Data-Driven Chopping*.

6.2 Detailed Experiments

We validate our proposed heuristics on the SSBM and TPC-H benchmark in terms of performance and caused IO on the PCIe bus. We investigate both effects—cache thrashing when a working set exceeds the co-processor cache and heap contention by excessive inter-operator parallelism—on the SSBM and TPC-H benchmark. For this, we perform one experiment per effect. We conduct an experiment where we increase the scale factor of both benchmarks (single user) and

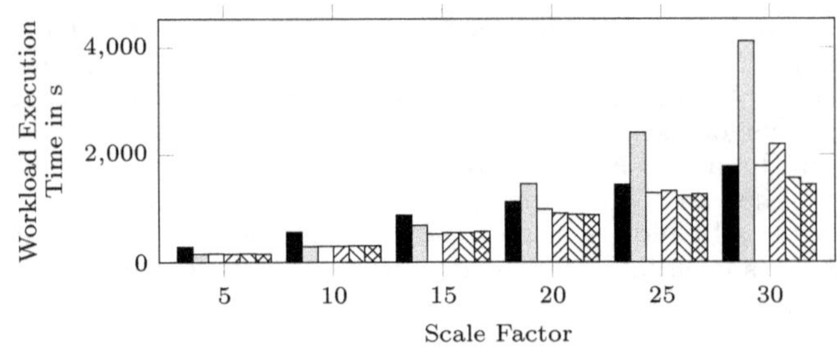

(a) Workload of SSBM queries.

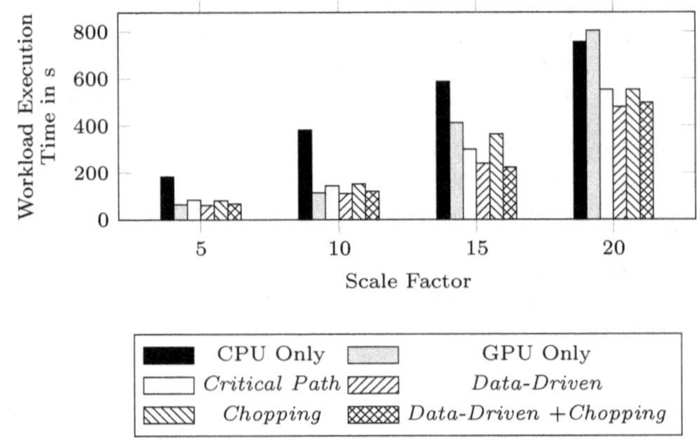

(b) Workload of selected TPC-H queries.

Figure 14: Average workload execution time of SSBM and selected TPC-H Queries. *Data-Driven* combined with *Chopping* can improve performance significantly and is never slower than any other heuristic.

measure performance and transfer times for inter-processor communication to investigate the cache thrashing effect. To understand how different execution and placement strategies react to heap contention situations, we conduct an experiment where we increase the number of concurrently running queries of both benchmarks and measure workload execution time and transfer times for inter-processor communication for a scale factor of 10.

As reference points, we included two heuristics for operator-driven data placement at compile-time to reflect the state of the art. The *GPU Preferred* heuristic executes all operators on the GPU, and only switches back to the CPU in case an operator runs out of memory. The *Critical Path* is the default iterative refinement optimizer of CoGaDB, which creates a hybrid CPU/GPU plan with the lowest response time. We describe *Critical Path* in detail in Appendix D. These heuristics all use operator-driven data placement at compile time. We compare these heuristics to the three basic variants of our proposal: *Data-Driven* at compile-time, *Chopping* with operator-driven data placement, and *Data-Driven Chopping*.

6.2.1 Scaling Database Size

To understand how different execution and placement strategies react to cache thrashing situations, we scale up the SSBM and TPC-H databases to increase the memory requirements of the working set. We show the results in Figure 14 for the SSBM and TPC-H benchmark. It is clearly visible that a GPU-only execution is not suitable for growing database sizes, as it is inferior to the remaining strategies. The reason is that a large portion of the execution time is spend on data

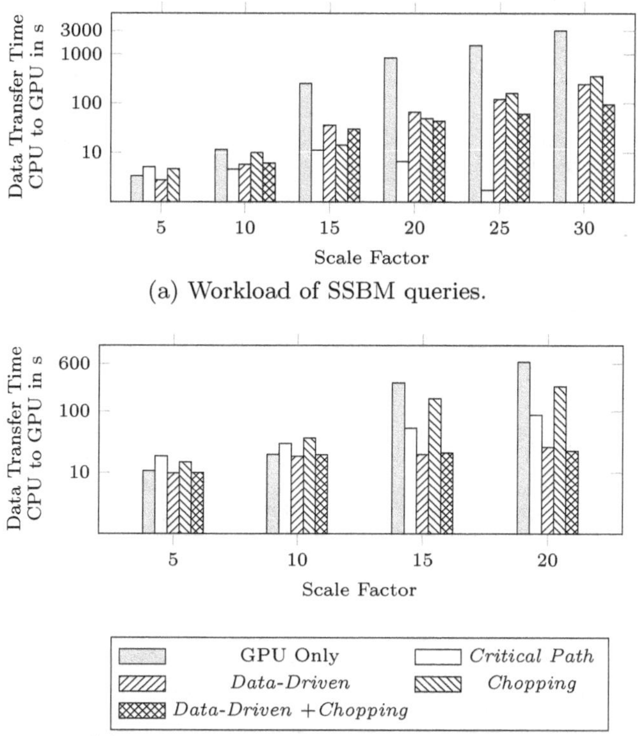

(a) Workload of SSBM queries.

(b) Workload of selected TPC-H queries.

Figure 15: Average data transfer time CPU to GPU of SSBM and selected TPC-H Queries. *Data-Driven* combined with *Chopping* saves the most IO.

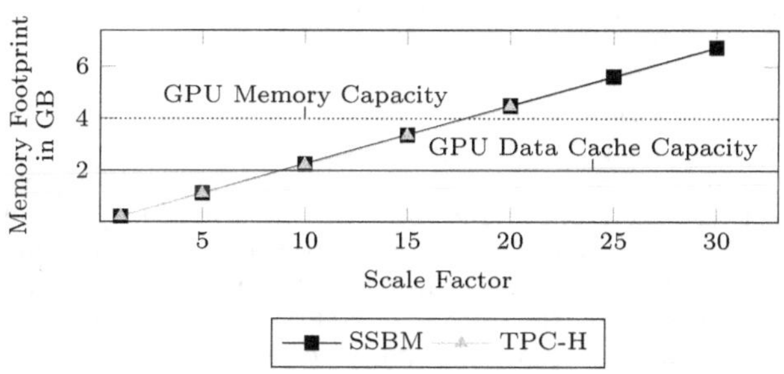

Figure 16: Memory footprint of workloads

transfers from CPU to GPU as illustrated by Figure 15. The performance of the GPU-only approach falls behind starting at scale factor 15 (SSBM and TPC-H). Figure 16 shows the memory footprint of the SSBM and TPC-H Workload. Starting from scale factor 15, it significantly exceeds the data cache, and thus, clearly shows the cache-thrashing effect.

As expected from our observations in the selection workload, *Data-Driven* and *Chopping* reduce the workload execution time compared to the GPU-only approach, however, *Data-Driven* can still slow down performance compared to a CPU-only approach. The combined *Data-Driven Chopping* approach can improve performance even when resources become scarce, and never performs worse than a CPU-only approach. Thus, *Data-Driven Chopping* fulfills our requirements for robust query processing.

Data-Driven saves data transfers from the CPU to the GPU, because *Chopping* runs into the cache thrashing effect while *Data-Driven* avoids this overhead. We can observe this effect in the increased copy times of *Chopping* compared to *Data-Driven* in the TPC-H workload (cf. Figure 15(b)). At

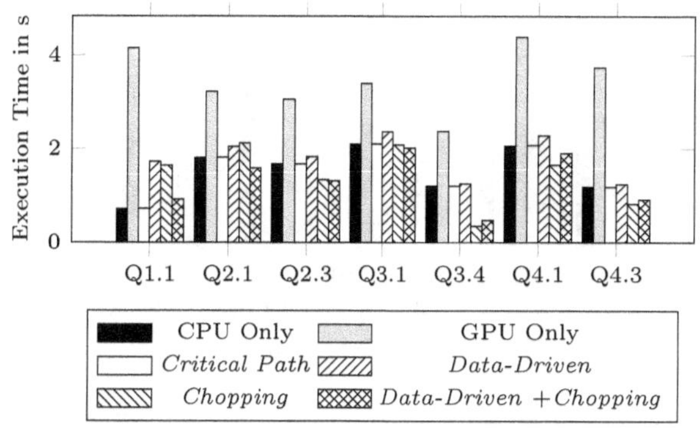

Figure 17: Query execution times for selected SSBM queries for a single user and a database of scale factor 30.

the same time, the data transfer time from GPU to CPU is larger for *Data-Driven* compared with *Chopping*, because *Data-Driven* alone cannot react to aborted operators.

According to the savings of IO time of *Chopping* compared with *Data-Driven*, we conclude that the increasing database size can also lead to the heap contention effect, where operators need to abort because they run out of heap memory. This situation is difficult to predict and *Chopping* provides a simple and cheap error handling.

To get a more detailed understanding of what happens when memory resources become scarce, we investigate the query run-time of selected SSBM queries at scale factor 30 and illustrate them in Figure 17. The GPU-Only approach slows down each query. *Critical Path* is always as fast as the CPU-Only approach, because it detected the performance degradation due to the co-processor and only uses the CPU. For low selectivity queries (Q1.1, Q2.1, Q3.1, Q4.1), *Data-Driven Chopping* has little impact on performance. However, for high selectivity queries (Q2.3, Q3.4, Q4.3) we observe a performance improvement of up to factor 2.5 (Q3.4). A detailed examination of the query plans revealed that the (pushed-down) selections are put on the GPU, and frequently the first join, which accelerates the query. Since the intermediate results are small, it is cheap to switch back to the CPU in case a required input column is not cached (e.g., a join column). The reason low selectivity queries cannot be accelerated as well is twofold. First, it is more costly to switch back to the CPU and second, larger intermediate results increase the probability of memory scarcity and hence, operator aborts.

Overall, we conclude that of the compared strategies, the combination *Data-Driven Chopping* achieves the best performance (Figure 14) and minimal IO (Figure 15).

6.2.2 Scaling User Parallelism

To show the heap contention effect, we use a SSBM and a TPC-H database with fixed size (scale factor 10) and increase the number of parallel running queries (users). For each workload, we execute all queries 100 times. We repeat the workload multiple times and present the average execution time. Note that the total number of queries in the workload is fixed, only the number of parallel running queries changes.

Parallel query execution slows down query processing by a factor of 1.24 for the SSBM workload and by a factor of 1.85 for the TPC-H workload compared to a naive use of the GPU, as we show in Figure 18. Compared to a GPU Only execution, *Data-Driven Chopping* achieves a speedup by a factor of 1.36 for the SSBM and 1.66 for the TPC-H workload and uses significantly less resources.

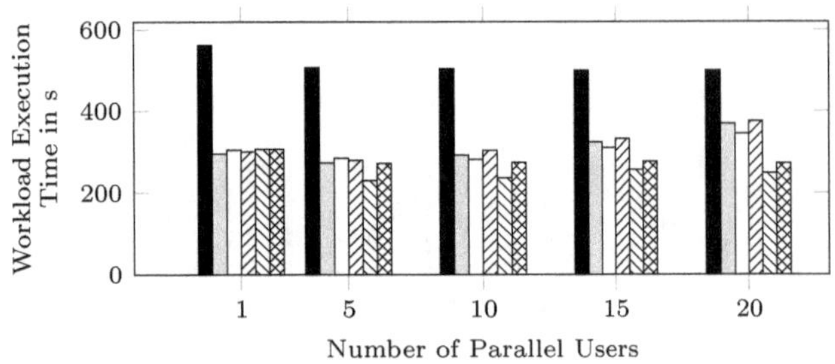

(a) Workload of SSBM queries.

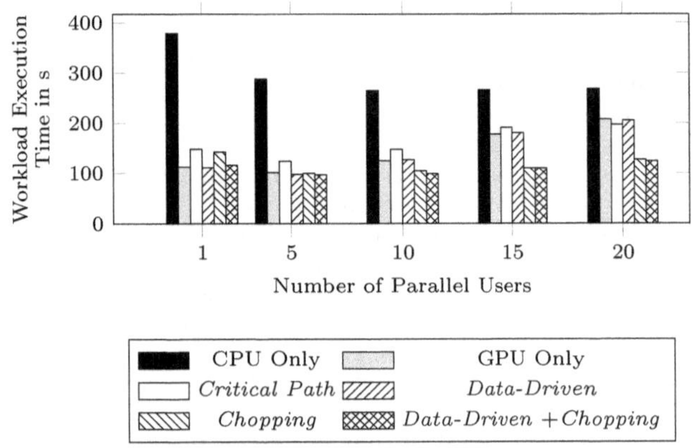

(b) Workload of selected TPC-H queries.

Figure 18: Average workload execution time of SSBM and TPC-H queries for varying parallel users. The dynamic reaction to faults of *Chopping* results in improved performance.

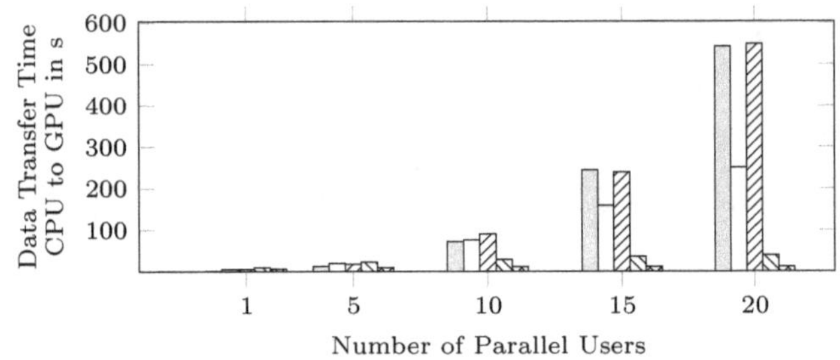

(a) Workload of SSBM queries

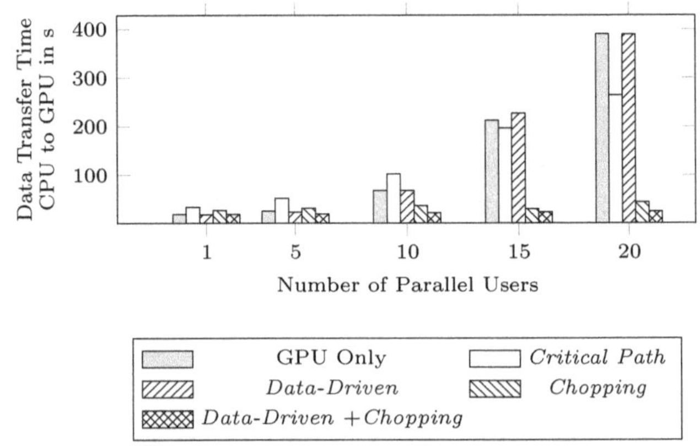

(b) Workload of selected TPC-H queries

Figure 19: Data transfer times CPU to GPU of SSBM and TPC-H workload for varying parallel users. *Chopping* reduces IO significantly especially with increasing number of parallel queries.

Chopping and *Data-Driven Chopping* reduce the required IO significantly—especially for workloads with many parallel users—as we show in Figure 19. *Data-Driven Chopping* reduces the time required for data transfers from CPU to GPU by a factor of 48 for the SSBM and 16 for the TPC-H workload. The main reason for the improved performance is the fine grained concurrency limitation of *Chopping*. However, run-time placement without parallelism control significantly reduces resource consumption as well.

To quantify the cost of aborted GPU operators, we measure the time from begin to abort of GPU operators and add them to a counter. We call this metric the *wasted time* and illustrate it for the SSBM experiments in Figure 20. *Chopping* and *Data-Driven Chopping* reduce the wasted time by up to a factor of 74. Note that both the copy time and wasted time can be larger than the overall workload execution time, because they reflect the total time, whereas the workload execution time represents the response time.

We show the execution time of selected SSBM queries for a workload serving 20 parallel users (cf. Figure 21). *Chopping* and *Data-Driven Chopping* are faster than the other heuristics for queries Q3.1, Q3.4, Q4.1 (up to a factor of 3.5 for Q3.4), competitive for queries 2.1, 2.3, 4.3, and slower for query Q1.1 (by a factor of 1.78 compared to GPU Only). As reference point, we use a GPU Only execution combined with an admission control mechanism that admits only a single query at a time. This way, intermediate results are consumed as fast as possible and heap contention is avoided. However, such admission control at query level increases query latencies (cf. Figure 21 and Figure 25 in the appendix). *Chopping* is either as fast as admission control (Q4.1 and Q4.2) or faster and improves query response times of up to a factor of 1.4. Compared to admission control, some queries are significantly faster using *Data-Driven Chopping* (Q3.4 by a factor of 3.6 and Q4.1 by a factor of 1.5), while other queries are slowed down (e.g., Q1.3 by a factor of 1.25). This is due to different operator placement enforced by the *Data-Driven* heuristic. With respect to the average query execution time, the average query response time of *Data-Driven Chopping* is improved by a factor of 1.1 and with *Chopping* it is improved by a factor of 1.2. By examining execution times of all queries, we observe that short running queries become slower to some degree, whereas long running queries are accelerated. This is not surprising as long running queries either include more operators or process more data, which both increases the probability of operator aborts and thus, benefit more from *Chopping*. Short running queries are not always executed at full speed but can be decelerated by the concurrency limitation of *Chopping*.

We conclude that heap contention occurs in complex workloads and can significantly decrease performance and increase resource usage. Furthermore, we have seen that *Chopping* and *Data-Driven Chopping* both significantly accelerate query processing and reduce resource consumption by avoiding heap contention.

During our experiments we also discovered that the heap contention effect can be much stronger in case the join order is sub-optimal, because the greater intermediate results increase processing time and the probability of operator aborts.

We confirm the observations of Wang that executing too many queries in parallel on GPUs degrades performance [35]. Our solution *Data-Driven Chopping* limits the use of the

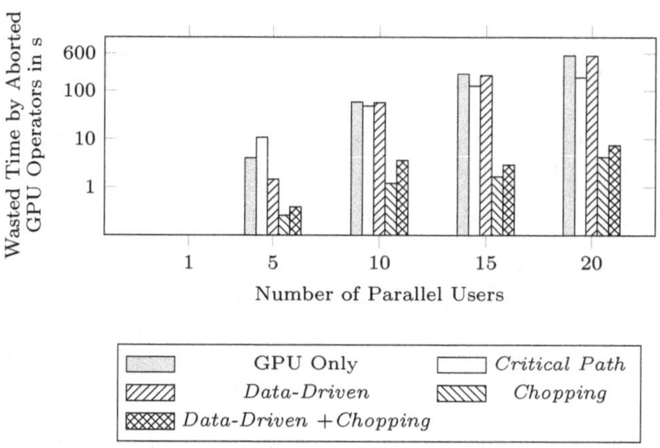

Figure 20: Wasted time by aborted GPU operators depending on the number of parallel users for the SSBM. With an increasing number of users, the wasted time increases significantly because of heap contention.

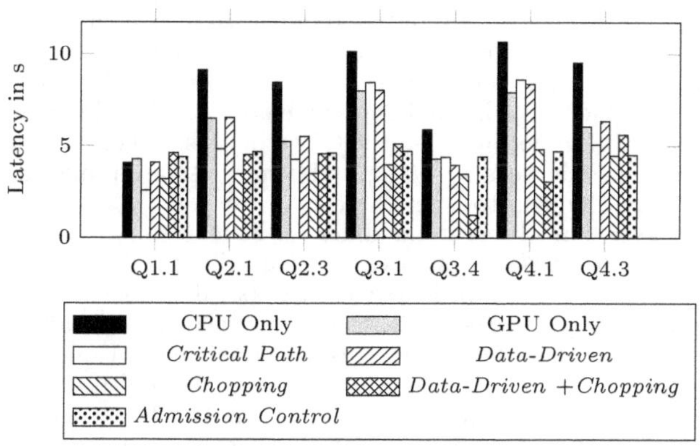

Figure 21: Latencies for selected SSBM queries for 20 users and a database of scale factor 10.

GPU to the degree where it is beneficial and thus, avoids heap contention.

6.3 Discussion

In all of our experiments, the strategy which combines *Data-Driven* with *Chopping* achieved the best overall result. Either it was the fastest strategy, or it was as fast as the other strategies while minimizing IO. This is not surprising as this is the only strategy that avoids the cache thrashing and the heap contention effect, and thus, achieves the most stable performance, especially when compared to the state-of-the-art heuristics, which use a operator-driven data placement at query compile-time. We also learned that cache thrashing has a much stronger effect on a complex query workload than heap contention.

Data-Driven Chopping improves several metrics at once:

1. **Worst-Case Execution Time:** *Data-Driven Chopping* improves performance when resources become scarce of up to factor 24 in our micro benchmarks and up to factor 2 for the SSBM and TPC-H workload.
2. **PCIe Traffic:** *Data-Driven Chopping* requires less IO (up to a factor of 48) on the PCIe bus. In database engines using block-oriented query execution, we can spend these resources to stream data blocks from CPU to the co-processor when the co-processor finished its local data.

Our results have several implications. We can use co-processors only for a part of the workload. We can improve the scalability by compressing the database, which shifts the point where performance breaks down to a larger scale factor or number of users. Thus, compression neither solves the cache thrashing nor the heap contention problem. However, it is common to use multiple GPUs in a single machine, which can handle larger databases and more parallel users. This scale up by multiple co-processors can help us to process workloads that have resource demands exceeding the resources of a single co-processor. Our *Data-Driven* strategy can support multiple co-processors by performing horizontal partitioning. However, the basic problems and their solutions stay the same. Additionally, our results show that GPUs—and other co-processors—alone are not a viable solution. CPUs and co-processors need to work together to perform query processing efficiently.

7. RELATED WORK

In this section, we discuss related work on co-processor-accelerated DBMSs and concurrent query processing.

7.1 Co-Processor-accelerated DBMSs

He and others developed the first GPU-accelerated database engine, namely GPUQP [13]. GPUQP can use CPU and GPU in the same query and uses a modified backtracking optimizer: Each query plan is decomposed into sub-plans with at most 10 operators. Then, the optimizer performs a backtracking search to find the optimal plan for each sub-plan. Finally, the physical query plan is created by combining the optimal sub-plans. GPUQP could afford to create many plan candidates, because it used analytical cost models, where each estimation can be computed in a couple of CPU cycles. However, for learning-based approaches, computing an estimation can take a non-negligible amount of time (in the order of several micro seconds). Since CoGaDB uses the learned cost models of HyPE during optimization, using backtracking or dynamic programming approaches is very expensive. In this work, we counter this drawback of learning-based cost models by introducing simple but efficient heuristics.

He and others investigated the performance of hash joins on a coupled CPU/GPU architecture [14]. For each step in the hash join, a certain part of the input data is placed on the CPU and on the GPU to fully occupy both processors and minimize execution skew.

Zhang and others developed OmniDB [38], a database engine that targets heterogeneous processor environments and focuses on hardware obliviousness, similar to Ocelot [15]. OmniDB schedules so called *work units* on the available processors. Each work unit is placed on the processor with the highest throughput, but only a certain fraction of the workload may be executed on each processor to avoid overloading. We were not able to include this heuristic in CoGaDB, because CoGaDB uses a bulk processor, whereas the heuristic of Zhang assumes a vector-at-a-time processing model.

Pirk and others propose the approximate and refine technique [30], where data is lossily compressed using the bitwise decomposition technique [31]. The idea is to compute an approximate result on lossily compressed data, which is cached on a co-processor. Then, the result is refined on the CPU, which has the missing information lost by the compression and filters out false positives. The technique completely avoids data transfer from the CPU to a co-processor, similar to our *Data-Driven* technique. However, approximate and refine requires a refinement step after each GPU operator. On the one hand, this distributes the load on CPU and GPU and allows for inter-device parallelism. On the other hand, the data transfer from the co-processor to the CPU is likely to become the bottleneck. *Data-Driven* avoids to copy back intermediate results if possible, but is also likely to require a larger device memory footprint. It would be worthwhile to compare these techniques in future work.

Karnagel and others extended the hardware-oblivious database engine Ocelot by their heterogeneity-aware operator placement [20], which uses a combination of analytical and learning-based cost models to predict the performance of operators, similar to He and others [13] and Yuan and others [37]. Karnagel and others place operators at run-time and use operator-driven data placement. However, they do not support inter-operator parallelism on a single processor.

Karnagel and others evaluated the impact of compile-time and run-time optimization with the Ocelot Engine [19]. They conclude that both approaches are similarly efficient, where run-time placement is easier to implement and global optimization achieves an overall more robust performance. We make similar observations in CoGaDB in case no memory thrashing or heap contention occurs. However, when hitting the resource limits of co-processors, the operator placement should be done at run-time.

Except some management tasks, GPUDB [37], MultiQx-GPU [35] and Red Fox [36] process queries only on the GPU, and hence, use no query optimization heuristic for operator placement. Ocelot is capable of running on all OpenCL capable processors, but Ocelot cannot make automatic placement decisions by itself [15]. For operator placement, Ocelot makes use of the HyPE optimizer [8].

Aside from GPUs, there are other co-processors to accelerate database query processing, such as MICs [18, 23], Cell Processors [16], and FPGAs [25].

7.2 Concurrent Query Processing

Parallel query processing on co-processors and its problems with resource contention is strongly related to concurrent query processing in general.

Harizopoulos and others contribute QPipe, a relational engine that uses *simultaneous pipelining* and focuses on parallel OLAP workloads [12]. Since concurrent queries are likely to access the same data and perform similar operators, it is possible to perform common disk accesses or to reuse common intermediate results. Since QPipe detects commonalities between queries at run-time, it does not need a multi-query optimizer. Our strategy *Data-Driven* shares the basic idea, because co-processor operators share the cached access structures of CoGaDB to avoid the data transfer overhead.

Arumugam and others developed the DataPath system, which uses a purely data-driven approach to push data to processors, where it is consumed by any interested computation [3]. This allows for heavy sharing of computational and memory resources and may be a viable way to use co-processors in case the database is orders of magnitudes larger than the co-processors memory.

Psaroudakis and others propose to decompose database operators into tasks, which can be efficiently executed on multi-socket, multi-core machines [33]. However, a fixed concurrency level is not optimal, and thus, needs to be adapted at run-time. Furthermore, they decompose complex operators into several tasks according to a certain task granularity to efficiently parallelize OLAP queries. These results can also benefit *Chopping*, and other run-time placement strategies, to adjust the concurrency in a workload, especially on a co-processor to find the optimal concurrency level, where co-processor operators seldom abort and we can sufficiently use the co-processor to accelerate query processing. The operator decomposition can also help us to process operators on CPUs and co-processors concurrently.

In a further study, Psaroudakis and others investigate under which conditions a data warehouse should use simultaneous pipelining and global query plans [32].

Leis and others present the Morsel framework, which multiplexes a query workload to a fixed set of worker threads at the granularity of blocks of tuples (morsels) [22]. Parallelism is achieved by processing different morsels in parallel by the same operator pipeline. These pipelines are created by just-in-time query compilation [27]. Furthermore, the Morsel framework is NUMA aware, because it prefers to work on morsels in local NUMA regions. Thus, it shares the idea of processing data locally similar to *Data-Driven* and also uses a thread pool pattern to avoid over-commitment similar to *Chopping*. Mühlbauer and others build a heterogeneity-aware operator placement on top of the Morsel framework to optimize databases for performance and energy efficiency on the ARM big.LITTLE processor [26].

Wang and others investigated concurrent query processing on GPUs in their system MultiQx-GPU [35]. They argue that we cannot utilize the PCIe bus bandwidth, device memory bandwidth, and compute utilization with a single query, and propose to execute queries concurrently on the GPU. However, due to the limited device memory, the DBMS needs to be careful to not overload the GPU, because otherwise the performance decreases. Wang and others use an admission control mechanism to steer the concurrency.

However, our observations differ for concurrent workloads for the *GPU Preferred* strategy, which achieved 62% better performance for a workload with ten parallel queries. We explain this difference by the differences in the database engines and their fault-tolerance mechanisms. Wang and others execute complete queries on the GPU, and use their cost-driven replacement technique to swap data to the CPU's main memory in case memory becomes scarce, which causes high PCIe bus traffic. CoGaDB also evicts cached data to successfully complete a query, but uses CPU and GPU to process queries. Otherwise, CoGaDB aborts an operator and restarts it on a CPU. With our *Data-Driven* heuristic, we avoid this data transfer overhead and can cheaply outsource load from the GPU in case it becomes overloaded. We expect similar results if our approaches are applied to other systems, such as Ocelot [15] or MultiQx-GPU [35].

8. SUMMARY

In this paper, we investigated robust query processing in heterogeneous co-processor environments. Since co-processors typically have a small dedicated memory, it is crucial to cache frequently-accessed data in the co-processor's memory. We identify two effects during query processing on co-processors that can lead to poor performance: Cache thrashing and heap contention.

We showed that placing operators on co-processors, where their input is cached and the remaining operators are processed on the CPU, is the key to overcome cache thrashing. The heap contention problem appears in parallel user workloads, where multiple operators use a co-processor. We can solve this issue by using a pool of worker threads that pulls operators to the co-processor, and at the same time dynamically reacts to operator faults (e.g., out of memory). We showed that our technique *Data-Driven Chopping* combines these approaches and achieves robust and stable query processing compared to the state of the art of query processing on co-processors.

9. REFERENCES

[1] CUDA C programming guide, CUDA version 6.5, 77–78. NVIDIA, 2014. http://docs.nvidia.com/cuda/pdf/CUDA_C_Programming_Guide.pdf.

[2] D. J. Abadi, S. R. Madden, and N. Hachem. Column-stores vs. row-stores: How different are they really? In *SIGMOD*, pages 967–980. ACM, 2008.

[3] S. Arumugam, A. Dobra, C. M. Jermaine, N. Pansare, and L. Perez. The DataPath system: A data-centric analytic processing engine for large data warehouses. In *SIGMOD*, pages 519–530. ACM, 2010.

[4] P. A. Boncz and M. L. Kersten. MIL primitives for querying a fragmented world. *The VLDB Journal*, 8(2):101–119, 1999.

[5] P. A. Boncz, M. Zukowski, and N. Nes. MonetDB/X100: Hyper-pipelining query execution. In *CIDR*, pages 225–237, 2005.

[6] S. Borkar and A. A. Chien. The future of microprocessors. *Communications of the ACM*, 54(5):67–77, 2011.

[7] S. Breß, F. Beier, H. Rauhe, K.-U. Sattler, E. Schallehn, and G. Saake. Efficient co-processor utilization in database query processing. *Information Systems*, 38(8):1084–1096, 2013.

[8] S. Breß, M. Heimel, M. Saecker, B. Kocher, V. Markl, and G. Saake. Ocelot/HyPE: Optimized data processing on heterogeneous hardware. *PVLDB*, 7(13):1609–1612, 2014.

[9] S. Breß, N. Siegmund, M. Heimel, M. Saecker, T. Lauer, L. Bellatreche, and G. Saake. Load-aware inter-co-processor parallelism in database query processing. *Data & Knowledge Engineering*, 93(0):60–79, 2014.

[10] L. Chen, X. Huo, and G. Agrawal. Accelerating mapreduce on a coupled cpu-gpu architecture. In *SC*, pages 25:1–25:11. IEEE, 2012.

[11] C. Gregg and K. Hazelwood. Where is the data? why you cannot debate CPU vs. GPU performance without the answer. In *ISPASS*, pages 134–144. IEEE, 2011.

[12] S. Harizopoulos, V. Shkapenyuk, and A. Ailamaki. QPipe: A simultaneously pipelined relational query engine. In *SIGMOD*, pages 383–394. ACM, 2005.

[13] B. He, M. Lu, K. Yang, R. Fang, N. K. Govindaraju, Q. Luo, and P. V. Sander. Relational query co-processing on graphics processors. In *ACM Trans. Database Syst.*, volume 34. ACM, 2009.

[14] J. He, M. Lu, and B. He. Revisiting co-processing for hash joins on the coupled CPU-GPU architecture. *Proc. VLDB Endow.*, 6(10):889–900, 2013.

[15] M. Heimel, M. Saecker, H. Pirk, S. Manegold, and V. Markl. Hardware-oblivious parallelism for in-memory column-stores. *PVLDB*, 6(9):709–720, 2013.

[16] S. Héman, N. Nes, M. Zukowski, and P. Boncz. Vectorized data processing on the Cell broadband engine. In *DaMoN*, pages 4:1–4:6. ACM, 2007.

[17] S. Idreos, F. Groffen, N. Nes, S. Manegold, K. S. Mullender, and M. L. Kersten. MonetDB: Two decades of research in column-oriented database architectures. *IEEE Data Eng. Bull.*, 35(1):40–45, 2012.

[18] S. Jha, B. He, M. Lu, X. Cheng, and H. P. Huynh. Improving main memory hash joins on Intel Xeon Phi processors: An experimental approach. *PVLDB*, 8(6):642–653, 2015.

[19] T. Karnagel, D. Habich, and W. Lehner. Local vs. global optimization: Operator placement strategies in heterogeneous environments. In *DAPHNE, EDBT/ICDT Workshops*, pages 48–55, 2015.

[20] T. Karnagel, M. Heimel, M. Hille, M. Ludwig, D. Habich, W. Lehner, and V. Markl. Demonstrating efficient query processing in heterogeneous environments. In *SIGMOD*, pages 693–696. ACM, 2014.

[21] K. Krikellas, S. Viglas, and M. Cintra. Generating code for holistic query evaluation. In *ICDE*, pages 613–624. IEEE, 2010.

[22] V. Leis, P. Boncz, A. Kemper, and T. Neumann. Morsel-driven parallelism: A NUMA-aware query evaluation framework for the many-core age. In *SIGMOD*, pages 743–754. ACM, 2014.

[23] M. Lu, L. Zhang, H. P. Huynh, Z. Ong, Y. Liang, B. He, R. Goh, and R. Huynh. Optimizing the mapreduce framework on Intel Xeon Phi coprocessor. In *Big Data*, pages 125–130. IEEE, 2013.

[24] T. Mostak. An overview of MapD (massively parallel database). White Paper, MIT, April 2013. http://geops.csail.mit.edu/docs/mapd_overview.pdf.

[25] R. Mueller, J. Teubner, and G. Alonso. Data processing on FPGAs. *PVLDB*, 2(1):910–921, 2009.

[26] T. Mühlbauer, W. Rödiger, R. Seilbeck, A. Kemper, and T. Neumann. Heterogeneity-conscious parallel query execution: Getting a better mileage while driving faster! In *DaMoN*, pages 2:1–2:10. ACM, 2014.

[27] T. Neumann. Efficiently compiling efficient query plans for modern hardware. *PVLDB*, 4(9):539–550, 2011.

[28] P. O'Neil, E. J. O'Neil, and X. Chen. The star schema benchmark (SSB), 2009. Revision 3, http://www.cs.umb.edu/~poneil/StarSchemaB.PDF.

[29] I. Pandis, R. Johnson, N. Hardavellas, and A. Ailamaki. Data-oriented transaction execution. *PVLDB*, 3(1-2):928–939, 2010.

[30] H. Pirk, S. Manegold, and M. Kersten. Waste not... efficient co-processing of relational data. In *ICDE*. IEEE, 2014.

[31] H. Pirk, T. Sellam, S. Manegold, and M. Kersten. X-Device Query Processing by Bitwise Distribution. In *DaMoN*, pages 48–54. ACM, 2012.

[32] I. Psaroudakis, M. Athanassoulis, and A. Ailamaki. Sharing data and work across concurrent analytical queries. *PVLDB*, 6(9):637–648, 2013.

[33] I. Psaroudakis, T. Scheuer, N. May, and A. Ailamaki. Task scheduling for highly concurrent analytical and transactional main-memory workloads. In *ADMS*, pages 36–45. VLDB Endowment, 2013.

[34] J. Sanders and E. Kandrot. *CUDA by Example: An Introduction to General-Purpose GPU Programming.* Addison-Wesley Professional, 1st edition, 2010.

[35] K. Wang, K. Zhang, Y. Yuan, S. Ma, R. Lee, X. Ding, and X. Zhang. Concurrent analytical query processing with GPUs. *PVLDB*, 7(11):1011–1022, 2014.

[36] H. Wu, G. Diamos, T. Sheard, M. Aref, S. Baxter, M. Garland, and S. Yalamanchili. Red Fox: An execution environment for relational query processing on GPUs. In *CGO*, pages 44:44–44:54. ACM, 2014.

[37] Y. Yuan, R. Lee, and X. Zhang. The yin and yang of processing data warehousing queries on GPU devices. *PVLDB*, 6(10):817–828, 2013.

[38] S. Zhang et al. OmniDB: Towards portable and efficient query processing on parallel CPU/GPU architectures. *PVLDB*, 6(12):1374–1377, 2013.

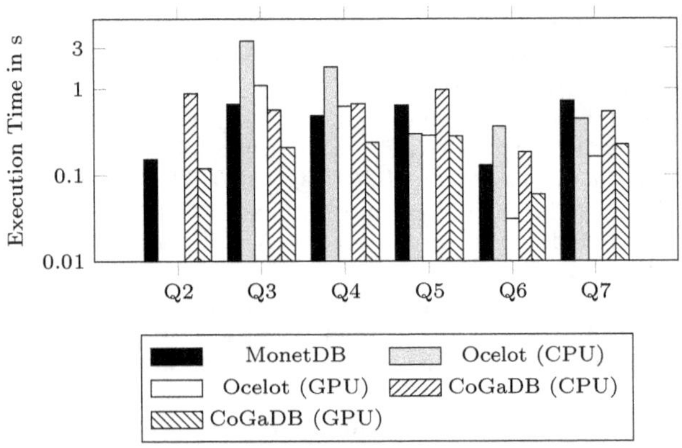

Figure 22: Query execution times for selected TPC-H queries for a single user and a database of scale factor 10.

APPENDIX

A. PERFORMANCE COMPARISON: OCELOT VERSUS CoGaDB

In this section, we conduct a performance comparison of CoGaDB and a state-of-the-art database engine with GPU support: Ocelot [15] (at revision 3e75851).[3] As Ocelot is an extension of MonetDB, we include measurements of MonetDB as well. Note that MonetDB, Ocelot, and CoGaDB exploit all cores of the CPU to maximize performance. For a fair comparison with CoGaDB, we optimized MonetDB/Ocelot as follows.

We set the databases to read-only mode and set the size of OIDs to 32 bit. Furthermore, we measured a warm system after the queries where run before to ensure that the database resides in memory. For all measurements with MonetDB/Ocelot, we used the benchmark scripts that are provided by the author of Ocelot as part of the source code.

We show the average query execution times for the TPC-H benchmark in Figure 22 and the SSBM in Figure 23. Both engines show that GPUs can significantly accelerate query processing. We will now discuss the performance for the GPU and CPU backends. Since we are interested in the raw query processing power, we choose a configuration with a single user and use databases with scale factor 10, where neither memory thrashing nor heap contention occurs. We omit SSBM Query 2.2 and TPC-H query 2 for Ocelot, as it does not support them.

For the SSBM workload, the GPU backends of Ocelot and CoGaDB perform equally well for queries Q1.1-Q1.3 and Q3.1-Q4.3. Ocelots GPU backend is faster for the queries Q2.1 and 2.3. As for the TPC-H workload, CoGaDB is faster for queries Q3 and Q4, equally fast for queries Q5 and Q7 and slower for query Q7. Thus, the GPU backends of Ocelot and CoGaDB are both highly optimized and competitive in performance.

As for the CPU backend, we see that Ocelot performs better than CoGaDB for all SSBM queries except Q1.1-1.3 and Q3.1. For queries Q4.1-Q4.3, the performance improvement is comparatively small. For the TPC-H queries, CoGaDB is faster or competitive to Ocelot for queries Q3,Q4,Q6, Q7 and slower for query Q5. Besides TPC-H query Q2, CoGaDB is never significantly slower than MonetDB, and for some queries even faster (e.g., SSBM Q4.1).

[3] https://bitbucket.org/msaecker/monetdb-opencl

We conclude that CoGaDB is competitive in performance to the MonetDB/Ocelot system and thus, is a suitable basis for our performance studies.

B. MICRO BENCHMARKS

In this section, we describe our micro benchmarks which show the cache thrashing and heap contention effects.

B.1 Serial Selection Workload

Our first benchmark shows the cache thrashing effect. For this, we execute queries serially and use multiple selection queries that access different input columns of the fact table from the star schema benchmark. We show the queries in Figure 1. A workload consists of 100 repetitions of these queries. We execute the workload multiple times and show the average execution time.

```
select * from order where quantity<1
select * from order where discount>10
select * from order where shippriority>0
select * from order where extendedprice<100
select * from order where ordtotalprice<100
select * from order where revenue<1000
select * from order where supplycost<1000
select * from order where tax>10
```

Listing 1: Serial Selection Queries. Note the interleaved execution. The order table is an alias for the lineorder table.

B.2 Parallel Selection Workload

Our second benchmark shows the heap contention effect. To show the problems of aborted co-processor operators, we use a more complex selection query, but filter only two columns which fit into the co-processors data cache (cf. Listing 2). The query is derived from query Q1.1 of the star schema benchmark. For each experiment, we execute 100 queries, but increase the number of parallel user sessions that execute the workload. Since all workloads contain the same amount work, an ideal system could execute all workloads in the same time. The only difference is that with increasing number of parallel users, the parallelism in the DBMS changes from intra-operator parallelism to inter-operator parallelism.

```
select * from order where discount
between 4 and 6 and quantity between 26 and 35
```

Listing 2: Parallel Selection Query

C. WORKLOADS

In this section, we briefly present the star schema benchmark and our modifications to the TPC-H benchmark.

C.1 Star Schema Benchmark

The *Star Schema Benchmark* (SSBM) is a popular OLAP benchmark, derived from the TPC-H benchmark by applying de-normalization. The SSBM is frequently used for performance evaluation, such as in C-Store [2] or GPUDB [37].

C.1.1 Schema and Data

The SSBM uses a classical star schema with one fact table *lineorder* and four dimension tables *supplier*, *part*, *date*, and *customer*. Similar to TPC-H, we can adjust the size of the database by a scale factor. If not defined differently, we use a scale factor of 10 (LINEORDER contains 60,000,000 tuples).

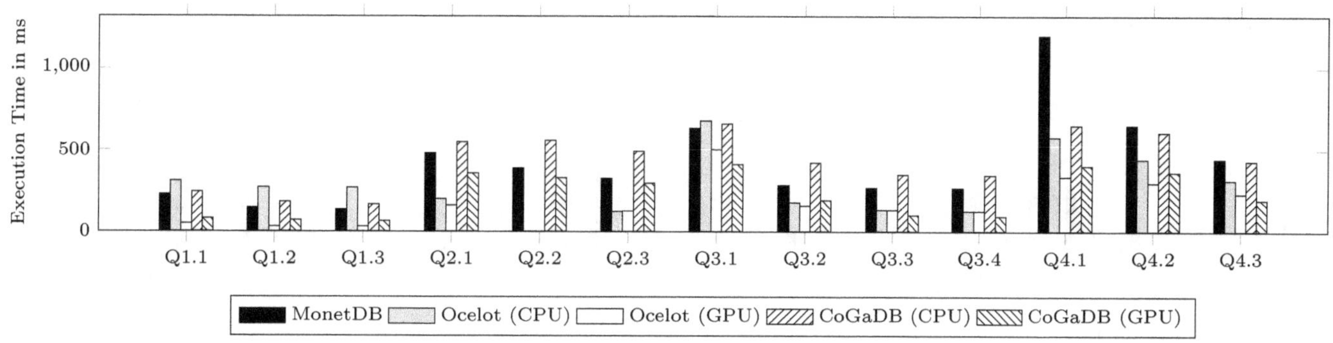

Figure 23: Query execution times for SSBM queries for a single user and a database of scale factor 10.

C.1.2 Queries

The SSBM defines 13 queries, which are grouped into four categories (flights). In each category, the basic query is the same, but different queries have different selectivities. One category basically models a drill-down operation in a data warehouse. Furthermore, the number of required join operations vary from 1 (category 1) to 4 (category 4) join operations. Therefore, with increasing category number, query complexity increases. For further details on the SSBM, we refer the reader to the work of O'Neil and others [28].

C.2 Modifications to TPC-H Benchmark

As the TPC-H benchmark is widely known, we will focus on our modifications to the workload. Our goal is to run a representative set of TPC-H queries that benchmark relational operators. Advanced capabilities such as case statements, joins with arbitrary join conditions, and substring functions are not in our scope and queries that use these features are omitted. Thus, we focused on the efficient support of six TPC-H queries (Q2-Q7) on CPU and GPU to evaluate the memory thrashing and heap contention effects.

D. CRITICAL PATH HEURISTIC

We now discuss the *Critical Path* heuristic for operator placement used by default in CoGaDB. *Critical Path* optimizes for response time and operates as classic cost-based optimizer, where multiple plan candidates are enumerated and the cheapest plan is selected for execution.

To achieve a low response time for queries, we need to optimize the *critical path*, which is the path from a leaf operator to the plan's root that takes the longest time to execute. As data transfers are expensive, we only consider plans where such a path is either completely executed on the CPU or the co-processor. For each binary operator, the processing on the co-processor is continued only if both child operators were executed on the co-processor.

This heuristic also significantly reduces the search space, as we have an exponential complexity in the number of leaf operators instead of an exponential complexity in the number of all operators. However, for large queries this can also become expensive, so we use an iterative refinement algorithm that prunes the search space further and runs for a fixed amount of iterations.

Based on these concepts, the *Critical Path* heuristic works as follows. Each leaf operator is assigned to the CPU and a pure CPU plan is created. From this initial plan, we first investigate all plans where a single leaf operator (and it's path to the first binary parent operator) is executed on the co-processor. For the fastest plan, one additional leaf operator is placed on the co-processor and the next iteration takes place.

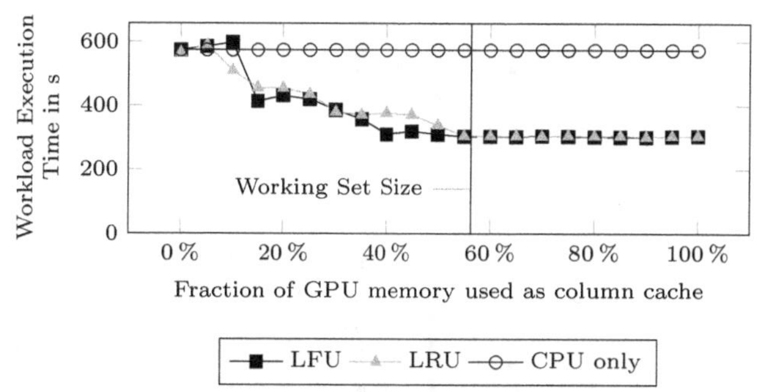

Figure 24: Execution time of a workload of interleaved SSBM queries with different placement strategies on a database of scale factor 10.

The additional reduction of the optimization space makes *Critical Path* quadratic in the number of leaf operators. The algorithm terminates if all plans of the reduced optimization space were examined or a fixed number of iterations has passed in case the plan contains too many leaf operators.

The *Critical Path* heuristic produces faster query plans than simulated annealing or genetic algorithms in most cases. Occasionally, the produced plans of simulated annealing or genetic algorithms are more efficient, but the plans produced by *Critical Path* are still competitive. Thus, the problem specific information of *Critical Path* provide an advantage over established optimization strategies that explore a larger part of the optimization space.

E. DATA PLACEMENT STRATEGIES

We compare a LFU and a LRU strategy in our data-driven strategy for a complete SSBM workload in Figure 24. The amount of GPU memory that is used as column cache is varied between 0% and 100%. If input data does not fit in the GPU memory, all processing on that data will be performed by the CPU. As expected, the execution times are improving until the working set fits entirely in the GPU memory, with no slowdown for cases where no column fits into the cache. The LFU strategy performs slightly better than the LRU strategy for corner cases, where different columns are cached first by LRU and LFU. This leads to a slight slowdown of LRU. Overall, we conclude that the background policy is effective for complex query workloads such as the SSBM and that the data placement strategy itself has only a minor impact on performance. Thus, the observed performance gain comes clearly from our data driven strategy.

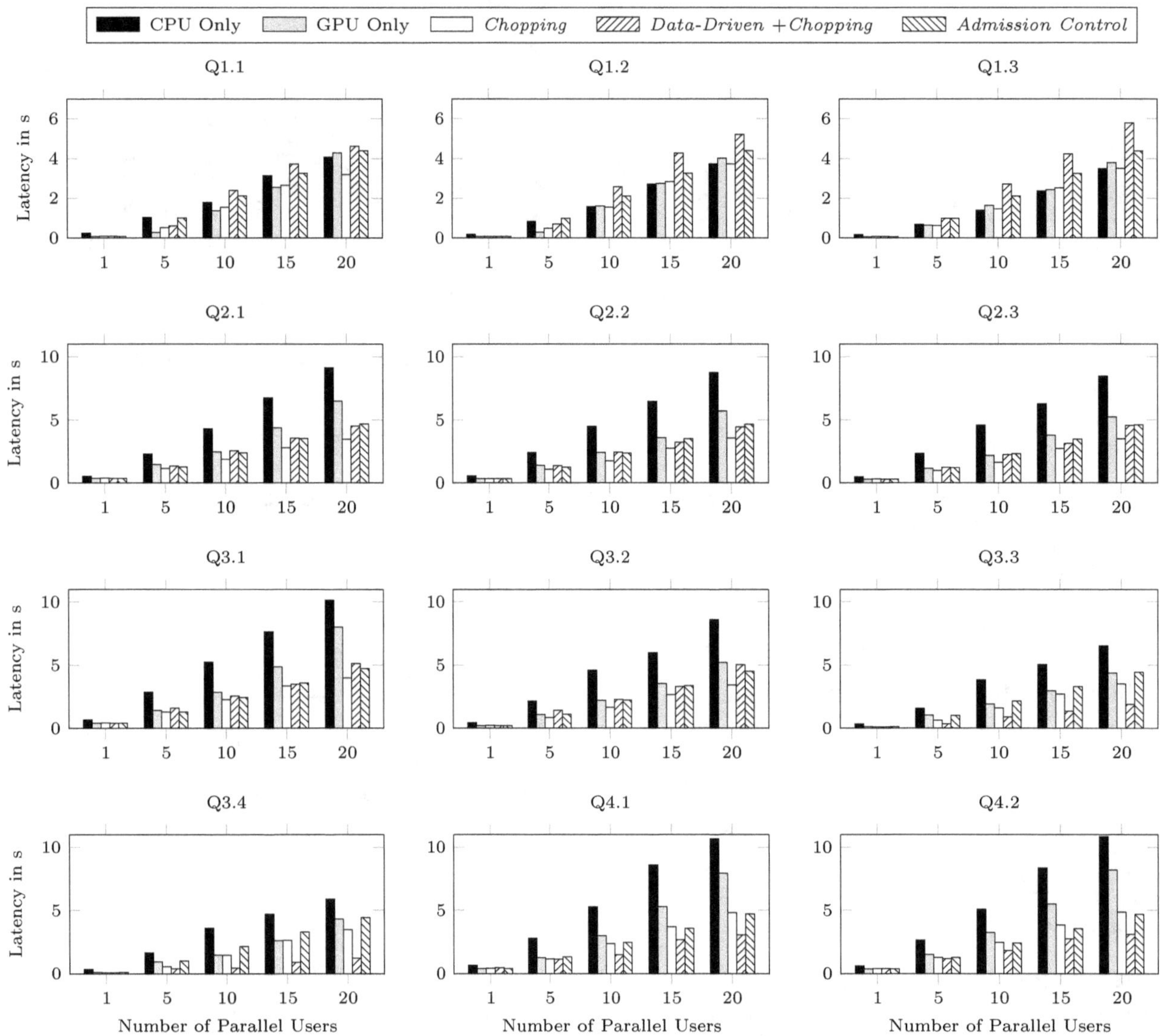

Figure 25: Latencies of all SSBM queries with a varying number of parallel users and a database of scale factor 10.

Acknowledgements

We thank the anonymous reviewers of SIGMOD for their helpful comments. We also thank Max Heimel from TU Berlin, David Broneske, Sebastian Dorok, and Andreas Meister from University of Magdeburg, and Thomas Lindemann and Michael Kußmann from TU Dortmund University for helpful feedback and discussions. The work has received funding from the Deutsche Forschungsgemeinschaft (DFG), Collaborative Research Center SFB 876, project C5 (http://sfb876.tu-dortmund.de/) and from the European Union's Horizon2020 Research & Innovation Program under grant agreement 671500 (project "SAGE").

How to Architect a Query Compiler

Amir Shaikhha, Yannis Klonatos, Lionel Parreaux, Lewis Brown,
Mohammad Dashti, and Christoph Koch
{firstname}.{lastname}@epfl.ch
École Polytechnique Fédérale de Lausanne

ABSTRACT

This paper studies architecting query compilers. The state of the art in query compiler construction is lagging behind that in the compilers field. We attempt to remedy this by exploring the key causes of technical challenges in need of well founded solutions, and by gathering the most relevant ideas and approaches from the PL and compilers communities for easy digestion by database researchers. All query compilers known to us are more or less monolithic template expanders that do the bulk of the compilation task in one large leap. Such systems are hard to build and maintain. We propose to use a stack of multiple DSLs on different levels of abstraction with lowering in multiple steps to make query compilers easier to build and extend, ultimately allowing us to create more convincing and sustainable compiler-based data management systems. We attempt to derive our advice for creating such DSL stacks from widely acceptable principles. We have also re-created a well-known query compiler following these ideas and report on this effort.

1. INTRODUCTION

Query compilation has been with us since the dawn of the relational database era: IBM's System R employed query compilation in its very first prototype, but this approach was quickly abandoned in favor of query *interpretation* [15]. Recently, query compilation has returned to the limelight, with commercial systems such as StreamBase, IBM Spade, Microsoft's Hekaton, Cloudera Impala, and MemSQL employing it. Academic research has also intensified [33, 2, 52, 56, 64, 53, 54, 55, 50, 84, 19, 62, 44, 6].

We can argue that, despite all this recent work, the state of the art in the design of query compilers lags behind the programming languages and compilers research field. To the best of our knowledge, all existing query compilers are *template expanders* at heart. A template expander is a procedure that, simply speaking, generates low-level code in one direct macro expansion step. While a query interpreter *calls* an operator implementation used inside a query plan, the template expander essentially *inlines* the operator code in the plan, for each operator, to obtain low-level code for the entire plan. We restrict our study to the actual compiler component of a possibly larger data management system. For instance, a system which first parses SQL into query plans and optimizes these Selinger-style, then feeds such plans to a compiler which generates LLVM bytecode, which is in turn lowered to machine code by LLVM, is still a template expander if that core compiler component – into which all of the DBMS engineering team's compiler efforts went – is sufficiently primitive, even if more than two languages and abstraction levels are present in the system as a whole.

Template expansion is a robust and intellectually accessible concept, but it has a number of drawbacks. The System R team reports that query compilation was abandoned in favor of interpretation since query compiler code was hard to maintain (cf. [15]). More fundamentally, template expanders make it impractical to support a range of sophisticated optimizations since multiple code transformers (with different optimization roles) have to be composed and inlined in all possible ways and orderings, causing a code size explosion in compiler code bases. Furthermore, template expanders make cross-operator code optimization impossible [50][1].

To illustrate the above-mentioned code explosion further, consider the example of a template expander that is to support two transformations: 1) pipelining (i.e. removing the need to materialize intermediate results between query operators) and 2) data-structure specialization (i.e. adapting the definition of a data structure to the particular context in which it is used). In order to perform these two optimizations together, one has to implement every combination of their respective cases. For example, if each optimization handles 3 different cases, one has to create a template expander with 9 cases to handle their combination. In general, the code complexity grows exponentially with the depth of the stack of desired transformations. Figure 1a illustrates this code explosion.

System R's initial query compiler as well as Hekaton are confirmed template expanders (cf., [15] and a private communication with the Hekaton team). While academic work makes numerous contributions to the practice of query compilers, it is fair to say that creating a query compiler that produces highly optimized code is a formidable challenge due to the needs to work with various Domain-Specific Languages (DSLs), understand their optimization potentials, and build on the wealth of algorithmic and systems results created by the research over multiple decades. The database community can profit from further tools and techniques from the compilers field.

In this paper, we provide, to the best of our knowledge, the first principled methodology for building query compilers.

We create tools and techniques to increase the *modularity* of query compiler components, to manage the complexity of these systems. Instead of using template expansion to directly gener-

[1]The key contribution of [64] is to show how a push operator interface can eliminate the need for cross-operator fusion transformers, making template expanders produce faster code.

SIGMOD'16, June 26-July 01, 2016, San Francisco, CA, USA

DOI: http://dx.doi.org/10.1145/2882903.2915244

ate low-level code from a high-level query plan, we propose **progressively lowering the level of abstraction** until we reach the lowest level, and only then generating low-level code. Each level of abstraction and each associated optimization can be seen as independent modules, enforcing the principle of *separation of concerns*. There are two kinds of code transformations, optimizations (where the source and target DSLs are the same) and lowerings. By supporting optimizations on every abstraction level, we obtain real power – moving to a lower-level DSL tends to expand the code size and there is a tradeoff between the search space for optimizations and the granularity of the DSL. Optimizations such as join reorderings are only feasible in high-level DSLs, while register allocation decisions can only be expressed in very low-level DSLs. We propose to use a stack of multiple internal DSLs, one for each such abstraction layer. We attempt to derive our advice for creating such DSL stacks from easily acceptable principles.

Returning to the above example, we can define a third intermediate abstraction level, a *data-structure aware DSL*, to place between the source and target languages. Pipelining transforms a high-level query plan to that intermediate language which has explicit constructs for the operations on the hash-table and list data structures. Then, data-structure specialization transforms the program from this language to low-level code by using an appropriate implementation of each data structure based on its context. Using this intermediate DSL and stepwise lowering, there is no longer any need to consider every combination of the two optimizations, as they no longer interfere by manipulating the same expression. As a result, the complexity of the query compiler code base is more manageable, as demonstrated in Figure 1b.

Creating a sophisticated query compiler is a challenging undertaking, and there are a number of results from the PL and compilers research communities that can help. We explore the key technical challenges in need of well founded solutions, and attempt to gather the most relevant ideas and solution approaches from the PL and compilers communities for easy digestion by database researchers. Specifically, we look at the choice of intermediate languages, how to maximize the separation of concerns among compiler optimizations and lowerings, implementation design choices, and several transformations expressible using this approach.

Throughout this paper, we use the Scala language for our examples and for embedding our DSLs, but nowhere does this paper specifically depend on this choice of programming language.

This is an atypical paper in that our main contributions are hard to experimentally validate. Our insights are based on building four distinct compiler-based data management systems over the past seven years, but creating query compilers with a maximally shared codebase for the multitude of alternatives discussed in this paper is beyond the resources of any research group.

Instead, we have re-created a well-known query compiler [50] following our ideas – our DSL stack with stepwise lowering – and report on this effort. We report on the productivity of creating this compiler using a suitable DSL compiler framework [1], and show that we are able to implement all the optimizations of [50] (and more), obtaining at least comparable and often better performance.

2. OVERALL DESIGN PRINCIPLES

2.1 Background

Most database management systems to date use high-level DSLs such as SQL to express queries. Those queries are transformed into optimized physical query plans, and then passed to an engine that interprets them. This approach pays the cost of interpretation overhead, and many low-level optimization opportunities are missed

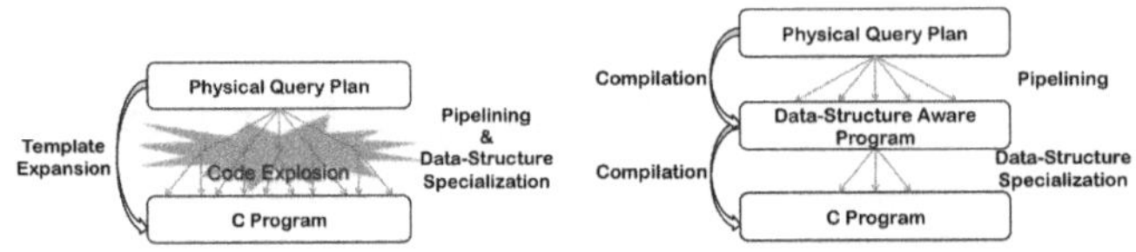

(a) Pipelining and data-structure specialization are applied concurrently. Hence, we should apply brute-force to all combinations, resulting in code explosion.

(b) Pipelining and data-structure specialization are applied sequentially. Hence, there is no need to consider all combinations, resulting in managed code base.

Figure 1: Handling concurrent optimizations in template expansion and progressive compilation approaches.

(e.g. function inlining), because they are not expressible in the high-level DSL of query plans. These sources of overhead may become especially significant for queries working with in-memory data, where computation is increasingly CPU-bound (rather than I/O-bound). To circumvent these limitations, query compilation aims to generate low-level code from the high-level query plans, allowing specific optimizations to be applied at this low-level representation[2].

However, by directly generating low-level code, we also miss optimization opportunities that are both not available at the high level, and hard to express at the low level – mainly because the locality of code patterns to match is lost. For example, loop fusion (i.e. replacing multiple loops with a single one) is not expressible in query plans, as there is no notion of loop at this abstraction level. Also, it is proven to be NP-complete [21, 48] and impractical in imperative languages such as C [26], the usual target of query compilers.

We propose the introduction of intermediate abstraction levels (referred to as *intermediate DSLs*) for expressing such optimizations. This has already been done in other domains, such as signal transforms and linear algebra. In these domains, we can cite the Σ-SPL [26] and Σ-LL [73] intermediate languages, which have been developed in Spiral [67] for expressing loop fusion optimizations.

In this work, we show that by using several abstraction levels and by doing *step-wise lowering* across them, we can express powerful optimizations (such as pipelining and data-structure synthesis) that are hard or impossible to express in existing query compilation approaches. The resulting set of DSLs, ordered from higher level to lower level, is referred to as the *DSL stack*.

2.2 Choosing The DSLs

Although the design space for a DSL stack may seem overwhelming, there are several constraints that make some design choices impractical, or even infeasible. These directions can be discarded. Among these constraints, there is an important principle for designing intermediate abstraction levels related to the expressive power of programming languages, in the sense of Felleisen [23]:

[2] In this work, we consider compilation as a form of *partial evaluation* [38]. A compiler-based approach can always delay some of this partial evaluation to runtime, in which case the nature of the system moves, at least in some aspect, from compilation to interpretation. A strict choice of either one or the other at design time is not, however, necessary. More concretely, there are scenarios where compilation staging, just-in-time compilation, or even interpretation are desirable: if some essential piece of information that can substantially speed up evaluation is not available at compile time, it is better to delay this partial evaluation until that information is available. The classical example is probably statistics for query optimization. Even a compilation-based query engine cannot afford to go without a query optimizer.

> **Expressibility principle:** *Any program written in a given DSL should be expressible in any of the lower-level DSLs as well. Therefore, by lowering the level of abstraction from the former to the latter, one should retain the same expressive power or gain more.*

Note that the converse does not need to hold: a program in a low-level DSL does *not* need to be expressible in higher-level DSLs. Based on the expressibility principle, we can start designing an appropriate DSL stack. For that, we need to answer the following questions: 1) What abstraction levels (DSLs) do we need? 2) On which abstraction level(s) should we put each transformation?

We propose a methodology that naturally answers both questions at the same time: to design a DSL stack, one should start from the simplest stack possible (a high-level DSL that maps directly to a low level one), then iteratively examine the desired transformations one by one and see if the existing DSL stack is sufficient for it or if a new abstraction level needs to be introduced.

Every transformation requires an input program in a *source language* and produces a program in a *target language*. If the source language and the target language are the same, the transformation is called an *optimization*, whereas if the target language is at lower level, it is called a *lowering* transformation. We will see in the next section why the source language is never going to be lower-level than the target language.

Optimizations are subject to the well-known *phase-ordering problem* [80]: most optimizations can produce opportunities for other optimizations that apply to the same language, but it is not clear how to order them optimally. This problem is still a topic of research in the Programming Language community, and no definitive answer has been formulated yet.[3] To mitigate this, we recursively apply optimizations inside the same abstraction level until we reach a fixed point,[4] where either no more optimizations can be applied or the application of an optimization does not yield structurally different code. On the other hand, lowering transformations are not subject to this issue, because they change the abstraction level of the program so previous optimizations are no longer applicable.

Note that lowering transformations should always be applicable, irrelevant of the input program. Otherwise, the transformation chains would be broken. In contrast, optimizations may or may not be applicable, depending on the information and patterns found in the program being optimized.

2.3 Constructing The Stack

For the DSL stack to be well-formed and to maximize the reuse of transformations, we need to ensure that transformations are not redundant. Each lowering transformation translates a DSL to the next lower-level DSL, and each high-level DSL program is, through a sequence of lowerings, eventually mapped to the target language. This requirement is summarized in the following principle:

> **Transformation cohesion principle:** *Between any two DSLs of different abstraction levels, there should be a unique path of lowering transformations translating programs in the higher-level DSL into programs in the lower-level one.*

[3] *Online* (or *local*) transformations do help removing ordering problems for a certain class of optimizations [39]. We provide facilities (cf. [13]) to encode them in our framework, but this is out of the scope of the current paper.

[4] Special care needs to be taken in the design of optimizations to ensure that iteratively applying them leads to termination.

Notice that this does not prevent having several different high-level front-end DSLs, or different low-level target languages. On the other hand, the principle implies that there can be no transformations from a given DSL a to a higher-level DSL b, as there would also need to be a path down from b to a, creating a loop, and thus an infinity of lowering paths from b to a, violating the principle.

Let us consider the case where we need to introduce a new abstraction level, which mainly happens when we have more than one lowering transformation between two particular DSLs. In such a case, we have to split either the source language or the target language into two separate languages. The new intermediate language should follow the expressibility principle, interpolating between the level above and below. Furthermore, the affected transformations should update their source or target languages: optimizations on the source and target languages, and the lowering transformations from the source to the target language. This update in the existing lowering transformations is necessary as, otherwise, the transformation cohesion principle would be violated.

Going back to our working example, consider a query compiler with SQL as the query language, C as the target language, and pipelining and data-structure specialization as transformations. First, we start from a two-level DSL stack, as shown in Figure 1a.

Second, we consider where to place the pipelining transformation. The information required for checking the applicability of pipelining is available in SQL. However, it is very hard to check such opportunities in a low-level language like C. Expressing a pipelined program is not possible in SQL. This requires the expressibility of a lower language, like C in this case. Hence, pipelining is a lowering transformation from SQL to C.

Finally, we examine the existing DSL stack (which is still two levels till now) for adding data-structure specialization. Similar to pipelining, this transformation is a lowering from SQL to C. This is because we need the high-level information available in SQL, but also a way to explicitly represent data structures (not possible in SQL). We now have two lowering transformations from SQL to C. This means we should break one of these languages into two languages to modularize these two transformations. In this case, we break C into two languages: 1) Data-structure-aware C, which is an extension to the standard C language with specific constructs for the data structures of a query engine, and 2) The standard C language. Data-structure specialization can now use data-structure-aware C as its source language and low-level C as its target language. At last, all transformations which had C as their source or target language should be updated accordingly. In this case, pipelining should update its target language in order to follow the transformation cohesion principle. Pipelining can be expressed in data-structure-aware C as well. Hence, the pipelining transformation is now a lowering transformation between SQL and data-structure-aware C. The new DSL stack is shown in Figure 1b.

In the next section, we further discuss the design space as well as compilation concerns for different DSL stacks.

3. DESIGN SPACE

3.1 Imperative vs. Declarative

So far, we have been referring to *high-level* and *low-level* languages without providing a clear definition for these terms. A more precise terminology would have us use *declarative* and *imperative* instead, although these do not always coincide. This dichotomy is not the only criterion to take into account while designing abstraction levels, but it does play a central role, as we will see. In a declarative language, programs are close to specifications of the results we want to compute, while in an imperative language, de-

Paradigm	Advantages
Declarative	✓ Concise programs ✓ Small search space of equivalent programs ✓ Simple to analyze and verify ✓ Simple to parallelize
Imperative	✓ Efficient data structures ✓ Precise control of runtime constructs ✓ More predictable performance

Table 1: Comparison of declarative and imperative languages

tails about how the result is computed are made explicit. The latter usually involves the use of side-effects like mutation. Table 1 summarizes the important differences between these two approaches.

Different mixes of declarative and imperative features in a DSL are amenable to different optimizations, and require different compilation techniques. Programs in high-level languages are smaller, and the search space of semantically equivalent programs is therefore more manageable. This allows us to use search strategies similar to the ones query optimizers use. These result in global optimizations that have more impact on the resulting program than optimizations on low-level programs, since an expression in a high-level program corresponds to many low-level expressions.

Moreover, high-level languages usually target specific domains – in our case, query processing. As a result, they need not be as complete and powerful as general-purpose languages: like SQL, they do not even need to be Turing-complete [59]. This allows compilers to provide more guarantees, and to perform better reasoning, static analysis, and optimization [83]. For example, it is feasible to statically reason about the runtime cost of a SQL query with typically good or acceptable accuracy. This is *not* possible in low-level Turing-complete languages without actually running the program [51].

Since low-level programs are larger, there is a large number of equivalent low-level programs. This makes the use of search techniques [51] impractical, preventing the global optimization of these programs. Instead, optimizing compilers usually perform only local optimizations (typically, so-called "peephole" optimizations, that only consider a small part of the program at a time).

In the rest of this section, we see how to design our intermediate DSLs to integrate more or less imperative and declarative features, depending on the type of optimizations we want to perform on them. Then, we discuss different possible Intermediate Representations (IRs) to encode programs written in these DSLs.

3.2 DSL Design and Optimization

Functional languages are a particularly important class of declarative languages. We use functional features to represent the declarative aspects of our DSLs for several reasons: first, these languages are easy to understand and to reason about, possibly reusing frameworks developed in the PL community [14]; second, functional constructs integrate well with imperative ones [65], supporting our goal of progressively turning programs from a declarative to an imperative form; finally, the hybrid Scala programming language, which we use in our framework, naturally allows such a mix of functional and imperative code.

Although functional programs are executable, they introduce a relatively heavy performance penalty and do not allow enough control on runtime constructs. This prevents the fine tuning of program performance. For example, standard functional data structures are immutable, and do not allow in-place modification of their elements, requiring copies instead. Without aggressive optimizations like deforestation [86], this translates into many unnecessary allocations and copies. Therefore, we need to lower these high-level declarative constructs into specific, optimized imperative representations. Such representations are close to the underlying architecture, providing opportunities for fine-grained performance tuning.

On the other hand, imperative programs that exhibit poor performance are harder to optimize. For example, detecting loop fusion opportunities is much harder in imperative programs than in functional ones. If the loops in an imperative program are not manually fused by the programmer, there is little chance that the compiler will be able to fuse them automatically. The reason is that optimizing imperative programs with side effects is notoriously hard [7], chiefly because the compiler has to reason about aliased mutable memory locations, a problem that has been shown to be intractable in general [69]. This has implications on low-level optimizations.

For example, consider a `for` loop written in C that only manipulates local variables. Modern compilers know how to optimize such constructs in near-optimal, almost unbeatable ways. But as soon as one introduces non-trivial function calls inside the loop, the compiler's bets are off and many automatic rewritings become impossible. Consider the following code:

```
for (int i = 0; i < size(str); i++) { str[i] = 'X'; }
```

In general, a compiler must not assume that it is safe to extract the call to `size(str)` out of the loop, because the way it is computed could be influenced by assignments performed inside the loop body. In fact, for the particular case where `str` is a simple C string, the compiler cannot know that we are not going to override the string termination character while iterating over the string (which would change the result of a subsequent call to `size`).[5] This would prevent the compiler from implementing resetting the characters of a string as an efficient `memset` instruction.

In this context, human expertise becomes important again. Based on domain-specific knowledge, one can make assumptions that low-level C compilers cannot, even after expensive program analyses that try to recover high-level information from the low-level code. Since we progressively lower abstraction one step at a time, we can exploit as many optimization opportunities as possible along the way. Our framework allows the expression of effectful computations, but can still reason about code that is known to be pure, and our transformations can leverage invariants that are known to hold in the intermediate DSLs.

Next, we discuss various intermediate representation choices for each abstraction level.

3.3 Intermediate Representation

Compilers usually convert input programs, given as text strings, into an *Intermediate Representation (IR)* which contains all essential information available about the program after parsing[6]. Optimizing compilers use IRs to facilitate the definition and application of optimizations.

The simplest form of an IR is an *Abstract Syntax Tree (AST)*. In database management systems, an AST represents a query in relational algebra or its physical plan. This representation is sufficient for performing algebraic rewrite rules on such algebraic languages without variable bindings. Examples of transformations include pushing down selections or changing the join order in relational algebra. As an example, Stratego [85] uses ASTs for its IR.

[5]A special case could be added in the compiler to handle this particular example, but this approach does not scale, as the general problem is undecidable.

[6]Observe that *different* DSLs or abstractions levels may use the *same* IR as their underlying data structure; however, the information (DSL constructs) encoded using these IRs may vary significantly.

However, there are optimizations that require more sophisticated IRs. For example, *Common Subexpression Elimination* (CSE) involves sharing leaves among sub-trees, which calls for a DAG rather than a tree representation, or equivalently a language with variable bindings (cf. [3, 30]).

Furthermore, as the language becomes more complicated (e.g., through the introduction of mutability), programs start requiring *data-flow analysis* [43, 42, 47] to check for the applicability of optimizations. Performing data-flow analysis for every independent optimization that requires it results in more analysis passes than necessary and is difficult to implement, debug, and maintain [79]. Hence, the need to replace plain ASTs with a data structure that stores the result of data-flow analysis, as a better representation on which to apply optimizations.

Several IRs have been proposed in the PL community for simplifying data-flow analysis and optimization. These IRs encode data-flow information by converting a given program into a *canonical representation*. For example, in all of these IRs, every subexpression in a program is bound to a local variable, and reassignment to these variables is not allowed (i.e. they are immutable) [14].

All DSLs in our stack use administrative-normal form (ANF) [25]. This form is better illustrated with an example. Consider the following expression which represents a part of an aggregation:

```
agg1 += R_A * R_B
agg2 += R_A * R_B * (1 - R_C)
agg3 += R_D * (1 - R_C)
```

After converting to ANF, all operators should accept either a constant or a local variable. Hence, every arithmetic operation is converted to a version which uses the local variable bound to its arguments. The ANF representation of this expression is as follows:

```
val x1 = R_A * R_B
agg1 += x1
val x2 = 1 - R_C
val x3 = x1 * x2
agg2 += x3
val x4 = R_D * x2
agg3 += x4
```

While converting a subexpression to an immutable variable, one can look up the mappings between the existing variable bindings and their corresponding subexpressions. If there is already a subexpression with the same operator and the same arguments, then the existing bound variable can be reused. This provides CSE *for free*. In the previous example, the expression `R_A * R_B` is computed once and is used twice for both `agg1` and `agg2`. The same happens for `1 - R_C` in both `agg2` and `agg3`. Observe that this optimization is only one of the advantages of the ANF form. Appendix A presents more information on ANF and several other well-known IRs in the PL community.

Finally, we encode additional information (other than data-flow information) about the expressions in the IR. There are cases in which we need some high-level information about the expressions which is not available in the current abstraction level. Such information can be guided through *annotations* from a higher level of abstraction. Note that since ANF assigns a unique symbol to each subexpression, this process is simplified by keeping a hash-table from these unique symbols to their associated annotations.

4. DSL STACK

In this section, we present the construction of our DSL stack by progressively refining a naïve two-level stack consisting of query plans and C, respectively the source and target languages commonly used in existing query compilers. We progressively add intermediate abstraction levels to perform new optimizations in a modular way, as described in Section 2. Finally, we demonstrate the straightforward addition of a new front-end language which

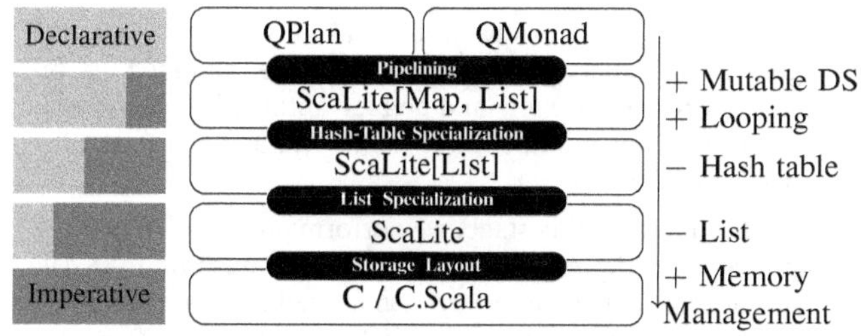

Figure 2: DSL Stack for Query Compilation

reuses the lower abstraction levels already defined in the DSL stack, thereby benefiting from all transformations that apply to them.

Scala DSLs. Figure 2 shows the final DSL stack. On the right, we show which constructs are added and removed by each intermediate DSL. Scala is the implementation language of the framework, and we use a subset of its features to encode intermediate DSLs as well. We refer to the main subset as ScaLite. We write ScaLite[X,Y,...] to denote ScaLite augmented with features X, Y, etc. QPlan and QMonad are Scala DSLs used as two possible front-ends for the DSL stack. ScaLite[Map, List] and ScaLite[List] are intermediate, data-structure-aware DSLs used for specializing the abstract *hash table* and *list* data structures. As we will see, we enforce more restrictions on higher-level DSLs, so that for example, restricted mutability makes ScaLite[Map, List] in fact *less* expressive than ScaLite[List], where mutable Maps can be implemented directly. In ScaLite, all data structure are completely implemented in the language itself, but the memory is assumed to be managed by the garbage collector of a runtime system (e.g. the JVM). Finally, C.Scala is another Scala DSL that expresses C constructs, and in particular memory manipulation constructs, so a program written in C.Scala is equivalent to a C program, modulo a straightforward syntactic transformation (called *stringification* or *unparsing*).

The advantage of using Scala to host these DSLs (we say they are *embedded* [36] in Scala) is that we benefit from its compilation tool-chain: parsing, type-checking, execution and debugging. Indeed, each DSL is executable as a Scala program, with low performance but improved debugging possibilities. Note that these DSLs could be designed in other programming languages (e.g. *quoted* DSLs [63] in Haskell) or as external DSLs if one is willing to build the compilation tool-chain from scratch.

Example Query. We use one query as a running example for demonstrating transformations. The query is shown in SQL and expressed in each intermediate DSL (with Scala syntax) in Figure 4.

4.1 Two-Level Stack (QPlan & C)

This is the two-level stack corresponding to existing query compilers, which are template-based.[7] The high-level DSL is an algebraic representation of query operators. A *query optimizer* typically finds the best query plan for a given SQL query, and produces a program in this declarative DSL. The low-level DSL is an architecture-dependent language that can express implementation details useful for tuning performance. Typical choices include C and LLVM IR.

QPlan. The QPlan DSL contains query plan operators typically encountered in various commercial database systems, including semi-, anti- and outer joins. These operators are sufficient for expressing a large class of SQL queries, including the 22 TPC-H [81] queries.

[7] A state-of-the-art database system will often manipulate SQL, relational algebra and basic query plans before handing the result to the query compiler, but these are not seen by the query compiler, and are thus not considered in this paper.

C.Scala. C.Scala is an extension of ScaLite with basic memory management constructs (e.g. `malloc` and `free`) and memory referencing constructs (pointers and pointer arithmetic). We use the GLib data structures to represent dynamic `Arrays` and sorted lists (as binary search trees).

Transformations. At this stage, we perform pipelining while producing C.Scala code, either by pulling [31] or pushing [64] data. With this approach, we remove many materialization points, which results in improved data locality and I/O costs. This transformation is discussed further in Section 5.1.

4.2 Three-Level Stack (+ ScaLite)

We saw in the introduction that this two-level stack with pipelining is not appropriate for adding a transformation that affects constructs that are also affected by pipelining. This is because both transformations interfere by manipulating related constructs at the same time (single compilation stage). Here, we want to introduce memory-management and layout optimizations. To resolve the problem as suggested in Section 2, we add a new intermediate DSL that can express pipelining, but does not contain memory management constructs yet.

ScaLite. The core of ScaLite is the simply-typed λ-calculus, which does not have recursion and mainly consists of constructs for function abstraction (a.k.a. λ abstraction) and for function application (invoking a function with an input parameter, possibly another function). ScaLite additionally supports control-flow constructs such as `if` statements and bounded loops (loops for which we statically know the maximum number of iterations). This DSL is not a purely functional language, as it also supports variables that are either immutable (as in `val x = e; f(x)`) or mutable (as in `var x = e1; f(x); x = e2`). It supports user-defined records and three data structures: fixed-size arrays, dynamic arrays, and sorted lists.

These make ScaLite a powerful enough low-level language satisfying the expressibility principle. The restrictions (bounded loops, no recursion) simplify program analysis.

Transformations. While lowering ScaLite programs to C.Scala, we enhance memory management. For example, we use memory pools to preallocate intermediate records. By using statistical information about the input, a worst-case estimate of the cardinality of elements is used to preallocate a memory pool, which obviates the need to perform a system call when allocating new memory. Another memory-management enhancement is to specialize the memory layout of data structures. For example, depending on the context, we represent an array of records either as: 1) an array of pointers to structs – a *boxed* [88] *layout*; 2) an array of structs [84]; or 3) a struct containing one array for each record field – a *columnar layout* [37, 75], which often has a positive impact on cache locality. These data-layout representations are demonstrated in Figure 3.

Figure 4g shows our working example in C.Scala. Line 1 explicitly specifies the representation of an array of records as an array of pointers to records. In line 2, we use the `malloc` function to allocate the array. In the rest of the program, we use arrows (`->`) to access the fields of a referenced record, as in C.

4.3 Four-Level Stack (+ ScaLite[Map, List])

Now, consider adding a transformation for data-structure specialization, which requires a data-structure-aware DSL, as explained in Section 2. Such a DSL has specific constructs for representing the operations of a set of data structures.

Hash tables and lists are two essential data structures for query engines [68]. Hash tables are used for implementing the aggregation and hash join operators, while lists are used for storing intermediate collections of records. There are two kinds of hash tables we are interested in: `HashMaps` associate every key to a single value, and are used for expressing aggregation operators; `MultiMaps` associate every key to a set or list of values, and are used for expressing hash join operators.

(a) Boxed layout (b) Row layout (c) Columnar layout

Figure 3: Different data-layout representations.

These data structures are specialized to efficient implementations, depending on the context in which they are used, which requires a prior analysis phase. This is not possible to do with naïve expansion strategies, like with C++ templates or C macros. It could also be interesting to consider other specialized data structures such as indexed trees to extend the DSL further. This can be useful for other workloads, which we leave as future work.

ScaLite[Map, List]. This DSL is an extension of ScaLite with the `HashMap`, `MultiMap`, and `List` data structures, as well as operations defined on them. For simplifying program analysis, we ensure that for every program in this DSL, the following invariant holds: hash-table data structures are not allowed to contain mutable elements, which means that the records we put into these hash tables should be immutable. This is because if we were allowed to read *and* write fields of an element obtained from a hash table, inferring the access patterns for this hash table would become significantly more complicated. Another way of expressing this invariant is to state that the DSL does not allow *nested mutability*.

Transformations. At this level, we can perform optimizations that use hash tables, such as *string dictionaries* [10]. This optimization maps string operations to integer operations and is discussed further in Section 5.3. Also, hash-table specialization is performed while lowering ScaLite[Map, List] programs. Access patterns are analyzed before this transformation in order to make informed *materialization* decisions and push some computations to a pre-processing phase, which is explained in more details in Section 5.2.

Figure 4d shows our working example in ScaLite[Map, List]. Implementing a hash join is done in two phases: the first phase (lines 3-12) iterates over the elements of the first relation and *builds* a hash table which groups these elements based on their join key; in the second phase, the algorithm *probes* the elements of the second relation and iterates over the corresponding elements of the first relation using the constructed hash table.

4.4 Five-Level Stack (+ ScaLite[List])

Directly translating hash tables to arrays is not necessarily optimal. We would like to translate them to lists first, so we can reuse the fine-grained, context-dependent lowering already defined that converts lists to arrays. Sometimes, it is better to lower lists to linked lists, whereas in some other cases, it is better to lower them to arrays. In order to do that, we add an abstraction level similar to the one above, but without hash tables.

ScaLite[List]. ScaLite[List] is also built atop ScaLite, but only adds constructs related to Lists. However, to encode `MultiMaps` using arrays of lists, we need to relax the restrictions imposed on ScaLite[Map, List]: if nested mutability was forbidden, there would be no way to express `MultiMaps` in a useful way, because we

```
SELECT COUNT(*)
FROM R, S
WHERE R.name == "R1"
  AND R.sid == S.rid
```

(a) The example query in SQL.

```
AggOp(
  HashJoinOp(
    SelectOp(R, "name", EQ,"R1"),
    S, "sid", "rid"), COUNT)
```

(b) The example query in QPlan.

```
R.filter(r =>
  r.name == "R1"
).hashJoin(S)(r => r.sid)(s => s.rid)
.count
```

(c) The example query in QMonad.

```
1  val hm = new MultiMap[Int, R]
2
3  for(r <- R) {
4    if(r.name == "R1") {
5
6
7      hm.addBinding(r.sid, r)
8
9
10
11   }
12 }
13 var count = 0
14 for(s <- S) {
15   hm.get(s.rid) match {
16     case Some(rList) =>
17       for(r <- rList) {
18         if(r.sid == s.rid)
19           count += 1
20       }
21     case None => ()
22   }
23 }
24 return count
```

(d) The example query in ScaLite[Map, List].

```
val MR: Array[List[R]] =
  new Array[List[R]](R_GROUPS)
for(r <- R) {
  if(r.name == "R1") {
    MR(r.sid) += r
  }
}
var count = 0
for(s <- S) {
  val rList = MR(s.rid)
  for(r <- rList) {
    if(r.sid == s.rid)
      count += 1
  }
}
return count
```

(e) The example query in ScaLite[List]. Note that List is a mutable data structure.

```
val MR: Array[R] =
  new Array[R](R_GROUPS)
for(r <- R) {
  if(r.name == "R1") {
    if(MR(r.sid) == null) {
      MR(r.sid) = r
    } else {
      r.next = MR(r.sid)
      MR(r.sid) = r
    }
  }
}
var count = 0
for(s <- S) {
  var r = MR(s.rid)
  while(r != null) {
    if(r.sid == s.rid)
      count += 1
    r = r.next
  }
}
return count
```

(f) The example query in ScaLite.

```
val MR: Array[Pointer[R]] =
  malloc[Pointer[R]](R_GROUPS)
for(r <- R) {
  if(r->name == "R1") {
    if(MR(r->sid) == null) {
      MR(r->sid) = r
    } else {
      r->next = MR(r->sid)
      MR(r->sid) = r
    }
  }
}
var count = 0
for(s <- S) {
  var r: Pointer[R] = MR(s->rid)
  while(r != null) {
    if(r->sid == s->rid)
      count += 1
    r = r->next
  }
}
return count
```

(g) The example query in C.Scala.

Figure 4: Representations of a query in different DSLs.

would not be able to update the set of elements associated with a particular key incrementally (a capability that was hidden behind the `MultiMap` interface of ScaLite[Map, List]).

Transformations. We perform list specialization while lowering from ScaLite[List] to ScaLite. Consider the case in which we lower lists to linked lists. In a typical scenario, lists are used for holding records. In that case, we use *intrusive linked lists*, which store the next pointer of each list node in the records themselves. This removes one level of indirection caused by the separate allocations of the container nodes and the records. On the other hand, since we are working with ScaLite, which only has bounded loops, it is sometimes possible to perform worst-case size analysis and obtain an estimate of the maximum cardinality of some lists. We consequently lower them to native static `Arrays`, instead of linked lists. This way, we benefit from the existing array layout optimizations provided for ScaLite down the DSL stack (e.g. columnar layout).

Figure 4e shows the working example in ScaLite[List]. Lines 1-2 contain the lowered representation of the `MultiMap` data structure. Line 7 shows the implementation of the `addBinding` method using the += method of List. Line 16 shows how we lower the `get` method of `MultiMap` by accessing a bucket in the lowered array.

4.5 Collection Programming Front-end

We refer to *collection programming* as the practice of preferring generic operations defined on collections like lists and associative maps (`filter`, `groupBy`, `sum`, etc.) rather than writing them out as loops. The user base of *collection programming* APIs is growing. These APIs improve the integration of applications with database back-ends by making them more seamless [61, 34, 33]. Thus, it makes sense to consider a DSL with a collection programming API as an alternative front-end for a query compiler.

QMonad. The QMonad DSL is a functional language inspired by Monad Calculus on lists [11, 12, 87], Query and Monoid Comprehensions [35, 82, 22] and other collection programming APIs like Spark *RDD*s [89]. In addition to standard collection operators (such as `map`, `filter`, `fold`, etc.), this DSL contains different join operators including semi-, anti-, and outer joins.[8]

Transformations. As we discussed in Section 3.2, declarative and functional languages are not appropriate for performance tuning. It is thus necessary to compile and optimize programs written in QMonad before executing them. Thankfully, by simply lowering those programs to ScaLite[Map, List], we can reuse the transformations provided by the lower level DSLs of our stack *for free*. To produce even faster code, we should perform pipelining to remove materialization points (pipeline breakers). This transformation has a similar effect to what we do for QPlan, by pushing or pulling data. Section 5.1 gives more detail about it.

Figure 4c shows our working example in QMonad. The `filter` method is a higher order function that corresponds to the selection operator in relational algebra. It takes the selection predicate as a parameter. The first parameter of the `hashJoin` method is the second relation, and the second and third parameters indicate the join keys of the first and second relations, respectively. The `count` method returns the number of elements in a list.

4.6 Extensibility

One of the main advantages of our DSL stack design is its extensibility in various dimensions. First, as we just saw, one can use another algebra as the front-end by replacing the front-end DSL (here, QMonad and QPlan). By providing a lowering transformation from the new algebra to one of our intermediate DSLs, the existing infrastructure generates optimized C code for that new front-end.

Second, user-defined functions (UDFs) can be added to input queries. There are two approaches for doing so: 1) expressing them in terms of our low-level DSLs – in this case, we miss high-

[8] Map and join expressions are expressively redundant with nested fold expressions, but represent an important performance choice, and are hard to reconstruct from folds.

```
       R.map(f).map(g)           ----------->     R.map(f o g)
              |                                        ^
              v                                        |
build { k1 =>                                    build { k1 =>
  (build { k2 =>                     (T)           R.foreach(e =>
    R.foreach(e => k2(f(e)))                          k1(g(f(e)))
  }).foreach(e => k1(g(e)))      ----------->     )}
}
(T): build(f1).foreach(f2) ~> f1(f2)
```

Figure 5: A simple example of loop fusion using short-cut fusion.

level optimization opportunities that could apply to them; 2) adding UDFs as constructs in a high-level DSL, and defining lowerings to immediately-lower DSLs in the appropriate phase. This approach works best if the user provides additional information (by using annotations, which was desribed in Section 3.3) about the additional language construct (e.g. their side-effects).

Third, we can change our target language without any need to change the higher-level DSLs, and still benefit from the optimizations provided in those higher-level DSLs. The only thing we need to do is to provide a lowering from ScaLite (or a higher-level DSL) to our desired target language, and then *unparse* the generated IR in a similar way as we unparse C.Scala to C. This approach works well as long as the underlying architecture is not changed. The extensibility of our DSL stack in the case of changing the target architecture (e.g. using a multi-core architecture instead of a single-core one) is discussed in Section 8.

5. TRANSFORMATIONS

In this section, we detail three transformations that were previously introduced, and which are expressed using the proposed DSL stack. First, we present the pipelining transformation used to improve data locality. Second, we present data-structure synthesis, which specializes and materializes data structures to improve query execution performances. Finally, we provide more details about the string dictionaries.

5.1 Pipelining – From Fusion to Push Query Engines

A query written using QMonad consists of chained invocations of higher-order functions such as `map`, `filter`, `flatMap`, etc. After naively generating low-level code for such queries (e.g. using template expansion), the generated code typically contains: 1) intermediate list constructions and destructions; and 2) loops corresponding to each higher-order function. Creating intermediate lists causes space and time overheads due to unnecessary allocations.

Loop fusion removes these overheads by removing the need to create intermediate lists. This is because in the fused version of the loops, the elements are pipelined from one operation to the next. Moreover, by merging several loops into a single loop, a single traversal is performed, reducing the iteration overhead.

The literature contains a very well-defined set of algebraic rewrite rules for Monad Calculus [11]. These rules are sufficient to express loop fusion for the Monad Calculus subset of QMonad. However, fusion is also needed outside of that subset. Since we add constructs to the language, we need to add the corresponding loop fusion rewrite rules. For this, it is important to be aware of relevant research that has been conducted in the PL community. In fact, it turns out that QMonad with n constructs needs $O(n^2)$ loop fusion rewrite rules, which is not scalable [27]. Ideally, one should need only $O(n)$ rewrite rules for a DSL with n constructs. Furthermore, there are cases in which the fusion of two operators in QMonad is not expressible in QMonad itself. Figure 4c shows a program that exhibits this property: the fusion of `filter` and `hashJoin` cannot

```
class QueryMonad[T] {
  /* These methods are both consumer and producer */
  def map[S](f: T => S): QueryMonad[S] = build { k =>
    for(e <- this) k(f(e))
  }
  def filter(p: T => Boolean): QueryMonad[T] = build { k =>
    for(e <- this) if(p(e)) k(e)
  }
  def hashJoin[S](list2: QueryMonad[S])
    (leftHash: T => Int)
    (rightHash: S => Int): QueryMonad[(T, S)] = build { k =>
    val hm = new MultiMap[Int, T]()
    for(e <- this)
      hm.addBinding(leftHash(e), e)
    for(e2 <- list2) {
      val key = rightHash(e)
      hm.get(key) match {
        case Some(list1) =>
          for(e1 <- list1)
            if(leftHash(e1) == rightHash(e2))
              k((e1, e2))
        case None => ()
      }
    }
  }
  /* This method is only a consumer */
  def count: Int = {
    var result = 0
    for(e <- this)
      result += 1
    result
  }
}
```

Figure 6: Producer-consumer encoding of QMonad operators. Note that in Scala, `for(e <- R) f(e)` is the same as `R.foreach(e => f(e))`.

be expressed using a single QMonad operator. This transformation needs to be expressed using operations provided by a lower level DSL. Hence, for these cases loop fusion is no longer an optimization but a lowering transformation (refer to Section 2).

Deforestation [86] is a well-known technique in the PL community that is used to remove intermediate data structures. This is the approach we use for performing loop fusion. There are several implementations of this technique, among which *short-cut fusion* (known as *cheap deforestation* or *foldr/build fusion*) [27, 28] has been proven to achieve pipelined query execution [35]. This approach requires defining every operator in the language using two primitive combinators: 1) a `build` combinator that *produces* a list; and 2) a `foldr` combinator that *consumes* a list. This way, the number of rewrite rules needed for QMonad with n constructs become $O(n)$ (the implementations of the n operators using the `build` and `foldr` combinators). Loop fusion is then achieved by eliminating adjacent occurrences of `build` and `foldr`.

We implement a variant of short-cut fusion [40] in which every operator is expressed using the *church-encoding of lists* [66], or *tranducers* [72] . For simplicity, we use the `foreach` operator and side effects, instead of the pure `foldRight` operator. This transformation is implemented as a lowering step from QMonad to ScaLite[Map, List]. Figure 6 shows the implementation of a few QMonad operators using `build` and `foreach`. Inlining this high-level implementation leads to pipelining transformation.

Figure 5 shows a simple example in which short-cut fusion is used to apply loop fusion (long path at the bottom). Transformation (T) is what allows us to transition from the code at the bottom-left corner to the code at the bottom-right. This example shows that short-cut fusion has the same impact as the corresponding algebraic rewrite rule from Monad Calculus (short path, on top).

Figure 4d shows the code resulting from the example in Figure 4c, after the pipelining. The `filter` operation is fused with the first loop of the `hashJoin` operation, which is responsible for creating a hash table based on the join key of the first relation. The `count` operation is fused with the second loop of `hashJoin`, which is responsible for iterating over the second relation and probing relevant partitions from the hash table. Our observations show that short-cut fusion has the same effect as the push-engines proposed in [64]. This is not a surprise, since every operator in the latter is modeled after a producer/consumer pattern, which directly corresponds to the foldr/build model described above.

After pipelining the query engine and lowering it to ScaLite[Map, List], there are new optimization opportunities to be applied on the resulting mutable data structures, as we saw in Section 4.3. Next, we discuss how to synthesize specialized data structures from ScaLite[Map, List] programs.

5.2 Specialized Data-Structure Synthesis

A pipelined query uses mutable data structures to perform in-place updates, instead of cloning the list every time a single element is updated. The resulting program is no longer in QMonad (or QPlan), but has been lowered to ScaLite[Map, List], and is thus no longer purely functional. This makes optimizations harder to express than in higher level, purely declarative DSLs, mainly because of the presence of side-effects. To resolve this issue, we enforce several restrictions on this DSL, which facilitate program analysis. For example, by not allowing nested mutability, we simplify side-effect analysis. This analysis helps identifying data dependencies among statements, after which we can safely reorder them without changing the semantics of the program.

`MultiMaps`, which are used to implement hash joins, can be specialized depending on the way they are used. For example, under circumstances described below, and if there is a one-to-one relationship between a write operation and its corresponding read, we can remove the `MultiMap` altogether. In Figure 7a, we iterate over a relation `R` and add its tuples into a `MultiMap`. We then access the relevant partitions of `R` while iterating over a second relation `S`. Instead of these two steps, we would like to directly access the elements of `R` while iterating over `S`. For it to be safe, such a transformation requires reordered statements to be free of data dependencies related to the two iterations, outside of read/write dependencies on the elements of the `MultiMap` we want to elide.

However, naïvely removing the intermediate `MultiMap` and substituting its read operation with an iteration over `R` clearly will not improve performance (it is equivalent to a nested loop join). Figure 7b shows the result of that naïve transformation. We can see that for each element of `S`, instead of iterating over the relevant tuples in `R`, we iterate over the whole relation. In order to correct this, we can materialize `R` based on the join key `sid`. First, we make sure `R` is not an intermediate relation, but an input relation (otherwise, the transformation is not applicable). Then, at query loading time, we materialize an array of lists which is indexed based on `sid`. As a result, we can now iterate only over the relevant parts of `R`, as is shown in Figure 7c.

Furthermore, in case `sid` is a primary key, the materialized data structure can be specialized further: since there will only be one tuple associated with each key (by definition of a primary key), there is no need for buckets anymore: a one dimensional array is sufficient, instead of an array of lists. We remove the corresponding bucket iteration in the main loop. Figure 7d shows the resulting code, in case the join key is a primary key.

Data-structure synthesis is not limited to `MultiMaps`. `HashMaps`, which are used to implement aggregations, can also be specialized. In that case, we synthesize materialized data structures which partition the `HashMaps` based on their grouping key, automatically inferring the grouping indices.

String Operation	C code	Integer Operation	Dictionary Type
equals	strcmp(x, y) == 0	x == y	Normal
notEquals	strcmp(x, y) != 0	x != y	Normal
startsWith	strncmp(x, y, strlen(y)) == 0	x>=start && x<=end	Ordered

Table 2: Mapping of string operations to integer operations through the corresponding types of string dictionaries. x and y are string arguments which are mapped to integers.

5.3 String Dictionaries

Operations on non-primitive data types, such as Strings, incur a very high performance overhead. This is true for two reasons: There is a function call associated with such operations, and most of these operations typically need to execute loops to process the encapsulated data types. Hence, such operations significantly affect branch prediction and cache locality.

For strings, we use String Dictionaries [10] to remove their abstraction overhead. One dictionary is maintained for every attribute of String type, which generally operates as follows. First, at data loading time, each string value of an attribute is mapped to an integer value. Then, at query execution time, string operations are mapped to their integer counterparts, as shown in Table 2. This mapping allows to significantly improve the query execution performance, as it completely eliminates underlying loops and, thus, significantly reduces the number of CPU instructions executed.

Special care is needed for string operations that require ordering. For example, Q14 of TPC-H needs to perform the `startsWith` string operations with a constant string. This requires that we utilize a dictionary that maintains the data in order; that is, if $string_x < string_y$ lexicographically, then $Int_x < Int_y$ as well. To do so, we take advantage of the fact that all input data is already materialized, and thus after computing the list of distinct values, we can then sort this list lexicographically, and then assign to the string attributes the integer value of the index in the corresponding sorted list for using during query execution. More specifically, the constant string is converted to a $[start, end]$ range, by iterating over the list of distinct values and finding the first and last strings which start or end with this string. Then, this range is used for lowering the operation, as shown in Table 2. This *two-phase* string dictionary allows to map all operations that require some notion of ordering.

Finally, it is important to note that string dictionaries, even though they significantly improve query execution performance, have a negative performance impact on data loading. In addition, string dictionaries can actually degrade performance when they are used for primary keys or for attributes that contain many distinct values. Thus, one should avoid using string dictionaries in such cases.

6. PUTTING IT ALL TOGETHER – THE DBLAB/LB QUERY ENGINE

We have implemented the DSLs of our multi-level stack and the associated transformers in DBLAB,[9] a framework for building efficient database systems via high-level programming. Using the components provided by DBLAB we have re-created the LegoBase [50] query engine. We refer to this re-implementation as DBLAB/LB.

First, developers write their queries in DBLAB/LB using one of the front-end languages of DBLAB/LB (QPlan or QMonad). DBLAB/LB uses the Yin-Yang [41] framework to construct the

[9] http://github.com/epfldata/dblab

```scala
val hm = new MultiMap[Int, R]
for(r <- R) {
  if(r.name == "R1")
    hm.addBinding(r.sid, r)
}
var count = 0
for(s <- S) {
  hm.get(s.rid) match {
    case Some(rList) =>
      for(r <- rList) {
        if(r.sid == s.rid)
          count += 1
      }
    case None => ()
  }
}
count
```

(a) The optimized version of the query in ScaLite[Map, List].

```scala
/*
The iteration over the first
relation is moved to the
next step.
*/
var count = 0
for(s <- S) {


  for(r <- R) {
    if(r.name == "R1")
      if(r.sid == s.rid)
        count += 1
  }

}
count
```

(b) Naïvely removing the `MultiMap` abstraction in ScaLite[List].

```scala
/* Precomputation */
val MR: Array[List[R]] =
  // Indexed R on sid

/* Actual Query Processing */
var count = 0
for(s <- S) {

  val rList = MR(s.rid)
  for(r <- rList) {
    if(r.name == "R1")
      if(r.sid == s.rid)
        count += 1
  }

}
count
```

(c) The optimized version of the query in ScaLite[List] when `R.sid` is a foreign key. Note that List is a mutable data structure.

```scala
/* Precomputation */
val MR: Array[R] =
  // Indexed R on sid

/* Actual Query Processing */
var count = 0
for(s <- S) {


  val r = MR(s.rid)
  if (r.name == "R1")
    if(r.sid == s.rid)
      count += 1

}

count
```

(d) The optimized version of the query in ScaLite[List] when `R.sid` is a primary key.

Figure 7: Representations of an example query after applying pipelining and data-structure synthesis.

corresponding IR from these queries. As already discussed in Section 4, the front-end languages are progressively lowered and optimized until they reach the abstraction level of the C programming language. Finally, the generated C programs are compiled using any traditional C compiler such as CLang or GCC. At this point, our stack has generated a stand-alone executable for the given query, which includes data loading and data processing and whose execution produces the final query results. The overall DSL code base (without the optimizations, whose lines of code are presented in Section 7) is around a thousand lines of Scala code.

DBLAB heavily relies upon the functionality provided by SC ("Systems Compiler") [1], a *generic* DSL compiler framework. SC provides a complete tool-chain for easily defining DSLs and the corresponding transformations as well as a number of *general-purpose* optimizations out-of-the-box. Note that applying one of the optimizations mentioned throughout this paper does not necessarily lead to performance improvements for a given query. In general, finding the combination of optimizations that leads to optimal performance is a very hard problem; for this reason, the SC DSL compiler does not try to automatically infer the optimal combination of optimizations for each incoming query. Instead, SC was designed so that it provides full control over the compilation process to the DSL developers, while hiding the complicated internal implementation details of the compiler itself. Like DBLAB/LB, SC is also written in Scala, and currently consists of around 27K LoC.

In this work, we extend the library of optimizations provided by SC with several *domain-specific* optimizations which we apply on and across the presented DSLs using the interfaces provided by SC. These domain-specific optimizations can be found in previous query compilation approaches, like those found in the HyPer [64] database, the HIQUE [56] query compiler and the LegoBase [50] query engine. More specifically, the DBLAB/LB DSL stack provides support for: 1) A push-based query engine [64], 2) Operator Inlining [64], 3) Specialization of hash-table data structures [50], 4) Control flow optimizations to improve branch prediction and cache locality [64], 5) String Dictionaries [10] [10], 6) Optimization of memory allocations, by converting *malloc* calls to using memory pools instead and, finally, 7) Standard compiler optimizations like Partial Evaluation, Function Inlining, Scalar Replacement, DCE and CSE [50].

[10]All performance numbers reported for LegoBase in [50] were obtained by including string dictionaries.

7. EXPERIMENTAL RESULTS

Our experimental platform consists of a server-type x86 machine equipped with two Intel Xeon E5-2620 v2 CPUs running at 2GHz each, 256GB of DDR3 RAM at 1600Mhz and two commodity hard disks of 2TB storing the experimental datasets. The operating system is Red Hat Enterprise 6.7. For compiling the generated programs throughout our evaluation we use version 2.9 of the CLang compiler with the default optimization flags. Finally, for C data structures we use the GLib library (version 2.42.1).

For our evaluation we use TPC-H [81], a benchmark suite which simulates data-warehousing and decision support; it provides a set of 22 queries which represent actual business analytics operations to a database with sales information. These queries have a high degree of complexity and express most SQL features.

As a reference point for all results presented in this section, we use the LegoBase query engine [50], an in-memory query execution engine written in the high-level programming language Scala. This is in contrast to the traditional wisdom which calls for the use of low-level languages for DBMS development. To avoid the overheads of a high-level language (e.g. complicated memory management) while maintaining nicely defined abstractions, LegoBase uses *generative programming* [70, 77] and compiles the Scala code to optimized, low-level C code for each SQL query. By programming databases in a high-level style and still being able to get good performance, the time saved can be spent implementing more database features and optimizations. LegoBase already significantly outperforms both a commercial in-memory database and an existing state-of-the-art query compiler.

Our evaluation is divided into three parts. First, we present experimental results which demonstrate that by utilizing our multilevel DSL stack, developers can build a query engine that matches or even significantly outperforms the LegoBase system. This is because, by splitting optimizations across different abstraction layers and separating concerns, it becomes easier to detect performance bottlenecks that are evasive otherwise. Note that some optimizations of the SC DSL stack are not compliant with the TPC-H rules. For this reason, we also present results for a TPC-H compliant set of optimizations[11]. Second, we examine how much memory footprint is required for running the optimized queries (generated with DBLAB/LB 5) and report on the compilation times. This is impor-

[11]To obtain this TPC-H compliant configuration we have disabled: 1) String Dictionaries 2) Data-Structure Partitioning 3) Automatic Index Inference and, finally, 4) Removing unused table attributes.

	Q1	Q2	Q3	Q4	Q5	Q6	Q7	Q8	Q9	Q10	Q11	Q12	Q13	Q14	Q15	Q16	Q17	Q18	Q19	Q20	Q21	Q22
LegoBase	168	108	195	283	2220	100	209	462	447	488	105	281	604	188	134	1326	75	245	371	495	669	191
DBLAB/LB 2	5936	1510	6176	12162	4904	580	4815	20069	27686	5500	797	3763	1846	1832	1633	16962	23765	6329	3075	1629	18636	1320
DBLAB/LB 3	1298	749	4978	10779	3514	289	2714	20069	27686	3411	339	3068	1002	1238	955	14956	18471	3055	3075	938	11595	885
DBLAB/LB 4	177	58	178	141	159	64	109	56	628	433	59	311	860	39	97	4285	38	198	64	194	385	91
DBLAB/LB 5	177	58	117	141	158	46	109	20	537	433	59	120	591	12	27	723	11	196	19	167	385	91
TPC-H Compliant	1298	611	4099	5628	2194	290	2745	6012	19944	3524	80	2567	855	446	1022	4285	4795	4228	2693	427	12070	900

Table 3: Performance results (in milliseconds) for TPC-H (scaling factor 8) for (a) the generated optimized C code of LegoBase [50], (b) the generated C code of DBLAB/LB using an increasing number of levels in our DSL stack and, finally, (c) the TPC-H compliant DSL stack.

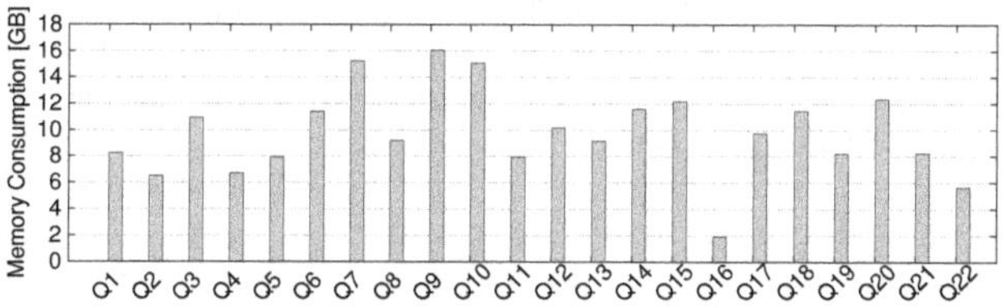

Figure 8: Memory consumption for generated C code of TPC-H.

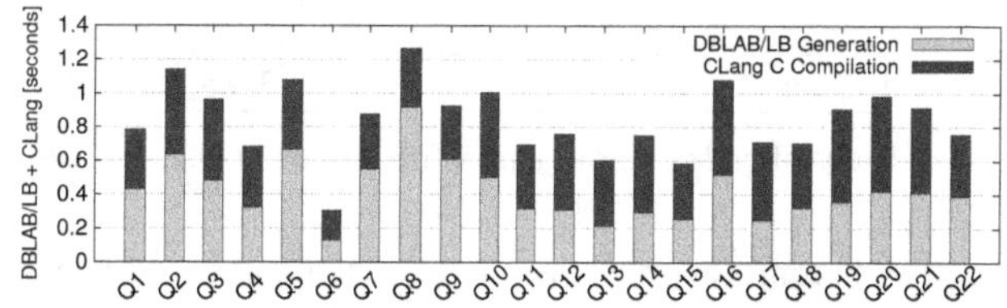

Figure 9: Compilation time for generated C code of TPC-H.

tant, as both these metrics are important indicators about whether our approach scales to large datasets and whether it is usable in practice. Finally, we are addressing the question of how much implementation effort is required for introducing additional abstraction layers or DSLs to an existing stack. We do so by reporting how many lines of code each optimization requires.

7.1 Performance Evaluation

In this section we experimentally evaluate the performance of the DBLAB/LB query compiler. Table 3 presents experimental results for all 22 queries of the TPC-H benchmark for both our system (while incrementally introducing DSLs and their corresponding optimizations as presented in Section 4) and LegoBase [50]. We observe the following three things.

DBLAB/LB achieves a speedup of up to 23× (Q8), with an average performance improvement of 5×. More specifically, for 20 out of 22 queries, DBLAB/LB significantly outperforms the state-of-the-art LegoBase system. This improvement was achieved by introducing optimizations related to removing intermediate materializations that have a significant negative performance impact at query execution. These materialization points (and other performance bottlenecks) were not easy to be detected in the complicated generated code of the original LegoBase system. In addition, we have introduced automatic inference of database indices, based on database statistics, a technique that provided significant performance improvements and was not expressed as a compiler optimization before. However, we also note that in cases where DBLAB/LB is slower than LegoBase (Q1, Q9), this is because the latter was more aggressively optimizing the data structures, e.g. by partitioning data using a composite set of attributes at data loading time. We plan to investigate such optimization opportunities, which are easily expressible with our DSL stack, in the future.

Second, Table 3 also presents a more detailed break-down of how performance improves as DSLs and their corresponding optimizations are introduced in DBLAB/LB. In general we observe that as more DSLs are introduced, performance can be significantly improved. More specifically, when moving from a three to a four-level DSL stack we get an additional 56× performance improvement. This is because the introduction of the additional DSL "unlocks" many optimization opportunities that were not expressible before with a three-level stack. Observe also that the introduction of additional DSLs does not always improve performance for all queries. For example, when moving from a two-level to a three-level DSL stack, performance is marginally improved (if at all) for 10 out of 22 queries. Yet, the introduction of an additional DSL significantly improves the performance of Q1. Thus, we see that it is definitely possible to express even query-specific optimizations with the DBLAB/LB DSL stack. More importantly, Table 3 clearly illustrates that performance is never negatively affected by the introduction of an additional DSL level, for all 22 TPC-H queries.

Finally, we observe that the TPC-H compliant set of DBLAB/LB optimizations typically leads to a better performance than that of a three-level DSL stack, however it does not outperform the four-level DSL stack. This is because, at the four-level stack we start introducing optimizations that are no-longer TPC-H compliant.

7.2 Memory and Compilation Overheads

Figures 8 and 9 show the memory consumption and compilation times, respectively, for all TPC-H queries (generated by DBLAB/LB with 5 DSL levels). For memory profiling we use Valgrind as well as a custom memory profiler, while the JVM is always first warmed up. Compilation time includes the time that (a) DBLAB/LB requires in order to perform program optimization and C code generation, as well as the (b) CLang compilation time.

First, we observe that the allocated memory is at most twice the size of the input data for most TPC-H queries. Second, the compilation time is divided almost equally between DBLAB/LB and CLang. These results suggest that our approach is usable in practice, as even for complicated, multi-way join queries both the memory footprint and the compilation time remain small. Observe that compilation overheads can be further reduced by generating LLVM code directly, a direction that we plan to investigate in the future.

7.3 Productivity Evaluation

In this section we investigate how hard it is to introduce new optimizations in the DSL stack of DBLAB/LB. This is a very important question, as it directly relates to the adaptivity of our proposed solution to new requirements not covered so far in our work. We address this question by presenting in detail our own experience with developing DBLAB/LB so far. More specifically, Table 4 presents the amount of code lines required in order to introduce new IR nodes for the associated transformations of each DSL in our stack. We make three observations.

First, it becomes clear from this table that new transformations can be introduced in DBLAB/LB with relative small programming

Column Store Transformer	184
Automatic Index Inference	318
Memory Allocation Hoisting	186
Pipelining in QPlan	0
Pipelining in QMonad	303
Horizontal Fusion in QMonad	152
Constant-Size Array to Local Vars	125
Flattening Nested Structs	118
Data-Structure Partitioning	505
Scala Constructs to C Transformer	1294
Total	3185

Table 4: Lines of code of several transformations in DBLAB/LB.

effort. This becomes evident when one considers complicated transformations like those of Automatic Index Inference and Horizontal Fusion[12] which can both be coded for merely $\sim$ 500 lines of code. More importantly, the overall coding effort of programming DSLs and their transformations in DBLAB/LB ($\sim$ 3.7KLoC) is almost the same as that reported by LegoBase ($\sim$ 4.8KLoC [50])[13]. Second, we see that pipelining in QPlan does not require any coding effort, while for QMonad it requires a transformation of $\sim$ 500 lines. This difference is due to the fact that QPlan inherently encodes a push engine; this is however not possible to do with the purely functional characteristics of QMonad. Finally, we observe that around half of the code-base concerns converting Scala code to C; however this is a naïve task to be performed by developers, as it usually results in a one-to-one translation between Scala and C constructs. More importantly, this is a task that is required to be performed only once for each language construct, and it needs to be extended *only* as new constructs are introduced in the low-level languages of DBLAB/LB.

8. OUTLOOK: PARALLELISM

One possible question regarding the extensibility of our approach would be adding parallelism to the query engine. There are many different variants of parallelization for database systems. Here, we focus only on the *intra-operator* (or *partitioned*) parallelism which can be achieved by (a) partitioning the input data of each operator in the operator tree, (b) applying the sequential operator implementations on each partition and, finally, (c) merging the result obtained on each partition [31]. Next, we show how our DSL stack can be enriched with parallelization through demonstrating the modifications needed for the DSLs and the transformations.

First, we present the required modifications for the DSLs in our stack. The parallelization logic is encoded in the QPlan DSL by adding the split and merge operators [60]. As these two operators are not expressible by middle level DSLs, the expressibility principle is violated. To solve this issue, the intermediate DSLs require an appropriate set of facilities for parallelism. This is achieved by adding threading facilities (i.e. forking and joining threads) to the ScaLite DSL. As ScaLite[List], ScaLite[Map, List], and C.Scala are extensions to ScaLite, these DSLs are also enriched with parallelism *for free*. The framework generates parallel code by unparsing the parallel C.Scala constructs to the corresponding C code (e.g. by using pthreads).

Second, we analyze what modifications are required for the transformations. If the queries are not using parallel physical query plans at all (e.g. there is no use of split and merge operators), then no change is required for the transformations. However, the generated code for a query with split and merge operators should use an appropriate set of parallelization constructs, as we described above. To do so, we add the implementation of these two operators using the threading constructs. This implementation leads to adjust the pipelining transformation rules for these two operators, as was described in Section 5.1. The merge operator needs special care based on the class of the aggregation (e.g. `SUM` is distributive and `AVG` is algebraic [32]). Apart from these two operators, there is no other modification needed for the existing query operators. Also, this modification is introduced only once and it is reused for all parallel physical query plans. Furthermore, as the rest of existing transformations are not modified, the generated code for each thread benefits from the optimizations provided for the sequential version of the DSL stack *for free*.

It has been shown that in some cases using shared data structures (which requires a locking mechanism) is better than using private data structures for each thread (which is the approach we demonstrated here) [16]. Also, there is a possibility of using lock-free data structures and work-stealing for scheduling the workload across the worker threads [57]. Finally, although we use hash partitioning, there are a number of other approaches for partitioning the input data (e.g. range partitioning, etc.): the performance of each scheme is dependent on the underlying workload scenario and data characteristics [60]. We plan to investigate these directions by employing program analysis and compilation techniques in the future.

9. CONCLUSIONS

In this paper we argue that it is time for a rethinking of how query compilers are designed and implemented. Current solutions are mainly using template expansion to generate low-level code from high-level queries in one single step. Our experience with systems built using this technique indicates that, in practice, it becomes very difficult to maintain and extend such query compilers over time; the complexity of their code-bases increases to unmanageable levels as more and more optimizations are added.

Our suggested approach advocates modularizing a query compiler by defining several abstraction levels. Each abstraction level is responsible for expressing *only* a subset of optimizations, a design decision which creates a separation of concerns between different optimizations. In addition, we propose *progressively* lowering the high-level query to low-level code through multiple abstraction levels. This allows for a more controlled code-generation approach.

We show that our approach, while introducing multiple abstraction layers, does not in fact negatively impact the performance of the generated code, but instead improves it. This is because it allows for expressing compiler optimizations that are already available in existing query compilers, but also *new* optimizations not available before. More importantly, it does so while actually providing for a great degree of programmer productivity, a property not found in any previous query compilation approach to date.

Acknowledgments

We thank Vojin Jovanovic and Manohar Jonalagedda for insightful discussions that helped to improve this paper. This work was supported by NCCR MARVEL and ERC grant 279804.

[12] To perform a good loop fusion, short-cut deforestation is not sufficient. Such techniques only provide *vertical* loop fusion, in which one loop uses the result produced by another loop. However, in order to perform further optimizations one requires to perform *horizontal* loop fusion, in which different loops iterating over the same range are fused into one loop [9, 29]. Good loop fusion is still an open research topic in the PL community [76, 18, 27].

[13] DBLAB/LB comes with additional optimizations not listed in Table 4; however their combined code size does not exceed 200LOC.

10. REFERENCES

[1] SC - Systems Compiler. http://data.epfl.ch/sc.

[2] Y. Ahmad and C. Koch. DBToaster: A SQL compiler for high-performance delta processing in main-memory databases. *PVLDB*, 2(2):1566–1569, 2009.

[3] A. V. Aho, R. Sethi, and J. D. Ullman. *Compilers, Principles, Techniques*. Addison wesley, 1986.

[4] A. W. Appel. SSA is functional programming. *SIGPLAN notices*, 33(4):17–20, 1998.

[5] A. W. Appel. *Compiling with continuations*. Cambridge University Press, 2006.

[6] M. Armbrust, R. S. Xin, C. Lian, Y. Huai, D. Liu, J. K. Bradley, X. Meng, T. Kaftan, M. J. Franklin, A. Ghodsi, and M. Zaharia. Spark SQL: Relational Data Processing in Spark. SIGMOD '15, pages 1383–1394, New York, NY, USA, 2015. ACM.

[7] K. Asai, H. Masuhara, and A. Yonezawa. Partial evaluation of call-by-value λ-calculus with side-effects. PEPM '97, pages 12–21. ACM, 1997.

[8] S. Bauman, C. F. Bolz, R. Hirschfeld, V. Kirilichev, T. Pape, J. G. Siek, and S. Tobin-Hochstadt. Pycket: A Tracing JIT for a Functional Language. ICFP 2015, pages 22–34. ACM, 2015.

[9] C. Beeri and Y. Kornatzky. Algebraic optimization of object-oriented query languages. In *ICDT '90*, volume 470, pages 72–88. 1990.

[10] C. Binnig, S. Hildenbrand, and F. Färber. Dictionary-based order-preserving string compression for main memory column stores. In *SIGMOD '09*, pages 283–296. ACM, 2009.

[11] V. Breazu-Tannen, P. Buneman, and L. Wong. *Naturally embedded query languages*. Springer, 1992.

[12] V. Breazu-Tannen and R. Subrahmanyam. *Logical and computational aspects of programming with sets/bags/lists*. Springer, 1991.

[13] J. Carette, O. Kiselyov, and C.-C. Shan. Finally tagless, partially evaluated: Tagless staged interpreters for simpler typed languages. *Journal of Functional Programming*, 19(05):509–543, 2009.

[14] M. M. Chakravarty, G. Keller, and P. Zadarnowski. A functional perspective on SSA optimisation algorithms. *Electronic Notes in Theoretical Computer Science*, 82(2):347–361, 2004.

[15] D. D. Chamberlin, M. M. Astrahan, M. W. Blasgen, J. Gray, W. F. King III, B. G. Lindsay, R. A. Lorie, J. W. Mehl, T. G. Price, G. R. Putzolu, P. G. Selinger, M. Schkolnick, D. R. Slutz, I. L. Traiger, B. W. Wade, and R. A. Yost. A history and evaluation of system R. *CACM*, 24(10):632–646, 1981.

[16] J. Cieslewicz and K. A. Ross. Adaptive aggregation on chip multiprocessors. VLDB '07, pages 339–350. ACM, 2007.

[17] C. Click and K. D. Cooper. Combining analyses, combining optimizations. *TOPLAS*, 17(2):181–196, Mar. 1995.

[18] D. Coutts, R. Leshchinskiy, and D. Stewart. Stream fusion. from lists to streams to nothing at all. In *ICFP '07*, 2007.

[19] A. Crotty, A. Galakatos, K. Dursun, T. Kraska, U. Çetintemel, and S. B. Zdonik. Tupleware:" big" data, big analytics, small clusters. In *CIDR*, 2015.

[20] R. Cytron, J. Ferrante, B. K. Rosen, M. N. Wegman, and F. K. Zadeck. Efficiently computing static single assignment form and the control dependence graph. *TOPLAS*, 13(4):451–490, 1991.

[21] A. Darte. On the complexity of loop fusion. *Parallel Computing*, 26(9):1175 – 1193, 2000.

[22] L. Fegaras and D. Maier. Optimizing object queries using an effective calculus. *ACM Trans. Database Syst.*, 25(4):457–516, Dec. 2000.

[23] M. Felleisen. On the expressive power of programming languages. In *ESOP'90*, pages 134–151. Springer, 1990.

[24] J. Ferrante, K. J. Ottenstein, and J. D. Warren. The program dependence graph and its use in optimization. *TOPLAS*, 9(3):319–349, July 1987.

[25] C. Flanagan, A. Sabry, B. F. Duba, and M. Felleisen. The essence of compiling with continuations. In *ACM Sigplan Notices*, volume 28, pages 237–247. ACM, 1993.

[26] F. Franchetti, Y. Voronenko, and M. Püschel. Formal loop merging for signal transforms. PLDI '05, pages 315–326.

[27] A. Gill, J. Launchbury, and S. L. Peyton Jones. A short cut to deforestation. FPCA, pages 223–232. ACM, 1993.

[28] A. J. Gill. *Cheap deforestation for non-strict functional languages*. PhD thesis, University of Glasgow, 1996.

[29] A. Goldberg and R. Paige. Stream processing. LFP '84, pages 53–62, New York, NY, USA, 1984. ACM.

[30] G. Graefe. Query evaluation techniques for large databases. *CSUR*, 25(2):73–169, June 1993.

[31] G. Graefe. Volcano-an extensible and parallel query evaluation system. *IEEE Transactions on Knowledge and Data Engineering*, 6(1):120–135, 1994.

[32] J. Gray, S. Chaudhuri, A. Bosworth, A. Layman, D. Reichart, M. Venkatrao, F. Pellow, and H. Pirahesh. Data cube: A relational aggregation operator generalizing group-by, cross-tab, and sub-totals. *Data Min. Knowl. Discov.*, 1(1):29–53, Jan. 1997.

[33] T. Grust, M. Mayr, J. Rittinger, and T. Schreiber. FERRY: database-supported program execution. SIGMOD 2009, pages 1063–1066. ACM.

[34] T. Grust, J. Rittinger, and T. Schreiber. Avalanche-safe LINQ compilation. *PVLDB*, 3(1-2):162–172, Sept. 2010.

[35] T. Grust and M. Scholl. How to comprehend queries functionally. *Journal of Intelligent Information Systems*, 12(2-3):191–218, 1999.

[36] P. Hudak. Building domain-specific embedded languages. *ACM Comput. Surv.*, 28(4es), Dec. 1996.

[37] S. Idreos, F. Groffen, N. Nes, S. Manegold, S. Mullender, M. Kersten, et al. Monetdb: Two decades of research in column-oriented database architectures. *IEEE Data Eng. Bull.*, 35(1):40–45, 2012.

[38] N. D. Jones, C. K. Gomard, and P. Sestoft. *Partial evaluation and automatic program generation*. Prentice Hall, 1993.

[39] S. Jones. Compiling haskell by program transformation: A report from the trenches. In H. Nielson, editor, *Programming Languages and Systems - ESOP '96*, volume 1058 of *Lecture Notes in Computer Science*, pages 18–44. Springer Berlin Heidelberg, 1996.

[40] M. Jonnalagedda and S. Stucki. Fold-based fusion as a library: A generative programming pearl. In *Proceedings of the 6th ACM SIGPLAN Symposium on Scala*, pages 41–50. ACM, 2015.

[41] V. Jovanovic, A. Shaikhha, S. Stucki, V. Nikolaev, C. Koch, and M. Odersky. Yin-Yang: Concealing the deep embedding of DSLs. GPCE 2014, pages 73–82. ACM, 2014.

[42] J. Kam and J. Ullman. Monotone data flow analysis frameworks. *Acta Informatica*, 7(3):305–317, 1977.

[43] J. B. Kam and J. D. Ullman. Global data flow analysis and iterative algorithms. *J. ACM*, 23(1):158–171, Jan. 1976.

[44] M. Karpathiotakis, I. Alagiannis, T. Heinis, M. Branco, and A. Ailamaki. Just-in-time data virtualization: Lightweight data management with vida. In *CIDR*, 2015.

[45] R. A. Kelsey. A correspondence between continuation passing style and static single assignment form. In *ACM SIGPLAN Notices*, volume 30, pages 13–22. ACM, 1995.

[46] A. Kennedy. Compiling with continuations, continued. In *ACM SIGPLAN Notices*, volume 42, pages 177–190, 2007.

[47] K. Kennedy. *A survey of data flow analysis techniques*. IBM Thomas J. Watson Research Division, 1979.

[48] K. Kennedy and K. McKinley. Maximizing loop parallelism and improving data locality via loop fusion and distribution. In *Languages and Compilers for Parallel Computing*, pages 301–320. Springer Berlin Heidelberg, 1994.

[49] W. Kim. On Optimizing an SQL-like Nested Query. *ACM Trans. Database Syst.*, 7(3):443–469, Sept. 1982.

[50] Y. Klonatos, C. Koch, T. Rompf, and H. Chafi. Building efficient query engines in a high-level language. *PVLDB*, 7(10):853–864, 2014.

[51] Y. Klonatos, A. Nötzli, A. Spielmann, C. Koch, and V. Kuncak. Automatic Synthesis of Out-of-core Algorithms. In *ACM SIGMOD*, pages 133–144, 2013.

[52] C. Koch. Incremental query evaluation in a ring of databases. PODS 2010, pages 87–98. ACM, 2010.

[53] C. Koch. Abstraction without regret in data management systems. In *CIDR*, 2013.

[54] C. Koch. Abstraction without regret in database systems building: a manifesto. *IEEE Data Eng. Bull.*, 37(1):70–79, 2014.

[55] C. Koch, Y. Ahmad, O. Kennedy, M. Nikolic, A. Nötzli, D. Lupei, and A. Shaikhha. DBToaster: higher-order delta processing for dynamic, frequently fresh views. *VLDBJ*, 23(2):253–278, 2014.

[56] K. Krikellas, S. Viglas, and M. Cintra. Generating code for holistic query evaluation. In *ICDE*, pages 613–624, 2010.

[57] V. Leis, P. Boncz, A. Kemper, and T. Neumann. Morsel-driven Parallelism: A NUMA-aware Query Evaluation Framework for the Many-core Age. SIGMOD '14, pages 743–754, New York, NY, USA, 2014. ACM.

[58] D. Leivant. Reasoning about functional programs and complexity classes associated with type disciplines. In *FOCS*, pages 460–469, Nov 1983.

[59] L. Libkin. Expressive Power of SQL. *Theor. Comput. Sci.*, 296(3):379–404, Mar. 2003.

[60] M. Mehta and D. J. DeWitt. Managing intra-operator parallelism in parallel database systems. In *VLDB*, volume 95, pages 382–394, 1995.

[61] E. Meijer, B. Beckman, and G. Bierman. LINQ: Reconciling Object, Relations and XML in the .NET Framework. SIGMOD '06, pages 706–706. ACM, 2006.

[62] F. Nagel, G. Bierman, and S. D. Viglas. Code generation for efficient query processing in managed runtimes. *PVLDB*, 7(12):1095–1106.

[63] S. Najd, S. Lindley, J. Svenningsson, and P. Wadler. Everything old is new again: Quoted domain-specific languages. PEPM 2016, pages 25–36, New York, NY, USA, 2016. ACM.

[64] T. Neumann. Efficiently Compiling Efficient Query Plans for Modern Hardware. *PVLDB*, 4(9):539–550, 2011.

[65] V. Pankratius, F. Schmidt, and G. Garreton. Combining functional and imperative programming for multicore software: An empirical study evaluating Scala and Java. In *ICSE 2012*, pages 123–133.

[66] B. C. Pierce. *Types and programming languages*. MIT press, 2002.

[67] M. Puschel, J. M. Moura, J. R. Johnson, D. Padua, M. M. Veloso, B. W. Singer, J. Xiong, F. Franchetti, A. Gacic, Y. Voronenko, et al. SPIRAL: code generation for DSP transforms. *Proceedings of the IEEE*, 93(2):232–275, 2005.

[68] R. Ramakrishnan and J. Gehrke. *Database Management Systems*. Osborne/McGraw-Hill, 2nd edition, 2000.

[69] G. Ramalingam. The undecidability of aliasing. *TOPLAS*, 16(5):1467–1471, Sept. 1994.

[70] T. Rompf and M. Odersky. Lightweight Modular Staging: A Pragmatic Approach to Runtime Code Generation and Compiled DSLs. *CACM*, 55(6):121–130, June 2012.

[71] B. K. Rosen, M. N. Wegman, and F. K. Zadeck. Global Value Numbers and Redundant Computations. POPL '88, pages 12–27. ACM, 1988.

[72] O. Shivers and M. Might. Continuations and transducer composition. PLDI '06, pages 295–307. ACM, 2006.

[73] D. G. Spampinato and M. Püschel. A basic linear algebra compiler. CGO '14, pages 23:23–23:32. ACM, 2014.

[74] J. Stanier and D. Watson. Intermediate representations in imperative compilers: A survey. *CSUR*, 45(3):26:1–26:27, July 2013.

[75] M. Stonebraker, D. J. Abadi, A. Batkin, X. Chen, M. Cherniack, M. Ferreira, E. Lau, A. Lin, S. Madden, E. O'Neil, P. O'Neil, A. Rasin, N. Tran, and S. Zdonik. C-store: A Column-oriented DBMS. VLDB '05, pages 553–564. VLDB Endowment, 2005.

[76] J. Svenningsson. Shortcut fusion for accumulating parameters & zip-like functions. ICFP '02, pages 124–132. ACM, 2002.

[77] W. Taha and T. Sheard. Multi-stage programming with explicit annotations. PEPM '97, pages 203–217, NY, USA, 1997. ACM.

[78] R. Tate, M. Stepp, Z. Tatlock, and S. Lerner. Equality saturation: A new approach to optimization. POPL '09, pages 264–276. ACM.

[79] L. Torczon and K. Cooper. *Engineering A Compiler*. Morgan Kaufmann Publishers Inc., 2nd edition, 2011.

[80] S.-A.-A. Touati and D. Barthou. On the decidability of phase ordering problem in optimizing compilation. In *Proceedings of the 3rd Conference on Computing Frontiers*, CF '06, pages 147–156, 2006.

[81] Transaction Processing Performance Council. TPC-H, a decision support benchmark. http://www.tpc.org/tpch.

[82] P. Trinder. Comprehensions, a Query Notation for DBPLs. In *Proc. of the 3rd DBPL workshop*, DBPL3, pages 55–68, San Francisco, CA, USA, 1992. Morgan Kaufmann Publishers Inc.

[83] D. Turner. Total functional programming. *Journal of Universal Computer Science*, 10(7):751–768, 2004.

[84] S. Viglas, G. M. Bierman, and F. Nagel. Processing Declarative Queries Through Generating Imperative Code in Managed Runtimes. *IEEE Data Eng. Bull.*, 37(1):12–21, 2014.

[85] E. Visser, Z. Benaissa, and A. Tolmach. Building program optimizers with rewriting strategies. ICFP '98, pages 13–26, 1998.

[86] P. Wadler. Deforestation: Transforming programs to eliminate trees. In *ESOP'88*, pages 344–358. Springer, 1988.

[87] P. Wadler. Comprehending monads. In *Proceedings of the 1990 ACM Conference on LISP and Functional Programming*, LFP '90, pages 61–78, New York, NY, USA, 1990. ACM.

[88] T. Würthinger, A. Wöß, L. Stadler, G. Duboscq, D. Simon, and C. Wimmer. Self-optimizing AST Interpreters. DLS '12, pages 73–82, New York, NY, USA, 2012. ACM.

[89] M. Zaharia, M. Chowdhury, T. Das, A. Dave, J. Ma, M. McCauley, M. J. Franklin, S. Shenker, and I. Stoica. Resilient Distributed Datasets: A Fault-tolerant Abstraction for In-memory Cluster Computing. NSDI'12. USENIX Association.

APPENDIX

In this section we provide more information in two areas. First, we discuss about other IRs introduced in the PL community, and compare those with the ANF IR used in DBLAB/LB. Second, we present more optimizations supported by the DBLAB/LB stack for a number of different database components.

A. MORE ON INTERMEDIATE REPRESENTATIONS

There are several IRs proposed in the PL community which simplify data-flow analysis, chief among them 1) SSA [71, 20], 2) CPS [5, 46], and 3) ANF [25]. Although it has been proven that these IRs are semantically equivalent [25, 4, 45], from a practical point of view there are advantages and disadvantages for using each one. Even in the PL community, there is no consensus on which IR is the best [46, 25, 14]. It is, however, undisputed in the PL community that a simple use of ASTs, the dominant choice in work by the database community, creates the problems mentioned before and is inferior to these three for many uses.

The reasons for using ANF can be summarized as follows: first, ANF simplifies data-flow analysis by allowing a single definition of variables [14], which has a great impact on simplifying optimizations that use data-flow information, such as CSE – indeed, it facilitates the mix of effectful and pure computations, and has been shown to make optimizing transformations and analyses easier to write [8]; second, both ANF and SSA preserve the natural organization of programs (called "direct-style"), making them more understandable than CPS (which uses "continuation-passing style", whereby functions call continuations instead of returning values [25]); third, as ANF is a direct-style representation of λ-calculus [25], there are very well-known frameworks for the analysis and verification of λ-calculus developed in the PL community [58]. Hence, reasoning about compiler optimizations in ANF is simpler [14]; finally, by converting many semantically equivalent programs into a canonical representation, expressing optimizations becomes simpler [49], as there is no more any need to express optimizations for all semantically equivalent cases: it suffices to only express one for the canonical form.

There are other IRs proposed in the literature, which mainly target optimizations for parallel architectures (e.g. PDG [24]), or are meant to help and combine compiler optimizations (e.g. a *sea of IR nodes* [17] and E-PEG [78]). However, these IRs complicate the debugging process of program compilation, and are seldom used in real-world, mainstream compilers [74]. Although we did not consider using these IRs, it would be an interesting direction for our future work, particularly when targeting parallel architectures.

B. DATA-STRUCTURE SPECIALIZATION

Data-structure specialization is crucial for achieving high-performance query execution, as it eliminates the unnecessary abstraction overhead of generic data structures like hash tables. Next, we present in more detail how our system performs such optimizations.

B.1 Indexing and Partitioning

The most important form of data-structure specialization concerns optimizing the data structures that hold the data of the *input* relations. This is true even for multi-way join-intensive queries. To enable several DBLAB/LB optimizations for these structures, developers must annotate the primary and foreign keys of their relations, at schema definition time. DBLAB/LB then creates optimized data structures for those relations, as follows.

First, for each input relation, DBLAB/LB creates a replicated data structure which is accessed in constant time through the primary key specified for that relation. There are two possibilities:

- For single-attribute primary keys, the value of this attribute in each tuple is used to place the tuple in a continuous 1D-array. This is easy to do for the relations with integer primary keys in the range of [1...*#num_tuples*]. However, even when the primary key is not in a continuous value range, DBLAB/LB currently makes an aggressive system memory trade-off to hold a sparse array for that primary key.
- For composite primary keys, DBLAB/LB does not create a 1D array and instead uses the foreign key for this purpose.

Second, DBLAB/LB replicates and repartitions the data of the input relations based on each specified foreign key. This basically leads to the creation of a two-dimensional array, indexed by the foreign key, where each bucket holds all the tuples having a particular value for that foreign key. We also apply the same partitioning technique for relations that have primary composite keys, as we mentioned above. We resolve the case where the foreign key is not in a contiguous value range by trading-off system memory, in a similar way to how we handled the primary keys.

This technique improves query performance, but trades-off memory consumption as a consequence. Observe that for relations that have multiple foreign keys, not all corresponding partitioned input relations need to be kept in memory at the same time, as an incoming SQL query may not use all of them. Thus, DBLAB/LB loads the proper partitioned table based on select and join conditions available in the given query only, and the attributes referenced on those conditions.

In addition to the aforementioned partitioning mechanism, the DBLAB/LB system re-uses this mechanism in order to create indices on attributes of `date` types. These are used to significantly speed up select predicates performed on such attributes.

These indices are automatically constructed at data loading time when an SQL query is given to the DBLAB/LB query compiler. These indices are created by repartitioning the data from the original relation array into a two dimensional array, where each bucket holds the tuples belonging to a specific year (or even a particular year-month combination).

As a result of these indices, the corresponding predicates on date attributes are converted into simple `if` conditions capturing whether the tuples belonging to a bucket should be processed or not. These indices are particularly important for scan operators that process large input relations.

B.2 Hash-Table Specialization

One of the most important data structures in query processing for handling different operators such as hash join and aggregation is the hash-table data structure. By default, DBLAB/LB uses GLib hash tables for generating C code out of the hash-table constructs of the Scala programming language. Independent of the language chosen, however, the overhead of using such generic data structures is significant for at least three reasons: (a) there typically exists data redundancy between the key and value stored in the map, (b) there are numerous function calls occurring for processing a single tuple, and, (c) resizing operations may be needed, so that the data structure remains efficient as more data is placed into it. DBLAB/LB avoids these issues by lowering hash tables to native arrays and linked lists and inlining the corresponding operations.

C. OPTIMIZING MEMORY HIERARCHY ACCESSES

Unused Struct Field Removal: DBLAB/LB provides an optimization for removing struct fields that are not accessed by a particular SQL query. DBLAB/LB optimizes data loading, so that it avoids loading into memory the values for the unnecessary fields. It does so, by analyzing the input code and removing the set of unused fields from the record definitions. This reduces memory pressure and improves cache locality.

The removal of unnecessary fields improves the performance of row layout the most. This is because of two reasons. First, even without field removal optimization the columnar layout is implicitly applying this optimization, as the unused columns are never cached, thus not negatively affecting cache locality. Second, for row layout the field removal optimization basically allows to store the record attributes in a more compact way in memory and hence, improves the cache locality for this layout.

Removing Unnecessary Let-Bindings: The SC DSL compiler uses the ANF IR (cf. Section 3.3) for applying transformations and while performing code generation. Although this IR simplifies analysis, transformations, and code generation for the compiler, it has the negative effect of introducing many unnecessary intermediate variables during code generation. We have observed that this form of code generation not only affects code compactness, but also significantly increases register pressure. To improve upon this situation, the SC DSL compiler removes any intermediate variable that satisfies the following three conditions: it (a) is set only once, (b) has no side effects, and, finally, (c) is initialized with a single value (and thus its initialization does not correspond to executing possible expensive computation). SC then replaces any appearance of this variable later in the code with its initialization value. We have observed that this optimization makes the generated code much more compact, reduces register pressure, and results in significant performance improvements. More importantly, we have observed that the granularity at which this optimization is applied does not allow this optimization to be detected by low-level compilers like LLVM.

Finally, the SC DSL compiler applies a technique known as *Scalar Replacement*. This optimization removes *structs* whose fields can be flattened to local variables. This optimization has the effect of removing a memory access from the critical path, since the field of a struct can be referenced immediately without requiring referencing the variable holding the struct itself. We have observed that this optimization significantly improves cache locality.

D. DOMAIN-SPECIFIC CODE MOTION

Domain-Specific Code Motion subsumes optimizations that remove code segments that have negative impact on query execution performance from the critical path, and instead execute the logic of those code segments during data loading. Thus, the optimizations in this category trade-off increased loading time for improved query execution performance. There are two main optimizations in this category, described next.

D.1 Hoisting Memory Allocations

Memory allocations can cause significant performance degradation in query execution. By taking advantage of type information available in each SQL query, we can completely eliminate such allocations from the critical path, as described next.

At query compilation time, information is gathered regarding the data types used throughout an incoming SQL query. This is done through an analysis phase, where the compiler collects all `malloc` expressions in the program, once the latter has been lowered to the C.Scala DSL (cf. Section 4.1). The obtained types may represent either the initial database relations or the intermediate results. Based on this information, the DBLAB/LB query compiler initializes memory pools during data loading, one for each type. For example, for TPC-H queries, DBLAB/LB generates pools for allocating the data types of all TPC-H relations, as well as supporting pools for specific operators, e.g. a pool for allocating the aggregate records.

Then, at query execution time, the corresponding `malloc` statements are replaced with references to those memory pools. We have observed that this optimization significantly reduces the number of CPU instructions executed, and significantly contributes to improving cache locality. We note that it is not sufficient to naïvely generate one pool per data-type in the order of their appearance, as there may be dependencies between types. This is particularly true for composite types, which need to reference the pools of the native types (e.g. the pool for Strings). We resolve such dependencies by first applying topological sorting on the obtained type information and then generating the pools in the proper order.

Finally, the size of these pools is estimated by performing worst-case cardinality analysis on a given query. Currently worst-case estimation is driven by two factors: (a) the collection of statistical metrics like cardinality estimation and attribute skew (e.g. number of distinct values per attribute) as well as (b) the usage of annotations that are specified by developers at schema definition time. As an example of the former, DBLAB/LB gathers information about how many distinct years exist in all attributes of date type (and utilizes this information in the join indices presented in Section B.1), while an example of the latter includes the definition by developers of *1-N* relationships when joining two relations. Based on this information, DBLAB/LB calculates the worst-case selectivity of even multi-way join queries.

As the cardinality is estimated in a worst-case scenario, the transformer may lead to allocation of much more space than what is actually needed. However, we have confirmed that our estimated statistics are accurate enough so that they do not unnecessarily create memory pressure, thus negatively affecting query execution performance. Furthermore, our general framework is not tied to this transformation. Hence, based on the workload we can use different variants of this transformation. For example, one could completely disable this transformation and leave the memory management to the runtime. Alternatively, one could preallocate certain amount of memory pools and in the case of overflowing the memory pool increasing its capacity by a certain factor (e.g. a factor of two) to amortize the runtime complexity.

D.2 Hoisting Data-Structure Initialization

Key-value stores are used in DBLAB/LB to calculate aggregations. During this evaluation, it is necessary to first check whether the corresponding key for the aggregation already exists in the aggregation data structure. If so, it would return the existing aggregation, otherwise it would insert a new aggregation into the data structure. This means, that *at least one* `if` condition must be evaluated for *every* tuple that is processed by the aggregate operator. We have observed that such `if` conditions, that exist purely for the purpose of data structure initialization, significantly affect branch prediction and overall query execution performance.

DBLAB/LB provides a transformation to remove such initialization of data structures from the critical path by taking advantage of domain-specific knowledge. For instance, if the key to the aggregation is a relation primary key, we know from data loading time the possible values this key can take. By doing so, we can initialize possible aggregations for each key with the value zero. Then, at query execution time, the corresponding `if` condition mentioned above no longer needs to be evaluated, as the aggregation already exists and can be accessed directly.

It is important to note that this optimization is not possible in its full generality, as it directly depends on the ability to predict the possible key values in advance, during data loading. Particularly for TPC-H, we note two things. First, there is no key that is the result of an intermediate join operator deeply nested in the query plan. Instead, TPC-H uses attributes of the original relations to access most data structures, attributes whose value range can be estimated accurately during data loading. Second, for TPC-H queries the value range is very small, typically ranging up to a couple of thousand sequential key values. These two properties combined allow to completely remove initialization overheads and the associated unnecessary computation for the TPC-H queries. As an example, this optimization improves the performance of TPC-H query 1 by 10%. The workload-specific information is guided through annotations (cf. Section 3.3). These annotations are used for checking the applicability of this optimization. If the given query does not have these properties (e.g. a query without the properties of the TPC-H queries mentioned above) the transformation is no longer applied. In other words, this transformation is smart enough to be applied only to queries which statisfy the mentioned properties.

E. FINE-GRAINED OPTIMIZATIONS

Finally, there is a category of fine-grained compiler optimizations that are applied last in the compilation process. These optimizations target optimizing very small code segments (even individual statements) under particular conditions. We briefly present three such optimizations next.

DBLAB/LB can transform arrays to a set of local variables. This lowering is possible only when (a) the array size is statically known at compile time, (b) the array is relatively small and, finally, (c) the index of every array access can be inferred at compile time (otherwise, the compiler is not able to know to which local variable this array access is mapped to). Second, the query compiler provides an optimization to change the boolean condition `x && y` to `x & y` where `x` and `y` both evaluate to boolean, an optimization which, according to our observations, improves branch prediction. However, to make sure that this optimization is semantic preserving, the second operand must not have any side-effect. Finally, the compiler can be instructed to apply tiling to `for` loops whose range are known at compile time (or can be accurately estimated). Based on our observations these fine-grained optimizations, which can be typically written in less than a hundred lines of code, significantly improve query execution performance. More importantly, since they have very fine-grained granularity, their application does not introduce additional performance overheads.

Automated Demand-driven Resource Scaling in Relational Database-as-a-Service

Sudipto Das Feng Li Vivek R. Narasayya Arnd Christian König

Microsoft Research
Redmond, WA 98052, USA
{sudiptod, fenl, viveknar, chrisko}@microsoft.com

ABSTRACT

Relational Database-as-a-Service (DaaS) platforms today support the abstraction of a *resource container* that guarantees a fixed amount of resources. Tenants are responsible for selecting a container size suitable for their workloads, which they can change to leverage the cloud's elasticity. However, automating this task is daunting for most tenants since estimating resource demands for arbitrary SQL workloads in an RDBMS is complex and challenging. In addition, workloads and resource requirements can vary significantly within minutes to hours, and container sizes vary by orders of magnitude both in the amount of resources as well as monetary cost. We present a solution to enable a DaaS to auto-scale container sizes on behalf of its tenants. Approaches to auto-scale stateless services, such as web servers, that rely on historical resource *utilization* as the primary signal, often perform poorly for stateful database servers which are significantly more complex. Our solution derives a set of robust signals from database engine telemetry and combines them to significantly improve accuracy of demand estimation for database workloads resulting in more accurate scaling decisions. Our solution raises the abstraction by allowing tenants to reason about monetary budget and query latency rather than resources. We prototyped our approach in Microsoft Azure SQL Database and ran extensive experiments using workloads with realistic time-varying resource demand patterns obtained from production traces. Compared to an approach that uses only resource utilization to estimate demand, our approach results in $1.5\times$ to $3\times$ lower monetary costs while achieving comparable query latencies.

Keywords

Relational database-as-a-service; elasticity; auto-scaling; resource demand estimation.

1. INTRODUCTION

Relational Database-as-a-Service (*DaaS*) is a rapidly growing business with offerings from major providers, such as Amazon's Relational Database Service (RDS), Microsoft's Azure SQL Database (Azure SQL DB), and Google's Cloud SQL. Many enterprises today deploy mission-critical databases in these DaaS environments.

SIGMOD'16, June 26-July 01, 2016, San Francisco, CA, USA

ISBN 978-1-4503-3531-7/16/06...$15.00

DOI: http://dx.doi.org/10.1145/2882903.2903733

Since these DaaS environments are multi-tenant, performance predictability through resource isolation has been identified as a critical requirement for such mission-critical databases [10, 15]. Commercial DaaS offerings now support resource isolation through logical or physical **containers**. The container can be a virtual machine (VM) [10, 20] dedicated to a tenant's database, such as in Amazon RDS, or a logical container, such as in Azure SQL Database [15]. Regardless of the specific container abstraction, a container guarantees a fixed set of resources, referred to as the **container size**.

A major attraction of DaaS is the promise of elasticity, pay-per-use, and high availability. DaaS platforms offer a collection of container sizes and supports elasticity by allowing a tenant to change the container size for their database over time.[1,2,3] Such container size changes can be performed relatively quickly (e.g., typically within minutes). Judiciously changing container sizes results in significant cost savings due to two reasons. First, the workload's resource requirements change over time. Our analysis of resource utilization from thousands of production tenant databases (details in Section 2.2) reveals that changes in resource requirements crossing container size boundaries are frequent, typically occurring in the order of minutes to a few hours. This is similar to resource demand variations observed in non-database workloads [8, 19]. Second, there are large differences in resources and cost between different container sizes. For example, at the time of writing, three orders of magnitude separate the cost of the smallest and largest containers in Azure SQL DB.

We focus on the "scale-up" form of auto-scaling, where the size of a *single* container is changed over time. This is different from the "scale-out" approach of auto-scaling [4,8,19,20] which changes the *number* of containers (e.g., VMs). The "scale-out" approach repartitions the workload as the number of containers change. This orthogonal "scale-up" approach is supported in today's DaaS and allows databases contained in a single server to leverage elasticity without partitioning the database. Even though the maximum container size is limited by the largest server in the service, based on current trends, large containers with $16 - 32$ cores, hundreds of Gigabytes of RAM and Terabytes of storage are sufficient for an overwhelming majority of tenants.

Today, to benefit from elasticity, a tenant has to determine when to scale the container size. Well-known application-agnostic approaches rely on resource utilization as the primary driver for scaling decisions. For instance, if resource utilization is high (e.g., 80% I/O utilization in the current container with 100 IOPS), then scale up the container; similarly, low resource utilization implies scale down. However, high resource utilization does not necessarily

[1] http://azure.microsoft.com/en-us/pricing/details/sql-database/
[2] https://developers.google.com/cloud-sql/pricing
[3] http://aws.amazon.com/rds/pricing/

mean that there is **demand** for more resources. That is, if allocated a larger container (e.g., with 200 IOPS), the workload will indeed consume the additional resources (i.e., number of I/Os will exceed 100 IOPS). *Since resource demand cannot be measured*, the problem is to *estimate* demand for database workloads. The challenge arises due to the complexity of database engines and how multiple resources interact. For example, if the offered load increases, it does not necessarily mean that that adding more resources will significantly improve query latencies, particularly if queries are mostly waiting for locks on shared data items. Similarly, adding more memory might reduce the need for I/O and increase the CPU demand since more data can be cached. When container sizes vary significantly in resources and cost, the penalty for incorrect demand estimation can be high – either poor performance if demand is underestimated or higher monetary cost if demand is overestimated. Most tenants of a DaaS cannot afford to hire sophisticated database administrators necessary to make judiciously scale resources.

We study the problem of how a DaaS platform can support robust auto-scaling functionality on the tenant's behalf by estimating resource demands for the tenant's workload. Any solution that the DaaS platform uses must be general enough for arbitrary, and often unseen, SQL workloads that the tenant's application may issue. Previous work on resource modeling in classic enterprise consolidation scenarios build resource models assuming the workload is known in advance [3,14,21] (e.g., the query classes and their relative frequencies are known). However, obtaining such a "representative" workload to train models specific to the workload is hard even with expert database administrators, and is infeasible for a DaaS platform which must support hundreds of thousands of tenants with very different requirements. Therefore, our auto-scaling solution leverages generic telemetry and execution characteristics of a tenant's workload that is available for all tenants and does not require tenant-specific human input.

Auto-scaling functionality supported today in commercial cloud platforms uses tenant-specified rules based on resource utilization.[4,5] We show that for database workloads, it is possible to significantly improve accuracy of demand estimation by deriving additional signals from database engine telemetry that goes well beyond resource utilization. For example, we show that *resource waits*, which is the amount of time a tenant's requests wait for a logical or physical resource, is an important signal since significant waits for resources might indicate the workload would benefit from more resources.

Our technique results in improved accuracy in demand estimation due to three key ideas. First, we derive statistically-robust signals that can tolerate noise, which is inevitable in system telemetry (Section 3). Second, we use domain knowledge of database engine internals to systematically design a decision logic to combine multiple signals to greatly reduce the fraction of inaccurate estimations of high (or low) demand (Section 4). Intuitively, if there are multiple weak signals of high demand for a resource (such as utilization and waits), it increases the likelihood of the demand actually being high. Third, we leverage the fact that a DaaS platform can observe telemetry of large numbers of tenants with very different workloads and resource demands. We analyze this service-wide telemetry to improve our demand-estimation logic, e.g., to determine meaningful and suitable thresholds for the input signals.

Besides estimating resource demands, an end-to-end auto-scaling solution must cater to a number of practical challenges. First, many tenants have a cost budget which is specified over a longer period of time such as a month, while container sizing actions occur more frequently, e.g., in minutes or hours. The challenge is to design an online budget allocation strategy that allows periods of high resource demand (where the budget is consumed at a rate higher that the average rate) while ensuring that the total cost does not exceed the budget. We borrow ideas from the traffic shaping problem in computer networks to address this problem (Section 5). Second, tenants may wish to specify latency goals for their applications. We use this input to further reduce costs. If latency goals are met, we allocate a smaller container even if there is demand for a larger container. Further, latency goals might not be met due to issues beyond resources, such as poorly-written application code. Therefore, we increase the container sizes *only* if there is resource demand, even when the latency goals are not being met. Note that tenants do not need to specify a throughput goal. When the offered load increases, the unmet resource demand and query latencies provide the necessary feedback to the auto-scaling logic. Our solution continuously monitors the resource demands and latency goals, and adjusts the container sizes in a closed loop. We present an end-to-end auto-scaling solution for relational DaaS that *helps the tenants achieve their desired latency goals while minimizing the costs and remaining within the specified budget* (Section 6). Such functionality raises the abstraction of a DaaS by allowing tenants to reason about budget and query latency rather than resource provisioning.

We prototype our solution in Microsoft Azure SQL Database and demonstrate the benefits using a variety of benchmark workloads and resource demand traces derived from production workloads. When compared to an approach that uses only resource utilization to estimate demand, our solution reduces the tenant's costs by $1.5\times$ to $3\times$ while resulting in similar 95th percentile latencies.

Following are the major contributions of this paper:

- By leveraging domain knowledge of database engines, we identify a set of statistically-robust signals and propose a decision logic to improve accuracy in estimating resource demands.
- We propose an end-to-end solution for auto-scaling in a DaaS that combines automatic estimated resource demands with tenant-specified budget constraints and latency goals.
- We demonstrate the cost-effectiveness and robustness of our approach by prototyping it in Microsoft Azure SQL Database and evaluation using a variety of benchmark workloads and resource demand patterns derived from production traces.

2. PROBLEM SETTING

2.1 Database-as-a-Service

We consider a relational DaaS such as Azure SQL Database. The DaaS offers a set of resource containers each with a fixed set of resources (e.g., two virtual cores, 4GB memory, 100 disk IOPS, and 1 TB disk space) and a cost per **billing interval** (e.g., 50 cents/hour).

We consider a setting where container sizes can be scaled independently in each resource dimension or in lock-step for all resources. Figure 1 demonstrates this scaling of container sizes using two resource dimensions CPU and Disk I/O as examples. Container sizes $(S, M, L, \ldots)$ scale both the CPU and Disk I/O in the same proportion. That is, M has $2\times$ larger allocation and L has $3\times$ larger allocation for both CPU and Disk IO compared to S. $S, M_C, L_C, \ldots$

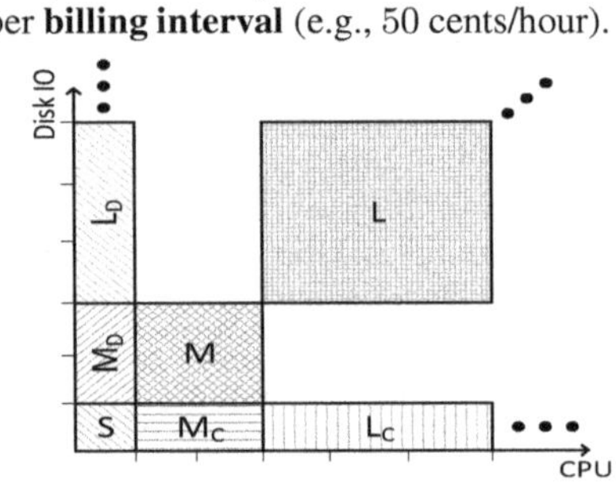

Figure 1: Container sizes in a DaaS with resources as dimensions.

[4]http://aws.amazon.com/autoscaling/

[5]https://cloud.google.com/compute/docs/autoscaler/

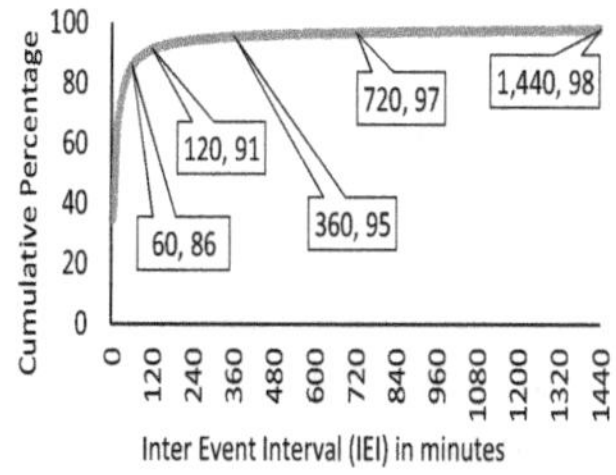

(a) CDF of IEI in minutes.

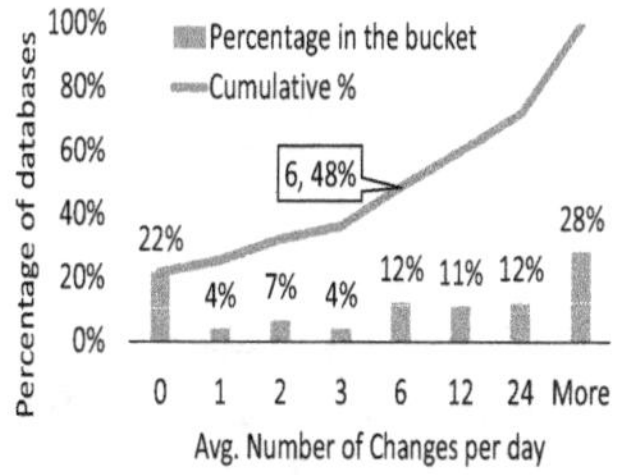

(b) Change frequency distribution.

Figure 2: Distribution of interval between changes (IEI) and the frequency of changes.

and $S, M_D, L_D, \ldots$ represent container scaling along CPU and Disk IO dimensions respectively. For instance, the standard tiers in Amazon and Azure proportionally increase resources while high memory, high CPU, and high I/O instances scale resources along a specific dimension. Workloads having demand in one resource can benefit if containers are scaled independently in each dimension.

2.2 Resource Demand Analysis in Production

To understand the importance of auto-scaling, we performed an offline analysis using week-long resource utilization traces for a few thousand tenant databases from production Azure DB clusters. We aggregated a tenant's resource utilization over 5 minute intervals for CPU, I/O, and memory. We then logically *assigned* the smallest container supported by the service that can meet the resource requirements for that interval as the tenant's container for that interval. We record a *change event* when a tenant's *assigned* container size changes between successive intervals. Intuitively, a change event indicates resource demand changes equivalent to a container resize. Since we did not actually change container sizes, we can only capture cases where demand is smaller or equal to the tenant's current container size. Thus, our analysis may even be an underestimation. We use the *Inter Event Interval* (IEI), the time between two successive change events, to characterize the changes in the tenant's resource demands.

Figure 2(a) plots the cumulative percentage distribution of the IEI for all databases in the service. That is, the data point of (60, 86) implies that among all container size changes detected across the service, 86% of the changes happen within 60 minutes of the previous change. From Figure 2(b) plots the percentage distribution of the number of changes per day. As is evident, more than 78% of tenants averaged at least one change event per day, more than 52% of tenants had 6 or more change events per day; and 28% of the tenants averaged more than 24 change events per day.

The key takeaway from this analysis is that an overwhelming majority of tenants in a DaaS experience significant resource demand variations (crossing container size boundaries) per day and these variations occur frequently. Therefore, an auto-scaling solution could potentially be of great value to such tenants.

2.3 Auto-scaling Knobs

For many tenants of DaaS, who are not sophisticated database administrators, it is challenging to reason about resource demands for their workload. By contrast, it is far easier for tenants to relate to application-level latency goals and monetary constraints such as a monthly budget for the database. By auto-scaling resources based on demand, we aim to bridge this gap.

In principle, an auto-scaling logic can automatically scale the container sizes purely based on demand. However, based on our analysis of various customer scenarios and talking to database administrators, we find that customers want knobs to tailor the behavior of this automated logic for their databases. A DaaS platform hosts variety of tenants, from small departmental applications with modest latency requirements to line-of-business applications requiring interactive query latency. While scaling purely based on demand might be desirable for performance-critical applications, it might not be cost-effective for budget-conscious tenants. To support a variety of tenant requirements, we expose a small set of *knobs*, which the tenants can *optionally* set, to control the costs and behavior of the auto-scaling logic.

Budget. Tenants with an operating budget for their databases can specify a budget for longer periods of time called the **budgeting period**, e.g., a month. The budget is treated as a hard constraint. When a budget is specified, the auto-scaling logic selects the smallest container sufficient to meet the resource demands and has cost less than the available budget. If the budget is not constrained, containers are selected based only on demand.

Latency goals. Applications having a latency goal for their database back-end can provide goals for the *average* or 95th percentile latency. The latency goals allow the auto-scaling logic to provide resources sufficient to achieve the latency goals, thus reducing costs when resource demands require a larger container size but the latency goals can be achieved using a smaller container size. For instance, an application involving interactive user activity might specify a 95th percentile latency of 100 ms. On the other hand, a small departmental web application may be content with an average latency of 1000 ms, thereby potentially achieving lower costs if the latency goals can be met with a smaller container. Latency goals of an application might not be met due to issues beyond resources, such as poorly-written application code. Therefore, latency goals are not a guarantee of performance, rather a knob to control costs.

Coarse-grained performance sensitivity. For tenants without precise latency goals, this coarse-grained knob indicates how latency-sensitive their application is. In principle, this knob can be a continuous value (e.g., between 0 and 1). However, for convenience, we expose a small set of discrete steps such as: `HIGH, MEDIUM, LOW` with the default value set to `MEDIUM`. Intuitively, for a tenant with `LOW` sensitivity, the auto-scaling logic will be less aggressive in scaling up (and more aggressive in scaling down) than for a tenant with `HIGH` sensitivity, thereby potentially reducing costs.

2.4 Solution Overview

The core of our solution is to improve the accuracy of *resource demand* estimation for a variety of SQL workloads that a DaaS serves. Figure 3 illustrates a simplified architecture of a DaaS. The service comprises a collection of servers that host the tenant databases and serve requests. Figure 3 hides other components of the service, such as the management servers, gateways and load balancers. Each database server in the service hosts a set of containers, one for each tenant database. The co-location of specific containers at a server is determined by the management fabric of the service. The DaaS collects detailed counters (called *production telemetry*) for each container.

The auto-scaling module has three major components. (a) The **Telemetry manager** (Section 3) collects telemetry for each tenant database. Its challenge is to select a subset from the hundreds of counters in the telemetry which can be used as signals to robustly-estimate demand. (b) The **Resource demand estimator** (Section 4) uses the signals from the telemetry manager to estimate the demand for each of the resources comprising the container. Signals collected from telemetry are at best weakly-predictive of resource demands. The main challenge is to accurately and robustly estimate demands for a variety of workloads. (c) The **Budget manager** (Section 5) is responsible for judiciously translating the budget for the budgeting period into a budget for each billing interval

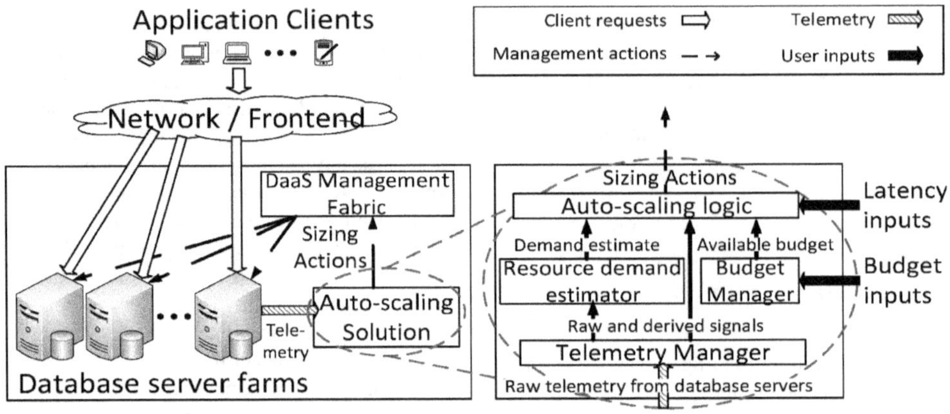

Figure 3: Simplified architecture of an auto-scaling solution for a DaaS.

for which a container is chosen. The main challenge is to design an online technique, i.e., one without knowledge of future workload patterns, which allocates enough budget for each billing interval that meets bursts in resource demands while ensuring the budget constraints for the longer budgeting period. The auto-scaling logic (Section 6) combines the three components to transform the raw telemetry and high-level tenant-specified knobs into container sizing actions supported by the DaaS, thus continuously and dynamically scaling container sizes in a closed loop as the tenant's resource demands vary over time.

3. TELEMETRY MANAGER

Mature DBMSs monitor and report hundreds of counters that comprise the production *telemetry*. The goal of the *telemetry manager* (TM) is to transform this raw telemetry into *signals* that can be used to estimate resource demands of a variety of workloads with high accuracy. First, we need to identify a small set of counters which are *predictive* of resource demand. We use domain knowledge of database engines to identify the relevant signals. As we will discuss later, these signals are at best weakly-predictive. The crux of our solution is to combine these weakly-predictive signals into robust and accurate resource demand estimation. In this section, we focus our discussion to telemetry available from Microsoft SQL Server, the engine hosting the tenant databases in Azure SQL DB. Note that many mature RDBMSs provide such telemetry. Hence, we expect many of our techniques to generalize to other systems.

Second, there is significant amounts of 'noise' in the telemetry arising from the inherent variance and spikes in workloads, transient system activities such as checkpoints interacting with workload, etc. Simple statistical measures such as *averages* can easily be 'dominated' by a few large outlier values. Therefore, as a general rule, we use statistical measures that are *robust* to outliers. We define robustness to outliers using the notion of the *breakdown point* of an estimator [18]. Intuitively, an estimator's breakdown point is the percentage of incorrect observations (e.g., arbitrarily large deviations) an estimator can handle before giving an incorrect result. *Example "breakdown point:"* Given m independent variables and their realizations $x_1, \ldots x_m$, we can use $\bar{x} = (\sum_{i=1}^{m} x_i)/m$ to estimate their mean. However, this estimator has a breakdown point of 0, because we can make $\bar{x}$ arbitrarily large just by changing any *one* of the x_i. In contrast, the median of a distribution has a breakdown point of 50%, which is the highest breakdown point possible.

The remainder of this section explains the signals we obtain from the telemetry. Some signals are robust aggregates on counters obtained from the raw telemetry, while other are derived robust statistical measures over the counters.

3.1 Signals from Raw Telemetry

Latency. The database servers track latency for every request completed for a tenant. We aggregate the latencies either to the percentile or the average as specified in the latency goals.

Resource Utilization. Resource utilization is a measure of how much the tenant's workload is currently using, and is an obvious signal for resource demand. The database server reports utilization for the key resources, such as CPU, memory, and disk I/O for each tenant. The TM collects these values at a fine granularity, such as once every few seconds, and computes robust statistical measures, such as the median, over different time granularities, ranging from minutes to hours, which comprise the utilization signals.

Wait Statistics. Resource utilization provides little information whether the workload needs more resources. By contrast, if a tenant's requests wait for a specific resource, it implies that the tenant has unmet demand for that resources. Mature DBMSs, such as Microsoft SQL Server, track the amount the time a tenant's request spends waiting within the database server. The TM tracks the magnitude of the wait times and the percentage waits, i.e., the time spent waiting for a resource as a percentage of the total waits for an interval of time. The TM exposes robust aggregates of these raw wait statistics as signals for demand estimation. Note that the magnitude and percentage waits are both important for demand estimation. For instance, we might observe large values of CPU waits. However, if CPU waits are insignificant compared to waits due to acquiring application-level locks, then even though there might be demand for more CPU, adding more CPU is not likely to significantly improve latencies. Similarly, CPU waits might comprise 100% of the waits. However, if the magnitude is small, then demand for CPU might not be high.

Microsoft SQL Server reports wait statistics categorized into more than 300 wait types.[6] Each wait type is associated to a (logical or physical) resource for which the request waited. Using rules, we map the wait times to the resource to determine the total time the tenant's requests waited for that resource. We classify waits into a broad set of classes for the key physical and logical resources: *CPU, memory, disk I/O, log I/O, locks,* and *system*. E.g., the *signal wait* time is the time when a thread has been signaled and ready to use to CPU to the time when it was actually allocated the CPU, and hence comprises CPU waits.

To demonstrate how wait statistics relate to and complement utilization, we analyzed the production telemetry from thousands of real tenant workloads. Figure 4 plots the CPU wait time (in ms) and Disk I/O wait time (in ms) in log scale vs. the percentage CPU utilization and percentage Disk I/O utilization respectively.

[6] http://msdn.microsoft.com/en-us/library/ms179984.aspx

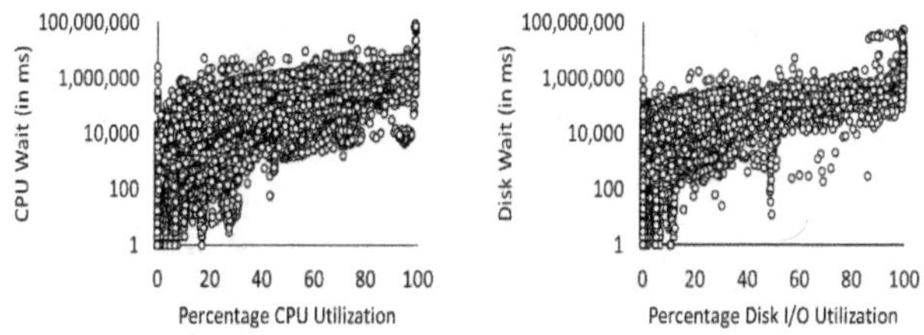

(a) CPU wait ms vs. % utilization. (b) Disk wait ms vs. % utilization.

Figure 4: Wait ms as a function of percentage utilization of CPU and Disk I/O.

Wait times are for five minute intervals; we report the median for both wait times and percentage utilization aggregated for an hour. As is evident from the figure, as the resource utilization increases, there is also an increasing trend in resource waits, though the wide "bandwidth" of the diagonal implies a weak correlation. Of particular interest is the observation that large values of resource utilization (e.g., 80) can correspond to small values of wait (e.g., $1,000$ ms), which corroborates our point that high utilization does not necessarily mean that requests are waiting due to unmet demand and hence can benefit from additional resources. Similarly, waits can be large (e.g., $1,000,000$ ms) for small utilization values (e.g., 20), which also shows that neither signal is sufficient by itself to robustly estimate demand.

3.2 Derived Signals

In addition to the (robustly-aggregated) "raw" telemetry information, we also want to analyze *trends* in latency, resource utilization etc., as well as *correlation* between signals, such as resource waits with performance. We track both correlation and trends as they serve different purposes. Trends identify changes to specific metrics (e.g., resource waits) over time, as these allow early identification of changes in the workload or its resource demands. Correlation characterizes the dependence between two signals (e.g., CPU waits and latencies). Large correlation values help us identify the main bottleneck(s) for a given workload, independently of whether there is an overall increase or decrease in these counters over time. These signals are particularly important if the tenants care about tail latencies (such as the 95th percentile), since tail latencies react faster to unmet demand.

3.2.1 *Robustly Identifying Trends over Time*

The first class of derived signals we use is trends in a subset of monitored counters–such as latency, resource utilization, or waits–over time. For instance, if there is a trend in the recent history that the latency is degrading with time, it might be an early signal that latency goals might be violated in the immediate future. Given the immediate time scale of our resource scaling actions, we focus on detecting short-term trends with sufficient confidence. Therefore, simple, but robust, linear models are sufficient for our purposes.

The challenge in detecting trends is the noise in the underlying data on which trends are computed. The data itself might be inherently noisy and there might not be a statistically-significant trend, in which case the trend must be ignored. In addition, the trend measure should be robust to outliers.

One common approach for detecting linear trends is the use of *linear least squares* regression to identify the trend line that minimizes the squared error of the value modeled by the line and the actual values. The coefficient of determination (denoted by the R^2 error) can be used to determine how good a fit the line is for the data and reject the trend if the fit is not good. However, the least squares linear regression technique has a small breakdown point, thus making the measure unsuitable for noisy data; a single large outlier point can significantly affect the line's slope.

To address the problem, we use the Theil-Sen estimator for robust detection of the trend line [25]. Given n tuples $\langle X, Y\rangle$, the Thiel-Sen estimator computes the slope of the line passing through each pair of tuples (x_i, y_i) and (x_j, y_j) as $m_i = \frac{y_j - y_i}{x_j - x_i}$ and uses the median of m_i as the slope of the trend line. It can be shown that this estimator has a breakdown point of 29%, making it robust to significant amount of noise in the telemetry data. While there exist estimators with even higher breakdown points, the Theil-Sen estimator has the advantages of being simple, efficient to compute, and not requiring additional tuning parameters.

We use the $O(n^2)$ slopes computed by the estimator in two ways. First, the median value is the slope of any existing trend in the data. Second, we use the set of slopes to test for the existence of a significant trend in the data. That is, if there is indeed a (linear) trend in the (non-noisy) data points, then this implies that (the vast majority of) the slopes between them have the same sign. Therefore, we only 'accept' a trend if at least $\alpha\%$ of the slopes are positive or $\alpha\%$ of the slopes are negative. In our implementation, we use $\alpha = 70$, which we have found to work well in practice.

3.2.2 *Robustly Detecting Correlation*

If there is demand for a resource which exceeds the allocation, making the resource a bottleneck, then in the time intervals preceding that event, there is typically an increase in the utilization of that resource or the wait times associated with that resource, or both. A strong correlation between the degrading latencies and the resource utilization and/or wait counters is indicative of demand in the resource which, if met, can significantly improve latencies. Therefore, we use this correlation measure as an additional signal.

We use the Spearman rank coefficient [22], denoted by ρ, as the correlation measure. Spearman's rank correlation is a statistical measure of the correlation of ranks or orders of two ranked data sets which assesses how well the relationship between two variables can be described using a monotonic function. That is, the dependence need not be linear for Spearman's coefficient to detect it, which makes it suitable for our case since for arbitrary database applications, the correlation of utilization, waits, and latencies is often non-linear. Given two ranked data sets X and Y, ρ is computed as the Pearson's coefficient on the ranks of the x and y values. The value of ρ lies between -1 and 1; $\rho = 1$ implies perfect correlation, $\rho = -1$ implies perfect negative correlation, and $\rho = 0$ implies no correlation between the two orders. A side-effect of using the Spearman coefficient is that outliers due to data noise become much less of an issue because we first map each value to the space of ranks, which bounds the degree to which an outlier value can deviate from the average.

4. RESOURCE DEMAND ESTIMATOR

Each signal obtained from the telemetry manager is weakly-predictive of resource demands, and hence cannot be used in isolation to estimate demand with high accuracy. Therefore, we need a technique to combine these signals to improve accuracy of demand estimation. Our observation is that if multiple weakly-predictive signals predict high demand for a resource, it increases the likelihood of the demand actually being high.

One approach is to use statistical learning techniques to infer a model using training data obtained from production telemetry. For instance, we could use machine learning techniques to estimate resource demand from the input signals. While such an approach is elegant and was one of the first approaches we tried, we found them to be prone to over-fitting. The general problem we face for any statistical technique that depends on customer workloads is that–when collecting training data–we can only observe a very small fraction of space of the possible customer workloads. When using a sufficiently-powerful statistical technique to combine different signals from production telemetry, we found the resulting model to have high prediction accuracy on the workload it had been trained on. However, the accuracy would degrade very significantly for other, unseen workloads. This is a major challenge for a relational DaaS platform which caters to a variety of applications and workloads. The tenant is free to execute any arbitrary SQL code and user defined functions which can be very different from what the model was trained on. Similar issues with statistical techniques were also reported in Li et al. [12]. Note that we do not claim that over-fitting is an inevitable side-effect of using fully-statistical learning techniques; they may be overcome with careful selection of features, the learners, and training data, something we would like to continue exploring in the future.

Our approach is to combine signals by leveraging domain knowledge of the internals of the database engine and how different resources interact. We propose a decision logic comprising a manually-constructed hierarchy of rules that use multiple signals to determine the resource demands of the tenant's workload. The core of the rule-based logic is a set of thresholds for each signal to determine the tenant's *state* in terms of each signal in isolation. Each rule combines the states obtained from each signal to determine the overall resource demand. By traversing this hierarchy of rules, the logic decides to add more resources (i.e., scale-up) if there is high demand or take away unused resources (i.e., scale-down) if the demand is low. Recall that given the discrete container sizes and that at any instant of time, the tenant is associated with a container size, our problem is to estimate if there is demand for a larger container or the demand can be met by a smaller container. When estimating demand, we determine in each resource dimension, how many steps in container sizes do we need to increase (or decrease). We use production telemetry across thousands of tenants to guide us through this process. By assigning container sizes to tenant's resource utilization values (similar to that in Section 2.2), we observed that of the total number of container size change events due to resource demands changing, 90% result in the container size changing by 1 step, and step sizes 1 and 2 together comprise 98% of the changes. Therefore, we constrain our problem to estimating demand to change container size by 0 (i.e., no change), 1, or 2 steps.

There are several pragmatic benefits of our approach. First, we found it to be robust when testing across a wide range of very different workloads. Second, once thresholds are applied to the signals, it transforms the signals from a continuous value domain to a categorical value domain where each category has easy-to-understand semantics. This makes the rules easier to construct, debug, maintain, extend, and explain. For instance, using categories with well-defined semantics allows the auto-scaling logic to provide an *"explanation"* of its actions. These explanations provide the (often unsophisticated) end-users with a simple reasoning for scaling actions. The container sizing decisions result from analyzing tens of signals. However, the model traverses a hierarchy of rules with well-understood semantics for each path. An explanation is a concise way of explaining the path the model traversed when recommending a container size. For instance, if the model identifies a CPU bottleneck which in turn scales up the container size, then an explanation of the form *"Scale-up due to a CPU bottleneck"* is generated. If the model recommended a scale-up but the budget constraints disallow it, then it can generate an explanation of the form *"Scale-up constrained by budget."* For an expert administrator, the model also exposes the raw telemetry as well as the signals used to facilitate detailed diagnostics.

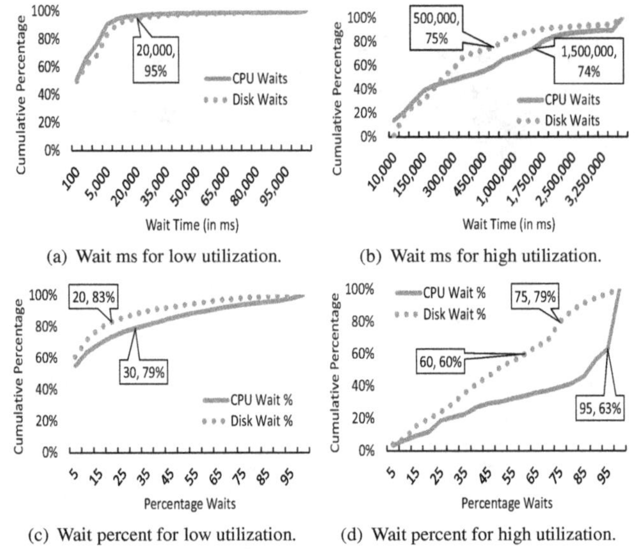

(a) Wait ms for low utilization. (b) Wait ms for high utilization.

(c) Wait percent for low utilization. (d) Wait percent for high utilization.

Figure 6: Distribution of wait ms and wait time for a resource as a percentage of total waits for CPU and Disk I/O.

We now explain the steps in resource demand estimation: determining the thresholds for each signal and how we leverage production telemetry from a DaaS to determine these thresholds, and some example rules to detect high and low demand.

4.1 Determining Thresholds

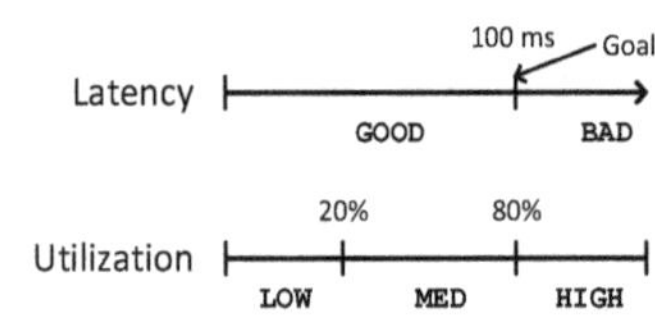

Figure 5: Categorizing signals using thresholds.

Setting thresholds for latencies and resource utilization is straightforward; Figure 5 illustrates this. If the tenant specifies a latency goal, it becomes the threshold to determine if the latency is GOOD (i.e., goals are met) vs. it is BAD, i.e., goals are not being met. Similarly, for the underlying database engine the DaaS platform utilizes, there already exist well-known thresholds and rules that system administrators use to categorize the resource utilization as LOW, MEDIUM, and HIGH (e.g., see Figure 5).

Waits associated with a resource can also be categorized as HIGH, MEDIUM or LOW. However, deriving thresholds to categorize waits is not as straightforward as latency and resource utilization. As can be seen from Figure 4, resource waits can be as large as $1,000$ seconds even with low utilization levels of 20% or 30% and waits can be as low as 1 second even for high utilization levels of 70% or 80%. Similar reasoning also applies for the percentage waits. It is imperative that we use a systematic approach for setting thresholds for the wait statistics in order that the categories are meaningful. We use production telemetry collected from thousands of real tenant's databases across the service to determine these thresholds. The rationale behind our approach is that if resource demands are high, wait for that resource will also be high. Since this correlation is weak, there can be occasional noise. However, if we analyze data from thousands of tenants, there should be a clear separation between waits for low and high demand; our analysis of production telemetry supports this hypothesis.

The first challenge is in determining the thresholds to categorize the resource wait times into HIGH, MEDIUM, and LOW. Figures 6(a) and 6(b) plot the cumulative distribution of the wait times (in ms) for CPU and Disk I/O for different levels of utilization for the corresponding resource. Wait times reported are for five minute intervals and we report the median over an hour. We separate the waits based on the utilization levels (low and high) of the corresponding resource, which we use as a proxy for high/low demand. Resource utilization is high if the average hourly utilization of that resource is more than 70% and low if the average hourly utilization is less than 30%. When the resource utilization is low, even the 90th percentile of both CPU and Disk I/O waits is about 20 seconds (see Figure 6(a)). On the other hand, when the resource utilization is high, the 75th percentile of Disk I/O waits is 500 seconds and that for CPU waits is 1500 seconds. Therefore, there exists a clear separation between the wait distributions for high and low utilization. We use percentile values from these distributions to categorize waits as `HIGH`, for instance if CPU waits exceed 1500 seconds, or `LOW` if it is less than 20 seconds. The percentiles shown in the figure are for illustration, the actual percentile is different for each container size, resources type, and cluster configuration.

The second challenge is to identify the thresholds for percentage waits to be `SIGNIFICANT` or `NOT SIGNIFICANT`. Again, we use production telemetry to set thresholds for percentage waits. Figures 6(c) and 6(d) plot the distribution of the percentage waits corresponding to CPU and Disk I/O. Similarly to the previous case, we plot separate distributions for low and high utilization levels for that resource. As is evident from Figure 6(c), the 80th percentile of percentage waits for CPU and Disk I/O is in the range $20\% - 30\%$ while the corresponding number for high utilization is in the range $70\% - 90\%$ which demonstrates this separation in values.

As the software evolves, new hardware SKUs are deployed in the data centers, and new container sizes are supported in the service, these thresholds need to be re-tuned. Updating these thresholds incrementally is automated through reports and alerts expressed over the aggregate telemetry collected from the service.

4.2 Detecting High Demand

We now explain how we use our knowledge of the database engine internals to craft a set of rules using the signals to estimate whether demand is high enough to require a scale-up. The first step is to identify the scenarios that correspond to high demand. A few *illustrative scenarios* are: (a) If utilization is `HIGH` and wait times are `HIGH` with `SIGNIFICANT` percentage waits. (b) If utilization is `HIGH`, wait times are `HIGH`, percentage waits are `NOT SIGNIFICANT`, and there is a `SIGNIFICANT` increasing trend over time in utilization and/or wait. (c) If utilization is `HIGH`, wait times are `MEDIUM`, percentage waits are `SIGNIFICANT`, and there is a `SIGNIFICANT` increasing trend over time in utilization and/or waits. Note that all of the scenarios combine two or more signals. Moreover, if one of the signals is weak (e.g., wait time in not `HIGH`), we consider additional signals (e.g., trends).

Note that we stated the scenarios in terms of the signals and their categories. In addition to being easy to explain, these scenarios can be directly encoded as predicate rules in the model which if true for a resource implies high demand for that resource.

Further note that memory and disk I/O interact. That is, if memory is a bottleneck, it will result in higher I/O utilization and waits. Since memory waits and tracked independent of I/O waits, if both resources are identified as a bottleneck, the model will recommend scaling-up both resources.

4.3 Detecting Low demand

Estimating whether demand is low is similar to high demand estimation, except that the tests are for the other end of the spectrum of categories for the signals. For instance, the rules test for `LOW` utilization or `LOW` waits, and non-positive trends in resource waits or utilization; we omit the rules for brevity. However, an interesting case is detecting low memory demand, which we discuss in the remainder of this subsection.

Memory utilization of a database server is rarely `LOW`. This is because the largest consumers of memory in a database server are the different caches, such as the buffer pool and the query plan cache, which do not voluntarily release memory. When all pages accessed are in memory, the waits associated with memory are also `LOW`. Therefore, estimating low memory demand using memory utilization and waits alone is hard since these signals do not accurately differentiate low demand from the case where there is demand but all requests are being met using memory already allocated to the tenant. For instance, if the tenant's working set fits in memory, it will result in low memory waits. However, when memory is reduced to a point where the working set does not fit in memory, there will be a significant increase in memory demand and subsequent impact on latency. Therefore, in addition to low memory waits, we must also account for the potential increase in number of disk I/Os and memory wait times as a result of reducing memory. Memory demand is low only if the expected increase in disk I/Os and wait times is below a threshold. Estimating this expected increase in I/Os when reducing memory for arbitrary database workloads is incredibly challenging.

We use a technique inspired by ballooning [3, 27] where we slowly reduce the memory allocated to a tenant to observe its impact on disk I/O. If the memory can be reduced all the way to the next smaller container size without causing a significant increase in disk I/O demand, we determine memory demand as low. If ballooning results in increase in disk I/O demand, we revert the tenant to the current memory allocation. Our challenge is to determine *when* to trigger ballooning so that the impact of latencies can be minimized. We trigger ballooning only when the demand for all other resources is `LOW`. While being conservative, in the absence of an accurate and versatile model to predict the impact of reducing memory on latencies, this strategy minimizes the risk of adversely affecting the tenant's query latencies.

5. BUDGET MANAGER

A tenant can specify a budget ($\mathbb{B}$) for a *budgeting period* comprising n billing intervals. The budget manager needs to determine the *available budget* (B_i) for each billing interval, which is considerably smaller than the budgeting period, such that $\sum_{i=1}^{n} B_i \leq \mathbb{B}$. Let C_{min} and C_{max} be the respective costs per billing interval for the cheapest and the most expensive containers. The budget manager must ensure $B_i \geq C_{min}$ in order still be able to allocate the cheapest container within the budget. The main challenge is in managing the surplus budget ($\mathbb{B} - n \times C_{min}$). The simplest approach is to spread the surplus equally among each interval. However, tenants' resource demands and workloads arrive in bursts, thus making the even-spread approach unsuitable. Moreover, since the budget allocation for an interval is online without any knowledge of the future workload arrival patterns, the allocation algorithm must balance meeting current demands while retaining sufficient budget for unanticipated bursts in future intervals.

We draw analogy of our budget management problem to the traffic shaping problem in computer networks [24]. A network router shapes a flow, allowing periodic bandwidth bursts, while providing a minimum steady bandwidth, and ensuring that the flow conforms to a total bandwidth allocation. We adapt the *token bucket algorithm* [24] for our problem of budget allocation. Figure 7 illustrates this algorithm which uses a fixed capacity bucket, of *depth* D, to hold tokens where D is the maximum burst size. The bucket is initialized with T_I tokens and periodically refreshed at a fixed rate, called the *fill rate* T_R, which is the guaranteed average bandwidth.

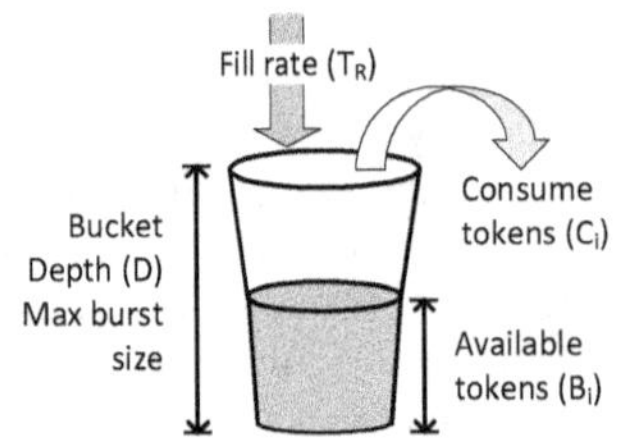

Figure 7: Token bucket.

We now describe how the budget manager configures the token bucket by setting T_R, T_I, and D to meet the requirements. At any instant, the number of tokens in the bucket is the available budget B_i. At the end of the ith billing interval, T_R tokens are added and C_i tokens are subtracted, where C_i is the cost for the ith interval. Setting $T_R = C_{min}$ ensures that $B_i \geq C_{min}$. Setting $D = \mathbb{B} - (n-1) \times C_{min}$ guarantees $\sum_{i=1}^{n} C_i \leq \mathbb{B}$. The value we set for T_I determines how aggressive we are in consuming the budget during periods of high demand. An aggressive bursting strategy sets $T_I = D$, i.e., start the budgeting period with a full bucket. If there is a sustained high demand such that the largest container is allocated for m intervals, the bucket will be empty when $m = \frac{\mathbb{B}-(n-m)\times C_{min}}{C_{max}}$. Starting from the $(m+1)^{th}$ interval to the nth interval, the available budget will be $B_i = C_{min}$ and the tenant can only use the cheapest container which might not be enough to meet the demands. An alternative is to set $T_I = K \times C_{max}$, where $K < m$ and set $T_R = \frac{\mathbb{B}-T_I}{n-1}$. This conservative setting ensures that the maximum usage burst is limited to at most K intervals of using C_{max} plus any surplus unused tokens unused from the past, i.e., this setting saves more for intervals later in the budgeting period at the expense of limiting costs early on. A service administrator can analyze the production telemetry to set a suitable value of K.

6. AUTO-SCALING LOGIC

The auto-scaling logic determines the container size for the next billing interval by monitoring latencies, resource demands, and the available budget. At the end of a billing interval, the auto-scaling logic determines if the tenant has high demand for a resource. If the latency is `BAD`, or there is a `SIGNIFICANT` increasing trend of latency with time, then the logic will recommend scaling-up if enough budget is available. If latency is `GOOD` and not degrading, and resource demands are `LOW`, then the logic recommends scale-down. Otherwise it takes no action.

The resource demand estimator determines if more (or less) of each resource resource is desired. The resource demand of each resource comprises the desired container size. The auto-scaling logic uses the available budget (B_i) and the desired container size to find the cheapest container, among the set of DaaS's containers, with resources greater or equal to the desired container on all resource dimensions and price $C_i \leq B_i$. If desired container is constrained by the available budget, then the most expensive container with price less than B_i is selected. This process is an iterative search over the set of containers supported by the DaaS. Since the resource demand estimation is for individual resources. Therefore, if the workload only has demand for one type of resource, such as CPU, then the estimation logic will only recommend increasing the CPU allocation in the desired container. If the DaaS supports scaling containers in each resource dimension, for instance Figure 1, the auto-scaling logic can leverage that.

If the container size recommended is different from the current container size, the model issues a container resize command to the management fabric of the DaaS which then executes the resize operation. This container resize operation is an online operation.

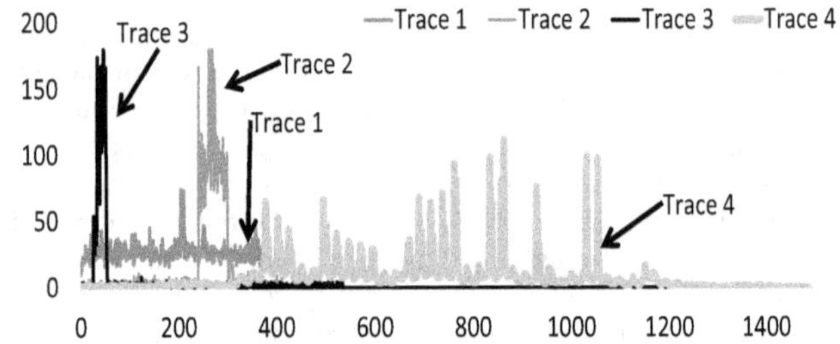

Figure 8: Traces derived from real-life workloads used for the experiments. Horizontal axis is time in minutes, vertical axis is number of concurrent requests per second.

7. EXPERIMENTAL EVALUATION

We prototyped our auto-scaling solution in Azure SQL Database which supports a set of fixed sized containers. In this section, we experimentally evaluate the effectiveness of our approach (henceforth referred to as **Auto** for brevity) using a variety of workloads and resource demand patterns derived from production traces. We compare our approach with a number of alternatives solution using **latency** (the 95th percentile latency of the workload), and **cost** incurred on behalf of the tenant. These experiments demonstrate that Auto's improved demand estimation accuracy results in significantly lower costs (in the range of $1.5\times$ to $8\times$) while achieving the desired latency goals for a wide variety of workloads and resource demand patterns, which also demonstrates its robustness.

7.1 Methodology

Our technique estimates the resource demand characteristics exhibited by any SQL workload and does not make any assumptions about the knowledge of the workload. We, therefore, expect our solution to to be effective for both transactional as well as data warehousing workloads. For brevity, we focus our experiments here on transactional workloads with time-varying resource demands. We use demand patterns derived from production workloads to control the load for some well-known benchmarks to create time-varying resource demands. Figure 8 plots four *"traces"* derived from real customer workloads in a production Daas. In each figure, the horizontal axis is time and the vertical axis is number of concurrent requests in the real workload.

Each trace is chosen to target a specific demand scenario. Trace 1 corresponds to a workload with steady demand. This trace is suitable for a static container size and the goal is to validate that an auto-scaling logic is at least competitive to a technique that knows the demand upfront and sets a static container size suitable for the demand. Traces 2 and 3 correspond to workloads which are mostly idle with one burst of resource demand; in trace 2 the burst lasts longer compared to trace 3. These demand patterns are suitable for an auto-scaling solution that reacts to the burst, scales up the container size during the period of high demand, and subsequently scales-down to save cost. Trace 4 exhibits lots of bursts in demand for short intervals. This workload is intended to stress-test the online auto-scaling solutions.

We use standard benchmark workloads to generate the actual user requests. The workload generator executes in steps in sync with the trace. At every step, the workload generator reads the number of requests from the trace to set the target number of requests/sec for the workload until the next step. At every step, the workload generator executes transactions from the benchmark workload and maintains the offered load as close as possible to the specified target. The workload generator executes the entire trace which comprises one run for that experiment. We use three types of workloads in our experiments: TPC-C, Dell DVD Store

(DS2),[7] and a synthetic micro-benchmark (CPUIO) that generates queries that are CPU-, disk I/O- and/or log I/O-intensive. Our goal of selecting these workloads is to generate a variety of transactions/query mixes ranging from short read/write transactions to lightweight analytical queries that scan parts of the data and computes aggregates. The CPUIO micro-benchmark allows us to execute queries that create demand for each of CPU, memory, and I/O while allowing us to alter the mix of the queries. The workload's working set is controlled by creating a hotspot in data accesses. This variety helps us evaluate the robustness of the solutions.

A tenant is an instance of one of these workloads and connects to its own database enclosed in a container. The auto-scaling module monitors the tenant's workload demands and sets the appropriate container size for the billing interval. We use a set of eleven container sizes modeled similar to ones supported by today's commercial offerings such as Microsoft Azure SQL DB, Amazon RDS, and Google Cloud SQL. The container sizes cover a large gamut of resource allocations all the way from half-a-core of CPU allocation for the smallest container to tens of CPU cores for the largest container. Other resources, such as memory and I/O, also have a similar spectrum; the cost of a container ranges from 7 units to 270 units for each billing interval.

For the purposes of experimentation, we compress the time scales for each workload trace as well as the billing interval. This compression makes the problem more challenging for an auto-scaling since changes in demands are more drastic. It also allows us to observe many instances of the container size changes without requiring to run the experiment for days. We use minutes as unit of time for the horizontal axis of each trace in Figure 8. This implies that an experiment on a trace takes from a few hours to up to a day depending on the length of the trace. We set the billing interval to one minute. Note that having a billing interval of a minute does not imply the auto-scaling module will change container sizes every minute—the auto-scaling module changes container sizes only when the demand changes, which we validate using the number of container size changes during an experiment.

7.2 Alternative Solutions

We compare Auto against a set of practical solutions which can be implemented in production today without requiring a deep understanding and knowledge of the application's workload. We compare Auto with two offline and one online solution. We also compare against a setting (called **Max**) where we statically set the tenant's container to the largest container supported by the DaaS. This results in the highest cost, but also provides a *gold standard* with the *best* performance for the workload.

7.2.1 Offline solutions

We use two offline solutions which have the luxury to observe the resource demands of the workload trace before making a choice of the container size. Since these techniques cannot dynamically adapt container sizes based on latency goals, we do not set any latency goal for these techniques. Once an offline solution selects a container size, we replay the exact same workload to measure the impact of container choice on latency.

Static. This solution simulates an approach a typical administrator who has knowledge about the historical resource demands for its application which s/he uses to statically set the container size. We execute the workload with **Max** to analyze the resource utilization and then set the container size to be the smallest container that can meet the historical utilization. We experiment with two settings for the container size: one using the 95th percentile resource utilization for the entire workload to configure the container for the **Peak**, and one using the *average* utilization to configure for the **Avg**.

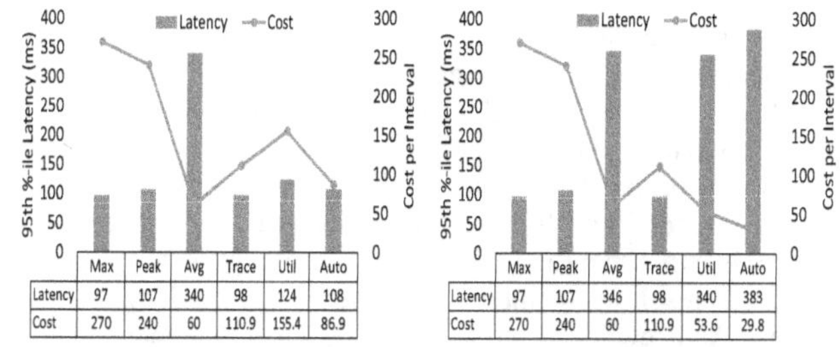

	Max	Peak	Avg	Trace	Util	Auto
Latency	97	107	340	98	124	108
Cost	270	240	60	110.9	155.4	86.9

(a) Goal: $1.25\times$ **Max** = 120 ms

	Max	Peak	Avg	Trace	Util	Auto
Latency	97	107	346	98	340	383
Cost	270	240	60	110.9	53.6	29.8

(b) Goal: $5\times$ **Max** = 485 ms

Figure 9: The impact of latency targets to trade costs with latency for a bursty resource demand (Trace 2) executing the CPUIO micro benchmark workload.

Trace. This solution simulates an offline approach which exactly *"knows"* the workload's resource demands and can generate a sequence of container size changes that *"hugs"* the resource utilization and demand curve. We generate this trace of hugging containers by executing the workload with **Max** to obtain the actual resource utilization of the workload. For a given billing interval, we then select the smallest container that meets the resource requirements for that interval. The output trace is of the form $\langle i, \text{Cont}_i \rangle$ where i is the billing interval and Cont_i is the container size for interval i. The exact workload is then repeated; during replay, at every interval i, the container size is set to Cont_i.

7.2.2 Online solutions

An online solution, such as Auto, estimates the resource demands and monitors performance to determine the container size. For these solutions, we specify a latency goal for the entire workload. We derive the latency goal from the 95th percentile latency measured by running the workload with **Max**, which corresponds to best latency. In one setting, we use $1.25\times$ latency with **Max** as the goal, and in another we use $5\times$ the latency with **Max** as the goal. Our evaluation primarily focuses on how the online solutions change container sizes based on resource demands and latency. We set the budget to the default value since it is intended as a tenant-specified safeguard and is not of interest for these experiments; experiments with budget constraint is omitted for brevity.

We compare against an online auto-scaling solution (**Util**) which uses the latency and the utilization of every resource to decide the container size. This solution emulates the auto-scaling offerings for VMs that today's cloud providers support, translated to our setting of determining container sizes instead of adding or removing VMs. This solution tracks latencies, and if latency is `BAD` and resource utilization is `GOOD` or `HIGH` then scales-up the container size. On the contrary, if performance is `GOOD` and resource utilization is `LOW`, it scales-down the container size.

7.3 End-to-End Results

We now report end-to-end results using a variety of resource demand traces and workloads. For the online techniques, latency goals are set for the 95th percentile for the entire workload; the offline techniques to not consider latency goals. Recall that use **Auto** to refer to our solution.

Figure 9 plots the cost and latencies for running the CPUIO workload using the demand pattern from Trace 2. The bars report the 95th percentile latency for the workload (in ms) and is plotted along the primary (left) vertical axis. The line reports the average cost per billing interval for each technique and is plotted along the secondary (right) vertical axis. The different sub figures correspond

[7]http://linux.dell.com/dvdstore/

to the different setting for the latency goals. Figure 9(a) reports the experiment where the latency goal was set to 1.25× the latency with Max (i.e., 120 ms) and Figure 9(b) reports the experiment where the latency goal was set to 5× the latency with Max (i.e., 485 ms). Recall that Trace 2 has one big burst of resource demand which is preceded and followed by periods of low activity. The goal of this experiment is to demonstrate that a good auto-scaling solution can result in *significant* cost savings while achieving good latencies. As is evident from Figure 9(a), when the tenant desires latencies close to that with Max, Auto helps the tenant achieve the latency goal with 2.75× lower cost when compared to allocation for the Peak (i.e., 95th percentile of resource utilization). Note that provisioning for Avg results in lower costs, but the latency is almost 3× worse compared to the goal. The other online solution Util results in about 1.8× higher cost compared to Auto. This demonstrates that reasoning about resource demands using multiple signals, such as utilization, resource waits, trends, and correlation can significantly lower costs of Auto while achieving good latencies within the tenant-specified goals. While not directly comparable, putting the results in perspective with the offline technique Trace, Auto results in a lower costs, though Trace achieves a slightly better latency. However, if the objective is achieve the least cost while meeting the goal, Auto's lower cost trumps Trace.

When the latency goal is set to 5× that with Max (Figure 9(b)), Auto results in 2× lower costs compared to Avg, about 8× lower costs compared to Peak, and about 1.8× lower cost compared to Util, all while meeting the tenant-specified latency goals. This experiment validates our claim that when the tenant's latency goals are less stringent, Auto reduces monetary costs even further. In terms of the number of container size changes, both Auto and Util made container size changes for about 11% of the total number of billing intervals during the experiment. In contrast, Trace, which hugs the demand curve, results in container size changes in about 15% of the billing intervals.

Figure 10 plots the latency and cost for the TPC-C workload using the demand pattern from Trace 4. In this experiment, the latency goal is set to 1.25× that of Max (i.e., 340 ms). Similar to the previous results, Auto results in significantly lower costs compared to all other alternatives while meeting the latency goal. Among the the techniques meeting the latency goal, Peak costs 2× more, Trace costs about 2.4×, and Util costs about 3.4× that of Auto.

To understand why Util costs 3.4× that of Auto, we report the container sizes, resource utilization, and the *performance factor* (which is the observed latency as a percentage of the goal, negative values imply the goal is not met) for both Util (Figure 13(a)) and Auto (Figure 13(b)). For ease of exposition, we only plot the CPU settings for the container and the CPU utilization (plotted along the primary vertical axis) since it is the dominant resource for this workload; the performance factor is plotted along the secondary vertical axis. Both CPU utilization and the container's Max CPU are expressed as percentage of the total server capacity on which the container is hosted. For both techniques, the performance factor is close to zero, which implies that performance is close to its goal. Both techniques are designed to keep a buffer for performance so that while they react to unanticipated resource demands, the tenant's performance does not significantly degrade beyond the goal. Therefore, both techniques will periodically scale up reacting to high resource demands and compensating for performance degradations for the period it takes to react to changes in demand. However, note that when Util decides to scale up, it ends up scaling much higher to compensate for the latency degradation—we see the container sizes as high as 70% of the server's CPU capacity. On the other hand, Auto's container size selection is in the range of 10% to

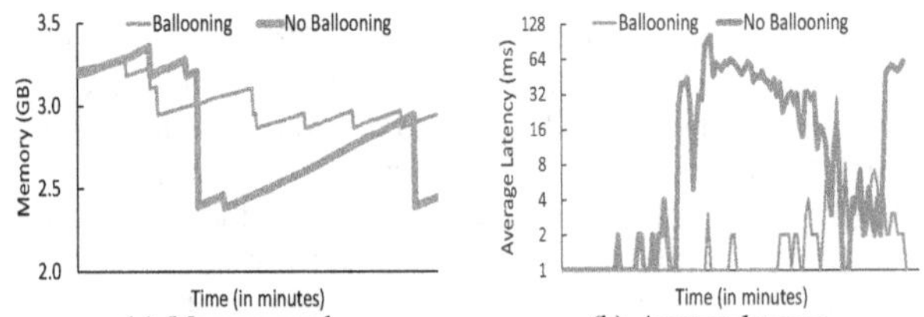

(a) Memory used (b) Average latency.

Figure 14: The impact of ballooning on end-to-end latency for CPUIO micro benchmark workload with a steady demand.

20% of the server's resources. Observe that even though the container sizes are large for Util, the CPU utilization continues to peak at about 10% for both techniques. This is because for this workload, the majority of time is spent on acquiring application-level locks and hence the workload's latencies cannot significantly benefit from the additional resources. This is evident from Figure 13(c) which reports the percentage waits for each wait category. Observe that lock waits (which are in a dark fill color) are more than 90% of the waits and dominate any other resource wait category. Auto uses the wait statistics and the correlation between resource waits and latencies to identify this bottleneck beyond resources and does not unnecessarily add resources. Based on this analysis, Auto selects smaller container sizes for most intervals which is enough to meet the resource demands for the workload while ensuring the latency remains close to the specified goal. This experiment demonstrates how domain knowledge of the internals of the database engines, using multiple signals, and reasoning about resource demand can significantly reduce costs while meeting the latency goals.

Figure 11 reports the latency and costs for the CPUIO workload with resource demand pattern driven by Trace 3 which is also a bursty workload. The latency goal is set to 5× Max (i.e., 500 ms). The benefits of Auto is also evident in this scenario where Peak incurs 4.5× higher cost, Avg incurs 1.5× higher cost, and Util results in 2.5× higher cost. Finally, Figure 12 reports the cost and latency for DS2 workload with an almost steady demand pattern driven by Trace 1. Even for this workload, which is perfect for a static container size, Peak incurs 1.5× higher cost, Avg incurs 1.2× higher cost, and Util incurs 1.5× higher cost compared to Auto. This demonstrates that not only is Auto beneficial for bursty workloads, it also results in significant reduction in costs while meeting the latency goals even for workloads with low variance in demand. These experiments demonstrates Auto excellent performance and robustness with a variety of workloads and resource demand patterns.

7.4 Ballooning and low memory demand

This experiment demonstrates the impact of using ballooning to avoid significant impact on the tenant's end-to-end latency due to incorrect estimation of low memory demand. We use the CPUIO workload with Trace 1 to generate a steady demand for all resources. The working set is close to 3GB and is controlled using a *hotspot* access distribution with more than 95% operations accessing data in the working set. Figure 14(a) plots the memory used by the tenant (in GB) as time progresses. The two lines correspond to Auto with and without ballooning. Once the workload reaches a steady state, the working set is cached in memory (with used memory $> 3GB$). Since the working set fits in memory, this corresponds to the hard case of detecting low memory demand. In the absence of ballooning, Auto changes the memory allocation to the next smaller container size (2.5GB) which causes a sharp drop in used memory (see Figure 14(a), thick orange line). This change causes the query latencies to increase two orders of magnitude; Figure 14(b) plots the average end-to-end query latency (in ms, log

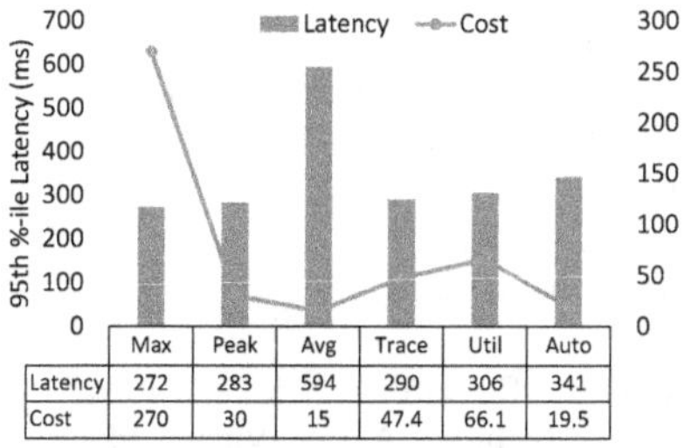

Figure 10: TPC-C, Trace 4, Latency goal: $1.25\times$ **Max = 340 ms.**

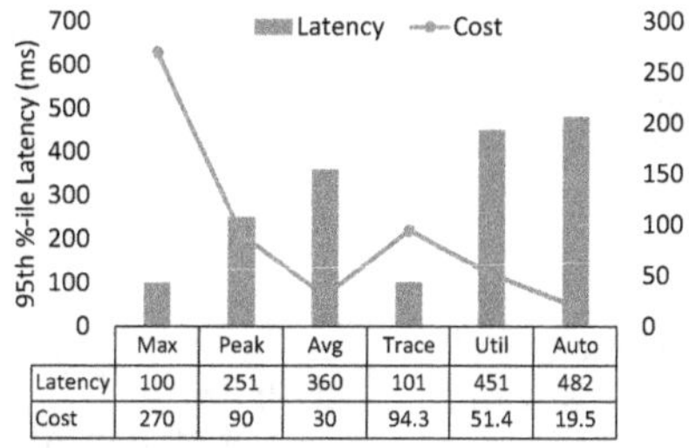

Figure 11: CPUIO, Trace 3, Latency goal: $5\times$ **Max = 500 ms.**

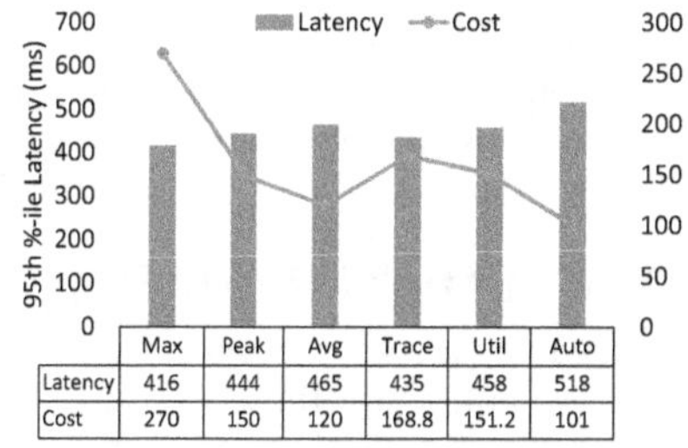

Figure 12: DS2, Trace 1, Latency goal: $1.25\times$ **Max = 520 ms.**

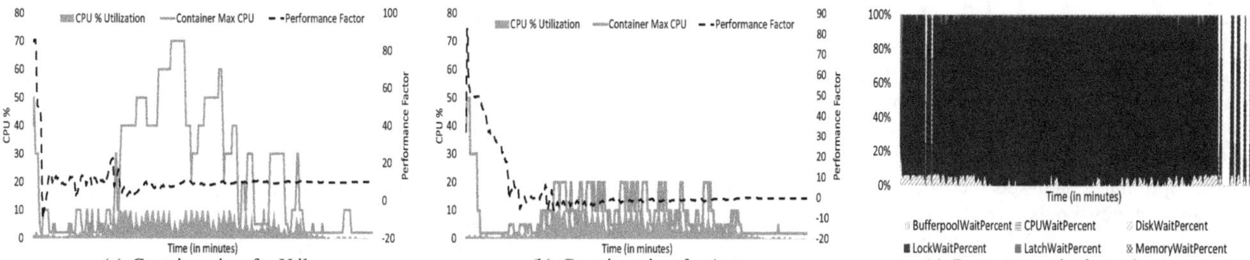

(a) Container sizes for Util (b) Container sizes for Auto (c) Percentage waits for each category

Figure 13: Drill down explaining the behavior of Util and Auto as time progressed through the experiment.

scale) as time progresses. Auto notices this increase in latency due to unmet disk I/O demand and reverts to the larger container. However, it takes a long time for the working set to be entirely cached in memory, which prolongs the impact on latency. By contrast, with ballooning, Auto starts the process of gradually reducing memory. However, it aborts before reaching the next smaller container, since it notices increased I/Os around the point where memory is reduced to $3GB$, which corresponds to the working set. Therefore, Auto equipped with ballooning results in minimal latency impact in the event of inaccurate low memory demand estimation.

8. RELATED WORK

Resource estimation, provisioning, and auto-scaling resources has been an active area of research in the database and the systems research communities. Existing approaches can be classified into black-box application-agnostic solutions, typically used for auto-scaling VMs that host a variety of applications, white-box and black-box modeling for database workloads typically for enterprise consolidation scenarios, and models for estimating resources for individual long-running data analysis queries.

There is a large body of work on application-agnostic techniques to auto-scale resources for any application running inside a VM such that a certain set of application SLOs can be achieved. Examples include CloudScale [19], AGILE [16], PRESS [9], AutoControl [17], AutoScale [8], CloudStone [13], SCADS [26], and Huber et al. [11]. Since these techniques are application-agnostic, they must rely on OS/hypervisor level counters to detect resource utilization and pressure. In contrast, our focus is on auto-scaling resources in a database server. As we show in this paper, by exploiting database-specific signals and building white-box models based on domain knowledge of database engine, we are able to significantly improve the accuracy in demand estimation, thereby lowering costs while achieving query latencies similar to approaches using generic resource utilization counters.

Resource modeling for database workloads in an enterprise workload consolidation scenario has also been studied. These solutions rely on a "representative workload" for each application to be provided upfront, which is then used to construct models that estimate the resources for that workload. Soror et al. [21] use the query optimizer's 'what-if' mode to estimate the impact of a particular resource on the performance. Kairos [3] replays the workload in a separate sandbox environment to model the resource utilization and demands. DBSeer [14] builds models to predict the resource utilization for a given set of transactions in an OLTP workload which can then be used to estimate resource requirements as the throughput of the workload changes (e.g., change in disk I/O if the throughput doubles). In contrast, since a DaaS is a platform to which tenants can and do submit arbitrary and ad-hoc queries, we are unable to make a closed-world assumption about knowledge of a "representative workload" to train our model. Thus, our resource demand estimation logic does not make assumptions that are specific to a workload, such as transaction types, or the fraction of each transaction type, and relies instead on exploiting correlation between lower-level counters that are generic to any database workloads. We do not require running the workloads in a sandbox environment, which is often infeasible in a DaaS setting. Due to the complexity of the problem and the inability to make a closed world assumption, instead of accurately predicting the resource requirements of a specific workload mix, we focus on a different problem of estimating if the current mix of workloads has demand a larger (or a smaller) container size in each resource dimension. Different from resource modeling, Pythia [6] targets the problem of modeling which combinations of tenants can be co-located at a server in a setting where tenant's workloads are not isolated using containers. The goal is to identify combinations of tenants which can be co-located without affecting each other's performance.

Accurately predicting resource usage for individual long-running queries is another area of active research [1, 2, 5, 7, 12]. These approaches typically rely on training statistical models on actual observations of resource consumptions for training queries executed in isolation. These models find applications in resource management and query scheduling in data warehouses with a fixed set of resources executing a handful of concurrent queries. By contrast, a typical tenant of a DaaS often executes hundreds of concurrent short-running queries typically finishing within milliseconds to seconds. The per-query models targeted a different setting and it is extremely challenging to generalize these models to estimate the resource requirements for the sum total of hundreds of concurrently executing queries. Instead of accurately estimating the resource requirements of tens or hundreds of concurrent queries, we focus on coarser-granularity estimation of whether the current workload mix has demand for the next larger (or smaller) container.

9. CONCLUDING REMARKS

Elasticity and pay-per-use are two key attractions of cloud platforms. Tenants can leverage this elasticity to reduce costs during periods of low demand and improve latencies during periods of high demand. We explored this problem of how a DaaS provider can efficiently and robustly support auto-scaling container sizes on behalf of its tenants. We demonstrated that resource utilization alone is not a good estimator for demand for a variety of database workloads. By using domain knowledge of database engines, we proposed a more accurate demand estimator that uses a statistically-robust set of signals, a decision logic to combine multiple signals, and a way to leverage the service-wide telemetry across thousands of tenants of a DaaS. Using a more accurate demand estimator coupled with optional tenant-specified inputs of monetary budget constraints and latency goals, we described an end-to-end auto-scaling solution for a DaaS. We prototyped our approach in Microsoft Azure SQL Database and demonstrated the cost effectiveness of our solution and robustness using a wide variety of benchmark workloads and resource demand traces derived from production. Our solution raises the abstraction for tenants of a DaaS by allowing them to reason about monetary budget and query latency rather than resource provisioning.

Acknowledgements

The authors would like to thank the anonymous reviewers, Pamela Bhattacharya, and Ishai Menache for useful feedback to improve this paper, Manoj Syamala and George Reynya for useful feedback to better understand the database engine internals, and Kukjin Lee for the help in analyzing production telemetry. Several members of the Microsoft Azure SQL Database group, including Peter Carlin, Miroslav Grbic, Veljko Vasic, and Petar Lotrean, have provided feedback that influenced our work.

10. REFERENCES

[1] M. Ahmad, S. Duan, A. Aboulnaga, and S. Babu. Predicting completion times of batch query workloads using interaction-aware models and simulation. In *EDBT*, pages 449–460, 2011.

[2] M. Akdere, U. Çetintemel, M. Riondato, E. Upfal, and S. B. Zdonik. Learning-based query performance modeling and prediction. In *ICDE*, pages 390–401, 2012.

[3] C. Curino, E. P. C. Jones, S. Madden, and H. Balakrishnan. Workload-aware database monitoring and consolidation. In *SIGMOD*, pages 313–324, 2011.

[4] S. Das, D. Agrawal, and A. El Abbadi. Elastras: An elastic, scalable, and self-managing transactional database for the cloud. *ACM Trans. Database Syst.*, 38(1):5, 2013.

[5] J. Duggan, U. Cetintemel, O. Papaemmanouil, and E. Upfal. Performance prediction for concurrent database workloads. In *SIGMOD*, pages 337–348, 2011.

[6] A. Elmore, S. Das, A. Pucher, D. Agrawal, A. E. Abbadi, and X. Yan. Characterizing Tenant Behavior for Placement and Crisis Mitigation in Multitenant DBMSs. In *SIGMOD*, pages 517–528, 2013.

[7] A. Ganapathi, H. Kuno, U. Dayal, J. Wiener, A. Fox, M. Jordan, and D. Patterson. Predicting multiple metrics for queries: Better decisions enabled by machine learning. In *ICDE*, pages 592–603, 2009.

[8] A. Gandhi, M. Harchol-Balter, R. Raghunathan, and M. A. Kozuch. Autoscale: Dynamic, robust capacity management for multi-tier data centers. *ACM Trans. Comput. Syst.*, 30(4):14:1–14:26, 2012.

[9] Z. Gong, X. Gu, and J. Wilkes. Press: Predictive elastic resource scaling for cloud systems. In *CNSM*, pages 9–16, 2010.

[10] D. Gupta, L. Cherkasova, R. Gardner, and A. Vahdat. Enforcing Performance Isolation Across Virtual Machines in Xen. In *Middleware*, pages 342–362, 2006.

[11] N. Huber, F. Brosig, and S. Kounev. Model-based self-adaptive resource allocation in virtualized environments. In *SEAMS*, pages 90–99, 2011.

[12] J. Li, A. C. König, V. R. Narasayya, and S. Chaudhuri. Robust estimation of resource consumption for SQL queries using statistical techniques. *PVLDB*, 5(11):1555–1566, 2012.

[13] H. C. Lim, S. Babu, and J. S. Chase. Automated control for elastic storage. In *ICAC*, pages 1–10, 2010.

[14] B. Mozafari, C. Curino, A. Jindal, and S. Madden. Performance and Resource Modeling in Highly-Concurrent OLTP Workloads. In *SIGMOD*, 2013.

[15] V. Narasayya, S. Das, M. Syamala, B. Chandramouli, and S. Chaudhuri. SQLVM: Performance Isolation in Multi-Tenant Relational Database-as-a-Service. In *CIDR*, 2013.

[16] H. Nguyen, Z. Shen, X. Gu, S. Subbiah, and J. Wilkes. Agile: Elastic distributed resource scaling for infrastructure-as-a-service. In *ICAC*, pages 69–82, 2013.

[17] P. Padala, K.-Y. Hou, K. G. Shin, X. Zhu, M. Uysal, Z. Wang, S. Singhal, and A. Merchant. Automated control of multiple virtualized resources. In *EuroSys*, pages 13–26, 2009.

[18] P. J. Rousseeuw and A. M. Leroy. *Robust Regression and Outlier Detection*. Wiley, 1987.

[19] Z. Shen, S. Subbiah, X. Gu, and J. Wilkes. Cloudscale: Elastic resource scaling for multi-tenant cloud systems. In *SOCC*, pages 5:1–5:14, 2011.

[20] P. Shivam, A. Demberel, P. Gunda, D. Irwin, L. Grit, A. Yumerefendi, S. Babu, and J. Chase. Automated and on-demand provisioning of virtual machines for database applications. In *SIGMOD*, pages 1079–1081, 2007.

[21] A. A. Soror, U. F. Minhas, A. Aboulnaga, K. Salem, P. Kokosielis, and S. Kamath. Automatic virtual machine configuration for database workloads. In *SIGMOD*, pages 953–966, 2008.

[22] C. Spearman. The proof and measurement of association between two things. *American J. of Psychology*, 15:72–101, 1904.

[23] A. J. Storm, C. Garcia-Arellano, S. S. Lightstone, Y. Diao, and M. Surendra. Adaptive self-tuning memory in db2. In *VLDB*, pages 1081–1092, 2006.

[24] A. S. Tanenbaum and D. J. Wetherall. *Computer Networks*. Pearson, 5th edition, 2011.

[25] H. Theil. A rank-invariant method of linear and polynomial regression analysis. *Nederl. Akad. Wetensch.*, 53, 1950.

[26] B. Trushkowsky, P. Bodík, A. Fox, M. J. Franklin, M. I. Jordan, and D. A. Patterson. The SCADS director: Scaling a distributed storage system under stringent performance requirements. In *FAST*, pages 163–176, 2011.

[27] C. A. Waldspurger. Memory resource management in vmware esx server. *SIGOPS Oper. Syst. Rev.*, 36(SI):181–194, 2002.

GPL: A GPU-based Pipelined Query Processing Engine

Johns Paul* Jiong He*
Nanyang Technological University, Singapore

Bingsheng He †
National University of Singapore

ABSTRACT

Graphics Processing Units (GPUs) have evolved as a powerful query co-processor for main memory On-Line Analytical Processing (OLAP) databases. However, existing GPU-based query processors adopt a *kernel*-based execution approach which optimizes individual kernels for resource utilization and executes the GPU kernels involved in the query plan one by one. Such a kernel-based approach cannot utilize all GPU resources efficiently due to the resource underutilization of individual kernels and memory ping-pong across kernel executions. In this paper, we propose *GPL*, a novel pipelined query execution engine to improve the resource utilization of query co-processing on the GPU. Different from the existing kernel-based execution, GPL takes advantage of hardware features of new-generation GPUs including concurrent kernel execution and efficient data communication *channel* between kernels. We further develop an analytical model to guide the generation of the optimal pipelined query plan. Thus, the *tile* size of the pipelined query execution can be adapted in a cost-based manner. We evaluate GPL with TPC-H queries on both AMD and NVIDIA GPUs. The experimental results show that 1) the analytical model is able to guide determining the suitable parameter values in pipelined query execution plan, and 2) GPL is able to significantly outperform the state-of-the-art kernel-based query processing approaches, with improvement up to 48%.

1. INTRODUCTION

Emerging hardware architectures have driven the database community to revisit and redesign database systems. As a powerful many-core accelerator, GPUs have recently been designed as a query co-processor and become an effective means to improve the performance of main memory databases for OLAP (e.g., [15, 16, 35, 37, 18]). However, existing GPU-based query processors adopt a *kernel*-based execution (KBE) approach which optimizes individual kernels for resource utilization and executes the GPU kernels involved in the query plan one by one. Note, a kernel is a program that runs in parallel on the GPU. The underlying rationale of existing query co-processing is, given that individual kernels are fully optimized, the overall query co-processing performance is optimized.

Despite the effectiveness of such kernel-based approaches on GPU-based query co-processing, we have identified a number of severe issues in performance and resource underutilization. First, executing one kernel at a time causes severe underutilization of GPU resources (e.g., memory bandwidth and computational power). Second, the inter-kernel communication is achieved through global memory or even host main memory in KBE. On the one hand, this explicitly materializes intermediate results across kernels, which increases GPU memory footprint. On the other hand, this causes significant overhead in memory ping-pong to global memory. Hence, KBE may incur serious performance degradations and low utilization on GPU resources (refer to Section 2.2). In this study, we investigate whether and how we can further improve the performance of GPU query co-processing by addressing the shortcomings of KBE.

Recently, some emerging hardware features have been introduced to new-generation GPUs. First, they support concurrent kernel executions. Early GPUs only support a single kernel running on the device. Recent GPUs from NVIDIA (Fermi or Kepler architectures) can support up to 16 kernels concurrently executed within the GPU. Second, a *channel* mechanism is supported for efficient data communication across kernels with proper tuning of configurations. These two hardware features change the assumptions of KBE, which opens new design space for query co-processing.

To take advantage of those emerging hardware features, we propose *GPL*, a novel pipelined query execution engine to improve the resource utilization of query co-processing on the GPU. Pipelined query execution is a widely adopted approach in existing database systems [41, 4]. However, it has never been developed for query co-processing. On new-generation GPUs, the support of concurrent kernel executions and channels enables the concurrent executions of operators in the pipeline and efficient intermediate result transfer among operators. Still, GPUs' special architectural characteristics and programming pattern make it challenging to implement an effective and efficient pipelined query execution engine on GPUs.

Firstly, it is challenging to fairly allocate GPU resources to concurrently running kernels. Imbalanced resource allo-

*Johns Paul and Jiong He contributed equally to this work.
†Work done while at Nanyang Technological University, Singapore.

SIGMOD'16, June 26-July 01, 2016, San Francisco, CA, USA
© 2016 ACM. ISBN 978-1-4503-3531-7/16/06...$15.00
DOI: http://dx.doi.org/10.1145/2882903.2915224

cation can seriously impact the efficiency of pipelined execution. The scheduling of workloads on GPUs is transparent to users without a fixed mapping between kernels and GPU resources, making resource allocation more difficult. Existing optimizations in pipelined execution such as preemption [22] are hardly applicable to tune the workload distribution, since current GPUs do not support preemption.

Secondly, various tuning knobs (such as the *tile* size) affect the efficiency of the pipelined execution. A more platform-dependent approach is needed to find the optimal pipelined execution plan across GPUs from different vendors including AMD and NVIDIA. Manually tuning the configuration for each hardware platform is ineffective and error-prone.

We have proposed a series of designs and optimizations in GPL to address the above challenges. Firstly, we adapt the number of work-groups to control the amount of resources allocated to each kernel in the pipeline execution. We adopt the tiling technique to logically partition the input data into smaller data tiles as inputs to the pipeline [41, 4]. Thus, workload imbalance can be minimized by adapting the tile size. Secondly, we further develop fine-grained and lightweight operators that are efficient for pipelined executions, rather than simply adopting the operator implementation of existing GPU-based query co-processors [15, 40, 16, 37, 35, 18]. Finally, to find the optimal configuration for the parameters of pipelined execution, we propose an analytical model that has taken all tuning knobs as well as hardware specifications into consideration. Thus, GPL is portable across various platforms with little modification.

We have conducted experiments with TPC-H queries on both AMD and NVIDIA GPUs, in comparison with the state-of-the-art kernel-based query processing approaches [15, 16, 18]. The experimental results show that 1) the analytical model is able to guide the selection of suitable parameter values in the pipelined query execution plan, and 2) GPL is able to achieve a much better resource utilization and significantly outperform the state-of-the-art kernel-based query processing approaches, with a performance improvement up to 48% on the AMD GPU. Experimental results for NVIDIA GPUs can be found in Appendix A. To the best of our knowledge, GPL is the first pipelined query execution engine on GPUs.

The contributions of this paper can be summarized as follows: (1) we have demonstrated severe resource underutilization of existing GPU-based query co-processors; (2) we have developed a novel pipelined query execution engine to improve resource utilization of query co-processing on the GPU; (3) we have proposed an analytical model that can determine the optimal configuration for the parameters of pipelined execution.

The remainder of this paper is organized as follows. In Section 2, we introduce the background on GPU architectures and pitfalls of KBE on GPUs as the motivations for the design and development of GPL. In Section 3, we elaborate the design and implementation details of GPL, followed by an analytical model in Section 4. We present the experimental results in Section 5. We review the related work in Section 6 and conclude our paper in Section 7.

2. BACKGROUND AND MOTIVATION

In this section, we first introduce the background on GPUs. Next, we elaborate the performance issues of current GPU query co-processors.

Table 1: Hardware specification.

	AMD	NVIDIA
#CU	8	15
Core frequency (MHz)	720	875
Private memory/CU (KB)	vector:64, scalar:8	64
Local memory/CU (KB)	32	48
Global memory (GB)	32	12
Cache (MB)	4	1.5
Concurrent kernels	2	16
Programming API	OpenCL	CUDA

2.1 Graphics Processing Units

GPUs are originally designed as co-processors for CPUs to process graphics tasks. In recent years, they have evolved into a powerful accelerator for many applications such as High Performance Computing (HPC) [25] and data processing (such as MapReduce [12] and key-value stores [39]).

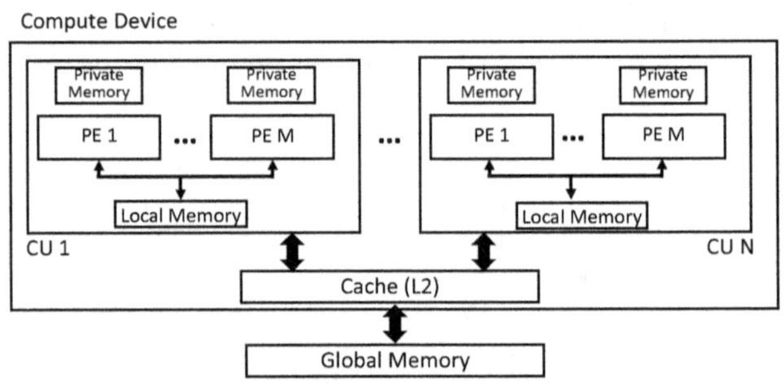

Figure 1: GPU Architecture.

Though the detailed components of GPUs from different vendors vary, their general architectural designs can be abstracted in the same model as shown in Figure 1. For illustration purposes, we use the terminology of AMD GPU and our design and implementation can be extended to NVIDIA GPUs with little modification. A GPU consists of multiple Compute Units (CUs), each of which is further composed of many vector Processing Elements (PEs). A program executed by the GPU is called a *Kernel*. Each PE executes its own instance of a kernel in a SIMD (Single Instruction Multiple Data) manner. Each PE has its own private memory (registers) and all PEs of a CU share a local memory, both of which are on-chip memory. Local memory is dedicated to one CU and invisible to all other CUs. Global memory is accessible to all CUs, and cache is placed between global memory and CUs to reduce the performance gap between PEs and global memory. The global memory for the AMD GPU is the main memory in the system, whereas the global memory for the NVIDIA GPU is within the GPU card.

The programmability of GPUs has been significantly improved by various programming frameworks like DirectCompute, CUDA and OpenCL. For illustration purposes, we use terms in OpenCL unless otherwise specified. A kernel execution consists of multiple work-groups, each of which further consists of multiple work-items. Each work-group is scheduled as the basic unit to one CU. Within a work-group, 64 work-items of that work-group are arranged together for actual execution on AMD GPU (denoted as a *wavefront*).

Recently, new-generation GPUs have been strengthened with various enhancements, including concurrent kernel execution and mechanisms for efficient communication between kernels. Table 1 shows the features of AMD and NVIDIA GPUs used in our experiments.

Concurrent execution. Early GPUs only support a single kernel execution. That is why most existing GPGPU applications focus on the implementations and optimizations in a single-kernel-based pattern [9, 14, 13]. Recent GPUs from AMD (GCN-based GPUs) have been enabled with concurrent kernel execution capability so that multiple kernels can be executed on the same GPU simultaneously. For example, AMD GPU support concurrent kernel execution with Asynchronous Compute Engines (ACEs) that manages multiple kernels in an interleaved fashion.

Efficient data communication across kernels. Efficient data communication among concurrent kernel execution is supported via *channel*. Vendors can have different terminology and mechanisms for channel. On AMD GPU, pipe is introduced in OpenCL 2.0. The main function of data channel is to pass data between concurrently running kernels without explicit materialization in global memory so that these kernels can communicate with each other in a finer-grained manner.

There are three key parameters for channel, including packet size, number of channels and the total size of data to be passed. Packet size is the basic unit of channel for data transfer between two kernels. The number of channels defines multiple channels that are able to transfer data more efficiently between two kernels. With appropriate channel settings, computations and memory accesses can be overlapped across kernels.

We conduct calibration experiments to have an in-depth understanding on relationship between channel configurations and the throughput. In the experiment, we set up a simple chain of two kernels, *producer* and *consumer*. The producer kernel generates N integers and passes them to the consumer kernel. The channel packet size is set as 16 bytes, which achieves the best efficiency in most scenarios. The results are shown in Figure 2, when N is varied from 512K to 8 million on AMD GPU. We find that both parameters of data channel configurations can affect the throughput significantly. Also, the input data size (N) impacts the throughput. When the input data is small, the channel is not fully utilized. When the input data is too large, the working set size is larger than the data cache. Cache thrashing occurs and the throughput degrades. On the tested AMD GPU, $N = 1$ million is the suitable size setting. Thus, a feasible solution is that, if the input data is larger than the suitable size setting, the input data is chunked with the suitable size setting prior to transferring via the channel. For a general approach across different platforms, we use calibrations on varying the three key parameters, and obtain the suitable parameter values. Particularly, we experimentally obtain the relationship between the three key parameters and the throughput as the input to our cost model to determine the suitable channel configuration.

In the following of the paper, we mainly concentrate our presentation on AMD GPU, and leave the detailed results of NVIDIA GPU to Appendix A.

2.2 Pitfalls of Existing Query Co-Processing

Existing query co-processors [15, 40, 16, 37, 35, 18] mostly rely on kernel-based executions (KBE). A relational operator is implemented with multiple kernels. For example, a selection in GDB [13] can be implemented with 3 kernels

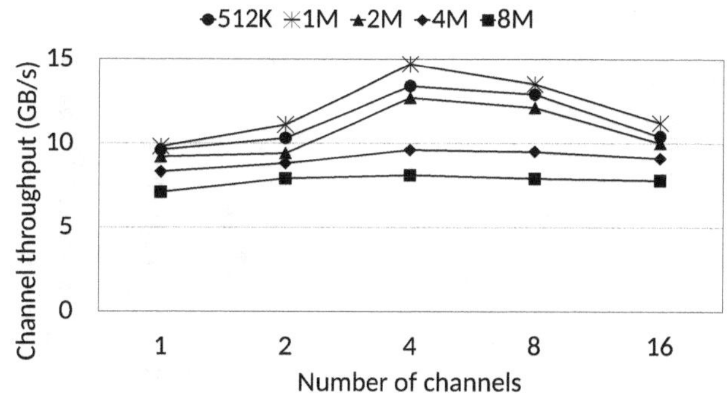

Figure 2: The relationship between channel configurations and throughput on AMD GPU for a packet size of 16 bytes.

including *map*, *prefix sum* and *scatter*. Existing query co-processors optimize the performance of individual kernels with various optimization techniques [14, 15] to exploit the GPU parallelism and to reduce the memory stalls of kernel execution. In KBE, each kernel is then executed on the GPU. Still, we observe serious performance pitfalls when evaluating an operator, even worse for a query. In the following, we summarize our observations, and present the experimental results from TPC-H queries with a scale factor of 10. More details on experimental setup can be found in Section 5.1.

To have a detailed understanding on the performance of KBE, we report various performance counters to comprehensively evaluate GPL on both platforms. Cache hit ratio measures the data locality exposed by data channels. Kernel occupancy is the ratio of in-flight wavefronts executed to the theoretical maximum wavefronts supported on each CU. It is a main indicator of the device utilization. We use the latest profiler from AMD (CodeXL) to obtain the above performance counters.

Observation 1: Explicit materialization of intermediate results across kernels not only generates a large amount of intermediate data, but also causes significant overhead in the communication between kernels. We have similar observations for all the tested queries and use TPC-H Q14 as an example for in-depth discussions. Figure 3 shows the normalized size of intermediate data generated by TPC-H Q14, with selections and joins. We normalize the intermediate data size to the input data size of the query. We also vary the selectivity and compare the results with the default. Specifically, we have changed the interval in the predicate of Q14 (*"l_shipdate >= date [DATE] and l_shipdate < date [DATE] + interval 1 month"*) to generate approximate selectivity ranging from 1% to 100% on *LINEITEM* relation (16.4% by default). The size of the intermediate data, which mainly include the tuples generated from the selection, and the intermediate results generated from the join (l_partkey = p_partkey), increases with the selectivity. After 75%, the intermediate results even exceed the original data input. Large intermediate results would waste global memory and cause memory access latency.

Such large intermediate results impose significant overhead in the communication between kernels. Figure 4 presents the cost of memory accesses through global memory, where the memory stall (Mem_cost) is directly obtained from hardware profiler. The global memory accesses not only incur high access overhead, but also sacrifice the overlapping opportunity between query co-processing and data trans-

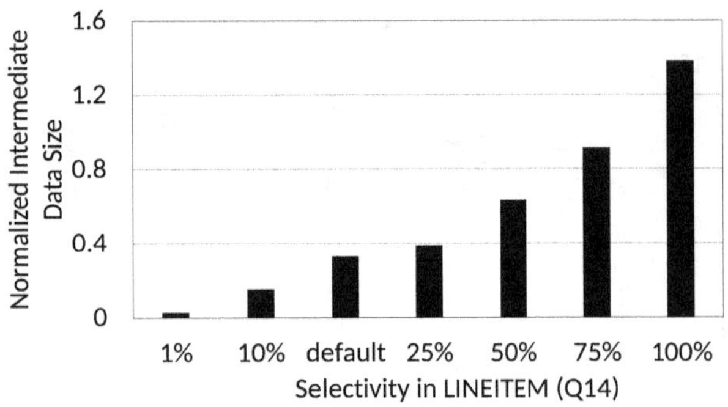

Figure 3: Size of intermediate results in KBE with varying selectivity (Q14).

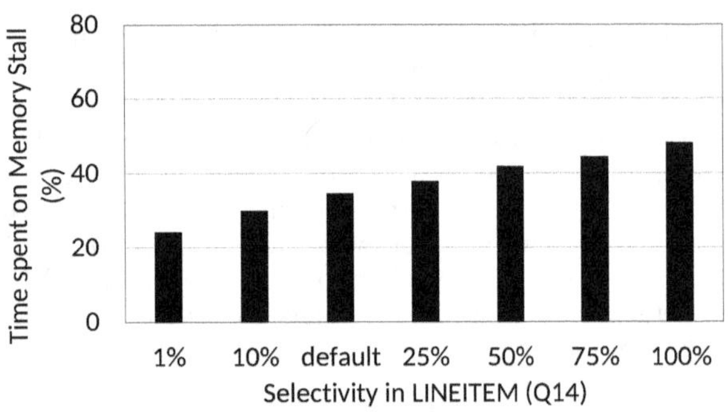

Figure 4: High communication cost in query execution with varying selectivity (Q14) on AMD GPU.

fers. Moreover, such bulky store/load operations are cache-unfriendly, generating more cache misses and degrading the query co-processing performance.

Observation 2: Processing one kernel at a time can lead to severe resource under-utilization of the GPU (e.g., memory bandwidth and computational power). We collect the resource utilization statistics of 5 TPC-H queries (Q5, Q7, Q8, Q9 and Q14) on AMD GPU in KBE approach and the average utilization results are presented in Figure 5. On AMD GPU, we use hardware counters *VALUBusy* and *MemUnitBusy* to evaluate the utilization of vector ALU and memory bandwidth. Also, we observe that the computation and memory utilization vary greatly among kernels. Within a query, some kernels may have high computation utilization but low memory utilization. Some other kernels favor more memory resources than computation resources. Thus, KBE barely can fully utilize both computation and memory resources of the GPU.

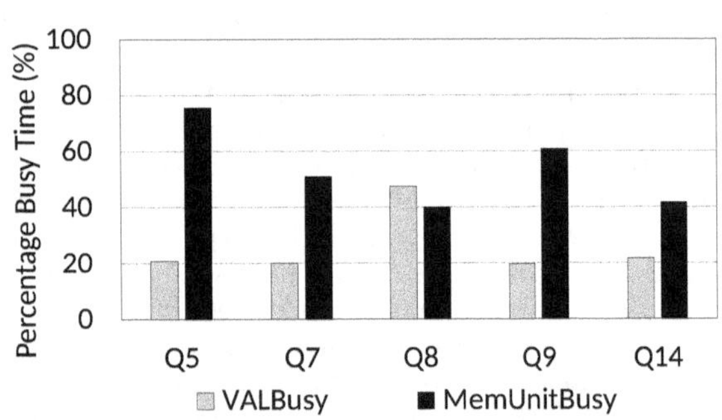

Figure 5: Low utilization of GPU resources in query execution on AMD GPU.

3. SYSTEM DESIGN AND IMPLEMENTATION

We develop a pipelined query processing engine named GPL to reduce inter-kernel communication overhead and improve resource utilization of query co-processing. GPL takes advantage of emerging GPU hardware features including channels and concurrent kernel execution to improve the resource utilization as well as to reduce memory overhead of the KBE approach. We note that, if we implement pipelined query processing on early GPUs with the support of only a single kernel, the intermediate results have to be materialized into the global memory and hence this system will suffer from similar performance bottleneck as KBE (as observed in Section 2).

In this section, we first show the overall architectural design of GPL. Then, we present the implementation of GPL operators. After that, we elaborate each key component of GPL with more details.

3.1 Architectural Design of GPL

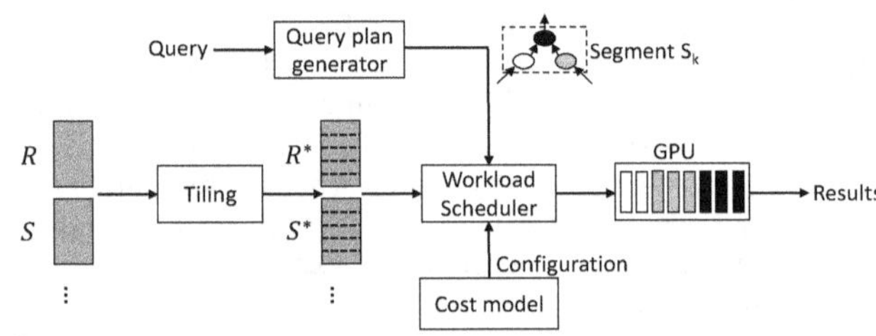

Figure 6: Architectural overview of GPL.

Figure 6 presents the main components of GPL. Like existing pipelined execution engines [41, 4], a query Q is firstly processed by the query plan generator to produce a segmented query plan tree. Specifically, it is processed according to its query plan tree T generated by Selinger-style optimizer [32]. Basically, T consists of a sequence of operators $(O(O_0, O_1, ..., O_i, ..., O_m))$. Such a sequence is produced by traversing T in post-order so that all child nodes precede before their parent nodes. We further denote the kernel sequence as $K(K_0, K_1, ..., K_j, ..., K_n)$, including blocking and non-blocking kernels. Because of the nature of blocking kernels, T is partitioned into a set of segments (S). Here, $S = \{S_0(K_0, ..., \hat{K}_p), ..., S_t(K_0, ..., \hat{K}_q)\}$ where S_i is a segment consisting of multiple kernels (K_0, K_1,...), and $\hat{K}_p$ and $\hat{K}_q$ are blocking kernels. We adopt an existing simple segment generation approach [23]. Each segment contains a sequence of non-blocking kernels, ending by a blocking kernel.

A segment is the basic unit for scheduling and execution in GPL. Each segment contains one or more kernels that are connected with channels, and simultaneously executed in pipelines. The input relations (e.g., R and S) are processed by tiling component to produce tiled relations (denoted as R^* and S^*), which are logically partitioned with nearly the same size. One tile is scheduled by workload scheduler as input to each segment. As we observed in Section 2.1, we need to determine the suitable tile size so that the channel and GPU resources can be fully utilized. Moreover, it also needs to consider the influences from data channel and concurrent kernel execution because they introduce additional cost such as pipelined execution delay. We propose a cost model that captures the characteristics of both queries and hardware.

The configuration produced from cost model can be used to guide the setting of parameter values of GPL. The amount of GPU resources allocated to each kernel is determined by the configuration to minimize the estimated execution time of individual segments. The workload scheduler component schedules the segments to GPU for execution one by one. Note, the output of a segment has to be materialized into the GPU global memory, which will be used as inputs for other segments.

3.2 Implementation of GPL Operators

GPL is based on an OpenCL-based query execution engine, OmniDB [40]. This section focuses on how GPL is developed from OmniDB. For the implementation details of individual operators/primitives, we refer readers to the previous studies [40, 15]. Even though GPL is based on OmniDB, our goal is to address the performance problem of kernel-based execution, which is adopted by most existing studies on GPU-based query co-processing, including OmniDB [40], Ocelot [18], and Red Fox [36]. We conjecture that the GPL design can improve the performance of all those systems. As a start, we have implemented GPL based on OmniDB, and leave the implementation on other systems as our future work.

OmniDB is not designed with pipelined execution capabilities. Our implementation specially maximizes the chances of non-blocking executions. Particularly, we reuse and modify the kernels and primitives in OmniDB to support pipelined execution if appropriate. In the following, we briefly describe the implementation details for selection, aggregation and hash joins. The implementation of other operators follows the same methodology.

Selection: We simplify the selection in OmniDB by removing prefix sum kernel. We only perform the map kernel on each tuple for evaluating the selection predicates, and send the satisfied tuple to the consumer kernel (if available) via channel.

Aggregation: In OmniDB, prefix scan is used to calculate the prefix sum in parallel upon an entire input. It is also used to implement aggregations. In GPL, we use an non-blocking approach by directly performing executions on the intermediate results from the channel packet by packet. Take the sum operator as an example. Upon receiving a packet, the kernel updates the partial sum by adding the values in the packet.

Hash join: We implement the simple hash join with two phases, i.e., hash build and hash probe separately based on existing code base [15] as primitives. Hash build is to build the hash table, and hash probe is to probe the hash table for matches. Both primitives are non-blocking. Still, it requires a blocking barrier after hash build. Partitioned hash joins can be implemented similarly, where the partition phase also can be implemented in a non-blocking manner.

Despite the similarities, the execution model of OmniDB and GPL are inherently different. We compare the query execution plans of both KBE and GPL in Figure 7 for an example query (Listing 1).

```
SELECT SUM(l_extendedprice * (1 - l_discount) * (1 +
    l_tax)) AS sum_charge
FROM LINEITEM
WHERE l_shipdate <= DATE '1988-11-01'
```

Listing 1: An example query.

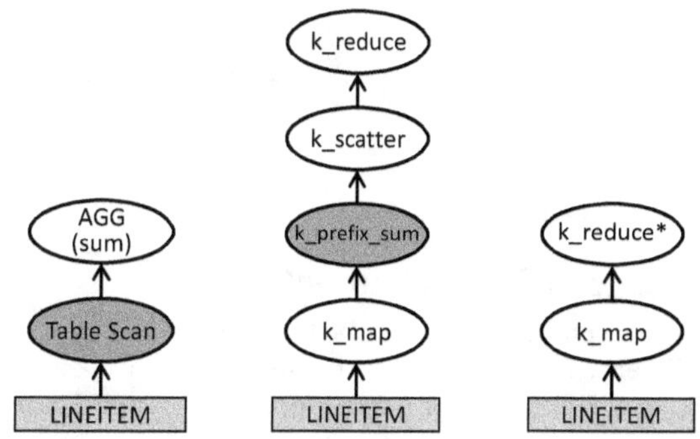

(a) Logical Plan (b) KBE (c) GPL

Figure 7: Comparison of query execution plan.

In the query plan, the shadowed ellipses represent the blocking operators and kernels. Blocking operators and kernels need to materialize the intermediate result in global memory. A blocking operator contains at least one blocking kernel. In conventional KBE implementations [15, 16, 13, 40], most operators are implemented in blocking fashion for intra-kernel parallelism. For instance, to filter tuples from *LINEITEM* that satisfy the predicate in the example query, the prefix sum kernel (*k_prefix_sum*) is used in KBE. As shown in Figure 7c, all kernels in the query plan are non-blocking, and can be executed concurrently on the GPU. Thus, the concurrent kernel execution can be exploited, rather than executing one kernel at a time in KBE. In GPL, after the *k_map* function is evaluated on each tuple of the input tile, the satisfied tuples are stored as a packet and passed to *k_reduce** together with *LINEITEM* via channel for further processing. The reduce kernel (*k_reduce**) directly performs the sum on each element in the packet.

3.3 Tiling

GPL adopts the tile-based pipelined execution model [41, 4]. Figure 8 compares the data storage in KBE (w/o tiling) and GPL, respectively. Without tiling, because KBE executes kernels one by one on the GPU, the GPU is entirely occupied by kernel K_j. Intermediate result R^* is produced and serves as the input to the next kernel K_{j+1}. With tiling in GPL, R is firstly partitioned into much smaller tiles. Tiles are processed one by one, immediately after the previous tile has been completely processed by K_j. The intermediate result r_i^* is passed to the next kernel via global memory (if K_{j+1} is blocking) or data channels (if K_{j+1} non-blocking).

The tile size is an important parameter for the efficiency of pipelined execution. Given a segment, the tile size determines the working set size of performing the pipelined execution as well as the amount of work on the GPU. Thus, on the one hand, small tile sizes cause resource underutilization of pipelined execution and dramatically degrade the data channel efficiency (as we observed in Section 2), and such an impact can be further exaggerated for deep pipelines. On the other hand, large tile sizes result in inefficient communications between kernels due to cache thrashing. Therefore, a carefully selected tile size is important in improving the data channel efficiency.

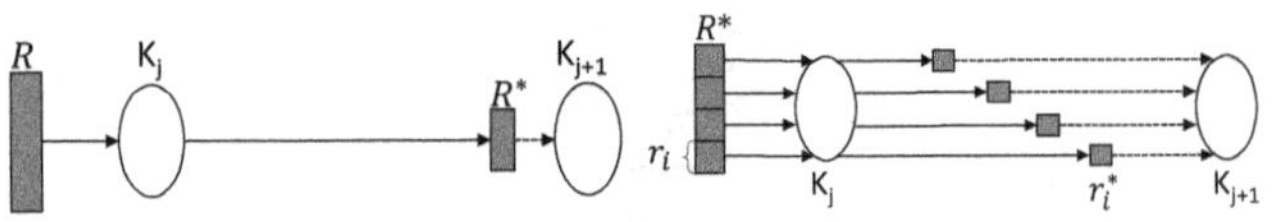

(a) KBE (b) GPL

Figure 8: Execution model of KBE and GPL.

3.4 Usage of Data Channels

With data channels, the data transfer in the pipeline is more efficient, further leading to fluent pipelined execution and higher GPU resource utilizations. In Figure 7, any arrows pointing to non-blocking nodes represent such data channels. That means, the output generated by the previous node directly passed via data channel to the next node, without materialization in the global memory.

Figure 9 presents the detailed mechanism of data passing between two kernels in the pipelined execution of GPL. For AMD data channel, the space is used on reservation basis by each work-group. Each time after one work-group in K_j has been finished, a synchronization operation is performed so that the next kernel K_{j+1} can fetch the results immediately. This light-weight synchronization guarantees data consistency as well as enables fine-grained coordination between connected kernels. In GPL, read and write operations are executed in the scope of a work-group. Each time a work-group of K_j that has finished its work is able to store its results into data channel, regardless of the progress of other work-groups. Once the corresponding work-group of K_{j+1} has received the data, it can start to execute without synchronization with other work-groups. In this way, GPL is able to establish a more fine-grained coordination between K_j and K_{j+1}. Moreover, data channel can expose more data locality. As the producer work-group stores its results into the channel, the consumer work-group can fetch them immediately. With a suitable tuning on the channel, it is very likely that the data still resides in cache.

In Section 2, we have observed that appropriate parameter settings are important for the throughput of data channels. Based on the cost model, we determine the optimal settings at various positions by capturing the dynamics among kernels (such as selectivity) and differences between hardware.

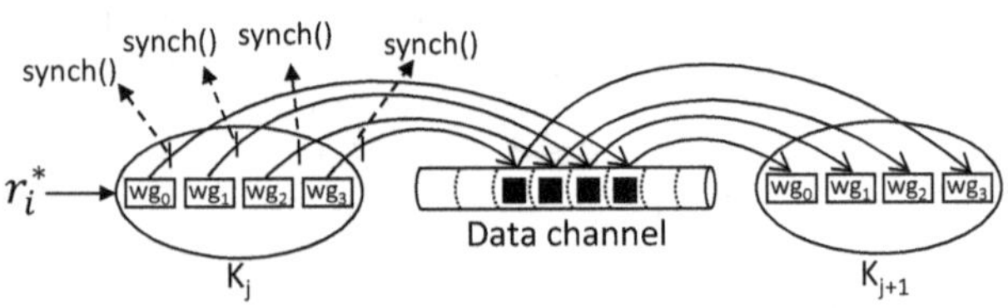

Figure 9: Fine-grained data passing between kernels w/ data channel.

3.5 Concurrent Kernel Execution

With concurrent kernel executions, the stages involved in the pipeline execution of a query segment are executed concurrently. Since stages can have different computation and memory characteristics, the GPU resources can be better utilized. We have designed a new execution paradigm combined with tiling technique to accommodate multiple kernels in a segment simultaneously. Figure 10 illustrates the workload distribution of three kernels K_i, K_j and K_k on the GPU. In KBE without concurrent execution, the workload scheduler distributes workload from one kernel each time

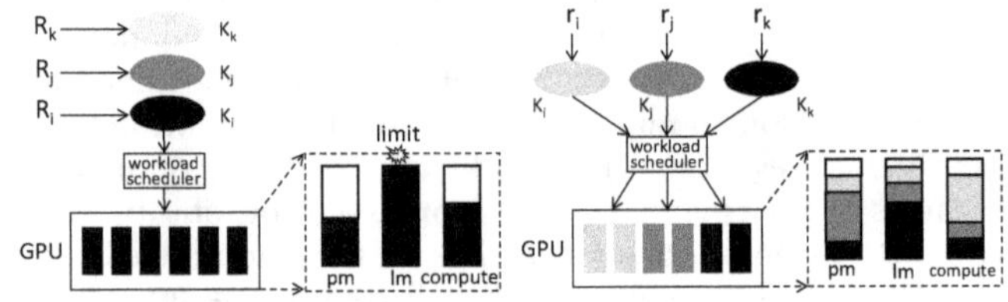

(a) w/o concurrent execution (b) w/ concurrent execution

Figure 10: Workload distribution w/o and w/ concurrent execution ("pm" and "lm" denote private memory and local memory, respectively).

onto all available GPU CUs. A single kernel cannot fully utilize all resources (e.g., private memory, local memory and compute units), as we have already observed in Section 2. If K_i is constrained by certain resource (e.g., local memory), the total active work-groups that can be scheduled for execution simultaneously is limited, leading to underutilization of all other resources (private memory and compute units). In contrast, in GPL the stages involved in the pipeline execution of a query segment are executed concurrently. Since stages can have different computation and memory characteristics, the GPU resources can be better utilized. In this way, each resource can be used to serve more kernels simultaneously, leading to a higher overall resource utilization.

We propose to control the resource allocation indirectly by adapting the work-group size as well as the total number of work-groups. The work-group size is fixed at 64 (wavefront size) to spawn more work-groups to gain scheduling flexibility. We leave choosing the optimal numbers of work-groups of each kernel according to the cost model.

4. ANALYTICAL MODEL

There are a number of parameters introduced in GPL. Inappropriate settings could cause significant performance loss. Without an automatic approach, it is impossible to evaluate and compare the performance of a large number of execution plans and to choose the most efficient execution plan. Therefore, we propose an analytical model to determine the optimal system configurations according to query and hardware information automatically.

4.1 Cost Model

There have been a number of studies on estimating the cost of individual database operators [13, 14, 15, 16]. We integrate existing methods into our cost model for estimations. However, additional factors related to tiling, data channel and GPU resource allocation need to be taken into consideration. The analytical model is designed to automatically determine these factors accurately without sacrificing performance.

We summarize all notations to be used in the cost model in Table 2. Notations are categorized into six groups: platform, profiling, program analysis, query optimizer, model output and calibration. *Platform input* notations are platform specific and can be obtained from its specification. Parameters from *Profiling input* are obtained by profiling tools such as CodeXL and Visual Profiler. Parameters from *program analysis* can be obtained from program analysis on the source code. Parameters from *query optimizer* are determined by query optimizer. Parameters from *calibration* are determined by calibration experiments. Parameters from *model output* are calculated as output in the cost model.

Table 2: Notations in the cost model

Notation	Definitions	Sources
$\#CU$	Number of CUs	platform input
w	Cycles to execute one instruction	
C	Concurrency degree	
mem_l	Global memory latency	
c_l	Data cache latency	
pm_{max}	Amount of available private memory per CU	
lm_{max}	Amount of available local memory per CU	
wg_{max}	Number of work-groups supported per CU	
$a\_wg\_K_i$	Number of active work-groups supported per CU for K_i	profiling input
$a\_CU\_K_i$	Number of active CUs for K_i	
$c\_inst\_K_i$	Number of compute instructions for K_i	
$m\_inst\_K_i$	Number of memory instructions for K_i	
cr_{K_i}	Data cache hit ratio for K_i	
pm_K_i	Private memory usage in each work-item for K_i	program analysis
lm_K_i	Local memory usage in each work-item for K_i	
r_{K_i}	Number of tiles processed by K_i	
set_l	Set of kernels that are leaf nodes in query plan tree	query optimizer
set_b	Set of kernels that have blocking kernels as child nodes	
wi_K_i	Work-group size in K_i	
λ_{K_i}	Ratio of intermediate data generated by K_i to Δ	
Γ	Relationship between data channel throughput and configuration	calibration
Δ	Tile size	model output
T_{K_i}	Execution time of kernel K_i per tile	
T_{S_k}	Execution time of segment S_k	
n	Number of data channels between two kernels	
p	Packet size of data channel (for AMD only)	
wg_K_i	Number of work-groups for K_i	
rep_K_i	Times for a CU to complete K_i	
c_K_i	Computation cycles of K_i	
m_K_i	Memory cycles of K_i	
$delay\_S_k$	Delayed cycles in segment S_k	

In the remainder of this section, we mainly present the model for the AMD GPU and we briefly describe the extensions needed for the NVIDIA GPU in Appendix A.

The data channels between running kernels pass data from one end to the other end in a fine-grained pattern so that the computation and data access latency can be largely overlapped. To quantitatively evaluate the performance of such data channels, we adopt a calibration-based approach to determine the relationship between the data channel throughput and three factors: data size, number of channels, size of packet (for AMD GPU). We find that for a given data size d, the channel throughput changes depending on the number of channels n and p. Thus, we conduct calibration with various data set sizes and data channel configurations to formulate the relationship between them as Γ in Eq. 1.

$$T = \Gamma(n, p, d) \tag{1}$$

Given a kernel K_i, the output data size can be calculated as $\Delta \times \lambda_{K_i}$ which is the amount of data K_i will send to K_{i+1}. λ_{K_i} is a kernel-specific parameter representing the data reduction ratio to the original tile size Δ and is obtained from the database query optimizer. For example, the output data size for a selection kernel depends on the selectivity. Given the output data size ($d = \Delta \times \lambda_{K_i}$), we search the data channel configuration that can maximize the data channel throughput from the relationship Γ. We denote the n_{max} and p_{max} to be the optimal values for n and p, respectively, for that channel setting.

To evaluate the cost of each segment, we categorize the cost into three parts: the computation cost (c_{K_i}), the memory cost (m_{K_i}) and the cost of delay ($delay_{S_k}$) between kernels of that segment due to imbalanced execution speed.

Computation cost: For each kernel executed on the GPU, the scheduling unit is work-group, which is further divided into execution unit wavefronts. As each work-item requests the same amount of resources (private memory and local memory) as well as the computation resources which is determined by the number of CUs that is assigned to that kernel, the total number of active work-groups ($a\_wg\_K_i$) as well as active CUs ($a\_CU\_K_i$) is constrained by the total available resources of each CU and the number of work-groups (wg_K_i) defined by programs. Given a segment S_k, Eq. 2 presents the resource limitations on private memory, local memory and CUs. The private memory (pm_K_i) and local memory (lm_K_i) required by each work-item of K_i can be obtained from analyzing the kernel code via program analysis. Particularly, the program analysis is performed in an off-line manner, with the source code of the kernel as input. The amount of private/local memory usage in each work item can be obtained from existing program analysis tools, such as AMD APP Profiler. This analysis is not restricted to certain query patterns.

$$\begin{cases} \sum^{S_k} pm\_K_i \times wi\_K_i \times wg\_K_i \leq pm_{max} \times \#CU \\ \sum^{S_k} lm\_K_i \times wi\_K_i \times wg\_K_i \leq lm_{max} \times \#CU \\ \sum^{S_k} wg\_K_i \leq wg_{max} \times \#CU \end{cases} \tag{2}$$

Under the condition in Eq. 2, the times (req_K_i) to complete all work-groups of K_i on the GPU is obtained in Eq. 3.

$$req\_K_i = \frac{wg\_K_i}{a\_wg\_K_i \times a\_CU\_K_i} \tag{3}$$

Thus, the total computation cost for kernel K_i on each CU is calculated based on the profiled statistics on the number of computation and memory instructions in Eq. 4. w is a platform-specific parameter to represent the number of cycles to issue and execute one instruction. In our experiments, w is 4 for both AMD and NVIDIA GPU. Due to the resource limitations, K_i can be finished in req_K_i times as in Eq. 3.

$$c\_K_i = (c\_inst\_K_i + m\_inst\_K_i) \times w \times req\_K_i \tag{4}$$

Memory cost: The memory cost consists of global memory access cost and data channel access cost. For those kernels in set_l, they suffer from long access latency as they have to fetch data from data tiles initially stored in global memory. Besides, given a blocking kernel K_i, its parent kernel K_j is a member of set_b. All kernels in set_b also suffer from global memory latency as their directly preceding blocking kernel materializes the intermediate results in the global memory. Thus, the memory cost for kernels in set_l and set_b is derived in Eq. 5. It consists of two parts: the cost of global memory accesses and the cost of L2 cache accesses. The number of memory accesses are calculated by cache hit ratio

(cr_{K_i}) and the total number of memory instruction derived from profiler.

$$m\_K_i = m\_inst\_K_i \times (1 - cr_{K_i}) \times mem\_l + m\_inst\_K_i \times cr_{K_i} \times c\_l, \forall K_i \in set\_l \cup set\_b \quad (5)$$

For the remaining kernels in the kernel set, the memory cost is from data channel access overhead. As the data to be passed to K_i over data channel is known ($\Delta \times \lambda(K_i)$), the memory cost for these kernels can be obtained as Eq. 6 based on Eq. 1.

$$m\_K_i = \frac{\Delta \times \lambda_{K_i}}{\Gamma(n_{max}, p_{max}, \Delta \times \lambda_{K_i})}, \forall K_i \in (K - set\_l \cup set\_b) \quad (6)$$

Therefore, the expected execution time for K_i is derived in Eq. 7 as the sum of computation time and memory access time.

$$T_{K_i} = c\_K_i + m\_K_i \quad (7)$$

Delay cost: Delay may be incurred between kernels as they form producer-consumer chain to achieve pipelined execution. The delayed cycles of the pipelined execution need to be minimized to maximize the efficiency of each segment. Eq. 8 calculates the total delayed cycles incurred within a segment S_k by calculating the absolute value of the difference between two connected kernels K_i and K_j. The actual execution time of segment S_k is shown in Eq. 9. Because of concurrent execution, the execution time of a segment is adjusted by $\frac{1}{C}$ where C is the concurrency degree of given platform (2 for the AMD GPU used in our study).

$$delay\_S_k = \sum^{S_k} abs(T_{K_i} * r_{K_i} - T_{K_j} * r_{K_j}) \quad (8)$$

$$T_{S_k} = \frac{1}{C} \times \sum^{S_k} T_{K_i} + delay\_S_k \quad (9)$$

The objectives of our analytical model is to minimize the total execution time of all kernels within a segment S_k. To minimize T_{S_k}, we extensively explore the search space by adapting three parameters, Δ, n, p and wg_K_i.

We have tried all means to reduce the solution space. In our query optimization, the solution space is for individual query segments. Moreover, for finding the optimal configuration of each query segment, we have used many effective approaches to reduce the solution space without significantly scarifying the solution quality. For each parameter, we search the value within the feasible range. For example, we find that the throughput of data channels continues to drop when the number of channels is over 16. Thus, n can be selected between 1 and 16. The wg_K_i represents the number of work-groups for each kernel. As work-groups can be scheduled to any CUs, we set wg_K_i integral multiple of $\#CU$. In this way, the search space and the overhead associated with query optimization can be dramatically reduced. In our experiments, the elapsed time for query optimization is generally smaller than 5ms, which is ignorable compared with the query processing time. With each set of these parameters, c_{K_i}, m_{K_i}, T_{K_i} and T_{S_k} also can be obtained accordingly. We determine the smallest T_{S_k} as the optimal pipelined execution plan.

4.2 An Example

We use an example query (Figure 7) to show pipelined plan generation on AMD GPU with our model.

The analytical model is applied to evaluate on a query segment. Apparently, *k_map* and *k_reduce** are in the same segment S_k as both of them are non-blocking kernels.

Next, by program analysis we can obtain statistics about the requirements for each type of resources, e.g., the local memory and private memory usage. All these statistics and parameter values need to satisfy conditions in Eq. 2.

After that, both kernels are launched together and *k_map* works on the first tile of $LINEITEM$. The tile size here is a variable but initiated with a default value. Once the first tile has been processed, CodeXL is used to collect runtime information such as $active\_wg\_K_i$, number of computation and memory instruction and cache hit cr_{K_i}. With these information, theoretical computation and memory access time can be calculated according to Eq. 3 to 6, depending on the platform we use. On AMD GPU, the data channel cost is determined by the size of data to be passed as well as the data channel configurations. Thus, estimated execution time of each kernel is a function of the number of work-groups for each kernel, tile size and data channel configurations.

Another cost is delay cost between two connected kernels if there is a difference between the estimated execution time of them. As in Eq. 9, T_{S_k} is a function of wg_K_i, Δ and data channel configurations. As the feasible range of these parameters has been constrained, the optimal parameter settings can be found through searching the solution space.

5. EXPERIMENTAL EVALUATIONS

We experiment with TPC-H queries to evaluate the efficiency and effectiveness of GPL. Our experiments have been conducted on AMD and NVIDIA GPUs. Furthermore, to give more in-depth understanding on the performance improvement, we further investigate hardware performance counters on cache, memory units and device utilization.

5.1 Experimental Setup

Hardware. We evaluate GPL on both AMD and NVIDIA GPU. Overall, we have similar findings on both GPUs. Here, we focus our discussions on the AMD GPU, and the detailed results on the NVIDIA GPU is presented in Appendix A. The AMD platform is a coupled CPU-GPU architecture (AMD A10 APU) in which the CPU and the GPU are integrated on the same die without PCI-e bus. More details about the processor specification of the AMD and NVIDIA GPU can be found in Table 1.

Workloads. We evaluate GPL on TPC-H queries (Q5, Q7, Q8, Q9, Q14) with the scale factor (SF) of 10 (by default). Detailed description of these TPC-H queries is given in Appendix B. The total size of the tables generated by the standard dbgen utility is around 10GB. Q14 has a single join operation, whereas other queries have multiple joins. Q8 and Q9 involve rather complicated subqueries, and others do not have. Those queries also have other common operators such as group-by and order-by.

The KBE approach [15, 16] is the baseline to compare with GPL. To have an in-depth understanding of the performance of pipeline executions, we further compare the performance of a GPL variant, namely GPL (w/o CE), by disabling concurrent execution and data channel in GPL. Thus, each tile is executed by corresponding kernels and the intermediate results have to be stored back to the global memory.

To show that the performance of GPL is comparable to state-of-the-art systems, we further compare GPL against

Ocelot [18]. Ocelot is a hardware oblivious extension for MonetDB [19], which is an in-memory column store database system. It replaces MonetDB's relational operators with OpenCL based operators which can run on a wide variety of devices that supports OpenCL. Ocelot supports all major relational operators (selection, projection, grouping and aggregation). However, in the current code base [31] it does not support data-types greater than 4 bytes in size or operators like multi-column sort. It also cannot support non-trivial string operations like inequality and sorting etc. Following the previous study [18], we have to slightly modify the TPC-H queries (as in Appendix B).

5.2 Model Evaluation

To validate the effectiveness of our cost model, we show the relative error associated with estimating the GPL runtime by our analytical model. The relative error is defined in Eq. 10, where $T_{measured}$ is the measured execution time for the query and $T_{estimated}$ is the estimated execution time by our analytical model for the same query.

$$relative\_error = \frac{|T_{measured} - T_{estimated}|}{T_{measured}} \quad (10)$$

The relative errors associated with performance estimation of all tested queries with the optimal configuration on AMD GPU are shown in Figure 11. As the results show, our cost model can predict relatively accurate system configurations for GPL. Specifically, the cost model is able to produce suggested values for parameters including tile size and number of work-groups for each kernel. Note, our prediction model generally underestimates the execution time. One possible reason is that, when we consider the concurrency degree of given platform in Eq. 9, we assume ideal parallelism, potentially leading to under-estimation.

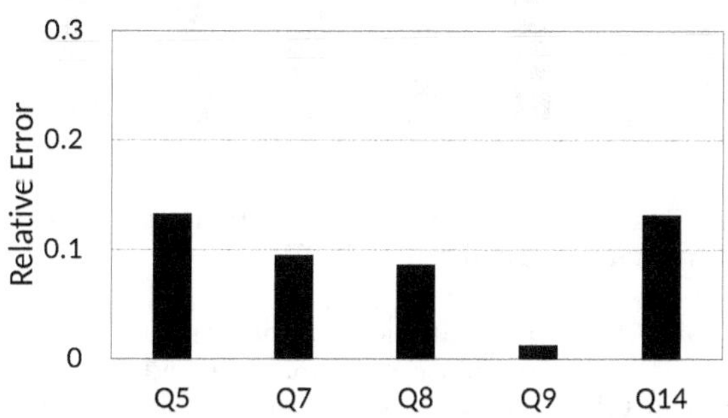

Figure 11: Relative error in estimating GPL runtime for TPC-H queries.

We take Q8 as an example to illustrate the effectiveness of our cost-based approach in determining the suitable parameter configuration. Similar results can be obtained from other queries. We study the detailed results on AMD GPU: 1) the relationship between tile sizes and overall query processing performance; 2) the relationship between resource allocations (number of work-groups assigned to each kernel) and delay cost.

Figure 12 presents the results of overall query processing performance when we vary the tile size from 256KB to 16MB while the other parameters are fixed to their default values. For better presentation, we normalize the execution time of all settings to that of 256KB. The star shows the optimal tile size estimated by the model. The results show that if the tile size is too small (resp. too large), the performance can be degraded due to inefficient resource utilization (resp. cache thrashing). Figure 13 shows that our cost model is able to capture this trend with very small relative errors and is able to estimate both the elapsed time and the optimal tile size accurately. The derived optimal tile size is 4MB, which is greatly different from the default size (1MB). The first query segment contains three kernels (2 *map* kernels K_0 and K_1, and 1 *hashbuild* kernel K_2). The optimal numbers of data channels between two *map* kernels and 1 *hashbuild* kernel are 4 and 2, respectively. Our cost model is able to capture the hardware characteristics as well as query statistics to give an accurate estimation.

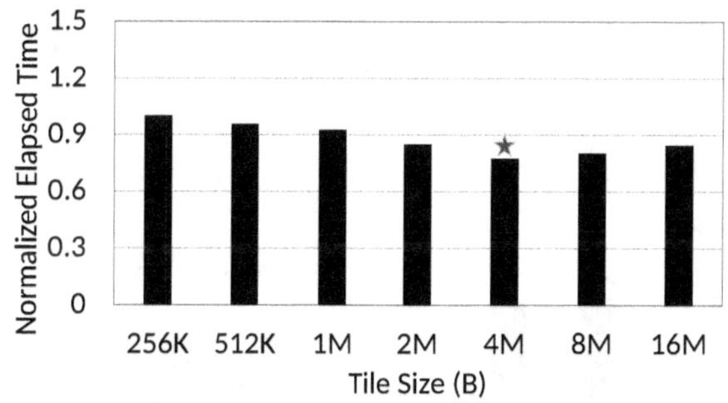

Figure 12: The overall query processing performance with varying tile sizes (Q8).

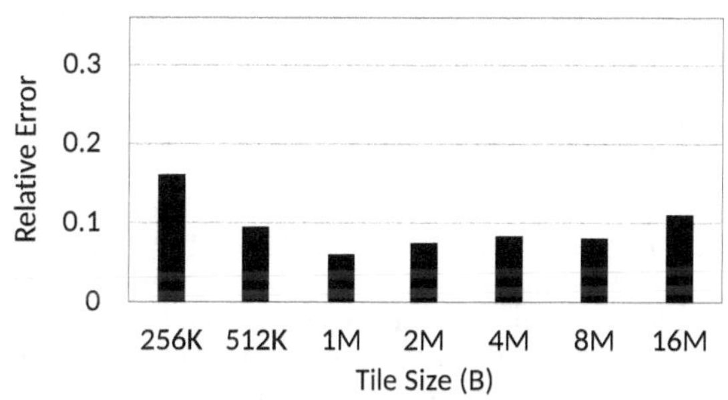

Figure 13: Relative error in estimating GPL runtime with varying tile sizes (Q8).

We further study the impact of the number of work-groups. We select a set of work-group settings (from S_1 to S_7). For each S_i (i $\in$ [1, 7]), where the number of work-groups assigned to each kernel is 2^{i-1} times of S_1. We set S_1 to be 2 for AMD GPU. Figure 14 shows the relative error in estimating the GPL runtime and Figure 15 shows the impacts of resource allocation imbalance on the overall query processing performance in terms of delay cost (normalized to the delay cost of S_1). The optimal settings derived by our cost model is S_4 (denoted by the star) for Q8 on AMD GPU, which is the setting with lowest delay overhead (Figure 15). The minimal delay overhead also corresponds to the lowest total query processing time. Note that the optimal setting varies for different queries. From the results, we find that our model is able to estimate the runtime of GPL with nominal error even with a varying number of work-groups. Also it can be seen that inappropriate resource allocations may result in serious delay overhead, especially in pipelined execution paradigm where any delay incurred along the pipeline can be exaggerated in the subsequent stages. Our model has captured this delay cost of pipelined execution. Thus, it is able to produce the optimal resource allocation for a given query that incurs minimum delay cost.

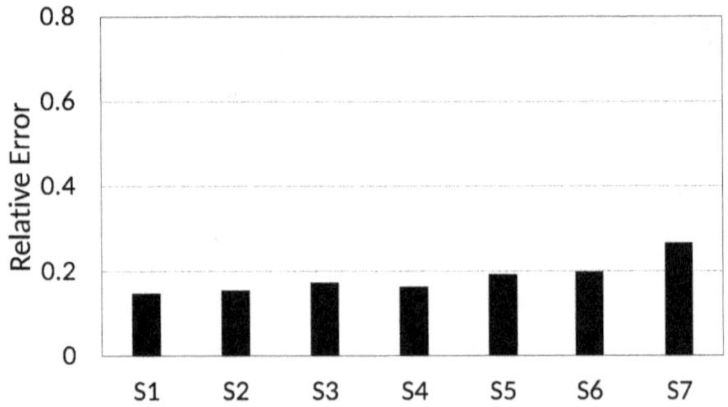

Figure 14: Relative error in estimating GPL runtime with varying number of work-groups (Q8).

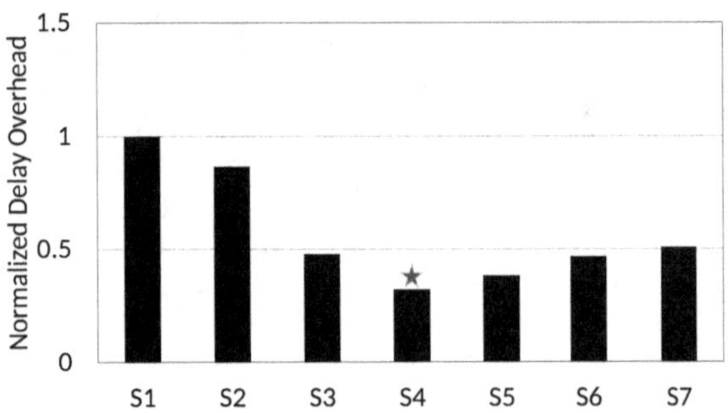

Figure 15: The delay cost with varying resource allocations (Q8).

5.3 Evaluation on GPL

5.3.1 Overall Comparison

Figure 16 shows the results for the TPC-H queries on AMD GPU. If tiling is applied without concurrent execution (GPL (w/o CE)), queries on AMD GPU suffer from performance degradation up to 31% on AMD. On the one hand, in the variant without concurrent execution, tiles are executed one by one as that in KBE. Thus, additional overhead is incurred by frequent kernel launches and large amount of intermediate data materialization. On the other hand, each time only one tile is processed by the GPU. Thus, insufficient data level parallelism would underutilize the GPU resources.

In GPL, concurrent execution as well as tiling are both applied together. By comparing query execution performance in KBE and GPL, we find that GPL outperforms KBE by over 48% on AMD GPU. Though applying only tiling would incur non-negligible overhead to query execution, combining tiling with data channels as well as concurrent execution can offset those overhead and even introduce more performance improvements over KBE approach. The main reasons include (1) the overhead of materialization of large intermediate results has been eliminated; (2) various types of kernels are executed concurrently. Thus, different types of GPU resources can be more efficiently utilized. It is even higher in NVIDIA GPU as it supports more concurrency.

5.3.2 Settlement of KBE Pitfalls

Pitfalls existing in KBE approach (Section 2.2) have negative impacts on the query execution performance. To understand the performance improvement as shown above, we

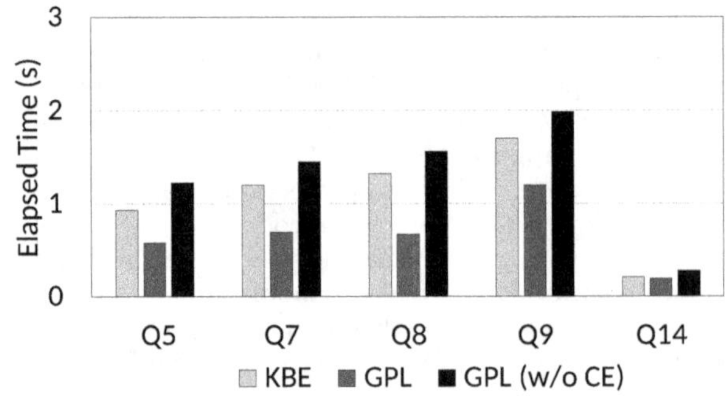

Figure 16: Comparison between KBE and GPL on AMD.

re-visit those pitfalls by examining them on both KBE and GPL designs.

Figure 17 shows the normalized size of intermediate results materialized in global memory in GPL. We normalize the results to the intermediate data size of KBE. In GPL, most intermediate results are passed through data channel in a fine-grained pattern so that the overhead can be overlapped with computation in concurrent kernel executions. Thus, intermediate results only need to be materialized in the global memory by blocking kernels like sort and hash build in GPL. However, all intermediate results in KBE need to be materialized in the global memory, resulting in high materialization overhead. The sizes of intermediate results materialized in the global memory in GPL are 15–33% of that of KBE.

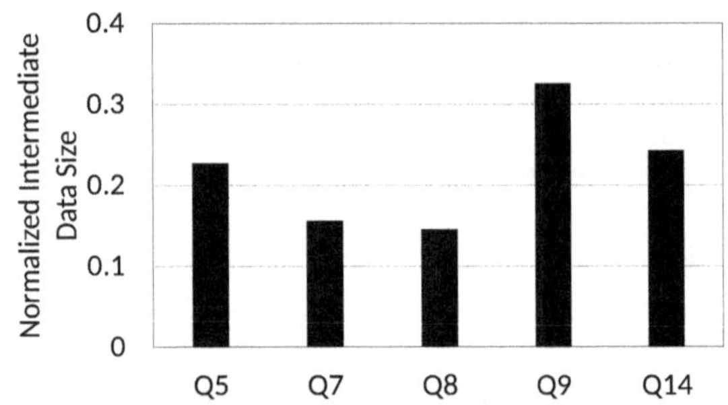

Figure 17: Reduced intermediate results materialized in the global memory (normalized to KBE).

We take Q14 as an example to demonstrate the reduction in the size of intermediate data materialized in the global memory in GPL, with varying selectivity ranging from 1% to 100%. The results are presented in Figure 18. Because of blocking kernels, intermediate data materialized in the global memory cannot be completely eliminated. However, the total size has been significantly reduced by data channel. When the selectivity is increased to 100%, the size of materialized intermediate results comes down from 1.38 times that of original input data in KBE to just 0.22 times that of the original input data in GPL. Therefore, more memory space can be saved and the overhead of global memory accesses is also reduced.

Figure 19 demonstrates the average resource utilization for various TPC-H queries on AMD GPU. Compared with KBE, GPL sustains steady and high resource utilization for memory and computation, because of finer-grained workload scheduling. Besides, the reduced memory stalls increases the efficiency of both memory and computation resources.

To examine the communication overhead among kernels,

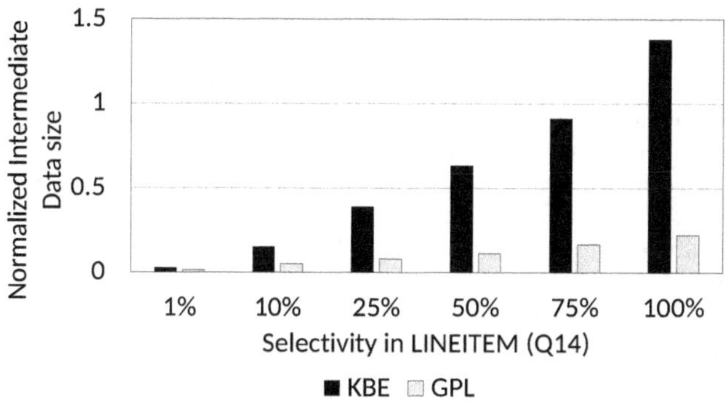

Figure 18: Size of intermediate results in GPL with varying selectivity (Q14).

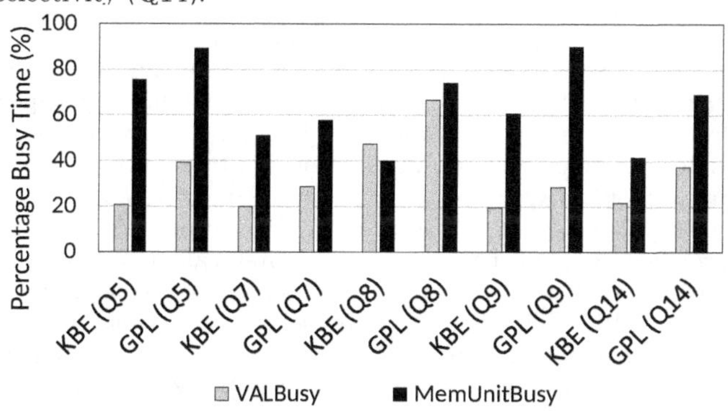

Figure 19: Improved GPU resource utilization on AMD GPU.

we show the query execution time breakdown with Q8 on AMD GPU in Figure 20. We have observed similar results for other queries. For GPL, two additional cost, the data channel access cost (*DC_cost*) and *Delay* cost existing in pipelines, are included into total query execution time. Thus, in GPL, the sum of memory cost, data channel cost and delay cost can be treated as the communication cost. The percentage of communication cost in GPL is up to 14% of the total execution time. However, it can be as high as 34% of the total execution time in KBE. On the other hand, GPL has better cache locality, resulting in an increase of 27% in cache hit ratio when compared to KBE (figures are omitted).

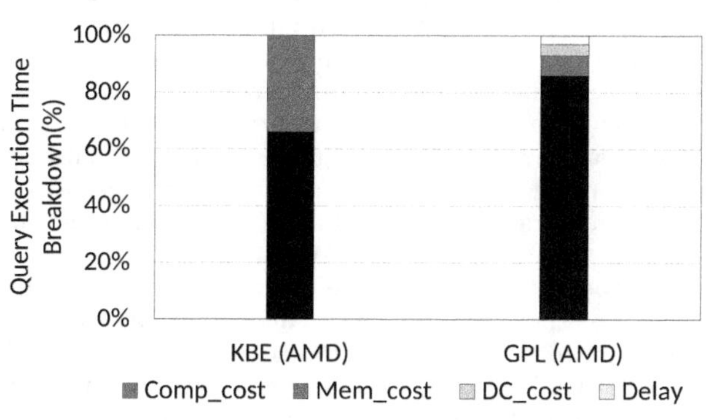

Figure 20: Query execution time breakdown (Q8) on AMD GPU.

5.4 Evaluation with Varying Data Sizes

We vary SF from 0.1 to 10, generating input data ranging from 100MB to 10GB. As the results show in Figure 21, when the data size increases, the performance improvement of GPL over KBE continues to increase on the AMD GPU. Moreover, the elapsed time increases of query execution in KBE are higher than those of GPL. As shown in Figure 10a, the KBE approach may be limited by a certain type of resource. Thus, simply increasing the data level parallelism cannot further improve the query execution performance in KBE. On the contrary, GPL leverages the increased data level parallelism and exploits the hardware strengths to overlap data accesses and computation for better performance.

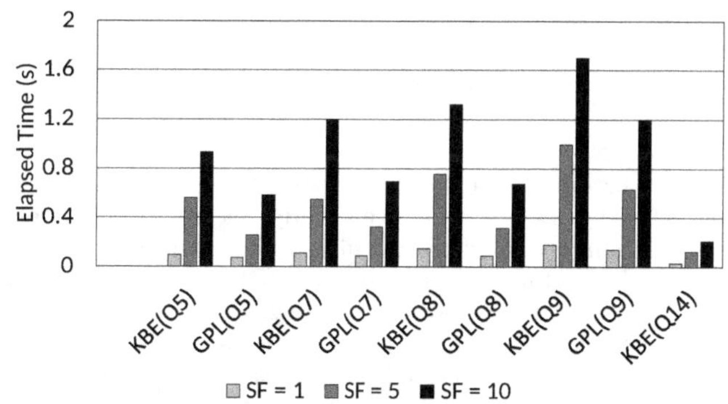

Figure 21: Query execution time on varying data size.

5.5 Performance Comparison with Ocelot

The comparison with Ocelot [18] was made for scale factors of 1, 5 and 10. Note, we cannot get the results for Q9 on Ocelot when the scale factor is 10. Figure 22 shows that, for most of the queries in our evaluation, GPL is comparable to or superior to Ocelot. For Q8 and Q9, GPL significantly outperforms Ocelot. GPL and Ocelot have comparable performance for other queries.

It would be a bit unfair to compare absolute execution time of Ocelot to that of GPL. On the one hand, since Ocelot is built on top of MonetDB, it can utilize optimizations like pre-fetching, data compression etc which are already implemented in MonetDB. Other major optimizations that are available in Ocelot include: 1) *Bitmaps.* The intermediate result of the selection operator is passed to the next operator as a bitmap in Ocelot. This helps Ocelot in reducing memory transactions when compared to GPL (the intermediate results are passed as integer arrays). 2) *Caching of hash tables.* Since generating hash tables is very costly, Ocelot's memroy manager keeps a cache of previously generated hash tables by saving the memory allocation time. So far, GPL does not have the above mentioned optimizations in Ocelot. On the other hand, GPL has more advanced pipelined query processing scheme, whereas Ocelot is still based on KBE. A more detailed study on how to extend our system with those advanced system features of Ocelot is our future work. Another future direction is to integrate GPL into Ocelot. Nevertheless, this comparison was made to show that the performance of GPL is comparable to, or even better than the state-of-the-art systems.

6. RELATED WORK

In-Memory Databases on CPUs. Larger main memory sizes drive database systems from disk-based design to in-memory design [34, 38, 19, 21]. As outlined in recent surveys [34, 38], in-memory databases have many challenges

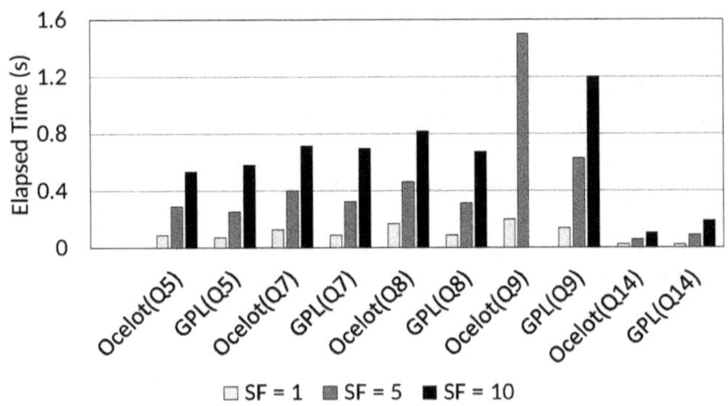

Figure 22: Query Execution Time for GPL and Ocelot on AMD GPU.

and opportunities for database research. We briefly review the related work relevant to this study, and refer the readers to those surveys for more details. Larger and faster caches reduce the performance gap between CPU and memory. A lot of cache-optimized algorithms (e.g., [1, 33, 24, 3, 7, 27]) have been developed to improve the cache locality. In our study, GPL takes advantage of channels to reduce the memory stalls. On the other hand, the emerging trend of multi-core and many-core processors enlarges the design space of in-memory databases with new optimization knobs such as data locality [8, 22] and SIMD [20, 29]. GPL is specifically designed for new-generation GPUs with the support of channels and concurrent kernel executions.

Pipelined Query Processing. Pipelined query processing has been extensively studied in relational database systems. Volcano [10] is a classic model to achieve pipelined execution paradigm in a tuple-at-a-time style. The simple execution pattern fails to utilize the CPU parallelism. Other later systems such as X100 [4] and Vectorwise [41] introduce vector processing capability to exploit the CPU parallelism. More recently, pipelined query processing has been explored on multi-core CPU [6] and NUMA architectures [22]. Particularly, Leis et al. proposes a morsel-driven query execution engine by dividing the input data into "morsels" as the basic scheduling unit and assigning them to each "worker" to exploit the thread parallelism. Our pipelined execution is similar to morsels and X100. Our work differs from theirs in two major aspects. First, the pipelined execution of GPL relies on kernels/primitives explicitly connected with channels, rather than a basic pipeline of operators. Second, GPL takes advantage of GPU hardware features, while their study does not. On the other hand, their study [22] targets at multi-core and NUMA systems and most techniques cannot be adopted into GPL. For example, preemption adopted in their study is not supported at current GPUs.

With the growing demands for concurrent query processing, identifying the opportunity of pipelining parallelism among many concurrent queries becomes an effective means to improve the query processing throughput. Harizopoulos et al. [11] designed a novel operator-centric relational query processing engine QPipe that can maximize the data and workload sharing among queries. Pandis et al. [26] designed DORA to decompose each transaction into smaller units and each unit is assigned to cores based on data locality. Both studies [11] and [26] try to achieve higher performance on CPUs by improving data sharing and data locality. With similar spirit on pipelined execution, GPL is specifically designed with the GPU hardware features in mind, to achieve higher resource utilization on GPUs. Giceva et al. [8] proposed a novel deployment algorithm to multi-core systems, by considering the behaviors of individual database operators and dataflow information. DataPath [2] introduces a novel push based data centric approach for CPUs. Different from previous studies, this paper advocates efficient pipelined execution on the GPU by taking advantage of emerging GPU features.

Query Co-Processing on GPUs. Query co-processing on GPUs has attracted much research attentions in recent years. He et al. [14, 13] conduct systematic studies on the implementations and optimizations of a query co-processing engine on GPUs. The same group further extends the study to coupled CPU-GPU architectures such as AMD Fusion [15, 16]. Yuan et al. [37] conducted a comprehensive study of complex database queries with different software optimizations and hardware configurations. A follow-up paper from the authors [35] proposed a prototype system to share GPU resources among multiple queries to improve system throughput. Recently, Pirk et al. [28] proposed a novel strategy to exploit GPUs in query co-processing. In their proposal, approximate results are first calculated on the GPU, and then the intermediate results are further refined on the CPU. Heimel et al. [18] developed a database engine based on a set of hardware-oblivious operators written in OpenCL to achieve cross-platform capability with minimal performance loss. Ocelot is built on top of MonetDB [19], which is an in-memory column based database. However, it does not support pipelined executions on the GPU. Jason et al. [30] studied a set of database primitives on the integrated GPU of a coupled architecture and show that transparent access to CPU virtual addresses and very low overhead of computation offloading are important for query co-processing performance. Heimel et al. [17] proposed a accelerated solution to quickly and accurately estimate the selectivity of multi-dimensional predicates. All the previous studies use the kernel-based execution which has performance pitfalls, as shown in Section 2. To the best of our knowledge, GPL is the first pipelined query execution engine on GPUs.

7. CONCLUSIONS

In this paper, we propose a novel GPU-based pipelined query execution engine (GPL) on GPUs to address low device utilization problem of existing query processing engines on GPUs. Specifically, we leverage emerging capabilities of GPUs, including channels and concurrent kernel execution, for the efficiency of pipelined query execution. The data channel is placed between two neighbouring kernels to reduce the data transfer overhead and enables a finer-grained concurrent kernel executions. We further propose an analytical model to determine the optimal system configurations such as tile size and resource allocation. We have conducted the experiments with TPC-H queries on both AMD and NVIDIA GPUs. The results show that GPL can significantly improve the query processing performance over the state-of-the-art kernel-based approaches, with improvement up to 48% on the AMD GPU.

Acknowledgement

This work is in part supported by Singapore Ministry of Education Academic Research Fund Tier 2 under Grant MOE2012-T2-2-067.

8. REFERENCES

[1] A. Ailamaki, D. J. DeWitt, M. D. Hill, and D. A. Wood. Dbmss on a modern processor: Where does time go? In *Proceedings of the 25th International Conference on Very Large Data Bases*, VLDB '99, pages 266–277, San Francisco, CA, USA, 1999. Morgan Kaufmann Publishers Inc.

[2] S. Arumugam, A. Dobra, C. M. Jermaine, N. Pansare, and L. Perez. The datapath system: A data-centric analytic processing engine for large data warehouses. In *SIGMOD*, 2010.

[3] C. Balkesen, J. Teubner, G. Alonso, and M. T. ÃŰzsu. Main-memory hash joins on multi-core CPUs: Tuning to the underlying hardware. In *Data Engineering (ICDE), 2013 IEEE 29th International Conference on*, pages 362–373, April 2013.

[4] P. A. Boncz, M. Zukowski, and N. Nes. Monetdb/x100: Hyper-pipelining query execution. *Conference on Innovative Data Systems Research (CIDR)*, 2005.

[5] Z. Chen, J. Xu, J. Tang, K. Kwiat, and C. Kamhoua. G-storm: GPU-enabled high-throughput online data processing in storm. In *Big Data (Big Data), 2015 IEEE International Conference on*, pages 307–312, Oct 2015.

[6] Y. Cheng and F. Rusu. Parallel in-situ data processing with speculative loading. In *SIGMOD*. ACM, 2014.

[7] J. Cieslewicz, W. Mee, and K. A. Ross. Cache-conscious buffering for database operators with state. In *Proceedings of the Fifth International Workshop on Data Management on New Hardware*, DaMoN '09, New York, NY, USA, 2009.

[8] J. Giceva, G. Alonso, T. Roscoe, and T. Harris. Deployment of query plans on multicores. *Proc. VLDB Endow.*, 8(3):233–244, Nov. 2014.

[9] N. K. Govindaraju, B. Lloyd, Y. Dotsenko, B. Smith, and J. Manferdelli. High performance discrete fourier transforms on graphics processors. In *Proceedings of the 2008 ACM/IEEE Conference on Supercomputing*, SC '08, Piscataway, NJ, USA, 2008.

[10] G. Graefe. Volcano - an extensible and parallel query evaluation system. *IEEE Trans. on Knowl. and Data Eng.*, 1994.

[11] S. Harizopoulos, V. Shkapenyuk, and A. Ailamaki. QPipe: A simultaneously pipelined relational query engine. In *SIGMOD*, 2005.

[12] B. He, W. Fang, Q. Luo, N. K. Govindaraju, and T. Wang. Mars: A mapreduce framework on graphics processors. In *Proceedings of the 17th International Conference on Parallel Architectures and Compilation Techniques*, PACT '08, pages 260–269, New York, NY, USA, 2008. ACM.

[13] B. He, M. Lu, K. Yang, R. Fang, N. K. Govindaraju, Q. Luo, and P. V. Sander. Relational query coprocessing on graphics processors. *ACM Trans. Database Syst.*, 34(4):21:1–21:39, Dec. 2009.

[14] B. He, K. Yang, R. Fang, M. Lu, N. Govindaraju, Q. Luo, and P. Sander. Relational joins on graphics processors. In *Proceedings of the 2008 ACM SIGMOD International Conference on Management of Data*, SIGMOD '08, pages 511–524, New York, NY, USA, 2008. ACM.

[15] J. He, M. Lu, and B. He. Revisiting co-processing for hash joins on the coupled CPU-GPU architecture. *Proc. VLDB Endow.*, 6(10):889–900, Aug. 2013.

[16] J. He, S. Zhang, and B. He. In-cache query co-processing on coupled CPU-GPU architectures. *Proc. VLDB Endow.*, 8(4):329–340, Dec. 2014.

[17] M. Heimel, M. Kiefer, and V. Markl. Self-tuning, GPU-accelerated kernel density models for multidimensional selectivity estimation. In *Proceedings of the 2015 ACM SIGMOD International Conference on Management of Data*, SIGMOD '15, New York, NY, USA, 2015.

[18] M. Heimel, M. Saecker, H. Pirk, S. Manegold, and V. Markl. Hardware-oblivious parallelism for in-memory column-stores. *Proc. VLDB Endow.*, 6(9):709–720, July 2013.

[19] S. Idreos, F. Groffen, N. Nes, S. Manegold, K. S. Mullender, and M. L. Kersten. Monetdb: Two decades of research in column-oriented database architectures. *IEEE Data Engineering Bulletin*, 35(1), 2012.

[20] S. Jha, B. He, M. Lu, X. Cheng, and H. P. Huynh. Improving main memory hash joins on intel xeon phi processors: An experimental approach. *Proc. VLDB Endow.*, 8(6):642–653, Feb. 2015.

[21] R. Kallman, H. Kimura, J. Natkins, A. Pavlo, A. Rasin, S. Zdonik, E. P. C. Jones, S. Madden, M. Stonebraker, Y. Zhang, J. Hugg, and D. J. Abadi. H-Store: A high-performance, distributed main memory transaction processing system. *Proc. VLDB Endow.*, 1(2), Aug. 2008.

[22] V. Leis, P. Boncz, A. Kemper, and T. Neumann. Morsel-driven parallelism: A numa-aware query evaluation framework for the many-core age. In *Proceedings of the 2014 ACM SIGMOD International Conference on Management of Data*, SIGMOD '14, pages 743–754, New York, NY, USA, 2014. ACM.

[23] G. Luo, J. F. Naughton, C. J. Ellmann, and M. W. Watzke. Toward a progress indicator for database queries. In *Proceedings of the 2004 ACM SIGMOD International Conference on Management of Data*, SIGMOD '04, New York, NY, USA, 2004. ACM.

[24] S. Manegold, P. A. Boncz, and M. L. Kersten. Optimizing database architecture for the new bottleneck: Memory access. *The VLDB Journal*, 9(3), Dec. 2000.

[25] J. D. Owens, D. Luebke, N. Govindaraju, M. Harris, J. KrÃijger, A. Lefohn, and T. J. Purcell. A survey of general-purpose computation on graphics hardware. *Computer Graphics Forum*, 2007.

[26] I. Pandis, R. Johnson, N. Hardavellas, and A. Ailamaki. Data-oriented transaction execution. *Proc. VLDB Endow.*, 3(1-2), Sept. 2010.

[27] H. Pirk, F. Funke, M. Grund, T. Neumann, U. Leser, S. Manegold, A. Kemper, and M. Kersten. CPU and cache efficient management of memory-resident databases. In *Data Engineering (ICDE), 2013 IEEE 29th International Conference on*, pages 14–25, April 2013.

[28] H. Pirk, S. Manegold, and M. Kersten. Waste not... efficient co-processing of relational data. In *2014 IEEE 30th International Conference on Data Engineering*, March 2014.

[29] O. Polychroniou, A. Raghavan, and K. A. Ross. Rethinking simd vectorization for in-memory databases. In *Proceedings of the 2015 ACM SIGMOD International Conference on Management of Data*, SIGMOD '15, pages 1493–1508, New York, NY, USA, 2015. ACM.

[30] J. Power, Y. Li, M. D. Hill, J. M. Patel, and D. A. Wood. Toward GPUs being mainstream in analytic processing: An initial argument using simple scan-aggregate queries. In *Proceedings of the 11th International Workshop on Data Management on New Hardware*, DaMoN'15, 2015.

[31] M. Saecker. Ocelot: A Hardware-Oblivious Database Engine. https://bitbucket.org/msaecker/monetdb-opencl.

[32] P. G. Selinger, M. M. Astrahan, D. D. Chamberlin, R. A. Lorie, and T. G. Price. Access path selection in a relational database management system. In *Proceedings of the 1979 ACM SIGMOD International Conference on Management of Data*, SIGMOD '79, 1979.

[33] A. Shatdal, C. Kant, and J. F. Naughton. Cache conscious algorithms for relational query processing. In *Proceedings of the 20th International Conference on Very Large Data Bases*, VLDB '94, pages 510–521, San Francisco, CA, USA, 1994. Morgan Kaufmann Publishers Inc.

[34] K.-L. Tan, Q. Cai, B. C. Ooi, W.-F. Wong, C. Yao, and H. Zhang. In-memory databases: Challenges and opportunities from software and hardware perspectives. *SIGMOD Rec.*, Aug. 2015.

[35] K. Wang, K. Zhang, Y. Yuan, S. Ma, R. Lee, X. Ding, and X. Zhang. Concurrent analytical query processing with GPUs. *Proc. VLDB Endow.*, July 2014.

[36] H. Wu, G. Diamos, T. Sheard, M. Aref, S. Baxter, M. Garland, and S. Yalamanchili. Red fox: An execution environment for relational query processing on GPUs. In *Proceedings of Annual IEEE/ACM International Symposium on Code Generation and Optimization*, CGO '14, pages 44:44–44:54, New York, NY, USA, 2014. ACM.

[37] Y. Yuan, R. Lee, and X. Zhang. The yin and yang of processing data warehousing queries on GPU devices. *Proc. VLDB Endow.*, 6(10):817–828, Aug. 2013.

[38] H. Zhang, G. Chen, B. C. Ooi, K. L. Tan, and M. Zhang. In-memory big data management and processing: A survey. *IEEE Transactions on Knowledge and Data Engineering*, 27(7):1920–1948, July 2015.

[39] K. Zhang, K. Wang, Y. Yuan, L. Guo, R. Lee, and X. Zhang. Mega-kv: A case for GPUs to maximize the throughput of in-memory key-value stores. *Proc. VLDB Endow.*, 8(11):1226–1237, July 2015.

[40] S. Zhang, J. He, B. He, and M. Lu. OmniDB: Towards portable and efficient query processing on parallel CPU/GPU architectures. *Proc. VLDB Endow.*, Aug. 2013.

[41] M. Zukowski, M. van de Wiel, and P. Boncz. Vectorwise: A vectorized analytical dbms. In *Data Engineering (ICDE), 2012 IEEE 28th International Conference on*, pages 1349–1350, April 2012.

APPENDIX

A. GPL ON NVIDIA GPU

As in case of the AMD GPU, the latest GPUs from NVIDIA (Fermi or Kepler architectures) have also been enabled with concurrent kernel execution capability so that multiple kernels can be executed on the same GPU simultaneously. They also have the ability to pass data directely from one kernel to another via Direct Data Transfer (DDT) [5]. All the techiques used by GPL on AMD GPU are applicable to NVIDIA GPU as well. To demonstrate that GPL works on platforms other than the AMD GPU mentioned in Section 5.1 we evaluate the performance of GPL on a NVIDIA GPU (Tesla K40) which is connected to the CPU with PCI-e 3.0 and has 12GB device memory. The data is initially loaded to the GPU and the cost of PCI-e data transfer overhead is omitted. The experimental results show that GPL is able to outperform existing kernel-based query processing approaches with performance improvement up to 47% on the NVIDIA GPU.

In Section A.1, we describe the relationship between channel configuration and throughput on NVIDIA GPU. Section A.2 describes how our analytical model (Section 4) can be adapted to NVIDIA GPU. Finally, we present our experimental results on NVIDIA GPU in Section A.3.

A.1 Kernel Communication on NVIDIA GPU

As mentioned in Section 2.1, calibration experiments were conducted to have an in-depth understanding on relationship between channel configurations and the throughput on the Telsa K40 GPU. Unlike the AMD GPU, the NVIDIA GPU do not need users to set the packet size. The results are shown in Figure 23, where N is varied from 512K to 8 million on the NVIDIA GPU. As seen in Section 2.1, we find that both parameters of kernel communication configurations can affect the throughput significantly.

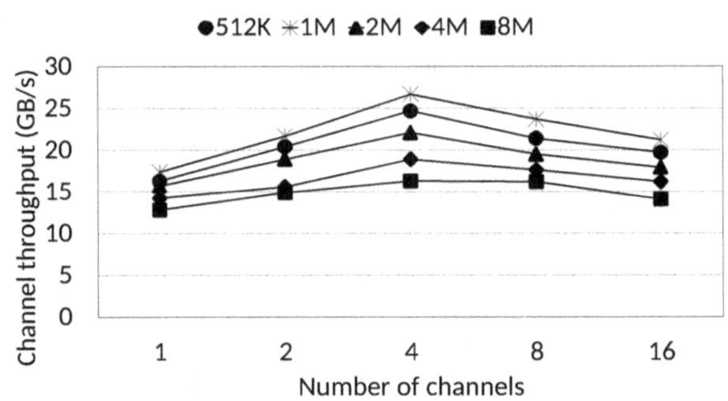

Figure 23: The relationship between kernel communication configurations and throughput on K40 GPU for a packet size of 16 bytes.

A.2 Model for NVIDIA GPU

The model described in Section 4.1 can be extended to NVIDIA GPU easily. The amount of private/local memory usage of each work item in NVIDIA GPU is obtained using the NVIDIA CUDA Occupancy Calculator. To adapt the cost model to NVIDIA GPU, only the data channel-related equations need to be modified accordingly. Specifically, the only parameters that can affect the throughput in of NVIDIA GPU are: (1) number of channels, (2) data size to be passed. Therefore as seen in Section 4.1 the relationship between them can be formulated as Eq. 11.

$$T = \Gamma(n, d) \tag{11}$$

The global memory access overhead in Eq. 6 is also adapted accordingly based on the adapted channel throughput.

$$m\_K_i = \frac{\Delta \times \lambda_{K_i}}{\Gamma(n_{max}, \Delta \times \lambda_{K_i})}, \forall K_i \in (K - set\_l \cup set\_b) \tag{12}$$

A.3 Experimental Evaluation

We experiment with TPC-H queries to evaluate the efficiency and effectiveness of GPL and our analytical model. We use the NVIDIA Visual Profiler to obtain values of the hardware counters on the NVIDIA GPU.

A.3.1 Model Evaluation

Figure 24 shows the *relative error* (defined in Section 5.2) made by the model for all tested queries with the optimal configuration. The relative error in the execution time estimation done by the model is very small for NVIDIA GPU as well. Taking Q8 as an example, we present the results for 1) the relationship between tile sizes and overall query processing performance; 2) the relationship between resource allocations (number of work-groups assigned to each kernel) and delay cost, on NVIDIA GPU. Figure 25 shows the relative error in estimating the optimal tile size and Figure 26 shows the change in runtime when we vary the tile size from 256KB to 16MB while the other parameters are fixed to their default values. These results show that our cost model is able to estimate the optimal tile size accurately (as indicated by the star) with very small relative error (Figure 26).

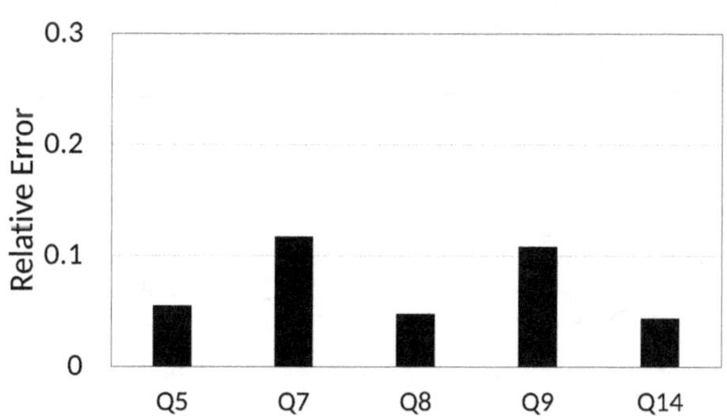

Figure 24: Relative error in GPL runtime estimation.

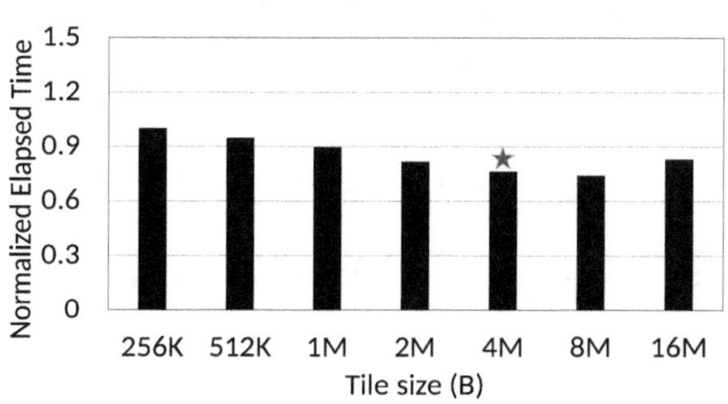

Figure 25: The overall query processing performance with varying tile sizes (Q8) on NVIDIA GPU.

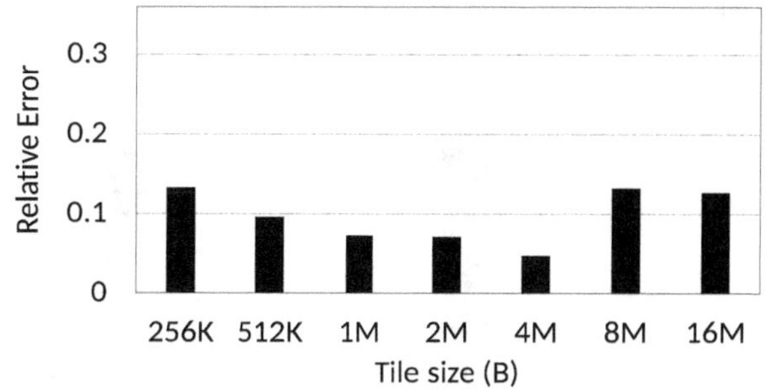

Figure 26: The overall query processing performance with varying tile sizes (Q8) on NVIDIA GPU.

We also study the impact of the number of work-groups on NVIDIA GPU. The results are simliar to those on the AMD GPU.

A.3.2 Evaluation of GPL

Runtime Comparison. Figure 27 show the runtime results for the TPC-H queries on NVIDIA GPU. It shows the runtime of GPL with concurrent execution enabled and GPL without concurrent execution. For better presentation, we normalize the execution time of every query with runtime of the KBE version of the same query. If tiling is applied without concurrent kernel execution then the queries show up to 1.15 times performance degradation on NVIDIA GPU. This is due to both insufficient data parallelism as well as due to the overhead incurred by frequent kernel launches which in turn is a result of input data tiling without using concurrent kernel execution. In GPL, both concurrent kernel execution and input data tiling are both applied together. The results show that GPL outperforms KBE by 50% on NVIDIA GPU.

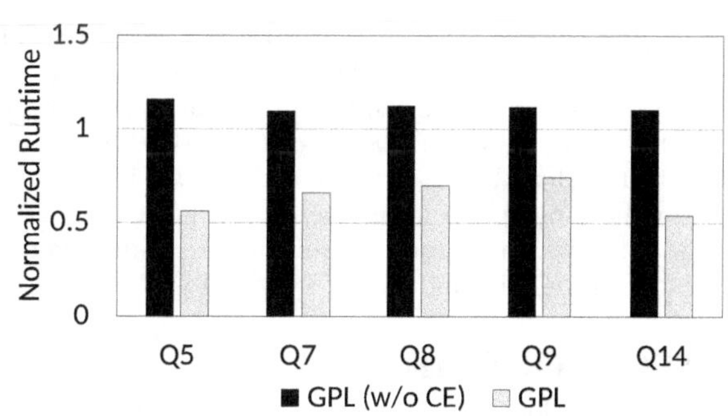

Figure 27: GPL execution time normalized to KBE on the NVIDIA GPU.

Resource Utilization. We take Q8 as an example to demonstrate higher resource utilization achieved by GPL on NVIDIA GPU. Figure 28 shows the average resource utilization achieved by both KBE and GPL for Q8 on the NVIDIA GPU. These results clearly shows that GPL is able to achieve higher average utilization of both memory and computational units when compared to KBE, on NVIDIA GPU.

Communication overhead. To examine the communication overhead among kernels on NVIDIA GPU, we show the breakdown of query execution time for Q8 in Figure 29. For GPL, the data channel access cost (*DC_cost*) and *Delay* cost existing in pipelines are included into total query execution time as mentioned in Section 5.3.1. In GPL communication

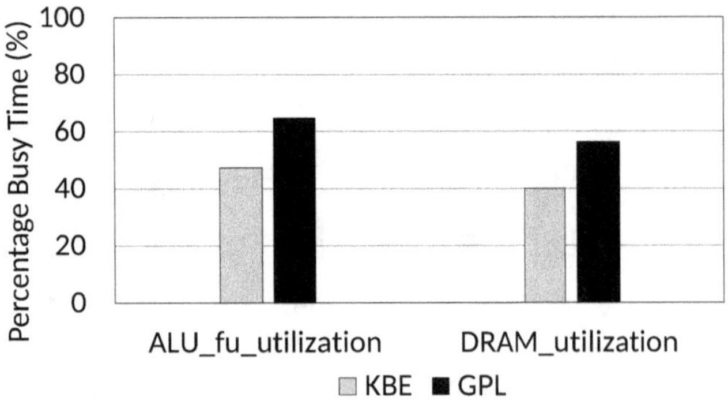

Figure 28: Improved GPU resource utilization (Q8) on the NVIDIA GPU.

cost is only 18% of the total execution time while in KBE it can go up to 32%.

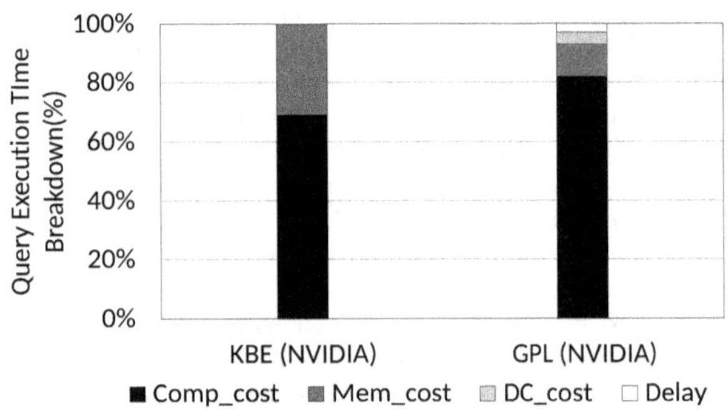

Figure 29: Improved GPU resource utilization (Q8) on the NVIDIA GPU.

Varying data sizes. GPL was also tested against KBE for different data sizes by varying the scale factor from 0.1 to 10 (Figures are omitted). The results are similar to those on the AMD GPU. When data size is small (100MB) GPL is only slightly faster than KBE. This is because an input which is too small cannot provide sufficient data level parallelism. Still, as data size increases, the performance improvement of GPL over KBE also increases.

B. TPC-H QUERIES

Since Ocelot does not support non-trivial string operations and multi-column sort, we used slightly modified versions of Q7, and Q9 to compare with Ocelot. Other queries are the same as those in the previous study [18]. The TPC-H queries used for comparison are given in Listings 2–6.

```
SELECT n_name,
    sum(l_extendedprice * (1 - l_discount)) as
         revenue
from customer, orders, lineitem, supplier, nation,
     region
where c_custkey = o_custkey
    and l_orderkey = o_orderkey
    and l_suppkey = s_suppkey
    and c_nationkey = s_nationkey
    and s_nationkey = n_nationkey
    and n_regionkey = r_regionkey
    and r_name = 'ASIA'
    and o_orderdate >= date '1994-01-01'
    and o_orderdate < date '1995-01-01'
group by n_name
order by revenue desc
```

Listing 2: Query 5

```
select supp_nation, cust_nation, l_year,
     sum(volume) as revenue
from ( select n1.n_name as supp_nation,
     n2.n_name as cust_nation,
     extract(year from l_shipdate) as l_year,
     l_extendedprice * (1 - l_discount) as volume
from supplier, lineitem, orders, customer, nation n1,
      nation n2
where s_suppkey = l_suppkey
    and o_orderkey = l_orderkey
    and c_custkey = o_custkey
    and s_nationkey = n1.n_nationkey
    and c_nationkey = n2.n_nationkey
    and ((n1.n_name='FRANCE' and n2.n_name='GERMANY')
    or (n1.n_name='GERMANY' and n2.n_name='FRANCE'))
    and l_shipdate between date '1995-01-01'
    and date '1996-12-31') as shipping
group by supp_nation, cust_nation, l_year
order by l_year
```

Listing 3: Query 7

```
select o_year, sum(case when nation = 'BRAZIL' then
    volume else 0 end) / sum(volume) as mkt_share
from (
    select extract(year from o_orderdate) as o_year,
         l_extendedprice * (1 - l_discount) as volume,
          n2.n_name as nation
    from part, supplier, lineitem, orders, customer,
         nation n1, nation n2, region
    where p_partkey = l_partkey
          and s_suppkey = l_suppkey
          and l_orderkey = o_orderkey
          and o_custkey = c_custkey
          and c_nationkey = n1.n_nationkey
          and n1.n_regionkey = r_regionkey
          and r_name = 'AMERICA'
          and s_nationkey = n2.n_nationkey
          and o_orderdate between date '1995-01-01'
          and date '1996-12-31'
          and p_type = 'ECONOMY␣ANODIZED␣STEEL'
) as all_nations
group by o_year
order by o_year
```

Listing 4: Query 8

```
select nation, o_year, sum(amount) as sum_profit
from (
    select n_name as nation, extract(year from
         o_orderdate) as o_year, l_extendedprice * (1
         - l_discount) - ps_supplycost * l_quantity as
          amount
    from part, supplier, lineitem, partsupp, orders,
         nation
    where s_suppkey = l_suppkey
          and ps_suppkey = l_suppkey
          and ps_partkey = l_partkey
          and p_partkey = l_partkey
          and o_orderkey = l_orderkey
          and s_nationkey = n_nationkey
          and p_partKey < 1000
) as profit
group by nation, o_year
order by o_year desc
```

Listing 5: Query 9

```
select 100.00 * sum(case when p_partKey then
     l_extendedprice * (1 - l_discount) else 0 end) /
     sum(l_extendedprice * (1 - l_discount)) as
     promo_revenue
from lineitem, part
where l_partkey = p_partkey
      and l_shipdate >= date '1995-09-01'
      and l_shipdate < date '1995-10-01'
```

Listing 6: Query 14

Towards a Hybrid Design for Fast Query Processing in DB2 with BLU Acceleration Using Graphical Processing Units: A Technology Demonstration

Sina Meraji #1, Berni Schiefer *2, Lan Pham *3, Lee Chu *4, Peter Kokosielis *5, Adam Storm *6

Cloud Innovation Lab, IBM Canada Ltd.
1 sinamera@ca.ibm.com

* *IBM DB2, IBM Canada Ltd.*
2 schiefer@ca.ibm.com
3 lpham@ca.ibm.com
4 leechu@ca.ibm.com
5 pkolosie@ca.ibm.com
6 ajstorm@ca.ibm.com

ABSTRACT

In this paper, we show how we use Nvidia GPUs and host CPU cores for faster query processing in a DB2 database using BLU Acceleration (DB2's column store technology). Moreover, we show the benef ts and problems of using hardware accelerators (more specif cally GPUs) in a real commercial Relational Database Management System (RDBMS). We investigate the effect of off-loading specif c database operations to a GPU, and show how doing so results in a signif cant performance improvement. We then demonstrate that for some queries, using just CPU to perform the entire operation is more benef cial. While we use some of Nvidia's fast kernels for operations like sort, we have also developed our own high performance kernels for operations such as group by and aggregation. Finally, we show how we use a dynamic design that can make use of optimizer metadata to intelligently choose a GPU kernel to run. For the f rst time in the literature, we use benchmarks representative of customer environments to gauge the performance of our prototype, the results of which show that we can get a speed increase upwards of 2x, using a realistic set of queries.

CCS Concepts

•Information systems → Query optimization;

Keywords

Query Optimization, GPU, DB2 BLU, Group by, Aggregation, Heterogeneous system

SIGMOD'16, June 26-July 01, 2016, San Francisco, CA, USA

DOI: http://dx.doi.org/10.1145/2882903.2903735

1. INTRODUCTION

In-memory columnar relational database management systems (RDBMSes) have been shown to be very performant for analytic query processing, as they can use the massive parallel processing of multi-core processors to quickly respond to user queries. As a result, in-memory columnar RDBMSes exist from multiple vendors, including HP (Vertica), SAP (HANA), Microsoft (SQL Server) and IBM (DB2). It has also been shown that hardware accelerators like GPUs, FPGAs and custom design ASICSs can be used to improve the performance of various applications [4, 5, 6, 7, 9, 11, 12, 13, 16, 24] . With that understanding, we have demonstrated two main achievements from our work. The f rst is to show that we can improve DB2 BLU query performance by using Nvidia GPUs. Improving performance through the use of a hardware accelerator requires some major changes in the software. As a result, our second achievement is the illustration of some of the challenges that arise when integrating such accelerators into a commercial database.

GPUs, such as those from Nvidia, are programmable hardware accelerators that provide massive parallel computing power. While GPUs have traditionally been used mostly for graphical applications, today's database applications (such as DB2 BLU) can exploit GPUs to off oad CPU computing intensive operations to run on the GPUs. The main goals of using GPUs for query processing in DB2 BLU are:

- Utilizing the massive parallel computing capability of GPU for DB2 engine operations that can be executed in parallel, thus reducing the runtime of such queries.
- Freeing up CPU cycles by off-loading CPU intensive operations to run in the GPU. The savings in CPU cycles can be applied to other running tasks in the system. This benef ts multiple concurrent user scenarios where the CPU savings from one query (while running in the GPU) can be applied to other running queries.

The amount of speed up we can achieve by using GPUs depends on the complexity of the operation, the size of the data, as well as the percentage of time the query spends within the costly operations such as sort, group by, aggregation, and join over the entire query.

Using GPUs to improve the performance of specif c database operations such as sort [6, 9, 11, 22], join[12, 13, 14], indexing[16, 17], compression[8, 19], and selection[10, 25] have been studied in various literature. Also techniques in [20] can be utilized for GPU aggregation operations. Moreover, [23] shows how GPUs can provide a cost-effective computing platform to support processing of large amounts of data streamed into a push-based database system. Based on this, the authors also provide some recommendations on how to design a query processing engine for such systems that run on GPUs. In [26] the authors show very preliminary work on a kernel- adapter based database engine named OmniDB which uses both the CPU and the GPU for query processing. [15] designs a database system that can eff ciently exploit highly heterogeneous hardware environments. The main contributions of our paper, in relation to previous work, are:

1. **Performance benef ts to using GPUs in conjunction with CPUs**- We demonstrate a design that uses both Nvidia GPUs and CPU cores for fast processing of database operations such as group by, aggregation and sort. In our design we show a hybrid approach that performs portions of the query processing in the CPU, and then uses the GPU to process certain compute intensive parts of the query.

2. **Eff cient integration of the Nvidia GPU to DB2 BLU run time**- One of the main bottlenecks in hardware accelerating our queries is in coming up with a data format that the accelerators can process eff ciently. This requires copying data to the hardware accelerator's memory, which would be the primary penalty to be paid. In our design however, we ensure we have the same number of data copies in our prototype as in the original DB2 BLU product. We also design our GPU kernels such that they can process DB2 BLU data with minimum conversion cost.

3. **Using heuristics to intelligently process queries**- That is, at runtime we can decide to use either the CPU, GPU, or both. We also use the meta-data which is generated during initial processing of query at DB2 BLU runtime, to tune/optimize the size of data structures on the GPU on-chip memory. To the best of our knowledge, none of the existing approaches use runtime meta-data to tune the size of data structures on the GPU.

4. **Multiple group by/aggregation GPU kernels**- In our design we have different group by/aggregation kernels while functionally these kernels perform the same operation, each kernel suits a specif c type of query. None of the existing techniques allows an accelerator kernel to be dynamically selected at runtime. We have implemented a software moderator that can intelligently make this decision at runtime based on factors such as the number of groups, the number of payloads, and the ratio of rows to number of groups. Moreover, if we have enough compute resources and memory on the GPU, we can use more than one kernel to execute the same query at the same time.

5. **Scheduling tasks across multiple GPUs**- We have built a simple scheduler which lets the DB2 BLU run time schedule tasks on the different GPUs. The scheduler takes into account parameters such as the resources required by the task and the resources currently available by each of the GPUs. This allows for f exibility in terms of hardware conf gurations, as the GPUs do not need to be homogenous in their specif cations.

The rest of this paper is organized as follows. In section 2 we discuss how we have changed the DB2 BLU engine to add support for Nvidia GPUs. Section 3 explains how we use a hybrid design to use both CPU and GPU for sorting. Fast group by/aggregation GPU kernels are studied in section 4. Section 5 shows our performance result on some standard benchmarks. Finally, section 6 concludes with our thoughts on the future of GPU acceleration in databases.

2. DB2 BLU WITH GPU INFRASTRUCTURE

In order to integrate the Nvidia GPUs to DB2 BLU, we need to make infrastructure changes in the DB2 BLU runtime code. The main components that are added to the DB2 BLU engine are: 1) memory management unit 2) support for multiple GPU devices 3) performance monitoring. We will brief y describe all three components in the following section.

2.1 Memory Management Unit

In this section we explain the changes we have made in DB2 BLU memory management unit to add GPU support.

2.1.1 Device Memory Reservation

Device memory reservation is important when there are multiple concurrent tasks (threads or processes) that request device memory from the same GPU device at the same time. If there are multiple concurrent tasks all entering GPU kernel execution at the same time, the contention for device memory between these tasks could lead to a memory allocation error during task execution. In such a scenario, the calling function would have to enter the expensive error code path to handle the out of memory error and roll back the operation to a consistent point, and then retry the operation. Moreover, implementing a memory reservation system would allow a GPU operation to complete if it could successfully satisfy all of its memory needs up front. We have implemented a simple memory reservation approach in which we track device memory usage by all consumers on a given GPU device, such that a task can query and reserve memory up front before proceeding to run the devices kernel code. Once the GPU kernel code execution is f nished, the reserved memory is released for use by other tasks. If a task fails to reserve the memory, it can then either 1) wait until device memory becomes available or 2) fall back and run the task on the CPU (host).

2.1.2 Host Memory Registration

Data transfers (memory copying) between the host and the GPU device can be very expensive if the memory is not registered (pinned) with the GPU device up front. If the host memory is registered with the GPU device, then the speed of data transfers from registered host memory can be more than 4X faster than the speed of data transfer from unregistered memory using PCI-e gen 3. For this reason, all memory that is allocated for GPU operations is preregistered with the GPU device(s) during the DB2 BLU start up phase. Registering the individual memory block can be very expensive. As a result, it is preferable to avoid the registration on each invocation of the kernel call. With our approach, the registration of all required memory is thus performed up front, using a single large memory segment. This allows subsequent memory requests on each kernel invocation to be accommodated through an allocation from this single large (registered) memory segment. When the GPU kernel f nishes its work and returns, the allocated memory is returned to the free pool of registered memory.

2.2 Support for Multiple GPU Devices

Our design supports multiple GPU devices by distributing workload to all of the available devices. To allow for good distribution, we must first track the number of outstanding jobs that are currently executing on the GPU devices, as well as track the amount of available memory on each device. In addition, we know the amount of memory that each kernel invocation call needs in advance. This can be calculated using the type of the query, size of the input data, and size of the internal data structures needed in the GPUs memory to perform the operation. After calculating the total memory size that a kernel invocation needs, we consult the GPUs to see if any of them has enough free resources to execute the given kernel call.

Supporting multiple GPU devices is highly important for 1) large workloads where the data set exceeds any single device's memory limit, and 2) scenarios in which multiple concurrent users are running on the system. In the case of large workloads, the input data is partitioned (typically using range partitioning) into multiple smaller chunks, and these smaller chunks are sent to some number of available GPU devices, to be operated on concurrently. The results are then merged together in the final step and returned back to the user. In the case of multiple concurrent users whose queries are able to exploit the GPUs, the set of queries can be scheduled to run on all GPUs and therefore fully utilize all available resources on the host.

2.3 Performance Monitoring

Monitoring the time spent inside the GPU and the time spent transferring data to and from the GPU is very important. This profiling information is mainly used to tune the kernel code in an effort to improve performance. In addition, this monitoring information can be used to optimize the implementation and therefore reduce the amount of data transferred between the host and the GPU device.

While there are existing tools (such as Nvidia's nvidia-smi tool) to monitor overall GPU performance and memory usage, they cannot profile detailed information about a GPU that is integrated to an existing application, which is the case in our implementation. As a result, we were forced to implement our own performance monitoring tooling. Our performance monitoring tool for the GPU is integrated with the existing DB2 BLU performance monitoring infrastructure and provides detailed information about the GPU related calls and kernels. This monitoring tooling was then used to tune the performance of the GPU kernels so that they could be compared with their CPU implementations.

3. OFFLOADING SORT DATA TO GPU

The DB2 BLU sort code receives incoming tuples for each column that is to be sorted. These tuples are stored in memory in a structure known as the Sort Data Store (SDS), which we refer to as the SDS buckets. Data in the SDS buckets remains unmodified and never moves during the sort. Since these tuples could be quite large, we do not want our swap operations during the sorting phase to have to move them around in memory. Instead, we have an intermediate structure that we call the partial key buffer.

Each partial key buffer entry consists of a 4 byte key and a 4 byte payload. The key is a partial binary sortable representation of the column that is being sorted, and subsequent fetches of the next partial key may be required to determine the final ordering. The payload is a pointer into the SDS bucket for the corresponding tuple. The payload is able to grow larger than 4 bytes, in cases where 4 bytes is not enough to address the number of rows in the SDS buckets.

DB2 BLU sort uses a job queuing system to represent each sorting task. Initially there is only one job, which represents the entire data set. When a job is started, it is taken off the queue and the host will generate (in parallel) a set of partial keys and payloads and populate the partial key buffer with this information. The DB2 BLU engine then determines if the job is a candidate for a GPU sort, based on the number of tuples in the job. For instance, if the number of input tuples is very small, there is no benefit in forwarding the sort job over to the GPU because the combined cost of the transfer time plus processing time overshadows the performance savings we would have gained from using the GPU to sort the job.

Though multiple threads are used to generate partial keys and payloads on the host side, only a single thread is needed to dispatch the job to the GPU. As explained in section 2-2, a scheduling algorithm is used to determine the GPU to which the job will be dispatched. Once a CPU thread has been chosen to dispatch the job to the GPU, the remaining CPU threads for this job are released since their work is complete. These released threads will process the next available job on the queue. We use the GPU Duane sort kernel[18] provided by Nvidia to perform the sort operation in the GPU. When the GPU returns from processing, it will have sorted the partial key buffer based upon the 4-byte partial key. This of course does not represent a completely sorted data set, since all we know up to this point is a partial ordering based upon the first 4 bytes. If there exists more than one tuple for which the first 4 bytes are identical, the next set of partial keys needs to be generated. We call such a group of tuples a duplicate range, which the GPU identifies for us. A new job is created for each duplicate range and is placed on the job queue. The sort is complete when there are no more jobs on the queue.

The job queuing system that we have in place is flexible to allow for concurrent jobs to be executed both by the GPU and the CPU. This allows for a truly hybrid sorting system and lets the host perform sorting where it does not make sense for the GPU to do so, such as for a small number of rows. This also facilitates load balancing where more threads can be directed at certain jobs.

Another feature of our sort design is that it is not dependent on the data type of the column being sorted, as we have transformed the underlying type into a binary stream that is sorted on 4 bytes at a time. Moreover, we have a merge free sort algorithm that uses both the CPU and GPU for sorting. Merging is a very costly step in all the sort algorithms that have a merge step. In our design, we remove the merging step by making conflict free partitions before sending sort jobs to the GPU.

4. GROUP BY / AGGREGATION

We have designed a hybrid hash-based group by/aggregation algorithm that utilizes features of DB2 BLU and Nvidia GPUs for fast query processing. Group by/aggregation can be very costly in all RDBMSes when there are a large number of grouping columns/keys and/or aggregation functions. However, for queries with a small number of input rows, using the GPU would be slower when compared to using only the CPU. One of the advantages of our design is that we can dynamically decide where to execute a group by/aggregation query based on its runtime features. In order to have these features, we made changes in the execution chain of group by/aggregation queries.

In all hardware accelerators, there are a limited (but usually large) number of compute resources. Knowing the query requirements in advance has a lot of benefits. We can 1) check to see if we have enough free resources on the GPU to execute the same query with different types of kernels 2) choose a suitable GPU kernel dynamically at run time. In addition, if we have enough resources on the

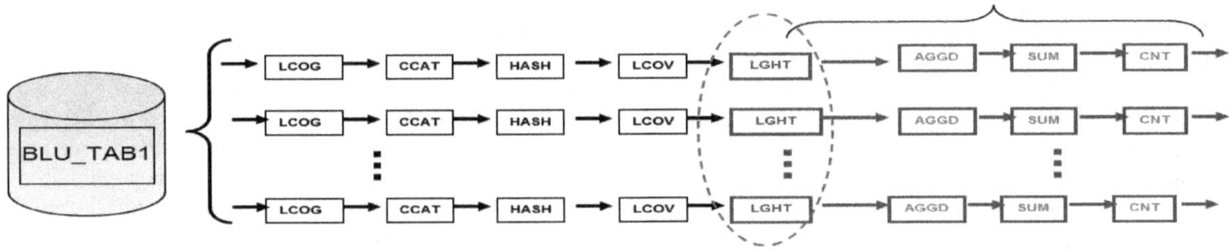

Figure 1: DB2-BLU Group by/Aggregation chain

GPU, we can run the query concurrently on two or more different kernels. This helps us f nd out the fastest kernel for a specif c query. We can then stop the other kernel(s) as soon as one of the kernels f nishes its job. This would give us more opportunity for faster processing of the query 3) add feedback logic to the design that informs a software moderator about the computation of the query using a specif c kernel. The moderator can then learn over time which of the kernels to use, given a specif c type of query. This feature is not yet implemented. Hence, we make use of metadata that is generated by the DB2 BLU runtime to accelerate query processing on the GPU. Such metadata includes the exact number of tuples, the estimated number of groups, and the number of aggregation functions. This information can help us call different kernels at runtime based on the type of the query.

In addition, this metadata allows us to optimize the size of the data structures we use in the GPU. This is very important because, as described, the GPU memory is very limited when compared to the host machine. The main data structure that we use to process the group by/aggregation queries in the hardware accelerator is a global hash table in the GPU memory. In our design we use the estimated number of groups to set the size of this hash table. If we do not know the number of groups then we need to set the size of hash table to be as big as the number of input rows which is much larger than number of groups in most queries. We describe our design in four main parts: 1) Changes we have made to the DB2 BLU runtime to integrate the GPU 2) The GPU run time 3) The group by kernels 4) The aggregation functions.

4.1 Eff cient Integration of GPU to DB2 BLU Runtime

Figure 1 shows the group by/aggregation chain in DB2 BLU. In the current design, group by/aggregation is performed in two phases. In the f rst phase, parallel threads read data from DB2 BLU tables and perform different operations on the data as depicted in f gure 1. When the f rst step f nishes, the f nal result is merged into a global hash table. The description of the different evaluators is as follows[21]:

LCOG, LCOV: Load grouping keys and payloads

CCAT: Concatenate keys for queries that group by on more than one column

HASH: Hash function that receives grouping keys and returns a hashed value

LGHT: First phase of BLU group by that creates groups in local hash tables

AGGD, SUM, CNT: Apply different aggregation functions

In our new design, as depicted in f gure 2, we moved some of these evaluators to the GPU and also added some new evaluators. As you can see, the LGHT and all aggregation functions are completely removed from the DB2 BLU group by evaluator chain. This is because we perform all of these operations in the GPU. We use CPU threads to load data and then use a simple hash function and KMV[2] algorithm to estimate the number of groups. We will use this estimate to tune the size of the GPU data structures.

Instead of having an LGHT evaluator, we have a simple MEMCPY evaluator that copies data to the pinned memory on the host machine. As explained, transfers to/from the GPU on-chip memory should be through the pinned memory because of its faster speed. After data is copied to the pinned memory, one of the CPU threads will call the GPU to perform the rest of operations. When the GPU f nishes its job, the result will be ready in the pinned memory. Details are in the next section. Moreover, we use input from the DB2 optimizer to choose a suitable group by/aggregation chain. The optimizer can provide some information like the number of groups/input rows before we start processing the group by chain. If the number of rows or groups (from the optimizer estimates) is smaller than a predef ned threshold (T1), we perform the entire computation in the host (i.e. in CPU, not GPU) using the DB2 BLU chains depicted in f gure 1. This optimization can be very benef cial for very small queries with small numbers of rows or groups. For these small queries, the cost of sending data to the GPU can be much more than the speed up we achieve by using the GPU. As a result, it is more suitable to perform the entire computation on the CPU for such small queries.

In contrast, if the number of rows is larger than a specif c threshold T1 while the number of groups is also larger than a threshold T2, we want to perform the entire computation on the GPU. This set of queries is very common and the GPU can be eff ciently used to improve the performance of these types of queries. We would like to emphasize that for queries with a very small number of rows or groups, the CPU is already very fast so there is no need to use the accelerator. As previously mentioned, we still use part of the original DB2 BLU group by chain to pass data to the accelerator, but the main computation is performed on the hardware accelerator. If the number of input rows is very large(larger than T3), the data will not f t in accelerator memory. In this case we will need to partition the data and use both the CPU and the GPU for query processing. In our current implementation, all of the large queries are processed in the CPU. This is depicted in f gure 3.

4.2 GPU Runtime

If it is decided that a query is to be executed on the GPU, only one of the CPU threads will launch the GPU runtime. As depicted in f gure 2, by this time all data have gone through the HASH evaluator. The HASH evaluator and KMV[2] algorithm together can help us to come up with a good estimate for the number of groups. Moreover, the exact number of input rows and aggregate functions is already determined by this point. All of the metadata is sent to the GPU runtime.

In the GPU, we use a hash based algorithm to perform the group by/aggregation operation. The details of the various group by and aggregation kernels are described in sections 4-3 and 4-4. In all of

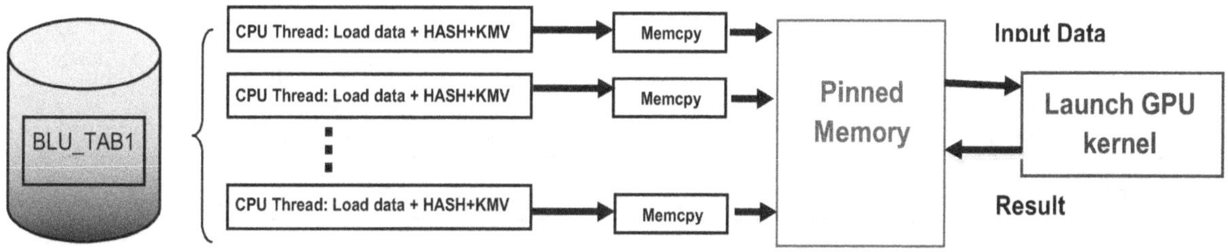

Figure 2: Group by/Aggregation chain in DB2-BLU with hardware accelerator

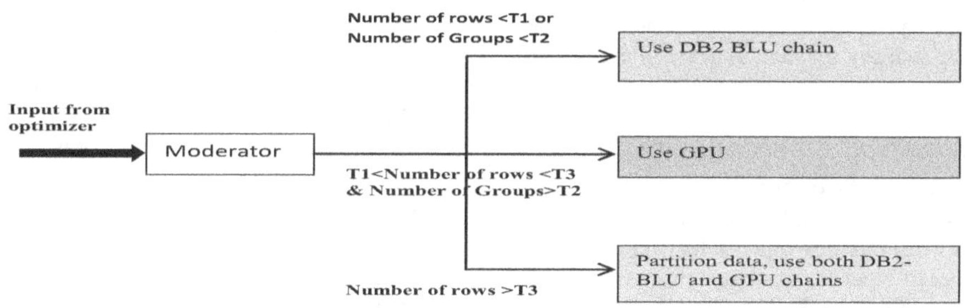

Figure 3: Using optimizer data to select the path for group by/aggregation queries

these hash based algorithms the size of the hash table is an important parameter that affects the performance of the system. Meanwhile, the estimated number of groups can be used to tune the size of the hash table. We also have an error detection code-path, so if the estimated number of groups is not correct (smaller than the exact number of groups) we could still process the query.

A moderator called the GPU moderator allows us to select an appropriate hardware accelerator kernel. The best kernel would be the one that can finish the computation in the fastest time using the fewest resources. However, there could be cases that the available resources on the GPU(compute resources, memory, cache, etc) is greater than what the query needs. For such scenarios, we can run the query using multiple kernels concurrently and then stop the computation in all kernels as soon as one of the kernels finishes its job. Furthermore, if we have multiple kernels running and the GPU becomes resource constrained (perhaps because new queries are sent to the GPU), we can terminate the kernels which have made the least amount of progress.

4.3 Group By Kernels

As explained, we use a hash based algorithm to perform the group by/aggregation operations in the GPU. We can have different implementations of hash-based algorithms based on: 1) number of input rows 2) estimated number of groups 3) number of aggregation functions. In the following we explain three different hash based group by/aggregation algorithms and show how we use them based on meta-data that the DB2 optimizer provides.

4.3.1 First Kernel: Regular Queries

These are queries that have neither a very small number of groups nor a large number of groups. They also do not have a very large number of aggregation functions. For these kinds of queries we use hash based group by/aggregation algorithm. We use the meta-data provided by the DB2 optimizer to set the size of global hash table in the GPU device memory to be slightly larger than the estimated number of groups. Each entry in the input table has one grouping key and can have N different payloads and corresponding N aggregation functions. The first step is to initialize the hash table using the size of the grouping keys and payloads, and also the type of aggregation functions. The data in the hash table should be 1, 2, 4, 8 or 16 byte aligned (Nvidia GPU requirement), so we may need to do some padding at the end of each row in the hash table. To initialize the hash table as quickly and as efficiently as possible, we create a hash table mask based on the size of the payloads and aggregation functions and then use parallel CUDA threads to copy that mask to the hash table. The initial value for the grouping portion of the mask is a sequence of Fs. If the size of the grouping key is M bits, then we will have M/4 Fs as the initial value of the grouping key in the mask. Then the initial value of payloads in the mask is determined based on payload type and the corresponding aggregation function. For instance, if we have a payload of type 32bit integer and SUM as the aggregation function for that payload, the initial value in the mask would be 0(32bits). As an example for a query like: Select SUM(C1), MAX(C2), MIN(C3) from table1 group by(C1) where C1 and C2 are 64 bit integers and C3 is 32 bit integer, the mask would be: FFFFFFFFFFFFFFFF,0,-9223372036854775808,2147483647,0 Where -9223372036854775808 is the smallest 64 bit integer number (initial value to perform MAX(C2)) and 2147483647 is the largest 32 bit integer(initial value to perform MIN(C3)). The 0s at the end are added for padding. After finding the mask, parallel threads will copy that to the hash table in parallel as it is shown in table 1.

After initializing the hash table, we launch CUDA threads to read data from the input table in parallel and insert groups to the hash table. Each CUDA thread reads a row and then uses a hash function and the grouping key to find the insertion location in the hash table. If the corresponding entry in the hash table is empty we use atomic operations to insert the key. In case the entry is occupied, we try to insert the key to the next empty slot in the hash table. If the keys are less than 64 bit, we use CUDA atomicCAS to insert the key. This guarantees that 2 different CUDA threads do not overwrite the same hash entry. If the key size is larger than 64 bit, we can not use CUDA atomic operations any more so we try to acquire a lock to get access to the entry and then insert the key. The hash function we use when the key size is larger than 64 bit is the Murmur hashing algorithm [3]. For keys smaller than 64 bit we use a mod hash function. We perform the aggregation right after

Table 1: Parallel insertion to the hash table

C1(64bit)	SUM(C1)(64bit)	MAX(C2)(64bit)	MIN(C3)(32bit)	Padding(32bit)
FFFFFFFFFFFFFFFF	0	-9223372036854775808	2147483647	0
FFFFFFFFFFFFFFFF	0	-9223372036854775808	2147483647	0
...	...	...	...	...
FFFFFFFFFFFFFFFF	0	-9223372036854775808	2147483647	0

the insertion/finding of grouping key in the hash table. If a thread discovers a key is already in the hash table, it updates the payload entries by applying the corresponding aggregation functions. We use either atomic operation or locks for that, as we will explain in section 4-4.

4.3.2 Second Kernel: Small Number of Groups

Queries with a very small number of groups are very common in real customer benchmarks. For example, grouping the employees of a company by their birth month would yield 12 unique values. However, if the number of input rows is large, processing such queries could be very costly. Moreover, Nvidia GPUs have Streaming Multiprocessors(SMX) where each SMX has its own 64KB configurable shared memory/L1 cache. We use this shared memory to perform partial grouping for queries with small numbers of groups. In order to have more space to keep groups/aggregated values in shared memory, we configure the shared memory/L1 cache to have 48KB as shared memory and 16KB as L1 cache.

Our algorithm has 2 main steps where in the first step, we perform a hash-based group by in the shared memory of the GPU using small hash tables that fit in the shared memory of GPU. This is similar to what we explained in section 4-3-1. Following that, the small hash tables in shared memory are merged to a global hash table in device memory. The main idea is to perform as many operations as we can in shared memory and then if it gets full, we can merge the partial result into a global hash table in the device memory. The reason we need to merge the result in the device memory is because the hash tables in different SMXs shared memories are totally separate. Basically, different threads perform group by in parallel on different chunks of input table tuples and generate partial group by results in the shared memory of different SMXs. Afterward the partial results are aggregated into the global hash table in device memory. The GPU runtime moderator will execute this kernel for all queries with small numbers of groups.

4.3.3 Third Kernel: Large Number of Aggregation Functions

The main structure of this kernel is the same as the one we explain in 4-3-1. This means that we use a hash table in the device memory of the GPU and then threads try to insert grouping keys into the hash table in parallel. However, the main difference is in the way that we perform the aggregation. Our experiments show that if the number of aggregation functions is large (more than 5), using atomic operations to perform these functions one by one can be time consuming. Moreover, as mentioned for some data types like 128bit Integer or Decimal data type, there is no CUDA atomic call, so we have to use locks. However, getting and releasing locks per aggregation operation can be costly when the number of aggregation functions is large. The other scenario in which the first kernel performs poorly is cases in which the ratio of number of rows/number of groups is small. As a result, the contention is very low and the cost of acquiring/releasing locks per aggregation function or atomic operation is high. For these kinds of queries we use a global lock approach where each thread locks the entire row of the hash table after it finds out that its key matches the key in the corresponding hash table entry. After getting the lock, the thread goes through all the aggregation functions and applies them one by one. Finally, the thread releases the lock so other threads that want to update the same hash table row can acquire the lock. If both 1) the number of aggregation functions is large 2) number of rows/number groups is small, this kernel would have very good performance.

4.4 Aggregations

As explained, aggregation happens immediately after we find a group in which a grouping key belongs to. This means that the same thread goes through all the aggregation functions and corresponding values in the hash table (and the input table row) and applies all the functions one by one. We use 2 main approaches to perform the aggregation: 1) Atomic CUDA calls: For large sets of data types and aggregation functions, we can use CUDA atomic function calls. This includes some common data types like 32bit, 64 bit integer and float and aggregation functions like Min, Max, Sum and Count. We can also use atomicCAS to perform atomic operations on 128bit double or 128bit integer data types as explained in Nvidia documents [1]. 2) Locks: For some data types like fixed/variable size string that can have sizes larger than 128bit, we have to use locks. This is because we do not have the support from Nvdia hardware/software to perform the atomic operation. As a result, the threads need to acquire a lock first, apply the aggregation function, and then finally release the lock so that other threads can use it. While with this approach we can functionally perform group by/aggregation queries that have large sizes on GPU, the performance is lower than the other data types because acquiring/releasing locks is very costly operation. As described in section 4-3-3, we can optimize this for some queries by locking per row instead of per payload.

5. PERFORMANCE RESULTS

In this section we describe some performance results we have achieved with our prototype. We have run unmodified customer representative benchmarks using a commercial RDBMS (DB2 BLU) offloading processing to a GPU. We believe this is the first time that such a test has been attempted. We will describe these benchmarks, show the performance numbers with and without GPU acceleration, and also study the performance of running a subset of the queries from these benchmarks on the GPU. Our tests are run on an IBM Power S824 system with 2 sockets (24 cores running SMT 4 for a total of 96 hardware threads, running at 3.92GHz), 512GB RAM, Ubuntu 14.04 LTS for the ppc64le architecture. We also have 2 NVIDIA K40 cards on the box. Each K40 has around 3000 cores and 12G of memory. Transfers to/from GPU are through PCI-e gen3.

5.1 Benchmarks

5.1.1 BD Insights Workload Description

Big Data Insights or BD Insights is a workload developed by

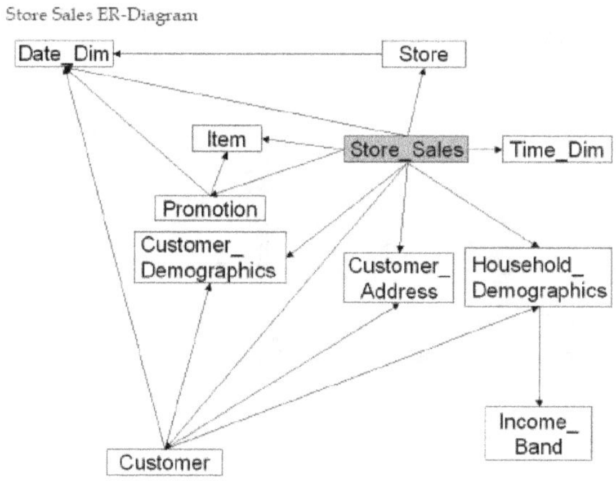

Figure 4: Store Sales fact table

IBM to model a day in the life of a customer representative business intelligence application.

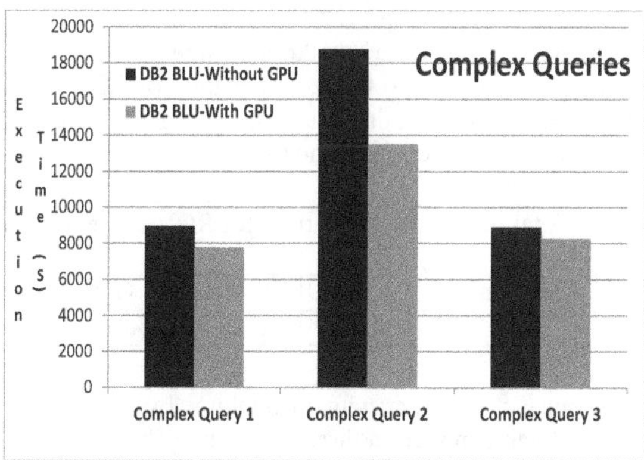

Figure 5: Complex queries in BD Insight benchmark

Database description: The data generator and database schema itself are derived from the industry TPC-DS Benchmark Standard (tpc.org). It represents a retail business and stores information about its merchandise sales through (1) its brick and mortar stores, (2) its online stores, and (3) through its catalog. The database also tracks customer demographic information, merchandise returns, inventory, and sales promotions among many other data points. There are seven fact tables in total and seventeen dimension tables in the schema. Figure 4 shows the star schema surrounding one of the fact tables which is called Store Sales in the database (representing merchandise sales from the brick & mortar stores).

BD Insights user description: The BD Insights workload has a separation of query types for three classes of typical business analytics users:

1. Returns Dashboard Analysts (Simple Queries): These users investigate the rate of merchandise returns and impact on the bottom line of the business. The queries can be characterized as short running against a narrow range of data, and likely to access a fact table.

2. Sales Report Analysts (Intermediate Queries): These users are generating sales reports to understand the prof tability of their retail enterprise. The queries used can be characterized as being intermediate in complexity with a broader range of data accessed.

3. Data Scientists (Complex Queries): These users are hand crafting deep-dive analytic queries that answer questions identif ed by sales report analysts and the returns dashboard analysts. The queries can be characterized as long running and complex using complicated SQL constructs over a large or full data range.

Overall, the BD Insights workload contains 100 distinct queries: 5 are complex, 25 are intermediate, and 70 are simple. The workload can be run in several modes with both single user and varying multi-user combinations using the Apache JMETER load driver as a front-end client. For the purposes of this test, the interest was in whether the GPU acceleration modif cations in DB2 would be able to functionally handle all of the queries, and then determine the query performance. The database was sized at 100GB so that it could fully f t in main memory, and would not overwhelm the memory available on the GPU cards.

5.1.2 Cognos ROLAP

Cognos ROLAP is an IBM internal analytical benchmark which simulates the core Business Intelligence(BI) workload from IBM Cognos suite. The Cognos ROLAP workload's schema and data generator are derived from the TPC-DS Benchmark Standard. In this particular instance, the queries were run against a BD Insights generated database. The Cognos ROLAP query set is composed of 46 complex analytical queries (a mix of join, group by, and sort), some of which include OLAP functions like RANK() that drive SORT. While the DB2 BLU engine is able to run all 46 queries, the prototype was only able to run 34 queries of these queries as the memory in the K40 GPU is limited, and 12 of the queries had memory requirements which exceeded the memory available.

5.2 Queries execution on the DB2 BLU with GPU

In this section we measure the performance of running BD Insight and Cognos ROLAP queries on DB2 BLU with GPU.

5.2.1 BD Insights Queries

Figures 5 and 6 show the execution of complex and intermediate queries on the GPU. The numbers in the Y axis of both charts shows the end to end execution time of the query i.e. what a real user would see. As you can see, our DB2 BLU with GPU prototype has done a good job of improving the performance of complex queries. The complex queries are heavy queries that have costly operations like join, group by, aggregation, sort, predicate evaluation, etc. The current prototype performs the bulk of each query in the CPU and only a subset on the GPU. With that in mind, we are able to improve the total execution time of complex queries by 20% which is promising for this type of benchmark.

However, the performance of our prototype is very close to baseline (DB2 BLU without GPU) as depicted in f gure 5. This may sound disappointing at f rst glance. However, after looking at the SQL of all these queries we found out that: 1) they have a small number of Group by, aggregation and sort queries 2) the execution time of most of the intermediate query is already very short in the baseline (the average query execution time is 30 sec). So there is really not much room for improvement for this set of queries. Moreover, if we off oad the Group by, aggregation, and sort components of these queries to the GPU, the execution time of all the queries will be larger than the baseline. This is because by off oading such small components, we will incur the relatively higher cost of transferring data to and from the GPU. However, using the optimizations explained in sections 3 and 4, we can f nd out about these short queries in advance and try to process them in the CPU instead

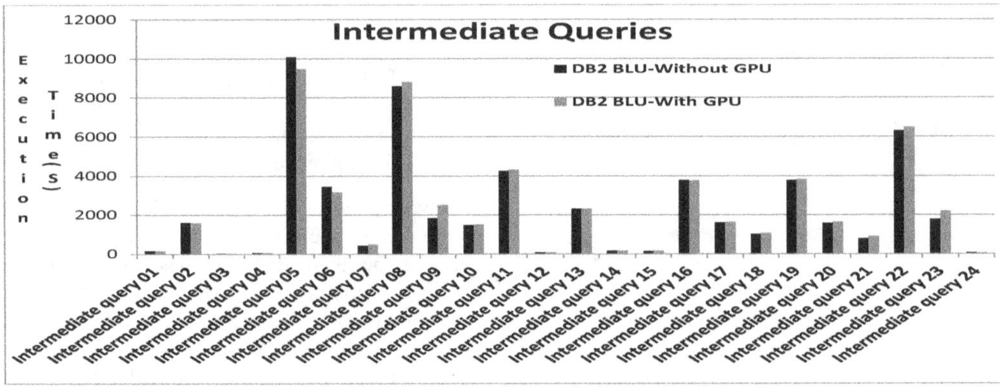

Figure 6: Intermediate queries in BD Insight Benchmark

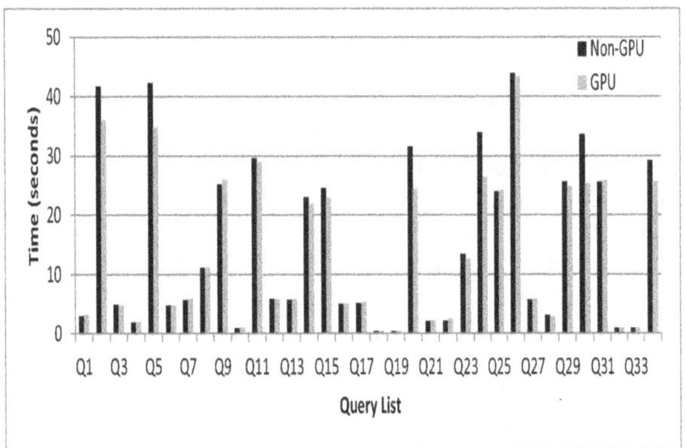

Figure 7: Query execution time for Cognos ROLAP benchmark

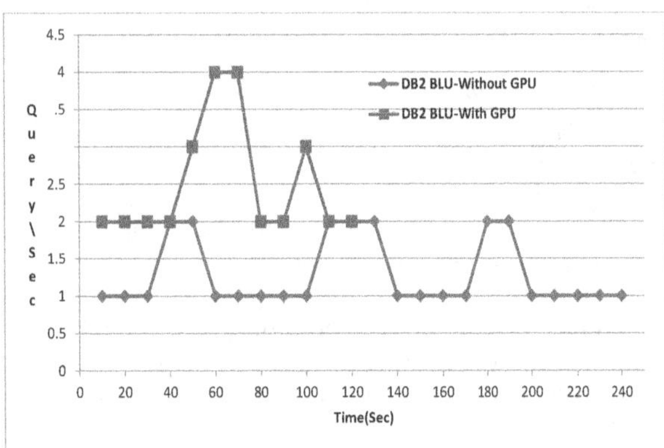

Figure 8: Concurrent query execution

of GPU. As a result, our prototype has performed well by keeping the execution time of all of these queries very close to the baseline. The remaining queries in the benchmark are simple queries that are very short (average is 150ms) and we do not send them to the GPU at all.

5.2.2 Cognos ROLAP

The Cognos ROLAP queries were run in two different modes: a serial run which aims to measure the query execution time, and a concurrent run where throughput was measured. Again, we compared our prototype (using GPU) with the standard DB2 BLU as the baseline (no GPU used). Table 2 shows the average serial execution of all 34 queries, with and without GPU. We run each query 5 times to eliminate the variation and get the average. As you can see, our GPU enabled prototype was able to save more than 8% of the total execution time. Figure 7 shows the per-query times during the run. Most of the queries take less time when GPU is used compared to the run with no GPU. The benef t of GPU off oading is apparent with longer running queries, but there is no benef t for shorter running queries (e.g. Q1 and Q4).

Table 2: Total query execution time for ROLAP benchmark

GPU On(ms)	GPU Off(ms)	GPU Gain
517133	474084	8.33%

We also measured the system throughput by running concurrent queries. Each connection thread continuously executed all the 34 Cognos ROLAP queries sequentially, and throughput (queries per Hour) is compared in Table 3. The throughput results show that the GPU benef ts are more pronounced in multi-user environments, rather than with higher degrees of parallelism. This is explainable because a single request launches a CUDA kernel and the parallelism in the GPU will be independent of the DB2 parallelism. However, more concurrent users means more parallel running CUDA kernels. So long as the GPUs have enough capacity to execute these kernels, DB2 can use the CPU capacity made available by off oading work to the GPUs.

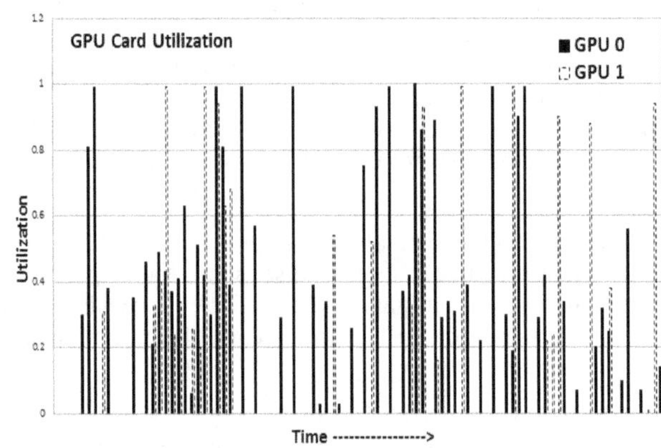

Figure 9: GPU utilization

Table 3: Throughput(Query/Sec for ROLAP benchmark)

#stream	#degree	GPU On	GPU Off	GPU Gain
1	24	403.96	385.51	4.79%
1	48	584.25	557.63	4.77%
1	64	630.9	602.1	4.78%
2	24	682.85	620.53	10.04%
2	48	868.09	773.46	12.23%
2	64	930.1	803.1	15.81%

5.3 Concurrent Query Execution

As already explained, we just run a subset of operations on the GPU in the current stage of our prototype i.e. queries that have group by, aggregation and sort operations. In order to better show how the GPU can help in accelerating the queries, we pick a set of queries where these three operations are represented heavily, moderately, or not at all. This test shows BLU with GPU acceleration handling cases of industry standard benchmark queries, handcrafted queries that would push the GPU to its limits, and queries where DB2 would decide to not use the GPU at all. It is a multi-user test to take advantage of CPU off oading and be more representative of real world workloads. The test was constructed using JMETER to have f ve thread groups of two threads each and thus 10 total users. The f rst three thread groups consist of complex queries sourced from the Cognos ROLAP workload that uses the GPU moderately (i.e. moderate use of group by, Aggregation and SORT processing) and a single BD Insights simple query that would not use the GPU. The fourth thread group consisted of two BD Insights complex queries (Complex Q1 and Q3) which would use the GPU moderately and one of the BD Insights simple queries which would not use the GPU. The f fth group contained two hand written queries that would perform group by and SORT on a large grouping set.

Figure 8 shows the elapsed time of running these queries with and without GPU. As you can see we can get almost a 2x speed up by using the GPU. This test demonstrates the impact of GPU acceleration for DB2 BLU analytic processing. The GPU heavy queries add a lot of processing cost to separate the groups and perform the aggregation for each group, as there are as many groups as there are rows in the table. Using a GPU kernel, this was off oaded and parallelized on an execution unit (2x K40s) that generally had the capacity to handle this type of work. The NVIDIA Tesla K40 has 2880 CUDA cores available for parallel batch jobs of a specif c nature (like group by), whereas the S824 had 24 cores that needed to handle all DB2 BLU processing. The GPU moderate queries would show about 15% benef t in standalone mode. The benef t comes from more parallelism in the CUDA kernel function than having DB2 sub-agent parallelism, which could be restricted due to degree, workload management, and CPU capacity. The Non-GPU queries performed similarly in both conf gurations, as would be the expectation. That leaves the majority of the benef t being due to off oad.

In f gure 9 we show the memory utilization for both GPUs that we have on our POWER 8 machine during the execution of queries. The GPU memory utilization characteristics for this workload shows a very spiky pattern. Clearly there is room for more GPU off-load, but it is also clear that at many points the workload is near GPU memory capacity. There were candidate queries for this test that were avoided simply due to the GPU memory restrictions, and no good way of handling them alternatively at the time.

6. CONCLUSION AND FUTURE WORK

In this paper, we have shown how we can improve the query processing time in DB2 BLU by using Nvidia GPUs. Moreover, we have provided realistic customer benchmarks on a commercial RDBMS with GPU acceleration, which has not been done before. We show a hybrid design that uses both CPU and GPUs for fast query processing. In our design we off oad specif c compute intensive operations like group by, aggregation and sort to GPU. Our main goals in doing this are: 1) To accelerate the computation of those specif c operations 2) To free up the CPU so that we can use it for other tasks. However, our experiments show that it is not always benef cial to off oad the operations to the GPU, because small data sets will perform optimally in the CPU. We have also discussed the necessary changes in the DB2 BLU runtime to integrate the GPUs. These changes included adding memory management, scheduling algorithms, and integration code for sort, group by, and aggregation operations. While we used Nvidia's fast sort kernel, we have also designed our very own group by/aggregation kernels. We show how we can use meta-data to tune the size of data structures in the GPU memory. As the memory in GPU is very limited, tuning the size of data structures is very important. Moreover, we demonstrated how we use meta-data to choose between these different kernels at run time to achieve the best performance.

Our performance results show a realistic representation of using GPU in a real RDBMS commercial tool. We show that the performance improvement was very signif cant for some queries, moderate for some other queries, and there were also queries that did not perform better when executed in the GPU. As mentioned, so far we have kernels for operations like group by, aggregation and sort. As one of our next steps, we would like to study the performance of other compute intensive operations (like join) on the GPU.

7. ADDITIONAL AUTHORS

Additional authors: Wayne Young (DB2, email: `wjyoung@ca.ibm.com`) and Chang Ge (DB2, email: `changge@ca.ibm.com`) and Geoffrey Ng (DB2, email: `Geoffrey@ca.ibm.com`) and Kajan Kanagaratnam (DB2, email: `kajanak@ca.ibm`).

8. REFERENCES

[1] *CUDA Atomic operations.* https://docs.nvidia.com/cuda/cuda-c-programming- guide/.

[2] *K-minimum values.* http://research.neustar.biz/tag/kmv/.

[3] *Murmur hashing algorithm.* https://en.wikipedia.org/wiki/MurmurHash.

[4] S. Breß, B. Köcher, M. Heimel, V. Markl, M. Saecker, and G. Saake. Ocelot/hype: Optimized data processing on heterogeneous hardware. *Proc. VLDB Endow.*, 7(13):1609–1612, Aug. 2014.

[5] S. Breßand G. Saake. Why it is time for a hype: A hybrid query processing engine for eff cient gpu coprocessing in dbms. *Proc. VLDB Endow.*, 6(12):1398–1403, Aug. 2013.

[6] D. Cederman and P. Tsigas. Gpu-quicksort: A practical quicksort algorithm for graphics processors. *J. Exp. Algorithmics*, 14:4:1.4–4:1.24, Jan. 2010.

[7] C. Dennl, D. Ziener, and J. Teich. Acceleration of SQL restrictions and aggregations through fpga-based dynamic partial reconf guration. In *21st IEEE Annual International Symposium on Field-Programmable Custom Computing Machines, FCCM 2013, Seattle, WA, USA, April 28-30, 2013*, pages 25–28, 2013.

[8] W. Fang, B. He, and Q. Luo. Database compression on

graphics processors. *Proc. VLDB Endow.*, 3(1-2):670–680, Sept. 2010.

[9] N. Govindaraju, J. Gray, R. Kumar, and D. Manocha. Gputerasort: High performance graphics co-processor sorting for large database management. In *Proceedings of the 2006 ACM SIGMOD International Conference on Management of Data*, SIGMOD '06, pages 325–336, New York, NY, USA, 2006. ACM.

[10] N. K. Govindaraju, B. Lloyd, W. Wang, M. Lin, and D. Manocha. Fast computation of database operations using graphics processors. In *Proceedings of the 2004 ACM SIGMOD International Conference on Management of Data*, SIGMOD '04, pages 215–226, New York, NY, USA, 2004. ACM.

[11] A. Greß and G. Zachmann. Gpu-abisort: Optimal parallel sorting on stream architectures. In *The 20th IEEE International Parallel and Distributed Processing Symposium (IPDPS '06)*, page 45, Apr. 2006.

[12] B. He, K. Yang, R. Fang, M. Lu, N. Govindaraju, Q. Luo, and P. Sander. Relational joins on graphics processors. In *Proceedings of the 2008 ACM SIGMOD International Conference on Management of Data*, SIGMOD '08, pages 511–524, New York, NY, USA, 2008. ACM.

[13] J. He, M. Lu, and B. He. Revisiting co-processing for hash joins on the coupled cpu-gpu architecture. *Proc. VLDB Endow.*, 6(10):889–900, Aug. 2013.

[14] T. Kaldewey, G. Lohman, R. Mueller, and P. Volk. Gpu join processing revisited. In *Proceedings of the Eighth International Workshop on Data Management on New Hardware*, DaMoN '12, pages 55–62, New York, NY, USA, 2012. ACM.

[15] T. Karnagel, M. Hille, M. Ludwig, D. Habich, W. Lehner, M. Heimel, and V. Markl. Demonstrating eff cient query processing in heterogeneous environments. In *Proceedings of the 2014 ACM SIGMOD International Conference on Management of Data*, SIGMOD '14, pages 693–696, New York, NY, USA, 2014. ACM.

[16] C. Kim, J. Chhugani, N. Satish, E. Sedlar, A. D. Nguyen, T. Kaldewey, V. W. Lee, S. A. Brandt, and P. Dubey. Fast: Fast architecture sensitive tree search on modern cpus and gpus. In *Proceedings of the 2010 ACM SIGMOD International Conference on Management of Data*, SIGMOD '10, pages 339–350, New York, NY, USA, 2010. ACM.

[17] E. W. B. L. J. Gosink, K. Wu and K. I. Joy. Bin-hash indexing: A parallel method for fast query processing.

[18] D. Merrill and A. Grimshaw. High performance and scalable radix sorting: A case study of implementing dynamic parallelism for GPU computing. *Parallel Processing Letters*, 21(02):245–272, 2011.

[19] M. A. O'Neil and M. Burtscher. Floating-point data compression at 75 gb/s on a gpu. In *Proceedings of the Fourth Workshop on General Purpose Processing on Graphics Processing Units*, GPGPU-4, pages 7:1–7:7, New York, NY, USA, 2011. ACM.

[20] O. Polychroniou and K. A. Ross. High throughput heavy hitter aggregation for modern simd processors. In *Proceedings of the Ninth International Workshop on Data Management on New Hardware*, DaMoN '13, pages 6:1–6:6, New York, NY, USA, 2013. ACM.

[21] V. Raman, G. Attaluri, R. Barber, N. Chainani, D. Kalmuk, V. KulandaiSamy, J. Leenstra, S. Lightstone, S. Liu, G. M. Lohman, T. Malkemus, R. Mueller, I. Pandis, B. Schiefer, D. Sharpe, R. Sidle, A. Storm, and L. Zhang. Db2 with blu acceleration: So much more than just a column store. *Proc. VLDB Endow.*, 6(11):1080–1091, Aug. 2013.

[22] N. Satish, C. Kim, J. Chhugani, A. D. Nguyen, V. W. Lee, D. Kim, and P. Dubey. Fast sort on cpus and gpus: A case for bandwidth oblivious simd sort. In *Proceedings of the 2010 ACM SIGMOD International Conference on Management of Data*, SIGMOD '10, pages 351–362, New York, NY, USA, 2010. ACM.

[23] Y.-C. Tu, A. Kumar, D. Yu, R. Rui, and R. Wheeler. Data management systems on gpus: Promises and challenges. In *Proceedings of the 25th International Conference on Scientif c and Statistical Database Management*, SSDBM, pages 33:1–33:4, New York, NY, USA, 2013. ACM.

[24] H. Wu, G. Diamos, T. Sheard, M. Aref, S. Baxter, M. Garland, and S. Yalamanchili. Red fox: An execution environment for relational query processing on gpus. In *Proceedings of Annual IEEE/ACM International Symposium on Code Generation and Optimization*, CGO '14, pages 44:44–44:54, New York, NY, USA, 2014. ACM.

[25] R. Wu, B. Zhang, M. Hsu, and Q. Chen. Gpu-accelerated predicate evaluation on column store. In *Proceedings of the 11th International Conference on Web-age Information Management*, WAIM'10, pages 570–581, Berlin, Heidelberg, 2010. Springer-Verlag.

[26] S. Zhang, J. He, B. He, and M. Lu. Omnidb: Towards portable and eff cient query processing on parallel cpu/gpu architectures. *Proc. VLDB Endow.*, 6(12):1374–1377, Aug. 2013.

An Experimental Comparison of Thirteen Relational Equi-Joins in Main Memory

Stefan Schuh, Xiao Chen, Jens Dittrich
Information Systems Group
Saarland University
http://infosys.cs.uni-saarland.de

ABSTRACT

Relational equi-joins are at the heart of almost every query plan. They have been studied, improved, and reexamined on a regular basis since the existence of the database community. In the past four years several new join algorithms have been proposed and experimentally evaluated. Some of those papers contradict each other in their experimental findings. This makes it surprisingly hard to answer a very simple question: what is the fastest join algorithm in 2015? In this paper we will try to develop an answer. We start with an end-to-end black box comparison of the most important methods. Afterwards, we inspect the internals of these algorithms in a white box comparison. We derive improved variants of state-of-the-art join algorithms by applying optimizations like software-write combine buffers, various hash table implementations, as well as NUMA-awareness in terms of data placement and scheduling. We also inspect various radix partitioning strategies. Eventually, we are in the position to perform a comprehensive comparison of thirteen different join algorithms. We factor in scaling effects in terms of size of the input datasets, the number of threads, different page sizes, and data distributions. Furthermore, we analyze the impact of various joins on an (unchanged) TPC-H query. Finally, we conclude with a list of major lessons learned from our study and a guideline for practitioners implementing massive main-memory joins. As is the case with almost all algorithms in databases, we will learn that there is no single best join algorithm. Each algorithm has its strength and weaknesses and shines in different areas of the parameter space.

1. INTRODUCTION

Database research is full of traditions. One of our most prominent traditions is to publish new join algorithms every year. And, yes, we mean equi-joins, on relational data; not some fancy approximate similarity join on probabilistic JSON data streams. Isn't this kind of magic that after 40 years of database research, there is still progress in an area that is at the core of almost every query plan? Shouldn't relational equi-join algorithms be a solved problem anyway? So, why should we care?

SIGMOD'16, June 26-July 01, 2016, San Francisco, CA, USA
© 2016 ACM. ISBN 978-1-4503-3531-7/16/06...$15.00
DOI: http://dx.doi.org/10.1145/2882903.2882917

When taking a deep look at the abundant recent related work on relational equi-joins from 2011 to 2015 [7, 6, 14, 3, 17, 4, 5], it quickly turns out that based on that literature it is surprisingly hard to decide which is the best join algorithm. For instance, it seems clear from [4] that a hash-based approach outperforms sort based approaches, at least on current hardware with the limited SIMD register width available today. However, for the different hash table-based join implementations it is unclear if hardware-conscious partition-based algorithm (the PRB-family of join algorithms) outperforms non-partitioning hardware-oblivious algorithms (the NOP-family of join algorithms) anyway. For instance, in 2011, the experiments in [7] show that NOP outperforms PRB. However, in 2013, the experiments in [4] show exactly the opposite: PRB outperforms NOP. In another work in 2013, [14] again, NOP outperforms PRB. So which algorithm is better? In odd years it is NOP? In even years it is PRB? The answer is: we do not know. The more interesting question is: why do those experiments report contradicting results? There are several reasons:

1. **different implementations** were used, e.g. in [7] a very basic NOP implementation was used where the concurrent chaining hash table was implemented using linked lists and two separate arrays were used for locks and head pointers. In contrast, [5] provided a more cache-efficient chaining hash table implementation which used a single array for both locks and tuples and removed head pointers. NOP from [14] implemented a lock free hash table by using linear probing and Compare-and-Swap instructions. Another example is PRB where [5] reimplemented the PRB algorithm from [7] since the implementation from [7] had too many function calls and pointer dereferencing in critical code paths.

2. **different optimizations** were applied to the different join algorithms, e.g. in [4, 6] software-write combine buffers were used for PRB, in [14, 7] they were not used, for [5] it is unclear wether software-write combine buffers were used for the results presented in the paper. Moreover, [14] used a linear probing hash-table as its hash-table implementation whereas [5, 4, 6] used chained hashing. In addition, [7, 4] did not consider NUMA-aware join processing at all, while in [14, 4] at least the join relations as well as working memory is distributed over all NUMA nodes.

3. **different performance metrics** were used, e.g. different definitions of "join throughput", e.g. in [4] it is defined as the number of join results produced per second, i.e. $Throughput = \frac{|R \bowtie S|}{|\text{total runtime}|}$. Notice, that this definition focusses on the amount of tuples output by the join algorithm. Hence, it is sensitive to the join selectivity. In contrast, in [14] throughput is defined as the ratio of the sum of the relation sizes and the total

runtime, i.e. $Throughput = \frac{|R| + |S|}{|\text{total runtime}|}$. This definition focusses on the input of the join algorithms. Hence, this definition is independent of the join selectivity. We will use the latter definition in our study.

4. **different machines**, e.g. the machine used in [7] is a single socket six-core Intel Xeon X5650 Nehalem. In contrast, [5] reports the results for several architectures with the best performance achieved on an eight-core Intel Xeon E5-2680 server. In [14] the authors used four eight-core Intel Xeon X7560 Nehalem CPUs in their experiments. Similarly, [5] used four eight-core Intel CPUs however with the Sandy Bridge architecture.

5. **difference of micro-benchmarks and real queries**, e.g. [7, 6, 5, 14, 3, 17, 4, 13] did not consider total query execution times of real world (or at least TPC-H) queries, that include several attributes that have to be considered for predicate evaluation after the join processing. However, simple techniques like selection push-down may considerably reduce the input sizes to a join algorithm (even though the unfiltered relations are huge). In such a situation the choice of the join algorithm may become less crucial. In addition, tuple reconstruction has been shown to have a substantial effect on the overall runtime of a query [2]. Whether a join is run with or without tuple reconstruction makes a huge difference in practice. However, none of these effects were evaluated in those works.

Any of these differences alone may have a substantial effect on the runtime of a join algorithm or its interpretation. Accumulating multiple of those differences makes a comparison very hard and comparing results from different papers becomes almost infeasible.

Therefore, we believe the time is ripe for a clean slate experimental comparison of relational equi-joins. This paper fills this gap. We will focus on hash-based join algorithms as almost all recent works suggest that these algorithms are the most promising ones. Still, we will use a modern sort-based approach as one baseline [4][1]. We do not further explore sort-based joins as the evidence from recent work suggests that sort-based joins cannot match the performance of other joins. We will evaluate all algorithms in the context of a modern NUMA (non-uniform memory access) architecture.

The algorithms we evaluate in our study are based on algorithms published in four recent papers [17, 4, 14, 5]. Notice that those papers in turn improve upon several other older papers [13, 7, 3]. We will introduce several variants of those algorithms. In total, in our study, we evaluate **thirteen different join algorithms**.

In this paper we make the following contributions:

1. **Black box Comparison.** We start with the core join algorithms from [14, 5, 17] which are already improved versions of join algorithms proposed in [7, 13] or have been shown to outperform join algorithms proposed in [3]. We will start with a black box end-to-end comparison of these four principal join algorithms in Section 4.

2. **White box Comparison.** We proceed by performing a white box comparison. We enable all optimizations mentioned in prior work and explore their effects on the runtime performance of the joins, see Section 5.1. We then proceed by evaluating the effect of different hash-table implementations in Section 5.2, for both NOP and PRB.

3. **Optimizing Join Algorithms.** In order to improve the join performance on NUMA architectures, we optimize the different versions of the PRB join algorithm. First, We will show how to make the partitioning phase NUMA-aware in Section 6.1 and also see that we can improve over PRB by 20%. Second, we will show in Section 6.2 that a NUMA-aware join task scheduling can also improve the performance by roughly 20%. These improvements are not cumulative as the NUMA-aware partitioning already makes use of all NUMA nodes in the join phase and therefore does not profit from a NUMA-aware scheduling.

4. **Comprehensive Comparison of Joins.** Finally, we will be in the position to perform a comprehensive comparison of all join algorithms, see Section 7. First, we define a common workload for all methods. We also do a reality check and use another meaningful baseline. For primary key columns it is common sense to use automatically generated integer IDs. This leads to a dense key domain of integers. For this distribution a simple array rather than a hash table may be a surprisingly good choice. Though the practicability of this approach may be questioned if the join key domain is sparse, it serves at least as a baseline on how good a join algorithm may get anyway. Additionally, for non-dense distributions a compressed array like the recently suggested [17] may be a good choice to avoid using a full-blown hash table.

   Second, we proceed by evaluating the page size of the virtual memory management on all phases of the different joins. This parameter has a surprising effect on runtime.

   Third, we look at the scalability of the join methods in terms of the input relation sizes. In this context we propose a strategy for choosing the right number of bits for partitioning the input relations in radix-based joins.

   Fourth, we explore the behavior of the join algorithms under moderately skewed and highly skewed data (Appendix A).

   Fifth, we examine the scalability of the different joins in terms of the number of threads and discuss possible reasons for the different scalability characteristics (Appendix B).

   Sixth, we evaluate the feasibility of using array joins in moderately dense domains (Appendix C).

   Seventh, we eveluate microarchitectural performance aspects (Appendix D).

5. **Effect on real queries.** We will evaluate the effect of the choice of the join algorithm in the context of a real TPC-H query in Section 8. We will start with a simple single join query, TPC-H Q19. We will analyze the portion of the query time spent in the actual join. We also provide an additional experiment changing the selectivity of Q19's predicates (see Appendix E). Additionally, see Appendices F and G.

6. **Key Lessons Learned.** Finally, we conclude by identifying the key lessons learned from our experimental study, see Section 9.

2. RELATED WORK

We focus on papers that discuss in-memory joins on multicore systems; we are aware that there is also a lot of related work on sorting, hashing or partitioning in memory, which is of course highly related to join processing. That work will be cited in other sections whenever appropriate. In the following we will discuss related work in chronological order.

[1]We also wanted to use a second sort-based baseline [14]. However, that code was not available.

Kim et. al. [13] revisited the sort vs hash argument in the context of main memory multi-core system by comparing a hash join and a sort-merge join that are optimized for modern multi-core systems. The hash join algorithm they introduced is called parallel radix hash join. Their experimental results showed that the parallel radix hash join outperforms the sort-merge join by a factor of two. They also developed an analytical model for the join performance and predicted that the sort-merge joins will become faster with the following two future hardware trends. First, *Wider SIMD instructions*: the sort-merge join algorithm scaled near-linearly with the width of SIMD instructions in their models, while the hash join algorithm hardly exploits the capability of SIMD instructions. Second, *Limited per-core bandwidth*: the hash join algorithm needs at least two pass partitioning for large data sets due to the limited number of TLB cache entries, which result in at least three trips to main memory, while the sort-merge join only needs two. With limited per-core bandwidth more memory trips would lead to worse performance.

Blanas et. al. [7] extended the categories of main memory multi-core join algorithms by introducing no-partitioning hash join. Unlike partition-based algorithm like parallel radix hash join [13], the no-partitioning hash join is a straightforward parallellised version of canonical (simple) hash join without partitioning the data at all. Blanas implemented the no-partitioning hash join with a lock-based concurrent chaining hash table and compared it with partition-based algorithms using three different partitioning algorithms: shared partitioning, independent partitioning, and the radix partitioning from Kim et. al. [13]. Their experimental results show that the no-partitioning hash join outperforms all partition-based hash joins for almost all data distributions and is only slightly slower than parallel radix hash join with uniform datasets.

A later work by Albutiu et. al. [3] on sort-merge join further extended the design space of main memory join algorithms by giving focus on optimizing for NUMA systems. The Massively Parallel Sort-Merge join (MPSM) proposed in their paper uses a carefully tuned memory access pattern and avoids inter-thread synchronization as much as possible. Their experimental results show that MPSM runs much faster than no-partitioning hash join [7] and radix hash join [15] (the latter implemented in Vectorwise on a 32-core, 4-socket machine). Unfortunately, the authors did not make their code available to us. Hence, we will use the sort-based join from Balkesen et. al. [4] as the sort-based baseline as it is freely available and additionally was shown to be superior to MPSM.

Balkesen et. al. [5] investigated the parallel radix hash join and no-partitioning hash join algorithms from Blanas et. al. [7] and proposed better variants for both algorithms. They achieved higher throughputs by improving the cache efficiency of the hash table implementations for both algorithms and adopting a better skew handling mechanism for parallel radix hash join. We discuss this algorithm (called PRB in our paper) in more detail in Section 3. In their experimental results, using their new implementations, the parallel radix hash join outperforms the no-partitioning hash join for almost all architectures and workloads — except on Niagara2, which has 8 threads per core, for a workload using a very large probe relation. This result is contradicting the conclusions made by Blanas et. al. [7].

The picture changed again when Lang et. al. [14] published their NUMA-aware no-partitioning hash join. In their results, their no-partitioning hash join method outperforms the parallel radix hash join from Balkesen et. al. [5] by a factor of more than two on a 4-socket machine with 64 hardware contexts. We discuss the no-partition algorithm (called NOP in our paper) from Lang et. al. in Section 3.

Another work by Balkesen et. al. [4] improved the sort-merge join from Kim et. al. [13] and their own parallel radix join from [5]. Their sort-merge join uses wider SIMD instructions and uses range partitioning to allow for efficient multithreading without heavy synchronization. We discuss the proposed sort-merge join (called MWAY in our paper) in more detail in Section 3. In their experimental results, in contrast to the prediction from Kim et. al. [13], wider SIMD instructions did not yet make sort-merge join superior to parallel radix hash join. In fact, in their experiments, parallel radix hash join still always outperforms sort-merge join.

While all the previous research focused on the runtime of join algorithms, the work from Barber [17] studied the memory-efficiency of hash join methods. They proposed a highly memory efficient linear probing hash table called concise hash table (CHT). We also discuss this algorithm (called CHTJ in our paper) in more detail in Section 3. They compared their method with the no-partitioning hash join and the parallel radix hash join from [5]. Their experimental results show that they can reduce the memory usage by one to three orders of magnitude with competitive performance.

Finally, there has been work optimizing joins for specialized architectures including GPUs, e.g. [12], hybrid CPU-GPU architectures, e.g. [10], and coprocessors attached through PCI express cards like Intel's Xeon Phi, e.g. [11, 18]. Though these are all interesting works they are way beyond the scope of this paper. We will focus on modern server CPUs which are still abundant.

3. FUNDAMENTAL REPRESENTATIVES OF MAIN-MEMORY JOIN ALGORITHMS

In summary, we can identify three fundamental classes of join algorithms into which the most recently published join algorithms fall. Namely: (1) partition-based hash joins, (2) no-partitioning hash joins, and (3) sort-merge joins.

In the following we will discuss one or two modern variants of each class in more detail. This discussion will serve as the starting point of our study.

Join Class	**Modern Variants Introduced in Paper**
Partition-based Hash Joins	[13],[7],[5],[4]
No-partitioning Hash Joins	[7],[5],[14],[17]
Sort-merge Joins	[13],[3],[4]

Table 1: Join algorithms from Section 2 and their assignment to classes

Table 1 shows this classification assigning the papers discussed in Section 2 to their corresponding class. Notice that some of those papers, e.g. [7], presented algorithms from multiple classes.

3.1 Partition-based Hash Joins

Core Idea: *Partition-based Hash Joins partition the input relations into small pairs of partitions (co-partitions) where one of the partitions typically fits into one of the caches. The overall goal of this method is to minimize the number of cache misses when building and probing hash tables.*

PRB is the two-pass parallel radix hash join described in [5]. A problem with partitioning joins is that different partitions will most likely reside on different memory pages. Thus, randomly writing tuples to a large number of partitions may cause excessive TLB

Join	Description	Paper	Code
Fundamental Classes of Join Algorithms (Section 3) &Black box comparison (Section 4)			
PRB	Basic two-pass parallel radix join without software managed buffer and non-temporal streaming	[5]	Original
NOP	No-partitioning hash join	[14]	Original
CHTJ	Concise hash table join	[17]	Own
MWAY	Multi-way sort merge join	[4]	Original
White box comparison (Section 5)			
NOPA	Same as NOP except using an array as the hash table	This	Modified
PRO	One-pass parallel radix join with software managed buffer and non-temporal streaming	[5]	Original
PRL	Same as PRO except using linear probing hashing instead of bucket chaining	This	Modified
PRA	Same as PRO except using arrays as hash tables	This	Modified
Optimizing Parallel Radix Join (Section 6)			
CPRL	Chunked parallel radix join with software managed buffer and non-temporal streaming	This	Own
CPRA	Same as CPRL except using arrays as hash tables	This	Own
PROiS	PRO with improved scheduling	This	Modified
PRLiS	Same as PROiS except using linear probing hashing instead of bucket chaining	This	Modified
PRAiS	PRA with improved scheduling	This	Modified

Table 2: reference table for the algorithms evaluated in this paper

misses. In order to fix this problem, **PRB** uses two-pass partitioning to guarantee that the number of partitions does not exceed the number of TLB entries. The first partitioning pass starts by assigning equal-sized regions (chunks) to each thread. The algorithm precomputes the output memory ranges of each target partition by building histograms. Hence, each thread knows where and how much to write for each partition without the need for further synchronization. After histograms have been built, each thread scans the input relation and writes each tuple to its destination region. The first partitioning pass already produces a considerable number of partitions. Therefore, in order to perform the second partitioning pass, entire sub-partitions (rather than chunks of a partition as done in the first partitioning pass) are assigned to worker threads by using a task queue. If required, skew handling may be done to break up larger partitions further by assigning multiple threads to an individual partition. In the join phase, each thread takes one co-partition at a time and runs a textbook hash join algorithm on it using a chained hash table.

3.2 No-partitioning Hash Joins

Core Idea: *No-partitioning hash joins concurrently build a single global hash table. Simultaneous multi-threading and out-of-order execution is used to hide cache miss penalties automatically. In contrast to partition-based joins, no knowledge about the hardware cache sizes or number of TLB entries is required for tuning.*

NOP is the no-partitioning hash join described in [14]. It uses a lock-free synchronization mechanism for a linear probing hash table using compare-and-swap. The algorithm starts by assigning equal-sized regions (chunks) to each thread. Each thread then inserts its chunk of the build relation into the global hash table. After all threads are done inserting, each thread starts probing its chunk of the probe relation against the global hash table.

For inserts into the global hash table, each thread uses an atomic Compare-and-Swap (CAS) operation. This is a transactional and conditional operation that is only executed if the slot contains the empty key; in that case the empty key is overwritten by the key to be inserted. Otherwise the operation returns false. As entries are never removed or overwritten in a slot, the thread can copy the payload to the bucket in an additional non-transactional operation. In addition to the lock-free hash table, another optimization of NOP is to interleave hash table allocation among all available NUMA nodes for better memory bandwidth utilization.

CHTJ is the concise hash table join described in [17]. At its core a Concise Hash Table (CHT) consists of four major components. First, an array A of size n storing all n inserted tuples without any additional empty slots. Second, a hash function $hash : Key \mapsto [8 \cdot n]^2$, where Key denotes the domain of the join keys and $[8 \cdot n]$ denotes the set of all integers in the range from 1 to $8 \cdot n$. Third, a bitmap B of size $8 \cdot n$. This bitmap marks if a certain hash bucket is occupied. Fourth, a population count array PC of size $n/4$ with a running sum of the population count of the bitmap, i.e. for for every 32 bits of the bitmap we count the number of elements stored up to that point. A CHT is a static structure that is bulkloaded once and then used for lookups only. Hence, this structure is very suitable for join processing. Notice that Google sparse hash map [8] is very similar to CHT, but additionally allows for inserts and deletes.

In a CHT, a lookup for a *key* works as follows: we first check if the bit $B(hash(key))$ is set. If that is the case, this implies that array slot $hash(key)$ is occupied. In other words: there *may* be a result. In that case, from the population count array PC we retrieve the population count from position $\lfloor hash(key)/32 \rfloor - 1$ and add it to the number of bits set in B within the range

$$[\lfloor hash(key)/32 \rfloor \cdot 32;\ hash(key) - 1].$$

In order to speed up this process B and PC are physically interleaved in the same structure.

CHTJ works as follows: first it radix-partitions the build input into a small number of partitions very similar to PRB. Second, one global CHT is allocated where each thread bulkloads its partition to a disjoint region in that CHT. Hence, there is no need for additional synchronization at this point. Fourth, the probe relation is handled similarly to NOP: each thread probes one chunk of the probe relation against the global CHT. Again, as no inserts are performed in the CHT at this point, there is no need for synchronization.

We classify CHTJ as a no-partition hash join even though the algorithm uses partitioning on the build input. However, that partitioning is only used to build the global CHT in parallel. Afterwards the algorithms is equal to NOP as discussed above. Moreover, in CHTJ the partitioning is not used to run independent joins on co-groups like in PRB.

3.3 Sort-merge Joins

Core Idea: *Sort-merge joins belong to the oldest join methods used in databases. The idea is to first sort both input relations on their join keys, if they are not yet sorted, and to use an efficient merge step afterwards to find all matching tuples. Sort-merge join algorithms can exploit and create so-called interesting orders. Even if the performance of a single join in a complex multi-join query would be suboptimal, the overall performance of the sort-merge join plan could be superior.*

MWAY is the m-way sort merge join described in [4]. It is also very similar to the method described in [13]. **MWAY** partitions the data very similar to **PRB**, however using only a single partitioning phase and creating only few partitions. In addition, software

[2]For simplicity we assume here that n is a power of 2.

write-combine buffers (see Section 5.1) are used. After partitioning, each partition will be merge-sorted independently by a separate thread. The merge-sort is implemented with bitonic sorting- and merge-networks. Both sort- and merge-networks are vectorized using SIMD instructions. In addition, multi-way merging is used to save memory bandwidth.

4. BLACK BOX COMPARISONS

In this section we want to compare the representatives of the fundamental join algorithms that were also compared in prior work. We want to identify some of the reasons for contradicting results in previous works. Table 2 lists all evaluated join algorithms and the abbreviations used. The *paper* column refers to papers where the specific algorithm was published and "this" means that the algorithm is proposed in this paper. The *code* column shows the implementation we used for each algorithm. There are three values for this column: "Original" means we use the implementation from authors of the paper, "Modified" means we modify the original implementation to get the new variant and "Own" means we implemented the algorithm from scratch.

For our experimental evaluations we use a setup that is similar to the one used throughout all mentioned previous join papers. The tuples of the join relations consist of two four byte attributes, namely the join key and the payload. Furthermore, the keys in the smaller relation are dense and unique, like in a primary key column. Throughout this study we use the same 60 core machine, see Section 7.1 for details. Unless stated differently, all algorithms use at most 32 threads even though our machine has 60 cores available. The reason is that the code of the MWAY algorithm only works with a power of two number of threads. In Section B we will increase the number of threads beyond 32 threads. We measure the throughput of a join as $(|R|+|S|)/t_{join}$, i.e. the total number of input tuples of both relations divided by the algorithm runtime.

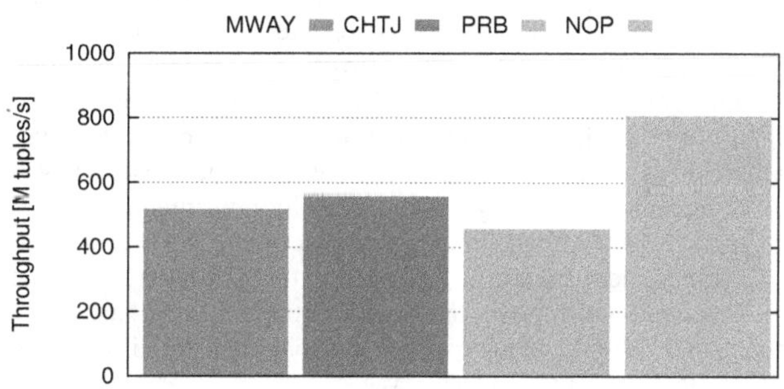

Figure 1: Black box comparison of the fundamental join representatives using 32 threads and relation sizes $|R| = 128M$ and $|S| = 1280M$.

Figure 1 shows the performance of this black box comparison in terms of throughput. We use inputs of size 128 million and 1280 million tuples respectively. These results are comparable to the results found in [14] and [17], but do not match the findings in [4] as for instance in that study the performance of PRB was found to be much better than MWAY.

To understand this inconsistency between results from prior work, we will take a closer look at the parallel radix partitioning join in the next section.

5. WHITE BOX COMPARISONS

From the prior publications it is not always clear what optimizations were used for the parallel radix join. We therefore take a closer look at different possible optimization for the different methods to make them more comparable.

Let's start by taking a closer look at the code for PRB provided by [1]. We see at least two optimizations that can be enabled.

5.1 Optimizing Radix Partitioning

NUMA-Awareness. The first option is the `-basic-numa` flag that equally allocates the partition buffer on all NUMA nodes, as otherwise the buffer will be allocated randomly over different NUMA regions. This option was most likely enabled in all related work as otherwise the performance of the join algorithm decreases considerably on NUMA machines. Turning on this option has another important effect:

Memory Allocation Locality. Before running the actual join, all physical pages will be allocated locally and mapped in the virtual memory table. Hence, we will not trigger page faults and consequent allocations while running a join algorithm. As database system always have a buffer manager anyways, we believe it is a fair assumption that memory buffers were already physically allocated. We already used this option in the previous section and we will also keep this option turned on throughout all following experiments.

Software Write-Combine Buffers. The second option provided by the code of [1] is the `-enable-swwc-part` flag[3]: this flag enables the use of software write-combine buffers (SWWCB) and non-temporal streaming instructions for the parallel partitioning algorithm. SWWCBs, aka software managed buffers, have been known for quite some time [20]. The idea is to allocate a small local buffer for each partition and first put tuples into buffers instead of directly flushing them to the output. This is similar to buffered writes in disk-based partitioning, however, *the size of each buffer is only one cache line*. SWWCB reduce the pressure on the TLB as

Algorithm 1 Partitioning with Software Write-Combine Buffers

```
for all tuple ∈ relation do
    partition ← hash(tuple.key);
    pos ← slots[partition] mod TuplePerCacheline;
    slots[partition]++;
    buffer[partition].data[pos] = tuple;
    if pos == TuplePerCacheline - 1 then
        dest ← slots[partition] - TuplePerCacheline;
        copy buffer[partition].data to output[dest];
```

the buffers are very likely to reside in cache and on very few pages while only a full buffer is flushed to main memory. If a buffer can hold N tuples, then the number of TLB misses will be reduced by a factor of N. Algorithm 1 illustrates how SWWCB works. Turning on this option has another important effect:

Non-temporal streaming. This is a technique allowing programmers to write half a cache line to DRAM bypassing all caches. It prevents polluting the caches with data that will never be read again. Recently, Schuhknecht et.al [21] performed an in-depth study of the effects of using both software write-combine buffers and non-temporal streaming on the single-threaded radix partitioning algorithm. We follow the guideline provided in that paper.

[3]To be fair with prior work that did not enable this feature in their comparisons. It is marked as experimental and we applied some fixes that removed minor race conditions that did not influence the performance.

After enabling all those features we obtain a much more efficient algorithm called **PRO** (Parallel Radix with Optimized partitioning).

Single-pass Partitioning. The original PRO used two-pass radix-partitioning. We ran micro-benchmarks on PRO comparing single-pass and two-pass partitioning and also determined the optimal number of partitions to use for partitioning. Figure 2 shows that a single-pass partitioning using 14 bits leads to the highest throughput. We will use this setting in the following for all variants of PRO.

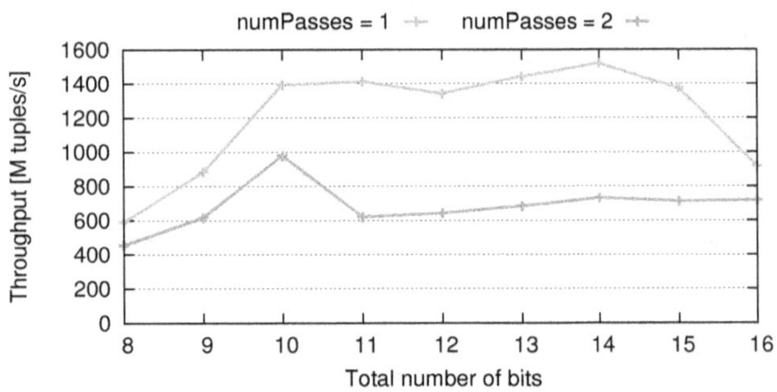

Figure 2: Throughput of PRO for different partition sizes and number of radix bits for partitioning (total join including partitioning and join phase); the two-pass algorithm divides the bits evenly over the two passes.

5.2 Choice of Hash Method

Linear vs Chained vs CHT. Another dimension that makes the available join algorithms harder to compare is the usage of different hash table implementations in the algorithms. All presented hash join methods use different hash table implementations. CHTJ of course uses a concise hash table; PRO uses a variant of chained hashing while the NOP algorithm uses linear probing to implement the hash table. We therefore also implemented a version of PRO that uses a linear probing hash table and call that method **PRL**. An in-depth study for different hashing strategies can be found in [19].

Arrays. When using unique and dense domains of join keys we can go one step further and use an even simpler hash table implementation — a simple array. Instead of storing key value pairs in a hash table we can simply use the key as an index in the array and store the value in that position. This assumption on the key domain may sound unrealistic on first sight, however, often joins are performed along 1:n or n:1 foreign key relationships using artificially created IDs (ID Integer PRIMARY KEY AUTOINCREMENT), this situation may occur frequently in practice. It can also be identified easily by the query optimizer through the available statistics. This simple array implementation can also be used in the NOP-family of joins and hence we get two new hash join variants called No Partition Array join (**NOPA**) and the Parallel Radix partition Array join (**PRA**). These joins are of course not as widely applicable as the other hash joins. We will also investigate the usefulness of these methods in the presence of holes in the key domain in Section C.

Performance Comparison. Considering the optimizations discussed in Sections 5.1 and 5.2, we take another look at the performance of the join algorithms and show their throughput in Figure 3. We can see that PRO clearly outperforms NOP and now the performance of PRO also resembles the results presented in [4]. However, surprisingly, there is almost no difference in runtime between PRA, PRO, and PRL. Therefore, we might conclude that the choice of the hash method does not have an effect on the runtime; however, later on we will learn that this conclusion would be wrong (see Section 6.2).

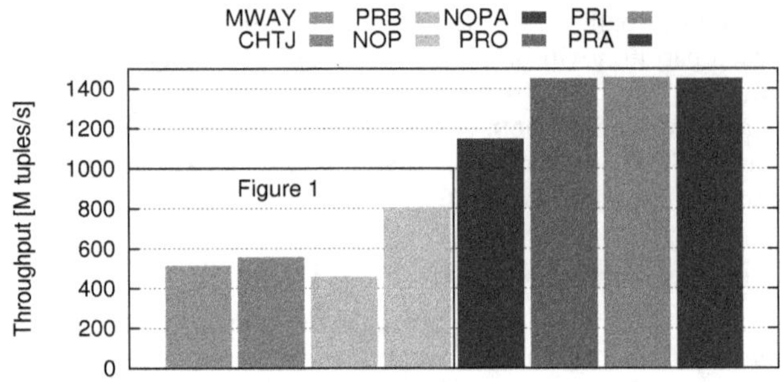

Figure 3: Join throughput including improved versions. We observe almost a twofold performance improvement over the black-box versions shown in Figure 1.

6. OPTIMIZING PARALLEL RADIX JOIN

We have observed in Figure 3 that the parallel radix partitioning joins PR* are providing the highest throughput so far. We are therefore looking for ways to further improve their performance. In the following, we will look at the partition phase and the join phase separately.

6.1 NUMA-aware Partitioning

First we investigate the partitioning phase. The Parallel Radix Partitioning algorithm is illustrated in Figure 4(a). It works as follows: (1) every thread sequentially reads a horizontal chunk of the input relation to create a local histogram. (2) a global thread merges the local histograms into a global histogram[4]. The goal is to exploit this global histogram later on as an index to the target partitions. To merge the local histograms, we need a synchronization barrier, as every thread has to complete the local histogram before the final output positions can be computed. (3) each thread reads again its horizontal local chunk of the input relation and partitions the data into its corresponding SWWCB. Each thread keeps as many SWWCB as it has target partitions. Whenever a SWWCB becomes full, it is flushed to the final output position in its target partition using non-temporal streaming. As the final output position of every partition was already determined in phase (2), no further synchronization is necessary. For the probe relation, phases (1)–(3) are executed similarly using the same partitioning function. Once both inputs have been partitioned, each pair of corresponding partitions is joined independently. This is done by building a hash table on the left input and probing the right input against that hash table. Hence, from a high-level perspective this join algorithm is a variant of Grace Hash Join applied to NUMA.

NUMA-partitioning is a task which triggers a considerable number of memory reads and writes, especially when writing out tuples to their destinations. However, in NUMA systems, careless memory access patterns can hurt the performance very badly as remote memory accesses have higher latency and lower bandwidth than local memory accesses. So we devoted our effort on analyzing memory access patterns of PRO and we found out that there are in particular random remote memory writes that we can avoid in this algorithm.

Figure 4(b) depicts the NUMA access pattern in a simplified case with four sockets, four threads, and four partitions when writing tuples to their target partitions. We see that the partitioning algorithm of PRO introduces many random **remote** writes when writing tuples to their corresponding partitions. Based on this observation,

[4]Technically, this may also be implemented by letting the threads merge their histogram independently as in phase (3) each thread only requires a subset of the global histogram.

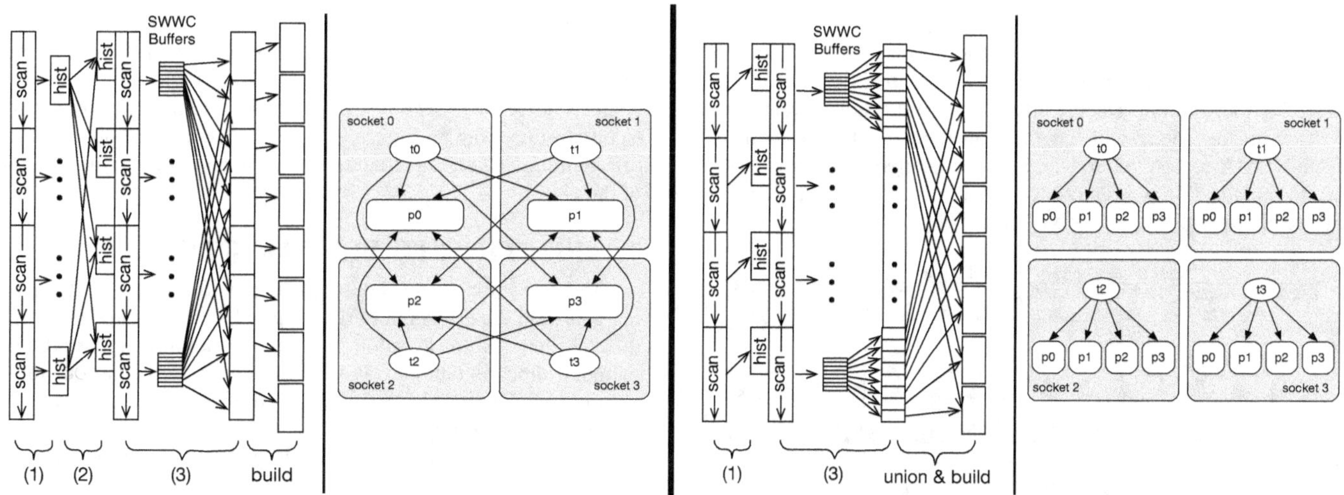

(a) Schematic view on build relation partitioning of PRO

(b) NUMA write pattern for PRO

(c) Schematic view on build relation partitioning of CPRL

(d) NUMA write pattern for CPRL

Figure 4: High-level schematic view and NUMA write pattern: PRO vs CPRL

we propose the Chunked Parallel Radix partition (**CPRL**) algorithm that eliminates remote writes when flushing tuples to partitions.

Figure 4(c) shows a high-level schematic view on our algorithm CPRL. Notice, that the histogram phase (1) is the same as in PRO. However in contrast to PRO, in CPRL we leave out phase (2), i.e. we do not compute a global histogram. We proceed directly with phase (3), i.e. each thread partitions its data locally within its chunk only based on its local histogram. On a high-level this can be viewed as running a single-threaded histogram-based radix-partitioning inside a chunk. For the probe relation phases (1)–(3) are executed similarly using the same partitioning function. Once both inputs have been partitioned, each pair of corresponding partitions, i.e. each co-partition, is joined independently. In contrast to PRO, at this point we neither have physically contiguous probe nor build partitions available. Hence, we first have to read the different chunks belonging to the build input from its (possibly NUMA-remote) sources. In that process, we directly load that data into a local hash table. Then we also read the different chunks belonging to the probe input from its (possibly NUMA-remote) sources and probe them directly against the hash table. Hence, from a high-level perspective this join algorithm is also a variant of Grace Hash Join applied to NUMA. However, in contrast to PRO, we do not require the inputs to each join to be physically contiguous in main memory. Therefore, CPRL trades small random writes to remote memory for large sequential reads from remote memory. Notice that CPRL uses the same linear probing hash table as PRL since it was easier to integrate our own linear hash table implementation. In addition, the linear hash table also provided a slightly better performance compared to the chained hash table implementation by Balkesen et. al. When we use arrays rather than hash tables in the join phase of the Chunked Parallel Radix join, we call it **CPRA**. Again, optimizations like software write-combine buffers and non-temporal store instructions are also used in this algorithm. The write pattern of CPRL is illustrated in Figure 4(d).

Let's compare the performance of PRO, PRL, and PRA with our proposed CPRL and CPRA. Figure 5 shows the end to end join processing time broken down into partition and join phase. We see that the CPR*-algorithms outperform the PR*-algorithms by $\sim$20%. We also observe that the partitioning times of the CPR*-algorithms are indeed reduced as expected. However, surprisingly

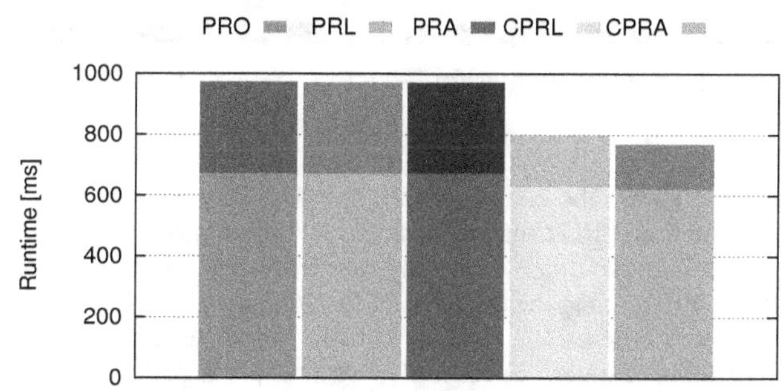

Figure 5: Runtime of PR* vs CPR*-algorithms. Relation sizes: $|R| = 128M$, $|S| = 1280M$. Lighter colors denote the partition phase and darker colors denote the join phase.

even the join time is reduced. This is counterintuitive to what we expected as we traded remote writes in the partitioning phase with remote reads from all sockets in the join phase. We will investigate the reason for this in the next section.

6.2 NUMA-aware Scheduling

All PR*- and CPR*-algorithms build co-partitions which eventually have to be joined independently. How are those individual joins scheduled? What effect does this schedule have on the overall performance of the join algorithms?

After partitioning, in both PR*- and CPR*-algorithms, all co-partitions are put into a LIFO-task queue (which is actually a stack), to be processed by different threads. Recall that the PR*-algorithms partitions an input array into p partitions where for any two partitions $i, j \in [0; p-1], i < j$ it holds that the starting address of partition j is greater than the starting address of partition i. In other words, the partition indices correlate with their virtual addresses. We observed that in all PR*- and CPR*-algorithms, co-partitions are inserted into the queue in ascending sequential indices order, i.e. for p co-partitions the insert order into the queue is $0, \ldots, p-1$. However, recall, that before executing any join, one quarter of each input relation is physically allocated on one of the NUMA-regions. In addition, any additional memory required for partititioning or building hash tables is also equally distributed across NUMA-regions. This memory allocation strategy was already present in the code used by [5]. Assume that the number of threads is considerably smaller than the number of partitions, i.e. $t << p$, typically $p = 16384$ and for our machine $t = 60$. This implies that the first $\lceil 16384/60 \rceil = 274$ partitions reside **on the same** NUMA-region. Hence, all of the first 60 threads removing tasks from the queue will have to read their input data from the same NUMA-region. Moreover, for three quarters of those threads, i.e. 45 threads, this is a remote NUMA-region. Similar bottlenecks can be observed for all other blocks of 274 partitions.

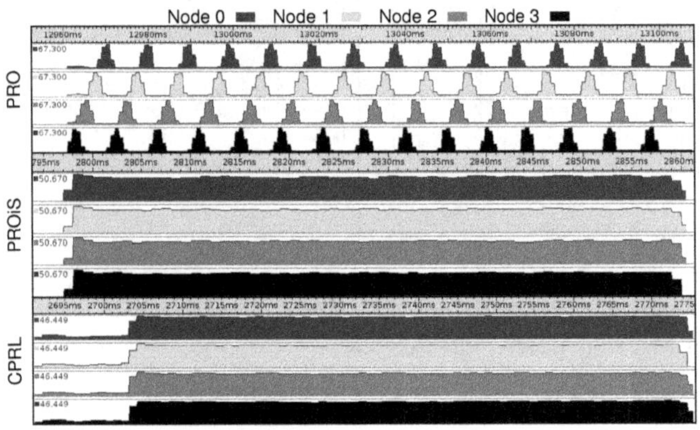

Figure 6: Bandwidth profiles for PRO, PROiS, and CPRL obtained with Intel VTunes

Figure 6 shows the bandwidth profile of PRO. We observe that most of the time PRO uses only a single NUMA-region.

We can improve this by carefully reordering the join tasks. We fixed this by changing the task scheduling strategy used by all PR*-algorithms as follows: we insert co-partitions into the task queue in a round-robin manner. Specifically, we first put a partition from the first NUMA region into the queue and then a partition from the second NUMA region and so on. An alternative would be to use a different queue for each NUMA-region. Like that it is very likely that all memory controllers are utilized simultaneously.

Figure 6 shows a bandwidth plot of the original PRO, the variant of PRO using improved scheduling, coined **PROiS**, as well as CPRL. In addition, we also introduce variants of PRL and PRA using improved scheduling called **PRLiS** and **PRAiS**. We observe that the improved scheduling of PROiS has a substantial effect on the total bandwidth utilization, i.e. all NUMA nodes are used at the same time. Even though the suboptimal scheduling is also used for CPRL, it does not affect the bandwidth utilization, as every partition has to be read from all NUMA nodes anyhow.

The improved scheduling results in a speedup of the join phase of PRL and PRA by more than a factor of 2, see Figure 7. As expected

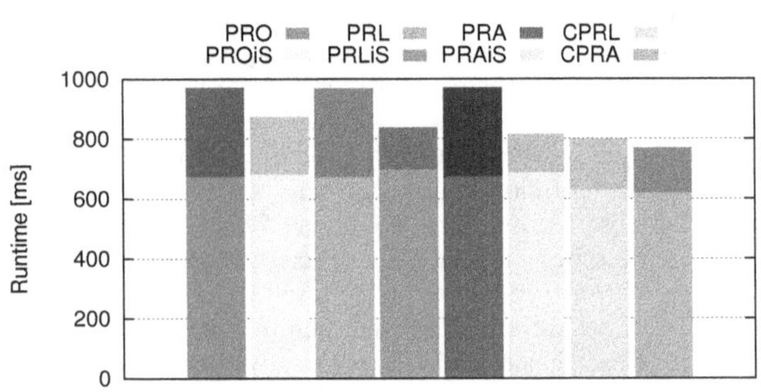

Figure 7: Runtime of PR* and CPR*-algorithms vs their variants with improved scheduling (PR*iS-algorithms). Relation sizes: $|R| = 128M$, $|S| = 1280M$. Lighter colors denote the partition phase and darker colors denote the join phase.

in Section 6.1, we can now observe that the join phase of the CPR*-algorithms is in fact slightly more expensive than the one of the PR*iS-algorithms. However, still, in total the CPR*-algorithms are slightly faster than the PR*iS-algorithms. Moreover, in contrast to our results from in Figure 3, we can now clearly observe that different hash table implementations have an effect on the runtime of the algorithms.

7. PUTTING IT ALL TOGETHER

After our initial black box comparison (Section 4), after having analyzed the effects of optimizing radix partitioning and using different hash tables (Section 5), and after optimizing the NUMA memory allocation and NUMA access pattern of the various radix algorithms (Section 6), we are finally in the position to perform a comprehensive comparison of *all* join algorithms.

In this section we will perform a large-scale experimental study of all thirteen algorithms mentioned above. Recall that Table 2 lists all algorithm abbreviations and their short descriptions. In the pdf of this paper all occurrences of algorithm abbreviations are hyperlinks pointing to their description. We evaluate all algorithms in the same benchmarking framework. Additional experiments including skewed data and semi-dense key domains can be found in the Appendix.

7.1 Settings

All our experiments are performed on a server with half a terabyte of main memory and four Intel Xeon E7-4870 v2 CPUs, clocked at 2.30 GHz (published in Q1 2014). This CPU has 30 hardware contexts executed on 15 physical cores that share a 30 MB L3 cache. Each core has one private 32 KB L1 data, one 32 KB instruction cache, and one 256 KB L2 data cache. Notice that the number of TLB entries when using 4 KB page is 256. However, if we use 2 MB pages, we only have 32 TLB-entries! The operating system we used is a 64-bit Debian 7 server with the kernel version of 3.2.0-4. The CPU supports AVX 1.0. Just like the original studies [13, 4, 3, 14, 6], we also assume a column-oriented storage model and adopt the configuration of using a <Key, Payload> pair as a tuple. We use a 4-byte integer key and a 4-byte integer payload to make a fair comparison between all methods, since some available implementations only work for this key size. We assume that the build relation follows a dense primary key distribution and the keys of the probe relation have a foreign key relationship to the keys of the build relation, if not mentioned otherwise. This setting was also used in the mentioned previous studies.

In the following experiments, we use the implementations of PRO, PRB, NOP from the original authors. PRA, PRL, PRAiS, PROiS, NOPA are implemented based on the authors' implementations. We implemented CPRL, CPRA, and CHTJ ourself from scratch. Since the build relation has dense primary keys, we use the identity hash function modulo the hash table size for all hash joins as it is very effective and efficient in this setting and was also used in the previous studies. Lang et. al. [14] additionally evaluated different hash functions like Murmur, CRC, and multiplicative hashing. We are not evaluating the effect of different hash functions on the join performance in this paper. All software is implemented in C/C++ and compiled by gcc/g++ version 4.7.2 with optimization level -O3.

7.2 Varying Page Sizes

The first dimension we want to explore is the page size of the virtual memory used for the join algorithms. As partitioning is very sensitive to TLB misses, this is a very important aspect. In the previous experiments we used huge page sizes for all allocations, i.e. 2 MB. To study the effect of the page size on the different algorithms we evaluate pages of 4 KB and 2 MB by switching the kernel setting transparent_hugepage/enabled between `never` and `always`. We also ensured that all allocations use the default `malloc` or `posix_memalign` methods.

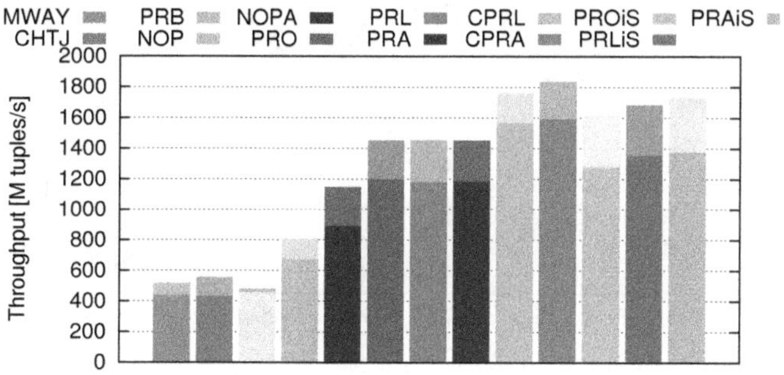

Figure 8: Performance of all thirteen join algorithms when using small (4 KB, dark color) and huge pages (2 MB, light color)

Figure 8 shows the performance of all thirteen join algorithms when using small (4 KB) and huge pages (2 MB). We observe that all algorithms except PRB improve by using huge pages. PRB is the only algorithm that has a slightly worse performance when using huge pages. This is due to the naive partitioning that does not use any software write-combine buffers for the different partitions. In each of the two radix passes PRB partitions along 7 bits = 128 partitions. The entries for all those pages fit into the TLB-cache when using small pages. However, when using huge pages, we only have 32 TLB-entries available. Hence, many write operations to partitions lead to TLB-misses. This effect is mitigated when using SWWCB as in PRO.

As some of the algorithms are clearly dominated by others, in the following, we do not report for results for PRB, PRO, PRL, and PRA anymore. In addition, for all following experiments we use huge pages.

7.3 Scalability in Dataset Size

The next dimension we will explore is the scalability in the size of the input data to the joins. We will explore two workloads: (1) the probe relation is ten times the size of the build relation. The factor ten is motivated by the typical ratio in the TPC-H benchmark and the observation that in a star schema, often used in OLAP applications, the dimension tables are typically much smaller than the fact table. (2) both relations have the same size. This is close to a worst case for hash joins, as the typically more expensive build phase is followed by a rather short probe phase. If the build relation becomes smaller than the probe relation, the optimizer should actually have switched the roles of the relations in the first place. At the same time, this case is close to a best case for sort-based methods, as sorting has super-linear costs and is therefore minimized if both relations have the same size. Previous studies [4, 14] also used similar workloads.

Fine-tuning the partition-based joins. When we started benchmarking the effects of scaling the input datasets, we quickly noticed that the radix-based algorithms are very sensitive to the number of bits used for partitioning. Recall, that in Section 5.1 we already explored this effect for *a fixed-size input dataset*. Following the results of our micro-benchmark in Figure 2 we assumed that when doubling the data size, we take one additional bit for partitioning and hence end up with the same partition size and obtain good performance. But is that really true? Let's take a second look:

Figure 11 shows the average partitioning time per tuple for a varying number of partitions and corresponding data set sizes. On the horizontal axis we use a log scale doubling the number of partitions at every tic. The number of partitions is chosen such that a chained hash table that is built on a single partition fits into L2 cache.

We observe that the average partition time per tuple stays almost constant up to including 2^{15} partitions. Starting with 2^{16} partitions the performance deteriorates. This can be explained with the size of the software write-combine buffers. Recall that we use 32 threads. If we create 2^{15} partitions using a single cache line per partition as an SWWCB, all SWWCBs together including other working variables, e.g. histograms, still fit into the shared last level cache (LLC). However, when using 2^{16} partitions, this is no longer the case.

We conclude from this experiment that partitioning data into too many partitions might overshadow the performance gains obtained in the join phase. We therefore micro-benchmarked the performance of all partition-based joins with a varying number of bits used for partitioning and show these results in Figure 9. In Figures 9(a)&(b) we choose the number of radix bits such that the hash table on a partition fits onto L2. In contrast, in Figures 9(c)&(d) we depict the number of radix bits actually leading to the lowest overall runtime. We can see that choosing the number of bits such that the partitions fit into L2 cache is close to the optimal choice as long as the SWWCBs still fit into the shared LLC. However, for larger datasets, we observe in Figure 9(b) that the partitioning costs increase sharply. Hence, we conclude that for these input sizes it is better to balance the partitioning cost with the join costs. The sweet spot for the number of bits used in partitioning seems to be the minimal number of bits such that the partitions still fit into the shared LLC.

Predicting the optimal number of radix bits. This leads to the following formula for the number of bits for partitioning n_p. Given the size of R as $|R|$, the size of a tuple of R as s_t, the intended load factor of the join hash tables l, the size of a partition buffer as s_b, the size of the L2 cache as $L2$, and the size per thread of the last level cache as LLC_t [5]:

$$n_p(|R|) = \begin{cases} \log_2\left(\frac{|R|\cdot s_t}{l\cdot L2}\right), & \frac{|R|\cdot s_b\cdot s_t}{L2\cdot l} < LLC_t \\ \log_2\left(\frac{|R|\cdot s_t}{l\cdot LLC_t}\right), & \text{otherwise} \end{cases} \quad (1)$$

Figure 12 shows the observed runtime for CPRL[6] when varying the number of radix bits from 8 to 18 bits (black points) versus the performance observed when setting the bits according to Equation (1) (red line). We can see that the number of bits computed by Equation (1) leads in almost all cases to the lowest runtime.

Back to Figure 9, we can also make an additional observation: we see that the different hash table implementations have an effect on the optimal number of bits for partitioning. This is reasonable, as the different hash table implementations differ in their space efficiency. For instance, array joins use a tight array that only keeps the payload, the key however is implicitly represented through the array index. In contrast, a linear probing hash table has to store the key explicitly.

Based on these results, from now on, we will use Equation (1) to set the bits of all PR*- and CPR*-algorithms and are in the position

[5] As the LLC is shared between cores, the available share per thread is dependent on the number of concurrently running threads.

[6] Similar results for the other algorithms are not shown due to space constraints.

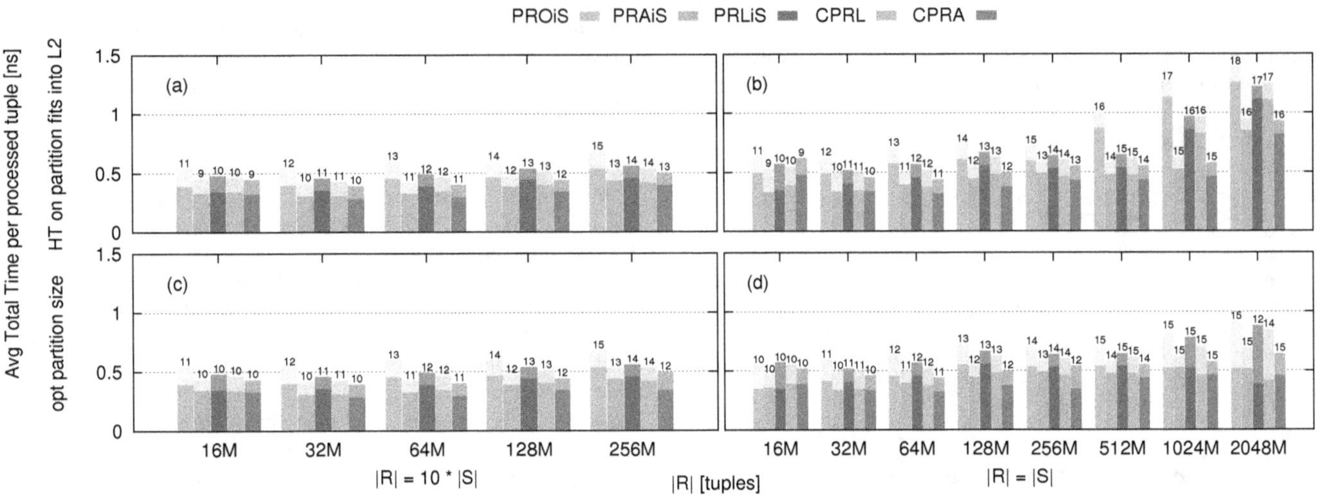

Figure 9: Average total time per tuple (partitioning and join) when varying the number of radix-bits used for partitioning. The dark color marks the time for partitioning; the light color marks the time for joining. In (a) and (b) we choose the number of radix bits such that the hash table on a partition fits onto L2. In contrast, in (c) and (d) we depict the number of radix bits leading to the lowest overall runtime. In particular for $|R| = |S|$ (right column) and $|R| \geq 512$ M tuples we see that our assumption, (a) and (b) diverges heavily from the optimal number of bits, (c) and (d). Notice that we can observe in (b) that the partitioning costs increase heavily whereas the join costs stay the same.

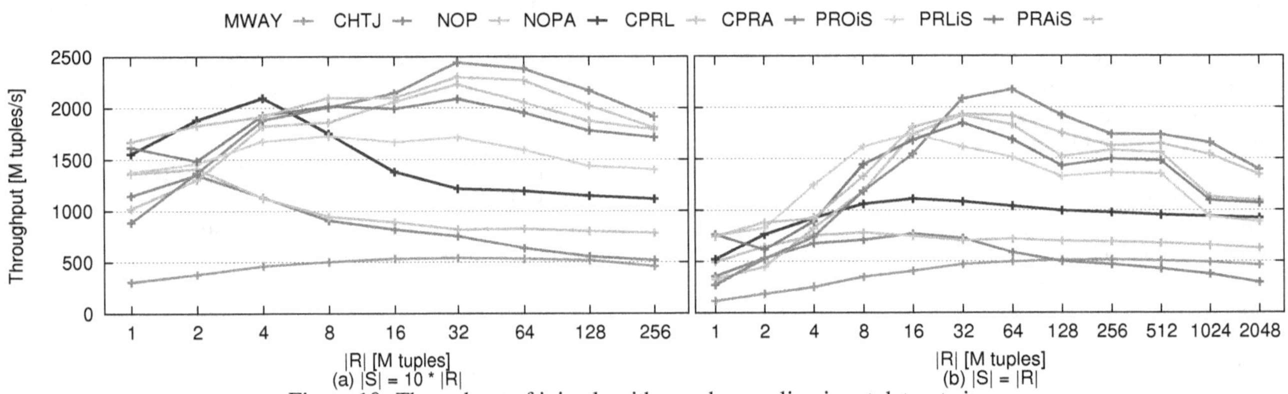

Figure 10: Throughput of join algorithms when scaling input dataset sizes

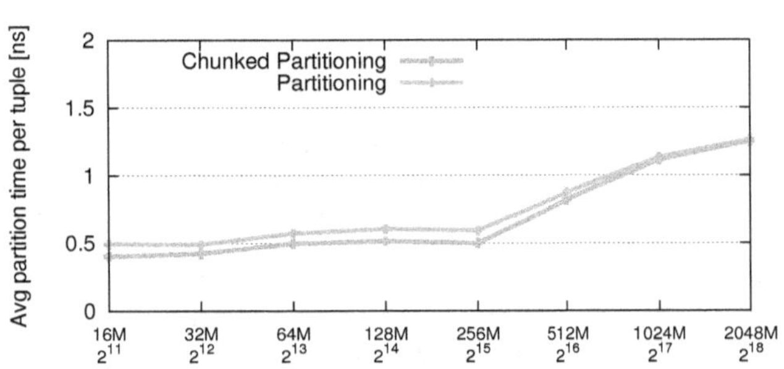

Figure 11: Scalability of the partition phase for chunked and non-chunked partitioning

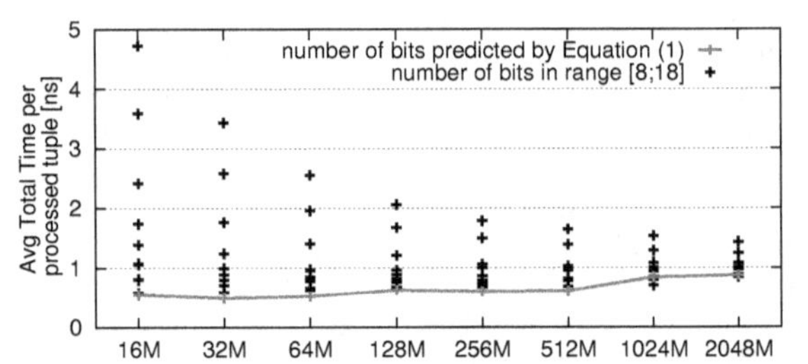

Figure 12: Runtime of CPRL when setting the number of partitioning bits according to Equation (1)

to evaluate the join performance when scaling the sizes of the input datasets.

Scalability results. Finally, Figure 10 contains the performance results for all join methods when scaling the input data size. For the partitioning joins we observe that for very small input sizes, i.e. up to 4M tuples, the various algorithms show similar performance. However, if we scale the input data to larger sizes, we observe that the PR*- and CPR*-algorithms outperform the NOP*-algorithms, CHTJ, and MWAY. In particular, for the NOP*-algorithms we can see from Figure 10 that the throughput is very good up to 4M. However, for larger inputs the throughput decreases. This matches our expectation since no-partitioning join methods need to build a big global hash table. With growing data sizes the global hash table won't fit into the LLC anymore, which in our case is just 30 MB. Hence, the bigger the build relation, the higher the probability for an LLC miss as well a TLB-miss. This effect can be observed very well in Figure 10(a): up to an input size for $|R| = 32$ M tuples there is a decrease in performance. Afterwards the performance does not deteriorate (visibly) anymore as almost all hash table accesses trigger LLC and TLB misses anyway (due to lacking spatial proximity in the caches). In other words, the NOP*-algorithms are already bound by this bottleneck.

The *inverse argument* to this holds for the PR*- and CPR*-algorithms. These algorithms perform *more* memory operations than the NOP*-algorithms. The underlying assumption of these algorithms, however, is that memory accesses to individual tuples may be very expensive, i.e. they may lead to a costly LLC miss. This effect is similar to external memory algorithms trying to avoid individual seeks on disk by bundling operations into larger granules. The PR*- and CPR*-algorithms try to access (and implicitly cache) memory according to larger granules, i.e. partitions and/or memory pages. This algorithmic pattern does not have much of an effect if the input data fits into LLC anyways (then, the underlying assumption of the algorithms simply does not hold). However, once the underlying assumption holds, i.e. the input data exceeds the size of the LLC, these algorithms can efficiently avoid costly DRAM accesses to individual tuples.

Notice that among the NOP*-algorithms, CHTJ is very sensitive to the data size as it needs at least two random accesses for every operation on its CHT. MWAY sort-merge join is another very stable algorithm, it even outperforms the CHTJ for large datasets.

8. EFFECTS ON REAL QUERIES

Up to now we focused on benchmarking raw performance of multithreaded joins. Like that we followed the micro-benchmarking philosophy of previous work [7, 6, 5, 14, 3, 17, 4, 13]. However, micro-benchmarks always trigger the same (and important) question: how big is the impact observed in micro-benchmarks in a larger context, e.g. when joins are used inside a larger query?

The development of a full-fledged multithreaded NUMA-aware query execution engine is beyond the scope of this paper. However, state-of-the-art main-memory databases use code compilation anyways [16], i.e. at query time they translate incoming SQL to machine code (a standalone program if you wish) and then execute that program kind of independently from the remaining system (if you do not require locking which is the case for us). Therefore we decided to simply emulate a column store in C++. Similar to MonetDB we represent every column as a separate array consisting of <virtual oid,value> pairs, where the virtual oid is given implicit by the position of the value in the array. More details can be found in Appendix F. We choose TPC-H query 19 (Listing 1 in Appendix F) as that query is the only query that contains a single join followed by an aggregation without any subqueries. This query joins the `Lineitem` table with the `Part` table.

Both tables are stored as a struct of arrays and additionally, we dictionary-compress all string columns. We used float values instead of arbitrary precision numeric values. All foreign and primary key columns are represented as <Key , Payload> pairs with the row ID as the payload, this made it easier to use the join implementations with minimal modifications.

On a high-level we execute this query according to the query execution plan depicted in Figure 13. We obtained this plan through textbook query optimization. Notice that the same plan is also used by HyperDB according to the explain functionality of their web interface [7]. In this plan, the selection, that was pushed down to the scan of the `Lineitem` table, has a selectivity of 3.57%. This means that for scale-factor 100 the build relation Part has 20 M tuples and the probe relation Lineitem has 600 M tuples (600 M$\cdot$ 3.57% = 21.42 M tuples after filtering), i.e. in the join both relations have roughly the same size.

[7]http://hyper-db.de/interface.html

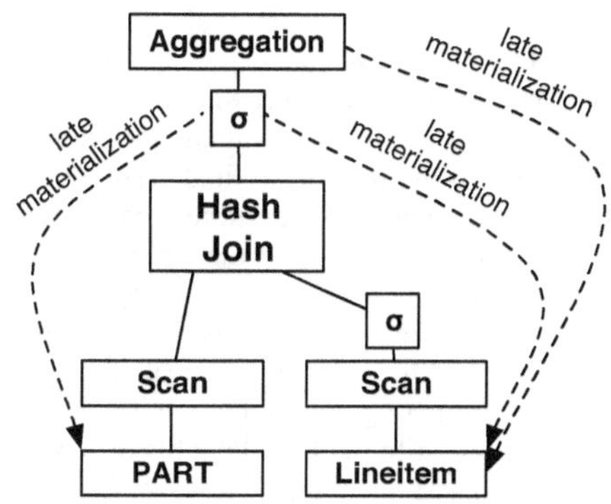

Figure 13: Optimized semi-physical query plan for TPC-H Q19 plus materialization strategy in the column store

For scale-factor=100 this corresponds to the results of our micro-benchmark of Figure 10(b) for $|R| \approx 20$ M tuples. Notice that the plan in Figure 13 is actually only *semi-physical* as it does not specify *when* to reconstruct tuples. We used late materialization, i.e. all attributes are only touched when required by an operation[8].

Figure 14 shows the runtime of Q19 for TPC-H for scale-factors 100. This figure includes a cost breakdown where the colored bars represent the time spent for the join. In contrast, the black bars represent the time spent in other parts of the query. We obtained the numbers for the colored bars by executing each join just like in the micro-benchmarks above, i.e. each of the four join algorithms receives a build input of 20 M tuples and a pre-filtered (and pre-materialized) probe input of 21.42 M tuples. The difference of the execution time of the query and the join smicro-benchmark yields the black bars[9].

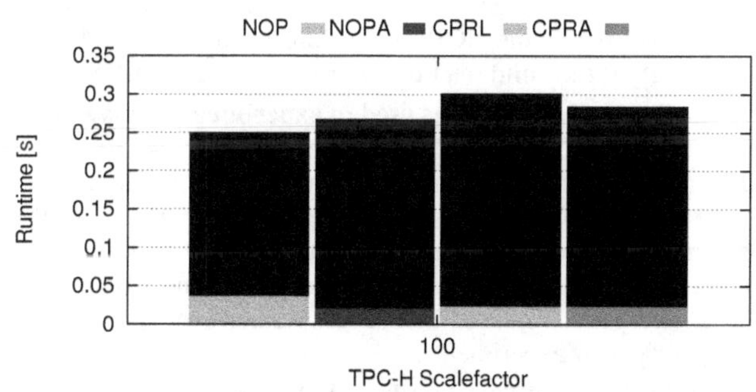

Figure 14: Runtime of TPC-H Query 19, colored bars mark the fraction of the time spent in the actual join; the black bars mark the time spent for the rest of the query.

We immediately observe that even for this relatively simple query a major part of the runtime is spent in the non-join parts of the query. The time spent in the actual join is only about 10%–15% of the total runtime! In addition, for some methods more time is spend outside the join than for others.

There are several reasons for this: First, the join key column is a primary dense key and the `Part` table is even generated in sorted order according to this key. This means that we have an ideal sequential access pattern for NOPA when building the join array (also compare our discussion in Section 5.2 as well as additional experimentation in Section C). Second, scanning and filtering 600 M tu-

[8]This strategy is also used by MonetDB.

[9]This method is not entirely fair as the join- and non-join parts of a query may overlap. However, it gives a good indication on how much of the total query time is actually due to the actual join.

ples from Lineitem down 21.42 M tuples simply eats up some time. Third, in contrast to the micro-benchmark experiments, for Q19 we have to access several attributes other than the join key. This happens in multiple places: in order to evaluate the complex predicate after the probe and to aggregate the final result, i.e. we have to perform implicit positional joins (for tuple reconstruction). In particular, In NOPA neither the `Lineitem` table nor the `Part` table have to be partitioned. Therefore, all other attributes *stay aligned with the join array and the probe relation.* This is especially beneficial for all attributes of the probe relation since they are accessed sequentially when evaluating the complex join predicate. In contrast, for the CPR*-algorithms those benefits do not apply. If we access attributes that are not the join key, we have to follow the row ids contained in the narrow join tuples. Those row-ids point to arbitrary locations after partitioning the data. This means that we pollute our cache and TLB with data from other attributes and lose locality in our accesses. Therefore, it would be beneficial to explore tuple reconstruction strategies for CPR*-joins in more detail.

9. LESSONS LEARNED

(1.) Don't use CPR* algorithms on small inputs. For input relations with less than 8 million tuples we do not observe a benefit of partitioning local chunks instead of the global relation. On the contrary, we even observe a performance degradation. This is mainly due to two things: (1) the overhead of creating all the threads does not pay off for the small input data. This is also true for all other presented algorithms. (2) the size of a chunk becomes smaller than a page. This leads to a random allocation of the pages to different NUMA nodes. Several threads will have to read from and write to remote memory, even though the main advantage of the CPR* algorithms over the PR* algorithms should be to avoid remote writes. For very small inputs the NOP* algorithms become very interesting, especially if the build relation starts to fit into the LLCs.

(2.) Clearly specify all options used in experiments. This sounds like common sense for any experimental study. Still, we list it here again as a gentle reminder since we ran into this problem when we were trying to interpret results from different papers. As the implementations provided by authors typically have multiple optimization options, it is sometimes hard to understand which optimizations were actually used in a paper. Rather over-specify than under-specify your experiments.

(3.) If in doubt, use a partition-based algorithm for large scale joins. In this paper, we have studied the performance of three variants of no-partitioning algorithm and eight variants of partition-based algorithms with different workloads by varying ratio between build and probe relations, data size, number of threads and skewness. **All** Partition-based algorithms outperform **all** no-partitioning algorithms in almost all except for only two cases. The first case is when the size of input relations scales to 32 GB where the worst partition-based algorithm is a little bit slower than the best no-partitioning algorithm. The second case is when the probe relation is highly skewed such that partition-base algorithms suffer from unbalanced loads between threads while no-partitioning algorithms have less cache misses. No-partitioning algorithms start outperforming partition-based algorithms only for a Zipf factor > 0.9.

(4.) Use huge pages. As we discussed in Section 7.2, all algorithms except PRB benefit from using huge pages. Using huge pages means less pages are needed for a certain amount of data, thus reduces the pressure on TLB system.

(5.) Use Software-write combine buffer. Software-write combine buffers are a very effective technique to reduce the number of TLB misses. Hence, using SWWCBs allows us to use single pass algorithm which accelerates partition-based algorithms.

(6.) Use the right number of partition bits for partition-based algorithms. Partition-based algorithms are very sensitive to choosing the right number of radix bits. For different data sizes, one has to choose different number of partition bits to get the optimal performance. As shown in Figure 9, choosing suboptimal number of bits can lead to performance degradation by up to a factor of 2.5.

(7.) Use a simple algorithm when possible. In our study, simple ideas turned out to be surprisingly efficient and effective. For instance, array joins are very efficient in the case of dense primary key distributions. They outperform other non-array variants under all workloads by up to 44%. Chunking is another simple idea we used to create faster join algorithms. Chunking eliminates remote memory writes in partition phase and improves the join performance by up to 26%.

(8.) Be sure to make your algorithm NUMA-aware. Back at the time when PRO and PRB [5] were published, the authors ran experiments on several single socket machines. These algorithms were designed for multicore systems but not yet for NUMA systems. Directly running these algorithms on NUMA systems will yield sub-optimal performance. We evaluated chunking to eliminate writes to remote memory and explored NUMA-aware scheduling to avoid bandwidth saturation on a single memory controller. These two optimizations improve the performance over non-NUMA-aware algorithms by up to 26% and 20%, respectively.

(9.) Be aware that join runtime$\neq$query time. Our experiments with a TPC-H query clearly indicated that the join time may actually only be a 10%–15% share of the total runtime of the query. We identified multiple reasons that lead to interesting avenues for future work. However, already at this point it again emphasizes that micro-benchmarks alone may be misleading in case we want to understand performance in a bigger context, e.g. an entire query.

10. CONCLUSIONS

In this paper, we evaluated thirteen main-memory join algorithms in a common setting. We resolved some contradicting results and showed that hardware-conscious partition-based approaches typically outperform hardware-oblivious no-partition based joins on modern multi-core NUMA architectures. At least this is the case if the probe relation is not highly skewed; for very skewed data the unpartitioned hash table can match or even outperform the partition-based approaches. We also presented new partition-based approaches, called CPRL and CPRA that often outperform the PR*-algorithms from prior work. Overall CPRL and CPRA achieve a remarkable join throughput of up to 3.4 billion input tuples per second.

So should we finally consider relational joins a solved problem? The bad news is, we will probably never be able to label it 100% solved as there will always be some fancy new SIMD instruction or whatever "new" hardware that may impact the relative performance differences. The good news, with this study we believe we made major steps forward in understanding the performance of state-of-the-art join algorithms as of 2015. However, as stated above, almost all previous works, e.g. [7, 6, 5, 14, 3, 17, 4, 13], evaluated micro-benchmarks only. We departed from that and evaluated the runtime of the most promising join algorithms when used in a simple TPC-H query. This initial experimentation already reveals that only a fraction of the query runtime may be spent in the actual join, a majority may be spent in other parts of the query including scanning, filtering, and tuple reconstruction. Hence, as future work we would like to evaluate the cross product of different join algorithms and the large space of tuple reconstruction algorithms, in particular for the very promising CPR*-family of join algorithms.

11. REFERENCES

[1] https://www.systems.ethz.ch/node/334.

[2] D.J. Abadi, D.S. Myers, D.J. DeWitt, and S.R. Madden. Materialization Strategies in a Column-Oriented DBMS. *ICDE*, pages 466–475, 2007.

[3] Martina-Cezara Albutiu, Alfons Kemper, and Thomas Neumann. Massively Parallel Sort-Merge Joins in Main Memory Multi-Core Database Systems. *PVLDB*, 5(10):1064–1075, 2012.

[4] Cagri Balkesen, Gustavo Alonso, Jens Teubner, and M Tamer Ozsu. Multi-Core, Main-Memory Joins: Sort vs. Hash Revisited. *PVLDB*, 7(1):85–96, 2013.

[5] Cagri Balkesen, Jens Teubner, Gustavo Alonso, and M Tamer Ozsu. Main-Memory Hash Joins on Multi-Core CPUs: Tuning to the Underlying Hardware. *ICDE*, pages 362–373, 2013.

[6] Cagri Balkesen, Jens Teubner, Gustavo Alonso, and M Tamer Ozsu. Main-Memory Hash Joins on Modern Processor Architectures. *TKDE*, 27(7):1754–1766, 2015.

[7] Spyros Blanas, Yinan Li, and Jignesh M Patel. Design and Evaluation of Main Memory Hash Join Algorithms for Multi-Core CPUs. *SIGMOD*, pages 37–48, 2011.

[8] Google Inc. Google Sparse and Dense Hashes. https://code.google.com/p/sparsehash/.

[9] Jim Gray, Prakash Sundaresan, Susanne Englert, Ken Baclawski, and Peter J Weinberger. Quickly Generating Billion-Record Synthetic Databases. *SIGMOD*, pages 243–252, 1994.

[10] Jiong He, Shuhao Zhang, and Bingsheng He. In-cache Query Co-processing on Coupled CPU-GPU Architectures. *PVLDB*, 8(4):329–340, 2014.

[11] Saurabh Jha, Bingsheng He, Mian Lu, Xuntao Cheng, and Huynh Phung Huynh. Improving Main Memory Hash Joins on Intel Xeon Phi Processors: An Experimental Approach. *PVLDB*, 8(6):642–653, 2015.

[12] Tim Kaldewey, Guy Lohman, Rene Mueller, and Peter Volk. GPU Join Processing Revisited. *DaMoN*, pages 55–62, 2012.

[13] Changkyu Kim, Tim Kaldewey, Victor W Lee, Eric Sedlar, Anthony D Nguyen, Nadathur Satish, Jatin Chhugani, Andrea Di Blas, and Pradeep Dubey. Sort vs. Hash Revisited: Fast Join Implementation on Modern Multi-Core CPUs. *PVLDB*, 2(2):1378–1389, 2009.

[14] Harald Lang, Viktor Leis, Martina-Cezara Albutiu, Thomas Neumann, and Alfons Kemper. Massively Parallel NUMA-aware Hash Joins. *IMDM*, pages 3–14, 2013.

[15] Stefan Manegold, Peter Boncz, and Martin Kersten. Optimizing Main-Memory Join on Modern Hardware. *TKDE*, 14(4):709–730, 2002.

[16] Thomas Neumann. Efficiently Compiling Efficient Query Plans for Modern Hardware. *PVLDB*, 4(9):539–550, 2011.

[17] R Barber G Lohman I Pandis, V Raman R Sidle, G Attaluri N Chainani S Lightstone, and D Sharpe. Memory-Efficient Hash Joins. *PVLDB*, 8(4):353–364, 2014.

[18] Orestis Polychroniou, Arun Raghavan, and Kenneth A. Ross. Rethinking SIMD Vectorization for In-Memory Databases. *SIGMOD*, pages 1493–1508, 2015.

[19] Stefan Richter, Victor Alvarez, and Jens Dittrich. A Seven-Dimensional Analysis of Hashing Methods and its Implications on Query Processing. In *PVLDB*, 2016.

[20] Nadathur Satish, Changkyu Kim, Jatin Chhugani, Anthony D. Nguyen, Victor W. Lee, Daehyun Kim, and Pradeep Dubey. Fast Sort on CPUs and GPUs: A Case for Bandwidth Oblivious SIMD Sort. *SIGMOD*, pages 351–362, 2010.

[21] Felix Martin Schuhknecht, Pankaj Khanchandani, and Jens Dittrich. On the Surprising Difficulty of Simple Things: the Case of Radix Partitioning. *PVLDB*, 8(9):934–937, 2015.

APPENDIX

A. SKEWED DATA DISTRIBUTIONS

Until now we only looked at uniformly distributed data sets. In the next set of experiments we use different skew factors for the probe relation. We used an algorithm proposed by Gray et. al. in [9] to quickly generate large amounts of skewed join keys. To achieve a more realistic distribution and to avoid that the key occurring most often, i.e. the smallest keys, are all in a single partition, we map the 10 smallest keys to random keys in the full domain. Figure 15 shows the performance of all algorithms with different zipf factors θ ranging from zero to 0.99. For every method we choose the number of threads such that the throughput was the highest. This means the no-partition algorithms make use of all hyper threads while the partition based algorithms only use a single thread per core to not pollute the private caches. We can see that lower levels of skew have no real impact on the performance of the algorithms.

When the skew factor is high we observe a shift in the throughput towards methods that do not partition the input. This has two reasons. First, the partition based methods have to handle skewed partition sizes, which is for now only handled automatically by a task queue. This means that the threads responsible for larger partitions are processing less partitions. We do not exploit the possibility to use multiple threads to process the join on the largest partitions in parallel. Second, a high skew factor makes the caches more effective, as the keys that are accessed most often are likely to be cached. For the partition based algorithms this effect is not helping, as the partitioning already makes the caches effective. We can see that the partition based approaches are still competitive with the no partition joins for the presented data size.

B. SCALABILITY IN NUMBER OF THREADS

In this section we explore the scalability of the different join methods in terms of multithreading. All previous experiments were run using 32 threads. As the implementation of MWAY only works with a power of two many threads, we cannot report numbers for MWAY with more than 32 threads[10].

We take as a starting point four threads where each thread is assigned to one of the four NUMA regions. From that starting point we increase the number of threads distributing threads evenly across NUMA regions.

Figure 16 shows the results when scaling the number of threads from 4 to 120. All methods achieve good performance when using all physical cores, i.e. 60 threads. All partitioned-based approaches perform worse when using hyper-threading. This is understandable, as then even the private caches have to be shared among the hyper-threads. Even for the NOP*-joins the benefit of hyper-threading is minimal. This is also understandable for our fast hash function, as we do not have many computations that could hide the memory latency. A more computationally intensive hash function could also benefit more from hyper-threads.

Table 3(a) shows a summary of the relative speedup for the join algorithms. We calculate the relative speedup as runtime($T > 4$ threads)/runtime(4 threads) where T is the number of threads used. Hence, the perfect speedup for $T = 60$ threads would be 15. Of course no method scales to this theoretically achievable perfect speedup, but CPRA and CPRL come close with a speedup of almost 12.

C. HOLES IN THE KEY RANGE

All previous experiments used a dense key range. In this section we want to study the effect of holes in the key range on the performance of the different join algorithms, especially on the array-based methods. We generate the build relation with a domain k times the size of $|R|$ for increasing values of k. Figure 17 shows the

[10] We also evaluated MWAY using 64 threads, but the results are not competitive and also not fair, as only four out of 60 cores have to work on two threads.

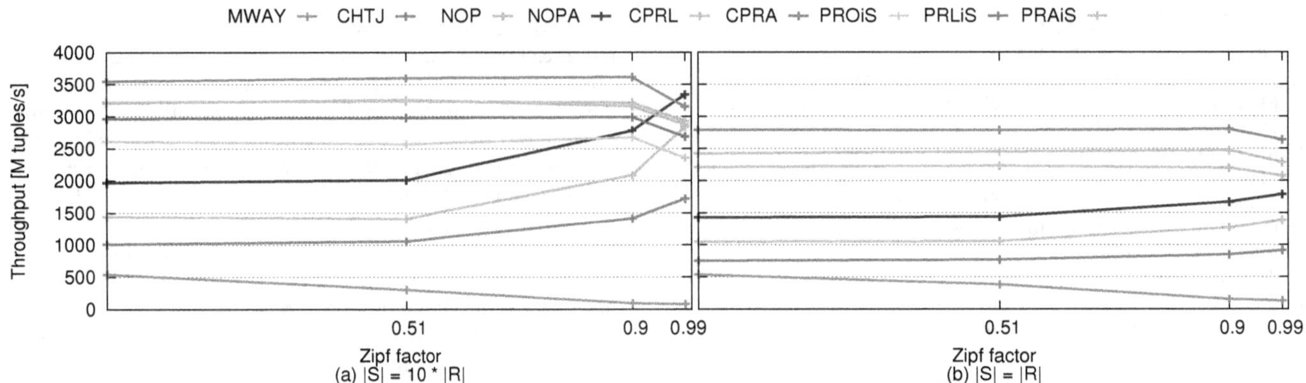

Figure 15: Throughput of join algorithms on skewed data. Relation size: $|R| = 128M$.

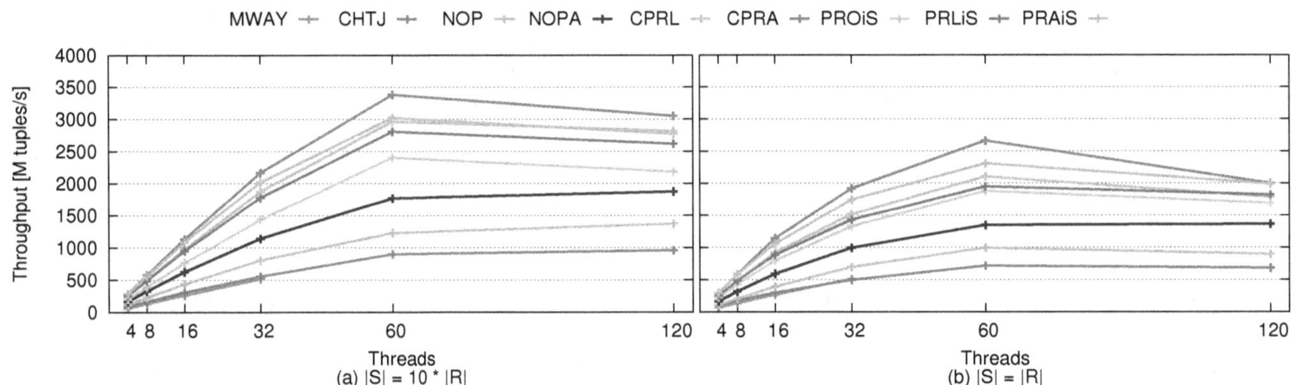

Figure 16: Throughput of join algorithms when scaling the number of threads. Size of relation $|R| = 128M$ tuples

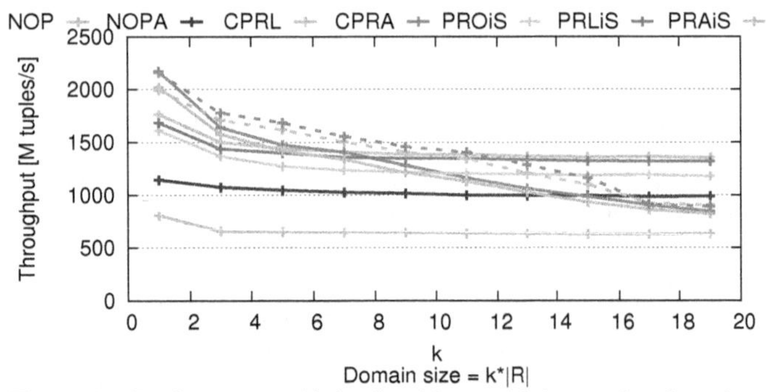

Figure 17: Performance of join algorithms with increasing domain size. $|R| = 128$ M and $|S| = 1280$ M. The dashed lines for CPRA and PRAiS denote the throughput when adapting the number of partitions to the domain size

performance of the different join algorithms for varying domain sizes $k \cdot |R|$. We can see that the performance of the NOPA join is not influenced that much. This is expected, even without any holes in the domain is it very unlikely that neighboring elements in the array are probed in a short enough sequence for the second tuple to still reside in the caches. This slight chance is simply eliminated in the case of very large domains, as neighboring elements are very unlikely to even be present at all. The size of the used array is of course growing linear with the domain size and occupies a larger and larger part of the available memory for the whole time of the join processing. The partition-based array joins on the other hand suffer greatly from large domains, as the array does no longer fit into the caches for larger and larger domains. A possible remedy for the partition-based methods is to use more fine grained partitioning in the case of larger domains, such that the array again fits into the cache. We applied this technique to PRAiS and CPRA and depicted the performance as dashed lines in Figure 17. Please note, that the main memory consumption of PRAiS and CPRA is much lower compared to NOPA as we only construct temporary arrays on small partitions, that can be freed after processing the co-partition join. On another note, all our hash table implementations suffer a small performance hit when increasing the domain, as now we can observe some collisions in the hash table when inserting and probing the join keys.

From the results it looks like NOPA stays very competitive for arbitrary large domains, as long as you are willing and able to pay the additional memory overhead. PRAiS and CPRA can also deal with domains that are reasonably dense, especially when adapting the partition strategy to the domain size.

D. MICRO-ARCHITECTURAL PERFORMANCE ASPECTS

We also measured the performance of all presented join algorithms with respect to the number of cache misses and the instructions per cycle (IPC) metric. Table 4 shows all measurements. The number of cache misses are measured in millions while the instructions retired (IR) count is given in billions. We see that the partition-based joins indeed lead to a dramatic reduction in cache misses and reach a cache hit rate of up to 99% for the join phase. Furthermore, the CHTJ suffers from roughly two times the number of cache misses compared to NOP, due to the additional bitmap lookup, as expected. We can also observe that the partition-based algorithms need more instructions to perform the join but they also have a much higher IPC rate, that allows them to perform the join faster than the no-partitioning joins. Please note, that the different amount of cache misses for PRA, PRL, PRO in the partition phase stem from the fact that we use 12, 13, or 14 radix bits respectively according to Equation (1).

Join	4 Threads [M/s]	60 Threads [M/s]	Relative Speedup: Total	Build or Partition Phase	Probe or Join Phase
CHTJ	87.3	945.7	10.8	8.4	10.9
NOP	122.1	1291.2	10.6	9.4	10.7
NOPA	176.2	1859.5	10.6	6.8	11.2
CPRL	264.3	3105.4	11.7	12.1	10.6
CPRA	300.1	3545.1	11.8	12.4	10.1
PROiS	212.0	2522.9	11.9	11.3	13.2
PRLiS	263.7	2944.0	11.2	11.3	10.8
PRAiS	302.3	3168.0	10.5	10.7	9.8

(a) With |R| = 128M and |S| = 1280M

Join	4 Threads [M/s]	60 Threads [M/s]	Relative Speedup: Total	Build or Partition Phase	Probe or Join Phase
CHTJ	96.6	751.6	7.8	8.5	7.7
NOP	109.8	1043.7	9.5	9.7	9.3
NOPA	173.0	1413.1	8.2	7.1	9.8
CPRL	260.2	2207.9	8.5	8.5	8.4
CPRA	304.9	2790.2	9.2	9.2	9.1
PROiS	234.2	1971.2	8.4	7.3	12.9
PRLiS	263.5	2046.0	7.8	7.3	10.4
PRAiS	312.3	2422.4	7.8	7.3	9.6

(b) With |R| = |S| = 128M

Table 3: Relative speedup when scaling from 4 to 60 threads.

Join	Sort or Build or Partition Phase: L2 Misses [M]	L3 Misses [M]	L2 Hit Rate	L3 Hit Rate	IR [B]	IPC	Probe or Join Phase: L2 Misses [M]	L3 Misses [M]	L2 Hit Rate	L3 Hit Rate	IR [B]	IPC
MWAY	430	388	0.64	0.10	260	1.36	10	10	0.01	0.04	17	1.78
CHTJ	559	353	0.20	0.37	15	0.40	1911	1561	< 0.01	0.18	29	0.25
PRB	558	555	< 0.01	0.01	65	0.33	59	40	0.98	0.33	30	1.46
NOP	394	393	0.38	< 0.01	8	0.36	957	955	0.39	< 0.01	20	0.39
NOPA	409	391	< 0.01	0.04	6	0.27	335	320	< 0.01	0.05	5	0.28
PRO	981	209	0.51	0.79	42	0.87	60	45	0.98	0.26	30	1.34
PRL	791	209	0.45	0.74	41	0.90	86	52	0.93	0.40	24	1.08
PRA	396	110	0.61	0.72	41	1.05	88	52	0.92	0.42	17	0.83
CPRL	730	193	0.47	0.74	43	1.06	72	25	0.94	0.65	29	2.26
CPRA	341	85	0.65	0.75	44	1.24	64	24	0.94	0.62	22	1.94
PROiS	976	209	0.51	0.79	40	0.83	31	13	0.99	0.59	30	2.10
PRLiS	788	209	0.45	0.73	40	0.87	55	23	0.95	0.58	24	2.28
PRAiS	398	110	0.61	0.72	40	1.00	63	31	0.94	0.50	17	1.80

Table 4: Performance counter for the join with |R| = 128M and |S| = 1280M and 32 threads.

E. VARYING THE SELECTIVITY OF THE SELECTION IN Q19

We also measure the query performance with a varying selectivity on the probe relation. Figure 18 shows that the partition based joins indeed outperform the no partition based joins when the actual probe relation in the join becomes large.

F. TPC-H QUERY USED

Listing 1 contains the full SQL code of TPC-H query 19.

Listing 1: TPC-H Query 19

```
select
        sum(l_extendedprice* (1 - l_discount)) as revenue
from
        lineitem,
        part
where
(
p_partkey = l_partkey
and p_brand = 'Brand#12'
and p_container in ('SM␣CASE', 'SM␣BOX', 'SM␣PACK', 'SM␣
    PKG')
and l_quantity >= 1 and l_quantity <= 1 + 10
and p_size between 1 and 5
and l_shipmode in ('AIR', 'AIR␣REG')
and l_shipinstruct = 'DELIVER␣IN␣PERSON'
)
or
(
 p_partkey = l_partkey
and p_brand = 'Brand#23'
and p_container in ('MED␣BAG', 'MED␣BOX', 'MED␣PKG', 'MED
    ␣PACK')
and l_quantity >= 10 and l_quantity <= 10 + 10
and p_size between 1 and 10
and l_shipmode in ('AIR', 'AIR␣REG')
and l_shipinstruct = 'DELIVER␣IN␣PERSON'
)
or
(
p_partkey = l_partkey
and p_brand = 'Brand#34'
and p_container in ('LG␣CASE', 'LG␣BOX', 'LG␣PACK', 'LG␣
    PKG')
and l_quantity >= 20 and l_quantity <= 20 + 10
and p_size between 1 and 15
and l_shipmode in ('AIR', 'AIR␣REG')
and l_shipinstruct = 'DELIVER␣IN␣PERSON'
)
```

Listing 2: Data-structures to represent the Lineitem and Parts tables

```
struct LineitemTable {
    size_t numTuples;
    float *l_extendedprice;
    float *l_discount;
    tuple_t *l_partkey;
    unsigned int *l_quantity;
    uint8_t *l_shipmode;
    uint8_t *l_shipinstruct;
};
struct PartTable {
    size_t numTuples;
    tuple_t *p_partkey;
    uint8_t *p_brand;
    uint8_t *p_container;
    unsigned int *p_size;
};
```

Our simulated column store represents the TPC-H tables as structs of column pointers as depicted in Listing 2. Please note, that we only represent the columns accessed in TPC-H Q19. The type

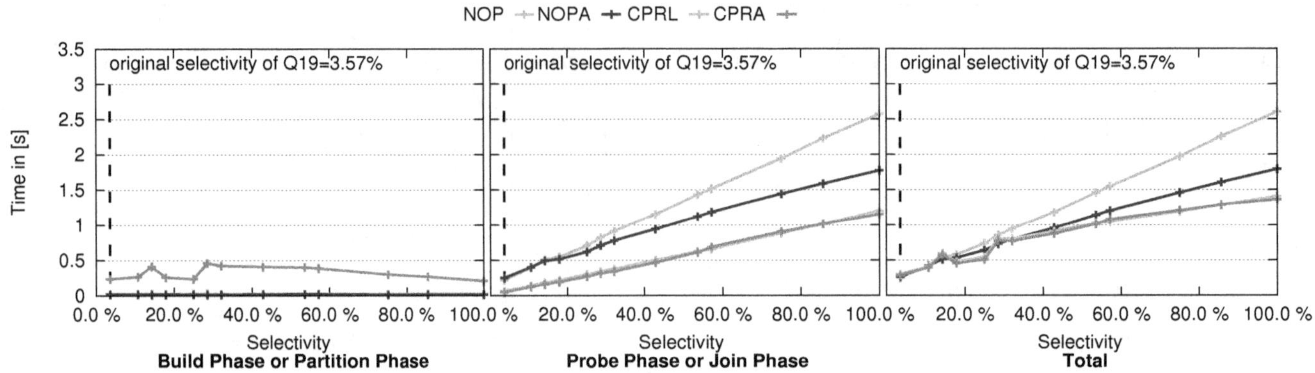

Figure 18: Runtime of TPC-H Query 19 (sf=100) when varying the selectivity of the pushed-down selection predicate

`tuple_t` is a <key,payload> pair with the rowID as the payload. We depict the filter predicate implementation in Listing 3.

Listing 3: Filter conditions

```
inline bool preJoin(LineitemTable *l, size_t rowID) {
    return (l->l_shipinstruct[rowID] == DELIVER_IN_PERSON
          &&
          (l->l_shipmode[rowID] ==AIR||l->l_shipmode[
              rowID] ==AIR_REG));
}
inline bool postJoin(LineitemTable *l, PartTable *p,
     size_t rowIDL, size_t rowIDP) {
    uint8_t p_brand = p->p_brand[rowIDP];
    uint8_t p_container = p->p_container[rowIDP];
    auto l_quantity = l->l_quantity[rowIDL];
    auto p_size = p->p_size[rowIDP];
    return (p_brand == BRAND12
           && (p_container == SM_CASE || p_container ==
               SM_BOX || p_container == SM_PACK ||
               p_container == SM_PKG)
           && l_quantity >= 1 && l_quantity <= 1 + 10
           && 1 <= p_size && p_size <= 5) ||
          (p_brand == BRAND23 &&
           (p_container == MED_BAG || p_container ==
               MED_BOX || p_container == MED_PKG ||
               p_container == MED_PACK)
           && l_quantity >= 10 && l_quantity <= 10 + 10
           && 1 <= p_size && p_size <= 10) ||
          (p_brand == BRAND34 &&
           (p_container == LG_CASE || p_container ==
               LG_BOX || p_container == LG_PACK ||
               p_container == LG_PKG)
           && l_quantity >= 20 && l_quantity <= 20 + 10
           && 1 <= p_size && p_size <= 15);
}
```

These predicates correspond one-to-one to the predicates in the SQL query depicted in Listing 1.

Listing 4 shows the pseudo code for the Q19 implementation using the NOP join. All threads build a hash table on `p_partkey` concurrently. Afterwards, every thread is responsible for a fixed chunk of tuples of the probe relation and first accesses the necessary attributes in `LineitemTable` to evaluate the preJoin predicate. All passing tuples from the `LineitemTable` are probed against the hash table and as soon as a join partner is found the postJoin predicate is evaluated. If the matched tuples pass this predicate, the `l_extendedprice` and `l_discount` attributes are immediately accessed and added to the final aggregate. With this execution strategy it is not necessary to materialize a join index for further processing. This execution strategy also corresponds to the strategy described for the HyperDB system [16].

Listing 4: Q19 Pseudo code for NOP

```
query_result_t
NOPQ19(LineitemTable *L, PartTable *P, int threadCount) {
parallelBuild(P,threadCount);
parallel for in chunks numTuples/threadCount
for (int i=0;i < L-> numTuples;++i) {
  if (preJoin(L,i)) {
    auto tuple=probe(L->l_partkey);
    if (postJoin(L,P,i,tuple.rowID)) {
      res+=L->l_extendedprice[i] * (1.0 - L->l_discount
          [i]);
    }}}}
```

G. FURTHER COST-BREAKDOWN OF Q19

We designed an additional experiment for NOP just to find out how much individual components of that query contribute to the overall runtime of that query. The core idea of this experiment is to start with the "naked join", i.e. the microbenchmark, and then gradually morph the microbenchmark into TPCH-Q19. Like that we see at each step the overhead introduced by that step.

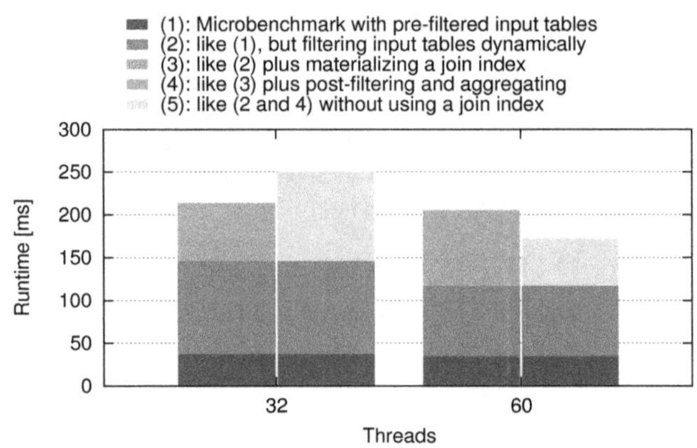

Figure 19: Additional cost-breakdown morphing a microbenchmark stepwise into Q19.

From the results in Figure 19, we can already learn many things:

(1.) Tuple reconstruction is **not** the main culprit for the overheads. In fact, for this query filtering the input rows eats up most of the additional time for both 32 and 60 threads.
(2.) Even writing out join results first into a join index and then doing all additional work like post-filtering, tuple reconstruction (in the same order as before!), and aggregating is faster than running all of this in a pipeline! But only for 32 threads! For 60 threads this does not hold anymore and the results turn upside down: here the overheads for creating and using a join index do not pay off anymore.
(3.) for 32 threads there is room for a tuple reconstruction algorithm, i.e. at most ~20% performance improvement seem possible (for a tuple reconstruction running in zero time).

Top-k Relevant Semantic Place Retrieval on Spatial RDF Data*

Jieming Shi
Department of Computer Science
University of Hong Kong
jmshi@cs.hku.hk

Dingming Wu
College of Computer Science & Software Engineering
Shenzhen University, China
dingming@szu.edu.cn

Nikos Mamoulis
Department of Computer Science and Engineering
University of Ioannina
nikos@cs.uoi.gr

ABSTRACT

RDF data are traditionally accessed using structured query languages, such as SPARQL. However, this requires users to understand the language as well as the RDF schema. Keyword search on RDF data aims at relieving the user from these requirements; the user only inputs a set of keywords and the goal is to find small RDF subgraphs which contain all keywords. At the same time, popular RDF knowledge bases also include spatial semantics, which opens the road to location-based search operations. In this work, we propose and study a novel location-based keyword search query on RDF data. The objective of top-k relevant semantic places (kSP) retrieval is to find RDF subgraphs which contain the query keywords and are rooted at spatial entities close to the query location. The novelty of kSP queries is that they are location-aware and that they do not rely on the use of structured query languages. We design a basic method for the processing of kSP queries. To further accelerate kSP retrieval, two pruning approaches and a data preprocessing technique are proposed. Extensive empirical studies on two real datasets demonstrate the superior and robust performance of our proposals compared to the basic method.

1. INTRODUCTION

With the proliferation of knowledge-sharing communities like Wikipedia and the advances in automated information extraction from the Web, large knowledge bases like DBpedia [5] and YAGO [12] are constructed and made available to the public. Such knowledge bases typically adopt the Resource Description Framework (RDF) data model, which represents the data as collections of $\langle subject, predicate, object\rangle$ triples. RDF models data as entities (subjects) which are linked to other entities and/or types or descriptions (i.e., objects could be entities, types, or literals). For instance, triple $\langle Montmajour\_Abbey, dedication, Saint\_Peter\rangle$ models the fact that Montmajour Abbey is dedicated to Saint Peter. Therefore, an RDF knowledge base can also be seen as a directed graph, where nodes are entities (or types/literals) and the edges are predicates which describe the relationships between nodes.

The English version of DBpedia currently describes 4.5M entities, roughly including 1,4M persons, 883K places, 411K creative works, 241K organizations, 251K species, etc. YAGO includes more than 10M entities (like persons, organizations, cities) and contains more than 120M facts about these entities. Data.gov [4] is the largest open-government, data-sharing website that has more than a thousand datasets in RDF format with a total of 6.4 billion triples to date, covering information from business, finance, health, education, local government, etc. Many excellent applications have been developed on top of these data [32], e.g., *Hospital Compare* [6], *Patients Like Me* [9], *Alternative Fueling Station Locator* [1], *Crime in Chicagoland* [3], *SpotCrime* [10].

Keyword Search on RDF Data. RDF data are traditionally accessed with the help of a structured query language, like SPARQL [50]. However, a standard SPARQL query over RDF data requires query issuers to fully understand the language itself and be aware of the data domain. Hence, SPARQL limits data access mostly to domain experts, since it is not friendly to common users. Given this, a *keyword search* model on RDF data emerged [23, 43, 52]. This model allows users to retrieve information from RDF knowledge bases without the direct use of SPARQL-like languages and without knowledge of the RDF data domain. RDF data belongs to the category of linked data and can be modeled as a directed graph with subjects and objects as vertices and predicates as directed edges. For the purpose of keyword search, this graph can be simplified [43] by eliminating outgoing edges from subjects which connect to types or literals and by collecting all the keywords in the URIs, types, and literals of such entities to form a *unified textual description* for each vertex. A keyword query retrieves a set of (small) subgraphs where the vertices of each subgraph collectively cover all the given keywords. Specifically, each of the retrieved subgraphs includes (i) a *root* node (which is central to the subgraph), (ii) a number of *keyword* nodes, each containing one of the query keywords, and (iii) the shortest paths that connect the keyword nodes to the root. The sum of the lengths of these paths define a *looseness* score for the subgraph [26, 43, 52]. Subgraphs of low looseness are more appropriate as keyword query answers and returned, because they represent a compact and coherent part of the knowledge base related to the keywords. This, in analogy to finding the smallest (tuple) subgraphs in relational keyword query search [35] and general keyword search on graphs [31].

Example 1 Figure 1(a) shows the graph representation of several triples extracted from DBpedia. Both circles and squares are vertices in the RDF graph, representing entities. The edges (labeled by predicates) model the relationships between entities. Each entity is associated to a textual description (document) extracted

*Work supported by grant 715413E from Hong Kong RGC, by EU grant 657347-LBSKQ, and by grant 61502310 from National Natural Science Foundation of China.

SIGMOD'16, June 26-July 01, 2016, San Francisco, CA, USA
© 2016 ACM. ISBN 978-1-4503-3531-7/16/06...$15.00
DOI: http://dx.doi.org/10.1145/2882903.2882941

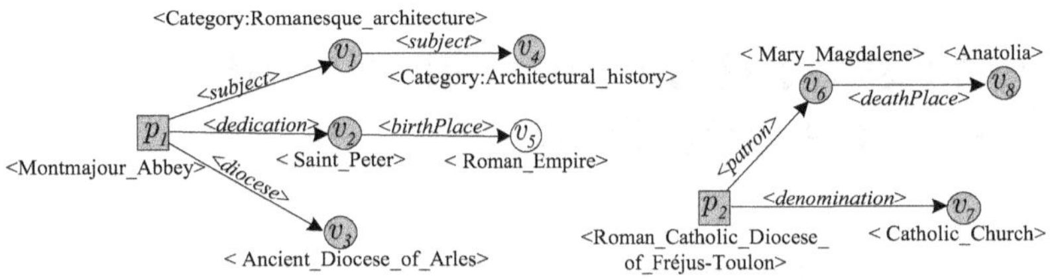

(a) RDF graph

p_1: {abbey, montmajour}
v_1: {architecture, romanesque, subject}
v_2: {catholic, dedication, peter, roman, saint}
v_3: {ancient, arles, diocese}
v_4: {architectural, history, subject}
v_5: {ancient, birthplace, empire, roman}
p_2: {catholic, diocese, roman}
v_6: {mary, magdalene, patron}
v_7: {catholic, church, denomination, history}
v_8: {anatolia, ancient, deathPlace, history}

(b) RDF documents

Figure 1: RDF example

from its URI, predicates, and literals [43]. Figure 1(b) displays the documents of all vertices in Figure 1(a) (due to space constraints, for each document, only some of the terms are shown). Consider an example keyword query $\{ancient, roman, catholic, history\}$. According to [31, 43], the top-1 answer to the keyword query is the subgraph consisting of vertices $\{p_2, v_6, v_7, v_8\}$ rooted at p_2, as well as the edges among them. This subgraph is the most compact one (i.e., it has the lowest looseness) among those whose vertices (i.e., their documents) collectively cover all query keywords. The looseness of the subgraph equals 3 and it is calculated as the sum of the lengths of the shortest paths from a common root vertex (i.e., p_2) to each matched vertex w.r.t each query keyword (i.e., p_2 for keywords $\{catholic, roman\}$, v_7 for keyword $\{history\}$, and v_8 for keyword $\{ancient\}$).

Spatial RDF data. Recently, RDF data have been enriched to include additional semantics. For example, YAGO2 [34] is an extension of the YAGO knowledge base that includes spatial and temporal knowledge. Enriched knowledge bases open the road to additional search and analysis operations, such as location-based retrieval. Indicatively, a key research direction of BBC News Lab is: *How might we use geolocation and linked data to increase relevance and expose the coverage of BBC News?* [2]. To fully utilize spatially enriched RDF data, the GeoSPARQL standard [14], defined by the Open Geospatial Consortium (OGC), extends RDF and SPARQL to represent geographic information and support spatial queries. RDF stores such as Virtuoso [11], Parliament [8], Strabon [42] are developed to support GeoSPARQL features. Recently, Liagouris et al. [46] extended the RDF-3X data store [48] such that the locations of spatial entities are encoded into their IDs; this facilitates efficient evaluation of spatial search operations in GeoSPARQL queries. Still, all these systems share the drawback of having to use a structured query language (SPARQL), which limits the access of common users to RDF data, as already discussed.

kSP Queries. In this paper we propose a novel way of searching spatial RDF data, namely the *top-k relevant Semantic Place retrieval* (kSP) query, which combines keyword search with location-based retrieval. kSP queries share the same motivation as RDF keyword queries; they are independent of the data domain and do not rely on structured languages such as SPARQL, which makes them friendly to ordinary users. They take a query location, a set of query keywords, and the number k of requested places as arguments, and they return as result the top-k *Tightest Qualified Semantic Places* (TQSP) according to a ranking function that considers both the spatial distance to the query location and the graph proximity of the occurrences of keywords in the RDF graph to the places. A *qualified semantic place* satisfies two conditions: (i) it is a tree rooted at a *place entity* (i.e., a vertex of the RDF graph associated to a spatial location, e.g., via hasGeometry predicates), (ii) the documents associated to all the vertices in the tree collectively cover all query keywords. In accordance to existing work on RDF keyword search [23,43,52], the *looseness* score of a qualified semantic place is measured by aggregating the graph distances between the place (root) and the occurrences of the covered keywords at the nodes of the tree. The kSP query returns the k places with the smallest *combined looseness and spatial distance* to the query location, based on an aggregate function (e.g., weighted sum).

Example 2 Consider again the RDF data in Example 1 and assume that the spatial coordinates of p_1 and p_2 in Figure 1(a) are as shown in Figure 2. Assume an 1SP query issued by a tourist at location q_1 in Figure 2 who wants to do field research related to keywords $\{ancient, roman, catholic, history\}$. The result would be the semantic place consisting of vertices $\{p_1, v_1, v_2, v_3, v_4\}$, rooted at p_1, indicating that Montmajour Abbey (p_1), is a promising site with respect to spatial distance and semantic relevance. If the tourist was at location q_2 in Figure 2, a 1SP query with the same keywords would retrieve the semantic place consisting of vertices $\{p_2, v_6, v_7, v_8\}$, rooted at p_2, i.e., Roman Catholic Diocese.

In simple words, the objective of a kSP query is to find places that are near a given query location and they are related to a set of search keywords. Compared to RDF keyword search, the kSP query has the following unique features: (i) it retrieves *semantic places*, i.e., only subgraphs rooted at a place entity, and (ii) it is query-location-aware. kSP queries find many applications, besides the one described in Example 2. For instance, they can be used by patients who want to find nearby hospitals which offer treatment for specific conditions, companies which want to investigate the business environment of some potential nearby sites, journalists who want to search for facts related to location-dependent subjects, etc.

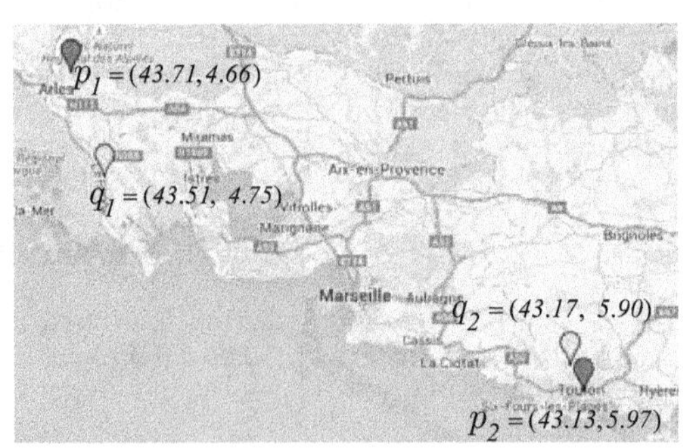

Figure 2: Map of places in Figure 1(a) and query points

Data Representation and Indexing. To our knowledge, this is the first work that proposes and studies kSP queries; therefore, no existing system and algorithm supports their evaluation. Typical RDF stores are designed for the efficient support of SPARQL queries, however, kSP queries require graph browsing and search operations (e.g., breadth first search). Therefore, we opt to represent the RDF data in their *native graph form* (i.e., using adjacency lists) in memory[1], as in [59]. In addition, in a preprocessing phase, we perform the following. First, we extract the document descriptions of all vertices and index them by an inverted file, which enables finding fast the vertices that contain a given keyword in their documents. Second, we store in a table, for each vertex, the document description and the spatial location (in case of a place entity), which makes it possible to directly access the keywords and location a vertex during graph browsing. Third, all place vertices are spatially indexed by an R-tree [29], which facilitates incremental nearest place retrieval from the query location.

Query Evaluation. A possible kSP query evaluation approach would be to extend the bottom-up algorithm for keyword search on graphs [31, 43]. For each query keyword t, the algorithm first determines the set of vertices whose documents contain t. From those vertices, it explores the graph by breadth first search and finds the first common vertex that all the query keywords can reach. If this common vertex is not a place vertex, the algorithm keeps running until a common place vertex is found. This vertex together with the shortest paths leading to vertices covering all keywords would form a qualified semantic place. By continuing this search it is possible to identify all TQSPs in increasing order of looseness. For each identified place, the spatial distance can be computed and the top-k TQSPs can be reported in the end. However, there is no obvious way of determining the top-k TQSPs before finding all qualified semantic places. Therefore, this method is expected to be slow; i.e., kSP queries cannot be efficiently evaluated by a straightforward extension of keyword search approaches [31, 43].

In brief, the challenges are twofold. First, not all vertices in the graph are candidate results since kSP queries look for spatial entities only. Second, the simple application of existing approaches on RDF keyword search (e.g., [31, 43]) is inefficient. As an alternative, we propose a Basic Semantic Place retrieval algorithm (BSP) that retrieves the place vertices in the RDF graph in ascending order of their spatial distances to the query location using the R-tree. For each retrieved place vertex p, BSP computes the corresponding TQSP, i.e., the smallest subtree of the RDF data graph, which is rooted at p and covers all query keywords. TQSP computation is done by browsing the graph from p in a BFS manner until the query keywords are covered. The top-k places are returned as the kSP results when there is no chance for the place vertices that have not been retrieved yet (based on lower bounds of their scores) to outrank the top-k places so far.

BSP is also inefficient because it computes the TQSP of each candidate place, an expensive operation for place vertices that either cannot cover all the query keywords or have worse ranking scores than the top-k places so far. Hence, we propose two approaches for pruning the search space. The first discards *unqualified* places which do not have a TQSP covering all query keywords. The second one prunes places by aborting their TQSP computation early, based on dynamically derived bounds on their looseness. The extension of BSP which applies the two pruning techniques is referred to as Semantic Place retrieval with Pruning (SPP). To further improve the performance of kSP search, we introduce a data preprocessing technique, which aggregates for each place and for sets of nearby places the keywords covered by the vertices in their α-radius neighborhoods (in the RDF data graph). By indexing the preprocessed data, we can define pruning rules for place vertices and for the R-tree nodes that spatially index them. We design a Semantic Place retrieval algorithm (SP) which applies these rules in addition to the pruning techniques of SPP. An extensive empirical study with two real data sets confirms the effectiveness and robustness of SP.

Outline. Section 2 introduces the definition of the kSP queries and relevant concepts. BSP is presented in Section 3. We present the pruning rules in Section 4 and the α-radius based bounds and related pruning techniques in Section 5. Our empirical study is reported in Section 6. Related work is reviewed in Section 7 and we conclude in Section 8.

2. PROBLEM DEFINITION

An RDF knowledge base can be modeled as a directed graph where each vertex v_i refers to an entity and edges represent triples that associate entities based on predicates. Some of the entities are associated to spatial coordinates. We call such entities *place vertices* or places for short. We use v to denote any vertex in the RDF graph, while p is especially used to denote place vertices. Each RDF triple corresponds to a directed edge from an entity (subject) to another entity (object). In accordance to previous work on RDF keyword search, we construct, for each entity, a document ψ from the entity's URI and literals. In addition, for each triple, the description of the predicate is added to the document of the object entity. A *semantic place* is a sub-tree of the RDF graph rooted at a place vertex. Given a place vertex as the root, multiple semantic places can be constructed. In other words, in the RDF graph, a place is associated to multiple semantics by being connected to different vertices.

Example 3 In Figure 1(a), the squares are place vertices and the circles are non-place vertices. Figure 1(b) shows (part of) the documents attached to the vertices. The tree consisting of vertices $\{p_1, v_1, v_2, v_3, v_4\}$ rooted at p_1 is a semantic place. The tree rooted at p_2 with vertices $\{p_2, v_6, v_7, v_8\}$ is another semantic place.

A *top-k relevant Semantic Place retrieval* (kSP) query q consists of three arguments: the query location $q.\lambda$, the query keywords $q.\psi$, and the number of requested semantic places k. A *qualified semantic place* w.r.t. a kSP query is formally defined in Definition 1. Generally speaking, the documents of the vertices in a qualified semantic place collectively cover all the query keywords.

Definition 1. **Qualified Semantic Place.** Given a kSP query q and a RDF graph $G = \langle V, E\rangle$, a qualified semantic place is a tree $T_p = \langle V', E'\rangle$ rooted at place vertex p, such that $V' \subseteq V$, $E' \subseteq E$, and $\cup_{v \in V'} v.\psi \supseteq q.\psi$.

For the ease of presentation, in the rest of the paper, a semantic place is also denoted by $\langle p, (v_1, v_2, \cdots)\rangle$, where p is the root and $(v_1, v_2, \cdots)$ includes all the other vertices. Given a kSP query, there may exist multiple semantic places with the same root p but different $(v_1, v_2, \cdots)$ sets. Following existing work on keyword search over graphs [31, 43], we define the looseness of a qualified semantic place in Definition 2.

Definition 2. **Looseness.** Given a qualified semantic place $T_p = \langle V', E'\rangle$, let $d_g(p, t_i) = \min_{v \in V' \wedge t_i \in v.\psi} d(p, v)$ be the length of the shortest path from root p to keyword $t_i \in q.\psi$, where $d(p, v)$ is the shortest path from p to v. The looseness of T_p is defined as $L(T_p) = 1 + \sum_{t_i \in q.\psi} d_g(p, t_i)$.

Looseness aggregates the proximity of the query keywords in the qualified semantic place in terms of graph distance. We add 1 to the sum of the paths from p to the nearest occurrence of each keyword for normalization purposes (as we will see later, the case

[1]Disk-based graph representations for RDF data (e.g., [60]) can also be used for larger-scale data.

of $L(T_p) = 0$ should be avoided in our raking function for kSP results). The smaller the looseness, the more relevant the root (i.e., the place) is to the vertices that cover the query keywords. Thus, given a place vertex p as the root, we seek for the *Tightest Qualified Semantic Place* (TQSP) for the given query keywords, which is the qualified semantic place rooted at p with the smallest looseness.[2]

Example 4 Assume that the given query keywords are $q.\psi = \{ancient, roman, catholic, history\}$. Based on the RDF example shown in Figure 1, multiple qualified semantic places can be found, such as $\langle p_2, (v_6, v_8)\rangle$, $\langle p_2, (v_6, v_7, v_8)\rangle$, and $\langle p_1, (v_1, v_2, v_3, v_4)\rangle$. The looseness of $\langle p_1, (v_1, v_2, v_3, v_4)\rangle$ is calculated by $1 + 1 + 1 + 2 + 1 = 6$, where $d_g(p_1, ancient) = 1, d_g(p_1, roman) = 1, d_g(p_1, catholic) = 1, d_g(p_1, history) = 2$. There are two qualified semantic places both rooted at p_2, but with different looseness, i.e., 5 for $\langle p_2, (v_6, v_8)\rangle$ and 4 for $\langle p_2, (v_6, v_7, v_8)\rangle$. Thus, the TQSP rooted at p_2 is $\langle p_2, (v_6, v_7, v_8)\rangle$.

Definition 3. **Top-k Relevant Semantic Place Retrieval.** Given a kSP query q on an RDF graph, the result of q includes k TQSPs minimizing ranking function $f(L(T_p), S(q,p))$, where $S(q,p)$ is the spatial distance between the query location and the root of the semantic place. Recall that each place p has a unique TQSP, therefore it may appear at most once in a kSP result.

The kSP query aims at finding the semantic places that (i) are spatially close to the query location, (ii) cover the query keywords, and (iii) have a tree in which the query keywords are closely connected. Without loss of generality, Euclidean distance $S(q,p)$ is used as spatial distance in this work. Ranking function $f(L(T_p), S(q,p))$ can be any monotonic aggregate function which considers both $L(T_p)$ and $S(q,p)$, such as:

$$f(L(T_p), S(q,p)) = \beta \times L(T_p) + (1 - \beta) \times S(q,p), \quad (1)$$

$$f(L(T_p), S(q,p)) = L(T_p) \times S(q,p). \quad (2)$$

The kSP evaluation approaches proposed in this paper are independent of how f is defined. In the rest of the paper, we use Equation (2) as the ranking function, because it is parameterless.

Example 5 Consider an example kSP query q with query location $q.\lambda = q_1$ as shown in Figure 2 and query keywords $q.\psi = \{ancient, roman, catholic, history\}$. Places p_1 and p_2 are located at $(43.71, 4.66)$ and $(43.13, 5.97)$, respectively in Figure 2. Based on the RDF graph in Figure 1(a) and the documents in Figure 1(b), place p_1 has $S(q_1, p_1) = 0.22$ and $L(T_{p_1}) = 1+1+1+2+1 = 6$. $f(L(T_{p_1}), S(q_1, p_1)) = L(T_{p_1}) \times S(q_1, p_1) = 1.32$. Place p_2 has $S(q_1, p_2) = 1.28$ and $L(T_{p_2}) = 0 + 0 + 1 + 2 + 1 = 4$. $f(L(T_{p_2}), S(q_1, p_2)) = 5.12$. Therefore, p_1 is returned as top-1 and p_2 ranks second for the kSP query q with $q.\lambda = q_1$ and $q.\psi = \{ancient, roman, catholic, history\}$.

If the query location of the kSP query q is changed to $q.\lambda = q_2$ and the query keywords are unchanged, then $S(q_2, p_1) = 1.35$, $L(T_{p_1}) = 6$, and $f(L(T_{p_1}), S(q_2, p_1)) = 8.10$. $S(q_2, p_2) = 0.08$, $L(T_{p_2}) = 4$ and $f(L(T_{p_1}), S(q_2, p_1)) = 0.32$. For the kSP query q with $q.\lambda = q_2$ and $q.\psi = \{ancient, roman, catholic, history\}$, p_2 is returned as the top-1 SP and p_1 ranks second.

[2]If multiple trees rooted at p have the same minimum looseness, we can: (1) break ties arbitrarily and select one of them to be the TQSP for p or (2) keep all trees with the same minimum looseness in a set. If we use option (2), the result of a kSP query would the top-k qualified semantic place sets. The methods proposed in this paper are applicable for both options. For the ease of presentation, we adopt option (1) in the rest of the paper.

3. BASIC METHOD: BSP

The most relevant existing work to our kSP queries are the top-k keyword queries on graphs [31,43]. Given a set of query keywords, the objective is to retrieve the top-k sub-trees of the RDF graph, such that the vertices of each tree collectively cover the query keywords, ranked by the looseness of the trees. A bottom-up algorithm is used to evaluate top-k keyword queries. For each query keyword t, the algorithm first determines the set of vertices whose documents contain t. From those vertices, it starts to explore the graph and finds the earliest common vertex that all the query keywords can reach. This way, candidate trees are found and the result is finalized by choosing the top-k less-looseness trees. However, this approach is not appropriate for our kSP queries. Firstly, we aim for semantic places that take place vertices as roots, however, the aforementioned algorithm cannot guarantee that the discovered trees are rooted at place vertices. Secondly, the ranking score of a semantic place depends on both its looseness and its spatial distance to the query location; even if a keyword query can identify candidate trees rooted at places, there is no obvious way of determining the top-k semantic places before getting all candidate trees, since a tree T_p with high $L(T_p)$ value but small spatial distance $S(p,q)$ to the query location q may outrank a tree $T_{p'}$ with low $L(T_{p'})$ but large spatial distance $S(p', q)$, and vice versa.

Obviously, a single TQSP computation is much more expensive compared to a single spatial distance computation. Therefore, using keyword query (keyword-first) methods to solve our problem would be inefficient. In view of this, we design methods that perform spatial search first, in order to avoid unnecessary TQSP computations. In this section, we propose a basic method for evaluating kSP queries. This method requires that we have preprocessed the RDF graph, extracted the places from it and spatially indexed them using an R-tree [29]. Like keyword search approaches, we also assume that the documents of the vertices in RDF graph are indexed by an inverted index [37]. Table 1 shows the inverted index for the documents in Figure 1(b). In addition, instead of storing and indexing the RDF data in a triples table format, which would enable efficient SPARQL query evaluation, we choose to store the RDF graph in memory in its native form (i.e., using adjacency lists, as in [59]), which enables efficient graph browsing operations (like BFS). Finally, we keep a table which helps to look-up fast the associated data (document, spatial coordinates) for each vertex, so there is no need to employ any special encoding scheme [46].

abbey: p_1	church: v_7	magdalene: v_6
anatolia: v_8	deathPlace: v_8	montmajour: p_1
ancient: v_3, v_5, v_8	dedication: v_2	patron: v_6
architectural: v_4	denomination: v_7	peter: v_2
architecture: v_1	diocese: v_3, p_2	roman: v_2, v_5, p_2
arles: v_3	empire: v_5	romanesque: v_1
birthplace: v_5	history: v_4, v_7, v_8	saint: v_2
catholic: v_2, p_2, v_7	mary: v_6	subject: v_1, v_4

Table 1: Inverted index of the documents in Figure 1(b)

Algorithm 1 shows the pseudo code of our Basic Semantic Place (BSP) search method for evaluating kSP queries. Initially, a top-k result queue H_k, which prioritizes identified semantic places by their ranking scores, is initialized (line 1). Given a kSP query q, the posting lists of the query keywords are loaded (lines 2–3). Then, the basic method applies the best-first search algorithm [33] on the R-tree to retrieve places in ascending order of their spatial distances to the query location (line 6). For each retrieved place p from the R-tree, BSP constructs the TQSP T_p rooted at p using function GETSEMANTICPLACE() (line 9). Then, T_p is inserted into the result queue H_k (line 13). A threshold θ is set as the ranking score of the kth semantic place in the result queue (line 14). For the next retrieved entry e from the R-tree (e may refer to a place or a node in the R-tree), if its minimum spatial distance to the query location is not smaller than the threshold, i.e., $S(q,e) \geq \theta$, the top-k result is finalized and the algorithm terminates (lines 7 and 15).

Correctness of Termination. For the next retrieved entry e, if $S(q,e) \geq \theta$, the spatial distances of all unprocessed places to the query location are not smaller than the threshold. This means that the ranking scores of all these places cannot be better than the current k^{th} candidate, given the fact that since $L(T_p) \geq 1$, we have $f(L(T_p), S(q,p)) \geq S(q,p)$. Hence, the current k candidates are correctly returned as the top-k TQSPs for q. Note that the termination condition is based on Equation 2; it can be easily adjusted if $f(L(T_p), S(q,p))$ is defined differently (e.g., using Equation 1).

Algorithm 1 BSP(q, R, G, I)

```
1: MinHeap H_k = ∅, ordered by f(L(T_p), S(q,p))
2: for each keyword t_i in q.ψ do
3:     Load posting list pl_i of t_i from I
4: Construct M_q.ψ
5: θ = +∞
6: while e=GETNEXT(R, q) do
7:     if S(q,e) ≥ θ then break
8:     if e refers to a place p then
9:         T_p = GETSEMANTICPLACE(q.ψ, p, G, M_q.ψ)
10:        if L(T_p) == +∞ then continue
11:        Compute the ranking score f of T_p
12:        if f < θ then
13:            H_k.add(T_p, f)
14:            Update θ
15: return H_k
```

Example 6 Consider a 1SP query q located at $q.\lambda = q_1$ in Figure 2 with query keywords $q.\psi$ = {*ancient, roman, catholic, history*}, applying on the RDF graph of Figure 1. Place p_1 is firstly retrieved from the R-tree and $L(T_{p_1}) = 6$ after calling function GETSEMANTICPLACE(). Therefore, the ranking score of T_{p_1} is $f = 1.32$. Next, T_{p_1} is added into H_k as the top-1 candidate and θ is updated to 1.32. Similarly, place p_2 is retrieved from the R-tree with $S(q_1, p_2) = 1.28 < \theta$. The TQSP rooted at p_2 is constructed with $L(T_{p_2}) = 4$ and its ranking score is $f = 5.12$. Finally, T_{p_1}, which has a smaller score, is returned as the top-1 result.

Before calling GETSEMANTICPLACE(), for the sake of efficiency, the loaded posting lists of the query keywords are converted into a map structure $M_{q.\psi}$ where keys are the vertices in these posting lists. For each key (vertex), its value is the set of query words appeared in the document of the vertex. Taking query keywords $q.\psi = \{ancient, roman, catholic, history\}$ as an example, according to the inverted index in Table 1, the content of $M_{q.\psi}$ is shown in Table 2. Usually the number of query keywords is small, therefore, $M_{q.\psi}$ is small and cheap to construct.

v_2: {catholic, roman}
v_3: {ancient}
v_4: {history}
v_5: {ancient, roman}
v_7: {catholic, history}
v_8: {ancient, history}
p_2: {catholic, roman}

Table 2: $M_{q.\psi}$ of the example in Figure 1

Function GETSEMANTICPLACE() constructs the TQSP T_p rooted at a place p w.r.t. query q. According to the definition of TQSP, T_p contains the shortest path from the root place to each query keyword. A naive way is to compute the shortest path from p to every vertex in the posting list pl_i of keyword t_i, and then choose the vertex with the smallest shortest path distance. For example, in Figure 1, in order to determine the shortest path from p_1 to keyword *ancient*, we need to compute the shortest path for pairs (p_1, v_3), (p_1, v_5) and (p_1, v_8), and then get $\langle p_1, v_3 \rangle$ as the shortest path from p_1 to keyword *ancient*. Apparently, when the RDF data graph is large, this approach would be expensive as it would require the computation of numerous and long shortest paths.

Instead, function GETSEMANTICPLACE() applies breadth first search (BFS) in the RDF graph, starting from the root place p, and checks whether each encountered vertex v contains any query keyword t using map $M_{q.\psi}$. Meanwhile, a keyword set B is maintained to record the undiscovered keywords during BFS. Algorithm 2 shows the pseudocode. TQSP T_p is initialized as empty (line 1), looseness $L(T_p)$ is set to 1 (line 2), and set B contains all the query keywords (line 3). BFS search starting from place p incrementally reports the next encounter vertex v (line 4). The query keywords $v.\psi_q$ associated with v can be obtained from $M_{q.\psi}$ (line 6). If B and $v.\psi_q$ share words, this means that the shortest paths from the root to some keywords in B have been identified (line 7). Then, T_p and its looseness are updated (lines 8) and these keywords are removed from B (line 9). If no more vertices are identified by BFS and B is not empty, there is no qualified semantic place rooted at p (line 10). As soon as B is empty (i.e., all query keywords have been covered), T_p is successfully constructed and returned.

Algorithm 2 GETSEMANTICPLACE($q.\psi, p, G, M_{q.\psi}$)

```
1: T_p = ∅
2: L(T_p) = 1
3: Set B = q.ψ
4: while v = BFS(G, p) and B ≠ ∅ do
5:     Add v to T_p
6:     v.ψ_q = M_q.ψ.get(v)
7:     if B ∩ v.ψ_q ≠ ∅ then
8:         L(T_p)+ = |B ∩ v.ψ_q| × d(p, v)
9:         B = B \ v.ψ_q
10: if B ≠ ∅ then L(T_p) = +∞ and T_p = NULL
11: return L(T_p) and T_p
```

Example 7 Given query keywords $q.\psi$ = {*ancient, roman, catholic, history*}, we illustrate function GETSEMANTICPLACE() (Algorithm 2) by constructing the TQSP for place p_1 in Figure 1. BFS firstly reports p_1 that is added to T_{p_1}. However, $B \cap p_1.\psi_q = \emptyset$, which means that there is nothing to do for p_1. Next, v_1 is visited by BFS, which again contains no keywords from B. When v_2 is visited, we have $B \cap v_2.\psi_q = \{catholic, roman\}$. Therefore, $L(T_{p_1})+ = 2 \cdot d(p, v_2) = 3$, and *catholic* and *roman* are removed from B. Similarly, after v_3 and v_4 have been processed, $L(T_{p_1})$ is updated to 6 and B becomes empty. Thus, $T_{p_1} = \langle p_1, (v_1, v_2, v_3, v_4) \rangle$ and $L(T_{p_1}) = 6$ are returned.

4. IMPROVED PRUNING: SPP

In the basic method, for each retrieved place p from the R-tree, function GETSEMANTICPLACE() is called to construct the TQSP T_p rooted at p. The effort of a TQSP construction is wasted under two circumstances: (i) T_p cannot cover all the query keywords, i.e., no qualified semantic place rooted at p can be obtained and (ii) the ranking score of T_p is no less than threshold θ (the ranking score of the kth candidate). For case (i), we design a reachability-based pruning rule that discards the places whose TQSP cannot be constructed. Using this rule, some places are pruned without calling function GETSEMANTICPLACE(). For case (ii), we derive a dynamic bound on the looseness of the TQSP under construction.

This bound is used to judge whether the unfinished TQSP has the potential to belong to the top-k result. This rule helps reducing the TQSP construction cost for some places that cannot enter the kSP result. Applying the two pruning techniques, we design a Semantic Place retrieval with Pruning algorithm (SPP).

4.1 Unqualified Place Pruning

A place p retrieved by the GETNEXT function of the basic algorithm may not form a qualified semantic place. This happens if it is not possible to reach vertices covering all query keywords by BFS from p. For example, consider place p_2 in Figure 1 and query keywords {*church*, *architecture*}; no qualified semantic place rooted at p_2 exists, since p_2 never reaches *architecture*. Formally:

PRUNING RULE 1. ***Unqualified Place Pruning.*** *Let $p \nrightarrow t$ denote that place p cannot reach keyword t in the RDF graph. Given query keywords $q.\psi$, place p is an unqualified place and can be pruned if $\exists t \in q.\psi, p \nrightarrow t$.*

Testing whether p can reach a keyword t in the graph can be implemented by reachability queries [20,39,40,53,58] that have been well studied in the literature. TF-Label [20] is the state-of-the-art algorithm for reachability queries, using which we can perform 1M reachability queries in a large graph within dozens of milliseconds. We use TF-Label as a independent component in our algorithm.

In the RDF graph, the documents of multiple vertices may share the same keyword t (as many as the length of the corresponding inverted list). For instance, in Figure 1(b), the documents of v_3, v_5, and v_8 all contain keyword *ancient*. Thus, in order to determine whether a place p can reach keyword *ancient*, in the worst case three reachability queries (i.e., to v_3, v_5, and v_8) have to be issued. In a very large data set, a huge number of reachability queries may have to be performed, which is inefficient. To reduce the number of reachability queries, we propose the following method. Firstly, a vertex v_t is constructed for each word t and added into the RDF graph. Edges are added from the vertices whose documents contain t to v_t. This way, for each query keyword t, it suffices to apply a single reachability query to v_t in order to find out whether any of the vertices whose documents contain t is reachable from the place vertex. Therefore, the number of required reachability queries for a place becomes at most equal to the number of query keywords. Secondly, based on the observation that infrequent query keywords have a high chance to make a place unqualified, we prioritize them when issuing reachability queries.

Pruning Rule 1 is used before calling function GETSEMANTICPLACE() (line 9 in Algorithm 1) to avoid unnecessary TQSP computations.

4.2 Dynamic Bound based Pruning

Function GETSEMANTICPLACE() constructs the TQSP T_p rooted at p in a BFS manner: starting from p its neighboring nodes are incrementally explored. During this process, some of the query keywords may be found early, while it may take time to find others. We derive a dynamic bound for the looseness of the TQSP T_p under construction in Lemma 1. This dynamic bound converges to the real looseness of TQSP as more keywords are covered.

LEMMA 1. ***Dynamic Bound on Looseness.*** *Given query keywords $q.\psi = \{t_1, ..., t_j, .., t_m\}$, without loss of generality, suppose that we have already discovered the first j query keywords during the BFS exploration starting from p. Let v be the next vertex encountered in the BFS process with graph distance $d(p, v)$. A lower bound of the looseness $L(T_p)$ is then $L_B(T_p) = \sum_{i=1}^{j} d_g(p, t_i) + d(p, v) \times (m - j)$.*

PROOF. Trivial due to the monotonicity of $L(T_p)$ w.r.t. the shortest paths to the first encounters of keywords. Vertex v is the next encountered vertex in the BFS process. Hence, all the undiscovered keywords cannot have a shorter graph distance from p than v does, i.e., $d_g(p, t_n) \geq d(p, v), j < n \leq m$. Therefore, we can have $L_B(T_p) = \sum_{i=1}^{j} d_g(p, t_i) + d(p, v) \times (m - j) \leq \sum_{i=1}^{m} d_g(p, t_i) = L(T_p)$. □

A TQSP T_p has a chance to be in the kSP result only if its ranking score is less than threshold θ. Definition 4 presents the looseness threshold for all TQSPs that have not been computed yet.

Definition 4. **Looseness Threshold.** Let θ be the ranking score of the kth TQSP found so far. The looseness threshold of any TQSP T_p is defined as $L_w(T_p) = \theta / S(q, p)$. If a TQSP has looseness no smaller than its $L_w(T_p)$, it cannot be in the kSP result.

Based on Lemma 1 and Definition 4, we introduce the dynamic bound based pruning rule in Pruning Rule 2.

PRUNING RULE 2. ***Dynamic Bound based Pruning.*** *For place p, as soon as $L_B(T_p) \geq L_w(T_p)$, the TQSP rooted at place p cannot be in the kSP result, and thus p can be pruned.*

PROOF. For the TQSP T_p rooted at p, if its best possible looseness $L_B(T_p)$ is no smaller than its looseness threshold $L_w(T_p)$, meaning that the ranking score of T_p must be no smaller than the current k^{th} candidate, then T_p cannot be in the result. □

By applying the two pruning rules, we can design algorithm SPP (Semantic Place search with Pruning), which is an extension of BSP. Algorithm 3 shows an improved version of function GETSEMANTICPLACE() (Algorithm 2) used in SPP. Algorithm 3 differs from Algorithm 2 in line 4 that computes the looseness threshold of the T_p to be constructed, line 7 that computes the dynamic bound on the looseness of T_p each time when BFS reports new vertex, and lines 8–9 that apply Pruning Rule 2 to prune places. Having Pruning Rules 1 and 2, SPP is Algorithm 1 with the following change. The looseness threshold in Definition 4 and Pruning Rule 2 guarantee that any place survived to the point when to be added to H_k must be ranked at least the kth position. Therefore, the *if* clause at line 12 of Algorithm 1 is not needed anymore.

Algorithm 3 GETSEMANTICPLACEP($q.\psi, p, G, M_{q.\psi}$)

```
1:  T_p = ∅
2:  L_B(T_p) = 1
3:  Set B = q.ψ
4:  Compute the looseness threshold L_w(T_p)
5:  while v = BFS(G, p) and B ≠ ∅ do
6:      Add v to T_p
7:      Compute the dynamic bound L_B(T_p)
8:      if L_B(T_p) ≥ L_w(T_p) then                ▷ Pruning Rule 2
9:          return +∞ and T_p = NULL
10:     v.ψ = M_{q.ψ}.get(v)
11:     if B ∩ v.ψ ≠ ∅ then
12:         B = B ∖ v.ψ
13: if B ≠ ∅ then L(T_p) = +∞ and T_p = NULL
14: return L_B(T_p) and T_p
```

Example 8 Consider a kSP query q located at $q.\lambda = q_1$ in Figure 2 with keywords $q.\psi$ = {*ancient, roman, catholic, history*}, requesting the top-1 TQSP in the RDF graph of Figure 1. Place p_1 is firstly retrieved from the R-tree. After applying Pruning Rule 1, we find that p_1 can reach all the query keywords and cannot be pruned. Then TQSP T_{p_1} rooted at p_1 is constructed and regarded as the top-1 candidate with ranking score 1.32. Threshold θ is set to 1.32. Next, place p_2 is retrieved from the R-tree, which again cannot be eliminated by Pruning Rule 1. Then, function GETSEMANTICPLACEP() is called to construct TQSP T_{p_2} rooted at p_2. The looseness threshold for T_{p_2} is calculated as $L_w(T_{p_2}) = \theta/S(q_1, p_2) = 1.32/1.28 = 1.03$. BFS starts to explore the graph starting from p_2; in the meanwhile, the dynamic bound on the looseness of T_{p_2} is computed. Initially, $L_B(T_{p_2})$=1. After p_2 is visited by BFS, $d(p_2, p_2) = 0$. By Lemma 1, $L_B(T_{p_2}) = 1 + d(p_2, p_2) \times |B| = 1$. Since $L_B(T_{p_2}) = 1 < L_w(T_{p_2})$, p_2 cannot be eliminated by Pruning Rule 2. Then, {*catholic*, *roman*} are removed from B since they are contained in p_2 itself. After v_6 is visited by BFS, $d(p_2, v_6) = 1$, and therefore, by Lemma 1, $L_B(T_{p_2})$ is increased by $|B| \times d(p_2, v_6)$ and becomes 3. According to Pruning Rule 2, $L_B(T_{p_2}) = 3 > 1.03 = L_w(T_{p_2})$ and T_{p_2} cannot be the top-1 result. Hence, function GETSEMANTICPLACEP() returns NULL before finishing the construction of T_{p_2} and is more efficient than function GETSEMANTICPLACE() in Algorithm 2.

5. α-RADIUS BASED BOUNDS

The pruning rules proposed in the previous section help discarding unqualified places and the places whose TQSPs cannot enter the kSP result. In this section, we propose new bounds on both the looseness and the ranking scores, for pruning not only individual places but also sets of places, i.e., R-tree entries and the corresponding sub-trees. We firstly introduce the α-radius word neighborhood in Definition 5, which is used for deriving the bounds.

Definition 5. **α-radius word neighborhood of place.** For place p, its α-radius word neighborhood $WN(p)$ contains the set of word-distance pairs $\{(t_i, d_g(p, t_i))\}$ where the shortest graph distance from p to each word t_i is no larger than α, i.e., $d_g(p, t_i) \leq \alpha$.

Based on the α-radius word neighborhood of individual places, we define the α-radius word neighborhoods of a set of places, i.e., a node in the R-tree, in Definition 6.

Definition 6. **α-radius word neighborhood of node.** For a set of places $\{p_j\}$ enclosed in a node N of the R-tree, the α-radius word neighborhood $WN(N)$ of N contains the set of word-distance pairs $\{(t_i, d_g(N, t_i))\}$ where the words in $WN(N)$ is the union of the words in $WN(p_j)$ of all places enclosed in N, and for each word t_i, $d_g(N, t_i) = \min_{p_j \in N} d_g(p_j, t_i)$. Obviously, $d_g(N, t_i) \leq \alpha$.

Construction of α-radius word neighborhood. In a preprocessing phase, the α-radius word neighborhoods of all places are computed first. For each place p, we explore the RDF graph in a breadth-first manner starting from p. Neighborhood $WN(p)$ is initialized as empty. When encountering a vertex v in the graph, for each word t appearing in v's document, if no corresponding pair for t is already in $WN(p)$, a new pair $(t, d(p, v))$ is added to $WN(p)$. After the α-radius word neighborhoods of all places have been constructed, the α-radius word neighborhoods of the nodes in the R-tree are computed in a bottom-up fashion from the leaf level to the root level. For each node N, let $\{e_i\}$ be the set of entries enclosed, where e_i refers to either a place or a node. Neighborhood $WN(N)$ is initialized as empty. For each pair $(t, d_g(e_i, t))$ in each $WN(e_i)$, if no corresponding pair for t is in $WN(N)$, $(t, d_g(e_i, t))$ is added to $WN(N)$ as $(t, d_g(N, t))$; otherwise, $d_g(N, t)$ is updated as $\min\{d_g(N, t), d_g(e_i, t)\}$.

Example 9 For $\alpha = 1$, part of the α-radius word neighborhoods of places p_1 and p_2 in Figure 1(a) are displayed in the first two rows of Table 3. '-' indicates that the place cannot reach the keyword within α-radius. Assuming that an R-tree node N contains p_1 and p_2, the α-radius $WN(N)$ is shown in the last row of the table.

$q.\psi$	abbey	...	ancient	catholic	roman	history	...
$d_g(p_1, t_i)$	0	...	1	1	1	-	...
$d_g(p_2, t_i)$	-	...	-	0	0	1	...
$d_g(N, t_i)$	0	...	1	0	0	1	...

Table 3: Example: 1-radius word neighborhoods

Based on the α-radius word neighborhoods of places, we derive bounds of the looseness and the ranking scores of TQSPs based on Lemmas 2 and 3. Lemmas 4 and 5 extend these bounds for sets of places rooted under R-tree nodes.

LEMMA 2. ***α-bound on the looseness of a place.*** *Let $WN(p)$ be the α-radius word neighborhood of place p. Given query keywords $q.\psi = \{t_1, \ldots, t_j, \ldots, t_m\}$, without loss of generality, assume that the first j keywords have corresponding pairs in $WN(p)$. The α-bound of the looseness of TQSP T_p rooted at p is $L_B^{\alpha}(T_p) = \sum_{i=1}^{j} d_g(p, t_i) + (\alpha + 1) \times (m - j)$ and $L_B^{\alpha}(T_p) \leq L(T_p)$.*

LEMMA 3. ***α-bound on the ranking score for places.*** *Let $L_B^{\alpha}(T_p)$ be the α-bound on the looseness of the TQSP T_p rooted at p. Given a kSP query q, the α-bound on the ranking score of T_p is $f_B^{\alpha}(p) = L_B^{\alpha}(T_p) \times S(q, p)$ and $f_B^{\alpha}(p) \leq f(L(T_p), S(q, p))$.*

LEMMA 4. ***α-bound on the looseness for nodes.*** *Let $WN(N)$ be the α-radius word neighborhood of node N. Given query keywords $q.\psi = \{t_1, \ldots, t_j, \ldots, t_m\}$, without loss of generality, assume that the first j keywords have corresponding pairs in $WN(N)$. The α-bound on the looseness of all the TQSPs T_p rooted at p enclosed in N is $L_B^{\alpha}(T_N) = \sum_{i=1}^{j} d_g(N, t_i) + (\alpha + 1) \times (m - j)$ and $\forall p_i \in N, L_B^{\alpha}(T_N) \leq L(T_{p_i})$.*

LEMMA 5. ***α-bound on the ranking score for nodes.*** *Let $L_B^{\alpha}(T_N)$ be the α-bound on the looseness of the TQSPs T_p rooted at places p enclosed in N. Given a kSP query q, the α-bound on the ranking score of all the T_p rooted at p enclosed in N is $f_B^{\alpha}(N) = L_B^{\alpha}(T_N) \times S(q, N)$, where $S(q, N)$ is the minimum spatial distance between q and N. $\forall p_i \in N, f_B^{\alpha}(N) \leq f(L(T_{p_i}), S(q, p_i))$.*

The proofs of Lemmas 2, 3, 4, and 5 are omitted for the interest of space. We proceed to introduce a pruning rule for places using Lemma 3 and a pruning rule for nodes using Lemma 5.

PRUNING RULE 3. ***Place pruning.*** *Given a kSP query q, let θ be the ranking score of the kth candidate TQSP and $f_B^{\alpha}(p)$ be the α-bound on the ranking score of the TQSP T_p rooted at p. If $f_B^{\alpha}(p) \geq \theta$, T_p cannot be the kSP result and p is pruned.*

PRUNING RULE 4. ***R-tree node pruning.*** *Given a kSP query q, let θ be the ranking score of the kth candidate TQSP and $f_B^{\alpha}(N)$ be the α-bound on the ranking score of the TQSPs T_p rooted at places p enclosed in N. If $f_B^{\alpha}(N) \geq \theta$, the TQSP rooted at any place enclosed in N cannot be the result and N is pruned.*

Example 10 Consider an R-tree node N formed by places p_1 and p_2 in Figure 1(a). For query keywords $q.\psi$ = {*ancient*, *roman*, *catholic*, *history*}, based on Table 3 and Lemma 4, $L_B^{\alpha}(T_N) = 1 + 0 + 0 + 1 + 1 = 3$. Assuming the minimum spatial distance from N to a query location $q.\lambda$ is 2, by Lemma 5, $f_B^{\alpha}(N) = 6$. If $\theta = 5$, according to Pruning Rule 4, $f_B^{\alpha}(N) > \theta$ which means all the places under N, i.e., p_1 and p_2 in this example, can be pruned.

Storage. The α-radius word neighborhoods of places and nodes can be modeled as vectors. They are indexed by an inverted file.

For a kSP query, part of the neighborhoods relevant to the query keywords, i.e., the posting lists of the query keywords, are loaded in the beginning query processing, to facilitate the computation of α-based bounds and the application of Pruning Rules 3 and 4.

Algorithm. By integrating the α-radius based bounds with the SPP algorithm, we design a Semantic Place retrieval algorithm (SP) for the processing of kSP queries, as described by Algorithm 4. SP has the following differences compared to SPP: (i) entries (referring to places and nodes) in the R-tree are processed in ascending order of their α-bounds on the ranking score rather than their spatial distance to the query location (lines 8 and 22), (ii) Pruning Rules 3 and 4 are used to discard places having no potential to be the result (line 21), and (iii) the termination condition is based on the α-bound on the ranking score rather than the spatial distance, which can be satisfied earlier (line 9).

Algorithm 4 SP(q, R, G, I, I^α)

```
1: MinHeap H_k = ∅, ordered by f(L(T_p), S(q,p))
2: for each keyword t_i in q.ψ do
3:     Load posting list pl_i of t_i from I
4:     Load posting list of t_i from I^α
5: Construct M_{q.ψ}
6: θ = +∞
7: Queue Q = (root)
8: while e=GETNEXT(Q, R, q) do
9:     if f_B^α(e) ≥ θ then break
10:    if e refers to a place p then
11:        if e is Unqualified then continue          ▷ Pruning Rule 1
12:        T_p = GETSEMANTICPLACEP(q.ψ, p, G, M_{q.ψ})
13:        if L(T_p) == +∞ then continue
14:        Compute the ranking score f of T_p
15:        H_k.add(T_p, f)
16:        Update θ
17:    else                                           ▷ e refers to a node N
18:        for each entry e in N do
19:            Compute α-bound on the looseness L_B^α(T_e) for e
20:            Compute α-bound on the ranking score f_B^α(e) for e
21:            if f_B^α(e) < θ then                   ▷ Pruning Rules 3 and 4
22:                Add (e, f_B^α(e)) to Q
23: return H_k
```

6. EXPERIMENTS

To evaluate the performance of methods BSP (Section 3), SPP (Section 4), and SP (Section 5), we conducted an empirical study using real datasets, under various settings.

6.1 Settings

Datasets. We extracted the data used in our experiments from well-known real RDF knowledge bases, namely DBpedia and Yago (version 2.5). In DBpedia, there are 8,099,955 vertices and 72,193,833 edges in the directed RDF graph, with a dictionary of 2,927,026 unique words. The documents of all vertices are organized by an inverted index. The average posting list length is 56.46, which means on average, a word appears in the documents of 56.46 vertices in the graph. Among all vertices, 883,665 are places with coordinates. In Yago, there are 8,091,179 vertices and 50,415,307 edges in the directed RDF graph, with a dictionary of 3,778,457 distinct words. The documents of all vertices are organized by an inverted index with average posting list length 7.83. Among all the vertices, 4,774,796 vertices are places with coordinates. The original DBpedia and Yago data graphs are highly connected, with many edges representing "sameAs" "linksTo" and "redirectTo" relationships, which introduce semantically meaningless paths. In the datasets we use, such edges are removed. As a result, DBpedia consists of a huge weak connected component (WCC) with 8,099,624 vertices and 145 tiny WCCs with less than 10 vertices each. Similarly, the resulting Yago graph has a huge WCC with 8,091,094 vertices and 4 tiny WCCs with average size around 20.

Queries. Generating kSP query locations and keywords totally at random reduces the probability of obtaining any results. Therefore, we tried to generate meaningful kSP queries, by following the spatial and keyword distribution of the datasets. For each generated query, we randomly select a place p in the RDF graph and then randomly select the query location from a large range around this place. From p, we explore the RDF graph in BFS manner and randomly select at least $|q.\psi|/2$ and at most $|q.\psi| \times factor$ vertices that are reachable from p ($factor \geq 1$). If there are less than $|q.\psi|/2$ vertices reachable from p, p is discarded to avoid the case that the subgraph around the query location is too limited. In this case, we randomly select another place and repeat the whole process. Among the selected $[|q.\psi|/2, |q.\psi| \cdot factor]$ vertices, we randomly choose at most $|q.\psi|$ vertices, and $|q.\psi|$ keywords are extracted from the documents of these vertices as the query keywords. We set $factor = 2$ which gives flexibility with respect to $|q.\psi|$ and is large enough to obtain many connected vertices from p, but not too large to obtain faraway vertices, which are less semantically relevant to p.

Parameter settings. Performance is evaluated by varying the number of requested TQSPs k, the number of query keywords $|q.\psi|$, α of the α-radius based bounds, and also the data size for scalability evaluation. By default, $k = 5, |q.\psi| = 5, \alpha = 3$. We vary one parameter while fixing the other two. Specifically, we report the result when parameter k varies in $\{1,3,5,8,10,15,20\}$, $|q.\psi|$ varies in $\{1,3,5,8,10\}$, and α varies in $\{1,3,5\}$. For each setting, we run 100 queries and measure the average runtime, number of TQSP computations, and number of R-tree nodes accessed.

Platform. All methods were implemented in Java and evaluated on a 3.4 GHz quad-core machine running Ubuntu 12.04 with 16 GBytes memory. For the two datasets, the sizes of the R-trees, the RDF graphs, and the inverted indexes are shown in Table 4. The R-tree and the RDF graph are assumed to be memory-resident. Although the inverted indexes used can also fit the main memory, we choose to follow the setting of commercial search engines, where the inverted index is disk-resident. The reason is that for each query, only a small portion of the inverted index is relevant and needs be kept in main memory. Besides, such a design is scalable when more textual data added to the RDF knowledge base.

Preprocessing costs. The time costs of constructing the indexes and the data structures used for pruning are shown in Table 5. To construct the R-tree, we inserted the places in it one-by-one, in order to achieve better quality. The cost can be drastically reduced if bulk loading was used [45]. The inverted index for the documents of all the vertices in the RDF graph takes a few minutes only to construct. The TFlabel index [20] for reachability queries, which facilitates Pruning Rule 1, is also constructed within reasonable time. The DBpedia data are richer in terms of text, therefore the times to build the corresponding inverted and TFlabel indices are higher compared to those for Yago. For alpha-radius preprocessing, there are two dominant cost factors: (i) the computation of α-radius Word Neighborhood (WN) for each place and R-tree node, and (ii) building the inverted index of the α-radius WNs. For DBpedia, the average keyword frequency is 56.46, which renders the α-radius WNs of DBpedia to be larger than 32GB. To build the inverted index for so large data without exceeding the available memory, we had to create inverted indexes for parts of the data and merge them together in the end, which explains the high cost of constructing the inverted index for DBpedia.

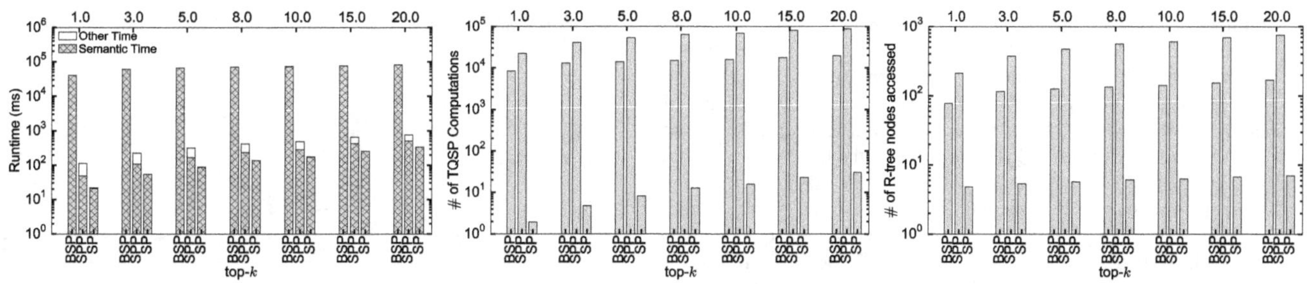

(a) runtime (b) number of TQSP computations (c) number of R-tree nodes accessed

Figure 3: Varying k on DBpedia.

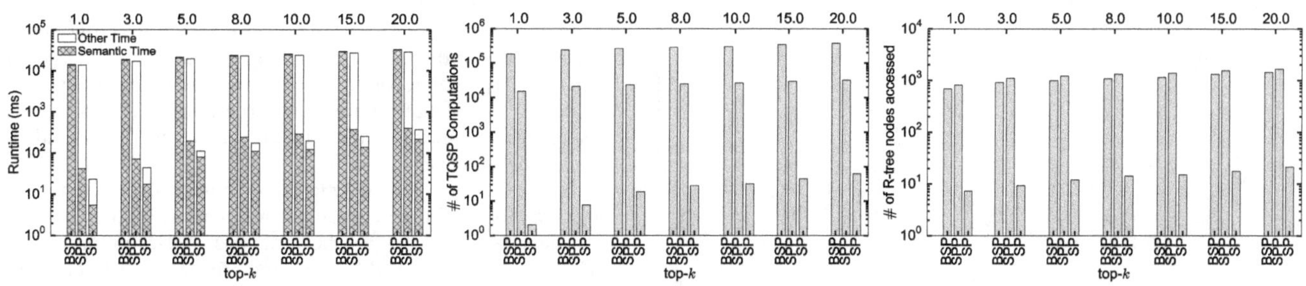

(a) runtime (b) number of TQSP computations (c) number of R-tree nodes accessed

Figure 4: Varying k on Yago.

Table 4: Storage Cost

Data	R-tree	RDF graph	Inverted index
DBpedia	50.54MB	607.95MB	1307.98MB
Yago	273.17MB	454.81MB	231.91MB

Table 5: Preprocessing and indexing time (minutes)

Dataset	R-tree	Inverted index	TFlabel index	$\alpha(=3)$-radius
DBpedia	3.17	4.61	22.60	1192.01
Yago	31.90	1.00	6.09	101.61

6.2 Efficiency Evaluation

BSP takes too long to finish for some queries because (i) the termination condition (line 7 of Algorithm 1) only uses spatial distance as a (very loose) lower bound, (ii) function GETSEMANTICPLACE wastes computational cost for places that are not qualified semantic places, and (iii) function GETSEMANTICPLACE wastes time on the construction of the TQSPs that cannot be part of the kSP result. Hence, in our experiments, we set the maximum runtime for the queries using BSP to 120 seconds and abort those that take longer time.

6.2.1 Varying k.

Figures 3 and 4 show the cost of all methods on dataset DBpedia and Yago, respectively. As expected, the runtime, the number of TQSP computations, and the number of R-tree nodes accessed all increase as k increases, since a larger number of requested semantic places requires exploring a larger search space.

On dataset DBpedia (Figure 3), SP is 240-1865 times faster than BSP and 2-5 times faster than SPP for all k. The performance gap is maintained as k increases. The runtime of SP stays under 500ms for all values of k. For all the methods, the cost of constructing TQSPs dominates the runtime (shown as the "semantic time" in Figure 3(a)). SPP includes other costs (i.e., "other time" in Figure 3(a)), which are mainly due to the reachability queries used in Pruning Rule 1. SP is the most efficient method in terms of both semantic time and other time, confirming the effectiveness of the proposed α-radius based bounds and Pruning Rules 3 and 4. SPP outperforms BSP because of Pruning Rules 1 and 2. As Figure 3(b) shows, SP only needs to compute the TQSPs for around 2-30 candidate places and accesses around 6 R-tree nodes on average, while SPP needs to compute tens of thousands TQSPs and access hundreds of R-tree nodes. Note that the numbers of TQSP computations and R-tree node accesses by BSP are smaller than the corresponding numbers by SPP, due to the 120 second time limit on BSP that that forces many queries to be terminated before finishing; this means that fewer places are processed in BSP compared to SPP, however, BSP may fail to return an answer, while SPP always computes the correct result. Furthermore, the runtime of SPP is much lower than that of BSP, which indicates that SPP takes less time to process more places than BSP does.

The results are similar on dataset Yago (Figure 4). Compared to DBpedia, the runtime gap between SPP and BSP decreases. However, the "semantic time" of SPP is 75-314 times less than the "semantic time" of BSP, which indicates that the pruning techniques in Section 4 reduce cost for TQSP computations significantly, but at the cost of performing reachability queries (i.e., the "other time" in Figure 4(a)). Yago contains more than 4.77M places, while DBpedia has 887K places. Therefore more reachability queries are issued on Yago compared to DBpedia, which leads to only a minor improvement of SPP over BSP on Yago. On the other hand, SP is robust in pruning a lot of places and nodes and achieves excellent performance on this large spatial RDF dataset.

6.2.2 Varying $|q.\psi|$.

Figure 5 compares the runtimes of all methods on DBpedia and Yago. In this and the subsequent experiments, we do not show the number of TQSP computations and the number of R-tree nodes accessed by the methods for the interest of space and because they do not give different insights compared to the previous experiment. Generally, the runtimes of all methods increase with the number of query keywords $|q.\psi|$, since more vertices in RDF graph need to be explored to discover TQSPs covering all the query keywords in $|q.\psi|$. Again, SP is significantly faster than the other methods and the performance gap widens with $|q.\psi|$. Due to the larger number of places in Yago, which require more reachability queries processed in SPP, the runtime gap between SPP and BSP on Yago is smaller than that on DBpedia. However, recall that BSP is terminated after 2 minutes, so it fails to produce results for a number of queries, while SPP is always correct. SPP has much lower "semantic time" than BSP, however, it performs numerous reachability queries, which eventually dominate its runtime cost.

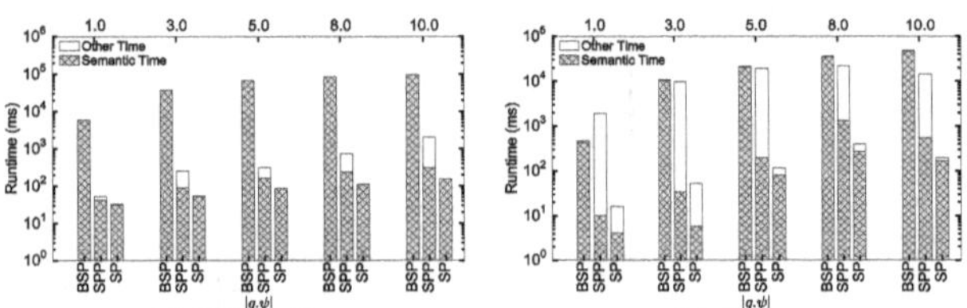

(a) DBpedia (b) Yago

Figure 5: Varying $|q.\psi|$

6.2.3 *Tuning* α

In the next experiment, we evaluate the effect of parameter α in SP. Table 6 displays the total space that the α-radius word neighborhoods occupy, for the two datasets and different values of α. As expected, the space increases with α. On both datasets, the space is moderate when $\alpha = 1, 2, 3$, but increases rapidly to 204.70GB on DBpedia and 30.63GB on Yago when $\alpha = 5$.

α	1	2	3	5
DBpedia (GB)	3.56	24.33	32.53	204.70
Yago (GB)	1.07	3.61	12.37	30.63

Table 6: α-radius word neighborhood size

We evaluate the performance of SP with $k = 1, 3, 5, 8, 10, 15, 20$ when varying α from 1 to 5 on DBpedia and Yago (Figure 6). The number of query keywords is fixed to $|q.\psi| = 5$. Note that with a larger α, the exploring direction of SP is more biased to TQSP looseness than spatial distance (Lemmas 2 and 4). On DBpedia data, when changing α from 1 to 5, the runtime of SP decreases, since large α values enable tighter bound derivations and facilitate the pruning of more pruned places and nodes. We also observed that the number of TQSP computations and the number of R-tree nodes accessed significantly decrease when changing α from 1 to 3, but remain stable when changing α from 3 to 5.

Yago has keyword frequency 7.83, which is much smaller than that of DBpedia (56.46), meaning that it is generally more difficult to find a query keyword that can be reached from a place candidate to construct TQSPs. Recall that TQSP computation takes too much time and the exploration direction is biased to it; thus, a larger α may increase rather than decrease the runtime of kSP queries. This is confirmed by the findings shown in Figure 6(b). When changing α from 1 to 3, the runtime of SP decreases significantly; the larger α value enables tighter bound derivations and more pruned places. However, the runtime increases when changing α from 3 to 5. Overall, based on the evaluation of different α values on the two datasets, we conclude that $\alpha = 3$ is a good choice w.r.t., both performance gains and the α-radius word neighborhood size (i.e., index size).

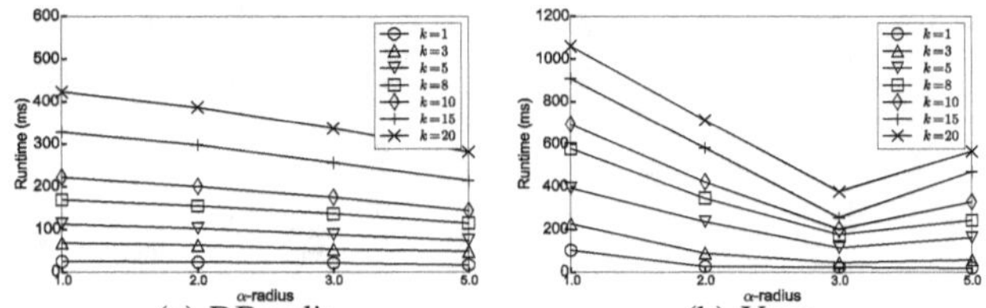

(a) DBpedia (b) Yago

Figure 6: Varying α

6.2.4 *Scalability*

In this section, we evaluate the performance of the three methods on datasets of different sizes. We adopt the random jump sampling method [44] with probability $c = 0.15$ on the Yago dataset to generate RDF graphs of different sizes (described in Table 7). The associated documents of the selected vertices are also included in each generated dataset.

Figure 7 shows the performance of all methods as a function of the graph size. To be consistent, we generate queries using the smallest dataset and apply the generated queries on all datasets. The runtime of BSP and SPP generally increases but not dramatically with the graph size. On the other hand, the runtime of SP slightly decreases as the graph becomes larger. The reason behind this behavior, as we found out by analyzing the results, is that with more edges (larger graph), the connectivity is better, which can make it easier to find good TQSPs without exploring too many places. This is especially true for SP, which takes advantage of the pruning rules and the α-radius bounds to prune places that are not associated with the keywords early.

# of vertices	# of edges	# of places
2,000,000	11,659,509	1,144,705
4,000,000	24,174,226	2,317,671
6,000,000	36,966,773	3,507,942
8,091,179	50,415,307	4,774,796

Table 7: Datasets extracted from Yago by Random Jump

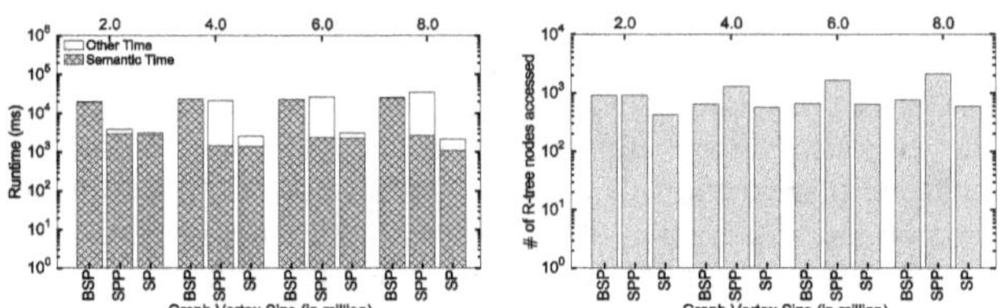

(a) runtime (b) R-tree node accessed

Figure 7: Varying graph size by random jump sampling (Yago).

6.2.5 *Results with Large Looseness*

In order to evaluate the robustness of SP for (hard) queries having results of large looseness, we conducted a set of experiments, in which the generated queries have these characteristics. For this purpose, we generated two types of queries: *Small distance large looseness* (SDLL) kSP queries have as results places that are near the query location and have large looseness; *Large distance large looseness* (LDLL) kSP queries have as results places that are quite far from the query location and have large looseness. To generate SDLL and LDLL queries, we followed a similar methodology as the one described in Section 6.1, with the following differences. First, in SDLL (LDLL) queries the query location is chosen to be near (far) from the place $p = (x, y)$ used to generate the query keywords. Specifically, in LDLL queries, the query location is a distant point location $(x, y + 90)$, increasing p's longitude by 90 degrees. Second, for both SDLL and LDLL queries, we choose infrequent words (with term frequency < 100) beyond 4 hops from p in the RDF graph as the query keywords. Due to (i) the low frequency of the selected words and (ii) the fact that similar places tend to be collocated [17, 18], the generated queries are anticipated to have as results places in the spatial neighborhood of p and with similar looseness as p (i.e., large looseness).

In order to confirm the correctness of our SDLL and LDLL query generators, we generated 100 queries in each of the two classes as well as 100 queries using the original query generator (Section 6.1). Then, for each query class (SDLL, LDLL, and O for our original generator), we averaged the spatial distance and the looseness of their top-k results, as shown in Figure 8. Observe, that the statistics are consistent with the intent of the generators. The results of SDLL and LDLL queries have smaller and larger, respectively, spatial distance compared to the results of O queries. At the same time, both SDLL and LDLL queries return results of much larger looseness compared to O queries.

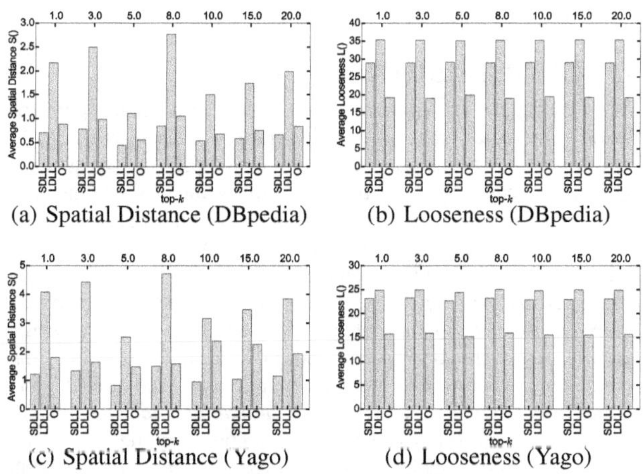

(a) Spatial Distance (DBpedia) (b) Looseness (DBpedia)

(c) Spatial Distance (Yago) (d) Looseness (Yago)

Figure 8: Average spatial distance and average looseness of the results by three classes of queries.

Figure 9 shows the runtime of BSP, SPP, SP for SDLL and LDLL kSP queries as a function of k. The relative performance of the algorithms is consistent with the previous experiments; SP is superior to SPP and outperforms BSP significantly. SDLL have similar cost as LDLL queries (slightly lower), which indicates that the dominant cost factor is not the spatial distance of the results, but their looseness. This can be also confirmed by comparing Figure 9 with Figure 3, which shows the evaluation cost of the original queries. For example, SP is 5-11 times slower on SDLL and LDLL queries compared to O queries. Still, SP achieves sub-second runtimes for k=5 even for these harder query classes and outperforms BSP by orders of magnitude.

6.2.6 Comparison with top-k aggregation

BSP and its optimized versions (SPP and SP) examine places in increasing spatial distance from the query location and compute their looseness as necessary, until the top-k places are confirmed. It is also possible to evaluate kSP queries by a hybrid approach that

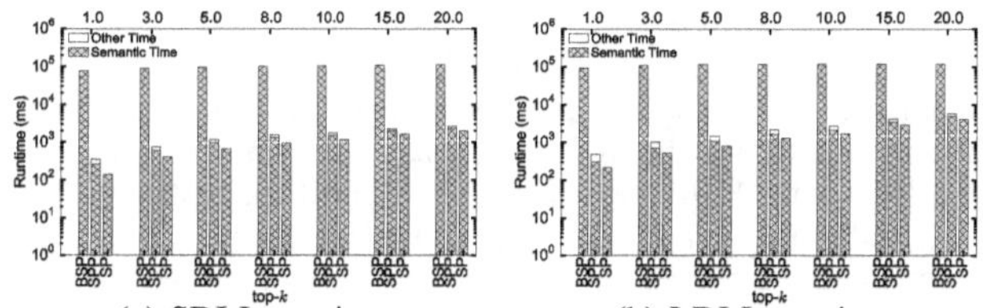

(a) SDLL queries (b) LDLL queries

Figure 9: Runtime of large-looseness queries (DBpedia).

combines two ranked lists of places: one that has qualified semantic places in increasing order of their looseness and one that has places in increasing order of their spatial distance to the query location. The first list can be incrementally generated by the extending the bottom-up RDF keyword search approach [43] (described in the Introduction) and the second by spatial nearest neighbor search. The two lists can be combined fast using the classic threshold algorithm (TA) of [25]: each time the next place is found by keyword search, its spatial distance is computed on-the-fly to complete its score; each time the next spatially nearest place is accessed, whether it is a qualifying semantic place (and its looseness) is computed by calling Algorithm 2. The algorithm terminates if the top-k TQSPs found so far cannot be outranked by the best possible place not found yet, according to the last incrementally computed spatial distance and looseness; i.e., the termination *threshold* of TA can obtained by applying f on these two values.

We implemented TA and compared it with our methods in Figure 10 for queries with various numbers of keywords $|q.\psi|$. On DBpedia, only when $|q.\psi| = 1$ TA performs better than BSP while being 8 times slower than SP. When $|q.\psi| \geq 3$, the runtime of TA increases significantly and TA becomes even slower than BSP. When $|q.\psi| \geq 3$, in order to find the semantic places in increasing looseness order, TA needs to start exploration from all the vertices containing any of the keywords and maintains $|q.\psi|$ queues to decide which vertex to explore next. TA also book-keeps for each vertex all the query keywords that have reached it (if a place has been reached by all query keywords, it becomes a semantic place and its looseness is calculated). These operations dominate the cost of TA, which spends a long time to rank the places by looseness. The results on Yago are similar to the DBpedia results. In addition, note that TA is slower than BSP for $|q.\psi| \geq 3$ for any value of k.

In summary, while it is extremely cheap to compute spatial distances and conduct spatial nearest neighbor search, it is expensive to conduct graph browsing and incremental ranking of places by looseness. This imbalance between the costs of computing spatial distance and looseness motivated the design of our algorithms, which prioritize the examination of places based on their spatial distances in order to minimize graph traversal operations.

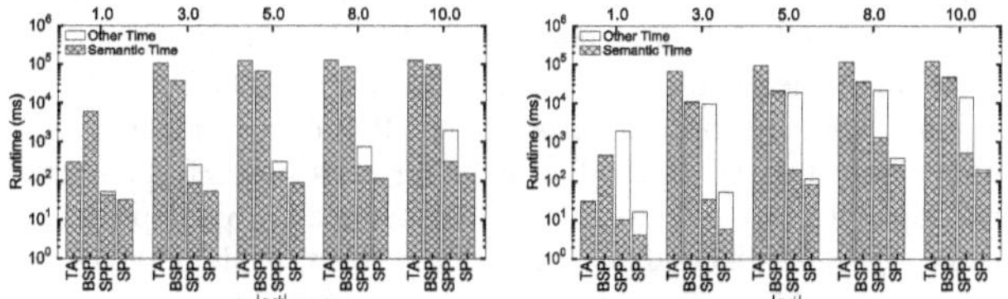

(a) DBpedia (b) Yago

Figure 10: Comparison with top-k aggregation (TA)

7. RELATED WORK

Keyword search on graph data. Due to its user-friendly query interface, keyword search is not only the de facto information retrieval method for the WWW data but also a popular querying mechanism for XML documents [21, 28], relational databases [13, 36], and graph data [22, 31, 41]. Traditional graph search algorithms convert queries into search over feature spaces, such as paths [51], frequent-patterns [57], and sequences [38], which focus more on the structure of the graph rather than the semantic content of the graph. Nevertheless, keyword search over graph data [13,21,22,28,31,36,41] determines a group of densely linked nodes in the graph by making use of both the content and the linkage structure. The overall quality of the results can be improved thanks to the re-enforcement between these two sources of information. Moreover, unexpected and interesting answers that are often difficult to be obtained via rigidly-formatted structured queries may be discovered by the keyword search. A recent survey about keyword search on schema graphs (e.g., relational data and XML documents) and schema-free graphs can be found in [56].

Keyword search on RDF data. RDF data are a special type of graph data, traditionally queried using structured query languages, like SPARQL. Recently, there has been increasing interest in keyword queries over RDF data. SPARQL queries are augmented with keywords for ranked retrieval of RDF data [24]. A keyword-based retrieval model over RDF graphs [23] identifies a set of maximal subgraphs whose vertices contain the query keywords. These subgraphs are ranked based on statistical language models (LMs) [49]. Top-k exploration of query candidates over RDF [52] first constructs a set of k query subgraphs based on the query keywords, and then let users choose the appropriate query graph. Query evaluation is performed using the underlying database engine. For the scalable and efficient processing of keyword queries on large RDF graphs, a summarization algorithm with pruning mechanisms on exploratory keyword search and its results is proposed [43]. Both [52] and [43] follow the definition of BLINKS [31] for the result subgraphs. k-nearest keyword (k-NK) search on RDF graphs [47] finds the k closest pairs of vertices, $(v_i\ ,\ u_i)$ that contain two given keywords q and w, respectively. SemDIS [30] demonstrates a system, where semantic associations are discovered in a large semantic metabase represented in RDF. Keyword query interpretation [26] personalizes the interpretation of a new query on RDF databases by a sequence of structured queries that correspond to the interpretations of keyword queries in the query history. Personalized keyword search on RDF [27] can personalize ranks based on the Ranking SVM approach that trains ranking functions with RDF-specific training features and utilizes historical user feedback. Diversified keyword search on RDF graphs [15] diversifies results by considering both the content and the structure of the results, as well as the RDF schema. A path-oriented RDF index for keyword search query [19] captures associations across RDF paths for improving the query execution performance.

Spatial RDF stores. Recently, there are many efforts toward the efficient storage and indexing of spatial RDF data. Parliament [8] is an implementation of GeoSPARQL. Strabon [42] employs a column-store approach to manage the RDF data in PostGIS, implementing two SO and OS indices for each property table, and uses spatial indexes on top of them. Brodt et al. [16] adopts a two-stage algorithm that either processes the non-spatial query components first and then verifies the spatial ones or the other way around to support spatial querying on RDF data. Geo-Store [54] uses a Hilbert space-filling curve to index the space and supports spatial range queries and NN search. S-Store [55] primarily indexes spatial RDF data based on their structure and uses their spatial locations to prune triples during search. In addition, several commercial systems, such as Oracle, Virtuoso [11], and OWLIM-SE [7], support spatial RDF data management, however, details about their internal design are not available. Recently, a spatial encoding scheme for RDF stores that supports efficient spatial data management was proposed in Liagouris et al. [46]. To our knowledge, no previous work on spatial RDF data management supports queries that combine spatial and keyword search.

Discussion. Our work differs significantly from existing work. Firstly, the kSP queries studied are schema-free; thus, query processing and optimization techniques in traditional RDF stores are inapplicable. Secondly, although keyword search on RDF data (i.e., one aspect of a kSP query) has been investigated in the literature, there is no direct way of extending the existing algorithms to process kSP queries. In fact, extensions are expected to be highly inefficient because they do not guide search based on the query location, as discussed in the beginning of Section 3. Thirdly, kSP queries enable users to search nearby places that semantically match their preferences (expressed by keywords). Such a functionality finds important and useful applications as discussed in Section 1, and cannot be achieved by other forms of queries in the literature. Fourthly, the query evaluation algorithms proposed in this paper are orthogonal to indexing and storage techniques for graph data, which can be applied to further improve the performance of kSP search on very large RDF data.

8. CONCLUSION

In this paper, we proposed a top-k relevant semantic place retrieval (kSP) query that takes as input a query location $q.\lambda$ and a set of query keywords $q.\psi$, and returns the top-k tightest qualified semantic places ranked by their spatial distance to $q.\lambda$ and their semantic looseness to $q.\psi$ over the RDF graph. kSP queries do not require the use of any structured query languages, thus they are user-friendly and do not rely on the knowledge of the RDF schema. Compared to existing keyword search, kSP queries are spatial-aware and support spatial-personalized search. After suggesting a baseline algorithm (BSP), we propose two pruning techniques that reduce the cost of computing the semantic relevance of each place to the query keywords; namely (i) an *unqualified place pruning* approach that discards places which do not cover the query keywords without computing their TQSPs, and (ii) a *dynamic bound based pruning* approach that early terminates the TQSP computation of a place if the place cannot enter the kSP result. To further boost efficiency, in Section 5, we introduce the concept of α-radius word neighborhood and propose α-radius bounds on both the looseness and the ranking scores that can be applied to prune not only individual places but also sets of places (i.e. R-tree nodes). The proposed techniques are evaluated on two large real RDF data sets, i.e., DBpedia and Yago. The results show that applying all techniques enables processing kSP in less than a second for most settings and outperforms the basic method by orders of magnitude.

In this paper, the RDF graph data assumed to be memory-resident. In the future, we plan to integrate and extend existing indexing and storage techniques for disk-resident graph data to develop a scalable solution. Our kSP definition follows directly from previous work of RDF keyword search [26, 31, 43, 52], where only incoming paths from keywords to the root node of a result subgraph are considered. In the future, we also plan to qualitatively evaluate an alternative definition of semantic places, where the keywords in outgoing paths from them are also considered (i.e., edge directions are disregarded).

9. REFERENCES

[1] Alternative fueling station locator. http://www.afdc.energy.gov/locator/stations/.

[2] Bbc lab post. http://www.bbc.co.uk/blogs/internet/entries/63841314-c3c6-33d2-a7b8-f58ca040a65b.

[3] Crime in chicagoland. http://crime.chicagotribune.com/.

[4] Data.gov. http://www.data.gov.

[5] Dbpedia. http://wiki.dbpedia.org.

[6] Hospital compare. http://health.data.gov/def/cqld.

[7] Owlim-se. http://owlim.ontotext.com/display/OWLIMv43/OWLIM-SE.

[8] Parliament. http://parliament.semwebcentral.org.

[9] Patients like me. www.patientslikeme.com.

[10] Spot crime. http://www.spotcrime.com/.

[11] Virtuoso. http://virtuoso.openlinksw.com.

[12] Yago. http://www.mpi-inf.mpg.de/departments/databases-and-information-systems/research/yago-naga/yago/.

[13] S. Agrawal, S. Chaudhuri, and G. Das. Dbxplorer: A system for keyword-based search over relational databases. In *ICDE*, pages 5–16, 2002.

[14] R. Battle and D. Kolas. Enabling the geospatial semantic web with parliament and geosparql. *Semantic Web*, 3(4):355–370, 2012.

[15] N. Bikakis, G. Giannopoulos, J. Liagouris, D. Skoutas, T. Dalamagas, and T. Sellis. Rdivf: Diversifying keyword search on RDF graphs. In *TPDL*, pages 413–416, 2013.

[16] A. Brodt, D. Nicklas, and B. Mitschang. Deep integration of spatial query processing into native RDF triple stores. In *SIGSPATIAL*, pages 33–42, 2010.

[17] X. Cao, G. Cong, and C. S. Jensen. Retrieving top-k prestige-based relevant spatial web objects. *PVLDB*, 3(1):373–384, 2010.

[18] X. Cao, G. Cong, C. S. Jensen, and M. L. Yiu. Retrieving regions of interest for user exploration. *PVLDB*, 7(9):733–744, 2014.

[19] P. Cappellari, R. D. Virgilio, A. Maccioni, and M. Roantree. A path-oriented RDF index for keyword search query processing. In *DEXA*, pages 366–380, 2011.

[20] J. Cheng, S. Huang, H. Wu, and A. W. Fu. Tf-label: a topological-folding labeling scheme for reachability querying in a large graph. In *SIGMOD*, pages 193–204, 2013.

[21] S. Cohen, J. Mamou, Y. Kanza, and Y. Sagiv. Xsearch: A semantic search engine for XML. In *VLDB*, pages 45–56, 2003.

[22] B. B. Dalvi, M. Kshirsagar, and S. Sudarshan. Keyword search on external memory data graphs. *PVLDB*, 1(1):1189–1204, 2008.

[23] S. Elbassuoni and R. Blanco. Keyword search over RDF graphs. In *CIKM*, pages 237–242, 2011.

[24] S. Elbassuoni, M. Ramanath, R. Schenkel, and G. Weikum. Searching RDF graphs with SPARQL and keywords. *IEEE Data Eng. Bull.*, 33(1):16–24, 2010.

[25] R. Fagin, A. Lotem, and M. Naor. Optimal aggregation algorithms for middleware. In *PODS*, 2001.

[26] H. Fu and K. Anyanwu. Effectively interpreting keyword queries on RDF databases with a rear view. In *ISWC*, pages 193–208, 2011.

[27] G. Giannopoulos, E. Biliri, and T. Sellis. Personalizing keyword search on RDF data. In *TPDL*, pages 272–278, 2013.

[28] L. Guo, F. Shao, C. Botev, and J. Shanmugasundaram. XRANK: ranked keyword search over XML documents. In *SIGMOD*, pages 16–27, 2003.

[29] A. Guttman. R-trees: A dynamic index structure for spatial searching. In *SIGMOD*, pages 47–57, 1984.

[30] C. Halaschek-Wiener, B. Aleman-Meza, I. B. Arpinar, and A. P. Sheth. Discovering and ranking semantic associations over a large RDF metabase. In *VLDB*, pages 1317–1320, 2004.

[31] H. He, H. Wang, J. Yang, and P. S. Yu. BLINKS: ranked keyword searches on graphs. In *SIGMOD*, pages 305–316, 2007.

[32] J. A. Hendler, J. Holm, C. Musialek, and G. Thomas. US government linked open data: Semantic.data.gov. *IEEE Intelligent Systems*, 27(3):25–31, 2012.

[33] G. R. Hjaltason and H. Samet. Distance browsing in spatial databases. *ACM Trans. Database Syst.*, 24(2):265–318, 1999.

[34] J. Hoffart, F. M. Suchanek, K. Berberich, and G. Weikum. YAGO2: A spatially and temporally enhanced knowledge base from wikipedia. *Artif. Intell.*, 194:28–61, 2013.

[35] V. Hristidis, L. Gravano, and Y. Papakonstantinou. Efficient ir-style keyword search over relational databases. In *VLDB*, pages 850–861, 2003.

[36] V. Hristidis and Y. Papakonstantinou. DISCOVER: keyword search in relational databases. In *VLDB*, pages 670–681, 2002.

[37] J. Inglis. Inverted indexes and multi-list structures. *Comput. J.*, 17(1):59–63, 1974.

[38] H. Jiang, H. Wang, P. S. Yu, and S. Zhou. Gstring: A novel approach for efficient search in graph databases. In *ICDE*, pages 566–575, 2007.

[39] R. Jin, N. Ruan, S. Dey, and J. X. Yu. SCARAB: scaling reachability computation on large graphs. In *SIGMOD*, pages 169–180, 2012.

[40] R. Jin, N. Ruan, Y. Xiang, and H. Wang. Path-tree: An efficient reachability indexing scheme for large directed graphs. *ACM Trans. Database Syst.*, 36(1):7, 2011.

[41] V. Kacholia, S. Pandit, S. Chakrabarti, S. Sudarshan, R. Desai, and H. Karambelkar. Bidirectional expansion for keyword search on graph databases. In *VLDB*, pages 505–516, 2005.

[42] K. Kyzirakos, M. Karpathiotakis, and M. Koubarakis. Strabon: A semantic geospatial DBMS. In *ISWC*, pages 295–311, 2012.

[43] W. Le, F. Li, A. Kementsietsidis, and S. Duan. Scalable keyword search on large RDF data. *TKDE*, 26(11):2774–2788, 2014.

[44] J. Leskovec and C. Faloutsos. Sampling from large graphs. In *KDD*, pages 631–636, 2006.

[45] S. T. Leutenegger, J. M. Edgington, and M. A. Lopez. STR: A simple and efficient algorithm for R-tree packing. In *ICDE97*, pages 497–506, 1997.

[46] J. Liagouris, N. Mamoulis, P. Bouros, and M. Terrovitis. An effective encoding scheme for spatial RDF data. *PVLDB*, 7(12):1271–1282, 2014.

[47] X. Lian, E. D. Hoyos, A. Chebotko, B. Fu, and C. Reilly. k-nearest keyword search in RDF graphs. *J. Web Sem.*, 22:40–56, 2013.

[48] T. Neumann and G. Weikum. RDF-3X: a risc-style engine for RDF. *PVLDB*, 1(1):647–659, 2008.

[49] J. M. Ponte and W. B. Croft. A language modeling approach to information retrieval. In *SIGIR*, pages 275–281, 1998.

[50] E. Prud'Hommeaux, A. Seaborne, et al. Sparql query language for rdf. *W3C recommendation*, 15, 2008.

[51] D. Shasha, J. T. L. Wang, and R. Giugno. Algorithmics and applications of tree and graph searching. In *PODS*, pages 39–52, 2002.

[52] T. Tran, H. Wang, S. Rudolph, and P. Cimiano. Top-k exploration of query candidates for efficient keyword search on graph-shaped (RDF) data. In *ICDE*, pages 405–416, 2009.

[53] S. J. van Schaik and O. de Moor. A memory efficient reachability data structure through bit vector compression. In *SIGMOD*, pages 913–924, 2011.

[54] C. Wang, W. Ku, and H. Chen. Geo-store: a spatially-augmented SPARQL query evaluation system. In *SIGSPATIAL*, pages 562–565, 2012.

[55] D. Wang, L. Zou, Y. Feng, X. Shen, J. Tian, and D. Zhao. S-store: An engine for large RDF graph integrating spatial information. In *DASFAA*, pages 31–47, 2013.

[56] H. Wang and C. C. Aggarwal. A survey of algorithms for keyword search on graph data. In *Managing and Mining Graph Data*, pages 249–273. 2010.

[57] X. Yan, P. S. Yu, and J. Han. Substructure similarity search in graph databases. In *SIGMOD*, pages 766–777, 2005.

[58] H. Yildirim, V. Chaoji, and M. J. Zaki. GRAIL: scalable reachability index for large graphs. *PVLDB*, 3(1):276–284, 2010.

[59] K. Zeng, J. Yang, H. Wang, B. Shao, and Z. Wang. A distributed graph engine for web scale RDF data. *PVLDB*, 6(4):265–276, 2013.

[60] L. Zou, J. Mo, L. Chen, M. T. Özsu, and D. Zhao. gstore: Answering SPARQL queries via subgraph matching. *PVLDB*, 4(8):482–493, 2011.

Local Similarity Search for Unstructured Text

Pei Wang
Nagoya University, Japan
wang@db.ss.is.nagoya-u.ac.jp

Chuan Xiao*
Nagoya University, Japan
chuanx@nagoya-u.jp

Jianbin Qin
UNSW, Australia
jqin@cse.unsw.edu.au

Wei Wang
UNSW, Australia
weiw@cse.unsw.edu.au

Xiaoyang Zhang
UNSW, Australia
xyzhang@cse.unsw.edu.au

Yoshiharu Ishikawa
Nagoya University, Japan
y-ishikawa@nagoya-u.jp

ABSTRACT

With the growing popularity of electronic documents, replication can occur for many reasons. People may copy text segments from various sources and make modifications. In this paper, we study the problem of local similarity search to find partially replicated text. Unlike existing studies on similarity search which find entirely duplicated documents, our target is to identify documents that approximately share a pair of sliding windows which differ by no more than τ tokens. Our problem is technically challenging because for sliding windows the tokens to be indexed are less selective than entire documents, rendering set similarity join-based algorithms less efficient. Our proposed method is based on enumerating token combinations to obtain signatures with high selectivity. In order to strike a balance between signature and candidate generation, we partition the token universe and for different partitions we generate combinations composed of different numbers of tokens. A cost-aware algorithm is devised to find a good partitioning of the token universe. We also propose to leverage the overlap between adjacent windows to share computation and thus speed up query processing. In addition, we develop the techniques to support the large thresholds. Experiments on real datasets demonstrate the efficiency of our method against alternative solutions.

Keywords

local similarity search; unstructured text; prefix filtering; k-wise signature

1. INTRODUCTION

One of the main issues accompanying the growing popularity of electronic documents is the existence of replication. People may borrow or plagiarize text segments from various sources and make modifications. Due the need in many applications, e.g., plagiarism detection and near-duplicate Web page detection, identifying replications between documents has attracted remarkable attention from research community, and many approaches were proposed in the last two decades, e.g., by similarity search and join [27, 10, 3, 4, 35, 33] or document fingerprinting [25, 6, 8, 29, 30, 18, 31]. For the body of work in similarity search and join, documents are regarded as (multi)sets of tokens or strings, and pairs of documents are identified if they satisfy a similarity constraint. For document fingerprinting, documents are usually divided into overlapping or non-overlapping text segments and then identical or similar segments are identified. However, in many cases of replication, only a small part of a document is copied and text laundering may happen, e.g., by reorganizing sentences, replacing words with synonyms, changing word order, etc. These replications are hardly detected by similarity search and join approaches since these methods measures the similarities of entire documents, which are relatively low when only a small part is replicated. Document fingerprinting approaches are also likely to miss these results because they are either susceptible to small modifications [25, 6, 8] or do not have any guarantee when detecting similar segments [30, 29, 18, 31].

Seeing the limitations of the existing work, we propose to study the local similarity search problem for unstructured text. Given a collection of data documents and a query document, our goal is to find the data documents that share with the query a sliding window of size w but differ by a small number of tokens which are constrained by a threshold τ. Sliding windows can effectively capture partial replications. We regard sliding windows as multisets of tokens and tolerate errors so that replications can be detected in spite of text laundering. Unlike the document fingerprinting methods without guarantee when modifications exist, we investigate exact solutions to the local similarity search problem.

An immediate solution to the problem is materializing all the windows in the documents as individual objects and invoking a set similarity join on two sets of windows, one from the data documents and the other from the query document. Many prevalent set similarity join methods are based on prefix filtering [10, 4, 35, 33] to find candidates that satisfy a necessary but less strict condition of the similarity constraint and then verify these candidates. Tokens in each object are sorted by a global order, and two objects must share a required amount of tokens in their first few tokens, called prefix, to become a candidate. To find candidates, an inverted index is built to map each token to a list of objects that have this token in their prefixes. Tokens are usually sorted by the order of increasing document frequency so that prefixes are composed

*corresponding author

SIGMOD'16, June 26-July 01, 2016, San Francisco, CA, USA

ISBN 978-1-4503-3531-7/16/06...$15.00

DOI: http://dx.doi.org/10.1145/2882903.2915211

of rare and hence selective tokens for fast query processing. However, for local similarity search, windows are much shorter than entire documents and thus the tokens in their prefixes are not so selective. In this case, they either have to use short prefixes but end up with large number of candidates, or use long prefixes but spend more in candidate generation due to the access to long postings lists in the inverted index. Either will result in poor performance. Another issue is that it is unknown how to share computation between overlapping windows by these methods, because prefixes can be different for adjacent windows though they share most of the tokens.

In this paper, we propose to solve the local similarity search problem by a novel way of leveraging prefix filtering. Unlike all the existing prefix filtering-based methods that take single tokens to index, we propose to index *k-wise signatures* which are combinations of k tokens in the prefix. Combining tokens significantly improves the selectivity and thus enables us to use long prefixes while accessing short postings lists. Since enumerating all possible k token combinations in the prefix results in large combination number and hence time-consuming signature generation, we divide the token universe into several partitions according to frequency and use different k's across these partitions. The corresponding prefix filtering condition is developed for k-wise signatures with the partitioning technique. The query processing cost is analyzed, and based on the cost model we propose a practical algorithm to find a good partitioning of the token universe. To take advantage of overlap between adjacent windows, we study how prefixes and candidates change for sliding windows, thereby developing an *interval sharing* technique to avoid unnecessary prefix computation and candidate generation as well as verification. For the case of large thresholds which may cause large number of combinations, we propose to further divide partitions and thus the combination number is reduced to be proportional to $\tau + 1$. Experiment results on publicly available datasets show that our method has superior performance to alternative solutions with up to 12x speedup.

We also note that tolerating errors in sliding windows will increase false positive for the task of detecting partial replications, whereas we aim at developing an efficient method to increase the recall. Additional post processing methods can be applied for the sake of high precision.

Our contributions can be summarized as:

- We study the problem of local similarity search to find sliding windows with a small amount of differences in unstructured text. It can capture partial replications with minor modifications which are hard to be detected by existing methods.
- We propose a prefix filtering-based method and address the major technical issue in adapting prefix filtering for local similarity search. Combinations of tokens are utilized for fast query processing and the token universe is partitioned to reduce the combination number. We propose a cost model based on which a practical partitioning algorithm is devised.
- We exploit the sharing of computation between adjacent windows to efficiently compute prefixes and candidates and perform verification for sliding windows.
- We conduct extensive experiments on real datasets. The proposed method is shown to be faster than alternative methods by up to an order of magnitude.

The rest of the paper is organized as follows: Section 2 defines the problem and introduces preliminaries. Section 3 presents the k-wise signature method with partitioning. Section 4 elaborates the interval sharing technique to share computation for overlapping windows. Cost analysis and token universe partitioning are covered by Section 5. Section 6 presents the technique to cope with large thresholds. Experimental results and analyses are reported in Section 7. Section 8 reviews related work. Section 9 concludes the paper.

2. PRELIMINARIES

2.1 Problem Definition

A document is defined as a sequence of tokens drawn from a finite universe $\mathcal{U} = \{ t_1, \dots, t_{|\mathcal{U}|} \}$. A token can be a word, a q-gram, etc. In our examples, we tokenize documents with whitespace as delimiters, but our algorithms are independent of the tokenization scheme. A window of size w is w consecutive tokens in a document d. $d[i]$ denotes the i-th token in d. $W(d,i)$ denotes the window starting with $d[i]$. We use the notation $x \sqsubseteq d$ to denote that x is a window of d. By neglecting the order of tokens in the original document, a window is transformed into a *multiset* of tokens. The overlap similarity measures the intersection of tokens in two windows x and y; i.e., $O(x,y) = |x \cap y|$. Note that multiplicities are considered when computing the overlap similarity. Let $mul(t,x)$ denote the multiplicity (number of occurrences) of a token in a window x. The multiplicity of t in $x \cap y$ is the smaller of $mul(t,x)$ and $mul(t,y)$. E.g., $\{ A, A, A, B \} \cap \{ A, A, B, B \} = \{ A, A, B \}$. If a window is drawn from a data document we call it a data window, and if it is drawn from a query document we call it a query window. The problem of local similarity search is defined as follows.

PROBLEM 1. *Given a collection of data documents $\mathcal{D}$, a query document q, a window size w, and a threshold θ, the problem of local similarity search is to find all pairs of windows $\langle x, y \rangle$, such that x is a data window, y is a query window, and their intersection is at least θ; i.e., $\{ \langle x, y \rangle \mid x \sqsubseteq d_i, d_i \in \mathcal{D}, y \sqsubseteq q, O(x,y) \geq \theta \}$.*

We may also define the threshold with dissimilarity; i.e., $\tau = w - \theta$, and our goal is to find the pair of windows $\langle x, y \rangle$ such that $w - O(x,y) \leq \tau$. For ease of exposition, we use the τ threshold instead of θ in the rest of the paper.

EXAMPLE 1. *Consider a data document d and a query document q,*

$$d = \text{“the lord of the rings”},$$
$$q = \text{“the lord and the kings”}.$$

$w = 4$, and $\tau = 1$. With the word-to-token mapping table,

Word	*the*	*lord*	*of*	*rings*	*and*	*kings*
Token	*A*	*B*	*C*	*D*	*E*	*F*
Window Freq.	*2*	*2*	*2*	*1*	*0*	*0*

The data document has two windows

$$W(d,1) = \{ A, B, C, A \},$$
$$W(d,2) = \{ B, C, A, D \}.$$

The query document has two windows

$$W(q,1) = \{ A, B, E, A \},$$
$$W(q,2) = \{ B, E, A, F \}.$$

$\langle W(d,1), W(q,1) \rangle$ is returned as the result of local similarity search because the $w - O(x,y) = 4 - 3 = 1 \leq \tau$.

2.2 Prefix Filtering

Similarity join [10] is an operation to take two relations as input and return pairs of objects from each relation that satisfy a similarity constraint. One may regard each window as an individual object and convert the local similarity search to a set similarity join on two relations $\mathcal{R}$ and $\mathcal{S}$, which consist of all the windows from the data and the query documents, respectively. Since similarity computation for all pairs of objects is time-consuming, many prevalent set similarity join algorithms are based on the filter-and-refine scheme to generate a set of promising candidates that satisfy necessary conditions for the similarity constraint and then verify them by similarity computation. Many of them [10, 4, 35, 33] utilize the prefix filtering principle for fast query processing:

LEMMA 1 (PREFIX FILTERING). *Consider two multisets x and y of size w. Both are sorted in a global order $\mathcal{O}$. Let the prefix of x be the first $(\tau + 1)$ tokens in x. If $w - O(x, y) \leq \tau$, the prefixes of x and y must share at least one token.*

For the global order $\mathcal{O}$, prefix filtering-based methods suggest sorting by increasing order of document frequency. In this way, prefixes tend to be composed of rare tokens, and thus the number of objects that share at least a token in prefixes (called candidates) tends to be small. For local similarity search, since each window is treated as an object, we sort the tokens in increasing order of window frequency, i.e., the number of windows in *data documents* that contain the token, and break tie by lexicographical order (after tokenization) and then increasing order of their positions in the original document. In this paper, we let $\mathcal{O}$ be this order unless otherwise stated. Consider a window x whose tokens are sorted by $\mathcal{O}$. $x[i]$ denotes the i-th token in x. $x[i\,..\,j]$ denotes the multiset of tokens from the i-th token to the j-th token in x. Given two tokens t_1 and t_2, $t_1 < t_2$ if t_1 precedes t_2 in $\mathcal{O}$.

In [35, 33], the prefix filtering is extended to k-prefix:

LEMMA 2 (EXTENDED PREFIX FILTERING). *Consider two multisets x and y of size w. Both are sorted in a global order $\mathcal{O}$. Let the k-prefix of x be the first $(\tau + k)$ tokens in x. If $w - O(x, y) \leq \tau$, then the k-prefixes of x and y must share at least k tokens.*

The condition of the k-prefix case is stricter than the 1-prefix case, and hence reduces the candidate number. In addition, an adaptive approach was proposed in [33] to optimize query processing performance by selecting an appropriate prefix length for each object using a cost model.

EXAMPLE 2. *Consider the windows and the window frequency table (note that window frequency only counts occurrences in data windows) in Example 1. $\mathcal{O}$ is $E < F < D < A < B < C$. We sort the tokens in each window in this order:*

$$W(d,1) = [\underline{A, A, B}, C],$$
$$W(d,2) = [\underline{D, A, B}, C],$$
$$W(q,1) = [\underline{E, A, A}, B],$$
$$W(q,2) = [\underline{E, F, A}, B].$$

The underlined tokens are 2-prefixes of these windows. $W(d,1)$ and $W(q,1)$ satisfy the similarity constraint. They share two tokens (two A's) in their 2-prefixes.

With the (extended) prefix filtering principle, one can design a similarity join-based algorithm [1] for local similarity search. The algorithm consists of two parts: the indexing part and the query processing part. In the indexing part, for each window in $\mathcal{R}$, the tokens in the prefix (can be 1-prefix, k-prefix, or adaptive prefix) are extracted, each token regarded as a *signature*. An inverted index is built offline, mapping each signature s to a list (called postings list) of windows whose prefixes contain s. In the query processing part, the windows in $\mathcal{S}$ are processed one by one in an index nested loops join manner, and there are three phases: (1) In the *signature generation phase*, signatures are generated in the same way as in the indexing part. (2) In the *candidate generation phase*, the inverted index is probed to find *candidate windows*, i.e., the windows in $\mathcal{R}$ that share required amount of tokens with the query window in their prefixes. (3) In the *verification phase*, candidate windows are verified and added to the result if they meet the similarity condition.

There are two main drawbacks of the similarity join-based algorithm: (1) Compared with similarity join on entire documents, windows size is smaller in local similarity search. Prefixes are likely to contain frequent tokens that are *not selective*, and this will result in the following dilemma: We either use short prefixes but end up with a time-consuming verification phase due to large number of candidate windows, or use long prefixes but need to access long postings lists which poses considerable overhead in the candidate generation phase. (2) Overlap exists between adjacent windows but they are processed individually without any share of computation, e.g., common tokens in prefixes as well as verification of adjacent windows. We proposed a new method to address the two issues in the next two sections.

3. k-wise SIGNATURE SCHEME

3.1 Combination of k Tokens

Unlike the similarity join-based algorithm that regards *single tokens* as signatures, e.g., [35, 33], we apply the prefix filtering in another way. Recall that extended prefix filtering requires that candidate windows share at least k tokens in their prefixes. For the k-prefix of each window, we pick the combination of k tokens in every possible way and generate signatures. An inverted index is built to map each signature to a list of windows that contain the signature, i.e., all the k tokens, in their prefixes. We use the index to find windows that share a common signature, hence at least k tokens in their prefixes. Since there are $(\tau + k)$ tokens in the k-prefix, the number of signatures for each window is $\binom{\tau+k}{k}$. We call this type of signatures *k-wise signatures*. Compared to single tokens, k-wise signatures are usually more selective and yield shorter postings lists in the index, thereby reducing the cost in the candidate generation phase. When $k = 1$, k-wise signatures become single tokens and the method is equivalent to standard prefix filtering (Lemma 1).

EXAMPLE 3. *Consider the four windows in Example 2. $\tau =$*

[1] Despite solving a search problem, we call it a join-based algorithm because it converts the search problem to a problem of joining two relations of windows.

1, and $k = 2$. The signatures for these windows are [2]*:*

$$S_{W(d,1)} = \{AA, AB, AB\},$$
$$S_{W(d,2)} = \{DA, DB, AB\},$$
$$S_{W(q,1)} = \{EA, EA, AA\},$$
$$S_{W(q,2)} = \{EF, EA, FA\}.$$

$W(d,1)$ and $W(q,1)$ share a common signature AA, and therefore share at least two tokens in their prefixes.

We compare the cost in the candidate generation phase. Using single tokens, the postings list of token A has two entries $W(d,1)$ and $W(d,2)$; E and F are not in the index. To process $W(q,1)$ and $W(q,2)$, $2+2=4$ entries are accessed. Using 2-wise signatures, the postings list of AA has one entry $W(d,1)$; EA, EF, and FA are not in the index. To process $W(q,1)$ and $W(q,2)$, 1 entry is accessed, and the cost is reduced by 3 from the single token case.

For the choice of k, a larger k decreases candidate generation cost as well as verification cost because signatures are more selective, resulting in shorter postings lists and less number of candidates. On the other hand, it increases signature generation cost due to more token combinations. According to our experiment results, setting k to 3 yields the best runtime performance for most w and τ settings.

3.2 Partition of Token Universe

Although using k-wise signatures reduces cost in the candidate generation phase, it increases the cost in the signature generation phase due to the enumeration of token combinations in prefixes. This renders it unable to scale up when τ or k increases. To remedy this, we observe that due to the power law distribution of token frequencies, the rarest tokens in prefixes are selective enough, and there is no need to combine them to k-wise signatures. Only the relatively frequent tokens (they are still uncommon when compared with the most popular tokens in a window) in prefixes need to be combined, and considering their frequencies we may use different k's for different tokens. This inspires our idea of partitioning token universe.

Consider a token universe $\mathcal{U}$ sorted by $\mathcal{O}$. It is divided into $k_{\max}$ disjoint partitions (empty partitions are allowed). For the tokens in the i-th partition, i-wise signatures are used and combinations are only generated from within. Note that if a window has less than i tokens in the i-th partition, we do not generate signatures for these tokens in this window. Intuitively, the rarest tokens are indexed in single tokens, while the most frequent tokens are indexed in $k_{\max}$-wise signatures. We say a token t's class (denoted by $class(t)$) is i if t is in the i-th partition of $\mathcal{U}$. We call this type of signatures partitioned k-wise signatures.

For the above partitioned k-wise signatures, we define candidate windows as the data windows that share with the query window at least one common signature generated from their respective prefixes. The prefix length for partitioned k-wise signatures needs to be computed, considering the possibility that a window may contain tokens in different classes. Since a pair of windows $\langle x, y\rangle$ satisfying the similarity constraint may differ by at most τ tokens, if a token of x is not in y, we call the token an *error* in x. Our goal is to find the shortest lengths l_x of x and l_y of y such that if there is no common signature generated from the tokens in $x[1\,..\,l_x]$ and $y[1\,..\,l_y]$, it will incur at least $\tau+1$ errors (in both x and y).

Algorithm 1: PrefixLength (x, τ)

```
cov = 0, n_i ← 0 (1 ≤ i ≤ k_max);
for l = 1 to w do
    i ← x[l]'s class;
    n_i ← n_i + 1;
    if n_i ≥ i then
        cov ← cov + 1;
        if cov = τ + 1 then break;
return l
```

We say a signature is *affected* by an error if the signature contains the error. Given a multiset of tokens, its *coverage* is defined as the minimum amount of errors required to affect all the signatures enumerated from these tokens.

LEMMA 3. *Consider n_i tokens in class i. The coverage of these tokens is captured by the following equation*

$$cov(i) = \begin{cases} n_i - i + 1 & , \textit{if } n_i \geq i \\ 0 & , \textit{otherwise.} \end{cases} \tag{1}$$

PROOF. For the case when $n_i \geq i$, if the number of errors is less than $(n_i - i + 1)$, there will be at least i common tokens, hence at least one common signature not affected. For the other case, since no signature can be generated, no error is needed. □

It can be seen that two signatures generated from different classes do not have any common tokens. Hence we have the following lemma.

LEMMA 4. *Consider a multiset which has n_i tokens in each class i ($1 \leq i \leq k_{\max}$). The coverage of these tokens is $\sum_{i=1}^{k_{\max}} cov(i)$.*

With the above lemma, we can design an algorithm (Algorithm 1) to compute the prefix length of a window x, whose tokens are already sorted by $\mathcal{O}$. First, the algorithm initializes as zero the coverage and a counter n_i for each class i. Then it iterates through the tokens in x. For each token $x[l]$ and its class i, it increments the corresponding counter n_i. The coverage is incremented if $n_i \geq i$. When the coverage reaches $\tau + 1$, it returns the current value of l as the prefix length. Although when $n_i < i$ no i-wise signatures are generated from the n_i tokens, these tokens are included in the prefix so that the prefix is still continuous [3]. The algorithm correctly computes the prefix length, as stated by the following theorem (proof is provided in Appendix B).

THEOREM 1. *Let l_x denote the prefix length of a window x, as output by Algorithm 1, and S_x be the set of signatures generated with the tokens in $x[1\,..\,l_x]$. If $w - O(x,y) \leq \tau$, $S_x \cap S_y \neq \emptyset$.*

EXAMPLE 4. *Consider the window in Figure 1. $\tau = 3$. We need a total coverage of 4. The number of tokens in the first three classes are 1, 3, and 1, respectively. Their coverages are 1, 2, and 0, respectively, which sum up to 3. Besides these five tokens, we need the first four tokens in class 4 to make the total coverage $\tau + 1$. Therefore the prefix length is 9.*

[2]We do not remove duplicate signatures because they are necessary to the correctness of the interval sharing technique which will be presented in Section 4.

[3]Including these tokens into the prefix is also necessary to guarantee the correctness of the interval sharing in Section 4.

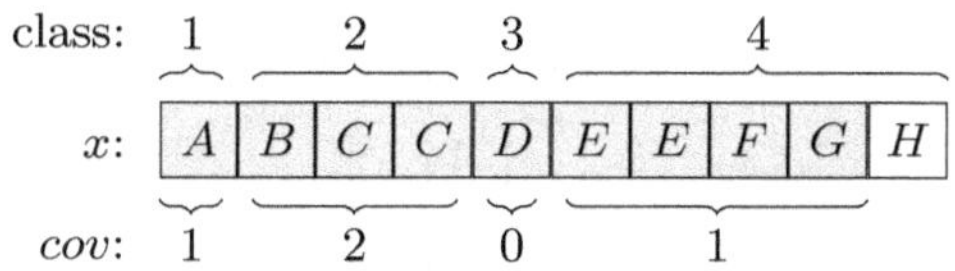

Figure 1: Example of Prefix Length (prefix tokens are shaded)

Algorithm 2: PartitionedKWise $(\mathcal{R}, \mathcal{S}, w, \tau, k_{\max})$

```
1  T ← ∅, I_i ← ∅;
2  foreach x ∈ R do
3      S ← GenSignature(x, τ, k_max);
4      foreach s ∈ S do
5          I_s ← I_s ∪ { x } ;            /* insert into index */
6  foreach y ∈ S do
7      A ← ∅;
8      S ← GenSignature(y, τ, k_max);
9      foreach s ∈ S do
10         foreach x ∈ I_s do
11             A ← A ∪ { x } ;            /* find a candidate */
12     foreach x ∈ A do
13         if w − O(x, y) ≤ τ then
14             T ← T ∪ { ⟨x, y⟩ };
15 return T
```

Supposing checking a token's class spends $O(1)$ time, the time complexity of Algorithm 1 is $O(l)$. Moreover, the prefix length of a window is upper-bounded by the following corollary, as derived from Lemmas 3 and 4.

COROLLARY 1. *A window's prefix length does not exceed* $\tau + 1 + \frac{k_{\max}(k_{\max}-1)}{2}$.

The upper bound is tight, because when there are $i-1$ tokens in class i ($1 \le i \le k_{\max}-1$), the prefix length reaches the upper bound. Corollary 1 also yields an upper-bound of the time complexity of Algorithm 1, which is $O(\tau + k_{\max}^2)$.

We call a token t a *covering* token if the coverage of the tokens in $class(t)$ is above zero, or a *non-covering* token otherwise. The following corollary states that the tokens in the highest class in the prefix are covering tokens.

COROLLARY 2. *Let h be the highest class in the prefix: $h = \max\{\, i \mid n_i > 0, 1 \le i \le k_{\max} \,\}$. The coverage of the tokens in class h is above zero.*

By replacing single tokens with partitioned k-wise signatures, we devise an algorithm (Algorithm 2) for local similarity search. Partitioned k-wise signatures are generated for indexing (Line 3) and signature generation (Line 8) by calling Algorithm 3, which computes the prefix length of a window and then combines tokens in each class i as i-wise signatures. In candidate generation, for each signature generated from a query window's prefix, we probe the inverted index and store the candidate windows in a set (Line 11). Then the candidate windows are verified by the similarity constraint (Line 13).

By Corollary 1, the completeness of the algorithm is stated by the following theorem.

THEOREM 2. *Algorithm 2 is complete and does not miss any result of local similarity search when* $w \ge \tau + 1 + \frac{k_{\max}(k_{\max}-1)}{2}$.

When $k_{\max} = 1$, only single tokens are used to generate signatures, and the prefix length returned by Algorithm 1 is exactly $\tau + 1$. Therefore, using standard prefix filtering is a special case of the partitioned k-wise algorithm.

Algorithm 3: GenSignature $(x, \tau, k_{\max})$

```
S ← ∅;
l ← PrefixLength(x, τ);
for i = 1 to k_max do
    P_i ← { t | t ∈ x[1 . . l] ∧ class(t) = i } ;   /* a multiset */
    S ← S ∪ { i-wise signatures generated from tokens in P_i };
return S
```

We analyze the cost of the partitioned k-wise algorithm and compare it with the algorithm generating the same set of candidate windows using single tokens, i.e., building index with single tokens for all the classes and finding the pairs of windows such that there exists a token class i in their prefixes where at least i tokens are shared. Assume that the cost of generating an i-wise signature is i and the cost of accessing each entry in a postings list is 1. For signature generation, the cost of the single token algorithm is $\sum_{i=1}^{k_{\max}} n_i$ and the partitioned k-wise algorithm is $\sum_{i=1}^{k_{\max}} i \cdot \binom{n_i}{i}$. Assume tokens are independent and the average length of postings list is $|\mathcal{R}| f_i$ for a single token in class i. For an i-wise signature, the expected length of its posting list is $|\mathcal{R}|(f_i)^i$. Hence for candidate generation, the cost of the single token algorithm is $\sum_{i=1}^{k_{\max}} n_i \cdot |\mathcal{R}| f_i$, and the partitioned k-wise algorithm is $\sum_{i=1}^{k_{\max}} \binom{n_i}{i} \cdot |\mathcal{R}|(f_i)^i$. The partitioned k-wise algorithm spends more on signature generation than the single token algorithm when $k_{\max} > 1$ and $n_i > i$, but saves candidate generation cost when $f_i < (\frac{n_i}{\binom{n_i}{i}})^{\frac{1}{i-1}}$.

The query processing performance of the partitioned k-wise algorithm depends on the partitioning of token universe. We leave this problem to Section 5 and investigate how to utilize the overlap of adjacent windows first.

4. INTERVAL SHARING

4.1 Signature Generation

Two adjacent windows $w(d, i)$ and $w(d, i+1)$ share $w-1$ tokens. It is very likely that they share most tokens in the prefixes. This motivates us to share signature generation for the adjacent windows.

We say a window x contains a signature s if s is generated from x's prefix. Instead of mapping a signature to a list of windows in the index, we choose to map a signature to a list of window intervals that contain this signature. A window interval is in the form of $d[u, v]$, representing that all the windows between $W(d, u)$ and $W(d, v)$, including both, contain the signature. For the sake of query processing performance, an interval is to be maximal; i.e., neither $W(d, u-1)$ nor $W(d, v+1)$ contains the signature. We slide through the document, open an interval of the signature when we reach $W(d, u)$, and close the interval when we leave $W(d, v)$. Then the interval $d[u, v]$ is inserted to the postings list of the signature.

For the first window of a document, its prefix is computed and signatures are generated by Algorithm 3. An interval is opened for each of these signatures. When a window slides to the next one, it can be observed that if none of the tokens in the prefix changes, no signature changes. Therefore intervals are only opened or closed when any token changes in the prefix. The intervals of signatures are all closed when we leave the last window of a document.

Based on the above observation, we design a prefix maintenance algorithm (pseudo-code provided in Appendix A). The basic idea is that when the window slides, we can exploit the current prefix to compute the new one rather than starting from scratch. Suppose x and x' are two adjacent windows. P denotes the prefix of x, whose length is l, and its coverage is denoted by $cov(P)$. Let t_1 be the first token of x and t_2 be the last token of x'; i.e., t_1 is the outgoing token and t_2 is the incoming token when the window slides. The algorithm takes x, l, t_1, and t_2 as input, and outputs a quadruple (x', l', S_o, S_c), where l' denotes the prefix length of x', and S_o and S_c denote the multisets of the signatures whose intervals are opened and closed while x slides to x', respectively. To compute the new prefix, our idea is to delete t_1 if it is in the current prefix, and insert t_2 if it precedes some token in the current prefix. Then we compute the coverage (either τ, $\tau+1$, or $\tau+2$) of the resulting prefix, and recover it to $\tau+1$ if not equal. To this end, we propose the notion of *temporary* prefix, denoted by P', to capture how the prefix changes with the slide. P' is first initialized as P. Then t_1 is deleted from P' if t_1 is a token of P', and t_2 is inserted into P' if it precedes the last token of P' in terms of the global order $\mathcal{O}$. Then we cope with the coverage of the resulting P'. The procedure is divided into the following cases.

- If $cov(P \backslash t_1) < \tau+1$, the coverage is below $\tau+1$ when t_1 is deleted. We check whether t_2 recovers the coverage to $\tau+1$.

  If so, it means that t_1 is replaced by t_2 in the prefix. Due to Corollary 2, we remove from P' the tokens in the highest class if they are non-covering, because t_1 may be in the highest class of P and its removal may cause the other tokens in this class to be non-covering. If $t_1 \neq t_2$, we close intervals for the signatures that contain t_1, generate signatures by combining t_2 and the tokens in the same class in P', and open intervals for them.

  Otherwise, it means that the removal of t_1 reduces the coverage but the inclusion of t_2 does not recover it. We need to include more tokens (denoted by ΔP) into the prefix to increase the coverage to $\tau+1$. If ΔP has tokens other than t_1 (note that t_1 may be a token of x' as well due to the multiplicity), we close intervals for the signatures that contain t_1, generate signatures by combining every token in ΔP and those in the same class in P', and open intervals for them.
- If $cov(P \backslash t_1) = \tau+1$, either t_1 is not in the prefix or the coverage remains $\tau+1$ when it is deleted. We check whether the coverage of P' exceeds $\tau+1$ due to t_2.

  If so, it means that the removal of t_1 does not affect the coverage but the inclusion of t_2 make it exceed $\tau+1$. We need to remove tokens (denoted by ΔP) from P' to decrease the coverage to $\tau+1$. The tokens in the highest class of P' are then removed if they are non-covering tokens. If ΔP has tokens other than t_2, we close intervals for the signatures that contain any token in ΔP, generate signatures by combining t_2 and the tokens in the same class in P', and open intervals for them.

  Otherwise, it means that neither t_1 and t_2 affects the coverage. No interval changes in this case.

EXAMPLE 5. *Figure 2 shows an example of the maintenance of prefix.* $w = 4$, *and* $\tau = 1$. d *is a document consisting of seven tokens. Suppose tokens are sorted in alphabetical order.* A, B, C, *and* D *are class 1 tokens.* E, F, *and* G *are class 2 tokens. Tokens in the prefix are underlined for each window.*

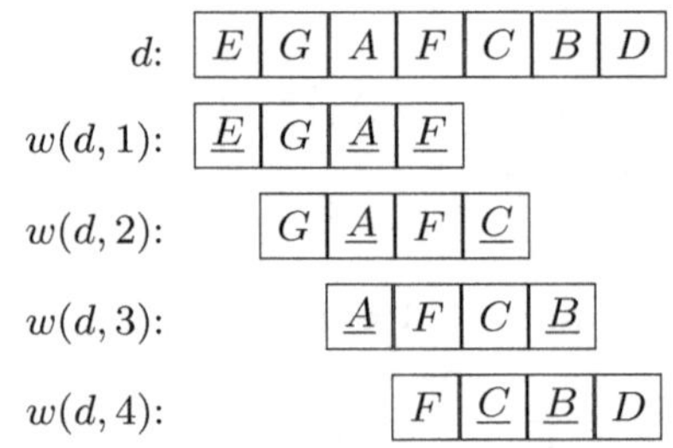

Figure 2: Example of Prefix Maintenance

Starting with $W(d,1)$, *the prefix is* $\{A, E, F\}$. *Signatures* A *and* EF *are generated, and intervals are opened for them. When the window slides to* $W(d,2)$, E *leaves the window. Since it is in the prefix of* $W(d,1)$, *the temporary prefix becomes* $\{A, F\}$. C *enters the window, and it is inserted into the temporary prefix because* $C < F$. *Now the coverage is* $\tau+1$. *We remove the highest class which consists of a non-covering token* F. *Hence the prefix of* $W(d,2)$ *is* $\{A, C\}$. *Because* $E \neq C$, *the interval of* EF *is closed, and the interval of* C *is opened. For* $W(d,3)$, G *leaves the window and it is not in the prefix of* $W(d,2)$. *The new token* B *is inserted into the temporary prefix because* $B < C$. *Since the coverage is* $\tau+2$, C *is removed to recover the coverage to* $\tau+1$. *Hence the prefix of* $W(d,3)$ *is* $\{A, B\}$. *The interval of* C *is closed, and the interval of* B *is opened. For* $W(d,4)$, A *leaves the window and it is in the prefix of* $W(d,3)$. *The temporary prefix becomes* $\{B\}$. *Then* D *is not inserted because* $D \not< B$. *Since the coverage is* τ, C *is included to recover it to* $\tau+1$. *Hence the prefix of* $W(d,4)$ *is* $\{B, C\}$. *Because* $A \neq C$, *the interval of* A *is closed, and the interval of* C *is opened. When reaching the end of* d, *we close the intervals of* B *and* C.

The signatures and their corresponding intervals are A : $\{d[1,3]\}$, EF : $\{d[1,1]\}$, C : $\{d[2,2], d[4,4]\}$, B : $\{d[3,4]\}$.

To efficiently implement the prefix maintenance algorithm, the tokens of window x can be stored in a binary search tree, so that the deletion of t_1 and the insertion of t_2 take $O(\log w)$ time. We do not materialize the prefix P or P' but record the prefix length l and l'. Hence checking if a token is in P' takes $O(\log w)$ time and any update on P' takes $O(1)$ time. By keeping track of the number of tokens in each class, any coverage-related operation takes $O(1)$ time. The loop of deleting the highest class from the temporary prefix is repeated at most ($k_{\max}$ - 1) times, hence taking $O(k_{\max})$ time in the worst case and $O(1)$ time in the average case. Ignoring the cost of generating signatures, the time complexity is $O(k_{\max} + \log w)$ in the worst case and $O(\log w)$ in the average case.

A subtle case is that the multiplicity of a token in the prefix may cause duplicate signatures in a window, and hence multiple opens or closes of an interval. E.g., $k_{\max} = 1$, and the prefixes of windows $W(d,1)$ to $W(d,5)$ are $\{A, B\}$, $\{A, A\}$, $\{A, B\}$, $\{A, B\}$, and $\{B, C\}$, respectively. The interval of signature A is opened at $W(d,1)$ and $W(d,2)$, and closed at $W(d,2)$ and $W(d,4)$, hence resulting in two overlapping intervals $d[1,4]$ and $d[2,2]$ which violate the maximality of an interval. To handle this case, we use a counter γ to store the times an interval has been opened. When it is opened for the first time, γ is initialized as 1. It is increased by 1 when an open occurs, and decreased by 1 when a close occurs. Only the first open (when $\gamma = 1$) and the last close (when $\gamma = 0$) are treated as "true" open and close of an interval, while the others are treated as "false" opens or closes. We only insert the interval into the index for a true close. In the above example, a true open occurs at $W(d,1)$ and a true close occurs at $W(d,4)$, hence resulting in a maximal interval $d[1,4]$. In the rest of the paper, we mean a true open or close when referring to an open or close of an interval unless otherwise noted, and the output of the prefix maintenance algorithm only involves signatures with true open or close intervals.

4.2 Candidate Generation

By utilizing index on window intervals, for a query window, we generate candidates in the form of $d[u,v]$ (called *candidate interval*), indicating that all the windows between $W(d,u)$ and $W(d,v)$, including both, share at least a signature with the query window in their prefixes.

We use the same method to generate signatures for both indexing and query processing. It can be seen that for two consecutive query windows $W(q,i)$ and $W(q,i+1)$, their candidate intervals are the same if the two windows generate the same set of signatures. We exploit this property and devise the partitioned k-wise algorithm equipped with interval sharing. The pseudo-code is shown in Algorithm 4.

To index data documents, it iterates through the data documents in $\mathcal{D}$, computes prefix and generates signatures for the first window of each document by Algorithms 1 and 3 (Line 4), and processes the other windows by the prefix maintenance algorithm (Line 6). Signatures are generated and corresponding window intervals are indexed (Line 8).

To process queries, we also call Algorithms 1 and 3 to compute prefix and generate signatures for the first query window (Line 10), and call the prefix maintenance algorithm to handle the other windows (Line 13). The candidate intervals of a query window $W(q,i)$ is stored in a multiset A_i. With the set of signatures whose intervals are open for the first query window, as returned by Algorithm 3, for each signature s in the set we probe the index to retrieve its (data) window intervals and insert them into A_1 (Line 11). For the other query windows, we monitor S_o and S_c output by the prefix maintenance algorithm, which are the multisets of the signatures whose intervals are opened and closed, respectively, while the query window slides. If S_o and S_c are both empty, indicating that $W(q,i)$ and $W(q,i+1)$ generate the same set of signatures, then $A_{i+1} = A_i$ (Line 14). Otherwise, we let $A_{i+1} = A_i$, probe the index for each signature in S_o (resp. S_c), and then insert into (resp. delete from) A_{i+1} the (data) window intervals retrieved from the index (Lines 15 – 16). Finally, we merge intervals in each A_i to eliminate the overlap among candidate intervals (Line 18) and perform verification (Line 20).

EXAMPLE 6. *Consider an index mapping two signatures s_1 and s_2 to the window intervals of d_1 and d_2:*

$$I_{s_1} = \{\, d_1[11,13], d_2[13,15] \,\},$$
$$I_{s_2} = \{\, d_1[12,14], d_2[11,14] \,\}.$$

Consider a query of three windows. Suppose both $W(q,1)$ and $W(q,2)$ generate a signature s_1, and $W(q,3)$ generates two signatures s_1 and s_2. Before merging, the candidate intervals of the three query windows are:

$$A_1 = \{\, d_1[11,13], d_2[13,15] \,\},$$
$$A_2 = \{\, d_1[11,13], d_2[13,15] \,\},$$
$$A_3 = \{\, d_1[11,13], d_2[13,15], d_1[12,14], d_2[11,14] \,\}.$$

We obtain A_1 by probing the postings list of s_1, and let $A_2 = A_1$ because they generate the same signature. For A_3, we probe the index and insert the window interval of s_2. After merging, A_3 becomes $\{\, d_1[11,14], d_2[11,15] \,\}$.

Algorithm 4: PartitionedKWiseInterval $(\mathcal{D}, q, w, \tau, k_{\max})$

```
1  T ← ∅, I_i ← ∅;
2  foreach d ∈ D do
3      x ← W(d, 1);
4      l ← PrefixLength(x, τ), S_o ← GenSignature(x, τ, k_max);
5      for i = 1 to |d| do
6          (x, l, S_o, S_c) ← MaintainPrefix(x, l, d[i], d[i + w]);
7          foreach s ∈ S_c and its interval [u, v] do
8              I_s ← I_s ∪ { d[u, v] };
9  y ← W(q, 1);
10 l ← PrefixLength(y, τ), S_o ← GenSignature(y, τ, k_max);
11 A_1 ← ⋃_{s∈S_o} I_s;
12 for i = 1 to |q| do
13     (y, l, S_o, S_c) ← MaintainPrefix(y, l, q[i], q[i + w]);
14     A_{i+1} ← A_i;
15     if S_o ≠ ∅ or S_c ≠ ∅ then
16         A_{i+1} ← (A_{i+1} \ ⋃_{s∈S_c} I_s) ∪ ⋃_{s∈S_o} I_s;
17 for i = 1 to |q| do
18     MergeInterval(A_i);
19     foreach d[u, v] ∈ A_i do
20         T ← T ∪ VerifyInterval(W(q, i), W(d, u..v));
21 return T
```

4.3 Verification

Because of the overlap between adjacent windows, the verification of a query window against a candidate interval can be performed in a rolling fashion. To compute the intersection of a query window y and a data window x, we use two hash tables to count the multiplicities of their tokens, and the intersection $O(x,y) = \sum_{t \in y} \min(mul(t,x), mul(t,y))$. For the next data window x', since only the multiplicities of the outgoing and the incoming tokens change, we can compute $O(x',y)$ with four operations on the two hash tables, including a deletion, an insertion, and two lookups. Similarly, for the next query window y', we can obtain its hash table by two operations on the existing hash table of y instead of counting multiplicities by starting from scratch.

The above method spends w hash table operations for the first query window, 2 for any other query window, and $2w + 4(v-u)$ for a candidate interval $d[u,v]$. Based on this observation, candidate intervals can be further merged if they are close to each other. Consider two candidate intervals $d[u_1,v_1]$ and $d[u_2,v_2]$, where $u_2 > v_1$. If $u_2 - v_1 < \frac{w}{2}$, they will be merged into $d[u_1,v_2]$ and verified. This is because there are $4w + 4(v_2 + v_1 - u_2 - u_1)$ hash table operations to process the two separate intervals, and $2w + 4(v_2 - u_1)$ for a merged interval. The latter is less than the former when $u_2 - v_1 < \frac{w}{2}$, even if the windows between $W(d, v_1+1)$ and $W(d, u_2-1)$ are not candidates. We integrate this method to the interval merge step (Line 18) in Algorithm 4.

Another optimization is that we can early terminate the verification of an interval seeing an already computed intersection. Consider a query window x and a window $W(d,j)$ from an interval $d[u,v]$. If $w - O(x, W(d,j)) = \tau + \delta$, where $\delta > 0$, then none of the windows between $W(d,j)$ and $W(d, j+\delta-1)$ is a result, because they differ by at most $\delta - 1$ tokens from $W(d,j)$ and thus at least $\tau + 1$ tokens from x. To exploit this observation, we skip verifying the remaining windows of the interval if $j + \delta > v$.

5. COST ANALYSIS AND TOKEN UNIVERSE PARTITIONING

We analyze the cost of Algorithm 4 and based on the analysis we devise the token universe partitioning algorithm.

5.1 Cost Analysis

For a given query q, the query processing cost consists of the costs in three phases: signature generation, candidate generation, and verification, i.e.,

$$C_{query\_proc}(q) = C_{sig\_gen}(q) + C_{cand\_gen}(q) + C_{verify}(q).$$

For the signature generation phase, we ignore the prefix computation costs of the algorithms compared and consider the costs of generating signatures only. A signature is generated when its interval is opened or closed (including false open and close). We assume that the cost of generating a signature s is $c_{comb} \cdot |s|$, i.e., the cost of combining a token multiplied by the number of constituent tokens in s. Then the signature generation cost of Algorithm 4

$$C_{sig\_gen}(q) = c_{comb} \cdot 2 \sum_{s \in S_{all}} |s|, \tag{2}$$

where S_{all} denotes the multiset [4] of signatures generated in the signature generation phase. We compare with Algorithm 2 which processes each window individually. Let $s.u$ and $s.v$ denote the two ends of a window interval that contains s. Algorithm 2's signature generation cost is $c_{comb} \cdot \sum_{s \in S_{all}} (s.v - s.u + 1)|s|$. Algorithm 4 saves signature generation cost for the signatures such that $s.v - s.u > 1$. In the worst case, nothing is shared in the prefixes of adjacent windows, and the signature generation cost of Algorithm 4 is twice as much as Algorithm 2.

The candidate generation cost of Algorithm 4 consists of two parts: accessing inverted index and merging candidate intervals. Index is accessed when the interval of a signature s is opened or closed (true open and close only). Merging only occurs if two adjacent windows have different candidate intervals. Assuming the cost of accessing an interval is c_{int}, the candidate generation cost

$$C_{cand\_gen}(q) = c_{int} \cdot (2 \sum_{s \in S_{true}} |I_s| + \sum_{i=1}^{|q|} 1_{S_i \neq S_{i-1}} \cdot \sum_{s \in S_i} |I_s|). \tag{3}$$

S_{true} denotes the multiset of signatures generated by a true open in the signature generation phase. $|I_s|$ denotes the number of window intervals in the postings list of s. S_i denotes the signatures whose intervals are open when the window slides to $W(q, i)$. $1_{S_i \neq S_{i-1}}$ is the indicator function that returns 1 if $S_i \neq S_{i-1}$ or 0 otherwise (S_0 is defined as an $\emptyset$). For Algorithm 2, the candidate generation cost is $c_{int} \cdot \sum_{i=1}^{|q|} \sum_{s \in S_i} |I'_s|$, where I'_s denotes the number of windows in the postings list of s. Hence Algorithm 4 saves cost for the signatures that are shared by more than two consecutive windows in both the query and the data windows. In the worst case, the candidate generation cost of Algorithm 4 is three times as much as Algorithm 2.

For verification, the first query window spends w operations to count its token multiplicities, and every other query window spends 2 operations, hence $2|q| - w$ operations in total. To count the token multiplicities of a candidate interval $d[u, v]$, there are $2w + 4(v - u)$ operations (early termination not considered). Assuming the cost of a hash table operation is c_{hash}, the verification cost of Algorithm 4

$$C_{verify}(q) = c_{hash} \cdot (2|q| - w + \sum_{i=1}^{|q|} \sum_{d[u,v] \in A_i} 2w + 4(v - u)), \tag{4}$$

where A_i denotes the set of candidate intervals of $W(q, i)$ after merging. When $w > 1$, this cost is always less than the cost of Algorithm 2, which is $c_{hash} \cdot (w|q| + \sum_{i=1}^{|q|} \sum_{d[u,v] \in A_i} 2w(v - u + 1))$, even if in the worst case.

5.2 A Greedy Partitioning Algorithm

Since the token universe partitioning can be done offline and queries are processed online, our goal is to optimize the query processing for multiple queries (denoted by a query workload $\mathcal{Q}$) rather than a single query. Instead of resorting to a straightforward equi-width partitioning, we leverage the above cost model and can formulate the token universe partitioning as an optimization problem.

Given a query workload $\mathcal{Q}$, the processing cost of each query is summed up to the total processing cost of the workload:

$$C_{workload}(\mathcal{Q}) = \sum_{q=1}^{|\mathcal{Q}|} C_{query\_proc}(q).$$

PROBLEM 2. *Given a token universe $\mathcal{U}$, a collection of data documents $\mathcal{D}$, a query workload $\mathcal{Q}$, and parameters w, τ, and $k_{\max}$, determine the global order $\mathcal{O}$ and divide the token universe into $k_{\max}$ partitions such that $C_{workload}(\mathcal{Q})$ is minimized.*

When $k_{\max} = 1$, this problem becomes finding the optimal global order for standard prefix filtering. It is likely to be intractable and hence most existing prefix filtering-based algorithms sort by increasing document frequency as a heuristic [10, 4, 35, 33] . The problem is harder when $k_{\max} > 1$. Moreover, the computation of $C_{workload}(\mathcal{Q})$ for a partitioning $\mathcal{P}$ incurs considerable overhead because we need to build index for $\mathcal{D}$ with respect to $\mathcal{P}$ and then process the queries in $\mathcal{Q}$ to sum up the cost. Seeing these factors, we design an algorithm to find a good partitioning while bounding the number of times computing $C_{workload}(\mathcal{Q})$.

Our algorithm is based on a greedy and two-level blocking strategy. We first choose to sort in $\mathcal{U}$ by increasing order of window frequency. Then we divide $\mathcal{U}$ into 1-wise and 2-wise tokens, find a best border which yields the smallest $C_{workload}(\mathcal{Q})$, and then divide the partition of 2-wise tokens into 2-wise and 3-wise tokens. This is repeated until $k_{\max}$ is reached. For a border of i-wise and $(i+1)$-wise tokens, there can be at most $|\mathcal{U}| + 1$ possibilities. Since computing $C_{workload}(\mathcal{Q})$ for such number of times is prohibitive for large $|\mathcal{U}|$, we choose to divide $\mathcal{U}$ into blocks of size B_1, and pick the block boundary which yields the smallest $C_{workload}(\mathcal{Q})$ if we divide the partition there. Denoting this block boundary by b_i, then we divide two adjacent blocks, $[b_{i-1}, b_i]$ and $[b_i, b_{i+1}]$, into sub-blocks of size B_2, and pick the best sub-block boundary as the partition boundary. The computation of $C_{workload}(\mathcal{Q})$ is invoked no more than $(k_{\max} - 1)(\lceil \frac{|\mathcal{U}|}{B_1} \rceil + 2\lceil \frac{B_1}{B_2} \rceil - 1)$ times.

Note that empty partitions are allowed by the greedy algorithm, and hence it is not mandatory to have i-wise tokens

[4] A signature may be generated multiple times. It is inserted into S when its interval is opened, including a false open.

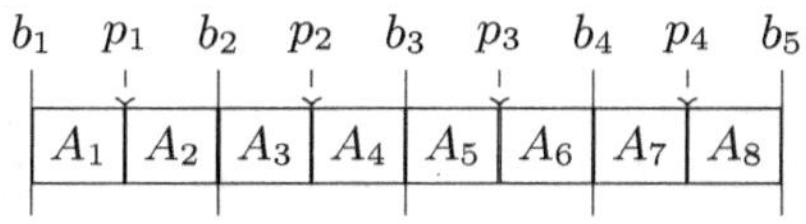

Figure 3: Greedy-and-Blocking Partitioning

for any $i \in [1, k_{\max}]$. We also argue that the reason why we choose to find a good partitioning by the cost model instead of simply setting a selectivity threshold is that combining any two tokens does not always make the selectivity approach the threshold due to the existence of correlations between tokens, e.g., "Kuala" and "Lumpur".

EXAMPLE 7. *Consider a universe consists of eight tokens, $k_{\max} = 3$, $B_1 = 2$, and $B_2 = 1$. The universe is divided into 4 blocks. Figure 3 shows the tokens and the block boundaries. We first divide the universe into 1-wise and 2-wise tokens. Suppose the costs of dividing at $b_1 \cdots b_5$ are 10, 8, 9, 10, 11, respectively. We pick the smallest one, b_2, and then divide $[b_1, b_2]$ and $[b_2, b_3]$ into sub-blocks of size B_2. Suppose the total costs of dividing at p_1 and p_2 are 9 and 7, respectively. p_2 is chosen to divide the universe, and thus $A_1 \cdots A_3$ are 1-wise tokens, and $A_4 \cdots A_8$ are 2-wise tokens. Then we proceed to divide the latter into 2-wise and 3-wise tokens. Suppose the total costs of dividing at p_2 and $b_3 \cdots b_5$ are 8, 8, 5, 7, respectively. We pick the smallest one, b_4, and then consider sub-block boundary p_3 and p_4. Suppose the costs of dividing at p_3 and p_4 are 4 and 6, respectively. p_3 is chosen to divide $A_4 \cdots A_8$. Finally, $A_1 \cdots A_3$ are 1-wise tokens, $A_4 \cdots A_5$ are 2-wise tokens, and $A_6 \cdots A_8$ are 3-wise tokens. The computation of $C_{workload}(\mathcal{Q})$ is invoked 13 times.*

In case that a historical query workload is not available, a portion of data documents can be sampled as a surrogate, denoted by $\mathcal{Q}'$. Its size is controlled by a sample ratio ρ; i.e., $|\mathcal{Q}'| = \rho \cdot |\mathcal{D}|$. We choose this option in our experiments.

6. COPING WITH LARGE THRESHOLDS

A large τ may cause large number of combinations in the signature generation. Assume in a window x, the $\tau+1$ coverage is equally distributed to the $k_{\max}$ partitions; i.e., each class in its prefix has a coverage of $\frac{\tau+1}{k_{\max}}$. For each class, there are $(\frac{\tau+1}{k_{\max}} + i - 1)$ tokens and thus $\binom{\frac{\tau+1}{k_{\max}}+i-1}{i}$ combinations generated. When $\tau = 99$, the total number of combinations generated from the prefix is 23,750 when $k_{\max} = 4$.

To scale up for large τ, recall in Section 3.2 we partition the token universe and tokens are only combined with others from the same partition. We further exploit this idea and divide each i-wise partition in the token universe into m equi-width sub-partitions. All these m sub-partitions use i-wise signatures, and combinations are only generated within each sub-partition. Since single tokens are used in 1-wise partition, we choose not to divide it into sub-partitions. To compute the prefix length, Lemmas 3 and 4 also apply for sub-partitions. Thus we modify Algorithm 1 by summing up the coverage in each sub-partition until it reaches $\tau + 1$.

EXAMPLE 8. *Consider the token universe in Figure 4. $k_{\max} = 3$, and the solid lines separate the three partitions. $\tau = 5$. Consider a window x. Before further partitioning, the prefix length is $4 + 5 = 9$ and there are $6 + 10 = 16$ combinations generated. When $m = 3$, 2-wise and 3-wise partitions are further divided into 3 sub-partitions, respectively, as shown by the dashed*

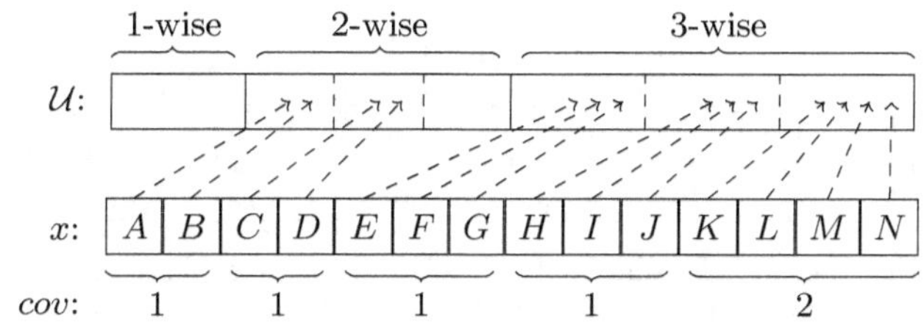

Figure 4: Example of Further Partitioning

lines. The arrows show which classes and which sub-partitions its tokens belong to. By further partitioning, the prefix length is increased to 2 + 2 + 3 + 3 + 4 = 14, but the number of combinations is reduced to 1 + 1 + 1 + 1 + 4 = 8.

Assume the above mentioned $\frac{\tau+1}{k_{\max}}$ coverage is equally distributed to the m sub-partitions. We need $(\frac{\tau+1}{m \cdot k_{\max}} + i - 1)$ tokens for each sub-partition of an i-wise partition, and thus in total $m(i-1)$ more tokens in each i-wise partition in the prefix. On the other hand, there are $m\binom{\frac{\tau+1}{m \cdot k_{\max}}+i-1}{i}$ combinations generated in each i-wise partition. In consequence, we trade prefix length for combination number. If we set m as $\alpha(\tau+1)$, the number of combinations will be $\alpha(\tau+1)\binom{\frac{1}{\alpha \cdot k_{\max}}+i-1}{i}$, hence proportional to $\tau + 1$ for a fixed i, as opposed to the exponential increase with τ before further partitioning. According to the experiments, $\alpha = 0.2$ gives best performance and we use this setting to compute token universe partitioning and process queries when τ is large.

To adapt Corollary 1 for sub-partitions, the upper bound of prefix length becomes $\tau + 1 + m\sum_{1}^{k_{\max}-1}$. For Corollary 2, in the highest class of a prefix, the last non-empty sub-partition of tokens has a coverage above zero.

7. EXPERIMENTS

7.1 Experiment Setup

The following algorithms are compared in the experiment.

- **Adapt** is a state-of-the-art algorithm for set similarity search and join [33]. It leverages extended prefix filtering and computes an appropriate prefix length for each query object using a cost model. To adapt the algorithm to local similarity search, we materialize the windows of data and query documents as its data and query objects, respectively.
- **Faerie** is a state-of-the-art algorithm for approximate dictionary-based entity extraction [13]. It finds approximate occurrences of the indexed entities in a query document. We materialize the windows of data documents as entities. The specific implementation we use considers only candidate windows of size w, and our overlap constraints are converted into corresponding equivalent Jaccard constraints.
- **FBW** is a Winnowing-family algorithm [31] which returns approximate answers to the problem of finding documents that share $w - q + 1$ consecutive token q-grams while tolerating $q\tau$ errors, where q is the q-gram length. We use its fingerprinting scheme to generate candidates and they are verified against our similarity constraint. q-gram length is set to 2 to balance the number of results and query processing time.
- **pkwise**, short for partitioned k-wise, is our proposed algorithm equipped with interval sharing for adjacent windows. We hash signatures into 4-byte integers. The number of sub-partitions m is set to 1 unless otherwise specified.

Table 1: Dataset Statistics

Dataset	$\|\mathcal{D}\|$	$\|\mathcal{Q}\|$	avg. $\|d\|$	avg. $\|q\|$	$\|\mathcal{U}\|$
REUTERS	7,791	1,000	237.2	231.1	33,260
TREC	185,666	1,000	198.2	214.1	148,244
PAN	10,483	1,000	27,026.8	721.6	1,846,623

Other methods for similarity search and join, e.g., [3, 4, 21, 35], and approximate entity extraction, e.g., [9], are not compared since prior work [35, 33, 13] showed they are outperformed by the above selected methods. We do not consider the method in [2] developed for approximate entity extraction because it relies on WtEnum [3] which enumerates minimal subset of entities whose sum of weights is no less than the threshold. By materializing query windows as entities, the number of subsets per window is $\binom{w}{w-\tau}$, which is prohibitive for local similarity search, e.g., 5.4×10^{20} when $w = 100$ and $\tau = 20$.

We select three publicly available datasets which were used in prior related studies:

- **REUTERS** is a set of 19K Reuters news stories [5]. We extract news body as documents.
- **TREC** is a set of references from MEDLINE. It is used for the TREC-9 Filtering Track Collections [6]. We extract the 233K paper abstracts as documents.
- **PAN** is used in the plagiarism detection task of PAN Workshop and Competition of 2010 (PAN-PC-10) [7]. It contains about 11K source documents and 16K suspicious documents that may contain plagiarism.

In order to make the numbers of documents in all the settings are the same, short documents with less than 100 tokens are removed from the corpora. For PAN, we use source documents as data documents and sample 1,000 queries from suspicious documents. Each query is composed of a number of paragraphs which contain true plagiarism. Non-English documents are removed. For REUTERS and TREC, we sample 1,000 documents as queries and take the rest as data documents. Table 1 shows statistics about the datasets.

Average query processing time is measured by varying τ while fixing w as 100, and by varying w while fixing τ as 5. For Adapt and Faerie, window materialization is not counted towards their index construction or query processing time.

The experiments were carried out on a PC with an Intel Xeon E5620 2.4GHz Processor and 96GB RAM, running Ubuntu 14.04.3. The algorithms were implemented in C++ and in a main memory fashion.

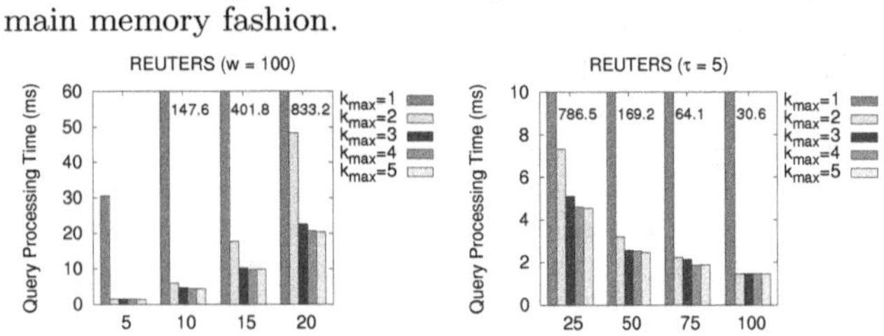

(a) REUTERS, vary τ (b) REUTERS, vary w

Figure 5: Effect of $k_{\max}$

We sample a subset of data documents as query workload Q' and partition token universe with the algorithm proposed in Section 5.2. The default value of $k_{\max}$ is 4. The values of c_{comb}, c_{int}, c_{hash} in Equations 2 – 4 are 10, 2, and 1, respectively. $B_1 = 0.1|\mathcal{U}|$ and $B_2 = 0.01|\mathcal{U}|$. Then we process the queries Q (different from Q') with the obtained partitioning results. As for the sample ratio of query workload, the experiment results show its effect on the query processing performance is not obvious. E.g., the average query processing times are 4.64, 4.44, 4.41, 4.39, and 4.39 milliseconds, respectively, when the sample ratio changes from 0.5% to 2.5% on REUTERS when $w = 100$ and $\tau = 10$. We choose 1% as the sample ratio.

[5]http://www.daviddlewis.com/resources/testcollections/reuters21578/

[6]http://trec.nist.gov/data/t9_filtering.html

[7]http://www.uni-weimar.de/en/media/chairs/webis/corpora/corpus-pan-pc-10/

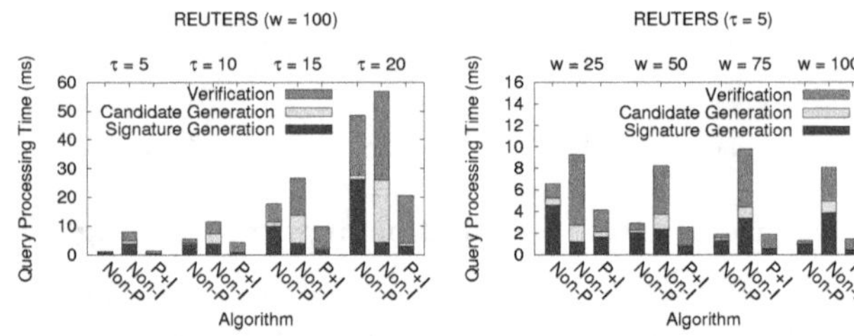

(a) REUTERS, vary τ (b) REUTERS, vary w

Figure 6: Effect of Partition & Interval

7.2 Effect of Partitioned k-wise Signatures

Figures 5(a) – 5(b) show the average query processing times with varying τ and w on REUTERS for $k_{\max} \in [1, 5]$. Note that the algorithm becomes standard prefix filtering when $k_{\max} = 1$. $k_{\max} = 1$ has the worst performance and is up to two orders of magnitude slower than the other $k_{\max}$ settings, especially for large τ or small w. The reason is that there are frequent tokens in its prefix and they cause large candidate numbers. When $w = 100$ and $\tau = 5$, a $k_{\max}$ of 2 or 3 is as good as 4 or 5. But when w decreases or τ increases, setting $k_{\max}$ as 4 or 5 runs 2 times faster than 2 or 3 because of looser similarity constraints which call for signatures with better selectivity. The results demonstrate that query performance can be improved by combining tokens. We set $k_{\max}$ as 4 in the rest of the experiments (on par with $k_{\max} = 5$ on query processing but faster on token universe partitioning).

We evaluate the effect of partition by comparing partitioned k-wise with non-partitioned k-wise, i.e., all signatures with a fixed number of tokens. The average query processing times with varying τ and w on REUTERS are shown in Figures 6(a) – 6(b). The running times are decomposed into three phases. The partitioned and the non-partitioned algorithms are denoted by P+I and Non-P, respectively. For partitioned k-wise, we set $k_{\max} = 4$. For non-partitioned k-wise, we choose $k = 3$ since it gives best performance for most w and τ settings. As seen from the figures, partitioned k-wise substantially saves signature generation time but spends more on verification time since 3-wise signatures are more selective than the mixture of 1 to 4-wise signatures. Considering the two effects, partitioned k-wise exhibits a reduction in overall query processing time in most cases. The speedup is more significant for larger τ or smaller w, and can be up to 2.4 times. We also observe an exception that non-partitioned k-wise spends slightly less time when $w = 100$ and $\tau = 5$. The reason is that both algorithms spend very short time on signature generation, and hence the gain of partitioned k-wise in this phase is small, resulting in an overall slower query processing.

7.3 Effect of Interval Sharing

We evaluate the effect of the interval sharing technique

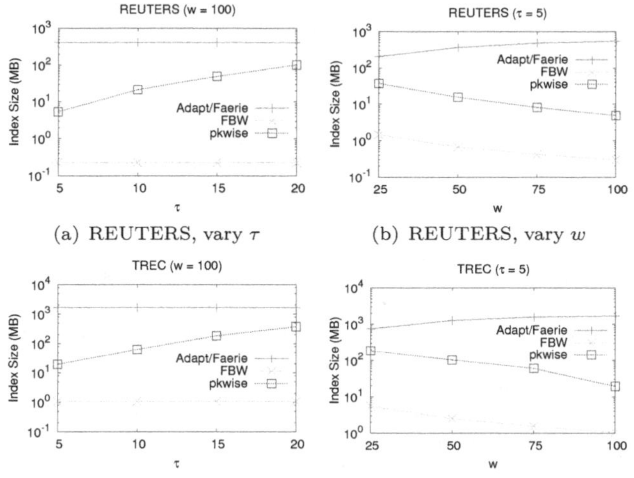

(a) REUTERS, vary τ (b) REUTERS, vary w

(c) TREC, vary τ (d) TREC, vary w

Figure 7: Comparison with Alternatives - Index

proposed in Section 4 and plot the average query processing times with varying τ and w on REUTERS in Figures 6(a) – 6(b). The algorithms with and without interval sharing are denoted by P+I and Non-I, respectively. By taking advantage of overlapping windows, the query processing time is reduced by 2.6 to 5.5 times by varying τ. By varying w, the speedup is 2.2 to 5.5 times, and different trends are observed for the algorithms with and without interval sharing. This is because for larger w and a fixed τ, the similarity constraint becomes tighter and thus candidate number decreases, but processing longer windows spends more time. The two factors result in the fluctuation of query processing time without interval sharing. When interval sharing is applied, processing continuous windows becomes faster and thus the effect of the first factor dominates. We also measure the average sharing by computing the Jaccard similarity between the prefixes of every two adjacent windows and taking the average. When $w = 100$ and τ grows from 5 to 20, the sharing in query windows slightly decreases from 0.966 to 0.963. When $\tau = 5$ and w grows from 25 to 100, the sharing in query windows increases from 0.872 to 0.966. A similar result is observed on the sharing in data windows. We also notice that when $w = 25$ and $\tau = 5$, the algorithm with interval sharing spends more time on signature generation. The reason is that window size is small and sharing is relatively low, and thus the gain from sharing does not counteract the overhead on maintaining prefixes and intervals. Nonetheless, candidate generation and verification still benefit from interval sharing, hence resulting in less overall query processing time in this setting. Another interesting result is that by indexing intervals instead of individual windows, index size is reduced by 3 to 14 times (e.g., from 77.4MB to 5.4MB when $w = 100$ and $\tau = 5$), and the reduction is more remarkable for larger w.

7.4 Comparison with Alternative Methods

Index sizes are compared first. Figures 7(a) – 7(d) show the index sizes of the algorithms with varying τ and w on REUTERS and TREC. Since Adapt and Faerie index all the tokens in each window, they have the same index sizes and they only vary with w. FBW's index size is significantly smaller than the exact algorithms due to its signature selection scheme. Among the exact algorithms, pkwise has the smallest index size, because (1) only the signatures generated from prefixes

Table 2: Index Construction Time (REUTERS)

w	τ	Adapt	Faerie	FBW	pkwise (part + index)
25	5	35s	28s	1.1s	303s + 10.3s
50	5	61s	47s	1.3s	172s + 4.9s
75	5	86s	66s	1.4s	147s + 3.7s
100	5	100s	72s	1.4s	133s + 2.9s
100	10	100s	72s	1.4s	377s + 4.7s
100	15	100s	72s	1.4s	859s + 9.5s
100	20	100s	72s	1.4s	2009s + 14.3s

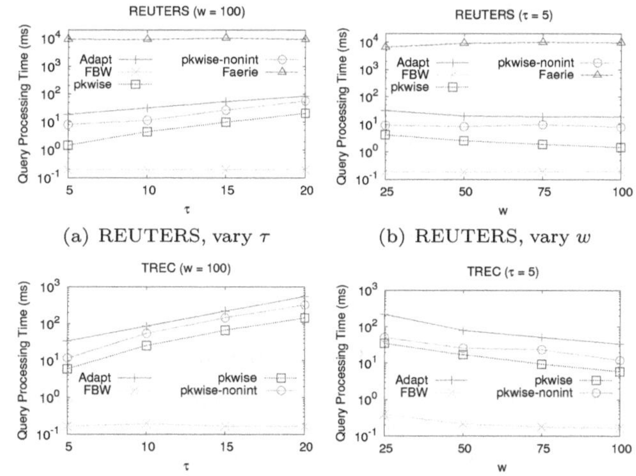

(a) REUTERS, vary τ (b) REUTERS, vary w

(c) TREC, vary τ (d) TREC, vary w

Figure 8: Comparison with Alternatives - Runtime

are indexed by pkwise, as opposed to Adapt and Faerie which index every token in every window, and (2) interval sharing further reduces pkwise's index size. The gap ranges from 3.5 to 76.1 times on REUTERS and 4.1 to 86.7 times on TREC.

The corresponding index construction times on REUTERS are shown in Table 2. For pkwise we decompose the time into two parts: computing token universe partitioning and indexing data documents. We observe that the indexing times of Adapt and Faerie only change with w. Both parts of pkwise's index construction time increase with looser similarity constraint (smaller w or larger τ). Despite more time consumption on the computation of partitioning, pkwise spends less time indexing the data documents than the other two exact algorithms. We argue that the computation of partitioning can be done offline and the output can be used on data documents with approximately the same token frequency distribution.

Figures 8(a) – 8(d) show the average query processing times of the algorithms on REUTERS and TREC by varying τ and w. Since the other competitors are not equipped with interval sharing, for the purpose of fair comparison, we also show pkwise's performance when interval sharing is disabled (denoted by pkwise-nonint). Faerie is unable to finish processing the 1,000 queries on TREC in 24 hours, and thus its performance is not shown on TREC. On REUTERS, Faerie is the least competitive and two to three orders of magnitude slower than the other algorithms. Although its candidate number is very close to the result number, its filtering is very time-consuming due to the heap-based candidate generation. This result suggests that Faerie is not efficient for local similarity search where windows are much longer than normal entities (on average less than ten tokens). For Adapt and pkwise, both times increase with τ and decrease with w. pkwise is always faster than Adapt. The speedup is 4.1 to 12.8 times on REUTERS and 3.3 to 6.3 times

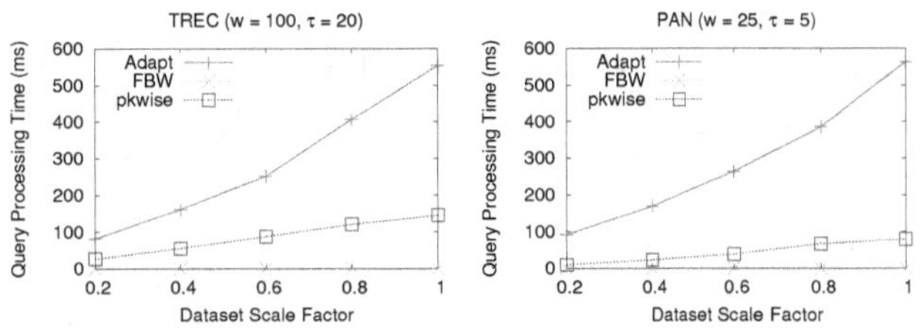

(a) TREC, vary $|\mathcal{D}|$ (b) PAN, vary $|\mathcal{D}|$

Figure 9: Scalability

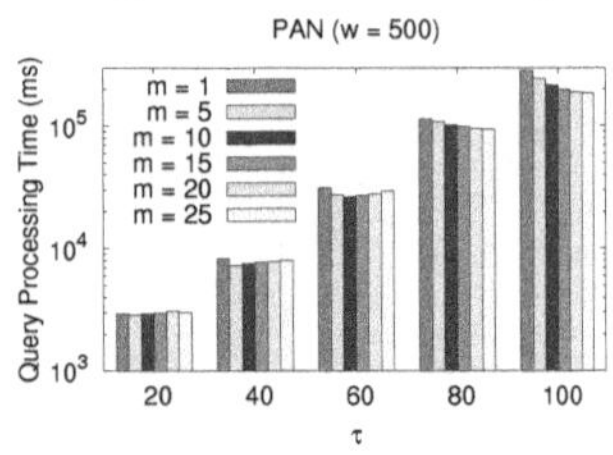

(a) PAN, vary τ

Figure 10: Large Thresholds

on TREC. The speedup not only comes from interval sharing but also partitioned k-wise signatures, as it can be seen that pkwise-nonint also outperforms Adapt (by up to 4.3 times) in every setting. Although FBW is significantly faster than the exact methods, it returns only 10.1% to 42.7% results, and the percentage is low for small w.

We evaluate the scalability of the algorithms with varying dataset size. 20% to 100% data documents are sampled from TREC and PAN. The query processing times ($w = 100$ and $\tau = 20$ on TREC and $w = 25$ and $\tau = 5$ on PAN) are given in Figures 9(a) – 9(b). Faerie is not shown due to its much longer query processing time. The times of the algorithms grow approximate linearly with the dataset size. pkwise has a slower growth rate than Adapt (3.8 and 7.1 times faster on TREC and PAN, respectively).

7.5 Large Thresholds

Figure 10(a) shows the average query processing time of pkwise on PAN with varying large thresholds when $w = 500$. The comparison with Adapt and Faerie is excluded because loading and indexing the materialized windows exceeds the main memory, and they are slower than pkwise on a sampled subset of 100 data documents when $w = 500$ and $\tau = 100$ by 4.4 and 213.7 times, respectively. We set the number of sub-partitions m to 1, 5, 10, 15, 20, and 25. With larger m, the number of combinations in signature generation is reduced but prefix length grows and thus selectivity is compromised. This effect can be seen: in most cases, the time first drops with m and then rebounds. Another trend is that the best m increases with τ: 1, 5, 10, 25, and 25 when $\tau = 20, 40, 60, 80$, and 100, respectively. Based on the results, we suggest users choose $m = 1$ when $m \leq 20$ and $m = 0.25 \cdot \tau$ when $m > 20$.

8. RELATED WORK

Similarity search and join have been studied by many researchers due to its importance in many applications, including near-duplicate document detection. To answer (multi)set similarity queries, many existing methods adopted the prefix filtering framework, which was proposed by Chaudhuri *et al.* [10] and later improved by subsequent studies [4, 35, 33]. Other methods include merging postings lists [27, 17, 21] and partitioning data by pigeon-hole principle [3], etc. Approximate solutions were also investigated; e.g., MinHash [7] and LSH [16, 28]. Another body of work studied the processing of string similarity queries by regarding documents as strings; e.g., [22, 34, 26, 12, 36]. Edit distance is usually adopted to capture the string similarity. We refer readers to [19] for an experimental comparison of prevalent methods.

Document fingerprinting methods have been extensively studied, aiming at finding near-duplicate documents or reused contents. Most proposed solutions can be divided into two categories: overlapping methods and non-overlapping methods, namely, by selecting overlapping or non-overlapping text segments as fingerprints. Notable overlapping methods are 0 mod p [25], super-shingles [8], Winnowing [29], Hailstorm [18], etc. Non-overlapping methods include hash breaking[6], DCT fingerprinting [30], qSign [20], learning hash code [37], etc. There are also methods using other features; e.g., I-Match [11] uses medium document frequency tokens and SpotSigs [32] selects tokens around stopwords.

While our paper and the above related studies focus on dealing with unstructured data, there are also a few studies on detecting copies in structured data [15, 5, 14, 24].

Token combinations (token sets) have been used to solve approximate ad-hoc entity extraction [2], error-tolerant set containment [1], and similarity queries on multi-attribute data [23]. The idea of partition and enumeration is used for similarity join [3]. We briefly discuss our differences: (1) To ensure the correctness, in [2] and [1], every minimal subset of entities or queries with sum of weight no less than the threshold is covered by at least one token set selected by a cost model. [3] resorts to pigeon-hole principle. Our method extends prefix filtering to enumerate token combinations. (2) In [3], records are converted to vectors and divided into two-level equi-sized partitions, and partition combinations are enumerated on the second level. In our method, token universe is partitioned using a cost model and we combine tokens rather than partitions. (3) [23] uses standard prefix filtering, and tokens of different attributes are organized in a tree and checked one by one to find candidates. We use hash values of token combinations to find candidates for a single attribute problem. (4) We take advantage of overlap between adjacent windows by interval sharing, which is not covered by the other methods.

9. CONCLUSION

We study the problem of local similarity search which identifies documents that share a common sliding window with the query but differ by at most τ tokens. Our solution is based on two observations: (1) token combinations are more selective than single tokens, and (2) overlap exist between adjacent sliding windows. We partition the token universe and consider using different numbers of tokens in a combination. A practical algorithm is devised to compute a good partitioning of the token universe. The techniques to support large thresholds are developed. Extensive experimental evaluation on real datasets demonstrates the superior query processing performance of the proposed method to alternative solutions.

Acknowledgements. Pei Wang, Chuan Xiao, and Yoshiharu Ishikawa are supported by JSPS Kakenhi 25280039 and 16H01722. Jianbin Qin and Wei Wang are supported by D2DCRC Grants DC25002 and DC25003. We thank the authors of [33] and [13] for kindly providing their source codes.

10. REFERENCES

[1] P. Agrawal, A. Arasu, and R. Kaushik. On indexing error-tolerant set containment. In *SIGMOD Conference*, pages 927–938, 2010.

[2] S. Agrawal, K. Chakrabarti, S. Chaudhuri, and V. Ganti. Scalable ad-hoc entity extraction from text collections. *PVLDB*, 1(1):945–957, 2008.

[3] A. Arasu, V. Ganti, and R. Kaushik. Efficient exact set-similarity joins. In *VLDB*, pages 918–929, 2006.

[4] R. J. Bayardo, Y. Ma, and R. Srikant. Scaling up all pairs similarity search. In *WWW*, pages 131–140, 2007.

[5] L. Blanco, V. Crescenzi, P. Merialdo, and P. Papotti. Probabilistic models to reconcile complex data from inaccurate data sources. In *CAiSE*, pages 83–97, 2010.

[6] S. Brin, J. Davis, and H. Garcia-Molina. Copy detection mechanisms for digital documents. In *SIGMOD Conference*, pages 398–409, 1995.

[7] A. Z. Broder. On the resemblance and containment of documents. In *SEQS*, pages 21–29, 1997.

[8] A. Z. Broder, S. C. Glassman, M. S. Manasse, and G. Zweig. Syntactic clustering of the web. *Computer Networks*, 29(8-13):1157–1166, 1997.

[9] K. Chakrabarti, S. Chaudhuri, V. Ganti, and D. Xin. An efficient filter for approximate membership checking. In *SIGMOD Conference*, pages 805–818, 2008.

[10] S. Chaudhuri, V. Ganti, and R. Kaushik. A primitive operator for similarity joins in data cleaning. In *ICDE*, pages 5–16, 2006.

[11] A. Chowdhury, O. Frieder, D. A. Grossman, and M. C. McCabe. Collection statistics for fast duplicate document detection. *ACM Trans. Inf. Syst.*, 20(2):171–191, 2002.

[12] D. Deng, G. Li, and J. Feng. A pivotal prefix based filtering algorithm for string similarity search. In *SIGMOD Conference*, pages 673–684, 2014.

[13] D. Deng, G. Li, J. Feng, Y. Duan, and Z. Gong. A unified framework for approximate dictionary-based entity extraction. *VLDB J.*, 24(1):143–167, 2015.

[14] X. Dong, L. Berti-Equille, Y. Hu, and D. Srivastava. Global detection of complex copying relationships between sources. *PVLDB*, 3(1):1358–1369, 2010.

[15] X. L. Dong, L. Berti-Equille, and D. Srivastava. Truth discovery and copying detection in a dynamic world. *PVLDB*, 2(1):562–573, 2009.

[16] A. Gionis, P. Indyk, and R. Motwani. Similarity search in high dimensions via hashing. In *VLDB*, pages 518–529, 1999.

[17] M. Hadjieleftheriou, A. Chandel, N. Koudas, and D. Srivastava. Fast indexes and algorithms for set similarity selection queries. In *ICDE*, pages 267–276, 2008.

[18] O. A. Hamid, B. Behzadi, S. Christoph, and M. R. Henzinger. Detecting the origin of text segments efficiently. In *WWW*, pages 61–70, 2009.

[19] Y. Jiang, G. Li, J. Feng, and W. Li. String similarity joins: An experimental evaluation. *PVLDB*, 7(8):625–636, 2014.

[20] J. W. Kim, K. S. Candan, and J. Tatemura. Efficient overlap and content reuse detection in blogs and online news articles. In *WWW*, pages 81–90, 2009.

[21] C. Li, J. Lu, and Y. Lu. Efficient merging and filtering algorithms for approximate string searches. In *ICDE*, pages 257–266, 2008.

[22] G. Li, D. Deng, J. Wang, and J. Feng. Pass-Join: A partition-based method for similarity joins. *PVLDB*, 5(1):253–264, 2012.

[23] G. Li, J. He, D. Deng, and J. Li. Efficient similarity join and search on multi-attribute data. In *SIGMOD Conference*, pages 1137–1151, 2015.

[24] X. Li, X. L. Dong, K. B. Lyons, W. Meng, and D. Srivastava. Scaling up copy detection. In *ICDE*, pages 89–100, 2015.

[25] U. Manber. Finding similar files in a large file system. In *USENIX Winter*, pages 1–10, 1994.

[26] J. Qin, W. Wang, C. Xiao, Y. Lu, X. Lin, and H. Wang. Asymmetric signature schemes for efficient exact edit similarity query processing. *ACM Trans. Database Syst.*, 38(3):16, 2013.

[27] S. Sarawagi and A. Kirpal. Efficient set joins on similarity predicates. In *SIGMOD Conference*, pages 743–754, 2004.

[28] V. Satuluri and S. Parthasarathy. Bayesian locality sensitive hashing for fast similarity search. *PVLDB*, 5(5):430–441, 2012.

[29] S. Schleimer, D. S. Wilkerson, and A. Aiken. Winnowing: Local algorithms for document fingerprinting. In *SIGMOD Conference*, pages 76–85, 2003.

[30] J. Seo and W. B. Croft. Local text reuse detection. In *SIGIR*, pages 571–578, 2008.

[31] Y. Sun, J. Qin, and W. Wang. Near duplicate text detection using frequency-biased signatures. In *WISE*, pages 277–291, 2013.

[32] M. Theobald, J. Siddharth, and A. Paepcke. Spotsigs: robust and efficient near duplicate detection in large web collections. In *SIGIR*, pages 563–570, 2008.

[33] J. Wang, G. Li, and J. Feng. Can we beat the prefix filtering?: an adaptive framework for similarity join and search. In *SIGMOD Conference*, pages 85–96, 2012.

[34] W. Wang, J. Qin, C. Xiao, X. Lin, and H. T. Shen. Vchunkjoin: An efficient algorithm for edit similarity joins. *IEEE Trans. Knowl. Data Eng.*, 25(8):1916–1929, 2013.

[35] C. Xiao, W. Wang, X. Lin, J. X. Yu, and G. Wang. Efficient similarity joins for near-duplicate detection. *ACM Trans. Database Syst.*, 36(3):15, 2011.

[36] X. Yang, Y. Wang, B. Wang, and W. Wang. Local filtering: Improving the performance of approximate queries on string collections. In *SIGMOD Conference*, pages 377–392, 2015.

[37] Q. Zhang, Y. Wu, Z. Ding, and X. Huang. Learning hash codes for efficient content reuse detection. In *SIGIR*, pages 405–414, 2012.

APPENDIX

A. PSEUDO-CODE OF PREFIX MAINTENANCE ALGORITHM

The pseudo-code of the prefix maintenance algorithm for signature generation is shown in Algorithm 5.

B. PROOFS

The proof of Theorem 1 is given below.

PROOF. We compare $x[l_x]$ and $y[l_y]$, the last tokens in x's and y's prefixes. Assume $x[l_x] \le y[l_y]$. If $S_x \cap S_y = \emptyset$, by Lemma 4, there must be at least $\tau + 1$ tokens in $x[1\,..\,l_x]$ but not in $y[1\,..\,l_y]$. Because $x[l_x] \le y[l_y]$, these tokens are not in $y[l_y + 1\,..\,|y|]$ either. Therefore, there must be at least $\tau + 1$ tokens in x but not in y, hence contradicting $w - O(x, y) \le \tau$. □

We give the proof of Corollary 1.

PROOF. $n_i - i + 1 \le 0$ when $n_i < i$. By Lemma 3, $\forall i, n_i - i + 1 \le cov(i)$. By Lemma 4 and Algorithm 1, $\sum_{i=1}^{k_{\max}} n_i - i + 1 \le \sum_{i=1}^{k_{\max}} cov(i) = \tau + 1$. Therefore $\sum_{i=1}^{k_{\max}} n_i \le \tau + 1 + \sum_{i=1}^{k_{\max}} (i - 1)$. The left side of the inequality is exactly the prefix length, and the right side equals to $\tau + 1 + \sum_{i=1}^{k_{\max}-1} i = \tau + 1 + \frac{k_{\max}(k_{\max}-1)}{2}$. □

We give the proof of Corollary 2.

PROOF. Assume that coverage of the tokens in class h is zero. Since the total coverage of the prefix is $\tau+1$, the tokens in class h can be removed from the prefix, and the total coverage is still $\tau + 1$. It contradicts that the prefix is shortest. □

C. EXTENSIONS TO WEIGHTED CASE

In the weighted case of local similarity search, each token t is assigned a weight $wt(t)$. Let $wt(x)$ denote the accumulated

Algorithm 5: MaintainPrefix (x, l, t_1, t_2)

```
P ← x[1..l], S_o ← ∅, S_c ← ∅;
if x is the last window then
    S_c ← signatures generated from P;
    return (∅, 0, S_o, S_c)
x' ← (x\t_1) ⊎ t_2, P' ← P;
if t_1 ∈ P then P' ← P'\t_1;
l' ← |P'|;
if t_2 < x[l'] then P' ← P' ⊎ { t_2 }, l' ← l' + 1;
if cov(P\t_1) < τ + 1 then
    if cov(P') = τ + 1 then
        while tail(P') are non-covering tokens do
            P' ← P'\tail(P');
        if t_1 ≠ t_2 then
            S_c ← signatures generated from P;
            S_o ← signatures composed of t_2 and tokens in P';
    else
        Δl ← min{ δ | cov(x'[l' + 1..l' + δ]) = 1 };
        ΔP ← x'[l' + 1..l' + Δl];
        P' ← P' ⊎ ΔP;
        if ΔP ≠ { t_1 } then
            S_c ← signatures generated from P and containing
              t_1;
            S_o ← signatures composed of any token in ΔP and
              those in P';
else
    if cov(P') > τ + 1 then
        Δl ← min{ δ | cov(x'[l' − δ..l']) = 1 };
        ΔP ← x'[l' − Δl..l'];
        P' ← P'\ΔP;
        while tail(P') are non-covering tokens do
            P' ← P'\tail(P');
        if ΔP ≠ { t_2 } then
            S_c ← signatures generated from P and containing
              any token in ΔP;
            S_o ← signatures composed of t_2 and tokens in P';
return (x', l', S_o, S_c)
```

weights of the tokens in x, i.e., $\sum_{t \in x} wt(t)$. Our goal is to find pair of windows such that the accumulated weights of their intersection is no less than a threshold; i.e., $\{ \langle x, y \rangle \mid x \sqsubseteq d_i, d_i \in \mathcal{D}, y \sqsubseteq q, wt(O(x, y)) \geq \theta \}$. Given a multiset of tokens, we define its weighted coverage as the minimum accumulated weights of the errors required to affect all the signatures enumerated from these tokens. For n_i tokens in class i, since we need at least $n_i - i + 1$ errors to affect all the signatures, the weighted coverage is the sum of the $n_i - i + 1$ smallest weights among the n_i tokens. Lemma 4 also holds for weighted case. Hence to compute the prefix length of x, we use Algorithm 1 to sum up the weighted coverage of tokens until the value reaches $wt(x) - \theta + \epsilon$, where ϵ is a small positive real number. The prefix maintenance algorithm (Algorithm 5) is also modified by replacing $\tau + 1$ with $wt(x) - \theta + \epsilon$. We also modify the verification algorithm to compute the accumulated weights of intersection.

D. MORE EXPERIMENTS

D.1 Token Universe Partitioning

We evaluate the token universe partitioning by comparing the greedy partitioning algorithm proposed in Section 5.2 with the equi-width partitioning. For equi-width partitioning, we choose the $k_{\max}$ that yields the fastest query processing speed. The average query processing times with varying τ and w on REUTERS are shown in Figures 11(a) – 11(b). The query processing with the greedy partitioning is always faster than the equi-width partitioning. The speedup varies from 2.0 to 4.7 times, and the gap is more significant when w is small.

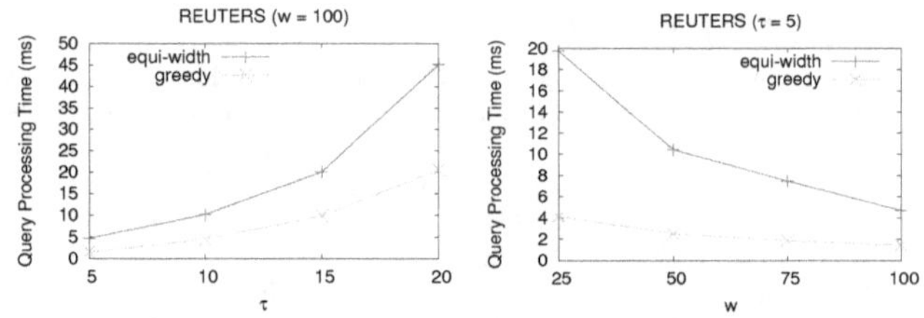

(a) REUTERS, vary τ (b) REUTERS, vary w

Figure 11: Token Universe Partitioning

Table 3: Precision/Recall on REUTERS and TREC

Algorithm	REUTERS (precision)	REUTERS (recall)	TREC (precision)	TREC (recall)
pkwise ($w = 25, \tau = 5$)	67.6%	86.1%	49.0%	85.7%
pkwise ($w = 50, \tau = 10$)	82.4%	53.5%	91.8%	57.1%
FBW ($w = 25, \tau = 5$)	81.5%	51.5%	75.5%	64.3%
FBW ($w = 50, \tau = 10$)	97.5%	10.0%	87.9%	28.6%

D.2 Quality of Local Similarity Search

We evaluate the quality of local similarity search by running pkwise and FBW with two parameter settings: (1) $w = 25$ and $\tau = 5$, and (2) $w = 50$ and $\tau = 10$. Adapt and Faerie are also exact algorithms, and thus they have the same precision and recall as pkwise.

To label the ground truth (plagiarism or text reuse) in REUTERS and TREC, we first retrieve a set of candidate document pairs that share at least ten consecutive tokens. Afterwards the candidates pairs are manually checked by our volunteers. The ground truth in PAN has already been included in the dataset.

The ground truth pair is in the form of $\langle d[u, v], q[u', v'] \rangle$, meaning that the text segment from the u'-th to the v'-the token of the query q is a plagiarism or reuse of the text segment from the u-th to the v-the token of a data document d. A ground truth pair $\langle d[u, v], q[u', v'] \rangle$ is regarded as identified, if there exists a result pair of local similarity search $\langle W(d', i), W(q', j) \rangle$, such that $d = d'$, $q = q'$, $[i, i + w - 1] \cap [u, v] \neq \emptyset$, and $[j, j + w - 1] \cap [u', v'] \neq \emptyset$; i.e., the result pair overlaps the region of the ground truth pair in both the data and the query documents. The recall is defined as the percentage of identified ground truth pairs. To measure precision, we say a token $q[i]$ in the query is positive if it is covered by a result pair of local similarity search. It is a true positive if it is covered by an identified ground truth pair. The precision is defined as the ratio between the numbers of true positives and all positives, i.e., the percentage of correctly identified text length.

Table 3 shows the precision and recall on REUTERS and TREC. Using the setting $w = 25$ and $\tau = 5$ yields lower precision but much higher recall than $w = 50$ and $\tau = 10$. The recall of pkwise can be up to around 86% on both datasets. Although FBW has higher precision, its recall is rather low, missing at least half true results on REUTERS and one third on TREC.

For a fair comparison of precision on PAN, we use entire suspicious documents as queries (on average 16K tokens per query). There are four types of plagiarism in PAN: artificial plagiarism generated by a computer program with no, low, or high obfuscation, and simulated plagiarism purposefully made by a human. We plot the precisions of four plagiarism types with the two parameter settings in Figures 12(a) – 12(b), and the recalls in Figures 12(c) – 12(d). The following observations are observed:

- The precisions are similar when using two different parameter settings. Both algorithms exhibit high precision on artificial plagiarism. We notice that the precision on plagiarism without obfuscation is lower than that with obfuscation. The reason is that without obfuscation the plagiarism exactly matches original text, while the windows within τ tokens left or right to the plagiarized text are also identified due to the errors allowed in the parameter settings. On simulated plagiarism, pkwise's precision is up to 50%, and it is better than FBW.
- Using the setting $w = 25$ and $\tau = 5$ achieves higher recall, especially for simulated plagiarism. The recall can be 100% for all types of artificial plagiarism and 91% for simulated plagiarism. pkwise exhibits higher recall than FBW (by up to 59%), especially for simulated and highly obfuscated artificial plagiarism. To see why FBW does not perform well for these two types of plagiarism, we notice that in these two types of plagiarism, there are uncommon wording and grammatical errors (e.g., "had make") whose frequencies are zero in the data documents. Since FBW selects least frequent q-grams as signatures, the q-grams containing these errors are chosen, and this will make the plagiarism missed by FBW.

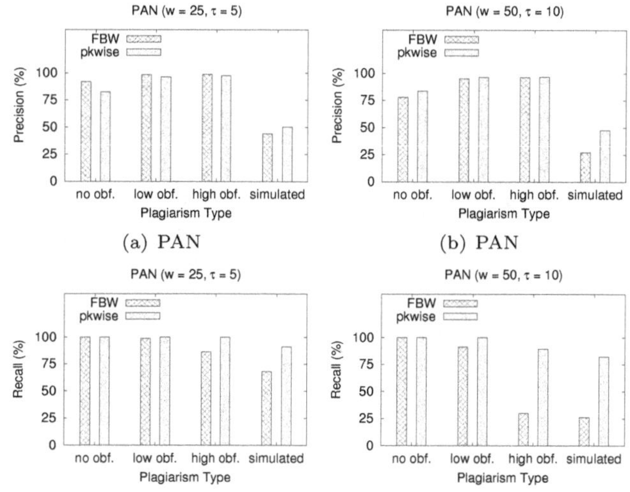

(a) PAN (b) PAN

(c) PAN (d) PAN

Figure 12: Precision/Recall on PAN

We note that the precisions (but not recalls) of the pkwise algorithm can be further enhanced by post-processing methods, e.g., machine learning-based and natural language processing-based techniques. In consequence, we suggest users choose $w = 25$ and $\tau = 5$.

Similarity Join over Array Data

Weijie Zhao[1] Florin Rusu[1,2] Bin Dong[2] Kesheng Wu[2]
[1]UC Merced, [2] Lawrence Berkeley National Laboratory
{wzhao23, frusu}@ucmerced.edu, {DBin, KWu}@lbl.gov

ABSTRACT

Scientific applications are generating an ever-increasing volume of multi-dimensional data that are largely processed inside distributed array databases and frameworks. Similarity join is a fundamental operation across scientific workloads that requires complex processing over an unbounded number of pairs of multi-dimensional points. In this paper, we introduce a novel distributed similarity join operator for multi-dimensional arrays. Unlike immediate extensions to array join and relational similarity join, the proposed operator minimizes the overall data transfer and network congestion while providing load-balancing, without completely repartitioning and replicating the input arrays. We define formally array similarity join and present the design, optimization strategies, and evaluation of the first array similarity join operator.

Categories and Subject Descriptors

H.2.4 [**Database Management**]: Systems—*query processing*

1. INTRODUCTION

In the era of data deluge, scientific applications collect and process massive amounts of data at an unprecedented scale. For example, projects in astronomy such as the Sloan Digital Sky Survey[1] (SDSS) and the Palomar Transient Factory[2] (PTF) record observations of stars and galaxies at nightly rates varying between 60 and 500 GB. The Large Synoptic Survey Telescope[3] (LSST), which is under construction, is expected to increase these volumes by two orders of magnitude—to 20 TB. Other scientific domains such as high-energy physics and genomics produce even larger datasets.

A common characteristic of these and many other scientific applications is that data are represented as *multi-dimensional arrays* rather than unordered sets—the case in the relational data model. Due to the inefficacy of traditional relational databases to handle ordered array data [10], numerous array processing solutions that implement a distributed multi-dimensional array data model have emerged [2, 43, 30, 47, 6, 8]. To cope with the massive data volumes, these systems partition the arrays across a *distributed shared-nothing cluster* and process the partitions concurrently.

Queries on arrays fall in two categories [41]. The first category consists of relational-style operations that can be executed efficiently by any traditional database. They include filtering, subsampling, join, and group-by aggregate. The second category contains array-specific operations such as smoothing, regridding, clustering, and cross-matching, which are not built-in operators in relational databases. These are supported as User-Defined Functions (UDF) in specialized array processing systems [2, 30, 8]. A common feature of the array-specific operations is that they apply a multi-dimensional shape to each cell of an array, essentially pairing the cell with other cells that are in its vicinity in the multi-dimensional array space. A subsequent function can be applied to the resulting group to generate a single aggregate value. To better illustrate this operation, we provide an example from astronomy.

Cross-matching astronomical catalogs. A set of observed celestial objects characterized by their position and the time of their observation is stored in a catalog, i.e., database. Given a newly extracted set of objects – from a new image – the goal in catalog matching [1] is to determine if they have appeared before in the catalog – they are matches of existing objects – or they are entirely new. Astronomical applications use the matches differently. For example, in the PTF project, matches are used to find transient objects [35], i.e., objects that are not permanent in the sky, such as supernovae and variable stars. Computing accurate matches is the most critical step in the PTF real-time transient detection pipeline because of the large number of potential candidates, i.e., $1 - 1.5$ million per night, and the limited time window for follow-up observations—several hours to a few days. Therefore, there has been considerable interest in developing efficient algorithms for the catalog matching problem [28, 45, 34]. Even with these algorithms, matching in PTF considers only a single catalog – the goal is to include several catalogs, e.g., SDSS, BOSS[4], NED[5] – and applies severe pruning and ranking to limit the number of matches. As a generalization, consider two distinct catalogs, e.g., PTF and SDSS, that store different properties of celestial objects. The cross-matching problem aims to create a single catalog that contains a unique instance of the objects in the two input catalogs that merges all their properties. In the PTF context, such a unified catalog has the potential to enhance the effectiveness of the real-time transient detection pipeline because it includes a larger number of properties. It is, therefore, a central piece of the PTF project.

In database jargon, catalog cross-matching corresponds to `FULL OUTER JOIN`. However, due to the uncertainty of astronomical

[1]www.sdss.org/dr12/
[2]www.astro.caltech.edu/ptf/
[3]www.lsst.org

SIGMOD'16, June 26-July 01, 2016, San Francisco, CA, USA
© 2016 ACM. ISBN 978-1-4503-3531-7/16/06...$15.00
DOI: http://dx.doi.org/10.1145/2882903.2915247

[4]https://www.sdss3.org/instruments/boss_spectrograph.php
[5]https://ned.ipac.caltech.edu/

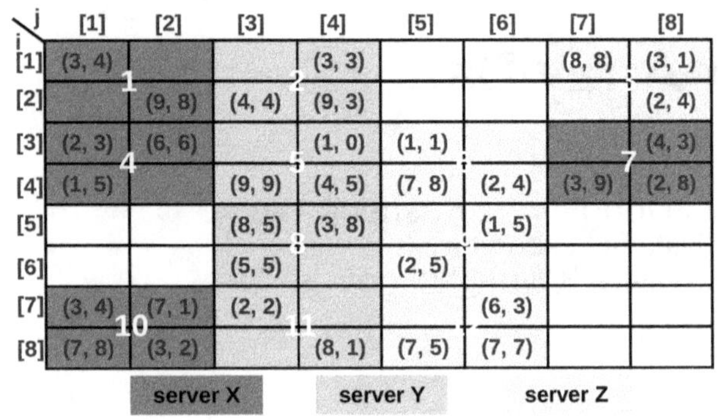

Figure 1: Array `A<v:int,u:int>[i=1,8,2;j=1,8,2]`.

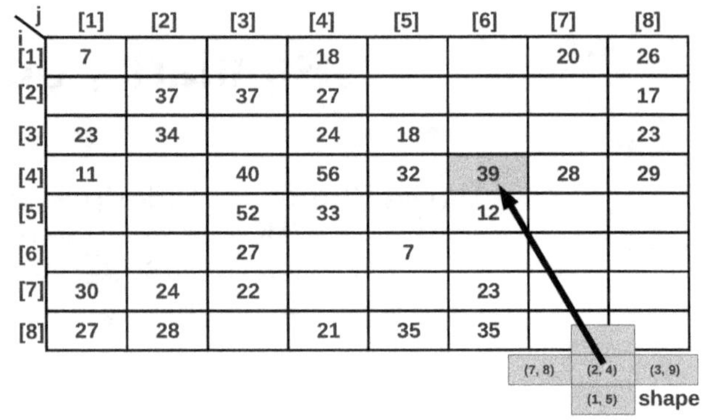

Figure 2: Result array of `APPLY(A, SUM(v+u), shape)`.

observations – the exact position of an object in the sky varies from one catalog to another – the matching is not exact, but rather approximate. For example, in the PTF transient detection pipeline, objects that are within 3 arcseconds of each other over the past hour are considered instances of the same celestial body. Thus, the join condition becomes a distance function inequality. This type of condition corresponds to similarity join [21].

An astronomical catalog can be represented as an array having dimensions the celestial coordinates *ra* and *dec*, and the *time* when the image is taken—a 3-D array `catalog[ra,dec,time]`. The range of each dimension is set according to the accuracy of the telescope. A cell in the array corresponds to an observed object, which is entirely identified by its index values in the array. As a result, distance-based similarity maps to a positional neighborhood relationship among array cells. The neighborhood of a cell can be expressed concisely as a shape array, defined as a collection of offsets in each dimension around the cell. Moreover, mapping from distance to shape array is a required step in similarity join whenever the input is array data. For example, in the PTF data, a cell corresponds to 1 arcsecond on *ra* and *dec*, and 1 minute on *time*. The shape array corresponding to identical objects defined above, e.g., within 3 arcseconds of each other over the past 60 minutes, is a $7 \times 7 \times 60$ cuboid with offsets $[-3:3, -3:3, -60:-1]$ on *ra*, *dec*, and *time*, respectively.

Problem statement & approach. In this paper, we investigate the design and implementation of an array similarity join operator for a distributed array database. Unlike previous work on relational data, we define similarity based on a shape array instead of a distance function. This novel formulation takes into consideration the discrete nature of array data and supports asymmetric similarity measures. We introduce a novel operator that builds upon existing array join algorithms [19, 3] by minimizing the overall data transfer and network congestion while providing load-balancing across the nodes that store data, but without completely repartitioning and replicating the arrays. In the query optimization phase, the operator computes an optimal execution plan for each of the worker nodes. The plan consists of three components—transfer graph, transfer schedule, and data access plan. Finding the optimal plan is challenging because it involves solving a complex non-linear optimization problem. Our solution is to decompose the original optimization problem into three separate sub-problems – one for each plan component – and solve them independently. The solution at each stage is taken as a pre-condition in the following stage. Even with these simplifications, finding the optimal solution at a stage cannot be done efficiently. We design graph-based heuristic algorithms that find competitive solutions much faster. At query execution, the array similarity join operator overlaps I/O – disk and network – with join computation which is heavily parallelized using a dynamic thread pool. Thus, several joins can be executed concurrently. This adds additional pressure on the I/O components – network, in particular – and makes their optimization critical.

Contributions. The main contributions of this work are:

- We define formally array similarity join with a shape array. As far as we know, this is the first array similarity join formulation that generalizes distance-based similarity. (Section 3)
- We introduce the first array similarity join operator that minimizes the overall data transfer and network congestion while providing load-balancing, but without completely repartitioning and replicating the arrays. Moreover, the array operator overlaps disk, network, and join computation in a multi-thread pipelined architecture. (Section 4.1-4.2)
- We model the query optimization of array similarity join as a vertex cover problem and introduce efficient algorithms to find optimal execution plans. (Section 4.3-4.5)
- We evaluate experimentally the proposed array similarity join operator and compare it against existing solutions on the PTF catalog consisting of 1 billion celestial objects. The results confirm the efficacy of the optimizations in reducing the overall data transfer as well as the execution time. (Section 5)

2. PRELIMINARIES

In this section, we introduce the Array Data Model (ADM), array joins, and similarity join over multi-dimensional data. These concepts are the foundation for array similarity join.

2.1 Array Data Model

A multi-dimensional array [41, 16, 19] is defined by a set of *dimensions* $\mathcal{D} = \{D_1, D_2, \ldots, D_d\}$ and a set of *attributes* $\mathcal{A} = \{A_1, A_2, \ldots, A_m\}$. These define the schema of the array. Each dimension D_i is a finite totally ordered discrete set. Without loss of generality, we assume that $D_i, i \in [1, d]$ is represented by the continuous range of integer values $[1, N]$. Each combination of dimension values $i_1, i_2, \ldots, i_d$, i.e., coordinates, defines a *cell*. All cells in a given array have the same type, given by the set of attributes $\mathcal{A}$. Each attribute has a scalar type, such as an integer or float. This is identical to the relational model. Based on these concepts, an array can be thought of as a function defined over dimensions and taking values attribute tuples:

$$Array : D_1 \times D_2 \times \cdots \times D_d \longmapsto (A_1, A_2, \ldots, A_m) \quad (1)$$

The cells for which the function is defined – occupied cells – contain data. The other cells are empty.

Chunking. Array databases apply chunking for storing, processing, and communicating arrays. A *chunk* groups several array cells into a single access – memory, I/O, network – and processing unit. To some extent, chunks are the equivalent of pages in relational databases. The main difference is the size—a page is in the order of kilobytes and a chunk is in the order of megabytes. While many strategies have been proposed in the literature – see [16] for a survey – *regular chunking* is the most popular in practice, e.g., SciDB. We adopt it in this paper. Chunks have the same dimensionality as the input array, are aligned with the dimensions, and have the same shape. There are many strategies to layout the array cells inside a chunk [16]. Without loss of generality, we adopt the *standard C-style ordering on the dimensions*, where the cells are sorted one dimension at a time, traversing the innermost dimension completely before increasing the outer dimension value. Dimensions are ordered according to the array schema. Array chunks are *vertically partitioned*, i.e., each attribute is stored in a separate set of pages, similar to column-oriented databases.

Shared-nothing architecture. We assume a distributed array database having a *shared-nothing architecture* over a cluster of *servers* or *nodes*, each hosting one instance of the query processing engine and having its local attached storage. The chunks of each array are stored across several servers, i.e., nodes, in order to support parallel processing. Unlike distributed systems such as Hadoop Map-Reduce, chunk replication is not a major concern. All servers participate in query execution and share access to a centralized system catalog that maintains information about active servers, array schemas, and chunk distribution. A *coordinator* stores the system catalog and manages the nodes and their access to the catalog. The coordinator is the single query input point into the system.

EXAMPLE 1 (ARRAY CHUNKING). *Figure 1 depicts a 2-D array with schema* `A <v:int,u:int> [i=1,8,2;j=1,8,2]` *given in AQL [25, 24]—the analogous of SQL for array databases. Array* `A` *has two dimensions,* `i` *and* `j`*, with values in* $[1\ldots8]$. *Each dimension has a chunk interval of* 2, *for a total of* 16 *chunks. The array has two attributes,* `v` *and* `u`*, of integer type. Out of the* 16 *chunks, only* 12 *contain data—colored and numbered in Figure 1. These chunks are distributed round-robin in row-major order over the* 3 *servers on which the array database runs. Only the cells that contain data are materialized on disk.*

2.2 Array Joins

Consider two d-dimensional arrays α and β given in the functional representation in Eq. (1):

$$\alpha : \{\mathcal{D}^\alpha = D_1^\alpha \times \cdots \times D_d^\alpha\} \longmapsto \{\mathcal{A}^\alpha = (A_1^\alpha, \ldots, A_m^\alpha)\}$$
$$\beta : \left\{\mathcal{D}^\beta = D_1^\beta \times \cdots \times D_d^\beta\right\} \longmapsto \left\{\mathcal{A}^\beta = (A_1^\beta, \ldots, A_m^\beta)\right\}$$

A join between arrays α and β, $\tau = \alpha \bowtie_P \beta$, is written in AQL as: `SELECT expression INTO` τ `FROM` α `JOIN` β `ON P`, where P is the join predicate which consists of pairs of attributes and/or dimensions from the two source arrays. The output is a new array $\tau : \mathcal{D}^\tau \longmapsto \mathcal{A}^\tau$ having the default schema:

$$\mathcal{D}^\tau = \mathcal{D}^\alpha \cup \mathcal{D}^\beta \qquad \mathcal{A}^\tau = \mathcal{A}^\alpha \cup \mathcal{A}^\beta \tag{2}$$

in which both the dimensions and the attributes from the input schemas are merged. Essentially, the result array has dimensionality equal to the sum of the dimensionality of the input arrays and each cell contains the union of the attributes. It is important to notice that the non-empty cells are given exclusively by the combination of non-empty cells in the input arrays. For example, cell [1,1,4,2] in the join result $A \bowtie A$ in Figure 1 is empty since cell [4,2] in `A` is empty. As is the case with the relational cross product, the default array join is not of particular practical importance since it requires the replication of array β for every chunk of α.

Duggan et al. [19] introduce a series of array equi-joins – *dimension:dimension*, *attribute:attribute*, and *attribute:dimension* – for the case in which predicate P contains only equality conditions. Out of the three types of array equi-join, dimension:dimension join is the most relevant for array databases since these do not provide any benefit for the other two types, compared to their relational counterparts.

2.3 Similarity Join

We consider the ϵ-join version [21] of similarity join. The input to ϵ-join is given by two d-dimensional datasets $A, B \in \mathbb{R}^d$. The goal is to find all the pairs of points $(\vec{a}, \vec{b})$, where $\vec{a} \in A$ and $\vec{b} \in B$, such that $||\vec{a} - \vec{b}|| < \epsilon$. This can be written formally as:

$$A \bowtie_\epsilon B = \left\{(\vec{a}, \vec{b}) : ||\vec{a} - \vec{b}|| < \epsilon; \vec{a} \in A, \vec{b} \in B\right\} \tag{3}$$

where $\vec{a} = (a_1, \ldots, a_d)$ and $\vec{b} = (b_1, \ldots, b_d)$ are d-dimensional points and $||\vec{a} - \vec{b}||$ is the distance between $\vec{a}$ and $\vec{b}$ measured using the generic L^p norm:

$$||\vec{a} - \vec{b}||^p = \left[\sum_{i=1}^{d} (a_i - b_i)^p\right]^{\frac{1}{p}} \tag{4}$$

with $p = 1, 2, \ldots, \infty$. L^2 corresponds to the familiar Euclidean distance, L^1 to the Manhattan distance, and L^∞ to the maximum distance in any dimension. Abstractly, similarity join can be represented as an array join between two d-dimensional arrays. These arrays are obtained by enforcing that each cell corresponds to a single point in the original dataset—ADM does not support attributes having container data type. As long as the original dataset does not contain duplicates, this can be achieved by increasing the resolution on dimensions.

3. ARRAY SIMILARITY JOIN

In this section, we define formally array similarity join with a shape array. To the best of our knowledge, we are the first to propose this novel operation. We show how standard similarity measures map into corresponding shape arrays and discuss the relationship of array similarity join with relational similarity join and array joins, respectively.

While ϵ-join is well-defined over relational tuples, it is not entirely extensible to arrays due to the discrete nature of the dimensions. Similarity join over arrays has to take into account the ordered structure imposed by dimensions. We define formally such an operation starting from the `APPLY` operators in the ArrayQL algebra [25] and AML [26], respectively. In the simplest form, `APPLY` applies a function given as argument to the attributes of each non-empty cell of an array. The output is an array with the same dimensionality, containing the result of the function in each cell. In a more general `APPLY` operator, the argument function is defined over an array shape and generates as output another shape. The function is applied to the shape centered on each cell in the array. The value of the output cell is a function of multiple adjacent cells in the input array. The most common case is when the output shape is a single array cell. In this case, there is a direct correspondence between the origin cell in the input array and the output cell. Figure 2 depicts the result of `APPLY(A, SUM(v+u), shape)` over array `A` in Figure 1. The sum of $v + u$ across all the cells

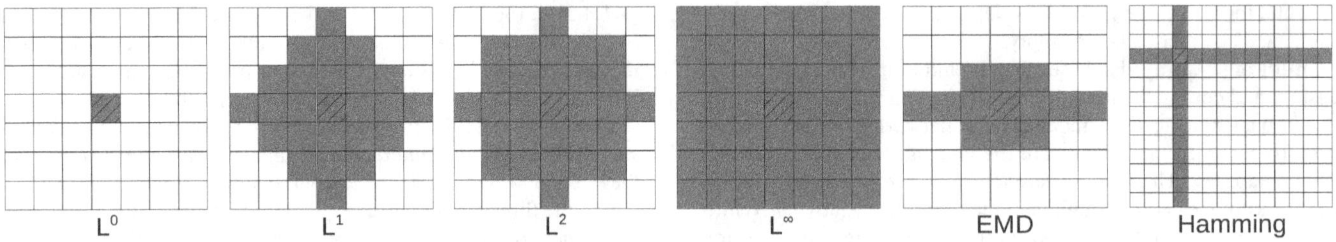

Figure 3: Mapping of similarity distance into shape array for $\epsilon = 3$ (L^0, L^1, L^2, L^∞, Earth Mover's Distance (EMD)) and $\epsilon = 1$ (Hamming).

within Manhattan distance of 1 – the shape is a symmetric cross – is computed for every non-empty cell. We show explicitly how the output for cell $[i = 4; j = 6]$ is generated in the figure.

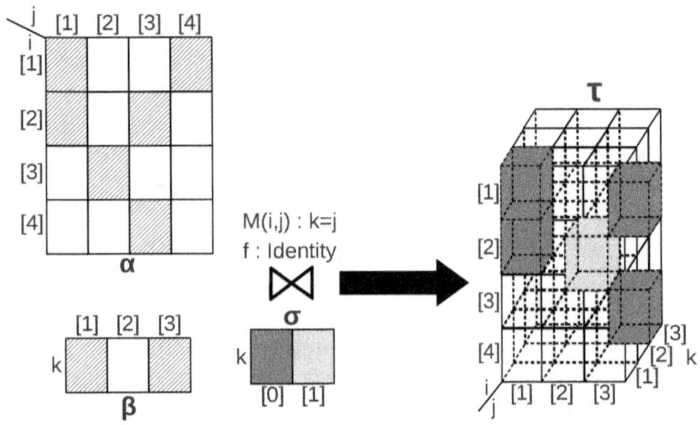

Figure 4: Array similarity join example:
`SELECT * INTO` τ `FROM` α `SIMILARITY JOIN` β
`ON` $(k = j)$ `WITH SHAPE` σ

DEFINITION 1 (ARRAY SIMILARITY JOIN). *Given two multi-dimensional arrays α and β in functional representation:*

$$\alpha : \{\mathcal{D}^\alpha = D_1^\alpha \times \cdots \times D_d^\alpha\} \longmapsto \{\mathcal{A}^\alpha = (A_1^\alpha, \ldots, A_m^\alpha)\}$$

$$\beta : \left\{\mathcal{D}^\beta = D_1^\beta \times \cdots \times D_d^\beta\right\} \longmapsto \left\{\mathcal{A}^\beta = (A_1^\beta, \ldots, A_m^\beta)\right\},$$

a mapping function $\mathcal{M} : \mathcal{D}^\alpha \longmapsto \mathcal{D}^\beta$, a shape array $\sigma : \mathcal{D}^\beta \longmapsto ()$, and a value function $f : \mathcal{A}^\alpha \cup \mathcal{A}^\beta \longmapsto \mathcal{A}^\tau$, let $\tau : \mathcal{D}^\alpha \cup \mathcal{D}^\beta \longmapsto \mathcal{A}^\tau$ be the result of the similarity join between α and β under $\mathcal{M}$, σ, and f, i.e., $\alpha \bowtie_{\sigma,f}^{\mathcal{M}} \beta$, written in AQL as:

`SELECT f INTO` τ
`FROM` α `SIMILARITY JOIN` β `ON` $\mathcal{M}$ `WITH SHAPE` σ

Function $\mathcal{M}$ maps a cell $\Upsilon \in \alpha$ to a cell $\Psi \in \beta$, while function f is defined over the set of attributes in the two input arrays. For each cell $\Upsilon \in \alpha$, array τ contains those non-empty cells in β that are in shape σ centered on Ψ, i.e., $\sigma(\Psi)$. The dimension of the τ cell is given by the concatenation of the Υ and $\sigma(\Psi)$ dimensions, while the value is computed by function $f(\Upsilon, \sigma(\Psi))$.

According to the definition, PTF catalog cross-matching corresponds to array similarity join between two 3-D arrays. While identity over *ra* and *dec* is an immediate choice for the mapping function, the mapping on *time* depends on the timestamps of the two catalogs. The shape array is centered on the mapped cell, e.g., same index for *ra* and *dec*, and the closest index on *time*. The actual shape is defined in the query, e.g., the $7 \times 7 \times 60$ cuboid with offsets $[-3 : 3, -3 : 3, -60 : -1]$ given in the introduction. Since the result is a 6-D array we cannot depict it graphically. Instead, we provide an illustrative example between a 2-D and a 1-D array corresponding to `[ra, dec]` and `[dec]`, respectively.

EXAMPLE 2. *Figure 4 depicts the result of the array similarity join between a 2-D array $\alpha[i = 1,4; j = 1,4]$ and a 1-D array $\beta[k = 1,3]$. The mapping function $\mathcal{M}$ maps a cell $(i,j) \in \alpha$ to the cell in β which has index $k = j$. This is the Ψ cell to which shape $\sigma[k = 0,1]$ is applied. The range of k in $\sigma[k = 0,1]$ determines the relationship between j and k in the join. In this case, a cell with index j from α is similar with cells having index $k = j$ or $k = j+1$ from β. The value function f concatenates the attributes of α and β into a single tuple. The schema of the result array is $\tau[i = 1,4; j = 1,3; k = 1,3]$. Since there is no valid mapping for $j = 4$, the range of j in τ is reduced to $[j = 1,3]$. There are 5 non-empty cells in τ—the non-empty cells in α and β are hatched. 4 of them – red in Figure 4 – correspond to the condition $k = j$. The only cell corresponding to condition $k = j + 1$ is $[i = 3; j = 2; k = 3]$—green in Figure 4.*

Mapping of similarity distance into shape array. Figure 3 depicts the shape array corresponding to several common similarity distances, e.g., L^p norms, Earth Mover's Distance (EMD), and Hamming, for a 2-D array. Other similarity measures, such as cosine and Jaccard similarity, do not have a suitable representation for array data. In all the figures, the Ψ cell is hatched. For the L^p norms, the size of the shape array increases as p increases. Since L^0 and L^∞ are defined as limits, we introduce special shapes for them. The shape array corresponding to L^0 is cell Ψ, while the shape array of L^∞ covers a square with side $(2\epsilon + 1)$. Although EMD and total variation distance (TVD) are defined for probability distributions, we can adapt them to arrays. The main characteristic of EMD is that dimensions are not symmetric. This can be seen in the corresponding figure, where the vertical dimension has priority. TVD is L^1 with distance 2ϵ. The shape for Hamming distance keeps the index of a dimension constant, while it covers the full range of the other dimension. It makes sense only for ϵ values smaller than the array dimensionality, otherwise it covers the entire array. The derived shapes can be generalized to higher dimensionality than 2-D.

Comparison with array joins. The array similarity join operator is a generalization of the dimension:dimension join [19] to more complex join predicates. dimension:dimension join is defined as a natural join with equality predicates. This corresponds to a mapping function $\mathcal{M} : (D_1^\beta = D_1^\alpha, \ldots, D_d^\beta = D_d^\alpha)$ and a similarity shape $\sigma\left[D_1^\beta = 0; \ldots; D_d^\beta = 0\right]$—the most primitive shape in a similarity join. The shape in Example 2 corresponds to the predicate `k=j OR k=j+1`, or, equivalently, `k≥j AND k<j+2`. None of these can be expressed as dimension:dimension equi-join.

Instead of expressing these predicates in a relational form, we generalize the array APPLY operator since it allows for complex predicates to be expressed concisely—and more intuitively. There are two modifications we make to the original APPLY which has a single array argument. First, we introduce a mapping function that assigns a unique cell Ψ in β to every cell Υ in α. Second, the shape σ is applied to Ψ rather than Υ—the case in APPLY.

Comparison with similarity join. Similarity join is defined only for sets of points having the same dimensionality. The proposed operator can handle arrays with any dimensionality. The relationship between points is expressed based on a distance function in the case of similarity join. While applicable to arrays – see the examples in Figure 3 – a distance function does not encode neighborhood relationships directly. This can introduce problems due to the discrete nature of the array dimensions and also requires mapping to array indices. Moreover, some complex shapes, e.g., arrays with empty cells or non-symmetric arrays, cannot always be expressed as a norm. The mapping function and similarity shape array in Definition 1 – on the other hand – can encode virtually any relationship between array cells.

4. ARRAY SIMILARITY JOIN OPERATOR

In this section, we present the first array similarity join operator for a distributed array database proposed in the literature. We begin with a high-level description of the operator's inner-workings that identifies the main processing stages. Then, we delve into the details of each stage and introduce our technical contributions.

High-level approach. Given two input arrays α and β chunked over the database servers, the goal is to compute optimally the result of their similarity join $\tau = \alpha \bowtie^{\mathcal{M}}_{\sigma,f} \beta$ as defined by the mapping function $\mathcal{M}$, the shape σ, and the value function f. Abstractly, the computation of τ requires three stages. First, for each chunk $\Upsilon \in \alpha$, the chunks $\Psi \in \beta$ that are in $\sigma(\mathcal{M}(\Upsilon))$ have to be identified. They can be located on one or multiple nodes in the cluster. This requires access only to the catalog metadata—considerably smaller in size. We assume the catalog can be stored in the memory of the coordinator and is properly indexed to efficiently identify the chunks in $\Psi \in \sigma(\mathcal{M}(\Upsilon))$. Second, chunks Υ and Ψ have to be transferred to the same node. In this case, network bandwidth is the resource to optimize. A special situation arises when the join is performed at a node that stores one of the chunks. In the third stage, function f is applied to compute the value of the output chunk in τ. This stage is computationally intensive, but fully parallelizable across chunks. Optimality, i.e., minimum processing time, is achieved when all the nodes perform the same amount of work or, equivalently, they operate on data having similar size—the workload is balanced. The execution of stage 2 and 3 can be overlapped across different chunks, reducing the overall optimization problem to minimizing the most expensive stage. We argue that network bandwidth – as the single common resource in a shared-nothing distributed architecture – has to be the primary optimization target, while load-balanced execution is secondary. Moreover, optimizing disk access to local chunks is paramount when the join is processed where chunks are stored.

4.1 Query Execution

The array similarity join operator functions as follows. The user submits a query to the coordinator node in charge of managing the workers and the metadata catalog. The coordinator computes an optimal execution plan for the query and sends it to the worker nodes. The workers process their share of chunks concurrently and asynchronously, informing the coordinator only when they finish.

The execution of the array similarity join operator follows closely the structural join [41]. The most significant difference is that the node which computes the join between two chunks is determined in the query optimization process—it is not the node that stores the chunk in array α. As a result, although the schema of the output array τ is well-defined at query time, the chunking of τ is known only at query execution. In general, τ is chunked along the array α dimensions—not necessarily regular. The actual shape of the chunks is determined by the shape array σ in the query. A chunk covers the full range of the dimensions in array β. In order to impose a specific chunking on array τ, schema alignment from shuffle join [19] is required. This is a costly operation that incurs complete data repartitioning and full replication of arrays α and β for every chunk in τ—the dimensionality of τ is the sum of the dimensionality of α and β, respectively. Due to the high cost, by default, there is no schema alignment in array similarity join.

Join algorithm. The most general algorithm to join two chunks is *nested-loop join*. It considers all the cell pairs and keeps only those that are similar. Since the cells $\Psi \in \beta$ that join with a cell $\Upsilon \in \alpha$ are structurally connected by the shape array σ and their number is typically much smaller than the number of cells in a chunk, more efficient join algorithms can be applied to identify similar cells. When the shape σ is convex, i.e., does not have holes, a *multi-dimensional index*, e.g., kd-tree or generalizations of quad-tree, can be built over the chunk in β. To find the similar cells corresponding to a cell $\Upsilon \in \alpha$, a range query with the predicate $\sigma(\mathcal{M}(\Upsilon))$ is executed over the index. As long as the index is queried a sufficiently large number of times, the construction cost is amortized. For the most general shape σ, *hash join* is likely the most efficient algorithm. A hash table is built over the chunk in β and is probed for each cell in $\sigma(\mathcal{M}(\Upsilon))$ corresponding to Υ. The proposed array similarity join operator chooses the join algorithm for each chunk pair at runtime. If the size of the chunks are below a specified threshold, nested-loop join is applied. Otherwise, index join is chosen for convex shapes, while hash join for non-convex.

Overlap I/O and processing through multi-threading. The array similarity join operator overlaps I/O – disk and network – with join computation at chunk granularity. Network transfer and local disk I/O are each handled by a separate thread. The join between two chunks is executed in a separate worker thread. The operator is configured with a pool of worker threads, allocated based on the number of CPU cores available in the system. Thus, several joins between pairs of chunks can be executed concurrently. All the threads – I/O and workers – execute asynchronously and coordinate through message exchange. The extensive degree of parallelism puts additional pressure on the I/O components – network, in particular – and makes their optimization even more critical. Thus, minimizing data transfer and network congestion are the primary objectives in the optimization of the array similarity join operator.

4.2 Query Optimization

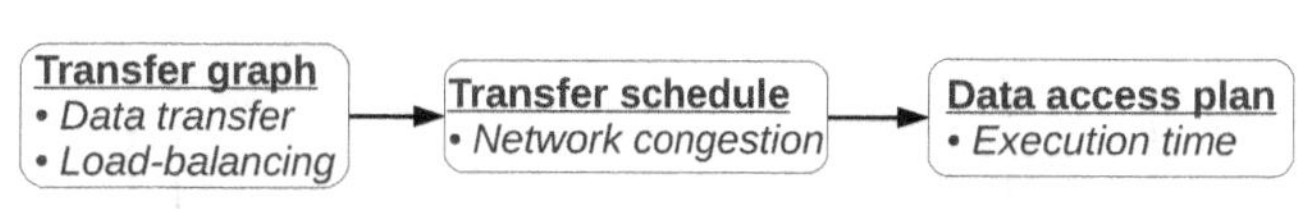

Figure 6: Query execution sub-plan for a node.

The coordinator is responsible for computing the optimal execution plan that minimizes the overall query processing time. The optimal plan is computed exclusively from the array similarity join query – the mapping function $\mathcal{M}$ and the shape array σ – and the catalog metadata which stores the location of the chunks and rele-

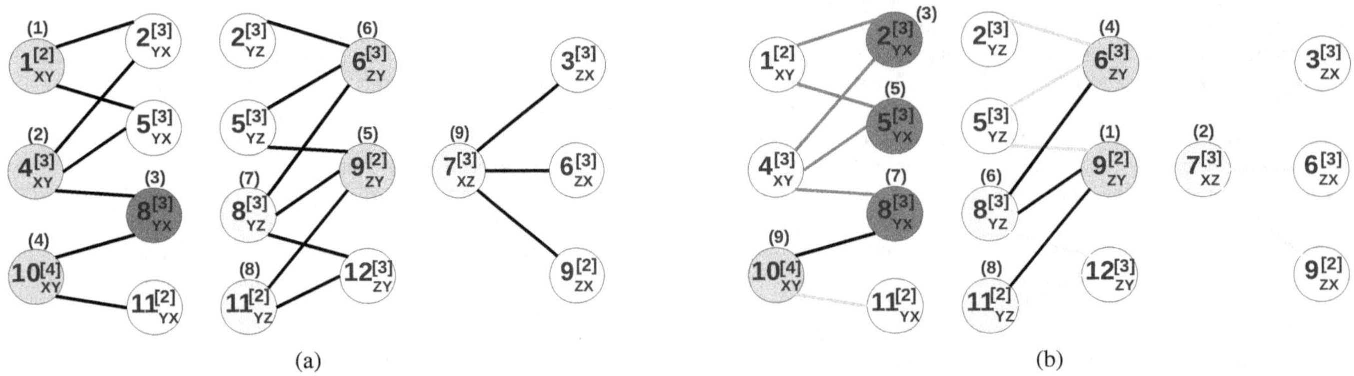

Figure 5: Optimal transfer graph: (a) HVC and (b) BHVC.

vant chunk statistics, such as the number of non-empty cells. The global plan consists of a detailed execution sub-plan (Figure 6) for each of the worker nodes.

The *transfer graph* specifies the chunks and the nodes where to send them, and the chunks to be received and from which nodes, respectively. This can be modeled through a series of binary variables x_{ijk} that specify that chunk i is sent from node j to node k. i ranges over the total number of chunks in α and β. However, x_{ijk} is set for a single j – the node where the chunk resides – and for the values of k on which there are chunks that join with chunk i.

The *transfer schedule* gives the order in which to send/receive chunks. It has two components: 1) the order of the nodes and 2) the order of the chunks assigned to a node. The optimal transfer schedule minimizes network congestion by enforcing only pairs of nodes to exchange data at any instant in time—a node receives data from a single other node. The objective function for the network transfer time is:

$$\min \left\{ \max_{ijk} \left\{ y_{ijkt} \cdot t \cdot T_{ntwk} \right\} \right\} \tag{5}$$

where y_{ijkt} specifies that chunk i is sent from node j to node k at time instant t. t takes values from 1 to the total number of chunks. Time-based permutations of the transfer graph variables x_{ijk} are encoded in the constraints on y_{ijkt}, i.e., $\sum_t y_{ijkt} = x_{ijk}, \forall i, j, k$. T_{ntwk} is the time to transfer a chunk between two nodes. It can be determined experimentally from the characteristics of the network.

The *data access plan* specifies the order in which to access local chunks when joining them with remote chunks. Since a local chunk joins with several remote chunks and a remote chunk joins with several local chunks, reducing I/O traffic – the assumption is that not all the local chunks fit in memory – plays an important role in minimizing query processing time. The objective function for disk access time is:

$$\min \left\{ \max_{k} \left\{ \sum_{tij} y_{ijk(t-1)} \sum_{i' \in \Psi_i} \left(1 - z_{i'j(t-1)}\right) \cdot T_{disk} \right\} \right\} \tag{6}$$

where z_{ijt} corresponds to local chunk i on node j being cached in memory at time instant t and T_{disk} is the time to load a chunk into memory. T_{disk} can be determined empirically.

Analytical cost model. The cost of an array similarity join query is the maximum between the network transfer time and the disk access time, i.e., $\max\{Eq. (5), Eq. (6)\}$, because these are overlapped. The cost does not include the join time. Since both disk and network are shared resources, while joins are processed in parallel across multiple threads, the computation is not the bottleneck, as long as sufficient threads are available in the system, e.g., we use 16 threads in the experiments. The cost also does not consider disk access time in network transfer time explicitly—before a chunk can be transferred from node j to node k, it has to be read from disk. This cost is accounted for in T_{ntwk}. In our model, data caching is employed only on the client side and exclusively for local chunks—it does not make sense to cache remote chunks since they are accessed once. Caching on the server side has to consider the access pattern from all the clients. Due to asynchronous execution, this is non-deterministic, thus, the benefits of optimization beyond standard LRU are unclear. We defer such an exploration to future work.

Challenges. The complete optimization formulation is given in Appendix A. Although it can be written as a linear integer program, finding the optimal network transfer schedule, i.e., Eq. (5), is known to be a combinatorially hard problem [33]. The disk access time objective, i.e., Eq. (6), is a quadratic integer optimization—an identically difficult problem. The number of variables in both these objectives is quadratic in the total number of chunks in the two arrays. When this number is in the order of thousands – the number of chunks in PTF is 200K – it is unfeasible to solve these optimizations in reasonable time since they contain billions of binary variables.

Solution. In these conditions, *our solution is to decompose the original optimization problem into a sequence of three separate sub-problems and solve them independently* (Figure 6). Notice, though, that solving each of the individual problems separately still poses significant challenges. First, we compute the optimal transfer graph, without considering the transfer schedule or the local data access plan. The graph guarantees minimal overall data transfer with a certain level of load-balancing. Second, the optimal transfer schedule is determined for the graph computed in the first stage. This schedule minimizes congestion over the network. The graph and the schedule target the network transfer time. Instead of computing which chunk goes to which node at which time instant, we first compute the assignment of chunks to nodes (transfer graph) and then the order only for those chunks assigned to a node (transfer schedule). Essentially, we introduce a new optimization problem over the x_{ijk} variables and take the result as a pre-conditioning for y_{ijkt}. Third, the local data access plan at each node is computed from the order in which remote chunks are received from other nodes. The data access plan targets the disk access time. By pre-conditioning Eq. (6) on y_{ijkt}, it becomes the well-known optimal cache replacement problem with a standard solution.

4.3 Transfer Graph Optimization

Consider x_{ijk} to be the variable obtained from y_{ijkt} by dropping index t. x_{ijk} specifies that chunk i is sent from node j to node k. With this simplification, minimizing the network transfer time becomes minimizing the amount of data each node has to send/receive. This can be written formally as:

$$\min \left\{ \max_j \sum_i \sum_k x_{ijk} \cdot s_i, \max_k \sum_i \sum_j x_{ijk} \cdot s_i \right\} \quad (7)$$

where s_i is the size of chunk i. While simpler, it turns out that solving this problem for a large number of chunks – while feasible – still takes minutes to hours. For example, CPLEX[6] takes more than 10 hours to compute the solution for joining two 3-D PTF arrays with 16 threads. This is not an acceptable optimization time since the actual execution takes less than 30 minutes (Section 5).

Our solution to solve this problem practically is to modify the objective to the total amount of data transfered over the network, i.e., $\min \sum_i \sum_j \sum_k x_{ijk} \cdot s_i$. This modified formulation can be mapped into a graph theoretical problem that can be solved efficiently. The main issue, though, is that it does not consider load-balancing—implicit in the original formulation in Eq. (7). We propose a novel graph-based algorithm for the modified formulation and show experimentally that is both close to optimal and provides load-balancing. Moreover, we show that the solutions to the original formulation and the proposed algorithm are similar.

The optimal transfer graph minimizes the overall data communicated over the network while guaranteeing a certain level of load-balancing. The graph encodes what chunks have to be communicated between nodes. Two chunks that have similar cells stored on separate nodes require network transfer. In order to determine these *chunk pairs* – in the worst case – the query optimizer has to compute $\sigma(\mathcal{M}(\Upsilon))$ for every cell in the α chunk. However, if the mapping function $\mathcal{M}$ preserves the order between cells along each of the dimensions, the chunks with potentially similar cells can be determined by computing $\sigma(\mathcal{M}(\Upsilon))$ only for the chunk corners.

Given potential chunk pairs and their node location, we build the transfer graph as follows. For each pair $\{v_i, \psi_j\}$, where v is a chunk in α stored on node i and ψ a chunk in β stored on node j, we create two vertices v_{ij} and ψ_{ji} connected by an edge. We assign a cost c proportional to the number of non-empty cells in the chunk to each vertex. c represents the amount of data that have to be transferred in order to evaluate similarity between cells in chunks v_i and ψ_j. It is important to notice that multiple vertices can be created for a single chunk if it is paired with chunks stored on different nodes. For chunks stored on the same node, multiple edges are created. An assumption embedded in the transfer graph is that chunk pairs can be joined only on the node that contains one of the chunks. This assumption is valid in array databases, where all the nodes store a relatively equal number of chunks [14].

EXAMPLE 3. *Figure 5 depicts the transfer graph for the array similarity self-join query* `SELECT * INTO` τ `FROM A` A_1 `SIMILARITY JOIN A` A_2 `ON` $(A_1.i = A_2.i$ `AND` $A_1.j = A_2.j)$ `WITH SHAPE` σ, *where A is the array in Figure 1 and* σ *is a* (3×3) *square centered on the cell. The notation for a vertex contains the chunk id – in white font in Figure 1 – the source and destination nodes, and the cost—in square brackets []. Node* $1_{XY}^{[2]}$ *corresponds to chunk 1 with 2 non-empty cells on node X being paired with chunks 2 and 5 on Y. Although the array has only 12 non-empty chunks, there are 18 vertices in the graph. This is because some chunks, e.g., chunk 2, are paired with chunks stored on multiple nodes, e.g., chunk 1 on X and chunk 6 on Z. There are 3 connected components in the graph—one for each pair of nodes.*

4.3.1 Vertex Cover

The *minimum weighted vertex cover of the transfer graph* corresponds to the minimum amount of data that have to be transferred for a given similarity join query modeled as a transfer graph. The minimum weighted vertex cover of a graph[7] is defined as the set of vertices with minimal total weight, i.e., cost, that cover all the edges. An edge is covered if at least one of its vertices is part of the solution set. In the case of the transfer graph, a selected vertex v_{ij} indicates that the corresponding chunk v is transfered from node i to node j. For general graphs, this is an NP-complete problem. However, there exist heuristics and approximation algorithms that provide constant-factor approximation ratio solutions.

Clarkson's heuristic for vertex cover (HVC) [9]. In this greedy algorithm, vertices are sorted according to the ratio $c/degree$, where *degree* is the number of incidental edges. This ratio represents the weight w of a vertex. At each iteration, the vertex with the minimum weight is selected and is eliminated from the graph together with all its incidental edges. This results in a reduction of the degree for all the adjacent vertices. Moreover, the weight of the selected vertex is subtracted from the cost of each adjacent vertex. HVC has a 2-approximation ratio. Figure 5a shows how HVC works for the transfer graph in Example 3. Vertices are selected independent of edges in this case. An important property of HVC is that it can be applied to each connected component separately.

4.3.2 Load-Balanced Vertex Cover

HVC does not consider load-balancing. In our case, this is a stringent requirement because, otherwise, a single or a few nodes have to do all the computation. This results in an increased execution time which, although not the primary optimization criterion, is still important. To cope with this problem, we introduce a new algorithm for minimum vertex cover that includes load-balancing in the vertex selection process. We start with the HVC algorithm and include penalties $p(v, recv) = recv(v.j) \cdot v.c \cdot |nodes|$ and $q(v, send) = send(v.j) \cdot v.c \cdot |nodes|$ in the weight w of each vertex $v_{ij}^{[c,w]}$. These penalties quantify the amount of data already assigned to the node corresponding to the destination (recv) and source (send) of the vertex, respectively. Constant r controls the penalty fraction assigned to each of these penalties. The modified objective gives higher priority to vertices on nodes that are assigned less data, even if their weight is larger. The pseudo-code for this new balanced heuristic vertex cover (BHVC) algorithm is presented in Algorithm 1. Line 3 selects the vertex with the minimum modified weight. The *for* loop in lines 4-8 updates the adjacent vertices, while lines 9 and 10 update the load of the destination/source node—initialized with 0.

Figure 5b depicts the output of BHVC on the transfer graph in Example 3. The main difference compared to HVC (Figure 5a) is that connected components are not considered independently. This is because each vertex assignment modifies the *recv* and *send* of the destination/source node. As a result, the assignment is done across components such that nodes always receive/send a similar amount of data. While HVC assigns 5 chunks to node Y and only 1 to X, with BHVC each node is assigned 3 chunks. However, BHVC

[6]http://www-01.ibm.com/software/commerce/optimization/cplex-optimizer/

[7]https://en.wikipedia.org/wiki/Vertex_cover

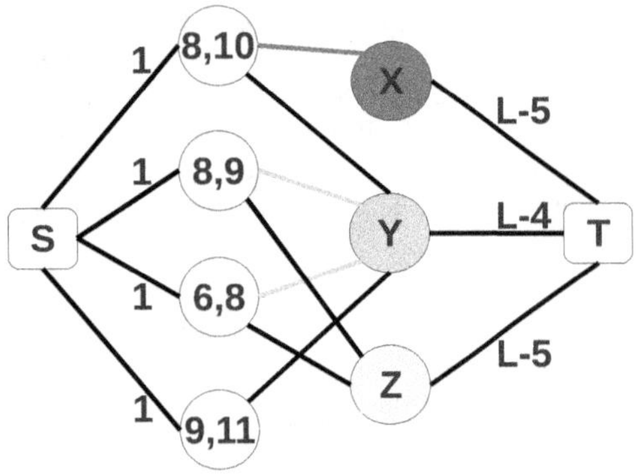

Figure 7: Assignment of chunk pairs to nodes. The non-colored vertices correspond to unassigned chunk pairs.

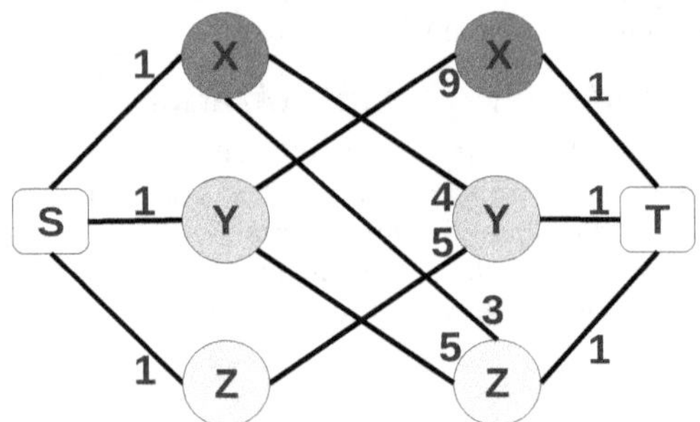

Figure 8: Transfer schedule network.

Algorithm 1 Balanced Heuristic Vertex Cover (BHVC)

Input: transfer graph $G(V, E)$
Output: balanced vertex cover $V' \subset V$

$load(n) \leftarrow 0, \forall n \in nodes$
while $E \neq \emptyset$ **do**
  select vertex $v_{ij}^{[c,w]}$ s.t.
  $argmin_{v \in V} \left\{ \frac{v.w + r \cdot p(v, recv) + (1-r) \cdot q(v, send)}{degree(v)} \right\}$
  for $(v, \psi) \in E$ **do**
    $E \leftarrow E \setminus (v, \psi)$
    $\psi.w \leftarrow \psi.w - \frac{v.w + r \cdot p(v, recv) + (1-r) \cdot q(v, send)}{degree(v)}$
    $degree(\psi) \leftarrow degree(\psi) - 1$
  end for
  $recv(v.j) \leftarrow recv(v.j) + v.c$
  $send(v.j) \leftarrow send(v.j) + v.c$
  $V' \leftarrow V' \cup v$
  $V \leftarrow V \setminus v$
end while

increases the total amount of data transferred by 1 array cell—from 25 to 26. r is set to 0.5 in this example.

4.3.3 Computation-to-Node Assignment

The minimum vertex cover of the transfer graph determines only the data transfer path, i.e., what nodes each chunk is sent to. It does not include information on which node two chunks are joined on. However, in the case of edges covered by a single vertex, the node on which the join is executed can be easily determined—it is the destination node of the covered vertex. For example, in Figure 5b chunks 1 and 2 are joined on node X. All the edges for which the assignment is immediate are colored in the color of the assigned node. The join corresponding to edges covered by two vertices can be computed on either of the two nodes storing the involved chunks.

In order to maintain load-balancing, a clever assignment strategy has to be devised. For this, we resort to the max-flow algorithm. We build a network consisting of a vertex for each unassigned chunk pair in the transfer graph and vertices for each of the processing nodes. Network edges connect only unassigned chunk pairs to nodes. These edges are assigned infinite capacity. A source vertex S has edges with capacity 1 to each chunk pair. A sink vertex T receives edges from each of the processing nodes. The capacity of these edges is to be determined by the assignment policy and it includes the already assigned chunk pairs. For example, the network in Figure 7 corresponds to the BHVC graph in Figure 5b in which 5 chunk pairs are already assigned to node X, 4 to node Y, and 5 to node Z, respectively. We want to assign the remaining 4 pairs, e.g., $(8, 10)$, $(8, 9)$, $(6, 8)$, and $(9, 11)$, such that the workload remains balanced. Let L be the maximum number of pairs assigned to a node in the final assignment. The minimum value of L for which a flow of size equal to the number of unassigned chunk pairs in this network exists, corresponds to a balanced assignment. This value can be found with a simple binary search over the interval $[1, \text{total number of chunk pairs}]$. For the network in Figure 7, L takes value 6 and the assignment of chunk pairs to nodes is color-coded. 6 chunk pairs have to be joined on each node.

4.4 Transfer Schedule Optimization

Given the solution to the transfer graph optimization, i.e., the chunks that have to be transferred between each two nodes x_{ijk}, the transfer schedule computes the order in which these chunks are sent/received, i.e., y_{ijkt}. For each node, we divide the transfer schedule into two components: 1) the order of the nodes and 2) the order of the chunks assigned to a node. We enforce that there is only node-to-node communication at any instant in time in order to minimizes network congestion.

Node order. We build a network in which there are two vertex instances corresponding to each node—one for sending and one for receiving. For each node pair that requires data transfer, an edge with capacity given by the total number of cells in the chunks to be transferred between them is added. The source and sink vertices are connected with each sending/receiving node instance by edges with capacity 1 (Figure 8). A max-flow in this network guarantees only node-to-node communication. At each step, the flown-through edge between nodes with the lowest capacity is removed and the process is repeated for the remaining graph. We stop when no edges exist between vertices corresponding to nodes. Figure 8 depicts the network for our running example. There is no edge between nodes Z and X since no chunks are sent from Z to X. A possible transfer schedule is: $\{(X \rightarrow Z, Y \rightarrow X, Z \rightarrow Y) : 3; (Y \rightarrow X, Z \rightarrow Y) : 2; (X \rightarrow Y, Y \rightarrow X) : 4; (Y \rightarrow Z) : 5\}$.

Chunk order. Given a set of chunks that have to be sent between two nodes, the question that arises immediately is in what order to do this? Consider the chunks sent from node Y to node X in Figure 5b. Chunk 2 and 5 have to be joined with chunk 1 and 4, while chunk 8 has to be joined with chunk 4 and 10, respectively. Since chunks on X have to be retrieved from disk, in the optimal case, each chunk is read only once, independent of the number of remote chunks it has to be joined with. Given that only a limited number of chunks can be cached in memory, it is impor-

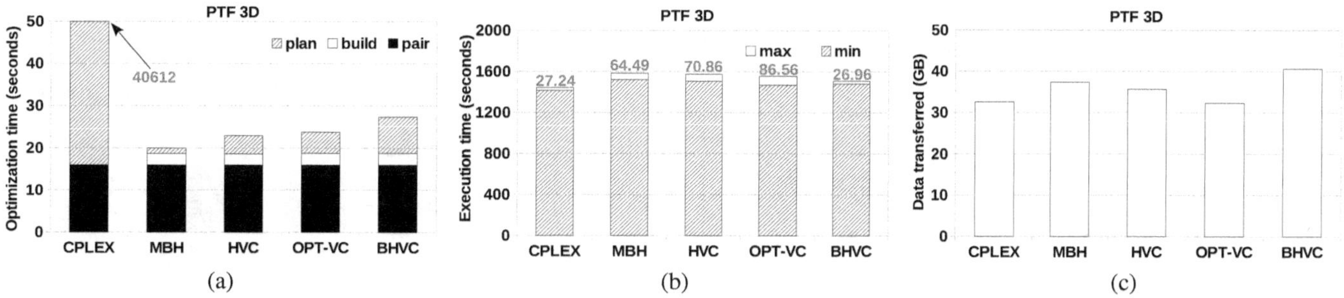

Figure 9: Transfer graph evaluation on PTF 3D query: (a) optimization time, (b) execution time, and (c) transferred data.

tant to use a chunk entirely once it is read. This can be achieved only if all the remote chunks that require the same local chunk are received (almost) contiguously. Our optimization framework does not guarantee this because chunks from different nodes are treated separately. However, we devise a solution that reorders the remote chunks from a node such that the number of local chunks they share is maximized. For a given remote chunk, the main idea is to choose another chunk from the same node that shares the largest number of local chunks. This can be found from the transfer graph. For example, the order 2, 5, 8 requires fewer disk accesses than 2, 8, 5 if only two local chunks can be stored in memory.

4.5 Data Access Plan Optimization

The last stage in the optimization process is to determine what local chunk to expel from memory. This problem arises whenever a remote chunk is joined with a local chunk that is not cached and the memory is full. The solution to this problem can be computed optimally since the transfer schedule specifies the incoming chunk order. Essentially, the chunk that will be used in the furthest future has to be expelled from memory. This minimizes the data access time from secondary storage, thus, the overall execution time. Following our running example, when chunk 8 is received at node X, local chunk 1 has to be removed from memory since chunk 4 has to be joined with 8.

5. EXPERIMENTAL EVALUATION

The objective of the experimental evaluation is to investigate the overall performance – as well as the impact of optimizations – of the proposed operator for two types of similarity queries over the PTF catalog. These are real queries executed in the PTF pipeline for transient detection. We use the LinkedGeoData[8] dataset in order to confirm the behavior of the proposed operator. Specifically, the experiments are targeted to answer the following questions:

- What is the effect of query optimization on execution time, amount of data transferred, network congestion, and data access plan at a node?
- What overhead is incurred by the optimization?
- How does the proposed BHVC algorithm compare against the original optimization formulation and HVC?
- What is the time distribution for a processing thread?
- How scalable is the array similarity join operator and how does it compare against state-of-the-art solutions?

Implementation. We implement the array similarity join operator as a `C++11` distributed multi-thread prototype on top of an array storage manager derived from ArrayStore [41]. The catalog is replicated at all the nodes in the cluster. The operator manages a pool of worker threads equal to the number of CPU cores in the system. Each worker is invoked with a pair of chunks that it has to join. The worker makes requests to the local and remote array storage managers. Once the chunks are received, the join is processed. This happens concurrently across all the workers. The optimization is executed at the coordinator as a separate process and the plans are distributed to the nodes. The code contains special function calls to harness detailed profiling data.

System. We execute the experiments on a 9-node cluster. The coordinator runs on one node while the other 8 nodes are workers. Each node has 2 AMD Opteron 6128 series 8-core processors (64 bit) – 16 cores – 28 GB of memory, and four 1 TB 7200 RPM SAS HDDs accessed independently. In the experiments, we use a single disk supporting buffered read rates of 120 MB/second on average per node. The number of worker threads is set to 16—the number of cores. Ubuntu 14.04.3 SMP 64-bit with Linux kernel 3.13.0-43 is the operating system. The nodes are mounted inside the same rack and are inter-connected through a Gigabit Ethernet switch. The network bandwidth on a link is similar to the disk bandwidth.

Methodology. We perform all experiments at least 3 times and report the average value as the result. We always enforce data to be read from disk, i.e., cold caches.

Data. We use two real datasets in our experiments. The *PTF catalog* consists of 1 billion time-stamped objects represented in the celestial coordinate system (ra, dec). The range of the time coordinate spans over 153,064 distinct values, while for *ra* and *dec* we use ranges of 100,000 and 50,0000, respectively. In array format, this corresponds to:

`PTF[time=1,153064;ra=1,100000;dec=1,50000]`

which is a sparse array with density less than 10^{-6}. Objects are not uniformly distributed over this array. They are heavily skewed around the physical location of the acquiring telescope—latitude corresponds to *dec*. After experimenting with several chunk sizes, we found that $(112, 100, 50)$ provides the best results. Due to the skew, there is considerable variance between the number of non-empty cells across chunks. However, the optimization algorithm takes this into account when assigning chunk pairs to nodes. Depending on how many attributes are stored for an object, the size of the catalog varies between 12 and 70 GB.

LinkedGeoData stores geo-spatial data used in OpenStreetMap[9]. We use the "Place" dataset which contains location information on roughly 3 million 2-D (long, lat) points-of-interest (POI). Since this is a too small dataset, we synthetically generate a larger dataset by adding 9 synthetic points with coordinates derived from each

[8]http://linkedgeodata.org

[9]www.openstreetmap.org

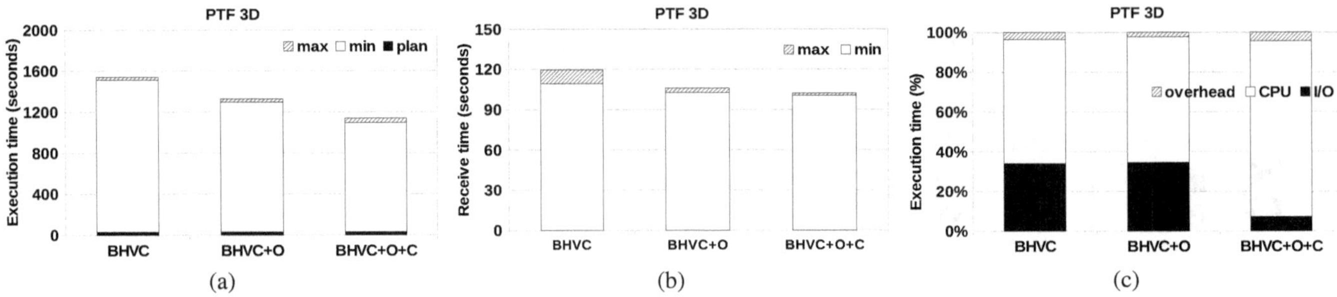

Figure 10: Query optimization evaluation on PTF 3D query: (a) execution time, (b) receiving time, and (c) thread time distribution.

original point using a Gaussian distribution with $\mu = 0$ and $\sigma = 10$ miles [36]. In array format, this corresponds to:

```
GEO[long=1,100000;lat=1,50000]
```

having chunk size of $(100, 50)$. Even with this replication, the size of GEO is still less than 1 GB.

Queries. In order to execute a real similarity join query, we create two separate instances of the datasets. They are treated as two independent arrays, even though special optimizations specific to self-join queries can be applied. We execute two types of queries – 2-D and 3-D – on PTF and 2-D on GEO. In PTF 2-D queries, the similarity shape is defined only over the (ra, dec) dimensions. The time is considered to be 0. This corresponds to finding objects within 10 arcseconds of each other in the same image. The similarity shape considers the 4 cells having L^1-norm of 1 from the origin cell. In 3-D queries, the time is part of the similarity shape, which includes the 26 cells having L^∞-norm of 1 from the center. The GEO 2-D query finds POIs within 1 mile of each other. The corresponding shape array is the L^2-norm equal to 4 (Figure 3). Since the results for all the queries follow similar patterns, we include below only the results for the PTF 3-D query. The results for the other two queries are in Appendix C.

5.1 Transfer Graph Evaluation

We evaluate the impact of the proposed BHVC algorithm on the overall execution time and amount of data transferred. We take as baseline the solution to the original network transfer time optimization formulation in Eq. (5). We solve this formulation using CPLEX with 16 threads and compare its optimization time to that of BHVC. In order to verify the ability of BHVC to provide load-balancing, we include in the comparison three algorithms for the vertex cover problem that minimize only the total amount of data transferred. The first algorithm is HVC (see Section 4.3.1). The minimum-bandwidth heuristic (MBH) [19] is a greedy algorithm that always transfers the smaller chunk in a pair to the larger one. This is done iteratively until all the edges are covered. Recall that vertices correspond to chunks and edges to chunk pairs in the transfer graph. The third algorithm is OPT-VC [18]. It computes the minimum weighted vertex cover of a bipartite graph using network max-flow. The transfer graph is bipartite by construction.

Optimization time. The time to compute the transfer graph is depicted in Figure 9a. The time to determine the chunk pairs is common across all the methods. In CPLEX, these are used to construct the linear program. The graph structure is built from the pairs in all the other methods. Even though it uses 16 threads, CPLEX cannot solve the linear program in less than 10 hours. This is because the number of chunk pairs in the PTF 3-D query is in the order of tens of thousands. The simple heuristics MBH and HVC are the fastest. BHVC takes a few seconds more than these methods – and OPT-VC – because it has to handle load-balancing, in addition to only minimizing the transferred data. The same trend is observed for the other two queries (Figure 14a and 15a).

Execution time. Figure 9b depicts query completion time both for the fastest as well as the slowest node in the cluster. The difference between the two is included in the figure. The optimization time is not included—only the transfer graph optimization is activated. As expected, the CPLEX solution has the fastest execution time. BHVC comes in a close second, while the other algorithms perform almost identical. When it comes to load-balancing, BHVC clearly shows its improvement over the algorithms that consider only the amount of data transferred. BHVC performs even better than CPLEX since minimizing the maximum data sent/received does not translate immediately into load-balancing.

Data transferred. OPT-VC is guaranteed to minimize the overall data transferred over the network. Figure 9c confirms this. The reason BHVC transfers the most data is because its goal is to obtain similar execution times across all the nodes. This requires additional data movement from the slower nodes to the faster ones in order to balance the overall load. We observe similar trends for the other two queries (Figure 14c and 15c).

5.2 Query Optimization Evaluation

We measure the effect each stage in the query optimization process has on execution time, receiving time as a surrogate for network congestion, and thread execution time distribution. We take as baseline the transfer graph generated by the BHVC algorithm and quantify the additional improvements brought by node and chunk reordering in the transfer schedule (O) and caching in local chunk accessing (C).

Execution time. Figure 10a depicts the impact on execution time of each stage in the optimization process. While the optimization time stays constant, schedule reordering and caching improve the execution time considerably. Schedule reordering enforces that only pairs of nodes communicate at every time instant. This reduces the traffic at each node and streamlines the communication. Intelligent caching at client reduces the number of requests made to the local storage manager. We also observe that these do not have a negative effect on load-balancing for any of the queries.

Receive time. The effect of schedule reordering on network congestion is depicted in Figure 10b. Since we cannot measure congestion directly, we measure the receive time at each node. We observe a significant reduction in receiving time when reordering is enabled across all the queries. Caching does not influence receiving time in any meaningful way.

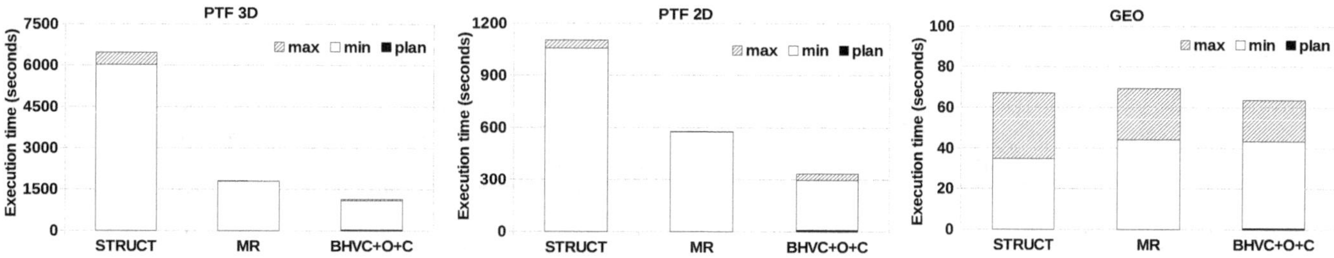

(a) (b) (c)

Figure 11: Algorithm execution time comparison: (a) PTF 3-D, (b) PTF 2-D, (c) GEO.

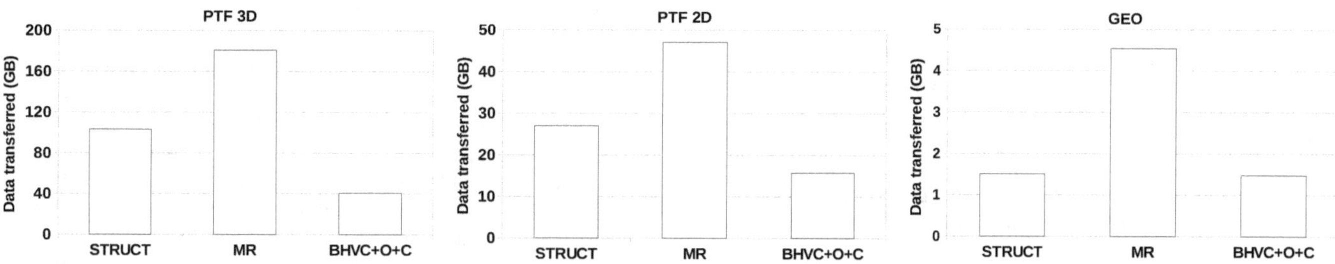

(a) (b) (c)

Figure 12: Algorithm data transferred comparison: (a) PTF 3-D, (b) PTF 2-D, (c) GEO.

Thread time distribution. Figure 10c shows the relative time distribution inside a worker thread. This is a good indicator of where the time is spent and where the bottlenecks are. Ideally, all the time should be spent in CPU processing. This is closely realized only when caching is active. The network traffic – not included in the figure – remains the bottleneck even in this situation. Schedule reordering plays a minimal role on thread time distribution.

5.3 Comparison with Related Algorithms

Since we are the first to introduce array similarity join, it is difficult to find appropriate candidate algorithms for direct comparison. In this situation, we adapt two classes of distributed algorithms to array similarity join. The first class is array join, while the second is relational similarity join. A complete description of these algorithms is given in Appendix B.

Structural join (STRUCT) [41] is the standard algorithm to implement dimension:dimension array join. It iterates over chunks of the outer array α. For each chunk, it looks-up the corresponding chunks in the inner array β, retrieves them all, and joins the outer chunk with each of the inner chunks in turn. The algorithm is applicable to array similarity join if the mapping function $\mathcal{M}$ preserves the adjacency relationship between cells. We implement structural join by having each of the nodes executing this algorithm concurrently on their share of the data. Moreover, we process multiple chunk pairs in parallel by assigning each of them to a separate worker from the thread pool.

MapReduce (MR) similarity join algorithms over relational multi-dimensional data [40, 37, 17, 36] are immediate instantiations of MapReduce join [4]. The most important challenge faced by these algorithms is how to choose the join units such that the amount of data that have to be replicated – thus, transferred over the network – is minimized. In the case of arrays, data are already chunked, thus, the join units are determined. The mapping of join units to reducers is done with a random hash function that partitions the join units uniformly. In our implementation, each reducer, i.e., worker from the thread pool, transfers its allocated join units and executes the join concurrently with the other reducers.

Figure 11 depicts the execution time of the three algorithms for the three queries considered. Including optimization time, BHVC is always the fastest—by as much as a factor of 2 over MR in the case of PTF 2-D. Even though it moves considerably more data, MR is faster than STRUCT. The reason is the better distribution of the workload across nodes. BHVC also transfers the least amount of data—a factor of 2.5 less than STRUCT in the case of PTF 3-D. These results prove that the proposed optimizations provide a significant improvement over state-of-the-art relational algorithms modified to work on array data.

5.4 Scalability

The speedup of the array similarity join operator is depicted in Figure 13 for the PTF 3-D query when executed over 2, 4, 6, and 8 nodes. The reason for the sub-linear speedup is that the bottleneck of the entire process is data access – disk or network – not the computation. However, a speedup of 3.64 out of 4 is obtained for 8 nodes. Due to less computation, the speedup for the other queries is worse – only around 2.6 – and we do not include it here.

5.5 Discussion

Based on the results presented above, we can answer the questions driving the experimental evaluation. The transfer graph optimization formulation cannot be solved by CPLEX in acceptable time—it takes more than the overall query execution. All the solutions that minimize the data transferred are scalable. However, only BHVC achieves load-balancing—at a small increase in op-

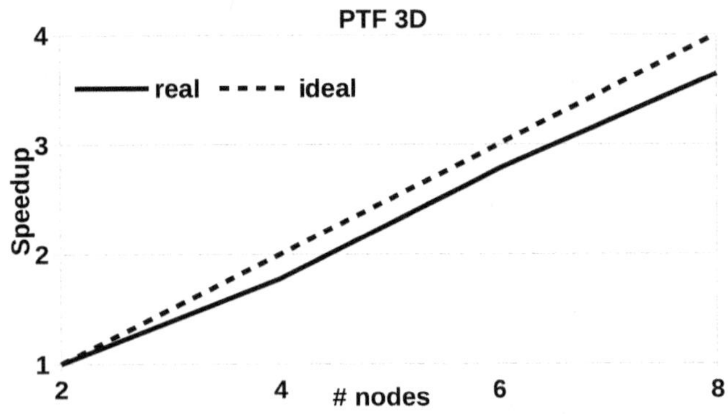

Figure 13: Speedup for the PTF 3-D query.

timization time and data transferred. The transfer schedule and caching reduce network congestion and increase the CPU utilization, respectively. They also improve the overall execution time by a significant margin. The proposed array similarity join operator is clearly more efficient – by at least a factor of 2 – than relational similarity operators modified to work with array data. As long as the query requires significant computation, the operator achieves close-to-linear speedup.

6. RELATED WORK

In this section, we discuss relevant work from array joins, relational similarity join, parallel similarity join, and spatial joins.

Array joins. The `APPLY` operator is part of original array algebra specifications [2, 26]. We define array similarity join as a generalization of the `APPLY` operator to two arrays. Positional array equi-joins are introduced in the first releases of the array database SciDB [30]. They are evaluated in the context of different chunking strategies in [41], where structural join is introduced. A complete formalization of array equi-joins and the shuffle join algorithm are given in [19], while a graph formulation is introduced in [3]. Array similarity join is not considered in any of the previous work. The proposed operator bears similarities to shuffle join [19] in allocating join units/chunk pairs to nodes based on an optimization process. However, the allocation is considerably more difficult in the case of similarity join. Moreover, our cost model considers disk access and overlapped network, I/O, and processing.

Relational similarity join. There is a significant amount of work on similarity join processing in the relational database literature [23, 39, 5, 38, 22, 21, 13, 20]. These algorithms can be separated into two categories—index-based and all-pairs [46]. ϵ-kdB tree [39] is the first high-dimensional index targeted at similarity join. It modifies the splitting criterion of kdB tree to take ϵ into account. In general, a new index has to be built for every similarity query. A parallel version of ϵ-kdB tree that requires complete data repartitioning is introduced in [38]. The ϵ Grid Ordering (EGO) family [5, 22, 21] of algorithms is a divide and conquer grid-based method. Points are mapped into grid cells and sorted before a recursive join is applied. This is done for every query. The effectiveness of the EGO-family of algorithms is heavily dependent upon the heuristic to prune the non-joinable sequences [22, 21, 13]. The Quickjoin algorithm [20] recursively partitions the data until each partition contains a few objects, at which point a nested-loop join is used. The data can be partitioned using a variety of techniques, such as ball partitioning or generalized hyperplane partitioning. Data at the border are replicated. While Quickjoin is perfect for self-join similarity queries, it encounters problems when handling join queries. The solution given in [20] is to put the points from the two sets together, execute Quickjoin on the merged dataset, but return only the results in which there is a point from each dataset. This is hardly efficient. Space filling curves algorithms such as ZC and MSJ [23], although simple, require space transformations and heavy preprocessing. These make them hard to parallelize.

Parallel similarity join. There has been considerable interest in parallelizing similarity join algorithms using the MapReduce framework [44, 29, 15, 27, 12]. MRSimJoin [40] is an extension of QuickJoin [20] to MapReduce. It is a divide-and-conquer algorithm that partitions the points iteratively into clusters until an in-memory similarity join algorithm can be executed on pair clusters. It uses pivot-based partitioning with random pivots extracted from one of the relations. While repartitioning is part of the MapReduce job, there is an unbounded number of such jobs because the exact partitioning cannot be controlled. ClusterJoin [36] introduces a set of bisector-based distance filters [7, 46] into MRSimJoin to generate more accurate partitions. MR-DSJ [37] and PHiDJ [17] are similarity self-join grid-based algorithms that extend EGO [5] to MapReduce. As is the case with all MapReduce solutions, complete data repartitioning is automatic. This is not necessary for arrays which are already chunked. The proposed array similarity join operator takes advantage of chunking to schedule join processing and to reduce data transfer. It is not clear how set [44], multiset [27], social image [48], and string [12] data can be represented as arrays in order to apply the array similarity join operator. These use different metrics and have special similarity join operators. We plan to explore these topics in future work.

Spatial join. In spatial join, pairs of overlapping objects have to be computed. This corresponds to cell overlapping in array similarity, i.e., L^0 norm. A standard approach is to decompose the space into grids and assign each object to all the grids it overlaps with [31]. The join is computed for each grid and duplicates are eliminated. Thermal-Join [42] introduces a non-uniform space partitioning that allows for overlapped objects to be identified without any computation. This approach does not work for array data unless a chunk contains a single cell. In general, while non-similar cells can be pruned away, similar cells require computation.

7. CONCLUSIONS AND FUTURE WORK

In this paper, we introduce the first array similarity join operator for a distributed array database. Unlike previous work on relational data, we define similarity based on a shape array instead of a distance function. This novel formulation takes into consideration the discrete nature of array data and supports asymmetric similarity measures. The proposed operator minimizes the overall data transfer and network congestion while providing load-balancing across the nodes that store data, but without completely repartitioning and replicating the arrays. Moreover, the array operator overlaps disk, network, and join computation in a multi-thread pipelined architecture. We model the query optimization of array similarity join as a vertex cover problem and introduce efficient algorithms to find optimal execution plans. We evaluate experimentally the proposed array similarity join operator and compare it against existing solutions on the PTF catalog consisting of 1 billion celestial objects. The results confirm the efficacy of the optimizations in reducing the overall data transfer as well as the execution time—by a factor of 2 or more. In future work, we plan to consider plans that assign computation to nodes that do not store the chunks in a join unit. While this makes the optimization harder, solutions similar to TrackJoin [32] can be devised. We also plan to consider other measures than L norms, e.g., Jaccard coefficient and cosine similarity.

Acknowledgments. This work is supported in part by the Director, Office of Laboratory Policy and Infrastructure Management of the U.S. Department of Energy under contract No. DE-AC02-05CH11231 and by a U.S. Department of Energy Early Career Award (DOE Career). Weijie Zhao and Florin Rusu have done part of this work while at Lawrence Berkeley Laboratory. We want to thank Peter Nugent from LBNL for providing us the PTF data used in the experiments. We also want to thank the anonymous reviewers for their insightful comments that improved the quality of the paper significantly.

8. REFERENCES

[1] A. Gal-Yam et al. Real-Time Detection and Rapid Multiwavelength Follow-Up Observations of a Highly Subluminous Type II-P Supernova from the Palomar Transient Factory Survey. *Astrophysical Journal*, 736(2), 2011.

[2] P. Baumann, A. Dehmel, P. Furtado, R. Ritsch, and N. Widmann. The Multidimensional Database System RasDaMan. In *SIGMOD 1998*.

[3] P. Baumann and V. Merticariu. On the Efficient Evaluation of Array Joins. geo-bigdata.github.io/2015/peter.pdf.

[4] S. Blanas, J. M. Patel, V. Ercegovac, J. Rao, E. J. Shekita, and Y. Tian. A Comparison of Join Algorithms for Log Processing in MaPreduce. In *SIGMOD 2010*.

[5] C. Bohm, B. Braunmuller, F. Krebs, and H.-P. Kriegel. Epsilon Grid Order: An Algorithm for the Similarity Join on Massive High-Dimensional Data. In *SIGMOD 2001*.

[6] J. B. Buck, N. Watkins, J. LeFevre, K. Ioannidou, C. Maltzahn, N. Polyzotis, and S. Brandt. SciHadoop: Array-based Query Processing in Hadoop. In *SC 2011*.

[7] S. Chaudhuri, V. Ganti, and R. Kaushik. A Primitive Operator for Similarity Joins in Data Cleaning. In *ICDE 2006*.

[8] Y. Cheng and F. Rusu. Formal Representation of the SS-DB Benchmark and Experimental Evaluation in EXTASCID. *Distrib. and Parallel Databases*, 2014.

[9] K. Clarkson. A Modification of the Greedy Algorithm for Vertex Cover. *IPL*, 16(1), 1983.

[10] P. Cudre-Mauroux, H. Kimura, K.-T. Lim, J. Rogers, S. Madden, M. Stonebraker, S. B. Zdonik, and P. G. Brown. SS-DB: A Standard Science DBMS Benchmark. http://www.xldb.org/science-benchmark/.

[11] D. J. DeWitt et al. The Gamma Database Machine Project. *IEEE Data Eng. Bull.*, 2(1):44–62, 1990.

[12] D. Deng, G. Li, S. Hao, J. Wang, and J. Feng. MassJoin: A MapReduce-based Algorithm for String Similarity Joins. In *ICDE 2013*.

[13] J.-P. Dittrich and B. Seeger. GESS: A Scalable Similarity-Join Algorithm for Mining Large Data Sets in High Dimensional Spaces. In *KDD 2001*.

[14] J. Duggan and M. Stonebraker. Incremental Elasticity For Array Databases. In *SIGMOD 2014*.

[15] F. Afrati et al. Fuzzy Joins using MapReduce. In *ICDE 2012*.

[16] F. Rusu and Y. Cheng. A Survey on Array Storage, Query Languages, and Systems. http://arxiv.org/abs/1302.0103, 2013.

[17] S. Fries, B. Boden, G. Stepien, and T. Seidl. PHiDJ: Parallel Similarity Self-Join for High-Dimensional Vector Data with MapReduce. In *ICDE 2014*.

[18] L. S. Goddard. *Mathematical Techniques of Operational Research*. 2014.

[19] J. Duggan, O. Papaemmanouil et al. Skew-Aware Join Optimization for Array Databases. In *SIGMOD 2015*.

[20] E. H. Jacox and H. Samet. Metric Space Similarity Joins. *ACM Transactions on Database Systems (TODS)*, 2007.

[21] D. V. Kalashnikov. Super-EGO: Fast Multi-dimensional Similarity Join. *VLDB Journal*, 4(2):561–585, 2013.

[22] D. V. Kalashnikov and S. Prabhakar. Fast Similarity Join for Multi-Dimensional Data. *Information Systems*, 32:160–177, 2007.

[23] N. Koudas and C. Sevcik. High Dimensional Similarity Joins: Algorithms and Performance Evaluation. In *ICDE 1998*.

[24] K.-T. Lim, D. Maier, J. Becla, M. Kersten, Y. Zhang, and M. Stonebraker. Array QL Syntax. http: //www.xldb.org/wp-content/uploads/2012/09/ArrayQL-Draft-4.pdf. [Online; January 2013].

[25] D. Maier. ArrayQL Algebra: version 3. http://www.xldb.org/ wp-content/uploads/2012/09/ArrayQL_Algebra_v3+.pdf. [Online; January 2013].

[26] A. P. Marathe and K. Salem. Query Processing Techniques for Arrays. *VLDB Journal*, 11(1):68–91, 2002.

[27] A. Metwally and C. Faloutsos. V-SMART-Join: A Scalable MapReduce Framework for All-Pair Similarity Joins of Multisets and Vectors. *PVLDB*, 5, 2012.

[28] M. A. Nieto-Santisteban, A. R. Thakar, and A. S. Szalay. Cross-Matching Very Large Datasets. In *National Science and Technology Council (NSTC) NASA 2006*.

[29] A. Okcan and M. Riedewald. Processing Theta-Joins using MapReduce. In *SIGMOD 2011*.

[30] P. Brown et al. Overview of SciDB: Large Scale Array Storage, Processing and Analysis. In *SIGMOD 2010*.

[31] J. Patel and D. DeWitt. Partition Based Spatial-Merge Join. In *SIGMOD 1996*.

[32] O. Polychroniou, R. Sen, and K. A. Ross. Track Join: Distributed Joins with Minimal Network Traffic. In *SIGMOD 2014*.

[33] W. Rodiger, T. Muhlbauer, P. Unterbrunner, A. Reiser, A. Kemper, and T. Neumann. Locality-Sensitive Operators for Parallel Main-Memory Database Clusters. In *ICDE 2014*.

[34] D. Rohde, M. Gallagher, and M. Drinkwater. Astronomical Catalog Matching as a Mixture-Model Problem. In *AIP 2012*.

[35] F. Rusu, P. Nugent, and J. K. Wu. Implementing the Palomar Transient Factory Real-Time Detection Pipeline in GLADE: Results and Observations. In *DNIS 2014*.

[36] A. D. Sarma, Y. He, and S. Chaudhuri. ClusterJoin: A Similarity Joins Framework using MapReduce. *PVLDB*, 7, 2014.

[37] T. Seidl, S. Fries, and B. Boden. MR-DSJ: Distance-based Self-Join for Large-Scale Vector Data Analysis with MapReduce. In *BTW 2013*.

[38] J. C. Shafer and R. Agrawal. Parallel Algorithms for High-dimensional Proximity Joins. In *VLDB 1997*.

[39] K. Shim, R. Srikant, and R. Agrawal. High-Dimensional Similarity Joins. In *ICDE 1997*.

[40] Y. N. Silva, J. M. Reed, and L. M. Tsosie. Mapreduce-based Similarity Join for Metric Spaces. In *Cloud-I 2012*.

[41] E. Soroush, M. Balazinska, and D. Wang. ArrayStore: A Storage Manager for Complex Parallel Array Processing. In *SIGMOD 2011*.

[42] F. Tauheedy, T. Heinis, and A. Ailamaki. THERMAL-JOIN: A Scalable Spatial Join for Dynamic Workloads. In *SIGMOD 2015*.

[43] A. R. van Ballegooij. RAM: A Multidimensional Array DBMS. In *EDBT 2004 Workshops*.

[44] R. Vernica, M. Carey, and C. Li. Efficient Parallel Set-Similarity Joins using MapReduce. In *SIGMOD 2010*.

[45] S. Wang, Y. Zhao, Q. Luo, C. Wu, and Y. Xu. Accelerating In-Memory Cross Match of Astronomical Catalogs. In *eScience 2013*.

[46] Y. Wang, A. Metwally, and S. Parthasarathy. Scalable All-Pairs Similarity Search in Metric Spaces. In *KDD 2013*.

[47] Y. Zhang, M. Kersten, M. Ivanova, and N. Nes. SciQL: Bridging the Gap between Science and Relational DBMS. In *IDEAS 2011*.

[48] Y. Zhuang, N. Jiang, Z.-A. Wu, J. Cao, and C. Ju. Efficient Batch Similarity Join Processing of Social Images based on Arbitrary Features. In *WWW 2015*.

APPENDIX

A. OPTIMIZATION FORMULATION

In this section, we provide the complete formulation for array similarity join optimization. We express the optimization as a constrained mixed integer program (MIP). In addition to the objective function presented in the cost model (Section 4), we include the relevant constraints. The binary variables are depicted in Table 1.

Variable	Significance
x_{ijk}	chunk i is sent from node j to node k
y_{ijkt}	chunk i is sent from node j to node k at time t
z_{ijt}	chunk i on node j is cached at time t

Table 1: MIP binary variables.

The cost of array similarity join has to be minimized:

$$\min \Big\{ \max_{ijk} \{y_{ijkt} \cdot t \cdot T_{ntwk}\}, \quad \max_{k} \Big\{ \sum_{tij} y_{ijk(t-1)} \sum_{i' \in \Psi_i} \left(1 - z_{i'j(t-1)}\right) \cdot T_{disk} \Big\} \Big\} \tag{8}$$

under the following set of constraints:

$$\begin{aligned}
C_1 &: x_{ijk} + x_{i'kj} = 1; \forall i, \forall i' \in \Psi_i, p(i) = j, p(i') = k \\
C_2 &: \sum_t y_{ijkt} = x_{ijk}; \forall i, \forall j, \forall k \\
C_3 &: \sum_{ijk} y_{ijkt} = 1; \forall t \\
C_4 &: \sum_{ik} y_{ijkt} = 1; \forall t, \forall j \\
C_5 &: \sum_{ij} y_{ijkt} = 1; \forall t, \forall k \\
C_6 &: \sum_i z_{ijt} \leq B; \forall t, \forall j \\
C_7 &: z_{i'jt} \leq z_{i'j(t-1)} + y_{ikjt}; \forall t, \forall k, \forall j, \forall i' \in \Psi_i
\end{aligned} \tag{9}$$

C_1 guarantees that every join unit is processed at a node that stores one of the chunks. C_2 connects variables x and y such that only chunks that are transferred are assigned a permutation position. C_3 ensures that a chunk is transferred to a remote node only once. C_4 guarantees that a node can send at most one chunk per time instant, while C_5 corresponds to receiving at most a chunk per time instant. C_6 is a bounding constraint limiting the size of the cache at a node. Finally, C_7 enforces that a chunk is cached only when it is required in a join at time t.

There are three parameters in this MIP optimization. T_{ntwk} is the time to transfer a chunk between two nodes. T_{disk} is the time to load a chunk into memory. B is the cache size. Their values can be determined based on an empirical calibration process.

B. BASELINE ALGORITHMS

In this section, we provide a detailed description of the state-of-the-art algorithms used for comparison with the proposed array similarity join operator. They are immediate extensions of algorithms for array join and similarity join, respectively. We discuss the advantages/disadvantages of each algorithm and provide a thorough comparison along several dimensions.

B.1 Structural Join

The standard algorithm to implement dimension:dimension, or structural, equi-join is a special form of nested-loop join operating at chunk level (see Algorithm 3 in [41]). The join iterates over chunks of the outer array α. For each chunk, it looks-up the corresponding chunks in the inner array β, retrieves them all, and joins the outer chunk with each of the inner chunks in turn. The join between two chunks is itself implemented as nested-loops iterating over chunk cells. If the cells in the chunks are sorted according to dimensions, the optimal merge join algorithm can be executed instead. The algorithm is immediately applicable to the array similarity join operator if the mapping function $\mathcal{M}$ preserves the adjacency relationship between cells. Identity function is one such example. Otherwise, cells have to be treated independently.

The structural join algorithm can be readily implemented in a distributed array database. Once the cells in $\sigma(\mathcal{M}(\Upsilon))$ are determined for an entire chunk – or all the chunks – the node identifies their location by querying the catalog on the coordinator. A message is sent to the corresponding node for every chunk and, when the chunk is received, the output cells in τ are computed. While the degree of parallelism across nodes is maximized, there are several problems with such an asynchronous decentralized approach. Although each node aims to minimize the amount of transferred data – it behaves locally optimal – there is no guarantee that the overall data are minimized. In fact, this is very unlikely since nodes do not coordinate at all. As a consequence, the actual data transfer can be severely imbalanced due to the contention for network bandwidth. In the extreme case, all the nodes in the cluster send/receive data to/from the same node. Load-balancing beyond what is achievable with a uniform chunk distribution to nodes is not considered at all in structural join.

B.2 MapReduce Similarity Join

In the structural join algorithm, the computation is executed exclusively at nodes storing chunks from the outer array α. Unless these chunks are distributed across the entire cluster, there will be nodes that do not participate in join processing. Moreover, if chunk distribution is not even, there will be load imbalance. MapReduce join [4] – as a direct extension of distributed Grace hash join [11] – guarantees that all the nodes in the cluster participate in join processing. Load-balancing is typically enforced at runtime through dynamic assignment of work – chunks to be joined – to nodes. The tradeoff to achieve these two goals is network traffic. MapReduce join is far from network-optimal because it transfers almost the full size of both arrays over the network [32]. Using pre-determined hash functions limits the probability that a hashed tuple will not be transferred over the network to $1/N$ on N nodes.

MapReduce join works as follows. The result array is divided into logical non-overlapping chunks, i.e., join units. These are computed from the schema of the result array—specified by the user, or inferred by the system in some restricted situations. Join units are computed at the coordinator and sent to all the nodes storing data from arrays α and β, or they are encoded directly into the Map hash function. Each node partitions the cells it stores over the join units. This is done concurrently across all the nodes. Cells Υ in α are assigned to a single join unit. Cells Ψ in β are assigned either to a single join unit – for equi-join – or they can be replicated in several units—for similarity join. The data alignment phase, i.e., shuffling, transmits all the partitions belonging to the same join unit to a single node for the computation of function f. In the case of distributed hash join, the assignment of join units to nodes is static and uniform. In MapReduce, tasks are assigned dynamically at runtime to better adapt to the processing capacity of the nodes, resulting in more adaptive load-balancing. The computation of f can start only after all the partitions are received.

MapReduce similarity join algorithms over multi-dimensional data [40, 37, 17, 36] are immediate instantiations of MapReduce join. They are readily applicable to arrays in which chunking is ignored. The most important challenge faced by these algorithms

	Structural Join	MapReduce Join	Shuffle Join	**Array Similarity Join**
Targeted join	general	equi-join	equi-join	**similarity join**
Data transfer	locally optimal	suboptimal	globally optimal	**globally optimal**
Network congestion	ignored	ignored	runtime global synchronization	**optimal scheduling**
Load-balancing	ignored	runtime reactive	static optimized	**static optimized**
Processing nodes	store one of α or β	all	all (store α or β preferred)	**store α or β**
Repartitioning	not required	complete	complete	**not required**
Replication	minimally required	suboptimal	suboptimal	**minimally required**

Table 2: Comparison of array similarity join algorithms.

is how to choose the join units such that the amount of data that have to be replicated – thus, transferred over the network – is minimized. MRSimJoin [40] uses pivot-based partitioning with random pivots extracted from array α. The points at the join unit border are replicated across all the neighboring units. This has the potential to degenerate into an unbounded number of data alignment rounds. ClusterJoin [36] introduces a series of filters to reduce the number of replicated points. Both these algorithms are extensions of QuickJoin [20] to MapReduce. MR-DSJ [37] uses grid-based partitioning, i.e., regular chunking across all dimensions, to compute join units. A join unit consists of a chunk and its neighbors—there are 2^d such neighbor chunks, where d is the number of dimensions. This results in a replication factor of 2^d for every cell. PHiDJ [17] reduces the replication factor in MR-DSJ by splitting the dimensions into several groups and executing MR-DSJ independently on each group. For k dimension groups, data are replicated only $k \cdot 2^{\frac{d}{k}}$ times. This reduction in replication – and amount of data transferred – translates into a corresponding exponential increase in computation—due to executing MR-DSJ k times.

B.3 Shuffle Join

None of the above algorithms optimize for the overall data transfer. In structural join, each node minimizes its local data receiving, while MapReduce join ignores communication completely. Shuffle join [19] aims to minimize the overall data transfer imposed by the execution of an array equi-join, while guaranteeing some form of load-balancing. It extends upon the track join minimal network traffic distributed hash algorithms introduced in [32]. The main idea is to consider the assignment of join units to nodes as a global optimization problem and solve it after all the nodes finish their local partitioning. The amount of data each node has in a join unit is the principal decision variable. Several algorithms are considered, including a simple minimum bandwidth greedy heuristic that assigns a join unit to the node storing the largest portion of cells in the unit; a tabu search algorithm that incorporates load-balancing into the minimum bandwidth heuristic; and an integer programming formulation that optimizes the end-to-end execution time. The proposed analytical cost model has the inherent limitation that communication and computation cannot be overlapped across the join units assigned to the same node. Moreover, the order in which a node has to send its partitions is not computed—it is arbitrary. A global synchronization mechanism that enforces a single node to transmit data to a destination at any given time instant is deployed in order to prevent network congestion. However, this can have the negative effect of stalling nodes.

B.4 Discussion

Table 2 summarizes the properties of the baseline algorithms for array similarity join in a distributed array database. It also includes the specific operator proposed in this work—in bold font. Structural join is the most general of these algorithms. MapReduce and shuffle join are in the same family of equi-join algorithms. Extensions to array similarity join and other types of join are possible, however, they incur costly modifications. Shuffle join is the only algorithm that aims to minimize the overall data transfer. MapReduce join incurs heavy all-to-all communication, while structural join targets only local optimizations at each node. Network congestion is addressed only by shuffle join through a runtime global synchronization mechanism that gives writing access on a link to a single sender. Load-balancing is supported as a runtime reactive process in MapReduce join. The approach in shuffle join is to embed load-balancing into the data transfer scheduling. Thus, only MapReduce and shuffle join include all the nodes – not only the ones storing the join arguments – in the processing. Since they are not specific to array similarity join, MapReduce and shuffle join require complete data repartitioning and mapping to the output array space. As a result, repartitioning incurs unnecessary data replication due to the output array having higher dimensionality than the input arrays. As shown in Table 2, the proposed array similarity join operator aims inherits the benefits of the baseline algorithms by minimizing the overall transfer and network congestion while providing load-balancing across the nodes that store data, but without completely repartitioning and replicating the arrays.

C. ADDITIONAL EXPERIMENTS

In this section, we include experimental results for the queries PTF 2-D and GEO. While the trend is similar to PTF 3-D, these results provide another reference point on the characteristics of the proposed array similarity join operator. They prove the benefits of the proposed operator over non-array similarity join operators applied to array data even when the number of join pairs is not extremely large (PTF 2-D) and the dataset size is rather small (GEO)—no parallel processing is required in this case.

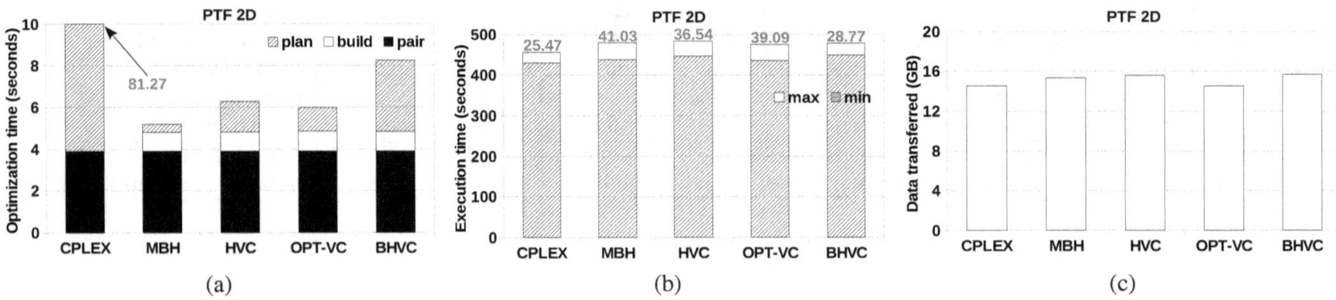

Figure 14: Transfer graph evaluation on PTF 2D query: (a) optimization time, (b) execution time, and (c) transferred data.

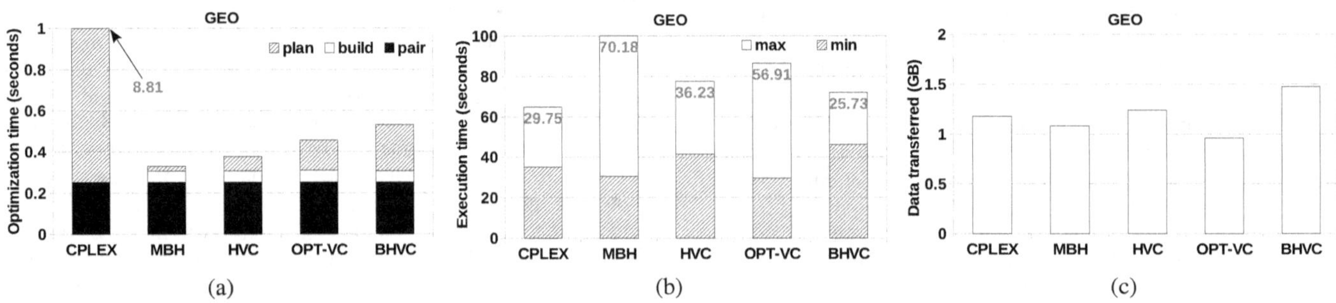

Figure 15: Transfer graph evaluation on GEO query: (a) optimization time, (b) execution time, and (c) transferred data.

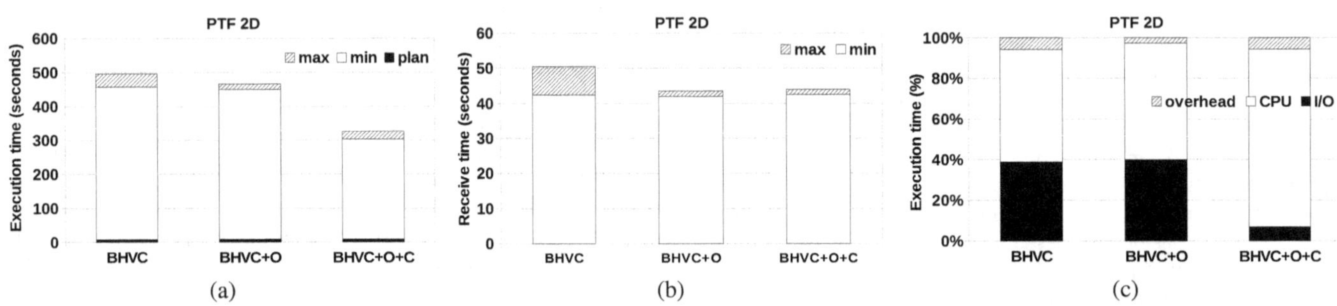

Figure 16: Query optimization evaluation on PTF 2D query: (a) execution time, (b) receiving time, and (c) thread time distribution.

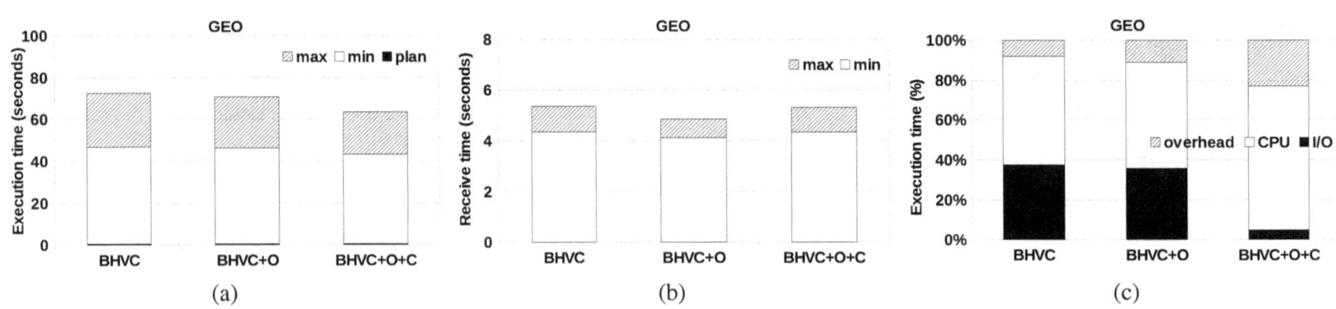

Figure 17: Query optimization evaluation on GEO query: (a) execution time, (b) receiving time, and (c) thread time distribution.

LazyLSH: Approximate Nearest Neighbor Search for Multiple Distance Functions with a Single Index

Yuxin Zheng†, Qi Guo†, Anthony K. H. Tung† and Sai Wu#
† School of Computing, National University of Singapore, Singapore
# College of Computer Science and Technology, Zhejiang University, China
†{yuxin, qiguo, atung}@comp.nus.edu.sg, #wusai@zju.edu.cn

ABSTRACT

Due to the "curse of dimensionality" problem, it is very expensive to process the nearest neighbor (NN) query in high-dimensional spaces; and hence, approximate approaches, such as Locality-Sensitive Hashing (LSH), are widely used for their theoretical guarantees and empirical performance. Current LSH-based approaches target at the ℓ_1 and ℓ_2 spaces, while as shown in previous work, the fractional distance metrics (ℓ_p metrics with $0 < p < 1$) can provide more insightful results than the usual ℓ_1 and ℓ_2 metrics for data mining and multimedia applications. However, none of the existing work can support multiple fractional distance metrics using one index. In this paper, we propose LazyLSH that answers approximate nearest neighbor queries for multiple ℓ_p metrics with theoretical guarantees. Different from previous LSH approaches which need to build one dedicated index for every query space, LazyLSH uses a single base index to support the computations in multiple ℓ_p spaces, significantly reducing the maintenance overhead. Extensive experiments show that LazyLSH provides more accurate results for approximate kNN search under fractional distance metrics.

CCS Concepts

•**Information systems** → **Nearest-neighbor search;**

Keywords

Locality sensitive hashing; Nearest neighbor search; ℓ_p metrics

1. INTRODUCTION

State-of-the-art kNN processing techniques have been proposed for low-dimensional cases. However, due to the "curse of dimensionality", the same techniques cannot be directly applied to high-dimensional spaces. It was shown that conventional kNN processing approaches become even slower than the naive linear-scan approach [18]. One compromise solution is to adopt the approximate kNN technique which returns k points within distance cR from a query point, where c is an approximation ratio and R is the distance between the query point and its true (k)th nearest neighbor. The intuition is that in high-dimensional spaces, approximate results are good enough for most applications.

Table 1: Classification accuracy

Dataset	Classification accuracy (%)						
	Real 1NN	LazyLSH (Approximate 1NN)					
	$\ell_{1.0}$	$\ell_{0.5}$	$\ell_{0.6}$	$\ell_{0.7}$	$\ell_{0.8}$	$\ell_{0.9}$	$\ell_{1.0}$
Ionos	90.9	**92.0**	91.7	91.7	91.7	91.7	91.5
Musk	93.5	**94.0**	93.8	93.5	93.4	93.4	93.5
BCW	92.8	**93.3**	**93.3**	93.1	93.0	92.6	92.8
SVS	67.5	67.8	**68.9**	67.8	67.4	67.2	67.5
Segme	91.9	92.1	92.1	**92.4**	92.3	92.1	91.9
Giset	96.2	94.9	95.7	96.4	96.4	**96.8**	96.5
SLS	90.0	87.8	88.3	88.7	89.2	**90.0**	89.8
Sun	9.5	9.0	9.3	9.3	9.4	9.4	**9.5**
Mnist	96.3	95.1	95.4	95.7	95.9	96.0	**96.2**

To process approximate kNN queries, several methods have been proposed [5, 26, 2, 33], among which, locality-sensitive hashing (LSH) [26] is widely used for its theoretical guarantees and empirical performance. In essence, the LSH scheme is based on a set of hash functions from the *locality-sensitive hash family* which guarantees that similar points are hashed into the same buckets with higher probabilities than dissimilar points. The LSH scheme was first proposed by Indyk et al. [26] for the use in the binary Hamming space, and later was extended for the use in the Euclidean space by Datar et al. [18] based on the p-stable distribution.

It was observed that the effectiveness of high-dimensional search is sensitive to the choice of distance functions [1]. Although the Manhattan (ℓ_1) and Euclidean (ℓ_2) metrics are widely used, it was shown that ℓ_p metrics with $0 < p < 1$, called *fractional distance metrics*, can provide more insightful results from both theoretical and empirical perspectives for data mining applications [1, 16] and content-based image retrievals [25]. Furthermore, it was shown that the optimal ℓ_p metric is application-dependent and required to be tuned or adjusted for each application [1, 16, 25, 20].

As an example, Table 1 shows the accuracy of the kNN classifier [17] under different ℓ_p metrics. We test *Mnist* [29], *Sun* [19] and seven datasets from the UCI ML repository[1]. The ground-truth classification results are provided by the datasets themselves. For each query point, we retrieve its

[1] http://archive.ics.uci.edu/ml/
The used datasets are: Ionosphere (Ionos), Musk, Breast Cancer Wisconsin (BCW), Statlog Vehicle Silhouettes (SVS), Segmentation (Segme), Gisette (Giset) and Statlog Landsat Satellite (SLS).

SIGMOD'16, June 26-July 01, 2016, San Francisco, CA, USA
© 2016 ACM. ISBN 978-1-4503-3531-7/16/06...$15.00
DOI: http://dx.doi.org/10.1145/2882903.2882930

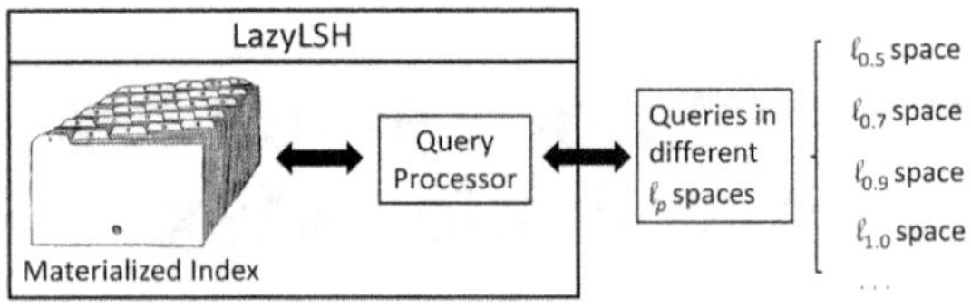

Figure 1: LazyLSH Overview

nearest neighbor and assign it to the same class tag as its nearest neighbor. For ℓ_p metrics ($0.5 \leq p \leq 1$), we compute the approximate 1NN using our LazyLSH technique proposed in the paper. For comparison, we also show the results of the 1NN classifiers where the 1NN is the true 1NN in the ℓ_1 space. We highlight the highest accuracy for LazyLSH in bold font. The results indicate that the best classification result may be obtained using different fractional distance metrics for different datasets. There is no way to know which fractional distance is optimal for a specific dataset. This finding is similar to the observations presented in [1, 25]. Therefore, before implementing a system, we need an approach that can explore the data using different distance metrics, such that we can select a proper one to achieve the best mining results.

Unfortunately, due to the lack of closed form density functions for p-stable distributions when $p \neq 1$ or 2, it is nontrivial to generate p-stable random variables and build an optimal index structure for fractional distance metrics. Moreover, the conventional approach of building one index for each possible value of p will incur very high costs in terms of computational time and space requirement (with the number of possible values of p being potentially infinite). To address this problem, in this paper, we propose LazyLSH to process approximate kNN queries in different ℓ_p spaces using only one single index.

LazyLSH builds an LSH index in a predefined ℓ_{p_0} space, which is referred to as the base space. Using this materialized index, LazyLSH can answer approximate kNN queries in a user-specific query space. The word "Lazy" is borrowed from the lazy learning algorithms [49] in which generalization beyond the training data is delayed until a query is issued. LazyLSH means that we do not build an index for every query space. Instead, we reuse the index constructed in the base space to answer queries in the query space. Our analysis shows that if two points are close in an ℓ_{p_1} space, then they are likely to be close in another ℓ_{p_2} space. We also find that a locality-sensitive hash function built in the base space is still locality-sensitive in the query space when certain conditions hold. With this observation, LazyLSH adopts the strategy of having "**one index for many fractional distance metrics**". Figure 1 illustrates this idea. A single materialized LSH index is built using a specific distance function, based on which, we can approximately process kNN queries for other fractional distance metrics.

In order to get more precise results, we propose a method called query-centric rehashing to search the base index and retrieve nearby objects. We further observe that during the processing of queries under different ℓ_p metrics, many common index entries are probed. This finding motivates us to optimize the processing of multiple queries under different ℓ_p metrics concurrently by sharing their I/Os.

We summarize the contributions of this paper as follows.

- We propose a novel method called LazyLSH to answer approximate nearest neighbor queries under multiple ℓ_p metrics. Compared to the costly naive method which builds an LSH index for every value of p to cover all possible fractional distance metrics, LazyLSH maintains only a single copy of LSH index in the base space, significantly reducing the storage overhead.

- We give a theoretical proof that when certain conditions hold, locality-sensitive hash function can be extended to support the fractional distance metrics. This is the first work that gives a theoretical bound for the approximate kNN processing using LSH with the fractional distance metric.

- We propose two novel optimization methods, namely query-centric rehashing and multi-query optimization, to improve the effectiveness and efficiency of performing queries.

- We experimentally verify the effectiveness and efficiency of our proposed LazyLSH using both synthetic and real datasets. Experimental results show that LazyLSH provides more accurate results for approximate kNN search under fractional distance metrics, and it can be used as the supervision to optimally choose the ℓ_p metric for different applications.

The rest of this paper is organized as follows. Section 2 briefly reviews the preliminaries on LSH. Section 3 presents the technical details of the proposed LazyLSH method. Section 4 shows the processing of approximate range queries and approximate kNN queries. Then, we experimentally evaluate the proposed method in Section 5 and discuss the related studies in Section 6. Finally, we conclude this paper in Section 7. For the ease of presentation, we summarize our notations in Table 2.

2. PRELIMINARY

Before delving into the details of LazyLSH, we first review some preliminary knowledge of the locality-sensitive hashing (LSH) method. We begin with the definition of the ℓ_p distance used in this paper.

DEFINITION 1 (ℓ_p DISTANCE). *The distance between any two d-dimensional points $\vec{o}$ and $\vec{q}$ in the ℓ_p space, denoted as $\ell_p(\vec{o}, \vec{q})$, is computed as:*

$$\ell_p(\vec{o}, \vec{q}) = \sqrt[p]{\sum_{i=1}^{d} |o_i - q_i|^p} \tag{1}$$

If $0 < p < 1$, $\ell_p(\vec{o}, \vec{q})$ is called the *fractional distance metric* [1]. In similarity search, if $\ell_p(\vec{o}, \vec{q}) \leq r$, we say the point $\vec{o}$ is within the *ball* of radius r centered at the point $\vec{q}$, denoted as $B_p(\vec{q}, r)$.

DEFINITION 2 (BALL $B_p(\vec{q}, r)$). *Given a point $\vec{q} \in \mathbb{R}^d$, and a radius r, the ball of radius r centered at point $\vec{q}$ in the ℓ_p space is defined as $B_p(\vec{q}, r) = \{\vec{v} \in \mathbb{R}^d | \ell_p(\vec{v}, \vec{q}) \leq r\}$.*

LSH methods try to map the points within a ball to the same hash bucket. Let $\mathcal{H}$ be a family of functions mapping $\mathbb{R}^d$ to some universe U. For any two points $\vec{o}, \vec{q} \in \mathbb{R}^d$, consider a process in which we choose a function h from $\mathcal{H}$ at

Table 2: Table of Notations

$\mathcal{D}$	database
d	dimensionality
$\vec{q}$	query point
$h_i^*(\cdot)$	based materialized hash function
$\vec{a}$	random vector in the hash function
b	offset in the hash function
c	approximation ratio
X	random variable
$\ell_p(\vec{o},\vec{q})$	the ℓ_p distance between $\vec{o}$ and $\vec{q}$
p	the subscript used in the ℓ_p space or ℓ_p distance
δ	radius in the ℓ_p space
r	radius in the ℓ_1 space
$\delta^\perp$	lower bound of the ℓ_1 distance given $\ell_p = \delta$
$\delta^\top$	upper bound of the ℓ_1 distance given $\ell_p = \delta$
$B_p(\vec{q}, r)$	the ball of radius r centered at $\vec{q}$ in the ℓ_p space
η	the number of required hash functions
θ	the collision count threshold

random, and analyze the probability of $h(\vec{o}) = h(\vec{q})$. The family $\mathcal{H}$ is called locality-sensitive if it satisfies the following conditions.

DEFINITION 3 (LOCALITY-SENSITIVE HASHING). *Let $d(\cdot,\cdot)$ be a distance function of a metric space. A family $\mathcal{H}$ is called (r, cr, p_1, p_2)-sensitive if for any two points $\vec{o},\vec{q} \in \mathbb{R}^d$, satisfying*
(1) if $d(\vec{o},\vec{q}) \le r$, then $Pr_{\mathcal{H}}[h(\vec{o}) = h(\vec{q})] \ge p_1$,
(2) if $d(\vec{o},\vec{q}) > cr$, then $Pr_{\mathcal{H}}[h(\vec{o}) = h(\vec{q})] < p_2$,
(3) $c > 1$, and
(4) $p_1 > p_2$.

Various LSH families have been discovered for different distance metrics [4]. In particular, the LSH family for the ℓ_p distance is found based on the p-stable distribution [18].

DEFINITION 4 (p-STABLE DISTRIBUTION). *A distribution G over $\mathbb{R}$ is called p-stable, if there exists $p \ge 0$ such that for any n real numbers $v_1, ..., v_n$ and i.i.d. random variables $X_1, ..., X_n$ with distribution G, the variable $\sum_i v_i X_i$ has the same distribution as the variable $(\sum_i |v_i|^p)^{1/p} X$, where X is a random variable with distribution G. It has been proved that stable distributions exist for $p \in (0, 2]$. In particular,*
- *The Cauchy distribution, with a density function $f(x) = \frac{1}{\pi}\frac{1}{1+x^2}$, is 1-stable;*
- *The Gaussian distribution, with a density function $f(x) = \frac{1}{\sqrt{2\pi}}e^{-x^2/2}$, is 2-stable.*

Using the p-stable distribution, one can generate a d-dimensional vector $\vec{a}$ by setting its element as a random value from the p-stable distribution. Given two points $\vec{v_1}, \vec{v_2} \in \mathbb{R}^d$, $(\vec{a}.\vec{v_1} - \vec{a}.\vec{v_2})$ is distributed as $\ell_p(\vec{v_1},\vec{v_2})X$, where X is a random variable with the same p-stable distribution. Based on the above observations, Datar et al. [18] proposed the following LSH family for the ℓ_p distance. A data point in $\mathbb{R}^d$ is projected onto a random line $\vec{a}$, which is segmented into equi-width intervals with length r_0. Formally, the proposed LSH function in the ℓ_p space is defined as:

$$h(\vec{v}) = \lfloor \frac{\vec{a}.\vec{v} + b}{r_0} \rfloor, \tag{2}$$

where the projection vector $\vec{a} \in \mathbb{R}^d$ is constructed by picking each coordinate from a p-stable distribution.

Given $\vec{v_1}, \vec{v_2} \in \mathbb{R}^d$, let $s = \ell_p(\vec{v_1},\vec{v_2})$. The probability that $\vec{v_1}$ and $\vec{v_2}$ collide under a hash function $h(\cdot)$, denoted as $p(s, r_0)$, can be computed as follows:

$$p(s, r_0) = \int_0^{r_0} \frac{1}{s} f_p(\frac{t}{s})(1 - \frac{t}{r_0})dt, \tag{3}$$

where $f_p(\cdot)$ is the probability density function of the absolute value of the p-stable distribution, and $p(s, r_0)$ is monotonically decreasing with s when r_0 is fixed [18]. As a result, the LSH family of the ℓ_p distance is $(1, c, p_1, p_2)$-sensitive with $p_1 = p(1, r_0)$ and $p_2 = p(c, r_0)$. For special cases such as p equals to 1 and 2, we can compute the probabilities using the corresponding density functions [18].
- For the Cauchy distribution ($p = 1$), we have

$$p(s, r_0) = 2\frac{\arctan(r_0/s)}{\pi} - \frac{1}{\pi(r_0/s)}\ln(1 + (r_0/s)^2) \tag{4}$$

- For the Gaussian distribution ($p = 2$), we have

$$p(s, r_0) = 1 - 2norm(-r_0/s) - \frac{2}{\sqrt{2\pi}(r_0/s)}(1 - e^{-(r^2/2s^2)}), \tag{5}$$

where $norm(\cdot)$ is the cumulative distribution function of the standard normal distribution.

The above LSH family was employed to process approximate nearest neighbor queries which are defined as:

DEFINITION 5 ($\mathcal{N}_p(\vec{q}, k, c)$ PROBLEM). *Given a dataset $\mathcal{D}$, a point $\vec{q} \in \mathbb{R}^d$, a cardinality k, an approximate ratio c, and an ℓ_p space, the c-approximate k nearest neighbors search returns a set of k points, $\mathcal{N}_p(\vec{q}, k, c) = \{\vec{o_1}, \ldots, \vec{o_k}\}$, where points are sorted in ascending order of their distances to $\vec{q}$ in the ℓ_p space, and $\vec{o_i}$ is a c-approximation of the real i^{th} nearest neighbor. Let $\vec{o_1^*}, \ldots, \vec{o_k^*}$ be the real kNNs in ascending order of their distances to $\vec{q}$. Then $\ell_p(\vec{o_i},\vec{q}) \le (c \times \ell_p(\vec{o_i^*},\vec{q}))$ holds for all $i \in [1, k]$.*

Several approaches were proposed to answer approximate nearest neighbor queries in the Euclidean space [18, 32, 45, 21, 43]. We briefly discuss two related methods: E2LSH [18] and C2LSH [21].

E2LSH: E2LSH [18] is the first proposed LSH method to answer the $\mathcal{R}_p(\vec{q},\ r,\ c)$ problem in the Euclidean space where $p = 2$, which is defined as:

DEFINITION 6 ($\mathcal{R}_p(\vec{q},\ r,\ c)$ PROBLEM). *Given a dataset $\mathcal{D}$, a query point $\vec{q} \in \mathbb{R}^d$, $\mathcal{R}_p(\vec{q},\ r,\ c)$ returns a point $\vec{o'} \in \mathcal{D}$, where $\vec{o'} \in B_p(\vec{q}, cr)$, if there exists a point $\vec{o} \in B_p(\vec{q}, r)$.*

As can be seen, the $\mathcal{R}_p(\vec{q},\ r,\ c)$ problem is a decision version of the $\mathcal{N}_p(\vec{q}, k, c)$ problem. E2LSH exploits LSH functions to address the $\mathcal{R}_2(\vec{q},\ r,\ c)$ problem in the following way. First, a set of m LSH functions $h_1(\cdot), \ldots, h_m(\cdot)$ are randomly chosen from an $(r,\ cr,\ p_1,\ p_2)$-sensitive family $\mathcal{H}$, and they are concatenated to form a compound hash function $g(\cdot)$, where $g(\vec{p}) = (h_1(\vec{p}), \ldots, h_m(\vec{p}))$ for a point $\vec{p} \in \mathbb{R}^d$. By using a compound hash function instead of a single LSH function, the probability that two faraway points collide can be largely reduced. Then, the hash function $g(\cdot)$ is used to map all the data to a hash table. The above two steps are repeated for L times and accordingly, L compound hash functions $g_1(\cdot), \ldots, g_L(\cdot)$ are used to produce L hash tables.

When a query $\vec{q}$ comes, the points from buckets $g_1(\vec{q}), \ldots, g_L(\vec{q})$ are retrieved until all the points or the first $3L$ points are found. For each retrieved point $\vec{v}$, it is returned if $\vec{v} \in B_2(\vec{q}, cr)$. An $\mathcal{N}_2(\vec{q}, k, c)$ query can be answered by issuing a series of $\mathcal{R}_2(\vec{q}, c, r)$ queries using gradually increasing search radii. For this purpose, hash tables with different radii must be built, incurring a high storage cost.

C2LSH: To avoid building many hash tables for different radii, C2LSH [21] is proposed by changing the original hash function to:

$$h(\vec{v}) = \lfloor \frac{\vec{a}.\vec{v} + b^*}{r_0} \rfloor, \quad (6)$$

where b^* is uniformly drawn from $\lfloor 0, c^{\lceil \log_c td \rceil}(r_0)^2 \rfloor$, c is the approximation ratio, t is the largest coordinate value, and d is the dimensionality of the data. It is proved that the hash function is $(1, c, p_1, p_2)$-sensitive.

First, a materialized index is built for a set of base LSH functions with a small interval r_0. Then, C2LSH reuses the materialized index to retrieve objects at different radii without explicitly building hash tables for different radii. This process is referred to as *virtual rehashing*. To answer an $\mathcal{R}_2(\vec{q}, r, c)$ query, C2LSH modifies the hash function as:

$$H^r(\vec{v}) = \lfloor \frac{h(\vec{v})}{r} \rfloor \quad (7)$$

Note that $H^r(\vec{v})$ is (r, cr, p_1, p_2)-sensitive. *Virtual rehashing* simplifies the process of retrieving the objects hashed to $H^r(\vec{q})$ by guaranteeing that it is identical to retrieving objects in the buckets within $[\lfloor \frac{h_{\vec{a},b}(\vec{v})}{r} \rfloor \times r, \lfloor \frac{h_{\vec{a},b}(\vec{v})}{r} \rfloor \times r + r - 1]$ in the base hash function.

In addition, C2LSH estimates the probability of being the nearest neighbor using the *collision count*. If the number of an object colliding with a query exceeds a certain threshold, namely the *collision count threshold* θ, the object is likely to be a neighbor. Such an object is considered as a candidate and retrieved for computing its real distance to the query.

As a result, an $\mathcal{N}_2(\vec{q}, k, c)$ query can be answered by C2LSH by issuing a set of $\mathcal{R}_2(\vec{q}, c, r)$ queries with increasing radii. C2LSH is claimed to be correct if these two properties hold with a constant probability.

- $\mathcal{P}_1$: If $\vec{v} \in B_2(\vec{q}, r)$, then the number of $\vec{v}$'s collision with the query $\vec{q}$ is at least θ.
- $\mathcal{P}_2$: The total number of false positives is smaller than $\beta|\mathcal{D}|$, where $|\mathcal{D}|$ is the cardinality of the database $\mathcal{D}$.

In $\mathcal{P}_1$, the number of collisions θ is related to the number of base hash functions, which is denoted as η. Given an error probability ε and a false positive rate β, θ and η must be carefully tuned for the best performance.

LEMMA 1. *If η and θ are set to:*

$$\eta = \lceil \frac{\ln \frac{1}{\varepsilon}}{2(p_1 - p_2)^2}(1+z)^2 \rceil, \text{ where } z = \sqrt{\frac{\ln \frac{2}{\beta}}{\ln \frac{1}{\varepsilon}}}, \quad (8)$$

$$\theta = \frac{zp_1 + p_2}{1+z}\eta, \quad (9)$$

then $Pr[\mathcal{P}_1] \geq 1 - \varepsilon$ and $Pr[\mathcal{P}_2] \geq 0.5$. [21]

Therefore, both $\mathcal{P}_1$ and $\mathcal{P}_2$ hold with a constant probability when the parameters are set as above, and C2LSH can correctly answer the $\mathcal{N}_2(\vec{q}, c, r)$ query.

3. LAZYLSH

In this section, we present LazyLSH as an efficient mechanism to process approximate kNN queries in different ℓ_p spaces. We begin with an overview, and then illustrate the technical details of LazyLSH.

3.1 Overview

In previous work such as E2LSH and C2LSH, an LSH index is built for the ℓ_2 space, while Aggarwal et al. [1] showed that the fractional distance metrics ($0 < p < 1$) provide more meaningful results and improve the effectiveness of information retrieval algorithms. Extending techniques in E2LSH and C2LSH to support an arbitrary fractional distance metric is not a trivial task. In this paper, we present LazyLSH, a novel approach that can process approximate nearest neighbor queries using different fractional distance metrics with a single LSH index.

LazyLSH is proposed based on the intuition that given $p, s > 0$, if two points are close in the ℓ_p space, then they are likely to be close in the ℓ_s space. Let $\epsilon = |p - s|$. The property holds with a higher probability for a smaller ϵ. This property can be extended as: the (r, cr, p_1, p_2)-sensitive hash function in the ℓ_p space is $(\delta, c\delta, p_1', p_2')$-sensitive in the ℓ_s space if certain conditions hold. We will give a detailed theoretical analysis for this property later in this section.

Using this property, LazyLSH can transform the hash functions between different ℓ_p spaces. LSH families for the ℓ_1 and ℓ_2 metrics have been well studied [4, 45, 21]. As the ℓ_1 metric is closer to the fractional distance metrics, in LazyLSH, we materialize the LSH index in the ℓ_1 space as our base index. We generate η_p base hash functions $h_1^*(\cdot)$, ..., $h_{\eta_p}^*(\cdot)$, where the setting of η_p will be discussed later. In particular, we construct $h_i^*(\cdot)$ as:

$$h_i^*(\vec{v}) = \lfloor \frac{\vec{a_i}.\vec{v} + b_i^*}{r_0} \rfloor, \quad (10)$$

where $\vec{a_i}$ is a random vector whose each entry is drawn from the 1-stable (Cauchy) distribution and the other parameters are the same as the ones in Equation 6. Each base hash function $h_i^*(\cdot)$ is $(1, c, p_1, p_2)$-sensitive in the ℓ_1 space, with $p_1 = p(1, r_0)$, $p_2 = p(c, r_0)$ as presented in Equation 4.

Using the materialized index, LazyLSH can answer $\mathcal{N}_p(\vec{q}, k, c)$ queries with probabilistic guarantees. For the ease of presentation, we first show our observation that an (r, cr, p_1, p_2)-sensitive hash function in the ℓ_p space is $(\delta, c\delta, p_1', p_2')$-sensitive in another ℓ_s space in this section. Then we illustrate how the LazyLSH method answers $\mathcal{R}_p(\vec{q}, r, c)$ and $\mathcal{N}_p(\vec{q}, k, c)$ queries in Section 4.

3.2 LSH in an ℓ_p Space

If there exists a point $\vec{o} \in B_p(\vec{q}, \delta)$, an $\mathcal{R}_p(\vec{q}, \delta, c)$ query returns a point $\vec{o'}$ if $\vec{o'} \in B_p(\vec{q}, c\delta)$. We observe that $B_p(\vec{q}, \delta)$ and $B_1(\vec{q}, r)$ share a lot of common areas if r is carefully tuned for δ. Figure 2 plots a $B_1(\vec{q}, r)$ ball in blue and a $B_p(\vec{q}, \delta)$ ball in red, where $0 < p < 1$. The shadow region represents the intersection of $B_1(\vec{q}, r)$ and $B_p(\vec{q}, \delta)$ which takes over a large portion of $B_p(\vec{q}, \delta)$. This observation motivates us to use a ball $B_1(\vec{q}, r)$ in the ℓ_1 space to approximate $B_p(\vec{q}, \delta)$ in the ℓ_p space for the query $\mathcal{R}_p(\vec{q}, \delta, c)$.

Given two points $\vec{q}, \vec{o} \in \mathbb{R}^d$, with $\ell_p(\vec{q}, \vec{o}) = \delta$. We can compute the lower bound and upper bound of δ in the ℓ_1 space, denoted as $\delta^\perp$ and $\delta^\top$ respectively. Figure 3 shows the geometric interpretations of $\delta^\perp$ and $\delta^\top$ for $0 < p < 1$ and $p > 1$. The values of $\delta^\perp$ and $\delta^\top$ are computed as:

$$\delta^\perp = \begin{cases} \frac{d \times \delta}{\sqrt[p]{d}} & \text{if } 0 < p < 1 \\ \delta & \text{if } p \geq 1 \end{cases} \qquad \delta^\top = \begin{cases} \delta & \text{if } 0 < p < 1 \\ \frac{d \times \delta}{\sqrt[p]{d}} & \text{if } p \geq 1 \end{cases} \quad (11)$$

Our goal is to use an ℓ_1 ball $B_1(\vec{q}, r)$ to approximate the

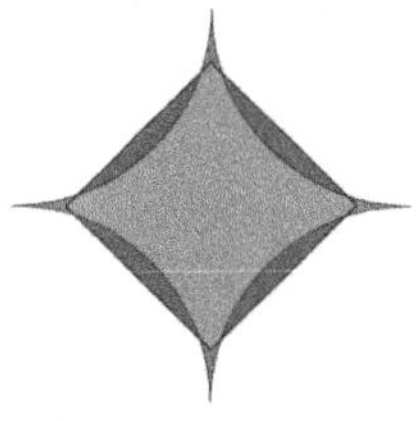

Figure 2: Use $B_1(\vec{q}, r)$ to approximate $B_p(\vec{q}, \delta)$ (Best viewed in color)

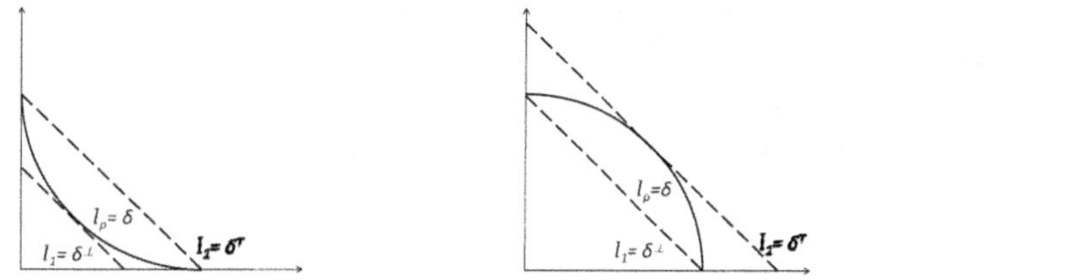

(a) $0 < p < 1$ (b) $p > 1$

Figure 3: Bounds of ℓ_p distance

ℓ_p ball $B_p(\vec{q}, \delta)$ specified by the query $\mathcal{R}_p(\vec{q},\ \delta,\ c)$. The radius r significantly affects the search performance. If $r < \delta^{\perp}$, we may fail to retrieve many candidate results, leading to many false negatives. On the other hand, if $r > \delta^{\top}$, many irrelevant objects are retrieved, generating many false positives. Therefore, a proper r should be chosen in the range of $[\delta^{\perp}, \delta^{\top}]$ for $B_1(\vec{q}, r)$ to approximate $B_p(\vec{q}, \delta)$.

Given a query $\mathcal{R}_p(\vec{q},\ \delta,\ c)$ and a based $(1, c, p_1, p_2)$-sensitive hash function $h_i^*(\cdot)$, we modify $h_i^*(\cdot)$ as follows:

$$h_i^r(\vec{v}) = \lfloor \frac{\vec{a_i}.\vec{v} + b_i^*}{r_0 r} \rfloor, \tag{12}$$

where r is in $[\delta^{\perp}, \delta^{\top}]$ as discussed above. It is easy to see that $h_i^r(\cdot)$ is $(r,\ cr,\ p(r, r_0 r),\ p(cr, r_0 r))$-sensitive in the ℓ_1 space, where $p(\cdot,\cdot)$ is defined in Equation 3. We further observe the following lemma.

LEMMA 2. *Let $p(s,r) = \int_0^r \frac{1}{s} f_p(\frac{t}{s})(1 - \frac{t}{r})dt$ as shown in Equation 3. For any real number $c > 0$, $p(s,r) = p(cs, cr)$.*

PROOF. See Appendix A.1. □

By Lemma 2, we get $p(r, r_0 r) = p(1, r_0) = p_1$ and $p(cr, r_0 r) = p(c, r_0) = p_2$, where p_1 and p_2 are the same as the ones defined in the base materialized hash function $h_i^*(\cdot)$.

Recall that our LSH index is built in the ℓ_1 space. The LSH family guarantees that close points in the ℓ_1 space are likely to be hashed into the same bucket. We are interested in whether an LSH function in the ℓ_1 space is still locality-sensitive in another ℓ_p space. Given an $(r,\ cr,\ p_1,\ p_2)$-sensitive hash function $h_i^r(\cdot)$ in the ℓ_1 space, we define the following events for any two points $\vec{o}, \vec{q} \in \mathbb{R}^d$:

$e_1 : h_i^r(\vec{o}) = h_i^r(\vec{q})$.
$e_2 : \ell_p(\vec{o}, \vec{q}) \leq \delta$. $\quad e_3 : \ell_p(\vec{o}, \vec{q}) > c\delta$,
$e_4 : \ell_1(\vec{o}, \vec{q}) \leq r$. $\quad e_5 : \ell_1(\vec{o}, \vec{q}) > cr$, where $c > 1$

To verify whether the modified hash function $h_i^r(\cdot)$ is locality-sensitive in the ℓ_p space, we need to calculate the probability of e_1 given e_2 and the probability of e_1 given e_3, i.e. $Pr(e_1|e_2)$ and $Pr(e_1|e_3)$ respectively. Let e^c represent the complementary of event e. By Bayes' Theorem, we compute a lower bound of $Pr(e_1|e_2)$:

$$\begin{aligned}
Pr(e_1|e_2) &= Pr(e_1 \wedge e_4|e_2) + Pr(e_1 \wedge e_4^c|e_2) \\
&= Pr(e_4|e_2)Pr(e_1|e_4 \wedge e_2) + Pr(e_4^c|e_2)Pr(e_1|e_4^c \wedge e_2) \\
&\quad (\text{Note: } Pr(e_1|e_4 \wedge e_2) \geq Pr(e_1|e_4) \geq p_1, \text{ and} \\
&\quad \ell_p(\vec{o}, \vec{q}) \leq \delta \text{ implies } \ell_1(\vec{o}, \vec{q}) \leq \delta^{\top}\ ) \\
&\geq Pr(e_4|e_2)p_1 + (1 - Pr(e_4|e_2))p(\delta^{\top}, r_0 r) \\
&= Pr(e_4|e_2)p_1 + (1 - Pr(e_4|e_2))p(1, \frac{r_0 r}{\delta^{\top}})
\end{aligned} \tag{13}$$

This is because $p(s,r)$ is monotonically decreasing with s when r is fixed. We infer $p(1, \frac{r_0 r}{\delta^{\top}}) \leq p_1$ from $\delta^{\perp} \leq r \leq \delta^{\top}$. For simplicity, we use p_1' to denote this lower bound. Consequently, we get $p_1' \leq p_1$. Similarly, we compute an upper bound of $Pr(e_1|e_3)$:

$$\begin{aligned}
Pr(e_1|e_3) =& Pr(e_1 \wedge e_5|e_3) + Pr(e_1 \wedge e_5^c|e_3) \\
=& Pr(e_5|e_3)Pr(e_1|e_5 \wedge e_3) + Pr(e_5^c|e_3)Pr(e_1|e_5^c \wedge e_3) \\
& (\text{Note: } Pr(e_1|e_5 \wedge e_3) \leq Pr(e_1|e_5) \leq p_2, \text{ and} \\
& \ell_p(\vec{o}, \vec{q}) > c\delta \text{ implies } \ell_1(\vec{o}, \vec{q}) > c\delta^{\perp}\ ) \\
\leq& Pr(e_5|e_3)p_2 + (1 - Pr(e_5|e_3))p(c\delta^{\perp}, r_0 r) \\
=& Pr(e_5|e_3)p_2 + (1 - Pr(e_5|e_3))p(c, r_0 r/\delta^{\perp}) \\
\leq& \begin{cases} p_2 & \text{if } p_2 \geq p(c, r_0 r/\delta^{\perp}), \text{ i.e. } r \leq \delta^{\perp} \\ p(c, r_0 r/\delta^{\perp}) & \text{otherwise} \end{cases} \\
& (\text{Note: we set } \delta^{\perp} \leq r \leq \delta^{\top}\ ) \\
=& p(c, r_0 r/\delta^{\perp})
\end{aligned} \tag{14}$$

Then, we use p_2' to denote $p(c, r_0 r/\delta^{\perp})$. Based on the above two inequalities, we have the following theorem:

THEOREM 1. *Given an $(r,\ cr,\ p_1,\ p_2)$-sensitive hash function $h_i^r(\cdot)$ in the ℓ_1 space, we find the following two conditions hold for a distance threshold δ in another ℓ_p space, where $\delta^{\perp} \leq r \leq \delta^{\top}$:*
(1) if $\ell_p(\vec{o}, \vec{q}) \leq \delta$, then $Pr[h_i^r(\vec{o}) = h_i^r(\vec{q})] \geq p_1'$,
(2) if $\ell_p(\vec{o}, \vec{q}) > c\delta$, then $Pr[h_i^r(\vec{o}) = h_i^r(\vec{q})] < p_2'$,
where p_1' and p_2' are stated as stated above.

$$p_1' = Pr(e_4|e_2)p_1 + (1 - Pr(e_4|e_2))p(1, \frac{r_0 r}{\delta^{\top}})$$
$$p_2' = p(c, r_0 r/\delta^{\perp})$$

3.3 Computing Internal Parameters

To ensure the correctness of LazyLSH, two parameters are required to be computed. One is the radius r of an ℓ_1 ball $B_1(\vec{q}, r)$ to approximate the ℓ_p ball $B_p(\vec{q}, \delta)$ for query $\mathcal{R}_p(\vec{q},\ \delta,\ c)$. The other is the number of required hash functions to be built, which is denoted as η_p. Then we present how to compute them.

Recall the definition of LSH, we must have $p_1' > p_2'$ so that the hash function $h_i^r(\cdot)$ is locality-sensitive in the ℓ_p space. By substituting p_1' and p_2', we have $p_2' = p(c, r_0 r/\delta^{\perp}) = p(c\delta^{\perp}/r, r_0) < p_1' \leq p_1 = p(1, r_0)$. Note that $p(s,r)$ is monotonically decreasing with s when r is fixed. Thus, we get $c\delta^{\perp}/r > 1$ as a necessary condition, which infers $r < c\delta^{\perp}$. Besides, we have $\delta^{\perp} \leq r \leq \delta^{\top}$ as we explained before. In summary, r must be chosen properly in the range of $[\delta^{\perp}, \min(\delta^{\top}, c\delta^{\perp})]$ in order for $p_1' > p_2'$ to hold. In details,

Algorithm 1: Sampling a point in $B_p(\vec{o}, 1)$ [13]

input : dimensionality d, ℓ_p space
output: a random point $\vec{y}$ in $B_p(\vec{o}, 1)$, where $\vec{o}$ is the origin

1 Generate d independent random real scalars $\xi_i \sim \tilde{G}(1, 1, p)$;
2 Construct a vector $\vec{x} \in \mathbb{R}^d$ of components $x_i = s_i \xi_i$, where s_i is an independent random sign;
3 Construct $z = w^{1/d}$, where w is a random variable uniformly distributed in the interval [0, 1] ;
4 **return** $\vec{y} = z \frac{\vec{x}}{\ell_p(\vec{x}, \vec{o})}$;

Algorithm 2: Calculating $Pr(\ell_1(\vec{o}, \vec{q}) \leq r | \ell_p(\vec{o}, \vec{q}) \leq 1)$

input : dimensionality d, ℓ_p space, the number of sample points n, the number of buckets b
output: an array p storing $Pr(\ell_1(\vec{o}, \vec{q}) \leq r | \ell_p(\vec{o}, \vec{q}) \leq 1)$ with different values of r

1 Initialize an array r of b dimensions recording the radii, $r[i] = \delta^{\perp} + (i+1) \times \frac{\min(\delta^{\top}, c\delta^{\perp}) - \delta^{\perp}}{b}$ for $0 \leq i < b$;
2 Initialize an array c of b dimensions to record the number of points in $B_1(\vec{o}, r)$, $c[i] \leftarrow 0$ for $0 \leq i < b$;
3 **for** $k \leftarrow 0$ **to** $n - 1$ **do**
4   $\vec{v} \leftarrow$ a random point in $B_p(\vec{o}, 1)$;
5   Compute $\ell_1(\vec{o}, \vec{v})$; /* $\vec{o}$ is the origin */
6   Find the minimal index j such that $r[j] \geq \ell_1(\vec{o}, \vec{v})$;
7   **for** $i \leftarrow j$ **to** $b - 1$ **do**
8     $c[i] \leftarrow c[i] + 1$;
9 **for** $i \leftarrow 0$ **to** $b - 1$ **do**
10   $p[i] \leftarrow \frac{c[i]}{n}$;
11 **return** p;

r is a parameter for the functions of p_1' and p_2'. p_2' can be simply computed using Equation 4 when we build the base LSH index in the ℓ_1 space, while computing p_1' is a nontrivial task. We begin with a lemma on the conditional probability.

LEMMA 3. *$Pr(\ell_s(\vec{x}, \vec{y}) \leq r | \ell_p(\vec{x}, \vec{y}) \leq \delta) = Pr(\ell_s(\vec{u}, \vec{v}) \leq cr | \ell_p(\vec{u}, \vec{v}) \leq c\delta)$ for any $s, p, c > 0$.*

PROOF. See Appendix A.2. □

Based on Lemma 3, we can reduce the problem of calculating $Pr(e_4|e_2)$ to the computation of $Pr(\ell_1(\vec{o}, \vec{q}) \leq r \mid \ell_p(\vec{o}, \vec{q}) \leq 1)$, where $\delta = 1$ and $\delta^{\perp} \leq r < \min(\delta^{\top}, c\delta^{\perp})$. $Pr(\ell_1(\vec{o}, \vec{q}) \leq r | \ell_p(\vec{o}, \vec{q}) \leq 1)$ can be computed as follows:

$$Pr(\ell_1(\vec{o}, \vec{q}) \leq r | \ell_p(\vec{o}, \vec{q}) \leq 1) = \frac{Vol(B_1(\vec{q}, r) \bigcap B_p(\vec{q}, 1))}{Vol(B_p(\vec{q}, 1))}, \tag{15}$$

where $Vol(\cdot)$ outputs the volume of a given shape.

The challenge, however, is that computing the volume of $(B_1(\vec{q}, r) \bigcap B_p(\vec{q}, 1))$ for a random p and r exactly is very expensive if not impossible. Alternatively, we use the Monte Carlo method [9] to estimate $Pr(\ell_1(\vec{o}, \vec{q}) \leq r | \ell_p(\vec{o}, \vec{q}) \leq 1)$. Basically, this estimation is done by randomly sampling points in $B_p(\vec{q}, 1)$ and then calculating the percentage of the sampled points in $B_1(\vec{q}, r)$. Suppose we randomly sample n points in $B_p(\vec{q}, 1)$, and find that m points are in $B_1(\vec{q}, r)$ as well. $\frac{m}{n}$ is roughly equal to $Pr(\ell_1(\vec{o}, \vec{q}) \leq r | \ell_p(\vec{o}, \vec{q}) \leq 1)$ if the number of samples is large enough.

$$Pr(\ell_1(\vec{o}, \vec{q}) \leq r | \ell_p(\vec{o}, \vec{q}) \leq 1) \approx \frac{m}{n}, \tag{16}$$

Note that the location of the center does not affect the probability. As a result, we sample points in $B_p(\vec{o}, 1)$, where $\vec{o}$ represents the origin. Given a d-dimensional space and a value of p, we can randomly sample points in $B_p(\vec{o}, 1)$ using Algorithm 1 [13]. In line 1, ξ_i is a random variable generated from a Generalized Gamma density function.

DEFINITION 7 (GENERALIZED GAMMA DENSITY [42]). *A random variable $x \in \mathbb{R}$ is generalized gamma distributed with three parameters $\alpha > 0$, $\lambda > 0$ and $\upsilon > 0$, denoted as $x \sim \tilde{G}(\alpha, \lambda, \upsilon)$, when x has the following density function:*

$$f(x) = \frac{\upsilon / \alpha^{\lambda}}{\Gamma(\lambda/\upsilon)} x^{\lambda - 1} e^{-(x/\alpha)^{\upsilon}}, x \geq 0. \tag{17}$$

A random Generalized Gamma variable $x \sim \tilde{G}(1, \lambda, \upsilon)$ can be obtained from a Gamma random variable $z \sim G(\frac{\lambda}{\upsilon}, 1)$ as $x = z^{1/\upsilon}$ [42].

The formula involves the gamma function $\Gamma(t)$ $(t > 0)$, which is computed as:

$$\Gamma(t) = \int_0^{\infty} x^{t-1} e^{-x} dx, t > 0. \tag{18}$$

Therefore, we can sample points in $B_p(\vec{o}, 1)$ using Algorithm 1. Next we compute $Pr(\ell_1(\vec{o}, \vec{q}) \leq r | \ell_p(\vec{o}, \vec{q}) \leq 1)$ w.r.t. different values of r. As r is chosen in $[\delta^{\perp}, \min(\delta^{\top}, c\delta^{\perp})]$, we divide $[\delta^{\perp}, \min(\delta^{\top}, c\delta^{\perp})]$ into b buckets. Thus, we get the length of each bucket: $\phi = (\min(\delta^{\top}, c\delta^{\perp}) - \delta^{\perp})/b$. Afterwards, we set r to $(\delta^{\perp} + \phi)$, $(\delta^{\perp} + 2\phi)$, ..., $\min(\delta^{\top}, c\delta^{\perp})$ respectively and compute $Pr(\ell_1(\vec{o}, \vec{q}) \leq r | \ell_p(\vec{o}, \vec{q}) \leq 1)$, as described in Algorithm 2.

We initialize a counter to record the number of sample points that are located in $B_1(\vec{o}, r)$ for each radius r (line 2). Then, we randomly sample n points in $B_p(\vec{o}, 1)$. For each sampled point $\vec{v}$, we calculate its distance $\ell_1(\vec{v}, \vec{o})$ to $\vec{o}$ in the ℓ_1 space. For all the radii r greater than $\ell_1(\vec{v}, \vec{o})$, we know that the sample point $\vec{v}$ is inside $B_1(\vec{o}, r)$. Then we add one to the corresponding counters (lines 6-8). After sampling n points, we output $Pr(\ell_1(\vec{o}, \vec{q}) \leq r | \ell_p(\vec{o}, \vec{q}) \leq 1)$ for different values of r (lines 9-11). Algorithm 2 is an offline process. The approximation is more accurate if we sample more points and maintain more buckets. In the experiments, we set the number of sample points n to 1,000,000 and the number of buckets b to 1000.

Once we get the value of $Pr(\ell_1(\vec{o}, \vec{q}) \leq r | \ell_p(\vec{o}, \vec{q}) \leq 1)$, which is equal to $Pr(e_4|e_2)$, we can compute p_1' and p_2' as shown in Equations 13 and 14. In particular, $p(\cdot, \cdot)$ is computed as the one in Equation 4, because we build the base index in the ℓ_1 space. Figure 4 plots the values of p_1' and p_2' w.r.t. r for $\ell_{0.5}$ in $\mathbb{R}^{128}$ when the approximate ratio c is set to 2. The x axis represents the ratio of r to $\delta_{\perp}$, i.e. $(\frac{r}{\delta_{\perp}})$. As can be seen in the figure, p_2' increases smoothly. In contrast, p_1' increases slowly at the beginning. When the ratio reaches 1.4, p_1' increases dramatically. When the ratio reaches around 1.55, p_1' exceeds p_2' and grows slowly at the end. We are interested in the cases when $p_1' > p_2'$.

Recall that a (1, c, p_1, p_2)-sensitive hash function requires $p_1 > p_2$. In addition, the number of base hash functions η must be set to a certain value to ensure the correctness of the algorithm, which is related to $(p_1 - p_2)$ as shown in Equation 8 [21]. Equation 8 shows that the greater $(p_1 - p_2)$ is, the less base hash functions are required, resulting in less storage overhead. Therefore, we choose an optimal radius r, denoted as $\hat{r}$, by maximizing $(p_1' - p_2')$.

$$\hat{r} = \arg\max_r \, (p_1' - p_2') \tag{19}$$

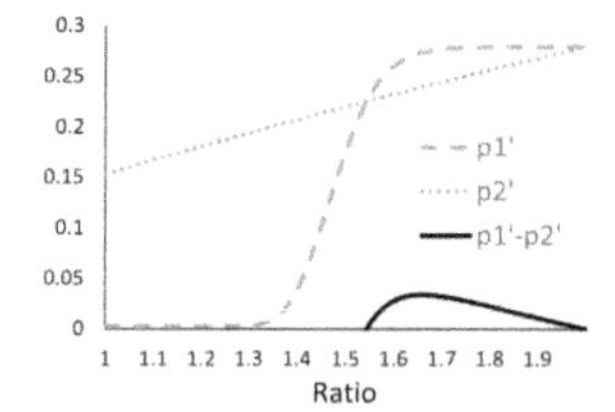

Figure 4: Values of p_1' and p_2' for $\ell_{0.5}$ in $\mathbb{R}^{128}$, $c = 2$

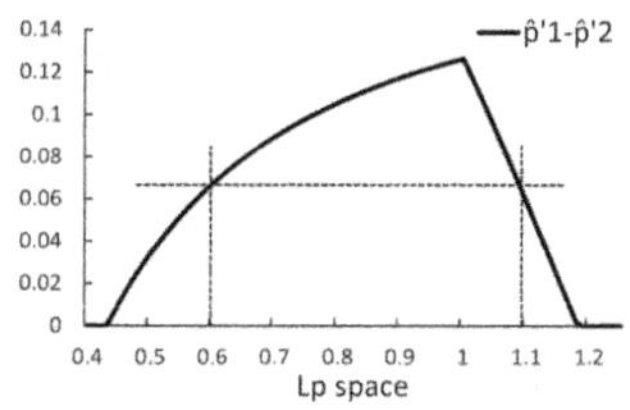

Figure 5: $(\hat{p}_1' - \hat{p}_2')$ w.r.t the ℓ_p spaces in $\mathbb{R}^{128}$, $c = 2$

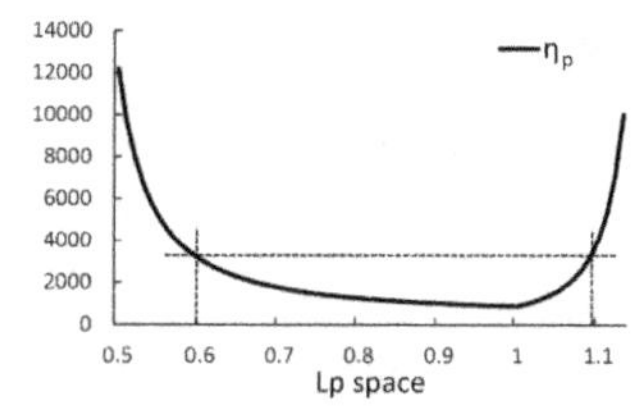

Figure 6: Number of hash functions required η_p in $\mathbb{R}^{128}$

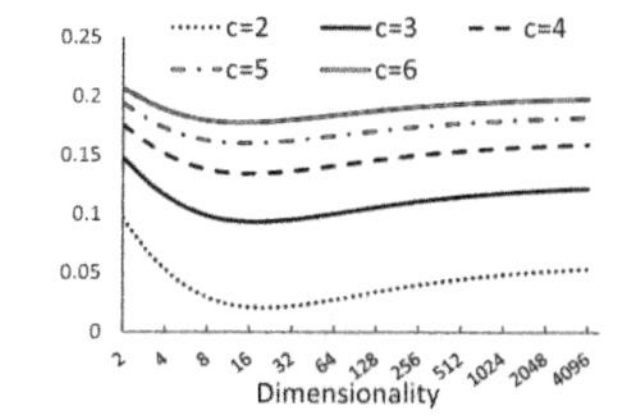

Figure 7: $(\hat{p}_1' - \hat{p}_2')$ w.r.t d in the $\ell_{0.5}$ space

For different ℓ_p spaces, the value of $\hat{r}$ varies. We pre-compute and save the values of $\hat{r}$ for different ℓ_p spaces, which is used when processing a query. Besides, we store the values of p_1' and p_2' when $r = \hat{r}$, which are denoted as $\hat{p}_1'$ and $\hat{p}_2'$ respectively. They are used to compute the number of required hash functions η_p when building the index and the collision count threshold θ_p in processing a query. Figure 5 plots $(\hat{p}_1' - \hat{p}_2')$ w.r.t. different ℓ_p spaces in $\mathbb{R}^{128}$, where the approximate ratio c is set to 2. When $p < 1$, $(\hat{p}_1' - \hat{p}_2')$ drops when p decreases. When $p < 0.44$, $\hat{p}_1'$ is always smaller than $\hat{p}_2'$, which indicates that the hash function built in the ℓ_1 space is no longer locality-sensitive in the corresponding ℓ_p space. When $p > 1$, $(\hat{p}_1' - \hat{p}_2')$ drops significantly when p increases. When $p > 1.18$, $\hat{p}_1'$ is always smaller than $\hat{p}_2'$.

Next, we calculate the number of required hash functions η_p for different ℓ_p spaces, which is computed as

$$\eta_p = \lceil \frac{\ln \frac{1}{\varepsilon}}{2(\hat{p}_1' - \hat{p}_2')^2}(1+z)^2 \rceil, \text{ where } z = \sqrt{\frac{\ln \frac{2}{\beta}}{\ln \frac{1}{\varepsilon}}}, \tag{20}$$

where ε and β are the same as the ones defined in Equation 8. Figure 6 plots η_p w.r.t. different ℓ_p spaces in $\mathbb{R}^{128}$, where $c = 2$, $\varepsilon = 0.01$ and $\beta = 0.0001$. When $p < 1$, η_p increases when p decreases, because η_p is inversely proportional to $(\hat{p}_1' - \hat{p}_2')$. Suppose we want to support a query $\mathcal{R}_{0.6}(\vec{q}, \delta, c)$ in the $\ell_{0.6}$ space. Correspondingly, at least $\eta_{0.6}$ hash functions are required to be materialized for the base index. Suppose we materialize $\eta_{0.6}$ hash functions as the base index. Using $\eta_{0.6}$ base hash functions, queries $\mathcal{R}_p(\vec{q}, r, c)$ can be answered in the ℓ_p spaces where $\eta_p \leq \eta_{0.6}$, as shown by the dashed line ($0.6 \leq p \leq 1.1$) in Figure 6.

4. QUERY PROCESSING

In this section, we discuss how to leverage LazyLSH to process approximate range queries ($\mathcal{R}_p(\vec{q}, \delta, c)$) and approximate nearest neighbor queries ($\mathcal{N}_p(\vec{q}, k, c)$) in different ℓ_p spaces.

4.1 Processing $\mathcal{R}_p(\vec{q}, \delta, c)$

Equation 20 indicates that we can find η_s and $\eta_{s'}$ with $s < s'$ and $\eta_s = \eta_{s'}$. Namely, two spaces share the same η value. This idea is also shown in Figure 5, where we get the same value of $|\hat{p}_1' - \hat{p}_2'|$ in $\ell_{0.6}$ and $\ell_{1.1}$. Suppose we have materialized η_s hash functions as the base index, where $0 < s < 1$. $\mathcal{R}_p(\vec{q}, \delta, c)$ queries can be answered in a series of ℓ_p spaces using the base index, where $s \leq p \leq s'$.

We use the $B_1(\vec{q}, \hat{r}\delta)$ ball in the ℓ_1 space to approximate the $B_p(\vec{q}, \delta)$ ball in the ℓ_p space as described in the previous section. We also pre-compute the corresponding $\hat{p}_1'$ and $\hat{p}_2'$ for the query ℓ_p space. To answer an $\mathcal{R}_p(\vec{q}, \delta, c)$ query, we

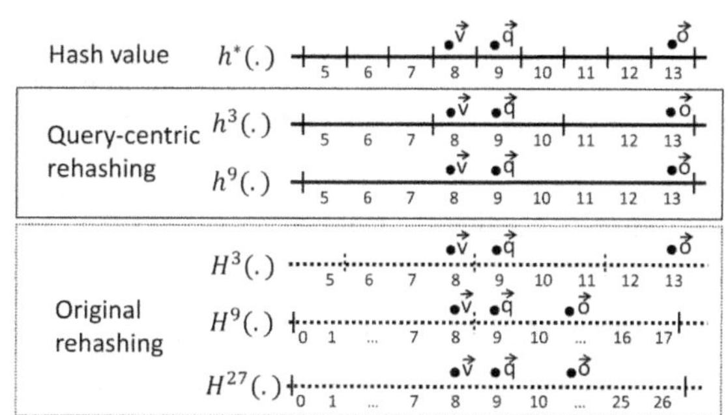

Figure 8: Query-centric rehashing

modify the base hash function $h_i^*(\cdot)$ as $h_i^{\hat{r}\delta}(\cdot)$

$$h_i^{\hat{r}\delta}(\vec{v}) = \lfloor \frac{h_i^*(\vec{v}) - (h_i^*(\vec{q}) \bmod \lfloor \hat{r}\delta \rfloor) + \lfloor \frac{3\hat{r}\delta}{2} \rfloor}{\hat{r}\delta} \rfloor \tag{21}$$

$(h_i^*(\vec{q}) \bmod \lfloor \hat{r}\delta \rfloor)$ can be viewed as a random integer as $\vec{q}$ is not known beforehand. Thus, $(\lfloor \frac{3\hat{r}\delta}{2} \rfloor - (h_i^*(\vec{q}) \bmod \lfloor \hat{r}\delta \rfloor))$ is a random positive integer, and $h_i^{\hat{r}\delta}(\cdot)$ is $(\hat{r}\delta, c\hat{r}\delta, p_1, p_2)$-sensitive in the ℓ_1 space. Based on Theorem 1, we know that $h_i^{\hat{r}\delta}(\cdot)$ is also $(\delta, c\delta, \hat{p}_1', \hat{p}_2')$-sensitive in the ℓ_p space if $\hat{p}_1' > \hat{p}_2'$.

Given a query $\mathcal{R}_p(\vec{q}, \delta, c)$ and the base hash functions, if an object collides with $\vec{q}$ more than θ_p times, the object is considered as a candidate. In particular, θ_p is defined as:

$$\theta_p = \frac{z\hat{p}_1' + \hat{p}_2'}{1+z}\eta_p, \tag{22}$$

The $\mathcal{R}_p(\vec{q}, \delta, c)$ query is processed by retrieving the objects that are hashed to the same bucket as $\vec{q}$ for $h_i^{\delta\hat{r}}(\cdot)$. We adopt the virtual rehashing method [21]. If a point $\vec{v}$ has the same hash value as the query, i.e. $h_i^{\delta\hat{r}}(\vec{v}) = h_i^{\delta\hat{r}}(\vec{q})$, we can get the value range of $h_i^*(\vec{v})$ by expanding the equation.

$$h_i^*(\vec{q}) - \lfloor \frac{\delta\hat{r}}{2} \rfloor \leq h_i^*(\vec{v}) \leq h_i^*(\vec{q}) + \lfloor \frac{\delta\hat{r}}{2} \rfloor \tag{23}$$

From the above equation, we observe that the points hashed into the range of $[\, h_i^*(\vec{q}) - \lfloor \frac{\delta\hat{r}}{2} \rfloor, h_i^*(\vec{q}) + \lfloor \frac{\delta\hat{r}}{2} \rfloor \,]$ in $h_i^*(\cdot)$ will collide with the query point which is mapped to the same bucket $h_i^{\delta\hat{r}}(\vec{q})$. We can see that the center of this range is the query point. Thus, we refer to the proposed hash function $h_i^{\hat{r}\delta}(\cdot)$ as the *query-centric rehashing* function.

Figure 8 presents the advantage of the proposed *query-centric rehashing* function. Suppose $\vec{q}$ is the query point. The first line represents the based hash function $h^*(\vec{q})$, where points $\vec{v}$, $\vec{q}$ and $\vec{o}$ are hashed to buckets 8, 9 and 13 respectively. The solid rectangle represents our proposed *query-centric rehashing* function for radius $r = 3, 9$, whereas the dashed rectangle represents the original rehashing function in Equation 7. For the *query-centric rehashing* function $h^r(\cdot)$, $\vec{q}$ and $\vec{v}$ are hashed to the same bucket when $r = 3$, while $\vec{q}$ and $\vec{o}$ are hashed to the same bucket when $r = 9$. In contrast, for $H^r(\cdot)$, $\vec{q}$ and $\vec{o}$ are hashed to the same bucket when $r = 9$, while $\vec{q}$ and $\vec{v}$ are hashed to the same bucket when $r = 27$. We notice that the query point $\vec{q}$ is actually closer to $\vec{v}$ compared with $\vec{o}$, and thus $\vec{q}$ should collide with $\vec{v}$ in the same bucket first. Our proposed *query-centric rehashing* function can hold this property while $H^r(\cdot)$ cannot. In particular, $H^r(\cdot)$ might perform poorly in some cases, for example, when a query point is hashed to the bucket whose id is a multiple of the radius.

Algorithm 3 shows the pseudo code of processing an $\mathcal{R}_p(\vec{q}, \delta, c)$ query. An object with collision count larger than θ_p is considered as a candidate and its real distance to the query is computed. The algorithm stops until $\beta|\mathcal{D}|$ candidates are found. The algorithm is sound if the following two properties hold with a constant probability.

1. $\mathcal{P}_1'$: If $\vec{v} \in B_p(\vec{q}, \delta)$, then the number of $\vec{v}$'s collision with the query $\vec{q}$ is at least θ_p.

2. $\mathcal{P}_2'$: The total number of false positives is smaller than $\beta|\mathcal{D}|$, where $|\mathcal{D}|$ is the cardinality of a database $\mathcal{D}$.

Corollary 1 guarantees the correctness of the algorithm.

COROLLARY 1. *Given a error probability ε and a false positive rate β, if η_p is set as the one in Equation 20, we have $Pr(\mathcal{P}_1') \geq (1 - \varepsilon)$ and $Pr(\mathcal{P}_2') \geq 1/2$*

PROOF. This is a corollary of Lemma 1 in [21]. We refer readers to [21] for more details. □

4.2 Processing $\mathcal{N}_p(\vec{q}, k, c)$

The nearest neighbor query can be processed in a similar way. Algorithm 4 presents the general idea which can be viewed as the processing of a set of $\mathcal{R}_p(\vec{q}, \delta, c)$ queries with increasing radii. We initialize the starting radius to be $\frac{1}{\hat{r}}$ and issue an $\mathcal{R}_p(\vec{q}, \delta, c)$ query. If not enough results are found, we increase the radius to be $c\delta$ and issue a new range query. The process continues until enough results are returned.

We iteratively retrieve the points that are hashed into the range of $[\ h_i^*(\vec{q}) - \lfloor\frac{\delta\hat{r}}{2}\rfloor, h_i^*(\vec{q}) + \lfloor\frac{\delta\hat{r}}{2}\rfloor\ ]$ for $h_i^*(\cdot)$, because they collide with the query point for the modified hash function. However, as we have visited the points that are hashed in $[\ h_i^*(\vec{q}) - \lfloor\frac{\delta\hat{r}}{2c}\rfloor, h_i^*(\vec{q}) + \lfloor\frac{\delta\hat{r}}{2c}\rfloor\ ]$ in the last iteration when the radius is (δ/c), we skip those IDs (line 10).

The algorithm stops if (1) we have obtained k candidates whose ℓ_p distance to q is smaller than $c\delta$, or (2) we have found more than $k + \beta|\mathcal{D}|$ candidates with collision count larger than θ_p (lines 15-16). The stop conditions are defined based on $\mathcal{P}_1'$ and $\mathcal{P}_2'$ respectively. In particular, $\mathcal{P}_1'$ guarantees that a candidate will be found, and $\mathcal{P}_2'$ ensures that there are no more than $\beta|\mathcal{D}|$ false positives. Therefore, we can stop the algorithm early and return the approximate kNNs of q in the ℓ_p space.

Algorithm 3: Answering $\mathcal{R}_p(\vec{q}, \delta, c)$

$T \leftarrow$ a hash table to record the collision count for each database object ;
$C \leftarrow$ a list to record the candidates ;
$\hat{r} \leftarrow$ the radius of $B_1(\vec{q}, \hat{r})$ to approximate $B_p(\vec{q}, 1)$;
for $i \leftarrow 0$ **to** $\eta_p - 1$ **do**
  Compute $h_i^{*\delta\hat{r}}(\vec{q})$;
  Read the IDs that are hashed in the range of $[\ h_i^*(\vec{q}) - \lfloor\frac{\delta\hat{r}}{2}\rfloor, h_i^*(\vec{q}) + \lfloor\frac{\delta\hat{r}}{2}\rfloor\ ]$ for $h_i^*(\cdot)$;
  foreach *object* $\vec{v} \in IDs$ **do**
    $T[\vec{v}] \leftarrow T[\vec{v}] + 1$;
    if $(T[\vec{v}] > \theta_p) \wedge (\vec{v} \notin C)$ **then**
      $C \leftarrow C \bigcup \{\vec{v}\}$;
      if $\ell_p(\vec{v}, \vec{q}) < c\delta$ **then**
        return $\vec{v}$;
      if $|C| > \beta|\mathcal{D}|$ **then**
        return NULL ;

Algorithm 4: Answering $\mathcal{N}_p(\vec{q}, k, c)$

1 $T \leftarrow$ a hash table to record the collision count for each database object ;
2 $C \leftarrow$ a list to record the candidates ;
3 $\hat{r} \leftarrow$ the radius of $B_1(\vec{q}, \hat{r})$ to approximate $B_p(\vec{q}, 1)$;
4 $\delta \leftarrow \frac{1}{\hat{r}}$;
5 **while** *TRUE* **do**
6   **for** $i \leftarrow 0$ **to** $\eta_p - 1$ **do**
7   **if** $\delta = \frac{1}{\hat{r}}$ **then**
8       $IDs \leftarrow$ the points that are hashed to $h_i^*(\vec{q})$;
9   **else**
10       $IDs \leftarrow$ the points that are hashed in $[\ h_i^*(\vec{q}) - \lfloor\frac{\delta\hat{r}}{2}\rfloor, h_i^*(\vec{q}) - \lfloor\frac{\delta\hat{r}}{2c}\rfloor - 1\ ]$ or $[\ h_i^*(\vec{q}) + \lfloor\frac{\delta\hat{r}}{2c}\rfloor + 1, h_i^*(\vec{q}) + \lfloor\frac{\delta\hat{r}}{2}\rfloor\ ]$ for $h_i^*(\cdot)$;
11   **foreach** *object* $\vec{v} \in IDs$ **do**
12       $T[\vec{v}] \leftarrow T[\vec{v}] + 1$;
13   **if** $(T[\vec{v}] > \theta_p) \wedge (\vec{v} \notin C)$ **then**
14         $C \leftarrow C \bigcup \{\vec{v}\}$;
15   **if** $(|\{\vec{o}|\vec{o} \in C \wedge \ell_p(\vec{o}, \vec{q}) < c\delta\}| \geq k) \vee (|C| > k + \beta|\mathcal{D}|)$ **then**
16   **return** the kNNs in C with the smallest ℓ_p distance to $\vec{q}$;
17   $\delta \leftarrow \delta * c$;

4.3 Multi-query Optimization

For the processing of queries under different ℓ_p metrics, the difference is that an object requires a different collision threshold to become a candidate. For fractional distance metrics, the smaller the p is, the larger the collision threshold is. This requires that more index entries are needed to be retrieved for the fractional distance metrics with a smaller p. The good news is that the index entries for a larger collision threshold (a smaller p) cover the index entries for a smaller collision threshold (a larger p), which means that no additional sequential I/O is required when we process queries in different ℓ_p spaces simultaneously for the same query point.

This finding motivates us to perform multiple queries under different ℓ_p metrics concurrently by sharing their I/Os. For example, suppose we need to answer queries $\mathcal{N}_p(\vec{q}, k, c)$ for $p = 0.5$, 0.6, 0.7, 0.8, 0.9 and 1.0. We can group them and answer them simultaneously. The I/O cost of processing these multiple queries is roughly the same as that of processing a single $\mathcal{N}_{0.5}(\vec{q}, k, c)$ query with additional random I/Os for retrieving candidates of other ℓ_p metrics.

5. EXPERIMENTS

In this section, we study the performance of LazyLSH with various datasets. We mainly focus on the following two issues: (1) How the index size changes with different parameter settings. (2) How LazyLSH performs with respect to the efficiency and effectiveness on various datasets.

Table 3: Parameter Settings for the synthetic datasets

Notation	Description	Values
$\|\mathcal{D}\|$	Cardinality	100k, 200k, <u>400k</u>, 800k, 1.6m
d	Dimensionality	100, 200, <u>400</u>, 800, 1600
c	Approximate ratio	2, <u>3</u>, 4, 5, 6
p	Supported ℓ_p space	<u>0.5</u>, 0.6, 0.7, 0.8, 0.9, 1.0

Table 4: Statistics of the real datasets and index sizes

Dataset	d	♯ points	value range	$\eta_{0.5}$	index size(MB)
Inria	128	4,455,041	[0, 255]	1358	23824
SUN	512	108,703	[0, 10,000]	916	1100
LabelMe	512	207,859	[0, 10,000]	959	2061
Mnist	784	60,000	[0, 255]	845	498

5.1 Datasets and Queries

In the experiments, synthetic datasets and four real datasets are used: **Mnist**[2] [29], **Inria**[3] [27], **LabelMe**[4] [37] and **Sun**[5] [48]. The statistics of the synthetic datasets and real datasets are summarized in Tables 3 and 4 respectively. We refer readers to Appendix B.1 for more details of the datasets and query sets.

5.2 Evaluation Metrics

We follow the previous methods [45, 21, 22, 43] and adopt three metrics in our evaluations.

Space Consumption. The space is measured by the number of required hash tables and the index size.

Query Efficiency. The query efficiency is measured by the average number of I/Os of answering a query. If a block of an inverted list (4KB per block) is loaded into memory, the number of simulated I/Os (sequential) is increased by 1. If an object is visited to compute its distance to the query, the number of simulated I/Os (random) is increased by 1.

Overall Ratio. The overall ratio is defined as how many times farther a reported neighbor is compared to the real nearest neighbor. Formally, for an $\mathcal{N}_p(\vec{q}, k, c)$ query, $\{\vec{o_1}, \ldots, \vec{o_k}\}$ are the reported results sorted in ascending order of their distances to $\vec{q}$. Let $\{\vec{o_1^*}, \ldots, \vec{o_k^*}\}$ be the true kNNs sorted in ascending order of their distances to $\vec{q}$. The overall ratio is calculated as: $\frac{1}{k}\sum_{i=1}^{k} \ell_p(\vec{o_i}, \vec{q})/\ell_p(\vec{o_i^*}, \vec{q})$.

The I/O cost and the overall ratio are averaged over queries. Unless otherwise specified, we materialize $\eta_{0.5}$ hash functions for the index so that queries can be answered in the ℓ_p spaces, where $0.5 \leq p \leq 1$. By default, queries are issued in the $\ell_{0.5}$ space.

Competitors. To the best of our knowledge, LazyLSH is the first work of supporting approximate nearest neighbor queries on multiple distance functions with a single index. There is no direct competitor of our approach. Alternatively, we modify C2LSH [21] and SRS [43] as competitors.

- *C2LSH*: We build the index of C2LSH in the ℓ_1 space. Then we retrieve $(k + 100)$ candidates in the ℓ_1 space, and select the top-k points from the candidate set with the smallest ℓ_p distance to the query.
- *SRS*: We build the index of SRS in the ℓ_2 space because SRS uses the 2-stable distribution. We retrieve the candidates in the ℓ_2 space, and select the top-k points from the candidate set with the smallest ℓ_p distance to the query. The number of projected dimensions in SRS is set to 6 as the experimental setting in [43]. The approximate ratio c is set to 3 for comparison.

[2] http://yann.lecun.com/exdb/mnist/

[3] http://lear.inrialpes.fr/~jegou/data.php

[4] http://labelme.csail.mit.edu/Release3.0/

[5] http://sundatabase.mit.edu/

Table 5: Index size w.r.t. different parameter settings

(a) Index size vs. the cardinality $|\mathcal{D}|$

$\|\mathcal{D}\|$	100k	200k	400k	800k	1.6m
$\eta_{0.5}$	923	979	1025	1071	1116
Size(MB)	1063	2211	4557	9250	18291

(b) Index size vs. the dimensionality d

d	100	200	400	800	1600
$\eta_{0.5}$	1223	1108	1025	966	879
Size(MB)	5011	4778	4557	4360	3997

(c) Index size vs. the approximate ratio c

c	2	3	4	5	6
$\eta_{0.5}$	7114	1025	570	425	355
Size(MB)	31609	4557	2531	1889	1577
I/Os	672184	77532	37252	24922	18712
Ratio	1.011	1.053	1.075	1.084	1.089

(d) Index size vs. the range of supported ℓ_p spaces

p	0.5	0.6	0.7	0.8	0.9	1.0
η_p	1025	711	579	507	462	432
Size(MB)	4557	3157	2576	2252	2051	1916

Implementation. Our algorithms were implemented in C++. All experiments were conducted on a PC with Intel Core i7-3770 CPU @ 3.40GHz, 8GB memory, 500GB hard disk, running Ubuntu 12.04LTS. The page size was set to 4 KB in the experiments.

5.3 Study on Synthetic Datasets

We use synthetic datasets to study the index size w.r.t. different parameter settings. As discussed in Section 3.3, the index size is affected by four parameters: (1) the cardinality of the dataset $|\mathcal{D}|$, (2) the dimensionality d, (3) the approximate ratio c, and (4) the range of supported ℓ_p spaces, where η_p hash functions are built for the base index. Table 3 shows the parameter settings of the synthetic datasets. The default values are underlined in the third column. We study the required index size w.r.t each parameter by varying one parameter and setting the other three parameters to the default values, as presented in Table 5.

Effect of the cardinality $|\mathcal{D}|$: Table 5a shows the index size w.r.t $|\mathcal{D}|$. When $|\mathcal{D}|$ increases, the number of required hash functions increases, and so does the index size.

Effect of the dimensionality d: Table 5b shows the index size w.r.t d. It is worth noting that the index size decreases when d increases. This is because η_p changes with $(\hat{p}_1' - \hat{p}_2')$ as shown in Equation 20 and $(\hat{p}_1' - \hat{p}_2')$ varies w.r.t different numbers of dimensions. Figure 7 shows the relationship between the value of $(\hat{p}_1' - \hat{p}_2')$ and the dimensionality. The solid line in this figure plots $(\hat{p}_1' - \hat{p}_2')$ when the approximate ratio $c = 3$. As can be seen, $(\hat{p}_1' - \hat{p}_2')$ first decreases rapidly with the dimensionality and reaches the smallest value when $d = 16$. Then $(\hat{p}_1' - \hat{p}_2')$ increases slowly when the dimensionality increases. This explains the reason why the index size decreases with d when $d > 100$ for the synthetic datasets.

Effect of the approximate ratio c: Table 5c shows the index size w.r.t c. When c increases, the index size decreases. The reason can be also explained by Figure 7. As shown in

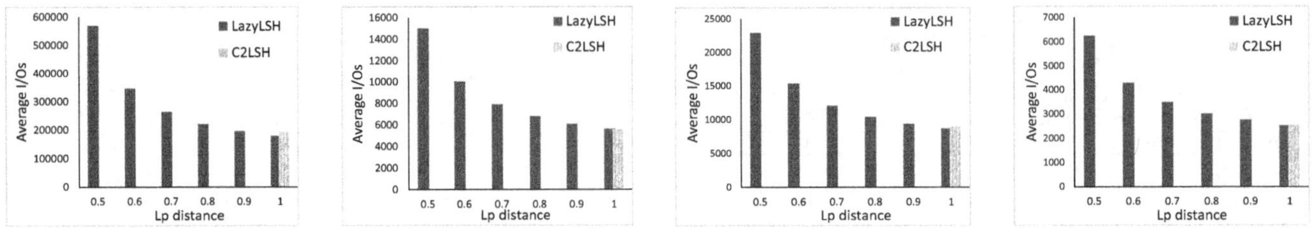

(a) Inria (b) SUN (c) LabelMe (d) Mnist

Figure 9: I/O costs on real datasets w.r.t. the ℓ_p distance

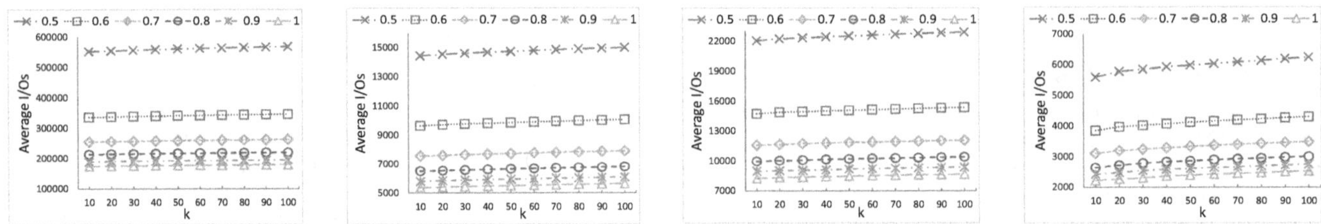

(a) Inria (b) SUN (c) LabelMe (d) Mnist

Figure 10: I/O costs on real datasets w.r.t. the value of k

the figure, for a fixed dimension, $(\hat{p}_1' - \hat{p}_2')$ increases when c increases, which leads to the smaller index size. When $c = 2$, the number of required hash functions $\eta_{0.5}$ is around seven times of $\eta_{0.5}$ for $c = 3$.

In addition, we test the number of I/Os and the overall ratio when processing approximate queries with different approximate ratio c. We notice that: (1) the number of I/Os decreases significantly as c increases. The number of I/Os when $c = 2$ is about nine times of that when $c = 3$, because of the difference in index size. (2) the overall ratio increases with c because a larger approximation ratio is applied, which means that we can get more accurate results when we use a smaller c. Therefore, c can be viewed as a parameter to be set as a trade-off between accuracy and efficiency (index size). To make it comparable to C2LSH, which used $c = 2$ or 3 in its experiment [21], we set $c = 3$ for LazyLSH in the rest of the experiments.

Effect of the range of supported ℓ_p spaces: Table 5d shows the index size w.r.t the range of supported ℓ_p spaces. To support a larger range of ℓ_p spaces, we need to materialize more hash functions. For instance, we need 2.37x hash functions to support queries in a range of ℓ_p spaces, where $0.5 \leq p \leq 1$, compared to the number of hash functions required for the ℓ_1 space.

5.4 Study on Real Datasets

5.4.1 *Index Size*

We first study the index size for the real datasets. We materialize $\eta_{0.5}$ hash functions as the base index so that queries $\mathcal{R}_p(\vec{q}, \delta, c)$ can be supported in a range of ℓ_p spaces, where $0.5 \leq p \leq 1$. Table 4 shows the number of hash functions required and the index size for the real datasets. When the dimensionality increases, fewer hash functions are required. This observation is consistent with the result of the synthetic datasets shown in Table 5b.

Next we study the performance of LazyLSH in terms of the I/O cost of processing a query.

5.4.2 *I/O Costs of Processing Queries*

I/O Costs w.r.t. the query ℓ_p space: Figure 9 plots the average I/Os of processing a query w.r.t. the ℓ_p space where the number of nearest neighbors k is set to 100. The query processing in the $\ell_{0.5}$ space incurs more I/O overhead than the ℓ_1 space. Generally, a smaller p will lead to a higher I/O cost. This is because the processing of queries in the $\ell_{0.5}$ space requires a higher collision threshold for an object to become a candidate and more index entries are required to be read. In the ℓ_1 space, the performance of LazyLSH is similar to C2LSH. The average I/O costs for these two methods are at the same level. However, C2LSH can only support queries in the ℓ_1 space, while in contrast, LazyLSH is designed to support queries in a larger range of ℓ_p distances. Please note that the I/O cost of SRS is not reported as the provided implementation[6] is in-memory and SRS is based on the ℓ_2 distance. Still, it is obvious that SRS can achieve the best performance in terms of the I/O cost as its index size is one order of magnitude smaller than that of C2LSH as reported in [43]. Even though SRS has a small I/O cost, its reliance on the 2-stable distribution in the ℓ_2 space constrains us from using its technique as the base index structure. We refer readers to Appendix C for more details.

I/O Costs w.r.t. the value of k: Figure 10 plots the average I/Os of processing a query w.r.t. the number of returned nearest neighbors. The horizontal axis k represents the number of returned nearest neighbors, ranging from 10 to 100. We observe that there is a slight increase of I/Os on all the four datasets when k increases. This indicates that users can issue a query with a larger k to get more precise nearest neighbors with a few additional I/Os.

I/O Costs w.r.t. the multiple-query optimization: One application of using LazyLSH is to select the optimal ℓ_p metric, which is shown to be highly application-dependent [20]. One way is to use classifications to select the best ℓ_p metric. In particular, we retrieve the approximate kNNs

[6]https://github.com/DBWangGroupUNSW/SRS

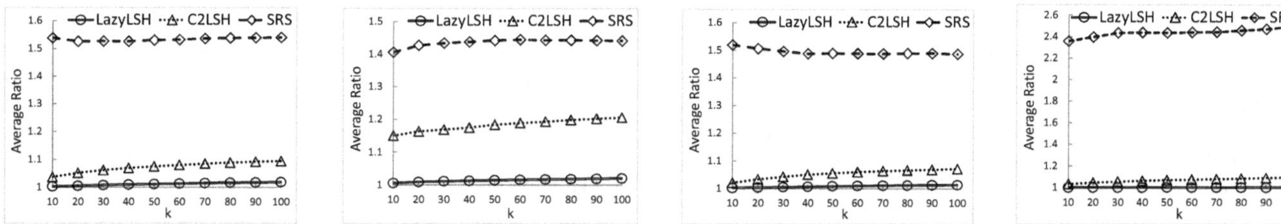

(a) Inria (b) SUN (c) LabelMe (d) Mnist

Figure 11: Average overall ratios on real datasets

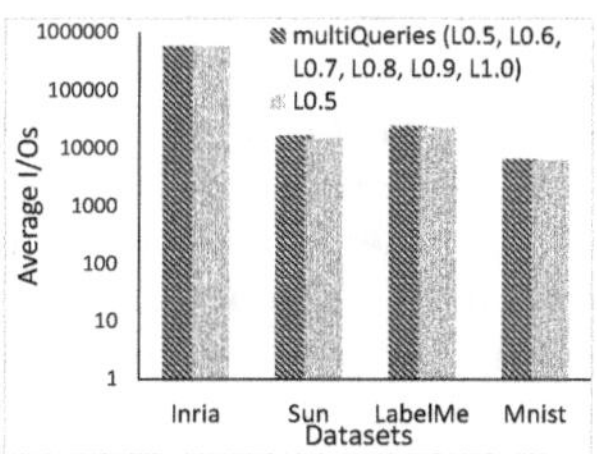

Figure 12: Multiple-query optimization

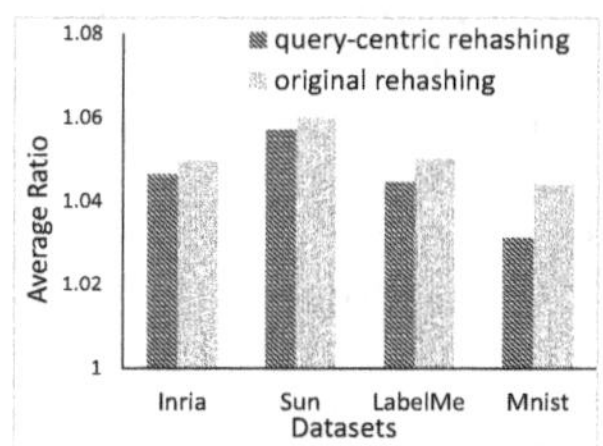

Figure 13: Impact of query-centric rehashing

in different ℓ_p spaces. Then we select the optimal ℓ_p metric with the highest classification accuracy as shown in Table 1. This approach requires performing approximate kNN queries in different ℓ_p spaces, which can be processed as the multi-query optimization in Section 4.3.

Figure 12 presents the I/O cost of processing a single query versus that of processing multiple queries concurrently. We try to find the kNNs of the same data point in different ℓ_p spaces (six queries in the $\ell_{0.5}$, $\ell_{0.6}$, $\ell_{0.7}$, $\ell_{0.8}$, $\ell_{0.9}$ and ℓ_1 spaces in this experiment). The queries of different ℓ_p spaces are processed together by sharing their I/Os, as they all probe many common hash buckets. As indicated in the figure, processing multiple queries concurrently only incurs a few more I/Os than processing a single query. This observation motivates us to process queries of different ℓ_p distances in a batch, instead of processing them individually. With the help of the multiple-query optimization, we can easily get the approximate kNNs of different ℓ_p metrics and choose the optimal ℓ_p metric for a particular dataset based on classification methods such as the kNN classifier as presented in Table 1 in the introduction. We also compare the running time of LazyLSH with that of the linear scan method, which is presented in Appendix B.2.

5.4.3 *Overall Ratio*

Overall Ratio for queries in fractional metrics: We then compare LazyLSH with the existing work in the context of the overall ratio. Figure 11 presents the average overall ratio for queries in the $\ell_{0.5}$ space. In general, LazyLSH outperforms C2LSH in terms of the overall ratio. In most cases, the overall ratio of LazyLSH is less than 1.02. In contrast, C2LSH does not perform well for queries in the $\ell_{0.5}$ space, because C2LSH is designed to answer queries in the ℓ_1 or ℓ_2 spaces and it is not optimized to answer queries for fractional distances. Therefore, LazyLSH has better performance in terms of the overall ratio.

Impact of the query-centric rehashing: Next we study the impact of the query-centric rehashing. To achieve a fair comparison, the queries are conducted in the same index with different rehashing methods. In particular, the queries are conducted in the ℓ_1 space and the approximate 100 NNs are returned. Figure 13 plots the average overall ratio for different rehashing methods. We notice that our query-centric rehashing method outperforms the original rehashing method on all the four datasets. This is because the query-centric rehashing method is likely to retrieve nearby points, while the original rehashing method may retrieve distant points in some cases as stated in Figure 8.

6. RELATED WORK

6.1 Similarity Search and kNN Processing

The similarity search problem is of fundamental importance to a variety of applications such as classification [17], clustering [35], semi-supervised learning [52], semi-lazy learning [51, 50], collaborative filtering [39] and near-duplicate detection [8]. Given a query object $\vec{q}$ represented as a high-dimensional vector, a typical similarity search retrieves the k-nearest neighbors (kNNs) of $\vec{q}$ using a specific distance function.

kNN search has been well studied in low-dimensional spaces [36, 38]. However, retrieving exact results becomes a nontrivial problem when the dimensionality increases due to the "curse of dimensionality". It has been shown that the average query time with an optimal indexing scheme is superpolynomial with the dimensionality [34]. When the dimensionality is sufficiently large, conventional kNN search approach becomes even slower than the linear scan approach [18]. To address the problem, approximate nearest neighbor search is introduced as an alternative solution, which trades off the accuracy to speed up the search. One typical solution is to employ the Locality-Sensitive Hashing (LSH) because of its precise theoretical guarantees and empirical performance.

6.2 Locality-Sensitive Hashing

LSH is first introduced by Indyk and Motwani [26]. The basic idea of LSH is that an LSH function produces a hash bit of a data point by projecting the data point to a random hyperplane. Statistics guarantees that the nearby points in the projected hyperplane are likely to be close to each other in the original space. In addition, multiple hash tables are built independently, aiming to enlarge the probability that similar data points are mapped to similar hash codes. Several LSH families have been discovered for metric distances [4], including the Hamming distance between binary vectors [26], the Jaccard distance between sets [11, 10], the arccos distance measuring the angles between vectors [14], the Manhattan distance [3, 18], and the Euclidean distance [18].

For the ℓ_p metrics, E2LSH [18] is the first LSH method that supports approximate nearest neighbor queries in the Euclidean space. The main drawback of E2LSH is that it needs to build multiple indexes with different radii, resulting in high maintenance overhead. To address the issue of high storage costs, multi-probe LSH [32] is proposed. It not only checks the data points that fall in the same bucket as the query point, but also probes multiple buckets that are likely to contain results in a hash table, which leads to the use of fewer hash tables. However, it still suffers from the need for building hash tables at different radii.

LSB-tree [45] is the first work that does not need to build hash tables at different radii. It groups hash values as a one-dimensional Z-order value and indexes it in a B-tree. Index entries for different radii can be retrieved in corresponding ranges in the B-tree. In addition, an LSB forest with multiple trees can be built to improve the search performance. C2LSH [21] further improves the LSB-tree method by introducing techniques of collision counting and virtual rehashing. C2LSH uses one hash function per hash table so that the number of hash buckets to read does not increase exponentially when the query radius increases. Furthermore, SRS [43] projects data points from the original high-dimensional space into a low-dimensional space via 2-stable projections. The major observation is that the ℓ_2 distance in the projected space over the ℓ_2 distance in the original space follows a chi-squared distribution, which has a sharp concentration bound. Therefore, SRS can index data points in the low-dimensional projected space and use the chi-squared distribution to perform queries. In this case, the index size is significantly reduced.

LSH variants are proposed to address the drawbacks of the traditional LSH methods. Traditional LSH methods suffer from the disadvantage of generating a large number of the false positives. To address this problem, BayesLSH [40] is proposed. It integrates the Bayesian statistics and performs candidate pruning and similarity estimation using LSH. It can quickly prune away false positives, which leads to a significant speedup. Traditional LSH methods also suffer from the disadvantage of accessing many candidates, which brings a larger number of random I/Os. To address this, SortingKeys-LSH [30] is presented to order the compound hash keys so that the data points are sorted accordingly in the index to reduce the I/O cost.

6.3 Fractional Distance Metric

Euclidean distance [15, 23, 41, 6, 36] is widely used in kNN search. However, it was shown that when the dimensionality is high, the Euclidean distance introduces the concentration problem [7]. Namely, the distance between any random pair of high-dimensional data points is almost identical. Therefore, the effectiveness of the Euclidean distance in the high-dimensional space is not clear [24, 1].

To address the concentration problem, one direction is to consider partial similarities, which have been drawn increasing attention in the last decade [28, 46, 12, 44]. Tung et al. [46] introduced the k-n-match model to discover the partial similarity in n dimensions, where n is a given integer smaller than the dimensionality and these n dimensions are determined dynamically to make the query and the returned results be the most similar. It has been shown that the k-n-match model yields better results than the traditional kNN query in identifying similar objects by partial similarities.

Another direction is to investigate different distance metrics. Aggarwal et al. [24, 1] examined the "curse of dimensionality" problem from the perspective of distance metrics. They found that the Manhattan distance (ℓ_1) metric is more effective than the Euclidean distance (ℓ_2) metric in the high-dimensional space. They further introduced and examined the fractional distance (ℓ_p for $0 < p < 1$) metrics, which are less concentrated. It was shown that the fractional distance metrics provide more meaningful results from both theoretical and empirical perspectives. Their experimental results verified that fractional distance metrics improve the effectiveness of standard clustering algorithms.

Later, fractional distance metrics have been applied to applications such as content-based image retrieval [25, 47]. The experiments showed that the performances of fractional distance metrics outperform the ℓ_1 and ℓ_2 metrics. In particular, the $\ell_{0.5}$ distance consistently outperforms both ℓ_1 and ℓ_2 metrics in their experiments. Still, the experimental results showed that the optimal ℓ_p metric is application-dependent and required to be learned for each dataset.

Recently, it was argued that the analysis of the concentration phenomenon is based on the assumption of independent and identically distributed variables [20], which might not be true in real datasets. The authors showed that the optimal ℓ_p metric is actually application-dependent. In order to explore the high-dimensional data, it is important to support different distance metrics. Hence, users can try and select the best ℓ_p metric for their applications. However, to the best of our knowledge, none of the existing LSH approaches can support multiple distance metrics. LazyLSH is the first work that supports approximate kNN processing in multiple fractional metrics using a single index. In this paper, we use the index structure of C2LSH as the base index structure. LazyLSH can also be used other LSH index structures as the base index, which is presented in Appendix C.

7. CONCLUSION

In this paper, we proposed an efficient mechanism called LazyLSH to answer approximate kNN queries under fractional distance metrics in high-dimensional spaces. We observed that an LSH function in a specific ℓ_p space can be extended to support queries in other spaces. Based on this observation, we materialized a base LSH index in the ℓ_1 space and used it to process approximate kNN queries in different ℓ_p spaces. We conducted extensive experiments on synthetic and real datasets, and the experimental results showed that LazyLSH provides accurate results and improves existing machine learning algorithms for retrieving approximate kNN under different fractional distance metrics.

8. ACKNOWLEDGEMENTS

The work by Anthony K.H. Tung was partially supported by NUS FRC Grant R-252-000-370-112. The work by Sai Wu was partially supported by the National Basic Research Program of China 973 (No. 2015CB352400). This research was carried out at the NUS-ZJU Sensor-Enhanced social Media (SeSaMe) Centre. It is supported by the Singapore National Research Foundation under its International Research Centre @ Singapore Funding Initiative and administered by the Interactive Digital Media Programme Office.

9. REFERENCES

[1] C. Aggarwal, A. Hinneburg, and D. Keim. On the surprising behavior of distance metrics in high dimensional space. In *ICDT*, volume 1973, pages 420–434. 2001.

[2] N. Ailon and B. Chazelle. Approximate nearest neighbors and the fast johnson-lindenstrauss transform. In *STOC*, pages 557–563, 2006.

[3] A. Andoni and P. Indyk. Efficient algorithms for substring near neighbor problem. In *SODA*, pages 1203–1212, 2006.

[4] A. Andoni and P. Indyk. Near-optimal hashing algorithms for approximate nearest neighbor in high dimensions. *COMMUNICATIONS OF THE ACM*, 51(1):117–122, 2008.

[5] S. Arya and D. M. Mount. Approximate nearest neighbor queries in fixed dimensions. In *SODA*, pages 271–280, 1993.

[6] N. Beckmann, H.-P. Kriegel, R. Schneider, and B. Seeger. The r*-tree: An efficient and robust access method for points and rectangles. In *SIGMOD*, pages 322–331, 1990.

[7] K. Beyer, J. Goldstein, R. Ramakrishnan, and U. Shaft. When is ąřnearest neighborąś meaningful? In *ICDT*, pages 217–235. 1999.

[8] M. Bilenko and R. J. Mooney. Adaptive duplicate detection using learnable string similarity measures. In *SIGKDD*, pages 39–48, 2003.

[9] K. Binder and D. Heermann. *Monte Carlo simulation in statistical physics: an introduction.* Springer Science & Business Media, 2010.

[10] A. Broder. On the resemblance and containment of documents. In *Compression and Complexity of Sequences 1997. Proceedings*, pages 21–29, 1997.

[11] A. Z. Broder, S. C. Glassman, M. S. Manasse, and G. Zweig. Syntactic clustering of the web. In *WWW*, pages 1157–1166, 1997.

[12] A. M. Bronstein, M. M. Bronstein, A. M. Bruckstein, and R. Kimmel. Partial similarity of objects, or how to compare a centaur to a horse. *International Journal of Computer Vision*, 84(2):163–183, 2008.

[13] G. Calafiore, F. Dabbene, and R. Tempo. Uniform sample generation in lp balls for probabilistic robustness analysis. In *CDC*, volume 3, pages 3335–3340, 1998.

[14] M. S. Charikar. Similarity estimation techniques from rounding algorithms. In *STOC*, pages 380–388, 2002.

[15] J. G. Cleary. Analysis of an algorithm for finding nearest neighbors in euclidean space. *ACM Trans. Math. Softw.*, 5(2):183–192, 1979.

[16] G. Cormode, P. Indyk, N. Koudas, and S. Muthukrishnan. Fast mining of massive tabular data via approximate distance computations. In *ICDE*, pages 605–614, 2002.

[17] T. Cover and P. Hart. Nearest neighbor pattern classification. *Information Theory, IEEE Trans. on*, 13(1):21–27, 1967.

[18] M. Datar, N. Immorlica, P. Indyk, and V. S. Mirrokni. Locality-sensitive hashing scheme based on p-stable distributions. In *SCG*, pages 253–262, 2004.

[19] M. Douze, H. Jégou, H. Sandhawalia, L. Amsaleg, and C. Schmid. Evaluation of gist descriptors for web-scale image search. In *CIVR*, pages 19:1–19:8, 2009.

[20] D. Francois, V. Wertz, and M. Verleysen. The concentration of fractional distances. *TKDE*, 19(7):873–886, 2007.

[21] J. Gan, J. Feng, Q. Fang, and W. Ng. Locality-sensitive hashing scheme based on dynamic collision counting. In *SIGMOD*, pages 541–552, 2012.

[22] J. Gao, H. V. Jagadish, W. Lu, and B. C. Ooi. Dsh: Data sensitive hashing for high-dimensional k-nnsearch. In *SIGMOD*, pages 1127–1138, 2014.

[23] A. Guttman. R-trees: A dynamic index structure for spatial searching. In *SIGMOD*, pages 47–57, 1984.

[24] A. Hinneburg, C. C. Aggarwal, and D. A. Keim. What is the nearest neighbor in high dimensional spaces? In *VLDB*, pages 506–515, 2000.

[25] P. Howarth and S. Rüger. Fractional distance measures for content-based image retrieval. In *ECIR*, pages 447–456, 2005.

[26] P. Indyk and R. Motwani. Approximate nearest neighbors: towards removing the curse of dimensionality. In *STOC*, pages 604–613, 1998.

[27] H. Jegou, M. Douze, and C. Schmid. Hamming embedding and weak geometric consistency for large scale image search. In *ECCV*, pages 304–317, 2008.

[28] L. J. Latecki, R. Lakaemper, and D. Wolter. Optimal partial shape similarity. *Image and Vision Computing*, 23(2):227 – 236, 2005.

[29] Y. Lecun, L. Bottou, Y. Bengio, and P. Haffner. Gradient-based learning applied to document recognition. *Proceedings of the IEEE*, 86(11):2278–2324, 1998.

[30] Y. Liu, J. Cui, Z. Huang, H. Li, and H. T. Shen. Sk-lsh: An efficient index structure for approximate nearest neighbor search. *PVLDB.*, 7(9):745–756, 2014.

[31] D. G. Lowe. Distinctive image features from scale-invariant keypoints. *Int. J. Comput. Vision*, 60(2):91–110, 2004.

[32] Q. Lv, W. Josephson, Z. Wang, M. Charikar, and K. Li. Multi-probe lsh: efficient indexing for high-dimensional similarity search. In *VLDB*, pages 950–961, 2007.

[33] M. Muja and D. G. Lowe. Fast approximate nearest neighbors with automatic algorithm configuration. *VISAPP (1)*, 2, 2009.

[34] V. Pestov. Lower bounds on performance of metric tree indexing schemes for exact similarity search in high dimensions. *Algorithmica*, 66:310–328, 2013.

[35] D. Ravichandran, P. Pantel, and E. Hovy. Randomized algorithms and nlp: Using locality sensitive hash function for high speed noun clustering. In *ACL*, pages 622–629, 2005.

[36] N. Roussopoulos, S. Kelley, and F. Vincent. Nearest neighbor queries. In *SIGMOD*, pages 71–79, 1995.

[37] B. C. Russell, A. Torralba, K. P. Murphy, and W. T. Freeman. Labelme: A database and web-based tool for image annotation. *Int. J. Comput. Vision*, 77(1-3):157–173, 2008.

[38] H. Samet. *Foundations of Multidimensional and Metric Data Structures.* Morgan Kaufmann Publishers Inc., 2005.

[39] B. Sarwar, G. Karypis, J. Konstan, and J. Riedl. Item-based collaborative filtering recommendation algorithms. In *WWW*, pages 285–295, 2001.

[40] V. Satuluri and S. Parthasarathy. Bayesian locality sensitive hashing for fast similarity search. *PVLDB*, 5(5):430–441, 2012.

[41] T. K. Sellis, N. Roussopoulos, and C. Faloutsos. The r+-tree: A dynamic index for multi-dimensional objects. In *VLDB*, pages 507–518, 1987.

[42] E. W. Stacy. A generalization of the gamma distribution. *The Annals of Mathematical Statistics*, pages 1187–1192, 1962.

[43] Y. Sun, W. Wang, J. Qin, Y. Zhang, and X. Lin. Srs: Solving c-approximate nearest neighbor queries in high dimensional euclidean space with a tiny index. *PVLDB*, 8(1):1–12, 2014.

[44] X. Tan, S. Chen, Z.-H. Zhou, and J. Liu. Face recognition under occlusions and variant expressions with partial similarity. *Information Forensics and Security, IEEE Transactions on*, 4(2):217–230, 2009.

[45] Y. Tao, K. Yi, C. Sheng, and P. Kalnis. Efficient and accurate nearest neighbor and closest pair search in high-dimensional space. *ACM Trans. Database Syst.*, 35(3):20:1–20:46, 2010.

[46] A. K. H. Tung, R. Zhang, N. Koudas, and B. C. Ooi. Similarity search: A matching based approach. In *VLDB*, pages 631–642, 2006.

[47] H. Wang, S. Zhang, W. Liang, F. Wang, and Y. Yao. Content-based image retrieval using fractional distance metric. In *IASP*, pages 1–5, 2012.

[48] J. Xiao, J. Hays, K. Ehinger, A. Oliva, and A. Torralba.

Sun database: Large-scale scene recognition from abbey to zoo. In *CVPR*, pages 3485–3492, 2010.
[49] M.-L. Zhang and Z.-H. Zhou. Ml-knn: A lazy learning approach to multi-label learning. *Pattern Recognition*, 40(7):2038 – 2048, 2007.
[50] J. Zhou and A. K. Tung. Smiler: A semi-lazy time series prediction system for sensors. In *SIGMOD*, pages 1871–1886, 2015.
[51] J. Zhou, A. K. Tung, W. Wu, and W. S. Ng. A ąřsemi-lazyąś approach to probabilistic path prediction in dynamic environments. In *SIGKDD*, pages 748–756, 2013.
[52] X. Zhu and A. B. Goldberg. Introduction to semi-supervised learning. *Synthesis lectures on artificial intelligence and machine learning*, 3(1):1–130, 2009.

APPENDIX

A. PROOF

A.1 Proof of Lemma 2

PROOF. We know:

$$p(cs, cr) = \int_0^{cr} \frac{1}{cs} f_p(\frac{t}{cs})(1 - \frac{t}{cr})dt$$

Let

$$x = t/c.$$

Then we get:

$$\begin{aligned} p(cs, cr) &= \int_0^{r} c\frac{1}{cs} f_p(\frac{cx}{cs})(1 - \frac{cx}{cr})dx \\ &= \int_0^{r} \frac{1}{s} f_p(\frac{x}{s})(1 - \frac{x}{r})dx = p(s, r) \quad \square \end{aligned}$$

A.2 Proof of Lemma 3

PROOF. For any $\vec{x}, \vec{y} \in \mathbb{R}^d$, let $\vec{u} = c\vec{x}$ and $\vec{v} = c\vec{y}$. Then, we have

$$\begin{aligned} \ell_s(\vec{u}, \vec{v}) =& (\sum_{i=1}^{d}(u_i - v_i)^s)^{1/s} \\ =& (\sum_{i=1}^{d}(cx_i - cy_i)^s)^{1/s} \\ =& c\ \ell_s(\vec{x}, \vec{y}) \end{aligned}$$

Therefore, we get $\ell_s(\vec{x}, \vec{y}) \leq r \iff \ell_s(\vec{u}, \vec{v}) \leq cr$. Similarly, $\ell_p(\vec{x}, \vec{y}) \leq \delta \iff \ell_p(\vec{u}, \vec{v}) \leq c\delta$. Note $\vec{u}$ and $\vec{x}$, $\vec{v}$ and $\vec{y}$ are one-to-one corresponding. Thus, we get

$$Pr(\ell_s(\vec{x}, \vec{y}) \leq r | \ell_p(\vec{x}, \vec{y}) \leq \delta) = Pr(\ell_s(\vec{u}, \vec{v}) \leq cr | \ell_p(\vec{u}, \vec{v}) \leq c\delta)$$

$\square$

B. MORE ON EXPERIMENTS

B.1 Datasets and Query sets

Synthetic datasets: We use synthetic datasets to study the influences of the dimensionality and the cardinality. We first fix the cardinality to be 40,000 and generate datasets with different dimensionality as {100, 200, 400, 800, 1600}. Then we fix the dimensionality to be 400 and generate datasets with different cardinality as {100k, 200k, 400k, 800k, 1.6m}. The value of each dimension is an integer randomly chosen from [0, 10000]. For each synthetic dataset, we randomly generate 50 query points as a query set.

Inria: The Inria dataset contains 1,491 holiday photos. 4,455,091 SIFT features [31] are extracted from the images, and each feature is represented as a 128-dimensional point. The value of each dimension is an integer in the range of [0, 255]. We randomly select 50 feature points as our query set and remove those features from the dataset during the query processing to avoid returning the same feature.

SUN: SUN is a dataset containing 108,753 images, each of which is attached with a class label to indicate which scene category the image belongs to. We obtain the GIST feature [19] of each image and generate a corresponding 512-dimensional data point. The value of each dimension is normalized to be an integer in the range of [0, 10,000]. We randomly pick 50 data points as a query set.

LabelMe: LabelMe is a dataset containing 207,909 images. We apply the processing method of SUN to the LabelMe dataset. Hence, the size of LabelMe is 207,859.

Mnist: Mnist is a dataset consisting of 60,000 pictures of handwritten digits. Each picture has a class label representing which digit the picture shows. Each picture is represented as a 784-dimensional point, of which each dimension is an integer ranging from 0 to 255. In addition, Mnist contains a test set of 10,000 points. We randomly choose 50 points to form a query set.

B.2 Additional experiments

This experiment analyzes the query time of LazyLSH versus that of the linear scan method. As presented in Table 1 and Section 5.4.2, we need to retrieve approximate kNNs in different ℓ_p spaces to test the accuracy of the kNN classifier in order to pick the optimal ℓ_p metric.

We first study the effect of the multi-query optimization in terms of query time. We use the synthetic dataset with cardinality of 400k and dimensionality of 400 in this experiment. We set the approximate ratio $c = 3, 4, 5, 6$ and the number of returned points $k = 100$. The result for $c = 2$ is skipped as the I/O cost for $c = 2$ is much higher than others as shown in Table 5c. The single query is performed in the $\ell_{0.5}$ space, and the multiple queries are preformed in the $\ell_{0.5}$, $\ell_{0.6}$, $\ell_{0.7}$, $\ell_{0.8}$, $\ell_{0.9}$ and ℓ_1 spaces using our multi-query optimization. Figure 14 shows that the average query time of the two methods. The query time of LazyLSH with $c = 4$ for the single query is at the same level as that of the linear scan. However, the running time of the linear scan method increases dramatically when multiple queries are answered. In contrast, the running time of LazyLSH for processing multiple queries remains at the same level as that for performing the single query. This finding is consistent to the result in Figure 12, because the number of I/Os increases by a small amount when processing multiple queries in a batch.

In addition, Figure 14 shows that the running time decreases as the approximate ratio c increases. In fact, the choice of c can be viewed as a trade-off between accuracy and query time. As it is shown in Figure 11, LazyLSH achieves the highest accuracy among the LSH competitors in performing approximate queries using fractional distance metrics. We are interested in how the accuracy changes given different settings of c. Figure 15 presents the average overall ratio of performing queries w.r.t c in different ℓ_p spaces. The overall ratio is fairly well. Even for $c = 6$, the overall ratio in the $\ell_{0.5}$ space is still smaller than 1.1. This finding indicates that we can set c to be larger for faster speed while the

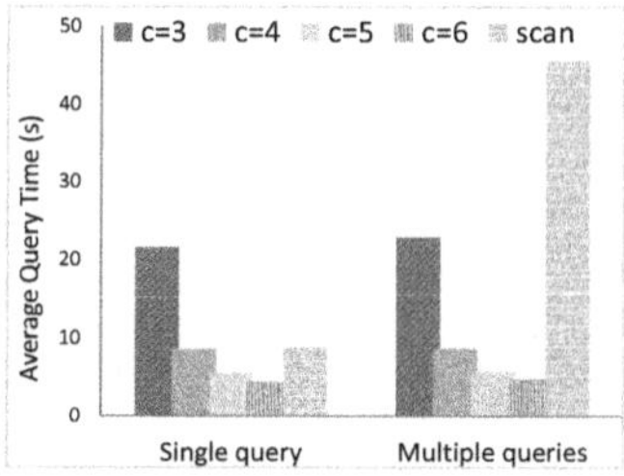

Figure 14: Query time with multi-query optimization

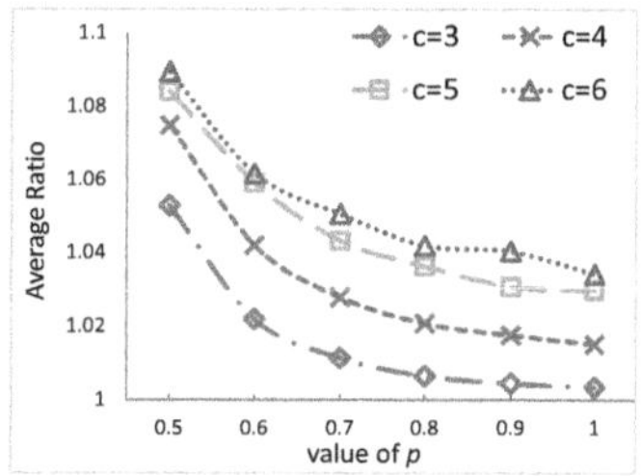

Figure 15: Average overall ratios w.r.t. c

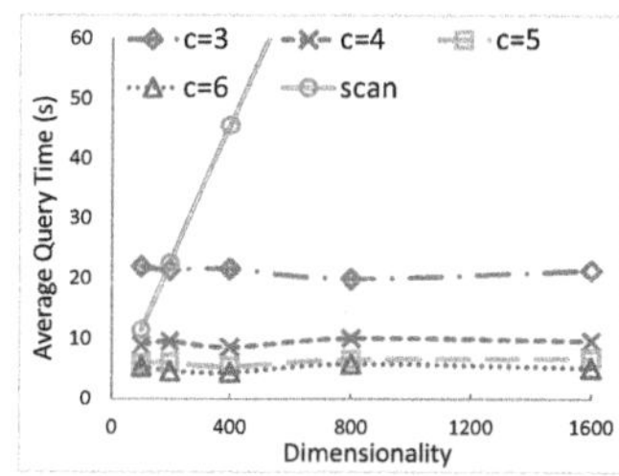

Figure 16: Average query time w.r.t. dimensionality

accuracy remains acceptable. We find that $c = 5$ or 6 might be good choices considering the trade-off between accuracy and query time.

Next we study the query time with respect to the dimensionality. We use the synthetic datasets with cardinality of 400k and dimensionality of 100, 200, 400, 800 and 1600. Figure 16 presents the average running time for processing multiple queries with different dimensionality. The average running time of the linear scan method increases linearly with the dimensionality because the CPU time of computing the distance to the query grows linearly. Please note that the results of the linear scan for $d = 800$ and 1600 are not shown for better viewing of the results of LazyLSH, and the results follow the trend. In contrast, the query time of LazyLSH remains at the same level for different dimensionality. When the approximate ratio is greater than or equal to 4, LazyLSH achieves better results in terms of query time compared to the linear scan method. In addition, LazyLSH gains more speedup when the number of dimensions increases, because the number of required hash functions does not increase linearly as presented in Table 5b. Again, the running time decreases given a larger approximate ratio c. In order to balance the accuracy and query time, we can use a larger c for those datasets with low dimensionality, and use a smaller c for those datasets with high dimensionality.

C. EXTENDING LAZYLSH TO OTHER EXISTING METHODS

LazyLSH is orthogonal to most previous work on LSH. LazyLSH targets at answering approximate nearest neighbor queries in different ℓ_p spaces using a single index. In this paper, the same index structure of C2LSH is used to process approximate nearest neighbor queries. Besides C2LSH, LazyLSH can also adopt other index structures. For instance, LazyLSH can be easily combined with the E2LSH structure. The difference is how to choose the optimal value of $\hat{r}$ in Equation 19. To fit the E2LSH structure and its variants [18, 30], we can choose $\hat{r}$ with a different optimization method. As stated in [18], $\rho = \frac{\ln 1/p_1'}{\ln 1/p_2'}$ is a parameter to be minimized in the algorithm. The smaller ρ is, the more precise results are returned. Therefore, we choose a radius r such that ρ is minimized, formally,

$$\hat{r} = \arg\min_r \rho = \arg\min_r \frac{\ln 1/p_1'}{\ln 1/p_2'}. \tag{24}$$

SRS [43] proposed a tiny index to support approximate nearest neighbor queries in the ℓ_2 space. It is reported that the index size of SRS is at least one order of magnitude smaller than that of C2LSH [21]. SRS projects data points from the original high-dimensional space into a low-dimensional space via 2-stable projections. The major observation is that the square of the ratio of the ℓ_2 distance between two points in the projected space to the ℓ_2 distance between them in the original space follows the standard chi-squared distribution. Therefore, SRS can index the data points in the low-dimensional projected space and process approximate nearest neighbor queries for high-dimensional points with theoretical guarantees based on the chi-squared distribution. However, such 2-stable projection restricts SRS to building its index in the ℓ_2 space. In contrast, our LazyLSH method is proposed based on the intuition that given $p > 0$ and $s > 0$, if two points are close in the ℓ_p space, then they are likely to be close in the ℓ_s space as well. Let $\epsilon = |p - s|$. The property holds with a higher probability for a smaller ϵ. In order to better support the approximate queries in fractional spaces, we materialize the base index in the ℓ_1 space.

To test whether the index built in the ℓ_2 space can answer approximate queries in fractional spaces, we try to use an ℓ_2 ball to approximate an $\ell_{0.5}$ ball. We set the approximate ratio $c = 3$. Our experimental result showed $p_1' < p_2'$ when the dimensionality is greater than five, which means that the LSH functions in the ℓ_2 space might not necessarily be locality-sensitive in the $\ell_{0.5}$ space when the dimensionality increases. Based on the analysis above, we conclude that it is hard to integrate SRS into LazyLSH to support queries in fractional distances because SRS has its restriction on building its index in the ℓ_2 space. However, if there is a subsequent method which can build a tiny index in the ℓ_1 space, it should be easy to extend LazyLSH to the method.

Set-based Similarity Search for Time Series

Jinglin Peng Hongzhi Wang Jianzhong Li Hong Gao
Harbin Institute of Technology
jlpengcs@gmail.com {wangzh,lijzh,honggao}@hit.edu.cn

ABSTRACT

A fundamental problem with time series involves k nearest neighbor (k-NN) query processing. However, existing methods are not fast enough for large datasets. In this paper, we propose a novel approach, STS3, for processing k-NN queries that transforms time series into sets and measures the similarity under the Jaccard metric. Our approach is more accurate than Dynamic Time Warping (DTW) in some suitable scenarios and is faster than most existing methods, due to the efficiency of similarity search for sets. In addition, we developed indexing, pruning and approximation techniques to improve the k-NN querying procedure. As shown in the experimental results, these techniques could accelerate the query processing effectively.

Keywords

time series; similarity search; k-NN; representation

1. INTRODUCTION

A time series is a sequence of data points measured in a fixed time interval. It is widely used in many applications such as financial data analysis [6], motion capture [10] and the tracking of moving objects [9]. In such applications, a k nearest neighbor (k-NN) similarity search of a time series is a basic operation that which aims at finding the time series in a set that are most k similar for a given query.

For example, the data in a electrocardiogram (ECG) could be modeled as a time series. In a computer-assisted diagnosis, a doctor may want to compare the ECG time series of a patient to the time series in a database and compare the k-NN time series to that of the patient to find candidates of diseases.

Due to its importance, some k-NN similarity search algorithms for time series have been proposed. Such algorithms are based on various similarity measures.

Similarity computation approaches aim to define and compute the similarity of time series. Some examples are Euclidean Distance (ED) [12], Longest Common Subsequence (LCSS) [30] and Dynamic Time Warping (DTW) [5].

Among these measures, the one with the most efficient search algorithm is ED. For two time series, S and Q, the computation complexity of ED is $O(n)$. However, the obvious drawbacks of ED are that it can only deal with time series of equal length and it is sensitive to noise. DTW and LCSS are more robust and can handle time series with various lengths, but their computations are expensive. The time complexity of DTW and LCSS restricted by the Sakoe-Chiba band [24] is $O(n\omega)$.

Although some indexing structures and pruning strategies have been proposed to accelerate DTW and LCSS, they do not solve the problem thoroughly. In LCSS, time series are indexed as MBRs (Minimum Boundary Rectangles) stored in an R-tree. When a query arrives, its Minimum Bounding Envelope (MBE) is constructed and split into MBRs. Then "similarity estimates are computed and the exact LCSS (or DTW) is performed only on the qualified sequences" [32]. Thus, by excluding the series that cannot be in k-NN, LCSS is accelerated. Similarly, DTW is quickly evaluated by its lower-bound functions, which cost less, [35] and some indexing techniques [26]. These acceleration strategies mainly depend on the rapid estimation of accurate distance, which is related to the specific data. Hence the acceleration is limited, and it may not achieve satisfactory efficiency in some cases.

To avoid the drawbacks of existing approaches and perform k-NN similarity search efficiently and effectively, we propose STS3, a novel algorithm for this problem. In our approach, we model time series as points on a plane. We further divide the plane into cells and the points in the same cell are treated as one element. Thus, during the processing, a time series is converted to a set of cells. The motivation for this conversion is to change the comparison of time series in quadratic time complexity into a comparison between sets, which can be accomplished in linear time. Thus, even without additional indexing and acceleration strategies, the similarity search is faster than early approaches.

To achieve higher performance, we design three filter strategies. The first one uses an inverted index to select candidates. The second one divides the plane into a scale and tries to prune candidates in this scale. The third one divides the plane into different scales in various rounds and only considers time series having maximal similarity to the query in each scale for processing in the next step, which achieves substantial filtering in each step.

The main contributions of this paper are as follows.

SIGMOD'16, June 26-July 01, 2016, San Francisco, CA, USA

DOI: http://dx.doi.org/10.1145/2882903.2882963

- We propose a novel approach that handles k-NN similarity search of time series by transforming time series to sets. To the best of our knowledge, this is the first work using set techniques to accelerate time series search.
- We propose three versions of STS3 to speed our approach up. The index-based STS3 uses an inverted list to index time series. The pruning-based STS3 prunes time series in a flexible scale, and the approximate STS3 filters time series in a coarse scale and then refines them. All three approaches can speed up the query processing effectively.
- To demonstrate the efficiency and effectiveness of the proposed approaches, we conduct extensive experiments on real data. The experimental results show that the proposed algorithm outperforms other approaches significantly in efficiency without significant loss of accuracy.

The rest of the paper is organized as follows. Background is discussed in Section 2. Section 3 describes our approach in detail, and the three speed-up techniques are demonstrated in Section 4. Section 5 extends our approach to handle situations outside of our assumptions. We discuss the pros and cons of our approach in Section 6. Our experimental results are presented in Section 7 and we discuss related work in Section 8. Section 9 concludes the paper.

2. BACKGROUND

In this paper, we investigate the problem of k-NN similarity search for time series. In this section, we introduce the definition of time series, the preprocessing approach and the assumptions used in this paper.

Definitions We define time series as follows.

DEFINITION 1. *A time series S is described as a sequence of pairs, i.e., $S = [(t_1, s_1), (t_2, s_2), ..., (t_n, s_n)]$, in which t_i is the time stamp of s_i, satisfying $t_i < t_j$ if $i < j$. s_i is a d-dimension data point.*

Preprocessing Before we process the time series, it is necessary to normalize them. The commonly used approach is z-normalization [17], shown as follows:

$$Norm(S) = \frac{S - mean(S)}{std(S)}$$

Assumptions For the convenience of our discussions, we make the following assumptions.

- All time series are z-normalized before processing and we use S to denote $Norm(S)$ throughout this paper.
- All time series are one dimensional sequences. For example, S=(2,3,4) denotes the time series S=((1,2),(2,3),(3,4)). That is, the time stamp is the sequential labeling and is omitted. Our method can be extended into multi dimensions, as will be shown in Section 5.1.
- We aim at NN search without special emphasis. The extension of our algorithm to k-NN search will be discussed in Section 5.2.
- All time series are limited by a fixed bound. This bound is used to convert the time series into sets, a process we will discuss in Section 3. Some time series may have points outside the bound. We provide solutions for these occurrences in Section 5.3.

3. STS3: A SET-BASED TIME SERIES SIMILARITY SEARCH ALGORITHM

In this section, we propose our novel method, Set-based Time Series Similarity Search (STS3).

3.1 Overview

To achieve high performance and balance search accuracy and efficiency, we develop a novel method to measure time series. Since in the normalization step, the scaling and shifting factors in the comparison are reduced, if two time series are similar, most of their corresponding segments should be similar. Furthermore, when we treat a time series as a set of points in a plane with time as t-axis and value as x-axis, the point sets corresponding to a pair of similar time series should contain many near points. Thus, we could use the number of near points in the point sets to measure the similarity of the time series.

With the consideration that near points are located in similar areas, we divide the plane into small cells and use the small cells containing points instead of the points themselves to represent the time series for the similarity search. The more cells two time series share, the more near points they have, and, correspondingly, the greater their similarity. In this way, we convert similarity search on time series to search on sets, which is more efficient for computation.

3.2 Set Representation for Time Series

In this section, we discuss how to represent a time series as a set of cells. Before beginning our discussion, however, we first provide these relevant definitions.

DEFINITION 2. *Given a set of time series D with a bound of D. bound(D)=$[(t_{min},x_{min}),(t_{max},x_{max})]$ is the minimum bounding rectangle in t-x plane covering D, in which t_{min}, x_{min}, t_{max} and x_{max} denote the minimal t and x values and the maximal t and x values in all time series in D, respectively.*

DEFINITION 3. *Given a time series S, a point p_i=(t_i,x_i) of S belongs to cell$_j$ or cell$_j$ is the corresponding cell of p_i, if $down_x < s_i \leq up_x$ and $left_t < i \leq right_t$, where the coordinates of the left-down and right-up of cell$_j$ are ($left_t$, $down_x$) and ($right_t$, up_x), respectively.*

Given a time series database D with bound(D), the zone in bound(D) is divided into cells, each of which are assigned an ID. For example, in Figure 1, the bound(D) is the minimal rectangle that contains the two time series. Then it is divided into cells with size $\sigma \times \varepsilon$, numbered from 1 to 6.

The generation of bound(D) is accomplished by scanning all points in D to find t_{min}, t_{max}, x_{min} and x_{max}.

With the generated bound, the cells are set to cover the bound with size $\sigma \times \varepsilon$. Since the goal of cell partition is measuring time series, it is necessary to ensure that similar time series have a greater number of common cells and to reduce the influence of time shift and value shift. While dividing the plane, we need two parameters, ε and σ, to tolerate time shift and value shift, respectively. These two parameters make our method robust.

After division, the cell IDs are assigned to the generated cells. i.e. the ID of a cell according to its row and column location in the grid is as follows:

$$ID = (row - 1) \times COLUMN\_NUM + column \quad (1)$$

where COLUMN_NUM is the number of columns in the grid. For example, in Figure 1, the number of columns is 3, so the ID of the cell in second row and first column of the grid is $(2-1) \times 3 + 1 = 4$.

Given a time series S, our algorithm generates its set representation by computing the cell IDs of all points. For a point (t, x) in S, the row and column of corresponding cell are $row = \frac{(x-x_{min})}{\sigma} + 1$ and $column = \frac{(t-t_{min})}{\varepsilon} + 1$, respectively.

Furthermore, the ID is computed using (1).

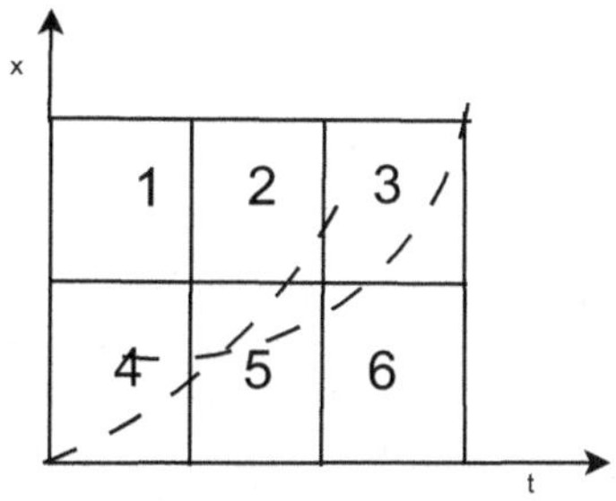

Figure 1: Grid Division

Algorithm 1 describes the procedure for transforming a time series S to the corresponding cell set S'. First, the columns of the grid are computed (Line 2). Then the cell ID of each point in S is computed (Lines 4-6). Finally all cell IDs are added to set S'(Line 7).

For a time series with n points, the time complexity of Algorithm 1 is O($nlogn$) with the set implemented by an order list for the convenience of linear-time intersection.

Algorithm 1: TimeSeriesTranstoSet

Input:
S: time series
BD: bound(D)
ε,σ: threshold
Output:
S': set presentation of S
1 $S' \leftarrow \Phi$;
2 $COLUMN\_NUM \leftarrow (BD.t_{max} - BD.t_{min}) \setminus \varepsilon$;
3 **for** *every point* s_i *of* S **do**
4 $row_i \leftarrow (x_i - BD.x_{min})/\sigma + 1$;
5 $column_i \leftarrow (t_i - BD.t_{min})/\varepsilon + 1$;
6 $number_i \leftarrow$ $(row_i - 1) \times COLUMN\_NUM + column_i$;
7 $S' \leftarrow S' \cup \{number_i\}$;
8 **end**
9 return S';

3.3 The STS3 Algorithm

When time series are converted into sets, their similarity can be computed with the Jaccard metric [19], which is one of the most popular similarities for sets. It is computed as follows: $Jaccard(S,Q) = \frac{|S \cap Q|}{|S \cup Q|}$.

In this section, we propose a naive version of the STS3 algorithm. As shown in Algorithm 2, this algorithm converts Q into cell set Q' (Line 2) and then scans the cell sets in D to find the one most similar to Q' (Lines 3-9).

The transformation cost from Q to set Q' is $O(nlogn)$. The Jaccard similarity computation cost of the sets is $O(|S|+|Q|)$ using a simple linear merge. Therefore, the time complexity of Algorithm 2 is $O(nlogn + \Sigma_{S\in D}|S| + |Q|)$.

Algorithm 2: Naive_STS3

Input:
Q:set representation of query time series
D:time series database with set representation
ε,σ:threshold
Output:
ans: NN results, $ans.TS$ denotes a time series and $ans.Jac$ denotes $Jaccard(Q, ans.TS)$
1 $ans \leftarrow null$;
2 $Q' \leftarrow TimeSeriesTranstoSet(S, bound(D), \varepsilon, \sigma)$;
3 **for** *every time series S' in D'* **do**
4 $Jac \leftarrow Jaccard(S', Q')$;
5 **if** *Jac>ans.Jac* **then**
6 $ans.TS \leftarrow Q'$;
7 $ans.Jac \leftarrow Jac$;
8 **end**
9 **end**
10 return ans;

4. EFFICIENT STS3 ALGORITHMS

In this section, we propose three efficient versions of STS3 algorithms, which are suitable for different scenarios. These are, specifically, the index-based algorithm is suitable for long time series, the pruning-based algorithm for short time series and the approximate algorithm for very long time series. To facilitate concise discussions, we use "time series" to denote the set presentation of time series in this section.

4.1 The Index-based STS3 Algorithm

Consider the procedure of naive STS3. During query processing, the Jaccard similarities of all time series in database D and the query Q have to be computed. Since most time series in D have little intersection with Q, it is unnecessary to compute the similarities for all of them. A natural way to avoid this is to use indexing to select the candidates efficiently. In this section, we propose the index-based STS3 algorithm for this purpose.

we use the inverted list [16] as the index for STS3. In the index-based STS3 algorithm, we use an inverted list IL with each entry as a pair (c, IL_c), where c is a cell and IL_c is the set of time series containing c. Intuitively, $S = \bigcup_{e\in Q} IL_e$ contains the time series intersecting with Q. Thus, the time series of processing can be limited.

Since the size of the intersection of S and Q is the number of times that S appears in all IL_e ($e \in Q$), we use a counter-array *intersection* with each entry *intersection*[S] counting the number of time series in S. The Jaccard similarities are computed according to *intersection* and the selection is performed correspondingly.

The pseudo code of the index-based STS3 is shown in Algorithm 3. First, we visit every cell e in Q. IL_e is scanned and the corresponding counter in *intersection* is refreshed for each element in it (Lines 1-5). After all counters are refreshed, the Jaccard similarity is computed directly from *intersection*, and the time series with the maximal similarity is returned as the answer (Lines 6-13).

Algorithm 3: Index_STS3

```
Input:
    Q:query time series
    D:time series database
    IL:inverted list for database
Output:
    ans: NN results, ans.TS denotes a time series and
    ans.Jac denotes Jaccard(Q, ans.TS)
for each element e in Q do
    for each time series t in IL_e do
        intersection[t] ← intersection[t] + 1;
    end
end
ans ← null;
for each time series t with non-zero intersection[t] do
    nowJac ← intersection[T]/(T.length + Q.length −
    intersection[T]);
    if nowJac > ans.Jac then
        ans.Jac ← nowJac;
        ans.TS ← t;
    end
end
return ans;
```

4.2 The Pruning-based STS3 Algorithm

In order to accelerate processing, we use a pruning strategy to filter time series. Our goal is to find a time series S with a maximal Jaccard similarity to query Q. Intuitively, when the length of S and Q are fixed, the larger $|S \cap Q|$ is, the larger Jaccard(S,Q) will be. For effective pruning, we require a fast evaluation of a tight upper bound of $|S \cap Q|$.

Unfortunately, it is hard to achieve both an accurate and efficient upper-bound evaluation. To balance the accuracy and efficiency, we set a parameter *scale* to make a flexible upper bound.

We divide the plane into zones, whose number is *scale*$\times$*scale*. An upper bound is computed for each zone, and the upper bounds of all zones are summed up. The trade-off between tightness and efficiency is tuned with the number of zones.

We use an example to illustrate this strategy. Figure 2(a) shows two time series. The plane is divided into 4 $\times$ 4 cells, and the set representations of time series 1 and 2 are (3,4,5,6,9,13) and (6,7,9,10,13), respectively. If we set *scale*=2, then we divide the plane into 2 $\times$ 2 zones, as shown in Figure 2(b). Cell 1,2,5,6 belongs to zone 1, cell 3,4,7,8 belongs to zone 2, cell 9,10,13,14 belongs to zone 3, and cell 11,12,15,16 belongs to zone 4. As shown in Figure 2(b), time series 1 has two cells in zone 1 whose cell IDs are 5 and 6 respectively, while time series 2 has one (cell ID 6). Hence the upper bound of their intersection in zone 1 is min(2,1)=1. Similarly, such upper bounds in zone 2, 3 and 4 are min(2,1)=1, min(2,3)=2 and min(0,0)=0, respectively. Hence an upper bound for intersection of the two time series is 1+1+2+0=4.

The whole algorithm is shown in Algorithm 4.

First, the plane is divided into zones. The number of cells in each zone of each time series in the database is recorded in Dzone, which is generated off line, and that of the query is recorded in Qzone (Lines 1-2). Each zone contains a subset of the time series S. We use S_i to denote the subset of S in $zone_i$. Since in $zone_i$, $min\{|S_i|, |Q_i|\}$ gives an upper

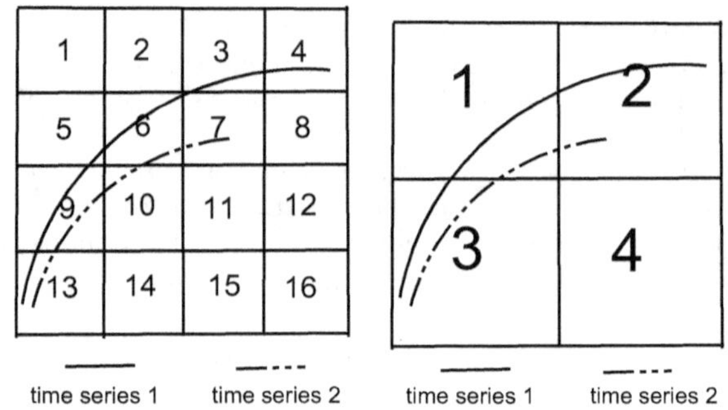

(a) 4 $\times$ 4 (b) 2 $\times$ 2

Figure 2: Two Time Series in the divided Plane

bound of $|S_i \cap Q_i|$, the upper bound of $|S \cap Q|$ is evaluated as the sum of all $min\{|S_i|, |Q_i|\}$ (Lines 6-8). After obtaining the upper bound, we use it for pruning (Lines 9-11). If the time series is not pruned, the Jaccard similarity is computed (Line 12). Finally, we find the NN answer (Lines 13-16).

Algorithm 4: Pruning_STS3

```
   Input:
       Q:query time series
       D:time series database
       scale:parameter
   Output:
       ans: NN results, ans.TS denotes a time series and
       ans.Jac denotes Jaccard(Q, ans.TS)
1  Dzone[N][i] ← number of elements of N in zone i;
2  Qzone[i] ← number of elements of Q in zone i;
3  ans ← null;
4  for each time series N in D do
5      LEN_NQ ← Q.length + N.length;
6      for i=1:scale × scale do
7          upBound ← the sum of
           min{Qzone[i], Dzone[N][i]};
8      end
9      if upBound/(LEN_NQ − upBound) < ans.Jac
       then
10         prune N;
11     end
12     Jac ← Jaccard(Q, N);
13     if Jac > ans.Jac then
14         ans.Jac ← Jac;
15         ans.TS ← N;
16     end
17 end
18 return ans
```

4.3 The Approximate STS3 Algorithm

The two algorithms above can obtain accurate results. However, for a large database, their efficiencies may be not sufficient. For such scenarios, we develop the approximate STS3 algorithm. This algorithm is pretty fast but may miss the time series that are most similar.

The approximate algorithm is based on the observation that if two time series are similar in a refined scale, then they are probably similar in a coarse scale. For example, in Figure 2(a), when the plane is divided into 4 × 4 cells, the set representations of time series 1, and time series 2 are (3,4,5,6,9,13) and (6,7,9,10,13), respectively. They are similar, with a Jaccard similarity of $\frac{3}{8}$. When the plane is divided in a coarse scale 2 × 2, as shown in Figure 2(b), both of set representations are (1,2,3), are still similar and even the same with a Jaccard similarity of 1.

Based on this observation, we can also select candidates in the coarse scale and then refine them in a more refined scale. With this approach, a greater number of similarity computations are performed in the coarse scale. As a result, the query processing is accelerated.

Our method is shown in Algorithm 5. First, the plane is divided into cells in scale from 2 to *maxScale*, an input parameter, and the set representation of each time series in the database in each scale is computed (Lines 1-5; this step is performed offline). A set *searchSet* for the candidate time series is initialized by all time series in the database (Line 6). Then in each scale, we compute the set representation of the query (Line 8) and maintain all time series with maximal similarity to Q, while removing others from *searchSet* (Lines 9-18). If the size of *searchSet* is 1, then we exit the loop (Lines 19-21). Finally, we scan all time series remaining in *searchSet* and return the one with maximal similarity to Q (Lines 24-30).

As the cost of high efficiency, the computation in the coarse scale may miss the time series that are most similar. For example, in Figure 3(a), time series 1 is the time series most similar to query. It has five elements in common with the query, while time series 2 has no elements in common with the query. But when the plane is divided into a coarse scale, as shown in Figure 3(b), time series 2 is more similar to the query since time series 2 shares more cells with the query in this scale. In this case, the time series that is most similar is missed. Fortunately, this situation is rare, since two similar time series have similar cell or zone distributions in both the refined and coarse scales with high possibility.

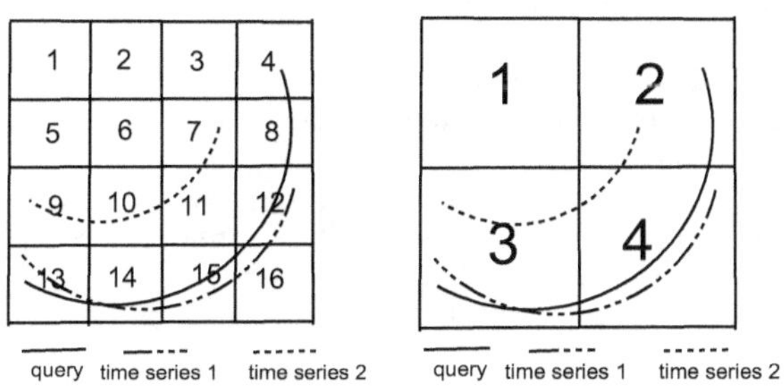

(a) 2 × 2 (b) 4 × 4

Figure 3: Example of Missing the Most Similar Time Series when Using the Approximate STS3 Algorithm

Algorithm 5: Approximate_STS3

```
  Input:
     Q:query time series
     D:time series database
     maxScale:parameter
  Output:
     ans: NN results, ans.TS denotes a time series and
     ans.Jac denotes Jaccard(Q, ans.TS)
1 for scale=2:maxScale do
2     for each time series T of D do
3         Ddivision[scale][T] ← set representation of T in
          scale division;
4     end
5 end
6 searchSet ← all time series of D;
7 for scale=2:maxScale do
8     nowQuery ← set representation of Q in scale
      division;
9     for each time series T in searchSet do
10        maxSim ←
          max{Jaccard(Ddivision[scale][T], nowQuery)}
11    end
12    newSearchSet ← null;
13    for each time series T in searchSet do
14        if Jaccard(Ddivision[scale][T], nowQuery) =
          maxSim then
15            newSearchSet.add(T);
16        end
17    end
18    searchSet ← newSearchSet;
19    if newSearchSet.size == 1 then
20        break;
21    end
22 end
23 ans ← null;
24 for each time series T in searchSet do
25    if Jaccard(T, Q) > ans.Jac then
26        ans.Jac ← Jaccard(T, Q);
27        ans.TS ← T;
28    end
29 end
30 return ans;
```

5. EXTENSIONS

In this section, we extend our approach to multi-dimensional time series and k-NN similarity search.

5.1 Multi-dimensional Time Series

When a time series is multi-dimensional, we only need to divide the multi-dimensional space into cells and give a unique ID to each cell to apply our approach. For example, if a time series is two dimensional, then we need three parametersâĂŤα_t, α_x, α_y- to divide t-x-y space into cubes and give each cube a unique ID to transform the time series into set. Thus, the cell ID of the cubic (t, x, y) is $\alpha_x\alpha_y(t-1)+\alpha_x(y-1)+x$.

With such cell IDs, the algorithms in Section 3 and Section 4 can be applied directly.

When a time series is in multi-dimensional, the computation of similarity is still efficient. The reason is that after the transformation into a set, the number of elements is smaller than the original points and the similarity of the sets can be computed in linear time.

However, when a time series is in multiple dimensions, the accuracy may be worse. For the sake of conciseness in this discussion, we analyze how the accuracy may change when a time series is two dimensional. The analysis for multiple dimensions is similar. We attempt to discuss the difference in optimal accuracy that the parameter can bring between the cases in one and two dimensions.

In the case of two dimensions, the impact of α_t on accuracy may not change compared to the impact in one dimension. The reason is that if a point has a shift in the t-axis in the t-x-y space, it probably has the same shift in the t-axis in the t-x plane and the t-y plane. For example, as shown in the experimental results in Section 7.3.1, the accuracies of three dimensions of cricket datasets are similar when α_t changes. Thus the optimal α_t of the t-x plane and the t-y plane may be close or even identical, bringing a good accuracy in t-x-y space.

When one parameter α_{xy} is used to control the shift of the x-axis and y-axis by setting α_x=α_y=α_{xy}, then the accuracy depends on the data and noise distribution. If the x-axis and y-axis have same data and noise distribution, the accuracy may not change much. The reason is that if the axes have the same distribution, the impact of α_{xy} on accuracy in the x-axis and y-axis will be similar. Therefore the α_{xy} that brings good accuracy to one axis may also be a good choice in the other, making the accuracy good in two dimensions. For example, in experiments in Section 7.3.1, the FacesUCR and FaceAll datasets have similar distributions and the results show that the impacts of α_{xy} on them are similar.

However, if the distribution of data and noise in the x-axis is different from that in the y-axis, then the α_{xy} that brings good accuracy to one axis may be a worse choice for the other, affecting the accuracy negatively.

When two parameters are used to control the shift of the x-axis and y-axis, the accuracy may decrease. This is because for the same training dataset, having more parameters usually causes overfitting, which decreases the accuracy.

5.2 k-NN Similarity Search

The extension from an NN similarity search to k-NN is straightforward. During the processing of k-NN similarity search, we use a min heap to maintain the greatest number of k similar time series instead of one. Specifically, with the naive STS3, we find the NN answer by the time series and judging whether its similarity is larger than the current best one (Lines 5-8 in Algorithm 2). For a k-NN query, this is changed to judge whether the similarity of the current time series is larger than the top element of the min heap. If it is, then the top element of the min heap is deleted and the current time series is added to the min heap. In the index-based and pruning-based STS3 Algorithms, the same change is made in Lines 9-12 in Algorithm 3 and Lines 13-16 in Algorithm 4, respectively. For the approximate STS3 algorithm in Algorithm 5, this change is made in Lines 25-28, and Line 19 changes the limiting condition to ($newSearchSet.size \leq k$) since we need to maintain at least k time series for the k-NN search.

5.3 Handling Out-of-Bound Points

In our assumption, all time series are limited in a bound. This assumption is reasonable. For the t-axis, in the real world the length of the time series is limited. For the x-axis, after z-normalization, the value obeys Gaussian distribution in most cases [23]. Therefore, a range large enough, such as (-3,3) will make almost all points fall into the bound [22].

For points outside the bound, which we call "out-points", we propose an effective strategy to handle them in this section. Since the bound is generated when the database D is constructed, out-points appear only in the query or in some updated time series in D. We discuss the handling strategy for each of these instances below.

5.3.1 For Out-points in the Query

Since the similarity is mainly determined by the common cells of Q and the time series in D, the cell IDs for the points of Q in bound(D), denoted by Q_{in}, should be uniform with those of D for the computation of common cells. For the points out of bound(D), denoted by Q_{out}, we just need to generate cell IDs different from those in bound(D).

With this in mind, the cell generation is divided into two steps for the points in Q_{in} and Q_{out}, respectively. For Q_{in}, the cell IDs are computed with the formula 1 in Section 3.2. For Q_{out}, which has no intersection with the time series in D, we only need to make the cell IDs different from those in D. Therefore, we generate the bound for Q_{out}, get the corresponding cell IDs for each point by formula 1, and add maxNumber to each ID, in which maxNumber is the maximal cell ID in bound(D). In this way, the cell IDs in Q_{out} are different from those in D.

The pseudo code of the algorithm is shown in Algorithm 6. In this algorithm, first we divide Q into Q_{in} and Q_{out} (Line 2). The set representation of Q_{in} is directly computed (Line 3). Then we transform Q_{out} into its set representation Q'_{out} (Line 4-5) and add maxNumber to each element of Q'_{out} (Lines 6-8). Finally we combine Q'_{in} and Q'_{out} to get the set representation of Q (Line 10).

Algorithm 6: Trans_outQuery_to_Set

Input:
Q:query time series
BD:bound(D)
ε,σ:threshold
Output:
Q':set presentation of Q

1 $Q' \leftarrow \Phi$;
2 Divide Q into Q_{in} and Q_{out};
3 $Q'_{in} \leftarrow TimeSeriesTranstoSet(Q_{in}, BD, \varepsilon, \sigma)$;
4 $BQ \leftarrow bound(Q_{out})$;
5 $Q'_{out} \leftarrow TimeSeriesTranstoSet(Q_{out}, BQ, \varepsilon, \sigma)$;
6 $maxNumber \leftarrow BD.rows \times BD.columns$;
7 **for** *every element t of* Q'_{out} **do**
8 | $t \leftarrow t + maxNumber$;
9 **end**
10 $Q' \leftarrow Q'_{out} \cup Q'_{in}$;
11 return Q';

5.3.2 For Out-points in the Updated Database

When time series in the updated database contain out-points, which are called out-TSs, it is straightforward to generate the new bound and recompute the set representations of all time series in database D. Such a strategy makes the updating expensive, however.

Thus, we use a "lazy" updating strategy. To be specific, we use a buffer to store the out-TSs. The bound of the buffer can be changed anytime when adding out-TSs to it, and we make sure that it is larger than the bound(D). When the buffer is full, the time series in the buffer are updated to D

and bound(D) is refreshed from the buffer. Then the cell IDs of time series in D are recomputed.

To ensure the correctness of the query processing, we handle the k-NN search in D first and then use the time series in the buffer to try to refresh the k-NN answer. Given a query Q, we compute its set representation with bound(D) and then handle the k-NN search in D. After that, we recompute the set representation of Q with bound(buffer) and compute the Jaccard similarity for Q and the time series in the buffer to try to refresh the k-NN answer. This procedure provides the final k-NN answer.

How does one decide the buffer size? In general, a small buffer may cause frequent database refreshing, while a large one will cost substantial time when time series in a buffer are used to refresh the k-NN answer. We have the following propositions, which we provide proofs for in Appendix A.

PROPOSITION 1. *The average refreshing cost of adding one time series to the database is proportional to the probability that the time series is out-TS and inversely proportional to the buffer size.*

PROPOSITION 2. *The average query cost of a time series is proportional to the sum of the buffer size and database size.*

The above propositions indicate that increasing the buffer size will increase the query time and decrease the refresh time. Therefore, in order to make the query and refresh times efficient, we suggest setting a small buffer size and a large bound, thus the buffer size and the probability that out-TS appears are small, which saves both query and refresh time.

6. DISCUSSIONS OF STS3

6.1 Efficiency

STS3 uses similarity of sets to replace similarity of time series in order to achieve high efficiency. In this section, we analyze the improvement of efficiency over DTW and LCSS.

Suppose we have two time series S and Q. Consider the procedures for DTW and LCSS restricted by the Sakoe-Chiba band [24]. These can be regarded as finding an optimal way to match points and computing the score of matched points as an evaluation of distance/similarity. In DTW, point S_i and point Q_j can be matched if $|i-j| <= \omega$ while in LCSS, they can be matched if $|i-j| <= \omega$ and $|S_i - Q_j| <= \epsilon$. Hence the points that can match a fixed point are not unique in both DTW and LCSS. Therefore, we need a principle to match all points. This principle is implemented through expensive dynamic programming, making DTW and LCSS costly.

In comparison, in STS3, the element that can match the fixed one is unique (the only one that has the same cell ID to it), so all we need to do is match all elements that can be matched. This procedure is handled by the Jaccard similarity, which can be computed in linear time. Therefore, our approach is theoretically efficient than DTW and LCSS.

6.2 Effectiveness

In this section, we discuss the effectiveness of STS3 and show some suitable scenarios for it.

Consider the accuracy of our approach. The major factor that affects accuracy is cell size. A small cell will lose the ability to hold shift. A large cell may cause different points to fall into the same cell and to be regarded as one point, which would overestimate the similarity. Therefore, when the noise of the data is great, the accuracy of our approach decreases. As a comparison, DTW does not depend on data distribution and has no such trouble.

We note therefore that in some cases the effectiveness of STS3 can be affected. Still, in some scenarios our approach is highly accurate. We discuss some examples below.

As discussed above, cell size is important for accuracy. In order to maximize accuracy, the cell size needs to balance the ability to hold shift and distinguish different time series.

One scenario satisfying the above condition is when time series have a slight shift in axis. If the shift is slight, a small cell size can hold it. Since the cell size is small, STS3 can distinguish different time series properly.

Another suitable scenario is when time series have a large global shift in the t-axis, only a few points have different values, and the values of other points are equal. If there is a large global shift in the t-axis, the cell has to be long enough to hold the shift. Although a long cell may increase the similarity of different time series, only a few points (those with different values) can be used to distinguish the different time series. Therefore, if the width of a cell is small, these points will probably fall into different cells and so distinguish different time series correctly. One specific application of such a scenario is determining similarities in the electricity consumption of different devices [21].

6.3 Determining Values for the Parameters

From the algorithm descriptions and above discussions, it should be clear that our approaches can perform better when the proper parameters are used. In this section, we discuss how to determine the parameters according to the training set.

σ and ϵ For specific applications, we can use a small amount of data to train the parameter. The series in the training dataset is labeled according to specific requirements, and is usually done manually. As an alternative, time series clustering algorithms such as [2] can be used to label the data. After that, experiments for accuracy are conducted with various parameters σ and ϵ. The parameters with the best accuracy are selected.

scale and *maxScale* *scale* (for the pruning-based STS3) and *maxScale* (for the approximate STS3) depends on the data. For *scale*, some queries are processed and the one returning maximal acceleration ratio is chosen. The range of *scale* is 2 to the square root of the time series length. For *maxScale*, it depends on the requirements and the one balancing the efficiency and accuracy in applications is chosen. A *maxScale* of 2 to 5 was usually enough in our tested cases.

7. EXPERIMENTS

To verify the effectiveness and efficiency of the proposed algorithms, we conduct extensive experiments.

All of our experiments are performed on a PC with quad core, 64-bit, 2.6 GHz CPU and 8 GB memory. The algorithms were implemented with JAVA. The operating system is Windows 7. We use runtime to measure the efficiency.

We use UCR datasets in [11] to test the accuracy of STS3. Without special emphasis, all other datasets are generated from an ECG dataset [23] that contains 20,140,000 points. The datasets are generated as follows. Given the number of time series in the database and queries, we first generate the database and then generate corresponding queries. All time series are generated by selecting l points in the order from the ECG dataset one by one and then z-normalizing them, where l is the given length of time series. The length of all time series in the database and queries is equal.

7.1 Preprocessing Time

Before using STS3, the time series need to be transformed into sets, whose cost is $O(nlogn)$. This experiment aims to test the preprocessing time on real datasets.

We use multiple representative data sets, including CBF, CinC_ECG_torso(CET) and ElectricDevices(ED). The information in the datasets and the parameters for STS3 are described in Table 1. The method used is the naive STS3 combined with an early-stopping strategy.

The transformation time for datasets and queries is shown in Table 2, as *offline time* and *online time*, respectively. For comparison, we also list query processing time as *query time*.

The results show that the transformation time of a query is very small compared to the query time. Thus, the major cost of querying is the computation of the similarity of the query and time series in the database. The experimental results show that transformation is valuable and costs little. In all the following experiments, the transformation time of the query is included in the runtime, that is, and we do not list it separately.

Table 1: Datasets Descriptions

Dataset	#query	#series	Length	(σ,ϵ)
CBF	30	900	128	(21,0.18)
CET	40	1380	1639	(76,0.82)
ED	7711	8926	96	(4,0.88)

Table 2: Series Transformation Time

Dataset	Offline Time	Online Time	Query Time
CBF	64	1	30
CET	121	3	35
ED	97	50	19,843

7.2 Comparisons

In this section, we compare our algorithm with ED, DTW, and LCSS in terms of efficiency and effectiveness.

7.2.1 *Efficiency*

To show the efficiency of STS3, we compare it to three representative approaches: ED, DTW and LCSS. We tested some optimization techniques based on these approaches. For DTW, we tested DTW with an LB_improved low boundary [18] and FastDTW [27]. For LCSS, we tested FTSE [22]. We used an early-stopping strategy in all techniques except for FastDTW, which uses a multi-layer filtering technique and cannot be stopped early.

The datasets used are the same as those in Section 7.1. The information on the datasets and the parameters for STS3 can be found in Table 1. The warping length for DTW used comes directly from UCR Archive [11]. FastDTW is implemented with Java-ML library [1]. The radius for FastDTW is set to 0, which gives it optimal speed. The warping length used for LCSS is 10% of the time series length and the ϵ is 0.5, as suggested in [31].

The runtime is shown in Table 3.

From the results, we observe that for these three datasets STS3 is faster than FTSE, FastDTW and LB_improved. For FTSE, before the computation of LCSS, it needs $O(n+m)$ time to build the intersection list. Hence it is slower than STS3. FastDTW is slower, it cannot use the early-stopping strategy. In addition, its time cost is $n(8r+14)$. When r=0, the constant cost is 14, larger than that of STS3 (which is 2). As for LB_improved, the cost of computing the envelope of the time series is $3n$, larger than STS3. Also, some time series cannot be pruned by LB_improved. Then the real and expensive DTW is computed for them. Hence it is slower than STS3 in these datasets.

As for ED, our approach is slightly faster than ED in two datasets. Theoretically our approach is slower than ED since we use linear intersection to compute the Jaccard similarity. However, when we transform the time series into sets, the length of the time series is usually reduced, which makes our approach faster sometimes than ED.

Table 3: Runtime of Different Approaches

Dataset	STS3	ED	FTSE	FastDTW	LB_improved
CBF	31	21	2262	2823	1155
CET	38	203	739753	110448	2106
ED	19893	28423	3506902	4023365	465266

7.2.2 *Effectiveness*

We use the datasets in the UCR Archive [11] to evaluate the accuracy of STS3. Each dataset has two parts, TRAIN and TEST, and each time series in the dataset is labeled. For each time series in TEST, an NN classification is performed on it and its class is computed as its nearest neighbor in TRAIN. The error rate is calculated as follows:

$$errorRate = \frac{number\ of\ wrongly\ classified\ time\ series}{total\ time\ series\ number\ of\ TEST}$$

We run experiments on the UCR Archive datasets with the different parameters ε and σ shown Table 5, where n is the length of the time series. The TRAIN dataset is divided into two parts in order to choose the optimal parameters, according to the principle that the number of time series belonging to same class is equal in each part.

In the interest of conserving, the error rate for all datasets is shown in Table 8 in Appendix B.2. For the convenience of our discussion, we extract some representative results to Table 4. The "tDTW" and "tSTS3" denote the train error rate for DTW and STS3, respectively.

From the results we observe that STS3 is as accurate as ED while DTW outperforms STS3 in 79.5% of the cases. We then examine why STS3 has better or worse accuracy, respectively.

In the suitable scenarios, described in Section 6.2, STS3 usually outperforms ED and sometimes outperforms DTW. For example, shapesAll(SA) and Herring(HE) are all image outline series. The shift in similar time series is slight, so STS3 can handle the shift and distinguish the different time series well. Therefore, STS3 outperforms DTW in HE. However, in SA, STS3 performs worse than DTW. The reason may be that SA has too many classes and this decreases the ability of grid to distinguish different classes.

Other examples include Computers (CP), RefrigerationDevices (RD) and ScreenType (ST). These datasets are the classifications for devices with similar electricity consumption usage patterns [21]. In the datasets, the time series have a global shift, but only a few points have different values. The value of others is 0. Hence, cells with long lengths and narrow widths can distinguish different time series well, achieving high accuracy.

From the results, we observe that in the above scenarios, the performance of STS3 in the Train dataset could be used to predict its performance in the TEST dataset. That is, if STS3 outperforms DTW in the TRAIN dataset, its probably outperform DTW in the TEST dataset.

Table 4: Error Rate in Part Datasets

Dataset	SA	HE	CP	RD	ST	PM	HO
ED	0.248	0.484	0.424	0.605	0.64	0.891	0.199
DTW	0.198	0.469	0.38	0.56	0.589	0.773	0.197
STS3	0.225	0.438	0.316	0.539	0.563	0.873	0.213
tDTW	0.188	0.484	0.248	0.331	0.456	0.785	0.100
tSTS3	0.263	0.161	0.185	0.29	0.425	0.758	0.065

We also find that most datasets in the UCR Archive do not fall within our suitable scenarios. For example, the phoneme(PM) dataset has a large amount of noise. The shift of points in similar time series is large, so the small cells cannot handle noise and the large cells cannot distinguish different time series. As a result, our approach does not perform as well as other approaches, as shown in Table 4.

Another example is the handoutlines(HO) dataset. It contains two classes and the time series belonging to the different classes are very similar. Since the cells cannot hold the shift, STS3 cannot distinguish different time series well in this situation. As a result, STS3 performs worse than ED and DTW, as shown in Table 4.

We also tested accuracy when the workload is relatively fixed. We use the TRAIN and TEST datasets to tune parameters and test the error rate of STS3 and DTW. The results are shown in Table 8 in Appendix B.2.

From these results, we conclude that STS3 outperforms DTW and ED when the workload is fixed. Hence it is also a good choice for that situation.

Table 5: Parameter Settings for STS3

Parameter	min Value	max Value	Step Size
σ	1	0.3*n	1
ε	0.02	1	0.02

7.3 The Impact of Parameters

In this section, we test the impact of parameters on our algorithms. The parameters include σ, ϵ, k, the number of time series in the database (*#series*), the length of each time series (*length*), the number of queries (*#query*), *scale* for the pruning-based STS3 and *maxScale* for the approximate STS3.

Without explicit explanation, the default settings of σ and ε are 3 and 0.58, which could achieve a large accuracy for the ECG200 dataset in [11]. Other default values are k=1 , *#series* =20,000, *length*=500. The parameters *scale* for the pruning-based STS3 and *maxScale* for the approximate STS3 vary from 2 to 50 and 2 to 10, respectively, and were chosen because they produce maximal speed-up rate.

7.3.1 The Impact of σ and ϵ on Accuracy

To explore the impact of σ and ϵ on accuracy, we fix the σ as the parameter bringing optimal accuracy and then vary ϵ to see how the accuracy changes. After that, we do the same with ϵ.

We observe that the trend depends on applications. As mentioned in Section 6.2, increasing the cell size may overestimate the similarity while decreasing the cell size will decrease the ability to handle shift. Hence, the impacts of σ and ϵ on accuracy mainly depend on the specific data.

For σ, if the data have a similar time shift, then the trends in accuracy are similar. This usually occurs in some multidimensional applications. In this case, if a point has time shift in one dimension, the time shift will also happen in other dimensions, so the trends are usually similar. For example, cricket_X, cricket_Y and cricket_Z are three dimensions of people mimicking the 12 gestures of a cricket umpire [7]. The figures for accuracy varying with σ are very similar, as shown in Figure 4(b)- 4(d).

As for ϵ, which controls the shift in the x-axis, it depends on the data and noise. For similar applications, the noise and data distributions are usually similar, so the figures are similar. For example, FacesUCR and FaceAll consist of time series transformed by the face images of 14 students in different situations [4]. Their figures for accuracy varying with ϵ are very similar, as shown in Figure 4(e)- 4(f).

7.4 The Impact of k on Efficiency

We test the efficiency of STS3 when parameter k changes. The results are shown in Figure 4(a). The time increases approximately logarithmically with k.This is because we use a heap to maintain the k-NN answer and the cost of updating heap is only $O(logk)$, which is pretty small.

7.4.1 The Impact of the Query Number on Efficiency

In this experiment, we test the impact of the query number on the efficiency by varying *#query* from 1000 to 8000.

The impacts on efficiency are shown in Figure 5(a). From the results we observe that the runtime of the pruning-based and the approximate STS3 increases linearly with *#query*. The approximate STS3 is the fastest one. The runtime of the index-based STS3 is not stable. When the query number is small, it is slow, but when the query number increases, it becomes fast. This is because in the index-based STS3, the cost of accessing entries in the inverted list dominates the runtime. Thus, when *#query* is small, a single query with small selectivity may have a large impact on the whole runtime, while a large *#query* could reduce the impact of a single query.

The parameters with the maximal speed-up rate for the pruning-based and approximate algorithms are shown in Table 6. From it, we observe that the parameter leading to maximal efficiency is relatively stable and robust for *#query*. That means when we choose parameters for these two algorithms, we could use some queries as a test and choose the parameters that produced maximal speed-up rate.

7.4.2 The Impact of Time Series Length on Efficiency

In this experiment, we test the impact of time series length on efficiency by varying *length* from 100 to 800. The results are shown in Figure 5(b).

From Figure 5(b) we observe that the approximate STS3

Table 6: Parameter Settings for Pruning and Approximate STS3 with Maximal Speed-up Rate

#query	1K	2K	3K	4K	5K	6K	7K	8K
scale	25	27	25	27	27	25	25	27
maxScale	7	5	6	6	6	7	7	7

is significantly faster than other algorithms in most cases and that the length of time series has little impact on it. Hence it is suitable to handle time series with long lengths. As for the index-based STS3, it is suitable for relatively long time series. The reason is that the number of cells is large for long series. Thus, each entry in the inverted list contains a small series. Accessing them is cheap. As for the pruning-based STS3, its runtime is around linear to *length*. When the time series is short, it runs fast while when the time series is long, it is slower than the index-based STS3. For a long series, effective pruning requires a large *scale*, which leads to a high computation cost. Thus the efficiency is affected. As a result, it is suitable for handling short time series, while the index-based STS3 is more suitable for long time series.

7.4.3 Scalability

In this experiment, we test the efficiency of three algorithms with *#series* ranging from 5000 to 30000. The experimental results are shown in Figure 5(c).

From Figure 5(c), we observe that the runtime of the approximate STS3 is around linear to database size. Because the approximate STS3 usually returns the answer within a few steps, its major cost depends on database size. The runtime of the index-based and pruning-based STS3s does not increase significantly, and even decreases sometimes, as the database size increases. For the index-based STS3, even for large datasets, only a small share of entries in the inverted lists are accessed. For the pruning-based STS3, it is because the pruning strategy could filter a large share of time series for large dataset.

7.4.4 The Impact of *scale* on Efficiency

In this experiment, we test the speed-up rate and pruning rate with different *scale* for the pruning-based STS3.

Results are shown in Figure 5(d).

As for the speed-up rate, we observe that it increases slowly at first, and then at some *scale* it reaches the peak, and then decreases slowly. This is because when *scale* is small, it cannot filter many time series and so the speed-up rate is relatively small. When it becomes too large, although the upper bound becomes tighter, the computation of upper bound becomes large, which leads to a slower speed-up rate. Only when *scale* is at some middle value can the pruning-based STS3 balance the efficiency and tightness of the upper bound, which leads to the maximal speed-up rate.

As for the pruning rate, we observe that it increases sharply with *scale* when *scale* is relatively small. After that, it increases slowly and is close to 1. Hence the *scale* bigger than the optimal *scale* cost much but does not bring large increase of pruning rate. As a consequence, the speed-up rate decreases.

7.4.5 The Impact of *maxScale*

In this experiment, we test the speed-up rate, the compression rate and the error rate of various *maxScales* for

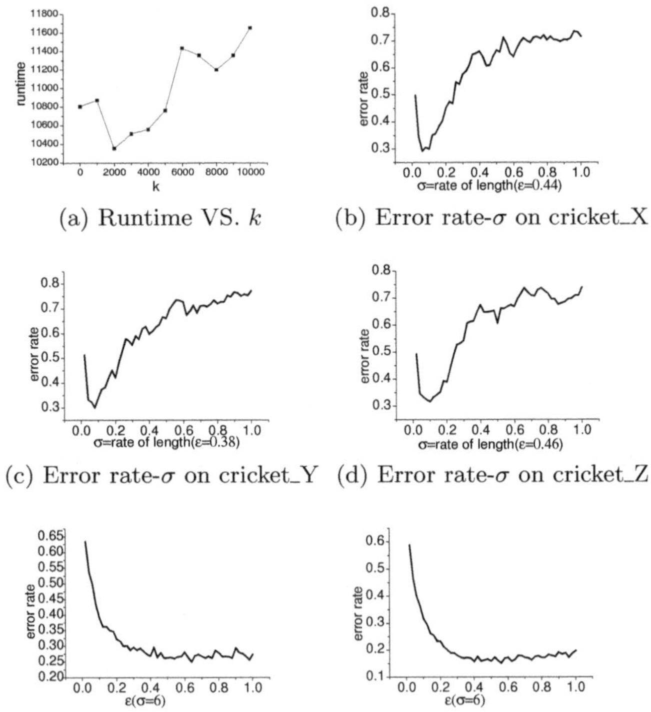

(a) Runtime VS. k (b) Error rate-σ on cricket_X

(c) Error rate-σ on cricket_Y (d) Error rate-σ on cricket_Z

(e) Error rate-ϵ on FaceAll (f) Error rate-ϵ on FacesUCR

Figure 4: Impact of Parameters on Accuracy-PartA

the approximate STS3. The *compression rate* is defined as the rate of set size after filtering and before filtering. The *Error rate* is defined as follows:

$$ErrorRate = \frac{approxDist - optimalDist}{optimalDist}[28]$$

.

The impact on the speed-up rate is shown in Figure 5(e). From this figure, we observe that the speed-up rate increases very fast at first and reaches a peak and then it decreases slowly. The reason is that many time series are filtered with a small *maxScale*, saving much time. When *maxScale* gets some value, after filtering, the number of time series remaining reaches the threshold. In this case, the growth of *maxScale* cannot filter more time series but cost much. As a consequence, the speed-up rate decreases.

Figure 5(f) shows the compression and error rate. For the compression rate, we observe that it decreases quickly and after a few steps it becomes a constant, which verifies our analysis about the speed-up rate. As for the error rate, it grows fast and then becomes stable. Additionally, the larger speed-up rate and the smaller compression rate are, the larger the error rate is. Another observation is that the error rate is generally smaller than 20%.

7.4.6 Comprehensive Comparison of Three STS3s

To make a comprehensive comparison of runtime and accuracy for the three versions of the STS3 algorithm, we conduct this experiment.

We use three datasets in the UCR Archive: ChlorineConcentration(CC), NonInvasiveFatalECG_Thorax1(NIFE) and ElectricDevices(ED). The information on the datasets and the settings of σ and ϵ are listed in Table 7. The param-

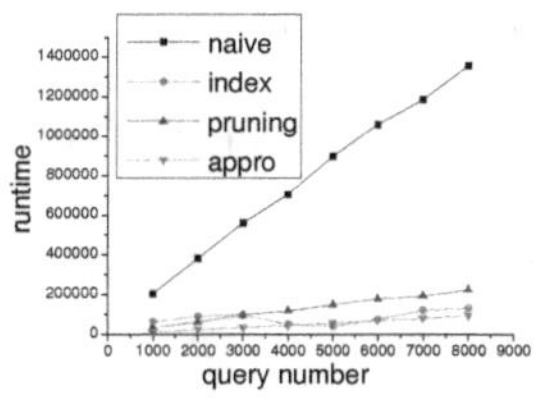

(a) Runtime VS. *#query*

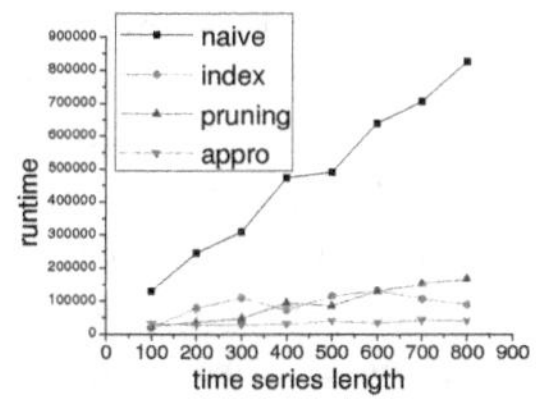

(b) Runtime VS. *length*

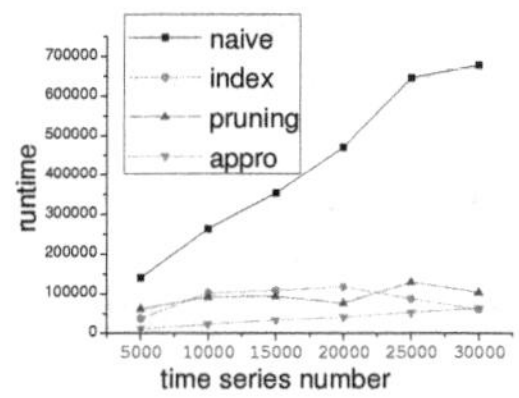

(c) Runtime VS. *#series*

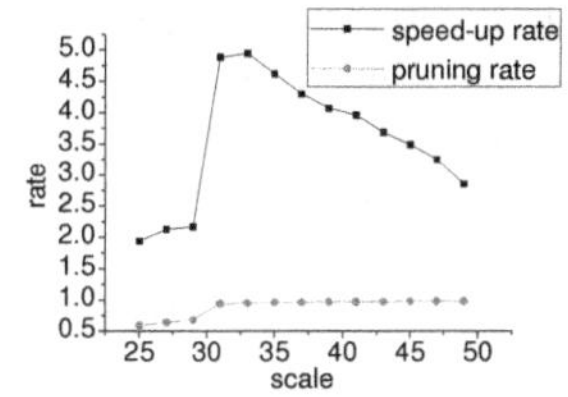

(d) The impact of *scale*

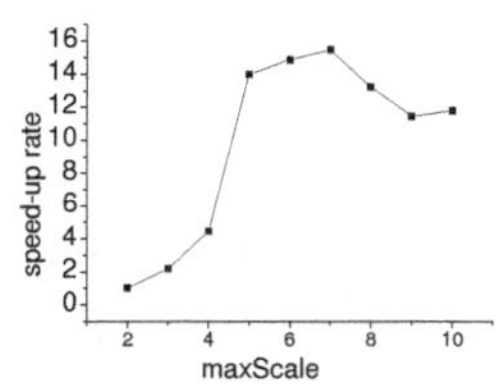

(e) Speed-up rate VS. *maxScale*

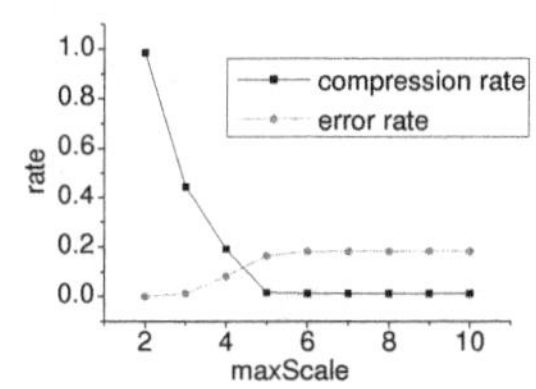

(f) Accuracy VS. *maxScale*

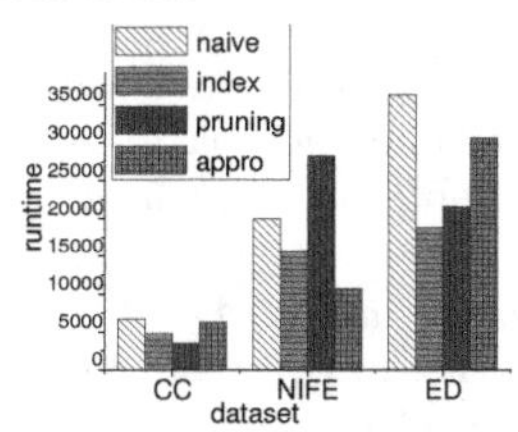

(g) Runtime of three STS3

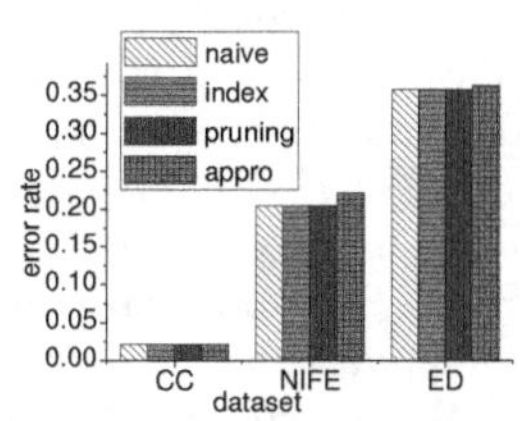

(h) Error rate of three STS3

Figure 5: Experimental Results for the Impact of Parameters-PartB

eter *scale* is set to 6 and *maxScale* is set to 4. Note that each dataset has two sub-datasets and we chose the one containing fewer time series as the query and the other as the database.

Table 7: Datasets of Comprehensive Comparison of Three STS3s

Dataset	#query	#series	length	(σ,ϵ)
CC	467	3840	166	(1,0.28)
NIFE	1800	1965	750	(7,0.14)
ED	7711	8926	96	(4,0.88)

The runtime is shown in Figure 5(g). From the results, we observe that the pruning-based STS3 has a slight advantage in CC, whose time series is relatively short. The approximate STS3 performs better in NIFE, whose time series is long. The index-based STS3 has a slight advantage in ED, whose database is large (since ED has a large number of queries and the time cost in computing set representations in different scales is expensive, which makes the pruning-based STS3 and the approximate STS3 slow).

The results for accuracy are shown in Figure 5(h). From the results, we observe that the accuracy of the approximate STS3 is only a little smaller than the other approaches, which demonstrates that the approximate STS3 misses the best solution only for a few cases.

8. RELATED WORK

Time series similarity search is mainly studied in two respects, time series representations and time series similarity measures with corresponding optimization techniques.

8.1 Time Series Representations

A straightforward representation for a time series is to divide the time series into pieces and use the average values to represent each piece [13, 14]. Piecewise aggregate approximation(PAA) [13] directly divides time series into equal sizes, which may miss some information such as maximums or minimums. [14] proposes an adaptive division method. It transforms time series by wavelet transformation and then divides time series into adaptive lengths according to the principle that minimizes the fitting.

Other representations include Discrete Fourier Transformation (DFT) [12], Single Value Decomposition (SVD) [12], Discrete Wavelet Transform (DWT) [29] and so on.

8.2 Time Series Similarity Measures

L_p-norm [3] is the most straightforward measure for time series. However, it can only handle time series with equal lengths and it is sensitive to noise. DTW is a classic speech recognition approach. Berndt and Clifford [5] introduced it to time-series data mining. It can handle time series with different lengths by allowing comparison one to many points and it is more robust than ED. DTW is a hot study domain. Much work has done on it. Low bounds and index techniques have been proposed to speed up DTW [15, 35, 23, 26]. A linear and approximate DTW algorithm named FastDTW has been proposed [27]. [25] proposed a very efficient algorithm named SPRING to handle subsequence similarity searches based on DTW.

Another idea is inspired by string measures such as the distance based on Long Common Subsequence (LCSS) [30, 33], Edit Distance on Real sequence (EDR) [9] and Edit Distance with Real Penalty (ERP) [8]. [22] proposes an algorithm to evaluate these measures efficiently and accurately. [32] proposes an index structure based on MBR, which supports multiple distance measures.

We also refer readers to [34] and [20]. [34] makes a comparison of different time-series measures while [20] makes a survey about time-series measures and their applications to time-series data mining.

9. CONCLUSIONS

In this paper, we propose a method, STS3, for processing k-NN search of time series. STS3 is faster than most existing methods. In addition, our experiments show that STS3 is more accurate than DTW in some suitable scenarios.

Furthermore, we propose three methods to speed up the k-NN query procedure and test their efficiency by experiment. Future work will include scaling our approach on large datasets by adopting a parallelized mechanism and developing a compression strategy for time series.

Acknowledgments. This paper was supported by NGFR 973 grant 2012CB316200, NSFC grant U1509216,61472099, 61133002 and National Sci-Tech Support Plan 2015BAH10F01. Hongzhi Wang is the corresponding author of this work. Hongzhi Wang and Jinglin Peng contributed to the work equally and should be regarded as co-first authors.

10. REFERENCES

[1] T. Abeel, Y. Van de Peer, and Y. Saeys. Java-ml: A machine learning library. *The Journal of Machine Learning Research*, 10:931–934, 2009.

[2] S. Aghabozorgi, A. S. Shirkhorshidi, and T. Y. Wah. Time-series clustering–a decade review. *Information Systems*, 2015.

[3] R. Agrawal, C. Faloutsos, and A. Swami. *Efficient similarity search in sequence databases.* Springer, 1993.

[4] M. G. Baydogan. *Modeling Time Series Data for Supervised Learning.* PhD thesis, 2012.

[5] D. J. Berndt and J. Clifford. Using dynamic time warping to find patterns in time series. In *KDD workshop*, 1994.

[6] A. Chakraborti, M. Patriarca, and M. S. Santhanam. Financial time-series analysis: a brief overview. *New Economic Windows*, 48(2):51–67, 2007.

[7] G. S. Chambers, S. Venkatesh, G. A. West, and H. H. Bui. Segmentation of intentional human gestures for sports video annotation. In *MMM 2004.*

[8] L. Chen and R. Ng. On the marriage of lp-norms and edit distance. In *VLDB 2004.*

[9] L. Chen, M. T. Özsu, and V. Oria. Robust and fast similarity search for moving object trajectories. In *SIGMOD 2005.*

[10] Y. Chen, G. Chen, K. Chen, and B. C. Ooi. Efficient processing of warping time series join of motion capture data. In *ICDE 2009.*

[11] Y. Chen, E. Keogh, B. Hu, N. Begum, A. Bagnall, A. Mueen, and G. Batista. The ucr time series classification archive, July 2015. www.cs.ucr.edu/~eamonn/time_series_data/.

[12] C. Faloutsos, M. Ranganathan, and Y. Manolopoulos. *Fast subsequence matching in time-series databases*, volume 23. ACM, 1994.

[13] E. Keogh, K. Chakrabarti, M. Pazzani, and S. Mehrotra. Dimensionality reduction for fast similarity search in large time series databases, 2000.

[14] E. Keogh, K. Chakrabarti, M. Pazzani, and S. Mehrotra. Locally adaptive dimensionality reduction for indexing large time series databases. *ACM SIGMOD Record*, 30(2), 2001.

[15] E. Keogh and C. A. Ratanamahatana. Exact indexing of dynamic time warping. *Knowledge and information systems*, 7(3), 2005.

[16] D. Knuth. Retrieval on secondary keys. *The art of computer programming: Sorting and Searching*, 3.

[17] E. Kreyszig. *Advanced Engineering Mathematics (Fourth ed.).* Wiley, 1979.

[18] D. Lemire. Faster retrieval with a two-pass dynamic-time-warping lower bound. *Pattern recognition*, 42(9), 2009.

[19] M. Levandowsky and D. Winter. Distance between sets. *Nature*, 234, 1971.

[20] T. W. Liao. Clustering of time series data-a survey. *Pattern recognition*, 38(11), 2005.

[21] J. Lines, A. Bagnall, P. Caiger-Smith, and S. Anderson. Classification of household devices by electricity usage profiles. In *IDEAL 2011.*

[22] M. D. Morse and J. M. Patel. An efficient and accurate method for evaluating time series similarity. In *SIGMOD 2007.*

[23] T. Rakthanmanon, B. Campana, A. Mueen, G. Batista, B. Westover, Q. Zhu, J. Zakaria, and E. Keogh. Addressing big data time series: Mining trillions of time series subsequences under dynamic time warping. *ACM Transactions on Knowledge Discovery from Data (TKDD)*, 7(3), 2013.

[24] H. Sakoe and S. Chiba. Dynamic programming algorithm optimization for spoken word recognition. *IEEE Transactions on Acoustics Speech & Signal Processing*, 26(1), 1978.

[25] Y. Sakurai, C. Faloutsos, and M. Yamamuro. Stream monitoring under the time warping distance. In *ICDE 2007.*

[26] Y. Sakurai, M. Yoshikawa, and C. Faloutsos. FTW: fast similarity search under the time warping distance. In *PODS 2005.*

[27] S. Salvador and P. Chan. Fastdtw: Toward accurate dynamic time warping in linear time and space. In *KDD workshop on mining temporal and sequential data.* Citeseer, 2004.

[28] S. W. Salvador. *Learning states for detecting anomalies in time series.* PhD thesis, Citeseer, 2004.

[29] Z. R. Struzik and A. Siebes. *Wavelet transform in similarity paradigm.* Springer, 1998.

[30] M. Vlachos, D. Gunopoulos, and G. Kollios. Discovering similar multidimensional trajectories. In *ICDE 2002.*

[31] M. Vlachos, M. Hadjieleftheriou, D. Gunopulos, and E. Keogh. Indexing multi-dimensional time-series with support for multiple distance measures. In *SIGKDD 2003.*

[32] M. Vlachos, M. Hadjieleftheriou, D. Gunopulos, and E. J. Keogh. Indexing multidimensional time-series. *VLDB J.*, 15(1), 2006.

[33] M. Vlachos, G. Kollios, and D. Gunopulos. Elastic translation invariant matching of trajectories. *Machine Learning*, 58(2-3), 2005.

[34] X. Wang, A. Mueen, H. Ding, G. Trajcevski, P. Scheuermann, and E. Keogh. Experimental comparison of representation methods and distance measures for time series data. *Data Mining and Knowledge Discovery*, 26(2), 2013.

[35] M. Zhou and M. H. Wong. Boundary-based lower-bound functions for dynamic time warping and their indexing. *Inf. Sci.*, 181(19), 2011.

APPENDIX

A. PROOF OF PROPOSITIONS IN SECTION 5.3.2

First we make some assumptions: (1) time series length is n, (2) the database contains M time series, (3) the buffer size is B (that is, it contains B time series) and (4) the probability of a time series added to the database breaking the bound is p.

Based on these assumptions, we prove the propositions.

Proof of Proposition 1: After adding $1/p$ time series to the database, there may be one series that breaks the bound. Then this series is added to the buffer. After adding about B/p time series the buffer is full and the database needs to be refreshed. The refreshing cost is $O(Mnlogn)$, so the average refreshing cost of adding one time series is $O(pMnlogn/B)$. Thus, Proposition 1 has been proved.

Proof of Proposition 2: The NN query time is $O(Mn)$ and $O((1+2+...+B)n/B) = O(Bn)$ in the database and buffer, respectively. As a result, the average query time for a time series is $O((M+B)n)$. Hence Proposition 2 has been proved.

B. SUPPLEMENTARY EXPERIMENTS

B.1 The Impact of σ and ϵ on Efficiency

In this experiment, we show the efficiency of the naive STS3 when three parameters change.

To show the impact of σ, we fix ϵ=0.5 and vary σ. The results are shown in Figure 6(a). From the figure, we observe that when σ grows, the runtime of STS3 decreases. This is because a big σ causes more points to locate in one cell and the cell number gets smaller.

We fix σ=20 and vary ε. The experimental results are shown in Figure 6(b). The trend is similar to Figure 6(a). The reason for this phenomenon is the same as that for σ.

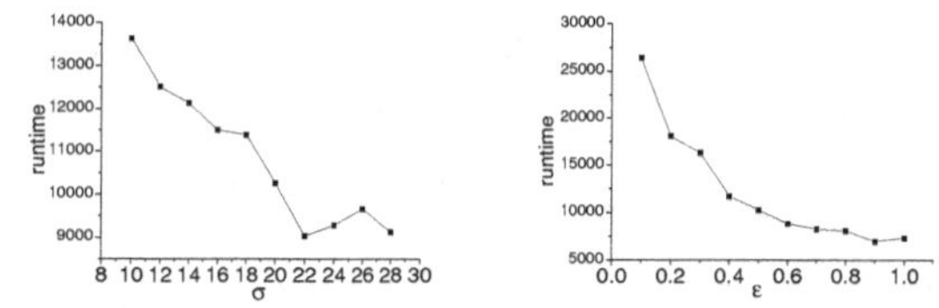

(a) Runtime VS. σ (b) Runtime VS. ε

B.2 The Whole Accuracy Comparison Result

This is the whole accuracy comparison result on UCR Archive datasets. Since our program will be terminated after one hour for each dataset, some datasets have no result and '-' is used to fill the blank. Since the runtime of LCSS in most datasets is over one hour, we do not list it in the table. The results of DTW are obtained directly from [11]. The meaning of each column is as follows:

1. Train-size: the number of time series in the TRAIN dataset.
2. Test-size: the number of time series in the TEST dataset.
3. TS-Len: the length of the time series.
4. #Classes: the number of different classes.
5. ED, DTW, STS3: the error rate of ED, DTW and STS3 when the TRAIN and TEST datasets are used to to train parameters and test the error rate, respectively.
6. DTWfixed, STS3fixed: the error rate of DTW and STS3 when the workload is relatively fixed. That is, the error rate when the TRAIN and TEST datasets are both used to train parameters.

Table 8: Error Rate of different Approaches in UCR Archive

Name	Train-size	Test-size	TS-Len	#Classes	ED	DTW	STS3	DTWfixed	STS3fixed
50words	450	455	270	50	0.369	0.242	0.299	0.235	0.270
Adiac	390	391	176	37	0.389	0.391	0.435	0.358	0.412
Beef	30	30	470	5	0.333	0.333	0.433	0.300	0.200
BeetleFly	20	20	512	2	0.250	0.300	0.200	0.250	0.000
BirdChicken	20	20	512	2	0.450	0.300	0.350	0.250	0.050
Car	60	60	577	4	0.267	0.233	0.300	0.217	0.183
CBF	30	900	128	3	0.148	0.004	0.157	0.002	0.001
ChlorineConcentration	467	3840	166	3	0.350	0.350	0.395	0.350	0.373
CinC_ECG_torso	40	1380	1639	4	0.103	0.070	0.063	-	0.018
Coffee	28	28	286	2	0.000	0.000	0.036	0.000	0.000
Computers	250	250	720	2	0.424	0.380	0.316	0.304	0.196
Cricket_X	390	390	300	12	0.423	0.228	0.308	0.221	0.277
Cricket_Y	390	390	300	12	0.433	0.238	0.326	0.233	0.279
Cricket_Z	390	390	300	12	0.413	0.254	0.300	0.223	0.272
DiatomSizeReduction	16	306	345	4	0.065	0.065	0.105	0.033	0.016
DistalPhalanxOutlineAgeGroup	139	400	80	3	0.218	0.228	0.233	0.200	0.155
DistalPhalanxOutlineCorrect	276	600	80	2	0.248	0.232	0.265	0.225	0.202
DistalPhalanxTW	139	400	80	6	0.273	0.272	0.308	0.273	0.213
Earthquakes	139	322	512	2	0.326	0.258	0.317	0.252	0.180
ECG200	100	100	96	2	0.120	0.120	0.160	0.100	0.070
ECG5000	500	4500	140	5	0.075	0.075	0.075	0.075	0.066
ECGFiveDays	23	861	136	2	0.203	0.203	0.225	0.165	0.096
ElectricDevices	8926	7711	96	7	0.450	0.376	-	-	-
FaceAll	560	1,690	131	14	0.286	0.192	0.267	0.183	0.250
FaceFour	24	88	350	4	0.216	0.114	0.114	0.114	0.057
FacesUCR	200	2050	131	14	0.231	0.088	0.195	0.077	0.150
FISH	175	175	463	7	0.217	0.154	0.246	0.149	0.194
FordA	1320	3601	500	2	0.341	0.341	-	-	-
FordB	810	3636	500	2	0.442	0.414	0.488	-	-
Gun_Point	50	150	150	2	0.087	0.087	0.227	0.027	0.027
Ham	109	105	431	2	0.400	0.400	0.429	0.400	0.276
HandOutlines	370	1000	2709	2	0.199	0.197	0.213	-	-
Haptics	155	308	1092	5	0.630	0.588	0.653	0.571	0.575
Herring	64	64	512	2	0.484	0.469	0.438	0.344	0.266
InlineSkate	100	550	1882	7	0.658	0.613	0.696	0.584	0.587
InsectWingbeatSound	220	1980	256	11	0.438	0.422	0.454	0.422	0.412
ItalyPowerDemand	67	1029	24	2	0.045	0.045	0.126	0.045	0.063
LargeKitchenAppliances	375	375	720	3	0.507	0.205	0.312	0.203	0.304
Lighting2	60	61	637	2	0.246	0.131	0.295	0.082	0.098
Lighting7	70	73	319	7	0.425	0.288	0.301	0.233	0.219
MALLAT	55	2345	1024	8	0.086	0.086	0.135	0.054	0.043
Meat	60	60	448	3	0.067	0.067	0.100	0.067	0.017
MedicalImages	381	760	99	10	0.316	0.253	0.357	0.246	0.316
MiddlePhalanxOutlineAgeGroup	154	400	80	3	0.260	0.253	0.218	0.248	0.200
MiddlePhalanxOutlineCorrect	291	600	80	2	0.247	0.318	0.327	0.247	0.237
MiddlePhalanxTW	154	399	80	6	0.439	0.419	0.456	0.414	0.353
MoteStrain	20	1252	84	2	0.121	0.134	0.167	0.121	0.113
NonInvasiveFatalECG_Thorax1	1800	1965	750	42	0.171	0.185	-	-	-
NonInvasiveFatalECG_Thorax2	1800	1965	750	42	0.120	0.129	-	-	-
OliveOil	30	30	570	4	0.133	0.133	0.200	0.133	0.100
OSULeaf	200	242	427	6	0.479	0.388	0.467	0.380	0.372
PhalangesOutlinesCorrect	1800	858	80	2	0.239	0.239	0.268	0.239	0.260
Phoneme	214	1896	1024	39	0.891	0.773	0.873	-	-
ProximalPhalanxOutlineAgeGroup	400	205	80	3	0.215	0.215	0.190	0.195	0.122
ProximalPhalanxOutlineCorrect	600	291	80	2	0.192	0.210	0.203	0.192	0.186
ProximalPhalanxTW	205	400	80	6	0.292	0.263	0.235	0.260	0.213
RefrigerationDevices	375	375	720	3	0.605	0.560	0.539	0.541	0.435
ScreenType	375	375	720	3	0.640	0.589	0.563	0.560	0.499
ShapeletSim	20	180	500	2	0.461	0.300	0.467	0.300	0.383
ShapesAll	600	600	512	60	0.248	0.198	0.225	0.192	0.198
SmallKitchenAppliances	375	375	720	3	0.659	0.328	0.363	0.307	0.328
SonyAIBORobotSurface	20	601	70	2	0.305	0.305	0.388	0.266	0.200
SonyAIBORobotSurfaceII	27	953	65	2	0.141	0.141	0.297	0.135	0.118
StarLightCurves	1000	8236	1024	3	0.151	0.095	-	-	-
Strawberry	370	613	235	2	0.062	0.062	0.062	0.057	0.046
SwedishLeaf	500	625	128	15	0.211	0.154	0.160	0.152	0.152
Symbols	25	995	398	6	0.100	0.062	0.210	0.050	0.052
synthetic_control	300	300	60	6	0.120	0.017	0.050	0.007	0.027
ToeSegmentation1	40	228	277	2	0.320	0.250	0.180	0.184	0.149
ToeSegmentation2	36	130	343	2	0.192	0.092	0.146	0.092	0.054
Trace	100	100	275	4	0.240	0.010	0.120	0.000	0.000
Two_Patterns	1,000	4,000	128	4	0.090	0.002	0.032	0.000	0.028
TwoLeadECG	23	1139	82	2	0.253	0.132	0.317	0.096	0.134
uWaveGestureLibrary_X	896	3582	315	8	0.261	0.227	0.253	-	-
uWaveGestureLibrary_Y	896	3582	315	8	0.338	0.301	0.323	-	-
uWaveGestureLibrary_Z	896	3582	315	8	0.350	0.322	0.332	-	-
UWaveGestureLibraryAll	896	3582	945	8	0.052	0.034	0.041	-	-
wafer	1,000	6,174	152	2	0.005	0.005	0.009	0.004	0.004
Wine	57	54	234	2	0.389	0.389	0.481	0.389	0.241
WordsSynonyms	267	638	270	25	0.382	0.252	0.346	0.251	0.312
Worms	77	181	900	5	0.635	0.586	0.558	0.530	0.459
WormsTwoClass	77	181	900	2	0.414	0.414	0.392	-	0.298
yoga	300	3000	426	2	0.170	0.155	0.196	0.151	0.162

Range-based Obstructed Nearest Neighbor Queries

Huaijie Zhu[†], Xiaochun Yang[†], Bin Wang[†], Wang-Chien Lee[‡]
[†]Northeastern University, China
[‡]Pennsylvania State University, University Park, PA 16802, USA
zhuhjneu@gmail.com, {yangxc, binwang}@mail.neu.edu.cn, wlee@cse.psu.edu

ABSTRACT

In this paper, we study a novel variant of obstructed nearest neighbor queries, namely, *range-based obstructed nearest neighbor* (RONN) search. A natural generalization of *continuous obstructed nearest-neighbor* (CONN), an RONN query retrieves the *obstructed nearest neighbor* for every point in a specified range. To process RONN, we first propose a *CONN-Based* (CONNB) algorithm as our baseline, which reduces the RONN query into a range query and four CONN queries processed using an R-tree. To address the shortcomings of the CONNB algorithm, we then propose a new *RONN by R-tree Filtering* (RONN-RF) algorithm, which explores effective filtering, also using R-tree. Next, we propose a new index, called *O-tree*, dedicated for indexing objects in the obstructed space. The novelty of O-tree lies in the idea of *dividing the obstructed space into non-obstructed subspaces*, aiming to efficiently retrieve highly qualified candidates for RONN processing. We develop an O-tree construction algorithm and propose a space division scheme, called *optimal obstacle balance* (OOB) scheme, to address the tree balance problem. Accordingly, we propose an efficient algorithm, called *RONN by O-tree Acceleration* (RONN-OA), which exploits O-tree to accelerate query processing of RONN. In addition, we extend O-tree for indexing polygons. At last, we conduct a comprehensive performance evaluation using both real and synthetic datasets to validate our ideas and the proposed algorithms. The experimental result shows that the RONN-OA algorithm outperforms the two R-tree based algorithms significantly. Moreover, we show that the OOB scheme achieves the best tree balance in O-tree and outperforms two baseline schemes.

Keywords

Nearest neighbor; Range-based nearest neighbor; Obstacle

1. INTRODUCTION

With the growing popularity of smart mobile devices and the rapid advance in wireless communication and positioning technologies, various spatial queries have been proposed to support the needs of mobile users. Range nearest neighbors (RNN) query [1, 3, 5, 10, 11, 14, 15] is a popular spatial query that retrieves the nearest neighbors to a spatial region where the mobile user is possibly located. It has been regarded as a fundamental query in support of various real applications, which have been discussed widely in the literatures [1, 3, 5, 10] and can be categorized into the following four use scenarios.

- Privacy-preserving. Mobile users are not willing to reveal their exact location information to location-based service providers, due to the concern of location privacy leaking. Spatial cloaking, a well-received privacy preserving technique, proposes to blur the user's exact location into a spatial region in order to satisfy the user's specified privacy requirements [9, 11, 12, 13, 14, 15, 16, 24, 27]. RNN facilitates search of the nearest neighbors with respect to the spatial region.
- Continuous queries. For services that facilitate continuous lookup of nearest neighbors while a user is moving around an area, it is inefficient to process individual NN queries against the whole data set at the server. To submit an RNN query to prefetch all possible nearest neighbors for this area as a candidate set is a better choice. As a result, NN queries issued for objects in this area can be processed locally against the candidate set, saving both computation and communication cost significantly [14, 15, 16].
- Batch processing. Consider the situation where very close NN queries are issued from many different users. Instead of processing these queries separately, it's more efficient to group spatially adjacent NN queries and process them in a batch. An RNN query with a spatial range bounding all the NN query points in the batch can be issued to obtain a candidate set and then the individual NN queries can be resolved with the candidate set returned by RNN [14].
- Location uncertainty. Due to the limitation of underlying positioning techniques (especially those network-based techniques relying on cellular and wifi access points) as well as the sampling imprecision caused by continuous motion, network delays, and frequent location updates (even for devices equipped with GPS), the location uncertainty of a mobile user remains an issue. To support such a user, an RNN query with a spatial region where the user location is guaranteed (to cope with the location uncertainty) can be issued to retrieve the NNs to the user [15, 16].

SIGMOD '16 June 26–July 1, 2016, San Francisco, USA

DOI: http://dx.doi.org/10.1145/2882903.2915234

Nevertheless, these prior RNN works mostly assume a plain space with no obstacles, and thus use Euclidean distance, the shortest distance between a data object and a query range, as the distance measure. While their contributions are significant to the field, there exists a gap to real-life applications, as the space we live in usually has obstacles instead of being plain. For example, a traveler drives around mountains and lakes; troops take detours to avoid enemy's ground; wireless communication messages may avoid routing through an area that suffers electromagnetic interference. Indeed, a recent trend in research of spatial queries is to consider the obstructed space where the *obstructed distance* [23], i.e., the shortest path between two points without crossing any obstacle, is adopted as the distance measure. For example, research studies on the *obstructed nearest neighbor* (ONN) query, which retrieves k ($k \geq 1$) NNs of a given query point in the obstructed space, are reported [23, 25]. Moreover, to support mobile applications, continuous obstructed nearest neighbor (CONN) query for finding nearest neighbors to a given line segment in the obstructed space is proposed [6]. The idea of *visibility graph* (VG) is also proposed to simplify the calculation of obstructed distance [4]. In addition, the problem of spatial clustering in the presence of obstacles is studied [21, 22]. The realistic needs and these research works for supporting mobile users in the obstructed space inspired our research presented in this paper.

Considering the problem of RNN under the context of obstructed space, in this paper, we propose a new spatial query, namely, *range-based obstructed nearest neighbor* (RONN) query.[1] Given a set of data objects P, and a set of obstacles O, an RONN query, specified by a query range R, retrieves all the nearest neighbors corresponding to every point in R based on obstructed distance.[2] An example of the RONN query is illustrated in Fig. 1. As shown, the circled points denote the data objects, the red line segments logically represent the obstacles and the rectangle at the center specifies a query range.[3] The result of this RONN search consists of the blue points. Notice that point p_7 is not in the result set owing to obstacle o_1. p_3 is not in the result set since p_4 is nearer to the query range than p_3. A major challenge faced in processing RONN lies in the adoption of the obstructed distance as a measure, which makes the existing techniques for conventional RNN inapplicable.

In this paper, we first propose a *CONN-Based* (CONNB) algorithm as the baseline to tackle the RONN problem. By reducing an RONN query to a range query and four CONN queries [6], we exploit an R-tree of data objects and obstacles to answer the query. Moreover, observing some shortcomings of the CONNB algorithm, we propose a new *RONN by R-tree Filtering* (RONN-RF) algorithm, which explores

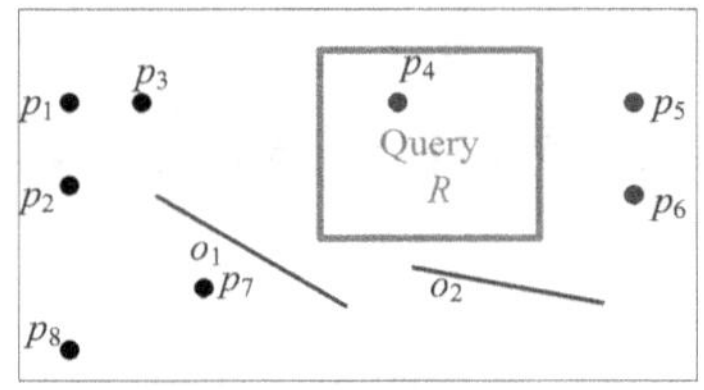

Figure 1: RONN search

effective filtering strategies to facilitate efficient query processing. Nevertheless, to process RONN, there exist two issues in R-tree due to the presence of obstacles. First, it requires multiple traversals of the R-tree for both RONN-RF and CONNB, i.e., as to be detailed later, RONN-RF needs to traverse R-Tree twice and CONNB requires five scans of the R-tree. Second, R-tree indexes both data objects and obstacles in the same Euclidean space, resulting in expensive online computation of obstructed distance during query processing.

To address the above two issues, we propose a new index, namely, *O-tree*, which organizes data objects and obstacles in a way that *non-obstructed subspaces* can be produced to alleviate the computation of obstructed distance. The novelty of O-tree lies in the idea of *dividing the obstructed space into non-obstacle subspaces*, aiming to efficiently retrieve highly qualified candidates for accelerating RONN processing. O-tree is constructed by sequentially selecting obstacles to find pivot points for space division recursively. Eventually, R-trees are embedded in the O-tree to handle the non-obstructed subspaces.

In order to build a balanced O-tree, we propose a notion of tree balance, namely, *obstacle balance*. Based on our analysis, we observe that the tree balance is primarily affected by the orders of obstacles being selected to build the O-index. Accordingly, we propose a space division scheme, namely, *optimal obstacle balance* (OOB). Moreover, we propose an efficient algorithm, called *RONN by O-tree Acceleration* (RONN-OA), which exploits O-tree to accelerate query processing of RONN. In addition, we extend O-tree for indexing polygons. At last, we conduct a comprehensive performance evaluation using both real and synthetic datasets to validate our ideas and evaluate the proposed algorithms.

The contributions made in this research are five-fold:

- We formalize the *Range-based Obstructed Nearest Neighbor* (RONN) query, a new variant of spatial queries in the obstructed space. To the best of our knowledge, this work is the first attempt to tackle the RONN problem.
- We propose two original RONN algorithms based on R-tree. The first one (CONNB) answers an RONN query with one range query and four CONN queries. The second one (RONN-RF) explores effective heuristics to facilitate efficient filtering by R-tree.
- As an alternative to R-tree, we propose a novel index (O-tree) by dividing the obstructed space into non-obstructed subspaces. This new index prevails R-tree in supporting efficient RONN query processing. In addition, we propose a space division scheme (OOB) for constructing the O-tree and study the tree balancing issue as an optimization problem. Moreover, we extend the O-tree to index obstacles as polygons (see Appendix).
- Based on O-tree, we propose a new algorithm (RONN-OA) for efficient query processing of RONN.

[1]To the best knowledge of the authors, the problem of RNN has not yet been addressed under the context of the obstructed space.

[2]Following the convention in spatial database research, we use a rectangle to represent the query range, which is assumed to be in parallel to x-axis or y-axis. Alternative representations of the query range will be explored in future works.

[3]Although an obstacle can be in any shape (e.g., triangle, pentagon, etc.), line segment is the basic unit of shapes, e.g., rectangular and polygon. for simplicity, we first follow the common assumption adopted in the literature of obstructed spatial queries to use *line segment* for obstacles. Later we also consider the polygons as an extension.

- We conduct extensive experiments to evaluate the proposed algorithms and schemes. The experimental result shows that the RONN-OA and RONN-RF algorithms significantly outperform the baseline algorithm (CONNB), with 360% and 300% improvement, respectively. Meanwhile, our study shows that OOB is the scheme of choice for space division in O-tree.

2. RELATED WORK

A lot of research effort related to our work, including *range based spatial queries*, *ONN queries*, and *spatial cloaking query* (for location privacy preservation), have been made in the field of spatial databases.

2.1 Range-based Spatial Queries

Many spatial queries have been studied over the years, e.g., range queries, nearest neighbor (NN) queries, continuous nearest neighbor (CNN) queries [18, 26, 20], *range nearest neighbor* (RNN) queries [10], and *range based skyline* (RSky) queries [16]. Among them, the "range-based" spatial queries are the most relevant to our work.

The notion of kRNN queries has been proposed to retrieve k nearest neighbors for every point in a specified range [10]. New algorithms are developed based on either planar geometry in two-dimensional space or linear programming in high-dimensional spaces. In addition, a solution-based auxiliary index, called *EXO-tree*, is developed to support a variety of NN queries, including traditional NN, CNN, and RNN searches. However, the design of EXO-tree does not consider the obstructed space and thus is not applicable to RONN.

Another relevant work is the RSky queries in mobile environment [16]. Two algorithms, namely, *I-SKY* and *N-SKY*, are proposed to find skyline objects in static and highly dynamic datasets, respectively. The authors also further consider the problem under the contexts of probabilistic and continuous queries. To process probabilistic RSky queries, they propose new pruning techniques to improve the computational efficiency. Moreover, they compute the valid scope for each skyline object to process continuous RSky queries efficiently. Again, the above RNN and RSky queries are considered only in non-obstructed space. In this work, we design a novel index for obstructed space to enhance query processing of RONN.

2.2 ONN Queries

Due to the impact of obstacles, a growing number of research lines considering the obstructed spatial space, including obstructed spatial queries, visible spatial queries, and obstructed spatial clustering, have been explored.

In obstructed spatial queries, Zhang et al. [25] propose algorithms for answering classical spatial queries, such as range queries, NN search, distance join queries, closest pair queries and distance semi-join queries, in the obstructed space. Xia et al. study the *obstructed nearest neighbor* (ONN) query which finds the kNNs of a given query point based on the obstructed distance [23]. This work adopts R-tree to index the data objects and obstacles in order to incrementally compute the obstructed distance by filtering out a large number of obstacles. Gao and Zheng study the continuous obstructed nearest neighbor (CONN) search [6]. As our baseline algorithm is to reduce an RONN to a range query and four CONN queries, we discuss some key ideas of this work in Section 3. RONN is fundamentally different from CONN as the RONN query is based on a range rather than a line segment.

Research works on visible spatial queries also consider the existence of obstacles. However, these queries adopt Euclidian distance instead of obstructed distance as the distance measure, i.e., two objects are visible to each other iff the straight line segment connecting them does not cross any obstacle. A visible nearest neighbors query returns the NNs visible to a given query point [19]. Gao explores the continuous visible nearest neighbor query which finds the visible NN of every point along a query line segment [7].

In addition, the problem of spatial clustering in the presence of obstacles has attracted considerable attention in recent years. It divides a set of two-dimensional data objects into smaller homogeneous groups (i.e., clusters) by taking into account the impact of obstacles or obstructed distance. A number of clustering algorithms with obstacle constraints have been reported in the literature [21, 22].

Although these works have considered the obstructed space or the impact of the obstacles, the RONN query has not been studied previously.

2.3 Spatial Cloaking Query

In location privacy preservation, several works propose to perform spatial cloaking for protecting users' exact location from leaking by specifying a *cloaked range*, instead of the exact query location. The spatial cloaking query calculates a safe region and provides all data objects inside the safe region (i.e. candidates) instead of a single exact answer [17].

Casper [17] blurs a user's exact location into a cloaked spatial range, in form of a rectangle, based on privacy requirements specified by the user. Accordingly, the server processes the query based on the cloaked spatial ranges. Gruteser, et al. [9] propose a Quadtree-based algorithm for spatial cloaking. It achieves identity anonymity in LBS by spatio-temporal cloaking based on a k-anonymity model, i.e., the cloaked location is made indistinguishable from the location information of at least k-1 other users. Gedik and Liu [8] propose a novel spatio-temporal cloaking algorithm, called CliqueCloak, which provides k-anonymity in LBSs for mobile users. The most close work to ours is [27]. Zhu et al. [27] construct a cloaked range corresponding to the exact location using a pyramid tree to address the obstructed nearest neighbor problem under the context of obstructed space. Different from the above cloaked ranged query techniques, RONN returns the nearest neighbors to every possible point in the cloaked range. We show the comparison results in Section 7.

3. PRELIMINARIES

In this section, we first introduce some background and definitions for our research. Then we formulate the RONN problem.

3.1 Background and Definitions

In this work, we focus on the *obstructed space*. We assume that there exists a set of data objects P and a set of obstacles O in the space. We assume that people moving from one point to another in the obstructed space follow the shortest path while avoiding the obstacles. In this space, a proper distance measure (other than Euclidean distance) is needed for obstructed spatial queries. Thus, we define the notion of *obstacle-free path* and use it to define the *obstructed distance* between two points.

Definition 1. (OBSTACLE-FREE PATH [23]). Consider two points p, p' in the obstructed space. An *obstacle-free path*, $\mathsf{P}(p,p') = \langle d_0, d_1, ..., d_n \rangle$ (where d_i is a point in the space and $d_0 = p, d_n = p'$), consists of n line segments of straightline subpaths $\langle d_0, d_1\rangle, \langle d_1, d_2\rangle, ..., \langle d_{n-1}, d_n\rangle$ that connect p and p'.[4]

Definition 2. (OBSTRUCTED DISTANCE [23]). Let the distance of an obstacle-free path $\mathsf{P}(p,p')$ be $|\mathsf{P}(p,p')| = \sum_{i\in[0,n-1]} dist(d_i, d_{i+1})$ where $dist(d_i, d_{i+1})$ is the Euclidean distance between d_i and d_{i+1}. The obstructed distance between p and p', denoted by $||p,p'||$, is the length of the *shortest obstacle-free path* (*shortest path* for short) from p to p', i.e., $\nexists \mathsf{P}(p,p'), |\mathsf{P}(p,p')| < ||p,p'||$.

Based on the notion of obstructed distance, we now define the *obstructed nearest neighbor* to a query point.

Definition 3. (OBSTRUCTED NEAREST NEIGHBOR). For a given query point q in the obstructed space, the data object $p \in P$ is the obstructed nearest neighbor (ONN) of q iff $\forall p' \in P - p, ||p,q|| \leq ||p',q||$.

By capturing the anticipated moving trajectory of a mobile user as a line segment, the idea of ONN can be extended to CONN as defined below.

Definition 4. (CONTINUOUS OBSTRUCTED NEAREST NEIGHBOR). Given a query line segment $\overline{q}$, the continuous obstructed nearest neighbors corresponding to $\overline{q}$, denoted by $CONN(\overline{q})$, is a subset of objects in P such that $\forall$ point $q \in \overline{q}$, $ONN(q) \in CONN(\overline{q})$.

Notice that the CONN of a line segment defined above is the union of ONN objects with respect to the (infinite number of) points on the line segment $\overline{q}$. Alternatively, $CONN(\overline{q})$ can be compactly represented as the union of CONNs corresponding to a sequence of line segments $\overline{q}_1$, $\overline{q}_2$, ..., $\overline{q}_t$ such that (i) $\overline{q}$ is the concatenation of $\overline{q}_1, \overline{q}_2, ..., \overline{q}_t$, (ii) there exists only one CONN, i.e., the ONN, for each $\overline{q}_i$ (where $i = 1..t$), and (iii) $ONN(\overline{q}_i) \neq ONN(\overline{q}_{i+1})$ (where $i = 1..t-1$).

Accordingly, the points $s_1, s_2, ..., s_{t-1}$ that split $\overline{q}$ as $\overline{q}_1$, $\overline{q}_2$, ..., $\overline{q}_t$, termed as *split points*, are defined below.

Definition 5. (SPLIT POINTS FOR CONN). Let the query line segment $\overline{q}$ be denoted by $\overline{ab}$, where a and b are the two end points of $\overline{q}$. Consider the $\overline{q}_1, \overline{q}_2, ..., \overline{q}_t$ associated with $CONN(\overline{q})$ where $\overline{q}_1 = \overline{as_1}, \overline{q}_2 = \overline{s_1s_2}, ..., \overline{q}_t = \overline{s_{t-1}b}$. The points $s_1, s_2, ..., s_{t-1}$ are split points of $\overline{ab}$. Moreover, let p_i and p_{i+1} be the ONNs to all the points along $\overline{s_{i-1}s_i}$ and $\overline{s_is_{i+1}}$, respectively. Then the obstructed distance from s_i to p_i and p_{i+1} are the same, i.e., $||p_i, s_i|| = ||p_{i+1}, s_i||$.

EXAMPLE 1. *Fig. 2 illustrates CONN. As shown,* $\{p_1, p_2, ..., p_6\}$ *are data objects,* $\{o_1, o_2, ..., o_4\}$ *are obstacles, and* $\overline{ab}$ *is the query line segment. The output of the CONN search is* $\{\langle p_1, \overline{as_1}\rangle, \langle p_2, \overline{s_1s_2}\rangle, \langle p_6, \overline{s_2s_3}\rangle, \langle p_3, \overline{s_3b}\rangle\}$*, where* s_1*,* s_2 *and* s_3 *are the split points. The split point* s_1 *for point* p_1 *and* p_2 *can be computed by a quadratic algorithm* [6].

The notion of CONN and split points are used to describe some of our algorithms built upon CONN.

[4]Note that there exists a straightline path between two points if and only if there is no obstacle blocking the path.

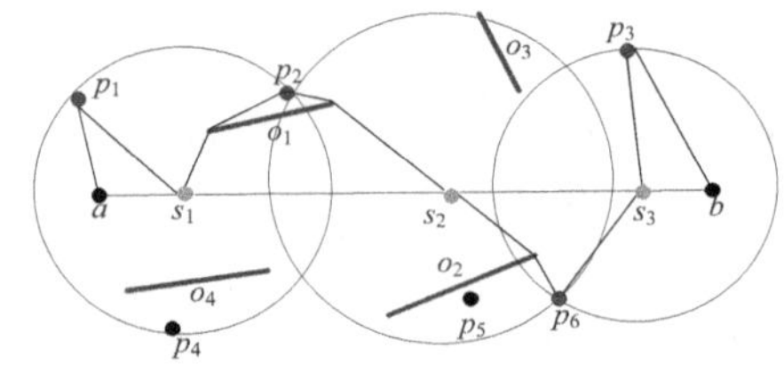

Figure 2: CONN search

3.2 Problem Formulation

In this section, we formally define the RONN query.

Problem Statement. *Given a set of data objects P and a set of obstacles O, a range-based obstructed nearest neighbor (RONN) query Q (specified by a rectangular range R), retrieves all the obstructed nearest neighbors of points in the query range, i.e.,* $RONN(Q) = \{ONN(p) | p \in R\}$.

4. R-TREE BASED QUERY PROCESSING

In this section, we propose two R-tree based algorithms for RONN query processing.

Given an RONN query Q, specified by a query range R, any object located inside R is automatically an RONN to the query. Thus, an idea to answer an RONN is to first issue a range query to find all "internal" RONNs located within R and then find the "external" RONNs located outside R. Intuitively, as indicated in Lemma 1, these external RONNs of R are the ONNs to the boundary of R.

LEMMA 1. *An object p is an external RONN of R if and only if 1) p is not located in R; and 2) p is an ONN for at least one point on the boundary of R.*

PROOF. For the necessary condition, it is inherent from the RONN definition that if p is an external RONN to R, then (1) and (2) above are satisfied.

Next, we prove the sufficient condition by contradiction. *Assume that there exists an RONN p outside R which is not the ONN to any point on the boundary of R.* Since p is an RONN, p is the ONN for at least one point m in R (see Fig. 3 for illustration). Let n be the intersection point of line segment $\overline{pm}$ and the boundary of R where n is located. Based on the assumption, as p is not the ONN of n (which is a point on the boundary), there must be another data object p' such that $||n,p'|| < ||n,p||$. Thus, $||n,p'|| + ||n,m|| < ||n,p|| + ||n,m||$. As a result, we have $||m,p'|| < ||m,p||$, which contradicts our assumption that p is the ONN of m. Therefore, the sufficient condition must hold.

Combine the cases of necessary and sufficient conditions, the proof completes. □

4.1 CONN-Based Algorithm

According to Lemma 1, this RONN query can be answered by issuing four CONN queries (using each edge of R as the query line segment) and one range query. The union set of data objects returned from the above five queries answers the RONN query. This *CONN-based* (CONNB) algorithm, serves as a baseline for comparison in our evaluation.

In CONNB, R-tree has been employed to index both data objects and obstacles. Accordingly, a quadratic algorithm proposed in [6] can be used to return the CONNs for each edge of R. As a result, CONNB is also quadratic.

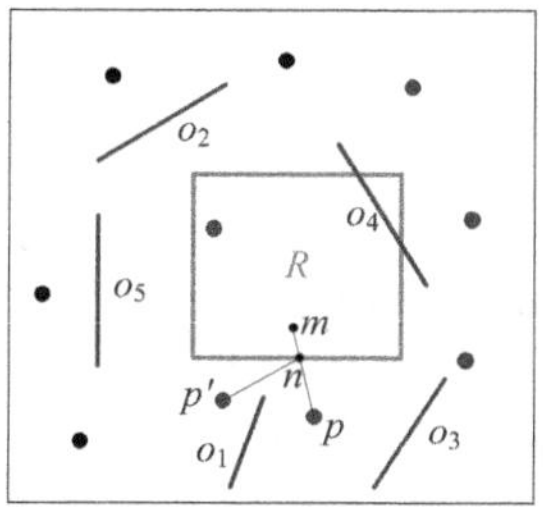

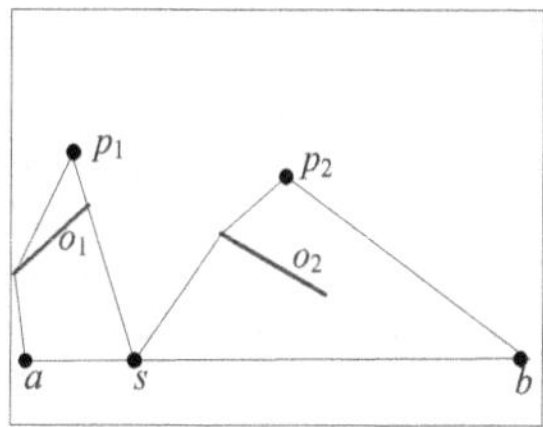

Figure 3: Illustration for Lemma 1

Figure 4: Maximum Obstructed Distance

4.2 R-tree Filtering Algorithm

The *CONNB* algorithm directly invokes range and CONN queries and thus does not explore some potential filtering strategies during query processing. Notice that some intermediate RONNs acquired during query processing may potentially disqualify certain RONN candidates located far away from the query range R. Thus, an idea to facilitate efficient filtering is to explore the RONNs using a distance-browsing approach to obtain RONNs in accordance with their minimal Euclidean distance to R. Accordingly, in this section, we propose a new RONN algorithm, called *R-tree Filtering Algorithm* (RONN-RF), which built upon R-tree to facilitate distance-based browsing and filtering.

To achieve our goal, RONN-RF maintains a number of *maximum obstructed distances*, one for each edge of the query range, from the set of intermediate RONNs to the query range R in order to filter out unqualified candidates. While using R-tree facilitates browsing of data objects in ascending order of their minimal Euclidean distance to R, a major challenge faced in answering the RONN query is the use of obstructed distance as a measure. Here we introduce the notion of *max obstructed distance of an object set to a line segment*, as defined below, for discussion of RONN-RF.

Definition 6. (MAXIMUM OBSTRUCTED DISTANCE OF AN RONN SET TO LINE SEGMENT). Given a set of intermediate RONNs P and a line segment $\overline{ab}$ on the obstacle space, we say that $||m, p_m||$ is the *maximum obstructed distance* from P to $\overline{ab}$, denoted by $max\_odis(P, \overline{ab})$, iff there exist a point m on $\overline{ab}$ such that $\forall$ point i on $\overline{ab}$, $||i, ONN_P(i)|| \leq ||m, ONN_P(p)||$ where $ONN_P(i)$ denotes the point in P serving as the ONN of point i.

EXAMPLE 2. *Consider* Fig. 4, *where $O = \{o_1, o_2\}$ is an obstacle set, $P = \{p_1, p_2\}$ is a set of intermediate ONNs obtained during query processing, and $\overline{ab}$ is a side edge of the query range. As shown, p_1 and p_2 are the RONNs for all points located on $\overline{as}$ and $\overline{sb}$, respectively. In this example, we have $max\_odist(p_1, \overline{as}) = ||p_1, s|| \leq ||p_2, b|| = max\_odist(p_2, \overline{sb})$, which thus is $max\_odis(P, \overline{ab})$.*

In RONN-RF, four *maximum obstructed distances* (MODs), one for each edge of the query range, are maintained to filter out unqualified objects from examination and to determine the terminating condition for query processing. RONN-RF first issues a range query to obtain the internal RONNs, which are used to initialize the four MODs.[5] Next, RONN-RF traverses the R-tree to visit the data objects in ascending order of their minimal Euclidean distances to query range R in order to determine whether they are ONNs to each edge. During the traversal of R-tree, a heap H is used to store the R-tree entries (including *minimum bounding boxes* (MBBs), data objects, and obstacles) in order to process them in ascending order of their minimum distances to R. Initially, H contains only the root entry. By de-heaping the entry e with the shortest distance to R, RONN-RF checks whether the minimal Euclidean distances from e to R is greater than all the current MODs. If this is true, e will be eliminated and a new entry is de-heaped. Otherwise, if e is an MBB (i.e., internal index node), all its child entries are pushed into H for further processing. On the other hand, if e is a leaf node of R-tree, there are two cases: (i) e is an obstacle: it is inserted into the visibility graph VG, which is used for computing the split points on edges for RONNs; and (ii) e is a data object: it updates RONN results and MODs corresponding to each edge by finding split points on edges of the range boundary (to be discussed further later). The above query processing steps (i.e., de-heaping a new entry from H and so on) are repeated until H becomes empty.

The operation of finding split points (called $FindSP$) plays an important role in query processing of RONN-RF. We follow the idea of CONN algorithm [6] to compute the split points for the query boundary. Notice that, instead of sequentially finding RONNs corresponding to each edge (as CONNB does), RONN-RF examines a data object corresponding to all edges simultaneously. This results in significant performance improvement, in addition to the major saving obtained from filtering out unqualified RONN candidates, because RONN-RF needs to scan R-tree only once instead of four times. Let $r_i (i = 1..4)$ denote the corner points of the query range R and $\overline{E_{ij}}$ denote the edge $\overline{r_i r_j}$. Given the intermediate RONN result set (RS_{ij}) and the visibility graph (VG) of obstacles visited so far, we are able to decide whether the data object under examination p is an RONN to $\overline{E_{ij}}$. If it is, we are able to obtain a list of split points that divide $\overline{E_{ij}}$ into line segments being corresponding to RONNs in RS_{ij}. Moreover, the MOD for $\overline{E_{ij}}$ is updated.

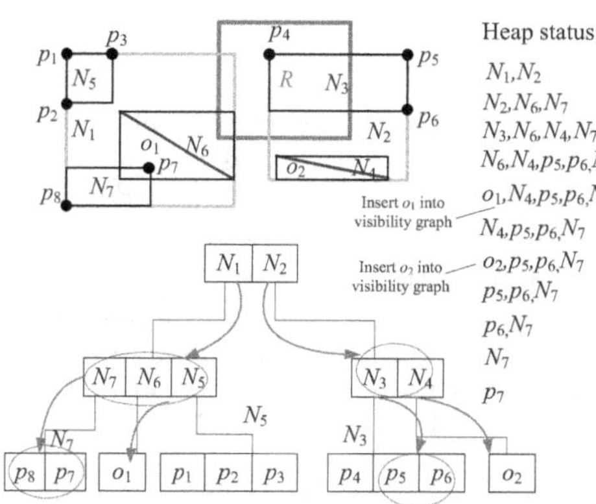

Figure 5: An example of RONN-RF

Fig. 5 shows an example for illustration of the RONN-RF algorithm. As shown, there are eight data objects $p_1, p_2, \ldots, p_8$ and two obstacles o_1 and o_2, maintained in an R-tree index. In the index, the root node contains two internal nodes N_1 and N_2 which cover N_5, N_6, N_7, and N_3, N_4, respectively. In turn, N_5 contains data objects p_1, p_2, and p_3, N_7 contains data objects p_7 and p_8, and N_3 contains

[5]These MODs are incrementally updated as the RONN answer set is refined during query processing.

data objects p_4, p_5, and p_6. On the other hand, N_6 and N_4 contains o_1 and o_2, respectively. Given a query range R (i.e., the red rectangle), RONN-RF first issues a range query to obtain the internal RONN p_4. Accordingly, it initializes the four MODs corresponding to each edge of R using p_4. Next, to identify external RONNs by traversing R-tree, we initialize H with N_1 and N_2, sorted in ascending order of their Euclidean distances to R.[6] We proceed to pop the top entry N_1 from H. As N_1 is an internal node, we compare the Euclidean distances of its child entries N_5, N_6 and N_7 with the maintained MODs and insert N_6 and N_7 back to H. Notice here that N_5 is filtered by the maintained MODs. Similarly, N_2 is de-heaped from H and then N_3, N_4 are inserted back. Continue with the process, N_3 is de-heaped and data objects p_5 and p_6 are inserted back. Here, since p_4 is already in the RONN result set, it is not put back to H. After that, we pop N_6 which contains an obstacle o_1. Thus, we insert o_1 into the visibility graph. Similarly, we handle N_4 and insert o_2 into visibility graph. Then p_5 is de-heaped as a data object and found to be an RONN (by updating current split points via VG). MODs corresponding to each edge of R are updated. Similarly, p_6 are included in the result set. Finally, we pop N_7 and insert p_7 into H because the Euclidean distance of p_8 is greater than some of the maintained MODs. p_7 is de-heaped as a data object but it can not update the current RONN results due to the blocking of obstacle o_1. At this stage, H becomes empty so the query processing ends. The final RONN result set includes p_4, p_5 and p_6.

As shown in the above example, we maintain four MODs, one for each edge. An RONN candidate is filtered only if all its Euclidean distances to the edges of query boundary are greater than the corresponding MODs. The filtering condition, as specified in Theorem 1, effectively reduces the search space of RONN solutions and thus alleviates significant computation overhead. Algorithm 1 presents the pseudo-code of RONN-RF. Notice that the main issue on R-tree is that the minimal Euclidian distance of accessing order is not very effective due to the affecting of obstacles, i.e., the minimal Euclidian distance of N_7 is very small but this is not the RONN result.

THEOREM 1. *Given a query range R and the current RONN result set RS, an entry e of R-tree is filtered iff for each edge $\overline{ab}$ of R, $min\_dist(e, \overline{ab}) > max\_odis(RS, \overline{ab})$.*

In Theorem 1, notice that $min\_dist(e, \overline{ab})$ is Euclidean distance, which is easy to compute. Moreover, it can filter distant data objects effectively because the Euclidean distance represents the lowerbound of obstructed distance from an entry e to the query range R.

Comparing to CONNB algorithm, the RONN-RF algorithm has two advantages: 1) RONN-RF needs only one traversal of R-tree to find the external RONNs while CONNB requires four scans of the R-tree; and 2) In traversal of the R-tree, RONN-RF explores effective heuristics to prune the RONN search space, while CONNB do not exploit intermediate (internal and external) RONNs for filtering in query processing.

[6]Notice that both N_1 and N_2 have Euclidean distances to some edges of R shorter than the current RONNs' MODs to these edges.

Algorithm 1: R-tree Filtering Algorithm (RONN-RF)

```
Input: Data objects and obstacles R-tree T, min-heap
       H = (root(T), 0), and query range R
Output: RONN results list RS
inRes ← Rangequery(T, R);/* internal RONNs*/
RS ← inRes; RS_k ← inRes ; k = 1, 2, 3, 4 /*storing
ONNs for four edges*/
over_k ← 0; k = 1, 2, 3, 4 /*Terminating signal for four
edges, 0 means query processing for the corresponding
edge is not over yet*/
while true do
    k ← 1;/*Starting from edge 1*/
    for Each edge E_ij of R do
        RS_k ← FindSP(E_ij, RS_k); /*Finding split
        points*/
        MOD_k ← max_odis(E_ij, RS_k);
        if H ≠ ∅ and H.head.key > MOD_k then
            over_k = 1. /* Processing for edge k is over*/
        if over_1&over_2&over_3&over_4 or H ≐ ∅ then
            return; /*There is no entry which will be an
            ONN for any edge*/
        k++;
    while H ≠ ∅ do
        de-heap the top entry (e, key) of H;
        if e is a data object then
            k ← 1;
            for key < MOD_k do
                insert e into RS_k;
                k++;
            break;
        else
            for each child entry e_i ∈ e do
                if min_dist(e_i, R) < MAX(MOD_k)
                then
                    insert e_i into H based on
                    min_dist(e_i, R).
    RS ← RS ∪ RS_k;
return RS;
```

5. O-TREE FOR OBSTRUCTED SPACE

As shown earlier, R-tree is used in CONNB and RONN-RF to index both data objects and obstacles in the obstructed space. While R-tree is a well-received index structure for spatial databases, however, it faces two issues in processing RONN queries due to the presence of obstacles. *One is the need for multiple traversals of R-tree in both RONN-RF and CONNB.* When doing internal RONN (range query) and external RONN query, RONN-RF needs to traverse R-tree twice and CONNB requires five scans of the R-tree. This inspires us to explore processing ideas that requires only one scan of the (indexed) data to process internal and external RONN queries all together. *The other issue is the expensive online computation of obstructed distance.* Note that R-tree is built based on the Euclidean space, i.e., Euclidean distance is used as the measure among data objects, obstacles and minimum bounding boxes (MBBs) in the index. As a result, R-tree-based RONN algorithms have to deal with expensive online computation of obstructed distance. Recall the example in Fig. 5. While p_1, p_2 and p_3 (actually N_5) have been effectively pruned early by RONN-RF, p_7 and p_8 have to be accessed since their Euclidean distances to R is small. This incurs expensive computation of their obstructed distances to R before they are eventually excluded from the answer. Thus, we aim to reduce access of data objects in online computation of obstructed distance.

To address these issues, we propose a novel index, called *O-tree*, to support efficient RONN query processing in the obstructed space. The novelty of O-tree lies in the idea of *dividing the obstructed space into non-obstructed subspaces* such that we can use R-tree to index the data objects associated with these subspaces. Our idea is to divide the space into four subspaces along the line of a selected obstacle and some perpendicular lines, e.g., its bisector. Recursively we divide the subspaces into more subspaces to build an index structure. The indexed subspaces may ideally consist of non-obstructed spaces which can facilitate efficient computation and pruning in query processing. While the idea is simple and elegant, the construction of O-tree still faces some design challenges, e.g., tree balance.

In the following, we first discuss the issues of space division in O-tree construction and propose a scheme to address this issue. At last, we present the O-tree construction algorithm.

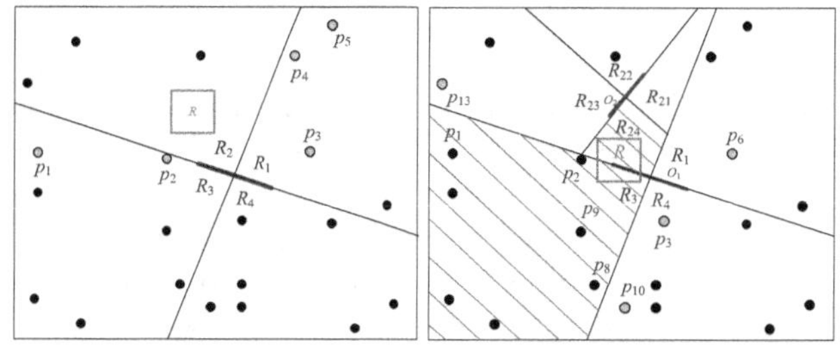

(a) One obstacle (b) Multiple obstacles

Figure 6: An example of space division

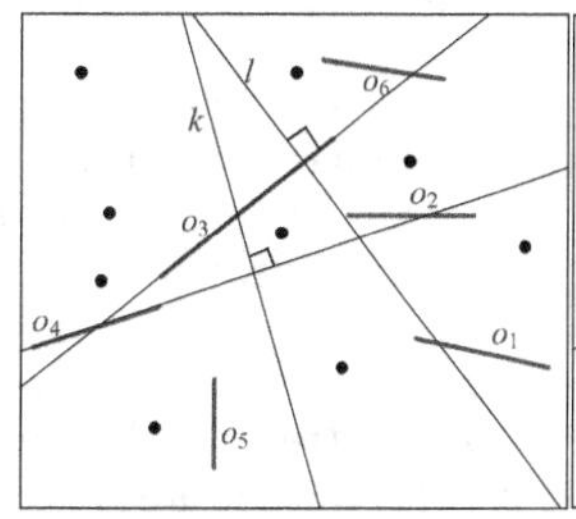

Figure 7: No strict obstacle balance

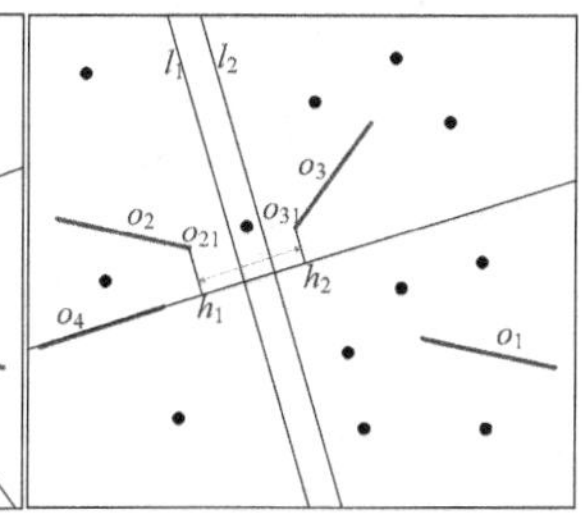

Figure 8: Illustration for equal perpendicular line

5.1 Space Division

As mentioned earlier, we aim to construct the O-tree by dividing an obstructed space into less obstructed subspaces (towards non-obstructed subspaces). Without loss of generality, we first consider an obstructed subspace with only one obstacle. Fig. 6(a) shows an example of such obstructed space. By dividing the space along the lines of the obstacle and its perpendicular bisector, we have four non-obstructed subspaces.

Following the design of conventional space-division based spatial indexes, e.g., Quad-tree or k-d tree, we use a subtree to cover the data objects located in each subspace (e.g., three black circles are covered in Region R_2). Nevertheless, this design inherently faces an issue in spatial query process, i.e., for a query point (a query range in the case of RONN) located close to the boundary of a region, the data objects located in neighbor regions need to be accessed. For example, in Fig. 6(a), not only the black circles in R_2 but also all the other grey circles in R_1, R_3 and R_4 need to be accessed to find the RONNs, which would obviously defeat the ultimate goal of our O-tree. To address this issue, we trade some storage overhead for processing efficiency in O-tree by including, for a giving region (subspace), all data objects that should be considered to answer any RONN query specified in the region. This set of additional data objects can be obtained by precomputing CONNs to the boundary line segments of the region during O-tree construction. Therefore, for the example in Fig. 6(a), O-tree stores the data objects denoted by both black circles in R_2 and the grey circles, $p_1, p_2, ..., p_5$. As such, all the candidate data objects for a given query range R can be quickly retrieved by accessing the regions intersected with R. This feature of O-tree is also applicable to the general case of a space with multiple obstacles. As shown in Fig. 6(b), only data objects associated with R_{24} and R_3 need to be examined in query processing (to be detailed in Section 6).

5.2 Optimal Obstacle Balance Scheme

Two key questions that may naturally arise during the discussion of space division earlier are:

- Which obstacle should be first selected to divide the space?
- For a given obstacle, is its perpendicular bisector the best choice to divide the space?

To answer these two questions, a fundamental yet closely related question is "How the divided spaces and thus the resultant O-tree are structured, if we choose obstacles in different orders with different "pivot points" to divide the space?" We argue that a balanced O-tree is desirable and thus propose a space division strategy to achieve tree balance. In O-tree, as obstacles are used to determine the pivot points for space division, we aim to maintain the *obstacle balance*, which is defined as follows:

Definition 7. (OBSTACLE BALANCE) Selecting one obstacle (obstacle line and its perpendicular line) to divide the space into four subspaces. In each dividing step, the obstacle balance is satisfied by the condition $|n_i - n_{i+1}| <= 1$ (n_i denotes the number of obstacles in each subspace), i.e., the difference of height of each branch is less than 1.

According to the above strict obstacle balance definition, can we always construct an obstacle balance tree? The answer is not. In fact, we can not always construct a balanced tree based on selection of obstacles and their perpendicular lines. (Sometimes there is no answer for the problem). Fig. 7 illustrates an example. From Fig. 7, we can see that if we choose o_4 (or o_3) to divide the space, there is no suitable perpendicular line to satisfy strict obstacle balance. The same situation still exists when choosing other obstacles to divide the space.

Since we can not always build a strictly balanced tree, we aim to build an optimal approximate balanced tree. Accordingly, in order to construct an optimal balanced tree, we propose a new space division scheme, called *optimal obstacle balance* (OOB) scheme, for O-tree. This scheme corresponds to an optimization problem which can be solved using enumeration.

Definition 8. (OPTIMIZATION PROBLEM) Select one obstacle (i.e., obstacle line) and one of its perpendicular lines to divide the space into four subspaces in each space dividing step. The goal is to minimize the objective function $\sum(|n_i - n_j|^2)$ $(i < j, i, j = 1, 2, 3, 4)$ where n_i, n_j denote the number of obstacles into two different subspaces.

The OOB scheme to choose an obstacle and a perpendicular line:

(1) there are n choices of obstacles to divide the space. This can be tried one at a time, so it takes $O(n)$ time.

(2) for a chosen obstacle, there are infinite choices to select a perpendicular line, which is obviously infeasible to enumerate one by one. So we aim to try some finite (a constant m) choices in selecting the best perpendicular line. Let's show an example in Fig. 8 for illustration. We project the endpoints of each obstacle on the chosen obstacle line. The projection of the endpoint o_{21} on obstacle line o_4 is h_1, while the projection of the endpoint o_{31} is h_2. We can see that there are also infinite perpendicular lines (such as l_1 and l_2) to choose from between h_1 and h_2. However, the objective score of choosing l_1 (or l_2) is the same as that of choosing perpendicular line through h_1 (or h_2). In other words, a certain range of perpendicular lines always equal to one perpendicular line through the projection of endpoints. We only need to compute the objective scores of the perpendicular lines through the projections of all endpoints to find the minimal score. As there are $2(n-1)$ perpendicular lines through all the endpoints, this step takes $O(2(n-1))$ time.

In total, this problem can be solved in $O(n * 2(n-1)) = O(n^2)$ time.

5.3 O-tree Index Structure

Based on the above discussion on space division, *O-tree* index first exploits obstacles to divide the obstructed space into a number of non-obstructed subspaces, which cover only data objects. Accordingly, we use R-tree to index the data objects in these Euclidean subspaces.

In summary, the O-tree index is structured as follows. The root node, denoting the whole obstructed space, points to four child nodes. Each of these child nodes denotes a region in the obstructed space. The internal nodes of *O-tree* maintain entries of $(reg, obs, optr_1, optr_2, optr_3, optr_4)$, while the leaf nodes contain entries of the form $(reg, rptr)$ where reg denotes a 2-dimensional polygon region, obs is the obstacle dividing the space, and $optr_i$ and $rptr$ denote pointers to O-tree and R-tree nodes, respectively. Fig. 9 illustrates the space divisions and the corresponding O-tree. Obstacle o_1 firstly divides the region into four subregions and the root has four child nodes (R_1, R_2, R_3, R_4). Next, R_3 is divided into four subregions (R_{31}, R_{32}, R_{33}, R_{34}) utilizing obstacle o_2, and the other three subregions directly form the leaf node. Internal node R_3 stores obstacle o_2, $optr$ pointing to four O-tree children R_{31}, R_{32}, R_{33}, and R_{34}. Leaf node R_{34} stores $rptr$ to an R-tree which contains N_1 and N_2. In turn, N_1 contains data objects p_3 and p_4, while N_2 contains p_5 and p_6. Similarly, R_{33} stores $rptr$ to another R-tree which contains N_2.

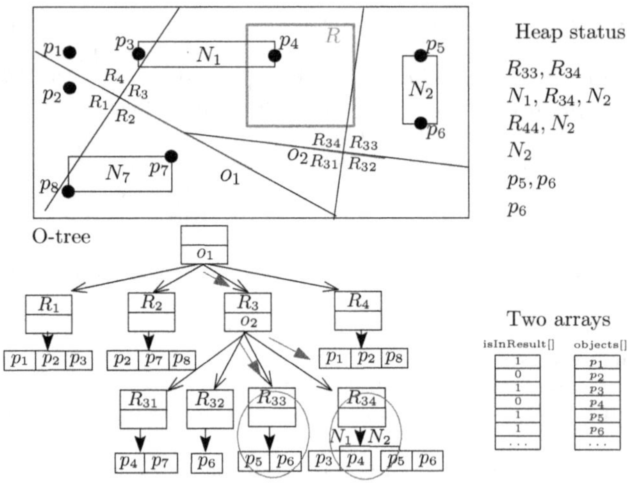

Figure 9: An example of O-tree

Reducing Data Redundancy Using Arrays for O-tree. As shown in Fig. 9, data objects p_1 and p_2 are stored twice in R-trees of nodes R_2 and R_3, respectively. The same case is for data objects p_5 and p_6. As there exists some data redundancy for O-tree index, two potential issues arise: (i) index size increases and (ii) possible redundant traversals of the same data object in query processing.

To reduce the index size, we store all the data objects in an array *objects* and store the array index like *id* for each object in our O-tree index. As shown in Fig. 9, there is an array *objects* for all the data objects. This reduces index size to some extent. As for traversal of data objects in the O-tree, if data object p is examined, we can check if its duplicate p' is already in the result set. We also build an array *isInResult* corresponding with *objects* array in Fig. 9. *isInResult* marks whether a data object is in result. As we can obtain the *id* of data object p from O-tree index, whether p is already in the result can be checked quickly. If p is not already in result, we mark it with $isInResult[id] = true$.

5.4 Building O-tree

In this section, we present our O-tree construction algorithm that performs space division recursively and fills its leaf nodes with R-trees containing data objects. The pseudo code of space division algorithm is shown in Algorithm 2.

Algorithm 2: Space division Algorithm

Input: A set of obstacles O, An O-tree node denoted by $Node$ (which contains information of its covered region, denoted by reg)
Output: The constructed O-tree denoted by $Node$

if $O \neq \varnothing$ **then**
  Use OOB scheme to decide one obstacle obs;
  Divide Region into four subregions and create four children $optrs$;
  for each $optr$ **do**
    Find all the obstacles O' inside the region of $optr$;
    Space_division(O', $optr$);

At first, we initialize the *root* node of O-tree with *reg* that covers the whole obstructed space. That is, the region of *root* covers all the points and obstacles. Then we recursively invoke the space division algorithm with Space_division(O, *root*) to build up the O-tree. As shown in Algorithm 2, if the current *O-tree* node has obstacles in its covered region, i.e., $O \neq \varnothing$, we utilize OOB scheme to choose one obstacle *obs* (Line 2). Then we divide the current node's region into four subregions and create four children nodes (Line 3). At last, we recursively invoke the Space_division algorithm to build up subtrees for the subregions. Finally, the subtrees are put together as an O-tree (Lines 4-6). After the O-tree is constructed, we then fill the leaf nodes of *O-tree* index with corresponding R-trees by invoking CLN algorithm.

We analyze the time complexity of *Space division* Algorithm. For each region, if there are n obstacles to divide the space, utilizing OOB scheme to do the optimal space division takes $O(n^2)$, and for its four children regions, it takes $O(4(\frac{n}{4})^2)$. So for all the space divisions, it takes $O(n^2 + 4(\frac{n}{4})^2 + 4(\frac{n}{4^2})^2 + ... + 4(\frac{n}{4^h})^2)$=$O(n^2)$, where h is the height of the tree.

Algorithm 3: Complete Leaf Nodes Algorithm (CLN)

Input: A set of points P, a set of obstacles O and O-tree node denoted by $Node$

Output: A *O-tree*

```
1 if Node is not Leaf Node then
2     for each child optr of Node do
3         CLN(P, O, optr);
4 else
5     Create an R-tree root node pointed by rptr for
      Node;
6     Find all the data objects inside region of ONode
      and insert them into the R-tree via rptr;
7     for each edge E̅_ij of the region of Node do
8         res ← CONN(E̅_ij, O, P);
9         insert res into the R-tree via rptr;
```

The pseudo code of the CLN algorithm is presented in Algorithm 3. The basic idea is to hang corresponding R-tree which contains ONNs of boundary and points inside with each leaf node. To complete the leaf node of O-tree with R-tree, we recursively traverse O-tree from the root. For each O-tree node, we check whether it is a leaf node. If not, we move on its children (Lines 1-3). If it is a leaf node, we create an R-tree for the O-tree node by inserting all the points inside this leaf node's region into the R-tree (Lines 5-6). At last, we compute the ONNs for each edge of the node's region [6] and insert them into the R-tree (Lines 7-9).

6. QUERY PROCESSING ON O-TREE

In this section, we first introduce a new RONN query processing algorithm, called *RONN-OA*, based on O-tree. Next, we analyze the time complexity of CONNB, RONN-RF and RONN-OA algorithms.

6.1 RONN-OA Algorithm

Similar to RONN-RF, RONN-OA maintains four maximum obstructed distances (MODs), one for each edge of the query range R, to filter out unqualified objects and to determine the terminating condition. RONN-OA first issues a range query to obtain the internal RONNs, which are used to initialize the four MODs. It is worth noting that the range query also returns the leaf nodes of O-tree that intersects with the query range. So the result of range query of RONN-OA Algorithm is different from that of range query of RONN-RF. Meanwhile, the obstacles visited in the process are retrieved to build a visibility graph (VG) for later RONN processing. Next, with the leaf nodes of O-tree obtained, RONN-OA continues to traverse the corresponding R-trees to access the data objects to find the external RONNs. During the traversal of R-trees, a heap H is used to store the R-tree entries. Initially, H contains only *the root entries of R-trees associated with the retrieved O-tree leaf nodes*. By de-heaping the entry e with the minimal distance to R, RONN-OA checks whether the minimal Euclidean distances from e to R is greater than all the current MODs. If this is true, e will be eliminated and a new entry is de-heaped. Otherwise, if e is an MBB (i.e., internal node of R-tree), all its child entries are examined for filtering based on Theorem 1 (as RONN-RF does) and inserted back to H for later processing. On the other hand, if e is a data object, RONN-OA examines it as an RONN candidate, and then updates RONN results and MODs as appropriate (corresponding to each edge by finding split points on edges of the range boundary, as discussed earlier for RONN-RF). The above query processing steps (i.e., de-heaping a new entry from H and so on) are repeated until H becomes empty. The pseudo-code of RONN-OA algorithm can be found in the Appendix A.

Recall the example in Figure 9. Given a query range R as specified by the red rectangle, RONN-OA first issues a range query to obtain the internal RONN p_4. At the same time, it will obtain the corresponding leaf nodes R_{11} and R_{14} that intersect with R. So we only need to traverse R_{11} and R_{14} for external RONN query. This filters a lot of data objects to accelerate RONN query processing. Obstacles o_1 and o_2 are also inserted into the visibility graph VG during the process of performing the range query. Accordingly, RONN-OA initializes the four MODs corresponding to each edge of R using p_4. Next, to traverse the R-trees corresponding to R_{11} and R_{14}, we initialize H with N_1 and N_2, sorted in ascending order of their Euclidean distances to R. We proceed to pop the top entry N_1 from H. As N_1 consists of p_3 and p_4, we check and filter p_3 by the maintained MODs. Meanwhile, we find p_4 is already the RONN result so it is not put back to H. Similarly, N_2 is de-heaped from H and then N_3, N_4 are inserted back. Continue with the process, N_3 is de-heaped and data objects p_5 and p_6 are inserted back. Then we pop p_5 and find it to be an RONN. Thus, we update MODs corresponding to each edge of R. Finally, p_6 is examined and included in the result set. At this stage, H becomes empty so the query processing ends. The final RONN result set includes p_4, p_5 and p_6. For the example, it is worth noting that p_7 and p_8, which need to be examined before eventually being excluded from the result set in RONN-RF, are not even considered in the processing due to the strength of O-tree.

THEOREM 2. *The RONN-OA algorithm retrieves exactly the ONN of every point on a given query range, i.e., the algorithm has no false misses and no false hits.*

Please see the proof in Appendix B.

6.2 Complexity Analysis

In this section, we analyze the time complexity of the three algorithms proposed in this paper. Let $|OT|$ be the size of O-tree, $|T|$ be the size of R-tree used in RONN-RF, $|T'|$ be the total size of R-trees maintained in the leaf nodes of O-tree, and $|VG|$ be the number of nodes in visibility graph. Moreover, let $n_{CONNB}, n_{RONN-RF}$ and $n_{RONN-OA}$ denote the number of data objects accessed during the external RONN search in CONNB, RONN-RF, and RONN-OA, respectively. The time complexity of these algorithms can be derived as follows.

Based on [6], the time complexity of the CONN algorithm is $O(n_{CONNB} \times \log|T| \times |VG| \times \log|VG|)$. Thus, we can easily deduce that the time complexity of our CONNB is $O(\log|T|+4\times n_{CONNB}\times\log|T|\times|VG|\times\log|VG|)=O(n_{CONNB}\times log|T| \times |VG| \times log|VG|)$.

The time complexity of RONN-RF is $O(\log|T|+n_{RONN-RF}\times \log|T| \times |VG| \times \log|VG|)= O(n_{RONN-RF} \times log|T| \times |VG| \times log|VG|)$ where $O(\log|T|)$ is for range query. Notice that $n_{RONN-RF}$ is the number of data objects accessed during external RONN query, which is much smaller than $4\times n_{CONNB}$ because RONN-RF traverses R-tree only once and filters a lot of unqualified results during traversal of R-trees.

Finally, for RONN-OA, it takes $O(\log|OT|)$ for obtaining the internal RONNs while obtaining the obstacles to construct the visibility graph VG for the query. Additionally, it traverses some R-trees to visit data objects in order to find external RONNs. For the $n_{RONN-OA}$ data objects accessed, RONN-OA takes $O(n_{RONN-OA}\times\log|T'|\times|VG|\times\log|VG|)$. Therefore, the time complexity is $O(\log|OT|+n_{RONN-OA}\times \log|T'|\times|VG|\times\log|VG|)= O(n_{RONN-OA}\times log|T'|\times|VG|\times log|VG|)$. From the above analysis, we may observe that the three algorithms have about the same order of complexity. However, the number of data objects accessed during query processing is a key factor contributing to the actual computational cost which is to be evaluated experimentally in Section 7.

7. EXPERIMENTS

We evaluate the performance of the proposed algorithms for the RONN query. All the algorithms were implemented in C++, while the experiments were conducted on an Intel Core 2 Duo 3.40 GHz PC with 4GB RAM.

We conduct experiments on three real datasets.

- ***Greece***. It consists of 22,650 MBRs of rivers (polylines) as obstacles and 5,921 locations of cities and villages (as the data objects).[7]
- ***Tiger Census Blocks***. It contains 556,696 census blocks (polygons) of Iowa, Kansa, Missouri, and Nebraska.[7]
- ***California Roads***. It contains the MBRs of 2,249,727 streets (polylines) of California.[7]

In addition, we construct synthetic datasets using SpatialDataGenerator.[7] We generated a synthetic dataset ***Uniform*** that contains 80,000 data objects and 20,000 line segments and rectangles as obstacles, respectively, following uniform distribution. Also we generate another 80,000 uniformed distributed data objects as the data of ***Tiger Census Blocks*** dataset. Finally, we randomly extract 500,000 streets from ***California Roads*** and generate two sets of 1 million data objects following uniform and zipf distributions to form two large-scale datasets ***UniformCA*** and ***ZipfCA***, respectively. All datasets are normalized to a $10,000 \times 10,000$ space in order to fit the search range.

[7]http://www.chorochronos.org.

Table 1: Parameter ranges and defaults values

Parameters	Range
♯ of obstacles ($\|O\|$)	1,000, 2,000, 4,000, **8,000**, 16,000, 500,000
♯ of data objects ($\|P\|$)	5,000, 20,000, 10,000, **40,000**, 80,000, 1,000,000
query size (*qsize*)	**100**, 200, 300, 400, 500

We conduct the performance evaluation in two aspects: (1) evaluating the efficiency of RONN algorithms – we compare the latency of the proposed RONN algorithms under various parameters (summarized in Table 7, numbers in bold are the default settings); and (2) evaluating the efficiency of O-tree – we compare the height, number of leaf nodes, index size and construction time of O-tree with respect to the space division strategies under comparison. Three different kinds of obstacles are indexed: (1) *line segment* obstacles (i.e., polylines in datasets); (2) *rectangle* obstacles (i.e., MBRs in the datasets); and (3) *polygon* obstacles. We randomly generate five groups of RONN queries with different query sizes where each group of queries consists of 50 RONN queries using SpatialDataGenerator.[8] In each experiment, we test one parameter at a time (other parameters are fixed at their default values). The reported experimental results are obtained by averaging the processing time of queries.

7.1 Efficiency of RONN Algorithms

In this section, we evaluate the efficiency of the proposed RONN algorithms, including CONNB, RONN-RF and RONN-OA. For CONNB and RONN-RF algorithms, data and obstacle sets are indexed with an R*-tree [2], where the page size is fixed at 4KB. For RONN-OA, we construct the O-tree index by adopting the proposed optimal obstacle balance (OOB) scheme for space division. We measure the average latency as the performance metric corresponding to three different parameters: (a) numbers of obstacles $|O|$; (b) numbers of data objects $|P|$; and (c) query size *qsize*. Accordingly, we test the three RONN algorithms using different datasets as described above.

Effect of the number of obstacles. In this experiment, we compare the average running time of three algorithms for processing RONN queries by increasing the number of obstacles. The average running time for finding internal RONNs and external RONNs, are depicted in Fig. 10. Fig. 10(a) shows the result on Uniform Segment dataset. As shown, it takes very little time to find the internal RONNs (too small to be seen), as the main cost in answering RONN queries is spent on external RONN search. RONN-OA and RONN-RF outperform CONNB significantly, with 360% and 300% improvement, respectively. On average, RONN-OA takes 50ms for each query. The excellent performance was achieved by the effective pruning facilitated by O-tree. As a result, RONN-OA searches a small number of R-trees for only once. RONN-RF also performs much better than CONNB because it traverses R-tree only once (instead of four times as CONNB does). The filtering in RONN-RF also helps. As expected, the performance becomes worse when the number of obstacles increases, especially in Greece Segment dataset, but all three algorithms scale well. The results obtained using the other three datasets are shown in Figs. 10(b)-(d). The observed trend and conclusion are consistent with

[8]Query size denotes the size of edges in query rectangle.

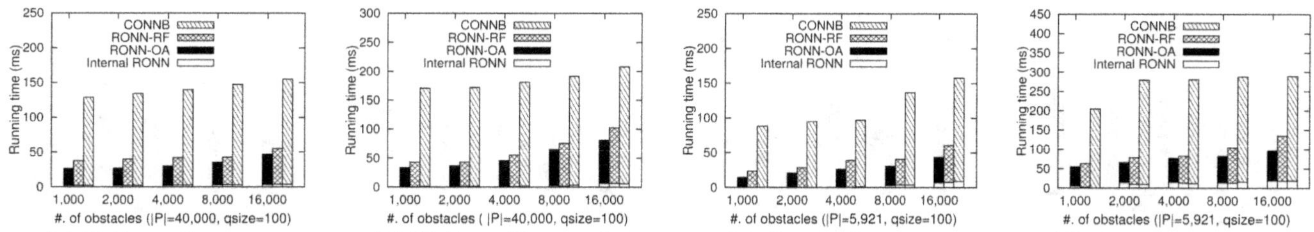

(a) Uniform Segment (b) Uniform Rectangle (c) Greece Segment (d) Greece Rectangle

Figure 10: Performance vs. $|O|$

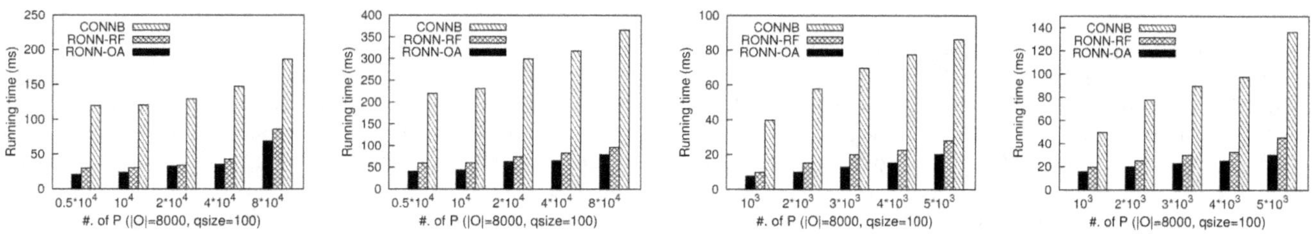

(a) Uniform Segment (b) Uniform Rectangle (c) Greece Segment (d) Greece Rectangle

Figure 11: Performance vs. $|P|$

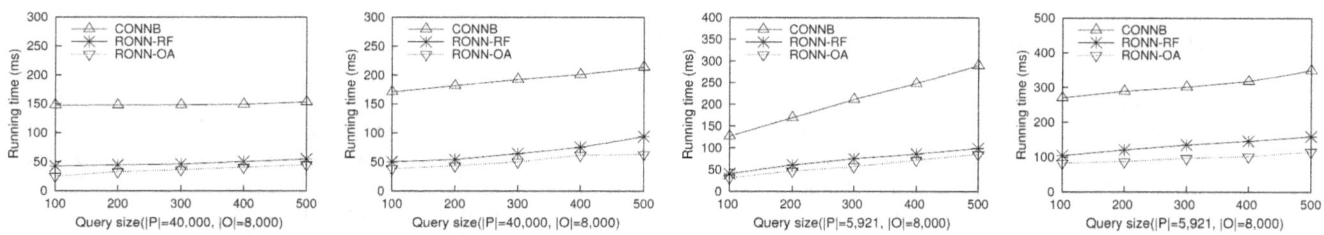

(a) Uniform Segment (b) Uniform Rectangle (c) Greece Segment (d) Greece Rectangle

Figure 12: Performance vs. query size

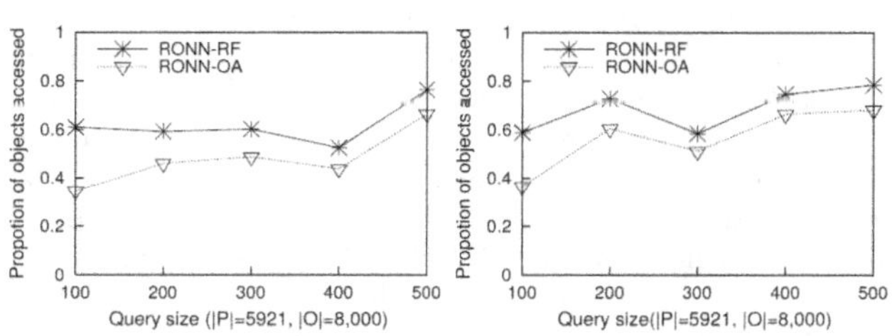

(a) Greece Segment (b) Greece Rectangle

Figure 13: Proportion of data objects accessed

Fig. 10(a). Compare with the obstacles represented as line segments, all the three algorithms spent longer time when obstacles are represented as rectangles. This is because more vertices of obstacles need to be inserted to their corresponding visibility graphs.

Effect of the number of data objects. Fig. 11 compares the performance of RONN algorithms by varying the number of data objects. For the Uniform dataset with segment and rectangle obstacles, respectively, all the three algorithms answer the query within half second. Both RONN-RF and RONN-OA are very efficient, cost less than 0.1 second when $|P|$ was 80,000. RONN-OA outperforms the two R-tree based algorithms significantly under various number of data objects because O-tree index provides good filtering ability. Moreover, the processing time of all three algorithms increases as the number of data objects increases. Also comparing Fig. 11(a) and Fig. 11(b), the three algorithms spent longer time when obstacles were represented as rectangles. The results on Greece dataset show that the three algorithms take less time compared with the Uniform dataset because the number of data objects in Uniform dataset is smaller.

Effect of query size. We then compare the RONN algorithms by varying query sizes and show the result in Fig. 12. For *Uniform* dataset, the results in Fig. 12(a) shows the superiority of RONN-OA over the two R-tree based algorithms. The search time of RONN-OA only takes about 35 ms, but the CONNB algorithm takes more than 150 ms, while RONN-RF takes almost 45 ms, because O-tree effectively divides the obstructed space into non-obstacle space. As a result, points in the non-obstacle spaces can be effectively filtered using R-trees. As Figs. 12(a) and 12(b) show, it takes more time to process rectangle dataset than line segment dataset. Similar results on *Greece* dataset are observed in Figs. 12(c) and 12(d).

Proportion of the number of data objects accessed. As mentioned in the complexity analysis earlier, the number of data objects accessed during query processing is a

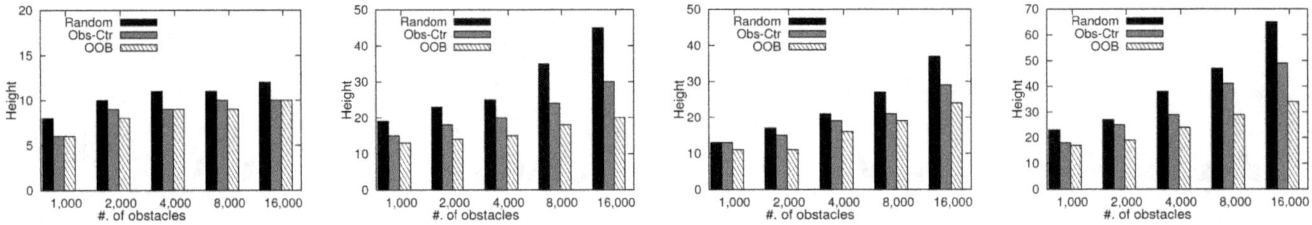

(a) Uniform Segment (b) Uniform Rectangle (c) Greece Segment (d) Greece Rectangle

Figure 14: The height of O-Tree vs. ♯ of O

key factor. We compare our RONN-OA and RONN-RF algorithm on proportion of the number of data objects accessed (dividing the number of data objects accessed by CONNB algorithm) by varying query size in Fig. 13. In Fig. 13(a), RONN-OA and RONN-RF, significantly outperforms CONNB, and RONN-OA outperforms RONN-RF because O-tree index can filter some data objects whose Euclidean distance to query range is small but obstructed distance to query range is big while R-tree can not filter such kind of data objects. The similar results are shown in on *Rectangle* dataset in Fig. 13(b).

7.2 Construction of the O-tree Index

As discussed in Section 5, space division is an essential issue in construction of O-tree. To achieve tree balance, we propose the optimal obstacle balance (OOB) scheme. In this section, we evaluate the performance of the OOB scheme, in comparison with the following two baseline schemes:

- *Random.* This scheme randomly chooses an obstacle for space division in construction of O-tree.
- *Obs-Ctr.* Obs-Ctr is to simply use the perpendicular bisector of selected obstacle as the perpendicular line for space division. It chooses the obstacle with the best score to divide the current space.

To compare these space division schemes, we use the heights and leaf nodes of the corresponding O-trees as performance metrics, as they reflect how balanced these O-trees are, i.e., the smaller the height and the number of leaf nodes are, the better the tree balance is. Additionally, we compare the size of the resulted index and their construction time.

Fig. 14 depicts the tree height of the space division schemes by varying the numbers of obstacles in four datasets. We can see that the OOB scheme outperforms the other two schemes in all circumstances using different datasets with different sizes of obstacle sets. The result also shows that Obs-Ctr is better than Random. When increasing the number of obstacles, the tree height for all schemes increases slowly in the experiment on uniform obstacle sets. However, for skewed datasets, i.e., *Greece* dataset, the impact of the number of obstacles is obviously more significant, especially on the Random and Obs-Ctr schemes. OOB performs the best because it achieves better obstacle balance in each space division step. In addition, the Obs-Ctr scheme performs better than the Random scheme in general, as they do achieve certain degree of obstacle balance. Moreover, by comparing Fig. 14(a) and Fig. 14(b), we observe that the tree height resulted from various schemes are higher on Rectangle dataset than on the Segment dataset, because these schemes deal with more obstacles on Rectangle dataset.

To evaluate those schemes more comprehensively, we further compare the number of leaf nodes in their resulted O-trees. With the growing numbers of obstacles, the number of leaf nodes in the tree is larger. And the number of leaf nodes using Random scheme increases faster than that using OOB or Obs-Ctr, showing OOB schemes achieving better tree balance. The corresponding experiment results and additional experimental results about index size and construction time can be found in Appendix D.

In summary, the height and the number of leaf nodes show that the proposed OOB scheme achieves the best tree balance among these three schemes.

8. CONCLUSION

In this paper, we formulate a new query, namely, *range-based obstructed nearest neighbor* (RONN) query, for finding nearest neighbors to a given spatial range in the obstructed space. We carry out a systematic study on the RONN query. First, we propose the CONNB algorithm as a baseline for the tackled RONN problem. To address the shortcomings of the CONNB algorithm, we further propose a new RONN-RF algorithm, that explores heuristics and filtering strategies via seamless integration of range and CONN queries to facilitate efficient query processing. Next, we propose a new index, called *O-tree*, dedicated for indexing objects in the obstructed space. The novelty of O-tree lies in the idea of *dividing the obstructed space into non-obstacle space*, aiming to exploit efficient query processing in non-obstacle subspaces. We propose a space division scheme OOB to address the tree balance problem. Moreover, we propose an efficient algorithm, called RONN-OA, which exploits O-tree to accelerate query processing of RONN. At last, a comprehensive performance evaluation is conducted to validate the proposed ideas and demonstrate the efficiency and effectiveness of the proposed index and algorithms.

This work may lead towards several new directions for future work, e.g., different shapes of query range, mobile obstacles, as well as parallel processing techniques.

9. ACKNOWLEDGMENTS

This work is partially supported by the NSF of China for Outstanding Young Scholars under grant No. 61322208, the National Basic Research Program of China (973 Program) under grant No. 2012CB316201, the NSF of China for Key Program under grant No. 61532021, and the NSF of China under grant Nos. 61272178 and 61572122. We are grateful to the anonymous reviewers for their constructive comments on this paper. Xiaochun Yang is the corresponding author of this work.

10. REFERENCES

[1] J. Bao, C.-Y. Chow, M. F. Mokbel, and W.-S. Ku. Efficient evaluation of k-range nearest neighbor queries in road networks. *MDM*, pages 115–124, 2010.

[2] N. Beckmann, H.-P. Kriegel, R. Schneider, and B. Seeger. The R*-tree: An efficient and robust access method for points and rectangles. *SIGMOD*, pages 322–331, 1990.

[3] N. Chan and T. Dang. On efficient processing of complicated cloaked region for location privacy aware nearest-neighbor queries. *International Conference on Information Communication Technology*, pages 101–110, 2013.

[4] M. de Berg, M. van Kreveld, M. Overmars, and O.Schwarzkopf. *Computational Geometry: Algorithms and Applications, Second Edition.* Springer-Verlag, Reading, Massachusetts, 2000.

[5] P. Galdames and Y. Cai. Efficient processing of location-cloaked queries. *IEEE INFOCOM*, 131(5):2480–2488, 2012.

[6] Y. Gao and B. Zheng. Continuous obstructed nearest neighbor queries in spatial databases. *SIGMOD*, pages 577–558, 2009.

[7] Y. Gao, B. Zheng, W.-C. Lee, and G. Chen. Continuous visible nearest neighbor queries. *EDBT 09*, pages 144–155, 2009.

[8] B. Gedik and L. Liu. A customizable k-anonymity model for protecting location privacy. *Distributed Computing Systems (ICDCS)*, pages 763–774, 2005.

[9] M. Gruteser and D. Grunwald. Anonymous usage of location-based services through spatial and temporal cloaking. *ACM MobiSys*, pages 763–774, 2003.

[10] H. Hu and D. L. Lee. Range nearest-neighbor query. *TKDE*, 18(1):78–91, 2006.

[11] C. H. J and J. R. Efficient processing of moving k-range nearest neighbor queries in directed and dynamic spatial networks. *Mobile Information Systems*, 2016.

[12] P. Kalnis, G. Ghinita, K. Mouratidis, and D. Papadias. Preventing location based identity inference in anonymous spatial queries. *TKDE*, 26(3):1719–1733, 2007.

[13] A. Khoshgozaran, C. Shahabi, and H. Shirani-Mehr. Enabling location privacy; moving beyond k-anonymity, cloaking and anonymizers. *Knowledge Information Systems*, 26(3):435–465, 2011.

[14] H.-I. Kim and J.-W. Chang. k-nearest neighbor query processing algorithms for a query region in road networks. *Journal of Computer Science and Technology*, 28(4):585–596, 2013.

[15] E. Lee, H. Cho, T. Chung, and K. Ryu. Moving range k nearest neighbor queries with quality guarantee over uncertain moving objects. *Information Sciences*, 325:324–341, 2015.

[16] X. Lin, J. Xu, and H. Hu. Range-based skyline queries in mobile environments. *TKDE*, 25(4):835–849, 2013.

[17] M. F. Mokbel, C. Y. Chow, and W. G. Aref. The New Casper: Query processing for location services without compromising privacy. *VLDB*, pages 763–774, 2006.

[18] K. Mouratidis, M. Yiu, D. Papadias, and N. Mamoulis. Continuous nearest neighbor monitoring in road networks. *VLDB*, pages 43–54, 2006.

[19] S. Nutanong, E. Tanin, and R. Zhang. Visible nearest neighbor queries. *DASFAA*, pages 876–883, 2007.

[20] Y. Tao, D. Papadias, and Q. Shen. Continuous nearest neighbor search. *VLDB*, pages 287–298, 2002.

[21] A. K. Tung, J. Hou, and J. Han. Spatial clustering in the presence of obstacles. *ICDE*, pages 322–331, 1990.

[22] X. Wang and H. J. Hamilton. Clustering spatial data in the presence of obstacles. *International Journal on Artificial Intelligence Tools*, 14(1-2):177–198, 2005.

[23] C. Xia, D. Hsu, and H. Tung. A fast filter for obstructed nearest neighbor queries. *BNCOD*, pages 203–215, November 2004.

[24] C. Zhang and Y. Huang. Cloaking locations for anonymous location based services: a hybrid approach. *Geoinformatica*, pages 159–182, 2009.

[25] J. Zhanga, D. Papadias, K. Mouratidis, and M. Zhu. Spatial queries in the presence of obstacles. *EDBT*, pages 366–384, 2004.

[26] B. Zheng, W.-C. Lee, and D. L. Lee. On searching continuous k nearest neighbors in wireless data broadcast systems. *IEEE Transactions on Mobile Computing*, 6(7):748–761, 2007.

[27] H. Zhu, J. Wang, B. Wang, and X. Yang. Location privacy preserving obstructed nearest neighbor queries. *Journal of Computer Research and Development*, 51(1):115–125, 2014.

APPENDIX

A. PSEUDO-CODE OF RONN-OA

Algorithm 4 depicts the pseudo-code of the RONN-OA Algorithm. It first issues an internal RONN query (see Algorithm 5) (Line 1). The corresponding leaf nodes intersect with the query range are returned. Notice that this is done simultaneously while traversing O-tree to perform the range query. With support of O-tree, CONN-OA avoids traversing O-tree from the root again (unlike what RONN-RF does to process the external RONN query). Lines 7-27 are very similar to the RONN-RF Algorithm. The main difference is that we initiate the min-heap with the root entries of R-trees associated with the found leaf nodes of O-tree in Line 1.

The range query used in RONN-OA is depicted in Algorithm 5. We recursively traverse O-tree to the leaf nodes. For each node visited, we first check whether its region intersects with the query range R (Line 1). If yes, we continue to check whether the node is a leaf node. There are two conditions: (i) if the node is a leaf node, we will traverse its associated R-tree to find data objects located in the query range and add them into the result set Res. Meanwhile, the leaf node itself is added to a leaf node list, namely, $LNodeList$ (Lines 2-4). (ii) if the node is not a leaf node, we will recursively search each of its child node (Lines 5-7).

B. PROOF OF THEOREM 2

Proof. We prove Theorem 2 by showing that the RONN-OA algorithm returns result with no false misses and no false hits.

(1) The result returned by the RONN-OA algorithm has no false misses. According to the RONN-OA algorithm, we know that an object p could be an answer to RONN only if (i) it is inside a region overlapped with the query range, or

Algorithm 4: RONN-OA Algorithm

```
Input: A O-tree OT, query range R, and min-heap H
Output: RONN results list RS
RQ(R, OT, InternalRes, LNodeList);
for k = 1 to 4 do
    RS_k ← InternalRes; over_k ← 0;
RS ← InternalRes;
for Each node n ∈ LNodeList do
    insert( n.rptr.root, mindist(n, R)) into H;
while true do
    k ← 1;
    for Each edge E_ij of R do
        RS_k ← FindSP(E_ij, RS_k);
        MOD_k ← max_odis(RS_k);
        if H.head.key > MOD_k then
            over_k = 1.
        if over_1&over_2&over_3&over_4 or H ≐ ∅ then
            return;
        k++;
    while H ≠ ∅ do
        de-heap the top entry (e, key) of H;
        if e is a data object then
            check whether e is in result RS; /* using
            isInResult array*/
            k ← 1;
            for key < MOD_k do
                insert e into RS_k; k++;
            break;
        else
            for each child entry e_i ∈ e do
                if mindist(e_i, R) < MAX(MOD_k) then
                    insert(e_i, mindist(e_i, R)) into H.
RS ← RS ∪ RS_k;
return RS;
```

Algorithm 5: O-tree::Range Query Algorithm (RQ)

```
Input: A query region R, a O-tree Node Node, and a
       Node list LNodeList.
Output: A set of data objects and LNodeList
if isIntersect(Node.reg, R) then
    if Node is leaf node then
        Res ← rangequery(R,Node.rptr);
        insert Node into LNodeList;
    else
        for Each optr of Node do
            RQ(R, optr, Res,LNodeList);
return Res and LNodeList;
```

(ii) it belongs the ONNs to the boundary line segments of a overlapped regions. Assume data object p does not satisfy the above two conditions but p is an answer to RONN. Then p is the nearest neighbor to any point inside the query range. Let q is a such point inside the query range. Moreover, q must exists inside a certain region R_i that are overlapped with the query range. From Lemma 1, we know that the ONN to q must be inside R_i or belong to the ONNs to the boundary of R_i. This contradicts with the assumption. Therefore, the returned results by RONN-OA has no false misses.

(2) The RONN-OA algorithm inserts all the data objects that satisfy the above two conditions into the heap for checking if it is an RONN answer. Hence, the algorithm has no false hits.

From (1) and (2) above, the proof completes. □

C. EXTENSION ON O-TREE

In this section, we extend the O-tree index for *polygons*. Fig. 15 shows an example of indexing a pentagon o_1. For space division, we can take each edge of the polygon as a separate obstacle line to divide the space. Then we can use the division schema for obstacles represented as line segments to divide the space. Firstly, we use the edge $\overline{ab}$ to divide the region into four subregions and the root has four child nodes (R_1, R_2, R_3, R_4). As R_1 can be divided into four subregions (R_{11}, R_{12}, R_{13}, R_{14}) utilizing the edge $\overline{ae}$, R_4 can be divided into four subregions using $\overline{cd}$, and the other two subregions can directly form the leaf node. At last, R_{11} and R_{42} can be divided into four subregions by $\overline{de}$ and $\overline{bc}$, respectively. An example of space division is shown on the top side of the figure, while the corresponding O-tree is depicted on the bottom side. Internal node R_1 stores obstacle $\overline{ae}$, and *optr* pointing to three O-tree children R_{11}, R_{12}, and R_{13}. Notice that O-tree does not store R_{14} since R_{14} locates inside the pentagon o_1. Internal node R_{11} stores obstacle $\overline{de}$, and *optr* pointing to two O-tree children R_{111} and R_{114}. Leaf node R_{12} stores *rptr* pointing to an R-tree which contains data objects p_3 and p_4. The other nodes is similar to Internal node R_{11} and leaf node R_{12}. Notice that when we use $\overline{ab}$ to divide the whole space, we choose the perpendicular bisector through the endpoint of $\overline{de}$ and $\overline{cd}$ to avoid splitting $\overline{de}$ and $\overline{cd}$ into more obstacles.

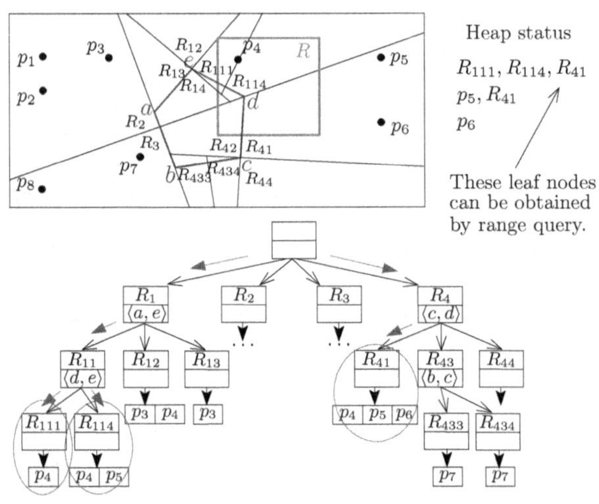

Figure 15: Index about polygon

Next, we introduce the RONN processing for polygon-shaped obstacles based on O-tree. Firstly, we issue a range query to obtain the interval RONN p_4. At the same time, it obtains the corresponding leaf nodes R_{111}, R_{114} and R_{44} that intersect with R. Then we follow the similar steps of RONN-OA shown in the heap status part of Fig. 15 until H

becomes empty so the query processing ends. Actually, the other data objects are filtered by internal RONN p_4 except p_5 and p_6 while searching O-Tree. Finally, the RONN result set includes p_4, p_5 and p_6.

While computing the ONNs with polygon obstacles, we observe a problem. As shown in Fig. 16, there is a rectangle obstacle o, and data objects p_1 and p_2. In our O-tree index of this rectangle obstacle, we take each edge of the rectangle as a separate line segment obstacle to perform space division and build O-tree index. However, in query processing, when we compute the obstructed distance of p_2 to p_1, we choose the distance of shortest path of $\langle p_2, b, d, p1\rangle$ instead of actual shortest path $\langle p_2, a, p1\rangle$. Actually, we can not go across from b to d. This is the *wrong crossing* problem.

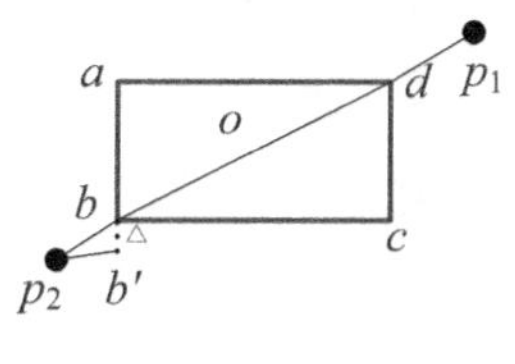

Figure 16: Wrong crossing

To avoid wrong crossing, we adopt an idea of Δ *shifting* to address the problem. As shown in Fig. 16, when going through p_2 to b (ending points of obstacle), we assume it goes through p_2 to b' which is obtained by shifting b with Δ distance (Note that Δ is relatively small here).

D. EXTRA EXPERIMENTAL RESULTS

To evaluate the experiments comprehensively, we list some extra experimental results.

D.1 Number of Leaf Nodes of O-tree

To evaluate the three space division schemes for building an O-tree more comprehensively, we further compare the number of leaf nodes in O-tree. As depicted in Fig.17(a), when increasing the numbers of obstacles, the number of leaf nodes in the tree become larger. In addition, the number of leaf nodes using Random scheme increases faster than that using OOB and Obs-Ctr. OOB scheme achieves the best tree balance. As expected, more division needed to be considered in *Uniform Rectangle* dataset, so the number of leaf nodes is much larger than that on *Uniform Segment* dataset. Figs.17(c) and 17(d) show the similar results on Greece datasets.

D.2 Index Size and Construction Time

Then, we show the index size and construction time of O-tree in Figs. 18(a)-(b) with respect to different numbers of obstacles on Uniform Segment dataset. For index size in Fig.18(a), O-tree generated using the OOB scheme only takes less than 10 MB, much smaller than the other two schemes. This result is consistent with the results on the height and the number of leaf nodes of O-trees. Additionally, the Random scheme results in largely varied sizes of O-trees. The construction times of index resulted from all space division schemes are shown in Fig. 18(b). Random is faster than the other two schemes because it takes no time to decide how to divide the space. However, this results an unbalanced tree which does not support RONN processing well. The other schemes take under 12 minutes to finish the index construction. In the last index comparison part of experiments, we compare O-tree performance of space division schemes when we assume each obstacle is an rectangle on Uniform dataset, and the experimental results are shown in Figs. 18(c)-(d) . O-tree index with line segment obstacles is more efficient for space division and building index in most cases. This is because if we take each rectangle obstacle as four line segment obstacles, many obstacles will be divided into more parts, and thus more difficult to deal with than the line segment obstacles.

D.3 Overlap of data objects stored in leaf nodes

We further evaluate the number of overlapped data objects among leaf nodes in O-tree. We compare the three space division schemes to see their effects on the number of overlapped data objects. Fig. 19 shows the comparison results. When increasing the number of obstacles, the number of overlapped objects increases. When the number of obstacles is less than 4,000, using OOB division scheme only produces less than 0.3 overlap. Random division scheme generates more overlap since it does not consider the density of the obstacles.

D.4 Comparison with Cloaking Query

Cloaking query in obstructed space [27] is the most related work to ours. Cloaking query is mainly proposed for protecting the query point so that the untrusted server cannot infer the correct query point among queries in the cloaked region. Due to the lack of the exact location information at the server, the anonymous query processor calculates a safe region and provides all data objects inside the safe region (i.e. candidates) instead of a single exact answer [17].

Different from cloaking query, an RONN query returns nearest neighbors to every query in the query region. A good point is that RONN can also protect the real query point and guarantees its returned result covering the exact answer to the protected query point in the query range. RONNA returns less number of points than the candidates returned by the cloaked query, therefore saving the communication cost as well as the post-processing time at client.

Fig. 18 shows the comparison between RONN-OA and cloaking query in obstructed space [27]. We use the number of returned points to represent communication cost. Fig. 20(a) shows that RONN incurs much less communication cost than cloaking query does. Fig. 20(b) shows that cloaking query runs a little faster than RONN-OA since it directly returns those candidates within the safe region without any examination. Notice that, more candidates returned from server require more cost for post-processing at client since the final answer should be refined and returned to the user. Fig. 20(c) shows the processing time at client.

D.5 Results on Polygon Obstacles

We also test the running time of our algorithms on *Tiger Census Blocks* datasets with polygon obstacles. They contain uniform and zipf distributed data objects datasets, respectively. Fig. 21 shows that RONN-OA and RONN-RF outperform CONNB significantly. The running time on uniform distributed dataset is faster than that on zipf distributed dataset, because the skewed data distribution makes the maximum obstructed distances (MODs) (i.e. filtering distance) longer than uniform data. Moreover, more data objects need to be examined.

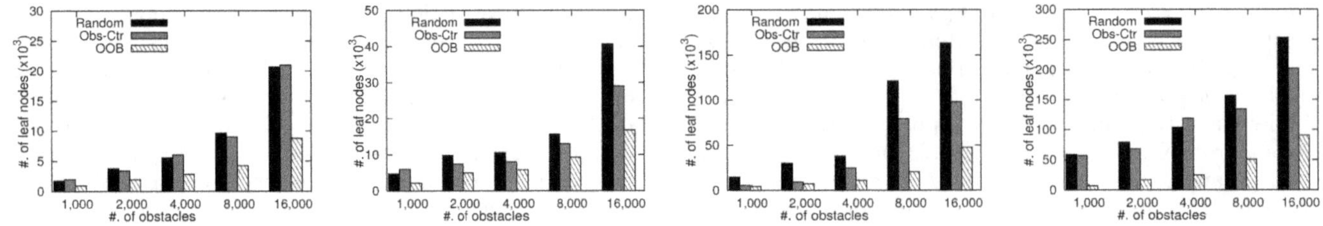

(a) Uniform Segment (b) Uniform Rectangle (c) Greece Segment (d) Greece Rectangle

Figure 17: The number of leaf nodes

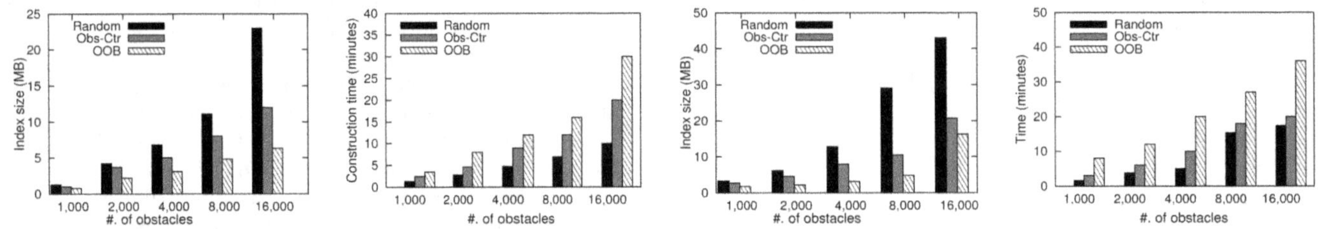

(a) Uniform Segment (b) Uniform Segment (c) Uniform Rectangle (d) Uniform Rectangle

Figure 18: Index size and construction time on Uniform Segment obstacles

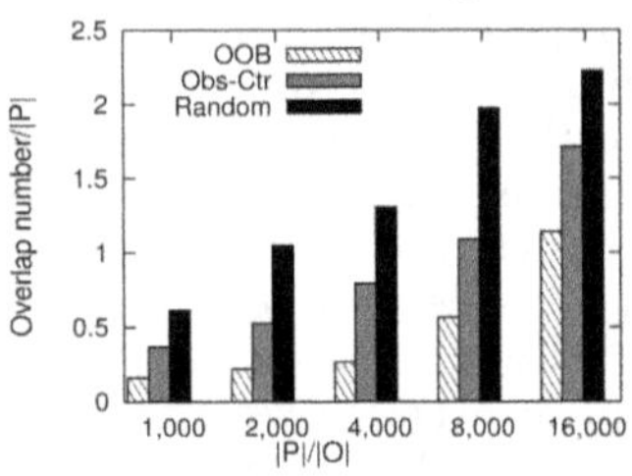

Figure 19: Data overlap

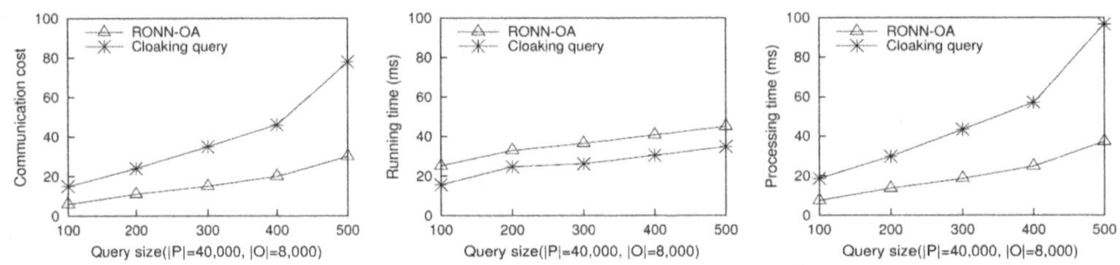

(a) Communication cost (b) Running time at server (c) Running time at client

Figure 20: Comparison with Cloaking query

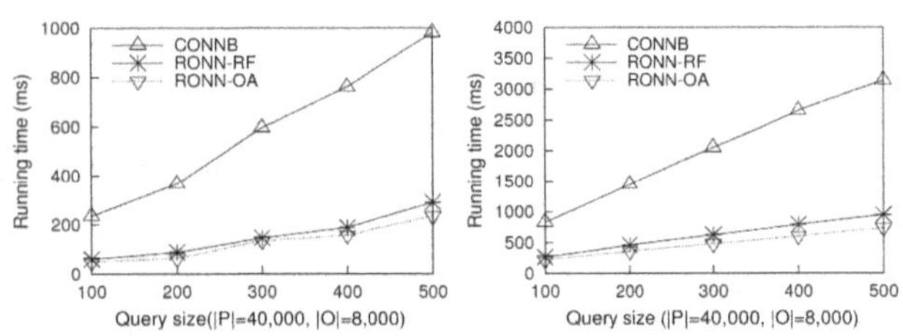

(a) Uniform Tiger (b) Zipf Tiger

Figure 21: Performance on polygon obstacles

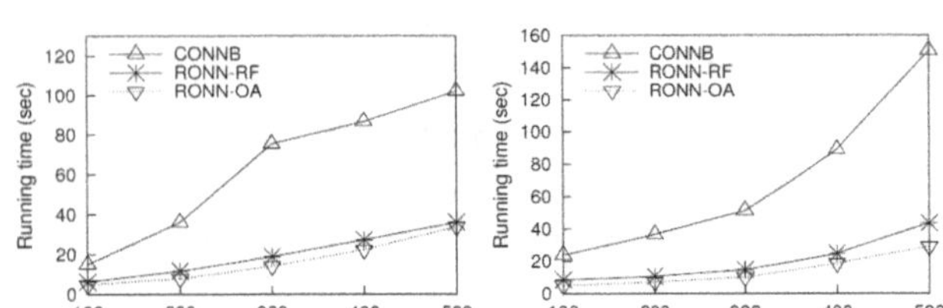

(a) (UniformCA) dataset (b) (ZipfCA) dataset

Figure 22: Performance on large datasets

D.6 Results on Large Datasets

We also evaluate the three algorithms on large datasets *UniformCA* and *ZipfCA* and show the experimental results in Fig. 22. The running time for the three algorithms were within 2 minutes on *UniformCA* dataset, faster than the time on *ZipfCA*.

Our RONN-OA and RONN-RF outperform the baseline algorithm CONNB with 405% and 300% improvement, respectively, which is consistent to the result on the other tested datasets. For example, when query size was 300, the running time was 75.3 seconds, 18.9 seconds, and 14 seconds for CONNA, RONN-RF, and RONN-OA, respectively. We can see that RONN-OA improves RONN-RF by 35% on the large dataset *UniformCA*.

Rheem: Enabling Multi-Platform Task Execution

Divy Agrawal[2*] Lamine Ba[1] Laure Berti-Equille[1] Sanjay Chawla[1] Ahmed Elmagarmid[1]
Hossam Hammady[1] Yasser Idris[1] Zoi Kaoudi[1] Zuhair Khayyat[4*] Sebastian Kruse[3*]
Mourad Ouzzani[1] Paolo Papotti[5*] Jorge-Arnulfo Quiané-Ruiz[1] Nan Tang[1] Mohammed J. Zaki[6*]

[1]Qatar Computing Research Institute, HBKU [2]University of California, Santa Barbara [3]Hasso Platner Institute
[4]King Abdullah University of Science and Technology [5]Arizona State University [6]Rensselaer Polytechnic Institute

ABSTRACT

Many emerging applications, from domains such as healthcare and oil & gas, require several data processing systems for complex analytics. This demo paper showcases RHEEM, a framework that provides multi-platform task execution for such applications. It features a three-layer data processing abstraction and a new query optimization approach for multi-platform settings. We will demonstrate the strengths of RHEEM by using real-world scenarios from three different applications, namely, machine learning, data cleaning, and data fusion.

1. NEED FOR FREEDOM

Following the philosophy "one size does not fit all", we have embarked on an endless race of developing data processing platforms for supporting different tasks, e.g., DBMSs and MapReduce-like systems. While these systems allow us to achieve high performance and scalability, users still face two major problems.

Platform Independence. Users are faced with a large number of choices on where to process their data. Each choice comes with possibly orders of magnitude differences in terms of performance. Moreover, whenever a new platform that achieves better performance than the existing ones becomes available, users are enticed to move to the new platform, e.g., Spark taking over Hadoop. Typically, such a move does not come without pain. Therefore, there is a clear need for a system that frees us from the burden and cost of re-implementing and migrating applications from one platform to another.

Multi-Platform Task Execution. Several complex data analytic pipelines are emerging in many different domains. These complex pipelines require combining multiple processing platforms to perform each task of the process and then integrating the results. Performing this combination and integration requires users to be intimate with the intricacies of the different processing platforms and to deal with their interoperability. There is a clear need for a system that eases the integration among different processing platforms by automatically dividing a task into subtasks and determining the underlying platform for each subtask.

Motivating Example. Let us illustrate these two problems by using an oil & gas use case [7]. A single oil company can produce more than 1.5TB of diverse data per day [3], which may be structured or unstructured. During the exploration phase, data has to be acquired, cleaned, integrated, and analyzed in order to predict if a reservoir would be profitable. Thousands of downhole sensors in exploratory wells produce real-time seismic data for monitoring resources and environmental conditions. Users integrate these data with the physical properties of the rocks to visualize volume and surface renderings. From these visualizations, geologists and geophysicists formulate hypotheses and verify them with machine learning methods. Thus, an application supporting such a complex analytic pipeline has to access several sources for historical data (relational, but also text and semi-structured), remove the noise from the streaming data coming from the sensors, possibly integrate a subset of these data sources, and run both traditional (such as SQL) and statistical analytics (such as machine learning algorithms) over different processing platforms.

Rheem. We recently presented a vision of RHEEM[1], our solution to tackle these two problems and thus provide data processing freedom [2]. We propose a three-level data processing abstraction that allows a large variety of applications to achieve processing *platform independence* as well as *multi-platform task execution*. The latter makes our proposal distinct from [5], which does not include an optimizer for automatic multi-platform task execution. Furthermore, in contrast to [6], RHEEM also considers the cost of data movement across underlying platforms. In this demonstration, we will showcase the benefits of RHEEM in terms of flexibility and efficiency. To prove its applicability, we will present three applications, namely, machine learning, data cleaning, and truth discovery.

2. RHEEM OVERVIEW

The current prototype of RHEEM provides two main concepts of the vision presented in [2]: the *data processing abstraction* and the *multi-platform task optimizer*. In this section, we start by describing the general architecture of RHEEM. We then briefly discuss its two main features.

*Work done while at QCRI.

[1]http://da.qcri.org/rheem/

SIGMOD'16, June 26-July 01, 2016, San Francisco, CA, USA

DOI: http://dx.doi.org/10.1145/2882903.2899414

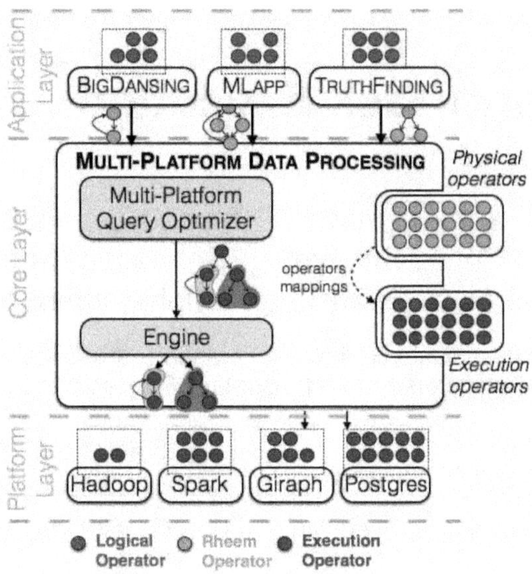

Figure 1: Rheem architecture.

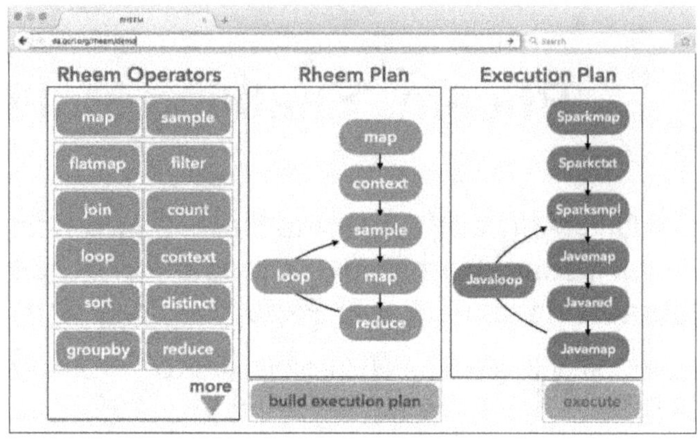

Figure 2: Rheem development interface.

2.1 Overview

Overall, our system provides a three-layer data processing abstraction that sits between user applications and data processing platforms such as Hadoop and Spark (see Figure 1): (i) an application layer that models all application-specific logic; (ii) a core layer that provides the intermediate representation between applications and processing platforms; and (iii) a platform layer that embraces the underlying processing platforms. The communication among these three layers is enabled by operators defined as user defined functions (UDFs). RHEEM provides a set of operators at each layer, namely, logical operators, Rheem operators, and execution operators. Using user-provided implementations of the logical operators specific to the application, the application layer produces a set of possible optimized Rheem plans. An application passes these Rheem plans to the core layer together with the cost functions to help the optimizer in choosing the best plan. These cost functions are obtained by applications and passed to the core layer as UDFs. At the core layer, RHEEM performs several multi-platform optimizations and outputs an execution plan. Then, the underlying processing platforms might further optimize a subplan for better performance. Notice that, in contrast to a DBMS, RHEEM decouples the core (physical) level from the execution one. This separation allows applications to express a Rheem plan in terms of algorithmic needs, without being tied to any platform.

These three layers allow RHEEM to provide applications with platform independence, which is exploited by the RHEEM optimizer to perform multi-platform task execution. Such execution is crucial to achieve the best performance at all times. In the following, we discuss in more details the data processing abstraction as well as the RHEEM optimizer.

2.2 Data Processing Abstraction

We now discuss how developers can define operators at the three levels of the RHEEM data processing abstraction.

Application Layer. A logical operator is a UDF that acts as an application-specific unit of data processing. Basically, it is a template where users provide the logic of their tasks. Such an abstraction enables both ease-of-use, by hiding underlying implementation details from the users (e.g., task parallelization), and high performance, by allowing several optimizations, e.g., seamless distributed execution. A logical operator works on data quanta; these are the smallest units of data from an input datasets. For example, a data quantum might represent a tuple in the input dataset or a row in a matrix. This fine-grained data model allows us to apply operators in a highly parallel fashion and thus achieve better performance.

To provide more insights about this layer, let us illustrate its use via a machine learning (ML) example. Consider a developer who wants to offer end users logical operators to implement various ML algorithms. He can define three basic operators: (i) Initialize, to initialize algorithm-specific parameters, e.g., initializing cluster centroids, (ii) Process, for the computations required by the ML algorithm, e.g., finding the nearest centroid of a point, and (iii) Loop, for specifying the stopping condition. Users can implement algorithms, e.g., SVM, K-means, and linear/logistic regression, using these operators.

Core Layer. This layer, which is at the heart of RHEEM, exposes a pool of Rheem operators. Each represents an algorithmic decision for executing an analytic task. A Rheem operator is a platform-independent implementation of a logical operator whereby a developer can deploy a new application on top of RHEEM. For example, in the above ML example, the application optimizer maps Initialize to a Map Rheem operator and Process to a GroupBy Rheem operator. The system also allows developers to define new operators as needed. Once an application has produced a Rheem plan, the system translates this plan into an execution plan by optimizing it according to the underlying processing platforms. Therefore, in contrast to DBMSs, RHEEM produces execution plans that can run on multiple platforms.

Platform Layer. An execution operator (in an execution plan) defines how a task is executed on the underlying processing platform. In other words, an execution operator is the platform-dependent implementation of a Rheem operator. For instance, consider again the above ML example, the MapPartitions and ReduceByKey execution operators for Spark are one way to perform Initialize and Process.

Defining mappings between Rheem and execution operators is the developers' responsibility whenever a new execution platform is plugged in. RHEEM relies on an internal mapping structure that models the correspondences between operators together with context information such as cost functions. The context is needed for the effective and efficient execution of each operator.

2.3 Multi-Platform Optimization

The optimizer is responsible for translating a given abstract RheemPlan (or a set of alternatives) into the most efficient ExecutionPlan. The resulting ExecutionPlan consists of a set of platform-specific subplans. Notice that this optimization problem is quite different from traditional database query optimization and thus poses several challenges. First, RHEEM itself is highly extensible and hence neither the RheemPlan operators nor the platforms are fixed. Second, the optimizer should be extensible on how to translate RheemPlans to platform-specific plans. Finally, RHEEM's data processing abstraction is based on UDFs, so operators appear to the optimizer as black-boxes; making cost and cardinality estimations harder.

RHEEM tackles these challenges as follows. First, it applies an extensible set of graph transformations to the RheemPlan to find alternative ExecutionPlans. Then, it compares those alternatives by using the ExecutionOperator's cost functions. These can either be given or learned, and are parameterized *w.r.t.* the underlying hardware (e.g., number of computing nodes for distributed operators). Because RHEEM data processing abstraction is based on UDFs, which are black-boxes for the optimizer, domain-specific optimizations have to be done in collaboration with applications. RHEEM lets applications expose semantic properties about their functions as in [10], and furthermore provides optimization hints (e.g., numbers of iterations), constraints (e.g., physical collocation of operators), and alternative plans. The optimizer uses those artifacts where available in a best-effort approach.

When the optimizer has decided upon an ExecutionPlan, the Engine executes that plan by (i) scheduling the different subplans, (ii) orchestrating the data flow across platforms, and (iii) collecting statistics of the execution to further improve its optimizations.

3. DEMONSTRATION

Our main goal in this demo is to show the benefits of RHEEM with respect to three main aspects: (i) diversity of applications, (ii) platform independence, and (iii) multi-platform execution. The audience will be able to interact with RHEEM directly through its GUI, as well as with applications, namely machine learning, data cleaning, and truth discovery, built on top of the system. The GUI enables users to drag-and-drop Rheem operators to create a physical plan and see how the RHEEM optimizer transforms it into an execution plan (see Figure 2).

3.1 Machine Learning

Many current applications, such as our oil & gas example, require highly efficient machine learning algorithms (MLAs) to perform scalable statistical analytics. However, ensuring high efficiency for MLAs is challenging because of (i) the amount of data involved and (ii) the number of times a MLA has to process the data. Simply distributing MLAs is not obvious due to their iterative nature. Hence, current distributed solutions suffer from performance bottlenecks. In addition, users have to deal with many physical details for implementing a MLA. Achieving high performance and ease-of-use are major lacunae that need to be urgently addressed. Finally, distributing an MLA is not always the best choice to proceed, especially if the data is small or the MLA is sequential. In this demo, we will show how RHEEM tackles the above problems through platform independence and multi-platform execution.

Scalable Clustering. We will consider the real case from a large airline based in the middle east to carry out large scale clustering for personalizing promotion offers to customers. For this, we will use the K-means algorithm and demonstrate the power of RHEEM to distribute the execution of a classical clustering algorithm depending on the dataset size. The audience will also be able to choose among a selection of input datasets are taken from UCI, a publicly available ML respository, and visually see the Rheem plans produced by the application as well as the execution plans produced. The goal of this use case is to show how platform independence not only frees the users from platform-specific implementation details but can also lead to huge performance benefits.

Multi-Platform Gradient Descent. We consider three variations of gradient descent (GD), namely batch GD (BGD), stochastic GD and mini-batch GD (MGD). The audience will be able to choose among these three methods to perform classification on a set of input datasets from UCI as well as tune some parameters such as the batch size. Depending on the chosen method and the size of the batch, the users will be able to see how a specific plan can run partly in Spark and partly in a JVM platform. The overall goal of this use case is to demonstrate how multi-platform execution achieves better performance.

Datasets. We will use a dataset from a large airline based in the middle east. The data is spread across intra-organizational boundaries making it impossible to create a unified dataset to apply a standard clustering algorithm. We will show how RHEEM operators can be used to decouple the algorithm design from the underlying processing platform which in turn can be decoupled from the precise data storage layout. The second set of datasets we will use is taken from UCI, a publicly available ML repository.

3.2 Data Cleaning

Data cleaning, which is detecting and repairing data errors, is critical in data management and data analytics. This is because high-quality business decisions must be made based on high-quality data. In response to the need of supporting heterogeneous and ad-hoc quality rules for various applications, we have built a commodity data cleaning system NADEEF [4]. We have further extended NADEEF using RHEEM [8]. In this demo, users will have the opportunity to experience how RHEEM can boost the performance of NADEEF through platform independence.

Rule Specification in Logical Level. Figure 3 displays the NADEEF GUI for specifying data quality rules. The users can either (a) load rules using rule classes e.g., CFDs, MDs or DCs; or (b) implement a customized rule by writing functions based on programming interface in a few lines of code.

Scalable NADEEF. We will first show how logical NADEEF operators can be mapped to RHEEM operators. Through these different operators, RHEEM frees NADEEF from platform-specific implementation details. That is, RHEEM will decide, based on the logical NADEEF operators, the best platform to execute this task for best performance. Moreover, to show extensibility, we extended the

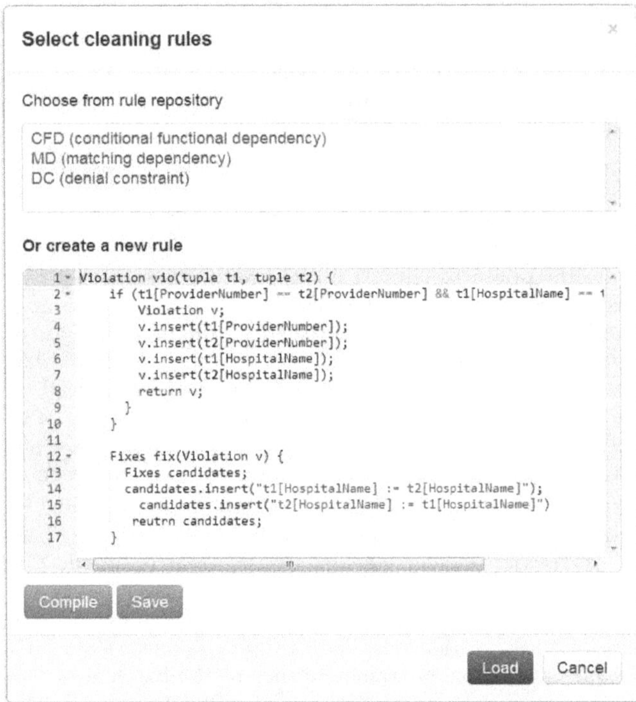

Figure 3: Rule specification in NADEEF.

set of physical RHEEM operators with a new join operator (called IEJoin [9]) to boost performance. This new operator provides a fast algorithm for joins containing only inequality conditions.

Datasets. We use three real-world large datasets. The first one is from an intelligence company that monitors over 700K Web sources. Errors are captured by temporal FD rules [1]. The second is a traffic data of Doha. Duplicates and erroneous readings are reported due to anomalies both in the detectors and in the Bluetooth devices. The third dataset comes from sensors reading from wells in an oil field. Erroneous readings need to be detected from different sensors in the Well during its normal operation, shutting, and opening . They are detected using different statistics-based data cleaning rules. We will demonstrate the significant performance gain (in orders of magnitude), by leveraging the easy mapping from NADEEF logical operators to RHEEM operators, and the platform independence of RHEEM to find the fastest execution plan.

3.3 Truth Discovery

Many real-world applications, e.g., our oil & gas use case, might face the problem of discovering the truth when merging conflicting information from a collection of heterogeneous sources. Such settings can use truth discovery algorithms that aim at resolving conflicts from different data sources in an automatic manner. Most of current truth discovery algorithms conduct an iterative process, which converges when a certain accuracy threshold or a given user-specified number of iterations is reached. As a result, some operations, such as the pairwise value similarity, highly impact the performance of truth discovery algorithms, limiting their scalability [11]. In fact, most truth discovery techniques are platform-dependent implementations with single-node execution. In this demo, we will use a typical data fusion scenario to demonstrate how RHEEM enables truth discovery algorithms to scale and be platform independent, with no additional effort.

Scalable Truth Discovery. We will show how a truth discovery application can be built on top of RHEEM, thanks to the flexibility of its operators. In particular, we will show how such an application can leverage the platform independence of RHEEM to overcome the common single-node execution of such algorithms. We will show how RHEEM leverages Spark by seamlessly distributing operations like value similarity.

Datasets. We showcase our scalable RHEEM truth discovery application using a large-size real-world biographical dataset. We show the improvement obtained from distributing RHEEM operations on SPARK against single-node execution on Java platform. Our dataset, whose entries (claims and sources) are extracted from several Wikipedia articles, contains over 10 millions values from one million sources.

4. REFERENCES

[1] Z. Abedjan, C. G. Akcora, M. Ouzzani, P. Papotti, and M. Stonebraker. Temporal rules discovery for web data cleaning. *PVLDB*, 9(4):336–347, 2015.

[2] D. Agarwal, S. Crawla, A. Elmagarmind, Z. Kaoudi, M. Ouzzani, P. Papati, J.-A. Quiané-Ruiz, N. Tang, and M. J. Zaki. Road to Freedom in Big Data Analytics. In *EDBT*, 2016.

[3] A. Baaziz and L. Quoniam. How to use big data technologies to optimize operations in upstream petroleum industry. In *21st World Petroleum Congress*, 2014.

[4] M. Dallachiesa et al. NADEEF: A Commodity Data Cleaning System. In *SIGMOD*, 2013.

[5] A. Elmore et al. A Demonstration of the BigDAWG Polystore System. In *VLDB 2015 (demo)*, 2015.

[6] I. Gog, M. Schwarzkopf, N. Crooks, M. P. Grosvenor, A. Clement, and S. Hand. Musketeer: All for One, One for All in Data Processing Systems. In *EuroSys*, 2015.

[7] A. Hems, A. Soofi, and E. Perez. How innovative oil and gas companies are using big data to outmaneuver the competition. Microsoft White Paper, http://goo.gl/2Bn0xq, 2014.

[8] Z. Khayyat, I. F. Ilyas, A. Jindal, S. Madden, M. Ouzanni, P. Papotti, J.-A. Quiané-Ruiz, N. Tang, and S. Yin. BigDansing: A System for Big Data Cleansing. In *SIGMOD*, 2015.

[9] Z. Khayyat, W. Lucia, M. Singh, M. Ouzzani, P. Papotti, J.-A. Quiané-Ruiz, N. Tang, and P. Kalnis. Lightning Fast and Space Efficient Inequality Joins. *PVLDB*, 8(13), 2015.

[10] A. Rheinländer, A. Heise, F. Hueske, U. Leser, and F. Naumann. SOFA: An extensible logical optimizer for UDF-heavy data flows. *Inf. Syst.*, 52:96–125, 2015.

[11] D. A. Waguih and L. Berti-Equille. Truth Discovery Algorithms: An Experimental Evaluation. *CoRR*, 1409.6428, 2014.

Emma in Action: Declarative Dataflows for Scalable Data Analysis

Alexander Alexandrov Andreas Salzmann
Georgi Krastev Asterios Katsifodimos Volker Markl

TU Berlin, Germany
firstname.lastname@tu-berlin.de

ABSTRACT

Parallel dataflow APIs based on second-order functions were originally seen as a flexible alternative to SQL. Over time, however, their complexity increased due to the number of physical aspects that had to be exposed by the underlying engines in order to facilitate efficient execution. To retain a sufficient level of abstraction and lower the barrier of entry for data scientists, projects like Spark and Flink currently offer domain-specific APIs on top of their parallel collection abstractions.

This demonstration highlights the benefits of an alternative design based on deep language embedding. We showcase Emma – a programming language embedded in Scala. Emma promotes parallel collection processing through native constructs like Scala's `for`-comprehensions – a declarative syntax akin to SQL. In addition, Emma also advocates quoting the entire data analysis algorithm rather than its individual dataflow expressions. This allows for decomposing the quoted code into (sequential) control flow and (parallel) dataflow fragments, optimizing the dataflows in context, and transparently offloading them to an engine like Spark or Flink. The proposed design promises increased programmer productivity due to avoiding an impedance mismatch, thereby reducing the lag times and cost of data analysis.

1. INTRODUCTION & MOTIVATION

The last decade was marked by a major shift in data analytics technology. Driven by the need to store and process in-situ data at scale, parallel dataflow engines like Hadoop MapReduce [2], Spark [3] and Flink [1] emerged as an alternative to parallel relational databases. The principle programming abstraction behind these systems is a distributed collection type equipped with second-order functions that encapsulate parallelism. Assembling dataflows by combining these functions offers flexibility, but is hindered by additional complexity as various physical execution aspects of the underlying engines have to be exposed in the API in order to facilitate efficient evaluation. Such issues are: (*i*) Multi-way joins need to be written as a cascade of binary `join` function applications. The resulting tree is mirrored at execution time, as no join order optimization is performed at this level; (*ii*) Parallel aggregates need to be written in a specific way using dedicated primitives like `reduceByKey` rather than the more general and intuitive `groupBy` followed by a `map`; (*iii*) Since dataflow expressions per default are lazy, the decision to materialize an intermediate result is made explicitly by the programmer with a `cache` primitive.

We end up in a situation with several well-known problems such as: (*i*) high barrier of entry due to the required level of understanding of the underlying execution model, (*ii*) hard to read and maintain code due to low level of abstraction, and (*iii*) missed opportunities for optimization due to hard-coded execution strategies. In [4] we present a more detailed discussion of the idiosyncratic code patterns resulting from these problems. The principle way to tackle these problems is by providing high-level programming abstractions on top of the low-level dataflow APIs. The merits of this approach are validated by the popularity of external domain-specific languages like Pig, Hive, and SystemML, on the one side, and internal domain-specific libraries like DataFrame APIs, GraphX, MLLib, and Mahout, on the other. Both strategies, however, do not resolve the need for declarative integration of parallel collection processing in a general-purpose language – external languages introduce a language barrier, while internal libraries introduce a domain or API barrier.

This demonstration aims to showcase the benefits of an alternative approach based on *deep language embedding* through quotation and meta-programming recently proposed in [5]. We show that the ability to manipulate the entire data analysis program at compile time has twofold impact. First, extending ideas explored by LINQ [10] and Ferry [7] to the field of parallel dataflow engines, it facilitates deep linguistic reuse of host language constructs like comprehension syntax for declarative, SQL-like dataflow definitions. Second, it allows for transparently decomposing the program code into a (sequential) driver and multiple (parallel) dataflow fragments. The identified dataflows can then be optimized jointly based on the surrounding driver context before being translated and offloaded to a co-processing parallel dataflow engine like Spark or Flink. The net effect is a high-level collection processing API where notions of parallelism associated with an underlying dataflow engine are hidden from the programmer.

SIGMOD'16, June 26-July 01, 2016, San Francisco, CA, USA

ISBN 978-1-4503-3531-7/16/06...$15.00

DOI: http://dx.doi.org/10.1145/2882903.2899396

2. FORMAL FOUNDATIONS

Parallel Bags and Folds. We use the theory of recursive data types to model the parallel collection types – `DataSet` in Flink and `RDD` in Spark – which form the core of the targeted parallel dataflow engines. Both types are oblivious with respect to element order and allow for duplicates and therefore can be accurately modeled by the algebraic data type Bag (as opposed to List which also models order or Set which does not model duplicates).

Depending on the constructor choice, there are two equivalent definitions of the recursive data type Bag A usually called *insert* and *union* representation [6]. We base our design on the latter, in which bags can be constructed in three ways: by a nullary constructor **emp** denoting the empty bag, an unary constructor **sng** x denoting a singleton bag, or a binary constructor **uni** xs ys denoting the (duplicate preserving) union of two other bags.

Union representation is better suited for our needs than the more widely used insert representation, as it allows us to characterize parallel collection processing by means of *structural recursion* (folds) – a method for defining functions on bags xs by means of recursive replacement of constructor applications with applications of compatible functions [9].

```
// structural recursion on union-style bags
def fold[A,B](e: B, s: A => B, u: (B,B) => B)
             (xs: Bag[A]) = xs match {
  case emp        => e
  case sng(x)     => s(x)
  case uni(ys,zs) => u(fold(e,s,u)(ys), fold(e,s,u)(zs))
}
```

The `fold` function takes three parameters: `e`, `s`, and `u`, substitutes them in place of the constructor applications in xs, and evaluates the resulting expression tree to get a final value $z \in$ B. To compute the sum of all elements, for example, we substitute with $\texttt{e} = 0$, $\texttt{s} = \texttt{id}$, and $\texttt{u} = +$:

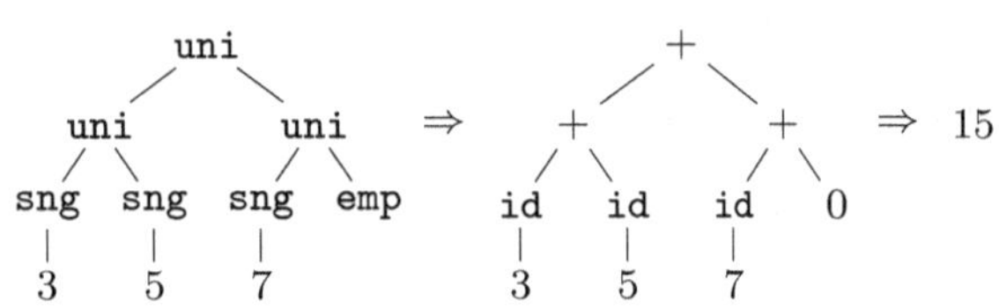

Aggregations like `min`, `max`, `sum`, and `count`, existential qualifiers like `exists` and `forall`, as well as collection processing operators like `map` and `filter` can be defined as folds.

Comprehension Syntax. Using the induced structural recursion scheme of union-style bags, we can define an algebraic structure known as *monad* on top of Bag A and enable declarative dataflow specification.

To illustrate the rationale behind the bag monad, consider two bags $xs = \{\{1, 2, 2, 3\}\}$ and $ys = \{\{1, 2\}\}$ with corresponding constructor application trees:

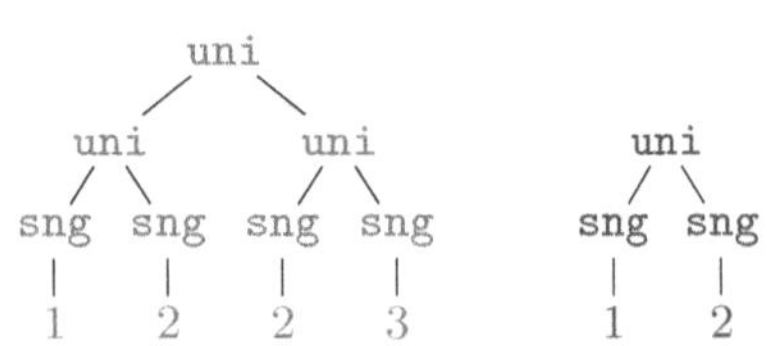

Now consider an example where we want to compute the bag of all pairs (x, y) where $x \in xs$, $y \in ys$ and $x = y$. If xs and ys were sets, we could describe this computation mathematically using set comprehension syntax:

$$\{ (x, y) \mid x \in xs,\ y \in ys,\ x = y \}$$

If xs and ys were relations in a database, we could write a select-from-where query:

```
SELECT x, y FROM xs as x, ys as y WHERE x = y
```

Modern functional languages like Scala allow us to use native comprehension syntax for arbitrary types, as long as those implement the so-called monad operators: `map`, `flatMap`, and `withFilter`. We can then formalize the intended computation as:

```
for (x <- xs; y <- ys; if x == y) yield (x, y)
```

At parse time, the `for`-comprehension syntax desugars into a chain of nested `flatMap` applications ending with a `map` and interleaved with `withFilter`. The above code becomes:

```
xs.flatMap(x =>
  ys.withFilter(y => x == y).map(y => (x, y)))
```

How should we interpret this desugaring in terms of the structural recursion scheme discussed above? The `map` part of the `flatMap` application operates on the level of the (red) xs tree – the tree shape is preserved and each value x is substituted with a copy of the entire ys tree. The inner `map` operates on the level of the ys trees and maps their y values to a (x, y) pair using the x from the outer `map`. We end up with an outer (red) bag of inner (blue) bags.

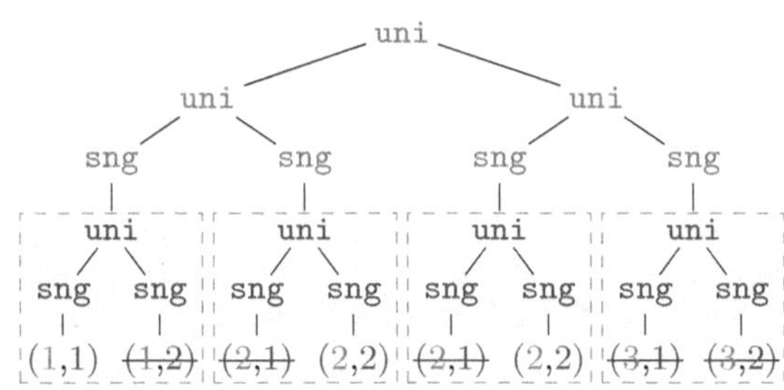

The `withFilter` application substitutes singleton bags that do not satisfy the $x = y$ predicate with `emp`, and the `flat` part of `flatMap` "forgets" the nested bag structure by inlining the inner trees into the outer one.

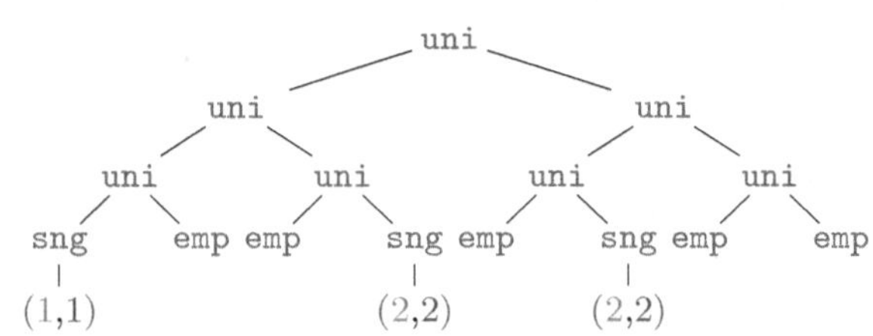

Theory to Practice. Bag comprehensions provide the key ingredient for solving two long-standing problems. First, as first-class citizen in a general-purpose source language, comprehension syntax offers direct means for declarative parallel collection processing that can be seen as a generalization of SQL. Second, as first-class citizen in an object language that can be manipulated trough meta-programming, comprehensions can serve as an entry point for the integration of

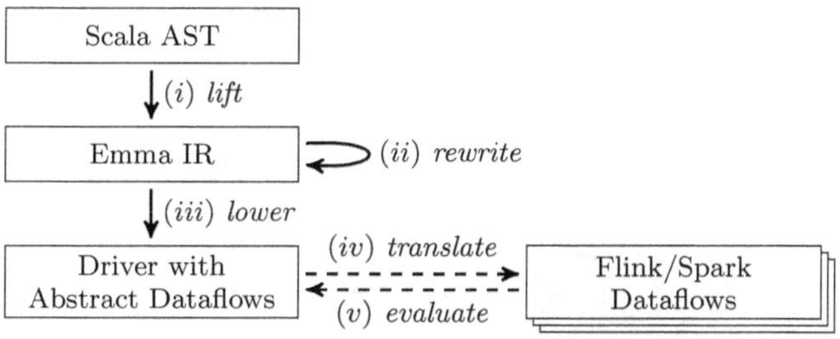

Figure 1: Emma compiler pipeline.

database optimization techniques into general-purpose languages. This allows for avoiding the naïve evaluation semantics by rewriting comprehended terms as join cascades [8].

3. EMMA: MAIN CONCEPTS & DESIGN

Based on the formal foundations outlined in Section 2, in [5] we proposed Emma – a declarative API for parallel collection processing deeply embedded in Scala. The core abstraction exposed by Emma is a generic type `DataBag` which models bags in union representation. In the following, we present the most distinguishing features by example.

Declarative SPJ Expressions. Binary operators like `join` and `cross` are not included in the API. Instead, the `DataBag` type implements the monad operators discussed in Section 2. This allows for writing dataflows in a declarative syntax similar to the `Select-Project-Join` style known from SQL. To illustrate this, consider the following code snippet taken from an Emma implementation of the Alternating Least Squares (ALS) algorithm as described by [11]. The code computes a collection of preference objects that associate users with the feature vectors and the ratings of their related (i.e. rated) items.

```
val prefs = for {
  user   <- users
  rating <- ratings
  item   <- items
  if rating.user == user.id
  if rating.item == item.id
} yield Pref(user, item.F, rating.value)
```

Multi-way joins like the example above are identified by the Emma compiler and translated as join cascades in the API of the backend engine.

Folds. Computing information from the contents of a `DataBag` is allowed only by means of structural recursion. To that end, we expose the `fold` operator from Section 2 as well as pre-defined aliases for commonly used folds (e.g. `count`, `exists`, `minBy`). Counting the number of users, for example, can be written as:

```
val N = users.fold(0, x => 1, (x, y) => x + y) // or
val N = users.count() // alias for the above
```

Nesting. The `groupBy` operator adds a level of nesting:

```
val ys: DataBag[Group[K, DataBag[A]]] = xs.groupBy(k)
```

The resulting bag contains groups of `values` that share the same `key` and `values` which again have type `DataBag[A]`. This is different from Spark and Flink, where the type of the group values is either `Iterable[A]` or `Iterator[A]` and nesting is not natively supported at the API level. The ability to nest `DataBag` instances allows for hiding the complexity of primitives like `groupByKey`, `reduceByKey`, and `aggregateByKey` behind an ubiquitous API in which bags can be processed in a nested manner. Continuing with the next step in the ALS example, the code that updates the user models from the preferences can be written as follows.

```
users = for { // update users
  (user, prefs) <- prefs.groupBy(p => p.user)
} yield { // calculate new feature vector per user
  val Vu = prefs.fold(V0)(p => p.F * p.rating, _ + _)
  val Au = prefs.fold(M0)(p => p.F outer p.F, _ + _)
  val Eu = E * (lambda * user.id)
  user.copy(F = inv(Au + Eu) * Vu)
}
```

As before, due to the fact that the whole expression can be manipulated at compile time, we can recognize nested `DataBag` patterns like the one above and rewrite them using more efficient primitives like `aggregateByKey`.

Coarse-Grained Parallelism Contracts. Dataflow APIs currently provide data-parallelism contracts at the operator level (e.g. `map` for element-at-a-time, `join` for pair-at-a-time, etc.). Emma takes a different approach as it's `DataBag` abstraction itself serves as a *coarse-grained* contract for data-parallel computation. The promise Emma gives to its users is to (*i*) discover all maximal `DataBag` expressions in a quoted code fragment, (*ii*) rewrite them logically in order to maximize the degree of data-parallelism, (*iii*) take a holistic approach while translating them as parallel dataflow expressions, and (*iv*) transparently place primitives that influence physical execution aspects like `broadcast` and `cache`.

Compiler Pipeline. Figure 1 depicts Emma's compiler pipeline. Scala expressions are quoted in a `parallelize` macro which exposes the Abstract Syntax Tree (AST) of the quoted code to the Emma compiler. The compiler first lifts the AST to a suitable intermediate representation (IR), and then performs joint logical and physical rewrites (e.g. inlining, fold-group fusion) on the identified dataflow fragments. The rewritten IR is finally lowered and compiled as a driver with abstract dataflow expressions. At runtime, these dataflow expressions are translated Just in Time (JIT) and evaluated on a target dataflow engine (Flink or Spark).

4. DEMONSTRATION

The demonstration is structured in three parts and showcases the main features of Emma highlighted in Sections 2 and 3 by example.

In Part ❶, we offer a gentle introduction to monads and introduce Emma's `DataBag` API. We demonstrate (*i*) the ability to use comprehension syntax instead of `join` cascades, (*ii*) the support for nesting, and (*iii*) `fold` as the main primitive for parallel computation. We compare the expressiveness offered by Emma against the parallel dataflow APIs targeted as a backend, SQL (as a de-facto standard for declarativity), as well as against domain-specific APIs offered by the backend engines (e.g. DataFrames in Spark, Table API in Flink).

In Part ❷, we showcase the compilation pipeline described in Section 3 and the core principles advocated by our design – coarse-grained parallelism contracts and coarse-grained quotation. To that end, we provide a graphical user interface (GUI) with two panes (Figure 2).

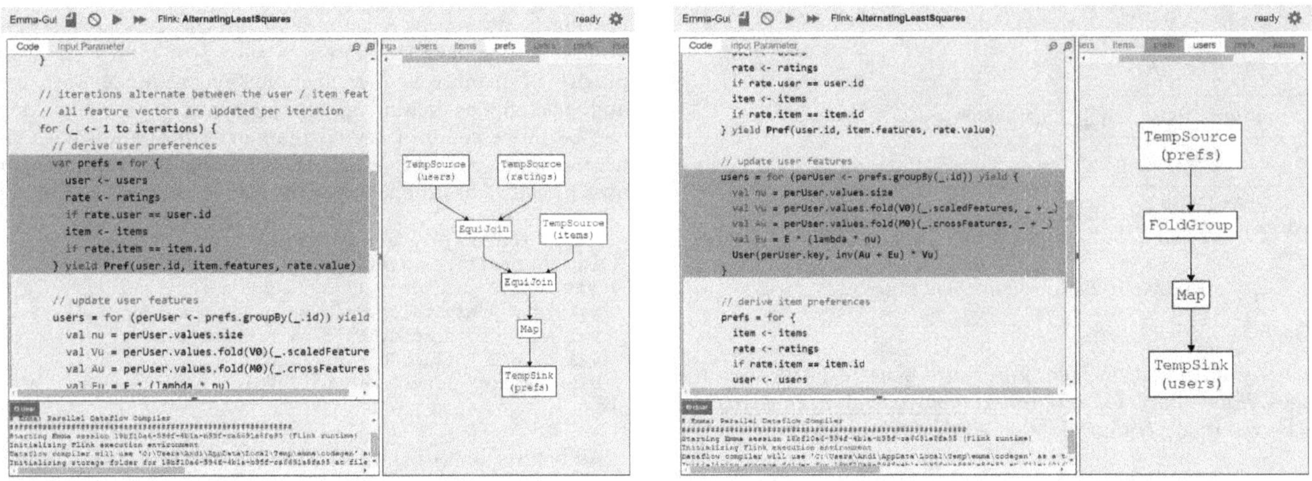

Figure 2: Two stages in the execution of an Alternating Least Squares algorithm in Emma.

Algorithm	Type/Domain
K-Means	Clustering
Naive Bayes	Classification
LabelRank	Semi-supervised classification
Alternating Least Squares	Collaborative filtering
Belief Propagation	Statistical inference
Graph Colouring	Graph analysis
Triangle Count	Graph analysis
Tic-Tac-Toe	Retrograde analysis
TPC-H Queries	Relational

Table 1: Example algorithms implemented in Emma.

1. On the left pane, audience members can select between several data-analysis algorithms written in Emma and review their source code (Table 1).

2. The algorithm code is quoted with a `parallelize` macro and transformed into an `Algorithm` object that can be evaluated by an Emma-supported runtime – we offer a choice between `Spark` or `Flink`. Execution is triggered by pressing a "Play" button from the GUI.

3. The GUI pauses before submitting the first dataflow, marks the corresponding `DataBag` term in the left pane, and shows the dataflow graph compiled by the Emma JIT component on the right pane. Optimizations performed by Emma are depicted on the visualized graph.

4. Upon renewed pressing of the "Play" button, the current dataflow and the subsequent driver expressions are evaluated. Execution halts at each subsequent dataflow in a manner similar to step 3.

5. A graph that marks adjacent dataflows is lazily constructed and visualized. The cycles and branches in the graph reflect the control-flow structure in the part of the code which constitutes the algorithm driver.

Finally, in Part ❸ we invite the audience to try out the Emma API and define other data analysis algorithms. The produced programs can be executed interactively from the GUI just as the predefined examples from Part ❷.

5. ACKNOWLEDGEMENTS

This work has been supported through grants by the German Science Foundation (DFG) as FOR 1306 Stratosphere, by the German Ministry for Education and Research as Berlin Big Data Center BBDC (ref. 01IS14013A), by the European Commission as Proteus (ref. 687691) and Streamline (ref. 688191), and by Oracle Labs.

6. REFERENCES

[1] Apache Flink Project. http://flink.apache.org.

[2] Apache Hadoop Project. http://hadoop.apache.org.

[3] Apache Spark Project. http://spark.apache.org.

[4] A. Alexandrov, A. Katsifodimos, G. Krastev, and V. Markl. Implicit parallelism through deep language embedding. *SIGMOD Record*, 2016 (to appear).

[5] A. Alexandrov, A. Kunft, A. Katsifodimos, F. Schüler, L. Thamsen, O. Kao, T. Herb, and V. Markl. Implicit parallelism through deep language embedding. In *SIGMOD Conference*, pages 47–61. ACM, 2015.

[6] P. Buneman, S. A. Naqvi, V. Tannen, and L. Wong. Principles of programming with complex objects and collection types. *Theor. Comput. Sci.*, 149(1):3–48, 1995.

[7] G. Giorgidze, T. Grust, T. Schreiber, and J. Weijers. Haskell boards the ferry - database-supported program execution for Haskell. In *IFL*, volume 6647 of *Lecture Notes in Computer Science*, pages 1–18. Springer, 2010.

[8] T. Grust and M. H. Scholl. How to comprehend queries functionally. *J. Intell. Inf. Syst.*, 12(2-3):191–218, 1999.

[9] G. L. S. Jr. Organizing functional code for parallel execution or, foldl and foldr considered slightly harmful. In *ICFP*, pages 1–2. ACM, 2009.

[10] E. Meijer, B. Beckman, and G. M. Bierman. LINQ: reconciling object, relations and XML in the .NET framework. In *SIGMOD Conference*, page 706. ACM, 2006.

[11] Y. Zhou, D. M. Wilkinson, R. Schreiber, and R. Pan. Large-scale parallel collaborative filtering for the Netflix Prize. In *AAIM*, volume 5034 of *Lecture Notes in Computer Science*, pages 337–348. Springer, 2008.

Wildfire: Concurrent Blazing Data Ingest and Analytics

Ronald Barber Matt Huras* Guy Lohman C. Mohan Rene Mueller
Fatma Özcan Hamid Pirahesh Vijayshankar Raman Richard Sidle
Oleg Sidorkin• Adam Storm* Yuanyuan Tian Pınar Tözün

IBM Research – Almaden *IBM Analytics •IBM DemandTec

ABSTRACT

We demonstrate Hybrid Transactional and Analytics Processing (HTAP) on the Spark platform by the Wildfire prototype, which can ingest up to ≈6 million inserts per second per node and simultaneously perform complex SQL analytics queries. Here, a simplified mobile application uses Wildfire to recommend advertising to mobile customers based upon their distance from stores and their interest in products sold by these stores, while continuously graphing analytics results as those customers move and respond to the ads with purchases.

1. INTRODUCTION

Traditionally, OLTP (On-Line Transactional Processing) systems have been separated from OLAP (On-Line Analytics Processing) systems because of the incompatibilty in their requirements: resource-hungry, long-running analytics queries interfere with the latency requirements of short-running transactions. However, recent advances in speeding up analytics queries [6, 7, 8, 9] now make it possible to combine these systems into one integrated system called Hybrid Transactional and Analytics Processing (HTAP). Doing so permits analytics to see the latest transactions, reducing the business risk of making wrong decisions, such as fraud detection, on stale data. It also dramatically increases business agility, permitting reports and analytics on operational data to perform real-time pricing, inventory, and supply-chain management. Thirdly, combining systems simplifies the system landscape and reduces operational costs.

Concomitantly, the increased availability of "Big Data" sources, tools, and processing power has spawned new applications that seek to understand and exploit individual customer behavior through analysis of that data. This analysis may include any combination of machine learning, graph processing, and stream processing, as well as more traditional forms of summarization, analytics, and reporting. Data volumes are increasingly driven by the wide deployment of inexpensive sensors, especially on mobile, geo-located platforms, which now generate large volumes of data at much higher rates than traditional transactional data, in aggregate exceeding millions of rows per second. These requirements have largely driven these new applications toward the Spark platform [10, 2], which offers: massively parallel execution on clusters of inexpensive commodity machines; in-memory processing that is 10x to 100x faster than Hadoop; flexible programming interfaces; and rich library support for machine learning, graph processing, and data streaming.

This demonstration presents Wildfire, which seeks to support this new class of scalable HTAP applications that require ultra-high data ingest rates in excess of 1 million inserts per second per node while concurrently performing analytics queries at speeds comparable to the latest Relational DBMS (RDBMS) engines [6, 7, 8, 9], about one half order of magnitude faster than existing Spark SQL [4]. We leverage the Spark infrastructure to provide a massively parallel and elastic HTAP solution that enables different types of analytics via the Spark ecosystem (Spark SQL, MLLib, GraphX, etc), but can also ingest data at very high rates. Our longer-term goal is to provide ACID transactions at these rates, and even to run analytics queries as part of such transactions (true HTAP).

To demonstrate Wildfire, we chose a hypothetical but plausible system that offers promotions to mobile customers whose new locations are continuously ingested. The promotions are offered as advertisements that are decided by a simulated machine learning model that is a function of the proximity of each user to store locations selling certain products, the remaining advertising budget for each store, the time since the last promotion displayed to that user, etc. The demo shows the rates at which user locations are ingested, while showing the results of several concurrently-executing analytic queries that summarize the data either geographically, by store, or by product category.

Our contributions include: (1) ingesting data to a distributed, persistent store (Solid-State Drives on commodity servers) at rates around 6 million / second / node; (2) concurrently performing multiple complex SQL analytic queries involving joins, grouping, and aggregation over this distributed data, using Spark SQL, as soon as it is persisted; and (3) simulating the exploitation of machine learning models derived from this data to make real-time business decisions based upon real-time location and budgetary information.

SIGMOD'16, June 26-July 01, 2016, San Francisco, CA, USA
© 2016 ACM. ISBN 978-1-4503-3531-7/16/06...$15.00
DOI: http://dx.doi.org/10.1145/2882903.2899406

2. WILDFIRE ARCHITECTURE

Figure 1 shows the current Wildfire architecture. We have a cluster of *Wildfire engines* running concurrently to

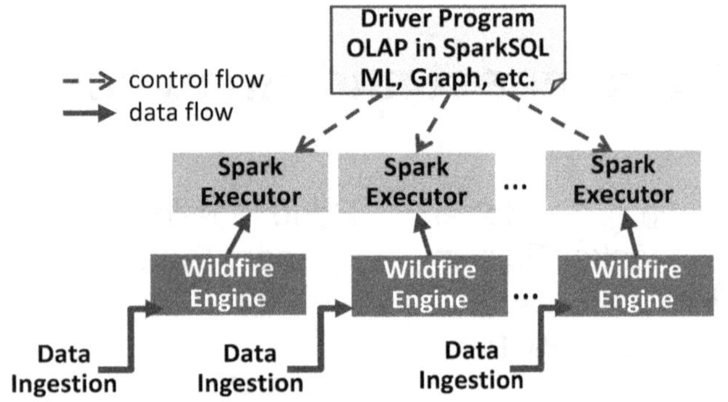

Figure 1: Wildfire Architecture for Demo.

ingest data and serve OLAP queries. Each table in our system is partitioned across the Wildfire engines, and each Wildfire engine ingests its partition of the data through a fast native API (marked as *Data Ingestion* in Figure 1). To enable distributed and complex analytics over large volumes of data, we integrate with Spark to run multiple Wildfire engines in a cluster, answering analytics queries through the Spark SQL interface. The Wildfire application *driver* runs in Spark and spawns *Spark executors* to coordinate the requests/results to/from the distributed Wildfire engines.

2.1 Wildfire Engine: Storage and Processing

Tables in Wildfire are stored in large blocks (up to 64 MB each) using a PAX layout [3] that is similar to Parquet [1]. As such, each block contains all column values for a given set of rows of the table, and the values are stored in column-major format within the block. Wildfire employs a block-local minus-coding scheme to compress the values in the block. The encoding is fixed in size (from 0 to 64 bits) within each block, and encoded values are written in fixed-sized chunks, with 512 values per chunk. The combination of the fixed-size encoding and chunking enables fast column scans on the encoded data. Given the PAX layout and local compression, the storage blocks are fully self-contained and portable. Therefore, these blocks are amenable to processing in a distributed compute environment such as Spark and storage within a cluster filesystem such as HDFS. In addition, one can efficiently append to an existing block and perform point-access to a data item in a block.

Wildfire uses a columnar query engine that has many similarities to the query engine of DB2 with BLU Acceleration [9]. Wildfire processes composite queries, such as joins, in multiple stages. Each stage scans a single input table. A query stage can have side-effects, for example by generating a hash table for the "build" of a hash join (to be probed during a subsequent stage that scans the outer table) or by inserting into another table. A query stage is executed as a sequence of operators, called *evaluators*. Evaluators employ vectorized processing, with each evaluator taking as input a set of vectors of values and producing one or more result vectors. Each query thread has its own evaluator sequence. Query threads perform work-stealing on the single input and fully process a batch of input rows through all evaluators before obtaining another batch.

To achieve high ingest rates, Wildfire provides a native request interface in the form of pre-compiled stored procedures for inserts to each table. In addition, the engine combines multiple insert requests and applies them in batched fashion using the vectorized processing described above. Blocks are appended to files when full or at the end of a batch insert.

Wildfire also uses non-partitioned hash joins and Concise Hash Tables, as described in [5]. In addition to column scans, hash joins, and inserts, Wildfire has support for many other evaluators, such as hash-based group by, predicate evaluation, expression evaluation, and updates of in-memory (non-persistent) indexes.

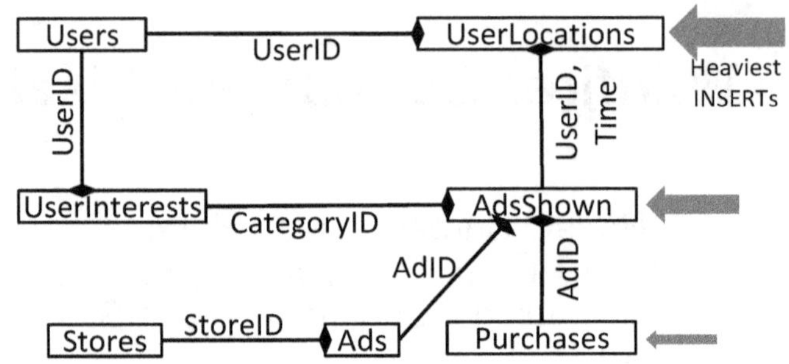

Figure 2: Wildfire Demo Application Schema.

2.2 Integration with Spark

To support distributed OLAP, we integrate the Wildfire engine into the Spark environment, as shown in Figure 1. We achieve this integration by implementing the Spark Data Sources API for Wildfire. Users issue their OLAP queries against the tables partitioned across the Wildfire engines through the Spark SQL interface, which submits the same query to all the Wildfire engines for processing and computes the final result. We configure the Spark driver to spawn one Spark executor for each Wildfire engine. To take advantage of locality, we also provide location hints to Spark so that the Spark executors are spawned on the same machines as the Wildfire engines. A submitted query is passed down from each Spark executor to its Wildfire counterpart through a TCP connection, and the Spark executor subsequently receives results back from the engine over the same connection. The final query result can then be further used for machine learning, graph, or other analyses supported by the Spark ecosystem.

3. DEMO

3.1 Application

To drive the demonstration of Wildfire, we have implemented a simplified application to offer promotions (advertisements) for products to mobile users whose locations are ingested at very high rates and stored persistently in solid-state drives (SSDs) by Wildfire. Which ad is shown to each user, and which products each user purchases, are also stored in separate tables.

3.1.1 Schema

Figure 2 provides the schema diagram for the application; each rectangle corresponds to a table, and edges represent joins between tables, labeled with the join column(s). Figure 2 also highlights those tables with the highest ingest rates. A fixed number (3 million) of `Users` move randomly within a region, providing new `UserLocations` at sub-second

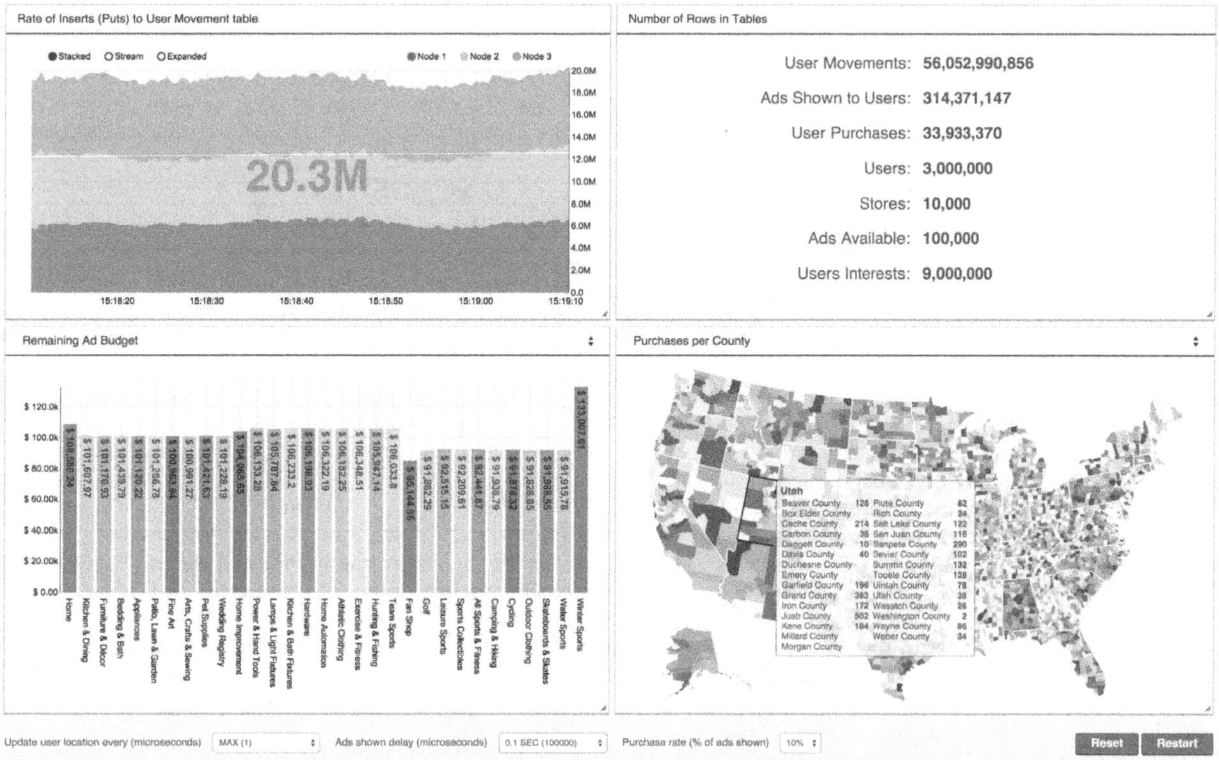

Figure 3: Wildfire Demo Live Screen.

intervals determined by a system parameter. An in-memory hash-index keeps the latest `UserLocation` for a `User`. A fixed number (10,000) of `Stores` at fixed locations in the region sell a different small subset of 100,000 products, each of which is advertised by an `Ad` and each of which fits into one of 31 broad categories. Each `User` has three `UserInterests` in buying products from these categories (so `UserInterests` table contains 9 M rows); these `UserInterests` and the strength of interest are different for each `User` and are pre-populated. Other system parameters, which the demo viewer may modify, control the rates at which `Ads` are shown to `Users` (5 secs. to 1 microsec.) and at what rate `Users` make `Purchases` (10% to 70% of AdsShown). `Users` are randomly partitioned, whereas `Stores` and `Ads` are replicated at each partition. All other tables are co-partitioned with the `Users`, based on the *UserID*.

3.1.2 Data Ingest (OLTP)

Each new `UserLocation` for a `User` is randomly generated as an azimuth and distance from the last `UserLocation`, without following a road network. These new `UserLocations` drive the highest ingest rates, in excess of 20 M rows per sec. at the most frequent update rate (1 microsec.).

As these `UserLocations` are ingested, a complex analytics query, `ShowAds`, runs continuously to determine which `Ads` to show to each `User` next. The results of `ShowAds`, described in Section 3.1.3, are inserted into the `AdsShown` table. To avoid bombardment of users with promotions, not every new `UserLocation` results in an `AdsShown` insert, so its ingest rate is significantly less than that of `UserLocation`.

Once an `Ad` is shown to a `User`, the `User` "clicks through" to purchase the product with some probability set by the system parameter, causing an insert into the `Purchases` table. That parameter therefore determines the relative size of `Purchases` to `AdsShown`.

3.1.3 Complex Analytics (OLAP) Queries

Concurrent with these high ingest rates, Wildfire continuously executes several complex analytics queries over the latest data, both to summarize it and to trigger events such as showing new promotions to users. The summarization queries, detailed in Section 3.2, are displayed in the lower two panes of the demo display. The query determining which promotions to show to users, `ShowAds`, is far more complex. It joins `Ads` having remaining budget (indexed in memory) to tables `Ads` and `Stores`, then grids each `Ad` by its `Store`'s location and `Ad`'s category that define a key for the `Ad` on this grid. The current `UserLocation` (another in-memory index) and `UserInterests` for which `Ads` haven't been shown recently (determined using a third index) define the lookup key over this grid. Each eligible `Ad` is then scored as a function of the precise distance from its `Store` to the current `UserLocation` and a weighting of the `UserInterest` categories. This function simulates the output from a machine learning model that would be continuously trained using earlier `Purchases`, but implementation of that model training is future work.

3.1.4 Setup

The demo runs the Wildfire prototype on three remote 2-socket servers with 14-core Intel Xeon E5-2683 processors (2GHz) with 384GB of RAM. The operating system is Ubuntu 15.04 with Linux kernel 3.19.0-30. Each node stores the data on, and reads it from, an Intel 750 Series SSD.

Each node runs one instance of our Wildfire engine and a Spark Executor, as shown in Figure 1. The application driver runs on one of the three nodes; it issues OLAP requests to, and combines the results from, the Spark Executor on each node. The data for ingestion is generated and inserted locally on each individual node. The demo user-interface is accessed through a web-browser, since the nodes are remote.

We pre-populate the `Users`, `Stores`, `Ads`, and `UserInterests` tables of the application (see Figure 2). These tables do not change after initial population, as Section 3.1 describes. The `UserLocations`, `AdsShown`, and `Purchases` tables grow as the demo runs.

3.2 What the Audience Sees

The demo screen is composed of four major panes, as shown in Figure 3. The upper half of the screen illustrates the ingest capabilities of Wildfire. The upper-left pane reports the aggregated ingest throughput of the `UserLocations` table, as well as the throughput per node, every second. The cardinalities of each table are shown in the upper-right pane. The last four rows in this pane indicate the cardinalities for the four pre-populated tables whose cardinalities do not change during the demo. The first three rows in this pane give the cardinalities of the tables whose cardinalities do change due to the insertion of new rows. These cardinalities are continuously combined from in-memory counts maintained on each node, and are updated every second on the demo screen.

The lower two panes of the display are dedicated to reporting summarization (analytics) queries that are run continuously over all the persisted data, including the recently ingested data, while concurrently running the ingest queries. The demo viewer may choose which query to run in each pane. Each such query is a *GROUP BY* query that either performs a *SUM* or *AVERAGE*, grouping the data by product categories (lower-left pane, displayed as a bar graph) or by U.S. county (lower-right pane, displayed as a heat map). For example, the lower-left pane summarizes how the *remaining ad budget*, *total sales (purchases)*, *total cost of ads*, etc. change per product category as we insert new data. From movements in the height of these bars, the demo viewer can readily discern this continuous analytics update using new data, when high rates of ingest occur, and how long it takes to (re-)run that query. The lower-right pane of the screen has a heat map to indicate the rate of *purchases* or *remaining ad budget* per county. Positioning the cursor on a state causes a pop-up that enumerates each county and the exact *purchase total or remaining ad budget* per county, as shown in Figure 3 for the state of Utah.

At the bottom of the display, a narrow pane permits the demo viewer to adjust the system parameters, such as the frequency with which new `UserLocations` are generated for each `User`, the frequency with which `Ads` are shown to `Users`, and the click-through percentage for `Purchases`.

We start our demo with a low ingest rate and then gradually increase this rate. This helps in observing how the insert throughput of the system increases, how dramatically the table cardinalities grow, and the results reported by the OLAP queries change under varying ingest pressure.

After demonstrating how the system behaves under different ingest rates, we will let the audience interact with our user interface if they wish. They can change the ingest rates further from the bottom of the screen, or choose different analytics queries to run from the drop-down menu at the top of the bar graph and heat map panes. Furthermore, they can restart the cluster services with or without resetting table data using the *Reset* or *Restart* buttons, respectively.

4. CONCLUSIONS

The Wildfire system demonstrates high-rate inserts (up to 20 million inserts per second on just 3 nodes) with concurrently executing analytics queries. The demo shows a Wildfire engine connected to a Spark Executor on each node to issue analytics queries through Spark's Data Sources API. The connection to Spark exposes the analytics capabilities of Wildfire to the entire Spark ecosystem, including Spark SQL, graph processing, and machine learning.

This demo is a snapshot of work in progress. We are working on extending its integration into Spark SQL, particularly on extensions to Spark's Catalyst optimizer to perform more complex push-down analysis, and generating compensation plans for the remaining portions of the analytics queries that are not pushed down into Wildfire. In addition, we are exposing the OLTP interface of the Wildfire engine to Spark, so that applications running inside Spark have access to the full HTAP functionality. Lastly, we are adding ACID transactions to the Wildfire engine.

5. REFERENCES

[1] Apache Parquet. https://parquet.apache.org/.

[2] Apache Spark. http://spark.apache.org/.

[3] A. Ailamaki, D. J. DeWitt, M. D. Hill, and M. Skounakis. Weaving Relations for Cache Performance. In *VLDB*, pages 169–180, 2001.

[4] M. Armbrust, R. S. Xin, C. Lian, Y. Huai, D. Liu, J. K. Bradley, X. Meng, T. Kaftan, M. J. Franklin, A. Ghodsi, and M. Zaharia. Spark SQL: Relational Data Processing in Spark. In *SIGMOD*, pages 1383–1394, 2015.

[5] R. Barber, G. Lohman, I. Pandis, V. Raman, R. Sidle, G. Attaluri, N. Chainani, S. Lightstone, and D. Sharpe. Memory Efficient Hash Joins. *PVLDB*, 8(4):353–364, 2014.

[6] P. Boncz, M. Zukowski, and N. Nes. MonetDB/X100: Hyper-Pipelining Query Execution. In *CIDR*, 2005.

[7] F. Färber, N. May, W. Lehner, P. Große, I. Müller, H. Rauhe, and J. Dees. The SAP HANA Database – An Architecture Overview. *IEEE DEBull*, 35(1), 2012.

[8] A. Lamb, M. Fuller, R. Varadarajan, N. Tran, B. Vandiver, L. Doshi, and C. Bear. The Vertica Analytic Database: C-store 7 Years Later. *PVLDB*, 5(12):1790–1801, 2012.

[9] V. Raman, G. Attaluri, R. Barber, N. Chainani, D. Kalmuk, V. KulandaiSamy, J. Leenstra, S. Lightstone, S. Liu, G. M. Lohman, T. Malkemus, R. Mueller, I. Pandis, B. Schiefer, D. Sharpe, R. Sidle, A. Storm, and L. Zhang. DB2 with BLU Acceleration: So Much More than Just a Column Store. *PVLDB*, 6:1080–1091, 2013.

[10] M. Zaharia, M. Chowdhury, T. Das, A. Dave, J. Ma, M. McCauly, M. J. Franklin, S. Shenker, and I. Stoica. Resilient Distributed Datasets: A Fault-Tolerant Abstraction for In-Memory Cluster Computing. In *NSDI*, pages 15–28, 2012.

Efficient Query Processing on Many-core Architectures: A Case Study with Intel Xeon Phi Processor

Xuntao Cheng[1] Bingsheng He[2] Mian Lu[3] Chiew Tong Lau[2]
Huynh Phung Huynh[4] Rick Siow Mong Goh[4]
[1]LILY, Interdisciplinary Graduate School, Nanyang Technological University
[2]Nanyang Technological University
[3]Huawei Singapore Research Centre
[4]IHPC, A*STAR, Singapore

ABSTRACT

Recently, Intel Xeon Phi is emerging as a many-core processor with up to 61 x86 cores. In this demonstration, we present PhiDB, an OLAP query processor with simultaneous multi-threading (SMT) capabilities on Xeon Phi as a case study for parallel database performance on future many-core processors. With the trend towards many-core architectures, query operator optimizations, and efficient query scheduling on such many-core architectures remain as challenging issues. This motivates us to redesign and evaluate query processors. In PhiDB, we apply Xeon Phi aware optimizations on query operators to exploit hardware features of Xeon Phi, and design a heuristic algorithm to schedule the concurrent execution of query operators for better performance, to demonstrate the performance impact of Xeon Phi aware optimizations. We have also developed a user interface for users to explore the underlying performance impacts of hardware-conscious optimizations and scheduling plans.

1. INTRODUCTION

Computer architectures have been evolving from multi-core processors to many-core processors with emerging architectural features. This calls for systematic rethinking on how to design and optimize database systems in the many-core era. Recently, Intel Xeon Phi is emerging as a many-core processor based on the Many Integrated Core architectures. Compared with other many-core processors (e.g., GPUs), Intel Xeon Phi is based on x86 CPUs. This allows easy deployments of conventional CPU-based programs on them. However, unlike conventional CPUs, it has some unique features such as 512-bit SIMD intrinsics and up to 61 x86 cores with SMT capabilities. These emerging architectural features offer exciting research opportunities to study parallel database performance on many-core processors.

Query processors have been utilizing the parallelism enabled by multi-cores to deliver high performance in query processing. With the trend towards many-core processors, we are facing with even more CPU cores. A naive scheduling is very likely to cause performance penalties and resource over-provisioning which eventually offsets the benefits of using more cores. Thus, it is necessary to systematically study query scheduling on many-core architectures.

To study efficient query processing on such a kind of many-core processors, we identify and apply Xeon Phi aware optimizations on query operators and achieve significant performance improvement. Based on these operators, we further design PhiDB by exploiting the hardware features of Xeon Phi such as SIMD intrinsics and prefetching. However, current query processors usually execute a single operator at a time. Such "operator-at-a-time" execution can underutilize the hardware resource of Xeon Phi. Thus, we design a scheduling algorithm to co-schedule query operators in a way that eligible operators are executed concurrently. We visualize performance impacts of architecture aware optimizations and scheduling plans by showing the execution diagram of all operators. With visualizations, users can observe the deployment and runtime statistics of query operators on Xeon Phi and the performance impact of the query scheduling optimization. Users can also enable or disable individual optimization techniques to compare their effectiveness. This visualization can further help developers to identify performance bottlenecks.

Our preliminary results demonstrate that the Xeon Phi aware optimizations improve the performance of query operator by 14-33%, compared with the baseline where no such architecture specific optimizations are applied. Our optimized query scheduler further improves the performance by about 30% taking advantage of concurrent execution of operators, compared with executing all the operators one at a time. Our study indicates that architecture aware optimizations are important for the database performance. Careful optimizations and redesign from the level of query operator to query optimization and scheduling are required for databases on future many-core processors.

SIGMOD'16, June 26-July 01, 2016, San Francisco, CA, USA

DOI: http://dx.doi.org/10.1145/2882903.2899407

2. PRELIMINARIES

In this section, we introduce the architecture of Intel Xeon Phi processors and related work.

2.1 Intel Xeon Phi Many-core Processor

We present PhiDB on a Xeon Phi 5110P processor featuring 60 Intel x86 in-order cores. All these cores share the same main memory in the Symmetric Multi-Processing (SMP) fashion. Up to 4 hardware threads are supported on each core. Thus, there are totally 240 threads. Each core has its L1 and L2 caches. All L2 caches are connected through a high-speed shared bus fabric. To hide the memory access overhead, Xeon Phi features hardware prefetchers at each L2 cache and supports software prefetching at both caches. Each core has a dedicated pipeline for 512-bit SIMD intrinsics. The next generation of Xeon Phi, as announced by Intel, is going to be available as a stand-alone processor with more cache, a total 16GB of main memory and higher processing power.

2.2 Related Work

Intel Xeon Phi has been widely used for high performance computing, scientific computing and MapReduce [7, 10, 13]. Many research efforts have been attracted to accelerate query processing on Xeon Phi taking advantage of its hardware characteristics. A Xeon Phi coprocessor has up to 61 x86 cores and supports 512-bit Single Instruction Multiple Data (SIMD) instructions. Utilizing such many cores and the advanced SIMD capability is important for database processing on Xeon Phi.

Optimizing and deploying databases on multi-core and many-core processors have always been a challenging task. Balkesen et al. studied main-memory hash joins extensively on multi-core CPUs considering a rich set of algorithmic alternatives and optimization techniques [1, 2]. We adopt their optimizations on hash join in the implementation of PhiDB. Optimizing database processing using SIMD has been a hot research topic. Chhugani et al. revisited the implementation of sort on multi-core CPUs utilizing SIMD intrinsics and achieved significant performance improvement [3]. Willhalm et al. accelerated full table scans in column-store data warehouse systems utilizing SIMD intrinsics' direct access to the main memory [14]. Feng et al. designed a set of bit-parallel algorithms for aggregations taking advantage of this intra-cycle parallelisms of CPUs [4]. Our previous work utilized the 512-bit SIMD for key hashing calculations, memory gather/scatter and the materialization of matched tuples resulting in significant performance improvement [9]. Hou et al. proposed a framework for the automatic SIMDization of parallel sorting which generates high-performance code for sort given any sorting network and SIMD instruction sets [8]. Polychroniou et al. presented the vectorized designs and implementations of database operators using many advanced SIMD operations such as gather/scatter intrinsics available on Xeon Phi [12].

3. DESIGN AND IMPLEMENTATION

In this section, we present the details of the design and implementation of PhiDB.

3.1 System overview

Figure 1 provides the system overview of PhiDB. It has 5 main components: **Query Parser**, **Query Optimizer**, **Query Execution Scheduler**, **Thread Pool** and **Query Processing Engine**. The query parser translates input queries into the *logical* query plan. The query optimizer tunes the concurrency level (the number of threads used) for each operator according to which operators are further divided into jobs. A job is to be executed by a single thread

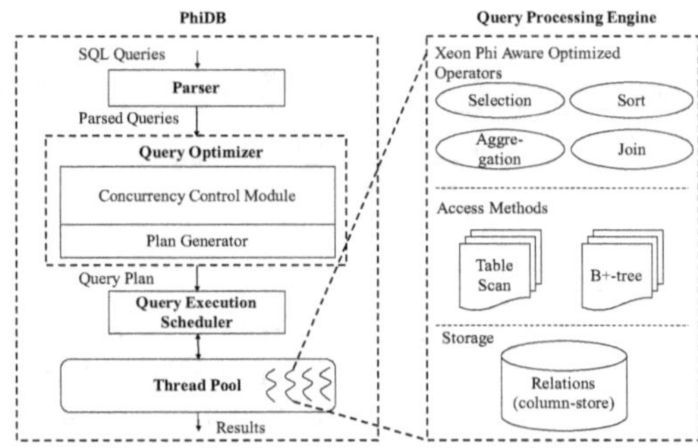

Figure 1: System overview of PhiDB

and it contains necessary information such as the assigned partition of input relations for the execution. The optimizer also decides which pairs of operators are to be executed concurrently and generates the final optimized scheduling plan. The query execution scheduler maintains a queue of operators according to such plan. In the thread pool, a thread *pulls* this queue for the next job when it becomes free and it executes the query engine to process each job. When all jobs of an operator are finished, the last thread serving that operator checks the DAG and pushes all operators with all their inputs ready into the queue. The query engine is divided into three layers: operators, access methods and the storage. All operators and access methods are optimized in a hardware-conscious way as introduced in Section 3.3. We start with EaseDB [5, 6], a query processor for in-memory databases on multi-core CPUs, and further enhance it with more recent query processing algorithms such as hash joins [1, 9]. We choose EaseDB because its cache-oblivious designs of data structures and operators, which optimizes the performance of relational query processing on all levels of a memory hierarchy, allow us to focus on the impacts of Xeon Phi-specific optimizations, rather than the memory hierarchy.

3.2 Preliminary Implementation

In this section, we introduce our preliminary implementation of key components in PhiDB.

Scheduling Optimization. We propose to execute multiple independent operators concurrently to accelerate query processing, because a single operator suffers from severe resource underutilization in our observations. Our proposed scheduling optimization examines ready-to-execute operators and co-schedule pairs of them for concurrent executions. However, to achieve the optimal optimization scheduling of query operators on many-core architectures is an NP-hard problem. Thus, we apply two heuristics to control the concurrency of query operators and optimize the query plan. Firstly, we concurrently execute memory-intensive and compute-intensive operators such as a selection and a join to alleviate the burden of the shared bus among cores. Secondly, we execute operators with small inputs first. These operators usually require fewer threads for their best performance, which brings more opportunities for concurrent executions.

Thread Pool. We implement a decentralized thread pool consisting of multiple software threads. Each software thread is pinned to a corresponding hardware context. Because there are 240 hardware contexts on Xeon Phi in total, we have 240 software threads in the pool. It is decentralized in the way that each thread *pulls* for new jobs autonomously when it becomes free rather than waiting for a centralized scheduler to assign jobs to them. This is to avoid the overhead caused by scheduling over a large number of threads on such many-core processors.

Query Engine. The query engine defines a set of optimized operators. For selection and aggregation, we take advantage of Xeon Phi's dual pipeline to use both the wide SIMD intrinsics and conventional scalar instructions to reduce memory stalls caused by memory accesses. For sort, we implement a bitonic sort and merge network because its fixed network topology and parallelism are ideal for SIMD intrinsics [3]. For joins, we adopt our implementations of both partitioned and non-partitioned hash joins as well as sort-merge joins in previous work [9].

3.3 Xeon Phi Aware Optimizations

Query operators defined in the query engine are optimized with Xeon Phi aware optimizations. The major techniques are SIMD vectorization, prefetching and huge pages.

SIMD Vectorization. Xeon Phi supports 512-bit SIMD intrinsics, which are important for programs to achieve high performance. On Xeon Phi, SIMD intrinsics are executed on a dedicated pipeline. Although cores on Xeon Phi are all in-order processors, after the issue of a SIMD intrinsic to its pipeline, the core pipeline is not stalled and proceeds to other instructions allowing SIMD intrinsics to overlap with others. Meanwhile, these SIMD intrinsics have rich functionalities. They can be utilized for parallel computations, complex bit operations and memory load/store which makes the use of SIMD has a large performance impact as shown in Section 4.2.

Prefetching. Xeon Phi supports both software and hardware prefetching. The software prefetcher at the L1 cache can guide the hardware prefetcher at the L2 cache to prefetch data more timely and avoid many unnecessary memory accesses [11]. This forms a two-level coordinated prefetching. For each operator, we manually tune the prefetching distance and have achieved a reasonable speedup.

Huge Page. Xeon Phi's TLB can be configured into both 4KB or 2MB. The 2MB configuration is usually addressed as the huge page. By configuring the TLB into 2MB, it can map up to 256MB of memory, which decreases page faults significantly on Xeon Phi. In our implementation, all memories are allocated in huge pages.

As a detailed example, we present the application of these three techniques in the hash join operator [9]. Key hashing is an important part for hash join. We use SIMD intrinsics to calculate the hashing of multiple keys in parallel. Since SIMD intrinsics are executed by dedicated pipelines other than the core pipelines, we further use SIMD intrinsics to conduct memory accesses including gather/scatter of keys and results materializations to reduce memory stalls. In both the build and the probe phase, we prefetch keys to accelerate the gather and the key hashing process. Gather is a very expensive memory operation. By determining the suitable prefetching distance, the memory access latency is largely hidden and its overhead is significantly reduced. Finally, we configure the TLB into 2MB and allocate memories in huge pages.

4. PLAN FOR DEMONSTRATION

In this section, we briefly present our setup and plan for the demonstration.

4.1 System Setup

We conduct our demonstration on a server equipped a Xeon Phi co-processor 5110P. PhiDB is a native application that runs entirely on the Xeon Phi. This means that all data are stored and processed on Xeon Phi. Other parts of the machine are not involved in the query processing. We adopt TPC-H queries as our evaluation benchmark for PhiDB. Input tables are generated by the TPC-H data generator with a scale factor of 5. We limit the scale factor to 5 so that the in-memory database can fit into the memory of Xeon Phi.

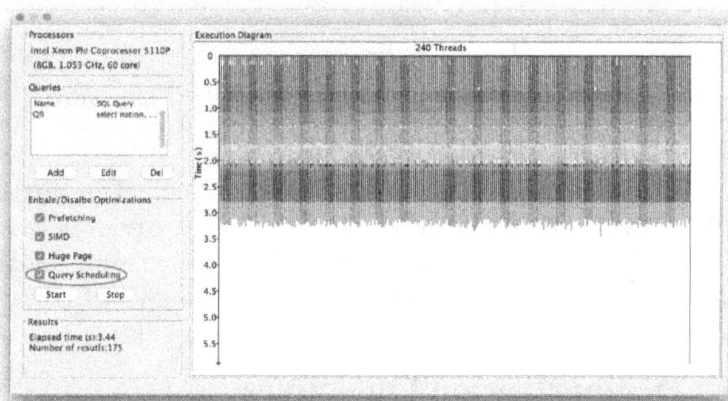

Figure 2: Screenshot of the GUI when executing Q9 in PhiDB with the query scheduling optimization enabled

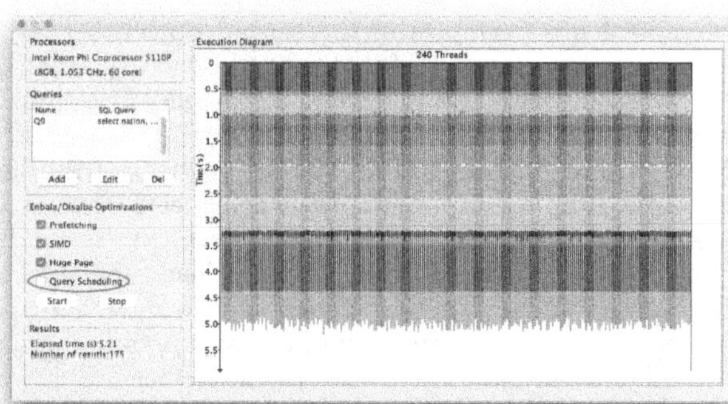

Figure 3: Screenshot of the GUI when executing Q9 *without* the query scheduling optimization

4.2 Visualization

The Graphics User Interface (GUI) is shown in Figure 2. At the left-hand side, users can add SQL queries for execution and choose to enable or disable Xeon Phi aware optimizations. If the "Query Scheduling" optimization is disabled, each operator uses the entire 240 threads, and essentially operators are executed one after another. Otherwise, operators may be executed concurrently for better performance. In the "Execution Diagram", the x-axis on top indicates the 240 threads on Xeon Phi and the y-axis at the left-hand side shows the execution time. We use different colors to represent the execution of different operators. From the diagram, we demonstrate the execution of each job, concurrently executed operators and idle states (spaces in the white color) caused by dependencies or stalls.

As a case study, the screenshots of execution diagram of Q9 with and without PhiDB's query optimization are

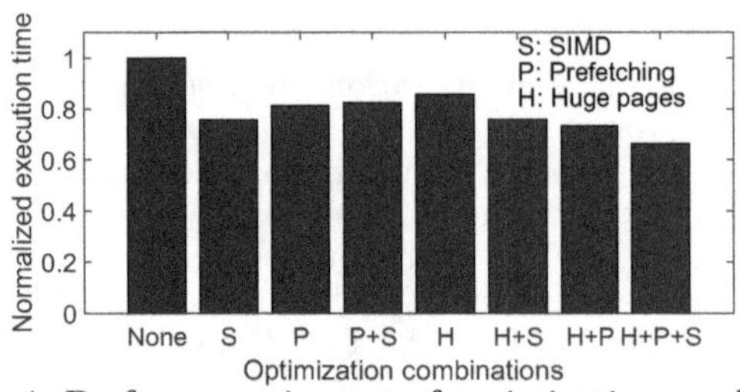

Figure 4: Performance impact of optimization combinations on Q9

shown in Figures 2 and 3, respectively. The same operators in both diagrams are colored in the same scheme. Q9 with PhiDB's query optimization is about 30% faster than that without it. Figure 3 shows that some operators consume more time when using 240 threads, which is an example of performance degradation caused by resource over-provisioning. Some are slower than those concurrent executions in Figure 2, which demonstrates the benefits of tunned concurrency among query operators.

4.3 Demonstration Objectives

This demonstration has two major goals.

Firstly, we aim to show the impact of Xeon Phi aware optimizations when one or more optimizations are enabled or disabled. We demonstrate the performance impact of the query optimization and runtime statistics with the GUI when executing TPC-H queries. The screenshots in Figures 2 and 3 are examples of the second objective. Now, we present one case study for the first objective. In Figure 4, we summarize the performance impact of optimization combinations. "S", "P" and "H" denote SIMD intrinsics, prefetching and huge pages enabled respectively (disabled otherwise). The execution time is normalized by that of "None" when all optimizations are disabled. SIMD intrinsics bring the highest performance improvement followed by prefetching and huge pages. In the demo, we show multiple screenshots similar to Figures 2 and 3, and present performance differences and their causes to the audience.

Secondly, we plan to demonstrate how to use this GUI to spot performance bottlenecks and assist the decision-making process for optimizations. For example, if we investigate Figure 3 carefully, we identify the performance problem that, at any time, Xeon Phi runs the workload with the same memory and computational characteristics (represented with the same color), and this execution cannot fully utilize the memory and computation resources. In the demonstration, we will also demonstrate the query plan and "where does time go" of evaluating a query.

5. SUMMARY

PhiDB demonstrates the preliminary design, implementation, and evaluation of databases on Intel Xeon Phi. We show that taking advantage of the hardware features is essential to the query processing performance. As the processors evolve from multi-core to many-core, we believe that a careful redesign and implementation of query processors become more and more desirable on future many-core processors. More work should be done along the direction. We will revisit different database system design such as row stores vs. column stores.

Acknowledgment

This work is supported in part by a Ministry of Education (MoE) AcRF Tier 2 grant. Xuntao's work is supported by the National Research Foundation, Prime Ministers Office, Singapore under its IDM Futures Funding Initiative and administered by the Interactive and Digital Media Programme Office (Grant No.: MDA/IDM/2012/8/8-2 VOL 01), LILY Center and Interdisciplinary Graduate School of NTU.

6. REFERENCES

[1] C. Balkesen, G. Alonso, J. Teubner, and M. T. Ozsu. Multi-core, main-memory joins: Sort vs. hash revisited. *VLDB*, 7(1), 2013.

[2] C. Balkesen, J. Teubner, G. Alonso, and M. Ozsu. Main-memory hash joins on modern processor architectures. *TKDE*, 2014.

[3] J. Chhugani, A. D. Nguyen, V. W. Lee, W. Macy, M. Hagog, Y.-K. Chen, A. Baransi, S. Kumar, and P. Dubey. Efficient implementation of sorting on multi-core simd cpu architecture. *VLDB*, 1(2), 2008.

[4] Z. Feng and E. Lo. Accelerating aggregation using intra-cycle parallelism. In *ICDE*. IEEE, 2015.

[5] B. He, Y. Li, Q. Luo, and D. Yang. Easedb: a cache-oblivious in-memory query processor. In *SIGMOD*. ACM, 2007.

[6] B. He and Q. Luo. Cache-oblivious databases: Limitations and opportunities. *TODS*, 33(2):8, 2008.

[7] A. Heinecke, K. Vaidyanathan, M. Smelyanskiy, A. Kobotov, R. Dubtsov, G. Henry, A. G. Shet, G. Chrysos, and P. Dubey. Design and implementation of the linpack benchmark for single and multi-node systems based on intel® xeon phi coprocessor. In *IPDPS*. IEEE, 2013.

[8] K. Hou, H. Wang, and W.-c. Feng. Aspas: A framework for automatic simdization of parallel sorting on x86-based many-core processors. In *ICS*. ACM, 2015.

[9] S. Jha, B. He, M. Lu, X. Cheng, and P. H. Huynh. Improving main memory hash joins on intel xeon phi processors: An experimental approach. *VLDB*, 8(6), 2015.

[10] M. Lu, L. Zhang, H. P. Huynh, Z. Ong, Y. Liang, B. He, R. S. M. Goh, and R. Huynh. Optimizing the mapreduce framework on intel xeon phi coprocessor. In *Big Data*. IEEE, 2013.

[11] S. Mehta, Z. Fang, A. Zhai, and P.-C. Yew. Multi-stage coordinated prefetching for present-day processors. In *SC*. ACM, 2014.

[12] O. Polychroniou, A. Raghavan, and K. A. Ross. Rethinking simd vectorization for in-memory databases. In *SIGMOD*. ACM, 2015.

[13] E. Saule, K. Kaya, and Ü. V. Çatalyürek. Performance evaluation of sparse matrix multiplication kernels on intel xeon phi. In *PPAM*. Springer, 2014.

[14] T. Willhalm, N. Popovici, Y. Boshmaf, H. Plattner, A. Zeier, and J. Schaffner. Simd-scan: ultra fast in-memory table scan using on-chip vector processing units. *VLDB*, 2(1), 2009.

ReproZip: Computational Reproducibility With Ease

Fernando Chirigati, Rémi Rampin, Dennis Shasha, and Juliana Freire
New York University
{fchirigati, remi.rampin, juliana.freire}@nyu.edu, shasha@cs.nyu.edu

ABSTRACT

We present ReproZip, the recommended packaging tool for the SIGMOD Reproducibility Review. ReproZip was designed to simplify the process of making an existing computational experiment reproducible across platforms, even when the experiment was put together without reproducibility in mind. The tool creates a self-contained package for an experiment by automatically tracking and identifying all its required dependencies. The researcher can share the package with others, who can then use ReproZip to unpack the experiment, reproduce the findings on their favorite operating system, as well as modify the original experiment for reuse in new research, all with little effort. The demo will consist of examples of non-trivial experiments, showing how these can be packed in a Linux machine and reproduced on different machines and operating systems. Demo visitors will also be able to pack and reproduce their own experiments.

Keywords

Computational Reproducibility; Provenance; ReproZip

1. INTRODUCTION

Reproducibility of computational experiments across platforms and time brings a range of benefits to science. First, reproducibility enables reviewers to test the outcomes presented in papers. Second, it allows new methods to be objectively compared against methods presented in reproducible publications. Third, researchers are able to build on top of previous work directly. Last but not least, recent studies indicate that reproducibility increases impact, visibility, and research quality [1, 26], and helps defeat self-deception [19].

In spite of its importance, achieving reproducibility has proved elusive for computational experiments, and this has led to a credibility crisis [10]. Ideally, researchers should create a compendium that encompasses all the components that are required to reproduce the experiment's results, including data, code, software, library dependencies, and information about the source computational environment (e.g., operating system and hardware architecture), i.e., the *provenance of the experiment*. As a computational experiment may consist of intricate chains of dependencies, manually creating such a compendium is a hard task at best and barely feasible most of the time.

There has been work on a plethora of tools that help create reproducible experiments and capture their provenance. Scientific workflow systems [6] represent an experiment as a dataflow (or workflow), stitching together its different steps and connecting data and processes in an executable representation. But adapting an experiment to run in these systems requires a steep learning curve that has hampered their adoption. Configuration management tools [3, 21, 22] automate the configuration of an experiment (e.g., installation of dependencies) by supporting the creation of "recipes" that can be reused every time a new machine needs to be configured; these scripts, however, need to be generated manually by researchers. Virtual machines (VMs) can be used to encapsulate the entire context of an experiment, providing an exact replica of the computational environment where the experiment took place. A drawback of virtual machines is that the derived images can be large, including a number of files that are not related to the experiment. Lighterweight solutions exist for deploying and maintaining software containers, such as Docker [9], but similar to VMs, the researcher is faced with the burden of ensuring that all necessary dependencies are in the container. Some computational platforms, such as Burrito [14] and Arnold [8], capture the provenance of all processes at the operating system (OS) level, recording detailed state information, but only allow experiments to be replayed in the same system. Last, there is a class of tools aimed at particular domains, e.g., GenePattern [12] is a genomic analysis platform, Madagascar [16] is used to analyze seismic data, Sumatra [7] is used for numerical computations, and noWorkflow [18] supports Python scripts only.

When using any of these solutions, making *existing* experiments reproducible is a time-consuming and error-prone process: researchers need to manually deploy dataflows, create configuration recipes, or transfer all the provenance to a VM. This difficulty discourages researchers from creating reproducible experiments, especially if the reason is solely for publication purposes [2, 5, 24].

In contrast to these approaches, `ReproZip` [4] provides a *lightweight* solution that makes experiments reproducible *without forethought*. Researchers can create an experiment without thinking about reproducibility and use `ReproZip` to

SIGMOD'16, June 26-July 01, 2016, San Francisco, CA, USA
© 2016 ACM. ISBN 978-1-4503-3531-7/16/06...$15.00
DOI: `http://dx.doi.org/10.1145/2882903.2899401`

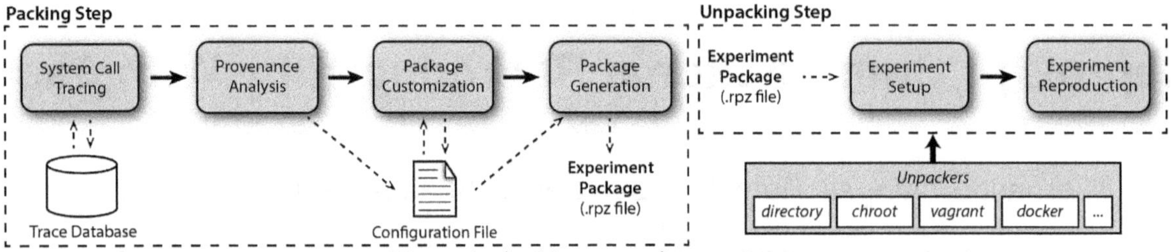

Figure 1: Architecture of ReproZip.

make it reproducible and portable to other machines immediately or many years later. ReproZip has been recommended for the SIGMOD Reproducibility Review.[1]

There are packaging systems that can help with reproducibility in the same *without-forethought* spirit as ReproZip, including CDE [13], PTU [20], and CARE [15]. They have the ability to create self-contained packages for the reproduction of existing Linux-based experiments. They do so by tracing the execution, intercepting system calls, and getting information related to the experiment. Using this provenance, all the necessary components of the experiment are copied to a package, which can then be sent to someone who wants to reproduce it. While reproducing an experiment, these tools dynamically change the system calls to point to the correct files included in the package.

Similar to these tools, ReproZip *automatically* and *transparently* captures the provenance of an existing experiment by tracing system calls, and uses this information to create a lightweight reproducible package that includes only the required files needed for its reproduction. However, ReproZip adds important features and contributions:

- *Portability:* Existing packaging systems have limited portability, as experiments can only be reproduced in environments with a compatible Linux kernel. In contrast, ReproZip provides *unpackers* that allow researchers to automatically create a VM or a Docker container encompassing the experiment, thus allowing it to be reproduced in different OS'es. ReproZip also generates a workflow specification for the experiment, which can be used to easily change parameters or modify the original dataflow.
- *Extensibility:* By implementing new unpackers, researchers can easily extend ReproZip to port experiments to other environments and systems (e.g., configuration "recipes" could be generated) while keeping compatibility with existing packaged experiments.
- *Modifiability:* ReproZip automatically identifies input files, parameters, and output files, allowing researchers to easily *modify* these for reuse purposes.
- *Usability:* Researchers have control over the collected trace and can customize the reproducible package. ReproZip also provides command-line interfaces that make it easier to setup, reproduce, and modify the original experiment.

The first (beta) version of ReproZip was developed in 2013 [4]. Since then, we have redesigned the system to be more general and cover a wider range of reproducibility requirements, and also to substantially improve its usability. In this demo, we describe ReproZip version 1.x. ReproZip can be downloaded from https://vida-nyu.github.io/reprozip, and a tutorial video on how to use the system is available at https://bit.ly/1N9QHCs.

[1] http://db-reproducibility.seas.harvard.edu/

2. SYSTEM ARCHITECTURE

ReproZip supports two main tasks (Figure 1): *packing*, which captures the dependencies for an experiment and creates a self-contained package, and *unpacking*, which supports the extraction of the package's content and the reproduction of the original experiment. In the following, assume a computational experiment E that runs on a single machine on OS S and that can be executed by running command line c.

2.1 Packing Experiments

The packing step is accomplished by four main modules: System Call Tracing, Provenance Analysis, Package Customization, and Package Generation (Figure 1). reprozip is the command-line tool responsible for this step.

System Call Tracing. To create a reproducible package, ReproZip needs to identify all the dependencies for E. Command c is prepended with reprozip trace, which runs E while tracing all the system calls; since this is done through ptrace, S must (currently) be a Linux-based OS. By tracing system calls, ReproZip can transparently capture all the provenance of E. For instance, execve is used to execute programs, open informs ReproZip which files are being opened, and read and write read from and write to a file, respectively. Therefore, ReproZip collects a plethora of information regarding E, including command-line arguments, environment variables, files read, and files written, and stores everything in a SQLite database.

The previous version of ReproZip used SystemTap [23] for tracing and MongoDB [17] for storage. While SystemTap is complex to install and update, ptrace is part of the Linux kernel. SQLite is also much lighter than MongoDB and part of the Python distribution. These changes were made to enhance usability, as the packing step no longer has external requirements.

Provenance Analysis. The provenance data is analyzed to detect the required components of E. For instance, given the files that were read and using the package manager of the OS, ReproZip can identify the *software packages* on which E depends. ReproZip also uses some heuristics to identify *input and output files*: files that were only read but that do not belong to any software package are considered input files; files that were only written are considered output files; files that were read and then written are considered stateful files (e.g., log or database files). This significantly improves the beta version of ReproZip, in which the provenance analysis is limited to detecting explicit input/output files and parameters from c. All the collected information is then written to a human-readable *configuration file*, which can be edited by researchers.

Package Customization. The configuration file contains all the required information for packing E, including: execution information (e.g., command, arguments, working directory, environment variables, and OS information), input

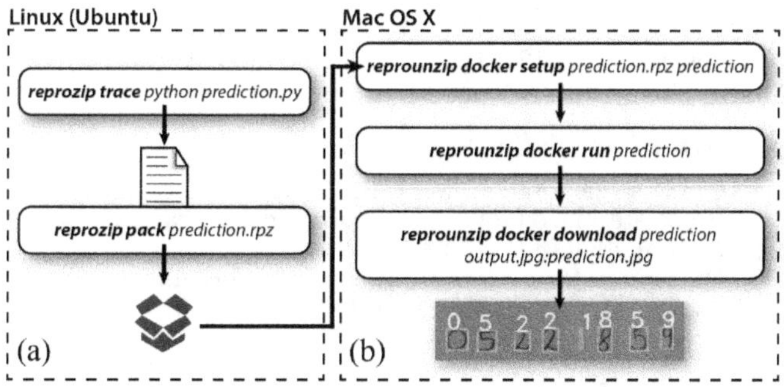

Figure 2: Packing (a) and unpacking (b) a computer vision experiment with `ReproZip`.

files, output files, and identified software packages. Even though this automatically-generated file is sufficient to create a working *experiment package*, researchers may edit this file (i) to modify command-line arguments; (ii) to modify environment variables; (iii) to remove big files that can be obtained elsewhere; (iv) to remove sensitive or proprietary information; or (v) to exclude software packages.

Package Generation. After tracing all the executions from E, analyzing the provenance data, and optionally editing the configuration file, the *experiment package* P can be created by running `reprozip pack`. The package is a `.rpz` file, which encompasses all the required data and information for reproducing the traced execution (e.g., input files, library dependencies, and binaries). P can then be sent to others so that E can be reproduced.

Example. *Figure 2(a) shows an experiment on Ubuntu that predicts the values of hand-writing digits from an input image and outputs a new image with the predictions. Packing this experiment is as easy as running two commands. While the full VM takes 4GB,* `prediction.rpz` *has 67MB, which is substantially lighter-weight for sharing.*

2.2 Unpacking Experiments

Given P, E can be reproduced by using the command-line tool `reprounzip`. Different *unpackers* are provided to reproduce the corresponding experiment.

2.2.1 Unpackers

The choice of an unpacker depends on the OS S' where E will be reproduced: S' can be either compatible with S ($S' \approx S$), or completely different from S ($S' \not\approx S$). An example of the former is when S' and S have compatible Linux kernels, while the latter scenario happens when S' is a Windows or a Mac OS X machine. Portability is a significant new feature of `ReproZip`, which previously could only unpack and reproduce experiments across Linux systems; more specifically, we only supported what is now the *directory* unpacker (see below) in our beta version [4].

$\boldsymbol{S' \not\approx S}$**.** There are two unpacking options: the *vagrant* and the *docker* unpackers. The *vagrant* unpacker allows E to be unpacked and reproduced inside a virtual machine automatically created through Vagrant [25]. Therefore, E can be reproduced on any system S' supported by this tool. The *docker* unpacker, on the other hand, unpacks and reproduces E in a Docker [9] container, either on the researcher's own machine, a remote one, or on a cloud provider. In both cases, `ReproZip` automatically selects a base system image that is the closest to S, but researchers can also explicitly choose their own.

$\boldsymbol{S' \approx S}$**.** `ReproZip` supports two additional unpackers: *directory* and *chroot*. The former unpacks E in a single directory: E can be reproduced directly from that directory. It does so by automatically setting up environment variables (e.g., `PATH`, `HOME`, and `LD_LIBRARY_PATH`) that point the experiment execution to the created directory, which has the same structure as in the original system S. Note that the created directory is *not* isolated from S'. In particular, should E use hardcoded absolute paths, they will hit the host system instead. This unpacker is meant for relatively well-behaved experiments that address files with relative paths only.

In the *chroot* unpacker, similar to the *directory* one, a directory is created from P. However, a full system environment is also built, which is then run with `chroot`, a Linux mechanism that changes the root directory for E to the created directory. Therefore, this unpacker works even in the presence of hardcoded absolute paths. Note as well that the unpacked software does not interfere with S' since E is isolated in that single directory.

`ReproZip` also has an option to natively install all the software packages. In this case, when reproducing E, both *directory* and *chroot* unpackers can use the installed dependencies, instead of the ones copied from inside P.

Extensions. If researchers need to port E to a different system not currently supported by `ReproZip`, they can easily create their own unpacker and attach it to the tool. `ReproZip` was redesigned in a way that makes it easy to create new extensions that will still support every package created in the past.

2.2.2 Modules

The unpacking step, regardless of the unpacker, consists of two main modules: Experiment Setup and Experiment Reproduction (Figure 1).

Experiment Setup. First, given P, the experiment needs to be extracted, and this is accomplished by running the `setup` command. While, for the *directory* and *chroot* unpackers, this command means copying E to a single directory (and creating a full system environment for the latter), a virtual machine and a Docker container are initialized with E for the *vagrant* and *docker* unpackers, respectively.

Experiment Reproduction. Once the package has been extracted, E can be reproduced by using the `run` command. The way E is reproduced depends on the chosen unpacker: for *directory*, the execution happens inside the experiment directory; for *chroot*, it happens inside the created file system; and for *vagrant* and *docker*, it is done inside the virtual image and the container, respectively. All the interaction with E is done through `reprounzip` and its command-line interfaces. Researchers do not need to know how to reproduce E or even how to use Vagrant or Docker, since `reprounzip` will perform the necessary steps automatically for them according to the selected unpacker. Such command-line interfaces were nonexistent in `ReproZip`'s beta version.

Example. *Figure 2(b) shows how to unpack—using the docker unpacker—*`prediction.rpz` *on a Mac OS X machine. The* `setup` *and* `run` *commands are the only steps necessary for reproducing the original experiment. Additionally, the command* `download` *(Section 2.2.3) may be used for retrieving the output file. The automatically-generated Docker image has 500MB. When using the vagrant unpacker, the virtual* *machine takes up 1.40GB, much lighter when compared to the original one (4GB) since the former encompasses only the files necessary for the reproduction.*

2.2.3 File and Dataflow Management

Recall that input and output files are identified based on heuristics. In the unpacking step, `ReproZip` uses this information to let researchers alter input files and retrieve the output files after E is reproduced. The command `showfiles` can be used to see which files are input and output, and the commands `upload` and `download` can be used to replace an input file and to retrieve an output file, respectively. This makes it easy to *reuse* E, or evaluate it on different inputs.

`ReproZip` can also derive a specification of the experiment workflow. The main programs of the experiment are wrapped in workflow modules that automatically take the command-line arguments and input files as inputs. Currently, `ReproZip` derives workflows for VisTrails [11]. Using this system, (i) the dataflow of an experiment can be understood; (ii) unpacked experiments can be executed; (iii) researchers can explore experiments and try different inputs; and (iv) researchers can extend the original workflow to explore different techniques and perform analyses, or modify the dataflow to reuse steps for their own research.

3. DEMONSTRATION

In our demonstration, we encourage visitors to bring their own experiments on their Linux machines, given that the execution takes no longer than a few minutes. They will:

- Install `ReproZip` on their machine S;
- Trace the execution of their experiment;
- Create a reproducible package;
- Transfer the package to a completely different machine S' (either a Mac OS X or a Windows machine);
- Replicate the experiment on S' and modify its inputs;
- Optionally generate a VisTrails workflow on S' to visualize the experiment dataflow and alter its pipeline.

In addition to the visitors' own experiments, we will have a number of real experiments from different domains, including computer vision, visualization (e.g., interactive and exploratory tools), and database research.

4. DISCUSSION AND FUTURE WORK

For experiments that run on Linux systems, `ReproZip` is a simple-to-deploy tool that makes an experiment reproducible across different platforms and long after it was created. Therefore, "*It's too difficult to reproduce*" can no longer be used as an excuse. The ability to pack software will, we believe, greatly contribute to scientific quality, allowing researchers to reuse the experiment produced by others, helping analyze the pipeline and dependencies of an experiment, and even helping industrial software developers deploy their software on new OS'es.

`ReproZip` supports a wide range of experiments, including client-server scenarios, experiments with databases, and graphical and interactive tools. Also, if experiment E requires multiple command-line executions (e.g., different execution paths, or a pipeline), each execution can be traced separately and the analyzed information can be added to a single configuration file, so that all the executions are included in the same package P. When unpacking P, researchers can select which runs to reproduce. We are currently working on support for experiments that run on distributed environments (e.g., MPI and Hadoop clusters).

Acknowledgments. This work was supported in part by NSF awards CNS-1229185 and CI-EN-1405927, and by the Moore-Sloan Data Science Environment at NYU.

5. REFERENCES

[1] C. G. Begley and L. M. Ellis. Drug development: Raise standards for preclinical cancer research. *Nature*, 483(7391):531–533, 2012.
[2] P. Bonnet et al. Repeatability and Workability Evaluation of SIGMOD 2011. *SIGMOD Rec.*, 40(2):45–48, 2011.
[3] Chef. `https://www.chef.io/`.
[4] F. Chirigati, D. Shasha, and J. Freire. Packing Experiments for Sharing and Publication. In *SIGMOD*, pages 977–980, 2013.
[5] C. Collberg, T. Proebsting, and A. M. Warren. Repeatability and Benefaction in Computer Systems Research. Technical Report TR 14-04, University of Arizona, 2015.
[6] S. B. Davidson and J. Freire. Provenance and Scientific Workflows: Challenges and Opportunities. In *SIGMOD*, pages 1345–1350, 2008.
[7] A. Davison. Automated Capture of Experiment Context for Easier Reproducibility in Computational Research. *Computing in Science Engineering*, 14(4):48–56, 2012.
[8] D. Devecsery, M. Chow, X. Dou, J. Flinn, and P. M. Chen. Eidetic systems. In *OSDI*, pages 525–540, 2014.
[9] Docker. `https://www.docker.com/`.
[10] D. Donoho, A. Maleki, I. Rahman, M. Shahram, and V. Stodden. Reproducible research in computational harmonic analysis. *Computing in Science & Engineering*, 11(1):8–18, Jan.-Feb. 2009.
[11] J. Freire, D. Koop, E. Santos, C. Scheidegger, C. T. Silva, and H. T. Vo. *The Architecture of Open Source Applications*, chapter VisTrails. Lulu Publishing, 2011.
[12] GenePattern. `http://www.broadinstitute.org/cancer/software/genepattern/`.
[13] P. Guo. CDE: A Tool For Creating Portable Experimental Software Packages. *Computing in Science & Engineering*, 14:32–35, 2012.
[14] P. J. Guo and M. Seltzer. BURRITO: Wrapping Your Lab Notebook in Computational Infrastructure. In *TaPP*, pages 7–7, 2012.
[15] Y. Janin, C. Vincent, and R. Duraffort. CARE, the Comprehensive Archiver for Reproducible Execution. In *TRUST*, pages 1:1–1:7, 2014.
[16] Madagascar. `http://www.ahay.org/wiki/Main_Page`.
[17] MongoDB. `http://www.mongodb.org/`.
[18] L. Murta, V. Braganholo, F. Chirigati, D. Koop, and J. Freire. noWorkflow: Capturing and Analyzing Provenance of Scripts. In *IPAW*, pages 71–83, 2015.
[19] R. Nuzzo. How scientists fool themselves, and how they can stop. *Nature*, 526(7572):182–185, 2015.
[20] Q. Pham, T. Malik, and I. Foster. Using Provenance for Repeatability. In *TaPP*, pages 2:1–2:4, 2013.
[21] Puppet. `http://puppetlabs.com/`.
[22] C. Ruiz, O. Richard, and J. Emeras. Reproducible Software Appliances for Experimentation. In *Testbeds and Research Infrastructure: Development of Networks and Communities*, volume 137, pages 33–42. 2014.
[23] SystemTap. `http://sourceware.org/systemtap/`.
[24] C. Tenopir, S. Allard, K. Douglass, A. U. Aydinoglu, L. Wu, E. Read, M. Manoff, and M. Frame. Data Sharing by Scientists: Practices and Perceptions. *PLoS ONE*, 6(6), 2011.
[25] Vagrant. `https://www.vagrantup.com/`.
[26] P. Vandewalle, J. Kovacevic, and M. Vetterli. Reproducible Research in Signal Processing. *Signal Processing Magazine, IEEE*, 26(3):37–47, 2009.

CLAMS: Bringing Quality to Data Lakes

Mina Farid
University of Waterloo
mfathy@uwaterloo.ca

Alexandra Roatiş
University of Waterloo
aroatis@uwaterloo.ca

Ihab F. Ilyas
University of Waterloo
ilyas@uwaterloo.ca

Hella-Franziska Hoffmann*
Thomson Reuters
hella.hoffmann@thomsonreuters.com

Xu Chu
University of Waterloo
x4chu@uwaterloo.ca

ABSTRACT

With the increasing incentive of enterprises to ingest as much data as they can in what is commonly referred to as "data lakes", and with the recent development of multiple technologies to support this "load-first" paradigm, the new environment presents serious data management challenges. Among them, the assessment of data quality and cleaning large volumes of heterogeneous data sources become essential tasks in unveiling the value of big data.

The coveted use of unstructured and semi-structured data in large volumes makes current data cleaning tools (primarily designed for relational data) not directly adoptable.

We present CLAMS, a system to discover and enforce expressive integrity constraints from large amounts of lake data with very limited schema information (e.g., represented as RDF triples). This demonstration shows how CLAMS is able to discover the constraints and the schemas they are defined on simultaneously. CLAMS also introduces a scale-out solution to efficiently detect errors in the raw data. CLAMS interacts with human experts to both validate the discovered constraints and to suggest data repairs.

CLAMS has been deployed in a real large-scale enterprise data lake and was experimented with a real data set of 1.2 billion triples. It has been able to spot multiple obscure data inconsistencies and errors early in the data processing stack, providing huge value to the enterprise.

1. INTRODUCTION

At present, data is viewed as a major enterprise asset, and tools for analyzing big data are highly coveted. To handle the scale of available data, businesses have shifted to a "load-first" approach. This has lead to an upward trend of maintaining data in its native format and storing it in large repositories referred to as "data lakes."[1]

The effectiveness of data analysis depends on the quality of the underlying data. Current data quality techniques [5] rely on the existence of a global schema and use it to define various integrity constraints. In load-first schema-later environments, most data is available in a plethora of local schemas, schema-less RDF triple formats, and comma-separated-value files. Analytics are performed on top of application-specific schemas that are defined much later in the stack. Waiting until a global schema is defined means propagating large volumes of erroneous data through multiple data processing layers via complex Extract-Transform-Load [2] operations. This complicates repairing and tracking errors to their original sources [1]. On the other hand, attempting to clean data in the lake directly after ingesting it from the sources is complicated by the lack of schema information and the limited number of integrity constraints that can be defined without a schema.

Denial Constraints (DCs) [4] are a state-of-the-art method to express data quality rules over relational data [5]. The literature has proposed efficient discovery [3] and enforcement [4] algorithms for DCs. However, these algorithms cannot be directly applied on data lakes because of (*i*) the schema-less nature of lake data; and (*ii*) the limited scalability of these algorithms to large datasets.

We present CLAMS, an interactive system that enables business users to design and enforce complex constraints over large unstructured and semi-structured datasets. In particular, CLAMS operates on large-scale data processing frameworks (specifically, Apache Spark) to manipulate massive datasets. The features of CLAMS include:

- Providing a data ingestion module to transform unstructured and semi-structured data into RDF triples, which are then loaded into HDFS;
- Specifying *expressive integrity constraints* over graph data through (*i*) automatic discovery and ranking of plausible quality constraints which get verified by the user; and (*ii*) a friendly and interactive UI for creating and modifying constraints guided by data sampling and summarization;
- Enforcing the specified constraints through scalable, distributed algorithms to detect data inconsistencies;
- Surfacing a ranked list of possible errors along with the lineage of the violating data for user inspection.

Our solution brings the enterprise one step closer to extracting value from its dark (limited-access) data.

2. CLAMS SYSTEM OVERVIEW

Figure 1 illustrates the system architecture of CLAMS. We give an overview of the different components, and then discuss the details of each component.

*Work done while at University of Waterloo
[1]http://www.gartner.com/newsroom/id/2809117

SIGMOD'16, June 26-July 01, 2016, San Francisco, CA, USA
© 2016 ACM. ISBN 978-1-4503-3531-7/16/06...$15.00
DOI: http://dx.doi.org/10.1145/2882903.2899391

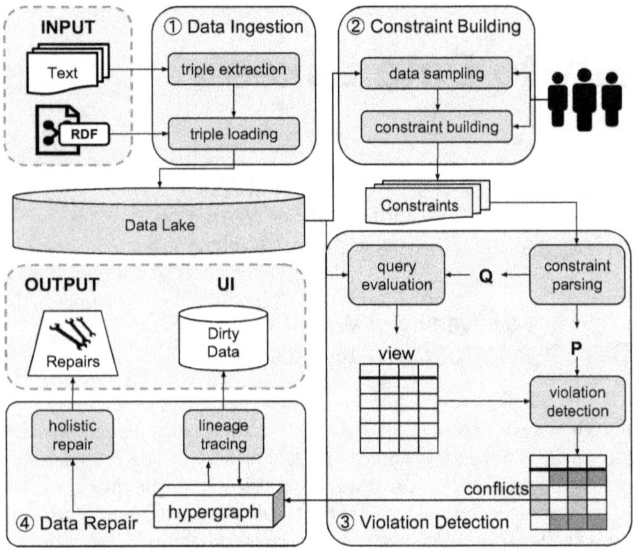

Figure 1: CLAMS System Architecture

- the *data ingestion* module ① loads datasets into HDFS, registers data sources for cleaning, and uses information extraction to produce semi-structured data (Section 2.1);
- the *constraint building* module ② offers an interactive UI to examine automatically discovered simple quality rules and guides the user in creating more complex ones (Section 2.2);
- the *violation detection* module ③ efficiently enforces a set of constraints over the registered data sources to detect data that does not conform to the specified constraints (Section 2.3);
- the *data repair* module ④ identifies the highly likely causes of errors and proposes solutions for cleaning them (Section 2.3).

2.1 Data Ingestion

At present, CLAMS uses the RDF data model for storing heterogeneous data. RDF is a graph-based data model, where facts are represented as *triples* (directed labeled edges between labeled nodes). Figure 2 shows a sample RDF dataset in its graph representation, using data from the New York Times[2] and GeoNames[3] datasets.

Heterogeneous information can be easily represented in this format. Also, no global schema is necessary to understand the data due to its human friendly readability.

Our conversation with multiple companies confirmed that RDF is indeed a common format to represent data coming from heterogenous data sources. Information extraction tools (e.g., Open Calais[4] of Thomson Reuters and IBM's AlchemyAPI[5]) may assist in extracting RDF triples from unstructured text and linking the extracted data to popular ontologies (e.g., DBpedia).

CLAMS ingests RDF data into HDFS. If the data is in a different format, CLAMS uses information extraction tools to extract RDF triples before loading them. Users can register HDFS datasets as resources, expanding the catalog of data sources on which constraints can be applied.

[2]http://data.nytimes.com/
[3]http://www.geonames.org/
[4]http://www.opencalais.com/
[5]http://www.alchemyapi.com/

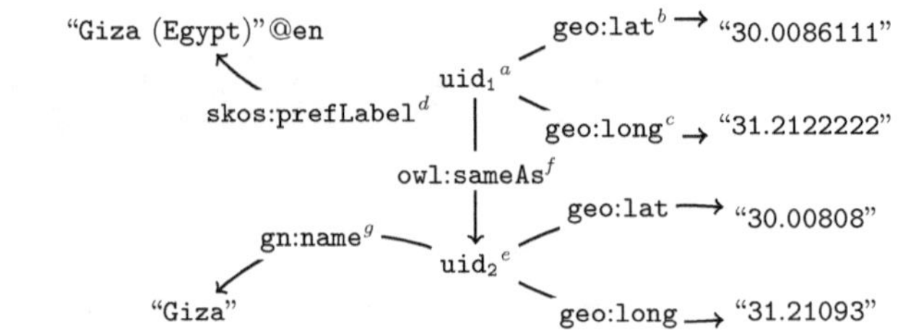

[a]http://data.nytimes.com/48075591700161033501
[b]http://www.w3.org/2003/01/geo/wgs84_pos#lat
[c]http://www.w3.org/2003/01/geo/wgs84_pos#long
[d]http://www.w3.org/2004/02/skos/core#prefLabel
[e]http://sws.geonames.org/360995/
[f]http://www.w3.org/2002/07/owl#sameAs
[g]http://www.geonames.org/ontology#name

Figure 2: Sample RDF Graph

Two identical locations must have the same latitude coordinates is represented as a CDC $c = (Q, \varphi)$, where:

```
Q = SELECT ?loc1 ?loc2 ?lat1 ?lat2
    WHERE { ?loc1 owl:sameAs ?loc2 .
            ?loc1 geo:lat ?lat1 .
            ?loc2 geo:lat ?lat2 }
```

$\varphi = \{\forall t \in Q(\mathcal{D}), \neg(t.lat1 \neq t.lat2)\}$

Figure 3: Sample Quality Constraint

2.2 Constraint Building

Definition of Constraints. In CLAMS, we define a *conditional denial constraint (CDC)* c over data model $\mathcal{M}$ as a pair (Q, φ), where Q is a query in language $\mathcal{L}$, and φ is a denial constraint over the relation defined by the answer of Q over $\mathcal{D}$, denoted $Q(\mathcal{D})$. The query Q in a CDC defines a relational view over the unstructured input dataset. Then, the denial constraint φ over the view expresses the set of conditions that represent a forbidden (incorrect) pattern for (sets of) tuples in $Q(\mathcal{D})$. We say that a dataset $\mathcal{D} \in \mathcal{M}$ *satisfies* a CDC $c = (Q, \varphi)$, denoted $\mathcal{D} \models c$, iff the answer to $Q(\mathcal{D})$ satisfies φ, denoted $Q(\mathcal{D}) \models \varphi$.

We will demonstrate the application of CDCs over heterogeneous datasets using the RDF data model and its query language, SPARQL. Figure 3 shows a simple constraint example over the RDF graph in Figure 2.

Note that while the set of predicates is limited by the DC formalism, the query Q allows the definition of constraints beyond DCs. Take for instance a graph reachability constraint stating a conflict of interest, e.g., a bank employee cannot be in charge of the account of a first-degree relative. In order to express that constraint, the reachability predicates are pushed into the query. Therefore, the query will represent the forbidden pattern while φ is void, signalling that every query answer is a violation of the CDC.

Constraint Discovery. The separation of a CDC into query and DC significantly complicates the discovery process. The space of possible DCs for a given schema is already massive [3]. Performing such a search for all possible schemas is unfeasible. We therefore limit our search to basic graph pattern (i.e., conjunctive) queries. This limitation allows for a manageable scope of potential schemas, with many repeating sub-patterns. Furthermore, CDC discovery is optimized by intertwining the search for relation schemas with the search for DC predicates.

The automatic constraint discovery uses multiple techniques to detect potential schemas in the data and discover constraints that may apply on them. The schema detection spans from using schema languages such as RDFS and OWL, to graph summaries and entity anchoring. DC predicate detection is based on state-of-the-art techniques [3], extended with attribute type inference and on-the-fly schema detection. CLAMS generates friendly natural English descriptions for the discovered constraints.

Constraint Building. CLAMS also provides an interactive interface to manually build more complex constraints. The system guides the user in the process of creating constraints by providing statistics about common types and properties in the dataset and their co-occurrence to assist in constructing the constraint queries.

2.3 Violation Detection and Holistic Repair

A violation of a CDC c is defined as a minimal set of triples that cannot coexist, and removing any triple from that set will resolve the violation. For example, the following triples from Figure 2 violate the CDC c from Figure 3. The set of triples $\{t_1, t_2, t_3\}$ forms a *single* violation of c.

t_1 : uid$_1$ owl:sameAs uid$_2$.
t_2 : uid$_1$ geo:lat "30.0086111" .
t_3 : uid$_2$ geo:lat "30.00808" .

Once we have detected all violations, possibly from multiple constraints, a *violation hypergraph* G is built. Each node in the hypergraph represents a triple, and each hyperedge represents a violation. Figure 4 shows a violation hypergraph with three violations V_1, V_2, V_3, where $V_1 = \{t_1, t_2, t_3\}$, $V_2 = \{t_1, t_2, t_4, t_5\}$, and $V_3 = \{t_1, t_6\}$.

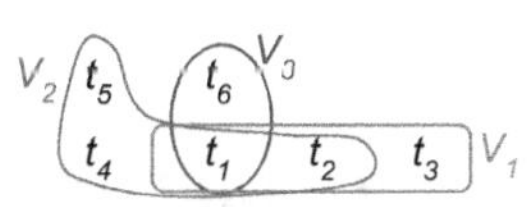

Figure 4: Example Hypergraph of three Violations

The hypergraph immediately reveals the number of violations a triple participates in, for example, t_1 is involved in three violations, while t_2 is involved in two violations. All nodes (triples) in the hypergraph are potential erroneous triples. We rank the potential erroneous triples by the number of violations each triple participates in. The intuition behind such ranking is that the more violations a triple is involved in, the more likely that triple is incorrect [4]. A visual interface is offered to the user, color coding the problematic triples by their participation in violations, as well as providing reasons to explain why these triples are erroneous [1]. The user gradually edits or remove triples from the graph until all the violations are solved. For example, triple t_1 in Figure 4 is first presented to the user. After examining the violations t_1 is involved in, the user might decide that t_1 is an erroneous triple and thus should be removed. Removing t_1 causes CLAMS to update the hypergraph. In this example, deleting t_1 causes all the hyperedges (i.e., violations)

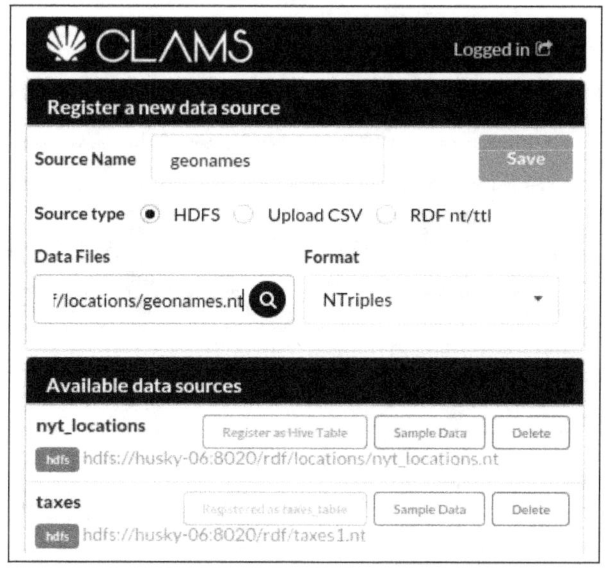

Figure 5: Data Source Registration

to be removed, eliminating the need for the user to further examine the rest of the triples.

2.4 Implementation Details

We designed and implemented the backend algorithms for constraint discovery and enforcement on the Apache Spark cluster computing framework to benefit from its efficient in-memory processing capabilities. Spark reads RDF data from HDFS, which represents our data lake, and distributes the algorithmic work among 10 worker nodes with a total of 832 GB RAM memory. We implemented a RESTful web services layer using Dropwizard[6] to communicate with Spark and HDFS. Dropwizard exposes our data quality algorithms as web services. When a request is received, we formulate and submit an appropriate Spark job to the cluster, and the results are written to HDFS. A user web application is built in JavaScript on top of Node.js[7] framework and it is responsible for providing an interactive UI to call the Dropwizard web services and manipulate catalog information.

3. DEMONSTRATION SCENARIO

The demonstration's audience will be able to use CLAMS to enforce quality constraints on RDF data. Participants may assess automatically discovered constraints or manually build constraints with the help of CLAMS's data exploration tool. After defining the constraints, the constraint enforcement algorithms of CLAMS run to detect violations and suggest repairs. Users can investigate the detected violations and provide repair feedback to the system.

In this section, we present a demonstration scenario to show the functionality of CLAMS in one possible application to enforce data quality constraints on the data lake.

Data Ingestion and Source Registration. The first step in our demonstration is to register the data sources that we will operate on.

[6]http://www.dropwizard.io/
[7]https://nodejs.org

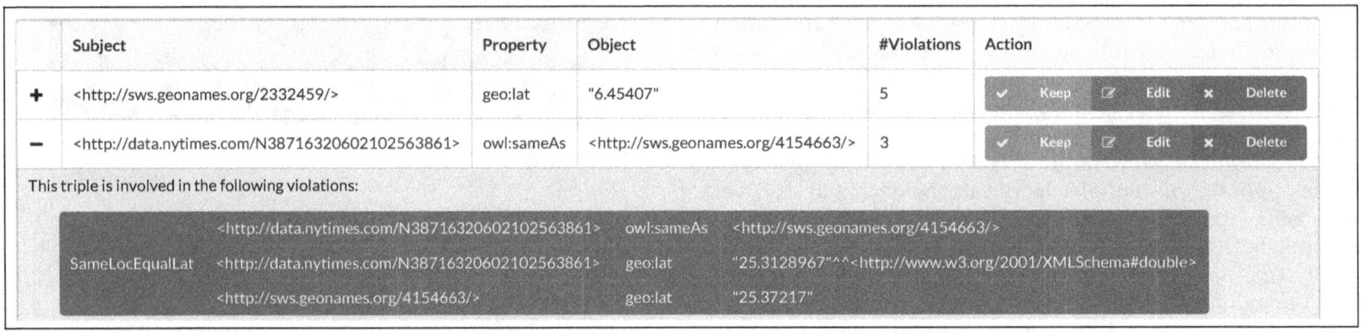

Figure 7: Detected Violations and User Feedback for Repair

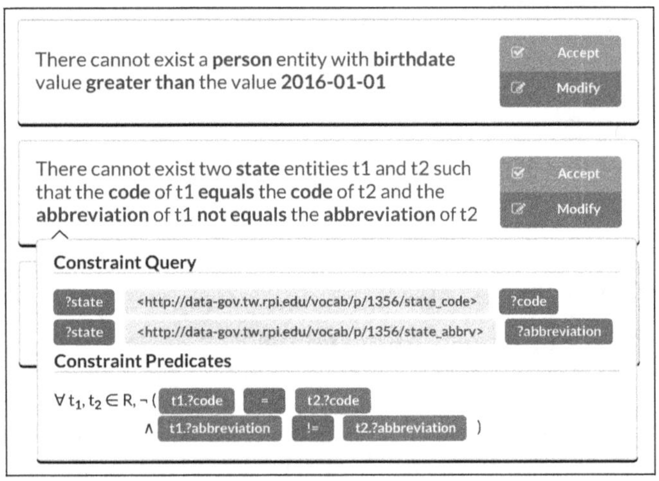

Figure 6: Discovered Constraints and User Verification

- Users can register RDF data (Figure 5) that is already loaded on HDFS (large datasets), upload RDF data files or select extractors for other data formats.
- CLAMS shows the registered datasets and allows users to see samples of them.

Discovering and Building Constraints. The next step is to define the constraints that apply on the dataset. CLAMS supports two methods to create constraints.

Discovered Constraints. First, users can trigger the automatic constraint discovery from the underlying datasets as explained in Section 2.2.

- The discovered constraints are presented to the user with simple English translations (Figure 6).
- Users can see the details of a constraint (its query and predicates) by hovering over it, and can modify it or directly add it (accept) to the system catalog.

User-Defined Constraints. The second approach is to use the interactive constraint building tool of CLAMS to explore a sample of the data and define manual constraints.

- Users interact with data to build the constraint query.
- Users define the constraint predicates based on the variables in the query. The predicates can be defined on a single tuple or on pairs of tuples.

Constraint Enforcement. Given a set of defined constraints and a set of registered data sources, users can run our constraint enforcement algorithm to detect violations.

- Users select the constraints to enforce and the data sources to enfoce them on, then start the constriant enforcement process.
- CLAMS runs the enforcement Spark jobs on the cluster and returns the detected violations (Figure 7).
- The system displays the violating RDF triples, ranked by their accumulated violations (cf. Section 2.3).
- Upon clicking on a triple, all the violations that this triple is involved in are displayed to the user.
- The user decides whether to keep, edit, or delete a triple from the data. If deleted, CLAMS excludes that triple when performing further constraint enforcement.

4. CONCLUSION

We presented CLAMS—a system to discover and to enforce quality constraints on large RDF datasets that reside in data lakes. CLAMS uses a new integrity constraint formalism to capture both relational model-like constraints and more expressive quality rules based on graph patterns. We showed how CLAMS holistically combines the signals from diverse constraints spanning over multiple datasets and utilize user feedback to obtain accurate repairs.

5. ACKNOWLEDGEMENTS

This work is generously funded by Thomson Reuters. The company has also provided us with valuable data that was used to validate CLAMS and feedback about the implemented prototype.

6. REFERENCES

[1] A. Chalamalla, I. F. Ilyas, M. Ouzzani, and P. Papotti. Descriptive and Prescriptive Data Cleaning. In *SIGMOD*, 2014.

[2] S. Chaudhuri and U. Dayal. An Overview of Data Warehousing and OLAP Technology. *SIGMOD Rec.*, 26(1):65–74, Mar. 1997.

[3] X. Chu, I. F. Ilyas, and P. Papotti. Discovering Denial Constraints. *Proc. VLDB Endow.*, 6(13):1498–1509, Aug. 2013.

[4] X. Chu, I. F. Ilyas, and P. Papotti. Holistic Data Cleaning: Put Violations Into Context. In *ICDE*, 2013.

[5] I. F. Ilyas and X. Chu. Trends in cleaning relational data: Consistency and deduplication. *Foundations and Trends in Databases*, 5(4):281–393, 2015.

FERARI: A Prototype for Complex Event Processing over Streaming Multi-cloud Platforms*

Ioannis Flouris* Vasiliki Manikaki* Nikos Giatrakos* Antonios Deligiannakis*
Minos Garofalakis* Michael Mock◇ Sebastian Bothe◇ Inna Skarbovsky♯
Fabiana Fournier♯ Marko Štajcer† Tomislav Križan† Jonathan Yom-Tov§
Taji Ćurin‡

*Technical University of Crete
{gflouris, manikaki, ngiatrakos, adeli, minos}@softnet.tuc.gr

♯IBM Research - Haifa
{fabiana, inna}@il.ibm.com

◇Fraunhofer IAIS
{michael.mock, sebastian.bothe}@iais.fraunhofer.de

§Technion, Israel Institute of Technology
jonyomtov@cs.technion.ac.il

†Poslovna Inteligencija
{marko.stajcer, tomislav.krizan}@inteligencija.com

‡T-Hrvatski Telekom
Taji.Curin@t.ht.hr

ABSTRACT

In this demo, we present FERARI, a prototype that enables real-time Complex Event Processing (CEP) for large volume event data streams over distributed topologies. Our prototype constitutes, to our knowledge, the first complete, multi-cloud based end-to-end CEP solution incorporating: a) a user-friendly, web-based query authoring tool, (b) a powerful CEP engine implemented on top of a streaming cloud platform, (c) a CEP optimizer that chooses the best query execution plan with respect to low latency and/or reduced inter-cloud communication burden, and (d) a query analytics dashboard encompassing graph and map visualization tools to provide a holistic picture with respect to the detected complex events to final stakeholders. As a proof-of-concept, we apply FERARI to enable mobile fraud detection over real, properly anonymized, telecommunication data from T-Hrvatski Telekom network in Croatia.

1. INTRODUCTION

Machine-to-Machine (M2M) synergies generate event data in high frequency in every modern Big Data system, from network health monitoring and mobile or sensor network deployments to computer clusters and smart energy grids. Besides M2M interactions, Internet-of-Things (IoT) platforms can offer advanced connectivity of devices and services that cover a variety of domains and applications, generating high volumes of event data streams and patterns of interest subjected to further study.

*This work was supported by the European Commission under ICT-FP7- FERARI-619491 (Flexible Event pRocessing for big dAta aRchItectures).

SIGMOD'16, June 26-July 01, 2016, San Francisco, CA, USA
© 2016 ACM. ISBN 978-1-4503-3531-7/16/06...$15.00
DOI: http://dx.doi.org/10.1145/2882903.2899395

Complex Event Processing (CEP) Engines [3, 5] aim at processing such event data streams efficiently and immediately recognizing interesting situations in real-time. Primitive events are atomic (i.e., non-decomposable) occurrences that stream into a CEP system, while complex events (CEs) are derived by the CEP Engine based on application-defined event patterns (rules) engaging other primitive and/or CE combinations. For instance, consider a number of telecommunication antennas in a simplified mobile fraud detection scenario. A mobile device exiting the realm of an antenna triggers the report of a corresponding primitive event with the duration of the ongoing call maintained by that particular cellular device as an attribute. The CE of a potential fraud case apparition may involve summing up the overall call duration for a certain cell phone number across visited antennas and assessing whether it exceeds a given threshold within a recent time window.

In large scale distributed CEP systems, centralizing all raw events is not possible, as this would create a bottleneck at the central site/cloud. Streaming event data arriving at multiple, potentially geographically dispersed, cloud platforms should be efficiently processed in situ (if possible) and then combined to provide holistic answers to global application queries. Efficient inter-cloud CEP is tightly coupled with the requirement for reduced communication since conventional communication links interconnect sites with distinct cloud deployments. Towards that end, query plans should be generated exploiting the potential for in-situ processing.

One step further, enabling CEP at vast scale involves scaling the amount of local processing performed within each site/cloud. With the emergence of streaming cloud platforms (such as Apache Storm [1]), CEP systems need to be adapted and redesigned to exploit *intra-cloud* parallelization and elastic resource consumption.

In this demo, we present FERARI, a prototype that enables real-time CEP for large volume event data streams over distributed topologies. The key characteristics that distinguish FERARI from conventional competitors that operate over cloud platforms (such as Esper [4]), is that FERARI takes advantage of both inter-cloud CEP by distributing the load over a set of streaming cloud platforms and parallelized, intra-cloud CEP where appropriate. However, FERARI's breakthrough is not limited to the above important charac-

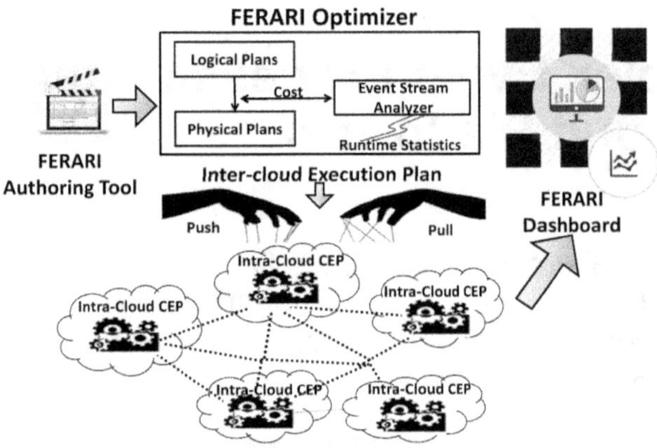

Figure 1: FERARI Architecture - The Big Picture

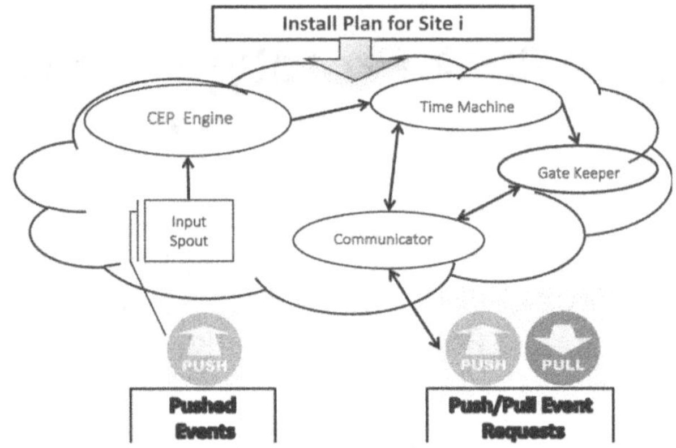

Figure 2: Intra-cloud FERARI Topology

teristic. FERARI constitutes, to our knowledge, the first complete, multi-cloud based, end-to-end CEP solution incorporating:

- a user-friendly, web-based query authoring tool,
- a powerful engine for efficient intra-cloud CEP, implemented on top of a state-of-the-art streaming cloud platform, namely Apache Storm [1],
- a CEP optimizer that orchestrates interactions among CEP Engines in different clouds, and chooses the best execution plan balancing requirements for both low latency and reduced inter-cloud communication,
- an analytics dashboard encompassing time series analysis, graph and map visualization tools to provide a holistic picture with respect to the detected CEs to final stakeholders.

As a proof-of-concept, we apply FERARI to enable mobile fraud detection using real rules and over real, anonymized, telecommunication data from T-Hrvatski Telekom network in Croatia.

2. FERARI ARCHITECTURE

The overall architecture of FERARI is illustrated is Figure 1, while Figure 2 and Figure 4 present intra-cloud processing modules in detail. Below, we present the main components of FERARI, along with our contributions.

CE Query Authoring Tool: In FERARI queries are formed using a web-based graphical user interface as shown in Figure 3. Our event query modeling approach is inspired by the CEP concepts discussed in [8, 9]. The query elements included in FERARI 's authoring tool involve [8, 9]:

- Event types - the events that are expected to be received as input or to be generated as CEs. An event type definition includes the event name and a list of its attributes.
- Producers - event sources and the way the CEP Engine gets events from them.
- Consumers - event consumers and the way they get derived events from the CEP Engine.
- Event Processing Agents (EPAs) - patterns of incoming events with specific context (see below) that detect situations and generate derived events.
- Temporal contexts - time windows in which EPAs are active.
- Segmentation contexts - semantic groupings of events.
- Composite contexts - synthesis of different contexts.
- Complex Event Definitions - Definition of the above concepts for CEs that are produced by EPAs.

An Event Processing Network (EPN), a conceptual query model describing the event processing flow execution, is then created. An EPN comprises a collection of EPAs, event producers and consumers. The network describes the flow of events originating at event producers and flowing through various event processing agents to eventually reach event consumers. The created query (EPN) is automatically transformed into a JSON file and is forwarded to FERARI's CEP optimizer upon query submission. It can easily be observed that directly coding a proper JSON file tailoring the above concepts to the desired query is a painful task. Therefore, our web-based authoring tool facilitates and speeds up this process. Query formulation using the authoring tool is oblivious to the details of the underlying multi-cloud setup. Users pose queries in a way that abstracts the details of the network of sites running cloud deployments. The EPN produced by the authoring tool may contain annotations, which are hints provided to the query optimizer, such as the optimization metric (i.e., minimize inter-site communication (default metric), maximum detection latency, etc).

FERARI Query Optimizer & Inter-cloud CEP: In our multi-cloud, distributed setup, different sites may observe only a subset of the event types that participate in the posed query. Therefore, the EPN received by the FERARI optimizer must be broken down into pieces involving different portions of the query. These parts of the EPN should be installed in, potentially overlapping, subsets of sites where relevant event types arrive. Furthermore, in order to enable the detection of CE pattern matches that encompass information across various sites, primitive or complex events need to be exchanged among the sites. For each EPA of the EPN that should be installed in a subset of sites, a sole site must be picked as the special one, responsible for synthesizing event information from other sites in the same subset to determine matches of event patterns.

In this context, our optimization approach uses the push/pull paradigm discussed in [6], but significantly extends these concepts by allowing the potential for EPAs to be installed at different clouds and by loosening the restricting assumption of having all sites in the network observe exactly the same event types. The main optimization goal is to produce Pareto optimal plans with respect to communication and latency. An optimal plan appropriately balances reduced communication, achieved by postponing push/pull activity regarding higher frequency events participating in a CE pattern until the occurrence of lower frequency ones, and event detection latency due to these postponed transmissions.

As shown in the middle top of Figure 1, the optimizer initially produces a set of logical plans. During logical plan generation, query rewriting procedures are applied on the posed query and subsets of sites where portions of the posed query need to be installed

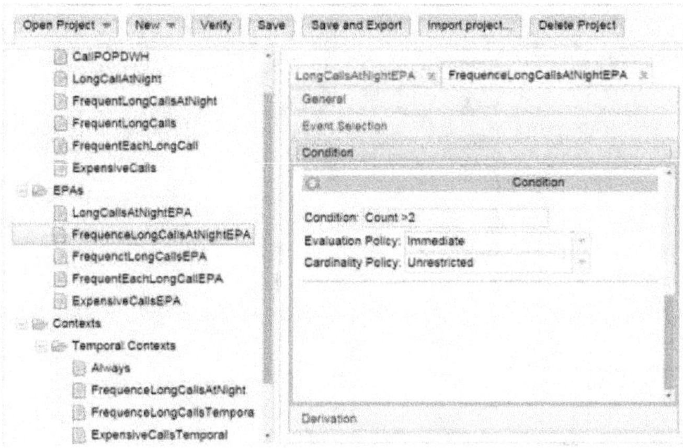

Figure 3: FERARI 's Authoring Tool

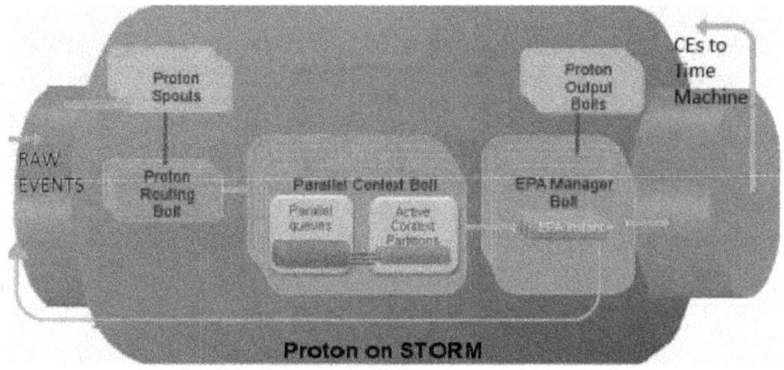

Figure 4: Intra-cloud FERARI - The CEP Engine

are determined. Furthermore, topological orderings of event types are created to later represent all possible sequences of push/pull activity during pattern matching checks. Based on the gathered statistics, physical plans are generated which include the best, in terms of Pareto optimality, EPA placement choice and the best order by which event tuples will be pulled from sites for each query portion and site subset. As soon as our optimizer comes up with the best possible plan, respective information is disseminated and properly transformed portions of the EPN are installed in each site running respective cloud platform deployments. To our knowledge, the FERARI optimizer is the only one incorporating the above advanced features for efficient plans in inter-cloud CEP processes.

FERARI Intra-cloud CEP: FERARI 's intra-cloud processing is built on top of a state-of-the-art streaming cloud platform, namely Apache Storm [1]. In other words, each site is assumed to run a Storm installation on which FERARI intra-cloud topology is created. A site's Storm topology, shown in Figure 2, is comprised of the following components [7]:

- Input Spout: A Storm spout where streaming tuples arrive or pushed events from other sites are fed into the CEP Engine.
- CEP Engine: Receives the input events from the Input Spout and having processed them according to the locally installed EPAs, emits derived events towards the Time Machine component. Details of our CEP Engine follow shortly.
- Time Machine: A Storm Bolt that buffers derived events from the CEP Engine.
- Gatekeeper: A Storm Bolt responsible for advanced calculations and distributed CE resolution procedures.
- Communicator: A Storm Bolt responsible for the push/pull based communication to/from sites in the same subsets, according to the parts of the query plan that are processed.

The CEP Engine module of our prototype, namely ProtonOnStorm [3], was built by IBM Research - Haifa within the scope of the FERARI project [2] and is an open source CEP Engine that extends the IBM Proactive Technology Online (Proton) standalone platform [3]. ProtonOnStorm's architecture is distributed across a number of Storm bolts (see Fig. 4) which allows for different degrees of parallelization in different modules. In that, ProtonOnStorm is a more elastic intra-cloud processing solution maximizing the potential for efficient intra-cloud CEP. Upon the reception of an incoming event, multiple independent parallel instances of the routing bolt of ProtonOnStorm, determine the metadata that should be assigned to the received event, the EPA name and the context name, which are added to the event tuple. ProtonOnStorm uses the STORM field grouping option on the metadata routing fields - the agent name and the context name- to route the information to the context processing bolt (see Fig. 4). After queuing the event instance in order to solve issues of out of order reception and parallelize processing of the same instance where possible by different EPAs, the event tuple is processed by the context service and the relevant context partition id is added to it. At this point, ProtonOnStorm uses the field grouping on context partition and agent name fields to route the event to specific instances of the relevant EPA, this way performing data segmentation. If a CE is detected that needs to be transmitted to a remote cloud, it will be routed to the Time Machine component (Fig. 2) and it will be pushed to the site responsible for synthesizing events from other sites in the same subset upon request, according to the inter-cloud execution plan.

FERARI Dashboard: The web-based dashboard of our prototype is generic enough to produce a wide variety of reports and analytic results that are useful from an application viewpoint, irrespectively of the actual details of the CEs, context or EPAs. It simply needs to be defined as an event consumer using a RESTful API [3]. FERARI Analytics come both in numerical, tabular format and graphical representations, while map visualization combines aggregate event statistics with their spatial reference, i.e., regarding the site of the multi-cloud platform where interesting situations occur.

3. DEMO SPECIFICATIONS

For the purposes of the demonstration, we will use a real, anonymized, dataset of call data coming from HT's network. HT data include around 2 TB of Call Detail Records (CDR), 600 GB of Postpaid usage and more than 1.5 TB of Prepaid CDR. In a simulated multi-cloud deployment, each site will be fed with a distinct local stream that comprises a set of calls recorded by a group of HT's telecommunication antennas, where groups are non-overlapping i.e., they share no antennas. During the demo, users will be able to interact with all the components of FERARI architecture in a real use case scenario involving mobile fraud detection.

CE Query Formation: we target at enabling both quick exploratory interaction with FERARI, as well as provide the potential for allowing users dig further into our prototype's querying and CEP capabilities. To achieve that, we use real (properly masked to comply with company policies) fraud detection rules from HT to a priori build a set of EPAs. In the pre-built scenario (see Fig. 3) users will be able to express their queries by combining the already available EPAs, defining event producers and consumers and visualizing the created EPN in FERARI 's authoring tool. Event patterns expressing masked HT's rules for mobile fraud detection involve:

- *LongCallAtNight:* Report long calls (defined as longer than X minutes) to premium locations during night hours (limited by a pair of timestamps).

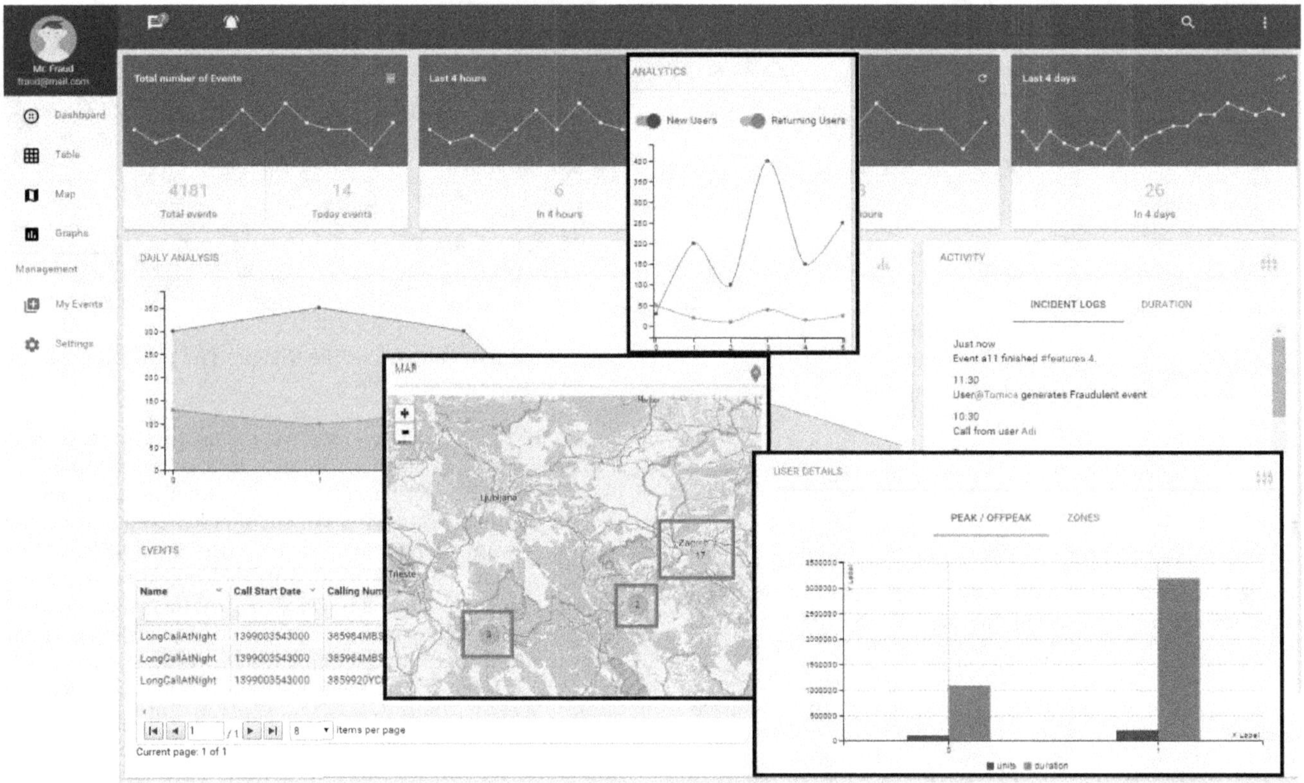

Figure 5: Screenshots of FERARI Dashboard

- *FrequentLongCallsAtNight:* Raise alarm upon the occurrence of at least Y calls made to premium locations during night hours, lasting longer than X minutes per calling number.
- *FrequentLongCalls:* Notify when at least Z calls made to a premium location sum up to at least X minutes duration in a day.
- *FrequentEachLongCall:* Notify when at least Z long, at least X minutes each, calls are made to a premium location in a day.
- *ExpensiveCall:* Every X minutes provide notifications in case calls dialed to premium locations sum up to more than a predefined cost per calling number.

Using the pre-built EPAs as a guide, users will also be able via the authoring tool to build their own, fraud detection related, queries modifying existing or define from scratch CEs, Contexts (temporal, segmentation or composite), EPAs and finalize their queries by graphically exploring the EPN that will be submitted to FERARI.

Assessing Inter- and Intra-cloud Internals: In order to fully assess the details of FERARI's deployment and the function of individual components beyond the application's viewpoint, interested users will be able to have access to logging information presented in a user-friendly way, which includes:

- FERARI optimizer's steps in choosing the best query plan as well as logical (including query rewriting in terms of the produced JSON file), physical plans and corresponding execution costs of other alternatives,
- real-time logs of inter-cloud push/pull communication according to the plan that has been prescribed by FERARI 's optimizer,
- real-time logs of intra-cloud activity via ProtonOnStorm's routing and EPA Manager bolts (Fig. 4).

CE Analytics: Real-time CE notifications will be provided via FERARI 's analytics platform. Nonetheless, the functionality of our prototype's dashboard includes much more than mere notifications of fraud event reports with detailed feature descriptions. Users will be able to access reports of numerical and graphical results about detected mobile fraud CEs as shown in Figure 5. More precisely, aggregate statistics of suspicious calls and user records will be provided at different temporal granularities in an online fashion (Fig 5). Furthermore, map visualization tools will account for the spatial dimension of the analysis, regarding the position of HT 's telecommunication antennas where fraud incidents occur or sets of antennas where suspicious users span as they commute.

4. REFERENCES

[1] Apache Storm project homepage. http://storm.apache.org/.

[2] Flexible event pRocessing for big dAta aRchItectures. the FERARI project. http://www.ferari-project.eu/.

[3] IBM Proactive Technology Online on STORM. https://github.com/ishkin/Proton.

[4] Storm-Esper. https://github.com/tomdz/storm-esper.

[5] J. Agrawal, Y. Diao, D. Gyllstrom, and N. Immerman. Efficient pattern matching over event streams. In *SIGMOD*, June 2008.

[6] M. Akdere, U. Çetintemel, and N. Tatbul. Plan-based complex event detection across distributed sources. In *PVLDB*, 2008.

[7] S. Bothe, V. Manikaki, A. Deligiannakis, and M. Mock. Towards flexible event processing in distributed data streams. In *Proc. of the Workshops of the EDBT/ICDT*, 2015.

[8] O. Etzion and P. Niblett. *Event Processing in Action*. Manning Publications Company, 2010.

[9] C. Moxey, M. Edwards, O. Etzion, M. Ibrahim, S. Iyer, H. Lalanne, M. Monze, M. Peters, Y. Rabinovich, G. Sharon, and K. Stewart. *A Conceptual Model for Event Processing Systems*. IBM Redguide publication, 2010.

Constance: An Intelligent Data Lake System

Rihan Hai
RWTH Aachen University
Aachen, Germany
hai@dbis.rwth-aachen.de

Sandra Geisler
RWTH Aachen University
Aachen, Germany
geisler@dbis.rwth-aachen.de

Christoph Quix
Fraunhofer FIT
St. Augustin, Germany
christoph.quix@fit.fraunhofer.de

ABSTRACT

As the challenge of our time, Big Data still has many research hassles, especially the variety of data. The high diversity of data sources often results in information silos, a collection of non-integrated data management systems with heterogeneous schemas, query languages, and APIs. *Data Lake* systems have been proposed as a solution to this problem, by providing a schema-less repository for raw data with a common access interface. However, just dumping all data into a data lake without any metadata management, would only lead to a 'data swamp'. To avoid this, we propose *Constance*[1], a Data Lake system with sophisticated metadata management over raw data extracted from heterogeneous data sources. Constance discovers, extracts, and summarizes the structural metadata from the data sources, and annotates data and metadata with semantic information to avoid ambiguities. With embedded query rewriting engines supporting structured data and semi-structured data, Constance provides users a unified interface for query processing and data exploration. During the demo, we will walk through each functional component of Constance. Constance will be applied to two real-life use cases in order to show attendees the importance and usefulness of our generic and extensible data lake system.

1. INTRODUCTION

Data lakes address the daunting challenge of Big Data: 'how to make an easy use of highly diverse data and provide knowledge?' Large amounts of data are available, but often the data is separated in information silos without or only with loose inter-connections. However, valuable insights are often only available upon the combination and integrated analysis of information in these silos. To meet this gap, *Data Lakes* (DLs) have been conceptualized as big data repositories which store raw data and provide functionality for on-demand integration with the help of metadata descriptions [1, 3, 9, 10]. DLs ingest raw data in its original format from heterogeneous data sources, fulfill their role as storage repositories, and allow users to query and explore them. As schema information, mappings, and other constraints are not defined explicitly or required initially for a DL, it is important to extract as much metadata as possible from the data sources during the ingestion phase. Metadata management is crucial for data reasoning, query processing, and data quality management. Without any metadata, the DL is hardly usable as the structure and semantics of the data are not known, which turns a Data Lake quickly into a 'data swamp'.

However, current proposals for DL systems lack details about the required metadata management features and methods for efficient integrated query processing, which hampers repeatable implementations. Furthermore, the DL systems put into practice now are often very application-specific solutions which have been crafted for the specific requirements of an organization. These specific solutions are based on generic software frameworks such as Hadoop and still require a lot of (wo)man power for adaptation and customization of the generic frameworks.

Therefore, in this paper we propose Constance as a first step towards a practical DL solution which can be used as the basis in several DL projects, because it provides a flexible, extensible framework for the data management problems within DL systems. In particular, Constance is a DL system which manages structural and semantic metadata, provides means to enrich the metadata with schema matching and schema summarization techniques, and offers a unified interface for query processing. To emphasize the importance of metadata in the maturation of a DL, in this demo we primarily focus on structured and semi-structured data accompanied by either explicit or implicit metadata. In contrast to other DL proposals [10, 2], Constance focuses more on data ingestion, metadata management, and query answering, but also provides basic security and provenance mechanisms. Before we go into more details of our proposal, we want to clarify two key points regarding the current DL debate [4]. First, a DL is more than just a storage repository on top of a Hadoop file system. Of course, Hadoop is good at managing the huge amount of data in a DL with its distributed and scalable file system; it also provides metadata management functions, but it does not provide all the metadata functionalities which are required for a DL. For

[1]Our system is named after Lake Constance, the largest lake in Germany (known as Bodensee in German). Shared by Switzerland, Germany and Austria, Lake Constance is an area with no borders, which is similar to our design philosophy for an open Data Lake.

SIGMOD '16, June 26–July 1, 2016, San Francisco, CA, USA.

DOI: http://dx.doi.org/10.1145/2882903.2899389

example, the DL architecture presented in [2] shows that a DL system is a complex eco-system of several components and that Hadoop provides only a part of the required functionality. Second, compared to data warehouse systems with a relational view of data, DLs need to handle more heterogeneous data sources including semi-structured and unstructured sources. Since the NoSQL movement introduced several new data models in the recent years, a DL system has to provide a flexible storage system which can handle these different data models efficiently in an integrated way.

Putting these ideas together, we propose in this paper *Constance*, which features the following concepts: (i) Constance provides a **metadata management system** which extracts explicit and implicit metadata from the imported data. (ii) Composed of semantic annotations, advanced modeling, and record linkage, Constance contributes **semantic metadata matching and enrichment**, therefore it improves the quality of data stored in the DL. (iii) For an easy use by both data experts and naive users, Constance supports a **formal structured query language** as well as simple **keyword queries**. Keyword queries are translated into a formal query by using a query formulation function. (iv) Constance provides an **integrated user interface**, which allows users to check the visualized impact of every schema management step, to query the data, and to monitor the **data quality** of the DL by user-defined quality metrics.

The rest of the paper is organized as follows: In Sec. 2, we give a system overview of Constance and its essential components. We present a brief walkthrough of a Constance workflow, combined with two real-life use cases in Sec. 3.

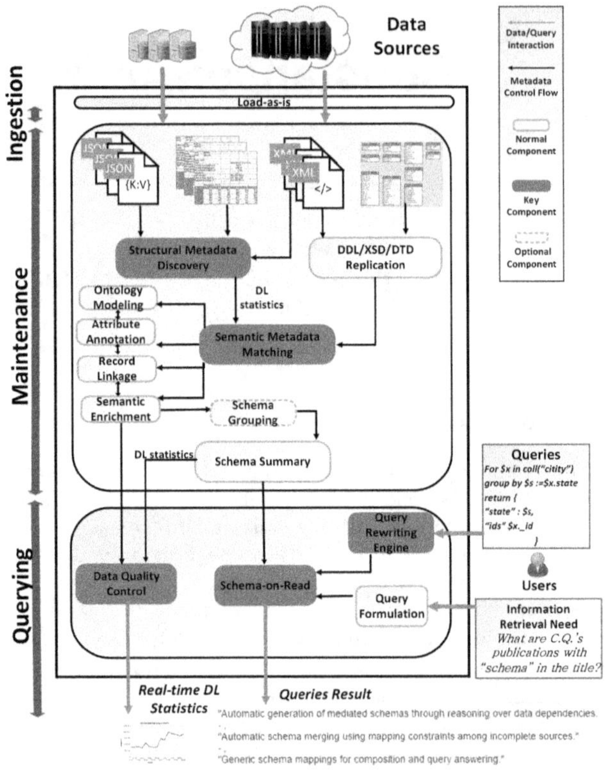

Figure 1: Constance System Overview

2. CONSTANCE OVERVIEW

Fig. 1 depicts the architecture of Constance, as well as its key components. Constance can be roughly divided into three functional layers: ingestion, maintenance, and querying. While the ingestion layer implements the interface between the data sources and Constance, the major human-machine interaction is enabled by the querying layer. In the middle are the components constituting the maintenance layer, which dynamically and incrementally extract and summarize the current metadata of the DL, and provide a uniform query interface.

2.1 Ingestion

The ingestion layer is responsible for importing data from heterogeneous sources into the DL system. Different from the traditional ETL process, Constance loads data in its original format without forcing expensive transformation or integration tasks. As shown in Fig. 1, regardless of the format of the source data (e.g., JSON, spreadsheets, XML or relational data), data is loaded and stored in Constance in its original format. Notably, for further metadata processing in the maintenance layer of the system, Constance extracts metadata from the data sources into a unified metamodel.

2.2 Maintenance

The components in this layer mainly contribute to Constance's metadata management functions. The backend of the maintenance layer provides the basic functions for data storage and efficient querying. Metadata is crucial for future querying. The first step of metadata management is extracting as much metadata as possible from the sources. For relational tables and some XML documents, explicit schema definitions (in SQL, XSD, or DTD) can be directly obtained from the source and integrated into the metamodel. The tricky part is semi-structured data (such as XML without XSD, JSON, or partially structured Excel or CSV files) which contains implicit schemata. Therefore, the component *Structural Metadata Discovery (SMD)* takes over the responsibility of discovering implicit metadata (e.g., entity types, relationship types, and constraints) from semi-structured data in a two-fold manner: (1) The SMD checks whether metadata is encoded inside the raw data file, in the filename, or the directories of the file system. An example is the self-describing spreadsheet in Fig. 1, where SMD extracts its schema (headers in columns and rows). (2) For semi-structured documents such as JSON or XML, SMD discovers "Has-a"-relationships and stores them in a path-like structure. Notably, as JSON records may not have sufficient relationships among documents, during run time Constance calculates frequencies of the entities which appeared in join conditions of user queries, and marks them as potential foreign key relationships and builds indexes on the corresponding attributes to improve the performance. This is the part we refer as 'incrementally maturing of a DL' as the metadata will be enriched in a pay-as-you-go fashion while users are using the system.

Another key component of Constance is the *Semantic Metadata Matching (SMM)* component, which consists of ontology modeling, attribute annotation, record linkage, and semantic enrichment. The output of this component can be observed in Fig. 2.b, which is a graph representation of the extracted metadata elements and their relationships. Semantic annotations about the meaning of certain metadata items can be added to the schema elements, and therefore, they can be exploited for querying. Using the semantic an-

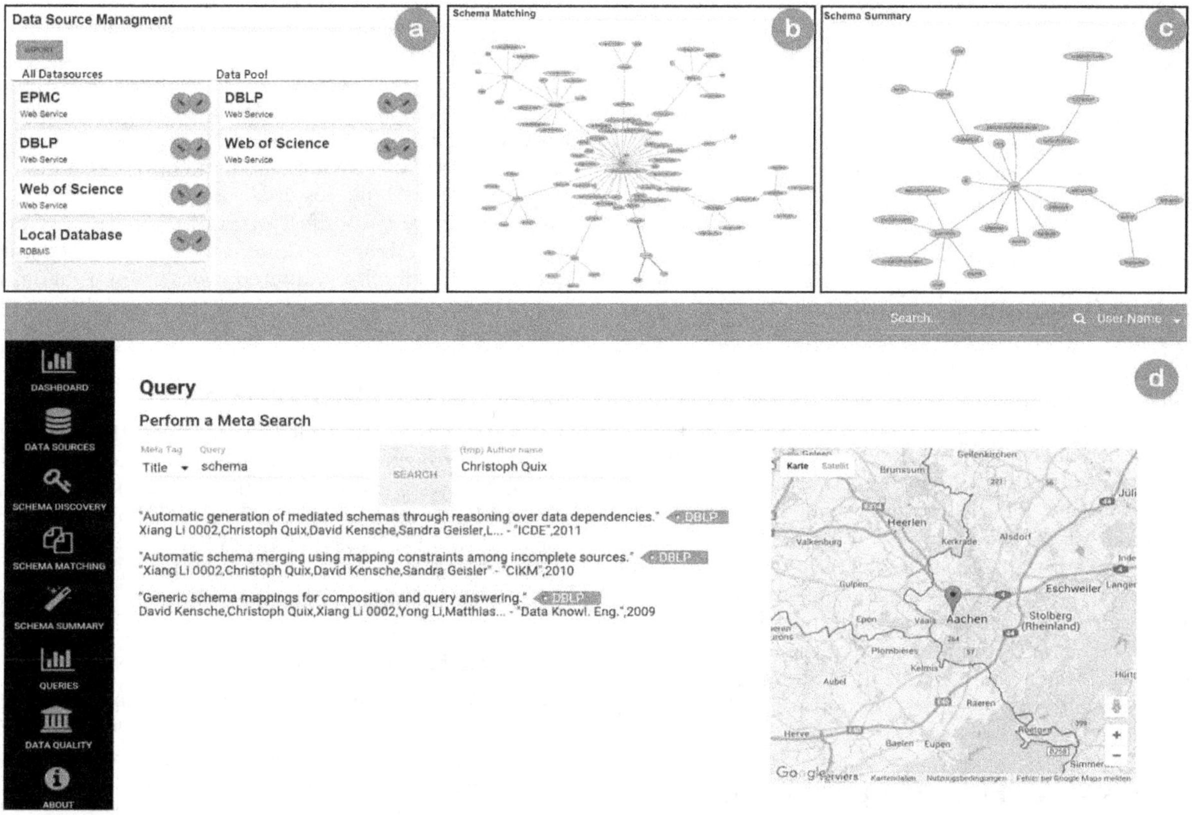

Figure 2: Major components of Constance user interface: (a) Data source management (b) Schema matching (c) Schema summary (d) Query Answering

notations, we perform a first shallow integration of the data as metadata elements with different labels (e.g., attributes 'dob' and 'DateOfBirth') can be linked if they are annotated with the same semantic element (e.g., 'foaf:birthday'). The user can then use the semantic term 'foaf:birthday' in a query; the query rewriting module of Constance rewrites the user query into a union of queries which use the schema elements from the sources. Semantic annotations are done with standardized domain-specific models or ontologies which provide a common, shared understanding for the domain.

As an optional step, *Schema Grouping* clusters the schemas and picks up the core of each cluster as its presentation. The necessity of grouping depends on the schema similarity calculated over the imported data sources. If the schemas are very distinctive or almost the same, schema grouping would not contribute much to the overall system improvement.

Based on the enriched and potentially grouped metadata, the *Schema Summary* component extracts a further compact structure of the currently managed schemata, which we refer to as *skeleton* [11], sketched in Fig. 2.c. Summarizing schemata is a method to filter the most important elements or relationships, respectively, within a complex schema. Elements and relationships used more frequently in instance data or queries are considered as more important.

2.3 Query Answering

All the above functions, eventually, serve for information retrieval, in the form of query answering. In common cases, users either input concrete queries in a particular query language, or they have an information retrieval need which supports the user in formulating a query starting from some keywords. Constance distributes the user need to the *Query Rewriting Engine* or *Query Formulation*, respectively. Constance currently implements a query language which is a subset of JSONiq (a query language for JSON-based systems which is similar to XQuery [5]) as this enables easy querying of semi-structured data in JSON. The semantic annotations mentioned above can be seen as simple global-as-view mappings, which means that a single user query might be rewritten into a union of queries over the sources in which the semantic terms are replaced with the original schema elements of the sources. We currently work on a more complex mapping and query language which is based on our previous work on second-order tuple generating dependencies for mappings between generic data models [8].

If the user prefers to start with keywords, the *Query Formulation* component supports users in creating formal queries that express the intended information requirement. The user will see only a simple natural language representation of the query. The entered values will be matched with metadata and data values. Depending on the matched items, the system will propose further related (meta)data items (e.g., if 'publication' has been recognized, the system might propose 'author' and 'title'). The goal is to have in the end a formal query expressed in our JSONiq-subset.

2.4 Data Quality Control

In addition to the advanced metadata management and querying functions, Constance provides also means for data quality management. The data quality model is based on our previous works for data warehouses [7] and data streams [6]. We define quality factors based on metrics which perform data quality measurements by executing queries (which return some aggregate value) or by invoking some specific functions (implemented as Java methods). The definition of quality metrics is application-specific and can be defined by the user for his/her DL instance. The values are presented in a summarized form in a data quality dashboard.

2.5 Extensibility and Flexibility

So far we have introduced the generic components of Constance. To apply it in real life projects, scenario-specific functionalities have to be integrated. Mostly notably in the raw data ingestion, the extractor components have to be adapted to some concrete data sources. We have developed an extensible and flexible framework for the ingestion phase in which the existing generic extractors can be adapted to new data source formats (e.g., by providing patterns for the data to be extracted from CSV or Excel files) or new extractors can be easily added using a plug-in mechanism.

On the querying side, the users might expect special ways of data visualization or data interaction of the query results. For example, as indicated in Fig. 2.d, fields referring to a geographic location (in this case, the author's affiliation) may be visualized in a map.

3. DEMONSTRATION WALKTHROUGH

Constance is a web-based application which follows Google's material design[2] for better user experience. Users can click on the button menu in the left, and switch among the key components, as shown in Fig. 2. To showcase the usefulness of Constance, we will demonstrate a typical workflow of Constance, derived from the medical engineering project *mi-Mappa*[3] which requires the integration of patent and publication data. Another use case is the integration of semi-structured data in the life science domain, which is currently being developed in the HUMIT project[4].

The demonstration will include the following scenarios:

Data Source Import Our demonstration begins with the data import. As shown in Fig. 2.a, users can import local files, databases, or remote data via web services. The imported data stores are shown in the left area as *All Data Sources* in the DL. Considering a running DL may contain a huge amount of data sources, while not all contribute to a certain analytical operation, users can select a subset of the data sources for the following step. This can be achieved by dragging and dropping the data sources from the left area to the right area 'data pool'. The selection can be also supported by queries over the data source metadata.

Schema Management Workflow By entering the Schema Discovery page, the schema discovery process is automatically performed and the extracted schema is visualized for the user. In the following Schema Matching step, Constance detects and equivalently maps entity types while users can see highlighted nodes, as shown in Fig. 2.b. Semantically equivalent entities, which come from different data sources and may vary by naming or structure, are replaced with one node and marked as yellow. After the execution of Schema Summary, a smaller set of nodes, representing a more concise set of the overall schema, is depicted in Fig. 2.c.

Querying In this section we will demonstrate how Constance retrieves information from its internal storage repository which has been filled by the data sources. As stated above, Constance provides two main options for querying, either using formal queries or keyword queries. The demo will show how these two different types of queries are processed in the system, how the queries are rewritten, and which queries will be finally evaluated over the internal data repository. Furthermore, we will show the possibilities to explore and browse the data as well as the metadata repository.

[2]https://www.google.com/design/spec/material-design/

[3]http://dbis.rwth-aachen.de/cms/projects/mi-mappa

[4]http://www.humit.de

4. ACKNOWLEDGMENTS

This work has been funded partially by the Klaus-Tschira-Stiftung (project mi-Mappa, http://www.dbis.rwth-aachen.de/mi-Mappa/, project no. 00.263.2015) and by the German Federal Ministry of Education and Research (BMBF) (project HUMIT, http://humit.de/, grant no. 01IS14007A) We would like to thank Patrick Schlesiona and David Kensche for their support and comments.

5. REFERENCES

[1] H. Alrehamy and C. Walker. Personal data lake with data gravity pull. In *Proc. IEEE BDCloud*, 2015.

[2] E. Boci and S. Thistlethwaite. A novel big data architecture in support of ads-b data analytic. In *Proc. ICNS*, 2015.

[3] M. Chessell, F. Scheepers, N. Nguyen, R. van Kessel, and R. van der Starre. Governing and managing big data for analytics and decision makers. www.redbooks.ibm.com/redpapers/pdfs/redp5120.pdf, 2014.

[4] J. Dixon. Data lakes revisited. https://jamesdixon.wordpress.com/2014/09/25/data-lakes-revisited/, September 2014.

[5] D. Florescu and G. Fourny. Jsoniq: The history of a query language. *IEEE Internet Computing*, 17(5):86–90, 2013.

[6] S. Geisler, S. Weber, and C. Quix. An ontology-based data quality framework for data stream applications. In *Proc. ICIQ*, 2011.

[7] M. Jarke, M. A. Jeusfeld, C. Quix, and P. Vassiliadis. Architecture and Quality in Data Warehouses: An Extended Repository Approach. *Information Systems*, 24(3):229–253, 1999.

[8] D. Kensche, C. Quix, X. Li, Y. Li, and M. Jarke. Generic schema mappings for composition and query answering. *Data Knowl. Eng.*, 2009.

[9] C. Quix, R. Hai, and I. Vatov. Gemms: A generic and extensible metadata management system for data lakes. In *CAISE FORUM*, 2016.

[10] I. Terrizzano, P. M. Schwarz, M. Roth, and J. E. Colino. Data wrangling: The challenging yourney from the wild to the lake. In *Proc. CIDR*, 2015.

[11] L. Wang, S. Zhang, J. Shi, L. Jiao, O. Hassanzadeh, J. Zou, and C. Wangz. Schema management for document stores. *PVLDB*, 8(9):922–933, 2015.

Exploring Privacy-Accuracy Tradeoffs using DPComp

Michael Hay*, Ashwin Machanavajjhala**, Gerome Miklau†, Yan Chen**, Dan Zhang†, George Bissias†

* Colgate University
Department of Computer Science
mhay@colgate.edu

** Duke University
Department of Computer Science
{ashwin,yanchen}@cs.duke.edu

† UMass Amherst
College of Computing and Information Sciences
{miklau,dzhang,gbiss}@cs.umass.edu

ABSTRACT

The emergence of differential privacy as a primary standard for privacy protection has led to the development, by the research community, of hundreds of algorithms for various data analysis tasks. Yet deployment of these techniques has been slowed by the complexity of algorithms and an incomplete understanding of the cost to accuracy implied by the adoption of differential privacy.

In this demonstration we present DPCOMP, a publicly-accessible web-based system, designed to support a broad community of users, including data analysts, privacy researchers, and data owners. Users can use DPCOMP to assess the accuracy of state-of-the-art privacy algorithms and interactively explore algorithm output in order to understand, both quantitatively and qualitatively, the error introduced by the algorithms. In addition, users can contribute new algorithms and new (non-sensitive) datasets. DPCOMP automatically incorporates user contributions into an evolving benchmark based on a rigorous evaluation methodology articulated by Hay et al. [4].

1. INTRODUCTION

Privacy concerns are a major obstacle to deriving the scientific insights now possible from increasing data collection and powerful new data analysis techniques. The goal of privacy technology is to permit data mining and analysis tasks to be safely carried out over a collection of sensitive records donated by individuals.

Differential privacy [2] has emerged as an important standard for protection of individuals' sensitive information. Differential privacy offers the compelling guarantee that the output the analyst receives is statistically indistinguishable (governed by a privacy parameter ϵ) from the output the analyst would have received if any one individual had opted out of the collection. Smaller ϵ implies less disclosure about any single individual.

General acceptance of differential privacy by researchers has led to a steady stream of research in the database community, as well as the data mining, theory, machine learning, programming languages, security, and statistics communities. For any given task (e.g., answering range queries or learning decision trees) there are a number of specialized differentially private algorithms for completing that task. They typically achieve privacy by adding noise. While smaller ϵ values generally result in more noise added, algorithms differ in how noise is added and its magnitude even for the same privacy level ϵ.

Despite maturing research efforts, the adoption of differential privacy by practitioners in industry, academia, or government agencies has so far been rare, with only a few examples to mention [3,6]. A major obstacle to practical adoption is that the "cost" of privacy, in terms of degraded accuracy, is difficult for practitioners to assess. This is because, for a given task:

- The research community has failed to clearly identify the state-of-the-art in terms of accuracy for a given privacy level (determined by ϵ), and
- Practitioners, who may not be experts in privacy (or even computer science), have no tools to try out state-of-the-art algorithms and understand the impact of noise on their data.

Assessing the accuracy of differentially private algorithms is complex for the following reasons. Theoretical bounds on error, when known, explain only worst case behavior and hide critical constant factors. Despite hundreds of papers on differentially private algorithms, there has been little attention paid to empirical evaluation methodology and no benchmarks have been established. Further, the accuracy of emerging algorithms has complex dependencies on the input data: an algorithm which offers state-of-the-art error rates on one dataset may substantially underperform a simple baseline technique on another dataset. Researchers have unfortunately reused a small collection of datasets for evaluation and it is therefore difficult to extrapolate performance from published results.

All of these factors mean a practitioner cannot easily identify the best algorithm for a particular task and dataset. She would have to survey literature from many different fields, and either extrapolate from multiple theoretical and empirical analyses, or implement all the algorithms and compare their performance. Moreover, there is a paucity of tools for helping practitioners understand the effect of noise on accuracy. For instance, the emphasis of published empirical evaluations often tends to be comparative (does algorithm $\mathbf{A}_{new}$ have lower error than algorithm $\mathbf{A}_{old}$?) rather than absolute (is the error in the output of $\mathbf{A}_{new}$ acceptable?); the latter being more important to the practitioner.

To address these important challenges we are building DPCOMP, a public web-based forum to support the principled evaluation of private data analysis and to encourage dissemination of related code and data. DPCOMP provides the infrastructure to rigorously evaluate a wide range of differentially private algorithms, for a wide range of tasks, and on a wide range of datasets. Users can view the results of careful, thorough empirical evaluation by interacting with dynamic visualizations. But most importantly, users can contribute datasets, task definitions, and algorithms to DPCOMP, triggering automatic evaluations and comparisons of empirical performance.

SIGMOD'16, June 26-July 01, 2016, San Francisco, CA, USA

DOI: http://dx.doi.org/10.1145/2882903.2899387

For the researcher, DPCOMP provides an evolving benchmark of datasets for various tasks, and a thorough comparison of existing techniques, illuminating performance gaps of existing techniques and open problems. For the practitioner, DPCOMP provides an easy way to explore the performance of state-of-the-art algorithms as well as tools to quantitatively and qualitatively assess the absolute error of algorithms.

Our proposed demonstration will present Version 1.0 of DPCOMP, which is focused on a limited but expressive class of data analysis tasks, in which sets of one- and two-dimensional counting queries are answered privately. Accurately supporting these tasks is essential for exploratory analysis on private data (e.g., summary statistics, marginal distributions), as well as building more complex privacy algorithms with these tasks as subroutines (e.g., density estimation, machine learning, log-linear modeling). DPCOMP utilizes a benchmark and a principled evaluation methodology that will be presented during the coinciding research track at SIGMOD 2016 [4]. This evaluation methodology has already revealed weaknesses and inconsistencies in the empirical evaluations of published algorithms. By adopting this methodology, DPCOMP provides a sound, reproducible view of the empirical performance of current privacy algorithms.

At the demonstration, an attendee can play the role of researcher or practitioner. As researcher, they can interactively visualize the complex relationships between privacy level ϵ, data characteristics, and accuracy on a large set of benchmark datasets. As practitioner, they may upload a new dataset and use DPCOMP to interactively explore privacy-accuracy tradeoffs and assess the usefulness of the private outputs on the chosen dataset.

2. BACKGROUND

Informally, an algorithm $\mathcal{A}$ is differentially private if its behavior is insensitive to small changes in the input database. Formally, $\mathcal{A}$ satisfies ϵ-differential privacy [2] if for all databases D and D' such that D' contains one additional record, and for any subset of outputs $S \subseteq Range(\mathcal{A})$, $Pr(\mathcal{A}(D) \in S) \leq e^{\epsilon} \times Pr(\mathcal{A}(D') \in S)$. An example of a differentially private algorithm is given below.

We use the term *task* to denote a certain analysis on the database. In DPCOMP Version 1.0, we focus on the following task: given a fixed set of attributes and a *workload* of multi-dimensional range-count queries over those attributes, compute answers to each of the queries. The number of attributes (aka dimensions) is small: we focus on the 1- and 2D cases. An algorithm for this task returns a vector of noisy answers. The main performance metric for these algorithms is error, which is measured as the L_2 distance between the true answers and the noisy answers. Notice that error is a random variable. In addition to reporting mean error, it is also important to estimate variance since an analyst only observes one output.

We give an example algorithm for the task of answering the workload of all range-count queries over a single attribute A. The PARTITION algorithm first constructs an equi-width histogram with each bucket containing k contiguous values from the domain of A and then computes the count of each bucket. To achieve privacy, it invokes the Laplace mechanism [2], which adds independent Laplace noise with scale $1/\epsilon$ to each bucket count. This noisy histogram can then be used to answer any range query in the workload by summing the appropriate noisy bucket counts. (Buckets on the range boundary only contribute a fraction of their count proportional to the number of values included in the range). To invoke this algorithm, one must specify, *a priori*, a value for k. Setting k to be large reduces the error due to noise (fewer noisy counts are summed) but coarsens the granularity of the histogram.

The core idea of PARTITION, grouping together sets of values, is one key idea underlying many of the algorithms proposed for this task (cf. [4]). However, the grouping strategies proposed are much more sophisticated than PARTITION and include adaptively selecting the partition based on the data (which is non-trivial and requires careful analysis to prove differential privacy).

The above example illustrates one of the aforementioned challenges with empirical evaluation: algorithm performance can be *data dependent*. In the case of PARTITION, the error decreases the more uniform the data distribution is within each bucket. This problem is further exacerbated by more sophisticated algorithms that respond adaptively to the data, making it hard to theoretically analyze performance.

In a companion paper [4], we identify 4 factors that influence the performance of differentially private algorithms: (i) ϵ, the privacy parameter, (ii) *scale*, the number of records in the database, (iii) *domain size*, the number of possible values each tuple in the database can take, and (iv) *shape*, or the empirical distribution of the data. The data generation procedure in [4] allows us to vary each of these parameters independently and thereby measure its effect on algorithm performance. In addition, we show that almost all private algorithms satisfy a property called *scale-epsilon exchangeability*, wherein for a fixed domain size and shape, increasing scale has an identical effect on error as increasing ϵ. Thus, two parameters, scale and ϵ, can be collapsed into a single one (the scale-ϵ product) which captures the strength of the "signal" from the data that competes with the "noise" injected by the algorithm.

3. THE DPCOMP SYSTEM

3.1 Vision and motivation

DPCOMP is a publicly-accessible web-based system designed to support a broad community of users: *data analysts* who are novice users of privacy mechanisms, *researchers* who develop new privacy algorithms, and *data owners* who manage sensitive data.

For a given data analysis task, DPCOMP automatically performs simulations of privacy algorithms running on real and synthetic datasets and presents a comprehensive analysis of algorithm performance. Users can assess accuracy of the output through various metrics, by comparison with informative baselines, and by visualizing the private output. Users can determine the best algorithm for their task and data, as well as the settings of privacy parameters that can be supported while retaining acceptable accuracy.

Users can also contribute to DPCOMP by uploading datasets, new algorithms, or new task descriptions. Doing so automatically triggers new simulations, the results of which are stored and made available to all users.

The main goals of DPCOMP are: (1) to improve the accessibility and transparency of privacy algorithms by allowing easy browsing, performance comparison, and download; (2) to provide a reproducible methodology for evaluating the performance of privacy algorithms (based on the principles and benchmark from [4]); and (3) to help guide future research by highlighting cases for which existing privacy algorithms do not provide acceptable accuracy.

DPCOMP was inspired by the MLCOMP website which was designed for "objectively comparing machine learning programs across various datasets" [5]. MLCOMP is useful because performance comparisons for algorithm selection for classical machine learning tasks has become complex for non-experts as well as algorithm designers. DPCOMP addresses a similar set of issues, but differs substantially from MLCOMP because our emphasis is solely on algorithms that offer formal privacy guarantees.

Note that it is *not* a goal of DPCOMP to host sensitive data sets. Instead, DPCOMP will provide a public environment in which to explore and evaluate private algorithms on *public* data. To support users with sensitive data, we instead make the entire infrastructure (task descriptions, algorithm implementations, and execution framework) available for local execution, so that users can easily reproduce results on their own sensitive datasets. (This will initially be done through an open-source code base; in future versions, a virtual machine image with code and data will be available.) Even though local execution is available, the public DPCOMP interface allows users to efficiently identify the algorithms likely to be best for their task.

3.2 Features of DPComp 1.0

Our proposed demonstration focuses on version 1.0 of DPCOMP which includes the following main capabilities and user-interactions:

Algorithm exploration DPCOMP will allow users to review the range of algorithms available for a task and to assess their performance as a function of both privacy parameters (i.e. epsilon), data parameters (e.g. scale, domain size, etc.) and algorithm parameters (i.e. internal divisions of the privacy budget, number of rounds of iterative algorithms, etc.). Results are provided in the form of dynamic, interactive plots showing not just comparisons of error rates for competing algorithms but also comparisons with natural baselines such as sampling error that help the user understand whether measured error rates are acceptable in practice.

Dataset contribution Data owners who wish to find an algorithm that works well on their data can submit (non-sensitive) sample data sets. Users can also design and submit synthetic datasets that either challenge existing algorithms or serve to distinguish competing algorithms. New datasets will automatically be tested on all applicable tasks and algorithms. As an important consequence, DPCOMP will thereby increase the variety of input data used for evaluation of algorithms.

Workload contribution Algorithms may perform better or worse on different workloads. Users can contribute workloads that distinguish the performance of competing algorithms. **Algorithm contribution** Privacy researchers can submit new algorithms to DPCOMP which will be automatically evaluated and compared against existing algorithms and baselines. Submitted programs will be required to conform to a standard API but may be implemented in any programming language. **Algorithm and benchmark download** Algorithms contributed to DPCOMP will be in the public domain and the DPCOMP website will support easy download of all implemented algorithms, along with datasets, workload definitions, and evaluation infrastructure (following [4]). This allows data owners to easily evaluate algorithms on their own sensitive data using their own systems.

3.3 System design of DPComp 1.0

DPCOMP is an extensible execution framework implemented in Python that schedules simulated trials on a large compute cluster with a total of 13,000 cores. Results are collected and stored in a cloud-based database system that underlies the web-based plotting and visualization components.

As an example, for the one-dimensional case, and before any user contributions, DPCOMP contains 14 published algorithms which are evaluated with respect to 2 workloads on 18 different source datasets across 4 domain sizes and 6 settings of scale/epsilon resulting in a total of $14 * 2 * 18 * 4 * 6 = 12,096$ experimental configurations. (The 2-D case has a similar number of configurations.) Because the privacy algorithms are randomized, to calculate high-confidence error measures, we run at least 25 trials of each configuration, resulting in approximately 300,000 independent trials. The computation time for each trial varies considerably across algorithms and algorithm parameters (between a few seconds and a few minutes, with an average of 22 seconds per trial) and also depends on the domain size and workload size. This amounts to 76 days of single-core computation time, which can be completed in under 2 hours using 1,000 cores.

In order to provide interactivity, DPCOMP performs selective, incremental evaluation, prioritizing simulations based on user requests and incrementally presenting partial results (e.g. from fewer than 25 trials) as they arrive. Specific examples are provided in the next section.

3.4 Features of DPComp 2.0 (Future work)

The future development of DPCOMP will include additional features not part of the proposed demonstration. First, we plan to expand our system to support additional private analysis tasks such as graph analysis, machine learning, and continual observation. Second, we will develop empirical methods for testing claimed privacy guarantees. DPCOMP Version 1.0 currently assumes that privacy claims are correct, which is acceptable since its current focus is on published algorithms for which privacy proofs are provided. Verifying that an arbitrary program is differentially private is not feasible, but we plan to develop black-box, empirical testing methods that can catch overt violations and errors. Third, we hope that DPCOMP may enable privacy contests which might, for example, challenge algorithm designers to achieve an accuracy target for a specific task and reward the winning algorithm. In the spirit of Kaggle [1], DPCOMP will be available to host competitions initiated by outside users.[1]

4. DEMONSTRATION EXPERIENCE

A demo attendee can choose one of two user experiences. They can play the role of a *researcher* who is interested in understanding the state of the art in differential privacy. As a researcher, the attendee can use DPCOMP to explore algorithm performance across a range of conditions and observe key relationships. Alternatively, the attendee can play the role of a *practitioner* who wants to perform a differentially private analysis on a particular dataset. They can use DPCOMP to find the algorithms that offer the best privacy-accuracy tradeoff for that dataset and also examine, both quantitatively and qualitatively, how the noise added for privacy impacts the usefulness of the analysis output.

Researcher experience The attendee will be directed to the DPCOMP "dashboard," which presents a summary of the complete set of empirical evaluations that have been computed by DPCOMP to date. The sheer volume of results presents an information visualization challenge. Our demo responds to this challenge in two ways. First, the visualizations are informed by our companion benchmark study [4] which relates algorithm performance to three properties of the input: scale-epsilon product, domain size, and data shape. The benchmark's data generator allows us to vary each of these properties independently, making it possible to measure and visualize the effect of each in isolation. The dashboard will have a separate figure for each property with menus and sliders to control the range of values for each. Second, the dashboard is interactive, allowing the user to do things such as focus on particular algorithms of interest, adjust the values of parameters, and link an algorithm's performance *across* multiple figures to see interaction effects between properties.

After the attendee has had a chance to become oriented to the

[1]Privacy competitions are a new phenomenon: e.g., a company called Hypios hosted a data anonymization contest (personal communication, 2013).

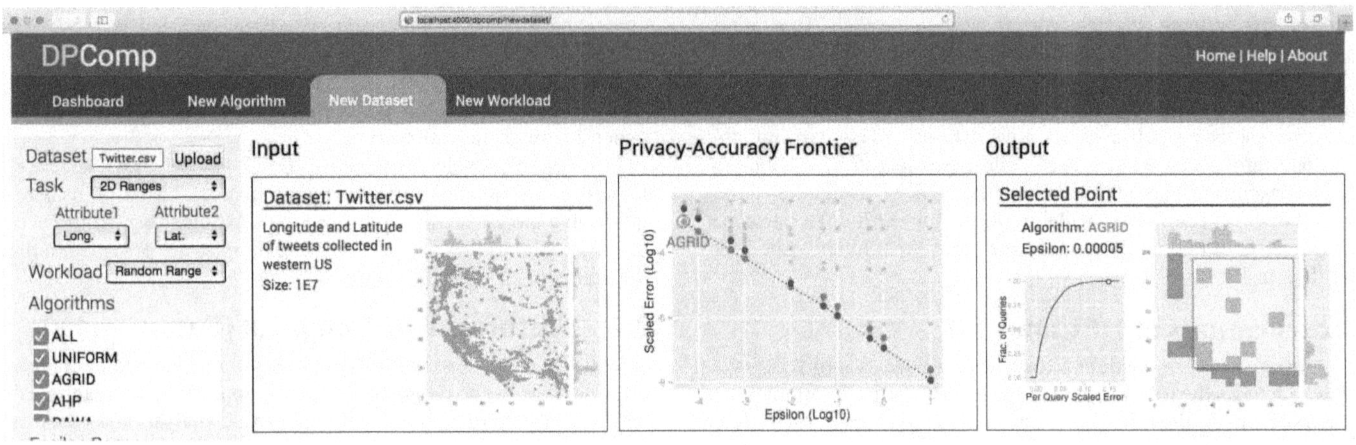

Figure 1: A screen shot of DPCOMP computing the privacy-accuracy frontier on a dataset uploaded by the user (details in Section 4).

dashboard, a demonstrator will guide the attendee to explore some interesting relationships. For example: (1) they will find that the performance "frontier" is diverse: no single algorithm dominates across all settings, but some algorithms do dominate for specific ranges of the input; (2) algorithm performance has a strong dependence on both epsilon and the scale of the data and that these two factors are exchangeable: if a given epsilon value is desired, utility can be improved by collecting more data; (3) in some cases, sophisticated algorithms do not outperform simple baselines.

Practitioner experience Given the realities of the SIGMOD demo setting, we do not expect attendees to come with a dataset in hand. Instead, to facilitate interaction, we will make available a set of datasets (in .csv format) that the attendee can upload to the system. (They could alternatively browse the web to find a dataset that is of interest and of suitable size and format for upload.)

Once the dataset is uploaded and the attendee has selected a task, the system will automatically evaluate all available algorithms on this new dataset for the given task. The system will compute and visualize the privacy-accuracy "frontier"—namely, for each setting of the privacy parameter ϵ, it will identify the set of algorithms that achieve highest accuracy on this dataset. (Using our execution framework, initial results can be obtained in under 30 seconds and additional trials are incrementally retrieved.) DPCOMP allows the attendee to explore points along the privacy-accuracy frontier, to get a qualitative sense of what the best algorithm can achieve at the given level of privacy.

An example screen of DPCOMP is shown in Fig. 1. Here, the user has uploaded `Twitter.csv`—a dataset of about 10^7 tweets collected using the Twitter API—and selected the task of answering 2D range queries over attributes corresponding to latitude and longitude. The user can specify other aspects of the evaluation, such as the workload, the set of algorithms, the range of ϵ, etc. DPCOMP computes and displays the privacy-accuracy frontier. Each point in this figure reports the error (y-axis) of a particular algorithm for the ϵ shown on the x-axis. Points associated with a particular algorithm are colored if the algorithm has the highest accuracy for at least one value of ϵ.

The user can click on a point along the frontier. In Fig. 1, the user has clicked on the point corresponding to the algorithm that achieves the lowest error at the smallest value of ϵ, which is the algorithm AGRID [7]. For the clicked point, a more detailed analysis is shown. First, it shows a visualization of the data released by the algorithm which can be compared against the input. (The visualization is a 2D histogram over the domain, which can be derived from the output of the algorithm. A point is drawn if the count of the corresponding histogram bucket is above a threshold.) In addition, the error distribution across queries in the workload is displayed. The attendee can click on a point in this inset figure and see the corresponding workload query. In this way, the attendee can get an intuition for which kinds of queries are answered most accurately.

The detailed view for the selected point shows AGRID at $\epsilon = 0.00005$. As is apparent from the visualization, AGRID dynamically partitions the data into a grid and summarizes the data at the grid level. Moreover, the visualization gives the practitioner qualitative feedback about the absolute error of an algorithm. A practitioner may decide $\epsilon = 0.00005$ is impractical from an accuracy standpoint, since even the best algorithm only preserves coarse statistics about the data. In addition, the highlighted range query suggests that some of the highest error queries are those that only partially overlap with dense regions.

In summary, DPCOMP will allow attendees to see that the state-of-the-art in differential privacy contains a diverse collection of algorithms, which can in some settings significantly outperform simple methods like the Laplace and exponential mechanisms. However, their performance depends in complex ways on 4 key characteristics of the input. DPCOMP helps the user identify the best algorithms for a given task and dataset. Further, it provides the user with not only a quantitative evaluation of error but also, through visualizations, a qualitative feel for how the noise added for privacy affects the analysis tasks.

Acknowledgments We appreciate the comments of the anonymous reviewers. This material is based upon work supported by the National Science Foundation under Grant Nos. 1012748, 1253327, 1408982, 1443014, 1409125, and 1409143.

5. REFERENCES

[1] Kaggle. www.kaggle.com, 2015.

[2] C. Dwork, F. M. K. Nissim, and A. Smith. Calibrating noise to sensitivity in private data analysis. In *TCC*, pages 265–284, 2006.

[3] Ú. Erlingsson, V. Pihur, and A. Korolova. Rappor: Randomized aggregatable privacy-preserving ordinal response. In *CCS*, 2014.

[4] M. Hay, A. Machanavajjhala, G. Miklau, Y. Chen, and D. Zhang. Principled evaluation of differentially private algorithms using DPBench. SIGMOD Conference, 2016.

[5] P. Liang and J. Abernathy. MLcomp. www.mlcomp.org, 2013.

[6] A. Machanavajjhala, D. Kifer, J. Abowd, J. Gehrke, and L. Vilhuber. Privacy: Theory meets practice on the map. In *ICDE*, 2008.

[7] W. Qardaji, W. Yang, and N. Li. Differentially private grids for geospatial data. In *ICDE*, 2013.

Interactive Search and Exploration of Waveform Data with Searchlight

Alexander Kalinin
Brown University
akalinin@cs.brown.edu

Ugur Cetintemel
Brown University
ugur@cs.brown.edu

Stan Zdonik
Brown University
sbz@cs.brown.edu

ABSTRACT

Searchlight [9] enables search and exploration of large, multi-dimensional data sets interactively. It allows users to explore by specifying rich constraints for the "objects" they are interested in identifying. Constraints can express a variety of properties, including a shape of the object (e.g., a waveform interval of length 10-100ms), its aggregate properties (e.g., the average amplitude of the signal over the interval is greater than 10), and similarity to another object (e.g., the distance between the interval's waveform and the query waveform is less than 5). Searchlight allows users to specify an arbitrary number of such constraints, with mixing different types of constraints in the same query.

Searchlight enhances the query execution engine of an array DBMS (currently SciDB) with the ability to perform sophisticated search using the power of Constraint Programming (CP). This allows an existing CP solver from Or-Tools (an open-source suite of operations research tools from Google) to directly access data inside the DBMS without the need to extract and transform it.

This demo will illustrate the rich search and exploration capabilities of Searchlight, and its innovative technical features, by using the real-world MIMIC II data set, which contains waveform data for multi-parameter recordings of ICU patients, such as ABP (Arterial Blood Pressure) and ECG (electrocardiogram). Users will be able to search for interesting waveform intervals by specifying aggregate properties of the corresponding signals. In addition, they will be able to search for intervals similar to already found, where similarity is defined as a distance between the signal sequences.

Categories and Subject Descriptors

H.2.4 [**Database Management**]: Systems—*query processing*

Keywords

Data exploration; Query processing; Constraint Programming; Array Databases; Interactive Results

SIGMOD'16, June 26-July 01, 2016, San Francisco, CA, USA
© 2016 ACM. ISBN 978-1-4503-3531-7/16/06...$15.00
DOI: http://dx.doi.org/10.1145/2882903.2899404

1. INTRODUCTION

In the era of big data, when the variety and volume of available data increases at a considerable pace, the need for ad-hoc analysis is becoming more and more evident. On the one hand, users often want to discover new knowledge hidden in the data, like interesting patterns or dependencies between attributes. For this, machine learning techniques have been used with great success in the recent years. On the other hand, users often have some idea about *what* they want to find, but have no idea *where* to look. The latter is clearly a *search* problem. An example might include a scientist who has a hypothesis and is looking for evidence to support it. In such a case she might want to find objects with specific properties, where the nature of the object and the properties depend on the area of research. While it might be possible to explore every possible object in the data and filter the required ones, this would certainly be infeasible in most common cases due to large search space size. The problem quickly gets out of hand when the user wants to try different properties or combinations of them, which is common for ad-hoc exploration. Moreover, the user might be more interested in getting *some* results quickly instead of *all* results after a considerable amount of time. Such interactivity is often unavailable in traditional DBMSs or might be hard to achieve for search queries due to their poor support in such systems.

Exploration via search queries. To give a more concrete example, let us assume a scientist working with the MIMIC database [2]. The data contains recordings of physiological signals from a number of ICU patients, including signal waveforms and accompanying metadata. The user might want to find waveform intervals satisfying some interesting properties, such as the average amplitude of the signal over the interval. Additionally, she might want to find intervals with waveforms similar to some pattern (possibly found via past queries). In this scenario the following types of queries are possible:

- *Basic search queries* search for an interval satisfying specified properties. For example, "find a time interval for patient 1 of length 10ms to 100ms where the average amplitude of the ABP (Arterial Blood Pressure) signal is below 20".
- *Complex search queries* involve multiple intervals and constraints tying them together. For example, the user might add this constraint to the previous query: "the difference between the maximum amplitude of the signal over the current interval and its left and right 100ms neighborhoods is greater than 10".

- *Similarity queries* involve searching for waveform intervals similar to the specified query waveform. It might have been obtained as a result of one of the previous search queries or found by looking at the data. In this case the user might ask for "waveform intervals with the distance from the query interval less than 20", where the distance is defined as Euclidean distance between the corresponding sequences of signal values.

In all these cases, the user should start getting results as quickly as possible. The user might not even be interested in the final result at all. She might quickly switch between queries, interrupt, refine and restart them.

Existing solutions. Traditional DBMSs have very limited support for exploration via search queries. For relational DBMSs there is a framework called Semantic Windows (SW) [8], which supports interactive execution of a limited subset of "Basic search queries" from the example above. Users can search for multidimensional regions satisfying common aggregate properties. SW does not provide any support for more complex constraints. When it comes to array DBMSs, the only option seems to use built-in analytical query operators or write complex scripts, combining several queries. For instance, SciDB has the `window()` operator, which computes aggregates for every possible sub-array of the specified size. This might allow users to find interesting sub-arrays. However, the operator processes sub-arrays sequentially, in the specific order, without any interactivity. Moreover, since it has to compute every possible sub-array, it is infeasible for large search spaces. For more complex search problems, containing multiple constraints, users would have to write several queries and perform some form of a "join" or concatenation between intermediate results.

Searchlight. *Searchlight* [9] enables users to express a variety of search problems written as constraint programs. Users can use traditional constraints and search heuristics available in CP systems. Additionally, they can define their own, which is essential for bringing search to different exploration domains. Under the hood, Searchlight efficiently connects the solver with the DBMS query execution engine, allowing the former to enjoy the benefits of such features as data buffering, access to DBMS query operators and efficient management of data. The search can run in the distributed environment, where multiple solvers work in parallel on different parts of the search space. Searchlight makes efficient use of the data distribution and networking capabilities present in distributed DBMSs.

Searchlight is implemented as a fusion between Google's Or-Tools [1], a suite of operations research tools, which contains a powerful CP solver, and SciDB [5, 3], an array DBMS. We demonstrate the practicality of our approach using the real-world MIMIC II [2] data set, allowing users to search for interesting waveform intervals defined by constraints, including complex neighborhood constraints and similarity.

2. SEARCHLIGHT OVERVIEW

In this section we briefly describe Searchlight, including its query model and system architecture. More thorough discussion of these topics, as well as the experimental evaluation, can be found in the Searchlight research paper [9].

2.1 Search Queries

Since Searchlight uses a CP solver to perform search, it takes queries in form of constraint programs. A query de-

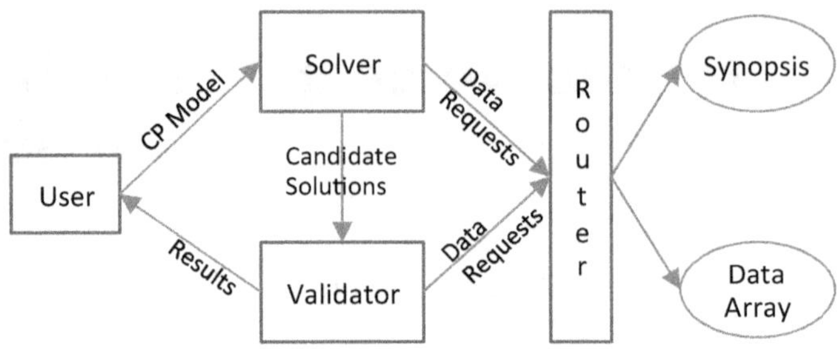

Figure 1: Two-level search query processing: the solver on the first level, the validator on the second level. The router routes data accesses to the synopsis or the array, depending on the context.

fines a number of *decision variables* and *constraints* over the variables. Revisiting the example from the Introduction, the user might study ABP signal recordings for a particular patient. If she wants to find an interval of length from 10ms to 100ms, she can specify two variables: $x \in [0, 3600000]$, denoting the start of the interval and $lx \in [10, 100]$, denoting the interval's length. The variables have *domains* associated with them, which define the search space. In this case we assume the patient's recording starts at time 0 and lasts for 1 hour. Then the user can specify the following constraints: $x + lx - 1 <= 3600000$, which keeps the entire interval inside the 1 hour recording, and $avg(x, lx, ABP) < 20$, which specifies the restriction for the average amplitude of the signal. The $avg()$ function is a Searchlight extension, used to access the ABP data in the DBMS.

2.2 Searchlight Query Processing

An overview of the Searchlight query processing is presented in Figure 1. The gist of our approach is two-level processing. At the first level, *Solvers* receive a constraint program, create the search model (i.e., decision variables and constraints) and perform *speculative* search on a *synopsis* instead of real data. The synopsis is a condensed representation of the data, containing information needed for verifying constraints, e.g., aggregate properties of different areas of the data, bitmaps for sparse areas, etc. As the result, the Solvers produce *candidate solutions* (*candidates*). Searchlight guarantees the absence of false negatives, however, the candidates might contain false positives. At the second level, *Validators* check the candidates over the original data, producing the real solutions. One of the most important features of the speculative search is the ability to prune parts of the data without reading the data itself, which significantly improves query completion times. The two-level processing is completely transparent for both Solvers and users, and is taken care by the *Router* component, which directs the API data calls to the appropriate data. Solvers and Validators do not require any additional knowledge about the query beyond general knowledge contained in the model.

2.3 Distributed Searchlight

Searchlight supports distributed query processing on both levels of the execution. At the first level, the query's search space is distributed among multiple Solvers on the same and different nodes, exploring both multi-core and multi-node parallelism. At the second level, Validators are assigned to different data partitions and are responsible for validating candidates referencing the corresponding data. Validators can redistribute data, if needed. There can be an arbitrary number of Solvers and Validators, since the two levels of query processing are completely disjoint, and no Solver-Validator collocation is needed.

When Searchlight distributes a query across multiple machines in a cluster, there might be a natural bias on each level. Some Solvers might produce more candidates than others, if they hit a "hot-spot" part of the search space. In the same way, since different Validators are responsible for different data partitions, some of them might have to validate more candidates than others. Searchlight supports both static and dynamic balancing on both levels. During the static phase the search space and the data is distributed between Solvers and Validators before the query begins. During the query execution Searchlight redistributes work between idle and busy Solvers to take care of the search bias. If some of the Validators become struggling with candidates and fall behind, Searchlight starts more CPU threads to help with the load. If increasing the number of threads does not help, Searchlight redistributes candidate solutions to idle Validators with possible data redistribution as the last resort. Since, both Solvers and Validators might use multiple threads Searchlight mediates resource utilization depending on the state of the query execution.

3. MIMIC DATA AND QUERIES

Searchlight uses SciDB [3, 5], an open-source array DBMS, as its underlying DBMS. An array is a collection of elements indexed by *dimensions*. Each element has its own tuple of *attributes*. We store the MIMIC II waveform data in a two-dimensional array indexed by the patient id and signal time. Each time point corresponds to 0.008s, since the measurements are taken with the frequency of 125Hz. The attributes represent signals stored for a particular patient at the particular time point. We store ABP (Arterial Blood Pressure), PAP (Pulmonary Artery Pressure)and ECG (electrocardiogram) for the purpose of the demonstration, although other signals can be easily added. If some signal was not recorded at the specified time for the specified patient, the value is considered *null* and is ignored during computations. Note, the original MIMIC data set might contain several recordings for a single patient. We have concatenated such recordings into a single timeline for each patient. To be able to find the original MIMIC record, we have an external index pointing to the original records.

Since Searchlight queries are constraint programs, let us discuss briefly how these programs might be composed for the MIMIC data. We use the following decision variables:

- id specifies the id of the patient. It can be set to the required value to explore a particular patient. Alternatively, it can be set to a suitable range.
- x defines the beginning of the resulting interval. x can be assigned a particular range, restricting the search to that range for each patient specified in the domain of id.
- lx denotes possible length of a resulting time interval. It can be set to a constant value to search for fixed length intervals, e.g., $lx = 125$ would look for 1 second intervals. Alternatively, it can be set to a range of suitable values, e.g., $lx \in [125, 1250]$ for 1-10 second intervals.

In addition, the user can use the following UDFs to access signal data in the DBMS:

- $avg/sum/count/min/max(id, x, lx, sig)$ compute the corresponding aggregate values for the specified signal and interval, e.g., $avg(id, x, lx, ABP)$ computes the average amplitude of the ABP signal over the specified interval.
- $sq\_dist(id, x, lx, sig, seq)$, which computes the squared Euclidean distance between the *sig*nal values of the interval (id, x, lx) and the sequence seq. This function allows users to search for waveforms similar to the specified by constraining the distance to be less than some value.

To express more complex queries involving multiple intervals, more variables can be defined. For example, if there is need to compare the ABP signal over the interval with the average signal over its 1 second left neighborhood, this can be achieved via $avg(id, ln, 125, ABP)$, where $ln = x - 125$ is a new variable. Instead the constant 125 another variable can be defined, similar to lx, to express a range of neighborhood lengths. One of the main ideas behind Searchlight is generality: Searchlight does not restrict users in terms of variables and constraints.

Section 2.2 mentioned the synopsis structure used at the first level of query processing. For MIMIC we use two types of synopsis: aggregate and DFT (Discrete Fourier Transform). The first one is an aggregate grid, where the waveform of each patient is divided into disjoint sub-intervals (cells), and each cells stores aggregate information (min/max, sum, count). This synopsis is based on Multi-Resolution Aggregate (MRA) structures [10]. The DFT synopsis is used for the *sq_dist* function and stores MBRs (Minimum Bounding Rectangles) for DFT traces of waveforms. This synopsis is based on the ST-index for subsequence matching [6].

4. DEMONSTRATION

We demonstrate all three types of queries described in the Introduction. The users do not directly write constraint programs, but use the GUI presented in Figure 2. The GUI converts the user-specified parameters into the constraint program and sends it to Searchlight. The GUI allows users to perform search queries over waveforms of all the patients loaded in the system. The user can specify the required length of the interval (including a range), the signal (e.g., ABP), the range of average values for the amplitude and the search range to restrict the timeline. She is also able to specify the *resolution* of the search, which restricts intervals to be aligned with the specified value. This might significantly improve query times, since increasing the resolution parameter results in decreasing the search space.

Searchlight is an interactive system. It starts outputting results in a table as soon as it finds them. The user can click on any results to asynchronously request the corresponding waveform. At any point during the query execution the user can interrupt the query and issue a new one.

To demonstrate more complex constraints, the GUI also allows users to search for anomalies, defined as the difference in the maximum signal amplitudes between the intervals and its neighborhoods. The user is able to specify the lengths of the neighborhoods and the required minimum differences of the maximum amplitude values.

The GUI also supports similarity queries (not shown in the Figure). When the user explores a visualized waveform, she can highlight a portion of it and ask for intervals with similar waveforms by specifying the maximum allowed distance between the corresponding sequences of signal values.

To compare the performance of Searchlight with the native SciDB, the users are able to run the same search queries

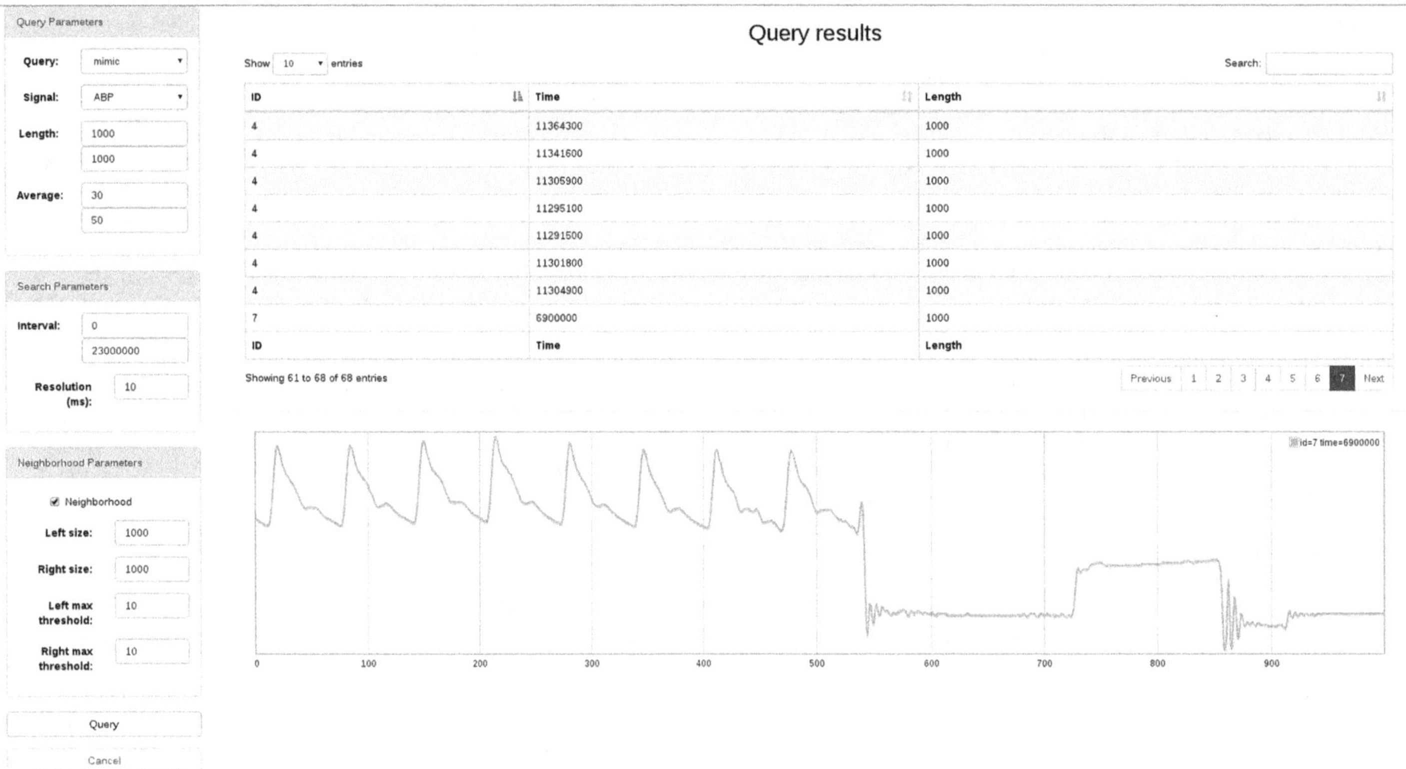

Figure 2: Searchlight GUI screenshot for exploring MIMIC.

on another screen by specifying parameters for predefined query scripts. The scripts access SciDB via its Python API and issue a series of AQL (Array Query Language) queries corresponding to the main search query.

5. DISCUSSION

There has been a growing interest in interactive query processing and data exploration, which resulted in a number of systems. Some systems, such as Tableau [4] or Dice [7], allow users to perform *navigation-like* data exploration with interactive speeds. Such exploration usually involves queries similar to SQL group-bys, joins, ranges, etc. In contrast, Searchlight performs *search* queries, expressed as a number of constraints for the result. We believe these systems can complement each other, where the user can use Searchlight to find interesting regions in the data, and then continue further with the navigational exploration.

Other systems, such as Rinse [11], allow users to execute specific search queries, such as sub-sequence matching. Rinse uses adaptive index building techniques, which significantly reduces index building times and makes the data quickly available for querying after the import. Searchlight can certainly benefit from similar techniques, for example by employing adaptive synopsis building. With respect to queries, however, Searchlight supports a richer set of constraints, going beyond sub-sequence matching.

6. ACKNOWLEDGEMENTS

This research was supported in part by the Intel Science and Technology Center for Big Data, NSF IIS-1111423, and NSF IIS-1526639.

7. REFERENCES

[1] Google or-tools. https://code.google.com/p/or-tools/.

[2] Multiparameter intelligent monitoring in intensive care (mimic ii). https://physionet.org/mimic2/.

[3] Scidb. http://www.scidb.org/.

[4] Tableau. http://www.tableau.com/.

[5] P. G. Brown. Overview of scidb: large scale array storage, processing and analysis. In *SIGMOD*, pages 963–968, 2010.

[6] C. Faloutsos, M. Ranganathan, and Y. Manolopoulos. Fast subsequence matching in time-series databases. In *SIGMOD*, pages 419–429, 1994.

[7] P. Jayachandran, K. Tunga, N. Kamat, and A. Nandi. Combining user interaction, speculative query execution and sampling in the dice system. *VLDB*, 7(13):1697–1700, 2014.

[8] A. Kalinin, U. Cetintemel, and S. Zdonik. Interactive data exploration using semantic windows. In *SIGMOD*, pages 505–516, 2014.

[9] A. Kalinin, U. Cetintemel, and S. Zdonik. Searchlight: Enabling integrated search and exploration over large multidimensional data. *VLDB*, 8(10):1094–1105, 2015.

[10] I. Lazaridis and S. Mehrotra. Progressive approximate aggregate queries with a multi-resolution tree structure. In *SIGMOD*, pages 401–412, 2001.

[11] K. Zoumpatianos, S. Idreos, and T. Palpanas. Rinse: Interactive data series exploration with ads+. *VLDB*, 8(12):1912–1915, 2015.

Ontology-Based Integration of Streaming and Static Relational Data with Optique

Evgeny Kharlamov[1] Sebastian Brandt[2] Ernesto Jimenez-Ruiz[1] Yannis Kotidis[3]
Steffen Lamparter[2] Theofilos Mailis[4] Christian Neuenstadt[5] Özguer Özçep[5] Christoph Pinkel[6]
Christoforos Svingos[4] Dmitriy Zheleznyakov[1] Ian Horrocks[1] Yannis Ioannidis[4] Ralf Möller[5]

[1] University of Oxford [2] Siemens CT [3] Athens University of Economics and Business
[4] University of Athens [5] University of Lübeck [6] fluid Operations AG

ABSTRACT

Real-time processing of data coming from multiple heterogeneous data streams and static databases is a typical task in many industrial scenarios such as diagnostics of large machines. A complex diagnostic task may require a collection of up to hundreds of queries over such data. Although many of these queries retrieve data of the same kind, such as temperature measurements, they access structurally different data sources. In this work we show how Semantic Technologies implemented in our system OPTIQUE can simplify such complex diagnostics by providing an abstraction layer—ontology—that integrates heterogeneous data. In a nutshell, OPTIQUE allows complex diagnostic tasks to be expressed with just a few high-level semantic queries. The system can then automatically enrich these queries, translate them into a collection with a large number of low-level data queries, and finally optimise and efficiently execute the collection in a heavily distributed environment. We will demo the benefits of OPTIQUE on a real world scenario from Siemens.

1. INTRODUCTION

Motivation. Real-time processing of streaming and static data is a typical task in many industrial scenarios such as diagnostics of large machines. This task is challenging since it often requires integration of data from multiple sources. For example *Siemens* runs service centres dedicated to diagnostics of thousands of power-generation appliances across the globe. One typical task for such centres is to detect in real-time potential faults caused by, e.g., an abnormal temperature and pressure increase. Such tasks require simultaneous processing of sequences of digitally encoded coherent signals produced and transmitted from thousands of power generating turbines, generators, and compressors installed in power plants, and of static data that includes the structure of relevant equipment, history of its exploitation and repairs, and even weather conditions. These data are scattered across a large number of heterogeneous data streams in addition to static DBs with hundreds of TBs of data.

Even for a single diagnostic task, such as checking if a given turbine might develop a fault, Siemens engineers have to analyse streams with temperature and other measurements from up to $2,000$ sensors installed in different parts of the turbine, analyse historical temperature data, compute temperature patterns, compare them to patterns in other turbines, compare weather conditions, etc. This requires to pose a collection of hundreds of queries, the majority of which are semantically the same (they ask about temperature), but syntactically different (they are over different schemata). Formulating and executing so many queries, and then assembling the computed answers, takes up to 80% of the overall diagnostic time [10].

Ontology-Based Integration Approach. In order to streamline the diagnostic process at Siemens, we propose a data integration approach based on Semantic Technologies. In this paper we will refer to our approach as *Ontology-Based Stream-Static Data Integration* (*OBSSDI*). It follows the classical data integration paradigm that requires the creation of a common 'global' schema that consolidates 'local' schemata of the integrated data sources, and mappings that define how the local and global schemata are related [8]. In *OBSSDI* the global schema is an *ontology*: a formal conceptualisation of the domain of interest that consists of a *vocabulary*, i.e., names of classes, attributes and binary relations, and *axioms* over the terms from the vocabulary that, e.g., assign attributes of classes, define relationships between classes, compose classes, class hierarchies, etc. The Siemens ontology that we developed [10] encodes generic specifications of appliances, characteristics of sensors, materials, processes, descriptions of diagnostic tasks, etc. *OBSSDI* mappings relate each ontological term to a set of queries over the underlying data. For example, the generic attribute *temperature-of-sensor* from the Siemens ontology is mapped to all specific data and procedures that return temperature readings from sensors in dozens of different turbines and DBs storing historical data, thus, all particularities and varieties of how the temperature of a sensor can be measured, represented, and stored are captured in these mappings.

In *OBSSDI* the integrated data can be accessed by posing queries over the ontology, i.e., *ontological queries*. These queries are *hybrid*: they refer to both streaming and static data. Evaluation of such queries in *OBSSDI* has three stages: *(i)* in the *enrichment* stage ontology axioms are used to expand the ontological query in order to access as much of relevant data as possible; *(ii)* in the *unfolding* stage the mappings are used to translate the enriched ontological query into (possibly many) queries over the data; and *(iii)* in the *execution* stage the unfolded queries are executed over the data.

The main benefit of *OBSSDI* is that the combination of ontologies and mappings allows to 'hide' the technical details of *how* the data is produced, represented, and stored in data sources, and to

SIGMOD'16, June 26-July 01, 2016, San Francisco, CA, USA

DOI: http://dx.doi.org/10.1145/2882903.2899385

show only *what* this data is about. This allows us to formulate the Siemens diagnostic task above using only one ontological query instead of a collection of hundreds data queries that today have to be written or configured by IT specialists. Note that this collection of queries does not disappear: the enrichment and unfolding stages of the evaluation by an *OBSSDI* system will automatically compute it from the the high-level ontological query. Another important benefit of *OBSSDI* is *modularity* and *compositionality* of its assets: each mapping relates one ontological term to the data, which allows the mappings to be constructed independently and on demand; and the same ontological term can be used in different queries, so defining mappings for even a few terms enables the evaluation of many different ontological queries.

OBSSDI extends existing semantic data integration solutions that either assume that data is in (static) relational DBs, e.g [3, 6], or streaming, e.g., [5, 17] but not of both kinds. *OBSSDI* also extends existing solutions for unified processing of streaming and static semantic data e.g. [7], since they assume that data is natively in the WC3 standardised RDF semantic data format while we assume the data to be relational and mapped to the semantic format.

Research Challenges. The benefits of *OBSSDI* come at a price. The main practical challenges for *OBSSDI* that are not addressed by existing Semantic Technologies include:

[C1] development of tools for semi-automatic support to construct high quality ontologies and mappings over relational and streaming data;

[C2] development of a query language over ontologies that combines streaming and static data, and allows for efficient enrichment and unfolding that preserves the semantics of ontological queries; and

[C3] development of a backend that can optimise large numbers of queries automatically generated via enrichment and unfolding, and efficiently execute them over distributed streaming and static data.

Construction of ontologies and mappings in *OBSSDI* is done independently and prior to query formulation and processing. Nevertheless, addressing C1 is practically important since such tools can dramatically speed up deployment and maintenance (e.g., adjustment to new query requirements) of *OBSSDI* systems. Addressing C2 is crucial since, to the best of our knowledge, no dedicated query language for hybrid semantic queries has the required properties. Addressing C3 is vital to ensure that *OBSSDI* queries are executable in reasonable time. Note that C3 is not trivial since even in the context where the data is only static and not distributed, query execution without dedicated optimisation techniques performs poorly since the queries that are automatically computed after enrichment and unfolding can be very inefficient, e.g., they may contain many redundant joins and unions [6].

Our Contributions. Besides proposing *OBSSDI*, we addressed the challenges C1-C3 and implemented our solutions in the OPTIQUE [11] system that has been successfully applied in several industrial contexts [12, 10, 2]. In order to address C1, we developed BOOTOX [9, 4], a system for "bootstrapping" *OBSSDI* assets by extracting, ontologies and mappings from static and streaming relational schema and data. In order to address C2, we introduced STARQL [19], a query language that allows for semantic queries over both streaming and static data. STARQL queries are expressed over OWL 2 QL ontologies, which are mapped to the underlying data via global-as-view mappings [8]. STARQL queries admit polynomial-time enrichment and can be unfolded into $\text{SQL}^{(+)}$ queries, i.e. SQL queries enhanced with operators for stream handling. Finally, in order to address C3, we introduced EXASTREAM [15, 18], a highly optimised engine capable of handling complex hybrid queries in real time. EXASTREAM supports parallel query execution and its Infrastructure as a Service architecture enables us to elastically scale the system to support user-demand in complex diagnostic scenarios. EXASTREAM incorporates several query optimisations such as adaptive main-memory indexing of stream measurements and native User Defined Functions that permit a user to express complex operators in a concise way. See Section 2 for more details on OPTIQUE solutions for C1-C3 challenges.

Demo Overview. Attendees will see how OPTIQUE simplifies diagnostics for Siemens: they will see how to set and monitor continuous diagnostic tasks as STARQL queries, how EXASTREAM can handle more than a thousand complex diagnostic tasks, and how to deploy OPTIQUE over Siemens data using BOOTOX. See Section 3 for more details on demo scenarios.

2. OPTIQUE SYSTEM

OPTIQUE is an integrated system that consist of multiple components to support *OBSSDI* end-to-end [11, 13]. For IT specialists OPTIQUE offers support for the whole lifecycle of ontologies and mappings: semi-automatic bootstrapping from relational data sources, importing of existing ontologies, semi-automatic quality verification and optimisation, cataloging, manual definition and editing of mappings. For end-users OPTIQUE offers tools for query formulation support, query cataloging, answer monitoring, as well as integration with GIS systems. Query evaluation is done via OPTIQUE's query enrichment, unfolding, and execution backends that allow to execute up to thousands complex ontological queries in highly distributed environments. In this section we give some details of three OPTIQUE components that address the C1-C3 challenges above.

Deployment Support. Our BOOTOX component extracts W3C standardised OWL 2 ontologies and R2RML mappings from relational streaming and static data. Consider, e.g., a class *Turbine*; a mapping for it is an expression: $\mathit{Turbine}(f(\vec{x})) \leftarrow \exists \vec{y}\, \mathtt{SQL}(\vec{x}, \vec{y})$, that can be seen as a view definition, where $\mathtt{SQL}(\vec{x}, \vec{y})$ is an SQL query, $\vec{x}$ are its output variables, $\vec{y}$ are its variables that are projected out and f is a function that converts tuples returned by `SQL` into identifiers of objects populating the class *Turbine*. Intuitively, mapping bootstrapping of BOOTOX boils down to discovery of 'meaningful' queries $\exists \vec{y}\, \mathtt{SQL}(\vec{x}, \vec{y})$ over the input data sources that would correspond to either a given element of the ontological vocabulary, e.g., the class *Turbine* or attribute *temperature-of-sensor*, or to a new ontological term. BOOTOX employs several novel schema- and data-driven query discovery techniques. E.g., BOOTOX can map two tables like `Turbine` and `Country` into classes by projecting them on primary keys, and the attribute `locatedIn` of `Turbine` into an object property between these two classes if there is either an explicit or implicit foreign key between `Turbine` and `Country`. For more complex mappings, BOOTOX requires users to provide a set of examples of entities from the class, e.g., *Turbine*, where each example is a set of keywords, e.g., $\{\mathit{albatros}, \mathit{gas}, \mathit{2008}\}$. Then the system turns these keywords into SQL queries by exploiting graph-based techniques similar to [16] for keyword-based query answering over DBs. Moreover, BOOTOX also allows us to incorporate third party OWL 2 ontologies in an existing OPTIQUE's deployment using ontology alignment techniques.

The ontological terms bootstrapped by means of BOOTOX provide the vocabulary for the formulation of STARQL ontological queries and the bootstrapped mappings. In the following we will discuss STARQL queries and how we process them.

```
CREATE STREAM   Str_out AS
CONSTRUCT       GRAPH NOW { ?c2 rdf:type :MonInc }
FROM            STREAM Str_Msmt [NOW-"PT10S"^^xsd:duration, NOW]->
                                "PT1S"^^xsd:duration,
                STATIC DATA sie:Static,
                ONTOLOGY sie:Ontology
USING           PULSE WITH START = "00:10:00CET", FREQUENCY = "1S"
WHERE           {?c1 a sie:Assembly. ?c2 a sie:Sensor.
                ?c1 sie:inAssembly ?c2.}
SEQUENCE BY     StandardSequencing AS seq
HAVING          MONOTONIC.HAVING(seq, ?c2, sie:hasValue)
```

```
CREATE AGGREGATE MONOTONIC.HAVING ($seq, $var, $attr) AS
      HAVING EXISTS ?k IN $seq: GRAPH ?k {$var sie:showsFault "true"}
      AND FORALL ?i, ?j  IN $seq:
           IF ( ?i < ?j < ?k  AND GRAPH ?i {$var $attr ?x}
           AND GRAPH ?j {$var $attr ?y}) THEN ?x < ?y
```

Figure 1: An example diagnostic task in STARQL, where the prefix *sie* stands for the URI of the Siemens ontology

Diagnostic Queries. In order to express diagnostic tasks we developed a query language STARQL [19] that allows us to perform complex semantic queries blending streaming with static data.

The syntax of STARQL extends so-called *basic graph patterns* of W3C standardised SPARQL query language for RDF databases. STARQL queries can express basic graph patterns, and typical mathematical, statistical, and event pattern features needed in real-time diagnostic scenarios. Moreover, STARQL queries can be nested, in the sense that the result of one query may be used in the construction of another query. STARQL has a formal semantics that combines open and closed-world reasoning and extends snapshot semantics for window operators [1] with sequencing semantics that can handle integrity constraints such as functionality assertions.

Due to the space limitation we cannot present STARQL in details. Instead, we will illustrate its main features on the following example diagnostic task: *Detect a real-time fault in a turbine caused by a temperature increase within 10 seconds.* This task can be expressed in STARQL over the Siemens ontology [10] as in Fig. 1 and it requires to combine streaming and static data. An output stream `S_out` is defined by the following language constructs: The `CONSTRUCT` specifies the format of the output stream, here instantiated by RDF triples asserting that there was a monotonic increase. The `FROM` clause specifies the resources on which the query is evaluated: the `ONTOLOGY`, `STATIC DATA`, and input `STREAM`(s), for which a window operator is specified with window range (here 10 sec) and with slide (here 1 sec). The `PULSE` declaration specifies the output frequency. In the `WHERE` clause, bindings for sensors (attached to the assembly structure of the turbine) are chosen. For every binding, the relevant condition of the diagnostic task is tested on the window contents. Here this condition is abbreviated by `MONOTONIC.HAVING(seq, ?c, sie:hasValue)` using a macro that is defined at the bottom of Fig. 1 in an `AGGREGATE` declaration. In words, the conditions asks whether there is some state `?k` in the window s.t. the sensor shows a failure message at `?k` and s.t. for all states before `?k` the attribute value `?attr` (in the example instantiated by `sie:hasValue`) is monotonically increasing.

STARQL has favourable computational properties [19]: despite its expressivity, answering STARQL queries is efficient since they can be efficiently enriched and then unfolded into efficient relational stream queries. STARQL query enrichment is polynomial-time in the size of the input ontology if the ontology is expressed in the OWL 2 QL ontology language and the queries are essentially conjunctive with value comparison and aggregates. STARQL unfolding is linear-time in the size of both mappings and query and enriched STARQL queries can be unfolded into relational stream queries. We developed a dedicated STARQL2SQL$^{(+)}$ translator that unfolds STARQL queries to SQL$^{(+)}$ queries, i.e. SQL queries enhanced with the essential operators for stream handling.

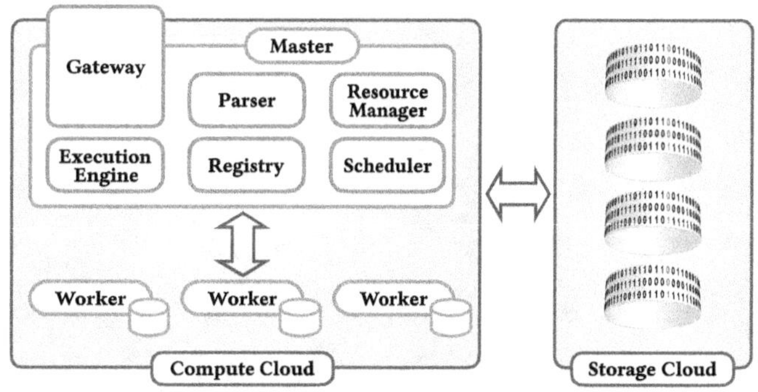

Figure 2: Distributed Stream Engine Architecture

Streaming and Static Relational Data Processing. Relational queries produced by the STARQL2SQL$^{(+)}$ translation, are handled by EXASTREAM, OPTIQUE's high-throughput distributed *Data Stream Management System* (*DSMS*). The EXASTREAM *DSMS* is embedded in EXAREME, a system for elastic large-scale dataflow processing in the cloud [18, 15] that is publicly available as an open source project under the MIT License. In the following, we present some key aspects of EXASTREAM.

EXASTREAM is built as a streaming extension of the SQLite *DBMS*, taking advantage of existing Database Management technologies and optimisations. It provides a declarative language, namely SQL$^{(+)}$, for querying data streams and relations that conform to the CQL semantics [1]. In contrast to other *DSMS*, the user does not need to consider low-level details of each query execution. Instead, the system's *query planner* is responsible for choosing an optimal plan depending on the query, the available stream/static data sources, and the execution environment.

EXASTREAM's optimizer makes it possible to process SQL$^{(+)}$ queries that blend streaming with static data. This has proven particularly useful in the Siemens use case since it allows us to combine streaming attributes (such as temperature measurements of a turbine) with metadata that remain invariant in time (such as the model or structure of a turbine) as well as archived stream data (such as past sensor readings, temperature measurements, etc.). Static relational tables may be stored in our system, or, they may be *federated* from external data-sources. Moreover, EXASTREAM allows defining database schemata on top of streaming and static data. This gives a wide range of opportunities for applying Semantic Web technologies and optimisations, e.g., bootstrapping techniques, that rely on these features.

EXASTREAM supports *parallelism* by distributing processing across different nodes in a distributed environment. Its architecture is shown in Figure 2. Queries are registered through the Asynchronous Gateway Server. Each registered query passes through the EXAREME parser and then is fed to the Scheduler module. The Scheduler places stream and relational operators on worker nodes based on the node's load. These operators are executed by a Stream Engine instance running on each node.

The EXASTREAM system natively supports *User Defined Functions* (*UDFs*) with arbitrary user code. The engine blends the execution of *UDFs* together with relational operators using JIT tracing compilation techniques. This greatly speeds up the execution as it reduces context switches and, most importantly, only the relevant execution traces are used, allowing the engine to perform optimizations at runtime that are not possible when the query is precompiled. *UDFs* allow us to express very complex dataflows using simple primitives. For OPTIQUE we used *UDFs* to implement communication with external sources, window partitioning on data streams, and data mining algorithms such as the *Locality-Sensitive Hashing* technique [14] for computing the correlation between values of multiple streams.

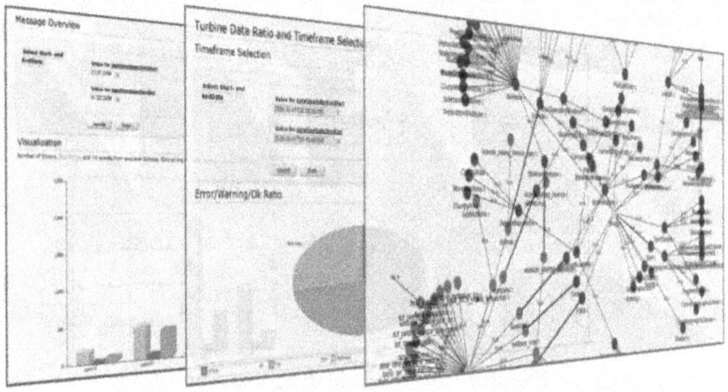

Figure 3: OPTIQUE screenshots

Whenever SQL abstractions are not sufficient (or efficient) for complex stream processing scenarios, we use standard SQL to combine data and process them with *UDFs*. Two main operators, implemented as *UDFs*, that incorporate the algorithmic logic for transforming SQLite into a *DSMS* are *timeSlidingWindow* and *wCache*:

- *timeSlidingWindow* groups tuples from the same time window and associates them with a unique window id,
- *wCache* acts as an index for answering efficiently equality constraints on the time column when processing infinite streams. The time column may be the *window identifier* produced by the *timeSlidingWindow* operator. *WCache* will then produce results to multiple queries accessing different streams.

The purpose of these *UDFs* is to perform the STARQL2SQL$^{(+)}$ translation, while they remain hidden from OPTIQUE's users.

In order to enable efficient processing of data streams of very high velocity we have implemented a number of optimisations in the stream processing engine. An optimisation that will be presented in the demo is *adaptive indexing*. With this technique EXASTREAM collects statistics during query execution and, adaptively, decides to build main-memory indexes on batches of cached stream tuples. These statistics are then used to expedite query processing during a complex operation (as in a join).

3. DEMONSTRATION SCENARIOS

We will demo the benefits of OPTIQUE on a real-world scenario from Siemens. In Figure 3 we presented some OPTIQUE screenshots about the deployment module and monitoring dashboards.

For the demonstration purpose we selected 20 diagnostic tasks typical for Siemens service centres and expressed these tasks in STARQL. An example diagnostic task is to calculate the Pearson correlation coefficient between turbine data streams. Then, we prepared a demo data set of streaming and static data from 950 turbines in the time from 2002 to 2011. This data is anonymised in a way that preserves the patterns needed for demo diagnostic tasks. During the demo we will 'play' the streaming data and thus emulate real time streams. Then, we distributed the demo-data in several installations with different number of nodes (VMs) ranging from 1 to 128, where each node has 2 processors and 4GB of main memory. To demonstrate diagnostics results we prepared a dedicated monitoring dashboard for each diagnostic task in the catalog. Dashboards show diagnostics results in real time, as well as statistics on streaming answers, relevant turbines, and other information that is typically required by the service engineers at Siemens. Finally, we deployed OPTIQUE over the Siemens data by bootstrapping ontologies and mappings and then manually post-processing and extending them so that they reach the required quality and contain necessary terms and mappings to cover 20 Siemens diagnostic tasks.

During the demo OPTIQUE will be available in three scenarios:

[S1] *Diagnostics with our deployment*: The attendees will be able to query our preconfigured Siemens deployment using diagnostic tasks from from the Siemens catalog and using their own STARQL queries, i.e., they will be able to create diagnostic tasks as parametrised continuous queries and register concrete instances of these tasks over specific data streams.

[S2] *Performance showcase of our deployment*: the attendees will be able to run various tests over our deployment using one of 128 preconfigured Siemens distributed environments and one of 10 test sets of queries. While running the tests they will monitor the throughput and progress of parallel query execution processes.

[S3] *Diagnostics with user's deployment*: the attendees will be able to deploy OPTIQUE over the Siemens data by bootstrapping ontologies and mappings, saving them, and observing and possibly improving them in dedicated editors. Then, they will query their deployed instance with diagnostic tasks from the Siemens catalog or their own STARQL queries.

Acknowledgements. This research has been partially supported by the EU project Optique (FP7-IP-318338), the Royal Society, the EPSRC grants Score!, DBonto, and MaSI[3].

4. REFERENCES

[1] A. Arasu et al. The CQL continuous query language: semantic foundations and query execution. *VLDBJ*, 15(2), 2006.

[2] A. Soylu et al. Ontology-based visual query formulation: An industry experience. In *ISVC*, 2015.

[3] C. Civili et al. MASTRO STUDIO: managing ontology based data access applications. *PVLDB*, 6(12), 2013.

[4] C. Pinkel et al. RODI: A benchmark for automatic mapping generation in relational-to-ontology data integration. In *ESWC*, 2015.

[5] J. Calbimonte. Enabling ontology-based access to streaming data sources. In *ISWC*, 2010.

[6] D. Calvanese et al. Ontop: Answering SPARQL Queries over Relational Databases. *Sem. Web. Journal*, 2015.

[7] D. L. Phuoc et al. A native approach for unified processing of linked streams and linked data. In *ISWC*, 2011.

[8] A. Doan, A. Y. Halevy, and Z. G. Ives. *Principles of Data Integration*. Morgan Kaufmann, 2012.

[9] E. Jiménez-Ruiz et al. BootOX: Practical Mapping of RDBs to OWL 2. In *ISWC*, 2015.

[10] E. Kharlamov at al. How Semantic Technologies Can Enhance Data Access at Siemens Energy. In *ISWC*, 2014.

[11] E. Kharlamov et al. Optique: Towards OBDA Systems for Industry. In *ESWC (Selected Papers)*, 2013.

[12] E. Kharlamov et al. Enabling Ontology Based Access at an Oil and Gas Company Statoil. In *ISWC*, 2015.

[13] E. Kharlamov et al. Optique: Ontology-based data access platform. In *ISWC (Posters & Demos)*, 2015.

[14] G. Nikos et al. In-network approximate computation of outliers with quality guarantees. *Inf. Sys.*, 38(8), 2013.

[15] H. Kllapi et al. Elastic Processing of Analytical Query Workloads on IaaS Clouds. *arXiv:1501.01070*, 2015.

[16] V. Hristidis and Y. Papakonstantinou. Discover: Keyword Search in Relational Databases. In *VLDB*, 2002.

[17] L. Fischer et al. Scalable linked data stream processing via network-aware workload scheduling. In *SSWKBS*, 2013.

[18] M. Tsangaris et al. Dataflow Processing and Optimization on Grid and Cloud Infrastructures. *IEEE D. Eng. Bull.*, 32, '09.

[19] Ö. Özçep et al. A Stream-Temporal Query Language for Ontology Based Data Access. In *KI*, 2014.

The CloudMdsQL Multistore System

Boyan Kolev, Carlyna Bondiombouy, Patrick Valduriez
Inria and LIRMM
Montpellier, France
firstname.lastname@inria.fr

Ricardo Jiménez-Peris
LeanXcale and UPM
Madrid, Spain

Raquel Pau
Sparsity Technologies
Barcelona, Spain

José Pereira
INESC TEC and U. Minho
Braga, Portugal

ABSTRACT

The blooming of different cloud data management infrastructures has turned multistore systems to a major topic in the nowadays cloud landscape. In this demonstration, we present a Cloud Multidatastore Query Language (CloudMdsQL), and its query engine. CloudMdsQL is a functional SQL-like language, capable of querying multiple heterogeneous data stores (relational and NoSQL) within a single query that may contain embedded invocations to each data store's native query interface. The major innovation is that a CloudMdsQL query can exploit the full power of local data stores, by simply allowing some local data store native queries (e.g. a breadth-first search query against a graph database) to be called as functions, and at the same time be optimized.

Within our demonstration, we focus on two use cases each involving four diverse data stores (graph, document, relational, and key-value) with its corresponding CloudMdsQL queries. The query execution flows are visualized by an embedded real-time monitoring subsystem. The users can also try out different ad-hoc queries, not necessarily in the context of the use cases.

Keywords

Cloud; multistore system; heterogeneous data stores; SQL and NoSQL integration.

1. INTRODUCTION

The blooming of different cloud data management infrastructures, specialized for different kinds of data and tasks, has led to a wide diversification of DBMS interfaces and the loss of a common programming paradigm. This makes it very hard for a user to integrate and analyze her data sitting in different data stores, e.g. RDBMS, NoSQL, and HDFS. For example, a media planning application, which needs to find top influencers inside social media communities for a list of topics, has to search for communities by keywords from a key-value store, then analyze the impact of influencers for each community using complex graph database traversals, and finally retrieve the influencers' profiles from an RDBMS and an excerpt of their blog posts from a document database. The CoherentPaaS project[1] addresses this problem, by providing a rich platform integrating different data management systems specialized for particular tasks, data and workloads. The platform is designed to provide a common programming model and language to query multiple data stores, which we herewith present.

The problem of accessing heterogeneous data sources has long been studied in the context of multidatabase and data integration systems [7]. More recently, with the advent of cloud databases and big data processing frameworks, the solution has evolved towards multistore systems that provide integrated access to a number of RDBMS, NoSQL and HDFS data stores through a common query engine. Data mediation SQL engines, such as Apache Drill, Spark SQL, and SQL++ provide common interfaces that allow different data sources to be plugged in (through the use of wrappers) and queried using SQL. The polystore BigDAWG [3] goes one step further by enabling queries across "islands of information", where each island corresponds to a specific data model and its language and provides transparent access to a subset of the underlying data stores through the island's data model. Another family of multistore systems [2,6] has been introduced with the goal of tightly integrating big data analytics frameworks (e.g. Hadoop MapReduce) with traditional RDBMS, by sacrificing the extensibility with other data sources. However, since none of these approaches supports the ad-hoc usage of native queries, they do not preserve the full expressivity of an arbitrary data store's query language. But what we want to give the user is the ability to express powerful ad-hoc queries that exploit the full power of the different data store languages, e.g. directly express a path traversal in a graph database. Therefore, the current multistore solutions do not directly apply to solve our problem.

In this demonstration, we present Cloud multidatastore query language (CloudMdsQL), a functional SQL-like language, designed for querying multiple heterogeneous databases (e.g. relational and NoSQL) within a single query containing nested subqueries [5]. Each subquery addresses directly a particular data store and may contain embedded invocations to the data store's native query interface. Thus, the major innovation is that a CloudMdsQL query can exploit the full power of local data stores, by simply allowing some local data store native queries (e.g. a breadth-first search query against a graph database) to be called as functions, and at the same time be optimized based on a simple cost model, e.g. by pushing down select predicates, using bind join, performing join ordering, or planning intermediate data

SIGMOD'16, June 26-July 01, 2016, San Francisco, CA, USA

ACM 978-1-4503-3531-7/16/06…$15.00 .
DOI: http://dx.doi.org/10.1145/2882903.2899400

[1] http://coherentpaas.eu

shipping. CloudMdsQL has been extended [1] to address distributed processing frameworks such as Apache Spark by enabling the ad-hoc usage of user defined map/filter/reduce operators as subqueries, yet allowing for pushing down predicates and bind join conditions.

2. LANGUAGE OVERVIEW

The CloudMdsQL language is SQL-based with the extended capabilities for embedding subqueries expressed in terms of each data store's native query interface. The common data model respectively is table-based, with support of rich datatypes that can capture a wide range of the underlying data stores' datatypes, such as arrays and JSON objects, in order to handle non-flat and nested data, with basic operators over such composite datatypes.

Queries that integrate data from several data stores usually consist of subqueries and an integration SELECT statement. A subquery is defined as a named table expression, i.e. an expression that returns a table and has a name and signature. The signature defines the names and types of the columns of the returned relation. Thus, each query, although agnostic to the underlying data stores' schemas, is executed in the context of an ad-hoc schema, formed by all named table expressions within the query. A named table expression can be defined by means of either an SQL SELECT statement (that the query compiler is able to analyze and possibly rewrite) or a native expression (that the query engine considers as a black box and delegates its processing directly to the data store). For example, the following simple CloudMdsQL query contains two subqueries, defined by the named table expressions `T1` and `T2`, and addressed respectively against the data stores `rdb` (an SQL database) and `mongo` (a MongoDB database):

```
T1(x int, y int)@rdb = ( SELECT x, y FROM A )
T2(x int, z array)@mongo = {*
  db.B.find( {$lt: {x, 10}}, {x:1, z:1, _id:0} )
*}
SELECT T1.x, T2.z
FROM T1, T2
WHERE T1.x = T2.x AND T1.y <= 3
```

The purpose of this query is to perform relational algebra operations (expressed in the main `SELECT` statement) on two datasets retrieved from a relational and a document database. The two subqueries are sent independently for execution against their data stores in order the retrieved relations to be joined by the common query engine. The SQL table expression `T1` is defined by an SQL subquery, while `T2` is a native expression (identified by the special bracket symbols `{* *}`) expressed as a native MongoDB call. Note that subqueries to some NoSQL data stores can also be expressed as SQL statements; in such cases, the wrapper must provide the mapping from relational operators to native calls. In our demonstration, unlike in the example above, we use an SQL wrapper to query MongoDB, which also benefits from subquery rewriting.

CloudMdsQL allows named table expressions to be defined as Python functions, which is useful for querying data stores that have only API-based query interface. A Python expression yields tuples to its result set much like a user-defined table function. It can also use as input the result of other subqueries. Furthermore, named table expressions can be parameterized by declaring parameters in the expression's signature. For example, the following Python expression uses the intermediate data retrieved by `T2` to return another table containing the number of occurrences of the parameter `v` in the array `T2.z`.

```
T3(x int, c int WITHPARAMS v string)@python = {*
  for (x, z) in CloudMdsQL.T2:
    yield( x, z.count(v) )
*}
```

A (parameterized) named table can then be instantiated by passing actual parameter values from another native/Python expression, as a table function in a `FROM` clause, or even as a scalar function (e.g. in the `SELECT` list). Calling a named table as a scalar function is useful e.g. to express direct lookups into a key-value data store.

Note that parametrization and nesting is also available in SQL and native named tables. In our demonstration, we give an example that involves the Sparksee graph database and we use its Python API to express subqueries that benefit from all of the features described above. In fact, our initial query engine implementation enables Python integration; however support for other languages (e.g. JavaScript) for user-defined operations can be easily added.

3. SYSTEM OVERVIEW

The query engine follows a mediator/wrapper architecture. The query compiler decomposes the query into a query execution plan (QEP), which appears as a directed acyclic graph of relational operators where leaf nodes correspond to subqueries for the wrappers to execute directly against the data stores.

3.1 Query Optimization

Before its actual execution, a QEP may be rewritten by the query optimizer. To compare alternative rewritings of a query, the optimizer uses basic cost information exposed by the wrappers in the form of cost functions or database statistics, and a simple cost model. In addition, the query language provides a possibility for the user to define cost and selectivity functions whenever they cannot be derived from the catalog, mostly in the case of using native subqueries.

CloudMdsQL uses bind join as an efficient method for performing semi-joins across heterogeneous data stores that uses subquery rewriting to push the join conditions. For example, the list of distinct values of the join attribute(s), retrieved from the left-hand side subquery, is passed as a filter to the right-hand side subquery. To illustrate it, let us consider the following CloudMdsQL query:

```
A(id int, x int)@DB1 = (SELECT a.id, a.x FROM a)
B(id int, y int)@DB2 = (SELECT b.id, b.y FROM b)
SELECT a.x, b.y FROM b JOIN a ON b.id = a.id
```

Let us assume that the optimizer has decided to use the bind join method and that the join condition will be bound to the right-hand side of the join operation. First, the relation `B` is retrieved from the corresponding data store using its query mechanism. Then, the distinct values of `B.id` are used as a filter condition in the query that retrieves the relation `A` from its data store. Assuming that the distinct values of `B.id` are b_1 ... b_n, the query to retrieve the right-hand side relation of the bind join uses the following SQL approach (or its equivalent according to the data store's query language), thus retrieving from `A` only the rows that match the join criteria:

```
SELECT a.id, a.x FROM a WHERE a.id IN (b1, …, bn)
```

The way to do the bind join analogue for native/Python queries is through the use of a `JOINED ON` clause in the named table signature. For example, if `A` is defined as the Python function below, as `A.id` participates in an equi-join, the values b_1 ... b_n will be provided to the Python code through the iterator `Outer`:

```
A(id int, x int JOINED ON id)@DB1 = {*
  for id in CloudMdsQL.Outer:
    yield ( id, db.get_x(id) )
*}
```

3.2 Query Engine Implementation

For the current implementation of the query engine, we modified the open source Apache Derby database to accept CloudMdsQL queries and transform the corresponding execution plan into Derby SQL operations. We developed the query planner and the query execution controller and linked them to the Derby core, which we use as the operator engine. Derby allows extending the set of SQL operations by means of `CREATE FUNCTION` statements. This type of statements creates an alias, with an optional set of parameters, to invoke a specific Java component as part of an execution plan. Thus, for each named table expression in a query, a table function is created dynamically, which invokes the corresponding wrapper as a Java class. Thus, Derby handles global execution, delegating local optimization and execution to the underlying data stores. As a second step, the query engine evaluates which named expressions are queried more than once and must be cached into the temporary table storage, which will be always queried and updated from the specified Java functions to reduce the query execution time. Finally, the last step consists of translating all operation nodes that appear in the execution plan into a Derby specific SQL execution plan.

4. DEMONSTRATION

The demonstration concentrates on two CloudMdsQL use case scenarios from different information systems: a social network analysis tool for marketing companies and a bibliographic recommendation system. The users will have the possibility to experience the use case scenarios through their web interfaces. They will be also able to try out custom CloudMdsQL queries, to follow their corresponding query execution plans, and to monitor their execution flow through X-Ray [4] – a subsystem of the CoherentPaaS platform for real-time visualization of performance and resource usage integrated with all the components of the platform (the query engine and the underlying data stores).

Scenario 1. The first use case aims at finding the *communities in a social network, for a specific set of topics, with their top influencers*. Marketing companies are interested in discovering the people they need to convince about the quality of a specific brand. The dataset of this use case is a sample of Twitter, but it allows working with other social networks like Facebook or blogs. The application runs a Twitter listener of a set of topics in real-time; it modifies the database for each tweet it receives. The schema of this application contains a generic entity called *Document* to store text-items (tweets, messages, etc.), which can appear *copies* or *references*. An *Entity* (person or company) is an *author* of a document or a *mention* of a social-network account. The people interactions in social networks with copies, references or mentions, can be understood as a set of graph of influences. In other words, we can infer who influences who and about what. These *Influences* and the *Communities* are incrementally computed when a new tweet comes to the application and thus, these concepts are part of the application schema.

The specification of the main query Q_1 the application uses is as follows: given a set of keywords k_1, k_2, k_3, find the 10 biggest communities and, for each community, find the 20 most influencers. For each of these influencers, the system must return the number of influenced entities inside the community, the influencer's id, name and account creation date and the last published document.

In order to implement this use case, we use a graph database (Sparksee) to store the graph of *Influences* and compute the *Communities*; a relational database (MonetDB) for all the basic information about *Entities* and *Documents* (only metadata); a document database (MongoDB) to store the *Document* contents; and a key-value data store (HBase) to index communities per keyword. Following the execution plan for the CloudMdSQL query Q_1, the query engine first invokes an HBase query to retrieve the communities preliminarily computed for a specific keyword; then, for each community, runs a Sparksee query using the Sparksee Python API to find the top 20 influencers, the number of influenced entities inside the community, and the maximum influence propagation depth. Finally, the basic information of each influencer (id, name, account creation date) and the last published document is retrieved by running queries to MonetDB and MongoDB. Figure 1 summarizes the described execution plan using a notation where each box represents a table expression as a data store subquery with its signature and a fragment, (pseudo)statement, or description of the subquery.

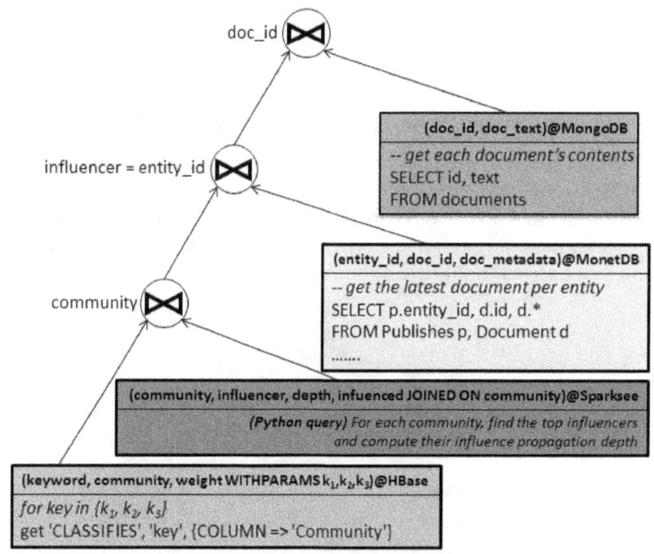

Figure 1. Execution plan for Q_1.

For this execution plan, the query optimization plays an important role to assign the bind join method to all the join operations. The reason is that the selected communities relevant to the keywords k_1, k_2 and k_3 are always a few, and thus the Sparksee query is evaluated only for a few communities, which significantly reduces the number of executions of expensive graph computations. Analogously, using bind join to retrieve the latest documents only for the filtered influencers increases the overall efficiency significantly by pushing bind join conditions to the MonetDB and MongoDB subqueries that take advantage of the existing indexes in both databases. Note that the MongoDB subquery is expressed in SQL, but the wrapper maps its sub-plan to a chain of invocations of MongoDB native API.

Within the results of this query, there is a nested level of information and the ranking of the suggested communities and influencers are important. For this reason, the Q_1 results are shown using a chart (see Figure 2) where the outer level of circles represents communities whereas the inner one corresponds to the influencers of those communities. The sizes of the community circles correspond to the relevance of the specified keywords with a community, while the sizes of the influencer circles correspond to the impact a person has on the community regarding the keywords.

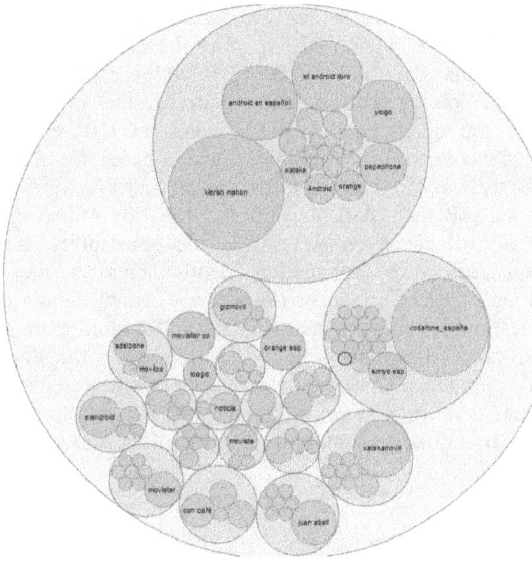

Figure 2. Visualization of communities and influencers.

The query execution can be monitored using the integrated system for real-time monitoring and analysis X-Ray (see Figure 3), where the user can view details for each operation running within the process, including relative start/end times of operation executions, intermediate cardinalities, rewritten queries, etc.

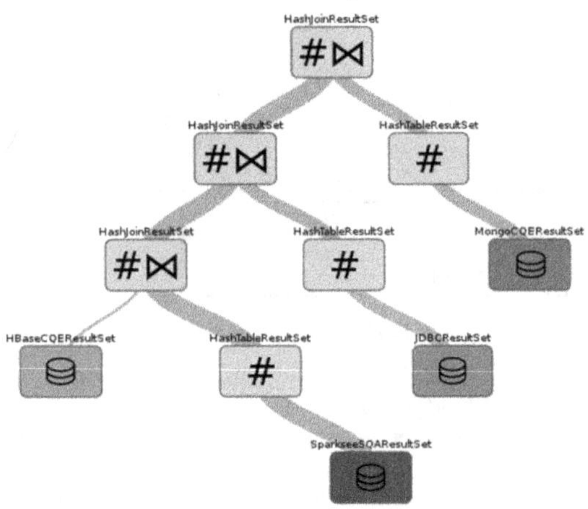

		Name	Operands	Rows	Start	End	Comment
1	#⋈	HashJoinResultSet	[2,4]	223	0.026	0.043	
2	#	HashTableResultSet	[3]	196	0.026	0.041	key=[0]
3		MongoCQEResultSet	[]	196	0.023	0.025	SELECT id,text FRC
4	#⋈	HashJoinResultSet	[5,7]	223	0.025	0.040	
5	#	HashTableResultSet	[6]	196	0.025	0.040	key=[0]
6		JDBCResultSet	[]	196	0.020	0.023	SELECT p.entity_id,
7	#⋈	HashJoinResultSet	[8,10]	223	0.026	0.040	
8	#	HashTableResultSet	[9]	223	0.000	0.003	key=[0]
9		SparkseeSQAResultSet	[]	223	0.003	0.020	<python query>
10		HBaseCQEResultSet	[]	78	0.000	0.003	get 'CLASSIFIES', 'k

Figure 3. Monitoring of the query execution.

Scenario 2. The second use case application recommends *reviewers for a specific European project* taking into account the DBLP and CORDIS knowledge base. DBLP is a bibliographic dataset focused in computer science that currently contains 1,8 million publications and 1 million authors. CORDIS is the European projects dataset, which currently contains 40000 projects and 1000 institutions. The main query Q_2 is one of the key functionalities of a system built by Sparsity-Technologies to offer recommendations for researchers. The system visualizes the results from a web browser using HTML5 because it provides a clear way to analyze the results.

The schema of this information system contains *Projects*, whose *participants* are *Institutions* and one of them is the *coordinator*. On the other hand, a part of the schema stores a bibliographic dataset, which contains *Documents* (papers) and their *authors* (*People*) with the corresponding *affiliations* (*Institutions*) for each year. This information system also *indexes Projects* and *Documents* by *Keywords*; analyzes which are the top *expert Institutions* and *People* for each *Keyword*.

The application and the query Q_2 use a graph database (Sparksee) to resolve the conflicting interests with the members of the project because graph databases are efficient solving paths/joins; a relational data store (LeanXcale) to store and retrieve the complete list of fields about the recommended reviewers; a key-value data store (HBase) to find the top experts in a list of topics taking advantage of a fast search by keywords; and a document data store (MongoDB) to retrieve the contents of the last paper produced by the suggested reviewers.

The specification of Q_2 is as follows: given a specific project p and a set of keywords k_1, k_2, k_3, find the people that have never worked in the same institutions as the participants of p that are also experts in k_1, k_2, k_3. For these people, return their name, last affiliation and last paper title.

5. ACKNOWLEDGEMENTS

This research has been partially funded by the European Commission under projects CoherentPaaS and LeanBigData (grants FP7-611068, FP7-619606), the Madrid Regional Council, FSE and FEDER, project Cloud4BigData (grant S2013TIC-2894), and the Spanish Research Agency MICIN project BigDataPaaS (grant TIN2013-46883).

6. REFERENCES

[1] Bondiombouy, C., Kolev, B., Levchenko, O., Valduriez, P. 2015. Integrating Big Data and Relational Data with a Functional SQL-like Query Language. *DEXA*, 170-185.

[2] DeWitt, D., Halverson, A., Nehme, R., Shankar, S., Aguilar-Saborit J., Avanes, A., Flasza, M., Gramling, J. 2013. Split Query Processing in Polybase. In *ACM SIGMOD* (2013), 1255-1266.

[3] Duggan, J., Elmore, A. J., Stonebraker, M., Balazinska, M., Howe, B., Kepner, J., Madden, S., Maier, D., Mattson, T., Zdonik, S. 2015. The BigDAWG Polystore System. *SIGMOD Rec.* 44, 2 (August 2015), 11-16. DOI=http://dx.doi.org/10.1145/2814710.2814713

[4] Guimarães, P., Pereira, J. 2015. X-Ray: Monitoring and Analysis of Distributed Database Queries, In *15th IFIP WG 6.1 International Conference, DAIS*, 80-93.

[5] Kolev, B., Valduriez, P., Bondiombouy, C., Jiménez-Peris, R., Pau, R., Pereira, J. 2015. CloudMdsQL: Querying Heterogeneous Cloud Data Stores with a Common Language. *Distributed and Parallel Databases*, pp 1-41, http://link.springer.com/article/10.1007%2Fs10619-015-7185-y

[6] LeFevre, J., Sankaranarayanan, J., Hacıgümüs, H., Tatemura, J., Polyzotis, N., Carey, M. 2014. MISO: Souping Up Big Data Query Processing with a Multistore System. In *ACM SIGMOD* (2014), 1591-1602.

[7] Özsu, T., Valduriez, P. 2011. *Principles of Distributed Database Systems* – Third Edition. Springer, 850 pages.

ActiveClean: An Interactive Data Cleaning Framework For Modern Machine Learning

Sanjay Krishnan
UC Berkeley
sanjay@eecs.berkeley.edu

Michael J. Franklin
UC Berkeley
franklin@berkeley.edu

Ken Goldberg
UC Berkeley
goldberg@berkeley.edu

Jiannan Wang
Simon Fraser University
jnwang@sfu.ca

Eugene Wu
Columbia University
ewu@cs.columbia.edu

ABSTRACT

Databases can be corrupted with various errors such as missing, incorrect, or inconsistent values. Increasingly, modern data analysis pipelines involve Machine Learning, and the effects of dirty data can be difficult to debug. Dirty data is often sparse, and naive sampling solutions are not suited for high-dimensional models. We propose ActiveClean, a progressive framework for training Machine Learning models with data cleaning. Our framework updates a model iteratively as the analyst cleans small batches of data, and includes numerous optimizations such as importance weighting and dirty data detection. We designed a visual interface to wrap around this framework and demonstrate ActiveClean for a video classification problem and a topic modeling problem.

1. INTRODUCTION

Model training on large and growing datasets is a key data management challenge with significant interest in both industry and academia [1, 2, 5]. While many scalable training frameworks abstract much of the crucial details of distributed Machine Learning (ML), they seldom offer the analyst support regarding constructing the model itself, such as which features to use or how to represent their data. The model construction process is still highly iterative often through trial-and-error. To further complicate matters, data are often *dirty*, including missing, incorrect, or inconsistent attributes, due to faulty sensors, software, time delays, or hardware. Thus, although part of the iterative process is tweaking the model parameters and features, a significant portion involves identifying and cleaning potentially dirty data. In our work, we focus on this latter issue. While data cleaning is an extensively studied problem, the high dimensionality of many models can amplify even a small amount of erroneous records [13], and the relative complexity (in comparison to SQL analytics) can make it difficult to trace the consequences of data error.

To highlight the importance of data cleaning in modern ML pipelines, we have noted the choice of data cleaning algorithm can

SIGMOD'16, June 26-July 01, 2016, San Francisco, CA, USA

DOI: http://dx.doi.org/10.1145/2882903.2899409

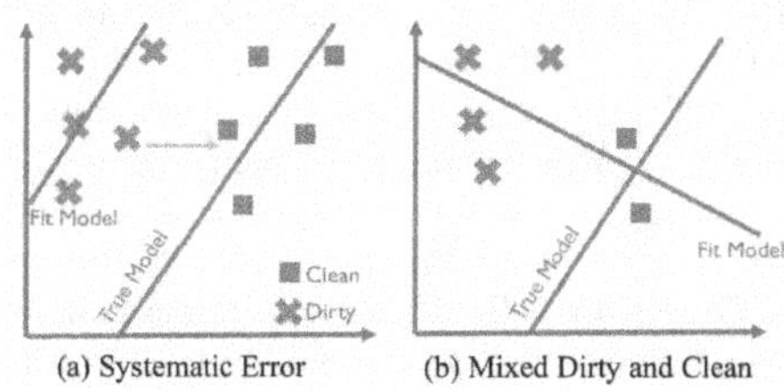

Figure 1: (a) Systematic corruption in one variable (axes) can lead to a shifted model (fitted lines). (b) Mixed dirty and clean data results in a less accurate model than no cleaning.

significantly affect results even when using robust statistical techniques [8, 9]. For instance, in one fraud prediction example, we found that applying Entity Resolution before model training improved true positive detection probabilities from 62% to 91%. Despite this importance, in theory and practice, the academic community has decoupled the data cleaning problem from featurization and ML. This disconnect is problematic because many ML techniques often make assumptions about independent and identically distributed data, which can be easily violated if the analyst applies data cleaning in an arbitrary way.

Consider an analyst training a regression model on dirty data. At first, she may not realize that there are outliers and train a preliminary model directly on the dirty data. As she starts to inspect the model and the data, she will soon realize that some records have large residual errors (i.e., not predicted accurately). Once she confirms that those records are indeed dirty, she has to design rules or scripts to fix or remove the offending records. After cleaning, she re-trains the model–iterating until she no longer finds dirty data. This iterative process is the de facto standard, and is in fact encouraged by the design of the increasingly popular interactive "notebook" ML development environments (e.g., IPython). This makes the implicit assumption that the models trained on partially clean data have meaningful predictive value. However, due to the well-known Simpson's paradox, models trained on a mix of dirty and clean data can have very misleading results even in simple scenarios (Figure 1).

In a parallel trend, the advent of techniques such as Deep Learning and Non-Parametric Bayesian Methods has lead to an explosion in the number of model parameters. It is now common to use 100,000s of features in image processing problems with Convolutional Neural Networks. Empirically, such feature spaces have facilitated breakthroughs in previously hard classification tasks such as image classification, robot actuation, and speech recognition. However, the pitfall is that higher dimensional models are harder to debug. Determining the combined effects of dirty data, model error, and counter-intuitive higher dimensional effects can be very challenging.

As it stands, there are two main problems in ML over dirty data, (1) correctness, and (2) dirty data identification. We address these two problems in a system called ActiveClean which facilitates interactive training-cleaning iteration in a safe way (with expected monotone convergence guarantees) and automatically selects the most valuable data for the analyst to inspect. ActiveClean builds on the algorithms described in our prior work [6, 12, 4, 7] and the details of the approach can be found in [8]. The selection technique applied in ActiveClean uses pointwise gradients to generalize the outlier filtering heuristics to select potentially dirty data even in complex models. The analyst initializes an ActiveClean with an ML model, a featurization function, and the base data, and the ActiveClean initially returns the model trained on the dataset. ActiveClean also returns a set of data sampled from the model that are possibly dirty. The analyst can apply any value transformations to the data and then prompt the system to iterate.

Intuitively, ActiveClean prioritizes data cleaning by identifying records, which if cleaned, are likely to change the analyst's model predictions. ActiveClean applies to a large class of models which can be represented as loss minimization problems solved by gradient descent. This captures SVMs, Linear Regression, Neural Networks (Deep Learning), and some types of topic modeling problems such as LDA (for a formal description see [8]). In our demonstration, we will show how ActiveClean facilitates debugging complex ML models to understand the effects of dirty data in two experimental scenarios:

EXAMPLE 1 (VIDEO SEGMENTATION WITH CNNS). *The JHU JIGSAWS Dataset is a corpus of surgical training 120 videos from between 1-5mins long. These videos are annotated by expert surgeons describing the gestures that occur in the video. Classifying video frames is an important task for segmentation and summarization of future videos. We would like a classifier that can predict these annotations. This can be done using Convolutional Neural Networks to featurize frames of the video and then applying a standard classifier like an SVM after the features are extracted. However, sometimes the annotations are incorrect and ActiveClean can be used to determine when the annotations are incorrect (correspond to the wrong gesture) and inconsistent (multiple gestures simultaneously).*

EXAMPLE 2 (TOPIC MODELING WITH LDA). *We have a corpus of reviews from Yelp and we wish to learn a topic model from this dataset. However, a substantial number of the reviews are spam that typically are soliciting traffic for a fraudulent website. These spam reviews can affect the distribution of words and affect any models learned from the data. However, some spam reviews are hard to detect automatically and require human validation. We can apply ActiveClean to efficiently estimate the topic model without having to validate every review.*

2. ARCHITECTURE AND OVERVIEW

We will first describe ActiveClean and overview the entire framework, and a detailed description of the research challenges and algorithms can be found in [8].

2.1 What Is New?

Machine learning, specifically active learning, has been applied in prior work to improve the efficiency of data cleaning [14, 15, 3]. Human input, either for cleaning or validation of automated cleaning, is often expensive and impractical for large datasets. An ML model can be used to extrapolate repairs to not-yet-cleaned data, and the goal of these approaches is to provide the cleanest possible dataset–independent of the subsequent analytics or query processing. Prior work studies how to *use machine learning models* to improve data cleaning. In contrast, ActiveClean explores how to control the impact of data cleaning for downstream machine learning models.

This new problem setting leads a question of correctness – if I incrementally clean subsets of my data, is the model I then train even correct? It also leads to optimization opportunities – how can the data cleaning step be made aware of the subsequent data analysis (e.g., the model that is trained) in such a way that the model will most quickly converge to the correct model? One of the primary contributions of this work is an incremental model update algorithm with correctness guarantees for the resulting mixture of dirty and clean data.

2.2 Problem Setup and Formalization

We assume that there is a featurizer $F(\cdot)$ that maps every record in a dataset $r \in R$ to a feature vector x and label y. This work focuses on a class of well-analyzed predictive analytics problems, ones that can be expressed as the minimization of loss functions, which will be trained on the output of applying $F(\cdot)$ to the records in R. For these labeled training examples $\{(x_i, y_i)\}_{i=1}^{N}$, the problem is to find a vector of *model parameters* θ by minimizing a loss function ℓ over all training examples:

$$\theta^* = \arg\min_{\theta} \sum_{i=1}^{N} \ell(x_i, y_i; \theta)$$

Where ϕ is a convex function in θ. Typically, a *regularization* term $r(\theta)$ is added to this problem. $r(\theta)$ penalizes high or low values of feature weights in θ to avoid overfitting to noise in the training examples.

$$\theta^* = \arg\min_{\theta} \sum_{i=1}^{N} \ell(x_i, y_i; \theta) + r(\theta) \tag{1}$$

In this work, without loss of generality, we will include the regularization as part of the loss function i.e., $\ell(x_i, y_i; \theta)$ includes $r(\theta)$. We note that designing ActiveClean for this form of machine learning model supports SVMs, Linear Regression, Logistic Regression, Neural Networks, Latent Dirichlet Allocation, and Gaussian Mixture Models.

2.3 Required User Input

In such a problem setting, ActiveClean takes as input four user-defined parameters. The first two are UDFs used to train models, and can be assumed to be readily available. The latter two consist of a user-tunable parameters with reasonable defaults, and a generic record cleaning function implemented by script or by manual effort:

Model: The user provides a predictive model (e.g., SVM) specified as a loss optimization problem $\ell(\cdot)$ and a featurizer $F(\cdot)$ that maps a record to its feature vector x and label y.

Gradient: The gradient function $\nabla\ell(\cdot)$ returns the gradient of the loss. For popular convex models such as SVMs and Linear Regression these functions are known and provided as part of the system. For more complex problems such Topic Modeling or Neural Network learning, we assume that this function (or an approximation of it) is expressed programmatically. There are many frameworks such as Torch, Theano, and TensorFlow, which can return such programs using symbolic differentiation.

Stopping Criteria: Data are cleaned in batches of size b and the user can change these settings if she desires more or less frequent model updates. We empirically find that a batch size of 50 performs well across different datasets and use that as a default. A cleaning budget k can be used as a stopping criterion once $C()$ has been called k times, and so the number of iterations of ActiveClean is $T = \frac{k}{b}$. Alternatively, the user can clean data until the model is of sufficient accuracy to make a decision.

Cleaning Function: We represent this operation as $C(\cdot)$ which can be applied to a record r (or a set of records) to recover the clean record $r' = C(r)$. Formally, we treat the $C(\cdot)$ as an expensive user-defined function (implemented as code or manual inspection) composed of deterministic schema-preserving map and filter operations applied to a subset of rows in the relation.

2.4 Basic Data Flow

The following pseudocode summarizes how ActiveClean works:

1. `Init(dirty_data, cleaned_data, dirty_model, batch, iter)`
2. For each t in $\{1, ..., T\}$
   (a) `dirty_sample = Sampler(dirty_data, sample_prob, detector, batch)`
   (b) `clean_sample = Cleaner(dirty_sample)`
   (c) `current_model = Updater(current_model, sample_prob, clean_sample)`
   (d) `cleaned_data = cleaned_data + clean_sample`
   (e) `dirty_data = dirty_data - clean_sample`
   (f) `sample_prob = Estimator(dirty_data, cleaned_data, detector)`
   (g) `detector = Detector(detector, cleaned_data)`
3. `Output: current_model`

The system first trains the model $\ell(\cdot)$ on the dirty dataset to find an initial model $\theta^{(d)}$ that the system will subsequently improve. The *Sampler* selects a sample of size b records from the dataset and passes the sample to the *Cleaner*, which executes $C(\cdot)$ on the whole sample and outputs their cleaned versions. The *Updater* uses the cleaned sample to update the weights of the model, thus moving the model closer to the true cleaned model (in expectation). Finally, the system either terminates due to a stopping condition (e.g., $C(\cdot)$ has been called a maximum number of times k, or training error convergence), or passes control to the *sampler* for the next iteration. ActiveClean assumes that *Init* and *Cleaner* are user-specified, and it implements all of the other functions.

2.5 Technical Details

We overview some of the research contributions, and the details can be found in [8].

Updater (Incremental Gradient Method): Rather than retraining, in ActiveClean, we start with a dirty model as an initialization θ_d, and then incrementally make an update using a gradient step.This process leverages the structure of the model rather than treating it as a black-box, and we apply convergence arguments from optimization theory.

Suppose, we model the cleaner $C(\cdot)$ as an oracle that maps a dirty example (x_i, y_i) to a clean example (x'_i, y'_i). Ideally, we would like to be able to solve the following problem:

$$\arg\min_{\theta \in \Theta} \sum_{i=1}^{N} \ell(C(x_i, y_i); \theta)$$

This minimization problem can be solved with an algorithm called Stochastic Gradient Descent, which iteratively samples data, estimates a gradient, and updates the current best model. We can represent the iterative cleaning process similarly where the gradient is

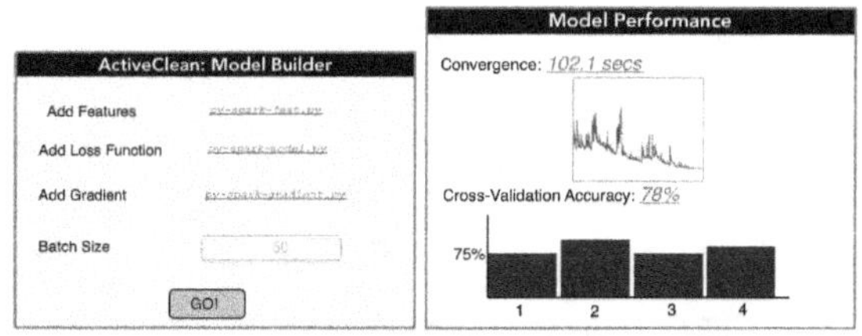

Figure 2: Initialization. The analyst loads user-defined model functions into ActiveClean and then trains an initial model on the dirty data

estimated from newly cleaned batches of data:

$$\theta^{(0)} \leftarrow \theta_d^* \quad \theta^{(t+1)} = \theta^{(t)} - \lambda \cdot \mathbf{w}$$

where $\mathbf{w}$ is an unbiased estimate of the gradient with $\mathbf{E}[\mathbf{w}] = \sum_i^N \nabla\ell(C(x_i, y_i); \theta^{(t)})$. If iterated to infinity, this procedure will converge to the correct value θ_c^* with rate $O(\frac{1}{t})$ for strongly convex functions and $O(\frac{1}{\sqrt{t}})$ for general convex functions and avoids the pitfalls of Simpson's paradox. There are some subtleties which we discuss in the technical report such as re-sampling already cleaned data and selecting batch sizes.

Sampler (Importance Sampling): We use an importance sampling technique to select a sample of likely dirty records. The necessary conditions for convergence are $\mathbf{E}[\mathbf{w}] = \sum_i^N \nabla\ell(C(x_i); \theta^{(t)})$ and there is nothing that enforces that we must uniformly sample the data. We can apply a technique called importance sampling which allows us to calculate expectations with respect to one distribution $q(\cdot)$ while sampling from another with the same support $p(\cdot)$, e.g., $\mathbf{E}_{X\ q}[X] = \sum_{x \in X} x \frac{q(x)}{p(x)}$, which leads the the following:

$$\mathbf{w} = \frac{|X|}{b} \sum_{i=1}^{b} \frac{1}{p(i)} \nabla\ell(C(x_i, y_i); \theta^{(t)})$$

While all of the distributions will have the same expected values, their variances will differ. We can show that an approximation for the distribution that minimizes the variance is simply: $p(i) \propto \|\nabla\ell(x_i, y_i; \theta^{(t)})\|$.

3. THE INTERFACE

Next, we will describe the components of the ActiveClean interface used in this demonstration.

3.1 Initialization

The analyst first uses the Model Builder (Figure 2, left panel) to specify and initialized the problem. She loads three user-defined functions written in PySpark [10] based on the descriptions in the previous section, and optionally tune the stopping criteria. Once the model is trained, the right panel will show summary information. The top shows Performance information, and plots the model's convergence as a function of iteration, The bottom shows model accuracy information and shows the cross-validation accuracy if it is a classification task and the hold-out residual error if it is a regression task.

3.2 Diagnose Interface

Suppose the analyst is unhappy with her model and wishes to understand why her prediction accuracy is poor. She can then open the Diagnose panel to understand why (Figure 3). When she opens the Diagnose panel, ActiveClean applies the importance sampling algorithm to select and visualize a subset of examples from the

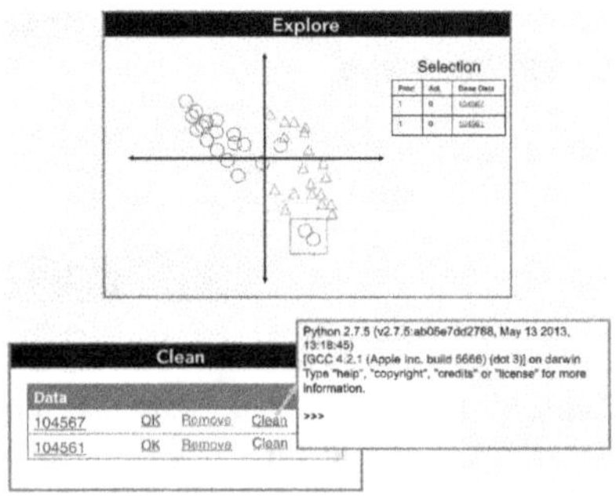

Figure 3: Diagnose Interface (above): The analyst can select and inspect suspect data. Cleaning Interface (below): The analyst can choose to remove data, write a custom cleaning operation, or automatically clean the data using an existing cleaning operation.

dataset. Since these points are in general high-dimensional, we apply T-SNE [11], a non-linear dimensionality reduction technique that is widely used to visualize complex data distributions, to visualize the points in a 2-D plot. The points are color coded to indicate the label in the case of classification. The analyst can select examples from the plot for further inspection.

3.3 Cleaning Interface

The Clean panel gives her the option to remove the dirty record, apply a custom cleaning operation (specified in Python), or pick from a pre-defined list of cleaning functions. Custom cleaning operations are added to the library to help taxonomize different types of errors and reduce analyst cleaning effort. This also provides a hint about which data are similarly corrupted (and thus fixed), we can guide future samples to draw similar data in future samples. We do this by training a classifier to learn the conditions for when the operation applies to a record; the details are described in our technical report [8].

Finally, after the data sample is cleaned, ActiveClean updates the current best model, and re-runs the cross-validation to visualize changes in the model accuracy. At this point, ActiveClean begins a new iteration by drawing a new sampling of records to show the analyst. Once ActiveClean satisfies the stopping conditions, the current best model parameters along with the (partially) cleaned dataset are returned to the analyst.

4. DEMONSTRATION PROPOSAL

In our demonstration, we will highlight both ActiveClean's overall efficacy on real large-scale scientific datasets, as well as provide the user with hands-on experience working in the clean-validate-retrain loop that is part of ActiveClean. Overall, the demo is intended to show how ActiveClean quickly improves the accuracy of the examples presented in the introduction.

To this end, we will first run a head-to-head comparison between ActiveClean and naive Active Learning in automatic mode – the participant will pick the example setting and see an animation as both algorithms proceed in real-time. The demo will automatically walk through all of the key panels of the interface, using full-scale instantiations of the models and datasets. As part of this process, both algorithms will select samples of dirty data points, automatically clean the points by replacing incorrect values with ground-truth, and retrain the model. The visualization of the cross-validation accuracy, as well as the diagnosis interface, will be updated in real time so that participants can visually compare the progress of both ActiveClean and the Active Learning algorithms in a real scenario.

After the automatic mode is complete, participants will have hands-on experience with ActiveClean. We will present a simplified dataset and model with artificial errors that is small enough to clean entirely in a minute or two. Participants will be able to train an SVM and manually clean samples of data using ActiveClean for a binary classification task. This will illustrate the tradeoffs and usability of the system.

5. CONCLUSION

Building and training high-quality machine learning models is hard, and doing so in the context of dirty data is painful. When presented with large, dirty datasets, practitioners often complain that it is difficult to know where to start the cleaning process. Worse, this process is often manual and makes fully cleaning the entire dataset impractical. Our key insight is that an important and broad class of predictive models, called loss models, *can* be cleaned progressively *with guarantees* by embedding the process into an incremental optimization loop controlled by a system such as ActiveClean. We hope to convey to the participants that the design of the ML development environment can be used to facilitate proper methodology.

This research is supported in part by NSF CISE Expeditions Award CCF-1139158, DOE Award SN10040 DE-SC0012463, and DARPA XData Award FA8750-12-2-0331, and gifts from Amazon Web Services, Google, IBM, SAP, The Thomas and Stacey Siebel Foundation, Apple Inc., Arimo, Blue Goji, Bosch, Cisco, Cray, Cloudera, Ericsson, Facebook, Fujitsu, Guavus, HP, Huawei, Intel, Microsoft, Pivotal, Samsung, Schlumberger, Splunk, State Farm and VMware.

6. REFERENCES

[1] U. Berkeley. Berkeley data analytics stack. https://amplab.cs.berkeley.edu/software/.

[2] A. Crotty, A. Galakatos, and T. Kraska. Tupleware: Distributed machine learning on small clusters. In *IEEE Data Eng. Bull.*, 2014.

[3] C. Gokhale, S. Das, A. Doan, J. F. Naughton, N. Rampalli, J. Shavlik, and X. Zhu. Corleone: Hands-off crowdsourcing for entity matching. In *SIGMOD*, 2014.

[4] D. Haas, S. Krishnan, J. Wang, M. J. Franklin, and E. Wu. Wisteria: Nurturing scalable data cleaning infrastructure. In *VLDB*, 2015.

[5] G. Inc. Tensorflow. https://www.tensorflow.org/.

[6] S. Krishnan, J. Wang, M. J. Franklin, K. Goldberg, and T. Kraska. Stale view cleaning: Getting fresh answers from stale materialized views. In *VLDB*, 2015.

[7] S. Krishnan, J. Wang, M. J. Franklin, K. Goldberg, T. Kraska, T. Milo, and E. Wu. Sampleclean: Fast and reliable analytics on dirty data. *IEEE Data Eng. Bull.*, 38(3):59–75, 2015.

[8] S. Krishnan, J. Wang, E. Wu, M. J. Franklin, and K. Goldberg. Activeclean: Interactive data cleaning while learning convex loss models. http://arxiv.org/abs/1601.03797v1.

[9] J. Mahler, S. Krishnan, M. Laskey, S. Sen, A. Murali, B. Kehoe, S. Patil, J. Wang, M. Franklin, P. Abbeel, and K. Y. Goldberg. Learning accurate kinematic control of cable-driven surgical robots using data cleaning and gaussian process regression. In *CASE*, 2014.

[10] P. Spark. Pyspark. https://spark.apache.org/docs/0.9.0/python-programming-guide.html.

[11] L. Van der Maaten and G. Hinton. Visualizing data using t-sne. In *JMLR*, 2008.

[12] J. Wang, S. Krishnan, M. J. Franklin, K. Goldberg, T. Kraska, and T. Milo. A sample-and-clean framework for fast and accurate query processing on dirty data. In *SIGMOD*, 2014.

[13] H. Xiao, B. Biggio, G. Brown, G. Fumera, C. Eckert, and F. Roli. Is feature selection secure against training data poisoning? In *ICML*, 2015.

[14] M. Yakout, L. Berti-Equille, and A. K. Elmagarmid. Don't be scared: use scalable automatic repairing with maximal likelihood and bounded changes. In *SIGMOD*, 2013.

[15] M. Yakout, A. K. Elmagarmid, J. Neville, M. Ouzzani, and I. F. Ilyas. Guided data repair. In *VLDB*, 2011.

Wander Join: Online Aggregation for Joins

Feifei Li [1], Bin Wu [2], Ke Yi [2], Zhuoyue Zhao [3]
[1]University of Utah [2]Hong Kong University of Science and Technology [3] Shanghai Jiao Tong University
lifeifei@cs.utah.edu {bwuac, yike}@cse.ust.hk zzy7896321@sjtu.edu.cn

ABSTRACT

Joins are expensive, and online aggregation over joins was proposed to mitigate the cost, which offers a nice and flexible tradeoff between query efficiency and accuracy in a continuous, online fashion. However, the state-of-the-art approach, in both internal and external memory, is based on ripple join, which is still very expensive and may also need very restrictive assumptions (e.g., tuples in a table are stored in random order). We introduce a new approach, *wander join*, to the online aggregation problem by performing random walks over the underlying join graph. We have also implemented and tested wander join in the latest PostgreSQL.

1. INTRODUCTION

Joins are the common operations in relational databases. In interactive data analytics, users often need the database system to quickly answer ad hoc queries with complex joins involving multiple tables over gigabetyes or even terabytes of data. For instance, the TPC-H benchmark specifies 22 queries, 17 of which are joins and the most complex one involves 8 tables. Unfortunately, even the leading relational database system may take hours to answer such complex queries, especially when working with large data.

A line of work known as "online aggregation" [8] was proposed, with the observation that users would prefer approximate answers with quality guarantees (in the form of confidence interval) if they can be returned much more quickly. The quality of the approximate answers improves over time. The user can immediately stop the query whenever the quality is satisfactory, saving a lot of computation resources.

```
SELECT SUM(l_extendedprice * (1 - l_discount))
FROM customer, orders, lineitem
WHERE c_mktsegment='BUILDING'
  AND c_custkey=o_custkey
  AND l_orderkey=o_orderkey
```

Consider the query above based on Q3 in TPC-H, which queries the total value of the orders placed by the customers in certain market segment. It involves natural joins over 3 tables. Running the full join to complete on TPC-H data with scale factor of 20 takes over 2 minutes while online aggregation achieves a 2.4% confidence interval within 1 second. If the user is satisfied with the result, he/she can stop the query. Or the user can wait for a bit longer to get a more accurate answer.

Prior work of online aggregation uses the ripple join algorithm to perform online aggregation over joins. However, no commercial or full-fledged open-source database systems have adopted ripple join due to its inherent limitations and weaknesses, which we will discuss in Section 2. We introduce a new approach called *wander join*, which outperforms ripple join significantly and is easy to implement in a full-fledged database engine. We implemented wander join in PostgreSQL. Users can pose online aggregation queries with new keyword `ONLINE` through PostgreSQL CLI. We also connected it to Apache Zeppelin, which allows users to see the convergence of estimators over time through a web interface.

We give the problem formulation and the background of online aggregation in Section 2. In Section 3 we describe the key ideas of wander join. In Section 4, we present the system implementation of wander join in PostgreSQL. In Section 5, we show some evaluation results to illustrate the performance advantage of wander join over ripple join and full join and present a demonstration plan of wander join. Lastly, we survey the related work in Section 6.

2. FORMULATION AND BACKGROUND

Problem formulation. The type of queries we aim to support is SQL queries of the form

SELECT g, AGG(expression)
FROM $R_1, R_2, \dots, R_k$
WHERE join conditions AND selection predicates
GROUP BY g

where `AGG` can be any of the standard aggregation functions (e.g. `SUM`, `AVG`, `COUNT`, `VARIANCE`) and `expression` can involve any attributes of the tables. The `join conditions` consist of equality or inequality conditions between pairs of the tables, and `selection predicates` can be applied to any number of the tables.

At any point in time during query processing, the algorithm should output an estimator $\tilde{Y}$ for `AGG(expression)` together with a confidence interval, i.e.,

$$\Pr[|\tilde{Y} - \texttt{AGG(expression)}| \leq \varepsilon] \geq \alpha.$$

Here, ε is called the *half-width* of the confidence interval

SIGMOD'16, June 26-July 01, 2016, San Francisco, CA, USA
© 2016 ACM. ISBN 978-1-4503-3531-7/16/06...$15.00
DOI: http://dx.doi.org/10.1145/2882903.2899413

and α the *confidence level.* The user should specify one of them and the algorithm will continuously update the other as time goes on. The user can terminate the query when it reaches the desired level. Alternatively, the user may also specify a time limit on the query processing, and the algorithm should return the best-effort estimate within the limit, together with a confidence interval.

Ripple join. The ripple join algorithm [6] is central to prior work on online aggregation over joins. It repeatedly takes independent random samples from each table in a round-robin fashion and stores them in the memory. When a new tuple is retrieved, it is joined with all tuples stored in the memory to get samples from the join results. Clearly, these samples are not independent, nonetheless the sample mean can still serve as an unbiased estimator but the formulas for confidence intervals are complex and differ from standard statistical formulas [5,7].

In spite of the nice properties of online aggregation, no commercial or full-fledged open-source database systems support this technique because of two weaknesses of the ripple join algorithm: (1) The performance highly depends on the fraction of the sampled tuples that actually join, which often can be extremely low in practice. (2) The algorithm requires that the tuples retrieved from the tables are in random order. However, tuples are usually clustered according to primary key to facilitate other operations. The system implementation of ripple join, DBO [4,13] actually has to be built from scratch (independent from any existing database engines) to support the random-order storage of tuples.

3. WANDER JOIN

In this section, we illustrate how wander join works by an example of the natural join between 3 tables R_1, R_2, R_3:

$$R_1(A,B) \bowtie R_2(B,C) \bowtie R_3(C,D), \tag{1}$$

where $R_1(A,B)$ means that R_1 has two attributes A and B, etc. The natural join returns all combinations of tuples from the 3 tables that have matching values on their common attributes. We assume that R_2 has an index on attribute B, R_3 has an index on attribute C, and the aggregation function is SUM(D).

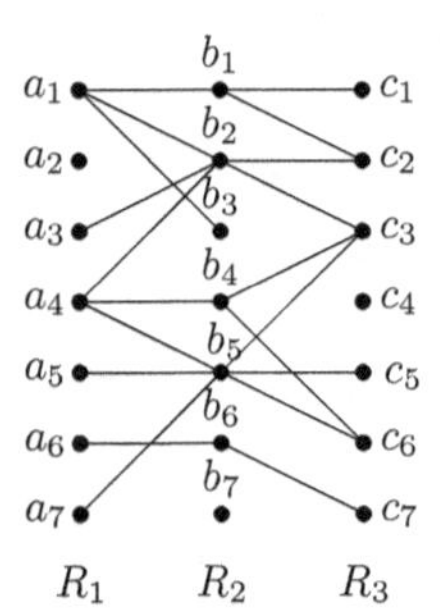

Figure 1: The 3-table join data graph: there is an edge between two tuples if they can join.

We model the join as a graph called *join data graph.* Figure 1 shows a possible join data graph of the 3-table natural join. Where each tuple is modeled as a vertex and there is an edge between two tuples whenever they can join, i.e. have the same value on their common attributes. Each join result is then represented by a path of length 2 from some vertex in R_1 to some vertex in R_3. Sampling a join result boils down to sampling such a path from the graph.

Sampling a path from the graph does not require the graph to be explicitly constructed. Rather, we first pick a vertex in R_1 uniformly at random and then perform a random walk towards R_3. In each step of the random walk, we sample from the tuples in the next table that can join the previous one uniformly at random, which can be done efficiently via a B-Tree index.

Different paths may have different probabilities to be sampled. It is obvious that sample mean is no longer an unbiased estimator. Fortunately, the *Horvitz-Thompson estimator* [9] can serve as an unbiased estimator. Suppose a path γ is sampled with probability $p(\gamma)$, whose value to be aggregated is $v(\gamma)$. Then $v(\gamma)/p(\gamma)$ is an unbiased estimator of the SUM aggregator. If the random walk gets stuck before the path is complete, we should return 0 as the estimator. The probability of a path γ can be easily computed on-the-fly as the path is sampled. Let $\gamma = (t_1, t_2, t_3)$ and $d_k(t_i)$ be the number of tuples in table k that can join t_i. Then the probability of the path γ is

$$p(\gamma) = \frac{1}{|R_1|} \cdot \frac{1}{d_2(t_1)} \cdot \frac{1}{d_3(t_2)} \tag{2}$$

With a number of independent unbiased estimators computed from the sampled paths, we can get an unbiased estimator with lower variance by taking the average. We omit the details for the formulas of variance and confidence interval for different aggregate operators in this demo paper, but they can be derived following similar techniques from [5].

4. WANDER JOIN IN POSTGRESQL

We implemented wander join in PostgreSQL by extending its parser, plan generator, and query exeuctor. We added serveral keywords to the SQL parser like ONLINE, WITHTIME, CONFIDENCE, REPORTINTERVAL. Following is the online aggregation query for the example based on Q3 of TPC-H:

```
SELECT ONLINE SUM(l_extendedprice * (1 - l_discount))
FROM customer, orders, lineitem
WHERE c_mktsegment='BUILDING'
  AND c_custkey=o_custkey
  AND l_orderkey=o_orderkey
WITHTIME 20 CONFIDENCE 95 REPORTINTERVAL 1
```

The above query tells the engine that it is an online aggregation query, such that the engine should report the estimations and their associated confidence intervals, calculated with respect to 95% confidence level every 1 second for up to 20 seconds.

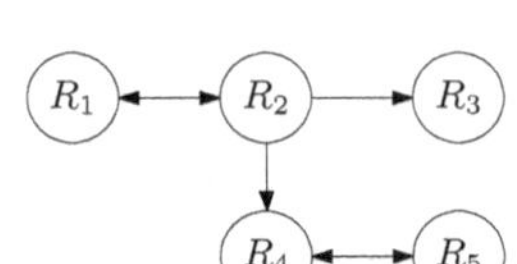

R_1, R_2, R_3, R_4, R_5
R_1, R_2, R_4, R_3, R_5
R_1, R_2, R_4, R_5, R_3
R_2, R_1, R_3, R_4, R_5
R_2, R_1, R_4, R_3, R_5
R_2, R_1, R_4, R_5, R_3
R_2, R_3, R_1, R_4, R_5
R_2, R_3, R_4, R_1, R_5
R_2, R_3, R_4, R_5, R_1
R_2, R_4, R_1, R_3, R_5
R_2, R_4, R_1, R_5, R_3
R_2, R_4, R_3, R_1, R_5
R_2, R_4, R_3, R_5, R_1
R_2, R_4, R_5, R_1, R_3
R_2, R_4, R_5, R_3, R_1

Figure 2: A directed join query graph and all its walk plans.

The online aggregation queries are passed to plan generator for wander join. The plan generator constructs the *join query graph* (or *query graph* in short), where each vertex represents a table and there is a *directed* edge from one table to another when there is an index on the join attribute of the second table. Figure 2 shows a possible query graph and all its walk plans. A walk plan is a walk order of the tables. We first try to find a valid walk order that for each table R_i (except the first one in the order), there exists a table R_j earlier in the order such that there is a join condition between R_i and R_j. In addition, R_i has an index on the join attribute. If it is not possible to find such a valid walk order, we relaxes the requirement by decomposing the graph into serveral components so that each component has a valid sub-walk order. All the join conditions not used in the walk and all the selection conditions will be verified as soon as tuples from the related tables are sampled. If the walk does not satisfy the conditions, it is treated as a failed walk and return an estimator of 0.

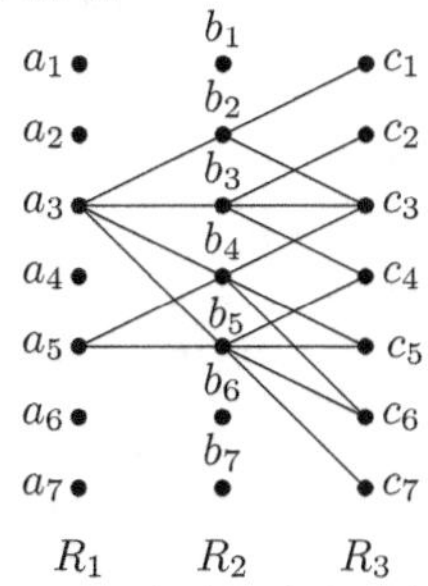

Figure 3: Structure of the join data graph has significant impact on different walk plans' performance.

Selection conditions, structures of the join data graph and different walk orders may greatly influence the success rate of the walk, i.e. the probability that the walk does not get stuck, which in turn influences how fast the estimator converges. Considering the join data graph in Figure 3, if we perform the random walk by the order $R1$, $R2$, $R3$, then the success probability is only 2/7, but if we follow the order $R3$, $R2$, $R1$, it is 100%. Even if the success rate is the same, different non-uniformity also influences the the speed of convergence. Instead of dealing with all the issues, we observe that the performance of the random walk is measured by the variance of the final estimator after a given amount of time. To find an optimal plan, we simply generate all the promising plans. Then we run some trial samples according to each of the plan and pick the best one to continue with. Note the total number of plans could be exponential in the number of tables but it is not a real concern because 1) the number of tables is usually small (up to 8 tables in TPC-H queries) 2) the trial samples can also be combined into the final estimator so that they are not wasted.

5. EVALUATION AND DEMO PLAN

5.1 Evaluation

We compared our system against the full join in PostgreSQL and the ripple join implemented in Turbo DBO [4], an improvement to the original DBO engine that extends ripple join to data on external memory with many optimizations. We used 95% as the default confidence level for both DBO and our system.

Due to the low-latency requirement for data analytical tasks and thanks to growing memory sizes, database systems are moving towards the "in-memory" computing paradigm.

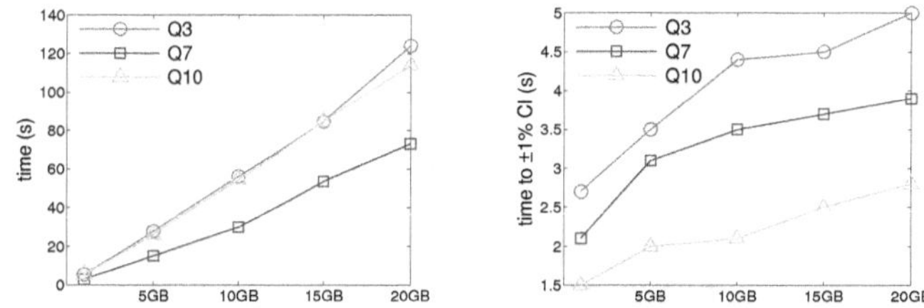

(a) PostgreSQL full join (b) Wander join in PG

Figure 4: Experimental results with sufficient memory: 32GB memory.

We first tested our PostgreSQL implementation of wander join when there is sufficient memory. We used a machine with 32GB memory and data sets of sizes up to 20GB. We ran 3 queries based on Q3, Q7 and Q10 in TPC-H benchmark using wander join, full join in PostgreSQL and Turbo DBO. As shown in Figure 4, the time of full join linearly clearly grows. The data size has a mild impact on the performance of wander join because the use of B-tree indices leads to logarithmical increase in access cost when data size grows. Nevertheless, the time growth is much slower than full join and the time to 1% confidence interval (CI) outperforms full join in PostgreSQL by more than one order of magnitude. We also ran Turbo DBO in this case but it turned out to be *even slower than full join in PostgreSQL*, so we do not show its results. Partly it is because DBO is designed for large data running with very small memory.

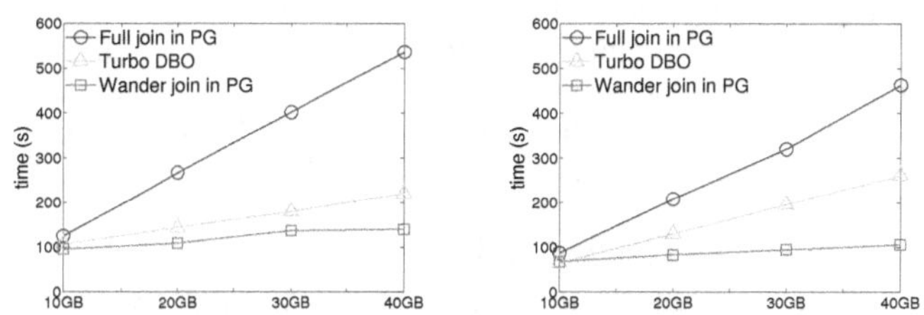

(a) Q3 (b) Q7

Figure 5: Experimental results with limited memory, 4GB memory (Wonder join in PG and Turbo DBO run to 1% confidence interval).

To compare our system and Turbo DBO in limited memory, we ran the queries again on a machine with only 4GB memory on data sized from 10GB to 40GB. As seen in Figure 5, our system outperforms both full join in PostgreSQL and Turbo DBO. Full join and Turbo DBO have a linear growth in time while our system's running time still grows mildly. Both DBO and our system run to 1% CI.

5.2 Demonstration Plan

We will have an end-to-end demonstration of online aggregation queries using wander join implemented in PostgreSQL over TPC-H dataset. We will also show the comparison of the performance of wander join in PostgreSQL, ripple join in DBO and full join in PostgreSQL.

Queries and dataset. The TPC-H benchmark used in our demonstration is a decision support benchmark. It features 8 tables: part, supplier, partsupp, nation, region, customer, orders, lineitem. The benchmark also features a set of business analysis queries (e.g. query of the value of goods shipped between two specific nations). We will prepare several online aggregation queries, e.g., Q3, Q7 and Q10 in TPC-H. Some queries will have multiple selection conditions and some will have groupby clause. Attendees can either use these ready-to-run queries or construct their own queries on

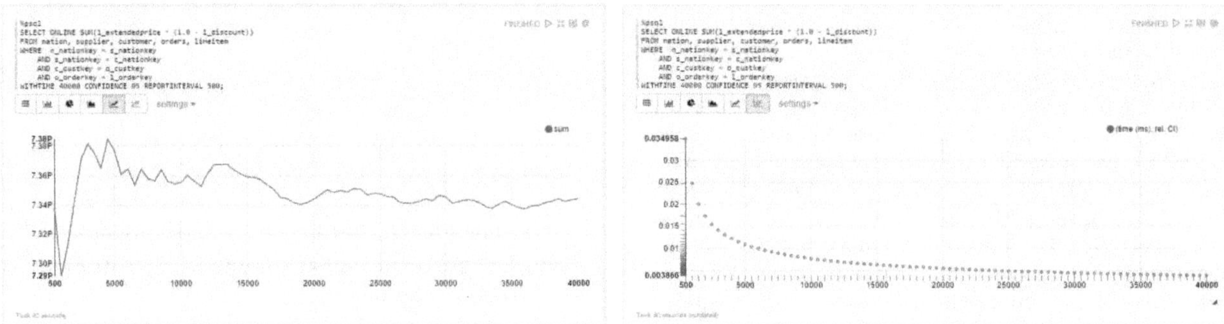

(a) Estimator converges over time. (b) (Relative) Confidence interval drops over time

Figure 6: Our web interface front-end for the demonstration of wander join in PostgreSQL.

the fly to test the system. We will preload TPC-H datasets with different scale factors.

Web interface for thed demo. We have connected PostgreSQL to Apache Zeppelin, which can show the query results in the form of table, line plot and other visualization representation. Figure 6 shows our web interface. Attendees can launch both online aggregation queries and normal queries through a query input form (more forms can be created on the fly). When launching online aggregation queries to PostgreSQL, our system will use wander join to execute the query. Attendees can see how the estimator converges over time as in Figure 6(a), or plot the relative confidence interval against elapsed time as in Figure 6(b).

We will also prepare the corresponding ready-to-run DBO queries. Attendees can see a side-by-side comparison of performance among wander join in PostgreSQL, ripple join in Turbo DBO and full join in PostgreSQL.

6. RELATED WORK

The concept of online aggregation was first proposed in [8]. In particular, related to our problem, online aggregation over joins was first studied in [6], where the ripple join algorithm was designed. Extensions to ripple join were done over the years [4, 12, 13, 15], in particular, to support ripple join in DBO for large data on external memory.

In addition to these efforts, there is an increasing interest in building sampling-based approximate query processing systems, e.g., represented by systems like BlinkDB, Monte-Carlo DB, Analytical Bootstrap, DICE and others [1–3, 10, 11, 14, 16–18], but these systems do not support online aggregations over joins.

7. ACKNOWLEDGMENT

Feifei Li is supported in part by NSF grants 1443046 and 1251019. Feifei Li is also supported in part by NSFC grant 61428204 and a Google research award. Bin Wu and Ke Yi are supported by HKRGC under grants GRF-621413, GRF-16211614, and GRF-16200415.

8. REFERENCES

[1] S. Agarwal, H. Milner, A. Kleiner, A. Talwalkar, M. I. Jordan, S. Madden, B. Mozafari, and I. Stoica. Knowing when you're wrong: building fast and reliable approximate query processing systems. In *SIGMOD*, pages 481–492, 2014.

[2] S. Agarwal, B. Mozafari, A. Panda, H. Milner, S. Madden, and I. Stoica. Blinkdb: queries with bounded errors and bounded response times on very large data. In *EuroSys*, pages 29–42, 2013.

[3] S. Agarwal, A. Panda, B. Mozafari, A. P. Iyer, S. Madden, and I. Stoica. Blink and it's done: Interactive queries on very large data. In *PVLDB*, volume 5, 2012.

[4] A. Dobra, C. Jermaine, F. Rusu, and F. Xu. Turbo charging estimate convergence in dbo. In *VLDB*, 2009.

[5] P. J. Haas. Large-sample and deterministic confidence intervals for online aggregation. In *Proc. Ninth Intl. Conf. Scientific and Statistical Database Management*, 1997.

[6] P. J. Haas and J. M. Hellerstein. Ripple joins for online aggregation. In *Proc. ACM SIGMOD International Conference on Management of Data*, pages 287–298, 1999.

[7] P. J. Haas, J. F. Naughton, S. Seshadri, and A. N. Swami. Selectivity and cost estimation for joins based on random sampling. *Journal of Computer and System Sciences*, 52:550–569, 1996.

[8] J. M. Hellerstein, P. J. Haas, and H. J. Wang. Online aggregation. In *Proc. ACM SIGMOD International Conference on Management of Data*, 1997.

[9] D. G. Horvitz and D. J. Thompson. A generalization of sampling without replacement from a finite universe. *Journal of the American Statistical Association*, 47:663–685, 1952.

[10] R. Jampani, F. Xu, M. Wu, L. L. Perez, C. Jermaine, and P. J. Haas. The monte carlo database system: Stochastic analysis close to the data. *ACM Trans. Database Syst.*, 36(3):18, 2011.

[11] P. Jayachandran, K. Tunga, N. Kamat, and A. Nandi. Combining user interaction, speculative query execution and sampling in the DICE system. *PVLDB*, 7(13):1697–1700, 2014.

[12] C. Jermaine, S. Arumugam, A. Pol, and A. Dobra. Scalable approximate query processing with the DBO engine. In *Proc. ACM SIGMOD International Conference on Management of Data*, 2007.

[13] C. Jermaine, S. Arumugam, A. Pol, and A. Dobra. Scalable approximate query processing with the DBO engine. *ACM TODS*, 33(4), Article 23, 2008.

[14] A. Klein, R. Gemulla, P. Rösch, and W. Lehner. Derby/s: a DBMS for sample-based query answering. In *SIGMOD*, 2006.

[15] G. Luo, C. J. Ellmann, P. J. Haas, and J. F. Naughton. A scalable hash ripple join algorithm. In *Proc. ACM SIGMOD International Conference on Management of Data*, 2002.

[16] S. Nirkhiwale, A. Dobra, and C. M. Jermaine. A sampling algebra for aggregate estimation. *PVLDB*, 6(14):1798–1809, 2013.

[17] K. Zeng, S. Gao, J. Gu, B. Mozafari, and C. Zaniolo. ABS: a system for scalable approximate queries with accuracy guarantees. In *SIGMOD*, pages 1067–1070, 2014.

[18] K. Zeng, S. Gao, B. Mozafari, and C. Zaniolo. The analytical bootstrap: a new method for fast error estimation in approximate query processing. In *SIGMOD*, pages 277–288, 2014.

PerNav: A Route Summarization Framework for Personalized Navigation

Yaguang Li[†], Han Su[†], Ugur Demiryurek[†], Bolong Zheng[‡], Kai Zeng[*], Cyrus Shahabi[†]

[†] University of Southern California, United States [*] Microsoft, United States [‡]University of Queensland, Australia
[†]{yaguang, hansu, demiryur, shahabi}@usc.edu [‡] b.zheng@uq.edu.au [*] kaizeng@microsoft.com

ABSTRACT

In this paper, we study a route summarization framework for Personalized Navigation dubbed *PerNav* - with which the goal is to generate more intuitive and customized turn-by-turn directions based on user generated content. The turn-by-turn directions provided in the existing navigation applications are exclusively derived from underlying road network topology information i.e., the connectivity of nodes to each other. Therefore, the turn-by-turn directions are simplified as metric translation of physical world (e.g. distance/time to turn) to spoken language. Such translation - that ignores human cognition about the geographic space - is often verbose and redundant for the drivers who have knowledge about the geographical areas. *PerNav* utilizes wealth of user generated historical trajectory data to extract namely "landmarks" (e.g., point of interests or intersections) and frequently visited routes between them from the road network. Then this extracted information is used to obtain cognitive turn-by-turn directions customized for each user.

Categories and Subject Descriptors

H.2.8 [**Database Applications**]: Spatial databases and GIS

1. INTRODUCTION

Navigation applications that find optimal routes and corresponding turn-by-turn directions in road networks are one of the fundamental and most used applications in wide variety of domains. While the problem of computing optimal path has been extensively studied and many efficient techniques have been developed over the past several decades, the turn-by-turn direction computation techniques have not changed. Meanwhile, with the ever-growing usage of navigation applications in mobile devices and car-navigation systems, plethora of user generated trajectory data became available. This data is particularly useful for producing more effective and cognitive turn-by-turn information.

SIGMOD'16, June 26-July 01, 2016, San Francisco, CA, USA

DOI: http://dx.doi.org/10.1145/2882903.2899384

Figure 1: Personalized Navigation Directions.

Taken Figure 1 as an example, suppose we plan to go to a restaurant for dinner. Figure 1(a) shows a route provided by navigation systems. With road network information, turn-by-turn navigation directions can be generated (Figure 1(b)). These turn-by-turn directions are computed by taking into account inherent cost measure (e.g., distance or travel time) and angle (e.g., left or right) between the nodes of the underlying road network. While verbose, it is hard to be laconic without losing route information if we only have road network data. However, experienced urban commuters (i.e., majority of the drivers on roads) have good knowledge about the city and will probably be familiar with a certain part, sometimes most parts, of the route, e.g., routes from home to nearby highways. Suppose the navigation software knows that a user frequently visit a cinema which shares a similar route with the restaurant, it can replace a large part of navigation instructions with a single sentence, e.g., in Figure 1(c), drive towards the cinema via I-10 (the name of a highway). Then for the parts of the route that are unfamiliar to the user, navigation software may continue using detailed turn-by-turn directions. In this way, by leveraging the wealth of user's historical trajectory data, we may be able to generate navigation directions that are both concise and intuitive.

To achieve this goal, however, we have to further address challenges in multiple spheres. First, how to effectively extract landmarks and routes from trajectories which usually come with noise and uncertainty? Second, how to utilize knowledge routes to generate personal navigation directions that are concise but convey enough information for user to interpret the route? - To address these challenges, we designed a prototype system called *PerNav* that produces turn-by-turn directions by leveraging the wealth of user's historical trajectory data. In particular, *PerNav* first extracts user's knowledge about the road network by leveraging trajectory calibration and trajectory clustering. Then for a given route, *PerNav* partitions it based on extracted knowledge using dynamic programming and branch-and-bound based approaches. The final step is to construct a personalized navigation directions based on the route partition. In summary, *PerNav* improves navigation applications in three ways. First, *PerNav* incorporates historical trajectory data to navigation applications to produce higher-quality personalized turn-by-turn directions for urban commuters. To our knowledge, this paper is the first to describe the use of trajectory data for generating personalized turn-by-turn directions. Second, *PerNav* offers network bandwidth reduction by significantly reducing the information transferred between the server and navigation clients. Third, *PerNav* allows user to customize the summary construction process with different detailed granularities.

The remainder of this paper is organized as follows. In Section 2, we formalize the problem and describe key techniques. In Section 3, we present our prototype system with real-world use cases. In Section 4, we review related work.

2. OVERVIEW

By referring to places and routes that are familiar to people, we can provide them an intuitive view about a new route. *PerNav* follows the same intuition to construct a higher level summary for a route generated by navigation software.

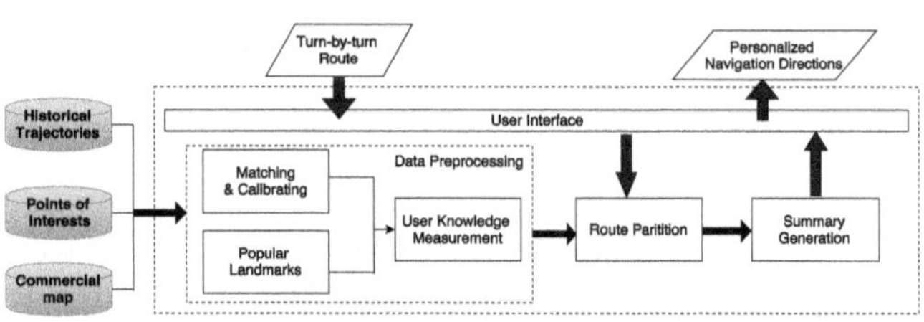

Figure 2: Framework overview of *PerNav*.

Figure 2 shows the overview of *PerNav*. The input of *PerNav* is a route and the output is a personalized navigation direction. This procedure mainly contains three steps, i.e., data preprocessing, route partition and summary generation. The first step for data preprocessing is offline while the last two steps are online. In the data preprocessing, *PerNav* will extract frequent visiting ⟨starting point, destination⟩ pairs and routes between them for every user, which are called the *knowledge* of users, from users' historical trajectories. Then given a route, *PerNav* partitions it based on extracted knowledge and the detail will be discussed in Section 2.3. The final step is to construct personalized navigation directions based on the route partition. In what follows, we will formalize the problem and describe the key technicals behind each step.

2.1 Preliminaries Concepts

We adopt the standard road network representation in which intersections are represented by nodes and roads are represented by links with attached features. Link is also known as road segment and we will use link and road segment interchangeably whenever the context is clear.

DEFINITION 1 (LANDMARK). *A landmark l is a geographical point in the space, which is stable and independent of user trajectories.*

A landmark can be either a Point of Interest (POI) or an intersection in the road network, and a route in the road network can be represented using landmarks.

DEFINITION 2 (ROUTE). *Formally, a route $\mathcal{R}$ in the road network is defined as a sequence of landmarks. $\mathcal{R} = [l_1, l_2, \cdots l_n]$. $\mathcal{R}(i)$ denotes the ith landmark, i.e., l_i. Every two adjacent landmarks are directly connected by a link in the road network. Thus $\mathcal{R}$ can also be considered as a sequence of links.*

In the road network, adjacent links usually share some features, e.g., street name, direction. Based on these features, we can divide the road network into disjointed routes, i.e., all the adjacent links with same features will be in the same route. As this type of route is independent of specific person, we call it *natural route* ($\mathcal{NR}$). For example, in Figure 1, S Atlantic Blvd is called a natural route. For a given route $\mathcal{R} = [l_1, l_2, \cdots l_n]$, we can use a sequence of natural routes $[\mathcal{NR}_1, \mathcal{NR}_2, \cdots, \mathcal{NR}_m]$ $(m \leq n)$, to represent it, which is known as the turn-by-turn manner, e.g., Figure 1(b), and this manner is widely used by existing navigation systems.

Moreover, there exists another type of route which is specific to individuals. In real life, urban commuters will get quite familiar with certain landmarks and routes between some of them, e.g., the route from home to work or the route from work to a shopping center. We call such a route *knowledge route* ($\mathcal{KR}$) for the urban commuter. In Figure 1(a), the route from home to the cinema is an example of knowledge route for the user.

Note that, a knowledge route usually contains multiple natural routes, i.e., $\mathcal{KR} = [\mathcal{NR}_i, \mathcal{NR}_{i+1}, \cdots, \mathcal{NR}_j]$. Thus, if this sequence of natural routes is a sub-sequence of $\mathcal{R}$, we can represent the route as:

$$\mathcal{R} = [\mathcal{NR}_1, \cdots, \mathcal{NR}_{i-1}, \mathcal{KR}, \mathcal{NR}_{j+1}, \cdots, \mathcal{NR}_k] \; k \leq m \leq n$$

which is called the personalized manner. Obviously, by using knowledge routes, the personalized manner becomes more concise, i.e., less number of the route-segments, and more familiar to the urban commuter than the turn-by-turn manner. In the following subsection, we will show how to extract and measure knowledge routes by analyzing user's historical trajectories.

2.2 User Knowledge Measurement

With historical trajectories, *PerNav* first employs trajectory calibration proposed in our previous research to map them into routes in the road network [8, 10]. Then stay points detection [15] is used to identify places that are familiar to user. These places are used to generate the description of knowledge routes. After that, *PerNav* groups trajectories into clusters [13]. In each cluster, the most representative route is extracted as a knowledge route connecting a source and a destination. Besides, for each knowledge route, we calculate a familiarity score $f(\mathcal{R}) \in [0,1]$, which indicates the user's familiarity of this knowledge route. $f(\mathcal{R})$ is affected by the following aspects: 1) The frequency this route is traversed. 2) The significance of start and end landmarks of this route. The significance of landmarks are calculated by leveraging a HITS-like algorithm [15] which models the travellers as authorities, landmarks as hubs, and check-ins as hyperlinks. In *PerNav*, normalized weighted sum of these two factors is used as the familiarity score. Note that, for a natural route, its familiarity to a user is 0 by default.

Given the familiarity of a route $\mathcal{R}$, we can derive the familiarity of its segments, i.e., *route segment.*

DEFINITION 3 (ROUTE SEGMENT). *A route segment* $\overline{RS} = \mathcal{R}(j,k) = [l_j, l_{j+1}, \cdots, l_k]$*, is defined as a sub-sequence of route* $\mathcal{R}$*. It can also be seen as a sequence of links connecting* l_j *and* l_k*.*

Based on the type of $\mathcal{R}$, a route segment can be either a *natural route segment* or a *knowledge route segment.* The familiarity of a route segment is calculated using Equation 1

$$f(\overline{RS}) = f(\mathcal{R}(\overline{RS})) \cdot g\Big(\frac{len(\overline{RS})}{len(\mathcal{R}(\overline{RS}))}\Big) \tag{1}$$

where $\mathcal{R}(\overline{RS})$ is the corresponding knowledge route of $\overline{RS}$, $\frac{len(\overline{RS})}{len(\mathcal{R}(\overline{RS}))}$ is the length ratio of $\overline{RS}$. $g(\cdot)$ is a monotonic convex function with $g(0) = 0$ and $g(1) = 1$. With the decrease of length ratio, the familiarity score decreases faster than a linear function which is more consistent with human being's cognition.

2.3 Knowledge-based Route Partition

Usually, if we want to describe a route, we will partition it into route segments and then give description for each of them.

DEFINITION 4 (ROUTE PARTITION). *For a route* $\mathcal{R}$*, a partition of it* $\mathbb{P}(\mathcal{R}) = \{\overline{RS}_1, \overline{RS}_2, \cdots, \overline{RS}_n\}$ *is such that:*

- $\bigcup_{i=1}^{n} \overline{RS}_i = \mathcal{R}$
- $\forall i,j\ \overline{RS}_i \cap \overline{RS}_j = \emptyset$

Each route segment $\overline{RS}_i$ *can be either a knowledge route segment or a natural route segment.*

For a route $\mathcal{R}$ in the road network, we can partition it in many ways resulting in possibly different navigation directions. Generally, we want the generated directions 1) be intuitive and easy for user to understand, i.e., utilizing knowledge routes with high familiarity in generated directions; and then 2) be concise, so it will be easy for human beings to read and share, i.e., minimize the number of route segments. With these objectives, we can evaluate the quality of a partition $\mathbb{P}$ by equation 2:

$$\mathcal{Q}_{\mathbb{P}(\mathcal{R})} = \sum_{\overline{RS}_i \in \mathbb{P}(\mathcal{R})} f(\overline{RS}_i) - \lambda|\mathbb{P}(\mathcal{R})| \tag{2}$$

$$\mathbb{P}_{opt}(\mathcal{R}) = \underset{\mathbb{P}(\mathcal{R})}{\operatorname{argmax}}\ \mathcal{Q}_{\mathbb{P}(\mathcal{R})} \tag{3}$$

where $f(\cdot)$ is the function to calculate the familiarity score in Equation 1, $|\mathbb{P}(\mathcal{R})|$ is the number of route segments in this partition, $\lambda \geq 0$ is used to constrain the number of segments in the generated route partition. We want to find the route partition $\mathbb{P}(\mathcal{R})_{opt}$ that maximize $\mathcal{Q}_{\mathbb{P}(\mathcal{R})}$.

The naïve approach is to enumerate all the possible combination of route segments and choose the one with maximum score. However, the time complexity is exponential in terms of the number of links in the route. In the following paragraphs, we will show that dynamic programming can be used to find the optimal route partition efficiently.

DEFINITION 5 (CONDITIONAL ROUTE PARTITION). *Given a route* $\mathcal{R} = [l_1, l_2, \cdots, l_n]$*, its conditional route partition* $\mathbb{P}(\mathcal{R}(1,i)|\mathcal{R}'(\cdot,\cdot))$ *is defined as route partitions with the last route segment, i.e.,* $\overline{RS}$*, coming from route* $\mathcal{R}'$*.*

Specially, $\mathbb{P}(\mathcal{R}(1,i)|\mathcal{R}'(j,k))$ represents the conditional route partition with the last route segment equals to $\mathcal{R}'(j,k)$.

LEMMA 1. *The optimal partition of a route is the best conditional optimal partition among all candidate routes for the last link.*

$$\mathbb{P}_{opt}(\mathcal{R}(1,i)) = \underset{\mathbb{P}}{\operatorname{argmax}}\ \mathcal{Q}\left(\mathbb{P}_{opt}(\mathcal{R}(1,i)|\mathcal{R}'(\cdot,\cdot)\right) \tag{4}$$
$$\mathcal{R}' \in \mathbb{R}(\mathcal{R}(i-1,i))$$

where $\mathbb{R}(\mathcal{R}(i-1,i))$ is the set of all the routes that contains link $\mathcal{R}(i-1,i)$. The proof is straightforward, as we enumerate all possible conditions and choose the best one.

LEMMA 2. *The conditional optimal route partition of a sub-route* $\mathcal{R}(1,i+1)$*, i.e.,* $\mathbb{P}_{opt}(\mathcal{R}(1,i+1)|\mathcal{R}'(\cdot,\cdot))$*, can be derived from conditional optimal route partitions of* $\mathcal{R}(1,i)$*, i.e.,* $\mathbb{P}_{opt}(\mathcal{R}(1,i)|\mathcal{R}''(\cdot,\cdot))$*.*

$$\mathbb{P}_{opt}(\mathcal{R}(1,i+1)|\mathcal{R}') = \underset{\mathcal{R}'' \in \mathbb{R}(\mathcal{R}(i-1,i))}{\operatorname{argmax}} \tag{5}$$
$$\mathcal{Q}\Big(\mathbb{P}_{opt}(\mathcal{R}(1,i)|\mathcal{R}''(\cdot,\cdot)) \cup (\mathcal{R}(i,i+1) \mapsto \mathcal{R}')\Big)$$

where $\mathbb{R}(\mathcal{R}(i-1,i))$ is the set of all the routes that contain link $\mathcal{R}(i-1,i)$, and $\mathbb{P}_{opt}(\mathcal{R}(1,i)|\mathcal{R}'') \cup (\mathcal{R}(i,i+1) \mapsto \mathcal{R}')$ means mapping the link $\mathcal{R}(i,i+1)$ to $\mathcal{R}'$ and merge it to the conditional optimal partition $\mathbb{P}_{opt}(\mathcal{R}(1,i)|\mathcal{R}'')$. Let $\Delta\mathcal{Q}(\mathcal{R}(i,i+1) \mapsto \mathcal{R}')$ denotes the score change after mapping the link $\mathcal{R}(i,i+1)$ to $\mathcal{R}'$. According to Equation 2, $\Delta\mathcal{Q}(\mathcal{R}(i,i+1) \mapsto \mathcal{R}')$ will be the same as long as the last segment of $\mathbb{P}$ is mapped to a route other than $\mathcal{R}'$. Thus, we can iteratively find the optimal partition using dynamic programming.

2.4 Summary Construction

After the partitioning step, a route $\mathcal{R}$ will become a sequence of route segments. Then *PerNav* will generate navigation directions by describing knowledge route segments and natural route segments respectively. As knowledge route $\mathcal{R}$ is familiar to user, we can describe it using some key features, e.g., the start/end landmark, the main highway, rather than describing all the natural routes in it. In order to construct more fluent summary sentences, we also define sentence templates, e.g., drive towards *POI name* via *most representative feature of the knowledge route.* The most significant POI within a certain distance is selected to generate the summary.

For natural routes, traditional turn-by-turn directions generations techniques can be used. Moreover, in *PerNav* user can specify the description granularity of directions. Under the configuration of the most detailed granularity, *PerNav* will generate descriptions for every single route segments.

The result will be similar to turn-by-turn directions provided by current navigation systems. With the decrease of detail level, less important route segments, i.e., low-level roads and short roads, will be omitted.

3. DEMONSTRATION

In this section, we will present a detailed demonstration plan and how user can interact with the system. *PerNav* has both web application and mobile application. Figure 3 shows GUI of the web application.

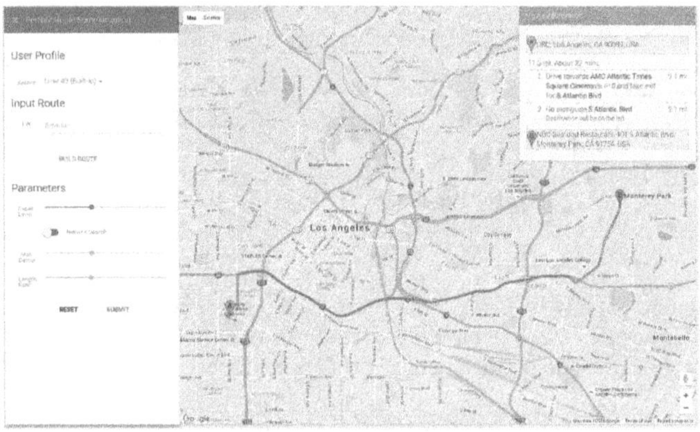

Figure 3: Main GUI

The left panel is for settings and query setup while the right panel is used for result visualization. Since *PerNav* requires historical trajectories information to work properly, we create several built-in profiles based on the following trajectory datasets: Geolife [14, 15], and Planet.gpx [1]. Geolife dataset consists of trajectories of 178 users over a period of four years while Planet.gpx contains the GPS traces uploaded by OpenStreetMap users within 7.5 years. Users can click to select which profile they prefer. Besides, users are allowed to create their own profiles. This can be done by specifying a set of ⟨source, destination⟩ pairs, a route connecting each pair and familiarity score of each route.

After choosing the profile, user can construct the input in following ways: 1) *PerNav* provides several built-in query routes for demonstration purpose; 2) user can interactively create a route by pinning and dragging. Then *PerNav* will generate a personalized route description with corresponding details visualized on the map. In addition, users are allowed to play with a set of parameters to customize the route summarization procedure.

4. RELATED WORK

The problem proposed in this work is relevant to trajectory processing and trajectory querying issues, including trajectory data mining [13, 5, 6], popular route discovery [7, 3], personalized route recommendation [2, 4, 9]. The method to discover personalized routes from trajectories is proposed in [2], while the approach to find popular routes is investigated in [3]. In [12, 4], algorithms to recommend routes based on historical trajectories are described. [11] proposes a system to construct summary for raw trajectory. However, none of these problems are same with ours. Our work is mainly regarding reinterpreting an existing route in a way that is intuitive to user and easy to follow, while the vast majority of existing works are dealing with general mining/prediction/recommendation problems.

Acknowledgment

This research has been funded by the USC Integrated Media Systems Center (IMSC) and unrestricted cash gifts from Oracle and Northrop Grumman Corporation.

5. REFERENCES

[1] OpenStreetMap. http://wiki.openstreetmap.org/wiki/Planet.gpx.

[2] K.-P. Chang, L.-Y. Wei, M.-Y. Yeh, and W.-C. Peng. Discovering personalized routes from trajectories. In *ACM SIGSPATIAL Workshop on Location-Based Social Networks*, pages 33–40. ACM, 2011.

[3] Z. Chen, H. T. Shen, and X. Zhou. Discovering popular routes from trajectories. In *ICDE*, pages 900–911. IEEE, 2011.

[4] D. Delling, A. V. Goldberg, M. Goldszmidt, J. Krumm, K. Talwar, and R. F. Werneck. Navigation made personal: Inferring driving preferences from gps traces. In *ACM GIS*. ACM, 2015.

[5] F. Giannotti, M. Nanni, F. Pinelli, and D. Pedreschi. Trajectory pattern mining. In *SIGKDD*, pages 330–339. ACM, 2007.

[6] J.-G. Lee, J. Han, X. Li, and H. Gonzalez. Traclass: trajectory classification using hierarchical region-based and trajectory-based clustering. *Proceedings of the VLDB Endowment*, 1(1):1081–1094, 2008.

[7] X. Li, J. Han, J.-G. Lee, and H. Gonzalez. Traffic density-based discovery of hot routes in road networks. In *SSTD*, pages 441–459. Springer, 2007.

[8] Y. Li, C. Liu, K. Liu, J. Xu, F. He, and Z. Ding. On efficient map-matching according to intersections you pass by. In *DEXA*, pages 42–56. Springer, 2013.

[9] S. Shang, R. Ding, B. Yuan, K. Xie, K. Zheng, and P. Kalnis. User oriented trajectory search for trip recommendation. In *EDBT*, pages 156–167. ACM, 2012.

[10] H. Su, K. Zheng, H. Wang, J. Huang, and X. Zhou. Calibrating trajectory data for similarity-based analysis. In *SIGMOD*, pages 833–844. ACM, 2013.

[11] H. Su, K. Zheng, K. Zeng, J. Huang, and X. Zhou. STMaker: a system to make sense of trajectory data. *VLDB*, 7(13):1701–1704, 2014.

[12] J. Yuan, Y. Zheng, X. Xie, and G. Sun. Driving with knowledge from the physical world. In *SIGKDD*, pages 316–324. ACM, 2011.

[13] Y. Zheng. Trajectory data mining: an overview. *ACM Transactions on Intelligent Systems and Technology (TIST)*, 6(3):29, 2015.

[14] Y. Zheng, X. Xie, and W.-Y. Ma. Geolife: A collaborative social networking service among user, location and trajectory. *IEEE Data Eng. Bull.*, 33(2):32–39, 2010.

[15] Y. Zheng, L. Zhang, X. Xie, and W.-Y. Ma. Mining interesting locations and travel sequences from gps trajectories. In *World Wide Web*, pages 791–800. ACM, 2009.

Making the Case for Query-by-Voice with EchoQuery

Gabriel Lyons, Vinh Tran, Carsten Binnig, Ugur Cetintemel, Tim Kraska
Brown University
firstname_lastname@brown.edu

ABSTRACT

Recent advances in automatic speech recognition and natural language processing have led to a new generation of robust voice-based interfaces. Yet, there is very little work on using voice-based interfaces to query database systems. In fact, one might even wonder who in her right mind would want to query a database system using voice commands!

With this demonstration, we make the case for querying database systems using a voice-based interface, a new querying and interaction paradigm we call *Query-by-Voice* (*QbV*). We will demonstrate the practicality and utility of *QbV* for relational DBMSs using a using a proof-of-concept system called *EchoQuery*. To achieve a smooth and intuitive interaction, the query interface of *EchoQuery* is inspired by casual human-to-human conversations. Our demo will show that voice-based interfaces present an intuitive means of querying and consuming data in a database. It will also highlight the unique advantages of *QbV* over the more traditional approaches, text-based or visual interfaces, for applications where context switching is too expensive, too risky or even not possible at all.

1. INTRODUCTION

Motivation: Recent advances in automatic speech recognition and natural language processing enabled a new generation of robust voice-based interfaces, such as Apple's Siri [3], Google Voice Action [4], and Amazon's Alexa Voice Service [1]. When used together with relational database systems, voice-based interfaces provide an intuitive way to query and consume data. A major advantage over classical query interfaces or even touch-based visual interfaces, such as Tableau [11] or Vizdom [7], is that voice-based interfaces are completely hands-free. As such, voice-based interfaces are superior in many situations where a context switch is either impossible or could cause a major distraction.

The medium of spoken-dialogue, although weak in information density, is strong in encouraging interactive use and engaging users into a "conversation" with the database system. Moreover, a voice-based interface also has also other benefits towards the general accessibility of information. Current database querying tools are inaccessible for people with disabilities that prevent them from using screens, keyboards, or even gestures. Having a voice-based interface for database querying enables people with disabilities to query data directly without having to use cumbersome and inefficient workarounds such as footmice, eyetrackers, or virtual keyboards in order to use SQL or any other query interface. Thus, we argue and demonstrate that a new querying paradigm, which we call *Query-by-Voice* (*QbV*), can be used profitably in such circumstances.

Contributions: In this demo, we present an end-to-end prototype system called *EchoQuery* that implements the *QbV* paradigm by offering a voice-based and hands-free interface to a relational database. Natural language interfaces to databases (NLIDBs) have been studied for several decades in the past [6] and recently gained more attention again [8, 9]. Different from our system, early NLIDBs have been very limited since they mainly focused on constructing interfaces for individual domains and not general purpose interfaces for exploring arbitrary data sets. More recent work [8, 9] to construct NLIDBs also provides a general purpose natural-language interface to query data sets independent from a certain domain. However, this work mainly focuses on the translation process from natural language (e.g., English) to SQL rather than building a full end-to-end *QbV*-system which is the scope of *EchoQuery*.

Another major difference from existing work is that the query interface of *EchoQuery* is inspired by regular human-to-human conversations in order to be natural for the user. The main features of the voice-based interface of *EchoQuery* are:

- **Hands-free Access**: *EchoQuery* does not require the user to press a button or start an application using a gesture or a mouse-click. Instead, users can interact with the database by solely using their voice at any time.
- **Dialogue-based Querying**: While traditional database systems provide a one-shot (i.e., stateless) query interface, natural language conversations are incremental (i.e., stateful) in nature. To that end, *EchoQuery* provides a stateful dialogue-based query interface between the user and the database where (1) users can start a conversation with an initial query and refine that query incrementally over time, and (2) *EchoQuery* can seek for clarification if the query is incomplete or has some ambiguities that need to be resolved.

SIGMOD'16, June 26-July 01, 2016, San Francisco, CA, USA

ISBN 978-1-4503-3531-7/16/06...$15.00

DOI: http://dx.doi.org/10.1145/2882903.2899394

- **Personalizable Vocabulary**: Domain experts often use their own terms to formulate queries, which might be different from the schema elements (i.e., table and column names) of a database. Learning the terminology of a user and its translation to the underlying schema is similar to the problem of constructing a schema mapping in data integration. *EchoQuery* constructs these mappings incrementally on a per-user basis by issuing clarification questions using its dialogue-based query interface.

In its current version, *EchoQuery* does not strive to be a system which attempts to translate arbitrary natural language statements into queries. Instead, *EchoQuery* exposes its query interface as a natural language based version (i.e., a spoken version) of SQL with a purposefully limited grammar. However, as we will see, this query interface allows non-trivial database queries.

Outline: The rest of this paper is organized as follows. Section 2 gives an overview of the architecture of *EchoQuery*. Section 3 then discusses details of *EchoQuery*'s interface. Finally, Section 4 presents the scenario that we plan to show in our demo. We recommend that the reviewers watch our demo movie to get an idea of *EchoQuery*.[1]

2. SYSTEM ARCHITECTURE

EchoQuery is built using a middleware approach over an existing relational database that provides a SQL interface. While the middleware implements our novel concepts for a voice-based database interface (i.e., hands-free access, dialog-based querying, personalizable vocabulary), the database system is used to efficiently store and query the data.

Figure 1 shows the system architecture of *EchoQuery*. As a frontend to the user, we currently use the *Echo*, a wireless speaker and voice command device from Amazon, and *Alexa* [2], the voice command service that powers the Echo. The main purpose of Alexa is twofold: Firstly, Alexa turns the voice input of the user into an audio request and sends it to the *Alexa Voice Service (AVS)* via an HTTP-request. Secondly Alexa also replays the audio response that is returned from AVS via an HTTP-response.

Moreover, the AVS is also the entry point to *EchoQuery*. AVS implements the speech recognition part of *EchoQuery* and maps voice commands to different intents. An intent in *EchoQuery* defines how the voice command of the user is handled. At the moment, *EchoQuery* implements three different intents: a *Query Intent*, a *Refine Intent*, and a *Clarify Intent*. In the following, we briefly discuss the tasks of each intent. A detailed discussion of each intent can be found later in Section 3.

Query Intent: This intent is used by *EchoQuery* to start a conversation with the user. In order to process an initial query request, the *Query Intent* first adds missing information that is not specified by the user (e.g., it infers missing join predicates or table names that are not specified when selecting columns). Afterwards, the completed query request is translated into an executable SQL query using the *Query Translator*.

Once the SQL query is executed the *Result Translator* takes the result table and renders a (textual) query response that is replayed to the user. It is important to note that the

[1]https://vimeo.com/151847274

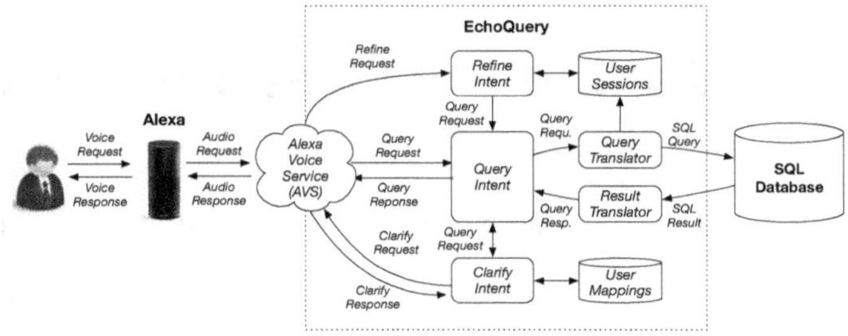

Figure 1: *EchoQuery* Architecture

result of the SQL query is not directly mapped into a textual query response one-by-one because the result might contain too many rows/columns to be efficiently consumable by the user. Therefore, the *Result Translator* might apply transformations that reduce the level of detail in the result (e.g., it returns only the count of rows as an answer instead of the result table content). If the user wants to know further details about the result, the user can use the *Refine Intent* to extract more details about the result or even to force *EchoQuery* to replay the full result.

Refine Intent: This intent is used by *EchoQuery* to answer a follow-up query in a conversation between the user and the database. In general, there are two purposes for which this intent is used for: (1) Extract some particular details of the result of the previous query (as discussed before). (2) Modify some parts of the previous query (e.g., apply or remove filter predicates, etc.). The *Refine Intent* therefore stores the last query of each user session.

Clarify Intent: If some information needed to actually execute a query request can not be automatically inferred or some information in the query request is ambiguous, the *Query Intent* calls the *Clarify Intent*. An example for this is, when the user refers to a column *name* that exists in multiple tables of the database schema. In that case, the *Clarify Intent* asks the user for more information to disambiguate the query request using a voice-based conversation (i.e., a clarify request is sent to Alexa for which the user has to provide a clarify response).

A second function of the clarify intent is that it learns the user terminology during the course of a conversation. Therefore, after asking the user for clarification, *EchoQuery* stores the mapping of the user terminology to schema elements (column or table names). That way, follow-up queries can use these stored mappings and execute the user queries without the need to ask the user for further clarification.

3. QUERY INTERFACE

EchoQuery's interaction model is composed of different *intents*, which implement the conversation between the user and our system.

3.1 Query Intent

The Query Intent is the primary intent that is typically used whenever a user starts a new conversation with *EchoQuery*. The input for this intent is called a query request.

Basic Query Requests: In its current version, *EchoQuery* supports simple non-aggregation and aggregation query requests using one of the aggregation type (COUNT, SUM,

AVG, MAX, MIN). In the current version of *EchoQuery*, a basic query request can contain either one or all result column(s), while allowing for multiple attributes in the where clause and also multiple group-by columns. To add or remove additional result columns, the Refine Intent must be used. We felt that this is more natural for the user when using a voice-based interface since results are replayed to the user via an audio channel.

The most basic query request is of the following form:

Get all {Table}(s)?
Get the {Column}(s) of {Table}(s)?
What is the {Aggregation} {Column}(s) of {Table}(s)?

Here {Column}(s) and {Table}(s) are elements of the database schema, while {Aggregation} refers to one of the spoken variants of the standard aggregation functions; i.e.,"total", "average", "minimum", and "maximum". COUNT aggregation queries, however, are formulated in a different way as they contain no column reference:

How many {Table}(s) are there?
What's the number of {Table}(s)?

There are many more variations of query requests that are not listed here. Given that, we can already see that even limited, the spoken SQL dialect of *EchoQuery* is quite intuitive. In the following, we consider how where and group-by clauses can be formulated in a query request.

Where Clauses: Where clauses can be added to a basic query request by appending:

... where {Table}(s) {Column}(s) {Comparator} {Value}?

Here {Column}(s) and {Table}(s) refer to elements of the database schema, while {Comparator} and {Value} refer to the comparison operator ("is", "is equal to", "is greater than", "is less than", etc.), and the value to compare the column against, respectively. When referring to a column the *{Table}(s)* phrase is optional in all query requests. For example, two equivalent query requests that use a simple where clause (one with and one without the table name) are:

How many orders are there where customer name is Sally?
How many orders are there where name is Sally?

Multiple where clauses are also supported, and can be added by adding "and" between clauses. At the moment, we only support conjunctive predicates for the where clause. We decided to not support arbitrary predicates in our initial version of *EchoQuery* since the semantics involving precedence of order of conjunctions and disjunctions would be hard to grasp for a non-expert user.

Moreover, it is important to note that join clauses between different tables used in the query request are not specified at all in our spoken SQL dialect. Instead, join paths are inferred using foreign-key relationships in the database schema. In the example above, *EchoQuery* uses the foreign-key relationship of the *Orders* table that refers to the *Customer* table. In case multiple join paths exist, *EchoQuery* asks the user for feedback using the Clarify Intent.

Group-by Clauses: Group-by clauses can be added to a query by adding one of the following variants to the beginning or end of a query request:

Grouped by {Table}(s) {Column}(s), ...
For each {Table}(s) {Column}(s), ...
..., grouped by {Table}(s) {Column}(s).
..., for each {Table}(s) {Column}(s).

For example, the following two queries are equivalent:

For each supplier name, what's the average price of orders?
What is the average price of orders, grouped by supplier name?

3.2 Refine Intent

After the user has formulated a query request using the Query Intent and thus opened a session with *EchoQuery*, the user can issue a refine request that triggers the Refine Intent to modify the last query of the session. Currently, possible modifications are to add/remove a result column and to add/change/remove where or group-by clauses.

Result Columns: The refine requests to add or remove a result column are of the following form:

Add {Table}(s) {Column}(s)
Drop {Table}(s) {Column}(s)

Similar requests can be also used to add or remove aggregation functions.

Where Clauses: A refine request can also be used to modify the where clause of the last query. To trigger the Refine Intent to modify the where clause, the user can use one of the following refine requests:

And {Predicate}
What if {Predicate}
Drop {Predicate}

While the And refine request is used to add a simple predicate to the current where clause, the What if request modifies a simple predicate with the given column name. Finally, the Drop request removes a simple predicate from the current where clause. An example of a refine request where the user adds an additional where clause is:

And where supplier name is Amazon.

Group-by Clauses: Similar refine requests can also be used to modify the group-by clause:

Also group by {Column}(s)
Instead group by {Clause}
Drop group by {Column}(s)

An example of refine request where the user adds an additional group-by attribute is:

Also group by supplier name.

A complete interaction with *EchoQuery* (EQ) using the Query Intent and Refine Intent might look like:

> *User: How many orders are there?*
> *EQ: There are six thousand rows in the orders table.*
> *User: And where customer name is Sally?*
> *EQ: There are three hundred rows in the orders table where customer name is Sally.*
> *User: Also group by supplier name?*
> *EQ: There are one hundred rows in the orders table where customer name is equal to Sally for the suppliers name Adobe, one hundred fifty rows for Amazon, and fifty rows for Apple.*

Another class of refine requests is used to extract more information about the previous result. This class of refine requests is useful, in case the last query result contains too many rows or columns to be consumable by the user using the voice-based result and *EchoQuery* thus only replays the number of rows as a voice-based result to the user. In the current version, this case is determined by some configurable and static thresholds. In future work, we plan to study results from perceptual science, of how much information a user can process efficiently using its auditory perception system, to make that decision.

In order to request more details about the previous result, the user can issue a refine request that starts with the phrase For the last result, ... Moreover, to be executable the user has to append a normal query request that asks for specific details. In effect, this is a query over the previous query's result. An example for this refine request is:

> *For the last result, how many rows are there where name is Sally*

Future work may include other ways of modifying a query using a refine request (e.g., to formulate arbitrary predicates). However, we can already see how using both the Query Intent and Refine Intent already results in quite a fluent and natural interaction between the user and *EchoQuery*.

3.3 Clarify Intent

This last intent illustrates an important capability of *EchoQuery*, namely asking questions back to the user in case a query or refine request can not be directly answered. This intent is applied in many different situations in *EchoQuery*.

In the following, we discuss the case where the user references a column without specifying which table it should be from, and our system is unable to infer which table the user is referencing. That is, there is more than one table with the same column name. A full discussion of all different cases which need clarification is beyond the scope of this demo.

In that case, instead of returning an error and having the user to start all over again with issuing a possibly lengthy Query Intent, *EchoQuery* asks the user for clarification:

> *By {ColumnUsage}, do you mean {Table1} {Column1}, ... , or {TableN} {ColumnN}?*

{ColumnUsage} here quotes the user's usage of the column to remind them which part of their query request *EchoQuery* is referring to and {Table1} {Column1}, ... , or {TableN} {ColumnN} lists the possible choices to disambiguate the initial query request. The user then responds with a clarify response to tell *EchoQuery* what they actually meant. In the example before, this could be in the form of:

> *I meant {Table}(s) {Column}(s)*

Once the user responds with this clarify response, the ambiguous query request is updated with this specific table. If there are more ambiguities in the query then *EchoQuery* will continue to ask further questions until they are resolved, otherwise the system continues as before. To avoid asking the same clarify requests over and over *EchoQuery* stores the answers of the users as mappings for future use.

In the following, we show an example of a complete dialogue involving a clarify request and response:

> *User: How many orders are there where name is Sally?*
> *EQ: By where name is equal to Sally, are you referring to parts name, suppliers name, or customers name?*
> *User: I meant customers name.*
> *EQ: There are three hundred rows in the orders table where customer name is Sally.*

4. DEMO SCENARIO

In our demo, we show all the before-mentioned features of *EchoQuery* and its query interface using the setup as depicted in Figure 1. For demoing our prototype of *EchoQuery*, we provide two databases that are preloaded: (1) A variant of the star schema benchmark database [10] where we replace the generated random values (e.g., random customer names) with more meaningful values. (2) The Multiparameter Intelligent Monitoring in Intensive Care (MIMIC II) dataset [5], which contains clinical data for ICU patients.

To get a good sense of how *EchoQuery* operates, we recommend seeing our demo video for the star schema benchmark database: https://vimeo.com/151847274.

5. REFERENCES

[1] Alexa Voice Service. https://developer.amazon.com/appsandservices/solutions/alexa/alexa-voice-service. Accessed: 2016-01-15.

[2] Amazon Echo / Alexa. http://www.amazon.com/echo. Accessed: 2016-01-15.

[3] Apple Siri. http://www.apple.com/ios/siri/. Accessed: 2016-01-15.

[4] Google Voice Action. https://developers.google.com/voice-actions/. Accessed: 2016-01-15.

[5] MIMIC II Dataset. http://mimic.physionet.org. Accessed: 2016-01-15.

[6] I. Androutsopoulos et al. Natural language interfaces to databases - an introduction. *Natural Language Engineering*, 1(1):29–81, 1995.

[7] A. Crotty et al. Vizdom: Interactive analytics through pen and touch. *PVLDB*, 8(12):2024–2035, 2015.

[8] F. Li et al. Constructing an interactive natural language interface for relational databases. *PVLDB*, 8(1):73–84, 2014.

[9] F. Li et al. Nalir: an interactive natural language interface for querying relational databases. In *International Conference on Management of Data, SIGMOD 2014, Snowbird, UT, USA, June 22-27, 2014*, pages 709–712, 2014.

[10] P. O'Neil et al. Star Schema Benchmark. http://www.cs.umb.edu/~poneil/StarSchemaB.PDF, 2007.

[11] P. Terlecki et al. On improving user response times in tableau. In *Proceedings of the 2015 ACM SIGMOD International Conference on Management of Data*, SIGMOD '15, pages 1695–1706, 2015.

QUEPA: QUerying and Exploring a Polystore by Augmentation

Antonio Maccioni
Roma Tre University
Rome, Italy
maccioni@inf.uniroma3.it

Edoardo Basili
Roma Tre University
Rome, Italy
basili@inf.uniroma3.it

Riccardo Torlone
Roma Tre University
Rome, Italy
torlone@inf.uniroma3.it

ABSTRACT

Polystore systems (or simply polystores) have been recently proposed to support a common scenario in which enterprise data are stored in a variety of database technologies relying on different data models and languages. Polystores provide a loosely coupled integration of data sources and support the direct access, with the local language, to each specific storage engine to exploit its distinctive features. Given the absence of a global schema, new challenges for accessing data arise in these environments. In fact, it is usually hard to know in advance if a query to a specific data store can be satisfied with data stored elsewhere in the polystore.

QUEPA addresses these issues by introducing *augmented search* and *augmented exploration* in a polystore, two access methods based on the automatic enrichment of the result of a query over a storage system with related data in the rest of the polystore. These features do not impact on the applications running on top of the polystore and are compatible with the most common database systems. QUEPA implements in this way a lightweight mechanism for data integration in the polystore and operates in a plug-and-play mode, thus reducing the need for ad-hoc configurations and for middleware layers involving standard APIs, unified query languages or shared data models. In our demonstration audience can experience with the augmentation construct by using the native query languages of the database systems available in the polystore.

1. INTRODUCTION

Polystores are the result of the "one size does not fit all" philosophy in a world where taking care of the peculiarities of different kind of data became necessary [5, 8]. Let us consider, as a practical example of a polystore environment, the databases of a company called ACME selling music online. As shown in Figure 1, each ACME department uses a storage system that best fits its specific business objectives: (i) the sales department requires ACID transactions and uses a relational database for the *purchases* and the *inventory* of products, as provided by sellers, (ii) a marketing department uses a document store for a music and customer *catalogue*, where each item is represented by a JSON document, and (iii) a business intelligence department uses a graph database for representing *similarities* among items. In addition, there exists a key-value store containing the products currently on *clearance*, which is shared among the three departments above.

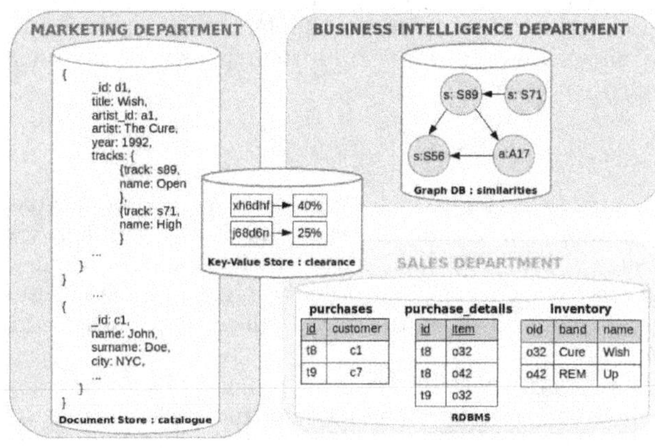

Figure 1: A polystore environment

In such scenario it is common that a user is only aware of a single database of the polystore but does not know anything about other databases (neither the content, nor the way to query them and, sometimes, not even their existence). This clearly poses new challenges for accessing and integrating data in an effective way. To recall a relevant discussion about polystores, the issue is that: *"if I knew what query to ask, I would ask it, but I don't"* [8].

QUEPA is a tool that shows a possible contribution to this problem by introducing *augmented search* and *augmented exploration*, two new methods to access a polystore based on the automatic enrichment of data extracted from a database with data that belong to the rest of the polystore.

Augmented search consists in the expansion of the result of a query over a local database with data that are relevant for the query but are stored elsewhere in the ploystore. For example, if Lucy, an employee of the sales department who only knows SQL, needs all the information available in ACME on the album "Wish", she submits the following query in *augmented* mode:

```
SELECT * FROM inventory
WHERE name like '%Wish%'
```


SIGMOD'16, June 26-July 01, 2016, San Francisco, CA, USA

ISBN 978-1-4503-3531-7/16/06...$15.00

DOI: http://dx.doi.org/10.1145/2882903.2899393

Taking advantage from a repository of metadata which stores the relationships between objects in different datastores, QUEPA returns the following augmented tuple revealing details about the product that are not in the database of the sales department, including the fact that such item is currently on clearance sale with a discount of 40%.

```
< o32, Cure, Wish >  ⇒  (clearance:  40%)
            ⇓
      (catalogue:  {title:  Wish,
                    artist_id:  a1,
                    artist:  The Cure,
                    year:  1992,
                    tracks:  { ...}
                   }
      )
```

Augmented exploration exploits the same infrastructure and provides a more interactive and flexible way to access data, which consists in a guided expansion of the result of a query over a local database with related data stored elsewhere in the polystore. For example, if Lucy submits the same query above in *exploratory* mode, QUEPA returns the following tuple, in which the links suggest that further information, related to the returned tuple, is available elsewhere and allows Lucy to decide which component of the query result to augment.

```
< o32, Cure, Wish >
```

This process is iterative and provides a method of database exploration [4], where the user can freely find her way through the polystore, similarly to what happens when we surf the Web. QUEPA is also able to suggest an initial result to start with, based on the most frequent items accessed in the past.

The majority of solutions to the problem of accessing data in polystores introduce a middleware approach, where a unified language, a common system interface or a universal data model is provided to address data heterogeneity [1, 2, 3]. These approaches introduce a generalization that not only adds computational overhead at runtime, but also hides the specificity and functionality these systems were adopted for [8]. Indeed, a middleware approach tends to vanish the expected benefits of a polystore and introduces an intrinsic complexity that increases when new database systems take part to the polystore. Conversely, QUEPA is a lightweight tool that does not add abstraction layers over a polystore, thus, it has a minimal impact on the applications running on top of the data sources. Moreover, the augmentation technique of QUEPA provides a soft mechanism for data integration in polystores that complements other approaches based on cross-db joins [5], it keeps data in the original format, allows the use of the original query languages or APIs and avoids any query translation. Finally, QUEPA is compatible with the most popular categories of modern database systems and it is easily extensible to work with additional systems.

Although it can be easily embedded on existing platforms that perform complex data operations over a polystore (e.g., [5]), we have implemented QUEPA as a stand-alone tool that exposes a set of primitives and connects to several database systems. We demonstrate this stand-alone version accessible through a web user interface.

In brief, the demonstration of QUEPA aims at showing the audience:

- the novel methods of augmented search and augmented exploration for accessing data scattered among heterogeneous database systems in a polystore;
- the advantages of the "Bring Your Own Language" approach for accessing a polystore, which allows the user to submit queries without the need to learn a new query language;
- the value of guaranteeing the exploitation of the complete functionality of each DBMS, which is the main motivation for adopting a polystore approach;
- the simplicity of operating, in this framework, in a plug-and-play mode, without ad-hoc configurations or additional code.

2. SYSTEM OVERVIEW

We briefly show our approach by explaining how each component of QUEPA works. As shown in Figure 2, the logical architecture of QUEPA relies on three main components: (a) an *augmenter*, which augments the result of local queries, (b) a link *repository*, which keeps track of meaningful relationships among data objects belonging to different stores, and (c) a link *collector*, which gathers such relationships. Each component is analyzed in more detail in the following of this section.

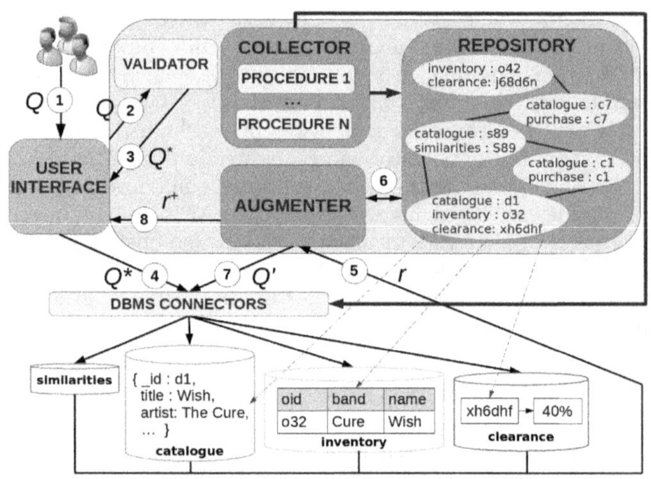

Figure 2: Architecture of QUEPA.

QUEPA exposes a set of primitives for a programmatic use of the augmentation construct. However, we have developed a light user interface that allows to use QUEPA via a web browser. Figure 3 and Figure 4 show two pages of this interface. The former allows users to submit an (augmented) query, specifying the target database in the polystore, and to visualize the augmented result composed of several data objects. The latter allows users to explore the polystore, by augmenting a single answer at a time.

Repository. QUEPA is based on a collection of relationships among related data objects in the polystore. Each database has one or many data collections (e.g., tables in a relational database), which are identified in the polystore

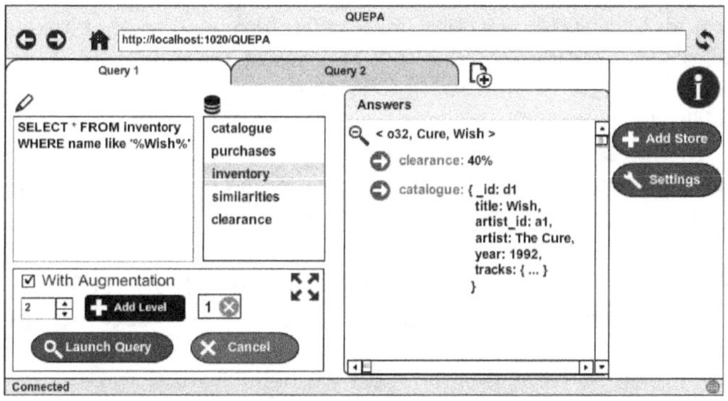

Figure 3: Interface for augmented search.

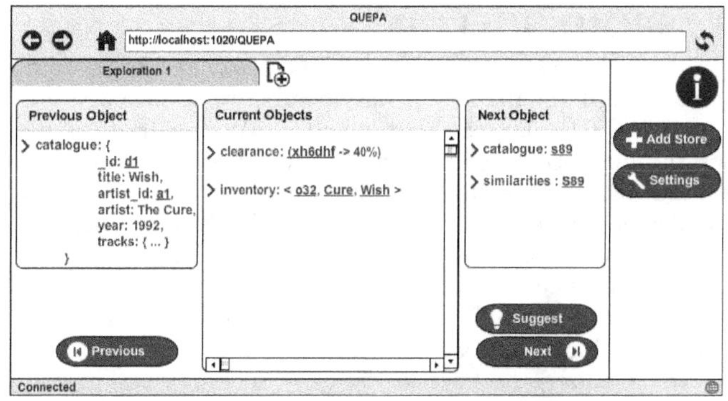

Figure 4: Interface for augmented exploration.

with a unique name. A data object is an atomic value set that can be uniquely identified inside a data collection. As a concrete example, tuples and JSON documents are data objects in relational databases and document stores, respectively. Each data object is represented in QUEPA with a key-value pair, where the key is the name of the data collection and the value is the (unique) identifier of the object, used in that data collection. A relationship indicates that two or more objects are related to each other. Relationships among objects capture either an identity or a reference. It turns out that the approach behind QUEPA is compatible with every database system whose data objects can be uniquely identified with a name and a key.

The set of all relationships in QUEPA forms an undirected graph. The nodes of the graph represent relationships that aim to capture identities in the polystore and are called *level 0* relationships. All key-value pairs that have been found to refer to the same conceptual object are stored in the same node. For example, in Figure 2 we have five *level 0* relationships, one of these is defined among three data objects: the tuple with key "o32" in the inventory, the document of the catalogue with id "d1" and the pair with key equal to "xh6dhf" in the clearances.

References among objects are represented by connecting with an edge the corresponding nodes of the graph. In this case we call them *level 1* relationships. Generalizing, the level of a relationship between two data objects is the length of the shortest path between the corresponding nodes in the graph. For example, the object with id "c1" in the *catalogue* is involved in a *level 3* relationship with the object "j68d6n" in the *clearance* database. Hence, the level of a relationship can be used to measure the distance between the result of a regular query and the data objects retrieved by the augmentation. For this reason, the augmentation is done with respect to a set of levels, as we will clarify below.

In the graph of relationships each data object of the polystore is represented in at most one *level 0* relationship (i.e. a key-value pair is unique over the entire graph). The graph of relationships is currently stored in the graph database management system Neo4j, which allows to easily manage a high number of relationships, but we are investigating different solutions for its implementation.

Collector. A fundamental task in QUEPA is the identification of the meaningful relationships among data objects in the polystore. This is a long standing problem, which is made even harder by the heterogeneity present in a polystore. Existing techniques usually require a *schema alignment* phase, where attributes of different schema are matched [7], followed by a *record linkage* phase (also known as entity resolution or duplicate detection), which serves to identify those objects that represent the same entity. Unfortunately, in a polystore, we cannot fully rely on state-of-the-art approaches because of the lack of necessary information (some of the stores are schema-less, others may not have any metadata associated to themselves) and of the different data models of the various systems involved. Therefore, we have opted for a combination of different techniques in the literature, with the goal of overcoming the limitations of each in our framework. The relationships are found transparently to the user and are progressively stored offline in the link repository by enforcing the constraints mentioned above. This aspect is, however, outside the scope of this demonstration.

Augmenter. When a user submits a query Q in augmented mode (step ① in Figure 2), QUEPA first checks, via a *validator* (step ②), whether the query involves only aggregate functions. In this case Q is computed without augmentation. In addition, the validator can rewrite Q into Q^* (step ③) by just adding all the identifiers of the data objects involved in the query that are not explicitly mentioned in Q, before its execution over the target database (step ④).

The result r of Q^* is then processed by the *augmenter* that computes the actual augmentation according to the level of relationship with the data objects in r (step ⑤). The default is 0 (that is, an augmented search returns, for each data object o in r, all the data objects in a *level 0* relationship with o) but, as also showed in Figure 3, the level of augmentation can be fixed by the user. In general, the *augmenter* is in charge of identifying all the relationships of the given level in the repository (step ⑥) and retrieving all the involved data objects by means of suitable queries to the corresponding databases in the polystore (step ⑦). This component has to account non-trivial algorithms for minimizing the number of accesses to the polystore needed to generate the current augmentation. Finally, the augmented answer r^+ is returned to the user (step ⑧).

In case of augmented exploration, the *augmenter* is in charge of retrieving and caching, in each step of the interaction with the user, all the data objects having either a *level 0* or a *level 1* relationship with the data objects in the current result (here the level of augmentation is transparent to the user). This information is suitably used by the user interface to build the output and to generate the next result according to the request of the user.

3. DEMO OUTLINE

In our demonstration we simulate the scenario of the running example in Figure 1. Specifically, we use a polystore for the ACME company that includes a MongoDB database for the marketing department, a MySQL database for the sales department, a Neo4j database supporting the business intelligence department and a shared Redis database. We have chosen these database systems because they are widely used within their respective category but, as previously mentioned, other database systems can be added to our framework with limited effort.

We have used the Last.fm dataset[1], included in The Million Song Dataset, to populate the *catalogue* and the *similarities* databases with 943.347 songs and 6.639.415 similarities , respectively. The MusicBrainz web services have been used to populate both the catalogue and the inventory with roughly 100.000 albums each. For the purpose of the demonstration, the content of these two databases does not overlap. In the generation of the albums, we have found many ambiguities due to different releases, special editions, etc. These ambiguities have been stored only in one of the two databases storing the albums. We have also used synthetic-data generators for populating the databases with user's profiles, products on clearance and purchases. We have generated in this way 20.000 user profiles, 40.000 products on clearance, 50.000 purchases of about 200.000 single albums sold.

We propose to the audience the following sequence of use cases that allow a comprehensive vision of the augmented construct and of the main functionality of QUEPA.

Scenario A: Plug-and-play. In this scenario we show how QUEPA can be used with a very simple configuration, which only requires to set the IP address of the underlying DBMSs. Audience can experience in this way the ability of QUEPA to easily collect a bunch of relationships, thus allowing to solve augmented queries without further human intervention. We then show more advanced configurations of the system that allow the user to gather more relationships and obtain a richer augmentation.

Scenario B: Bring Your Own Language (BYOL). This demo scenario focuses on query augmentation. A participant to the demonstration can choose the DBMS she/he is more expert in, among those available. As a result, QUEPA shows the structure of the chosen database so that she/he can submit meaningful queries. It is then possible to compare the results of the query with and without augmentation. Finally, we show the different results that can be obtained by varying the level of augmentation.

Scenario C: Augmented exploration. In this scenario, we ask the participant to submit a query in exploratory mode and after getting the results, we ask him/her to freely click on the links made available by the system to retrieve further information on that component of the result. This interaction can proceed as long as new data is found. During this exploration the system keeps track of the history of the navigation, so that the participant to the demo can go back to the previously visited data objects (see Figure 4).

We also demonstrate the ability of QUEPA to suggest the most promising links to follow according to the number of data objects that can be reached from them. Suggestions are also available without submitting a query, so that users who are totally unaware of the content of the polystore or do not know any of the local query languages can still interact with the system [4, 6].

In this scenario the level of augmentation is not visible to the user and the exploration proceeds, in each step, through the *level 0* and *level 1* relationships of the data objects in the current result.

Scenario D: Promotions of relationships. This last scenario serves to show one of the methods for collecting relationships. This procedure is currently the most involved among those implemented, and we believe that, since it requires human interaction, it can be more appealing to the audience. It relies on a simple, yet effective, adaptive learning mechanism, based on crowdsourcing, that allows the promotion of a *level n* relationship in the link repository to a *level m* relationship (with $m < n$).

More specifically, when a user interaction involve an augmentation, either in a search or in an exploration, she/he is following a path in the graph of the relationships. QUEPA keeps track of the most visited paths by the crowd. When a path is visited more times than a threshold (which we set to a low value for the demonstration purposes), the system connects the sink with the source of that path. As an example, in Figure 5 we have four nodes that are, supposedly, visited in sequence many times until reaching the given threshold. It can be concluded that this path of the graph is meaningful for the users and for this reason the dashed line is added to the link repository.

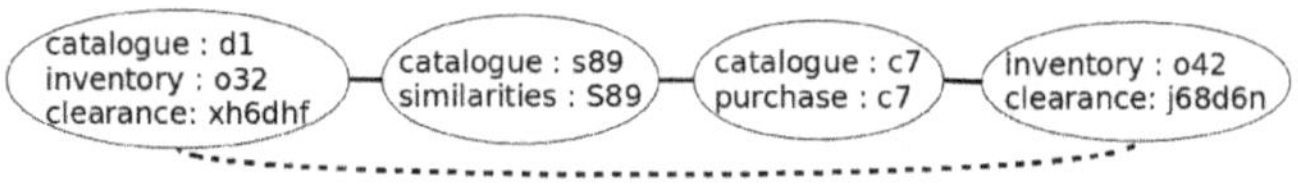

Figure 5: Promotion of relationships.

It follows that, in QUEPA, the graph of relationships evolves over time according to the behaviour of the users and so does the augmented result of the queries. This feature is demonstrated by showing the audience how the graph of the relationships evolves as soon as queries are performed and how these changes affect the augmentation process of QUEPA.

4. REFERENCES

[1] Apache MetaModel. http://metamodel.apache.org/, (accessed January, 2016).

[2] UnQL: Unstructured Data Query Language. http://www.couchbase.com/press-releases/unql-query-language, (accessed January, 2016).

[3] P. Atzeni, F. Bugiotti, and L. Rossi. Uniform access to nosql systems. *Inf. Syst.*, 43:117–133, 2014.

[4] M. Buoncristiano et al. Database challenges for exploratory computing. *SIGMOD Record*, 44(2):17–22, 2015.

[5] J. Duggan et al. The BigDAWG polystore system. *SIGMOD Record*, 44(2):11–16, 2015.

[6] K. Morton, M. Balazinska, D. Grossman, and J. D. Mackinlay. Support the data enthusiast: Challenges for next-generation data-analysis systems. *PVLDB*, 7(6):453–456, 2014.

[7] R. Pottinger and P. A. Bernstein. Schema merging and mapping creation for relational sources. In *EDBT*, pages 73–84, 2008.

[8] M. Stonebraker. The case for polystores. http://wp.sigmod.org/?p=1629, July, 2015.

[1]http://labrosa.ee.columbia.edu/millionsong/lastfm

REACT: Context-Sensitive Recommendations for Data Analysis

Tova Milo
Tel Aviv University, Tel Aviv, Israel
milo@post.tau.ac.il

Amit Somech
Tel Aviv University, Tel Aviv, Israel
amitsome@mail.tau.ac.il

ABSTRACT

Data analysis may be a difficult task, especially for non-expert users, as it requires deep understanding of the investigated domain and the particular context. In this demo we present **REACT**, a system that hooks to the analysis UI and provides the users with personalized recommendations of analysis actions. By matching the current user session to previous sessions of analysts working with the same or other data sets, **REACT** is able to identify the potentially best next analysis actions in the given user context. Unlike previous work that mainly focused on individual components of the analysis work, **REACT** provides a holistic approach that captures a wider range of analysis action types by utilizing novel notions of similarity in terms of the individual actions, the analyzed data and the entire analysis workflow.

We demonstrate the functionality of **REACT**, as well as its effectiveness through a digital forensics scenario where users are challenged to detect cyber attacks in real life data achieved from honeypot servers.

1. INTRODUCTION

Exploratory data analysis has evolved significantly since the emergence of the "Big Data" era. Data analysis software platforms (such as Tableau, Splunk and IBM InfoSphere) are gradually replacing traditional tools, allowing easy-to-use data exploration, visualization and mining, in big data environments, even for users lacking knowledge of SQL and programming languages. Yet, data analysis can be a difficult process, especially for non-expert users, as it requires deep understanding of the investigated domain and the particular context. Users therefore may skip significant analysis actions or overlook important aspects of the data [7].

In this demo we present **REACT**, a system that assists data analysts by providing personalized recommendations of relevant data analysis actions. **REACT** exploits previous experience of other analysts working with the same or other data sets that it records. Given the specific context of the user (the analysis actions performed thus far, the results obtained, the properties of the data set at hand, etc.) it uses the recorded information to suggest the next best analysis action to the user in the current context of their session.

Time	Source	Destination	Protocol	Length
0.000000000	172.16.254.128	216.58.208.206	SSL	55
0.000363000	216.58.208.206	172.16.254.128	TCP	60
0.289945000	172.16.254.128	216.58.208.226	TCP	55
0.293835000	216.58.208.226	172.16.254.128	TCP	60
3.464487000	172.16.254.128	8.8.8.8	DNS	73
3.482495000	8.8.8.8	172.16.254.128	DNS	89
3.483014000	172.16.254.128	216.58.208.227	TCP	66
3.483412000	172.16.254.128	216.58.208.227	TCP	66
3.495475000	216.58.208.227	172.16.254.128	TCP	60

Figure 1: Parsed Network Capture File

Generating adequate data analysis recommendations is a theoretical and practical challenge. Ideally, the recommended action should be given with respect to the users' level of expertise, methodology and their thinking process. It should be comprehensible at the current point in the analysis session, and most importantly, should result in a new view of the information, pointing out interesting aspects of the data objects in a way that the users did not see before. Furthermore, it should be presented to the user in reasonable time, i.e., before she decides herself on the next action.

Previous work suggests the use of recommendations in the domain of exploratory data analysis but mostly focuses on one specific aspect of the process. Some works (e.g. [3], [6]) focus on *data retrieval*, providing SQL query recommendations with auto-completion features; other works (e.g.[5]) focus on *data presentation* via OLAP operations, presenting a recommender system for data-cube queries; systems for *data visualization* recommendations were presented e.g. in [10]. While these works all make a notable contribution, user studies show that data analysis sessions interleave actions of all types with dependency of one action on the results of previous actions of the same or different type [1]. Thus, as advocated in the white paper of [7], a more holistic approach is required to fully capture the essence of the analysis work. It should also be noted that most of the previous work assumes an environment with a single data source queried by multiple users. Current big data settings support a large number of data sources and there is an important need to transfer experience gained with one data source to others.

REACT, to our knowledge, is the first one to provide a holistic approach that exploits user experience (in terms of both the individual analysis actions, their workflow, and the analyzed data), on similar-but-not-necessarily-identical data sources, for generating context sensitive recommendations.

In a nutshell, given a repository of recorded analysis sessions and the state of a user within its current session, **REACT**

SIGMOD'16, June 26-July 01, 2016, San Francisco, CA, USA

DOI: http://dx.doi.org/10.1145/2882903.2899392

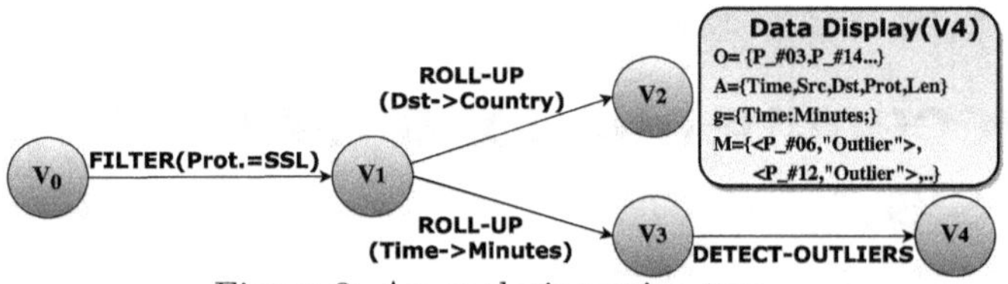

Figure 2: An analysis session tree.

operates as follows: First, it identifies previously performed similar sub-sessions, based on notions of *data-similarity* and *analysis actions-similarity* that we define. From these we retrieve a set of candidate next actions. Since the actions may be diverse and operate on distinct data sets, rather than looking at the individual frequent actions, our next step is to identify common generalized *action templates*. Finally, by considering the properties of the current data set, we instantiate the templates with actual parameters to obtain *concrete action recommendations* that have the potential to highlight new and interesting point-of-views of the given data source.

Our solution makes three primary contributions: (i) A generic data model that captures the nature of exploratory data analysis, including: data retrieval, cube operations and data mining, and can be expanded for visualization as well. Therefore `REACT` is easily adjustable to state-of-the-art data analysis platforms. (ii) Our system engine can identify similar analysis session patterns, made over different data sources. This novel approach significantly increases the pool of relevant actions for the recommendation process. (iii) Our system groups and then generalizes individual analysis actions performed by users, in order to find better recommendation candidates. This makes `REACT` a good fit for practical scenarios where there are many data sources and the chances for multiple users to perform the exact same actions are slim.

To demonstrate the functionality of `REACT`, our scenario of choice is digital forensics in the context of cyber security threat detection. Participants will be invited to take part in numerous forensics challenges from the HoneyNet project[1], for identifying malware communication, APT (advanced persistent threats), or exploits in the provided data. The participants will be asked to solve analysis challenges of increasing level of difficulty and we will compare the time it takes to complete them with and without the assistance of `REACT`. We will also provide a "behind the scenes" view of the system, demonstrating the operation of the underlying algorithms and their key components.

The remainder of this paper is structured as follows: Section 2 provides an overview of the data model and some theoretical background. A description of the system architecture and flow is presented in Section 3. Section 4 describes the demonstration scenario in more detail.

2. TECHNICAL BACKGROUND

We briefly review the technical background underlying `REACT`. We start with the data model, then overview the main algorithms for computing analysis recommendations.

Data source. A typical data analysis session starts when a data analyst inquires into a matter (e.g. *Detect a backdoor communication session within a network capture file*, as illustrated in Figure 1). Initially, she parses the traffic capture to a tabular format and loads the data to an analysis UI. Then, she executes a series of analysis tasks, to fulfill her assignment.

We abstractly model a data source by a triplet $\mathcal{D} = (\mathcal{O}, \mathcal{A}, \mathcal{H})$, where $\mathcal{O}$ is a set of data objects, $\mathcal{A}$ is a domain of attribute names and $\mathcal{H}$ is a set of semantic hierarchies, one per attribute name, that defines an abstraction refinement order on the attribute values. For example, semantic hierarchies that can be employed for the *time* and *IP* attributes of the data source in Figure 1 are: $hours \leq minutes \leq seconds$ and $country \leq city \leq IP$.

Data Display, Analysis actions, Analysis tree. Inspired by [1], we assume that an analyst performs actions of three main categories: ***data retrieval*** actions, performed to select and filter the relevant data objects for the current assignment (e.g. `FILTER` BY "protocol=*HTTP*"); ***data representation*** operations are performed to alter the point-of-view of the data objects and include OLAP cube exploration, sort, highlight, and alike (e.g., `ROLL-UP` 'session time' FROM *'seconds'* TO *'days'*) and ***data mining*** tasks such as clustering and outlier detection (e.g., *CLUSTER BY 'source IP address'*).

At each point of the analysis we are given some *Data Display* $D = (O, A, g, M)$, where $O \subseteq \mathcal{O}$ is the current subset of data objects and $A \subseteq \mathcal{A}$ are the attributes being considered. g denotes the current group-by preferences for the objects, identifying one abstraction level per attribute (and possibly a corresponding aggregate function) and represents the cube point-of-view of the current display (e.g. in the current example g can be $\{\langle$ *Time*:Minuetes;IP:country $\rangle$, 'avg_length':`AVG`(*length*)$\}$). Finally, M associates a (possibly empty) set of labels with each object, originating from data mining operations (Refer to Figure 2 for an example).

We assume a domain $\mathcal{T}$ of analysis actions that an analyst can perform on the data display through a given UI. Examples are `FILTER BY`, `ROLL-UP`, `CLUSTER BY`, etc. Each action $t \in \mathcal{T}$, takes some parameters (e.g. the filtering selection criteria, roll up attributes, clustering function, etc.) and, given as input some data display, generates a corresponding new display. We use $t(p)$ to denote the action $t \in \mathcal{T}$ with its concrete parameters p. We may *generalize* a concrete action $t(p)$ into an *action template* $t'(p')$ by replacing the action name or some of the parameter tokens in p by new variable names. For example, the two concrete filtering actions `FILTER`($length \geq 48$) and `FILTER`($length = 5$) may both be generalized to the action template `FILTER`($length$ $\texttt{x}_1$ $\texttt{x}_2$) where $\texttt{x}_1$ generalizes '='; and $\geq$ and $\texttt{x}_2$ generalizes '48' and '5'.

Generalization defines a partial order among templates. We write $t'(p') \leq t(p)$ if $t'(p')$ equals $t(p)$ or generalizes it. Given two actions $t_1(p_1)$, $t_2(p_2)$, we say that a template $t'(p')$ is their most specific generalization if it generalizes the two and there is no other template $t''(p'')$ s.t. $t'(p') \leq t''(p'')$. W.l.o.g. we will assume below that all actions have the same number of parameters/tokens. All results generalize to the general case via padding.

In our analysis we will be interested in action templates that occur frequently. Given a set T of concrete actions and some threshold Θ, we say that an action template $t'(p')$ is *frequent* in T if $\frac{|\{t(p)|t(p)\in T, t'(p')\leq t(p)\}|}{|T|} > \Theta$. In particular, we will be interested in the most specific such templates. We say that $t'(p')$ is *maximal-frequent* if it is frequent and there is no other frequent template $t''(p'')$ s.t. $t'(p') \leq t''(p'')$.

Analysis sessions work intuitively like website navigation sessions - at each point of the session one may backtrack

[1]http://honeynet.org

to a previous data display and take an alternative navigation path. We thus model an analysis session as an ordered labeled tree whose nodes are the data displays. The edges outgoing each node are labeled by the performed action and lead to the resulting data display node. The order captures the execution time-line. See Figure 2 for an illustration of an analysis session tree.

2.1 Generating recommendations

Given a repository of previously performed sessions (modeled as trees, as described above), and the current user session (modeled as well as a tree) we first search the repository to identify the top-k similar subtrees. Then we use them to generate next-action recommendations.

Identifying similar subtrees. Our notion of subtree similarity is based on *edit distance*: An *edit script* is constructed from edit operations that can be applied on nodes and on edges: *delete/add* a node or an edge, and *alter* the label of a node or an edge. Each operation has a cost, and the edit distance is the cumulative cost of edits required to transform one tree into another. Add/delete operations have a unit cost, whereas the cost of an alter operation for node/edge labels reflect the similarity between the data displays and analysis actions that they represent, respectively. Next, We intuitively define these similarity notions.

Data display similarity. Recall that different analysts may operate on distinct data sources (as well as on distinct sets of objects in the same source), yet we would like to benefit from the users' experience across data sources and sets. Given two data displays, we first employ schema matching [8] to match (when possible) between the attribute of the two displays. We then compare the content of the matched attributes. Since the objects being examined may be very different, and thus also the attribute domains, rather than comparing the actual value distributions we characterize their structure via the standard notion of entropy and compare the resulting entropy values. Finally, given two data displays, their overall similarity score (whose exact formula is omitted for space constraints) incorporates (1) the schema similarity matching score, (2) the attributes entropy similarity, (3) the similarity in the group-by preferences (defined by their distance in the abstraction hierarchy) and (4) the similarity in mining labels (defined via Dice coefficient, which is a standard similarity measure for multisets).

Actions similarity. We measure the similarity between two concrete analysis actions $t_1(p_1)$ and $t_2(p_2)$ by the sum of their distances from their common most specific generalization[2]. For instance, in our example above, the distance between FILTER($length \geq 48$) and FILTER($length = 5$) is 4, given that FILTER(*length* x_1 x_2) is their most specific common generalization.

Optimized search algorithm. To find the top-k similar trees we employ a refinement of the subtree similarity search algorithm in [2] with the edit distance computation method suggested in [11]. First, as [11] supports edit operations on nodes only, we replace each edge in our trees by an edge-node-edge triplet, assigning the edge label to the corresponding node. Second, since the algorithm in [2] is linear in the data size, and the number of recorded analysis sessions may be large, to allow for instant response time we preprocess the data, clustering similar analysis trees together. We compare the user tree only to the center of each cluster, and further explore cluster members (within a bounded radius from the center) only for the most similar ones.

[2]normalized by the maximal distance between a concrete action and a template where all tokens are variable

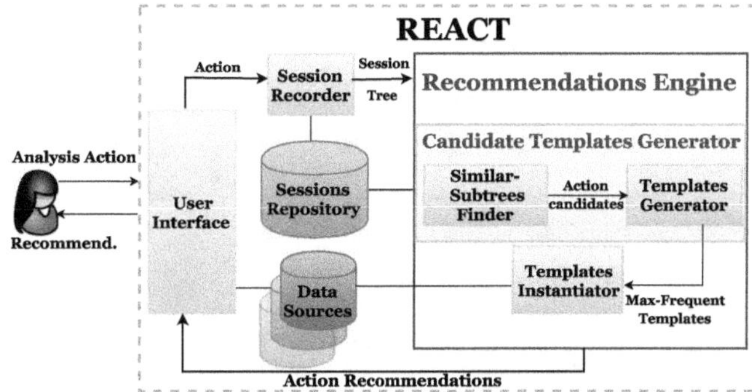

Figure 3: The system architecture.

From a storage (and computation) perspective it is important to note that the data displays need not be fully recorded to enable this computation. Indeed, for each node we only record the set of attribute names along with the entropy value for each attribute, and the attribute names (resp. mining labels) in g and M. Schema matching may also be precomputed for all data sources.

Generating recommendations. Once the set of similar trees is identified, we use them to decide on the best next action. This is done in three steps.

First we consider the nodes (in the retrieved set of similar subtrees) that correspond to the current user node. We take the edges (actions) outgoing these nodes and form a multiset consisting of candidate actions. Since the actions may be diverse and operate on distinct data sets, our next step is to identify common generalized action templates. Formally, the *maximal-frequent* action templates as defined above.

Finally, by considering the properties of the current data set, we instantiate the templates with actual parameters to obtain *concrete action recommendations* that are relevant to the given user and have potential to highlight new and interesting point-of-views of the data source. For that we employ notions presented in [4] to formulate an interestingness measure. Given an action template, the domain of instantiations that we consider for its variables, consist of the common instantiations in the actions that it generalizes (mapped to the current schema). For each such full instantiation, we calculate its interestingness by executing the action (using the measure mentioned above), and select the top-k most interesting such instantiations.

3. SYSTEM OVERVIEW

We implemented REACT in Python 2.7, as an intermediate plug-in between an analysis UI (Bootstrap 3) and the data source layer. The main system components and workflow are illustrated in Figure 3). A user analyzes data via a UI (see Figure 4) to which REACT is plugged in. Her analysis actions are passed from the UI to the *Session Recorder* which incrementally constructs the current session's tree representation and updates the *Sessions Repository* correspondingly. It then passes the session tree as input to the *Recommendations Engine* which works as follows. Given the current session tree, the *Candidate Templates Generator* calls the *Similar-Subtrees Finder* that searches the *Sessions Repository* for similar sub-sessions. It extracts from them a list of *Action Candidates* and passes them to the *Templates Gen-*

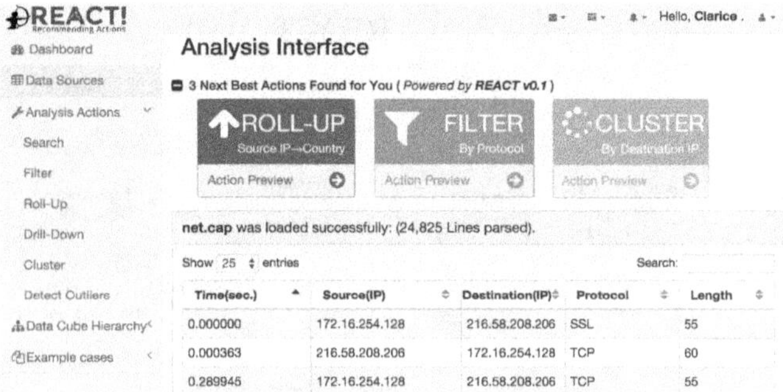

Figure 4: Analysis UI powered by REACT recommendations

REACT! Recommendation #1 Preview

ROLL-UP Source(IP)→(Country)

Showing results sample:

Count	Source(Country)	Destination(IP)	Protocol	Length(avg.)
338	Latvia	172.16.254.128	HTTP	144
122	United States	172.16.254.124	TCP	60
4	Russia	172.16.254.124	DNS	14
231	Israel	172.16.254.126	SSL	188

Figure 5: Action preview (Corresponding to Figure 4)

erator. The latter generalizes the actions to obtain a set of *maximal-frequent templates*. The templates are then passed to the *Templates Instantiator* that instantiates them into a set of explicit "most relevant" actions. To identify these actions it executes the candidate instantiations over the data source and measures the potential *interestingness* of the results. Finally, the selected *Action Recommendations* are returned to the user via the UI (Figure 4) where she can preview the recommendation results set (Figure 5).

4. DEMONSTRATION

We demonstrate the functionality of REACT, as well as its effectiveness, in the context of digital forensics in cyber security. Note that when solving cases of network breeches and malware attacks, forensics researchers often have to dive into a vast amount of machine generated data coming from multiple sources (e.g. network traffic files, system logs, memory dumps, etc.). This is a particularly suitable setting for demonstrating the capabilities of REACT as it includes all the challenges that the system addresses: The data sources vary from one investigation to another, and furthermore, even when working on the same data, users have different goals, as well as a distinct expertise and methodology.

We will begin with an overview of the system and its user interface, then invite the participants to take part in solving several forensics challenges from the HoneyNet project, published in the past few years. Each challenge has a distinct goal and data set, e.g., identifying malware communication in network traffic capture files, tracing APT (advanced persistent threat) activity in *syslog* messages and spotting exploits in memory dump files. The participants will be given analysis tasks in an increasing difficulty level and will be asked to perform the analysis actions via a dedicated UI.

To demonstrate the effectiveness of REACT, participants will be split into two groups, one working with the full fledged system, and another working with a degenerated version of the system that does not provide recommendations. We will record the time to completion of both user groups and present the average difference, demonstrating the superior success rates and speedup that REACT achieves.

Users working with the full system will be guided by REACT in performing the analysis actions required to complete the task. Within each analysis session, REACT will generate personalized recommendations using a sessions repository consisting of previous sessions recording tasks performed by users over the available data sources. We will complement the demonstration by providing a "behind the scenes" view of the system. Following the analysis work of participants, we will show how the system finds similar sessions, then generalizes the identified candidate actions into action templates and finally how it instantiates the templates to obtain a personalized recommendation to fit the user's context.

Related Work. As mentioned previously, there has been much work on recommender systems [9], and explicitly for data analysis [3] but they focus mostly on one specific aspect of the process. Our holistic approach incorporates these facets into a comprehensive solution. Our architecture is modular and can employ complimentary measures of similarity and interestingness depicted e.g. in [4]. Analysis recommendation systems often assume that users are working on the same data source/set of objects with a sufficient number of sessions that one can learn from [6]. However, this may not be the case in current distributed settings and our work allows to leverage sessions over multiple sources.

Acknowledgments. We thank Daniel Deutch and Amir Gilad for their insightful comments. This work has been partially funded by the European Research Council under the FP7, ERC grant MoDaS, agreement 291071 and by a grant from the Blavatnik Interdisciplinary Cyber Research Center.

5. REFERENCES

[1] R. Amar, J. Eagan, and J. Stasko. Low-level components of analytic activity in information visualization. In *INFOVIS*. IEEE, 2005.

[2] N. Augsten, D. Barbosa, M. Böhlen, and T. Palpanas. Tasm: Top-k approximate subtree matching. In *ICDE*, 2010.

[3] G. Chatzopoulou, M. Eirinaki, and N. Polyzotis. Query recommendations for interactive database exploration. In *SSDBM*, 2009.

[4] L. Geng and H. J. Hamilton. Interestingness measures for data mining: A survey. *CSUR*, 38(3):9, 2006.

[5] A. Giacometti, P. Marcel, and E. Negre. *Recommending multidimensional queries*. Springer Berlin Heidelberg, 2009.

[6] N. Khoussainova, Y. Kwon, M. Balazinska, and D. Suciu. Snipsuggest: Context-aware autocompletion for sql. *PVLDB*, 2010.

[7] J. Liu, A. Wilson, and D. Gunning. Workflow-based human-in-the-loop data analytics. In *HCBDR*, 2014.

[8] T. Sagi and A. Gal. Schema matching prediction with applications to data source discovery and dynamic ensembling. *PVLDB*, 2013.

[9] M. Sarwat, J. Avery, and M. F. Mokbel. Recdb in action: recommendation made easy in relational databases. *PVLDB*, 2013.

[10] M. Vartak, S. Rahman, S. Madden, A. Parameswaran, and N. Polyzotis. Seedb: efficient data-driven visualization recommendations to support visual analytics. *PVLDB*, 2015.

[11] K. Zhang and D. Shasha. Simple fast algorithms for the editing distance between trees and related problems. *SIAM*, 1989.

PerfEnforce Demonstration: Data Analytics with Performance Guarantees

Jennifer Ortiz, Brendan Lee, Magdalena Balazinska
Computer Science and Engineering Department, University of Washington
Seattle, Washington, USA
{jortiz16, lee33, magda}@cs.washington.edu

ABSTRACT

We demonstrate PerfEnforce, a dynamic scaling engine for analytics services. PerfEnforce automatically scales a cluster of virtual machines in order to minimize costs while probabilistically meeting the query runtime guarantees offered by a performance-oriented service level agreement (SLA). The demonstration will show three families of dynamic scaling algorithms –feedback control, reinforcement learning, and online machine learning– and will enable attendees to change tuning parameters, performance thresholds, and workloads to compare and contrast the algorithms in different settings.

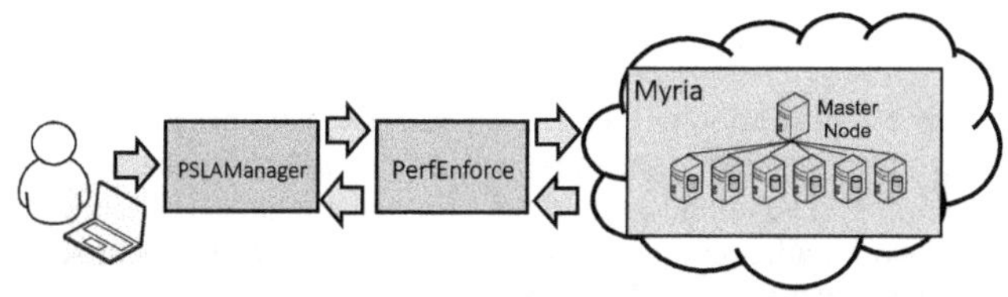

Figure 1: PerfEnforce deployment: PerfEnforce sits on top of an elastically scalable big data management system (*e.g.*, Myria in the demonstration) in support of performance-oriented SLAs for cloud data analytics (*e.g.*, PSLAManager in the demonstration).

1. INTRODUCTION

A variety of data analytics systems are available as cloud services today, including Amazon Elastic MapReduce (EMR) [1], Redshift [1], Azure's HDInsight [2], and others. With these services, users have access to compute clusters that come pre-packaged with data analytics tools. With most of these services, users select and pay for a given cluster configuration: *i.e.*, number and type of service instances. It is well known, however, that users often have difficultly selecting configurations that meet their needs. Frequently, users need to test many configurations before finding a suitable one [6]. Some database cloud services such as Amazon RDS [1] and Azure [2] offer the ability to scale a database application automatically, but they require users to manually specify the scaling conditions, which requires deep expertise and planning. Recent work offers solutions for automatic cluster resizing but either focuses on transaction processing [8, 3] or requires a known and profiled workload [6, 10].

An alternate approach is to enable users to purchase not a cluster size but a performance level. In Personalized Service Level Agreements [12], we developed an approach where users purchase service tiers with query time guarantees. Similarly, the XCloud system [13] supports SLAs with customer-specific performance criteria. The challenge behind selling performance-focused SLAs for data analytics is in guaranteeing the query runtimes advertised in the SLAs.

SIGMOD'16, June 26-July 01, 2016, San Francisco, CA, USA

ISBN 978-1-4503-3531-7/16/06. . . $15.00

DOI: http://dx.doi.org/10.1145/2882903.2899402

We design the PerfEnforce system to address the above need. PerfEnforce works in support of performance-centric SLAs for data analytics services. PerfEnforce targets services such as EMR or Redshift, where each user runs the service in his or her own cluster of virtual machines. Figure 1 shows the overall system architecture. In our approach, the user purchases a service tier with an SLA that specifies query runtimes. These runtimes correspond to query time estimates for specific cluster sizes, which define the tiers of service. Once the user selects a service tier, the cloud service instantiates the corresponding cluster. As the user executes queries, prediction inaccuracies and interference from other tenants using the service can cause query times to differ from the estimated ones purchased by the user. To meet the terms of the performance-based SLA, PerfEnforce automatically re-sizes the cluster allocated to the user. PerfEnforce seeks to minimize the cluster size allocated to the user subject to probabilistically satisfying the query time guarantees in the SLA. In the demonstration, we use the PSLAManager [12] to generate performance-based SLAs and the Myria system [5] as the elastically scalable data processing engine.

Several systems have recently studied performance guarantees through dynamic resource allocation in storage systems [9] using feedback control, or in transaction processing systems [8] using reinforcement learning. In this demonstration, we show how applying these techniques enables PerfEnforce to effectively scale the cluster by adding or removing nodes. In PerfEnforce, we also develop a third technique based on online machine learning. In contrast to feedback control and reinforcement learning, which are *reactive* methods, online machine learning enables PerfEnforce to change the cluster size *before* running an incoming query, which can improve QoS. As the user runs more queries in the session, this approach continuously improves the query runtime prediction model. In addition, it can compensate for early prediction errors using a control technique. This demonstration will show how the three techniques trade off QoS and cost given different databases and query workloads as exemplified in Figure 3.

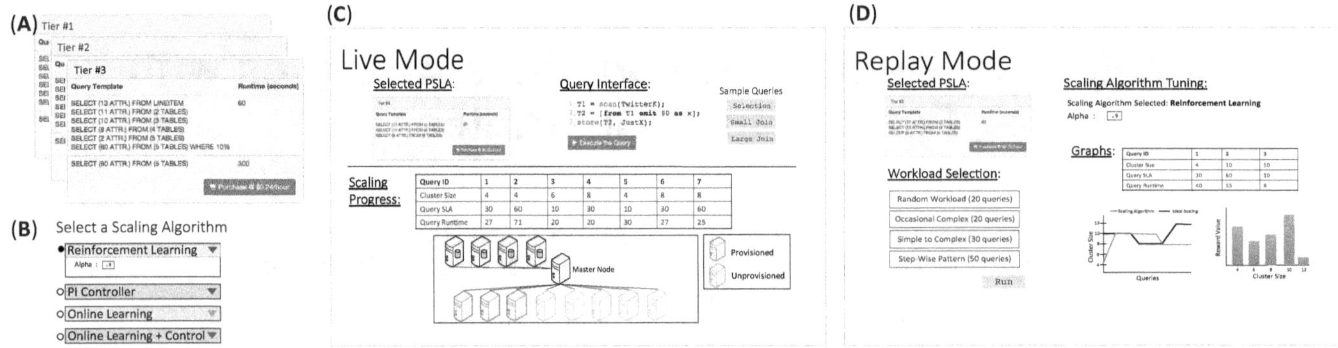

Figure 2: Demonstration screenshot described in Section 2.

The demonstration will enable attendees to experiment with the three cluster-scaling algorithms and experience their benefits and limitations. The attendees will select a performance agreement, a query workload, and the scaling algorithm. They will then observe how the selected algorithm changes the cluster size dynamically and the resulting query performance. Attendees will also be able to adjust tunable parameters for these algorithms. The demonstration will run as an Amazon EC2 cluster in one of two modes: *live* and *replay*. In the live mode, PerfEnforce will add and remove virtual machines (VMs) as the system executes queries on real data. The replay mode will enable the demonstration of PerfEnforce on longer queries and bigger workloads by showing only the cluster resizing decisions without actually re-sizing the cluster nor executing queries. Replay will use previously recorded query runtimes.

The demonstration will make two contributions: It will show PerfEnforce in action running queries on real data in the Amazon EC2 cloud. It will also enable attendees to experience different auto-scaling algorithms including feedback control and reinforcement learning used in prior work, as well as PerfEnforce's new approach based on a combination of online machine learning and feedback control.

2. DEMONSTRATION DETAILS

The demonstration starts with 10GB of TPC-H Star Schema Benchmark (TPC-H SSB) data [11] stored in Amazon S3 [1].

- *Selecting a Performance-Centric SLA:* The attendee first selects a service tier available in the SLA generated by our PSLAManager system for the TPC-H SSB dataset as shown in Figure 2 (A). Each service tier corresponds to a configuration of the service and comes with a price, representing the cost of the underlying cluster configuration. The query templates in each tier are grouped by time thresholds, representing the runtime guarantee for those queries. The demonstration uses a set of 5 tiers representing configurations of 4, 6, 8, 10 and 12 workers.

- *Scaling Algorithm:* The user selects and tunes the scaling algorithm that PerfEnforce will use as shown in Figure 2 (B). Available scaling algorithms include reinforcement learning, feedback control, online machine learning and online machine learning combined with feedback control. The scaling algorithm affects the number of queries that meet their SLA and the cloud cost of executing queries.

After making these selections, the user can then execute queries in either *live* or *replay mode*.

Live Mode: In this mode, the user experiences PerfEnforce as a live service. Starting from the purchased configuration, PerfEnforce executes queries and resizes the cluster by spinning up and shutting down service instances. As shown in Figure 2 (C), the user sees three screens: the chosen SLA tier, a query interface to write new queries or select pre-defined queries, and a visualization of the current cluster size including a table describing the query runtime, the SLA runtime, and the cluster size for the current and past queries.

Replay Mode: In the Replay Mode, the user sees four screens. The first screen shows the selected SLA tier. The second one, enables the user to select a pre-defined query workload. For example, one workload runs small queries followed by more complex ones. Another workload is a sequence of random queries. Once the user picks a workload, the system "runs" the queries by reusing their previously recorded runtimes. For each replayed query, the bottom right screen shows a table of the (previously measured) real query runtime, the SLA runtime, and the cluster size. The last screen also shows a set of graphs that vary with the selected scaling technique. If the user selects reinforcement learning, the graphs dynamically show how the reward changes over time for each cluster state. For feedback control, the graphs show the error for each current window as well as the history. For online machine learning, the interface shows predictions of the model compared to the real runtime of the query. In the tuning screen, the user can tune the scaling parameters again if desired.

3. THE PERFENFORCE SYSTEM

Figure 1 shows how PerfEnforce interacts with the other components of a cloud data analytics service. When a user begins her query session, she first purchases a performance tier from the cloud service provider. In our implementation, we use the PSLAManager system [12] to generate these performance tiers.

The PSLAManager from our prior work helps users select a service configuration by displaying a personalized service level agreement (PSLA). A PSLA is based on the user's data (the user provides the schema and basic statistics). Each PSLA tier corresponds to a cluster configuration but the user only sees an hourly price, a set of query templates, and a set of query runtimes. Intuitively, if a tier cost is cheaper, the configuration is smaller, and query latencies are larger. PerfEnforce can be extended to work with other SLA managers.

Once the user purchases a tier of service, PerfEnforce spins up the corresponding cluster and ingests the user's data. For this work, we use Myria as our data analytics cloud service. Myria is a shared-nothing parallel database system [5]. The Myria system has a master node that is responsible for sending queries to the worker nodes. The worker nodes ingest the data such that the first four workers each contain one quarter of the data. The first six workers each have one sixth of the data and so on. Each worker stores its data locally using an independent relational management system (RDBMS) instance for local storage. To scale the cluster dynamically, PerfEnforce schedules queries on the first N of the 12 workers. The remaining workers are not used and can be stopped but they need to preserve the locally stored data in case the cluster needs to grow.

As the user executes queries, the responsibility of the PSLAManager is to notify PerfEnforce about the query time guarantee associated with each user query to drive PerfEnforce's cluster re-sizing decisions.

3.1 Problem Description

PerfEnforce's goal is to minimize the number of cluster instances subject to probabilistically meeting the query runtime guarantees of the SLA tier selected by the user. The challenge is that query runtimes in SLAs are based on estimates, which are not always accurate due to cardinality estimation errors, differences between the training and user datasets, and limitations of the features used in the model. Query runtime prediction is not a contribution of our work. Instead, we focus on scaling the system in order to meet the guarantees in the selected SLA.

More formally, given a query session Q, with queries q_0 through q_n and a cluster C, PerfEnforce trades-off two competing goals: quality of service (QoS) and cost. We define cost as $\sum_{q=0}^{n}(\text{size}(C_q))$, where $\mathtt{size}(C_q)$ is the number of instances in the cluster used to execute query q. We define QoS as $\frac{1}{n}\sum_{q=0}^{n} g(q_i)$ where $g(q) = \{1 \ if \ t_{sla}(q) \geq t_{real}(q) \ ; \ 0 \ otherwise\}$. Here, $t_{sla}(q)$ and $t_{real}(q)$ are the SLA and actual runtimes of a query q, respectively.

QoS and cost are at odds with each other and their combination defines the SLA offered to the user. In this demonstration, instead of picking a specific SLA level (*e.g.*, 90% of queries should meet their SLA), we demonstrate how well different cluster-scaling algorithms can operate the cluster as close as possible to a point where resources are neither wasted nor missing: For each query, we compute the ratio between $t_{real}(q)$ and $t_{sla}(q)$, $\frac{t_{real}(q)}{t_{sla}(q)}$, and strive to achieve a ratio as close to 1 as possible. If this ratio is above 1, the cluster is underprovisioned. A ratio below 1 indicates that the cluster is in an overprovisioned state. In the next section, we describe how each algorithm effectively attempts to reach this goal.

3.2 Scaling Algorithms

We demonstrate the following four cluster-scaling algorithms.

3.2.1 Reactive Scaling Algorithms

We first describe reactive scaling algorithms. These algorithms take action after they witness either a good or bad event. In PerfEnforce, we implement proportional integral control and reinforcement learning as our reactive methods.

Proportional Integral Control Feedback control [7] is a commonly used approach to regulate a system in order to ensure that it operates at a given reference point. This approach has successfully been applied in various contexts including dynamically scaling data storage engines [9]. We use a proportional-integral controller (PI) as a method that helps PerfEnforce react based on the magnitude of the error while avoiding oscillations over time.

At each time step, t, the controller produces an actuator value $u(t)$ that causes the system to produce an output $y(t+1)$ at the next time step. The goal is for the system output $y(t)$ to be equal to some desired reference output $r(t)$. In an integral controller, the actuator value depends on the accumulation of past errors of the system. This can be represented as:

$$u(t+1) = u(t) + k_i e(t) \tag{1}$$

where $e(t) = y(t) - r(t)$, with $r(t)$ being the target system output and $y(t)$ being the observed output. k_i represents the gain of the integral control. Ideally, this parameter is tuned in such a way that helps drive $e(t)$ to 0.

In our scenario, the actuator value $u(t)$ is the discrete number of VMs provisioned. It is initialized to the cluster size corresponding to the SLA tier that the user purchased.

As for the system output, $y(t)$, we use the average ratio of the real query runtime $t_{real}(q)$ over the query runtime promised in the SLA, $t_{sla}(q)$, over some time window of queries $w(t)$.

$$y(t) = \frac{1}{|w(t)|} \sum_{q \in w(t)} \frac{t_{real}(q)}{t_{sla}(q)} \tag{2}$$

where $|w(t)|$ is the number of queries in $w(t)$.

Our target operating point is thus $r(t) = 1.0$ and the error $e(t) = y(t) - r(t)$ captures a percent error between the current and desired average runtime ratios. Because the number of VMs to add and remove given such a percent error depends on the cluster size, we add that size to the error computation as follows: $e(t) = (y(t) - r(t))u(t)$.

Integral control alone may be slow to react to changes in the workload. Therefore, we also introduce a proportional control component, to yield a PI controller with the following formulation:

$$u(t+1) = u(0) + \sum_{x=0}^{t} k_i e(x) + k_p e(t) \tag{3}$$

Reinforcement Learning As our second reactive method, we use reinforcement learning (RL). This approach has successfully been applied in the TIRAMOLA system, which supports elastic scaling of NoSQL databases [8].

With reinforcement learning, we model cluster scaling as a Markov decision process, where at each state s_1, the model makes a probabilistic decision to move to another state, s_2. The goal is to move to a state with the highest reward, $R(s)$. As the system moves between states, the model learns and updates the values of the rewards. In our setting, each cluster configuration represents a state in the model. We define the reward function to be the real-to-SLA runtime ratio. Our goal is to favor states with the reward closest to 1.0, where the real query runtimes are closest to the SLA runtimes (see Section 3.1). In RL, every time the system transitions to a state s, it updates the reward function for that state. In our setting, we use the following equation, where $R(s')$ denotes the updated reward for state s:

$$R(s') = \alpha * (\frac{t_{real}(q)}{t_{sla}(q)} - R(s)) + R(s) \tag{4}$$

α is the learning rate, which controls how fast learning takes place: *i.e.*, how much to update the reward based on the observed runtime value, $t_{real}(q)$, for the latest query q executed in state s.

At the initialization of the model, every state must begin with a defined reward value, $R(s)$, in order to determine which state to move to. This implies that the system must have prior knowledge about the performance of real query runtimes for each configuration. In PerfEnforce, we choose to make no assumptions about runtimes and initialize the reward for each state to 1.0. However, we do know that reward values will be lower for larger cluster sizes. To capture this information, we maintain a set of states called *active states*. When the query session begins, *active states* only contains the cluster size purchased by the user. If the reward for the current state goes above 1.0, we add the next larger cluster size to the active states, unless it was already in that set. If the reward for the current state goes below 1.0, we similarly add the next smaller cluster size. We repeat the process until all cluster sizes have been added.

3.2.2 Proactive Scaling Algorithms

Instead of approaches that react to runtime errors such as the PI controller and reinforcement learning, we also explore an approach that makes use of a predictive model. For each incoming query, PerfEnforce predicts the runtime for the query for each configuration and switches to the cheapest configuration that meets the SLA.

PerfEnforce first builds an offline model. For training data, we use the Parallel Data Generation Framework tool [14] to generate a 10GB dataset with a set of 2500 queries. Training data consists of query plan features including the estimated max cost, estimated number of rows, estimated width, and number of workers.

We observe that we can significantly improve this offline model if we incorporate information about specific queries that the user executes on his data. We achieve this goal by using an online machine learning model: as the user executes queries, PerfEnforce improves the model in an online fashion. We use the MOA (Massive Online Analysis) tool for online learning [4].

Online Learning (OL). We use the perceptron algorithm for the online model. The perceptron algorithm works by adjusting model weights for each new data point. We find that it adapts more quickly to new information than an active-learning based approach. PerfEnforce initiates the perceptron model by learning from the training set. For the first query, PerfEnforce uses this model to predict a runtime for each possible configuration. The cluster size with the closest runtime to the query's SLA is chosen. Once the system runs the query and knows the real runtime, it adds this information to the model.

Online Learning with Control Buffer We find that it takes a few queries before perceptron is able to start improving prediction accuracy. We find that we can not simply increase the learning rate as it causes significant oscillations in the predictions. Instead, to ensure high quality of service even early on in a query session, we add a buffer based on the observed prediction errors. We call this method online learning with control buffer (OL+B). We predict the runtime of the next query $t_{pred}(q_{t+1})$ as follows:

$$\begin{aligned} t_{pred}(q_{t+1}) = &\text{Perceptron}(q_{t+1}) \\ &+ k_p * Avg_{wt}(\max(0, \text{PercentError}(t_{real}(q_t)), \\ &\text{Perceptron}(q_t))) \end{aligned} \tag{5}$$

Where Perceptron$(t+1)$ is the runtime prediction for query $t_{pred}(q_{t+1})$. PerfEnforce adjusts that runtime if the previous window of queries resulted in a positive percent error. Based on this adjusted prediction, PerfEnforce allocates the cluster size with the predicted runtime closest to the SLA deadline.

3.2.3 Comparing Scaling Algorithms

Figure 3 shows the average performance of each algorithm on three sets of random query workloads. Each workload contains 100 queries. On the x-axis, we measure a normalized value of money saved. This value is derived from the cost for each query, C_q. We calculate the money saved compared with using the largest, 12-node cluster, for each query. On the y-axis, we measure the percent of queries that meet their deadline, essentially showing the *QoS*.

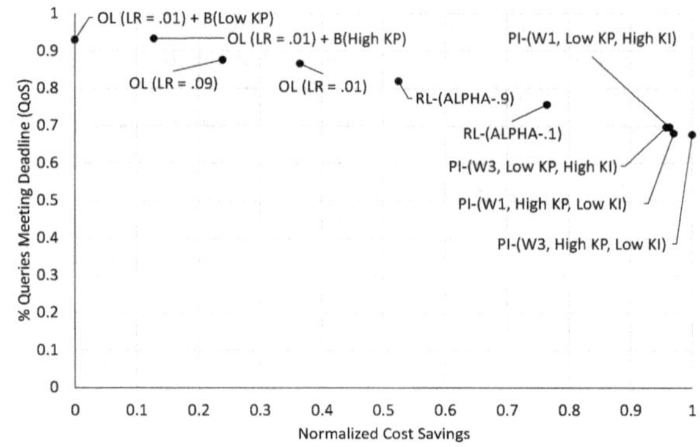

Figure 3: Example Trade-off between Scaling Algorithms

As the graph shows, no method clearly dominates the others. For Proportional Integral Control (PI), we vary the query window sizes, W, and use a combination of either high or low values for the gain parameters. From these experiments, higher k_i values result in a slightly higher QoS than using higher k_p. For reinforcement learning (RL), we end up with a higher QoS (75% - 82%) than the PI control methods. We find that Online learning (OL) yields the highest QoS (above 85%) for several learning rates, LR. Finally, Online Learning with Control Buffer(OL+B), has better QoS compared to OL but at an even higher cost. In this experiment, both OL and OL+B techniques provide the highest QoS, while PI control leads to largest cost savings.

4. CONCLUSION

In this demonstration, we introduce the PerfEnforce system. Based on the user's performance-centric SLA, PerfEnforce scales the system in order to achieve good QoS at a low cost. PerfEnforce can scale the system using a variety of scaling algorithms. In this demonstration, the user will observe and tune the algorithms on a running cloud service.

Acknowledgements This project was supported in part by NSF grants IIS-1247469 and IIS-1524535, gifts from Amazon, the Intel Science and Technology Center for Big Data, and Facebook. J. Ortiz was supported in part by an NSF graduate fellowship. We also thank Joseph L. Hellerstein for insightful discussions.

5. REFERENCES

[1] Amazon AWS. http://aws.amazon.com/.

[2] Microsoft azure. http://azure.microsoft.com/en-us/.

[3] S. Barker et al. Shuttledb: Database-aware elasticity in the cloud. In *ICAC '14*.

[4] A. Bifet et al. Moa: Massive online analysis. In *Journal of Machine Learning Research*, 2010.

[5] D. Halperin et al. Demonstration of the Myria big data management service. In *SIGMOD*, 2014.

[6] H. Herodotou et al. No one (cluster) size fits all: automatic cluster sizing for data-intensive analytics. In *Proc. of the 23rd SOSP Symp.*, 2011.

[7] P. K. Janert. *Feedback Control for Computer Systems*. O'Reilly Media, Inc., 2013.

[8] I. Konstantinou et al. TIRAMOLA: elastic nosql provisioning through a cloud management platform. In *Proc. of the SIGMOD Conf.*, 2012.

[9] H. Lim et al. Automated control for elastic storage. In *ICAC 2010*.

[10] H. A. Mahmoud et al. Cloudoptimizer: multi-tenancy for i/o-bound OLAP workloads. In *edbt13*, 2013.

[11] P. O'Neil, E. O'Neil, and X. Chen. The star schema benchmark. http://www.cs.umb.edu/~poneil/StarSchemaB.PDF.

[12] J. Ortiz et al. Changing the face of database cloud services with personalized service level agreements. 2015.

[13] O. Papaemmanouil. Supporting extensible performance slas for cloud databases. In *Proc. of the 28th ICDE Conf.*, 2012.

[14] T. Rabl et al. A data generator for cloud-scale benchmarking. TPCTC'10. Springer-Verlag.

High-Performance Geospatial Analytics in HyPerSpace

Varun Pandey
Tobias Mühlbauer

Andreas Kipf
Thomas Neumann

Dimitri Vorona
Alfons Kemper

Technische Universität München
{pandey, kipf, vorona, muehlbau, neumann, kemper}@in.tum.de

ABSTRACT

In the past few years, massive amounts of location-based data has been captured. Numerous datasets containing user location information are readily available to the public. Analyzing such datasets can lead to fascinating insights into the mobility patterns and behaviors of users. Moreover, in recent times a number of geospatial data-driven companies like Uber, Lyft, and Foursquare have emerged. Real-time analysis of geospatial data is essential and enables an emerging class of applications. Database support for geospatial operations is turning into a necessity instead of a distinct feature provided by only a few databases. Even though a lot of database systems provide geospatial support nowadays, queries often do not consider the most current database state. Geospatial queries are inherently slow given the fact that some of these queries require a couple of geometric computations. Disk-based database systems that do support geospatial datatypes and queries, provide rich features and functions, but they fall behind when performance is considered: specifically if real-time analysis of the latest transactional state is a requirement. In this demonstration, we present *HyPerSpace*, an extension to the high-performance main-memory database system HyPer developed at the Technical University of Munich, capable of processing geospatial queries with sub-second latencies.

CCS Concepts

•Information systems → Database query processing;

Keywords

geospatial data processing; indexing schemes

1. INTRODUCTION

There has been a rapid advancement in research areas such as machine learning and data mining, which can be attributed to the growth in the database industry and advances in data analysis research. This has resulted in a need for systems that can extract useful information and knowledge from data. Data scientists use various data mining tools on top of databases for this purpose. To achieve lower latencies and minimize transmission costs between the database and external tools, it is necessary to move computation closer to the data. The current trend in database research is to integrate these various analytical functionalities that are useful for knowledge discovery into the database kernel. The goal is to have a full-fledged general-purpose database that allows big data analysis along with conventional transaction processing.

At the same time, there has been an emergence of data-driven applications. Companies like Uber, Lyft, and Foursquare have a need to create real-time applications, including alerting systems, that consider the most current state of their data, enabling *real world awareness*. Some of these applications have been enabled by the advent of the Internet of Things and the massive amounts of geotagged sensor data it generates.

There are publicly available datasets that can help in geospatial exploration. The New York City (NYC) Taxi Rides [6] dataset is a good example, but is only a sample of what is captured by the aforementioned companies. The dataset contains approximately 1.1 billion taxi rides taken in the city since 2009. This represents about 470,000 taxi rides everyday in one of the most densely populated cities in the world. Uber, a popular on demand car service available via a mobile application, has also made a subset of the taxi rides available for the cities of San Francisco and NYC. For NYC, Uber published data containing around 19 million rides for the periods from April to September 2014 and from January to June 2015 [9]. Ever since the datasets were published, there have been multiple static analyses on these datasets [10, 2, 9]. The authors of [1] present a comprehensive system built from scratch for storing, querying, and visualizing geospatial data using kd-trees. Their system takes two seconds to execute a query that returns 100,000 taxi trips, which is too slow to address real-time workloads. MemSQL has some real-time capabilities [7] and is one of the first main-memory database systems (MMDBs) to deeply integrate geospatial support. The current database systems do not offer the performance required by real-time applications, and companies are often forced to build their own solutions [4]. We estimate that a 10x performance improvement is needed in general-purpose database systems to enable such applications/analytics.

We want to offer high-performance geospatial processing in a general-purpose database system that meets the require-

SIGMOD'16, June 26-July 01, 2016, San Francisco, CA, USA

ISBN 978-1-4503-3531-7/16/06...$15.00

DOI: http://dx.doi.org/10.1145/2882903.2899412

ments of real-time workloads, which can be used by emerging applications and data scientists alike without having to build their own system or use external tools for data analytics. Recent advancements in MMDBs research make it possible to efficiently create snapshots of the current database state. With our proposed system called *HyPerSpace*, we built a first prototype into that direction. Our goal is to drastically improve the performance of geospatial data processing in relational database systems by carefully using advanced encoding schemes and index structures. In our demo, we will present a web-based prototype called *HyPerMaps* that shows that it is possible to have an interactive analysis on geographical data using a general-purpose database system instead of a custom hand-written solution.

PostGIS [8] is a spatial database extension for the PostgreSQL object-relational database system. It adds support for geographic objects allowing users to formulate geospatial queries in SQL. PostGIS adds two popular spatial datatypes to PostgreSQL: *geometry* and *geography*. The *geometry* datatype treats the earth as a two dimensional flat surface. The earth is projected onto a plane and geographical coordinates are mapped to a two dimensional cartesian coordinate system. When evaluating spatial predicates such as *ST_Covers*, *ST_Intersects* and spatial measurements such as *ST_Area*, *ST_Distance*, this datatype allows for high efficiency, however, it comes with a drawback. Since it treats the earth as a two dimensional plane, the computations are not precise over a large area as the spherical nature of the earth is not considered. To put this into context, consider an example of the shortest distance between two points. In a 2D cartesian plane, the shortest distance between two points is a straight line, while on a spheroid the shortest distance between two points is a geodesic (shortest distance on the great circle). In contrast to *geometry*, the *geography* datatype treats the earth as a three dimensional spheroid and all the computations are based on the spheroid. The computations are precise since they are done on a spheroid, but they are very slow compared to those on *geometry*.

We implemented the *geography* datatype and the corresponding geospatial predicates, such as *ST_Covers*, in the high-performance MMDB HyPer [3][1]. HyPer belongs to an emerging class of hybrid databases, which enable *real world awareness* in real time by evaluating OLAP queries directly in the transactional database. In HyPer, OLAP is decoupled from mission-critical OLTP either by using the *copy on write* feature of the virtual memory management or *multi version concurrency control* [5]. These snapshotting mechanisms enable *HyPerSpace* to evaluate geospatial predicates on rapidly changing datasets. We achieve much better performance compared to an open-source database PostgreSQL, a commercially available MMDB (System A), and a successful key-value store (System B). This demonstration presents *HyPerSpace* and showcases that an interactive analysis of huge amounts of rapidly changing geospatial data is indeed possible.

2. HYPERSPACE

Similar to what PostGIS is to PostgreSQL, *HyPerSpace* is a geospatial extension to HyPer. For geospatial data processing in *HyPerSpace*, we make use of the Google S2 geometry library[2]. This is not novel, since System B also uses the S2 library for evaluating geospatial predicates. The novelty of our system is the integration of geospatial functionalities into a high-performance MMDB with snapshotting mechanisms which makes it possible to evaluate geospatial predicates on rapidly changing datasets.

At the moment, we support the three geospatial datatypes `Point`, `LineString`, and `Polygon`. Most of the geospatial processing is done using the S2 library.

S2 decomposes the earth into a hierarchy of cells. It considers earth of radius 1, and encloses it in a cube that completely covers it. S2 projects a point on the earth's surface onto one of the cube's faces and finds the cell that contains it. The faces of the cube are the top level cells, which can be recursively divided into four children to obtain lower level cells. There are 30 levels in total, and cells at the same level cover equivalent areas on earth (e.g., level 30 cells cover approximately $1cm^2$ each). The cells are enumerated using the Hilbert space-filling curve. The Hilbert curve is hierarchical in nature and fits well with the decomposition of earth into cells. Hilbert space-filling curves are fast to encode/decode and they have a very desirable spatial property: they preserve spatial locality. This means that the points on earth that are close to each other are also close on the Hilbert curve. The enumeration of the cells gives a compact representation of each cell in a 64 bit integer called *CellId*. A *CellId* thus uniquely identifies a cell in the cell decomposition. Similarly, other spatial datatypes like `LineString` and `Polygon` can be approximated using cells.

The enumeration of cells in S2 is hierarchical, which means that a parent cell shares its prefix with its children. To check if a cell is contained in another, we simply need to compare their prefixes, which is a bit operation. This enables one to index points based on their *CellIds* and thus be able to retrieve points contained in a certain cell by performing a prefix lookup on the index. B tree data structures are a good choice to index *CellIds*, since they support fast prefix lookups (essentially range scans). Additionally, B trees allow for high update rates, which is an essential requirement for real-time workloads.

3. EVALUATION

All experiments were run *single threaded* on an Ubuntu 15.04 machine with an Intel Xeon E5-2660 v2 CPU (2.20 GHz, 3.00 GHz maximum turbo boost) and 256 GB DDR3 RAM and all reported performance results are averages over ten runs.

For evaluation, we used the NYC Taxi Rides dataset consisting of approximately 1.1 billion rides taken in the city from January 2009 until June 2015. The dataset includes the pickup and dropoff locations (latitudes and longitudes), pickup and dropoff times, and various details about the trip, such as distance, payment type, number of passengers, various taxes, tolls, surcharge, tip amount, and total fare. For privacy reasons, it does not contain details about drivers or passengers. The exact route taken for the trip is also not available. We needed to clean the dataset as some of the pickup or dropoff locations did not make sense as they were way outside NYC. We cleaned such records from the dataset and only considered rides that originated between longitude values -70.00 and -80.00, and latitude values 35.00

[1]When saying HyPer, we are referring to the research version of HyPer developed at the Technical University of Munich.

[2]https://code.google.com/archive/p/s2-geometry-library/

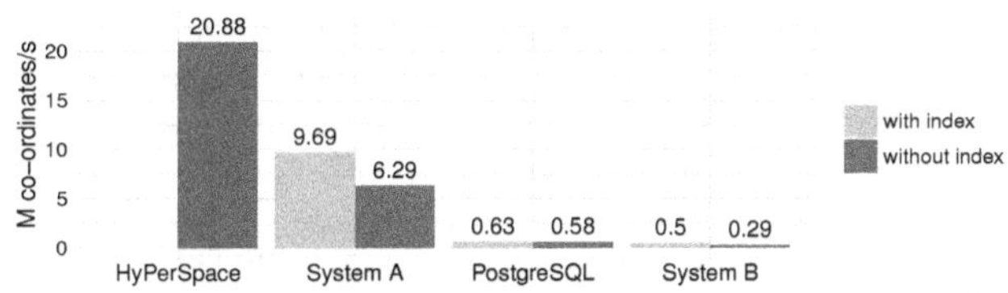

Figure 1: *HyPerSpace* vs. related systems: throughput of *ST_Covers* using lat/long co-ordinates

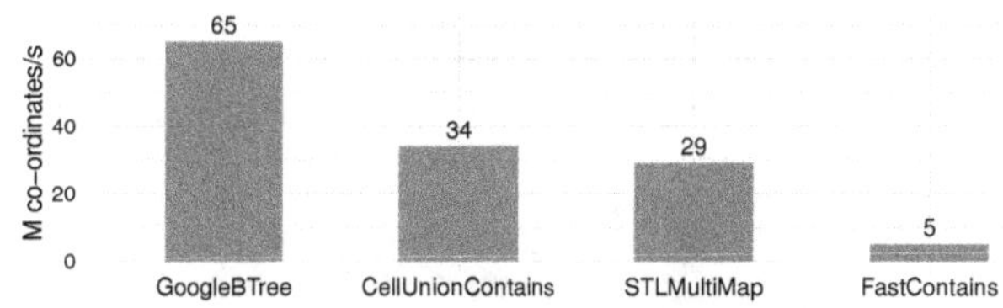

Figure 2: Microbenchmark results: throughput of *ST_Covers* using lat/long co-ordinates

and 45.00. For evaluation, we made use of the taxi data for the month of January 2015. The cleaned dataset for January 2015 contains a total of 12505344 records.

We compared *HyPerSpace* with the following related systems: System A, System B, and PostgreSQL 9.4.5 (postgis-2.2.0). Since PostgreSQL does not support intra-query parallelism, we configured all systems to run single threaded. For evaluation purposes, we find how many rides originated from Midtown Manhattan in January 2015. In SQL notation, the following query is issued:

```
select count(*)
from   nyc,pickups_jan_2015
where  ST_Covers(nyc.geog,pickups_jan_2015.geog)
       and borough='Manhattan'
       and neighborhood='Midtown';
```

With the exception of System B, with NoSQL syntax, the query looks similar on all systems.

Figure 1 shows the throughput of the *ST_Covers* predicate for all of the systems. System A, System B, and PostgreSQL achieve better performance when using appropriate index structures. Particularly System B, which also makes use of the Google S2 geometry library, benefits from its index on points. System B's index is basically a B tree on the 64bit *CellIds*. System B computes an exterior covering of the polygon using the S2 library. That covering consists of cells at various levels (i.e., of different sizes). For each cell of this covering, it then performs a prefix lookup in the B tree (essentially a range scan) and evaluates qualifying points for actual containment in the polygon. System B suffers heavily from its document-based storage layout, since it needs to parse GeoJSON documents at runtime.

HyPerSpace completes the query in 550ms and thus achieves more than twice the performance of its closest competitor, which is System A with an index on points (1290ms). We have not evaluated *HyPerSpace* with an index on points yet, but ran multiple microbenchmarks outside of *HyPerSpace*. All microbenchmarks were implemented in C++11 and compiled with gcc 4.9.2 with `-O3` and `-march=native` settings. We compared the implementation *CellUnionContains* that we used in *HyPerSpace* as well as *FastContains*, which is a modified version of the `S2Loop.Contains` implementation that skips the initial bounding box check, to the two index-based implementations *GoogleBTree* and *STLMultiMap*.

Figure 2 shows the throughput of the *ST_Covers* predicate for the different implementations. *GoogleBTree*, which is an implementation similar to System B's index, completes the workload in 191ms. In the *GoogleBTree* implementation, we first compute exterior and interior coverings for the given polygon and then perform a range scan in a Google B tree[3] for each cell of the exterior covering. For each qualifying point, we check whether the point is contained in the interior covering, which is essentially a binary search on a sorted vector of *CellIds*. Only if a point qualifies the exterior, but not the interior covering, an exact containment check using our modified implementation of the `S2Loop.Contains` function needs to be performed. The other index-based implementation *STLMultiMap* takes twice as long (425ms) as *GoogleBTree* to complete the workload, even though it uses the same approach. In C++11, the `stl::multi_map` interface that we used in this case is implemented by a RB tree, which is less efficient for range scans. It is well known that a B+ tree would yield even higher rates for range scans than a B tree. However, for the sake of expediency and reproducibility of our measurements, we have used the B tree implementation provided by Google instead of a custom B+ tree implementation. Once we integrate this approach into *HyPerSpace*, we will make use of an optimized B+ tree implementation. The difference in performance between the two implementations *GoogleBTree* and *STLMultiMap* shows that the overall runtime of this approach is heavily influenced by the actual index structure used.

The approach *CellUnionContains* completes the workload in 367ms, compared to 550ms when implemented within *HyPerSpace*. The overhead is mostly caused by function calls that are issued for each of the 12M points. *CellUnionContains* is a straightforward approach. It first computes the bounding box and exterior and interior coverings for the given polygon. For each of the points, *CellUnionContains* then performs the following steps: First, it checks whether the point is within the bounding box. If that is the case, it checks for containment in one of the cells of the exterior covering. Analogous to the containment check for the interior covering, this essentially comes down to a binary search. Then the *CellUnionContains* approach continues analogous to the *GoogleBTree* approach by checking the interior covering and performing the exact containment check if necessary. By properly using the S2 mechanisms, our *CellUnionContains* approach achieves a slightly better performance than the index-based *STLMultiMap* approach, even though we have to loop over all of the 12M points.

4. DEMONSTRATION

We created an interactive web interface, called *HyPerMaps*, that demonstrates the outstanding geospatial processing performance of *HyPerSpace* on the NYC Taxi Rides dataset. The user interaction concept of *HyPerMaps* is designed to minimize the requirement of users' expertize with the explored data. The ability of *HyPerSpace* to answer

[3]https://code.google.com/archive/p/cpp-btree/

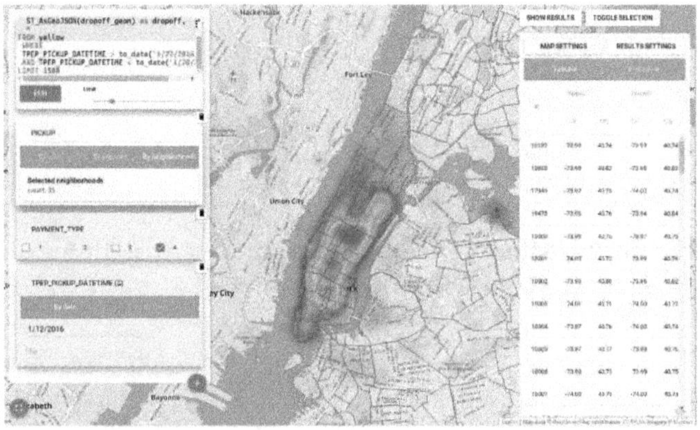

Figure 3: Interactive visualization of a real-time replay of NYC taxi rides using *HyPerMaps*

queries with typically sub-second latency enables tight feedback loops. It supports users during query formulation and encourages an iterative approach. During filtering of the data, users can rely on datatype dependent elements, which provide context-based information like value distributions or geographic locations in real time. Users can draw polygons on the map to filter points geographically. Subsequently, users can combine different graphical and textual representations to create an informative and intuitive visualization. During this data exploration process, *HyPerMaps* will automatically compute updated results reflecting the current state of the user interface as well as the underlying dataset.

Figure 3 shows *HyPerMaps* visualizing the taxi dataset. On the left, various tiles allow users to specify filters on the data, which will be immediately translated into SQL code as illustrated on the top. This binding works in both directions—manually written SQL code will be translated into corresponding tiles. Users can choose between a heat map and pins to display selected points on the map. On the right, *HyPerMaps* shows aggregated information about selected points in tabular or in chart form.

During the demonstration, we will run a *HyPerSpace* instance on a demonstration laptop with three of data being replayed at various speeds. We will motivate our demonstration by showing a scenario of a hotel owner wanting to install a shuttle bus for his or her guests to allow them to save money on their arrival, departure, and daily travels by not having to take expensive taxis. The hotel owner will select the taxi pickup area of his hotel by drawing a polygon on *HyPerMaps*, which boils down to a similar database query that we previously used for the evaluation of the different systems. Then, common dropoff areas of the taxi rides originating from this area will be displayed and the hotel owner can retrieve aggregate information for each of these areas. *HyPerMaps* will compute how much money and CO_2 emissions would be saved on aggregate if the hotel owner would install a shuttle to one of these dropoff areas. Additionally, we will demonstrate various scenarios showing that recently ingested data will be immediately reflected in *HyPerMaps*, thereby enabling *real world awareness* in real time.

5. TAKE-AWAY MESSAGE

In this paper, we presented *HyPerSpace*, a geospatial extension to the MMDB HyPer. Our implementation of the *ST_Covers* predicate achieves a much lower latency than corresponding implementations in related systems, without using any index structures. Additionally, we found that using index structures optimized for range scans such as B trees or B+ trees on *CellIds*, can yield even lower latencies. In our demo, we will show that it is indeed possible to build real-time visualizations on geographical data using a general-purpose database system instead of a custom hand-written solution that takes much longer to build and is harder to maintain. The novelty of our system is the integration of geospatial functionalities into a high-performance MMDB that allows for efficient snapshotting of the current database state. Our contribution also includes the careful use of the features of the Google S2 geometry library, thereby achieving much lower latencies than related systems. This makes it possible to evaluate geospatial predicates on high throughput data streams in real time. To demonstrate this, we created a web interface that allows users to interactively explore the NYC Taxi Rides dataset while the data is being replayed at various speeds. Our demo shows that features (such as value distributions) of the entire dataset, including the most current data, can be used to populate UI elements, thereby supporting users in creating meaningful (aggregated) real-time visualizations.

6. ACKNOWLEDGEMENTS

This work is part of the TUM Living Lab Connected Mobility (TUM LLCM) project and has been funded by the Bayerisches Staatsministerium für Wirtschaft und Medien, Energie und Technologie (StMWi).

7. REFERENCES

[1] N. F. Ferreira, J. Poco, H. T. Vo, J. Freire, and C. T. Silva. Visual Exploration of Big Spatio-Temporal Urban Data: A Study of New York City Taxi Trips. In *IEEE Transactions on Visualization and Computer Graphics*, pages 2149–2158, December 2013.

[2] R. Fischer-Baum and C. Bialik. *Uber Is Taking Millions Of Manhattan Rides Away From Taxis.* http://fivethirtyeight.com/features/uber-is-taking-millions-of-manhattan-rides-away-from-taxis/.

[3] A. Kemper and T. Neumann. HyPer: A Hybrid OLTP & OLAP Main Memory Database System Based on Virtual Memory Snapshots. In *ICDE*, pages 195–206, Apr. 2011.

[4] J. Miranda. *Uber Unveils its Realtime Market Platform.* http://www.infoq.com/news/2015/03/uber-realtime-market-platform/.

[5] T. Neumann, T. Mühlbauer, and A. Kemper. Fast Serializable Multi-Version Concurrency Control for Main-Memory Database Systems. In *SIGMOD*, SIGMOD '15, pages 677–689, New York, NY, USA, 2015. ACM.

[6] *TLC Trip Record Data.* http://www.nyc.gov/html/tlc/html/about/trip_record_data.shtml.

[7] G. Orenstein. *Real-Time Geospatial Intelligence with Supercar.* http://blog.memsql.com/real-time-geospatial-intelligence-with-supercar/.

[8] *PostGIS.* http://postgis.net/.

[9] T. Schneider. *Analyzing 1.1 Billion NYC Taxi and Uber Trips, with a Vengeance.* http://toddwschneider.com/posts/analyzing-1-1-billion-nyc-taxi-and-uber-trips-with-a-vengeance/.

[10] C. Wong. *FOILing NYC's Taxi Trip Data.* http://chriswhong.com/open-data/foil_nyc_taxi/.

What Makes a Good Physical plan? — Experiencing Hardware-Conscious Query Optimization with Candomblé

Holger Pirk
MIT CSAIL
holger@csail.mit.edu

Oscar Moll
MIT CSAIL
orm@csail.mit.edu

Sam Madden
MIT CSAIL
madden@csail.mit.edu

ABSTRACT

Query optimization is hard and the current proliferation of "modern" hardware does nothing to make it any easier. In addition, the tools that are commonly used by performance engineers, such as compiler intrinsics, static analyzers or hardware performance counters are neither integrated with data management systems nor easy to learn. This fact makes it (unnecessarily) hard to educate engineers, to prototype and to optimize database query plans for modern hardware. To address this problem, we developed a system called *Candomblé* that lets database performance engineers interactively examine, optimize and evaluate query plans using a touch-based interface. Candomblé puts attendants in the place of a physical query optimizer that has to rewrite a physical query plan into a better equivalent plan. Attendants experience the challenges when ad-hoc optimizing a physical plan for processing devices such as GPUs and CPUs and capture their gained knowledge in rules to be used by a rule-based optimizer.

1. INTRODUCTION

Hardware conscious database tuning is often regarded like a dark art – understood by few, difficult to learn and a discipline in which tiny details can have surprisingly large effects. Figure 1 illustrates how simple choices such as the way the output of a selection is materialized can have significant effects on query performance. In the figure, we see the penalty on query runtime if we use a branching over a branch-free implementation of the select operator: When branches are least predictable (50% selectivity) the penalty is slight on a GPU (Nvidia Titan X) but significantly negative on CPUs (an Intel(R) Xeon(R) CPU E3-1270 v5).

While sensitivity to parameters seems an inherent feature of the field of hardware-conscious optimization, our work addresses the other two problems: understanding and learning curve. These problems are, to a large extent, due to the lack of proper tools: the available tools are usually not integrated with the data management system but inherited from the programming language and the computer architecture.

SIGMOD'16, June 26-July 01, 2016, San Francisco, CA, USA

ISBN 978-1-4503-3531-7/16/06...$15.00

DOI: http://dx.doi.org/10.1145/2882903.2899410

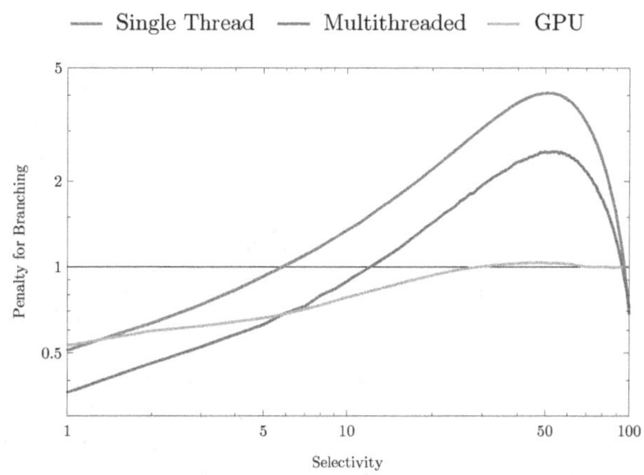

Figure 1: The penalty for branching selections is hardware as well as data dependent

In the light of the increasing importance of hardware-conscious optimization on database performance, many recent approaches have blurred the line between data processors and compilers: systems like HyPeR [3], Legobase [2] and TupleWare [1] compile declarative queries into imperative code at runtime and rely on the underlying compiler to optimize it. This way, the low-level optimizer can make decisions with full knowledge about the hardware it is optimizing for. Unfortunately, this approach has a significant shortcoming: the low-level compiler is not aware of properties of the data that is to be processed by the generated code. This prevents a number of optimizations of which predication (the one applied for Figure 1) is one example. Other examples include the selection of appropriate parallelization strategies, materialization points, hash-functions and collision handling.

To address this problem, we developed Voodoo, a *virtual* database kernel based on a unified algebra for physical and logical optimization. The Voodoo kernel is "virtual" in the sense that it generates efficient executable machine code for variety of different hardware platforms, both sequential as well as parallel. In addition, Voodoo provides fine grained control over low-level tuning through the use of RISC-style[1] plan operators. Through these techniques, Voodoo achieves performance that is competitive and sometimes superior to

[1]Reduced Instruction Set Computing [4]

that of existing "hand-optimized" systems such as HyPeR and Tupleware "on their home turf", i.e., classic multicore processors running TPC-H [5]. In addition, Voodoo code can also run on massively parallel processors and, thus, significantly outperform existing CPU-oriented systems.

While Voodoo allows expressing and executing efficient plans for relational query processing on different hardware, it still relies on a hardware-conscious optimizer to generate an appropriate plan. Fortunately, we found that appropriate plans on these different devices are often similarly shaped and can, thus, be enumerated efficiently. So, while Voodoo makes it possible to express, enumerate and execute plans, it takes a hardware-conscious cost model to select an appropriate plan. In the absence of that, we currently rely on rule-based optimization. However, Voodoo's RISC operators are an easily comprehensible way to represent virtually every static [2] aspect of the query evaluation process such as join or grouping strategies. We propose to exploit this property to illustrate the challenges of hardware-conscious optimization but also the level of tunability that is offered by a RISC-style plan algebra.

Purpose of the Demonstration

The purpose of the demonstration is for the attendants to experience the challenges of hardware-conscious optimization without the need to learn to use specialized tools. To that end, we demonstrate a touch-based visual query builder that allows users to examine, optimize and evaluate the query plan by tuning operator parameters as well as by manipulating the plan structure itself. Through this UI, users will experience how a) local changes to operators can have broader impact on the plan and b) seemingly unnecessary operators can improve performance by, e.g., increasing locality or enabling intermediate reuse. We also demonstrate that a compact RISC-style plan algebra is a useful intermediate stage on the way to executable machine code, allowing effective tuning without suffering from prohibitive interpretation overhead.

2. THE VOODOO SYSTEM

Before presenting the specific demonstration, let us briefly discuss the architecture of our system (see Figure 2). Our demonstration is built on the Voodoo database kernel [5] which provides the query execution layer in the DBMS stack. While Voodoo can be used as a standalone library, it is designed to serve as a drop-in replacement for existing database kernels: for our prototype we replaced the execution layer of MonetDB with Voodoo. By reusing the MonetDB SQL compiler, we allow users to formulate ad-hoc queries in SQL. We extract the relational algebra plan that is generated by MonetDB and compile it to the Voodoo plan algebra (see Section 2.1). This plan is passed through an extensible rule based optimizer before being sent to the interactive plan optimization component that is the heart of our demonstration. At this point, the evaluation process blocks until the user finishes her interactive optimization pass and sends the plan back for execution. At that point, the Voodoo program is evaluated by either compiling and running it using the OpenCL Backend on a CPU, a GPU or using the Interpreter Backend (which provides interactive debugging but inferior performance).

[2] as opposed to runtime aspects such as aspects like load-balancing or memory allocation

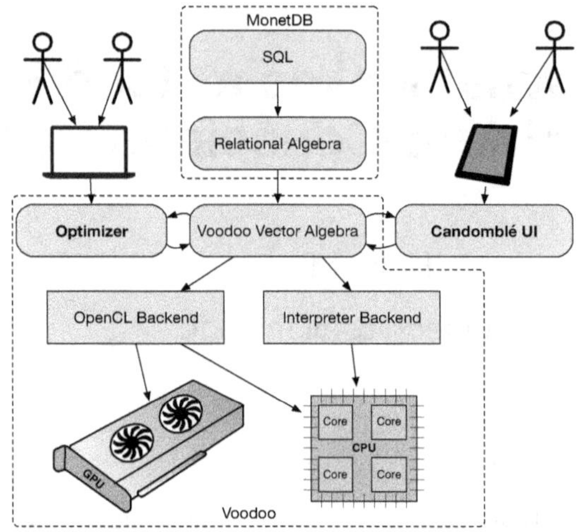

Figure 2: The Voodoo System Architecture

To effectively optimize a Voodoo program, the attendants need a basic understanding of our operator model. For the demo, we will provide a poster that briefly explains the operators. Fortunately, as we illustrate in the next section, the operator model is very simple.

2.1 The Voodoo Algebra

The goal of the Voodoo Vector Algebra is to expose a maximum amount of control to the optimizers while abstracting away hardware specifics. To achieve this level of control, we follow an approach that differs from most "classic" database algebras: Traditional algebras start with a a high-level algebra (usually relational algebra) and carefully lower the level of abstraction by a) introducing multiple alternatives for a given logical operator, b) introducing designated physical operators such as partitioning or sorting and c) annotating operators with auxiliary information such as sizes of hash-buckets or the number of sorted runs to generate. The goal of these algebras is to introduce just as many physical concepts as necessary to perform the desired optimizations while maintaining a plan that is as high-level as possible.

In contrast, Voodoo is designed using a different approach: we start with low-level design concepts that are similar to those found in computer architecture design (RISC, SIMD, ...) and carefully raise the level of abstraction. The design goal is to abstract the specifics of the hardware to allow efficient reasoning about the plan without obstructing the potential for hardware-specific optimization. By that we make every intermediate step of the query execution process explicit and, thus, tunable. This is captured in three guiding principles in our design of Voodoo:

No Implicit State The key design decision in Voodoo is the lack of hidden operator state. Where existing dataflow models, such as Spark RDDs and most database kernels, have hidden per-operator state, Voodoo exposes all generated data structures. This makes Voodoo both portable and tunable. It is tunable because if the optimizer decides that a certain step in a complex operator is unnecessary or shared with other operators, it can simply remove it or share the code that creates it. It is portable, because all state needs to be declared up front, which allows Voodoo to run plans in execution environments that prevent dynamic memory (re-)allocation such as GPUs.

Leanness Voodoo follows the design principle of *Reduced Instruction Set (RISC)* [4]. This decision is strongly tied to the previous: complex operators are prone to maintain implicit state which violates the first principle. We also aspired to keep the language free of redundancy: there should not be more than one way of expressing the same algorithm.

Static Critical Path The third distinguishing property of Voodoo is a *Static Critical Path*. In Voodoo, runtime decisions about operator execution (such as scheduling or load balancing) is outside the control of the optimizer. For our purposes the main advantage of this approach is that it provides portability and performance: by making the critical path of the program entirely static, we keep it free from hazards such as function calls or preemption. This allows good (and predictable) performance on classic CPUs as well as the efficient execution of Voodoo code on massively parallel processors that suffer significant performance degradation when execution paths diverge at runtime.

2.1.1 Primitive Operators

The Voodoo primitive operators are similar to SIMD CPU operations albeit on variable sized vectors: like CPUs, Voodoo implements operators that only create a single output *of known size* and no auxiliary data structures. Additionally, Voodoo operators have no side effects and variables can only be assigned once. Voodoo contains two kinds of data processing operations: the first kind are *data-parallel operations* such as arithmetics and logics but also `scatter` (write data values to specified positions) and `gather` (read values from specified positions). The second kind are *fold operations* that are not fully data parallel. This comprises all operations in which an output value depends on more than one value of the input vector. Naturally, this includes aggregations but also others such as order preserving selections or partitioning. While not entirely data-parallel, *Fold operations* can still be parallelized by logically partitioning the input. To designate logical partitions, Voodoo allows the creation of *Control Vectors*: virtual vectors that are merely used as partition ids when operating on data vectors. When compiling the plan, Voodoo maintains metadata about the *Control Vectors* and uses it as tuning hints (much like `#pragmas` in imperative languages). *Control Vectors* are never translated into executable code.

2.1.2 Macros

In addition to the primitive operators, Voodoo allows the definition of macros: complex operators that are comprised of primitives. Macros can be expanded in the UI to perform optimization of their implementation. While users can define their own macro operators, Voodoo comes with a library of standard operators for common data processing operations such as nested-loop joins, hash-building and -probing as well as partitioning. Since these operators are expandable, attendees are free to investigate and even optimize the *Voodoo Standard Library*.

3. DEMONSTRATION

A Voodoo query plan can be interpreted as a dataflow DAG where the vertices represent operators and edges represent data dependencies between operators.

We believe that the most approachable way to interact with such query plan DAGs is through a graphic interface. Consequently, we implemented *Candomblé* a touch-based user interface providing a plan visualizer (see Figure 3) that allows both the manipulation of operator parameters as well as the manipulation of the plan shape by adding, removing and reconnecting operators. Operators can be added to the plan by dragging an edge from an existing operator to an operator-class in the roster (on the right of the screens in Figure 3). Since most operators take more than one input, the user may have to draw more than one line before an operator is instantiated.

To familiarize the attendee with the Voodoo algebra before letting him explore freely, we divide our demonstration into two parts: a guided tour through the user interface by means of an example followed by a challenge.

3.1 The Guided Tour

To demonstrate the usage of the Candomblé UI for hardware-conscious optimization, we start by walking the user through the steps our rule-based optimizer takes.

Starting with an initial sequential plan that is generated from an SQL query we guide the user to speed up an aggregation through parallelization. The work flow in Figure 3 shows the steps the user needs to take. The initial plan contains a selection and a global sum operator over the selected values. To speed up the computation of this sum, we can split the sum into two hierarchical phases: The first will partition the input into multiple independent chunks (introduced Fig. 3a), and compute their subtotals (Fig. 3b) in parallel. In the final stage a global sum operator will sequentially merge the results from the separate chunks into one final answer (in Fig. 3c). However, since the optimal performance of the plan usually depends on size of the partitions, the user can drill into the partition-step (Fig. 3d), and tune the partition size (Fig. 3e). The system will provide live update on the performance (see Fig. 3d) as well as result correctness.

3.2 The Challenge

While we believe that the guided tour provides an insight into the difficulties of hardware-conscious optimization, we hope to entice attendants to try to beat our rule-based optimizer by tuning plans using our UI. However, the challenge is not as simple as it sounds: since Voodoo has the ability to run queries on different hardware platforms with varying costs for synchronization, materialization and even arithmetics on different datatypes[3], an optimal query plan for one platform may not translate to an optimal one for another. The attendants can experiment with tuning techniques such as a) eliminate redundant computation in an existing plan by sharing intermediates, b) replacing multiplications with bit shifts, c) pushing aggregations through joins (in Voodoo-terms: replacing Add(Gather(A,X), Gather(B,X)) with Gather(Add(A,B),X)) or d) switch a selection from branching to branch-free or vice-versa.

[3]On GPUs, for example, floating point arithmetic is usually cheaper than integer arithmetic

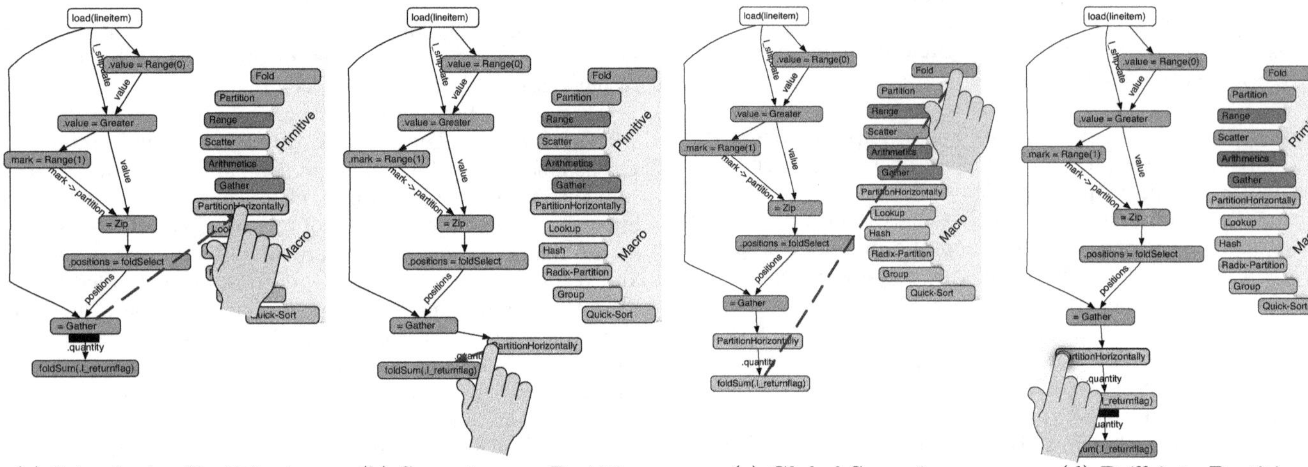

(a) Introducing Partitioning (b) Summing per Partition (c) Global Summing (d) Drill into Partition

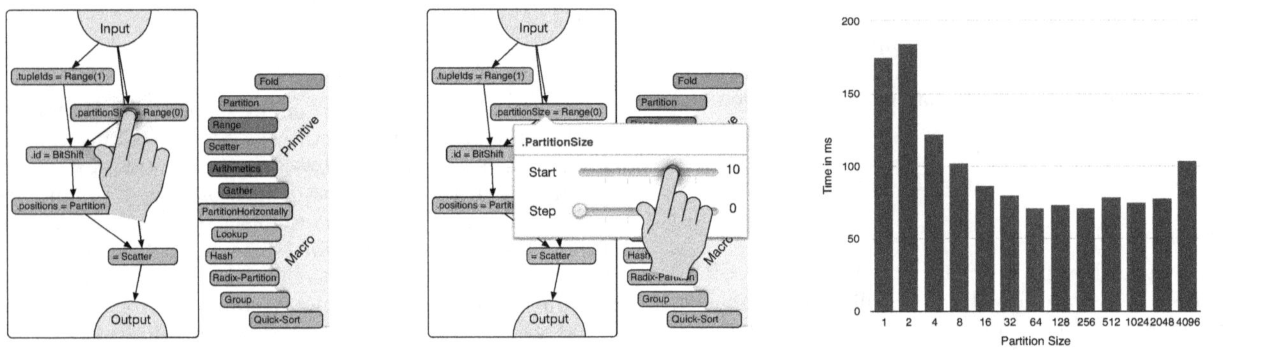

(e) Select Partition Size Control Vector (f) Tune Partition Size (g) Impact of the Partition Size (on CPU)

Figure 3: The Interaction Flow: Introducing a 2 level hierarchical aggregation

3.3 Further exploration of rule based optimizations

In addition to manually changing sections of the graph, we allow the user to define new simple, i.e., wild-card free, rule-based optimizations and apply them to the full plan DAG as well as other queries. She does so by selecting a set of adjacent operators through a circling gesture which is then used as an example for a more generic pattern. The sytem hightlights other matches of this pattern throughout the DAG. The user can then continue to refine the pattern or move on to specify a transformation for that pattern through the Voodoo UI similar to Figure 3e. In the latter case, the UI compiles the proposed transformation into a pass over the expression DAG, executes it and displays the transformed graph as well as the new performance results.

4. CONCLUSION & FUTURE BENEFIT

We believe that Voodoo is a good abstraction of executable machine code for the purpose of implementing and tuning data-intensive algorithms. It provides a simple operator model that allow efficient examination, optimization and evaluation of a physical query plan. However, it also gives fine grained control over virtually every (static) aspect of the query plan.

In addition to these benefits, we feel that the Candomblé UI is well suited to educate students, engineers and even non-experts about the challenges and benefits of hardware-conscious optimization. To facilitate this, both Voodoo and the *Candomblé UI* will be available in open source upon demonstration. We hope and invite others to use Voodoo as well as the Candomblé UI for teaching and prototyping.

5. REFERENCES

[1] Crotty, A., Galakatos, A., Dursun, K., Kraska, T., Cetintemel, U., and Zdoni, S. Tupleware:" big" data, big analytics, small clusters. In *CIDR* (2015).

[2] Klonatos, Y., Koch, C., Rompf, T., and Chafi, H. Building efficient query engines in a high-level language. *PVLDB* (2014).

[3] Neumann, T. Efficiently compiling efficient query plans for modern hardware. *PVLDB* (2011).

[4] Patterson, D. A., and Ditzel, D. R. The case for the reduced instruction set computer. *SIGARCH Comput. Archit. News* (October 1980).

[5] Pirk, H., Moll, O., Zaharia, M., and Madden, S. Voodoo - a vector algebra for portable database performance on modern hardware. In *Submitted for Review* (2016).

SnappyData: A Hybrid Transactional Analytical Store Built On Spark*

Jags Ramnarayan[1] Barzan Mozafari[1,2] Sumedh Wale[1] Sudhir Menon[1]
Neeraj Kumar[1] Hemant Bhanawat[1] Soubhik Chakraborty
Yogesh Mahajan Rishitesh Mishra Kishor Bachhav

[1]SnappyData Inc., Portland, OR [2]University of Michigan, Ann Arbor, MI

[1] {jramnarayan,barzan,swale,smenon,nkumar,hbhanawat}@snappydata.io
[2] mozafari@umich.edu

ABSTRACT

In recent years, our customers have expressed frustration in the traditional approach of using a combination of disparate products to handle their streaming, transactional and analytical needs. The common practice of stitching heterogeneous environments in custom ways has caused enormous production woes by increasing development complexity and total cost of ownership. With SnappyData, an open source platform, we propose a unified engine for real-time operational analytics, delivering stream analytics, OLTP and OLAP in a single integrated solution. We realize this platform through a seamless integration of Apache Spark (as a big data computational engine) with GemFire (as an in-memory transactional store with scale-out SQL semantics).

In this demonstration, after presenting a few use case scenarios, we exhibit SnappyData as our our in-memory solution for delivering truly interactive analytics (i.e., a couple of seconds), when faced with large data volumes or high velocity streams. We show that SnappyData can exploit state-of-the-art approximate query processing techniques and a variety of data synopses. Finally, we allow the audience to define various *high-level accuracy contracts (HAC)*, to communicate their accuracy requirements with SnappyData in an intuitive fashion.

1. INTRODUCTION

Many of our customers, particularly those active in financial trading or IoT (Internet of Things), are increasingly relying on applications whose workflows involve (1) continuous stream processing, (2) transactional and write-heavy workloads, and (3) interactive SQL analytics. These applications need to consume high-velocity streams to trigger real-time alerts, ingest them into a write-optimized store, and perform OLAP-style analytics to derive deep insight quickly.

*For a detailed paper, see [13].

SIGMOD/PODS'16 June 26 - July 01, 2016, San Francisco, CA, USA

ACM ISBN 978-1-4503-3531-7/16/06.

DOI: http://dx.doi.org/10.1145/2882903.2899408

While there have been a flurry of data management solutions designed for one or two of these tasks, there is no single solution that is apt at all three.

SQL-on-Hadoop solutions (e.g., Hive, Impala, and Spark SQL) use OLAP-style optimizations and columnar formats to run OLAP queries over massive volumes of static data. While apt at batch-processing, these systems are not designed as real-time operational databases, as they lack the ability to mutate data with transactional consistency, use indexing for efficient point accesses, or handle high-concurrency and bursty workloads.

Hybrid Transaction/Analytical Processing (HTAP) systems support both OLTP and OLAP queries by storing data in dual formats—row-oriented fashion (on disk or traditional database cache buffers) and compressed in-memory columns—but need to be used alongside a streaming engine (e.g., Storm [14], Kafka, Confluent) to support streaming processing.

Finally, stream processors (e.g., Samza [1]) provide some form of state management, but only allow support simple analytics over data streams. This is because complex analytics require the same optimizations used in a OLAP engine [7, 10], such as columnar formats and efficient operators for joining, grouping, or aggregating large histories. For example, many of our customers in Industrial IoT derive insight by ingesting unbounded streams of data at very high speeds, while running continuous analytical queries on windows correlated with large quantities of history.

Consequently, the demand for mixed workloads has resulted in several composite data architectures, exemplified in the "lambda" architecture, requiring multiple solutions to be stitched together—an exercise that can be hard, time consuming and expensive.

For instance, in capital markets, a real time market surveillance application has to stream in trades at very high rates and detect abusive trading patterns (e.g., insider trading). This requires correlating large volumes of data by joining a stream with historical records, other streams, and financial reference data (which may change throughout the trading day). A triggered alert could in turn result in additional analytical queries, which need to run on both the ingested and historical data. Trades arrive on a message bus (e.g., Tibco, IBM MQ, Kafka) and are processed using a stream processor (e.g., Storm) or a homegrown application, writing state to a key-value store (e.g., Cassandra) or an in-memory data grid (e.g., GemFire). This data is also stored in HDFS and analyzed periodically using SQL-on-Hadoop OLAP engines.

Increased TCO (total cost of ownership) — This heterogeneous architecture, which is far too common among our customers, has several drawbacks (D1–D3) that significantly increase the total cost of ownership for these companies.

D1. Increased complexity: The use of incompatible and autonomous systems has significantly increased the total cost of ownership for these companies. Developers have to master disparate APIs, data models, configurations and tuning options for multiple products. Once in production, operational management is a nightmare. Diagnosing the root cause of problems often requires hard-to-find experts that have to correlate logs and metrics across different products.

D2. Lower performance: The required analytics necessitates data access across multiple non-colocated clusters, resulting in several network hops and multiple copies of data. Data may also need to be transformed when dealing with incompatible data models (e.g., turning Cassandra ColumnFamilies into domain objects in Storm).

D3. Wasted resources: With data getting duplicated, increased data shuffling wastes network bandwidth, CPU cycles and memory.

Lack of Interactive Analytics — Achieving interactive SQL analytics has remained an on-going challenge, even for modest volumes of data. Unfortunately, any analytical query that requires distributed shuffling of the records can take tens of seconds to minutes, hardly permitting interactive analytics (e.g., for exploratory analytics). Moreover, distributed clusters can be shared by hundreds of users concurrently running such queries.

Our Goal — *We aim to deliver interactive-speed analytics with modest investments in cluster infrastructure and far less complexity than today.* SnappyData fulfills this promise by (i) enabling streaming, transactions and interactive analytics in a single unifying system—rather than stitching different solutions—and (ii) delivering true interactive speeds via a state-of-the-art approximate query engine that can leverage a multitude of synopses as well as the full dataset.

Our Approach — We envision a single unified, scale out database cluster that ingests static data sets (e.g., from HDFS), acquires updatable reference data from enterprise databases, manages streams in memory, while permitting both continuous SQL analytics on the streams and interactive queries on entire data (acquired from streams, HDFS or enterprise DBs). To achieve this goal, our approach consists of a deep integration of Apache Spark, as a computational framework, and GemFire, as an in-memory transactional store, as described next.

Best of two worlds — Spark offers an appealing programming model to both modern application developers and data scientists. Through a common set of abstractions, Spark programmers can tackle a confluence of different paradigms (e.g., streaming, machine learning, SQL analytics). Spark's core abstraction, a Resilient Distributed Dataset (RDD), provides fault tolerance by efficiently storing the lineage of all transformations instead of the data. The data itself is partitioned across nodes and if any partition is lost, it can be reconstructed using the lineage information. The benefit of this approach is avoiding replication over the network and operating on data as a batch for higher throughput. While this approach provides efficiency and fault tolerance, it also requires that an RDD be immutable. In other words, Spark is simply designed as a computational framework, and therefore (i) does not have its own storage engine, and (ii) does not support mutability semantics.

On the other hand, GemFire is an in-memory data grid, which manages records in a partitioned row-oriented store with synchronous replication. It ensures consistency by integrating a *dynamic group membership service* (GMS) and a *distributed transaction service* (DTS). Data can be indexed and updated in a fine grained or batch manner. Updates can be reliably enqueued and asynchronously written back out to an external database. Data can also be persisted on disk using append-only logging with offline compaction for fast disk writes.

Therefore, to combine the best of both worlds, SnappyData seamlessly fuses the Spark and GemFire runtimes, adopting Spark as the programming model with extensions to support mutability and HA (high availability) through GemFire's replication and fine grained updates. For instance, when ingesting a stream, we process the incoming stream as a batch, avoid replication, and replay from the source on a failure. Here, the processed state could be written into the store in batches to avoid a tuple-at-a-time replication. Recovery from failure will thus be limited to the time needed to replay a single batch.

Challenges — Spark is designed as a computational engine for processing batch jobs. Each Spark application (e.g., a Map-reduce job) runs as an independent set of processes (i.e., executor JVMs) on the cluster. These JVMs are reused for the lifetime of the application. While, data can be cached and reused in these JVMs for a single application, sharing data across applications or clients requires an external storage tier, such as HDFS. We, on the other hand, target a real-time, "always-on", operational design center—clients can connect at will, and share data across any number of concurrent connections. This is similar to any operational database on the market today. Thus, to manage data in the same JVM, our first challenge is to alter the life cycle of these executors so that they are *long-lived* and *de-coupled from individual applications.*

A second but related challenge is Spark's design for how user requests (i.e., jobs) are handled. A single driver orchestrates all the work done on the executors. Given our need for high concurrency and a hybrid OLTP-OLAP workload, this driver introduces (i) a single point of contention for all requests, and (ii) a barrier for achieving high availability (HA). Executors are shutdown if the driver fails, requiring a full refresh of any cached state.

Spark's primary usage of memory is for caching RDDs and for shuffling blocks to other nodes. Data is managed in blocks and is immutable. On the other hand, we need to manage more complex data structures (along with indexes) for point access and updates. Therefore, another challenge is merging these two disparate storage systems with little impedance to the application. This challenge is exacerbated by current limitations of Spark SQL—mostly related to mutability characteristics and conformance to SQL.

Finally, Spark's strong and growing community has zero tolerance for incompatible forks. This means that no changes can be made to Spark's execution model or its semantics for existing APIs. In other words, our changes have to be an extension.

Contributions — SnappyData makes the following contributions to deliver a unified and optimized runtime.

(a) **Marrying an operational in-memory data store with Spark's computational model.** We introduce a number of extensions to fuse our runtime with that of Spark. When Spark executes tasks in a partitioned manner, it keeps all available CPU cores busy. We extend this design by allowing low latency and fine grained operations to interleave and get higher priority, without involving the scheduler. To support high concurrency, we also extend the runtime with a "Job Server" that decouples applications from data servers, while sharing state across many clients and applications.

(b) **Unified API for OLAP, OLTP, and streaming.** We extend Spark's API to (i) allow for OLTP operations, e.g., transactions and inserts/updates/deletions on tables, (ii) be conformant with SQL standards, e.g., allowing tables alterations, constraints, indexes, and (iii) support declarative stream processing in SQL.

(c) **Optimized Spark applications** Our deeply integrated store eliminates the need for an external one (e.g., a KV store) for Spark applications. This improves overall performance by minimizing network traffic and serialization costs. In addition, by promoting colocated schema designs, in many scenarios SnappyData eliminates the need for shuffling altogether.

(d) To deliver analytics at truly interactive speeds, we have equipped SnappyData with state-of-the-art AQP techniques [4, 5] as well as several novel features. Unlike previous AQP engines [2, 3, 6, 9, 15], Instead of overwhelming end users with numerous statistics, we provide an intuitive means for expressing accuracy requirements as *high-level accuracy contracts (HAC)* [11]. SnappyData is also the first AQP engine to offer automatic bias correction for arbitrarily complex SQL queries. Finally, while traditional load shedding techniques are restricted to simple queries [12], SnappyData provides error estimates for arbitrarily complex queries on streams.

2. SYSTEM OVERVIEW

2.1 System Architecture

Figure 1 depicts the core components of SnappyData, where Spark's original components are highlighted in gray. To simplify, we have omitted standard components, such as security and monitoring.

The storage layer is primarily in-memory and manages data in either row or column formats. The column format is derived from Spark's RDD caching implementation and allows for compression. Row oriented tables can be indexed on keys or secondary columns, supporting fast reads and writes on index keys.

We support two primary programming models—SQL and Spark's API. SQL access is through JDBC/ODBC and is based on Spark SQL dialect with several extensions. One could perceive SnappyData as a SQL database that uses Spark API as its language for stored procedures. We provide

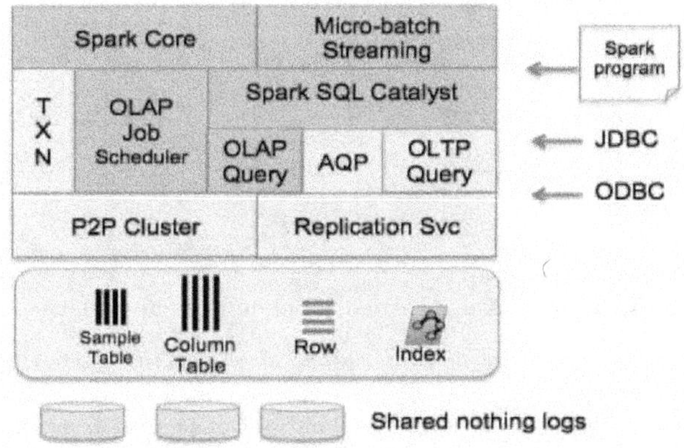

Figure 1: SnappyData's core components

a glimpse over our SQL and programming APIs. Our stream processing is primarily through Spark Streaming, but it is integrated and runs *in-situ* with our store.

The OLAP scheduler and job server coordinate all OLAP and Spark jobs and are capable of working with external cluster managers, such as YARN or Mesos. We route all OLTP operations immediately to appropriate data partitions without incurring any scheduling overhead.

To support replica consistency, fast point updates, and instantaneous detection of failure conditions in the cluster, we use a P2P (peer-to-peer) cluster membership service that ensures view consistency and virtual synchrony in the cluster. Any of the in-memory tables can be synchronously replicated using this P2P cluster.

In addition to the "exact" dataset, data can also be summarized using *probabilistic* data structures, such as stratified samples and other forms of synopses. Using our API, applications can choose to trade accuracy for performance. SnappyData's query engine has built-in support for approximate query processing (AQP) and will exploit appropriate probabilistic data structures to meet the user's requested level of accuracy or performance.

2.2 Data Ingestion Pipeline

SnappyData focuses on use cases that involve stream ingestion and interactive analytics with transactional updates. The steps to support these tasks are depicted in Figure 2, and explained below.

Step 1. Once the SnappyData cluster is started and before any live streams can be processed, we ensure that the historical and reference datasets are readily accessible. The data sets may come from HDFS, enterprise relational databases (RDB), or disks managed by SnappyData. Immutable batch sources (e.g., HDFS) can be loaded in parallel into a columnar format table with or without compression. Reference data that is often mutating can be managed as row tables.

Step 2. We rely on Spark Streaming's parallel receivers to consume data from multiple sources. These receivers produce a DStream, whereby the input is batched over small time intervals and emitted as a stream of RDDs. This batched data is typically transformed, enriched and emitted as one or more additional streams. The raw incoming stream may be persisted into HDFS for batch analytics.

Step 3. Next, we use SQL to analyze these streams. As DStreams (RDDs) use the same processing and data model as data stored in tables (DataFrames), we can seamlessly combine these data structures in arbitrary SQL queries (re-

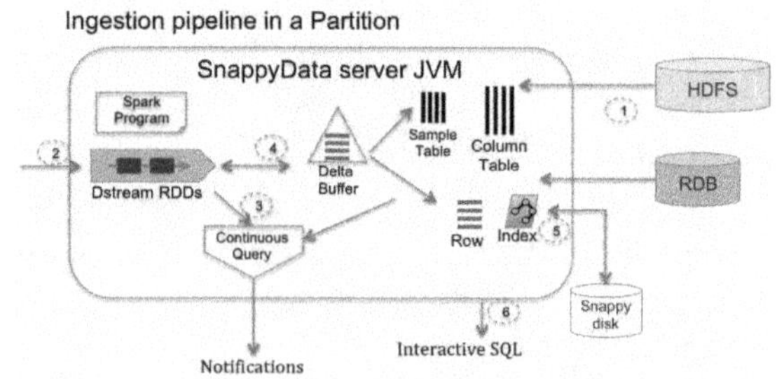

Figure 2: Data ingestion pipeline in SnappyData

ferred to as continuous queries as they execute each time the stream emits a batch). When faced with complex analytics or high velocity streams, SnappyData can still provide answers in real time by resorting to approximation.

Step 4. The stream processing layer can interact with the storage layer in a variety of ways. The enriched stream can be efficiently stored in a column table. The results of continuous queries may result in several point updates in the store (e.g., maintaining counters). The continuous queries may join, correlate, and aggregate with other streams, history or reference tables. When records are written into column tables one (or a small batch) at a time, data goes through stages, arriving first into a delta row buffer that is capable of high write rates, and then aging into a columnar form. This delta row buffer is merged during query execution.

Step 5. To prevent running out of memory, tables can be configured to evict or overflow to disk using an LRU strategy. For instance, an application may ingest all data into HDFS while preserving the last day's worth of data in memory.

Step 6. Once ingested, the data is readily available for interactive analytics using SQL. Similar to stream analytics, SnappyData can again use approximate query processing to ensure interactive analytics on massive historical data in accordance to users' requested accuracy.

3. DEMONSTRATION DETAILS

Our demonstration scenario imagines the audience as users of a energy management system, monitoring in real time, metrics from thousands to millions of smart meters to understand load distribution, outliers, trends and so on. We organize our demonstration into two phases:

1. A brief introduction to the main system functionalities, in which we will exhibit the key components and features of our system.
2. A hands-on phase where the audience is invited to directly interact with the system and test its capabilities.

Our primary goal with this demonstration is to decisively show that curated sampled data sets and synopsis data structures can be extremely effective in providing quick responses to arbitrary analytic class queries at interactive speeds. We show side by side comparison to native Spark in-memory performance.

For interactive analytics on historical data, we store meter readings for households and businesses for the last few years and permit our demonstration users to try out queries using Apache Zeppelin—a web based notebook for interactive analytics (see Figure 3). They would be able to create our CMS (count-min-sketch [8]) based structures for managing time series meter readings across multiple dimensions or create one or more stratified samples.

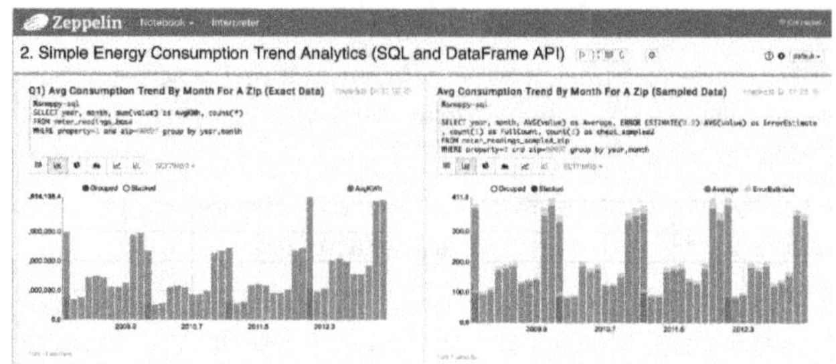

Figure 3: A screenshot of the demonstration scenario using Zeppelin and SnappyData

The demonstration is divided into 3 different notebooks. The first notebook introduces the APIs for sampling structures, loading data, and monitoring memory utilization. Moreover, the users will be given an opportunity to define their own HACs and observe their impact on the cardinality, accuracy, and response time of of various analytical queries.

The second notebook demonstrates the power of sampling and summary structures on already ingested data. The third notebook demonstrates the use of SQL-based "continuous queries" for detecting complex patterns in streaming data over arbitrary time windows. User will be able to choose various forms of exact or approximate answers using our CMS-based structures. For instance, energy utilization pattern over few mins correlated with similar periods in the past may predict future demand and enable outage management.

Bibliography

[1] Apache Samza. http://samza.apache.org/.

[2] Fast, approximate analysis of big data (yahoo's druid). http://yahooeng.tumblr.com/post/135390948446/data-sketches.

[3] Presto: Distributed SQL query engine for big data. https://prestodb.io/docs/current/release/release-0.61.html.

[4] S. Agarwal, H. Milner, A. Kleiner, A. Talwalkar, M. Jordan, S. Madden, B. Mozafari, and I. Stoica. Knowing when you're wrong: Building fast and reliable approximate query processing systems. In *SIGMOD*, 2014.

[5] S. Agarwal, B. Mozafari, A. Panda, H. Milner, S. Madden, and I. Stoica. BlinkDB: queries with bounded errors and bounded response times on very large data. In *EuroSys*, 2013.

[6] S. Agarwal, A. Panda, B. Mozafari, A. P. Iyer, S. Madden, and I. Stoica. Blink and it's done: Interactive queries on very large data. *PVLDB*, 2012.

[7] L. Braun et al. Analytics in motion: High performance event-processing and real-time analytics in the same database. In *SIGMOD*, 2015.

[8] G. Cormode and S. Muthukrishnan. An improved data stream summary: the count-min sketch and its applications. *Journal of Algorithms*, 55, 2005.

[9] J. M. Hellerstein, P. J. Haas, and H. J. Wang. Online aggregation. In *SIGMOD*, 1997.

[10] E. Liarou et al. Monetdb/datacell: online analytics in a streaming column-store. *PVLDB*, 2012.

[11] B. Mozafari and N. Niu. A handbook for building an approximate query engine. *IEEE Data Engineering Bulletin*, 2015.

[12] B. Mozafari and C. Zaniolo. Optimal load shedding with aggregates and mining queries. In *ICDE*, 2010.

[13] J. Ramnarayan, B. Mozafari, S. Menon, et al. Snappydata: Streaming, transactions, and interactive analytics in a unified engine. http://web.eecs.umich.edu/ mozafari/php/data/uploads/snappy.pdf, 2016.

[14] A. Toshniwal et al. Storm@twitter. In *SIGMOD*, 2014.

[15] K. Zeng, S. Gao, J. Gu, B. Mozafari, and C. Zaniolo. Abs: a system for scalable approximate queries with accuracy guarantees. In *SIGMOD*, 2014.

SourceSight: Enabling Effective Source Selection

Theodoros Rekatsinas
Stanford University
thodrek@cs.stanford.edu

Amol Deshpande
University of Maryland
amol@cs.umd.edu

Xin Luna Dong
Google Inc.
lunadong@google.com

Lise Getoor
UC Santa Cruz
getoor@soe.ucsc.edu

Divesh Srivastava
AT&T Labs-Research
divesh@research.att.com

ABSTRACT

Recently there has been a rapid increase in the number of data sources and data services, such as cloud-based data markets and data portals, that facilitate the collection, publishing and trading of data. Data sources typically exhibit large heterogeneity in the type and quality of data they provide. Unfortunately, when the number of data sources is large, it is difficult for users to reason about the actual usefulness of sources for their applications and the trade-offs between the benefits and costs of acquiring and integrating sources. In this demonstration we present SOURCESIGHT, a system that allows users to interactively explore a large number of heterogeneous data sources, and discover valuable sets of sources for diverse integration tasks. SOURCESIGHT uses a novel multi-level source quality index that enables effective source selection at different granularity levels, and introduces a collection of new techniques to discover and evaluate relevant sources for integration.

1. INTRODUCTION

Data integration remains among the most cost-intensive tasks in data management, because of the considerable computation and human-curation costs involved in the process [8] and, often times, the monetary cost involved in acquiring data [1]. With a rapid increase in the number of data sources available for consumption, facilitated in part by the rise of data markets [1] and public dataset repositories [2], an additional challenge faced by a user is to *identify* the sources that are truly valuable and appropriate for her application. This gives rise to the natural question of how can one discover *the most valuable sources* for integration, i.e., sources that maximize the user's benefit (i.e., the utility of the data in the final integration result) at the minimum cost.

Several approaches have been proposed to help users reason about the value of integrating multiple sources: (i) *cost-oriented* techniques that focus on characterizing solely the cost of integration, and (ii) *value-oriented* techniques that reason about the trade-off between the benefit and cost of integration. Techniques from the first category reason about the effort required to perform schema-matching, data-cleaning and data-transformation when integrating multiple sources [8]; however, these techniques do not estimate the actual benefit of integration [14]. Existing value-oriented techniques focus on the marginal benefit of integrating a new source [6, 13]. Nevertheless, they typically assume that users have already identified *all* sources relevant to their application and do not allow users to explore and identify which sources are the most valuable for their desired *integration task*, nor do they support diverse integration tasks across multiple users.

To understand these limitations, consider companies, such as Dataminr, Bloomberg, Thomson-Reuters, etc., that integrate data streams from multiple news sources into unified real-time feeds for clients in finance, the public sector, news, security and crisis management. Each client-specific task is associated with a different *integration task*, i.e., multiple news sources are combined together to construct the necessary feeds. Moreover, client-tasks are diverse and can be characterized by a set of named entities, such as people, locations, or specific topics, such as finance or terrorism etc. Due to the large number of sources it is unlikely that users know in advance all sources that provide valuable data for their task. Thus, it is essential to allow multiple users to discover and select sources based purely based on their integration task description.

Recent research has shown that carefully selecting data sources can dramatically improve the quality of integrated data both in terms of accuracy [6] and timeliness [13, 15]. This can, in turn, improve the performance of intelligence applications, such as disease outbreak forecasting [15], or demonstration and civil unrest monitoring [12], or can help businesses minimize the monetary cost of their integration pipelines by enabling them to detect and acquire only the most valuable sources for their applications [6].

Motivated by the above, we recently introduced our vision for a *data source management system* [14] that enables users to discover the most valuable sources for their applications. In this demonstration proposal, we present SOURCESIGHT, a fully functional prototype of such a data source management system. We also discuss extensions to our initial design that allow a user to evaluate the effectiveness of the system (Section 3.5) at selecting sources automatically. The core of the system is built around *source selection* [6] allowing one to reason about the trade-offs between the benefit and cost of integration. The benefit of integration can be quantified using a variety of metrics, such as coverage, accuracy, timeliness and bias [14]. The cost of integration is quantified using a model similar to that of Dong et al. [6]; other cost models [8] can be seamlessly incorporated in our system. SOURCESIGHT offers a number of unique features:

(1) Users can describe the domain of their integration task using a keyword-based interface and explore sources as well as similar integration tasks relevant to their task.

(2) Given an integration task, users can perform source selection using a variety of quality metrics. SOURCESIGHT casts source

SIGMOD '16, June 26–July 1, 2016, San Francisco, CA, USA.

DOI: http://dx.doi.org/10.1145/2882903.2899403

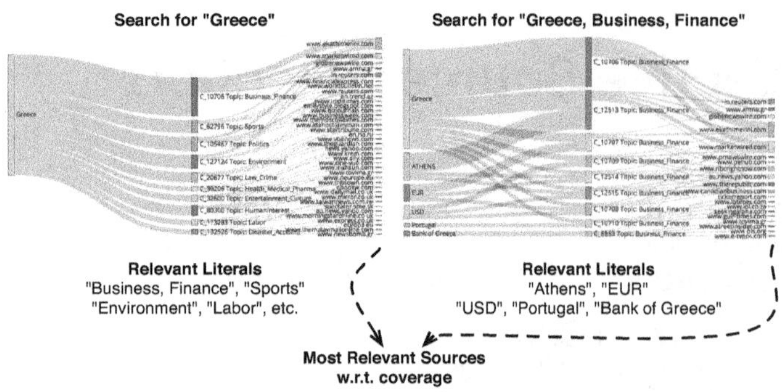

Figure 1: Discovering relevant sources and refining an integration task with SOURCESIGHT.

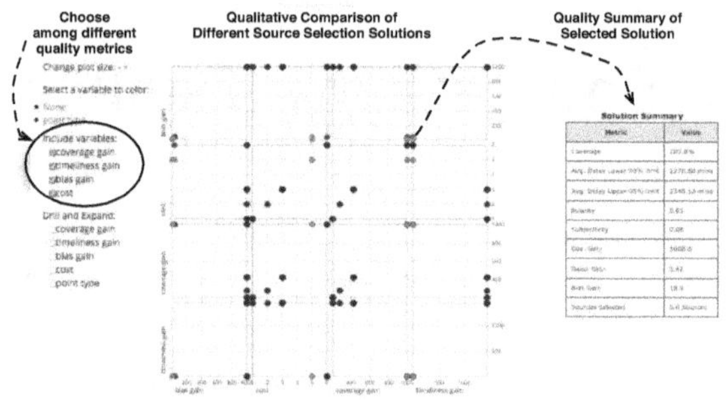

Figure 2: SOURCESIGHT's interface for exploring different source selection solutions.

selection as a multivariate optimization problem to help users understand the actual trade-offs between different quality metrics and proposes different sets of sources to be used when different weights are assigned to different quality metrics.

(3) Finally, the system allows users to interactively edit the recommended solutions by adding or deleting sources. Users can also perform a qualitative comparison between different sets of sources. This is crucial for evaluating the solutions recommended by SOURCESIGHT and aids the users to understand why a particular set of sources was proposed by the system.

Related work. Over the past few years, the research community has introduced a number of techniques to support search over large numbers of datasets in the form of Web tables [10, 4]. Unlike SOURCESIGHT, these techniques focus on providing rankings of datasets and are agnostic to the cost or benefit of integrating multiple datasets. Apart from Web table search, more generic data search systems, such as Microsoft's Power BI[1], have been recently proposed. Nonetheless, while facilitating data integration, they do not help analysts to understand the quality of data sources.

2. DISCOVERING VALUABLE SOURCES

Consider a user who wants to find sources relevant to an integration task, e.g., a data scientist exploring datasets in a repository such as DataHub [2] or a journalist compiling information from multiple news sources in a repository such as EventRegistry[2]. While users can provide a keyword-based description of their task, they may not know all the relevant sources. Our goal is twofold:

First, users should be able to provide a keyword-based description of their task and *discover* sources relevant to it. Further, it would be beneficial to explore related and more specialized task descriptions as the set of relevant sources may change significantly. SOURCESIGHT is the first system that unifies these two aspects of source exploration into a common interface. Figure 1 shows an example use-case where a journalist wants to write an overview article about the socio-economic situation in Greece. The journalist starts by requesting news sources relevant to the keyword "Greece". Apart from presenting the relevant sources, SOURCESIGHT additionally recommends that it might be beneficial to explore related and more specialized descriptions, such as "Greece and Business and Finance" or "Greece and Labor", as the set of relevant sources may change significantly. Based on these recommendations the user can revise her integration task description and obtain a new more focused set of relevant sources.

Second, sources discovered in the previous step may exhibit large heterogeneity. They may provide stale or erroneous data [5, 9], they may contain duplicate data [3, 9] at different costs, and may exhibit schema or instance heterogeneity. Given this diversity in the sources, the users need to be able to reason about the utility of integrating together a *set* of sources; a user should be able to find a set of sources that satisfy any cost constraints that she has, and if integrated together will maximize the *benefit* of integration.

To support this, SOURCESIGHT allows users to perform *source selection* [6], i.e., choose a subset of sources among a set of relevant sources S identified using keyword search and exploration. Let $B(\bar{S}, I)$ denote the benefit of integrating sources $\bar{S}$ with respect to an integration task I, and let $C(\bar{S})$ denote the total integration cost for $\bar{S}$. Source selection finds a set of sources S_I such that $S_I = \arg\max_{\bar{S} \subseteq S} B(\bar{S}, I) - C(\bar{S})$. To quantify the benefit of integration, SOURCESIGHT uses a range of rigorous data quality metrics, such as *coverage*, *accuracy*, *timeliness* and *bias* [14].

Given this variety of quality metrics, SOURCESIGHT provides the user with multiple source selection solutions that correspond to different weighting configurations for the available quality metrics. This allows users to explore different trade-offs amongst the available quality metrics and identify the set of sources that best satisfies their quality requirements (see Figure 2).

3. SOURCESIGHT DESIGN

Recently, we put forward our vision about the functionalities and architecture of data source management systems for effective source selection [14]. SOURCESIGHT is a realization of such a system. Next, we present SOURCESIGHT's architecture, how it implements (Sections 3.3 and 3.4) the functionalities described in [14], and new functionalities (Section 3.5) SOURCESIGHT provides.

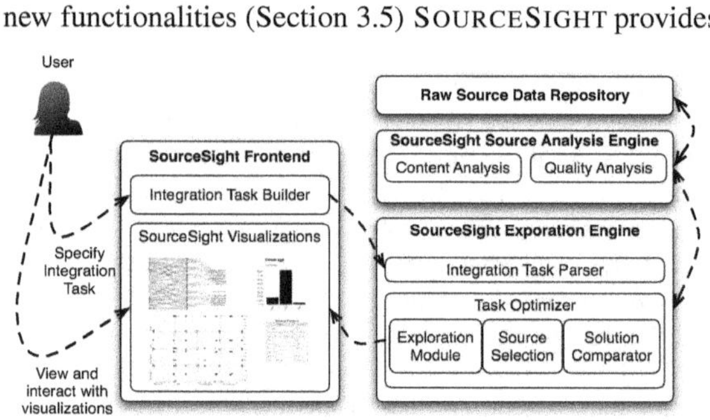

Figure 3: SOURCESIGHT architecture.

3.1 Architecture overview

SOURCESIGHT is built as a layer on top of a data source repository that stores the raw data of data sources. Acquisition of the data sources is out of the scope of this work. The system consists of three components: a front-end, a source analysis engine and an exploration engine (Figure 3). The basic operations of SOURCESIGHT can be divided into an *offline* phase and an *online* phase. In the offline phase, the source analysis module constructs an index describing both the content and the quality of each source with

[1] http://www.microsoft.com/en-us/powerbi

[2] http://eventregistry.org/

respect to multiple quality metrics. This index is used during the online phase to serve user requests. We discuss the indexing technique in more detail in Section 3.2. In the online phase, users interact with SOURCESIGHT via its front-end module and user requests are served by the exploration engine. Users can specify a desired integration task by providing a keyword-based description of their integration task. Once a description is provided, users can choose among three main functionalities: They can (i) choose to explore which keywords and sources are most relevant to their task, (ii) choose to perform source selection, or (iii) choose to perform a qualitative comparison between different sets of sources constructed either manually or automatically via source selection.

3.2 Reasoning about the content of sources

We assume that each entry in a source (e.g., a tuple in a table or a news article in a news media source) is associated with a set of *context literals* and all context literals come from a *literal dictionary* V. We assume that V is hierarchically structured and edges between literals can encode containment, equivalence and other semantic relations. For example, V can be a knowledge base with literals corresponding to *real-world entities* and *concepts*. Figure 4 shows an example knowledge base with concept literals being hierarchically structured (e.g., "Country" is subsumed by "Location") and entity literals being semantically associated with concept literals (e.g., "USA" has a specific "Population"). Dictionary V allows us to identify the domains covered by each source by analyzing the union of context-literal sets for the entries of the source.

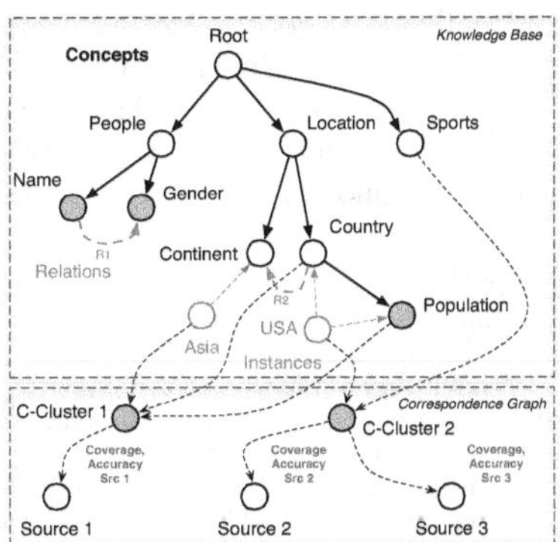

Figure 4: An example knowledge base with the corresponding correspondence graph.

To reason about the content and quality of different sources we augment V with a *correspondence graph* [14]. An example of a correspondence graph is shown in Figure 4. The nodes in the correspondence graph are either data sources (*source nodes*) or clusters of literals as dictated by the available sources (*c-cluster nodes*). The edges in the correspondence graph connect each source node with c-cluster nodes and c-cluster nodes with the corresponding literals in the knowledge base. In the example above, there are two c-cluster nodes, one corresponding to the population of countries in Asia and one to sports in the USA (i.e., "USA and Sports"). The edges connecting c-cluster nodes to literals follow conjunctive semantics. Each edge from a source to a c-cluster node is annotated with a quality profile of that source for that specific c-cluster, and each c-cluster node is associated with local information about the dependencies of the data sources that are connected to it.

The correspondence graph serves as a content and quality index for the available sources. To construct it we first learn the latent c-cluster nodes and then compute the quality profiles and data source dependencies for each c-cluster node. To discover the literals associated with each source entry we use Thomson Reuters' Open Calais[3], an API for semantic annotations with respect to multiple knowledge bases including DBpedia, Freebase and others. To construct the c-cluster nodes we adopt a frequent pattern mining approach based on the FP-growth algorithm [7]. This allows discovering domains that are prevalent in multiple sources. After discovering the c-cluster nodes, we compute the quality of each source with respect to each c-cluster node it is connected to. To do this, we collectively analyze the content of all sources connected to a c-cluster node to form a single dataset characterizing the content of the c-cluster and then each individual source is compared with the combined data to compute its quality [14].

3.3 Specifying an integration task

SOURCESIGHT allows users to specify an integration task $I = (I_d, I_c)$ by providing a description that corresponds to a context-literal set I_d defining the *domain* of the task and potentially a set of integration cost constraints I_c. The system recommends literals and sources that are related to their keyword search, enabling them to either explore sources relevant to their search or refine their initial task description by considering related literals.

Relevant context-literals are all literals that are related to literals in I_d either via V or via the correspondence graph. The former accounts for semantic relations across literals while the second accounts for co-occurrence of literals in a source. Similarly, relevant sources to task I are all data sources that provide entries whose context-literal set is a subset of I_d or related to I_d via the literal dictionary V (e.g., using equivalence or containment relationships).

SOURCESIGHT offers a unified interface for users to explore both context-literals and sources related to their desired integration task (see Figure 1). Given an integration task description I_d, SOURCESIGHT returns the set of top relevant literals to the search of the user as well as the most relevant sources with respect to coverage or other metrics for the specified keyword search. The user can then select any of the recommended sources to view a summary of the literals that the source covers as well as a quality summary of the source for the corresponding keyword search. Users can also choose to update their integration task description I_d by including new relevant context-literals to I_d.

3.4 Multivariate source selection

Given an integration task $I = (I_d, I_c)$, the user can perform source selection with respect to the context-literals I_d and the constraints I_c. As discussed in Section 2, SOURCESIGHT considers multiple quality metrics to quantify the benefit of integration. The system casts source selection as a multi-objective optimization problem and finds the set of *Pareto optimal* solutions corresponding to the source selection problem at hand.

Discovering all the solutions on the Pareto front is expensive as one needs to reason about all the potential trade-offs amongst the available quality metrics. To address this issue we use a sampling strategy to discover solutions that correspond to different quality trade-offs. Let Q be the set of quality metrics under consideration and $B_q(\cdot)$ be an oracle computing the benefit of integration with respect to quality metric $q \in Q$ for any set of sources. We compute the total benefit of integration as a weighted linear combination of the individual benefit of each quality metric, i.e., $B(\cdot) = \sum_{q \in Q} w_q \cdot B_q(\cdot)$. Given this definition of the total benefit of integration, we sample different combinations of the weights w_q and solve source selection for each of those. Finally, we identify the Pareto optimal solutions amongst the sampled solutions.

The sampled solutions are presented to the user in a way that makes it easy to compare the quality of each solution. The corre-

[3]http://www.opencalais.com/

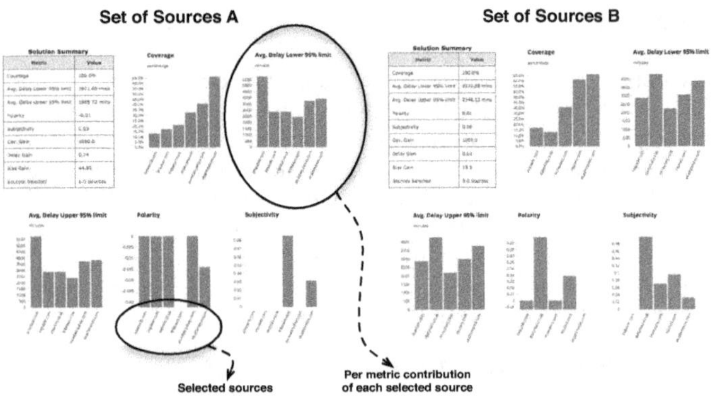

Figure 5: Comparing sets of sources.

sponding interface is shown in Figure 2. Users can select a particular solution and view a concise summary of the benefit and cost of integration achieved by it. Users can also drill down and expand only on a subset of the available quality metrics to fully understand specific trade-offs across different solutions. Finally, users can view a detailed description of a source selection solution with information about the sources included in the result and their individual contributions to the quality of the final integration result.

3.5 Comparing sets of sources

SOURCESIGHT enables users to understand why a particular set of sources was recommended to them and evaluate its performance. Users can perform a qualitative comparison between two sets of sources with respect to the same integration task (Figure 5). They are also able to examine how two sets of sources compare against each other with respect to individual quality metrics, as well as the total integration benefit and cost. The sets of sources to be compared can correspond to recommended solutions from source selection or can be manually constructed by the user as follows: (i) users can start from a returned source selection solution and add new sources or remove already included sources, or (ii) users can manually select individual sources and construct their own set. The former allows them to examine the neighborhood of the returned solution but also serves as a mechanism of convincing the user of the value achieved by the output of source selection. To enable the latter, SOURCESIGHT provides users with the top-k most relevant sources for their integration task with respect to each individual quality metric.

4. DEMO DETAILS

We will demonstrate the functionality of SOURCESIGHT through hands-on experience with two real-world scenarios. With the data stored on a remote server, users will interact with the system via a web interface. Our goals are two fold: (i) demonstrate the utility of SOURCESIGHT in exploring and selecting beneficial sources for integration, and (ii) demonstrate the effectiveness of automatic source selection for diverse integration tasks.

Scenarios. The first scenario corresponds to that of identifying the most valuable news data sources providing events for different locations, people, etc. The underlying data consists of event extractions collected from EventRegistry, a repository that monitors news media from all over the world. The dataset contains 15,000 data sources which correspond to news domains and quality metrics such as coverage, timeliness or position bias of the articles that are inherently relevant. EventRegistry gets updated at fixed intervals by ingesting feeds of newly extracted news articles. EventRegistry is the right fit to demonstrate the usefulness and practicality of SOURCESIGHT due to the large number of data sources available, the available updates over time, and the heterogeneity that the sources exhibit both with respect to their domains and their quality. We plan to use a recent snapshot retrieved from EventRegistry containing at least six months of news article data.

The second scenario corresponds to that of enriching an existing genomics knowledge base recording the interactions between genes and phenotypes. Constructing knowledge bases by analyzing vast amounts of scientific literature is gaining more and more traction in several domains [11]. However, a critical pain point in those applications is identifying the most relevant scientific articles to analyze and extract information from so that the coverage and accuracy of the knowledge base is improved. To demonstrate this scenario we will use the abstracts of scientific articles collected by PubMed and we will consider expanding a knowledge base constructed by DeepDive[4]. The total number of articles is 359,324 and each article corresponds to a data source. The goal of this scenario is to demonstrate how users can use source selection techniques to identify the most valuable sources that will improve the quality and expand a running integrated dataset.

Demonstrating Utility. Attendees will be able to describe ad-hoc tasks or use pre-formulated integration tasks in SOURCESIGHT. Then they will have the opportunity to evaluate the source exploration and source selection functionalities offered by SOURCESIGHT. Our goal is for users to understand the trade-offs between different quality metrics of sources in both datasets we have described above and understand how SOURCESIGHT can guide them to select the most suitable set of sources for their application needs.

Demonstrating Effectiveness. For this part of the demo users will mainly interact with the third functionality of SOURCESIGHT, i.e., comparing and contrasting sets of sources. Attendees will compare sets of sources provided by source selection with manually created sets of sources and understand the quality differences across them.

5. REFERENCES

[1] M. Balazinska, B. Howe, and D. Suciu. Data markets in the cloud: An opportunity for the database community. *PVLDB*, 2011.

[2] A. Bhardwaj, S. Bhattacherjee, A. Chavan, A. Deshpande, A. J. Elmore, S. Madden, and A. G. Parameswaran. Datahub: Collaborative data science & dataset version management at scale. In *CIDR*, 2015.

[3] M. Bronzi, V. Crescenzi, P. Merialdo, and P. Papotti. Extraction and integration of partially overlapping web sources. *PVLDB*, 2013.

[4] A. Das Sarma, L. Fang, N. Gupta, A. Halevy, H. Lee, F. Wu, R. Xin, and C. Yu. Finding related tables. In *SIGMOD*, 2012.

[5] X. L. Dong, A. Halevy, and C. Yu. Data integration with uncertainty. *VLDB Journal*, 2009.

[6] X. L. Dong, B. Saha, and D. Srivastava. Less is more: selecting sources wisely for integration. *PVLDB*, 2012.

[7] J. Han, J. Pei, and Y. Yin. Mining frequent patterns without candidate generation. In *SIGMOD*, 2000.

[8] S. Kruse, P. Papotti, and F. Naumann. Estimating data integration and cleaning effort. In *EDBT*, 2015.

[9] X. Li, X. L. Dong, K. Lyons, W. Meng, and D. Srivastava. Truth finding on the deep web: is the problem solved? *PVLDB*, 2013.

[10] G. Limaye, S. Sarawagi, and S. Chakrabarti. Annotating and searching web tables using entities, types and relationships. *PVLDB*, 2010.

[11] F. Niu, C. Zhang, C. Ré, and J. Shavlik. Deepdive: Web-scale knowledge-base construction using statistical learning and inference. In *VLDS*, 2012.

[12] N. Ramakrishnan, C. Lu, M. Marathe, A. Marathe, A. Vullikanti, S. Eubank, S. Leman, M. Roan, J. Brownstein, K. Summers, et al. Model-based forecasting of significant societal events. *Intelligent Systems, IEEE*, 30:86–90, 2015.

[13] T. Rekatsinas, X. L. Dong, and D. Srivastava. Characterizing and selecting fresh data sources. In *SIGMOD*, 2014.

[14] T. Rekatsinas, X. L. Dong, L. Getoor, and D. Srivastava. Finding Quality in Quantity: The Challenge of Discovering Valuable Sources for Integration. In *CIDR*, 2015.

[15] T. Rekatsinas, S. Ghosh, S. Mekaru, E. Nsoesie, J. Brownstein, L. Getoor, and N. Ramakrishnan. Sourceseer: Forecasting rare disease outbreaks using multiple data sources. In *SDM*, 2015.

[4]http://deepdive.stanford.edu/

BART in Action: Error Generation and Empirical Evaluations of Data-Cleaning Systems

Donatello Santoro
University of Basilicata, Italy

Patricia C. Arocena*
University of Toronto, Canada

Boris Glavic
Illinois Inst. of Technology, US

Giansalvatore Mecca
University of Basilicata, Italy

Renée J. Miller*
University of Toronto, Canada

Paolo Papotti
Arizona State University, US

ABSTRACT

Repairing erroneous or conflicting data that violate a set of constraints is an important problem in data management. Many automatic or semi-automatic data-repairing algorithms have been proposed in the last few years, each with its own strengths and weaknesses. BART is an open-source error-generation system conceived to support thorough experimental evaluations of these data-repairing systems. The demo is centered around three main lessons. To start, we discuss how generating errors in data is a complex problem, with several facets. We introduce the important notions of detectability and repairability of an error, that stand at the core of BART. Then, we show how, by changing the features of errors, it is possible to influence quite significantly the performance of the tools. Finally, we concretely put to work five data-repairing algorithms on dirty data of various kinds generated using BART, and discuss their performance.

1. INTRODUCTION

Data quality is a very important concern in data management. To date, many (disparate) automatic and semi-automatic data-cleaning algorithms have been proposed in the database community [10]. These algorithms come from different inspirations. Most of them are *constraint-based*: they assume that the target database comes with a set of data-quality rules – for example, functional dependencies (FDs) or conditional functional dependencies (CFDs) – and data is repaired to remove violations to these constraints. Others rely on statistical measures of data quality or statistics combined with constraints [13].

Due to the richness of research proposals, it is important to conduct thorough and fair experimental evaluations to assess each tool's potential. In fact, other fields in the data quality landscape, like *entity resolution* and *record linkage*, have worked to develop consolidated tools and benchmarks for empirically evaluating algorithms. Thorough evaluation of data-cleaning systems requires systematic control over the amount of errors in a dataset, and over how hard these errors are to repair. Dirty datasets must be paired with a ground-truth clean dataset to enable evaluation of the quality of a repair produced by a cleaning algorithm. To support rigorous empirical evaluations, an error-generation system must be able to generate multiple dirty versions of a dataset with low user effort, and scale to large datasets.

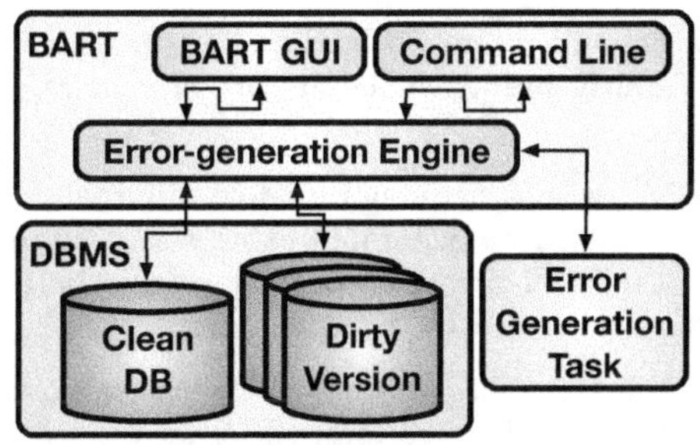

Figure 1: Bart System Overview

Bart. BART[1] [1] is the first error-generation tool explicitly conceived to support empirical evaluations of data-repairing algorithms as per the requirements outlined above. It takes as input a clean database and a set of data-quality rules, and injects errors into the database. Rules are expressed using the powerful language of *denial constraints* [11] and errors can be of several kinds, such as typos, duplicated values, nulls, and outliers. We show the major components of the system in Figure 1. A user interacts with BART by creating error-generation tasks, using a GUI or CL interface. These tasks are then interpreted by BART's error-generation engine to create dirty versions of a clean database.

The system provides the highest possible level of control over the error-generation process. Among other parameters, it allows users to choose the percentage of errors, whether they want a guarantee that errors are detectable using the given constraints, and even provides an estimate of how hard it will be to restore the database to its original clean state. BART is open-source: its codebase is available on GitHub[2]

*Supported in part by NSERC.

SIGMOD'16, June 26-July 01, 2016, San Francisco, CA, USA
© 2016 ACM. ISBN 978-1-4503-3531-7/16/06... $15.00
DOI: http://dx.doi.org/10.1145/2882903.2899397

[1] BART: Benchmarking Algorithms for data Repairing and Translation

[2] https://github.com/dbunibas/BART

Player	Name	Season	Team	Stadium	Goals
t_1 :	Giovinco	2013-14	Juventus	Juv.Stadium	3
t_2 :	Giovinco	2014-15	Toronto	BMO Field	23
t_3 :	Pirlo	2014-15	Juventus	Juv.Stadium	5
t_4 :	Pirlo	2015-16	N.Y.City	Yankee St.	0
t_5 :	Vidal	2014-15	Juventus	Juv.Stadium	8
t_6 :	Vidal	2015-16	Bayern	Allianz Ar.	3

Figure 2: Example Clean Database

and can be further extended by the community to develop new features and functionalities.

Demonstration Overview. The demonstration will convey three primary insights about the system.

(*i*) First, we will discuss how the fine control over the features of errors distinguishes BART from previous error-generating techniques used in evaluating data-repairing systems.

(*ii*) Then, we will discuss how the characteristics of errors may significantly influence the quality of repairs generated by a system.

(*iii*) Finally, we will demonstrate five different algorithms in action on dirty data generated using BART, to reveal new insights on their (relative) performance as the characteristics of the errors are varied by BART.

Overall, the attendees will learn how the availability of a tool like BART may help to level the field and raise the bar for evaluation standards in data cleaning.

The paper is organized as follows. Section 2 introduces the main motivation for the system, and the notions of detectability and repairability of errors. Section 3 provides an overview of the system and of its main use cases. Finally, Section 4 discusses the organization of the demo, and the main lessons that can be learned from it.

2. CONCEPT AND MOTIVATION

Assume we are given a database about soccer players, shown in Figure 2, and we want to assess the performance of repair algorithms according to a few data-quality rules.

(*i*) A first FD stating that Name and Season are a key for the table: d_1 : Name, Season $\rightarrow$ Team, Stadium, Goals.

(*ii*) And, a second FD stating that Team implies Stadium: d_2 : Team $\rightarrow$ Stadium.

We specify these rules in BART using the language of *denial constraints*. Denial constraints are a very expressive language, capable of capturing most data-quality rules used for data-repairing, including FDs, CFDs, cleaning equality-generating dependencies, editing rules, fixing rules, and ordering constraints [10]. For the sake of simplicity, here we omit the technical details about the syntax and semantics of denial constraints, and show example data-quality rules in the more familiar syntax of FDs.

To evaluate data-repair systems, we proceed as follows.

(*i*) We start with a clean instance I, like the one in Figure 2, and the set of constraints $\Sigma = \{d_1, d_2\}$ discussed above.

(*ii*) We inject errors by applying a set of *cell changes*; each cell change ch $= \langle t_i.A := v \rangle$ updates the value of attribute A in tuple t_i to a new value v, e.g, $\langle t_1.\text{Season} := \text{2011-12} \rangle$. By applying a set of cell changes Ch to I, we obtain a new instance $I_d = Ch(I)$, named the *dirty* instance.

(*iii*) We run a data-repairing algorithm over I_d to obtain a repaired instance I_{rep}. We measure the quality of the algorithm using precision and recall. Intuitively, we count how many changes in Ch have been restored to their original values in I_{rep}. Further details are in the full paper [1].

We want now to emphasize how different ways to change the cells of the clean instance may lead to errors that show completely different features when considered from the perspective of a data-repairing tool.

2.1 Detectability

When evaluating a constraint-based repair algorithm, we want to make sure the errors we inject are detectable by the system in question. After all, an error that cannot be detected, cannot be repaired. To reason about detectability, we need a notion for determining whether a cell change is involved in a constraint violation. Consider the following cell change: ch$_1$ $= \langle t_1.\text{Season} := \text{2012-13} \rangle$ that updates tuple t_1 as follows:

Player	Name	Season	Team	Stadium	Goals
t_1 :	Giovinco	**2012-13**	Juventus	Juv.Stadium	3

This change does not introduce a violation to any of the constraints in Σ, i.e., after the cell change the modified database instances does fulfill all the constraints. Therefore, any data-repairing tool that relies on the constraints to detect dirtiness in the database will not be able to detect the change. We call this an *undetectable change*.

More formally, a cell change ch $= \langle t_i.A := v \rangle$ in Ch introduces a *detectable error* in I for constraint dc if: (*i*) cell $t_i.A$ is *involved in a violation* with dc in instance I_d, and (*ii*) cell $t_i.A$ was not involved in a violation with dc in instance I. Here "involved in a violation" is defined based on the fact that a constraint can be associated with a query that returns sets of cells that cause a violation. We call this type of queries *violation-detection* queries. A cell is involved in a violation with a constraint dc if it is in the result of the violation-detection query for dc [1]. For example, the violation-detection query for d_2 is $Q_{d_2}(i, i', t, a, a') = \text{Player}(i, n, s, t, a, g),\ \text{Player}(i', n', s', t, a', g'),\ a \neq a',\ i \neq i'$. This query returns the Team and Stadium attributes of pairs of Player tuples with the same team, but different stadiums.[3] Using the tuple *id*'s, sets of cells involved in violations can be determined based on the result of this query.

In addition to generating changes to the clean database that are detectable using the constraints Σ, BART may also be configured to generated random changes. Generating detectable changes requires BART to reason efficiently and holistically about a set of changes to ensure that they are detectable using a given set of constraints.

Interestingly, this latter requirement significantly increases the complexity of the error-generation process. In fact, generating a given number of errors in a clean database that are detectable using a set of constraints Σ is an NP-complete problem [1]. To deal with this complexity BART implements several novel optimizations [1] that balance the need for control over the nature of errors and scalability.

2.2 Repairability

An alternative change that indeed introduces a detectable error is the following: ch$_2$ $= \langle t_1.\text{Season} := \text{2014-15} \rangle$. After

[3]We assume every tuple has a unique identifier that per convention is the first attribute. Queries are expressed in a notation similar to Datalog.

this update, tuples t_1 and t_2 violate FD d_1, which states that Name and Season are a key for the table:

Player	Name	Season	Team	Stadium	Goals
t_1 :	Giovinco	**2014-15**	Juventus	Juv.Stadium	3
t_2 :	Giovinco	2014-15	Toronto	BMO Field	23

This change is easily detected using the constraints. Still, it is quite difficult for an automatic data-repairing algorithm to restore the database to its clean state. Notice, in fact, that after this change, the original value 2013-14 has been removed from the active domain of the dirty database. A correct repair cannot be found by any repair algorithm that uses the values in the database as the candidates for repair.

BART uses the notion of *repairability* of an error to characterize this aspect. In the case above, it would assign repairability 0 to change ch_2. Different detectable changes may have quite different repairability values.

As an example, consider now change $ch_3 = \langle t_1.\text{Stadium} :=$ Delle Alpi$\rangle$. The change is detectable using FD d_2. In addition, the redundancy in the dirty database may be used to repair the database:

Player	Name	Season	Team	Stadium	Goals
t_1 :	Giovinco	2013-14	Juventus	**Delle Alpi**	3
t_3 :	Pirlo	2014-15	Juventus	Juv.Stadium	5
t_5 :	Vidal	2014-15	Juventus	Juv.Stadium	8

The new, dirty tuple t_1 is involved in two violations to d_2, one with t_3, another with t_5. In both cases, the change is in violation with Juv.Stadium. By a straightforward probabilistic argument, BART would calculate a 2/3 repairability for this error, and rank it as a medium-repairability error.

Errors may have higher repairability, even 1 in some cases. Consider, for example, an additional rule d_3: $\text{Team}[Juventus]$, $\text{Season}[2013-14] \rightarrow \text{Stadium}[Juv.Stadium]$. This CFD rule states unequivocably that Juventus has played its home games for season 2013–14 in the Juventus Stadium. Since this knowledge is part of the constraint, the dirty cell can easily be restored to its original, clean state.

2.3 Other Kinds of Errors

To conclude this discussion about the features of errors, we notice that the notions of detectability and repairability, that are centered around detecting violations to constraints, are not the only ones supported by BART.

Consider, for example, change $ch_4 = \langle t_1.\text{Goals} := 123\rangle$. This change is not detectable using the constraints. However, it might be detected by a statistics-based data-repairing algorithm, because it introduces an *outlier* into the distribution of values of the Goals attribute. BART can be configured in order to generate changes of this kind as well.

3. OVERVIEW OF THE SYSTEM

BART provides users with the graphical user interface shown in Figure 3 to handle error-generation tasks. An *error-generation task*, **E** is composed of four key elements: (*i*) a database schema S; (*ii*) a set Σ of denial constraints (DCs) encoding data quality rules over S; (*iii*) an instance I of S that is clean with respect to Σ; (*iv*) a set of configuration parameters Conf (shown in Figure 3.1) to control the error-generation process. These parameters specify, among other things, which relations can be changed, how many errors should be introduced, and how many of these errors should be detectable. They also let the user control the degree of repairability of the errors.

Based on this, BART supports several uses cases. The main one consists of generating a desired degree of detectable errors for each constraint. In addition, users may also specify a range of repairability values for each constraint; BART will estimate the repairability of changes, and only generate errors with estimated repairability within that range.

In addition to detectable errors, BART may also generate random errors of several kinds: *typos* (e.g., 'databse'), *duplicated values*, *bogus* or *null values* (e.g., '999', '***'). Random errors may be freely mixed with constraint-induced ones. Finally, BART can introduce outliers in numerical attributes.

BART provides sophisticated features to analyze the characteristics of errors that are introduced in the data. It generates charts to analyze the number of errors detected by each constraint, and their estimated repairability (shown in Figure 3.3). It also offers a versioning system, that allows users to generate different dirty databases for the given scenario, and compare the characteristics of their errors.

Finally, BART offers a flexible set of metrics to measure the quality of the repairs generated by a data-repairing tool. In fact, different algorithms can repair data in different ways. For example, some algorithms can produce repairs that mark dirty cells using a variable, while others always restore the dirty instance with a constant value. Different metrics have been proposed and are implemented in BART to uniformly evaluate these heterogenous changes in the data [2, 9].

4. DEMONSTRATION

The demo will be centered around the empirical evaluation of several data-repairing algorithms over dirty data generated using BART. We will use two publicly available tools, Llunatic [9] and Nadeef [6], to run four rule-based data-repairing algorithms: (*i*) Greedy [3, 5]; (*ii*) Holistic [4]; (*iii*) Llunatic [8]; and (*iv*) Sampling [2]. In addition, we will evaluate (*v*) SCARE [14], a statistics-based tool.

The tools will be tested with several repair tasks, based on synthetic and real datasets, some of them constraint-based and some statistics-based. We briefly list them here: (*i*) Employees is a synthetic scenario in the full paper [1]; (*ii*) Customers is a synthetic scenario from Geerts et al. [8]; (*iii*) Tax is a synthetic scenario from Fan et al. [7]; (*iv*) Bus is a real-world scenario from Dallachiesa et al. [6]; and (*v*) Hospital is a real-world scenario used in several data-repairing papers (e.g., [6, 8]).

Datasets and constraints have been chosen to exhibit different characteristics. Some have high redundancy in their data. Others contain numerical attributes, and constraints containing ordering ($<$, $>$) comparisons. Some datasets have *master-data* [12] and CFDs, while others have only FDs. All these differences help to validate our techniques and the tools under exam.

Notice the purpose of this evaluation is not to assess the quality of the repair algorithms, rather to show how BART can be used to uncover new insights into the data-repairing process. Some important insights are the following.

Lesson 1: Data-repairing is not yet Mature. We expect that a wide degree of variability in quality among all algorithms will emerge from our evaluations. This variability does not clearly emerge from evaluations reported in the literature, an observation that suggests there is no definitive data-repairing algorithm yet.

Lesson 2: Repairability Matters. We will observe different trends with respect to repairability. Typically, repair algorithms return very good repairs when sufficient infor-

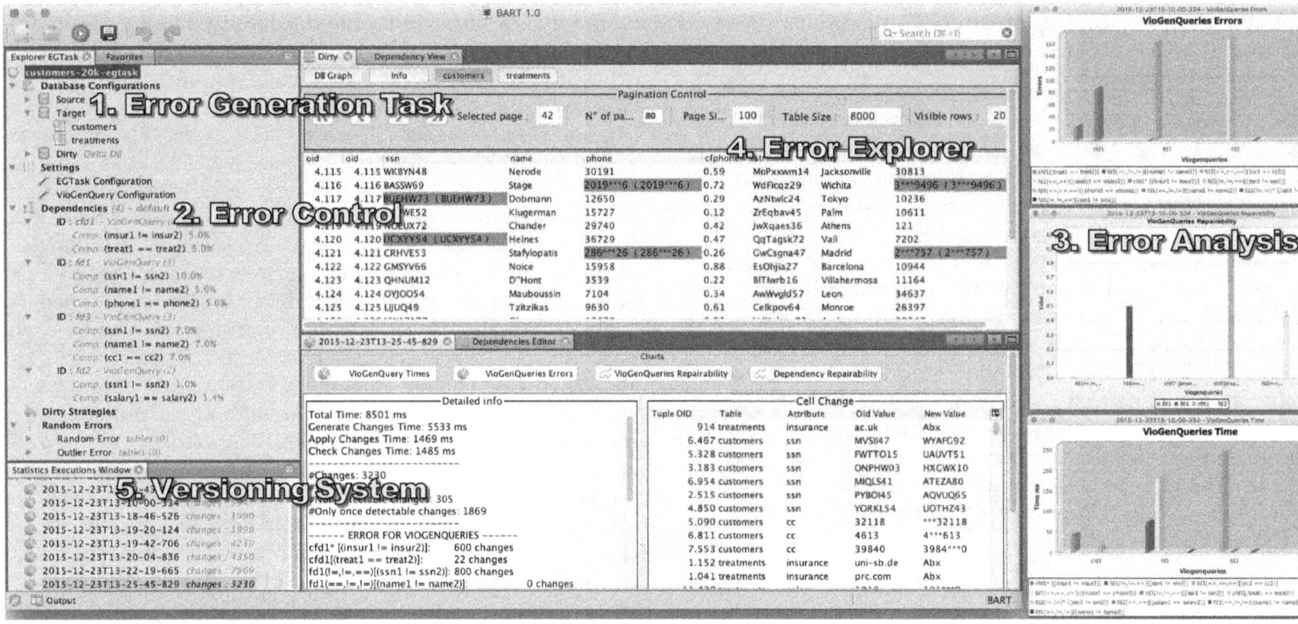

Figure 3: User Interface

mation is available (i.e., high repairability); however, their quality tends to degrade quickly as repairability decreases.

A key observation is that repairability has a strong correlation with the quality of the repairs. In this respect, we believe it nicely captures the *"hardness"* of the data-repairing problem and it helps in getting a concrete intuition of the power and the limits of existing solutions.

Lesson 3: We Need to Document Our Dirty Data. We may conclude that tools exhibit quite different performance on data-repairing problems of different nature, and the repairability is a natural proxy to characterize how *"difficult"* a data-repairing problem is.

In light of this and to level the field, we believe it is crucial to have at our disposal systematic error-generation tools and to properly document the characteristics of the dirty data used in empirical evaluations of data-repairing solutions. BART is a concrete step in this direction.

Lesson 4: Generating Errors is Hard. The problem of systematically generating errors, however, is not an easy one. We will show how different configurations of the error-generation task affect the overall scalability of the system, and discuss the main optimizations that BART relies on in order to tame the complexity of the process.

5. REFERENCES

[1] P. C. Arocena, B. Glavic, G. Mecca, R. J. Miller, P. Papotti, and D. Santoro. Messing-Up with BART: Error Generation for Evaluating Data Cleaning Algorithms. *PVLDB*, 9(2):36–47, 2015.

[2] G. Beskales, I. F. Ilyas, and L. Golab. Sampling the Repairs of Functional Dependency Violations under Hard Constraints. *PVLDB*, 3(1):197–207, 2010.

[3] P. Bohannon, M. Flaster, W. Fan, and R. Rastogi. A Cost-Based Model and Effective Heuristic for Repairing Constraints by Value Modification. In *SIGMOD*, pages 143–154, 2005.

[4] X. Chu, I. F. Ilyas, and P. Papotti. Holistic Data Cleaning: Putting Violations into Context. In *ICDE*, pages 458–469, 2013.

[5] G. Cong, W. Fan, F. Geerts, X. Jia, and S. Ma. Improving Data Quality: Consistency and Accuracy. In *VLDB*, pages 315–326, 2007.

[6] M. Dallachiesa, A. Ebaid, A. Eldawy, A. K. Elmagarmid, I. F. Ilyas, M. Ouzzani, and N. Tang. NADEEF: a Commodity Data Cleaning System. In *SIGMOD*, pages 541–552, 2013.

[7] W. Fan, F. Geerts, X. Jia, and A. Kementsietsidis. Conditional Functional Dependencies for Capturing Data Inconsistencies. *ACM TODS*, 33, 2008.

[8] F. Geerts, G. Mecca, P. Papotti, and D. Santoro. Mapping and Cleaning. In *ICDE*, pages 232–243, 2014.

[9] F. Geerts, G. Mecca, P. Papotti, and D. Santoro. That's All Folks! LLUNATIC Goes Open Source. *PVLDB*, 7(13):1565–1568, 2014.

[10] I. F. Ilyas and X. Chu. Trends in cleaning relational data: Consistency and deduplication. *Foundations and Trends in Databases*, 5(4):281–393, 2015.

[11] A. Lopatenko and L. Bravo. Efficient Approximation Algorithms for Repairing Inconsistent Databases. In *ICDE*, pages 216–225, 2007.

[12] D. Loshin. *Master Data Management.* Knowl. Integrity, Inc., 2009.

[13] N. Prokoshyna, J. Szlichta, F. Chiang, R. J. Miller, and D. Srivastava. Combining quantitative and logical data cleaning. *PVLDB*, 9(4):300–311, 2015.

[14] M. Yakout, L. Berti-Équille, and A. K. Elmagarmid. Don't be SCAREd: Use SCalable Automatic REpairing with Maximal Likelihood and Bounded Changes. In *SIGMOD*, pages 553–564, 2013.

RxSpatial: Reactive Spatial Library for Real-Time Location Tracking and Processing

Youying Shi[1], Abdeltawab M. Hendawi[2], Hossam Fattah[3], Mohamed Ali[1]
[1]Center for Data Science, Institute of Technology, University of Washington, WA, USA
[1]{youyings, mhali}@uw.edu
[2]Department of Computer Science, University of Virginia, VA, USA
hendawi@virginia.edu
[3]Microsoft Corporation, WA, USA
hofattah@microsoft.com

ABSTRACT

Current commercial spatial libraries have implemented strong support for functionalities like intersection, distance, and area of various stationary geospatial objects. The missing point is the support for moving objects. Performing moving object real-time location tracking and computation on the server side of GIS applications is challenging because of the large numbers of moving objects to be tracked, the time complexity of spatial computation, and the real-time requirements. In this Demo, we present the *RxSpatial* Library, a real time reactive spatial library that consists of (1) a front-end, a programming interface for developers who are familiar with the Reactive framework and the Microsoft Spatial Library, and (2) a back-end for processing spatial operations in a streaming fashion. Then we provide demo scenarios that show how *RxSpatial* is employed in real-world applications. The demo scenarios include criminal activity tracking, collaborative vehicle system, performance analysis and visualization of the library's internal algorithms.

1. INTRODUCTION

In many time sensitive GIS applications, real-time location tracking enables immediate feedback when certain conditions are met, (e.g., entering a risky region [8]). For instance, in some child safety systems, children wearing smart devices are tracked. When they get near forbidden or dangerous areas, the application needs to send an alert to parents on time so that they can stop the children from getting hurt. In the scenario of autonomous vehicle clusters, where a cluster of driverless cars are on the way heading to the same direction, every car is a moving object to be tracked. If any car is too far away from the cluster or too close to its neighboring cars, actions should be taken to adjust its movement. In advertising applications, when a driver is close to a shopping mall, coupons, recommendations, and possibly a parking spot information needs to reach his smart device. In social networks, when a friend is nearby, it would be good to receive a push notification of the friend's location information. In safe routing engines [8], the commuters' location information and the disastrous weather zone require real-time processing to generate a reasonable life saving emergency route to evacuate. To fulfill the needs of these applications, this paper introduces the *Reactive eXtension Spatial library*, *RxSpatial* for short. *RxSpatial* offers a front-end programming interface for developers. This front-end provides new interface that is called *RxGeography* that is derived from the IObservable interface of the Microsoft Reactive Framework [11]. RxGeography implements modified versions of the methods found in the STGeography class in the SQL Spatial Library. For example, the STGeography class implements a method called STIntersection to detect if two 'stationary' geography objects intersect. The RxGeography implements a method called RxIntersects to continuously monitor and detect the intersection between a moving object (represented by an RxGeography object) and a stationary object (represented as STGeography). It also implements a method called RxRxIntersection to continuously monitor and detect the intersection of two moving objects,(i.e., both of them are represented as RxGeography).

In addition to the programming interface front-end, the *RxSpatial* library provides a back-end for processing spatial operations in a streaming fashion. The contribution at the back end level lies in the incremental stream processing of various geospatial operations. As an example, to detect the intersection of a moving ob ject and a set of geofences, the intersection operation is not carried over from scratch between the moving object's location and all geofences upon the receipt of a location update. Instead, the intersection operation is incrementally evaluated to make use of as much computations as possible from the previous step. This is achieved by mapping each moving object to an Observable (i.e., IObservable interface) and each location update for a moving object triggers the geospatial computation module of the observers who have subscribed this object's movements. Then, the location, direction and speed of the moving object are used on top of multidimensional index structure to efficiently process various geospatial operations.

Fortunately, we release the *RxSpatial* library equipped with the RUM-Tree [12] as the core spatial index. RUM-Tree is chosen based on its ability to handle moving objects update in an efficient way compared to other conventional index structures, e.g., R-trees and quad trees. Furthermore, the geospatial computation in the *RxSpatial* library is powered by the spatial data types supported in the Microsoft SQL Server Spatial Library [2]. It provides optimized data types such as SqlGeometry and SqlGeography to store and query objects in flat and geodetic spaces, respectively. Various methods are provided to handle these spatial data types. The SQL Server Spatial Library adheres to the Open Geospatial Consortium "Simple Feature Access specification" [10] which is inherited by our proposed *RxSpatial* library. Moreover, the *RxSpatial* library provides strong support for asynchronous program devel-

SIGMOD'16, June 26-July 01, 2016, San Francisco, CA, USA

 ISBN 978-1-4503-3531-7/16/06. . . $15.00
DOI: http://dx.doi.org/10.1145/2882903.2899411

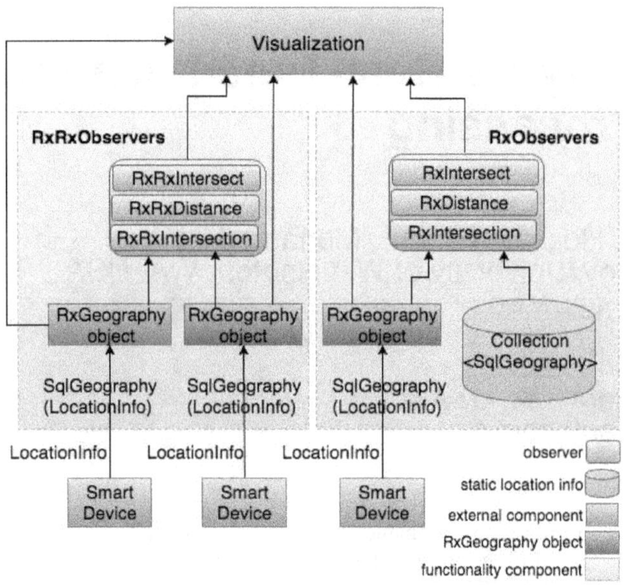

Figure 1: The Architecture of The *RxSpatial* Library.

opment and event-based programs, with a smooth learning curve. Developer is able to represent asynchronous data streams with Observable objects [3]. This is enabled through the use of SqlGeography object as input to the onNext API supported by Microsoft Reactive Extension(Rx) [11]. Thus, the *RxSpatial* library can query the asynchronous data streams using LINQ [1]. It is also able to parameterize the concurrency issues related to the asynchronous data streams using Schedulers. To illustrate the usability of the proposed *RxSpatial* library, we describe two real-world applications; monitoring criminal activity system, and collaborative vehicle system.

2. ARCHITECTURE

Figure 1 provides a high level description of the *RxSpatial* architecture. Location data streams are continuously fed to the server from registered smart devices. Standing spatial queries are also registered within the system. For the sake of this demo, the query result is sent to a visualization module. The *Reactive Spatial Library* mainly introduces two types of observers: *RxObservers* and *RxRxObservers*. *RxObservers* monitor the relationship (e.g., intersection or distance) between one static (i.e., non moving) object and a non-static (moving) object. *RxRxObservers* monitor the relationship between two moving objects.

An RxGeography object and a moving object have one-to-one correspondence. A moving object's location is represented in the library by an RxGeography object. RxGeography comes with an interface for observers (both RxObservers and RxRxObservers) to subscribe to the location updates of its moving object. When a location update of a smart device is received, the new location is stored inside the RxGeography object. Then, it is propagated to all subscribing observers.

2.1 RxObservers

Any observer that monitors the status between a moving object and a non-moving object is called *RxObservers*. It stores the location data of a pre-stored static location G locally. It is triggered by the event of a location update from the moving object that is being monitored. As a naming convention, there is just one 'Rx' in the name of any type of RxObservers because there is only one moving object involved. *RxObservers* comes with three different types; each of them utilizes different APIs provided by the SQL Server Spatial Library: (i) *RxIntersect* observer that outputs

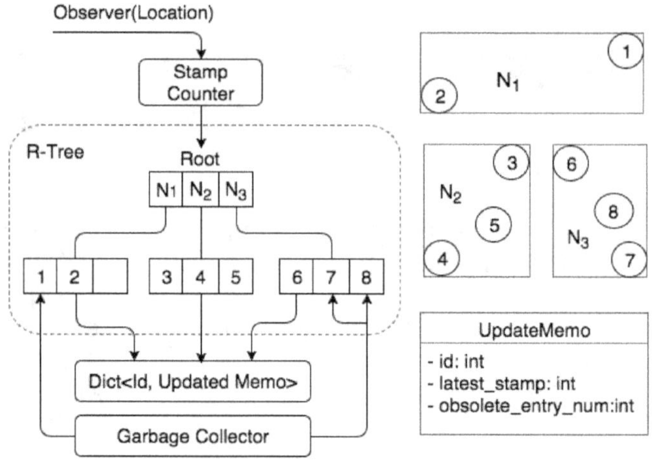

Figure 2: Integrating RUM-Tree (R-Tree With Updated Memo) Inside *RxSpatial.*

a boolean value. This internally calls the STIntersect API, e.g., G.STIntersect(g) indicates whether a static object G intersects a moving object g, (ii) *RxDistance* observer that outputs a double value, e.g., G.STDistance(g) computes the distance between G and g , and (iii) *RxIntersection* observer that outputs a SqlGeography object, e.g., G.STIntersection(g) computes the intersection region between G and g.

In the RxGeography class, calling RxIntersect, RxDistance, RxIntersection APIs subscribes the *RxObserver* of the corresponding operation type to the movement of this RxGeography object. Every time a new location is fed to the RxGeography object; each *RxObserver* will be notified by calling the OnNext API. This will recompute the corresponding computation, and then new update is streamed to the final output.

2.2 RxRxObservers

Any observer that monitors the relationship between two moving objects is called *RxRxObserver*. *RxRxObserver* is triggered by the event of a location update from anyone of the two observed moving objects. As a naming convention, there are two 'Rx's in the name of any type of RxRxObserver because there are two RxGeography objects involved in the operation. Three different variations of the *RxRxObservers* are currently implemented in the *RxSpatial* library. Each one of them internally dispatches a corresponding API provided by the SQL Server Spatial Library. The variations are: (i) *RxRxIntersect* observer that outputs a boolean, e.g., g_1.STIntersect(g_2) checks whether g_1 intersects g_2, (ii) *RxRxDistance* observer that outputs a double, e.g., g_1.STDistance(g_2) computes the distance between g_1 and g_2, and (iii) *RxRxIntersection* observer that outputs a SqlGeography object, e.g., g_1.STIntersection(g_2) gets intersection region between g_1 and g_2, where g_1 and g_2 are both moving objects.

In RxGeography class, by calling RxRxIntersect, RxRxDistance, and RxRxIntersection APIs, the *RxRxObserver* of the specified type can subscribe the movement of this RxGeography object. By OnNext API, new location update will be fed to the observed RxGeography object. Then, each *RxRxObserver* will be notified with this update to do the consequent computation.

As mentioned earlier, the main users of this library are developers. The advantage of designing the architecture in this way is that all the internal interfaces, observers and data structure do not need to be maintained by the application developer. This isolation allows developers to use the *RxSpatial* with little knowledge about the structure of the underlying SQL Spatial library.

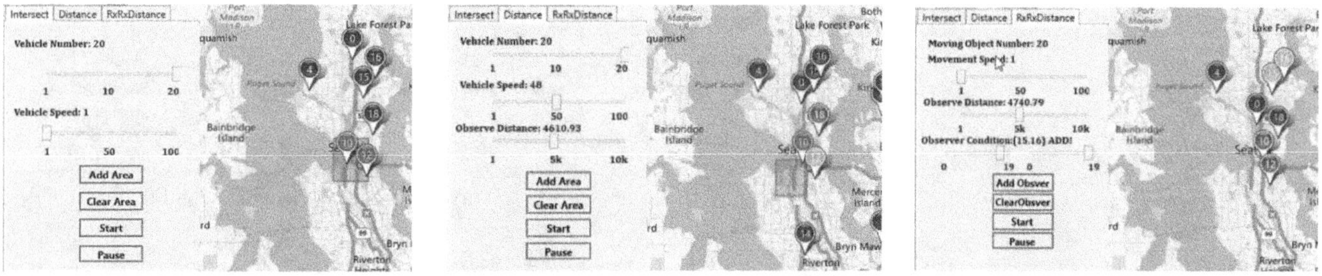

(a) Restricted Region Enter Tracking. (b) Restricted Region Proximity Tracking. (c) Mutual Proximity Tracking.

Figure 3: Using the *RxSpatial* Library For Geofencing And Proximity Distance Operations In Criminal Activity Tracking System.

2.3 Data Structure

The data structure we chose is RUM-Tree, R-Tree with update memos. RUM-tree is used to store observer objects. It consists of three main components: a stamp counter, a R-Tree and update memos. We use stamp counter to add stamp to each insert/delete operation; the observer objects themselves are stored in an R-Tree; 'update memos' act as a memory-based auxiliary structure that help differentiate obsolete objects from the new ones. The 'update memos' are dictionaries whose keys are the unique object ids. Each update memo consists of three parts: a unique object id, the newest stamp of this object id, and the total number of obsolete objects with the same object id that required to be removed in garbage collection stage.

An insertion operation is executed when we store a new observer into the RUM-Tree. It is performed as follows: firstly the observer object is assigned an id; then we add 1 to the stamp counter and the observer is assigned with the current stamp. After that the observer would be inserted into R-tree and stored into a R-Tree node together with its stamp, indexed by its location; then a automatic check would be performed by the library to check whether this id is stored in the Update memos. If this id was found in the Update memos, the library would get the corresponding Update memos, modify the latest stamp with the current stamp and increment the obsolete entry number. On the other hand, if this id wasn't found in the Update memos, the id and Update memo pair would be inserted into the Update memo dictionary for reference by the library, the latest stamp in this Update memo entry would be set to the current timestamp, and the obsolete entry number would be set to 1, which means one Observer with this id would need to be removed.

An update operation is executed when the location of one observer is modified. It is performed with the following two steps: firstly the old entry of this observer is deleted from the RUM-Tree; then an insertion operation is performed. The deletion operation is as following steps: first the library would check whether the object id of this observer already exist in the Update memo dictionary. If it was found in the dictionary, the library would modify the corresponding Update memo with the latest stamp and add increment the obsolete entry number. Otherwise the id and Update memo pair would be inserted to Update memo dictionary by the library for reference; it would also set the latest stamp and set obsolete entry number to 1. We would be able to save the time needed to search and remove the old observer in the R-Tree, therefore speed up the deletion operation. After the deletion operation, the insertion operation is the same. Thus the overall update operation cost of RUM-Tree is less than R-Tree.

Figure 2 demonstrates how observers are organized in RUM-Tree. The area is partitioned into three Rectangles: N_1, N_2 and N_3; location 1 and 2 are in N_1. location 3, 4 and 5 are in N_2. Location 6, 7 and 8 are in N_3.In this example, observer1 moved from location 1 in N_1 to 6 in N_3; observer2 moved from location 7 in N_3 to 2 in N_1; observer3 moved from location 8 in N_3 to location 3 in N_2. When a location update with new location 2 was sent from observer1, whose old location is 7, to RUM-Tree, the following steps are executed: firstly the stamp counter is increased and the new stamp is assigned to observer1; secondly; the library would check whether the update memo entry of observer1 exist: if the update memo entry exits, the library would update its stamp and increment the obsolete entry number by 1; Otherwise the library would create a new update memo entry for observer1, assign the newest stamp to the update memo and assign 1 to the obsolete entry, as only one node with exact same id needs to be deleted; then the library would put observer1 in an appropriate node. When a location update in n3 was sent to RxGeography object, the library would notify each observer except for the obsolete ones. In the described case, observer1 in location 6 would get the notification but observer2 and observer3 will not, as 7 and 8 are obsolete areas.

3. DEMO SCENARIOS

In this section, we demonstrate two application scenarios, i.e., *Monitoring Criminal Activity* and *Collaborative Vehicle System*, supported by our proposed Reactive Spatial library, (*RxSpatial*). In addition, we will depict an internal inspection of the system and give glances on the performance evaluation. The (*RxSpatial*) library and the application scenarios in this demo are implemented in C#, in Visual Studio 2013, and running on Windows 8.1. This demonstration is based on real GPS data streamed out of ankle bracelets [9] for the *Monitoring Criminal Activity* scenario. Two sets of moving objects on the Washington state USA [5, 4, 6, 7] are used for the *Collaborative Vehicle System* and the performance examination.

In the application snapshots, figures 3 and 4, we can notice that a numbered push pin represents a moving object. A blue pin means this moving object does not trigger anything or it is not even watched by anything. A pin with other colors means that moving object has some active condition. The control panel is on the left side of each figure. The function of buttons and scroll bars are as follows. *Start*: to start the objects movement, *Pause*: to pause the movement, *Vehicle speed*: to control the moving speed of pins, *Vehicle number*: to control the number of moving objects on the map, *Observer Distance*: to define the distance between observer and observed object which could trigger the watch notification, *Add Area*: to draw a rectangle in the map to add a stationary RxObserver, *Clear Area*: to remove all observers already added, and *Add Obsver*: to add a pair of mutually observing observers in RxRxObservers when the user selects the id of a pair of push pins and clicks the *Add Obsver* button. The color code of the push pin depends on the application scenario.

3.1 Monitoring Criminal Activity

The criminal justice system sometimes requires an offender on probation or on bail to have an ankle bracelet to track his location. Every criminal is designated a restriction area which he is supposed

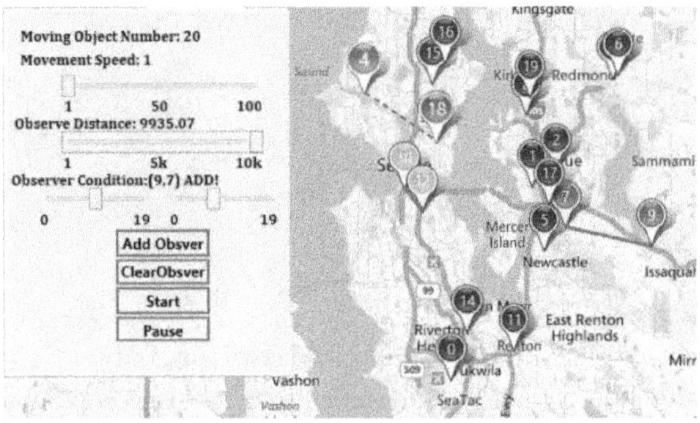

Figure 4: Distance Monitoring in Collaborative Vehicle Sys.

to stay away from. Sometimes, some offenders are not supposed to meet with each other. Figure 3(a) demonstrates restricted region tracking scenario: the gray rectangle indicates a restricted region where certain criminals, (i.e., push pins), are not supposed to enter. When the offenders 10 and 12 enter the restricted region, this act will trigger an alert.

Figure 3(b) demonstrates restricted region proximity tracking scenario where certain criminals are not supposed to get close to the restricted region. We can see that the offender 18 gets in the watching distance of the restricted region and thus triggers the watch notification. Offender 12 gets close enough to the restricted area, and then triggering security notification. When offender 10 gets in the restricted area, this will trigger enter notification.

Figure 3(c) demonstrates mutual proximity tracking scenario: Criminal 10 and criminal 12 are not supposed to meet each other. Here in this figure, they are close enough and likely to meet, so the watch notification is triggered. Offender 15 and offender 16 are not supposed to meet either; in this figure they are so close that security notification is triggered.

3.2 Collaborative Vehicle System

In this part, we are going to demonstrate the distance control in collaborative vehicle system. One scenario is data sharing which can only be guaranteed when the distance between cars is within a working distance. Examples include, the in-front road status and yielding for coming car message at the left turn can be shared from the leading car to following car. In Figure 4, each pin represents a car in the collaborative vehicle system. The collaboration status is tracked between 4 and 18, 10 and 12, and 7 and 9. The dotted line between car 4 and 18, and the gray color of pins, show that the cars 4 and 18 are watching the movement of each other. But the connection between them is not strong enough as the distance exceeds a limit. The solid thick line between 10 and 12 and the yellow color of pins show that they are within a stable working distance. The thin line between 7 and 9, and the green color of pins show that they are within a working distance but are likely to disconnect if they get further apart. The blue color of other cars show that they did not intend to watch the movement of any cars, so they are not trying to connect and thus no need to audit the connections.

3.3 Performance Test Result Visualization Demo

In this part, we are going to have a control panel to visualize the performance of the system. Audience will have the ability to decide to examine the RxObserver or RxRxObserver. They can choose x-axis type and y-axis type and other parameters as well. The x-axis types are Update Interval, Observer Number per Object, or Moving Object Number, and the y-axis types could be Average processing time, or Max number of moving objects supported by the system. For example, the control panel configured like Figure 5(a) will generate the results charted in Figure 5(b).

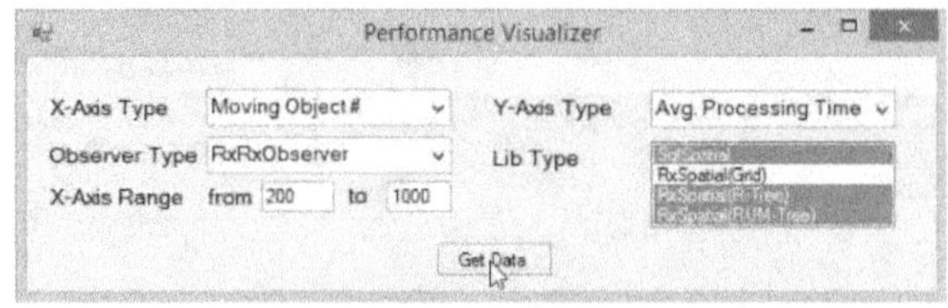

(a) Performance Visualizer control.

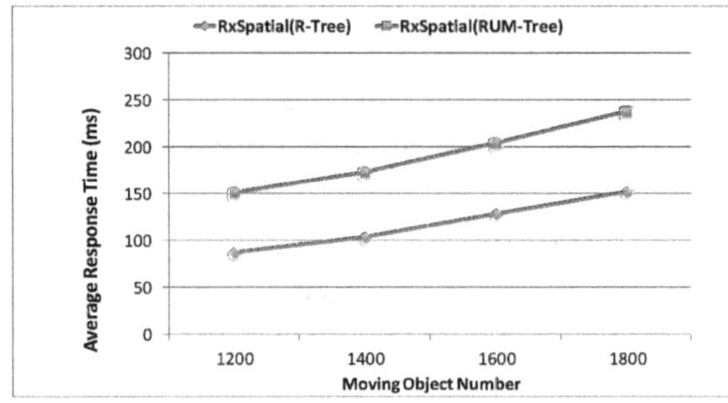

(b) Performance Visualizer Chart.

Figure 5: Performance Visualizer.

4. REFERENCES

[1] V. S. 2015. LINQ (Language-Integrated Query). https://msdn.microsoft.com/en-us/library/bb397926.aspx, Dec. 2015.

[2] S. S. 2016. Microsoft SQL Server Spatial Libraries. https://msdn.microsoft.com/en-us/library/bb933790.aspx, Dec. 2015.

[3] N. F. 4.6 and 4.5. IObservable Generic Interface. https://msdn.microsoft.com/library/dd990377.aspx, Dec. 2015.

[4] A. M. Hendawi, J. Bao, and M. F. Mokbel. iRoad: A Framework For Scalable Predictive Query Processing On Road Networks. In *VLDB*, Riva Del Garda, Italy, Aug. 2013.

[5] A. M. Hendawi, J. Bao, M. F. Mokbel, and M. Ali. Predictive Tree: An Efficient Index for Predictive Queries On Road Networks. In *ICDE*, Seoul, South Korea, Apr. 2015.

[6] A. M. Hendawi, A. Khot, A. Rustum, A. Basalamah, A. Teredesai, and M. Ali. COMA: Road Network Compression For Map-Matching. In *MDM*, Pennsylvania, USA, June 2015.

[7] A. M. Hendawi, E. Sturm, D. Oliver, , and S. Shekhar. CrowdPath: a framework for next generation routing services using volunteered geographic information. In *SSTD*, Munich, Germany, Aug. 2013.

[8] Y. Li, S. George, C. Apfelbeck, A. M. Hendawi, D. Hazel, A. Teredesai, and M. Ali. Routing Service With Real World Severe Weather. In *ACM SIGSPATIAL GIS*, Texas, USA, Nov. 2014.

[9] D. Mohammed, F. Olajumoke, J. Lars, S. Niko, Y. Brett, N. Joe, and A. Mohamed. Safe step: a real-time GPS tracking and analysis system for criminal activities using ankle bracelets. In *ACM SIGSPATIAL*, pages 512–515, Florida, USA, Nov. 2013.

[10] OGC. Open Geospatial Consortium. http://www.opengeospatial.org, Dec. 2015.

[11] RX. Microsoft Reactive Extensions. https://msdn.microsoft.com/en-us/data/gg577609.aspx, Dec. 2015.

[12] X. Xiaopeng and A. W. G. R-trees with update memos. In *IEEE ICDE*, pages 22–22, Georgia, USA, Apr. 2006.

Web-based Benchmarks for Forecasting Systems - The ECAST Platform

Robert Ulbricht
Robotron Datenbank-Software GmbH
Dresden, Germany
robert.ulbricht@robotron.de

Claudio Hartmann
Technische Universität Dresden
Dresden, Germany
claudio.hartmann@tu-dresden.de

Martin Hahmann
Technische Universität Dresden
Dresden, Germany
martin.hahmann@tu-dresden.de

Hilko Donker
Robotron Datenbank-Software GmbH
Dresden, Germany
hilko.donker@robotron.de

Wolfgang Lehner
Technische Universität Dresden
Dresden, Germany
wolfgang.lehner@tu-dresden.de

ABSTRACT

The role of precise forecasts in the energy domain has changed dramatically. New supply forecasting methods are developed to better address this challenge, but meaningful benchmarks are rare and time-intensive. We propose the ECAST online platform in order to solve that problem. The system's capability is demonstrated on a real-world use case by comparing the performance of different prediction tools.

CCS Concepts

•Information systems → Expert systems; •Applied computing → Forecasting;

Keywords

Time Series Forecasting; Benchmark; Transparency

1. INTRODUCTION

Forecasting time series is traditionally an important issue for any industry. It has always been the case that in corporate areas like production, distribution or pricing, many decisions have to be made based on uncertain data. This explains why countless methods and solutions have been published by the multitude of different communities active in that field of research. For example, considering only top-ranked energy journals[1], since 2005 more than 200 articles have been published related to the forecasting of renewable energy supply from fluctuating sources like solar and wind power. But choosing the optimal solution for a specific forecasting problem remains a formidable and work-intensive task, mainly caused by their poor qualitative comparability: First of all, evaluations are almost always conducted on dissimilar data sets, which means that they vary in aspects like the measurement quality of individual observation points, the amount of used time series and their completeness, individual characteristics like patterns, aggregation or normalization, or their geographical origin. Another source of bias emerges from the experimental setup, as different values are used for environmental parameters like forecasting horizon, the length of training histories or evaluation periods. Next, different statistical error metrics are applied to measure the accuracy of forecasts, which is a separate research topic as shown by e.g. Chen and Yang [1] or Hyndman and Koehler [3] to mention a few. Finally, conclusions can also suffer from the authors somehow 'personal' point of view. Experimental results may be optimized towards the desired findings by using only very few and specific test cases or compared against too simple baselines, so incredibly low errors or high improvement factors are achieved but are hardly reproducible in practice.

Besides literature, methods can be compared in forecasting competitions. Although they present a more practical alternative, they do have some drawbacks: Intensive efforts are required for preparing and participating alike, thus making them rather rare events. For the famous *M-Competitions* founded by Makridakis [6], the latest activities date back to the year 2005. A much more recent approach is the *Global Energy Forecasting Competition (GEFCom)*, started in 2012 and running every two years since then. The insights published by Hong et al. [2] show that such approaches have difficulties with the simulation of real-world situations where forecasts have to be provided on a rolling basis for intra-day or day-ahead periods. This results in a shift of the forecast origin with newly arriving observation data, thus leading to multiple time-intensive evaluation phases. Although repeatedly requested in the past, e.g. for the energy domain by Madsen et al. [5] or Kostylev and Pavlovski [4], there is still

[1]based on SCImago Journal & Country rank

SIGMOD'16, June 26-July 01, 2016, San Francisco, CA, USA
© 2016 ACM. ISBN 978-1-4503-3531-7/16/06...$15.00
DOI: http://dx.doi.org/10.1145/2882903.2899399

no reliable and internationally admitted reference model nor industry standard available for such benchmarks. For example something like the well-established TCP-H standard, the state-of-the-art benchmark for database performance evaluation [7], remains an unsolved research gap for the forecasting community. For the above mentioned reasons, it becomes obvious that interested parties like software providers or application users can hardly compare the quality of forecasting methods without implementing them, collecting interesting use cases, and conducting intensive evaluations. This, besides being a resource-intensive task, can only be successful if the descriptions provided for the proposed solutions turn out to be clear and detailed enough. The constantly high number of new articles and reviews proves the unbroken public interest in that field, at the same time it underlines the strong need for consolidated results. We believe that following a system integration approach can solve that problem, as this is a straightforward way to tackle one of the major challenges: To provide transparency by bringing together representative use cases, homogenous evaluation criteria, and competing tools or algorithms in one public place, anytime available for everybody.

In this paper, we demonstrate the ECAST platform to cope with the problem of qualitative evaluation of competing forecasting methods as discussed earlier in this introduction. The remainder of the paper is organized as follows: In Section 2 we describe the system's core features and components before we demonstrate the functionality in Section 3. Finally, we summarize our work and show directions for future developments in Section 4. For additional material and direct access to the platform, we refer to the REEF project web site[2].

2. SYSTEM DESCRIPTION

In this section we explain the general idea behind ECAST and the system's architecture. Originally, ECAST was designed as a tool for energy forecasting automation and later expanded to allow for benchmarking forecasting practices in any domain. As a consequence, it combines functionality for task automation, data handling and result representation as shown in Figure 1. In order to define a new experiment, users can choose among the available use cases and predictors or upload their own time series and methods. All necessary parameters are defined via the web-interface. This includes the data to be used for training and forecasting and the experimental conditions, e.g. the forecasting horizon or the evaluation criteria. Hereby, the system can support the user by recommending the initial values. Once an experiment is defined, all corresponding tasks are generated and executed sequentially by a background batch process. Results are stored in the use case repository and immediately displayed in the interface. Further, users can compare the ranking of the obtained output compared to all experiments formerly conducted on that time series.

In short, ECAST helps making results transparent and reproducible. Any personal bias is eliminated by such a neutral tool. It prevents users from battling with large amounts of locally stored CSV-files. Finally, due to the consequent

[2]https://wwwdb.inf.tu-dresden.de/research-projects/projects/reef/

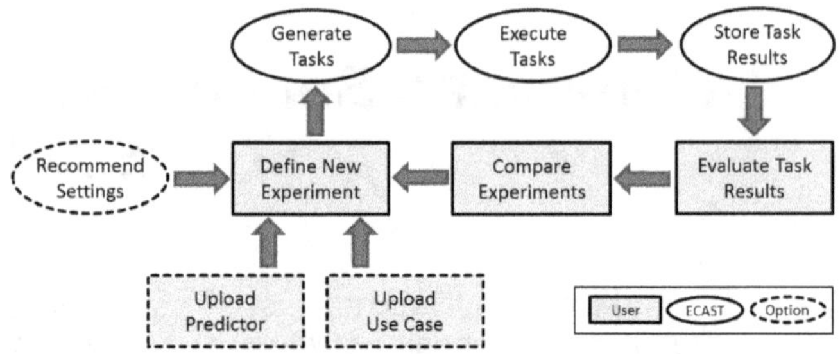

Figure 1: Task Automation Chain

employment of web technology, ECAST is easy accessible, always available and does not require installation or configuration before usage.

The ECAST platform is composed of the four main components as displayed in Figure 2: (1) A *Use Case Repository (UCR)* as the central data storage unit, (2) the *Core Logic Component (CLC)* as a container to encapsulate all necessary functions, (3) the *Prediction-Interface (API)* as the connector to the forecasting methods and finally (4) the *Web User Interface (GUI)* used for interaction and result presentation.

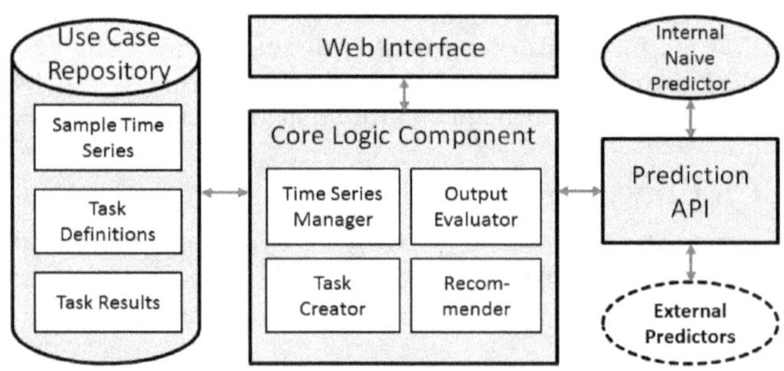

Figure 2: ECAST System Architecture

(1) Use Case Repository. The UCR is the central data storage unit. In its relational data structure we store the reference parameters used for system and experiment configuration, all time series and their associated context information, the generated tasks for the experiments and the output obtained from the predictors. The latter includes the forecasted values, the errors and the experiments' computation time. We implemented the data model in a PostgreSQL database.

(2) Core Logic Component. The CLC is the heart of the system. It contains all functions needed for configuration, handling input and output data and task automation procedures. The implementation is split into separate modules as displayed in Figure 2: First, the *Time Series Manager* is responsible for data preparation and transformation. All incoming time series are converted into the platform's internal format. Next, the *Recommender* queries the repository in order to find the optimal parameter settings for a new experiment. It compares the target time series to all stored use cases based on their structural similarity and the provided context information. Then, it selects the experiments with the lowest error values ever conducted on that data and offers the associated parameters as default setting for the user. The *Task Creator* converts all forecast queries belonging to an experiment definition into individual tasks. This means that the chosen settings and parameters are persisted and stored until their final execution. Depending on the definition, a single forecast query can lead to multiple tasks, for example by including various predictors, different forecasting horizons and a variable training history length. Finally, the *Output Evaluator* computes different statistical error metrics to evaluate the accuracy of obtained forecasts.

(3) Prediction API. The API realizes the connection to the predictors. This includes commercial or scientific standalone forecasting tools as well as algorithms scripted in the statistical language *R* In both cases, the API calls the forecasting method, delivers training and evaluation data and sets the values for all available parameters, if any. With this input data, ECAST is able to externally set the configuration for the supported predictors, execute the training of the model and finally the calculation of the forecast. Subsequently, the API returns the forecasted values and the total computation time consumed by the called predictor.

(4) Web User Interface. The GUI is primarily designed to facilitate experiment definition and for result presentation. Consequently, it supports the user during the selection of the uses case, the predictors to be assessed, their parameters and the experimental conditions. In the post-experimental phase, the interface plots the original and the forecasted time series. Visual inspection of time series is common and hard to replace by analytic algorithms, as skilled users often posses expert knowledge which helps to reveal unusual data points. The GUI also displays accuracy values and all parameters and features used in each experiment.

Figure 3: Data Selection in ECAST

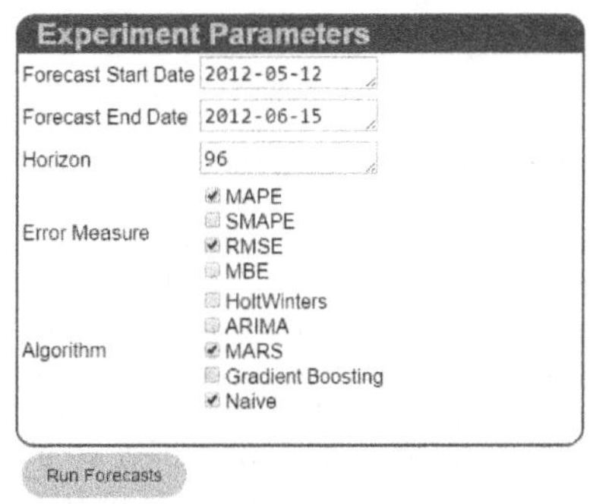

Figure 4: Experiment Definition in ECAST

3. DEMONSTRATION

In this section we describe the platform's core features and give a brief walk-through, based on an exemplary energy forecasting scenario.

3.1 Experiment Definition

First, we start by searching the UCR for publicly available data sets we may access. Using the filter functions, we find a data set from the energy production domain having a history length of more than one year and set up a new experiment. We select the external influences which we think will have a positive effect on the forecasting result. As shown in Figure 3, ECAST lists all recorded external influences related to the target time series, such that we can see if the desired information is available or not. In this example we decide to include the observation values for global irradiation, outside air temperature, and wind speed.

In the next step we set the parameters for the experiment (compare Figure 4). We begin with the start and the end dates for the evaluation period, and the horizon which determines how many values we want to predict. Afterwards we choose the error measures we are interested in and decide for MAPE and RMSE, since these are widely used in the energy domain. Finally, we choose the forecasting algorithms we want to evaluate, in our example the MARS algorithm (implemented in the Earth-Package for *R*) and the naive predictor, which is used as base line. As we have included multiple algorithms, they will be executed one after another in separate tasks but using identical parameters. On top of that, ECAST will show all experiments that were already conducted on the currently used data set. This helps to find available experimental results and setting up new experiments which are directly comparable to the previous one by using identical parameters but different forecasting methods. During the set-up process the system supports the user by recommending a pre-selection of forecasting algorithms which performed well on similar data sets based on the results already present in the UCR. The user can modify these recommendations at will. The completely parametrized experiment is subsequently executed by ECAST and the results are stored in the UCR In case we had started by uploading a new data set via a csv-file, the only limitation would be that ECAST would not be able to compare the results with previous experiments.

3.2 Result Presentation

The results of the experiment are presented as shown in Figure 5: The diagram section shows the forecasted values of the selected algorithms next to the original time series.

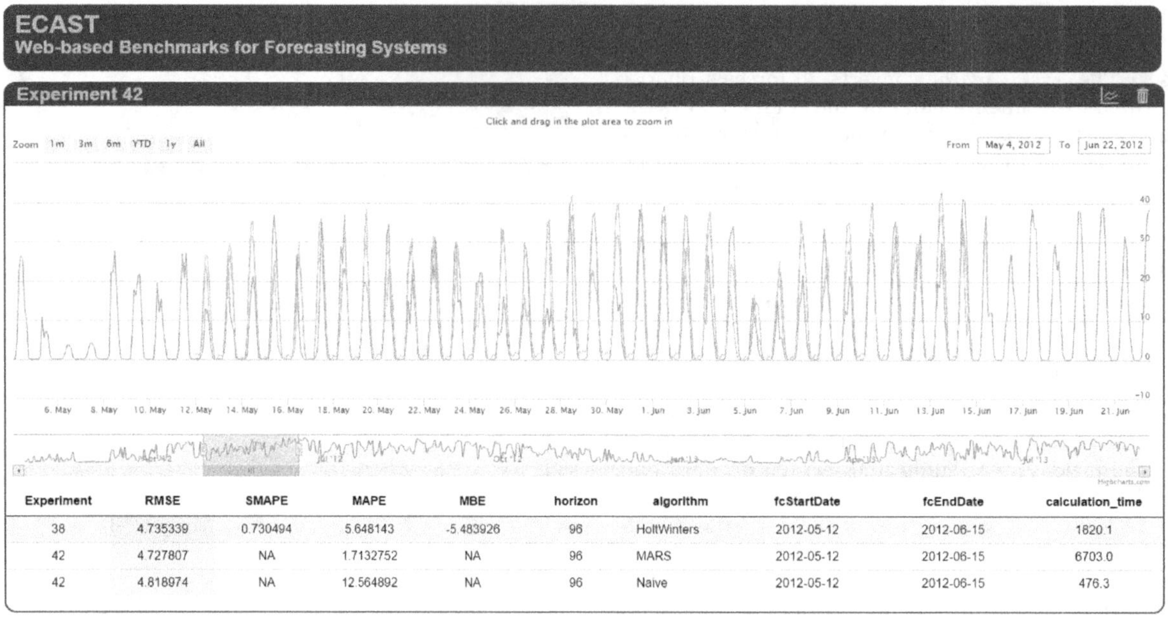

Experiment	RMSE	SMAPE	MAPE	MBE	horizon	algorithm	fcStartDate	fcEndDate	calculation_time
38	4.735339	0.730494	5.648143	-5.483926	96	HoltWinters	2012-05-12	2012-06-15	1820.1
42	4.727807	NA	1.7132752	NA	96	MARS	2012-05-12	2012-06-15	6703.0
42	4.818974	NA	12.564892	NA	96	Naive	2012-05-12	2012-06-15	476.3

Figure 5: Result Presentation in ECAST

This allows for visual exploration of the results to see where the forecast algorithms perform best. The table section in the lower part contains the error measures that were calculated during the experiments, which allows a quick first comparison of the evaluated algorithms. Additionally, older experiments conducted on this data set can be loaded into the table. In this case, we observe that experiment no. 38 using the HoltWinters algorithm obtained almost similar results to the current experiment (no. 42) in terms of RMSE, but under-performs in terms of MAPE. Any of these experiments can be chosen to be displayed next to the current one for a more detailed visual comparison in the diagram area.

Now, with this information we are able to decide whether we are satisfied with the performance of the chosen algorithm or not. For example, if the visual exploration shows that the deviation of the forecasted values from the original time series is too high for the time stamps with the highest energy production, although the average RMSE error is satisfying we might want to start another experiment. In this case we can start over using different algorithms or external influences. The ECAST system even allows it for experienced users to upload their own forecasting algorithms written in *R* and use them in the experiments.

4. SUMMARY AND OUTLOOK

In this demonstration we have shown that ECAST is an open and easy-to-use platform for time series forecasting. It supports the user with automated tasks, provides real-world use cases and offers sophisticated pre- and post-processing procedures, thus making complex benchmarks much more efficient. In the future, we plan to integrate additional logical modules like an Ensembler, to build flexible hybrid models by using appropriate combination criteria, or a Feature Optimizer to allow for an automatic creation and optimal pre-selection of external influences for the models to be built.

Acknowledgment

The work presented in this paper was funded by the European Regional Development Fund (EFRE) under co-financing by the Free State of Saxony and Robotron Datenbank-Software GmbH. We gratefully acknowledge the contributions of Lucas Bruenings and Johannes Wilke.

5. REFERENCES

[1] Z. Chen and Y. Yang. Assessing forecast accuracy measures. Technical Report 2004-2010, Iowa State University, Department of Statistics & Statistical Laboratory, 2004.

[2] T. Hong, P. Pinson, and S. Fan. Global Energy Forecasting Competition 2012. *International Journal of Forecasting*, 30(2):357–363, 2013.

[3] R. J. Hyndman and A. B. Koehler. Another look at measures of forecast accuracy. *International Journal of Forecasting*, 22(4):679–688, 2006.

[4] V. Kostylev and A. Pavlovski. Solar Power Forecasting Performance - Towards Industry Standards. In *1st Int. Workshop on the Integration of Solar Power into Power Systems*, Aarhus, Denmark, 2011.

[5] H. Madsen, G. Kariniotakis, H. Nielsen, T. Nielsen, and P. Pinson. A Protocol for Standardizing the Performance Evaluation of Short-Term Wind Power Prediction Models. Anemos project, European Commission, 2004.

[6] S. Makridakis and M. Hibon. The M3-Competition: results, conclusions and implications. *International Journal of Forecasting*, 16:451–476, 2000.

[7] R. Nambiar, M. Poess, A. Masland, H. R. Taheri, M. Emmerton, F. Carman, and M. Majdalany. TPC Benchmark Roadmap 2012. In *Selected Topics in Performance Evaluation and Benchmarking*, pages 1–20. Springer Berlin Heidelberg, 2013.

Energy Elasticity on Heterogeneous Hardware using Adaptive Resource Reconfiguration LIVE

Annett Ungethüm, Thomas Kissinger, Willi-Wolfram Mentzel, Dirk Habich, Wolfgang Lehner
Database Technology Group
Technische Universität Dresden
01062 Dresden, Germany
{firstname.lastname}@tu-dresden.de

ABSTRACT

Energy awareness of database systems has emerged as a critical research topic, since energy consumption is becoming a major limiter for their scalability. Recent energy-related hardware developments trend towards offering more and more configuration opportunities for the software to control its own energy consumption. Existing research so far mainly focused on leveraging this configuration spectrum to find the most energy-efficient configuration for specific operators or entire queries. In this demo, we introduce the concept of *energy elasticity* and propose the *energy-control loop* as an implementation of this concept. Energy elasticity refers to the ability of software to behave energy-proportional and energy-efficient at the same time while maintaining a certain quality of service. Thus, our system does not draw the least energy possible but the least energy necessary to still perform reasonably. We demonstrate our overall approach using a rich interactive GUI to give attendees the opportunity to learn more about our concept.

Keywords

Energy, Adaptivity, Heterogeneity, Energy Elasticity

1. INTRODUCTION

Energy consumption is becoming a major limiter for scalability on today's server systems and thus for the data management software running on such hardware. For that reason, energy awareness of database systems was identified as a critical research topic some years ago [1], but the absence of energy-aware hardware strongly limited the optimization potential of the software [5]. Recently, energy-related technology that originates from the mobile devices sector started to make its way into desktop and server systems. Those hardware developments, especially a more fine-grained dynamic voltage and frequency scaling (DVFS) as well as sleep states, allow an energy-proportional behavior of the hardware. However, to fully utilize these energy control knobs offered by the hardware, software has to make appropriate use of them. Following the current hardware development trends, even an ARM big.LITTLE-like design, which adds stripped versions of traditional fat cores to the system, will appear in future server systems opening up an additional dimension for the energy optimization process.

SIGMOD '16 June 26–July 1, 2016, San Francisco, CA, USA

ISBN 978-1-4503-3531-7/16/06. . . $15.00
DOI: http://dx.doi.org/10.1145/2882903.2899390

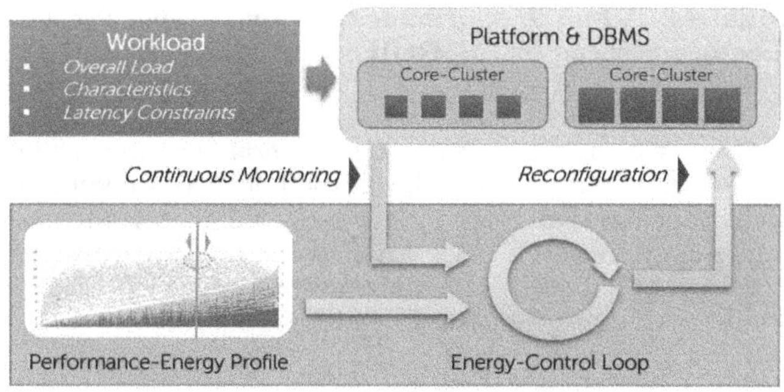

Figure 1: Architectural Overview.

In this demo, we propose the *energy-control loop*, which addresses the topic of software-controlled hardware reconfigurations at runtime for data management systems running on a single heterogeneous server system optionally employing a big.LITTLE design. While existing works [3, 4] mainly try to find the most energy-efficient configuration for a given workload, our approach not only aims at achieving *energy-proportionality*, but also considers *energy-efficiency* as a secondary optimization target. This way, our energy-control loop is able to run the system in an energy-efficient configuration while still being able to maintain certain query latency constraints, especially in times of heavy load. Since the workload is a moving target, the loop is continuously running and adapts the hardware configuration. We call this concept *energy elasticity*.

Figure 1 shows the overall architectural overview of the system. The platform that is running the DBMS is exposed to a dynamic workload and has to fulfill certain soft constraints in terms of maximum query response time respectively query latency. While processing the workload, the *energy-control loop* is continuously monitoring the DBMS to detect the required performance demand that is necessary to meet the latency constraints. If this performance demand increases or decreases, the loop applies another energy-efficient configuration suitable for this case at runtime. This config-

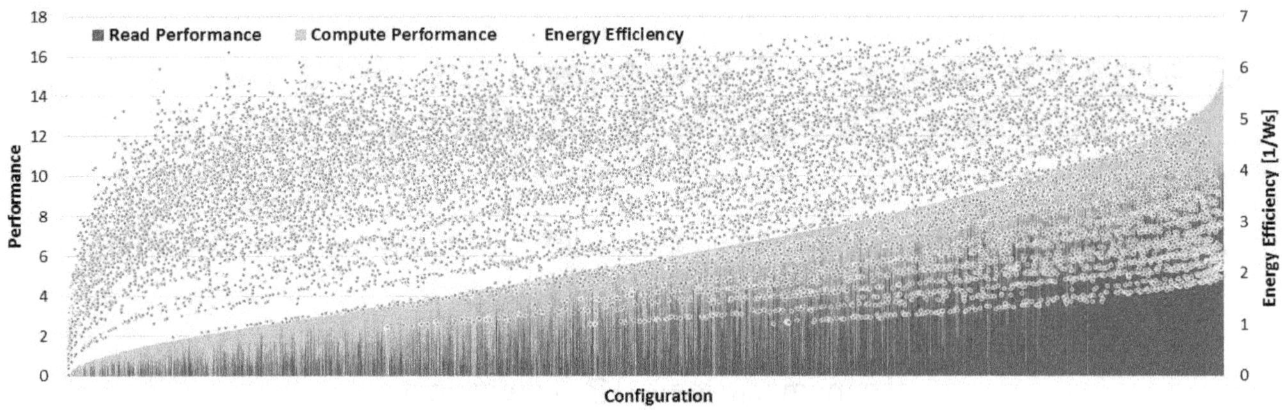

Figure 2: Full *Performance-Energy Profile* for mixed sequential read and compute workloads for 200MHz frequency steps on ODROID-XU3 (four big cores and four LITTLE cores).

uration is found by scanning the *performance-energy profile*, which is a precalculated collection of all possible hardware configurations and their corresponding performance and energy-efficiency. Hence, all configurations which do not meet the requested performance are neglected regardless of their energy-efficiency.

2. ENERGY ELASTICITY

With the term *energy elasticity*, we refer to the ability of software to (1) behave *energy-proportional* and (2) *energy-efficient* at the same time while (3) maintaining a certain quality of service. Up to now, research mostly focused on finding the most energy-efficient configuration for a specific query offering a binary decision between a responsive performance mode or a slower energy-efficient query processing mode.

Our approach breaks with this binary decision and allows the database system to scale between both processing modes and is thus primarily enabling fine-grained energy proportionality meaning that system load and energy consumption strongly correlate with each other. The main indicator for the selection of the proper hardware configuration is the tolerated average query latency and thus the amount of performance that is necessary to hold this constraint. Besides solely aiming for energy proportionality, our *energy-control loop* applies the most energy-efficient hardware configuration that is able to meet the given query latency respectively performance demands.

2.1 Energy Profile

The operation of the *energy-control loop* depends on the existence of an energy-profile for the target platform. Such an energy profile has to be produced once and usually behaves equally for the same hardware platform. An energy profile basically consists of exploration points that contain the specific configuration as well as energy and performance measurements. A configuration itself usually comprises:

(1) A list of active cores with benchmark/operator type mapping.
(2) The frequencies for all available cores, because the frequency of sleeping cores sometimes influences the performance and power consumption of others.

To produce an energy profile for a platform, all reasonable configurations have to be generated and benchmarked. For instance, the ODROID-XU3 as our demo platform features one cluster of four LITTLE ARM Cortex A7 (frequency range from 200MHz to 1.4 GHz) and one cluster of four big ARM Cortex A15 (frequency range from 200MHz to 2 GHz) as well as a Mali GPU, which will not be subject of the demo. Both core clusters implement the same instruction set architecture (ISA) but differ from each other in their instruction execution pipeline, last level cache size, and frequency range. This platform allows 24 active core combinations and 70 frequency combinations (200 MHz steps; shared clock per core cluster) which amounts to a total configuration space of 1680 exploration points. However, the quality of the energy profile also depends on the characteristics of the benchmark that is executed for the different configurations. For modern in-memory database systems, the result of a benchmark usually depends on its memory access pattern. Here, we distinguish between sequential reads (e.g., column scans), random access reads (e.g., index lookups), and compute-bound issuing mostly no memory accesses as well as sequential writes and random access writes. Adding different benchmark types that simulate certain database operators, exponentially increases the configuration space and thus the amount of exploration points requiring a sampling-based benchmarking approach.

For our demo, we demonstrate a data processing system that is limited to a workload that is composed of basic sequential reads (i.e., column aggregations) and compute-bound operators. Figure 2 visualizes the full energy profile for our demo setup using the mentioned benchmark respectively operator types. The configurations are ordered by their overall performance (measured in the number of performed scans respectively computations), which is the sum of the compute and sequential read performance (normalized to the single LITTLE core performance to make both benchmarks comparable). An example configuration for the ODROID-XU3 platform looks like this:

(1) Cluster 1 (2x seq. read, 1x compute, 1x sleep),
Cluster 2 (2x compute, 2x sleep)
(2) Cluster 1 (800 MHz),
Cluster 2 (1,000 MHz)

The energy consumption was measured using the sum of all built-in power sensors. Using the normalized benchmark performance result and the measured energy consumption,

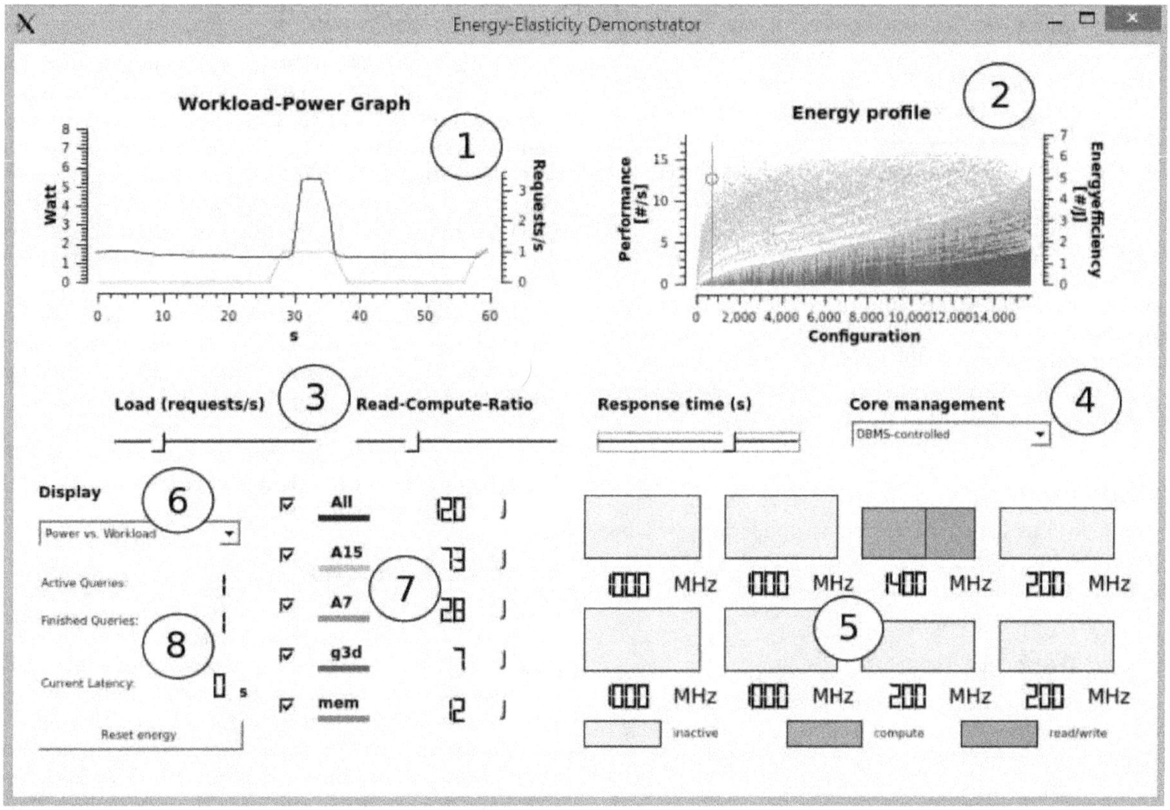

Figure 3: A Screenshot of our Demo Application.

the energy efficiency is calculated as $performance/energy$. The chart shows a nearly linear performance scaling and a high variety regarding the energy efficiency of the configurations.

2.2 Energy-Control Loop

The *energy-control loop* is designed following the principle of a reactive control loop. Every time the loop is triggered, it firstly collects the current monitoring information that basically includes the current latencies for the different query classes (read or compute intensive on our case). Afterwards, it compares the latencies with the given latency constraints for the query classes and either demands less or more read respectively compute performance. Using this reduced or increased performance demands, it searches the energy profile for configurations that fulfill those demands for both query classes and selects the configuration that requires the least energy.

Finally, the *energy-control loop* applies the new hardware configuration using the facilities exposed by the operating system. Additionally, the loop instructs the database operator scheduler to schedule queries of a respective query class on the cores as specified by the configuration. Since the loop executes a pretty lightweight process, it can be triggered multiple times per second and is thus very responsive to cope with highly volatile workload characteristics.

3. DEMONSTRATION

In this section, we explain our overall demonstration setup and discuss the interactive opportunities that our demo GUI offers to the attendees of the demo.

3.1 Setup

For this demonstration we employ an ODROID-XU3, which is based on the ARM big.LITTLE design, running an Ubuntu 14 Linux. As already mentioned, the chip features one cluster of four LITTLE ARM Cortex A7 (maximum frequency of 1.4 GHz) and one cluster of four big ARM Cortex A15 (maximum frequency of 2 GHz) as well as a Mali GPU, which will not be subject of the demo. The SoC containing both core clusters is a Samsung Exynos 5422 operating in the heterogeneous multi-processing mode (HMP), which allows us to simultaneously schedule threads on both kinds of cores and thus to selectively power specific core combinations.

In contrast to its predecessors, the ODROID-XU3 also contains four current and voltage sensors. They are used in this demo for individually measuring the power consumption of the A15 and A7 clusters, the GPU, and the DRAM. The average of the measurements is periodically written to dedicated system files every 0.26 s.

Because of the absence of built-in sensors, existing works [2, 3] used a power meter between the wall socket and the AC input of the board to quantify power consumption. This approach has two major disadvantages: First, the power consumption of the A15 and A7 clusters cannot be analyzed independently from each other or from the other elements on the board (e.g. ethernet interface and USB controller) Second, the consumption of the wall plug transformer is included in the measurement. However, energy conversion efficiency varies not only between different wall plug transformers, it is also dependent on the drawn power. Thus, an overhead is created which is not constant. As already mentioned, this setup does not consider the fixed base power consumption of auxiliary components which effectively shortens the absolute energy efficiency range of the power profile, however, the most energy-efficient configurations will stay the same.

The demo software itself runs a basic database system that allows column aggregations and compute-intensive queries. The user is able to interactively adjust the workload in terms of overall system load, query mix, and desired query latency. The *energy-control loop* automatically applies the appropriate hardware configuration and thus implements *energy-elasticity*. The monitoring information is gathered from the database system and is visualized in the demo UI.

3.2 Walkthrough

Figure 3 shows a screenshot of our demo application, which is composed of the following configuration options and visualizations.

The Power and Workload Monitor

The attendee is able to choose whether he wants to watch the detailed power monitoring information, which displays the power consumption for each component individually, or the overall power consumption in comparison to the current workload (6) to get an impression of how quickly and accurately the *energy-control loop* adapts the hardware configuration. The selected curves are shown in (1) and are updated smoothly in real-time. In the detailed power view, the graph for each hardware component can be enabled or disabled individually. Additionally, the total energy consumption for each element is shown (7). The energy calculation begins at the start of the application and can be reset at any time. This way, the attendee is able to quantify the overall energy savings made by our approach.

Workload Selection

We provide three options for changing the workload (3). The first one is the overall system load, i.e., the number of incoming queries per second, which affects the performance that is required to meet the latency constraint. The second one is the read-compute ratio, which is the ratio of read-intensive and compute-intensive queries. Since the required performance varies depending on the workload characteristics, this option affects the resulting hardware configuration when we apply our concept of *energy-elasticity*.

However, usually there is a limit for the response time a user regards as acceptable, i.e., he demands a minimum execution performance. For this reason the average response time can be manipulated, too, as a third option, which effectively enables *energy elasticity*, because otherwise the system would stay either in full performance or the most energy-efficient mode. This way it could either not maintain the required average query latency or is at risk of choosing a configuration which draws more energy than necessary. To observe the query processing state and get an impression of the current degree of adaptation, the number of active and finished queries as well as the currently measured response time is displayed (8).

Resource Configuration

According to the requested performance, our application shows the current configuration that was picked from the energy profile (2) and chooses the most energy-efficient configuration within a range of the desired performance. In the energy profile the performance is shown in ascending order. The dots represent the respective energy efficiency. A vertical line marks the configuration which is currently in use. Additionally, the energy efficiency is highlighted with a circle.

The individual core usage (5) shows the characteristics of the current configuration. The user can observe which cores are active, how the compute- and read-intensive operations are distributed and at which frequency the cores are running.

For comparative purposes the *energy-control loop* can be disabled (4). In this case the management of the CPUs (i.e., the scheduling and frequency settings) is completely left to the operating system.

4. CONCLUSIONS

In this demo proposal, we addressed the challenge of achieving both facets of energy awareness – *energy-proportionality* and *energy-efficiency* – simultaneously while still regarding user-defined query latency constraints. We presented how to implement this concept of *energy elasticity* using the lightweight *energy-control loop* which depends on an energy profile. The *energy-control loop* leverages the configuration opportunities offered by modern hardware, which is reconfigured at runtime to adapt its power consumption proportionally to the current workload. For demonstration purposes, we employ a portable heterogeneous platform and a rich interactive GUI to give attendees the opportunity to gain more insight into our approach.

5. ACKNOWLEDGMENTS

This work is partly funded by the German Research Foundation (DFG) in the Collaborative Research Center 912 "Highly Adaptive Energy-Efficient Computing".

6. REFERENCES

[1] S. Harizopoulos, M. A. Shah, J. Meza, and P. Ranganathan. Energy Efficiency: The New Holy Grail of Data Management Systems Research. In *CIDR*, 2009.

[2] D. Loghin, B. M. Tudor, H. Zhang, B. C. Ooi, and Y. M. Teo. A performance study of big data on small nodes. *Proceedings of the VLDB Endowment*, 8(7):762–773, 2015.

[3] T. Mühlbauer, W. Rödiger, R. Seilbeck, A. Kemper, and T. Neumann. Heterogeneity-Conscious Parallel Query Execution: Getting a better mileage while driving faster! In *DaMoN*, 2014.

[4] I. Psaroudakis, T. Kissinger, D. Porobic, T. Ilsche, E. Liarou, P. Tözün, A. Ailamaki, and W. Lehner. Dynamic Fine-Grained Scheduling for Energy-Efficient Main-Memory Queries. In *DaMoN*, 2014.

[5] D. Tsirogiannis, S. Harizopoulos, and M. A. Shah. Analyzing the Energy Efficiency of a Database Server. In *SIGMOD*, 2010.

QFix: Demonstrating Error Diagnosis in Query Histories

Xiaolan Wang
School of Computer Science
University of Massachusetts
xlwang@cs.umass.edu

Alexandra Meliou
School of Computer Science
University of Massachusetts
ameli@cs.umass.edu

Eugene Wu
Computer Science
Columbia University
ewu@cs.columbia.edu

ABSTRACT

An increasing number of applications in all aspects of society rely on data. Despite the long line of research in data cleaning and repairs, data correctness has been an elusive goal. Errors in the data can be extremely disruptive, and are detrimental to the effectiveness and proper function of data-driven applications. Even when data is cleaned, new errors can be introduced by applications and users who interact with the data. Subsequent valid updates can obscure these errors and propagate them through the dataset causing more discrepancies. Any discovered errors tend to be corrected superficially, on a case-by-case basis, further obscuring the true underlying cause, and making detection of the remaining errors harder.

In this demo proposal, we outline the design of QFix, a *query-centric* framework that derives explanations and repairs for discrepancies in relational data based on potential errors in the queries that operated on the data. This is a marked departure from traditional *data-centric* techniques that directly fix the data. We then describe how users will use QFix in a demonstration scenario. Participants will be able to select from a number of transactional benchmarks, introduce errors into the queries that are executed, and compare the fixes to the queries proposed by QFix as well as existing alternative algorithms such as decision trees.

1. INTRODUCTION

Data errors are a pervasive, expensive, and time consuming problem that afflicts the vast majority of data-driven applications. For example, errors in retail price data cost US consumers $2.5 billion each year [5]. In aggregate, studies estimate data errors to cost the US economy more than $600 billion per year [4]. Despite the costliness of data errors, studies have found that a significant fraction of time in data analysis — up to 80% [8] — is devoted to cleaning and wrangling [7] the data into a structured and sufficiently clean form to use in downstream applications.

In response, both industry and academia have focused on data cleaning solutions to mitigate this problem. ETL-type systems [10, 13] focus on cleansing the data before it

SIGMOD'16, June 26-July 01, 2016, San Francisco, CA, USA

ISBN 978-1-4503-3531-7/16/06...$15.00

DOI: http://dx.doi.org/10.1145/2882903.2899388

Initial database: D_0

ID	tax	income	pay
t1	950	9500	8550
t2	22500	90000	67500
t3	21500	86000	64500

Final database: D_3

ID	tax	income	pay
t1	950	9500	8550
t2	27000	90000	63000
t3	25800	86000	60200
t4	21625	86500	64875

Query Log: Q

Q_1
```
UPDATE Salary
SET tax = 0.3*income
WHERE income > 85700
```

Q_2
```
UPDATE Salary
SET pay = income - tax
```

Q_3
```
INSERT INTO Salary VALUES
(4, 21625, 86500, 64875)
```

Figure 1: Q_1 updates the tax amount with 30% tax rate for high income employees using an incorrect predicate. The error is propogated by Q_2 to the *pay* field in the database. Finally, a benign insert query Q_3 inserts correct salary information. The final database state contains a mixture of incorrect and correct salary data.

is loaded into the database using a set of pre-defined rules; outlier and anomaly detection algorithms [1] are used to identify errors in the database after the data has been loaded; while recent approaches use downstream applications such as interactive visualizations [7, 16], application queries [11], or data-products to facilitate error detection and correction algorithms. In each of these cases, the focus of error diagnosis and cleaning has been *data centric*, in the sense that the process is meant to identify and directly fix data values.

These efforts have largely ignored an important source of errors — *queries*. Mistakes in queries can introduce errors that spread throughout the database due to subsequent, possibly correct updates. Consider the following example:

EXAMPLE 1 (SALARY UPDATE ERROR). *A manager updates the employees' financial records to set the tax rate to 30% for high income employees who earn more than $87500. She submits the update through a form in the salary accounting application, but incorrectly types $85700 for the income threshold. Later queries that insert new paychecks, compute tax calculations, and aggregate department salaries, end up propagating this error to other records in the database, resulting in incorrect paychecks and employee dissatisfaction. Figure 1 illustrates this example where Q_1, Q_2, and Q_3 are executed on an initial salary database D_0. The error in the predicate of Q_1 is propagated to other fields in the table, by other correct queries.*

By the time some errors in the database are identified, possibly by employees reporting incorrect paystubs, it is difficult to (a) identify all other errors in the database, and (b) trace these errors back to the erroneous update. Such problems can occur in any data processing system with a dynamic database: errors can be introduced by adhoc queries executed by a system administrator, web-based forms that construct queries based on user input, stored procedures that use human input to fill the parameter values, or even queries with automatically generated parameters if there is a chance of errors in the code or data used for the parameter generation.

Although existing data-centric cleaning techniques may help identify and correct these reported errors directly, this is suboptimal because it treats the symptom — the errors in the current database state — rather than the anomalous queries that are the underlying cause. In practice, only a subset of the paystub errors will be reported, thus fixing the reported errors on a case-by-case basis will likely obscure the root problem, making it more difficult to find both the erroneous query and the other affected data. Furthermore, a data-centric approach must repair *all errors* — a non-repaired value such as the incorrect tax rate may continue to introduce errors in the database through future queries (e.g., inserting incorrectly computed paychecks based on the still-incorrect tax rate).

For these reasons, traditional data cleaning approaches may be helpful for finding errors in the data, but are not designed to diagnose causes of the errors when they are rooted in incorrect queries. There has been some work along a similar spirit, but not directly for this problem. For example, integrity constraint-based methods [9] reject some improper updates if the data will fall outside predefined ranges. Certificate-based verification [2] handles a broader class of erroneous queries, but relies on asking users queries prior to executing the update, which renders application-generated updates infeasible. Several techniques have proposed diagnoses that describe structural sources of errors either in the form of predicates most correlated with the errors [16] or common components of a workflow that caused the errors [14], but not at the level of query identification.

Ultimately, query-centric cleaning and repair is challenging because an error introduced by a query can be obscured by, or propagated throughout the database by subsequent queries. This alludes to several factors that make even identifying problematic queries difficult:

1. **Butterfly effect:** An error in even a single query can affect a large number of records, as documented in several real-world cases [6, 12, 17]. Even if a single record is incorrect, its value may be used as part of the `WHERE` or `SET` clauses of subsequent valid queries that introduce additional errors that are seemingly unrelated.

2. **Partial information:** In most practical settings, we cannot assume that we can identify all errors in the database — for example, not all employees will complain about their incorrect paystubs. More likely, we only have access to a subset of the data errors, and must use them to extrapolate the queries that affected a possibly larger set of data. A diagnostic tool that can reduce the entire transaction log to the most likely candidate queries and propose fixes is needed to make this process manageable.

3. **Multiple types of errors:** An erroneous query can cause multiple types of data errors. For example, a record that should not exist may have been accidentally inserted, or conversely a record that should exist was unintentionally deleted. Similarly, attribute values may be incorrectly updated, updated when they should not have been, or not updated when they should have. Any combination of these error types may be present in the current state of the database, and although they may not be obviously related to each other, they must be addressed in a holistic manner.

In this demo proposal, we outline the design of QFix, a framework that derives explanations and repairs for discrepancies in relational data based on potential errors in the queries that operated on the data, and describe how users will use QFix in a demonstration scenario. In contrast to existing approaches in data cleaning that aim to detect and correct errors in the data directly, the goal of QFix is to identify the problematic queries that introduced errors into the database. These diagnoses both *explain* how errors were introduced to a dataset, and also lead to the identification of additional discrepancies in the data that would have otherwise remained undetected. Participants will be able to select from a number of transactional benchmarks to generate a query workload, introduce errors into the queries that are executed, and compare the fixes to the queries proposed by QFix against existing alternative algorithms such as decision trees.

2. THE QFix ARCHITECTURE

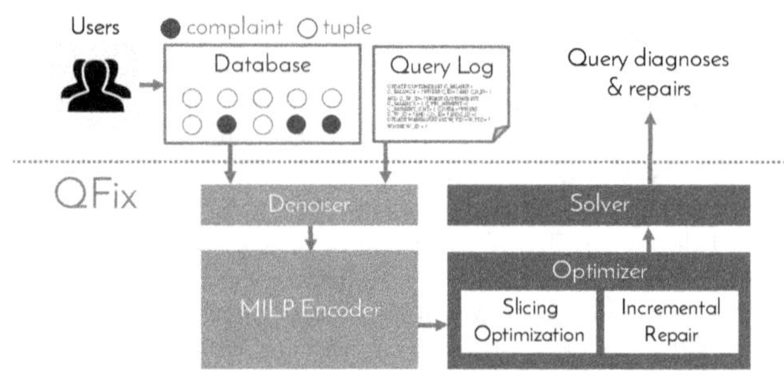

Figure 2: QFix architecture diagram

Figure 2 shows QFix's major components. QFix takes as input a query log containing UPDATE, INSERT and DELETE queries, the database, along with a set of identified data errors (called *complaints*). These complaints are pairs of tuple id of tuples that are wrong, along with an estimate of their correct values (e.g., 21500 as tuple t_3's tax value in Example 1). QFix uses this information to trace the causes of the errors and output the most likely set of queries in the log (*diagnoses*), along with proposed *repairs* of these queries.

To achieve this, QFix first performs an optional outlier removal step to deal with potential false positives in the complaints. Then the *MILP Encoding* component transforms the query diagnosis problem into a Mixed Integer Linear Program (MILP) that is further optimized through slicing and incremental repair techniques, before being sent to an industrial MILP solver. The output of the solver constitutes solutions to the query diagnosis problem.

3. PROBLEM AND SOLUTION SKETCH

3.1 Problem Outline

We assume a query log Q containing a sequence of update, insert and delete queries $q_1, \ldots q_n$ that have been executed on an initial database state D_0. For simplicity, we assume that the database is a single relation with attributes $A_i, \ldots, A_m$, though this single-relation restriction is not a requirement for QFix. Let $D_i = q_i(\ldots q_1(D_0))$ be the the database state output after executing queries q_1 though q_i on D_0. Thus, the final database state is simply the application of the query log to the initial state: $D_n = Q(D_0) = q_n(\ldots q_1(D_0))$. We assume that UPDATE and DELETE queries use predicates composed of conjunctive and disjunctive range clauses of the form $\langle A_j\ op\ ?\rangle$, where $op \in \{=,>,<,\leq,\geq,\neq\}$ and ? is a constant value. We also assume that SET clauses are of the form $\langle A_j = A_i + ?\rangle$ (relative update) or $\langle A_j = ?\rangle$ (constant update).

Queries in Q are possibly erroneous and introduce errors in the data. We assume there is a true sequence of queries $Q^* = \{q_1^*, \ldots, q_n^*\}$ that generate a true sequence of database states $\{D_0, D_1^*, \ldots, D_n^*\}$. The true query log and database states are unknown, and our goal is to find and correct errors in Q to retrieve the correct database state D_n^*.

To do so, QFix takes as input a set of identified or user-reported data errors, called a *complaint set* and denoted as $\mathcal{C}$. A complaint $c \in \mathcal{C}$ corresponds to a tuple in D_n along with its true attribute value assignments. For example, $\mathcal{C} = \{c_1\}$, where $c_1 = (t3, \{tax = 21500\}, \{income = 86000\}, \{pay = 64500\})$ forms the *complaint set* with incorrect *tax* and *pay* attribute for the query log Q in Example 1. A complaint can also model addition or removal of tuples: $c = (\perp, t^*)$ means that t^* should be added to the database, while $c = (t_i, \perp)$ denotes that t_i should be removed.

Our goal is to derive a diagnosis as a log repair $Q' = \{q_1', \ldots, q_n'\}$, such that $Q'(D_0) = D_n^*$. In this work, we focus on errors produced by incorrect parameters in queries, so our repairs focus on altering query constants rather than query structure. Therefore, each query $q_i' \in Q'$ has the same structure as q_i (e.g., the same number of predicates, the same variables and operators in the WHERE clause), but possibly different parameters. For example, a good log repair for the example of Figure 1 is $Q' = \{q_1', q_2, q_3\}$, where q_1'=`UPDATE Taxes SET tax = 0.3 * income WHERE income >= 87500`.

Problem definition

We now formalize the problem definition for diagnosing data errors using query logs. A diagnosis is a log repair Q' that resolves all complaints in the set $\mathcal{C}$ and leads to a correct database state D_n^*.

DEFINITION 2 (OPTIMAL DIAGNOSIS). *Given database states D_0 and D_n, a query log Q such that $Q(D_0) = D_n$, a set of complaints $\mathcal{C}$ on D_n, and a distance function d, the optimal diagnosis is a log repair Q', such that:*

- *$Q'(D_0) = D_n^*$, where D_n^* has no errors*
- *$d(\mathcal{Q}, \mathcal{Q}^*)$ is minimized*

Where $d(\mathcal{Q}, \mathcal{Q}^*)$ measures the changes made in the repaired query log. Informally, we seek the minimum changes to the log $\mathcal{Q}$ that would result in a clean database state D_n^*. Obviously, a challenge is that D_n^* is unknown, unless we know that the complaint set contains all of, and only, true complaints.

3.2 Solution Sketch

Our general strategy is to translate the starting and ending database states, D_0 and D_n, the query log Q, and complaint set $\mathcal{C}$ into a mixed-integer linear program (MILP) and solve the resulting program using a generic solver. Briefly, a linear program is a minimization problem consisting of a set of constraints in the form of linear equations, along with an objective function that is minimized; an MILP is a linear program where only a subset of the undetermined variables are required to be integers, while the rest are real valued.

To achieve this translation, we model each query as a linear equation that computes the output tuple values from the inputs or previous database state, and transforms the equation into a set of of linear constraints. In addition, the constant values in the queries are parameterized into a set of undetermined variables, while the database state is encoded as constraints on the initial and final tuple values. Finally, the undetermined variables are used to construct an objective function that prefers value assignments that minimize both the amount that the queries change and the number of non-complaint tuples that are affected.

Due to space constraints, we will walk through an example of how the query `UPDATE Taxes SET tax = 0.3*income WHERE income>85700`, when applied to t_3^{old} to produce t_3^{new}, is translated into a set of constraints as detailed below.

First, we can rewrite the query as a conditional statement:

$$t_3^{new}.tax = \begin{cases} 0.3 * t_3^{old}.rate & \text{if } p \\ t_3^{old}.tax & 1 - \text{p} \end{cases}$$

where

$$p = t_3^{old}.income > 85700$$

This is equivalent to the following linearized form. In addition, we add constraints on the starting and ending value for the *rate* attribute: If $t_3^{new}.tax$ was specified in $\mathcal{C}$, then the provided value is used instead of the value in the database:

$$\begin{aligned} t_3^{new}.tax &= (0.3 * t_3^{old}.income) \times p + t_3^{old}.tax \times (1-p) \\ p &= t_3^{old}.income > 85700 \\ t_3^{old}.tax &= 30 \\ t_3^{new}.tax &= 25 \end{aligned}$$

In the above formulation, all variables are determined and is trivially solvable. Instead, we replace the constaints 0.3 and 85700 with undetermined variables v_1 and v_2, so that solving the constraints will reassign those query constants to new values that result in the desired value for $t_3^{new}.rate$. Note that the initial range $[minval, maxval]$ of the undetermined variables could be defined based on the valid range of the corresponding attribute(s), or, as a heuristic, based on the empirical distribute of the attribute values in the database.

Extending this process to all tuples and all queries in the log describes the naive encoding procedure that solves the OPTIMAL DIAGNOSIS problem. However, the size of the resulting constraint problem increases at a rate of $O(|D| \times |Q| \times \#\text{attributes})$, rendering it infeasible for all but the smallest databases and query logs.

QFix uses four additional optimizations not presented in this paper to scale to large query log and database sizes. The first three are called *Slicing* optimizations that reduce each of the components in the problem size: *Tuple-slicing*; *Query-slicing*; *Attribute-slicing*. MILP solvers typically (though not guaranteed) take a much longer time as the size of the MILP problem increases, thus each of the slicing techniques reduces the problem and speeds up the solver time. Our technical report [15] shows, among other results, that our optimizations can achieve up to 40× speedups over the basic approach.

The final optimization serves to reduce the number of undetermined variables that the MILP solver must provide a solution for. The cost of the solver, in our experiments, increases exponentially with the number of undetermined variables. To this end, QFix uses an incremental algorithm that tries to fix the queries in the query log one at a time.

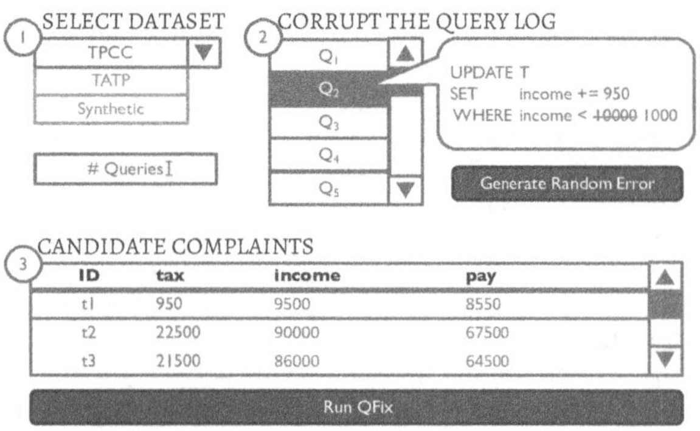

Figure 3: Users introduce errors to benchmark workloads.

These optimizations enable QFix to propose a solution within several seconds for thousands of queries and tuples on common transaction benchmarks in OLTPBench [3].

4. DEMONSTRATION OUTLINE

The objective of this demonstration is to show how QFix can quickly and accurately detect and propose fixes to errors in a query log, and compare its results to alternatives that use existing techniques.

Figures 3 and 4 show screenshots of the initial and results pages. Each step is annotated with a circled number, which we detail below.

Step 1 (Select Dataset): Participants may first choose from a dropdown menu containing a number of transaction workload generators from the benchmarks in OLTPBench [3]. Since most transactional benchmarks focus on point update queries, we additionally include a synthetic workload generator that includes range updates, as well as insert and delete queries. The text box on the right side allows users to specify the number of queries to generate in the workload.

Step 2 (Corrupt the Query Log): Once the workload generator is specified, the Query Log component of the interface renders a scrollable list containing all of the queries. Users can either let the system to inject errors randomly by clicking the "Random Error" button or manually add errors. To introduce errors, the interface allows users to select any editable query in the log and shows the selected query in an editable popup so that users can edit the queries. For example, in the figure, the user has edited query Q_2 and reduced the threshold from $income < 10,000$ to $income < 100$.

Step 3 (Form a Complaint Set): The modified query cause the state of the database at the end of the workload to differ from the result of the original workload. The candidate complaints table lists the tuples that are different and highlights the attribute values in those tuples as red text. For instance, $t_1.tax$, $t_1.income$ and $t_1.pay$ are all errors introduced by the modified query. Users can select individual attribute values or entire tuples to add to the complaint set that is used as input to the QFix algorithms. When she is satisfied, the user clicks `Run QFix` to execute the baseline QFix, the optimized QFix, and alternative algorithms.

Step 4 (View Log Repairs): The result page lists the original query ID and text at the top. The ID is important because some proposed fixes may identify an incorrect query. Below the original query, the interface shows each of the proposed fixes as columns. For example, Figure 4 shows that both the QFix and alternative fixes identified the correct query Q_2, however QFix only took 0.2 seconds to run, and correctly fixed Q_2, whereas the alternative took 10 sec, incorrectly selected Q_5, and proposed an incorrect fix.

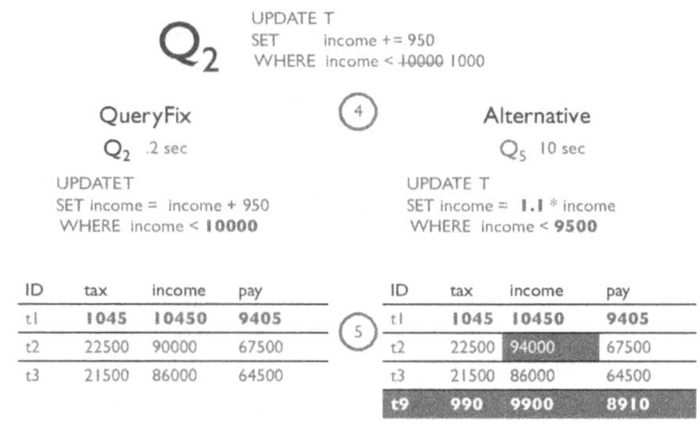

Figure 4: Comparisons between proposed fixes.

Step 5 (Validate Repairs): The bottom tables show the effects of the fixes on the complaints from step 3. Correctly fixed attribute values are highlighted in blue, unfixed errors are shown as red text, while incorrectly fixed values are highlighted with a red background. Finally, it is possible for proposed fixes to *introduce* new errors, which are shown as entire rows that are highlighted with a red background.

Acknowledgements. This material is based upon work supported by the National Science Foundation under grants IIS-1421322 and IIS-1453543.

5. REFERENCES

[1] V. Chandola, A. Banerjee, and V. Kumar. Outlier detection: A survey. *ACM Computing Surveys*, 2007.
[2] S. Chen, X. L. Dong, L. V. Lakshmanan, and D. Srivastava. We challenge you to certify your updates. In *SIGMOD*, 2011.
[3] D. E. Difallah, A. Pavlo, C. Curino, and P. Cudre-Mauroux. Oltp-bench: An extensible testbed for benchmarking relational databases. In *VLDB*, 2013.
[4] W. W. Eckerson. Data quality and the bottom line. *TDWI Report, The Data Warehouse Institute*, 2002.
[5] W. Fan, F. Geerts, and X. Jia. A revival of integrity constraints for data cleaning. In *VLDB*, 2008.
[6] B. Grady. Oakland unified makes $7.6M accounting error in budget; asking schools not to count on it. In *Oakland*, 2013.
[7] S. Kandel, A. Paepcke, J. Hellerstein, and J. Heer. Wrangler: interactive visual specification of data transformation scripts. In *CHI*, 2011.
[8] S. Kandel, A. Paepcke, J. M. Hellerstein, and J. Heer. Enterprise data analysis and visualization: An interview study. *IEEE Trans. Vis. Comput. Graph.*, 2012.
[9] N. Khoussainova, M. Balazinska, and D. Suciu. Towards correcting input data errors probabilistically using integrity constraints. In *MobiDE*, 2006.
[10] R. Krishnamurthy, Y. Li, S. Raghavan, F. Reiss, S. Vaithyanathan, and H. Zhu. Systemt: a system for declarative information extraction. *SIGMOD Record*, 2009.
[11] S. Krishnan, J. Wang, M. J. Franklin, K. Goldberg, T. Kraska, T. Milo, and E. Wu. Sampleclean: Fast and reliable analytics on dirty data. *arXiv*, 2015.
[12] M. Sakal and L. Raković. Errors in building and using electronic tables: Financial consequences and minimisation techniques. In *Strategic Management*, 2012.
[13] C. Thomsen and T. B. Pedersen. A survey of open source tools for business intelligence. *Data Warehousing and Knowledge Discovery*, 2005.
[14] X. Wang, X. L. Dong, and A. Meliou. Data x-ray: A diagnostic tool for data errors. In *SIGMOD*, 2015.
[15] X. Wang, A. Meliou, and E. Wu. Qfix: Diagnosing errors through query histories. *CoRR*, abs/1601.07539, 2016.
[16] E. Wu and S. Madden. Scorpion: Explaining away outliers in aggregate queries. In *PVLDB*, 2013.
[17] J. Yates. Data entry error wipes out life insurance coverage. In *Chicago Tribune*, 2005.

CoDAR: Revealing the Generalized Procedure & Recommending Algorithms of Community Detection *

Xiang Ying[1], Chaokun Wang[1], Meng Wang[1], Jeffrey Xu Yu[2], Jun Zhang[1]
[1] School of Software, Tsinghua University, Beijing 100084, China
[2] The Chinese University of Hong Kong, Hong Kong, China
{yingx14, meng-wang12, zhang-jun10}@mails.tsinghua.edu.cn, chaokun@tsinghua.edu.cn, yu@se.cuhk.edu.hk

ABSTRACT

Community detection has attracted great interest in graph analysis and mining during the past decade, and a great number of approaches have been developed to address this problem. However, the lack of a uniform framework and a reasonable evaluation method makes it a puzzle to analyze, compare and evaluate the extensive work, let alone picking out a best one when necessary. In this paper, we design a tool called CoDAR, which reveals the generalized procedure of community detection and monitors the real-time structural changes of network during the detection process. Moreover, CoDAR adopts 12 recognized metrics and builds a rating model for performance evaluation of communities to recommend the best-performing algorithm. Finally, the tool also provides nice interactive windows for display.

Keywords

Community detection, Procedure monitoring, Algorithm recommendation

1. INTRODUCTION

Community detection has arisen as one of the popular topics in graph mining, and is also widely applied in other fields, such as social network analysis, biological data analysis. Finding inherent communities in a network is an interesting as well as a challenging task, mainly due to the obscure definition of a community, diverse problem-solving perspectives, multiple evaluation criterions and the lack of a reliable ground-truth for a real-world network.

Over the past decade, the extensive research work has promoted the prosperity of the family of community detection approaches. Given the diversity of the existing approaches to this problem, e.g. different similarity measurements of nodes, links or other structures in a network, it is usually difficult to understand, analyze and evaluate the approaches of various categories. According to these points, how to choose the most appropriate approach in specific scenarios is also becoming a more and more intractable problem. In addition, since there exists no quantitative definition of communities, we always have no idea about to what extent a community assignment is good enough. Therefore, an intelligent evaluation method is quite necessary and beneficial in the performance evaluation of community detection.

*Corresponding author: Chaokun Wang.

SIGMOD'16, June 26-July 01, 2016, San Francisco, CA, USA

ISBN 978-1-4503-3531-7/16/06. . . $15.00

DOI: http://dx.doi.org/10.1145/2882903.2899386

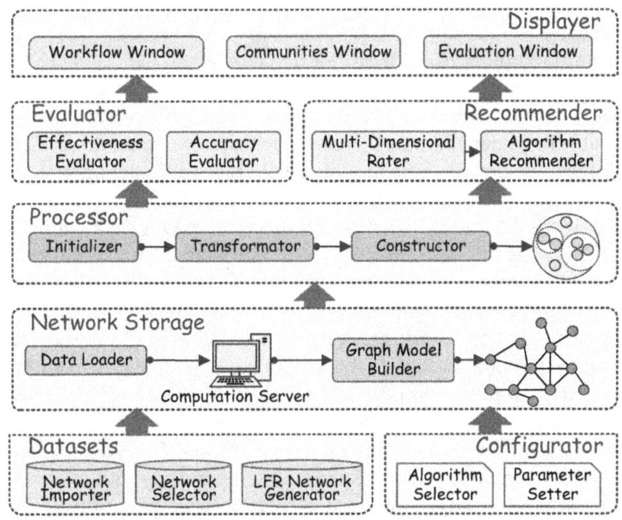

Figure 1: The system architecture of CoDAR

In this paper, we present a tool called **CoDAR**, which is the visualization and an extension of our work [6]. **CoDAR** provides **Co**mmunity **D**etection **A**lgorithm **R**ecommendation for users and it can also reveal the generalized procedure of community detection. More specifically, CoDAR possesses the following advantages:

- Firstly, CoDAR integrates 10 state-of-the-art algorithms of community detection studied in [6], providing a set of useful detection approaches for users to analyze and utilize.
- Moreover, it dives deep into the workflow of community detection, reveals the generalized procedure of community detection upon our proposed framework [6], and monitors the dynamic changes of network structures.
- Besides, based on 12 recognized evaluation metrics, CoDAR builds a rating model by learning different weight factors of different metrics, to measure the performance of communities produced by different algorithms.
- Finally, the tool is built with a friendly user interface, providing multiple windows for display.

2. OVERVIEW OF CODAR

The core computing modules of CoDAR have been implemented in standard C++. The tool is built with dynamic and interactive data visualizations using D3.js library (http://d3js.org/). Considering the

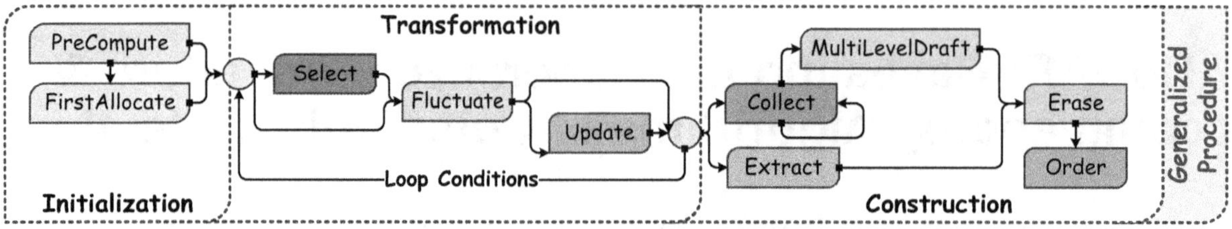

Figure 2: The generalized procedure of community detection

fundamental functions and workflow of CoDAR, it consists of the following seven modules, as shown in Fig. 1:

Datasets. CoDAR embeds the LFR Network Generator [3] to produce customized synthetic networks, provides various real-world networks (http://snap.stanford.edu/data/) by the Network Selector , and supports data importing by users as well.

Configurator. The Algorithm Selector integrates 10 state-of-the-art community detection approaches, covering different categories, such as hierarchy clustering, label propagation, matrix blocking and clique percolation. Based on the features of datasets, e.g. the average node degree or node scale, the Parameter Setter adjusts the requisite parameters of each algorithm automatically.

Network Storage. The network file is stored on the Computation Server by the Data Loader. The Graph Model Builder converts the data file to graph, and records attributes of nodes, edges and other related structures during the whole computation.

Processor. The Initializer, Transformator and Constructor correspond to the three phases of the generalized procedure of community detection in our proposed framework [6]. More details of the framework are discussed in Sec. 3.1.

Evaluator. To make performance evaluation, CoDAR employs 12 goodness metrics (see in Sec. 3.2.1), measuring both *effectiveness* (without ground-truth) and *accuracy* (with ground-truth) of the detected communities. These metrics show different preferences for different structural characteristics, quantifying how "good" the communities found by different algorithms are.

Recommender. Based on the evaluation of each algorithm, the Multi-Dimensional Rater aims at integrating the scores of these metric functions to give an overall score of each algorithm. More than a simple "average" method, CoDAR builds a rating model, learning the appropriate values of the weight factors of different metrics, to recommend the best-performing algorithm for users.

Displayer. CoDAR provides a user-friendly interface, including three visual windows. The Workflow Window shows the dynamic changes of structures in the network during detection process, the Communities Window gives an intuitive view of the detected communities, and the Evaluation Window presents the score of each metric function.

3. SYSTEM FEATURES

CoDAR possesses good skills in exploring in-depth knowledge of community detection. The features of our tool mainly embody two aspects. On the one hand, it uncovers the generalized procedure of community detection, and presents the real-time changes of the structural information to users. On the other hand, CoDAR provides a comprehensive comparison of the communities produced by different algorithms to pick out the best-performing algorithm.

3.1 Generalized Procedure

Since the problem of community detection can be solved from diverse ways, it is a puzzle to understand, analyze and compare the great number of existing approaches of different categories. Here, we recapped our procedure-oriented framework for community detection proposed in our latest work [6], which consists of the following parts. More details of the framework are available in [6].

Firstly, the framework contains two fundamental concepts to enlighten us on the community structure: the **Propinquity Measure**, which estimates the nearness of the network elements, and the **Revelatory Structure**, which provides yet another way to organize the elements. Moreover, we formulate a generalized procedure in this framework, which decomposes the process of community detection into three phases and a series of key steps, as shown in Fig. 2. Besides, CoDAR monitors the dynamic status of the procedure and provides insight into a general procedure of community detection:

Initialization. Network elements, such as nodes, links or other structures, get their initial propinquity via PRECOMPUTE and form a primary community assignment via FIRSTALLOCATE.

Transformation. Inner structures and relations underlying the network elements are transformed iteratively, and the result is gradually clarified in this phase. SELECT, FLUCTUATE and UPDATE consist of the main steps in each iteration. First of all, candidate elements in the network are picked out from the network in SELECT. Then, in FLUCTUATE, the correlated parts in the revelatory structure with these elements are fluctuated to make the communities more apparent. Following these transformations, the propinquity of other involved elements is recomputed in UPDATE. Three kinds of loop conditions are employed in this phase, and they are usually designed specifically in different approaches.

Construction. The final result can be obtained by refining the revelatory structure output in the previous phase. If there are multiple results, COLLECT first gets each of them, and then chooses the best one via MULTILEVELDRAFT. If there is no obvious result, EXTRACT is employed to filter the communities out. Eventually, tiny communities are removed by ERASE, and the rest communities are sorted via ORDER by the scale.

3.2 Algorithm Recommendation

Since CoDAR integrates various existing algorithms, users may be interesting in the algorithm which produces the most appropriate community assignment. The problem is how we can pick out the best-performing algorithm under the current circumstance (i.e. a given dataset). CoDAR makes the algorithm recommendation via a comprehensive performance evaluation and a multi-dimensional rating method.

3.2.1 Performance Evaluation

CoDAR inherits 12 metrics in performance evaluation to measure the quality of the communities produced by an algorithm. Fig. 3 shows these metrics, which are widely used in recent work: {*CC*, *S*, *Q*, *Jaccard*, F_{same}, *NMI*} [6], {F_1, *NMI*} [4], {*D*, *CC*, *Q*} [7], {*DBI*, *SI*, *MNI*} [1], {*Q*, *ARI*, *P*} [2], {*Q*, *Jaccard*, F_{same}} [5]. They can be grouped into two basic categories, i.e. **Accuracy** and **Effectiveness**. The former is used only when the ground-truth (the authentic communities) can be acquired, while the latter is not confined to the ground-truth. Moreover, according to the structural characteristics these metrics mainly embody, we can divide them

Categories	Metrics	Formula
Effectiveness		
Inner Relationship	Density	$D = \frac{1}{K}\sum_i \frac{\lvert E_i\rvert}{\lvert C_i\rvert\cdot(\lvert C_i\rvert-1)}$
Inner Relationship	Cluster Coefficient	$CC = \frac{1}{K}\sum_i \frac{1}{\lvert C_i\rvert}\sum_{v\in C_i} \frac{\lvert e_{ts}: v_s, v_j \in N_v \cap C_i,\ e_{ts}\in E_i\rvert}{d_v\cdot(d_v-1)}$
In/Out Relationship	Strength	$S = \frac{1}{K}\sum_i [s(C_i) + \frac{1}{2}w(C_i)]$
In/Out Relationship	Modularity	$Q = \sum_{i=1}^{K}\left[\frac{\lvert E_i^{in}\rvert}{\lvert E\rvert} - \left(\frac{2\lvert E_i^{in}\rvert + \lvert E_i^{out}\rvert}{2\lvert E\rvert}\right)^2\right]$
Distance	Davies Bouldin Index	$DBI = \frac{1}{K}\max_{i\neq j}\left[\frac{\bar{d}(C_i)+\bar{d}(C_j)}{d(C_i,\ C_j)}\right]$
Distance	Silhouette Index	$SI = \frac{1}{K}\sum_i \frac{1}{\lvert C_i\rvert}\sum_{v\in C_i}\frac{d(v,C_{cloest})-d(v,C_i)}{max\{d(v,C_{cloest}),\ d(v,C_i)\}}$

Categories	Metrics	Formula
Accuracy		
Shared Node Pairs	Jaccard Index	$Jaccard = {}^{a}/_{a+b+c}$
Shared Node Pairs	Adjusted Rand Index	$ARI = \frac{\binom{2}{n}(a+d)-[(a+b)(a+c)+(c+d)(b+d)]}{\binom{2}{n}^2-[(a+b)(a+c)+(c+d)(b+d)]}$
Shared Nodes	Average F_1-Score	$F_1 = \frac{1}{2K}\sum_i \max_j \frac{2\lvert C_i\cap C_j'\rvert}{\lvert C_i\rvert+\lvert C_j'\rvert} + \frac{1}{2K'}\sum_j \max_i \frac{2\lvert C_i\cap C_j'\rvert}{\lvert C_i\rvert+\lvert C_j'\rvert}$
Shared Nodes	Purity	$P = \frac{1}{2}\sum_i \max_i \lvert C_i \cap C_j'\rvert$
Shared Nodes	Cross Common Fraction	$F_{same} = \frac{1}{2}\sum_i \max_j \lvert C_i\cap C_j'\rvert + \frac{1}{2}\sum_j \max_i \lvert C_i \cap C_j'\rvert$
Shared Nodes	Normalized Mutual Information	$NMI = \frac{-2\sum_{i,j} N_{ij}\log\frac{N_{ij}N_t}{N_{i.}N_{.j}}}{\sum_i N_{i.}\log\frac{N_{i.}}{N_t}+\sum_j N_{.j}\log\frac{N_{.j}}{N_t}}$

Figure 3: Categories of evaluation metrics for detected communities (C, C': detected communities, real communities; $K = |C|$; E^{in}, E^{out}: links in or out of C_i; N_v: neighbors of node v; $d_v = |N_v|$; $s(C_i) = 1$ or $w(C_i) = 1$ if C_i is strong or weak; $\overline{d}(C_i)$: diameter of C_i; $d(C_i, C_j)$: average distance between C_i and C_j; $d(v, C_i)$: average distance from v to C_i; $C_{closest}$: the nearest community to v; a: the number of node pairs in the same community in both C and C', b: the number of node pairs which are in the same community in C but in different communities in C', and c vice versa, d: the number of node pairs in different communities in both C and C'; $N_{ij} = |C_i \cap C_j'|$, $N_{i.} = \sum_j N_{ij}$, $N_{.j} = \sum_i N_{ij}$, $N_t = \sum_i \sum_j N_{ij}$)

into five subcategories: (1) **Inner Relationship** usually measures the tightness of the links inside a community; (2) **In/Our Relationship** captures the intuition that good communities are well-separated from the rest of the network; (3) **Distance** focuses on the closeness of different communities, based on the shortest path among nodes; (4) **Shared Node Pair** characterizes the proportion of the number of node pairs which are correctly classified in the detected communities. (5) **Shared Nodes** captures the fraction of shared nodes in a generated community and an authentic one.

It is easy to see that evaluation metrics of accuracy usually derive from the proportion of shared nodes or node pairs in C and C', while metrics of effectiveness are designed differently indeed and may have their own preference on some specific structural features.

3.2.2 *Learning to Rate & Recommend*

The metrics of effectiveness with different structural preferences are all based on their own premise, showing different characteristics a good community assignment may possess. Actually, a result produced by an algorithm may fit one metric well but show poor performance with another metric. With such diverse standards, a simple way to make the overall rating is to get the average score of all the metric functions. However, since we have no priori knowledge of the potential preferences, treating these metrics equally may be unfair to a reasonable judgement. Best of all, taking the scores of the accuracy metrics as the baseline, a "smart" rating model is able to learn the proportions of the opinions from these effectiveness metrics, which we should adopt in the evaluation. Specifically, CoDAR builds the following rating model:

Suppose that M and N are numbers of selected evaluation metrics of accuracy and effectiveness respectively. For a given network g, a selected algorithm a, a group of normalized score of M effectiveness metrics $\{s_m^E(a) | 1 \leq m \leq M\}$, and a group of score of N accuracy metrics $\{s_n^A(a) | 1 \leq n \leq N\}$, the overall score of algorithm a on network g is made up of two parts, and can be defined as

$$S(a) = S^E(a) + S^A(a) = \sum_{m=1}^{M} \theta_m \cdot s_m^E(a) + \frac{1}{N}\sum_{n=1}^{N} s_n^A(a), \quad (1)$$

where θ_m is the weight factor of the m-th effectiveness metric, $0 \leq \theta_m \leq 1$ and $\sum_{m=1}^{M} \theta_m = 1$. Then, CoDAR recommends the best-performing algorithm $\hat{a}$ with the highest overall score to users:

$$\hat{a} = \{a_j | j = \arg\max_j S(a_j)\}. \quad (2)$$

Actually, a group of desired weight factors should indicate a group of reasonable proportions of different characteristics involved in the metrics. Taking $\Theta = \{\theta_1, \theta_2, ..., \theta_M\}$ as parameters, CoDAR learns the optimized parameters $\hat{\Theta}$ with a training set using authentic community assignments of different datasets generated by the LFR Network Generator [3].

Given a set $G_t = \{t_i | 1 \leq i \leq T\}$, containing the ground-truth of T networks, we can get the estimation model of Θ as

$$\hat{\Theta} = \arg\min_{\Theta} \sum_{i=1}^{T} (f(\mathbf{x}_i; \Theta) - y_i)^2 + \lambda |\Theta|^2, \quad (3)$$

where $\mathbf{x}_i = (s_1^E(t_i), s_2^E(t_i), ..., s_M^E(t_i))$ is the effectiveness vector of t_i, $f(\mathbf{x}_i; \Theta) = \sum_{m=1}^{M} \theta_m \cdot s_m^{t_i}$, $y_i = \frac{1}{N}\sum_{n=1}^{N} s_n^A(t_i)$ is the average accuracy of t_i. The second is a regular term which can avoid over-fitting.

The optimized parameters can be learned through a gradient descent method. Moreover, since CoDAR allows users to import their own datasets, with the increasing number of the cases executed in the tool, the weights of different metrics can get adjusted continually and become more and more precise.

4. DEMONSTRATION

In this demonstration, we plan to show how CoDAR works in two typical scenarios.

4.1 Monitoring Detection Procedure

CoDAR integrates 10 state-of-the-art algorithms of community detection for users to analyze, compare and evaluate. Users can take an algorithm as an example, e.g. the MB-DSGE algorithm [6], from the algorithm set which is shown in the left sidebar in Fig. 4. The right sidebar of this page provides three different ways to set the dataset, as discussed in Sec. 2. After choosing a real-world network, e.g. the NCAA Football network [2], users can click the button "Compute" to run the algorithm. During the whole detection process, CoDAR is able to monitor the current status of the detection process and show the dynamic structural changes of the network.

The top of the page shows the generalized procedure of community detection, and the current status FLUCTUATE is highlighted in a different color. The status changes dynamically as the procedure continues, intuitively reflecting the workflow of a community detection approach. The center network shows the current network

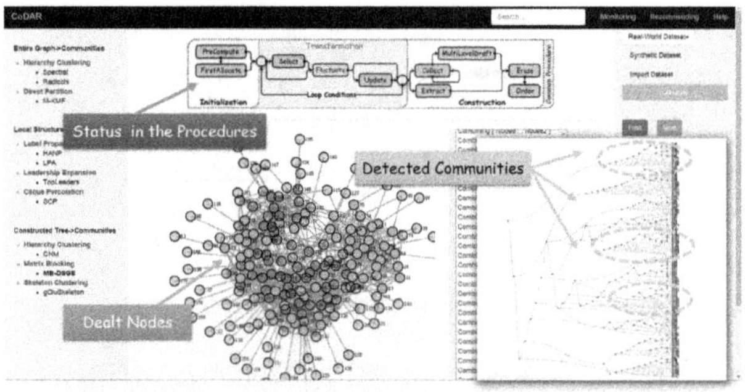

Figure 4: A snapshot of the generalized procedure

under the step FLUCTUATE during an intermediate iteration, and the dealt nodes in the network are highlighted in green.

The floating figure at the bottom right corner in Fig. 4 shows the status under EXTRACT, where communities are found in the revelatory structure (the hierarchy tree) in this algorithm. At this point, leaf nodes in each branch stand for members of a same group, and groups with higher density than a predefined threshold are extracted as communities.

4.2 Recommending the Best Approach

When users need to find the intrinsic community structure in a given network, CoDAR is useful in recommending the best algorithm of community detection as well as the corresponding community assignment. Here, they choose a batch of optional algorithms in CoDAR, e.g. CNM, Spectral, HANP and M-KMF [6], which address this problem in different perspectives, including hierarchy clustering (agglomeration and division), label propagation, and direct partitioning, as shown in the left sidebar in Fig. 5. The selected algorithms to be evaluated are highlighted in red. First of all, CoDAR proceeds an underlying step, in which the corresponding requisite parameters of each algorithm get automatically adjusted to appropriate values based on the characteristics of networks, such as the average degree of nodes. Then, the tool finds different community assignments using the selected algorithms.

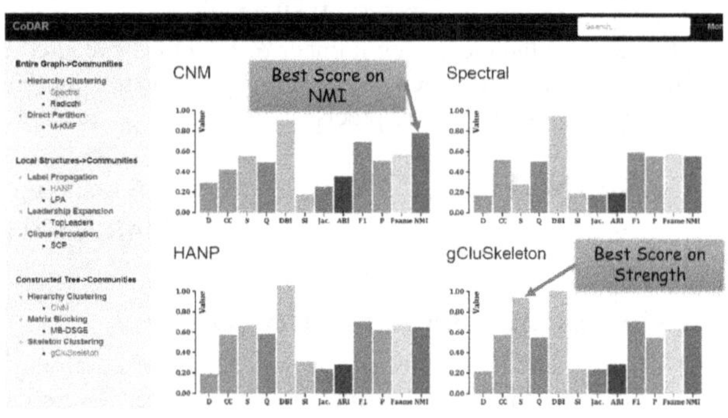

Figure 5: Scores of 12 evaluation metrics w.r.t. 4 algorithms

The evaluation results of these algorithms under the 12 metrics are shown in Fig. 5. Scores of the same metric are shown in the same color, which is convenient for users to concentrate on the differences of each metric among these algorithms. Based on the scores of different quality functions, we can find that CNM prefers to produce communities with high *NMI* while gCluSkeleton tends to form communities with high strength. Therefore, users may be confused about which algorithm produces the best communities on the current network on earth.

Next, after user pressing the button "Show Best", CoDAR gathers the scores of different metrics, makes a multi-dimensional rating, and returns the best result to users. Fig. 6 is the final page with

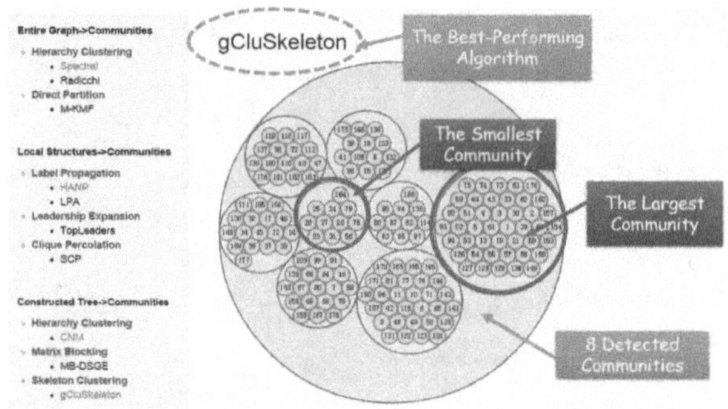

Figure 6: Communities produced by the best-performing algorithm

the recommended results, where the output communities lie in the right part. We can find that gCluSkeleton is the best-performing algorithm on the NCAA football network.

Besides, we can see the scale of each community intuitively from Fig. 6. We can find that gCluSkeleton outputs 8 communities with different sizes. The largest community has 44 members and the smallest one has only 11 members.

5. CONCLUSIONS

CoDAR is a practical tool which explores in-depth knowledge of community detection. On the one hand, it reveals the generalized procedure of community detection to users. On the other hand, it evaluates the performance of different algorithms and recommends the best one to users. Moreover, different display windows under special scenarios intuitively demonstrate the effects of the tool. CoDAR also verifies that our proposed framework of community detection is sound, modularized and easy to be extended. We will improve the scalability of CoDAR in the future.

6. ACKNOWLEDGMENTS

This work was supported by the National Natural Science Foundation of China (No. 61373023, No. 61170064) and the National High Technology Research and Development Program of China (No. 2013AA013204).

7. REFERENCES

[1] J. Huang, H. Sun, Q. Song, H. Deng, and J. Han. Revealing density-based clustering structure from the core-connected tree of a network. *TKDE*, 25(8):1876–1889, 2013.

[2] R. R. Khorasgani, J. Chen, and O. R. Zaïane. Top leaders community detection approach in information networks. In *SNA-KDD*. Citeseer, 2010.

[3] A. Lancichinetti, S. Fortunato, and F. Radicchi. Benchmark graphs for testing community detection algorithms. *Physical review E*, 78(4):046110, 2008.

[4] A. Prat-Pérez, D. Dominguez-Sal, and J.-L. Larriba-Pey. High quality, scalable and parallel community detection for large real graphs. In *WWW*, pages 225–236. ACM, 2014.

[5] U. N. Raghavan, R. Albert, and S. Kumara. Near linear time algorithm to detect community structures in large-scale networks. *Physical Review E*, 76(3):036106, 2007.

[6] M. Wang, C. Wang, J. X. Yu, and J. Zhang. Community detection in social networks: an in-depth benchmarking study with a procedure-oriented framework. *Proceedings of the VLDB Endowment*, 8(10):998–1009, 2015.

[7] J. Yang and J. Leskovec. Defining and evaluating network communities based on ground-truth. In *ICDM*, pages 745–754. IEEE, 2012.

DB-Risk: The Game of Global Database Placement

[Demonstration proposal]

Victor Zakhary Faisal Nawab Divyakant Agrawal Amr El Abbadi
Department of Computer Science
University of California, Santa Barbara
Santa Barbara, CA 93106
{victorzakhary,nawab,agrawal,amr}@cs.ucsb.com

ABSTRACT

Geo-replication is the process of maintaining copies of data at geographically dispersed datacenters for better availability and fault-tolerance. The distinguishing characteristic of geo-replication is the large wide-area latency between datacenters that varies widely depending on the location of the datacenters. Thus, choosing which datacenters to deploy a cloud application has a direct impact on the observable response time. We propose an optimization framework that automatically derives a geo-replication placement plan with the objective of minimizing latency. By running the optimization framework on real placement scenarios, we learn a set of placement optimizations for geo-replication. Some of these optimizations are surprising while others are in retrospect straight-forward. In this demonstration, we highlight the geo-replication placement optimizations through the DB-Risk game. DB-Risk invites players to create different placement scenarios while experimenting with the proposed optimizations. The placements created by the players are tested on real cloud deployments.

Keywords

Geo-replication, transactions, placement

1. INTRODUCTION

Cloud applications strive for a 24/7 service with fast response time. Geo-replication has become necessary to achieve these objectives; a 24/7 service might be disrupted when datacenter-scale outages occur. Geo-replication helps alleviate this disruption by allowing requests to be directed only to operating datacenters. Fast response time is a challenge when the cloud application's user base is dispersed across the world. Geo-replication brings data closer to the user and increases the level of read availability.

When geo-replicating a cloud application, the system administrator is faced with an important design decision: at which datacenters should the data be placed? Cloud providers offer more than a few datacenters for deployment (*e.g.*, Amazon AWS hosts applications in 10 datacenters around the world each with multiple availability zones). With multiple cloud providers, the possibilities for geo-replicated deployments are the subsets of tens of datacenters. The placement decision affects many performance characteristics.

In this work, we focus on the effect of geo-replication placement on the response time for transactional workloads with serializability as the correctness guarantee. The response time of transactions on geo-replicated data is directly affected by the *deployment topology*, which we define as the relative locations of datacenters and the communication latencies between them. The topology affects response time differently for different replication protocols. Our study focuses on majority protocols, but can be applied on centralized protocols, coordination-free techniques [2], and Helios [3]; a recent geo-replication proposal.

We propose an optimization framework to make geo-replication placement decisions. The optimization framework, *framework* for short, constructs a model of the system. The model includes the topology, workload, and user distribution. Then, the model is used in an optimization problem formulation with the objective of minimizing **transaction latency** in addition to adhering to fault-tolerance and quality-of-service guarantees.

The framework has been built to allow *breaking* the rules of the replication protocols. Thus, the framework could yield outcomes with "tweaks" that are not part of the original protocol. Sometimes these tweaks are not feasible. But other times, these tweaks are viable optimizations to the original protocol that will result in better transaction latency. Some of the viable optimizations were more common than others, and upon closer examination it becomes clear that they exemplify a set of best practices, or optimizations, for geo-replication placement. We present three of the optimizations that we have found to be rewarding in geo-replication. The first optimization is quite novel while the other two optimizations were introduced before. The three optimizations, altogether, achieve in some deployments the minimum transaction latency.

We propose the game DB-Risk[1] to demonstrate the challenges in geo-replication placement, and showcase our framework and geo-replication placement optimizations. The players are presented with a geo-replication environment with clients distributed globally. Players then compete by

[1]The game and name are inspired from the famous game "Risk: The Game of Global Domination".

SIGMOD'16, June 26-July 01, 2016, San Francisco, CA, USA
© 2016 ACM. ISBN 978-1-4503-3531-7/16/06...$15.00
DOI: http://dx.doi.org/10.1145/2882903.2899405

placing their replicas at datacenters with the objective of minimizing the transaction response time for clients. The game proceeds in multiple rounds with the opportunity to apply a subset of the geo-replication optimizations to lower the response time. The winner is the player who places replicas to achieve the lowest response time. DB-Risk is augmented with our framework to compare the winner's placement to the calculated optimal placement. We also incorporate a real deployment on Amazon AWS to validate the performance of the chosen placements.

2. BACKGROUND

System model. Our model of geo-replication consists of a topology of datacenters and clients executing transactional workload. Data is fully replicated to a subset of datacenters. Users issue transactions that consist of read and write operations. Each client execute transactions back-to-back. The execution of transactions depends on the replication protocol. We focus in this work on majority based protocols. Next is a description of the variation we use for the majority protocol.

Majority. We adopt a variant of the majority protocol. A client executes a transaction by performing the reads and buffering the writes. Read requests are sent to a majority of datacenters. The highest version read is used. After executing reads and writes a vote request is sent to datacenters. The vote request consists of the read versions and the buffered write operations. Each datacenter, upon receiving a vote request, attempts to lock objects that are being written. Additionally, it verifies that the read versions were not overwritten. If both are successful, the datacenter sends back a positive vote. Otherwise, a negative vote is sent. The client commits the transaction if a majority of positive votes is received and aborts the transaction otherwise. The client sends the decision *to all replicas*. Once a majority acknowledges the receipt of the decision, the transaction terminates. The transaction latency is the time from the beginning of executing operations until terminating the transaction. We define the commit latency as the time spent committing the transaction, which is equivalent to the transaction latency without the time spent reading the data values.

Cost of coordination. A central concern of this work is optimizing transaction latency by finding the best replica placement. In an earlier work, we have found that the sum of transaction latencies at any two datacenters cannot be smaller than the RTT between these datacenters [3].

Related work. Geo-replication and data placement are areas that have undergone extensive research. Recent works study the problem of data placement for geo-replication [1, 4, 5, 8, 9]. Spanstore [8] is the closest work to our optimization framework. It tackles the data placement problem in geo-replication using an optimization formulation. Ping et. al. [4, 5] propose the use of a utility function to derive a placement that balances between speed and availability. Volley [1] analyzes usage logs and leverages an optimization formulation to place data partitions. Unlike our optimization framework, these works do not support a multi-access transactional workload with strong consistency. Sharov [6] optimizes for transactional workloads using leader based protocols. The optimization focuses on the leader placement, the leader and replica roles, and replica location, roles, and the leader. A transactional workload requires more complex coordination between replicas to detect conflicts. Our framework is designed to engage in the design decisions the optimization techniques to be used in the majority based replication protocols, and illuminates unintuitive optimizations to achieve a better performance.

3. GEO-REPLICATION PLACEMENT

Where copies of data are placed is a critical design decision that affects, among others, the performance of the application. It turns out that it is not straight forward to devise a placement strategy on geo-replicated data. The optimal placement depends on the workload patterns, user base, in addition to monetary and even geo-political considerations. However, even in the simple case of a uniform workload with no restrictions, monetary or otherwise, the placement problem is still complex. The reason of this complexity stems from two characteristics: (1) we consider a transactional workload, which require replicas to coordinate to detect conflicts. (2) The topology of replicas in geo-replication is more complex than traditional replication; each link in the topology could have a significantly different communication latency. These two characteristics decides which replication protocol performs better and should be chosen. Even if we have a finite set of replication protocols to consider (we focus here on majority protocols), each protocol comes with many variations. The large design space makes it difficult to know the combination of a placement strategy and replication protocol variations that will lead to the best performance.

Optimization Framework

To address the large space of placements and replication protocol variations, we developed an optimization framework. The framework takes as input the replicas network topology, workload parameters, and availability constraints. It searches through the space of placements and protocol variations and chooses the ones that minimizes transaction's response latency. The straight-forward way to search through the possible space of replication protocol variations is to hard-code as many of them as possible. However, hard-coding restricts the space of possible variations. What we do instead is only hard-code a single variation of each family of protocols. Then, we intentionally allow the optimization framework to break some of the protocol's behavior. It is possible that the resulting "tweaks" are not feasible, leading to violation of correctness. But it is also possible that we arrive to the right tweaks that will optimize the performance of the replication protocol. In our study, we have repeatedly seen a set of optimizations reoccur. Some of them are straight-forward and some of them are surprising. Next, we summarize the derived placement optimizations for geo-replicated systems.

Placement Optimizations

Here we summarize the geo-replication placement optimizations that we learned from the optimization framework. For the rest of this discussion we assume that data is fully replicated.

Commit hand-off. In a fully-replicated system, a client accessing data typically sends the commit request to the local, or closest, replica. Our optimization framework shows that this is not always the best practice in a geo-replicated environment; it is sometimes better to send the commit request to a datacenter other than the local one. For example, consider Figure 1 that shows an example of geo-

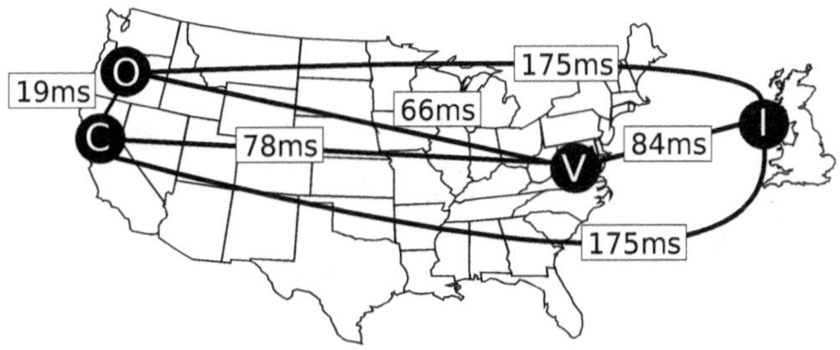

Figure 1: An example of replicating to four datacenters in Oregon (O), Virginia (V), California (C), and Ireland (I)

replication: four datacenters in Oregon (O), Virginia (V), California (C), and Ireland (I). The communication Round-Trip Times (RTTs) between the datacenters are shown in the figure. The RTTs between Ireland and the other datacenters are significantly higher than the remaining RTTs. Assume that a majority protocol is used to commit transactions in this scenario. The commit latency of a majority protocol is two RTTs to the closest majority. Thus, the commit latency of clients in Oregon is $132ms$, in California and Virginia is $156ms$, and in Ireland is $350ms$.

The large latency of clients in Ireland is due to the common convention that driving the transaction commitment from the local datacenter is the best practice. However, running this scenario in our optimization framework shows that this convention is not always true. In fact, clients in Ireland are in a better position sending their commit requests to Virginia. Committing a transaction in Virginia takes $156ms$. And sending the request from Ireland to Virginia and waiting for the decision to be sent back takes $84ms$. This means that the commit latency becomes the sum of the two latencies, which is equal to $240ms$. Compared to the original commit latency, this is a 31% improvement in commit latency of clients in Ireland. An insight from the optimization framework led to an improvement in commit latency with a simple change to the original protocol.

Passive replicas. Our second optimization is a byproduct of the commit hand-off optimization. In the scenario in Figure 1, when applying the hand-off optimization, clients at Ireland send their commit requests to Virginia. Clients in other datacenters send commit requests to their local replicas. This means that the replica at Ireland does not receive commit requests. With this knowledge, it is easy to observe that the demand placed on Ireland is lower than the other datacenters. For most of the time, Ireland will only serve read requests and receive the outcome of transactions and not drive the commitment of transactions. Thus, less resources need to be provisioned in Ireland and more resources need to be provisioned elsewhere.

When the framework recommends the hand-off optimization, it is sometimes accompanied by an interesting side effect. The side effect is that the replica that is not receiving commit requests becomes a *passive replica*. A passive replica is a replica that serves read requests but does not engage in the commit protocol. This means that it does not become part of the majority protocol, but more like a cache of data used for reading. In the example in Figure 1, this means that the majority protocol will involve getting votes only from Oregon, Virginia, and California. The number of replicas to constitute a majority has thus been lowered from three replicas when four datacenters were involved to two replicas now that only three replicas are involved. This makes the commit latency lower, since each replica needs to get votes from only one other replica. This makes the commit latency of Oregon and California $38ms$, of Virginia $132ms$, and of Ireland $216ms$. Making Ireland a passive replica reduced the average latency by 39%. It is important to note that this optimization is allowed in this scenario only if the system is required to tolerate only a single datacenter failure.

Optimistic reading. A conventional majority protocol reads from a majority of replicas to ensure that the most recent version is read. However, it is possible to optimistically read from the local replica only, and then validate the read in a majority of replicas in the commit phase [7]. The choice of whether to read optimistically or from a majority is controlled by a trade-off between the latency of read operations and contention. An optimistic read lowers the read latency but it increases contention because the version at the local replica might be stale. Reading from a majority requires a larger latency but ensures getting the most recent version. Running our optimization framework on various geo-replication scenarios reveals that optimistic reads are more favorable. It turns out that due to the large communication latencies between datacenters, a read from a majority is susceptible to a close contention level to the level when reading optimistically. Thus, there was no significant benefit in reading from a majority compared to reading optimistically, while an optimistic read enjoyed the benefit of a low latency.

4. THE DB-RISK GAME

We propose DB-Risk, a game to motivate thinking about the challenges of data placement in geo-replicated environments. It also showcases the capabilities of our optimization framework and the derived geo-replication placement optimizations. The game is designed to be played by two players to introduce a competitive element. The game assumes a majority protocol is used. An actual deployment of the majority protocol and placement optimizations are deployed on Amazon AWS to validate the players choices.

Summary. In DB-Risk, players place replicas in datacenters around the world with the aim of minimizing the transaction latency. The players also choose from the set of placement optimizations to enhance the transaction latency. The winner is the player with a placement and set of optimizations that achieve the lowest average transaction latency.

Rules. The game begins by showing a map similar to the map shown in Figure 2. The map shows a datacenter icon for each location that a player can choose. These datacenter locations correspond to actual datacenter locations of Amazon AWS. Players take turns choosing datacenters. Each datacenter can be chosen only once; a datacenter cannot host both players. The game proceeds in three rounds. The first round starts after placing data on datacenters. The average latency is calculated and displayed for each player. Before the second round, the players are given the opportunity to choose one *advantage card*. There are four advantage cards: three correspond to the placement optimizations and one card allows coordination-free execution of transactions [2]. The coordination-free card affects a randomly assigned per-

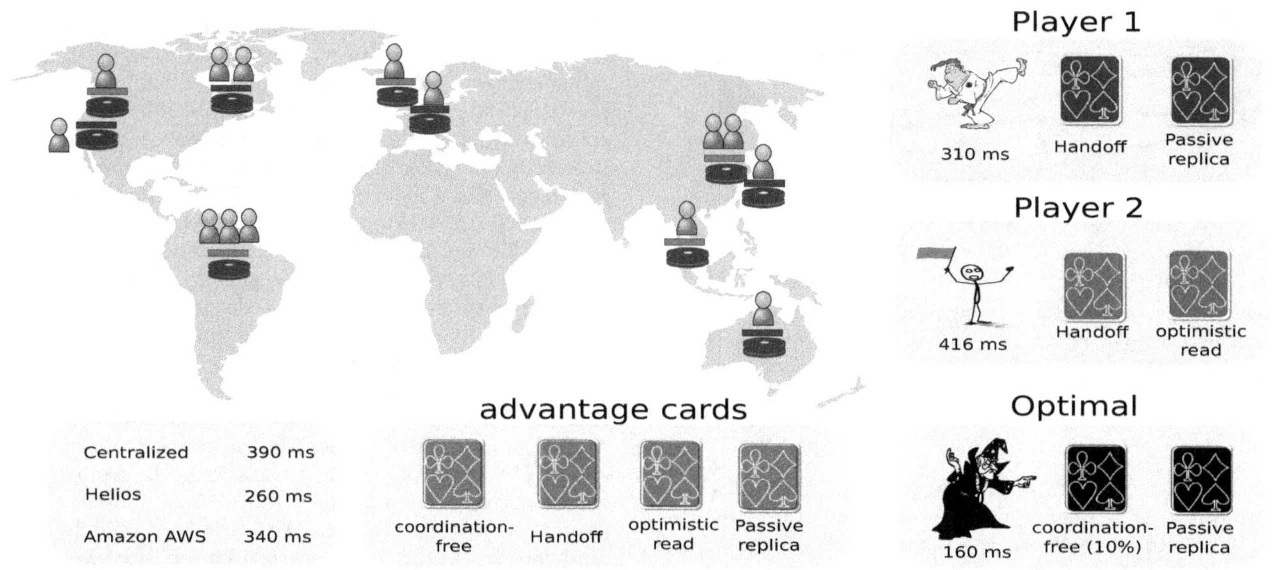

Figure 2: Two players place their application in datacenters and choose optimizations to win with the lowest average transaction latency

centage of the transactions. Then, the new average transaction latency is shown for both players. The third round is identical to the second round. The players choose another placement optimization and the final average transaction latencies are shown. The winner of the game is the player with the lower average transaction latency.

Comparisons. After announcing the winner, the optimization framework shows the optimal placement and the set of placement optimizations used to minimize transaction latency. In addition, the optimization framework also calculates the optimal placement for the centralized protocol and Helios (lower-bound latency) [3], and shows the transaction latency attained by them.

Validation. During the game, the transaction latencies are calculated using the system model in the optimization framework. But, for each game, the winning deployment is validated on a real deployment of the majority protocol and placement optimizations on Amazon AWS.

5. CONCLUSION

In geo-replication, the location of replicas plays a significant role in performance. We have developed an optimization framework that derives the optimal placement of replicas. Unlike prior work, our optimization framework models a transactional workload. Additionally, our framework is designed to engage in the design decisions of the replication protocol. Geo-replication placement optimizations are derived using the optimization framework. Most surprising is the hand-off optimization, which shows that sometimes it is rewarding to send commit requests to a farther datacenter rather than the local one. We proposed DB-Risk, a game to motivate the placement problem and to showcase our optimization framework and placement optimizations.

6. ACKNOWLEDGMENTS

This work is partially supported by NSF Grants 1018637, 1528178, and 1442966.

7. REFERENCES

[1] S. Agarwal et al. Volley: Automated data placement for geo-distributed cloud services. In *NSDI*, 2010.

[2] P. Bailis, A. Fekete, M. J. Franklin, A. Ghodsi, J. M. Hellerstein, and I. Stoica. Coordination avoidance in database systems. In *VLDB*, 2014.

[3] F. Nawab, V. Arora, D. Agrawal, and A. El Abbadi. Minimizing commit latency of transactions in geo-replicated data stores. In *SIGMOD*, 2015.

[4] F. Ping, J.-H. Hwang, X. Li, C. McConnell, and R. Vabbalareddy. Wide area placement of data replicas for fast and highly available data access. In *the International Workshop on Data-intensive Distributed Computing (DIDC)*, 2011.

[5] F. Ping, X. Li, C. McConnell, R. Vabbalareddy, and J.-H. Hwang. Towards optimal data replication across data centers. In *the Distributed Computing Systems Workshops (ICDCSW)*, 2011.

[6] A. Sharov, A. Shraer, A. Merchant, and M. Stokely. Take me to your leader!: online optimization of distributed storage configurations. *Proceedings of the VLDB Endowment*, 8(12):1490–1501, 2015.

[7] R. H. Thomas. A majority consensus approach to concurrency control for multiple copy databases. *ACM TODS*, 1979.

[8] Z. Wu, M. Butkiewicz, D. Perkins, E. Katz-Bassett, and H. V. Madhyastha. Spanstore: Cost-effective geo-replicated storage spanning multiple cloud services. In *SOSP*, 2013.

[9] Z. Ye, S. Li, and X. Zhou. Gcplace: Geo-cloud based correlation aware data replica placement. In *Symposium on Applied Computing*, 2013.

Quegel: A General-Purpose System for Querying Big Graphs

Qizhen Zhang Da Yan James Cheng
Department of Computer Science and Engineering
The Chinese University of Hong Kong
{qzzhang, yanda, jcheng}@cse.cuhk.edu.hk

ABSTRACT

Inspired by Google's Pregel, many distributed graph processing systems have been developed recently to process big graphs. These systems expose a vertex-centric programming interface to users, where a programmer thinks like a vertex when designing parallel graph algorithms. However, existing systems are designed for tasks where most vertices in a graph participate in the computation, and they are not suitable for processing light-workload graph queries which only access a small portion of vertices. This is because their programming model can seriously under-utilize the resources in a cluster for processing graph queries.

In this demonstration, we introduce a general-purpose system for querying big graphs, called **Quegel**, which treats queries as first-class citizens in the design of its computing model. Quegel adopts a novel *superstep-sharing* execution model to overcome the weaknesses of existing systems. We demonstrate it is user-friendly to write parallel graph-querying programs with Quegel's interface; and we also show that Quegel is able to achieve real-time response time in various applications, including the two applications that we plan to demonstrate: point-to-point shortest-path queries and XML keyword search.

1. INTRODUCTION

Graph data are very common in real-life applications nowadays, such as online social networks, mobile communication networks and the Semantic Web. These graphs often contain billions to trillions of vertices and edges, and require dedicated infrastructure for efficient processing. Pregel [7] and Pregel-like systems [1, 3, 11, 10, 6] have become popular in recently years due to their user-friendly programming paradigm and good horizontal scalability. In a Pregel-like system, a programmer only needs to specify the behavior of one generic vertex, and the execution of the specified computation logic on all vertices is automatically scheduled by the system, which also handles other issues such as fault tolerance and horizontal scalability.

However, existing Pregel-like systems are designed for graph-analytic tasks with *heavy-weight* workload, where most part of a graph or the entire graph is accessed. For example, the PageRank algorithm of [7] accesses all vertices in each iteration. However, many real-world applications involve various types of graph querying, whose computation is *light-weight* as they only need to access a small portion of the input graph. For instance, in our collaboration with researchers in a large online shopping platform, we have seen huge demands for querying different aspects of big graphs for all sorts of analysis to boost sales and improve customer experience. A particular example is that they need to frequently examine the *shortest-path distance* between some users in a large network extracted from their online shopping data. In this case, *point-to-point shortest-path* (PPSP) queries studied in this work is much more efficient than *single-source shortest-path* (SSSP) [7] because only the paths between the queried users are of interest.

The importance of querying big graph has also been recognized in some recent work [5]. The work identifies two kinds of systems: (1) those for offline graph analytics (e.g, Pregel and GraphLab) and (2) those for online graph querying, including Horton [9] and G-SPARQL [8]. However, the online systems are only tailored for specific queries, and so far, there lacks a *general-purpose framework* that allows users to easily design distributed algorithms for efficiently answering various types of queries on big graphs.

While we may also answer graph queries using an existing Pregel-like system, this approach suffers from the following weaknesses. There are two solutions to utilizing an existing Pregel-like system for processing queries on demand:

- to process queries one by one, which results in a low throughput since the communication workload of one query is usually too light to fully utilize the network bandwidth and there can be many synchronization barriers; or
- to hardcode a program to process a batch of queries together and to take care of the stop conditions manually, which is not user-friendly and may suffer from the straggler problem towards the end of the processing, since most queries may have finished their processing.

There is also no obvious solution to using graph indexing to process queries in existing Pregel-like systems.

To address the above limitations, we developed **Quegel**, a distributed graph-querying engine, which treats queries as first-class citizens: users only need to write a Pregel-like algorithm for processing a generic query, and the system automatically schedules the processing of multiple incoming queries on demand. As a result, Quegel is able to answer a query as long as it can be processed by a Pregel-style algorithm (but with much better performance). Quegel adopts a novel *superstep-sharing execution model* to effectively utilize the cluster resources, and uses many other optimization techniques to improve system performance and reduce memory consumption. Quegel also provides a convenient inter-

SIGMOD'16, June 26-July 01, 2016, San Francisco, CA, USA
 ISBN 978-1-4503-3531-7/16/06...$15.00
DOI: http://dx.doi.org/10.1145/2882903.2899398

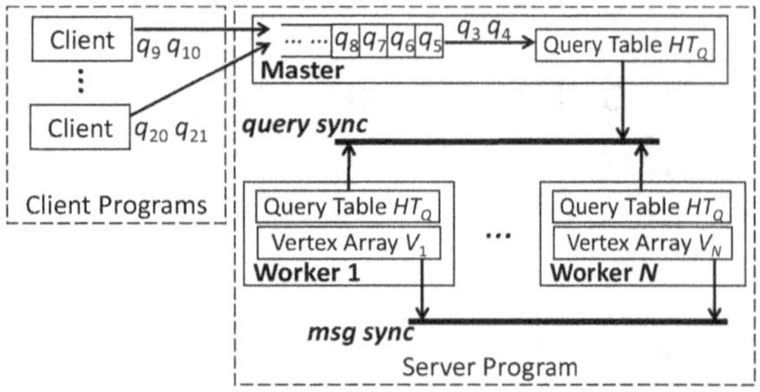

Figure 1: System architecture of Quegel

face for constructing graph indexes, which can significantly improve query performance. To our knowledge, Quegel is the first general-purpose programming framework for querying big graphs at interactive speeds on a distributed cluster.

The rest of this paper is organized as follows. Section 2 introduces the system design of Quegel, and illustrates how the *superstep-sharing execution model* efficiently processes multiple queries on demand, and manages memory space efficiently. Section 3 presents the programming interface of Quegel, and demonstrates it is easy to program graph-querying algorithms in Quegel. Finally, in Section 4, we compare the performance of Quegel with the state-of-the-art vertex-centric systems, and introduce our demonstration plan.

2. THE QUEGEL SYSTEM

Due to space limit, we refer readers to the full paper of Quegel [12] for more details of Quegel.

System Architecture. Quegel follows a Client/Server architecture. There is a server program that is responsible for loading the input graph and processing incoming graph queries. Users submit their queries to the client programs, which then send them to the server. Quegel supports an arbitrary number of clients. The architecture of Quegel is shown in Figure 1. The server program consists of a master and a cluster of workers. The master keeps receiving incoming queries and appending them to a query queue. Queries are periodically fetched from the queue to be processed, whose information is maintained in a query table HT_Q. The HT_Q of master is synchronized to all workers at each communication barrier for processing, as indicated by "query sync" in Figure 1. Meanwhile, vertices on different workers exchange messages with each other, as indicated by "msg sync".

The server program is deployed on top of Hadoop Distributed File System (HDFS). Initially, the server program loads an input graph G from HDFS, i.e., it distributes vertices into main memories of the workers. After the graph is loaded, if users have enabled graph indexing, each worker will build an index from its local vertices. Then, the server program receives incoming queries and processes them with the user-defined computing logic in a similar way as in Pregel. To interact with the server program, users may either type their queries in a client console, or submit a file containing a batch of queries.

Application Scenarios. Quegel adopts a novel *superstep-sharing* execution model to address the problems of existing systems mentioned in Section 1. Before introducing the execution model of Quegel, we first present the design goals of Quegel. Since it is difficult to achieve both high querying throughput and short response time in querying a big graph, we target at two big graph querying scenarios as follows, both of which are common in real world applications.

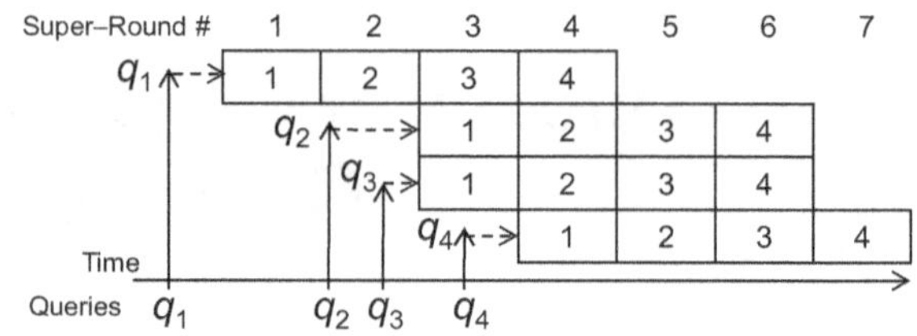

Figure 2: Illustration of superstep-sharing

Scenarios (i): Interactive Querying, in which a user submits a query, checks the result, and then submits another refined query again, until he/she obtains the desired result. In this scenario, a query is expected to be answered at interactive speed. For example, consider a data scientist in a social media company, who interacts with its social network to study user behaviors. However, no existing Pregel-like system can meet this requirement.

Scenarios (ii): Batch Querying, in which a user submits a batch of queries to the system, and these queries need to be answered in a reasonable amount of time. For example, consider the vertex-pair sampling approaches for estimating graph metrics (e.g., diameter, betweenness centrality), where a large number of PPSP queries need to be answered. Quegel is up to two orders of magnitude faster than existing systems for batch querying, and can thus provide more accurate estimates of the various graph metrics.

Superstep-Sharing. To meet the requirements of both scenarios mentioned above, Quegel adopts a novel *superstep-sharing execution model*. In this model, each iteration is called a **super-round**. In a super-round, Quegel evaluates all queries in HT_Q by one superstep (hence the name *superstep-sharing*); while from the perspective of a query, it is processed one superstep after another like in Pregel. Quegel numbers the superstep of each query separately, and thus if two queries are submitted at two different super-rounds, their superstep numbers are different in the same super-round.

Figure 2 illustrates the execution process of superstep-sharing, in which four queries q_1, q_2, q_3 and q_4 are submitted to Quegel at different time. Assume that all the four queries need 4 supersteps to be processed. At the first two super-rounds, there is only one query q_1, which executes two supersteps. Since q_2 and q_3 are received when Quegel is processing super-round 2, at the beginning of super-round 3, they are fetched from the query queue of the master for processing together with q_1 (note that in this super-round, the superstep number of q_1 is 3, while the superstep number of q_2 and q_3 are 1). When Quegel is processing this super-round, q_4 is appended to query queue. When super-round 4 begins, q_4 is fetched for processing along with the other three queries. In this super-round, q_1 executes its last superstep, q_2 and q_3 execute their second superstep, and q_4 executes its first superstep.

When processing a super-round, different workers run in parallel, where each worker evaluates every query $q \in HT_Q$. If q has not been answered yet, the worker performs the user-defined vertex-centric computation on each of its vertices that are activated by q; otherwise, the worker reports the results of q and and releases the resources occupied by q. Messages (resp. aggregator and control information) of all queries are only synchronized at the end of a super-round, as illustrated by "msg sync" (resp. "query sync" for query-specific aggregators and control information) in Figure 1.

Benefits of Superstep-Sharing. For interactive querying where queries are processed one at a time, the superstep-sharing model

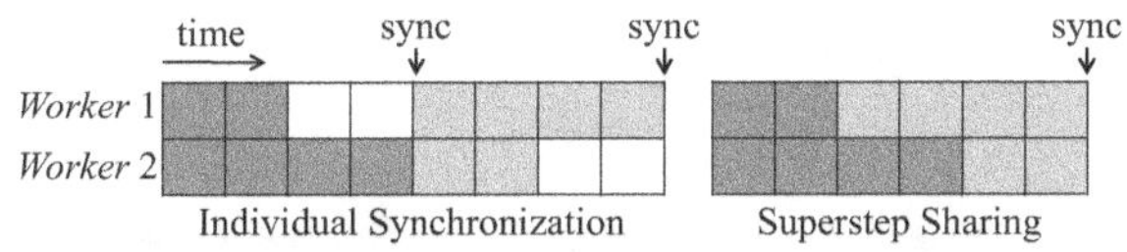

Figure 3: Load balancing of superstep-sharing

uses all the resources of the cluster to process each query as in Pregel. However, Quegel has a shorter query latency since the graph is already memory-resident, and graph indexing is supported.

For batch querying, superstep-sharing combines the workloads of multiple queries together in each super-round to better utilize the cluster resources. This model is more efficient than answering queries one after another (as in existing Pregel-like systems), since only one synchronization barrier is required in each super-round. In other words, in a super-round, the messages of multiple queries can be sent in one batch to better utilize the network bandwidth. The superstep-sharing model also significantly reduces the synchronization cost. Note that since the workload of processing each query is light, performing a synchronization barrier for each query is relatively expensive.

Superstep-sharing also results in a more balanced workload distribution. We explain the reason with the example given in Figure 3, which shows the execution of two queries in one superstep in a cluster of two workers. The first query (darker shading) takes 2 time units on Worker 1 and 4 time units on Worker 2, while the second query (lighter shading) takes 4 time units on Worker 1 and 2 time units on Worker 2. The figure on the left of Figure 3 shows the case where the second query needs to wait for the synchronization of the first query before starting its processing. Thus, 8 time units are required in total. In contrast, by using superstep-sharing as illustrated in the figure on the right of Figure 3, only 6 time units are required.

System Design. Three kinds of data are managed in Quegel: (i) *V-data*, whose value only depends on a vertex, for example, the adjacency list of the vertex. (ii) *VQ-data*, whose value depends on both a vertex and a query, e.g., the distance of a vertex from the source in a PPSP query. (iii) *Q-data*, whose value depends on a query, such as the superstep number of each query.

As shown in Figure 1, in Quegel, each worker keeps a hash table HT_Q that holds the Q-data of every query in evaluation. When a new query q is fetched from the master for processing, its Q-data is inserted into HT_Q of every worker; correspondingly, after q is finished with evaluation, its Q-data is removed from the tables. Similarly, each vertex maintains its VQ-data by a lookup table LUT_v, where $LUT_v[q]$ refers to the VQ-data for query q. To reduce memory consumption, Quegel allocates a VQ-data to a vertex v for query q only if q accesses v in its processing.

3. PROGRAMMING INTERFACE

To write a program in Quegel, a programmer only needs to (1) subclass the base classes of Quegel with proper template arguments, and (2) implement the user-defined functions (UDFs) to specify the application logic. There are two important base classes in Quegel, *Vertex* and *Worker*, which we introduce next.

Vertex Class. The *Vertex* class has an UDF *compute*(.) for programmers to specify the computation behavior of a vertex. In *compute*(.), function *get_query()* may be called to get the content of q, the query currently being processed (e.g., source and destination vertices in a PPSP query). There are also interfaces for users to

```
class BFSVertex:public Vertex<VertexID, int, BFSValue, char, intpair>{
    virtual void compute(MessageContainer& messages){
        if(superstep()==1) {
            broadcast message to neighbors
        }
        else if(qvalue()==INT_MAX){
            //step i marks all vertices (i-1) hops away from src
            qvalue()=superstep()-1;
            if(id == get_query().v2) force_terminate();  //dst reached
            else {
              broadcast message to neighbors
            }
        }
        vote_to_halt();
    }
};

class BFSWorker:public Worker<BFSVertex>{
    virtual BFSVertex* toVertex(char* line){
        parse line to vertex object and return
    }
    virtual intpair toQuery(char* line){
        parse line to (src, dst) and return
    }
}
```

Figure 4: Code snippet of implementation of BFS for PPSP

access the VQ-data of the current vertex (e.g., the vertex value for query q) or update it (e.g., vote the vertex to halt). One may also obtain other Q-data of the current query q, such as q's superstep number, and may call *force_terminate()* to terminate the processing of q. The vertex class takes the form *Vertex*<I, V^Q, V^V, M, Q>, where the five template arguments are given as follows: (1) <*I*> specifies the type (e.g., int) of vertex ID. (2) <V^Q> specifies the type of the VQ-data of a vertex. (3) <V^V> specifies the type of V-data of a vertex. (4) <M> specifies the type of messages exchanged between vertices. (5) <*Q*> specifies the query content type (e.g., for a PPSP query, <*Q*> is a pair of source and destination vertices).

Worker Class. Worker class provides UDFs to specify the format of data input and output, including how to parse a query string into a query content, how to parse an input line from HDFS into a vertex object, how to save the VQ-data of a query (i.e., query results) to HDFS, how to construct a local index from the vertices of a worker, etc. The worker class takes the form of *Worker*<T_{vtx}, T_{idx}>, where <T_{vtx}> specifies the user-defined subclass of *Vertex*, and <T_{idx}> specifies the optional index class.

The interface of Quegel is easy to use. For example, to implement a breadth-first search (BFS) based algorithm for answering PPSP queries, users only need to define the subclasses of *Vertex* and *Worker* as illustrated in Figure 4. The code for the Quegel system and various applications on top of it can be found in [2].

4. THE DEMONSTRATION

In this section, we present our demonstration plan, including the settings of demonstration, and the demonstration scenarios.

4.1 Settings of Demonstration

Environment. We will run the Quegel applications in a cluster of 21 machines (with 1 serving as the master), each with two 2.0GHz Intel Xeon E5-2620 CPUs and 48GB DDR3 RAM. The machines are connected by Gigabite Ethernet, running 64-bit CentOS 6.5 with Linux kernel 2.6.32. The HDFS is from Apache Hadoop 2.7.1.

Applications. To demonstrate the efficiency of Quegel for querying big graphs, we have implemented many graph querying algorithms in Quegel, two of which are given as follows (others include point-to-point reachability queries, terrain shortest path queries, graph keyword queries, etc.). Table 1 shows the real graph datasets we will use in our demonstration.

Table 1: Graph Datasets (M=million)

Dataset	$\|V\|$	$\|E\|$	Max Deg	Avg Deg
Twitter	52.58 M	1963 M	0.78 M	37.34
BTC	164.7 M	772.8 M	1.64 M	4.69
LiveJ	10.69 M	224.6 M	1.05 M	21.01

(a) Datasets for PPSP Queries

Dataset	$\|V\|$	Doc Size	Graph Size
DBLP	81.85M	1.4 GB	4.9 GB
XMark	170.53 M	5.5 GB	14 GB

(b) Datasets for XML Keyword Search

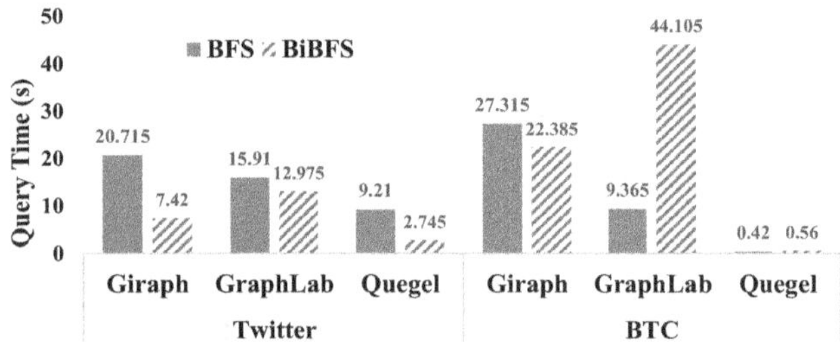

Figure 5: Performance comparison on *Twitter* and *BTC*

(i) PPSP Queries. We implemented three algorithms to answer PPSP queries: BFS, bidirectional BFS (abbr. *BiBFS*) and *Hub*^{2}-*Labeling* (abbr. *Hub*^{2}) [4]. *Hub*^{2} uses a graph index and achieves much better performance than *BFS* and *BiBFS*, and while it is easy to implement *Hub*^{2} using Quegel, it is not clear how to implement it in existing vertex-centric systems.

(ii) XML Keyword Search. This application requires each worker to construct a local inverted index on its vertices, to map each keyword to those vertices that contain it. The indexing can be easily implemented in Quegel, and then queries can be evaluated by starting message propagation from the matched vertices.

System Comparison. To give the audience an idea about the performance of Quegel, we compare Quegel with two state-of-the-art systems, Giraph [1] and GraphLab [3], by running *BFS* and *BiBFS* on the two datasets *Twitter* and *BTC* for solving 20 randomly-generated PPSP queries. Figure 5 shows the average query performance of the systems, which shows that Quegel is much faster than Giraph and GraphLab. In fact, when *Hub*^{2} is used in Quegel, we can answer multiple PPSP queries in a second. More performance results can be found in the full Quegel paper [12].

4.2 Demonstration Scenarios

For the demo, we built a web interface (of brower/server architecture) on top of the Quegel system, and we call the website *Quegel Demo*. A user inputs his/her graph queries into a browser, which transmits them to the web server of *Quegel Demo*. *Quegel Demo* then submits those queries to our Quegel backend, and whenever a query gets answered, *Quegel Demo* sends the results back to the browser for display.

The web interface of *Quegel Demo* allows users to select the desired querying application and dataset to start the Quegel server program. After the program is started, a user can submit queries through a webpage. *Quegel Demo* allows users to customize the visualization module of each specific application. For example, for PPSP queries, we implemented a module for displaying the shortest path (see Figure 6), while for XML keyword search, the visualization module displays the results as tree fragments. We provide over 10 scenarios for demonstration in *Quegel Demo*.

The target audience of this demo includes anyone who is interested in querying big graphs, and *Quegel Demo* supports many attendees to participate at the same time. The participants can simply

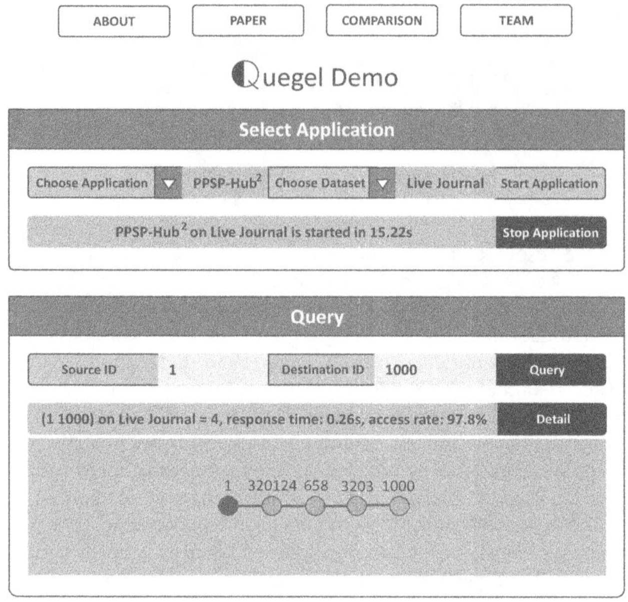

Figure 6: A screenshot of Quegel Demo

select their interested applications on a webpage of *Quegel Demo*, and type their queries into the browser. *Quegel Demo* will process these queries in parallel and respond to users at interactive speeds. Users can see the visualized query results and the reported performance statistics on the webpage.

Acknowledgments. We thank the reviewers for their valuable comments. The authors are supported by the Hong Kong GRF 2150851.

5. REFERENCES

[1] Apache Giraph: http://giraph.apache.org.

[2] Quegel: http://www.cse.cuhk.edu.hk/quegel/.

[3] J. E. Gonzalez, Y. Low, H. Gu, D. Bickson, and C. Guestrin. Powergraph: Distributed graph-parallel computation on natural graphs. In *OSDI*, pages 17–30, 2012.

[4] R. Jin, N. Ruan, B. You, and H. Wang. Hub-accelerator: Fast and exact shortest path computation in large social networks. *CoRR*, abs/1305.0507, 2013.

[5] A. Khan and S. Elnikety. Systems for big-graphs. *PVLDB*, 7(13):1709–1710, 2014.

[6] Y. Lu, J. Cheng, D. Yan, and H. Wu. Large-scale distributed graph computing systems: An experimental evaluation. *PVLDB*, 8(3):281–292, 2014.

[7] G. Malewicz, M. H. Austern, A. J. C. Bik, J. C. Dehnert, I. Horn, N. Leiser, and G. Czajkowski. Pregel: a system for large-scale graph processing. In *SIGMOD*, pages 135–146, 2010.

[8] S. Sakr, S. Elnikety, and Y. He. G-SPARQL: a hybrid engine for querying large attributed graphs. In *CIKM*, pages 335–344, 2012.

[9] M. Sarwat, S. Elnikety, Y. He, and M. F. Mokbel. Horton+: A distributed system for processing declarative reachability queries over partitioned graphs. *PVLDB*, 6(14):1918–1929, 2013.

[10] D. Yan, J. Cheng, Y. Lu, and W. Ng. Blogel: A block-centric framework for distributed computation on real-world graphs. *PVLDB*, 7(14):1981–1992, 2014.

[11] D. Yan, J. Cheng, Y. Lu, and W. Ng. Effective techniques for message reduction and load balancing in distributed graph computation. In *WWW*, pages 1307–1317, 2015.

[12] D. Yan, J. Cheng, M. T. Özsu, F. Yang, Y. Lu, J. C. S. Lui, Q. Zhang, and W. Ng. A general-purpose query-centric framework for querying big graphs. *PVLDB*, 9(7):564–575, 2016.

Introduction to Spark 2.0 for Database Researchers

Michael Armbrust[1], Doug Bateman[1], Reynold Xin[1], Matei Zaharia[1,2]
[1]Databricks, [2] MIT CSAIL
{michael, doug.bateman, rxin, matei}@databricks.com

1. INTRODUCTION

Originally started as an academic research project at UC Berkeley, Apache Spark is one of the most popular open source projects for big data analytics. Over 1000 volunteers have contributed code to the project; it is supported by virtually every commercial vendor; many universities are now offering courses on Spark.

Spark has evolved significantly since the 2010 research paper: its foundational APIs are becoming more relational and structural with the introduction of the Catalyst relational optimizer, and its execution engine is developing quickly to adopt the latest research advances in database systems such as whole-stage code generation.

This tutorial is designed for database researchers (graduate students, faculty members, and industrial researchers) interested in a brief hands-on overview of Spark. This tutorial covers the core APIs for using Spark 2.0, including DataFrames, Datasets, SQL, streaming and machine learning pipelines. Each topic includes slide and lecture content along with hands-on use of a Spark cluster through a web-based notebook environment.

In addition, we will dive into the engine internals to discuss architectural design choices and their implications in practice. We will guide the audience to "hack" Spark by extending its query optimizer to speed up distributed join execution.

2. TARGET AUDIENCE

The target audience for this tutorial is anyone with an interest in Spark and more generally big data processing. The audience is expected to have a basic understanding of database systems, and bring a laptop with Chrome/Safari browser in order to complete the hands-on exercise.

Upon completion of the tutorial, the audience should walk away with a good understanding of the state-of-the-art in Spark in order to build research projects or create educational materials.

3. TUTORIAL OUTLINE

This tutorial is divided into four parts. We first introduce Spark 2.0 and the main programming abstraction it offers, followed by discussions on engine internals. A large fraction of the tutorial features hands-on coding exercises.

SIGMOD '16, June 26–July 1, 2016, San Francisco, CA, USA.

ACM 978-1-4503-3531-7/16/06...$15.00
DOI: http://dx.doi.org/10.1145/2882903.2912565

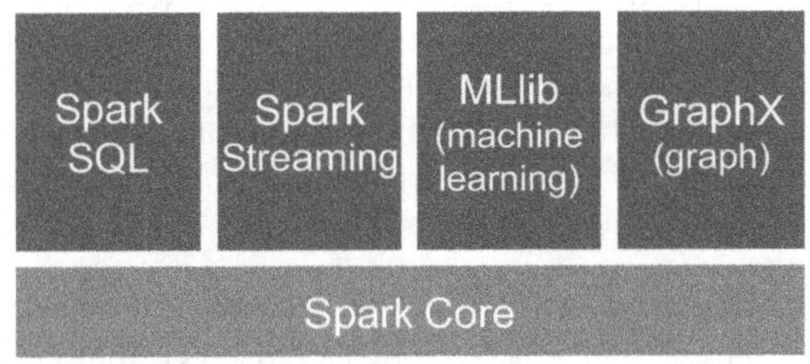

Figure 1: Spark software stack, showing the various libraries implemented over the core engine.

3.1 Spark from an end-user's perspective

We will first introduce Spark, its history, and many of the projects in the Spark ecosystem [6, 3, 5, 1, 4, 2].

We will then focus on the main APIs in Spark 2.0, including the typed Dataset API and the untyped DataFrame API for both interactive data analysis and production data engineering. This module comes with hands-on exercise in the Databricks cloud Spark platform using notebooks.

3.2 Catalyst query optimizer

Catalyst is an extensible optimizer in Spark that builds on the functional programming constructs in Scala. CatalystâĂŹs extensible design had two purposes. First, we wanted to make it easy to add new optimization techniques and features to Spark SQL, especially for the purpose of tackling various problems we were seeing with big data (e.g., semistructured data and advanced analytics). Second, we wanted to enable external developers to extend the optimizer. For example, by adding data source specific rules that can push filtering or aggregation into external storage systems, or support for new data types. Catalyst supports both rule-based and cost-based optimization.

In this module, we will explain the internals of the Catalyst optimizer, and conduct a hands-on exercise to enhance the optimizer to conduct more efficient range joins.

3.3 Streaming and machine learning

This module covers two additional components in Spark: streaming and machine learning.

Structured Streaming is a new stream processing framework in Spark 2.0. It allows users to specify stream processing logic in the same way as batch analytics, and the engine leverages the Catalyst query optimizer to automatically incrementalize the execution on streams.

MLlib is an open-source distributed machine learning library built on Spark. MLlib provides efficient functionality for a wide range of learning settings and includes several underlying statistical, optimization, and linear algebra primitives. Shipped with Spark, MLlib supports several languages and provides a high-level API that leverages SparkâĂŹs rich ecosystem to simplify the development of end-to-end machine learning pipelines.

3.4 Engine internals

This module dives into the execution engine internals, covering some of the recent development in Spark, including runtime code generation, memory management, and scheduling.

4. PRESENTERS - BIOS

Michael Armbrust leads the development of Spark SQL, a project he created in 2014 that became the most popular component of Spark. He received his PhD from UC Berkeley in 2013, and was advised by Michael Franklin, David Patterson, and Armando Fox. His thesis focused on building systems that allow developers to rapidly build scalable interactive applications, and specifically defined the notion of scale independence. His interests broadly include distributed systems, large-scale structured storage and query optimization.

Doug Bateman is the Director of Training at Databricks and teaches advanced Spark classes for Databricks' customers. He has taught 800+ classes on Java, Spring, Hibernate, Python, and Android and 15+ years of software engineering experience.

Reynold Xin is a cofounder and Chief Architect for Spark at Databricks. Prior to Databricks, he was pursuing a PhD at the UC Berkeley AMPLab, advised by Michael Franklin. While at Berkeley, he worked on CrowdDB, Shark and GraphX. He also set the 2014 world record in 100 TB sorting (Daytona Gray), beating the previous 2013 Hadoop record by 30X on per-node efficiency.

Matei Zaharia is an assistant professor of computer science at MIT and CTO of Databricks, the company commercializing Apache Spark. He started the Spark project during his PhD at UC Berkeley. He is broadly interested in large-scale computer systems and networks, and has also contributed to projects including Mesos, Hadoop, Tachyon and Shark. Matei received the 2014 ACM Doctoral Dissertation award for his research on Spark, as well as best paper awards at NSDI and SIGCOMM.

Acknowledgments: We would like to thank Alexandros Labrinidis and Sam Madden for their feedback and help with this tutorial.

5. REFERENCES

[1] M. Armbrust, T. Das, A. Davidson, A. Ghodsi, A. Or, J. Rosen, I. Stoica, P. Wendell, R. Xin, and M. Zaharia. Scaling spark in the real world: performance and usability. *Proceedings of the VLDB Endowment*, 8(12):1840–1843, 2015.

[2] M. Armbrust, R. S. Xin, C. Lian, Y. Huai, et al. Spark SQL: Relational data processing in Spark. In *SIGMOD*, pages 1383–1394, 2015.

[3] J. E. Gonzalez, R. S. Xin, A. Dave, D. Crankshaw, M. J. Franklin, and I. Stoica. Graphx: Graph processing in a distributed dataflow framework. In *OSDI 2014*, pages 599–613.

[4] X. Meng, J. Bradley, B. Yavuz, E. Sparks, S. Venkataraman, D. Liu, J. Freeman, D. Tsai, M. Amde, S. Owen, et al. Mllib: Machine learning in apache spark. *arXiv preprint arXiv:1505.06807*, 2015.

[5] S. Venkataraman, Z. Yang, E. L. Davies Liu, H. Falaki, X. Meng, R. Xin, A. Ghodsi, M. Franklin, I. Stoica, and M. Zaharia. Sparkr: Scaling r programs with spark. In *SIGMOD*, 2016.

[6] R. S. Xin, J. Rosen, M. Zaharia, M. J. Franklin, S. Shenker, and I. Stoica. Shark: SQL and rich analytics at scale. In *SIGMOD 2013*.

Design Tradeoffs of Data Access Methods

Manos Athanassoulis
Harvard University
manos@seas.harvard.edu

Stratos Idreos
Harvard University
stratos@seas.harvard.edu

ABSTRACT

Database researchers and practitioners have been building methods to store, access, and update data for more than five decades. Designing *access methods* has been a constant effort to adapt to the ever changing underlying hardware and workload requirements. The recent explosion in data system designs – including, in addition to traditional SQL systems, NoSQL, NewSQL, and other relational and non-relational systems – makes understanding the tradeoffs of designing access methods more important than ever. Access methods are at the core of any new data system. In this tutorial we survey recent developments in access method design and we place them in the design space where each approach focuses primarily on one or a subset of read performance, update performance, and memory utilization. We discuss how to utilize designs and lessons-learned from past research. In addition, we discuss new ideas on how to build access methods that have tunable behavior, as well as, what is the scenery of open research problems.

1. INTRODUCTION

Access Methods and Data Systems. A skey aspect of all data management systems is the *access methods* they employ. An access method is a collection of *algorithms and data structures for organizing and accessing data* [36]. Finding the proper physical design (through static autotuning [19], online tuning [13], or adaptively [38]) has been a key data management research challenge for several decades. The way we physically organize data on storage devices (disk, flash, memory, caches) defines and restricts the possible ways that we can read and update it. For example, a scan access method in a modern main-memory read optimized column-store consists of an array of dense values and a cache conscious for-loop access pattern [1]. Traditional data management systems access the base data through their scan and index access methods, however, applications, use cases, and the system design itself are becoming more complex. As a result, an increasing number of new access method designs and variations of existing have been proposed.

The recent explosion of applications has led to the development of relational and non-relational data systems typically categorized under the SQL, NoSQL, and newSQL terminology [59]. Regardless how a system is categorized, its core functionality is storing and accessing data. Thus, designing the right access methods still remains a key challenge. Given the broad spectrum of workloads and applications today, it is more important than ever to both learn from past work and to keep inventing new solutions. Helping with this task is exactly the goal of this tutorial.

Design Tradeoffs. A close look at existing proposals on access methods reveals that each is confronted with the same fundamental challenges and design decisions again and again. In particular, there are three quantities and design parameters that researchers always try to minimize: (i) the read overhead (**R**), (ii) the update overhead (**U**), and (iii) the memory (or storage) overhead (**M**), henceforth called the *RUM overheads* [6]. Deciding which overhead(s) to optimize for and to what extent, remains a prominent part of the process of designing a new access method, especially as hardware and workloads change over time. For example, in the 1970s one of the critical aspects of every database algorithm was to minimize the number of random accesses on disk; fast-forward 40 years and a similar strategy is still used, only now we minimize the number of random accesses to main memory. Today, different hardware runs different applications but the concepts and design choices remain the same. New challenges, however, arise from the exponential growth in the amount of data generated and processed, and the wealth of emerging data-driven applications, both stressing existing access methods. The three RUM overheads form a design space with a three-way balance: optimizing for any two overheads negatively impacts the third [6].

Similar tradeoffs are typically observed for access methods designed for domain-specific use cases. We identify three broad classes: (i) high-dimensional data, (ii) time-series data, and (iii) graph data. Typically the relevant workloads are not transactional in the same way that relational and key-value data are required to be.

Tutorial Outline and Goals. This tutorial gives a comprehensive introduction to the design tradeoffs of access methods, discussing the basic methodologies used to optimize for each. Specifically it includes the following sections:

1. Introduction: We start with an introduction of access method design and how this affects data systems design and broadly data management research. We give specific

SIGMOD '16, June 26–July 01, 2016, San Francisco, CA, USA
© 2016 ACM. ISBN 978-1-4503-3531-7/16/06...$15.00
DOI: http://dx.doi.org/10.1145/2882903.2912569

examples both from research and industry (including both startups and established companies).

2. Design Tradeoffs: We dissect the key tradeoffs of access method design: read performance, update performance, and memory. We present the intuition behind the fact that we cannot optimize, at the same time, for all three goals. Orthogonally to whether the access methods are designed for reads, updates, or memory utilization, we highlight that there are common high-level concepts across all three groups: (a) logarithmic design, (b) continuous reorganization, (c) space-efficient design.

3. Logarithmic Design: We start by presenting a common theme among several access methods: their logarithmic design. We cover how such access methods are designed to be optimized for reads [8, 28, 30, 47, 64, 67], for updates [17, 45, 49, 65, 72, 85], and for memory [9, 21, 48, 50, 57, 69].

4. Continuous Reorganization: We continue with another common theme, workload-driven continuous reorganization which can be used either when optimizing for read performance [30, 31, 32, 33, 35, 38, 39, 40, 41, 71] or, with differential updates, for update performance [2, 4, 5, 29, 37, 42, 73, 75].

5. Space-Efficient Designs: We conclude the discussion for the design tradeoffs presenting how space-efficient access methods are used to offer good read performance when the workload permits [11, 15, 16, 22, 63, 66, 82, 83], and how we can trade memory utilization for performance with approximate indexing and data skipping techniques [3, 27, 52, 58, 77, 86].

6. Other Access Method Classes: We dedicate a part of this tutorial to three additional access method classes. In particular, we present the core principles of access method designs for (i) high-dimensional data, (ii) time-series data, and (iii) graph data. We conclude this part by highlighting the RUM tradeoffs in the key solutions for these data types.

7. Open Research Challenges: Finally, we discuss open problems in access method design as they manifest in modern data systems, including ideas about declarative and shape-shifting access methods.

2. DESIGNING ACCESS METHODS

In order to understand the design space, we introduce the audience to the different design elements used in access methods. Typically, each design element offers specific behavior (e.g., read-friendly), however in multiple cases it can be multi-faceted and offer different optimizations. Table 1 shows the classification of the papers we discuss. We discuss three main design elements of access methods, logarithmic design, continuous reorganization, and space efficiency, and we see how each of them affects the read, the update, and the memory overhead. The key point of this presentation is the clustering of the presented access methods in terms of techniques, in order to argue about the fundamental tradeoffs. That way we can learn how to navigate this access method design "space" of read-optimized, update-optimized and memory-optimized designs.

2.1 Logarithmic Design

We first introduce the generic concept of logarithmic design used by several data structures, like B-Trees, Tries and variations of them. The key idea is to organize metadata in a way that the search cost of a specific element is logarithmic to the size of the dataset. We differentiate between access methods with logarithmic design optimized for reads and for updates.

Optimizing Reads. Tree-based access methods are typically optimized for read performance. Logarithmic-time structures such as B-Trees [30], and Tries [28, 47, 61] offer fast read access but increase space overhead. Tries, in particular, typically suffer from space inefficiency. Adaptive Radix Tree [47] overcomes the shortcoming of prior tries by offering update-friendly, and space-efficient trie indexing. The key insight is that instead of following a common node design throughout the tree, each node is locally adapted to what is needed based on the density of the domain for the corresponding values. Such data structures are the state-of-the-art used by widely adopted commercial or open-source data management systems. SB-Tree [64] is designed to support high-performance sequential disk access for long range retrievals. It assumes an array of disks from which it retrieves data or intermediate nodes should they not be in memory, by employing multi-page reads during sequential access to any node level below the root. The bounded disorder access method is introduced as a generic framework for access methods [52, 53]. The method aims at increasing the ratio of file size to index size (i.e., to decrease the size of the index) by building a shallow tree to create range partitioning in wide ranges and using hashing for distributing the keys in a multi-bucket node, corresponding to each range. The bounded disorder access method does not decrease the index size too aggressively for good reason; since, by doing that it would cause more random accesses on the storage medium, which is assumed to be traditional hard disks. On the contrary, the goal is to guarantee that point queries would get read overhead similar to the what a hash index offers, and range queries would get read overhead similar to what a B^+-Tree index offers.

Optimizing Updates. We then continue to discuss how logarithmic access methods can be used to efficiently treat updates. Logarithmic access methods for updates typically follow a hierarchical log-structured approach. When the top level receives enough updates it is merged with lower levels and these updates gradually propagate in the tree. A prime example which has been used as inspiration for multiple follow-up approaches is the Log-Structure Merge Tree (LSM-Tree) [65]. An LSM-Tree is comprised of a number of exponentially growing levels; each level is k times larger than the previous. Incoming data are buffered and when the buffer is filled they are sorted and written on the first level of the tree. When k such buffers accumulate, the sorted buffers are merged and written out in the next level, a process that keeps repeating. That way, the number of physical writes per insert is kept low and the typically efficient sequential write on the device can be exploited. More recently, a number of access methods use the logarithmic method to offer a tradeoff between reads and updates [9, 37, 49, 72, 75, 85]. In addition to LSM [65], the Partitioned B-tree (PBT) [29], and the Positional Delta Tree (PDT) [37] offer good performance under updates but increase the read costs and the space overhead. Fractal-Tree and FD-Tree [9, 49] use fractional cascading [20] to restrict the number of reads to one per level. LSM-Trie [85] merges less greedily by using T substructures in each level. That way it reduces write-amplification by a factor of T, at the expense of losing the ability to do range-queries. BigTable uses LSM-Trees

	Logarithmic Design	*Continuous Reorganization*	*Space Efficient*
Read	Trees/Tries/Skiplists [8, 28, 30, 47, 64, 67]	Cracking/Adaptive Indexing [30, 31, 32, 33, 35, 38, 39, 40, 41, 71]	Bitmaps/Hash Index [11, 15, 16, 22, 63, 66, 82, 83]
Update	Log-Structured Trees [17, 45, 49, 65, 72, 85]	Differential Updates [2, 4, 5, 29, 37, 42, 73, 75]	
Memory	Cache Optimizations [9, 21, 48, 50, 57, 69]		Approximate/Data Skipping [3, 27, 52, 58, 77, 86]

Table 1: Classification of access method designs. Each row corresponds to the main optimization goal and each column corresponds to the underlying design element. Some approaches may fit in multiple cells; we discuss this in detail in the tutorial content but for simplicity we list them in the cell that fits the motivation of each design.

with a fixed size ratio equal to ten between adjacent levels [17]. Bigtable also uses Bloom filters to avoid reading unnecessary levels. These Bloom filters are tuned statically and uniformly across levels, a decision which can be further optimized with careful tuning. In addition, Cassandra [46], LOCS [81], VT-Tree [75], and bLSM [72] build on top of BigTable, LevelDB, and LSM-Trees to provide logarithmic access method design. LOCS [81] is a version of LevelDB that utilizes SSD parallelism. VT-Tree [75] avoids repeatidly writing sorted data by stitching non-overlapping runs. bLSM [72] restricts the number of levels, restricting read and write performance irrespectively of the workload.

Optimizing for Memory. Several approaches leverage knowledge about the memory hierarchy. Fractal Prefetching B^+-Trees [21] use different node sizes for disk-based and in-memory processing in order to have the optimal for both cases. Cache-sensitive B^+-Trees [69] physically cluster sibling nodes together to reduce the number of cache misses, and decrease the node size using offsets rather than pointers. SB-Trees [64] operate in an analogous way when the index is disk-based, while BW-Tree [48] and Masstree [57] present a number of optimizations related to cache memory, main memory and flash-based secondary storage. SILT [50] combines write-optimized logging, read-optimized immutable hashing, and, a sorted store, carefully designed to balance the tradeoffs of the various memory levels.

2.2 Continuous Reorganization

In the next part we present the notion of continuous reorganization, which we see in many workload-driven approaches. This approach is taken by query-driven adaptive indexing and by differential updates. While the goal of the adaptive indexing is classically optimizing for read performance, the latter aims at offering efficient updates.

Optimizing Reads. Adaptive indexes are flexible data structures designed to actively balance the tradeoffs. Most existing data structures provide tunable parameters that can be used to balance the tradeoffs offline, however, adaptive data structures balance the tradeoffs online across a larger area of the design space.

Notable proposals are Database Cracking [38], which reorganizes the data in memory to match how queries access data, and adaptive indexing [31, 33] that follows the same principle as database cracking by focusing the index optimization on key ranges used in actual queries. The hybrid, Adaptive Merging [41] balances the read performance versus the overhead of creating an index. Although much more flexible than traditional data structures, existing adaptive data structures cannot cover the whole tradeoff spectrum as they are typically designed for a particular type of hardware and application.

Optimizing Updates. Differential files is the first access method that proposed to store only differential updates instead of in-place updates [73]. The fundamental idea is to consolidate updates and apply them in bulk.

Differential updates have been further studied in the context of updating analytical datasets with the stepped-merge algorithm [42] and the Materialized Sort-Merge (MaSM) [4, 5] algorithm. The stepped-merge algorithm stores updates lazily by maintaining updates in memory in sorted runs, and eventually forming a B^+-Tree of these updates using an external merge-sort. MaSM operates at a similar level, where updates are kept in sorted runs on flash devices and merged only once more before being migrated to the main data, forming large immutable sorted runs. The stepped-merge approach aims at minimizing random I/O requests. On the other hand, the MaSM algorithms focus on minimizing memory consumption and unnecessary writes on flash at the expense of more, yet efficient, random read I/O requests.

2.3 Space-Efficient Designs

The third category to discuss is the space-efficient design elements. We distinguish between designs that (i) have small size but they support fewer types of queries, (ii) have small size because they exploit underlying data organization, and (iii) offer approximate indexing.

Optimizing Reads. Hash Indexing is a typical example of an access method that has small size because it trades functionality (i.e., trade how large is the variety of types of queries it efficiently supports, for size). Next, we discuss bitmap indexing. It is typically used for large data sets. It leverages fast bitwise operations [15, 16, 63, 66, 82], and, today, is commonly used for a number of applications ranging from scientific data management [83] to analytics and data warehousing [18, 55, 70, 78, 79, 84]. Bitmap indexes are utilized by several popular database systems, including open-source systems like PostgreSQL and commercial systems like Oracle [74], SybaseIQ [55, 66], and DB2 [14]. While bitmap indexes typically are designed for read performance, UpBit offers efficient updates at the expense of additional metadata and a small penalty in read performance [7].

Optimizing for Memory. We discuss two main categories for access methods that optimize for memory size by exploiting existing structure of data (due to data generation or data preparation): data skipping and approximate indexing.

Existing structure in data can be utilized by light-weight access methods that can skip touching non-qualifying data via simple checks. At its core, data skipping is a form of scan enhancement. Zonemaps [27, 68, 80, 86] and Column Imprints [77] are prime examples where we maintain metadata for zones of a column, such as min/max information, and a scan uses that metadata to decide whether to scan a zone or not. Such approaches work quite well when data is clustered or fully sorted.

Approximate indexing capitalizes on existing structure of the data in a similar way, but it can be equally efficiently used both for point reads, and for range queries. BF-Tree [3] implements approximate indexing using probabilistic data structures like Bloom filters [11] in order to be able to tune accuracy of the index as a function of the size of the index structure. In addition to Bloom filters, approximate indexing can use other probabilistic data structures like quotient filters [10] and cuckoo filters [26].

3. OTHER ACCESS METHOD CLASSES

In this tutorial we primarily focus on the design elements and tradeoffs of access methods in one-dimensional, key-value or relational data. However, there is a wealth of use cases that face similar tradeoffs and design decisions and require different, typically specialized solutions. We present a representative subset.

First, spatial and other high-dimensional data require access methods that can navigate efficiently a high-dimensional space addressing the "curse of dimensionality" in the context of access methods [56]. While this dimension is not present for one-dimensional data, most of the other observations and design decisions are shared. A second class is time-series data. While time-series can be represented and stored by relational systems, typically specialized time and data series systems offer better performance by taking into account the fundamental characteristics of time series: there is always a sorted dimension (time or simply measurement id), and data are appended either in the form of new – more recent – data items, or new data series. A third class that we identify is access methods for graph based data. We see similar tradeoffs between read, update, and memory performance for all three classes, having however, a varying degree of similarity to the design elements we outline in this tutorial.

3.1 High-Dimensional Access Methods

Spatial and other high-dimensional data (two or more dimensions) have long been attracting specialized solutions. A key insight which has been used as the baseline to build upon is R-Trees [34] which use a hierarchy of minimum bounding rectangles (MBR). An R-Tree shares the main properties of a B^+-Tree: it is a balanced search tree and it is designed for storage on disk. As the number of dimensions increases the efficiency of an R-Tree is dramatically reduced facing the "curse of dimensionality". Similarly to the case of access methods for uni-dimensional data, access methods for high-dimension data face the RUM tradeoffs. Typically, we cannot quantify the read cost with accuracy and we rely on experimental estimations [12]. Due to the aforementioned "curse of dimensionality", however, it often makes sense to break the space into small MBRs in order to have less overlap, leading to more metadata needed for the indexing structure, facing one of the RUM tradeoffs. On the other hand, in this case updating the index is more expensive. A high-dimensional update-friendly access method typically allows for higher overlap between MBRs, making, as a result, reads more expensive, facing yet again, a RUM tradeoff. After the initial proposal of R-Trees, a number of follow up approaches have been proposed, offering domain specific optimizations and a different designs in terms of the balance of RUM tradeoffs, surveyed in detail [12, 56, 60, 62].

3.2 Time-Series Access Methods

The key insight for efficient time series data processing is the representation of the series through segmented means [44, 87], which allowed for space-efficient representation at the expense of accuracy. Using this representation allowed Lin et al. [51] to introduce the Symbolic Aggregate approXimation (SAX), which in turn was later extended to an indexable representation called iSAX [76]. The main challenge iSAX faces is that of building time. In order to address the long index building time ADS follows the approach of query-driven *continuous reorganization* to offer fast build time with small memory footprint at the expense of gradually decreasing query latency [88], an approach that manages to offer overall better workload latency as it cleverly takes into account past queries to add structure gradually. The updates in time-series workloads are significantly different than in relational systems. Typically, the aforementioned approaches treat updates that are in effect new time-series in a large collection of time series leaving old data unaffected and requiring append-only style of updates. Irrespectively of the update scheme, both iSAX and ADS add indexing metadata in order to facilitate read queries making the update more expensive; in essence optimizing for read performance at the expense of both index size and update overhead.

3.3 Graph Access Methods

In graph storage systems we do not typically have a clear distinction between the access methods and the system. The reason is twofold; first, the graph representation plays a big role in performance and each representation may require a very different way to access the data; second, there has been a much smaller effort in standardization when compared with relational systems, hence allowing more native solutions which do not adhere to a global standard. However, the increased interest in graph-based data analysis has lead to the development of a number of approaches that face similar tradeoffs than the ones described in this tutorial.

Similar to the time-series data, graph data are heavily impacted by the data representation. A space efficient graph representation is the compressed spared row (CSR) representation [25] which typically offers immutable data, a key difference from relational data. LLAMA, a recently proposed graph analytics tool, however, allows operating on multi-version CSR data, in essence allowing operating on graphs in the presence of incremental data ingest and mutation [54]. LLAMA in essence exchanges additional storage needs (multiple versions) for efficient support of updates balancing off the RUM tradeoffs in a similar way that RUM Conjecture anticipates them to balance for any access method.

Summary. In this section, we briefly summarize the core design decisions for each access method class, demonstrating that similar tradeoffs as with one-dimensional data do exist. However, covering extensively the design choices and the tradeoffs of access methods of these three classes requires a separate detailed study.

4. OPEN PROBLEMS

The final part of the tutorial presents open problems. A recurring theme of this tutorial is that by studying and classifying all the access method designs, we identify different strategies to achieve a specific optimization goal, e.g., optimize for read performance. In fact there are two fundamentally different ways to reach a static point in the read/update/memory design space: either by using a static design, or by using an adaptive design which eventually leads to the desired design point. A number of new research directions build upon this concept. For example, *how can we build access methods that support a dynamic optimization goal, which is reached either by a static or an adaptive to the workload design [6, 43]?* In addition, *can we build an "access method design optimizer" to help us choose the right access method given specific hardware and workload properties [6]?* Similar directions are taken at the system level. For example, *can we build a declarative storage engine that does not have to chose between being either row-oriented or column-oriented [23, 24]?* In the final part of the tutorial, we discuss these open problems and we highlight opportunities for innovation.

5. BIOGRAPHIES

Manos Athanassoulis is a postdoctoral researcher fellow at DASlab, the Data Systems Laboratory, at Harvard SEAS. Manos works on designing data systems and access methods for dynamic environments that workload and hardware constantly change. Manos received his undergraduate and Masters' degree from the University of Athens, Greece, and his Ph.D. from Ecole Polytechnique Fédérale de Lausanne, Switzerland. In 2011 he interned at IBM Research, New York. Manos is the recipient of a Postdoc Mobility Fellowship from the Swiss National Science Foundation, a "Best of VLDB" selection for 2010, and an IBM Ph.D. Fellowship.

Stratos Idreos is an assistant professor of Computer Science at Harvard University where he leads DASlab, the Data Systems Laboratory, at Harvard SEAS. Stratos works on data systems architectures with emphasis on designing systems for big data exploration. For his doctoral work on Database Cracking, Stratos won the 2011 ACM SIGMOD Jim Gray Doctoral Dissertation award and the 2011 ERCIM Cor Baayen award as "most promising European young researcher in computer science and applied mathematics" from the European Research Council on Informatics and Mathematics. In 2010 he was awarded the IBM zEnterpise System Recognition Award by IBM Research, and in 2011 he won the VLDB Challenges and Visions best paper award. In 2015 he received an NSF CAREER award and the 2015 IEEE TCDE Early Career Award from the IEEE Technical Committee on Data Engineering.

Acknowledgments. We thank the reviewers and the members of DASlab for their valuable feedback. This work is supported by SNSF Grant No. P2ELP2_158936 and by NSF Grant No. IIS-1452595.

6. REFERENCES

[1] D. J. Abadi et al. The Design and Implementation of Modern Column-Oriented Database Systems. *Found. Trends Databases*, 5(3):197–280, 2013.

[2] D. Agrawal, D. Ganesan, R. Sitaraman, Y. Diao, and S. Singh. Lazy-Adaptive Tree: An Optimized Index Structure for Flash Devices. *PVLDB*, 2(1):361–372, 2009.

[3] M. Athanassoulis and A. Ailamaki. BF-Tree: Approximate Tree Indexing. *PVLDB*, 7(14):1881–1892, 2014.

[4] M. Athanassoulis, S. Chen, A. Ailamaki, P. B. Gibbons, and R. Stoica. MaSM: Efficient Online Updates in Data Warehouses. In *SIGMOD*, 2011.

[5] M. Athanassoulis, S. Chen, A. Ailamaki, P. B. Gibbons, and R. Stoica. Online Updates on Data Warehouses via Judicious Use of Solid-State Storage. *TODS*, 40(1), 2015.

[6] M. Athanassoulis, M. S. Kester, L. M. Maas, R. Stoica, S. Idreos, A. Ailamaki, and M. Callaghan. Designing Access Methods: The RUM Conjecture. In *EDBT*, 2016.

[7] M. Athanassoulis, Z. Yan, and S. Idreos. UpBit: Scalable In-Memory Updatable Bitmap Indexing. In *SIGMOD*, 2016.

[8] R. Bayer and K. Unterauer. Prefix B-trees. *TODS*, 2(1):11–26, 1977.

[9] M. A. Bender, M. Farach-Colton, J. T. Fineman, Y. R. Fogel, B. C. Kuszmaul, and J. Nelson. Cache-Oblivious Streaming B-trees. In *SPAA*, 2007.

[10] M. A. Bender et al. Don't Thrash: How to Cache Your Hash on Flash. *PVLDB*, 5(11):1627–1637, 2012.

[11] B. H. Bloom. Space/Time Trade-offs in Hash Coding with Allowable Errors. *CACM*, 13(7):422–426, 1970.

[12] C. Böhm, S. Berchtold, amd D. A. Keim. Searching in High-dimensional Spaces: Index Structures for Improving the Performance of Multimedia Databases. *Comp. Surv.*, 33(3):322–373, 2001.

[13] N. Bruno and S. Chaudhuri. An Online Approach to Physical Design Tuning. In *ICDE*, 2007.

[14] M. Cain and K. Milligan. IBM DB2 for i indexing methods and strategies. *IBM White Paper*, 2011.

[15] C.-Y. Chan and Y. E. Ioannidis. Bitmap index design and evaluation. *SIGMOD Rec.*, 27(2):355–366, 1998.

[16] C.-Y. Chan and Y. E. Ioannidis. An efficient bitmap encoding scheme for selection queries. *SIGMOD Rec.*, 28(2):215–226, 1999.

[17] F. Chang et al. Bigtable: A Distributed Storage System for Structured Data. In *OSDI*, 2006.

[18] S. Chaudhuri and U. Dayal. An Overview of Data Warehousing and OLAP Technology. *SIGMOD Rec.*, 26(1):65–74, 1997.

[19] S. Chaudhuri and V. R. Narasayya. An Efficient Cost-Driven Index Selection Tool for Microsoft SQL Server. In *VLDB*, 1997.

[20] B. Chazelle and L. Guibas. Fractional Cascading: I. A Data Structuring Technique. *Algorithmica*, 1(2):133–162, 1986.

[21] S. Chen, P. B. Gibbons, T. C. Mowry, and G. Valentin. Fractal prefetching B+-Trees. In *SIGMOD*, 2002.

[22] G. Cormode and S. Muthukrishnan. An improved data stream summary: The count-min sketch and its applications. *Journal of Algorithms*, 55(1):58–75, 2005.

[23] P. Cudré-Mauroux, E. Wu, and S. Madden. The Case for RodentStore: An Adaptive, Declarative Storage System. In *CIDR*, 2009.

[24] J. Dittrich and A. Jindal. Towards a One Size Fits All Database Architecture. In *CIDR*, 2011.

[25] J. Dongarra, P. Koev, X. Li, J. Demmel, and H. van der Vorst. 10. Common Issues. In *Templates for the Solution of Algebraic Eigenvalue Problems: A Practical Guide*, page 22. 2000.

[26] B. Fan, D. G. Andersen, M. Kaminsky, and M. Mitzenmacher. Cuckoo Filter: Practically Better Than Bloom. In *CoNEXT*, 2014.

[27] P. Francisco. The Netezza Data Appliance Architecture: A Platform for High Performance Data Warehousing and Analytics. *IBM Redbooks*, 2011.

[28] E. Fredkin. Trie memory. *CACM*, 3(9):490–499, 1960.

[29] G. Graefe. Sorting And Indexing With Partitioned B-Trees. In *CIDR*, 2003.

[30] G. Graefe. Modern B-Tree Techniques. *Found. Trends Databases*, 3(4):203–402, 2011.

[31] G. Graefe, F. Halim, S. Idreos, H. Kuno, and S. Manegold. Concurrency control for adaptive indexing. *PVLDB*, 5(7):656–667, 2012.

[32] G. Graefe, F. Halim, S. Idreos, H. A. Kuno, S. Manegold, and B. Seeger. Transactional support for adaptive indexing. *VLDBJ*, 23(2):303–328, 2014.

[33] G. Graefe and H. Kuno. Self-selecting, self-tuning, incrementally optimized indexes. In *EDBT*, 2010.
[34] A. Guttman. R-Trees: A Dynamic Index Structure for Spatial Searching. In *SIGMOD*, 1984.
[35] F. Halim, S. Idreos, P. Karras, and R. H. C. Yap. Stochastic Database Cracking: Towards Robust Adaptive Indexing in Main-Memory Column-Stores. *PVLDB*, 5(6):502–513, 2012.
[36] J. M. Hellerstein, M. Stonebraker, and J. R. Hamilton. Architecture of a Database System. *Found. Trends Databases*, 1(2):141–259, 2007.
[37] S. Héman, M. Zukowski, and N. J. Nes. Positional update handling in column stores. In *SIGMOD*, 2010.
[38] S. Idreos, M. L. Kersten, and S. Manegold. Database Cracking. In *CIDR*, 2007.
[39] S. Idreos, M. L. Kersten, and S. Manegold. Updating a cracked database. In *SIGMOD*, 2007.
[40] S. Idreos, M. L. Kersten, and S. Manegold. Self-organizing tuple reconstruction in column-stores. In *SIGMOD*, 2009.
[41] S. Idreos, S. Manegold, H. Kuno, and G. Graefe. Merging What's Cracked, Cracking What's Merged: Adaptive Indexing in Main-Memory Column-Stores. *PVLDB*, 4(9):586–597, 2011.
[42] H. V. Jagadish, P. P. S. Narayan, S. Seshadri, S. Sudarshan, and R. Kanneganti. Incremental Organization for Data Recording and Warehousing. In *VLDB*, 1997.
[43] O. Kennedy and L. Ziarek. Just-In-Time Data Structures. In *CIDR*, 2015.
[44] E. J. Keogh, K. Chakrabarti, M. J. Pazzani, and S. Mehrotra. Dimensionality Reduction for Fast Similarity Search in Large Time Series Databases. *KAIS*, 3(3):263–286, 2001.
[45] B. C. Kuszmaul. A Comparison of Fractal Trees to Log-Structured Merge (LSM) Trees. *White Paper*, 2014.
[46] A. Lakshman and P. Malik. Cassandra - A Decentralized Structured Storage System. *SIGOPS Op. Sys. Rev.*, 44(2):35–40, 2010.
[47] V. Leis, A. Kemper, and T. Neumann. The Adaptive Radix Tree: ARTful Indexing for Main-Memory Databases. In *ICDE*, 2013.
[48] J. J. Levandoski, D. B. Lomet, and S. Sengupta. The Bw-Tree: A B-tree for new hardware platforms. In *ICDE*, 2013.
[49] Y. Li, B. He, J. Yang, Q. Luo, K. Yi, and R. J. Yang. Tree Indexing on Solid State Drives. *PVLDB*, 3(1-2):1195–1206, 2010.
[50] H. Lim, B. Fan, D. G. Andersen, and M. Kaminsky. SILT: a memory-efficient, high-performance key-value store. In *SOSP*, 2011.
[51] J. Lin, E. J. Keogh, S. Lonardi, and B. Y.-c. Chiu. A symbolic representation of time series, with implications for streaming algorithms. In *DMKD*, 2003.
[52] W. Litwin and D. B. Lomet. The Bounded Disorder Access Method. In *ICDE*, 1986.
[53] D. B. Lomet. A simple bounded disorder file organization with good performance. *TODS*, 13(4):525–551, 1988.
[54] P. Macko, V. J. Marathe, D. W. Margo, and M. I. Seltzer. LLAMA: Efficient graph analytics using Large Multiversioned Arrays. In *ICDE*, 2015.
[55] R. MacNicol and B. French. Sybase IQ Multiplex - Designed For Analytics. In *VLDB*, 2004.
[56] Y. Manolopoulos, A. Nanopoulos, A. N. Papadopoulos, and Y. Theodoridis. *R-Trees: Theory and Applications*. Springer, 2006.
[57] Y. Mao, E. Kohler, and R. T. Morris. Cache craftiness for fast multicore key-value storage. In *EuroSys*, 2012.
[58] G. Moerkotte. Small Materialized Aggregates: A Light Weight Index Structure for Data Warehousing. In *VLDB*, 1998.
[59] C. Mohan. Tutorial: An In-Depth Look at Modern Database Systems. In *EDBT*, 2014.
[60] M. F. Mokbel, T. M. Ghanem, and W. G. Aref. Spatio-Temporal Access Methods. *IEEE DEBULL*, 26(2):40–49, 2003.
[61] D. R. Morrison. PATRICIA - Practical Algorithm To Retrieve Information Coded in Alphanumeric. *Journal of the ACM*, 15(4):514–534, 1968.
[62] L.-V. Nguyen-Dinh, W. G. Aref, and M. F. Mokbel. Spatio-Temporal Access Methods: Part 2 (2003 - 2010). *IEEE DEBULL*, 33(2):46–55, 2010.
[63] P. E. O'Neil. Model 204 Architecture and Performance. In *HPTS*, 1987.
[64] P. E. O'Neil. The SB-Tree: An Index-Sequential Structure for High-Performance Sequential Access. *Acta Informatica*, 29(3):241–265, 1992.
[65] P. E. O'Neil, E. Cheng, D. Gawlick, and E. J. O'Neil. The log-structured merge-tree (LSM-tree). *Acta Informatica*, 33(4):351–385, 1996.
[66] P. E. O'Neil and D. Quass. Improved query performance with variant indexes. *SIGMOD Rec.*, 26(2):38–49, 1997.
[67] W. Pugh. Skip lists: a probabilistic alternative to balanced trees. *CACM*, 33(6):668–676, 1990.
[68] V. Raman et al. DB2 with BLU acceleration: so much more than just a column store. *PVLDB*, 6(11):1080–1091, 2013.
[69] J. Rao and K. A. Ross. Making B+- trees cache conscious in main memory. In *SIGMOD*, 2000.
[70] P. Russom. High-Performance Data Warehousing. *TDWI Best Practices Report*, 2012.
[71] F. M. Schuhknecht, A. Jindal, and J. Dittrich. The Uncracked Pieces in Database Cracking. *PVLDB*, 7(2):97–108, 2013.
[72] R. Sears and R. Ramakrishnan. bLSM: A General Purpose Log Structured Merge Tree. In *SIGMOD*, 2012.
[73] D. G. Severance and G. M. Lohman. Differential files: their application to the maintenance of large databases. *TODS*, 1(3):256–267, 1976.
[74] V. Sharma. Bitmap Index vs. B-tree Index: Which and When? *Oracle White Paper*, 2005.
[75] P. Shetty, R. P. Spillane, R. Malpani, B. Andrews, J. Seyster, and E. Zadok. Building Workload-Independent Storage with VT-trees. In *FAST*, 2013.
[76] J. Shieh and E. J. Keogh. \emph{i}SAX: indexing and mining terabyte sized time series. In *SIGKDD*, 2008.
[77] L. Sidirourgos and M. L. Kersten. Column Imprints: A Secondary Index Structure. In *SIGMOD*, 2013.
[78] K. Stockinger. Bitmap Indices for Speeding Up High-Dimensional Data Analysis. In *DEXA*, 2002.
[79] M. Stonebraker et al. C-Store: A Column-oriented DBMS. In *VLDB*, 2005.
[80] L. Sun, M. J. Franklin, S. Krishnan, and R. S. Xin. Fine-grained Partitioning for Aggressive Data Skipping. In *SIGMOD*, 2014.
[81] P. Wang et al. An Efficient Design and Implementation of LSM-Tree based Key-Value Store on Open-Channel SSD. In *EuroSys*, 2014.
[82] H. K. T. Wong, H.-F. Liu, F. Olken, D. Rotem, and L. Wong. Bit Transposed Files. In *VLDB*, 1985.
[83] K. Wu et al. FastBit: interactively searching massive data. *J. of Physics: Conference Series*, 180(1):012053, 2009.
[84] M.-C. Wu and A. P. Buchmann. Encoded Bitmap Indexing for Data Warehouses. In *ICDE*, 1998.
[85] X. Wu, Y. Xu, Z. Shao, and S. Jiang. LSM-trie: An LSM-tree-based Ultra-Large Key-Value Store for Small Data Items. In *ATC*, 2015.
[86] R. S. Xin et al. Shark: SQL and Rich Analytics at Scale. In *SIGMOD*, 2013.
[87] B.-K. Yi and C. Faloutsos. Fast Time Sequence Indexing for Arbitrary Lp Norms. In *VLDB*, 2000.
[88] K. Zoumpatianos, S. Idreos, and T. Palpanas. Indexing for interactive exploration of big data series. In *SIGMOD*, 2014.

Data Cleaning: Overview and Emerging Challenges

Xu Chu* Ihab F. Ilyas* Sanjay Krishnan# Jiannan Wang$

*University of Waterloo #UC Berkeley $Simon Fraser University

*{x4chu,ilyas}@uwaterloo.ca #sanjaykrishnan@berkeley.edu $jnwang@sfu.ca

ABSTRACT

Detecting and repairing *dirty* data is one of the perennial challenges in data analytics, and failure to do so can result in inaccurate analytics and unreliable decisions. Over the past few years, there has been a surge of interest from both industry and academia on data cleaning problems including new abstractions, interfaces, approaches for scalability, and statistical techniques. To better understand the new advances in the field, we will first present a taxonomy of the data cleaning literature in which we highlight the recent interest in techniques that use constraints, rules, or patterns to detect errors, which we call qualitative data cleaning. We will describe the state-of-the-art techniques and also highlight their limitations with a series of illustrative examples. While traditionally such approaches are distinct from quantitative approaches such as outlier detection, we also discuss recent work that casts such approaches into a statistical estimation framework including: using Machine Learning to improve the efficiency and accuracy of data cleaning and considering the effects of data cleaning on statistical analysis.

1. INTRODUCTION

It is becoming easier for enterprises to store and acquire the large amounts of data. These data sets can facilitate improved decision making, richer analytics, and increasingly, provide training data for Machine Learning. However, data quality remains to be a major concern, and *dirty data* can lead to incorrect decisions and unreliable analysis. Examples of common errors include missing values, typos, mixed formats, replicated entries of the same real-world entity, and violations of business rules. Analysts must consider the effects of dirty data before making any decisions, and as a result, data cleaning has been a key area of database research (see Johnson and Dasu [44] and Rahm and Do [63]).

Over the past few years, there has been a surge of interest from both industry and academia on different aspects of data cleaning including new abstractions [10, 30, 77, 22, 33, 14, 73], interfaces [1, 26], approaches for scalability [75, 45, 3, 53, 67], and crowdsourcing techniques [35, 69, 62, 18, 82, 23, 37, 60, 61, 76, 71, 78]. One of the key differentiating factors is how to *define* data error (i.e., error detection). Quantitative techniques, largely used for outlier detection, employ statistical methods to identify abnormal behaviors and errors (e.g., *"a salary that is three standard deviation away from the mean salary is an error"*). On the other hand, qualitative techniques use constraints, rules, patterns to detect errors (e.g., *"there cannot exist two employees of the same level, the one who is located in NYC is earning less than the one not in NYC"*). Once the errors are detected, repair can be performed using scripts, human crowds or experts, or a hybrid of both. Quantitative data cleaning techniques have been extensively covered in multiple surveys [2, 65, 40] and tutorials [48, 17], but there have been fewer surveys of qualitative data cleaning [44]. Accordingly, this tutorial focuses on the subject of qualitative data cleaning (in terms of both detection and repair), and we argue that much of the recent interest in data cleaning has a similar focus [14, 22, 33, 26, 73, 21, 82, 23, 10, 30, 77].

In the first part of the tutorial, we overview qualitative data cleaning with a taxonomy of error detection and error repairing approaches. We will describe the state-of-the-art techniques and also highlight their limitations with a series of illustrative examples. This section will focus on rule-based data cleaning techniques, where integrity constraints (ICs) are used to express data quality rules; any part of the data that does not conform to a given set of ICs is considered erroneous (also known as a violation of ICs). These rules can capture a wide variety of errors including duplication, inconsistency, and missing values. We conclude by discussing the challenges raised by "big data" era, and recent proposals for scalable data cleaning techniques. Most of the materials in the first part of the tutorial come from our survey in *Foundations and Trends in Databases* [41].

In the second part of the tutorial, we describe a statistical perspective on qualitative data cleaning, where approaches either use techniques from Machine Learning to improve accuracy or efficiency or consider the effects of cleaning on subsequent numerical queries. We present these approaches within the same overall taxonomy of data cleaning and show that many qualitative techniques are amenable to such statistical analysis. By considering the qualitative models in a rigorous statistical framework, we can understand the trade-off between cleaning and the ultimate accuracy of inferences made from the data. The materials for this section are inspired by our work on the SampleClean project [51].

Tutorial Structure: The intended audience are members of the academic and industrial research community. We will not require any prior background knowledge about data cleaning research, but assume familiarity with database research concepts. A basic understanding of the concepts and concerns in modern data analytics (e.g., training v.s. test data) will also be helpful. The tutorial is 3 hours split into two 1.5 hour sections.

SIGMOD'16, June 26-July 01, 2016, San Francisco, CA, USA

 ISBN 978-1-4503-3531-7/16/06... $15.00

DOI: http://dx.doi.org/10.1145/2882903.2912574

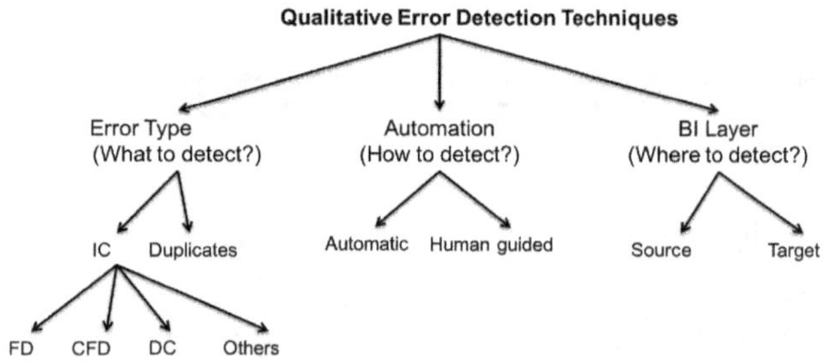

Figure 1: Classification of qualitative error detection techniques.

	Error Type What		Automation How		BI Layer Where	
	IC	Data deduplication	Automatic	Human involved	Source	Target
FDs value modification [13]	✓		✓		✓	
Holistic data cleaning [22]	✓		✓		✓	
CrowdER [74]		✓		✓	✓	
Corleone [35]		✓		✓	✓	
Causality Analysis [58]	✓			✓		✓
Scorpion [79]	✓			✓		✓
DBRx [16]	✓		✓			✓

Table 1: A sample of qualitative error detection techniques.

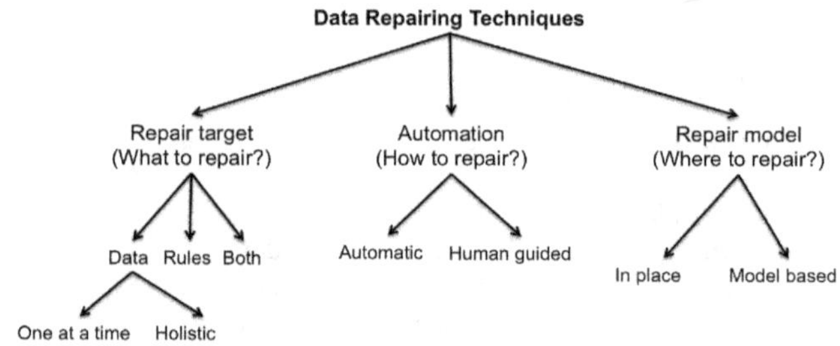

Figure 2: Classification of data repairing techniques.

2. DATA CLEANING OVERVIEW

Since data cleaning usually consists of two stages: error detection and error repairing, we will discuss a variety of techniques for qualitative error detection (Section 2.1), as well as various techniques for error repairing (Section 2.2). These techniques will be explained with a motivating example highlighting many different data quality problems, such as duplicates, missing values, integrity constraints violations, and outliers.

2.1 Qualitative Error Detection

Given a dirty database instance, the first step is to detect anomalies or errors. Figure 1 illustrates our taxonomy of qualitative error detection. There are three main questions that every technique needs to address: (1) "What to Detect", (2) "How to Detect", and "Where to Detect".

• *Error Type (What to Detect?)* Qualitative error detection techniques can be classified according to which type of errors are captured. In other words, what languages are used to describe patterns or constraints of a legal data instance. A large body of work uses integrity constraints (ICs), a fractional of first order logic, to capture data quality rules that the database should conform to, including functional dependencies (FDs) [13], and denial constraints (DCs) [22]. While duplicate records can be considered a violation of an integrity constraint (key constraint), we recognize the large body of work that focuses on this problem and we discuss it as a separate error type from other types of integrity constraints.

Manual designing such ICs or patterns require great domain expertise, and is time-consuming, automatic discovery techniques are essential and have been proposed for various ICs [21]. We classify the IC discovery techniques into schema-driven approaches and instance driven approaches, and we will discuss and compare these two approaches.

• *Automation (How to Detect?)* We classify proposed approaches according to whether and how humans are involved in the error detection process. Most techniques are fully automatic, for example, detecting violations of functional dependencies [13], while other techniques involve humans, for example, to identify duplicate records [74].

• *Business Intelligence Layer (Where to Detect?)* Errors can happen in all stages of a business intelligence (BI) stack, for example, errors in the source database are often propagated through the data processing pipeline. While most error detection techniques detect errors in the original database, some errors can only be discovered much later in the data processing pipeline [16], where more semantics and business logic are available, for example, constraints on total budget can only be enforced after aggregating cost and expenses.

Table 1 shows a sample of detection techniques, which cover all categories of the proposed taxonomy. We will give one or more example error detection techniques in each category in detail in the tutorial.

2.2 Error Repairing

Given a relational database instance I of schema R and a set of data quality requirements expressed in a variety of ways, data repairing refers to the process of finding another database instance I' that conforms to the set of data quality requirements. This problem has been extensively studied and Figure 2 depicts our taxonomy of the proposed data repairing techniques. Similar to error detection, there are three main questions that every technique needs to address: (1) "What to Repair?", (2) "How to Repair?", and (3) "Where to Repair?". In the following, we classify the techniques on these axes, and discuss the impact on the design and efficiency of the techniques.

• *Repair Target (What to Repair?)* Repairing algorithms make different assumptions about the data and the quality rules: (1) trusting the declared integrity constraints, and hence, only data can be updated to remove errors [22]; (2) trusting the data completely and allowing the relaxation of the constraints [36], for example, to address schema evolution and obsolete business rules; and finally (3) exploring the possibility of changing both the data and the constraints [11]. For techniques that trust the rules, and change only the data, they can be further divided according to the driver to the repairing exercise, that is, what types of errors they are targeting. A majority of techniques repair the data with respect to one type of errors only (one at a time), while other emerging techniques consider the interactions among multiple types of errors and provide a holistic repair of the data (holistic).

• *Automation (How to Repair?)* We classify proposed approaches with respect to the tools used in the repairing process. More specifically, we classify current repairing approaches according to whether and how humans are involved. Some techniques are fully automatic, for example, by modifying the database, such that the distance between the original database I and the modified database I' is minimized according to some cost function. Other techniques

	Repair target What				Automation How		Repair model Where	
	Data - One at a time	Data - Holistic	Rules	Both	Automatic	Human involved	In place	Model based
FDs value modification [13]	✓				✓		✓	
FDs hypergraph [46]	✓				✓		✓	
CFDs value modification [25]	✓				✓		✓	
Holistic data cleaning [22]		✓			✓		✓	
LLUNATIC [33]		✓			✓		✓	
Record matching and data repairing [31]		✓			✓		✓	
NADEEF [26]		✓			✓		✓	
Generate optimal tablaux [36]			✓		✓		✓	
Unified repair [19]				✓	✓		✓	
Relative trust [11]				✓	✓		✓	
Continuous data cleaning [73]				✓	✓		✓	
Potter's Wheel [64]	✓					✓	✓	
GDR [82]	✓					✓	✓	
KATARA [23]	✓					✓	✓	
DataTamer [69]	✓					✓	✓	
Editing rules [30]	✓					✓	✓	
Sampling FDs repairs [10]	✓				✓			✓
Sampling Duplicates [12]	✓				✓			✓

Table 2: A sample of data repairing techniques.

involve humans in the repairing process either to verify the fixes, to suggest fixes, or to train machine learning models to carry out automatic repairing decisions [82].

• *Repair Model (Where to Repair?)* We classify proposed approaches based on whether they change the database in-situ, or build a model to describe the possible repairs. Most proposed techniques repair the database in-situ, thus destructing the database. For none in-situ repairs, a model is often built to describe the different ways to repair the underlying database. Queries are answered by these models using, for example, sampling from all possible repairs and other probabilistic query answering mechanisms [10].

Table 2 shows a sample of data repairing techniques using the taxonomy. We will discuss one or more example error repairing techniques in each category in detail in the tutorial.

3. DATA CLEANING FROM A STATISTICAL PERSPECTIVE

As analytics become increasingly complex, it is important to understand the statistical implications of data cleaning. In this part of the tutorial, we will discuss approaches that either use techniques from Machine Learning to improve accuracy or efficiency, or consider the effects of cleaning on subsequent numerical queries. We will focus on deduplication (Duplication Error), repairing missing and incorrect values (Attribute Error), and the removal of erroneous or irrelevant data (Relevant Error). We will build on the taxonomy presented in the previous part, and overview recently proposed data cleaning algorithms and systems based on their relationship with statistics (Table 3).

3.1 Data Cleaning with Statistics

There are several techniques to improve the efficiency or accuracy of data cleaning algorithms using statistical methods such as Machine Learning.

Active Learning in Crowdsourcing: Crowdsourcing is widely applied in industry for data cleaning [56]. In academia, there is a growing consensus that crowds are difficult to scale [35, 69, 62, 18, 82, 23, 37, 60, 61], and as a result several recent works employ Active Learning to prioritize queries to the crowd [38, 35, 59]. The basic idea is to formulate the human-input to data cleaning as labels for a supervised learning technique (such as an SVM or Random Forest), and Active Learning is a class of algorithms that select the most informative labels to acquire.

Other Statistical Methods: There have also been several works that use statistical techniques to more accurately clean a dirty database, and this section of the tutorial will highlight a few of the seminal results. The Eracer project showed how data cleaning on dirty relations could be posed as a two-step learning problem: first learning a graphical model to represent the relation and message-passing algorithm to resolve inconsistencies [57]. Furthermore, in the sensor network literature (refer to a 2007 survey [6] and a 2010 survey [54]) there are several examples of statistical outlier detection and mitigation techniques. Finally, Yakout et al. [81] employ Machine Learning to improve the reliability of data cleaning.

3.2 Data Cleaning for Statistical Analysis

While larger datasets can facilitate training more sophisticated ML models, systematic data errors, i.e., corruption that affect particular records disproportionately, can make model training unreliable. It has repeatedly been found that ML problems are highly sensitive to dirty data, even when using robust techniques [52, 55, 49, 80], and the high-dimensionality of these models lead to counter-intuitive effects when trained after some types of data cleaning procedures [52]. For example, in one fraud prediction example, simply merging inconsistent attributes before SVM model training improved true positive detection probabilities from 62% to 91% [52]. This tutorial section studies the link between data cleaning and the subsequent analytics, and surveys works that try to analyze the effects of data cleaning on the analytics.

Aggregate Queries: The tutorial will first overview recent results on cleaning samples of data to estimate aggregate query results. SampleClean [75, 51] notes that for aggregates such as `sum`, `count`, and `avg` there are diminishing returns for data cleaning, and it often suffices to clean small samples of data to estimate results with high accuracy. This problem was further extended to study aggregate queries on materialized views [50]. We will also briefly describe the related fields of query-driven cleaning and consistent query answering [9, 7, 4] as these works have studied the problem of how inconsistencies affect individual queries.

Machine Learning: SampleClean was extended to study data cleaning that precedes Machine Learning model training in a system called ActiveClean [52]. ActiveClean employs selection techniques for the most valuable data and techniques to incrementally update ML models given newly clean data. One of the interesting findings of this work is that progressive data cleaning and model training do not commute in an expected way. Suppose $k \ll N$ records are cleaned, but all of the remaining dirty records are retained in the dataset. Aggregates over mixtures of different populations of data can result in spurious relationships due to the well-known phenomenon called Simpson's paradox [68]. Some of these problems are not apparent in 1D analytics such as `sum`, `count`, and `avg`, but can lead to subtle biases in higher-dimensional statistical analysis.

Adaptive Data Analysis: In a recent development, the statistics community has studied some of these problems in a field called "Adaptive Data Analysis", and we will also overview some of that work [66, 29]. Concepts such as Multiple Hypothesis Testing and False Discovery Rate are highly relevant to the design of analysis tools [66, 29]. These works consider the problem of false discoveries, where analysts discover non-existent trends in a dataset due to statistical chance. In the tutorial, we will discuss recent results and new opportunities for the database community to build these techniques into new tools.

Type of Error	Operation	Uses Statistics	For Statistics
Attribute Error	Value Imputation	[57, 72, 8, 81, 62, 23]	[75, 52, 43, 24]
	Data Repairing	[1, 57, 8, 37]	[75, 52]
Duplication Error	Entity Resolution	[39, 24, 81, 69]	[35, 37]
Relevance Error	Error/Outlier Removal	[27, 70, 28, 15, 34]	[52]

Table 3: We categorize the capabilities of recently proposed data cleaning algorithms and systems (some may fit in multiple categories). "Uses Statistics" are the ones that use a statistical model (e.g., a Probabilistic Graphical Model) to identify and correct errors. "For Statistics" are the ones that are explicitly designed to support data cleaning for aggregate analytics and advanced statistical analytics.

4. NEW CHALLENGES

We highlight many emerging trends in data cleaning research. Both Part 1 and Part 2 of the tutorial will go through some of them.

Scalability. Scaling data cleaning techniques to the large and rapidly growing datasets of the Big Data era will be an important challenge. Current techniques include blocking for duplicate detection [5], sampling for data cleaning [75], and distributed data cleaning [47, 45, 20].

User Engagement. Although much research has been done about involving humans to perform data deduplication, for example, through active learning, involving humans in other data cleaning tasks, such as repairing IC violations, and taking user feedback in discovering of data quality rules, is yet to be explored.

Semi-structured and unstructured data. A significant portion of data is residing in semi-structured formats, e.g., JSON, and unstructured formats, e.g., text documents. Data quality problems for semi-structured and unstructured data remain largely unexplored.

New Applications for Streaming Data. There is a renewed interest in considering data collected from vast collections of sensors and mobile devices. Gartner estimates that there will be 26 billion devices on the Internet-of-Things (IoT) by 2020 [32]. 5-10 years ago the data management and quality challenges from distributed sensors was an important research topic, e.g., [54, 27, 42, 43]. However, most of the prior work on data cleaning in this domain has relied on many quantitative such as outlier detection. One avenue for future work is to consider how qualitative data cleaning approaches will work on distributed streams of data.

Growing Privacy and Security Concerns. Finally, there are significant concerns about data privacy as increasingly more individual data are collected by enterprises. Data cleaning is by nature a task that requires examining and searching through raw data, which may be restricted in some domains including finance and medicine. An important challenge will be to reconcile the need for data provenance, access to unaggregated data, and privacy.

5. CONCLUSION

Detecting and repairing *dirty* data is one of the perennial challenges in data analytics, and failure to do so can result in inaccurate analytics and unreliable decisions. Over the past few years, there has been a surge of interest from both industry and academia on different aspects of this problem including new abstractions, interfaces, and approaches for scalability. This tutorial focused on qualitative data cleaning which uses constraints, rules, or patterns to detect errors. While this subject has traditionally been distinct from quantitative statistical approaches for cleaning, we described the growing relationship between the two branches of literature. Most of the materials for this tutorial can be found in *Foundations and Trends in Databases* [41], and in an overview of the *SampleClean* project [51].

6. REFERENCES

[1] Trifacta. http://www.trifacta.com.

[2] C. C. Aggarwal. *Outlier Analysis*. Springer, 2013.

[3] Y. Altowim, D. V. Kalashnikov, and S. Mehrotra. Progressive approach to relational entity resolution. *PVLDB*, 7(11), 2014.

[4] H. Altwaijry, S. Mehrotra, and D. V. Kalashnikov. Query: A framework for integrating entity resolution with query processing. *PVLDB*, 9(3):120–131, 2015.

[5] R. Ananthakrishna, S. Chaudhuri, and V. Ganti. Eliminating fuzzy duplicates in data warehouses. In *PVLDB*, pages 586–597, 2002.

[6] M. Balazinska, A. Deshpande, M. J. Franklin, P. B. Gibbons, J. Gray, M. H. Hansen, M. Liebhold, S. Nath, A. S. Szalay, and V. Tao. Data management in the worldwide sensor web. *IEEE Pervasive Computing*, 6(2):30–40, 2007.

[7] M. Bergman, T. Milo, S. Novgorodov, and W. C. Tan. Query-oriented data cleaning with oracles. In *SIGMOD*, 2015.

[8] L. Berti-Equille, T. Dasu, and D. Srivastava. Discovery of complex glitch patterns: A novel approach to quantitative data cleaning. In *ICDE*, pages 733–744, 2011.

[9] L. E. Bertossi. Consistent query answering in databases. *SIGMOD Record*, 35(2):68–76, 2006.

[10] G. Beskales, I. F. Ilyas, and L. Golab. Sampling the repairs of functional dependency violations under hard constraints. *PVLDB*, 3(1-2):197–207, 2010.

[11] G. Beskales, I. F. Ilyas, L. Golab, and A. Galiullin. On the relative trust between inconsistent data and inaccurate constraints. In *ICDE*, pages 541–552, 2013.

[12] G. Beskales, M. A. Soliman, I. F. Ilyas, and S. Ben-David. Modeling and querying possible repairs in duplicate detection. *PVLDB*, pages 598–609, 2009.

[13] P. Bohannon, W. Fan, M. Flaster, and R. Rastogi. A cost-based model and effective heuristic for repairing constraints by value modification. In *SIGMOD*, pages 143–154. ACM, 2005.

[14] P. Bohannon, W. Fan, F. Geerts, X. Jia, and A. Kementsietsidis. Conditional functional dependencies for data cleaning. In *ICDE*, pages 746–755, 2007.

[15] L. Cao, D. Yang, Q. Wang, Y. Yu, J. Wang, and E. A. Rundensteiner. Scalable distance-based outlier detection over high-volume data streams. In *ICDE*, pages 76–87, 2014.

[16] A. Chalamalla, I. F. Ilyas, M. Ouzzani, and P. Papotti. Descriptive and prescriptive data cleaning. In *SIGMOD*, pages 445–456, 2014.

[17] S. Chawla and P. Sun. Outlier detection: Principles, techniques and applications. In *PAKDD*, 2006.

[18] Z. Chen and M. Cafarella. Integrating spreadsheet data via accurate and low-effort extraction. In *KDD*. ACM, 2014.

[19] F. Chiang and R. J. Miller. A unified model for data and constraint repair. In *ICDE*, pages 446–457, 2011.

[20] X. Chu, I. F. Ilyas, and P. Koutris. Distributed Data Deduplication. Technical Report CS-2016-02, University of Waterloo, 2016.

[21] X. Chu, I. F. Ilyas, and P. Papotti. Discovering denial constraints. *PVLDB*, 6(13):1498–1509, 2013.

[22] X. Chu, I. F. Ilyas, and P. Papotti. Holistic data cleaning: Putting violations into context. In *ICDE*, pages 458–469, 2013.

[23] X. Chu, J. Morcos, I. F. Ilyas, M. Ouzzani, P. Papotti, N. Tang, and Y. Ye. KATARA: A data cleaning system powered by knowledge bases and crowdsourcing. In *SIGMOD*, pages 1247–1261, 2015.

[24] Y. Chung, M. L. Mortensen, C. Binnig, and T. Kraska. Estimating the impact of unknown unknowns on aggregate query results. *CoRR*, abs/1507.05591, 2015.

[25] G. Cong, W. Fan, F. Geerts, X. Jia, and S. Ma. Improving data quality: Consistency and accuracy. In *PVLDB*, pages 315–326. VLDB Endowment, 2007.

[26] M. Dallachiesa, A. Ebaid, A. Eldawy, A. Elmagarmid, I. F. Ilyas, M. Ouzzani, and N. Tang. Nadeef: a commodity data cleaning system. In *SIGMOD*, pages 541–552, 2013.

[27] A. Deligiannakis, Y. Kotidis, V. Vassalos, V. Stoumpos, and A. Delis. Another outlier bites the dust: Computing meaningful aggregates in sensor networks. In *ICDE*, pages 988–999, 2009.

[28] A. Deshpande, C. Guestrin, S. Madden, J. M. Hellerstein, and W. Hong. Model-driven data acquisition in sensor networks. In *PVLDB*, pages 588–599, 2004.

[29] C. Dwork, V. Feldman, M. Hardt, T. Pitassi, O. Reingold, and A. L. Roth. Preserving statistical validity in adaptive data analysis. In *STOC*, pages 117–126, 2015.

[30] W. Fan, J. Li, S. Ma, N. Tang, and W. Yu. Towards certain fixes with editing rules and master data. *PVLDB*, 3(1-2):173–184, 2010.

[31] W. Fan, J. Li, S. Ma, N. Tang, and W. Yu. Interaction between record matching and data repairing. In *SIGMOD*, pages 469–480. ACM, 2011.

[32] Gartner. Forecast: The internet of things, worldwide. https://www.gartner.com/doc/2625419/forecast-internet-things-worldwide-.

[33] F. Geerts, G. Mecca, P. Papotti, and D. Santoro. The llunatic data-cleaning framework. *PVLDB*, 6(9):625–636, 2013.

[34] D. Georgiadis, M. Kontaki, A. Gounaris, A. N. Papadopoulos, K. Tsichlas, and Y. Manolopoulos. Continuous outlier detection in data streams: an extensible framework and state-of-the-art algorithms. In *SIGMOD*, pages 1061–1064, 2013.

[35] C. Gokhale, S. Das, A. Doan, J. F. Naughton, N. Rampalli, J. Shavlik, and X. Zhu. Corleone: Hands-off crowdsourcing for entity matching. In *SIGMOD*, 2014.

[36] L. Golab, H. Karloff, F. Korn, D. Srivastava, and B. Yu. On generating near-optimal tableaux for conditional functional dependencies. *PVLDB*, 1(1):376–390, 2008.

[37] D. Haas, S. Krishnan, J. Wang, M. J. Franklin, and E. Wu. Wisteria: Nurturing scalable data cleaning infrastructure. *PVLDB*, 8(12), 2015.

[38] D. Haas, J. Wang, E. Wu, and M. J. Franklin. Clamshell: Speeding up crowds for low-latency data labeling. *PVLDB*, 9(4):372–383, Dec. 2015.

[39] A. Heise, G. Kasneci, and F. Naumann. Estimating the number and sizes of fuzzy-duplicate clusters. In *CIKM Conference*, 2014.

[40] J. M. Hellerstein. Quantitative data cleaning for large databases. *United Nations Economic Commission for Europe (UNECE)*, 2008.

[41] I. F. Ilyas and X. Chu. Trends in cleaning relational data: Consistency and deduplication. *Foundations and Trends in Databases*, 5(4):281–393, 2015.

[42] S. R. Jeffery, G. Alonso, M. J. Franklin, W. Hong, and J. Widom. A pipelined framework for online cleaning of sensor data streams. In *ICDE*, 2006.

[43] S. R. Jeffery, M. N. Garofalakis, and M. J. Franklin. Adaptive cleaning for RFID data streams. In *Proceedings of the 32nd International Conference on Very Large Data Bases, Seoul, Korea, September 12-15, 2006*, pages 163–174, 2006.

[44] T. Johnson and T. Dasu. Data quality and data cleaning: An overview. In *SIGMOD*, page 681, 2003.

[45] Z. Khayyat, I. F. Ilyas, A. Jindal, S. Madden, M. Ouzzani, P. Papotti, J. Quiané-Ruiz, N. Tang, and S. Yin. Bigdansing: A system for big data cleansing. pages 1215–1230, 2015.

[46] S. Kolahi and L. V. S. Lakshmanan. On approximating optimum repairs for functional dependency violations. In *ICDT*, pages 53–62, 2009.

[47] L. Kolb, A. Thor, and E. Rahm. Dedoop: efficient deduplication with hadoop. *PVLDB*, 5(12):1878–1881, 2012.

[48] H.-P. Kriegel, P. Kröger, and A. Zimek. Outlier detection techniques. In *Tutorial at SIGKDD*, 2010.

[49] S. Krishnan, J. Patel, M. J. Franklin, and K. Goldberg. A methodology for learning, analyzing, and mitigating social influence bias in recommender systems. In *RecSys*, 2014.

[50] S. Krishnan, J. Wang, M. J. Franklin, K. Goldberg, and T. Kraska. Stale view cleaning: Getting fresh answers from stale materialized views. *PVLDB*, 8(12), 2015.

[51] S. Krishnan, J. Wang, M. J. Franklin, K. Goldberg, T. Kraska, T. Milo, and E. Wu. Sampleclean: Fast and reliable analytics on dirty data. *IEEE Data Eng. Bull.*, 38(3):59–75, 2015.

[52] S. Krishnan, J. Wang, E. Wu, M. J. Franklin, and K. Goldberg. Activeclean: Interactive data cleaning while learning convex loss models. In *Arxiv: http://arxiv.org/pdf/1601.03797.pdf*, 2015.

[53] Z. Li, S. Shang, Q. Xie, and X. Zhang. Cost reduction for web-based data imputation. In *Database Systems for Advanced Applications*, pages 438–452. Springer, 2014.

[54] S. Madden. Database abstractions for managing sensor network data. *Proceedings of the IEEE*, 98(11):1879–1886, 2010.

[55] J. Mahler, S. Krishnan, M. Laskey, S. Sen, A. Murali, B. Kehoe, S. Patil, J. Wang, M. Franklin, P. Abbeel, and K. Y. Goldberg. Learning accurate kinematic control of cable-driven surgical robots using data cleaning and gaussian process regression. In *CASE*, 2014.

[56] A. Marcus and A. Parameswaran. Crowdsourced data management: Industry and academic perspectives. *Foundations and Trends in Databases*, 6(1-2):1–161, 2013.

[57] C. Mayfield, J. Neville, and S. Prabhakar. ERACER: a database approach for statistical inference and data cleaning. In *SIGMOD*, 2010.

[58] A. Meliou, W. Gatterbauer, S. Nath, and D. Suciu. Tracing data errors with view-conditioned causality. In *SIGMOD*, pages 505–516, 2011.

[59] B. Mozafari, P. Sarkar, M. J. Franklin, M. I. Jordan, and S. Madden. Scaling up crowd-sourcing to very large datasets: A case for active learning. *PVLDB*, 8(2), 2014.

[60] A. Parameswaran, H. Garcia-Molina, H. Park, N. Polyzotis, A. Ramesh, and J. Widom. Crowdscreen: Algorithms for filtering data with humans.

[61] A. Parameswaran and N. Polyzotis. Answering queries using humans, algorithms and databases. 2011.

[62] H. Park and J. Widom. Crowdfill: collecting structured data from the crowd. In *SIGMOD*, 2014.

[63] E. Rahm and H. H. Do. Data cleaning: Problems and current approaches. *IEEE Data Eng. Bull.*, 23(4), 2000.

[64] V. Raman and J. M. Hellerstein. Potter's wheel: An interactive data cleaning system. In *VLDB*, pages 381–390, 2001.

[65] P. J. Rousseeuw and A. M. Leroy. *Robust regression and outlier detection*, volume 589. John Wiley & Sons, 2005.

[66] D. Russo and J. Zou. Controlling bias in adaptive data analysis using information theory. *CoRR*, abs/1511.05219, 2015.

[67] G. Simoes, H. Galhardas, and L. Gravano. When speed has a price: Fast information extraction using approximate algorithms. *PVLDB*, 6(13):1462–1473, 2013.

[68] E. H. Simpson. The interpretation of interaction in contingency tables. *Journal of the Royal Statistical Society. Series B (Methodological)*, 1951.

[69] M. Stonebraker, D. Bruckner, I. F. Ilyas, G. Beskales, M. Cherniack, S. B. Zdonik, A. Pagan, and S. Xu. Data curation at scale: The data tamer system. In *CIDR*, 2013.

[70] S. Subramaniam, T. Palpanas, D. Papadopoulos, V. Kalogeraki, and D. Gunopulos. Online outlier detection in sensor data using non-parametric models. In *PVLDB*, pages 187–198, 2006.

[71] Y. Tong, C. C. Cao, C. J. Zhang, Y. Li, and L. Chen. Crowdcleaner: Data cleaning for multi-version data on the web via crowdsourcing. In *ICDE*, pages 1182–1185, 2014.

[72] R. Verborgh and M. De Wilde. *Using OpenRefine*. Packt Publishing Ltd, 2013.

[73] M. Volkovs, F. Chiang, J. Szlichta, and R. J. Miller. Continuous data cleaning. In *ICDE*, pages 244–255, 2014.

[74] J. Wang, T. Kraska, M. J. Franklin, and J. Feng. Crowder: Crowdsourcing entity resolution. *PVLDB*, 5(11), 2012.

[75] J. Wang, S. Krishnan, M. J. Franklin, K. Goldberg, T. Kraska, and T. Milo. A sample-and-clean framework for fast and accurate query processing on dirty data. In *SIGMOD*, 2014.

[76] J. Wang, G. Li, T. Kraska, M. J. Franklin, and J. Feng. Leveraging transitive relations for crowdsourced joins. In *SIGMOD*, pages 229–240, 2013.

[77] J. Wang and N. Tang. Towards dependable data repairing with fixing rules. In *SIGMOD*, pages 457–468. ACM, 2014.

[78] S. E. Whang, P. Lofgren, and H. Garcia-Molina. Question selection for crowd entity resolution. *PVLDB*, 6(6):349–360, Apr. 2013.

[79] E. Wu and S. Madden. Scorpion: Explaining away outliers in aggregate queries. *PVLDB*, 6(8):553–564, 2013.

[80] H. Xiao, B. Biggio, G. Brown, G. Fumera, C. Eckert, and F. Roli. Is feature selection secure against training data poisoning? In *ICML*, 2015.

[81] M. Yakout, L. Berti-Equille, and A. K. Elmagarmid. Don't be scared: use scalable automatic repairing with maximal likelihood and bounded changes. In *SIGMOD*, 2013.

[82] M. Yakout, A. K. Elmagarmid, J. Neville, M. Ouzzani, and I. F. Ilyas. Guided data repair. *PVLDB*, 4(5):279–289, 2011.

Biographies

Xu Chu

Xu Chu is a PhD student in the Cheriton School of Computer Science at the University of Waterloo. His main research interests are data quality and data cleaning. He won the prestigious Microsoft Research PhD fellowship in 2015. Xu has also received Cheriton Fellowship from the University of Waterloo 2013-2015.

Ihab F. Ilyas

Ihab Ilyas is a professor in the Cheriton School of Computer Science at the University of Waterloo. He received his PhD in computer science from Purdue University, West Lafayette. His main research is in the area of database systems, with special interest in data quality, managing uncertain data, rank-aware query processing, and information extraction. Ihab is a recipient of the Ontario Early Researcher Award (2009), a Cheriton Faculty Fellowship (2013), an NSERC Discovery Accelerator Award (2014), and a Google Faculty Award (2014), and he is an ACM Distinguished Scientist. Ihab is a co-founder of Tamr, a startup focusing on large-scale data integration and cleaning. He serves on the VLDB Board of Trustees, and he is an associate editor of the ACM Transactions of Database Systems (TODS).

Sanjay Krishnan

Sanjay Krishnan is a Computer Science PhD candidate in the Algorithms, Machines, and People Lab (AMPLab) and in the Berkeley Laboratory for Automation Science and Engineering at UC Berkeley. His research studies techniques for data analytics on dirty data and data representation problems in physical systems.

Jiannan Wang

Jiannan Wang is an Assistant Professor of Computing Science at Simon Fraser University. His research is focused on developing algorithms and systems for extracting value from dirty data. Prior to that, he was a postdoc in the AMPLab at UC Berkeley. He obtained his PhD from the Computer Science Department at Tsinghua University. During his PhD, he has been a visiting scholar at Chinese University of Hong Kong and UC Berkeley, and an intern at Qatar Computing Research Institute. His PhD research work was supported from a Google PhD Fellowship, a Boeing Scholarship, and a New PhD Researcher Award by Chinese Ministry of Education. His PhD dissertation won the China Computer Federation (CCF) Distinguished Dissertation Award. His similarity-join algorithm won first place of EDBT String Similarity Search/Join Competition.

Querying Geo-Textual Data: Spatial Keyword Queries and Beyond

Gao Cong
Nanyang Technological University
Singapore
gaocong@ntu.edu.sg

Christian S. Jensen
Aalborg University
Denmark
csj@cs.aau.dk

ABSTRACT

Over the past decade, we have moved from a predominantly desktop based web to a predominantly mobile web, where users most often access the web from mobile devices such as smartphones. In addition, we are witnessing a proliferation of geo-located, textual web content. Motivated in part by these developments, the research community has been hard at work enabling the efficient computation of a variety of query functionality on geo-textual data, yielding a sizable body of literature on the querying of geo-textual data.

With a focus on different types of keyword-based queries on geo-textual data, the tutorial also explores topics such as continuous queries on streaming geo-textual data, queries that retrieve attractive regions of geo-textual objects, and queries that extract properties, e.g., topics and top-k frequent words, of the objects in regions. The tutorial is designed to offer an overview of the problems addressed in this body of literature and offers an overview of pertinent concepts and techniques. In addition, the tutorial suggests open problems and new research direction.

1. INTRODUCTION

In part due to the proliferation of GPS-equipped mobile devices, notably smartphones, massive volumes of geo-located, or geo-tagged, text content is becoming available on the Web. Examples of such content include points of interest (POIs) with descriptive text, geo-tagged micro-blog posts (e.g., tweets), geo-tagged photos with text tags (e.g., as found at Flickr and Instagram), check-ins from location-based social networks (e.g., FourSquare), geo-tagged news, and geo-tagged web pages.

We refer to such data as geo-textual, or spatio-textual, data. As stated, massive volumes of such data are available. For example, Foursquare hosts over 87 million locations around the world with over 8 billion check-ins[1]. Further, new geo-textual data is being generated, and the volumes of geo-textual data are expected to grow at an accelerated pace as mobile devices continue to proliferate.

Geo-textual data can be divided into (i) streaming geo-textual data that arrives at a high rate, exemplified by geo-tagged tweets and (ii) static geo-textual data that is relatively stable, exemplified by collections of POIs.

The development described above also motivates increased research on the management of geo-textual data in the data management, data mining, and information retrieval communities. On the one hand, compared with traditional spatial data, the textual component greatly enriches the data. On the other hand, the spatial component of geo-textual data also adds a new and semantically rich aspect to textual data.

The tutorial first covers keyword-based querying of geo-textual data and then covers related functionality. A brief overview of the scope of the tutorial follows.

Spatial keyword queries. Many types of spatial database queries have been revisited for geo-textual data; and keyword queries have also been revisited in the context of geo-textual data. The resulting studies give prominence to spatial keyword queries that combine spatial functionality (e.g., range and nearest neighbor queries) with keyword queries. A typical spatial keyword query finds the objects that best match the location and keywords in the query. To address different use cases, many types of spatial keyword queries and accompanying indexing and query processing techniques have been proposed.

Querying geo-textual streams. Geo-textual data may arrive at a high rate (e.g., geo-tagged tweets or photos) and can then be modeled as a data stream. In such streaming settings, continuous queries are of particular interest. Here, users may want to be notified when interesting geo-textual objects arrive. For example, a user may want to be notified when tweets arrive that contain the term "flu" and are posted from within 5 km of the user's home.

Exploratory search and mining. Exploratory search [41] helps users search, navigate, and discover new facts and has grown in prominence. Here, querying and browsing are typically combined to enable investigation and foster learning. Geo-textual data contains both structured and unstructured data and can be readily presented on a map. One approach to enabling exploratory search on geo-textual data is to conduct search or mining of geo-textual data in a user-specified region interactively, such as finding the top-k most frequent terms in a region. Another approach is to interactively find regions with particular, user-specified properties.

[1] https://foursquare.com/about accessed January 2016.

SIGMOD'16, June 26-July 01, 2016, San Francisco, CA, USA
 ISBN 978-1-4503-3531-7/16/06...$15.00
DOI: http://dx.doi.org/10.1145/2882903.2912572

In the reminder, we review the topics covered and also cover future directions.

2. SPATIAL KEYWORD QUERIES

We briefly review different types of spatial keyword queries and indexing techniques.

2.1 Standard Queries

Standard queries generalize fundamental queries from spatial databases and information retrieval. In spatial databases, the arguably most fundamental queries are range and k nearest neighbor queries. In information retrieval, queries may be Boolean, returning results that contain query keywords, or ranking-based, returning the k objects that are most similar to query keywords according to some text similarity function.

The content that is queried is a set $\mathcal{D}$ of objects. An object $p \in \mathcal{D}$ has two attributes: $\langle \lambda, \psi \rangle$, where λ encodes a geo-location and ψ is a text value. These objects are digital, are often assumed to be available on the web, and typically represent a physical, geo-located entity that may be of potential interest to a user. The objects are also called places, POIs, geo-textual objects, or web objects. Standard queries return a set or ranked list of objects from $\mathcal{D}$.

We cover several types of standard queries. Let ρ be a spatial region, λ be a point location, ψ be a set of keywords, and k be the number of objects to return.

1. A *Boolean range query* $q = \langle \rho, \psi \rangle$ returns all objects in $\mathcal{D}$ that are located in region ρ and that contain all the keywords in ψ.

2. A *Boolean kNN query* $q = \langle \lambda, \psi, k \rangle$ returns up to k objects from $\mathcal{D}$, each of which contains all the keywords in ψ, ranked in increasing spatial distance from λ.

3. A *top-k range query* $q = \langle \rho, \psi, k \rangle$ returns up to k objects from $\mathcal{D}$ that are located in the query region ρ, now ranked according to their text relevance to ψ.

4. Finally, a *top-k kNN query* $q = \langle \lambda, \psi, k \rangle$ retrieves k objects from $\mathcal{D}$, ranked according to a score that takes into consideration both spatial proximity and text relevance.

We name the above queries by following the work [4]; the queries may be named differently in other studies [10,13,19, 21,27,29,43,50,61,65,67].

2.2 Beyond Single Object Result Granularity

In some scenarios, a user's needs are not met best by a query result that returns a set or ranked list of geo-textual objects from $\mathcal{D}$, each of which aims to satisfy the user's needs. Instead, the user's needs may be better satisfied by an aggregation of several objects that are near each other, meaning that the possible answers are subsets of $\mathcal{D}$, sets of subsets of $\mathcal{D}$, or ranked lists of subsets of $\mathcal{D}$.

For example, several objects may combine to collectively meet the user's needs, while no individual object meets the needs well. Consider a query with keywords "hotel, pub, beach." Perhaps no nearby single place is a good match for this combination of keywords. Instead, a group of three places that are close to each other and are close to the query location may combine to provide a result that meets the user's needs better than any single object.

The *m-closest keywords* (mCK) query [26,63,64] retrieves a set of objects with text descriptions that combine to contain a set of m query keywords, while also minimizing the maximum distance between any two objects in the result set. Apart from retrieving a set of objects satisfying the user needs, the mCK query can also be used for geo-tagging a document or a photo with textual tags.

The *collective keyword* query [6,7,37] further generalizes the mCK query. A query q takes a location λ and a set of keywords ψ as arguments. Its search space is all subsets of the set of objects $\mathcal{D}$, and it returns a set of objects such that (i) the textual descriptions of the objects collectively cover ψ, (ii) the result objects are all close to λ, and (iii) the result objects are close to each other.

The *top-k groups* query [2,47] aims to support users who wish to explore different objects. For example, a user may want to explore different restaurants before deciding where to have dinner. Given a query location and query keywords, the query retrieves a ranked list of k groups, or sets, of objects that score the best according to a ranking function that takes into account the diameter of the group, the group's distance to the query location, and the relevance of the group's objects to the query keywords. Unlike in the collective keyword query, where result objects combine to be an answer, each object in a result group is a possible answer.

The *keyword-aware route planning* query [5,60] retrieves a route that covers all query keywords and perhaps satisfies a certain constraint (e.g., distance), while optimizing an objective, e.g., the popularity of the route.

2.3 Other Queries

Generalizations of many other types of spatial queries are revisited in the context of geo-textual data, including the following.

1. *Moving continuous queries* [54,57–59]. This type of query enables a mobile user (e.g., a pedestrian or driver) to be continuously aware of the k geo-textual objects that best match a query with respect to location and text relevancy. In addition to static POIs, the objects may model users that play the role of service providers and thus offer moving services, with textual descriptions, to other users.

2. *Why-not queries* [14,15]. When issuing a top-k NN query, a user may expect some known object to be in the result of the query. Should such an object be missing from the result, a why-not query offers an explanation of why the expected object is missing and suggests a similar query with revised parameters that includes the missing object in its result.

3. *Reverse kNN queries* [18,38]. Different from a traditional user, a business may be interested in finding users or business objects that have a query object in their lists of top-k objects ranked by a ranking function that takes both spatial proximity and text relevance into consideration. This query is called a reverse spatial and textual kNN query.

4. *Similarity join queries* [3,22]. Given a set of geo-textual objects, a distance threshold, and a text similarity threshold, the spatio-textual similarity join query

finds all pairs of objects such that the distance between each pair is smaller than the distance threshold and their text similarity exceeds a threshold.

2.4 Querying in Road Networks

The proposals reviewed above generally assume a Euclidean space setting. Other proposals (e.g., [8,44,62]) on efficiently processing of spatial keyword queries assume a spatial-network setting and define spatial distance as road network distance, which is more computationally expensive to compute than Euclidean distance. A distributed solution [39] is proposed to process Boolean range queries and spatial group keyword queries on road networks.

2.5 Indexing Techniques

A common challenge in answering the kinds of spatial keyword queries covered above is to develop index structures and algorithms that enable efficient query processing. The tutorial does not cover algorithms, but it offers a brief coverage of indexing techniques for geo-textual data and related techniques used in open sources/commercial systems.

Existing spatial-keyword indexing techniques usually combine a spatial index and a text index so that both textual and spatial information can be utilized to prune the search space when processing spatial keyword queries. The existing indices can be categorized according to the spatial index they utilize: (i) R-tree based indices [21,27,29,43,55,56,67]; (ii) grid or quad-tree based indices [20,34,50,61,65]; and (iii) space filling curve based indices [16,19]. Using the text index employed, indexing techniques can also be classified as inverted file based (e.g., [67]) and signature-file based (e.g., [29]). In addition, some techniques (e.g., [67]) loosely combine a spatial and a text index, while other others integrate them tightly, resulting in hybrid index structures (e.g., [29]), and yet another approach captures an object's spatio-textual part as a compact bit string that can be indexed using a standard index [46] such as a B-tree.

3. QUERYING GEO-TEXTUAL STREAMS

Streaming geo-textual data, exemplified by streams of geo-tagged microblog posts, is an increasingly available and thus important type of data that is attracting increasing interest. Most of existing research on querying geo-textual data streams aims to develop efficient solutions to handling a large number of spatial-keyword subscription, or continuous, queries over geo-textual streams. We cover recent studies on querying geo-textual data streams.

Boolean subscription queries. Several proposals [11, 35, 53] consider Boolean subscription queries over streaming data, where both spatial and keyword conditions serve as Boolean filters. These proposals adopt slightly different settings.

For example, the keyword condition in one study [11] supports both Boolean AND and Boolean OR semantics, while the other studies [35,53] focus on Boolean AND. The geo-textual objects in one study [35] can be associated with regions, while the geo-textual objects in the other studies have point locations. These proposals present solutions to indexing and grouping subscription queries such that a group of subscriptions can be processed together over the geo-textual data stream, rather than being processed individually, which will be computationally expensive. In addition to being able to efficiently process a large number of subscription queries over geo-textual data streams where geo-textual objects arrive at a high rate, such solutions should be capable of efficiently handling the arrival of new subscriptions and the expiry or discontinuation of existing subscriptions.

Similarity based subscription queries. Instead of employing Boolean conditions in subscription queries, several recent studies [12,28] employ similarity notions in subscription conditions. In one study [28], a subscription condition can be defined on the spatial-keyword similarity between an incoming geo-textual object and a subscription. Thus, if the similarity exceeds a threshold, the condition is satisfied, and the object is emitted as a result of the subscription.

In contrast, another study [12] aims at maintaining the top-k best objects for each subscription over a stream of geo-textual objects, where the ranking score for each object is computed by considering text relevance, spatial proximity, and the freshness of the object. In yet another study [25], a different type of subscription query is proposed, where the user of each subscription query moves.

Other queries There exists little work on supporting one-time queries on geo-textual data streams. A system [40] is built to support querying geo-textual data within given spatial and temporal ranges.

4. EXPLORATORY SEARCH AND MINING

We proceed to outline studies on exploring geo-textual data. We group them into two categories.

Region search. Given a collection of geo-textual objects, the region search problem is to identify a region, that satisfies a user-specified condition (e.g., involving the size and shape of the region) and that maximizes some aggregate score (e.g., a SUM function) of the objects inside it, for user exploration. Based on a returned result, users may want to modify the query parameters and issue a new region search query.

Given a set $\mathcal{D}$ of geo-textual objects and a rectangle r of a given size (length and width), the *Maximizing Range Sum* (MaxRS) problem is to find a location for r that maximizes the sum of the scores of all the objects covered by r. The problem was first studied in the computational geometry community. Imai et al. [30] propose an $O(n \log n)$ optimal algorithm, where n is the number of objects in $\mathcal{D}$; Nandy and Bhattacharya [42] propose a line-sweeping-based algorithm with the same complexity. An external memory algorithm for the MaxRS problem has also been proposed [17], as has an approximate algorithm for the problem [49]. In recent work [23], the aggregate score functions in the region search problem are defined to be submodular monotone set functions, rather than SUM as used in MaxRS query. These existing studies on region search consider a collection of static geo-textual objects.

The problem of finding a region that does not exceed a given size and that contains objects with the maximum sum of scores is also studied in a road network setting [9]. Here, vertices are created for all geo-textual objects, and weights are associated with vertices that denote the relevance to query keywords of an object. A region is a connected subgraph, and subgraph size is formalized as the sum of the lengths of the edges in in the subgraph. The goal is then to find a qualifying subgraph where the sum of the vertex weights is maximal.

The above studies do not aim at supporting interactive

exploration. In contrast, Alexander et al. [31] propose semantic window to study the region search problem for interactive data exploration of multidimensional data, in which a user explores a data space by posing a number of queries that find rectangular regions of interest.

Region exploration. The problem of region exploration is to explore and discover properties of user-specified regions. Based on the returned results, users may interactively specify different regions and pose a different region exploration queries. Region exploration over geo-textual data is a relatively new research topic. Given a user-specified region, one study [48] considers the problem of retrieving the top-k frequent words over the geo-textual data stream for the region. Another study considers the problem of selectivity estimation [52] for a user-specified region. Based on pre-computed probabilistic topic models for each grid cell, a recent study [66] proposes an approach to efficiently discover topics for a user-specified region. Additionally, event detection [1] is performed for a given region over text streams [51]. Feng et al. [24] propose a system called StreamCube designed to enable exploration of events over the spatio-temporal Twitter stream by clustering hashtags. Sankaranarayanan et al. [45] develop a news processing system, called TwitterStand, to continuously acquire breaking news from tweets. In TwitterStand, tweets falling into a specified region are clustered, and each cluster of tweets is associated with a set of geographical locations.

5. FUTURE DIRECTIONS

While good progress has already been made, research on geo-textual data has just begun, and there are many opportunities for continued research. Here, we discuss some of the possible directions.

Effective ranking and user evaluation. Numerous signals are in play when search engines perform ranking of web pages, such as the quality of a web page, click through, and diversity. It is natural to consider whether the signals used for conventional web-page ranking can be useful for the ranking of geo-textual data. Further, geo-textual data contains new features that can be considered for ranking, such as the popularity or rating of a POI.

Reliable evaluation of ranking proposals for geo-textual objects is essential in order to make progress. There is often no mathematical definition of the right, or best, result. Rather, the utility of a result is user dependent, and we need to determine how useful users will find a result. It is thus challenging to establish a reliable ground truth for the results of ranking queries, and user evaluation is an important ingredient when attempting to evaluate the effectiveness of a proposal for the ranking of geo-textual objects. Being able to assess how good ranking functions are will enable better and more complex ranking function [32]. This may in turn call for new indexing and query processing techniques.

Personalized spatial keyword queries. The existing work on spatial keyword queries does not consider personalization. On the other hand, work on personalized location recommendation [36] does not consider spatial keyword search, but instead aims to understand users' topical interests and mobility preference from users' historical geo-textual data. It is of interest to attempt to bridge this gap, thus enabling personalized search.

Querying and mining geo-textual data streams. It is an open problem to effectively and efficiently support continuous queries on geo-textual streams. For example, instead of receiving individual tweets from a stream, users may want to be notified in real time of relevant trending events or even of casual relationships among events. Furthermore, high velocity geo-textual data streams call for distributed solutions. Additionally, geo-textual data streams can be integrated with static geo-textual data, such as POIs. By bridging dynamic geo-textual data streams and static geo-textual data, exciting opportunities for data analytics emerge.

Exploratory search and mining. Being a new topic for geo-textual data, many research problems remain open within the scope of this topic. For example, what are interesting exploratory search and mining tasks on geo-textual data? What factors should be considered in such tasks, e.g., diversity [33]? How can the tasks be performed efficiently? How can interactive exploratory search and mining be performed efficiently?

6. REFERENCES

[1] H. Becker, M. Naaman, and L. Gravano. Learning similarity metrics for event identification in social media. In *WSDM*, pages 291–300, 2010.

[2] K. S. Bøgh, A. Skovsgaard, and C. S. Jensen. GroupFinder: A new approach to top-k point-of-interest group retrieval. *PVLDB*, 6(12):1226–1229, 2013.

[3] P. Bouros, S. Ge, and N. Mamoulis. Spatio-textual similarity joins. *PVLDB*, 6(1):1–12, 2012.

[4] X. Cao, L. Chen, G. Cong, C. S. Jensen, Q. Qu, A. Skovsgaard, D. Wu, and M. L. Yiu. Spatial keyword querying. In *ER*, pages 16–29, 2012.

[5] X. Cao, L. Chen, G. Cong, and X. Xiao. Keyword-aware optimal route search. *PVLDB*, 5(11):1136–1147, 2012.

[6] X. Cao, G. Cong, T. Guo, C. S. Jensen, and B. C. Ooi. Efficient processing of spatial group keyword queries. *ACM Trans. Database Syst.*, 40(2):13, 2015.

[7] X. Cao, G. Cong, C. S. Jensen, and B. C. Ooi. Collective spatial keyword querying. In *SIGMOD*, pages 373–384, 2011.

[8] X. Cao, G. Cong, C. S. Jensen, and M. L. Yiu. Retrieving regions of interest for user exploration. *PVLDB*, 7(9):733–744, 2014.

[9] X. Cao, G. Cong, C. S. Jensen, and M. L. Yiu. Retrieving regions of interest for user exploration. *PVLDB*, 7(9):733–744, 2014.

[10] A. Cary, O. Wolfson, and N. Rishe. Efficient and scalable method for processing top-k spatial Boolean queries. In *SSDBM*, pages 87–95, 2010.

[11] L. Chen, G. Cong, and X. Cao. An efficient query indexing mechanism for filtering geo-textual data. In *SIGMOD*, pages 749–760, 2013.

[12] L. Chen, G. Cong, X. Cao, and K. Tan. Temporal spatial-keyword top-k publish/subscribe. In *ICDE*, pages 255–266, 2015.

[13] L. Chen, G. Cong, C. S. Jensen, and D. Wu. Spatial keyword query processing: An experimental evaluation. *PVLDB*, 6(3):217–228, 2013.

[14] L. Chen, X. Lin, H. Hu, C. S. Jensen, and J. Xu. Answering why-not questions on spatial keyword top-k queries. In *ICDE*, pages 279–290, 2015.

[15] L. Chen, X. Lin, H. Hu, C. S. Jensen, and J. Xu. Answering why-not spatial keyword top-k queries via keyword adaption. In *ICDE*, to appear, 2016.

[16] Y. Chen, T. Suel, and A. Markowetz. Efficient query processing in geographic web search engines. In *SIGMOD*, pages 277–288, 2006.

[17] D.-W. Choi, C.-W. Chung, and Y. Tao. A scalable algorithm for maximizing range sum in spatial databases. *PVLDB*, 5(11):1088–1099, 2012.

[18] F. Choudhury, J. S. Culpepper, T. Sellis, and X. Cao. Maximizing bichromatic reverse spatial and textual k nearest neighbor queries. *PVLDB*, 9(6):456–467, 2016.

[19] M. Christoforaki, J. He, C. Dimopoulos, A. Markowetz, and T. Suel. Text vs. space: efficient geo-search query processing. In *CIKM*, pages 423–432, 2011.

[20] G. Cong, H. Lu, B. C. Ooi, D. Zhang, and M. Zhang. Efficient spatial keyword search in trajectory databases. *CoRR*, abs/1205.2880, 2012.

[21] G. Cong, C. S.Jensen, and D. Wu. Efficient retrieval of the top-k most relevant spatial web objects. *PVLDB*, pages 337–348, 2009.

[22] J. Fan, G. Li, L. Zhou, S. Chen, and J. Hu. SEAL: spatio-textual similarity search. *PVLDB*, 5(9):824–835, 2012.

[23] K. Feng, G. Cong, S. S. Bhowmick, W.-C. Peng, and C. Miao. Towards best region search for data exploration. In *SIGMOD*, to appear, 2016.

[24] W. Feng, C. Zhang, W. Zhang, J. Han, J. Wang, C. Aggarwal, and J. Huang. STREAMCUBE: hierarchical spatio-temporal hashtag clustering for event exploration over the Twitter stream. In *ICDE*, pages 1561–1572, 2015.

[25] L. Guo, D. Zhang, G. Li, K. Tan, and Z. Bao. Location-aware pub/sub system: When continuous moving queries meet dynamic event streams. In *SIGMOD*, pages 843–857, 2015.

[26] T. Guo, X. Cao, and G. Cong. Efficient algorithms for answering the m-closest keywords query. In *SIGMOD*, pages 405–418, 2015.

[27] R. Hariharan, B. Hore, C. Li, and S. Mehrotra. Processing spatial-keyword (SK) queries in geographic information retrieval (GIR) systems. In *SSDBM*, page 16, 2007.

[28] H. Hu, Y. Liu, G. Li, J. Feng, and K. Tan. A location-aware publish/subscribe framework for parameterized spatio-textual subscriptions. In *ICDE*, pages 711–722, 2015.

[29] I.D.Felipe, V.Hristidis, and N.Rishe. Keyword search on spatial databases. In *ICDE*, pages 656–665, 2008.

[30] H. Imai and T. Asano. Finding the connected components and a maximum clique of an intersection graph of rectangles in the plane. *Journal of Algorithms*, 4(4):310–323, 1983.

[31] A. Kalinin, U. Cetintemel, and S. Zdonik. Interactive data exploration using semantic windows. In *SIGMOD*, pages 505–516, 2014.

[32] I. Keles, S. Šaltenis, and C. S. Jensen. Synthesis of partial rankings of points of interest using crowdsourcing. In *GIR*, pages 15:1–15:10, 2015.

[33] H. A. Khan, M. A. Sharaf, and A. Albarrak. Divide: efficient diversification for interactive data exploration. In *SSDBM*, pages 15:1–15:12, 2014.

[34] A. Khodaei, C. Shahabi, and C. Li. Hybrid indexing and seamless ranking of spatial and textual features of web documents. In *DEXA (1)*, pages 450–466, 2010.

[35] G. Li, Y. Wang, T. Wang, and J. Feng. Location-aware publish/subscribe. In *KDD*, pages 802–810, 2013.

[36] X. Li, G. Cong, X. Li, T. N. Pham, and S. Krishnaswamy. Rank-GeoFM: A ranking based geographical factorization method for point of interest recommendation. In *SIGIR*, pages 433–442, 2015.

[37] C. Long, R. C. Wong, K. Wang, and A. W. Fu. Collective spatial keyword queries: a distance owner-driven approach. In *SIGMOD*, pages 689–700, 2013.

[38] J. Lu, Y. Lu, and G. Cong. Reverse spatial and textual k nearest neighbor search. In *SIGMOD*, pages 349–360, 2011.

[39] S. Luo, Y. Luo, S. Zhou, G. Cong, and J. Guan. Distributed spatial keyword querying on road networks. In *EDBT*, pages 235–246, 2014.

[40] A. Magdy, L. Alarabi, S. Al-Harthi, M. Musleh, T. M. Ghanem, S. Ghani, and M. F. Mokbel. Taghreed: a system for querying, analyzing, and visualizing geotagged microblogs. In *SIGSPATIAL*, pages 163–172, 2014.

[41] G. Marchionini. Exploratory search: From finding to understanding. *Commun. ACM*, 49(4):41–46, Apr. 2006.

[42] S. C. Nandy and B. B. Bhattacharya. A unified algorithm for finding maximum and minimum object enclosing rectangles and cuboids. *Computers & Mathematics with Applications*, 29(8):45–61, 1995.

[43] J. B. Rocha-Junior, O. Gkorgkas, S. Jonassen, and K. Nørvåg. Efficient processing of top-k spatial keyword queries. In *SSTD*, pages 205–222, 2011.

[44] J. B. Rocha-Junior and K. Nørvåg. Top-k spatial keyword queries on road networks. In *EDBT*, pages 168–179, 2012.

[45] J. Sankaranarayanan, H. Samet, B. E. Teitler, M. D. Lieberman, and J. Sperling. Twitterstand: news in tweets. In *SIGSPATIAL*, pages 42–51, 2009.

[46] A. Skovsgaard and C. S. Jensen. Top-k point of interest retrieval using standard indexes. In *SIGSPATIAL*, pages 173–182, 2014.

[47] A. Skovsgaard and C. S. Jensen. Finding top-k relevant groups of spatial web objects. *VLDB J.*, 24(4):537–555, 2015.

[48] A. Skovsgaard, D. Sidlauskas, and C. S. Jensen. Scalable top-k spatio-temporal term querying. In *ICDE*, pages 148–159, 2014.

[49] Y. Tao, X. Hu, D.-W. Choi, and C.-W. Chung. Approximate maxrs in spatial databases. *PVLDB*, 6(13):1546–1557, 2013.

[50] S. Vaid, C. B. Jones, H. Joho, and M. Sanderson. Spatio-textual indexing for geographical search on the web. In *SSTD*, pages 218–235, 2005.

[51] M. Walther and M. Kaisser. Geo-spatial event detection in the Twitter stream. In *ECIR*, pages 356–367, 2013.

[52] X. Wang, Y. Zhang, W. Zhang, X. Lin, and W. Wang.

Selectivity estimation on streaming spatio-textual data using local correlations. *PVLDB*, 8(2):101–112, 2014.

[53] X. Wang, Y. Zhang, W. Zhang, X. Lin, and W. Wang. AP-Tree: Efficiently support continuous spatial-keyword queries over stream. In *ICDE*, pages 1107–1118, 2015.

[54] D. Wu, B. Choi, J. Xu, and C. S. Jensen. Authentication of moving top-k spatial keyword queries. *IEEE Trans. Knowl. Data Eng.*, 27(4):922–935, 2015.

[55] D. Wu, G. Cong, and C. S. Jensen. A framework for efficient spatial web object retrieval. *VLDB J.*, 21(6):797–822, 2012.

[56] D. Wu, M. L. Yiu, G. Cong, and C. S. Jensen. Joint top-k spatial keyword query processing. *IEEE Trans. Knowl. Data Eng.*, 24(10):1889–1903, 2012.

[57] D. Wu, M. L. Yiu, and C. S. Jensen. Moving spatial keyword queries: Formulation, methods, and analysis. *ACM Trans. Database Syst.*, 38(1):7, 2013.

[58] D. Wu, M. L. Yiu, C. S. Jensen, and G. Cong. Efficient continuously moving top-k spatial keyword query processing. In *ICDE*, pages 541–552, 2011.

[59] X. Xie, P. Jin, M. L. Yiu, J. Du, M. Yuan, and C. S. Jensen. Enabling scalable geographic service sharing with weighted imprecise voronoi cells. *IEEE Trans. Knowl. Data Eng.*, 28(2):439–453, 2016.

[60] B. Yao, M. Tang, and F. Li. Multi-approximate-keyword routing in GIS data. In *SIGSPATIAL*, pages 201–210, 2011.

[61] C. Zhang, Y. Zhang, W. Zhang, and X. Lin. Inverted linear quadtree: Efficient top k spatial keyword search. In *ICDE*, pages 901–912, 2013.

[62] C. Zhang, Y. Zhang, W. Zhang, X. Lin, M. A. Cheema, and X. Wang. Diversified spatial keyword search on road networks. In *EDBT*, pages 367–378, 2014.

[63] D. Zhang, Y. M. Chee, A. Mondal, A. K. H. Tung, and M. Kitsuregawa. Keyword search in spatial databases: Towards searching by document. In *ICDE*, pages 688–699, 2009.

[64] D. Zhang, B. C. Ooi, and A. K. H. Tung. Locating mapped resources in web 2.0. In *ICDE*, pages 521–532, 2010.

[65] D. Zhang, K.-L. Tan, and A. K. H. Tung. Scalable top-k spatial keyword search. In *EDBT*, pages 359–370, 2013.

[66] K. Zhao, L. Chen, and G. Cong. Topic exploration in spatio-temporal document collections. In *SIGMOD*, to appear, 2016.

[67] Y. Zhou, X. Xie, C. Wang, Y. Gong, and W.-Y. Ma. Hybrid index structures for location-based web search. In *CIKM*, pages 155–162, 2005.

Provenance: On and Behind the Screens

Melanie Herschel
Institute for Parallel and Distributed Systems
University of Stuttgart
Stuttgart, Germany
melanie.herschel@ipvs.uni-stuttgart.de

Marcel Hlawatsch
Visualization Research Center
University of Stuttgart
Stuttgart, Germany
marcel.hlawatsch@visus.uni-stuttgart.de

ABSTRACT

Collecting and processing *provenance*, i.e., information describing the production process of some end product, is important in various applications, e.g., to assess quality, to ensure reproducibility, or to reinforce trust in the end product. In the past, different types of provenance meta-data have been proposed, each with a different scope. The first part of the proposed tutorial provides an overview and comparison of these different types of provenance.

To put provenance to good use, it is essential to be able to interact with and present provenance data in a user-friendly way. Often, users interested in provenance are not necessarily experts in databases or query languages, as they are typically domain experts of the product and production process for which provenance is collected (biologists, journalists, etc.). Furthermore, in some scenarios, it is difficult to use solely queries for analyzing and exploring provenance data. The second part of this tutorial therefore focuses on enabling users to leverage provenance through adapted visualizations. To this end, we will present some fundamental concepts of visualization before we discuss possible visualizations for provenance.

1. PROVENANCE TYPES AND VISUALIZATIONS

Provenance generally refers to any information that describes the production process of an end product, which can be anything from a piece of data to a physical object (food, chemical compound, business report, etc.). Thus, in general, provenance information includes meta-data about entities, processes, activities, and persons involved in the production process. As discussed below, provenance information exists under various forms, i.e., different *provenance types* exist. Essentially, these different types have been motivated by varying application requirements and usage scenarios.

Visualization deals with the visual representation of data. Since the visual channel is the largest information channel of the human, visualization enables the analysis and exploration of large amounts of data, especially when combined with suitable interaction methods. Considering the variety of provenance types, it is clear that there is no single visualization concept that can represent all types of provenance in the best possible way. To be most efficient, the visualization must be developed and adapted to each type of provenance and each type of application. This tutorial therefore presents general visualization concepts and approaches applicable to provenance data. The goal is to provide basic knowledge for designing, developing, and applying provenance visualization.

Structure. In the remainder of this section, we provide some background on both provenance and visualization in the context of provenance. Section 2 summarizes the learning objectives and the tutorial outline. Tutorial format and audience are covered in Section 3 before the tutorial's instructors are briefly introduced in Section 4.

1.1 Provenance Types

As mentioned above, different types of provenance have been proposed, guided by varying application needs. We classify the prevalent types of provenance into four main types of provenance, namely *data provenance*, *workflow provenance*, *information systems provenance*, and *provenance meta-data*. Roughly speaking, these four types form a type hierarchy, as illustrated in Figure 1. Essentially, as we move up from one level to a more specific level of the provenance type hierarchy, the more specialized the provenance type becomes, i.e., its domain reduces, meaning that either the set of possible processes or the set of possible provenance data models reduces, as illustrated in Table 1.

We now briefly introduce the different types in more detail, starting with the most general one.

SIGMOD'16, June 26-July 01, 2016, San Francisco, CA, USA
 ISBN 978-1-4503-3531-7/16/06...$15.00
DOI: http://dx.doi.org/10.1145/2882903.2912568

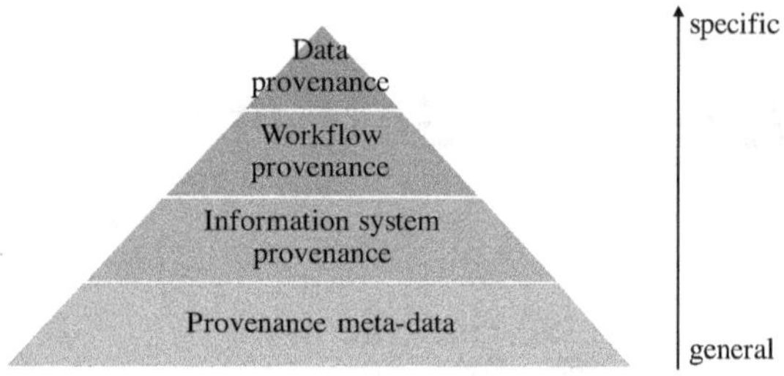

Figure 1: Provenance type hierarchy.

Prov. type	Process type	Prov. data model
data provenance	structured query language	based on specific data model and query language of corresponding process type
workflow prov.	workflows	standards-based
information system provenance	processes supported by information systems	standards-based
prov. meta-data	anything	anything

Table 1: Restrictions on process type and provenance data model on provenance (prov.) types.

Provenance meta-data. Provenance meta-data can be any type of data describing the source, the process of acquisition, the context or environment of acquisition etc. of some data. This most general type of provenance provides users with the widest degree of freedom to model, store, or access the provenance of any type of end product or production process. We distinguish provenance meta-data from other meta-data based on its intended purpose. Indeed, whereas general meta-data aims at assigning meaning to data, provenance information is descriptive of the data derivation process [13]. Note that these meta-data types may overlap. For instance, the resolution of a digital photograph can be seen as meta-data translating the quality of the photograph. At the same time, it is a key parameter in the process of taking and post-processing the photograph. Without further restrictions, provenance meta-data can be modeled, stored, or queried in any conceivable way, justifying the generality of this first type of provenance. This type of provenance, for instance, applies on proprietary solutions for provenance management (e.g., Informatica Big Data Management, IBM InfoSphere Information Governance Catalog, SAS Lineage).

Information system provenance. The problems of proprietary solutions for provenance management, in particular the interoperability between different information systems, have initiated standardization efforts on both the syntax (e.g., XML [5] or RDF [29]) and semantics of provenance meta-data (e.g., [11, 21]). One significant result of these efforts is a W3C standard, W3C PROV [20], that includes a clearly defined data model, ontology, and mechanisms for accessing and querying provenance. In summary, information system provenance covers provenance for various different types of production processes supported by information systems that complies with some standard representation of provenance. As we further move up the provenance hierarchy, the processes for which provenance are collected become more specific.

Workflow provenance. Due to requirements such as documentation, repeatability, accountability, or parameter evaluation, provenance has become an integral part of workflow management tools (as surveyed for instance in [12, 14]). To represent provenance, these typically rely on a standard representation of provenance for better exchange and interoperability, which are already at the heart of information systems provenance. What distinguishes workflow provenance from information system provenance is the restriction to a very specific family of processes, i.e., workflows. This specialization entails a specialization of the semantics of provenance meta-data. In particular, when considering workflow provenance, we distinguish between retrospective and prospective workflow provenance or different provenance granularities.

Data provenance. Data provenance (surveys include [10]) allows to track the processing of individual data items (e.g., tuples) at the "highest resolution", i.e., the provenance itself is at the level of individual data items (and the operations they undergo). Collecting data provenance typically applies on structured data models and declarative query languages or dataflow languages with clearly defined semantics of individual operators or functions (SQL [16], Spark [19]). This is necessary to either recover data provenance of individual data items after running a data transformation, or to extend data items or operators to pass on their provenance annotation as the data is processed. Clearly, the data model of the generated provenance meta-data highly depends on the data model of the processed data and the semantics of operators of the data manipulation language.

As we will discuss in more detail in Section 2, this tutorial's first learning objective is to give the audience an introduction to the four introduced types of provenance. Thus, this tutorial provides an in-depth survey on provenance. Additionally, we will discuss details of selected provenance methods to allow for a more informed decision when faced with a problem or application that may benefit from provenance.

1.2 Visualization

The primary goal of visualization is to find a suitable visual representation of data that provides the viewer with the information she requires or is interested in. This requires usually emphasizing or hiding parts or aspects of the data. To be effective, the visualization must be designed and adapted for the specific application, its data, and its context. It is therefore not possible to find a single visualization method that represents all the different types of provenance in an effective and useful way. Thus, this tutorial will introduce common visualization concepts and principles with the goal to provide the audience with basic knowledge to select or develop provenance visualization for their application.

Perceptual aspects. Human perception is an important aspect when developing a visualization because it influences how the visual information is processed and interpreted by the viewer [28]. Three Important topics in this context are (i) the usage and the effect of colors [6], (ii) issues with 3D perception and reasons why information visualization typically uses only 2D representations [26], and (iii) the usefulness of animation [27].

Visual metaphors. There are established and common visual metaphors for different classes or aspects of data. For instance, relational data or graphs can be represented with node-link diagrams, adjacency matrices, or adjacency lists [18]. There are different ways to represent the time dimension of temporal data, e.g., by using a spatial dimension or animation [1]. Glyphs are a powerful visual metaphor that can encode many different data dimensions [4]. Furthermore, the visualization can make use of different layouts for the data dimensions, e.g., Cartesian or radial layouts [8].

Presentation and interaction concepts. There are some basic principles for the presentation of the data and how the user can interact with the visualization. Multiple coordinated views can be used to provide different visual representations for the same data to combine the advantages of different visualization methods [22]. The different views must be synchronized, i.e., if something is changed in one view, the other views must be updated accordingly. Strongly related to this is the concept of "brushing and linking" [7]: selecting data elements in one view also highlights them in the other views. Another concept is "overview first, details on demand" [24]. Intuitively, the idea is to initially provide an overview of the data and then allow the user to interactively explore and analyze parts of it in detail.

By providing an overview on these important visualization aspects, this tutorial will support the attendees in selecting an appropriate visualization method for their type of provenance (Section 1.1) and application. Furthermore, it will help them to assess the suitability of existing provenance visualization methods for their applications.

Provenance visualization. Examples for such visualization methods include our work [17] on visualizing workflow provenance, VisTrails [9], or the work by Shrinivasan and Wijk [25] on supporting analytical reasoning. A recent survey [23] provides further examples.

2. TUTORIAL OUTLINE

The goal of the tutorial is twofold. First, it aims at giving an introduction and general understanding of provenance types and techniques to obtain provenance information. Second, it provides an introduction to visualization in general and its application to provenance. With such a broad survey, this tutorial will equip non-experts with the essential knowledge necessary to begin research in the field of provenance in general, with an emphasis on provenance exploration, analysis, and processing based on visual user interaction. More specifically, after attending the tutorial, we expect the audience to:

- Obtain a general understanding of types of provenance and typical applications leveraging these different types. Thus, when confronted with a problem requiring or benefiting from provenance, adequate solutions may be developed more rapidly, accurately, and systematically.
- Get a deeper understanding of basic methods and algorithms employed to represent and obtain provenance information as well as an overview of the state of the art of more advanced methods.
- Understand the importance of visualization to represent and interact with data and know which visualization concepts and techniques are best amenable to provenance-based applications.

To achieve these learning objectives, we propose the following tutorial outline.

1. Motivation and provenance overview. We begin the tutorial with a motivation for provenance metadata, based on multiple real-life applications from various domains. Possible domains include business analytics, source code auditing, scientific data processing, query debugging and fixing, or visualization. Based on these use-cases, we introduce the provenance type hierarchy depicted in Figure 1. We show examples of systems operating at each of these levels (including those in our introduction) and clearly highlight the differences distinguishing the different provenance types, along the lines briefly covered in Section 1.1.

2. Provenance types. The remainder of the first part of the tutorial delves into details of individual provenance types, primarily focusing on workflow provenance and data provenance. The most general provenance type that essentially represents a "placeholder" for further provenance types as well as information system provenance will be briefly covered through a high-level discussion and illustration. For the remaining provenance type, we begin with the summary of an in-depth survey of the state of the art, based on novel classifications. For instance, data provenance research may be classified as illustrated in Figure 2, significantly extending the classification previously proposed in [10]. We then discuss selected solutions representative of each provenance type in a bit more detail. Whereas workflow provenance will be detailed as proposed in [9, 2], our discussion of data provenance will introduce provenance semi-rings (how-provenance) [15] and their missing-data provenance counterpart [3].

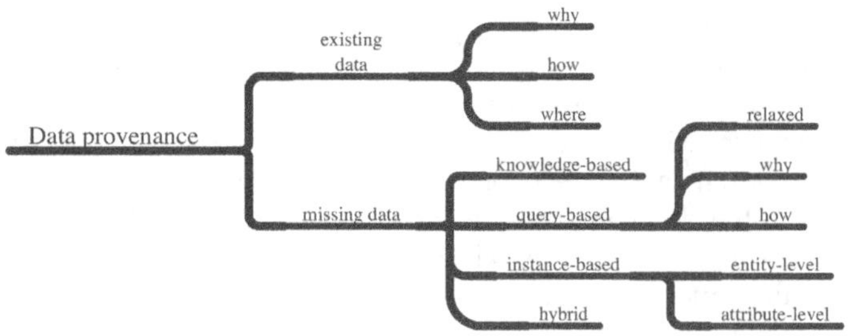

Figure 2: Data provenance survey classification.

3. Visualization basics The second part of the tutorial is related to visualization. We first discuss basic information visualization concepts applicable to provenance data as introduced in Section 1.2. These include perceptual aspects related to color, 2D and 3D representations, and animation. We discuss different visual metaphors, like glyphs or graph representations, that can be and have been used to represent provenance data. We exemplify possible mappings of the temporal dimension and different visualization layout strategies. Furthermore, we introduce common presentation and interaction concepts like multiple coordinated views. Some of these concepts are then demonstrated in the following step-by-step example of provenance visualization.

4. Visualization for provenance. On the example of our work [17], we will demonstrate how to design and develop a suitable visualization for workflow provenance (Figure 3). We will discuss different design choices and what visualization methods are suitable for the considered application scenario.

5. Open research issues. After surveying the state of the art, we will discuss selected open research issues at the intersection of provenance and visualization. Some of these are ongoing research within a national collaborative research center[1]. In particular, we will provide details and food for thought on (i) provenance visualization quality quantification and its potential uses, (ii) visualization-guided pay-as-you-go provenance computation and collection, and (iii) semi-automatic provenance visualization optimization.

3. EXPECTED AUDIENCE

The target audience for this ninety minute tutorial consists of both students and researchers with a general interest in the research fields of provenance and visualization, both being listed as SIGMOD 2016 topics of interest. Additionally, provenance is a relevant field for further areas of interest to SIGMOD, including data warehousing, database monitoring and tuning, database usability, information extraction, information retrieval,

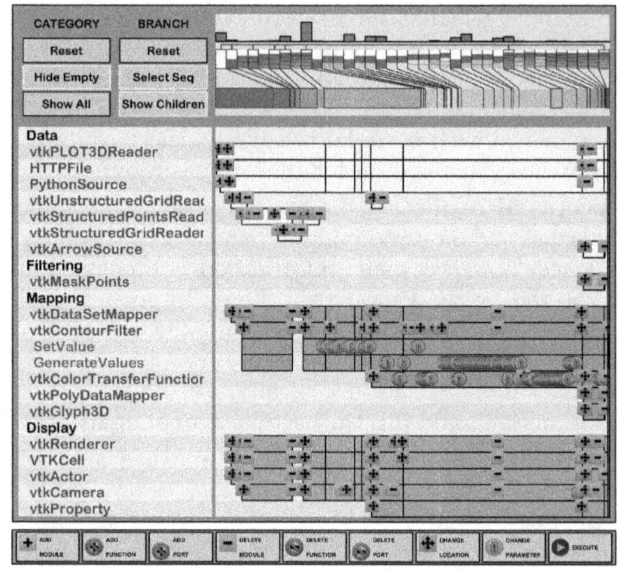

Figure 3: Provenance visualization example. The visualization shows the changes in a visualization workflow made by the user when using VisTrails [9].

knowledge discovery, data integration and cleaning, scientific databases, and uncertain databases.

As prior knowledge, we expect basic knowledge on databases (which any SIGMOD attendee typically has). Building on this knowledge, we will provide a brief self-sufficient motivation and introduction to essential preliminaries of provenance to enable non-specialists to follow the subsequent detailed discussion. Given the scope of SIGMOD, we do not expect any prior knowledge on visualization and will devote more time to the introduction of fundamental concepts.

4. BIOGRAPHIES

Melanie Herschel is a professor at the University of Stuttgart. Her primary research interests include provenance, data integration, entity resolution, and data engineering. Currently, she is a primary investigator within the Collaborative Research Center "Quantitative Methods for Visual Computing" (SFB-TRR 161), where she explores synergies between visualization and provenance. She is also the leading scientist of the Nautilus project, leveraging provenance for query debugging and semi-automatic fixing. Recently, she has been the area co-chair at ICDE 2015 and the publicity chair of SIGMOD 2016.

Marcel Hlawatsch has a PhD in computer science and works at the Visualization Research Center of the University of Stuttgart (VISUS), Germany, as a research associate. His research topics cover, amongst others, the visualization of provenance data, (dynamic) graphs, and eye tracking data. He is also the manager of the Collaborative Research Center "Quantitative Methods for

[1]Collaborative Research Center "Quantitative Methods for Visual Computing" (SFB-TRR 161): http://www.sfbtrr161.de

Visual Computing" (SFB-TRR 161) at the University of Stuttgart funded by the German research foundation DFG.

Acknowledgements. The authors thank the German Research Foundation (DFG) for financial support within projects B01 and D03 of SFB/Transregio 161.

5. REFERENCES

[1] W. Aigner, S. Miksch, H. Schumann, and C. Tominski. *Visualization of Time-Oriented Data*. Human–Computer Interaction Series. Springer London, 2011.

[2] Y. Amsterdamer, S. B. Davidson, D. Deutch, T. Milo, J. Stoyanovich, and V. Tannen. Putting lipstick on pig: Enabling database-style workflow provenance. *Proceedings of the VLDB Endowment (PVLDB)*, 5(4), 2011.

[3] N. Bidoit, M. Herschel, and A. Tzompanaki. Efficient computation of polynomial explanations of why-not questions. In *International Conference on Information and Knowledge Management, (CIKM)*, 2015.

[4] R. Borgo, J. Kehrer, D. H. Chung, E. Maguire, R. S. Laramee, H. Hauser, M. Ward, and M. Chen. Glyph-based visualization: Foundations, design guidelines, techniques and applications. *Eurographics State of the Art Reports*, 2013.

[5] R. Bose and J. Frew. Composing lineage metadata with XML for custom satellite-derived data products. In *International Conference on Scientific and Statistical Database Management (SSDBM)*, 2004.

[6] C. A. Brewer. Color use guidelines for data representation. *Section on Statistical Graphics, American Statistical Association*, 1999.

[7] A. Buja, J. A. McDonald, J. Michalak, and W. Stuetzle. Interactive data visualization using focusing and linking. In *International Conference on Visualization (VIS)*, 1991.

[8] M. Burch and D. Weiskopf. On the benefits and drawbacks of radial diagrams. In W. Huang, editor, *Handbook of Human Centric Visualization*. Springer New York, 2014.

[9] S. P. Callahan, J. Freire, E. Santos, C. E. Scheidegger, C. T. Silva, and H. T. Vo. Vistrails: Visualization meets data management. In *Proceedings of the 2006 ACM SIGMOD International Conference on Management of Data*, 2006.

[10] J. Cheney, L. Chiticariu, and W. C. Tan. Provenance in databases: Why, how, and where. *Foundations and Trends in Databases*, 1(4), 2009.

[11] P. P. da Silva, D. L. McGuinness, and R. McCool. Knowledge provenance infrastructure. *IEEE Data Engineering Bulletin*, 26(4), 2003.

[12] S. B. Davidson and J. Freire. Provenance and scientific workflows: challenges and opportunities. In *International Conference on Management of Data, (SIGMOD)*, 2008.

[13] E. Deelman, G. B. Berriman, A. L. Chervenak, Ó. Corcho, P. T. Groth, and L. Moreau. Metadata and provenance management. In A. Shoshani and D. Rotem, editors, *Scientific Data Management: Challenges, Technology, and Deployment*. Chapman & Hall/CRC, 1st edition, 2009.

[14] J. Freire, D. Koop, E. Santos, and C. T. Silva. Provenance for computational tasks: A survey. *Computing in Science and Engineering*, 10(3), 2008.

[15] T. J. Green, G. Karvounarakis, and V. Tannen. Provenance semirings. In *Principles of Database Systems (PODS)*, 2007.

[16] M. Herschel. A hybrid approach to answering why-not questions on relational query results. *ACM Journal on Data and Information Quality (JDIQ)*, 5(3), 2015.

[17] M. Hlawatsch, M. Burch, F. Beck, J. Freire, C. Silva, and D. Weiskopf. Visualizing the evolution of module workflows. In *International Conference on Information Visualisation (IV)*, 2015.

[18] M. Hlawatsch, M. Burch, and D. Weiskopf. Visual adjacency lists for dynamic graphs. *IEEE Trans. on Visualization and Computer Graphics*, 20(11), 2014.

[19] M. Interlandi, K. Shah, S. D. Tetali, M. Gulzar, S. Yoo, M. Kim, T. D. Millstein, and T. Condie. Titian: Data provenance support in spark. *Proceedings of the VLDB Endowment (PVLDB)*, 9(3), 2015.

[20] P. Missier, K. Belhajjame, and J. Cheney. The W3C PROV family of specifications for modelling provenance metadata. In *Conference on Extending Database Technology (EDBT)*, 2013.

[21] L. Moreau, B. Clifford, J. Freire, J. Futrelle, Y. Gil, P. Groth, N. Kwasnikowska, S. Miles, P. Missier, J. Myers, B. Plale, Y. Simmhan, E. Stephan, and J. V. den Bussche. The open provenance model core specification (v1.1). *Future Generation Computer Systems*, 27(6), 2011.

[22] C. North and B. Shneiderman. Snap-together visualization: can users construct and operate coordinated visualizations? *International Journal of Human-Computer Studies*, 53(5), 2000.

[23] E. Ragan, A. Endert, J. Sanyal, and J. Chen. Characterizing provenance in visualization and data analysis: An organizational framework of provenance types and purposes. *IEEE Trans. on Visualization and Computer Graphics*, 22(1), 2016.

[24] B. Shneiderman. The eyes have it: a task by data type taxonomy for information visualizations. In *IEEE Symposium on Visual Languages 1996*, 1996.

[25] Y. B. Shrinivasan and J. J. van Wijk. Supporting the analytical reasoning process in information visualization. In *SIGCHI Conference on Human Factors in Computing Systems*, 2008.

[26] M. Tory, A. E. Kirkpatrick, M. S. Atkins, and T. Moller. Visualization task performance with 2d, 3d, and combination displays. *IEEE Trans. on Visualization and Computer Graphics*, 12(1), 2006.

[27] B. Tversky, J. B. Morrison, and M. Betrancourt. Animation: can it facilitate? *International Journal of Human-Computer Studies*, 57(4), 2002.

[28] C. Ware. *Information Visualization: Perception for Design*. Information Visualization: Perception for Design. Morgan Kaufmann, 2013.

[29] J. Zhao, C. Wroe, C. A. Goble, R. Stevens, D. Quan, and R. M. Greenwood. Using semantic web technologies for representing e-science provenance. In *International Semantic Web Conference (ISWC)*, 2004.

Microblogs Data Management Systems: Querying, Analysis, and Visualization

Mohamed F. Mokbel Amr Magdy

Department of Computer Science and Engineering
University of Minnesota, Minneapolis, MN, USA
{mokbel,amr}@cs.umn.edu

ABSTRACT

Microblogs data, e.g., tweets, reviews, news comments, and social media comments, has gained considerable attention in recent years due to its popularity and rich contents. Nowadays, microblogs applications span a wide spectrum of interests, including analyzing events and users activities and critical applications like discovering health issues and rescue services. Consequently, major research efforts are spent to manage, analyze, and visualize microblogs data to support different applications. In this tutorial, we give a 1.5 hours overview about microblogs data management, analysis, visualization, and systems. The tutorial gives a comprehensive review for research on core data management components to support microblogs queries at scale. This includes system-level issues and on-going work on supporting microblogs data through the rising wave of big data systems. In addition, the tutorial reviews research on microblogs data analysis and visualization. Through its different parts, the tutorial highlights the challenges and opportunities in microblogs data research.

1. INTRODUCTION

Microblogs data, e.g., tweets, reviews, news comments, and social media comments, has become very popular in recent years. Everyday, over billion users post more than four billions microblogs [10, 43] on Facebook and Twitter. Such tremendous amounts of user-generated data have rich contents, e.g., news, updates on on-going events, reviews, and discussions in politics, products, and many others. The richness of microblogs data has motivated researchers and developers worldwide to take advantage of microblogs to support a wide variety of practical applications, including social media analysis [44], discovering health-related issues [33], real-time news delivery [4], rescue services [9], and geotargeted advertising [30]. The distinguished nature of microblogs data, that includes large data sizes and high velocity, has motivated researchers to develop new techniques for data management to support microblogs analysis and visualization at scale.

This research is capitally supported by NSF grants IIS-0952977, IIS-1218168, IIS-1525953, CNS-1512877, and the University of Minnesota Doctoral Dissertation Fellowship.

SIGMOD '16, June 26–July 1, 2016, San Francisco, CA, USA.

© 2016 ACM. ISBN 978-1-4503-3531-7/16/06. . . $15.00

DOI: http://dx.doi.org/10.1145/2882903.2912570

In this tutorial, we aim to provide a comprehensive review for almost all existing techniques and systems for microblogs data management, analysis, and visualization, since the inception of Twitter in 2006. Figure 1 depicts a summary of the techniques and systems that will be covered in this tutorial in a timeline format. The horizontal axis in Figure 1 represents the year of publication or system release for each technique/system, while the vertical axis represents the research topic. The techniques are then classif ed into three categories: (1) techniques that deal with real-time data, i.e., very recent data, depicted by a f lled black circle, (2) techniques that deal with historical data, depicted by a blank circle, and (3) techniques that deal with both real-time and historical data, depicted by a blank triangle.

Figure 2 gives the detailed tutorial outline and timing that lasts for **1.5 hours**. The f rst f ve minutes will be an introduction to the world of microblogs and a motivation for the need for research in data management. Following that quick introduction, the rest of the tutorial is divided into four parts: (1) microblogs data analysis (20 minutes), (2) microblogs data management (30 minutes), (3) microblogs data visualization (15 minutes), and (4) microblogs systems (20 minutes). The following sections describe the contents and scope of each part.

2. PART 1: MICROBLOGS DATA ANALYSIS

This part covers the literature for microblogs data analysis that are depicted in the f rst four rows of Figure 1. As shown in Figure 2, this part will take 20 minutes in total, where f ve minutes will be dedicated for each of the following four types of analysis:

- **Event detection and analysis** [1, 11, 36, 38, 42, 44]: This work exploits the fact that microblogs users post many updates on on-going events. Such updates are identif ed, grouped, and analyzed to discover events in real time [1, 36] or analyze long term events [11, 38, 42, 44], e.g., elections.
- **Recommendation** [7, 14, 32]: This work exploits microblogs user-generated contents as means for catching user preferences. The main tasks is to recommend real-time news to read [32], authority users to follow [7], or users who share similar interests [14].
- **Sentiment and semantic analysis** [3, 27, 29]: This work quantif es positive and negative opinions in social media discussions as a pre-processing step for this data to be used in other analysis tasks, e.g., product review or election candidate surveying.
- **User analysis** [14, 17, 20, 45]: This work is mainly interested in analyzing user information to identify top inf uential

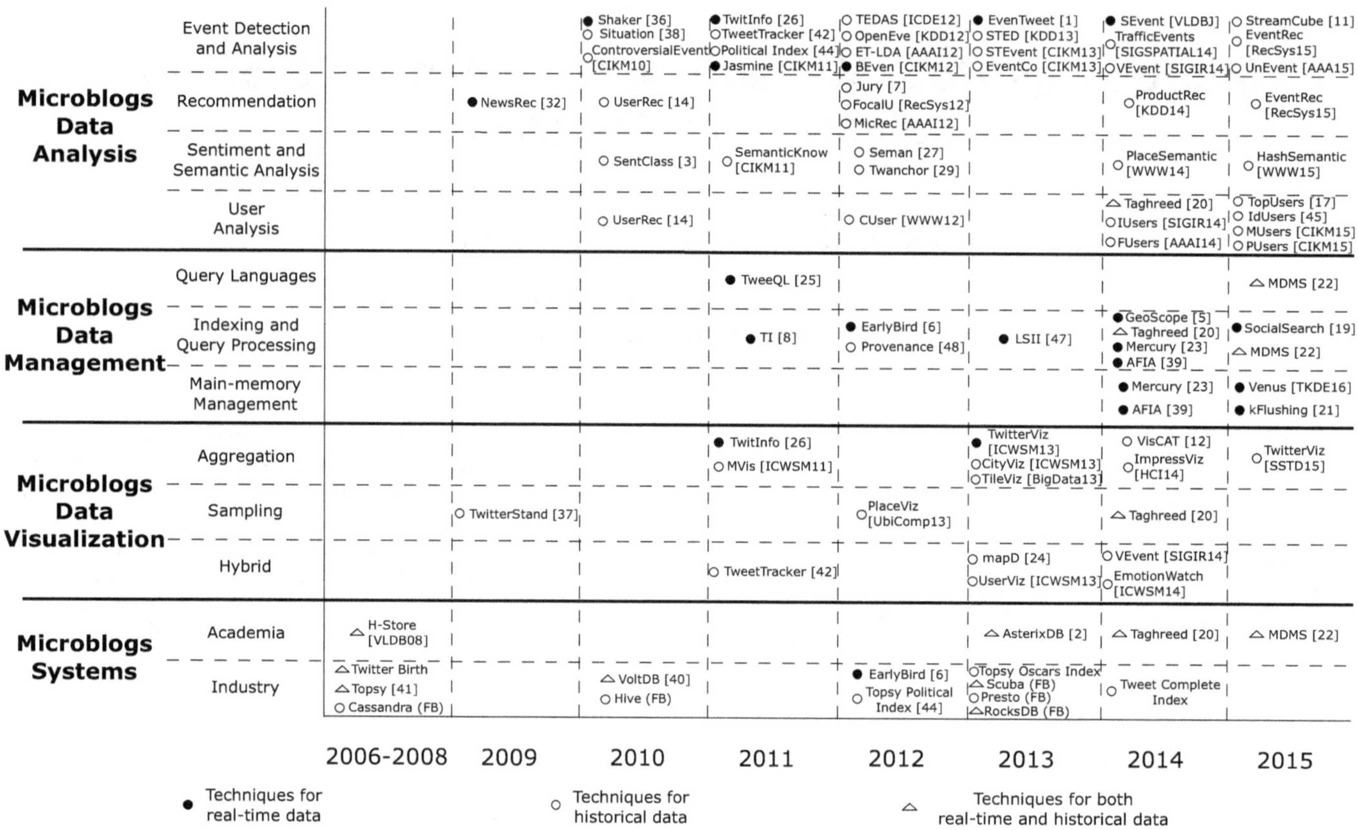

Figure 1: Microblogs Timeline

users in certain regions or topics [17, 20, 45], or discover users with similar interests [14]. Such users, or group of users, can be used in several scenarios, including posting ads and enhancing their social graph.

Other analysis tasks are addressed on microblogs data in both academic community, e.g., news extraction [32, 37], topic extraction [15, 34], and automatic geotagging [16, 18, 35, 49], and industrial community, e.g., geo-targeted advertising [30] and generic social media analysis [41, 50]. However, for limited time budget and audience engagement, we outline the main performed analysis that span a wide variety of interests and applications.

3. PART 2: MICROBLOGS DATA MANAGEMENT

This part of the tutorial covers existing work for microblogs data management that are depicted in the f fth to seventh rows of Figure 1. As shown in Figure 2, this part will take 30 minutes in total, and include the following three data management areas:

- **Query languages** [22, 25]: This work provides generic query languages that support SQL-like queries on top of microblogs. This facilitates basic Select-Project-Join operators that are able to support a variety of queries, either on top of Twitter APIs [25] or in core systems that supports microblogs data management [22].
- **Indexing and query processing**: This work includes various indexing techniques that have been proposed to index incoming microblogs either in memory [5, 6, 20, 23, 39, 47, 48] or in disk [8, 20]. This includes keyword search based on temporal ranking [6, 8], single-attribute search based on generic ranking functions [47], spatial-aware search that exploits location information in microblogs [23], personalized social-aware search that exploits the social graph and produces user-specif c search results [19], and aggregate queries [5, 39] that f nd frequent keywords and correlated locations instead of individual microblog items. Each search technique comes with its index and query processor, and tackles certain limitations in its preceding techniques.
- **Main-memory management** [21, 23, 39]: This work includes techniques that optimize for main-memory consumption and utilization. In recent microblogs indexing and query processing techniques, almost all of them depend on main-memory to host microblogs in their index structures. Thus, some techniques are equipped for main-memory management such that memory resources are eff ciently utilized, either for aggregate queries [39] or basic search queries that retrieve individual data items [21, 23].

4. PART 3: MICROBLOGS DATA VISUALIZATION

This part covers existing work for microblogs data visualization that are depicted in eighth to tenth rows of Figure 1. As shown in Figure 2, this part will take 15 minutes in total, and divides visualization techniques in microblogs into three areas:

- **Aggregation-based Visualization** [12, 26, 46]: This work overcomes the diff culty of visualizing tremendous amount

Introduction and Background (5 minutes)

- Importance and applications of microblogs
- Research literature outline

Part 1: Microblogs Data Analysis (20 minutes)

- Event detection and analysis (5 minutes)
- Recommendation (5 minutes)
- Sentiment and semantic analysis (5 minutes)
- User analysis (5 minutes)

Part 2: Microblogs Data Management (30 minutes)

- Query languages (5 minutes)
- Indexing and query processing (20 minutes)
  - Keyword search (5 minutes)
  - Generic search (5 minutes)
  - Spatial-aware search (5 minutes)
  - Social-aware search (5 minutes)
- Main-memory management (5 minutes)

Part 3: Microblogs Data Visualization (15 minutes)

- Aggregation-based Visualization (5 minutes)
- Sampling-based Visualization (5 minutes)
- Hybrid Visualization (5 minutes)

Part 4: Microblogs Systems (20 minutes)

- Challenges and motivational case studies (5 minutes)
- Microblogs in existing big data systems (15 minutes)
  - Twitter: Digesting, indexing, and querying tweets
  - AsterixDB: Persisting fast data
  - VoltDB: Transactions on fast data
  - Taghreed: Querying, analyzing, and visualizing microblogs

Figure 2: Detailed Outline and Timing of 1.5 hours Tutorial

of data through showing only aggregate information that summarize the large amounts of microblogs data and its contents. Such aggregation is application-dependent and is usually performed based on major attributes, like temporal aggregation [46], spatial aggregation [12, 46], or keyword aggregation [26].

- **Sampling-based Visualization** [20, 37]: This work selects only a sample of microblogs and visualize them to users. The sample of data is of interest to the application, which can be selected based on some relevance criteria, e.g., tweets with news stories [37], or based on interest in certain attribute(s) [20].

- **Hybrid Visualization** [24, 42]: This work combines both aggregation and sampling in visualizing microblogs of interest. The two steps are either used simultaneously with the purpose of interest in certain data items, e.g., analyzing certain events [42], or used sequentially [24, 31] with purpose of bounding the number of microblogs to visualize.

5. PART 4: MICROBLOGS SYSTEMS

This part highlights the current state and the challenges of managing microblogs data through existing big data systems [2, 6, 28, 20, 40], depicted in the last two rows in Figure 1. As shown in Figure 2, this part will take 20 minutes and will give a brief ng on system challenges and motivational case studies. Then, we highlights the data management technologies in the following four systems:

- **Twitter** [6, 28]: Twitter is the most famous microblogging service provider worldwide. Every now and then, Twitter reveals technical details about its underlying systems components. We give a comprehensive review about the data management aspects of Twitter systems, per their published papers [6, 28].

- **AsterixDB** [2]: AsterixDB is a generic big data management system that can support various data sources. Recently, AsterixDB has extended its components to support fast data [13], e.g., microblogs, natively in the system. We review the fast data support in AsterixDB, which shows the challenges in persisting fast data in existing systems.

- **VoltDB** [40]: VoltDB is an emerging big data management system that is mainly optimized for database transactions on fast data, e.g., microblogs. We review the challenges of supporting transactional applications on fast data and solutions at the system level.

- **Taghreed** [20]: Taghreed is the f rst end-to-end holistic system to support microblogs data management. It supports different types of queries on both very recent data as well as historical data. We review the main components of Taghreed system highlighting its distinguishing properties to handle microblogs data.

6. INTENDED AUDIENCE

This tutorial targets researchers and developers who are interested in analyzing, processing, and building applications on microblogs data. Our tutorial gives extensive survey on core components that manages microblogs data at scale, highlighting challenges and opportunities in this area. In addition, we highlight the major analysis tasks that have been conducted on microblogs, along with detailed explanation for different visualization techniques that are used to show their output. Hence, attending this tutorial would help the audience to get more familiar with the state-of-the-art research on microblogs and identify the possible opportunities for future work.

7. PREVIOUS TUTORIALS

Mohamed Mokbel and Amr Magdy have a similar 90-minute tutorial to be presented in IEEE International Conference on Data Engineering (ICDE) on May 2016. There are two main differences between the two tutorials: (1) Part 3 of this tutorial (visualization) is completely new and was not proposed nor will be presented in the ICDE tutorial. (2) While the ICDE tutorial mainly focus on the data analysis part, this tutorial gives less focus on data analysis in favor of the data management part and the new visualization part.

8. PRESENTERS BIOGRAPHY

Amr Magdy is a f fth year Ph.D. student at the Department of Computer Science and Engineering, University of Minnesota. He received his M.Sc. at the same department in 2013. His main research interest is microblogs data management. He has been selected as a f nalist for Microsoft Research PhD Fellowship 2014-2016 for his work in microblogs research and has been awarded the University of Minnesota Doctoral Dissertation Fellowship in 2015 for his dissertation focus on microblogs. His research work on microblogs has been incubated by Bing GeoSpatial team and has been selected among best papers in ICDE 2014. During his PhD, he has collaborated with Microsoft Research in Redmond in joint research on microblogs from which they got three publications and working on the fourth. Amr is also the main architect and developer for Taghreed system; the f rst holistic system for microblogs data management. Amr has published extensively in the area of microblogs data in top research venues, including IEEE ICDE, ACM SIGSPATIAL, IEEE TKDE, and IEEE MDM.

Mohamed F. Mokbel is an associate professor at University of Minnesota. His current research interests focus on database systems, GIS, and big spatial data. His research work has been recognized by f ve best paper awards and by the NSF CAREER award 2010. Mohamed is/was General co-chair of SSTD 2011, Program co-chair of ACM SIGSPATIAL GIS 2008-2010, and IEEE MDM 2011, 2014, Tutorial co-chair for ICDE 2014, and Sponsorship Co-Chair for ACM SIGMOD 2015-2016. He is in the editorial board of ACM Transactions on Database Systems, VLDB Journal, ACM Transactions on Spatial Algorithms and Systems, and GeoInformatica. Mohamed has held various visiting positions at Microsoft Research-Redmond and Hong Kong Polytechnic University. Mohamed is a founding member of ACM SIGSPATIAL and is currently serving as an elected chair of ACM SIGSPATIAL for the term 2014-2017. For more information, please visit: www.cs.umn.edu/∼mokbel

References

[1] H. Abdelhaq, C. Sengstock, and M. Gertz. EvenTweet: Online Localized Event Detection from Twitter. In *VLDB*, 2013.

[2] S. Alsubaiee and et. al. AsterixDB: A Scalable, Open Source BDMS. *PVLDB*, 7(14), 2014.

[3] A. Bermingham and A. F. Smeaton. Classifying Sentiment in Microblogs: Is Brevity an Advantage? In *CIKM*, 2010.

[4] After Boston Explosions, People Rush to Twitter for Breaking News. http://www.latimes.com/business/technology/la-f -tn-after-boston-explosions-people-rush-to-twitter-for-breaking-news-20130415,0,3729783.story, 2013.

[5] C. Budak, T. Georgiou, D. Agrawal, and A. E. Abbadi. GeoScope: Online Detection of Geo-Correlated Information Trends in Social Networks. In *VLDB*, 2014.

[6] M. Busch, K. Gade, B. Larson, P. Lok, S. Luckenbill, and J. Lin. Earlybird: Real-Time Search at Twitter. In *ICDE*, 2012.

[7] C. C. Cao, J. She, Y. Tong, and L. Chen. Whom to Ask? Jury Selection for Decision Making Tasks on Micro-blog Services. *PVLDB*, 5(11), 2012.

[8] C. Chen, F. Li, B. C. Ooi, and S. Wu. TI: An Eff cient Indexing Mechanism for Real-Time Search on Tweets. In *SIGMOD*, 2011.

[9] Sina Weibo, China Twitter, comes to rescue amid f ooding in Beijing. http://thenextweb.com/asia/2012/07/23/sina-weibo-chinas-twitter-comes-to-rescue-amid-f ooding-in-beijing/, 2012.

[10] Facebook Statistics. http://newsroom.fb.com/company-info/, 2015.

[11] W. Feng, J. Han, J. Wang, C. Aggarwal, and J. Huang. STREAMCUBE: Hierarchical Spatio-temporal Hashtag Clustering for Event Exploration Over the Twitter Stream. In *ICDE*, 2015.

[12] T. Ghanem, A. Magdy, M. Musleh, S. Ghani, and M. Mokbel. VisCAT: Spatio-Temporal Visualization and Aggregation of Categorical Attributes in Twitter Data. In *SIGSPATIAL*, 2014.

[13] R. Grover and M. Carey. Data Ingestion in AsterixDB. In *EDBT*, 2015.

[14] J. Hannon, M. Bennett, and B. Smyth. Recommending Twitter Users to Follow Using Content and Collaborative Filtering Approaches. In *RecSys*, 2010.

[15] L. Hong, A. Ahmed, S. Gurumurthy, A. J. Smola, and K. Tsioutsiouliklis. Discovering Geographical Topics In The Twitter Stream. In *WWW*, 2012.

[16] Y. Ikawa, M. Enoki, and M. Tatsubori. Location Inference Using Microblog Messages. In *WWW*, 2012.

[17] J. Jiang, H. Lu, B. Yang, and B. Cui. Finding Top-k Local Users in Geo-Tagged Social Media Data. In *ICDE*, 2015.

[18] G. Li, J. Hu, J. Feng, and K. Tan. Effective Location Identif cation from Microblogs. In *ICDE*, 2014.

[19] Y. Li, Z. Bao, G. Li, and K.-L. Tan. Real Time Personalized Search on Social Networks. In *ICDE*, 2015.

[20] A. Magdy, L. Alarabi, S. Al-Harthi, M. Musleh, T. Ghanem, S. Ghani, and M. Mokbel. Taghreed: A System for Querying, Analyzing, and Visualizing Geotagged Microblogs. In *SIGSPATIAL*, 2014.

[21] A. Magdy, R. Alghamdi, and M. F. Mokbel. On Main-memory Flushing in Microblogs Data Management Systems. In *ICDE*, 2016.

[22] A. Magdy and M. Mokbel. Towards a Microblogs Data Management System. In *MDM*, 2015.

[23] A. Magdy, M. F. Mokbel, S. Elnikety, S. Nath, and Y. He. Mercury: A Memory-Constrained Spatio-temporal Real-time Search on Microblogs. In *ICDE*, 2014.

[24] MapD. http://www.mapd.com/, 2013.

[25] A. Marcus, M. S. Bernstein, O. Badar, D. R. Karger, S. Madden, and R. C. Miller. Tweets as Data: Demonstration of TweeQL and TwitInfo. In *SIGMOD*, 2011.

[26] A. Marcus, M. S. Bernstein, O. Badar, D. R. Karger, S. Madden, and R. C. Miller. Twitinfo: Aggregating and Visualizing Microblogs for Event Exploration. In *CHI*, 2011.

[27] E. Meij, W. Weerkamp, and M. de Rijke. Adding Semantics to Microblog Posts. In *WSDM*, 2012.

[28] G. Mishne, J. Dalton, Z. Li, A. Sharma, and J. Lin. Fast Data in the Era of Big Data: Twitter's Real-time Related Query Suggestion Architecture. In *SIGMOD*, 2013.

[29] G. Mishne and J. Lin. Twanchor Text: A Preliminary Study of the Value of Tweets as Anchor Text. In *SIGIR*, 2012.

[30] New Enhanced Geo-targeting for Marketers. https://blog.twitter.com/2012/new-enhanced-geo-targeting-for-marketers.

[31] One Million Tweet Map. http://onemilliontweetmap.com/, 2016.

[32] O. Phelan, K. McCarthy, and B. Smyth. Using Twitter to Recommend Real-Time Topical News. In *RecSys*, 2009.

[33] Public Health Emergency, Department of Health and Human Services. http://nowtrending.hhs.gov/, 2015.

[34] D. Ramage, S. T. Dumais, and D. J. Liebling. Characterizing Microblogs with Topic Models. In *ICWSM*, 2010.

[35] C. Safran, V. M. García-Barrios, and M. Ebner. The Benef ts of Geo-Tagging and Microblogging in m-Learning: a Use Case. In *MindTrek*, 2009.

[36] T. Sakaki, M. Okazaki, and Y. Matsuo. Earthquake Shakes Twitter Users: Real-Time Event Detection by Social Sensors. In *WWW*, 2010.

[37] J. Sankaranarayanan, H. Samet, B. E. Teitler, M. D. Lieberman, and J. Sperling. TwitterStand: News in Tweets. In *GIS*, 2009.

[38] V. K. Singh, M. Gao, and R. Jain. Situation Detection and Control using Spatio-temporal Analysis of Microblogs. In *WWW*, 2010.

[39] A. Skovsgaard, D. Sidlauskas, and C. S. Jensen. Scalable Top-k Spatio-temporal Term Querying. In *ICDE*, 2014.

[40] M. Stonebraker and A. Weisberg. The VoltDB Main Memory DBMS. *IEEE Data Engineering Bulletin*, 36(2):21–27, 2013.

[41] Topsy Analytics: Find the insights that matter. www.topsy.com, 2014.

[42] TweetTracker: track, analyze, and understand activity on Twitter. tweettracker.fulton.asu.edu/, 2014.

[43] Twitter Statistics. https://about.twitter.com/company, 2015.

[44] Topsy Analytics for Twitter Political Index. topsylabs.com/election/.

[45] N. Vesdapunt and H. Garcia-Molina. Identifying Users in Social Networks with Limited Information. In *ICDE*, 2015.

[46] I. Weber and V. R. K. Garimella. Visualizing User-Def ned, Discriminative Geo-Temporal Twitter Activity. In *ICWSM*, 2014.

[47] L. Wu, W. Lin, X. Xiao, and Y. Xu. LSII: An Indexing Structure for Exact Real-Time Search on Microblogs. In *ICDE*, 2013.

[48] J. Yao, B. Cui, Z. Xue, and Q. Liu. Provenance-based Indexing Support in Micro-blog Platforms. In *ICDE*, 2012.

[49] R. Zhang, X. He, A. Zhou, and C. Sha. Identif cation of Key Locations based on Online Social Network Activity. In *ASONAM*, 2014.

[50] J. Zhao, J. C. Lui, D. Towsley, P. Wang, and X. Guan. Sampling Design on Hybrid Social-Aff liation Networks. In *ICDE*, 2015.

The Challenges of Global-scale Data Management

Faisal Nawab Divyakant Agrawal Amr El Abbadi

Department of Computer Science
University of California, Santa Barbara
Santa Barbara, CA 93106
{nawab,agrawal,amr}@cs.ucsb.edu

ABSTRACT

Global-scale data management (GSDM) empowers systems by providing higher levels of fault-tolerance, read availability, and efficiency in utilizing cloud resources. This has led to the emergence of global-scale data management and event processing. However, the Wide-Area Network (WAN) latency separating data is orders of magnitude larger than conventional network latencies, and this requires a reevaluation of many of the traditional design trade-offs of data management systems. Therefore, data management problems must be revisited to account for the new design space. In this tutorial we survey recent developments in GSDM focusing on identifying fundamental challenges and advancements in addition to open research opportunities.

1. INTRODUCTION

Internet applications strive for high-performance 24/7 service to users dispersed around the world. Achieving this is threatened by complete datacenter outages and the physical limitations of both the datacenter infrastructure and wide-area communication. To overcome these challenges, systems are increasingly being deployed in multiple datacenters spanning large geographic regions. The replication of data across datacenters (geo-replication) allows requests to be served even in the event of complete datacenter-scale outages. Likewise, distributing the processing and storage across datacenters brings the application closer to users and sources of data, enabling higher levels of availability and performance. Additionally, extremely large applications consume huge amounts of resources. These resources vary and include computing infrastructure in addition to power and real-estate. Globally distributing the computing infrastructure of large applications allows them to utilize resources beyond the restrictions of a single datacenter or cloud provider.

Moving to global-scale data management (GSDM), despite its benefits, raises many novel challenges that are not faced by traditional deployments. The large WAN communication latency is orders of magnitude larger than traditional communication latency (See Figure 1). This invalidates the traditional space of design trade-offs and makes the WAN latency a significant bottleneck. Likewise, WAN bandwidth (~100 Tbps [3]) is larger than traditional networks bandwidth. However, big data applications transfer large volumes of data reported to be in the order of hundreds of TBs per day and projected to be increasing in the future [62]. These increasing demands will lead to a bottleneck in WAN communication. The design of efficient mechanisms that better utilize the WAN links are necessary to avoid limiting the growth of global-scale big data applications. Also, due to privacy legislation concerns in some parts of the world, there is a direction to limit control on where data is placed and at what level of privacy it is stored [1, 2]. These restrictions affect the design of global-scale data placement and task scheduling.

SIGMOD'16, June 26-July 01, 2016, San Francisco, CA, USA

DOI: http://dx.doi.org/10.1145/2882903.2912571

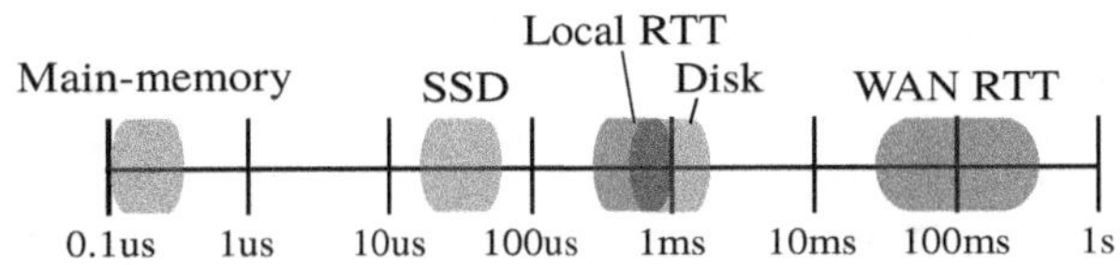

Figure 1: Latency of the Wide-Area Network Round-Trip Time communication (WAN RTT) compared to memory access latency [50] and network latency within the datacenter (local RTT)

Building GSDM systems requires a rethinking of data management problems in light of the new design trade-offs and constraints. In this tutorial we survey recent work in building GSDM systems. We focus on exposing the salient features of GSDM systems that make them different, and also identify the short- and long-term research opportunities in this space.

2. TUTORIAL INFORMATION

The target audience are database researchers and practitioners with basic knowledge of transactions. Some knowledge of replication, stream processing, or analytics is helpful but not necessary. For newcomers, the tutorial introduces GSDM as an emerging framework with unique research challenges and novel system designs. For researchers experienced in GSDM, the tutorial provides a broader view of GSDM research beyond the work within the databases community. Generally, we aim to enable data researchers to extend their work and expertise to a global-scale framework.

We present the challenges and design principles of GSDM. The development of GSDM research is presented in chronological order, emphasizing the trends that led to the current state-of-the-art. We then extend these trends to project the upcoming challenges and opportunities of GSDM. To provide more depth to the presented topics, for each part we highlight and discuss in more details one or two representative systems. Each work that we discuss in detail is underlined in this proposal.

The tutorial is divided into three sections: (1) The system model and unique characteristics of GSDM (Section 1), (2) Data access technology (Section 3.1) that includes principles and system designs of data access to geo-distributed storage, and (3) Event processing (section 3.2) that includes global-scale stream processing and analytics. The target length of the tutorial is 3 hours.

3. TUTORIAL OUTLINE

3.1 Data access

Data access is the ability to read and modify data objects typically via put and get operations or groups of operations forming a transaction. This section surveys literature on methods to access globally-distributed data. Globally-distributed data is either geo-replicated where data objects are replicated in multiple datacenters, geo-distributed where different partitions of the data exist in different datacenters, or a combination of both.

The central problem tackled by data access of globally-distributed data is managing the consistency-performance trade-off that is amplified due to large wide-area latency. To guarantee consistent outcomes, coordination between distributed components is necessary. This coordination is expensive due to WAN links, and thus affects performance immensely. The first reaction to the new trade-off was the abandonment of strong notions of consistency in favor of performance [10, 16, 19]. Systems that adopt this approach provide weak guarantees like eventual consistency and single-key atomicity. These guarantees were sufficient for many applications, however, it turns out that many use-cases require stronger notions of consistency. In addition, developing applications on top of weakly consistent data is error-prone and less natural to developers.

The need for stronger forms of consistency on globally-distributed data sparked a trend to explore different points in the consistency-performance trade-off spectrum. The goal is to explore existing consistency notions, that are weaker than expensive strong consistency, and extend them in ways suitable for globally-distributed data. Causal consistency, inspired by the causal ordering principle [35], preserves causal relations between operations. Causal consistency is attractive for GSDM because it does not require coordination between replicas. Thus, causally consistent systems that are built for globally-distributed data, do not suffer significantly from the cost of wide-area latency [11, 20, 40, 41, 44]. For example, COPS and Eiger [40, 41] are scalable causally consistent systems that offer single-key operations in addition to read-only or write-only transactional access. COPS extends the notion of causal consistency and proposes Causal+ consistency that, in addition to causality, guarantees data convergence.

Snapshot Isolation (SI) [13] guarantees that transactions always read a consistent snapshot and ensures the absence of write-write conflicts. SI can lead to better performance compared to stronger notions of consistency like serializability specially for read-intensive workloads [13]. Many solutions leverage SI for GSDM [18, 21, 38, 39, 57]. Walter [57] extends the notion of SI and proposes Parallel SI (PSI). PSI redefines snapshot reads and write-write conflicts to accommodate the new environment of globally-distributed data. With PSI, Walter is able to replicate data asynchronously while still providing strong guarantees within each site. In the original SI, asynchronous replication is not possible.

Strong consistency guarantees, such as serializability [14] and linearizability [27], require extensive coordination between globally-distributed data. Despite their performance implications, industry and academia have recently shown that strong guarantees are needed for a wide range of applications. This has started a movement towards preserving strong consistency guarantees while trying to reduce the cost of coordination on performance. Paxos [36] is a fault-tolerant consensus protocol that has been used to implement GSDM systems that provide strong guarantees, such as megastore [12] and Paxos-CP [48]. Later though, it was shown to perform better as a synchronous communication layer integrated with a transaction commit protocol [17, 23, 42]. For example, Spanner [17] and Replicated Commit [42] commit transactions using variants of Two-Phase Commit (2PC) and Strict Two-Phase Locking (S2PL) and leverage Paxos to replicate across datacenters. Paxos, however, requires two rounds of communication to commit, which is a cost amplified by WAN latency. This led to efforts to optimize the cost of Paxos by the use of leases to eliminate the cost of the first round of communication and by adopting Fast Paxos [37] that allows committing with a single round to a super majority [32, 47].

The existing 2PC and Paxos protocols require one round of communication at least to commit a transaction. Nawab et. al. explored breaking the round-trip barrier by decoupling consistency from fault-tolerance [43, 45]. Message Futures [43] reserves commit points for future transactions to achieve low commit latency. Commit points are represented as logical timestamps in shared replicated logs. Because transactions can use previously assigned commit points, they can commit in less than a round-trip time. Helios [45] detects conflicts using timestamp-based conflict detection. For each transaction, it calculates time ranges at which conflicts might occur. The transaction commits once it verifies that there are no conflicting transactions in these time ranges. The calculation of time ranges leverages a theoretical result on lower-bound transaction latency that leads to close to optimal transaction latency.

The use of timestamps and time synchronization has been explored for GSDM systems [17, 20, 21, 45]. Spanner [17] provides external consistency guarantees by leveraging accurate time synchronization using specialized infrastructure such as atomic clocks. Without accurate time synchronization, other systems resort to loosely-synchronized clocks methods [20, 21, 45].

To commit arbitrary transactions with strong consistency guarantees, the cost of coordination is inevitable [45]. However, coordination-free execution is possible for some types of transactions [9, 52, 66]. This is possible by inferring application-level invariants of transactions correctness and then exploring whether a coordination-free execution is permissible. Transaction Chains [66] derives an execution plan of distributed transactions that allows for a fast response time. A client needs to wait for the execution of the transaction at only a single site, rather than waiting for the execution at all accessed sites. Often, the first site is local to the client, making the response latency unaffected by the WAN latency.

Placement of data and workers has a significant effect on GSDM systems performance [4, 22, 49, 53, 54, 62, 63, 65]. In this part of the tutorial we discuss how placement plays a role in general data access systems. SPANStore [63] proposes an optimization formulation of placement to minimize monetary cost. SPANStore's formulation considers constraints on fault-tolerance, consistency requirements, and performance SLOs. Sharov et al. [54] propose an optimization formulation for placement with an objective of minimizing latency. What distinguishes this work is that it considers transactional access to storage.

Global-scale placement depends on the workload, which includes the location of users and the type of requests being issued. A successful placement needs to correctly estimate workload and adapt to workload changes. A correct estimation of the workload has to be done using an accurate system model and using efficient log and trace collection and analysis. Adapting to workload changes is more challenging, since the new workload characteristics potentially lead to choosing a significantly different configuration. SPANStore changes configurations in an epoch-based fashion. Violations might occur while changing configurations, but are rare since they only occur at epoch boundaries.

The dynamic and variable nature of workload and communication links in GSDM led to work on dynamic techniques for GSDM systems [7,58,64]. Variability of the communication link leads to the reordering and delaying of sent messages. CosTLO [64] proposes adding redundancy in messaging to lower the latency variance. GSDM systems trade-off consistency and performance and could be locked in their initial protocol choice. Pileus and Tuba [7, 58] allow applications to dynamically control the consistency-performance trade-off by declaring their consistency and latency priorities. The application's priorities then influence the decision on which servers to access. Stronger consistency requires accessing more servers and thus increases latency. In turn, more relaxed consistency requires accessing lesser number of servers and thus decreases latency.

3.2 Event processing

Global-scale applications receive and generate large volumes of data across datacenters. It is reported that the amount of data processed by large web applications is in the order of 10s to 100s of TBs per day [62]. This has led to the design of many GSDM systems for stream processing and data pipelining from Google [5, 6, 24, 55, 56], Twitter [33, 60], Facebook [59], and LinkedIn [8]. These systems are designed to support the high volume and velocity of events while conserving availability and high performance. In addition, they guarantee correctness of computations that use the streamed data. Correctness invariants vary depending on the application, but the following correctness conditions are common: (1) *At-most-once semantics*, which means that no event is processed more than once, and (2) *Near-exact semantics*, which means that with no significant delay, all events will be processed. These correctness conditions, albeit simple, are challenging on the scale of global web applications where streams might be significantly reordered and delayed. Photon [6] is a system deployed at Google to join global-scale continuous streams. To tolerate failures, an event can be processed at any of the operating datacenters. To guarantee at-most-once semantics, before a joiner starts processing an event it ensures that the event has not been processed before. It does so by using a logically centralized Paxos process for the event's unique ID.

In addition to processing streams and managing data pipelines, GSDM systems often perform analytical and machine learning queries on data to extract insight and business knowledge. Global-scale analytics — as opposed to traditional analytics within a datacenter — face novel challenges. Until recently, global-scale analytics were performed by pulling all data to a central location [61]. This, however, consumes the WAN links, which causes monetary loss and poses a physical constraint on throughput. Additionally, data movement could be constrained due to emerging data sovereignty legislation and privacy concerns. Recent solutions address the challenges of global-scale analytics [15,25,26,28,30,31, 46,49,51,61,62]. Geode [62] and PIXIDA [31] are two systems that propose a query planning and replication framework that targets reducing the bandwidth cost between datacenters. Additionally, Geode uses optimizations such as aggressive caching and measurement collection that allow for the reuse of past queries. Unlike Geode and PIXIDA, Iridium [49] aims to minimize the latency of global analytics by deriving the placement of both data and tasks. Geode, PIXIDA, and Iridium derive their solutions using an optimization formulation. They all face a common problem of the intractability of optimization solvers with 10s of datacenters. To overcome this, Geode and Iridium leverage a greedy heuristic and PIXIDA proposes a flow-based approximation algorithm.

4. OUTLOOK

Modern web applications require higher levels of fault-tolerance and availability. Also, they are increasingly consuming larger volumes of data. Globally deploying web applications is a necessary step towards fulfilling these requirements. However, GSDM has unique characteristics that change the traditional space of design trade-offs. Most notably are the WAN link characteristics. The cost of coordination has been amplified due to WAN latency, and the WAN bandwidth, albeit large, is limited as it serves a large number of data-intensive applications. Additionally, regulatory constraints may limit the control of data management systems.

Leveraging advances in WAN research from the networking community is an important step towards building efficient GSDM systems. Networking techniques, like Software-defined Networking (SDN), are now being applied to the context of WANs (*e.g.*, BwE [34] and B4 [29]). A promising opportunity is to develop GSDM systems that integrate these advances. Also, adopting privacy-preserving techniques for GSDM is an important endeavour to address the geo-political regulatory concerns on data usage. However, current privacy-preserving protocols are communication-intensive and rely on redundancy that cause over-utilization of network bandwidth. As such, this makes these protocols especially inappropriate for GSDM. We expect a proliferation of studies on the trade-off between privacy and performance at the global scale.

The unique challenges of GSDM introduce inefficiencies to existing designs across various data management problems. The opportunity is for researchers to explore the implications of transforming their work from a local traditional computing framework to the global scale.

5. BIOGRAPHICAL SKETCHES

Faisal Nawab is a doctoral student at the University of California at Santa Barbara. His current research work is in the areas of global-scale data management, big data analytics, and data management on emerging non-volatile memory technology.

Divyakant Agrawal is a Professor of Computer Science at the University of California at Santa Barbara. His current interests are in the area of scalable data management and data analysis in Cloud Computing environments, security and privacy of data in the cloud, and scalable analytics over big data. Prof. Agrawal is an ACM Distinguished Scientist (2010), an ACM Fellow (2012), and an IEEE Fellow (2012).

Amr El Abbadi is a Professor of Computer Science at the University of California, Santa Barbara. Prof. El Abbadi is an ACM Fellow, AAAS Fellow, and IEEE Fellow. He was Chair of the Computer Science Department at UCSB from 2007 to 2011. He has served as a journal editor for several database journals and has been Program Chair for multiple database and distributed systems conferences. Most recently Prof. El Abbadi was the co-recipient of the Test of Time Award at EDBT/ICDT 2015. He has published over 300 articles in databases and distributed systems and has supervised over 30 PhD students.

6. ACKNOWLEDGMENT

This work is supported by NSF grants IIS 1018637, 1528178, and 1442966 and is partially funded by a gift grant from NEC Labs America.

7. REFERENCES

[1] Amazon web services. whitepaper on eu data protection. https://d0.awsstatic.com/whitepapers/compliance/AWS_EU_Data_Protection_Whitepaper.pdf. 2015.

[2] European commission press release. commission to pursue role as honest broker in future global negotiations on internet governance. http://europa.eu/rapid/press-release_IP-14-142_en.htm. 2014.

[3] Global internet geography. https://www.telegeography.com/research-services/global-internet-geography/. 2015.

[4] AGARWAL, S., DUNAGAN, J., JAIN, N., SAROIU, S., WOLMAN, A., AND BHOGAN, H. Volley: Automated data placement for geo-distributed cloud services. In *NSDI* (2010).

[5] AKIDAU, T., BALIKOV, A., BEKIROĞLU, K., CHERNYAK, S., HABERMAN, J., LAX, R., MCVEETY, S., MILLS, D., NORDSTROM, P., AND WHITTLE, S. Millwheel: fault-tolerant stream processing at internet scale. In *VLDB* (2013).

[6] ANANTHANARAYANAN, R., BASKER, V., DAS, S., GUPTA, A., JIANG, H., QIU, T., REZNICHENKO, A., RYABKOV, D., SINGH, M., AND VENKATARAMAN, S. Photon: Fault-tolerant and scalable joining of continuous data streams. In *SIGMOD* (2013).

[7] ARDEKANI, M. S., AND TERRY, D. B. A self-configurable geo-replicated cloud storage system. In *OSDI* (2014).

[8] AURADKAR, A., BOTEV, C., DAS, S., DE MAAGD, D., FEINBERG, A., GANTI, P., GAO, L., GHOSH, B., GOPALAKRISHNA, K., HARRIS, B., ET AL. Data infrastructure at linkedin. In *ICDE* (2012).

[9] BAILIS, P., FEKETE, A., FRANKLIN, M. J., GHODSI, A., HELLERSTEIN, J. M., AND STOICA, I. Coordination avoidance in database systems. In *VLDB* (2014).

[10] BAILIS, P., AND GHODSI, A. Eventual consistency today: limitations, extensions, and beyond. *Communications of the ACM 56*, 5 (2013), 55–63.

[11] BAILIS, P., GHODSI, A., HELLERSTEIN, J. M., AND STOICA, I. Bolt-on causal consistency. In *SIGMOD* (2013).

[12] BAKER, J., ET AL. Megastore: Providing scalable, highly available storage for interactive services. In *CIDR* (2011).

[13] BERENSON, H., BERNSTEIN, P., GRAY, J., MELTON, J., O'NEIL, E., AND O'NEIL, P. A critique of ansi sql isolation levels. In *SIGMOD* (1995).

[14] BERNSTEIN, P. A., HADZILACOS, V., AND GOODMAN, N. *Concurrency Control and Recovery in Database Systems*. Addison-Wesley, 1987.

[15] CANO, I., WEIMER, M., MAHAJAN, D., CURINO, C., AND FUMAROLA, G. Towards geo-distributed machine learning. In *Workshop on Machine Learning Systems at NIPS* (2015).

[16] COOPER, B. F., RAMAKRISHNAN, R., SRIVASTAVA, U., SILBERSTEIN, A., BOHANNON, P., JACOBSEN, H.-A., PUZ, N., WEAVER, D., AND YERNENI, R. Pnuts: Yahoo!'s hosted data serving platform. *VLDB* (2008).

[17] CORBETT, J., DEAN, J., EPSTEIN, M., FIKES, A., FROST, C., FURMAN, J., GHEMAWAT, S., GUBAREV, A., HEISER, C., HOCHSCHILD, P., ET AL. Spanner: Google's globally-distributed database. In *OSDI* (2012).

[18] DAUDJEE, K., AND SALEM, K. Lazy database replication with snapshot isolation. In *VLDB* (2006).

[19] DECANDIA, G., HASTORUN, D., JAMPANI, M., KAKULAPATI, G., LAKSHMAN, A., PILCHIN, A., SIVASUBRAMANIAN, S., VOSSHALL, P., AND VOGELS, W. Dynamo: amazon's highly available key-value store. In *ACM SIGOPS* (2007).

[20] DU, J., ELNIKETY, S., ROY, A., AND ZWAENEPOEL, W. Orbe: Scalable causal consistency using dependency matrices and physical clocks. In *SoCC* (2013).

[21] DU, J., ELNIKETY, S., AND ZWAENEPOEL, W. Clock-si: Snapshot isolation for partitioned data stores using loosely synchronized clocks. In *SRDS* (2013).

[22] ENDO, P. T., DE ALMEIDA PALHARES, A. V., PEREIRA, N. N., GONCALVES, G. E., SADOK, D., KELNER, J., MELANDER, B., AND MÅNGS, J.-E. Resource allocation for distributed cloud: concepts and research challenges. *Network, IEEE* (2011).

[23] GLENDENNING, L., BESCHASTNIKH, I., KRISHNAMURTHY, A., AND ANDERSON, T. Scalable consistency in scatter. In *SOSP* (2011).

[24] GUPTA, A., YANG, F., GOVIG, J., KIRSCH, A., CHAN, K., LAI, K., WU, S., DHOOT, S. G., KUMAR, A. R., AGIWAL, A., BHANSALI, S., HONG, M., CAMERON, J., SIDDIQI, M., JONES, D., SHUTE, J., GUBAREV, A., VENKATARAMAN, S., AND AGRAWAL, D. Mesa: Geo-replicated, near real-time, scalable data warehousing. *Proc. VLDB Endow. 7*, 12 (Aug. 2014), 1259–1270.

[25] HEINTZ, B., CHANDRA, A., AND SITARAMAN, R. K. Optimizing grouped aggregation in geo-distributed streaming analytics. In *HPDC* (2015).

[26] HEINTZ, B., CHANDRA, A., AND SITARAMAN, R. K. Towards optimizing wide-area streaming analytics. In *IEEE Workshop on Cloud Analytics* (2015).

[27] HERLIHY, M. P., AND WING, J. M. Linearizability: A correctness condition for concurrent objects. *ACM TOPLAS 12*, 3 (1990), 463–492.

[28] HUNG, C.-C., GOLUBCHIK, L., AND YU, M. Scheduling jobs across geo-distributed datacenters. In *SoCC* (2015).

[29] JAIN, S., KUMAR, A., MANDAL, S., ONG, J., POUTIEVSKI, L., SINGH, A., VENKATA, S., WANDERER, J., ZHOU, J., ZHU, M., ET AL. B4: Experience with a globally-deployed software defined wan. In *SIGCOMM* (2013).

[30] JONATHAN, A., CHANDRA, A., AND WEISSMAN, J. Awan: Locality-aware resource manager for geo-distributed data-intensive applications.

[31] KLOUDAS, K., MAMEDE, M., PREGUIÇA, N., AND RODRIGUES, R. Pixida: optimizing data parallel jobs in wide-area data analytics. In *VLDB* (2015).

[32] KRASKA, T., PANG, G., FRANKLIN, M. J., MADDEN, S., AND FEKETE, A. Mdcc: Multi-data center consistency. In *EuroSys* (2013).

[33] KULKARNI, S., BHAGAT, N., FU, M., KEDIGEHALLI, V., KELLOGG, C., MITTAL, S., PATEL, J. M., RAMASAMY, K., AND TANEJA, S. Twitter heron: Stream processing at scale. In *SIGMOD* (2015).

[34] KUMAR, A., JAIN, S., NAIK, U., RAGHURAMAN, A., KASINADHUNI, N., ZERMENO, E. C., GUNN, C. S., AI, J., CARLIN, B., AMARANDEI-STAVILA, M., ET AL. Bwe: Flexible, hierarchical bandwidth allocation for wan distributed computing. In *SIGCOMM* (2015).

[35] LAMPORT, L. Time, clocks, and the ordering of events in a distributed system. *Commun. ACM 21*, 7 (July 1978), 558–565.

[36] LAMPORT, L. The part-time parliament. *ACM Trans. Comput. Syst.* (1998).

[37] LAMPORT, L. Fast paxos. *Distributed Computing* (2006).

[38] LIN, Y., ET AL. Middleware based data replication providing snapshot isolation. In *SIGMOD* (2005).

[39] LIN, Y., ET AL. Enhancing edge computing with database replication. In *SRDS* (2007).

[40] LLOYD, W., FREEDMAN, M. J., KAMINSKY, M., AND ANDERSEN, D. G. Don't settle for eventual: scalable causal consistency for wide-area storage with cops. In *SOSP* (2011).

[41] LLOYD, W., FREEDMAN, M. J., KAMINSKY, M., AND ANDERSEN, D. G. Stronger semantics for low-latency geo-replicated storage. In *NSDI* (2013).

[42] MAHMOUD, H. A., NAWAB, F., PUCHER, A., AGRAWAL, D., AND EL ABBADI, A. Low-latency multi-datacenter databases using replicated commits. In *VLDB* (2013).

[43] NAWAB, F., AGRAWAL, D., AND EL ABBADI, A. Message futures: Fast commitment of transactions in multi-datacenter environments. In *CIDR* (2013).

[44] NAWAB, F., ARORA, V., AGRAWAL, D., AND ABBADI, A. Chariots: A scalable shared log for data management in multi-datacenter cloud environments. EDBT.

[45] NAWAB, F., ARORA, V., AGRAWAL, D., AND EL ABBADI, A. Minimizing commit latency of transactions in geo-replicated data stores. In *SIGMOD* (2015).

[46] OKTAY, K. Y., MEHROTRA, S., KHADILKAR, V., AND KANTARCIOGLU, M. Semrod: Secure and efficient mapreduce over hybrid clouds. In *SIGMOD* (2015).

[47] PANG, G., KRASKA, T., FRANKLIN, M. J., AND FEKETE, A. Planet: making progress with commit processing in unpredictable environments. In *SIGMOD* (2014).

[48] PATTERSON, S., ELMORE, A. J., NAWAB, F., AGRAWAL, D., AND ABBADI, A. E. Serializability, not serial: Concurrency control and availability in multi-datacenter datastores. *PVLDB* (2012).

[49] PU, Q., ANANTHANARAYANAN, G., BODIK, P., KANDULA, S., AKELLA, A., BAHL, P., AND STOICA, I. Low latency geo-distributed data analytics. In *SIGCOMM* (2015).

[50] QURESHI, M. K., GURUMURTHI, S., AND RAJENDRAN, B. Phase change memory: From devices to systems. *Synthesis Lectures on Computer Architecture 6*, 4 (2011), 1–134.

[51] RABKIN, A., ARYE, M., SEN, S., PAI, V. S., AND FREEDMAN, M. J. Aggregation and degradation in jetstream: Streaming analytics in the wide area. In *NSDI* (2014).

[52] ROY, S., KOT, L., BENDER, G., DING, B., HOJJAT, H., KOCH, C., FOSTER, N., AND GEHRKE, J. The homeostasis protocol: Avoiding transaction coordination through program analysis. In *SIGMOD* (2015).

[53] SHANKARANARAYANAN, P., SIVAKUMAR, A., RAO, S., AND TAWARMALANI, M. Performance sensitive replication in geo-distributed cloud datastores. In *DSN* (2014).

[54] SHAROV, A., SHRAER, A., MERCHANT, A., AND STOKELY, M. Take me to your leader!: online optimization of distributed storage configurations. *Proceedings of the VLDB Endowment 8*, 12 (2015), 1490–1501.

[55] SHUTE, J., OANCEA, M., ELLNER, S., HANDY, B., ROLLINS, E., SAMWEL, B., VINGRALEK, R., WHIPKEY, C., CHEN, X., JEGERLEHNER, B., ET AL. F1: the fault-tolerant distributed rdbms supporting google's ad business. In *SIGMOD* (2012).

[56] SHUTE, J., VINGRALEK, R., SAMWEL, B., HANDY, B., WHIPKEY, C., ROLLINS, E., OANCEA, M., LITTLEFIELD, K., MENESTRINA, D., ELLNER, S., ET AL. F1: A distributed sql database that scales. In *VLDB* (2013).

[57] SOVRAN, Y., POWER, R., AGUILERA, M. K., AND LI, J. Transactional storage for geo-replicated systems. In *SOSP* (2011).

[58] TERRY, D. B., PRABHAKARAN, V., KOTLA, R., BALAKRISHNAN, M., AGUILERA, M. K., AND ABU-LIBDEH, H. Consistency-based service level agreements for cloud storage. In *SOSP* (2013).

[59] THUSOO, A., SHAO, Z., ANTHONY, S., BORTHAKUR, D., JAIN, N., SEN SARMA, J., MURTHY, R., AND LIU, H. Data warehousing and analytics infrastructure at facebook. In *SIGMOD* (2010).

[60] TOSHNIWAL, A., TANEJA, S., SHUKLA, A., RAMASAMY, K., PATEL, J. M., KULKARNI, S., JACKSON, J., GADE, K., FU, M., DONHAM, J., ET AL. Storm@ twitter. In *SIGMOD* (2014).

[61] VULIMIRI, A., CURINO, C., GODFREY, B., KARANASOS, K., AND VARGHESE, G. Wanalytics: Analytics for a geo-distributed data-intensive world. In *CIDR* (2015).

[62] VULIMIRI, A., CURINO, C., GODFREY, B., PADHYE, J., AND VARGHESE, G. Global analytics in the face of bandwidth and regulatory constraints. In *NSDI* (2015).

[63] WU, Z., BUTKIEWICZ, M., PERKINS, D., KATZ-BASSETT, E., AND MADHYASTHA, H. V. Spanstore: Cost-effective geo-replicated storage spanning multiple cloud services. In *SOSP* (2013).

[64] WU, Z., YU, C., AND MADHYASTHA, H. V. Costlo: Cost-effective redundancy for lower latency variance on cloud storage services. In *NSDI* (2015).

[65] ZAKHARY, V., NAWAB, F., AGRAWAL, D., AND EL ABBADI, A. Db-risk: The game of global database placement. In *SIGMOD* (2016).

[66] ZHANG, Y., POWER, R., ZHOU, S., SOVRAN, Y., AGUILERA, M. K., AND LI, J. Transaction chains: achieving serializability with low latency in geo-distributed storage systems. In *SOSP* (2013).

Semistructured Models, Queries and Algebras in the Big Data Era *

[Tutorial Summary]

Yannis Papakonstantinou
Computer Science and Engineering, UCSD
yannis@cs.ucsd.edu

ABSTRACT

Numerous databases promoted as SQL-on-Hadoop, NewSQL and NoSQL support semi-structured, schemaless and heterogeneous data, typically in the form of enriched JSON. They also provide corresponding query languages. In addition to these *genuine JSON databases*, relational databases also provide special functions and language features for the support of JSON columns, typically piggybacking on non-1NF (non first normal form) features that SQL acquired over the years. We refer to SQL databases with JSON support as *SQL/JSON databases*.

The evolving query languages present multiple variations: Some are superficial syntactic ones, while other ones are genuine differences in modeling, language capabilities and semantics. Incompatibility with SQL presents a learning challenge for genuine JSON databases, while the table orientation of SQL/JSON databases often leads to cumbersome syntactic/semantic structures that are contrary to the semistructured nature of JSON. Furthermore, the query languages often fall short of full-fledged semistructured query language capabilities, when compared to the yardstick set by XQuery and prior works on semistructured data (even after superficial model differences are abstracted out).

We survey features, the designers' options and differences in the approaches taken by actual systems. In particular, we first present a SQL backwards-compatible language, named *SQL++*, which can access both SQL and JSON data. SQL++ is expected to be supported by Couchbase's CouchDB and UCI's AsterixDB semistructured databases. Then we expand SQL++ into the *Configurable SQL++*, whereas multiple possible (and different) semantics are formally captured by the multiple options that the language's semantic configuration options can take. We show how appropriate setting of the configuration options morphs the Configurable SQL++ semantics into the semantics of 10 surveyed languages, hence providing a compact and formal tool to understand the essential semantic differences between different systems. We briefly comment on the utility of formally capturing semantic variations in polystore systems.

Finally we discuss the comparison with prior nested and semistructured query languages (notably OQL and XQuery) and describe a key aspect of query processor implementation: set-oriented semistructured query algebras. In particular, we transfer into the JSON era lessons from the semistructured query processing research of the 90s and 00s and combine them with insights on current JSON databases. Again, the tutorial presents the algebras' fundamentals while it abstracts away modeling differences that are not applicable.

1. INTRODUCTION

This is a summary of the SIGMOD 2016 tutorial. *The reader is referred to* ***http://db.ucsd.edu/TutorialSIGMOD16/*** *for the complete material, which includes the full presented slideware and extended companion papers.*

2. TOPIC AND AUDIENCE OF THIS TUTORIAL

Numerous databases promoted as SQL-on-Hadoop, NewSQL and NoSQL support Big Data applications. These databases generally support the 3Vs.(i) Volume: amount of data (ii) Velocity: speed of data in and out (iii) *Variety*: semi-structured, schemaless and heterogeneous data, which is the focus of this tutorial. Due to the Variety requirement, many databases have adopted semi-structured data models, which are generally slightly different subsets of enriched JSON. The databases provide corresponding query languages.

In addition to these *genuine JSON databases* that utilize variants of JSON as their data model, relational databases also provide special functions and language features for the support of JSON columns, often piggybacking on non-1NF (non first normal form) features that SQL acquired over the years. We refer to SQL databases with JSON support as *SQL/JSON databases*.

In total, the tutorial's evolving companion survey discusses the following as of April 2016 (and potentially more by the time the reader accesses it).

1. Apache Hive [34] (description of Hive largely applicable to Cloudera Impala [11] also)
2. IBM Jaql [7]
3. Apache Pig [26]

*Supported by NSF IIS129263, NSF SHB1237174, Informatica Inc. gift and Couchbase Inc. gift.

SIGMOD'16, June 26-July 01, 2016, San Francisco, CA, USA

ISBN 978-1-4503-3531-7/16/06...$15.00
DOI: http://dx.doi.org/10.1145/2882903.2912573

4. Apache Cassandra CQL [22]
5. MongoDB [25]
6. Couchbase's N1QL [13, 9]
7. JSONiq [17]
8. AsterixDB's AQL [6]
9. Google Big Query (aka Dremel [23])
10. Mongo JDBC [35] (a JDBC driver provided by the UnityJDBC middleware for SQL-compliant access to MongoDB)
11. SQL-92 - as the anchor of SQL compliance

Myriads of developers and researchers currently use genuine JSON databases as well as SQL/JSON databases. Database builders and researchers work on expanding the databases' query language abilities. Both parties face the challenges described below regarding surveying and comparing models and query languages, past and present. This tutorial provides a deep understanding of the current data models and query languages of genuine JSON and SQL/JSON databases, hence enabling comparisons.

The tutorial does not limit itself to the current status of JSON querying: The database builders and researchers need to draw lessons from the rich body of past research on nested [19, 32, 2], object-oriented [4] and semistructured data models and querying [14, 8, 31], which have been a topic of intense database research: They were first researched in the form of labeled graphs in the mid-90s. Then semistructured data research boomed in the form of XML and its labeled tree abstraction. The current industrial boost to semistructured data emerged primarily from startups, often on the mobile and web space, that utilize Javascript and JSON.[1] Many of the important language design issues of the first eras must be recalled in the new era of semistructured data.

Similarly, when it comes to implementations, we discuss set-at-a-time algebras for semistructured and object-oriented data, in the interest of transferring into the new space time-tested lessons on algebra-based relational query processing as well as lessons from set-at-a-time algebras from past research on nested relational algebra, OQL and XQuery [10, 37, 12, 5, 18, 30, 24, 3, 1, 36, 33, 21, 29, 20, 16, 38].

More broadly, we compare SQL (which we use as a baseline) with the recent crop of semistructured databases and connect the recent activity around JSON querying to the (much richer) past activity on nested relational, OQL and XML/labeled tree models and respective query languages and implementations.

3. CHALLENGES IN COMPREHENDING THE SPACE OF SEMISTRUCTURED DBS

A first challenge is that the evolving query languages have many variations. Some variations are due to superficial syntactic differences that simply create "noise" when one tries to understand and compare systems. However, other variations are genuine differences in query language capabilities and semantics.

Indeed, the evolving query languages of both the genuine semistructured databases and the SQL/JSON databases fall short of full-fledged semi-structured query language capabilities.[2] The designers of the new query languages can gain by understanding and picking the salient features of past full-fledged *declarative* query languages for non-relational data models: OQL [4], the nested relational model [19, 32, 2], XQuery, and other XML query languages [31, 14, 8].

Part of the confusion around current genuine JSON query languages is derived from the lack of compatibility with the well known SQL. In the interest of broadening the audience, this tutorial assumes that the audience is well-aware of SQL and the standard material of graduate textbooks on SQL system implementation. The tutorial does not assume knowledge of other query languages. Consequently we explain the JSON model and query languages as minimal extensions to SQL.S

Similarly, part of the confusion and the large semantics behind SQL/JSON is due to the retrofit of SQL for JSON columns, while certain limitations of SQL (such as the need of a schema) remain in place. Again, the tutorial does not require knowledge of non-1NF, often proprietary, features that have been added to SQL. Rather it only requires textbook SQL-92 language and teaches the non-1NF concepts.

A final challenge in understanding the new space of semistructured data is the lack of a succinct, mathematically clear, formal syntax and semantics by the vendors.

In summary, the mentioned challenges and confusions hurt researchers and developers:

1. They inhibit a deep understanding of the capabilities and important idiosyncracies of the various query languages. Potential users can be lost in superficial details and miss fundamental points.

2. They impede progress towards declarative languages and systems for querying semi-structured data. Language designers and query processor implementors need to appreciate the available options, in order to proceed to well-designed fully-fledged languages and efficient implementations thereof.

4. A SYSTEMATIC SURVEY OF MODEL AND LANGUAGE OPTIONS AND VARIATIONS

Step 1: Extending the relational model and SQL for semistructured As discussed above, part of the confusion is derived from the lack of compatibility with the well known, baseline SQL, which both researchers and practitioners generally understand. Therefore, the first step of this tutorial towards explaining the large space of current and past works is the introduction of *Configurable SQL++*. Neglecting temporarily the "configurable" aspect (discussed in Step 2), one may think of SQL++ as a semi-structured query language, based on extending SQL with a minimal number of features.

[1] Their JSON motivation is essentially the same one that the early semistructured research works had: flexible, schemaless data. Douglas Crockford's book "Javascript: The Good Parts" characteristically muses about JSON that "the less we need to agree on in order to interoperate, the more easily we can interoperate".

[2] Most genuine semistructured databases also fall significantly short of full-fledged SQL capabilities, which is not surprising since many commercial JSON databases started as key-value and document-oriented databases.

SQL++ is *backwards compatible* with the "textbook" SQL-92 and mostly backwards compatible with other relevant features of the SQL standard. (The cases where it is not, such as differences in type coercion, lend themselves to interesting discussed comparisons.) Hence SQL++ can be easily understood by SQL programmers and researchers.

The enabler of the relatively easy extension from SQL to genuine JSON database capability is that the semi-structured SQL++ data model is a superset of both JSON and the SQL data model. One should think of JSON objects as tuples. Then the SQL++ model can be thought of as expanding JSON with bags (as opposed to having JSON arrays only) and enriched values, i.e., atomic values that are not only numbers and strings (vendors have already made this extension). Vice versa, one may think of SQL++ as expanding SQL with JSON features: arrays, heterogeneity, and the possibility that any value may be an arbitrary composition of the array, bag and tuple constructors, hence enabling arbitrary nested structures, such as arrays of arrays. Consequently, the SQL++ query language inputs and outputs SQL++ data. Notice that there was no such straightforward correspondence between the XML model and relational, primarily due to the lack of explicit tuples in XML.

Then we incorprorate into SQL++ salient features of past full-fledged *declarative* query languages for non-relational data models: SQL non-1NF features (starting with SQL 2003), OQL, the nested relational model and query languages, and XQuery (and other XML-based query languages). For example, in the spirit of XQuery, JSONiq and OQL, SQL++ is a fully composable and semi-structured language, hence being able to input and output nested and heterogeneous structures. In this tutorial, a new student/researcher of semistructured data, who missed the OQL and XQuery eras, will be able to absorb the essential teachings of XQuery while they are succinctly cast as a *minimally modified SQL*. We describe these modifications next, which will enable an audience member with SQL background to comprehend the fundamentals of the extension to genuine JSON databases with minimal effort.

Minimal semantics changes Instead of inventing (or re-inventing) multiple syntactic/semantic features for the same fundamental functions (something that, as we show, occassionally happens in SQL/JSON databases), the extension from SQL to SQL++ is most often achieved simply by *removing* semantic restrictions of SQL. Here are a few examples:

1. Unlike SQL's `FROM` clause variables, which bind to tuples only, the FROM clause variables of SQL++ bind to any JSON element.
2. SQL++ is fully composable in the sense that subqueries can appear anywhere, potentially creating nested results when they appear in the `SELECT` clause.
3. While correlation of the subqueries in a `FROM` clause is not allowed in SQL-92, the SQL++ subqueries of a `FROM` clause may be freely correlated with (earlier defined) variables of the same `FROM` clause.
4. The groups created by the `GROUP BY` are directly usable in nested queries - as opposed to SQL's approach where they may only participate in aggregate functions in very limited and particular ways. Interestingly, the SQL++ approach ends up explaining in a simple, formal way even SQL's grouping and aggregation.
5. Unlike SQL, the SQL++ semantics do not require schema or any homogeneity on the input data.

A complete specification of SQL++ can be found in [27]. Notice that features 2 to 4 above are also present in SQL 2003, which includes many 1NF features. In the interest of unifying genuine JSON databases with non-1NF features of SQL, this tutorial explains such features using SQL++, which leads to syntax and semantics succinct and significantly shorter than the SQL 2003 specification. A key methodology that leads to short, succinct semantics is the staging, which reminds of XQuery's specification: First we define an *SQL++ core*. Consequently, additional features and SQL compatibility is achieved as syntactic sugar over the core.

Besides restriction removals, some extensions are also presented. For example, pivoting the tuples' attribute/value pairs to columns is a feature of some databases. Therefore, SQL++ can allow a pair of variables of the `FROM` clause to range over the attribute name and attribute value pairs of input tuples. Similarly, when a `FROM` clause ranges over an array, SQL++ allows a pair of variables to capture the data at an array position and the index of this position. In this way SQL++ seamlessly expands the logic of SQL to "schema" inspection and arrays.

SQL++ shows positive early adoption signs: Couchbase and UCI's AsterixDB are in the process of adopting SQL++.[3] An earlier version of SQL++ has been used by the federated query processor of the UCSD FORWARD application development platform `http://forward.ucsd.edu/sqlpp`.

After having taught Step 1, we will show that multiple model and language differences are superficial syntactic differences.

Step 2: Substantial Semantic Differences between Databases However, not all differences are superficial. Furthermore, this tutorial does not suggest that SQL++ (or some close descendant thereof) will become a standard and remove the many variations that are now found in this space. If nothing else, the gap between genuine JSON databases and SQL/JSON is relatively deep as SQL/JSON is very much based on tables and semantics around tables. Furthermore, via communication with genuine JSON database vendors we recognize that a model and query language standard is premature for such a young and fast-evolving area. Yet, the language designers and researchers need to know now the design options that are available to them and the options that have been used by others, especially as it pertains to the handling of semi-structured aspects (semantics for missing attributes, heterogeneous types, etc), which are not captured by the SQL backwards compatibility. Towards this goal the tutorial utilizes an extension of SQL++ into Configurable SQL++, which is essentially a guery language generator. Depending on the options that are chosen for various features, different capabilities are assumed and different semantics emerge.

The Configurable SQL++ explains the multiple options that language designers have and the options they have chosen in current systems. The Configurable SQL++ includes *configuration options* that describe

1. which features are supported and

[3]The tutorial's author has collaborated with the AsterixDB and Couchbase teams on specifying SQL++.

2. (for the supported features) different options of language semantics that formally capture the variations of existing database query languages.

One particular example where configuration options capture differences concisely, is the behavior of paths of the various query languages in the absence of information. For example, consider a JSON object `{a:1, b:2}` and a path that navigates into the absent path `c`. Languages differ on what is the result of `c`. Is it an error? Is it a special value? If it is a special value, how does it behave in other features of the query language? Is the query writer given control on what special value may emerge or whether an error will be thrown? A configuration option captures these differences precisely.

By appropriate choices of configuration options, the Configurable SQL++ semantics morphs into the semantics of other query languages. Hence, the audience will be able to understand the essential differences between the various query languages, without being swamped by their superficial syntactic differences. Given the time constraints, the comparisons will be mostly around the SQL standard, three well known databases (Cassandra CQL, MongoDB, Couchbase N1QL) and one academia-originating system (AsterixDB AQL). Selected features will be explained as particular settings of various configuration options. The reader can find the "configuration options" surveying approach, as well as coverage of additional databases, in the companion documents of this tutorial at **http://db.ucsd.edu/TutorialSIGMOD16/**.

We expect that some of the results listed in the feature matrices describing configuration options will change in the next years as the space evolves rapidly. Despite the forthcoming changes, we expect Configurable SQL++ to remain a standing tool in understanding the space, since by understanding each database's capabilities in terms of applicable options, the reader can focus on the fundamental differences of the databases. To further facilitate understanding of Configurable SQL++ and the effect of the various configuration options, we provide a web-accessible reference implementation of Configurable SQL++ at `http://forward.ucsd.edu/sqlpp`.

Finally, with respect to configurability, we note the potential applicability of the formal capture (by the Configurable SQL++) of capability and semantic differences in the area of polystore querying and query rewriting [15].

Step 3: Additional Features We will also discuss features, many of which coming from XQuery, that have not been captured by configuration options and are not present in current industrial languages. These will prompt a more open-ended discussion of language designs and tradeoff's. A notable one is type coercion - the approaches and the pros and cons.

Step 4: Set-at-a-time Algebras It is desirable that the processing of semistructured queries by genuine JSON databases leverages existing SQL query processing techniques. A distinguishing feature of SQL query processing is the utilization of algebraic plans that consist of set-at-a-time operators. The tutorial shows next that SQL++ query processing can be based on a *SQL++ algebra*, which is a set-at-a-time algebra that extends the relational algebra. The point is particularly relevant to genuine JSON databases, as they evolve from key-value stores to full-blown databases.

The SQL++ algebra is representative of multiple algebras that were proposed and used in the context of semistructured and nested data. It combines ideas that had first appeared in the context of set-at-a-time algebras for XQuery and OQL. Nested relational algebras are also explained as a subset of the SQL++ algebra.

In the interest of capturing multiple algebraic approaches, we present a non-minimal set of algebraic operators, along with algebraic equivalences that explain how certain operators can be replaced by others. The provided equivalences explain how the various approaches connect to each other, while the commentary highlights the tradeoffs.

Open Issues Finally, we emphasize open issues in the expansion from structured to semistructured querying (dealing with lack of typing, potential expansions to include graphs) and briefly discuss interoperability challenges induced by language differences.

5. OTHER DATA

Prerequisite Knowledge The attendees must have solid knowledge of SQL-92, since it is the baseline upon which the semistructured aspects are then added. Also solid knowledge of relational algebra. Knowledge of SQL-2003 and/or XQuery are a plus but not required.

Relevant Aspects of Presenter's Bio Yannis Papakonstantinou is a Professor of Computer Science and Engineering at UCSD. A common theme of his research is the extension of database platforms and query processors beyond centralized relational databases and into semistructured databases, integrated views of distributed databases and web services, textual data and queries involving keyword search. His research has received more than 12,500 citations, according to Google Scholar, most of which refer to his work on semistructured data, semistructured query processing and related middleware.

In addition to his academic activity in middleware, semistructured data and query processing, Yannis was the Chief Scientist of Enosys Software, which built and commercialized an early Enterprise Information Integration platform for structured and semistructured data, utilizing XML and XQuery. The Enosys Software was OEM'd and sold under the BEA Liquid Data and BEA Aqualogic brand names, eventually acquired in 2003 by BEA Systems.

Acknowledgments The presenter thanks his coauthors of [28] and [27], on which most of this tutorial presentation is based on.

Many of the language-related aspects of the proposed tutorial have been presented by Yannis Papakonstantinou during the past year at talks at the following companies and universities that develop NoSQL databases, SQL-on-Hadoop databases or middleware that operates over them: Amazon, Couchbase, MapR, Informatica (which develops middleware for data warehousing and virtual databases over SQL, NoSQL, Hadoop-on-SQL and NewSQL databases), Pivotal. The above talks led to very useful feedback.

6. REFERENCES

[1] S. Abiteboul and N. Bidoit. Non first normal form relations: An algebra allowing data restructuring. *JCSS*, 33(3):361–393, 1986.

[2] S. Abiteboul, P. C. Fischer, and H.-J. Schek, editors. *Nested Relations and Complex Objects*, volume 361 of *Lecture Notes in Computer Science*. Springer, 1989.

[3] A. Arion, V. Benzaken, I. Manolescu, Y. Papakonstantinou, and R. Vijay. Algebra-based identification of tree patterns in XQuery. In *FQAS*, pages 13–25, 2006.

[4] F. Bancilhon, S. Cluet, and C. Delobel. A query language for the O2 object-oriented database system. In *DBPL*, pages 122–138, 1989.

[5] C. Beeri and Y. Tzaban. SAL: An algebra for semistructured data and XML. In *WebDB*, 1999.

[6] A. Behm, V. R. Borkar, M. J. Carey, R. Grover, C. Li, N. Onose, R. Vernica, A. Deutsch, Y. Papakonstantinou, and V. J. Tsotras. ASTERIX: towards a scalable, semistructured data platform for evolving-world models. *Distributed and Parallel Databases*, 29(3):185–216, 2011.

[7] K. S. Beyer, V. Ercegovac, R. Gemulla, A. Balmin, M. Y. Eltabakh, C.-C. Kanne, F. Özcan, and E. J. Shekita. Jaql: A scripting language for large scale semistructured data analysis. *PVLDB*, 4(12):1272–1283, 2011.

[8] A. Bonifati and S. Ceri. Comparative analysis of five XML query languages. *SIGMOD Record*, 29(1):68–79, 2000.

[9] D. Borkar, R. Mayurum, G. Sangudi, and M. Carey. Have your data and query it too: From key-value caching to big data management. In *SIGMOD Conference*, 2016.

[10] Z. Chen, H. Jagadish, L. Lakshmanan, and S. Paparizos. From tree patterns to generalized tree patterns: On efficient evaluation of XQuery. In *VLDB*, 2003.

[11] Cloudera Impala. http://www.cloudera.com/content/cloudera/en/products-and-services/cdh/impala.html.

[12] S. Cluet and G. Moerkotte. Nested queries in object bases. Technical report, 1995.

[13] Couchbase. http://www.couchbase.com/.

[14] A. Deutsch, M. F. Fernández, D. Florescu, A. Y. Levy, and D. Suciu. A query language for XML. *Computer Networks*, 31(11-16):1155–1169, 1999.

[15] J. Duggan, A. J. Elmore, M. Stonebraker, M. Balazinska, B. Howe, J. Kepner, S. Madden, D. Maier, T. Mattson, and S. B. Zdonik. The bigdawg polystore system. *SIGMOD Record*, 44(2):11–16, 2015.

[16] T. Fiebig, S. Helmer, C. Kanne, G. Moerkotte, J. Neumann, R. Schiele, and T. Westmann. Anatomy of a native XML base management system. *VLDB J*, 11(4), 2002.

[17] D. Florescu and G. Fourny. JSONiq: The history of a query language. *IEEE Internet Computing*, 17(5):86–90, 2013.

[18] D. Florescu, C. Hillery, D. Kossmann, P. Lucas, F. Riccardi, T. Westmann, M. Carey, and A. Sundararajan. The BEA streaming XQuery processor. *VLDB Journal*, 13, 2004.

[19] G. Jaeschke and H.-J. Schek. Remarks on the algebra of non first normal form relations. In *PODS*, pages 124–138. ACM, 1982.

[20] H. V. Jagadish, S. Al-Khalifa, A. Chapman, L. V. S. Lakshmanan, A. Nierman, S. Paparizos, J. M. Patel, D. Srivastava, N. Wiwatwattana, Y. Wu, and C. Yu. TIMBER: A native XML database. *VLDB Journal*, 11(4):274–291, 2002.

[21] H. V. Jagadish, L. V. S. Lakshmanan, D. Srivastava, and K. Thompson. TAX: A tree algebra for XML. In *DBPL*, 2001.

[22] A. Lakshman and P. Malik. Cassandra: a decentralized structured storage system. *Operating Systems Review*, 44(2):35–40, 2010.

[23] S. Melnik, A. Gubarev, J. J. Long, G. Romer, S. Shivakumar, M. Tolton, and T. Vassilakis. Dremel: Interactive analysis of web-scale datasets. *PVLDB*, 3(1):330–339, 2010.

[24] P. Michiels, G. A. Mihaila, and J. Siméon. Put a Tree Pattern in Your Algebra. In *ICDE*, 2007.

[25] MongoDB. http://www.mongodb.org/.

[26] C. Olston, B. Reed, U. Srivastava, R. Kumar, and A. Tomkins. Pig Latin: a not-so-foreign language for data processing. In *SIGMOD Conference*, pages 1099–1110, 2008.

[27] K. W. Ong, Y. Papakonstantinou, and R. Vernoux. SQL++: An expressiveness benchmark of SQL-on-Hadoop, NoSQL and NewSQL databases, 2015. http://db.ucsd.edu/wp-content/uploads/pdfs/375.pdf.

[28] K. W. Ong, Y. Papakonstantinou, and R. Vernoux. The SQL++ query language: Configurable, unifying and semi-structured. *CoRR*, abs/1405.3631, 2015. http://arxiv.org/abs/1405.3631.

[29] Y. Papakonstantinou, V. R. Borkar, M. Orgiyan, K. Stathatos, L. Suta, V. Vassalos, and P. Velikhov. XML queries and algebra in the Enosys integration platform. *Data Knowl. Eng.*, 44(3):299–322, 2003.

[30] C. Re, J. Siméon, and M. Fernández. A complete and efficient algebraic compiler for XQuery. In *ICDE*, 2006.

[31] J. Robie, D. Chamberlin, M. Dyck, and J. Snelson. XQuery 3.0: An XML query language, W3C candidate recommendation, 2013. http://www.w3.org/TR/2013/PR-xquery-30-20131022/.

[32] M. A. Roth, H. F. Korth, and A. Silberschatz. Extended algebra and calculus for nested relational databases. *ACM Trans. Database Syst.*, 13(4):389–417, 1988.

[33] C. Sartiani and A. Albano. Yet another query algebra for XML data. In *IDEAS*, 2002.

[34] A. Thusoo, J. S. Sarma, N. Jain, Z. Shao, P. Chakka, N. Zhang, S. Anthony, H. Liu, and R. Murthy. Hive - a petabyte scale data warehouse using Hadoop. In *ICDE*, pages 996–1005, 2010.

[35] JDBC driver for MongoDB. http://www.unityjdbc.com/mongojdbc/mongosqltranslate.php.

[36] S. D. . Viglas, L. Galanis, D. J. DeWitt, D. Maier, and J. F. Naughton. Putting XML query algebras into context. Available at: http://www.cs.wisc.edu/niagara/Publications.html.

[37] X. Zhang, B. Pielech, and E. Rundensteiner. Honey, I shrunk the XQuery!: An XML algebra optimization approach. In *WIDM*, 2002.

[38] X. Zhang and E. Rundensteiner. XAT: XML algebra for Rainbow system. Technical Report. WPI-CS-TR-02-24, July 2002.

Automatic Entity Recognition and Typing in Massive Text Data

Xiang Ren† Ahmed El-Kishky† Heng Ji ‡ Jiawei Han†
† University of Illinois at Urbana-Champaign
‡ Computer Science Department, Rensselaer Polytechnic Institute
† Urbana, IL, USA ‡ Troy, NY, USA
†{xren7, elkishk2, hanj}@illinois.edu ‡jih@rpi.edu

ABSTRACT

In today's computerized and information-based society, individuals are constantly presented with vast amounts of text data, ranging from news articles, scientific publications, product reviews, to a wide range of textual information from social media. To extract value from these large, multi-domain pools of text, it is of great importance to gain an understanding of entities and their relationships. In this tutorial, we introduce data-driven methods to recognize typed entities of interest in massive, domain-specific text corpora. These methods can automatically identify token spans as entity mentions in documents and label their fine-grained types (*e.g.*, people, product and food) in a scalable way. Since these methods do not rely on annotated data, predefined typing schema or hand-crafted features, they can be quickly adapted to a new domain, genre and language. We demonstrate on real datasets including various genres (*e.g.*, news articles, discussion forum posts, and tweets), domains (general vs. biomedical domains) and languages (*e.g.*, English, Chinese, Arabic, and even low-resource languages like Hausa and Yoruba) how these typed entities aid in knowledge discovery and management.

1. INTRODUCTION

Recognizing some limitations in organizing large-scale textual data, we motivate the necessity of powerful and scalable methods for entity recognition and typing as database technology is applied to modern-day massive text data.

Motivation

We motivate this tutorial by starting with identifying the key aspects that have led to the success in database technology and suggesting a similar approach to handling the modern day explosion of unstructured big-data.

Entity recognition/typing and structured analysis of massive text corpora. The success of database technology is largely attributed to the efficient and effective management of structured data. The construction of a well-structured database is often the premise of consequent applications. Although the majority of existing data generated in our society is unstructured, big data leads to big opportunities to uncover structures of real-world entities, such as people, products and organizations, from massive amount but interrelated unstructured data. By mining token spans of entity mentions in documents, labeling their structured types and inferring their relations, it is possible to construct semantically rich structures and provide conceptual summarization of such data. The uncovered structures will facilitate browsing information and retrieving knowledge that are otherwise locked in the data.

Several techniques we discussed have already gained some publicity or application within industry. Our phrase mining tool, SegPhrase [27], won the grand prize of Yelp Dataset Challenge[1] and was adopted in TripAdvisor's new feature[2]. Our entity recognition and typing tool, ClusType [33], was shipped to facilitate products in Microsoft Bing Ads team. Our Entity Discovery and Linking system [17] won first place at NIST TAC-KBP Tri-lingual Entity Discovery and Linking Evaluation.

Example: Automatically recognizing and typing entities in Yelp reviews. In a business review corpus like Yelp reviews, entities such as `food`, `restaurant`, `location` and `event` are mentioned in the documents. For example, from the sentences "*The best BBQ I've tasted in Washington! I had the pulled pork sandwich with coleslaw for lunch.*", it is desirable to identify "*BBQ*", "*pulled pork sandwich*", and "*coleslaw*" as `food`, and "*Washington*" as location. Furthermore, the label of "*coleslaw*" can be refined as `salad` (and "*pulled pork sandwich*" as `sandwich`). However, existing work encounters several challenges when handling such a *domain-specific* text corpus.

1. The lack of annotated data for domain-specific corpora presents a major challenge for adapting traditional supervised named-entity recognition techniques. Fortunately, a number of semantically rich knowledge-bases are available, which provides chances for *automatically* recognizing entities by *distant supervision*.

2. The automatically generated training data by distant supervision may introduce noisy labels—labels that are irrelevant to the local context of entity mention. It is

SIGMOD'16, June 26-July 01, 2016, San Francisco, CA, USA

DOI: http://dx.doi.org/10.1145/2882903.2912567

[1] http://www.yelp.com/dataset_challenge
[2] http://engineering.tripadvisor.com/using-nlp-to-find-interesting-collections-of-hotels/

necessary to conduct label noise reduction on the training data by leveraging corpus-level statistics.

3. Many entity detection tools such as noun phrase chunkers are trained on general-domain corpora (*e.g.*, news articles), but they do not work effectively nor efficiently on domain-specific corpora such as Yelp reviews (*e.g.*, "*pulled pork sandwich*" cannot be detected). A domain-agnostic phrase mining algorithm is required to efficiently generate entity mentions with minimal linguistic assumptions.

4. Entity surface names are often ambiguous—multiple entities many share the same surface name (*e.g.*, "*Washington*" may refer to the U.S. government, the capital city or a sport team). Although the contexts surrounding each entity mention provide clues on its types, challenges arise due to the diversity on paraphrasing. With data redundancy in a massive corpus, it is possible to disambiguate entities and resolve synonymous contexts using correlated textual information structured in an information network for holistic analysis.

What will be covered?

Preliminaries: We introduce the audience to the broad subject of entity recognition by providing motivation in the context of *information extraction for knowledge base population* . Within this context introduce entities, types, extracting these entities from within text itself, and examples validating the necessity for entity disambiguation and resolution. We then introduce several different applications to latent entity discovery in data. In particular, we will introduce and explain grouping latent entities by concepts, by topics, and even extracting and understanding relationships between entities.

Entity Mention Detection: In this part of our presentation, we introduce the problem of identifying entity mentions. We formulate the problem and discuss three main schools of thought in tackling the problem.

1. **Supervised Methods:** We begin by introducing IOB, a common representation that transforms entity mention detection into classification. Then, beginning with classical (non-sequential) models, we outline a variety of methods including unigram and higher-order chunkers, SVM's, maximum entropy models, and ensemble methods. We then introduce sequential models for entity mention detection and outline a progressive array of methods from generative to discriminative models.
2. **Unsupervised Methods:** We follow on by introducing two main classes of unsupervised approaches: chunking grammar approaches and methods that draw upon large-text corpora and their relative merits and broad spectrum of applications. We then focus on applications of ToPMine for topical phrase mining and noun-collocation mining.
3. **Distantly / Weakly Supervised Methods:** We focus on a variety of methods including incorporating outside information via dictionary. We mainly emphasize SegPhrase, an approach for extracting high-quality phrases and entity mentions with minimal supervision.

Entity Recognition in Individual Documents: Within the context of entity recognition in individual documents (as opposed to large text collections), we discuss how this objective differs in the general and domain-specific case.

1. **General Text:** In the context of general text recognition, we discuss introduce many named entity recognition (NER) methods. We discuss entity recognition as sequence labeling as well as the coarse types and manually-annotated corpora these models leverage.
2. **Domain Text:** In the context of domain-specific extraction, we discuss several approaches. We discuss twitter in the context of Tweet segmentation and chunking as well as LabeledLDA based on Freebase. In addition to twitter we discuss entity recognition in product reviews and biomedical text data.

Entity Recognition in Large Domain-Specific Corpora: We contrast single-document cases to the context of large single-domain corpora. Starting with semi-supervised approaches, we present sequence-labeling models and models that combine local and global features. We transition to weakly supervised approaches and their merits -discussing pattern-based bootstrapping methods, SEISA: Set expansion, and a variety of probabilistic modeling methods as well as graph-based label propagation approaches. We then discuss several approaches for distantly supervised entity recognition. These methods include state of the art approaches such as FIGER which performs sequence labeling with automatically annotated data , SemTagger - a contextual classifier that uses seed data , APOLLO which performs label propagation on graphs, and ClusType which employs relation phrase-based clustering for effective entity recognition.

Case Study and Evaluations We conclude our tutorial by demonstrating the capabilities of many of the tools and methods mentioned on a variety of test cases and metrics. We begin by evaluating tools and methodologies for entity recognition. We introduce a variety of evaluation metrics and public datasets, and evaluate a variety of general-domain NER systems including the Stanford Named Entity Recognizer, Illinois Named Entity Tagger, FIGER, and other Named Entity Recognition in NLP toolkits. We then present a few case-studies on two real-world datasets consisting of news articles and tweets. In particular we focus on entity mention detection in these datasets and typing these extracted entity mentions.

Why a tutorial at SIGMOD 2016

In today's era of 'big data', people are exposed to an explosion of information in the form of documentary data collections, ranging from the scientific knowledge of all humanity, to the daily life of individuals. Most of these collections are unstructured or loosely structured. Effective detection, extraction, and typing of entity structures is key to inducing structure and understanding from messy and scattered raw data. This tutorial will present an organized picture of recent research on entity mention detection, entity typing, and general text extraction algorithms. We will show how exciting and surprising knowledge can be discovered from your own not so well-structured raw data.

Audience and Prerequisites

Researchers and practitioners in the field of database systems, information extraction, data mining, text mining, information retrieval, web search, and information systems. While the audience with a good background in these areas would benefit most from this tutorial, we believe the material to be presented would give general audience and newcomers an introductory pointer to the current work and important research topics in this field, and inspire them to learn more. Only preliminary knowledge about text mining, information extraction, data mining, algorithms, and their applications are needed.

2. TUTORIAL OUTLINE

This tutorial presents a comprehensive overview of the techniques developed for automatic entity recognition and typing in recent years. We will discuss the following key issues.

1. Preliminaries of Entity Recognition and Typing
   (a) Entities that are explicitly typed and linked externally with documents.
      i. Wikilinks and ClueWeb corpora
   (b) Entities that can be extracted within text.
   (c) Entity disambiguation and resolution.
      i. MENED: Mining evidence outside referent knowledge bases
2. Entity Mention Detection
   (a) Unsupervised Entity Mention Detection
      i. ReVerb: A pattern-based approach for matching entities and relations
      ii. Significance detection of phrases and entities in a corpus
      iii. Jointly identifying significant phrases for entities and relations
   (b) Supervised Entity Mention Detection
      i. Jointly extracting entities and relations
      ii. MaxiEnt markov models for information extraction and segmentation
      iii. Semi-supervised text chunking for entity candidate generation
      iv. Ranking for entity mention
   (c) Distantly / Weakly Supervised Methods
      i. SegPhrase: Weakly supervised phrase extraction and segmentation
      ii. Exploiting dictionaries: Combining semi-markov extraction process with data integration
3. Entity Recognition in Single Text Documents
   (a) Traditional supervised named entity recognition (NER) systems
      i. Entity recognition and typing as a sequence labeling task
      ii. Classic coarse types and manually-annotated corpora
      iii. Sequence labeling models
   (b) Entity recognition in tweets
      i. Tweet segmentation and chunking
      ii. LabeledLDA based on Freebase
      iii. Segment ranking
   (c) Entity recognition in product reviews
   (d) Entity recognition in biomedical text
4. Entity Recognition in A Large, Domain-specific Corpus
   (a) Semi-supervised approaches
      i. Combining local and global features
   (b) Weakly-supervised approaches
      i. Pattern-based bootstrapping methods
      ii. SEISA: A set expansion method
      iii. Probabilistic modeling methods
      iv. Graph-based label propagation
      v. Extracting entities from web tables
   (c) Distantly-supervised approaches
      i. SemTagger: Seed-based contextual classifier for entity typing
      ii. APOLLO: Label propagation on graphs
      iii. ClusType: Effective entity recognition by relation phrase-based clustering
   (d) Fine-grained typing approaches
      i. FIGER: Multi-label classification with automatically annotated data
      ii. HYENA: Hierarchical classification for fine-grained typing
      iii. WSABIE: Embedding method for fine-grained typing
   (e) Label noise reduction in distant supervision
      i. Noisy candidate types in automatically generated training data
      ii. Simple pruning heuristics
      iii. Partial-label learning methods
      iv. Label noise reduction by heterogeneous partial-label embedding
   (f) Liberal entity recognition and typing
      i. Three-level semantic representation
      ii. Joint hierarchical clustering and linking algorithm
5. Evaluations of entity recognition
   (a) Evaluation metrics and public datasets
   (b) Public general-domain NER systems
   (c) Shared tasks on entity recognition
6. Case studies: news articles and tweets.
   (a) Entity recognition in these datasets
      i. Detect entity mentions in these datasets
      ii. Typing entity mentions in these datasets
   (b) Integrating entities in both datasets
7. Recent progress and research problems on entity recognition

Tailor of the Tutorial for Different Durations. The duration of the tutorial is flexible from a full presentation of 3 hours or compressed into 1.5 hours. The outline presented here is for the full length tutorial. For shorter duration of the tutorial, we plan to cut the detection of entity mentions by half, cut entity recognition in single, general-domain text document in half, and cut the case studies section.

3. ABOUT THE INSTRUCTORS

Xiang Ren is a Ph.D. candidate of Department of Computer Science at Univ. of Illinois at Urbana-Champaign. His research focuses on knowledge acquisition from text data and mining linked data. He is the recipient of the 2016 Google PhD Fellowship in Data Management and Databases, was the recipient of C. L. and Jane W.-S. Liu Award and Yahoo!-DAIS Research Excellence Award in 2015, and received the Microsoft Young Fellowship from Microsoft Research Asia in 2012.

Ahmed El-Kishky is a Ph.D. candidate at Univ. of Illinois at Urbana-Champaign. His research interests include mining large unstructured data, text mining, learning to rank, and network mining. He is the recipient of both the National Science Foundation Graduate Research Fellowship and National Defense Science and Engineering Fellowship.

Jiawei Han is an Abel Bliss Professor at the Department of Computer Science, UIUC. His research areas encompass data mining, data warehousing, database systems, and information networks, with over 700 publications. He is Fellow of ACM, Fellow of IEEE, Director of IPAN (2009-2016), supported by Network Science Collaborative Technology Alliance program of the U.S. Army Research Lab, and the co-Director of KnowEnG: a Knowledge Engine for Genomics, one of the NIH supported Big Data to Knowledge (BD2K) Centers.

Heng Ji is an Edward P. Hamilton Development Chair Associate Professor of Computer Science Department of Rensselaer Polytechnic Institute. Her research interests focus on Natural Language Processing and its connections with Data Mining and Vision. She received "AI's 10 to Watch" Award by IEEE Intelligent Systems in 2013 and NSF CAREER award in 2009. She coordinated the NIST TAC Knowledge Base Population task in 2010, 2011, 2014, 2015 and 2016.

4. AUTHORS' RELATED TUTORIALS

1. **Conference tutorial:** Xiang Ren, Ahmed El-Kishky, Chi Wang and Jiawei Han. "Automatic Entity Recognition and Typing from Massive Text Corpora: A Phrase and Network Mining Approach." KDD 2015.

2. **Conference tutorial:** Jiawei Han, Heng Ji and Yizhou Sun. "Successful Data Mining Methods for NLP." ACL 2015.

3. **Conference tutorial:** Han, Jiawei, Chi Wang, and Ahmed El-Kishky. "Bringing structure to text: Mining phrases, entities, topics, and hierarchies" KDD 2014.

4. **Conference tutorial:** Dan Roth, Heng Ji, Ming-Wei Chang and Taylor Cassidy. "Wikification and Beyond: The Challenges of Entity and Concept Grounding." ACL 2014.

5. **Conference tutorial:** Jiawei Han and ChiWang, "Mining Latent Entity Structures from Massive Unstructured and Interconnected Data", SIGMOD 2014.

6. **Conference tutorial:** Tim Weninger, and Jiawei Han, "Information Network Analysis and Extraction on the World Wide Web", WWW 2013.

7. **Conference tutorial:** Tim Weninger and Jiawei Han, "Exploring Structure and Content on the Web: Extraction and Integration of the Semi-Structured Web", WSDM 2013.

8. **Conference tutorial:** Yizhou Sun, Jiawei Han, Xifeng Yan, and Philip S. Yu, "Mining Knowledge from Interconnected Data: A Heterogeneous Information Network Analysis Approach", VLDB 2012.

The above are the related tutorials given by the authors. Several of our early tutorials were on mining heterogeneous information networks. However, the power of such mining comes from structures of such networks (entities and links). Recent advances in information extraction and typing makes it possible to construct these networks from the raw data. This tutorial presents this new line of research from shallow information extraction to deep network analysis through mining latent entity structures from text and constructing a structured database for knowledge discovery.

5. ACKNOWLEDGMENTS

Research was sponsored in part by the U.S. Army Research Lab. under Cooperative Agreement No. W911NF-09-2-0053 (NSCTA), National Science Foundation IIS-1017362, IIS-1320617, and IIS-1354329, HDTRA1-10-1-0120, and grant 1U54GM114838 awarded by NIGMS through funds provided by the trans-NIH Big Data to Knowledge (BD2K) initiative (www.bd2k.nih.gov). The views and conclusions contained in this document are those of the author(s) and should not be interpreted as representing the official policies of the U.S. Army Research Laboratory or the U.S. Government. The U.S. Government is authorized to reproduce and distribute reprints for Government purposes notwithstanding any copyright notation hereon.

References

[1] R. K. Ando and T. Zhang. A high-performance semi-supervised learning method for text chunking. In *ACL*, 2005.

[2] K. Bollacker, C. Evans, P. Paritosh, T. Sturge, and J. Taylor. Freebase: a collaboratively created graph database for structuring human knowledge. In *SIGMOD*, 2008.

[3] A. Carlson, J. Betteridge, R. C. Wang, E. R. Hruschka Jr, and T. M. Mitchell. Coupled semi-supervised learning for information extraction. In *WSDM*, 2010.

[4] W. W. Cohen and S. Sarawagi. Exploiting dictionaries in named entity extraction: combining semi-markov extraction processes and data integration methods. In *SIGKDD*, 2004.

[5] M. Collins. Ranking algorithms for named-entity extraction: Boosting and the voted perceptron. In *ACL*, 2002.

[6] J. R. Curran and S. Clark. Language independent ner using a maximum entropy tagger. In *HLT-NAACL*, 2003.

[7] B. B. Dalvi, W. W. Cohen, and J. Callan. Websets: Extracting sets of entities from the web using unsupervised information extraction. In *WSDM*, 2012.

[8] L. Dong, F. Wei, H. Sun, M. Zhou, and K. Xu. A hybrid neural model for type classification of entity mentions. In *IJCAI*, 2015.

[9] A. El-Kishky, Y. Song, C. Wang, C. R. Voss, and J. Han. Scalable topical phrase mining from text corpora. *VLDB*, 2015.

[10] O. Etzioni, M. Cafarella, D. Downey, A.-M. Popescu, T. Shaked, S. Soderland, D. S. Weld, and A. Yates. Unsupervised named-entity extraction from the web: An experimental study. *Artificial intelligence*, 165(1):91–134, 2005.

[11] A. Fader, S. Soderland, and O. Etzioni. Identifying relations for open information extraction. In *EMNLP*, 2011.

[12] J. R. Finkel, T. Grenager, and C. Manning. Incorporating non-local information into information extraction systems by gibbs sampling. In *ACL*, 2005.

[13] V. Ganti, A. C. König, and R. Vernica. Entity categorization over large document collections. In *SIGKDD*, 2008.

[14] A. Gattani, D. S. Lamba, N. Garera, M. Tiwari, X. Chai, S. Das, S. Subramaniam, A. Rajaraman, V. Harinarayan, and A. Doan. Entity extraction, linking, classification, and tagging for social media: a wikipedia-based approach. *VLDB*, 6(11), 2013.

[15] S. Gupta and C. D. Manning. Improved pattern learning for bootstrapped entity extraction. In *CONLL*, 2014.

[16] Y. He and D. Xin. Seisa: set expansion by iterative similarity aggregation. In *WWW*, 2011.

[17] Y. Hong, D. Lu, D. Yu, X. Pan, X. Wang, Y. Chen, L. Huang, and H. Ji. Rpi_blender tac-kbp2015 system description. In *Proc. Text Analysis Conference (TAC2015)*, 2015.

[18] R. Huang and E. Riloff. Inducing domain-specific semantic class taggers from (almost) nothing. In *ACL*, 2010.

[19] H. Ji and R. Grishman. Knowledge base population: Successful approaches and challenges. In *ACL*, 2011.

[20] D. S. Kim, K. Verma, and P. Z. Yeh. Joint extraction and labeling via graph propagation for dictionary construction. In *AAAI*, 2013.

[21] Z. Kozareva, K. Voevodski, and S.-H. Teng. Class label enhancement via related instances. In *EMNLP*, 2011.

[22] C. Li, J. Weng, Q. He, Y. Yao, A. Datta, A. Sun, and B.-S. Lee. Twiner: named entity recognition in targeted twitter stream. In *SIGIR*, 2012.

[23] Q. Li and H. Ji. Incremental joint extraction of entity mentions and relations. In *ACL*, 2014.

[24] Y. Li, C. Wang, F. Han, J. Han, D. Roth, and X. Yan. Mining evidences for named entity disambiguation. In *SIGKDD*, 2013.

[25] G. Limaye, S. Sarawagi, and S. Chakrabarti. Annotating and searching web tables using entities, types and relationships. *VLDB*, 3(1-2):1338–1347, 2010.

[26] X. Ling and D. S. Weld. Fine-grained entity recognition. In *AAAI*, 2012.

[27] J. Liu, J. Shang, C. Wang, X. Ren, and J. Han. Mining quality phrases from massive text corpora. In *SIGMOD*, 2015.

[28] A. McCallum, D. Freitag, and F. C. Pereira. Maximum entropy markov models for information extraction and segmentation. In *ICML*, volume 17, pages 591–598, 2000.

[29] D. Nadeau and S. Sekine. A survey of named entity recognition and classification. *Lingvisticae Investigationes*, 30(1):3–26, 2007.

[30] N. Nguyen and R. Caruana. Classification with partial labels. In *SIGKDD*, 2008.

[31] K. Nigam and R. Ghani. Analyzing the effectiveness and applicability of co-training. In *CIKM*, 2000.

[32] L. Ratinov and D. Roth. Design challenges and misconceptions in named entity recognition. In *ACL*, 2009.

[33] X. Ren, A. El-Kishky, C. Wang, F. Tao, C. R. Voss, and J. Han. Clustype: Effective entity recognition and typing by relation phrase-based clustering. In *SIGKDD*, 2015.

[34] A. Ritter, S. Clark, O. Etzioni, et al. Named entity recognition in tweets: an experimental study. In *EMNLP*, 2011.

[35] W. Shen, J. Wang, and J. Han. Entity linking with a knowledge base: Issues, techniques, and solutions. *TKDE*, 27(99):1–20, 2014.

[36] P. P. Talukdar, T. Brants, M. Liberman, and F. Pereira. A context pattern induction method for named entity extraction. In *CONLL*, 2006.

[37] J. Tang, M. Qu, and Q. Mei. Pte: Predictive text embedding through large-scale heterogeneous text networks. In *SIGKDD*, 2015.

[38] J. Turian, L. Ratinov, and Y. Bengio. Word representations: a simple and general method for semi-supervised learning. In *ACL*, 2010.

[39] W. Wu, H. Li, H. Wang, and K. Q. Zhu. Probase: A probabilistic taxonomy for text understanding. In *SIGMOD*, 2012.

[40] M. Yakout, K. Ganjam, K. Chakrabarti, and S. Chaudhuri. Infogather: entity augmentation and attribute discovery by holistic matching with web tables. In *SIGMOD*, 2012.

[41] R. Yangarber, W. Lin, and R. Grishman. Unsupervised learning of generalized names. In *COLING*, 2002.

[42] D. Yogatama, D. Gillick, and N. Lazic. Embedding methods for fine grained entity type classification. In *ACL*, 2015.

[43] M. A. Yosef, S. Bauer, J. Hoffart, M. Spaniol, and G. Weikum. Hyena: Hierarchical type classification for entity names. In *COLING*, 2012.

Big Graph Analytics Systems

Da Yan
The Chinese University of Hong Kong
yanda@cse.cuhk.edu.hk

Yingyi Bu
Couchbase, Inc.
yingyi@couchbase.com

Yuanyuan Tian
IBM Almaden Research Center, USA
ytian@us.ibm.com

Amol Deshpande
University of Maryland
amol@cs.umd.edu

James Cheng
The Chinese University of Hong Kong
jcheng@cse.cuhk.edu.hk

ABSTRACT

In recent years we have witnessed a surging interest in developing Big Graph processing systems. To date, tens of Big Graph systems have been proposed. This tutorial provides a timely and comprehensive review of existing Big Graph systems, and summarizes their pros and cons from various perspectives. We start from the existing vertex-centric systems, which which a programmer thinks intuitively like a vertex when developing parallel graph algorithms. We then introduce systems that adopt other computation paradigms and execution settings. The topics covered in this tutorial include programming models and algorithm design, computation models, communication mechanisms, out-of-core support, fault tolerance, dynamic graph support, and so on. We also highlight future research opportunities on Big Graph analytics.

CCS Concepts

•Mathematics of computing → Graph algorithms; •Networks → Cloud computing; •Theory of computation → Graph algorithms analysis; •Computing methodologies → Parallel computing methodologies; •Computer systems organization → Parallel architectures;

Keywords

Graph; system; platform; Pregel; GraphLab; vertex-centric

1. INTRODUCTION

With the increasing popularity of online social networks and the prevalence of mobile communication networks and other types of information networks, there has been a great interest in developing efficient and scalable techniques to study these networks, modeled as graphs. In particular, many Big Graph systems have been developed in recent years, which provide a user-friendly, unified framework for programmers to implement parallel algorithms for all kinds of graph analytics. As graph data continue to proliferate in many real world applications, more Big Graph systems are expected to emerge in the near future. However, the sudden emergence of so many Big Graph systems easily overwhelms both researchers and general users who are interested in developing new systems or in using these systems for graph analytics.

This tutorial provides a comprehensive survey of the existing Big Graph systems. For each work (or system), we highlight the key ideas and features of its design, and summarize its strengths and weaknesses. The goal of this tutorial is three-fold. With an in-depth analysis of the various techniques adopted by existing systems, we aim to (1) help system researchers avoid reinventing the wheel, but instead, develop new ideas in system design; (2) help system practitioners apply useful existing techniques to their systems to improve system performance; and (3) help general users understand the pros and cons of different systems and select the right system for their particular graph analytics tasks.

While the existing Big Graph systems can be categorized in various ways, this tutorial categorizes these systems mainly according to their *programming models*, *execution models*, and *execution settings*. We emphasize them dimensions since user-friendliness in programming is one important feature of modern Big Graph systems, while the execution model and settings are critical to the efficiency of graph computation.

Features of Big Graph Systems. We first consider the computation model. Vertex-centric computation is probably the most popular computation model for iterative graph computations, where a programmer only needs to specify the behavior for one generic vertex, and the systems automatically apply the user-defined logic to different vertices in a graph to complete the computation. There also exist graph-parallel systems that adopt other computation models. For example, Giraph++ [9] and Blogel [12] extend the vertex-centric computation model with a novel block-centric computation model, to avoid incurring communication for the computation within a subgraph block. GRACE [11] applies a similar idea to improve the hit rate of CPU caches. Among others, PEGASUS [5] and GBASE [4] model graph computation by (generalized) matrix-vector multiplications; while Green-Marl [3] and Galois [6] let users specify the computation logic by a domain-specific language (DSL). N-Scale [7] adopts a subgraph-centric model where users define

SIGMOD'16, June 26-July 01, 2016, San Francisco, CA, USA

DOI: http://dx.doi.org/10.1145/2882903.2912566

computation logic on a subgraph of interest, and the model is better at solving graph problems whose outputs are a set of possibly overlapping subgraphs, such as graph matching and motif mining. There are also systems that use Datalog for Big Graph analytics, such as SociaLite [8].

Other features of big data systems include (1) whether the execution is synchronous or asynchronous, (2) the support for topology mutation, i.e., the deletion and addition of edges and vertices; (3) the support for dynamic graphs with frequent updates, such as in Kineograph [1], TIDE [10], and Chronos [2]; and (4) the support for out-of-core execution. Finally, in terms of hardware platforms, while most graph systems are designed to run on a cluster, there are a few systems designed to run in a single machine or to run with SSDs or GPUs.

2. TARGET AUDIENCE

The target audience for this tutorial includes all who are interested in graph analytics and its applications.

3. TUTORIAL OUTLINE

The preferred duration of this tutorial is 3 hours, which covers two parts that consist of 6 topics (see below). Each part takes around 1.5 hours. Part I covers Topics 1 and 2, and Part II covers Topics 3, 4, 5 and 6.

3.1 Topic 1: Pregel-Like Systems

In this topic, we first review the computation model of Pregel, and introduce how to design Pregel algorithms that have performance guarantees. We then review existing Pregel-like systems that optimizes the basic model of Pregel from various aspects, including communication mechanisms, load balancing, computation model, support for asynchronous execution, and fault tolerance.

3.2 Topic 2: Shared Memory Abstraction

In this topic, we review vertex-centric Big Graph systems that adopt the shared memory abstraction. We first review the pioneering system GraphLab, as well as its improved version, PowerGraph. We then introduce three important systems that adopt shared memory abstraction: GraphChi, X-Stream and VENUS. These systems are designed to perform out-of-core graph processing on a single PC.

3.3 Topic 3: Matrix-Based Systems

In this topic, we first review three matrix-based systems that rely on MapReduce for execution: PEGASUS, GBASE and SystemML. We then review three single-machine systems that adopt a vertex-centric programming model but perform matrix-based execution: GraphMat, GraphTwist and GridGraph.

3.4 Topic 4: Single-Machine Systems

While Topics 2 and 3 already covered some single-machine systems, this topic review more single-machine systems that can be classified into three categories: (1) out-of-core systems that process graphs on SSD(s); (2) in-memory systems for multi-core execution, which emphasize more on ease of programming and high parallelism; (3) systems for execution with GPU(s).

3.5 Topic 5: Subgraph-Based Systems

This topic reviews the two recent systems that adopt a *overlapping subgraph-centric* model, NScale and Arabesque. These systems target graph analysis tasks whose output size can be exponential in the graph size (e.g., graph matching and finding motifs), or tasks which require reasoning about neighborhoods or connected components, neither of which can be well-solved by vertex-centric systems. We also point out the inefficiencies of these systems in constructing subgraphs for processing, and identify the opportunities for further research in this field.

3.6 Topic 6: DBMS-Based Systems

In this topic, we discuss connections between DBMS-style recursive query processing and Big Graph analytical systems. We revisit recent research projects that are "resurging" Datalog in the context of scalable Big Graph analytics, discuss existing dataflow-based graph systems, and dataflow systems for incremental graph processing.

4. OPEN PROBLEMS

We end our tutorial with a discussion of open problems in developing Big Graph analytics platforms. Despite the plurality of graph systems, very few support the analysis of temporal graphs that dynamically change over time. More work can be done in this area, especially for efficiently supporting dynamic graphs with frequent vertex and edge deletions. Also, existing systems for graph matching and motif finding all suffer from various performance problems, thus a more efficient framework for the overlapping subgraph-centric model remains to be found. Another interesting open problem is to study how the various models can be integrated together to solve complicated real-life problems that involve graph ETL (extract, transform, and load) and computation tasks of all kinds.

5. ACKNOWLEDGMENTS

Da Yan and James Cheng are supported by the Hong Kong GRF 2150851. Amol Deshpande is supported by NSF under grant IIS-1319432, and an IBM Collaborative Research Award.

6. REFERENCES

[1] R. Cheng, J. Hong, A. Kyrola, Y. Miao, X. Weng, M. Wu, F. Yang, L. Zhou, F. Zhao, and E. Chen. Kineograph: taking the pulse of a fast-changing and connected world. In *EuroSys*, pages 85–98, 2012.

[2] W. Han, Y. Miao, K. Li, M. Wu, F. Yang, L. Zhou, V. Prabhakaran, W. Chen, and E. Chen. Chronos: a graph engine for temporal graph analysis. In *EuroSys*, pages 1:1–1:14, 2014.

[3] S. Hong, H. Chafi, E. Sedlar, and K. Olukotun. Green-marl: a DSL for easy and efficient graph analysis. In *ASPLOS*, pages 349–362, 2012.

[4] U. Kang, H. Tong, J. Sun, C. Lin, and C. Faloutsos. GBASE: a scalable and general graph management system. In *SIGKDD*, pages 1091–1099, 2011.

[5] U. Kang, C. E. Tsourakakis, and C. Faloutsos. PEGASUS: A peta-scale graph mining system. In *ICDM*, pages 229–238, 2009.

[6] D. Nguyen, A. Lenharth, and K. Pingali. A lightweight infrastructure for graph analytics. In *SOSP*, pages 456–471, 2013.

[7] A. Quamar, A. Deshpande, and J. Lin. Nscale: Neighborhood-centric analytics on large graphs. *PVLDB*, 7(13):1673–1676, 2014.

[8] J. Seo, S. Guo, and M. S. Lam. Socialite: Datalog extensions for efficient social network analysis. In *29th IEEE International Conference on Data Engineering, ICDE 2013, Brisbane, Australia, April 8-12, 2013*, pages 278–289, 2013.

[9] Y. Tian, A. Balmin, S. A. Corsten, S. Tatikonda, and J. McPherson. From "think like a vertex" to "think like a graph". *PVLDB*, 7(3):193–204, 2013.

[10] W. Xie, Y. Tian, Y. Sismanis, A. Balmin, and P. J. Haas. Dynamic interaction graphs with probabilistic edge decay. In *ICDE*, pages 1143–1154, 2015.

[11] W. Xie, G. Wang, D. Bindel, A. J. Demers, and J. Gehrke. Fast iterative graph computation with block updates. *PVLDB*, 6(14):2014–2025, 2013.

[12] D. Yan, J. Cheng, Y. Lu, and W. Ng. Blogel: A block-centric framework for distributed computation on real-world graphs. *PVLDB*, 7(14):1981–1992, 2014.

7. BIOGRAPHIES

Dr. YAN, Da is with the Department of Computer Science and Engineering at the Chinese University of Hong Kong. He is the winner of the 2015 Hong Kong Young Scientist Award.

Dr. Yingyi Bu is a senior software engineer in Couchbase Inc. He is the recipient of a Google PhD fellowship award and a Yahoo! key scientific challenge award.

Dr. Yuanyuan Tian is a Research Staff Member at IBM Almaden Research Center, USA. Her research interests include large scale machine learning, graph analytics, SQL on Hadoop, and big data federation. She is the recipient of the Distinguished Achievement Award from the Univeristy of Michigan.

Dr. Amol Deshpande is an Associate Professor of Computer Science at the University of Maryland at College Park. His research interests include graph data management, adaptive query processing, data streams, sensor networks and statistical modeling of data. He is a recipient of the NSF CAREER Award.

Dr. James Cheng is with the Department of Computer Science and Engineering at the Chinese University of Hong Kong. His research focuses on big data infrastructures, distributed computing systems, and large-scale network analysis.

Constructing Join Histograms from Histograms with q-error Guarantees

Kaleb Alway*
David R. Cheriton School of Computer Science
Faculty of Mathematics, University of Waterloo
kpalway@uwaterloo.ca

Anisoara Nica
SAP SE
Waterloo, Ontario, Canada
Anisoara.Nica@sap.com

ABSTRACT

Histograms are implemented and used in any database system, usually defined on a single-column of a database table. However, one of the most desired statistical data in such systems are statistics on the correlation among columns. In this paper we present a novel construction algorithm for building a *join histogram* that accepts two single-column histograms over different attributes, each with q-error guarantees, and produces a histogram over the result of the join operation on these attributes. The join histogram is built only from the input histograms without accessing the base data or computing the join relation. Under certain restrictions, a q-error guarantee can be placed on the produced join histogram.

It is possible to construct adversarial input histograms that produce arbitrarily large q-error in the resulting join histogram, but across several experiments, this type of input does not occur in either randomly generated data or real-world data. Our construction algorithm runs in linear time with respect to the size of the input histograms, and produces a join histogram that is at most as large as the sum of the sizes of the input histograms. These join histograms can be used to efficiently and accurately estimate the cardinality of join queries.

Keywords

Query Optimization; Histogram; Cardinality Estimation

1. INTRODUCTION

In this paper we use a general notion of q-error. As defined in Moerkotte et al. [1], an estimate $\hat{f}$ of a value f is said to be θ, q-acceptable if either $f \leq \theta \wedge \hat{f} \leq \theta$ or $||\hat{f}/f||_Q \leq q$, where $||x||_Q = max(x, 1/x)$. Note that when the parameter θ is zero, the notion of θ, q-acceptability is the same as a plain q-error bound. We consider the statistical question of cardinality estimation of a join query of the form:

*The student author and the adviser Dr. Anisoara Nica worked on this project during Fall 2015 co-op term at SAP Waterloo, Canada.

SIGMOD/PODS'16 June 26 - July 01, 2016, San Francisco, CA, USA

ACM ISBN 978-1-4503-3531-7/16/06.

DOI: http://dx.doi.org/10.1145/2882903.2914828

$Join(J) = \Pi_{R.A}(\sigma_{(R.A=T.B)\wedge p_1(R.A)\wedge p_2(T.B)}(R \times T))$
where:

- The column $R.A$ has a θ_1, q_1-acceptable histogram H_1
- The column $T.B$ has a θ_2, q_2-acceptable histogram H_2
- $p_1(R.A)$ and $p_2(T.B)$ are *histogram-SARGable* predicates on columns $R.A$ and $T.B$, i.e., predicates for which the selectivity estimation can be computed using the histograms H_1 and H_2, respectively. For example, a *histogram-SARGable* predicate on the column $R.A$ is $(R.A\varphi c)$ with $\varphi \in \{<, \leq, =, \geq, >\}$ and c a constant.

We assume that the histograms H_1 and H_2 satisfy some general properties, namely, the histograms must be able to provide a θ, q-acceptable estimate $\hat{f}_{v_i}$ for each value v_i in the column domain, which approximates the frequency f_{v_i}, i.e. the number of times v_i occurs in the column.

Our objective is to construct a histogram H for the column J of the join relation $Join(J)$, using the input histograms H_1 and H_2, without computing the join query or accessing the base data of the relations R and T. We study under what conditions the join histogram is also θ, q-acceptable.

2. θ, q-ACCEPTABLE JOIN HISTOGRAM

The first step in our algorithm is to restrict both input histograms by applying the *histogram-SARGabale* predicates $p_1(R.A)$ and $p_2(T.B)$, as well as restricting their domains to the ranges present in the active domains of both columns.

Therefore we can theoretically assume a common domain $V = \{v_1, \cdots, v_k\}$, with $v_1 < \cdots < v_k$, such that each v_i is in the range of the active domain of both $R.A$ and $T.B$, and satisfies the filter predicates $p_1(R.A)$ and $p_2(T.B)$. The frequency of any individual element v_i in $R.A$, $\hat{f}_1(v_i)$, can be estimated using H_1. Similarly, we can attain a frequency estimate for v_i in $T.B$, $\hat{f}_2(v_i)$, using H_2. Let $f_1(v_i)$ and $f_2(v_i)$ denote the corresponding precise frequencies.

The theoretical estimate for the frequency of v_i in the join result is $\hat{f}(v_i) = \hat{f}_1(v_i)\hat{f}_2(v_i)$. The following result allows us to place a loose θ, q-acceptability bound on this estimate:

LEMMA 2.1. *If $\hat{f}_1, \hat{f}_2$ are estimates for f_1, f_2, θ_1, q_1-acceptable and θ_2, q_2-acceptable, respectively, then $\hat{f}_1\hat{f}_2$ is a $\theta_1\theta_2, q'$-acceptable estimate for $f_1 f_2$, $q' = \max(\theta_1 q_2, \theta_2 q_1, q_1 q_2)$.*

We define $f^i \stackrel{def}{=} f(v_i)$, $f^+(v_m, v_n) \stackrel{def}{=} f^+(m, n) \stackrel{def}{=} \sum_{m \leq i \leq n} f^i$,

and similarly, $\hat{f}^+(v_m, v_n) \stackrel{def}{=} \hat{f}^+(m, n) \stackrel{def}{=} \sum_{m \leq i \leq n} \hat{f}^i$.

Our join histogram algorithm is based on the construction algorithm described in [1], with the following important adjustment which makes possible the building of the join his-

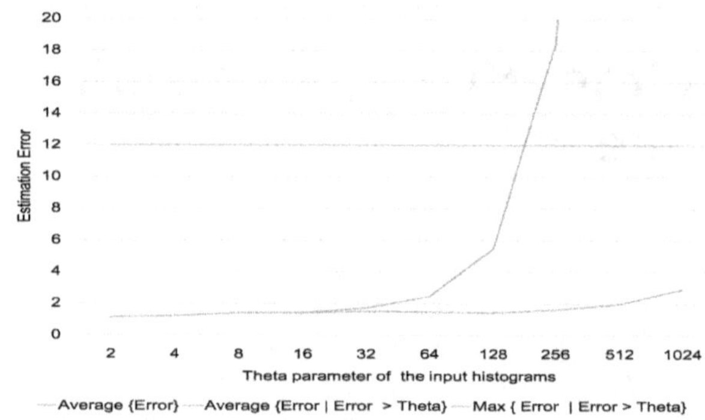

Figure 1: Estimation error using join histograms built from $\theta, 2$-acceptable histograms ($\theta \in \{2, 4, \ldots, 1024\}$); Query: $\sigma_{c_1 \le J \le c_2} Join(J)$; $e = \dfrac{\text{real number of rows}}{\text{estimated number of rows}}$: Estimation Error $= \max(\ e,\ \frac{1}{e}\ )$

togram without accessing the base data: instead of using the true frequency value f^+ when checking our error bounds, we treat $\hat{f}^+$ as the true frequency as these can be obtained only from the input histograms. This algorithm yields a sequence of θ, q-acceptable buckets, each with a different θ, q, having an "estimate of an estimate", as the frequencies used to construct these buckets are the estimated frequencies computed from the input histograms.

The following lemma allows us to place a bound on the resulting join histogram's error.

LEMMA 2.2. *If $\hat{f}$ is a θ, q-acceptable estimate for f and $\bar{f}$ is a θ', q'-acceptable estimate for $\hat{f}$, then $\bar{f}$ is a $\theta\theta', q''$-acceptable estimate for f, with $q'' = \max(qq', q'\theta, q\theta')$*

Lemma 2.2 shows that it is possible to construct a join histogram that is θ, q-acceptable for finite values of θ and q.

We now give some interesting details of our construction algorithm when join columns are dictionary-encoded[1]. Consider the scenario where the columns $R.A$ and $T.B$ are dictionary-encoded by ordered dictionaries and the histograms H_1 and H_2 are built on the dictionary values as described in [1]. For any range of actual domain values $[l, u]$, there are corresponding ranges $[i_1, j_1]$ for $R.A$ and $[i_2, j_2]$ for $T.B$ which are the minimum ranges containing dictionary entries mapping to an element in the range $[l, u]$. Let's assume that $j_1 - i_1 > j_2 - i_2$. In this discussion, we make the following two theoretical assumptions:

1 For every $n \in [i_2, j_2]$, $\exists m \in [i_1, j_1]$ such that $D_2(n) = D_1(m)$, where D_1 and D_2 are the dictionaries for $R.A$ and $T.B$ respectively. In other words, every distinct value of $T.B$ in $[l, u]$ also occurs in $R.A$[2].

2 If $[i, j]$ is covered by a single bucket in a histogram H, then for any $m \in [i, j]$, $\hat{f}(m) = \dfrac{\hat{f}^+(i, j)}{j - i}$.

By the Lemmas 2.1 and 2.2, we can compute an error-bounded frequency for the join result on the range $[l, u]$ with the sum $\sum_{n=i_2; D_2(n)=D_1(m)}^{j_2} \hat{f}_2(n)\hat{f}_1(m)$. Using the second assumption, when $[l, u]$ is contained in a single bucket, this simplifies to:

$$\hat{f}(l, u) = \sum_{n=i_2}^{j_2} \frac{\hat{f}_1^+(i_1, j_1)}{j_1 - i_1} \frac{\hat{f}_2^+(i_2, j_2)}{j_2 - i_2} = \frac{\hat{f}_1^+(i_1, j_1)\hat{f}_2^+(i_2, j_2)}{j_1 - i_1}$$

This tight bound motivates our construction algorithm **buildJoinHistogram** to generate buckets in H_J corresponding to maximum intervals $[l, u]$ contained in exactly one bucket in both histograms H_1 and H_2.

buildJoinHistogram(H_1, H_2, D_1, D_2)
Output: Join histogram H_J for the column J in $Join(J)$
index i_1, i_2, j_1, j_2, value l, u, vector *buckets*, bucket b
$initJoinIteration(i_1, j_1, i_2, j_2)$
while $i_1 < H_1.maxValue() \wedge i_2 < H_2.maxValue()$ **do**
$findNextBoundaries(i_1, j_1, i_2, j_2, l, u)$ // find next $[l, u]$
$b.begin = l$, $b.end = u$
$b.count = H_1.getCardinality([i_1, j_1]) \cdot \frac{H_2.getCardinality([i_2, j_2])}{\max(j_1 - i_1, j_2 - i_2)}$
$b.distinct = \min(j_1 - i_1, j_2 - i_2)$
$buckets.push(b)$
end while
$H_J.initBuckets(buckets)$
return H_J

The main idea of the algorithm is to iterate over the buckets of H_1 and H_2 by looking up the dictionary values stored at the next bucket boundary and comparing them to find the largest valid range for the next bucket to add to H_J.

Our final algorithm prototypes a set of improvements such as dropping the assumption 1., and applying a post-construction optimization where adjacent buckets in H_J are merged as long as the q-error is maintained.

Figure 1 depicts the experimental results for estimation errors using join histograms built by our algorithm. We use a combination of real-world data and randomly generated data. The input histograms were constructed with $q = 2$, and θ varied in the range 2 to 1024. A join histogram was built for the join relation $Join(J) = \sigma_{R.A=T.B}(R \times B)$ (i.e., without filter predicates). This means that each bucket has $\theta^2, 2\theta$-acceptable upper bounds (by Lemma 2.1). We run a set of range queries of the form $Q(c_1, c_2) = \sigma_{c_1 \le J \le c_2} Join(J)$ and record the actual number of rows, and the estimated number of rows computed using the join histogram. The estimation error is computed as $\max(\ e,\ \frac{1}{e}\ )$ where $e = \dfrac{\text{real number of rows}}{\text{estimated number of rows}}$.

For large θ, when the actual number of rows in $Q(c_1, c_2)$ is less than θ^2, the average q-error is large as well, as the estimation from the join histogram is bound by θ^2. As θ grows larger, most range queries contain fewer than θ^2 elements, so the average q-error of all queries rises rapidly. However, as shown by these experiments, the real q-error observed using the join histograms is often much lower than the theoretical q-error bounds established on the join histogram's estimates.

3. REFERENCES

[1] G. Moerkotte, D. DeHaan, N. May, A. Nica, and A. Boehm. Exploiting ordered dictionaries to efficiently construct histograms with q-error guarantees. In *ACM SIGMOD*, pages 361–372, 2014.

[1] We have also extended this algorithm to work on histograms built directly on the domain values, but leave its details out of this discussion.

[2] This assumption was relaxed in our implementation.

Graph Summarization for Geo-correlated Trends Detection in Social Networks

Colin Biafore Faisal Nawab
Department of Computer Science
University of California, Santa Barbara
Santa Barbara, CA 93106
colinbiafore@umail.ucsb.edu nawab@cs.ucsb.com

ABSTRACT

Trends detection in social networks is possible via a multitude of models with different characteristics. These models are pre-defined and rigid which creates the need to expose the social network graph to data scientists to introduce the human-element in trends detection. However, inspecting large social network graphs visually is tiresome. We tackle this problem by providing effective graph summarizations aimed at the application of geo-correlated trends detection in social networks.

1. INTRODUCTION

Graphs are used to model many real-world applications such as social networks and biological networks. Nodes in the graph represent objects being modeled and edges represent relationships between nodes. There could be many types of nodes and edges with different attributes in a single graph.

We focus in this work on the problem of detecting geo-correlated trends in social networks [2–4]. Thus, each node in the graph represents either a person in the social graph or a post (*e.g.*, tweet). Geo-correlation leverages the First Law of Geography that states: "Everything is related to everything else, but near things are more related than distant things".

A trend is not a concept that can be defined exactly—trends are manifested in different ways and forms. This leads to many diverse models of trends in social networks [2–4], each with different characteristics. We aim at providing a framework to enable data scientists to explore social network graphs with the purpose of detecting trends. Introducing the human element will provide data scientists with the freedom to infer trends themselves, without the restrictions of pre-defined models. We are encouraged by the success of human-driven data analysis to detect trends [1] and the success of human-assisted methods to search graphs [5].

Social networks are often very large with thousands to millions of nodes and edges. Thus, visual inspection to extract information from the social network graph is an arduous, if not an unattainable, task. Graph summarization techniques are useful to help extracting and understanding information from graph data [6, 7]. Rather than providing statistics to describe graphs, these techniques produce small graphs that preserve the information of the full graph. They also allow the user to control the resolution of these summarization graphs by "drill-down" and "roll-up" operations.

This work leverages the research in graph summarization for the specific application of detecting geo-correlated trends in social networks. We propose summarization methods that are curated to our application.

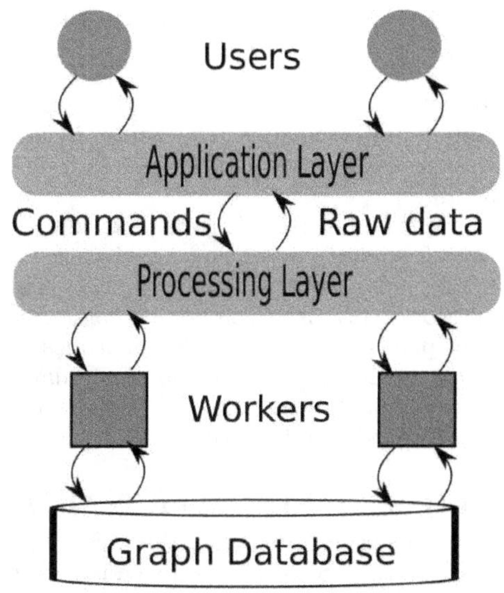

Figure 1: The architecture of the trends detection framework

2. FRAMEWORK

The architecture of our framework consists of four layers depicted in Figure 1. The application layer receives user actions that were performed in the framework's interface. The application layer transforms these actions to meaningful queries and commands to be passed down to lower layers. The application layer also transforms raw data to a presentable format to be displayed back to users. The processing layer is responsible of creating executions to answer users actions. Executions are passed down to workers that query a graph database. Workers cooperate to produce re-

SIGMOD'16 June 26 - July 01, 2016, San Francisco, CA, USA

ACM ISBN 978-1-4503-3531-7/16/06.
DOI: http://dx.doi.org/10.1145/2882903.2914832

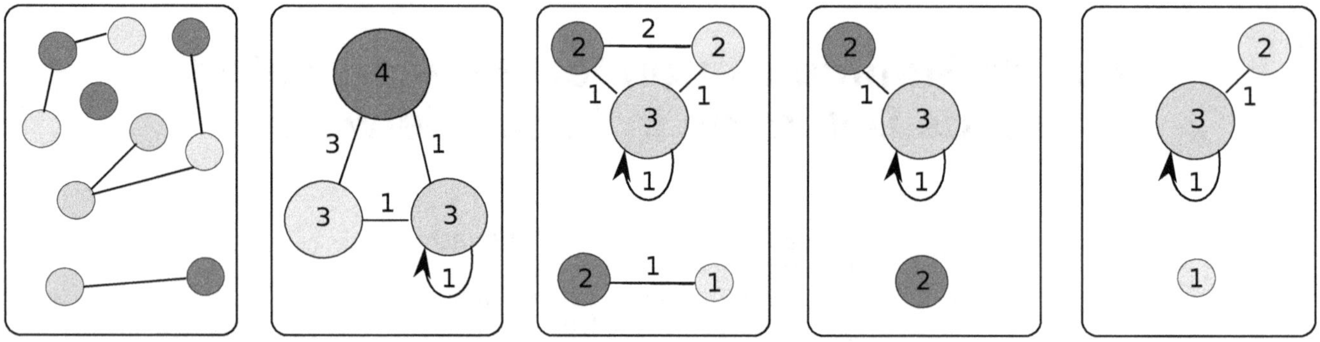

(a) Node type reduction (b) Frequency display (c) Locality display (d) Slicing (Slice 1) (e) Slicing (Slice 2)

Figure 2: A depiction of the summarization graph after applying each presented method

sults in parallel. And some workers work continuously to produce guiding and predictive information in addition to receiving streams from online social networks to be incorporated in the graph.

The raw graph G consists of nodes and edges. A node represents either a person or a post. An edge exists between two person nodes if there is a connection between them in the social network. Also, a person node is connected to post nodes that the person authored. Nodes and edges have other characteristics and labels that can be manipulated by the user. We focus on the location of posts as they are essential for our geo-correlated trends detection.

3. GRAPH SUMMARIZATION METHODS

Now, we present graph summarization methods that targets the application of geo-correlated trends detection. We demonstrate how the methods affect the summarization graph in Figure 2.

Node type reduction. The full graph contains authors and posts. Our first method, node type reduction, reduces the number of node types. The graph resulting after applying this method contain nodes that represent *topics*. Topics are defined by the users where a post can be mapped to a single or multiple topics. For example, topics can be hash tags mentioned in a post, or they can be the sentiment of the post. In Figure 2(a), for example, the summarization graph has three topics shown by the colors red, blue, and gray, that may represent three hash tags. Nodes capture what the user chose to be the topic of interest. Edges captures the relationship between the authors of posts that resulted in topics. For example, the edge between the red and gray nodes in the bottom means that the posts that resulted in these two topic nodes were authored by persons that are connected in the original graph.

Frequency display. The next method groups topic nodes that are similar to each other. Figure 2(b) shows a grouping of topic nodes that are identical. We call these the frequency nodes. An edge between two frequency nodes represents the edges in the original topics graph. For example, there are three edges between red and blue nodes in the original graph shown as an edge with weight 3 between the red and blue frequency nodes. The user can also control the frequencies that are displayed so that only topics with high frequency are shown.

Locality display. To capture the spatial aspect of topics, we introduce the location display method. This method partitions the graph according to the location of posts. The user has control on what defines a locality by setting a threshold distance—if two posts are within this distance then they are in the same locality. Figure 2(c) shows an example of partitioning the frequency graph into two localities. The top locality represents 7 topic nodes and the lower locality represents 3 topic nodes. Users can then drill down and view different localities individually.

Graph slicing. Graph slicing divides the graph into slices of topics. A slice of the graph contains the nodes representing a subset of the topics. Slices are generated to try to capture topics that might have a relation to each other. This might yield a topic to be in multiple slices. An example of slicing the locality graph in Figure 2(c) is to two slices: slice 1 that contains the red and gray topics (Figure 2(d)) and slice 2 that contains the blue and gray topics (Figure 2(e)).

4. ACKNOWLEDGMENT

This work is supported by NSF grant IIS 1018637, 1528178, and 1442966 and is partially funded by a gift grant from NEC Labs America.

5. REFERENCES

[1] Eighteen hours to thirty six hours entering #tripoli. http://r-shief.org/ eighteen-hours-to-thirty-six-hours-entering-tripoli/. 08-29-2011.

[2] C. Budak, D. Agrawal, and A. El Abbadi. Structural trend analysis for online social networks. *Proceedings of the VLDB Endowment*, 4(10):646–656, 2011.

[3] L. Hong et al. Discovering geographical topics in the twitter stream. In *Proceedings of the 21st international conference on World Wide Web*, pages 769–778. ACM, 2012.

[4] T. Lappas et al. On the spatiotemporal burstiness of terms. *Proceedings of the VLDB Endowment*, 5(9):836–847, 2012.

[5] A. Parameswaran et al. Human-assisted graph search: it's okay to ask questions. *Proceedings of the VLDB Endowment*, 4(5):267–278, 2011.

[6] Y. Tian et al. Efficient aggregation for graph summarization. In *SIGMOD*, 2008.

[7] N. Zhang, Y. Tian, and J. M. Patel. Discovery-driven graph summarization. In *ICDE*. IEEE, 2010.

M3: Scaling Up Machine Learning via Memory Mapping

Dezhi Fang
College of Computing
Georgia Institute of Technology
dezhifang@gatech.edu

Duen Horng Chau
College of Computing
Georgia Institute of Technology
polo@gatech.edu

ABSTRACT

To process data that do not fit in RAM, conventional wisdom would suggest using distributed approaches. However, recent research has demonstrated virtual memory's strong potential in scaling up graph mining algorithms on a single machine. We propose to use a similar approach for general machine learning. We contribute: (1) our latest finding that memory mapping is also a feasible technique for scaling up general machine learning algorithms like logistic regression and k-means, when data fits in or exceeds RAM (we tested datasets up to 190GB); (2) an approach, called M3, that enables existing machine learning algorithms to work with out-of-core datasets through memory mapping, achieving a speed that is significantly faster than a 4-instance Spark cluster, and comparable to an 8-instance cluster.

CCS Concepts

•Software and its engineering → Virtual memory; •Computing methodologies → Machine learning;

1. INTRODUCTION

Leveraging virtual memory to extend algorithms for out-of-core data has received increasing attention in data analytics communities. Recent research demonstrated virtual memory's strong potential to scale up graph algorithms on a single PC [4, 3]. Available on almost all modern platforms, virtual memory based approaches are straight forward to implement and to use, and can handle graphs with as many as 6 billion edges [3]. Some single-thread implementations on a PC can even outperform popular distributed systems like Spark (128 cores) [4]. Memory mapping a dataset into a machine's virtual memory space allows the dataset to be treated identically as an in-memory dataset. The algorithm developer no longer needs to explicitly determine how to partition the (large) dataset, nor manage which partitions should be loaded into RAM, or unloaded from it. The OS performs similar actions on the developer's behalf, through paging the dataset in and out of RAM, via highly optimized OS-level operations.

SIGMOD/PODS'16 June 26 - July 01, 2016, San Francisco, CA, USA

ACM ISBN 978-1-4503-3531-7/16/06.

DOI: http://dx.doi.org/10.1145/2882903.2914830

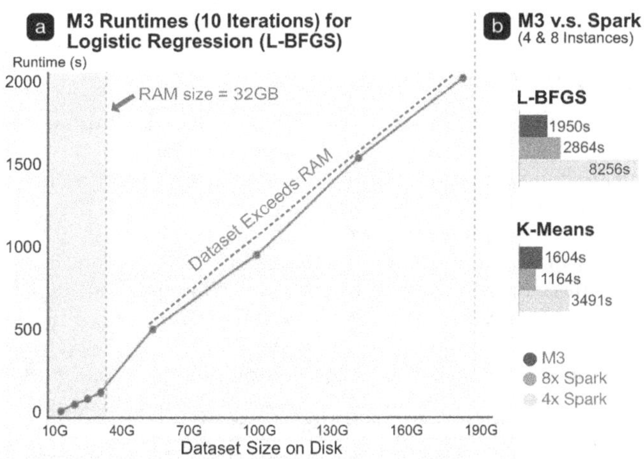

Figure 1: a: M3 runtime scales linearly with data size, when data fits in or exceeds RAM. b: M3's speed (one PC) comparable to 8-instance Spark (orange), and significantly faster than 4-instance Spark (light orange).

2. SCALING UP USING M3

As existing works focused on graph algorithms such as PageRank and finding connected components, we are investigating whether a similar virtual memory based approach can generalize to machine learning algorithms at large.

Inspired by prior works on graph computation, our M3[1] approach uses memory mapping to amplify a single machine's capability to process large amounts of data for machine learning algorithms. As memory mapping a dataset allows it to be treated identically as an in-memory dataset, M3 is a transparent scale-up strategy that developers can easily apply, requiring minimal modifications to existing code. For example, Table 1 shows that with only minimal code changes and a trivial helper function, existing algorithm implementation can easily handle much larger, memory-mapped datasets.

Modern 64bit machines have address spaces large enough to fit large datasets into (up to 1024PB). Because the operating system has access to a variety of internal statistics on how the mapped data is being used, the access to such data can be further optimized by the operating system via

[1] M3 stands for Machine Learning via Memory Mapping.

Original	M3
`Mat data;`	`double *m = mmapAlloc(file, rows * cols);` `Mat data(m, rows, cols);`

Table 1: M3 introduces minimal changes to code originally using in-memory data structure, enabling it to work with much larger memory-mapped data.

methods including least recent used caching and read-ahead to achieve efficiency [1].

To test the feasibility of M3, we minimally modified mlpack, an efficient machine learning library written in C++ [2]. Memory mapping can be easily applied to other languages and algorithm libraries.

3. EXPERIMENTS

Our current evaluation focuses on: (1) understanding of how M3 scales with increasing data sizes; and (2) how M3 compares with distributed systems such as Spark, as prior work suggested the possibility that a single machine can outperform a computer cluster [4].

Experiment Setup. All tests with M3 are conducted on a desktop computer with Intel i7-4770K quad-core CPU at 3.50GHz (8 hyperthreads), 4×8GB RAM, 1TB SSD of OCZ RevoDrive 350. We used Amazon EC2 `m3.2xlarge` instances for Spark experiments. Each instance has 8 vCPUs (hyperthreads of an Intel Xeon core) with 30GB memory and 2×80GB SSDs. The Spark clusters are created by Amazon Elastic MapReduce and the datasets are stored on the cluster's HDFS.

Dataset. We used the *Infimnist*[2] dataset, an infinite supply of digit images (0–9) derived from the well-known MNIST dataset using pseudo-random deformations and translations. Each image is 28×28 pixel grayscale image (784 features; each image is 6272 bytes). We generated up to 32M images, whose dense data matrix representation contains 23.5 billion entries, amounting to 190GB. Smaller datasets are subsets of the full 32M images.

Algorithms Evaluated. We selected *logistic regression* (L-BFGS for optimization) and k-means, since they are commonly used classification and clustering algorithms.[3]

3.1 Key Findings & Implications

1. M3 scales linearly when data fits in RAM and when out-of-core, for logistic regression (Figure 1a). The dotted vertical line in the figure indicates RAM size (32GB). M3's runtime scales linearly both when the dataset fits in RAM (yellow region in Fig. 1a), and when it exceeds RAM (green dotted line), at a higher scaling constant, as expected.

Looking at M3's resource utilization, we saw that M3 is I/O bound: disk I/O was 100% utilized while CPU was only utilized at around 13%. This suggests strong potential for M3 reaching even higher speed if we use faster disks, or configurations such as RAID 0.

2. M3's speed (one PC) is comparable to 8-instance Spark and significantly faster than 4-instance Spark for logistic regression (L-BFGS) and k-means (Figure 1b). This result echoes prior works focusing on graph computation that suggests cluster may not be necessary for moderately-sized datasets [4, 3]. Our result extends those findings to two general machine learning methods.

For *logistic regression* (with 10 iterations of L-BFGS), M3 is about 30% faster than 8-instance Spark. 4-instance Spark's runtime was 4.2X that of M3. For *k-means* (10 iterations, 5 clusters), M3 ran at a speed comparable to 8-instance Spark (1.37X), and more than twice as fast as 4-instance Spark.

Certainly, using more Spark instances will increase speed, but that may also incur additional overhead (e.g., communication between nodes). Here, we showed that for moderately-sized datasets, single-machine approaches like M3 can be attractive alternatives to distributed approaches.

4. CONCLUSIONS & ONGOING WORK

We are taking a first major step in assessing the feasibility of using virtual memory as a fundamental, alternative way to scale up machine learning algorithms. M3 adds an interesting perspective to existing solutions primarily based on distributed systems.

We contribute: (1) our latest finding that memory mapping could become a feasible technique for scaling up general machine learning algorithms when the dataset exceeds RAM; (2) M3, an easy-to-apply approach that enables existing machine learning implementations to work with out-of-core datasets; (3) our observations that M3 on a PC can achieve a speed that is significantly faster than a 4-instance Spark cluster, and comparable to an 8-instance cluster.

We will extend our M3 approach to a wide range of machine learning (including online learning) and data mining algorithms. We plan to extensively study the memory access patterns and locality of algorithms (e.g., sequential scans vs random access) to better understand how they they affect performance. We plan to develop mathematical models and systematic approaches to profile and predict algorithm performance and energy usage based on extensive evaluations across platforms, datasets, and languages.

5. ACKNOWLEDGMENTS

We thank Dr. Ryan Curtin and Minsuk (Brian) Kahng for their feedback. This work was supported by NSF grants IIS-1217559, TWC-1526254, IIS-1563816, and by gifts from Google, Symantec, Yahoo, eBay, Intel, Amazon, LogicBlox.

6. REFERENCES

[1] S. Boyd-Wickizer, A. T. Clements, Y. Mao, A. Pesterev, M. F. Kaashoek, R. Morris, N. Zeldovich, et al. An analysis of linux scalability to many cores. In *OSDI*, volume 10, pages 86–93, 2010.

[2] R. R. Curtin, J. R. Cline, N. P. Slagle, W. B. March, P. Ram, N. A. Mehta, and A. G. Gray. mlpack: A scalable C++ machine learning library. *Journal of Machine Learning Research*, 14:801–805, 2013.

[3] Z. Lin, M. Kahng, K. M. Sabrin, D. H. P. Chau, H. Lee, and U. Kang. Mmap: Fast billion-scale graph computation on a pc via memory mapping. In *Big Data (Big Data), 2014 IEEE International Conference on*, pages 159–164. IEEE, 2014.

[4] F. McSherry, M. Isard, and D. G. Murray. Scalability! but at what cost? In *15th Workshop on Hot Topics in Operating Systems (HotOS XV)*, 2015.

[2] http://leon.bottou.org/projects/infimnist

[3] We are primarily interested in runtimes, so we did not perform image pre-processing.

K-means Split Revisited: Well-grounded Approach and Experimental Evaluation

Valentin Grigorev
Saint-Petersburg State University
v.grigoriev@2013.spbu.ru

George Chernishev
Saint-Petersburg State University
g.chernyshev@spbu.ru

ABSTRACT

R-tree is a data structure used for multidimensional indexing. Essentially, it is a balanced tree consisting of nested hyper-rectangles which are used to locate the data. One of the most performance sensitive parts of this data structure is its split algorithm, which runs during node overflows. The split can be performed in multiple ways, according to many different criteria and in general the problem of finding an optimal solution is NP-hard. There are many heuristic split algorithms.

In this paper we study an existing k-means node split algorithm. We describe a number of serious issues in its theoretical foundation, which made us to re-design k-means split. We propose several well-grounded solutions to the re-emerged problem of k-means split. Finally, we report the comparison results using PostgreSQL and contemporary benchmark for multidimensional structures.

Keywords

R-tree; R-tree split; k-means; Multidimensional Indexing

1. INTRODUCTION AND THE PROBLEM

R-tree [5] and its variants [6] are popular data structures used for multidimensional indexing in many industrial applications [2]. The plain R-tree is more interesting to us because of their widespread industry adoption [6].

The split algorithm is a very performance sensitive part of the R-tree. It can be performed in multiple ways, the quality of resulting tree may differ by several times. The problem was proved to be NP-hard, so all of the existing algorithms (several dozens) rely on some heuristic.

In this paper we address the k-means R-tree split algorithm. To the best of our knowledge the idea to use clustering for R-tree node split was proposed for the first time in the paper [3]. Authors have adapted the popular k-means clustering algorithm for this problem. This is a beautiful idea which was adopted by the industry even outside the DBMS or GIS applications.

SIGMOD '16, June 26–July 1, 2016, San Francisco, CA, USA.

ACM ISBN 978-1-4503-3531-7/16/06.

DOI: http://dx.doi.org/10.1145/2882903.2914833

Let's mathematically describe the problem of clustering for hyper-rectangles in a most abstract fashion [4].

Let X be the finite multiset of hyper-rectangles in $\mathbb{R}^d$, $\{X_j\}_{j=1\dots k}$ be a partition of X, $X_j = \{\mathbf{x^j_1}, \dots, \mathbf{x^j_{n_j}}\}$ and D be a distance between hyper-rectangles. Let $\mathbf{c}$ be a centroid of cluster X_j, i. e. hyper-rectangle that minimizes function:

$$S_p(X_j, \mathbf{c}) = \begin{cases} (\sum\limits_{i=1}^{n_j} D(\mathbf{x^j_i}, \mathbf{c})^p)^{1/p} & for\ p < \infty \\ \max\limits_{i=1\dots n_j} D(\mathbf{x^j_i}, \mathbf{c}) & for\ p = \infty \end{cases} \tag{1}$$

So, clustering of hyper-rectangles is the following optimization problem:

$$\arg\min_{X_j \subset X} \sum_{j=1}^{k} S_p(X_j, \mathbf{c_j}) \tag{2}$$

where $\mathbf{c_j}$ is a centroid of X_j.

K-means is an iterative algorithm for solving this optimization problem. In order to employ it one has to choose in a consistent fashion parameter p, distance D and a function, that calculates cluster centroid. Then k-means can be considered fully defined for rectangles.

Let's review how this problem was solved in the original k-means split paper [3].

Authors of [3] set $p = 2$ and chose as the metric the diagonal length of the minimum bounding rectangle containing the respective objects:

$$D(\mathbf{x_1}, \mathbf{x_2}) = \sqrt{\sum_{i=1}^{d} (max(b^j_1, b^j_2) - min(a^j_1, a^j_2))^2}, \tag{3}$$

where $\mathbf{x_i} = \prod\limits_{j=1}^{d} [a^j_i, b^j_i]$

Furthermore, the proposed mean of a rectangle set (or the centroid) is a point, which is defined as follows:

$$\mathbf{c_j}(\mathbf{x_1}, \dots, \mathbf{x_n}) = \frac{\sum\limits_{i=1}^{n} \frac{a^j_i + b^j_i}{2} \mu(\mathbf{x_i})}{\sum\limits_{i=1}^{n} \mu(\mathbf{x_i})}, \ j = 1..d \tag{4}$$

where μ is a volume of hyper-rectangle. In other words it's essentially a center of gravity of cluster members, where mass of each rectangle is equal to its volume.

However, this approach has some fundamental issues. Firstly, (3) isn't really a metric because it violates the first axiom of metric:

$$d(x, y) \geq 0, \ and\ d(x, y) = 0\ iff\ x = y \tag{5}$$

It is unclear whether this function can be used as a metric in k-means clustering algorithm. Unfortunately, paper [3] does not provide any hints.

The centroid definition leads to more serious issues. The formula (4) demonstrates three issues: 1) it is not consistent with the mean value of a point set; 2) it is not consistent with degenerate rectangles, since their contribution to the formula is zero; 3) if all rectangles are degenerate, the formula instructs us to divide by zero which is unacceptable.

Finally, it is not clear whether this centroid function is consistent with chosen metric, i.e. whether it satisfies (2) or minimizes any other cost function. Most importantly, it is not proven that the k-means algorithm converges under these conditions.

2. SOLUTION

To the best of our knowledge there were no clustering algorithms specialized for hyper-rectangles when original k-means split was being developed.

Proper solution of aforementioned problems was proposed by Marie Chavent et al. in the series of papers about clustering of hyper-rectangles, that was summarized in [4]. In our paper we adopt those results to k-means split.

There are a lot of metrics that could be used for hyper-rectangles. We are interested in two types — Hausdorff distance based on L_∞ and coordinate-wise distances, based on the following distances between intervals: L_1 combination of Hausdorff distances, L_2 combination of L_2 distances, L_∞ combination of Hausdorff distances.

In these cases (with $p = \infty, 1, 2, \infty$, respectively) we have explicit formulas for distance and centroids, so they can be computed efficiently.

3. EXPERIMENTS

We have implemented k-means split on the base of "cube" extension for the PostgreSQL DBMS. This R-tree implementation is based on the GiST interface, thus we were restricted to 2-means algorithm.

Experimental evaluation was performed on PC with following parameters: 4-core processor Intel®Core™i7 2.20GHz, 8 Gb RAM, running Linux Ubuntu 14.04.3 LTS, PostgreSQL 9.4.5. For performance evaluation we have used some of "rea" datasets from the benchmark [1] used in recent R-tree studies [2].

The k-means split variations with different metrics from the previous section were evaluated. Version with coordinate-wise distance based on L_2 combination of L_2 distance between intervals was found to be the most efficient:

$$D(\mathbf{x_1}, \mathbf{x_2}) = \sqrt{\sum_{j=1}^{d} (a_1^j - a_2^j)^2 + (b_1^j - b_2^j)^2}$$

$$\widetilde{\mathbf{c}}_\mathbf{j} = \left[\frac{1}{n}\sum_{i=1}^{n} a_i^j, \frac{1}{n}\sum_{i=1}^{n} b_i^j\right], \; j = 1..d$$

where $\mathbf{x_i} = \prod_{j=1}^{d} [a_i^j, b_i^j]$

Due to the lack of space we do not present all of experiments.

Finally, we compared the winning variant with the PostgreSQL implementation of Guttman's Quadratic Split [5]. The results are presented in the Table 1.

Table 1: Experimental results (milliseconds)

		PG default	k-means	speedup
rea02	build	$60510.3 \pm 1.3\%$	$36816.3 \pm 0.5\%$	1.6
	QR1	$16862.0 \pm 1.3\%$	$16090.5 \pm 1.3\%$	1.0
	QR100	$7401.8 \pm 1.3\%$	$7304.2 \pm 0.2\%$	1.0
	QR1000	$19750.3 \pm 0.6\%$	$19789.1 \pm 0.7\%$	1.0
rea03	build	$519482.1 \pm 1.6\%$	$197558.4 \pm 0.5\%$	2.6
	QR1	$1317888.0 \pm 6.2\%$	$838620.9 \pm 3.9\%$	1.6
	QR100	$297591.3 \pm 3.9\%$	$180884.8 \pm 2.5\%$	1.6
	QR1000	$290002.7 \pm 2.0\%$	$216493.6 \pm 1.0\%$	1.3
rea05	build	$20327.9 \pm 0.6\%$	$8625. \pm 0.9\%$	2.4
	QR1	$31515.0 \pm 3.1\%$	$11889.6 \pm 5.8\%$	2.7
	QR100	$14689.8 \pm 4.0\%$	$4566.3 \pm 2.9\%$	3.2
	QR1000	$12541.3 \pm 3.3\%$	$5977.1 \pm 1.5\%$	2.1
rea09	build	$1924.2 \pm 0.5\%$	$807.3 \pm 0.6\%$	2.4
	QR1	$1930.3 \pm 3.3\%$	$1715.8 \pm 3.0\%$	1.1
	QR100	$1084.4 \pm 0.9\%$	$970.8 \pm 2.1\%$	1.1
	QR1000	$1295.0 \pm 0.8\%$	$1216.7 \pm 0.9\%$	1.1

For each dataset/query/split combination we executed benchmark 10 times and calculated 95% confidence interval.

4. CONCLUSIONS

In this paper we presented a well-grounded algorithm for R-tree split based on k-means algorithm. We have approached the rectangles clustering problem as the problem of selection of consistent configuration of p, distance and centroid functions. Using the recent advances in geometry we have selected a number of such configurations. Then, we have evaluated the found configurations on real data distributions of the standard multidimensional indexing benchmark. Results show that our k-means generally outperforms standard Guttman's quadratic split in terms of build time as well as query processing. The best improvement on the processing stage was achieved on datasets of medium dimensionaly (3 and 5). Build time improved almost twice on all datasets.

5. ACKNOWLEDGMENTS

We would like to thank Kirill Smirnov for his valuable comments on this work.

6. REFERENCES

[1] N. Beckmann and B. Seeger. A benchmark for multidimensional index structures. http://www.mathematik.uni-marburg.de/~rstar/benchmark/distributions.pdf, 2008.

[2] N. Beckmann and B. Seeger. A revised R*-tree in comparison with related index structures. ACM SIGMOD, pages 799–812, 2009.

[3] S. Brakatsoulas et al. Revisiting R-Tree Construction Principles. ADBIS, pages 149–162, 2002.

[4] M. Chavent and J. Saracco. On central tendency and dispersion measures for intervals and hypercubes. *Communications in Statistics—Theory and Methods*, 37(9):1471–1482, 2008.

[5] A. Guttman. R-trees: a dynamic index structure for spatial searching. *SIGMOD Rec.*, 14(2):47–57, 1984.

[6] A. N. Papadopoulos et al. R-Tree (and Family). In L. Liu and M. T. Özsu, editors, *Encyclopedia of Database Systems*, pages 2453–2459. 2009.

Main Memory Adaptive Denormalization

Zezhou Liu
Harvard University
zezhouliu@college.harvard.edu

Stratos Idreos
Harvard University
stratos@seas.harvard.edu

ABSTRACT

Joins have traditionally been the most expensive database operator, but they are required to query normalized schemas. In turn, normalized schemas are necessary to minimize update costs and space usage. Joins can be avoided altogether by using a denormalized schema instead of a normalized schema; this improves analytical query processing times at the tradeoff of increased update overhead, loading cost, and storage requirements.

In our work, we show that we can achieve the best of both worlds by leveraging partial, incremental, and dynamic denormalized tables to avoid join operators, resulting in fast query performance while retaining the minimized loading, update, and storage costs of a normalized schema.

We introduce adaptive denormalization for modern main memory systems. We replace the traditional join operations with efficient scans over the relevant partial universal tables without incurring the prohibitive costs of full denormalization.

1. INTRODUCTION

Normalized schemas are standard in database systems [3][4]. Normalization leads to many desirable characteristics such as enabling efficient and accurate updates, minimizing data redundancy, reducing storage requirements and loading costs [4][6]. However, normalization requires join operations with expensive data access patterns and computational costs to operate over the normalized schema. Despite advances in modern hardware capabilities and join algorithms, the join operator continues to dominate query processing time even in systems that are well-tuned for high performance [1][2][5].

For example, Figure 1 compares a state-of-the-art hardware optimized hash join implementation [1] over a normalized schema against a fast scan (multi-core, numa-aware, SIMD) over a denormalized one. Within the time needed to join just 100 million tuples over the normalized schema we can scan and perform a logical join across more than 100 times the data in the denormalized schema.

Contributions. In this paper we introduce the idea of adaptive denormalization, in which the base data lies in a normalized state while hot data is adaptively and partially denormalized on-demand. This allows our system to operate within a given memory budget and mitigate the negative side-effects of denormalization while still producing the performance gains of denormalized systems. We show that adaptive denormalization achieves performance gains of orders of magnitudes over systems that use strict normalized schemas.

SIGMOD'16 June 26 - July 01, 2016, San Francisco, CA, USA

ACM ISBN 978-1-4503-3531-7/16/06.

DOI: http://dx.doi.org/10.1145/2882903.2914835

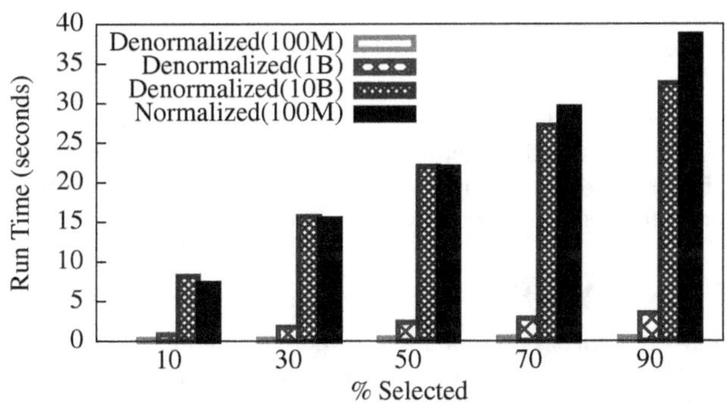

Figure 1: In the time it takes to join inputs of 100 million rows in a normalized schema, we can perform a (logical) join by scanning over 10 billion rows in denormalized schema. The disparity is larger when a higher percentage of rows are selected.

2. ADAPTIVE DENORMALIZATION

Adaptive denormalization achieves the best characteristics of both normalization and denormalization by exploiting embarrassingly parallel scans over a denormalized schema to process join queries while still achieving the efficient space utilization, updates, and loading time characteristics found in normalized schemas.

Adaptive denormalization maintains data in a normalized state and denormalizes only regions of the data as they are queried and to only data that has not yet been denormalized by previous queries. As a result, future queries on any previously queried range can be answered with scans, thereby avoiding expensive join operations. These denormalized regions form partial universal tables – auxiliary data structures that are maintained alongside the underlying normalized data.

By denormalizing only the data that is touched, we limit the extra storage requirements to only attributes of interest. Furthermore, adaptive denormalization operates within the given memory budget by dropping regions of the partial universal table in response to memory pressures. Moreover, denormalizing during query processing amortizes the overhead and cost of denormalization across many queries. Loading costs are the same as in normalized schemas. Since the denormalized data is logically separated into partial universal tables, updates can be applied lazily to only the partial universal tables that are required by the query, fur-

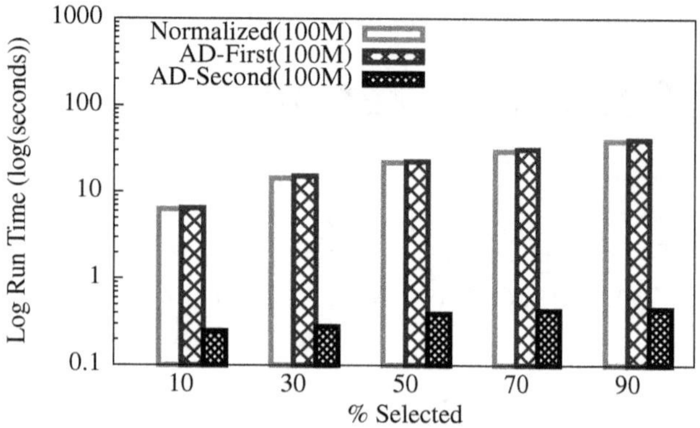

Figure 2: Adaptive denormalization (AD) improves significantly over repeated join patterns without penalizing the first join queries.

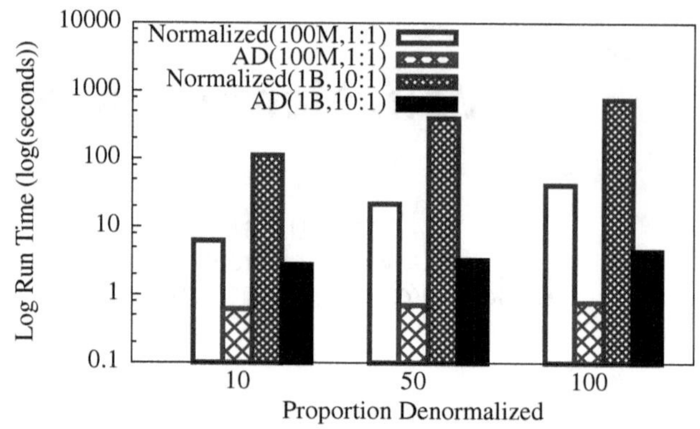

Figure 3: Adaptive denormalization (AD) achieves significant benefits even when the required data is only partially denormalized.

ther mitigating update costs that might otherwise be prohibitive in a fully denormalized system. These properties allow us to leverage the benefits of both denormalization and normalization without suffering the negative characteristics.

3. ANALYSIS

In this section we present a brief experimental analysis to show the performance advantages of adaptive denormalization over traditional join operations over normalized schemas.

Experimental Setup. We run our experiments on an in-memory column store prototype with modern multi-core scan and hash joins implementations. We evaluate our system on a 4-way Intel Xeon E7-4820 configuration with 64 hardware threads and 1 TB of main memory. We evaluate our system on synthetic workloads to meet certain selectivity, input size, and join output size criteria. We use 8-byte ints generated from random uniform distributions, which we tune to control the sizes of input columns and join outputs.

Performance Gains of Adaptive Denormalization. A query benefits from adaptive denormalization if its results are partially contained in the universal tables, since the query can be evaluated with fast sequential scans and only require joins for the parts where the data is being queried for the first time. Joins can be avoided altogether if the universal table contains all the data necessary to answer the query. Figure 3 reveals that this strategy results in orders of magnitudes in speed-up, especially when the join operation is large and the data is already contained in the universal table. For example, the joins over a normalized schema between 100M tuples with 100M tuples for a join output of 100M (output:input ratio of 1:1), requires 38.6 seconds, whereas a scan over the equivalent denormalized 100M output tuples requires only 0.45 seconds.

This speed-up is further magnified as the size of the join output increases. In Figure 3 we see that at a join output size of 1B (output:input ratio of 10:1), the traditional operator takes 6 minutes, whereas adaptive denormalization takes only 5.1 seconds. Figure 3 also shows that there are benefits even when only part of the query is contained in the current denormalized tables.

Small Overhead of Adaptive Denormalization. The overhead of adaptive denormalization can be separated into performance and storage overhead. The performance overhead results from the additional book-keeping required to track which parts of the queries can be answered using the partial universal table and which parts still need to be joined. Figure 2 compares the performance of a join over a normalized schema with that of our modified adaptive denormalization join when the universal table is empty and a join cannot be avoided (Normalized vs AD-First). In these cases, the overhead still represents only 5-10% of total query time.

Storage overhead results from the additional storage required for the partial universal tables. However, adaptive denormalization operates within the given memory budget by dropping regions of the partial universal table if they are no longer needed by the workload. This is an inexpensive solution since future reconstruction is relatively cheap as shown in the aforementioned performance overhead. Our lazy update technique also makes update overhead small; further details are left for a full future paper.

4. CONCLUSION & FUTURE WORK

Joins have been one of the primary performance bottlenecks in relational database systems for the past five decades. In this paper, we show how to effectively eliminate join costs for the hot part of the workload. We present adaptive denormalization to provide a way to achieve the best of both schemas: faster query processing via scans instead of joins as in a denormalized schema and at the same time minimum loading, storage and update overheads as in a normalized schema. Arbitrary joins, not just equi-joins, can benefit from this technique as long as subsequent queries share the same join condition. We show how adaptive denormalization in a modern column-store achieves gains of orders of magnitude over traditional strict systems that rely on normalized data or on a priori full denormalization.

Our ongoing plans include work on handling updates with limited impact on read and write performance and evaluating our system on real workloads. We also work on handling some limitations of adaptive denormalization, such as cases when performing a scan on the Universal Table is slower than its equivalent join.

Acknowledgements. The authors of this paper would like to thank Michael Kester and Wilson Qin, members of the Harvard DASlab, for their help on this project.

This work is partially supported by NSF Grant No. IIS-1452595.

5. REFERENCES

[1] C. Balkesen, G. Alonso, J. Teubner, and M. T. Özsu. Multi-core, main-memory joins: Sort vs. hash revisited. *PVLDB*, pages 85–96, 2013.

[2] C. Balkesen, J. Teubner, G. Alonso, and M. T. Özsu. Main-memory hash joins on multi-core cpus: Tuning to the underlying hardware. In *ICDE*, pages 362–373, 2013.

[3] E. F. Codd. A relational model of data for large shared data banks. *Commun. ACM*, pages 377–387, 1970.

[4] G. Gottlob, R. Pichler, and V. Savenkov. Normalization and optimization of schema mappings. *VLDB*, pages 277–302, 2011.

[5] V. Raman et al. Constant-time query processing. In *ICDE*, pages 60–69, 2008.

[6] G. Sanders and S. Shin. Denormalization Effects on Performance of RDBMS. In *HICSS*, pages 9–17, 2001.

Adaptive Data Skipping in Main-Memory Systems

Wilson Qin
Harvard University
wilsonqin@college.harvard.edu

Stratos Idreos
Harvard University
stratos@seas.harvard.edu

ABSTRACT

As modern main-memory optimized data systems increasingly rely on fast scans, lightweight indexes that allow for data skipping play a crucial role in data filtering to reduce system I/O. Scans benefit from data skipping when the data order is sorted, semi-sorted, or comprised of clustered values. However data skipping loses effectiveness over arbitrary data distributions. Applying data skipping techniques over non-sorted data can significantly decrease query performance since the extra cost of metadata reads result in no corresponding scan performance gains. We introduce *adaptive data skipping* as a framework for structures and techniques that respond to a vast array of data distributions and query workloads. We reveal an *adaptive zonemaps* design and implementation on a main-memory column store prototype to demonstrate that adaptive data skipping has potential for 1.4X speedup.

1. INTRODUCTION

Data Skipping. Modern main-memory optimized systems use scans with lightweight data skipping methods for fast data filtering. These systems maintain lightweight statistics such as minima and maxima values describing virtual zones - contiguous regions of a data column. A scan can then use the metadata to determine the relevance of a zone for a query and decide whether to skip or scan its underlying data. When used appropriately in conjunction with a priori user knowledge about query workloads and datasets, data skipping techniques can drastically improve scan performance by reducing the magnitude of records scanned at a smaller space and maintenance overhead than traditional indexing techniques [6, 8]. Data skipping techniques have been implemented for many modern systems including Netezza [3], Oracle [2], IBM DB2 [7], MySQL [1], Cloudera Impala [5], Hadoop [4], Shark [9], and Brighthouse [8].

Problem with Generalization. Current data skipping techniques do not generalize to all combinations of query workloads and datasets. Techniques typically work well on data columns that are sorted, semi-sorted, or locally clustered, but are ineffective when operating over arbitrary data distributions. Consider for example an attribute with a two value domain. With a column on this random uniform attribute, many zones will contain both values. Minima and maxima metadata that indicate which values are included in each zone are of no use to the query workload. In these cases gains from data skipping disappear as the system is penalized with the extra cost of metadata scan without resulting gains from skipping underlying data. The result is even worse performance than a full scan that uses no additional structure.

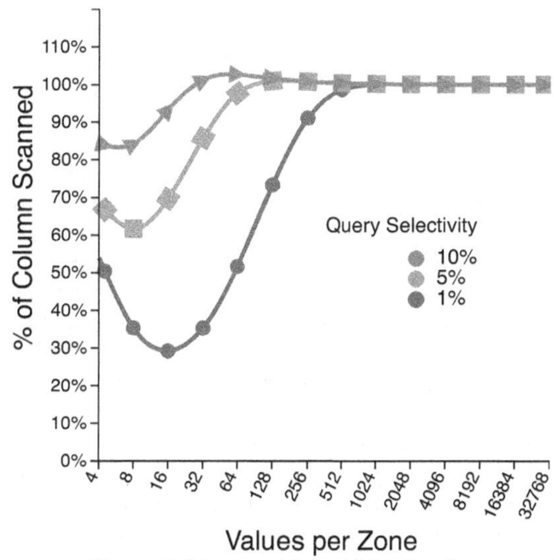

Figure 1: No general data skipping "sweet spot".

End of Static Layout Fits All. The effectiveness of data skipping layouts is strongly affected by variation in data distributions and query workloads. In Figure 1 we illustrate the performance effects of varying zone sizes when a random uniform dataset limited to a domain of 100 values is queried by a workload targeting low values at varying levels of selectivity. The data layout is unsorted and maintains zone minima and maxima. Figure 1 reveals that queries are not equally responsive to the same zonemap layouts; a layout that works for one distribution and workload can lose effectiveness in another case. This variation in zonemap effectiveness indicates the potential for dynamic structures beyond static layouts that can adapt to a changing query workload over time.

Our Contribution. In this paper we study data skipping on columnar main-memory data systems. We introduce adaptive data skipping as a framework for generalizing data skipping to a wide variety of scenarios. Adaptive data skipping leverages dynamic data layout to skip more data for future queries even when there is no order in the data. We show an adaptive zonemap design and implementation with potential for 1.4X speedup over standard data skipping techniques.

SIGMOD/PODS'16 June 26 - July 01, 2016, San Francisco, CA, USA

ACM ISBN 978-1-4503-3531-7/16/06.

DOI: http://dx.doi.org/10.1145/2882903.2914836

2. ADAPTIVE DATA SKIPPING

Adaptive data skipping is a robust data skipping framework applicable to a much wider array of data distributions and ad-hoc query workloads than standard data skipping methods. The core idea behind adaptive data skipping is incremental and on demand refinement of the underlying data (and metadata) during query processing. Metadata statistics can be created and improved on by manipulating a column's underlying data. Adaptive data skipping improves data zones at query time by reorganizing the data layout to maintain useful zone statistics with tighter domain bounds. This adaptive reorganization operates on hot zones during scan time, dynamically dividing or merging zones as needed.

Adaptive Zonemap Prototype. Adaptive zonemaps operate by gradually reducing the amount of excess non-qualifying values that must be scanned for any query. Data layout reorganization occurs at both the underlying data and metadata levels. Data values are relocated to create more order within zones. Large hot zones incur splitting into smaller zones to tune zone minima and maxima. This allows adaptive improvement which makes metadata relevant throughout the lifetime of any query workload, enabling data skipping methods with self-improving performance. Additionally adaptive data skipping allows for all columns to have a zonemap, but only the columns that are targeted by queries incur the costs of materialization. Thus, adaptive data skipping eliminates the previous need for a priori knowledge of which columns to build a zonemap on. By constantly improving the zone layout as well as metadata relevance adaptive data skipping addresses generalized data skipping performance in the long term.

Analysis. We now provide a proof of concept performance analysis. We use a main-memory column-store prototype on a 4-way Intel Xeon E7-4820 configuration with 64 hardware threads and 1 TB of main memory. The system uses bulk processing and late materialization for queries, storing columns as fixed-width and dense arrays. Column and metadata values are assumed to fit in memory. For experimentation, we use a synthetic dataset of 8-byte integers generated with random uniform distribution on a domain of 10^5, producing columns of 10^9 values. We evaluate a synthetic query workload on the system comparing the performance of a scan, zonemap (zone size 2048), and adaptive zonemap. We run 150 select queries of random selectivity over a single column and report the performance of the select operator.

Figure 2 shows the results from the last five queries of the workload which specifically target outlier values. The standard zonemap has large zones of size 2048, but its performance is plagued by an interspersion of outliers that appear in nearly all zones (at a frequency of 1 in 500 values). The adaptive zonemap begins with zones of size 2048, but periodically splits hot zones into smaller zones (size 32) and recomputes metadata for new zones. While the standard zonemap struggles to improve on the plain scan, we see that our adaptive zonemap clearly outperforms both scan and the standard zonemap by nearly 1.4X. By continuously refining the zones to match the access patterns, adaptive zonemaps minimize the amount of data they need to touch.

3. SUMMARY AND FUTURE WORK

In this paper, we demonstrate an initial step towards adaptive data skipping to solve the problem of lightweight zonemap-style indexes being useful only for specific data workloads and data orders. We reveal adaptive zonemaps as an implementation of adaptive data skipping. Adaptive zonemaps refine the underlying data incrementally and on demand to match the incoming workload with relevant data zones. Early results show 1.4X performance improvement over standard zonemaps in a main-memory column-store for handling arbitrary data workloads where no initial value order exists. We are currently working on several open topics towards fully materializing adaptive data skipping. For example, a sample of important open topics include studying alternate data reorganization strategies, utilizing adaptive data skipping across numerous columns, and finding the right balance of column optimization at system initialization (given certain idle time) to provide robust future performance.

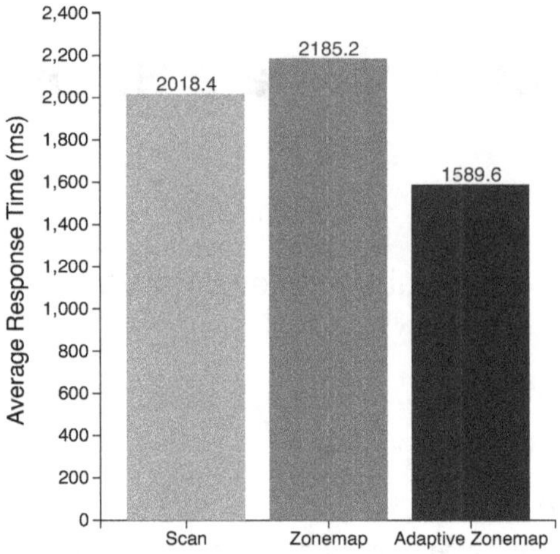

Figure 2: Adaptive Zonemaps provide 1.4X benefit in average response time speedup.

4. ACKNOWLEDGMENTS

This work is partially supported by NSF Grant No. IIS-1452595. The authors would like to thank Michael S. Kester, Zezhou Alex Liu, and other members of Harvard DASlab for their help and feedback on this project.

5. REFERENCES

[1] Mysql 5.5 reference manual.

[2] Oracle database data warehousing guide.

[3] The Netezza FAST Engines Framework: A Powerful Framework for High-Performance Analytics. *Netezza Corporation*, 2007.

[4] M. Y. Eltabakh, F. Özcan, Y. Sismanis, P. J. Haas, H. Pirahesh, and J. Vondrak. Eagle-eyed elephant: Split-oriented indexing in hadoop. In *Proceedings of the International Conference on Extending Database Technology (EDBT)*, pages 89–100, 2013.

[5] M. Kornacker, A. Behm, V. Bittorf, T. Bobrovytsky, C. Ching, A. Choi, J. Erickson, M. Grund, D. Hecht, M. Jacobs, et al. Impala: A modern, open-source sql engine for hadoop. *Proceedings of the Conference on Innovative Data Systems Research (CIDR)*, 2015.

[6] J. K. Metzger, B. M. Zane, and F. D. Hinshaw. Limiting scans of loosely ordered and/or grouped relations using nearly ordered maps. *US Patent US6973452 B2*, 2005.

[7] V. Raman, G. M. Lohman, T. Malkemus, R. Mueller, I. Pandis, B. Schiefer, D. Sharpe, R. Sidle, A. Storm, L. Zhang, G. Attaluri, R. Barber, N. Chainani, D. Kalmuk, V. KulandaiSamy, J. Leenstra, S. Lightstone, and S. Liu. DB2 with BLU acceleration: so much more than just a column store. *Proceedings of the VLDB Endowment*, 6(11):1080–1091, 2013.

[8] D. Slezak, J. Wroblewski, V. Eastwood, and P. Synak. Brighthouse: an analytic data warehouse for ad-hoc queries. *Proceedings of the VLDB Endowment*, 1(2):1337–1345, 2008.

[9] R. S. Xin, J. Rosen, M. Zaharia, M. J. Franklin, S. Shenker, and I. Stoica. Shark: SQL and Rich Analytics at Scale. In *Proceedings of the ACM SIGMOD International Conference on Management of Data*, pages 13–24, 2013.

Searching Web Data using MinHash LSH

BiChen Rao
University of Toronto
erao@cs.toronto.edu

Erkang Zhu
University of Toronto
ekzhu@cs.toronto.edu

ABSTRACT

In this extended abstract, we explore the use of MinHash Locality Sensitive Hashing (MinHash LSH) to address the problem of indexing and searching Web data. We discuss a statistical tuning strategy of MinHash LSH, and experimentally evaluate the accuracy and performance, compared with inverted index. In addition, we describe an on-line demo for the index with real Web data.

1. INTRODUCTION

Numerous datasets are published on the Web and can be used freely. The Web Data Common Web Table project extracted over 200 millions tabular datasets from HTML pages on the Web [6]. With the large amount of data available, it is difficult for researchers to discover datasets covering similar topics that are relevant to their interests, due to heterogeneous sources and schemas and the lack of search infrastructure. Datasets can be huge in size and the number of datasets is usually massive, causing additional challenges for Web data search.

When searching for datasets, we can use the Jaccard distance between *attributes* of the datasets as a relevance measure. An attribute is a set of values. It may be a column of a tabular dataset, or a full path in a semi-structured dataset. Due to the massive size and number of attributes, computing Jaccard distance directly using data values can be very expensive. We can represent an attribute with a fixed-size summary called *MinHash*, which has been used to reduce the memory usage of attributes and increase the query and insertion speed [2]. However, over millions of attributes, linear scan over MinHashes is still very slow. MinHash LSH can be used to index the MinHashes of attributes [5]. Similar attributes can be searched by querying a number of hash tables whose hash keys are concatenations of hash values in MinHash, in sub-linear time with respect to the number of attributes. SimHash is an alternative LSH index that also supports sub-linear search time [3], however, a recent paper showed that MinHash LSH is more computationally efficient than SimHash [7].

SIGMOD/PODS'16 June 26 - July 01, 2016, San Francisco, CA, USA

ACM ISBN 978-1-4503-3531-7/16/06.

DOI: http://dx.doi.org/10.1145/2882903.2914838

In this extended abstract, we present a new evaluation of MinHash LSH with a statistical tuning strategy proposed by Dong et al. [4] using real Web data.

2. TUNING MINHASH LSH

Minhash LSH has two parameters: L the number of hash tables and M the size of the hash key, which is a concatenation of M hash values in MinHash. The parameters typically need to be hand-tuned in order to balance accuracy and performance.

We used a statistical tuning strategy based on the one proposed by Dong et al. for Euclidean distance [4]. In order to use this strategy, the following distributions need to be obtained from the data: (1) the distribution of all-pair squared Jaccard distance, and (2) given K, the distribution of squared Jaccard distance for the 1st to K^{th} ranked attributes. The tuning is formulated as an optimization problem, where the objective is to minimize *selectivity*, which is defined as the number of matches returned by LSH divided by the total number of attributes in the index, while maintaining a minimum level of *recall*. In other words, we want to minimize the processing cost for the returned matches without loosing too much accuracy. The selectivity can be expressed as:

$$selectivity = \int_0^{1.0} \rho(\sqrt{x}) f(x) dx \qquad (1)$$

And the recall can be expressed as:

$$recall = \frac{1}{K} \sum_{k=1}^{K} \int_0^{1.0} \rho(\sqrt{x}) f_k(x) dx \qquad (2)$$

f is the squared Jaccard distance distribution of all-pairs and f_k is the squared Jaccard distance distribution of the Kth result. ρ is the probability of LSH returning the result given the distance to the the query data. ρ can be obtained using a closed form equation given M and L.[8].

3. EXPERIMENTAL EVALUATION

To evaluate the accuracy and performance of MinHash LSH index with the statistical tuning strategy, we downloaded the English relational subset of the 2015 Web Data Common Web Table [6]. It contains 51 million tables and 262,893,349 attributes in total.

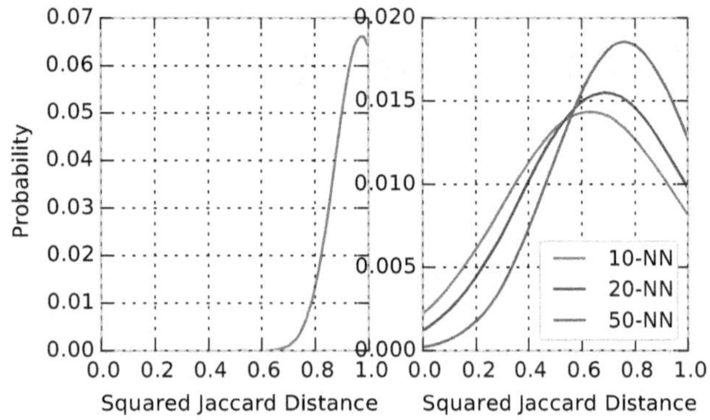

Figure 1: Squared Jaccard Distance Distribution for Attributes in Web Table

K	Precision	Recall	F Score
10	0.716	0.584	0.643
30	0.738	0.564	0.639
50	0.775	0.583	0.665

Table 1: Precision, Recall and F-score for different Ks

Accuracy. We take a random sample of 1,000 tables to estimate the distributions required for index tuning. The all-pair square Jaccard distance distribution is plotted on left side of Figure 1. The right side of Figure 1 shows the squared Jaccard distance distributions for the 10th, 20th, and 50th rank in the top-K matches. We fit the distributions with gamma functions, and use the fitted gamma functions to approximate the probability density functions of the original distributions. For index tuning, we choose the minimum recall to be 0.6. The optimal parameters are $M = 2$ and $L = 256$. We build the index using 1,000 random selected tables. Table 1 presents the average precision and recall of 1,000 randomly selected query attributes. We can see the recall is very close to the minimum recall set in index tuning.
Performance. An alternative search index is inverted index. In our experiment, the inverted index is constructed by building a mapping from data value to attributes. For query, MinHash LSH has a time complexity of $O(L \cdot M)$ since it only needs to query L hash tables to retrieve the appropriate attributes, and each hash key is a concatenation of M hash values. The inverted index has a time complexity of $O(log(N) \cdot q)$ where N is the number of indexed attributes and q is the number of distinct data values in the query attribute. For each data value, the index finds all attributes that contain it. Figure 2 shows the query time of inverted index vs. MinHash LSH with respect to increasing number of indexed attributes. The query time of the MinHash LSH index stays constant, while the query time of the inverted index increases. Thus, the result confirms the previous analysis.

4. DEMO

A demo of the MinHash LSH index with Web Table data can be accessed at `vldb.cs.toronto.edu:4001`. User can upload a CSV file through the web interface and find tables that contain similar columns as the input CSV.

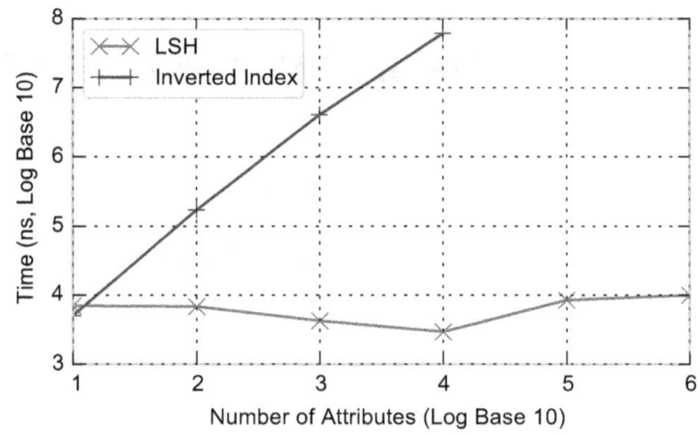

Figure 2: MinHash LSH with Tuning vs Inverted Index Performance

5. CONCLUSION

We have shown that MinHash LSH is very efficient for searching datasets, and a statistical tuning strategy can be used to balance the performance and recall accuracy. Alternative LSH indexes such as LSH Forest [1] can be used to improve recall. Furthermore, set containment is sometimes preferred over Jaccard distance as a relevance measure, and LSH Ensemble [8] can be used for set containment search. Applying the statistical tuning strategy to LSH Ensemble is another potential direction of research.

6. REFERENCES

[1] Mayank Bawa, Tyson Condie, and Prasanna Ganesan. LSH Forest: Self-tuning Indexes for Similarity Search. In *WWW*, pages 651–660. ACM, 2005.

[2] A. Broder. On the Resemblance and Containment of Documents. In *SEQUENCES*, pages 21–. IEEE Computer Society, 1997.

[3] Moses Charikar. Similarity Estimation Techniques from Rounding Algorithms. In *STOC*, pages 380–388. ACM, 2002.

[4] Wei Dong, Zhe Wang, William Josephson, Moses Charikar, and Kai Li. Modeling LSH for Performance Tuning. In *CIKM*, pages 669–678. ACM, 2008.

[5] Piotr Indyk and Rajeev Motwani. Approximate Nearest Neighbors: Towards Removing the Curse of Dimensionality. In *STOC*, pages 604–613. ACM, 1998.

[6] Oliver Lehmberg, Dominique Ritze, Robert Meusel, and Christian Bizer. A Large Public Corpus of Web Tables Containing Time and Context Metadata. In *WWW (Companion Volume)*, pages 75–76. ACM, 2016.

[7] Anshumali Shrivastava and Ping Li. In Defense of Minhash over Simhash. In *AISTATS*, volume 33 of *JMLR Proceedings*, pages 886–894. JMLR.org, 2014.

[8] Erkang Zhu, Fatemeh Nargesian, Ken Q. Pu, and Renée J. Miller. LSH Ensemble: Internet Scale Domain Search. *CoRR*, abs/1603.07410, 2016.

Research Contribution as a Measure of Influence

[Extended Abstract]

Lais M. A. Rocha, Mirella M. Moro
Universidade Federal de Minas Gerais, Belo Horizonte, Brazil
{laismota,mirella}@dcc.ufmg.br

ABSTRACT

We propose the 3c-index that measures the influence degree of researchers by evaluating the links they establish between communities. We evaluate its performance against well known metrics. The results show 3c-index outperforms them in most cases and can be employed as a complementary metric to assess researchers' productivity.

CCS Concepts

•Information systems → Content ranking; •Human-centered computing → Social network analysis;

Keywords

Bibliometry; Research performance; Ranking strategy

1. INTRODUCTION

Studies have analyzed academic social networks to uncover information about their participants (researchers, professors, etc.) and relationships (advirsorship, coauthorship, etc.). They have considered performance of each researcher individually as well as measured the influence degree among research areas and contributions from researchers, providing meaningful visions of academia [1, 6, 7, 8].

We focus on the propagation of influence through the concept of *communities* formed by researchers who share common interests. Specifically, each researcher has a base community where he/she presents greater influence. Then, we follow the ideas of diversity and novelty [2] and consider that when a researcher works on a community (besides the base one), he/she transfers new knowledge to that community, then increasing the overall research quality. Our goal is to measure the *influence degree* by evaluating such links between different communities exploring two social concepts: closure as the potential knowledge acquired and brokerage as the potential for sharing information. We then propose an indicator, the **3c-index** (*Cross-Community Contribution*), to aggregate the score of the researcher in the base community and the influence transfer among communities.

SIGMOD/PODS'16 June 26 - July 01, 2016, San Francisco, CA, USA

ACM ISBN 978-1-4503-3531-7/16/06.

DOI: http://dx.doi.org/10.1145/2882903.2914834

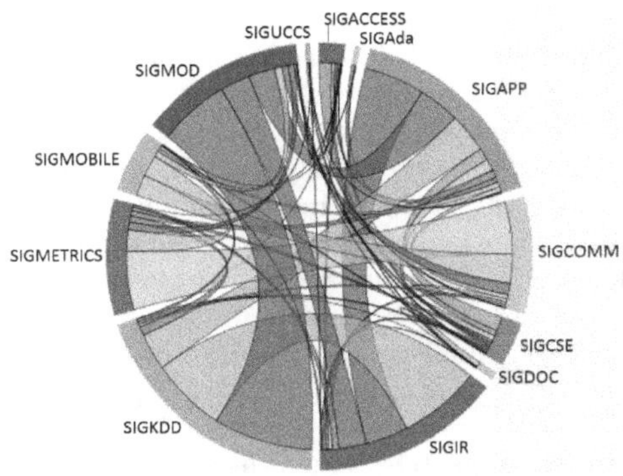

Figure 1: Knowledge transfer among SIGs showing, for instance, a significant transfer between SIGMOD-SIGKDD and a smaller one between SIGIR-SIGMOD.

2. RELATED WORK

In academic networks, ranking researchers on their importance is hard. One of the first studies on such importance is Granovetter's [3], which introduced the idea of *weak ties* as links that join different groups by building bridges within the network. Then, Newman [7] measures the influence on the information flow among individuals through high scores of *brokering*. Likewise, Burt [2] calls *brokers* the people who build social capital through structural holes in the networks. For ranking, Haveliwala [4] measures domain-specific importance using biased PageRank vectors, and Lima et al. [5] create a generic strategy for researchers from multiple areas by projecting productivity under a single perspective.

Overall, the aforementioned studies (among many others) emphasize the importance of building bridges and connecting distant network nodes. In academic social networks, researchers who connect different groups should bring more influence to those groups. Hence, this work aims at measuring such influence by considering his/her specific area and the knowledge transfer to other areas.

3. TECHNICAL OVERVIEW

In general, researchers have one or a group of areas of expertise. The knowledge transfer among research areas is fundamental for improving Science, because it enables the application of well-known and proved ideas from one context to solve problems on other domains of knowledge. Here, we define the **3c-index** as a metric that relates the knowledge transfer within different communities. This new index measures the influence of researchers according to their specialities (defined as influence degree) to other contexts.

The *3c-index* quantifies the influence degree in terms of percentile ranks and by rewarding important links that act as bridges. Formally, let p_i^c be the percentile ranking for a researcher i in the community c defined by: $p_i^c = \frac{l_i^c + 0.5e_i^c}{N^c}$, where N^c is the number of researchers in community c, l_i^c and e_i^c are the number of such researchers with a score lower than or equal to that of researcher i, respectively. For example, in a community with 100 researchers, the researcher at position 10th in the rank has $l_i^c = 89$ and $e_i^c = 1$, then producing a percentile rank of 90%. After calculating the p_i^c for all communities in which a researcher publishes, we define the *base community* b_i as the one with the researcher's largest percentile, i.e., $b_i = \arg\max_{c \in C} p_i^c$. Then, the influence degree $infd_i^c$ is defined as the difference between the percentiles attained, i.e., $infd_i^c = b_i - p_i^c$. Here, a community corresponds to all authors who published in a SIG (ACM Special Interest Groups) (Figure 1), and $infd_i^c = 0$ for the base community because it has no knowledge *tranfer*.

Finally, *3c-index* combines the scores from the base community to the contribution across communities. For a set of communities, a normalization factor accounts for their distinct profiles (e.g., size, number of citations, etc). As Lima et al. [5], we consider the percentile ranks of researchers *mapped* to their base community. The *3c-index* of a researcher i is then defined as $3c\text{-}index(i) = f_b(b_i) + \sum_{c \in C}(b_i - p_i^c) f_b(p_i^c)$, where $f_b(x)$ is the projection function that maps the percentile x to the respective value ranking on the researcher's base community b. The score considers both base community information and the scores on other communities. Also, the ranking strategy allows different metrics in the projection function, such as number of citations, volume of publications and h-index, giving flexibility to 3c-index.

4. RESULTS AND CONCLUSION

We built a dataset from DBLP and Google Scholar in January 2015, with 18,511 authors and about 100 thousand papers with more than a half million citations. Our evaluation validates 3c-index against a ground truth of 137 (out of 18,511) ACM Awards winners, i.e., a perfect top-50 ranking has 50 winners of ACM Awards. We compare the ranking results to those by citations, volume, h-index and ca-index (cross-area) [5]. We use the normalized Discounted Cumulative Gain (nDCG), which measures the ranking quality according to a graded scale with a log-based discount factor to penalize relevant items in lower positions. We consider the *nDCG@k* for a rank cutoff k varying from 1 to 50.

Influential Researchers. Table 1 shows the researchers ranked by 3c-index. The 3c-volume and 3c-h-index rank first researchers (names in bold) that are recognized in their communities: five for 3c-volume and four for 3c-h-index. Instead, 3-citation ranks two outstanding researchers. The 3c-index ranks well-known researchers at the first positions.

3c-index against Baselines. Figure 2a compares 3c-index (with h-index as its score function) and three standard metrics. It summarizes the good performance of our ranking strategy for almost the entire range of k.

3c-index against ca-index. ca-index follows three properties [5]: *plurality* as researcher's productivity is assessed in all areas of her publications; *diversity* as each research area profile is considered; and *equality* as all areas are regarded as equally important. In fact, the *equality* property puts SIGUCCS with equally importance as SIGMOD, which

Table 1: Researchers best ranked according to 3x-index in SIGs. In bold, the winners of ACM Awards, ♯*ACM fellow*, ‡*ACM distinguished scientist*, †*ACM senior member*.

Position	3c-citation	3c-volume	3c-h-index
1st	**Scott Shenker**♯	**W. Bruce Croft**♯	**Jiawei Han**♯
2nd	Ion Stoica♯	**Christos Faloutsos**♯	**Christos Faloutsos**♯
3rd	M. Frans Kaashoek♯	**Surajit Chaudhuri**♯	**Scott Shenker**♯
4th	David R. Karger♯	**Jiawei Han**♯	**W. Bruce Croft**♯
5th	Sylvia Ratnasamy	**Scott Shenker**♯	ChengXiang Zhai‡
6th	Mark Handley	ChengXiang Zhai‡	**Surajit Chaudhuri**♯
7th	Paul Francis	Philip S. Yu♯	Wei-Ying Ma‡
8th	Richard M. Karp♯	Zheng Chen†	Zheng Chen†
9th	**Jon M. Kleinberg**♯	Divesh Srivastava♯	Philip S. Yu♯
10th	Dina Katabi♯	Leif Azzopardi	Divesh Srivastava♯

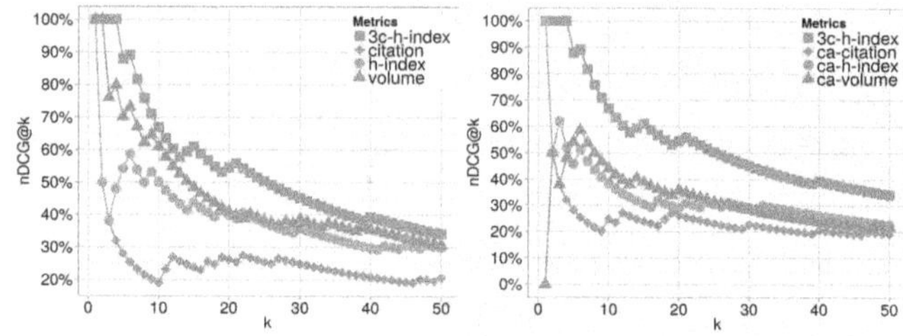

(a) 3c-index versus Baselines (b) 3c-index versus ca-index

Figure 2: Results for 3c-index versus baselines and ca-index.

may have negatively affected its behavior. Hence, ca-index is not indicated to be used in a *closed community perspective*; however, it is still good for assessing research in multiple area scenario. Figure 2b shows the results of the ranking produced by 3c-index and ca-index using score given by the same baselines. It emphasizes the good performance of our proposed index comparing with the ca-index.

Our approach has best results to measure research contribution across communities, surpassing previous metrics. Overall, *3c-index* successfully measured the impact of researchers' contributions based on the publications by community. As future work, we plan to expand *3c-index* by considering the researchers' contributions through areas.

Acknowledgments

Work in collaboration with Thiago H. P. Silva and Ana Paula C. Silva, funded by CNPq. A complete version of this work is available at [8].

5. REFERENCES

[1] M. A. Brandão and M. M. Moro. Analyzing the strength of co-authorship ties with neighborhood overlap. In *DEXA*, pages 527–542, 2015.

[2] R. S. Burt. Structural Holes and Good Ideas. *American Journal of Sociology*, 110(2):349–399, 2004.

[3] M. S. Granovetter. The Strength of Weak Ties. *American Journal of Sociology*, 78(6):1360–1380, 1973.

[4] T. H. Haveliwala. Topic-sensitive pagerank. In *WWW*, pages 517–526, 2002.

[5] H. Lima et al. Aggregating Productivity Indices for Ranking Researchers Across Multiple Areas. In *JCDL*, pages 97–106, Indianapolis, USA, 2013.

[6] S. L. Montolio, D. Dominguez-Sal, and J. L. Larriba-Pey. Research endogamy as an indicator of conference quality. *ACM SIGMOD Record*, 42(2):11–16, 2013.

[7] M. Newman. Who is the best connected scientist? a study of scientific coauthorship networks. *Complex networks*, pages 337–370, 2004.

[8] T. H. P. Silva, L. Mota, A. P. C. Silva, and M. M. Moro. 3c-index: Research Contribution across Communities as an Influence Indicator. *JIDM*, 6(3):192–205, 2015.

Vectorizing an In Situ Query Engine

Panagiotis Sioulas
University of Athens
panossioulas@gmail.com

Anastasia Ailamaki
École Polytechnique Fédérale de Lausanne
anastasia.ailamaki@epfl.ch

ABSTRACT

Database systems serve a wide range of use cases efficiently, but require data to be loaded and adapted to the system's execution engine. This pre-processing step is a bottleneck to the analysis of the increasingly large and heterogeneous datasets. Therefore, numerous research efforts advocate for querying each dataset *in situ*,i.e., without pre-loading it in a DBMS. On the other hand, performing analysis over *raw data* entails numerous overheads because of the potentially inefficient data representations.

In this paper, we investigate the effect of vector processing on raw data querying. We enhance the operators of a query engine to use SIMD operations. Specifically, we examine the effect of SIMD on two different cases: the scan operators that perform the CPU-intensive task of input parsing, and the part of the query pipeline that performs a selection and computes an aggregate. We show that a vectorized approach has a lot of potential to improve performance, which nevertheless comes with trade-offs.

1. INTRODUCTION

As the size of data and its variety continue to grow at rapid rates, loading entire datasets in a DBMS prior to querying them constitutes a bottleneck, incurred before any queries can be launched over the datasets. In addition, many practitioners avoid the use of DBMS altogether due to vendor lock-in concerns. They avoid storing their data in proprietary, DBMS-specific file formats because they still want to launch external scripts or other programs over their data. Consequently, numerous systems advocate querying data in their raw representation, without loading them in a DBMS a priori [1,2,3,4,5].

On the other hand, DBMS load data in a compact, well-engineered representation to minimize access costs. Querying raw data introduces various overheads. For verbose, textual file formats, every query has to re-parse the input data, identify tokens per "tuple ", convert raw data fields, etc. To minimize the costs, systems querying raw data use various techniques, such as specialized index structures [1,2,4] and parallelism [3,5]. The former techniques target scenarios where data accesses are meant to be judicious, whereas the latter attempt to load the raw data with a negligible loading cost.

This work focuses on how judicious data accesses can be further sped up through the use of vectorization [5]. We therefore use a pipelined query engine as the starting point, and extend it to be able to access raw CSV data with the use of *positional maps*[1]. Positional maps are auxiliary structures that capture the position of raw data fields in a CSV file. For example, for every row in a CSV file, the positional map for it captures the positions of the 1st, 6th, 11th, … fields. The system can thus use the known positions to navigate in the raw file with reduced cost, avoiding parsing from scratch. Then, we extend the query engine with SIMD processing primitives to further reduce processing costs, which allow performing the same operation for a vector of data at a time, thus taking advantage of data level parallelism.

Contributions. In this paper, we examine SIMD optimizations on a query engine for raw data. We develop a SIMD-powered scan operator for CSV data, and an aggregation operator that also performs data filtering. Our results show that SIMD-aware operators outperform their scalar counterparts in the majority of cases. There are cases, however, where combining scalar and vectorized code is more beneficial.

SIGMOD'16, June 26 - July 01, 2016, San Francisco, CA, USA
ACM 978-1-4503-3531-7/16/06.
http://dx.doi.org/10.1145/2882903.2914829

2. OPTIMIZED OPERATORS

Scan. The query engine we use converts judiciously only the data fields necessary to answer the current query. Therefore, a typical invocation of a scan operator for CSV files involves a combination of field skips and conversions of target fields per CSV record. A skip searches for a delimiter, either forwards or backwards in the file, using a character-to-character comparison; the delimiter denotes the end of a field. The single-character comparisons can be vectorized by loading N bytes at a time in SIMD registers and comparing them in vector-sized chunks [5]. The result of the SIMD comparison is a mask vector that can be converted to a single integer bitmask, with set bit positions corresponding to delimiter offsets. The number of trailing zeroes in this bitmask equals the offset of the delimiter. The search for the next field continues from the last delimiter found.

For relatively short fields, consecutive loads of the SIMD registers and comparisons overlap. The result is performance degradation, because we have to fill the SIMD registers repeatedly for short fields. As bitmasks hold the position of all delimiters in a chunk, this inefficiency can be avoided by reusing the bitmask's data rather than discarding it. A persistent bitmask can be used as previously, shifted appropriately for each skip to reflect the current position until it is depleted. Then, the next bitmask is computed. For instance, a "0001001001000000" bitmask produced by a 16 byte scan can be exploited for 3 skips, each consuming up to the rightmost set bit by shifting 7, 3 and 3 bits to the right respectively, before scanning forward again. This method implies a one-way traversal compared to the scalar version.

SIMD-aware scans are mostly useful when fully converting the data input. When, however, they are combined with a positional map for judicious data accesses, the persistent bitmask is always relative to the current position in the file and is made irrelevant by jumps. For this approach to operate correctly, the bitmask info has to be reset after using the index. By accessing data only to retrieve specific values, the code path becomes more complex. Thus, the benefit from vectorization is smaller.

Aggregations. Analytical queries typically include a series of filtering predicates and the calculation of some aggregate expressions. We therefore examine an operator that combines a selection and an aggregation step. For each record, the necessary columns are loaded, the condition is computed and, if true, the code branches to the aggregation. We have added a SIMD-aware

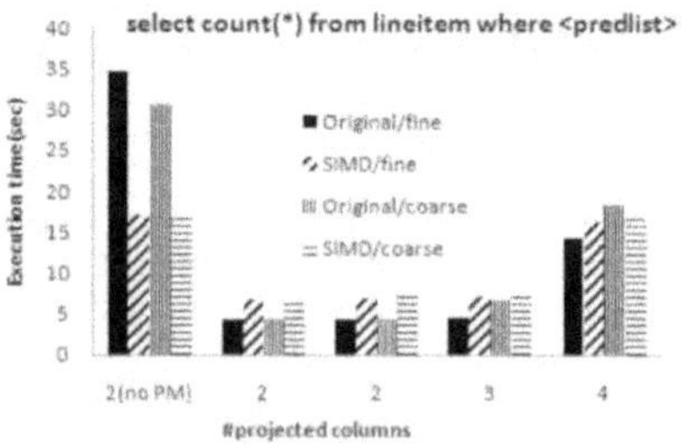

Figure 1: Scan w/ coarse/fine grained PM

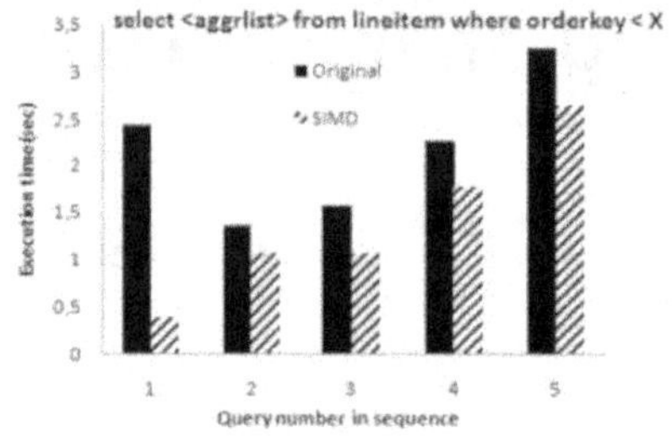

Figure 2: Aggregation pipelines

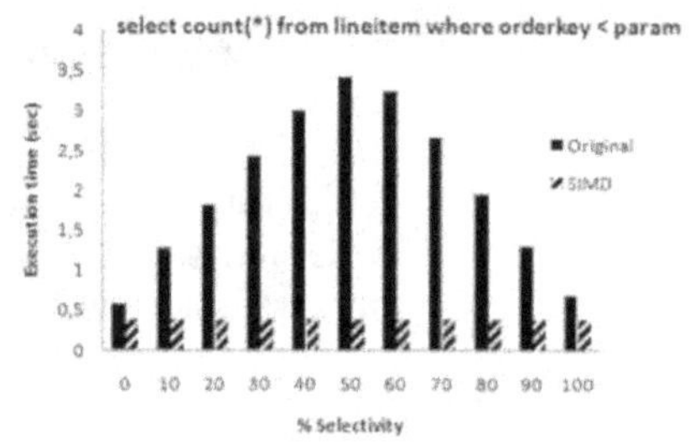

Figure 3: Misprediction sensitivity

version of the aggregation operator, which works with a vector of data at a time.

SIMD, however, is incompatible with aggregation by branching. The vectorized alternative is predication. The selection predicate results in a mask vector, applied to the entire input. In the end, the elements of the partial results are aggregated together to produce the result. As the overall operator supports multiple aggregations at once, this process takes place for each one of them.

3. EXPERIMENTAL EVALUATION

Experimental Setup. We evaluate the impact of our optimizations to the raw data querying engine using a server with 2 Intel Xeon E5-2650L v3 processors running at 1.8 GHz. These processors support 256-bit wide AVX2 SIMD instructions .The system has 384GB of DRAM and 2TB SATA3 HDD. We use the *LineItem* table from the TPC-H benchmark as the schema for the input datasets.

Scan. In this experiment, we evaluate the vectorized version of the scan operator. The input file uses the CSV file format and contains 60 million rows that require 7.2GB on disk. The workload consists of 5 queries and we clear the caches before running the first query. The first 3 queries in the sequence project 2 columns, while Q4 and Q5 project 3 and 4 columns respectively. We repeat the experiment with a positional map that contains one entry per 3 columns, and a coarser-grained version that uses one entry per 5 columns.

Figure 1 plots the execution time per query using either of the fine-and coarse-grained settings. In both cases, the positional map is populated during the execution of the first query and reused subsequently. The first query benefits greatly from the use of SIMD instructions, which decrease the execution time by 1.8-2x depending on the type of the positional map. However, the next two queries that project the same columns are 60% slower when using SIMD. These queries represent the ideal case for the original version of the scan operator as they can fully reuse the positional map for direct access to the raw data. On the other hand, the SIMD version encounters short sequences that create delays in the pipeline. When projecting additional columns, the benefits of SIMD depend on the position of the attributes relative to the state of the positional map. This trade-off can be observed in the query that projects 4 columns. Overall, utilizing SIMD efficiently requires tuning all parameters of the scan operator.

Aggregations. In this experiment, we evaluate the vectorized version of the aggregation pipeline. The input files use a binary columnar representation of the table with 600 million rows. The workload consists of 5 queries and we clear the caches before running the first query. All queries apply a filtering predicate with 30% selectivity on the *orderkey* attribute, and also vary the type of the aggregation operator and the columns it accesses. Q1 uses a simple "COUNT(*)" aggregation while Q2 uses "MAX(quantity)". Q3 combines the two aggregation operators, while Q4 and Q5 each add additional MAX operator on a different column to the preceding query in the sequence.

Figure 2 plots the execution time of the original and vectorized version of the system for the sequence of queries. In all cases, the SIMD version reduces execution time by a factor of 1.2-6x. The biggest improvement is observable in the Q1 COUNT query. This effect is due to the very high branch misprediction rate of 0.447 for the original version, whereas the SIMD version does not perform branches. High branch misprediction causes the execution time of Q1 to be higher than Q3, even though Q3 is essentially an extended version of Q1 that calculates more aggregates. We further examine Q1 in Figure 3, where we vary selectivity: For selectivities closer to 50%,we observe even higher performance improvement, which corroborates the finding of a related study [7]. When the pipelines include multiple operators, this effect is masked by other instructions required to compute the additional aggregations. Overall, the use of SIMD improves robustness by removing sensitivity to selectivity.

4. CONCLUSIONS

In this paper, we quantify the opportunities for applying vectorization techniques to raw data querying. We study two components of the system, the scan operator and the aggregation pipeline, and examine the trade-offs involved in using SIMD-powered vectorized execution. We show that the performance of the vectorized scan operator depends on both the positional map settings and the attribute layout, while the vectorized aggregations are more robust. In the future, we will apply vectorization techniques to other operators and fine-tune them to amortize the trade-offs.

5. REFERENCES

[1] I. Alagiannis, R. Borovica, M. Branco, S. Idreos and A. Ailamaki. NoDB:Efficient Query Execution on Raw Data Files. In SIGMOD, 2012.

[2] S. Blanas, K. Wu, S. Byna, B. Dong and A. Shoshani. Parallel data analysis directly on scientific file formats. In SIGMOD, 2014.

[3] Y. Cheng and F. Rusu. Parallel in-situ data processing with speculative loading. In SIGMOD, 2014.

[4] M. Karpathiotakis, M. Branco, I. Alagiannis and A. Ailamaki. Adaptive Query Processing on RAW Data. In PVLDB, 7(12): 1119-1130, 2014.

[5] T. Mühlbauer, W. Rödiger, R. Seilbeck, A. Reiser, A. Kemper and T. Neumann. Instant loading for main memory databases. In PVLDB, 6(14): 1702-1713, 2013.

[6] O. Polychroniou, A. Raghavan and K.A. Ross. Rethinking SIMD Vectorization for In-Memory Databases. In SIGMOD, 2015.

[7] J. Sompolski, M. Zukowski and P. A. Boncz. Vectorization vs compilation in query execution. In DaMoN, 2011.

Exploring Visualization of Data Transforms

[Extended Abstract]

Larry Xu
UC Berkeley
larry.xu@berkeley.edu

ABSTRACT

In the context of data exploration, users often interact with relational database systems in an interactive query session to form useful insights. Each query a user executes can potentially transform a resultset in complex ways. We explore some of the challenges in understanding these transformations, and how these challenges can be solved through more informative visual representations of data transforms. We present the concept of "tweening" of resultsets as a method of incrementally visualizing data transformations, and explore approaches towards generating these resultset tweens. Through a series of user studies, we evaluate tweening as an effective method of understanding the changes that result from data transformations.

1. INTRODUCTION

There has been a great deal of research on visual interfaces to databases, resulting in the creation of many tools for specifying queries and visualizing results. These visualization tools can greatly improve the usability of database systems, but despite all of the benefits these tools provide, users can still have difficulty understanding how a query specifically affects its results. The visual difference between the input and output of a query transformation can be significant and difficult to comprehend. In our work we focus on the design and evaluation of techniques to bridge the gap between these input and output visualizations, so that users can understand the effects of their queries in a more detailed and intuitive manner.

In a typical relational database setting, a user will write a sequence of queries which explore the structure and content of the data being analyzed. The user enters a feedback loop where each query result reveals more information to help the user write their next query until the desired results are found. Each query iteratively transforms a single resultset, but it can be difficult to understand how the data is being manipulated and filtered as these transformations occur. This interface lacks data lineage information that describes how the data changes throughout the transformation[1]. These problems are not only prevalent when writing a sequence of queries; even individual queries that cause large complex transformations, such as aggregations or pivots, can be difficult to comprehend.

To help users understand data transformations we introduce the concept of "tweening" of resultsets. The concept of tweening stems from the world of animation. It is the process of generating intermediate frames between two or more key frames to give the appearance of a smooth transition. This technique has been widely used in animation, and we believe that it can be adapted towards creating animated visualizations of data transformations. Previous research has shown that animated data visualizations can help in decision making[2] and reducing a user's cognitive load[3]. Furthermore, animated visualizations provide additional data lineage information that traditional interfaces lack.

2. RESULTSET TWEENING

We discuss the concept of resultset tweening by first defining a query session for the purposes of interactive data exploration, followed by different approaches to generating a tweening sequence.

2.1 Query Session

We define a query session as a series of queries on the same relation. A query Q transforms resultset R_{old} into a new resultset R_{new} where Q is a standard SQL query and each resultset is tabular data visually represented as a standard two-dimensional grid. Hence, a resultset tween for query Q visualizes an incremental transformation from R_{old} to R_{new}.

2.2 Approach

A resultset tween can be represented as an ordered sequence of visual operations. Each operation modifies the visual representation of a resultset through structural transforms (e.g. insertions and deletions) or visual cues (e.g. highlights and annotations). A comprehensive set of visual operations can be defined in a formal grammar which expresses the entire space of data transforms on resultsets. Figure 1 showcases a simple tween example where a resultset is modified through a series of such visual operations.

There are multiple approaches that can be used to generate a tweening sequence for a data transform. First we consider a result-based approach which analyzes only the differences between two resultsets (a table diff) without considering the underlying queries which created those resultsets. By mapping a table diff to a sequence of cell/row/column inser-

SIGMOD'16 June 26 - July 01, 2016, San Francisco, CA, USA

ACM ISBN 978-1-4503-3531-7/16/06.

DOI: http://dx.doi.org/10.1145/2882903.2914837

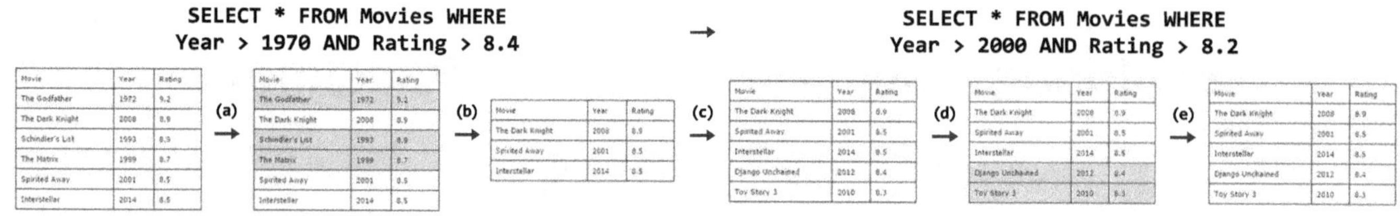

(a) emphasize(positions={rows:[1,3,4]}, cause='delete')

(b) delete(positions={rows:[1,3,4]})

(c) insert(positions={rows:[4,5]}, data=[['Django Unchained',2012,8.4], ['Toy Story 3',2010,8.3]])

(d) emphasize(positions={rows:[4,5]}, cause='insert')

(e) deemphasize(positions={rows:[4,5]})

Figure 1: Frames of a sample tweening sequence for a query change in the WHERE clause highlighting the addition and deletion of rows from the original table. The visual interface should animate the tween to produce a smooth transition.

tion, deletion, and reorder operations, we can automatically generate a tween between any two resultsets. This approach works well for very simple resultset transforms, however can create inaccurate visual tweens for more complex types of transformations such as aggregations or pivot operations.

Instead, we consider a query-based approach to tweening that analyzes differences in the underlying query structure combined with a rulebase to accurately generate a tweening sequence. This approach breaks down the two queries Q_{old} and Q_{new} into a query diff Δ_Q that specifies which SQL clauses changed, and uses rules to determine which visual operations to use for the tween. Each rule maps a type of SQL clause change to an ordered set of visual operations.

3. EVALUATION

To evaluate the effectiveness of tweening as a method of visualizing data transformations, we conducted a set of user studies that quantify how well users understand certain properties of a data transformation after being exposed to a resultset tween. For each study, we employed a between-subjects design with two groups, a "tween" group and a "non-tween" group, where the users of each group are shown a tweened and non-tweened visualization, respectively. We deployed each study as a separate task on Amazon Mechanical Turk, ensuring that each user participated in at most one study to prevent any biases from completing multiple studies.

3.1 User Studies

We designed 3 studies that show the user an example transformation that is the result of a query change:

- Study 1 - Change in SELECT clause
- Study 2 - Change in WHERE clause
- Study 3 - Change in SELECT and WHERE clauses

We then ask the user to identify how many rows and/or columns were added or removed in the process. We scored the user responses by summing the absolute differences of the response and expected answer for each question. After collecting a sample distribution of scores for the "tween" group and the "non-tween" group, we ran a Mann-Whitney U test to detect whether the two distributions differed significantly. Table 1 shows the results of a one-tailed test for the 3 different studies we ran. The results suggest that the users in the "tween" group were able to more accurately judge the number of rows and columns that were modified.

Table 1: Mann-Whitney U Test Statistics

Study	Tween Users	Non-tween Users	U	p-value
1	20	20	118	0.02391
2	17	20	103	0.00917
3	18	20	121	0.08528

4. CONCLUSIONS AND FUTURE WORK

The analysis reveals that resultset tweening can be an effective means of portraying a visual representation of the transformations that occur in an interactive query session. The query-based tweening approach described in this paper presents a good first step towards automatically generating tweening sequences. With a proper visual grammar and rulebase it can readily be adapted into existing data visualization tools like Tableau or d3.js to animate SQL transformations. Further exploration into the factors that comprise a "useful" tween and ways to optimize the generation of tweening sequences via visual cost models would be appropriate next steps to furthering our understanding of resultset tweens. More research experimenting with tweening for large resultsets that cannot fit well on screen could further the practicality of tweening as well.

5. ACKNOWLEDGMENTS

I would like to thank Joseph Hellerstein, Arnab Nandi, and Meraj Khan for their guidance and fundamental contributions to this research project. This report serves as a summary of our collective efforts in working on this project, as well as my own personal contributions as an undergraduate researcher working with them.

6. REFERENCES

[1] J. Cheney, L. Chiticariu, and W.-C. Tan. Provenance in databases: Why, how, and where. *Foundations and Trends in Databases*, 1(4):379–474, 2009.

[2] C. Gonzalez. Does animation in user interfaces improve decision making? In *Proceedings of the ACM SIGCHI Conference on Human Factors in Computing Systems*, pages 27–34, 1996.

[3] G. G. Robertson, S. K. Card, and J. D. Mackinlay. Information visualization using 3d interactive animation. *Communications of the ACM*, 36(4):57–71, 1993.

Minimizing *Average Regret Ratio* in Database

Sepanta Zeighami
Hong Kong University of Science and Technology
Clear Water Bay, Kowloon, Hong Kong
szeighami@connect.ust.hk

Raymond Chi-Wing Wong
Hong Kong University of Science and Technology
Clear Water Bay, Kowloon, Hong Kong
raywong@cse.ust.hk

ABSTRACT

We propose "average regret ratio" as a metric to measure users' satisfaction after a user sees k selected points of a database, instead of all of the points in the database. We introduce the average regret ratio as another means of multi-criteria decision making. Unlike the original k-regret operator that uses the maximum regret ratio, the average regret ratio takes into account the satisfaction of a general user. While assuming the existence of some utility functions for the users, in contrast to the top-k query, it does not require a user to input his or her utility function but instead depends on the probability distribution of the utility functions. We prove that the average regret ratio is a supermodular function and provide a polynomial-time approximation algorithm to find the average regret ratio minimizing set for a database.

1. INTRODUCTION

Representing a set of points with a few data points which best satisfy users' expectations is a problem with many applications. As an example, consider a website that allows users to find and book hotels. Imagine the case that users' preferences are not known. The user may not know exactly what kind of a room he or she is looking for, or may not be willing to input his or her preferences. Besides, the website owner may want to give suggestions to a user before he or she inputs his or her criteria. A problem now will be that which hotels should be shown to the user.

This problem has been treated in the literature using different approaches. Skyline queries proposed by Borzsony et al. [1], which select the points to be in the *skyline* of a dataset, and top-k queries, which select k points based on a specific user's preferences, are two ways of addressing the problem.

Another approach towards the problem is using the idea of *regret ratio*. The regret ratio of a user after seeing a subset of the points in a database is a measure of how disappointed the user is with the selected points. Hence, the regret ratio measures how "unhappy" a user is with a subset of points. As such, minimizing the regret ratios of the users is a suitable means of selecting representative points from a database.

In this paper, we use the idea of the regret ratio to select a few representative points from a database. We propose the measure of *average regret ratio* which evaluates how well the points are selected by calculating the average of the regret ratios of all the users. Using the average regret ratio, we can measure how users, on average, feel about the points. Hence, we can select the points that will on average be the most suitable for the users by minimizing the average regret ratio. In addition, the selection of the points using the average regret ratio, unlike the top-k queries, does not require the users to input their preferences, and in contrast to the skyline queries, returns a fixed number of points independent of the number of criteria involved.

Regret ratio has been used by Nanongkai et al. [4] who introduced the k-regret operator, an operator which outputs k points from a database to minimize the maximum regret ratio of a user. However, the k-regret operator suffers from the drawback that it only considers the regret ratio of the most unhappy user, and will be skewed towards the least satisfied users only, ignoring the other users. Hence, with only few very dissatisfied users and many satisfied ones, the maximum regret ratio may not be an accurate measure of the satisfaction of the users. On the other hand, the average regret ratio will not be biased towards a few dissatisfied users, and will give a better impression of how a user in general feel towards the selected points.

In what follows, we use the minimization of the average regret ratio to select k data points from a database. For this, we first define the average regret ratio formally and discuss how it can be calculated. Then, we present an algorithm that returns k data points which minimize the average regret ratio to within a small factor of the best possible solution and we present our experimental results on how well the algorithm works in comparison with other existing methods.

2. PROBLEM DEFINITION

To define the problem, we need to introduce a few concepts. First, we assume that the happiness of the users can be expressed using a utility function. Hence, a utility function, f, is a mapping $f : R_+^d \to R_+$ where $f(p)$ is the utility of a point p for a user with the utility function f. A utility function shows how "happy" a user is with a data point. Then, we define the regret ratio of a user with the utitliy function f after seeing a subset S of a database D to be $rr_D(S, f) = \frac{\max_{p \in D} f(p) - \max_{p \in S} f(p)}{\max_{p \in D} f(p)}$. As such, the regret ra-

SIGMOD/PODS'16 June 26 - July 01, 2016, San Francisco, CA, USA

ACM ISBN 978-1-4503-3531-7/16/06.

DOI: http://dx.doi.org/10.1145/2882903.2914831

tio measures how dissapointed (or unhappy) a user is after seeing a subset of the database, by calculating the maximum possible utility or satisfaction the user can gain from seeing the subset and the original database. Then, we can define the average regret ratio as $arr_D(S) = \int_{f \in F} rr_D(S, f)\eta(f)df$, where $\eta(f)$ is the probability distribution function of the utility functions of different users and F is the set of all of the utility functions. The average regret ratio, therefore, is the expected regret ratio of a user. With this, the general problem of selecting k representative points from a database can be written as follows.

Problem Definition. Given a d-dimensional database D of size n, a set F of utility functions of size N, the probability distribution function of the utility functions $\eta(.)$ and an integer k, find a set S, where $S \subseteq D$, of cardinality k for which $arr_D(S)$ is the least. i.e.

$$S = argmin_{S' \subseteq D, |S'| = k} arr_D(S')$$

3. CALCULATION OF THE AVERAGE REGRET RATIO

The calculation of the average regret ratio, $arr_D(\cdot)$, involves calculating the average of the regret ratios of all the utility functions. If the set of the utility functions is defined on a discrete space, we can calculate the average regret ratio by summing for all the utility functions their regret ratios multiplied by their probabilities. But, if the distribution of the utility functions is continuous, the calculation of the average regret ratio requires the calculation of a d-dimensional integral. Since the calculation of such an integral is costly, we use a sampling approach instead. We select N utility functions based on the probability distribution of the utility functions and calculate the average regret ratio by taking the average of regret ratios for these N sampled utility function. For this, we need to choose a value for N that approximates the true value of the average regret ratio with a high confidence and within a reasonable error parameter. We prove that given a confidence parameter $\sigma \in [0, 1]$ and an error parameter $\epsilon \in [0, 1]$, if the sampling size N is at least $\frac{3ln(\frac{1}{\sigma})}{\epsilon^2}$, then with the confidence of at least 1 - σ, the calculated average regret ratio is within ϵ of its true value.

4. ALGORITHM

We provide an approximation algorithm that outputs k points from a dataset that minimize the average regret ratio of a user. We first prove that the average regret ratio is a monotonically non-increasing supermodular set function. Based on this and an algorithm suggested by Il'ev [2] for minimizing a supermodular set function, we propose a greedy algorithm that minimizes the average regret ratio. This greedy algorithm initializes the solution set S to be equal to the dataset D. Then, it iterates from n to $n - k$ and at each iteration removes the point from S whose removal increases the average regret ratio the least. If Alg is the solution returned by this algorithm and Opt is the optimal solution, and $h(S) = arr_D(S)$, then, $\frac{h(Alg)}{h(Opt)} \leq \frac{e^t - 1}{t}$, where $t = \frac{s}{1-s}$ and s is h's steepness, where steepness is the maximum possible marginal decrease of a function.

The calculation of the average regret ratio based on the method explained above takes time $O(dnN)$ and there are $O(n^2)$ iterations in the greedy algorithm. So, the total running time of the algorithm is $O(dNn^3)$. This, however, can be improved empirically using an R*-tree data structure and by means of heuristics. For instance, at each iteration of the algorithm, instead of going through all the N users to calculate the average regret ratio, we can keep track of the users whose regret ratio changes in each iteration of the algorithm, and calculate the regret ratios only for those users.

5. EXPERIMENTS

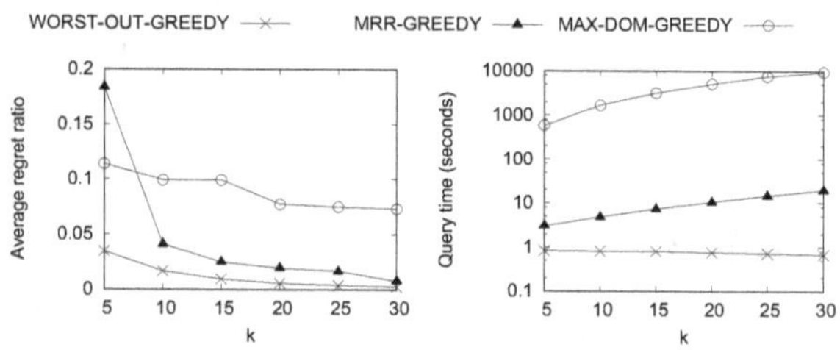

Figure 1: ***Results on the House-6d dataset, varying** k*

We ran experiments on real and synthetic datasets to measure how well our proposed algorithm works in comparison with other existing algorithms. The algorithms were implemented in C++ and were run on machines with 2.26GHz CPUs and 32GB RAM. For the sake of space, we only present one of the results here. A real dataset with 127,931 points in 6 dimensions called *House-6d* (http://www.ipums.org) was used in the experiment, with 10,000 utility functions sampled from a uniform distribution on the linear class of the utility functions (note that the distribution of the utility functions in real world can be obtained from search logs or rating systems, by recording users' activities and using machine learning techniques). The algorithm proposed by us is called WORST-OUT-GREEDY and the two other algorithms are MRR-GREEDY, proposed by Nanongkai et al. [4], designed for the *maximum regret ratio* operator and MAX-DOM-GREEDY proposed by Lin et al. [3], which selects k points that dominate the most number of points in the skyline of the dataset.

As illustrated by Figure 1, WORST-OUT-GREEDY results in a very low average regret ratio and the average regret ratio for the algorithm MRR-GREEDY drops drastically when k, the number of the selected points, increases. Besides, MAX-DOM-GREEDY results in a larger average regret ratio. The running time of MAX-DOM-GREEDY is smaller than a second for all values of k, while the running time of MRR-GREEDY increases to more than 10 seconds when k increases. However, MAX-DOM-GREEDY has a much larger running time.

References

[1] S. Borzsony, D. Kossmann, and K. Stocker. The skyline operator. *ICDE*, 2001.

[2] V. P. Il'ev. An approximation guarantee of the greedy descent algorithm for minimizing a supermodular set function. *Discrete Applied Mathematics*, 114(1-3):131–146, October 2001.

[3] X. Lin, Y. Yuan, Q. Zhang, and Y. Zhang. Selecting stars: The k most representative skyline operator. *ICDE*, 2007.

[4] D. Nanongkai, A. D. Sarma, A. Lall, R. J. Lipton, and J. Xu. Regret-minimizing representative databases. *VLDB*, 2010.

Author Index

www.ingramcontent.com/pod-product-compliance
Lightning Source LLC
LaVergne TN
LVHW080106011026
849160LV00013B/1040